THE YEAR'S WORK 2002

The Year's Work
in English Studies
Volume 83

Covering work published in 2002

OXFORD

UNIVERSITY PRESS

Great Clarendon Street, Oxford OX2 6DP, UK

Oxford University Press is a department of the University of Oxford.
It furthers the University's objective of excellence in research, scholarship,
and education by publishing worldwide in

Oxford New York

Athens Auckland Bangkok Bogotá Buenos Aire Cape Town
Chennai Dar es Salaam Delhi Florence Hong Kong Istanbul Karachi
Kolkata Kuala Lumpur Madrid Melbourne Mexico City Mumbai Nairobi
Paris São Paulo Shanghai Taipei Tokyo Toronto Warsaw

Oxford is a registered trade mark of Oxford University Press
in the UK and in certain other countries

British Library Cataloguing in Publication Data

Data available

ISSN 0084 4144
ISBN 0 1985 6624 7

1 3 5 7 9 10 8 6 4 2

Typeset by Hope Services (Abingdon) Ltd
Printed in Great Britain
on acid-free paper by
Biddles Ltd., King's Lynn

The English Association

The object of The English Association is to promote the knowledge and appreciation of English language and its literatures.

The Association pursues these aims by creating opportunities of co-operation among all those interested in English; by furthering the recognition of English as essential in education; by discussing methods of English teaching; by holding lectures, conferences, and other meetings; by publishing several journals, books, and leaflets; and by forming local branches overseas and at home. English Association Fellowships recognize distinction and achievement in the field of English worldwide.

Publications

The Year's Work in English Studies. An annual narrative bibliography which aims to cover all work of quality in english studies published in a given year. Published by Oxford University Press.

The Year's Work in Critical and Cultural Theory. An annual narrative bibliography which aims to provide comprehensive cover of all work of quality in critical and cultural theory published in a given year. Published by Oxford University Press.

Essays and Studies. A well-established series of annual themed volumes edited each year by a distinguished academic. The 2004 volume is *Contemporary British Women Writers* edited by Dr Emma Parker, University of Leicester and published by Boydell & Brewer.

English. This internationally-known journal of the Association is aimed at teachers of English in universities and colleges, with articles on all aspects of literature and critical theory and an extensive reviews section. Three issues per year.

Use of English. The longest-standing journal for English teachers in schools and colleges. Three issues per year.

English 4–11. Designed and developed by primary English specialists to give practical help to primary and middle school teachers. Three issues per year.

English Association Studies. A new monograph series published in association with Boydell & Brewer.

Issues in English. Occasional pamphlet series.

Membership

Membership information can be found at http://www.le.ac.uk/engassoc or please write to The English Association, University of Leicester, University Road, Leicester LE1 7RH, UK or email: engassoc@le.ac.uk.

The Year's Work
in English Studies

Subscriptions for Volume 83

Institutional (combined rate to both *The Year's Work in English Studies* and *The Year's Work in Critical and Cultural Theory*) print and online: £217/$347.

Personal rates: as above.

Please note: £ Sterling rates apply in Europe, US$ elsewhere. All prices include postage, and for subscribers outside the UK delivery is by Standard Air. There may be other subscription rates available. For a complete listing, please visit www.ywes.oupjournals.org/subinfo.

Online Access

For details please email Oxford University Press Journals Customer Services on: jnls.cust.serv@oup.co.uk.

Order Information

Full prepayment, in the correct currency, is required for all orders. Orders are regarded as firm and payments are not refundable. Subscriptions are accepted and entered on a complete volume basis. Claims cannot be considered more than FOUR months after publication or date of order, whichever is later. All subscriptions in Canada are subject to GST. Subscriptions in the EU may be subject to European VAT. If registered, please supply details to avoid unnecessary charges. For subscriptions that include online versions, a proportion of the subscription price may be subject to UK VAT. Personal rate subscriptions are only available if payment is made by personal cheque or credit card and delivery is to a private address.

Methods of payment. Payment may be made by cheque (payable to Oxford University Press) in £ Sterling drawn on a UK bank or in US$ drawn on a US bank, bank transfer (£ Sterling – Barclays Bank plc, Oxford City Office, PO Box 333, Oxford, OX1 3HS, UK. Bank sort code: 20-65-18, Account No. 70299332, IBAN number GB89BARC20651870299332, Swift code BARCGB22), or by credit card (Mastercard, Visa, Switch or American Express).

Back Issues

The current plus two back volumes are available from Oxford University Press. Previous volumes can be obtained from the Periodicals Service Company, 11 Main Street, Germantown, NY 12526, USA. Email: psc@periodicals.com; tel: +1 (518) 537 4700; fax: +1 (518) 537 5899.

Further information. Journals Customer Service Department, Oxford University Press, Great Clarendon Street, Oxford OX2 6DP, UK. Email: jnls.cust.serv@oup-journals.org; tel (and answerphone outside normal working hours): +44 (0) 1865 353907; fax: +44 (0) 1865 353485. *In the US, please contact:* Journals Customer Service Department, Oxford University Press, 2001 Evans Road, Cary, NC 27513, USA. Email: jnlorders@oupjournals.org; tel (and answerphone outside normal working hours): 800 852 7323 (toll-free in USA/Canada); fax: 919 677 1714. *In Japan, please contact:* Journals Customer Services, Oxford University Press, 1-1-17-5F, Mukogaoka, Bunkyo-ku, Tokyo, 113-0023, Japan. Email: okudaoup@po.iijnet.or.jp; tel: (03) 3813 1461; fax: (03) 3818 1522.

The Year's Work in English Studies (ISSN 0084 4144) is published annually by Oxford University Press, Oxford, UK. Annual subscription price is £217/$347. *The Year's Work in English Studies* is distributed by Mercury International, 365 Blair Road, Avenel, NJ 07001, USA. Periodicals postage paid at Rahway, NJ and at additional entry points.

US Postmaster: send address changes to *The Year's Work in English Studies*, c/o Mercury International, 365 Blair Road, Avenel, NJ 07001, USA.

The Table of Contents email alerting service allows anyone who registers their email address to be notified via email when new content goes online. Details are available at http://www3.oup.co.uk/yes/etoc.html.

Permissions

For permissions requests, please visit www.oupjournals.org/permissions.

Advertising

Inquiries about advertising should be sent to Helen Pearson, Oxford Journals Advertising, PO Box 347, Abingdon OX14 1GJ, UK. Email: helen@oxfor-dads.com; tel/fax: +44 (0) 1235 201904.

Disclaimer

Contents

Abbreviations

1. Journals, Series and Reference Works

1650–1850	*1650–1850 Ideas, Aesthetics, and Inquiries in the Early Modern Era*
A&D	*Art and Design*
A&E	*Anglistik und Englishunterricht*
AAA	*Arbeiten aus Anglistik und Amerikanistik*
AAAJ	*Accounting, Auditing and Accountability Journal*
AAR	*African American Review*
ABäG	*Amsterdamer Beiträge zur Älteren Germanistik*
ABC	*American Book Collector*
ABELL	*Annual Bibliography of English Language and Literature*
ABM	*Antiquarian Book Monthly Review*
ABQ	*American Baptist Quarterly*
ABR	*American Benedictine Review*
ABSt	*A/B: Auto/Biography Studies*
AC	*Archeologia Classica*
Academy Forum	Academy Forum
AcadSF	Academia Scientiarum Fennica
ACar	*Analecta Cartusiana*
ACF	*Annali, Facolta di Lingue e Litterature Straniere di Ca' Foscari*
ACH	*Australian Cultural History*
ACLALSB	*ACLALS Bulletin*
ACM	*Aligarh Critical Miscellany*
ACS	*Australian–Canadian Studies: A Journal for the Humanities and Social Sciences*
Acta	Acta (Binghamton, NY)
AdI	*Annali d'Italianistica*
ADS	*Australasian Drama Studies*
AEB	*Analytical and Enumerative Bibliography*
Æstel	*Æstel*
AF	*Anglistische Forschungen*
AfricanA	*African Affairs*
AfrSR	*African Studies Review*
AgeJ	*Age of Johnson: A Scholarly Annual*
Agenda	*Agenda*
Agni	*Agni Review*
AH	*Art History*
AHR	*American Historical Review*

AHS	*Australian Historical Studies*
AI	*American Imago*
AICRJ	*American Indian Culture and Research Journal*
AIQ	*American Indian Quarterly*
AJ	*Art Journal*
AJGLL	*American Journal of Germanic Linguistics and Literatures*
AJIS	*Australian Journal of Irish Studies*
AJL	*Australian Journal of Linguistics*
AJP	*American Journal of Psychoanalysis*
AJPH	*Australian Journal of Politics and History*
AJS	*American Journal of Semiotics*
AKML	Abhandlungen zur Kunst-, Musik- and Literaturwissenschaft
AL	*American Literature*
ALA	African Literature Association Annuals
ALASH	*Acta Linguistica Academiae Scientiarum Hungaricae*
Albion	*Albion*
AlexS	Alexander Shakespeare
ALH	*Acta Linguistica Hafniensia; International Journal of Linguistics*
Alif	*Journal of Comparative Poetics* (Cairo, Egypt)
ALitASH	*Acta Literaria Academiae Scientiarum Hungaricae*
Allegorica	*Allegorica*
ALR	*American Literary Realism, 1870–1910*
ALS	*Australian Literary Studies*
ALT	*African Literature Today*
Alternatives	*Alternatives*
AmasJ	*Amerasian Journal*
AmDram	*American Drama*
Americana	*Americana*
AmerP	*American Poetry*
AmerS	*American Studies*
AmLH	*American Literary History*
AmLS	American Literary Scholarship: An Annual
AMon	*Atlantic Monthly*
AmPer	*American Periodicals*
AmRev	*Americas Review: A Review of Hispanic Literature and Art of the USA*
Amst	*Amerikastudien/American Studies*
AN	Acta Neophilologica
Anaïs	*Anaïs*
AnBol	*Analecta Bollandiana*
ANF	*Arkiv för Nordisk Filologi*
Angelaki	*Angelaki*
Anglia	*Anglia: Zeitschrift für Englische Philologie*
Anglistica	*Anglistica*
Anglistik	*Anglistik: Mitteilungen des Verbandes Deutscher Anglisten*
AnH	*Analecta Husserliana*

AnL	*Anthropological Linguistics*
AnM	*Annuale Mediaevale*
Ann	*Annales: Économies, Sociétés, Civilisations*
ANQ	*ANQ: A Quarterly Journal of Short Articles, Notes and Reviews* (formerly *American Notes and Queries*)
AntColl	*Antique Collector*
AntigR	*Antigonish Review*
Antipodes	*Antipodes: A North American Journal of Australian Literature*
ANZSC	*Australian and New Zealand Studies in Canada*
ANZTR	*Australian and New Zealand Theatre Record*
APBR	*Atlantic Provinces Book Review*
APL	*Antwerp Papers in Linguistics*
AppLing	*Applied Linguistics*
APR	*American Poetry Review*
AQ	*American Quarterly*
Aquarius	*Aquarius*
AR	*Antioch Review*
ArAA	*Arbeiten aus Anglistik und Amerikanistik*
Arcadia	*Arcadia*
Archiv	*Archiv für das Stadium der Neueren Sprachen und Literaturen*
ARCS	*American Review of Canadian Studies*
ArdenS	Arden Shakespeare
ArielE	*Ariel: A Review of International English Literature*
ArkQ	*Arkansas Quarterly: A Journal of Criticism*
ArkR	*Arkansas Review: A Journal of Criticism*
ArQ	*Arizona Quarterly*
ARS	Augustan Reprint Society
ARSR	*Australian Religion Studies Review*
ArtB	*Art Bulletin*
Arth	*Arthuriana*
ArthI	*Arthurian Interpretations*
ArthL	*Arthurian Literature*
Arv	*Arv: Nordic Yearbook of Folklore*
AS	*American Speech*
ASch	*American Scholar*
ASE	*Anglo-Saxon England*
ASInt	*American Studies International*
ASoc	*Arts in Society*
Aspects	*Aspects: Journal of the Language Society* (University of Essex)
AspectsAF	*Aspects of Australian Fiction*
ASPR	*Anglo-Saxon Poetic Records*
ASSAH	*Anglo-Saxon Studies in Archaeology and History*
Assaph	*Assaph: Studies in the Arts (Theatre Studies)*
Assays	*Assays: Critical Approaches to Medieval and Renaissance Texts*

ASUI	*Analele Stiintifice ale Universitatii 'Al.I. Cuza' din Iasi (Serie Noua), e. Lingvistica*
ATQ	*American Transcendental Quarterly: A Journal of New England Writers*
AuBR	*Australian Book Review*
AuFolk	*Australian Folklore*
AuFS	*Australian Feminist Studies*
AuHR	*Australian Humanities Review*
AuJL	*Australian Journal of Linguistics*
AUMLA	*Journal of the Australasian Universities Language and Literature Association*
AuS	*Australian Studies*
AuSA	*Australian Studies* (Australia)
AusCan	*Australian–Canadian Studies*
AusPl	*Australian Playwrights*
AusRB	*Australians' Review of Books*
AuVSJ	*Australasian Victorian Studies Journal*
AuWBR	*Australian Women's Book Review*
AvC	*Avalon to Camelot*
AY	*Arthurian Yearbook*
BakhtinN	*Bakhtin Newsletter*
BALF	*Black American Literature Forum*
BAReview	*British Academy Review*
BARS Bulletin	*British Association for Romantic Studies Bulletin & Review*
BAS	*British and American Studies*
BASAM	*BASA Magazine*
BathH	*Bath History*
BayreuthAS	Bayreuth African Studies
BB	*Bulletin of Bibliography*
BBCS	*Bulletin of the Board of Celtic Studies*
BBCSh	BBC Shakespeare
BBN	*British Book News*
BBSIA	*Bulletin Bibliographique de la Société Internationale Arthurienne*
BC	*Book Collector*
BCan	*Books in Canada*
BCMA	*Bulletin of Cleveland Museum of Art*
BCS	*B.C. Studies*
BDEC	*Bulletin of the Department of English* (Calcutta)
BDP	*Beiträge zur Deutschen Philologie*
Belfagor	*Belfagor: Rassegna di Varia Umanità*
BEPIF	*Bulletin des Itudes Portugaises et Brésiliennes*
BFLS	*Bulletin de la Faculté des Lettres de Strasbourg*
BGDSL	*Beiträge zur Geschichte der Deutschen Sprache und Literatur*
BHI	*British Humanities Index*
BHL	*Bibliotheca Hagiographica Latina Antiquae et Mediae Aetatis*

BHM	Bulletin of the History of Medicine
BHR	Bibliothèque d'Humanisme et Renaissance
BHS	Bulletin of Hispanic Studies
BI	Books at Iowa
Bibliotheck	Bibliotheck: A Scottish Journal of Bibliography and Allied Topics
Biography	Biography: An Interdisciplinary Quarterly
BIS	Browning Institute Studies: An Annual of Victorian Literary and Cultural History
BJA	British Journal of Aesthetics
BJCS	British Journal of Canadian Studies
BJDC	British Journal of Disorders of Communication
BJECS	British Journal for Eighteenth-Century Studies
BJHP	British Journal for the History of Philosophy
BJHS	British Journal for the History of Science
BJJ	Ben Jonson Journal
BJL	Belgian Journal of Linguistics
BJPS	British Journal for the Philosophy of Science
BJRL	Bulletin of the John Rylands (University Library of Manchester)
BJS	British Journal of Sociology
Blake	Blake: An Illustrated Quarterly
BLE	Bulletin de Littérature Ecclésiastique
BLJ	British Library Journal
BLR	Bodleian Library Record
BN	Beiträge zur Namenforschung
BNB	British National Bibliography
BoH	Book History
Bookbird	Bookbird
Borderlines	Borderlines
Boundary	Boundary 2: A Journal of Postmodern Literature and Culture
BP	Banasthali Patrika
BPMA	Bulletin of Philadelphia Museum of Art
BPN	Barbara Pym Newsletter
BQ	Baptist Quarterly
BRASE	Basic Readings in Anglo-Saxon England
BRH	Bulletin of Research in the Humanities
Brick	Brick: A Journal of Reviews
BRMMLA	Bulletin of the Rocky Mountain Modern Language Association
BRONZS	British Review of New Zealand Books
BSANZB	Bibliographical Society of Australia and New Zealand Bulletin
BSE	Brno Studies in English
BSEAA	Bulletin de la Société d'Études Anglo-Américaines des XVIIe et XVIIIe Siècles

BSJ	*Baker Street Journal: An Irregular Quarterly of Sherlockiana*
BSLP	*Bulletin de la Société de Linguistique de Paris*
BSNotes	*Browning Society Notes*
BSRS	*Bulletin of the Society for Renaissance Studies*
BSSA	*Bulletin de la Société de Stylistique Anglaise*
BST	*Brontë Society Transactions*
BSUF	*Ball State University Forum*
BTHGNewsl	*Book Trade History Group Newsletter*
BTLV	*Bijdragen tot de Taal-, Land- en Volkenhunde*
Bul	*Bulletin (Australia)*
Bullán	*Bullán*
BunyanS	*Bunyan Studies*
BuR	*Bucknell Review*
BurlM	*Burlington Magazine*
BurnsC	*Burns Chronicle*
BWPLL	Belfast Working Papers in Language and Linguistics
BWVACET	*Bulletin of the West Virginia Association of College English Teachers*
ByronJ	*Byron Journal*
CABS	Contemporary Authors Bibliographical Series
CahiersE	*Cahiers Élisabéthains*
CAIEF	*Cahiers de l'Association Internationale des Études Françaises*
Caliban	*Caliban* (Toulouse, France)
Callaloo	*Callaloo*
CalR	*Calcutta Review*
CamObsc	*Camera Obscura: A Journal of Feminism and Film Theory*
CamR	*Cambridge Review*
CanD	*Canadian Drama / L'Art Dramatique Canadienne*
C&L	*Christianity and Literature*
C&Lang	*Communication and Languages*
C&M	*Classica et Medievalia*
CanL	*Canadian Literature*
CAnn	*Carlyle Annual*
CanPo	*Canadian Poetry*
CapR	*Capilano Review*
CARA	Centre Aixois de Recherches Anglaises
Carib	*Carib*
Caribana	*Caribana*
CaribW	*Caribbean Writer*
CarR	*Caribbean Review*
Carrell	*Carrell: Journal of the Friends of the University of Miami Library*
CASE	Cambridge Studies in Anglo-Saxon England
CaudaP	*Cauda Pavonis*
CBAA	*Current Bibliography on African Affairs*
CBEL	*Cambridge Bibliography of English Literature*

CCRev	*Comparative Civilizations Review*
CCrit	*Comparative Criticism: An Annual Journal*
CCTES	*Conference of College Teachers of English Studies*
CCV	*Centro de Cultura Valenciana*
CDALB	*Concise Dictionary of American Literary Biography*
CDCP	Comparative Drama Conference Papers
CDIL	*Cahiers de l'Institut de Linguistique de Louvain*
CdL	*Cahiers de Lexicologie*
CE	*College English*
CEA	*CEA Critic*
CEAfr	*Cahiers d'Études Africaines*
CE&S	*Commonwealth Essays and Studies*
CentR	*Centennial Review*
Cervantes	*Cervantes*
CF	*Crime Factory*
CFM	*Canadian Fiction Magazine*
CFS	*Cahiers Ferdinand de Saussure: Revue de Linguistique Générale*
Chapman	*Chapman*
Chasqui	*Chasqui*
ChauR	*Chaucer Review*
ChauS	*Chaucer Studion*
ChauY	*Chaucer Yearbook*
ChH	*Church History*
ChildL	*Children's Literature*
ChiR	*Chicago Review*
ChLB	*Charles Lamb Bulletin*
CHLSSF	*Commentationes Humanarum Litterarum Societatis Scientiarum Fennicae*
CHR	*Camden History Review*
CHum	*Computers and the Humanities*
CI	Critical Idiom
CILT	Amsterdam Studies in the Theory and History of the Language Sciences IV: Current Issues in Linguistic Theory
Cinéaste	*Cinéaste*
CinJ	*Cinema Journal*
CIQ	*Colby Quarterly*
CISh	Contemporary Interpretations of Shakespeare
Cithara	*Cithara: Essays in the Judaeo-Christian Tradition*
CJ	*Classical Journal*
CJE	*Cambridge Journal of Education*
CJH	*Canadian Journal of History*
CJIS	*Canadian Journal of Irish Studies*
CJL	*Canadian Journal of Linguistics*
CJR	*Christian–Jewish Relations*
CK	*Common Knowledge*
CL	*Comparative Literature* (Eugene, OR)
CLAJ	*CLA Journal*

CLAQ	*Children's Literature Association Quarterly*
ClarkN	*Clark Newsletter: Bulletin of the UCLA Center for Seventeenth- and Eighteenth-Century Studies*
ClassW	*Classical World*
CLC	*Columbia Library Columns*
CLE	*Children's Literature in Education*
CLIN	*Cuadernos de Literatura*
ClioI	*Clio: A Journal of Literature, History and the Philosophy of History*
CLQ	*Colby Library Quarterly*
CLS	*Comparative Literature Studies*
Clues	*Clues: A Journal of Detection*
CMCS	*Cambridge Medieval Celtic Studies*
CML	*Classical and Modern Literature*
CN	*Chaucer Newsletter*
CNIE	*Commonwealth Novel in English*
CogLing	*Cognitive Linguistics*
Cognition	*Cognition*
ColB	*Coleridge Bulletin*
ColF	*Columbia Forum*
Collections	*Collections*
CollG	*Colloquia Germanica*
CollL	*College Literature*
Com	*Commonwealth*
Comitatus	*Comitatus: A Journal of Medieval and Renaissance Studies*
Commentary	*Commentary*
Comparatist	*Comparatist: Journal of the Southern Comparative Literature Association*
CompD	*Comparative Drama*
CompLing	*Contemporary Linguistics*
ConfLett	*Confronto Letterario*
ConL	*Contemporary Literature*
Connotations	*Connotations*
ConnR	*Connecticut Review*
Conradian	*Conradian*
Conradiana	*Conradiana: A Journal of Joseph Conrad Studies*
ContempR	*Contemporary Review*
Coppertales	*Coppertales: A Journal of Rural Arts*
Cosmos	*Cosmos*
Costume	*Journal of the Costume Society*
CP	*Concerning Poetry*
CQ	*Cambridge Quarterly*
CR	*Critical Review*
CRCL	*Canadian Review of Comparative Literature*
CRev	*Chesterton Review*
CRevAS	*Canadian Review of American Studies*
Crit	*Critique: Studies in Modern Fiction*
CritI	*Critical Inquiry*

Criticism	*Criticism: A Quarterly for Literature and the Arts*
Critique	*Critique* (Paris)
CritQ	*Critical Quarterly*
CritT	*Critical Texts: A Review of Theory and Criticism*
CrM	*Critical Mass*
CRNLE	*CRNLE Reviews Journal*
Crossings	*Crossings*
CRUX	*CRUX: A Journal on the Teaching of English*
CS	*Critical Survey*
CSASE	Cambridge Studies in Anglo-Saxon England
CSCC	*Case Studies in Contemporary Criticism*
CSELT	Cambridge Studies in Eighteenth-Century Literature and Thought
CSLBull	*Bulletin of the New York C.S. Lewis Society*
CSLL	*Cardozo Studies in Law and Literature*
CSML	Cambridge Studies in Medieval Literature
CSNCLC	Cambridge Studies in Nineteenth-Century Literature and Culture
CSPC	Cambridge Studies in Paleography and Codicology
CSR	Cambridge Studies in Romanticism
CSRev	*Christian Scholar's Review*
CStA	*Carlyle Studies Annual* (previously *CAnn*)
CTR	*Canadian Theatre Review*
Cuadernos	*Cuadernos de Literatura Infantil y Juvenil*
CulC	*Cultural Critique*
CulS	*Cultural Studies*
CulSR	*Cultural Studies Review*
CUNY	*CUNY English Forum*
Current Writing	*Current Writing: Text and Reception in Southern Africa*
CV2	*Contemporary Verse 2*
CVE	*Cahiers Victoriens et Edouardiens*
CW	*Current Writing: Text and Perception in Southern Africa*
CWAAS	*Transactions of the Cumberland and Westmorland Antiquarian and Archaeological Society*
CWS	*Canadian Woman Studies*
DA	*Dictionary of Americanisms*
DAE	*Dictionary of American English*
DAEM	*Deutsches Archiv für Erforschung des Mittelalters*
DAI	*Dissertation Abstracts International*
DAL	*Descriptive and Applied Linguistics*
D&CN&Q	*Devon and Cornwall Notes and Queries*
D&S	*Discourse and Society*
Daphnis	*Daphnis: Zeitschrift für Mittlere Deutsche Literatur*
DC	Dickens Companions
DerbyM	*Derbyshire Miscellany*
Descant	*Descant*
DFS	*Dalhousie French Studies*
DHLR	*D.H. Lawrence Review*

DHS	*Dix-huitième Siècle*
Diac	*Diacritics*
Diachronica	*Diachronica*
Dialogue	*Dialogue: Canadian Philosophical Review*
Dickensian	*Dickensian*
DicS	*Dickinson Studies*
Dictionaries	*Dictionaries: Journal of the Dictionary Society of North America*
Dionysos	*Dionysos*
Discourse	*Discourse*
DisS	*Discourse Studies*
DLB	*Dictionary of Literary Biography*
DLN	*Doris Lessing Newsletter*
DM	*Dublin Magazine*
DMT	Durham Medieval Texts
DNB	*Dictionary of National Biography*
DOE	*Dictionary of Old English*
Dolphin	*Dolphin: Publications of the English Department* (University of Aarhus)
DOST	*Dictionary of the Older Scottish Tongue*
DownR	*Downside Review*
DPr	*Discourse Processes*
DQ	*Denver Quarterly*
DQR	*Dutch Quarterly Review of Anglo-American Letters*
DQu	*Dickens Quarterly*
DR	*Dalhousie Review*
Drama	*Drama: The Quarterly Theatre Review*
DrS	*Dreiser Studies*
DS	*Deep South*
DSA	*Dickens Studies Annual*
DU	*Der Deutschunterricht: Beiträge zu Seiner Praxis und Wissenschaftlichen Grundlegung*
DUJ	*Durham University Journal*
DVLG	*Deutsche Vierteljahrsschrift für Literaturwissenschaft und Geistesgeschichte*
DWPELL	*Dutch Working Papers in English Language and Linguistics*
EA	*Études Anglaises*
EAL	*Early American Literature*
E&D	*Enlightenment and Dissent*
E&S	*Essays and Studies*
E&Soc	*Economy and Society*
EAS	*Essays in Arts and Sciences*
EASt	*Englisch Amerikanische Studien*
EBST	*Edinburgh Bibliographical Society Transactions*
EC	*Études Celtiques*
ECan	*Études Canadiennes/Canadian Studies*
ECCB	*Eighteenth Century: A Current Bibliography*

ECent	*Eighteenth Century: Theory and Interpretation*
ECF	*Eighteenth-Century Fiction*
ECI	*Eighteenth-Century Ireland*
ECIntell	*East-Central Intelligencer*
ECLife	*Eighteenth-Century Life*
ECN	*Eighteenth-Century Novel*
ECon	*L'Époque Conradienne*
ECr	*L'Esprit Créateur*
ECS	*Eighteenth-Century Studies*
ECSTC	Eighteenth-Century Short Title Catalogue
ECW	*Essays on Canadian Writing*
ECWomen	*Eighteenth-Century Women: Studies in their Lives, Work, and Culture*
EDAMN	*EDAM Newsletter*
EDAMR	*Early Drama, Art, and Music Review*
EDH	*Essays by Divers Hands*
EdL	*Études de Lettres*
EdN	*Editors' Notes: Bulletin of the Conference of Editors of Learned Journals*
EDSL	*Encyclopedic Dictionary of the Sciences of Language*
EEMF	Early English Manuscripts in Facsimile
EF	*Études Francaises*
EHR	*English Historical Review*
EI	*Études Irlandaises* (Lille)
EIC	*Essays in Criticism*
EinA	*English in Africa*
EiP	*Essays in Poetics*
EIRC	*Explorations in Renaissance Culture*
Éire	*Éire-Ireland*
EiTET	*Essays in Theatre / Études Théâtrales*
EJ	*English Journal*
EJES	*European Journal of English Studies*
ELangT	*ELT Journal: An International Journal for Teachers of English to Speakers of Other Languages*
ELet	*Esperienze Letterarie: Rivista Trimestrale di Critica e Cultura*
ELH	*English Literary History*
ELing	*English Linguistics*
ELL	*English Language and Linguistics*
ELN	*English Language Notes*
ELR	*English Literary Renaissance*
ELS	*English Literary Studies*
ELT	*English Literature in Transition*
ELWIU	*Essays in Literature* (Western Illinois University)
EM	*English Miscellany*
Embl	*Emblematica: An Interdisciplinary Journal of English Studies*
EMD	*European Medieval Drama*

EME	*Early Modern Europe*
EMedE	*Early Medieval Europe* (online)
EMLS	*Early Modern Literary Studies* (online)
EMMS	*Early Modern Manuscript Studies*
EMS	*English Manuscript Studies, 1100–1700*
EMu	*Early Music*
EMW	Early Modern Englishwomen
Encult	*Enculturation: Cultural Theories and Rhetorics*
Encyclia	*Encyclia*
English	*English: The Journal of the English Association*
EnT	*English Today: The International Review of the English Language*
EONR	*Eugene O'Neill Review*
EPD	*English Pronouncing Dictionary*
ER	*English Review*
ERLM	*Europe-Revue Littéraire Mensuelle*
ERR	*European Romantic Review*
ES	*English Studies*
ESA	*English Studies in Africa*
ESC	*English Studies in Canada*
ESQ	*ESQ: A Journal of the American Renaissance*
ESRS	*Emporia State Research Studies*
EssaysMedSt	*Essays in Medieval Studies*
EST	*Eureka Street*
ET	*Elizabethan Theatre*
EuroS	*European Studies: A Journal of European Culture, History and Politics*
EWhR	*Edith Wharton Review*
EWIP	*Edinburgh University, Department of Linguistics, Work in Progress*
EWN	*Evelyn Waugh Newsletter*
EWPAL	*Edinburgh Working Papers in Applied Linguistics*
EWW	*English World-Wide*
Excavatio	*Excavatio*
Exemplaria	*Exemplaria*
Expl	*Explicator*
Extrapolation	*Extrapolation: A Journal Science Fiction and Fantasy*
FC	*Feminist Collections: A Quarterly of Women's Studies Resources*
FCEMN	*Mystics Quarterly* (formerly *Fourteenth-Century English Mystics Newsletter*)
FCS	*Fifteenth-Century Studies*
FDT	Fountainwell Drama Texts
FemR	*Feminist Review*
FemSEL	*Feminist Studies in English Literature*
FFW	*Food and Foodways*
FH	*Die Neue Gesellschaft / Frankfurter Hefte*
Fiction International	*Fiction International*

FilmJ	Film Journal
FilmQ	Film Quarterly
FiveP	Five Points: A Journal of Literature and Art (Atlanta, GA)
FJS	Fu Jen Studies: Literature and Linguistics (Taipei)
FLH	Folia Linguistica Historica
Florilegium	Florilegium: Carleton University Annual Papers on Classical Antiquity and the Middle Ages
FMLS	Forum for Modern Language Studies
FNS	Frank Norris Studies
Folklore	Folklore
FoLi	Folia Linguistica
Forum	Forum
FranS	Franciscan Studies
FreeA	Free Associations
FrontenacR	Revue Frontenac
Frontiers	Frontiers: A Journal of Women's Studies
FS	French Studies
FSt	Feminist Studies
FT	Fashion Theory
FuL	Functions of Language
Futures	Futures
GAG	Göppinger Arbeiten zur Germanistik
GaR	Georgia Review
GBB	George Borrow Bulletin
GBK	Gengo Bunka Kenkyu: Studies in Language and Culture
GEGHLS	George Eliot–George Henry Lewes Studies
GeM	Genealogists Magazine
Genders	Genders
Genre	Genre
GER	George Eliot Review
Gestus	Gestus: A Quarterly Journal of Brechtian Studies
Gettysburg Review	Gettysburg Review
GG@G	Generative Grammar in Geneva (online)
GHJ	George Herbert Journal
GissingJ	Gissing Journal
GJ	Gutenberg-Jahrbuch
GL	General Linguistics
GL&L	German Life and Letters
GlasR	Glasgow Review
Glossa	Glossa: An International Journal of Linguistics
GLQ	A Journal of Lesbian and Gay Studies (Duke University)
GLS	Grazer Linguistische Studien
GR	Germanic Review
Gramma	Gramma: Journal of Theory and Criticism
Gramma/TTT	Tijdschrift voor Taalwetenschap
GrandS	Grand Street
Granta	Granta
Greyfriar	Greyfriar Siena Studies in Literature

GRM	*Germanisch-Romanische Monatsschrift*
GSE	Gothenberg Studies in English
GSJ	*Gaskell Society Journal*
GSN	*Gaskell Society Newsletter*
GURT	*Georgetown University Round Table on Language and Linguistics*
HamS	*Hamlet Studies*
H&T	*History and Theory*
HardyR	*Hardy Review*
Harvard Law Review	*Harvard Law Review*
HatcherR	*Hatcher Review*
HBS	Henry Bradshaw Society
HC	*Hollins Critic*
HCM	*Hitting Critical Mass: A Journal of Asian American Cultural Criticism*
HE	*History of Education*
HEAT	*HEAT*
Hecate	*Hecate: An Interdisciplinary Journal of Women's Liberation*
HEdQ	*History of Education Quarterly*
HEI	*History of European Ideas*
HeineJ	*Heine Jahrbuch*
HEL	*Histoire Épistémologie Language*
Helios	*Helios*
HEng	*History of the English Language*
Hermathena	*Hermathena: A Trinity College Dublin Review*
HeyJ	*Heythrop Journal*
HFR	*Hayden Ferry Review*
HistJ	*Historical Journal*
History	*History: The Journal of the Historical Association*
HistR	*Historical Research*
HJR	*Henry James Review* (Baton Rouge, LA)
HL	*Historiographia Linguistica*
HLB	*Harvard Library Bulletin*
HLQ	*Huntingdon Library Quarterly*
HLSL	(online)
HNCIS	Harvester New Critical Introductions to Shakespeare
HNR	Harvester New Readings
HOPE	*History of Political Economy*
HPT	*History of Political Thought*
HQ	*Hopkins Quarterly*
HR	*Harvard Review*
HRB	*Hopkins Research Bulletin*
HSci	*History of Science*
HSE	*Hungarian Studies in English*
HSELL	*Hiroshima Studies in English Language and Literature*
HSJ	*Housman Society Journal*
HSL	*University of Hartford Studies in Literature*

HSN	*Hawthorne Society Newsletter*
HSSh	*Hunganan Studies in Shakespeare*
HSSN	*Henry Sweet Society Newsletter*
HT	*History Today*
HTR	*Harvard Theological Review*
HudR	*Hudson Review*
HumeS	*Hume Studies*
HumLov	*Humanistica Lovaniensia: Journal of Neo-Latin Studies*
Humor	*Humor: International Journal of Humor Research*
HUSL	*Hebrew University Studies in Literature and the Arts*
HWJ	*History Workshop*
HWS	History Workshop Series
Hypatia	*Hypatia*
IAL	*Issues in Applied Linguistics*
IAN	*Izvestiia Akademii Nauk SSSR* (Moscow)
I&C	*Ideology and Consciousness*
I&P	*Ideas and Production*
ICAME	*International Computer Archive of Modern and Medieval English*
ICS	*Illinois Classical Studies*
IEEETrans	*IEEE Transactions on Professional Communications*
IF	*Indogermanische Forschungen*
IFR	*International Fiction Review*
IGK	*Irland: Gesellschaft und Kultur*
IJAES	*International Journal of Arabic-English Studies*
IJAL	*International Journal of Applied Linguistics*
IJB	*International Journal of Bilingualism*
IJBEB	*International Journal of Bilingual Education & Bilingualism*
IJCL	*International Journal of Corpus Linguistics*
IJCT	*International Journal of the Classical Tradition*
IJECS	*Indian Journal for Eighteenth-Century Studies*
IJES	*Indian Journal of English Studies*
IJL	*International Journal of Lexicography*
IJPR	*International Journal for Philosophy of Religion*
IJSL	*International Journal of the Sociology of Language*
IJSS	*Indian Journal of Shakespeare Studies*
IJWS	*International Journal of Women's Studies*
ILR	*Indian Literary Review*
ILS	*Irish Literary Supplement*
Imago	*Imago: New Writing*
IMB	*International Medieval Bibliography*
Imprimatur	*Imprimatur*
Indexer	*Indexer*
IndH	*Indian Horizons*
IndL	*Indian Literature*
InG	*In Geardagum: Essays on Old and Middle English Language and Literature*

Inklings	*Inklings: Jahrbuch für Literatur and Ästhetik*
Ioc	*Index to Censorship*
Inquiry	*Inquiry: An Interdisciplinary Journal of Philosophy*
Interlink	*Interlink*
Interpretation	*Interpretation*
Interventions	*Interventions: The International Journal of Postcolonial Studies*
IowaR	*Iowa Review*
IRAL	*IRAL: International Review of Applied Linguistics in Language Teaching*
Iris	*Iris: A Journal of Theory on Image and Sound*
IS	*Italian Studies*
ISh	*Independent Shavian*
ISJR	*Iowa State Journal of Research*
Island	*Island Magazine*
Islands	*Islands*
Isle	*Interdisciplinary Studies in Literature and Environment*
ISR	*Irish Studies Review*
IUR	*Irish University Review: A Journal of Irish Studies*
JAAC	*Journal of Aesthetics and Art Criticism*
JAAR	*Journal of the American Academy of Religion*
Jacket	*Jacket*
JADT	*Journal of American Drama and Theatre*
JAF	*Journal of American Folklore*
JafM	*Journal of African Marxists*
JAIS	*Journal of Anglo-Italian Studies*
JAL	*Journal of Australian Literature*
JamC	*Journal of American Culture*
JAmH	*Journal of American History*
JAmS	*Journal of American Studies*
JAPC	*Journal of Asian Pacific Communication*
JArabL	*Journal of Arabic Literature*
JAS	*Journal of Australian Studies*
JASAL	*Journal of the Association for the Study of Australian Literature*
JAStT	*Journal of American Studies of Turkey*
JBeckS	*Journal of Beckett Studies*
JBS	*Journal of British Studies*
JBSSJ	*Journal of the Blake Society at St James*
JCAKSU	*Journal of the College of Arts* (King Saud University)
JCanL	*Journal of Canadian Literature*
JCC	*Journal of Canadian Culture*
JCF	*Journal of Canadian Fiction*
JChL	*Journal of Child Language*
JCL	*Journal of Commonwealth Literature*
JCP	*Journal of Canadian Poetry*
JCPCS	*Journal of Commonwealth and Postcolonial Studies*
JCSJ	*John Clare Society Journal*

JCSR	*Journal of Canadian Studies / Revue d'Études Canadiennes*
JCSt	*Journal of Caribbean Studies*
JDECU	*Journal of the Department of English* (Calcutta University)
JDHLS	*D.H. Lawrence: The Journal of the D.H. Lawrence Society*
JDJ	*John Dunne Journal*
JDN	*James Dickey Newsletter*
JDTC	*Journal of Dramatic Theory and Criticism*
JEBS	*Journal of the Early Book Society*
JEDRBU	*Journal of the English Department* (Rabindra Bharati University)
JEGP	*Journal of English and Germanic Philology*
JEH	*Journal of Ecclesiastical History*
JELL	*Journal of English Language and Literature*
JEn	*Journal of English* (Sana'a University)
JEngL	*Journal of English Linguistics*
JENS	*Journal of the Eighteen Nineties Society*
JEP	*Journal of Evolutionary Psychology*
JEPNS	*Journal of the English Place-Name Society*
JES	*Journal of European Studies*
JETS	*Journal of the Evangelical Theological Society*
JFR	*Journal of Folklore Research*
JGE	*Journal of General Education*
JGenS	*Journal of Gender Studies*
JGH	*Journal of Garden History*
JGL	*Journal of Germanic Linguistics*
JGN	*John Gower Newsletter*
JH	*Journal of Homosexuality*
JHI	*Journal of the History of Ideas*
JHLP	*Journal of Historical Linguistics and Philology*
JHP	*Journal of the History of Philosophy*
JHPrag	*Journal of Historical Pragmatics*
JHSex	*Journal of the History of Sexuality*
JHu	*Journal of Humanities*
JHuP	*Journal of Humanistic Psychology*
JIEP	*Journal of Indo-European Perspectives*
JIES	*Journal of Indo-European Studies*
JIL	*Journal of Irish Literature*
JIPA	*Journal of the International Phonetic Association*
JIWE	*Journal of Indian Writing in English*
JJ	*Jamaica Journal*
JJA	*James Joyce Annual*
JJB	*James Joyce Broadsheet*
JJLS	*James Joyce Literary Supplement*
JJQ	*James Joyce Quarterly*
JKS	*Journal of Kentucky Studies*
JL	*Journal of Linguistics*

JLH	*Journal of Library History, Philosophy and Comparative Librarianship*
JLLI	*Journal of Logic, Language and Information*
JLP	*Journal of Linguistics and Politics*
JLS	*Journal of Literary Semanitcs*
JLSP	*Journal of Language and Social Psychology*
JLVSG	*Journal of the Longborough Victorian Studies Group*
JMemL	*Journal of Memory and Language*
JMEMS	*Journal of Medieval and Early Modern Studies*
JMGS	*Journal of Modern Greek Studies*
JMH	*Journal of Medieval History*
JML	*Journal of Modern Literature*
JMMD	*Journal of Multilingual and Multicultural Development*
JMMLA	*Journal of the Midwest Modern Language Association*
JModH	*Journal of Modern History*
JMRS	*Journal of Medieval and Renaissance Studies*
JMS	*Journal of Men's Studies*
JNLH	*Journal of Narrative and Life History*
JNPH	*Journal of Newspaper and Periodical History*
JNT	*Journal of Narrative Theory* (formerly *Technique*)
JNZL	*Journal of New Zealand Literature*
Jouvert	*Jouvert: A Journal of Postcolonial Studies*
JoyceSA	*Joyce Studies Annual*
JP	*Journal of Philosophy*
JPC	*Journal of Popular Culture*
JPCL	*Journal of Pidgin and Creole Languages*
JPhon	*Journal of Phonetics*
JPJ	*Journal of Psychology and Judaism*
JPrag	*Journal of Pragmatics*
JPRAS	*Journal of Pre-Raphaelite and Aesthetic Studies*
JPsyR	*Journal of Psycholinguistic Research*
JQ	*Journalism Quarterly*
JR	*Journal of Religion*
JRAHS	*Journal of the Royal Australian Historical Society*
JRH	*Journal of Religious History*
JRMA	*Journal of the Royal Musical Association*
JRMMRA	*Journal of the Rocky Mountain Medieval and Renaissance Association*
JRSA	*Journal of the Royal Society of Arts*
JRUL	*Journal of the Rutgers University Libraries*
JSA	*Journal of the Society of Archivists*
JSaga	*Journal of the Faculty of Liberal Arts and Science* (Saga University)
JSAS	*Journal of Southern African Studies*
JScholP	*Journal of Scholarly Publishing*
JSem	*Journal of Semantics*
JSoc	*Journal of Sociolinguistics*
JSSE	*Journal of the Short Story in English*

JSTWS	*Journal of the Sylvia Townsend Warner Society*
JTheoS	*Journal of Theological Studies*
JVC	*Journal of Victorian Culture*
JWCI	*Journal of the Warburg and Courtauld Institutes*
JWH	*Journal of Women's History*
JWIL	*Journal of West Indian Literature*
JWMS	*Journal of the William Morris Society*
JWSL	*Journal of Women's Studies in Literature*
KanE	*Kansas English*
KanQ	*Kansas Quarterly*
KB	*Kavya Bharati*
KCLMS	King's College London Medieval Series
KCS	*Kobe College Studies* (Japan)
KJ	*Kipling Journal*
KN	*Kwartalnik Neoflologiczny* (Warsaw)
KompH	*Komparatistische Hefte*
Kotare	*Kotare: New Zealand Notes and Queries*
KPR	*Kentucky Philological Review*
KR	*Kenyon Review*
KSJ	*Keats–Shelley Journal*
KSR	*Keats–Shelley Review*
Kuka	*Kuka: Journal of Creative and Critical Writing* (Zaria, Nigeria)
Kunapipi	*Kunapipi*
KWS	*Key-Word Studies in Chaucer*
L&A	*Literature and Aesthetics*
L&B	*Literature and Belief*
L&C	*Language and Communication*
L&E	*Linguistics and Education: An International Research Journal*
Landfall	*Landfall: A New Zealand Quarterly*
L&H	*Literature and History*
L&L	*Language and Literature*
L&LC	*Literary and Linguistic Computing*
L&M	*Literature and Medicine*
L&P	*Literature and Psychology*
L&S	*Language and Speech*
L&T	*Literature and Theology: An Interdisciplinary Journal of Theory and Criticism*
L&U	*Lion and the Unicorn: A Critical Journal of Children's Literature*
Lang&S	*Language and Style*
LangF	*Language Forum*
LangQ	*USF Language Quarterly*
LangR	*Language Research*
LangS	*Language Sciences*
Language	*Language* (Linguistic Society of America)
LanM	*Les Langues Modernes*

LATR	*Latin American Theatre Review*
LaTrobe	*La Trobe Journal*
LB	*Leuvense Bijdragen*
LBR	*Luso-Brazilian Review*
LCrit	*Literary Criterion* (Mysore, India)
LCUT	*Library Chronicle* (University of Texas at Austin)
LDOCE	*Longman Dictionary of Contemporary English*
LeedsSE	*Leeds Studies in English*
Legacy	*Legacy: A Journal of Nineteenth-Century American Women Writers*
L'EpC	*L'Epoque Conradienne*
LeS	*Lingua e Stile*
Lexicographica	*Lexicographica: International Annual for Lexicography*
Lexicography	*Lexicography*
LFQ	*Literature/Film Quarterly*
LH	*Library History*
LHY	*Literary Half-Yearly*
Library	*Library*
LibrQ	*Library Quarterly*
LIN	*Linguistics in the Netherlands*
LingA	*Linguistic Analysis*
Ling&P	*Linguistics and Philosophy*
Ling&Philol	*Linguistics and Philology*
LingB	*Linguistische Berichte*
LingI	*Linguistic Inquiry*
LingInv	*Linvisticæ Investigationes*
LingP	*Linguistica Pragensia*
Lingua	*Lingua: International Review of General Linguistics*
Linguistics	*Linguistics*
Linguistique	*La Linguistique*
LiNQ	*Literature in Northern Queensland*
LIT	*LIT: Literature, Interpretation, Theory*
LitH	*Literary Horizons*
LitI	*Literary Imagination: The Review of the Association of Literary Scholars and Critics*
LitR	*Literary Review: An International Journal of Contemporary Writing*
LittPrag	*Litteraria Pragensia: Studies in Literature and Culture*
LJCS	*London Journal of Canadian Studies*
LJGG	*Literaturwissenschaftliches Jahrbuch im Aufrage der Görres-Gesellschaft*
LJHum	*Lamar Journal of the Humanities*
LMag	*London Magazine*
LockeN	*Locke Newsletter*
LocusF	*Locus Focus*
LongR	*Long Room: Bulletin of the Friends of the Library* (Trinity College, Dublin)
Lore&L	*Lore and Language*

LP	*Lingua Posnaniensis*
LPLD	*Liverpool Papers in Language and Discourse*
LPLP	*Language Problems and Language Planning*
LR	*Les Lettres Romanes*
LRB	*London Review of Books*
LSE	Lund Studies in English
LSLD	Liverpool Studies in Language and Discourse
LSoc	*Language in Society*
LSp	*Language and Speech*
LST	Longman Study Texts
LTM	Leeds Texts and Monographs
LTP	*LTP: Journal of Literature Teaching Politics*
LTR	*London Theatre Record*
LuK	*Literatur und Kritik*
LVC	*Language Variation and Change*
LWU	*Literatur in Wissenschaft und Unterricht*
M&Lang	*Mind and Language*
MÆ	*Medium Ævum*
MAEL	Macmillan Anthologies of English Literature
MaComère	*MaComère*
MagL	*Magazine Littéraire*
Mana	*Mana*
MAS	*Modern Asian Studies*
M&H	*Medievalia et Humanistica*
M&L	*Music and Letters*
M&N	*Man and Nature / L'Homme et la Nature: Proceedings of the Canadian Society for Eighteenth-Century Studies*
Manuscripta	*Manuscripta*
MAR	*Mid-American Review*
Margin	*Margin*
MarkhamR	*Markham Review*
Matatu	*Matatu*
Matrix	*Matrix*
MBL	*Modern British Literature*
MC&S	*Media, Culture and Society*
MCI	Modern Critical Interpretations
MCJNews	*Milton Centre of Japan News*
McNR	*McNeese Review*
MCRel	*Mythes, Croyances et Religions dans le Monde Anglo-Saxon*
MCV	Modern Critical Views
MD	*Modern Drama*
ME	*Medieval Encounters*
Meanjin	*Meanjin*
MED	*Middle English Dictionary*
MedFor	*Medieval Forum* (online)
Mediaevalia	*Mediaevalia: A Journal of Mediaeval Studies*
MedPers	*Medieval Perspectives*

MELUS	*MELUS: The Journal of the Society of Multi-Ethnic Literature of the United States*
Meridian	*Meridian*
MESN	*Mediaeval English Studies Newsletter*
MET	Middle English Texts
METh	*Medieval English Theatre*
MFF	*Medieval Feminist Forum* (formerly *Medieval Feminist Newsletter*)
MFN	*Medieval Feminist Newsletter* (now *Medieval Feminist Forum*)
MFS	*Modern Fiction Studies*
MH	*Malahat Review*
MHL	Macmillan History of Literature
MHLS	*Mid-Hudson Language Studies*
MichA	*Michigan Academician*
MiltonQ	*Milton Quarterly*
MiltonS	*Milton Studies*
MinnR	*Minnesota Review*
MissQ	*Mississippi Quarterly*
MissR	*Missouri Review*
Mittelalter	*Das Mittelalter: Perspektiven Mediavistischer Forschung*
MJLF	*Midwestern Journal of Language and Folklore*
ML	*Music and Letters*
MLAIB	*Modern Language Association International Bibliography*
MLing	*Modelès Linguistiques*
MLJ	*Modern Language Journal*
MLN	*Modern Language Notes*
MLQ	*Modern Language Quarterly*
MLR	*Modern Language Review*
MLRev	*Malcolm Lowry Review*
MLS	*Modern Language Studies*
M/M	*Modernism/Modernity*
MMD	Macmillan Modern Dramatists
MMG	Macmillan Master Guides
MMisc	*Midwestern Miscellany*
MOCS	*Magazine of Cultural Studies*
ModA	*Modern Age: A Quarterly Review*
ModET	*Modern English Teacher*
ModM	*Modern Masters*
ModSp	*Moderne Sprachen*
Mo/Mo	*Modernism/Modernity*
Monist	*Monist*
MonSP	*Monash Swift Papers*
Month	*Month: A Review of Christian Thought and World Affairs*
MOR	*Mount Olive Review*
Moreana	*Moreana: Bulletin Thomas More* (Angers, France)
Mosaic	*Mosaic: A Journal for the Interdisciplinary Study of Literature*

MoyA	*Moyen Age*
MP	*Modern Philology*
MPHJ	*Middlesex Polytechnic History Journal*
MPR	*Mervyn Peake Review*
MQ	*Midwest Quarterly*
MQR	*Michigan Quarterly Review*
MR	*Massachusetts Review*
MRDE	*Medieval and Renaissance Drama in England*
MRTS	Medieval and Renaissance Texts and Studies
MS	*Mediaeval Studies*
MSC	Malone Society Collections
MSE	*Massachusetts Studies in English*
MSEx	*Melville Society Extracts*
MSh	Macmillan Shakespeare
MSNH	Mémoires de la Société Néophilologique de Helsinki
MSpr	*Moderna Språk*
MSR	Malone Society Reprints
MSSN	*Medieval Sermon Studies Newsletter*
MT	*Musical Times*
MTJ	*Mark Twain Journal*
MusR	*Music Review*
MW	*Muslim World* (Hartford, CT)
MysticsQ	*Mystics Quarterly*
Mythlore	*Mythlore: A Journal of J.R.R. Tolkein, C.S. Lewis, Charles Williams, and the Genres of Myth and Fantasy Studies*
NA	*Nuova Antologia*
Names	*Names: Journal of the American Name Society*
NAmR	*North American Review*
N&F	*Notes & Furphies*
N&Q	*Notes and Queries*
Narrative	*Narrative*
Navasilu	*Navasilu*
NB	*Namn och Bygd*
NCaS	New Cambridge Shakespeare
NCBEL	*New Cambridge Bibliography of English Literature*
NCC	*Nineteenth-Century Contexts*
NCE	Norton Critical Editions
NCFS	*Nineteenth-Century French Studies*
NCL	*Nineteenth-Century Literature*
NConL	*Notes on Contemporary Literature*
NCP	*Nineteenth-Century Prose*
NCS	New Clarendon Shakespeare
NCSR	New Chaucer Society Readings
NCSTC	Nineteenth-Century Short Title Catalogue
NCStud	*Nineteenth-Century Studies*
NCT	*Nineteenth-Century Theatre*
NDQ	*North Dakota Quarterly*
NegroD	*Negro Digest*

NELS	*North Eastern Linguistic Society*
Neoh	*Neohelicon*
Neophil	*Neophilologus*
NEQ	*New England Quarterly*
NERMS	*New England Review*
NewA	*New African*
NewBR	*New Beacon Review*
NewC	*New Criterion*
New Casebooks	New Casebooks: Contemporary Critical Essays
NewComp	*New Comparison: A Journal of Comparative and General Literary Studies*
NewF	*New Formations*
NewHR	*New Historical Review*
NewR	*New Republic*
NewSt	*Newfoundland Studies*
NewV	*New Voices*
NF	*Neiophilologica Fennica*
NfN	*News from Nowhere*
NFS	*Nottingham French Studies*
NGC	*New German Critique*
NGS	*New German Studies*
NH	*Northern History*
NHR	*Nathaniel Hawthorne Review*
NIS	*Nordic Irish Studies*
NJL	*Nordic Journal of Linguistics*
NL	*Nouvelles Littéraires*
NLAN	*National Library of Australia News*
NL&LT	*Natural Language and Linguistic Theory*
NLH	*New Literary History: A Journal of Theory and Interpretation*
NLitsR	*New Literatures Review*
NLR	*New Left Review*
NLS	*Natural Language Semantics*
NLWJ	*National Library of Wales Journal*
NM	*Neuphilologische Mitteilungen*
NMAL	*NMAL: Notes on Modern American Literature*
NMer	New Mermaids
NMIL	*Notes on Modern Irish Literature*
NMS	*Nottingham Medieval Studies*
NMW	*Notes on Mississippi Writers*
NN	*Nordiska Namenstudier*
NNER	*Northern New England Review*
Nomina	*Nomina: A Journal of Name Studies Relating to Great Britain and Ireland*
NoP	*Northern Perspective*
NOR	*New Orleans Review*
NorfolkA	*Norfolk Archaeology*
NortonCE	Norton Critical Edition

Novel	*Novel: A Forum on Fiction*
NOWELE	*North-Western European Language Evolution*
NPS	New Penguin Shakespeare
NR	*Nassau Review*
NRF	*La Nouvelle Revue Française*
NRRS	*Notes and Records of the Royal Society of London*
NS	*Die neuren Sprachen*
NSS	New Swan Shakespeare
NTQ	*New Theatre Quarterly*
NVSAWC	*Newsletter of the Victorian Studies Association of Western Canada*
NwJ	*Northward Journal*
NWR	*Northwest Review*
NWRev	*New Welsh Review*
NYH	*New York History*
NYLF	New York Literary Forum
NYRB	*New York Review of Books*
NYT	*New York Times*
NYTBR	*New York Times Book Review*
NZB	*New Zealand Books*
NZListener	*New Zealand Listener*
OA	Oxford Authors
OB	*Ord och Bild*
Obsidian	*Obsidian II: Black Literature in Review*
OBSP	Oxford Bibliographical Society Publications
OED	*Oxford English Dictionary*
OENews	*Old English Newsletter*
OET	Oxford English Texts
OH	*Over Here: An American Studies Journal*
OHEL	Oxford History of English Literature
OhR	*Ohio Review*
OLR	*Oxford Literary Review*
OnCan	*Onomastica Canadiana*
OPBS	*Occasional Papers of the Bibliographical Society*
OpenGL	Open Guides to Literature
OpL	*Open Letter*
OPL	Oxford Poetry Library
OPLiLL	*Occasional Papers in Linguistics and Language Learning*
OPSL	*Occasional Papers in Systemic Linguistics*
OralT	*Oral Tradition*
Orbis	*Orbis*
OrbisLit	*Orbis Litterarum*
OS	Oxford Shakespeare
OSS	Oxford Shakespeare Studies
OT	*Oral Tradition*
Outrider	*Outrider: A Publication of the Wyoming State Library*
Overland	*Overland*
PA	*Présence Africaine*

PAAS	Proceedings of the American Antiquarian Society
PacStud	Pacific Studies
Paideuma	Paideuma: A Journal Devoted to Ezra Pound Scholarship
PAJ	Performing Art Journal
P&C	Pragmatics and Cognition
P&CT	Psychoanalysis and Contemporary Thought
P&L	Philosophy and Literature
P&P	Past and Present
P&R	Philosophy and Rhetoric
P&SC	Philosophy and Social Criticism
PAPA	Publications of the Arkansas Philological Association
Papers	Papers: Explorations into Children's Literature
PAPS	Proceedings of the American Philosophical Society
PAR	Performing Arts Resources
Parabola	Parabola: The Magazine of Myth and Tradition
Paragraph	Paragraph: The Journal of the Modern Critical Theory Group
Parergon	Parergon: Bulletin of the Australian and New Zealand Association for Medieval and Renaissance Studies
ParisR	Paris Review
Parnassus	Parnassus: Poetry in Review
PastM	Past Masters
PaterN	Pater Newsletter
PAus	Poetry Australia
PBA	Proceedings of the British Academy
PBerLS	Proceedings of the Berkeley Linguistics Society
PBSA	Papers of the Bibliographical Society of America
PBSC	Papers of the Biographical Society of Canada
PCL	Perspectives on Contemporary Literature
PCLAC	Proceedings of the California Linguistics Association Conference
PCLS	Proceedings of the Comparative Literature Symposium (Lubbock, TX)
PCP	Pacific Coast Philology
PCRev	Popular Culture Review
PCS	Penguin Critical Studies
PEAN	Proceedings of the English Association North
PE&W	Philosophy East and West: A Quarterly of Asian and Comparative Thought
PELL	Papers on English Language and Literature (Japan)
Pequod	Pequod: A Journal of Contemporary Literature and Literary Criticism
Performance	Performance
Peritia	Peritia: Journal of the Medieval Academy of Ireland
Persuasions	Persuasions: Journal of the Jane Austen Society of North America
Philosophy	Philosophy
PHist	Printing History

Phonetica	*Phonetica: International Journal of Speech Science*
PHOS	Publishing History Occasional Series
PhRA	*Philosophical Research Archives*
PhT	*Philosophy Today*
PiL	*Papers in Linguistics*
PIMA	*Proceedings of the Illinois Medieval Association*
PinterR	*Pinter Review*
PJCL	*Prairie Journal of Canadian Literature*
PLL	*Papers on Language and Literature*
PLPLS	*Proceedings of the Leeds Philosophical and Literary Society, Literary and Historical Section*
PM	*Penguin Masterstudies*
PMHB	*Pennsylvania Magazine of History and Biography*
PMLA	*Publications of the Modern Language Association of America*
PMPA	*Proceedings of the Missouri Philological Association*
PNotes	*Pynchon Notes*
PNR	*Poetry and Nation Review*
PoeS	*Poe Studies*
Poetica	*Poetica: Zeitschrift für Sprach- und Literaturwissenschaft* (Amsterdam)
PoeticaJ	*Poetica: An International Journal of Linguistic-Literary Studies* (Tokyo)
Poetics	*Poetics: International Review for the Theory of Literature*
Poétique	*Poétique: Revue de Théorie et d'Analyse Littéraires*
Poetry	*Poetry* (Chicago)
PoetryCR	*Poetry Canada Review*
PoetryR	*Poetry Review*
PoetryW	*Poetry Wales*
POMPA	*Publications of the Mississippi Philological Association*
PostS	*Past Script: Essays in Film and the Humanities*
PoT	*Poetics Today*
PP	Penguin Passnotes
PP	*Philologica Pragensia*
PPMRC	*Proceedings of the International Patristic, Mediaeval and Renaissance Conference*
PPR	*Philosophy and Phenomenological Research*
PQ	*Philological Quarterly*
PQM	*Pacific Quarterly* (Moana)
PR	*Partisan Review*
Pragmatics	*Pragmatics: Quarterly Publication of the International Pragmatics Association*
PrairieF	*Prairie Fire*
Praxis	*Praxis: A Journal of Cultural Criticism*
Prépub	*(Pré)publications*
PRev	*Powys Review*
PRIA	*Proceedings of the Royal Irish Academy*

PRIAA	Publications of the Research Institute of the Abo Akademi Foundation
PRMCLS	*Papers from the Regional Meetings of the Chicago Linguistics Society*
Prospects	*Prospects: An Annual Journal of American Cultural Studies*
Prospero	*Prospero: Journal of New Thinking in Philosophy for Education*
Proteus	*Proteus: A Journal of Ideas*
Proverbium	*Proverbium*
PrS	*Prairie Schooner*
PSt	*Prose Studies*
PsyArt	*Psychological Study of the Arts* (hyperlink journal)
PsychR	*Psychological Reports*
PTBI	Publications of the Sir Thomas Browne Institute
PubH	*Publishing History*
PULC	*Princeton University Library Chronicle*
PURBA	*Panjab University Research Bulletin (Arts)*
PVR	*Platte Valley Review*
PWC	*Pickering's Women's Classics*
PY	*Phonology Yearbook*
QDLLSM	*Quaderni del Dipartimento e Lingue e Letterature Straniere Moderne*
QI	*Quaderni d'Italianistica*
QJS	*Quarterly Journal of Speech*
QLing	*Quantitative Linguistics*
QQ	*Queen's Quarterly*
QR	*Queensland Review*
QRFV	*Quarterly Review of Film and Video*
Quadrant	*Quadrant* (Sydney)
Quarendo	*Quarendo*
Quarry	*Quarry*
QWERTY	*QWERTY: Arts, Littératures, et Civilisations du Monde Anglophone*
RadP	*Radical Philosophy*
RAL	*Research in African Literatures*
RALS	*Resources for American Literary Study*
Ramus	*Ramus: Critical Studies in Greek and Roman Literature*
R&C	*Race and Class*
R&L	*Religion and Literature*
Raritan	*Raritan: A Quarterly Review*
Rask	*Rask: International tidsskrift for sprong og kommunikation*
RB	*Revue Bénédictine*
RBPH	*Revue Belge de Philologie et d'Histoire*
RCEI	*Revista Canaria de Estudios Ingleses*
RCF	*Review of Contemporary Fiction*
RCPS	*Romantic Circles Praxis Series* (online)
RDN	*Renaissance Drama Newsletter*

RE	*Revue d'Esthétique*
ReAL	*Re: Artes Liberales*
REALB	*REAL: The Yearbook of Research in English and American Literature* (Berlin)
ReAr	*Religion and the Arts*
RecBucks	*Records of Buckinghamshire*
RecL	*Recovery Literature*
RECTR	*Restoration and Eighteenth-Century Theatre Research*
RedL	*Red Letters: A Journal of Cultural Politics*
REED	Records of Early English Drama
REEDN	*Records of Early English Drama Newsletter*
ReFr	*Revue Française*
Reinardus	*Reinardus*
REL	*Review of English Literature* (Kyoto)
RELC	*RELC Journal: A Journal of Language Teaching and Research in Southeast Asia*
Ren&R	*Renaissance and Reformation*
Renascence	*Renascence: Essays on Values in Literature*
RenD	*Renaissance Drama*
Renfor	*Renaissance Forum* (online)
RenP	*Renaissance Papers*
RenQ	*Renaissance Quarterly*
Rep	*Representations*
RePublica	*RePublica*
RES	*Review of English Studies*
Restoration	*Restoration: Studies in English Literary Culture, 1660–1700*
Rev	*Review* (Blacksburg, VA)
RevAli	*Revista Alicantina de Estudios Ingleses*
Revels	Revels Plays
RevelsCL	Revels Plays Companion Library
RevelsSE	Revels Student Editions
RevR	Revolution and Romanticism, 1789–1834
RFEA	*Revue Française d'Études Américaines*
RFR	*Robert Frost Review*
RG	*Revue Générale*
RH	*Recusant History*
Rhetorica	*Rhetorica: A Journal of the History of Rhetoric*
Rhetorik	*Rhetorik: Ein Internationales Jahrbuch*
RHist	*Rural History*
RHL	*Revue d'Histoire Littéraire de la France*
RHT	*Revue d'Histoire du Théâtre*
RIB	*Revista Interamericana de Bibliografía: Inter-American Reviews of Bibliography*
Ricardian	*Ricardian: Journal of the Richard III Society*
RL	Rereading Literature
RLAn	*Romance Languages Annual*
RLC	*Revue de Littérature Comparée*

RLing	*Rivista di Linguistica*
RLit	*Russian Literature*
RLM	*La Revue des Lettres Modernes: Histoire des Idées des Littératures*
RLMC	*Rivista di Letterature Moderne e Comparate*
RLT	*Russian Literature Triquarterly*
RM	*Rethinking Marxism*
RMR	*Rocky Mountain Review of Language and Literature*
RM	*Renaissance and Modern Studies*
RMSt	*Reading Medieval Studies*
Romania	*Romania*
Romanticism	*Romanticism*
RomN	*Romance Notes*
RomQ	*Romance Quarterly*
RomS	*Romance Studies*
RoN	*Romanticism on the Net*
ROO	*Room of One's Own: A Feminist Journal of Literature and Criticism*
RORD	*Research Opportunities in Renaissance Drama*
RPT	Russian Poetics in Translation
RQ	*Riverside Quarterly*
RR	*Romanic Review*
RRDS	Regents Renaissance Drama Series
RRestDS	Regents Restoration Drama Series
RS	*Renaissance Studies*
RSQ	*Rhetoric Society Quarterly*
RSV	*Rivista di Studi Vittoriani*
RUO	*Revue de l'Université d'Ottawa*
RUSEng	*Rajasthan University Studies in English*
RuskN	*Ruskin Newsletter*
RUUL	*Reports from the Uppsala University Department of Linguistics*
R/WT	*Readerly/Writerly Texts*
SAC	*Studies in the Age of Chaucer*
SAD	*Studies in American Drama, 1945–Present*
SAF	*Studies in American Fiction*
Saga-Book	*Saga-Book (Viking Society for Northern Research)*
Sagetrieb	*Sagatrieb: A Journal Devoted to Poets in the Pound–H.D.–Williams Tradition*
SAIL	*Studies in American Indian Literatures: The Journal of the Association for the Study of American Indian Literatures*
SAJL	*Studies in American Jewish Literature*
SAJMRS	*South African Journal of Medieval and Renaissance Studies*
Sal	*Salmagrundi: A Quarterly of the Humanities and Social Sciences*
SALCT	*SALCT: Studies in Australian Literature, Culture and Thought*

S&S	*Sight and Sound*
SAntS	*Studia Anthroponymica Scandinavica*
SAP	*Studia Anglica Posnaniensia*
SAQ	*South Atlantic Quarterly*
SAR	*Studies in the American Renaissance*
SARB	*South African Review of Books*
SASLC	Studies in Anglo-Saxon Literature and Culture
SatR	*Saturday Review*
SB	*Studies in Bibliography*
SBHC	*Studies in Browning and his Circle*
SC	*Seventeenth Century*
Scan	*Scandinavica: An International Journal of Scandinavian Studies*
ScanS	*Scandinavian Studies*
SCel	*Studia Celtica*
SCER	*Society for Critical Exchange Report*
Schuylkill	*Schuylkill: A Creative and Critical Review* (Temple University)
SCJ	*Sixteenth Century Journal*
SCL	*Studies in Canadian Literature*
ScLJ	*Scottish Literary Journal: A Review of Studies in Scottish Language and Literature*
ScLJ(S)	*Scottish Literary Journal Supplement*
SCLOP	*Society for Caribbean Linguistics Occasional Papers*
SCN	*Seventeenth-Century News*
ScottN	*Scott Newsletter*
SCR	*South Carolina Review*
Screen	*Screen* (London)
SCRev	*South Central Review*
Scriblerian	*Scriblerian and the Kit Cats: A Newsjournal Devoted to Pope, Swift, and their Circle*
Scripsi	*Scripsi*
Scriptorium	*Scriptorium: International Review of Manuscript Studies*
ScTh	*Scottish Journal of Theology*
SD	*Social Dynamics*
SDR	*South Dakota Review*
SECC	*Studies in Eighteenth-Century Culture*
SECOLR	*SECOL Review: Southeastern Conference on Linguistics*
SED	*Survey of English Dialects*
SEDERI	*Journal of the Spanish Society for Renaissance Studies (Sociedad Española de Estudios Renacentistas Ingleses)*
SEEJ	*Slavic and East European Journal*
SEL	*Studies in English Literature, 1500–1900* (Rice University)
SELing	*Studies in English Linguistics* (Tokyo)
SELit	*Studies in English Literature* (Tokyo)
SELL	*Studies in English Language and Literature*
Sem	*Semiotica: Journal of the International Association for Semiotic Studies*

Semiosis	*Semiosis: Internationale Zeitschrift für Semiotik und Ästhetik*
SER	*Studien zur Englischen Romantik*
Seven	*Seven: An Anglo-American Literary Review*
SF&R	Scholars' Facsimiles and Reprints
SFic	*Science Fiction: A Review of Speculative Literature*
SFNL	*Shakespeare on Film Newsletter*
SFQ	*Southern Folklore Quarterly*
SFR	*Stanford French Review*
SFS	*Science-Fiction Studies*
SH	*Studia Hibernica* (Dublin)
ShakB	*Shakespeare Bulletin*
ShakS	*Shakespeare Studies* (New York)
Shandean	*Shandean*
Sh&Sch	*Shakespeare and Schools*
ShawR	*Shaw: The Annual of Bernard Shaw Studies*
Shenandoah	*Shenandoah*
SherHR	*Sherlock Holmes Review*
ShIntY	*Shakespeare International Yearbook*
Shiron	*Shiron*
ShJE	*Shakespeare Jahrbuch* (Weimar)
ShJW	*Deutsche Shakespeare-Gesellschaft West Jahrbuch* (Bochum)
ShLR	*Shoin Literary Review*
ShN	*Shakespeare Newsletter*
SHR	*Southern Humanities Review*
ShS	*Shakespeare Survey*
ShSA	*Shakespeare in Southern Africa*
ShStud	*Shakespeare Studies* (Tokyo)
SHW	*Studies in Hogg and his World*
ShY	*Shakespeare Yearbook*
SiAF	*Studies in American Fiction*
SIcon	*Studies in Iconography*
SidJ	*Sidney Journal*
SidN	*Sidney Newsletter and Journal*
Signs	*Signs: Journal of Women in Culture and Society*
SiHoLS	*Studies in the History of the Language Sciences*
SiM	*Studies in Medievalism*
SIM	*Studies in Music*
SiP	Shakespeare in Performance
SiPr	Shakespeare in Production
SiR	*Studies in Romanticism*
SJS	*San José Studies*
SL	*Studia Linguistica*
SLang	*Studies in Language*
SLCS	*Studies in Language Companion Series*
SLI	*Studies in the Literary Imagination*
SLJ	*Southern Literary Journal*

SLRev	*Stanford Literature Review*
SLSc	*Studies in the Linguistic Sciences*
SMC	*Studies in Medieval Culture*
SMed	*Studi Medievali*
SMELL	*Studies in Medieval English Language and Literature*
SMLit	*Studies in Mystical Literature* (Taiwan)
SMRH	*Studies in Medieval and Renaissance History*
SMRT	*Studies in Medieval and Renaissance Teaching*
SMS	*Studier i Modern Språkvetenskap*
SMy	*Studia Mystica*
SN	*Studia Neophilologica*
SNNTS	*Studies in the Novel* (North Texas State University)
SO	*Shakespeare Originals*
SOA	*Sydsvenska Ortnamnssällskapets Årsskrift*
SoAR	*South Atlantic Review*
SoC	*Senses of Cinema* (online)
Sociocrit	*Sociocriticism*
Socioling	*Sociolinguistica*
SocN	*Sociolinguistics*
SocSem	*Social Semiotics*
SocT	*Social Text*
SohoB	Soho Bibliographies
SoQ	*Southern Quarterly*
SoR	*Southern Review* (Baton Rouge, LA)
SoRA	*Southern Review* (Adelaide)
SoSt	*Southern Studies: An Interdisciplinary Journal of the South*
Soundings	*Soundings: An Interdisciplinary Journal*
Southerly	*Southerly: A Review of Australian Literature*
SovL	*Soviet Literature*
SP	*Studies in Philology*
SPAN	*SPAN: Newsletter of the South Pacific Association for Commonwealth Literature and Language Studies*
SPAS	*Studies in Puritan American Spirituality*
SPC	*Studies in Popular Culture*
Spectrum	*Spectrum*
Speculum	*Speculum: A Journal of Medieval Studies*
SPELL	*Swiss Papers in English Language and Literature*
Sphinx	*Sphinx: A Magazine of Literature and Society*
SpM	*Spicilegio Moderno*
SpNL	*Spenser Newsletter*
Sprachwiss	*Sprachwissenschalt*
SpringE	*Spring: The Journal of the e.e. cummings Society*
SPub	*Studies in Publishing*
SPWVSRA	*Selected Papers from the West Virginia Shakespeare and Renaissance Association*
SQ	*Shakespeare Quarterly*
SR	*Sewanee Review*
SRen	*Studies in the Renaissance*

SRSR	*Status Report on Speech Research* (Haskins Laboratories)
SSEL	Stockholm Studies in English
SSELER	Salzburg Studies in English Literature: Elizabethan and Renaissance
SSELJDS	Salzburg Studies in English Literature: Jacobean Drama Studies
SSELPDPT	Salzburg Studies in English Literature: Poetic Drama and Poetic Theory
SSELRR	Salzburg Studies in English Literature: Romantic Reassessment
SSEng	*Sydney Studies in English*
SSF	*Studies in Short Fiction*
SSL	*Studies in Scottish Literature*
SSR	*Scottish Studies Review*
SSt	*Spenser Studies*
SStud	*Swift Studies: The Annual of the Ehrenpreis Center*
Staffrider	*Staffrider*
StaffordS	*Staffordshire Studies*
STAH	*Strange Things Are Happening*
STGM	Studien und Texte zur Geistegeschichte des Mittelalters
StHR	*Stanford Historical Review*
StHum	*Studies in the Humanities*
StIn	*Studi Inglesi*
StLF	*Studi di Letteratura Francese*
StQ	*Steinbeck Quarterly*
StrR	*Structuralist Review*
StTCL	*Studies in Twentieth-Century Literature*
StTW	*Studies in Travel Writing*
StudWF	*Studies in Weird Fiction*
STUF	*Sprachtypologie und Universalienforschung*
Style	*Style* (De Kalb, IL)
SUAS	*Stratford-upon-Avon Studies*
SubStance	*SubStance: A Review of Theory and Literary Criticism*
SUS	*Susquehanna University Studies*
SussexAC	*Sussex Archaeological Collections*
SussexP&P	*Sussex Past & Present*
SVEC	*Studies on Voltaire and the Eighteenth Century*
SWPLL	*Sheffield Working Papers in Language and Linguistics*
SWR	*Southwest Review*
SwR	*Swansea Review: A Journal of Criticism*
Sycamore	*Sycamore*
Symbolism	*Symbolism: An International Journal of Critical Aesthetics*
TA	*Theatre Annual*
Tabu	*Bulletin voor Taalwetenschap, Groningen*
Takahe	*Takahe*
Talisman	*Talisman*
T&C	*Text and Context*
T&L	*Translation and Literature*

T&P	Text and Performance
TAPS	Transactions of the American Philosophical Society
TCBS	Transactions of the Cambridge Bibliographical Society
TCE	Texas College English
TCL	Twentieth-Century Literature
TCS	Theory, Culture and Society: Explorations in Critical Social Science
TCWAAS	Transactions of the Cumberland and Westmorland Antiquarian and Archaeological Society
TD	Themes in Drama
TDR	Drama Review
TEAS	Twayne's English Authors Series
Telos	Telos: A Quarterly Journal of Post-Critical Thought
TennEJ	Tennessee English Journal
TennQ	Tennessee Quarterly
TennSL	Tennessee Studies in Literature
TeReo	Te Reo: Journal of the Linguistic Society of New Zealand
TSLL	Texas Studies in Language and Literature
Text	Text: Transactions of the Society for Textual Scholarship
TH	Texas Humanist
THA	Thomas Hardy Annual
Thalia	Thalia: Studies in Literary Humor
ThC	Theatre Crafts
Theater	Theater
TheatreS	Theatre Studies
Theoria	Theoria: A Journal of Studies in the Arts, Humanities and Social Sciences (Natal)
THES	Times Higher Education Supplement
Thesis	Thesis Eleven
THIC	Theatre History in Canada
THJ	Thomas Hardy Journal
ThN	Thackeray Newsletter
ThoreauQ	Thoreau Quarterly: A Journal of Literary and Philosophical Studies
Thought	Thought: A Review of Culture and Ideas
Thph	Theatrephile
ThreR	Threepenny Review
ThS	Theatre Survey: The American Journal of Theatre History
THSLC	Transactions of the Historic Society of Lancashire and Cheshire
THStud	Theatre History Studies
ThTop	Theatre Topics
THY	Thomas Hardy Yearbook
TiLSM	Trends in Linguistics: Studies and Monographs
TiP	Theory in Practice
Tirra Lirra	Tirra Lirra: The Quarterly Magazine for the Yarra Valley
TJ	Theatre Journal
TJS	Transactions (Johnson Society)

TJAAWP	*Text: Journal of the Australian Association of Writing Programs*
TkR	*Tamkang Review*
TL	*Theoretical Linguistics*
TLR	*Linguistic Review*
TLS	*Times Literary Supplement*
TMLT	*Toronto Medieval Latin Texts*
TN	*Theatre Notebook*
TNWSECS	*Transactions of the North West Society for Eighteenth Century Studies*
TP	*Terzo Programma*
TPLL	*Tilbury Papers in Language and Literature*
TPQ	*Text and Performance Quarterly*
TPr	*Textual Practice*
TPS	*Transactions of the Philological Society*
TR	*Theatre Record*
Traditio	*Traditio: Studies in Ancient and Medieval History, Thought, and Religion*
Transition	*Transition*
TRB	*Tennyson Research Bulletin*
TRHS	*Transactions of the Royal Historical Society*
TRI	*Theatre Research International*
TriQ	*TriQuarterly*
Trivium	*Trivium*
Tropismes	*Tropismes*
TSAR	*Toronto South Asian Review*
TSB	*Thoreau Society Bulletin*
TSLang	Typological Studies in Language
TSLL	*Texas Studies in Literature and Language*
TSWL	*Tulsa Studies in Women's Literature*
TTR	*Trinidad and Tobago Review*
TUSAS	Twayne's United States Authors Series
TWAS	Twayne's World Authors Series
TWBR	*Third World Book Review*
TWQ	*Third World Quarterly*
TWR	*Thomas Wolfe Review*
Txt	*Text: An Interdisciplinary Annual of Textual Studies*
TYDS	*Transactions of the Yorkshire Dialect Society*
Typophiles	Typophiles (New York)
UCrow	*Upstart Crow*
UCTSE	*University of Cape Town Studies in English*
UCWPL	*UCL Working Papers in Linguistics*
UDR	*University of Drayton Review*
UE	*Use of English*
UEAPL	*UEA Papers in Linguistics*
UES	*Unisa English Studies*
Ufahamu	*Ufahamu*
ULR	*University of Leeds Review*

UMSE	*University of Mississippi Studies in English*
Untold	*Untold*
UOQ	*University of Ottawa Quarterly*
URM	*Ultimate Reality and Meaning: Interdisciplinary Studies in the Philosophy of Understanding*
USSE	*University of Saga Studies in English*
UtopST	*Utopian Studies*
UTQ	*University of Toronto Quarterly*
UWR	*University of Windsor Review*
VCT	Les Voies de la Création Théâtrale
VEAW	Varieties of English around the World
Verbatim	*Verbatim: The Language Quarterly*
VIA	*VIA: The Journal of the Graduate School of Fine Arts* (University of Pennsylvania)
Viator	*Viator: Medieval and Renaissance Studies*
Views	*Viennese English Working Papers*
VIJ	*Victorians Institute Journal*
VLC	*Victorian Literature and Culture*
VN	*Victorian Newsletter*
Voices	*Voices*
VP	*Victorian Poetry*
VPR	*Victorian Periodicals Review*
VQR	*Virginia Quarterly Review*
VR	*Victorian Review*
VS	*Victorian Studies*
VSB	*Victorian Studies Bulletin*
VWM	*Virginia Woolf Miscellany*
WAJ	*Women's Art Journal*
WAL	*Western American Literature*
W&I	*Word and Image*
W&L	*Women and Literature*
W&Lang	*Women and Language*
Wasafiri	*Wasafiri*
WascanaR	*Wascana Review*
WBEP	Wiener Beiträge zur Englischen Philologie
WC	World's Classics
WC	*Wordsworth Circle*
WCR	*West Coast Review*
WCSJ	*Wilkie Collins Society Journal*
WCWR	*William Carlos Williams Review*
Wellsian	*Wellsian: The Journal of the H.G. Wells Society*
WEn	*World Englishes*
Westerly	*Westerly: A Quarterly Review*
WestHR	*West Hills Review: A Walt Whitman Journal*
WF	*Western Folklore*
WHASN	*W.H. Auden Society Newsletter*
WHR	*Western Humanities Review*
WI	*Word and Image*

WLA	Wyndham Lewis Annual
WL&A	War Literature, and the Arts: An International Journal of the Humanities
WLT	World Literature Today
WLWE	World Literature Written in English
WMQ	William and Mary Quarterly
WoHR	Women's History Review
WolfenbütteleB	Wolfenbüttele Beiträge: Aus den Schätzen der Herzog August Bibliothek
Women	Women: A Cultural Review
WorcesterR	Worcester Review
WORD	WORD: Journal of the International Linguistic Association
WQ	Wilson Quarterly
WRB	Women's Review of Books
WS	Women's Studies: An Interdisciplinary Journal
WSIF	Women's Studies: International Forum
WSJour	Wallace Stevens Journal
WSR	Wicazo Sa Review
WTJ	Westminster Theological Journal
WTW	Writers and their Work
WVUPP	West Virginia University Philological Papers
WW	Women's Writing
WWR	Walt Whitman Quarterly Review
XUS	Xavier Review
YCC	Yearbook of Comparative Criticism
YeA	Yeats Annual
YER	Yeats Eliot Review
YES	Yearbook of English Studies
YEuS	Yearbook of European Studies/Annuaire d'Études Européennes
YFS	Yale French Studies
Yiddish	Yiddish
YJC	Yale Journal of Criticism: Interpretation in the Humanities
YLS	Yearbook of Langland Studies
YM	Yearbook of Morphology
YNS	York Note Series
YPL	York Papers in Linguistics
YR	Yale Review
YULG	Yale University Library Gazette
YWES	Year's Work in English Studies
ZAA	Zeitschrift für Anglistik und Amerikanistik
ZCP	Zeitschrift für celtische Philologie
ZDA	Zeitschrift für deutsches Altertum und deutsche Literatur
ZDL	Zeitschrift für Dialektologie und Linguistik
ZGKS	Zeitschrfit für Gesellschaft für Kanada-Studien
ZGL	Zeitschrift für germanistische Linguistik
ZPSK	Zeitschrift für Phonetik, Sprachwissenshaft und Kommunikationsforschung

ZSpr	*Zeitschrift für Sprachwissenshaft*
ZVS	*Zeitschrift für vergleichende Sprachforschung*

Volume numbers are supplied in the text, as are individual issue numbers for journals that are not continuously paginated through the year.

2. Publishers

AAAH	Acta Academiae Åboensis Humaniora, Åbo, Finland
AAH	Australian Academy of Humanities
A&B	Allison & Busby, London
A&R	Angus & Robertson, North Ryde, New South Wales
A&U	Allen & Unwin (now Unwin Hyman)
A&UA	Allen & Unwin, North Sydney, New South Wales
A&W	Almqvist & Wiksell International, Stockholm
AarhusUP	Aarhus UP, Aarhus, Denmark
ABC	ABC Enterprises
ABC CLIO	ABC CLIO Reference Books, Santa Barbara, CA
Abbeville	Abbeville Press, New York
ABDO	Association Bourguignonne de Dialectologie et d'Onom-astique, Dijon
AberdeenUP	Aberdeen UP, Aberdeen
Abhinav	Abhinav Publications, New Delhi
Abingdon	Abingdon Press, Nashville, TN
ABL	Armstrong Browning Library, Waco, TX
Ablex	Ablex Publishing, Norwood, NJ
Åbo	Åbo Akademi, Åbo, Finland
Abrams	Harry N. Abrams, New York
Academia	Academia Press, Melbourne
Academic	Academic Press, London and Orlando, FL
Academy	Academy Press, Dublin
AcademyC	Academy Chicago Publishers, Chicago
AcademyE	Academy Editions, London
Acadiensis	Acadiensis Press, Fredericton, New Brunswick, Canada
ACarS	Association for Caribbean Studies, Coral Gables, FL
ACC	Antique Collectors' Club, Woodbridge, Suffolk
ACCO	ACCO, Leuven, Belgium
ACMRS	Arizona Center for Medieval and Renaissance Studies
ACP	Another Chicago Press, Chicago
ACS	Association for Canadian Studies, Ottawa
Adam Hart	Adam Hart Publishers, London
Adam Matthew	Adam Matthew, Suffolk
Addison-Wesley	Addison-Wesley, Wokingham, Berkshire
ADFA	Australian Defence Force Academy, Department of English
Adosa	Adosa, Clermont-Ferrand, France
AEMS	American Early Medieval Studies

AF	Akademisk Forlag, Copenhagen
Affiliated	Affiliated East–West Press, New Delhi
AFP	Associated Faculty Press, New York
Africana	Africana Publications, New York
A–H	Arnold–Heinemann, New Delhi
Ahriman	Ahriman-Verlag, Freiburg im Breisgau, Germany
AIAS	Australian Institute of Aboriginal Studies, Canberra
Ajanta	Ajanta Publications, Delhi
AK	Akadémiai Kiadó, Budapest
ALA	ALA Editions, Chicago
Al&Ba	Allyn & Bacon, Boston, MA
Albatross	Albatross Books, Sutherland, New South Wales
Albion	Albion, Appalachian State University, Boone, NC
Alderman	Alderman Press, London
Aldwych	Aldwych Press
AligarhMU	Aligarh Muslim University, Uttar Pradesh, India
Alioth	Alioth Press, Beaverton, OR
Allen	W.H. Allen, London
Allied Publishers	Allied Indian Publishers, Lahore and New Delhi
Almond	Almond Press, Sheffield
AM	Aubier Montaigne, Paris
AMAES	Association des Médiévistes Angliciste de l'Enseignement Supérieur, Paris
Amate	Amate Press, Oxford
AmberL	Amber Lane, Oxford
Amistad	Amistad Press, New York
AMP	Aurora Metro Press, London
AMS	AMS Press, New York
AMU	Adam Mickiewicz University, Posnan
Anansi	Anansi Press, Toronto
Anderson-Lovelace	Anderson-Lovelace, Los Altos Hills, CA
Anma Libri	Anma Libri, Saratoga, CA
Antipodes	Antipodes Press, Plimmerton, New Zealand
Anvil	Anvil Press Poetry, London
APA	APA, Maarssen, Netherlands
APH	Associated Publishing House, New Delhi
APL	American Poetry and Literature Press, Philadelphia
APP	Australian Professional Publications, Mosman, New South Wales
Applause	Applause Theatre Book Publishers
Appletree	Appletree Press, Belfast
APS	American Philosophical Society, Philadelphia
Aquarian	Aquarian Press, Wellingborough, Northants
ArborH	Arbor House Publishing, New York
Arcade	Arcade Publishing, New York
Archon	Archon Books, Hamden, CT
ArchP	Architectural Press Books, Guildford, Surrey
ArdenSh	Arden Shakespeare

Ardis	Ardis Publishers, Ann Arbor, MI
Ariel	Ariel Press, London
Aristotle	Aristotle University, Thessaloniki
Ark	Ark Paperbacks, London
Arkona	Arkona Forlaget, Aarhus, Denmark
Arlington	Arlington Books, London
Arnold	Edward Arnold, London
ArnoldEJ	E.J. Arnold & Son, Leeds
ARP	Australian Reference Publications, N. Balwyn, Victoria
Arrow	Arrow Books, London
Arsenal	Arsenal Pulp Press
Artmoves	Artmoves, Parkdale, Victoria
ASAL	Association for the Study of Australian Literature
ASB	Anglo-Saxon Books, Middlesex
ASECS	American Society for Eighteenth-Century Studies, c/o Ohio State University, Columbus
Ashfield	Ashfield Press, London
Ashgate	Ashgate, Brookfield, VT
Ashton	Ashton Scholastic
Aslib	Aslib, London
ASLS	Association for Scottish Literary Studies, Aberdeen
ASP	Australian Scholarly Publishing
ASU	Arizona State University, Tempe
Atheneum	Atheneum Publishers, New York
Athlone	Athlone Press, London
Atlantic	Atlantic Publishers, Darya Ganj, New Delhi
Atlas	Atlas Press, London
Attic	Attic Press, Dublin
AuBC	Australian Book Collector
AucklandUP	Auckland UP, Auckland
AUG	Acta Universitatis Gothoburgensis, Sweden
AUP	Associated University Presses, London and Toronto
AUPG	Academic & University Publishers, London
Aurum	Aurum Press, London
Auslib	Auslib Press, Adelaide
AUU	Acta Universitatis Umensis, Umeå, Sweden
AUUp	Acta Universitatis Upsaliensis, Uppsala
Avebury	Avebury Publishing, Aldershot, Hampshire
Avero	Avero Publications, Newcastle upon Tyne
A-V Verlag	A-V Verlag, Franz Fischer, Augsburg, Germany
AWP	Africa World Press, Trenton, NJ
Axelrod	Axelrod Publishing, Tampa Bay, FL
BA	British Academy, London
BAAS	British Association for American Studies, c/o University of Keele
Bagel	August Bagel Verlag, Dusseldorf
Bahri	Bahri Publications, New Delhi
Bamberger	Bamberger Books, Flint, MI

B&B	Boydell & Brewer, Woodbridge, Suffolk
B&J	Barrie & Jenkins, London
B&N	Barnes & Noble, Totowa, NJ
B&O	Burns & Oates, Tunbridge Wells, Kent
B&S	Michael Benskin and M.L. Samuels, Middle English Dialect Project, University of Edinburgh
BAR	British Archaelogical Reports, Oxford
Barn Owl	Barn Owl Books, Taunton, Somerset
Barnes	A.S. Barnes, San Diego, CA
Barr Smith	Barr Smith Press, Barr Smith Library, University of Adelaide
Bath UP	Bath UP, Bath
Batsford	B.T. Batsford, London
Bayreuth	Bayreuth African Studies, University of Bayreuth, Germany
BBC	BBC Publications, London
BClarkL	Bruccoli Clark Layman
BCP	Bristol Classical Press, Bristol
Beacon	Beacon Press, Boston, MA
Beck	C.H. Beck'sche Verlagsbuchandlung, Munich
Becket	Becket Publications, London
Belin	Éditions Belin, Paris
Belknap	Belknap Press, Cambridge, MA
Belles Lettres	Société d'Édition les Belles Lettres, Paris
Bellew	Bellew Publishing, London
Bellflower	Belflower Press, Case University, Cleveland, OH
Benjamins	John Benjamins, Amsterdam
BenjaminsNA	John Benjamins North America, Philadelphia
BennC	Bennington College, Bennington, VT
Berg	Berg Publishers, Oxford
BFI	British Film Institute, London
BGUP	Bowling Green University Popular Press, Bowling Green, OH
BibS	Bibliographical Society, London
Bilingual	Bilingual Press, Arizona State University, Tempe
Bingley	Clive Bingley, London
Binnacle	Binnacle Press, London
Biografia	Biografia Publishers, London
Birkbeck	Birkbeck College, University of London
Bishopsgate	Bishopsgate Press, Tonbridge, Kent
BL	British Library, London
Black	Adam & Charles Black, London
Black Cat	Black Cat Press, Blackrock, Eire
Blackie	Blackie & Son, Glasgow
Black Moss	Black Moss, Windsor, Ontario
Blackstaff	Blackstaff Press, Belfast
Black Swan	Black Swan, Curtin, UT
Blackwell	Basil Blackwell, Oxford

BlackwellR	Blackwell Reference, Oxford
Blackwood	Blackwood, Pillans & Wilson, Edinburgh
Bl&Br	Blond & Briggs, London
Blandford	Blandford Press, London
Blaue Eule	Verlag die Blaue Eule, Essen
Bloodaxe	Bloodaxe Books, Newcastle upon Tyne
Bloomsbury	Bloomsbury Publishing, London
Blubber Head	Blubber Head Press, Hobart
BM	Bobbs-Merrill, New York
BMP	British Museum Publications, London
Bodleian	Bodleian Library, Oxford
Bodley	Bodley Head, London
Bogle	Bogle L'Ouverture Publications, London
BoiseSUP	Boise State UP, Boise, Idaho
Book Guild	Book Guild, Lewes, E. Sussex
BookplateS	Bookplate Society, Edgbaston, Birmingham
Boombana	Boombana Press, Brisbane, Queensland
Borealis	Borealis Press, Ottawa
Borgo	Borgo Press, San Bernardino, CA
BostonAL	Boston Athenaeum Library, Boxton, MA
Bouma	Bouma's Boekhuis, Groningen, Netherlands
Bowker	R.R. Bowker, New Providence, NJ
Boyars	Marion Boyars, London and Boston, MA
Boydell	Boydell Press, Woodbridge, Suffolk
Boyes	Megan Boyes, Allestree, Derbyshire
Br&S	Brandl & Schlesinger
Bran's Head	Bran's Head Books, Frome, Somerset
Braumüller	Wilhelm Braumüller,Vienna
Breakwater	Breakwater Books, St John's, Newfoundland
Brentham	Brentham Press, St Albans, Hertfordshire
Brepols	Brepols, Turnhout, Belgium
Brewer	D.S. Brewer, Woodbridge, Suffolk
Brewin	Brewin Books, Studley, Warwicks
Bridge	Bridge Publishing, S. Plainfield, NJ
Brill	E.J. Brill, Leiden
BrillA	Brill Academic Publishers
Brilliance	Brilliance Books, London
Broadview	Broadview, London, Ontario and Lewiston, NY
Brookside	Brookside Press, London
Browne	Sinclair Browne, London
Brownstone	Brownstone Books, Madison, IN
BrownUP	Brown UP, Providence, RI
Brynmill	Brynmill Press, Harleston, Norfolk
BSA	Bibliographical Society of America
BSB	Black Swan Books, Redding Ridge, CT
BSP	Black Sparrow Press, Santa Barbara, CA
BSU	Ball State University, Muncie, IN
BuckUP	Bucknell UP, Lewisburg, PA

Bulzoni	Bulzoni Editore, Rome
BUP	Birmingham University Press
Burnett	Burnett Books, London
Buske	Helmut Buske, Hamburg
Butterfly	Butterfly Books, San Antonio, TX
BWilliamsNZ	Bridget Williams Books, Wellington, New Zealand
CA	Creative Arts Book, Berkeley, CA
CAAS	Connecticut Academy of Arts and Sciences, New Haven
CAB International	Centre for Agriculture and Biosciences International, Wallingford, Oxfordshire
Cadmus	Cadmus Editions, Tiburon, CA
Cairns	Francis Cairns, University of Leeds
Calaloux	Calaloux Publications, Ithaca, NY
Calder	John Calder, London
CALLS	Centre for Australian Language and Literature Studies, English Department, Universty of New England, New South Wales
Camden	Camden Press, London
C&G	Carroll & Graf, New York
C&W	Chatto & Windus, London
Canongate	Canongate Publishing, Edinburgh
Canterbury	Canterbury Press, Norwich
Cape	Jonathan Cape, London
Capra	Capra Press, Santa Barbara, CA
Carcanet	Carcanet New Press, Manchester, Lancashire
Cardinal	Cardinal, London
CaribB	Caribbean Books, Parkersburg, IA
CarletonUP	Carleton UP, Ottawa
Carucci	Carucci, Rome
Cascadilla	Cascadilla Press, Somerville, MA
Cass	Frank Cass, London
Cassell	Cassell, London
Cavaliere Azzurro	Cavaliere Azzurro, Bologna
Cave	Godfrey Cave Associates, London
CBA	Council for British Archaeology, London
CBS	Cambridge Bibliographical Society, Cambridge
CCEUCan	Centre for Continuing Education, University of Canterbury, Christchurch, New Zealand
CCP	Canadian Children's Press, Guelph, Ontario
CCS	Centre for Canadian Studies, Mount Allison University, Sackville, NB
CDSH	Centre de Documentation Sciences Humaines, Paris
CENS	Centre for English Name Studies, University of Nottingham
Century	Century Publishing, London
Ceolfrith	Ceolfrith Press, Sunderland, Tyne and Wear
CESR	Société des Amis du Centre d'Études Supérieures de la Renaissance, Tours

CETEDOC	Library of Christian Latin Texts
CFA	Canadian Federation for the Humanities, Ottawa
CG	Common Ground
CH	Croom Helm, London
C–H	Chadwyck–Healey, Cambridge
Chambers	W. & R. Chambers, Edinburgh
Champaign	Champaign Public Library and Information Center, Champaign, IL
Champion	Librairie Honoré Champion, Paris
Chand	S. Chand, Madras
ChelseaH	Chelsea House Publishers, New York, New Haven, and Philadelphia
ChLitAssoc	Children's Literature Association
Christendom	Christendom Publications, Front Royal, VA
Chronicle	Chronicle Books, London
Chrysalis	Chrysalis Press
ChuoUL	Chuo University Library, Tokyo
Churchman	Churchman Publishing, Worthing, W. Sussex
Cistercian	Cistercian Publications, Kalamazoo, MI
CL	City Lights Books, San Francisco
CLA	Canadian Library Association, Ottawa
Clarendon	Clarendon Press, Oxford
Claridge	Claridge, St Albans, Hertfordshire
Clarion	Clarion State College, Clarion, PA
Clark	T. & T. Clark, Edinburgh
Clarke	James Clarke, Cambridge
Classical	Classical Publishing, New Delhi
CLCS	Centre for Language and Communication Studies, Trinity College, Dublin
ClogherHS	Clogher Historical Society, Monaghan, Eire
CLUEB	Cooperativa Libraria Universitaria Editrice, Bologna
Clunie	Clunie Press, Pitlochry, Tayside
CMAP	Caxton's Modern Arts Press, Dallas, TX
CMERS	Center for Medieval and Early Renaissance Studies, Binghamton, NY
CML	William Andrews Clark Memorial Library, Los Angeles
CMST	Centre for Medieval Studies, University of Toronto
Coach House	Coach House Press, Toronto
Colleagues	Colleagues Press, East Lansing, MI
Collector	Collector, London
College-Hill	College-Hill Press, San Diego, CA
Collins	William Collins, London
CollinsA	William Collins (Australia), Sydney
Collins & Brown	Collins & Brown, London
ColUP	Columbia UP, New York
Comedia	Comedia Publishing, London
Comet	Comet Books, London
Compton	Compton Press, Tisbury, Wiltshire

Constable	Constable, London
Contemporary	Contemporary Books, Chicago
Continuum	Continuum Publishing, New York
Copp	Copp Clark Pitman, Mississuaga, Ontario
Corgi	Corgi Books, London
CorkUP	Cork UP, Eire
Cormorant	Cormorant Press, Victoria, BC
Cornford	Cornford Press, Launceston, Tasmania
CornUP	Cornell UP, Ithaca, NY
Cornwallis	Cornwallis Press, Hastings, E. Sussex
Coronado	Coronado Press, Lawrence, KS
Cosmo	Cosmo Publications, New Delhi
Coteau	Coteau Books, Regina, Saskatchewan
Cowley	Cowley Publications, Cambridge, MA
Cowper	Cowper House, Pacific Grove, CA
CPP	Canadian Poetry Press, London, Ontario
CQUP	Central Queensland UP, Rockhampton
Crabtree	Crabtree Press, Sussex
Craftsman House	Craftsman House, Netherlands
Craig Pottoon	Craig Pottoon Publishing, New Zealand
Crawford	Crawford House Publishing, Hindmarsh, SA
Creag Darach	Creag Durach Publications, Stirling
CreativeB	Creative Books, New Delhi
Cresset	Cresset Library, London
CRNLE	Centre for Research in the New Literatures in English, Adelaide
Crossing	Crossing Press, Freedom, CA
Crossroad	Crossroad Publishing, New York
Crown	Crown Publishers, New York
Crowood	Crowood Press, Marlborough, Wiltshire
CSAL	Centre for Studies in Australian Literature, University of Western Australia, Nedlands
CSLI	Center for the Study of Language and Information, Stanford University
CSP	Canadian Scholars' Press, Toronto
CSU	Cleveland State University, Cleveland, OH
CTHS	Éditions du Comité des Travaux Historiques et Scientifiques, Paris
CUAP	Catholic University of America Press, Washington, DC
Cuff	Harry Cuff Publications, St John's, Newfoundland
CULouvain	Catholic University of Louvain, Belgium
CULublin	Catholic University of Lublin, Poland
CUP	Cambridge UP, Cambridge, New York, and Melbourne
Currency	Currency Press, Paddington, New South Wales
Currey	James Currey, London
CV	Cherry Valley Edition, Rochester, NY
CVK	Cornelson-Velhagen & Klasing, Berlin
CWU	Carl Winter Universitätsverlag, Heidelberg

Da Capo	Da Capo Press, New York
Dacorum	Dacorum College, Hemel Hempstead, Hertfordshire
Daisy	Daisy Books, Peterborough, Northampton
Dalkey	Dalkey Archive Press, Elmwood Park, IL
D&C	David & Charles, Newton Abbot, Devon
D&H	Duncker & Humblot, Berlin
D&M	Douglas & McIntyre, Vancouver, BC
D&S	Duffy and Snellgrove, Polts Point, New South Wales
Dangaroo	Dangaroo Press, Mundelstrup, Denmark
DavidB	David Brown Books
Dawson	Dawson Publishing, Folkestone, Kent
DawsonsPM	Dawsons Pall Mall
DBAP	Daphne Brasell Associates Press
DBP	Drama Book Publishers, New York
Deakin UP	Deakin UP, Geelong, Victoria
De Boeck	De Boeck-Wesmael, Brussels
Dee	Ivan R. Dee Publishers, Chicago, IL
De Graaf	De Graaf, Nierwkoup, Netherlands
Denoël	Denoël S.A.R.L., Paris
Dent	J.M. Dent, London
DentA	Dent, Ferntree Gully, Victoria
Depanee	Depanee Printers and Publishers, Nugegoda, Sri Lanka
Deutsch	André Deutsch, London
Didier	Éditions Didier, Paris
Diesterweg	Verlag Moritz Diesterweg, Frankfurt am Main
Dim Gray Bar Press	Dim Gray Bar Press
Doaba	Doaba House, Delhi
Dobby	Eric Dobby Publishing, St Albans
Dobson	Dobson Books, Durham
Dolmen	Dolmen Press, Portlaoise, Eire
Donald	John Donald, Edinburgh
Donker	Adriaan Donker, Johannesburg
Dorset	Dorset Publishing
Doubleday	Doubleday, London and New York
Dove	Dove, Sydney
Dovecote	Dovecote Press, Wimborne, Dorset
Dovehouse	Dovehouse Editions, Canada
Dover	Dover Publications, New York
Drew	Richard Drew, Edinburgh
Droste	Droste Verlag, Düsseldorf
Droz	Librairie Droz SA, Geneva
DublinUP	Dublin UP, Dublin
Duckworth	Gerald Duckworth, London
Duculot	J. Duculot, Gembloux, Belgium
DukeUP	Duke UP, Dublin
Dundurn	Dundurn Press, Toronto and London, Ontario
Duquesne	Duquesne UP, Pittsburgh
Dutton	E.P. Dutton, New York

DWT	Dr Williams's Trust, London
EA	English Association, London
EAS	English Association Sydney Incorporated
Eason	Eason & Son, Dublin
East Bay	East Bay Books, Berkeley, CA
Ebony	Ebony Books, Melbourne
Ecco	Ecco Press, New York
ECNRS	Éditions du Centre National de la Recherche Scientifique, Paris
ECW	ECW Press, Downsview, Ontario
Eden	Eden Press, Montreal and St Albans, VT
EdinUP	Edinburgh UP, Edinburgh
Edizioni	Edizioni del Grifo
EEM	Eastern European Monographs, Boulder, CO
Eerdmans	William Eerdmans, Grand Rapids, MI
EETS	Early English Text Society, c/o Exeter College, Oxford
1890sS	Eighteen-Nineties Society, Oxford
Eihosha	Eihosha, Tokyo
Elephas	Elephas Books, Kewdale, Australia
Elibank	Elibank Press, Wellington, New Zealand
Elm Tree	Elm Tree Books, London
ELS	English Literary Studies
Ember	Ember Press, Brixham, South Devon
EMSH	Éditions de la Maison des Sciences de l'Homme, Paris
Enitharmon	Enitharmon Press, London
Enzyklopädie	Enzyklopädie, Leipzig
EONF	Eugene O'Neill Foundation, Danville, CA
EPNS	English Place-Name Society, Beeston, Nottingham
Epworth	Epworth Press, Manchester
Eriksson	Paul Eriksson, Middlebury, VT
Erlbaum	Erlbaum Associates, NJ
Erskine	Erskine Press, Harleston, Norfolk
EscutchP	Escutcheon Press
ESI	Edizioni Scientifiche Italiane, Naples
ESL	Edizioni di Storia e Letteratura, Rome
EUFS	Éditions Universitaires Fribourg Suisse
EUL	Edinburgh University Library, Edinburgh
Europa	Europa Publishers, London
Evans	M. Evans, New York
Exact Change	Exact Change, Boston
Exile	Exile Editions, Toronto, Ontario
Eyre	Eyre Methuen, London
FAB	Free Association Books, London
Faber	Faber & Faber, London
FAC	Fédération d'Activités Culturelles, Paris
FACP	Fremantle Arts Centre Press, Fremantle, WA
Falcon Books	Falcon Books, Eastbourne

FALS	Foundation for Australian Literary Studies, James Cook University of North Queensland, Townsville
F&F	Fels & Firn Press, San Anselmo, CA
F&S	Feffer & Simons, Amsterdam
Farrand	Farrand Press, London
Fay	Barbara Fay, Stuttgart
F–B	Ford–Brown, Houston, TX
FCP	Four Courts Press, Dublin
FDUP	Fairleigh Dickinson UP, Madison, NJ
FE	Fourth Estate, London
Feminist	Feminist Press, New York
FictionColl	Fiction Collective, Brooklyn College, Brooklyn, NY
Field Day	Field Day, Derry
Fifth House	Fifth House Publications, Saskatoon, Saskatchewan
FILEF	FILEF Italo–Australian Publications, Leichhardt, New South Wales
Fine	Donald Fine, New York
Fink	Fink Verlag, Munich
Five Leaves	Five Leaves Publications, Nottingham
Flamingo	Flamingo Publishing, Newark, NJ
Flammarion	Flammarion, Paris
FlindersU	Flinders University of South Australia, Bedford Park
Floris	Floris Books, Edinburgh
FlorSU	Florida State University, Tallahassee, FL
FOF	Facts on File, New York
Folger	Folger Shakespeare Library, Washington, DC
Folio	Folio Press, London
Fontana	Fontana Press, London
Footprint	Footprint Press, Colchester, Essex
FordUP	Fordham UP, New York
Foris	Foris Publications, Dordrecht
Forsten	Egbert Forsten Publishing, Groningen, Netherlands
Fortress	Fortress Press, Philadelphia
Francke	Francke Verlag, Berne
Franklin	Burt Franklin, New York
FreeP	Free Press, New York
FreeUP	Free UP, Amsterdam
Freundlich	Freundlich Books, New York
Frommann-Holzboog	Frommann-Holzboog, Stuttgart
FS&G	Farrar, Straus & Giroux
FSP	Five Seasons Press, Madley, Hereford
FW	Fragments West/Valentine Press, Long Beach, CA
FWA	Fiji Writers' Association, Suva
FWP	Falling Wall Press, Bristol
Gale	Gale Research, Detroit, MI
Galilée	Galilée, Paris
Gallimard	Gallimard, Paris
G&G	Grevatt & Grevatt, Newcastle upon Tyne

G&M	Gill & Macmillan, Dublin
Garland	Garland Publishing, New York
Gasson	Roy Gasson Associates, Wimbourne, Dorset
Gateway	Gateway Editions, Washington, DC
GE	Greenwich Exchange, UK
GIA	GIA Publications, USA
Girasole	Edizioni del Girasole, Ravenna
GL	Goose Lane Editions, Fredericton, NB
GlasgowDL	Glasgow District Libraries, Glasgow
Gleerup	Gleerupska, Lund
Gliddon	Gliddon Books Publishers, Norwich
Gloger	Gloger Family Books, Portland, OR
GMP	GMP Publishing, London
GMSmith	Gibbs M. Smith, Layton, UT
Golden Dog	Golden Dog, Ottawa
Gollancz	Victor Gollancz, London
Gomer	Gomer Press, Llandysul, Dyfed
GothU	Gothenburg University, Gothenburg
Gower	Gower Publishing, Aldershot, Hants.
GRAAT	Groupe de Recherches Anglo-Américaines de Tours
Grafton	Grafton Books, London
GranB	Granary Books, New York
Granta	Granta Publications, London
Granville	Granville Publishing, London
Grasset	Grasset & Fasquelle, Paris
Grassroots	Grassroots, London
Graywolf	Graywolf Press, St Paul, MI
Greenhalgh	M.J. Greenhalgh, London
Greenhill	Greenhill Books, London
Greenwood	Greenwood Press, Westport, CT
Gregg	Gregg Publishing, Surrey
Greville	Greville Press, Warwick
Greymitre	Greymitre Books, London
GroC	Grolier Club, New York
Groos	Julius Groos Verlag, Heidelberg
Grove	Grove Press, New York
GRP	Greenfield Review Press, New York
Grüner	B.R. Grüner, Amsterdam
Gruyter	Walter de Gruyter, Berlin
Guernica	Guernica Editions, Montreal, Canada
Guilford	Guilford, New York
Gulmohar	Gulmohar Press, Islamabad, Pakistan
Haggerston	Haggerston Press, London
HakluytS	Hakluyt Society, c/o British Library, London
Hale	Robert Hale, London
Hall	G.K. Hall, Boston, MA
Halstead	Halstead Press, Rushcutters Bay, New South Wales
HalsteadP	Halstead Press, c/o J. Wiley & Sons, Chichester, W. Sussex

Hambledon	Hambledon Press, London
H&I	Hale & Iremonger, Sydney
H&L	Hambledon and London
H&M	Holmes & Meier, London and New York
H&S	Hodder & Stoughton, London
H&SNZ	Hodder & Stoughton, Auckland
H&W	Hill & Wang, New York
Hansib	Hansib Publishing, London
Harbour	Harbour Publishing, Madeira Park, BC
Harman	Harman Publishing House, New Delhi
Harper	Harper & Row, New York
Harrap	Harrap, Edinburgh
HarrV	Harrassowitz Verlag, Wiesbaden
HarvardUP	Harvard UP, Cambridge, MA
Harwood	Harwood Academic Publishers, Langhorne, PA
Hatje	Verlag Gerd Hatje, Germany
HBJ	Harcourt Brace Jovanovich, New York and London
HC	HarperCollins, London
HCAus	HarperCollins Australia, Pymble, New South Wales
Headline	Headline Book Publishing, London
Heath	D.C. Heath, Lexington, MS
HebrewUMP	Hebrew University Magnes Press
Heinemann	William Heinemann, London
HeinemannA	William Heinemann, St Kilda, Victoria
HeinemannC	Heinemann Educational Books, Kingston, Jamaica
HeinemannNg	Heinemann Educational Books, Nigeria
HeinemannNZ	Heinemann Publishers, Auckland (now Heinemann Reed)
HeinemannR	Heinemann Reed, Auckland
Helm	Christopher Helm, London
HelmI	Helm Information
Herbert	Herbert Press, London
Hermitage	Hermitage Antiquarian Bookshop, Denver, CO
Hern	Nick Hern Books, London
Heyday	Heyday Books, Berkeley, CA
HH	Hamish Hamilton, London
Hilger	Adam Hilger, Bristol
HM	Harvey Miller, London
HMSO	HMSO, London
Hodder, Moa, Beckett	Hodder, Moa, Beckett, Milford, Auckland, New Zealand
Hodge	A. Hodge, Penzance, Cornwall
Hogarth	Hogarth Press, London
HongKongUP	Hong Kong UP, Hong Kong
Horsdal & Schubart	Horsdal & Schubart, Victoria, BC
Horwood	Ellis Horwood, Hemel Hempstead, Hertfordshire
HoughtonM	Houghton Mifflin, Boston, MA
Howard	Howard UP, Washington, DC
HREOC	Human Rights and Equal Opportunity Commission, Commonweath of Australia, Canberra

HRW	Holt, Reinhart & Winston, New York
Hudson	Hudson Hills Press, New York
Hueber	Max Hueber, Ismaning, Germany
HUL	Hutchinson University Library, London
HullUP	Hull UP, University of Hull
Humanities	Humanities Press, Atlantic Highlands, NJ
Huntington	Huntington Library, San Marino, CA
Hutchinson	Hutchinson Books, London
HW	Harvester Wheatsheaf, Hemel Hempstead, Hertfordshire
HWWilson	H.W. Wilson, New York
Hyland House	Hyland House Publishing, Victoria
HyphenP	Hyphen Press, London
IAAS	Indian Institute of Aveanced Studies, Lahore and New Delhi
Ian Henry	Ian Henry Publications, Hornchurch, Essex
IAP	Irish Academic Press, Dublin
Ibadan	Ibadan University Press
IBK	Innsbrucker Beiträge zur Kulturwissenschaft, University of Innsbruck
ICA	Institute of Contemporary Arts, London
IHA	International Hopkins Association, Waterloo, Ontario
IJamaica	Institute of Jamaica Publications, Kingston
Imago	Imago Imprint, New York
ImperialWarMuseum	Imperial War Museum Publications, London
IndUP	Indiana UP, Bloomington, IN
Inkblot	Inkblot Publications, Berkeley, CA
IntUP	International Universities Press, New York
Inventions	Inventions Press, London
IonaC	Iona College, New Rochelle, NY
IowaSUP	Iowa State UP, Ames, IA
IOWP	Isle of Wight County Press, Newport, Isle of Wight
IP	In Parenthesis, London
Ipswich	Ipswich Press, Ipswich, MA
IrishAP	Irish Academic Press, Dublin
ISI	ISI Press, Philadelphia
Italica	Italica Press, New York
IULC	Indiana University Linguistics Club, Bloomington, IN
IUP	Indiana University of Pennsylvania Press, Indiana, PA
Ivon	Ivon Publishing House, Bombay
Jacaranda	Jacaranda Wiley, Milton, Queensland
JadavpurU	Jadavpur University, Calcutta
James CookU	James Cook University of North Queensland, Townsville
Jarrow	Parish of Jarrow, Tyne and Wear
Jesperson	Jesperson Press, St John's, Newfoundland
JHall	James Hall, Leamington Spa, Warwickshire
JHUP	Johns Hopkins UP, Baltimore, MD
JIWE	JIWE Publications, University of Gulbarga, India
JLRC	Jack London Research Center, Glen Ellen, CA

J-NP	Joe-Noye Press
Jonas	Jonas Verlag, Marburg, Germany
Joseph	Michael Joseph, London
Journeyman	Journeyman Press, London
JPGM	J. Paul Getty Museum
JT	James Thin, Edinburgh
Junction	Junction Books, London
Junius-Vaughan	Junius-Vaughan Press, Fairview, NJ
Jupiter	Jupiter Press, Lake Bluff, IL
JyväskyläU	Jyväskylä University, Jyväskylä, Finland
Kaibunsha	Kaibunsha, Tokyo
K&N	Königshausen & Neumann, Würzburg, Germany
K&W	Kaye & Ward, London
Kangaroo	Kangaroo Press, Simon & Schuster (Australia), Roseville, New South Wales
Kansai	Kansai University of Foreign Studies, Osaka
Kardo	Kardo, Coatbridge, Scotland
Kardoorair	Kardoorair Press, Adelaide
Karia	Karia Press, London
Karnak	Karnak House, London
Karoma	Karoma Publishers, Ann Arbor, MI
Katha	Katha, New Delhi
KC	Kyle Cathie, London
KCL	King's College London
KeeleUP	Keele University Press
Kegan Paul	Kegan Paul International, London
Kenkyu	Kenkyu-Sha, Tokyo
Kennikat	Kennikat Press, Port Washington, NY
Kensal	Kensal Press, Oxford
KentSUP	Kent State University Press, Kent, OH
KenyaLB	Kenya Literature Bureau, Nairobi
Kerosina	Kerosina Publications, Worcester Park, Surrey
Kerr	Charles H. Kerr, Chicago
Kestrel	Viking Kestrel, London
K/H	Kendall/Hunt Publishing, Dubuque, IA
Kingsley	J. Kingsley Publishers, London
Kingston	Kingston Publishers, Kingston, Jamaica
Kinseido	Kinseido, Tokyo
KITLV	KITLV Press, Leiden
Klostermann	Vittorio Klostermann, Frankfurt am Main
Kluwer	Kluwer Academic Publications, Dordrecht
Knopf	Alfred A. Knopf, New York
Knowledge	Knowledge Industry Publications, White Plains, NY
Kraft	Kraft Books, Ibadan
Kraus	Kraus International Publications, White Plains, NY
KSUP	Kent State UP, Kent OH
LA	Library Association, London

LACUS	Linguistic Association of Canada and the United States, Chapel Hill, NC
Lake View	Lake View Press, Chicago
LAm	Library of America, New York
Lancelot	Lancelot Press, Hantsport, NS
Landesman	Jay Landesman, London
L&W	Lawrence & Wishart, London
Lane	Allen Lane, London
Lang	Peter D. Lang, Frankfurt am Main and Berne
LehighUP	Lehigh University Press, Bethlehem, PA
LeicAE	University of Leicester, Department of Adult Education
LeicsCC	Leicestershire County Council, Libraries and Information Service, Leicester
LeicUP	Leicester UP, Leicester
LeidenUP	Leiden UP, Leiden
Leopard's Head	Leopard's Head Press, Oxford
Letao	Letao Press, Albury, New South Wales
LeuvenUP	Leuven UP, Leuven, Belgium
Lexik	Lexik House, Cold Spring, NY
Lexington	Lexington Publishers
LF	LiberFörlag, Stockholm
LH	Lund Humphries Publishers, London
Liberty	Liberty Classics, Indianapolis, IN
Libris	Libris, London
LibrU	Libraries Unlimited, Englewood, CO
Liguori	Liguori, Naples
Limelight	Limelight Editions, New York
Lime Tree	Lime Tree Press, Octopus Publishing, London
LincolnUP	Lincoln University Press, Nebraska
LITIR	LITIR Database, University of Alberta
LittleH	Little Hills Press, Burwood, New South Wales
Liveright	Liveright Publishing, New York
LiverUP	Liverpool UP, Liverpool
Livre de Poche	Le Livre de Poche, Paris
Llanerch	Llanerch Enterprises, Lampeter, Dyfed
Locust Hill	Locust Hill Press, West Cornwall, CT
Loewenthal	Loewenthal Press, New York
Longman	Addison Longman Wesley, Harlow, Essex
LongmanC	Longman Caribbean, Harlow, Essex
LongmanF	Longman, France
LongmanNZ	Longman, Auckland
Longspoon	Longspoon Press, University of Alberta, Edmonton
Lovell	David Lovell Publishing, Brunswick, Australia
Lowell	Lowell Press, Kansas City, MS
Lowry	Lowry Publishers, Johannesburg
LSUP	Louisiana State UP, Baton Rouge, LA
LundU	Lund University, Lund, Sweden
LUP	Loyola UP, Chicago

Lutterworth	Lutterworth Press, Cambridge
Lymes	Lymes Press, Newcastle, Staffordshire
MAA	Medieval Academy of America, Cambridge, MA
Macmillan	Macmillan Publishers, London
MacmillanC	Macmillan Caribbean
Madison	Madison Books, Lanham, MD
Madurai	Madurai University, Madurai, India
Maecenas	Maecenas Press, Iowa City, Iowa
Magabala	Magabala Books, Broome, WA
Magnes	Magnes Press, The Hebrew University, Jerusalem
Mainstream	Mainstream Publishing, Edinburgh
Maisonneuve	Maisonneuve Press, Washington, DC
Malone	Malone Society, c/o King's College, London
Mambo	Mambo Press, Gweru, Zimbabwe
ManCASS	Manchester Centre for Anglo-Saxon Studies, University of Manchester
M&E	Macdonald & Evans, Estover, Plymouth, Devon
M&S	McClelland & Stewart, Toronto
Maney	W.S. Maney & Sons, Leeds
Manohar	Manohar Publishers, Darya Gan, New Delhi
Mansell	Mansell Publishing, London
Manufacture	La Manufacture, Lyons
ManUP	Manchester UP, Milwaukee, WI
Mardaga	Mardaga
Mariner	Mariner Books, Boston, MA
MarquetteUP	Marquette UP, Milwaukee, WI
Marvell	Marvell Press, Calstock, Cornwall
MB	Mitchell Beazley, London
McDougall, Littel	McDougall, Littel, Evanston, IL
McFarland	McFarland, Jefferson, NC
McG-QUP	McGill-Queen's UP, Montreal
McGraw-Hill	McGraw-Hill, New York
McIndoe	John McIndoe, Dunedin, New Zealand
McPheeG	McPhee Gribble Publishers, Fitzroy, Victoria
McPherson	McPherson, Kingston, NY
MCSU	Maria Curie Sk³odowska University
ME	M. Evans, New York
Meany	P.D. Meany Publishing, Port Credit, Ontario
Meckler	Meckler Publishing, Westport, CT
MelbourneUP	Melbourne UP, Carlton South, Victoria
Mellen	Edwin Mellen Press, Lewiston, NY
MellenR	Mellen Research UP
Menzies	Menzies Centre for Australian Studies
MercerUP	Mercer UP, Macon, GA
Mercury	Mercury Press, Stratford, Ontario
Merlin	Merlin Press, London
Methuen	Methuen, London
MethuenA	Methuen Australia, North Ryde, New South Wales

MethuenC	Methuen, Toronto
Metro	Metro Publishing, Auckland
Metzler	Metzler, Stuttgart
MGruyter	Mouton de Gruyter, Berlin, New York, and Amsterdam
MH	Michael Haag, London
MHRA	Modern Humanities Research Association, London
MHS	Missouri Historical Society, St Louis, MO
MI	Microforms International, Pergamon Press, Oxford
Micah	Micah Publications, Marblehead, MA.
MichSUP	Michigan State UP, East Lansing, MI
MidNAG	Mid-Northumberland Arts Group, Ashington, Northumbria
Mieyungah	Mieyungah Press, Melbourne University Press, Carlton South, Victoria
Milestone	Milestone Publications, Horndean, Hampshire
Millennium	Millennium Books, E.J. Dwyer, Newtown, Australia
Millstream	Millstream Books, Bath
Milner	Milner, London
Minuit	Éditions de Minuit, Paris
MIP	Medieval Institute Publications, Western Michigan University, Kalamazoo
MITP	Massachusetts Institute of Technology Press, Cambridge, MA
MLA	Modern Language Association of America, New York
MlM	Multilingual Matters, Clevedon, Avon
MLP	Manchester Literary and Philosophical Society, Manchester
Modern Library	Modern Library (Random House), New York
Monarch	Monarch Publications, Sussex
Moonraker	Moonraker Press, Bradford-on-Avon, Wiltshire
Moorland	Moorland Publishing, Ashbourne, Derby
Moreana	Moreana, Angers, France
MorganSU	Morgan State University, Baltimore, MD
Morrow	William Morrow, New York
Mosaic	Mosaic Press, Oakville, Ontario
Motilal	Motilal Books, Oxford
Motley	Motley Press, Romsey, Hampshire
Mouton	Mouton Publishers, New York and Paris
Mowbray	A.R. Mowbray, Oxford
MR	Martin Robertson, Oxford
MRS	Medieval and Renaissance Society, North Texas State University, Denton
MRTS	MRTS, Binghamton, NY
MSUP	Memphis State UP, Memphis, TN
MtAllisonU	Mount Allison University, Sackville, NB
MTP	Museum Tusculanum Press, University of Copenhagen
Mulini	Mulini Press, ACT
Muller	Frederick Muller, London
MULP	McMaster University Library Press

Murray	John Murray, London
Mursia	Ugo Mursia, Milan
NAL	New American Library, New York
Narr	Gunter Narr Verlag, Tübingen
Nathan	Fernand Nathan, Paris
NBB	New Beacon Books, London
NBCAus	National Book Council of Australia, Melbourne
NCP	New Century Press, Durham
ND	New Directions, New York
NDT	Nottingham Drama Texts, c/o University of Nottingham
NEL	New English Library, London
NELM	National English Literary Museum, Grahamstown, S. Africa
Nelson	Nelson Publishers, Melbourne
NelsonT	Thomas Nelson, London
New Endeavour	New Endeavour Press
NeWest	NeWest Press, Edmonton, Alberta
New Horn	New Horn Press, Ibadan, Nigeria
New Island	New Island Press
NewIssuesP	New Issues Press, Western Michigan University
NH	New Horizon Press, Far Hills, NJ
N-H	Nelson-Hall, Chicago
NHPC	North Holland Publishing, Amsterdam and New York
NicV	Nicolaische Verlagsbuchhandlung, Berlin
NIE	La Nuova Italia Editrice, Florence
Niemeyer	Max Niemeyer, Tübingen, Germany
Nightwood	Nightwood Editions, Toronto
NIUP	Northern Illinois UP, De Kalb, IL
NUSam	National University of Samoa
NLA	National Library of Australia
NLB	New Left Books, London
NLC	National Library of Canada, Ottawa
NLP	New London Press, Dallas, TX
NLS	National Library of Scotland, Edinburgh
NLW	National Library of Wales, Aberystwyth, Dyfed
Nodus	Nodus Publikationen, Münster
Northcote	Northcote House Publishers, Plymouth
NortheasternU	Northeastern University, Boston, MA
NorthwesternUP	Northwestern UP, Evanston, IL
Norton	W.W. Norton, New York and London
NorUP	Norwegian University Press, Oslo
Novus	Novus Press, Oslo
NPF	National Poetry Foundation, Orono, ME
NPG	National Portrait Gallery, London
NPP	North Point Press, Berkeley, CA
NSP	New Statesman Publishing, New Delhi
NSU Press	Northern States Universities Press
NSWUP	New South Wales UP, Kensington, New South Wales
NT	National Textbook, Lincolnwood, IL

NUC	Nipissing University College, North Bay, Ontario
NUP	National University Publications, Millwood, NY
NUSam	National University of Samoa
NUU	New University of Ulster, Coleraine
NWAP	North Waterloo Academic Press, Waterloo, Ontario
NWP	New World Perspectives, Montreal
NYPL	New York Public Library, New York
NYUP	New York UP, New York
OakK	Oak Knoll Press, New Castle, DE
O&B	Oliver & Boyd, Harlow, Essex
Oasis	Oasis Books, London
OBAC	Organization of Black American Culture, Chicago
OberlinCP	Oberlin College Press, Oberlin, OH
Oberon	Oberon Books, London
O'Brien	O'Brien Press, Dublin
OBS	Oxford Bibliographical Society, Bodleian Library, Oxford
Octopus	Octopus Books, London
OdenseUP	Odense UP, Odense
OE	Officina Edizioni, Rome
OEColl	Old English Colloquium, Berkeley, CA
Offord	John Offord Publications, Eastbourne, E. Sussex
OhioUP	Ohio UP, Athens, OH
Oldcastle	Oldcastle Books, Harpenden, Hertfordshire
Olms	Georg Olms, Hildesheim, Germany
Olschki	Leo S. Olschki, Florence
O'Mara	Michael O'Mara Books, London
Omnigraphics	Omnigraphics, Detroit, MI
Open Books	Open Books Publishing, Wells, Somerset
Open Court	Open Court Publishing, USA
OpenUP	Open UP, Buckingham and Philadelphia
OPP	Oxford Polytechnic Press, Oxford
Orbis	Orbis Books, London
OregonSUP	Oregon State UP, Corvallis, OR
Oriel	Oriel Press, Stocksfield, Northumberland
Orient Longman	Orient Longman, India
OrientUP	Oriental UP, London
OriginalNZ	Original Books, Wellington, New Zealand
Ortnamnsarkivet	Ortnamnsarkivet i Uppsala, Sweden
Orwell	Orwell Press, Southwold, Suffolk
Oryx	Oryx Press, Phoenix, AR
OSUP	Ohio State UP, Columbus, OH
OTP	Oak Tree Press, London
OUCA	Oxford University Committee for Archaeology, Oxford
OUP	Oxford UP, Oxford
OUPAm	Oxford UP, New York
OUPAus	Oxford UP, Melbourne
OUPC	Oxford UP, Toronto
OUPI	Oxford UP, New Delhi

OUPNZ	Oxford UP, Auckland
OUPSA	Oxford UP Southern Africa, Cape Town
Outlet	Outlet Book, New York
Overlook	Overlook Press, New York
Owen	Peter Owen, London
Owl	Owl
Pace UP	Pace University Press, New York
Pacifica	Press Pacifica, Kailua, Hawaii
Paget	Paget Press, Santa Barbara, CA
PAJ	PAJ Publications, New York
Paladin	Paladin Books, London
Palgrave	Palgrave, NY
Pan	Pan Books, London
PanAmU	Pan American University, Edinburgh, TX
P&C	Pickering & Chatto, London
Pandion	Pandion Press, Capitola, CA
Pandora	Pandora Press, London
Pan Macmillan	Pan Macmillan Australia, South Yarra, Victoria
Pantheon	Pantheon Books, New York
ParagonH	Paragon House Publishers, New York
Parnassus	Parnassus Imprints, Hyannis, MA
Parousia	Parousia Publications, London
Paternoster	Paternoster Press, Carlisle, Cumbria
Patten	Patten Press, Penzance
Paulist	Paulist Press, Ramsey, NJ
Paupers	Paupers' Press, Nottingham
Pavilion	Pavilion Books, London
PBFA	Provincial Booksellers' Fairs Association, Cambridge
Peachtree	Peachtree Publishers, Atlanta, GA
Pearson	David Pearson, Huntingdon, Cambridge
Peepal Tree	Peepal Tree Books, Leeds
Peeters	Peeters Publishers and Booksellers, Leuven, Belgium
Pelham	Pelham Books, London
Pembridge	Pembridge Press, London
Pemmican	Pemmican Publications, Winnipeg, Canada
PencraftI	Pencraft International, Ashok Vihar II, Delhi
Penguin	Penguin Books, Harmondsworth, Middlesex
PenguinA	Penguin Books, Ringwood, Victoria
PenguinNZ	Penguin Books, Auckland
Penkevill	Penkevill Publishing, Greenwood, FL
Pentland	Pentland Press, Ely, Cambridge
Penumbra	Penumbra Press, Moonbeam, Ontario
People's	People's Publications, London
Pergamon	Pergamon Press, Oxford
Permanent	Permanent Press, Sag Harbor, NY
Perpetua	Perpetua Press, Oxford
Petton	Petton Books, Oxford
Pevensey	Pevensey Press, Newton Abbot, Devon

PH	Prentice-Hall, Englewood Cliffs, NJ
Phaidon	Phaidon Press, London
PHI	Prentice-Hall International, Hemel Hempstead, Hertfordshire
PhilL	Philosophical Library, New York
Phillimore	Phillimore, Chichester
Phoenix	Phoenix
Piatkus	Piatkus Books, London
Pickwick	Pickwick Publications, Allison Park, PA
Pilgrim	Pilgrim Books, Norman, OK
PIMS	Pontifical Institute of Mediaeval Studies, Toronto
Pinter	Frances Pinter Publishers, London
Plains	Plains Books, Carlisle
Plenum	Plenum Publishing, London and New York
Plexus	Plexus Publishing, London
Pliegos	Editorial Pliegos, Madrid
Ploughshares	Ploughshares Books, Watertown, MA
Pluto	Pluto Press, London
PML	Pierpont Morgan Library, New York
Polity	Polity Press, Cambridge
Polygon	Polygon, Edinburgh
Poolbeg	Poolbeg Press, Swords, Dublin
Porcepic	Press Porcepic, Victoria, BC
Porcupine	Porcupine's Quill, Canada
PortN	Port Nicholson Press, Wellington, NZ
Potter	Clarkson N. Potter, New York
Power	Power Publications, University of Sydney
PPUBarcelona	Promociones y Publicaciones Universitarias, Barcelona
Praeger	Praeger, New York
Prestel	Prestel Verlag, Germany
PrestigeB	Prestige Books, New Delhi
Primavera	Edizioni Primavera, Gunti Publishing, Florence, Italy
Primrose	Primrose Press, Alhambra, CA
PrincetonUL	Princeton University Library, Princeton, NJ
PrincetonUP	Princeton UP, Princeton, NJ
Printwell	Printwell Publishers, Jaipur, India
Prism	Prism Press, Bridport, Dorset
PRO	Public Record Office, London
Profile	Profile Books, Ascot, Berks
ProgP	Progressive Publishers, Calcutta
PSUP	Pennsylvania State UP, University Park, PA
Pucker	Puckerbrush Press, Orono, ME
PUF	Presses Universitaires de France, Paris
PurdueUP	Purdue UP, Lafayette, IN
Pushcart	Pushcart Press, Wainscott, NY
Pustet	Friedrich Pustet, Regensburg
Putnam	Putnam Publishing, New York
PWP	Poetry Wales Press, Ogmore by Sea, mid-Glamorgan

QED	QED Press, Ann Arbor, MI
Quarry	Quarry Press, Kingston, Ontario
Quartet	Quartet Books, London
QUT	Queensland University of Technology
RA	Royal Academy of Arts, London
Rainforest	Rainforest Publishing, Faxground, New South Wales
Rampant Lions	Rampant Lions Press, Cambridge
R&B	Rosenklide & Bagger, Copenhagen
R&L	Rowman & Littlefield, Totowa, NJ
Randle	Ian Randle, Kingston, Jamaica
RandomH	Random House, London and New York
RandomHAus	Random House Australia, Victoria
Ravan	Ravan Press, Johannesburg
Ravette	Ravette, London
Rawat	Rawat Publishing, Jaipur and New Delhi
Reaktion	Reaktion Books, London
Rebel	Rebel Press, London
Red Kite	Red Kite Press, Guelph, Ontario
Red Rooster	Red Rooster Press, Hotham Hill, Victoria
Red Sea	Red Sea Press, NJ
Reed	Reed Books, Port Melbourne
Reference	Reference Press, Toronto
Regents	Regents Press of Kansas, Lawrence, KS
Reichenberger	Roswitha Reichenberger, Kessel, Germany
Reinhardt	Max Reinhardt, London
Remak	Remak, Alblasserdam, Netherlands
RenI	Renaissance Institute, Sophia University, Tokyo
Research	Research Publications, Reading
RETS	Renaissance English Text Society, Chicago
RH	Ramsay Head Press, Edinburgh
RHS	Royal Historical Society, London
RIA	Royal Irish Academy, Dublin
RiceUP	Rice UP, Houston, TX
Richarz	Hans Richarz, St Augustin, Germany
RICL	Research Institute for Comparative Literature, University of Alberta
Rivers Oram	Rivers Oram Press, London
Rizzoli	Rizzoli International Publications, New York
RobartsCCS	Robarts Centre for Canadian Studies, York University, North York, Ontario
Robinson	Robinson Publishing, London
Robson	Robson Books, London
Rodopi	Rodopi, Amsterdam
Roebuck	Stuart Roebuck, Suffolk
RoehamptonI	Roehampton Institute London
Routledge	Routledge, London and New York
Royce	Robert Royce, London
RS	Royal Society, London

RSC	Royal Shakespeare Company, London
RSL	Royal Society of Literature, London
RSVP	Research Society for Victorian Periodicals, University of Leicester
RT	RT Publications, London
Running	Running Press, Philadelphia
Russell	Michael Russell, Norwich
RutgersUP	Rutgers UP, New Brunswick, NJ
Ryan	Ryan Publishing, London
SA	Sahitya Akademi, New Delhi
Sage	Sage Publications, London
SAI	Sociological Abstracts, San Diego, CA
Salamander	Salamander Books, London
Salem	Salem Press, Englewood Cliffs, NJ
S&A	Shukayr and Akasheh, Amman, Jordon
S&D	Stein & Day, Briarcliff Manor, NJ
S&J	Sidgwick & Jackson, London
S&M	Sun & Moon Press, Los Angeles
S&P	Simon & Piere, Toronto
S&S	Simon & Schuster, New York and London
S&W	Secker & Warburg, London
Sangam	Sangam Books, London
Sangsters	Sangsters Book Stores, Kingston, Jamaica
SAP	Scottish Academic Press, Edinburgh
Saros	Saros International Publishers
SASSC	Sydney Association for Studies in Society and Culture, University of Sydney, New South Wales
Saur	Bowker-Saur, Sevenoaks, Kent
Savacou	Savacou Publications, Kingston, Jamaica
S-B	Schwann-Bagel, Düsseldorf
ScanUP	Scandinavian University Presses, Oslo
Scarecrow	Scarecrow Press, Metuchen, NJ
Schäuble	Schäuble Verlag, Rheinfelden, Germany
Schmidt	Erich Schmidt Verlag, Berlin
Schneider	Lambert Schneider, Heidelberg
Schocken	Schocken Books, New York
Scholarly	Scholarly Press, St Clair Shores, MI
ScholarsG	Scholars Press, GA
Schöningh	Ferdinand Schöningh, Paderborn, Germany
Schwinn	Michael Schwinn, Neustadt, Germany
SCJP	Sixteenth-Century Journal Publications
Scolar	Scolar Press, Aldershot, Hampshire
SCP	Second Chance Press, Sag Harbor, NY
Scribe	Scribe Publishing, Colchester
Scribner	Charles Scribner, New York
Seafarer	Seafarer Books, London
Seaver	Seaver Books, New York
Segue	Segue, New York

Semiotext(e)	Semiotext(e), Columbia University, New York
SePA	Self-Publishing Association
Seren Books	Seren Books, Bridgend, mid-Glamorgan
Serpent's Tail	Serpent's Tail Publishing, London
Sessions	William Sessions, York
Seuil	Éditions du Seuil, Paris
7:84 Pubns	7:84 Publications, Glasgow
Severn	Severn House, Wallington, Surrey
SF&R	Scholars' Facsimiles and Reprints, Delmar, NY
SH	Somerset House, Teaneck, NJ
Shalabh	Shalabh Book House, Meerut, India
ShAP	Sheffield Academic Press
Shaun Tyas	Paul Watkins Publishing, Donington, Lincolnshire
Shearwater	Shearwater Press, Lenah Valley, Tasmania
Sheba	Sheba Feminist Publishers, London
Sheed&Ward	Sheed & Ward, London
Sheldon	Sheldon Press, London
SHESL	Société d'Histoire et d'Épistemologie des Sciences du Langage, Paris
Shinozaki	Shinozaki Shorin, Tokyo
Shinshindo	Shinshindo Publishing, Tokyo
Shire	Shire Publications, Princes Risborough, Buckinghamshire
Shoal Bay Press	Shoal Bay Press, New Zealand
Shoe String	Shoe String Press, Hamden, CT
SHP	Shakespeare Head Press
SIAS	Scandinavian Institute of African Studies, Uppsala
SIL	Summer Institute of Linguistics, Academic Publications, Dallas, TX
SIUP	Southern Illinois University Press
Simon King	Simon King Press, Milnthorpe, Cumbria
Sinclair-Stevenson	Sinclair-Stevenson, London
SingaporeUP	Singapore UP, Singapore
SIUP	Southern Illinois UP, Carbondale, IL
SJSU	San Jose State University, San Jose, CA
Skilton	Charles Skilton, London
Skoob	Skoob Books, London
Slatkine	Éditions Slatkine, Paris
Slavica	Slavica Publishers, Columbus, OH
Sleepy Hollow	Sleepy Hollow Press, Tarrytown, NY
SLG	SLG Press, Oxford
Smith Settle	Smith Settle, W. Yorkshire
SMUP	Southern Methodist UP, Dallas, TX
Smythe	Colin Smythe, Gerrards Cross, Buckinghamshire
SNH	Société Néophilologique de Helsinki
SNLS	Society for New Language Study, Denver, CO
SOA	Society of Authors, London
Soho	Soho Book, London
SohoP	Soho Press, New York

Solaris	Solaris Press, Rochester, MI
SonoNis	Sono Nis Press, Victoria, BC
Sorbonne	Publications de la Sorbonne, Paris
SorbonneN	Publications du Conseil Scientifique de la Sorbonne Nouvelle, Paris
Souvenir	Souvenir Press, London
SPA	SPA Books
SPACLALS	South Pacific Association for Commonwealth Literature and Language Studies, Wollongong, New South Wales
Spaniel	Spaniel Books, Paddington, New South Wales
SPCK	SPCK, London
Spectrum	Spectrum Books, Ibadan, Nigeria
Split Pea	Split Pea Press, Edinburgh
Spokesman	Spokesman Books, Nottingham
Spoon River	Spoon River Poetry Press, Granite Falls, MN
SRC	Steinbeck Research Center, San Jose State University, San Jose, CA
SRI	Steinbeck Research Institute, Ball State University, Muncie, IN
SriA	Sri Aurobindo, Pondicherry, India
Sri Satguru	Sri Satguru Publications, Delhi
SSA	John Steinbeck Society of America, Muncie, IN
SSAB	Sprakförlaget Skriptor AB, Stockholm
SSNS	Scottish Society for Northern Studies, Edinburgh
StanfordUP	Stanford UP, Stanford, CA
Staple	Staple, Matlock, Derbyshire
Starmont	Starmont House, Mercer Island, WA
Starrhill	Starrhill Press, Washington, DC
Station Hill	Station Hill, Barrytown, NY
Stauffenburg	Stauffenburg Verlag, Tübingen, Germany
StDL	St Deiniol's Library, Hawarden, Clwyd
Steel Rail	Steel Rail Publishing, Ottawa
Steiner	Franz Steiner, Wiesbaden, Germany
Sterling	Sterling Publishing, New York
SterlingND	Sterling Publishers, New Delhi
Stichting	Stichtig Neerlandistiek, Amsterdam
St James	St James Press, Andover, Hampshire
St Martin's	St Martin's Press, New York
StMut	State Mutual Book and Periodical Source, New York
Stockwell	Arthur H. Stockwell, Ilfracombe, Devon
Stoddart	Stoddart Publishing, Don Mills, Ontario
StPB	St Paul's Bibliographies, Winchester, Hampshire
STR	Society for Theatre Research, London
Strauch	R.O.U. Strauch, Ludwigsburg
Studio	Studio Editions, London
Stump Cross	Stump Cross Books, Stump Cross, Essex
Sud	Sud, Marseilles
Suhrkamp	Suhrkamp Verlag, Frankfurt am Main

Summa	Summa Publications, Birmingham, AL
SUNYP	State University of New York Press, Albany, NY
SUP	Sydney University Press
Surtees	R.S. Surtees Society, Frome, Somerset
SusquehannaUP	Susquehanna UP, Selinsgrove, PA
SussexAP	Sussex Academic Press
SussexUP	Sussex UP, University of Sussex, Brighton
Sutton	Alan Sutton, Stroud, Gloucester
SVP	Sister Vision Press, Toronto
S–W	Shepheard–Walwyn Publishing, London
Swallow	Swallow Press, Athens, OH
SWG	Saskatchewan Writers Guild, Regina
Sybylla	Sybylla Feminist Press
SydneyUP	Sydney UP, Sydney
SyracuseUP	Syracuse UP, Syracuse, NY
Tabb	Tabb House, Padstow, Cornwall
Taishukan	Taishukan Publishing, Tokyo
Talonbooks	Talonbooks, Vancouver
TamilU	Tamil University, Thanjavur, India
T&F	Taylor & Francis Books
T&H	Thames & Hudson, London
Tantivy	Tantivy Press, London
Tarcher	Jeremy P. Tarcher, Los Angeles
Tartarus	Tartarus Press
Tate	Tate Gallery Publications, London
Tavistock	Tavistock Publications, London
Taylor	Taylor Publishing, Bellingham, WA
TaylorCo	Taylor Publishing, Dallas, TX
TCG	Theatre Communications Group, New York
TCP	Three Continents Press, Washington, DC
TCUP	Texas Christian UP, Fort Worth, TX
TEC	Third Eye Centre, Glasgow
Tecumseh	Tecumseh Press, Ottawa
Telos	Telos Press, St Louis, MO
TempleUP	Temple UP, Philadelphia
TennS	Tennyson Society, Lincoln
TexA&MUP	Texas A&MUP, College Station, TX
Text	Text Publishing, Melbourne
TextileB	Textile Bridge Press, Clarence Center, NY
TexTULib	Friends of the University Library, Texas Tech University, Lubbock
The Smith	The Smith, New York
Thimble	Thimble Press, Stroud, Gloucester
Thoemmes	Thoemmes Press, Bristol
Thornes	Stanley Thornes, Cheltenham
Thorpe	D.W. Thorpe, Australia
Thorsons	Thorsons Publishers, London
Times	Times of Gloucester Press, Gloucester, Ontario

TMP	Thunder's Mouth Press, New York
Tombouctou	Tombouctou Books, Bolinas, CA
Totem	Totem Books, Don Mills, Ontario
Toucan	Toucan Press, St Peter Port, Guernsey
Touzot	Jean Touzot, Paris
TPF	Trianon Press Facsimiles, London
Tragara	Tragara Press, Edinburgh
Transaction	Transaction Publishers, New Brunswick, NJ
Transcendental	Transcendental Books, Hartford, CT
Transworld	Transworld, London
TrinityUP	Trinity UP, San Antonio, TX
Tsar	Tsar Publications, Canada
TTUP	Texas Technical University Press, Lubbock
Tuckwell	Tuckwell Press, East Linton
Tuduv	Tuduv, Munich
TulaneUP	Tulane UP, New Orleans, LA
TurkuU	Turku University, Turku, Finland
Turnstone	Turnstone Press, Winnipeg, Manitoba
Turtle Island	Turtle Island Foundation, Berkeley, CA
Twayne	Twayne Publishing, Boston, MA
UAB	University of Aston, Birmingham
UAdelaide	University of Adelaide, Australia
UAlaP	University of Alabama Press, Tuscaloosa
UAlbertaP	University of Alberta Press, Edmonton
UAntwerp	University of Antwerp
UArizP	University of Arizona Press, Tucson
UArkP	University of Arkansas Press, Fayetteville
UAthens	University of Athens, Greece
UBarcelona	University of Barcelona, Spain
UBCP	University of British Columbia Press, Vancouver
UBergen	University of Bergen, Norway
UBrno	J.E. Purkyne University of Brno, Czechoslovakia
UBrussels	University of Brussels
UCalgaryP	University of Calgary Press, Canada
UCalP	University of California Press, Berkeley
UCAP	University of Central Arkansas Press, Conway
UCapeT	University of Cape Town Press
UChicP	University of Chicago Press
UCDubP	University College Dublin Press
UCL	UCL Press (University College London)
UCopenP	University of Copenhagen Press, Denmark
UDelP	University of Delaware Press, Newark
UDijon	University of Dijon
UDur	University of Durham, Durham, UK
UEA	University of East Anglia, Norwich
UErlangen-N	University of Erlangen-Nuremberg, Germany
UEssex	University of Essex, Colchester
UExe	University of Exeter, Devon

UFlorence	University of Florence, Italy
UFlorP	University of Florida Press
UFR	Université François Rabelais, Tours
UGal	University College, Galway
UGeoP	University of Georgia Press, Athens
UGhent	University of Ghent
UGlasP	University of Glasgow Press
UHawaiiP	University of Hawaii Press, Honolulu
UIfeP	University of Ife Press, Ile-Ife, Nigeria
UIllp	University of Illinois Press, Champaign
UInnsbruck	University of Innsbruck
UIowaP	University of Iowa Press, Iowa City
UKanP	University of Kansas Press, Lawrence, KS
UKL	University of Kentucky Libraries, Lexington
ULavalP	Les Presses de l'Université Laval, Quebec
ULiège	University of Liège, Belgium
ULilleP	Presses Universitaires de Lille, France
ULondon	University of London
Ulster	University of Ulster, Coleraine
U/M	Underwood/Miller, Los Angeles
UMalta	University of Malta, Msida
UManitobaP	University of Manitoba Press, Winnipeg
UMassP	University of Massachusetts Press, Amherst
Umeå	Umeå Universitetsbibliotek, Umeå
UMichP	University of Michigan Press, Ann Arbor
UMinnP	University of Minnesota Press, Minneapolis
UMirail-ToulouseP	University of Mirail-Toulouse Press, France
UMIRes	UMI Research Press, Ann Arbor, MI
UMissP	University of Missouri Press, Columbia
UMP	University of Mississippi Press, Lafayette
UMysore	University of Mysore, India
UNancyP	Presses Universitaires de Nancy, France
UNCP	University of North Carolina Press, Chapel Hill, NC
Undena	Undena Publications, Malibu, CA
UNDP	University of Notre Dame Press, Notre Dame, IN
UNebP	University of Nebraska Press, Lincoln
UNevP	University of Nevada Press, Reno
UNewE	University of New England, Armidale, New South Wales
UnEWE, CALLS	University of New England, Centre for Australian Language and Literature Studies
Ungar	Frederick Ungar, New York
Unicopli	Edizioni Unicopli, Milan
Unity	Unity Press, Hull
UnityP	Unity Press Woollahra
Universa	Uilgeverij Universa, Wetteren, Belgium
UNMP	University of New Mexico Press, Albuquerque
UNorthTP	University of North Texas Press
UNott	University of Nottingham

UNSW	University of New South Wales
Unwin	Unwin Paperbacks, London
Unwin Hyman	Unwin Hyman, London
UOklaP	University of Oklahoma Press, Norman
UOslo	University of Oslo
UOtagoP	University of Otago Press, Dunedin, New Zealand
UOttawaP	University of Ottawa Press
UPA	UP of America, Lanham, MD
UParis	University of Paris
UPColardo	UP of Colorado, Niwot, CO
UPennP	University of Pennsylvania Press, Philadelphia
UPittP	University of Pittsburgh Press, Pittsburgh
UPKen	University Press of Kentucky, Lexington
UPMissip	UP of Mississippi, Jackson
UPN	Université de Paris Nord, Paris
UPNE	UP of New England, Hanover, NH
Uppsala	Uppsala University, Uppsala
UProvence	University of Provence, Aix-en-Provence
UPSouth	University Press of the South, NO
UPValéry	University Paul Valéry, Montpellier
UPVirginia	UP of Virginia, Charlottesville
UQDE	University of Queensland, Department of English
UQP	University of Queensland Press, St Lucia
URouen	University of Rouen, Mont St Aignan
URP	University of Rochester Press
USalz	Institut für Anglistik und Amerikanstik, University of Salzburg
USantiago	University of Santiago, Spain
USCP	University of South Carolina Press, Columbia
USFlorP	University of South Florida Press, Florida
USheff	University of Sheffield
Usher	La Casa Usher, Florence
USPacific	University of the South Pacific, Institute of Pacific Studies, Suva, Fiji
USQ, DHSS	University of Southern Queensland, Department of Humanities and Social Sciences
USydP	University of Sydney Press
USzeged	University of Szeged, Hungary
UtahSUP	Utah State UP, Logan
UTampereP	University of Tampere Press, Knoxville
UTas	University of Tasmania, Hobart
UTennP	University of Tennessee Press, Knoxville
UTexP	University of Texas Press, Austin
UTorP	University of Toronto Press, Toronto
UTours	Université de Tours
UVerm	University of Vermont, Burlington
UVict	University of Victoria, Victoria, BC
UWalesP	University of Wales Press, Cardiff

UWAP	University of Western Australia Press, Nedlands
UWarwick	University of Warwick, Coventry
UWashP	University of Washington Press, Seattle
UWaterlooP	University of Waterloo Press, Waterloo, Ontario
UWI	University of the West Indies, St Augustine, Trinidad
UWIndiesP	University of West Indies Press, Mona, Jamaica
UWiscM	University of Wisconsin, Milwaukee
UWiscP	University of Wisconsin Press, Madison
UWoll	University of Wollongong
UYork	University of York, York
Valentine	Valentine Publishing and Drama, Rhinebeck, NY
V&A	Victoria and Albert Museum, London
VanderbiltUP	Vanderbilt UP, Nashville, TE
V&R	Vandenhoeck & Ruprecht, Göttingen, Germany
Van Gorcum	Van Gorcum, Assen, Netherlands
Vantage	Vantage Press, New York
Variorum	Variorum, Ashgate Publishing, Hampshire
Vehicule	Vehicule Press, Montreal
Vendome	Vendome Press, New York
Verdant	Verdant Publications, Chichester
Verso	Verso Editions, London
VictUP	Victoria UP, Victoria University of Wellington, New Zealand
Vieweg	Vieweg Braunschweig, Wiesbaden
Vikas	Vikas Publishing House, New Delhi
Viking	Viking Press, New York
VikingNZ	Viking, Auckland
Virago	Virago Press, London
Vision	Vision Press, London
VLB	VLB Éditeur, Montreal
VP	Vulgar Press, Carlton North, Australia
VR	Variorum Reprints, London
Vrin	J. Vrin, Paris
VUUP	Vrije Universiteit UP, Amsterdam
Wakefield	Wakefield Press
W&B	Whiting & Birch, London
W&N	Weidenfeld & Nicolson, London
Water Row	Water Row Press, Sudbury, MA
Watkins	Paul Watkins, Stanford, Lincsolnshire
WB	Wissenschaftliche Buchgesellschaft, Darmstadt
W/B	Woomer/Brotherson, Revere, PA
Weaver	Weaver Press
Webb&Bower	Webb & Bower, Exeter
Wedgestone	Wedgestone Press, Winfield, KS
Wedgetail	Wedgetail Press, Earlwood, New South Wales
WesleyanUP	Wesleyan UP, Middletown, CT
West	West Publishing, St Paul, MN
WHA	William Heinemann Australia, Port Melbourne, Victoria

Wheatsheaf	Wheatsheaf Books, Brighton
Whiteknights	Whiteknights Press, University of Reading, Berkshire
White Lion	White Lion Books, Cambridge
Whitston	Whitston Publishing, Troy, NY
Whittington	Whittington Press, Herefordshire
WHP	Warren House Press, Sale, Cheshire
Wiener	Wiener Publishing, New York
Wildwood	Wildwood House, Aldershot, Hampshire
Wiley	John Wiley, Chichester, New York and Brisbane
Wilson	Philip Wilson, London
Winter	Carl Winter Universitätsverlag, Heidelberg, Germany
Winthrop	Winthrop Publishers, Cambridge, MA
WIU	Western Illinois University, Macomb, IL
WL	Ward Lock, London
WLUP	Wilfrid Laurier UP, Waterloo, Ontario
WMP	World Microfilms Publications, London
WMU	Western Michigan University, Kalamazoo, MI
Woeli	Woeli Publishing Services
Wolfhound	Wolfhound Press, Dublin
Wombat	Wombat Press, Wolfville, NS
Wo-No	Wolters-Noordhoff, Groningen, Netherlands
Woodstock	Woodstock Books, Oxford
Woolf	Cecil Woolf, London
Words	Words, Framfield, E. Sussex
WP	Women's Press, London
WPC	Women's Press of Canada, Toronto
WSUP	Wayne State UP, Detroit, MI
WVUP	West Virginia UP, Morgantown
W-W	Williams-Wallace, Toronto
WWU	Western Washington University, Bellingham
Xanadu	Xanadu Publications, London
YaleUL	Yale University Library Publications, New Haven, CT
YaleUP	Yale UP, New Haven, CO and London
Yamaguchi	Yamaguchi Shoten, Kyoto
YorkP	York Press, Fredericton, NB
Younsmere	Younsmere Press, Brighton
Zed	Zed Books, London
Zell	Hans Zell, East Grinstead, W. Sussex
Zena	Zena Publications, Penrhyndeudraeth, Gwynedd
Zephyr	Zephyr Press, Somerville, MA
Zomba	Zomba Books, London
Zwemmer	A. Zwemmer, London

3. Acronyms

AAVE	African-American Vernacular English

AmE	American English
AusE	Australian English
BrE	British English
DP	Determiner Phrase
ECP	Empty Category Principle
EFL	English as a Foreign Language
EIL	English as an International Language
ELT	English Language Teaching
eModE	early Modern English
ENL	English as a Native Language
EPNS	English Place-Name Society
ESL	English as a Second Language
ESP	English for Special Purposes
HPSG	Head-driven Phrase Structure Grammar
LF	Logical Form
LFG	Lexical Functional Grammar
ME	Middle English
MED	Middle English Dictionary
NZE	New Zealand English
ODan	Old Danish
OE	Old English
OED	Oxford English Dictionary
OF	Old French
ON	Old Norse
OT	Optimality Theory
PDE	Present-Day English
PF	Phonological Form
PP	Prepositional Phrase
SABE	South African Black English
SAE	South African English
TMA	Tense, Mood and Aspect
UG	Universal Grammar

Preface

The Year's Work in English Studies is a narrative bibliography that records and evaluates scholarly writing on English language and on literatures written in English. It is published by Oxford University Press on behalf of the English Association.

The Editors and the English Association are pleased to announce that this year's Beatrice White Prize has been awarded to Ian C. Cunningham and Andrew G. Watson for their editorial work on the fifth volume of Neil Ripley Ker's *Medieval Manuscripts in British Libraries* published by Clarendon Press (ISBN 0 1981 8277 5).

The authors of *YWES* attempt to cover all significant contributions to English studies. Writers of articles can assist this process by sending offprints to the journal, and editors of journals that are not readily available in the UK are urged to join the many who send us complete sets of current and back issues. These materials should be addressed to The Editors, *YWES*, The English Association, The University of Leicester, University Road, Leicester LEI 7RH, UK.

Our coverage of articles and books is greatly assisted by the Modern Language Association of America, who annually supply proofs of their *International Bibliography* in advance of the publication of each year's coverage.

The views expressed in *YWES* are those of its individual contributors and are not necessarily shared by the Editors, Associate Editors, or the English Association.

We would like to acknowledge a special debt of gratitude to Gill Mitchell and Carole Bookhamer for their efforts on behalf of this volume.

The Editors

I

English Language

CAMILLA VASQUEZ, JEROEN VAN DE WEIJER, BETTELOU
LOS, WIM VAN DER WURFF, BEÁTA GYURIS, JULIE
COLEMAN, EDWARD CALLARY, LIESELOTTE ANDERWALD,
ANDREA SAND, PETRA BETTIG AND CLARA CALVO

This chapter has eleven sections: 1. History of English Linguistics; 2. Phonetics and Phonology; 3. Morphology; 4. Syntax; 5. Semantics; 6. Lexicography, Lexicology, and Lexical Semantics; 7. Onomastics; 8. Dialectology and Sociolinguistics; 9. New Englishes and Creolistics; 10. Pragmatics and Discourse Analysis; 11. Stylistics. Section 1 is by Camilla Vasquez; section 2 is by Jeroen van de Weijer; sections 3 and 4 are by Bettelou Los and Wim van der Wurff; section 5 is by Beáta Gyuris; section 6 is by Julie Coleman; section 7 is by Edward Callary; section 8 is by Lieselotte Anderwald; section 9 is by Andrea Sand; section 10 is by Petra Bettig; section 11 is by Clara Calvo.

1. History of English Linguistics

The dating of the second version of Ben Jonson's *English Grammar* is discussed in a brief article by Derek Britton (*N&Q* 49[2002] 331–4). The original version of Jonson's *Grammar* was destroyed by fire in 1623, and the second version was published in 1640, subsequent to Jonson's death in 1637. Using biographical evidence to challenge the commonly held scholarly opinion, which dates the *Grammar* to the 1630s, Britton suggests instead an earlier dating. He argues convincingly that, among other factors, the stroke that Jonson suffered in 1628, which left him partially paralysed, would have made it difficult for Jonson to write the *Grammar* in his final years. Britton notes that it seems far more likely that Jonson would have taken up writing the second version of the *Grammar* shortly after the fire, at a time when he could more easily recall the contents of the original *Grammar*.

In her article, 'Out in Left Field: Spelling Reformers of the Eighteenth Century' (*TPS* 100[2002] 5–23), Joan C. Beal observes that while the middle of the eighteenth century saw few spelling reformers, there were 'small clusters of work on spelling reform' (p. 7) around the beginning and the end of the century. Beal centres her discussion primarily on three spelling reformers from the end of the century: Abraham Tucker, Thomas Spence, and James Elphinston. Because there was no unified spelling reform movement at the time and the three men were unacquainted with one another, Beal attempts to find some common link or 'common denominator' between them. Spence and Elphinston had more in common with one another than with Tucker: both were teachers, and both were somewhat zealous in the mission for spelling reform. Tucker, in contrast, was 'a country gentleman', and in terms of his interest in spelling reform, is described by Beal as more of a 'dilettante' than Spence and Elphinston. Using network theory, Beal argues that all three men were potential innovators due to their non-mainstream or marginal place in society. She concludes by pointing out another possible connection among the three men and their interest in spelling reform: John Locke's writings, which were generally influential on eighteenth-century linguistic thought, and which advocated that 'written language should conform to spoken usage' (p. 20).

Ingrid Tieken-Boon van Ostade and Randy Bax, 'Of Dodsley's Projects and Linguistic Influence: The Language of Johnson and Lowth' (*HLSL* 2[2002]), also use social network analysis to study linguistic change and linguistic influence, focusing on Robert Dodsley's friendship with Samuel Johnson and Robert Lowth. The authors provide examples of Hester Thrale's correspondence with Johnson, which seem to indicate that Thrale was influenced by Johnson's spelling system, thereby attesting to Johnson's role of 'early adopter' within the social network, who set the norm for others. Due to his social and geographical mobility, Lowth, in contrast, is presented as 'a linguistic innovator', who functioned as a sort of 'bridge' between the upper classes and 'all those who wished to improve themselves through their language'. Lowth's relationships with others in his social network are based on an analysis of epistolary formulas found in his personal correspondence. Robert Lowth is also the topic of another article by Ingrid Tieken-Boon van Ostade, which is concerned with 'Robert Lowth and the Strong Verb System' (*LangS* 24[2002] 459–69). She focuses, in particular, on Lowth's discussion of two strong verb forms: past tense and past participle. Comparing his treatment of strong verbs to those of his contemporaries, she observes that Lowth 'can be regarded as the first grammarian to actually condemn the use of a single form for the past tense and for the past participle and to take a truly prescriptive point of view in this matter' (p. 463). Most interesting is Tieken-Boon van Ostade's analysis of the language of Lowth's personal correspondence. She finds that, in eleven instances, Lowth confounded past tense with past participle; however, these occurrences appeared only in his informal letters to his wife and close friends, and never in his more formal correspondence. Tieken-Boon van Ostade calls for the publication of a collection of Lowth's letters, which would facilitate the systematic analysis of Lowth's own language and allow for a comparison of the ways in which Lowth's own language 'differed from the linguistic norm he presented in his grammar' (p. 467).

Linda Mitchell's *Grammar Wars: Language as Cultural Battlefield in 17th and 18th Century England* represents an important contribution to scholarship not only on the history of English linguistics, but also on social, cultural, and intellectual history in the seventeenth and eighteenth centuries. Mitchell describes this period as a time of linguistic change and innovation, with grammar at the centre of many controversies, which often extended far beyond grammar. In her introduction, Mitchell observes that 'any given grammar text was almost always engaged in one of five controversies [which are treated successively in five chapters] at the time: standardization, pedagogy, writing instruction, universal language, and social position' (p. 14). In her first chapter, Mitchell explores the complex ways in which grammar was understood during this period, focusing on three key themes: the relationships between English grammar and Latin grammar, the emergence of two 'factions' of grammarians (prescriptivists and descriptivists), and the 'inversion of linguistic authority' from grammarians to lexicographers. The impact of the shift from Latin 'as the language of the educated' (p. 46) to English 'as the language of primary use' (p. 46) on pedagogic practices is addressed in chapter 2. Chapter 3 includes a discussion of the integration of the teaching of writing into many grammars of the period, including the influence of rhetoric and the introduction of letter-writing exercises in grammar texts. In chapter 4, Mitchell takes up the changing meaning of 'universal language': from the seventeenth-century's interest in the creation of artificial languages, to the resulting eighteenth-century search for elements which were common to all languages. Mitchell's final chapter is concerned with the production of grammars designed for two new audiences: foreigners and women. She concludes with a summary of related further topics for exploration and provides an extensive bibliography of primary and secondary sources. (Due to its late publication date in December 2001, this title was unavailable for review in the previous edition of *YWES*.)

Manfred Görlach's *Explorations in English Historical Linguistics* brings together three of the author's papers written in 2000–2001, which cover distinct yet related topics. This volume represents an important contribution to the history and historiography of English, and throughout the papers Görlach points out areas that are in need of further research. In chapter 1, Görlach explores the contribution of translations to the development of the English language, from Old English up to the nineteenth century. Under the subheading for each period, Görlach discusses the linguistic consequences of biblical, literary, and poetic translations. English etymology is the topic taken up in chapter 2. Görlach notes that the study of etymology has long been neglected in studies of historical English linguistics. Historical sociolinguistic concerns such as standardization are the focus of chapter 3, the title of which is 'Correctness and the History of English'. *A Re-view of Reviews* represents a selected collection of forty reviews written by Görlach. A complete bibliography of Görlach's nearly 750 reviews is included as an appendix. The forty reviews are organized into chapters around four topics: Medieval Studies; Historical Linguistics and the History of English; Dialectology and Sociolinguistics; and Contact Linguistics and Lexicography.

2. Phonetics and Phonology

A number of articles discuss general phonological concepts on which English phonology bears. Natasha Warner, 'The Phonology of Epenthetic Stops: Implications for the Phonetics-Phonology Interface in Optimality Theory' (*Linguistics* 40[2002] 1–27), discusses stop insertion, which has been described for many languages including English (e.g. the [p] sound in *dream*[p]*t* is an epenthetic stop). This phenomenon is well understood as mistiming of the changes in place, voicing, and velic closure. In her article, Warner also seeks to account for

quantitative differences of stop insertion in different environments, and discusses
the implications of the process for the phonetics-phonology interface as modelled in
OT.

The interface between phonology and morphology is dealt with by Luigi Burzio
in 'Missing Players: Phonology and the Past-Tense Debate' (*Lingua* 112[2002]
157–99) on the basis of the observation that morphological irregularity correlates
inversely with phonological regularity, e.g. regular past tense formation may result
in phonologically ill-formed syllables (e.g. *peeped* with a long vowel in a doubly
closed syllable) while irregular past tense formation results in phonologically well-
formed syllables (e.g. *kept* with a short vowel in the same context). This observation
was not straightforwardly captured in earlier models, Burzio argues. In his own
model, underlying representations in the traditional sense do not exist. In
'Segmental Contrast Meets Output-to-Output Faithfulness' (*LingB* 11[2002] 163–
81) Burzio also underscores the importance of 'other' existing surface forms in the
optimization process.

Daniel Silverman's 'Dynamic versus Static Phonotactic Conditions in Prosodic
Morphology' (*Linguistics* 40[2002] 29–59) discusses the concept of complementary
distribution, making use, among others, of New York tensing data, in which [æ] is
tensed and diphthongized preceding a certain class of segments in the same syllable,
so that the vowel in *man* is different from that in *manager*.

A number of articles broaden our knowledge of particular dialects and varieties of
English. In Britain, Klaske van Leyden, in 'The Relationship between Vowel and
Consonant Duration in Orkney and Shetland Dialects' (*Phonetica* 59[2002] 1–19),
discusses the Shetland dialect, in which closed monosyllables generally contain
either a short vowel followed by a long consonant, or a long vowel followed by a
short consonant. This correlation is attributed to the Scandinavian substrate of the
dialect, which shows the same correlation. In an investigation of this feature for
Shetland and Orkney dialects, as well as of Standard Scottish English and Standard
Norwegian, van Leyden finds that the relation is strongest in Shetland and resembles
the Norwegian situation. The influence of the Scottish Vowel Length Rule is also
taken into account. With respect to Received Pronunciation (RP), Anne Fabricius's
'Weak Vowels in Modern RP: An Acoustic Study of happY-tensing and KIT/schwa
Shift' (*LVC* 14[2002] 211–37), considers variation in weak vowels, such as the final
vowel in words like *happy*. Is this still the [ɪ]-type vowel that was prescribed in
traditional RP, or has it becomes tense [i] instead? Fabricius finds that many
younger speakers settle upon an intermediate phonetic value, and discusses the
implications of her findings for discussions of dialect levelling in Britain.

On the other side of the Atlantic, Christine Mallinson and Walt Wolfram's
'Dialect Accommodation in a Bi-Ethnic Mountain Enclave Community: More
Evidence on the Development of African American English' (*LSoc* 31[2002] 743–
75) lists, among other things, phonological characteristics of the language variety
discussed: consonant cluster reduction, reduction of syllable-final stops, rhoticity,
/ai/ monophthongization, and its overall vowel system in the Appalachian region of
western North Carolina. Thomas E. Murray, in 'Language Variation and Change in
the Urban Midwest: The Case of St. Louis, Missouri' (*LVC* 14[2002] 347–61),
presents and discusses a number of phonological features characteristic of the St
Louis variety of English, bearing on the place of this variety in the American dialect
situation.

On the topic of American English in general, Bryan Gick's 'An X-Ray Investigation of Pharyngeal Constriction in American English Schwa' (*Phonetica* 59[2002] 38–48) shows that there is a mid-pharyngeal constriction in this vowel, which contradicts views that schwa should be a vowel without an articulatory target or place features. The article also investigates the relation of schwa with the segment /r/. Lisa Lavoie's 'Some Influences on the Realization of *for* and *four* in American English' (*JIPA* 32[2002] 175–202) presents a good review of reduction phenomena related to speech style, and examines in minute phonetic detail the different factors that play a role in the realization of the function word *for* and the content word *four*.

Careful phonetic studies with respect to vowel-to-vowel co-articulation were done by Patrice Speeter Beddor, James D. Harnsberger, and Stephanie Lindemann in 'Language-Specific Patterns of Vowel-to-Vowel Coarticulation: Acoustic Structures and their Perceptual Correlates' (*JPhon* 30[2002] 591–627). They report on production and perception experiments that suggest that vowel-to-vowel co-articulation effects are different between languages (they compare English and Shona), and that listeners make use of these differences in perception.

Finally, there are a number of articles which deal with language acquisition. Allyson Carter and Cynthia G. Glopper, 'Prosodic Effects on Word Recognition' (*L&S* 45[2002] 321–53), find that English children's reduction of certain syllables is mirrored by English adult outputs to a large extent. Both maintain well-formed prosodic structures and preserve prominent syllables: the children while acquiring the language, and the adults in an experimental setting. A difference between both categories of speakers exists as well, however: in English, adults tend to preserve word-initial syllables while the children tend to preserve word-final ones. This is attributed to a shift in bias at some point in time from the right to the left edge of the word. David Snow and Heather L. Balog's 'Do Children Produce the Melody before the Words? A Review of Developmental Intonation Research' (*Lingua* 112[2002] 1025–58) is an attempt to find out when babies begin to acquire the highly complex system of intonation, with special attention to the difference between intonation rooted in emotion and physiology, and intonation that is used for grammatical purposes such as phrase-marking. It is very difficult to tease both types apart, and the difficulties that had to be overcome in carrying out the experiment reported on underline the importance of this study.

3. Morphology

We begin with two excellent textbooks. *An Introduction to English Morphology*, by Andrew Carstairs-McCarthy, has appeared in the Edinburgh series of Textbooks on the English Language. It has chapters on words (types, tokens, lexical items), roots and affixes (bound and free, allomorphs), inflection (regular and irregular, nominal, verbal and adjectival), derivation (by conversion and affixation), compounds/blends/phrasal words, word structure (with the affix as head, with multiple affixation, and with bracketing paradoxes), productivity (in shape and meaning), the history of English word formation (the Germanic, Greek, and Romance contributions, the diachronic development), and words in languages in general (comparative concerns). The author has managed to make the material both clear and challenging; exercises and recommended reading for each chapter help to achieve this. For more advanced students, a textbook has come out in Arnold's Understanding Language series: *Understanding Morphology* by Martin Haspelmath. The first chapter explains what morphology is and introduces the distinction between analytic and (poly)synthetic; chapter 2 clears the ground by introducing basic terms (morphemes, lexemes, bases and roots, reduplication, etc.). The remaining chapters deal with morphological issues: the role of the lexicon; morphological rules; grammaticalization and reanalysis; inflection and derivation; morphological trees and productivity, inflectional paradigms, diagnostics for word division, free versus bound forms, lexical integrity, output constraints, morphophonology, level I and level II affixes, and valence-changing operations, to name just a few. Data are drawn from a wide variety of languages, there is a glossary, and each chapter concludes with a brief summary and exercises.

Among general morphological issues, the extent to which morphology mirrors syntax—or is even produced by syntax—has continued to occupy several minds. Joseph Emonds sees 'A Common Basis for Syntax and Morphology: Tri-Level Lexical Insertion' (in Boucher, ed., *Many Morphologies*, pp. 235–62). He points out that the Right Hand Head Rule of morphology is also encountered in many syntactic phrases (*very proud, mere boys*, (*he*) *angrily spoke*), and goes on to suggest that the heads of words are also the heads of phrases. Another similarity is found in bound morphemes and grammatical words: both typically express general, cognitive meanings. As a consequence, Emonds proposes that bound morphemes can be inserted not only lexically, but also at LF or PF (depending on their properties). A further broad similarity is discussed in Anna Maria di Sciullo's 'The Asymmetry of Morphology' (in Boucher, ed., pp. 1–28), which takes affixes to be heads, projecting a specifier and complement; different affixes impose different requirements on the configurations in these positions. This is applied to the affixes -*er*, -*able* and others, and also to the set of WH-*ever* forms.

The nature of the influence that word forms and meanings have on each other, and the proper way to represent it, is also still a big issue in morphology. Gary Libben and Roberto G. de Almeida ask: 'Is there a Morphological Parser?' (in Bendjahballah, Dressler, Pfeiffer, and Voeikova, eds., *Morphology 2000*, pp. 213–25). Their answer is: yes, and it is always on (i.e. there is pre-access as well as post-access parsing, at least in visual word recognition); evidence comes from an experiment in which a word like *banking* acted as a stimulus not only for *teller* (due to shared semantics of the whole word) but also for *river* (due to shared semantics of part of the word). Mary L. Hare, Michael Ford, and William D. Marslen-Wilson study 'Ambiguity and Frequency Effects in Regular Verb Inflection' (in Bybee and Hopper, eds., *Frequency and the Emergence of Linguistic Structure*, pp. 181–200); on the basis of experimental evidence, they argue that the past tense of regular verbs too must be lexically represented (since more frequent regular verbs are accessed faster than infrequent ones). A different approach is advocated by Laura M. Gonnerman and Elaine S. Andersen in 'Graded Semantic and Phonological Similarity Effects in Morphologically Complex Words' (in Bendjahballah *et al.*, eds., pp. 137–148). They argue for a distributed connectionist account of morphology to explain priming effects which show that both semantic and phonological similarity have scale-like rather than categorical effects. Adam Albright looks at 'The Lexical Bases of Morphological Well-Formedness' (in Bendjahballah *et al.*, eds., pp. 5–15). Experimental acceptability ratings show that it is type rather than token frequency that matters for novel verb forms (such as the past tense of *cleef—cleft*? or *cleefed*? and for *spling—splinged*? *splung*? *splang*? or *splought*?). In a non-derivational approach to word formation, Luigi Burzio considers 'Surface-to-Surface Morphology: When Your Representations Turn into Constraints' (in Boucher, ed., pp. 142–77). He also proposes that word shape is influenced by similar words in the lexicon (e.g. *remEdiable* does not follow the stress pattern of *rEmedy* because of the attraction by *remEdial*) and shows how word formation rules can be replaced by constraints as in Optimality Theory.

'Locatum and Location Verbs in Lexeme–Morpheme Base Morphology' by Mark Volpe (*Lingua* 112[2002] 103–19) presents a reanalysis of locatum/location verbs like *shelve* within the framework of L–MBM. Unaccusatives are studied in two articles by Bożena Cetnarowska: 'Unaccusativity Mismatches and Unaccusativity Diagnostics from Derivational Morphology' (in Boucher, ed., pp. 48–81) and 'Adjectival Past-Participle Formation as an Unaccusativity Diagnostic in English and in Polish' (in Bendjahballah *et al.*, eds., pp. 59–72). She shows that adjectival past participle formation (*the vanished treasure* vs. **the slept children*) and *re*-prefixation (*re-appear* vs. **re-laugh*) are reliable diagnostics for unaccusativity, once the semantic and pragmatic restrictions on these processes are recognized (e.g. for participle formation, the verb must be telic, and the resulting participle must be informative, as in ?*rested children* vs. *well-rested children*). The exact nature of the lexical entry for middle verbs is scrutinized in Christian Bassac and Pierette Bouillon's 'Middle Transitive Alternations in English: A Generative Lexicon Approach' (in Boucher, ed., pp. 29–47); the crucial element in the analysis is the inclusion of two sub-events, with an adverbial and negation licensing a shift to the second sub-event.

We turn to inflection. The article 'Accounting for the Position of Verbal Agreement Morphology with Psycholinguistic and Diachronic Explanatory Factors' by A. Enrique-Arias (*SLang* 26[2002] 1–31) argues that the position of agreement inflections can be accounted for by the fact that their diachronic origin is a relatively mobile source (unstressed pronouns) and by the assumption of a psycholinguistic principle which prevents fusion of grammatical markers to complex sequences of inflections. Julia Schlüter, in 'Morphology Recycled: The Principle of Rhythmic Alternation at Work in Early and Late Modern English Grammatical Variation' (in Fanego, López-Couso, and Pérez-Guerra, eds., *English Historical Syntax and Morphology*, pp. 255–81) argues that the rhythmic ideal of a strict alternation of strong and weak beats may have been a influential factor in morpheme loss once the decline of inflectional morphology in English was well under way. Though also on an inflectional affix, a very different tack is taken by Yael Sharvit and Penka Stateva in 'Superlative Expressions, Context, and Focus' (*Ling&P* 25[2002] 453–504): they argue that superlative morphemes cannot be interpreted DP-externally, and develop a DP-internal account.

In trying to determine the typical results of derivational processes, Laurie Bauer examines 'What You Can Do with Derivational Morphology' (in Bendjahballah *et al.*, eds., pp. 37–48). Some processes that are common among the forty-two languages examined are the formation of abstract and personal nouns from verbs, of diminutives from nouns, of abstract nouns from adjectives, of causative verbs, of adverbs from nouns, and so on. The material shows a certain amount of geographical clustering, but no clear implicational patterns. Noting the rarity of verbs derived from nouns (cf. *to clear* 'make clear', *to enlarge* 'make large', but not **to enthrone* 'to make into a throne' or **to hospitalize* 'to make into a hospital'), Mark Baker focuses 'On Category Asymmetries in Derivational Morphology' (in Bendjahballah *et al.*, eds., pp. 17–35). His solution lies in a novel theory of lexical categories, in which nouns crucially bear a referential index, which would have to be lost for successful derivation to take place. Mark Aronoff and Nanna Fuhrhop, in 'Restricting Suffix Combinations in German and English: Closing Suffixes and the Monosuffix Constraint' (*NL&LT* 20[2002] 451–90), present an account of the restrictions on combining derivational suffixes.

Laurie Bauer, in 'Why Are We Linguists and Not Linguisticians?'(in Lentz and Möhlig, eds., *Of Dyuersitie & Chaunge of Language*, pp. 27–32) tries to trace the semantic and pragmatic factors that have governed the fortunes of the *-ician* suffix. Dieter Kastovsky's 'The Derivation of Ornative, Locative, Ablative, Privative and Reversative Verbs in English'(in Fanego, López-Couso, and Pérez-Guerra, eds., pp. 99–109) describes the development of prefixes *be-*, *en-*, *dis-*, *un-*, *de-* and the suffixes *-ify*, *-ize*, *-ate*, *-en* in the history of English. Peter Hallmann compares 'Passive in Arabic and English' (in Bendjahballah *et al.*, eds., pp. 149–60), arguing that the passive participle in both languages is formed by a derivational process converting a verb into an adjective, but that this process is excluded by the presence of agentivity (hence the restriction to passives and unaccusatives). Knud Sørensen, in 'Particle + Verb-Stem Nouns' (in Lentz and Möhlig, eds., pp. 47–54) investigates combinations like *downturn*, *input* compared to *lookout* and *spinoff* and their productivity in the history of English. Ursula Lenker, in 'Is It, Stylewise or Otherwise, Wise to Use *-wise*? Domain Adverbials and the History of English *-wise*' (in Fanego, López-Couso, and Pérez-Guerra, eds., pp. 157–80) charts the development of this suffix to a viewpoint adverbial in PE, parallel to *-(c)ally*.

A few items discuss compounding. Roberto G. de Almeida and Gary Libben, in 'Compound Pre-Access Decomposition: Effects of Constituent Disruption' (*FoLi* 36[2002] 97–115), report on three experiments in which specific characters in the data were blanked out, which seem to show that compound processing is not dependent on accurate recognition of constituent morphemes. This points to a dual-route approach as the more likely model. Dieter Kastovsky's 'The "Haves" and the "Have-Nots" in Germanic and English: From *Bahuvrihi* Compounds to Affixal Derivation' (in Lentz and Möhlig, eds., pp. 33–46) traces the development of possessive compounds like *barefoot* 'having bare feet', which are adjectives and not, as expected by the right-headedness of Germanic compounds, nouns. 'The Emergence of the Verb–Verb Compound in Twentieth-Century English and Twentieth-Century Linguistics' by Benji Wald and Lawrence Besserman (in Minkova and Stockwell, eds., *Studies in the History of the English Language: A Millennial Perspective*, pp. 417–47) discusses combinations such as *freeze-dry* and *stir-fry*, which are a relative innovation. 'On the Structure of Acronyms and Neighbouring Categories: A Prototype-Based Account' (*ELL* 6[2002] 31–60), by Paula López Rúa, explores initialisms (acronyms, clippings, blends, and abbreviations).

We finish with some remaining items on historical issues. 'Diachronic Word-Formation and Studying Changes in Productivity over Time: Theoretical and Methodological Considerations', by Claire Cowie and Christianne Dalton-Puffer (in Díaz Vera, ed., *A Changing World of Words: Studies in English Historical*

Lexicography, Lexicology and Semantics, pp. 410–37), addresses the general question of how morphological productivity can be established for a historical stage of a language, in this case English. 'Inflections in the Two Manuscripts of Layamon's Brut', by Jacek Fisiak and Marcin Krygier (*LangS* 24[2002] 231–45), compares the strong verb system and personal pronoun usage in the two manuscripts and confirms the general view that the language of the Caligula manuscript is the most archaic. Laura Wright, in 'Some Morphological Features of the Norfolk Guild Certificates of 1388/9: An Exercise in Variation' (in Fisiak and Trudgill, eds., *East Anglian English*, pp. 79–162), looks at the distribution of eleven morphological features in London and Norfolk. Terttu Nevalainen, Helena Raumolin-Brunberg, and Peter Trudgill, in 'Chapters in the Social history of East Anglian English: The Case of the Third-Person Singular' (in Fisiak and Trudgill, eds., pp. 189–204) chart the variation between *-th* and *-s* and conclude that *-s* was not generalized in East Anglia until the seventeenth century, some forty years later than London. Muriel Norde, in 'The Final Stages of Grammaticalization: Affixhood and Beyond' (in Wischer and Diewald, eds., *New Reflections on Grammaticalization*, pp. 45–65), includes interesting cases of inflectional affixes becoming derivational affixes, which could be argued to be a case of degrammaticalization. Peter Kitson's 'Topography, Dialect, and the Relation of Old English Psalter Glosses (I)' (*ES* 83[2002] 474–503) is the first part of a detailed investigation into the stemma of the OE Psalter MSS, based on regional vocabulary for *brook*, *stream*, *spring*, etc. as well as regional morpho-syntactic differences, e.g. the case governed by the preposition *between*: dative (Wessex) or accusative (elsewhere).

4. Syntax

(a) Modern English

Howard Jackson's *Grammar and Vocabulary: A Resource Book for Students* is one of the impressively structured books in the Routledge English Language Introductions which can be worked through not only in the usual linear fashion but also by reading, say, the fifth unit in each of the four main sections, 'Introduction', 'Development', 'Exploration', and 'Extension'. This would mean reading in sequence, for instance, the sections 'Word Structure', 'Making New Words', 'Types of Word Structure', and 'Lexicalisation'. Such a 'flexi-text' approach is extremely useful for filling in particular gaps, like morphology, basic syntax, or word categories, in an individual student's knowledge. The final section, 'Exploration', consists of readings from the work of well-known experts in the various fields. Each unit comes with exercises and keys ('commentaries'), and there is a glossary.

A slim and useful student textbook for English syntax is *An Introduction to English Syntax* by Jim Miller. Although most of the examples are from English, the book introduces general concepts which provide the necessary tools for a basic syntactic analysis of any language. The book concentrates on topics that will remain useful to the student who does not go on to study linguistics but, say, literature or EFL teaching. Apart from the expected chapters on constituents and their functions, word classes, clauses, and so on, the book also includes a chapter on thematic roles, a chapter on case, gender, and mood, and one on aspect, tense and voice. A set of exercises is appended to every chapter, and there are appendices on notations to mark head–dependency relations and simple tree structures. Also a textbook, but of a pedagogical grammatical rather than theoretical kind is Lachlan Mackenzie's *Principles and Pitfalls of English Grammar*, a comparative Dutch–English grammar for first-year students in higher education. The second edition, published this year, has ironed out some infelicities but retains all the strengths of the first edition: it is still a thorough and patient pedagogical description of all the main areas of grammar, which also provides the student with enough linguistic terminology to talk and think sensibly about the topics dealt with.

Gunnel Tottie, *An Introduction to American English*, is an excellent introductory work which does not restrict itself to the linguistic features of the American language (including semantics and word-formation) and how these contrast with British English (pronunciation, vocabulary), but also provides socio-cultural background information: historical background, administration, everyday life, names (John Doe and Jane Roe), metaphors, pragmatics (the use of *uh* or *uh-uh*, openings and closings including those of typical American telephone conversations, thanking), varieties, language politics, and the 'ecology' of American English. Every chapter offers its own section of recommended reading and relevant websites, and some provide ideas for text corpora assignments. The book could be used in undergraduate courses but is also extremely useful as background reading for teachers of English.

African American English: A Linguistic Introduction by Lisa J. Green offers a descriptive grammar of AAE. It is beginning to be recognized that AAE speakers are at a disadvantage in the educational system because teachers tend to see their variety as just 'bad English' instead of a language in its own right. This affects the teacher's attitude towards the student, with a resultant negative expectation, and has a demoralizing effect on students, who sense the teacher's disdain for something that is an integral part of their identity. The aim of the book is not to discourage teachers from teaching their students Standard English, but to have them refrain from constantly 'correcting' the student's ordinary speech. By describing the features of AAE, the book shows that AAE has a grammar of its own. The first chapter describes some salient points of the AAE lexicon. Chapter 2 describes the use of verbal aspectual markers 'be', 'bin', 'dɔn', 'finna', 'steady', 'come'. Chapter 3 deals with negation, existential 'it' and 'dey', question formation, relative clauses and the preterite *had*. Chapter 4 looks at the phonology and prosodic features like stress and intonation. Chapter 5 examines speech events and rules of interaction, and the various modes of verbal repartee, stylized boasts, exchanges of inventive derogatory remarks ('playing the dozens'), and other strategies to impress, persuade, or manipulate people; it also includes a section on the conventions of AAE church services, with their practice of call and response between preacher and congregation. Chapters 6 and 7 deal with AAE in literature and in the media. The final chapter discusses approaches, attitudes, and education. This chapter provides concrete advice on how teachers can teach their AAE-speaking students Standard English without devaluing the language skills they learn at home. Exercises are provided at the end of each chapter.

A textbook of a more theoretical nature is Jae Jung Song's *Linguistic Typology: Morphology and Syntax*, which covers the typological ground in a very readable and accessible manner. The overall approach is Greenbergian, but European approaches (the Leningrad school; the Cologne UNITYP work; and the Prague school) are also briefly described. The topics dealt with include the staple typological issues: after an introduction on universals, typological axioms and problems, and the sampling of languages, there are chapters on basic word order (the object-verb versus verb-object types; explanations in terms of branching direction; the hypothesis of Early Immediate Constituents; the relation between word and morpheme order), case marking (the different systems encountered; the theories developed to make sense of them; the relations between case marking and discourse; argument-changing operations; head versus dependent marking), relative clauses (the different strategies, the accessibility hierarchy, relations with word order), causatives (the various types; the expression of the causee), and applications of typology (in historical linguistics and in studies of language acquisition). Altogether, this is a fine work and it seems to us that it more than fulfils the author's hope, expressed in the preface, that the book will meet a need among students of linguistics.

Among the general works, pride of place this year must be given to Ray Jackendoff for his *Foundations of Language: Brain, Meaning, Grammar, Evolution*. Jackendoff has taken up the challenge of relating language and thought to the real world. The achievements of neuroscience and those of the linguistic enterprise intersect when language in all its aspects is investigated from the viewpoint of psychology, biology, philosophy, and evolutionary theory. Part I, 'Psychological and Biological Foundations', discusses the complexity of language, and language as a mental phenomenon. Jackendoff clarifies the competence/performance debate and concludes that these concepts should be taken as a methodological convenience, 'not as a firewall to protect a certain form of inquiry', p. 34). The connection between the two (i.e. between linguistic structure and language processing) is a running motif throughout the book. The concept of Universal Grammar (UG) is re-examined in the light of evidence from both inside and outside linguistics (language impairments and brain injury or genetic defects). The second part of the book presents a theory of grammar that goes beyond syntax but tries to integrate the various subfields—phonology, morphology, semantics—into one architecture: this is linguistic structure, i.e. 'competence'. The problem of lexical storage versus rule-derivation—i.e. which items are irregular and have to be listed and which are regular and can be derived from rules, although there is evidence that many of these are also stored—is important for our understanding of language-processing and 'performance', and chapter 7, 'Implications for Processing' shows how the proposed architecture translates into a processing model. The final chapter of part II, 'An Evolutionary Perspective on the Architecture', argues that UG is best regarded as consisting of layered subcomponents, some of which are more vulnerable (to late language learning, to aphasia) than others, which may point to them being relative evolutionary innovations. Language evolution, then, can be seen as an incremental build-up of refinements of pre-existing interfaces between components. Part III, 'Semantic and Conceptual Foundations', looks at how meaning can be handled in the parallel architecture. Syntax alone does not determine semantics (as in much generative thinking), but neither does semantics entirely determine syntax (as is often asserted in Cognitive Grammar). An absolute must for anyone interested in language.

William Croft, unhappy with the endless cycle of new and revised syntactic theories that for all their claims of universality still fall into the trap of trying to fit the world's languages into the mould of 'Standard Average European', has offered his own approach to syntax in *Radical Construction Grammar: Syntactic Theory in Typological Perspective*. Radical Construction Grammar (RCG) builds upon concepts from Cognitive Grammar and Construction Grammar, and, like these, takes syntax (but also morphology and idioms) to be made up of conventionalized routines of pairing form and meaning. Constructions in RCG are the primitive elements of syntactic representation, and grammatical categories like 'noun', 'verb' or functions like 'subject' or 'object' are derivatives, not primitives. All constructions are language-specific, none can claim universality. One of the advantages of the approach is that a language is described with as few presupposed ideas about structure, grammatical functions, or word categories as possible. This extremely interesting and thought-provoking book discusses data from a wide range of languages and includes a section 'Frequently Asked Questions' as part of its argumentation, answering questions like 'How can you have a syntactic theory without atomic primitive units?' and 'How can I use RCG for grammatical description if all categories are construction-specific and constructions are language-specific?'

William Croft does not stand alone in his rejection of word categories as primitives of linguistic theory. In 'No Nouns, No Verbs: Psycholinguistic Arguments in Favor of Lexical Underspecification'(*Lingua* 112[2002] 771–91), David Barner and Alan Bale use arguments from research in neuro-linguistics and developmental psychology to conclude that a theory without lexical categories provides a better account of creative language use and category-specific neurological deficits, and offers a natural solution to the bootstrapping problem in language acquisition. That category labels like Adjective, Noun, and Verb are not linguistic primitives is also argued by Artemis Alexiadou in *Functional Structure in Nominals: Nominalization and Ergativity*. They are created by the syntax, more specifically by the functional projections DP, AspectP, and vP and their feature specifications. These feature specifications allow Alexiadou to posit a typology of derivational processes denoting events in terms of functional architecture. The striking parallels between nominalizations in nominative-accusative languages and those in ergative languages suggest that nominalizations are unaccusative systems. The investigation unearthed further parallels between possessor subjects in nominalizations (*John's destruction of the city*) and *have*-perfects, and between *by*-phrase possessors (*the destruction of the city by John*) and *be*-perfects, where the agent is introduced as a PP.

A volume that will be cheered by some and booed by others, because it defends a thesis that is widely disbelieved, is Enfield, ed., *Ethnosyntax: Explorations in Grammar and Culture*. In his introduction (pp. 3–30) the editor provides a definition of ethno-syntax (the connections between cultural knowledge, attitudes, and practices on the one hand and the morpho-syntax of a language on the other), distinguishes various types, sketches ethno-syntactic methodology (paying special attention to the dangers besetting this approach), and points out a route along which culture can enter syntax (the process of grammaticalization by which pragmatic—culturally determined—implications get reinterpreted as semantics). The papers that follow illustrate these various points; we only mention here the ones that deal with English facts or make points of obvious interest for the study of English. Anthony V.N. Diller and Wilaiwan Khanittanan, in 'Syntactic Enquiry as a Cultural Activity' (pp. 31–51), argue that notions of acceptability represent institutionally situated judgements; specifically, they can be the result of linguistic education. Cliff Goddard's 'Ethnosyntax, Ethnopragmatics, Sign—Functions, and Culture' (pp. 52–73) is an exploration of the role of indexicality and iconicity in ethno-syntax. The paper on 'Culture, Cognition, and the Grammar of "Give" Clauses' by John Newman (pp. 74–95) finds connections between culture and the (complex) structure of 'give' clauses in some respects, but apparent arbitrariness in others. Andrew Pawly examines 'Using *He* and *She* for Inanimate Referents in English: Questions of Grammar and World View' (pp. 110–37). Tasmanian and US English show a surprising degree of convergence in their use of these pronouns for salient entities in animated discourse: portable objects get *he* if viewed with detachment, *she* if not; plants and animals get *he*; everything else gets *she*. A danger for the unwary ethno-syntactician is dealt with by Ronald Langacker in 'A Study in Unified Diversity: English and Mixtec Locatives' (pp. 138–61). Since Mixtec lacks PPs, instead using noun–noun compounds, it might be thought there is some basic cognitive or cultural difference between English and Mixtec speakers in the area of location; however, Langacker shows that both the English and Mixtec systems follow from well-established principles of cognitive grammar and grammaticalization theory, making clear that any ethno-syntactic effort must involve prior linguistic analysis. Lastly, there is Anna Wierzbicka, the inventor of the term ethno-syntax, with 'English Causative Constructions in an Ethnosyntactic Perspective: Focusing on *Let*' (pp. 162–203). From the many uses of *let*, she deduces the two meanings of 'refraining from doing something to others' and 'cooperation', and then links these to the Anglo-American cultural emphasis on personal autonomy, freedom, and equality.

John McWhorter, in *The Power of Babel: A Natural History of Language*, manages to present an account of his fascination for the diversity of human languages that is eminently readable for linguists and non-linguists alike. The book could be used as a textbook or sourcebook for courses on language change, as much of the discussion focuses on the propensity of human languages for 'morphing' into something completely different with the passage of time. The book does not feature the traditional concerns of language change textbooks—glottochronology, neogrammarians, Labov—but is probably more likely to make people interested in the subject of linguistics than such, more traditional, works. It intelligently and thoroughly addresses some typical non-linguist preoccupations, like the lack of hard-and-fast demarcations of what constitutes a language or a dialect, or the impossibility of ever reconstructing 'Proto-World', the ultimate ancestor, or why some languages have evolved such extremely complex systems: tonicity, sixteen 'genders', the Celtic consonant mutations. The issue of learnability is also much to the fore. McWhorter's thesis is that baroque complexity arises simply because it can: the powerful language acquisition device of children allows really complex systems to be still learnable. It becomes a different matter when the language in question has to be acquired through socio-historic accident by adult learners; the result is that the language inevitably loses some of its more *recherché* features—and McWhorter presents concrete examples of this process. The book includes a discussion of the problem of language death threatening so many of the world's languages today, as well as a realistic view of the kind of measures that can be taken considering the typical scenario of language death, particularly in the Third World—with massive urban migration leading to a situation in which people are far more likely to find a partner outside their original speech community, making it very impracticable to hand their native language down to their children and completely impossible to preserve it intact for their grandchildren.

David Crystal's *Language Death* can in some ways be regarded as a complementary volume to his *English as a Global Language* (CUP [1997]). Its chapter titles give a good idea of the content and structure of the book—each title is in the form of a question: 'What is Language Death?', 'Why Should We Care?', 'Why Do Languages Die?', 'Where Do We Begin?' and 'What Can Be Done?'. Complex issues are presented clearly and poignantly: how an indigenous language may be increasingly restricted to fewer and fewer domains—'folklorized'—by being officially marginalized by the dominant culture; how speakers themselves are made to feel ashamed of their own language; how people make a conscious decision to stop using their language, or not to pass it on to their children. Of the many things that can be done (like ensuring that the speakers of the endangered language have enough food, shelter, and health to survive at all), setting up new academic centres specifically for the study of the endangered language has proved to be a way of giving these languages an institutionalized presence, and thus prestige, the first prerequisite for language survival. Crystal stresses that an unyielding, condemnatory purism which does not allow the endangered language to change like any other language is yet another factor working against its survival.

We turn to corpus work. Susan Hunston's *Corpora in Applied Linguistics* is an introduction to corpus linguistics. The first half of the book discusses the scope and limitations of corpus studies, how to evaluate a corpus on content, size, and representativeness, the sort of research that can be carried out with its help, corpus annotation, and which methods of analysis can be used. The second half provides a detailed overview of how corpus linguistics can be useful in a variety of domains: the design of language-teaching materials, English for specific purposes, testing, lexicology, stylistics, and language variation, to name a few. The book touches upon interesting issues like the usefulness of corpus linguistics in 'forensic linguistics', where doubt was cast on the authenticity of a police confession because a corpus comparison brought to light the unnaturalness of the language as a sample of verbatim informal speech. The book provides a good overall view of the uses and concerns of corpus linguistics, with an emphasis on teaching.

In this it is quite different from another introductory work on corpus linguistics, *English Corpus Linguistics: An Introduction* by Charles F. Meyer, which introduces corpora from a purely linguistic point of view, as a step-by-step guide to constructing a corpus for linguistic purposes. The first chapter includes an upfront discussion of the strained relationship of corpus linguists who are perfectly happy to aim for descriptive adequacy, and the generative school who aim at explanatory adequacy and have less use for the ragged fringes of language that do not allow generalizations. Chapters 2 to 4 are the 'manual part': planning a corpus, collecting and computerizing data samples, and annotating (tagging and parsing) the result. Chapter 5, 'Analyzing a Corpus', gives guidance on determining whether a corpus is suitable for answering a particular research question, extracting information from a corpus and determining whether, and which, statistical tests are appropriate to the extracted information. The final chapter is about future prospects in corpus linguistics in view of the greater possibilities offered by technological advances. The book could be used as a student textbook: each chapter is provided with study questions at the end. One of the book's special features is the extensive list of existing corpora at the end, with details of where to find them.

Much in the same vein, but restricting itself to one particular corpus and therefore more like a manual, is *Exploring Natural Language: Working with the British Component of the International Corpus of English* by Gerald Nelson, Sean Wallis and Bas Aarts. It is the first of a series of handbooks on working with the various corpora in the International Corpus of English (ICE), a sub-series planned within the Varieties of English Around the World series. Part I, 'Introducing the Corpus', presents the ICE-GB Grammar and its tagging and parsing systems; part II, 'Exploring the Corpus', introduces the ICE Corpus Utility Program, which allows the user to construct queries. Queries that take a long time will be done in the background, so that the user does not have to stop work while the program 'thinks'. The possibilities offered by the Utility Program are impressive, especially with respect to syntactic queries. It is unfortunate that the book suffers from the sort of defect that can make computer manuals so infuriating; when 'fuzzy tree fragments', an important facility for putting together a query about a syntactic structure, are first introduced, the book goes straight on to describing how such a query is made without any explanation about what FTFs are or why one would want to use them. This information is not provided until forty-five pages later. Part III, 'Performing Research with the Corpus', presents six case studies and includes a chapter on experimental design which also incorporates chi-square tests and methodological problems. Part IV, 'The Future of the Corpus', outlines future plans. This book is a must for anyone who wants to explore the immense possibilities of the ICE-GB. It may be a good idea, nevertheless, not to restrict one's search to a single corpus. As Hideshi Takaie points out in 'A Trap in Corpus Linguistics: The Gap between Corpus-Based Analysis and Intuition-Based Analysis' (in Saito, Nakamura, and Yamazaki, eds., *English Corpus Linguistics in Japan*, pp. 111–30), data from different corpora often show surprising disparities (and not only in the rather obvious case when one of the corpora consists of intuitions).

The corpus formed by the definition sentences in the *Collins Cobuild Student's Dictionary* is exhaustively analysed in Geoff Barnbrook's *Defining Language: A Local Grammar of Definition Sentences*. After chapters dealing with monolingual English dictionaries in general (the type of linguistic information they contain, their definitions, the history of the genre, their conceptualization of meaning), with grammars and parsers, and with sub-languages (one of which is 'definition sentences', a text type that lends itself well to the development of a local grammar), Barnbrook proceeds to a taxonomy of the Cobuild definition types (four of them are encountered in the material) and a description of the grammar and parser that he has constructed for them. The book ends with a chapter containing an evaluation and implications (for the further study of this and related sub-languages and for the practical task of dictionary-making). All in all, this is a useful study of material that is consulted innumerable times by language learners.

We also include here a collection of articles using the multi-dimensional approach to textual variation, developed and popularized by Douglas Biber, by which linguistic co-occurrence patterns are established and then functionally interpreted. The book, entitled *Variation in English: Multi-Dimensional Studies*, is edited by Susan Conrad and Douglas Biber, who between them are also the (co-)authors of eight of the fourteen articles. The focus in the articles is of course not on individual syntactic features but on their patterning as groups, as found in texts of various types. Among the texts examined are the transactions of the Royal Society from 1675 till 1975, speech-based and written registers from the same period, texts about American nuclear arms policy, textbooks and journal articles in biology and history, medical research articles, oral proficiency samples, male and female dialogue in *Star Trek* and in dramatic dialogue, British versus American spoken materials, written and spoken texts by schoolchildren, eighteenth-century speech-based and written texts, and complex versus less complex registers. From these contributions (and several others, dealt with in the following subsection) it is clear that Biber's approach has by now firmly established itself as the main method for investigating overall use of language in different registers.

There are of course also shorter pieces reporting corpus ideas and findings. Paul Rayson, Andrew Wilson, and Geoffrey Leech report on 'Grammatical Word Class Variation within the British National Corpus Sampler' (in Peters, Collins, and Smith, eds., *New Frontiers of Corpus Research*, pp. 295–306). Comparison of simple part-of-speech frequencies is used to determine to what extent different mediums (speech and writing) and genres vary in this respect. Norma A. Pravec presents an international 'Survey of Learner Corpora' (*ICAME* 26[2002] 81–114), i.e. corpora that have been compiled with the written text of learners of English as a second or foreign language. 'Exploitation and Assessment of a Business English Corpus through Language Learning Tasks' by Alejandro Curado Fuentes (*ICAME* 26[2002] 5–31) discusses important factors for the optimal design of such a corpus. 'Lexical Constellations: What Collocates Fail to Tell' by Pascual Cantos and Aquilino Sánchez (*IJCL* 6[2002] 199–228) investigates the way words form complex network-like structures or units: lexical constellations. What matters is not the span, but the lexical hierarchy which collocates with a form within a linguistic unit. 'Contrastive and Comparable Corpora: Quantitative Aspects' by Anatole Shaikevich (*IJCL* 6[2002] 229–55) introduces the terminological distinction between these corpus types and demonstrates DSAT methodology (distributional statistical analysis of texts), a formal approach to the study of text corpora. 'The IJS-ELAN Slovene-English Parallel Corpus' by Tomaž Erjavec (*IJCL* 7[2002] 1–20) describes this annotated parallel corpus, which was compiled to be a widely distributable dataset for language engineering and for translation and terminology studies. 'In Search of Representativity in Specialised Corpora: Categorisation through Collocation' by Geoffrey Williams (*IJCL* 7[2002] 43–64) demonstrates a non-subjective, corpus-directed system of internal selection using lexical criteria to measure the representativity of special language corpora. Thomas A. Upton, in 'Understanding Direct Mail Letters as a Genre' (*IJCL* 7[2002] 65–85), identifies key patterns in the rhetorical structure of fundraising discourse. 'The Contribution of Verbal Semantic Content: Towards Term Recognition' by Eugenia Eumeridou, Blaise Nkwenti-Azeh, and John McNaught (*IJCL* 7[2002] 87–106) demonstrates the importance of contextual information for automatic term recognition, a natural language-processing technology used for updating terminologies and thesauri, machine translation, information retrieval, document indexing, etc.

From corpora, we turn to specific theories. There is no shortage of generative work this year. A slim but very useful first introduction has appeared by Elly van Gelderen, *An Introduction to the Grammar of English: Arguments and Socio-Historical Background*. The first chapter describes briefly but lucidly some basic tenets about knowledge of language and universal grammar; the next chapters prepare the ground by acquainting the student with the necessary tools: the concept of lexical and grammatical categories, phrases, constituent functions, finite and non-finite clauses; and chapters 9 and 10 tackle the internal structure of the complex NP. Trees are binary and do not contain bar-levels as yet, with the exception of NP and S. The final chapter presents movement (*wh*-, topicalization) in a very basic, non-technical way. There is a comprehensive glossary. Every chapter ends with exercises and keys; every two or three chapters there is a useful review section. The book is enlivened throughout with relevant illustrations and examples, including comic strips, cartoons, and poems.

Somewhat more ambitious than van Gelderen's work is Geoffrey Poole's *Syntactic Theory*, a carefully crafted introduction to the underlying ideas, theoretical concepts, and formal machinery of the generative enterprise. In view of its advanced nature, minimalist work is not touched on; instead, what the student gets is an overview of the achievements of government-binding theory. There are chapters (nearly all including in-text and additional exercises) on phrase structure, functional categories, theta-theory and case, binding theory, movement, logical form, empty categories, the empty category principle, and verb-raising. Throughout, the emphasis is on the reasoning behind the analysis rather than on the mechanisms adopted to give it a shape, making this a very suitable introductory text for students with minimal prior exposure to formal linguistics (this, at least, is what our own experience has been; we may perhaps add that it included an inspiring guest-lecture about the material by the author himself). More ambitious in certain ways, but for this reason probably too challenging for some students, is Andrew Carnie's *Syntax: A Generative Introduction*. This is a much bigger book, which covers much the same ground as Poole's work, but in addition includes separate chapters on minimalism, lexical-functional grammar, and head-driven phrase structure grammar. Moreover, Carnie evinces a greater desire to tell the readers about all the puzzles, refinements, alternatives, and technical terminology that have accrued over the years—this has its dangers, but it will certainly make anyone that emerges from his book in one piece well equipped to tackle the original literature.

Juan Uriagereka's *Derivations: Exploring the Dynamics of Syntax* is a collection of papers the author has written over the last few years, often in collaboration with others. After an introduction on the differences between representational and derivational systems, and a defence of minimalism (an elaboration of Uriagereka's reply to the Lappin, Levine, and Johnson attack on minimalism, see *YWES* 81[2002] 23), the papers are loosely divided into two sections: 'Syntagmatic Issues' and 'Paradigmatic Concerns'. The papers in the first part focus on the general architecture of minimalism, e.g.: 'Multiple Spell-Out', 'Cyclicity and Extraction Domains', 'Minimal Restrictions of Basque Movements', 'Labels and Projections: A Note on the Syntax of Quantifiers', 'Formal and Substantive Elegance in the Minimalist Program: On the Emergence of Some Linguistic Forms'. The second part moves on to discussing the derivation of particular structures in a wider linguistic and philosophical context, e.g.: 'From Being to Having' (the syntax and semantics of possession), 'Two Types of Small Clauses: Towards a Syntax of Theme/Rheme Relations', 'Parataxis', 'WARPS: Some Thoughts on Categorization'.

Further work within the minimalist framework is found in Epstein and Seely, eds., *Derivation and Explanation in the Minimalist Program*. The editors provide an introduction (pp. 1–18) in which they emphasize the meta-theoretical arguments in favour of minimalism, such as the need in science to guard against a proliferation of assumptions, principles, levels, and machinery whose total complexity matches or even exceeds that of the facts to be explained (compare also András Kertész, 'On the Contribution of Metascience to Cognitive Linguistics: A Case Study' (*LingB* 190[2002] 207–27), which offers a philosopher's view of the aims and problems of linguistics, with Cognitive Linguistics as its case study). Most of the papers that follow in the Epstein and Seely volume argue for a derivational approach to syntactic structure, but Michael Brody, 'On the Status of Representations and Derivations' (pp. 19–41), continues his campaign in defence of representationalism. He points out, for example, that the apparent contrast between the complex representational definition of c-command and its simple derivational counterpart (where it follows from the workings of the basic process of Merge) evaporates once it is realized that, representationally, c-command can be defined in terms of a sister and all its terms (though Brody goes on to argue that the whole concept is redundant anyway). A more mainstream minimalist contribution is 'Eliminating Labels' by Chris Collins (pp. 42–64), in which an attempt is made to do away with labels for phrasal category labels, necessitating changes in several areas where they used to be appealed to (X-bar theory, selection, and the PF interface). The editors themselves contribute 'Rule Application as Cycles in a Level-Free Syntax' (pp. 65–89), in which they suggest that the Spell-Out should take place as part of every syntactic operation, not just when a CP or vP are merged (as Noam Chomsky has proposed). John Frampton and Sam Gutmann propose that there should be a 'Crash-Proof Syntax' (pp. 90–105), i.e. that all constraints should be met during the derivation rather than be checked afterwards—they discuss the obvious problems posed for this by the case filter and chain condition. Norbert Hornstein and Juan Uriagereka argue for the existence of 'Reprojections' (pp. 106–32), whereby a VP can become a QP at LF, solving certain blocking effects of quantifiers. A minimalist analysis of binding principles B and C is developed by Richard Kayne in 'Pronouns and their Antecedents' (pp. 133–66); antecedent and pronoun are generated together as one phrase, with subsequent movement of the antecedent, as in *John$_i$ thinks that (t_i, he) is smart*. The same approach is used by Jan-Wouter Zwart in his 'Issues Relating to a Derivational Theory of Binding' (pp. 269–304), but here, the focus is on binding principle A. In Hisatsugu Kitahara's 'Scrambling, Case, and Interpretability' (pp. 167–83), scrambling is argued to be Match-driven movement. Long A-bar binding is examined by James McCloskey in 'Resumption, Successive Cyclicity, and the Locality of Operations' (pp. 184–226); he proposes that intermediate positions in an A-bar chain can be filled either to bona-fide movement but also by direct Merge of an operator. Norvin Richards considers 'Very Local A' Movement in a Root-First Derivation' (pp. 227–48). Using a system whereby a tree is built from the top down, he proposes an account of A-bar movement blocked by an A-position (as in **Which violin is that sonata hard to imagine John playing t on t*). The problem of raising over an experiencer (as in *they seem to each other t to admire this artist*), in apparent violation of the minimal link condition, is investigated by Esther Torrego in 'Arguments for a Derivational Approach to Syntactic Relations Based on Clitics' (pp. 249–68); the solution involves consideration of the exact status of the experiencer.

Robert Frank's *Phrase Structure Composition and Syntactic Dependencies* aims to make the Tree Adjoining Grammar (TAG) formalism accessible to a wider audience and to incorporate it into current models of syntactic theory. The TAG conception of syntactic derivation was first defined in the 1970s, and further developed since, but never systematically presented to a larger public, as in this work. TAG offers a derivational machinery that is directly compatible with the Minimalist Program as long as the restriction is taken on board that derivations are not permitted to manipulate structures beyond a certain size. A fundamental difference between the two approaches is the domain in which transformations, i.e. syntactic dependencies, can apply. The fundamental hypothesis in TAG is that every syntactic dependency is expressed locally within a single elementary tree; Frank's derivation of these elementary trees makes use of the Minimalist concepts of Merge and Move, although he explicitly states that other formalisms (e.g. Lexical-Functional Grammar or Relational Grammar) probably work equally well. TAG derivations which combine these elementary trees make use of two notions: Adjoining and Substitution. The book concentrates on two types of dependencies to illustrate the workings of the TAG formalism: *wh*-movement and raising.

In 'The Formal Origins of Syntactic Theory' (*Lingua* 112[2002] 827–48) Marcus Tomalin explores the influence of mathematics (especially Hilbertian Formalism) on the development of syntactic theory in the twentieth century. Francis Cornish, in '"Downstream" Effects on the Predicate in Functional Grammar Clause Derivations' (*JL* 38[2002] 247–78), deals with the dynamic, retroactive effects within a clause derivation of various 'downstream' specifications (i.e. at subsequent levels in the derivation) on the semantic structure and aspectual character of the predicator at the 'nuclear', 'core', and 'extended' predication layers within standard Functional Grammar. Frederick J. Newmeyer, in 'Optimality and Functionality: A Critique of Functionally-Based Optimality-Theoretic Syntax' (*NL&LT* 20[2002] 43–80), points out some basic weaknesses of such an approach to syntax, most importantly that it incorrectly locates the form–function interface in the mental grammar itself rather than in language use and acquisition. Joan Bresnan and Judith Aissen's rebuttal of Newmeyer's criticisms follow in 'Optimality and Functionality: Objections and Refutations' (*NL&LT* 20[2002] 81–95), which in turn sparks Newmeyer's 'A Rejoinder to Bresnan and Aissen' (*NL&LT* 20[2002] 97–9).

If anyone is not sure what these objections, refutations, and rejoinders are all about, they should read Legendre, Grimshaw, and Vikner, eds., *Optimality-Theoretic Syntax*. This large volume (nearly 550 pages) will give the reader a good idea not only of what OT is about in general terms, but also of how it can be insightfully applied to syntactic phenomena. After an introduction by Legendre dealing with the nature and architecture of OT, constraint conflict, ranking, reranking, and violation, the role of economy, optionality and ineffability, there are fifteen chapters, on a wide range of issues and languages. We just mention here the ones in which English data play a role (but recommend the others as well). Peter Ackema and Ad Neeleman's chapter is called 'Competition between Syntax and Morphology' (pp. 29–60); it considers the extent to which morphological forms, such as (synthetic) compounds and inflected elements, can be said to compete with syntactic formations. Eric Baković and Edward Keer contribute 'Optionality and

Ineffability' (pp. 97–112), dealing with *that/wh/*zero variability in English COMPs. Gereon Müller writes about superiority effects and much else in 'Order Preservation, Parallel Movement, and the Emergence of the Unmarked' (pp. 279–313). Structural focus phenomena in various languages are the topic of Vieri Samek-Lodovici's 'Cross-Linguistic Typologies in Optimality Theory' (pp. 315–53). Margaret Speas looks at the distribution of PRO in her 'Constraints on Null Pronouns' (pp. 393–425). Sten Vikner analyses 'V°-to-I° Movement and Its Insertion in Optimality Theory' (pp. 427–64), also paying attention to the elements filling COMP. The other papers do not directly address issues in English syntax, but the wide array of topics discussed (subjects and markedness, pronouns, scrambling, word order, clitics, verb-second and second-position clitics, voice systems, anaphora, and case patterns) shows, if nothing else, that OT syntax is turning into a force to reckon with.

We have arrived at the individual elements of the clause, beginning with noun phrases. 'Orality and Noun Phrase Structure in Registers of British and Kenyan English' by Diana Hudson-Ettle and Tore Nilsson (*ICAME* 26[2002] 33–61) investigates the correlation between noun phrase complexity and orality in two different varieties of English. 'Alternate Construals, Iconicity, and Grounding: The Case of Nominals with the Noun *Part*' (*Fol* 36[2002] 313–34), by Elżbieta Górska, explores the selection of zero or indefinite article in pairs like *The engine is part of the car* and *The engine is a part of the car*. Omission of the article will also turn a title like *the Chairman* into a pseudo-title like *Chairman Brown*; Charles F. Meyer looks at 'Pseudo-Titles in the Press Genre of Various Components of the International Corpus of English' (in Reppen, Fitzmaurice, and Biber, eds., *Using Corpora to Explore Linguistic Variation*, pp. 147–66), and finds that this construction, though originating in AmE, is now most common in NZE and Philippine English, with quite long specimens sometimes being encountered there. 'A Categorial Treatment of Adverbial Nouns' by Neal Whitman (*JL* 38[2002] 561–97) discusses NPs like *this week* that can act as adverbs without being preceded by a preposition, and presents an analysis in a categorial grammar framework.

Anette Rosenbach, in *Genitive Variation in English: Conceptual Factors in Synchronic and Diachronic Studies*, investigates the variation between constructions such as *the girl's eyes* and *the eyes of the girl* and identifies a number of possible competing motivations: animacy, topicality, and the type of possessive relation. One chapter is devoted to how variation is handled by the various approaches (generative and optimality theory, sociolinguistic and corpus-linguistic approaches, functionalism, and cognitive linguistics). In order to predict, rather than determine post hoc, what the relevant factors will be in an empirical study, a functional approach is decided on because the choice between the two forms appears to be guided mostly by cognitive-psychological factors. The notions of naturalness and iconicity are narrowly defined in terms of human conceptualization and processing. The resulting preference theory incorporates economy considerations, and the idea of hierarchically ordered competing motivations. The predictions of this preference theory are then tested in an experimental study, first synchronically, and then diachronically (one generation). Rosenbach suggests in the final chapter that Bresnan's (and associates') Stochastic OT could be an excellent tool here because of its probabilistic content and its assumption that categorical differences in some languages can show up as statistical preferences in others. 'Determiners in

Genitive Constructions', by Nicholas Sobin (*Lingua* 112[2002] 597–618), supports earlier claims that the overt determiner which may appear in a possessive DP (e.g. *the* in *the girl's truck*) has a 'low' source and proposes a Spec-head agreement analysis to counter the problem of controlling D-selection among the projected D-positions in a DP-recursive analysis of possessive expressions.

Susan Strauss, in '*This*, *That*, and *It* in Spoken American English: A Demonstrative System of Gradient Focus' (*LangS* 24[2002] 131–52), provides an alternative analysis, rejecting the traditional proximal/distal distinction, for the demonstrative system of reference in spontaneous oral discourse, based on interaction between participants and the role of focus. We also insert here Catie Berkenfield's 'The Role of Frequency in the Realization of English *That*' (in Bybee and Hopper, eds., *Frequency and the Emergence of Linguistic Structure*, pp. 281–307), which shows that there is an increase in frequency from demonstrative to complementizer to relative *that*, with concomitant shortening and centralization of the vowel.

Lieven Vandelanotte argues, in 'Prenominal Adjectives in English: Structures and Ordering' (*FoLi* 36[2002] 219–58), that there is a class of adjectives—represented by *fucking* in *read the fucking manual* which behaves more like a sentential adverb: 'For God's sake, read the manual!', and by adjectives like *so-called*, *putative*, *alleged* and the like—that are best described in terms of scoping or framing rather than in terms of constituency or dependency. More on adjectives can be found in Shunji Yamazaki's 'Distribution of Frequent Adjectives in the Wellington Corpus of Written New Zealand English' (in Saito *et al.*, eds., pp. 63–75); as might be expected, different text types have different adjectival profiles, and there is a wide variation in the syntactic roles of adjectives. Modification of nouns in general is studied in Toshihiko Kubota's 'Lexical Richness and Semantic Loading Capacity of Nouns'(in Saito *et al.*, eds., pp. 93–110); the hypothesis is that lexically rich nouns (e.g. *dalmatian*) will be modified less often than lexically poorer nouns (*dog*, or *animal*). Cobuild Corpus data tend to support this idea, though factors such as real-world interest of the referent can cause exceptions. Chris Barker, in 'The Dynamics of Vagueness' (*Ling&P* 25[2002] 1–36), provides an explicit formal analysis of how a use of a vague gradable adjective (e.g. *tall*) affects shared knowledge in a developing discourse.

'The Indefinites *Some* and *Any* in Linguistic Theory and Actual Usage', by Bengt Jacobsson (*SN* 74[2002] 1–14), examines the logic-inspired terminology used in most treatments of *some* and *any*, and takes a fresh look at their distribution, especially in negative environments. The findings of William Philip's study, 'Dutch Teenagers' SLA of English *Any*' (*LIN* 19[2002] 129–38), suggest that the subjects of his experiment are actively constructing a grammar of English rather than attempting to derive one from their L1. Edward L. Keenan, in 'Some Properties of Natural Language Quantifiers: Generalized Quantifier Theory' (*Ling&P* 25[2002] 627–54), describes the advances that have been made in this field over the last twenty-five years.

From noun phrases, we turn to subjects, on which an assorted array of articles has appeared this year. 'Extraposed Subjects vs. Postverbal Complements: On the So-Called Obligatory Extraposition', by Aimo Seppänen and Jennifer Herriman (*SN* 74[2002] 30–59), argues that the ungrammaticality of sentences like **that the boys were tired seemed (to me)* is not due to obligatory extraposition but follows naturally from the fact that *seem* is a copula. 'Pronouns and Case', by Fred Weerman and Jacqueline Evers-Vermeul (*Lingua* 112[2002] 301–38), argues that subjects are DPs and that objects are extended with a Case Phrase. Several peculiar characteristics of Dutch and English pronouns follow from this theory. Klaus-Michael Köpcke and Klaus-Uwe Panther, in 'Zur Identifikation leerer Subjekte in infinitivischen Komplementsätzen—ein semantisch-pragmatisches Modell' (*FoLi* 36[2002] 191–218), argue that the interpretation of empty elements (like PRO) is only minimally guided by syntactic principles. They propose a cognitively based theory of obligatory control. The frequency of specific subject–verb combinations is investigated in Joanne Scheibman's 'Local Patterns of Subjectivity in Person and Verb Type in American English Conversation' (in Bybee and Hopper, eds., pp. 61–89). Common patterns are *I* with a cognition verb in the present tense (*I think* etc.); *I* + action verb in the past tense (*I went* etc.); *you know*; *you* +(modal+) action verb; third person + relational verb (*that is terrible*). The conclusion is that subjective concerns play a large role in conversation. The special status of the subject as compared with other clausal arguments is scrutinized in Susan Rothstein's monograph *Predicates and their Subjects*. She takes the view that subjects are required by syntactic predicates, since these are unsaturated, making them the only non-lexical argument-selecting elements. This means that, unlike a lot of other work, Rothstein's proposal takes the notion of subject to be not a pragmatic or semantic one, but a syntactic one: it represents the structurally most prominent argument. The semantics of the subject–predicate relation is explored in detail, as is the special case of copular sentences, and of *be* in general. Throughout, pleonastics play an important role in the argumentation; their occurrence in object position (e.g. *she regretted it that she was so late*) is argued to be only apparent, since items like this bear a theta-role.

After the subject comes the verb. Takeshi Okada examines 'Conjugational Patterns and Text Categories in the LOB Corpus' (in Saito *et al.*, eds., pp. 43–62), with the aim of establishing to what extent specific verbs are attested with all possible inflected forms or only a subset of them. The verb *say*, for example, is highly frequent, but 60 per cent of all its tokens are past tense, making its other forms much less frequent; other verbs lack certain attestations altogether, leading to important implications for foreign learners. Chiara Finocchiaro and Gabriele Miceli, in 'Verb Actionality in Aphasia: Data from Two Aphasic Subjects' (*FoLi* 36[2002] 335–56), found that one of their aphasic subjects had preserved the category 'state verbs' significantly better than other categories, whereas their other subject had preserved 'process verbs' best, from which they conclude that actional category information is a fundamental organizational principle of semantic knowledge of verbs in the brain. Paul Hopper, in 'Hendiadys and Auxiliation in English' (in Bybee and Noonan, eds., *Complex Sentences in Grammar and Discourse*, pp. 145–73) presents a corpus investigation of expressions like *you have to start and think about how this will be* instead of auxiliary constructions like *start thinking* and formulates their function in the discourse. Peter Trudgill, Terttu Nevalainen, and Ilse Wischer, in 'Dynamic *have* in North American and British Isles English' (*ELL* 6[2002] 1–15), suggest that the different use of *do*-support with the verb *have* in the two varieties is connected to the fact that *have* does not feature in set expressions in AmE as much as in BrE (BrE *I had a shower* versus AmE *I took a shower*), possibly because of language contact with German or Yiddish.

Markku Filppula's 'A Tale of Two Perfects: A Case of Competition between Grammars?' (in Lentz and Möhlig, eds., pp. 66–76) investigates structures like *I had him cornered* and *he had a bible given him*, which exhibit different control relations. Geoffrey Sampson, in 'Regional Variation in the English Verb Qualifier System' (*ELL* 6[2002] 17–30), explores the well-known use of past tense forms for past participles in non-standard dialects. Many of these non-standard past tenses can be explained as the result of non-standard systems of verb qualifiers (TMA markers), including the peculiar orthographic practice of some writers of spelling unstressed *have* as *of*. The present perfect remains a puzzling category. As Norbert Schlüter, 'Temporal Specification of the Present Perfect: A Corpus-Based Study' (in Peters *et al.*, eds., pp. 307–15), points out, pronouncements about it are usually based on intuition rather than real data. Schlüter remedies this by providing data from the Brown, LOB, and London–Lund corpora which show that: (1) one out of three present perfect tokens co-occurs with a temporal adverbial; (2) the adverbial is most often a single adverb; but (3) the most frequent adverbial has the structure *ever since* ... ; and (4) no great differences between AmE and BrE are apparent in this area of grammar. An aspectual category that may be 'Ever Moving On?' is 'The Progressive in Recent British English', as studied by Nicholas Smith (in Peters *et al.*, eds., pp. 317–30). Using the 1960s Brown and LOB corpora and their 1990s counterparts Frown and FLOB, Smith finds that the progressive is indeed moving on, especially in the present tense and in main clauses. However, to what extent this development in written texts is reflected in any corresponding development in speech remains to be established.

Modal verbs and modality have inspired several researchers as well. Annabel Cormack and Neil Smith have studied 'Modals and Negation in English' (in Barbiers, Beukema, and van der Wurff, eds., *Modality and its Interaction with the Verbal System*, pp. 133–63). They distinguish three types of negation— metalinguistic negation, sentential negation, and VP negation—and show that modals always scope under the first and over the second, but that there is variation for the second type of negation. Graeme Kennedy examines 'Variation in the Distribution of Modal Verbs in the British National Corpus' (in Reppen *et al.*, eds., pp. 73–90), finding 1.45 million tokens altogether, with *will*, *would*, *can*, and *could* accounting for 73 per cent of the total; the highest frequencies are found in spoken texts. Roberta Facchinetti has studied '*Can* and *Could* in Contemporary British English: A Study of the ICE-GB Corpus' (in Peters *et al.*, eds., pp. 229–46). Both modals are extremely frequent, but the author makes clear that there are several unexpected syntactic and semantic distinctions between them. The emerging modals *gonna*, *gotta*, and *wanna* are dealt with by Manfred Krug in 'Frequency, Iconicity, Categorization: Evidence from Emerging Modals' (in Bybee and Hopper, eds., pp. 309–35). These items are not only among the thirty most frequent verbs in spontaneous conversation, they also have a shared phonological pattern, making their development an example of increased economy and iconicity at the same time.

No *YWES* volume would be complete without negation. Jaakko Hintikka, in 'Negation in Logic and in Natural Language' (*Ling&P* 25[2002] 585–600), argues that, in natural language, contradictory negation may occur within the scope of a quantifier and yields an interpretation that cannot be handled by the normal first-order semantics. Lee Davies, in 'Specific Language Impairment as Principle Conflict: Evidence from Negation' (*Lingua* 112[2002] 281–300), presents the results from an experimental study which assesses SLI children's ability to judge the grammaticality of a range of negative constructions. Jong-Bok Kim and Ivan A. Sag, in 'Negation without Head Movement' (*NL&LT* 20[2002] 339–412), present an analysis of negation in French and English in a constraint-based account that dispenses with head movement. *Negation in Non-Standard British English: Gaps, Regularizations and Asymmetries*, by Lieselotte Anderwald, is a comparative study of negation patterns in standard and non-standard varieties of British English with data from large text corpora and dialect atlases. After an overview of negation patterns in the standard and in regional varieties, the investigation concentrates on those features of modern non-standard English that are not regionally restricted. Many non-standard variant patterns can be interpreted as attempts to fill system gaps (*amn't*, epistemic *mustn't*) or repair irregularities (*have* negated without a form of *do*) in the standard. The persistence of negative concord (*I couldn't do nothing about it*), one of the best-known features of non-standard English, is surprising in view of the stigma it carries, but not in view of the typological fact that negative concord is the more frequent pattern in the languages of the world. There is also a functional explanation in that the negation of the sentence would otherwise be expressed solely by the unstressed contraction *n't*. *Ain't*/*in't*, historically regular developments from *aren't* and *isn't*, shows evidence of the trend towards a single negator for a range of verb forms. Third person singular *don't* for *doesn't* parallels the use of *ain't* in that it is becoming a kind of invariant negation marker for the present tense for all persons. Cross-linguistically, there is a strong tendency for languages with special negative auxiliaries to generalize one form. Finally, the generalization of one form of *be* for the past tense—either with *was* for positives and *weren't* for negatives, or *was*/*wasn't* or *were*/*weren't* for these respective functions—is also supported by cross-linguistic findings. Grammatical distinctions (such as number) easily fuse in a marked environment (negation). Unmarked values (here: affirmative) typically exhibit more distinct forms in the paradigm than marked values.

Objects and other complements of the verb are also well represented this year. The use of *You and I* as object is dealt with by Joyce Tang Boyland in 'Hypercorrect Pronoun Case in English? Cognitive Processes that Account for Pronoun Usage' (in Bybee and Hopper, eds., pp. 383–404), where the high frequency and therefore automatization of this phrase is held up as the main causative factor. The opposite phenomenon of *whom* in subject function is also dealt with—it is shown to be common only in pushdown relatives (*someone whom he feels is worth listening to*). Seppo Kittilä's 'Remarks on the Basic Transitive Sentence' (*LangS* 24[2002] 107–30) discusses the parameters that affect transitivity and proposes a new prototype. Sandra A. Thompson and Paul J. Hopper examine their own prototype approach to transitives in 'Transitivity, Clause Structure, and Argument Structure: Evidence from Conversation' (in Bybee and Hopper, eds., pp. 27–60). They find that their (small) corpus of American conversations mostly has clauses that are low in transitivity, and relate this to the nature of typical conversations (which are not about events, but about attitudes, properties, and assessments). In 'Transitivity Revisited as an Example of a More Strict Approach in Typological Research', by Gilbert Lazard (*FoLi* 36[2002] 141–90), the author argues for falsifiable theories on cross-linguistic universals.

D.J. Allerton, in *Stretched Verb Constructions in English*, investigates the relation between VPs like *accuse somebody* (*of something*), *approve* (*of*) *something* versus their longer, 'stretched' parallels *make an accusation against somebody* and *give one's approval for something* using items from a large database. Similar parallels, though less easy to detect, are pairs like *Sebastian indulged in some acting at college* and *Sebastian acted at college* (p. 73) and *Sybil recorded some achievements last year* and *Sybil achieved some successes last year* (p. 93). The investigation probes deeply into the syntactic structure of the stretched VP and its simpler parallel, as well as the nature and semantic 'eventive' contribution of the nominalizing suffixes that play a role here (*-ion*, *-age*, *-al*, etc.) and zero-derivation. Striking is the near-absence of the classic *nomen actionis* suffix *-ing*, eventive suffix *par excellence*. The other constituents of the stretched verb construction, i.e. modifiers and qualifiers (*make a quick adjustment to* beside *adjust something quickly*), postmodifying PPs and the syntactic/semantic contribution of the light ('thin' in Allerton's terminology) verbs themselves, all receive extensive treatment. Although many of these 'thin' verbs are of high frequency and quite freely collocate, there are some notable exceptions of verbs that are unique or nearly unique to one particular deverbal noun, e.g. *dance* in *dance attendance on* and *lodge* in *lodge an appeal*. An interesting finding is that a large proportion (two-fifths) of stretched verb constructions differ in *aktionsart* from their simple counterparts: *applaud* versus *burst into applause*, *assassinate* versus *carry out the assassination* (p. 205).

Nicole Dehé's *Particle Verbs in English: Syntax, Information Structure and Intonation* is a welcome addition to the huge literature on phrasal verbs. Dehé proposes a syntactic analysis in Minimalist terms and rejects approaches in which objects and particle constitute a Small Clause, or approaches that analyse the particle as a functional head. She has an important contribution to make to the ongoing debate on the structure, analysis, and history of phrasal verbs in that she has performed a detailed examination of the two orders, the 'continuous' order encountered in *he wiped off the table* and the 'discontinuous' order encountered in *he wiped the table off*. On the basis of experimental studies she identifies information structural needs (and the relation of accent placement and focus) as the overriding factor that determines which of the two orders is selected. Taking the continuous order as underlying, she argues that particle stranding—i.e. the discontinuous order—is triggered by a focus feature.

Teruhiko Fukaya writes 'On Viewing Reflexives in the Bank of English: Their Distribution and Frequency' (in Saito *et al.*, eds., pp. 77–91), a study of the construction *find* + reflexive + complement (as in *I found myself getting angry*, and *he found himself pushed down*). Especially common in books (rather than magazines or speech), the construction typically involves a negative and unexpected situation, and this is reflected in the nature of its collocates in the material. In 'The Dual Status of Middle-Distance Reflexives' (*JL* 38[2002] 71–86), Ping Xue and Fred Popowich argue that these reflexives, a subset of the 'picture of' reflexives, can either be syntactically bound or be interpreted according to pragmatic and discourse conditions.

Next, it is adverbs and adverbials. Charles J. Fillmore, in 'Mini-Grammars of Some Time-When Expressions in English' (in Bybee and Noonan, eds., pp. 31–59), presents an analysis of expressions like *recently* or *on the morning of Christmas Day* in a simplified version of Construction Grammar. 'The Functions of *Actually* in a Corpus of Intercultural Conversations', by Winnie Cheng and Martin Warren (*IJCL* 6[2002] 257–80), compares the frequency and functions of this word in native and non-native speakers of English in Hong Kong and tentatively offers a motivation for the differences in terms of different conceptions of the notion of face. An even shorter expression is investigated by He Anping in 'On the Discourse Marker *So*' (in Peters *et al.*, eds., pp. 41–52); in the course of trying to account for the overuse of *so* by Chinese learners of English, Anping presents data on its use in corpora of native English (it turns out to be characteristic of spoken English, and to favour sentence-medial position). Items like *wow, absolutely, sure, right* and *fine* are studied by Michael McCarthy in 'Good Listenership Made Plain: British and American Non-Minimal Response Tokens in Everyday Conversation' (in Reppen *et al.*, eds., pp. 49–71); the two varieties show some differences in the frequency of individual items, but they behave in similar ways overall.

Thomas Ernst, in *The Syntax of Adjuncts*, presents a scope-based theory of the syntax of adverbial adjuncts to account for the distribution and position of the various adjunct types. The hierarchical arrangement of adverbials is primarily determined by the interaction of compositional rules and lexico-semantic requirements of individual adjuncts, as semantic representations are built up according to syntactic structure, and relatively little 'pure' syntax is involved. His theory also makes use of Directionality Principles, i.e. the parameterization of the basic direction of complements, and Weight Theory, because the 'weight' of the adverbial constituent in the sentence also influences position. The two basic classes of adverbials, predicational adjuncts and functional adjuncts, differ in the way in which they are licensed and hence in their distributional properties. The former observe a strict hierarchy. Manner and measure adverbials occur adjoined to VP or PredP, as they involve event-internal modification; the same goes for subject-oriented adverbs if they have manner-readings (*Vera withdrew all her funds from the bank craftily*). If they have clausal readings, however (as in *Craftily, Vera withdrew all her funds from the bank*), they are adjoined to a higher position. Speaker-oriented adverbs cannot adjoin below aspectual auxiliaries (except when raising of the auxiliary allows the latter's base position to mark its scope). Evidentials (such as *clearly*) are the only adverbials in this group that can occur below negation because only they combine with propositions to yield events rather than propositions. The functional adjuncts, on the other hand, like time-related adjuncts, frequency adjuncts, and clausal functional adjuncts (purpose, causal, conditional, concessive, etc.) have on the whole greater freedom of position and may in principle adjoin to any functional projection, although co-occurrence with particular aspects, tenses, or negation may induce semantic clashes that rule out certain combinations.

Naomi Hallan presents 'Paths to Prepositions? A Corpus-Based Study of the Acquisition of a Lexico-Grammatical Category' (in Bybee and Hopper, eds., pp. 91–120). Her findings are that the prepositions *over* and *on* feature few or no clear PP uses in child English, instead occurring in combinations like *over (t)here, come over*, and *all over the place*. This of course casts doubt on the idea that the spatial meaning of these and other prepositions is central. 'The Theoretical Status of Prepositions: The Case of the "Prospective Use" of *In*', by Franck Lebas (in Feigenbaum and Kurzon, eds., *Prepositions in their Syntactic, Semantic and Pragmatic Context*, pp. 59–73), focuses on examples like *He will arrive in three hours* and proposes an Extrinsic Properties Theory of prepositions. David S. Brée and Ian E. Pratt-Hartmann, in 'Temporal Semantics of Prepositions in Context' (in

Feigenbaum and Kurzon, eds., pp. 75–113), explore how the temporal semantics of prepositions and verbs interact to determine the interval in which the main proposition in a sentence holds. In the same volume (pp. 115–26), Ian Pratt-Hartmann and Nissim Francez, in 'Prepositions and Context', examine the semantics of spatial PPs in sentences which report the occurrence of events, states, or activities. Cliff Goddard, in '*On and On*: Verbal Explication for a Polysemic network' (*CogLing* 13[2002] 277–94), analyses prepositional *on*-constructions in terms of Anna Wierzbicka's 'natural semantic metalanguage' framework. Arnim von Stechow, in 'Temporal Prepositional Phrases with Quantifiers: Some Additions to Pratt and Francez (2001)' (*Ling&P* 25[2002] 755–800), discusses the semantics of cascades of temporal PPs like *during every meeting on a Monday before Christmas*.

We've come to subordinate clauses. Joan Bybee, in 'Main Clauses Are Innovative, Subordinate Clauses Are Conservative' (in Bybee and Noonan, eds., pp. 1–17), presents the interesting finding—in view of the diachrony of word order patterns in English—that word order changes tend to affect main clauses first. Main clauses are pragmatically richer, containing the focused information and the possibility of setting off old from new information, while subordinate clauses contain supplementary material or material that has been previously presented. Nevertheless, Carol Lord, in 'Are Subordinate Clauses More Difficult?' (in Bybee and Noonan, eds., pp. 223–33), is able to give a positive answer to that question on the basis of corpus of students' answers to mathematics word problems with and without subordinate clauses. In 'Combining Clauses into Clause Complexes: A Multi-Faceted View' (in Bybee and Noonan, eds., pp. 235–319), Christian M.I.M. Matthiessen sketches a complex 'ecological' account of clause combining by considering functions in areas like interpersonal relations, genres, and registers. Etsuyo Yuasa and Jerry M. Sadock, in 'Pseudo-Subordination: A Mismatch between Syntax and Semantics' (*JL* 38[2002] 87–111), present mismatches of the type *You drink one more can of beer and I'm leaving* and argue that a theory like Autolexical Grammar (Sadock [1991]) can account for them. Subordination and the problems it presents to the hearer are investigated in Emanuel A. Schegloff's 'Overwrought Utterances: "Complex Sentences" in a Different Sense' (in Bybee and Noonan, eds., pp. 321–36); cued by the difficulties of the hearer, speakers simplify their utterances.

In '"Object Complements" and Conversation: Towards a Realistic Account', by Sandra Thompson (*SLang* 26[2002] 125–63), the standard view of complements as subordinate clauses in a grammatical relation with a complement-taking predicate is argued to be better understood in terms of epistemic/evidential/evaluative formulaic fragments expressing speaker stance towards the content of a clause.

An empirically oriented piece on relative clauses is Hans Martin Lehmann's 'Zero Subject Relative Constructions in American and British English' (in Peters *et al.*, eds., pp. 163–77), on constructions like *I have a home help ø does my shopping*. Interestingly, the American corpus examined (*c.*5 million words of speech) contained far fewer tokens than the British one (equally large): 94 to 205. With respect to syntactic context, there was a fairly wide spread, and, with regard to age, there was a slant towards older speakers (suggesting that there is still change going on, with AmE being far ahead of BrE). In another relative piece, Pieter de Haan asks and asserts that '*Whom* is not Dead?' (in Peters *et al.*, eds., pp. 215–28). After reviewing a recent web discussion about this question, de Haan presents corpus data that make clear that *whom* is still alive, continuing to pop up in various text types (mostly, but not exclusively, of a formal written nature); its favoured environment (*c*.20 per cent of all tokens) is the phrase *all/some/many/both/one of whom*. Dana McDaniel, Helen E. Stickney, Sadie Fowler, and Cecile McKee, in 'What's Thats?' (*ES* 83[2002] 51–69), discuss a less respectable relative usage: *thats* instead of *whose* in sentences like *This is the girl thats hat is red* in certain varieties of American English. We have seen two generative pieces on relative clauses. 'The Comp-Trace Effect, the Adverb Effect and Minimal CP', by Nicholas Sobin (*JL* 38[2002] 527–60), argues that (1) adverbs may undergo lexical adjunction to a complementizer and (2) the CP layer may be contracting or folding in rather than expanding. This may explain the COMP-trace effect, the adverb effect, and other aspects of the behaviour of complementizers in relative constructions and in complement constructions. 'C, T, and the Subject: *That*-t Phenomena Revisited', by Anna Roussou (*Lingua* 112[2002] 13–52), attempts a new (Minimalist) analysis in which the *that*-trace effect is a result of the Agr-features of T[ense] failing to be lexicalized.

A full descriptive and theoretical account of adverbial clauses of various types is presented by María Jesús Pérez Quintero in *Adverbial Subordination in English: A Functional Approach*. After outlining the relevant elements of the theory adopted (Functional Grammar as developed by Simon Dik and his associates in Amsterdam), the semantics and expression formats of the adverbial clauses in the material (selected from the LOB corpus) are dealt with, and it is shown that there is a correlation between form and meaning: the use of a finite/non-finite adverbial clause signals the position of the clause on the four semantic hierarchies distinguished (entity type, time dependency, factuality, presupposition). The book finishes with recommendations on how to incorporate the results more directly in the theoretical framework. Although the inclusion in this study of fourteen different adverbial types (means, time, manner, comparison, purpose, consequence, addition, cause, condition, etc. etc.) inevitably leads to a lack of attention to fine detail, and although the framework adopted is not widely known, the book as a whole offers a clear and consistent perspective on selected aspects of its topic.

Christopher Kennedy, in 'Comparative Deletion and Optimality in Syntax' (*NL&LT* 20[2002] 553–621), investigates the syntax of sentences like *My sister drives as carefully as I drive*. Christopher Potts, in 'The Syntax and Semantics of *As*-Parentheticals' (*NL&LT* 20[2002] 623–89), investigates the syntax and semantics of phrases like *as you know* in *Ames, as you know, was a spy*. Barbara Dancygier, in 'Mental Space Embeddings, Counterfactuality, and the Use of *Unless*' (*ELL* 6[2002] 347–77), argues for an account of irrealis *unless*-sentences in terms of epistemic distance and mental space embeddings. John Haiman and Tania Kuteva, in 'The Symmetry of Counterfactuals' (in Bybee and Noonan, eds., pp. 101–24), investigate the phenomenon that protasis and apodosis of a conditional sentence tend to use the same tense forms.

We finish this section with some work on clausal operations. 'Interpreting Interrogatives as Rhetorical Questions', by Chung-hye Han (*Lingua* 112[2002] 201–29), demonstrates various differences between the two structures with respect to e.g. negative polarity licensing, and suggests that the compositional semantics of the rhetorical question falls out as a result of directly mapping a pragmatic, post-LF representation onto the semantic interpretation (for more details on the semantics, see also Section 5). Victoria Escandell-Vidal, in 'Echo-Syntax and Metarepresentations' (*Lingua* 112[2002] 871–900), relates the syntactic properties of echo-questions to their semantics and their distribution, making use of Minimalist syntax and Dan Sperber and Deirdre Wilson's Relevance theory. John Haiman, in 'Systematization and the Origin of Rules: The Case of Subject-Verb Inversion in Questions' (*SLang* 26[2002] 573–93), discusses the, originally, functional basis of subject-verb inversion in questions against the more general background of conventionalizing and systematization processes in language change. Adele Goldberg, in 'Surface Generalizations: An Alternative to Alternations' (*CogLing* 13[2002] 326–56), argues against the practice of relating two constructional patterns to each other in terms of alternations (as in the locative alternation or the dative alternation) as it obscures the clear differences between them.

(b) Early Syntax

Albert C. Baugh and Thomas Cable's classic, *A History of the English Language*, is now in its fifth edition. The changes have been relatively minor—the chapter topics are the same (with just a bit of expansion here and there), and the student will still find in this work a history with an overall orientation towards external events rather than hard linguistic change. As the preface states, no use has been made of '[linguistic] ideas that come and go' (p. xiv), which may sound entirely justified for a textbook on the history of English but of course also betrays a rather bleak view of (historical) linguistics as a scientific enterprise. Still, the generous annotated bibliographies after each chapter include some of the hard linguistic work on the history of English that has been done over the last twenty or so years, and it has to be kept in mind that the book is meant to be comprehensible and informative also for complete beginners, an aim in which this edition succeeds just as well as its predecessors.

Two handy new student textbooks have appeared, *An Introduction to Old English* by Richard Hogg and *An Introduction to Middle English* by Simon Horobin and Jeremy Smith in the Edinburgh Textbooks on the English Language series. Richard Hogg's introduction presents the cultural background to the people and the texts, a linguistic analysis of the language (noun and adjective declension, weak and strong verbs, noun phrases and verb phrases, clauses, vocabulary/derivational morphology) and a chapter on variety (prose, poetry, dialects). The final chapter, 'The Future', provides a recapitulation of the previous chapters and a brief description of developments in ME. Exercises are included after every chapter, and the book contains a OE–PDE glossary, a glossary of linguistic terms, and an annotated bibliography with suggestions for further reading. Horobin and Smith's textbook is divided into three parts. The first part gives a first glimpse of the language, discusses (very briefly) the problems of transmission, and covers editorial practices, the status of English compared to other languages (Latin, French), the literature, the diversification into dialects, and standardization of speech and writing. Part II focuses on Chaucer's language, with an introduction to the relation between spellings and sounds, the lexicon, and a chapter on syntax and morphology. The final chapter discusses language change, and looks at three editorial problems. Every chapter is provided with exercises and recommended reading. The appendices include samples of ME texts and keys to exercises.

Also suitable for use as a textbook is Norman F. Blake's *A Grammar of Shakespeare's Language*, a solid exploration of the syntax and morphology of the language of Shakespeare's canon. The book provides a number of well-argued alternative readings for a number of Shakespearian cruces. The introductory chapters set out the necessary background of the status of the First Folio and the 'bad' and 'good' quartos and the increased interest in English as a literary language at the close of the sixteenth century on the evidence of the flurry of books on vocabulary, grammar, and rhetoric that were published at the time. Shakespeare makes a number of oblique references to some of these in his works. This is followed by chapters on the noun group; the verb group; adverbials, interjections, conjunctions, and prepositions; concord, negation, ellipsis, and repetition; clause organization; and sentence structure. There is chapter on discourse and register, which pays attention to forms of address, parting formulae, discourse markers like *well, I say, look you*, including *why* (a conciliatory word expressing agreement or understanding), *what* (indicates impatience or irritation), and *when* (possibly expressing frustration and anger) which may give modern editors trouble distinguishing them from the corresponding interrogative adverbs. As the plays consist largely of dialogue, there is also a chapter on pragmatic features of conversation, such as Grice's maxims and politeness phenomena. Although the book is clearly theoretically informed, the terminology is traditional and so accessible to all readers.

Chambers, Trudgill, and Schilling-Estes, eds., *The Handbook of Language Variation and Change*, is extensively discussed in Section 8 below. The book also has much to offer for the historical linguist. Especially useful are Edgar W. Schneider's chapter 'Variation and Change in Written Documents' (pp. 67–96), which is concerned with evaluating the validity of certain written texts (letters, interview transcripts) as truly representative of the speech of the individual. Matthew J. Gordon's chapter, 'Investigating Chain Shifts and Mergers' (pp. 244–66), illustrates the value of studying such changes in progress for our understanding of the mechanisms behind them. Gillian Sankoff's chapter, 'Linguistic Outcomes of Language Contact' (pp. 638–68), presents an overview of research in this area. And finally, Alison Henry, in 'Variation and Syntactic Theory' (pp. 267–82), argues that the variability in core syntax exhibited by a single individual has implications for syntactic theory, which will have to incorporate variability into its system. Language acquisition is the key: a child must be able to acquire a grammar from the output of different speakers, and, in order to function in the community, the grammar so acquired must be able to generate various styles.

The following articles also deal with general topics in the study of change, though each addresses rather different issues. Elizabeth Closs Traugott, in 'From Etymology to Historical Pragmatics' (in Minkova and Stockwell, eds., pp. 19–49) presents a survey and discussion of the insights about the motivation of language change in historical linguistic work in the last century, with pointers to the future. David W. Lightfoot, in 'Myths and the Prehistory of Grammars' (*JL* 38[2002] 113–36), argues that one can no more reconstruct the syntax of a proto-language than one can reconstruct last week's weather, and for the same reason: both reflect chaotic systems. The same volume contains Lyle Campbell and Alice C. Harris's reaction, 'Syntactic Reconstruction and Demythologizing "Myths and the Prehistory of grammars"' (*JL* 38[2002] 599–618), which in turn is followed by David Lightfoot's reaction 'More Myths' (*JL* 38[2002] 619–26). Guy Deutscher's 'On the Misuse of the Notion of "Abduction" in Linguistics' (*JL* 38[2002] 469–85) argues that the interpretation of abduction in (historical) linguistics is based on a critical misunderstanding of the original concept as it appears in the philosophy of Charles Peirce. The term 'abductive change' is neither adequate nor necessary for classifying linguistic innovations.

Herbert Schendl, in 'Mixed-Language Texts as Data and Evidence in English Historical Linguistics' (in Minkova and Stockwell, eds., pp. 51–78), presents a survey of recent research into historical code-switching. He also presents an empirical study in 'Code-Switching in Medieval English Poetry' (in Kastovsky and Mettinger, eds., *Language Contact in the History of English*, pp. 305–35). The results show a surprising correspondence to tendencies observed in the modern code-switching literature. Laura C. Wright, in 'Models of Language Mixing: Code-Switching Versus Semicommunication in Medieval Latin and Middle English Accounts' (in Kastovsky and Mettinger, eds., pp. 363–76), looks at code-switching in medieval accounts, which commonly mixed Latin and English, and Anglo-Norman and English, on an orderly basis.

More code-switching in *Language and History in Viking Age England: Linguistic Relations between Speakers of Old Norse and Old English* by Matthew Townend, who explores the issues of mutual intelligibility, borrowing, and substrate influence in the Danelaw area in the late OE period from every possible angle. The two languages were of course related, and still very similar at that point; but were they similar enough to be mutually intelligible? Townend makes an informed guess on the basis of what happened to English place names in the Danelaw area that the same principle of phonemic substitution may have been involved here as has been reported from PDE dialect studies: increased contact leads to familiarity with each other's speech, and to the development of simple translation procedures that make sense of regular correspondences between the various phonemes of the two languages. Other evidence is literary (while references to interpreters are common in OE texts, no such reference is ever found in the context of Anglo-Norse contact), historical/archaeological, and linguistic (loanwords). Modern insights into bilingualism and dialect shift are applied intelligently to throw light on a situation of which we can have no direct knowledge. The author concludes that intelligibility, though far from perfect, was probably adequate. Norse and English may originally have been adstratal, i.e. enjoying more or less equal prestige, and it took a while for the Norse language in England to die out (eleventh to twelfth centuries). It is through language shift—Norse speakers going over to English, so basically a situation in which Norse was a substrate—rather than borrowing by English speakers into English, that the majority of Norse loans entered ME. This tallies with the fact that they retained their Norse phonology. This is in sharp contrast to earlier (OE) borrowings from Norse that tend to show English phonology rather than Norse. A good example is Norse *reynar* 'reindeer', which was borrowed in OE as *hranas* on the basis of regular phonological and morphological correspondences (*a* for *ey*, *as* for *ar*) and re-borrowed in early Middle English as *reyne(dere)*, with the Norse phonology intact. Townend's findings are specifically of interest because they provide some background for the traditional assumptions about the influence of ON on OE/ME morphology and syntax.

And there is more on language contact. David Burnley, in 'French and Frenches in Fourteenth-Century London' (in Kastovsky and Mettinger, eds., pp. 17–34), reconstructs the attitudes of fourteenth-century Londoners towards French. In the same volume (pp. 131–60), Raymond Hickey, in 'Language Contact and Typological Difference: Transfer between Irish and Irish English', discusses the sociolinguistic background, and transfer on various linguistic levels, including syntax. Thomas Kohnen, in 'The Influence of "Latinate" Constructions in Early Modern English: Orality and Literacy as Complementary Forces' (in Kastovsky and Mettinger, eds., pp. 171–94), charts the rise of various participial constructions in various text types and argues that they spread to informal text types along with other stylistic norms of formal, prestigious texts. Gillis Kristensson, in 'Language in Contact: Old East Saxon and East Anglian' (in Fisiak and Trudgill, eds., 63–77), discusses some geographical details of the Anglo-Saxon invasion and its linguistic consequences. The same author grapples with the immigration patterns into London from the surrounding counties, particularly Norfolk, in 'Sociolects in Fourteenth-Century London' (in Fisiak and Trudgill, eds., pp. 71–7).

Text types have been studied from various perspectives. Satoru Tsukamoto contributes 'Syntactic Annotation and Text Classification: A Study Using the Penn-Helsinki Parsed Corpus of Middle English' (in Saito *et al.*, eds., pp. 249–71). The frequencies of nouns, verbs, conjunctions, and clause types are used to classify texts, with results that sometimes (but by no means always) coincide with the externally based text groupings adopted in the corpus itself. With the exception of *The Battle of Maldon*, OE poetry is notoriously difficult to date. Historical linguists may therefore be interested to learn of Geoffrey Russom's 'Dating Criteria for Old English Poems' (in Minkova and Stockwell, eds., pp. 245–65). Terttu Nevalainen, in 'What's in a Royal Letter? Linguistic Variation in the Correspondence of King Henry VIII' (in Lentz and Möhlig, eds., pp. 169–79), compares the linguistic features in both holograph letters (e.g. his love-letters to Anne Boleyn) and more official secretarial letters of this monarch. 'Servant or Patron? Jacob Tonson and the Language of Deference and Respect', by Susan Fitzmaurice (*LangS* 24[2002] 247–60), shows how the language in the correspondence of the members of the Kit-Cat Club (founded in 1700 by Jacob Tonson) reveals their linguistic acknowledgement of the very real position of power (as a 'patron broker') occupied by Tonson.

Several studies have looked at specific periods and/or genres using the multi-dimensional approach developed in the 1980s by Douglas Biber. In a small-scale but thorough study, Christer Geisler has been 'Investigating Register Variation in Nineteenth-Century English: A Multi-Dimensional Comparison' (in Reppen *et al.*, eds., pp. 249–71). Overall, there is a gradual increase in involvement (Biber's dimension 1), and the registers of letters, drama, and fiction become more personal and non-abstract (dimension 5); scientific writing remains fairly stable throughout the century. A slice of late ModE is investigated in this way by Ingrid Westin in her *Language Change in English Newspaper Editorials*, an account of the language of editorials in *The Times*, the *Daily Telegraph*, and the *Guardian* from 1900 to the 1990s. Using a selection of the linguistic features found to be discriminatory in earlier work, Westin establishes that the editorials have become less narrative, more interactional, but also more lexically specific and diverse, and informationally dense. With respect to the individual newspapers, the *Guardian* was found to be more conversational and narrative than the other two, perhaps as a reflection of the type of readership aimed at. Given the nature of the material, no conclusions about categorical grammatical change are possible, yet Westin's data show clearly that the twentieth century saw a marked increase in the acceptability of all kinds of colloquial devices in what is still a rather formal type of writing. A briefer account of the same material is given in 'A Multi-Dimensional Study of Diachronic Variation in British Newspaper Editorials' by Ingrid Westin and Christer Geisler (*ICAME* 26[2002] 133–52).

Bernd Heine and Tania Kuteva have written a *World Lexicon of Grammaticalization,* in which the most salient generalizations of grammaticalization processes, several hundred in all, are listed in alphabetical order, e.g. *ablative > agent, change-of-state > future, child > diminutive, neck > locative, need > obligation, possessive > perfect,* etc. Every process is illustrated with examples from a wide range of languages; an appendix gives information about which family or phylum each language belongs to. More on grammaticalization as a *process* is to be found in the proceedings of a conference on this topic held in Potsdam in 2001 (Wischer and Diewald, eds., *New Reflections on Grammaticalization*). In his contribution, 'New Reflections on Grammaticalization and Lexicalization' (pp. 1–18), Christian Lehmann discusses the relation between these two concepts. Wallace Chafe's 'Putting Grammaticalization in its Place' (pp. 395–412) is a more philosophical piece about the relation between thought and language. Marianne Mithun, in 'An Invisible Hand at the Root of Causation: The Role of Lexicalization in the Grammaticalization of Causatives' (pp. 237–57), describes the development of causative morphology from lexical items, particularly those meaning 'hand', containing means or manner affixes. Johan van der Auwera, in 'More Thoughts on Degrammaticalization' (pp. 19–29), defines the concept and makes an inventory of its properties. 'Grammaticalization within a Theory of Morphocentricity', by Jurgen Klausenburger (pp. 31–43), presents a theoretical approach in which morphological structure is taken to be central. Grammaticalization contexts are discussed in Bernd Heine's 'On the Role of Context in Grammaticalization' (pp. 83–101) and Gabriele Diewald's 'A Model for Relevant Types of Contexts in Grammaticalization' (pp. 103–20).

'*Really worthwhile* or *not really significant*? A Corpus-Based Approach to the Delexicalization and Grammaticalization of Intensifiers in Modern English', by Gunter Lorenz (in Wischer and Diewald, eds., pp. 143–61), demonstrates that intensifiers like *absolutely*, *ab fab*, or *bloody* are drawn from five 'resources' which he calls SCALAR, SEMANTIC FEATURE COPYING, EVALUATIVE, COMPARATIVE, and MODAL. More about the history of intensifiers is found in 'Fairly Pretty or Pretty Fair? On the Development and Grammaticalization of English Downtoners', by Terttu Nevalainen and Matti Rissanen (*LangS* 24[2002] 359–80), which also tries to establish whether adverb formation in -*ly* is regular enough to constitute an inflectional process in Modern English. Dagmar Barth-Weingarten and Elizabeth Couper-Kuhlen, in 'On the Development of Final *Though*: A Case of Grammaticalization?' (in Wischer and Diewald, eds., pp. 345–61), try to trace the development of this lexical item from concessive to discourse marker as in *listen, another factor though you brought up...* (taken from a discussion from a radio talk show). Mitsumi Uchida contributes 'From Participles to Conjunctions: A Parallel Corpus Study of Grammaticalization in English and French' (in Saito *et al.*, eds., pp. 131–46), investigating the process by which detached participles, as in *No news was received, causing everyone to be fidgety*, developed; the verb in question is usually one of 'causing'; the main clause is often passive or non-agentive in some other way.

Matters of word order are prominent this year. 'Internal and External Forces Again: Changes in Word Order in Old English and Old Irish', by Raymond Hickey (*LangS* 24[2002] 261–83), discusses the possible causes for the typological reorientation that affected these languages (Old Irish went from SOV to VSO, Old English from SOV to SVO). More about OE word order in Susan Pintzuk's 'Morphological Case and Word Order in Old English' (*LangS* 24[2002] 381–95), which concludes that case marking has no effect on the position of objects in OE, and that a formal syntactic account with case marking linked to feature strength fails to make the correct predictions for the diachronic trends. Some of this material also appears in Pintzuk's 'Verb-Object Order in Old English: Variation as Grammatical Competition' (in Lightfoot, ed., *Syntactic Effects of Morphological Change*, pp. 276–99). Here, she explains in greater detail why an analysis is to be preferred which works in terms of grammar competition (with two underlying orders being available, and scrambling from post- to pre-verbal position being restricted to pronouns and quantified elements). Carola Trips contributes *From OV to VO in Early Middle English*, a detailed study of the period when the change in canonical word order is usually said to have taken place. Her starting hypothesis is that the change was triggered by language contact with the Scandinavians, and she presents various types of supporting evidence for this, especially from the *Ormulum*. Thus, northern texts not only showed high percentages of VO order, but they also adopted other features of Scandinavian, such as general verb-second (where OE and more southern ME texts have various exceptions to this rule) and stylistic fronting. The absence of Scandinavian object shift from the ME texts might be thought to cast doubt on the borrowing hypothesis, but Trips elegantly demonstrates that this phenomenon is a more recent innovation in Scandinavian anyway. To model the variation in the ordering of object and verb found in her data, Trips adopts the grammar competition model developed by Anthony Kroch, and also applied to the OE data by Susan Pintzuk. The survival of OV order in late ME, which is known to involve mainly negative objects in clauses with a modal, is the topic of Frits Beukema and Wim van der Wurff's 'Modals, Objects and Negation in Late Middle English' (in Barbiers *et al.*, eds., pp. 75–102). The authors present data from various texts showing that the use of OV order is attested not just with one or two modals, but with all of them, making this a possible diagnostic for late ME modalhood (or at least auxiliarihood); like Cormack and Smith (Section 4(*a*)) they find that the scope of modality and (VP) negation varies.

The relative order of the direct object and indirect object in OE, and the introduction of the *to*-variant in early ME, are addressed in two articles. Chiara Polo looks at 'Double Objects and Morphological Triggers for Syntactic Case' (in Lightfoot, ed., pp. 124–42), arguing that the order DO-IO still occurred with full NPs when they had lost dative case marking. However, pronouns retained it, and this was apparently enough to trigger syntactic dative case on full NPs as well. The decline of morphological dative on pronouns coincides with, and triggers, the decline of the DO-IO order with all types of objects. A somewhat different story is told by Thomas McFadden (in Lightfoot, ed., pp. 107–23), who argues that the DO-IO order had oblique case for the IO, and was replaced in early ME by the DO its NP variant, since oblique case was no longer available.

Issues of verb movement form another important topic in the history of English syntax. 'Word Order in Old English Prose and Poetry: The Position of Finite Verb and Adverbs', by Ans van Kemenade (in Minkova and Stockwell, eds., pp. 355–71), draws attention to a marked difference between the two text types: negative-initial clauses in poetry (here *Beowulf*) often fail to have verb-fronting. Eric Haeberli addresses 'Inflectional Morphology and the Loss of Verb-Second in English' (in Lightfoot, ed., pp. 88–106). On the basis of comparative data, he argues that the loss of verb-second in English (which, following work by others, he dates to the fifteenth century) was caused by the loss of empty expletives (itself due to the loss of agreement morphology). 'Word Order in Different Text Types in Early Modern English', by Bjørg Bækken (*SN* 74[2002] 15–29), investigates the use of inversion in different types of writing and in different authors in the Early Modern English period; apart from anything else, the findings show that the conventional dating of the loss of inversion is too early. Verb movement of the V-to-I type is the topic of Michio Hosaka's 'Adverbial Positions and Verb Movement in Middle English and Early Modern English' (in Saito *et al.*, eds., pp. 195–210). Data on the position of *oft(en)* fail to clearly support the idea that V-to-I was lost at the end of the sixteenth century; in a more theoretical vein, it is proposed that V-to-I was lost due to the rise of Aux.

We turn to noun phrases. Cynthia L. Allen has been working on various aspects of ME possessives for several years now, and she informs us about her findings in three articles this year. In 'Case and Middle English Genitive Noun Phrases' (in Lightfoot, ed., pp. 57–80), she traces the history of the construction *the king's son William* 'King William's son', which arose in early ME; Allen attributes it to the loss of agreement (rather than case) and sets it in the context of other possessive developments at the time. Allen's 'On the Development of *A Friend of Mine*' (in Fanego, López-Couso, and Pérez-Guerra, eds., pp. 23–41) describes the diachronic stages which led to the construction and offers insights into the discourse motivations behind the choice for *that nose of yours* instead of plain *your nose*, which may also have been a factor in its development. Allen's third possessive piece is 'The Development of "Strengthened" Possessive Pronouns in English' (*LangS* 24[2002] 189–211), which looks at forms like *hers* and *hern*. They resulted in a processing advantage, as they signal to the hearer that no head NP is following. 'Historical Shifts in Modification Patterns with Complex Noun Phrase Structures: How Long Can You Go without a Verb?', by Douglas Biber and Victoria Clark (in Fanego, López-Couso, and Pérez-Guerra, eds., pp. 43–66), investigates complex NPs like *the penny-pinching circumstances that surrounded this international event* on the basis of diachronic and synchronic corpora. They report quite marked changes in informationally written registers (e.g. newspaper reports and medical prose) over the last hundred years, resulting in a much more compressed style of presentation. 'Grammaticalization versus Lexicalization Reconsidered: On the *Late* Use of Temporal Adverbs', by Laurel J. Brinton (in Fanego, López-Couso, and Pérez-Guerra, eds., pp. 67–97), investigates the once widespread use of such adverbs (*my late father*, *the then practice*), which seem to present a challenge to concepts such as grammaticalization and lexicalization.

The shift from *thou* to *you* remains one of the most intriguing developments in the history of English. Ulrich Busse has studied part of it in great detail in his *Linguistic Variation in the Shakespeare Corpus: Morpho-Syntactic Variability of Second*

Person Pronouns. After an introduction motivating the study and setting out its theoretical background (a combination of corpus linguistics, socio-historical linguistics, and historical pragmatics) and a chapter containing a very useful review of previous research on the personal pronouns in eModE, Busse explores in detail the distribution of *you* and *thou* in the Shakespeare corpus, their co-occurrence with nominal address forms (as in *you knave*), the use of *pray you* and *prithee*, the possible correlation with specific verbs or verb classes, the use of *thy* versus *thine*, and the form *ye.* The findings resist easy summary and we refer the reader to Busse's own recapitulations; one point that we mention here is the persistent tendency for minority forms to survive in certain fixed collocations (as in *thine own, thine eye, hark ye, look ye*). Ingrid Tieken-Boon van Ostade, in '*You was* and Eighteenth-Century Normative Grammar' (in Lentz and Möhlig, eds., pp. 88–102), argues that this form represents a brief transitional stage in the shift of *thou* to *you* as the canonical form for the second person singular. Bettelou Los turns to a pronoun that was lost much earlier in 'The Loss of the Indefinite Pronoun *Man*: Syntactic Change and Information Structure' (in Fanego, López-Couso, and Pérez-Guerra, eds., pp. 181–202). She argues that one of the factors in the demise of this pronoun was the loss of V2 in the main clause; the latter development transformed the role of subject NPs, which became the only expression of an unmarked theme (in the sense of M. Halliday [1994]). This in turn promoted the use of agentless passives instead of active sentences with *man*.

'The Origin of Definite Article Reduction in Northern English Dialects: Evidence from Dialect Allomorphy', by Mark J. Jones (*ELL* 6[2002] 325–45), finds evidence against the traditional hypothesis that this reduction is linked to the regional change of *þe* to *te* in Middle English, though no alternative explanation suggests itself. 'Explaining the Creation of Reflexive Pronouns in English', by Edward L. Keenan (in Minkova and Stockwell, eds., pp. 325–54), traces the development of the *-self* pronouns. Nikolaus Ritt, in 'The Spread of Scandinavian Third Person Plural Pronouns in English: Optimisation, Adaptation and Evolutionary Stability' (in Kastovsky and Mettinger, eds., pp. 279–304), looks at the spread of these pronouns from a functional perspective. Aimo Seppänen, in 'On Analysing the Pronoun *It*' (*ES* 83[2002] 442–62), states the case against the view recently put forward by Gunther Kaltenböck that a unified treatment of *it* as a referential pronoun is possible even for weather *it* and anticipatory *it.* Isabel Moskowich-Spiegel Fandiño and Begoña Crespo García, in 'Adjectival Forms in Middle English: Syntactic and Semantic Implications' (*SN* 74[2002] 161–70), report the not very surprising finding that attributive adjectives occurred mainly prenominally in late Middle English.

Next, it is subjects. The development of dative experiencers (*me hungreth*) into nominative experiencers (*I hunger*) is studied by Susana Bejar, in 'Movement, Morphology, and Learnability' (in Lightfoot, ed., pp. 307–325). She argues that this change was due not to case syncretism but to the emergence of A-movement, which itself resulted from the interplay of requirements of the language acquisition device (having to do with the functional category TP) and the earlier reanalysis of constructions like *him rued that fall* (NOM) into *him rued that fall* (ACC). 'Synchronic and Diachronic Aspects of Overt Subject Raising in English', by Tomoyuki Tanaka, argues that restrictions in the distribution of unaccusative subjects in the course of the diachronic development of English, as in *there arrived three students*, are the result of the loss of rich verbal agreement. 'Subject Control and Coreference in Early Modern English Free Adjuncts and Absolutes', by Carmen Río-Rey (*ELL* 6[2002] 309–23), concludes that the PE distinction between these two clauses is far less clear in eModE. Minoji Akimoto, in 'Two Types of Passivization of "V+NP+P" Constructions in Relation to Idiomatization' (in Fanego, López-Couso, and Pérez-Guerra, eds., pp. 9–22), reports on a diachronic investigation into two rival passivization patterns of composite predicates: *Advantage was taken of the students* versus *The students were taken advantage of*. '*Thank You* and *Thanks* in Early Modern English', by Mattias Jacobsson (*ICAME* 26[2002] 63–80), presents a corpus study of these expressions of gratitude and concludes that they had not yet developed the discourse marking features of today's BrE. 'Lexical Analysis of Middle English Passive Constructions', by Junichi Toyota (in Díaz Vera, ed., pp. 572–610) investigates verbal passives, adjectival passives (as in *he was surprised at the result*), and resultative passives (as in *he was displeased*), as well as the competitors of *by* in the agentive phrase: *from*, *mid*, *through*, and *of*. 'Detransitivization in the History of English from a Semantic Perspective', by Ruth Möhlig and Monika Klages (in Fanego, López-Couso, and Pérez-Guerra, eds., pp. 231–54), investigates the emergence of intransitive counterparts to transitive verbs—*wash*, *open*, generics (like *he is wise who reads*), and middles (*this book reads well*)—from a functional viewpoint. Arie Verhagen, in 'From Parts to Wholes and Back Again' (*CogLing* 13[2002] 403–39), argues that the usage-based conception of linguistic structure also operated in the historical development of some conceptually but not formally complex conceptual structures.

Modal and aspectual properties of the verb groups have also been investigated. Manfred Krug's 'A Path to Volitional Modality' (in Fanego, López-Couso, and Pérez-Guerra, eds., pp. 131–55) traces the development of the verb *want* and argues that its semantic development of 'lack'/'need' to 'desire' and hence to volitional and even obligation modality (*you want to be careful*) was motivated by the conventionalization of pragmatic inferences. 'Pragmatic Uses of SHALL Future Constructions in Early Modern English', by Maurizio Gotti (in Minkova and Stockwell, eds., pp. 301–22), compares these uses in eModE texts to the pragmatic values assigned to *shall* in grammars of the same period. Susan Fitzmaurice, in 'Politeness and Modal Meaning in the Construction of Humiliative Discourse in an Early Eighteenth-Century Network of Patron–Client Relationships' (*ELL* 6[2002] 239–65), shows that the choice of modal verb is influenced by the letter-writer's estimation of how he stands with his patron. Silvia Molina-Plaza, in 'Modal Change: A Corpus Study from 1500 to 1710 Compared to Current Usage' (in Díaz Vera, ed., pp. 539–62), gives an overview of the changes in the expression of modality since that period. Ian Roberts and Anna Roussou's 'The History of the Future' (in Lightfoot, ed., pp. 23–56) views the rise of the English modals (*will*, *shall*, but also non-futurate ones) as a case of grammaticalization, involving reanalysis of an original verb, generated inside the VP and subsequently moved to a higher functional position, into an auxiliary merged directly in the functional domain; a similar development affected the Romance and Greek markers of future.

Anneli Meurman-Solin, in 'The Progressive in Older Scots' (in Fanego, López-Couso, and Pérez-Guerra, eds., pp. 203–29) traces the use of the progressive variants *be doand*, *be doing* and *be in/a doing* from 1450 onwards and the linguistic factors underlying their distribution. Rajend Mesthrie, in 'Endogeny Versus Contact Revisited: Aspectual Busy in South African English' (*LangS* 24[2002] 345–58) considers the *busy*-construction as in SAE *It is busy snowing here at the moment* and concludes that it shows varying degrees of grammaticalization into a progressive marker in AmE, BrE, and SAE. Larisa Oldireva Gustafsson, in *Preterite and Past Participle Forms in English 1680–1790: Standardisation Processes in Public and Private Writing*, presents a corpus study on qualitative and quantitative changes in the various spellings of regular past tenses (e.g. *fixed, fix'd, fixd, fixt*, and *fix't*) and the use of preterite and past participle forms of irregular verbs (e.g. the preterite variants *drunk* and *writ* and the past participle variants *drank* and *wrote*). The corpus findings are compared to the evidence of contemporaneous grammars, rhetoric books, and dictionaries. Gustafsson found that, with respect to the regular verbs, the spellings that were later to become standard (i.e. *-ed*) were already largely established in public writings. This was not yet the case with the irregular verbs. In private writings (letters), we find some measure of standardization particularly of the irregular verbs, whereas the standardization of past forms of the regular verbs appears to be lagging behind somewhat. When the factors of time, register, text type, and grammatical category are taken into account, the picture becomes more diffuse. Registers of writing, public and private, differed in their response to the pressures of standardization, and so did individual practices of language users. A different perspective on this question is offered by Ingrid Tieken-Boon van Ostade, in 'Robert Lowth and the Strong Verb System' (see Section 1 above).

Arguing for subtle differences in interpretation of aspect in historical data is always an unenviable task. Jeong-Hoon Lee, in 'The "Have" Perfect in Old English: How Close was it to the Modern English Perfect?' (in Minkova and Stockwell, eds., pp. 373–97), tries to argue that there has not been a change in the uses of the perfect since OE. His greatest problem is of course the continuative perfect, especially in view of the fact that the presence of durative time adverbials is in itself not enough to diagnose a continuative. A straightforward formal difference is addressed by K. Aaron Smith, in 'The Role of Frequency in the Specialization of the English Anterior' (in Bybee and Hopper, eds., pp. 361–82), which deals with the replacement of the *be*-perfect by the *have*-perfect. 'English *Do*: On the Convergence of Languages and Linguists', by Johan van der Auwera and Inge Genee (*ELL* 6[2002] 283–307), evaluates the various hypotheses of a Celtic origin of periphrastic *do*, and linguists' emotive attitudes to this issue.

'Corpus-Provoked Questions about Negation in Early Middle English', by Margaret Laing (*LangS* 24[2002] 297–321), discusses formal variation in early ME negation patterns (*ne* on its own, *ne ... naht* or *nat/not* on its own), including some rarer constructions, notably with *but* ('nothing except'), and possible syntactic constraints on their use. A negative polarity item is the focus of Yoko Iyeiri's 'Development of *Any* from Middle English to Early Modern English: A Study Using the Helsinki Corpus of English Texts' (in Saito *et al.*, eds., pp. 211–23); she finds that *any* is already common around 1380, and spreads most quickly in legal texts and official documents. Later developments in negative sentences are the topic of Susan Fitzmaurice's 'The Textual Resolution of Structural Ambiguity in Eighteenth-Century English: A Corpus-Linguistic Study of Patterns of Negation' (in Reppen *et al.*, eds., pp. 227–47); she wonders whether authors exploited the use of *do* to avoid the ambiguity inherent in sentences like *Leonora stayed not to make him any reply*. The findings suggest they didn't.

Christian Mair, in 'Three Changing Patterns of Verb Complementation in Late Modern English: A Real-Time Study Based on Matching Text Corpora' (*ELL* 6[2002] 105–31), examines grammatical variation in non-finite complementation patterns. Hideo Nishimura has looked at 'Degree Adverbs in the Corpus of Early English Correspondence Sampler' (in Saito *et al.*, eds., pp. 183–93); the findings are that the decline of the degree adverb *full* (its place being taken by *right*) is well under way already before 1500, and that by 1500, *very* is becoming predominant (not only in simple frequency but also in the number of collocations that it enters into). While degree adverbs form a small set, Masahiro Hori's 'Collocational Patterns of -*ly* Manner Adverbs in Dickens' (in Saito *et al.*, eds., 149–63) finds not only run-of-the-mill items like *really*, *anxiously*, *certainly*, but also unique formations like *metropolitaneously*, *mouldily*, *uvularly*, and many more; these can actually be considered a typical marker of Dickens's style.

Sebastian Hoffmann investigates several corpora from 1650 till today in 'In (Hot) Pursuit of Data: Complex Prepositions in Late Modern English' (in Peters *et al.*, eds., pp. 127–46). Once Hoffmann has caught them, the complex prepositions (275 in all, not counting two-word combinations like *instead of*) are counted, classified, and interpreted in terms of a grammaticalization process, whereby they initially appear with modifiers but later tend to lose these, as rigidification and conventionalization set in.

We finish with contributions on subordinate clauses. Christine Johansson looks at 'Pied Piping and Stranding from a Diachronic Perspective' (in Peters *et al.*, eds., pp. 147–62), finding that in relative clauses in the Penn-Helsinki Corpus of ME, *wh*-forms seldom feature stranding (perhaps not surprising for what was after all a new relativizer), though some mixed constructions appear (*of which he spoke of* (*it*)). Genitives and partitives did not occur in the pattern *the voices of which*, instead taking *of which the voices*. Norihiko Otsu, in 'On the Presence or Absence of the Conjunction *þæt* in Old English, with Special Reference to Dependent Sentences Containing a *gif*-Clause' (*ELL* 6[2002] 225–38), argues that the emergence of the zero complementizer has its origins in direct speech. The same author also writes 'On the Absence of the Conjunction *That* in Late Middle English' (in Saito *et al.*, eds., pp. 225–34), finding support in this material for the same conclusion: in this period, it is very clear that *that*-omission is most frequent in speech-related texts. 'Historical *That* and Indirect Questions in Modern English', by Jon L. Erickson (in Lentz and Möhlig, eds., pp. 55–65), provides a minimalist diachronic account of *that* and zero in such questions. '"Without Except(ing) Unless …"': On the Grammaticalisation of Expressions Indicating Exception in English', by Matti Rissanen (in Lentz and Möhlig, eds., pp. 77–87), discusses the grammaticalization of such elements. Merja Kytö and the late Andrei Danchev, in 'The Middle English "*For To* + Infinitive" Construction' (in Kastovsky and Mettinger, eds., pp. 35–55), discuss possible Scandinavian influence in the emergence and spread of this construction.

5. Semantics

Sebastian Löbner's *Understanding Semantics* is one of the best of the many textbooks published in the past few years aiming to serve as a first introduction to the discipline. Its high quality can be seen especially in the excellent balance it achieves between a (relatively) theory-neutral and sufficiently detailed presentation of the major concepts in linguistic semantics and in the overview it offers of some dominant semantic theories of the recent past and present. Part I introduces the reader to the major concepts and central phenomena investigated in linguistic semantics. Chapter 1 defines the subject matter of the discipline, surveys the various levels of meaning, and discusses the principle of compositionality, together with its implications. Descriptive meaning (which conveys factual information) is contrasted to social and expressive meaning in chapter 2. Lexical versus sentential ambiguity is dealt with in chapter 3, and the basics of a truth-conditional approach to meaning in chapter 4, while chapter 5 discusses some basic meaning relations (hyponymy, or various types of semantic oppositions). Chapter 6, on 'Predication', introduces the reader to the major concepts of sentence semantics. In part II, three theoretical approaches to the study of meaning are introduced. The emphasis falls not on a detailed explication of the particulars of these theories, but on providing a sense of the types of explanations they lend themselves to, which is done with the help of toy theories for particular phenomena formulated in the spirit of these approaches. The theories investigated include structuralism (presented together with more recent examples of 'feature semantics'), cognitive semantics, and formal semantics. A separate chapter discusses the issue of language comparison and the nature of semantic universals. Each chapter is supplemented by learning aids, such as a checklist of terms, notes, suggestions for further reading, and some well-chosen exercises, which all contribute to making it an extremely user-friendly textbook for both undergraduate and postgraduate courses. The fact that Löbner's book not only presents material to be acquired by the students, but also helps them to acquire the means to evaluate competing semantic theories, makes it superior to its predecessors.

Féry and Sternefeld, eds., *Audiatur Vox Sapientiae*, is a Festschrift dedicated to Arnim von Stechow, one of the most influential linguists of our time. Most papers in the volume discuss fascinating new results in subfields to which Arnim von Stechow himself also made significant contributions. Related to one of the leitmotifs of his work, the situational dependence of reference, three essays are devoted to the semantics of English *again* and German *wieder*. Sigrid Beck and William Snyder, in 'The Resultative Parameter and Restitutive *Again*' (pp. 48–69), show that the parameter related to the availability of an interpretation principle accounting for the interpretation of resultative constructions (e.g. as in *Mary beat the metal smooth*), proposed in von Stechow [1995], is also sensitive to the availability of the restitutive interpretation of *again* (which, for example, corresponds to the following reading of *Sally walked to the summit again*: 'Sally walked to the summit, and she had been there before'). Cathrine Fabricius-Hansen, in '"Wi(e)der" and "Again(st)"' (pp. 101–30), argues for a true polysemy of the lexical items in the title, whereas Wolfgang Klein accounts for the semantics of a monosemous *wieder* by assuming that the semantic representation of a verb may contain one or two time variables. In '(A)Temporal Complements' (pp. 240–58), Graham Katz investigates the temporal interpretation of infinitival complements of verbs like *believe* vs. *expect* in a framework in which tenses display both anaphoric and operator-like properties. Fascinating reactions to von Stechow's [1999] ExtendedNow-Theory on the German perfect are presented in Renate Musan's 'Narrowing down the

ExtendedNow' (pp. 372–91) and Monika Rathert's 'Anteriority Versus the Extended-Now: Theories of the German Perfect' (pp. 410–26). Thomas Ede Zimmermann, 'Unspecificity and Intensionality' (pp. 514–33), argues against the conviction that unspecificity and intensionality are independent of each other. Manfred Krifka's contribution to the volume, 'For a Structured Meaning Account of Questions and Answers' (pp. 287–359), is related to another achievement by von Stechow, the structured meaning approach to focus interpretation. It compares the approach developed independently by von Stechow and Joachim Jacobs to another powerful theory, Rooth's alternative semantics, with respect to their predictions on the interpretation of question-answer dialogues, concluding that the former fares much better in accounting for the new set of data. Von Stechow's work on the syntax/semantics interface is reflected in Cécile Meier's 'Multihead Comparatives and Result Clause Constructions with "Split Antecedents"' (pp. 348–71), and Irene Heim's 'Degree Operators and Scope' (pp. 214–39), both on the comparative, as well as in Kjell Johan Sæbø's 'Necessary Conditions in a Natural Language' (pp. 427–49), which addresses the semantics of conditionals with an expression of necessity in the matrix and an expression of intention in the conditional clause.

The papers in Hasselgård, Johansson, Behrens, and Fabricius-Hansen, eds., *Information Structure in a Cross-Linguistic Perspective*, address the issue of how text production is influenced by how a message is presented in terms of given/new information, focus, cohesion, and point of view. They do this by contrasting corpus-based empirical data from English, German, and/or one of the Scandinavian languages on the distribution of clause connectives, adverbials, modals, or certain parallel constructions (e.g. clefts). The papers by Valéria Molnár ('Contrast—From a Contrastive Perspective', pp. 147–61) and Jorunn Hetland ('Accent and the Notion of Contrast: A Cross-Linguistic Approach', pp. 163–78), however, address more theoretical questions on the nature of contrast, as well as on its relation to other information structural notions and to pitch accent, respectively.

The Noun Phrase, by J. Rijkhoff, is a valuable empirical and theoretical study of the structure of this constituent, based on an impressively large body of data from fifty-two languages. Chapters 2 to 6 provide a cross-linguistic account of the semantic and morpho-syntactic properties of the NP. The author proposes a classification of nouns into six noun types (or nominal subcategories), including general nouns, sort nouns, mass nouns, set nouns, singular object nouns, and collective nouns. Various systems of classifying nouns are reviewed, including classifier systems, noun class systems (including genders), and classifications based on the number of arguments as well as on morphological and phonological properties. Noun modifiers are classified into three groups, depending on whether they specify the Quality, Quantity, or Locality of the noun referent. Chapter 7 argues that the underlying structure of NPs can be represented in a typologically correct way in terms of a hierarchically nested layered structure in the framework of Simon Dik's [1997] theory of Functional Grammar. The layered structure of NPs is said to be analogous to the internal structure of clauses. Chapters 8 to 10 aim to provide a cross-linguistically adequate account of the internal syntax of simple NPs, concentrating primarily on the relative order of the determiner, numeral, adjective, and noun.

Preyer and Peter, eds., *Logical Form and Language*, is a splendid collection which brings together philosophers of language and linguists with the aim of taking a new look at the nature of logical form and its interactions with grammar and meaning from various theoretical perspectives. Among the studies with the most direct application to present-day natural language semantics, the following are particularly worthy of attention. Paul M. Pietroski, in 'Function and Concatenation' (pp. 91–117), argues for an approach in which the semantic contribution of syntactic branching is taken to be predicate conjunction and not function application. James Higginbotham's 'Why is Sequence of Tense Obligatory?' (pp. 207–27) proposes a new account of the asymmetry between the available temporal interpretations of complement clauses (as in *Gianni said that Maria was ill,* which is ambiguous between two readings: Maria's illness may be simultaneous with or happen at some time before the event of 'saying') and those in object relatives (as in *Gianni saw [a woman who was ill]*, where the ambiguity can be threefold: the woman's illness may be simultaneous with, it may happen at some time before, or at any time prior to, the event of 'seeing'). Richard Larson's 'The Grammar of Intensionality' (pp. 228–62) defends the view that intensionality phenomena are connected to a particular grammatical environment, namely, complement clauses, by showing that phenomena that are often cited as counter-examples to this view are in fact either clausal (i.e. the so-called intensional transitives, as in *Max wants a werewolf*) or non-intensional (adverbial modifiers as in *Olga allegedly dances,* and adjectival modifiers as in *Olga is an alleged dancer*). Barry Schein's 'Events and the Semantic Content of Thematic Relations' (pp. 263–344) takes a new look at the question of whether the thematic roles appearing in the logical form of sentences should be considered absolute or relativized to event concepts. Schein proposes an extension of event mereology with so-called 'scenes', which are more fine-grained than events. Jason Stanley's paper 'Nominal Restriction' (pp. 365–88) argues against the view that the number of ways in which extra-linguistic context can affect interpretation seriously undermines any attempt at a systematic theory of meaning for natural language, by showing that what appear to be different effects of context in the interpretation of three different types of constructions are in fact reducible to the same mechanism, which he calls 'Nominal Restriction'.

Hoeksema, Rullmann, Sánchez-Valencia, and van der Wouden, eds., *Perspectives on Negation and Polarity Items*, presents some fascinating new developments in one of the favourite topics of recent research in natural language syntax and semantics. Several papers in this collection discuss polarity sensitivity and, more specifically, the question of which semantic features license polarity items. Jay David Atlas's 'Negative Quantifier Noun Phrases: A Typology and an Acquisition Hypothesis' (pp. 1–22) proposes a hierarchy of negative quantifier NPs, according to which—among downwards monotonic NPs—the anti-additive ones (e.g. *no animals*) are to be considered more negative than anti-multiplicative ones (*not all animals*). Anastasia Giannakidou's study of 'Polarity Items and the (Non)Veridicality Hypothesis' (pp. 99–127) is a summary of the already influential theory of the author. This theory is based on the claim that limited distribution phenomena in Greek, which are traditionally assumed to be polarity-sensitive, are in fact sensitive to (non)veridicality and can be accounted for in terms of licensing and anti-licensing dependencies. Christopher Kennedy's contribution, 'On the Monotonicity of Polar Adjectives' (pp. 201–21), argues for representing the polarity sensitivity of polar adjectives (as in *It is difficult/*easy for Tim to admit that he has ever been wrong*) in terms of a model in which gradable adjectives denote relations between individuals and intervals on a scale. Other papers in the collection are devoted to the issue of what types of expressions are sensitive to polarity, such as the one by Johan van der Auwera ('On the Typology of Negative Modals', pp. 23–48), which reports the results of a cross-linguistic study of the lexicalization patterns of negative modals (i.e. combinations of negation and modality) in twenty-nine (Indo) European languages. Gabriel Falkenberg's 'Lexical Sensitivity in Negative Polarity Verbs' (pp. 79–97) investigates negative polarity verbs in German, and classifies them into four categories, referred to as abstentives, attractives, privatives, and verbs of care. Anita Mittwoch, in 'Perfective Sentences under Negation and Durative Adverbials: A Double-Jointed Construction' (pp. 265–82), examines two conflicting analyses of negative sentences containing the temporal connective *until*, as in *Mary didn't work until May 1st,* where the scope of the adverb and negation are reversed with respect to each other; she argues that, given the grammar of English, both should be considered correct.

Two volumes in the series Typological Studies in Language published by Benjamins deserve a closer look. The first, Baron, Herslund, and Sørensen, eds., *Dimensions of Possession,* investigates the various structures used for expressing the notion of possession. The most frequent among these are the genitive, and constructions with verbs meaning 'have', in a wide variety of languages, including Cahuilla, Danish, Nyulnyulan languages, Russian, French, Spanish, Spanoghe-Portuguese, and Classical Latin. The basic difference between the different constructions used is whether they are predicative or attributive, as stated by Michael Herslund and Irène Baron in their introduction (pp. 1–25). In the former case, the prime examples of which are the 'have' and 'belong' constructions, the possessive relation is explicitly asserted, and expressed by the verb; in the latter, the possessive relation is captured by a nominal, but this relation, they claim, is merely presupposed, which is the reason why these constructions (e.g., *John's book*) are much more polysemous than the corresponding predicative ones. The contributions to the other Benjamins volume, Feigenbaum and Kurzon, eds., *Prepositions in their Syntactic, Semantic and Pragmatic Context,* are concerned with the study of prepositions in English, French, Hebrew, the English-based creole Bislama, modern Judaeo-Greek (a sociolect of Greek spoken by Romaniote Jews), and Maltese. From the point of view of non-lexical semantics, two studies deserve particular attention: David S. Brée and Ian E. Pratt-Hartmann, in 'Temporal Semantics of Prepositions in Context' (pp. 75–113), investigate whether the interaction of the temporal semantics of prepositions and verbs in (the process of) determining whether the interval in which the main proposition in a sentence holds, is simply additive or rather interactive, while Ian Pratt-Hartmann and Nissim Francez, on 'Prepositions in Context' (pp. 115–26), argue for an approach which takes aspectual class distinctions into account when determining the interpretation of spatial adverbials.

Portner and Partee, eds., *Formal Semantics: The Essential Readings,* is an absolute must for any postgraduate student of linguistics or anyone interested in what formal semantics is all about. The volume contains almost all of the classic papers that constitute the major milestones in the development of the discipline, starting from the great paper by the 'founder' of the field, Richard Montague: 'The Proper Treatment of Quantification in Ordinary English' (pp. 17–34). The development of NP semantics is represented by the 'Unified Analysis of the English Bare Plural', by Greg N. Carlson (pp. 35–74), 'Generalized Quantifiers and Natural

Language', by Jon Barwise and Robin Cooper (pp. 75–126), and 'The Logical Analysis of Plurals and Mass Terms: A Lattice-Theoretical Approach', by Godehard Link (pp. 127–46). Robert C. Stalnaker's 'Assertion' (pp. 147–61), and David Lewis's 'Scorekeeping in a Language Game' (pp. 162–77) are important contributions to philosophical pragmatics, and regarded as foundational works for the field dynamic semantics; the most important early achievements in this field are represented by David Lewis's 'Adverb of Quantification' (pp. 178–88), Hans Kamp's 'A Theory of Truth and Semantic Representation' (pp. 189–222), and two papers by Irene Heim: 'File Change Semantics and the Familiarity Theory of Definiteness' (pp. 223–48) and 'On the Projection Problem for Presuppositions' (pp. 249–60). The semantics of the TMA system is discussed in the foundational papers 'Toward a Semantic Analysis of Verb Aspect and the English "Imperfective" Progressive', by David R. Dowty (pp. 261–88), 'The Notional Category of Modality', by Angelika Kratzer (pp. 289–323), and 'The Algebra of Events', by Emmon Bach (pp. 324–33). 'Generalized Conjunction and Type Ambiguity', by Barbara H. Partee and Mats Rooth (pp. 334–56), as well as 'Noun Phrase Interpretation and Type-Shifting Principles', by Barbara H. Partee (pp. 357–81), are the first systematic discussions of an approach which formally captures the fact that certain phrases can have different but logically related meanings. Important foundational contributions to the semantics of questions are represented by the papers 'Syntax and Semantics of Questions', by Lauri Karttunen (pp. 382–420), and 'Type-Shifting Rules and the Semantics of Interrogatives', by Jeroen Groenendijk and Martin Stokhof (pp. 421–56). William A. Ladusaw's paper 'On the Notion *Affective* in the Analysis of Negative-Polarity Items' (pp. 457–70) is a first illustration of the fact that a model-theoretic property can play a role in determining the distribution of linguistic forms.

Another collection, *The Compositionality Papers*, by the philosophers Jerry A. Fodor and Ernest Lepore, containing reprinted papers (sometimes in a revised form), needs a brief acknowledgement here since it discusses issues highly relevant to natural language semantics, namely, the property of compositionality characterizing systems of representation.

Turning to articles in journals, it is to be noted that much attention has been paid in 2002 to the semantics of questions. Building on the observation that ordinary questions and rhetorical questions do not pattern alike with respect to various well-formedness conditions (e.g., negative polarity licensing), Chung-hye Han, in 'Interpreting Interrogatives as Rhetorical Questions' (*Lingua* 112[2002] 201–29), proposes that the representation over which well-formedness conditions are stated should be the output of a post-LF derivation, determined via interaction with pragmatics. Sigrid Beck and Yael Sharvit, in 'Pluralities of Questions' (*JSem* 19[2002] 105–57), take a new look at the quantificational variability data first discussed by Berman (1991)—for example, sentences like *Mary mostly knows who cheated*, under the reading 'For most people who cheated, Mary knows that they cheated'— and argue that the domain of the adverb of quantification in these sentences is a division of the original question into subquestions. The paper by R. Nelken and N. Francez, Bilattices and the Semantics of Natural Language Questions' (*Ling&P* 25[2002] 37–64), calls into question the traditional assumption, according to which questions are inherently intensional entities, and puts forward an extensional theory of questions in which the domain of type **t** is reinterpreted as a 'bilattice'. Yael Sharvit's 'Embedded Questions and "De Dicto" Readings' (*NLS* 10[2002] 97–123) is concerned with the interpretation of *wh*-complements of veridical question-embedding verbs such as *know* or *surprise*.

A special issue of the *Journal of Semantics* (19:iii[2002]), edited by Klaus von Heusinger and Kerstin Schwabe, is devoted to the issue of specificity, a concept central to the interpretation of indefinite NPs, which emerged in the 1960s as a result of transferring the *de re–de dicto* distinction from definite NPs to the domain of indefinites. As the guest editors state in their brief introduction, a specific reading of an indefinite can pre-theoretically be defined as a reading which expresses 'certainty of the speaker about the identity of the referent'. Work on the semantics of specific indefinites in the past few decades has made it evident that a successful analysis of their meaning has to integrate the contribution of factors like scope, domain restriction, information structure, and referential dependency, and has to account for the place of specificity in the interpretation process as well as its representation. Donka Farkas's 'Specificity Distinctions' (*JSem* 19:iii[2002] 213–43) proposes an approach which treats determiners as lexically encoding instructions for the evaluation of variables introduced by their determiner phrases (DPs). For definite DPs this value is assumed to be fixed, whereas with indefinites there is variation concerning the choice of value for the variable. In 'Specificity and Definiteness in Sentence and Discourse Structure' (*JSem* 19:iii[2002] 245–74), Klaus von Heusinger argues against the view that specific expressions are a subclass of indefinite NPs. He proposes that definiteness expresses the discourse pragmatic property of familiarity, whereas specific NPs are those referentially anchored to another discourse object, and thus the two concepts are independent of each other. Finally, Paul Portner's 'Topicality and (Non-)Specificity in Mandarin' (*JSem* 19:iii[2002] 275–87) investigates complex interactions between indefinites, topics, and specificity, while Roger Schwarzschild, in 'Singleton Indefinites' (*JSem* 19:iii[2002] 289–314), explores the consequences of the view that the apparent scope-taking abilities of indefinites can be explained in terms of quantifier domain restriction.

A special issue of *Theoretical Linguistics* (28:i[2002]), also edited by von Heusinger and Schwabe, is concerned with the interactions between information structure and sentence type. Franz-Josef d'Avis's 'On the Interpretation of *Wh*-Clauses in Exclamative Environments' (*TL* 28:i[2002] 5–31) argues for the view that root *wh*-exclamatives in German are of the same semantic type as *wh*-interrogatives. Hans-Martin Gärtner, 'On the Force of V2 Declaratives' (*TL* 28:i[2002] 33–42), evaluates two rival analyses for embedded German V2 declaratives that share properties with both subordinate relative clauses and main clauses. And lastly, Ingo Reich's 'Question/Answer Congruence and the Semantics of *Wh*-Phrases' (*TL* 28:i[2002] 73–94) argues for analysing *wh*-phrases as functional expressions with an indefinite core, and not as indefinites, in the spirit of Karttunen [1977].

In 'Topic, Focus, and the Interpretation of Bare Plurals' (*NLS* 10[2002] 125–65), Ariel Cohen and Nomi Erteschik-Shir argue for the position that focus structure determines the interpretation of bare plurals, namely, that topic bare plurals are interpreted generically, whereas focused bare plurals are interpreted existentially. Two papers are concerned with the interpretation of 'donkey' in sentences such as *Every farmer who owns a donkey beats it*. Barbara Abbott's 'Donkey

Demonstratives' (*NLS* 10[2002] 285–98) argues for a new way of paraphrasing donkey pronouns (like the *it* in the above example) in terms of demonstrative phrases (e.g. *that donkey*). Bart Geurts, in 'Donkey Business', (*Ling&P* 25[2002] 129–56), discusses the phenomenon that certain aspects of world knowledge seem to play a role in the interpretation of donkey-sentences with non-intersective determiners (like *every* or *most*) but not in that of sentences with intersective determiners.

Further papers that merit attention include Markus Egg's 'Semantic Construction for Reinterpretation Phenomena' (*Linguistics* 40[2002] 579–609), which proposes a compositional semantics for structures whose full meaning can only be determined on the basis of extra-linguistic knowledge (i.e. structures in need of reinterpretation) with the help of the representational language CLLS (Constraint Language for Lambda Structures). Greg Carlson and Francis Jeffry Pelletier, in 'The Average American Has 2.3 Children' (*JSem* 19[2002] 73–104), propose an account of the meaning of 'average'-NPs not referring to anything concrete in the world, which can, however, be integrated into a standard account of the semantics for definite NPs. Marcus Kracht's 'On the Semantics of Locatives' (*Ling&P* 25[2002] 157–232) suggests a model-theoretic approach to the semantics of locative expressions that assumes that the meaning of these expressions involves two layers—these in fact also surface morphologically in many languages—the first defines a location, and the second a type of movement to that location. Roger Schwarzschild and Karina Wilkinson, in 'Quantifiers in Comparatives: A Semantics of Degree Based on Intervals' (*NLS* 10[2002] 1–41), put forth a new analysis for structures with a quantifier in the scope of a comparative, as in *Irving was closer to me than he was to most of the others*, based on intervals. Matthew Whelpton's 'Locality and Control with Infinitives of Result' (*NLS* 10[2002] 167–210) presents an analysis of rationale clause indefinites. We close with Mats Dahllöf, who, in 'Token Dependency Semantics and the Paratactic Analysis of Intensional Constructions' (*JSem* 19[2002] 333–68), introduces Token Dependency Semantics, a surface-oriented and token-based framework for compositional truth-conditional semantics.

6. Lexicography, Lexicology, and Lexical Semantics

A range of interesting dictionaries appeared this year. Christopher Stray's *English Slang in the Nineteenth Century* is a collection, in five handsomely bound volumes, of reprints of nineteenth- and early twentieth-century slang dictionaries. The greater availability of these texts is much to be applauded, but the selection of dictionaries is eclectic, to say the least. It includes two dictionaries called *Gradus ad Cantabrigiam,* one produced by 'A Pembrochian', and the other by 'A Brace of Cantabs', and the anonymous *Mushri–English Pronouncing Dictionary*, which lists the slang used at Winchester school. Stray includes both the reprinted seventh edition from 1901 and his own edited version, which contains a detailed introduction and notes. The inclusion of Hotten's *Slang Dictionary* is unproblematic, but the *Lexicon Balatronicum* is treated here as if it were a nineteenth-century dictionary by Francis Grose (who died in 1791). George William, Lord Lyttelton's *Contributions Towards a Glossary of the Glynne Language* documents the language used by the Glynne family of Hawarden, spread by marriage to the Lytteltons and the

Gladstones. It is an interesting work, parodying the developing discipline of comparative philology, but perhaps not a slang dictionary in the strictest sense. Bath Charles Smart and Henry Thomas Crofton's *The Dialect of the English Gypsies* is clearly not a slang dictionary even in the widest sense. In his introduction, Stray works to justify his selection and asserts that these dictionaries chart the movement from enthusiastic amateur to systematic scholar. He argues convincingly that they demonstrate the importance of slang in reflecting and reinforcing institutional identity.

Paul Beale's edition of Partridge's *Dictionary of Slang and Unconventional English* was issued in paperback this year. There is a brief foreword by David Crystal, including an account of Partridge's life, followed by lengthy and useful prefatory material, including Partridge's own preface to the first edition. This, the eighth edition of the dictionary, conflates the original 1937 edition with all subsequent published and unpublished addenda. Beale makes some deletions, explained and justified in the preface, and discusses Partridge's criteria for dating usages. The appendix includes a table showing the development of the phonetic alphabet, and discussion of the development of several categories of slang, including army slang, nicknames for football teams, Australian surfing talk, and so on. Beale updates Partridge's notes and adds a few categories of his own.

R.W. Holder's *How Not To Say What You Mean: A Dictionary of Euphemisms* is the third edition of his variously entitled *Dictionary of American and British Euphemisms* [1987] and *Dictionary of Euphemisms* [1995]. As in earlier editions, the thematic index is an extremely useful way of accessing the alphabetically listed entries. Richard A. Spears's *Slang and Euphemism* is also a third edition, revised and abridged. He provides a list of entries containing synonyms to allow the user to locate alternative terms. This is rather more time-consuming than Holder's approach, but does provide more material. Spears gives more historical information and includes more obsolete terms. His dictionary would be the better of the two for reference, but Holder's includes citations and thus makes for more interesting browsing. They are both very good value for money.

Peter Novobatzky and Ammon Shea's *Depraved and Insulting English* makes no pretence to scholarly exhaustiveness. It is a lively, anecdotal, and well-illustrated collection bringing together two earlier works that treated abusive and offensive terms separately. James Morton's *Gang Slang: A Dictionary of Criminal and Sexual Slang* concentrates on criminal and sexual terms. The two domains do not always sit easily together, but the book is an invaluable source for modern cant. John Ayto's *The Oxford Dictionary of Rhyming Slang* can be recommended on the grounds of its excellent introduction. In it, Ayto discusses the popularity of rhyming slang lists as 'more souvenirs than practical dictionaries' (p. vii) and traces the interest in rhyming slang to its humorous rather than secretive use. He divides his examples into 'museum pieces', 'fixtures in … the passive vocabulary of British English speakers', and new coinages (p. x), but wonders whether it isn't 'all really part of a giant ongoing word-game, whose product is more droll artefact than linguists' lexeme' (p. xii), arguing that normal lexicographic rules of authenticity are not relevant to this field. From the vocabulary of rhyming slang, Ayto produces a prototypical rhyming slangster, and he goes on to discuss the methods by which rhyming slang is produced. Entries are arranged thematically, with discursive commentary and citations. To round off this dictionary section, we note that Jessy

Randall has reproduced a 1901 Colorado slang glossary, in 'The Slang of the Day' (*Verbatim* 27:i[2002] 9–11).

Dictionary researchers have also been busy. Howard Jackson's *Lexicography: An Introduction* is a readable account of lexicography for an undergraduate audience. He begins by discussing some of the difficulties faced by a lexicographer in deciding what is a word, and talks briefly about various possible sources of new vocabulary and about word meaning. He considers dictionary typology and contents, and gives an account of the history of English lexicography, beginning with OE glossaries and ending with current electronic dictionaries. He goes on to consider dictionary users, questions of definition, and the information that dictionaries include on spelling, pronunciation, grammar, usage, etc. A separate chapter is devoted to etymology, with the emphasis on how to interpret etymological information in dictionaries and on why it should be included at all. Learners' dictionaries also merit a brief chapter of their own, concentrating on the work of Hornby, Palmer, West, and their successors. The final chapters deal with alternatives to the alphabet as a principle of organization, and the processes of compiling and also of criticizing dictionaries. Jackson also published *Grammar and Vocabulary: A Resource Book for Students* this year. While it is a useful introduction to basic grammar, *Lexicography* has more to say about vocabulary.

Anne McDermott questions the received wisdom that hard-word lexicographers merely anglicized the headwords in English–Latin dictionaries, in 'Early Dictionaries of English and Historical Corpora: In Search of Hard Words' (in Díaz Vera, ed. *A Changing World of Words*, pp. 197–226). Rowena Fowler looks at Woolf's use of dictionaries and dictionaries' use of Woolf, in 'Virginia Woolf: Lexicographer' (*ELN* 39:iii[2002] 54–70). In 'Public Political Vocabulary: Model of a Dictionary' (in Gottlieb, Mogensen, and Zettersten, eds., *Symposium on Lexicography X. Proceedings of the Tenth International Symposium on Lexicography*, pp. 173–84), Olga Karpova and Svetlana Manik look at the treatment of terms such as *ethnic cleansing* and *affirmative action* in English and Russian dictionaries, and suggest some areas for improvement.

Gabriele Stein's *Better Words: Evaluating EFL Dictionaries* is a collection of ten essays from the last quarter of the twentieth century (two of which are previously unpublished), which aims 'to help teachers and learners alike' (p. x). She begins by looking at the history and development of the English dictionary, and then focuses on the use of EFL dictionaries in teaching and learning. Unlike many researchers in this area, she argues that bilingual dictionaries are useful to language learners, and cannot be entirely replaced by monolingual learners' dictionaries. With this in mind, she proposes the features required in a bilingual dictionary: that it should have a restricted defining vocabulary; that the section alphabetized by the English word should be fully explanatory while the section alphabetized by the other language should be indexical; that meanings and senses should be given in the mother tongue; that grammatical information should be explicit; that illustrative citations should be translated; and that illustrations should be provided wherever possible. Stein notes that research into word formation has had little effect on modern English lexicography. She prefaces her examination of recent developments in EFL dictionaries with a consideration of their history in the 1930s and goes on to look at the use of EFL dictionaries by language learners and teachers. Two interesting chapters look at the use of illustrations in learners' dictionaries. Stein argues that the illustrations, while sometimes amusing, may not always be useful to the dictionary-user. She also considers the inclusion of cultural material and gives an account of the use of illustrations in English learners' dictionaries, starting with Huloet's *Abecedarium* [1552], and concentrating on EFL dictionaries. These chapters include some of the same material, which emphasizes that, fascinating as this volume is, it is a collection of papers rather than a coherent monograph.

Kurt Opitz's 'The Dictionary of Connotations: A Viable Proposition?' (in Gottlieb, Mogensen, and Zettersten, eds., pp. 261–5), is best illustrated by an example. He proposes that an entry for garden, a term with largely positive connotations, would run '*beauty*, innocence; man-made, *protection*' (p. 264). In the same volume, Geart van der Meer, in 'Metaphors: How Do Dictionaries Scramble Out of This Morass of Meaning?' (pp. 231–42), argues that frequency should not be the only consideration in ordering literal and figurative senses in learners' dictionaries. Ksenija Leban proposes the production of a specialized learners' dictionary in 'Towards a Slovene–English False-Friend Dictionary' (pp. 185–97). Leban argues that specialized works are more useful than general bilingual dictionaries, which attempt to meet the requirements of all users. Wlodzimierz Sobkowiak, in 'On the Phonetics of *Trans-* in EFL Dictionaries' (pp. 293–301), argues that EFL dictionaries are inconsistent in their treatment of pronunciation and morphology, and their interaction. Tadamasa Nishimura, 'Japanese Learners' Problems in Using English–Japanese Dictionaries' (pp. 243–51), looks at some users' complaints about bilingual dictionaries. Still in the same volume, Yoshiaki Otani asks 'Who Uses English–Japanese Dictionaries and When?' (pp. 267–72), and concludes that they are unlikely to be used by any but the most advanced learners of Japanese, so the market is restricted to Japanese-speakers learning English. Finally in this volume, Arne Zettersten and Hanne Lauridson describe the production of their two-volume *English–Danish Dictionary* in 'From Projection to Reception—On the Process of Bilingual Dictionary Making' (pp. 325–30). Frawley, Hill, and Munro, eds., *Making Dictionaries: Preserving Indigenous Languages of the Americas* includes fascinating accounts of a variety of dictionary projects and the practical and theoretical problems they encountered. Ten issues summarized in the preface are relevant to all dictionary makers and researchers, and are summarized under the headings: 'Entries', 'Theory', 'Literacy', 'Graphics', 'Role of the Community', '*E pluribus unum*', 'History', 'Technology', 'Lexicographic Tradition', and 'Rules Shall Be Known by their Violation'. Chapters concentrate on different aspect of individual dictionaries. Unfortunately there is not room to discuss them all here, but Leanne Hinton and William F. Weigel's 'A Dictionary for Whom? Tensions between Academic and Nonacademic Functions of Bilingual Dictionaries' (pp. 155–70) is particularly interesting. It argues that the needs of linguists and the native community are so different that lexicographers have to negotiate carefully between the two. Mary L. Clayton and R. Joe Campbell provide a fascinating account of 'Alonso de Molina as Lexicographer' (pp. 336–90), charting his production of three bilingual Nahuatl–Spanish dictionaries in the mid- to late sixteenth century.

A number of studies are concerned with the *OED*. Philip Durkin looks at 'Layamon in the Third Edition of the *Oxford English Dictionary*' (in Allen, Perry, and Roberts, eds., *Layamon: Contexts, Language, and Interpretation*, pp. 203–10). Michael Heaney and John Forrest provide 'An Antedating for the "Morris Dance"'

(*N&Q* 49[2002] 190–3). Colin Wilcockson antedates the *OED* entry for *breaking the ice* (*N&Q* 49[2002] 323–4), and Greg Crossan identifies Thomas Lovell Beddoes's *Death's Jest-Book* as a useful text for *OED* antedatings (*N&Q* 49[2002] 486–9). The *Oxford English Dictionary News* continues to chart the progress of *OED3* and to review its history. Interesting features include Peter Gilliver on 'J.R.R. Tolkien and the *OED*' (*OEDNews* 2:xxi[2002] 1–3), Catherine Bailey on revising the shorter *OED*: 'The essence of the *OED*' (*OEDNews* 2:xxii[2002] 1–2), and Emma Lenz and Sarah Williams on 'Mining the Web' (*OEDNews* 2:xxiii[2002] 2–3). In 'Changing Documentation in the Third Edition of the *Oxford English Dictionary*: Sixteenth-Century Vocabulary as a Test Case' (in Fanego, Méndez-Naya, and Seoane, eds., *Sounds, Words, Texts and Change. Selected Papers from 11 ICEHL*, pp. 65–81), Philip Durkin looks at the pitfalls of using dictionary data for research into changes in vocabulary.

Paul Baker's *Polari: The Lost Language of Gay Men* is an interesting, but flawed, account of 'a secret language mainly used by gay men and lesbians, in London and other UK cities with an established gay subculture, in the first 70 or so years of the twentieth century' (p. 1), a definition which he goes on to deconstruct. Polari came to wider notice through its use on the BBC radio comedy *Round the Horne*, and fell from use during the 1970s. Baker is interested in its use in constructing gay identities, and in the reasons for its decline. He begins by looking at the historical origins of polari, looking at linguistic precursors, such as cant, the lingua franca of sailors in the eighteenth and nineteenth centuries, rhyming slang, backslang, and Romany, and also at social contexts in which such a specialized form could develop, including the eighteenth-century Molly-houses, the theatre, and 1960s drug culture. The accounts of non-standard Englishes are largely derivative and sometimes wrong. Baker writes in detail about Julian and Sandy's use of a sanitized and simplified version of polari on *Round the Horne*, and then discusses the various causes of its decline during the 1970s, which was largely due to 'the gradual change in how gay identity was perceived, both by the gay subculture and by mainstream society' (p. 124). Chapter 7 discusses the revival of interest in polari since the mid-1990s. The appendix contains a glossary of polari terms, with pronunciation indicated. Baker prefers 'a shaky etymology [to] none at all' (p. 196).

Kyo Kageura's *The Dynamics of Terminology. A Descriptive Theory of Term Formation and Terminological Growth* argues that 'a theoretical work on terminology should, as a logical requirement, be accompanied by a concrete description of the terminology of a domain' (p. 4). Kageura remarks that terminology combines the flexibility of natural language with features of the rigidity and systematicity of artificial languages. Traditionally, work in terminology has given primacy to concepts over terms, has excluded morphological and syntactic study, and has adopted a synchronic approach. In contrast, Kageura's own study concentrates on 'the dynamic potentiality observed in the formation patterns of terms within the system of terminology at a synchronic slice' (p. 40). He argues that the study of terminology should deal not with individual terms or arbitrarily selected examples, but with the terminology of a domain in its totality. His discussion of Japanese terminological data in the field of documentation leads into the development of a 'theoretico-descriptive framework for the study of the dynamics of terminology' (p. 2), which will be of interest to scholars of the terminology of any language.

Seija Kerttula's *English Colour Terms: Etymology, Chronology, and Relative Basicness* is a wide-ranging diachronic study of an enormous field, referring to work by anthropologists, psychologists, and sociolinguists, as well as historical linguists. She addresses three central hypotheses of colour-term studies: that OE treats colour in terms of brightness; that colour terminology changed after the Norman Conquest; and that this change can be analysed by examining the origins and development of English colour terms. The main body of the text consists of chronological lists of colour terms with brief comments regarding register, etymology, and frequency. Observations about groups of colour terms, such as 'the black-related colour terms', are drawn together at the end of each section. Later chapters deal with colour terms grouped by their 'pre-colour meanings', such as brightness, the names of animals, plants, minerals, and so on, and grouped by their language sources. Kerttula then applies Berlin and Kay's criteria for primacy to the colour terms of English: the primacy of the colour sense, frequency, application, and derivational productivity. Kerttula concludes that, although brightness was emphasized in OE, hue terms did occur. The Conquest then accelerated the movement towards hue terms, and French terms came to dominate the field. During the seventeenth century, new colour terms were largely English or Latin. By the twentieth century, colour terms were generally created from native words. Thus cultural influences and universal tendencies both contributed to the development of the colour terminology of English.

In contrast, Joan Ann Tietz's *A Thousand Years of Sweet: A Semantic and Cultural Study* is a thorough and detailed study of a single lexeme, its compounds and derivatives. It also covers common phrases, such as *life is sweet, sweetness and light, sweet Fanny Adams*, and *sweet and sour*. The book is divided into three parts, covering the periods 1000–1500, 1500–1900, and 1900–2000. Within each part are chapters discussing the use of *sweet* for taste, smell, sound, and 'in an abstract way in metaphorical extension to cover visual experience, non-sensory experience and human propensity and behaviour' (p. 1). Tietz argues that *sweet* meant 'pleasant-tasting/smelling' rather than 'sweet-tasting/smelling' in its earliest period. During this period, though not later, *sweet* was also used with reference to spiritual comfort. She finds that harmlessness is first implied in *sweet* in the nineteenth century, giving rise to negative terms in the twentieth.

Díaz Vera, ed., *A Changing World of Words*, includes a number of articles covering a broader semantic field but more restricted time period. In 'The Semantic Architecture of the Old English Verbal Lexicon: A Historical-Lexicographical Proposal', Javier E. Díaz Vera looks particularly at the field of TOUCHING in OE (pp. 47–77), while Małgorzata Fabiszak provides 'A Semantic Analysis of FEAR, GRIEF and ANGER Words in Old English' (pp. 255–74). Caroline Gevaert brings together historical, cognitive, and prototype semantics, to explore 'The Evolution of the Lexical and Conceptual Field of ANGER in Old and Middle English' (pp. 275–99). Pamela Faber and Juan Gabriel Vázquez González write about 'Adapting Functional-Lexematic Methodology to the Structuring of Old English Verbs: A Programmatic Proposal' (pp. 78–108). In 'A Morphodynamic Interpretation of Synonym and Polysemy in Old English' (pp. 332–52), Manuela Romano Pozo attempts 'a preliminary description and representation of the structure, membership/synonymic relations and polysemy of the semantic field of FRIENDSHIP in Old English' (p. 333).

Several studies in Díaz Vera, ed., consider the role played by loanwords. In 'Words of EMOTION in Old and Middle English' (pp. 484–99), Michiko Ogura notes that loanwords shared semantic space with native words in this field for some time before they superseded them. Janne Skaffari uses the Helsinki Corpus to study loanwords in ME, in '"Touched by an Alien Tongue": Studying Lexical Borrowings in the Earliest Middle English' (pp. 500–21). In 'Words for MAN in the Transmission of *Piers Plowman*' (pp. 375–409), Merja Black Stenroos draws some tentative conclusions about frequency, distribution, and scribal behaviour. Finally, another paper interested in loanwords is Bernhard Diensberg's 'Old French Loanwords of Germanic Origin Borrowed into English' (in Gottlieb *et al.*, eds., pp. 91–106), which proposes a classification system.

Díaz Vera, ed., also contains papers geared more towards the theoretical background of lexical change. 'The HORSE Family: On the Evolution of the Field and its Metaphorization Process' (pp. 229–54) is Isabel de la Cruz and Cristina Tejedor's contribution to research into metaphors. Päivi Koivisto-Alanko considers 'Prototypes in Semantic Change: A Diachronic Perspective on Abstract Nouns' (pp. 300–31), in her prototype-theoretical study of the noun *wit* in PDE. 'The Cognitive Etymological Search for Lexical Traces of Conceptual Mappings: Analysis of the Lexical-Conceptual Domain of the Verbs of POSSESSION' (pp. 438–63) is Eulalio Fernández-Sánchez's demonstration of 'the psychological adequacy of the Functional-Lexematic architecture of the lexicon' (p. 447).

Still in the historical domain, Bammesberger looks at 'Old English *Ealuscerwen* in *Beowulf* 769a' (*RES* 53[2002] 469–74), and concludes that it means 'a dispensation of good luck'. Gunnar Persson uses prototype theory and frame semantics to explore the semantic development of *spinster*: 'From "Spinning Woman" to "Old Maid" to What?' (in Gottlieb *et al.*, eds., pp. 273–83). Maria Luisa Maggioni looks at 'Linguistic Economy and Lexical Innovation: The Case of Doublets in John Trevisa's Translation of *De Proprietatibus Rerum* (Books I–II)' (in Iamartino, Bignami, and Pagetti, eds., *The Economy Principle in English: Linguistic, Literary, and Cultural Perspectives*, pp. 204–12). Norman Blake's 'Towards a Dictionary of Shakespeare's Informal English' (in Gottlieb *et al.*, eds., pp. 1–18) considers approaches to the study of informal language in Shakespeare's plays. He gives a further account of the project in 'On Shakespeare's Informal Language' (*JHPrag* 3[2002] 179–204). Maurizio Gotti discusses the main processes of word formation involved in 'The Origin of 17th Century Canting Terms' (in Díaz Vera, ed., pp. 163–96). In the same volume, Claire Cowie and Christiane Dalton-Puffer consider 'Diachronic Word-Formation and Studying Changes in Productivity over Time: Theoretical and Methodological Considerations' (pp. 410–37). They argue that derivational morphology has been neglected in diachronic studies of the lexicon in favour of the study of loanwords.

Moving now to the present day, Andrejs Veisbergs looks at the treatment of 'Euphemisms in General Monolingual Dictionaries' (in Gottlieb *et al.*, eds., pp. 303–11) and concludes that the subject needs more attention. Jessy Randall discusses terms for pregnancy in 'Anything But Pregnant: A Compendium of Colloquialisms' (*Verbatim* 27:ii[2002] 4–6), many of which are euphemistic. In 'Words: The Stealth Weapon of War' (*Verbatim* 27:iii[2002] 28–9), Howard Richler looks at the language used by Palestinians and Israelis to describe their own and each other's activities. Erin McKean considers *leet*, a code or jargon used in computer gaming, in 'L33t-sp34k' (*Verbatim* 27:i[2002] 13–4). Greg Costikyan builds on McKean's paper in his 'Talk Like a Gamer' (*Verbatim* 27:iii[2002] 1–6). Gabriella Mazzon's 'How R U Feeling, θ or λ? Exploring Netspeak and the New Economy of Writing' (in Iamartino *et al.*, eds., pp. 213–19) looks at the use of meaning shifts, acronyms, and emoticons in computer language. In the same volume, Maria Grazia Guido's '"B S U R, B :)! U C? I M :) 2! TT4N {{}}. AFK": A Reassessment of the Principle of Economy in the Pragmatic Use of Syllabic Notations, Acronyms and Emoticons in English-Internettese Discourse' (pp. 187–203) argues that this development is imperialistic and sometimes sexist. Nick Humez discusses 'Weird Tools, Improbable Jobs' (*Verbatim* 27:ii[2002] 18–19), and laments the loss of such specialist terms as *snath wrench* and *nurling iron*. In 'Jumpers and Rounders and Tops, Oh My' (*Verbatim* 27:iv[2002] 14), Allison Whitehead reveals some of the acronyms and jargon used by those working on the London Underground. Mat Coward's 'Horribile Dictu' (*Verbatim* 27:i[2002] 15) discusses the use of slang in formal contexts. In 'Certain Somebodies' (*Verbatim* 27:i [2002] 20–3), Nick Humez examines generic names for rhetorical use, such as *John Doe*, *Tommy Atkins*, and *Jack Tar*. Finally, in 'The Sneeze: More Than Just Ac-Choo and Bless You' (*Verbatim* 27:iv[2002] 7–10), Jessy Randall looks at terms for sneezing and responses to it.

Alison Wray's *Formulaic Language and the Lexicon* considers the status of formulaic sequences in the lexicon. She defines her subject thus: 'a sequence, continuous or discontinuous, of words or other elements, which is, or appears to be, prefabricated: that is, stored and retrieved whole from memory at the time of use, rather than being subject to generation or analysis by the language grammar' (p. 9). Chapters discuss methods by which formulaicity can be identified, defining what it is, its occurrence in adult and child first- and second-language acquisition, and in aphasic language. The last section of the book aims to provide an integrated model, bringing all these perspectives together, without obscuring the differences between them. Wray emphasizes the role of formulaic sequences in expressing personal identity and group membership as well as in reducing a speaker's 'processing load' (p. 92). Formulaic sequences, far from being marginal to language and language study, are actually extremely common. She concludes that speakers adopt different approaches for different purposes. Young children may treat as formulaic, sequences that are not. Older children and adult second-language learners opt for an analytic approach, whereas adult first-language speakers use 'holistic processing' (p. 279).

Steven Jones's *Antonymy: A Corpus-Based Perspective* begins with an account of recent research, emphasizing disparities in the conclusions reached and providing corpus citations to support his criticisms. The study is based on a 3,000-sentence corpus from the *Independent* newspaper, containing a pre-selected sample of fifty-six antonymous pairs. The pairs were selected with reference to previous work, but largely intuitively, with an attempt to cover different types of antonymy. Frequency was not a factor in the selection of pairs, but more sentences were included for the commonest antonyms. Jones categorizes the functions of the co-occurring antonyms as ancillary, coordinated, comparative, distinguished, transitional, negated, extreme, and idiomatic antonymy, and goes on to explore these categories in more detail. He finds that in over three-quarters of his sentences, antonyms were used to signal contrast or inclusivity. Jones also looks at the relative frequency of terms in antonym pairs, the sequence in which they co-occur, and the relationship between word class and antonymy. Chapter 10 is an interesting discussion of how pairs developing antonymy might be identified using lexico-syntactic frameworks, and Jones closes with a new definition of antonymy: 'Antonyms are pairs of words which contrast along a given semantic scale and frequently function in a coordinated and ancillary fashion such that they become lexically enshrined as "opposites"' (p. 179). Sándor Martsa's 'Homonymy vs Polysemy: Conversion in English' (in Gottlieb *et al.*, eds., pp. 211–29) looks at words that challenge the current understanding of these terms.

7. Onomastics

Thomas E. Murray's 'A New Look at Address in American English: The Rules Have Changed' (*Names* 50[2002] 43–61) is a welcome redaction of a forty-year-old, now classic study of address in American English. Murray's essay clearly demonstrates (once again) the relevance and importance of onomastics as a device for gaining insights into social structure and social dynamics. The earlier study, by Roger Brown and Marguerite Ford, which appeared in the *Journal of Abnormal and Social Psychology* (62[1961] 375–85), showed that in the middle of the twentieth century there were primarily two choices of terms of address: address by given name or address by title plus surname. The selection was based upon the social constructs of intimacy and status: mutual use of given name implied intimacy and use of title plus surname reflected status differences based upon age and occupation. Murray's redaction shows that Americans' concepts of distance, formality, intimacy, and status changed dramatically in the last half century. In particular, address by given name was found to be appropriate over a wider range of occupations; address by given name was now appropriate over a greater age range as well; and new acquaintances were looked upon as intimates within a shorter period of time. In addition (and perhaps more surprising), the rules for address by children had changed. For Brown and Ford, any adult could be expected to be addressed by title plus surname, but for Murray this rule had been relaxed to the point where any adult with whom a child felt comfortable was regularly addressed by given name only.

The American Name Society was founded in Detroit in 1951. As part of the year-long celebration of the society's golden anniversary, Leonard R.N. Ashley, a past president and member of the governing board for many years, prepared a personal, anecdotal history of his forty-plus years with ANS. This reflection was published as 'The American Name Society: The First 50 Years' (*Names* 50[2002] 63–72). Since it is a reminiscence, the article will not be summarized, but I point out that it will appeal to anyone interested in the events and particularly the personalities which shaped the organization, especially in its formative years.

As part of a larger study on religion in American life, 'Names of Chicago's Churches: A Tale of (at Least) Two Cultures' (*Names* 50[2002] 83–103), the distinguished cultural geographer Wilbur Zelinsky collected and analysed the names of more than 4,500 houses of worship in the greater Chicago area, looking in particular at the differences in naming between Black and non-Black congregations. Zelinsky found both quantitative and qualitative differences in naming between the cultures, with those of the Black congregations much more varied and thus more interesting. Quantitatively the names of Black churches are longer than those of the non-Black churches and among other differences they make use of complete declarative sentences as components of the names, something very rare in onomastics; the only analogue which comes to mind is Puritan naming practices of the seventeenth century. What is there about religion which makes this practice attractive? Examples given by Zelinsky include 'God is in Control Healing & Deliverance Church', and 'God Never Fails Ministries'. Qualitatively, the names of Black churches reflect two 'overarching themes': 'sheer emotional and verbal exuberance', and 'an aspiration toward a loftier plane of grace that is tinged with a certain spiritual-cum-material expansionism'. Examples of emotional and verbal exuberance are the many uses of 'Hope', 'Joy', 'Care', and 'Brotherly Love', and examples of the 'loftier plane of grace,' are formatives such as 'Greater', 'Monumental', 'Universal', and 'Everlasting'. Zelinsky sees in these naming patterns confirmation of the 'coexistence and quasi-autonomy of two cultural worlds within the United States: the African American and the majoritarian White Euro-American' (p. 100). I cannot praise this article too highly; it is a model investigation which should be carefully read and studied by everyone interested in the social dimensions of names, in other words all onomasts.

D.K. Tucker continued his investigations into the statistical properties of name distributions. In 'Distribution of Forenames, Surnames, and Forename-Surname Pairs in Canada' (*Names* 50[2002] 105–32) Tucker provides frequency distributions, appropriately graphed by a semi-logarithmic plot. The most popular 1 per cent of Canadian surname types account for more than 60 per cent of all names; conversely 90 per cent of surname types (the rare names) account for only 12 per cent of all surnames. In fact 75 per cent of the population is covered by a mere 2.84 per cent of surname types. Tucker also supplies lists of the most frequently occurring names and name combinations. Of the hundred most popular Canadian surnames, the most frequent are (in order) Smith, Brown, Tremblay, Martin, Roy, Wilson, Gagnon, Johnson, Campbell, and Cote. Only Tremblay and Cote are French; Martin is both French and non-French. Readers are referred to Tucker's article for extensive lists and analyses.

Vivian de Klerk's essay, 'Changing Names in the "New" South Africa' (*Names* 50[2002] 201–21), compared first-name changes in South Africa in 2000 with those of 1997 and found it 'remarkable in light of concerted national efforts to encourage the African Renaissance' (p. 201) that there was a marked increase in the number of African-language speakers who overtly favoured English when changing their names. The favoured mechanisms were adding an English name to an existing African name, deleting an African name, or reversing the order of names so that an English name came first.

Douglas A. Galbi, in 'Long Term Trends in the Frequencies of Given Names' (*Names* 50[2002] 105–32), looked at several measures of name concentration and dispersion in the United Kingdom over the past thousand years. While it is generally acknowledged that given names, especially for females, have become more diverse over the years, it was unknown when or where, and especially why, this trend began. Galbi shines considerable light into this previous darkness. He shows that, in the UK at least, the early nineteenth century proved to be the watershed; new naming patterns evolved at that time which were different from those which had characterized the previous eight centuries. Thus it appears that industrialization was revolutionary in more ways than one. Since the nineteenth century, the relative popularity of the most frequent names has declined; for centuries prior to that time the most popular given names were not only more stable but in retrospect quite rigid. Especially noteworthy is Galbi's claim that 'significant social, political, and religious changes in England prior to 1800 seem to have had little effect of the overall distribution of name frequencies ... By the middle of the 13th century, the distribution of name frequencies was more like that of 1800 than it was of the late 20th century.' The radical shift in naming patterns beginning in the nineteenth century may be seen as another manifestation of the far-ranging changes wrought by the Industrial Revolution, which restructured the British economy and many aspects of British society as well.

The 2002 issue of *Onoma* was devoted to Nordic onomastics; therefore, even though there are several articles of general interest, such as those dealing with standardization of names, changes in personal naming patterns in the Nordic countries, and the much-neglected area of urban toponymy, they will not be summarized here. However, there is one article which I cannot pass over without comment since it has a great deal to say about how onomastics is practised in different parts of the world; this is Katharina Leibring's essay 'Cattle Names in the Nordic Countries' (*Onoma* 37[2002] 81–92). The naming of animals (with the very limited exception of racehorses) has never held much interest for onomasts in North America, who rarely study the naming of pets, much less that of farm animals. For many years I have been befuddled by the indifference shown by American and Canadian scholars to what is a rich and largely untapped source of data (although annually becoming less so as animal husbandry becomes more standardized and regimented and as some groups of farm animals disappear entirely. Because of the now near-exclusive use of artificial insemination, bulls, for one, have all but disappeared from the family farm). My concerns aside, and of interest to a review of English onomastics, Leibring gives a nice summary of cattle-naming in northern Europe from the eighteenth to the twentieth centuries, noting that traditionally animals were named characteristically, e.g. 'mottled', 'born in the morning', given praiseworthy names, e.g. 'princess', or uncommon personal names, e.g. 'Zeus'. What is of interest is how the naming patterns have recently changed, especially in the latter decades of the last century. Cows are now given usual female names, especially those drawn from popular English-speaking culture, e.g. 'Lady Diana', 'Madonna', and from American television programmes, e.g. 'Sue Ellen' and 'Dallas'. Finally, as Leibring notes, the use of names for cows is being replaced by numbers, something which happened to most (unfortunate) bulls decades ago.

The two numbers of *Onomastica Canadiana* for 2002 were devoted to the memory of Frank Hamlin, who died in June 2002. Hamlin was a noted Romance scholar, specializing in French and Provençal. In 1998 the French Ministry of Culture awarded him the title Chevalier de l'Ordre des Arts et des Lettres for his contributions to French culture. Because Hamlin's work was largely in French onomastics (and written in French), much of *Onomastica Canadiana*'s tribute to him is likewise in and on French. I will, therefore, exclude these articles from this summary, with the following exception since it is concerned with English onomastics. Tim Nau, in 'The Relationship of the Signatures of 18th Century American Men to their Names' (*OnCan* 84[2002] 83–94), notes that until the nineteenth century it was common for American men to abbreviate one or another of their forenames and to give their surname in full, e.g. 'G^o Washington', 'Th

Jefferson'. Nau argues that only a small portion of these abbreviations can be explained as graphic representations of spoken hypocoristic forms, such as Fred for Frederick or Sam for Samuel; rather, abbreviations such as Step for Stephen, Jon:th for Jonathan, and Edwd for Edward can be explained only by the visual impact of the abbreviation, an abstract picture as it were, and in this way the abbreviations are related to and in some cases descendants of monograms, rubrics, and coats of arms.

Nomina contains a number of articles on place names and personal names. Victor Watts, in 'Medieval Field-Names in Two South Durham Townships' (*Nomina* 25[2002] 53–64) uses field names to determine the extent of Scandinavian influence in County Durham, particularly in Billingham and Wolviston, in the Middle Ages, noting that it was 'severely restricted', since the names retained their 'underlying English character' (p. 58). David Postles's 'Bynames of Location with the Suffix *-by* Revisited' (*Nomina* 25[2002] 5–11) provides a chronological and geographical perspective for such names as *Southiby* for one who lived in the southern part of the village and *Estiby* for one who lived in the eastern part, reporting that this practice was most common in the East and West Ridings of Lincolnshire, particularly in the fourteenth century, by the end of which it had become less common and was largely confined to the East Riding. David N. Parsons's '*Anna, Dot, Thorir* … Counting Domesday Personal Names' (*Nomina* 25[2002] 29–52) is an intriguing article which argues for the use of statistical methods applied to onomastic databases, such as (in this case) the Domesday Book of 1086. Parsons concludes by comparing his work, drawn from the eleventh century, with that of Cecily Clark, drawn from the twelfth and thirteenth centuries. The comparisons of the Scandinavian proportion of the name-stock over at least a century show 'a remarkable continuity in naming patterns'. Furthermore, and something which is often overlooked in historical onomastics, 'the study of personal names can inform the study of place-names' (p. 52). Peter R. Kitson, in 'How Anglo-Saxon Personal Names Work' (*Nomina* 25[2002] 91–131), claims that about 1950 marked the end of an older period of naming, which was replaced by a contemporary one characterized by film names and non-Christian immigrant names. Kitson states that an older pattern of biblical names, and names of non-biblical saints and kings, had held true, especially for boys, since about the thirteenth century. Using the lineage of the royals of Wessex as a database, Kitson claims that, in Anglo-Saxon days, and with some gender differences, names tended to be broken up into their constituent morphemes and recombined rather than reused as units. First elements of di-thematic names were common between the sexes, e.g. Ælf 'elf', Ēad 'felicity', while the second elements differed, with men's names being drawn from the class of masculine nouns and women's names from feminine nouns; thus the names of both sexes were semantically transparent, although arbitrary. Kitson's article can usefully be compared with Galbi's, mentioned above.

I will close this brief review of the year's work in onomastics by considering what I believe are the two most potentially influential publications of the year, both dealing with theoretical concerns, and both touching on issues which are vitally important if onomastics is to progress as a science, but which onomasts in English-speaking countries have been reluctant to confront and in fact have assiduously avoided, much to the detriment of the discipline. The first of these is Wilbur Zelinsky's 'Slouching Toward a Theory of Names: A Tentative Taxonomic Fix' (*Names* 50[2002] 243–62). Zelinsky makes a convincing argument that onomastics has not advanced significantly beyond the 'primitive level' of attempting to specify the object of concern, i.e., the distinction between proper nouns and common nouns, and has certainly not yet reached even the first rung of the scientific ladder, that of establishing a generally agreed upon taxonomy, which is necessary for the collection of information and the organization of data. A taxonomy would also serve to define the discipline and provide a basis for considering serious and fundamental theoretical questions concerning names and naming. Zelinsky offers what he calls 'a preliminary typology of names', wherein he attempts to identify and organize the universe of what is named. The major sections of the typology are worth mentioning here: Deities, Biota, Places, Events, Social Entities, Enterprises, Artifacts, and Unclassifiable. These are presented with numerous sub-classifications and references. The efficacy and importance of such a classification is obvious. Although the typology is tentative and offered by Zelinsky more as a means to further discussion than as a finished product, it raises important issues for onomastics, and its mere existence sets a research agenda if only by the lacunae within categories. To mention several—probably trivial—examples which come quickly to mind: first, many (most?) of the world's cultures name the months of the year and the days of the week, but far fewer name the years (Chinese does) and I would imagine that even fewer (none?) name the weeks of the month. We need data on what parts of the calendar are named and by whom. Of greater interest: is there a developmental sequence in the naming of chronologies (as there is in colour terminology, for instance) or is the process essentially random? I think not, but I have no evidence. Second, in some cultures primary residences are named; in others, such as the US, they are usually not, although second homes, vacation cottages, and even camping trailers often are. Large plantations are apparent exceptions, although ranches are not, since many states have laws requiring that they be named. Again, what are the parameters or social constraints on the naming of domiciles? Finally, some body parts are named, at least informally; most are not. One is named far more often than any other. Why should this be? Since this is a family publication I will not mention that (those) part(s), but for interested persons, *Lady Chatterley's Lover* would be a good place to start. What would a sub-typology of body-part naming look like? Is it universal or culture specific? Without a comprehensive typology, based on scientific principles of classification, the important questions cannot even be framed in a way which would facilitate research. Zelinsky would be the first to admit that his taxonomy is incomplete and in need of improvement, but it does provide a framework and guidance for what is of great importance and sorely needed in onomastics. Zelinsky is to be commended for this path-breaking effort.

Shawn M. Clankie's *A Theory of Genericization on Brand Name Change* is an important book in the development of onomastics. Clankie is concerned with an old onomastic chestnut, one which has heretofore been treated as trivial by both onomasts and linguists, namely proper names which become common nouns. In general the process by which, say, Coke came to be the name for any soft drink (or at least any cola drink) while Pepsi did not, was seen as haphazard; some brand names just happened to become generic while others did not. Clankie's theoretical contribution to onomastics is to show that, far from being random, the journey from brand name to generic is governed by a number of social and linguistic constraints, and in the process Clankie provides both a scientific footing and a framework for looking at names in society. Names of all sorts (personal names, geographic names, product names) are in constant competition with one another and Clankie shows that there are general principles which have a great deal to say about which names will be winners and which will be losers. There is, in this case, a structured process by which a proper noun (really a proper adjective, as Clankie demonstrates) breaks loose from its status as an individual designator and becomes the designator of a class of similar items. In this instance, genericization tends to take place when the following conditions obtain: (1) when the brand name is that of an innovative product; thus the brand name will become associated with and ultimately synonymous with that product; (2) when the brand name is shorter than one of a number of brand names associated with a particular product; and (3) when the brand name is associated with a single product rather than several. Not only does Clankie provide insights into the process of genericization, he gives to onomastics a theory (that a small set of principles govern much of naming behaviour) and a procedure whereby these principles can be rigorously tested. Clankie's study and Zelinsky's taxonomy are ground-breaking efforts with great potential for influencing the form and practice of onomastic study. They deserve careful consideration by all students of names and naming.

8. Dialectology and Sociolinguistics

General publications in sociolinguistics are dominated this year by Chambers, Trudgill, and Schilling-Estes, eds., *Handbook of Language Variation and Change*. Much more narrowly restricted to Labovian-style variationist sociolinguistics than the *Handbook of Sociolinguistics* (edited by Florian Coulmas [1997]) in the same series, this volume is nevertheless almost 300 pages longer, and contains some of the best overview articles to be found in the field at the moment. The list of contributors almost constitutes a *Who's Who* in (English) sociolinguistics, with the notable exception of William Labov. His spirit is, however, present, 'imbuing every page' (dedication), and indeed the whole volume is dedicated to him. The contributions are sensibly grouped into five parts, ranging from questions of 'Methodologies' (seven chapters) over 'Linguistic Structure' (four chapters) and 'Social Factors' (predictably the longest with twelve chapters) to 'Contact' (three chapters) and finally 'Language and Societies' (three chapters). All contributions are up to date, yet suitable as introductory reading at undergraduate and graduate level. In contrast to other handbooks in the series, all contributions have their own section of references, thus making each chapter suitable to be read on its own. Because of their outstanding importance, all contributions will be briefly reviewed in this general section.

J.K. Chambers gives an excellent introduction on the evolution of the field of sociolinguistics in the introductory chapter, 'Studying Language Variation: An Informal Epistemology' (pp. 3–14). Crawford Feagin guides the reader who is interested in collecting spoken data in her personal and often anecdotal overview of what to consider in 'Entering the Community: Fieldwork' (pp. 20–39). The use of written data is the subject of Schneider's 'Investigating Variation and Change in Written Documents' (pp. 67–96). It provides a useful categorization of written sources from transcripts and recalled data to semi-literate letters, contemporary commentaries, and, of course, literary sources. Laurie Bauer writes on 'Inferring

Variation and Change from Public Corpora' (pp. 97–114), defining both 'corpus' and 'public' on the way. Thus provided with the basic materials, we can proceed to the next section, 'Evaluation'. Robert Bayley introduces 'The Quantitative Paradigm' (pp. 117–41), considering both theoretical principles and practical applications (VARBRUL and general logistic regression models). John R. Rickford discusses 'Implicational Scales' (pp. 142–67) complete with their weaknesses and caveats. Erik R. Thomas writes on 'Instrumental Phonetics' (pp. 168–200), a subdiscipline that even many experienced sociolinguists will not be entirely familiar with, and where a basic introduction is particularly welcome. (Similar in some respects is Thomas's call for more studies of speech perception in 'Sociophonetic Applications of Speech Perception Experiments' (AS 77[2002] 115–47), giving a good overview of the work done so far in the field and indeed providing guidelines of how to proceed.) While the 'Evaluation' section is more geared towards the technical side of data-handling, theory is dealt with in the following contributions. Arto Anttila extends the currently fashionable OT to variation in 'Variation and Phonological Theory' (pp. 206–43); basically he seems to propose the not so new concept of parallel grammars in a more sophisticated guise, but admits that it is not clear yet what the wider implications of the various models are. Also on a phonological topic, Matthew J. Gordon 'Investigat[es] Chain Shifts and Mergers' (pp. 244–66), introducing the new concept of a near-merger, where perception and production can be shown not to pattern together. Neatly, this concept can explain why and how some mergers may split again, sometimes after a considerable time, as in the historical case of *meat* and *mate*. As one of the few syntacticians in the Chomskyan school working on dialect data, Alison Henry presents a chapter on 'Variation and Syntactic Theory' (pp. 267–82) and deplores the fact that the considerable implications linguistic variability has for syntactic theory 'have scarcely been taken into account in the development of that theory' (p. 280); unfortunately a publication in this handbook will hardly remedy this situation (given that generative syntacticians are unlikely to use it as a resource). A different emphasis, the importance of a sound theory for the study of variation, could have given this contribution more relevance for the intended audience, students and practitioners of sociolinguistics. Finally in this section, Ronald Macaulay gives an overview of studies in 'Discourse Variation' (pp. 283–305), moving into more qualitatively oriented work. The following section, 'Social Factors', the longest and possibly the one best suited as preparatory reading for various sociolinguistic courses, has an excellent overview of studies in 'Real and Apparent Time', by Guy Bailey (pp. 312–32), with all the pitfalls and drawbacks various proposals have. Nevertheless, from his own extended studies, Bailey comes to the conclusion that apparent time developments have in many cases proved to be good indicators of actual language change. Julie Roberts presents a more peripheral field with her contribution on 'Child Language Variation' (pp. 333–48), yet not irrelevant, as even preschool children have been shown to participate in ongoing sound change. 'Patterns of Variation Including Change' are discussed by J.K. Chambers (pp. 349–72), where he points to the interesting fact that phonological variables tend to be diffusely distributed across social classes, while morphosyntactic variables tend to act as 'categorical distinguishers' (p. 350). Incidentally, it is in this chapter that the concept of 'age grading' is hidden (in case any readers were wondering). Natalie Schilling-Estes 'Investigat[es] Stylistic Variation' (pp. 375–401), leading the reader through various ethnographic and sociolinguistic approaches to this important variable. (More on style will be found in Eckert and Rickford, eds., below.) Sharon Ash addresses one of the most central concepts of Labovian sociolinguistics, 'Social Class' (pp. 402–22), where she also discusses rival concepts like the linguistic marketplace. Jenny Cheshire gives a much-needed wide-ranging overview of 'Sex and Gender in Variationist Research' (pp. 423–43), managing to include in barely twenty pages the major paradigmatic shifts as well as the landmark studies conducted in this field. Carmen Fought presents 'Ethnicity' (pp. 444–72), dealing mainly with non-white ethnic groups in the US. Norma Mendoza-Denton discusses 'Language and Identity' (pp. 475–99), and Kirk Hazen presents a rather neglected topic, 'The Family' (pp. 500–25), a more prominent object of sociolinguistic investigation so far having been the peer group rather than the family. Hazen suggests, however, that 'families and their linguistic influence ... should be integrated into the description of the speech community' (p. 518). Miriam Meyerhoff moves away from strict Labovian sociolinguistics in her contribution on 'Communities of Practice' (pp. 528–48), and Lesley Milroy writes on 'Social Networks' (pp. 549–72), a concept no one can be better suited to report on. The central sociolinguistic concept of 'The Speech Community' in more general terms is summed up by Peter L. Patrick (pp. 573–97), curiously placed at the very end of the section. Sociolinguistic work on language variation through dialect and language contact is the subject of the fourth part, started off by David Britain on the important variable of 'Space and Spatial Diffusion' (pp. 603–37), illustrating major concepts with data from the English Fenlands (more on which below). Gillian Sankoff introduces 'Linguistic Outcomes of Language Contact' (pp. 638–68), stressing that nonce borrowings in the minority language seem to constitute the major gateway first to phonetic and then to grammatical changes. Paul Kerswill discusses the contact-induced rapid change known as 'Koineization and Accommodation' (pp. 669–702). Kerswill distinguishes regional koinés (which tend not to displace the original dialects which have contributed to them) and immigrant koinés (or new dialects), which serve as the vernacular of a new community, which is where we can observe these rapid processes. The last section, on 'Language and Societies', has some interesting wider-ranging chapters. Peter Trudgill, for example, suggests a 'Linguistic and Social Typology' (pp. 707–28), if tentatively, linking insights from linguistic typology and Milroy's social network concept. Trudgill proposes that isolated communities can preserve more 'marked' features through being close-knit and through their isolation, as they are not in need of accommodation: 'lack of contact favours lack of change' (p. 709). At the same time, close-knit networks can enforce norms and thus enforce relative linguistic homogeneity. (For a different view, see Schilling-Estes's important contribution below). Sali Tagliamonte introduces 'Comparative Sociolinguistics' (pp. 729–63), which involves comparison across corpora or across speech-communities; her chapter is ideally suited as a basic introduction to some very important quantitative concepts (what to count and why). The final, slightly moribund, chapter in this handbook is entitled 'Language Death and Dying', by Walt Wolfram (pp. 764–87), who discusses several types of language death and its causes, both non-linguistic and linguistic, as well as models that can describe language loss, the linguistic levels that are affected, and the variability and complexity that occurs in language obsolescence—as dying varieties are by no means homogeneous or simplified. This concludes our overview of the *Handbook of Language Variation and Change*.

In the area of textbooks, there is one new addition to the field and one slightly revised edition of a 'classic', each tailored to different needs and suitable for classroom teaching for different purposes. The new addition is Peter Stockwell's *Sociolinguistics: A Resource Book for Students*, at 200 pages a rather small book with a very interesting concept. The content is divided into four sections (A to D) and includes fourteen units, covering expected topics like 'accent and dialect', 'social class', 'age and gender', and the like. Students are expected to read the short general introduction to a unit in section A first (comprising about two pages), and proceed to the relevant 'development' unit in section B, where the same topic is expanded with more detail as well as examples. Section C then 'guides the student through their own investigation of the field', and section D finally provides excerpts from more theoretical texts. This is an original idea, and the content is refreshingly original as well—for example, we find investigations of the sociolinguistic situation on football terraces, and a questionnaire study of attitudes to (German) pronouns of address. On the other hand, the fact that expected 'classics' of sociolinguistics are only briefly mentioned or referred to in 'further reading' sections makes the use of this book as the only textbook basis of a university class debatable. The revised classic mentioned above is Ronald Wardhaugh's *An Introduction to Sociolinguistics*, now in its fourth edition (the third edition is only five years old). The book has been changed and expanded in a myriad of (minor) ways, a page here, a quotation there, without, however, altering the overall design or the (high) quality of the contents. If anything, Wardhaugh's *Introduction* is now even more readable than it was before. One example may suffice: chapter 5, 'Speech Communities', no longer starts straight away with Chomsky's concept of the ideal speaker-hearer; instead, Wardhaugh has inserted a whole page on the question of groups, which may serve as an accessible introduction to the more theoretical core of this chapter.

An important and long-announced contribution to a much-neglected sociolinguistic variable is Eckert and Rickford, eds., *Style and Sociolinguistic Variation*, which provides a good overview of the various definitions of style that have been around for the last forty years or so. The contributions are divided into anthropological approaches (with contributions by Judith Irvine, Susan Ervin-Tripp, Richard Bauman, and Ronald Macaulay), 'Attention Paid to Speech' (perhaps the section most directly relevant to Labovian sociolinguistics), 'Audience Design and Self-Identification', and 'Functionally Motivated Situational Variation'. Labov himself presents 'The Anatomy of Style-Shifting' (pp. 85–108), including his 'decision tree' of how to separate careful and casual speech. John Baugh comments on Labov's methodology in 'A Dissection of Style-Shifting' (pp. 109–18) and in particular criticizes the use of reading passages and word lists to effect a careful style as this is clearly inappropriate for illiterate informants. Penelope Eckert, in 'Style and Social Meaning' (pp. 119–26), comments on Labov's decision tree and cautions researchers that attention paid to speech can actually result in more, rather than less, vernacular speech. In part III, Allan Ball is 'Back in Style: Reworking Audience Design' (pp. 139–69), refining ideas that are critically evaluated by Malcah Yaeger-Dror, who points out that it is not at all clear whether some central variables, such as topic, setting, footing, etc., are really primitive. Nikolas Coupland argues against unidimensional models of style shifting as these do not take account of the active role of the speaker in self-construction, in 'Language, Situation and the Relational Self: Theorizing Dialect-Style in Sociolinguistics' (pp. 185–210). Howard Giles, in 'Couplandia and Beyond' (pp. 211–19), on the other hand, argues against this extreme deconstructionist position and calls for attention to intentions (speakers' as well as hearers'). John Rickford, in 'Style and Stylizing from the Perspective of a Non-Autonomous Sociolinguistics' (pp. 220–31) also questions Coupland's emphasis on self-stylization, as this may very well be a characteristic of the public performances that Coupland takes as his basis for investigation. The final section is concerned with Finegan and Biber's distinction of registers and is thus not directly relevant to sociolinguistics.

Moving to more technical questions, Edgar W. Schneider provides an overview of 'Quantitative Techniques in the Analysis of Dialect Data' (in Kastovsky, Kaltenböck, and Reichl eds., *Anglistentag 2001: Proceedings*, pp. 75–87), showing that new techniques can lead to surprisingly relevant results when applied to 'old' dialect data, as for example data from the American Atlas projects. Going into much more technical detail, any reader interested in VARBRUL should consult John Paolillo, *Analyzing Linguistic Variation: Statistical Models and Methods*. Written for the statistically uninitiated, the book tries to clear VARBRUL of the nimbus of being an insider-only computer program, knowledge of which is transmitted, and kept, in informal networks. Paolillo uses previously published data, e.g. Labov's department store data, to guide the reader through the technical and theoretical possibilities of VARBRUL analyses. However, despite the intended readership, the discussion does get technical rather quickly, so that true beginners might well get stuck at the data-coding stage.

Gender is an important topic this year and features in several publications. General in outlook for example is Ann Weatherall's *Gender, Language and Discourse*, written, however, more from a psychological than a sociolinguistic perspective. In particular, Weatherall investigates gender as a 'socially constructed category' (p. 97). I must add, however, that this book is not much more than elaborate stock-taking—important as this may be—tracing the study of gender in discourse studies through ethno-methodology and conversation analysis to the social constructivism dominant in many fields today. More narrowly sociolinguistic in nature, and therefore preferable to Weatherall as an introductory text, Natalie Schilling-Estes gives a good historical overview of the study of gender in (American) sociolinguistics in 'American English Social Dialect Variation and Gender' (*JEngL* 30[2002] 122–37), at the same time tracing the development of the concept of gender as biologically given to gender as a social construct in communities of practice.

Gender as a meta-topic is the subject of Bonnie McElhinny, Marijke Hols, Jeff Holtzkener, Susanne Unger, and Claire Hicks, in 'Gender, Publication and Citation in Sociolinguistics and Linguistic Anthropology: The Construction of a Scholarly Canon' (*LSoc* 32[2002] 299–328), where they find some striking imbalances: journals with the largest number of women on the editorial board tend to publish more women's work, only 5 per cent of publications centre on gender, and only a fifth of textbooks are written by women. Men cite women's work over 10 per cent less frequently than women do, and theories seem to be regarded as an almost exclusively male domain. The authors conclude that in general, citation cannot be counted as an objective measure towards a scholar's standing. In contrast, a purely syntactic topic is the subject of Britta Mondorf's 'Gender Differences in English Syntax' (*JEngL* 30[2002] 158–80). Based on the (unfortunately quite dated) London Lund Corpus, Mondorf finds that women actually use more adverbial clauses than men—in particular those that signal limited commitment to the truth—and especially use them in postposition, where epistemic grounding is similarly limited. Another linguistic asymmetry is addressed by Robert Sigley and Janet Holmes, who are 'Looking at *girls* in Corpora of English' (*JEngL* 30[2002] 138–57). In a diachronic comparison of British English (the LOB Corpus from 1961 vs. FLOB from 1991), the authors find that *girl* referring to adult women has decreased sharply since 1961. Moving into discourse studies, Susan A. Speer investigates sexism 'in action' in 'Sexist Talk: Gender Categories, Participants' Orientations and Irony' (*JSoc* 6[2002] 347–77), concerned with men's and women's non-participation in sports and leisure activities. On a specifically non-sexist theme, Maciej Baronowski shows that *they* has taken over from *he* as the generic pronoun in 'Current Usage of the Epicene Pronoun in Written English' (*JSoc* 6[2002] 378–97), especially in British English, while American English is still a little more conservative.

Another more general topic is the subject of a special edition of the *Journal of Sociolinguistics* (6:i[2002]) on dialect contact, edited by Lesley Milroy. As most contributions are regional in nature, they are discussed below in the regional sections. The introduction by Milroy gives a concise overview of the development of this young research area: 'Introduction: Mobility, Contact and Language Change—Working with Contemporary Speech Communities' (*JSoc* 6[2002] 3–15). J.K. Chambers, in 'Dynamics of Dialect Convergence' (*JSoc* 6[2002] 117–30), makes the important point that 'mobility is the most effective leveller of dialect and accent' (p. 117), distinguishing in particular immigrants, immigrants' offspring, and newcomers (measured by his Regionality Index, cf. *YWES* 81[2002] 93). Natalie Schilling-Estes reports 'On the Nature of Isolated and Post-Isolated Dialects: Innovation, Variation and Differentiation' (*JSoc* 6[2002] 64–85). Drawing on data from Smith Island, Maryland, and the Lumbee Native Americans in Robeson County, North Carolina, she argues that, contrary to received wisdom (and contrary to Trudgill's *Handbook* article quoted above), isolated communities may be very heterogeneous as well as linguistically innovative, as dialect levelling typically results from pressures that come with dialect contact. Close-knit networks allow the transmission of intricate patterns of variation instead.

Perceptual dialectology, or the study of attitudes to dialects, again plays an important role in publications this year, and several introductions to the field have appeared, all by Dennis R. Preston. The first is an article under the heading of 'Language with an Attitude' (in Chambers *et al.*, eds., pp. 40–66). A more technical overview is 'Perceptual Dialectology: Aims, Methods, Findings' (in Berns and van Marle, eds., *Present-Day Dialectology: Problems and Findings*, pp. 57–104). Finally, more suitable to a non-technical audience is 'The Story of Good and Bad English in the United States' (in Watts and Trudgill, eds., *Alternative Histories of English*, pp. 132–51), which also takes into account some historical data. On the subject of attitudinal studies, a range of regional investigations is published in the second volume of Long and Preston, eds., *Handbook of Perceptual Dialectology*. Although this second volume concentrates on areas and countries 'overlooked' in the first volume, some contributions also deal with English in Britain or America, and they will be discussed in the regional sections below.

Turning to historical sociolinguistics now, this relatively new cross-over area continues to produce interesting publications. One of these is the collection of original essays in Watts and Trudgill, eds., *Alternative Histories of English*, individual contributions to which are also discussed below and in the next section, on world Englishes. Jim Milroy discusses the myth of Standard English in 'The Legitimate Language: Giving a History to English' (pp. 7–25), especially how ideologies of purity and continuity have influenced the perception and historiography of Old and Middle English. Richard Watts traces the eighteenth-century British obsession with 'politeness', and how 'polite language' came to be equal to 'standard English', in 'From Polite Language to Educated Language: The Re-Emergence of an Ideology' (pp. 155–72), explaining why Standard English is still linked to access to political and cultural power. Standardization and language purism are incidentally also discussed in Peter Hohenhaus, 'Standardization, Language Change, Resistance and the Question of Linguistic Threat: 18th Century English and Present-Day German' (in Linn and McLelland, eds., *Standardization: Studies from the Germanic Languages*, pp. 153–78).

William A. Kretzschmar Jr., in 'Dialectology and the History of the English Language' (in Minkova and Stockwell eds., pp. 79–108) cautions the historical linguist that a defence of the Neogrammarian position of the exceptionlessness of sound change is unwarranted in the light of dialect data. Instead, Kretzschmar proposes an asymptotic curve (few very frequent variants, many rare variants) as a much more flexible model for language variation and change. Linking history and gender, Terttu Nevalainen considers 'Women's Writing as Evidence for Linguistic Continuity and Change in Early Modern English' (in Watts and Trudgill eds., 191–209), based on the Corpus of Early English Correspondence; women's writing is generally considered to be closer to spoken language, and it can in fact be shown that women lead a range of supra-local morphological changes. Nevalainen also discusses 'Language and Woman's Place in Earlier English' more generally (*JEngL* 30[2002] 181–99), showing that many stereotypes we have of women (talkativeness, use of colour terms, more standard speech) cannot actually be historically supported. A final contribution to the field of historical sociolinguistics comes from Colette Moore, 'Writing Good Southerne: Local and Supralocal Norms in the Plumpton Letter Collection' (*LVC* 14[2002] 1–17). Moore focuses on changes in written norms in the history of English, investigating three morphosyntactic variables (3sg present tense endings, 3pl *be*, and the Northern Subject Rule) in the (northern) Plumpton letters from the fifteenth and sixteenth centuries, in which northern and southern forms were in competition.

Turning to the regional contributions now, we start our overview with Great Britain and Ireland, proceeding roughly in north-to-south order, looking at some general publications first. The second edition of Storry and Childs, eds., *British Cultural Identities*, makes interesting, if not essential, background reading for Great Britain. The book has been thoroughly updated, as indeed topics like 'youth culture and style' must have changed rapidly over the last five years or so (the first edition was from 1997). Of most interest to sociolinguists will be chapter 6, 'Ethnicity and Language', by Gerry Smyth (pp. 209–38), who finds that 'in British English, a growing informality is apparent' (p. 214), and that the homogeneity of English is challenged not only through the 'New Englishes' but already from within the state. A good short introduction to various regional varieties is provided by Tom

McArthur in the *Oxford Guide to World English*, where he introduces not only the very general terms 'Northern' and 'Southern' English, but looks in some more detail at London, the West Country, the West Midlands, and East Anglia, as well as Yorkshire and Lancashire, and at Cumbrian and Geordie for England, and of course Scots, Welsh English, and Irish English. McArthur's presentation is well informed and eminently readable, so that these eighty pages might well be used as an informal introduction to dialect divisions in undergraduate classes.

The only longer publication on Irish English this year is Simone Zwickl, *Language Attitudes, Ethnic Identity and Dialect Use across the Northern Ireland Border: Armagh and Monaghan*. Although these two towns are only roughly fifteen miles apart, they are separated by the political border between Northern Ireland and the Republic of Ireland, and Zwickl investigates how far this border correlates with different attitudes to the local dialect. Perhaps privileged as an outsider in this difficult political situation, Zwickl manages to elicit an enormous range of material. Combining quantitative and qualitative methods, she finds that in Armagh (Northern Ireland) religious denomination is more of a dividing factor, with the Catholics identifying strongly with the Irish language (despite or perhaps because of a lack of widespread competence in it) and with the local dialect. The Protestants in Monaghan (Republic of Ireland), on the other hand, have the highest rates of approval for Standard English, probably using this variety to create a positive self-image. Zwickl claims that, 'although the border did not have a massive impact on the knowledge and use of dialect words, it has caused divergence in attitudes to language' (p. 241). Based on data from Limerick, Fiona Farr and Anne O'Keeffe examine '*Would* as a Hedging Device in an Irish Context' (in Reppen *et al.*, eds., pp. 25–48), and find that, in Irish English, hedges involving *would* are used more frequently than in British or American English, due to the fact that 'hedges had a broader pragmatic function for speakers of Irish English' (pp. 44–5), i.e. differences in socio-cultural norms. Raymond Hickey has added to the field *A Source Book for Irish English*, including an introduction to Irish English and an overview of research themes. The main part, however, comprises an extensive bibliography of around 400 pages, plus a historical timeline and various maps. The enterprise becomes even more valuable and variable through the additional publication of the contents on CD-ROM, with an accompanying database manager that allows access to the material in a variety of ways. The author promises to update the bibliography every one or two months on his home page, and this compilation is thus an up-to-date 'must have' for anyone interested in the study of Irish English.

Historical Scots is, as usual, the subject of Anneli Meurman-Solin, who looks at 'The Progressive in Older Scots' (in Fanego, López-Couso, and Pérez-Guerra, eds., *English Historical Syntax and Morphology*, pp. 203–29), in particular the ousting of participle forms in *-and* in favour of the Anglo-English norm in *-ing*, a change that took place between 1500 and 1640. Her electronic corpora of Older Scots suggest that this change progressed through particular contexts and genres, at the same time also ruling out a possible (Celtic) substrate influence on the progressive. Speaking of possible Celtic substrate for at least some varieties of English, researchers will welcome the new publication of Ball, ed. (with James Fife), *The Celtic Languages*, now also available in paperback. While part I, 'Historical Aspects', may have a curiosity value for anyone who ever wondered about a possible Celtic influence on the formation of Old English, parts II to IV might be more relevant to researchers of

Irish, Scottish, and Welsh English (and possible Manx), as they contain good overviews of the history, phonology, morphology, and syntax as well as some comments on the lexicon of Irish (Gaelic) (by Gearóid McEoin, pp. 101–44), Scottish Gaelic (by William Gillies, pp. 145–227), and Manx (by George Broderick, pp. 228–85), as well as Welsh (by T. Arwyn Watkins, pp. 289–348) and Cornish (by Ken George, pp. 410–68). Part IV contains contributions on the sociolinguistic situation of Modern Irish, Scottish Gaelic, and Welsh, and thus nicely complements studies on (Celtic) English varieties.

Charles Jones provides an attractive brief introduction to *The English Language in Scotland: An Introduction to Scots*, in particular the syntax, sounds, and vocabulary of Scots (or Scottish English). A large part of the book is also dedicated to social and regional variation inside Scotland, as well as the (probably obligatory) representation of Scots in literature, and some account of the external history of English in Scotland. Although this book is written primarily with a non-linguistic audience in mind, it is nevertheless very useful as a brief overview of this interesting variety and should be highly useful in the classroom. More detail on a specific Scottish variety is provided by J. Derrick McClure in *Doric: The Dialect of North-East Scotland*. McClure gives a historical overview of the Scots spoken roughly between Aberdeen and Inverness. As this book has appeared in Benjamin's Text series, it is perhaps not surprising that it consists mostly of dialect texts. Nevertheless, apart from the general introduction as well as the glossary, especially the carefully transcribed spoken texts might be useful for more dialectological purposes. Situated in roughly the same area, Colleen M. Fitzgerald investigates 'Vowel Harmony in Buchan Scots English' (*ELL* 6[2002] 61–79) in syllables without primary stress. Fitzgerald finds that vowel height is indeed predictable from the preceding stressed vowel and concludes that vowel harmony actually operates in this north-eastern dialect of Scottish English. Moving south a little, Ronald Macaulay asks: 'Extremely Interesting, Very Interesting or Only Quite Interesting?' in his investigation of 'Adverbs and Social Class' (*JSoc* 6[2002] 398–417). Based on data from Ayr, but probably more widely relevant, Macaulay finds that his middle-class informants use more adverbs in -*ly* as well as hedges, whereas working-class narratives are characterized by accumulation of details as well as movement rules. Far less useful from a dialectological point of view is the use of dialect in writing, which is the subject of Annette Hagan's detailed investigation in *Urban Scots Dialect Writing*. Hagan concentrates on the depiction of Glaswegian Scots in five literary texts from the twentieth century, and comes to the tentative conclusion that 'the more recent a passage, the more convincing it is in terms of its speech realism' (p. 299).

Moving south of the border, but remaining with the subject of written dialect texts, Bill Griffiths provides a (short) dictionary and a volume of dialect texts in the two-volume *North East Dialect: Survey and Word List* and *North East Dialect: The Texts*, himself unabashedly 'Northern' (e.g. in the preface we read 'The book has selled well', a past tense form specific to the north-east and the Scottish Lowlands). While this collection is not aimed at a linguistic audience, the *Survey and Word List* in particular is sufficiently technical in detail that it might be a useful resource in dialect work. The 'North' is generally quite well represented in dialect studies this year: a (stereotyped) phonological/morphological feature is the subject of Mark J. Jones's 'The Origins of Definite Article Reduction in Northern English Dialects:

Evidence from Dialect Allomorphy' (*ELL* 6[2002] 325–45), where he calls into question the usual derivation of the clitic article *t'* from a reduction of ME *þe* on distributional grounds. Katie Wales illustrates present and past attitudes to 'Northern' English in '"North of Watford Gap": A Cultural History of Northern English (from 1700)' (in Watts and Trudgill, eds., pp. 45–66). Her contribution is nicely complemented by Keith Williamson's 'The Dialectology of "English" North of the Humber, *c*.1380–1500' (in Fanego, Méndez-Naya, and Seoane, eds., pp. 253–86), where the author finds striking dialect differences between Scottish and English as early as late ME. Also on a northern theme, Dominic Watt presents evidence of accent levelling in '"I don't speak with a Geordie accent, I speak, like, the northern accent": Contact-Induced Levelling in the Tyneside Vowel System' (*JSoc* 6[2002] 44–63). In data from Newcastle from the PVC project (Phonological Variation and Change in Contemporary Spoken British English, cf. *YWES* 80[2001] 75), Watt finds that in the FACE and GOAT vowels, younger speakers use the less regionally marked variant instead of the highly localized ones.

Intensifiers are discussed in much detail by Rika Ito and Sali Tagliamonte, in '*Well* Weird, *Right* Dodgy, *Very* Strange, *Really* Cool: Layering and Recycling in English Intensifiers' (*LSoc* 32[2002] 257–79). These intensifiers are attested historically since ME, but the authors find that in their data from York, intensifiers are used more by the younger generation, and that the younger speakers are shifting from *very* to the more commonly used *really*. *Really* is discussed in another contribution by the same authors, 'Think *Really Different*: Continuity and Specialization in the English Dual Form Adverbs' (*JSoc* 6[2002] 236–66). Based on the same data, Tagliamonte and Ito analyse the variation between adverbs in -*ly* and -Ø. If the highly frequent *really* is discounted, -Ø can be described as the continuation of a concrete, objective meaning from historical foundations. Probably the most detailed morpho-syntactic study on British dialects this year is *Negation in Non-Standard British English* by Lieselotte Anderwald. Based on the spoken sections of the British National Corpus Anderwald investigates (purportedly) non-regional phenomena like negative concord, *ain't*, and third person singular *don't*, as well as variation in the past tense paradigm of BE. Despite accepted authorities, almost all phenomena (except for *don't*) show a striking regional distribution, a phenomenon worthy of further investigation (for more details, see Section 4(*a*)). Based on the same material, Geoffrey Sampson finds striking differences in the occurrence of verb phrases in 'Regional Variation in the English Verb Qualifier System' (*ELL* 6[2002] 17–30). Sampson shows that the perfect especially is very rare in the south of England, in fact as rare as in Irish English, and suggests that the perfect as a category is missing from the underlying non-standard grammar here as well.

The English south has received comparatively less attention this year. The formation of a new dialect in the Midlands is the subject of Judy Dyer's 'We All Speak the Same Around Here: Dialect Levelling in a Scottish-English Community' (*JSoc* 6[2002] 99–116), which concentrates on Corby, Northamptonshire, where a Scottish company from Glasgow constructed an iron and steel works in 1933 and recruited many Scottish workers. Dyer finds that today, Corby speakers speak mostly a mixed dialect where historically Scottish features have been reassigned to index local identity. David Britain investigates 'Diffusion, Levelling, Simplification and Reallocation in Past Tense BE in the English Fens' (*JSoc* 6[2002] 16–43), the area of England that separates East Anglia from the Midlands. The current system is mixed, with *was* used for all persons in positive contexts, *weren't* in negative ones. From various historical and dialectological sources, Britain concludes that this mixed system is due to dialect contact, as the Fens traditionally seem to have had a system that levelled all persons to *were/weren't*. Based on narratives from sixteen middle-class boys and girls from Reading, Jenny Cheshire and Ann Williams discuss 'Information Structure in Male and Female Adolescent Talk' (*JEngL* 30[2002] 217–38) and find that, both in the introduction of Brand New Entities into the talk and in Turn-Final Discourse Markers, the boys are more concerned with referentially orientated components, whereas the girls use more affectively oriented components. Linking Reading with Milton Keynes (and the northern town Hull) Paul Kerswill and Ann Williams discuss 'Dialect Recognition and Speech Community Focusing in New and Old Towns in England: The Effects of Dialect Levelling, Demography and Social Networks' (in Long and Preston, eds., *Handbook of Perceptual Dialectology*, pp. 173–204). Their informants had to identify the regional origin of taped voices, and while it is clear that familiar dialects are identified most correctly, their data show that Hull is the most focused (and easily recognizable) accent, with recognition intact across generations, whereas Reading seems to be influenced by London more and more, and older speakers are (mis-)identified as 'West Country', a 'perceptual dislocation' (p. 202). Milton Keynes finally, having started out with diverse accents, is slowly becoming more focused.

Anne Fabricius documents 'Ongoing Change in Modern RP: Evidence for the Disappearing Stigma of T-Glottalling' (*EWW* 23 [2002] 115–36) in a study of ex-public school students at Cambridge. Fabricius finds word-final preconsonantal t-glottalling in all speakers, while pre-*pausal* t-glottalling has not moved out from London further than the Home Counties, and pre-*vocalic* t-glottalling is still largely restricted to London speakers. (Another study of (some of) the same subjects by Fabricius is discussed in Section 2 above). London teenagers have been recorded in the COLT corpus, which is the subject of *Trends in Teenage Talk: Corpus Compilation, Analysis and Findings* by Anna-Brita Stenström, Gisle Andersen and Ingrid Kristine Hasund. The authors introduce the corpus (compilation, speakers, and conversations) as well as the use of slang, swearing, and dirty language. The second half of this book adds some linguistic studies. For example, the authors find that their teenagers use quotative *go* almost twice as often as *say*, but that *go* is characteristic of lower social class and of middle and late adolescence, dropping sharply almost to zero for young adults. This interesting sub-chapter on non-standard grammar is unfortunately condensed into only six pages, which obviously cannot do justice to the twenty-one(!) morphosyntactic features identified. (Annoyingly, non-concord (*we was*, *he don't*) is repeatedly referred to as *negative* concord, and there are some other unfortunate mistakes.) As in York, the intensifier *really* is much more frequent than *very*, but is itself topped by *right* by the London teenagers. *Contra* Tagliamonte and Ito above, Stenström *et al.* propose the use of *real* for *really* as an American import, without, however, giving any conclusive evidence for this derivation. The authors also find that teenagers use invariant tags (like *innit*, *right*, *yeah*, or *okay*) far more than adults, with a wider range of functions. Ritual conflict, interestingly between girls, is the subject of the last chapter, which may be a feature of ethnicity, as both girls investigated are black. In contrast to boys' ritual insults, girls do not seem to compete, but rather stand up to people and answer back when being attacked.

Peter Trudgill, Terttu Nevalainen, and Ilse Wischer span the Atlantic in 'Dynamic *Have* in North American and British Isles English' (*ELL* 6[2002] 1–15), connecting the facts that American English (in contrast to BrE) requires *do* support for *have* (*Do you have any coffee?*) and uses *take* rather than *have* in constructions like *have a shower*. The authors claim, on the basis of historical and dialectal evidence, that American English never acquired the more dynamic meanings of *have*, which might explain both phenomena. This contribution has taken us to North America. Very little has been published on English in Canada this year. One notable exception is Tom McArthur, who in the *Oxford Guide to World English* naturally also deals with English in Canada (pp. 207–25), discussing in some detail Quebec English, Atlantic Canada (Maritimes and Newfoundland) and General Canadian. Although this (sub)chapter is strongest on history and politics, it also contains useful sections on pronunciation, grammar, and vocabulary and is thus a nicely readable, up-to-date introduction to Canadian English. The only other two contributions in this area come, first, from Ruth King and Sandra Clarke, who discuss 'Contesting Meaning: *Newfie* and the Politics of Ethnic Labelling' (*JSoc* 6[2002] 537–56). The label *Newfie* (for *Newfoundlander*) is a relatively recent innovation and perceived as derogatory by some, positive by others. Newfoundland, Canada's newest and poorest province, has a strong regional identity, not least linguistically, and the authors show how the negative perception of *Newfie* goes hand in hand with a rejection of the stereotypes (by outgroups), whereas a positive perception is partly due to less experience of the out-group usage, but may also be caused by denying the intent or the impact of the stereotype. Secondly, a wider group of speakers is investigated by Meghan McKinnie and Jennifer Dailey-O'Cain, in 'Perceptual Dialectology of Anglophone Canada from the Perspectives of Young Albertans and Ontarians' (in Long and Preston, eds., pp. 277–94), who find that in terms of pleasantness, correctness, and similarity, ratings are quite similar across informants; no Canadian region is rated as either very unpleasant or very incorrect.

Moving to English in the US, Tom McArthur can also be quoted as a good introduction to US dialect divisions, as the third chapter of his *Oxford Guide to World English* is exclusively concerned with 'The Americas' (pp. 163–244) (including the section on Canada reviewed above). Refreshingly, McArthur presents a comprehensive overview of several dialects, rather than relying on the usual emphasis on Southern States English and AAVE. He also deals with the North, the Midland, Western, Yiddish, and 'Spanglish' (perhaps better known as Chicano English), and with the controversy surrounding the term 'General American'. On an almost classic topic, Renée Blake and Meredith Josey have conducted a fascinating follow-up study on 'The /ay/ Diphthong in a Martha's Vineyard Community', asking: 'What Can We Say 40 Years after Labov?' (*LSoc* 32[2002] 451–85). They find that due to economic and ideological change (tourism is now the main source of income on the island, most islanders are middle-class, close-knit networks have loosened, and mainlanders are not perceived as the 'other' any longer); /ay/ is no longer as centralized phonetically as Labov found it to be, and islanders do not identify with the notion of 'the fishermen'. Instead, the authors find evidence for Canadian Raising on Martha's Vineyard, a change they characterize as 'ideology-free', as it no longer constitutes a marker of social identity. A curious phonetic phenomenon is the subject of Bryan Gick's 'The American Intrusive *l*' (*AS* 77[2002] 167–83), a relatively recent feature that may have developed in two places independently (Texas/Oklahoma and on the mid-Atlantic) and is used in place of the more common intrusive *r*. Also on a phonological topic, Barbara Johnstone, Neeta Bhasin, and Denise Wittkofski investigate '"Dahntahn" Pittsburgh: Monophthongal /aw/ and Representations of Localness in Southwestern Pennsylvania' (*AS* 77[2002] 148–77), a dialect feature that indexes Pittsburgh identity, and whose persistence may in fact be linked to its stereotypical status. Also on the mid-Atlantic, Charles T. Scott investigates 'American English "Short a" Revisited: A Phonological Puzzle' (*AS* 77[2002] 358–69), i.e. the difference between *can* (container) and *can* (modal verb)—a puzzle that seems, however, a puzzle for American speakers only. A syntactic topic not documented so far is 'The Case of *Like* + Past Participle in American English', examined by Thomas E. Murray and Beth Lee Simon (*AS* 77[2002] 32–69), i.e. constructions like *The baby likes cuddled*. Various ways of collecting data show that this (rare) phenomenon is concentrated in the US Midlands, and that it may be of Scotch-Irish origin. Moving west a little, one of the authors, Thomas E. Murray, also depicts 'Language Variation and Change in the Urban Midwest: The Case of St. Louis, Missouri' (*LVC* 14[2002] 347–61), which has traditionally been described as a Northern island in a sea of Southern (or South Midland) forms. Murray finds that, indeed, a trend towards more Northern forms seems to have been accelerating over the last generation. 'Attitudes Toward Midwestern American English', the area widely believed to be where Standard American English is spoken, are examined in more detail by Nancy Niedzielski (in Long and Preston, eds., pp. 321–7). Niedzielski explains the continuation of this belief in the face of a dramatic phonetic shift like the Northern Cities Chain Shift (NCCS) and various morphological non-standard features in the framework of social constructivist theory. Thus, Detroiters actually hear standard vowels even when confronted with NCCS systems because they hold on to their identity of being SAE speakers, and the author has apparently 'narrowly escaped fist-fights for even suggesting' otherwise (p. 326). Malcah Yaeger-Dror, Lauren Hall-Lew, and Sharon Deckert investigate contraction strategies in '*It's not* or *isn't it*? Using Large Corpora to Determine the Influences on Contraction Strategies' (*LVC* 14[2002] 79–118). They try to separate factors like register and speaker stance, which undoubtedly influence the choice of contraction type, from clearly dialect-related factors. Not unexpectedly, 'the more carefully scripted speech is, the more likely full form is to be used' (p. 96). For conversational data, especially *isn't*/*aren't* run counter to expectations, and auxiliary contraction is actually preferred, at least in the south-east and the south-west of the US.

The western US is notoriously under-represented in dialectology, but Carmen Fought goes some way to remedy the situation, at least for attitude studies, with her contribution on 'California Students' Perceptions of, You Know, Regions and Dialects?' (in Long and Preston, eds., pp. 113–34), California of course being the home of the notorious 'valley girl' and the 'surfers'. Fought finds that her Californian informants have only a 'highly nebulous' (p. 132) concept of the Midwest as a dialect area, and, not surprisingly, that the South is the most prominent dialect label. The most correct (or 'proper') English is interestingly perceived to be spoken on the East Coast, not the West or the Midwest. In the same volume, Betsy E. Evans, 'An Acoustic and Perceptual Analysis of Imitation' (pp. 95–112), provides evidence that dialect imitation does not have to be restricted to only a few stereotypical features. She investigates the vowel system of a 29-year-old Northern speaker in his imitation of a Southern dialect for systematic evidence of the Southern Vowel Shift and finds both acoustic and perceptual evidence for the accuracy of the imitation. Unfortunately Evans does not consider whether her informant is perhaps bidialectal (he grew up in the South Midlands) rather than just imitating a dialect.

Turning now to AAVE, the study of this variety has a strong historical focus this year. Scholars on the history of AAVE will welcome the reprint of Lorenzo Dow Turner's *Africanisms in the Gullah Dialect*. Although this has of course not changed since its first publication in 1949, it is now freely available again, and the reprint has a valuable introduction both to Gullah and to the impact of Turner's original study of it written by Katherine Wyly Mille and Michael B. Montgomery. Shana Poplack, Gerard van Herk, and Dawn Harvie report on an interesting project in '"Deformed in the Dialects": An Alternative History of Non-Standard English' (in Watts and Trudgill, eds., pp. 87–110). In the Ottawa Grammar Resource on Early Variability in English, they have compiled all historical references to grammatical variation (e.g. from reference grammars, style manuals, etc.) between 1577 and 1898, which they use to show that the non-standard features of early AAE, especially in the past tense forms, can be traced back to widespread variation in Early Modern English in Britain.

The historical focus is mainly supplied by two monograph publications. The first is Alexander Kautzsch, *The Historical Evolution of Earlier African American English: An Empirical Comparison of Early Sources*. Kautzsch concentrates on actual historical material, using a wide range of transcripts (Rawick's ex-slave narratives, the WPA project, ex-slave recordings, and Hyatt's hoodoo-interviews) for his morphosyntactic analyses of negation patterns, the copula, and relativization. In an ingenious twist, Kautzsch looks at his material not only per subcorpus, per state, etc. (as would be expected—and which incidentally makes rather tedious reading), but mixes his corpora and divides his speakers by birth decades, which gives him an enormous apparent time range of informants, from 1833(!) to 1924. This arrangement allows him to make much more confident statements on historical developments in actual AAE than has previously been possible. Despite this neat idea, the data are comparatively messy, and, especially for the evolution of the copula and for relativization strategies, no clear developments can be traced. On the other hand, this is perhaps not too surprising when we consider the socio-political situation of the slaves, in which linguistic uniformity across several states can hardly be expected. Nevertheless, some interesting results obtain: Kautzsch finds for example that the use of *ain't* for *didn't*, one of the hallmarks of Present-Day AAVE, is not a historical feature of AAE; in general, Kautzsch's study supports the idea that (the relatively homogeneous) AAE as we know it today is a phenomenon of the late nineteenth and early twentieth centuries. For those readers interested in a short summary of his main findings Alexander Kautzsch's 'Combining Early Sources: A New Approach to the Historical Study of African American English' (in Kastovsky et al., eds., pp. 56–73) can be recommended.

The second monograph comes from Walt Wolfram's research group on an AAE enclave community in Hyde County: Walt Wolfram and Erik R. Thomas, *The Development of African American English*. After a careful methodological discussion of the use of enclave communities in the resolution of the Anglicist–

Creolist debate, Wolfram and Thomas dedicate the analytical part of the book to several morphosyntactic features (past tense BE, copula absence), vowels, consonants, the difficult topic of intonation, and a discussion of some individual speakers. The authors stress in particular that the selection of diagnostic structures might affect one's conclusions considerably, and that the range of features under investigation should therefore be as broad as possible—a principle admirably realized in this work. In fact, Wolfram and Thomas question both a neo-Anglicist position and a pure Creolist position on the origin of AAVE, and argue that the evolution of any vernacular norm has a linguistic dimension, a sociohistorical and a sociolinguistic component, and of course an ideological dimension. The data from Hyde County suggest that AAE must have been closer to the regional European American varieties than contemporary AAVE, but that there were indisputable substratal effects from the early contact situation. Wolfram and Thomas's study is complemented by Christine Mallinson and Walt Wolfram, 'Dialect Accommodation in a Bi-Ethnic Mountain Enclave Community: More Evidence on the Development of African American English' (*LSoc* 31[2002] 743–75), based on data from Beech Bottom in the Appalachian mountains. Again the authors discuss both morphosyntactic and phonological variables. They find that the African Americans have accommodated extensively to the local norms for most vernacular features, although there is still an ethnic divide with regard to 3sg -*s*, copula absence, and consonant cluster reduction, an argument for these three features being the historical norm for AAVE.

Moving to Present-Day AAVE, Julie Sweetland provides an interesting study on the 'Unexpected but Authentic Use of an Ethnically-Marked Dialect' (*JSoc* 6[2002] 514–36), namely the use of AAVE by a white female, who can be described as an in-group member despite her race, nicely illustrating the dictum that race is (among other things) linguistically constituted. AAVE in Detroit is the subject of Bridget L. Anderson, 'Dialect Levelling and /ai/ Monophthongization among African American Detroiters' (*JSoc* 6[2002] 86–98). Levelling of /ai/ in pre-voiceless position (e.g. *tight*) is usually associated only with white Southerners, but Anderson argues that, in this community, it might have arisen through contact—and solidarity—with White Appalachian migrants. The remaining publications on Present-Day AAE are dominated by a new generation of female African American linguists, which gives the field a decidedly new, and often very personal, tone. Lisa J. Green has written the first introductory textbook on AAE, *African American English: A Linguistic Introduction*. She deals with important distinguishing characteristics of AAE in detail but also discusses more discourse-oriented features like speech events and rules of interaction, as well as the (often inaccurate) use of AAE in literature, in the media, and in education (for more details on this book, see Section 4(*a*)). A second highlight is Marcyliena Morgan's *Language, Discourse and Power in African American Culture*. In some fine-tuned analyses, Morgan succeeds in making rap lyrics comprehensible to outsiders (such as the present reviewer), introduces the reader to the different verbal styles of AAE, shows how ignorance of essential parts of AAE grammar (e.g. the recent past *had gone* mistaken for StE past perfect) can lead to dire consequences like dismissal, discusses Black women's language, and shows the AAE (as well as Spanish) influence on urban youth culture (of Blacks and non-Blacks alike), in particular in the field of hiphop. The final chapter deals with language, discourse and power in the context of schools. The book is imbued with the extreme verbal creativity, love of language, and intelligence of its performers, and the personal stance of the author makes her analyses always accessible and comprehensible. Much like Morgan's analysis, hiphop lyrics are also the subject of H. Samy Alim, 'Street-Conscious Copula Variation in the Hip Hop Nation' (AS 77[2002] 288–304). Alim, however, approaches the subject from a quantitative perspective and compares copula absence across informal interviews and the lyrics, finding that this feature in particular is used to construct a street-conscious identity.

The result of possibly an even more personal project, *Sista, Speak! Black Women Kinfolk Talk About Language and Literacy*, by Sonja L. Lanehart, collects interviews and statements from five African American women (the author, her grandmother, mother, aunt, and sister) on the topic of language and literacy, and links them carefully to each woman's life story. It quickly becomes clear how, even within the same generation in the same family, different educational and social opportunities can lead to very different linguistic abilities, and in return how the ideology of Standard English and the lack of appreciation for AAVE has led to very different self-images, self-confidence, and educational achievements for these five women.

Patricia Cukor-Avila looks at quotatives in '*She say, she go, she be like*: Verbs of Quotation Over Time in African American English' (AS 77 [2002] 3–31) in the small rural Texan town of 'Springville'. Her longitudinal study shows that *be like* is used only by the younger generation, thus possibly diffusing from urban to rural speakers. Unfortunately, her study cannot yet resolve the interesting question of whether *be like* is age-graded, or whether this change is here to stay.

Finally, some publications on the fringes of sociolinguistics should be noted here. A small-scale study on the role of language and political arguments is the subject of Julie Lindquist, *A Place to Stand: Politics and Persuasion in a Working-Class Bar*, where the bar is also, according to the chapter headings, 'A Place to Be' and 'A Place to Tell It'. Lindquist shows in particular the role of political arguments in constituting the working-class identity of her informants: 'as a kind of cultural currency, arguments are a locally legitimate, covertly prestigious way to achieve distinction' (p. 152). Going well beyond established sociolinguistic techniques, this book is sociolinguistic only in its broadest sense. Also on the fringes of a narrower conception of sociolinguistics is Diane Boxer, *Applying Sociolinguistics: Domains and Face-to-Face Interaction*, which would squarely fall into pragmatics in the European classification. Boxer investigates face-to-face interaction in the family, in the social domain, in education, in religion, in the workplace, and finally in cross-cultural interactions. It is particularly interesting (if not wholly unexpected) that gendered and generational roles are not only *revealed* in family talk, but of course also perpetuated, even and especially as 'the values reflected in such talk may ... be subtle and below the level of consciousness of the participants' (p. 212).

9. New Englishes and Creolistics

As in 2001, we find a wealth of publications on English as a world language or international English. We will turn to monographs first. Janina Brut-Griffler discusses the historical, political, ideological, and educational aspects of this phenomenon in *World English: A Study of its Development.* Working within the framework of applied linguistics, her interest is not in the linguistic forms of World English, but rather in how it affects speech communities which have become bilingual or multilingual or are undergoing a language shift. Tom McArthur's *Oxford Guide to World English* combines historical and political information on the spread of English with a brief description of the many varieties spoken and written around the world. The book obviously draws on his previous work *The English Languages* (cf. *YWES* 79[2000] 2–3), both in content and presentation, but has been supplemented in order to provide a more comprehensive survey of English worldwide. However, those mainly interested in the New Englishes must note that more than half of the volume is devoted to English in Great Britain, the United States, and Canada. McArthur gives a brief overview of the development of English in each area under discussion, followed by a short list of linguistic features, usually including phonology, morpho-syntax, and lexicon, and a few short text samples. His book can thus be used as a reference work or introductory textbook, which might have been improved by a more comprehensive bibliography or suggestions for further reading.

The other two monographs dealing with international English also sketch the spread of English around the world, but their main concern is the linguistic description of the varieties discussed. Laurie Bauer promises *An Introduction to International Varieties of English*, but he limits the scope of his book in his introductory chapter to the so-called 'inner circle varieties', namely the English spoken in Britain (including Scotland, Wales, and Ireland), the United States, Canada, South Africa, Australia, and New Zealand. Since these varieties were formed under similar conditions, Bauer then proceeds to discuss shared processes in the development of the lexicon, the morpho-syntax, and the phonology of the varieties under analysis. He also discusses language attitudes and standard versus non-standard usage in the former colonies. The similarities discussed in his book lead Bauer to the conclusion that the imminent break-up of English as predicted by McArthur [1998] into mutually unintelligible languages is definitely not about to happen in the case of the L1 varieties. Peter Trudgill and Jean Hannah's *International English: A Guide to the Varieties of Standard English* in its fourth edition also includes West Indian English and a number of L2 varieties, such as East and West African English, Indian, Singaporean, and Philippines English. In the case of the West Indies, they discuss English-based creoles as well as the standard varieties spoken there, but this is not the case for West Africa. Information on the phonology, morpho-syntax, and lexicon is given for all varieties, but unfortunately no text samples, only single words or sentences. In the case of British, American, and Canadian English, regional variation is also discussed. There is also a chapter on lesser-known varieties, such as the English spoken on the Miskito Coast in Nicaragua or the Falkland Islands, but for these varieties no linguistic features are given. The bibliography is lamentably short and dated for a book that is intended as a textbook or reference work.

Ismail S. Talib's *The Language of Postcolonial Literatures: An Introduction* is clearly geared towards a non-linguistic audience, since the linguistic content is treated on a very basic level. Talib sketches the development of (global) English and then discusses the problems of linguistic and cultural decay after the advent of English in the (former) colonies, language attitudes and literary criticism throughout the English-speaking world. Talib's book is of more interest to students of stylistics; for more details see Section 11.

Manfred Görlach presents the fourth 'Englishes' volume, *Still More Englishes*: as before, this is a collection of (mainly) previously published and some original work on various varieties of English. Of the nine chapters, the first three are of interest to those working on New Englishes: 'Global English(?)' traces the development and effects of English as a world language; 'The Problem of Authentic Language' addresses issues of data collection and interpretation; and 'Language and Nation: Linguistic Identity in the History of English' discusses the tensions between the use of English and nationalism in countries like the US and Canada, and in the Caribbean, West Africa, South Africa, India, and South-East Asia. Most useful despite its personal bias, finally, is the appendix: 'An Annotated Bibliography of EWL'.

Next, we will have a look at the articles published this year on New Englishes. Peter Trudgill records 'The History of the Lesser-Known Varieties of English' (in Watts and Trudgill, eds., pp. 29–44), including, among others, the English spoken in Newfoundland, Bermuda, the Lesser Antilles, the Bahamas, Central America, St. Helena, the Pitcairn Islands, the Falkland Islands, Tristan da Cunha, and the Bonin Islands. Surprisingly, he also includes varieties like Indian English or Kenyan English in this chapter. The role of World Englishes in education is the topic of a symposium on 'World Englishes and Teaching English as a Foreign Language' published in *World Englishes* (21[2002] 421–56), in which educators report on various approaches to include New Englishes and EFL varieties in the TESOL curricula. In 'Predicting Challenges to English as a Global Language in the 21st Century' (*LPLP* 26[2002] 129–57), Paul Bruthiaux examines the criteria a potential global language must fulfil and comes to the conclusion that the predominance of English is likely to continue. On a more feature-oriented level, Charles F. Meyer looks at 'Pseudo-Titles in the Press Genres of Various Components of the International Corpus of English' (in Reppen *et al.*, eds., pp. 147–66), based on data from the ICE corpora from Great Britain, East Africa, Jamaica, New Zealand, the Philippines, Singapore, and the United States. With regard to lexicography, Tony T.N. Hung argues for a systematic approach in handling the pronunciation of '"New English" Words in International English Dictionaries' (*EnT* 72:iv[2002] 29–34).

As was the case last year, there is continued interest in language contact phenomena. Two monographs have been published on this topic, namely Donald Winford's *An Introduction to Contact Linguistics* and Carol Myers-Scotton's *Contact Linguistics: Bilingual Encounters and Grammatical Outcomes*. Winford's book is devised as a comprehensive textbook for advanced students of linguistics which covers all aspects of lexical borrowing, various types of structural diffusion in situations of language maintenance, social and linguistic aspects of code-switching, the development of mixed languages, individual and group SLA, language shift, and first-language attrition and language death, as well as pidginization, and creole formation, in great detail. The textbook character is enhanced by many examples, exercises, chapter summaries, and an ample bibliography. In most chapters, Winford critically evaluates previous research in the field and presents his readers with different approaches to each topic, for example Poplack's Interacting Grammars and Myers-Scotton's Matrix Language Frame model in the case of code-switching. His book is thus a well-rounded overview of all the issues relevant in the field of contact linguistics. Carol Myers-Scotton's *Contact Linguistics*, on the other hand, is an elaboration of her Matrix Frame Model and the more recent 4-M and Abstract-level models with the aim of widening their scope from code-switching to include other areas of language contact, such as grammatical convergence, mixed languages (which she calls 'split languages'), and creole formation. Both Winford and Myers-Scotton argue that all language contact phenomena are due to the same underlying processes, but their explanations of these processes differ greatly. While Winford leans more towards universal SLA processes, Myers-Scotton regards her models derived from code-switching research as best suited for accounting for all types of language contact phenomena. Two contributions in Chambers *et al.*, eds. (cf. Section 8 for a comprehensive review) are also of importance, namely Gillian Sankoff's discussion of 'Linguistic Outcomes of Language Contact' (pp. 638–68) and Paul Kerswill's overview of 'Koineization and Accommodation' (pp. 669–702), which both concentrate on the typical results of these language contact phenomena.

Moving on to the southern hemisphere varieties, I have noticed that the contributions on AusE are mostly concerned with gender issues. June Luchjenbroers looks at 'Gendered Features of Australian English Discourse: Discourse Strategies in Negotiated Talk' (*JEngL* 30[2002] 200–16) between young academics, and Anna Wierzbicka detects 'Sexism in Grammar: The Semantics of Gender in Australian English' (*AnL* 44[2002] 143–77) in the use of the pronouns *he* and *she* for inanimate referents, especially in (non-standard) Tasmanian English. In 'Looking at *girls* in Corpora of English' (*JEngL* 30[2002] 138–57), Robert Sigley and Janet Holmes find that the meanings of the lexemes *boy* and *girl* in British (LOB and FLOB), American (Brown and Frown) and New Zealand (WWC) corpora reveal a number of sexist usages. Timothy Jowan Curnow asks 'Can You Be Gay and Lesbian in Australian English?' (*AJL* 22[2002] 23–33), and documents the lexicalization of the phrase *gay and lesbian* on the basis of a corpus of Australian TV broadcasts.

Concerning other issues in AusE, Joanne Winter reports on 'Discourse Quotatives in Australian English: Adolescents Performing Voices' (*AJL* 22[2002] 5–21) in comparison to data from Great Britain, the USA, and Canada. Barbara M. Horvath and Ronald J. Horvath study 'The Geolinguistics of /l/ Vocalization in Australia and New Zealand' (*JSoc* 6[2002] 319–46) in nine different localities, identifying Christchurch as the place of origin of this change and relating factors contributing to its spread. Laurie Bauer and Winifred Bauer ask 'Can We Watch Regional Dialects Developing in Colonial English? The Case of New Zealand' (*EWW* 23[2002] 169–93), reporting on a survey of primary school children who were found to use regionally varied vocabulary items. They proceed to discuss a hypothesis for the development of regional variation in colonial varieties, as is already witnessed in AusE. They also report on the use of 'Adjective Boosters in the English of Young New Zealanders' (*JEngL* 30[2002] 244–57), drawing on data from the same survey. David Britain and Andrea Sudbury note that 'There's Sheep and There's Penguins: Convergence, "Drift" and "Slant" in New Zealand and Falkland Island English' (in Jones and Esch, eds., *Language Change: The Interplay of Internal, External and Extralinguistic Factors*, pp. 209–40), pointing out that, despite their isolation, both varieties have developed identical grammatical features, such as plural existentials with singular verbs. Elizabeth Gordon and Andrea Sudbury also stress the similarities between AusE, NZE, and SAE, which they discuss in 'The History of

Southern Hemisphere Englishes' (in Watts and Trudgill, eds., pp. 67–86). Apart from the historical account of the development of the English-speaking population in these colonies, they also comment on the shared phonological features, lexicon, and grammar of their varieties, as well as various theories put forward to explain their linguistic origins. Finally, Peter Mühlhäusler records 'Changing Names for a Changing Landscape: The Case of Norfolk Island' (*EWW* 23[2002] 59–91), and provides insight into the different naming practices of various social groups, such as colonial administrators, settlers and, more recently, tourism promoters.

With regard to English in Asia we note a new area of interest, namely English in Hong Kong and China. Kingsley Bolton is the editor of a volume on *Hong Kong English: Autonomy and Creativity*, which covers the sociolinguistics of Hong Kong English (HKE), several linguistic features, Hong Kong English literature, and resources for further research. The majority of the contributions have been previously published (*WEn* 19:iii[2000]) but were unavailable for review, and will therefore be covered presently. In his survey of 'The Sociolinguistics of Hong Kong and the Space for Hong Kong English' (pp. 29–56; *WEn* 19[2000] 265–85), Kingsley Bolton relates not only the history of this variety but also issues of language planning and language attitudes and a number of linguistic features which underscore the linguistic autonomy of HKE. Amy B.M. Tsui and David Bunton report on 'The Discourse and Attitudes of English Teachers in Hong Kong' (pp. 57–78; *WEn* 19[2000] 287–303) on the basis of over 1,000 messages on language issues in a teachers' computer network, which clearly indicate that HKE is not viewed favourably by this group. David C.S. Li looks at 'Cantonese–English Code-Switching Research in Hong Kong: A Survey of Recent Research' (pp. 79–100; *WEn* 19[2000] 305–22), identifying contexts in which the Cantonese press will resort to English, namely for purposes of euphemism or punning. Chan Yuen-Ying traces the development of 'The English-Language Media in Hong Kong' (pp. 101–16; *WEn* 19[2000] 323–35). In the section on language form, Tony T.N. Hung works 'Towards a Phonology of Hong Kong English' (pp. 119–40; *WEn* 19[2000] 337–56), showing that HKE speakers produce fewer vowel and consonant contrasts than native speakers of English. Nikolas Gisborne examines 'Relative Clauses in Hong Kong English' (pp. 141–60; *WEn* 19[2000] 357–71), trying to establish how much the HKE system is different from its Cantonese substrate and other varieties of English. Phil Benson provides information on 'Hong Kong Words: Variation and Context' (pp. 161–70; *WEn* 19[2000] 373–80), covering the semantics, pragmatics, and sociolinguistic contexts for a number of HKE lexemes. In the resource section, Kingsley Bolton and Gerald Nelson provide tools for 'Analysing Hong Kong English: Sample Texts from the International Corpus of English' (pp. 241–64). Shirley Geok-lin Lim explores 'Cultural Imagination and English in Hong Kong' (pp. 265–80), and Kingsley Bolton presents 'Researching Hong Kong English: Bibliographical Sources' (pp. 281–92; *WEn* 19[2000] 445–52), including publications and online sources on the sociolinguistics and applied linguistics of HKE, as well as on creative writing. Finally, Kingsley Bolton and Shirley Lim speculate on 'Futures for Hong Kong English' (pp. 295–313; *WEn* 19[2000] 429–43).

Kingsley Bolton, Gerald Nelson, and Joseph Hung report on 'A Corpus-Based Study of Connectors in Student Writing: Research from the International Corpus of English in Hong Kong (ICE-HK)' (*IJCL* 7[2002] 165–82), which reveals that Hong

Kong students and British students alike tend to over-use certain connectors, while no significant evidence of under-use could be found. John Flowerdew, David C.S. Li, and Sarah Tran discover 'Discriminatory News Discourse: Some Hong Kong Data' (*D&S* 13[2002] 319–45), examining reportage and editorials of the *South China Morning Post* by means of critical discourse analysis.

A special issue of *WEn* (21:ii[2002]), edited by Kingsley Bolton, covers English in China. Together with Q.S. Tong the editor also provides the introduction: 'Interdisciplinary Perspectives in English in China' (*WEn* 21[2002] 177–80). Of the thirteen articles in this volume, four are of importance for linguists. Kingsley Bolton's overview of 'Chinese Englishes: From Canton Jargon to Global English' (*WEn* 21[2002] 181–99) covers the history of English in China beginning in the seventeenth century. Guo Zhongshi and Huang Yu investigate 'Hybridized Discourse: Social Openness and Functions of English Media in Post-Mao China' (*WEn* 21[2002] 217–30), while Agnes Lam looks at 'English in Education: Policy Changes and Learners' Experiences' (*WEn* 21[2002] 245–56). Finally, Bob Adamson, Kingsley Bolton, Agnes Lam, and Q.S. Tong have compiled 'English in China: A Preliminary Bibliography' (*WEn* 21[2002] 349–55).

A special issue on 'Maintaining and Setting Standards and Language Variation in the Asian Pacific region' appeared in *JAPC* and includes various contributions on HKE and Asian Englishes in general. David Coniam and Peter Falvey's 'Selecting Models and Setting Standards for Teachers of English in Hong Kong' (*JAPC* 12[2002] 13–38) presents the government's benchmarking initiative, which was explicitly based on an educated Hong Kong variety rather than a native English model. David Bunton and Amy B.M. Tsui, on the other hand, hold in their paper on 'Setting Language Benchmarks: Whose Benchmark?' (*JAPC* 12[2002] 63–76) that the benchmarks for language teachers are largely exo-normative and do not correspond to the reality of spoken English in Hong Kong. Sarah Kaur Gill reports on 'Language Policy and English Language Standards in Malaysia: Nationalism and Pragmatism' (*JAPC* 12[2002] 95–115), while Agneta M.-L. Svalberg examines a linguistic detail of 'Language Standards and Language Variation in Brunei Darussalam: The Understanding of *Would* by Native and Non-Native Speakers of English' (*JAPC* 12[2002] 117–41). Bob Adamson and Ora Kwo are concerned with the Chinese government's efforts in 'Constructing an Official English for China, 1949–2000' (*JAPC* 12[2002] 159–83) on the basis of school syllabi and official textbooks which implement a British English norm.

Manfred Görlach addresses the question of 'English in Singapore, Malaysia, Hong Kong, Indonesia, the Philippines … a Second or Foreign Language?' (in Görlach, ed., pp. 99–117). He assesses the historical development and present situation of English in each of these countries, pointing out that the traditional labels are no longer appropriate in some cases, as, for example, Singapore English is on the verge of becoming an ENL variety. This is a situation the Singaporean government would rather prevent, because it poses a threat to the bilingual education policy which assigns a mother tongue on the basis of ethnicity and treats English as a neutral second language for all Singaporeans, as Lionel Wee relates in his article 'When English Is Not a Mother Tongue: Linguistic Ownership and the Eurasian Community in Singapore (*JMMD* 23[2002] 282–95). Xu Daming and Li Wei, on the other hand, conclude that 'Managing Multilingualism in Singapore' (in Wei, Dewaele, and Housen, eds., *Opportunities and Challenges of Bilingualism*, pp. 275–

95) is very effective since the government treats multilingualism as an economic resource.

Three articles discuss English in India. Stephen Evans reports on 'Macaulay's Minute Revisited: Colonial Language Policy in Nineteenth-Century India' (*JMMD* 23[2002] 260–81), relating the Anglicist vs. Orientalist debate of the time and pointing out the short-term and long-term consequences of Macaulay's 'Minute'. Raja Ram Mehrotra presents characteristic register features of 'English in Private Letters in India' (*EnT* 18:iv[2002] 39–44), while Chandrika K. Rogers looks at stative verbs, prepositional verbs, and present and past perfect tense in her analysis of 'Syntactic Features of Indian English: An Examination of Written Indian English' (in Reppen *et al.*, eds., pp. 187–202).

The bulk of the publications dealing with English in Africa are concerned with SAE. Two books bearing the title *Language in South Africa* have appeared, and since they approach their topic from different angles they complement each other, offering a comprehensive view of the linguistic situation in South Africa. The volume edited by Rajend Meshtrie has a clearly linguistic focus. It contains structural descriptions of all language groups spoken in South Africa and discusses aspects of language contact, gender, language change, and language shift, as well as issues of language planning, policy, and education. The most important contributions for scholars interested in the New Englishes include, first of all, Rajend Meshtrie's introductory 'South Africa: A Sociolinguistic Overview' (pp. 11–26), which sets the scene for the individual linguistic profiles. Roger Lass writes on 'South African English' (pp. 104–26), giving a brief historical overview, a detailed discussion of its socio-phonology, and a very brief account of its morpho-syntax. In the section on language contact, William Bradford and J.S. Claughton report on 'Mutual Lexical Borrowings among Some Languages of Southern Africa: Xhosa, Afrikaans and English' (pp. 199–215) on a more general level, while K. McCormick discusses concrete cases of 'Code-Switching, Mixing and Convergence in Cape Town' (pp. 216–34). S. Slabbert and R. Finlayson look at 'Code-Switching in South African Townships' (pp. 235–57). In the section on new varieties of English, Rajend Meshtrie analyses the change 'From Second Language to First Language: Indian South African English' (pp. 339–55), not only accounting for the language shift, but also explaining the sociolinguistic continuum of this variety. Vivian de Klerk and David Gough examine the historical context, the demographic and linguistic features as well as language attitudes towards 'Black South African English' (pp. 356–78). Finally, three contributions are concerned with issues of language planning. T.G. Reagan looks at 'Language Planning and Language Policy: Past, Present and Future' (pp. 419–33), Sarah Murray addresses 'Language Issues in South African Education: An Overview' (pp. 434–48), and Kathleen Heugh reports on 'Recovering Multilingualism: Recent Language Policy Developments' (pp. 449–75).

These issues are also the focus of Vic Webb's monograph *Language in South Africa: The Role of Language in National Transformation, Reconstruction and Development*, in which he presents a sociolinguistic profile of South Africa and examines the macro-contexts of language planning, and the role of language in administration, nation-building, education, and economic development. He reports on efforts at promoting the Bantu languages and introduces all the institutions concerned with language management. His evaluation of the present situation is not very encouraging because he regards the planning situation as not very effective, despite the efforts which have been made by the present government. A special issue of *WEn* (21:i [2002]) is also devoted to SAE. The editor, Nkonko M. Kamwangamalu, describes 'The Social History of English in South Africa' (*WEn* 21[2002] 1–8). Pat Hill and Susan van Zyl report on 'English and Multilingualism in the South African Engineering Workplace' (*WEn* 21[2002] 23–35) in Witwatersrand, showing how English, Afrikaans, and a number of African languages are all used by the engineers in the course of their work. Vic Webb provides insights into the role of 'English as a Second Language in South Africa's Tertiary Institutions: A Case Study at the University of Pretoria' (*WEn* 21[2002] 49–61), showing that students tend to fail fewer courses if they are taught in their L1. Susan Coetzee-van Rooy looks at 'Cultural Identity Profiles of Afrikaans and Southern Sotho Learners of English: Resource or Hazard?' (*WEn* 21[2002] 63–81), identifying complex patterns which are the basis of several recommendations to improve the teaching of English in South Africa. Elizabeth de Kadt examines 'Gender and Usage Patterns of English in Southern African Urban and Rural Contexts' (*WEn* 21[2002] 83–97), based on a study of schoolchildren from one urban and one rural school in KwaZulu-Natal. Rajend Meshtrie analyses 'Mocklanguages and Symbolic Power: The South African Radio Series *Applesammy and Naidoo*' (*WEn* 21[2002] 99–112) from the 1940s in comparison to authentic SA Indian English data. Johann L. van der Walt and Bertus van Rooy detect a movement 'Towards a Norm in South African Englishes' (*WEn* 21[2002] 113–28), based on production and perception data from speakers of SA Black English (SABE). Daan Wissing is also concerned with 'South African Black English: A New English? Observations from a Phonetic Viewpoint' (*WEn* 21[2002] 129–44), pointing out that speakers of Bantu languages tend to lack certain vowel contrasts of Standard English, but that there are generally no major differences in the pronunciation of SABE of speakers with different L1s. Finally, Bertus van Rooy also reports on 'Stress Placement in Tswana English: The Makings of a Coherent System' (*WEn* 21[2002] 145–60). Using an OT approach on a corpus of 333 polysyllabic words, he finds that there is lexical stress for function words, but a coherent system of stress placement for content words, thus rejecting two previous hypotheses on the subject. Rajend Meshtrie's contribution, 'Building a New English Dialect: South African Indian English and the History of Englishes' (in Watts and Trudgill, eds., pp. 111–33), combines general reflections on the introduction of English in a colonial context and its consequences with a detailed account of the history of SA Indian English. Meshtrie has also done a follow-up study on 'Endogeny versus Contact Revisited: Aspectual *busy* in South African English' (*LangS* 24[2002] 345–58), concluding that Lass and Wright's 1986 paper (*EWW* 7[1986] 201–23) is generally in line with the data in his corpus, but that evidence from other varieties of English suggests that the influence from Afrikaans is weaker than postulated by Lass and Wright. Isabel Diaz and Antonio Lillo present '*Betty Boop's Ready!* Some Aspects of South African Rhyming Slang' (*EnT* 18:ii[2002] 21–7), pointing out that some of the items used in SAE are imported from British, American, or Australian usage while others are local coinages. Liesel Hibbert's paper, 'English in South Africa: Parallels with African American Vernacular English' (*EnT* 18:i[2002] 31–6), compares SABE and AAVE in terms of history, status, and functions. Vivian de Klerk proposes 'Starting with Xhosa English ...

Towards a Spoken Corpus' (*IJCL* 7[2002] 21–42), which is intended to eventually become part of a corpus of spoken SABE because the current SAE component of the International Corpus of English comprises speakers of all sociolinguistic backgrounds and is thus not representative of any variety of SAE in particular. Vivian de Klerk also writes on 'Xhosa as a "Home Appliance"? A Case Study of Language Shift in Grahamstown' (in Wei *et al.*, eds., pp. 221–48) on the basis of quantitative and qualitative research carried out in 1998. Finally, Nkonko M. Kamwangamalu has conducted a questionnaire survey on 'Code-Switching, Code-Crossing, and Identity Construction in a Society in Transition, South Africa' (in Duszak, ed., *Us and Others: Social Identities across Languages, Discourses and Cultures*, pp. 187–210), and arrives at the conclusion that, while code-switching is common, code-crossing is still rare, in his view due to the continued legacy of apartheid.

There are also some publications dealing with other varieties of English in Africa. Jean-Paul Kouega presents a questionnaire survey on the 'Uses of English in Southern British Cameroons' (*EWW* 23[2002] 93–113), outlining the domains in which English prevails and those in which it competes with Pidgin English, French, or local languages. Kari Dako examines 'Code-Switching and Lexical Borrowing: Which is What in Ghanaian English?' (*EnT* 18:iii[2002] 48–54) on the basis of criteria established by Poplack and Sankoff, citing examples of lexical items which are fully integrated in Ghanaian English. Diana Hudson-Ettle reports on 'Nominal *that* Clauses in Three Regional Varieties of English: A Study of the Relevance of Text Type, Medium and Syntactic Function' (*FoLi* 36[2002] 258–73), comparing data from the Kenyan subcorpus of ICE-East Africa with data from ICE-GB and ICE-NZ. In collaboration with Tore Nilsson, Hudson-Ettle also looks at 'Orality and Noun Phrase Structure in Registers of British and Kenyan English' (*ICAME* 26[2002] 33–62), particularly NP premodification, on the basis of four text types from the Kenyan component of ICE-East Africa and two British English corpora, the Uppsala Press Corpus and the Uppsala Corpus of Travel Texts. Almost 3,000 kilometres off the shores of South Africa, Daniel Schreier takes us to the 'Terra Incognita in the Anglophone World: Tristan da Cunha, South Atlantic Ocean' (*EWW* 23[2002] 1–29), outlining the development of this little-known variety, as well as a structural profile and a discussion of various linguistic features with regard to their possible sources.

Moving on to Caribbean English, we welcome the new paperback edition of the *Dictionary of Jamaican English* by Frederic G. Cassidy and Robert B. LePage. This edition means that this invaluable classic is now more widely available to interested scholars and laypersons. The dictionary covers the whole linguistic continuum in Jamaica, from Jamaicanisms in the acrolect to Jamaican Creole lexemes. The spelling system devised by Cassidy and Le Page has long become the standard orthography for the (scholarly) writing of Jamaican Creole. An in-depth study of one area of lexicography is presented in Mervyn C. Alleyne's study of *The Construction of Race and Ethnicity in the Caribbean and the World*, which traces the development and semantic extensions of terms denoting race (like *black* or *white*) in the Caribbean, especially with regard to Puerto Rico, Martinique, and Jamaica. Christian Mair identifies 'Creolisms in an Emerging Standard: Written English in Jamaica' (*EWW* 23[2003] 31–58), presenting data from internet databases and from ICE-Jamaica in order to arrive at a classification of creolisms in written Jamaican

English. Peter L. Patrick and Esther Figuera present the first systematic analysis of 'Kiss-Teeth' (*AS* 77[2002] 383–97), a paralinguistic gesture and its related ideophones (*chups!*) and interjections (*cho!* or *kst!*) which are very frequent in all parts of the Caribbean (both in creole and acrolectal English usage), as well as in AAVE and Gullah.

Turning to creolistics, we find a collection of papers from a symposium on *Pidgin and Creole Linguistics in the Twenty-First Century*, edited by Glenn Gilbert. The contributors comment on the state of the art and the future of creolistics, arriving at quite different conclusions. Jeff Siegel stresses the importance of 'Applied Creolistics in the 21st Century' (pp. 7–48), showing that there is still a lot to be done in terms of the status of pidgins, creoles, and other minority languages in the legal and educational systems. Jacques Arends's paper links 'The Historical Study of Creoles and the Future of Creole Studies' (pp. 49–68). Peter Bakker identifies 'Some Future Challenges for Pidgin and Creole Studies' (pp. 69–92), especially in the area of comparing pidgins, creoles, and mixed languages on a structural level. Michael Aceto is in favour of 'Going Back to the Beginning: Describing the (Nearly) Undocumented Anglophone Creoles of the Caribbean' (pp. 93–120), such as the varieties spoken in Antigua, Bermuda, Carriacou, the Caymans, Dominica, Grenada, Montserrat, the Virgin Islands and several others. John Holm contributes aspects of 'The Study of Semi-Creoles in the 21st Century' (pp. 173–97), focusing on the comparative work of the CUNY research group. Two contributions are concerned with structural developments in creole languages, especially with regard to the formation of inflectional morphology: Anand Seya reports on 'Future Developments in Creole Languages: Moving Away from Analyticity' (pp. 199–228) and Ingo Plag writes 'On the Role of Grammaticalization in Creolization' (pp. 229–46). Claire Lefebvre is concerned with 'The Field of Pidgin and Creole Linguistics at the Turn of the Millennium: The Problem of the Genesis and Development of PCs' (pp. 247–85), stressing the relevance of dialect levelling with regard to her theory of relexification. As in his monograph mentioned above, Donald Winford places 'Creoles in the Context of Contact Linguistics' (pp. 287–354). Finally, Mikael Parkvall is of the opinion that creolists are 'Cutting off the Branch' (pp. 355–67) on which they are sitting by establishing that 'there is nothing structurally peculiar about creole languages' (p. 362). Parkvall recommends that researchers take up issues like the systematic comparison of pidgins, creoles, and other language contact phenomena in order to justify the continued existence of the discipline. The much-debated question of 'Which Route(s) to Creole Genesis' (*JPCL* 17[2002] 265–71) is taken up again by Sarah G. Thomason, who discusses all the hypotheses which have been brought forward previously', finally arguing in terms of paying more attention to SLA research. John H. McWhorter, on the other hand, presents 'The Rest of the Story: Restoring Pidginization to Creole Genesis Theory' (*JPCL* 17[2002] 1–48), taking up an idea that goes back to Hall's life-cycle model and pointing out features which never occur in pidgins and only develop gradually in creoles. Michel de Graff gives a detailed account of 'Relexification: A Reevaluation' (*AnL* 44[2002] 321–414), once again painstakingly compiling counter-evidence against Lefebvre's model. He claims that the underlying assumptions of relexification theory are inconsistent with the sociohistorical and linguistic profiles of Haitian Creole, that the structural properties of Haitian Creole cannot be reconciled with a relexification process, and that relexification is incompatible with our current knowledge about language acquisition.

Of the individual pidgins and creoles under analysis, the Atlantic varieties receive most attention. Susanne Mühleisen presents a comprehensive study of *Creole Discourse: Exploring Prestige Formation and Change across Caribbean English-Lexicon Creoles*. In the first three chapters, Mühleisen covers various theoretical approaches to language prestige, proposing a combination of Foucauldian theory and micro-level textual analysis. In the remaining chapters, she provides three test cases for her model, namely an empirical study of Caribbean creole speakers in London on the basis of informant interviews, a historical study of creole representations in writing (mainly in literature), and a historical account of changing creole representations in translation. She concludes that micro-level changes in the use of creole in the areas covered by her test cases form a 'productive force in the negotiation of language prestige' (p. 263), resulting in higher prestige of the formerly stigmatized creoles. Hubert Devonish's *Talking Rhythm Stressing Tone: The Role of Prominence in Anglo-West African Creole Languages* compares the suprasegmental features of English-based creoles in the Caribbean, South America, and West Africa with special attention given to the evolution of the phonological and suprasegmental systems of the Caribbean creoles, particularly Guyanese Creole, early Saramaccan, and the West African varieties Krio, Cameroon Pidgin, and Nigerian Pidgin within the framework of segmental prominence. Mark Sebba and Shirley Tate analyse '"Global" and "Local" Identities in the Discourses of British-Born Caribbeans' (*IJB* 6[2002] 75–89), pointing out that for these speakers, the Creole (a British variety of Jamaican Creole) signals a global identity, while their variety of English is used as a local (e.g. London, Manchester) identity marker. Michael Aceto analyses 'Ethnic Personal Names and Multiple Identities in Anglophone Caribbean Speech Communities in Latin America' (*LSoc* 31[2002] 577–608) on the basis of data collected on the island of Bastimentos, Panama, where nearly every Afro-Panamanian resident has two names, an official Spanish name and a Creole-derived ethnic name, as in *Liliana* and *Yaya*. He discusses naming practices in general and presents previous research on alternative naming practices in Jamaica, Suriname, St. Lucia, Carriacou, Barbados, the Bermudas, and Belize, and among the Gullah speakers on the Sea Islands off the Carolina and Georgia coast.

Moving on to work on individual creoles, Eithne B. Carlin and Jacques Arends have edited the *Atlas of the Languages of Suriname*, which is divided into three sections. The first deals with the Amerindian peoples and languages (e.g. Arawak), the second with the creole languages (Sranan, Saramaccan, and Ndyuka), and the third with the Eurasian languages (e.g. Surinamese Dutch) spoken in Suriname. With regard to the creole languages, Jacques Arends provides 'The History of the Surinamese Creoles I: A Sociohistorical Survey' (pp. 115–30) and Norval Smith reports on 'The History of the Surinamese Creoles II: Origin and Differentiation' (pp. 131–52), looking at the linguistic aspects. Adrienne Bruyn gives a synchronic account of 'The Structure of the Surinamese Creoles' (pp. 153–82), and the section is completed by Jacques Arends's evaluation of 'Young Languages, Old Texts: Early Documents in the Surinamese Creoles' (pp. 183–205). All contributions contain many illustrations and linguistic examples, which make the *Atlas* an excellent source of reference for anyone interested in the Surinamese creoles and the wider linguistic situation in this multilingual country. Bettina Migge's study of a historical variety of a Surinamese creole, 'The Origins of the Copulas (d/n)a and de in Eastern Maroon Creole' (*Diachronica* 19[2002] 81–153), suggests that the functional properties of these copulas go back to substrate influence from Gbe, while their form is derived from English *that* as a resumptive pronoun and locative *there*. Peter Patrick discusses issues related to 'Caribbean Creoles and the Speech Community' (*SCLOP* 30[2002] 1–27) on the basis of urban Jamaican Creole, addressing topics such as the creole continuum model, the nature of the mesolect, and the benefits of the 'acts of identity' model by LePage and Tabouret-Keller. With regard to specific features of Atlantic creoles, Jack Sidell looks at 'Habitual and Imperfective in Guyanese Creole' (*JPCL* 17[2002] 151–89), pointing out the various grammatical strategies for conveying habituality (preverbal *a*, *doz*, *ustu*), progressivity (preverbal *a* and *-ing*), and imperfectivity (preverbal *a*) and the conditioning factors for their respective use. Michael Aceto also presents the first linguistic account of 'Barbudan Creole English: Its History and Some Grammatical Features' (*EWW* 23[2002] 223–50). He has compiled the basic facts about the linguistic history of this small island in the Lesser Antilles, which was first colonized by speakers of English in the seventeenth century and is today a semi-autonomous dependency of neighbouring Antigua. The descriptive part of Aceto's article is based on a corpus of spontaneous conversations and interviews with eleven informants, and covers preverbal markers, contraction, pronouns, plural markers, the copula, and a few lexical archaisms. Finally in this section, we welcome a contribution on a West African pidgin, namely Dagmar Deuber's '"First year of nation's return to government of make you talk your own make I talk my own": Anglicisms versus Pidginization in News Translations into Nigerian Pidgin' (*EWW* 23[2002] 195–222). On the basis of a corpus of various text-types, Deuber analyses various discourse strategies employed in Nigerian Pidgin broadcast news which are translated from an English version of the news. The different strategies (Anglicisms, pidgin circumlocutions, translations, or idiomatic renditions) were judged by speakers of Nigerian Pidgin by means of an elicitation questionnaire, which yielded that respondents favoured texts in which neither the use of Anglicisms nor the various attempts at pidginization are over-represented.

To round off this section, let me turn to the Pacific pidgins. Geoff P. Smith presents *Growing Up with Tok Pisin: Contact, Creolization and Change in Papua New Guinea's National Language* based on data from young native speakers of Tok Pisin (TP). Smith starts out with an overview of previous research on TP, the sociolinguistic situation in Papua New Guinea, and the historical development of TP. The second chapter is devoted to research methodology, including information on his informants, data collection, and interpretation. The following chapters contain a description of TP phonology, including regional variation, suprasegmentals, and phonological influence of English, morphology, lexicon and word formation, syntax, including TMA marking, verb serialization, relativization and complementation, and discourse processes. Smith carefully compares his data with earlier research and always indicates regional preferences and the ratio of innovations versus conservative standard usage. The most important results of his study are the processes of 'phonological streamlining' (p. 201), which occur in the speech of L1 speakers, contracting function words, and those of morpho-syntactic elaboration and change. Smith's book also contains longer transcribed speech samples from various regions, an extensive bibliography, and numerous illustrations. It is an excellent documentation of the state of TP as an L1.

Peter Mühlhäusler sheds light on 'Pidgin English and the Melanesian Mission' (*JPCL* 17[2002] 237–63) in the nineteenth century, examining mission documents for evidence of the use of Pidgin English in the Pacific as well as in terms of language attitudes. Miriam Meyerhoff examines 'Formal and Cultural Constraints on Optional Objects in Bislama' (*LVC* 14[2002] 323–46), which include discourse factors (e.g. given information), syntactic factors (e.g. grammatical role), and social factors (e.g. age), as well as the transfer of substrate features (e.g. animacy or inalienable possession). While the social factors were found to be insignificant, the type of antecedent and the semantic feature of inalienable possession appear to be the main factors favouring zero-objects. Dennis Kurzon writes on '"Preposition" as Functor: The Case of *Long* in Bislama' (in Feigenbaum and Kurzon, eds., pp. 233–48), pointing out the complex semantic and syntactic functions of *long*, which can also be used to form compound prepositions and to introduce verbal complements.

10. Pragmatics and Discourse Analysis

This year's literature published in the field of pragmatics and discourse analysis testifies to the ever-increasing interest in discourse markers. In *English Discourse Particles: Evidence from a Corpus*, Karin Aijmer investigates the distribution and function(s) of *now, oh* and *ah, just, sort of, and that sort of thing*, and *actually*. She uses the London–Lund Corpus of Spoken English as well as some additional data from the Lancaster–Oslo/Bergen Corpus and the Bergen Corpus of London Teenager Language. Her choice of discourse particles to be examined is based on their frequency of occurrence in the corpus. Two concepts are fundamental to Aijmer's study: indexicality and grammaticalization. Aijmer claims that discourse particles are indexical on an interpersonal level—pointing, for instance, to the speaker's attitude towards the hearer—and on a textual level—pointing to the discourse following or preceding the utterance. She also notes that discourse particles have been grammaticalized to a higher or lower degree, and that during this process they have acquired certain properties. Among these are formal properties pertaining to syntax, style, lexis, and prosody. On the basis of the two concepts, the author analyses the use and functions of individual discourse particles and attempts to establish their core function and meaning.

Finding the 'Basic Meanings of *You Know* and *I Mean*' (*JPrag* 34[2002] 727–47) is the aim of Jean E. Fox Tree and Josef C. Schrock. Their motivation for this is the large number of different and partly contradictory descriptions of the functions not only of *you know* and *I mean*, but of discourse markers in general. The authors claim that once the basic meanings of discourse markers have been determined, their usage can be understood and explained. Jesús Romero Trillo studies discourse markers from quite a different perspective. He is interested in 'The Pragmatic Fossilization of Discourse Markers in Non-Native Speakers of English' (*JPrag* 34[2002] 769–84). For his investigation, the author uses corpora of spoken English produced by native and non-native speakers of two age-groups, namely children and adults. He finds that the use of discourse markers by the adult non-native speakers shows a lack of pragmatic competence and that pragmatic competence is not acquired at the same rate as grammatical competence. This leads him to demand that non-native speakers should be instructed in the use of pragmatic markers much more intensively.

Diane Blakemore's *Relevance and Linguistic Meaning: The Semantics and Pragmatics of Discourse Markers* begins with the somewhat startling statement that 'the aim of this book is to show that there is no justification for writing a book about discourse or discourse markers at all' (p. 1). She qualifies this, however, by adding that there is no justification for writing such a book from the perspective of those who, like Blakemore, follow a relevance theoretic approach to utterance interpretation. What she finds objectionable are two assumptions underlying work on discourse markers: 'the assumption that linguistic meaning can be non-truth conditional and the assumption that there are expressions that mark connections in discourse' (p. 2). The first assumption is addressed by the author in relation to the view that truth-conditional meaning is semantic meaning and non-truth-conditional meaning is pragmatic meaning. Blakemore argues that this view cannot be upheld because semantic representations produced by the grammar are linguistically underdetermined, due, for instance, to lexical ambiguity or indexical indeterminacy, and thus do not encode truth conditions. She offers a different approach to linguistic meaning, based on a previously developed concept of procedural and conceptual encoding. A consequence of this new approach is that a single class of discourse markers cannot be established. Turning to the second assumption, Blakemore proposes that discourse markers should not be analysed as markers of connections in discourse but rather as contributors to the cognitive processes that are the object of study for relevance theorists.

Some of the topics covered by Diane Blakemore are also present in Robyn Carston's *Thoughts and Utterances: The Pragmatics of Explicit Communication*, namely the semantics/pragmatics distinction and linguistic underdeterminacy. Carston first explores the disparity between linguistic meaning and speaker meaning, using her underdeterminacy thesis, which says that 'linguistic meaning underdetermines what is said' (p. 19). She argues that linguistic underdeterminacy is universal, that is, linguistic expressions never fully encode the thoughts they are used to express. She goes on to discuss the explicit/implicit distinction, presenting and commenting upon currently held views on this, and then examines two specific cases: 'and' and negation. Both, Carston claims, are cases of pragmatic enrichment: pragmatic inference can contribute to a proposition expressed in different ways, and enrichment is one of them; thus, pragmatic inference does not necessarily result in implicature but also contributes to explicature.

Jennifer M. Saul takes up Carston's underdeterminacy thesis and analysis of 'and' in 'What Is Said and Psychological Reality: Grice's Project and Relevance Theorists' Criticisms' (*Ling&P* 25[2002] 347–72). Besides these issues she also discusses some aspects of Dan Sperber and Deirdre Wilson's criticism of Grice, for instance those concerning indexical reference and disambiguation. Saul argues that their criticism is based on a fundamental misunderstanding of Grice, who did not, Saul emphasizes, aim to describe the process of utterance interpretation.

In Vanderveken and Kubo, eds., *Essays in Speech Act Theory*, written from the perspectives of philosophy, psychology, computer science, and linguistics, Marc Dominicy and Nathalie Franken, 'Speech Acts and Relevance Theory' (pp. 263–83), examine how speech act theory and relevance theory can be used to study imperative sentences. They suggest that speech act theory can account for instances such as advice, permission, or good wishes in imperative form, whereas relevance theory might be better suited to an analysis of echoicity and irony. Jacques Moeschler's paper in this volume is concerned with 'Speech Act Theory and the Analysis of Conversations: Sequencing and Interpretation in Pragmatic Theory' (pp. 239–61). It is meant as a contribution to the debate concerning the potential use of speech act theory to analyse conversation. He discusses one of the possible approaches and the problems connected with it, namely the interpretation and the sequencing problem, both of which, he claims, can be solved within relevance theory.

In her study of *The Familiar Letter in Early Modern English: A Pragmatic Approach*, Susan M. Fitzmaurice makes use of speech act theory and relevance theory to build a framework for the analysis of a corpus of letters, real as well as fictional ones, written in the seventeenth and eighteenth centuries. In the first two of four chapters of analysis, Fitzmaurice's focus is on the letter-writer. She examines the 'epistolary acts' of advising and of seeking and dispensing patronage, paying special attention to the illocutionary force and perlocutionary effect of these acts. In the next two chapters, she turns to the reader/interpreter. First, she uses one-sided correspondence, including fictional letters, to see how the interpreter is constructed by the letter-writer, and how this construction influences the writing and produces an image of the writer. Following this, the author presents both sides of a correspondence to show how the addressee's response to a letter allows conclusions as to the reading and interpreting processes that are performed, and how this performance as well as the writing of a return letter is determined by the addressee's perspective rather than the thought of what the writer's perspective might be.

The following articles go back even further in history. Teresa Sánchez Roura investigates 'The Pragmatics of *Captatio Benevolentiae* in the Cely Letters' (*JHPrag* 3[2002] 253–72). Her focus is on the politeness strategies employed with this type of expression, which she classifies as a face-threatening act. She argues that the choice of both the topics that are mentioned by the correspondents and their politeness strategies is dependent on the relative closeness of the correspondents and on their social standing. In '"Yf ye wyll bergayne wullen cloth or othir marchandise ...": Bargaining in Early Modern Language Teaching Textbooks' (*JHPrag* 3[2002] 273–97), Monika Becker examines the structure of sales talk. Having argued for the value of this type of discourse for studies in historical pragmatics (although the dialogues in the textbooks are fictitious, they should be seen as 'relatively' authentic representations), she goes on with a discussion of the structural elements of sales talk and their functions, suggesting that the findings are also relevant for the analysis of everyday discourse.

Litosseliti and Sunderland, eds., *Gender Identity and Discourse Analysis*, offers a number of articles. In an introductory chapter, the editors give an overview of the development of gender and language study and discuss salient concepts such as identity, discourse and communities of practice. They especially emphasize a concept that is shared by all the contributors to the book: the concept of gender (identity) as something variable and dynamic and shaped by language. In 'Stunning, Shimmering, Iridescent: Toys as the Representation of Gendered Social Actors' (pp. 91–108), Carmen Rosa Caldas-Coulthard and Theo van Leeuwen investigate toys—representing social actors—and descriptive texts and images of these toys. The display of gender divisions manifest in names, descriptions and visual representations as well as kinetic design of toys is judged as potentially damaging in its influence on children. Lia Litosseliti, '"Head to Head": Gendered Repertoires in Newspaper Arguments' (pp. 129–48), provides an analysis of moral arguments in a debate published in a weekly column in the *Guardian*. The debate is one in a series; it has two participants, who contribute in the form of letters. The author focuses on how gender assumptions influence the structure of arguments and how in turn gender is produced. Gender representation and teacher talk used in connection with language textbooks are the objects of investigation in Jane Sunderland, Maire Cowley, Fauziah Abdul Rahim, Christina Leontzakou, and Julie Shattuck's contribution 'From Representation towards Discursive Practices: Gender in the Foreign Language Textbook Revisited' (pp. 223–55). The authors state that it has been shown in other studies that in recent textbooks stereotypical gender representations are less frequent than they used to be. That is why the authors are not so much interested in textbooks but rather in the actual use of them in language education; in particular, they examine the role of teachers in endorsing, challenging, or shaping gender identities. In the data that Jane Sunderland uses in 'Baby Entertainer, Bumbling Assistant and Line Manager: Discourses of Paternal Identity in Parentcraft Texts' (pp. 293–324), she finds traditional gender images represented, especially that of the mother as the main parent and the part-time father. These pictures, the author admits, may be more or less close to reality, but they do nothing towards showing possible or already existing alternatives.

Marjorie Harness Goodwin examines the processes involved in 'Building Power Asymmetries in Girls' Interaction' (*D&S* 13[2002] 715–30). She focuses on initiating moves made by girls to establish a powerful position within a group of girls of the same age or within a group of younger girls, and the reactions to these moves. She finds behaviour oriented towards disagreement and rudeness rather than politeness and agreement. This leads her to propose a reconsideration of the characterization of same-sex female talk as cooperative and polite, a characterization, she claims, that is based mainly on studies of male–female interaction and thus should not be generalized. The notion of participant orientation in conversation analysis is the topic of Susan Ehrlich's study of 'Legal Institutions, Nonspeaking Recipiency and Participants' Orientations' (*D&S* 13[2002] 731–47). Ehrlich analyses the speech of the complainants, the defendant, and the lawyers, the 'speaking participants', in a sexual assault trial, paying special attention to the strategies employed by the defendant to downplay or eliminate his agency in the events that led to the trial. She finds that, although the interaction of the speaking participants is oriented to the trial and not to gender, gendered categories are made explicit by the 'nonspeaking recipient', the judge. The author argues, therefore, that this wider context of the interaction has to be taken into account to understand how 'gendering' works.

This section will conclude with a discussion of some more studies of institutional discourse. Roberta Piazza investigates 'The Pragmatics of Conducive Questions in Academic Discourse' (*JPrag* 34[2002] 509–27) to set up a model suitable for identifying differing degrees of conduciveness. Factors which contribute to the interpretation of a question as more or less conducive include prosody, change or maintenance of topic, repetition, and the power relationship between speaker and hearer, but especially the hearer's answer. Academic discourse is also dealt with by Bethan Benwell and Elizabeth H. Stokoe, in 'Constructing Discussion Tasks in

University Tutorials: Shifting Dynamics and Identities' (*DisS* 4[2002] 429–53). One aspect of their study was the structure of the tutors' turns spent on setting a task, which they found to consist of a sequence of three parts, referring to 'work-to-come', 'work-thus-far' and 'work-at-hand'. The second aspect was the students' display of resistance to the tasks set by the tutors (silence, laughter, or interruption, for instance) and the tutors' reactions to this. The authors suggest that a wider social and cultural context needs to be considered to explain their findings. Scott Jacobs discusses the conflicting aims of mediators in 'Maintaining Neutrality in Dispute Mediation: Managing Disagreement While Managing Not To Disagree' (*JPrag* 34[2002] 1403–26). On the one hand, mediators have to take a neutral stance in a dispute; on the other, they must try to lead the disputants towards consensus. Jacobs identifies three main strategies employed by mediators: asking questions with a 'leading quality', summarizing the disputants' positions in such a way as to steer the argument in a particular direction, and agreeing with both parties to introduce necessary information at the same time. In 'Resisting the Incitement to Talk in Child Counselling: Aspects of the Utterance "I Don't Know"' (*DS* 4[2002] 147–68), Ian Hutchby demonstrates the difficulties of interpreting the uses children may make of the utterance 'I don't know' in counselling sessions. It may just be a statement of really not knowing something or it may be used strategically to avoid answering questions. Focusing on the case of a 6-year-old boy whose parents have separated, Hutchby shows that the interpretation of the utterance 'I don't know' may be decisive for the success or failure of the counselling session.

11. Stylistics

Cognitive approaches to literature were overwhelmingly present in last year's volume of *Language and Literature* (*L&L* 10[2001]) and now seem ubiquitous in stylistics. A students' introduction, a collection of essays, and three special issues in three different journals—'Literature and the Cognitive Revolution' (*PoT* 23:i[2002]); 'Cognitive Approaches to Figurative Language' (*Style* 36:iii[2002]); and 'Special Issue: Metaphor Identification' (*L&L* 11:i[2002])—suggest that cognitive stylistics is already a full-fledged field. Peter Stockwell's *Cognitive Poetics: An Introduction* provides much more than its title announces because, rather than being a basic undergraduate textbook, it contains a comprehensive overview of the interface between cognitive linguistics and literature. After an introduction subtitled 'Body, Mind and Literature', the reader finds chapters on deixis, cognitive grammar, scripts and schemas, discourse worlds, conceptual metaphor, parable, and text worlds, which explore a wide range of literary texts including, among other things, the OE poem *The Dream of the Rood*, the ME *Sir Gawain and the Green Knight*, poems by George Herbert, John Keats, and Ted Hughes, Emily Brontë's *Wuthering Heights*, Oscar Wilde's *The Importance of Being Earnest*, and science fiction. Written in lively and stimulating prose, Stockwell's *Introduction* fulfils its pedagogical aims by attaching to each chapter a final section entitled 'Explorations', which contains an ample choice of activities inviting students and lecturers to apply the conceptual frameworks introduced to a selection of literary texts. His book will no doubt arouse interest in and promote addiction to the growing field of cognitive stylistics. Semino and Culpeper, eds.,

Cognitive Stylistics: Language and Cognition in Text Analysis, proves that cognitive poetics can no longer be seen as an emergent area of literary studies. All the contributors to this collection of essays aim to show what the combination of cognitive psychology and cognitive linguistics can do for the linguistic analysis of literary texts. The issues they address and the phenomena dealt with are varied; the range of historical periods and genres is equally diverse, including texts by Christine de Pizan and Milton side by side with Stephen King and Bob Dylan. Most of the contributors are well-known scholars in the field: both editors contribute individual chapters that stand next to essays by Catherine Emmott, Margaret Freeman, Willie van Peer, Gerard Steen, and Peter Stockwell. As a whole, it presents an excellent state of the art of the field and will very likely encourage further research in cognitive stylistics.

The editors of *Poetics Today*'s special issue (*PoT* 23:i[2002]) on cognitive approaches to literature, Alan Richardson and Francis F. Steen, have grouped contributions in two sections: 'Toward an Integrated Cognitive Poetics' mostly deals with theoretical issues, and 'Cognitive Historicism: Situating the Literary Mind' contains practical applications of the blending of cognitive science and literary studies. The first section includes a contribution by Mark Turner, 'The Cognitive Study of Art, Language and Literature' (*PoT* 23:i[2002] 9–20), on how the cognitive turn the humanities are experiencing today is part of a larger turn in the contemporary study of human beings, both in the humanities and the sciences, which has its roots in Greek rhetoric. Paul Hernadi, in 'Why Is Literature: A Coevolutionary Perspective on Imaginative Worldmaking' (*PoT* 23:i[2002] 21–42), writes on literature's role in the co-evolution of human nature and cultures. Ellen Spolsky, 'Darwin and Derrida: Cognitive Literary Theory as a Species of Post-Structuralism' (*PoT* 23:i[2002] 43–62), deals with the relation of evolutionary cognitive perspectives to post-structuralist theory and deconstruction. Reuven Tsur shows, in 'Some Cognitive Foundation of "Cultural Programs"' (*PoT* 23:i[2002] 63–89), how cultural and literary forms are constrained by cognitive processes with specific reference to versification. The second section begins with Francis F. Steen, 'The Politics of Love: Propaganda and Structural Learning in Aphra Behn's *Love-Letters between a Nobleman and his Sister*' (*PoT* 23:i[2002] 92–122), on the apparent contradiction between Behn's feminist social agenda and her reactionary political attitudes in relation to the struggle between king and parliament in the 1680s, which is accounted for by Behn's use of the psychology of transgressive love. Next follows Lisa Zunshine, 'Rhetoric, Cognition, and Ideology in A. L. Barbauld's *Hymns in Prose for Children* (1781)' (*PoT* 23:i[2002] 123–39), which proposes a hybridization of cultural studies and cognitive science by means of a cognitive reading of Anna Laetitia Barbauld's writings for children. The section closes with Alan Richardson's 'Of Heartache and Head Injury: Reading Minds in *Persuasion*' (*PoT* 23:i[2002] 141–60), showing how Jane Austen's last completed novel displays an innovative narrative style and a new approach to characterization that relate the novel to the exploration of subjectivity conducted by both Romantic poets and contemporary brain scientists. The special issue ends with an interesting essay by Tony E. Jackson, 'Issues and Problems in the Blending of Cognitive Science, Evolutionary Psychology, and Literary Study' (*PoT* 23:i[2002] 162–79), which serves as respondent to the previous seven articles and looks for the spanner in the interdisciplinary works that blend cognitive science, evolutionary psychology, and literary studies.

Style's issue on cognitive approaches to figurative language (*Style* 36:iii[2002]) contains one article on apostrophe, another one on allegory, and eight articles on metaphor, showing the perhaps excessive attention this area of literary studies receives in cognitive stylistics, to the detriment of other literary phenomena. Alan Richardson, in 'Apostrophe in Life and in Romantic Art: Everyday Discourse Overhearing, and Poetic Address' (*Style* 36 [2002] 363–85), explores, with the help of recent work in cognitive rhetoric, the continuity, rather than the disjunction, between figurative language and everyday linguistic usage as exemplified by the use of apostrophe. Michael Sinding's 'Assembling Spaces: The Conceptual Structure of Allegory' (*Style* 36[2002] 503–23) shows how blending theory can resolve traditional puzzles in the interpretation of allegories. Gerard J. Steen, in 'Identifying Metaphor in Language: A Cognitive Approach' (*Style* 36[2002] 386–407), presents a five-step procedure for metaphor identification based on a theoretical framework which is both cognitive-linguistic and social-scientific, and applies it to Tennyson's 'Now Sleeps the Crimson Petal'. Craig A. Hamilton's 'Mapping the Mind and the Body: On W.H. Auden's Personifications' (*Style* 36[2002] 408–27), looks into Auden's peculiar personification metaphors for the mind and the body with the help of conceptual metaphor and conceptual blending theory. Chanita Goodblatt and Joseph Glicksohn, in 'Metaphor Comprehension as Problem Solving: An Online Study of the Reading Process' (*Style* 36[2002] 428–45), combine literary criticism and cognitive psychology by proposing a Gestalt-Interactionist theory of metaphor, which aims to provide empirical support to explain metaphor comprehension as problem-solving; they do so with the help of a flow-chart that depicts the reading process. Jim Swan, in '"Life without Parole": Metaphor and Discursive Commitment' (*Style* 36[2002] 446–65), questions theories of metaphor as embodied schema (Lakoff and Johnson) and conceptual integration (Turner and Fauconnier), arguing in favour of the role played by top-down judgement from an intuitive subject in the interpretation of figurative thought. Margaret H. Freeman, in 'Cognitive Mapping in Literary Analysis' (*Style* 36[2002] 466–83), applies analogical mapping, conceptual metaphor, and conceptual integration networks to poems by Dickinson in order to argue that authors and readers share implicit cognitive mapping strategies when they write and interpret literary texts. Patrick Colm Hogan argues, in 'A Minimal, Lexicalist/Constituent Transfer Account of Metaphor' (*Style* 36[2002] 484–502), that the constituent transfer approach to metaphor can account for both literal and metaphorical interpretation more elegantly than the cognitive metaphor approach. Raymond W. Gibbs Jr. and Nicole L. Wilson's contribution, 'Bodily Action and Metaphorical Meaning' (*Style* 36[2002] 524–40), is an exploration of how people's understanding of metaphorical language is often constrained by the ways in which we move and experience our bodies; it shows how phenomenological experience, concrete and abstract concepts, and conventional and poetic metaphors are related. Dylan Glynn's 'LOVE and ANGER: The Grammatical Structure of Conceptual Metaphors' (*Style* 36[2002] 541–59) applies one of the basic tenets of cognitive linguistics, the interdependence of meaning and form, to the study of conceptual metaphors in two conceptual domains, LOVE and ANGER, stressing the importance of morpho-syntactic considerations when dealing with the conceptual make-up of a domain.

The special issue on metaphor identification in this year's volume of *Language and Literature* (*L&L* 11:i[2002]) opens with an address by the issue editor Gerard Steen explaining the origin of the PALA Special Interest Group in Metaphor, one of whose aims is the production of a reliable procedure for the identification of metaphors. In addition, in 'Towards a Procedure for Metaphor Identification' (*L&L* 11[2002] 17–33) Steen introduces his 'stepwise procedure' for metaphor identification using the notion of metaphorical propositions to link linguistic metaphors and metaphorical mappings, and applies this procedure to Robert Browning's 'Parting at Morning.' Peter Crisp's 'Metaphorical Propositions: A Rationale' (*L&L* 11[2002] 7–16), introduces the approach to metaphor analysis shared by all contributors to the issue, which combines the tools of propositional analysis developed by discourse psychology with the cross-domain mapping used in cognitive semantics to explain metaphor activity. In 'Linguistic Metaphor Identification in Two Extracts from Novels'(*L&L* 11[2002] 35–54), John Heywood, Elena Semino, and Mick Short explore metaphor identification in fiction with examples taken from Sara Maitland's *Three Times Table* and Salman Rushdie's *The Moor's Last Sigh*, in order to find a means of relating linguistic metaphors in texts to the conceptual metaphors of cognitive linguistics and to probe into the different aesthetic effects achieved by metaphor in two very different kinds of fiction. Peter Crisp, John Heywood, and Gerard Steen combine their strength to detect recurring structural patterns of metaphor usage in 'Metaphor Identification and Analysis, Classification and Quantification' (*L&L* 11[2002] 55–69), and propose a taxonomy of metaphorical mappings. The issue is rounded off with a series of invited comments on metaphor identification from different perspectives: Andrew Goatly from the point of view of text-linguistics (*L&L* 11[2002] 70–4); Zoltán Kövecses from the point of view of cognitive-linguistics (*L&L* 11[2002] 74–8); Raymond W. Gibbs, Jr. represents psycholinguistics (*L&L* 11[2002] 78–84); and Graham Low and Lynne Cameron represent applied linguistics (*L&L* 11[2002] 84–90). If this year's abundant cognitive meal leaves stylistic readers craving for afters, attention could be turned to James W. Underhill, 'Meaning, Language, and Mind: An Interview with Mark Turner' (*Style* 36[2002] 700–17), Craig A. Hamilton and Ralf Schneider's 'From Iser to Turner and Beyond: Reception Theory Meets Cognitive Criticism' (*Style* 36[2002] 640–39), and Hans Adler and Sabine Gross's 'Adjusting the Frame: Comments on Cognitivism and Literature' (*PoT* 23[2002] 195–220).

Two very different books published this year, one on Shakespeare and eModE grammar and the other on postcolonial language, will be of interest to readers of this section. N.F. Blake's *A Grammar of Shakespeare's Language* provides a very useful description of Shakespearian language which helps to explain language use in his plays and poems both stylistically and diachronically. Blake provides his readers with the kind of linguistic information which is often lacking in the commentary of most available editions of Shakespeare's works (for more details on this book see Section 4(*b*)). Ismail Talib, in *The Language of Postcolonial Literatures: An Introduction*, provides a collection of stimulating thoughts about the complex relation between language and literature in the postcolonial condition. An attempt to define English literature by reference to nation, ethnicity, or language is doomed to failure, and this complicates the ways in which postcolonial writers (in Ireland, Scotland, and Wales as much as in South Africa, the US, Canada, Australia, or New Zealand or former British colonies in the Caribbean, Asia, or Africa) deal with a

language which is sometimes both the language of the colonizer and their own
mother-tongue. Exploring the language of postcolonial literatures raises questions
about dialect and 'standard' English that Talib does not ignore, showing how the
relationship of postcolonial writers—from Mark Twain and James Joyce to
contemporary writers—with the language they write in is often a troubled one.
Stylistic choices such as the use of the f-word in recent Scottish fiction or the lack of
number concordance in *Huckleberry Finn* are discussed next to the presence of
native and aboriginal languages inside an English text. Although its attempt to
encompass a very wide spectrum of issues sometimes leaves the reader wishing for
greater depth in analysis and commentary, this is a very useful study of the
relationship between literature and language in a postcolonial world that will be of
interest not only to those specializing in non-English varieties of literature in
English but to anyone who is aware of the importance of language variation
(whether geographical, social, historical, or ethnic) for a full understanding of any
literary text.

Although the focus of Sánchez Macarro, ed., *Windows on the World: Media
Discourse in English*, is not the literary text, the methods of linguistic analysis
deployed in the contributions to this volume will be of interest even to those working
on literary stylistics. Articles in this collection deal with a diverse range of media
texts and genres. Ronald Carter and Michael McCarthy's 'From Conversation to
Corpus: A Dual Analysis of a Broadcast Political Interview' (pp. 15–39) analyses a
political interview with Tony Blair, broadcast on BBC Radio 4, with a combination
of conversation analysis and corpus linguistics. In 'Elusive Masculinities: Locating
the Male in the Men's Lifestyle Magazine' (pp. 41–62), Bethan Benwell shows how
the magazine discourse of masculinity in men's magazines such as *GQ*, *Loaded*,
Arena, *Maxim* and *FHM* is built up out of in-group humour, irony, and a reluctance
to adopt clear ideological positions. Luis Pérez González studies how language use
is being adapted to computer-based media by language users, with examples from
electronically mediated interaction in emergency calls, in 'New Media, New
Behaviours: Emerging   Conversational   Patterns   in   Computer-Mediated
Communication' (pp. 63–90). Anne O'Keeffe, in 'Exploring Indices of National
Identity in a Corpus of Radio Phone-In Data from Irish Radio' (pp. 91–113),
analyses data from the Irish phone-in programme *Liveline* to explore traces of self-
representation and national identity; Phoebe Chang's 'Who's Behind the Personal
Pronouns in Talk Radio? *Cartalk*, a Case Study' (pp. 115–52) also deals with a radio
phone-in programme, *Cartalk*, broadcast on National Public Radio in the US, to
study the use of personal pronouns and their frequency. In '*Heroes* and *Villains*:
Theory-Building in Tabloid Talkshow Storytelling' (pp. 153–75), Carmen Gregori
Signes explores confrontation talk and storytelling in TV tabloid talk-shows,
showing how narratives in these programmes differ from traditional storytelling as
they are mostly constructed by elicitation, through question-answer sequences.
Gordon Tucker, in 'Towards a Semantics of Sun Exposure: The Lexicogrammatical
Construal of Tanning and Burning' (pp. 177–202), examines the semantics of sun
exposure through a corpus study of the lexemes *tan*, *suntan*, and *sunburn* in lexico-
grammatical patterns of transitivity and nominalization. Soledad Pérez de Ayala, in
'Unstable Relationships in Advertising: A Changing Text' (pp. 203–37), dissects an
advertising campaign conducted through personal mailing, in which a leading
international magazine tries to persuade a customer to renew their yearly

subscription, to show how an attractive identity for the customer who renews subscription is constructed through the choice of grammatical subject, mood, and modality. Karen J. O'Keeffe's 'The Quality Press in Ireland: A Linguistic Analysis of Two Text-Types' (pp. 239–63) examines editorials and on-the-spot news reports in two Irish newspapers (*The Irish Times* and *The Examiner*) with the help of Biber's multi-feature/multi-dimensional analytic framework. Claudia Rausell Köster and Pau Rausell Köster show how consumer's reaction to advertisements containing untruths can turn advertising into a challenging discourse in 'Advertising and Consumption: A New Field for Social Participation?' (pp. 265–80). Finally, Margit Böck and Gunther Kress, in 'Unequal Expectations: Child Readers and Adult Tastes' (pp. 281–301), discuss the different expectations children and adult readers entertain about reading books and how they are related to recent transformations in mass media, which have altered the place, value, function, and use of the book.

Pedagogical stylistics has seen an important contribution to the available choice of textbooks with Peter Verdonk's *Stylistics*, which foregrounds the practical analysis of texts over the long-winded discussion of theoretical concepts. Stylistics is introduced as a means of accounting, through detailed analysis, for the diverse interpretations and different kinds of literary effect to be found in a given text. The initial chapters offer a definition of style and stylistics, a discussion of the relation of style to context, and a distinction between representational and referential uses of language. In later chapters, texts by John Betjeman, Kazuo Ishiguro, James Joyce, and Virginia Woolf are analysed in relation to point of view, deixis, given-new information, modality, and speech and thought presentation. Verdonk then shows how the different analytical frameworks introduced in his book can be applied to a sonnet by Seamus Heaney. As in other volumes of the Oxford Introductions to Language Study series, this textbook also includes a collection of key readings, an annotated list of references, and a glossary that students and teachers alike will find very useful. The vitality of Routledge's Intertext series is exemplified by the second edition of Angela Goddard's *The Language of Advertising*, which has been updated to take into account new developments in the field, including internet advertising and how it influences printed texts, new activities for students, and a revised further reading list. A very welcome addition to the series is Jill Marshall and Angela Werndly's *The Language of Television*, which continues the useful work this series has done in the past to provide concise and easily accessible guidebooks to the language of different registers of written and spoken English. It contains a thorough analysis of the grammar of television, with chapters that present ways of examining television genres, live and reported talk, and media discourse. As with previous volumes in the series, self-contained sections introducing concepts and analytical techniques are accompanied by activities and discussion, turning it into a useful tool in courses taught in both media and English studies. Shlomith Rimmon-Kenan's second edition of *Narrative Fiction: Contemporary Poetics* incorporates a revised reading list and a wholly new chapter entitled 'Towards ... Afterthought, Almost Twenty Years Later', offering an assessment of changes experienced by the discipline of narratology from its 'classical' structuralist origins to a new 'post-classical' phase, in which cultural and historical narratologies have turned into an interdisciplinary and context-oriented project. This year's pedagogical output is completed with Daniel Chandler's *Semiotics: The Basics*, a very valuable introduction to key concepts in semiotics that students will treasure and lecturers will reluctantly lend to others. The printed version has a companion volume in its version on the web, which, as the author explains in his introduction, is constantly being updated and contains further material.

Two articles on drama published this year should be foregrounded, given the scanty attention the field of stylistics pays to this type of literary text. Norman Blake's 'On Shakespeare's Informal Language' (*JHP* 3[2002] 179–204) discusses what kind of data should be collected in a dictionary of Shakespearian informal language, and analyses the Nurse's idiolect in a scene from *Romeo and Juliet* to illustrate several categories of informal lexical terms that could be included in such a lexicographical work. Susan M. Fitzmaurice's '"Plethoras of Witty Verbiage" and "Heathen Greek": Ways of Reading Meaning in English Comic Drama' (*JHP* 3[2002] 31–60) explores a range of English comic texts, from Ben Jonson and William Wycherley to Steven Berkoff. She studies the pragmatic features that operate in comic drama, showing that conversational implicatures are often situation-based rather than code-based.

Unlike drama, poetic texts have always attracted the attention of those interested in the interface between language and literature. Laura Hidalgo Downing continues her work on negation (see *YWES* 81[2002] 97–8) in 'Creating Things That Are Not: The Role of Negation in the Poetry of Wislawa Szymborska' (*JLS* 31[2002] 113–32), and explores the role negation plays in the creation of counterfactual realities, showing that a negative sub-world in Szymborska's poems offers a reality which contrasts with the existing one in the text world. Raymond W. Gibbs, Jr., 'Identifying and Appreciating Poetic Metaphor' (*JLS* 31[2002] 101–12), offers two empirical studies on how readers identify metaphors in poetic texts, and demonstrates that metaphor identification does not interfere with the enjoyment of a literary text; rather, it enhances its appreciation and triggers readers' emotional reactions to poems. In 'Processing of Obscure Poetic Texts: Mechanisms of Selection' (*JLS* 31[2002] 133–70), Iris Yaron reports on experiments conducted to discover the strategies adopted by readers when processing difficult poems that are also culturally valued texts; she concludes that, in dealing with obscure poems, readers activate selection processes and pay more attention to strange terms, ignoring ordinary vocabulary. Aided by direct speech, questions, and affective signification, Ming-Yu Tseng, in 'On the Interplay between Speech and Writing: Where Wordsworth and Zen Discourse Meet' (*JLS* 31[2002] 171–98), explores the speech–writing interface in the discourse of Wordsworth's poetry and Zen koans, a genre unique to Zen Buddhism, which shares with the Romantic English poet an interest in the growth of the individual mind. With a view to redressing the scant notice literary criticism has taken of rhythmic and linguistic forms in poetry, Richard D. Cureton proposes a componential theory of rhythm in 'Temporality and Poetic Form' (*JLS* 31[2002] 37–59), applying it to Robert Frost's poem 'Nothing Gold Can Stay'. Metrical stylistics has produced two articles this year. Nigel Fabb's 'The Metres of "Dover Beach"' (*L&L* 11[2002] 99–117) is a study in generative metrics that applies the Bracketed Grid theory of metrical form to Matthew Arnold's famous poem to show that the four different line lengths present in its metrical shape can be generated by variants of the same basic metre, the iambic pentameter. Martin J. Duffell's 'The Italian Line in English after Chaucer' (*L&L* 11[2002] 291–305) suggests that the mixture of French (or pausing) and Italian (or running) lines is a distinguishing feature of the English iambic pentameter.

Fiction continues to be the literary mode which attracts most attention in current stylistics. Aiming to explore the link between the early English novel and journalism from a linguistic perspective, Joe Bray's 'Embedded Quotations in Eighteenth-Century Fiction: Journalism and the Early Novel' (*JLS* 31[2002] 61–75) shows how Lovelace reports speech in Richardson's *Clarissa*, concluding that the use of embedded quotations enables him to distort Clarissa's words. Charles Forceville, in 'The Conspiracy in *The Comfort of Strangers*: Narration in the Novel and the Film' (*L&L* 11[2002] 119–35), offers a comparison of Ian McEwan's novel with Paul Schrader's film version of it and Harold Pinter's script to show how the narrative ambiguity achieved in the novel through the use of free indirect speech is reproduced in the film with a variety of audio-visual resources that build up the cinematic point of view. Florencia Cortés-Conde and Diana Boxer's 'Bilingual Word-Play in Literary Discourse: The Creation of Relational Identity' (*L&L* 11[2002] 137–51), approaches the stylistic effects of bilingual literary discourse in a work by the Chicana writer Sandra Cisneros (*Woman Hollering Creek*), showing how bilingualism enables the existence of *fluid* identities and 'in-group' humour. In 'Such Words in his Things: The Poetry of Bacon's New Science' (*L&L* 11[2002] 195–215), Francis Wilson makes a strong case for the role played by figurative language in Bacon's new science through an examination of his utopian narrative *New Atlantis* in connection with the other Baconian work with which it was published, *Sylva Sylvarum*. Ernest W.B. Hess-Lüttich applies linguistic tools of dialogue analysis to a novel by Theodor Fontane, in '"Evil Tongues": The Rhetoric of Discreet Indiscretion in Fontane's *L'Adultera*' (*L&L* 11[2002] 217–30) in order to show how the use of gossip in fiction enables an author to sketch characters indirectly, offer literary means for the negotiation of social relationships, and assess the society of the time critically. Conrad's short story 'Typhoon' and the presentation of temporal data in fictional narratives is the focus of Ken Ireland's 'Temporal Traps: Simultaneous Phase and Narrative Transitions in Conrad' (*L&L* 11[2002] 231–42), which provides a thorough study of Conrad's narrative technique in the light of similar devices employed by Joyce, Hardy, Moore, Maupassant, and Flaubert. Siobhan Chapman combines Uspenksy's notion of point of view with Geoffrey Leech and Mick Short's cline of speech presentation and Bakhtin's concept of 'voice-images' in '"From their Point of View": Voice and Speech in George Moore's *Esther Waters*' (*L&L* 11[2002] 307–23). He compares Moore's novel to Hardy's *Tess of the D'Urbervilles* to show how Esther's 'voice' is heard throughout the narrative beyond the representation of her own speech since it acts as focalizer. Speech and thought presentation is also the concern of Mick Short, Elena Semino, and Martin Wynne, in 'Revisiting the Notion of Faithfulness in Discourse Presentation Using a Corpus Approach' (*L&L* 11[2002] 325–55); they re-examine, using a corpus-based approach, the issue of faithfulness to an original in reporting and (re-)presenting discourse. Göran Nieragden, in 'Focalization and Narration: Theoretical and Terminological Refinements' (*PoT* 23[2002] 685–97), proposes a revision of the hierarchical levels of focalization and narration and argues that a greater refinement in the degrees of characters' and narrators' involvement in narrative could provide a more flexible typology. In 'From "Under the Rose" to *V*.: A Linguistic Approach to Human Agency in Pynchon's Fiction' (*PoT* 23[2002] 633–56), M. Angeles Martínez explores linguistic differences in two fictional narratives, one of Pynchon's short stories and the revision of it in his novel *V.*, showing the resulting changes in transitivity, which affect the reader's conceptualization of fictional characters. Finally, Bronwen E. Thomas, in 'Multiparty Talk in the Novel: The Distribution of Tea and Talk in a Scene from Evelyn Waugh's *Black Mischief* (*PoT* 23[2002] 656–84), examines the dynamics of multi-party talk, as opposed to group talk, in which participants share goals with a modicum of cohesion present, to show the need for a reassessment of how fictional discourse should be discussed.

Discourse is also the focus of Encarnación Hidalgo-Tenorio's '"I Want To Be a Prime Minister"; or What Linguistic Choice Can Do for Campaigning Politicians' (*L&L* 11[2002] 243–61), a study of the discursive practices of Spanish politicians in the 2000 electoral campaign in Andalusia, which shows how both gender and political stance can influence politicians' discourse choices, suggesting that linguistic features of the winning candidate's speech may have contributed to his success. Two other articles with a more theoretical orientation deserve attention. In 'A Systems Model of the Evolution of Literary Paradigms' (*JLS* 31[2002] 19–36), Piotr Sadowski applies Marian Mazur's cybernetic theory of autonomous systems to a model that aims to account for the evolution of literary paradigms in a macro-historical perspective, from the prehistoric magico-religious beginning of literature to the present Western scientific age. Willie van Peer's 'On the Origins of Style' (*JLS* 31[2002] 1–18) takes as a departure point an experiment showing how computers can perceive stylistic variation better than humans; he next moves on to an assessment of the state of the art in stylistics, and concludes that more interdisciplinarity is required, suggesting how research in stylistics can benefit from sociology and evolutionary psychology. Other articles that readers of this section may find of interest are John Burrows, 'The Englishing of Juvenal: Computational Stylistics and Translated Texts' (*Style* 36[2002] 677–99), which examines fifteen English versions of Juvenal's tenth satire looking for the 'stylistic signature' of the translator; László Halász, Mick Short, and Ágnes Varga, 'A Cross-Cultural Study of Fictional and Non-Fictional Text Understanding' (*Poetics* 30[2002] 195–219), which examines how English, Hungarian, and German senior secondary-school students react to three different text-types (novel, newspaper report, and autobiography); and David S. Miall and Don Kuiken, 'A Feeling for Fiction: Becoming What We Behold' (*Poetics* 30[2002] 221–41), a study of readers' responses to a short story by Sean O'Faoláin, which suggests that during literary reading aesthetic and narrative feelings contribute to the production of metaphors of personal identification that affect self-understanding.

The debate on critical discourse analysis (CDA), which sprouted in the pages of *Language and Literature* in 1995 with a polemical article by Widdowson attacking CDA's practice (see *YWES* 76[1997]), and continued in the following years in the Notes and Discussion section of the same journal (see *YWES* 77[1998] and 78[1999]), emerges afresh with Jean-Jacques Weber's 'The Critical Practices of Henry Widdowson' (*L&L* 11[2002] 153–60) and Widdowson's own views in 'Verbal Art and Social Practice: A Reply to Weber' (*L&L* 11[2002] 161–7). Weber takes issue with the version of literary criticism Widdowson uses to question the practice of CDA; according to Weber, Widdowson makes an unsatisfactory division between literary and non-literary texts, between reference and representation, and favours a reading of literary texts which decontextualizes them. Widdowson's reply to Weber clarifies his position with regard to CDA's practice—which he sees as producing partial interpretations of texts—and to the stylistic analysis of literary texts—which he thinks should differ from the stylistic analysis of non-literary texts since literature is verbal art and literary stylistics should therefore account for its linguistic texture in order to unravel its aesthetic effects.

As in previous years, the last issue of *Language and Literature* ends with Geoff Hall's review article, 'The Year's Work in Stylistics: 2001' (*L&L* 11[2002] 357–72), which continues to provide readers of this section with an alternative source of information and Hall's excellent critical insight. His reflections on the pre-eminence of cognitive approaches in today's stylistics and his invitation to enhance the hybridity of mainstream literary and stylistic studies provide substantial food for thought.

Books Reviewed

Aijmer, Karin. *English Discourse Particles: Evidence from a Corpus.* Studies in Corpus Linguistics 10. Benjamins. [2002] pp. xvi + 299. €95 ISBN 9 0272 2280 0 (Europe), $95 ISBN 1 5881 1284 5 (US).

Alexiadou, Artemis. *Functional Structure in Nominals: Nominalization and Ergativity.* Linguistik Aktuell 42. Benjamins. [2001] pp. vii + 231. €90 ISBN 9 0272 2763 2.

Allen, Rosamund, Lucy Perry, and Jane Roberts, eds. *Layamon: Contexts, Language, and Interpretation.* KCL Centre for Late Antique and Medieval Studies. [2002] pp. xii + 438. £21 ISBN 0 9539 8381 1.

Allerton, D.J. *Stretched Verb Constructions in English.* Routledge Studies in Germanic Linguistics 7. Routledge. [2002] pp. xiii + 299. £65 ISBN 0 4152 5733 6.

Alleyne, Mervyn C. *The Construction of Race and Ethnicity in the Caribbean and the World.* UWIndiesP. [2002] pp. x + 266. £34.50 ISBN 9 7664 0114 4.

Anderwald, Lieselotte. *Negation in Non-Standard British English: Gaps, Regularizations and Asymmetries.* Routledge Studies in Germanic Linguistics 8. Routledge. [2002] pp. xv + 232. £65 ISBN 0 4152 5874 X.

Ayto, John, *The Oxford Dictionary of Rhyming Slang.* OUP. [2002] pp. xvii + 309. pb £9.99 ISBN 0 1928 0122 8.

Baker, Paul, *Polari: The Lost Language of Gay Men.* Routledge. [2002] pp. viii + 215. £55 ISBN 0 4152 6180 5.

Ball, Martin J., and James Fife, eds. *The Celtic Languages.* Routledge. [2002] pp. xi + 682. pb £22.99 ISBN 0 4152 8080 X.

Barbiers, Sjef, Frits Beukema, and Wim van der Wurff, eds. *Modality and its Interaction with the Verbal System.* Linguistik Aktuell 47. Benjamins. [2002] pp. ix + 288. €98 ISBN 9 0272 2768 3.

Barnbrook, Geoff. *Defining Language: A Local Grammar of Definition Sentences.* Studies in Corpus Linguistics 11. Benjamins. [2002] pp. xvi + 28. €88 ISBN 9 0272 2281 9.

Baron, Irène, Michael D. Herslund, and Finn Sørensen, eds. *Dimensions of Possession.* TSLang 47. Benjamins. [2001] pp. vi + 335. €95 ISBN 9 0272 2951 1.

Bauer, Laurie. *An Introduction to International Varieties of English*. EdinUP. [2002] pp. viii + 135. hb £35 ISBN 0 7486 1337 4, pb £10.99 ISBN 0 7486 1338 2.

Baugh, Albert C., and Thomas Cable. *A History of the English Language*, 5th edn. Routledge. [2002] pp. xvi + 447. pb £16.99 ISBN 0 4152 8099 0.

Bendjahballah, S., W.U. Dressler, O.E. Pfeiffer, and M.D. Voeikova, eds. *Morphology 2000: Selected Papers from the 9th Morphology Meeting, Vienna, 24–28 February 2000*. CILT 218. Benjamins. [2002] pp. vii + 317. €105 ISBN 9 0272 3725 5.

Berns, Jan, and Jaap van Marle, eds. *Present-Day Dialectology: Problems and Findings*. Trends in Linguistics 137. MGruyter. [2002] pp. vi + 365. €98 ISBN 3 1101 6781 6.

Blake, Norman F. A. *Grammar of Shakespeare's Language*. Palgrave. [2001] pp. xvi + 416. hb £55 ISBN 0 3337 2590 5, pb £18.99 ISBN 0 3337 2591 3.

Blakemore, Diane. *Relevance and Linguistic Meaning: The Semantics and Pragmatics of Discourse Markers*. CUP. [2002] pp. 208. £47.50 ISBN 0 5216 4007 5.

Bolton, Kingsley, ed. *Hong Kong English: Autonomy and Creativity*. HKUP. [2002] pp. viii + 332. HK$225 (US$29.95) ISBN 9 6220 9553 4.

Boucher, Paul, ed. *Many Morphologies*. Cascadilla. [2002] pp. xv + 267. hb $68.95 ISBN 1 5747 3125 4, pb $28.95 ISBN 1 5747 3025 8.

Boxer, Diana. *Applying Sociolinguistics: Domains and Face-to-Face Interaction*. Impact: Studies in Language and Society 15. Benjamins. [2002] pp. ix + 244. €40 ISBN 9 0272 1851 X (Europe), $39.95 ISBN 1 5881 1198 9 (US).

Brutt-Griffler, Janina. *World English: A Study of its Development*. MlM. [2002] pp. xiii + 215. hb £49.95 (US$74.95) ISBN 1 8535 9578 0, pb £16.95 ($24.95) ISBN 1 8535 9577 2.

Busse, Ulrich. *Linguistic Variation in the Shakespeare Corpus: Morpho-Syntactic Variability of Second Person Pronouns*. Pragmatics and Beyond. ns 106. Benjamins. [2002] pp. xiv + 339. €88 ISBN 9 0272 5346 3.

Bybee, Joan, and Paul Hopper, eds. *Frequency and the Emergence of Linguistic Structure*. TSLang 45. Benjamins. [2001] pp. vii + 492. hb €124.79 ISBN 9 0272 2947 3, pb €43.11 ISBN 9 0272 2948 1.

Bybee, Joan and Michael Noonan, eds. *Complex Sentences in Grammar and Discourse: Essays in Honor of Sandra A. Thompson*. Benjamins. [2002] pp. viii + 363. €110 ISBN 9 0272 2585 0.

Carlin, Eithne B., and Jacques Arends, eds. *Atlas of the Languages of Suriname*. KITLV Leiden. [2002] pp. xii + 345. €37.50 ISBN 9 0671 8196 X.

Carnie, Andrew. *Syntax: A Generative Introduction*. Introducing Linguistics. Blackwell. [2002] pp. xv + 390. pb £17.99 ISBN 0 6312 2544 7.

Carstairs-McCarthy, Andrew. *An Introduction to English Morphology*. Edinburgh Textbooks on the English Language. EdinUP. [2002] pp. viii + 151. pb £10.99 ISBN 0 7486 1326 9.

Carston, Robyn. *Thoughts and Utterances: The Pragmatics of Explicit Communication*. Blackwell. [2002] pp. 432. hb £60 ISBN 0 6311 7891 0, pb £19.99 ISBN 0 6312 1488 7.

Cassidy, Frederic G., and Robert B. LePage, eds. *A Dictionary of Jamaican English*. UWIndiesP. [2002] pp. lxiv + 509. pb £22.95 ISBN 9 7664 0127 6.

Chambers, J.K., Peter Trudgill, and Natalie Schilling-Estes, eds. *Handbook of Language Variation and Change*. Blackwell Handbooks in Linguistics. Blackwell. [2002] pp. 807. £85 ($124.94) ISBN 0 6312 1803 3.

Chandler, Daniel. *Semiotics: The Basics*. Routledge. [2002] pp. xx + 273. hb £45 ISBN 0 4152 6593 2, pb £9.99 ISBN 0 4152 6594 0.

Chantrell, Glynnis, ed., *The Oxford Dictionary of Word Histories*. OUP. [2002] pp. viii + 560. £17.99. ISBN 0 1986 3121 9.

Clankie, Shawn M. *A Theory of Genericization on Brand Name Change*. Studies in Onomastics 6. Mellen. [2002] pp. iv + 244. $109.95 ISBN 0 7734 6955 9.

Conrad, Susan, and Douglas Biber, eds. *Variation in English: Multi-Dimensional Studies*. Studies in Language and Linguistics. Longman. [2001] pp. viii + 255. pb £30.99 ISBN 0 5823 0741 4.

Croft, William. *Radical Construction Grammar: Syntactic Theory in Typological Perspective*. OUP. [2001] pp. 352. hb £49.50 ISBN 0 1982 9955 9, pb £22.50 ISBN 0 1982 9954 0.

Crystal, David. *Language Death*. CUP. [2002] pp. 208. hb £13.95 ISBN 0 5216 5321 5, pb £9.95 ISBN 0 5210 1271 6.

Dehé, Nicole. *Particle Verbs in English: Syntax, Information Structure and Intonation*. Linguistik Aktuell 59. Benjamins. [2002] pp. x + 302. €108 ISBN 9 0272 2780 2.

Devonish, Hubert. *Talking Rhythm Stressing Tone: The Role of Prominence in Anglo-West African Creole Languages*. Arawak Publications, Kingston (Jamaica). [2002] pp. viii + 207. £15.95 ISBN 9 7681 8925 8.

Díaz Vera, Javier E., ed., *A Changing World of Words: Studies in English Historical Lexicography, Lexicology and Semantics*. Rodopi. [2002] pp. xix + 610. €125 ISBN 9 0420 1330 3.

Duszak, Anna, ed. *Us and Others: Social Identities across Languages, Discourses and Cultures*. Benjamins. [2002] pp. viii + 522. € 35 ($135) ISBN 9 0272 5118 5, ISBN 1 5881 1205 5.

Eckert, Penelope, and John R. Rickford, eds. *Style and Sociolinguistic Variation*. CUP. [2001] pp. xv + 341. hb £45 ($65) ISBN 0 5215 9191 0, pb £15.95 ($23) ISBN 0 5215 9789 7.

Enfield, N.J., ed. *Ethnosyntax: Explorations in Grammar and Culture*. OUP. [2002] pp. ix + 325. £45 ISBN 0 1992 4906 7.

Epstein, Samuel David, and T. Daniel Seely, eds. *Derivation and Explanation in the Minimalist Program*. Generative Syntax. Blackwell. [2002] pp. xii + 317. pb £19.99. ISBN 0 6312 2733 4.

Ernst, Thomas. *The Syntax of Adjuncts*. Cambridge Studies in Linguistics 96. CUP. [2002] pp. xii + 555 . £70 ISBN 0 5217 7134 X.

Fanego, Teresa, Belén Méndez-Naya, and Elena Seoane, eds. *Sounds, Words, Texts and Change: Selected Papers from 11 ICEHL, Santiago de Compostela, 7–11 September 2000*. CILT 224. Benjamins. [2002] pp. viii + 310. €109 ISBN 9 0272 4732 3 (Europe), $109 ISBN 1 5881 1196 2 (US).

Fanego, Teresa, María José López-Couso, and Javier Pérez-Guerra, eds. *English Historical Syntax and Morphology: Selected Papers from 11 ICEHL, Santiago de Compostela, 7–11 September 2000*. CILT 223. Benjamins. [2002] pp. viii + 297. €109 ISBN 9 0272 4931 5 (Europe), $109 ISBN 1 5881 1192 X (US).

Feigenbaum, Susanne, and Dennis Kurzon, eds. *Prepositions in their Syntactic, Semantic and Pragmatic Context*. TSLang 50. Benjamins. [2002] pp. vi + 302 . €100 ISBN 9 0272 2956 2.

Féry, Caroline, and Wolfgang Sternefeld, eds. *Audiatur Vox Sapientiae. A Festschrift for Arnim von Stechow*. Studia Grammatica 52. Akademie Verlag. [2001] pp. 541. €84.80 ISBN 3 0500 3672 9.

Fisiak, Jacek and Peter Trudgill, eds. *East Anglian English*. Brewer. [2001] pp. xii + 264. pb £55. ISBN 0 8599 1571 9.

Fitzmaurice, Susan M. *The Familiar Letter in Early Modern English: A Pragmatic Approach*. Pragmatics & Beyond ns 95. Benjamins. [2002] pp. viii + 263. €100 ISBN 9 0272 5115 0 (Europe), $100 ISBN 1 5881 1186 5 (US).

Fodor, Jerry A., and Ernest Lepore. *The Compositionality Papers*. Clarendon. [2002] pp. vi + 220. hb £40 ISBN 0 1992 5215 7, pb £14.99 ISBN 0 1992 5216 5.

Frank, Robert. *Phrase Structure Composition and Syntactic Dependencies*. Current Studies in Linguistics 38. MITP. [2002] pp. xiv + 324. £27.95 ISBN 0 2620 6229 1.

Frawley, William, Kenneth C. Hill, and Pamela Munro, eds., *Making Dictionaries: Preserving Indigenous Languages of the Americas*. UCalP. [2002] pp. xi + 449. pb $24.95 ISBN 0 5202 2996 7.

Gelderen, Elly van. *An Introduction to the Grammar of English: Syntactic Arguments and Socio-Historical Background*. Benjamins. [2002] pp. xxiv + 2000. pb €33 ISBN 9 0272 2586 9.

Gilbert, Glenn. *Pidgin and Creole Linguistics in the Twenty-First Century*. Lang. [2002] pp. vi + 379. £43 ($67.95) ISBN 0 8204 5149 5.

Goddard, Angela. *The Language of Advertising*, 2nd edn. Intertext. Routledge. [2002] pp. xii + 131. hb £40 ISBN 0 4152 7802 3, pb £9.99 ISBN 0 4152 7803 1.

Görlach, Manfred. *A Re-View of Reviews*. Winter. [2002] pp. 227. €25 ISBN 3 8253 1319 0.

Görlach, Manfred. *Explorations in English Historical Linguistics*. Winter. [2002] pp. x + 226. €25 ISBN 3 8253 1320 4.

Görlach, Manfred. *Still More Englishes*. VEAW G28. Benjamins. [2002] pp. xiv + 240. €80 ISBN 9 0272 4887 (Europe), $72 ISBN 1 5881 1263 2 (US).

Gottlieb, Henrik, Jens Erik Mogensen, and Arne Zettersten, eds., *Symposium on Lexicography X. Proceedings of the Tenth International Symposium on Lexicography May 4–6, 2000 at the University of Copenhagen*. Niemeyer. [2002] pp. xvii + 330. pb €92 ISBN 3 4843 9109 X.

Green, Lisa J. *African American English: A Linguistic Introduction*. CUP. [2002] pp. xii + 285. hb £47.50 ISBN 0 5218 1449 9, pb £16.95 ISBN 0 5218 9138 8.

Griffiths, Bill. *North East Dialect: Survey and Word List*. Centre for Northern Studies, University of Northumbria. [2002] pp. 145. pb £7.99 ISBN 0 9511 4728 5.

Griffiths, Bill. *North East Dialect: The Texts*. Centre for Northern Studies, University of Northumbria. [2002] pp. 144. pb £8.99 ISBN 0 9545 0010 5.

Gustafsson, Larisa Oldireva. *Preterite and Past Participle Forms in English, 1680–1790: Standardisation Processes in Public and Private Writing*. Studia Anglistica Upsaliensia 120. Uppsala. [2002] pp. 306. 245kr. ISBN 9 1554 5254 X.

Hagan, Annette I. *Urban Scots Dialect Writing*. Lang. [2002] pp. 345. pb £34 ISBN 3 9067 6839 2.

ENGLISH LANGUAGE 103

Haspelmath, Martin. *Understanding Morphology*. Understanding Language. Arnold. [2002] pp. xiii + 290. hb £50 ISBN 0 3407 6026 5, pb £14.99 ISBN 0 3407 6025 7.

Hasselgård, Hilde, Stig Johansson, Bergljot Behrens, and Cathrine Fabricius-Hansen, eds. *Information Structure in a Cross-Linguistic Perspective*. Language and Computers: Studies in Practical Linguistics 39. Rodopi. [2002] pp. xiii + 228. €55 ISBN 9 0420 1469 5.

Heine, Bernd, and Tania Kuteva. *World Lexicon of Grammaticalization*. CUP. [2002] pp. xii + 387. hb £47.50 ISBN 0 5218 0339 X, pb £17.95 ISBN 0 5210 0597 3.

Hickey, Raymond. *A Source Book for Irish English*. Library and Information Sources in Linguistics. Benjamins. [2002] pp. xii + 541. €150 ISBN 9 0272 3753 0 (Europe) ISBN 1 5881 1209 8 (US).

Hoeksema, Jack, Hotze Rullmann, Víctor Sánchez-Valencia, and Ton van der Wouden, eds. *Perspectives on Negation and Polarity Items*. Linguistik Aktuell. Benjamins. [2001] pp. xi + 366. €115 ISBN 9 0272 2761 6.

Hogg, Richard. *An Introduction to Old English*. Edinburgh Textbooks on the English Language. EdinUP. [2002] pp. ix + 163. hb £35 ISBN 0 7486 1329 3, pb £10.99. ISBN 0 7486 1328 5.

Holder, R.W. *How Not To Say What You Mean: A Dictionary of Euphemisms*, 3rd edn. OUP. [2002] pp. xx + 501. £9.99 ISBN 0 1986 0402 5.

Horobin, Simon and Jeremy Smith. *An Introduction to Middle English*. Edinburgh Textbooks on the English Language. EdinUP. [2002] pp.182. hb £35 ISBN 0 7486 1480 X, pb £10.99 ISBN 0 7486 1481 8.

Hunston, Susan. *Corpora in Applied Linguistics*. Cambridge Applied Linguistics. CUP. [2002] pp. 288. hb £40 ISBN 0 5218 0171 0, pb £14.95 ISBN 0 5218 0583 X.

Iamartino, Giovanni, Marialuisa Bignami, and Carlo Pagetti, eds. *The Economy Principle in English: Linguistic, Literary, and Cultural Perspectives. Proceedings of the XIX Conference of the Associazione Italiana di Anglistica (Milan, 21–23 October 1999)*. Edizioni Unicopli. [2002] pp. 680. pb €39 ISBN 8 8400 0785 7.

Jackendoff, Ray. *Foundations of Language: Brain, Meaning, Grammar, Evolution*. OUP. [2002] pp. xix + 477. hb £25 ISBN 0 1982 7012 7, pb £17.50 ISBN 0 1992 6437 6.

Jackson, Howard. *Lexicography: An Introduction*. Routledge. [2002] pp. x + 190. pb £15.99 ISBN 0 4152 3173 6.

Jackson, Howard. *Grammar and Vocabulary: A Resource Book for Students*. Routledge. [2002] pp. xvii + 202. pb £14.99 ISBN 0 4152 3171 X.

Jones, Charles. *The English Language in Scotland: An Introduction to Scots*. Tuckwell. [2002] pp. viii + 120. £12.99 ($19.95) ISBN 1 8623 2206 6.

Jones, Mari C., and Edith Esch, eds. *Language Change: The Interplay of Internal, External and Extralinguistic Factors*. MGruyter. [2002] pp. ix + 338. $97 (€88) ISBN 3 1101 7202 X.

Jones, Steven, *Antonymy. A Corpus-Based Perspective*. Routledge. [2002] pp. xviii + 193. £55 ISBN 0 4152 6374 3.

Kageura, Kyo, *The Dynamics of Terminology: A Descriptive Theory of Term Formation and Terminological Growth.* Benjamins. [2002] pp. viii + 322. €92 ISBN 9 0272 2328 9 (Europe), $92 1 588 11314 0 (US).

Kastovsky, Dieter, and Arthur Mettinger, eds. *Language Contact in the History of English.* Studies in English Medieval Language and Literature 1. Lang. [2001] pp. 410. pb €46.80 ISBN 3 6313 6243 9.

Kastovsky, Dieter, Gunther Kaltenböck, and Susanne Reichl, eds. *Anglistentag 2001 Wien: Proceedings.* Wissenschaftlicher Verlag Trier. [2002] pp. xiii + 454. pb €60 ISBN 3 8847 6551 5.

Kautzsch, Alexander. *The Historical Evolution of Earlier African American English: An Empirical Comparison of Early Sources.* Topics in English Linguistics. MGruyter. [2002] pp. xv + 335. €68 ($82) ISBN 3 1101 7301 8.

Kerttula, Seija, *English Colour Terms. Etymology, Chronology, and Relative Basicness.* SNH. [2002] pp. 364. pb $45 ISBN 9 5190 4017 X.

Lanehart, Sonja L. *Sista, Speak! Black Women Kinfolk Talk About Language and Literacy.* UTexP. [2002] pp. x + 252. hb £48 ISBN 0 2927 4728 4, pb £19.95 ISBN 0 2727 4729 2.

Legendre, Géraldine, Jane Grimshaw, and Sten Vikner, eds. *Optimality-Theoretic Syntax.* Language, Speech, and Communication. MITP. [2001] pp. xviii + 584. hb $105 ISBN 0 2621 2235 9, pb $42 ISBN 0 2626 2138 X.

Lentz, Katja, and Ruth Möhlig, eds. *Of Dyuersitie & Chaunge of Language: Essays Presented to Manfred Görlach on the Occasion of his 65th Birthday.* Anglistische Forschungen 308. Winter. [2002] pp. 420. €50 ISBN 3 8253 1322 0.

Lightfoot, David W. *Syntactic Effects of Morphological Change.* Oxford Linguistics. OUP. [2002] pp. xi + 409. pb £25 ISBN 0 1992 5069 3.

Lindquist, Julie. *A Place to Stand: Politics and Persuasion in a Working-Class Bar.* OUP. [2002] pp. viii + 204. pb £25 ISBN 0 1951 4138 9.

Linn, Andrew R., and Nicola McLelland, eds. *Standardization: Studies from the Germanic Languages.* CILT. Benjamins. [2002] pp. xii + 258. €89 ISBN 9 0272 4747 1 (Europe), $89 ISBN 1 5811 1366 3 (US).

Litosseliti, Lia, and Jane Sunderland, eds. *Gender Identity and Discourse Analysis.* Benjamins. [2002] pp. viii + 336. €99 ISBN 9 0272 2692 X (Europe), $99 ISBN 1 5881 1213 6 (US).

Löbner, Sebastian. *Understanding Semantics.* Understanding Language. Arnold. [2002] pp. xii + 260. hb £45 ISBN 0 3407 3197 4, pb £14.99 ISBN 0 3407 3198 2.

Long, Daniel, and Dennis R. Preston, eds. *Handbook of Perceptual Dialectology.* Benjamins. [2002] pp. xxv + 412. €174 ISBN 9 0272 2185 5 (Europe), $174 ISBN 1 5561 9757 8 (US).

McArthur, Tom. *Oxford Guide to World English.* OUP. [2002] pp. xiv + 501. hb £19.99 ISBN 0 1986 6248 3, pb £9.99 ISBN 0 1986 0771 7.

McClure, J. Derrick. *Doric: The Dialect of North-East Scotland.* Varieties of English Around the World T8. Benjamins. [2002] pp. 219. €110 ISBN 9 0272 4717 X (Europe), $100 ISBN 1 5881 1130 X (US).

Mackenzie, J. Lachlan. *Principles and Pitfalls of English Grammar*, 2nd edn. Coutinho. [2002] pp. 242. pb €24.50 ISBN 9 0628 3321 7.

McWhorter, John H. *The Power of Babel: A Natural History of Language.* Heinemann. [2002] pp. 327. ISBN 0 4340 0789 7.

Marshall, Jill, and Angela Werndly. *The Language of Television.* Intertext. Routledge. [2002] pp. x + 117. hb £40 ISBN 0 4152 8794 4, pb £9.99 ISBN 0 4152 5119 2.

Meshtrie, Rajend, ed. *Language in South Africa.* CUP. [2002] pp. xvii + 485. £50 ($75) ISBN 0 5217 9105 7.

Meyer, Charles F. *English Corpus Linguistics: An Introduction.* Studies in English Language. CUP. [2002] pp. 220, hb £45 ISBN 0 5218 0879 0, pb £15.95. ISBN 0 5210 0490 X.

Miller, Jim. *An Introduction to English Syntax.* Edinburgh Textbooks on the English Language. EdinUP. [2002] pp. xvi + 190. hb £35 ISBN 0 7486 1254 8, pb £10.99 ISBN 0 7486 1253 X.

Minkova, Donka and Robert Stockwell. *Studies in the History of the English Language: A Millennial Perspective.* Topics in English Linguistics 39. MGruyter. [2002] pp. vi + 496. €98 ($118) ISBN 3 1101 7368 9.

Mitchell, Linda C. *Grammar Wars: Language as Cultural Battlefield in 17th and 18th Century England.* Ashgate. [2001] pp. vii + 218. $79.95 ISBN 0 7546 0272 9.

Morgan, Marcyliena. *Language, Discourse and Power in African American Culture.* CUP. [2002] pp. xiv + 180. hb £42.50 ($58) ISBN 0 5218 0671 2, pb £15.95 ($21) ISBN 0 5210 0149 8.

Morton, James, *Gang Slang: A Dictionary of Criminal and Sexual Slang.* Virgin Books. [2002] pp. 184. pb £5.99 ISBN 0 7535 0699 8.

Mühleisen, Susanne. *Creole Discourse: Exploring Prestige Formation and Change across Caribbean English-Lexicon Creoles.* CLL 24. Benjamins. [2002] pp. xiii + 331. €110 ISBN 9 0272 5246 7, $110 ISBN 1 5881 1297 7 (US).

Myers-Scotton, Carol. *Contact Linguistics: Bilingual Encounters and Grammatical Outcomes.* OUP. [2002] pp. 448. hb $98 ISBN 0 1982 9952 4, pb $29.95 ISBN 0 1982 9953 2.

Nelson, Gerald, Sean Wallis, and Bas Aarts. *Exploring Natural Language: Working with the British Component of the International Corpus of English.* Varieties of English around the World, General Series 29. Benjamins. [2002] pp. xvii + 342. hb €95 ISBN 9 0272 4888 5, pb €55 ISBN 9 0272 4889 3.

Novobatzky, Peter, and Ammon Shea, *Depraved and Insulting English.* Harcourt. [2002] pp. xi + 256. pb $13 ISBN 0 1560 1149 2.

Paolillo, John C. *Analyzing Linguistic Variation: Statistical Models and Methods.* CSLI Lecture Notes 114. CSLI. [2002] pp. xi + 268. hb $65 ISBN 1 5758 6275 1, pb $25 ISBN 1 5758 6276 X.

Partridge, Eric. *A Dictionary of Slang and Unconventional English*, edited by Paul Beale. Routledge. [2002] pp. xxxiv + 1,400. pb £25 ISBN 0 4152 9189 5.

Pérez Quintero, María Jesús. *Adverbial Subordination in English: A Functional Approach.* Language and Computers 41. Rodopi. [2002] pp. xiv + 216. €50 ISBN 9 0420 1360 5.

Peters, Pam, Peter Collins, and Adam Smith, eds. *New Frontiers of Corpus Research: Papers from the Twenty-First International Conference on English Language Research on Computerized Corpora, Sydney 2000.* Language and Computers 36. Rodopi. [2002] pp. 332. €80 ISBN 9 0420 1237 4.

Poole, Geoffrey. *Syntactic Theory.* Modern Linguistics. Palgrave. [2002] pp. xvi + 316. pb £18.99 ISBN 0 3337 7097 8.

Portner, Paul, and Barbara H. Partee, eds. *Formal Semantics: The Essential Readings*. Blackwell. [2002] pp. x + 470. hb £65 ISBN 0 6312 1541 7, pb £19.99 ISBN 0 6312 1542 5.

Preyer, Gerhard, and Georg Peter, eds. *Logical Form and Language*. Clarendon. [2002] pp. x + 522. hb £55 ISBN 0 1992 4460 X, pb £19.99 ISBN 0 1992 4555 X.

Reppen, Randi, Susan M. Fitzmaurice, and Douglas Biber, eds. *Using Corpora to Explore Linguistic Variation*. Studies in Corpus Linguistics 9. Benjamins. [2002] pp. xi + 274. €95 ISBN 9 0272 2279 7.

Rijkhoff, J. *The Noun Phrase*. Oxford Studies in Typology and Linguistic Theory. OUP. [2002] pp. xiii + 428. hb £57.50 ISBN 0 1982 3782 0, pb £24.50 ISBN 0 1992 6964 5.

Rimmon-Kenan, Shlomith. *Narrative Fiction: Contemporary Poetics*, 2nd edn. Routledge. [2002] pp. xii + 193. hb £55 ISBN 0 4152 8021 4, pb £9.99 ISBN 0 4152 8022 2.

Rosenbach, Anette. *Genitive Variation in English: Conceptual Factors in Synchronic and Diachronic Studies*. Topics in English Linguistics 42. Mouton. [2002] pp. xii + 361. ISBN 3 1101 7370 0.

Rothstein, Susan. *Predicates and their Subjects*. Studies in Linguistics and Philosophy 74. Kluwer. [2001] pp. xv + 349. €145 ISBN 0 7923 6409 0.

Saito, Toshio, Junsaku Nakamura, and Shunji Yamazaki, eds. *English Corpus Linguistics in Japan*. Language and Computers 38. Rodopi. [2002] pp. xii + 340. €70 ISBN 9 0420 1369 9.

Sánchez Macarro, Antonia, ed., *Windows on the World: Media Discourse in English*. Universitat de Valencia. [2002] pp. 304. pb €19 ISBN 8 4370 5446 X.

Semino, Elena, and Jonathan Culpeper, eds. *Cognitive Stylistics: Language and Cognition in Text Analysis*. Benjamins. [2002] pp xvi + 333. hb €95 ISBN 9 0272 3331 4, pb €33 ISBN 9 0272 3332 2

Smith, Geoff P. *Growing Up with Tok Pisin: Contact, Creolization and Change in Papua New Guinea's National Language*. Battlebridge. [2002] pp. xi + 244. £18 ISBN 1 9032 9206 9.

Song, Jae Jung. *Linguistic Typology: Morphology and Syntax*. Longman Linguistics Library. Longman. [2001] pp. xix + 406. pb £19.99 ISBN 0 5823 1221 3.

Spears, Richard A. *Slang and Euphemism*, 3rd edn. Signet. [2002] pp. xxvii + 412. pb $7.99 ISBN 0 4512 0371 2.

Stein, Gabriele. *Better Words. Evaluating EFL Dictionaries*. UExe. [2002] pp. x + 246. £39.50 ISBN 0 8598 9719 2.

Stenström, Anna-Brita, Gisle Andersen, and Ingrid Kristine Hasund. *Trends in Teenage Talk: Corpus Compilation, Analysis and Findings*. Studies in Corpus Linguistics 8. Benjamins. [2002] pp. xi + 228. €63 ISBN 9 0272 2278 9 (Europe), $63 ISBN 1 5881 1252 7 (US).

Stockwell, Peter. *Cognitive Poetics: An Introduction*. Routledge. [2002] pp. x + 193. hb £55 ISBN 0 4152 5894 4, pb £16.99 ISBN 0 4152 5895 2.

Stockwell, Peter. *Sociolinguistics: A Resource Book for Students*. Routledge English Language Introduction. Routledge. [2002] pp. xv + 213. hb £50 ISBN 0 4152 3452 2, pb £14.99 ISBN 0 4152 3453 0.

Storry, Mike, and Peter Childs, eds. *British Cultural Identities*, 2nd edn. Routledge. [2002] pp. xiv + 303. hb £60 ISBN 0 4152 7860 0, pb £15.99 ISBN 0 4152 7861 9.

Stray, Christopher, ed., *English Slang in the Nineteenth Century.* 5 vols. Thoemmes/ Edition Synapse. [2002] £395. ISBN 1 8550 6952 0.

Talib, Ismail S. *The Language of Postcolonial Literatures: An Introduction.* Routledge. [2002] pp. vii + 182. hb £55 ISBN 0 4152 4018 2, pb £17.99 ISBN 0 4152 4019 0.

Tietz, Joan Ann. *A Thousand Years of Sweet: A Semantic and Cultural Study.* Lang. [2001] pp. viii + 268. pb £30 ISBN 3 6313 7789 4.

Tottie, Gunnel. *An Introduction to American English.* Blackwell. [2002] pp. xx + 293. hb £55 ($64.95) ISBN 0 6311 9791 5, pb £15.99 ($29.95) ISBN 0 6311 9792 3.

Townend, Matthew. *Language and History in Viking Age England: Linguistic Relations between Speakers of Old Norse and Old English.* Studies in the Early Middle Ages 6. Brepols. [2002] pp. xii + 248. €60 ISBN 2 5035 1292 5.

Trips, Carola. *From OV to VO in Early Middle English.* Linguistik Aktuell 60. Benjamins. [2002] pp. xiii + 356. €120 ISBN 9 0272 2781 0.

Trudgill, Peter, and Jean Hannah, eds. *International English: A Guide to the Varieties of Standard English,* 4th edn. Arnold. [2002] pp. xv + 153. £14.99 ($21.95) ISBN 0 3408 0834 9.

Turner, Lorenzo D. *Africanisms in the Gullah Dialect* [1949]. With a new introduction by Katherine Wyly Mille and Michael B. Montgomery. USCP. [2002] pp. lxi + 321. pb $21.95 ISBN 1 5570 3452 4.

Uriagereka, Juan. *Derivations: Exploring the Dynamics of Syntax.* Routledge Leading Linguists 9. Routledge. [2002] pp. x + 366. £70 ISBN 0 4152 4776 4.

Vanderveken, Daniel, and Susumu Kubo, eds. *Essays in Speech Act Theory.* Pragmatics & Beyond ns 77. Benjamins. [2002] pp. vi + 328. €83 ISBN 9 0272 5093 6 (Europe), $83 ISBN 1 5561 9835 3 (US).

Verdonk, Peter. *Stylistics.* Oxford Introductions to Language Study. OUP. [2000] pp. xiii + 124. pb £8.30 ISBN 0 1943 7240 5.

Wardhaugh, Ronald. *An Introduction to Sociolinguistics,* 4th edn. Blackwell Textbooks in Linguistics. Blackwell. [2002] pp. vi + 408. hb £65 ($69.95) ISBN 0 6312 2539 0, pb £15.99 ($34.95) ISBN 0 6312 2540 4.

Watts, Richard, and Peter Trudgill, eds. *Alternative Histories of English.* Epilogue by David Crystal. Routledge. [2002] pp. xiii + 280. hb £60 ISBN 0 4152 3356 9, pb £17.99 ISBN 0 4152 3357 7.

Weatherall, Ann. *Gender, Language and Discourse.* Routledge. [2002] pp. ix + 177. hb £45 ISBN 0 4151 6905 4, pb £16.99 ISBN 0 4151 6906 2.

Webb, Vic. *Language in South Africa: The Role of Language in National Transformation, Reconstruction and Development.* Impact 14. Benjamins. [2002] pp. xxviii + 356. €110 ISBN 9 0272 1849 8 (Europe), $99 ISBN 1 5881 1189 X (US).

Wei, Li, Jean-Marc Dewaële, and Alex Housen, eds. *Opportunities and Challenges of Bilingualism.* MGruyter. [2002] pp. xii + 346. €98 ($118) ISBN 3 1101 7305 0.

Westin, Ingrid. *Language Change in English Newspaper Editorials.* Language and Computers 44. Rodopi. [2002] pp. xvi + 204. €50. ISBN 9 0420 0863 6.

Winford, Donald. *An Introduction to Contact Linguistics.* Blackwell. [2002] pp. xvii + 416. hb £55 ($69.95) ISBN 0 6312 1250 7, pb £17.99 ($34.95) ISBN 0 6312 1251 5.

Wischer, Ilse, and Gabriele Diewald, eds. *New Reflections on Grammaticalization.* TSLang 49. Benjamins. [2002] pb €65 ISBN 9 0272 2955 4.

Wolfram, Walt, and Erik R. Thomas. *The Development of African American English.* Blackwell. [2002] pp. xv + 237. hb £55 ISBN 0 6312 3086 6, pb £19.99 ISBN 0 6312 3087 4.

Wray, Alison, *Formulaic Language and the Lexicon.* CUP. [2002] pp. xii + 332. £47.50 ($65) ISBN 0 5217 7309 1.

Zwickl, Simone. *Language Attitudes, Ethnic Identity and Dialect Use Across the Northern Ireland Border: Armagh and Monaghan.* Belfast Studies in Language, Culture and Politics. Queen's University Belfast. [2002] pp. xviii + 281. £29.95 ISBN 0 8538 9834 0.

II

Old English Literature

STACY S. KLEIN AND MARY SWAN

This chapter has ten sections: 1. Bibliography; 2. Manuscript Studies, Palaeography, and Facsimiles; 3. Social, Cultural, and Intellectual Background; 4. Literature: General; 5. The Exeter Book; 6. The Poems of the Vercelli Book; 7. The Junius Manuscript; 8. The *Beowulf* Manuscript; 9. Other Poems; 10. Prose. Sections 1, 2, and 3 are by Mary Swan; section 4 is by Mary Swan and Stacy Klein; sections 5 to 9 are by Stacy Klein; section 10 is by Mary Swan with additional material by Stacy Klein.

1. Bibliography

The *Old English Newsletter* 33:ii[2000] was published in 2002, and contains the Year's Work in Old English Studies [1998]. Volume 35:iii[Spring 2002] includes news of conferences and publications. The seventeenth progress report of the Fontes Anglo-Saxonici project (*OENews* 35:iii[2002] 8–9) is contributed by Peter Jackson, and the third annual report on the Anglo-Saxon Plant Name Survey by C.P. Biggam (*OENews* 35:iii[2002] 10–11). This volume also contains Abstracts of Papers in Anglo-Saxon Studies. Volume 35:iv[Summer 2002] contains the Old English Bibliography for 2001 and the Research in Progress listings. Volume 36:i[Fall 2002] includes notes on forthcoming conferences, news of publications, and reports on the *Dictionary of Old English* and the Friends of the DOE fundraising campaign. Martin K. Foys contributes his annual article on digital resources: '*Circolwyrde 2002*: New Electronic Resources for Anglo-Saxon Studies' (*OENews* 36:i[2002] 11–16), Malcolm Godden and Rohini Jayatilaka report on 'The Fontes Anglo-Saxonici Database: The Stand-Alone Version' (*OENews* 36:i[2002] 17–23), and Matthew Z. Heintzelman describes 'English Resources at the Hill Monastic Library' (*OENews* 36:i[2002] 24–31).

    ASE 31[2001] 275–368 contains the bibliography for 2001.

2. Manuscript Studies, Palaeography, and Facsimiles

Two major additions to the range of facsimiles of illuminated manuscripts from Anglo-Saxon England are published. The second volume of Richard Gameson's magnificently produced *The Codex Aureus: An Eighth-Century Gospel Book* is published this year [2002]. This is the last volume to be published in the Early English Manuscripts in Facsimile series, which has played a vital part in enabling and encouraging Anglo-Saxonists to pay attention to the physical detail of manuscripts. In this second volume of the Codex Aureus facsimile, Gameson supplies notes on details of the physical fabric of the manuscript, and follows these with the facsimile of the gospels of Mark, Luke, and John. Andrew Prescott provides a concise and useful introduction to *The Benedictional of St Æthelwold: A Masterpiece of Anglo-Saxon Art. A Facsimile*, which serves to set in context the very high-quality, full-colour and actual-size facsimile of the whole manuscript.

The seventh volume in the Anglo-Saxon Manuscripts in Microfiche Facsimile series, *Anglo-Saxon Bibles and the 'Book of Cerne'*, is published this year, with descriptions by A.N. Doane. It includes the following manuscripts and manuscript fragments: Cambridge, Corpus Christi College 557; Cambridge, University Library L1.1.10; Lawrence, Kansas, Kenneth Spencer Research Library, Pryce C2:1, C2:2, P2A:1; London, British Library Cotton, Claudius B.iv; Cotton Vespasian D.xxi; Harley 3376; Royal 1 B.vii; Royal 1 D.ix; Oxford, Bodleian Library Auct. D.2.14 (2698); Auct. D.5.3 (277688); Lat. Misc. a.3, fo. 49; and Laud Misc. 509 (1042). The accompanying booklet includes full codicological descriptions of all the manuscripts, and notes on their history and contents. The fiches in this volume include supplemental fiches to volume 6 (Christine Franzen, *Worcester Manuscripts* [1998]: *YWES* 81[2002] 133).

Richards, ed., *Anglo-Saxon Manuscripts: Basic Readings*, first published in 1994, was issued in paperback in 2001. Mary Richards's introduction, 'Basic Readings in Anglo-Saxon Manuscripts', surveys the essays in the volume, all but three of which (those by Rumble and Pfaff, and Kiernan's 'Old Manuscripts/New Technologies') were originally published in a variety of journals, collections of essays, and other studies. The volume's contents are: 'Using Anglo-Saxon Manuscripts' by Alexander R. Rumble; 'Self-Contained Units in Composite Manuscripts of the Anglo-Saxon Period' by P.R. Robinson; 'Old Manuscripts/New Technologies' by Kevin S. Kiernan; 'N.R. Ker and the Study of English Medieval Manuscripts' by Richard W. Pfaff; 'Further Addenda and Corrigenda to N.R. Ker's *Catalogue*' by Mary Blockley; 'Surviving Booklists from Anglo-Saxon England' by Michael Lapidge; 'English Libraries Before 1066: Use and Abuse of the Manuscript Evidence' by David N. Dumville; 'Orality and the Developing Text of Cædmon's *Hymn*' by Katherine O'Brien O'Keeffe; 'The Construction of Oxford, Bodleian Library, Junius 11' by Barbara Raw; 'The Eleventh-Century Origin of *Beowulf* and the *Beowulf* Manuscript' by Kevin S. Kiernan; 'The Structure of the Exeter Book Codex (Exeter, Cathedral Library, MS.3501)' by Patrick W. Conner; 'The Compilation of the Vercelli Book' by D.G. Scragg; 'History of the Manuscript', 'Punctuation' (both on Ælfric's First Series of *Catholic Homilies* in London, British Library, Royal 7.C.xii fols. 4–218), and 'The Production of an Illustrated Version' (on *The Old English Illustrated Hexateuch*), all by Peter Clemoes; and 'The Publication of Alfred's *Pastoral Care*' by Kenneth Sisam.

Michelle P. Brown's 2000 Jarrow Lecture, *'In the beginning was the Word':
Books and Faith in the Age of Bede*, is published this year, and presents some of her
very important new findings on the production and preparation of the Lindisfarne
Gospels. Brown situates the Gospels as an element of the cult of Cuthbert, and also
considers the practical prerequisites for the production of this book, and of the
Cuthbert Gospel, the early Lives of Cuthbert, and the Ceolfrith bibles. On the
subject of the making of the Lindisfarne Gospels, Brown describes, and provides
illustrations of, the drypoint sketches and layout markings which reveal the ongoing
process of invention and innovation in the manuscript. She stresses signs of the
influence of Wearmouth/Jarrow on the Gospels' imagery and text, and argues that
the three houses are 'working together to establish a new identity for Northumbria,
and thereby for England' (p. 25).

Richard Gameson offers new studies of two manuscripts. He considers 'The
colophon of the Eadwig Gospels' (*ASE* 31[2002] 201–22)—manuscript Hanover,
Kestner-Museum, WM XXIa, 36—by surveying what is known of Eadwig's career,
and comparing this manuscript with other examples of his work. He concludes that
the Eadwig Gospels might have been commissioned and written for export. In 'The
Insular Gospel Book at Hereford Cathedral' (*Scriptorium* 56[2002] 48–79),
Gameson examines Hereford Cathedral Library manuscript P.1.2 in terms of its
fabric, text, script, decoration, and Anglo-Saxon additions of a record of an
eleventh-century lawsuit, and provides a translation of the two added Old English
documents.

Peter S. Baker explains 'How to Cheat at Editing: The Domitian Bilingual
Chronicle, Anno 679' (*ANQ* 15:ii[2002] 8–13). This is London, British Library,
Cotton Domitian A.viii, fos. 30–70—the bilingual Latin and Old English F-version
of the *Anglo-Saxon Chronicle*. Baker uses it to demonstrate editorial strategies for
dealing with text which not only does not make sense when transcribed, but which
is also not aligned with an annal number in the manuscript. E.G. Stanley ventures
into 'Palaeographical and Textual Deep Waters: <a> for <u> and <u> for <a>, <d>
for <ð> and <ð> for <d> in Old English' (*ANQ* 15:ii[2002] 64–72) by examining
examples of these letter forms in *Beowulf*. He considers the implications of these
examples for the dating of *Beowulf*, and decides that sure conclusions are not yet
reached.

Michelle Brown studies 'Female Book-Ownership and Production in Anglo-
Saxon England: The Evidence of the Ninth-Century Prayerbooks' (in Kay and
Sylvester, eds., *Lexis and Texts in Early English: Studies Presented to Jane Roberts*,
pp. 45–67), with reference to literary, hagiographical, and historical evidence for
female literacy. Examples examined include the works of Boniface and his
correspondents Leoba and Eadburh; the writings of Bede, Aldhelm, and Asser; and
archaeological evidence from Whitby and Barking. Particular attention is paid to
three early ninth-century Mercian prayerbooks, manuscripts London, British
Library Harley 7653 and 2965, and Royal 2.A.xx. Brown presents important indirect
evidence for female ownership of all three of these books.

Cassidy and Wright, eds., *Studies in the Illustration of the Psalter*, includes three
essays of relevance to Anglo-Saxon manuscripts. In 'The Book of Kells and the
Corbie Psalter (with a Note on Harley 2788)' (pp. 12–23), a slightly altered version
of the original, published in Bernard, Ó Cróinín, and Simms, eds., *A Miracle of
Learning: Studies in Manuscripts and Irish Learning* (London [1998], pp. 29–39),

Bernard Meehan draws on a comparison of the first two manuscripts to propose new readings of some scenes depicted in the Book of Kells illustrations. Peter Kidd offers 'A Re-examination of the Date of an Eleventh-Century Psalter from Winchester (British Library, MS Arundel 60)' (pp. 42–54). Basing his argument on a red cross inscribed against the year 1073 in the Easter table of this manuscript, Meehan highlights the danger of 'the assumption that "Anglo-Saxon" decoration and the use of Old English indicates a pre-Conquest date and that Norman-influenced decoration in England dates from after the Conquest' (p. 44), and puts forward two possible contexts for the production of the psalter: the commemoration of the death of Walkelin, bishop of Winchester, in 1098, and Riwallon's appointment as abbot of New Minster in 1072. A report on 'A Handlist of Anglo-Saxon Manuscripts' was given by Helmut Gneuss (in Herren, McDonough, and Arthur, eds., *Latin Culture in the Eleventh Century*, pp. 345–52) before the publication of his Handlist in book form in 2001 (*YWES* 82[2003] 116).

3. Social, Cultural, and Intellectual Background

Janet L. Nelson's 1991 Royal Historical Society presidential address, 'England and the Continent in the Ninth Century: I, Ends and Beginnings' (*TRHS* 12[2002] 1–21) opens with an overview of the ways in which the historiography of the earlier Middle Ages has been shaped by 'periodisation, History's handy organiser, but also its bane' (p. 3). Nelson shows how recent work on the ninth century has provided a more complex picture, and offers a detailed reading of the pontificate of Leo III as a moment when 'England and the Continent meet, figuratively speaking, in Rome' (p. 1). Ann Williams's R. Allen Brown Memorial Lecture, 'Thegnly Piety and Ecclesiastical Patronage in the Late Old English Kingdom', is published this year (*Anglo-Norman Studies* 24[2002] 1–24). Williams summarizes the documentary evidence for bequests to churches by Anglo-Saxon thegns, much of which only survives in later copies. She then focuses on the relationship between eleventh-century wealthy thegns and the churches which stand on land owned by them, and notes that all surviving guild statutes from the tenth and eleventh centuries are for guilds associated with churches.

Pauline Stafford identifies some important 'Political Ideas in Late Tenth-Century England: Charters as Evidence' (in Stafford, Nelson, and Martindale, eds., *Law, Laity and Solidarities: Essays in Honour of Susan Reynolds*, pp. 68–82). The charters in question date from the 990s, are in the name of Æthelred II, and restore lands and liberties to churches. Stafford's careful analysis of these texts demonstrates how valuable charters can be as indicators of mentalities: she shows that all of these Æthelred charters promote an image of the king's youth as a time of ignorance and mistakes, which he now wishes to reverse, and that they thus seek to rewrite the later 980s and revise the king's reputation. Hans Sauer discusses Anglo-Saxon evidence for the language used by—and on behalf of—the rulers of England, in 'The English Kings and Queens and the English Language' (in Lenz and Möhlig, eds., *Of Dyuersitie & Chaunge of Langage: Essays Presented to Manfred Görlach on the Occasion of his 65th Birthday*, pp. 180–98). In 'Where Did All the Charters Go? Anglo-Saxon Charters and the New Politics of the Eleventh Century' (*Anglo-Norman Studies* 24[2002] 109–27), Charles Insley contemplates the question of why the solemn diploma ceases to be used after the mid- to late eleventh century, and also the ideological and practical functions of charters.

Almost the whole of the period, and all of Britain, are encompassed in Edward James's *Britain in the First Millennium*. After chapters dealing with the period of Roman occupation, James turns to the Migration Period, the post-Roman kingdoms, the missionary Church, the eighth century, Viking attack and settlement, and, in the Epilogue, includes some remarks on the Norman Conquest. James's incorporation of all of Britain into his survey is valuable because it sets out an understanding of Anglo-Saxon England in its immediate geographical and cultural contexts. Another wide-ranging study with plenty of relevance to the contexts and connections of Anglo-Saxon textual culture is Lineham and Nelson, eds., *The Medieval World*, and in particular 'Powerful Women in the Early Middle Ages: Queens and Abbesses', by Pauline Stafford (pp. 398–415). Lisa M. Bitel's *Women in Early Medieval Europe, 400–1100* aims to provide 'not just a history of women, but a history of the early European Middle Ages through the eyes of women' (p. 12). Many Anglo-Saxon women, and much Anglo-Saxon evidence, are included in Bitel's study, which is organized thematically, and covers landscape, invasion, migration, barbarian queens, religion, kinship, marriage, motherhood, mobility, and fame.

Religious developments are the subject of a good number of new pieces of work this year. Penance is particularly popular, and Philip G. Rusche's focus is on 'St. Augustine's Abbey and the Tradition of Penance in Early Tenth-Century England' (*Anglia* 20[2002] 159–83). Rusche notes evidence for the use of penitential manuals in England in the period between the ninth-century Viking invasions and the Benedictine Reform, in the form of entries from a glossed copy of *The Penitential of Halitgar* and from the *Penitential of Theodore*, which are preserved in two texts copied by a single scribe in St Augustine's Abbey, Canterbury, in the 930s and 940s. Brad Bedingfield analyses the evidence for 'Public Penance in Anglo-Saxon England' (*ASE* 31[2002] 223–55) in a range of mostly slightly later texts, including works by Wulfstan and Ælfric, an anonymous homily for Ash Wednesday in Cambridge, Corpus Christi College MS 190, the Penitentials of Theodore and Pseudo-Egbert, the Rule of Chrodegang, the *Regularis Concordia*, Pontificals, and the text of the liturgy. He concludes that this rite was 'a powerful and malleable penitential option' in Anglo-Saxon England (p. 255).

'Saint Basil in Anglo-Saxon Exeter' is the subject of Gabriella Corona's article (*N&Q* 49[2002] 316–20). Corona notes the inclusion of a relic of Basil in the Æthelstan relic list, and the fragment of a Latin Life of Basil in the tenth-century Exeter manuscript Exeter Cathedral Library FMS/3. She proposes that this text might have reached England through Æthelstan's importing of relics and books from northern France, and might very soon have been copied there, and interprets its copying in Exeter as a sign of close links with Continental Europe. The Æthelstan relic list also features in Mary Swan's 'Remembering Veronica in Anglo-Saxon England' (in Treharne, ed., *Writing Gender and Genre in Medieval Literature: Approaches to Old and Middle English Texts*, pp. 19–39). Swan tracks evidence for narratives about Veronica in pre-Conquest England, and suggests that the two surviving Old English texts which incorporate parts of this story, and other evidence, including charms and recipes and a relic list entry, indicate that the story of Veronica's miraculous cloth might have been known in Exeter by the late Anglo-Saxon period.

Francesca Tinti tracks the trajectory 'From Episcopal Conception to Monastic Compilation: Hemming's Cartulary in Context' (*EMedE* 11[2002] 233–61). She analyses the composition of this text—a late eleventh-century cartulary from Worcester—in the context of the Worcester monastic community at this date, and especially the relationship of the monastic community to the bishop of Worcester. Tinti argues that the Cartulary shows that this relationship had changed between Wulfstan's initial suggestion that the Cartulary be composed and the succession of Samson in 1096, and that in late eleventh-century Worcester 'the monastic community started to emerge as a distinctive institutional body' (p. 257).

Julie Coleman continues her work on Old English as a key to social categorizations, and specifically to concepts related to women, with 'Lexicology and Medieval Prostitution' (in Kay and Sylvester, eds., pp. 69–87). She notes that the extensive lexis of terms for prostitution in Old English is mostly recorded in a restricted range of text glosses, glossaries, translations, and 'non-native contexts' (p. 69), and speculates that the Danelaw might have provided the social conditions for an identifiable culture of prostitution, and that this might account for Scandinavian-associated terms such as *horcwene* and *portcwene*.

New work on material culture continues to enrich our understanding of the context of Anglo-Saxon literature. The sixth volume of the Corpus of Anglo-Saxon Stone Sculpture, *Northern Yorkshire*, edited by James Lang, was published in 2001. Like the other volumes in the series, it provides the invaluable service of setting out photographs of every surviving piece of sculpture in the area so that scholars can note the range of styles and the potential functions of the items. The photographs form the final section of the volume, which opens with chapters which summarize earlier research, outline the historical background, regional geology, Anglian and Anglo-Scandinavian period forms and ornament, the schools of sculpture identified, and the inscriptions on the sculpture. These chapters are followed by the catalogue of items, which gives detailed measurements, descriptions, and notes on probable date and function. A now lost piece of Anglo-Saxon architectural sculpture, described in the *Liber Eliensis*, is discussed in Virginia Blanton-Whetsell's '*Tota integra, tota incorrupta*: The Shrine of St. Æthelthryth as Symbol of Monastic Autonomy' (*JMEMS* 32[2002] 227–67). Blanton-Whetsell explores the situating of Æthelthryth's corpse as a symbol in the *Liber Eliensis*, and argues that, in this collection of texts, the monks of Ely exploit the meanings of female bodies and female space in order to 'deliberately rewrite their situation, illustrating their community as a physical part of the saint's corporate body in order to appear to be the victims of aggression during the Norman invasion' (p. 222).

Christopher Pickles's *Texts and Monuments: A Study of Ten Anglo-Saxon Churches of the Pre-Viking Period* draws together in its analysis documentary, archaeological, and architectural evidence for the churches in question: St Mary's Abbey, Abingdon; Beverley Minster; Canterbury Cathedral; Canterbury Abbey of SS Peter and Paul; Glastonbury Abbey; Hexham Abbey; Monkwearmouth; Jarrow; York Minster; York *Alma Sophia* monastic church; and York St Michael. Comparative evidence from mainland European churches is presented, and the texts of almost all the English documentary evidence are provided, along with modern English translations.

In 'The Bayeux "Tapestry": Invisible Seams and Visible Boundaries' (*ASE* 31[2002] 257–73), Gale R. Owen-Crocker's focus is on the range of edges in the

Tapestry: the increasingly carefully worked seams which join the panels, the borders which mark its top and bottom edges, and its now lost end. She shows that 'the manufacture of the hanging was a learning process' (p. 258), and stresses the integrity of the design of the whole. Owen-Crocker also published 'Anglo-Saxon Women: The Art of Concealment' (*LeedsSE* 33[2002] 31–51), in which she studies a variety of Anglo-Saxon objects inscribed with individual names, including the Cuthbert embroideries, the Alfred Jewel, finger rings, a brooch, seals, knives, the Coppergate helmet, the Brussels Cross, grave slabs, and stone sculpture. She finds that inscriptions of women's names are often on the back of the object in question, and interprets this as 'a power and self-recognition in these women, which is otherwise hidden from history' (p. 43).

Places and identities are of central concern in a number of new pieces of work on the social context of Anglo-Saxon England. Greta Austin's 'Marvelous Peoples or Marvelous Races? Race and the Anglo-Saxon *Wonders of the East*' (in Jones and Sprunger, eds., *Marvels, Monsters and Miracles: Studies in the Medieval and Early Modern Imaginations*, pp. 25–51) focuses on the version of the *Wonders of the East* in MS London, British Library Cotton Tiberius B.v. Austin shows how 'the *Wonders* can be seen to take the theological position that the marvelous peoples were human and could, therefore, be saved' (p. 50), and argues that modern definitions of race do not fit the categories used in this version of the text, and that 'race' is not an accurate translation of either of the two related terms used in the text: 'genus' and 'cyn'.

In 'Beverly, *Inderauuda* and St John: A Neglected Reference' (*NH* 28[2001] 315–16), John Blair's starting-point is the different versions given by Bede and the Old English text on the resting places of the saints of the burial place of Bishop John of Hexham. He offers evidence from a liturgical calendar written in the mid- or late ninth century in support of the argument advanced by Richard Morris and David Palliser for *Inderauuda* being Beverly. N.J. Higham examines 'Britons in Northern England in the Early Middle Ages: Through a Thick Glass Darkly' (*NH* 28[2001] 5–25). In opening, he notes how the surviving textual evidence for this region and period is so limited that it is very difficult to historicize Britons or non-Christians. He then uses the surviving sources of relevant information to argue that 'British cultural identity may have been far more durable, and far more widespread, in early Northumbria than we imagine' (p. 24). Andrew C. Breeze makes a number of new observations about the geography and territorial politics of early Anglo-Saxon England. In 'Seventh-Century Northumbria and a Poem to Cadwallon' (*NH* 28[2001] 145–52), he draws attention to a Welsh source of information on Northumbria. Breeze provides a modern English translation of the poem, argues that it is indeed of seventh-century origin, and stresses its importance to historians of Northumbria. In 'The Battle of *Alutthèlia* in 844 and Bishop Auckland' (*NH* 29[2002] 124–5), Breeze examines the evidence for the whereabouts of this battle of Rædwulf with a pagan army, and argues for Bishop Auckland as the most likely solution. In 'The Celtic Names of Blencow and Blenkinsopp' (*NH* 29[2002] 291–2), he proposes translations of 'hollow of (the) summit' and 'ridge-top valley', respectively. In 'The Kingdom and Name of Elmet' (*NH* 29[2002] 157–71), Breeze surveys the standard historical sources for Elmet and scholarship on them. He then uses Celtic philology to examine the possible meaning of 'Elmet', and translates two Welsh poems, probably sixth-century, on Gwallog and Madgog, lords of Elmet. In

'The Early Medieval Shires of Yeavering, Breamish and Bamburgh' (*Archaeologia Aeliana* 30[2002] 53–73), Colm O'Brien demonstrates how post-Conquest records of tenure and taxation can shed light on early medieval shire organization, and in particular on the now lost shires of Bamburgh, *Bromic* and *Gefrin*.

Alexander R. Rumble's *Property and Piety in Early Medieval Winchester: Documents Relating to the Topography of the Anglo-Saxon and Norman City and its Minsters* provides scholars with a wealth of documents in edited and translated form, and also with a context in which to read them in the form of the introductory discussions of manuscript sources, authenticity, and the evidence in the documents for historical topography and the history of the city. The volume also includes a useful set of Latin and Old English word-lists, and indexes of biblical references, personal and place names, and references to Anglo-Saxon charters.

The defining and redefining of Englishness continues to be a popular topic for new work. Nicholas Brooks looks to 'Canterbury, Rome and the Construction of English Identity' (in Smith, ed., *Early Medieval Rome and the Christian West*, pp. 221–45) and argues that 'Canterbury's prolonged campaign of *imitatio Romae* was an essential element in the process of English ethnogenesis, that is in a programme of constructing a single *gens Anglorum* ... from a mixed British and Anglo-Saxon population' (p. 222). Alan Thacker goes 'In Search of Saints: The English Church and the Cult of Roman Apostles and Martyrs in the Seventh and Eighth Centuries' (in Smith, ed., pp. 247–77), in order to investigate how the cult of saints developed in this period. He argues that Roman saints and cult forms were introduced into England by Roman missionaries, and that these influenced the beginnings of the development of saints' cults in Anglo-Saxon England, which were only later influenced by Gallic models.

D.M. Hadley's 'Viking and Native: Re-thinking Identity in the Danelaw' (*EMedE* 11[2000] 45–70) surveys the use of ethnic and linguistic labels in the literature of Anglo-Saxon and Anglo-Scandinavian England, and examines the evidence of place names, personal names, and material culture. Hadley argues that ethnic identity seems to have become relevant at particular times, and that research should focus on new ruling elites rather than on the scale of Scandinavian settlement. David N. Dumville examines 'Images of the Viking in Eleventh-Century Latin Literature' (in Herren, McDonough, and Arthur, eds., pp. 250–63), with particular reference to Æthelweard's *Chronicon* and Abbo of Fleury's *Passio Sancti Eadmundi*. Matthew Townend's *Language and History in Viking Age England: Linguistic Relations between Speakers of Old Norse and Old English* offers a wealth of material relevant to the understanding of how English and Anglo-Scandinavian identities are interrelated. Townend surveys the evidence for language contact and the evolution of Viking Age Norse and English, and provides detailed analyses of Scandinavianized Old English place names, and evidence for and descriptions of Anglo-Norse contact in literary texts. In conclusion, he makes a case for 'a situation of adequate mutual intelligibility between speakers of Old Norse and Old English, rather than one involving widespread bilingualism or the use of interpreters' (p. 210).

Archaeology and settlement studies are combined in Geake and Kenney, eds., *Early Deira: Archaeological Studies of the East Riding in the Fourth to Ninth Centuries*, to shed new light on this part of Anglo-Saxon England. The volume contains a preface by Martin Carver; 'Anglo-Saxon Yorkshire: Current Research

Problems' by Philip Rahtz; 'Early Medieval Burials in East Yorkshire: Reconsidering the Evidence' by S.J. Lucy; 'West Heslerton Settlement Mobility: A Case of Static Development' by Dominic Powlesland; 'Anglo-Saxon Settlements and Archaeological Visibility in the Yorkshire Wolds' by Julian D. Richards; 'King Edwin of the Deiri: Rhetoric and the Reality of Power in Early England' by N.J. Higham; 'Middle Anglo-Saxon Metalwork from South Newbald and the "Productive Site" Phenomenon in Yorkshire' by Kevin Leahy; 'Northumbrian Coinage and the Productive Site at South Newbald ("Sancton")' by James Booth; 'The Case for Archaeological Research at Whitby' by Jennie Spofford; 'Monuments from Yorkshire in the Age of Alcuin' by Jim Lang; 'Where are Yorkshire's "Terps"? Wetland Exploitation in the Early Medieval Period' by Robert Van de Noort, and 'The Bioarchaeology of Anglo-Saxon Yorkshire: Present and Future Perspectives' by Keith Dobney, Allan Hall, and Harry Kenward.

Sam Lucy tracks the movement 'From Pots to People: Two Hundred Years of Anglo-Saxon Archaeology' (in Hough and Lowe, eds., *'Lastworda Best': Essays in Memory of Christine E. Fell with her Unpublished Writings*, pp. 144–69). In particular, she deals with the debates about the study of fifth- and sixth-century landscape, settlement, cemeteries, and artefacts, and with the implications of the interdependence of historical and archaeological investigation. Crabtree, ed., *Medieval Archaeology: An Encyclopedia*, includes many entries of relevance to Anglo-Saxonists. Those relating to Anglo-Saxon England are easily found via the index of site entries by country, and the subject guide, both of which form part of the introduction to the volume, and also in the very useful overall index to the volume.

More work on Anglo-Saxon texts and traditions in the post-Conquest period is published this year. Jennifer Ramsay offers 'A Possible "Tremulous Hand" Addition to *The Grave* in MS Bodley 343' (*N&Q* 49[2002] 177–80). The writing in question is three verses which are added to *The Grave*. The development of Anglo-Saxon saints' cults after the Conquest is the subject of David Cox's 'St Oswald of Worcester at Evesham Abbey: Cult and Concealment' (*JEH* 53[2002] 269–85). Cox shows that the altering of the Evesham chronicle, the *Gesta abbatum*, in the twelfth or thirteenth century, in order to remove references to the tenth-century reform of the abbey by Oswald, may indicate a desire by the monks of Evesham to dissociate their house from Worcester, and thus to protect their case for exemption from the authority of the bishops of Worcester. He contrasts this political distancing from Oswald with the continuing veneration of the saint's relic at Evesham. A translation of the second version of William of Malmesbury's *The Deeds of the Bishops of England (Gesta Pontificum Anglorum)* is produced this year by David Preest. This, and David Rollason's edition and translation of Symeon of Durham's *Libellus de Exordio atque Procursu istius hoc est Dunhelmensis Ecclesie: Tract on the Origins and Progress of this the Church of Durham*, should serve to bring to wider attention these works, which are of great interest for their account of Anglo-Saxon ecclesiastical politics. Timothy Graham considers 'William L'Isle's Letters to Sir Robert Cotton' (in Treharne and Rosser, eds., *Early Medieval English Texts and Interpretations: Studies Presented to Donald G. Scragg*, pp. 353–80), which show L'Isle's interest in Old English, and also reveal how Cotton developed his library, and ways in which it was used. Graham edits seven letters from L'Isle to Cotton, and provides a commentary on each of them.

4. Literature: General

A milestone in Anglo-Saxon literary studies is reached with the publication of Biggs, Hill, Szarmach, and Whatley, eds., *Sources of Anglo-Saxon Literary Culture*, volume 1: *Abbo of Fleury, Abbo of Saint-Germain-des-Prés and Acta Sanctorum*. This volume sets the tone for the rest of the eagerly awaited SASLC series, with scrupulously detailed, clear, concise, and well-organized entries on texts which were available to Anglo-Saxon authors. It will act as an impetus to important new work on the transmission of narrative, ideas, and traditions.

ANQ 15:ii[Spring 2002] is devoted to articles on Old English topics, which are reviewed in the appropriate sections of this chapter. J.R. Hall provides an overview of them all in 'Nota Bene: Preface to a Collection of Notes by Various Hands on Various Old English Texts' (*ANQ* 15:ii[2002] 3–7).

The influence of Latin textual and linguistic traditions on Anglo-Saxon literature is the topic of a number of new articles this year. The place of 'Persius's *Satires* in Anglo-Saxon England' is investigated by Phillip Pulsiano (*Journal of Medieval Latin* 11[2001] 142–55). Pulsiano assesses the relationship of the commentary on the *Satires* in manuscripts from Anglo-Saxon England with other versions, and concludes that the *Satires* were known in England at least from the seventh century, were probably introduced through Theodore and Hadrian's Canterbury school, and were well used by prominent Anglo-Saxon authors, including Aldhelm and Alcuin. David Howlett discusses '"Tres Linguae Sacrae" and Threefold Play in Insular Latin' (*Peritia* 16[2002] 94–115) from the fifth to the twelfth centuries, making reference to a range of texts by Anglo-Saxon authors, including Aldhelm and Aedeluald, and the inscriptions on the Franks Casket and the Ruthwell monument.

Martha Bayless encourages scholars to pay attention to 'Alcuin's *Disputatio Pippini* and the Early Medieval Riddle Tradition' (in Halsall, ed., *Humour, History and Politics in Late Antiquity and the Early Middle Ages*, pp. 157–78) by highlighting its relationship to wisdom dialogues, curiosity dialogues, and riddle collections, its varied contents and lively style, and by providing the text of the riddles in the *Disputatio*, along with a translation into modern English, and a commentary.

Michael Lapidge and Jill Mann's 'Reconstructing the Anglo-Latin Aesop: The Literary Tradition of the "Hexametrical Romulus"' (in Herren, McDonough, and Arthur, eds., pp. 1–33) sets out the evidence for 'Aesop' being studied in Anglo-Saxon England. They cite a reference to Aesop in Bede's *De Tabernaculo*, an entry in Patrick Young's seventeenth-century catalogue of Worcester Cathedral Library to a manuscript containing two Old English homilies and a text of 'Aesop', and an Old English translation of an Aesop moral in a composite homily on the Harrowing of Hell in MS Junius 121, written at Worcester in the third quarter of the eleventh century, and argue that the Hexametrical Romulus, which is preserved in a late eleventh-century English manuscript, was composed in Anglo-Saxon England, and that it also provides evidence to support the existence of an Anglo-Latin prose version of this text.

E.G. Stanley sets out to define 'Linguistic Self-Awareness at Various Times in the History of English from Old English Onwards' (in Kay and Sylvester, eds., pp. 237–53), and explores the significance of language in concepts of nationhood and ethnicity, and the ways in which linguistic sensitivity is place- and time-specific.

Robert Stanton's *The Culture of Translation in Anglo-Saxon England* is a major contribution to our understanding of Anglo-Saxon textual practices, and in particular of the ways in which vernacular literature was shaped by its contact with Latin. As he notes in his introduction, 'Translation is a productive cultural practice in that it defines an attitude to received authority and sets the terms under which authority can be reproduced and shifted from one social group to another' (p. 1). This construction and transmission of authority is then analysed in detail in the central chapters of his study, which deal in turn with 'Interpretation, Pedagogy, and Anglo-Saxon Glosses', 'King Alfred and Early English Translation', 'Bible Translation and the Anxiety of Authority', and 'Ælfric and the Rhetoric of Translation'.

Eight unpublished writings by Christine E. Fell are included in Hough and Lowe, eds., *'Lastworda Betst'*. They are: 'Words and Women in Anglo-Saxon England', 'Old English *bearmteag*', 'Mild and Bitter: A Problem of Semantics', 'Some Questions of Layout and Legal Manuscripts', 'Crook-Neb'd Corslets and Other Impedimentia', 'Wax Tablets of Stone', 'Runes and Riddles in Anglo-Saxon England', and 'Introduction to *Anglo-Saxon Letters and Letter-Writers*', which includes sample translations from the draft of this book, on which Fell was working at the time of her death. Other essays in this collection are reviewed in the appropriate parts of this chapter.

This year has seen the publication of several new anthologies and reference guides that are well suited for teaching purposes. Treharne and Wu, eds., *Old and Middle English Poetry*, is a short anthology of medieval poetry, approximately half of which is devoted to Old English texts placed alongside modern English translations. The anthology opens with an introduction by Treharne, which offers valuable historical and literary background, as well as brief remarks on manuscript culture and poetic form. Kevin Crossley-Holland's *The Anglo-Saxon World*, which has long served as a useful edition of modern English translations of Old English poetry and prose, has appeared in a new edition. The new anthology contains the same texts as the 1982 edition but features an updated introduction and eight colour illustrations. Michael Swanton's *English Poetry Before Chaucer* offers close readings of English poems produced between the seventh and thirteenth centuries. The book is a revised and expanded version of Swanton's *English Literature Before Chaucer* [1987]. Individual chapters offer literary analysis and historical context for *Widsith*, *Deor*, *Waldere*, *The Fight at Finnsburh*, *Beowulf*, *Cædmon's Hymn*, *Genesis A*, *Exodus*, *The Dream of the Rood*, *The Wanderer*, *The Seafarer*, *The Ruin*, *The Phoenix*, *Guthlac A*, *Judith*, and *The Battle of Maldon*. Chapters 1–5 deal with Old English texts, the appendix deals with early English prosody, and the endmatter contains brief discussions of various writers, texts, and sources. This is a useful book for scholars looking for a quick and accessible guide to the major critical issues and problems raised by individual Old English texts.

Lambdin and Lambdin, eds., *A Companion to Old and Middle English Literature*, is a reference guide to medieval literature organized by genre. Each chapter offers a critical history of the particular genre in question and a bibliography. Individual chapters that discuss Anglo-Saxon texts include 'Old English and Anglo-Norman Literature' by Robert Thomas Lambdin and Laura Cooner Lambdin; 'Religious and Allegorical Verse' by Gwendolyn Morgan; 'Alliterative Poetry in Old and Middle English' by Scott Lightsey; 'The Beast Fable' by Brian Gastle; 'Chronicle' by

Emma B. Hawkins; 'Epic and Heroic Poetry' by John Michael Crafton; 'The Epic Genres and Medieval Epics' by Richard McDonald; 'Hagiographic, Homiletic, and Didactic Literature' by John H. Brinegar; 'Lyric Poetry' by Sigrid King; 'Riddles' by Michelle Igareshi; and 'Visions of the Afterlife' by Ed Eleazar.

Antonina Harbus has produced two important monographs this year. *Helena of Britain in Medieval Legend* offers rich material for scholars interested in the numerous Anglo-Saxon discussions of St Helena. Moving from late antiquity to the twentieth century, Harbus traces the origins, development, political exploitation, and decline of the legend regarding Helena's British origins, and argues that the legend contributed to the promotion of her cult as a saint and to her continuing appeal over time. Anglo-Saxonists will be particularly interested in chapter 1, which offers a detailed discussion of late Roman historical sources that consider Helena's life, and also chapter 2, which analyses Helena's appearance in Anglo-Saxon and Frankish writings. Although Anglo-Saxon texts never explicitly refer to Helena's British origins, they nevertheless frequently claim that Constantine was born in Britain, a belief that may have arisen on account of Old English translators' misconstrual of the Latin *creatus* (*imperator*) 'raised up (as emperor)' as *accened* 'born'. Harbus maintains that '[t]he imperfect grasp of Latin by writers of Old English adaptations may very well supply the key to the origin of the British Helena legend' (p. 43), and suggests that the legend probably originated in Anglo-Saxon England rather than in late antiquity. Harbus's *The Life of the Mind in Old English Poetry* seeks 'to investigate the emphasis on the mind in the poetic traditions of Anglo-Saxon England, and to outline the model of the mind on which this poetic discourse was structured' (p. 13). Beginning with a detailed discussion of the vocabulary used to refer to the mind and its functions in Old English, Harbus proceeds to examine the mind as depicted in wisdom poetry, poetic saints' lives, elegies, and *Beowulf*. She counters common understandings of Old English poetry as presenting only types rather than unique subjectivities, and shows that particular viewpoints were encapsulated through a poetic emphasis on the mental arena. Harbus argues further that Anglo-Saxon literary culture privileges the universality of mental experience by envisaging mental life as perceptible to both the self and to others, and she shows that the Anglo-Saxons viewed poetry as an important means of self-expression.

R.M. Liuzza, ed., *Old English Literature*, brings together twenty-one essays that have long been recognized as some of the best work in Anglo-Saxon studies. They include 'The Cultural Construction of Reading in Anglo-Saxon England' by Nicholas Howe; 'Anglo-Saxon Lay Society and the Written Word' by Susan Kelly; 'The Making of *Angelcynn*: English Identity before the Norman Conquest' by Sarah Foot; 'Orality and the Developing Text of Cædmon's *Hymn*' by Katherine O'Brien O'Keeffe; 'Reading Cædmon's "Hymn" with Someone Else's Glosses' by Kevin S. Kiernan; 'Birthing Bishops and Fathering Poets: Bede, Hild, and the Relations of Cultural Production' by Clare A. Lees and Gillian R. Overing; 'Kinship and Lordship in Early Medieval England: The Story of Sigeberht, Cynewulf, and Cyneheard' by Stephen D. White; 'The Thematic Structure of the *Sermo Lupi*' by Stephanie Hollis; 'Social Idealism in Ælfric's *Colloquy*' by Earl R. Anderson; 'The Hero in Christian Reception: Ælfric and Heroic Poetry' by Jocelyn Wogan-Browne; 'Didacticism and the Christian Community: The Teachers and the Taught' by Clare A. Lees; 'The Editing of Old English Poetic Texts: Questions of Style' by Roy F.

Leslie; 'Anglo-Saxons on the Mind' by M.R. Godden; '*Sundor æt Rune*: The Voluntary Exile of *The Wanderer*' by Robert E. Bjork; 'From Plaint to Praise: Language as Cure in "The Wanderer"' by Margrét Gunnarsdóttir Champion; 'The Form and Structure of *The Seafarer*' by Peter Orton; 'En/closed Subjects: *The Wife's Lament* and the Culture of Early Medieval Female Monasticism' by Shari Horner; 'The Devotional Context of the Cross before A.D. 1000' by Sandra McEntire; 'Stylistic Disjunctions in *The Dream of the Rood*' by Carol Braun Pasternack; 'God, Death, and Loyalty in *The Battle of Maldon*' by Fred C. Robinson; and 'Maldon and Mythopoesis' by John D. Niles. This diverse collection opens with an introduction by Liuzza that contextualizes the various essays and offers insight into the problems and pleasures of studying Anglo-Saxon literature.

Claire A. Lees and Gillian R. Overing, 'The Clerics and the Critics: Misogyny and the Social Symbolic in Anglo-Saxon England' (in Fenster and Lees, eds., *Gender in Debate from the Early Middle Ages to the Renaissance*, pp. 19–39), explores evidence for debates about gender in Anglo-Saxon textual culture. Beginning from the premise that Anglo-Saxon writers do not routinely use the genre of debate as a vehicle for exploring and enforcing gender norms, Lees and Overing consider how Anglo-Saxon culture may contribute to our understanding of debates about women in the later Middle Ages.

Several works from this year discuss Old English verse form, linguistics, and relations between linguistics and metrics. In a 'A Bard's-Eye View of the Germanic Syllable' (*JEGP* 101[2002] 305–28), Geoffrey Russom engages the long-standing problem of why rules of alliterative metre have proven so difficult to identify, and proposes that recent developments in phonological theory can help to solve problems. He focuses on problems with Sievers's two-stress hypothesis, in the hope of 'using new kinds of metrical evidence to obtain a simpler and more consistent account of the Germanic syllable' (p. 306). Rachel Mines offers 'An Examination of Kuhn's Second Law and its Validity as a Metrical-Syntactical Rule' (*SP* 99[2002] 337–55). Focusing on a sample set of eighteen Old English poems, Mines shows that Kuhn's second law—that a clause upbeat must contain at least one clause-particle and may not consist solely of phrase-particles—is violated in between 1 and 5 per cent of main clauses. She argues that Kuhn's second law 'is neither a metrical rule nor a special rule of poetic syntax', and proposes that '[t]he fact that phrase-particles tend not to occur alone in Old English clause upbeats can be alternatively explained in terms of the Old English lexicon and syntactical rules that occur also in the prose' (p. 355). Göran Kjellmer studies '*Gēata Lēod*: On the Partitive Genitive in Old English Poetry' (*Anglia* 119[2001] 596–605), and questions why the partitive genitive is more commonly found in Old English poetry than in prose. Considering a sample set of Old English poetic and prose texts, Kjellmer finds that the very late Old English poem *The Battle of Maldon* contains fewer partitive genitives than earlier poems, and argues that chronology (that is, the fact that most Old English poetry was likely to have been composed earlier than the prose) plays an important part in underlining the distinction between the styles of prose and verse texts. Minkova and Stockwell, eds., *Studies in the History of the English Language: A Millennial Perspective*, contains several essays on historical linguistics that are relevant to Anglo-Saxon studies: Thomas Cable, 'Issues for a New History of English Prosody' (pp. 125–51); Geoffrey Russom, 'Dating Criteria for Old English Poems' (pp. 244–65); Ans van Kemenade, 'Word Order in Old English Prose and

Poetry: The Position of Finite Verbs and Adverbs' (pp. 355–71); and Jeong-Hoon Lee, 'The "Have" Perfect in Old English: How Close was it to the Modern English Perfect?' (pp. 373–97).

Several important items from last year escaped notice. Mary Blockley's *Aspects of Old English Poetic Syntax: Where Clauses Begin* investigates the ways in which Old English poetry and prose signal the beginning and ending of clauses. Focusing on four of the most common and most syntactically important words in Old English (*ond*, *þa*, *ac*, and *þæt*), as well as such aspects of clauses as verb-initial order, negative contraction, and unexpressed but understood subjects, Blockley elucidates how these words and structures mark the relationships between phrases and clauses. She draws on a range of poetic and prose writings to shed fresh light on the rules that govern syntactic relationships and to show how understandings of clause boundaries crucially affect our interpretation of Old English texts.

Clare A. Lees and Gillian R. Overing's *Double Agents: Women and Clerical Culture in Anglo-Saxon England* offers a substantial contribution to our understanding of women's relationship to culture in Anglo-Saxon England. Departing from former studies that seek to examine women as they are depicted in historical and literary texts, this book investigates how textual forms and literary representations are themselves partly responsible for the absence and presence of women in the historical record. Drawing on both contemporary critical theory and a host of Anglo-Saxon texts, Lees and Overing raise questions about the place of Anglo-Saxon literature in cultural studies at large, and show how Anglo-Saxonists might productively engage with larger critical conversations about culture, subjectivity, and identity without sacrificing historical particularity. Individual chapters deal with Bede and patristic understandings of maternity, women's relationship to orality and literacy, gendered sanctity, and the female body as a site for patristic metaphor. Anglo-Saxonists will be especially interested in the discussion of Wisdom in Pseudo-Bede's *Collectanea*, a recently edited text that has heretofore received little attention.

Nicole Guenther Discenza examines 'Wealth and Wisdom: Symbolic Capital and the Ruler in the Translational Program of Alfred the Great' (*Exemplaria* 13[2001] 433–67). Focusing mainly on the prologues of the Alfredian translations, especially the preface to the *Pastoral Care*, Discenza argues that these texts 'constantly slip … back and forth between the idea of wisdom as wealth and the idea that wisdom supplants wealth' (p. 466). The Alfredian translations and prefaces thus 'attempted to revalue wisdom and wealth, making "wisdom" a commodity whose worth the Anglo-Saxons could recognize as easily as they recognized the value of gold' (p. 467).

The year 2001 also saw the issuing of a sixth edition of Bruce Mitchell and Fred C. Robinson's *A Guide to Old English*. The sixth edition adds two texts, *Wulf and Eadwacer* and *Judith*, as well as a paragraph on *Judith* 186b–95a in the section on punctuation. It also contains minor variations and additions to keep the book up-to-date. Otherwise, most of the book remains unchanged.

The study of Anglo-Saxon literature features in all of the essays in Treharne, ed., *Vital Signs: English in Medieval Studies in Twenty-First Century Higher Education*. Treharne's own contribution, 'Introduction: The Current State of Medieval Studies' (pp. 1–5), surveys the political climate for the teaching of Old English in universities in Britain and Northern Ireland, and counters the view that the study of medieval

English is in decline. Wendy Scase, in 'Medieval Studies and the Future of English' (pp. 7–15), addresses the ways in which the study of early English is contributing to the development of the discipline of English 'as the discipline responds to and engages with intellectual, cultural and social change' (p. 15). Richard K. Emerson assesses 'Medieval Studies at the Beginning of the New Millennium' (pp. 17–27) in terms of the engagement of scholars of medieval English with critical theories, new technologies, and pedagogy, and urges further scholarly engagement with popular medievalism. Robert E. Bjork sets out 'The Portfolio for Medieval Studies' (pp. 29–34), identifies three 'health indicators' (p. 29)—organizations, publications, and electronic resources—and concludes that diversification and flexibility are important, and that signs for the future are good.

5. The Exeter Book

Several essays have appeared on *The Wanderer*. Andy Orchard argues for 'Re-Reading *The Wanderer*: The Value of Cross-References' (in Hall, ed., *Via Crucis*, pp. 1–26). He examines intertextual links between *The Wanderer* and such texts as *The Dream of the Rood*, *Deor*, *Homiletic Fragment 2* (from the Exeter Book), Vercelli Homily 10, and the Lord's Prayer, and argues that these cross-references are the deliberate work of a highly skilled poet who sought to create a 'heroic homily' (p. 26) that would blend imagery, themes, thoughts, and structuring techniques from both secular poetic and homiletic prose traditions. Recognition of these intertextual echoes is invited through intratextual echo and repetition. Rosemary Greentree, 'The Wanderer's Horizon: A Note on *ofer waþema gebind*' (*Neophil* 86[2002] 307–9), reconsiders the idea of frozen waves that is commonly associated with the phrase *ofer waþema gebind*. She argues that a consideration of seafaring conditions, namely, the restricted field of vision available to people rowing on the sea, offers another plausible explanation for the idea of being bound by waves.

The female-voiced elegies in The Exeter Book continue to generate exciting new work. Pat Belanoff's '*Ides … geomrode giddum*: The Old English Female Lament' (in Klinck and Rasmussen, eds., *Medieval Woman's Song: Cross-Cultural Approaches*, pp. 29–46) offers an important contribution to our understanding of the gendered nature of lament in Old English poetry. Placing *Wulf and Eadwacer* and *The Wife's Lament* alongside such male-voiced laments as *The Wanderer* and *The Seafarer*, Belanoff argues that the female-voiced laments contain various features which distinguish them from male-voiced laments: an intense focus on the present, a sense of the impossibility of consolation, and a strict adherence to the individual rather than the generalized voice. However, Belanoff also identifies striking differences between the two female-voiced laments, and she argues that, while the speaker of *The Wife's Lament* has been immobilized by sorrow, the woman in *Wulf and Eadwacer* has been mobilized by her sorrow to look forward to violent action. Such differences between the two poems render the language and thematics of *The Wife's Lament* closer to the elegiac tradition, and *Wulf and Eadwacer* closer to the heroic. Alaric Hall considers 'The Images and Structure of *The Wife's Lament*' (*LeedsSE* 33[2002] 1–29). Focusing on the poem's punctuation, structure, and analogues, Hall argues that '[t]he situations of the speaker and her *freond* are, then, neither merely gloomy landscapes, nor purely pathetic fallacy: they involve distinct motifs, possibly including "women's/lovers' lament" figures, describing environments with images not only of misery, but also, it seems, inversions of the paradisical—images of the hellish' (p. 22). Thomas D. Hill reconsiders possible meanings for the phrase "'Leger weardiað": *The Wife's Lament* 34b' (*ANQ* 15[2002] 34–7). Pointing to the fact that *leger* is cognate with Old Norse-Icelandic *legr* and that *leir* is well attested in Middle English in the sense of 'bed', Hill argues that the phrase *leger weardiað* refers to the sharing of a bed rather than a grave or sickbed.

In another article, 'The Old English Dough Riddle and the Power of Women's Magic: The Traditional Context of Exeter Book Riddle 45' (in Hall, ed., pp. 50–60), Thomas D. Hill explores literary and folkloric analogues to Riddle 45. Hill reminds us that, while some of the Exeter Book riddles derive from the Latin riddle tradition, Riddle 45 more closely parallels accounts of women and dough found in later English folk tradition and in early medieval accounts of ritual magic. Although these analogues exhibit a wide range of attitudes towards women's use of dough, they nevertheless display a shared sense of dough as a rich symbol of female power within the home.

Dieter Bitterli's 'Exeter Book Riddle 15: Some Points for the Porcupine' (*Anglia* 120[2002] 461–87) re-examines solutions commonly proposed to Riddle 15 (badger, fox), arguing that, while the porcupine is not indigenous to England, it nevertheless appears in numerous Latin texts that inform the Anglo-Saxon riddling tradition and is the most likely solution to Riddle 15.

In 'A Reconsideration of the Structure of *Guthlac A*: The Extremes of Saintliness' (*JEGP* 101[2002] 185–200), Manish Sharma argues that 'each of the three critical episodes of *Guthlac A* depicts an approach to a threshold' (p. 200), and that the poem should thus be read as 'essentially tripartite in structure' (p. 186). Focusing on 'the binding motif of physical and spiritual "ascension" that runs throughout the poem' (p. 200), Sharma maintains that the structure of *Guthlac A* renders Guthlac 'inextricably associated with limits, and [emphasizes] his status as a figure upon the extreme boundaries of the human' (p. 200). The poet's use of scenes dealing with liminality and boundary-crossing thus 'sharpens the presentation of the struggle between the demonic and the saintly' and highlights the sense of the saint as distinct from the rest of mankind (p. 200).

Bruce Mitchell's '*Phoenix* 71–84 and 424–42: Two Syntactical Cruces Involving Punctuation' (*ANQ* 15[2002] 38–46) sheds new light on the punctuating of two difficult passages in *The Phoenix*. Reviewing previous editorial attempts to punctuate these passages, Mitchell repunctuates them, and offers detailed discussion of his rationale for doing so. Sachi Shimomura's 'Visualizing Judgment: Illumination in the Old English *Christ III*' (in Hall, ed., pp. 27–49) considers the allegorization of light and brightness in *Christ III*. By contextualizing the poet's use of light imagery within biblical, patristic, and secular Anglo-Saxon discussions of light and brightness, Sachimura shows that *Christ III* contains a 'rhetorical transformation that literalizes Christ as the illuminator of the Last Judgment' (p. 48). It is thus the light of the Son which reveals the deeds of the blessed, and the light of the sun which reveals those of the damned. For Sachimura, light imagery functions as a crucial means of identifying the *Christ III* poet's theologies of vision and judgement.

6. The Poems of the Vercelli Book

Charles D. Wright finds 'More Old English Poetry in Vercelli Homily XXI' (in Treharne and Rosser, eds., pp. 245–62). He begins by showing how the rigid scholarly demarcation between poetry and prose has hindered the recognition and study of the full extent of surviving Old English poetry. The passage in Vercelli Homily XXI which Wright identifies and edits here runs from lines 128 to 141 of the homily as edited by Scragg. Its topic is the rebel angels, and Wright defines its rhetoric and form as 'self-consciously "poetical"' (p. 261), and suggests that it offers evidence for a now lost, separate, Old English poem.

7. The Junius Manuscript

Much work has appeared this year on the Junius manuscript. Liuzza, ed., *The Poems of MS Junius 11: Basic Readings*, brings together fourteen important essays on Junius 11: 'Confronting *Germania Latina*: Changing Responses to Old English Biblical Verse' by Joyce Hill; 'The Old English Epic of Redemption: The Theological Unity of MS Junius 11' by J.R. Hall; '"The Old English Epic of Redemption": Twenty-Five-Year Retrospective' by J.R. Hall; 'Some Uses of Paronomasia in Old English Scriptural Verse' by Roberta Frank; 'Tempter as Rhetoric Teacher: The Fall of Language in Old English *Genesis B*' by Eric Jager; 'Conspicuous Heroism: Abraham, Prudentius, and the Old English Verse *Genesis*' by Andrew Orchard; 'Christian Tradition in the Old English *Exodus*' by James W. Earl; 'The Patriarchal Digression in the Old English *Exodus*, Lines 362–446' by Stanley R. Hauer; 'The Lion Standard in *Exodus*: Jewish Legend, Germanic Tradition, and Christian Typology' by Charles D. Wright; 'The Structure of the Old English *Daniel*' by Robert T. Farrell; 'Style and Theme in the Old English *Daniel*' by Earl R. Anderson; 'Nebuchadnezzar's Dreams in the Old English *Daniel*' by Antonina Harbus; 'The Power of Knowledge and the Location of the Reader in *Christ and Satan*' by Ruth Wehlau; and 'The Wisdom Poem at the End of MS Junius 11' by Janet Schrunk Ericksen. All of these essays have previously been published, except for J.R. Hall's retrospective and Janet Schrunk Ericksen's contribution, which was commissioned for this volume. Liuzza provides a lucid introduction that summarizes the contributions of the individual essays, as well as the ways in which they engage with one another. Leslie Lockett offers 'An Integrated Re-examination of the Dating of Oxford, Bodleian Library, Junius 11' (*ASE* 31[2002] 141–73). Reminding us that efforts to date Junius 11 through individual features have produced discrepant results, Lockett offers an integrated analysis of the manuscript that brings together evidence provided by each datable feature of the codex: codicological evidence, line drawings, use of colour, palaeographical features, and punctuation. She concludes that Junius 11 ought to be redated to the period c.960– c.990, and reminds us that integrated and spectrum-based methods of dating may shed new light on other Anglo-Saxon manuscripts.

Paul G. Remley writes on '*Daniel*, the *Three Youths* Fragment and the Transmission of Old English Verse' (*ASE* 31[2002] 81–140). Reminding us that scholars have often looked to the rare, parallel passages in *Daniel* (ll. 279–439) and *The Canticles of the Three Youths* (long known as *Azarius*) as evidence for Anglo-

Saxon scribal practice and literate transmission, Remley seeks to 'improve our understanding of the *Daniel–Three Youths* variants by identifying some discernible points of scribal intervention in the parallel texts, as well as some thoroughly revised passages of verse' (p. 84). He concludes that the transmitted texts of *Daniel* and *The Three Youths* go back to a common antecedent text produced before the period of vigorous Benedictine reforms, and he suggests numerous transmissional stages after the emergence of this text, involving physical damage to the exemplar, comprehensive textual restoration, and several additional types of textual alteration.

Damian Love's 'The Old English *Exodus*: A Verse Translation' (*Neophil* 86[2002] 621–39) offers a verse translation of *Exodus* that 'adopts the stress metre and alliterative scheme of the original' (p. 620). Love also provides notes that discuss relevant themes and historical events, and a brief bibliography. Thomas D. Hill writes on 'Pilate's Visionary Wife and the Innocence of Eve: An Old Saxon Source for the Old English *Genesis B*' (*JEGP* 101[2002] 170–84). Pointing to parallels between the vision of Eve in *Genesis B* and that of Procla (Pilate's wife) in *The Heliand*, Hill suggests that the *Genesis B*-poet may have regarded the Procla narrative as an appropriate model for his account of Eve's temptation, and as an attractive means of explaining how Eve could have assumed the role of tempter without any malice or ill-will.

Carole Hough re-examines '*Christ and Satan* line 406b' (*N&Q* 49[2002] 6–8) and proposes that the manuscript reading *7 ne moste Efe þa gyt* 'but Eve was not yet allowed ...' ought to be restored. Pointing out that both the Tironian note *7* and the written conjunction *and*/*ond* frequently carry an adversative sense, Hough argues that we need not read the Tironian note *7* in this line as a contraction for *ac*.

8. The *Beowulf* Manuscript

The *Beowulf* manuscript continues to inspire rigorous scholarship, with much of this year's work centred on translations. *Beowulf: A Prose Translation* offers a new critical edition by Nicholas Howe of E. Talbot Donaldson's classic prose translation. In addition to useful explanatory notes, Howe also provides annotations for technical terms and historical figures, and has added new material to the 'Contexts' section. The edition includes a new final section, 'Criticism', which brings together seven important essays on *Beowulf*. The selection is limited to essays published after 1980 'so that readers can be exposed to the current conversation in the field about *Beowulf*' (p. ix). Essays include 'Appositive Style and the Theme of *Beowulf*' by Fred C. Robinson; 'The *Beowulf* Poet's Sense of History' by Roberta Frank; 'Reconceiving *Beowulf*: Poetry as Social Praxis' by John D. Niles; '*Beowulf* and the Psychology of Terror' by Michael Lapidge; '"Þæt wæs geomuru ides!" A Female Stereotype Examined' by Joyce Hill; 'The Female Mourner at Beowulf's Funeral: Filling in the Blanks/Hearing the Spaces' by Helen Bennett; and 'The Uses of Uncertainty: On the Dating of *Beowulf*' by Nicholas Howe. The edition concludes with a short bibliography that directs readers to earlier *Beowulf* criticism.

Beowulf: A Verse Translation offers a new critical edition by Daniel Donoghue of Seamus Heaney's poetic translation. Heaney's translation is accompanied by a translator's introduction and a final essay by Donoghue, both of which address the process of translation and situate Heaney's *Beowulf* in the context of his life and work. The edition also provides a 'Contexts' section designed to introduce students to the cultural and historical milieu of *Beowulf*, thirty-six illustrations, and eight critical essays. Essays include '*Beowulf*: The Monsters and the Critics' by J.R.R. Tolkien; 'The Interlace Structure of *Beowulf*' by John Leyerle; 'The Structural Unity of *Beowulf*: The Problem of Grendel's Mother' by Jane Chance; 'The *Beowulf* Poet's Sense of History' by Roberta Frank; 'The Tomb of *Beowulf*' by Fred C. Robinson; 'The Christian Language and Theme of *Beowulf*' by Thomas D. Hill; 'Archaeology and *Beowulf*' by Leslie Webster; and 'The Philologer Poet: Seamus Heaney and the Translation of *Beowulf*' by Daniel Donoghue. Louis J. Rodrigues's *Beowulf and the Fight at Finnsburh: A Modern English Verse Rendering* offers a new verse translation of *Beowulf* in parallel-text format. The translation is 'intended for a non-academic audience' (p. vi), and offers accessible commentary, glossaries, genealogies, and name-indices, as well as a number of black and white drawings.

R.M. Liuzza's 'Lost in Translation: Some Versions of *Beowulf* in the Nineteenth Century' (*ES* 83[2002] 281–95) begins with a brief review of the textual history of *Beowulf* and subsequently considers the poem's reception and translation in the nineteenth century. Focusing on the work of John Josiah Conybeare, J.M. Kemble, Henry Wadsworth Longfellow, William Morris, and others, Liuzza charts how nineteenth-century translations of *Beowulf* were conditioned by contemporary social and political developments. These local analyses enable Liuzza to argue that all translations are acts of recovery driven by the dual urges to recapture the spirit of a vanished and irrecoverable original and to respond to the literary demands of one's own time. As Liuzza writes, 'A translation is successful or not, not by virtue of its accuracy or fidelity to its indecipherable cause, but by how well it makes the poem seem like a living thing rather than a dead one' (p. 295).

Several articles this year focus on the natural and supernatural worlds. Margaret Gelling investigates 'The Landscape of *Beowulf*' (*ASE* 31[2002] 7–11), with particular attention to the poet's use of such landscape terms as *hlið*, *hop*, and *gelad*. Although rarely attested in other literary sources, these terms are well evidenced in place names, and Gelling argues that attending to place-name usage may help us to better understand how landscape terms are used in *Beowulf*. Michael Swisher's 'Beyond the Hoar Stone' (*Neophil* 86[2002] 133–6) considers the formulaic phrase *se harne stan* 'the hoar stone' as a 'boundary marker separating the known natural world from the dangerous supernatural one' (p. 133). He focuses mainly on the phrase as used in *Beowulf*, with some attention to its appearance in Blickling Homily 17 and *Andreas*. Roberta Frank gives us some 'North-Sea Soundings in *Andreas*' (in Treharne and Rosser, eds., pp. 1–11), by drawing on skaldic poetry to offer clarification of the Old English poem's imagery.

A striking number of this year's essays focus on monsters and animal imagery. Frederick M. Biggs examines 'Beowulf's Fight with the Nine Nicors' (*RES* 53[2002] 311–28) and the implications of the nine sea-beasts, who comprise the major discrepancy between Beowulf's and Unferth's accounts of the competition with Breca. Biggs argues that the poet's early account of sea-beasts offers a paradigm for understanding how monsters function throughout the poem as literary constructs that offer commentary on human actions. In 'From "Whale-Road" to "Gannet's Bath": Images of Foreign Relations and Exchange in *Beowulf*' (*RMSt* 28[2002] 59–86), Robert L. Schichler considers the three sea-kennings with animal elements found in *Beowulf*. Highlighting the idea of the sea as a path with the capacity to either facilitate or hinder foreign relations and social exchange, Schichler argues that the *Beowulf*-poet employs a succession of sea-kennings to construct a distinct shift in foreign relations as we move from Scyld's to Hrothgar's reigns: 'from one marked by intimidation and forced tribute, to one rooted in friendship and free exchange' (p. 60). John Tanke's 'Beowulf, Gold-Luck, and God's Will' (*SP* 99[2002] 356–79) focuses on the dragon's treasure and the curse laid upon it. Tanke investigates possible meanings for the hapax legomenon *goldhwæte* (l. 3074a), and argues that 'the poet has conceived of the curse in a thoroughly plausible, pagan-Germanic context as a protective spell laid upon a sacrificial treasure, and that death and not damnation is the fate assigned to its victim' (p. 358).

Gale R. Owen-Crocker continues her work on death and burial in *Beowulf* with 'Horror in *Beowulf*: Mutilation, Decapitation and Unburied Dead' (in Treharne and Rosser, eds., pp. 81–100). Focusing on deaths in the poem which are presented as being so unnatural that the body cannot be buried with the proper funeral rites, Owen-Crocker highlights evidence for Anglo-Saxon sensitivities, and the poem's exploitation of them to produce horror in its audience.

The poem's many feuds continue to generate interest. Michael Pantazakos's 'From Epic to Romance: The Literary Transformation of Private Blood Feud into Societal *Ressentiment*' (*Comitatus* 3[2002] 37–57) offers a 'comparative literary critique of ... the *Chanson de Roland* and *Beowulf*' (p. 37) to argue for a connection between literary and social changes in the late eleventh century. Pointing to this period as one that witnessed the transformation of epic into romance as well as increased anti-Semitism, Pantazakos suggests that the movement towards romance was enacted and expressed as a new form of anti-Semitism that resulted from changing world-values, namely, an increasing tendency to reject private blood feud in favour of a kind of social *ressentiment*, or revenge directed against an innocent other rather than against the true source of one's wrath. Lidan Lin writes on 'The Narrative Strategy of Double Voicing in *Beowulf*' (*NDQ* 69[2002] 40–9), with particular attention to the poem's digressions on feuds. Lin argues that feud digressions, such as the Finnsburh episode, create a 'unified counter-heroic narrative constantly competing for authority with the heroic narrative' (p. 40).

As usual, there is a substantial amount of new work on poetic form, style, and metrics. In *The Indeterminacy of Beowulf*, Johann Köberl takes a fresh look at some of the indeterminacies, ambiguities, and ambivalences that have engaged *Beowulf* scholars for many years. Focusing on syntactic, lexical, and thematic contradictions within the text, Köberl suggests that readers ought to embrace these ambiguities as part of its aesthetic appeal rather than looking for resolution, and that we 'might want to see structures—such as ambiguity, a high-lighting of transitionality, or an open-ended questioning of values—that permit a continual discourse on, and therefore a continual recreation of, *Beowulf*, thus deferring *ad infinitum* any final resolutions' (p. 178).

John Harkness offers some 'Observations on Appositions in *Beowulf*' (*JIEP* 43[2002] 79–88), with particular attention to where appositions fall in the poetic half-line. Defining apposition as 'coreferent, parallel, unconjoined lexical noun phrases in the same clause' (p. 79), Harkness shows that the majority of such appositions begin in the second half-line, with the second element of apposition in the following first half-line, and he offers several possible explanations for this phenomenon. John D. Sundquist discusses 'Relative Clause Variation and the Unity of *Beowulf* (*JGL* 14[2002] 243–69). He argues that aspects of various relative clause types in *Beowulf* are unique in the Old English poetic and prose corpus and consistent throughout all three proposed parts of the poem. Sundquist thus concludes that quantitative data on relative clause variation provides additional evidence that *Beowulf* is a unified poem and that it is not the work of multiple authors. Michael Getty studies *The Metre of Beowulf: A Constraint-Based Approach*. Getty's goal is 'to present a theory of the metrical system behind the Old English alliterative poem *Beowulf* (p. 1), and he writes for an audience of both generative linguists and traditional metrists willing to consider an alternative to Sievers, Kuhn, and Bliss. This book offers detailed analyses of Old English stress phonology and metrical structure at the level of the foot, the half-line, and the line. Getty argues that Old English poetry does not constitute a language of its own, but merely a kind of tidying-up of the prose language, which occurs 'according to a set of conditions on form which, by and large, can be justified quite independently of any need to understand the metre' (p. 5).

The numerous analogues to *Beowulf* continue to intrigue scholars. Alexander M. Bruce's *Scyld and Scef: Expanding the Analogues* examines the identity and textual functions of Scyld and Scef, two figures who are most well known from the opening of *Beowulf*. The book begins with a foreword by Paul Szarmach, and then proceeds to part I, an analysis of Scyld and Scef in Anglo-Saxon poetry, early English genealogies, English records from the twelfth to the fifteenth centuries, Icelandic sources, and Danish texts. In part II, Bruce presents primary texts and translations of the forty-three extant references to Scyld and Scef. Dean Swinford studies 'Form and Representation in *Beowulf* and *Grettis Saga*' (*Neophil* 86[2002] 613–20). While previous studies have identified plot similarities between Beowulf's battle with Grendel and Grettir's battle with Glámr, Swinford focuses on generic distinctions between the two battles to show that 'the dimensions of psychological horror conveyed by Grendel are clearly lacking from the saga's depiction of Glámr' (p. 619). He argues that such distinctions point to different conceptions of heroic action and to varying cultural expectations of Anglo-Saxon and Old Norse audiences.

As in past years, Alfred Bammesberger offers helpful textual notes on difficult lines. In 'The Syntactic Analysis of *Beowulf*, Lines 750–754' (*Neophil* 86[2002] 303–6), he re-examines the syntax of lines 750–4 and argues that they are correctly translated: 'At once the keeper of crimes realized that he had never met a greater grip in another man of the corners of the earth, of the world. He became terrified in spirit. Yet he was not able to get away any sooner' (p. 305). In 'An Unnecessary Emendation (*Beowulf*, line 1763a)' (*N&Q* 49[2002] 174–5), he suggests that the phrase *adl oððe ecg* 'illness or the sword' ought not to be emended to *adl oððe ece* 'illness or pain'. In 'OE *Ænegum* in *Beowulf*' (*N&Q* 49[2002] 312–14), he suggests that the phrase *ænegum men* actually represents (normalized) *āngan menn*, that the phrase ought to be translated as 'to one man alone' and that the emphasis thus lies on Beowulf fighting alone. In 'Beowulf's Death' (*N&Q* 49[2002] 314–15), he argues that the manuscript reading *hwæðre* in line 2819b makes good sense and ought not to be emended to *hræðre*. In 'Grendel's Death (*Beowulf* 850–852)' (*Neophil* 86[2002] 467–9), he suggests that *him* in line 852b (*þær him hel onfeng*) does not refer to Grendel but to either his 'life' (singular) or to his 'life and soul' (plural). In 'Old English *Ealuscerwen* in *Beowulf* 769a' (*RES* 53[2002] 469–74), he contends that *ealuscerwan* ought to be translated as 'a dispensation of good luck' and that the noun *-ealu* ought not to be identified as the noun for 'ale'. Bammesberger also revisits the question of 'Where Did Hrothgar Deliver his Speech?' (*ES* 83[2002] 1–5). Drawing on an earlier suggestion made by Leslie Webster, Bammesberger argues that the phrase *on stapole* (l. 926a) ought to be translated 'at the pillar' and that Hrothgar's speech took place outside Heorot, at a large pillar-like structural support to the building which may have also had ceremonial functions.

Other brief analyses of difficult lines and phrases have also appeared. Sarah M. Elder offers 'A Note on the Meaning of *Beowulf*, Lines 1288–1295' (*N&Q* 49[2002] 315–16). Elder argues that *se broga* (l. 1291b) refers to Grendel's mother, and that the half-line is thus correctly translated as 'when that monstrous thing perceived him', rather than 'when the terror seized him'. Carl T. Berkhout writes on '*Beowulf* 2200–08: Mind the Gap' (*ANQ* 15[2002] 51–8). He briefly reviews debates on the textually mutilated condition of fol. 179, and considers 'why both sides of 179, along with the first three lines on the verso of 180, might have been erased or partially erased in the first place' (p. 52). In 'An Aspirin for *Beowulf*: Against Aches and Pains—*ece* and *wærc*' (*ANQ* 15[2002] 58–63), Roberta Frank considers recent calls for emendation of *ecg* 'sword' (l. 1763a) and *weorc* 'work' (ll. 1418b, 1638b, and 1721b) to *ece* 'ache' and *wærc* 'pain'. Frank offers a detailed discussion of the various Anglo-Saxon uses and contexts for these words, and concludes that the drive towards such emendations is inadvisable and may simply result from a modern sensibility in which language is seen as a harmonious mathematical system.

E.L. Risden, 'Teaching Anglo-Saxon Humor, or Yes, Virginia, There Is Humor in *Beowulf*' (*SMRT* 9[2002] 21–38), suggests that focusing on humour in Old English poetry may help to increase interest in medieval poetry. Risden argues that Anglo-Saxon humour ought to be understood as 'a sudden pleasing mental catharsis experienced in safety' (p. 29), and identifies examples of humour in *Beowulf*, the Riddles, and *Juliana*.

Drout, ed., *Beowulf and the Critics*, is a critical edition of the two earlier and heretofore unpublished versions of Tolkien's landmark essay '*Beowulf*: The Monsters and the Critics'. Labelling the two versions 'A' and 'B', Drout shows how they differ from the final, far shorter version delivered to the British Academy in 1936, and he suggests that Tolkien wrote the longer texts in the early 1930s and may have delivered them as a series of lectures at Oxford. Drout provides a description of the manuscript containing the two longer works, complete textual and explanatory notes, and an introduction that discusses the place of Tolkien's scholarship in literary studies and in *Beowulf* scholarship.

Interest in gender issues keeps *Judith* at the centre of scholarly investigation. In 'Five Textual Notes on the Old English *Judith*' (*ANQ* 15[2002] 47–51), Fred C. Robinson offers fresh insight into five problematic aspects of the poem: the Old English poet's omission of Judith's dressing herself in fine clothes, Holofernes' *fleohnet*, Judith's prayers, the responses of the retainers to Holofernes' confinement, and their efforts to rouse him. Hugh Magennis explores 'Gender and Heroism in the Old English *Judith*' (in Treharne, ed., *Writing Gender and Genre*, pp. 5–18). Magennis considers the ways in which Judith departs from gender roles typically ascribed to women in heroic poetry, while nevertheless retaining a recognizable femininity which renders her naturally unsuited to the task of defending Bethulia.

Magennis argues that the poet maintains a sense of Judith as female, thereby heightening the sense of difficulty in her achievement and the profound faith that enables it. An item from last year that escaped notice was Lori Ann Garner's 'The Art of Translation in the Old English *Judith*' (*SN* 73[2001] 171–83). Focusing on the battle scenes, Holofernes' feast and descent into hell, and Judith's relationship with her maid, Garner sheds new light on the poet's manipulation of his Latin sources and on how these scenes would have registered in Anglo-Saxon culture.

For work on the *Passion of Saint Christopher*, see Section 10 below.

9. Other Poems

The Battle of Maldon continues to intrigue scholars. Michael Matto's 'A War of Containment: The Heroic Image in *The Battle of Maldon*' (*SN* 74[2002] 60–75) investigates images of containment and bounded spaces as recurring motifs in *Maldon*. Matto argues that the poet uses containment imagery to schematize the conflicts between two different heroic ideals: an ideal that views social order as a product of 'containment and the attendant processes of restraint, intake, and metered release' (p. 69) and an ethos 'that is based not in containment but in individual action, loyalty, and vengeance' (p. 63). In 'Wistan's Parentage' (*N&Q* 49[2002] 175–6), Carole Hough offers fresh insight into lines 297b–300 of *Maldon*. Hough reminds us that the Anglo-Saxons frequently formed names for both men and women by combining elements of the mother's and father's names. Since *Wistan* is a reduction of *Wigstan*, Wistan's mother may have been *Wigelines* and his father *Þurstan*, and lines 300a and 298a ought to be recognized as containing these names.

Jonathan Watson's 'The Finnsburh Skald: Kennings and Cruces in the Anglo-Saxon Fragment' (*JEGP* 101[2002] 497–519) focuses on the phrases *Celæs borð* (l. 29a) and *Hwearflacra hrær* (l. 34a), both of which appear in the *Finnsburh* fragment. Watson rejects the usual explanation of these unintelligible phrases as a product of the unsure hand of George Hickes, and proposes, instead, that they 'point toward a shared Scandinavian identity ... [and] are mythological kennings consistent with those found in Old Norse verse' (p. 498). Watson suggests further that the *Finnsburh* fragment 'probably reflects a Viking-Age rendering of the Danish ancestral past' (p. 519).

Paul E. Szarmach's 'Meter 20: Context Bereft' (*ANQ* 15[2002] 28–34) shows how the valuation of Bodley 180 over the fire-damaged Cotton Otho A.vi may obscure our understanding of Meter 20 in the Old English *Boethius*.

Alfred Bammesberger claims that there has been 'A Doubtful Reconstruction in the Old English Ruthwell Crucifixion Poem' (*SN* 74[2002] 143–5). Challenging two readings in David Howlett's 1976 reconstruction of the poem, Bammesberger argues that *gastæ* must be replaced by *gast*, and *sendæ* by *onsendæ* or possibly *ondsende*.

'Crook-Neb'd Corslets and Barefaced Cheek' (in Hough and Lowe, eds., pp. 189–97) are the subject of Tania Styles's development of the reading proposed by Christine Fell (published in the same volume, and reviewed in Section 4 above) for *geapneb*, a *hapax legomenon* in *Waldere*. Styles discusses the historical semantics of *neb*, including in her examination its use in Old English homilies, and proposes a new sense for this term and its derivatives: imprudence

Paul Cavill examines the relationship between 'Bede and Cædmon's *Hymn*' (in Hough and Lowe, eds., pp. 1–17), by assessing the evidence for the opposing views that the Old English *Hymn* is a back-formation from Bede's Latin version, and that Bede constructed his Latin version as a paraphrase of an earlier Old English one. His conclusion is that the latter is the more likely of the two possibilities.

D.R. Howlett offers a study of 'The Verse of Æthelweard's Chronicle' (*Bulletin du Cange* 58[2000] 219–24) which proposes some changes to the last lines of the relevant section in Campbell's edition, gives a new translation of the section, and shows the influence of the 'Insular tradition of metrical experiment' (p. 224) on Æthelweard's poetry.

10. Prose

Bede and his works continue to attract new analysis. In 'Discovering the Calendar (*annalis libellus*) Attached to Bede's Own Copy of *De temporum ratione*' (*AnBol* 120[2002] 5–64), Paul Meyvaert re-examines the manuscripts of *De temporum ratione*, and concludes that '*DTR* stands apart in Bede's works as the product of his classroom teaching' (p. 42), and that Bede copied entries from the *Codex cosmographiorum* into his calendar. Daniel Paul O'Donnell assesses 'The Accuracy of the "St Petersburg Bede"' (*N&Q* 49[2002] 4–6), and finds that, despite the presence of many more errors than previous scholars have acknowledged, this version of the *Historia ecclesiastica* is indeed early and accurate. Scott DeGregorio's '"Nostrorum socordiam temporum": The Reforming Impulse of Bede's Later Exegesis' (*EMedE* 11[2002] 107–22) examines examples of Bede's commentaries from different periods of his career in their social and political context. DeGregorio draws attention to how intertextual and socially involved Bede's later writings are.

In 'A Northumbrian Phrase in the Formation of the Hieronymian Martyrology: The Evidence of the Martyrology of Tallaght' (*AnBol* 120[2002] 311–63), Pádraig Ó Riain argues that the Echternach version of the Martyrology of Tallaght, and also the three versions produced at St-Wandrille or St Servatius, St-Avold, and Sens, all use a Northumbrian/English exemplar.

Two of the essays in Treharne and Rosser, eds., *Early Medieval English Texts*, deal with Alfredian texts. In 'Editions of Alfred: The Wages of Un-influence' (pp. 135–49), Paul E. Szarmach evaluates 'the lamentable state of the texts that comprise the Alfredian corpus' (p. 135), and names as contributory factors to this lack of sustained scholarly interest modern disciplinary divides between history and literature, failure to recognize Alfred as a poet, failure to credit ninth-century Anglo-Saxon authors with philosophical interests, a lack of clarity in Anglo-Saxon studies about what should constitute an edition, and the declining value attributed to the work of editing. 'Book Divisions and Chapter Headings in the Translations of the Alfredian Period' are the subject of Janet Bately's analysis (pp. 151–66). Through an examination of manuscripts of a range of Alfredian translations, Bately shows the extent to which editors of the texts have imposed their own divisions, that Anglo-Saxon scribes of the texts are much less interested in dividing them up, and that where contents lists, titling, and numbering do exist in manuscript, there is no sign of a uniform approach. Alfred P. Smyth publishes *The Medieval Life of King Alfred the Great: A Translation and Commentary on the Text Attributed to Asser*. The commentary in the volume engages further with the arguments about the reliability of the Life, the identity of Asser as its author, the style of the text, and its use of the *Anglo-Saxon Chronicle*, and Smyth advances a case for the Life being written at Ramsey in *c*. a.d. 1000.

O'Neill, ed., *King Alfred's Old English Prose Translations of the First Fifty Psalms*, offers a welcome new edition of the prose psalms contained in the Paris Psalter. O'Neill includes discussions of the manuscript, sources, translation and style, language, and authorship. The text of the psalms is supplemented by extensive commentary, a glossary, and a select bibliography. [SK]

Studies on Ælfric and his work continue to multiply this year. Hugh Magennis examines 'Warrior Saints, Warfare, and the Hagiography of Ælfric of Eynsham' (*Traditio* 56[2001] 27–51). Magennis addresses the potential conflict between secular heroism and sanctity, and focuses on Ælfric's Lives of Martin, Oswald, Edmund, Sebastian, and the Forty Soldiers to argue that, in content and style, they represent 'a kind of managed popularization of the cult of saints' (p. 50). In 'Ælfric on the Creation and Fall of the Angels' (*ASE* 31[2002] 175–200), Michael Fox notes Ælfric's numerous treatments of this subject, and how his interpretation of it differs from his main authorities, and traces Ælfric's increasing 'need for scriptural authority' (p. 200) on this matter.

Several of the contributors to Hall, ed., *Via Crucis*, write on Ælfric's hagiography. Dabney Anderson Bankert's 'Reconciling Family and Faith: Ælfric's *Lives of Saints* and Domestic Dramas of Conversion' (pp. 138–57) focuses on two Lives which have conversion as a central theme—those of Agnes and Gallicanus—and shows how Ælfric uses the pairing of these stories to construct models which will appeal in particular to lay members of his audience. E. Gordon Whatley also considers Ælfric's interaction with lay readers in '*Pearls before Swine*: Ælfric, Vernacular Hagiography, and the Lay Reader' (pp. 158–84). After surveying Ælfric's expressed views and anxieties about lay access to vernacular translations of Latin texts, and his manipulation of his own sources in the *Catholic Homilies* so that what he considers to be problematic elements are counterbalanced, Whatley turns to the *Lives of Saints*, and shows how these too are refashioned from their sources into narratives acceptable in Ælfric's mind for reading by his lay patrons.

Six of the essays in Treharne and Rosser, eds., *Early Medieval English Texts*, also focus on Ælfric. Malcolm Godden considers 'Ælfric as Grammarian: The Evidence of his *Catholic Homilies*' (pp. 13–29). He considers the evidence for changes made by Ælfric to the text of the *Catholic Homilies*, notes the lack of signs that these changes were consistent, or part of a systematic revision of the whole work, and concludes that 'Ælfric was primarily a stylist rather than a grammarian or even a pedagogue' (p. 29). Mechthild Gretsch compares 'Ælfric's *Sanctorale* and the Benedictional of Æthelwold' (pp. 31–50) in order to discern something of the rationale behind Ælfric's selection of saints for his hagiographical writings. Gretsch surveys the evidence for 'political and ethical motivation' (p. 34) on Ælfric's part, and for influence being brought to bear on him by the patrons and commissioners of his work, and then goes on to examine the compare the saints in the Benedictional of Æthelwold and the subjects of Ælfric's hagiography, to characterize the Benedictional as a book which 'furnishes much of the ideological background of Edgar's rule and coronation, and hence may have always been intended for public display in the church on certain occasions' (p. 50), and to propose that it may have influenced Ælfric's choice of subjects. Joyce Hill furthers her work on 'Ælfric's Authorities' (pp. 51–65) with a study of homilies VII, X, and XVII in Pope's edited collection of *Supplementary Homilies*, which aims to show 'the problems to be faced and the predispositions to be overcome in negotiating the intertextual minefield' (p. 59), and which confirms the importance of Carolingian compilers as sources of Ælfric's exegetical writings. Mary Clayton offers 'An Edition of Ælfric's *Letter to Brother Edward*' (pp. 263–83). Clayton's edition is accompanied by a modern English translation, and is preceded by a discussion of the text in which she argues convincingly for Ælfric's authorship of it, and presents it as offering 'a fascinating insight into the views of an English person around the last millennium, reacting to the spread of Danish ways in England' (pp. 263–4). Jonathan Wilcox's 'The Transmission of Ælfric's *Letter to Sigefyrth* and the Mutilation of London, British Library, Cotton Vespasian D. xiv' (pp. 285–300) traces Ælfric's composition of this text, his reworking of it into a homily, the popularity of the text as a treatise on virginity, the survival of part of the preface to the *Letter to Sigefyrth* in Vespasian D.xiv, and the impact on that manuscript of sixteenth- and seventeenth-century readers, including Robert Cotton, whom Wilcox shows to have been most probably responsible for the excision of the rest of the *Letter*. Michael Lapidge examines the evidence for 'Ælfric's Schooldays' (pp. 301–9) by scrutinizing the Latin preface to his *Grammar*, in which reference is made to the pronunciation of *brittonice*. Lapidge compares this assertion to the description in Latin poems composed at Æthelwold's school at Winchester of a Welsh schoolmaster named Iorwerth, and argues that Ælfric's Preface supports the case for Iorwerth being at Winchester in the time of Æthelwold, and thus being an influence on Ælfric's education.

A post-Conquest copy of one of Ælfric's probable sources is examined by Joana Proud in 'The Cotton-Corpus Legendary into the Twelfth Century: Notes on Salisbury Cathedral Library MSS 221 and 222' (in Treharne and Rosser, eds., pp. 341–52). Proud analyses this late eleventh-century manuscript for information on 'the ways that scribes responded to the demand for Latin hagiography in the period 1060–1200' (p. 342), and argues that the adaptation of the collection to include more English saints was a gradual process begun by Ælfric in his adaptation of parts of it into English, but then not resumed until the augmentation of the Latin collection with the addition of English saints' lives in twelfth-century copies. Kathy Lavezzo offers interesting insights into 'Another Country: Ælfric and the Production of English Identity' (*NML* 3[for 1999; published 2002] 67–93). Focusing on Ælfric's narration of the encounter with the English slave-boys in his homily on Gregory, Lavezzo shows how Ælfric 'presents a fantasy of English-Christian belonging' (p. 70).

Ælfric's language is also scrutinized this year. Alfred Bammesberger surveys the use of 'OE *bysegan* in Ælfric's *Catholic Homilies*, ii.440.20' (*N&Q* 49[2002] 9–10), and suggests a translation of 'chores'. In 'Speaking *Brittonice*: Vowel Quantities and Musical Length in Ælfric's *Grammar*' (*Peritia* 16[2002] 26–39), Melinda J. Menzer studies Ælfric's statement on the pronunciation of short vowels. She argues that he is drawing on the systems of *musica* and *grammatica*, and notes that his attribution of short pronunciation to the Welsh might indicate differences between Latin pronunciation in different parts of Britain.

Wulfstan is also the subject of new studies, including two essays in a collection on the year a.d. 1000. Mary P. Richards writes on 'Wulfstan and the Millennium' (in Frassetto, ed. *The Year 1000: Religious and Social Response to the Turning of the First Millennium*, pp. 41–8). Richards focuses on those of Wulfstan's eschatological sermons which reveal his millenarian concerns, contrasts them with the eschatological writings of Ælfric, and emphasizes how Wulfstan's 'criticisms and warnings become ever sharper as he seeks to end the current crisis' (p. 46). Nancy E. Atkinson and Dan E. Burton's examination of 'Harrowing the Houses of the Holy: Images of Violation in Wulfstan's Homilies' (in Frassetto, ed., pp. 49–62) shows how Wulfstan's eschatological homilies respond to the conflict between the English and the Danes, promote the idea of the violation of the English clergy by Vikings, and thus position the English clergy as potential national saviours.

Andy Orchard comments 'On Editing Wulfstan' (in Treharne and Rosser, eds., pp. 311–40), using Bethurum XXI as an example of the problems generated by earlier editorial treatments of the different versions of this text, which typifies the tendency of Wulfstan and other Anglo-Saxon writers to adapt and recycle his prose. Orchard emphasizes the value of a manuscript-centred approach to editing Wulfstan's works, and in the appendix to his article provides an edition and literal modern English translation of Bethurum XXI from manuscript London, British Library Cotton Nero A.i. The balance of 'Germanic Tradition and Latin Learning in Wulfstan's Echoic Compounds' is assessed by Don W. Chapman (*JEGP* 101[2002] 1–18). Chapman concedes that these compounds seem at first sight to be drawn from native, Germanic style, but argues that they also echo learned, Latinate style, that Wulfstan would have been aware of both of these connections, and that he is 'enhancing native idiom from an awareness derived from Latin learning' (p. 18).

In 'The Division of the Ten Commandments in Anglo-Saxon England' (*NM* 103[2002] 227–40), Aaron J. Kleist opens by noting differences of opinion over the numbering of the Commandments, and then turns to an analysis of five Anglo-Saxon texts which order them: *Solomon and Saturn I*, Wulfstan's *De christianitate*, and three texts by Ælfric: the Second Old English Letter for Wulfstan, *Decalogus Moysi*, and *Dominica in media quadragesime*. He shows that Wulfstan's *De christianitate* draws on Ælfric, and that all five texts represent a single tradition of the Decalogue, under the influence of Ælfric.

New studies of the anonymous prose homiletic corpus appear this year. Don Chapman's analysis of 'Poetic Compounding in the Vercelli, Blickling, and Wulfstan Homilies' (*NM* 103[2002] 409–21) builds on studies of compounding in poetic texts, contrasts it with the use of the technique in prose, and finds that the homiletic tradition shows 'an independent creativity with the resources of the language' (p. 419). The relationship between 'Vercelli Homily 6 and the Apocryphal Gospel of Pseudo-Matthew' is assessed by Frederick M. Biggs (*N&Q* 49[2002] 176–8), in the light of the possibility that the whole of this apocryphal gospel might have circulated in Anglo-Saxon England. Charles D. Wright publishes three more important studies of the Vercelli Homilies. He assesses 'Vercelli Homilies XI–XIII and the Anglo-Saxon Benedictine Reform: Tailored Sources and Implied Audiences' (in Muessig, ed., *Preacher, Sermon and Audience in the Middle Ages*, pp. 203–27). Through a combined attention to codicology, internal references, and treatment of sources, Wright is able to construct a convincing hypothesis of an intended audience of secular clerics. In 'The Old English "Macarius" Homily,

Vercelli Homily IV, and Ephrem Latinus, *De paenitentia*' (in Hall, ed., pp. 210–34), Wright explores the relationship between these two Old English homilies, and identifies the Latin source of their shared introductory section. Wright's 'More Old English Poetry in Vercelli Homily XXI' (in Treharne and Rosser, eds., pp. 245–62) is reviewed in Section 6 above. Jane Roberts offers 'Two Readings in the Guthlac Homily' (in Treharne and Rosser, eds., pp. 201–10)—Vercelli Homily XXIII—by examining emendations made in D.G. Scragg's 1992 edition of the text. She concludes that in the first case, 'big fer[c]ede' (ll. 81–2), Scragg is correct, and that in the second, '[h]recetunge' (l. 126), it is possible that the reading 'ræscetunge' might be the correct one. Paul E. Szarmach edits and analyses the adaptations of Alcuin's *Liber de virtutibus et vitiis* in 'Pembroke College 25, Arts. 93–95' (in Hall, ed., pp. 295–325), a manuscript which contains an intermediate source linking Alcuin's *Liber* and Vercelli Homily XX.

Patrizia Lendinara's '*frater non redimit, redimet homo* … : A Homiletic Motif and its Variants in Old English' (in Treharne and Rosser, eds., pp. 67–80) examines the use of this motif—which emphasizes that no one will be able to receive help from relatives or friends on Judgement Day—in a number of anonymous Old English homilies. Lendinara finds parallels for the motif in lines 97–102 of *The Seafarer*, in the Old High German poem *Muspilli*, and in Otfried's *Evangelienbuch*, explores a range of possible sources for it, and shows how it is reshaped in Old English texts to fit an Anglo-Saxon cultural context. Frederick M. Biggs offers 'Comments on the Codicology of Two Paris Manuscripts (BN Lat. 13,408 and 5574)' (in Hall, ed., pp. 326–30), both of which are in Latin, and the latter of which is of particular interest to Anglo-Saxonists because its script and contents, including some saints' lives, suggest English production.

Two editions of anonymous Old English hagiographic texts by Phillip Pulsiano are published this year. In 'The Passion of Saint Christopher' (in Treharne and Rosser, eds., pp. 167–210) Pulsiano discusses this text, found in MS London, British Library, Cotton Vitellius A.xv and also once in MS Cotton Otho B.x, and edits it from Vitellius A.xv with notes and a glossary. 'The Old English Life of Saint Pantaleon' (in Hall, ed., pp. 61–103), in MS London, British Library, Cotton Vitellius D.xvii, is edited by Pulsiano along with the Anglo-Latin version of the narrative which is closest to the probable source of the Old English. The edition is preceded by a discussion of the development of the tradition of the narrative about St Pantaleon.

Hugh Magennis produces a very welcome addition to the corpus of edited Old English saints' lives in *The Old English Life of St Mary of Egypt*. The edition, which is based on the text in London, British Library, MS Cotton Julius E.vii, is preceded by a clear introduction to the narrative of the legend, its transmission, the Old English versions and the relationship between them, the question of sources, and the language, style, and register of the Old English version. The edition is made particularly useful for undergraduate students by the inclusion of facing-page translation into modern English, and for scholars at all levels by the provision of the surviving Latin text closest to the probable source, which is also accompanied by a modern English translation.

Thomas N. Hall edits 'The Earliest Anglo-Latin Text of the *Trinubium Annae* (*BHL* 505zl)' (in Hall, ed., pp. 104–37) from MS Cambridge, St John's College 35, written in the late eleventh or early twelfth century at Bury St Edmunds, and also the

Old English version of the *Trinubium* from MS London, British Library Cotton Vespasian D.xiv, produced in Canterbury or Rochester in the second quarter of the twelfth century. Hall also traces the development of narratives about St Anne and her family, and in particular her three marriages; reconstructs the context for the production of the Bury text as part of a well-developed Marian cult; and proposes that a copy closely related to the Bury text was the immediate source of the Old English version.

Ted Johnson South edits *Historia de Sancto Cuthberto: A History of Saint Cuthbert and a Record of his Patrimony* from a text produced in the late Anglo-Saxon or early Anglo-Norman period. The introduction to the edition deals with the context for the composition of the text, sources available to its author, surviving manuscripts and their interrelationships, the date of composition, and previous scholarship on the text. The edition is accompanied by a facing-page translation into modern English, and the appendices supply editions of related texts, discuss estate structure in the *Historia*, and provide a catalogue of place names in the text.

Hagiography and its context of production are the subject of Pauline Head's 'Who Is the Nun from Hildeheim? A Study of Hugeburc's *Vita Willibaldi*' (*MÆ* 71[2002] 29–46). This saint's life was written between 776 and 786 in Heidenheim, by an Anglo-Saxon nun called Hugeburc, traces of whose identity are, Head argues, woven into the narrative. Head shows Hugeburc to have constructed a parallel between the life of her subject and her own life as a pilgrim and missionary, and thus responded to the ongoing redefinition of 'the boundaries of gender and vocation' (p. 41). Jane Roberts studies 'The Case of the Miraculous Hand in the Old English Prose Life of Guthlac' (*ANQ* 15:ii[2002] 17–22) by comparing it to Felix's *Vita sancti Guthlaci*. Roberts notes that the Old English Life, in MS London, British Library, Cotton Vespasian D.xxi, shares one particularly striking difference from Felix's Life with an eleventh-century office for Guthlac from Worcester, and speculates that the Vespasian redactor might have been influenced by a liturgical text in making this change. 'Job and Jacob in the Old English *Life of Malchus*', a text surviving in a mid-eleventh-century Worcester manuscript, is the subject of Michael S. Armstrong's investigation (*N&Q* 49[2002] 10–12). Armstrong accounts for the apparent confusion of Job and Jacob in the text by tracing a hypothetical error in the Latin exemplar, and the Old English translator's response to this. John Edward Damon considers the possibility of 'Sanctifying Anglo-Saxon Ealdormen: Lay Sainthood and the Rise of the Crusading Ideal' (in Hall, ed., pp. 185–209), by focusing on five ealdormen from the late tenth and early eleventh centuries— Byrhtnoth, Æthelwine of East Anglia, Æthelweard of Wessex, Leofric of Mercia, and Waltheof of Northumbria—whose lives were represented in literature. He concludes that the representation of all these men's lives was influenced by hagiographical conventions, and that Waltheof came closest to being treated as a saint.

New editions of liturgical texts continue to appear. Nicholas Orchard describes *The Leofric Missal* as '[f]or the most part ... not really a missal at all', but rather a 'combined sacramentary, pontifical and ritual' (p. 1) in MS Oxford, Bodleian Library, Bodley 579. In the first volume of his edition, Orchard discusses the manuscript and its history, untangles the layers of annotation and augmentation added to it between the early tenth and late eleventh centuries, and provides a number of useful collation tables and indexes. The second volume contains the edited text. Phillip Pulsiano's posthumously published edition of *Old English Glossed Psalters: Psalms 1–50* gives an introductory survey of the relevant manuscripts, explains the presentation and arrangement of material in the edition, and sets out notes on the scribal hands and their representation in the edition which follows. The volume's appendices contain the Blickling Psalter red ink glosses and folio references for the psalm verses.

Lisi Oliver provides welcome new editions and modern English translations of the laws of Æthelberht, Hloþhere and Eadric, and Wihtred in *The Beginnings of English Law*. The volume opens with a useful introduction to the historical context of the laws, the twelfth-century manuscript in which they survive (Rochester, Cathedral Library A.3.5), the language of the texts, and their chronology. Each of the main chapters of the volume contains the edition and translation of one of the three laws, supplementing these with detailed commentary. The volume's appendices include diplomatic transcriptions of the laws.

C.P. Biggam explains the relationship between '*Ualdenegi* and the Concept of Strange Eyes' (in Kay and Sylvester, eds., pp. 31–43), with reference to an entry in the Third Erfurt Glossary: the Latin lemma *cessius* (*caseius*), the Latin interpretation *glaucus*, and the Old English interpretation *ualdenegi*.

Pettit, ed., *Anglo-Saxon Remedies, Charms, and Prayers: From British Library MS Harley 585: The Lacnunga*, provides an important contribution to the study of Anglo-Saxon medicine and folklore in his two-volume edition and translation of the *Lacnunga*. Volume 1 includes a detailed discussion of BL MS Harley 585 and the sources, analogues, cultural context, and language of the *Lacnunga*. The text is accompanied by facing-page translations, as well as a full glossary of Old English and Old Irish words. Volume 2 is devoted to extensive commentary and a bibliography. [SK]

Concepts of the past, and of its relevance to Anglo-Saxon identity, are the subject of three articles this year. Daniel Anlezark surveys references to 'Sceaf, Japheth and the Origins of the Anglo-Saxons' (*ASE* 31[2002] 13–46) in Anglo-Saxon texts including *Exodus*, the Old English *Consolation of Philosophy*, the *Anglo-Saxon Chronicle*, Æthelweard's *Chronicon*, Ælfric's homilies *De initio creaturae*, *Dominica XXI post Pentecosten*, and *Dominica II post Aepiphania Domini*, and his Old English version of Alcuin's *Interrogationes Sigeuulfi in Genesin*, and notes the contrast between those texts which uphold the idea that the kings of Wessex are descended from Noah's ark-born son, and Ælfric's writings, which reject the existence of this son. Malcolm Godden examines 'The Anglo-Saxons and the Goths: Rewriting the Sack of Rome' (*ASE* 31[2002] 47–68), tracing accounts of this event from the fifth to the tenth centuries through the works of Augustine, Orosius, Bede, Gildas, Alcuin, the Old English *Consolation of Philosophy*, the *Anglo-Saxon Chronicle*, and Æthelweard's *Chronicon*. He shows how the significance of the sack of Rome developed for the Anglo-Saxons, and in particular how 'in the Alfredian circle at least Goths could be an honourable ancestry' (p. 68). Alice Sheppard's 'Noble Counsel, No Counsel: Advising Ethelred the Unready' (in Hall, ed., pp. 393–422) presents a carefully worked-out argument for a single chronicler composing all of the *Anglo-Saxon Chronicle* Æthelred annals as a single narrative, either at the end of Æthelred's or the beginning of Cnut's reign. She compares these *Chronicle* entries with works for Cnut written by Wulfstan, and shows how the chronicler 'builds a unifying identity for Cnut's nobles and the conquered Anglo-Saxons' (p.

397). Nicole Guenther Discenza approaches Anglo-Saxon identity from a slightly different angle to Godden and Lavezzo. In 'The Old English *Bede* and the Construction of Anglo-Saxon Authority' (*ASE* 31[2002] 69–80), she investigates the ways in which 'the Old English *Bede* authorizes itself not through any overt claims in an original preface but through strategic translations of the Latin preface and of the text itself' (p. 69), and also how, unlike other Alfredian translations, the text does not announce itself as the work of a translator, but instead 'Bede speaks to the reader directly in Old English' (p. 79).

M. Bradford Bedingfield's *The Dramatic Liturgy of Anglo-Saxon England* has at its core an analysis of the *Regularis Concordia*, the liturgical manuscripts of the late tenth and eleventh centuries, and Old English preaching texts of the same period. Acknowledging the longstanding scholarly tendency to claim that the tenth-century English Church is the point of origin of liturgical drama, Bedingfield highlights evidence for liturgical innovation in this period, but is careful not to equate this with drama. He finds, instead, that the *Regularis Concordia* and the other texts he studies represent 'something of a turning point in the stability and vigour of liturgical and devotional experience in Anglo-Saxon England' (p. 2).

Joyce Hill also continues to produce new insights into the *Regularis Concordia*. In two articles, her focus is on the version of the text in the early eleventh-century manuscript Cambridge, Corpus Christi College 201. 'Lexical Choices for Holy Week: Studies in Old English Ecclesiastical Vocabulary' (in Kay and Sylvester, eds., pp. 117–27) deals with the unusual lexical choices made by the Old English translator. The lexical choices are compared with those made by the Old English gloss-translator of the *Regularis Concordia* in London, British Library, Cotton Tiberius A.iii, a mid-eleventh-century Canterbury manuscript. Hill also evaluates the use of the words of 'Provost and prior in the *Regularis Concordia*' (*ANQ* 15:ii[2002] 13–17). She shows that the rank of 'provost' is not clear in the Old English version, and that 'prior' is not consistently recognized here as a title of office, and thus reminds us that 'we have to keep an open mind about what might be signified by apparently familiar terms' (p. 17).

R.M. Liuzza's 'The Devil and his Father: A Case of Editorial Irresponsibility in the Old English Gospels' (*ANQ* 15:ii[2002] 22–8) draws on his work editing the texts of the Old English Gospels, in the course of which he identified many 'bad translations', some of which he thinks might be evidence for the existence of 'unorthodox nontraditional readings and understandings of the Gospels' (p. 22). The specific example Liuzza discusses in this essay is from the Old English version of John 8:44, and he notes that there exists a tradition, referred to in writings including those of Augustine and Origen, and *Juliana*, of reading this line in the way the Old English translation reads it. Mary Garrison studies 'The Bible and Alcuin's Interpretation of Current Events' (*Peritia* 16[2002] 68–84) and identifies 'a turning-point in his outlook' (p. 68) in 796, at which point—after learning of a number of events which he found shocking, including the murder of Æthelred of Northumbria—he begins to assign a clear providential meaning to the Viking attack on Lindisfarne.

Three new articles on Gildas, with Anglo-Saxon import, are published this year. David Howlett's 'The Prophecy of Saxon Occupation in Gildas, *De Excidio Britanniae*' (*Peritia* 16[2002] 156–60) notes that this passage preserves the earliest written word of Old English, and also suggests that it might have influenced the composer of Æthelberht's law-code. Alex Woolf draws attention to the same passage in 'An Interpolation in the Text of Gildas's *De Excidio Britanniae*' (*Peritia* 16[2002] 161–7), and argues that it might have been interpolated, possibly in Canterbury. Alf Siewers's 'Gildas and Glastonbury: Revisiting the Origins of Glastonbury Abbey' (in Hall, ed., pp. 423–32) surveys interpretations of the archaeological evidence for early British Christianity in general, and at Glastonbury in particular, and argues that these reinforce Gildas's account of Christianity coming to Britain by a.d. 37, and that the 'Glastonbury legend as myth may reflect an historically plausible memory of contact between Irish-Welsh migrants and a remnant of earlier Romano-British Christianity' (p. 432).

Anglo-Saxon teaching texts continue to attract attention. David W. Porter edits *'Excerptiones de Prisciano': The Source for Ælfric's Latin–Old English Grammar*. The introduction to the edition includes discussion of the manuscripts, their relationships and provenance, the content and organization of the *Excerptiones de Prisciano*, and the history of the study of Priscian. The edited text is supplemented with a facing-page modern English translation, and is followed by a commentary. In '*Anima quae pars*: A Tenth-Century Parsing Grammar' (*Journal of Medieval Latin* 12[2002] 181–204), Don Chapman provides an edition and discussion of a text from MS Worcester Cathedral Library Q.5, probably written at Christ Church, Canterbury.

Post-Conquest transmission of Old English generates more new scholarship. Loredana Teresi's '*Be Heofonwarum 7 be Helwarum*: A Complete Edition' (in Treharne and Rosser, eds., pp. 211–44) presents an edition and glossary of this homily, which is preserved in MSS Cambridge, Corpus Christi College 302 (first half of the twelfth century) and London, British Library, Cotton Faustina A.ix (late eleventh to early twelfth century), along with a discussion of the two manuscripts and their relationship, the homily's theme, and the sort of milieu in which it could have been composed, which she speculates might be 'Irish-influenced ... sometime before the end of the eleventh century, possibly in Anglia or in a scriptorium where WS was not powerfully influential'. Alexander R. Rumble's '*Interpretationes in latinum*: Some Twelfth-Century Translations of Anglo-Saxon Charters' (in Treharne and Rosser, eds., pp. 101–17) examines 'the tension in the relationship between English and Latin' (p. 103) after 1066, as witnessed in Latin translations of Old English charters. Rumble sorts the charters in question into three categories, describes the examples of each, comments on the translation of Old English technical terms, on the influence of a glossary circulating in the twelfth century which contained Old English technical terms, on the case of Winchester Cathedral Priory, and on the palaeographical response in the twelfth century to Anglo-Saxon scripts.

Books Reviewed

Alexander, Michael. *A History of Old English Literature*. Broadview. [2002] pp. xviii + 299. pb £12.99 ($22.95) ISBN 1 5511 1322 8.
Bedingfield, M. Bradford. *The Dramatic Liturgy of Anglo-Saxon England*. Boydell. [2002] pp. ix + 246. £45 ($75) ISBN 0 8511 5873 0.

Biggs, Frederick M., Thomas D. Hill, Paul E. Szarmach, and E. Gordon Whatley, eds. *Sources of Anglo-Saxon Literary Culture*, vol. 1: *Abbo of Fleury, Abbo of Saint-Germain-des-Prés and Acta Sanctorum*. MIP. [2001] pp. xlvi + 548. $40 ISBN 1 5804 4073 8.

Bitel, Lisa M. *Women in Early Medieval Europe, 400–1100*. CUP. [2002] pp. xv + 326. £42.50 ISBN 0 5215 9207 0.

Blockley, Mary. *Aspects of Old English Poetic Syntax: Where Clauses Begin*. UIllP. [2001] pp. xii + 248. $39.95 ISBN 0 2520 2606 3.

Brown, Michelle P. *'In the beginning was the Word': Books and Faith in the Age of Bede*. Jarrow Lecture 2000, St Paul's Church, Jarrow. [2002] pp. 37 + 9 plates. £4 ISBN not given.

Bruce, Alexander M. *Scyld and Scef: Expanding the Analogues*. Routledge. [2002] pp. xiii + 209. $85 ISBN 0 8153 3904 6.

Cassidy, Brendan, and Rosemary Muir Wright, eds. *Studies in the Illustration of the Psalter*. Shaun Tyas. [2000] pp. x + 86 + 64 plates. £19.95 ISBN 1 9002 8942 3.

Crabtree, Pam J., ed. *Medieval Archaeology: An Encyclopedia*. Garland. [2001] pp. xxi + 426. £80 ISBN 0 8153 1286 5.

Crossley-Holland, Kevin, ed. and trans. *The Anglo-Saxon World*, rev. edn. Boydell. [2002] pp. 275 + 8 colour plates. £30 ($50) ISBN 0 8511 5885 4.

Doane, A. N. *Anglo-Saxon Manuscripts in Microfiche Facsimile*, vol. 7: *Anglo-Saxon Bibles and 'The Book of Cerne'*. ACMRS. [2002] pp. x + 78. £58 ($90) ISBN 0 8669 8229 9.

Donaldson, E. Talbot, trans. *Beowulf: A Prose Translation*, ed. Nicholas Howe. 2nd edn. Norton. [2002] pp. xvi + 198. pb $ 9.38 ISBN 0 3939 7406 5.

Drout, Michael, ed. *Beowulf and the Critics by J.R.R. Tolkien*. MRTS 248. ACMRS. [2002] pp. xix + 461. £33 ($38) ISBN 0 8669 8290 6.

Fenster, Thelma S., and Clare A. Lees, eds. *Gender in Debate from the Early Middle Ages to the Renaissance*. Palgrave [2002] pp. xi + 292. $59.95 ISBN 0 3122 3244 6.

Frassetto, Michael, ed. *The Year 1000: Religious and Social Response to the Turning of the First Millennium*. Palgrave. [2002] pp. xi + 278. $59.95 ISBN 1 4039 6029 1.

Gameson, Richard, ed. *The Codex Aureus: An Eighth-Century Gospel Book. Part II*. EEMF 29. R&B. [2002] pp. 16 + 137 plates. hb €1297 ISBN 8 7423 0537 3, pb €1112 ISBN 8 7423 0535 7.

Geake, Helen, and Jonathan Kenny, eds. *Early Deira: Archaeological Studies of the East Riding in the Fourth to Ninth Centuries AD*. Oxbow. [2000] pp. xi + 140. £28 ISBN 1 9001 8890 2.

Getty, Michael. *The Metre of Beowulf: A Constraint-Based Approach*. MGruyter [2002] pp. x + 368. €88 ISBN 3 1101 7105 8.

Hall, Thomas N., ed., with assistance from Thomas D. Hill and Charles Wright. *Via Crucis: Essays on Early Medieval Sources and Ideas in Memory of J.E. Cross*. WVUP. [2002] pp. xvii + 449. pb $45 ISBN 0 9370 5858 0.

Halsall, Guy, ed. *Humour, History and Politics in Late Antiquity and the Early Middle Ages*. CUP. [2002] pp. xiv + 208. £37.50 ISBN 0 5218 1116 3.

Harbus, Antonina. *Helena of Britain in Medieval Legend*. Brewer. [2002] pp. viii + 215. £44 ($75) ISBN 0 8599 1625 1.

Harbus, Antonina. *The Life of the Mind in Old English Poetry*. Costerus ns 143. Rodopi. [2002] pp. ix + 220. pb €45 ($56) ISBN 9 0420 0814 8.

Heaney, Seamus, trans. *Beowulf: A Verse Translation*, ed. Daniel Donoghue. Norton. [2002] pp. xxiii + 256. pb $11.88 ISBN 0 3939 7580 0.

Herren, Michael W., C.J. McDonough, and Ross G. Arthur, eds. *Latin Culture in the Eleventh Century*. 2 vols. Proceedings of the Third International Conference on Medieval Latin Studies. Cambridge, 9–12 September 1998. Publications of the Journal of Medieval Latin 5/1 and 5/2. Brepols. [2002] pp. xx + 519 (vol. 1), pp. vii + 520 (vol. 2). €50 ISBN 2 5035 1255 0.

Hough, Carole, and Kathryn A. Lowe, eds. *'Lastworda Best': Essays in Memory of Christine E. Fell with her Unpublished Writings*. Shaun Tyas. [2002] pp. xv + 298. £35 ISBN 1 9002 8953 9.

James, Edward. *Britain in the First Millennium*. Arnold. [2001] pp. x + 310. £19.99 ISBN 0 3405 8687 7.

Johnson South, Ted, ed. *Historia de Sancto Cuthberto: A History of Saint Cuthbert and a Record of his Patrimony*. Brewer. [2002] pp. x + 155. £45 ISBN 0 8559 1627 8.

Jones, Timothy S., and David A. Sprunger, eds. *Marvels, Monsters, and Miracles: Studies in the Medieval and Early Modern Imaginations*. MIP. [2002] pp. xxv + 306. £24 ISBN 1 5804 4066 5.

Klinck, Anne L., and Ann Marie Rasmussen, eds. *Medieval Woman's Song: Cross-Cultural Approaches*. UPennP. [2002] pp. viii + 279. £35 ($49.95) ISBN 0 8122 3624 6.

Köberl, Johann. *The Indeterminacy of Beowulf*. UPA. [2002] pp. xiv + 226. pb $35 ISBN 0 7618 2321 2.

Lambdin, Laura Cooner, and Robert Thomas Lambdin, eds. *A Companion to Old and Middle English Literature*. Greenwood. [2002] pp. xi + 433. $74.95 ISBN 0 3133 1054 8.

Lang, James. *Northern Yorkshire*. Corpus of Anglo-Saxon Stone Sculpture 6. OUP. [2001] pp. xvi + 540. £130 ISBN 0 1972 6256 2.

Lees, Clare A., and Gillian R. Overing. *Double Agents: Women and Clerical Culture in Anglo-Saxon England*. UPennP. [2001] pp. x + 244. £35 ($49.95) ISBN 0 8122 3628 9.

Lenz, Katja, and Ruth Möhlig, eds. *Of Dyuersitie & Chaunge of Langage: Essays Presented to Manfred Görlach on the Occasion of his 65th Birthday*. Anglistische Forschungen 308. Winter. [2002] pp. xxx + 389. €50 ISBN 3 8253 1322 0.

Lineham, Peter, and Janet L. Nelson, eds. *The Medieval World*. Routledge. [2001] pp. xx + 745. £25 ISBN 0 4153 0234 X.

Liuzza, R. M., ed. *The Poems of MS Junius 11: Basic Readings*. Routledge. [2002] pp. xxi + 328. $95 ISBN 0 8153 3862 7.

Liuzza, R. M., ed. *Old English Literature: Critical Essays*. YaleUP. [2002] pp. xxxviii + 479. $26 ISBN 0 3000 9139 7.

Magennis, Hugh, ed. *The Old English Life of Saint Mary of Egypt*. UExe. [2002] pp. xii + 260. £13.99 ISBN 0 8598 9672 2.

Minkova, Donka, and Robert Stockwell, eds. *Studies in the History of the English Language: A Millennial Perspective*. MGruyter. [2002] pp. vi + 496. hb €98 ISBN 3 1101 7368 9, pb €36.95 ISBN 3 1101 7591 6.

Mitchell, Bruce, and Fred C. Robinson. *A Guide to Old English.* 6th edn. Blackwell. [2001] pp. xviii + 400. pb £19.99 ($38.95) ISBN 0 6312 2636 2.

Muessig, Carolyn, ed. *Preacher, Sermon and Audience in the Middle Ages.* Brill. [2002] pp. xix + 322. €126 ISBN 9 0041 1416 5.

Oliver, Lisi. *The Beginnings of English Law.* UTorP. [2002] pp. xiv + 297. £40 ISBN 0 8020 3535 3.

O'Neill, Patrick P., ed. *King Alfred's Old English Prose Translations of the First Fifty Psalms.* MAB 104. MAA. [2001] pp. vii + 362. $50 ISBN 0 9156 5113 0.

Orchard, Nicholas, ed. *The Leofric Missal.* 2 vols. HBS. [1999–2000 (vol. 1); 2001–2 (vol. 2)] pp. xii + 387 (vol. 1), vii + 514 (vol. 2). £40 ($70) per volume. ISBN 1 8705 5217 9 (vol. 1), 1 8702 5218 7 (vol. 2).

Pettit, Edward, ed. and trans. *Anglo-Saxon Remedies, Charms, and Prayers. From British Library MS Harley 585: The Lacnunga.* 2 vols. Mellen. [2001] pp. lxiii + 276 (vol. 1). pp. 404 (vol. 2). £74.95 ($119.95) ISBN 0 7734 7555 9 (vol. 1), £79.95 ($129.95) ISBN 0 7734 7557 5 (vol. 2).

Pickles, Christopher. *Texts and Monuments: A Study of Ten Anglo-Saxon Churches of the Pre-Viking Period.* BAR Series 277. Archaeopress. [1999] pp. ix + 316. £37 ISBN 0 8605 4941 0.

Porter, David W., ed. *'Excerptiones de Prisciano': The Source for Ælfric's Latin–Old English Grammar.* Brewer. [2002] pp. xiv + 408. £60 ($110) ISBN 0 8599 1635 9.

Preest, David, trans. *The Deeds of the Bishops of England (Gesta Pontificum Anglorum)* by William of Malmesbury. Boydell. [2002] pp. xv + 320. £25 ($39.95) ISBN 0 8511 5884 6.

Prescott, Andrew. *The Benedictional of St Æthelwold: A Masterpiece of Anglo-Saxon Art. A Facsimile.* BL. [2002] pp. 27 + 120 plates. £50 ISBN 0 7123 4755 0.

Pulsiano, Phillip, ed. *Old English Glossed Psalters Psalms 1–50.* UTorP. [2001] pp. lv + 742. £65 ISBN 0 8020 4470 0.

Richards, Mary P., ed. *Anglo-Saxon Manuscripts: Basic Readings.* Routledge. [2001] pp. xv + 401. pb £15.99 ISBN 0 8153 3567 9.

Rodrigues, Louis J. *Beowulf and the Fight at Finnsburh: A Modern English Verse Rendering.* RunetreeP. [2002] pp. vii + 179. ISBN 1 8985 7708 0.

Rollason, David, ed. and trans. *Libellus de Exordio atque Procursu istius hoc est Dunhelmensis Ecclesie; Tract on the Origins and Progress of this the Church of Durham,* by Symeon of Durham. OUP. [2000] pp. xcvi + 353. £65 ISBN 0 1982 0207 5.

Rumble, Alexander R. *Property and Piety in Early Medieval Winchester: Documents Relating to the Topography of the Anglo-Saxon and Norman City and its Minsters.* Winchester Studies 4:3. The Anglo-Saxon Minsters of Winchester. Part III. Clarendon. [2002] pp. xxiv + 253. £120 ISBN 0 1981 3413 4.

Smith, Julia M.H., ed. *Early Medieval Rome and the Christian West: Essays in Honour of Donald A. Bullough.* Brill. [2000] pp. xxxii + 446. €109 ($136) ISBN 9 0041 1716 4.

Smyth, Alfred P. *The Medieval Life of King Alfred the Great: A Translation and Commentary on the Text Attributed to Asser.* Palgrave. [2002] pp. xx + 280. £35 ISBN 0 3336 9917 3.

Stafford, Pauline, Janet L. Nelson, and Jane Martindale, eds. *Law, Laity and Solidarities: Essays in Honour of Susan Reynolds.* ManUP. [2001] pp. ix + 274. £16.99 ISBN 0 7190 5836 8.

Stanton, Robert. *The Culture of Translation in Anglo-Saxon England.* Brewer. [2002] pp. x + 198. £40 ($70) ISBN 0 8599 1643 X.

Swanton, Michael. *English Poetry Before Chaucer*, rev. edn of *English Literature Before Chaucer* (Longman [1987]). UExe. [2002] pp. ix + 379. hb £47.50 ISBN 0 8598 9633 1, pb £15.99 ISBN 0 8598 9681 1.

Townend, Matthew. *Language and History in Viking Age England: Linguistic Relations between Speakers of Old Norse and Old English.* Brepols. [2002] pp. xv + 248. £42 ISBN 2 5035 1292 5.

Treharne, Elaine, ed. *Vital Signs: English in Medieval Studies in Twenty-First Century Higher Education.* Issues in English 2. EA. [2002] pp. iii + 36. £5 ISBN 0 9002 3220 X.

Treharne, Elaine, ed. *Writing Gender and Genre in Medieval Literature.* Brewer. [2002] pp. 142. £30 ISBN 0 8599 1760 6.

Treharne, Elaine and Susan Rosser, eds. *Early Medieval English Texts and Interpretations: Studies Presented to Donald G. Scragg.* ACMRS. [2002] pp. xix + 391. £36 ($40) ISBN 0 8669 8295 7.

Treharne, Elaine and Duncan Wu, eds. *Old and Middle English Poetry.* Blackwell. [2002] pp. vii + 174 hb £40 ($52.95) ISBN 0 6312 3073 4, pb £9.99 ($18.95) ISBN 0 6312 3074 2.

III

Middle English: Excluding Chaucer

DORSEY ARMSTRONG, NICOLE CLIFTON, JURIS LIDAKA,
MARION TURNER, GREG WALKER AND K.S. WHETTER

This chapter has eight sections: 1. General and Miscellaneous; 2. Women's Writing; 3. Alliterative Verse and Lyrics; 4. *Piers Plowman*; 5. Romance; 6. Gower, Lydgate, Hoccleve; 7. Malory and Caxton; 8. Drama. Section 1 is by K.S. Whetter, with additional material by Juris Lidaka; section 2 is by Marion Turner, with additional material by K.S. Whetter; sections 3 and 4 are by Nicole Clifton; sections 5 and 6 are by Juris Lidaka; section 7 is by Dorsey Armstrong; section 8 is by Greg Walker.

1. General and Miscellaneous

Once again, this section begins with manuscripts and texts. Alixe Bovey's *Monsters and Grotesques in Medieval Manuscripts* is more of a guidebook than a scholarly study, but it contains a wealth of information, and the fifty colour illustrations of various monsters and fabulous creatures are magnificent. The images in question come from British Library manuscripts with both Continental and Insular origins, and from variegated sources ranging from the late tenth century to *c*.1500: Augustine, Mandeville, Pliny, Alexander romances, the Smithfield Decretals, and the Luttrel Psalter all make appearances. Partly the argument and images confirm the stereotype of 'beyond here be monsters': medieval travel and the widening of boundaries did nothing to dispel the notion of the monstrous—and monstrously inhabited—unknown. At the same time, medieval audiences were obviously entranced and terrified by these unknown creatures, some of which, like dragons, are terrible, while others, like unicorns, are 'beautiful' (p. 23).

Thirty-three years after the first volume and ten years after the fourth, I.C. Cunningham and A.G. Watson have provided the fifth volume, *Indexes and Addenda* to N.R. Ker's majestic *Medieval Manuscripts in British Libraries*. Ker died in 1982, but his papers were sufficiently complete for the third volume, covering Lampeter to Oxford, to be issued the very next year, tidied up by Andrew Watson. Here, we finally have the ease of access needed for the whole set, but as a reminder that there is always more to do, if not re-do, the book begins with addenda and corrigenda that run to twenty-six pages. Addenda in English (most of which are generally known) include Lydgate, the *Brut*, Chaucer, the *Prick of Conscience*, fragments of a Robin Hood play and a commonplace book, the *Brut Chronicle to 1377*, medical materials, and a physician's handbook. Corrigenda include some notices of sales and of more recent catalogues; though addenda are indexed in the rest of the volume, corrigenda are not. The indexes run to eleven in all, the longest being the first two: 'Authors, Subjects, and Titles' and 'Names', meaning those of scribes, owners, etc. Some standard indices include *secundo folios*, manuscripts cited, and separate ones for bibles and liturgies. There is also an iconographic index, which should be very helpful to those working in the visual arts, and one for origins and dates of manuscripts. Readers of *YWES* who wish to find works in English can use the index of 'Languages other than Latin', with six items in Old English separated from two columns'-worth in 'English' (and six in Anglo-Norman from over two columns of French) and the index of *incipits* for non-Latin languages, in addition to one for Latin. The addenda include references to the *Index of Middle English Verse* and its *Supplement*, and these plus the *Index of Middle English Prose* are cross-listed in the 'Index of Repertories Cited'. Naturally, there will be errors and peculiarities; a quick spot check found that a Bartholomaeus Anglicus, said to be found in volume 3, page 252 (top) was actually at the top of page 552, and that the *South English Legendary* is not indexed among titles but evidently subsumed under 'SAINTS ... Collections', while the *Gesta Romanorum* (even in English) is explicitly indexed under 'TALES'. These small glitches notwithstanding, it is a relief to have this volume at last, since the many treasures of the catalogue could be accessed otherwise only through careful scrutiny of each page and item. [JL]

In *Textual Situations*, meanwhile, Andrew Taylor focuses on three specific manuscripts (Bodleian MS Digby 23, British Library MS Harley 978, and British Library MS Royal 10.E.4) to draw attention to 'the way in which the material support of the medieval text, which is not just the manuscript but also the social conventions that surround it, differs from that of the printed book' (p. 2). In doing so, Taylor hopes to counter what he sees as the general suppression of codicological evidence and to emphasize the need for greater collaboration when studying manuscript miscellanies. Thus he traces the early readers of the three manuscripts under consideration and argues for the ways in which print culture often blinds us to the oral aspects of medieval reading and the differences between manuscript and print culture. More specific Middle English material is found in chapter 3's opening account of Harley's 'Sumer is icumen in' and its accompanying Latin hymn. Taylor lauds musicologists for recognizing the 'corporeal materiality' (p. 83) of this lyric, a recognition which does not extend to the rest of Harley's contents. Throughout, quotations are offered in both original language and translation, Taylor's prose is clear and jargon-free, and various arguments are augmented by plates. Curiously, though, the acknowledgements, including the statement that parts of the study represent earlier articles, come at the end of the book. Pedants will also object to the occasional use of *book* for what are, strictly speaking, *incunabula*.

Richard Newhauser, 'A Middle English Poem on the Fleeting Nature of Material Wealth' (*MÆ* 71[2002] 74–81), points to the existence of a Middle English quatrain deriding materialism written on folio 125^r of Cambridge, Pembroke College, MS 229, a collection of Latin theological tracts. Newhauser then studies the hand, context, and cognates of the poem, pointing to similar verses in British Library MS Royal 17 B.xvii. Finally, in 'Notes on Cambridge University Library MS Ff.1.6' (*N&Q* 49 [2002] 439–42), Simone Celine Marshall highlights gaps in the 1977 facsimile of the Findern manuscript (MS Ff.1.6 of the title). The problems include missing folios and incorrect foliation, dropped *IMEV* descriptions, misattributions of the material by Chaucer and Lydgate, and insufficient description of marginalia.

Moving from manuscripts to editions, there are two relevant EETS volumes this year. The first is Seymour, ed., *The Defective Version of Mandeville's Travels*. The Defective Version is so named for its 'Egypt Gap', the loss of material (probably an entire quire) dealing with Egypt (p. xi). It is, however, 'the oldest English translation of the [Anglo-Norman] Insular Version' of the *Travels* (p. xi); this Insular Version is itself based on the Continental Version. Despite its lacuna, the Defective Version of the *Travels* quickly established itself as the principal English text. Seymour tentatively suggests a translation date of *c.*1385 (p. xiii), and believes that the extant chapter divisions roughly follow the translator's own. Both the Middle English translator's source, in the form of an Anglo-Norman Insular manuscript, and his English holograph are lost. Seymour therefore proposes 'to recover as far as possible the substance of the earliest extant Middle English translation of *Mandeville's Travels*' (p. xxvi); a procedure, he convincingly argues, which is best done through following the most reliable extant manuscript of subgroup 1 rather than by attempting to reconstruct the missing holograph. Seymour makes an equally sound case for using Queen's College, Oxford MS 383 as the base-text, and for using MS Arundel 140—the main manuscript of subgroup 2 of the *Travels*—for correcting omissions. The convenient chapter numbers of his edition are also 'based on those of subgroup 2' (p. xxix). The result is a clear and reasonably clean text, with collations and variants recorded in footnotes, as well as in the apparatus. In addition to the introduction, much of which is devoted to detailing manuscript affiliations and collation procedures, the textual apparatus has two principal forms: the textual commentary, which offers further readings from the Anglo-Norman version which are useful in reconstructing the Middle English Defective Text and revealing its origins; and the appendix, which records twelve extracts from each of Pynson's *incunabulum* (itself edited by Kohanski in 2001 [*YWES* 82[2003] 139]) and twenty-three manuscripts. The textual commentary also offers some variant English readings, and there is in addition a full literary commentary (pp. 137–73). Seymour is a Mandeville authority, and the result is an excellent text and apparatus.

The second relevant EETS title is Easting, ed., *The Revelation of the Monk of Eynsham*. The *Revelation* is a fifteenth-century English prose translation of the twelfth-century Latin *Visio monachi de Eynsham*, 'one of the most extensive accounts we have among medieval visions of the other world' (p. xcvii). *Revelation* is further important for being the latest and longest Middle English other-world vision, and—it is claimed—the sole pre-1500 printed vision (though Easting then confusingly lists a number of fifteenth-century cognates (p. xix)). Easting offers a parallel Latin–English text: the heretofore incompletely edited C-text of the *Visio* from Bodleian Library MS Selden Supra 66, and the *Revelation*, from British Library IA.55449, one of two extant English *incunabula* (the other being in the Bodleian). This is the first complete Middle English edition of *Revelation* in over a hundred years, and the Latin text is offered as being 'closest to that used by the [Middle English] translator' (p. xcviii). Neither author nor visionary is explicitly identified in the texts, but their names are given in a roughly contemporary manuscript *incipit*; Easting therefore cautiously promulgates the traditional view that the *Visio* was authored *c.*1196 by Adam of Eynsham, recording the vision of his younger brother Edmund. The identity of the Middle English translator is unknown, but Easting 'locates the text ... in the Kidderminster area' (p. li) and gives some attention in the apparatus to language, vocabulary, and lexicological matters. There are also details of and a commentary on the *Revelation*, its chronology, and context, as well as the vision itself and the relationship between the Latin and English texts. It is emphasized that the proper title is *Eynsham*, not *Evesham*. The Middle English text is clean and readable; the commentary highlights both textual and critical matters; appendix 1 covers variants and appendix 2 is lexicological, linking the *Revelation*'s vocabulary to (omissions in) the *OED* and *MED*.

Another extremely full apparatus accompanies Thomas Usk's *Testament of Love*, edited by Gary W. Shawver. More accurately, this is Shawver's updated edition of (his tutor) John Leyerle's doctoral dissertation, undertaken with Leyerle's support. Although there is a 1998 TEAMS text (*YWES* 79[2000] 174–5), Shawver and Leyerle herald their edition as the first published critical edition of the *Testament* since Skeat. For better or worse, the only copy-text available is the version of the *Testament* printed by Thynne, in this case the British Library copy of Thynne's *Workes of Geffray Chaucer* [1532]. Although 'the *Testament* is primarily a historical apologia' rather than autobiography (p. 8), it does contain autobiographical elements that have helped scholars to outline Usk's career. Most significantly, we know that Usk was a close member of John of Northampton's circle from at least the 1380s. Due to this involvement and Northampton's opposition to the London mayor, Usk was imprisoned in 1384, where he drafted his *Appeal*, a 'formal accusation against Northampton' (p. 14). Shawver and Leyerle make a strong case for dating the *Testament* to this period, composed partially in prison as a justification-cum-apology for turning against Northampton. Usk was later tried by the king, but managed briefly to prosper, working for Richard before falling foul of the Merciless Parliament in 1388, whereupon he was executed. The introduction also details Usk's major sources. Since expansion of abbreviations and normalizations are silent, the text proper is mostly clean and readable. The exception is the problematic third book, where Shawver and Leyerle accept but modify the Bradley–Skeat shift; here the necessarily more 'speculative' emendations are denoted by braces { } (p. 277). In themselves these are relatively innocuous; but Shawver and Leyerle have also attempted to counter the difficulties of Usk's prose and meaning in Book III by offering, in parallel to Usk's text, Latin and English passages from the appropriate sections of the source: St Anselm's *De concordia*. This results in frequent 'gaps in Usk's text so that both facing-page texts can be quoted in full' (p. 283). This is fully acknowledged and apologized for in the opening commentary to III. 3, but the result is definitely distracting. Whether it is equally beneficial will ultimately depend upon individual readers' sentiments. The apparatus is generally clean and extremely helpful.

More student-friendly than these titles are two TEAMS texts. Robert Hasenfratz's edition of *Ancrene Wisse* has plentiful on-page glossing, modern letters, capitalization and punctuation, and normalization and regularization of *u/v* and *i/j*. Hasenfratz offers 'a reading text of the entire Corpus [manuscript]' (p. 1; cf. p. 43) of *Ancrene Wisse* (here dated to 1225–40). The introduction includes overviews of anchoritic life, anchorholds, and thirteenth-century spirituality, including the observation that the thirteenth century in particular saw more female than male anchorites. Hasenfratz argues that the prohibitions in *Ancrene Wisse* against worldly affairs, correspondence, and monetary transactions indicate 'that many anchorites became something like spiritual celebrities' (p. 7). He further suggests that *Ancrene Wisse* is in English instead of Latin because it was composed for lay women with limited Latin. There is also a lengthy discussion of what Tolkien termed *Ancrene Wisse*'s 'AB language' (p. 21), as well as its sources and related texts. It is not clear, however, whether Hasenfratz is supporting Augustinian or Dominican or collaborative authorship. Equally irritating is the fact that the complex stemma (pp. 28–9) precedes the key explaining which letter represents which manuscript. Hasenfratz closes the introduction by emphasizing that his edition is based on the Corpus manuscript not out of the 'best text' belief that it most represents authorial intention (p. 43), but rather because it is 'one of the most interesting versions' of what can be considered the varied and evolving *Ancrene Wisse* textual tradition. The text (with its ample on-page glossing) is followed by explanatory notes (outlining such matters as organization, sources, allusions, and criticism), textual notes (outlining variants and emendations), appendices, and glossary. The text is extremely readable, but I failed to find any explanation as to why Latin phrases appear in bold. I randomly compared a number of passages against Tolkien's edition (which was reprinted by Boydell & Brewer in 2000) and found justifications for any discrepancies in the textual notes. The one exception is *u ther-of* (p. 94, l. 390), where Tolkien reads *nu* instead of *u*.

The second relevant TEAMS title is Salisbury, ed., *The Trials and Joys of Marriage*. This is an anthology of diverse texts, authors, and genres, some obscure, some better known, ranging from the late thirteenth to the early sixteenth centuries. Some of the selections include, or are extracted from, *Dame Sirith*, *Interludium de clerico et puella*, *The Wright's Chaste Wife*, *A Talk of Ten Wives*, the tales of Felicianus, Godfridus, and the 'Punished of Adulterers' from *Gesta Romanorum*, *How the Goode Wife Taught Hyr Doughter*, and *How the Goode Man Taght Hys Sone*. Such disparate material is unified by the theme of marriage: not all texts adopt the same approach to marriage, but marriage and its tribulations appear in one form or another throughout. In her introduction Salisbury surveys attitudes to marriage and love in writings from classical, biblical, Church, and romance sources, arguing that the variegated views 'allow us to interrogate the traditional assumptions that shape the idea of the medieval household' (p. 1). The volume is then innocuously divided into three sections: 'Satire and Fabliaux in Verse and Prose' (the longest section); 'Didactic Prose and Exempla'; and 'Select Lyrics of the Fourteenth and Fifteenth Centuries' (the shortest section). In accordance with TEAMS practice there is ample on-page glossing. In the first two sections each text is immediately followed by a short bibliography of manuscripts, editions, and (where relevant) studies, as well as textual notes. The final section presents its nine lyrics consecutively, two or even three to a page, before offering the relevant bibliography and notes as one unit. There is also a small glossary. All of this is very student-friendly, and the usual TEAMS editorial policies (outlined above), together with silent expansions, result in an eminently readable text. In fact, the text is arguably misleadingly clean: students will only be aware of emendation and variation if they consult the notes, but since initially students probably only want text, not variants, this is a minor complaint.

W.R.J. Barron and Glyn S. Burgess have coordinated the work of many hands in *The Voyage of Saint Brendan: Representative Versions of the Legend in English*

Translation. The volume includes translations of the *Voyage* in Latin, Anglo-Norman, Dutch, German, Venetian, Occitan, Catalan, Norse, and Early and Late Middle English, which come from the *South English Legendary* and Caxton's *Golden Legend*. The last five selections are accompanied by editions of the original texts *en regarde*, because those texts might not be readily available. Each version is preceded by a usually generous introduction, following a formula to cover bibliographic background, authorship, date, content, structure, sources, genre, and author's purpose. The physical design shows good consideration for legibility, though concession to space means that texts with facing translations do not match up well across the spread. Footnotes are used sometimes in the introductions, but endnotes are used for the texts and translations; this is an interesting way to provide more complete information in the introductions, for those who want it, while ensuring that the bulky notes for sources, comments, and textual matter do not interrupt smooth reading of the texts. A general bibliography, subdivided in its parts for the specific versions included, closes the volume. [JL]

Murdoch and Tasioulas, eds., *The Apocryphal Lives of Adam and Eve: Edited from the Auchinleck Manuscript and from Trinity College, Oxford MS 57*, will appeal to students and scholars both of Middle English and the Old Testament. The editors present two independent texts from the apocryphal but popular Adam and Eve tradition: the early fourteenth-century Auchinleck *Life of Adam*, a fragmentary Middle English text in rhyming couplets, and the *c*.1375 Middle English *Canticum de Creatione*, from Trinity College, Oxford, in tail-rhyme. Like all stories in the Adambook tradition, both texts recount aspects of Adam and Eve's penance and attempts to regain Paradise. As expected, the introduction gives details of the manuscripts, as well as the textual and literary traditions, including the fact that the *Life of Adam* and *Canticum* represent different versions of the Adambook tradition. The texts are related, however, by virtue of being the sole surviving English verse variants of this tradition and because they probably ultimately derive from an insular Latin *Vita Adæ* tradition. Both texts are very clean and readable. Codicological and emendatory matters are given in footnotes, with more detailed textual notes (many dealing with the question of sources) appearing at the end of the volume. There is a lot of untranslated Latin in these textual notes. Together with the lack of marginal glosses, this makes the volume less attractive to students. However, the volume would be far bulkier with translations, and there is a full and user-friendly Middle English glossary. The text is not only readable, but reasonably priced; since the last edition was 1878, this is, all things considered, a fine volume.

Cooper, ed., *The Wycliffe New Testament (1388)*, is, as the subtitle makes clear, a modernized text of the 1388 'Later Version' (p. vii) English Bible based on British Library Royal MS I.C.viii. The introduction immediately acknowledges that Wyclif inspired but did not translate the Bible attributed to him. Cooper also offers a short overview of Wyclif and Lollardy, as well as praise for what are considered the translation's legion of merits. It is in order to maximize the enjoyment of these merits that the text is modernized; there are also marginal glosses of archaic words, though there is no italicization or indication of which word the gloss explains. Since the edition is clearly directed towards readers unfamiliar (or unwilling to cope) with Middle English, it is difficult to say whether the intended audience will recognize which archaic word the gloss accompanies. The order of the books 'follow[s] exactly the preferred order of the Lollard Bible' (p. xiii), and includes Paul's Epistle to the Laodiceans, which the Lollards accepted as 'genuine' (p. xiii).

Since understanding of the *South English Legendary* will remain incomplete while its edition(s) remain incomplete, Michael S. Nagy, 'Saint Æþelberht of East Anglia in the *South English Legendary*' (*ChauR* 37[2002] 159–72), offers an edition (and list of variants) of the *SEL*'s Life of St Æþelberht, together with an analysis of its literary and political contexts. Richard Beadle, 'Fifteenth-Century Political Verses from the Holkham Archives' (*MÆ* 71[2002] 101–21), presents 'for the first time' (p. 101) an edition of and commentary upon the tail-rhyme verses in the title, taken from the verso side of Deed 116 in the Holkham archives. The text relates events from 1450 to 1461, but Beadle dates it to the 'aftermath' (p. 113) of Towton (1461). With apologies to the authors and interested readers, I have not been able to see R.F.S. Hamer and V.D. Russell's EETS edition of *Supplementary Lives in Some Manuscripts of the Gilte Legend* [2000], nor the EETS edition of *The English Text of the Ancrene Riwle: The 'Vernon' Text* [2000] by A. Zettersten and B. Diensberg.

In explicitly textual studies, Bengt Lindstrom, 'Additional Remarks on the Middle English *Genesis and Exodus*' (*N&Q* 49[2002] 180–4), examines nine textual cruces from *Genesis and Exodus*, suggesting in each case one or more of the following: meanings of disputed words or passages, sources, and emendation. The arguments are convincing, but would benefit from some sort of thesis statement.

In critical studies, Sebastian I. Sobecki, 'Mandeville's Thought of the Limit: The Discourse of Similarity and Difference in *The Travels of Sir John Mandeville*' (*RES* 53[2002] 329–43), applies Foucauldian thoughts of 'transgression' (p. 330) and 'limit' (p. 331) to the *Travels*, convincingly arguing that Mandeville acts as intermediary between the reader and Other. By being open-minded towards difference and critical of Western religion, Mandeville subtly negotiates the limits of Same and Other. Limits of another sort, endings, are the focus of Thomas R. Liszka's 'The Dragon in the *South English Legendary*: Judas, Pilate, and the "A(1)" Redaction' (*MP* 100[2002] 50–9). Liszka notes that important *SEL* manuscripts contain lives of Judas and Pilate, and argues that the '"A(1)" redactor' (p. 54) placed these at the close of the collection as a unifying 'damned souls section' (pp. 50, 53).

Cheryl Taylor, in 'A Contemplative Community? The *Cloud* Texts and *Scale 2* in Dialogue' (*Parergon* 19:ii[July 2002] 81–99), argues that the intertextual echoes between *The Cloud of Unknowing* and Walter Hilton's *Scale 2* stem from a common devotional culture, and that, more specifically, while Hilton at times follows the thinking or doctrine of *Cloud*, his principal concern is to render it 'more conventional and ... accessible' (p. 93). The date and authorship of the entire *Cloud* corpus are the subject of Annie Sutherland's 'The Dating and Authorship of the *Cloud* Corpus: A Reassessment of the Evidence' (*MÆ* 71[2002] 82–100). Sutherland agues that *Cloud* was composed by the 1380s at the latest, and uses the corpus's biblical quotations to corroborate Carthusian authorship, simultaneously rejecting the authenticity of *Spirites* and *Benjamin minor*. [KW]

Sarah Salih, 'Queering *Sponsalia Christi*' (*NML* 5[2002] 155–75), focuses on the presentation of virgin brides of Christ in *Þe Wohunge of ure Lauerd* and the Katherine Group. Salih argues that medieval virginity can include 'desire for God' (p. 156 *et passim*) and could upset gender roles. Her argument, while interesting, is more convincing in its early stages. The Katherine Group is also the subject of Julie Hassel's stimulating *Choosing Not To Marry: Women and Autonomy in the*

Katherine Group. Although she raises issues of reading, audience, and context, Hassel's principal argument is that the Katherine Group does not so much emphasize the 'sacred benefits' of virginity (p. 1) as the deleterious effects of marriage. The Katherine Group, she argues, is 'profoundly non-mystical' (p. 1), demonstrating female power. Like much modern criticism, Hassel is lamentably over-fond of contractions, and her text would benefit from a brief conclusion, and from quoting *Hali Meiðhad* from the critical edition cited elsewhere in the same chapter, rather than from an anthology. These minor complaints aside, this is an intriguing and generally well-written study, with a clear thesis. Hassel suggests in chapter 1 that, while the Katherine Group was composed by a man for a female audience, the texts all manage 'to empower women' (p. 4), simultaneously promoting Church-endorsed views of Christianity. She urges that the Katherine Group be considered separately from *Ancrene Wisse*, and surveys modern gender theory and medieval attitudes to ascetic virginity as useful paradigms for approaching the group. Chapter 2 examines English anchoritism during the eleventh to thirteenth centuries, and suggests that the initial audience for the group were women practising 'domestic monasticism' (p. 23). Chapter 3 argues that *Hali Meiðhad* belittles marriage, presenting it as an obstacle to 'medieval woman's autonomy' (pp. 35–6). Further, even a good marriage is but a pale imitation of marriage to God, and is both physically and spiritually draining. In chapter 4 Hassel argues that the Katherine *vitae* offer models of empowerment and self-definition in which Katherine, Margaret, and Juliana each play a key role in orchestrating their own lives, faiths, and martyrdoms. She uses the power of the saints to challenge the view that *Katherine* is misogynistic. Finally, it is argued that *Sawles Warde* reduces and complicates simple male–female binaries, revealing once again the negative aspects of marriage versus the positive possibilities afforded the virgin. Female religious are also the subject of Bella Millett's '*Ancrene Wisse* and the Life of Perfection' (*LeedsSE* 33[2002] 53–76). Millett questions the prevailing view that the *Ancrene Wisse* anchoresses became coenobites. Rather, it is persuasively suggested that monastic restrictions and financial burdens meant the women would remain religious solitaries, but not members of a formal order. Hence the implications within *Ancrene Wisse* that anchorites are superior to coenobites. [KW].

Paul Hardwick's 'Breaking the Rules that "ben not writen": Reginald Pecock and the Vernacular' (*Parergon* 19:ii[July 2002] 101–18), convincingly examines Pecock's 'use of the vernacular' (p. 102) and the role it played in his fall from grace. According to Hardwick, Pecock gets into trouble by accepting the existence of English bibles and an intelligent, occasionally literate, laity, and especially for trying to provide that laity with vernacular instruction.

Community is linked to appropriation in Rhonda Knight's 'Stealing Stonehenge: Translation, Appropriation, and Cultural identity in Robert Mannyng of Brunne's *Chronicle*' (*JMEMS* 32:i[Winter 2002] 41–58), which highlights the relationship between appropriation and English cultural and national identity in Mannyng's presentation of Merlin's cannibalistic seizure of Stonehenge. All of *New Medieval Literatures* 5 [2002] purports to focus on themes of origins and 'fundamental conditions: death, pain, time and memory' (p. 1). Although Christopher Baswell's 'Aeneas in 1381' (*NML* 5[2002] 7–58), a study of origins and social upheaval in fourteenth-century views of the *Aeneid*, is not all relevant here, his examination of the complex interactions between city officials, potentially rebellious commons, and aristocracy in England c.1377–87 is. Similarly, Robert Mills's 'A Man Is Being Beaten' (*NML* 5[2002] 115–53), a Freudian reading of hagiographic and iconographic representations of pain, might, I suppose, be applied to sundry Middle English texts. Mills argues for the voyeuristic and '"positive" aspects of pain' (p. 117) in, amongst other things, Julian's *Shewings*. Also heavily Freudian is D. Vance Smith's 'Crypt and Decryption' (*NML* 5[2002] 59–85), an arguably over-specialized approach to the problems of coping with death and 'memorialization' (pp. 68, 72) presented by the body of the pagan judge in *St Erkenwald*.

In *Incest and the Medieval Imagination*, Elizabeth Archibald 'explore[s] medieval uses of the incest motif in a variety of literary genres' (p. 1). The examples are diverse, including Latin, German, and French, as well as Middle English texts, but the popularity of the incest theme as well as the comprehensiveness of Archibald's survey justify its inclusion here. Chapter 1 reviews Graeco-Roman, Judaic, and patristic influences on medieval incest law, changing medieval legislation, and various views of incest. Like rape, *incest* had a wider range of meaning in the Middle Ages than today, and definitions of kinship were extremely inclusive. Chapter 2 highlights the influence of classical myth and the most popular classical incest tales in the Middle Ages. Chapter 3 focuses on mother–son incest in texts covering Judas, Gregorius, and Middle English romances such as *Eglamour*. For a medieval audience, this form of incest was the most egregious. Chapter 4 looks at the most common literary type, father–daughter incest, concentrating on both consummated and unconsummated or 'Flight from Incest' (p. 147) narratives. Finally, chapter 5 traces sibling and related types of incest. Sibling incest is rarer than the other medieval types, but appears in such prominent hero tales as those of Sigurd, Charlemagne, and Arthur. Archibald focuses on Arthur, but gives evidence of other examples as well. Amidst sundry other matters Archibald concludes that the Church used incest to emphasize humanity's sin as well as God's grace, that the Virgin Mary was presented as 'both mother and daughter of … Christ' (p. 238), and that incest was a common medieval theme, but also one particularly well suited to literary treatment. This interesting book is well laid out, with a clear and jargon-free argument and a wide range of illustrative texts. Archibald acknowledges at the outset that, given the breadth of material involved, she can only hope to illumine the variety and popularity of the motif, perhaps providing a foundation for future study. She is thus occasionally less specific than certain readers might like, but this itself testifies to her success in laying such foundations: this is now the port of entry for any study of the medieval incest theme.

Monstrous appetites are also the subject of McAvoy and Walters, eds., *Consuming Narratives*, a collection of essays on the dialectic between gender and appetite, and especially monstrosity, self, and consumption in the Middle Ages and Renaissance. Of the relevant Middle English papers not reviewed elsewhere in this chapter, Diane Watt, in 'Consuming Passions in Book VIII of John Gower's *Confessio Amantis*', pursues a psychoanalytical reading of power, familial relations, and monstrous appetite in Gower's Apollonius story. Ruth Evans highlights (anti-misogynistic aspects of) connections between female sexuality, 'the supernatural [and] … originary myths' (p. 182) in 'The Devil in Disguise: Perverse Female Origins of the Nation'. Her principal texts are *Sir Orfeo*, the *Wife of Bath's Tale*, the York play *Joseph's Trouble about Mary*, and the Albina legend *De Origine Gigantum*. The book is divided into three sections, each of which begins, somewhat curiously, with a 'response' (p. 8) to the papers that follow. The essays are clearly written, with a number of cross-references and some acknowledgement of the volume's occasionally disparate viewpoints. Although this is an interesting collection, the introduction is repetitive, and this repetition is exacerbated by the fact that the three responses also serve as introductions to their respective sections.

An engaging collection of essays which will interest scholars of either law or literature—and the growing number of critics studying both—is Steiner and Barrington, eds., *The Letter of the Law: Legal Practice and Literary Production in Medieval England*, a disparate study of the intersections of law and literature. In their introduction Steiner and Barrington emphasize not only this intersection, but also the consequences of such mixture for the English literary tradition. The volume as a whole, it is suggested, argues that 'Middle English literature (understood here as encompassing approximately 1225 to 1475) developed in *dialogue* with legal discourse, practices, and material culture' (p. 4; original emphasis). Relevant essays not reviewed elsewhere in this chapter are: 'Land, Lepers and the Law in *The Testament of Cresseid*' (pp. 40–66), in which Jana Mathews examines Henryson's *Testament of Cresseid* as a study of 'the law of personhood' (p. 42); 'Language on Trial: Performing the Law in the N-Town Trial Play' (pp. 115–35), in which Emma Lipton focuses on the concern with language and law and drama and court in the N-Town *Trial of Mary and Joseph*; 'Robin Hood: Thinking Globally, Acting Locally in the Fifteenth-Century Ballads' (pp. 12–39), in which Christine Chism argues (insufficiently) for a fifteenth-century date for the *Gest of Robin Hood*, *Robin Hood and the Monk*, and *Robin Hood and the Potter*, and (more successfully) that the ballads criticize 'the localization [and abuse] of law enforcement' (p. 13) consequent upon monarchical expansion. Like other essays in this collection, Chism's will interest both legal and literary critics; it should be noted, however, that much of her paper is devoted more to a study of brotherhood and power than the law. Bruce Holsinger makes an interesting case for *The Owl and the Nightingale*'s concern with jurisdiction, liturgy, and the law, in 'Vernacular Legality: The English Jurisdictions of *The Owl and Nightingale*' (pp. 154–84), all in the context of vernacular poetics. In 'Inventing Legality: Documenting Culture and Lollard Preaching' (pp. 185–201), Steiner argues that fabricated Christian charters were used by Lollard and 'heterodox' (p. 186 *et passim*) religious to criticize indulgences, orthodox belief, and textuality in the fourteenth century. Finally, Frank Grady, in 'The Generation of 1399' (pp. 202–29), highlights a peculiar Lancastrian style and political concern in *Mum and the Sothsegger*, *Richard the Redeless* and Gower's *Cronica*. There is also an appendix with Andrew Galloway's translation of Favent's record of the 1386 parliament. The index is full but incomplete (the entries on Salter and Wallace, for example, miss several appearances by each).

The development of Middle English as a discipline is the focus of David Matthews's *The Making of Middle English*. Or rather, since 'there was no discipline of Middle English before 1868' (p. xxvi), and since even Skeat's chair was in Anglo-Saxon, Matthews strives to reclaim the 'material history' (p. xvii) of the formulation of early Middle English studies. He focuses on personalities, contexts, and apparatuses as much as texts and manuscripts. The key dates of the full title are the first publication of Thomas Percy's *Reliques* in 1765, and the death of Furnivall and final emergence of Middle English as a (British) university discipline in 1910. Matthews divides the book into two parts, the first highlighting connections between literary study and the antiquarian self, and the second emphasizing Middle English and nationalism, but in fact these associations run through the entire study. Chapter 1 looks at connections between Thomas P(i)ercy's 'self-fashioning' and the beginnings of Middle English, together with Percy's rewriting of his Folio. Joseph Ritson, Percy's personal and professional enemy, is the principal subject of chapter 2, which highlights Ritson's similarities to, as well as his differences from, his peers. Percy's notion of the minstrel influenced Walter Scott, whose 'aesthetic' and 'social' personae (p. 56) are examined in chapter 3, together with Scott's edition of *Tristrem*. Chapter 4 focuses on gentlemen's literary clubs, which tended to valorize the historio-nationalistic aspects of Middle English (especially romance) while deriding its literary value. Chapter 5 illuminates Madden's approximation of editorial standards together with his continuities to his peers. Editorial standards (or their absence) and high (not always quality) production also figure in chapter 6's study of Furnivall and his contexts and achievements, including the establishment of the Early English Text Society in 1864. There is also a penultimate chapter on early Chaucer studies and Middle English, again with parts played by Furnivall and Skeat, amongst others, and which emphasizes Chaucer's early stature independent of Middle English. This is followed by a brief conclusion. Overall, although Matthews's introduction is laboured, the individual chapters are surprisingly engaging. The volume would benefit from a bibliography, but is throughout well documented. *Making Middle English* will interest scholars of Middle English, of romance, and of eighteenth- and nineteenth-century antiquarianism.

Matthews follows this text with a companion volume, *The Invention of Middle English*, which is essentially an addendum to the previous book. *Invention* is an anthology of primary sources extracted from the contexts and personalities outlined in *Making*. Surveying writings from George Hickes (1642–1715) to Walter William Skeat (1835–1911), Matthews hopes to show 'how the modern study of Middle English became the way it is', emphasizing in particular 'the peculiar turns Middle English studies has taken' (p. 8). Matthews's *terminus ad quem* of the 1870s creates some curious absentees, notably Furnivall, who features so prominently in *Making*, but these later writings are, claims Matthews, typically available elsewhere. Each author is given a brief biographical and, where appropriate, bibliographical introduction. This is very helpful, as is the rough division between language (in part 1) and criticism (in the lengthier part 2), and the chronological arrangement of entries within each section. Matthews also acknowledges (p. 14), but nonetheless presents for assessment, antiquarian views which will now often seem hostile or even wrong-headed. On the other hand, despite the brief thematic pointer at the bottom of page 13, the lack of an index is somewhat annoying. Foreign writers like Grimm and Koch are cited both in the original and translation; throughout, Matthews retains the spelling and punctuation of his originals, but otherwise has cut and annotated extensively. The result is a heavily edited series of extracts, but since any other option would make the book entirely unwieldy, this seems appropriate. As with *The Making of Middle English*, *The Invention of Middle English* will interest scholars and teachers of Middle English, of the history of the language, and of medievalism generally.

Rather different in approach is Francisco Alonso-Almeida and Mercedes Cabrera-Abreu's 'Formulation of Promise in Medieval English Medical Recipes: A Relevance-Theoretic Approach' (*Neophil* 86[2002] 137–54). The authors argue that written texts can be assessed by their 'pragmatic features' (p. 137) and by relevance theory, and apply such an interpretation to 'the formulation of promise' (p. 137) formulae found in medieval medical recipes. More wide-ranging is the continued proliferation of literary handbooks and histories, the most relevant example here being James Simpson's *Oxford English Literary History*, volume 2: *1350–1547: Reform and Cultural Revolution*. Chapter 1 argues that 'English literary history begins' (p. 11) with John Leland and John Bale. Chapter 2 re-examines the 'periodization' (p. 43) which presents Lydgate as 'dull' (p. 45) and medieval, in contrast to the view of Chaucer as the palmary pre-Reformation author. Chapter 3 focuses on anti-imperial strains in fourteenth- and fifteenth-century tragic martial narratives, contrasting with sixteenth-century pro-imperial Virgilian translations. The discussion of the elegiac in chapter 4 argues for the influence of Ovid throughout this period, and especially examines love poetry from 1370 to 1390 and 1530 to 1550. Chapter 5 looks at political writing. Chapter 6 examines romance and Chaucer's comedies, including their political ramifications, and is entitled 'The Comic' to reflect romance's happy ending. Chapter 7 focuses on religious literature, especially *Piers*, chapter 8 is called 'Moving Images', but might better be termed 'Affective Images' to reflect its focus on devotional writing and *vitae*, and chapter 9 turns to biblical translations and literary treatments like *Piers*, *Pearl*, and Julian's *Shewings*. Chapter 10 highlights the ways in which medieval drama is a product not of ecclesiastical but of lay culture. This is followed by a short summing up, a brief regnal list, short author biographies and bibliographies, a list of further reading, and a bibliography and index. The division of secular literature by genre is useful, especially given Simpson's desire to downplay the differences between medieval and Renaissance. This also allows for the discussion of the same author or text in more than one category. Readers will note their own favourite absentees (one of mine would be the stanzaic *Morte Arthur*, especially as the alliterative *Morte Arthure* does appear), and one might question the claim that Malory's final tale was 'completed by 1469' (p. 104), especially as this contradicts the 1469–71 designation given in the author biography (p. 583), as well as the more traditional 1469–70 date. There are also places where Simpson perhaps presses too far in the laudable attempt to downplay the periodic distinction between medieval and Renaissance. But overall these are minor quibbles in an engaging and erudite study.

Another new handbook is Lambdin and Lambdin, eds., *A Companion to Old and Middle English Literature*. This reference guide's strongest feature is that it (likewise) divides and discusses Old and Middle English literature by genre, with an eye also to the socio-historical contexts of particular texts and types. Although this context is stronger in some chapters than others, each chapter offers a definition of its genre(s) and overviews of key literary texts (where relevant, in both Old and Middle English), as well as a critical survey and select bibliography. There is also a general bibliography and index. This is valuable and user-friendly organization, especially for students, and the editors rightly acknowledge that 'medieval author[s] knew the artistic conventions and structures of typical literary types' (pp. ix–x). It goes too far, though, to suggest (pp. x–xi) that medieval authors always clearly followed convention. There are some further troubling curiosities: *epic*, for instance, gets two different chapters, both of which ignore the fact that epic need not be in verse (*contra* pp. 211, 232–33). Malory's *Morte Darthur* is also here classified as an epic (p. 251; not in the index), with no indication that such a view is contentious.

This is all the more puzzling considering that the romance chapter defines the *Morte* as 'the high point of Middle English prose romance' (p. 368). Neither critic offers a cross-reference, and the second, more usual, classification is contradicted by the first (and vice versa). It is also lamentable (however grammatically correct it may be) that Malory's work is referred to throughout as *Morte d'Arthur* (e.g. pp. 250, 368, 370), and completely unjustified that the alliterative *Morte Arthure* is likewise styled *Morte d'Arthur* (e.g. pp. 251, 359). Other classifications are less problematic, and, despite its errors, this is, overall, a useful and occasionally illuminating companion. The entire chapter-genre divisions run thus: Old English and Anglo-Norman; Religious and Allegorical Verse; Alliterative Poetry; Balladry; Beast Fable; Breton Lay; Chronicle; Debate Poetry; Drama; Dream Vision; Epic and Heroic Poetry; Epic Genre and Medieval Epics; Fabliau; Hagiographic, Homiletic, and Didactic Literature; Lyric; Parody; Riddles; Romance; Visions of the Afterlife. The illustrative texts cannot be comprehensive, but they are wide-ranging and judicious.

Deliberately more restricted in range is Michael Swanton's *English Poetry Before Chaucer*, a revision of his *English Literature Before Chaucer* [1987]. The scope of this companion is Old and Middle English poetry from the seventh to thirteenth centuries, and translations are given for all primary materials. Swanton argues for connections between the periods discussed rather than discontinuities, as well as for the sophistication of early English poets and the plurality of their reception. He is against more fanciful criticism, and claims, somewhat disingenuously given the verve and idiosyncrasy of some of his interpretations, that his own readings 'offer merely a series of starting-points' (p. ix). Chapter 1 introduces the historical and cultural milieu of the period in question, giving lucid overviews of Heroic Age Britain, the rise of English Christianity, chivalry, *fin amor* (dealt with briefly enough to annoy the increasing number of scholars and teachers who object to courtly love), 1066 and its consequences, the rise of towns and schools, and the twelfth-century Renaissance. Of the relevant material, chapter 6 offers the intriguing but contentious idea that '*romans* ... seems to have applied to Continental story-material of the type enjoyed by the new aristocracy, whereas *geste* ... is commonly used of indigenous tales' (p. 209). The focus is mostly on romance, but there is a reading of the fabliau *Madame Sirith*, a tale, says Swanton, dominated by 'sex and stupidity' (p. 245), and one which might best be considered a comic dramatic monologue 'based on a lost dramatic original' (p. 249). Chapter 7 focuses on a variety of lyrics, including *The Owl and the Nightingale*. Swanton is perhaps stronger on the Old than Middle English material, and the book is lopsided: chapters 2 to 5 deal with Old English material, excepting Layamon, who appears with Old English heroic texts in chapter 5, while only two chapters are devoted to Middle English. There are also some textual infelicities, as when Chaucer is cited from Robinson rather than the Riverside. However, Swanton's readings are often excellent and witty, there is immense learning, and reference is made to a vast range of primary materials. There are new headers, a helpful chronology and contexts chart, a fully updated bibliography, and notes on various authors and texts.

A useful and up-to-date historical companion to late medieval literature and culture classes is Michael Hicks's *English Political Culture in the Fifteenth Century*. Chapter 2 emphasizes the cultural differences and perceptions that encompass 'Political Culture' (p. 3), and offers overviews of fifteenth-century religion, women, and monarchy and government, as well as the concepts of worship and service. Chapter 3 explores more fully the English monarchy in the fifteenth century. Chapter 4 examines the aristocracy, including the ideas of chivalry, lineage and heritage. Chapter 5 focuses on the estates, clergy, townspeople, and peasants. Chapter 6 looks at the participants and procedures of central government. Chapter 7 highlights 'alternative perceptions of class, place and … constitutional concepts' (p. 117), including law and treason. Chapter 8 illumines bastard feudalism and argues that 'Indentured retainers' (p. 151) were actually quite rare in the fifteenth century because of their expense. Chapter 9 looks at 'Provincial Communities' (p. 164), chapter 10 turns to the workings of government and politics in both peace and trouble, and chapter 11 focuses on fifteenth-century civil wars, which Hicks divides into five categories: popular unrest; 'Lollard uprisings' (p. 204); small-scale feuds; '*coups*' (p. 204); and outright rebellions. In addition to brief opening and closing chapters there is also a full index. Since the book is available in paperback, and since it both covers the basic concepts and sheds new light on some old issues, it is a valuable companion to the student of literature—or history, for that matter.

Book-length studies of King Arthur's historicity likewise continue apace with N.J. Higham, *King Arthur: Myth-Making and History*. The worthiest and most original part of Higham's argument are the middle three chapters on Gildas, *Historia Brittonum*, and *Annales Cambriae*. Chapter 2 (pp. 38–97) emphasizes the ways in which the different political and ideological agenda of Roman and medieval authors, notably Gildas, create, pillory, or valorize particular nations and identities, especially those of Britain. Chapter 3 (pp. 98–169) traces the political and cultural trends and ambitions in eighth-century England and Wales to highlight Anglo-Saxon colonialism and the withering of Welsh power and culture. Against this background, *Historia Brittonum* is a highly politicized history of a nation designed to refute Gildas and Bede and to aggrandize the British rather than English peoples, particularly the king of Gwynedd. Higham claims a biblical source for the phrase *dux bellorum*, which is designed to present Arthur 'as the British Joshua' (p. 143). Chapter 4 (pp. 170–217) examines the social, cultural, and political context of *Annales Cambriae*, again with an eye to Welsh partisanship and the promotion of a specific king. As is obvious from this review, Higham's principal focus is not the historicity of Arthur but 'the *idea* of King Arthur' (p. 3; original emphasis) and the uses to which he is put by various political factions, particularly the ways in which Arthur is constructed and used in *Historia Brittonum* and *Annales Cambriae*. Chapter 1 (pp. 10–37) sets everything in motion with an extremely thorough survey of the historical Arthur debate, chapter 5 (pp. 218–66) offers a brief overview of pre-1100 Arthuriana before tracing Arthur's status as cultural and royal figure being used as a model for English kings from the Normans to Tudors, and chapter 6 (pp. 267–74) gives an excellent summary of the entire book. There is less in these flanking chapters that is original, but each offers a valuable and well-read summary, covering both older and more recent criticism. Overall, Higham discounts any post-Badon British peace and thus any strong evidence for Arthur's existence. Rather, he supports O.J. Padel's view of 'the folkloric re-imagining of a legendary figure of Romano-British history' (p. 96).

This section closes, again, with a tangential item, Alcuin Blamires and Gail C. Holian's *The Romance of the Rose Illuminated*. Although the focus is not Middle English, the *Rose*'s importance to Middle English literature and letters justifies its inclusion here. The introduction makes clear Blamires and Holian's enquiry: the illuminations of seven specific *Rose* manuscripts now in the National Library of Wales. Blamires and Holian then review the principal characters and events of the poem to establish where illustrations usually occur, but note that different manuscripts illustrate the same scene in different ways. Although the illustrations may well instigate interpretation, Blamires and Holian argue that this response aspect is *'accidental'* (p. xxxvi; original emphasis) since illuminators were not deeply versed in their texts or literary analysis. Chapter 1 then surveys and critiques the major iconographic studies of the *Rose*, suggesting, amidst much else, that the images of 'Oiseuse/Ease with mirror and comb' signify 'female beauty' (p. 12), while the illustrations of Pygmalion represent a 'problematization' of male desire. Chapter 2's principal focus (and interest) is a detailed commentary on the Welsh manuscripts' illuminations, which are taken in complete sequence, from 'frontispieces' (p. 31), through the vices on the Garden Wall (the second most commonly decorated portion of the *Rose*), to the Dreamer's greeting by Oiseuse/ Ease, and the various events and figures in the Garden. This includes illustration of Jean's arrival as author. The final figure considered, and the last decoration in the Welsh manuscripts, is Pygmalion. Chapter 3 is by Daniel Huws, who gives a professional description of the seven manuscripts and their collector. There are forty-nine colour plates keyed to the commentary, some of which reproduce the same figure from different manuscripts, and sixteen black and white decorations from other manuscripts. My major complaint is that the illustrations come *en masse* in chapters 2 and 3, so that readers must constantly flip back and forth between image and commentary. It would be much better to have them accompanying the relevant discussions. Otherwise, this is an important book which will interest scholars of the *Rose* and its (Middle English) tradition and heritage, as well as art historians and iconographers.

2. Women's Writing

Two excellent books published this year—Rebecca Krug's *Reading Families: Women's Literate Practice in Late Medieval England* and Mary Erler's *Women, Reading, and Piety in Late Medieval England*—examine what Krug terms 'the ordinariness of (which is not to say insignificance of) medieval women's relationship to written texts' (p. 16). Rather than examining the writings of female 'authors', both books instead explore the ways in which literate practice was embedded into the lives of some medieval women.

Reading Families focuses on two women, Margaret Paston and Margaret Beaufort, and two communities, the Norwich Lollards and the Bridgettines at Syon. Krug argues that medieval women's engagement with texts and literate practice was not revolutionary, but was encouraged and sanctioned by their family relationships. She is interested both in the ways in which family structures shaped women's relationships with texts and writing, and in the ways in which women used the family as an imaginative category through which they could interpret the world. The chapter which focuses most directly on women's writing is chapter 1: 'Husbands and Sons: Margaret Paston's Letter-Writing'. Krug argues that Margaret Paston wrote letters not because it was a normal thing to do, but because of the family that she had married into, emphasizing the Pastons' interest in documents, and the family's expectation of female letter-writing. An interesting argument is developed concerning the ways in which Margaret's stance, as reflected in her letters, changed during her life as she metamorphosed from wife (authorized by her husband) to mother and widow (disempowered somewhat by her son). Krug makes fascinating observations about the position of the scribe, and the public nature of even the most apparently private letters written at this time (notably Margery Brews's famed Valentine). This chapter also emphasizes Margaret's belief in texts, and her 'sense that reality could be fixed through textual transformation' (p. 59). Other parts of *Reading Families* are also concerned with women's writing; for example, in chapter 2, 'Margaret Beaufort's Literate Practice: Service and Self-Inscription', Krug discusses the 'imaginative insertion of one's own person and interests into the words of the text' (p. 67) that can be seen in annotations and additions to books used by women. This book also explores the abjurations of the Norwich Lollards, pointing out, for example, that Hawisia Moon links spatial domesticity with spiritual birth in her confession. More generally, Krug addresses the issue of why there is not more literature by women extant from the late medieval period, and concludes that women 'responded to writing dynamically, not in terms of "consumption" and "production" of discrete texts but as forces that shaped their familial lives' (pp. 210–11).

While Krug emphasizes the importance of the patriarchal family in shaping women's relationships to literate practice (p. 11), Erler is interested in 'the narrative of women's connection, even their friendship' (p. 138). She stresses the interactions between secular and religious life, and focuses on examining the histories of seven women readers (none of whom is married—each is either widowed, divorced, or religious). Erler's book is primarily about women's reading and book ownership, but it is peppered with the written words of medieval women. There are many references to and quotations from sources such as wills, letters, and annotations. Thus we hear about Katherine Chadderton's letter to her brother, George Plumpton, requesting a book (p. 25), about Eleanor Fettyplace's note now pasted in the cover of a missal, attesting to her ownership (p. 95), and about a devotional tract written by a Syon nun for one of her companions (p. 19). Erler uses a lot of sixteenth-century material, and discusses the importance of printing for medieval women. This book also includes three useful appendices entitled 'Surviving Religious Women's Books not Listed in Ker-Watson or Bell', 'Multiple Book Ownership by Religious Women', and 'Surviving Copies of Various Incunabula in Female Ownership'.

Both *Reading Families* and *Women, Reading, and Piety* discuss letters by medieval women, and 2002 saw the publication of a valuable resource for anyone interested in such letters: Crawford, ed., *Letters of Medieval Women*, which collects together a diverse range of documents. This book is suitable for the non-specialist, while also being of great interest to scholars of the period. Letters originally in Latin, French, and Middle English are all translated into modern English and there is a good general introduction covering issues such as the material conditions of letter-writing, the roles that women could take in medieval society, hospitality, the household, widowhood, land ownership, etc. Several black and white plates are included, mainly representing images from manuscripts. The letters are not arranged chronologically or by subject, but by the identity of the letter's intended recipient. Thus chapters include '"Dear and wellbeloved father": Women and their Parents' and '" I recommend me to you in my most hearty manner": Women and their Patrons, Friends and Servants'. Each letter is preceded by an explanation of the identity and position of the writer and recipient and, where relevant, the background details of the matters to which the letter refers. The earliest letter dates from 1130; the latest from 1506. Although most extant letters by medieval women are written by noble- or gentlewomen, this does not mean that the perspective of or the subject matter covered in the letters is unvaried. On the contrary, reading these letters allows one to view snapshots of different aspects of medieval women's lives—and indeed of medieval society. Some letters deal with high politics, others with local lawsuits, others with financial need, others with love. While some are short and prosaic, others—most notably the fabulously vituperative and descriptive letter by Joan Armburgh to John Horell (pp. 199–201)—employ extensive imagery and clearly draw on literary sources. This rich volume does much to illuminate medieval women's lives and throws light on the diversity of reasons that women had for writing letters.

Julian of Norwich's *Revelations of Divine Love* has been discussed from a range of perspectives this year. Alexandra Barratt's 'Julian of Norwich and the Holy Spirit, "Our Good Lord"' (*MysticsQ* 28[2002] 78–84) focuses on the necessity of treating Julian not as 'woman of our time' but as 'a woman of the later fourteenth and early fifteenth century' (p. 83). She emphasizes the importance of examining the language that Julian uses in its social context, concentrating on Julian's use of the phrase 'good lord' to refer to the Holy Spirit. Barratt's article discusses the negative connotations of good lordship, its associations with livery and maintenance, bastard feudalism and corruption, and good lordship's contrary, positive associations with guaranteeing social order. The idea of the Holy Spirit as 'feudal lord and patron' (p. 81) is then related to the Greek term *parakletos*, used four times in St John's Gospel, meaning literally 'advocate'. Barratt stresses that Julian is 'uncritical of the concept of "good lordship"' (p. 83). Similarly, in 'Consuming the Body of the Working Man in the Later Middle Ages' (in McAvoy and Walters, eds., pp. 42–53), Isabel Davis argues that Julian has an essentially conservative social position that 'reinforces class inequality' (p. 49). Davis too focuses on the social contexts and nuances of Julian's writings, discussing the body of the working man in the famous parable of the lord and the servant, and in depictions of Christ. Davis examines Julian's text alongside other contemporary texts such as *Piers Plowman*, describing the ways in which the working man is associated with food, pain, and corporeality in texts of the late fourteenth century, and particularly exploring the 'work/pain nexus' (p. 46) in such depictions. These two articles both aim to place the images and language used by Julian in historical and social context.

A discussion of the literary context of Julian's text is provided by Tarjei Park's *Selfhood and 'Gostly Menyng' in Some Middle English Mystics: Semiotic Approaches to Contemplative Theology*. This monograph covers the writings of Walter Hilton and the *Cloud of Unknowing* author as well as those of Julian, and investigates 'how their language *works*' (p. iii; emphasis in original). Park argues that Julian's work 'is of a greater flexibility and multivalence than that of Walter Hilton or the *Cloud*-author' (p. 169), suggesting that 'much of Julian's text might be seen as the disruption of the formulaic' (p. 172). He discusses in detail the position of the 'self' in Julian's writings, exploring the meaning of substance and sensuality, and emphasizing Julian's overwhelming interest in integration and wholeness (pp.

174, 206). Park also discusses such crucial issues as the idea that sin is 'behovabil' (p. 210), ultimately writing that 'for Julian, union with God *is already achieved*. The constitutional union is prior to the "work" of contemplation' (p. 220). Julian's work is again placed alongside that of Walter Hilton and the *Cloud* author, as well as the work of Ignatius of Loyola and John of the Cross in John D. Green's *A Strange Tongue: Tradition, Language, and the Appropriation of Mystical Experience in Late Fourteenth-Century England and Sixteenth-Century Spain*, a book which focuses on the practice and development of 'discernment of spirits' in late fourteenth-century England and sixteenth-century Spain.

Liz Herbert McAvoy has published two articles on Julian of Norwich this year. One, 'Julian of Norwich and a Trinity of the Feminine' (*MysticsQ* 28[2002] 68–77), appears alongside Barratt's article on the Holy Spirit discussed above. McAvoy discusses the way in which Julian uses the discourse of sin as a constructive way to redemption, and focuses on the image of the female body in Julian's text. She describes Julian's engagement with Mary Magdalen and discusses the parallel experiences of contemplatives and prostitutes, arguing that both emerged in numbers from the increasing urbanization of English society. In particular, McAvoy is concerned with Christ's femininity in Julian's writings. McAvoy again discusses the 'gynaecentric metaphors contained within a suffering and bleeding Christic body' in '"Ant nes he him seolf reclus i marie wombe?" Julian of Norwich, the Anchorhold and Redemption of the Monstrous Female Body' (in McAvoy and Walters, eds., pp. 128–43: 135; alongside Davis's article, discussed above). This article discusses discourses of enclosure, and the feminine spaces of enclosure. In both articles, McAvoy also draws attention to Margery Kempe, discussing her meeting with Julian ('Julian of Norwich and a Trinity of the Feminine', p. 68), and men's desire to enclose Margery ('Julian of Norwich, the Anchorhold and Redemption of the Monstrous Female Body', p. 131).

A third article in McAvoy and Walters also makes some mention of Julian: Sue Niebrzydowski's 'Monstrous (M)othering: The Representation of the Sowdanesse in Chaucer's *Man of Law's Tale*' (pp. 196–207) briefly discusses Julian's description of the idea of good motherhood in her development of the concept of Christ as mother (p. 197). This concept is discussed in the context of contemporary feminist theological debate in Kerry Dearborn, 'The Crucified Christ as the Motherly God: The Theology of Julian of Norwich' (*ScTh* 55[2002] 283–302), and Dearborn also comments on other uses of the idea of Christ as mother. Another article in the same journal—Marilyn McCord Adams, 'Horrors in Theological Context' (*ScTh* 55[2002] 468–79)—also refers to Julian of Norwich. Roberta Bondi's 'A Conversation with Julian of Norwich on Religious Experience' (*Spiritus* 2[2002] 83–98) is a personal religious response to Julian's text and to the idea of revelation. Two other books which are concerned with Julian of Norwich have been published this year but were not available for review: Elizabeth Ruth Obbard's *Medieval Women Mystics: Gertrude the Great, Angela of Foligno, Birgitta of Sweden, Julian of Norwich: Selected Spiritual Writings*, and Rosemary Radford Ruether's *Visionary Women: Three Medieval Mystics*.

Julian of Norwich appears in Diane Krantz, 'The Changing Feminine Archetype in Julian of Norwich's Long Text: A Psychology of Enclosure' (in Spivack and Herold, eds., *Archetypal Readings of Medieval Literature*, pp. 65–91). Krantz focuses on images of the Jungian Feminine and Great Mother in Julian's *Shewings*, arguing that Julian's Jesus appears as Great Mother and that Julian comes to identify herself as Divine Feminine. Ultimately, the two are linked and conflated by enclosure. [KW]

This year has seen the publication of an important new book on Margery Kempe, Anthony Goodman's *Margery Kempe and her World*. Written from a strongly social and historical perspective, this book focuses on mentalities, arguing that Margery's *Book* 'is unique in the nature and richness of the testimony it gives as a construction of a town dweller's mentality in medieval England' (p. 3). Part of The Medieval World series, this book could be used by both the undergraduate student and the professional academic. It includes useful apparatus, including plates and illustrations, a chronology of Margery Kempe's life, maps, and a glossary. The chapters cover a range of perspectives on Margery's life and writings: 'Lynn and the Brunham Family', 'Margery and Urban Gender Roles', 'Ecclesiastical Authority and Religious Culture in Lynn', 'The Piety of the *Book of Margery Kempe*', 'English Travels and Contexts', 'A Wider World', 'Great Cities and Sacred Soil'. Written with detailed historical knowledge, the book is dense with nuggets of information. Thus, the Kempes' marriage is placed alongside a case concerning an unconsummated marriage that was presented before Bishop Arundel's commissaries in Lynn in 1436 (p. 76), and Christ's comment to Margery in the *Book* that she will be gnawed by people as rats gnaw stockfish (p. 20) is contextualized by explaining that the storage of stockfish in Lynn attracted rats and the Black Death. Goodman carefully reconstructs place, describing the local politics and tensions of Lynn, as well as the churches that Margery knew, and also dwells on the cities that she visited, exploring what one might have experienced in places such as Venice, Rome, and the Holy Land in the fifteenth century. This book also views Margery in other perspectives, discussing, for example, Continental mysticism, Julian of Norwich, and the textual history of the *Book* in its manuscript and early printed forms. While Goodman emphasizes the vibrancy of Margery's *Book* and its value as an exposition of states of mind in Lynn in the 1430s, he is also careful to point out its limitations, discussing in the Conclusion what it omits and glosses over. Goodman's work will be of great use and interest to literary and historical scholars alike.

Margery's text is placed alongside other contemporary writing in Sarah Salih's 'Staging Conversion: The Digby Saint Plays and *The Book of Margery Kempe*' (in Riches and Salih, eds., *Gender and Holiness: Men, Women, and Saints in Late Medieval Europe*, pp. 121–34). Building on comments by Caroline Walker Bynum and Dyan Elliot, Salih argues that, contrary to the general rule that while men experience sudden conversion, women's experience is described as continuous and unified, Margery Kempe is attached to scenes of sudden conversion. Salih compares scenes of conversion in the *Book* with scenes in the Digby plays of St Mary Magdalen and St Paul, using the writings of Althusser and Butler to discuss subjectivity and interpellation. Salih goes on to suggest that, while Paul remains masculine, vocal, and active both before and after conversion, Margery and Mary Magdalen have to become 'differently feminine' (p. 131) as they pass through the feminine to their 'public apostolate' (p. 127). Finally, Salih speculates that the *Book of Margery Kempe* could itself have influenced the Digby playwright. Several other articles in Riches and Salih, eds., also discuss Margery. Two articles draw on Salih's earlier work on Margery and virginity: Samantha J.E. Riches, 'St George as a Male

Virgin Martyr' (pp. 65–85) and Katherine J. Lewis, 'Becoming a Virgin King: Richard II and Edward the Confessor' (pp. 86–100). Miriam Gill's 'Female Piety and Impiety: Selected Images of Women in Wall Paintings in England after 1300' (pp. 101–20) refers to Margery's retrospective attitude to her brewing as greed in the context of depictions of the fraudulent alewife, and P.H. Cullum, in 'Gendering Charity in Medieval Hagiography' (pp. 135–51), comments on Margery's being propositioned on her way to Evensong.

Like Salih, Fiona Somerset also uses the work of Judith Butler to comment on Margery, in 'Excitative Speech: Theories of Emotive Response from Richard Fitzralph to Margery Kempe' (in Blumenfeld-Kosinski, Robertson, and Warren, eds., *The Vernacular Spirit: Essays on Medieval Religious Literature*, pp. 59–79). Drawing on Butler's 'Excitable Speech', Somerset argues that Margery Kempe is a 'vernacular theorist of excitative speech' (p. 70) describing the way in which her own outbursts of weeping tend to be provoked by 'emotionally provocative language linked to Christ's Passion' (p. 73). Margery Kempe is also the subject of an article by A.C. Spearing in a special section of a journal themed 'The Margins and Setting of Life-Narrative': '*The Book of Margery Kempe*; Or The Diary of a Nobody' (*SoR* 38[2002] 625–35). Spearing ultimately compares Margery's *Book* to the Victorian *Diary of a Nobody*, arguing that, although it is tempting to read the *Book* as posturing, it demands a more serious response. Cristina Mazzoni's 'Of Stockfish and Stew: Feasting and Fasting in the Book of Margery Kempe' (*FFw* 10[2002] 171–82) examines encounters with and images of food in Margery's text. This article describes Margery's attitude to food as 'reverent' (p. 182), exploring both the way in which food and fasting are important in Margery's life, and her use of images of food. Mazzoni discusses, for example, Margery's desire to nourish and to mother Mary by giving her gruel and wine, and the use of images such as that of 'love as sticky stockfish' (p. 181). She contrasts Margery's attitude to food with that of 'holy anorexics', arguing that, for Margery, food is an object of desire, not revulsion.

Margery Kempe is the focus of Naoë Kukita Yoshikawa's 'Margery Kempe's Mystical Marriage and Roman Sojourn: [The] Influence of St Bridget of Sweden' (*RMSt* 28[2002] 39–57). Yoshikawa makes a strong case for Bridgettine influence in the parallels between Margery's and Bridget's revelations, the echoes of Bridgettine noviciate ceremony found in Margery's account of herself as bride, as well as in the pilgrimage route itself. Margery Kempe also appears very briefly in Claire Sponsler's 'In Transit: Theorizing Cultural Appropriation in Medieval Europe' (*JMEMS* 32:i[Winter 2002] 17–39), as do Chaucer and the *Play of the Sacrament*. Sponsler's focus is more on theories of appropriation and bricolage (and how appropriation can reveal cultural history) than Middle English, but she does argue for the work of Margery's scribes as being itself 'creative' (p. 25). [KW]

Jocelyn Wogan-Browne's 'Analytical Survey 5' (*NML* 5[2002] 229–97) provides an excellent overview and bibliography of the Anglo-American scholarly construction and study of 'Female Reading Communities' in medieval England (p. 229), including studies of book ownership and female religious. Women readers are also the subject of C. Annette Grisé's 'Women's Devotional Reading in Late-Medieval England and the Gendered Reader' (*MÆ* 71[2002] 209–25). Grisé argues that the stereotypes of author and reader in *The Myroure of Oure Ladye*, *De institutione inclusarum*, *Formula noviciorum*, *Disce mori*, *Deuot Treatyse of the*

Tree, The Tretyse of Love, and *Speculum devotorum* both 'reassert traditional gender hierarchies' (p. 221) and legitimatize and empower certain female behaviour. [KW]

The boundaries of what we might consider as 'women's writing' are explored by Judith M. Bennett in 'Ventriloquisms: When Maidens Speak in English Songs, c.1300–1550' (in Klinck and Rasmussen, eds., *Medieval Woman's Song: Cross-Cultural Approaches,* pp. 187–204). In the context of a volume focusing on 'medieval woman's song' across the early and late medieval periods and in various European contexts, Bennett discusses English female-voice songs in the late Middle Ages, suggesting that women may have written some of these songs, and that the distinction between composition and performance was often blurred at this time. Another volume, Spearing, ed., *Medieval Writings on Female Spirituality,* also focuses on examining English women's writing in the Continental context. This is a book of translations of extracts from the work of Hildegard of Bingen, Christina of Markyate, Hadewijch, Christine the Astonishing, Mary of Oignes, Elizabeth of Spaalbeck, Marguerite Porete, Bridget of Sweden, Julian of Norwich, an anonymous female writer, and Margery Kempe. This Penguin Classics volume is a useful introductory book: it includes short bibliographies for each writer, and a good introduction. Spearing also places Margery Kempe and Julian of Norwich not only in the Continental context, but also alongside the work of an anonymous English woman, author of 'A Revelation of Purgatory', which adds an interesting point of comparison.

Jennifer Ward's *Women in Medieval Europe, 1200–1500,* part of the six-volume Longman History of European Women, refers to many English women writers, including Margaret Paston, Margery Kempe, Julian of Norwich, Hawisia Moon, and Margery Baxter. This year has seen the reissue of Henrietta Leyser's well-known book, *Medieval Women: Social History of Women in England, 450–1500,* which also includes discussion of a variety of women writers, in particular Margery Kempe and Julian of Norwich.

3. Alliterative Verse and Lyrics

The Siege of Jerusalem has been popular this year, inspiring two articles and a book chapter. The chapter is in Christine Chism's *Alliterative Revivals,* a book dealing mainly with romance; Chism sees the poem as negotiating anxieties of Jewish origin for the Christian faith, and trying to change these into 'imperial and economic certainties' through a crusading ethos (p. 155). Jonathan Watson, in 'The Minimistic Imagination: Scribal Invention and the Word in the Early English Alliterative Tradition' (*OT* 17[2002] 290–309), focuses on scribal variations within a passage describing night falling in the *Siege* in order to show that 'the tension between oral and literate signification remains alive' (p. 290) into the fifteenth century. Words containing a series of minims, such as dimmed/dinned, give rise to variants that in turn condition other elements of the passage, developing motifs traceable through other ME and OE texts as scribes become, at least temporarily, performers. Taking a much wider view, Roger Nicholson, in 'Haunted Itineraries: Reading the *Siege of Jerusalem*' (*Exemplaria* 14[2002] 447–84), argues that, despite modern critical distaste, the poem's medieval popularity requires examination. Nicholson suggests that it speaks to battles of the 1390s against Turkish incursions, and that the poem was possibly dedicated to Henry Bolingbroke. Nicholson explores the text's various borders, both generic and physical (as in breached bodies and walls). Its real target, he argues, is Jerusalem rather than the Jews, who replace Saracens; the poem thereby offers 'a glimpse into the furnace where bad faith itself is being formed' (p. 484). Combining close reading, historical situation, and Kristeva's theories of abjection, this essay significantly illumines a problematic work.

A few pieces in *Medium Ævum* 71[2002] deal with Middle English verse. In '"As dewe in Aprille": "I syng of a mayden" and the Liturgy' (*MÆ* 71[2002] 66–73), Michael Steffes notes various biblical, homiletic, and liturgical images of dew falling, arguing that because 'the liturgy provides its own commentary' (p. 69) and because its repetition through the calendar encouraged internalizing and meditating on its images, the liturgy for 25 March (Feast of the Annunciation) is a likely source for the lyric's line about dew. Richard Newhauser studies the manuscript contexts of a quatrain in 'A Middle English Poem on the Fleeting Nature of Material Wealth' (*MÆ* 71[2002] 74–81), focusing on its marginal appearance in a preacher's anthology where, he suggests, it shows a reader's response to Peter of Limoges. Richard Beadle's 'Fifteenth-Century Political Verses from the Holkham Archive' (*MÆ* 71[2002] 101–21) presents a new discovery in Middle English verse: tail-rhyme verses written between April and October 1461, after the battle at Towton, won by Yorkist forces. They lament trouble in England and ask their audience to pray for four men bringing succour to the land. The verses appear on the back of a list of lands held by John Sewale; the language shows a number of distinctive Norfolk traits.

Karin Boklund-Lagopoulou's *'I have a yong suster': Popular Song and the Middle English Lyric* combines a structuralist approach with study of manuscript context to analyse the workings of 'non-courtly, non-ecclesiastical' medieval ballads and potential ballads (pp. 21–2). Boklund-Lagopoulou studies the lyrics of Oxford, Bodleian Library MS Rawlinson D.913 (including 'Irlaunde' and 'Maiden in the mor lay'); 'Judas'; lyrics from London, British Library MS Sloane 2593; outlaw ballads, including but not limited to Robin Hood material; comic ballads such as 'King John and the Bishop'; ballads of the Otherworld, such as 'Thomas of Erceldoune'; historical ballads; and items from Richard Hill's commonplace book (Oxford, Balliol College MS 354). She suggests that much of the appeal of Middle English lyric, 'its musicality, sense of rhythm, economy of language, simplicity of expression' (p. 234), comes from a basis in folk songs. While the structural analysis does help to make sense of some enigmatic lyrics, many of the author's conclusions must remain tentative.

4. Piers Plowman

William Elford Rogers's *Interpretation in 'Piers Plowman'* explores 'how things get done in the poem', rather than 'what the poem is about' (p. 16), doing so through the principles of originality, (inter)textuality, and recursiveness. His first chapter, significantly shorter than the other two, draws on exegetical readings of the Tower of Babel to interpret the beginning and end of the poem as displaying the world as 'conflicting texts' (p. 28). Chapter 2 studies the competing discourses of Holy Church, Anima, and Need, arguing that the poem is always dramatic, rather than 'driving toward conceptual coherence' (p. 81). The third multi-part chapter focuses on Piers and the dreamer as 'reciprocally determining' private symbols (p. 175), studying their significance and interrelationship in the pardon scene, in debates with the various figures associated with learning or thought, in the explication of the Tree of Charity, and in the events of Holy Week. Each chapter includes up to three bibliographical essays in which Rogers explains how his work relates to that of other critics; this organization can lead to a sense of anticlimax at the end of sections and chapters, and especially at the end of the book, where a more developed conclusion would be welcome.

In *The Charters of Christ and 'Piers Plowman': Documenting Salvation*, Jill Keen considers *Piers*'s effective and ineffective allegorical legal documents in the context of other Middle English fictional legal 'documents of salvation' (p. 2). She distinguishes four types of document purporting to come from Jesus, of which the first two are charters either of enfeoffment or of pardon; such charters form the bulk of material analysed in the first two chapters. Keen then considers Favel's charter to Fals—a 'clearly wicked document' though its form is valid (p. 60)—and Truth's pardon, 'invalid in its unjust intent' (p. 74) before analysing the documents from Spes, Peace, and Piers in C.XIX–XXI, accepted by other characters though their legal form is less clear. Piers's pardon 'fulfils not only the promises, but also the fears of the earlier documents' (p. 100).

Yearbook of Langland Studies 16[2002] leads off with Lawrence Warner's argument for a radical revision to received views of the production and circulation of A, B, and C versions, 'The Ur-B *Piers Plowman* and the Earliest Production of C and B' (*YLS* 16[2002] 3–39). Warner contends that Langland's original B-text was shorter than the version which, since Skeat, has been known as B, and that a version of C circulated before any B manuscripts. The argument develops through a comparison of National Library of Wales MS 733B (formerly considered an AC text) to the groups RF and W+ (or alpha and beta). The two groups of B-texts show different influences from C material, which Warner attributes to loose sheets of Langland's revisions coming into the hands of different scribes. Appendices contain the full sets of manuscript agreements that underpin the argument.

Thorlac Turville-Petre also focuses on manuscript traditions in 'Putting It Right: The Corrections of Huntington Library MS. Hm 128 and BL Additional MS. 35287' (*YLS* 16[2002] 41–65). Scribal practices reveal information about linguistic usage and readerly expectations. For the scribes and correctors of Hm 128, it appears that final -*e* 'perhaps was rather like … the apostrophe today' (p. 51), a convention of written language causing much anxiety and confusion, while the corrector of BL Add. 35287 (M) understood (or learned) where <e> belonged. Turville-Petre suggests that Hm was written for a religious house that wanted an accurate text, while M may have been 'adapted … as an exemplar for texts for the London market' (p. 63).

'Green and Filial Love: Two Notes on the Russell–Kane C Text: C.8.215 and C.17.48' (*YLS* 16[2002] 67–83) is Thomas D. Hill's tribute to the Russell–Kane edition. The first note queries a reading from R–K, while the second upholds a departure from the Pearsall and Schmidt editions. Hill argues that Langland coined the term 'filial', and that scribes unfamiliar with the term altered it. He then explores the patristic background of the phrase 'grene loue' and pursues it into the texts of later commentators and poets.

Traugott Lawler, in 'The Secular Clergy in *Piers Plowman*' (*YLS* 16[2002] 85–117), tackles the question of 'when Langland was talking to the clergy' (p. 85) and which members of it he had in mind. Disagreeing with Scase and Clopper, he claims that the secular clergy—priests, curators, parsons, preachers, teachers, loresmen, in Langland's terminology—play an important part in Langland's vision of society and religion. Langland considers separately the regular clergy, under the rules of an order. Lawler pays particular attention to B.XI.154–319 and B.XV, and their C counterparts. In a detailed response to this essay (pp. 118–29), Míceál F. Vaughan appreciates Lawler's marshalling of evidence but argues that '"priest" and "religious" are not comprehensively opposed terms, or vocations' (p. 119); further, actions (verbs) being more important than names (nouns) in *Piers*, it may be irrelevant that friars who preach are not called preachers. Vaughan similarly objects to applying other general terms (such as charity) too narrowly, as Piers the Plowman must represent 'EveryChristian' (p. 127).

Margaret Kim's 'Hunger, Need, and the Politics of Poverty in *Piers Plowman*' (*YLS* 16[2002] 130–68) studies the relations between politics and religion, concentrating on depictions of the poor. Following a brief survey of critical literature, she discusses Augustine's treatment of Lucifer's fall (which Langland echoes) and its implications for worldly politics. She then explores the political and moral implications of Hunger's and Need's interactions with poor people: 'tame projection[s] of dominant-class ideology' (p. 165) as Hunger acts on Piers' orders, but assertive activists in Need's speech.

Ralph Hanna presents, somewhat tentatively, 'Two New(?) Lost *Piers* Manuscripts(?)' (*YLS* 16[2002] 169–77) from an assessment of Sir Richard Brereton's goods in 1558. The tentativeness is because the entries could refer to Crowley's prints, and because, if manuscripts, one may be known already. Considering Brereton's reading interests and the provenance of many works in his library, Hanna suggests that one of Brereton's two *Piers* copies might be the one Ralph Coppinger lent to a 'Mr. Le of Addyngton' (p. 176), if Coppinger meant to write 'Adlyngton'.

Thomas D. Hill analyses Langland's treatment of 'The Swift Samaritan's Journey: *Piers Plowman* C XVIII–XIX' (*Anglia* 120[2002] 184–99), noting that, as well as heightening drama, Langland's emphasis on haste has exegetical and homiletic parallels: symbolically, then, Will and readers should hurry on their spiritual journey. Ambrose, Jerome, and Gilbert de Hollandia provide analogues for the wounded man's nakedness, and for treatment of Abraham and Moses.

Two essays dealing with *Piers* appeared in Dimmick, Simpson, and Zeeman, eds., *Images, Idolatry, and Iconoclasm in Late Medieval England: Textuality and the Visual Image*. David Aers tackles 'The Sacrament of the Altar in *Piers Plowman* and the Late Medieval Church in England'(pp. 63–80), arguing that this critically neglected element of Langland's theology is 'profound and coherent' (p. 80), worked out against the complex religious and social debates of the late fourteenth century. Although in passus 7 Piers seems to suggest that outer signs and community are unnecessary, Ymaginatif and Liberum Arbitrium create expectations that the sacrament of the altar will be revisited, which Christ as the Samaritan satisfies, and Conscience underlines, in C.XXI.385–90. In 'Langland's Ymaginatif: Images and the Limits of Poetry' (in Dimmick et al., eds., pp. 81–94), Ralph Hanna studies Ymaginatif as a pragmatic figure interested in the uses of learning rather than in creative endeavour. Ymaginatif counsels Will to read, not meddle with makings; he urges doing well by applying one's learning. Hanna analyses Ymaginatif's analogies and allusions, claiming that he participates more in popular and grammar-school discourses than in theological or scholastic argument. The icon Hanna attacks is that of 'Langland as poetic theorist ... suspiciously like ourselves' (p. 93).

Lynn Staley discusses Haukyn the Active Man, among other figures, in 'The Man in Foul Clothes and a Late Fourteenth-Century Conversation about Sin' (*SAC* 24[2002] 1–47). She also considers *Cleanness, St. Erkenwald*, Julian of Norwich's *Showings*, Chaucer's *Canon's Yeoman's Tale*, and a sermon by Richard Fitzralph as she pursues connections among their treatment of a figure based on Matthew 22:1–14. Haukyn seems to speak for this silent, shamefaced figure; the Active Man 'had a catalytic effect', Staley argues, on both Julian and on the 'shifting, confessional performance of the Canon's Yeoman' (p. 47), while *Erkenwald* responds both to *Cleanness* and to *Piers*.

'The Prophecies of *Piers Plowman* in Cambridge University Library MS Gg.4.31', by Bryan P. Davis (*JEBS* 5[2002] 15–36), examines the index, marginalia, and glosses of this manuscript. The apparatus appears to have been influenced by the changes brought about by the new print culture. While the manuscript's planner took note of such 'conventional interests' as 'estates satire and anticlericalism' (p. 24), he seems to have been most interested in sections that could be read, in the early sixteenth century, as prophecy.

Dee Dyas revisits the opening lines of the Prologue to *Piers* in 'A Pilgrim in Sheep's Clothing? The Nature of Wandering in *Piers Plowman*' (*ELN* 39:iv[2002] 1–12) to connect wandering, as well as working, with the Fall of Man. Lines from Genesis, Psalms, and Chronicles show humans as exiles. Further, Will's wandering 'as I a sheep were' (*PP* Prol. 2) suggests going astray and requiring rescue. These lines from the Prologue introduce themes taken up later in the poem.

'On the Grammar and Rhetoric of Language Mixing in *Piers Plowman*' (*NM* 103[2002] 33–50), by Helena Halmari and Robert Adams, examines Langland's use of Latin and French to show both that his macaronic language corresponds to current theoretical expectations for language-mixing (even though these are based mainly on conversation), and that it is 'Langland's way of asserting personal and social identity' with his intended audience (p. 35). After analysing various types of sentence that syntactically intermix English and Latin, the authors conclude that these insertions, by referring to Scripture and religious disputations, help to establish Langland's clerical authority.

5. Romance

As usual, textual matters first. Una O'Farrell-Tate has edited *The Abridged English Metrical Brut: Edited from London, British Library MS Royal 12 C.XII* because, though incomplete (ending with the beheading of Gaveston), this manuscript has various important features, apart from the possibility that, as Zettl concluded in 1935, it was a copy of the author's own. There are seven manuscripts of the work, but many of the textual details are unique to this one, such as the brief comment that Arthur survived for ten years after the battle with Mordred. The manuscript is not the earliest, but is known for the main scribe, also the scribe of Harley 2253, who copied this *Brut* as 'the earliest item copied into the manuscript *c.* 1316' (p. 52). The generous introduction is followed by the text; footnotes dealing with textual and codicological matters; tables of kings' names in the seven manuscripts, with two French texts, and historical kings; glossaries of words and proper names; and a bibliography.

In '"The Chronicles of Saints and Kings of England": Two Occurrences of the Middle English Prose *Brut*'s "Peculiar Version" in MSS of the early *Canterbury Tales*' (*JEBS* 5[2002] 145–9), Daniel W. Mosser briefly describes the new copies in the Cardigan manuscript and British Library MS 2864, finding them related to each other, with two of the three other known copies forming a separate branch and the third sharing readings from both. Mosser also comments on similar textual relationships in copies of Lydgate's *Siege of Thebes* and Chaucer in these manuscripts, and queries how the exemplars for the three texts circulated and were related.

Elaine Barber's *The Arthurian Bibliography IV: 1993–1998* represents the principal bibliographic publication of the year, with nearly 4,000 entries sorted by author and then by date, with a short subject index added. As with previous volumes, entries from individual issues of the *Bibliographical Bulletin of the International Arthurian Society* (*BBSIA*) were retyped into a spreadsheet (not a database) with some cross-checking, but not full reconciliation of entries from various contributors or volumes to a single standard style, though some non-English terms have been Anglicized and some personal names have been regularized to one form. Since the *BBSIA* plays catch-up at times, some entries prior to 1993 are included, such as *Arthurian Literature* for 1989 and later (no. 148 ff.). One can always quibble with subject indexes: E. Jane Burns's 'Which Queen? Guinevere's Transvestism in the French Prose *Lancelot*' (no. 587) does not show up under 'transvestism' or 'transvestites' in the subject index, for there are no such entries; Paul Zumthor is listed as a subject, but the only reference is to a book entitled *Images d'auteur dans le roman médiéval [XIIe–XIIIe siècles]*. Of greater interest to *YWES* readers will be curiosities such as *The Wedding of Sir Gawain and Dame Ragnell* having eight items listed but none of those appearing under 'Gauvain'. Checks against the online *International Medieval Bibliography*, the *MLA*, and *Iter* confirm the usual advice: one should not rely on a single bibliographic source for complete coverage of a matter, nor assume that it would index its entries correctly. Each of these three tools included materials not referenced in one or more of the others. Thus researchers in the romances would be amiss to ignore this handy summary of the *BBSIA*.

Turning to character, John C. Ford busies himself 'Contrasting the Identical: Differentiation of the "Indistinguishable" Characters of *Amis and Amiloun*' (*Neophil* 86[2002] 311–23). Despite the text's own initial stress on their many shared traits, the romance's plot does carefully make them complementary opposites: Amiloun is more chivalric and Amis more courtly, or perhaps a better description is of a more masculine Amiloun paired with a more feminine Amis. Furthermore, the 2000 conference on Romance in Medieval England, held at Reading, appears to have focused on character, as announced in the introduction to the proceedings: Hardman, ed., *The Matter of Identity in Medieval Romance*. Tony Davenport's 'Abbreviation and the Education of the Hero in *Chevalere Assigne*' (pp. 9–20) starts from the often noted topos of *abbreviatio* among versions of the *Chevalere Assigne* and notes how the English version does actually emphasize three scenes of dialogue which tend to teach the young hero how to be an adult—one with the hermit, the second with his father, and the third with the anonymous knight— through formulaic question-and-answer format. Joanne A. Charbonneau raises far more questions than answers while ringing changes in 'From Devil to Saint: Transformations in *Sir Gowther*' (pp. 21–8). Corinne Saunders discusses the relationship between providence and 'Desire, Will and Intention in *Sir Beves of Hamtoun*' (pp. 29–42), with regard to both Beves and Josian.

The last romance also lies at the heart of Jessica Brantley's 'Images of the Vernacular in the Taymouth Hours' (*EMS* 10[2002] 83–113). Produced in around 1330, the book of hours pictures a portion of *Bevis of Hamtoun* wherein Josiane is unharmed by a pair of lions that kill Boneface, but is killed by Beves, who refused her help. Unlike the text of the romance, these pictures give her half the narrative space and have her render spiritual aid by praying. This is probably a link to the book's female owner's lesson about prayer itself as a valid activity, and the link between the visual and the vernacular should prompt us to think again about how manuscripts were read. According to Graham N. Drake's 'Not Safe Even in Their Own Castles: Reading Domestic Violence Against Children in Four Middle English Romances' (in Salisbury, Donavin, and Llewelyn Price, eds., *Domestic Violence in Medieval Texts*, pp. 139–63), *King Horn*, *Havelok the Dane*, *Bevis of Hampton*, and *Athelston* appealed to their audiences in part through their use of parental fear and a sense of pathos in relation to suffering or abused children. When such outrages occur in the sanctity of the home, righteous indignation follows, as the changing readership would sympathize with bad fosterage or apprenticeship and forced marriage.

Women feature in further studies. In '"Born to Thralldom and Penance": Wives and Mothers in Middle English Romance' (*E&S* 55[2002] 41–59), David Salter begins with the medieval hints that romances might have been considered a feminine genre and reviews how women in the romances are typically defined by their relationships to husbands and children. He then examines this in *Octavian* and *Kyng Alisaunder*, concluding that—despite the apparent dissimilitude of the unnamed Empress and Olympias—the romances display typical attitudes about women. *Octavian* exonerates the passive Empress and blames her active mother-in-law, while *Kyng Alisaunder* 'exposes the ambivalence and emotional uncertainty of medieval romance in its representation of women' (p. 59). Second, Sheryl L. Forste-Grupp's 'A Woman Circumvents the Laws of Primogeniture in *The Weddynge of Sir Gawen and Dame Ragnell*' (*SP* 99[2002] 105–22) continues a trend of discovering political statements in the romances. Three groups of lines appear to be anomalous: Arthur's having given Sir Gromer Somer Joure's lands to Gawain, Ragnell's being Gromer's sister, and her bearing Gawain a son, Gyngolyn (ll. 55–9, 473–6, and 799–801). How Arthur took the lands in question is not explained, though Forste-Grupp presents some possibilities, yet Ragnell is effectively able to return them to her family through the marriage and son, though not to Gromer's side. Third, Eve Salisbury's 'Chaucer's "Wife," the Law, and the Middle English Breton Lays' (in Salisbury et al., eds., pp. 73–93) notes that Alisoun's relationship with Jankyn bears some resemblance to the 'battered women's syndrome', and that though her tale seems to close with the hag's supremacy in marriage it actually says that the wife 'obeyed him in everything' (l. 1255). She then places the wife and her tale within canon law and its practice, remarking on the relationship between rape and marriage. *Raptus* also is a feature of *Sir Orfeo, Sir Degaré, Sir Gowther*, and Thomas Chestre's *Sir Launfal*, which appear to confirm medieval public attitudes about sexuality, rape, and the status of peasant women. Such attitudes can lead to the kind of psychological abuse seen in the *Franklin's Tale*.

Also in Salisbury et al., eds., on the relationships among plots and women, Amanda Hopkins shows the device of 'Female Vulnerability as Catalyst in the Middle English Breton Lays' (pp. 43–58), such as those by Marie de France, but principally *Emaré, Sir Gowther, Sir Degaré, The Erle of Tolous*, and *Sir Orfeo*. Again working from lays, this time Thomas's *Tristan, The Romance of Horn, Eliduc, Boeve de Haumtone*, and *Le Bel Inconnu*, Morgan Dickson lays out the relationships between 'Female Doubling and Male Identity in Medieval Romance' (pp. 59–72); the doubled women show how attractive the hero is and allow him to prove himself, emphasizing also how men have roles outside marriage while women do not. Examining more than just plots, Marianne Ailes, 'Ganelon in the Middle English *Fierabras* Romances' (pp. 73–85), considers how the three versions (*Firumbras, Sir Ferumbras*, and *The Sowdone of Babylone*) relate to the French texts, including the *Chanson de Roland*. The Middle English versions focus more on plot and thus simplify character, but—though the authors seem unaware of *Roland*—Ganelon is a bit more than the archetypal traitor.

Thematic concerns are the matter of Judith Weiss's 'Emperors and Antichrists: Reflections of Empire in Insular Narrative, 1130–1250' (in Salisbury et al., eds., pp. 87–102), for the 'constant interpenetration of the historical and the eschatological led to varied, ambivalent and contradictory depictions of empire' (p. 88). Arthurian narratives often contain emperors, and England's changeable relations with the Hohenstaufen emperors may have influenced some thinking in these and other tales, as well as prophetic writing, in Anglo-Norman and even in Latin. Working from thematic elements that could be historical allusions, interpretations, or even misunderstandings, John Simons argues for 'A Byzantine Identity for *Robert of Cisyle*' (pp. 103–11), in that the tale may have been originally in Greek, set at midsummer's eve, with Pope Urban being Urban II, Robert being one of the Norman lords of Sicily (Roger Borsa or Roger I), and Valemounde being Bohemund, the changes in personal names due to pronunciation difficulties across languages. A different source for a hero is posed in Rhiannon Purdie's 'Generic Identity and the Origins of *Sir Isumbras*' (pp. 113–24); more specifically, Purdie wonders if the poet was struck by a similarity between the legend of St Eustace and *Guillaume d'Angleterre*, though both occur together only in a Spanish manuscript, evidently drawn from French versions.

In the same volume, but on a more bibliographic note, Maldwyn Mills, 'Generic Titles in Bodleian Library MS Douce 261 and British Library MS Egerton 3132A' (pp. 125–38) points out that the romances of Isenbras, Degore, Gawayne, Eglamoure, and Robert the Devil that E.B. copied from printed sources into these manuscripts are labelled 'hystorye', 'treatyse', 'jeaste', just by the title *Syr Eglamoure of Artoys*, and 'lyfe', respectively, and discusses these generic descriptors with regards to these and other works, the discussion extending briefly into modern generic description. Some of these romances overlap into print, as A.S.G. Edwards's 'William Copland and the Identity of Printed Middle English Romance' (pp. 139–47) shows in its survey of Copland's extensive repertoire of printed romances which follow de Worde's example and which are more numerous than his contemporaries' output. Copland also paid more attention to physical attributes, tending towards folios for verse and quartos for prose and adding illustrations. Finally, Roger Dalrymple's '*Amoryus and Cleopes*: John Metham's Metamorphosis of Chaucer and Ovid' (pp. 149–62) looks at how Metham retold Ovid's tale of Pyramus and Thisbe with a weighty eye on Chaucer's *Troilus*. Acknowledging Metham's stylistic and rhythmic missteps, Dalrymple endeavours to reveal Metham's debt and attempted improvements upon Chaucer, by his time filtered through Lydgate.

Layamon was a growth industry this year, including his language. In 'Inflections in the Two Manuscripts of Layamon's Brut' (*LangS* 24[2002] 231–45), Jack Fisiak and Marcin Krygier use 3,432 lines of text to analyse strong verbs and personal pronouns to demonstrate that the Caligula manuscript is much more archaic or conservative, though it is not certain whether this is due to time or dialectal distance. Michael A. Faletra's 'Once and Future Britons: The Welsh in Lawman's *Brut*' (*M&H* 28[2002] 1–23) sees Layamon's archaic language and style, which avoid French influences, as paralleling his vision of ancient Britons and of contemporary Welsh resistance to Norman hegemony. In contrast to Geoffrey of Monmouth, Layamon closes with the Britons coming together in Wales, awaiting God's will. This image is also implied by Layamon's reintroduction of Merlin's prophecies from Geoffrey of Monmouth, over Wace's omission. Layamon's ecumenical acceptance of various people is signalled by the four fishes in the rectangular, elf-dug lake in Scotland: they live in one pool, yet they are separate but equal. Separately, Alice Sheppard's 'Love Rewritten: Authorizing History in the Prologue to Layamon's *Brut*' (*Mediaevalia* 23[2002] 99–121) reviews how the foundation story emphasizes 'love' as the proper social bond between a lord and his followers, and then lets lordship turn to patronage with the historian as the patron of his text; Layamon thereby helps the provincial landowners of his audience link themselves to the court.

Further, a revised dissertation, Kelley M. Wickham-Crowley's *Writing the Future: Layamon's Prophetic History*, brackets her material with an introductory literature review and an appended summary of Layamon's *Brut*. The first of three parts explores the relationship Layamon depicts between one's language and one's heritage, and thereby one's duty versus betrayal or treachery. The second part displays Layamon's self-consciousness about language in both oral and written versions, evident through his puns in rhymes and half-rhymes, his distinction between the 'bookish' Christians and the illiterate pagans, and his dialogic relationship with the reader (we get more Bakhtinian here), with an excursion into likely Welsh influence, including triads. Finally, Merlin's prophecies in the historical past are divinely sanctioned, so his prophesying the return of the British Arthur for the English is taken not as supernaturally dubious but as historically possible; this aspect of Layamon's preaching salvation history was politically untenable for an English audience, and explains why the *Brut* did not become popular. Thomas J. Harford's *A Comprehensive Study of Layamon's 'Brut'* appears to be a very lightly revised publication of his 1999 thesis. The title is deceptive, for Harford's intent is solely to discuss Layamon as a writer of history, explicating the strategies Layamon applied to 'the narrative's polyvocality in his attempt to bestow authority on his entire project' (p. 6): his archaizing style, etymologizing toponyms, use of the multiple meanings of *runen* as a theme, representing prophecy, and framing exile stories.

Layamon's biggest appearance this year is in Allen, Perry, and Roberts, eds., *Layamon: Contexts, Language, and Interpretation*, the proceedings of Layamon 2000, held at King's College, London. We are informed that the spelling of his name used in *YWES*—with a y rather than a yogh—'is no longer in general use', yet three of the papers prefer Otho's version 'Lawman'. The papers published are organized in three parts, following the subtitle. First, in 'Contexts' we find the two plenary talks: Eric Stanley's 'Layamon: Priest and Hagiographer' (pp. 3–24), masterfully surveying the author in his milieu and his reception, followed by Daniel Donoghue's questioning survey of 'Lawman, Frederic Madden and Literary History' (pp. 25–38), asking first why Madden chose to edit the *Brut* and then moving into his scholarship and its influence, and extending even into periodization.

Then the papers commence, beginning with local geography. Carole Weinberg's 'Marginal Illustration: A Clue to the Provenance of the Cotton Caligula Manuscript of Layamon's *Brut*?' (pp. 39–52) finds similarities with an Augustinian psalter from Bristol now in Krivoklát Castle, and with a Benedictine psalter from Gloucester in Queens' College, Cambridge, both of which were in the diocese of Worcester, *c.* 1260–90. John Frankis broadens the context in 'Towards a Regional Context for Lawman's *Brut*: Literary Activity in the Dioceses of Worcester and Hereford in the Twelfth Century' (pp. 53–78), because Lawman's Areley Kings 'is only a couple of miles from the medieval diocesan boundary between Worcester and Hereford' (pp. 53–5). According to Frankis, before 1250 Worcester literary activity seems largely to be Anglo-Saxon antiquarianism concentrated in the Cathedral priory; Hereford had greater imaginative diversity and variety. Thus his alliterative line is grounded in Worcester, but his elves and underworld seem more indebted to Walter Map or William of Malmesbury. Cyril Edwards looks more closely at 'Layamon's Elves' (pp. 79–96) and their sources and analogues: the fairy godmothers at Arthur's birth, the elvish smith, the elves in the loch, and those in Avalon.

Ireland and Brittany occupy the next few offerings. Andrew Breeze's 'Merlin, Stonehenge, and the Hill of Uisneach, Ireland' (pp. 97–101) briefly shows why the hill outside Killare (Geoffrey of Monmouth's *in Killarao monte*) is a reasonable site for the original home of Stonehenge: it is 'placed in the no-man's-land where the ancient provinces met' (p. 99), where the fires of Beltain could be seen throughout Ireland, and thus its political and religious significance runs deeper than Christianity. However, Herbert Pilch's 'Layamon's Presentation of Ireland and the Irish' (pp. 103–15) classifies the scant information available to show how Layamon probably had no personal knowledge of them but depicted them as 'alien barbarians' (p. 103). Elizabeth J. Bryan turns to the colonial discourse of 'The Afterlife of Armoriche' (pp. 117–55) to discuss political aspirations within the work and how these were read symbolically outside it. The section closes with W.R.J. Barron on 'The Idiom and the Audience of Layamon's *Brut*' (pp. 157–84), casting his net widely to catch clues to why the archaizing poet may have had a similarly archaizing audience.

The second section, 'Language', opens with Richard Dance, 'Interpreting Layamon: Linguistic Diversity and Some Cruces in Cotton Caligula A. ix, with Particular Regard to Norse-Derived Words' (pp. 187–202), more generally on Norse and with some helpful clues from AB language. Philip Durkin notes that Layamon's full vocabulary should be available electronically in 'Layamon in the Third Edition of the *Oxford English Dictionary*: A Brief Report' (pp. 203–10); full spelling variants should be there, and the dates for the manuscript texts will be adjusted to *c*.1275 for the Caligula and *c*.1300 for the Otho. Michiko Ogura's tests concerning 'Verbs of Motion In Layamon's *Brut*' (pp. 211–25) are fairly indecisive about the time difference between the two versions, for some spelling and lexical choices could easily be contemporary during a period of change, but Caligula seems more variable while Otho seems more uniform. In 'Language, Genre, and Register: Factors in the Use of Simple Demonstrative Forms in the South-West Midlands of the Thirteenth Century' (pp. 227–39), Robert McColl Millar uses linguistic data from multiple works to argue that roughly contemporary texts may display varying degrees of archaism or modernity depending on their literary register. Gloria Mercatanti looks briefly at 'Some Rhetorical Devices of the Latin Tradition in Layamon's *Brut*' (pp. 241–9) as they appear in the preface and Arthur's second dream, showing first his familiarity with them and second his novel use of them. Finally in this part, Rosamund Allen's '"Nv seið mid loft-songe": A Re-Appraisal of Lawman's Verse Form' (pp. 251–82) analyses sample passages from the beginning, middle, and end of both manuscripts and compares the results with sources and near-contemporary practices to conclude that his verse is brilliantly flexible across alliteration, chime, and various rhymes.

The third section, 'Interpretation', begins with James Noble's 'Layamon's Arthur: *Aðelest kingen*' (pp. 285–97), which finds that the only significant expansions of Wace concern treason: Arthur's dream of the destruction of his hall and his own razing of Winchester. Temperance, moderation, and measure are themes investigated by Lucy Hay in 'Measures of Kingship in Layamon's *Brut*' (pp. 299–312), most apparent in the contrast between decent Elidur and his dishonourable father Morpidus, brothers, and nephews. Joseph D. Parry takes 'Lawman's Vortigern: The Problem of Knowledge and the Problem of Evil' (pp. 313–33) to examine how wilful choice of evil is a powerful corruption that endangers its own social fabric, made worse all the more because Vortigern is always 'war' of his choices. Marie-Françoise Alamichel's '"Ænne swiðe sellichne mon": Arthur and the Apocalypse in Layamon's *Brut*' (pp. 335–50) begins with seven largely prophetic passages (the fairy gifts are only mentioned here) to argue that Layamon was influenced by apocalyptic motifs, which themselves lead to new creations. In 'Cannibal Cultures and the Body of Text in Layamon's *Brut*' (pp. 351–69), Kelley M. Wickham-Crowley notes that the poets' and warriors' feeding off Arthur is metaphorical eucharistic sharing, but Cadwathlan's eating Brien's thigh is symptomatic of Layamon's discomfort over his cannibalizing Welsh history and when even priority in insular Christianity, though usually the cannibals or those eaten (as in *Richard Coer de Lion*) are subhuman 'others'. However, in 'The Life of Brian: A Loyal Retainer and a Loving Subject' (pp. 385–411), Lucy Perry finds Cadwathlan's action eucharistic in a love-triangle with Brien and Edwin, with Layamon's general avoidance of the word 'sodomy' providing him with some freedom to explore male relationships. Kenneth J. Tiller's 'Romancing History: Masculine Identity and Historical Authority in Layamon's Prologue (Cotton MS Caligula A. Ix ll. 1–35)' (pp. 371–83) focuses on the elements of male gender and how gazing at something tends to seduce the gazer. Finally, turning to Wace, Wayne Glowka's 'Masculinity, Male Sexuality, and Kingship in Wace's *Roman de Brut*' (pp. 413–31) marshals cases that show that sexual excess and military prowess and leadership are incompatible, and that ideally a ruler would be prudent in choosing when to have sex to ensure domestic and dynastic prosperity.

Several articles range more broadly. The stanzaic *Morte Arthur* is usually considered a romance, but K.S. Whetter, 'The Stanzaic *Morte Arthur* and Medieval Tragedy' (*RMSt* 28[2002] 87–111), re-examines the structure, theme, and genre of the poem to suggest instead that it is a hybrid *tragic romance* genre, a genre which considerably influenced Malory. [KW]

In 'Vision and History: Prophecy in the Middle English Prose *Brut* Chronicle' (*Arth* 12[2002] 25–49), Tamar Drukker discusses various features of prophecy and prophets, working from an understanding that the compilers' audience would have an implicit grasp of biblical prophecy and thus would use that to interpret how they relate to the *Brut*. Carole Weinberg's 'The Giant of Mont-Saint-Michel: An Arthurian Villain' (*BJRL* 84:iii[2002] 9–23) begins with the superficial parallels between Jack the Giant-Killer's story and Arthur's, then moves into more subtle ones shared by Geoffrey of Monmouth's Brutus and Joshua, as both clear their promised lands of giants. The giant at Mont-Saint-Michel is particularly vile, and 'therefore validates Arthur's eminence at both the personal and national level' (p. 16); his story continues into the *Brut* and to Layamon, who makes him demonic rather than monstrous. One should have ambiguity in mind when reading Geoffrey, according to Sjoerd Levelt's '"This book, attractively composed to form a consecutive and orderly narrative": The Ambiguity of Geoffrey of Monmouth's *Historia regum Britanniae*' (in Kooper, ed., *The Medieval Chronicle II*, pp. 130–43); indeed, his history subverts the historical tradition from within. Virginie Greene's 'Qui croit au retour d'Arthur?' (*Cahiers de Civilisation Médiévale* 45[2002] 321–40) ranges widely among materials in Latin and Romance, and matters pertaining to Wales and Brittany, concluding that belief in his return is presented as a stereotype, held by others, but not by authors.

Language issues attract new research. Jenifer Sutherland finds a strong relationship between 'Rhyming Patterns and Structures of Meaning in the Stanzaic *Morte Arthur*' (*Arth* 12[2002] 1–24). There are even rhymes associated with the four main characters, thus aiding readers or listeners in comprehending the development of the structure: *-ake* for Launcelot, *-ayne* for Gawain and Agravain, and *-ene* for Guenivere. A number of rhymes are structurally or thematically important, and it is good to see attention paid to formal features the poet knew better than we. An interesting approach to an old conundrum is Karen Hunter Trimnell's '"And shold have been oderwyse understond": The Disenchanting of Sir Gromer Somer Joure' (*MÆ* 71[2002] 294–301). Considering pronunciation rather than literary antecedents first, she reconstructs how the name sounded and finds a similar-sounding name in Goumerés sans Mesure of *L'Âtre périlleux*, who bears only some resemblance to Sir Gromer Somer Joure, but was apparently known as hostile to Gawain. She also extends the discussion to Malory's name (or names) Grummor Grummorsom, and reminds us that the oral circulation of names could differ interestingly from the literary traditions of texts.

Only two articles focus on *Havelok the Dane*. First, Seth Lerer proposes for '*Havelok*, Line 1158: An Emendation' (*N&Q* 49[2002] 13–14), where a one-syllable word is missing, 'smoþe', which does occur in alliterative collocations, thus having Godrich speaking 'smooth and slick' to his daughter. Second, in a new online journal, Donna Crawford got physical with 'The Vulnerable Body of *Havelok the Dane*' (*Medieval Forum* 1[2002]). Havelok's body represents the kingdom as in any king's two bodies, and any body's vulnerability and state display, even if they do not justify, social power (such as in his 'kynemark'). Politics is also the subject of Roger Nicholson's 'Haunted Itineraries: Reading the *Siege of Jerusalem*' (*Exemplaria* 14[2002] 447–84), where various 'borders' are 'symptomatic of political stress' (p. 451), primarily the body as border, but including the *Siege* as crossing several genre borders. Nicholson locates the *Siege* within the crusading polemic against the Turks in the 1390s and within Kristeva's work on abjection.

Working primarily with the early Latin Arthurian sources but continuing through the nineteenth century, N.J. Higham's *King Arthur* opens with a curious polarity: 'On the one side, belief in Arthur as a real figure in real time and space has become deeply entrenched. On the other, several scholars have urged caution or even sought to argue the negative, that no historical Arthur ever existed' (p. 1). Despite a penchant for entrenchment, Higham explores the idea of Arthur, using Gildas to portray how fifth- and sixth-century Britons perceived their national identity, then the *Historia Brittonum* as their providential history, with Arthur playing Joshua to St Patrick's Moses, as viewed through a contemporary political lens, since a contemporary dynastic and political agenda colours the *Annales Cambriae*. From such beginnings, it is no surprise that later versions prismatically refract and refocus the partial sources, selecting and amplifying what their own times prefer to have displayed before them.

Ranging more equally from medieval through modern is a collection of essays based upon presentations at Camelot 2000: A Millennial Conference on the Arthurian Legends: Lupack, ed., *New Directions in Arthurian Studies*. Unlike many 'New ...' volumes, this one begins with a retrospect on previous scholarship, 'Arthurian Research in a New Century: Prospects and Projects', by Norris J. Lacy (pp. 1–20). Lacy bemoans the continuing second-class citizenship of editing in academia, but finds hope in new scholarly endeavours, despite popular hype that baldly ignores learned caveats. The next two articles both concern Malory: P.J.C. Field's 'Malory and his Audience' (pp. 21–32), partly a revision of his essay in W.R.J. Barron, ed., *The Arthur of the English* (see *YWES* 80[2001] 165–6), exploring the implications of what Malory could have imagined his audience to be, based on several comments in his text and on his use of sources but extending to his narrative skill. Derek Brewer's 'The Paradoxes of Honour in Malory' (pp. 33–47) lists ten contradictions of potentially honourable behaviour and then ranges broadly among conflicting actions and beliefs in Malory. Shifting to another medieval language, Siân Echard begins '"Hic est Arthur": Reading Latin and Reading Arthur' (pp. 49–67) by reminding us of the social register of Latin versus the vernacular and of how the early Latin comments on vernacular tales of Arthur match the register. Geoffrey of Monmouth's portrayed use of the ancient British book inverts the usual topoi and attitudes, questioning received opinion regarding orality and textuality; this new attitude recurs afterwards in interesting ways in *De ortu Waluuanii*, William of Rennes' *Gesta regum Britannie*, and *Arthur and Gorlagon*. Finishing up the medieval portion of the book is another retrospect: Robert J. Blanch and the late Julian N. Wasserman's 'Judging Camelot: Changing Critical Perspectives in *Sir Gawain and the Green Knight*' (pp. 69–81), which looks over the second half of twentieth-century scholarship with an emphasis on evaluations of the Camelot of the poem. Since recent decades have read *Gawain* in the context of MS Cotton Nero A.x, they suggest that the future might restore it to the realm of romances and especially of Gawain-works, whence new readings could arise.

The volume then skips to just after the middle of the nineteenth century with David Staines, 'Tennyson's Guinevere and her *Idylls of the King*' (pp. 83–95). The *Idylls* are a cycle with Arthur as a centrepiece against which the others are viewed, but it was through Guinevere that Tennyson found the best embodiment for his vision of Camelot and its lesson for us: too late, she learned to see the ideal in the real, and then the contrast between the two benighted petty reality. Raymond H. Thompson moves to modern fantasy novels in 'Darkness over Camelot: Enemies of the Arthurian Dream' (pp. 97–104), looking briefly at external invaders, internal dissent, and personal ambivalence. Barbara Tepa Lupack's 'King Arthur and Black American Popular Culture' (pp. 105–21) is a brief but tantalizing overview of late nineteenth- and mainly twentieth-century African American novels, with some poems, and it extends into television and theatre films as well as comic books, culminating in a recounting of the Post Office Knights of the Round Table in Chicago, originating during the Depression and continuing to the present.

A third retrospect and prospect is Bonnie Wheeler's 'The Project of Arthurian Studies: Quondam et Futurus' (pp. 123–34), looking back at Arthurian studies as a field and then forward by way of various schools of criticism, with comments on editing and translating and an excursus on 'Arthurian Aryanism', an anthropological approach that bears on concepts of ethnicity. Kevin J. Harty moves from the familiar past to the present in '"Arthur? Arthur? Arthur?"—Where Exactly Is the Cinematic Arthur to be Found?' (pp. 135–48), discussing the Arthurian aspects of M. Night Shyamalan's *The Sixth Sense* and, less surprisingly, *Knightriders*, *Four Diamonds*, and *The Mighty*. Finally, in 'Merlin in the Twenty-First Century' (pp. 149–62), Peter H. Goodrich has a concluding retrospect that swiftly skips through more chronological and generic ground than the former articles did, and he predicts that the future will continue past presentations of Merlin as a 'strange attractor': atavism, anachronism, avatar, adaptation, and commodity.

Masaji Tajiri, *Studies in the Middle English Didactic Tail-Rhyme Romances* (Eihosha [2002]), was not available for review.

6. Gower, Lydgate, Hoccleve

(a) Gower

Two theoretically influenced articles on Gower appear in the same journal. First, in 'Gower's Boat, Richard's Barge, and the True Story of the *Confessio Amantis*: Text and Gloss' (*TSLL* 44[2002] 1–15), Frank Grady takes his cue from new historicist use of anecdotes and 'close reading' to make Gower's staged meeting with Richard, the Arion tale, and the *Westminster Chronicle*'s accounts of Richard's other barge incidents into a re-vision of Gower's intentions, as well as those of the critics, with some commentary on his own travail. Following hard upon this, Robert Epstein unites the 'Literal Opposition: Deconstruction, History, and Lancaster' (*TSLL* 44[2002] 16–33), observing that Gower's changes in the dedicatees of the *Confessio Amantis* and use of the initials R and H in the *Cronica Tripartita* define Henry IV in his very opposition to Richard II. Hoccleve similarly defines Henry V through opposition with the Lollards and Oldcastle, as do the *Gesta Henrici Quinti* and Usk's *Chronicon*. All these oppositions, however, rely on mirror-like reversals, wherein the fair image is a foul reflection and vice versa. That is, 'identity is represented as relational rather than absolute', just as language and signification are relational.

In a similar vein, though more tightly written and extensively buttressed, is Andrew Galloway's 'The Literature of 1388 and the Politics of Pity in Gower's *Confessio Amantis*' (in Steiner and Barrington, eds., *The Letter of the Law*, pp. 67–104). Galloway reviews the accounts of the Merciless Parliament in light of their narrative techniques and political leanings, emphasizing the ad hoc nature of the proceedings and subsequent difficulties with legal corruption presented as grants of mercy, or pity (he adds a translation of Thomas Favent's narrative in an appendix, pp. 231–52). Gower's *Cronica tripertita* resembles the Westminster chronicle in tone and the prophecies of Merlin in some aspects of style, with *pietas* a major theme, a term translated in the *Confessio amantis* as 'pity'. Written in 1400, the *Cronica* can clearly display Gower's evaluation of Richard's *pietas*, while the *Confessio* is far more circumspect a decade earlier, implying at least that royal pity is but 'predicated on a suspension of cruelty' (p. 93). Richard's use of general pardons seemed unpredictable and was largely self-serving. A number of Gower's tales examine true versus false pity; for example, the discussion of royal policy in book 7 includes a use of 'appeal' reminiscent of the Appellants', differing in that the appealing Pagan leaves both mercy and vengeance in the hands of his God. The final tale of Apollonius uses pity and mercy in various ways, with echoes of 1388: customers are made impotent by Thais' pitiful complaints in the brothel, and the traitor's execution of Dionise and her husband, who feigned pity, is sanctioned as divine providence, 'Which doth mercy forth with justice' (8.1957). Finally, the Lover in his self-pity is seen as a traitor to love; the assembled throng clamours for Venus to pity him, yet his punishment is castration by the blind, groping Cupid.

At the end of the volume is Frank Grady's 'The Generation of 1399' (pp. 202–29), which groups together *Mum and Sothsegger*, *Richard the Redeless*, and Gower's *Cronica tripertita* as Lancastrian poems not just because of their dates but also because they are openly partisan in politics and use 'certain formal poetic devices and structural traits' (p. 206), for example referring to individuals by means of allegories and, more importantly, departing from dream visions into a documentary mode. Politics is also the interest of Lynn Arner in 'History Lessons from the End of Time: Gower and the English Rising of 1381' (*ClioI* 31[2001–2] 237–55), which examines Nebuchadnezzar's dream as an appeal to former rebels and sympathizers to realign themselves with the status quo. Given the statue as a teleological model of history, any change represents long spans of time, within which quick political activities are futile. Being at the end of time, Gower's England faces only destruction with change, so stability through conservatism is the wisest course. It is the weakness of the lowest social orders, figured by the feet, that will cause society's destruction.

Sexual attitudes and behaviour attracted the attention of other writers. According to Michael Hanrahan in 'Speaking of Sodomy: Gower's Advice to Princes in the *Confessio Amantis*' (*Exemplaria* 14[2002] 423–46), sodomy—a sin that could not be named (though it was)—included any vice that seemed unnatural, including simony, usury, and heresy, as well as unspecified sexual practices. Nevertheless, it was often a charge laid against certain groups, including bad counsellors, and individuals, including the deposed Richard II. Hanrahan considers book VII of the *Confessio* in this context, finding that lechery was considered to feminize men and led rulers to risk deposition. More in line with postmodern theory is Georgiana Donavin's 'Taboo and Transgression in Gower's "Appolonius of Tyre"' (in Salisbury et al., eds., pp. 94–121). The laws meant to preserve domestic harmony lead to domestic violence, for, as theory shows, in forbidding an activity, a taboo creates a desire for it. Particularly here, incest—named only through euphemism—in book VIII draws attraction to itself by its very prohibition. Jenny Rebecca Rytting's 'In Search of the Perfect Spouse: John Gower's *Confessio Amantis* as a Marriage Manual' (*DR* 82[2002] 113–26) summarizes the virtues illustrated in the marriage stories through good and bad examples.

(b) Lydgate
Reserving the text for a forthcoming TEAMS edition of *Saints' Legends from Middle English Collections* edited by himself, Anne B. Thompson, and Robert K. Upchurch, E. Gordon Whatley discusses 'John Lydgate's *Saint Austin at Compton*: The Poem and its Sources' (in Echard and Wieland, eds., *Anglo-Latin and its Heritage: Essays in Honour of A.G. Rigg on his 64th Birthday*, pp. 191–227). In the poem, St Augustine of Canterbury reconciles a dead British lord with the priest who excommunicated him 150 years previously for non-payment of tithes, with the reanimated corpse scourged by the resuscitated priest. The genesis for Lydgate's rendering might be a tithing dispute centred around a London Franciscan, William Russell, in the late 1420s, but the main source comes from a Latin miracle Whatley edits from nine manuscripts as an appendix.

Following somewhat in the tradition of his recent Chaucer manuscript catalogues, M. C. Seymour discusses and describes 'Some Lydgate Manuscripts: The Siege of Thebes' (*EBST* 6:v[2002 for 1995–7] 149–77). He offers a regrouping of Erdmann's 1925 classification and discusses the possible origin of the poem and format of the original manuscript, adding comments on material support and early owners. The bulk of the article is a series of twenty-seven descriptions, each ranging over codicology, contents, scribes, and history. Both the *Siege of Thebes* and the *Troy Book* are surveyed briefly in the context of Statius, Boccaccio, and Chaucer by Robert R. Edwards in 'Medieval Literary Careers: The Theban Track' (in Cheney and de Armas, eds., *European Literary Careers: The Author from Antiquity to the Renaissance*, pp. 104–28).

Several studies touched on Lydgate's 'Verses on the Kings of England'. First, Paul Acker discusses and edits some previously unpublished 'Texts from the Margin: Lydgate, Recipes, and Glosses in Bühler MS 17' (*ChauR* 37[2002] 59–85). The Lydgate text is a copy of the first redaction of the 'Verses', copied early in the second quarter of the fifteenth century into a manuscript of Petrus Crescentius' *Liber ruralium commodorum*. Acker argues that some of the recipes were copied in between 1457 and 1463. Second, Henk Dragstra asks a simple question, '"This myghti William": Why Did Lydgate Write his "Verses on the Kings of England since William the Conqueror"?' (in Kooper, ed., pp. 65–77). Taking it as an occasional poem for the knighting of Henry VI in Westminster Hall, Dragstra observes that the statues there would have provided kings' portraits missing from the poem; when the knighting was moved up in time and performed in Leicester, the poem lost its occasion. Third, Matthew Spencer and Christopher J. Howe ask 'How Accurate Were Scribes? A Mathematical Model' (*L&LC* 17[2002] 311–22). Using mathematics and mathematical software, they pose that it is possible to derive a 'relationship between the total number of manuscripts in the tradition' of a work and 'the number of copying events (copy distance) separating a randomly chosen pair of manuscripts' (p. 312), after which the formulae can produce an average of copy distance and of the probability of change. When this was applied to the thirty-five manuscripts of Lydgate's 'Kings of England', the average copy distance worked out to be 4.8, and there was a 0.022 probability of change (both numbers rising if more manuscripts are estimated to have existed).

That article is related to one written slightly earlier, though rather late in publication, and involving additional authors: Linne R. Mooney. Adrian C. Baybrook, Christopher J. Howe, and Matthew Spencer's 'Stemmatic Analysis of Lydgate's "Kings of England": A Test Case for the Application of Software Developed for Evolutionary Biology to Manuscript Stemmatics' (*Revue d'Histoire des Textes* 31[2001] 275–97), which compares fairly traditional stemmatic analysis with two programs: PAUP* and SplitsTree. Preparing the text meant identifying the common readings as well as the instances and the nature of variants: inversions, major versus minor omissions, additions, etc. However, the software required the text to be replaced by one-character symbols representing agreement or the type or instance of a type of variant, so that a line of seven words was recoded as a line of eleven symbols. Both programs produced results resembling those of traditional analysis, with PAUP* displaying an 'unrooted tree' graph (much like a vine with multiple branches but no originating root) and SplitsTree displaying a starburst structure. When the types of variants were assigned different explicit numeric weights, just as editors assign implicit weights, the computer programs resembled human decisions more closely, although SplitsTree decided one manuscript was related to a different family. One wishes the authors had gone on to establish the text of Lydgate's poem and then seen how well the programs would identify the root and subsequent stemma, or at least variant families, but perhaps they will treat this in a future article testing Peter Robinson's Collate program. At least it would be good if the analysis included a discussion of whether the additional steps required for computer analysis seemed worth the investment, and of how the programs perform when an established text is the base against which variants are measured. The authors already note that work is needed on determining the numeric weights to assign variants.

Sue Bianco's 'New Perspectives on Lydgate's Courtly Verse' (in Cooney, ed., *Nation, Court and Culture: New Essays on Fifteenth-Century English Poetry*, pp. 95–115) continues from an earlier article placing Lydgate's verse into the French *dits amoureux* tradition (see *YWES* 80[2001] 171), this time working with the *Complaynt of a Loveres Lyfe* and *The Temple of Glass*. The *Complaynt* is about the exiled Bolingbroke, and is addressed to the Percies of Northumberland. The *Temple*, however, concerns the marriage of Henry IV and Joan of Navarre, and Lydgate uses Venus to moral ends. In the same volume, Julia Boffey also treats of the *Temple of Glass*, but together with the anonymous *Assembly of Ladies*, in her '"Forto compleyne she had gret desire": The Grievances Expressed in Two Fifteenth-Century Dream-Visions' (pp. 116–28). The two are similar in their portrayal of social harmony obtained through due process intended to find concord.

In 'A False Caxton "Embleme" in the *OED*' (*W&I* 18[2002] 123–5), Ayers Bagley points out that the *Oxford English Dictionary* mistakenly used a Roxburgh Club reprint to furnish a fifteenth-century symbolic sense of 'emblem', citing the opening line of Lydgate's *Chorle and Byrd*. The citation is of Lydgate in an 1818 source, which is the date of the reprint, wherein the opening line omits an anticipated capital E and was read '[E]mblemes of olde likenes and figures | Which prouyd ben fructuous of sentence'. However, the first two extant letters are 'ro' misread as 'm' and Lydgate's text is known to begin with the word 'Problemes'.

(c) Hoccleve
There are very few holograph manuscripts from the Middle Ages, but Hoccleve has provided us with no less than four, and we have several examples of his acting as scribe for work by others. Three of these manuscripts are for his own verse in Middle English, and those portions are now presented in Burrow and Doyle's *Thomas Hoccleve: A Facsimile of the Autograph Verse Manuscripts*: Huntington Library HM 111 and 744 and Durham University Library Cosin V.III.9. The fourth is, of course, his formulary (British Library MS Add. 24062), and there is at least one draft of a letter in the Public Records Office (PRO E28/29 (no. 30)). The three come somewhere between 1422 and 1426, but Burrow and Doyle are unable to find any order for them in that time frame. In 1978 Parkes and Doyle proposed that HM 111 and 744 could originally have been meant to go in one book, a suggestion based on the size and contents, and there was some discussion of this in the intervening years, but here Burrow and Doyle note that the base ruling differs somewhat, and that after production their histories diverge enough to make it more likely that they were designed to be compatible but not intended to be together. The introduction begins with the contents and descriptions of the manuscripts, then moves on to a careful discussion of Hoccleve's handwriting, abbreviations, and punctuation. Then the plates begin, similar in colour to those of the EETS facsimile of Digby 86—that is, a brownish grey which allows details and contrasts to appear rather clearly, including the relative darkness of the leaves themselves. HM 744 is not reproduced in full because it was put together with twenty-four leaves of other material in the third quarter of the fifteenth century, apparently by the Filer family. With this excellent reproduction to hand, it will be much easier for the dubious to test recent editions using Hoccleve's spellings (see *YWES* 80[2001] 172–3).

Continuing from his work on the facsimile, in 'Hoccleve's Questions: Intonation and Punctuation' (*N&Q* 247[2002] 184–8), John Burrow demonstrates the need for more careful examination of medieval punctuation. Hoccleve uses only virgules and the *punctus elevatus* (with or without the lower point), but no *punctus interrogativus*, and marks only 41 of 265 questions, always with a *punctus elevatus*. Of these 41, 38 are *yes/no* questions (86 out of all 265), which nowadays are distinguished by a rise in pitch at the end, unlike *wh-* questions, which usually fall but do have versions that rise and would be interpreted differently. For example, 'Would you like tea or coffee?' may be intoned to mean either a choice between the two drinks or just a request about a hot, caffeinated beverage. Most of Hoccleve's *yes/no* questions are rhetorical, and sometimes recapitulatory. Two of the remaining three marked questions are rhetorical *wh-* questions with 'no one' as the expected reply, and the third is a delicate *wh-* question asking about the state of Hoccleve's marriage. From all these, Burrow concludes that Hoccleve's punctuated questions were intended to show rising pitch, resembling modern usage.

Looking at Hoccleve and manuscripts from another direction, John J. Thompson's 'Thomas Hoccleve and Manuscript Culture' (in Cooney, ed., pp. 81–94) considers the purpose of the late autograph manuscripts as autobiographical recycling, aided in that purpose by the introductory headings, to promote his literary career, just as this was aided by the circulation of some Hoccleve works together with Chaucer's. We cannot know how deeply that was influenced by Hoccleve's participation in the London book trade as a scribe, but he did direct poems to Marleburgh and Carpenter, whose direct involvement or patronage are well known. The manuscripts also imply that scribes or the trade linked the *Regiment* with the *Series*.

Unsurprisingly, politics has generated new work. John Bowers asks a simple question in 'Thomas Hoccleve and the Politics of Tradition' (*ChauR* 36[2001–2] 352–69): since Hoccleve framed himself as literary heir to his 'maistir Chaucer' and (unlike Lydgate) was already in London and Westminster, why was he 'excluded from the literary tradition that he himself did so much to formulate'? He endorsed the right party lines, worked on important manuscripts of Chaucer and Gower, and even directed his works to various elite figures. The answer could lie in Hoccleve's own lifestyle as a loner and misfit, which would bias readers against his attempts to provide advice. His choice of using London as a setting may have brought local topical factionalism to mind, and he apparently lacked sufficient skill in 'imaginative storytelling'. These and other stylistic features made Hoccleve's work seem more Langlandian, though not embracing as broad a range of society or themes. And in directing his *Regiment* too specifically to Henry IV, Hoccleve helped ensure its relevance would pass with that Henry. In 'Hoccleve, the Virgin, and the Politics of Complaint' (*PMLA* 117[2002] 1172–87), Jennifer E. Bryan claims that 'The Complaint of the Virgin' encapsulates the way in which a marginalized female voice is necessary for the powerful centre. Mary's pleas concerning Jesus and his body are grounded in a privacy opened to voyeuristic public view; her pain is not that of a mother but, to Bryan, a spurned, jealous lover, who loses her self through the loss of Jesus. The complaint, or confession, made public helps reaffirm the social contract. Finally, J.A. Burrow's 'Hoccleve and the "Court"' (in Cooney, ed., pp. 70–80) swiftly reviews the close relationship the office of the privy seal had to the court, and thereby reminds us how Hoccleve's works do function as courtly when they are petitionary and didactic (most obviously the *Regiment of Princes*) and when they celebrate state occasions (for example the shorter poems numbered IV–VI and VIII in Furnivall); though he was in the court, he was not of it.

7. Malory and Caxton

As has been the case in recent years, Malory's text has received considerable treatment from scholars interested in gender and feminist theory. In 'The Writable Lesbian and Lesbian Desire in Malory's *Morte Darthur*' (*Exemplaria* 14[2002] 239–70), Kathleen Coyne Kelly uses Terry Castle's theory of the 'apparitional lesbian' as a starting point from which to analyse the episode of the Leprous Lady and Percivale's sister. Kelly argues that this moment represents an instance of the *gynesocial*—significantly distinct from *homosocial*—which threatens the heteronormative patriarchal order of the Arthurian community. While acknowledging the difficulties inherent in attempting to find evidence of the lesboerotic in Malory's text, Kelly suggests that, when approached from this perspective, the anxieties of masculine patriarchy become more clearly visible.

Another article that engages Malory from the perspective of gender and feminist criticism is Olga Burakov Mongan's 'Between Knights: Triangular Desire and Sir Palomides in Sir Thomas Malory's *The Book of Sir Tristram de Lyones*' (*Arth* 12:iv[2002] 75–90), Drawing on the theories of Eve Sedgwick and René Girard, Mongan argues that in the erotic triangles depicted in the *Book of Sir Tristram*— Mark, Tristram, Isode and Tristram, Isode, Palomides—it is the relationships of the male rivals to one another that are of greatest significance. The 'feminine' corner of the triangle, Isode, is primarily important in that she facilitates the interaction of the men who contest for her. Dorsey Armstrong's 'Gender and Fear: Malory's Lancelot and Knightly Identity' (in Scott and Kosso, eds., *Fear and its Representations in the Middle Ages and the Renaissance*, pp. 255–73) also examines representations of masculinity in Malory. Armstrong argues that the figure of Lancelot demonstrates that fear of loss of masculine identity is the single most important factor driving the performance of masculine knighthood.

The particular relationship between the feminine and chivalry is explored by Kenneth Hodges in 'Swords and Sorceresses: The Chivalry of Malory's Nyneve' (*Arth* 12:ii[2002] 78–96). Noting that Malory considerably expanded the role of Nyneve from that found in his sources, Hodges suggests that Nyneve plays a much more direct role in the defining and shaping of chivalric ideals in Malory than has hitherto been recognized. Arguing that the traditional view of Nyneve—as opposite or foil to Morgan le Fay—is too simplistic, Hodges traces how her character functions as participant in, rather then merely external guardian of, chivalry in the *Morte*. In '"Always to do ladies, damosels, and gentlewomen succor": Women and the Chivalric Code in *Malory's Morte Darthur*' (*Midwest Studies in Philosophy* 26[2002] 1–12), Felicia Ackerman suggests that the institution of the Pentecostal Oath in Malory brings with it some unexpected advantages for women. Noting that the 'ladies' clause' of the oath ensures that women in the *Morte Darthur* are able to command the service of the greatest knights of the land simply by asking, Ackerman goes on to point out that, even when clauses of the chivalric code conflict, the dilemma is usually resolved in favour of the feminine.

Two articles focus their attention on the figure of Lancelot in 'The Book of Sir Launcelot and Queen Guenevere'. In 'Disarming Lancelot' (*SP* 99[2002] 380–403), Elizabeth Scala discusses two instances of disarming, one literal and one figurative, to argue that Lancelot's arms paradoxically signify his identity at exactly the moment when he believes them to be most insignificant. Noting that Malory's text is unlike other chivalric literature in that it has no arming scene, Scala suggests that the moments of disarming in the text are significant in that they serve to disarm the reader as well. Central to Scala's argument is an analysis of the 'Fair Maid of Astolat', an episode that also figures significantly in Timothy D. O'Brien's 'Hand Imagery, Masculinity, and Narrative Authority in *The Book of Sir Launcelot and Queen Guinevere*' (*ELN* 39:iii[2002] 1–18). Building on the work of earlier scholars who have examined representations of the body in Malory, O'Brien points out that

Malory makes more frequent use of hand imagery than do his sources. Arguing that the hand figures significantly in Lancelot's struggle to adhere to his many and conflicting loyalties, O'Brien further suggests that the hand is critically important in the construction of knightly gendered identity.

In 'Pledging Troth in Malory's *Tale of Sir Gareth*' (*JEGP* 101[2002] 19–40), Karen Cherewatuk analyses this section of the *Morte Darthur* in terms of fifteenth-century marriage practices, particularly as evidenced in the Paston letters. Cherewatuk argues that it is important to see the relationship of Gareth and Lyonesse as reflecting both medieval canon law and the ideals of the late medieval gentry. Cherewatuk points out that, although it is a union ostensibly based on mutual affection, the marriage of Gareth and Lyonesse has greater significance for Malory's audience as an alliance between two noble and wealthy lineages. Thomas A. Prendergast also deals with the topic of marriage, but his article 'The Invisible Spouse: Henry VI, Arthur, and the Fifteenth Century Subject' (*JMEMS* 32[2002] 305–26) focuses specifically on the royal marriage of Henry VI to Margaret of Anjou, arguing that Malory's fictional depiction of the turmoil surrounding Guenevere reflects the very real anxieties surrounding Henry's relationship to Margaret. As he delineates the complex relationships between king and queen and king and subjects both in Malory's text and in late fifteenth-century England, Prendergast suggests that the king's legitimacy 'lies not in what people can see, but in what remains hidden or private' (p. 306), and that the visibility of the queen's body is threatening to the king's sovereignty. In 'Edward IV and the Alchemists' (*HT* 52:viii[2002] 10–17) Jonathan Hughes explores Edward IV's obsession with alchemy, contending that Malory's text both reacts to and comments upon the conflict and turmoil that marked Edward's reign, seeing in the story of the Fisher King a comment upon the consecutive imprisonments of Henry and Edward VI, and in the negative portrayal of Guenevere a comment upon Edward's queen, Elizabeth Woodville. In 'The Idea of Family in Chrétien de Troyes and Sir Thomas Malory' (*Arth* 12:iv[2002] 91–9), Jerome Mandel describes the ideal 'family' in both twelfth-century France and fifteenth-century England, but argues that the different representations of family in Chrétien and Malory function primarily to serve the aesthetic needs of the text rather than to reflect historical reality. Mandel contends that the family unit in Malory produces tensions and conflicts that drive the narrative of the text, while the family in Chrétien offers an alternative to the chivalric activity of romance.

Three articles discuss the use and impact of Malory in the twentieth century. In 'From Children's Story to Adult Fiction: T.H. White's *The Once and Future King*' (*Arth* 12:ii[2002] 97–119) Heather Worthington argues that White's work is the last successful adaptation of Malory's work, noting that later treatments of the legend tend to take a more primitive Britain as their setting. Worthington contends that the two most significant aspects of White's work—the evolution of Arthur from child to adult and the representation of the feminine as both dangerous and marginal—mirror the narrative structure and thematic concerns of Malory's text. In 'Faulkner's "fabulous immeasurable Camelots": *Absalom, Absalom!* and *Le Morte Darthur*' (*SLJ* 34:ii[2002] 45–63), Hagood Taylor contends that Faulkner's story of the life of Thomas Sutpen is a retelling of Malory's version of the Arthurian legend. In particular, Taylor explores how in Faulkner's creation of a mythic 'Old South' the author deliberately uses the tensions and conflicts of Malory's Camelot as a template. In 'Martin, Darwin, Malory and Pushkin: The Anglo-Russian Culture of *Glory*' (in Grayson et al., eds., *Nabokov's World, I: The Shape of Nabokov's World*, pp. 159–72), Charles Nicol argues that the character of Martin Edelweiss in Vladimir Nabokov's novel *Glory* reflects the author's own experience of British literature in his childhood and of Russian literature as an adult. Contending that the Russian character of Martin is deliberately connected to the English writer Malory, and that the English character of Darwin is associated with the Russian writer Pushkin, Nicol analyses the interaction of the two characters to suggest that the theme of knighthood is a critically important element in the novel.

By far the most significant contribution to Malory studies in 2002 is Catherine Batt's *Malory's Morte Darthur: Remaking Arthurian Tradition*. Taking as her starting point Malory's famously original and puzzling 'May passage', Batt argues that this contribution by Malory to the Arthurian legend is indicative of Malory's method in reworking (mostly) French sources into a narrative that prominently features an 'English' perspective. Batt suggests that this reworking creates a text that exists somewhere between French and English treatments of the legend, and, further, that this 'in-betweenness' produces an anxious relationship among Malory's subject, imagined audience, and narrator. This anxiety, Batt contends, is most clearly displayed in the text's representations of masculinity, particularly in the figure of Lancelot. Taking care to situate the *Morte* in its fifteenth-century historical context and in terms of its relationship to earlier versions of the Arthurian legend, Batt argues that, 'through the meeting of English and French traditions, Malory makes his Arthurian book the site for interrogating—rather than celebrating—ideas of identity, nation, narrative, and history' (p. 35). Maintaining historical grounding while making expert use of current critical theory, Batt goes on to trace how the violence that drives the narrative progress of the *Morte* problematizes ideals of heroism, masculinity, and social order. Batt's study divides the *Morte* into five sections: the early episodes that include Merlin; the Roman War, Launcelot, and Gareth's tales; the *Tristram* section; the Grail Quest; and finally, the concluding scenes from the 'May passage' to Malory's parting words to his readers. In her analysis Batt not only displays an impressive grasp of Arthurian literature in all its forms, but also carefully locates the *Morte* within the broader tradition of medieval romance in general. A significant contribution to Malory studies, Batt's book is no less valuable to Caxton scholars, in that she spends considerable time scrutinizing Caxton's treatment of the text and the understanding of 'audience' such treatment suggests.

Robert Costomiris examines the way in which early printers attempted to become 'a second author' (p. 3) of Chaucer's texts in 'Sharing Chaucer's Authority in Prefaces to Chaucer's Works from William Caxton to William Thynne' (*JEBS* 5[2002] 1–13). Costomiris argues that in the preface to his second printing of Chaucer's *Canterbury Tales* [1483], Caxton demonstrates a deliberate emulation of Chaucer's language and style in an attempt represent himself as *the* authority on Chaucer; subsequent printers Pynson and de Worde also made use of Caxton's preface because they found that when it came to selling books 'Caxton's authority virtually outstripped Chaucer's s' (p. 10). Costomiris contends that William Thynne's preface to Chaucer's works participates in this tradition but expands upon it by including the king (Henry VIII) in the authorial position shared by writer and printer.

In a brief but fascinating article, 'A False Caxton "Embleme" in the *OED*' (*WI* 18:ii[2002] 123–5), Ayers Bagley convincingly argues that the *OED*'s attribution of the word 'emblem' to Caxton's printing of Lydgate's *Chorle and Birde* is in error, and is a misreading of the word 'problem' as it is rendered, without the initial capital, in the 1818 *Roxburghe* facsimile of Caxton's incunabula.

Caxton is mentioned briefly in articles by A.S.G. Edwards and Richard Altick. In 'William Copland and the Identity of Printed Middle English Romance' (in Hardman, ed., pp. 139–47), Edwards discusses Copland's decision to print many of Caxton's romances, including the *Morte Darthur*. A reprinted article by Altick traces the rise of literacy in England from Caxton onwards: 'The English Common Reader: From Caxton to the Eighteenth Century' (in Finkelstein and McCleery, eds., *The Book History Reader*, pp. 340–9).

Yuri Fuwa, 'An Unhappy Hero: Mordred, Arthur's Incestuous Son' (*Iris* 23[2002] 27–36), was not available for review.

8. Drama

The quantity of monographs available for review this year has been rather smaller than last year's bumper crop, but the quality of those books which have appeared remains impressively high. Scholars and students alike will welcome the publication of Clifford Davidson's *History, Religion, and Violence: Cultural Contexts for Medieval and Renaissance English Drama*. Gathering together thirteen of Professor Davidson's articles, many rewritten in the light of subsequent research, the volume is characterized by his meticulous and enthusiastic interdisciplinarity as well as his lifelong commitment to documenting the intellectual and material contexts of early drama. In addition to a number of essays on Shakespeare and the Elizabethan theatre, there are two sections dealing respectively with 'Violence and the Mysteries' and 'Cultural Contexts for Early Drama'. In the first the focus is variously on depictions of Cain, the sacrifice of Isaac, nudity, and sacred blood, while in the latter the opposition of Carnival and Lent, anti-theatrical prejudices, images and idolatry, saints plays, and representations of Doomsday feature prominently. Another very welcome publication is Elizabeth Baldwin's *Paying the Piper: Music in Pre-1642 Cheshire, with a Contribution on Music in the City by David Mills*. Growing out of the archival research associated with the REED project, Baldwin's study examines the evidence of and for (primarily secular) musical activity in the county prior to the English Civil War. The section 'Music in the City' by David Mills rounds the volume off into a comprehensive report on the findings of years of archival research, describing the performers themselves, the instruments they played, and the auspices under which they played them. In addition, valuable appendices print inventories of goods left by musicians, and the names of all the known Cheshire musicians in the period.

The third and final volume covering the Bodleian Library in the excellent *Index of English Manuscripts from the Time of Chaucer to Henry VIII*, produced under the general editorship of Kathleen Scott, has now appeared, covering the manuscripts from e Museo to Wood. Among the various maps, diagrams, and sketches listed (and in some cases illustrated) is one in particular that will interest scholars of the drama: a fascinating representation of what appears to be Annas and Caiaphas wearing headgear of the Old Law, respectively an antique mitre and a patriarch's hat (p. 139).

An insight into the spiritual life of women in the pre-Reformation period can be gained from the text of *Here begynneth the Rule of Seynt Benet*, an English translation of the Benedictine Rule for women undertaken by Richard Fox, the early Tudor bishop of Winchester, at the request of several senior religious women of his diocese. The Rule, published in 1516–17, is here newly edited with an additional critical introduction and contextual apparatus by Barry Collet and published as *Female Monastic Life in Early Tudor England, with an Edition of Richard Fox's Translation of the Benedictine Rule for Women, 1517*. The text reveals a good deal about both the conventionality and the vitality of the regular religious life of the period, as well as about the regulation of female spirituality in particular.

Invaluable as both a teaching aid and a research tool where secular ecclesiastical practice is concerned are the introductory essays in Heffernan and Matter, eds., *The Liturgy of the Medieval Church*. Most obviously useful to drama scholars is Thomas P. Campbell's essay, 'Liturgical drama and Community Discourse' (pp. 619–44), but also of interest are the chapters on 'Architecture as Liturgical Setting', by Elizabeth C. Parker (pp. 273–326); 'The Liturgical Vessels and Implements', by Elizabeth Parker McLachlan (pp. 369–431); 'The Liturgy and Vernacular Literature', by Evelyn Birge Vitz (pp. 551–618); 'The Music of the Liturgy', by Gabriela Initchi (pp. 645–72); and the concluding overview provided by C. Clifford Flanigan, Kathleen Ashley, and Pamela Sheingorn, 'Liturgy as Social Performance: Expanding the Definitions' (pp. 695–714). Also focused on the liturgical drama is Dunbar H. Ogden's volume, *The Staging of Drama in the Medieval Church*. This large-format, illustrated book offers both an overview of the development of the liturgical drama in medieval western Europe and close studies of particular themes and traditions: stage space and movement, 'special effects', costumes, acting styles, and music. Informative and provocative, the study will be useful both for advanced undergraduate courses in search of an engaging introduction to the genre, and to research seminars interested in the ongoing debates concerning the origins and development of religious drama.

Also both thought-provoking and entertaining by turns are the stories related and analysed in Jody Ender's new study *Death by Drama and Other Medieval Urban Legends*. As her title suggests, Enders examines a range of anecdotes and narrative vignettes concerning mishaps, scandalous behaviour, and odd and macabre occurrences related to dramatic performances in the medieval period in the light of the modern concept of the urban legend. Like the contemporary (not always) metropolitan descendants of the folk myth, these stories suggest a good deal about the anxieties and aspirations of the communities that produced and circulated them. As Enders shows, they provide valuable and often poignant insights into particular medieval attitudes towards gender, class, and political affiliation, as well as towards dramatic representation and performance more generally. Drawn almost exclusively from French drama, these stories have a far wider resonance, charting the mysterious, powerful processes by which theatre and life become momentarily confused or blur into one another, and one has a startling and disruptive impact on the other. Whether it is when the play devils or madmen prove to be genuinely demonic or dangerously deranged and wreak havoc among the spectators, or when the beautiful female saints (or their male performers) become so attractive that they seduce the audiences or their fellow actors, in each case these narratives suggest new insights into medieval notions of belief and scepticism, social and spiritual identity, and the nature of 'acting' as a personal and cultural impulse.

Two historical studies published this year throw interesting sidelights on the drama. Scholars interested in the Cornish material will profit greatly from reading Mark Stoyle's shrewd, insightful monograph, *West Britons: Cornish Identities and the Early Modern British State*. Clearly and elegantly written, this book devotes considerable attention to the questions of what made Cornwall distinctive, culturally and politically, in the sixteenth and seventeenth centuries, throwing considerable light back onto the medieval period in the process. Equally illuminating are a number of the essays collected in Highley and King, eds., *John Foxe and his World*. Anthony Martin's essay, 'The End of History: Thomas Norton's "v periods" and the Pattern of English Protestant Historiography' (pp. 37–53), examines a less well known work of the co-author of *Gorboduc*, while Christopher Warner's 'Elizabeth I, Saviour of Books' (pp. 91–101) studies that still more *sui generis* dramatist, John Bale's, introduction to the *Scriptorum illustrium majoris Brytanniae ... catologus*, and Tom Betteridge, in 'Truth and History in Foxe's *Acts and Monuments*' (pp. 145–59), looks at iconoclasm and idolatry in the illustrations to Foxe's 'Book of Martyrs'.

Among the best of the articles in specialist journals available as this chapter went to press, Jane Tomie's 'Mrs Noah and Didactic Abuses' (*Early Theatre* 5:i[2002] 11–36) offers a shrewd and informative rereading of the treatment of Noah's wife in the York, Chester, and Towneley plays, suggesting how ambivalences about female recalcitrance and the violence it both provokes and seems to justify colour each of them in different ways. The articles published in the latest issue of *European Medieval Drama* (volume 5 [2002 for 2001], edited by Jelle Koopmans and Bart Ramakers) continue to expand that journal's admirable aim to promote the widest geographical coverage of early drama, both across Europe and beyond. Thus there are pieces on Croatian drama: 'When and How Does God Appear? The Divine on the Croatian Medieval Stage', by Zrinka Pulišelić (*EMD* 5[2002] 43–52); on Hispano-Mexican: Catherine Raffi-Meroud, 'Théâtre religieux en Nouvelle Espagne (Mexique) au XVIe siècle: Le Thèâtre d'évangélisation' (*EMD* 5[2002] 53–67), and Óscar Armando Garcia, 'Adaptation d'un appareil scénique médiéval dans la représentation de l'Assomption de la Vierge à Tlaxcala, Mexique (XVIe siècle)' (*EMD* 5[2002] 69–82); and on Bolivian drama: Max Harris, 'A Bolivian Morality Play: Saint Michael and the Sins of the Carnival Virgin' (*EMD* 5[2002] 83–98), in addition to the more familiar material on French, Dutch, and English theatre. The essays on strictly English material, all focused on the broad theme of visual culture, are J.-P. Debax, 'From the Throne of God to the Throne of Man: Thrones as Prop and Allegory in Tudor Drama' (*EMD* 5[2002] 17–26); Alexandra F. Johnston, 'Gendering Abstractions: The Portrayal of Women in *The Castle of Perseverance*' (*EMD* 5[2002] 123–34); and David Mills, '"Education, Education, Education!": Nice Wanton and the Allegorical Tradition' (*EMD* 5[2002] 191–203). 2002 and 2003 publications on the *Gawain*-poet and on Middle Scots Poetry will be reviewed in YWES 84.

Books Reviewed

Allen, Rosamund, Lucy Perry, and Jane Roberts, eds. *Layamon: Contexts, Language, and Interpretation*. KCL. [2002] pp. xii + 440. £21 ISBN 0 9539 8381 1.

Archibald, Elizabeth. *Incest and the Medieval Imagination*. Clarendon. [2001] pp. xvi + 296. £52.50 ISBN 0 1981 1209 2.

Baldwin, Elizabeth. *Paying the Piper: Music in Pre-1642 Cheshire, with a Contribution on Music in the City by David Mills*. EDAM Monographs 29. MIP. [2002] pp. 287. hb $30 ISBN 1 5804 4040 1, pb $15 ISBN 1 5804 4045 X.

Barber, Elaine, comp. *The Arthurian Bibliography IV: 1993–1998*. Brewer. [2002] pp. xxii + 464. £80 ($110) ISBN 0 8599 1633 2.

Barron, W. R. J., and Glyn S. Burgess, eds. *The Voyage of Saint Brendan: Representative Versions of the Legend in English Translation*. UExe. [2002] pp. xii + 378. £45 ($75) ISBN 0 8598 9656 0.

Batt, Catherine. *Malory's Morte Darthur: Remaking Arthurian Tradition*. Palgrave. [2002] pp. xxiii + 264. £32.50 ($55) ISBN 0 3122 2998 4.

Blamires, Alcuin, and Gail C. Holian. *The Romance of the Rose Illuminated: Manuscripts at the National Library of Wales, Aberystwyth*. MRTS 223. MRTS. [2002] pp. xxxviii + 138 + 49 colour plates + 16 b/w figures. £42 ISBN 0 8669 8265 5.

Blumenfeld-Kosinski, Renate, Duncan Robertson, and Nancy Bradley Warren, eds. *The Vernacular Spirit: Essays on Medieval Religious Literature*. Palgrave. [2002] pp. 324. £32.50 ($65) ISBN 0 3122 9385 2.

Boklund-Lagopoulou, Karin. *'I have a yong suster': Popular Song and the Middle English Lyric*. FCP. [2002] pp. 269. £47.25 ISBN 1 8518 2627 0.

Bovey, Alixe. *Monsters and Grotesques in Medieval Manuscripts*. BL and UTorP. [2002] pp. 64 + 50 colour illus. pb £7.95 ($CAN19.95) ISBN 0 7123 4745 3 (BL), ISBN 0 8020 8512 1 (UTorP).

Burrow, J. A., and A.I. Doyle, eds. *Thomas Hoccleve: A Facsimile of the Autograph Verse Manuscripts*. EETS ss 19. OUP. [2002] pp. xl + 382(unnumbered). £80 ISBN 0 1972 2420 2.

Cheney, Patrick, and Frederick A. de Armas, eds. *European Literary Careers: The Author from Antiquity to the Renaissance*. UTorP. [2002] pp. x + 366. $CAN65 ISBN 0 8020 4779 3.

Chism, Christine. *Alliterative Revivals*. UPennP. [2002] pp. 329. $57.50. ISBN 0 8122 3655 6.

Collett, Barry, ed. *Female Monastic Life in Early Tudor England, with an Edition of Richard Fox's Translation of the Benedictine Rule for Women, 1517*. The Early Modern Englishwoman, 1500–1750. Ashgate. [2002] pp. 190. £40 ISBN 1 8401 4609 5.

Cooney, Helen, ed. *Nation, Court and Culture: New Essays on Fifteenth-Century English Poetry*. FCP. [2002] pp. 192. £55 ISBN 1 8518 2566 5.

Cooper, W. R., ed. *The Wycliffe New Testament (1388): An Edition in Modern Spelling, with an Introduction, the Original Prologues and the Epistle to the Laodiceans*. BL. [2002] pp. xvi + 528. £20 ISBN 0 7123 4728 3.

Crawford, Anne, ed. *Letters of Medieval Women*. Sutton. [2002] pp. x + 262. £20 ISBN 0 7509 2798 4.

Cunningham, I. C., and A.G. Watson. *Indexes and Addenda*, vol. 5 of N.R. Ker, *Medieval Manuscripts in British Libraries*. Clarendon. [2002] pp. xiv+501 £150 ISBN 0 1981 8277 5.

Davidson, Clifford. *History, Religion, and Violence: Cultural Contexts for Medieval and Renaissance English Drama*. Ashgate. [2002] pp. 318. £52.50 ISBN 0 8607 8882 2.

Dimmick, Jeremy, James Simpson, and Nicolette Zeeman, eds. *Images, Idolatry, and Iconoclasm in Late Medieval England: Textuality and the Visual Image*. OUP. [2002] pp. xiii + 250. £45. ISBN 0 1981 8759 9.

Easting, Robert, ed. *The Revelation of the Monk of Eynsham*. EETS 318. OUP. [2002] pp. c + 278. £50 ISBN 0 1972 2321 4.

Echard, Siân, and Gernot R. Wieland, eds. *Anglo-Latin and its Heritage: Essays in Honour of A.G. Rigg on his 64th Birthday*. Publications of the Journal of Medieval Latin 4. Brepols. [2001] pp. xviii + 280. €50 ISBN 2 5035 0838 3.

Enders, Jody, *Death by Drama and Other Medieval Urban Legends*. UChicP. [2002] pp. 432. £24.50 ISBN 0 2262 0787 0.

Erler, Mary C. *Women, Reading, and Piety in Late Medieval England*. CSML. CUP. [2002] pp. xii + 228. £45 ISBN 0 5218 1221 6.

Finkelstein, David, and Alistair McCleery, eds. *The Book History Reader*. Routledge. [2002] pp. x + 390. £65 ($90) ISBN 0 4152 2657 0.

Goodman, Anthony. *Margery Kempe and her World*. Longman. [2002] pp. xx + 274. pb £15.99 ($21.95) ISBN 0 5823 6808 1.

Grayson, Jane, et al., eds. *Nabokov's World, I: The Shape of Nabokov's World*. Palgrave. [2002] pp. xvii + 237. $69.95 ISBN 0 3339 6415 2.

Green, John D. *A Strange Tongue: Tradition, Language, and the Appropriation of Mystical Experience in Late Fourteenth-Century England and Sixteenth-Century Spain*. Peeters. [2002] pp. viii + 227. €30 ISBN 9 0429 1236 7.

Hardman, Philippa, ed. *The Matter of Identity in Medieval Romance*. Brewer. [2002] pp. xii + 166. £40 ($70) ISBN 0 8599 1761 4.

Harford, Thomas J. *A Comprehensive Study of Layamon's 'Brut'*. Studies in Medieval Literature 21. Mellen. [2002] xii + 182 pp. £64.95 ($99.95) ISBN 0 7734 7097 2.

Hasenfratz, Robert, ed. *Ancrene Wisse*. TEAMS. MIP. [2000] pp. xii + 690. pb $30 ISBN 1 5804 4070 3.

Hassel, Julie. *Choosing Not To Marry: Women and Autonomy in the Katherine Group*. Studies in Medieval History and Culture. Routledge. [2002] pp. xiv + 140. £45 ISBN 0 4159 3784 1.

Heffernan, Thomas J., and E. Ann Matter, eds. *The Liturgy of the Medieval Church*. MIP. [2001] pp. 778. pb $30 ISBN 1 5804 4008 8.

Hicks, Michael. *English Political Culture in the Fifteenth Century*. Routledge. [2002] pp. xviii + 262. hb £55 ISBN 0 4152 1763 6, pb £15.99 ISBN 0 4152 1764 4.

Higham, N. J. *King Arthur: Myth-Making and History*. Routledge. [2002] pp. xi + 303. $27.95 ISBN 0 4152 1305 3.

Highley, Christopher, and John N. King, eds. *John Foxe and his World*. St Andrews Studies in Reformation History. Ashgate. [2002] pp. 350 + 1 colour and 40 b/w illus. £55 ISBN 0 7546 0306 7.

Keen, Jill Averil. *The Charters of Christ and 'Piers Plowman': Documenting Salvation*. Lang. [2002] pp. 122. £29 ISBN 0 8204 4006 X.

Klinck, Anne L., and Ann Marie Rasmussen, eds. *Medieval Woman's Song: Cross-Cultural Approaches*. UPennP. [2002] pp. viii + 280. £35 ($49.95) ISBN 0 8122 3624 6.

Kooper, Erik, ed. *The Medieval Chronicle II*. Proceedings of the 2nd International Conference on the Medieval Chronicle Driebergen/Utrecht 16–21 July 1999. Costerus ns 144. Rodopi. [2002] pp. vi + 280. €55 ($65) ISBN 9 0420 0834 2.

Krug, Rebecca. *Reading Families: Women's Literate Practice in Late Medieval England*. CornUP. [2002] pp. xiv + 238. $45. ISBN 0 8014 3924 8.

Lambdin, Laura Cooner, and Robert Thomas Lambdin, eds. *A Companion to Old and Middle English Literature*. Greenwood. [2002] pp. xiv + 434. £48.50 ISBN 0 3133 1054 8.

Leyser, Henrietta. *Medieval Women: Social History of Women in England 450–1500*. Phoenix. [2002] pp. 688. pb £6.99 ISBN 1 8421 2621 0.

Lupack, Alan, ed. *New Directions in Arthurian Studies*. Brewer. [2002] pp. x + 168. £40 ($70) ISBN 0 8599 1642 1.

McAvoy, Liz Herbert, and Teresa Walters, eds. *Consuming Narratives: Gender and Monstrous Appetite in the Middle Ages and Renaissance*. UWalesP. [2002] pp. xii + 257. pb £15.99 ISBN 0 7083 1742 1.

Matthews, David. *The Making of Middle English, 1765–1910*. Medieval Cultures 18. UMinnP. [1999] pp. xxxvii + 234. $39.95 ISBN 0 8166 3185 9.

Matthews, David. *The Invention of Middle English: An Anthology of Primary Sources*. Brepols. [2000] pp. xii + 244. €55 ISBN 2 5035 0769 7.

Murdoch, Brian, and J.A. Tasioulas, ed. *The Apocryphal Lives of Adam and Eve: Edited from the Auchinleck Manuscript and from Trinity College, Oxford, MS 57*. UExe. [2002] pp. viii + 159. pb £16.99 ISBN 0 8598 9698 6.

Obbard, Elizabeth Ruth. *Medieval Women Mystics: Gertrude the Great, Angela of Foligno, Birgitta of Sweden, Julian of Norwich: Selected Spiritual Writings*. New City. [2002] pp. 168. pb $13.95 ISBN 1 5654 8157 7.

O'Farrell-Tate, Una, ed. *The Abridged English Metrical Brut: Edited from London, British Library MS Royal 12 C.XII*. MET 32. Winter. [2002] pp. 144. €39 ISBN 3 8253 1290 9.

Ogden, Dunbar H. *The Staging of Drama in the Medieval Church*, UDelP [2002] pp. 251 + 40 b/w illus. £33 ISBN 0 8741 3707 8.

Park, Tarjei. *Selfhood and 'Gostly Menyng' in Some Middle English Mystics: Semiotic Approaches to Contemplative Theology*. Mellen. [2002] pp. xiv + 314. £74.95 ($119.95) ISBN 0 7734 7507 9.

Riches, Samantha J.E., and Sarah Salih, eds. *Gender and Holiness: Men, Women, and Saints in Late Medieval Europe*. Routledge. [2002] pp. xiv + 200. £58 ISBN 0 4152 5821 9.

Rogers, William Elford. *Interpretation in 'Piers Plowman'*. CUAP. [2002] pp. x + 300. $64.95 ISBN 0 8132 1092 5.

Ruether, Rosemary Radford, ed. *Visionary Women: Three Medieval Mystics*. Fortress. [2002] pp. 96. pb $6 ISBN 0 8006 3448 9.

Salisbury, Eve, ed. *The Trials and Joys of Marriage*. TEAMS. MIP. [2002] pp. x + 278. pb $18 ISBN 1 5804 4035 5.

Salisbury, Eve, Georgiana Donavin, and Merrall Llewelyn Price, eds. *Domestic Violence in Medieval Texts*. UFlorP. [2002] pp. x + 354. $59.95 ISBN 0 8130 2442 0.

Scott, Anne, and Cynthia Kosso, eds. *Fear and its Representations in the Middle Ages and the Renaissance*. Arizona Studies in the Middle Ages and the Renaissance 6. Brepols. [2002] xxxvii + 350. $63 ISBN 2 5035 1207 0.

Scott, Kathleen L., Lynda Dennison, and Michael T. Orr, eds. *An Index of Images in English Manuscripts from the Time of Chaucer to Henry VIII: Fascicle III: The Bodleian Library, Oxford, MSS e Museo-Wood*. HM. [2002] pp. 129 + 12 b/w plates. $60 ISBN 1 8725 0127 3.

Seymour, M. C., ed. *The Defective Version of Mandeville's Travels*. EETS 319. OUP. [2002] pp. xxx + 234. £50 ISBN 0 1972 2322 2.

Simpson, James. *The Oxford English Literary History*, vol. 2: *1350–1547: Reform and Cultural Revolution*. OUP. [2002] pp. xviii + 661. £30 ISBN 0 1981 8261 9.

Spearing, Elizabeth, ed. *Medieval Writings on Female Spirituality*. Penguin. [2002] pp. i + 268. pb $14 ISBN 0 1404 3925 0.

Spivack, Charlotte, and Christine Herold, eds. *Archetypal Readings of Medieval Literature*. Studies in Medieval Literature 22. Mellen. [2002] pp. 264. £69.95 ISBN 0 7734 6966 4.

Steiner, Emily, and Candace Barrington, eds. *The Letter of the Law: Legal Practice and Literary Production in Medieval England*. CornUP. [2002] pp. ix + 257. £30.50 ISBN 0 8014 3975 2.

Stoyle, Mark. *West Britons: Cornish Identities and the Early Modern British State*. UExe. [2002] pp. 262. £40 ISBN 0 8598 9687 0.

Swanton, Michael. *English Poetry Before Chaucer*, rev. edn of *English Literature Before Chaucer* (Longman [1987]). UExe. [2002] pp. ix + 379. hb £47.50 ISBN 0 8598 9633 1, pb £15.99 ISBN 0 8598 9681 1.

Taylor, Andrew. *Textual Situations: Three Medieval Manuscripts and their Readers*. UPennP. [2002] pp. vi + 300. £32.50 ISBN 0 8122 3642 4.

Usk, Thomas. *Testament of Love*, ed. Gary W. Shawver, based on the edition of John F. Leyerle. UTorP. [2002] pp. xii + 356. £80 ($125) ISBN 0 8020 5471 4.

Ward, Jennifer. *Women in Medieval Europe, 1200–1500*. Longman. [2002] pp. viii + 322. pb £16.99 ISBN 0 5822 8827 4.

Wickham-Crowley, Kelley M. *Writing the Future: Layamon's Prophetic History*. UWalesP. [2002] pp. x + 182. £37.50 ISBN 0 7083 1714 6.

IV

Middle English: Chaucer

VALERIE ALLEN AND MARGARET CONNOLLY

This chapter has four sections: 1. General; 2. *Canterbury Tales*; 3. *Troilus and Criseyde*; 4. Other Works. The ordering of individual tales and poems within the sections follows that of the *Riverside Chaucer*.

1. General

Mark Allen and Bege K. Bowers remain responsible for co-ordinating the production of 'An Annotated Chaucer Bibliography 1999' (*SAC* 24[2002] 455–561); for the electronic version consult the New Chaucer Society webpage: <http://ncs.rutgers.edu or http://uchaucer.utsa.edu>. Additionally this year Bege K. Bowers and Mark Allen offer the *Annotated Chaucer Bibliography, 1986–1996*, a substantial tome that collects all of the bibliographical information accumulated about Chaucer over the eleven years mentioned in the title. Essentially this reproduces material previously assembled for the annual *Studies in the Age of Chaucer* bibliography, but it will be a useful single volume for scholars whose institutional libraries do not subscribe to *SAC*, and it also takes its place in the long tradition of comprehensive Chaucer bibliographies which was begun by Eleanor Prescott Hammond in the early years of the twentieth century.

Another addition to the reference shelf is *Chaucer's Church: A Dictionary of Religious Terms in Chaucer*, compiled by Edward E. Foster and David H. Carey. This handy little book lists all terms that have a specific religious meaning as well as terms with secular meanings if these also have important religious implications; typical entries range from *dortour* and *semycope* to *bigamye* and *lust*; saints and biblical figures are also included. Foster and Carey state that they aim to be informative but not comprehensive. They use the *Riverside Chaucer* as a base, but do not cite line references, since they expect users to turn from Chaucer's text to their own work. Exactly who is intended to use this volume is not quite clear. The definitions range from the blindingly obvious to the mildly informative, so the book's best audience would be students, but it is priced above this level, unless intended for library purchase only, and in fact students would find other non-specialized glossaries just as useful.

From the patently obvious attempts of Lydgate et al. to write themselves into the pilgrimage and even become Chaucer, literary reception of Chaucer has been shaped by the desire to commune directly with and speak for Chaucer, observes Stephanie Trigg in *Congenial Souls: Reading Chaucer from Medieval to Postmodern*. Even modern critique of the poet, which has moved from the intimacy of imitation and maintains a fashionable distance from, for example, anti-feminist or anti-Semitic strains in the text, covertly, even furtively, participates in this desire to belong to a Chaucer club of congenial souls, who have, it might be added, historically all been male. Is it still possible to be a postmodern reader and to have a soul congenial to Chaucer's, as Dryden termed it? Trigg judiciously avoids simplistic answers, although her confident sense that the business of Chaucer criticism is alive, well, and of relevance suggests an affirmative reply to the question. Trigg's book takes a step back from Chaucer's work to meditate on the practices and assumptions through history that have shaped the Chaucerian reader's identity. Her 'texts' are the readers of Chaucer's work; indeed there is no sustained, direct 'reading' of his poetry at any point. The omission is deliberate, both opening up a space for self-reflection and implying that any understanding of Chaucer's work is in fact the *history* of the understanding of Chaucer's work. The chapters thus tell the story in loose chronological order of that process, from the manuscript tradition of the fifteenth century, where differences are already discernible between the knowing Ellesmere, which already memorializes Chaucer as absent, and the more innocent and workmanlike Hengwrt, which seems closer to the poet's intentions; to the early printed editions of the sixteenth (see *YWES* 80[2001] 187); to Dryden, who ushers in the era of modern critical reception of Chaucer; to the rise of the professional critic. There is no one who will not be prompted to stop and think at some point in this book.

L.O. Aranye Fradenburg's *Sacrifice Your Love: Psychoanalysis, Historicism, Chaucer* is as much about psychoanalysis and historicism as it is about Chaucer. Fradenburg's writing is characteristically difficult; her engagement with theory cuts deep (Freud, Lacan, and Slavoj Žižak are regularly quoted), and her attempt is at all times to think medieval and modern categories of thought in terms of each other. The main theme of her book is the hidden connection, masquerading as opposition, between desire and the ethics of sacrifice and obligation. One will see at once the rub between this approach and the division laid out by Patterson last year (*YWES* 82[2003] 215) between the scholarly 'discipline' of historicism and the enthusiasms of psychoanalysis. In chapter 1, specifically on the relationship between the two, historicism is described as bearing the 'ethical burden ... to put aside our modernity' (p. 45) in search of the 'alterity of the past' (p. 48). But since, according to the Lacanian model of identity, 'the subject only comes into being *by* being split' (p. 8) and thus 'there is no pure self' (p. 31), then the same holds true for history. The present does not stand in relation to the (medieval) past as identity stands to difference; rather, the present is already foreign to itself, and one need not seek it in the past; the excavation into the strangeness of the past in the name of historical ascesis is a projection of our fantasies, desires, and griefs. New material relating to Chaucer comes in chapter 3, 'The Ninety-Six Tears of Chaucer's Monk', in which Fradenburg considers how the Monk collects, remembers, and shows off by narration the catastrophes of tragedy. For chapters on Chaucer from this work which were previously published, see *YWES* 80[2001] 206–7 and 78[1999] 244, 259.

Richard Utz tackles head on the thorny topic of philology, a term that never has translated well from German into English, in *Chaucer and the Discourse of German Philology: A History of Reception and an Annotated Bibliography of Studies, 1793–1948*. The volume has been heralded by some earlier publications (last year, reviewed below, and *YWES* 79[2000] 201) but here the material is collected and expanded. Utz begins his analysis by considering how the cool reception by philologists of Nietzsche's *Birth of Tragedy* even then betrayed the discipline's self-conscious seriousness and embarrassment with the enthusiasms of poetry. Yet despite the sorry reputation *Chaucerphilologie* has acquired as drudgery or, worse, covert right-wing nationalism, Utz claims its centrality and relevance, and calls for its inclusion in the pluralist canons of literary theory. Bluntly put, his question to medievalists is why Latin and Old French should be considered linguistic professional requirements, and German merely optional. For those of us whose German remains plodding, the volume contains many critical passages translated for the first time into English from or about the giants of the discipline: Jacob Grimm, Karl Lachmann, Julius Zupitza, and the overlooked John Koch. Utz's immersion in the critical literature enables a telling of the story of *Chaucerphilologie* in all its nuances, including its ties to Prussian supremacism, and the foibles of its doyens (a chapter on Zupitza and ten Brink is highly readable). Much has recently been written about the English Chaucerians who mapped the texts and manuscripts—Henry Bradshaw, Frederick Furnivall, and W.W. Skeat—but this worthy tome supplies the German background and context to the scholarship that we usually take as our *terminus a quo*. An annotated bibliography of nearly 150 pages offers a valuable digest of Chaucer scholarship published in German throughout the nineteenth and earlier part of the twentieth centuries. Utz concludes the volume by suggesting continuities between the fuss about Nietzsche's *Birth of Tragedy* and recent debates about 'new' philology and the divide between philology and theory; in this, Utz implies, philology then as now remains intrinsic to our subject.

Continuing the international theme, Warren S. Ginsberg considers *Chaucer's Italian Tradition*, of which some parts have appeared earlier: (*YWES* 79[2000] 216 and 77[1998] 43). Pre-empting an obvious question, namely, 'What Italian tradition?', Ginsberg adopts a notion of influence that accommodates both the (Italian) features Chaucer leaves out and the way in which he filters one poet through another; most notoriously, Dante through Boccaccio. 'The gravitational pull of each writer's manner of meaning follows and modifies the orbit of the others' (p. ix). Although he mentions his debt to theorists such as Walter Benjamin and Hans Robert Jauss, Ginsberg sounds rather more under the influence of T.S. Eliot, whose thoughts about tradition seem to be echoed here. The obvious recent contender in the debate about Chaucer and Italy is David Wallace's *Chaucerian Polity* (*YWES* 78[1999] 240–1), for whom the cultural boundary between England and Italy was far more permeable than Ginsberg will allow. Much, then, of the early part of the book is devoted to explaining how Italian literature initially assumes a presence in Chaucer's writing; as he frequently observes, Chaucer paradoxically manages to convey a radically different aesthetic than Dante even when Dante's influence is at its greatest. Moreover, Chaucer's reception of the Italian tradition was itself filtered through his prior reception of the French tradition. After Italy, France, and even England, no longer appear as they did, and thus Florence makes Chaucer a closer observer of London life. Chaucer's developing sense of city-space, captured in the urban mode of *Troilus and Criseyde*, becomes one of the most defining features of his Italian legacy. Ginsberg's meditations on the city that 'is not Florence, nor London, and is both' (p. 147) keep step with those of David Wallace, who also wrote about the London that was present by its absence in Chaucer's poetry (*YWES* 73[1994] 151). For Ginsberg, however, Italy represented difference to Chaucer in a way that the home turf of France never did. The disconnectedness Chaucer must inevitably have felt as a visitor to Italy becomes an aesthetic principle within his later work, and it is in this sense, then, that Ginsberg speaks of an Italian tradition that is ever new.

James Simpson's volume in the Oxford English Literary History series, *Reform and Cultural Revolution*, covering the years 1350–1547, makes significant mention of Chaucer, but the thematic organization of the book means that these references are scattered throughout. In the chapter entitled 'The Elegiac', Simpson grants a great deal of space to works which range from the brief poem 'A Complaint to Pity' to *Troilus*, but most attention here is given to the dream visions. *Troilus* surfaces again in passing, and references to the *Canterbury Tales* are ubiquitous, particularly in the chapters entitled 'The Comic' and 'The Political'. In truth it is hard to find a section in this book where Chaucer is not mentioned in one guise or another, and there is also a useful and succinct entry on him in the list of 'Author Bibliographies'.

Chaucer is given significant attention in Elizabeth Scala's study of *Absent Narratives, Manuscript Textuality, and Literary Structure in Late Medieval England*, which also covers Gower, the *Gawain*-poet, and Malory. Scala focuses on missing stories, that is, stories implied or mentioned but not actually told in the texts she examines. She finds this absence to be a frequent feature of late medieval narrative, and imaginatively links this to the circumstances of textual production, attempting to combine manuscript study with postmodern theory. In her introduction she sets forth the conditions of medieval textuality and manuscript culture and then reads one of Chaucer's earliest poems, the *Book of the Duchess*, as a case study. Various absences are identified here: for example, in addition to Blanche's notorious absence from the narrative, Scala reminds us that some sections of the poem itself are known only from Thynne's edition and not from the three surviving manuscripts; notably the missing lines contain much of what we know (or think we know) about the narrator and his concerns. Chapter 2, which has previously appeared in article form (*YWES* 76[1997] 192) ostensibly concentrates on the *Squire's Tale*, but in fact in its discussion of the missing story of Canacee and the suppressed narrative of incest it has much to say about the *Man of Law's Tale* as well. Arguing that the Squire, contrary to received critical wisdom, is actually a very accomplished narrator, Scala moves on in the third chapter to link his fragmentary tale to the perfectly ordered tale of the Knight, and also in passing discusses the tales of the Miller and the Reeve. She suggests that the *Canterbury Tales* should be regarded as a family romance, with the *Knight's Tale* functioning as its primal scene; all the tales that follow are merely 'troubled versions of and versions troubled by the "Knight's Tale"' (p. 132). In conclusion she argues that absent narratives offer a method of reading structurally and thus encourage us to read beyond the author in late medieval manuscript culture. This is an ambitious and accomplished study, but Scala is not always successful in drawing the links she promises with the conditions of medieval writing.

In *Chaucer and Boccaccio: Antiquity and Modernity*, Robert R. Edwards contends that the historical context of Chaucer's poetry is textuality and literary relations, and that the most illuminating way to read his work is via his relation to other writers. Boccaccio is the writer from whom Chaucer takes the most and is therefore an appropriate base for Edwards's study. Although, as he admits, his survey is necessarily selective (he does not deal extensively, for example, with the *Monk's Tale*), the book nevertheless covers a great deal of ground. In terms of antiquity Edwards considers Chaucer's engagement with the stories of Thebes, Troy, and Rome, through three initial chapters that focus on *Anelida and Arcite*, the *Knight's Tale*, *Troilus and Criseyde*, and the *Legend of Good Women*. In the first chapter Edwards analyses how Chaucer uses Statius's *Thebaid* and Boccaccio's *Teseida* as sources for the *Knight's Tale*, reading the latter against the *Teseida* in order to show how Chaucer refashions and interrogates the medieval aristocratic context devised by Boccaccio. In the second chapter Edwards turns to *Troilus and Criseyde*, Chaucer's most profound exploration of classical antiquity, indicating how closely Chaucer works with his Boccaccian source text, and arguing that in *Troilus* the twin necessities of history and desire unfold in a significant tension with poetic assertions of choice. Overall these opening chapters claim that Chaucer displays antiquity from a dominant position, featuring male aristocratic subjects who face the convergence of history and desire. In chapter 3 Edwards suggests that this dominant perspective of antiquity is challenged by the *Legend of Good Women*, whose stories offer a view of history that locates the causes of catastrophe internally. The chapter ends with a coda on Christian antiquity and some remarks on the figures of Cecilia and Custance; this forms a pleasing link to the second part of the book, which deals with the twin aspect of modernity and which focuses inevitably on the *Canterbury Tales*. Edwards defines Chaucer's modernity as essentially based on contract and negotiation. In chapter 4 he analyses Chaucer's revival of the fabliau form, discussing the tales of the Miller, Reeve, Shipman, and Pardoner. Edwards finds that the important values in the tales of the Miller and Reeve are gain and mobility, which serve to establish a set of social relations based on individual agency and self-interest. The pressure of mercantile exchange on the traditional structures of household, marriage, and friendship are sketched in the *Shipman's Tale*, and the *Pardoner's Tale* also absorbs a mercantile ethic, which it carries to its spiritual conclusion.

The final two chapters concentrate on tales from the marriage group, the *Clerk's Tale* and the *Franklin's Tale*, as Edwards examines what happens when a courtly world with fixed and traditional hierarchies is disrupted by the values of contract and exchange. In the *Clerk's Tale* Chaucer finds a middle ground between Boccaccio's hermeneutic multiplicity and Petrarch's closure, and although his version is resolutely conservative in maintaining hierarchical rule, it allows natural nobility to be accommodated in the structures of power. The *Franklin's Tale* looks back nostalgically to a mythologized feudal world but the defining terms of social relations in this story belong to an emergent mercantile culture. Both of these chapters have previously appeared in print, for which see, respectively, *YWES* 77[1998] 213 and 81[2002] 246–7. For other previously published sections see *YWES* 72[1993] 139 and 73[1994] 162. The book is strongly argued throughout, so its lack of a separate conclusion is perhaps not a weakness.

Jill Mann's study *Feminizing Chaucer* first appeared as *Geoffrey Chaucer* in 1991 (*YWES* 73[1994] 152). Its new title reflects Mann's belief that the ethos pervading Chaucer's work is a feminized one, and that women are central to his imaginative vision and his exploration of various ethical problems. It also signals more honestly that the author's interpretation of Chaucer's work stems from a feminist viewpoint, a point underlined forcefully by the new preface, which succinctly surveys developments in Chaucerian gender studies over the past decade. Otherwise not much is new in the 2002 edition; some updating of references, footnotes, and bibliography has been undertaken, and there is one new section 'Excursus: Wife-Swapping in Medieval Literature' (pp. 152–73), which augments the discussion of the *Franklin's Tale*, but otherwise the central substance of the 1991 text remains unchanged. Its reissue is welcome, however, since it has already earned its place on recommended reading lists, and Mann's addition of the admittedly brief overview of gender studies will only increase its attractiveness in this regard. Richard West's readable biography, *Chaucer 1340–1400*, which first appeared in 2000 (*YWES* 81[2002] 230) is this year issued in paperback, as is Peter Brown's *A Companion to Chaucer*, also first published in 2000 (*YWES* 81[2002] 233–4).

Kathryn L. Lynch, ed., *Chaucer's Cultural Geography* brings together in one volume a number of landmark essays in the subject, along with some new pieces, the first of which is Kenneth Bleeth's 'Orientalism and the Critical History of the *Squire's Tale*' (pp. 21–31). Here Bleeth charts the construction of the Orient as exotic with the simultaneous expansion of colonialist presence, and notes how recent is our coming to consciousness of that assumption of exoticism—an awareness greatly indebted to the work of Edward Said. Suzanne Conklin Akbari also contributes a new piece, with 'Orientation and Nation in Chaucer's *Canterbury Tales*' (pp. 102–34). Although Orientalism is a late invention, made possible by colonialism, nationalism was already a concern of Chaucer and his world. Akbari eschews the modern, post-religious definition of nationalism in search of a more fluid notion of place and identity, which is captured in Chaucer's frequent use of the term *degree*. Lynch's introduction is also worth a look: in it she advances a view of space in Chaucer that is more organic and contingent than our modern, punctual topographies. *Mapamounde* means both a map and the world itself, suggesting a less abstract organization of space. Her introduction is followed with a short selected bibliography. The following are reprinted: John M. Fyler, 'Domesticating the Exotic in the *Squire's Tale*' (pp. 32–55; *YWES* 69[1990] 189); Vincent J. Dimarco, 'The Historical Basis of Chaucer's *Squire's Tale*' (pp. 56–75); Kathryn L. Lynch, 'East Meets West in Chaucer's *Squire's* and *Franklin's Tales*' (pp. 76–101; *YWES* 76[1997] 192–3); Dorothee Metlitzki, who writes on the *Canon Yeoman's Tale* in 'Scientific Imagery in Chaucer' (pp. 135–51; *YWES* 58[1979] 70–1); Katharine Slater Gittes, 'The *Canterbury Tales* and the Arabic Frame Tradition' (pp. 152–73; *YWES* 64[1975] 149); Louise O. Fradenburg, 'Criticism, Anti-Semitism, and the *Prioress's Tale*' (pp. 174–92; *YWES* 70[1991] 225); Sylvia Tomasch, '*Mappae Mundi* and "The Knight's Tale": The Geography of Power, the Technology of Control' (pp. 193–224; *YWES* 73[1994] 159); Sheila Delany, 'Geographies of Desire: Orientalism in Chaucer's *Legend of Good Women*' (pp. 225–47); Susan Schibanoff, 'Worlds Apart: Orientalism, Antifeminism, and Heresy in Chaucer's *Man of Law's Tale*' (pp. 248–80; *YWES* 77[1998] 235); and Derek Pearsall, 'Chaucer and Englishness' (pp. 281–301), who argues that there is no one less interested in quintessential Englishness than Chaucer. His Englishness expresses his sense of internationalism, and faith in the ability of England to assume its position in Europe.

Pearsall and Wu, eds., *Poetry from Chaucer to Spenser*, is a cut-down, cut-price version of Pearsall's excellent anthology *Chaucer to Spenser* (*YWES* 80[2001] 184). As part of Blackwell's Essential Literature series its virtues are cited as 'authoritative selection, compactness and ease of use' (p. viii), and it promises to be a useful aid to students 'hard-pressed for time'. Since the real problem is that students are generally hard-pressed for money, it is hard to avoid drawing the conclusion that the publishers have encouraged the cutting and pasting of the most obvious texts from Pearsall's more substantial volume into a cheaper and therefore more marketable book. In terms of selection, 'authoritative' seems to mean highly canonical, and this volume is likely to suit only the most cursory and old-fashioned of introductory survey courses covering medieval and early modern literature. All the Chaucerian offerings are from the *Canterbury Tales*, comprising the *General Prologue*, the *Wife of Bath's Prologue and Tale*, and the *Pardoner's Tale*; all are complete, except for the last, which has ninety lines cut from the middle. Compactness and ease of use may turn out to be contradictory virtues. The texts are supported by only the briefest of glosses to problematic words; similarly brief are suggestions for further reading (all published by Blackwell), and the six-page introduction written by Wu, in which Chaucer gets four paragraphs rather than the single paragraph allocated to other authors.

N.S. Thompson contributes an entry on 'Geoffrey Chaucer (c.1340–1400)' to Parini, ed., *British Writers, Retrospective*, supplement 7 (pp. 33–50). Beginning with Chaucer's literary reputation amongst men of letters, Thompson tracks Chaucer's fall from Lydgate's 'noble Rhetor' to Byron's 'obscene and contemptible' poet. Changing fashions aside, Chaucer can be described, argues Thompson, as the 'founder of English realism' (p. 33). A biographical review follows—in which, incidentally, Thomson claims that Chaucer and his wife were not as separated as has been suggested—and then discussion of Chaucer's early work. Although the ordering of material is driven by a loose chronological sequence, the movement from dream vision (of which the *Legend of Good Women* is certainly late enough to be contemporaneous with some parts of the *Tales*) to *Troilus and Criseyde*, described as a 'laboratory situation for looking at love' (p. 45), to the *Canterbury Tales* invites us to regard the last as expressing Chaucer at his most authentic and his evolution to realism at its zenith. It is perhaps unfair to Chaucer's contemporaries to assert that the *Tales* investigates the possibilities of literature before people were even asking what literature was. The lyrics and non-poetical works are dispatched quickly, and the entry concludes with a selected bibliography.

There are two pieces on Chaucer in Salisbury, Donavin, and Price eds., *Domestic Violence in Medieval Texts*. The first essay, by Eve Salisbury, 'Chaucer's "Wife", the Law, and the Middle English Breton Lays' (pp. 73–93), is concerned to show how literature can underwrite and reinforce the law. Salisbury reads thirteenth- and fourteenth-century rape laws against the *Wife of Bath's Tale* and several Middle English Breton lays. She notes that the Knight's sentence in the tale duplicates the penalties required by ecclesiastical law, where rape was regarded as a species of lechery and its punishment as a type of penance. Conversely secular laws on rape were harsh. Salisbury shows how Alisoun reveals the grey areas between these two components of the medieval legal system and exposes the inadequacies in the prosecution of sexual crimes. In the second essay, 'Reframing the Violence of the Father: Reverse Oedipal Fantasies in Chaucer's *Clerk's*, *Man of Law's*, and *Prioress's Tales*' (pp. 122–38), Barrie Ruth Straus contends that these three Chaucerian saints' lives articulate a profound cultural anxiety about paternity. In a discussion informed by psychoanalytic theory Straus focuses on the psychic rather than physical violence inherent in the symbolic structure of the family. A third essay in the collection, 'The "Homicidal Women" Stories in the *Roman de Thèbes*, the *Brut Chronicles*, and Deschamps's "Ballade 285"' by Anna Roberts (pp. 205–22) contains only passing reference to Chaucer.

Chaucer features in two of the twelve essays on career criticism in Cheney and de Armas, eds., *European Literary Careers: The Author from Antiquity to the Renaissance*. In 'Medieval Literary Careers: The Theban Track' (pp. 104–28) Robert R. Edwards discusses Dante, Marie de France, Statius, Boccaccio, Chaucer, and Lydgate. He looks briefly at *Anelida and Arcite* and the *Knight's Tale*, claiming that Chaucer reconceives Boccaccio by making his narrative more Statian. Overall he argues that invention and rewriting were the most important factors in shaping medieval poetic careers. Patrick Cheney has more to say about Chaucer in '"Novells of his devise": Chaucerian and Virgilian Career Paths in Spenser's *Februarie* Eclogue' (pp. 231–67). He shows how Spenser surveys available career routes in his 1579 poem, but then rejects these authoritative models in favour of his own programme of pastoral, love lyric, epic, and hymn.

The Festschrift for Matsuji Tajima—Iyeiri and Connolly, eds. *'And gladly wolde he lerne and gladly teche': Essays on Medieval English Presented to Professor Matsuji Tajima on his Sixtieth Birthday*—contains fourteen essays on literary and linguistic topics, five of which pertain to Chaucer. Sadahiro Kumamoto investigates 'The Function of Word Classes and the Import of French in Middle English Poetry: A Comparative Study of *The Romaunt of the Rose-A* and *Le Roman de la Rose*' (pp. 95–107), finding wide differences when rhymes involve verbs and adverbs, and also that the use of pronouns in the rhyme position is entirely confined to the English text. Yoko Iyeiri looks at 'The Development of Non-Assertive *any* in Later Middle English and the Decline of Multiple Negation' (pp. 127–43). She examines the occurrence of *any* in four Middle English texts, including the *Canterbury Tales*, and discovers that the term occurs more frequently in negative contexts in the more formal tales such as those of the Knight, Clerk, and Parson, and the *Tale of Melibee*. Thomas Cable laments the deterioration in the understanding of Chaucer's metre in 'Fifteenth-Century Rhythmical Changes' (pp. 109–25), and contends that the lack of critical attention to the loss of final -*e* in the fifteenth century has resulted in the misreading of the poetry of Lydgate, Hoccleve, Barclay, and Hawes. Two further essays concentrate on Troilus. First, in 'Modality and Ambiguity in Chaucer's *trewely*: With a Focus on *Troilus and Criseyde*' (pp. 73–94), Yoshiyuki Nakao tabulates the frequency of epistemic *trewely* in Chaucer's major works, comparing the semantic frequency of the word in Chaucer with several other contemporary poetic texts. The significance of the modal adverb *trewely* in Troilus is given particular scrutiny, as is its role in developing readers' awareness of Criseyde's *untrouthe*. Secondly, Joseph Witting writes on 'Troilus and the Law of Kind' (pp. 181–94). He examines one of the Boethian passages in *Troilus* Book IV (ll. 958–

1078), comparing its context in the poem with that in the source text, and arguing that the impact of the borrowing is to make the Christian import of the closing lines of the poem already implicit at this earlier stage.

Another Festschrift volume that arrived too late for review last year, and that shares the opening of its title with Iyeiri and Connolly, is Witalisz, ed., *'And gladly wolde he lerne and gladly teche': Studies on Language and Literature in Honour of Professor Dr. Karl Heinz Göller.* The collection contains nineteen essays, which span medieval and modern literature and linguistics; two of these focus on Chaucer. In the first, Marta Kapera considers the different characterizations of 'Traitor Calchas in Chaucer's and Shakespeare's Versions of the Troilus-Criseyde/Cressida Story' (pp. 9–16). In the second, 'Editing Chaucer: John Koch and the Forgotten Tradition' (pp. 17–26), Richard Utz compiles a bio-bibliographical study of this now largely overlooked German editor of Chaucer, arguing that Koch exerted a tremendous influence on Chaucerian textual scholarship between the 1880s and 1930s. Richard Utz also offers a more generalized survey of German academia in his article 'When Dinosaurs Ruled the Earth: A Short History of German *Chaucerphilologie* in the Nineteenth and Early Twentieth Century' (*PhiN* 21[2002] 54–62). He charts German disdain for those untrained in philology and textual criticism, and the prolific work of German scholars in editing early English texts. He also notes that the very success of philological methodology in Germany led to its eventual downfall: postwar British and American scholars abandoned this mode of research precisely because of its German associations. Michael Kensak offers a brief 'In Memoriam: Emerson Brown, Jr.' (*ChauR* 37[2002] 190–4), which contains a bibliography of his works.

Jay Ruud's essay 'Declaiming Chaucer to a Field of Cows: Three Twentieth-Century Glimpses of the Poet' (in Olive and Sprunger, eds., *Proceedings of the Tenth Annual Northern Plains Conference on Earlier British Literature*, pp. 8–21), offers close readings of three poems that all take Chaucer as their subject. The poems in question are sonnets by Benjamin Bradley [1922] and E.E. Cummings [1950], and Ted Hughes's poem 'Chaucer' published in *Birthday Letters* [1998]; texts are not included, though this would have been helpful. Ruud's analysis consists partly of close reading in the new-critical style, and partly of reception study, and it demonstrates, even if only accidentally, how critical preoccupation with Chaucer has evolved during the course of the century. Karen Hodder explores Chaucer's nineteenth-century reception in '"Dispersing the Atmosphere of Antiquity and Attempting the Impossible": R.H. Horne's *Geoffrey Chaucer Modernized*' (*BC* 51[2002] 222–39). This select anthology of Chaucer's poetry was 'a resounding publishing failure' (p. 222) in its day, but is interesting now because of its two most eminent poet-contributors: William Wordsworth and Elizabeth Barrett. Hodder looks generally at the process of adapting Chaucer for a 'modern' audience, and surveys the collaborative effort involved in the production of this volume before assessing the merits of the two poets' contributions. Their translations are situated in a long tradition of *imitatio* and poetic craft-learning; for Barrett this apprenticeship also constituted the means of admission to an otherwise exclusively masculine poetic club.

Lynn Staley's description of 'The Man in Foul Clothes and a Late Fourteenth-Century Conversation About Sin' (*SAC* 24[2002] 1–47) is centred on the biblical figure of the inappropriately dressed wedding guest (Matthew 22). She argues that fourteenth-century writers use this figure not just as a symbol of impurity but also as a means of exposing defects in the institutional Church and to explore issues of sin and judgement generally. Her discussion posits connections between certain fourteenth-century texts; these include *Piers Plowman* and the *Canterbury Tales* since she believes that the character of the Canon's Yeoman may have been inspired by Langland's Haukyn. Biblical influence on Chaucer and other writers is also investigated by Rodney Delasanta in a broad-ranging article, 'Putting Off the Old Man and Putting on the New: Ephesians 4:22–24 in Chaucer, Shakespeare, Swift, and Dostoevsky' (*C&L* 51[2002] 339–62). Delasanta takes St Paul's image of disrobing the Old Man and robing the New as his essay's organizing metaphor, and traces the impact of its transmission in the *Pardoner's Tale*, *King Lear*, *Gulliver's Travels*, and *The Brothers Karamazov*. With regard to Chaucer, he argues that, although the Pardoner presents himself as a young man, his choice of the character of the old man in his tale reveals his *alter ego* and demonstrates that the Pauline imperative of putting off the old and taking on the new is not easily achieved. He also notes that Chaucer made use of other Pauline passages in his work, and that this particular passage would have been familiar from the Sarum epistle reading for the nineteenth Sunday after Trinity.

William Kamowski reconsiders the claim for a Wycliffite Chaucer in 'Chaucer and Wyclif: God's Miracles Against the Clergy's Magic' (*ChauR* 37[2002] 5–25). Concentrating on Fragments III, VI, and VIII of the *Canterbury Tales* he demonstrates Chaucer's tendency to contrast ancient scenes of moral victory with contemporary scenes of moral failure; genuine miracles are old and remote, whereas those of the contemporary Church are fake. Therein lies Chaucer's affinity with Wycliffite theology, but Kamowski finds this no reason to label Chaucer a Wycliffite, regarding him instead as an orthodox voice for protest and reform.

Robin R. Hass looks at medieval representations of the female body in '"A picture of such beauty in their minds": The Medieval Rhetoricians, Chaucer, and Evocative *Effictio*' (*Exemplaria* 14[2002] 383–422). In an article informed by the modern theories of Foucault, Barthes, de Lauretis, and Mulvey, he analyses the thinking of such medieval theoreticians as Matthew of Vendôme and Geoffrey of Vinsauf before attending to Chaucer's descriptions of three female figures in the *Canterbury Tales*: Alisoun (the *Miller's Tale*), Virginia, and the unnamed maiden in the *Wife of Bath's Tale*. Much of his discussion focuses on rape and sexual violence, and so, unsurprisingly, he concludes with reference to Chaucer's alleged involvement with Cecily Chaumpaigne.

Of related interest is Mary-Jo Arn's article 'Thomas Chaucer and William Paston Take Care of Business: HLS Deeds 349' (*SAC* 24[2002] 237–67), describing a fifteenth-century property transaction involving Thomas Chaucer.

The marketing of Chaucer's works by fifteenth- and sixteenth-century printers is considered by Robert Costomiris in 'Sharing Chaucer's Authority in Prefaces to Chaucer's *Works* from William Caxton to William Thynne' (*JEBS* 5[2002] 1–13). He argues that the growth of Chaucer's authority may be perceived through the language deployed in the printers' prefaces to his works. Caxton adopted a laudatory formula that allowed him to borrow Chaucer's authority, a strategy repeated by Pynson and de Worde; only Thynne departs from this template. Martha Driver offers a generously illustrated study, 'Mapping Chaucer: John Speed and the Later Portraits' (*ChauR* 36[2002] 228–49). Beginning with a survey of Speed's life and various careers (as tailor, artist, map-maker, historian), Driver moves on to consider his image of Chaucer in the context of his interests in history and genealogy. Noting that Chaucer is symbolized emblematically and heraldically in the portrait, Driver concludes that Speed's presentation renders the poet a key figure in the national political identity of the Elizabethan age.

Simone Marshall offers some 'Notes on Cambridge University Library MS Ff.1.6' (*N&Q* 49[2002] 439–41), alerting readers to a number of problems with the published facsimile of the manuscript (ed. R. Beadle and A.E.B. Owen [1977]). She also lists marginalia visible in the facsimile, but has not consolidated her research by consulting the original manuscript. Estelle Stubbs tentatively identifies 'A New Manuscript by the Hengwrt/Ellesmere Scribe? Aberystwyth, National Library of Wales, MS. Peniarth 393D' (*JEBS* 5[2002] 161–7), finding similarities in script and layout between this copy of *Boece* and the famous copies of the *Canterbury Tales*. And Daniel W. Mosser locates hitherto unknown copies of '"The Chronicles of Saints and Kings of England": Two Occurrences of the Middle English Prose *Brut*'s "Peculiar Version" in MSS of the *Canterbury Tales*' (*JEBS* 5[2002] 145–9). The manuscripts in question are University of Texas HRC pre-1700 MS 143 (the 'Cardigan MS') and British Library Egerton MS 2864.

In 'Chaucer and Genre: A Teaching Model for the Upper-Level Undergraduate Course' (*SMART* 9[2002] 45–60), Tison Pugh describes an introductory approach to Chaucer that is based on genre and close reading. The course portfolio offered negotiates Chaucer's work in what we assume to be a reverse chronological order (*Canterbury Tales*, *Troilus and Criseyde*, dream visions). With its initial concentration on romance and fabliau, and its incorporation of modern film, it contains few surprises except, perhaps, in its insistence that upper-level undergraduates find the dream visions difficult and specifically 'weird'. Pugh's account of questions raised in class is useful, as is the listing of various 'medieval' films, but otherwise what is outlined here is essentially a very simplistic pedagogical approach. In another discussion of teaching practice Richard E. Zeikowitz advocates 'Befriending the Medieval Queer: A Pedagogy for Literature Classes' (*CE* 65[2002] 67–80). He defines 'queer' as signifying any non-normative behaviour, relationship, or identity, and investigates three 'monstrous' medieval characters: Grendel, the Green Knight, and the Pardoner, demonstrating how each might be viewed via a queer-informed pedagogy. The Pardoner, for example, may be seen as a sexual being who is constructed to pose a threat to normative society and to culturally defined masculine men. The article concludes with descriptions of student homework assignments.

A collection of twenty papers, Saito, Nakamura, and Yamazaki, eds., *English Corpus Linguistics in Japan*, contains an essay by Yoshiyuki Nakao on 'The Semantics of Chaucer's *Moot/Moste* and *Shal/Sholde*: Conditional Elements and Degrees of their Quantifiability' (pp. 235–47). Nakao describes the effect of propositional, clause structure, and pragmatic factors on Chaucer's use of the modals *moot/moste* and *shal/sholde*, and examines the extent to which these conditions are quantified or to which they can be tagged in an electronic text. Because some external causals are undistinguished and unmarked, and therefore cannot be easily quantified, Nakao concludes that the semantics of Chaucer's modals can only be made comprehensible through the balanced interaction of computer-readable data and readers' input.

A collection of conference papers, Minkova and Stockwell, eds., *Studies in the History of the English Language: A Millennial Perspective*, contains a debate on the nature of iambic pentameter and Chaucer's use of it. Thomas Cable begins the debate in his essay on 'Issues for a New History of English Prosody' (pp. 125–51), in which he surveys developments in English metrical study during the twentieth century, focusing particularly on the emergence of iambic pentameter between Chaucer and Donne. Having analysed stress shift, metrical pause, and ictus, his conclusion (self-described as 'eccentric', p. 147), is that Chaucer wrote not in iambic pentameter but in what he terms an alternating metre. In a counterpoint paper, 'Chaucer: Folk Poet or Littérateur?' (pp. 153–75), Gilbert Youmans and Xingzhong Li respond to Cable by revoicing the traditional view that Chaucer wrote iambic pentameter. Using a framework consistent with Optimality Theory, they find that Chaucer conforms more closely than Shakespeare does to the alternating stress pattern WSWS, which is statistically normative in all iambic pentameter verse, and they decide, in answer to the question posed by their title, that Chaucer was indeed a littérateur. The editors then allow Cable 'A Rejoinder to Youmans and Li' (pp. 177–82), in which he summarizes the differences between his theory of pentameter and that of the generativists, as represented by Youmans and Li. The intricacies of iambic pentameter have attracted more interest elsewhere. In a technical and broad-ranging essay charting 'The Italian Line in English after Chaucer' (*L&L* 11[2002] 291–305), Martin J. Duffell argues that English iambic pentameter has other important features in addition to the five parameters identified by parametric theory. He focuses on one of these features, the mixture of pausing and running lines, which he terms French and Italian respectively, and analyses the extent to which each occurs in the verse of eighteen poets from Chaucer to Browning by means of statistical sampling. In Chaucer he detects a growing preference for the Italian line, a tendency upheld by the Scots Chaucerians such as Dunbar and Douglas but not by other English poets until Spenser and Shakespeare.

S.C.P. Horobin examines the language of 'Chaucer's Norfolk Reeve' (*Neophil* 86[2002] 609–12), identifying in his speech some distinctive features characteristic of the Norfolk dialect. He argues that the dialect of the pilgrim character himself has been overlooked as critics, led by Tolkien, have concentrated on Chaucer's representation of the northern dialect in the students' dialogue in his tale. Horobin's findings accord perfectly with Pearcy's consideration (see below) of a northernism uttered by the Reeve. Luisella Caon investigates 'Final -e and Spelling Habits in the Fifteenth-Century Versions of the *Wife of Bath's Prologue*' (*ES* 83[2002] 296–310), using the CD-ROM of the *Wife of Bath's Prologue* to achieve a systematic analysis. She finds that final -e is preserved in all copies of the *Prologue*, and that its transmission is far from haphazard, as was previously believed. Whereas some scribes retain a conservative spelling, others use final -e as a marker of vowel length, and others either delete or add final -e ubiquitously. Her findings point to a systematic use of this spelling feature in the fifteenth century amongst Chaucerian scribes and printers.

Studies in the Age of Chaucer contains a 'Colloquium: Chaucer and the Future of Language Study' (*SAC* 24[2002] 299–354) with contributions by six academics. All of the speakers consider the supposed uniqueness of Chaucer's poetic achievement and the privileged place that he enjoys in the medieval literary canon. Christopher Cannon begins the debate by attempting to define 'What Chaucer's Language Is'

(*SAC* 24[2002] 301–8), using the two examples of Chomsky and Muscatine to demonstrate the fracture between linguistics and literary criticism in Chaucer studies. Linguistic methodology has proved unacceptable to Chaucerian literary critics, who have resisted the notion that Chaucer's language might be reduced to a simple set of rules. In conclusion Cannon outlines some directions for the future study of Chaucer's language, including a suggestion for an approach based on philosophical principles. Ralph Hanna's contribution 'Chaucer and the Future of Language Study' (*SAC* 24[2002] 309–15), which shares the title of the overall debate, pays detailed attention to Cannon's monograph *The Making of Chaucer's English: A Study of Words* [1998] (see *YWES* 79[2000] 204–5). Pointing out that such a study could only have been undertaken by someone with an extensive knowledge of non-Chaucerian language, Hanna appeals for more cooperation between language study and Chaucerian literary history. He also critiques Cannon's work, arguing that Chaucer's language, especially in its relation to Anglo-Norman and Continental French, may be more innovative than Cannon allows, and noting some aspects of lexical study which might be developed further. Tim William Machan's sensible essay focuses on 'Politics and the Middle English Language' (*SAC* 24[2002] 317–24). Machan surveys the grand claims that have been made for Chaucer as the father of English poetry and the inventor of English, and demonstrates how unlikely it is that such claims might be true. Rather than depending upon the agency of individuals, the 'very long and very gradual shift to English as the language of both prestige and common written usage' (p. 323) was effected through institutional and historical contexts. In the next contribution to the discussion, 'Tolkien, Philology, and *The Reeve's Tale*: Towards the Cultural Move in Middle English Studies' (*SAC* 24[2002] 325–34), Wendy Scase also takes the notion of Chaucer as the 'father' of English literary language as her point of departure, and in common with other speakers in the debate she is alert to the rupture between Chaucer studies and the rest of Middle English literature, and between language and literature more generally. As her title indicates, she discusses the *Reeve's Tale*, an example used in previous analyses of Chaucer's language by J.R.R. Tolkien and David Burnley. Scase notes that Burnley sought to reunite language study with literary and cultural history via linguistic pragmatics, and proposes extending his method to effect what she terms the 'cultural move' of returning Chaucer to Middle English.

Jeremy J. Smith's paper, 'Chaucer and the Invention of English' (*SAC* 24[2002] 335–46) differs from the others in this colloquium in having something concrete to say about Chaucer's language. Giving a clear account of the development of late medieval English, Smith discusses the linguistic resources available to Chaucer and how he engaged with these materials. He thus sets Chaucer in his linguistic context, reminding us that London in the fourteenth and fifteenth centuries was a veritable linguistic melting-pot of immigrants who brought with them different speech, usages, and cultures. Finally, in 'The New Medievalization of Chaucer' (*SAC* 24[2002] 347–54), Stephanie Trigg warns that we can no longer safely rely upon Chaucer to 'save' medieval studies. She argues that our pedagogic habit of placing Chaucer on courses to entice student choice and our reliance on him as approachable and readable for beginners have served only to reinforce the false distinction between Chaucer studies and the rest of Middle English literature.

2. *Canterbury Tales*

It is good to know that Chaucer is still an inspiration to (dramatic) poets. John Guare publishes his new play *Chaucer in Rome*, in which a painter visits Rome as a prize for his painting, but has to be treated over there for skin cancer caused by paint toxins. His crisis of identity coincides with a flood of pilgrims visiting Rome for the year 2000. The blurb on the back cover describes the play as an 'expansive rumination on art, religion, and the price one pays for celebrity'. The Canterbury theme is only loosely employed, but the play constitutes a serious moment in modern popular reception of Chaucer, and could possibly offer itself as a comparison piece as a class assignment. An Afterword offers some excerpts from Guare's journal on how the play came about.

A landmark in Chaucer studies this year is the first volume of Correale and Hamel, eds., *Sources and Analogues of the 'Canterbury Tales'*. Bryan and Dempster's *Sources and Analogues of Chaucer's 'Canterbury Tales'* appeared in 1941 (*YWES* 22[1943] 51), so a new edition is by now much needed. Although much of Bryan and Dempster's scholarship is retained, there are many changes: some new sources and analogues for the *Friar's Tale* and the *Second Nun's Tale*; re-editions of texts from manuscripts known to have been closer to what Chaucer actually accessed (the *Man of Law's Tale*, and *Wife of Bath's Prologue*); some casualties from the first edition, such as Sercambi's *Novelle*, too late to have been used by Chaucer; and modern English translations of all material in foreign languages, an expansion that has required a second volume. In this first volume are covered: the frame, by Helen Cooper (*YWES* 78[1999] 242); the *Reeve's Tale*, by Peter G. Beidler, who edits *Le Meunier et les .II. clers*; the *Cook's Tale*, by John Scattergood, who writes a general essay in the absence of any known source; the *Friar's Tale*, by Peter Nicholson, who supplies a small group of Latin exempla as analogues; the *Clerk's Tale*, by Thomas J. Farrell and Amy W. Goodwin, who present texts of the Griselda story; the *Squire's Tale*, by Vincent DiMarco, who supplies a wide range of material on motifs and themes found in Chaucer's tale; the *Franklin's Tale*, by Robert R. Edwards, who offers chronicles and Jerome's anti-feminist polemic in addition to Boccaccio's *Filocolo*; the *Pardoner's Prologue and Tale*, by Mary Hamel, who gives the *Roman de la Rose* for the *Prologue* and for the tale and a wide range of exempla and *florilegia*, as well as an Italian play of St Anthony; the *Tale of Melibee*, by William R. Askins, who supplies both French and Latin versions of Albertano of Brescia's *Liber consolationis et consilii*; the *Monk's Tale*, by Thomas H. Bestul, who gives French, Italian, and Latin analogues in addition to Boccaccio's *De Casibus virorum illustrium*; the *Nun's Priest's Tale*, by Edward Wheatley, whose main material comes from the *Roman de Renart*; the *Second Nun's Prologue and Tale*, by Sherry L. Reames, who offers Latin hymns and excerpts from Dante's *Paradiso* and the *Legenda aurea*; and finally the *Parson's Tale*, by Richard Newhauser, who includes a meditation of Anselm of Canterbury along with the expected Raymund of Pennaforte's *Summa de paenitentia*. Apart from reflecting the latest findings of source material, this edition widens its usefulness in offering translations, and is a welcome new tool of research. We look forward to volume 2.

Marijane Osborn, in *Time and the Astrolabe in the 'Canterbury Tales'*, turns Chaucer's seemingly pedestrian interest in the gadget into a dominating presence. Carefully differentiating her work from numerology or astrology, Osborn never or rarely loses contact with the practical mechanics of the astrolabe, which are explained in the first chapter. One example of this occurs in chapter 2, in which she suggests that the steed of brass in the *Squire's Tale* resembles the astrolabe, which, in certain illustrations, has a horse-shaped pin that holds together its separate plates. No esoteric interpretation necessarily follows from this; Osborn's point is that Chaucer's work is full of learned allusions that function more like private jokes for a knowing audience or little Lewis than as hermeneutic code. Chaucer's references to John Somer and Nicholas of Lynn, who dedicated their works to Joan of Kent and John of Gaunt respectively, point to other very specific and technical references designed to delight certain readers. The main function of the astrolabe is to locate objects in the sky and use the bearings from them to determine time or location on earth. Nowadays, the zodiacal names for the divisions of the ecliptic, which means the annual path of the sun, have been dropped, resulting in the linguistic distance between navigator and astrologer. But in Chaucer's time astronomical description and astrological prediction shared a vocabulary, creating an ambivalence that Chaucer puts to good use. Osborn finds that astrolabic evidence generally supports the theory, articulated by Bradshaw, that local geography organizes the sequence of tales; yet evidence for the artificial single-day trip is also present, and has obvious symbolic appeal. Open-minded in the face of conflicting evidence, she recognizes that, despite her reluctance to take the exegetical path, there is much to be said for the astrolabic horizon of the pilgrimage being transcended by a higher temporal scheme. This conflict is already present in the *Knight's Tale*, where, Osborn argues (chapter 5), the astrolabe serves as the actual plan for the amphitheatre, and symbolizes human time and destiny, eventually overruled by a providential scheme unmeasurable by any instrument. There are no short cuts through this book, and the material in chapter 1 is especially hard going. That said, the technicalities are what open up the complex possibilities, and in reading the book we are reminded again of Chaucer's endless magpie curiosity.

In 2000 Sheila Delany edited a special issue of *Exemplaria*, on medievalism and the Jews. Now her edited collection of essays for Routledge's Multicultural Middle Ages series, *Chaucer and the Jews: Sources, Contexts, Meanings*, furthers the work of the *Exemplaria* issue, which contained no Chaucer. Fed up with ventriloquizing Catholic doctrine, Delany describes in her introduction her gradual recognition of the absent presence of Jews in an England that had expelled them in 1290, and her resulting liberation from the invisible theological norms that had fettered her teaching and thinking about Chaucer studies. Delany's introduction bears much of the freshness and directness of her early feminist and Marxist criticism, although its promise is only partially borne out by the rest of the collection.

The anthology is divided into three parts: 'Chaucer's Texts', 'Chaucerian Contexts', and 'Chaucer, Jews, and Us'. Under the first heading comes Christine M. Rose's 'The Jewish Mother-in-Law: Synagoga and the *Man of Law's Tale*' (pp. 3–23), the essay being published in 1998. Rose argues that the cultural matrix of the *Man of Law's Tale* encodes Jew and Muslim as Semitic other, that the mother-in-law *v.* Constance opposition functions similarly to that between Synagoga and Ecclesia. Such iconographic representations of Old and New Church were available to Chaucer at Chartres, Saint-Denis, and Bury St Edmunds and in a presentation play of Philippe de Mézières. Historian William Chester Jordan makes his first foray into literary criticism in 'The Pardoner's "Holy Jew"' (pp. 25–42). Given that the Jews were actually against veneration of relics, it was absurd that the bone brandished by the Pardoner allegedly came from a sheep owned by a holy Jew. The allusion resonates with the view of the Jew as alien and a dabbler in occult arts. Jerome Mandel finds no satire in the reference to '"Jewes werk" in *Sir Thopas*' (pp. 59–68). Jews enjoyed a reputation as fine craftsmen, albeit not specifically as workers of armour, and thus the workmanship of Thopas's 'fyn hawberk' is a general allusion to Jewish skill and the beauty of the armour. Two reprinted essays complete this section: Sheila Delany's 'Chaucer's Prioress, the Jews, and the Muslims' (pp. 43–57; *YWES* 80[2001] 202); and Sylvia Tomasch's 'Postcolonial Chaucer and the Virtual Jew' (pp. 69–85; *YWES* 81[2002] 235).

In the second part the lens takes a wider sweep, and in many ways this is the most informative and useful section. Mary Dove writes about 'Chaucer and the Translation of the Jewish Scriptures' (pp. 89–107). Although historically it was the Jews who were deemed blind literalists and thus bad readers of the Scriptures, the prefatory comments of the Wycliffite Bible demonstrate anxiety over anyone reading aright, cleric, lewd, or Jew. The Jew, with his long tradition of talmudic exegesis, emerges as a more faithful reader of Scripture than the Christian January, who reads the Song of Songs carnally. Dove concludes by speculating that Chaucer may have read parts of the Wycliffite Bible, had his own reservations about reading Hebrew Scripture without interpretative gloss, and shared the translator's respect for Jewish reading practices. In 'Reading Biblical Outlaws: The "Rise of David" Story in the Fourteenth Century' (pp. 109–32) Timothy S. Jones finds similarities between David and Robin Hood as good outlaws, as opposed to bad outlaws, such as Cain or Lucifer. There is little application to Chaucer. In 'Robert Holcot on the Jews' (pp. 133–44) Nancy L. Turner notes the negative stereotype Holcot promotes, and how from his commentary on the apocryphal Wisdom of Solomon, a text Chaucer is thought to have known, Chaucer may have learned to see Jews as envious, cruel, and vaguely unhuman. Denise L. Despres considers the more subtle representations of Jews who refuse both scriptural and usurious stereotype in 'The Protean Jew in the Vernon Manuscript' (pp. 145–64). Noting that Chaucer does not employ such protean depictions amounts to much the same thing as saying that he does employ cheap stereotypes. Elisa Narin van Court has a reprinted essay, '*The Siege of Jerusalem* and Augustinian Historians: Writing about Jews in Fourteenth-Century England' (pp. 165–84; *YWES* 76[1997] 142). Anthony P. Bale considers the enduring appeal of stories about Jews murdering children in '"House-Devil, Town Saint": Anti-Semitism and Hagiography in Medieval Suffolk' (pp. 185–210); in particular he considers the cult of Robert, a child said to have been murdered by Jews of Bury St Edmunds.

Three essays comprise the third and final section. Colin Richmond's reprinted essay 'Englishness and Medieval Anglo-Jewry' (pp. 213–27; not covered in *YWES* 73[1994]), exposes the ideological constructedness of the equation between Englishness and non-Jewishness. Gillian Steinberg talks about her experiences 'Teaching Chaucer to the "Cursed Folk of Herod"' (pp. 229–36). Steinberg teaches Chaucer to an orthodox all-male class at New York's Yeshiva University. The poet's anti-Semitism is not strong enough to ban him from the curriculum, but the dirty bits do cause problems. The students' concern about non-Jews reading Chaucer's anti-Semitic *Prioress's Tale* curiously parallels Wycliffite concern about Christian misreading of the Scriptures. The last essay comes from Judith S. Neaman, who strikes an offputtingly evangelical note in 'Positively Medieval: Teaching as a Missionary Activity' (pp. 237–45). Neaman teaches orthodox Jewish women, who, like their male counterparts, find altogether too much information about body functions in Chaucer's poetry. Her secular mission is to reveal Chaucer's 'undisputed literary genius' (pp. 244–5) to them, and to get them to consider whether Chaucer was a conservative advocate of fourteenth-century attitudes or a liberalizing humanist.

In 'The Mercantile (Mis)Reader in *The Canterbury Tales*' (*SP* 99[2002] 17–32), Roger A. Ladd argues that merchants in the *Tales* fail to distinguish the *fruyt* of truth from the *chaf* of narrative. The merchant from whom the Man of Law claims he received his tale of Custance commodifies the tidings he tells, creating a rift between moral tale and amoral teller; the pilgrim Merchant mimics the language of the Clerk, who satirizes modern marriage, but misses the Clerk's meaning; and the merchant of the *Shipman's Tale* is blind to the reality of his wife's business transactions. Avoiding the frontal assault of estates satire, Chaucer nonetheless portrays merchants throughout his poem as unable to perceive or transmit *sentence*.

Two pieces on the *Canterbury Tales* are included in the collection of nineteen essays, Mullini, ed., *Tudor Theatre, For Laughs(?), Pour Rire(?)*, which focuses on the theme of laughter on the Tudor stage. First, Greg Walker considers 'Laughable Men: Comedy and Masculinity from Chaucer to Shakespeare' (pp. 1–20). Beginning with the *Miller's Tale* Walker traces some well-worn male stereotypes (the *senex amans*, the sexually predatory trickster, and the squeamish male) from the fabliau tradition down to the sixteenth century. Second, Maria Katarzyna Greenwood writes about 'Garlands of Derision: The Thematic Imagery in Chaucer's *The Knight's Tale* and Shakespeare's *A Midsummer Night's Dream*' (pp. 21–39). Greenwood distinguishes between the use of garlands in the different contexts of courtship, victory, and artistic endeavour, and analyses how the image is variously used by Chaucer and Shakespeare to invite either admiration or derisive laughter.

Periodically in the Chaucer discussion groups comes a trouncing of Pier Paolo Pasolini's film adaptation, *I racconti di Canterbury*, as cheap caricature. Kathleen Forni offers a more thoughtful and sympathetic understanding of this innovative filmmaker's intentions: 'A "Cinema of Poetry": What Pasolini Did to Chaucer's *Canterbury Tales*' (*LFQ* 30[2002] 256–63). In keeping with his Marxism and sharp sense of sexual politics, Pasolini exposes the queer subtext of the tales, and celebrates a pre-capitalist and unfettered sexuality. The sadistic end of Perkyn Revelour is surprisingly close to the spirit of Rawlinson Poetry 141, which causes the trickster to be 'honged hye', or of Bodley 686, where he is 'y-dampned to presoun perpetually'. See also the online journal, *Senses of Cinema* (*SoC* 19[2002] no pagination), in which Gino Moliterno reviews Pasolini's *The Canterbury Tales*, which was the second film in the 'Trilogy of Life', the first being *Il Decameron* [1970] and the third *Il Fiore di Mille e una Notte* [1974]. As with Forni, Moliterno shows the sympathy and open-mindedness to poetic licence that the film deserves. Let's hope Chaucer discussion groupies read these pieces before their next ritual declamation. The cinematic theme is strong this year, with an entire issue of *Studies in Medievalism*, edited by Tom Shippey and Martin Arnold, devoted to the meeting of screen, fiction, and the medieval. Here Nickolas Haydock writes about 'Arthurian Melodrama, Chaucerian Spectacle, and the Waywardness of Cinematic Pastiche in *First Knight* and *A Knight's Tale*' (*SiM* 12[2002] 5–38). Glaring anachronisms in the films, argues Haydock, are signs of an ironically knowing, postmodern revisitation of the past. The tendency to pastiche, in both senses of 'assemblage' and 'forgery', is closer to the poetics of Chaucer's *Knight's Tale* than medievalists care to admit. The egregious ways in which the historical is exposed as rhetorical in the films strikes a parallel to, for example, the Hoccleve portrait of Chaucer, which is both historical and highly mannered. Chaucer's own use of spectacle in the *Knight's Tale* well conveys his awareness of the rhetorical construction of power. Moving over to fiction, William Calin asks 'What *Tales of a Wayside Inn* Tells Us about Longfellow and about Chaucer' (*SiM* 12[2002] 197–213). For Longfellow, the golden Middle Ages, reflected in his *Tales*, offered him a nostalgic site from which to react against modernity, capitalism, optimism, and grasping materialism.

Move over Homer, says Helen Cooper, and make room for 'Joyce's Other Father: The Case for Chaucer' in Boldrini, ed., *Medieval Joyce* (pp. 143–63). Joyce is known to have been reading the *Canterbury Tales* during his revision of *Ulysses*, and Cooper draws our attention to the encyclopaedicism, naturalism, multiple perspectives and self-referentiality that mark the two works. Her comparison between the two authors is not sustained in any single instance but rather developed over an accretion of lesser points of connection. Her analysis concludes in an assertion we do not hear so often nowadays: that Chaucer is a modernist in all but the chronological sense, and that it took English literature 200 years to catch up with him.

By means of J.L. Austin's speech act theory, and commissive utterances, which in linguistics refer to utterances that obligate the speaker to a certain course of action, Marie Nelson looks at the language of promise (*biheste*) and obligation (*dette*) in '"Biheste is detter": Marriage Promises in Chaucer's *Canterbury Tales*' (*PLL* 38[2002] 167–99). What emerges from considering the conjugal promises exchanged in the tales of the Clerk, Wife of Bath, Merchant, Franklin, Shipman, and Second Nun is Chaucer's sensitivity to the nuances of sincerity, reciprocity, and legal obligation. With this, compare Conor McCarthy on 'Love, Marriage, and Law: Three Canterbury Tales' (*ES* 83[2002] 504–18). Although Walter and Griselda exchange mutual vows, there is an element of coercion in Griselda's complaisance that undermines the consensual requirement of marriage. January's marriage is less a remedy for sin than an excuse for it. Common law forbade married women from making contracts, and Dorigen's promise to Aurelius is both irregular and suggests that she has not accepted Arveragus's full sovereignty. Viewed from the perspective of law, the *Franklin's Tale* only compounds problems rather than solving them, as the traditional marriage-group theory proposes.

Claire M. Waters pits the disembodied Parson against an overly physical Pardoner in 'Holy Duplicity: The Preacher's Two Faces' (*SAC* 24[2002] 75–113). In the contrast between the two she finds a duality attested elsewhere between the deathless and absolute body of institutional authority and the mortal, fallible body of that authority's human representative. The bodiless piety of the Parson is an impossibility, for preaching is a material and local event, executed by bodies that are incontrovertibly male. The bulk of Waters's essay is occupied with preaching treatises by Maurice of Sully, Humbert of Romans, Thomas of Chobham, and Alan of Lille; in her consideration of the *Tales*, she points out the Parson's own individuality, distinct from his office, and presents both Parson and Pardoner less as moral alternatives than as supplements of each other.

William Sayers argues for a greater complexity of characterization for Chaucer's pilgrim in 'Chaucer's Shipman and the Law Marine' (*ChauR* 37[2002] 145–58). Read against the background of the *Rôles d'Oléron*, articles that dealt with contentious cases of maritime law, recorded in the fourteenth-century *Oak Book of Southampton*, the Shipman's questionable practices are only hinted at. Law and conscience must take second place to craft and exigency. Shipman and Knight together are the most travelled pilgrims, and represent the great agendas of Christian mission and capitalist trade.

Richard Firth Green considers the legal vocabulary of 'Palamon's Appeal of Treason in the *Knight's Tale*' (in Steiner and Barrington, eds., *The Letter of the Law: Legal Practice and Literary Production in Medieval England*, pp. 105–14). Departing from his source in Boccaccio, Chaucer depicts his knights in dispute, the juridical nuances of which Green expounds carefully and clearly. He notes the correspondence between the fictive tournament and the trial by battle that concluded the case of John Annesley *v.* Thomas Katrington in 1380. From then on, the Court of Chivalry extended its jurisdiction to cover offences properly pursued under common law, and charges of treason were increasingly used as cover for private disputes. Unease at the Court of Chivalry's abuse of legal prerogative and Richard II's exploitation of it are expressed in both attempted parliamentary reform and Chaucer's conclusion to the knights' tournament, where Arcite, who wins the trial by battle, dies before enjoying his prize of Emily as wife. This is a fine piece of scholarship; informative, intelligent, and illuminating.

To a collection devoted to *A History of English Laughter: Laughter from Beowulf to Beckett and Beyond*, edited by Manfred Pfister, Andrew James Johnson contributes an analysis of 'The Exegetic of Laughter: Religious Parody in Chaucer's *Miller's Tale*' (pp. 17–33). Here every biblical resonance is explored: Absolon's name, the Flood, Song of Songs, God's *pryvetee*, and Alison as parodic type of the Virgin Mary. It is not only exegetical abuse but the exegetic act itself that is laughed at, argues Johnson, and Chaucer treads a delicate line between laughter that is contained and laughter that is subversive. Expanding on one of the biblical threads traced by Johnson, Louise M. Bishop, in '"Of Goddes pryvetee nor of his wyf": Confusion of Orifices in Chaucer's *Miller's Tale*' (*TSLL* 44[2002] 231–46), continues the debate over what exactly Absolon kissed in the darkness. Bishop refers us to Exodus 33:18–23, in which God shows his backside to Moses, and to St Augustine's commentary on the passage. Moses' request to behold God's face is a forbidden enquiry into divine *pryvetee*, and God's revealed *posteriora* is a symbol of circumscribed knowledge. Chaucer, rather cheekily, makes a covert allusion to such mystery in the confusion of Alison's orifices. 'Chaucer's Absolon and Boccaccio's *Decameron*' are brought into relation by John Finlayson (*NM* 103[2002] 403–7), who finds a closer resemblance between the priest of *Decameron* VIII.2 and Absolon than between the priest and Daun John of the *Shipman's Tale*, with whom he is usually compared. The 'heroine', Monna Belcolore, sounds like Alison, proffering further evidence for a connection with the *Miller's Tale*. There is, however, concludes Finlayson, no reason why Chaucer should not have used Boccaccio's tale in two different places. In a partial replication of his essay published this same year (reviewed above), Greg Walker, in 'Rough Girls and Squeamish Boys: The Trouble with Absolon in *The Miller's Tale*' (in Treharne, ed., *Writing Gender and Genre in Medieval Literature: Approaches to Old and Middle*

English Texts, pp. 61–91), notes the liminal position Absolon assumes between lover and husband, man and woman, adult and child, and between fabliau, romance, and biblical narrative. In keeping with the volume's emphasis on genre and gender, Walker suggests that Chaucer's satirical intentions with regard to Absolon are aimed at undoing traditional and stereotypical gender assumptions operating within the various literary genres.

Dalhousie Review 82:i is a special issue on medieval studies, of which two articles relate to Chaucer. Under the section entitled 'Household' comes a consideration by Elizabeth Edwards of 'The Economics of Justice in Chaucer's *Miller's* and *Reeve's Tales*' (*DR* 82[2002] 91–112). Translated into fiscal terms, jealousy is a kind of hoarding, licentiousness an over-spending, and *quyting* an equivocation between repayment and repayment with interest. Everyone in the tale has to pay up or is paid back, except Alison, who is associated with surplus. Edwards turns attention away from *pryvetee* to *foyson*. Her argument works well for the *Miller's Tale* but much less so for that of the Reeve.

Rodney Delasanta spots 'The Mill in Chaucer's *Reeve's Tale*' (*ChauR* 36[2002] 270–6) as an apocalyptic image. Since the clerks filch both the flower of the daughter's virginity and flour made into bread, the mill is a clear enough image in the tale for *swyvyng*. Delasanta notes the iconographic use of the 'Mystic Mill' (p. 272) as a type for the grinding down of the Old Law into the food of the New. As is so often the case in Chaucerian fabliau, the sexual or scatological allusions disclose a theological meaning in keeping with the occasion of pilgrimage. Roy J. Pearcy asks what exactly is *digne* about stagnant, smelly ditch water in 'A Northern Idiom in RvT: 3964, "As digne as water in a dich"' (*ChauR* 36[2002] 370–3). Pearcy suggests that the phrase does not mean that the miller's wife was as 'worthy as stinking ditch water' (i.e. not worthy at all) but 'as worthy as ditch water is stinking' (i.e. very worthy). Since contemporaneous northern texts render southern *digne* as the grapheme *deyne*, a pun is created with *deyne/dain*, meaning 'stinking'. Where Hengwrt and Ellesmere record *digne*, Harley 7334, Lansdowne 851, Helmingham, and Cambridge Dd.4.24 all preserve the superior reading of northern *deyn(e)* or *deigne*.

'"Wel bet is roten appul out of hoord": Chaucer's Cook, Commerce, and Civic Order' (*SP* 99[2002] 229–46), by Craig E. Bertolet, presents a contrast between the gastronomic ethics of the Franklin, for whom food is a pleasure and a good, and the Cook, for whom food—of doubtful quality—is business. The Cook's proverb in reference to Perkyn is ironic: one rotten apple spoils the hoard; one bad apprentice spoils the business and guild community; and one *mormel* spoils the appetite. The Cook attempts to appear an honest trader, but his own sententious narrative gives him away. Olga Burakov argues that 'Chaucer's *Cook's Tale*' is central to his biblical poetics (*Expl* 61[2002] 2–5). The tale begins with Perkyn Revelour in an edenic setting, which was lost through his theft of the forbidden fruit of the money-box, and it concludes—inasmuch as it does conclude—with his exile from his master's shop into a new residence with the Eve-like woman who supports herself through prostitution. It is not impossible, but the biblical analogy seems too general to apply.

Kathy Lavezzo contributes to the debate about cultural geography in 'Beyond Rome: Mapping Gender and Justice in *The Man of Law's Tale*' (*SAC* 24[2002] 149–80). As medieval *mappae mundi* illustrate, England is on the world's edge, and it is this sense of his own land as on the margins of law that comes across in Chaucer's tale. England, visited by Custance, bearer of Roman Christian law, has a privileged relation to Christianity. Yet the erasure of women in the tale suggests the desire of the Man of Law, and his English legal compatriots, to move beyond the reach of Rome and 'rehabilitate marginality in the name of English sovereignty' (p. 176). By sometimes disconnected stages, Maura Nolan considers the uneasy relationship between legal and poetic discourse in '"Acquiteth yow now": Textual Contradiction and Legal Discourse in the Man of Law's Introduction' (in Steiner and Barrington, eds., pp. 136–53), noting that critics read the tale in terms of one or the other, but that neither works entirely. The general requirement for the pilgrims to 'quit' each other puts two discursive systems, the legal and the poetic, into operation. The tensions between narrating modes are reflected in the conflicting manuscript evidence of what has become known as the epilogue, in which the Host reacts to the Man of Law's story, although the speaker is designated variously and the ordering of the tale problematic.

Alcuin Blamires offers informed analysis in 'Refiguring the "Scandalous Excess" of Medieval Woman: The Wife of Bath and Liberality' (in Fenster and Lees, eds., *Gender and Debate from the Early Middle Ages to the Renaissance*, pp. 57–78). Blamires returns us to Aristotelian ethics in noting that excess, like defect, is vicious in relation to the virtuous mean. Women are notoriously defective in reason and excessive in passion. Blamires considers contemporary rebuttals by writers such as Christine de Pizan, who counterclaims, for example, that women's avarice is just prudence and their extravagance liberality—a rhetorical strategy he terms 'redoctrination'. He then considers light and heat as metaphors for liberality and finds it to be more a female than male virtue. Aware that equating generosity with women is just another essentializing move, Blamires nonetheless reckons that any challenge to misogyny is worth hearing about. The problem of voice that Elaine Treharne addresses in 'The Stereotype Confirmed? Chaucer's Wife of Bath' (in Treharne, ed., pp. 93–115) is readily evident from her opening quote from Hélène Cixous, '"I write woman: woman must write woman. And man, man"' (p. 93). Despite the Wife's imprisonment within masculine language, Chaucer nonetheless attempts to create a female voice and language. Quoting Otto Jespersen and drawing from sociolinguistics, Treharne examines assumptions about female discourse as garrulous, circular, and gossipy, and finds them both reaffirmed and challenged in the Wife's speech, which, though larded with intensifiers and euphemisms, poses pertinent questions.

Patricia Clare Ingham considers the politics of genre in 'Pastoral Histories: Utopia, Conquest, and the *Wife of Bath's Tale*' (*TSLL* 44[2002] 34–46). She notes how in the post-Glyn Dwr years, anti-vaticination laws forbade Welsh prophecies of the Breton hope, namely, the prophecy of Merlin predicting Welsh recovery of insular British kingship, and suggests that Chaucer uses traditions of pastoral history important to Welsh group fantasies of sovereign rule. Ingham questions 'realist' history and its relentless demand for accuracy, for by discounting the relevance of failed sovereign dreams in favour of the tyranny of what actually happened, history occludes utopian fantasies of the subordinated. The essay clearly partakes in the psychoanalysis *v.* historicism debate, and is echoed in Elizabeth Scala's essay in the same issue, 'Historicists and their Discontents: Reading Psychoanalytically in Medieval Studies' (*TSLL* 44[2002] 108–31), in which she asserts that 'it is *only* psychoanalysis that can rescue historicism from the blindness it displays in relation to its own desires and its own historical moment' (p. 110). Martin Puhvel revisits the notion that the Wife of Bath bumped off husband number four in 'The Death of Alys of Bath's "Revelour" Husband' (*NM* 103[2002] 329–40), and suggests not only that she did so without Jankyn's help but also that she may have done in Jankyn himself. Puhvel draws attention to hints of this within the text, such as the violence of her curses, and also claims from outside the text her similarity to Alice Kyteler of Kilkenny, accused of witchcraft. Apart from sharing a name, the two women are much married, and have a connection with textiles, the Kyteler family originally being Flemish merchants. Finally, Chaucer was deputy forester near Bath, the city to which Alice Kyteler was thought to have fled. Peter G. Beidler takes issue with 'Fire in the House: Ralph Waldo Emerson's Misreading of Lines 1139–45 in Chaucer's *Wife of Bath's Tale*' (*ChauR* 37[2002] 86–94). Where the hag's point is that *gentilesse* remains *gentilesse* whether observed or not, Emerson says the difference is that between being observed by many or just a few. Emerson's larger intention in 'The Poet' is to exemplify how the initial imaginative impact of a trope is of more value than its precise sense, and in this he follows his own patrician aesthetic, but Beidler finds the misreading irresponsible and Emerson to be the first of 'many modern misreaders' of Chaucer (p. 93).

'Present Panic in *The Merchant's Tale*', by Glenn Burger (*SAC* 24[2002] 49–73), considers the role marriage plays in hegemonizing sex and gender norms and in constructing lay subjectivity. Indeed, conjugality is central to and instrumental in constructing bourgeois identity. Somewhere in the middle, in between the conjugal nightmare of the Wife's unruliness and the oppressive tyranny of Walter in the *Clerk's Tale*, the Merchant's henpecked self-commentary stands as an early articulation of middle-class identity. Despite January's status as knight, his self is asserted through the paraphernalia of privacy and interiority associated with a mercantile rather than aristocratic class—the garden, key, exclusive access to May's body, the bedchamber, etc.

'Chaucer's *Squire's Tale*: Animal Discourse, Women, and Subjectivity' are the combined topic of Lesley Kordeki's article (*ChauR* 36[2002] 277–97). Seated in the lap of sympathetic Canacee, who identifies with her story, the dolorous falcon plaining her betrayal brings together the non-human, the feminine, and human subjectivity. It is significant, observes Kordeki, that in Chaucer's three tales involving talking animals, the tales of the Man of Law, the Nun's Priest, and the Squire, rhetorical exuberance is excessive, as if in them Chaucer is more acutely aware of his own style and voice.

In 'Dorigen's Lament and the Resolution of the *Franklin's Tale*' (*ChauR* 36[2002] 374–90) Warren S. Smith continues his thesis, advanced earlier, that the Wife rebuts St Jerome's anti-feminist polemics in *Adversus Jovinianum* (*YWES* 78[1999] 247), by applying it to the *Franklin's Tale*. Where Jerome is self-contradictory and satirical in his treatment of female morals and nature, Dorigen adopts a more considered, serious, and sympathetic position. The body of the essay involves line-by-line comparisons between Jerome's and Chaucer's exempla. Smith divides Dorigen's lament into two sets of eleven examples; one set of women who committed suicide to avoid male oppression and the other set of women renowned for their love for their husbands. Paul Battles considers the enigmatic clerk of Orléans in 'Magic and Metafiction in the *Franklin's Tale*' (in Jones and Sprunger, eds., *Marvels, Monsters, and Miracles; Studies in the Medieval and Early Modern Imaginations*, pp. 243–66). Much of the essay is spent reviewing critical commentary about the figure; to the interpretation of the illusionist clerk as a portrait of the artist Battles prefers that of surrogate Franklin. Food and hospitality link the clerk with the tale's narrator, although the Franklin remains at a distance from the magician's tricks. Aurelius as surrogate Squire sustains the parallel between tale and Canterbury frame. The dramatic exchange between Franklin and Squire is mediated through the narration of the tale, which shows that Aurelius can only achieve *gentilesse* once he submits himself to the greater power of the clerk. In 'A Perfect Marriage on the Rocks: Geoffrey and Philippa Chaucer, and the *Franklin's Tale*' (*ChauR* 37[2002] 129–44), Craig R. Davis notes the analogue between Arveragus's marriage above his station and Chaucer's to Philippa Roet. The rocks expose Dorigen's immature reluctance to accept the consequences of having married a lesser knight, namely, that Arveragus must go abroad to gain repute. Chaucer's duties as royal agent and Philippa's as lady-in-waiting presumably kept them apart. But true love marks the unequal fictional match, and the couple work their problems out. Chaucer, suggests Davis, is not idealizing his own marriage so much as suggesting that forbearance must overrule. Perhaps a little sheepishly, Davis agrees with Kittredge's contention that the tale is invested with a special seriousness on Chaucer's part. Andrew Breeze takes a philological turn in considering 'The Name of Kayrrud in the *Franklin's Tale*' (*ChauR* 37[2002] 95–9), which refers to Arveragus's home. To date, the word has been thought either to mean 'red house' or, emending to 'Kairiud' from manuscript variants of *caere iuda*, to refer to Kérity, a fishing village in Brittany. Breeze declines both Kayrrud and Kérity, arguing that Kairiud, as it stands, can be translated from Old Breton as 'fortress of lords' and refers to no scruffy fishing village. Chaucer's knowledge both of Breton language and terrain is greater than hitherto appreciated. For Chaucer's knowledge of Breton terrain, see also an essay by Friedman (*YWES* 77[1998] 238).

Michael Uebel discusses 'Public Fantasy and the Logic of Sacrifice in the *Physician's Tale*' (*ANQ* 15:iii[2002] 30–3). Struck by a recent television episode in which a father commits murder in order to protect his daughter from ritual circumcision, Uebel ponders the spectre of violence that seems to haunt the condition of virginity. Virginius's infanticide is a personal sacrifice committed for the sake of a public investment in female chastity. In relating virginity to death, Uebel might have recollected Howard Bloch's well-known essay on the tale, in which he asserts that the 'only good virgin is a dead virgin' (p. 120) (*YWES* 70[1991] 223–4).

Richard Firth Green reiterates his earlier argument that effeminacy in the Middle Ages was the mark of a womanizer rather than of queerdom or eunuchry (*MÆ* 71[2002] 307–9). Having been taken to task for lack of contemporary evidence, Green triumphantly cites a piece of mid-fourteenth-century Latin invective from London, British Library, MS Cotton Titus A.xx fo. 96ʳ, in which the emasculated Frenchman affects many of the postures of the Pardoner. Short and sweet as Green's note is, it is another instance of rumblings noted last year (*YWES* 82[2003] 215–16) against the assumption of the Pardoner's queerdom and its centrality to his characterization. Robert G. Twombly compares '*The Pardoner's Tale* and Dominican Meditation' (*ChauR* 36[2002] 250–69), finding in the tale's Old Man something like the kind of dramatized envisaging of one's own death prescribed in

Dominican discourses of self-examination and *artes moriendi*. For all the Pardoner's false spirituality, he tells a tale cautioning against the dangers of not recognizing death. The second essay pertaining to Chaucer in *Dalhousie Review*'s special issue is by Richard E. Zeikowitz, who maintains that the Pardoner is 'Silenced But Not Stifled: The Disruptive Queer Power of Chaucer's Pardoner' (*DR* 82[2002] 55–73). Zeikowitz aligns his arguments with those of Dinshaw, Kruger, and Burger in noting the heteronormative policing of the Pardoner's sexuality, but maintains that the Pardoner is empowered rather than victimized in the text. In his showdown with the Host, the Host's reaction is hysterical, inadvertently disclosing his envy of the Pardoner's queer phallus, which represents the best of all possible worlds, the combination of maternal ur-phallus and male phallus.

In 'Mercantile Ideology in Chaucer's *Shipman's Tale*' (*ChauR* 36[2002] 311–28) Helen Fulton argues that, viewed in the context of pre-capitalist urban government, the merchant's behaviour appears much less positive than it does in other readings, which are driven by capitalist assumptions about the naturalness of economic growth. This context is the struggle for urban control between merchants, who made their money from trade, and the gentry, especially the non-landowning kind like Chaucer himself. In exchanging currencies without productivity, the merchant's profiteering smacks of usury, and this, along with his accumulation of wealth without dispense for the common good leaves his integrity and moral ability to govern open to question. John Finlayson continues his consideration of Italian influence in 'Chaucer's *Shipman's Tale*, Boccaccio, and the "Civilizing" of Fabliau' (*ChauR* 36[2002] 336–51). Boccaccio's disgust at women who sell their sexual favours is evident in *Decameron* VIII.1 and 2, the generally acknowledged sources for Chaucer's tale, but Chaucer's critique is more veiled, and his fabliau more worldly and cynical. Finlayson interprets money in the tale as itself morally neutral, put to good mercantile ends in the merchant's case and bad in his wife's. In this he and Fulton will find much to disagree on. One of the narratives that may yet find its way into volume 2 of *Sources and Analogues* is 'The Legendary Don Juan: A Possible Source for Chaucer's *The Shipman's Tale*' (*JSSE* 39[2002] 11–21), in which Raychel Haugrud Reiff suggests that Chaucer's multiple references by name to the monk as 'Daun John' are pointed. Although the Don Juan legend does not appear in print until Tirso de Molina's work in the seventeenth century, his story seems to have circulated in folklore for a long time before, and Chaucer may well have known the legend.

Michael Calabrese asks large and pertinent questions about the purpose of literary criticism in 'Performing the Prioress: "Conscience" and Responsibility in Studies of Chaucer's *Prioress's Tale*' (*TSLL* 44[2002] 66–91). Without relapsing into apoliticism but in quest of an ethical disinterestedness, he asks whether literary criticism should be used as a political platform. Calabrese is wary of the urge to equate thirteenth-century anti-Semitism with the twentieth-century Holocaust, and finds in it the same flattening of history of which the Prioress herself is guilty, when she dispatches 150 years as just 'a litel while ago'. Would, concludes Calabrese, that we were as alert to our own 'affective poetics' (p. 84) as we are to the Prioress's. Anne Marie D'Arcy offers a broad survey of the '"Cursed folk of Herodes al new": Supersessionist Typology and Chaucer's Prioress' (in Treharne, ed., pp. 117–36). Although there are many local points of insight and interest, such as in her connection between the Prioress's mawkish sentimentality and the affective mysticism of the late fourteenth century, a dominant argument is not apparent. Treharne, in her introduction, says that the essay challenges conventional wisdom on the *raison d'être* of the work, but how this is done remains unclear.

In 'The Escape of Chaucer's Chauntecleer: A Brief Revaluation' (*ChauR* 36[2002] 329–35), Marc M. Pelen expands the exegetic reading of the cock's fall as the fall of man by noting that Chauntecleer actually escapes, thereby conflating lapsarian and redemption narratives into the one event. P.J.C. Field queries the identity of the mysterious 'my lord' in 'The Ending of Chaucer's *Nun's Priest's Tale*' (*MÆ* 71[2002] 302–6). Finding neither any of the pilgrims, nor St Paul, nor a contemporary dignitary a satisfactory option, Field plumps for Christ.

In 'Performing Feminine Sanctity in Late Medieval England: Parish Guilds, Saints' Plays, and the *Second Nun's Tale*' (*JMEMS* [2002] 269–303), Catherine Sanok contrasts the fulsome account in the *Chronicle of London* of a performance of a St Katherine pageant in honour of the marriage of Catherine of Aragon to Prince Arthur in 1501 with an earlier sparse reference to another St Katherine pageant in 1393. The voice of Cecilia preaching, as well as that of the Second Nun, is taken over by male authority, much as civic authority wrests sponsorship of the female saints' plays from parish guilds for their own ends. The Second Nun's curious reference to herself as a 'sone of Eve' reminds us that a man ultimately performs both tale and teller. Despite much quoting of authority, Sanok's argument rests on the over-simple logic that historical chronicle records the voice of political authority, and that its absence of information about the performance of saints' pageants signals the subversive potential of those narratives. It is 'The Unhidden Piety of Chaucer's "Seint Cecilie"' that strikes Joseph L. Grossi, Jr (*ChauR* 36[2002] 298–309), who compares Chaucer's rendition with that of Jacobus de Voragine's life of the saint from the *Legenda aurea*. Where Jacobus emphasizes her patrician heritage, Chaucer stresses Cecilia's equality with the disenfranchised members of the early Church. She shows more social commitment than the pagan Rome she opposes, suggesting perhaps a piety that Chaucer celebrates without irony and holds up as example to a papacy signally lacking in the virtue.

Stephen D. Powell, in 'Game Over: Defragmenting the End of the *Canterbury Tales*' (*ChauR* 37[2002] 40–58), considers the relationship between Fragments XI and X. The geographical and chronological inconsistencies between the prologues of Manciple and Parson support the assumption that something is missing from between the two fragments, but Powell thinks that they are of a piece, hence his project to 'defragment' them. Most of the manuscripts and all the earliest printed editions presented them as a single entity. Powell reviews arguments for and against fragmentation, and argues that the tales of Parson and Manciple are aesthetically linked by contrast and reversal rather than by continuity, revealing a 'more Christian and more doctrinal Chaucer' (p. 55) than modern criticism usually allows.

3. *Troilus and Criseyde*

George Krapp's quasi-translation *Troilus and Cressida* [1932] is reissued this year, accompanied with an introduction by Peter G. Beidler and notes by Cindy L. Vitto. Krapp's 'translation' is more of a modernization, and if it takes some of the pain out of reading the original for today's undergraduate, it takes out less than it would have in 1932. Vitto's notes, however, are helpful if brief.

Troilus is one of two Middle English poems (*Sir Gawain and the Green Knight* is the other) analysed by John Burrow in his study of *Gestures and Looks in Medieval Narrative*. Burrow is interested in the role of non-verbal communication in medieval literature, and he spends some time at the beginning of the book explaining how many different forms such 'language' might take. He quickly finds that visible signs, that is gestures and looks, are the forms most frequently represented in his source texts, and after devoting two general chapters to a survey of these, in which other Chaucerian texts (principally sections of the *Canterbury Tales* and the *Book of the Duchess*) get various mentions, he moves on to consider *Troilus* in more detail. Burrow compares *Troilus* with its source, finding that Chaucer's longer poem makes significantly more of non-verbal messages between its characters than is the case in *Il Filostrato*. Examining the evidence of rituals of greeting and parting as exemplified in the two works, Burrow notes that Chaucer has added some kisses and deleted others, but concludes that in general Chaucer's Troy seems to be governed by the same code of manners as Boccaccio's. As well as movements such as kneeling, bowing, and handclasping, Burrow analyses those gestures expressive of distress and sorrow, again finding that in this respect Chaucer follows his source closely, though he also notes that the repertoire of actions involved was highly conventional and would have been well known to both authors from French narratives. On the other hand, an aspect of gestural behaviour not at all represented in *Il Filostrato* is the more informal register of emotions used in private exchanges between Criseyde and Pandarus, and Chaucer also introduces many more significant instances of looking between the protagonists. Overall Burrow identifies some cross-cultural differences between the two poets, but in the end he chimes with the conclusion of previous critics such as Windeatt that, in terms of polite social exchange, Chaucer's London was a formal, rather old-fashioned place.

Marion Turner examines Usk's adaptation of Chaucer's poetry in '"Certaynly his noble sayenges can I not amende": Thomas Usk and *Troilus and Criseyde*' (*ChauR* 37[2002] 26–39). Working from the passages listed by Usk's editors, Turner looks at the effects of Usk's recontextualizations, noting that Usk often changes the signification of Chaucer's words by placing them in a spiritual rather than sexual context. At the same time Usk's aims in writing are for political advancement; Turner claims that the *Testament of Love* is factional and partisan, and that its use of *Troilus and Criseyde* exemplifies Usk's attempts to situate himself within the Ricardian literary community. In '*Amoryus and Cleopes*: John Metham's Metamorphosis of Chaucer and Ovid' (in Hardman, ed., *The Matter of Identity in Medieval Romance*, pp. 149–62), Roger Dalrymple shows how Metham's poem contributes to our understanding of the fifteenth-century reception of *Troilus and Criseyde*. By selectively recasting scenes and romance motifs from *Troilus*, Metham's poem succeeds in harmonizing some of the central tensions of Chaucer's poem, notably its conflicting conceptions of love, competing patterns of tragic action, and the uneasy relationship between its Christian narrator and pagan protagonists. In resolving these antagonisms Metham aligns himself with other fifteenth-century Chaucerians who tended to eschew the more open-ended aspects of Chaucer's works. Seth Lerer discusses 'Latin Annotations in a Copy of Stowe's Chaucer and the Seventeenth-Century Reception of *Troilus and Criseyde*' (*RES*

53[2002] 1–7). He dates and identifies the annotations as quotations from Virgil and Seneca and suggests that their inscription testifies to a growing association of Chaucer with writers of classical antiquity.

Colin Wilcockson considers 'The Woodbind and the Nightingale Images in *Troilus and Criseyde* Book II, Lines 918–924 and Book III, Lines 1230–1239' (*N&Q* 49[2002] 320–3), and suggests that Chaucer's poem contains allusions to two of Marie de France's *lais*, *Chievrefeuille* and *Laüstic*. Nancy Ciccone is also alert to the influence of Chaucer's sources in 'Saving Chaucer's Troilus "With desir and reson twight"' (*Neophil* 86[2002] 641–58), where she attempts to redress the critical balance of sympathy for Troilus by reminding us of the context of his philosophical deliberations. She argues that Troilus's reasoning follows the prescribed rules of a rough syllogistic format dictated by medieval academic protocol, but that this fails to offer any practical wisdom. As a result Troilus is caught in a double bind that emotionally and intellectually paralyses him, though Ciccone would have us believe that this is the process that also humanizes him.

Roy J. Pearcy stops short of claiming to have discovered new source materials in his essay '"And Nysus doughter song with fressh entente": Tragedy and Romance in *Troilus and Criseyde*' (*SAC* 24[2002] 269–97). Instead he proposes that Chaucer was familiar with 'some concept of a skeletal but exemplary tragic *mythos* circulating among fourteenth-century *litterati*' (p. 290) and that this influenced his development of the story of the two lovers. Pearcy describes episodes from three little-known texts: the encounter between the maid Marion de la Bruere and Sir Ernalt de Lyls in the Anglo-Norman prose romance *Fouke le Fitz Waryn*; the story of Scylla and Minos from the *Ovid Moralisé*; and the story of the murderous washerwoman told by John of Garland in *The Paristiana Poetria*. He finds that all of the elements of the tragic motif as exemplified in these stories are present either overtly or implicitly in Chaucer's text, and, although he has to acknowledge— weakly—that there is no evidence that Chaucer knew these texts at all, he argues nevertheless that Criseyde is the tragic heroic counterpart to these three female figures. Similarly in '"Al this peynted process": Chaucer and the Psychology of Courtly Love' (*ES* 83[2002] 391–8), Damian Love tries (not entirely successfully) to read *Troilus and Criseyde* in the light of Augustine's *Confessions*, suggesting that the complex love affair depicted in Chaucer's poem subverts the boundaries between sacred and profane love.

Molly Murray explores 'The Value of "Eschaunge": Ransom and Substitution in *Troilus and Criseyde*' (*ELH* 69[2002] 335–58), drawing coherent and illuminating parallels between the exchange of Criseyde for Antenor and the medieval chivalric practice of ransom. She details the principles and methods of medieval ransom, and explains how its practice could be both lucrative and productive. Negotiations for ransom were typically protracted and complex, an aspect which is reflected in the poem by the multiple perspectives attached to Criseyde's proposed exchange. Having explored other substitutions and changes embedded in the narrative, Murray reaches a startling conclusion about the poem's message, which is that arbitrary human change is what provides life with significance and that tragedy consists in the ending of all possibilities for change. Her argument is coherent and compelling, and she even manages to incorporate the poem's Christian coda into her disquisition on ransom.

4. Other Works

Steven Davis explores Chaucer's relationship to his sources in 'Guillaume de Machaut, Chaucer's *Book of the Duchess*, and the Chaucer Tradition' (*ChauR* 36[2002] 391–405). Setting Chaucer alongside Machaut, and looking primarily at the *Dit dou Vergier* and the *Remede de Fortune*, Davis examines the *Book of the Duchess* as an example of poetic misprision. By charting Chaucer's adaptation of three Machauldian motifs—his creative refashioning of classical and vernacular literary traditions, his relation to a system of courtly patronage, and his use of the intercalated lyric—Davis argues that Chaucer defines the French poetic tradition as two-dimensional and lacking in serious historical reference, a view which has persisted in the history of the Chaucer criticism.

Jay Ruud considers fourteenth-century theories of knowledge in 'Realism, Nominalism, and the Inconclusive Ending of the *Parliament of Fowls*' (*InG* 23[2002] 1–28), and makes the surprising claim that Boethius has been overlooked amongst studies of the poem's sources. John Scattergood offers a convincing solution to some problematic lines in 'Making Arrows: *The Parliament of Fowls*, 211–217' (*N&Q* 49[2002] 444–7).

Helen Phillips pays detailed attention to language in a thought-provoking article 'Register, Politics, and the *Legend of Good Women*' (*ChauR* 37[2002] 101–28), arguing that Chaucer has been regarded as apolitical because critics have looked in the wrong places for evidence of his engagement with contemporary issues. She suggests that the sociolinguistic register of Chaucer's poetry may hold the key to his politics, and by way of a case study examines the F and G prologues to the *Legend of Good Women* for instances of topical Ricardian diction. En route she charts many of the differences between the two versions of the prologue, and usefully offers alternative identifications of the texts cited in G as evidence of female fidelity. In an informative essay, 'Laboring in the God of Love's Garden: Chaucer's Prologue to *The Legend of Good Women*' (*SAC* 24[2002] 115–47) Kellie Robertson reconsiders what Chaucer's life may have been like between 1385 and 1389 when, according to his biographers, he was languishing in the backwaters of Kent. She argues that these years did not provide time out from political controversy, and that Chaucer's service as a JP would have brought him into close contact with labour regulations that were deeply unpopular. She goes on to read the prologue to the *Legend of Good Women* as a significant literary statement about the late medieval controversy over labour, finding links here with *Piers Plowman* and other alliterative dream vision poems.

Daniel Wakelin identifies a fifteenth-century reader of *Boece* in 'William Worcester Reads Chaucer's *Boece*' (*JEBS* 5[2002] 177–9), recognizing the antiquary's hand in an inscription in Cambridge, Pembroke College, MS 215.

Richard P. Horvath writes on 'Chaucer's Epistolary Poetic: The Envoys to Bukton and Scogan' (*ChauR* 37[2002] 173–89), arguing that these minor poems are less occasional than has been supposed, and that their aspect is more public than private. Horvath claims that the envoys use the conventions of letter-writing to communicate generally rather than just with individuals, and that they share a hybrid quality as objects of courtly making that are also able to envisage their own posterity.

Much the biggest event this year in this miscellaneous section is Sigmund's Eisner's edition of a *Treatise on the Astrolabe*, the first part of the sixth volume in

the Variorum series. Together with Osborn's *Time and the Astrolabe in the
'Canterbury Tales'*, this book brings Chaucer's *Treatise* centre-stage and makes it
the year of the astrolabe. A picture tells a thousand words, it is said, and the pictures
of the Painswick Astrolabe, front and back, help greatly while progressing through
the opening, densely packed pages on the construction and history of the
planispheric astrolabe. Next comes a critical commentary on the text of the *Treatise*,
in which the date, authorship, the identity of little Lewis, and sources are reviewed.
The historical survey of commentary (pp. 22–40) enables one to review at a sweep
the changing and unchanging attitudes towards the work. In the long section on the
thirty-two extant manuscripts of the *Treatise*, Eisner explains the rationale behind
his decision to create a conflate base-text of Oxford, Bodleian Library, Bodley 619
and Oxford, Bodleian Library, Digby 72, which together represent the two
manuscript traditions, each of which contains material not in the other. The
variorum editions are known for generosity of space in their layout of material, and,
especially with a work like this which requires slow and attentive reading, the
wealth of explanatory figures occurring every couple of pages proves invaluable in
explaining the text and bringing this instrument to life. Perhaps more than the poetic
texts, where critical vogues come and go, the fortunes of the *Treatise* have remained
relatively constant, evoking admiration from a respectful if uninterested distance.
The condensation of scholarship in this volume will be of lasting value, and will, it
is hoped, make the *Treatise* more read and more talked about than it has been.

Books Reviewed

Boldrini, Lucia, ed. *Medieval Joyce*. European Joyce Studies 13. Rodopi. [2002] pp.
  235. $50 ISBN 9 0420 1409 1.
Bowers, Bege K., and Mark Allen, eds. *Annotated Chaucer Bibliography 1986–
  1996*. UNDP. [2002] pp. 719. £66.95 ISBN 0 2680 2016 7.
Brown, Peter, ed. *A Companion to Chaucer*. Blackwell. [2002] pp. xvii + 515. pb
  $34.95 ISBN 0 6312 3590 6.
Burrow, John. *Gestures and Looks in Medieval Narrative*. CSML 48. CUP. [2002]
  pp. xi + 200. £40 ($55) ISBN 0 5218 1564 9.
Cheney, Patrick, and Frederick A. de Armas, eds. *European Literary Careers: The
  Author from Antiquity to the Renaissance*. UTorP. [2002] pp. x + 366. $65 ISBN
  0 8020 4779 3.
Correale, Robert M., and Mary Hamel, eds. *Sources and Analogues of the
  'Canterbury Tales'*, vol. 1. Chaucer Studies 28. Brewer. [2002] pp. xii + 623. $50
  ISBN 0 8599 1628 6.
Delany, Sheila, ed. *Chaucer and the Jews: Sources, Contexts, Meanings*. Routledge.
  [2002] pp. xi + 258. $90 ISBN 0 4159 3882 1.
Edwards, Robert R. *Chaucer and Boccaccio: Antiquity and Modernity*. Palgrave.
  [2002] pp. xv + 205. £47.50 ISBN 0 3339 7008 X.
Eisner, Sigmund, ed. *A Variorum Edition of the Works of Geoffrey Chaucer*, vol. 4:
  The Prose Treatises. Part One, A Treatise on the Astrolabe. UOklaP. [2002] pp.
  xxiv + 358. $75 ISBN 0 8061 3413 5.

Fenster, Thelma S., and Clare A. Lees, eds. *Gender and Debate from the Early Middle Ages to the Renaissance*. Palgrave. [2002] pp. 292. $55 ISBN 0 3122 3244 6.

Foster, Edward E., and David H. Carey. *Chaucer's Church: A Dictionary of Religious Terms in Chaucer*. Ashgate. [2002] pp. ix + 149. £35 ISBN 0 7546 0674 0.

Fradenburg, L. O. Aranye. *Sacrifice Your Love: Psychoanalysis, Historicism, Chaucer*. Medieval Cultures 31. UMinnP. [2002] pp. 327. hb $59.95 ISBN 0 8166 3645 1, pb $19.95 (£14) ISBN 0 8166 3646 X.

Ginsberg, Warren. *Chaucer's Italian Tradition*. UMichP. [2002] pp. xiv + 297. $60 ISBN 0 4721 1234 1.

Guare, John. *'The House of Blue Leaves' and 'Chaucer in Rome': Two Plays by John Guare*. Overlook. [2002] pp. 184. $17.95 ISBN 1 5856 7291 2.

Hardman, Phillipa, ed. *The Matter of Identity in Medieval Romance*. B&B. [2002] pp. xi + 165. £40 ($70) ISBN 0 8599 1761 4.

Iyeiri, Yoko, and Margaret Connolly, eds. *'And gladly wolde he lerne and gladly teche': Essays on Medieval English Presented to Professor Matsuji Tajima on his Sixtieth Birthday*. Kaibunsha. [2002] pp. xiv + 270. $65 ISBN 4 8757 1577 3.

Jones, Timothy S., and David A. Sprunger, eds. *Marvels, Monsters, and Miracles: Studies in the Medieval and Early Modern Imaginations*. Studies in Medieval Culture 42. WMU. [2002] pp. xxv + 306. $20 ISBN 1 5804 4065 7.

Krapp, George, trans. *Geoffrey Chaucer: 'Troilus and Cressida'*. Random. [2002] pp. xxii + 311. pb $9.95 ISBN 0 3757 5736 8.

Lynch, Kathryn L., ed. *Chaucer's Cultural Geography*. Routledge. [2002] pp. 319. $95 ISBN 0 4159 3001 4.

Mann, Jill. *Feminizing Chaucer*. Chaucer Studies 30. B&B. [2002] pp. xxi + 194. pb £16.99 ($29.95) ISBN 0 8599 1613 8.

Minkova, Donka, and Robert Stockwell, eds. *Studies in the History of the English Language: A Millennial Perspective*. Mouton. [2002] pp. vi + 496. $127.40 ISBN 3 1101 7368 9.

Mullini, Roberta, ed. *Tudor Theatre: For Laughs(?), Pour Rire(?). Puzzling Laughter in Plays of the Tudor Age / Rires et Problèmes dans le Théâtre des Tudor*. Centre d'Études Supérieures de la Renaissance. Lang. [2002] pp. xxii + 345. pb £36 ISBN 3 9067 6901 1.

Olive, Barbara, and David Sprunger, eds. *Proceedings of the Tenth Annual Northern Plains Conference on Earlier British Literature*. Concordia College, Moorhead, MN. [2002] pp. 107. pb $5 ISBN not listed.

Osborn. Marijane. *Time and the Astrolabe in the 'Canterbury Tales'*. UOklaP. [2002] pp. xvii + 350. £49.95 ($69.95) ISBN 0 8061 3403 8.

Parini, Jay, ed. *British Writers, Retrospective*, Supplement 7. Scribner. [2002] pp. lxxi + 509. $181.25 ISBN 0 6843 1228 X.

Pearsall, Derek, and Duncan Wu, eds. *Poetry from Chaucer to Spenser*. Blackwell. [2002] pp. viii + 181. hb £40 ISBN 0 6312 2986 8, pb £9.99 ISBN 0 6312 2987 6.

Pfister, Manfred, ed. *A History of English Laughter: Laughter from Beowulf to Beckett and Beyond*. Rodopi. [2002] pp. x + 201. $35 ISBN 9 0420 1288 9.

Saito, Toshio, Junsaku Nakamura, and Shunji Yamazaki, eds. *English Corpus Linguistics in Japan: Language and Computers*. Studies in Practical Linguistics 38. Rodopi. [2002] pp. xii + 340. $66 ISBN 9 0420 1369 9.

Salisbury, Eve, Georgiana Donavin, and Merrall Llewelyn Price, eds. *Domestic Violence in Medieval Texts*. UFlorP. [2002] pp. viii + 354. hb £48.50 ISBN 0 8130 2442 0.

Scala, Elizabeth. *Absent Narratives, Manuscript Textuality, and Literary Structure in Late Medieval England*. Palgrave. [2002] pp. xix + 284. £35 ISBN 0 3122 4043 0.

Shippey, Tom, with Martin Arnold, eds. *Film and Fiction: Reviewing the Middle Ages*. Studies in Medievalism 12. Brewer. [2002] pp. 257. $60 ISBN 0 8599 1772 X.

Simpson, James. *The Oxford English Literary History*, vol. 2: *1350–1547, Reform and Cultural Revolution*. OUP. [2002] pp. xvii + 661. £30 ISBN 0 1981 8261 9.

Steiner, Emily, and Candace Barrington, eds. *The Letter of the Law: Legal Practice and Literary Production in Medieval England*. CornUP. [2002] pp. viii + 257. hb $45 ISBN 0 8014 3975 2, pb $19.95 ISBN 0 8014 8770 6.

Treharne, Elaine, ed. *Writing Gender and Genre in Medieval Literature: Approaches to Old and Middle English Texts*. E&S 55. Brewer. [2002] pp. 142. $50 ISBN 0 8599 1760 6.

Trigg, Stephanie. *Congenial Souls: Reading Chaucer from Medieval to Postmodern*. Medieval Cultures 30. UMinnP. [2002] pp. xxiv + 280. hb $57.95 ISBN 0 8166 3822 5, pb $22.95 ISBN 0 8166 3923 3.

Utz, Richard. *Chaucer and the Discourse of German Philology: A History of Reception and an Annotated Bibliography of Studies 1793–1948*. Making the Middle Ages 3. Brepols. [2002] pp. xxi + 446. $83 ISBN 2 5035 1086 8.

West, Richard. *Chaucer 1340–1400*. Constable & Robinson. [2002] pp. 320. pb £7.99 ISBN 1 8411 9463 8.

Witalisz, Wladyslaw, ed. *'And gladly wolde he lerne and gladly teche': Studies on Language and Literature in Honour of Professor Dr. Karl Heinz Göller*. Wydawnictwo Uniwersytetu Jagiellonskiego. [2001] pp. 216. pb 38 zloty ISBN 8 3233 1472 1.

V

The Sixteenth Century: Excluding Drama after 1550

ROS KING AND JOAN FITZPATRICK

This chapter has three sections: 1. General; 2. Sidney; 3. Spenser. Section 1 is by Ros King; sections 2 and 3 are by Joan Fitzpatrick.

1. General

This year again it is historical work on the English Reformation that has the greatest significance for anyone working on any aspect of the sixteenth century. Without a complex understanding of the relationships between both individual conviction and the public expression of religious orthodoxy, and between religion and the politics of control and social change, we are unlikely to get much further in our work on the artistic culture of the period.

The writing of doctrinal and ecclesiastical history over the last half-century is in itself so mutable that all of the books on this topic reviewed here usefully provide overviews as part of their introductory chapters. The problem, of course, is that the subject itself is not yet history. The effects of the Reformation are still with us, informing current beliefs and stirring prejudice. Judgements are likely to be more than usually affected by inner convictions. It is therefore, I feel, incumbent on all writers on this subject to declare their personal interest and background of belief. Eamon Duffy's personal sympathy for the 'old' religion, for instance, is well known; most writers allude to it while withholding their own beliefs, which is a trifle unfair. As an atheist, then, I am both glad of and intrigued by the inadvertently secularizing effect of the establishment of the Church of England. For me it is the inadvertencies that make the story so compelling; secularism is not the normal goal of state religion.

As Stephen Alford, in *Kingship and Politics in the Reign of Edward VI*, makes clear, the Church of England was established within a political system of *counselled* monarchy, which was remarkably permeable by able men from outside the aristocratic class. He notes that many of our preconceptions about Edward's reign stem from features found in near-contemporary histories (in particular John Hayward's *Life and Reign of Edward VI*, framed to imitate events in the *Annales* of

Tacitus) and finds that the reign's reputation for faction is 'an issue of historiography rather than history' (p. 31). Alford is also at pains to humanize more recent accounts of formal mid-Tudor bureaucracy. He traces networks of kin, friendship, and patronage in court circles, and amongst those responsible for the explosion of Protestant printed books in the first years of the reign, as well as between court and print shop. The arms of Katherine Brandon, the evangelical duchess of Suffolk, twice appear in books published by the printer John Day and his business associate William Seres in 1548, while her sons, Charles and Henry, shared their education with Richard Grafton, the king's printer. Seres was at one time a servant in William Cecil's household. Perhaps this interconnectedness is not so surprising in such a small population of educated people, but it reveals the possibility of a certain kind of politics. Alford argues that frank counsel given in confidence whereby the king rules by God's law is what underpins contemporary views of good government. Although he does not explore this area, the concept of counsel is immensely important for those of us interested in the role of literary culture in the Tudor courts. Drama in particular, which by its very nature gives voice to conflict of opinion but in which the answer is often left for the individual viewer to determine, need no longer be regarded as variously subversive or contained (as in so much new historicist criticism) but as creating a vehicle for dialogue in which dangerous matters can be legitimately aired. This book contains fascinating material and is a very much easier read than Alford's *The Early Elizabethan Polity: William Cecil and the British Succession* (republished in paperback this year), but it could still have benefited from redrafting. It too often contains phrases familiar from previous chapters that directly or implicitly recall earlier arguments, a structure which this reader, at any rate, found irritating and confusing.

We are now beginning to see that to ask whether the Reformation, in England at least, came 'from above' or 'from below' is to ask the wrong question. During the first hundred years of its existence, the curious hybrid that is now the Anglican Church embodied at different times the entire gamut of possible doctrinal orthodoxies. Its continued existence was the result of a series of peculiar accidents and political struggles that were played out for most of the sixteenth and seventeenth centuries around the dual, indeed deeply contradictory, imperative that the head of the Church of England was an unordained, imperial monarch and that that monarch was, despite strenuous efforts by various incumbents to the contrary, ultimately unable to rule without parliamentary consent. The rhetoric of the one true catholic church that could not err was employed by religious zealots and political opportunists on all sides. People on all sides, too, were struggling for a multiplicity of 'reforms'. It has never been more important to understand this complexity than it is now at this time of current concern, and muddle, about religious differences and fundamentalisms on a global level.

The multifacetedness of the history of the development of Protestantism in England therefore lends itself to a collection of essays by different authors, particularly when that collection has been so well structured as Marshall and Ryrie, eds., *The Beginnings of English Protestantism*. It is clear that the contributors to this volume do not always entirely agree with each other, but that agreements and disagreements alike are acknowledged, engaged with, and footnoted is one of the volume's strengths. The two editors, besides collaborating on the introduction, which sets out the multiplicity of 'Protestantisms and their Beginnings' each also contribute individual chapters. Marshall ('Evangelical Conversion in the Reign of Henry VIII') explores the language of conversion biographies and autobiographies, attempting to distinguish the level of actual personal experience within conventional phrases and formats. Ryrie ('Counting Sheep, Counting Shepherds') asks 'Did the English jump into their peculiar Reformation, or were they pushed?' He explores the concatenation of imperatives that led to people willingly changing their faith: 'one did not become an evangelical because one broke a fast, much less because one accepted official relaxation of fasts. However, by breaking a fast ... one aligned one's life with those who were preaching in defence of what you had done and against those who had denounced it' (p. 103). Richard Rex ('Friars of the English Reformation') explores the probability that large numbers of well-educated Catholic friars such as the Observant Franciscans, who were already used to preaching and most active in their pursuit of the reform of the Church from within, became preachers in the new religion. More than a hundred were released from their vows by Cranmer and licensed for the secular priesthood. While there are many reasons for friars abandoning their calling—not least the fact that they were now deprived of the alms by which they lived—the personal scruples of those who took the opportunity to marry is worthy of examination. As he points out, although they were now legally entitled to do so, marriage for such people would still entail breaking an oath. This would be so much easier for those who had come to believe that celibacy was 'an insupportable burden imposed upon the flesh by Antichrist in order to drive religious souls to despair'. He suggests that those ex-friars deprived of their benefices under Mary because of their marriages are likely to have been men who had 'moved a considerable way towards protestantism' (p. 48).

Susan Wabuda, who also has a chapter in this volume on the effects of the Reformation on women ('Sanctified by the Believing Spouse: Women, Men and the Marital Yoke in the Early Reformation'), devotes an entire book, *Preaching during the English Reformation*, to the largely Catholic origins of preaching. She explores the tension inherent in Protestant belief in the unique value of God's word printed in the vernacular and the need for 'direction in the correct understanding of what the Word meant'. Many pulpits were torn down along with the rood screens, while some evangelicals took to going out to preach on horseback: 'Perhaps the willingness to sacrifice the long-established preaching place in the effort to sustain the sermon has been one of the little-noticed paradoxes of the English Reformation' (pp. 105–6).

Book history is of course a vital part of Reformation studies. Andrew Pettegree, 'Printing and the Reformation: The English Exception' (in Marshall and Ryrie, eds.), points out that, although early English printed books are amongst the most studied by bibliographers, England in the early years of printing history occupied the outer, slower ring of a definitely 'two-speed Europe' and that by 'England' what is really meant in the context of printing is London and Westminster—a small and compact industry that is relatively easy to study. By contrast, the books that 'would form the backbone of scholarly collections were almost all imported' from the great centres of Latin printing (Venice and Paris, later Antwerp, Basle, and Lyons), and continued to be so even after printing had been well established in England. The wool trade ensured the presence of English merchants in Antwerp (where, initially, there was freedom to print vernacular religious works), and abetted the smuggling of banned books into England. In the middle years of Edward VI's reign, after a crackdown by Charles V, many of these printers fled to England. John N. King's chapter 'John Day', also in this volume, examines the operation of Day's print shop where several of these émigrés were employed. Like Alford, he too explores Day's social networks, including the Brandon connection, and prints several of the same illustrations.

Andrew McRae's *God Speed the Plough: The Representation of Agrarian England, 1500–1660* (1996, but published in paperback for the first time this year) begins with the problem of the fluidity of interpretation in times of religious change. Thomas More had prevented the translation into English of his *Utopia* precisely because he did not want to see its potentially radical politics applied to conditions in England. When, sixteen years after his death, the book was finally published in English, his critique of the greed of 'Abbottes, holy men god wote' and the effects on the countryside of enclosure for sheep farming rather than tillage was appropriated to the service of the reformers in ways which, as McRae says, could only have appalled him. With the straightforward morality of traditional Christian teaching against covetousness and greed so bound up in practice with the economics of landholding, and the pragmatics of social control at odds with concern for rural poverty, there is a constant tension between sowing the seeds of the true religion (whatever brand that is) and ploughing the furrow of reform that makes complaint literature of the Tudor period a complex problem of interpretation. Religious and economic radicalisms were inevitably at odds: biblical fundamentalism versus the growth of the market economy.

The comparative deluge of Protestant texts that suddenly poured from English printing presses during the reign of Edward VI included the first printed text of *Piers Plowman*, published and with added marginal notes by Robert Crowley that were designed to 'reshape the poem as a proto-Protestant prophecy'. Crowley himself was also a prolific author of evangelical polemic in a variety of literary forms: prose, verse, and dramatic dialogues. McRae tells a fascinating story about the changes in direction in complaint literature during the sixteenth century as well as the usage of the term 'commonwealth', for, in Sir Thomas Smith's *Discourse of the Commonweale* (*c*.1549, although not printed for another forty years), 'the juxtaposed complaints of the landlord, craftsman and merchant simply belie the Husbandman's attempts to explain his own problems as the result of covetousness and oppression' (p. 55). On his return from Marian exile, Robert Crowley had to revise his previous approach to fit the 'new environment of the Elizabethan Church', for now the necessity of maintaining social distinction meant that riches had to be seen as 'the gyft of God' (p. 61). There was no significant attempt to revive the mid-Tudor tradition of complaint after Elizabeth's accession. Indeed 'the bulk of religious writing published under Elizabeth subverted the predominantly social vision of the Edwardian Protestants' (p. 69). McRae identifies (if slightly apologetically) the 'unsettling spectre of communist thought' behind much of the agrarian, Protestant literature of the period. He traces the development of this via a brief survey of Elizabethan and Jacobean satirical drama (in which he says the countryside is 'ridiculed as the home of the peasant and the boor', p. 97) and discusses the writings of Gerard Winstanley, before considering the chorographical studies of the later sixteenth and early seventeenth centuries whereby national observers and historians such as Leland and Camden, as well as local landholders, described and mapped the countryside, creating a sense of national identity even while confirming it as parcels of private property.

Peter Lake's *The Antichrist's Lewd Hat: Protestant, Papists and Players in Post-Reformation England* (with Michael Questier) starts with the cheap print of Reformation literature, but follows a different trajectory into the seamier reaches of town life where 'the irruptive force of God's providence jostled for space with scenes of graphic violence and implicitly explicit sex' within the text and woodcut of the murder pamphlet (p. xiii). Lake explores how this hitherto neglected genre was used for publicity purposes by Protestant, Puritan, and Catholic alike, as well as being turned to salacious effect on the public stage in the hope of profit. He in turn has produced a Bible-sized tome which revels in the minutiae of its subject in a relaxed and often racy tone, and demonstrates that 'providentialism was anything but a protestant, still less a puritan monopoly, as the origin of some of these stories in catholic sources shows quite nicely' (p. 253). All sides of the religious divide 'knew how to skewer a soul in distress' for their own propagandist purposes (p. 228).

Melanie Ord, 'Classical and Contemporary Italy in Roger Ascham's *The Scholemaster* (1570)' (*RS* 16[2002] 201–26), strives to see Ascham's work as a whole, stressing that his insistence on the importance of correct grammar, the 'right ordering of sentences', and well-directed classical reading in a school education in England is directly counterbalanced by his fears of the dangers of allowing young men to travel indiscriminately to Catholic Italy. Ascham saw moral degeneracy as much in careless, 'wandering' study as in undirected travel. He too had a religious project, objecting to translations by 'sutle and secrete Papistes at home' that attempted to seduce young minds to a wanton disregard of '"severe" books' thereby seeking 'to attract Englishmen to Catholicism by first undermining their moral fibre' (pp. 209–10).

A slightly different view of the relationship between sixteenth-century Italy and England can be found in Cinzia M. Sicca's 'Consumption and Trade of Art between Italy and England in the First Half of the Sixteenth Century: The London House of the Bardi and Cavalcanti Company' (*RS* 16[2002] 163–201). Collation of the twenty-seven surviving registers of the Bardi and Cavalcanti company with the English State Papers and the Privy Purse expenses of both Henry VIII and his daughter the Princess Mary provides detailed information about running a successful international company in the sixteenth century. This includes bookkeeping practices, the structure of the parent company and its dealings with subsidiaries abroad, shipping insurance, and the activities of shareholders, as well as the taste for imported luxuries such as the most favoured patterns and colours of expensive cloths at both the English and the papal courts. Cavalcanti arrived in England in 1509, the year of accession of Henry VIII, perhaps as part of a diplomatic attempt by Cardinal Giovanni de' Medici to win the young king to the papal side against France. He quickly became indispensable in England, exporting wool, importing much of the military equipment that Henry needed for his role in the anti-French League, and apparently supplying many of the textiles for his appearance at the Field of the Cloth of Gold. Extraordinarily, he was simultaneously a gentleman usher of the Apostolic Chamber.

Michael Spiller's lively little book on the sonnet is likely to prove a godsend to those teaching introductions to Renaissance literature. Belied by its rather solid and conventional Eng. Lit. title, *Early Modern Sonneteers: From Wyatt to Milton*, it actually does more than it says on the tin, supplying brief, readable chapters on the idea and invention of the sonnet, as well as on the two most famous Italian exponents of the form, Dante and Petrarch, and short biographies of all the writers included in the book: Wyatt, Surrey, Sidney, Spenser, Drayton, Shakespeare, Donne, Herbert, Milton, of course, but also Anne Locke, Mary Wroth, and William Drummond. A short chapter, in which two or more sonnets are analysed in detail, is devoted to each writer. The fact that Spiller feels able to say that one particular sonnet sequence is 'truly awful', 'bumpy and unpredictable' (p. 46) is bound to endear him to students.

Raphael Lyne describes his *Ovid's Changing Worlds: English Metamorphoses, 1567–1632* as a 'book about what four renaissance writers do to Ovid, and what he does to them' as they attempt to forge both national and literary identities. Framed by chapters devoted to the translations of the *Metamorphoses* by Arthur Golding [1567] and George Sandys [1632], the two central chapters are devoted to Ovidian 'subtexts' and metamorphoses in *The Faerie Queene* and, following on from that, Drayton's use of Ovid and of Spenser's riparian chorography in *Poly-Olbion*, and his imitation of the *Heroides* in the *Heroical Epistles*. The research for this book no doubt constituted an exhaustive Ph.D. thesis in its tracing of textual correspondences, but it is difficult to see what it all adds up to. Indeed Lyne himself does not always seem to know. The concluding chapter, in devoting some pages to a somewhat cursory look at Ovidian references in *Cymbeline*, refers to such borrowings as 'a bit of a blind alley ... bereft of function and functionally bereft' (p. 267), although to my mind this is because the function needs further exploration.

By contrast, Jason Scott-Warren's nicely illustrated *Sir John Harington and the Book as Gift* explores the 'endlessly metamorphosing' significances incorporated not only within Harington's language but also in the contexts created when he customized printed copies of his longer works with scribal annotation and collections of his epigrammatic poems before giving them away. These volumes and the letters that accompanied them function as 'self-presentation' in the pursuit of patronage, preferment, and a family legacy. Scott-Warren thereby exposes the underbelly of Elizabethan social networks and, in the light of Harington's political satire on a jakes, is understandably unable to resist punning chapter headings such as 'Privy Politics', 'The Excremental Society', and 'Out of the Closet'. He paints a vivid picture of a fascinating individual, but explicitly warns us against being tempted to want to make him 'one of the family' (p. 99), although, on the evidence offered, Harington seems merely more wittily forthright in the expression of his opinions and his problems with his mother-in-law than most. If he was largely disappointed in his pursuit of greater influence at court, it can only have been because his wit made him too much of a loose cannon. This book too is interesting on the complex issue of conformity in the 1590s. The copy of the *New Discourse* held at Princeton includes annotations in Harington's hand identifying the owners of the great houses listed in the work as belonging to 'hospitable' housekeepers. All were 'known, or suspected, to be Catholic' (and, of course, the giving of hospitality to the poor is one of the good 'works' for which Catholics might expect reward in heaven), but all lived their lives 'in the hope that Catholics might conform to and be tolerated by the secular establishment' (pp. 86, 88). 'The building and hospitable housekeeping which Harington demands of his ideal readers and critics can thus be taken to symbolize a gentry status that cuts across religious divisions. Gentility entails allegiance to crown, commonwealth, and political nation, and it calls for a (small-c) "catholic" practice of hospitality' (p. 94).

Maps and Memory in early Modern England: A Sense of Place by Rhonda Lemke Sanford is part of a new series entitled Early Modern Cultural Studies, edited by Ivo Kamps, and designed to reflect the fact that 'literary criticism, literary theory, historiography, and cultural studies have become so interwoven that we can now think of them as an eclectic and only loosely unified (but still recognizable) approach to formerly distinct fields of inquiry such as literature, society, history and culture' (p. xii). Eclecticism is indeed necessary to describe a culture that had not yet divided into our traditional academic disciplines, but it puts an extra burden on modern historians of culture, who need to be adept in all those traditional techniques—and more. Sanford devotes the first chapter of her book to demonstrating how a map can, of course, never exactly equate with the area mapped: choices have to be made in order to reduce the reality of the place to a small-scale, conventionalized representation of the features of that place that most concern the map-maker and his clients. Sometimes the features that seem most important are not readily visible on the ground, for example marks of current ownership such as coats of arms, or of historical occupation with inscriptions of the names of ancient tribes. Sanford's desire, however, to map early modern maps onto modern politically correct ideologies in mapping theory sometimes bears an uncanny resemblance to Captain Fluellen's chorographical comparison of the birthplaces of Henry V and Alexander the Great: both with rivers and 'salmons in both' (*Henry V*, IV.vii.32). Having pointed out the importance of centrality in mapping convention from the earliest times, and with recourse to Leonardo's famous drawing of a human figure inscribed in a circle and a square in which the genitals are the mid point, she describes John Case's *Sphaera Civitatis*, in which the head and shoulders of Queen Elizabeth appear behind a quasi-Ptolemaic 'map' of state power. Wanting to reinforce the idea of the permeability of land gendered female, and therefore its capacity to be raped or taken, she identifies the concentric circles as representations of the 'officers of the Court of Star Chamber' making 'invasion' of the 'royal body', and locates the central circle, labelled 'Iustitia Innobilis', 'where the queen's genitals might be inferred beneath the cosmographic image' and thus reminiscent of the *hortus conclusus* of ideal femininity, 'also a commonly used emblem of the queen's virginity and of England the island' (p. 57). In fact, the queen's titles occupy the outer, celestial, sphere of this map; the sphere of the fixed stars is made to represent *proceres* (the nobles or other celebrated men, including even masters in the arts or sciences), *heroes* (the military men), and *consiliarii* (councillors) of the state. The seven planetary spheres are labelled with concepts ranging from majesty to eloquence, all attributes of the just monarchy ruled according to law, so that the earthly sphere is appropriately filled with justice for all, not just the nobility (*innobilis*). By my reckoning, Sanford has also located the queen's genitals just slightly above where her knees would be. A number of her literary readings (of the Thames and Medway marriage in *The Faerie Queene*, *Cymbeline*, 'To Penshurst', Elizabeth's coronation entry, and Whitney's 'Wyll and Testament' to the City of London, among others) follow similar patterns.

The technique of suggestive correspondence is present in Valerie Traub's *The Renaissance of Lesbianism in Early Modern England*, although handled with both more panache and more accuracy of observation. In a critique of Louis Montrose's analysis of the Armada portrait of Elizabeth with its bow (which he refers to as a 'virgin knot') and drop-pearl jewel positioned just at the pointed base of the stomacher, Traub, who has amassed a fascinating array of medical literature to arrive at a finely nuanced study of female sexuality and its meanings during the period, is struck by the ambiguity of the combination of knot and glistening pearl. She states, 'the drop pearl in the Armada portrait emblematises the erotic self-assertion of the most powerful woman in the realm, figuratively announcing Elizabeth's sovereign right to her own pleasures. This self-assertion is reinforced by the painting's composition, which utterly defies any logic of penetration ... a visual address that simultaneously solicits and prohibits the spectator's access' (p. 130). Incorporating a discreet and quite critical use of Freud throughout, the book looks in detail at a number of plays including, very usefully, those of John Lyly. A chapter devoted to recounting retellings of Ovid's Calisto myth in sixteenth- and seventeenth-century texts including Cavalli's 1651 opera, however, would perhaps have benefited from more of the subtle intertextuality evident elsewhere in the book. Calisto's sense of 'guilt' after her rape by Jove in the guise of Diana comes direct from Ovid and is not just found in Golding's translation, while prior knowledge of the original (or of Golding) by contemporary readers would surely have lent added piquancy to the quite substantial alterations made by Warner in *Albion's England* or Heywood in *Troia Britannica*. There is an issue here in the difference between translation and adaptation, which might interfere with Traub's tracing of the rise of the femme. The placing of individual sexual desire within a frame of the historical development of sexuality is perhaps even more fraught with difficulty than the charting of individual religious belief. Traub is referring to the mid- to late seventeenth century when she states that 'female pleasure began to be psychologized' and 'The development of a new marital regime in which erotic desire became the *sine qua non* of conjugal life did not happen overnight' (p. 268). John Harington's unusually explicit epigrams, however, and his complaints that his long-suffering (or insufferable, depending on your point of view) wife was in a strop with him (Scott-Warren, pp. 108–18) suggest to me an even longer time-frame. Nevertheless Traub's book is valuable because it is so alive to contradictions within broad historical changes.

The definition of both correspondence and difference across an extensive period of historical time is an important feature of Meg Twycross's and Sarah Carpenter's book, *Masks and Masking in Medieval and Early Tudor England*. The wearing of masks as part of theatrical performance has recently re-entered British theatre practice and is usually described with reference to the Continental *commedia dell' arte* or classical Greek traditions. But this book explores the ubiquitous presence of the masked face in early English theatre and attempts to trace the relationship between that and the mask as a generic theatrical form. It distinguishes between English and Continental theatre traditions, and disentangles practice and signification from semantic similarity: 'A *mumming* did not mean the same to a fifteenth-century English tradesman as a *mommerij* did to his courtly German contemporary' (p. 2). Not only that, but a 'mumming encounter between friends may be very different from one between strangers' (p. 6), while the 'same mask can mean different things in different contexts' (p. 7). The very heterogeneity of the subject (rightly) demands a complexity of approach: 'no one explanation or theory can account for all its different manifestations' (p. 3), and the authors carefully distinguish between a range of different political and social significations for the disruptive and celebratory effects of mask and carnival. The book is accordingly divided into four parts: 'Popular Masking', 'Courtly Masking', 'Theatrical Masking', and a final section labelled 'Theory and Practice'. This has separate chapters devoted to 'Ideas and Theories', 'Materials and Methods' (which details some techniques of construction), and finally 'Terminology', which usefully explores the etymologies of the words so repeatedly—and so differently—used in the records. The authors are careful in their use of sources: 'Preachers, antiquaries, and poets may show articulate interest in the facts or moral significance of masking without necessarily having much experience of contemporary practice' (p. 280). In trying to pinpoint historically specific meaning, however, they do not stint to draw modern parallels and analogies. Far from reducing the material to some vague 'presentism', this serves to highlight the possibilities of difference. It also raises interesting questions of relevance to modern performance practice and its over-reliance on the theory and practice of Stanislavski. Wearing a mask focuses attention on the role rather than the performer. It allowed one performer to undertake a number of roles within a single interlude while several different performers might undertake one role across the span of a processional mystery cycle. But it does not mean that the spectator's emotional response to the events of the play or cycle are thereby dissipated or lessened. This book's twenty-year gestation period shows in the subtlety of its approach, its detailed, rigorously researched content, and the clarity with which it is written, a combination rarely achieved in today's RAE-driven British academy.

Anne Lancashire's *London Civic Theatre* deals with theatrical entertainment and civic processions from Roman times to Elizabeth's accession. Lancashire too is rigorous in her attention to the precise forms of language used in the financial account books, which are so often our only source of information about such events. Her text, however, is in parts a difficult read, with parenthesis nested within parenthesis and a peculiar use of the colon as if research notes have simply been transcribed. This is a tremendous shame since the content is so important.

Lancashire is extremely careful not to extrapolate too far beyond concrete positive evidence for any particular practice while recognizing that the extant records may not tell the full story. It is always more difficult for modern historians to identify the continuing existence of something that was regarded as usual practice, since people usually only record the unfamiliar. Accordingly, she carefully explores the possible reasons for the demise of the Midsummer Watch—the night-time processions of the lord mayor and the watch with lights and pageants on the eves of St John and St Peter—and questions the date given for its abolition in the much later historical description found in Stow's *Survey of London*. Although she acknowledges the conventional explanation that 'some stridently Protestant Londoners' might have welcomed the putting down of a festival associated with saints' days, she adduces a range of other documentary evidence to suggest that the watch was an increasing financial burden on the City in the late 1530s and that it began to get confused with Henry's request for an annual military muster. Rather than being cancelled, 'the Watch had to be maintained, and pretty well at its current level: so as not to give the king indirect control over London civic pageantry funding'. The activities associated with this procession thereafter seem to have been diverted towards developing both the City's May games and the lord mayor's investiture (pp. 169–70). The story thus supplies an interesting footnote to the larger political tensions between Crown and people that are being noted in the work on the Reformation with which I began. Simple religious difference is generally too easy an answer, and problems are likely to be both political and economic.

2. Sidney

In a valuable addition to the genre of Sidney biography, John Considine considers a range of what he refers to as 'contemporary testimonies' in order to answer the question posed by his essay 'How Much Greek Did Philip Sidney Know?' (*SidJ* 20:ii[2002] 57–78). Sidney's writings themselves tell us little about his proficiency in Greek without an English translation, but the documents considered by Considine in this essay undermine the traditional notion of Sidney as a scholar. The documents are an exchange of letters between Sidney and Hubert Languet in January and February 1574, dedications to Sidney of works edited and published by Henri Estienne in 1576 and 1581, and four panegyrics: a poem by Janus Dousa the younger, written in 1585 or 1586, an elegy by Jerome Lisle de Groslot written in 1586, an elegy by Nathanael Dod written in 1586 or 1587, and a biography by Thomas Moffet written in 1593. Considine shows that Sidney was introduced to the Greek language between 1564 and 1582, during his education at Shrewsbury and Oxford but that, as his letters to Languet suggest, he had forgotten much of what he learned by 1574. In the same year Sidney might have begun studying Greek again and, by the winter of 1574 to 1575, Henri Estienne thought him interested enough eventually to be able to read it without translation. However, there is no further evidence to indicate that Sidney was interested in the language and in 1579 praise of his linguistic ability made no reference to Greek. Furthermore, asserts Considine, those claims that Sidney knew Greek, made in panegyrics on him between 1585 and 1593, are wholly unreliable. Based on the evidence detailed here, Considine comes to the important conclusion that Sidney's interest in Greek was 'far from scholarly' and that Sidney was 'by no means learned' (p. 77).

Sidney's beliefs are the subject of Robert E. Stillman's essay which challenges Alan Sinfield's influential reading of Sidney's *Defence* as a work of Soviet-style propaganda on behalf of the Puritan faction which he believed was an ideologically driven vehicle related to the absolutist aspirations of the Elizabethan state: 'The Truths of a Slippery World: Poetry and Tyranny in Sidney's *Defence*' (*RenQ* 55[2002] 1287–1319). Stillman argues that Sidney's *Defence* 'needs to be recontextualized as a governing body of assumptions about the nature of knowledge that Sidney derived from the revival of natural law theory among an intellectual elite closely associated with the late Philip Melanchthon (1497–1560)—the so-called Philippists—and the early proponents of tyrannomachist political philosophy' (p. 1291). Via detailed reference to the evidence gathered together here, in particular the writings of Melanchthon and his followers (including Sidney's mentor and friend Hubert Languet), Stillman makes a convincing case for the politics of Sidney's *Defence*, and in particular his identification of tyranny with self-love, being best understood via this identifiable network of cosmopolitan Protestant humanists. Stillman's essay for *Spenser Studies*, 'Deadly Stinging Adders: Sidney's Piety, Philippism, and the *Defence of Poesy*' (*SSt* 16[2002] 231–69), is also concerned with the influence of the Philippists on Sidney's prose text and takes issue with those critics who have defined the *Defence* as a Calvinist text, again emphasizing the humanist trajectory of that particular school of philosophy, in particular its positive attitude to human agency.

Sidney's *Arcadia* was the focus for a number of articles this year. H.R. Woudhuysen, 'A New Manuscript Fragment of Sidney's *Old Arcadia*: The Huddleston Manuscript' (*EMS* 11[2002] 52–69), adds considerably to our knowledge of a fragment of a previously unrecorded manuscript of the first version of Sidney's *Old Arcadia* recently discovered by Steven W. May. The fragment comes from one of the volumes of the Huddleston papers in the Cambridge County Record Office and was used to reinforce the lower cover of a vellum-bound account of a terrier listing the possessions of Sir Edmund Huddleston. Sidney's poem was copied on to a single recto page which was then discarded because the scribe made an error. Woudhuysen claims that the manuscript 'has various features which are highly unusual' (p. 54) and goes on to demonstrate that its scribe was the same man who wrote the Huddleston terrier, John Paxton, estate steward to Huddleston. Woudhuysen outlines the biography of Paxton and his employer, in particular the strong Catholic loyalties of the Huddleston family. It is unclear how Paxton or Huddleston got hold of the manuscript of *Old Arcadia* in order to make a copy, since 'no direct links between the family and Philip Sidney or his friends and family can be traced; nor do there seem to be any obvious associations between the Huddlestons and the known owners of other Sidney manuscripts' (pp. 63–4), but it is possible that the Huddlestons knew the Rich family (Sidney's Stella) since they lived about ten miles apart. The terrier is dated 10 May 1580, but 'it is a fair copy and so could have been written and bound at any date after then' (p. 65), and the curious numbering of the poems in the fragment makes it possible that the *Old Arcadia* poems 'were at some stage arranged in a different order from the familiar one' (p. 66). Woudhuysen concludes that, if this fragment was copied directly from Sidney's papers, it 'provides additional evidence that he wanted the work published in manuscript'; however, if it is the copy of a copy we can infer that the text was common enough that a family with no apparent links to Sidney had access to it. It also fits a repeated pattern: that 'among earliest readers of Sidney's romance were minor gentry … [with] Roman Catholic associations' (p. 66).

R.W. Maslen, 'Sidneian Geographies' (*SidJ* 20:ii[2002] 45–55), suggests that Sidney's choice of the title 'duke' for Basilius in the *Old Arcadia*, rather than the more obvious 'king' (the meaning of his name in Greek), can be traced to his sources. Richard Eden's *The Decades of the Newe Worlde or West India* [1555], a translation of Peter Martyr's history of the Spanish conquest of the New World, *De orbe novo decades* [1516], was revised by Richard Wills in 1577 and reprinted as part of a larger volume, *The History of Travayle in the West and East Indies*. Eden and Wills included accounts of efforts by Europeans to find a north-east passage to Cathay and in these are references to Duke Basilius of Moscovia, also known as Vasily III, father of Ivan the Terrible. Maslen believes that Basilius of Moscovia provided inspiration for the paranoid duke in the *Old Arcadia*, most evident in the historical duke's 'obsessive preoccupation with the vexed question of his title' (p. 50) and the 'elaborate dispute over "title" that dominates the trial scene at the end of *The Old Arcadia*' (p. 52). Maslen also notes Wills's debt to Strabo, who, inspired by Homer's *Odyssey*, praised the disciplines of poetry and geography as equally useful in his *Geographia* and thinks it possible that Strabo provided Sidney 'with the theoretical justification for the fusion of real and imaginary persons and places ... which characterizes the Arcadia' (p. 55). Wills's *History of Travayle* might have provided Sidney with 'a mental map' of the world which, combined with his own experiences of travelling, would allow him to gain 'geographical knowledge on a level with that of Homer', and Maslen rightly argues that the 'links between ancient and early modern writers on the poetics of geography deserve fuller consideration than they have yet received' (p. 55).

Several essays on the *Arcadia* were concerned with gender, its female readership, or sexuality. Marea Mitchell, '"Strange but Vain Conceits": Re-writing Romance in the Arcadias' (*SidJ* 20:ii[2002] 1–20), considers the reworking of two important and related stories dealing with love and romance by Sidney in the *New Arcadia* and by several female authors from the seventeenth to the nineteenth centuries. Dicus's account of Cupid, which originated in the *Old Arcadia*, is reworked by Sidney in Miso's story from the *New Arcadia*. Although both stories depict Cupid as threatening, the latter advises 'not so much to abjure love and all its workings' (p. 7) but to avoid 'the loss of self' which love entails (p. 7). Most significantly perhaps, the revised story is spoken by a woman rather than an old man and, moreover, a woman from the lower classes who is one of the 'sexually experienced, desiring women' in the *New Arcadia* (p. 8). The tale that is told by Mopsa, Miso's daughter, is a 'hyper-romantic' tale which contrasts with her mother's 'worldly cynicism', and Mitchell asserts that mother and daughter convey the range of Renaissance romance and anti-romance which can be found in Sidney's text: put simply, politics dominates in *Old Arcadia* but love takes centre-stage in its revision. Mopsa's tale is revised and enlarged by the female authors Anna Weamys [1651], D. Stanley [1725], Hain Friswellin [1867], and Emily Henrietta Hickey [1881], all of whom change the gender and class connotations of Sidney's original story. The rewriting of Mopsa's tale suggests 'a kind of feminization and domestication of romance' (p. 19) which entails a shift from the chivalric and medieval, emphasis on action, and formal eclogues to character development, interiority and the role of story-telling in the development of relationships which has as much to do with the expectations of an increasingly female audience as the sex of the author.

Julie Crawford, 'Sidney's Sapphics and the Role of Interpretive Communities' (*ELH* 69[2002] 979–1007), claims that critics have neglected the significance of Sidney's use of 'sapphics', the poetic ode named after the female poet Sappho, in the *Old Arcadia*. In one particular episode from the poem the Amazon Cleophila (cross-dressed as the hero Pyrocles) sings sapphics to the woman she loves, and the form appears elsewhere in the poem. Crawford argues that, although the content of Cleophila's song is highly conventional, Sidney's use of the sapphic form is radical since his sapphics 'are not merely metrical experiments' but rather 'invoke and enact female agency, desire and homoeroticism' (p. 979). Crawford considers the textual means by which Sappho and sapphics circulated in the early modern period and suggests that, although critics tend to focus on Sidney as an explicitly homosocial writer, his use of sapphics, a form long used 'to flatter or solicit the pleasure of women' (p. 986), may have been a deliberate attempt to appeal to the women readers who dominated his literary coterie.

Sue Starke, '"The Majesty of Unconquered Virtue": Pamela and the Argument of Feminine Nobility in Sidney's *New Arcadia*' (*EIRC* 28[2002] 181–206), takes exception to the traditional critical view of the sisters Pamela and Philoclea in the *Arcadia*s which reads them as a rhetorical exercise in antithesis, arguing rather that the reader is expected to judge, not merely distinguish between, these two models of femininity. Via detailed reference to Old and New *Arcadia*s Starke presents a solid argument for the younger sister Philoclea being inferior to her elder, not merely because of age. That the sisters should offer distinct models of femininity is evident in the *Old Arcadia*, argues Starke, but is also present in the revised version, which 'offers a crucial supplement to their histories in Sidney's earlier fiction' and provides the reader with 'a vastly more confident and positive view of female chastity as a moral and political force' (p. 182). Relating the experiences of the two young women in the face of adversity to contemporary notions about appropriate behaviour for aristocratic women, Starke concludes that Pamela rather than Philoclea is celebrated because, unlike her submissive sister, she displays 'a strong sense of her own value and prerogative' (p. 203), primarily through her successful use of rhetoric, and as such provides a strong model of aristocratic womanhood for subsequent writers of pastoral romance.

Stephanie Chamberlain, 'Wife and Widow in Arcadia: Re-envisioning the Ideal' (*CollL* 29:ii[2002] 80–98), also problematizes the traditional dichotomizing of Sidney's heroines in the *Arcadia*. By reference to a real-life case and early modern behaviour manuals for women, Chamberlain points out that, although the virtuous Parthenia and the malevolent Cecropia might appear to conform to the early modern female type and anti-type, closer inspection reveals a more complex attitude to female agency, with the behaviour of each figure violating what is expected.

Benjamin Scott Grossberg, 'Politics and Shifting Desire in Sidney's *New Arcadia*' (*SEL* 42:i[2002] 63–83) considers the significance of three curious figures from Sidney's *New Arcadia*, the two shepherds, Claius and Strephon, and the shepherdess, who 'are not crucial to Sidney's dramatic arc' and so 'must serve a critical function thematically'. For Grossberg, Sidney uses these figures and 'an idealized Arcadia' to show how 'both the homoerotic bonds and the potential violence of patriarchy were supposed to be contained in the Elizabethan adaptation of chivalry' (p. 65). For Grossberg Urania represents Elizabeth I, who also functioned as a 'bridge for homoerotic contact' in a court where male–male relations were ordered, but this cannot be sustained in either Arcadia or the Elizabethan court: 'given the realities of conflicting desire and a fallible queen figure, the state proves unable to contain male–male relations and erupts into civil war' (p. 65). In what Grossberg calls 'the second Arcadia', which takes place in Basilius's woods, there is a shift since 'no presiding figure appears to effectively order male–male relations or to ensure that male–female relations are subjugated to the needs of patriarchy' (p. 72). Basilius fails because, like his consort Gynecia, he focuses on 'heteroerotic desire, rather than regulating male–male desire' (p. 74), a shift also evident in the two princes, Musidorus and Pyrocles. In the *New Arcadia* the patriarchal state dissolves, undermined by a heteroerotic drive which Grossberg relates to Elizabeth I's desire to regulate her courtiers' marriages, and Sidney makes what Grossberg terms 'a harsh comment on the effectiveness of the Elizabethan medieval revival to contain male–male relations' (p. 80).

Most scholars believe that the proposed match between Queen Elizabeth and the duke of Alençon forms a backdrop for Sidney's *Arcadia*s, but Jonathan Gibson, 'Sidney's *Arcadia*s and Elizabethan Courtiership' (*EIC* 52:i[2002] 36–55), claims that a neglected aspect of the dispute's influence on Sidney is the relationship between Sidney's *Arcadia*s and the writings of his court rival Edward DeVere, seventeenth earl of Oxford. Oxford's advocacy of the French match was connected to the revival of the French-influenced Petrarchan lyric, a genre which complicated patronage negotiations, making it 'impossible to tell whether the speaker of a poem is in love or seeking political favour' (p. 39). Gibson contends that the *Arcadia*s might be read as 'an attack on the slippery nature of "Oxfordian" court writing' and that the 'moral seriousness' of Sidney's text constitutes 'an implicit rebuke' to the 'opportunistic' 'new lyrical' writings favoured by Oxford (p. 39). Also evident in Sidney's *Arcadia*s, claims Gibson, is a concern about a courtier's control over his text and the problem of being vulnerable to misinterpretation or manipulation. Using examples from both the Old and New *Arcadia*s, Gibson outlines how the former 'tries to circumvent the problems of Elizabethan courtiership' while the latter provides 'a darker, more pessimistic view of human agency' (p. 39).

The proposed French match was of interest also to Peter Beal who, in 'Philip Sidney's Letter to Queen Elizabeth and That "False Knave" Alexander Dicsone' (*EMS* 11[2002] 1–51), considers a new manuscript of Sidney's letter to Queen Elizabeth arguing against her proposed marriage to the duc d'Alençon (duc d'Anjou) in 1579, held in the National Library of Scotland. Although there are multiple surviving manuscripts, none of them authorial and containing many variant readings, this one is notable because it is one of a few that can be dated with any certainty (not much later than the 1580s) and because its textual variants may illuminate 'the divergences in early transmission' (p. 1). Its original owner was Alexander Dicsone, an active member of Sidney's circle, who was commissioned by Sidney or his uncle to write for them. Dicsone, a Scottish writer, intellectual, and traveller who worked as royal propagandist for James VI was a double-agent who also worked for leading members of the Scottish Catholic aristocracy as well as the English and French governments. In 1595 Dicsone was accused of passing sensitive state papers and information to the French, and on 9 August of that year wrote a letter (reproduced here in an appendix) defending himself against the allegation. Dicsone was accepted into the circle of Leicester and Sidney and so 'had access to the kind of political materials which then circulated within the relatively confined purview of the Court' (p. 32). Citing various examples, Beal claims that the manuscript owned by Dicsone might be based upon authorial readings 'before they were eliminated by subsequent revision by Sidney and his immediate circle when the process of composition was still effectively in progress' (p. 19). He also suggests that Walsingham (sent by the queen on missions to negotiate the marriage) and not Leicester, as is usually thought, was responsible for appointing Sidney as spokesman for the Leicester–Walsingham faction.

Although critics have recognized that Sidney's poem 'Now was our heav'nly vault deprived of the light' comments upon his relationship with the queen, they have not noted the political impetus of the allusion. In 'Temples Defaced and Altars in the Dust: Edwardian and Elizabethan Church Reform and Sidney's "Now was our heav'nly vault deprived of the light"' (*SSt* 16[2002] 197–229), Barbara Brumbaugh claims that Sidney's poem, which was transferred from Philisides in the *Old Arcadia* to Amphialus in the *New Arcadia*, contains distinct criticism of Elizabeth's approach to religion and nostalgia for the reign of her brother, Edward VI. Brumbaugh shows that a brief period of happiness during the youth of Amphialus, the poem's narrator, is associated with what was considered by fervent Protestants as a golden era under Edward, replaced by the inadequate leadership of the nation's Church under Elizabeth. Further criticism of Elizabeth is evident in Amphialus's difficulties with Diana and Venus, who represent Elizabeth as distinct from Mira, the True Church. That Sidney was critical of Elizabeth's rule is confirmed by his letters, and more likely if we consider that his family prospered under the reign of Edward.

Sidney's sonnet sequence inspired two notable essays this year. Using Byron's *Don Juan* as a rather appropriate starting point, Erik Gray, 'Sonnet Kisses: Sidney to Barrett Browning' (*EIC* 52:ii[2002] 126–42), explores the paradox of the kiss in a range of sonnets. In Byron's poem the paradox, or irony, is that the kiss 'extinguishes the very feature that gave rise to the desire to kiss' (p. 127), that is, the smile of the beloved. Similarly in Sidney's *Astrophil and Stella*, which contains 'the first major sonnet-kiss in English' (p. 127), the features of Stella admired by Astrophil—her eyes, her cheeks, the sound of her voice—are obliterated by a kiss, which is more desirable than sexual intercourse, an act which would not obliterate the features. The paradox of all post-Petrarchan sequences, claims Gray, is their claim to originality while 'deploying the most codified and imitative of all lyric conventions' (p. 128). Just as the sonneteer 'borrows or deflects another's language from its original context' (p. 129) so too the kiss is always borrowed, indeed kissing 'is not the primary function of the lips' (p. 129). Moreover a kiss, like a sonnet, 'is both the result and the initiator of desire' (p. 130): the aim of the sonnet is not closure since consummation with the beloved will not occur, and so kissing is often figured as a lesson, repeated as 'a preparation for greater things' (p. 131). Gray concludes his essay by considering the sonnet-kiss in the Victorian period, which saw its development from 'a simple, pretty paradox' (p. 132) in the Renaissance to an action characterized by awkwardness and morbidity.

Rebecca Laroche, '"O Absent Presence", Sidney is Not Here: The Lament for Astrophil and the Stellar Presence of a Woman Writer' (*SidJ* 20:ii[2002] 21–44), considers a range of elegies on Sidney which manipulate the lover–beloved paradigm of Sidney's *Astrophil and Stella*. After his premature death Sidney displaced Stella as the object of desire in writings that may be read as continuations of his own sonnet sequence, especially since Stella's absence from the final poems prefigures the absence of the poet in death. In the elegiac writings of members of Sidney's coterie—Mary Sidney Herbert, Edmund Spenser, Walter Ralegh, Edward Dyer, Fulke Greville, and Thomas Nashe, amongst others—'the conventional sonnet relationship of male lover addressing female beloved becomes malleable as the elegists substitute the departed poet for the absent beloved' (p. 22), an explicit fusion of the elegiac and erotic, not hitherto emphasized by critics.

The Versifications of the Psalms of David, begun by Philip Sidney and completed by his sister Mary Sidney Herbert, is the topic of Michael Brennan's lengthy and engaging essay, 'The Queen's Proposed Visit to Wilton House in 1599 and the "Sidney Psalms"' (*SidJ* 20:i[2002] 27–53). It is not clear whether the Sidneys intended their work on the Psalms 'merely as a self-reflective exercise in metrical virtuosity, only to be circulated among friends and relatives in manuscript' (p. 39) or whether they were interested in publication. The Sidneys certainly considered their work on the Psalms an important project: in *A Defence of Poetry* Sidney 'asserted the absolute pre-eminence of the Psalms of David as poetry' (p. 37) and the work by

Philip and Mary, using the French Psalter of 1562 as their primary literary model, demonstrates their metrical inventiveness (p. 38). Brennan suggests that Mary may have been 'actively involved ... in considering the wider dissemination of the Sidney palms through print' (p. 29) and had planned to present the Psalms, together with three of her own original poems, to Queen Elizabeth during the monarch's visit to her home, Wilton House. Although Mary had connections in the printing world, printing patents, which would enable the printing of English versions of the Psalms, were granted only at royal discretion, and a visit by Elizabeth would have provided the perfect opportunity for initiating the venture. The cancellation of the queen's visit, coupled with subsequent changes in printing legislation, apparently halted proceedings; the Psalms would not be published until 1823.

3. Spenser

As might be expected, a number of articles on *The Faerie Queene* appeared in this year's contributions to the study of Spenser. Roger Kuin, 'The Double Helix: Private and Public in *The Faerie Queene*' (*SSt* 16[2002] 1–22), uses Judith A. Swanson's 1992 analysis of Aristotle's virtues to trace the pattern of private and public, or politic, virtues in Spenser's epic poem. Swanson believed that for Aristotle private and public virtues were not distinct but overlapped, virtue was action rather than a quality of character, and privacy allowed such virtues to be undertaken free from public demands. For Kuin, categories of private and public function as 'constitutive genetic codes of the text as a text of moral education' (p. 4), and he uses the model of the double helix to consider these categories, which he believes to be both distinct and intertwined in every book of poem. Kuin considers a number of the poem's cruxes, for example Book I is private and yet Lucifera's palace is a very public place, which Kuin interprets as a warning to the reader that in court politic virtues depend on the exercise of private ones. Kuin also considers Book V, which has always seemed to be the most public book of the poem, a view which is complicated by Aristotle's view of justice as a private virtue. The double helix's central space is occupied by core or key roles: the principal figure here is Arthur, although for a number of books Archimago and Duessa play similar parts and 'may be engaged at any moment in either of the codes' (p. 6). Arthur functions as a key 'for he enters every book and both codes, which shows him to be situated in the core' but, unlike Archimago and Duessa, he is easy to decode: the *Letter to Raleigh* claims he is 'Magnificence', and he thus represents all private and public moral virtues, culminating in the figure of Elizabeth. For Kuin the model of double helix is helpful 'in the *making sense* which is, for Spenser, the attentive reader-disciples' necessary (and virtuous) activity' (p. 6), and he ends this valuable essay by pondering how, following the Aristotelian model, Spenser might have completed his unfinished poem.

In an essay which engages with recent debates about Spenser's alleged republican tendencies, Louis Montrose, 'Spenser and the Elizabethan Political Imaginary' (*ELH* 69[2002] 907–46), situates Spenser's poetry within the context of contemporary attitudes toward monarchical power and gender. Taking John Knox's infamous denunciation of female rulers as his starting point, Montrose notes that it 'encapsulates certain persistent thematic, imagistic, and rhetorical elements that are writ large across Spenser's *Faerie Queene*', a text which 'narrativizes the monstrous regiment of women in numerous variations' (p. 909). Montrose, who considers key episodes featuring Belphoebe and Acrasia from Book II of *The Faerie Queene*, reads Spenser's writing, in particular his use of myth and blazon, as part of a culture of unsolicited public advice to the monarch, encoded to varying degrees, which sought 'to improve the system of which she was the centre, not to destroy it' (p. 915). Spenser neither celebrated the cult of Elizabeth nor promoted what we might recognize as a republican agenda but rather, claims Montrose, 'employed the resources of misogyny to further the political agenda of a limited monarchy' (p. 939).

Laurel L. Hendrix's fascinating and well-researched essay, 'Pulchritudo Vincit? Emblematic Reversals in Spenser's House of Busirane' (*SSt* 16[2002] 23–54), considers the significance of Spenser's revision of the 1590 ending of Book III in the 1596 edition of *The Faerie Queene*—which undoes the hermaphroditic figure of an embracing Amoret and Scudamour following her release from imprisonment by Busirane—via contrasting representations of love. In the House of Busirane Spenser employs a series of traditional and conflicting emblems of Cupid: he is the armed tyrant, as in many emblems, but also a symbol of regenerative love, as in Spenser's own Garden of Adonis in Book III, which 'follows a longstanding epigrammatic and emblematic tradition' (p. 28). As Hendrix notes, although we might understand the punishment of the proud Mirabella in Book VI it is not clear why Amoret, who loves Scudamour 'chastely and steadfastly' (p. 32), should be punished by a martial Cupid. Hendrix explains that Spenser distinguishes between Venus and armed Cupid as symbols of love, and when Venus adopts Amoretta (little love) this female unarmed love takes the place of her lost child Cupid. Amoretta is an Anteros figure (representing reciprocal love), and is thus a counter-example to the martial Eros. In the House of Busirane, Eros dominates and subdues Anteros, and love is redefined as lust for power. Scudamour means 'shield of love', and is thus associated with Cupid's emblem of 'maisterie' on his shield, so although Scudamour laments Amoret's plight he is largely responsible for it. Curiously, the binding of Amoret reverses the tradition where the martial Cupid 'is bound, scourged, and tempered' (p. 36) and, according to this tradition, Spenser's Amoret must be unbound for virtuous love to triumph. It is Britomart, Amoret's champion, who 'acts as a catalyst, setting in motion the emblematic reversals necessary for the achievement of these imperatives' (p. 39). In freeing Amoret, Britomart restrains Cupid's proxy, Busirane, and acts herself as Amoret's proxy, Anteros; Spenser thus alludes to Venus and plays upon the topos of *pulchritudo vincit*, beauty's conquering power. Beauty is a weapon, but for Amoret it also makes her the victim of 'maisterie'. Britomart, however, asserts beauty's might against Busirane and 'embodies a militant feminine principle which contrasts with the passive, vulnerable beauty and femininity embodied in Amoret' (p. 41). Spenser thus transforms the power of beauty: what is traditionally a passive feminine grace becomes an active virtue. In the 1596 ending of Book III Hendrix identifies 'an important shift' in Spenser's poetics where, instead of the hermaphrodite, we get 'the most blatant narrative rupture of the entire poem' (p. 47). Rather than being entwined in a mutual embrace, Amoret is subject to 'maisterie' in the temple of Venus (*FQ* IV.ix.38–41). Hendrix concludes that, in deferring the lovers' union, Spenser undoes the closure of the 1590 narrative: there is no defeat of martial Eros, no consummation of reciprocal love, and he delimits Beauty's power, later to be embodied in the more sinister Radigund, where Britomart will become a traditional emblem of *pulchritudo vincit* and women's power is limited to men's hearts.

In an informative and nicely argued piece William C. Johnson, 'Spenser's Hermetic Tricksters in *The Faerie Queene* III and IV' (*ES* 83[2002] 338–55), traces the figure of the trickster in those books of *The Faerie Queene* centred on chastity and friendship: Books III and IV respectively. For Johnson, tricksters are introduced by Spenser in order to create 'humorous disorder even as they parody and present more serious matters' (p. 338). The trickster is informed by a range of sources, erudite and popular, and Johnson lists his characteristics as defined by fellow critic William G. Doty: he is a marginal figure with paradoxical qualities, has connections with relationships and the erotic, functions as a creator and restorer, engages in deceit and theft, comedy and wit, and is associated with hermeneutics, the art of interpretation, a word possibly derived from Hermes, himself a trickster figure. Trickster narratives both define and violate boundaries, and the function of the trickster is to remind those around him that 'the periphery, not the center, of our attention may very well be what is most important' (p. 339). The most significant trickster figure in Book III is the Squire of Dames, who 'has a penchant for sly jokes … an affinity for travelers and thieves, an ability for quick wit and smooth talking' (p. 340), and who is replaced by a number of 'figurative offspring and substitutes' (p. 340) such as the False Florimell and Paridell. Johnson traces the workings of such figures, describing their impact on the narrative in terms of a learning process about the reality of human nature and the workings of the world, something Britomart must tackle if she is to emerge as a fully developed heroic figure.

Spenser's source material also informs a short but important article by Mathew Steggle, 'Weighing Winged Words: An Intertext in *The Faerie Queene* V.ii' (*SSt* 16[2002] 273–6). This considers the episode where Artegall encounters the Giant who weighs justice in Book V, and argues for a hitherto unacknowledged source for the 'winged words' escaping from the Giant's scales (V.ii.44.8–9). Critics are alert to the biblical and epic allusions of the image, but Steggle makes a convincing case for Aristophanes' play *Frogs* as a source or, more specifically, an intertext for the image of weighing words in particular, which allows for a reading of the passage in Spenser as comic.

Cora Fox, 'Spenser's Grieving Adicia and the Gender Politics of Renaissance Ovidianism' (*ELH* 69[2002] 385–412), is concerned with Spenser's debt to Ovid's tale of Hecuba's grief and transformation in the *Metamorphoses*, which he imitated in the story of Adicia, wife of the evil Souldan in Book V of *The Faerie Queene*, a woman who runs mad with grief and rage when her husband is killed and is metamorphosed into a tiger. In a thought-provoking analysis of this neglected episode Fox contends that Spenser not only engages with Ovid's text as 'an archive of myths' and as a way of underpinning his writing via classical allusion but also 'wrestles more broadly with Ovid's often anti-authoritarian politics' (p. 385). Spenser was interested not only in Ovid's stories but also his representation of gender politics and female subjectivity. Adicia is unlikely to represent any particular contemporary woman, but rather the episode in which she appears, which represents her transformation as a result of excessive affect, interrogates the social role of powerful female figures and the consequence of excessive female emotion.

George F. Butler, ('Spenser, Milton, and the Renaissance Campe: Monsters and Myths in *The Faerie Queene* and *Paradise Lost*' (*MiltonS* 40[2002] 19–37), points out that Milton's depiction of Sin and Death in *Paradise Lost* is indebted to Spenser's Error, and that both authors were indebted to Campe, a little-known monster from classical mythology. Butler traces references to Campe in works by several classical authors, most of which would have been available to Milton and Spenser, but 'the most vivid' (p. 21) of which is the description of Campe in the *Dionysiaca*, written around ad 470 by the Byzantine poet Nonnos of Panopolis. Citing John Steadman, Butler notes that Spenser's monster, like Nonnos' Campe, 'is part woman, with serpentine and canine attributes' (p. 27), and Milton's sin continues this tradition. Spenser's depiction of Error undoubtedly influenced Milton's story of Satan's rebellion and the error of Adam and Eve: the Wandering Wood is a kind of hell and Error is linked to the Fall in an episode which prefigures Redcrosse's battle with the dragon in the fallen Eden.

Wendy Olmsted, 'Elizabethan Rhetoric, Ideology, and Britomart's Sorrow By the Sea' (*Exemplaria* 14:i[2002] 167–200), argues that in *The Faerie Queene* readers are encouraged to examine alternative viewpoints in a poem which is less concerned with advocating a particular stance on any given issue than on generating enquiry into the complex ideas surrounding it. Of particular interest to Olmsted is Spenser's account of Britomart's sorrow by the sea, which 'produces analogies and disanalogies with contemporary intertexts that suggest her fears, generated by misogynist discourses of the time' (pp. 172–3). Among the contemporary intertexts that inform Olmsted's detailed and critically informed essay are Petrarch's sonnet 189 from the *Rime Sparse* and the *Elizabethan Homily on Marriage*, both of which serve to facilitate multiple, sometimes conflicting, positions which suggest the allegory's preoccupation with rhetorical debate.

The focus of Clare R. Kinney's fascinating article, '"What S/he Ought to Have Been": Romancing Truth in *Spencer Redivivus*' (*SSt* 16[2002] 125–37), is Edward Howard's translation of Book I of *The Faerie Queene*, published in 1687. Howard's proclaimed purpose was to improve upon what he referred to as Spenser's 'obsolete Language and manner of Verse' (p. 125), and although he insisted that his translation 'entirely preserv'd' Spenser's 'matter and design' (p. 126), except where abbreviation was called for in an effort to improve, it does in fact insert new material and, most significantly, presents a striking refiguring of Spenser's Una. Via detailed comparisons between Howard's dire translation and Spenser's original, Kinney details how Howard's presentation of Spenser's allegory 'strips Una of her theological rigor and her command of scripture' (p. 131) and is clearly a precursor to the nineteenth-century sentiment which would accentuate and idealize the conventional feminine attributes of Spenser's female protagonists. This is a welcome and lively analysis of Howard's effort which, as Kinney points out, has hitherto received little critical attention.

Staying with translation, Jialuan Hu, 'Spenser in Chinese Translation' (*SSt* 16[2002] 139–49), agrees with the general precept of Chinese translators that the Chinese version of a text 'should approximate the original both in rhythm and in rhyme', but notes the difficulty of translating Spenser's lengthy *Faerie Queene* when metrical verse in Chinese 'is often associated with classical poems which are most commonly arranged in lines of either five or seven characters' (p. 140). Using examples from *The Faerie Queene* to illustrate, Hu proposes that a solution to the problem would be to use the pauses that occur naturally in the Chinese language to correspond to the foot in English verse and to follow the rhyme scheme of the original, although this is by no means a simple task. This is a thoughtful essay, but Hu's point that the extent to which a Chinese version succeeds 'must be left for the judgment of the Chinese reader' (p. 148) highlights the essay's main fault: unless the reader is proficient in Chinese (and, alas, this reviewer is not) she must trust Hu's analysis of examples given.

D. Allen Carroll, 'Thomas Watson and the 1588 MS Commendation of *The Faerie Queene*: Reading the Rebuses' (*SSt* 16[2002] 105–23), elaborates upon the case made by Joseph Black for Thomas Watson being author of an anonymous manuscript poem about *The Faerie Queene* dated 1588. Black's essay, '"Pan is hee": Commending *The Faerie Queene*' (*SSt* 15[2001]; see *YWES* 82[2003] 242), cited various reasons for Watson as a candidate for authorship but, claims Carroll, was 'overly cautious' in one particular respect (p. 106). Carroll here expands upon evidence for his idea, mentioned by Black, that the sketches at the head and foot of the poem 'reveal obliquely and playfully who was responsible for the text' (p. 106) by detailing how the sketches provide three rebuses on the name 'Thomas Watson' and two on the title of his major work *Hekatompathia* [1582].

Although the main books of *The Faerie Queene* dominated this year's contributions to the study of Spenser, the Mutabilitie Cantos also featured and, again, Spenser's sources were a focus. Angus Fletcher, 'Marvelous Progression: The Paradoxical Defense of Women in Spenser's Mutabilitie Cantos' (*MP* 100:i[2002] 5–23), claims that Spenser 'was particularly interested in the philosophical potential of poetry' and the Mutabilitie Cantos 'represent the culmination of this interest, exploiting the deep connection between wonder and philosophical affirmation to lead the reader through a sequence of thought that results in a moment of marvelous resolution'. Recently critics have tended to situation the Cantos within the tradition of jurisprudence, but Fletcher argues persuasively that they are modelled on the ironic defence of women, a rhetorical tradition of misogyny often used to instruct young lawyers. Such defences grew out of a popular tradition of misogyny, and Fletcher traces parallels between Spenser's Cantos and a ballad attributed to Chaucer, printed in Stow's 1561 edition of his works, although Spenser's poem is derived not only from one source but from 'a set of expectations developed by a large body of similar works' (p. 10). Fletcher disagrees with Elizabeth Fowler's claim that a major literary precedent of Spenser's Cantos is Chaucer's *Parlement of Foules*, but does agree that Spenser's decision to model them on the form of an ironic defence is innovative, and that by doing this 'Spenser develops a novel, pedagogic function for the marvelous within poetry' (p. 15). Spenser, like other English poets of his time, was influenced by the theories of poetry developed in sixteenth-century Italy, where the marvellous was particularly associated with two things, novelty (the contradiction of expectation) and suspension (rhetorical and physiological). The first published commentary on *The Faerie Queene*, Kenelm Digby's *Observations* [1644], is like the Mutabilitie Cantos in that both 'perform in practice what the theoretical framework of Sidney's *Apologie* argues is impossible, demonstrating a method of reading poetry that contains the progressions and affirmations typically associated with philosophy' (p. 23), although, crucially, Spenser does not equate philosophy and poetry but rather subordinates the former to poetic ends.

In a short but valuable note, Kathryn Walls, 'Divine Resorts: Arlo Hill and Mount Thabor in Spenser's Mutabilitie Cantos' (*ELN* 40:ii[2002] 1–3), claims that Spenser's description of Mount Arlo in canto vi of the Mutabilitie Cantos 'anticipates and reinforces' (p. 3) his allusion to the transfiguration of Christ on Mount Thabor when describing the Goddess Nature in canto vii of the same. Although critics have commented on Spenser's reference to Christ's transfiguration, none before Walls has focused on the setting for this event. Walls claims that Spenser was probably informed by Stephen Batman's 1582 modernization of John Trevisa's late fourteenth-century English translation of *De Proprietatibus Rerum*, Bartholomaeus Anglicus's medieval encyclopedia, which describes Mount Thabor's natural perfection. Tracing parallels between Batman's translation and Spenser's description of Arlo Hill before it was cursed by Diana, Walls concludes that Arlo Hill 'is cast in the image of Mount Thabor' (p. 2), both being holy and fertile islands honoured by the presence of gods and goddesses, especially the Goddess Nature. Unfortunately Walls makes the mistake of referring to Book VI, canto vi when describing Arlo Hill rather than the correct Book VII, canto vi, a minor error in an otherwise fine piece.

The *Shepheardes Calender* also featured in a number of this year's contributions. In an original and thoughtful piece, 'The Politics of Time in Edmund Spenser's English Calendar' (*SEL* 42:i[2002] 1–24), Alison A. Chapman notes that, despite its title, critics have paid little attention to the calendrical structure of Spenser's first major work. Rather than recognizing *The Shepheardes Calender* as a 'highly politicized reorganization of annual time published during an era obsessed with time and forms of time reckoning' (p. 1), critics have read it as natural and conventional, despite the fact that 'no precedent exists in pastoral poetry for his text's monthly arrangement' (p. 2). Chapman points out that for early moderns the calendar, far from being 'natural', was 'the site of fierce debate as different ideological and political interests vied for control over its timetable' (p. 2). The calendar was contested in two ways: by Pope Gregory's desire to eliminate ten days from it in order that it should conform to celestial motions, and by the contemporary refashioning of the liturgical calendar to limit the number of holy days. Spenser's poem was written during the period of debate about Gregorian reform which involved his two employers, Bishop Young and Robert Dudley, earl of Leicester. The main aim of E.K.'s discussion of the calendar is to defend January rather than March as first month of year, but 'he derives the text's privileging of January from native English practice instead of from papal mandate' (p. 9): in Spenser's Anglicized calendar, 'English shepherds follow temporal rhythms sanctioned by local customs and speak in the tongue of their native vernacular' and the text is given 'a specifically English geography' by reference to English places (p. 10). Chapman contends that the centrality also of England's queen as shepherd/monarch constitutes implicit counselling of Elizabeth by Spenser to protect English Protestants against Catholic doctrine and the pope's calendar reform. Chapman also argues for the influence of Foxe's *Actes and Monuments* [1563], already recognized as source for *The Faerie Queene*, on *The Shepheardes Calender*. Although for most early modern reformers calendar reform meant removing Catholic saints, some, including Foxe, 'replaced the traditional canon with new Protestant names', both the well known and those 'of lesser renown', and a similar process can be seen in Spenser's text, which 'is filled with the names of English shepherds ... prominent figures of the Reformation' such as Archbishop Edmund Grindal and Queen Elizabeth, as well as 'humble, unknown shepherds—such as Thomalin and Willye of the "March" eclogue' (p. 13). The choice of April for the queen's month distances her from feasts of the Virgin Mary, and that April was also the month of St George suggests 'Elizabeth as the nation's new patron saint' (p. 16), perhaps prefiguring George's transformation in *The Faerie Queene* from Catholic saint to Protestant knight. Chapman asserts that the historical specificity of Protestant calendars 'worked to dissolve the aura of timelessness that had enveloped the medieval calendar saint' whereby the calendar instead became 'a vehicle for commentary on localized, recent events' (p. 18). As well as being a structure for organizing the year, 'calendar' also meant 'guide, directory: an example, model', and by calling his text a 'calendar' Spenser makes it 'the "guide" or "example" for English poetry' (p. 19) which became the poetic standard for subsequent generations of writers. Moreover, Spenser inserts himself in calendar as Colin Clout, which 'suggests that the sheer skill of the new Protestant poet renders him as "canonical" as even the new Protestant martyr or the immemorial Catholic saint' (p. 19).

In 'Diggon Davie and Davy Dicar: Edmund Spenser, Thomas Churchyard, and the Poetics of Public Protest' (*SSt* 16[2002] 151–65) Scott Lucas presents an analysis of the relationship between Thomas Churchyard's poem 'Davy Dycars Dreame' and the September eclogue of Spenser's *Shepheardes Calender*. Churchyard's poem can be read as an attack on the counsellors of Edward VI, and it was read as such by Thomas Camell, who publicly denounced it in his poetic response, 'To Davy Dycars Dreame'. Churchyard, who did not want to retract the point made in his poem but did not want to suffer as a result of its dangerous message, answered Camell by drawing attention to 'those attributes of its rhetorical structure' (p. 154) that protected him. As Lucas points out in this lucid and thoughtful essay, Spenser's September eclogue contributes to the debate: Diggon Davie is similar to Thomas Churchyard himself, and Spenser protects himself by casting his protest in a literary form and providing comments from the poem's 'readers', Hobinoll and E.K., who distance the author from his creation. Lucas emphasizes the contribution made by Spenser to the genre of protest verse by his 'bringing together, improving upon, and displaying in concise form the scattered commentary and rhetorical structures of the Davy Dicar poems' (p. 161) in an eclogue which exemplifies the protective strategies available to poets. Lucas also usefully reprints a copy of Churchyard's poem as an appendix.

Lee Piepho, '*The Shepheardes Calender* and Neo-Latin Pastoral: A Book Newly Discovered to have been Owned By Spenser' (*SSt* 16[2002] 77–103), surveys a volume (now two volumes) of Continental Latin poetry held in the Folger Shakespeare Library which contains copies of Latin works by the German humanist poets Georgius Sabinus and Petrus Lotichius Secundus. A nineteenth-century note on the flyleaf claims that the volume in which the two texts were originally bound belonged to either Spenser or Gabriel Harvey, and in 1980 Peter Beal discovered that the volume contained 'the only extent autograph manuscript of a literary text made by Spenser, copies of a letter and two poems on a blank leaf between the two texts' (p. 78). Yet Beal questioned Spenser's ownership of the volume, claiming that the relevant pages were inserted at a later stage, an assertion denied by Piepho, who cites as evidence for Spenser's ownership the collation of the Sabinus collection and the choice of texts copied out. According to Piepho, Beal is wrong about the later insertion since the leaf containing the transcriptions 'is the concluding blank leaf of the first of the two bound texts' (p. 79). He admits that the case for ownership of Lotichius 'is less certain', but considers it unlikely that Spenser would have bothered copying out a letter and an epigram related to Lotichius if he had no interest in the poet. Piepho believes that the volume belonged to Spenser and, moreover, is relevant to the literary context underlying *The Shepheardes Calender*. He gives a useful account of the collections: one of Sabinus's eclogues, an allegory involving animals, 'is much more straightforward than Spenser's beast fables', and Lotichius's 'more ambitious and interesting work' is an eclogue about hunters not shepherds, making it part of a 'comparatively rare' genre (p. 81). Most significantly, however, Piepho thinks that the epithalamions written by Sabinus and Lotichius may have influenced Spenser's adaptations of the genre in the April eclogue of his pastoral poem. That neither German poet wrote ecclesiastical satire, a form used by Spenser in his poem, shows that English writers, unlike their German counterparts, 'linked discussion of church reform with the language of pastoral literature' (p. 85). Piepho's essay includes a lengthy appendix which provides a complete list of contents for the two collections, although an English translation of the Latin would have proved useful, as would a translation of the extract from Lotichius's second eclogue reproduced on page 82.

Recent studies which acknowledge Spenser's equivocal attitude to Ireland form the context for Christopher Warley's worthy consideration of Spenser's conflicted and contradictory ideas about social distinction in his sonnets, '"So plenty makes me poore": Ireland, Capitalism, and Class in Spenser's *Amoretti* and *Epithalamion*' (*ELH* 69[2002] 567–98). Warley's main point is that Spenser, like the speaker in these poems, 'tries to create his own social authority by mimicking an idealized conception of nobles, especially nobles in Ireland' (p. 567). Like other sonnet sequences of the period, Spenser's poems seek to reinforce royal authority but, citing Louis Montrose, Warley suggests that Spenser's position in Ireland offered an 'alternative center' which implicitly challenged the centrality of the court (p. 568). In the *Amoretti* and *Epithalamion* the speaker imagines himself 'as a noble lord controlling a virtually feudal estate, and the primary vehicle used for this fantasy is his attempt to control his female poetic object' (p. 569). Crucially, Warley detects an inherent contradiction related to Spenser's life in Ireland: although Ireland was represented as uncivil, it was a place where the New English could live out 'an ideal of feudal land possession and social distinction' (p. 571). Spenser's political connections allowed him to participate in the Munster plantation, a government enterprise aimed at the social elite, and the speaker of the poems is keen to distinguish himself from the wealth of merchants, claiming social superiority and ascribing nascent capitalism to them. Spenser's Munster estate represented his upward mobility but also, contradictorily, 'the limits placed on that mobility by its basis in emergent capitalist land relations' (p. 573). Unlike the merchants who deal in mutable, material things, the speaker's lady is constant, and possession of her marks his social distinction. Warley draws a parallel between the speaker's desire for a constant lady and the Old English, who possessed their estates 'free from the vicissitudes of exchange and from the new, civilized English mode of agricultural production' (p. 581), although, contradictorily, the New English seek to destroy this. Warley detects similar tensions within sonnet 75 which reflect Spenser's social position: he longs for the feudal life enjoyed by the Old English but at the same time seeks to eliminate it. Warley argues that, rather than resolving the historical paradox of the *Amoretti*, as many critics have argued, the *Epithalamion* rearticulates it. In the latter sequence Spenser's preoccupation with social standing is again evident, and he adopts a genre usually reserved for royalty and aristocracy. His construction of a social hierarchy in stanza 11 is not only a reaction against Elizabeth's court, and thus a celebration of his domestic domain, but a reaction against the bourgeois 'merchant daughters' and a desire 'to be like either the Old English—an English lord over an Irish estate—or like Elizabeth herself, a mini-monarch' (p. 587). The speaker defines his masculinity, nationality, and social class against these feminized merchants, but, as in sonnet 15 of the *Amoretti*, 'the blazon always threatens to expose the speaker's economic similarity to merchants' daughters' and his control of the queen 'ultimately depends upon his control of a commodity and the violation of the idealized feudal position he desires to occupy' (p. 588). The song itself becomes a commodity and 'creates the spectacle that marks the speaker's social superiority' (p. 589), but the fact that he has to write it himself marks the insecurity of his socio-economic position and masculinity.

Following in the footsteps of Don Cameron Allen, who challenged assertions by previous critics that Spenser's *Muiopotmos, Or The Fate of the Butterflie* was a less than serious work, Eric C. Brown, 'The Allegory of Small Things: Insect Eschatology in Spenser's Muiopotmos' (*SP* 99:iii[2002] 247–67), considers the poem's allegory to be as resistant to literal readings as *The Faerie Queene*. Brown contends that the poem 'joins a tradition of works in which the slightest of creatures, namely insects, represent allegorically and often anagogically the most extreme of human conditions'. Far from being a poem concerned with trivial matters, a fight between a butterfly and a spider, it considers death and the Last Judgement and presents a common Renaissance paradox: 'small things are not small at all' (p. 249). Clarion, the butterfly, represents the vulnerable Christian soul which must be ever watchful against sin, here represented by the spider, 'a type of apocalyptic beast' (p. 264). This well-researched essay is a welcome analysis of a neglected work in the context of contemporary attitudes to theology in general and eschatology in particular.

We saw that the process of translation featured in two essays on *The Faerie Queene*, and it is also the subject of A.E.B. Coldiron's study, 'How Spenser Excavates Du Bellay's *Antiquitez*: Or, the Role of the Poet, Lyric Historiography, and the English Sonnet' (*JEGP* 101:i[2002] 41–67), which considers Spenser's translation of Du Bellay's sonnets in the light of Du Bellay's condemnation of translation as inevitably inferior in his *Deffence*. Using a range of examples, Coldiron shows that Spenser does not translate Du Bellay in any straightforward manner but rather 'creates a new way of writing the lyric sequence, and a newly optimistic view of the poet's role in history' so that his translation of Du Bellay is not the 'profanation' (p. 42) identified by Du Bellay but rather an innovative and subtle reshaping of his source which is of particular appeal to an English Renaissance audience.

Drawing upon a range of contemporary writings but with a particular focus on Spenser, Barbara Fuchs, 'Spanish Lessons: Spenser and the Irish Moriscos' (*SEL* 42:i[2002] 43–62), alerts readers to the complex relationship between Spain and England—both 'imperial actors' on the world's stage (p. 43)—during hostilities between the two countries. Fuchs argues convincingly that early modern England's antagonism towards Spain 'via the widely disseminated Black Legend of Spanish Cruelty' (p. 44) has led critics to overlook the many connections between the two countries, and that 'Ireland functions as a key site for analyzing England's tortuous relationship to Spain as both model and rival' (p. 44). Fuchs traces what she refers to as the 'fascinating similarities' (p. 46) between England's desire to control Ireland and the Spanish project in Granada against the Moriscos, or little Moors. In both cases there was a distinct fear of hybridity, and they shared a myth of reconquest which downplayed their colonial objectives: the English notion that they were restoring the rule of ancient Britons over Ireland was echoed in 'the Spanish Reconquista of peninsular territory from the Moors' (p. 46). Although Spanish activities against the Moriscos could be explicitly evoked as a model for English activities in Ireland after peace with Spain, such identifications were not possible when Spain was England's enemy, but Fuchs identifies what she considers 'a highly elliptical allusion' (p. 51) to the parallels between the two countries in Spenser's *A View of the Present State of Ireland* and *The Faerie Queene*, Book V. In the former text Irenius rejects Irish claims to Spanish ancestry and aligns the Spanish with the Moors, but Fuchs notes an apparent unease, a hesitancy, and repeated qualifications which suggest that 'the English are to the Irish as the Spanish are to the Moriscos' (p. 53). Fuchs proceeds to offer two examples from Book V of Spenser's epic poem where the 'problematic identification' (p. 53) between England and Spain is evident: Artegall's defeat of that 'cursed cruell Sarazin' Pollente (V.ii.4) and Arthur's defeat of the Souldan (V.viii.40–1). In the former episode Artegall 'is fighting an islam closely identified with Spain' but Spenser's source for the episode, Ariosto's *Orlando Furioso*, makes Artegall 'akin to a Spanish knight, removing Moorish obstacles to safe passage' (p. 54). Furthermore, Pollente's fall into the Irish River Lee suggests the 'equation of England and Spain in a highly convoluted form: there is no overt identification of Moors with Irishmen, but instead an oblique suggestion that England can learn territorial control from Spain's war against the Moors' (p. 54). In the episode featuring Arthur's defeat of the Souldan, Fuchs notes that critics usually identify the Souldan as Philip II, but little attention has been given to the Souldan as Islamic. In Arthur's defeat of the Souldan he is referred to as the 'infant', and Fuchs draws attention to the Spanish context of that word which referred to 'a prince or princess of Spain or Portugal', making Arthur 'at once a British prince defeating Spain and a Spanish prince defeating Moors—a complex, and empowering, identification for an imperial England' (p. 57).

Thomas Herron, 'The Spanish Armada, Ireland, and Spenser's *The Faerie Queene*' (*NewHR* 6:ii[2002] 82–105) points out that, although the Souldan episode has long been identified as an allegory for the defeat of the Spanish Armada, the Irish context of the episode has not been emphasized. Herron here elaborates upon a point made by Raymond Jenkins in 1938: that the group of damaged ships from the defeated Armada that crashed along Ireland's northern and western coasts in 1588 'possibly inspired the lines which picture the demolition of the chariot of the Soldan' (p. 79). Although critics have acknowledged the episode's Spanish context, Herron provides evidence of its 'Irish and specifically Connaught, historical and mythical connections' (p. 95), among them the likelihood that the Souldan functions as an exaggeration of traditional Irish lords. Herron is keen to emphasize the 'hybrid Irish-Spanish threat' which the Soldan represents, and this well-researched essay makes a valuable contribution to the substantial body of critical material which acknowledges the importance of Ireland to Spenser's imaginative creations.

Staying with Spain, Frank Ardolino, 'The Effect of the Defeat of the Spanish Armada on Spenser's *Complaints*' (*SSt* 16[2002] 55–75), presents a solid case for his argument that throughout Spenser's *Complaints* run allusions to the English defeat of the Spanish Armada in 1588. Ardolino agrees with those critics who believe the *Complaints* 'can best be viewed within a specific Protestant apocalyptic context' (p. 57) and, via reference to contemporary commentators as well as to Spenser's use of imagery, notes that they form part of the visionary rhetoric which perceived the defeat of Spain, at the hands of the small and 'divinely favoured' (p. 60) nation of England, in the context of the demise of Babylon and Rome.

Pamela Coren, 'Maximal and Minimal Texts: Shakespeare v. The Globe' (*ShSurv* 52[1999] 68–87), presents a convincing revaluation of Gary Waller's claim that Mary Sidney, not Spenser, authored an untitled poem published in a collection of seven elegies in 1595. Various authors have pointed to evidence for Spenser's authorship of the poem, known as 'The Doleful Lay of Clorinda', and Coren too believes that the Lay was written by Spenser. Waller criticized those who use features of style to argue for Spenser's authorship and, claims Coren, 'attributes the Spenserian feel of the Lay to its genre, using the formula "features common to a host of Elizabethan pastoral elegies"' (p. 27). Rather than listing individual parallels, Coren compares the stanzas of the Lay to stanzas from a range of Spenser's minor poems and, displaying her findings in the form of a table, argues that the 'syntax, phrasing, and rhythm is Spenser's throughout' (p. 29). Furthermore, she believes that 'The "Spenserian" sound of the Lay is undeniable, and it is the sound of an individual voice as much as of a convention.' She considers one of Mary Sidney's poems, 'To the Angell Spirit', in detail, and cites other critics who agree that there is 'a very different poet here' from the one who wrote the Lay (p. 30). For the Lay to have been authored by Sidney would have involved her parodying Spenser, which is most unlikely, as is imitation in a poem which is an elegy to her brother. Coren disputes Waller's claim that Sidney requested the return of the Lay from Sir Edward Wotton so it could be passed to Spenser for publication, since the poem requested could just as easily have been another, and she also questions Waller's assertion that the printer's layout of the volume proves his attribution, since space inserted by the printer throughout seems fairly random and of little significance, not an indication of her authorship. Social decorum would make it unlikely for Sidney to offer her poem for commercial publication, and it forms part of a tradition of 'inscribing lament in the female voice' (p. 37) seen elsewhere in Spenser's writing, for example in *The Faerie Queene*.

Of significant interest this year was a group of articles focusing on Spenser's representation of the sacraments. Margaret Christian, 'Spenser's Theology: The Sacraments in *The Faerie Queene*' (*Reformation* 6[2002] 103–7), provides a useful introduction and overview of these pieces which, she informs us, 'emerged from a round table discussion at the 1998 Sixteenth Century Studies Conference in Toronto'. In the first essay, 'Sacramental Parody in *The Faerie Queene*' (*Reformation* 6[2002]109–14), John N. King considers a range of allusions to the mass in *The Faerie Queene*, especially Book I, and argues that Spenser's approach to the sacraments was essentially Calvinistic. In keeping with Protestant theology, Spenser allegorizes only two of the seven sacraments, and his poem reveals 'hard opposition to the ritual, worship and sacerdotalism of the Church of Rome' (p. 111) via parody of the mass. James Schiavoni, 'Sacrament and Structure in *The Faerie Queene*' (*Reformation* 6[2002] 115–18), focuses on Books I and II of Spenser's epic poem and suggests that his approach to the sacraments is Augustinian. According to Schiavoni, the images and structures of these two books 'reflect two distinctions in Augustinian thought' which influenced the most theological parts of *The Faerie Queene*: that 'between sacramental efficacy and predestination' and that 'between spiritual guild and concupiscence' (p. 118). For H.L. Weatherby, 'Spenser and the Sacraments' (*Reformation* 6[2002] 119–23), *The Faerie Queene* indicates that Spenser is anti-Roman but holds an essentially a Catholic view of baptism, marriage, and the eucharist. Focusing on Redcrosse, the Knight of Holiness in *The Faerie Queene*, and the presentation of the marriage service in the *Epithalamion*, Weatherby argues that, although Spenser should not be thought of as a 'Church papist' or crypto-Catholic, neither was he 'consistently Protestant in his every address to religious matters' (p. 122).

Carol V. Kaske's essay, 'The Eucharistic Cup: Romanist, Establishment and Communitarian' (*Reformation* 6[2002] 125–32), makes important links between Duessa's golden cup in Book I of *The Faerie Queene* and that administered by the good Cambina in Book IV. According to Kaske, Spenser encourages his readers to condemn Duessa's magic cup, which represents transubstantiation, and to praise the good cup of Cambina, which symbolizes the eucharist. Following upon C.S. Lewis's admonition that we should not be surprised to find Catholic elements in the Protestant allegory of *The Faerie Queene*, Clinton Allen Brand, 'Sacramental Initiation and Residual Catholicism in the Legend of Holiness' (*Reformation* 6[2002] 133–44) considers Spenser's representation of the sacraments in the last three cantos of Book I. Brand detects in these cantos a residual Catholicism, and argues that Spenser's anti-Romanism was not incompatible with 'nostalgia for elements of the "old religion" and his longing for the beauty, coherence and efficacy of sacramental presence' (p. 144). Kenneth Borris, 'The Sacraments in *The Faerie Queene*' (*Reformation* 6[2002] 145–54), considers sacramental symbolism in a range of episodes from *The Faerie Queene* and is particularly interested in the representation of the sacraments of baptism and the eucharist. For Borris the poem features 'a composite heroism' (p. 145) since patron knights and other good characters express aspects of Arthurian and Christian virtue. Darryl Gless's essay, 'Acts of Construction: The Sacraments and Spenser' (*Reformation* 6[2002] 155–61), sounds a note of caution by warning readers to be alert to the complexity of the Protestant doctrine with which Spenser was familiar before coming to confident conclusions about the doctrinal position of *The Faerie Queene* or its author. Gless notes that the contemporary concept of holiness was complex and that 'Spenser's use of sacramental ideas and images contributes in numerous deft, specific, yet elusive ways to a rich poetic exploration of an especially capacious virtue' (p. 161). Lastly, Anne Lake Prescott's 'Why Arguments Over Communion Matter to Allegory; or, Why Are Catholics like Orgoglio' (*Reformation* 6[2002] 163–78), considers Spenser's *Faerie Queene* in the light of contemporary debates about the sacraments and finds in both a focus on the nature of signs, space, bodies, and time, each of which is discussed in a separate section. Prescott notes that the cannibalistic giant Orgoglio in Book I of Spenser's poem 'recalls the giants of anti-Catholic polemic' (p. 166) who can be aligned with the god-eating papists of Catholic doctrine. Prescott also provides a useful appendix containing the views of Theodore Beza, who 'insists that Catholics ignorantly collapse sign and signifier into each other' (p. 163), a view shared by, among others, Thomas Cranmer.

Three important books on Spenser were published this year. The focus of Judith Owens's monograph *Enabling Engagements: Edmund Spenser and the Poetics of Patronage* is Spenser's negotiation with the process of patronage and the court. Owens's point is that Spenser actively resisted the pull of the court, and her study of the political dynamics of royal entertainments and the treatises of Richard Mulcaster in the introductory chapter provides an original context from which to explore Spenser's attitude to authority and agency. Chapter 2 provides a detailed reading of *The Shepheardes Calender* and proposes that in this first important work Spenser is concerned 'to preserve poetic and moral autonomy', his 'anti-courtly poetics' emphasizing 'selfhood, private experience, romantic love' in an effort to challenge 'the pressures in patronage designed to mould the court-centred, laureate poet' (p. 40). It is in his connection with the patrons E.K. and Hobbinol that Spenser's resistance to laureateship, via Colin, emerges most fully, and their conceptions of the poet, claims Owens, are opposed from the January eclogue onwards. In chapter 3 Owens rightly notes that the commendatory verses appended to the first instalment of *The Faerie Queene* have hitherto received little attention from the critics, and she presents an analysis of Spenser's inauguration as national poet in relation to contexts which lie beyond the confines of the court: London's commercial and market forces as well as Ireland. Spenser's Irish tenure is also brought into focus in chapter 4, which considers the Irish context of the 1590 dedicatory sonnets and notes that, far from being merely complimentary, they engage with issues of political moment, for example criticism of Ralegh's Petrarchan politics and poetics which are aligned to the court and which Spenser considers inadequate for Ireland's reformation. Ralegh also figures in chapter 5, which again considers the limitation of his Petrarchan poetics in the context of Ireland, this time via the figure of Timias in Book III of *The Faerie Queene*. This is an insightful and engaging work which adds to our understanding of the tension between patronage and authorial autonomy and Spenser's troubled relationship with the court.

Bart Van Es's fine monograph, *Spenser's Forms of History*, which grew out of his doctoral research, reads Spenser's poetical and prose works alongside a wide range of historical and quasi-historical sources: the chronicle, chorography, antiquarianism, euhemerism, analogy, and prophecy. Although Spenser has long been recognized as the 'poet historical' he termed himself, Van Es is keen to point out that there is more to him than *The Faerie Queene*'s providential patterns in history which is the usual focus for critics. Van Es's introduction acknowledges how recent scholarship has expanded our ways of reading Spenser via history, and promises to build upon this in an original way by widening the domain of history, making reference to texts by Spenser not usually considered in this context, and by focusing on 'form' or genre: for Van Es the word 'form', like the word 'historical', is neither specifically Elizabethan nor modern but something between the two, and it is the nebulous quality of the concept which informs his approach. Chapter 1 concentrates on the chronicles and the tensions inherent in Spenser's use of the term 'monument' in his translations of Du Bellay, his own *Ruines of Time*, and the 'monuments' that occur in Arthur's chronicle from Book II of *The Faerie Queene*. Chapter 2 builds upon these tensions and is alert to the multi-vocality of the chorographic texts echoed by Spenser in Books III and IV of *The Faerie Queene*, *Colin Clouts Come Home Againe*, and *Prothalamion*. In a welcome reading of Spenser's neglected river-marriage canto in Book IV of *The Faerie Queene* Van Es highlights Spenser's ability to make use of ancient history in his take on contemporary colonial projects. Chapter 3 asserts that the classification 'antiquarian tract' has more validity than is usually acknowledged by critics, and reads James Ware's 1633 edition of Spenser's *View* in the context of the Elizabethan College of Antiquaries, drawing useful parallels between the political significance of both, as well as considering Spenser's Mutabilitie Cantos as a way of interrogating the influence of the past upon present monarchical power. Chapter 4 deals with euhemerism, a method used by Elizabethan historiographers which found moral and historical truth in pagan myths which they defined as allegories; Spenser's ambiguous position as a 'poet historical' is explored via several episodes from his epic poem with a particular focus on the figure of the giant. Chapter 5 concentrates on Spenser's debt to historical analogy, the comparison between contemporary figures and historical personages, which could operate as praise or criticism, typified in the mirror created for Elizabeth in *The Faerie Queene*. The final chapter looks at the practice of political prophecy and shows how existing histories which served the interests of Elizabeth might be manipulated in order to produce subversive manuscript prophecies at sensitive political moments. Here Van Es demonstrates the influence of astrological prophecy on *The Shepheardes Calender*, the *Letters* between Spenser and Harvey, and the prophecy delivered to Britomart in Books III and V of *The Faerie Queene*, concluding that prophecy is a particularly dangerous form of historical narrative. On the whole this book represents a useful corrective to our rather narrow conception of history and succeeds in being alert to the instability of genre while presenting cogent and sensitive readings of a wide range of Spenser's writings.

Richard McCabe's study *Spenser's Monstrous Regiment: Elizabethan Ireland and the Poetics of Difference*, explores Spenser's career and writings in the context of Irish as well as English voices. As McCabe points out in his introduction, there have been many studies on Spenser and Ireland but 'Gaelic Ireland has been all but ignored' and studies have been 'rigidly anglophone despite their avowed hostility to anglocentrism' (p. 2). McCabe's decision to include Gaelic literature, especially bardic poetry, in his analysis of Spenser is a welcome addition to the critical focus Ireland has brought to Spenser studies, but it might be argued that an important reason for the previous exclusion of texts written in Gaelic has been a pragmatic one: it is unlikely that academics specializing in English Renaissance literature will also be proficient in Gaelic, and indeed McCabe makes use of translations throughout which, it might also be noted, are unlikely to be held in most university libraries outside Ireland. Nevertheless he is right to indicate the irony of an interest in Spenser's Irish context which all but ignores the Irish language and literature around him, and so this study makes an important contribution to the field. The book is divided into six parts, each containing two or three chapters, and although some section headings and chapter titles make the contents of each fairly clear ('*The Faerie Queene* 1590', 'The Response to *A View*'), others are more esoteric ('Arms and the Woman', 'Salvagesse sans finesse'). Another criticism is that McCabe includes a list of primary sources at the back of the book, with critical sources cited in footnotes; this reviewer would have preferred one or other style to be used. On the whole, though, McCabe's persuasive readings of Spenser's poetry and prose in a Gaelic context are written with a historian's sensitivity to Spenser's milieu, and reading the landscape of Ireland and its Celtic voices against Spenser's unease about Elizabeth's rule works well.

Books Reviewed

Alford, Stephen. *The Early Elizabethan* Polity: *William Cecil and the British Succession Crisis, 1558–1569*. CUP. [1998] pp. xii + 271. hb £47.50 ISBN 0 5216 2218 2, pb £18.99 ISBN 0 5218 9285 6.

Alford, Stephen. *Kingship and Politics in the Reign of Edward VI*. CUP. [2002] pp. xiii + 233. £40 ISBN 0 5216 6055 6.

Lake, Peter, with Michael Questier. *The Antichrist's Lewd Hat: Protestant, Papists and Players in Post-Reformation England*. YaleUP. [2002] pp. xxxiv + 731. $50 ISBN 0 3000 8884 1.

Lancashire, Anne. *London Civic Theatre: City Drama and Pageantry from Roman Times to 1558*. CUP. [2002] pp. xix + 355. £50 ISBN 0 5216 3278 1.

Lyne, Raphael. *Ovid's Changing Worlds: English Metamorphoses, 1567–1632*. OUP. [2001] pp. 303. £40 ISBN 0 1981 8704 1.

Marshall, Peter, and Alec Ryrie, eds. *The Beginnings of English Protestantism*. CUP. [2002] pp. xi + 242. hb £40 ISBN 0 5218 0274 1, pb £14.99 ISBN 0 5210 0324 5.

McCabe, Richard. *Spenser's Monstrous Regiment: Elizabethan Ireland and the Poetics of Difference*. OUP. [2002] pp. 220. £45 ISBN 0 1981 8734 3.

McRae, Andrew. *God Speed the Plough: The Representation of Agrarian England, 1500–1660*. CUP. [1996] pp. xv + 335. hb £55 ISBN 0 5214 5379 8, pb £29.99 ISBN 0 5215 2466 0.

Owens, Judith. *Enabling Engagements: Edmund Spenser and the Poetics of Patronage*. McG-QUP. [2002] pp. 192. $65 ISBN 0 7735 2331 6.

Sanford, Rhonda Lemke. *Maps and Memory in Early Modern England: A Sense of Place*. Palgrave. [2002] pp. xiv + 225. £35 ISBN 0 3122 9455 7.

Scott-Warren, Jason. *Sir John Harington and the Book as Gift*. OUP. [2001] pp. 273. £45 ISBN 0 1992 4445 6.

Spiller, Michael. *Early Modern Sonneteers: From Wyatt to Milton*. Northcote in association with the British Council. [2001] pp. xv + 112. pb £9.99 ISBN 0 7463 0936 8.

Traub, Valerie. *The Renaissance of Lesbianism in Early Modern England*. CUP. [2002] pp. xvi + 492. hb £65 ISBN 0 5214 4427 6, pb £22.99 ISBN 0 5214 4885 9.

Twycross, Meg, and Sarah Carpenter. *Masks and Masking in Medieval and Early Tudor England*. Ashgate. [2002] pp. x + 428. £47.50 ISBN 0 7546 0230 3.

Van Es, Bart. *Spenser's Forms of History*. OUP. [2002] pp. 242. £40 ISBN 0 1992 4970 9.

Wabuda, Susan. *Preaching During the English Reformation*. CUP. [2002] pp. ix + 203. £40 ISBN 0 5214 5395 X.

VI

Shakespeare

GABRIEL EGAN, PETER J. SMITH, LUCY MUNRO, DONALD
WATSON, JAMES PURKIS, ANNALIESE CONNOLLY, ANDREW
HISCOCK, STEPHEN LONGSTAFFE, JON ORTEN AND CLARE
MCMANUS

This chapter has four sections: 1. Editions and Textual Matters; 2. Shakespeare in
the Theatre; 3. Shakespeare on Screen; 4. Criticism. Section 1 is by Gabriel Egan;
section 2 is by Peter J. Smith; section 3 is by Lucy Munro; section 4(a) is by Donald
Watson, section 4(b) is by James Purkis, section 4(c) is by Annaliese Connolly,
section 4(d) is by Andrew Hiscock, section 4(e) is by Stephen Longstaffe, section
4(f) is by Jon Orten, and section 4(g) is by Clare McManus.

1. Editions and Textual Matters

First, a correction. In last year's review, the introduction to John D. Cox and Eric
Rasmussen's Arden Shakespeare *3 Henry VI* was criticized for offering the example
of Q1 *King Lear* as a 'bad' quarto that had, since the heyday of new bibliography,
been rehabilitated (p. 164); this reviewer complained that no one had ever made the
claim that it was a 'bad' quarto (p. 265). In fact, Leo Kirschbaum claimed it as a
'bad' quarto in 1938 ('A Census of Bad Quartos', *RES* 14[1938] 20–43), and W.W.
Greg concurred in 1942 (*The Editorial Problem in Shakespeare: A Survey of the
Foundations of the Text*, pp. 49–101). The claim has resurfaced occasionally since
then, as I should have known.

Books outweighed journal articles this year: five major scholarly editions
appeared, and Brian Vickers published two door-stopper monographs on
Shakespeare, Co-author: A Historical Study of Five Collaborative Plays and
*'Counterfeiting' Shakespeare: Evidence, Authorship, and John Ford's 'Funerall
Elegye'*. For the Oxford Shakespeare, Colin Burrow edited *The Complete Sonnets
and Poems*, Charles Whitworth edited *The Comedy of Errors*, and Roger Warren
edited *King Henry VI Part 2*. For the Arden Shakespeare, Charles Forker edited
King Richard II and David Scott Kastan edited *King Henry IV Part 1*. Burrow's is a
huge book and the hardbound review copy was not well printed, using cheaper paper
than is normal for this series and showing the kind of horizontal discontinuities

produced by a worn-out office inkjet printer. Happily, a copy consulted in the Shakespeare Institute library had neither of these flaws, although it did have a number of pages of either poor registration or cavalier cropping that reduced either the top or bottom margin to almost nothing. At 158 pages Burrow's introduction is longer than usual for the series, but then it has much more to cover than a single play edition would. The edition includes poems that Burrow thinks are probably not by Shakespeare but which his early readers thought were his, and Burrow describes the 'chief aim' of the edition as being to ask 'What sort of poet was Shakespeare?' (p. 1). This strikes an odd note as a *raison d'être*, since editors usually think of that question as secondary to a chief aim of presenting the works to modern readers.

By putting the narrative poems in the same covers as the sonnets, Burrow hopes to encourage readers to think of them together as an oeuvre and he suspects that Heminges and Condell left them out of the 1623 Folio because they were men of the theatre and because the poems were selling well in their own right. Perpetuating this split in the canon, eighteenth-century editions of the complete works tended to make the poems an add-on in the last volume of a series. In the poems taken as an oeuvre Burrow sees a thematic connection, for they 'repeatedly meditate on the perverse effects and consequences of sexual desire, on sacrifice and self-sacrifice, on the ways in which a relationship of sexual passion might objectify or enslave both the desirer and the desired, and they repeatedly complicate simple binary distinctions between male and female' (p. 5). Moreover, they not only show another side to the theatrical Shakespeare with which we are familiar, but in fact show 'the foundational thought which underpins his dramatic works'.

Burrow's introduction is divided into a section for each major poetic work, starting with *Venus and Adonis* and proceeding chronologically. Richard Field was an obvious choice as printer of *Venus and Adonis* for he specialized in high-quality reproduction of poetical works and what we would call literary theory. Q1 of 1593 is the only substantive printing—all others are derivative—and paradoxically, the success of the poem made it peripheral to the canon, as it was too popular in its own right to be included in the Folio (p. 7). Burrow interprets the flood of Stationers' Register entries of plays in 1594 as the players 'attempting to use print to realize their assets' during plague closure (p. 9) without responding to Peter W.M. Blayney's now often-quoted objection that the flood comes a little too late for that and must in fact be part of an advertising campaign to announce the reopening of the theatres after the plague subsided ('The Publication of Playbooks', in John D. Cox and David Scott Kastan, eds., *A New History of Early English Drama* [1997]). Burrow surveys the dedication and concludes that Shakespeare ceased to have anything to do with Southampton in 1594, who was not the W.H. of the sonnets' dedication (pp. 10–15); one minor slip here is that Alan Bray's name is misspelled Allan Bray (p. 14 n. 2). Burrow sees *Venus and Adonis* as part of a new tradition of stand-alone erotic poems made from tales in Ovid's *Metamorphoses* and gives a highly intelligent literary-critical reading of it (pp. 20–40). *Lucrece* was also printed by Richard Field, but not for himself but for John Harrison, and like *Venus and Adonis* it was dedicated to Southampton. Burrow reports of the 1594 quarto that 'There are two different states of several gatherings of Q1, one unrevised (Qa) and the other which contains a number of "press variants" (Qb)' (p. 42), but presumably he means different states of several formes (individual sides of a sheet, not the whole sheet) since, as R.B. McKerrow long ago pointed out (*The Devil's Charter*, pp. xiii–

xviii), the forme was the unit of press-correction. If it so happens that both sides of a sheet show the same state of press correction (either unrevised or revised), as Burrow seems to imply by writing about 'different states of several gatherings' and that the Bodleian and Yale copies 'retain earlier readings in sigs. B, I, and K; other copies contain early readings in sigs. I and/or K' (p. 42 n. 3), Burrow ought to explain how he thinks such an unlikelihood occurred. It would seem to require that, after the first forme was wrought off, the sheets containing the revised state of that forme were kept separate from the rest in order that they might be perfected using only the revised state of the forme printed on the other side. Burrow lists the lines affected by press correction (24, 31, 50, 125, 126, 1182, 1335, 1350) and, importantly, concludes that some might have been made with reference to authorial copy.

Burrow notes that the Argument differs from the poem itself in details of the story, and focuses on the republican outcome, while the poem ends with the personal: 'Tarquin's everlasting banishment'. Of course, that distinction is partly created by the editing, for no possessive apostrophe appears in the quarto's last line ('Tarqvins'), and one could argue, as Katherine Duncan-Jones did in an article reviewed here last year ('Ravished and Revised: The 1616 *Lucrece*', *RES* 52[2001] 516–23), that editors should end the poem with 'Tarquins' everlasting banishment' on the evidence of the Argument itself. For Burrow, however, the differences between the Argument and the poem derive from Shakespeare's interest in the multiple perspectives one can take on a single story, encompassing the personal and the social (pp. 48–50). Burrow's literary criticism of *Lucrece* is excellent throughout and draws on the important scholarship of Heather Dubrow and Nancy Vickers, and he documents well the Elizabethan laws and prejudices about rape—a personal violation, and separately an attack on another man's property—and the extraordinary fact that conception 'proved' consent; thus a victim's suicide could be a way to forestall others concluding from conception that she had consented (pp. 66–8).

Burrow sees *The Passionate Pilgrim* [1599] as William Jaggard's attempt to persuade the buying public that he had 'hitherto hidden works of Shakespeare the poet' (p. 5), and outlines four possible ways that a couple of Shakespeare's sonnets (nos. 138 and 144) got into this collection of twenty poems that Burrow reproduces in its entirety (pp. 76–7). We should not, Burrow thinks, simply take Thomas Heywood's word for it (in *Apology for Actors* [1612]) that Shakespeare was angry at William Jaggard over *The Passionate Pilgrim*, for this could be just exaggeration motivated by Heywood's ongoing battle with Jaggard over *Troia Britannica* (pp. 78–9). Burrow surveys the other poems in *The Passionate Pilgrim* and concludes on purely artistic and stylistic grounds that none of them is by Shakespeare. Maintaining the characteristic Oxford tradition, Burrow rejects the familiar name of the poem *The Phoenix and Turtle* as something not used until 1807 and instead adopts its first line ('Let the bird of loudest lay') as its title (pp. 82–90). The poem appears as fifth in a group of fourteen poems by Marston, Chapman, Jonson, and an unknown man, all appended to 'a long, digressive narrative poem called *Love's Martyr* by an obscure poet called Robert Chester' printed in 1601 by Richard Field; the group of fourteen appeared with its own title page within the book. Burrow's literary criticism of 'Let the bird' finds that it is dark and elusive and that no one can fathom it. In an uncharacteristic slip, Burrow here refers to the 'prologue to Act 5 of *Henry V*' (p. 88) when of course he means the chorus.

The largest section of Burrow's introduction is, naturally, given to the sonnets (pp. 91–132). To contextualize the publishing history, Burrow claims that for early modern readers 'authorial ownership of intellectual property was an emergent concept (if that)' and that 'Copy in this period belonged to the printer who entered it as his or hers in the Stationers' Register' (p. 96). As we shall see, Brian Vickers has challenged this claim about the emergent concept of intellectual property (forever emergent, yet never said to have actually emerged), and certainly the claim about 'copy' is contestable. If one means by 'copy' the physical document embodying a work to be printed, that could of course belong to anyone. If one means, however, 'these words in this order' then, as we shall see, Vickers has strong arguments to show that this always attached to authors. However, if one means 'the *right* to print these words in this order' (or indeed, any other words that come close to the same meaning or story) then, yes, Stationers' Register entry was a way to prove priority in connection with the Stationers' Company's 'first come first served' regulations. Burrow thinks that we should read the cryptic dedication of the sonnets in the light of contemporary poetic play with anonymity and address: 'Poems do not target their addressees with exact precision in this period. They were addressed to the person who found themselves addressed by them' (pp. 101–2).

Burrow gives a useful survey of stylometric analysis of sonnets, especially MacDonald P. Jackson's work on early/late rare word occurrence (pp. 103–6). From the differences between numbers 138 and 144 as they appear in *The Passionate Pilgrim* and as they appear in the sonnets, Burrow concluded that, like other sonneteers, Shakespeare revised his poems, and Burrow chooses to print a manuscript version of sonnet 2 as well as the quarto version, just in case the former represents an early authorial version, although he does not really think it does (pp. 106–7). Burrow is particularly animated by names, observing that the so-called 'young man' of the sonnets is never called that in them (p. 123) and that nor is the Dark Lady. The latter is only called that 'by the prurient in order to make her sound both sexy and upper-crust, and (within careful racially determined limits) exotic' (p. 131). This seems a bit harsh: until not long ago polite children were told to address any woman they did not know as 'lady'. Regarding sexual orientation, Burrow offers the standard post-Foucauldian line ('no one in the period would have sought to define their identity by their sexual activity', p. 125), supported by citations of Alan Bray and Bruce Smith, but since one of his themes in his introduction is the multiplicity of readings they stimulate Burrow might have mentioned the increasingly popular counter-view that we have all been misled by Foucault on this point. (Another small slip in connection with this: Jonathan Goldberg's book is called *Queering the Renaissance* not *Queering the English Renaissance*, p. 126 n. 2.)

Burrow thinks that *A Lover's Complaint* rightly occupies its place after the sonnets in the 1609 quarto, although a recent article by Brian Vickers in the *Times Literary Supplement*, to be reviewed next year, claims that it is not by Shakespeare at all but by John Davies of Hereford. An entire section of Burrow's introduction is given over to 'Poems Attributed to Shakespeare in the Seventeenth Century' (pp. 146–58) in which he explains why some non-Shakespearian works are included in this book, albeit relegated to an appendix. The point is 'to show the kinds of poems which Shakespeare was thought to have written by his contemporaries and near-contemporaries' (p. 147). Weighing the evidence, Burrow observes that, while printers obviously stood to gain from putting a false name on a book, 'scribes and copyists of manuscript miscellanies did not have a financial stake in misascription'. Surely they did if there was a market in circulating manuscripts, as Vickers points out in connection with Gary Taylor's claim for 'Shall I die?'. Burrow comes clean and admits that he thinks *A Funerall Elegye* and 'Shall I die?' are not by Shakespeare, but only in the case of the former is he convinced strongly enough to exclude it from the book. Of course, *A Funerall Elegye* was not actually attributed to Shakespeare—Burrow's criterion for admittance—but rather to 'W.S.', and with commendable frankness Burrow admits that 'the criteria for including poems in this edition have been determined in this way partly because I find the attribution of *A Funerall Elegye* to Shakespeare improbable' (p. 154). Burrow surveys reasons to think *A Funerall Elegye* is by John Ford and observes that the tests (specifically, Ward E.Y. Elliott and Robert J. Valenza's) that reject it also reject *A Lover's Complaint*, and comments that this 'may be an indication of the difficulty of adjusting such tests to take account of inflexions to a dominant style which can result from genre and conscious pastiche' (p. 155). This rather misses the fundamental point of such tests, which is to exclude that which varies with genre and imitation and detect those things that do not change. Burrows also thinks that stylometry is a limited tool when 'the theoretical pool of authors is not limited, and where the full extent of that pool is not knowable', to which one might well respond that unless the author of *A Funerall Elegye* published nothing else, his work will be somewhere in Chadwyck-Healey's Literature Online (LION) database. It would be worth someone's time to check how may poets in LION only ever published one work, although presumably one would be hampered by the difficulty of determining whether many things currently attributed to 'Anon' are in fact by the same writer.

In particular editorial choices Burrow is generally unsurprising. Lines 1013–14 of *Venus and Adonis* he renders as 'Tells him of trophies, statues, tombs, and stories | His victories, his triumphs, and his glories', whereas Q has a comma after 'stories'. Taking it out, Burrow, following Malone and agreeing with Charles Jaspar Sisson (*New Readings in Shakespeare*, p. 207) and the Oxford *Complete Works*, makes 'stories' a verb. The press corrections in *Lucrece* Burrow treats individually and on their particular merits. Thus his line 31 is 'What needeth then apology be made', which is the Qa reading, while Qb has 'apologies'. Since the 'correction' to 'apologies' could be attributed to the press corrector, Sisson thought there was 'no need for it'. Likewise at line 50 Burrow gives 'When at Collatium this false lord arrived', the Qa reading, instead of the press-corrected Qb reading of 'Collatia', the classically more correct form; Burrow clearly agrees with Sisson that it was an educated press-corrector's alteration. Sisson thought that accepting this point entailed rejecting other Qb corrections, including those in lines 125–6 that Burrow renders as 'And every one to rest themselves betake, | Save thieves, and cares, and troubled minds that wake', in which 'themselves betake' and 'minds that wake' are the Qb readings and Qa has 'himself betake' and 'minds that wakes'. Sisson thought Qa's 'minds that wakes' typically Shakespearian and nothing for editors to get upset about, while finding Qb's 'every one … themselves' awkward, but Burrow (here departing from the Oxford *Complete Works*) pointed out that 'Shakespeare often takes indefinite pronouns (here *every one*) to imply more than one person' (p. 250) and hence the press-corrected text might also reflect what Shakespeare wrote. Press corrections are a tricky business, and arguably the criterion should be 'does this correction look clearly more likely to be authorial than compositorial?' Since press correction was usually done without reference to copy, the uncorrected state is, on average, more likely to be right and one should, Fredson Bowers argued ('The Problem of the Variant Forme in a Facsimile Edition', *Library* 7[1952] 262–72), only use the corrected state when one is certain that it resulted from consultation of copy.

In sonnet 39 Burrow follows Q in printing 'Which time and thoughts so sweetly dost deceive', as Sisson argued and against Malone and the Oxford *Complete Works* in which singular present indicative 'dost' was changed to the plural 'doth' to suit the plural subject of the verb, 'time and thoughts'. Sisson argued that 'O absence' three lines earlier is the antecedent of an understood (not expressed) 'thou' that is the singular subject of the verb 'deceive' (hence singular 'dost deceive') of which 'time and thoughts' are the object. Elsewhere a couple of recent suggestions are not actioned, so that in sonnet 69 Burrow prints 'Then, churls, their thoughts' and does not mention N.F. Blake's suggestion ('Shakespeare's Sonnet 69', *N&Q* 45[1998] 355–7) that this is a genitive form equivalent to 'churls' thoughts', and in sonnet 106 he prints 'They had not skill enough your worth to sing' rather than Q's 'still enough' that Kenji Go has defended ('Unemending the Emendation of "Still" in Shakespeare's Sonnet 106', *SP* 98[2001] 114–42). Burrow's sonnet 146 begins 'Poor soul, the centre of my sinful earth, | Spoiled by these rebel powers' where Q notoriously begins the second line by repeating the last three words of the first. Burrow credits 'This edition' as the first to use his emendation, and attributes the idea to '(*conj.* Spence)', but there is no Spence in the list of works cited and of abbreviations, yet elsewhere—such as *Lucrece* line 1662 'wreathèd] DYCE 1866 (*conj.* Walker)'—one finds the person, here W.S. Walker, in the list of abbreviations.

The introduction to Charles Whitworth's edition of *The Comedy of Errors* for The Oxford Shakespeare is short and mostly concerned with the genre and the sources of the play (pp. 1–79). Whitworth finds the play 'too well plotted' to be very early Shakespeare (such as *The Two Gentlemen of Verona* and *The Taming of the Shrew* and the Henry VI plays) and observes that its preservation of the unities would have appealed to the classically educated audience at the presumed Inns of Courts performance and to the queen, who also would have liked his recently published poetry (pp. 6–7). Whitworth summarizes internal evidence for the date of composition using the stylometric tables in the *Textual Companion* to the Oxford *Complete Works* and, like Burrow (see above), takes the standard line that plays were sold to publishers when a company was short of cash (pp. 8–11). Whitworth suspects that it was the plays' availability in clean Ralph Crane manuscript copy that probably made Heminges and Condell put *The Tempest*, *The Two Gentlemen of Verona*, *The Merry Wives of Windsor*, and *Measure for Measure* first in the 1623 Folio, since these would thereby form a good opening impression upon the reader. Then came *The Comedy of Errors*, copy for which is 'generally accepted' to be 'authorial manuscript, or holograph (foul papers)' (p. 12). The general reader probably should be told that Whitworth's word 'or' here means 'also known as'. Whitworth acknowledges Paul Werstine's demurral from the view that 'foul papers' were something too untidy to perform from, but he falls back on the 'orthodox opinion of Chambers, McKerrow and Greg' that there is no evidence that authorial papers were played from. (In truth, finding quotations that show those three men agreeing on this matter would not be straightforward.) However, since *The Comedy of Errors* was performed 'only on a few special occasions', the authorial papers could have served 'as promptbook on those rare occasions', and Whitworth gives the standard new bibliographical reasons for seeing the Folio copy as 'foul papers' (p. 13).

In the section 'Farce, City Comedy and Romance' (pp. 42–59) Whitworth makes much of the frequency with which certain words occur, and here some problems emerge. For example, 'the words *conjure* and *conjurer* together occur six times in *Errors*, more than in any other play in the canon (including all cognate forms of the words)' (pp. 41–2). I count five occurrences in the dialogue of *The Contention of York and Lancaster* (I.ii.76, I.ii.99, II.i.173, IV.ii.92, V.i.197) if we include *conjuration* as cognate, and two more in stage directions (I.iv.0, II.iii.0). Perhaps Whitworth should have made clear if he meant just in dialogue. Still, if we include *conjuration* then *Henry V* has six dialogue occurrences too (I.ii.29, II.i.52, III.i.7, V.ii.286, V.ii.290, V.ii.291) and so does *Romeo and Juliet* (II.i.6, II.i.16, II.i.17, II.i.26, II.i.29, V.iii.68) and clearly such assertions depend in part upon the choice of edition used for the counting; mine are all from the electronic edition of the Oxford *Complete Works*. Whitworth observes that '*witch* and *witches* together occur six times in the play' (p. 42), with which I agree but notice that there are the same number in *1 Henry VI* if we include *bewitched* (I.vii.6, I.vii.21, II.i.18, III.iv.3, III.vii.58, V.iv.5), and seven in *The Contention of York and Lancaster* (I.i.155, I.ii.75, I.ii.91, II.i.173, II.iii.7, II.iii.8, III.ii.116) even if we exclude stage directions and speech prefixes and exclude an occurrence of *witched* (III.ii.119), and fully nine just in the dialogue in *The Merry Wives of Windsor* (IV.ii.78, IV.ii.89, IV.ii.158, IV.ii.164, IV.ii.171, IV.ii.178, IV.ii.179, IV.v.109, IV.v.113). On the same page, Whitworth claims that '*sorcerer(s)/sorceress* [occurs] three times (more than in any other play except *The Tempest*)' but in fact *1 Henry VI* has three occurrences of *sorcerers/sorceress* (I.i.26, III.iv.3, V.vi.1) plus one of *sorcery* (II.i.15), and that '*Devil/devil*'s occurs seven times'. This last claim is true, but what is its relevance when there are twenty-four occurrences in the dialogue of *1 Henry IV* (I.ii.6, I.ii.113, I.ii.116, I.ii.118, I.ii.120, I.ii.122, I.iii.114, I.iii.123, I.iii.251, II.v.225, II.v.340, II.v.371, II.v.452, II.v.492, III.i.54, III.i.55, III.i.56, III.i.59, III.i.66, III.i.153, III.i.226, IV.i.58, IV.ii.19, IV.ii.50) and twenty-seven in the dialogue of *Othello* (I.i.91, I.i.111, II.i.114, II.i.227, II.i.245, II.iii.277, II.iii.289, II.iii.290, II.iii.301, II.iii.342, III.iii.481, III.iv.42, III.iv.134, III.iv.181, IV.i.6, IV.i.8, IV.i.42, IV.i.145, IV.i.240, IV.i.244, IV.ii.38, V.ii.140, V.ii.142, V.ii.227, V.ii.284, V.ii.293, V.ii.307)? On page 43 Whitworth claims that '*Beat, beaten* and *beating*, always in the primary sense of physical blows (as opposed to the beating of the heart, for example, or of the sea upon the rocks), occur a total of fourteen times in *Errors*, more than in any other play in the canon'. Whitworth seems to be including stage directions here ('There is further vigorous action in ... '), in which case *Coriolanus* has the highest count, eighteen occurrences in all (I.iii. 48, I.iv.29, I.v.7, I.v.12, I.v.13, I.vii.40, I.xi.8, II.iii.216, III.i.228, III.i.242, III.iii.83, IV.v.50, IV.v.52, IV.v.122, IV.vi.56, V.iv.49, V.vi.110, V.vi.150), and even if he means only in dialogue, thirteen of these examples stand. I suspect that Whitworth took his numbers from Marvin Spevack's 'Harvard' Concordance since it agrees with all his figures quoted while Bartlett's Concordance, for example, gives eleven for *beat/ beaten/beating* rather than Whitworth's claimed fourteen. Of course, Spevack's Concordance is based on the Riverside Shakespeare edited by Gwynne Blakemore Evans, which is considerably different in hundreds of substantive readings from the Oxford *Complete Works*, which one would expect a book in this series to be using.

The foregoing quibbles do not constitute an attack on the substance of Whitworth's introduction, which ranges across an admirably broad collection of materials germane to the play. In particular editorial choices too Whitworth is incisive. At I.i.17 he prints 'Syracusan' instead of F's 'Syracusian', explaining this as being 'in the interest of consistency with the noun form *Syracusa*' and points out that an *-ian* ending can be one or two syllables. At I.i.41 Whitworth restores the correct name to the city of Epidamnus (the Latin nominative form), rejecting F's 'Epidamium' and Pope's—and indeed Sisson's (1:88) and the Oxford *Complete Works*'—declined form 'Epidamnum'. In an explanatory note Whitworth remarks that Shakespeare probably wrote 'Epidamium' or 'Epidamnium', so clearly his aim is not simply to try to recover the name of the town that Shakespeare thought he had set his play in but rather its true name. At I.i.54–5 Whitworth prints 'A mean young woman was deliverèd | Of such a burden, male twins, both alike' where F has 'A meane woman was deliuered | Of such a burthen Male, twins both alike'. Whitworth's 'mean young' is his own solution to the line, being metrically short, and other editors have proposed their own, none of which has much to recommend it over the others. For the punctuation of 'burden, male twins, both' Whitworth points out that the phrase 'burden male' has no examples in *OED*, and indeed I have checked LION too and can confirm that it seems unique.

At II.i.110–14 Whitworth prints 'I see the jewel best enamellèd | Will lose his beauty; and though gold bides still | That others touch, yet often touching will | Wear gold, and so no man that hath a name | By falsehood and corruption doth it shame' where F has 'I see the Iewell best enameled | Will loose his beautie: yet the gold bides still | That others touch, and often touching will, | Where gold and no man that hath a name, | By falshood and corruption doth it shame'. This mostly relies on Theobald, but Whitworth makes the pragmatic observation that it does not much matter what an actress says here 'so long as she conveys Adriana's anguish at her husband's imagined infidelity and his apparent unconcern about his sullied reputation'. Indeed, Whitworth suggests that one might simply cut these lines in performance, as directors have on occasion done. For the speeches at V.i.347–52 Whitworth gives a long note defending the ordering in F against claims that the Duke should not interpose himself between the Abbess's entreaty ('if thou be'st the same Egeon, speak') and Egeon's response ('If I dream not, thou art Emilia').

Finally for the Oxford Shakespeare, Roger Warren edits *2 Henry VI* and in 'A Note on Titles' (p. x) clarifies that he reserves the titles of *1*, *2*, and *3 Henry VI* for the Folio texts and reserves *The Contention of York and Lancaster* and *Richard Duke of York/True Tragedy* for the 1594 quarto and 1595 octavo respectively. This in essence is a gentle remonstrance for the Oxford *Complete Works*' muddying of the waters by printing essentially the Folio texts under their original stage titles. In his introduction Warren explores the phenomenon that each of the three Henry VI plays stands on its own yet is enriched by being read or seen in relation to the others (pp. 1–6) and his expected tour of the stage history (pp. 6–26) is enlivened by personal experiences of working in the theatre. A section on 'Origins' (pp. 27–32) reports how the raw materials appeared in Hall and Holinshed, but the section on 'History and Pseudo-History' (pp. 32–6) strikes an odd note with the claim about Shakespeare that, 'in the early 1590s, as he was starting out his writing career, there was no such genre' as the history play (p. 35). It is hard to think what else but 'history plays' would be an adequate description of *The Famous Victories of Henry V* (first performed 1583–8), the anonymous *Richard III* (first performed 1588–94), Marlowe's *Edward II* (first performed 1591–3), the anonymous *Jack Straw* (first performed 1590–3), the anonymous *Richard II Part 1* (first performed 1591–5), or Heywood's *Edward IV Parts 1 and 2* (first performed 1592–9). If Warren rejects the generic and/or dating claims that I have here drawn from Alfred Harbage's *Annals of English Drama*, it would be interesting to hear why. Indeed, in a ground-breaking study of one company Scott McMillin and Sally-Beth MacLean wrote of 'the innovation of carrying English history into the popular theatre' that 'the Queen's men appear to have been first' (*The Queen's Men and their Plays*, p. 167), and listed amongst their repertory *The Famous Victories of Henry V* (Stationers' Register entry 1594, printed 1598 with the Queen's men's name on the title page), *The Troublesome Reign of King John* (printed 1591 with the Queen's men's name on the title page), and *The True Tragedy of Richard III* (printed 1594 with the Queen's men's name on title page), all of which contradicts Warren's claim that the history play genre did not exist when Shakespeare started his career in the early 1590s.

An interesting intersection of criticism and editing occurs in relation to the Jack Cade rebellion. Because the Bakhtinian carnivalesque (as made relevant to the rebellion by the scholarship of Stephen Longstaffe) is universally mocking, even of its own participants and the leader of the rebellion, Warren reports (p. 52) that he decided not to put the rebels' mocking comments on their leader at IV.ii.31–58 into asides, as editors usually do. Warren's section on 'Date and Chronology' (pp. 60–74) is typically thorough, although unusually he seems to treat *Greene's Groatsworth of Wit* as though it were written by Greene himself. Warren notes that the play that Henslowe recorded as 'ne' on 3 March 1592 was 'harey the vj' and 'since one motive for publication [of *Richard Duke of York*] must have been to cash in on the play's success, it could only have done that if it had used the title under which it was performed—which cannot therefore have been *Harry VI*' (p. 61). The logic is faulty here, for Henslowe was under no obligation to record the proper stage title, and indeed we know of several plays where his form of the title does not match the one used in publication, as Charles Edelman shows in relation to *The Battle of Alcazar/Muly Molocco* (see below). Since Henslowe's play cannot, by Warren's logic, be *Richard Duke of York* it cannot by the same token be *The Contention of York and Lancaster*, so it must be *1 Henry VI*. But 'ne' does not necessarily mean 'new', Warren points out, and 'perhaps sometimes [indicated] a newly revised or even newly licensed' play. Hence, he argues (pp. 65–71), the order of composition might have been *1, 2, 3 Henry VI*, whereas most scholars think that *1 Henry VI* was 'ne[w]' in March 1592 and hence there was not enough time to compose *2* and *3 Henry VI* after the first one and in time for the entry of Greene's Groatsworth (with its allusion to *3 Henry VI*) in the Stationers' Register in September 1592. He is, of course, quite right to be suspicious of the claim that Henslowe's 'ne' meant 'new', for it might just as well have indicated that a particular play was performed at Henslowe's Newington Butts theatre, as Winifred Frazer observed ('Henslowe's "Ne"', *N&Q* 38[1991] 34–5). Warren skilfully deals with the remaining objections against *1*, *2*, and *3 Henry VI* being the order of composition, including the one that trilogies just were not done, two-parters being the rule (pp. 71–4). But he leaves out the fact that the preparations for the printing of the 1623 Folio included the first-time entry in the Stationers' Register on 8 November 1622 of 'The thirde parte of Henry the sixte'. This cannot be what we now call *3 Henry VI* because this had already been printed in 1595 as *Richard Duke of York*, so it is most likely *1 Henry VI* considered as the third part of the series in order of composition, not in order of historical events. Likewise on 19 April 1602 Millington transferred his rights in 'The first and Second parte of HENRY the VJ[t][h]' to Pavier, who later printed *The Contention of York and Lancaster* and *Richard Duke of York*, which suggests that what we now call *2 Henry VI* was originally the first part of a two-parter and *3 Henry VI* was its completion.

Warren's 'Textual Introduction' (pp. 75–100) is of greatest interest to this survey, and in it he points out that Steven Urkowitz (like others who attack the theory of memorial reconstruction) 'creates an entirely false antithesis' in suggesting that memorial reconstruction implies a perfect original desecrated by the reconstructors (p. 78). The strongest reason for believing that the 1594 quarto of this play was a memorial reconstruction is York's garbling of his own genealogy in a way that simply cannot be attributed to an author, and Warren observes also that Q's version of the queen's speech to Suffolk (I.iii.43–65) contains several bits that in F are in different places. It is inherently unlikely that Shakespeare subsequently took this speech apart and highly likely that we see here an actor undertaking 'a piece of cobbling, attempting to reconstruct a dimly remembered speech with material from disparate places' (p. 81). The illogical action of Q's version of the rest of that scene (including an unmotivated exit and re-entrance for Duke Humphrey of Gloucester) when read against the perfectly logical F version makes it clear that it is a garbled recollection, and likewise Q's version of the witchcraft scene has 'borrowings of phrases from other plays known to the actors', namely Marlowe's *Doctor Faustus* and *Tamburlaine* (pp. 81–3). In Q's version of III.ii Margaret says that, wherever in the world Suffolk is, she will 'haue an Irish that shall find thee out', whereas F has the obviously correct 'an Iris'. Warren reckons the reporter is recalling a messenger's news about Irish rebellion in the previous scene: 'It is inconceivable that an *author* could have written this as an alternative version'. But Q does not simply report the version that was eventually printed in F, for there must also have been revision between composition (reflected in F) and performance (reflected in Q). For example, F gives little space for Somerset and Buckingham's part in the plot against Duke Humphrey and in planning the response to the Irish rebellion: they are present in the latter half of III.i but say almost nothing. Q seems to fix this, to integrate them into the scene by having the queen address them by name and by giving the otherwise silent Buckingham something to say.

More complicatingly still, F also contains signs of subsequent authorial revision. Warren offers the example of Q's '*Elnor* What hast thou conferd with *Margery Iordane*, the | cunning witch of *Ely*' against F's '*Elia*. What saist thou man? Hast thou as yet confer'd | With *Margerie Iordane* the cunning Witch'. If F simply represents authorial papers and Q performance, who would have put in the historically correct detail of where Jordan was from? As McKerrow argued, it is hard to imagine a playwright sprinkling that sort of detail into a play already written, since it would take extensive digging in his sources. Warren thinks it more likely that 'of Ely' was cut to make F's 'absolutely regular iambic pentameter' and 'more incisive' line; so here F is the revised text (p. 88). Likewise, when Cade orders Lord Saye's execution, Q contains historical details from Hall (about 'the Standard in Cheapside' and 'Mile End Green') that F omits. Unless we think (as indeed William Montgomery did for the Oxford *Complete Works*) that someone went to Hall and put such details into the performances that underlie Q, we must suppose instead that someone (and Warren thinks it is Shakespeare) omitted them from the text underlying F. Another example is a reference to the historical fact of Cardinal Beaufort's bastardy, present in Q and absent from F. Q shows that it got performed, so either it was added into the play during rehearsal (most unlikely) or it was removed from the manuscript underlying F. This might have happened through censorship, but Warren thinks it happened when 'Shakespeare, revising and/or copying his manuscript, cut the passage to shorten a scene that contains quite enough bickering between Humphrey and the Cardinal' (p. 90). Once we accept that F contains post-performance authorial revisions, all the Q/F differences come up for question: should we follow Q on the grounds that it is what was first performed or F because that is what Shakespeare later decided he wanted? Warren surveys the Q/F differences (pp. 90–7), trying to determine which might be things that got added to/ cut from the play during rehearsal (and hence into Q) and things that Shakespeare changed when copying up his authorial papers to make the manuscript that eventually produced F. Here Warren reminds the reader of one possible occasion for the authorial revisions (mentioned earlier, pp. 73–4, but only here explicitly now tied to the argument about revision in F): a revival of the Henry VI plays around the end of the 1590s to run with the Henry IV and V plays.

Thankfully, Warren offers a summary of his views on the complex situation (pp. 98–100): Q and F show 'signs of two different kinds of revision of the play as originally written. Q seems to report changes to it made in rehearsal, F to reflect changes made in a later revision, probably for a revival'. But the authorial revisions reflected in F do not incorporate those made during rehearsal (indeed, that is how come we can detect them at all in Q) so Shakespeare seems not to 'have thought sufficiently well of them to include them in the revision detectable in F'. Warren's new bibliographical thinking is apparent: 'The Folio text was printed from an authorial manuscript, as its vague and "permissive" stage directions make clear: for example, Jack Cade's first entry is accompanied with the "infinite numbers" (4.2.30.2/TLN 2351) characteristic of a dramatist writing impressionistically rather than with a strict regard for theatrical practicalities.' Honigmann showed that in making his own fair copy a dramatist might introduce all sorts of minor changes, and indeed the deletion of chronicle details that are in Q and not in F could easily be explained this way. But against the idea that F was printed from an authorial fair copy is the fact that Henry calls his Queen Margaret 'Nell', which is in fact Humphrey's pet name for his wife Eleanor; surely Shakespeare would have spotted his slip and fixed it? Unless, Warren argued in an article reviewed here two years ago ('The Quarto and Folio Texts of *2 Henry VI*: A Reconsideration', *RES* 51[2000] 193–207), Shakespeare did his revision on his original manuscript (rather than copying it out fair) and did not even look at the bits he knew were all right such as Act III. Warren reports that 'The text in this edition is based firmly on that in the Folio, as representing Shakespeare's latest thoughts on the play, and unlike the Oxford *Complete Works* only incorporates material from the Quarto to correct obvious errors (for example, to supply the missing line at IV.i.49), with one important exception: since the Quarto reports an Elizabethan performance, its interesting and often extensive stage directions are incorporated into this edition where they supplement the rather meagre information given in the Folio ones (for example, at the opening of the play).'

Warren accepts that F was set directly from a quarto (probably Q3) at certain points, and thinks these three to be particularly clear examples: '2.1.112–149.2/TLN 858–904; 2.3.58.1–2.4.0.2/TLN 1115–70; and 4.5.0.1–4.6.0.2/TLN 2598–2614' (p. 99). This is a shorter list than that produced by William Montgomery for the Oxford *Complete Works* (TLN 63–79, 795–6, 858–904, 1115–70, 2598–2639) but is wholly a subset of it. The important point is that, where F was printed from Q, the latter is the only substantive text and should be any editor's control text, but Warren unaccountably departs from this principle. To be fair, Montgomery did too, claiming that he had decided to take Q as the 'only substantive text' for these passages and 'treat any departures from it—including those we adopt from F—as emendations' (*Textual Companion*, p. 176). But in the detailed textual notes Montgomery suddenly introduced the idea that F's copy was not simply an example of Q3 but 'an annotated copy', which would explain why F during these passages does not always follow Q1 or Q3. Montgomery did not tell the reader where he thought these annotations came from, although in his notes to II.iii.76–83 and II.iii.91–103 he wondered aloud whether it was 'perhaps corrected by recourse to foul papers'. To give such credence to F's substantive differences from Q3 is in fact not to treat it as his 'only substantive text' at all, and casts doubt on Montgomery's procedure of joining those individual occasions where Q3 seems to influence F into whole stretches where Q3 is supposed to be F's copy. Warren certainly prefers F over Q even in those sections that he declares are 'particularly clear' cases of F being printed from Q, as when he prints 'But cloaks and gowns before this day, a many' (II.i.113) where Q1-3 have 'ere' instead of F's 'before'. Again at II.i.132 Warren gives 'O master, that you could!' following F instead of Q's 'I would you could'. In the second of Warren's three stretches of clear use of Q copy for F, he nonetheless has Peter leave his hammer to Will and his apron to Robin (as F does) instead of the other way around (as Q does).

The third of Warren's three stretches of Q copy for F begins with the opening stage direction of IV.v that he renders as '*Enter Lord Scales [and Matthew Gough] upon the Tower, walking. Then enters two or three Citizens below*'. In a note to this Warren writes: 'Since the texts (and even the layout) of F and Q3 are almost identical at this point, F was probably set from Q3 here (see Textual Introduction, pp. 99–100); neither mentions Scales by name. The reporter of Q may have omitted a line or phrase identifying Scales, or he may simply have known who Scales was through rehearsal discussion, while the audience may not even have needed to know his name: his essential dramatic function is to be an authority figure defending the Tower.' (Warren actually means that no one mentions Scales's name *in dialogue*.) The evidence that F was set from a quarto (not specifically Q3, as Warren implies) is indeed the closeness in the phrasing ('upon … walking') of a stage direction, which a memorially reconstructed text and an authorial copy are unlikely to agree upon by chance. But the evidence that the quarto used for F was *specifically* Q3 comes from something else not mentioned by Warren: had it been Q1 or Q2 it would be bizarre to change 3–4 citizens (the Q1-2 reading) to 2–3 citizens (the F reading).

Q3 omits to say how many citizens, and since this is obviously an omission (a citizen almost immediately speaks) the Folio compositor probably rectified this himself, guessing at the number of citizens and guessing (from the dramatic context) that they enter below. This was the argument in Montgomery's Ph.D. thesis and repeated in the *Textual Companion* (p. 177). Warren keeps the F reading, which by this argument is of course a non-Shakespearian interpolation, and even keeps the un-Shakespearian phrasing 'enters' that Montgomery pointed out only occurs elsewhere in the parts of the Shakespeare canon thought to have been printed from scribal copy or not written by Shakespeare. (Actually, Montgomery garbled this point, writing that 'enters' occurs in 'quarto and Folio *Contention* 2.4.83.3/1019.3' but he must have meant II.iii.58.3 and in any case the important point is the ungrammatical use of this word, here at the beginning of IV.v and previously in 'Enters a Messenger' near the end of I.i in Q1, corrected in Q3.) For the rest of this scene, IV.v, that Warren thinks was printed in F from Q, he nonetheless follows F for substantive variants, giving 'The rebels have essayed to win the Tower' (IV.v.8) where Q1-3 have 'attempted to win'.

Generally Warren's editorial choices are properly explained, but not always. At I.iii.92 he prints: 'That she will light to listen to their lays', where F has 'listen to the lays'. Warren, following Rowe and the Oxford *Complete Works*, here departs from his copy (F) in a matter of substance yet there is no mention of it in the collation, nor an explanatory note. At III.i.260 he prints 'As Humphrey, proved by reasons, to my liege', adding commas around 'proved by reasons' that are not in F. Warren says that he punctuates lightly (p. 102), but these commas shut down a possible different interpretation. In Warren's reading Humphrey has shown himself ('proved') to be an enemy to the king just as the fox proves himself an enemy to the flock (two lines earlier), whereas Sisson argued (2:77) that Humphrey had earlier proved something to the king (III.i.168–71), namely that reasons will be found to get rid of him and that 'A staff is quickly found to beat a dog', and that Suffolk is here 'sardonically' recalling that moment. Sisson's reading might be thought somewhat strained, but by punctuating even more lightly than he has Warren might have left the matter open.

For the Arden Shakespeare, Charles Forker gives *King Richard II* a huge introduction covering 'Politics' (pp. 5–55), 'Language' (pp. 55–90), 'Afterlife' (pp. 90–111), 'The Date' (pp. 111–20), 'Probable Venues of Performance' (pp. 120–3), 'Sources' (pp. 123–64), and 'Text' (pp. 165–9). This last is just a summary, however, and there is a full appendix (pp. 506–41) for the detailed 'Textual Analysis'. Under 'Politics' Forker considers Ernst Kantorowicz's reading of the play as 'a tragedy of royal christology' about the dual nature of king and man, but fails to make the connection necessary for those unfamiliar with these concepts: Christ's dual nature as deity and man. Perhaps it seems too obvious to Forker, and indeed sometimes his choices of what needs explaining are curious. For example, under 'Afterlife' he lists places where *Richard II* has been performed: 'Athens, Avignon, Berlin, Bonn, Bratislava, Braunschweig, Bucharest, Dublin, Hamburg, Kampala (Uganda), Marseilles, Milan, Munich, Verona and Zurich' (p. 100). What kind of reader does Forker expect will recognize the German spelling of the small town of Brunswick (Braunschweig) but needs to be told which country contains the much larger capital city of Kampala? Under 'Probable Venues' Forker makes a slight slip in writing that the Swan drawing shows no central opening between the left and right doors 'such as the Globe possessed' (p. 122) when in fact we do not know whether the Globe possessed one, and the Swan drawing is one of the major pieces of evidence in that particular puzzle. Also unreliable is his comment that, 'According to the computer-based findings of Donald Foster', Shakespeare played Gaunt and the head Gardener and an anonymous lord in IV.i and maybe also the Groom, for which Forker cites Foster's article in *Shakespeare Newsletter* [1995] that, in the light of Foster's subsequent exposure as a charlatan, nobody should trust. A final small slip is Forker's repetition of the familiar error of claiming that the opening moments of *Hamlet* dramatize a violation of military protocol because the relieving sentinel challenges the man on duty (p. 126 n. 1). As Charles Edelman has privately pointed out, even if the protocol were strict on this matter (and it is not), no one watching the opening moments of the play could spot which man is relieving which.

In his summary of the textual situation, Forker reports that Q1 (printed 1597) is the 'basic text' except for the deposition scene (IV.i.155–318) that first appeared in a reliable form in F, Q4-1608's version of it being unreliable. Thus there is no early text of roughly equal authority to the one chosen as Forker's control text, and hence this edition does not include (as some Ardens do) a facsimile reprint of the one not chosen. Forker writes that 'Q is apparently the text closest to Shakespeare's holograph' (p. 165) and perhaps was printed directly from it. F seems to be printed from a copy of Q3 (printed 1598) that had been extensively annotated by reference 'to the theatre promptbook and augmented from the same source by a manuscript insertion of the missing abdication episode'. Forker thinks that the deposition scene was always performed, but 'was considered too dangerous to print in 1597'. For bits where F's wordings not in Q have been included in this edition, Forker uses the convention of wrapping the superscript letter 'F' around them (^{F}xxx xxxx^F) just as R.A. Foakes did for his Arden 3 *King Lear* (p. 167). Forker gives an intelligent explanation of his decision to retain Richard's speech prefix as 'King Richard' right to the end of the play, even though Bolingbroke changes to 'King Henry' in V.iii: one of the play's themes is precisely the question of whether both can be king at once, or whether the office is indivisible (p. 168).

Forker's appendix 1 goes into the detail underlying this summary of the textual situation, such as the nature of the copy underlying F. Was it a whole copy of Q3 or a one whose missing final leaves were supplied from a copy of Q5? Everyone agrees that some promptbook influence on the Q3 used to print F occurred, since F's version of the deposition is not simply a reprint of the one in Q4-5, and F restores a number of good Q1 readings that got corrupted in Q2 and Q3, and that it has cuts that seem theatrically authoritative. Regarding terminology, Forker acknowledges William Long's objection to use of the word 'promptbook' and although he agrees that 'playbook' is better, 'the older term has been so commonly used by scholars that it is difficult to avoid it' (p. 508 n. 1). Of course, if anyone has the power to change misleading terminology it is the editors of major critical editions, whom one might hope would take a more adventurous position than Forker's. Additional reasons for thinking that a promptbook influenced F is that it improves on its quarto copy's speech prefixes and stage directions in ways that we can imagine occurring during rehearsal, as when it is realized that Gaunt is needed at the beginning of I.ii so had better exit before the end of I.i. Corroborating the theatrical influence is F's substitution of safe words (such as 'heaven') for its quarto copy's oaths (such as 'God') in line with the 1606 act that applied to performance but not to printing. In all, F has what Jowett and Gary Taylor picturesquely termed 'sprinklings of authority' (pp. 509–15).

Forker believes that Q1 simply omitted to print the deposition scene that was in its manuscript copy, although he footnotes David Bergeron's argument that it might in fact have been written later than the rest of the play. Q1 seems to be authorial in its imprecise and theatrically pointless stage directions (of the kind 'enter xxxx with news'), and in its variant speech prefixes; was the copy authorial papers or scribal copy of them? We cannot tell: certain features (such as the use of abbreviations) seem authorial, while others (such as the preference for *Oh* instead of Shakespeare's habitual *O*) seem scribal (pp. 518–20). What of the nature of the text used to annotate Q3? Forker reports Jowett and Taylor's hypothesis, based on the clustering of Q5 readings at the end of the Folio text, that the last leaf of the promptbook went missing and was replaced with a transcript from Q5, and that this promptbook was used to annotate an example of Q3 to make copy for F. A problem, Forker observes, is the unlikelihood that 'the annotator of Q3 would trouble to introduce a cluster of such unimportant readings from Q5, even if these had somehow got into the promptbook' (p. 523). Forker praises Jowett and Taylor's work on just how heavily, and where, the annotator of Q3 (using the promptbook as his authority) did his annotating: evenly in stage directions and speech prefixes but in dialogue he was more interventionist in the first third or so of the play. For a modern editor, then, the problem when using Q1 as the basic text is which of the F variants to prefer on the grounds that they have promptbook authority (p. 524). Indeed, how authoritative *is* a promptbook? Obviously there is bound to be an element of subjectivity, and Forker lists the major F variants from Q3 that he adopts—that is, where he lets F, differing from its copy Q3, overrule his basic text Q1—chosen on the criterion of having 'garnered the approval of a significant number of modern editors' (p. 525). (Where F differs from Forker's basic text Q1 but follows Q3, that is probably because F is simply reprinting Q3.) Forker's appeal to a consensus of editors is most odd: a kind of editing by committee. Lest that seems harsh, I quote Forker being quite explicit: 'The "corrections" of Q3 discussed in the preceding paragraphs (including modifications of the SDs and the introduction of dubiously authorial act and scene divisions) represent something like a consensus of twentieth-century editorial judgement on which F readings should be admitted into a modern critical editions of *Richard II*' (p. 528). Although Forker mentions a couple of moments where he breaks with tradition, especially when he is unconvinced that just because something got in the promptbook and thence into F, it had authorial sanction, he is not one of the 'cultural contextualists' for whom a play is inherently an overdetermined collaboration (p. 529).

Alan Craven's Ph.D. on the printing of Q1 revised Charlton Hinman's compositor attribution, giving more of the play to compositor A (57½ pages) and less to compositor S (15 pages). Compositor A did all of the reprint Q2, and from his departures from his copy (Q1) in that task we can determine his habits, which add up to a lot of unauthoritative departures from copy (pp. 537–8). For this reason, Craven advocated greater editorial intervention in Q1 (when used as the basis of a modern edition) than one would otherwise want to perform, on the grounds that Q1 probably has lots of compositor A's errors in it. But Peter Davison pointed out the slenderness of the evidence on which we make the compositorial identifications, and did not think the errors in Q2 were as many as Craven saw: some are defensible alternatives, others may have come from the Q1 being used as copy having uncorrected sheets in it. Still, observes Forker, whether compositor A or S is responsible for Q1's errors, there are enough errors in Q2 (printed from known Q1 copy) to suggest that the printing of Q1 brought in considerable compositorial error, and for this reason he incorporates six of Craven's thirteen suggested departures from Q1, moments when the compositor probably erred from his copy (pp. 539–40).

At I.iii.26 Forker prints 'Marshal, ask of yonder knight in arms' where Q and F have (modernized) 'Marshal, ask yonder knight in arms'. Forker's note surveys some possibilities, but having accepted that 'Shakespeare occasionally introduces short lines for variety' Forker gives no reason for adding the word *of* (which is his own) rather than following what Q and F agree upon; and this is not one of his six moments of claimed compositorial slip. At I.iii.239–42 Forker has Gaunt say 'O, had it been a stranger, not my child, | To smooth his fault I should have been more mild. | A partial slander sought I to avoid, | And in the sentence my own life destroyed'. These four lines are in Q1-3 but omitted in F, and the Oxford *Complete Works* omitted them too on the grounds that the comparison of Q3 with the promptbook (to prepare Q3 to be copy for F) showed that they had been cut in performance. Forker's approach conflates Q3 and F, accepting F's reading wherever it adds something to the play (such as fuller stage directions) but ignoring its evidence where it takes material away. This is not really reasonable use of F, for it treats the text as a pot to be filled as much as possible rather than a dramatic product where sometimes 'less' (textually) is 'more' (dramatically). The same point is true of the other passages that the Oxford *Complete Works* prints as 'Additional' and Forker incorporates in his main text. At II.i.114 Richard cuts off the dying Gaunt's words in a celebrated dramatic moment: '[Gaunt] And thou— | King Richard A lunatic lean-witted fool'. A modernized form of Q1 would be 'And thou | King Richard A lunatic … ', while F has 'And— | King Richard And thou … '. Forker is following Capell's emendation (that is, using Q's words but adding a dash), but for no other reason than that it 'clarifies the dramatic interruption'. Yet F makes sense, and since F here seems to emend Q3—presumably by reference to the promptbook—the logical thing to do would be follow F.

Forker's interventions are occasionally justified by judgements about what Shakespeare ought to have written, so that at III.ii.35 he has '[Aumerle] Grows strong and great in substance and in power', which is the Q1 reading, even though F here departs from its copy to have 'in friends'; this Forker rejects because it seems 'distinctly weaker'. Likewise, at III.ii.37–8 Forker has Richard say 'That when the searching eye of heaven is hid | Behind the globe and lights the lower world', where Q and F agree on 'eye of heaven is hid | Behind the globe, that lights the lower world', meaning 'the searching eye of heaven … that lights the lower world'. Forker uses Hanmer's emendation of 'that' to 'and' because it 'clarifies the syntax and makes the sentence more readily intelligible in the theatre'. This seems to go beyond the editor's job, for both textual authorities agree on a syntax that is awkward to us but entirely acceptable by Elizabethan standards, so it is hard to see the need to emend. A further example is at III.ii.84, when Forker has Richard 'Awake, thou coward Majesty, thou sleepest!', which is essentially Q's reading, even though F departs from its copy Q3—presumably on promptbook authority—to give 'sluggard Majesty'. Forker's reason for not following F here is that it 'weakens the speech'. It is hard to find an authority strong enough to shake Forker's faith in his own judgement, since at III.ii.202–3 he prints 'And all your southern gentlemen in arms | Upon his party', the Q1 reading, rather than F's departure from Q3 of 'Upon his faction'. Forker admits that F's reading 'presumably comes from the promptbook', but he still will not adopt it because it 'seems more specific and perhaps more limiting'. In general the convention of wrapping superscript 'F' around words taken from the Folio works well, although for consistency Forker puts the entire deposition scene (IV.i.153–318) inside such a pairing; across twenty-one pages the convention fails to signal its meaning to the reader. The only literal fault I could find was at V.vi.25 n., where Q3's 'reverend' is given as 'rverend'.

The final edition reviewed this year follows historically and dramatically from Forker's: David Scott Kastan's *King Henry IV Part 1*. By comparison with Part 2, which was not reprinted between its first printing in 1600 and the 1623 Folio, Part 1 went through nine editions between 1598 and 1630: it was a bestseller (pp. 1–2). Kastan notes that, when it was published, what we call the first part of *Henry IV* was simply called *Henry IV* and only the second part got explicitly called the second (p. 18). That is true, but it is not quite as surprising as Kastan seems to think: Henslowe followed this practice and Hollywood does today (*Rocky*, *Rocky II*). Kastan's account of Falstaff/Oldcastle is much as in one of his recent books (*Shakespeare After Theory*, pp. 93–108), and addresses the tricky question of why Shakespeare might mock a Protestant martyr. The answer is that by the 1590s the Lollards were seen as extremists of the Puritan kind, and hence mocking them could be a moderate Protestant thing to do (pp. 51–62). In an uncharacteristic slip, Kastan reproduces the wrong picture for his caption 'Frontispiece of Kirkman, *The Wits*, 1662' (p. 82) using the coarse copy of 1672 rather than the original, as can be seen by comparison with John Astington's reproductions in an article that got to the bottom of this matter ('*The Wits* Illustration, 1662', *TN* 47[1993] 122–40).

With admirable succinctness, Kastan keeps his discussion of 'The Play on the Page' to thirteen pages (pp. 106–18), noting that Q2-8 and F 'are all derived from the 1598 quartos' (that is Q0, existing only in a fragment, and Q1) and that F was printed from Q5 of 1613 (p. 111). There must have been some outside influence on F, however, for it removes Q5's oaths in line with the 1606 act. Jowett and Taylor saw in this the unmistakable influence of a playhouse manuscript, for only there would the oaths have been altered to meet the act's requirements, but Kastan wonders if perhaps Heminges and Condell might have editorially removed the oaths when preparing Q5 as the F copy, perhaps 'to bring the printed text in line with the play as it had been performed' (p. 113). Indeed, had a promptbook been used to annotate an example of Q5, it is a wonder that the stage directions were not tidied up more than they are in F. Crucially, to Kastan's mind, F gives the 'But this our purpose is a twelue month old' (I.i.28), which regularizes Q5's faulty metre of 'But this our purpose is twelue month old'. Were a promptbook or other authoritative manuscript used to do the annotating of Q5 to make it ready to be copy for F, we would expect F to have the correct reading that we find in Q1: 'But this our purpose now is twelue month old' (pp. 114–15). Thus F is merely a derivative text with no independent authority, and hence Q0 is the substantive text for what little of the play it has, and Q1 is substantive for the rest. However, F's departures from Q5 'do demand careful consideration' because Heminges and Condell knew the play in performance (p. 116). Comparing Q1 to its copy Q0, we can see that Q1 was carefully printed, but the quartos' stage directions are 'insufficiently specific to cue performance' so the quartos do not derive from 'the theatre company's prompt copy' (p. 117). Like almost everyone these days, Kastan notes Long's objections to the term 'promptbook' and his article showing that stage directions were not necessarily tidied in theatrical manuscripts ('Stage-Directions: A Misinterpreted Factor in Determining Textual Provenance', *Text* 2[1985] 121–37), but then continues as though these things do not matter. Firmly in new bibliographical territory, Kastan decides that the manuscript used to print Q might have been authorial papers but finds that the lack of Shakespearian preferences—*betwixt* where he preferred *between*, *prithee* where he preferred *pray thee*—suggests rather that it was a scribal copy of authorial papers (p. 118).

Kastan's section on 'Editorial Procedures' (pp. 119–31) is somewhat longer than one would expect, mostly because it is taken up with a detailed study of the effects of modernization (pp. 119–26). Commendably, Kastan writes 'I have … departed from Q0 and Q1 only when they are evidently in error', which he thinks makes him 'more conservative than many editors' (p. 119). Much concerned with the forms of names, Kastan retains the Anglicization of the name Glyndŵr as Glendower because 'for Shakespeare "Glendower" exists as he is written', already inserted in this form into English history. Kastan uses the name Bardoll because he is never Bardolph (or Bardolfe) in a sixteenth- or seventeenth-century quarto of this play. Only in F does he get the 'f' ending and apparently that was a matter of 'bringing it into line with the spelling in *2 Henry IV*, *Henry V* and *Merry Wives*'. In *Shakespeare After Theory* Kastan made an innovative argument against the Oxford *Complete Works*' restoration of Oldcastle's name in *1 Henry IV*: that might well have been Shakespeare's first intention for this character, but it was also his intention to have the same name in both parts of the play (*Shakespeare After Theory*, p. 95). I suppose one might argue that Bardolph deserves the same uniform treatment rather than being Bardoll in Part 1 and Bardolph in Part 2. There is little to be said about Kastan's particular editorial choices, based as they are on a sound conservative principle of following Q. In a note to line III.i.226 about the music that Glendower conjures up, Kastan writes that 'Hotspur … is presumably aware, as is the audience of the play, that the musicians in the theatre company are most likely sitting behind a curtain in the music gallery and so might indeed be said to "Hang in the air", 221'. Actually, Richard Hosley long ago showed that in stage directions for music the location changed from 'within' (that is, inside the tiring house) to 'above' around 1609, presumably when the King's men altered the practices at their open-air Globe playhouse to match the practices at the indoor Blackfriars ('Was There a Music-Room in Shakespeare's Globe?', *ShS* 13[1960] 113–23). Unless we think they altered their practices twice, the strong likelihood is that at the Theatre and the Curtain (where *1 Henry IV* was first performed) the music room was also inside the tiring house, not in 'the music gallery' as Kastan supposes. On a couple of occasions Kastan might have stuck with a quarto reading but does not. At IV.i.20 he has a messenger say 'His letters bear his mind, not I, my lord' where Q1 has 'His letters beares his mind, not I my mind'. Sisson (2:36) pointed out that the quarto reading make perfect sense: 'It is not my job to carry my own opinions to you, just letters.' Likewise, at V.iii.22 Kastan has Douglas say to the slain Blount 'A fool go with thy soul, whither it goes!' where Q1 has 'Ah foole, goe with thy soule whither it goes'; Sisson pointed out (2:38) that Q1 makes perfect sense: 'You and your soul, dead Blount, go together to wherever you are going.'

Brian Vickers's *Shakespeare, Co-Author* is divided in two parts, moving from the general ('Elizabethan Drama and the Methodology of Authorship Studies', pp. 1–134) to the specific ('Shakespeare as Co-Author', pp. 135–500). In a brief survey of early printings of Shakespeare, Vickers claims that 'A "booke" was the term used to describe a playhouse manuscript or prompt-book, prepared by or for the "book holder", who acted as stage manager and prompter' (p. 6). Actually, Henslowe frequently referred to what he bought from a dramatist as 'the booke', and such a thing certainly had yet to be theatricalized; there are nine examples within two pages of Foakes's edition (*Henslowe's Diary, Edited with Supplementary Material, Introduction and Notes*, pp. 96–7). Vickers calls Henslowe's Diary 'a business record' (p. 20), which it is, but it also has spells, medical treatments, and card tricks in it. Occasionally an error might be due to over-zealous copy-editing, such as the failure to capitalize the name of The Theatre in Shoreditch (p. 7). Vickers shows that naming a sole dramatist was, in the early part of the period, considered unimportant, and naming joint dramatists even less so, but over time both kinds of naming became more usual (pp. 10–17). Collaborations were less likely to reach print, but by the time of the 1623 Folio it was not unusual to acknowledge co-authorship. Perhaps in constructing 'Shakespeare' in F, Heminges and Condell decided not to acknowledge his collaborations, but we do not have to follow them, Vickers points out. Vickers thinks that Shakespeare demonstrably collaborated 'in at least seven surviving plays' (p. 19), and it would have been a courtesy to here name them for the reader. By G.E. Bentley's calculation about 15–20 per cent of all plays were collaborative, and of the professional plays as many as 50 per cent 'incorporated the writing at some date of more than one man' (that is, including those that got subsequently reworked by someone other than the original writer) and in Henslowe's Diary the proportion reaches 66 per cent.

Vickers uncritically repeats W.W. Greg's view of what a playhouse 'plot' was for (p. 21) and surveys the scant evidence for the unit of division between collaborators, usually the 'act' as frequently mentioned in Henslowe's Diary (pp. 27–9). The discussion here really ought to have addressed the problem that before 1609 the open-air amphitheatres, for which many of the dramatists were writing, did not use act intervals. Did they think in acts anyway? In a chapter on 'Identifying Co-Authors' (pp. 44–134) Vickers surveys methods of making attributions from internal evidence, including pause pattern tests and proclitic and enclitic microphrases. He gives a scathing summary of the faults in Gary Taylor's *Textual Companion* to the Oxford *Complete Works* concerning function word frequencies as a means of determining authorship, and does the same to the faults in the stylometric methods of A.Q. Morton and his followers G. Harold Metz and Thomas Merriam, and ending with the off-the-spectrum craziness of Barron Brainerd. Against all this Vickers contrasts the entirely reasonable work of Ward Elliott and Robert Valenza and the Claremont McKenna 'Shakespeare Authorship Clinic' and the sociolinguistics of Jonathan Hope that tracks changes in usage over time and between different social groups, as in 'you' instead of 'thou' being educated, urban youth-speak more likely to come from a Fletcher than a Shakespeare (pp. 116–19). A particularly good marker is 'auxiliary *do*', the absence of which (the 'unregulated' form, as in 'Went you home?' instead of our 'Did you go home?') was old-fashioned. Shakespeare's rate of regulation never exceeded 84 per cent, while six other dramatists Hope compared him to never fell below 85 per cent. Unaccountably in the middle of discussing Hope's work on the choice of *thou/you*, Vickers starts referring to 'T/V choice' (p. 124) without mentioning that it comes from the linguists' convention of using 'T' for the informal form (from the French 'tu') and 'V' for the formal form (from the French 'vous'). Vickers has a high opinion of the work of Gregor Sarrazin on the words that Shakespeare dropped from and added to his vocabulary over his career, which showed that each play really does have most 'rare word' links with other plays composed at the same time, and MacDonald Jackson's sophistications of this (pp. 129–32), as reviewed here last year.

Turning to Shakespeare, Vickers revises his count of co-authored plays to eight by adding *Edward III*. Of these, the collaboration with Middleton on *Timon of Athens* (pp. 244–90) is not of itself going to surprise anyone, nor is the collaboration with Wilkins on *Pericles* (pp. 291–332), nor with Fletcher on *Henry VIII* and *The Two Noble Kinsmen* (pp. 333–432). Vickers begins with his most surprising claim, that Peele wrote part of *Titus Andronicus* (pp. 148–243). The date of *Titus* is no longer set by the 'ne' record in Henslowe for 23 (read 24) January 1593, since Frazer (discussed above in connection with Roger Warren's edition of *2 Henry VI*) showed that it could mean 'performed at Newington' (p. 149). Vickers accepts June Schlueter's argument, which would take the Peacham picture away from Shakespeare's play, but neglects to mention Stanley Wells's immediate objection ('Letter to the Editor: "The Longleat Drawing"', *TLS* 23 April[1999] 17), or Richard Levin's subsequent demolition of Schlueter's position ('The Longleat Manuscript and *Titus Andronicus*', *SQ* 53[2002] 323–40); the latter probably came too late for the book. Vickers gives a brief history of more than 300 years of critical dislike of the play (pp. 150–5) and moves on to the tangible evidence. T.M. Parrott compared the rate of feminine endings in Shakespeare (8–12 per cent on average) with other dramatists who used them much less, and noticed that Act I of *Titus* has only about 3.6 per cent; Parrott also noticed verbal parallels between Act I and the works of Peele, and the rest with Shakespeare (pp. 156–60). Peele coined the word 'palliament', meaning robe, in his poem *The Honour of the Garter* [1593] and it appears also in Act I of *Titus* but nowhere else in Shakespeare or indeed anyone else. Philip Timberlake's 1931 book on feminine endings showed that differing definitions of this phenomenon give different counts, but that *Titus* I.i, II.i, and IV.i have far too few, howsoever counted, to be by Shakespeare, and the rest of the play has far too many to be by anyone else (p. 163). Because Hereward T. Price misrepresented Timberlake's findings, no one paid serious attention to his work until MacDonald Jackson confirmed it in 1979. Vickers is a master of rhetoric and sometimes needs to be watched closely, as when he admits that a dramatist might alter a co-author's work, but 'all the historical evidence reviewed in Chapter 1 indicates that co-authors normally contributed whole acts, or at least whole scenes, and the piecemeal over-writing [Shakespeare redoing Peele] that Dover Wilson claimed to discover seems improbable' (p. 181). Actually, there was little historical evidence about the unit of collaboration in chapter 1, and it was all confined to pages 27–34.

Vickers is particularly scathing about scholarly avoidance of the fairly obvious (and forever evidentially growing) fact that *Titus* was co-authored with Peele. Eugene Waith for the Oxford Shakespeare pretended that it was not and the Oxford *Complete Works* did not mention it, although Taylor had become convinced and said so in the *Textual Companion*. (In fact, the electronic edition of the Oxford *Complete*

Works, published in 1989, does mark the editors' doubts about Shakespeare's authorship of Act I and scenes II.i and IV.i, but the reader has to know that that is what is meant by the arcane electronic tag '<?A Shakespeare>'.) Vickers roundly castigates Alan Hughes's New Cambridge Shakespeare and Jonathan Bate's Arden 3 Shakespeare editions of *Titus*, the latter especially for relying on A.Q. Morton's discredited work, and Sonia Massai's New Penguin edition for simply reporting that 'Bate distances himself' from the view that Peele wrote Act I (pp. 192–210). Vickers is occasionally so rude about other scholars' ignorance that it is tempting to respond in kind, and opportunities certainly present themselves. To claim that permissive phrasing 'has long been understood as typifying an author's stage directions in its vagueness (since those involved in theatrical productions need to specify just which actors/characters are involved)' (p. 121) is to show ignorance of an entire field of textual-theatrical scholarship led by Paul Werstine and William Long that is firmly ranged against what Vickers thinks 'long … understood'. As an example, Vickers offers the permissive direction for the entrance of 'as many as can be' in the first act of *Titus* and in Peele's *Edward I* that Jackson thought unique in the canon of English Renaissance drama from 1576 to 1642. When Vickers repeated this claim on Hardy Cook's SHAKSPER email discussion list (archived at www.shaksper.net) I supplied him with references to five further examples, two anonymous, and one each by Armin, Chettle, and the Fletcher–Massinger collaboration (posting SHK 14.0994 on 20 May 2003).

Vickers's chapter '*Timon of Athens* with Thomas Middleton' offers nothing new but a summary of the arguments that he thinks have been under-examined by the scholarly community. An odd comment occurs in a footnote that claims he has 'twice attempted to obtain Dr [R.V.] Holdsworth's permission to read his thesis, but without success' (p. 280 n. 30). I should have thought anyone could just go to the University of Manchester library where it resides and read it there if the authorities will not let it be posted elsewhere. The chapter on *Pericles* follows the same trajectory, but here Vickers lays into the New Cambridge Shakespeare edition by two professors of drama, Doreen Del Vecchio and Anthony Hammond, for its ignorance of much of the authorship scholarship and for their misrepresentation of the little they knew. The implication is that the shift towards stage-centred thinking in Shakespeare studies has been at the cost of some English literature specialist skills ('the stage is not in any case a court of appeal in authorship studies, for quite different concerns are involved', p. 329), but one could argue with equal force about Vickers's ignorance of developments in thinking about matters theatrical. At the start of the sixth chapter, on collaboration with Fletcher, Vickers tacitly admits that the book has become formulaic ('a by now familiar pattern', p. 333) in its movement from nineteenth-century pioneering work on authorship, later consolidated, denied, or overlooked by the 'Shakespeare "conservators"', and now reconfirmed by fresh scholarship. Here, however, Vickers is hamstrung by the lack of opposing voices— even E.K. Chambers could see that *Henry VIII* was collaborative—so he starts to invent them. A sustained attack on Gordon McMullan's Arden 3 edition of *Henry VIII* is pure 'straw man', as is the complaint that Literary Theory (Vickers's capitals) has banished the concept of the author. The final chapter, 'Plot and Character in Co-Authored Plays: Problems of Co-ordination' (pp. 433–500) is a survey of traditional scholarship on organic unity, and shows scant familiarity with recent critical and historical work, which failing in others is one of Vickers's chief bugbears. For example, Vickers quotes without demur the view of J.Q. Adams that 'Henslowe continually oppressed by hard dealings' the Lady Elizabeth's men and had a policy of keeping them in debt (p. 433), which no one familiar with recent work on the subject—or even passingly familiar with Foakes's scholarship—would accept.

The second appendix of Vickers's book is called 'Abolishing the Author? Theory *versus* History' (pp. 506–41), and in it he exercises his familiar antipathy to theory while making a number of substantial points that could in fact be usefully corrective of it. Michel Foucault's claim (in 'What is an Author?') that from the seventeenth century onwards scientific texts were essentially anonymous is not true: Kepler, Galileo, Descartes, and Newton were scientific authors, and likewise his claim that before then poetic texts were effectively anonymous is in complete ignorance of the classical world's concept of the author (pp. 509–17). Ninety per cent of all books published in England from 1475 to 1641 (30,000+ items) have authors specifically thanking their patrons, which is not the behaviour of 'Anon.', and publishers often boasted that the author's permission had not been received, hence an *unauthorized* publication depending on the notion of an author who will be displeased. Vickers offers a most useful survey of the evidence that plagiarism was recognized and detested (pp. 522–7), and then gets personal. Jeffrey Masten is excoriated for swallowing Foucault's nonsense about the invention of the author and moving it back to Shakespeare's time, and for not engaging with the practicalities of collaboration at all; rather (and this complaint has some merit), Masten simply repeats the mantra that we cannot separate out who wrote what, and that collaboration preceded single authorship. It is fair of Vickers to complain that Masten is evasive about just when the 'author-function' emerged: in Masten, it is forever 'emergent' but never comes out (p. 531). Somewhat unfair, however, is the claim that Masten entirely imposes homoerotic interest on the texts that he reads and links them to collaboration without justification. Appropriately, Vickers ends with a strike that rebounds on him, quoting Masten repeating the word 'homosocial' and commenting 'Michel Foucault, thou art mighty yet' (p. 535). Vickers seems not to know that the term is not Foucault's but Eve Kosofsky Sedgwick's. Physician, heal thyself.

Vickers's other book this year, *'Counterfeiting' Shakespeare*, is longer still and much better. The 'counterfeiting' of his title is not the creation of false documents but the venial sin of 'presenting anonymously authored work as Shakespeare's' (p. xii). The subtitle makes clear that Vickers is concerned with Donald Foster's since retracted claim that *A Funerall Elegye* is by Shakespeare, but in fact the retraction came while the book was in production. Indeed, in a letter to the *Times Literary Supplement* on the day that this review was completed (16 January 2004) Vickers claimed that Foster used bullying tactics to hold up Cambridge University Press's publication of this book in order to be able to concede defeat to Gilles Monsarrat (whose article is reviewed below) rather than to Vickers. In a stop-press note (p. xxi), Vickers mentions that Foster announced his submission in a posting to the SHAKSPER email discussion but gives the wrong date (it was 12 June 2002, not 13 June) and the wrong SHAKSPER index number (it was 13.1514, not 13.1519). Limbering up for his attack on Foster, Vickers begins with the relatively easy target of Gary Taylor's attribution of 'Shall I die' to Shakespeare, made using just printed concordances, whereas these days full-text computer databases would be employed (pp. 1–53). Like *Shakespeare, Co-Author*, *'Counterfeiting' Shakespeare* is divided into two parts: the first (pp. 55–260) on what is wrong with Foster's attribution of *A Funerall Elegye* to Shakespeare, and the second (pp. 261–464) on why we should think it was really by Ford. Key pieces of evidence that Vickers reviews are by now familiar: the poem gets wrong the length of William Peter's marriage at the time of his death (three years, not nine), Gilbert Shakespeare was buried the same week as William Peter—so it is hard to imagine Shakespeare taking time to honour a man he hardly (if at all) knew—and that the initials 'W.S.' should raise immediate suspicions for they never appeared on a genuine Shakespeare work and were used several times on things we know were not his. The chapter 'Parallels? Plagiarism?' (pp. 80–99) shows that none of Foster's claimed links between *A Funerall Elegye* and Shakespeare stand up: they are all commonplaces or simple misreadings of the texts, and the next chapter shows that Foster's grasp of 'Vocabulary and Diction' (pp. 100–20), especially Shakespeare's, was woefully inadequate to the task. Foster chose a list of 'function words' (ones that add no poetic content and the relative frequencies of which are stable across the Shakespeare canon), starting with *and*, *but*, *not*, *so*, *that*, *by*, *in*, *to*, and *with*, but he made the fatal error (pointed out by MacDonald Jackson in 1989) of paring this list down by eliminating the last four and so entirely distorted the picture (pp. 114–19)

Foster's database of 'representative' English Memorial Verse 1610–13 was horribly unrepresentative, and hence Foster convinced himself that using 'who' for an inanimate antecedent (as in 'hopes ... who') when personification is not being used ('stars ... who') was distinctly Shakespearian; it is not. Foster was also wildly inaccurate in summarizing the findings of A.C. Partridge and Charles Barber (pp. 121–38). Charles Bathurst established that three aspects of Shakespeare's prosody changed over his career—he moved the caesura, he made fewer pauses at the end of a line, and he used more double endings (p. 139)—and by contrast Foster's analysis of the poetic structure of *A Funerall Elegye* (and its likeness to Shakespeare's sonnets) is a catalogue of half-truths (pp. 141–4). To make his claims about the 'Funerall Elegye''s enjambment, Foster blamed George Eld's compositors for heavily punctuating W.S.'s lightly pointed text, but Vickers thinks that there is no reason to suppose that the copy was lightly pointed and that most evidence indicates that compositors usually respected copy punctuation (p. 146). This is not quite true, since Joseph Moxon advised that compositors should improve punctuation if necessary, and Vickers appears to concede this point in a footnote (p. 151 n. 16) that cites D.F. McKenzie showing that Pavier's compositor B added heavy punctuation, especially at the ends of lines. Vickers objects to Foster's claim that 'As a measure of style any reasonable definition is adequate so long as the same criterion is used throughout', thinking rather that one needs sensitivity to historical differences, specifically here between syntactic enjambment and non-punctuated lines (p. 147). This objection Vickers seems to have forgotten 350 pages (!) later when he writes in support of F.E. Peirce's claim that '"the value of any criterion depends largely on the consistency with which" it is used' (p. 499), which is much the same thing as Foster claimed. One reason why there are so many pages in Vickers's book is that the publisher has permitted slack writing, such as 'wrote a *particular* poem in *Anno Domini* 1612' (p. 147): the words I have emphasized could go without hardship.

Foster edited ' A Funerall Elegye' to remove most of the end-line punctuation, and then showed that in not having it (that is, in having enjambed lines) the poem was like late Shakespeare. Put the punctuation back in, as Vickers has done, and its rate of enjambment looks like Shakespeare in 1599, which is of course impossible given the date of Peter's death (p. 152). Piling up the evidence, Vickers shows that the poem's rate of feminine endings, 11.6 per cent of lines, is far below the 30+ per cent of late Shakespeare, that the frequency of hexameter lines, 0.35 per cent, is far below the 2 per cent average of late Shakespeare, and that the pause patterns too are markedly different from late Shakespeare (pp. 153–9). The pioneer of pause-pattern analysis was Ants Oras, who 'showed that Shakespeare's early plays favour a caesura after the fourth foot; by 1600 the fourth and sixth positions are equally favoured, while in the later period the sixth position is dominant, with the unstressed seventh position gaining importance' (p. 156). The point is a good one, although Vickers surely means the fourth syllable not foot; pity the proof-reader of a 568-page monograph. Driving the final quantitative nails in, Vickers shows that study of proclitic and enclitic micro-phrases (that is, an unstressed monosyllable leaning forward to the stressed syllable following it, or backward to the stressed syllable preceding it) puts *A Funerall Elegye* impossibly far from Shakespeare (pp. 160–2). The rest of this section gilds the lily with chapters showing that the hendiadys Foster saw in *A Funerall Elegye* just is not there and that he did not really understand the rhetorical term properly (pp. 163–88), and that Foster is terrible at statistics (pp. 189–203). Most of the second part of the book, showing that Ford wrote *A Funerall Elegye*, is not directly relevant to this review. In chapter 10, however, Vickers shows that many habits that Foster claimed were distinctly Shakespearian—such as the coining of *un-* words, the making of compound words, the use of 'very' as a restrictive adjective ('the very man'), and elliptic use of 'can' (as in 'I can not more')—are found in abundance in Ford, and Vickers adds more things of his own that Ford and *A Funerall Elegye* share (pp. 302–62). Chapter 11 (pp. 363–431) completes the argument with a list of all the Ford parallels that Vickers found in *A Funerall Elegye*.

In an 'epilogue' with the surprisingly trendy title of 'The Politics of Attribution' (pp. 422–65), Vickers considers the fascinating question of how Foster's nonsense was taken so seriously for so long. Or, what is wrong with the academy? Here Vickers examines the kudos Foster earned from identifying Joe Klein as the author of *Primary Colors*—there were hardly a lot of candidates in that case—and most shockingly his shameful intrusion in the JonBenét Ramsey murder case, first blaming the victim's half-brother, who was never a suspect, then asserting the innocence of the mother, then asserting the guilt of the mother (pp. 458–62). Vickers finds a way to link the themes of this book—the academy's systemic failure in the case of *A Funerall Elegye*—to his particular bugbear of 'the "social agendas" of race, gender, and class' and uses John M. Ellis's false analogy with Darwinian 'fitness': adverse criticism picks off the weakest elements of an intellectual species and 'keep[s] it strong', without which 'the species degenerates' (p. 463). The analogy is false because species do not degenerate without predators, and this view of 'species health' has disturbing overtones of social Darwinism. Also, the opposition of political criticism with pure, disinterested research is false: many who consider themselves politically motivated in their criticism feel that their politics is best served by truthful models of the world, and that those schools of criticism that deny that they are political just want everyone to treat their politics as simple statements about reality and not a form of politics at all. In a final Vickersian paradox, he seems to accept a form of this argument, that what we call truth is often just whatever the powerful have got everyone to accept as truth, quoting C.S. Peirce making precisely this point (p. 465)

On to the year's articles. The journal *Studies in Bibliography* seems to arrive at most libraries at least a couple of years after the date on the spine, so it has not been noticed before within this reviewer's stint for *YWES*, which began with work published in 1999. Volume 52 (for 1999) is now available, but contains nothing of relevance to this review. Volume 53 (for 2000) begins with, of all things, a new essay by R.B. McKerrow, 'The Relationship of English Printed Books to Authors' Manuscripts During the Sixteenth and Seventeenth Centuries (The 1928 Sandars Lectures)', ed. Carlo M. Bajetta (*SB* 53[2000] 1–65) that is of great historical interest but does not fall within the scope of this review of work newly done. As reported last year, the journal *Analytical and Enumerative Bibliography* has closed. The 2002 issues of the journal *The Library* contained nothing of interest to this review. Volumes 14 and 15 of *Text* allegedly contain work published in 2001 and 2002 and hence relevant to this review, but the industry of the librarians of the Shakespeare Institute of the University of Birmingham (United Kingdom) has failed to elicit a copy of either from the publishers (UMichP) and review of this work will be held over until such time as it may be seen. Likewise, the most recent *Shakespearean International Yearbook* was dated the end of the last millennium and more recent volumes will be noticed when (if?) they ever appear.

Two articles in *Review of English Studies* were relevant this year. The first is Gilles Monsarrat's demonstration that *A Funerall Elegye* is not by Shakespeare but by Ford: '*A Funeral Elegy*: Ford, W.S., and Shakespeare' (*RES* 53[2002] 186–203). This we can tell from certain phrases that are seldom or never used by Shakespeare but are common in Ford; presumably 'W.S.' was a man who wanted to honour William Peter so he got Ford to do it as a job of work. In the second article, '*The True Tragedy of Richard Duke of York* and *3 Henry VI*: Report and Revision' (*RES* 53[2002] 8–30), Randall Martin expands upon the arguments in his Oxford Shakespeare edition of *3 Henry VI* (reviewed here last year), and specifically that memorial reconstruction and revision separate the octavo and Folio versions. Neither phenomenon on its own can account for the O/F relationship, and the case for memorial reconstruction is clinched by the misreporting of the marriage regarding Lord Scales. In O the complaint is about Scales's marriage to the daughter of Lord Bonfield and in F it is the marriage of Scales's daughter to the new queen's brother and Bon*ville*'s daughter's marriage to the new queen's son. As Peter Alexander observed, the whole point is the king's favouring of the queen's relatives, so O's version makes no sense (pp. 10–11). Steven Urkowitz defended O as still making theatrical sense, but overlooked Alexander's crucial point that Bonfield does not exist in the chronicles, and Martin thinks the name came from another play (accidentally remembered by the actor), *George a Greene* (p. 12). Likewise Lord Cobham getting the (historically incorrect) personal name Edmund Brooke in O makes no sense other than as an actor's mistake or interpolation, and there are examples in O of characters anticipating what they come to know only later in the play, which is just the sort of trick memory plays (pp. 13–14). Here Martin gives more evidence than he presented in his play edition: O (sig. A7r) has York say he is going to St Albans and staying at Sandall castle, all in one speech, and the Keeper spots deposed Henry VI in disguise before he has spoken (which is impossible), while F has him rightly overhear the ex-king and learn who he is from his own mouth (pp. 14–16). Some inartistic internal repetitions in O also betray its memorial-reconstruction origins, and Martin here repeats his argument—rather more clearly than in the play edition—that O used mostly Hall for its history and F used mostly Holinshed. Even bits that we cannot relate to Hall or Holinshed show a general pattern of artistic reshaping of MSO to make MSF, and O and F are really different plays separated by authorial revision.

The most important article this year is by Lukas Erne and appeared in *Shakespeare Quarterly*: 'Shakespeare and the Publication of his Plays' (*SQ* 53[2002] 1–20). The substance of it is that we have no reason to suppose that Shakespeare was indifferent to the publication of his plays: companies appear to have favoured printing about two years after composition, but they were at the mercy of the market, which Blayney has shown was not good for playtexts. Alexander Pope started the myth that Shakespeare did not care about publishing his plays ('And grew Immortal in his own despight') and it is still often repeated, although in 1965 E.A.J. Honigmann suggested we think again. In the light of Blayney's fresh view of the economics of publishing plays, we can revisit E.K. Chambers's assertion that a company would fear that publication would give its plays to rivals, and A.W. Pollard's that publication would hurt playhouse attendance. After all, *The Spanish Tragedy* was much printed and apparently stayed popular in performance. Richard Dutton suggested that it was the work of 'contracted "ordinary poets"' that the companies wanted to keep out of print, but if so they failed miserably: only eight non-Shakespearian Chamberlain's men plays from 1594–1603 reached print, while in the same period twelve of Shakespeare's plays for that company were printed. Of course, judging whose plays were printed from the evidence of what has survived is unsafe: Shakespeare quartos may well have been valued more, so had a better chance of surviving. My list of the Shakespeare plays printed between 1594 and 1603 is: *Titus Andronicus, 2 Henry VI, 3 Henry VI, Richard II, Richard III, Romeo and Juliet, 1 Henry IV, Love's Labour's Lost, Henry V, 2 Henry IV, Much Ado About Nothing, A Midsummer Night's Dream, The Merchant of Venice, The Merry Wives of Windsor*, and *Hamlet*, a total of fifteen. Erne excludes *Edward III* but includes the lost *Love's Labour's Won*, so how does he get his figure of twelve plays? Presumably by excluding *Titus Andronicus, 2 Henry VI*, and *3 Henry VI* as not being written for the Chamberlain's men; life would be easier if the reader did not have to guess such details. Even discounting the so-called 'bad' quartos, Erne points out that there are a lot of Shakespeare printings to account for. Chambers and Andrew Gurr accounted for the publications around the turn of the century with the need for money to build the Globe and Fortune, but Neil Carson's analysis of the Henslowe Diary shows that, while £5 or £8 might be paid for a script, £20 or £30 might be paid for costumes and other necessaries, and Blayney reckons that about 30 shillings were paid by a stationer for a play to print. In any case, as Erne argues, Shakespeare and his fellows were not hard up in the late 1590s, to judge by Shakespeare's purchases and James Burbage's will.

Erne sets himself the task of examining the first twelve plays Shakespeare wrote for the Chamberlain's men (p. 6), but frustratingly he does not state what he thinks those twelve plays are. He excludes *The Comedy of Errors* because he thinks it predates Shakespeare's joining the company, but does not explain how come *Titus Andronicus* and perhaps the early histories are not excluded for the same reason. In case the reader has retained a firm grasp of the lists that Erne is juggling, he switches at this point (p. 7) to the 'bad' quartos of plays written in the 1590s (*Romeo and Juliet*, *The Merry Wives of Windsor*, *Henry V*, and perhaps *Love's Labour's Lost*) and argues that Shakespeare would surely have preferred good texts to get printed. Well, answering himself, Erne observes that in the cases of *Romeo and Juliet*, *Hamlet*, and *Love's Labour's Lost* the 'bad' quartos were indeed followed by good. (If you are wondering what *Hamlet* has to do with this—were we not confining ourselves to the 1590s for a moment?—then that makes two of us.) Erne wisely does not rest too heavily on this *post hoc ergo propter hoc* argument: in the case of *Romeo and Juliet* the stationer owning the good manuscript may have got it *before* the bad quarto appeared even though he published his good manuscript *after* the bad, although Erne offers no reasons to prefer this 'may have' to its opposite. In the case of *Hamlet*, the guess that the good manuscript underlying Q2-1604 changed hands before the printing of Q1 is 'a strong, indeed the strongest, possibility' because James Roberts (who published Q2) entered *Hamlet* in the Stationers' Register on 26 July 1602, before Q1—printed by Valentine Simmes, Nicholas Ling, and John Trundle, without Stationers' Register entry—appeared in 1603.

Actually, Roberts did not publish Q2 *Hamlet*, for its title page says 'Printed by I[ames] R[oberts] for N[icholas] L[ing]', which means that Ling published it and Roberts was just the printer; Erne goes on to account for this. Erne finds that one theory fits these facts best: 'Ling and Trundell seem to have licensed but not entered their manuscript [that is, MSQ1] and had it printed without anyone realizing that Roberts had once entered a different version. Having found out about Ling and Trundle's unintentional breach, Roberts could have caused them trouble but may have preferred to negotiate an advantageous deal with his neighbors in Fleet Street, selling to Ling and Trundle his longer and better manuscript and having them pay him to print it' (p. 7).

In the case of *Love's Labour's Lost* there is no extant bad quarto, but Q1's title page implies that one once existed by describing the text as 'Newly corrected and augmented'. But that claim is also made on the title page of Q3 *Richard III*, where it is 'demonstrably misleading' (*Textual Companion*, p. 270), and Werstine has shown that the Q1 *Love's Labour's Lost* copy appears to have been print, not manuscript, so there was a good Q0. So, in each of these three cases (*Romeo and Juliet*, *Hamlet*, and *Love's Labour's Lost*), it seems that the Chamberlain's men sold a good manuscript before the first edition, rather than that they reacted to the bad quarto by selling a good manuscript to supersede it. At least, that is what Erne thinks he has shown, but in fact he offers no evidence for his chronology in the case of *Romeo and Juliet*. He has a workable (but not the only) hypothesis for *Hamlet*, and has shown that there was no bad quarto of *Love's Labour's Lost* in the first place; this does not amount to showing that a good manuscript was sold before a bad quarto came out. What of the 'bad' quartos which were not superseded by good ones, *Henry V* and *The Merry Wives of Windsor*? Erne knows that it will not do to argue that the non-superseding of these shows the company's indifference to printing, for it may rather have been that they sold poorly and no publisher had reason to invest in a subsequent edition. Having dealt with four of the twelve plays (*Romeo and Juliet*, *The Merry Wives of Windsor*, *Henry V*, *Love's Labour's Lost*), Erne comments that 'Of the eight other plays Shakespeare is likely to have written for his company from 1594 until close to the turn of the century'—yes, yet another way of defining an unstated list—*Love's Labour's Won* (if it ever existed) cannot be discussed because lost and

King John did not get printed until 1623 (pp. 8–9). Perhaps in the case of *King John* the company feared infringing the *Troublesome Reign* quarto of 1591.

The other six Shakespeare plays (*Richard II*, *A Midsummer Night's Dream*, *The Merchant of Venice*, *1 Henry IV*, *2 Henry IV*, and *Much Ado About Nothing*—that is, the remaining six of the first twelve that Shakespeare wrote for the Chamberlain's men—*were* in fact printed between 1597 and 1600. For these Erne thinks we should look at the underlying copy of the printing to see if the players sold their manuscripts to the printer. The copy is uncertain for *Richard II* and *The Merchant of Venice* (authorial manuscript, or faithful transcript of it), for *1 Henry IV* is probably scribal transcript of authorial manuscript, and is probably author's manuscript for *A Midsummer Night's Dream*, *2 Henry IV*, and *Much Ado About Nothing* (pp. 9–10). Erne acknowledges recent objections to the new bibliography that gives us these conclusions, but points out that there is nothing to 'contradict the interpretation that any one of them [that is, the copy manuscripts] may (though not necessarily all of them must) have been in the possession of the Lord Chamberlain's Men and/or their playwright before being sold to a stationer'. Looking at the likely dates of composition and of entrance in the Stationers' Register, Erne finds roughly a two-year wait in each case. Leaving aside the corrupt *Pericles*, only two more of Shakespeare's plays were printed in his lifetime—*Troilus and Cressida* and *King Lear*—and again there is a two-year gap between composition (1601 and 1605, respectively) and Stationers' Register entry (1603 and 1607, respectively). One could quibble with some of the dates here, but mostly not by more than a year or so. Erne sees the danger of circularity in his method: some of the datings are dependent on assumptions about the unlikelihood of the players letting the printers get the plays, but he admits that in the case of *A Midsummer Night's Dream* 'there's nothing beyond style to suggest a particular date' (p. 11). He has to say that, for the usual dating of 1595 is a full five years before the first printing, bucking his trend and prompting him to wonder if its being written for a private wedding and not publicly performed until some time later solves the problem.

Erne sums up crisply: 'of Shakespeare's first dozen or so plays written for the Lord Chamberlain's Men, not a single one that could legally have been printed remained unprinted by 1602' (p. 12) and the typical vector was the company selling a manuscript to a printer two years after first performance. Why wait two years? Because that was about the time to publicly promote a revival of a play (pp. 14–15). For some reason the printing of Shakespeare plays fell off after 1600: thirteen plays in twenty-four editions from 1594 to 1600 (more than three a year) whereas only five plays in nineteen editions from 1601 to 1616 (just over one a year). Blayney suggested that perhaps the market was glutted around 1600 (twenty-seven plays entered in the Stationers' Register between May 1600 and October 1601), and publishers were finding that they did not sell as hoped. The remainder of Erne's article deals with small objections that might be made to his main thesis, and he concludes by observing, as Blayney does, that we have been looking at play publication from the wrong end (writers and companies) rather than from the end of stationers, publishers, and booksellers. The essential error, revealed by Blayney's scholarship, was that we assumed that demand for printed plays exceeded supply, but in fact it did not. Once we refocus our attention in the light of this, we can address some old problems with fresh insight: why are plays too long to be performed in two hours, what lies behind the 'bad' or short quartos, and how was a play text 'socialized'?

One of those questions is addressed with fresh evidence by Jesus Tronch-Pérez, who shows that a Spanish case of memorial reconstruction of a play gives comfort to the theory that Q1 *Hamlet* was made this way: 'A Comparison of the Suspect Texts of Lope de Vega's *La Dama Boba* and Shakespeare's *Hamlet*' (*ShY* 13[2002] 30–57). Memory man Luís Remírez signed his reconstructed copy of Lope de Vega's play *La dama boba* and we have Lope's autograph copy and a published version. Folio *Hamlet* deviates from Q2 *Hamlet* in much the way the memorial reconstruction of *La dama boba* deviates from Lope's holograph, and Q1 *Hamlet* is quite different again, so at first it looks like Folio *Hamlet* is a memorial reconstruction. But with a study of how the variants do their differing, this changes: whereas 45 per cent of Folio *Hamlet* differences from Q2 are 'indifferent', 36.5 per cent change the meaning, and 18.5 per cent are uses of synonyms, in the memorial reconstruction of Lope's play nearly half the substitutions are 'words of related meaning and paraphrases', 'indifferent' variants count for 36.5 per cent, and 15 per cent actually change the meaning. Compared to Q2, Q1 *Hamlet* too mostly contains changes that preserve the meaning and least numerous are those changes that alter the meaning; thus the Lope memorial reconstruction is like Q1 *Hamlet*, and this is especially true of those parts of Act I involving Marcellus and, to a slightly lesser extent, his allegedly doubled role of Voltemar. The memory man Remírez sometimes brings forward a word that should occur later (sometimes much later) in the play, and Folio *Hamlet* does this in respect of Q2 and so does Q1, and Q1 repeatedly uses stock phrases in relation to a certain idea ('the cause and ground' of Hamlet's madness), and so does Remírez (pp. 44–6). Tronch-Pérez concludes:

> Of the textual features I have analysed in all three texts, Remírez's version of *La dama boba* has many more in common with the First Folio *Hamlet* than with the First Quarto *Hamlet*. ... This shows that Remírez's memorial reconstruction was of such good quality that it resembled more the variant textual versions of Shakespeare's multiple-text plays such as *King Lear*, *Richard III* and *Hamlet* than the 'bad' quarto versions, and that it would not be judged a 'bad' or suspect text unless we had the external documentary evidence that indicates the contrary. (p. 52)

But the Spanish memorial reconstruction and Q1 *Hamlet* do have things in common: 'In three kinds of textual alteration, both DB and Q1 interestingly show higher frequency than F1 does: synonymic and near-synonymic substitutions (from single words to paraphrase of several lines), internal repetitions of single words and phrases (including quasi-formulaic expressions), transposition of single words, phrases and lines' (p. 53). Importantly, Q1 *Hamlet* resembles the Spanish memorial reconstruction 'in those segments in which the alleged reporter Marcellus intervenes'. This does not prove that Q1 *Hamlet* is a memorial reconstruction, nor that the parts of Q1 *Hamlet* unlike the Spanish memorial reconstruction are not due to memorial reconstruction: the internal evidence is simply inconclusive, and in the Spanish case we have reliable external evidence that tells us it is a memorial reconstruction. Thus, 'Q1's explanation as a memorial reconstruction, based on internal evidence alone, remains a probable, but unproved, hypothesis' (p. 54), and importantly the recollections of a man consciously attempting to memorize a play would necessarily be different from the memory of a man performing in it and only later attempting to recall the text.

Three articles from *Shakespeare Survey* were relevant this year. In the first, 'How Shakespeare Knew *King Leir*' (*ShS* 55[2002] 12–35), Richard Knowles argues that Shakespeare might have seen *King Leir* in the 1590s but it did not much affect his writing until it was published in 1605, whereupon it became a source for Shakespeare's *King Lear*. Henslowe's Diary records 'Kinge Leare' performed on 6 and 8 April 1594, and it was entered in the Stationers' Register on 14 May 1594 by Edward White and again on 8 May 1605 by Simon Stafford and then the same day transferred to John Wright, who had Stafford print it later in 1605. Many commentators have thought *King Lear* little indebted to *Leir*, but Knowles lists the similarities of plot and argues that they show Shakespeare's 'recent and detailed' knowledge of the source—most of them are not in the other sources—and there are quite a few verbal parallels too (pp. 14–17). McMillin and MacLean thought that Shakespeare was in the Queen's men (who played *Leir*), but if so it is hard to understand how come his pre-1594 plays (the murky period) were performed by Strange's men (*1 Henry VI*, *Titus Andronicus*), Pembroke's men (*2 and 3 Henry VI*, *The Taming of the Shrew*, and *Titus Andronicus*), and Sussex's men (*Titus Andronicus*). More likely, thinks Knowles, he moved between these companies and never played in *Leir* (p. 18). Scholarly claims that *Leir* influenced lots of other Shakespeare plays have been grossly inflated, and Knowles sees no such influence at all, and even if accepted, there is no certainty that Shakespeare was the borrower rather than the lender.

Knowles takes care to demolish claimed echoes of *Leir* in Shakespeare's plays other than *King Lear*, for example by showing that malapropism existed well before he wrote it for the Watch in *Much Ado About Nothing* (pp. 22–7). In any case there is no obvious means by which *Leir* might have influenced Shakespeare: no edition was printed from 1594 (recorded performance) to 1605, although if Shakespeare was in Sussex's men in April 1594, when they were sharing the Rose with the Queen's men—as Henslowe's column heading of plays performed by 'the Quenes men and my lord of Susexe to gether' is usually taken to mean—then he might have seen it. But this would not give the occasion for repeated and sustained influence for the next ten years that some scholars have claimed. Nor could he have had access to the manuscript: White would have kept the one he registered in 1594. Henslowe wrote that in May 1594 the Queen's men 'brocke & went into the contrey to playe', which is a bit ambiguous ('broke' and carried on playing?), but they certainly did not disappear as a company but rather toured successfully for another decade, so they are unlikely to have given up the playbook of one of their most successful plays since they would need the licensed copy if challenged about their authority to play it on tour. Probably what they sold in 1594 was an authorial or scribal copy of their licensed playbook. Henslowe must have had faith in the Queen's men's provincial future, for he lent his nephew Francis Henslowe £15 to buy a share in them. The Queen's men disbanded with their patron's death in 1603, and that is probably when they sold off the licensed playbook of *Leir* and hence Stafford got it. This cannot have been the same manuscript that Edward White registered in 1594 because (1) White did not transfer it to anyone, and (2) White's heirs continued to claim ownership of it long after his death (p. 30). The fact that the 1605 edition of *Leir* does not mention the company or the venue is also consistent with the copy coming from the disbanded Queen's men; they had not been in London for over a decade and there would be no advantage in harking back to 1594 when they last were. Hence the title page's simple claim that the play was 'divers and sundry times lately acted'.

On the other hand, what got printed does not seem to be a battered and presumably written-over licensed playbook (marked for a reduced company on tour) but rather a clean, pre-theatrical text for a full-sized company. And what of the fact that Wright was formerly White's apprentice? Wright had only just got his freedom, so he is hardly likely to have risked his whole future on a piracy of his master's possession. Knowles's ingenious hypothesis is that Stafford got hold of a manuscript from the disbanded Queen's men, went to register it, and found that White had registered the play eleven years before. Stafford went to White, who did 'two good deeds at once': he allowed Stafford to print it, if he made Wright (White's newly freed apprentice) the publisher; then White handed over his own manuscript (the one he registered in 1594) and that is what got printed; hence the 1605 printing is not like what we would expect from a manuscript that has been used on tour for a decade. Or perhaps White just let Stafford's compositor look at his 1594 manuscript to check readings. There is no evidence that any of the newly formed Chamberlain's men of 1594 came from the Queen's men, so in all of this theatre and textual history there is no obvious means for Shakespeare to get hold of a manuscript of *Leir*. The obvious impetus for his doing his *Lear* play was simply the publication of *Leir* in 1605.

The second piece from *Shakespeare Survey* is Sonia Massai's '"Taking Just Care of the Impression": Editorial Intervention in Shakespeare's Fourth Folio, 1685' (*ShS* 55[2002] 257–70), which claims that the Third Folio copy for the Fourth Folio was editorially annotated, probably by Nahum Tate, and hence Rowe should not be counted the first editor of Shakespeare. Massai lists occasions when F4 speculatively emends its copy, F3, to produce really rather good (even F1) readings in place of bad; but this was not done by reference to F1 since 'on other occasions mistakes first introduced in F2 or F3 are not emended according to F1' and Massai points out that the F3/F4 corrections she has noted could not happen during stop-press correction (pp. 260–1). An example: F4 wrongly calls a character in *Coriolanus* 'Titus Lucius' where F1-3 had the correct 'Titus Lartius'; the change probably happened because in F1-3 this man is addressed (wrongly) as 'Titus Lucius'. It is unlikely that a compositor of F4 adopted 'Lucius' (which is what he set) throughout his work, and against his F3 copy, on the basis of this one line of dialogue. More likely his F3 copy was annotated with all the 'Lartius' readings changed to 'Lucius' readings. Similarly, elsewhere in F4 *Coriolanus* speech prefixes are altered (that is, the F3 speech prefix is overruled) to make them match names as spoken in dialogue.

Some F4 plays were much more altered (in respect of their F3 copy) than others, which also suggests not correction in the three printing houses (which would tend to be uniform across plays printed in each house) but editorial intervention at the level of F3 copy and varying according to 'the editor's familiarity with a specific text, or the intrinsic quality of his copy-text'. Confirming this is the 'consistency of procedures' across the division of labour in printing F4 between the three printing houses: compared the F3 copy, commas are used to improve syntax, apostrophes are used to mark contractions and possession, and spelling is modernized. To show that this is not simply what anyone printing in the 1680s would do with copy from the 1660s, Massai looked at *The Northern Lass* (printed 1663 and 1684) and *A Jovial Crew* (printed 1661 and 1684) and found that the changes between F3 and F4 are much more numerous than the changes in these two Brome plays. It is clearly intentional editorial change, not a shift in the general climate (p. 262). Looking at other printings of *belles-lettres* there appears to be a nascent 'editor' function in the sixteenth and seventeenth centuries, even though it did not become a distinct job title until the early eighteenth century. As the 'literary author as sole originator of his meanings' came to be constructed in the seventeenth century, there was some reluctance to admit that editing had taken place, and Massai quotes prefaces that refer to the need to make sure that printers do not mangle the author's words (p. 265). Writers tended not to mention editorial annotation of copy prior to printing because it was 'ideologically controversial' although necessary, and increasingly printing houses built up communities of scholarly freelancers who worked on copy prior to printing, as when Nicholas and John Okes hired Thomas Heywood (whose plays they had printed) to work on others' plays, including making choice of copy, making explanatory notes, and indices. Henry Herringman, one of the F4 publishers, probably had the services of John Dryden, and another Herringman reprint, *Cutter of Cole-man Street* (1663 and 1693), has levels of editorial intervention similar to those that Massai has found between F3 and F4, and in particular such features as making speech prefixes match what someone is called in dialogue (p. 268). The likeliest candidate for the secret editor of F4 is Nahum Tate, for Dryden was at the time working for another publisher, had in past passed work on to Tate, and we know that Tate subsequently did editorial work for Herringman. F4 *Coriolanus* has 'Commons' where F3 has 'Commoners', which Massai thinks would be a typical intervention from Tate, for he does not characterize the populace as a rabble in his own adaptations of Shakespeare.

Finally from *Shakespeare Survey* comes Michael Cordner's 'Actors, Editors, and the Annotation of Shakespearean Playscripts' (*ShS* 55[2002] 181–98), an argument that modern editions are not as stage-aware as their creators would like to think and are far too quick to close down meanings rather than explore the multiple performance possibilities latent in the words. Standards for annotation in a Shakespeare edition are, Cordner observes, almost never discussed, and being stage-centred should not just mean thinking about action but should also include thinking about words as actions. Cordner catches René Weiss and Philip Edwards offering glosses that assert the superiority of one possible interpretation of a particular moment over another without saying why it should be preferred. Shakespeare probably wrote knowing that the full semantic possibilities of the words he was using were not available to his imagining let alone his control: the actors' craft (including intonation, stress, timing, blocking) brings out different ones, often differing between performances. In particular Cordner objects to R.A. Foakes's glossing of Antipholus of Syracuse's statement that in looking for his mother and brother he will 'lose myself' as perhaps meaning 'lose my wits', on the grounds that at that this stage in the play (I.ii) there is no reason to suppose he will lose his wits, and comments:

To a spectator already acquainted with the play, the phrase may acquire proleptic irony, given the strange experiences which await the character, and which will in due course lead him to doubt both his own and the Ephesians' sanity. But that is a layer of dramatic implication quite distinct from anything the actor of the Syracusan Antipholus can here represent his character as consciously intending; and those layers should be systematically distinguished by the annotator. (p. 190)

On close inspection, this comment is awfully carefully phrased (a model for editors?), for it allows that the actor might convey the proleptic irony—why should not the dramatist and players aim to entertain those who see the play more than once?—but that this conveyance is not the same as what the actor 'represent[s] his character as consciously intending'.

F. Elizabeth Hart, 'The "Missing" Scene in Act 2 of *Pericles*' (*ELN* 40:ii[2002] 4–12), argues that there is no missing music scene in the quarto of *Pericles*, as has often been claimed, because what the sources have has been replaced with a dancing scene instead. The morning after the revels, Simonides thanks Pericles for making beautiful music, but the audience did not see him do this, or hear it. The sources have the hero and his future wife, the king's daughter, in a harp-playing contest, and the Oxford *Complete Works* used Wilkins's 1608 novella to put in a bit of Pericles playing, but the New Cambridge editors think this hubris. Hart agrees, because Shakespeare makes the female body itself be a musical instrument (Antiochus's daughter as a 'faire Violl' in the first scene), and there are father–daughter pairings at the beginning (Antiochus and daughter), middle (Simonides and daughter), and end (Pericles and Marina) of the play. There are other symmetries between the beginning of the play and its middle—rather than incoherences derived from dual authorship—such as enflaming, tournamenting, and the playing of a woman like the playing of an instrument, discordant in the case of Antiochus and harmonious in the case of Simonides 'arranging' his daughter for Pericles. Where some editors think there is a missing scene there is a dance, and this Hart thinks is deliberate: instead of a divisive competition of producing music there is a unifying consumption of it. This is a 'condensation of energy' and a 'conservation of energy' by which 'Musical mastery is condensed into metaphor, in which form it offers rich meaning but never threatens to monopolize stage dynamics' (p. 9). Thus Hart sees no missing scene, although one cannot help wondering why Simonides makes a reference to *playing* music, so calculated to make readers, audiences, and editors think that something has fallen out.

In an article from *Literary and Linguistic Computing*, 'Pause Patterns in Shakespeare's Verse: Canon and Chronology' (*L&LC* 17[2002] 36–47), MacDonald P. Jackson uses new statistical analyses of old data to show that the Oxford *Complete Works*' chronology of Shakespeare's plays is essentially right. Ants Oras measured where the pause tended to fall in Shakespeare's line (after the first, second, third, fourth, fifth, sixth, seventh, eighth, or ninth syllable) across his career, and found that, like his fellow dramatists, Shakespeare moved away from the standard pause after the fourth syllable (the dominant pattern until near the end of the sixteenth century) and started to put the pause in the second half of the line. Oras published the findings as a book with charts in 1960, and Jackson has done statistical analysis on it to make a matrix of 'Pearson product moment correlation coefficients' that show how similar each play's pause pattern is to each other play's pause pattern. Jackson offers a table that shows for each play its Oxford-assigned year and then the five other plays with the closest pause patterns to it; as we would expect, the plays composed around the same time tend to be alike. This strongly confirms the Oxford chronology, although, as Jackson notes, that chronology is in part determined using Oras's work. Where there is mixed authorship (as in *1 Henry VI*, *Titus Andronicus*, and *Timon of Athens*) clouding the issue—since Oras took the whole play in all cases except *Pericles*, *Henry VIII*, and *Two Noble Kinsmen*—the pattern is not much disturbed. This is because Shakespeare followed the general climate of change (that is, all the dramatists changed together) in respect of pause patterns. *King John* has strong links with *A Midsummer Night's Dream* [1595], *Romeo and Juliet* [1595], *Love's Labour's Lost* [1594–5], *The Comedy of Errors* [1594], and *Richard II* [1595], so it can be dated about 1595 if the Oxford dating of these other plays is right; hence *Troublesome Reign* [printed 1591] was a source not a copy of *King John*. *The Merchant of Venice* has links with *1 Henry IV* [1596–7], *Much Ado About Nothing* [1598], *Henry V* [1598–9], *Julius Caesar* [1599], and *As You Like It* [1599–1600, not '1599–60' as given here], and hence perhaps it should be dated after the three Falstaff plays, not before them.

The Merry Wives of Windsor*, oddly, has links with a lot of plays widely separated in time, perhaps because it has so little verse (240 lines), and this is a test that relies on verse. Likewise *2 Henry IV* has widely spread links and is more than half prose, although the averages of the widely separated dates for these two plays come out fairly near the Oxford chronology figures. But for *Troilus and Cressida* the average of the link-plays' dates is 1597, which is rather earlier than previously thought, and the play might have been misdated. Also oddly, *Othello* [1603–4] and *All's Well that Ends Well* [1604–5] are close in the chronology but do not appear in one another's list of the five other plays most like it in its pause pattern. *Othello* is most like *Hamlet* [1600–1], so perhaps holding on until Richard Knolles's *History of the Turks* [1603] came out—because it is a presumed source—is an error: details of the Turkish fleet's movements could have reached England before this book. Similarly, perhaps *All's Well* should be moved a little later to get within the era of the plays it is most like. All this bears also on authorship: the first two acts of *Pericles* (Wilkins's alleged work) link to middle-period Shakespeare [1597–1604], whereas the other three acts link to Shakespeare's late plays, just as we would expect if in 1607 he wrote Acts III–V but not I–II. Confirming this is the likeness of Acts I–II with other of Wilkins's work of the same period. Likewise, the alleged Fletcher scenes in *Henry VIII* link with the alleged Fletcher scenes in *Two Noble Kinsmen* more highly than with any wholly Shakespearian play, although the next closest thing they are like is the Shakespeare scenes in *Henry VIII*, and the same is true of alleged Fletcher scenes in *The Two Noble Kinsmen*. In short Fletcher and Shakespeare are 'clearly distinguishable in their pause patterns', and Oras was probably right in thinking that pause patterns were an unconscious phenomenon. *King John* still remains a problem: if *Troublesome Reign* is a borrower from it, then the whole first half-dozen of Shakespeare's plays need to be shunted about three years earlier than they currently are reckoned to be.

Two articles of interest appeared in *Papers of the Bibliographical Society of America*. In the first, 'Act Divisions in the Shakespeare First Folio' (*PBSA* 96[2002] 219–56), James Hirsh argues that the Jaggards, not the King's men, were

responsible for the division of the 1623 Folio texts into acts, and that most of the
work was carried out by Ralph Crane. The 'act' does seem to be the sub-unit of a
play, but not forming one-fifth as we might think, to judge from the evidence of
Jaques's 'His acts being seven ages' and the division of *Pericles* by eight choruses.
Certainly act intervals spread from the Blackfriars to the open-air theatres after
about 1607, but only slowly, and moreover 'The main venue, and the one from
which the shareholders derived most of their profits, remained the Globe' (p. 224).
It would indeed be interesting to see evidence for this statement, as it runs counter to
the overwhelming evidence that the actors always wanted to be indoors in the
affluent districts; Hirsh offers nothing to support his surprising claim. Hirsh finds no
evidence that Shakespeare changed his style to suit division into five units, and
thinks that *The Winter's Tale* is in essentially two parts. So, if Shakespeare did not
start to write in acts even after 1607, where did the act divisions in twenty-eight of
the Folio's thirty-six plays come from? It cannot be a theatre person, because some
of the divisions are rather inept, and Hirsh conjectures two patterns of division based
on very simple principles. Pattern A plays are *The Tempest*, *The Two Gentlemen of
Verona*, *The Merry Wives of Windsor*, *Measure for Measure*, *The Comedy of Errors*,
Much Ado About Nothing, *As You Like It*, *Twelfth Night*, *The Winter's Tale*, *1 Henry
IV*, *2 Henry IV*, *Henry V*, *Henry VIII*, *Titus Andronicus*, *Julius Caesar*, *Macbeth*,
Othello, and probably *The Merchant of Venice* (eighteen plays), while Pattern B
plays are *Love's Labour's Lost*, *A Midsummer Night's Dream*, *All's Well That Ends
Well*, *King John*, *Richard II*, *1 Henry VI*, *Richard III*, *Coriolanus*, and *The Taming
of the Shrew* (nine plays), leaving *Cymbeline* and *King Lear* to their own anomalous
patterns, and seven plays (*2 Henry VI*, *3 Henry VI*, *Troilus and Cressida*, *Romeo and
Juliet*, *Timon of Athens*, *Antony and Cleopatra*, and *Hamlet*) with no divisions. The
rules are mechanical ones of the kind 'look for scene breaks', 'even out the chunks',
and 'do not put an interval before an alarum or excursion direction'. Although he
probably did not count lines, Divider A's results add up to Hinman Through Line-
Numbering counts, being almost perfectly divided by five, while Divider B was less
finicky about numerical proportionality in his divisions and more interested in
starting acts with large entrances.

As one might imagine, Hirsh has to give Divider B responsibility for *A
Midsummer Night Dream*'s direction 'They sleepe all the Act' since he has already
ruled out Shakespeare as its author. Hirsh calculates the chances that the patterns
were arrived at by artistic means and that the rules he has constructed just happen to
fit as well, and they are small for any one play and virtually nil for so many together.
After some categorical statistical statements, Hirsh perhaps anxiously writes that his
argument is 'at least as reasonable and as firmly grounded in hard evidence as the
arguments that scholars have been making for generations about the methods of
compositors who worked on the Folio' (p. 244), which is true but not much of a
recommendation. Five of the Pattern A plays (*The Tempest*, *The Two Gentlemen of
Verona*, *The Merry Wives of Windsor*, *Measure for Measure*, and *The Winter's Tale*)
are known to have been printed from Crane transcripts, and he is the obvious
candidate for being Divider A since the chances of all five of Crane's transcripts
randomly being assigned to Divider A are small and he certainly did not scruple
about 'literary embellishments', as Jowett called them. Crane's habits with his
literary transcripts of non-Shakespearian drama seem to fit the Divider A pattern
too. Hirsh ends by speculating (rather wildly) about the availability of Dividers A

and B during the print-run of the Folio in order to explain why some plays were divided and others not.

In the second article from *Papers of the Bibliographical Society of America*, 'What Price Shakespeare? James Orchard Halliwell-Phillipps and the Shilling Shakespeares of the 1860s' (*PBSA* 96[2002] 23–47), Marvin Spevack surveys nineteenth-century attempts to produce cheap single-volume editions of the complete works. Spevack focuses particularly on James Orchard Halliwell-Phillipps's plans, hatched in 1863, for a shilling edition that never materialized, in part it seems because the editor himself had conflictual feelings about the kind of people who would buy it. Others' plans for a shilling-Shakespeare succeeded, and Spevack usefully contextualizes them within patrician ideals about bringing all English-speaking men together, and within laissez-faire economics that were almost bound to succeed: someone would inevitably work out how to get the thing made for almost no cost.

Spevack is a veteran of computer applications to Shakespeare, and elsewhere argues that the machines have not delivered what we wanted and that literary scholars need to shape what their software providers create ('Shakespeare@computer.horizons', *ShN* 52[2002] 61, 82–4, 86). Although Spevack's concordance was completed nearly forty years ago, no one has yet done anything more interesting with this kind of approach. The only intelligent contribution that Spevack thinks he made to the concordance was the algorithm for working out how much context to give for each hit, and he was disappointed that no reviewer commented on this. Modern technology has given us much more data and made it available more quickly, but where we are woefully lacking (because the computer people do not really care about it) is in the *organization* of data in meaningful ways. (I would take slight exception to that comment, since web-crawler indexing software underlying search engines is remarkably efficient and, incredibly, one generally does find what one wants.) In the early 1970s we thought that we would eventually have a systematized Shakespeare data centre holding all the data organized coherently, but the new technology has not brought this. Rather, there are scraps of data indifferently organized and in lots of different places, and much of the software upon which we rely imposes structures on the data that the users remain unaware of. Spevack discusses the problems of hand-tagging for content and imagines the process being computerized, in the course of which he, rather confusingly for most people, mentions TEI without glossing this as the Text Encoding Initiative. More importantly, he does not address the argument that some, such as Peter Robinson, are making the case that perhaps we should not worry about tagging at all but rather make our search engines better at understanding texts that are not tagged. Elsewhere, in 'A Victorian at Work: Halliwell's Folio Edition of Shakespeare' (in Moisan and Bruster, eds., *In the Company of Shakespeare: Essays on English Renaissance Literature in Honor of G. Blakemore Evans*), Spevack offers a detailed history of James Orchard Halliwell-Phillipps's work getting his sixteen-volume 'Folio' edition of Shakespeare [1853–65] completed.

John V. Robinson, 'Hamlet's Evil Ale: *Hamlet* I.iv.36–38' (*HSt* 24[2002] 10–25), thinks that Hamlet's 'dram of eale' should be emended to 'dram of ale'. In Jonson's *Bartholomew Fair*, Northern says 'the eale's too meeghty' ('the ale's too mighty'), and although Robinson notices that it is a drunken scene he wonders why no other dialect-speaking character in the play says 'eale' to mean 'ale'. (I would hazard the answer that the spelling was meant to indicate a northern English pronunciation, and that only Northern speaks this way.) Robinson thinks 'eale' in Q2 is a 'compositor's error' for 'ale', and he takes trouble to explain what I would have thought well known, that 'dram' means a small serving of spirits. Thus 'the dram of eale | Doth all the noble substance of a doubt | To his own scandle' (Q2, sig. D1v) should be emended to 'The dram of ale doth all the noble substance often doubt to his own scandal', meaning that 'people doubt [are sceptical of] the power of liquor, and it often leads to their ruin'. Robinson explains his hypothesized 'ale' to 'eale' compositorial error by pointing out that Shakespeare's handwriting had an 'f' with a final flourish that looked like an 'e', so 'of ale' could easily be read as 'of eale'. He is right that Hand D of *Sir Thomas More* has this flourish, but although it looks like an 'e' to us, it looks nothing like the 'e' that Hand D writes, whether initially, medially, or terminally. Robinson imagines that the compositor was overworked and inexperienced, but the point of John R. Brown's compositorial study, which he cites, was that the same two men who set Q2 *Hamlet* had previously printed *The Merchant of Venice*, so they were not inexperienced.

David Haley, '"The cause of this defect": The Dram of Eale' (in Anderson and Lull, eds., *'A Certain Text': Close Readings and Textual Studies in Shakespeare and Others*), thinks that we should emend Q2 *Hamlet* to read 'the dram of esill | Doth all the noble substance often sour'. Haley uses the example of Cassio, whose honour is lost by drinking, to illuminate Hamlet's 'dram of eale' speech, the link between the Ghost (which is what the characters are waiting for) and drinking being that both involve spirits. Wine is the 'noble substance' that gets tainted, and Haley uses a bit of Nashe's *Pierce Pennilesse* that he thinks inspired this speech to help make sense of what Shakespeare wrote. The suggestion that 'of a doubt' is a compositor's mistake for 'often dout' (that is, the bad thing extinguishes the good) is not much help, Haley decides, because the sense is clearly of transforming good to bad, not extinguishing it. Haley considers the palaeographical possibilities for misreading, and then gives them over to suggest that 'of a doubt' was in Shakespeare's manuscript 'often sour', even though he admits in a footnote that the long 's' that would begin 'sowre' (the likely spelling) really could not be misread as a 'd'. It is vinegar that sours wine, Haley asserts, and later in Q2 *Hamlet* (the 'eat a crocodile' speech, on sig. M4v) Shakespeare spells it 'Esill', and Haley makes a not unreasonable palaeographic case for 'Esill' being set as 'eale'. In the same volume, Janis Lull, 'Thirteen Ways of Looking at a Blooper: Some Notes on the Endless Editing of *Richard III*', offers what looks like an essay about editing but turns out to be about the resonances of Buckingham's dying words on All Souls' Day and how this relates to *Richard III*'s parade of dead souls before the battle of Bosworth field. More relevantly, the book also carries Linda Anderson's argument about the cast size for the first quarto of *The Merry Wives of Windsor*: '"Who's in, who's out": Stage Directions and Stage Presences in *The Merry Wives of Windsor*, Q1'. This is normally assumed to be a touring text, and Anderson notices that the stage directions for servants doing things outside their normal duties are accurate and explicit, but those for them doing their usual duties are haphazard and in several cases manifestly wrong. Perhaps 'The adapter and the audience may simply have assumed that servants would accompany their masters onstage whether or not they had any part to play in the action' (p. 70). This sounds profligate because we tend to assume that on tour the companies used the minimum possible number of actors for each play, but

Anderson makes the incisive point that the minimum needed for the largest-cast play would determine the number of actors actually present on the tour, and other plays in the tour's repertory could use more than the minimum number of actors needed for each play instead of having men idle.

William B. Hunter wrote the only two articles of relevance from *American Notes and Queries*. In the first, 'Heminge and Condell as Editors of the Shakespeare First Folio' (*ANQ* 15:iv[2002] 11–19), he argues that perhaps Heminges and Condell themselves emended the quartos that became Folio copy, using their knowledge of performance of these plays. Folio *Titus Andronicus* differs from the quarto only in scenes in which Marcus is present, perhaps because the actor playing him annotated the Q copy that made F. Hunter tries to apply this principle to *Love's Labour's Lost* and *Much Ado About Nothing*, and as one might expect it gives him explanatorial carte blanche: when the 'correction' is right, the actor is remembering what he performed, when 'wrong' he is misremembering. Strangely, Hunter seems to think that the error in the *Much Ado About Nothing* quarto's direction 'Enter Leonato, his brother, his wife, Hero his daughter, and Beatrice his neece, and a kinsman' (sig. B3^r) is that of Hero being called Leonato's wife. The problem, of course, is that of Leonato having a wife at all. In his second article, 'New Readings of *A Midsummer Night's Dream*' (*ANQ* 15:iv[2002] 3–10), Hunter argues that Shakespeare revised *A Midsummer Night's Dream* for different weddings, creating some of the textual muddles we have, and that Heminges played Egeus and annotated Q2 to make F's copy. Hunter recaps his own work elsewhere on the play being an occasional piece for a wedding in 1594 and revived for another wedding in 1596, and how its content fits the known time-schemes of the performances. Like David Wiles, Hunter thinks that *Romeo and Juliet* must come earlier because *Pyramus and Thisbe* is clearly a parody of it, and a parody cannot come before what it parodies. (This is surely a weak argument: both can be different workings of essentially the same source material.) The play's multiple endings—the mechanicals' dance, then Theseus' epilogue sending everyone to bed, then the fairies' masque, and finally Puck's epilogue—come from the different performances at court, where Puck's 'gentles' would be inappropriate, and on the public stage, where it would not. Hunter's best point is that the play as we have it has an oddity in Hippolyta's part. She is in the first scene but says almost nothing (surprisingly for an Amazon in a scene where a woman is being compelled to obey a man) and then she reappears in Act IV, where she speaks a considerable amount. Hunter thinks there was more for Hippolyta and that it has dropped out in revision. The beginning of the play also has Philostrate, who in F never reappears (Egeus takes over as Master of the Revels), and this too Hunter reckons to result from authorial revision. Hunter takes a guess—that is all it is—that Heminges did the textual work on the Folio's copy by annotating an example of Q2 using his memories of being in it. Thus it was he who put in the actor's name 'Tawyer' and changed all the Philostrate speech prefixes to Egeus (as it was when he played it, the Philostrate name coming in later revision and then getting into Q2), but he missed one.

Jeremy Ehrlich, 'The Search for the *Hamlet* "Director's Cut"' (*ES* 83[2002] 399–406), notes that if, as many believe, Q1 *Hamlet* is based on a recollection of a markedly different version of the play from that we know from Q2/F, we could for sport put F's words into Q1's structure, character names, and pattern of cuts. To do so would be to eliminate some of the linguistic flaws of recollection and thereby inch a little closer to the lost, different version. After all, the remembering actor is not likely to have invented the order of scenes and the plot of the play he was recalling, and the majority of his errors would have hurt only the language. Noticeably, F's verse lines make neater patterns when Q1's cuts are applied to them than they do in F, particularly by the elimination of unmetrical short lines. Could the adapter who made the good text that is buried under Q1's misrememberings have been trying to tidy the verse? Ehrlich ends with the quite reasonable complaint that 'identifying what we do not know about early printed texts' has too often put a brake on 'speculative projects' that would be revealing.

Finally, the round-up of material in *Notes and Queries*. Andrew Breeze, in 'Welsh Tradition and the Baker's Daughter in *Hamlet*' (*N&Q* 49[2002] 199–200), thinks that Ophelia's 'the owl was a baker's daughter' (IV.v.41–2) comes from a medieval Welsh tale circulating in various forms about a girl punished for sexual betrayal. He has not got any substantial evidence for this other than the fact that there was a Welsh story about a girl turned into a owl; unfortunately she was not a baker's daughter. Charles Edelman, '*The Battle of Alcazar, Muly Molocco*, and Shakespeare's *2* and *3 Henry VI*' (*N&Q* 49[2002] 215–18), shows that Peele's play *The Battle of Alcazar* is the same as the *Muly Molocco* that Henslowe's records show was played fourteen times between February 1592 and January 1593. The quarto of *The Battle of Alcazar* has two stage directions that call for 'chambers' to be 'discharged', and the only other plays of the period that use this phrasing are the quartos of Shakespeare's *2 Henry VI* and *3 Henry VI*, both Strange's men's plays from around 1591. This link of discharged chambers suggests that *The Battle of Alcazar* was also a Strange's men's play, and that the 1594 quarto of it with these stage directions was based on copy written by the same person who wrote the *2 Henry VI* and *3 Henry VI* directions. Thus *The Battle of Alcazar* is the same as *Muly Molocco* that Henslowe records, and the reason why the main character is much more often called by his alternative name of 'Abdelmelec' than 'Muly Molocco' is that it sounds better and scans much more easily.

Thomas Merriam, 'Faustian Joan' (*N&Q* 49[2002] 218–20), thinks that Marlowe wrote the Joan-as-witch scene in *1 Henry VI*. The penultimate appearance of Joan la Pucell (or 'de Pucell', as Merriam unaccountably calls her) has her addressing her diabolical helpers and offering her soul, and it shares quite a few words and phrases with Marlowe's works, especially *Doctor Faustus*. Merriam claims that the appearance of devils onstage in *1 Henry VI* 'is unique in Shakespeare', but that is true only if we forget about the conjuring of Asnath in *The Contention of York and Lancaster*, its sequel. Merriam uses '1st Principal Component' and '2nd Principal Component' without explaining what these terms mean, nor the difference between them, and there is not even a citation telling the reader where to find an explanation. Worse, there is something strangely wrong with the graph that Merriam thinks explains it all: the horizontal access (labelled '1st PRINCIPAL COMPONENT (ALL)')—the one that Merriam says is all that matters for distinguishing authorship—goes in six uniform steps of 0.2, left from 0.8 to –0.4, which is fair enough, but then takes another six uniform steps to get to –1.5 (should be –1.6). Likewise, it goes in six uniform steps (of 0.2?) right from 0.8 to 1.9 (should be 2.0) and then a further six uniform steps to get to 3.0, which should be 3.1, or the previous mark should have been 1.8. In short, this is not a linear scale but has been made to look like one by small tweaks; this does not encourage confidence. David

Farley-Hills, 'The Theatrical Provenance of *The Comedy of Errors*' (*N&Q* 49[2002] 220–2), thinks that the placing of entrance and exit directions shows that *The Comedy of Errors* was written for indoor hall performance. Mariko Ichikawa showed that on the open-air stages Shakespeare's major characters were usually allowed four lines to enter or exit to or from their place on the stage (front centre), and that minor characters—who tend to stay in the background—are usually allowed two lines. We have always suspected that *The Comedy of Errors* was written for the smaller stage of an indoor hall performance, where entrances and exits could have been made much more quickly, and indeed the play is anomalous in giving characters less than the usual four lines. Farley-Hills refers to Ichikawa's 'unpublished doctoral thesis', but it has since appeared as a splendid book (*Shakespearean Entrances*).

J.J.M. Tobin, 'More Evidence for a 1594 *Titus*' (*N&Q* 49[2002] 222–4), thinks that *Titus Andronicus* borrows from the Epistle to the Reader in Nashe's *Christ's Tears Over Jerusalem* [1594], which itself responds to criticism of Nashe's *Unfortunate Traveller* [also 1594], so Shakespeare cannot have written the play earlier than that year. The epistle refers to criticism that Nashe makes up -*ize* verbs such as 'tyrannize', which appears twice in *Titus Andronicus*, and that Nashe makes compound nouns, as does Shakespeare. Tobin cites a few, not terribly close, verbal parallels between *Christ's Tears* and Shakespeare's play, and makes an argument for the direction—Shakespeare borrowing from Nashe—that I cannot understand and that he does not seem to find convincing either: 'it is certainly possible that Nashe borrowed from Shakespeare'. Adrian Streete, 'Charity and Law in *Love's Labour's Lost*: A Calvinist Analogue' (*N&Q* 49[2002] 224–5), notes that Berowne's 'charity itself fulfils the law' (*LLL* IV.iii.337) is usually taken to be a biblical allusion (Romans 13:8 or 13:10), but in fact it is not directly from Scripture but from Calvin's *Sermons* [1549], which was itself alluding to the Bible. As Streete observes, early modern writers could use Calvin without getting partisan about his doctrines. Randall Martin, 'Catholic Ephesians in *Henry IV, Part Two*' (*N&Q* 49[2002] 225–6), glosses the page's report that Falstaff sups in Eastcheap with 'Ephesians … of the old church' (*2 Henry IV* II.ii.142) as meaning 'with Catholics'. The Geneva Bible likened Catholicism to the old cult of Eastern Diana/Artemis worship—connoting fertility, not chastity as in the West—at Ephesus, whose adherents resented Paul's first-century mission to replace it with Christianity. Naseeb Shaheen, 'Biblical References in *Julius Caesar*' (*N&Q* 49[2002] 226–7), objects to the Arden 3 editor David Daniell finding in Luke 1:8 the source for Cassius's 'Will you go see the order of the course' (*JC* I.ii.25), since it comes from North's Plutarch describing the same moment. Shaheen suggests that a faint memory of another line in Luke ('as his course came in order') in a totally unrelated context might also have shaped Shakespeare's phrasing.

William Poole, '*Julius Caesar* and *Caesar's Revenge* Again' (*N&Q* 49[2002] 227–8), supports others' recent arguments that the anonymous *Tragedy of Caesar and Pompey*, performed at Trinity College Oxford, is a source for *Julius Caesar*. Poole spots a new link: 'To grace in captive bonds his chariot wheels' (*JC* I.i.34), said of Pompey, has 'grace[d]', 'captive', and 'chariot wheels' in common with one of Pompey's speeches from the other play. Tiffany Stern, 'The "Part" for Greene's *Orlando Furioso*: A Source for the "Mock Trial" in Shakespeare's *Lear*?' (*N&Q* 49[2002] 229–31), has a new source for the mock trial: Greene's mad-for-jealousy character Orlando Furioso—much more known than Ariosto's Italian or Harington's English versions—was frequently alluded to, and is the only role for which we have a surviving actor's 'part'. This contains a mock trial by mad Orlando that Stern thinks similar to Lear's; could Child Rowland be Orlando? Stern assumes that because the 'part' was 'found among Alleyn's effects' it must be his, but in fact David Kathman will shortly publish an article showing that at least one other document in the Dulwich cache, the plot of 2 Seven Deadly Sins, got there decades after Alleyn's death. The editors of Notes and Queries might have tidied some of Stern's phrasing, such as the comment that we have the 'part' and a play quarto 'both of which differ significantly from each other'; as opposed to only one of them differing? Stern rightly condemns W.W. Greg's explanation that the 'part' is 'good' and the quarto is 'bad' and wonders if the differences come from revisions associated with Greene's double-selling of the play, first to the Queen's and then to the Admiral's men.

MacDonald P. Jackson, 'Dating Shakespeare's Sonnets: Some Old Evidence Revisited' (N&Q 49[2002] 237–41), reports that fresh processing of rare-word analysis undertaken by J.A. Fort in the 1930s produces the same links between certain runs of Shakespeare's sonnets and certain groups of Shakespeare's plays that Jackson found and reported in an article reviewed here last year. Interestingly, Fort himself did not read his data this way and remained convinced that all the sonnets were written 1593–6. Kenji Go, '"I am that I am" in Shakespeare's Sonnet 121 and 1 Corinthians 15:10' (N&Q 49[2002] 241–2), notes that 'I am that I am' (sonnet 121 line 9) is generally taken to be from Exodus 3:14, but since these are God's words that would seem to make the poet sound 'smug, presumptuous, and stupid', as Stephen Booth put it. In fact the phrase also occurs in 1 Corinthians 15:10, which would have been familiar from prescribed pulpit reading, and in which context it shows St Paul's humility, not megalomania; Iago's 'He's that he is' (Othello IV.i.270) is a witty parody of Paul's phrase. Bryan Crockett, 'From Pulpit to Stage: Thomas Playfere's Influence on Shakespeare' (N&Q 49[2002] 243–5), argues not very convincingly that some lines for which we already have Shakespeare's sources actually come from hearing and/or reading the charismatic preacher Thomas Playfere.

2. Shakespeare in the Theatre

The accent of Wells and Stanton, eds., The Cambridge Companion to Shakespeare on Stage, is on the modern. Of the fifteen essays here collected, only the first five deal with pre-twentieth-century topics. Gary Taylor's 'Shakespeare Plays on Renaissance Stages' (pp. 1–20) refutes the separation between page and stage: 'we mislead ourselves if we imagine a play moving from text to stage' (p. 1). Pointing out that the acting companies rather than the author appeared on the title pages of early editions, Taylor argues that they had a much greater ownership of the texts and consequently were more involved in the script's composition than modern notions of authorship might suggest. Shakespeare's plays are thus seen to be collaborative enterprises with 'his fellow-actors [filling] in those obvious blanks' (p. 4), playing women, or characters of different race. Taylor insists that this is a theatre of convention rather than illusion: 'Shakespeare wrote for stages where racial and ethnic differences were mimicked by Anglo-Saxon actors for Anglo-Saxon audiences' (p. 11). In 'Improving Shakespeare: From the Restoration to Garrick' (pp. 21–36), Jean I. Marsden describes the revulsion from Shakespeare's barbarism felt by a neoclassical aesthetic which looked towards the Aristotelian unities and rewrote Shakespeare's plots in order to make them comply. Thus the sixteen-year gap in *The Winter's Tale* or the geographical oscillation of *Antony and Cleopatra* put them beyond the pale and they were not staged. Of course such rewrites were topically inflected, with John Crowne, for instance, adapting the *Henry VI* plays at the beginning of the 1680s 'graphically [to] display the evils of civil war brought on by rebellious factions and the dangers of a court filled with Catholic advisors' (p. 27). Shakespeare's cultural elevation to the status of 'England's answer to Homer' (p. 30) prompted the return of unadapted scripts, a movement championed by David Garrick. Jane Moody opens her 'Romantic Shakespeare' (pp. 37–57) with the assertion that 'Performing Shakespeare in the Romantic age became an intensely political business' (p. 37). John Philip Kemble's productions of the 1790s are described as 'a magnificent and spectacular advertisement for the political establishment' (p. 44) which prompted William Hazlitt to react against these productions (notably Kemble's *Coriolanus*) and to conclude that the plays should rather be used to interrogate contemporary injustices. Unsurprisingly, Hazlitt warmed to the radical performances given by Edmund Kean, writing ironically: 'We wish we had never seen Mr Kean. He has destroyed the Kemble religion; and it is the religion in which we were brought up' (p. 50). Moody concludes, 'Edmund Kean's performances had fractured the moral and political certainties of the Kemble era' (p. 56).

Edmund's son, Charles Kean, is identified in Richard W. Schoch's 'Pictorial Shakespeare' (pp. 58–75) as 'the most ardent and aggressive historiciser of Shakespeare in the British theatre' (p. 61). This emphasis on historical authenticity and pictorial detail is identified as part of a nineteenth-century obsession with visual artefacts: 'the Victorians were insatiable consumers of pictures' (p. 58). Technological developments (not least the invention of gaslight) allowed further realization of pictorial settings. Schoch argues that this pictorialism actualizes Shakespeare's intentions since 'Shakespeare himself wanted such effects but his theatre did not possess the resources required to achieve them ... that is, pictorial Shakespeare is true to the intentions of the playwright' (p. 69). As the century progressed, however, the pictorialism found its way through to the cinema while theatre retreated to modernism, moving away from illusionism to formalism. In 'Reconstructive Shakespeare: Reproducing Elizabethan and Jacobean Stages' (pp. 76–97), Marion O'Connor considers this Victorian pictorialism to be the style against which the staging experiments of William Poel *et al.* were conducted. The search for Elizabethan stage conditions was championed not by scholars, 'let alone academics, but theatre practitioners with antiquarian inclinations and associations' (p. 76). The quest for 'authenticity' has given rise to a surprising number of Globe reconstructions, including Earl's Court [1912], Chicago [1934], and San Diego [1935], as well as Los Angeles, Odessa, Texas, and Cedar City, Utah. Such reconstructions are expensive and specialist and O'Connor asserts that the 'commercial success of Globe 3 is against historical odds' (p. 90), though she notes the proximity of Tate Modern which is partly responsible for turning Southwark into a 'culture-vulture circuit' (p. 92). Robert Smallwood is unimpressed, noting the

Globe's 'propensity to pander to the lowest common denominator of taste in its audiences [though whether this] is a passing phase or an incurable malady, it is too early to say' (p. 113). His essay, 'Twentieth-Century Performance: The Stratford and London Companies' (pp. 98–117), is a thorough and fluent piece. Despite the unpopularity of the Royal Shakespeare Theatre ever since it opened in 1932, Stratford retains its unique importance as the only consistently influential site of Shakespearian performance in England outside the capital. Smallwood charts the decline of the West End actor-manager and the rise of director's theatre, which 'has brought us a very long way from the massively cut texts, generously interrupted with intervals, and from the Shakespeare of the scene painters, with which the [twentieth] century began' (p. 109).

A pair of essays follows: 'The Tragic Actor and Shakespeare' (pp. 118–36) and 'The Comic Actor and Shakespeare' (pp. 137–54) by Simon Williams and Peter Thomson respectively. The first is sentimental and strangely nebulous: 'When the actor plays the poetry, he plays both what is known to the character and what is not known. What is not known provides the symbolic content of the role, but as the action advances the hero comes to know more of this symbolic plane and the actor should therefore increasingly point towards general truths rather than only to individual experience' (p. 119). As if this is not mysterious enough, he writes of the death of Ferdinand Fleck's eighteenth-century Macbeth: 'Macbeth's evil was sensed as being incorporated into the benign wholeness of the universe' (p. 126). It would be difficult enough to make sense of this description of a contemporary performance, let alone one over two centuries old. Thomson's companion piece is rather more down to earth as he stresses the importance of the relationship between comic actor and audience and the theory of humours, though his assertion that Will Kemp may have 'made a theatrical feature of his buttocks' (p. 142) is offered without much in the way of evidence! Penny Gay's 'Women and Shakespearean Performance' (pp. 155–73) charts the rise of the female actor from the Restoration to the present day. While this increasing presence has of course been assisted by social and political progress, Gay also emphasizes the contribution of psychoanalysis to the art of acting, with its stress on characterization and 'complex psychological (i.e. individual, rather than socially determined) motivations' (p. 168). Gay's essay ends with the overly optimistic description of 'a concept of gender that no longer confines men or women to predetermined roles, either in life or on the stage' (p. 172).

'International Shakespeare' (pp. 174–93) is the collection's finest essay, in which Anthony B. Dawson asks 'what kind of intercultural dilemmas does the internationalisation of Shakespeare pose in the theatre, which is after all, or was until very recently, an institution of deep cultural specificity and locatedness?' (p. 179). In answering this question, Dawson sensitively rejects the pat notion of Shakespeare as a colonialist weapon, arguing instead that 'theatres in diverse parts of the globe have embraced his work as deeply relevant to their own diverse cultural situations, even at times as liberatory' (p. 177). International Shakespeare is a good deal more complex than post-colonial critics would have us believe, and Dawson discusses 'something of that need for otherness, not simply as a way of defining self or effacing difference, but as a means of braiding the local and the foreign in order to acknowledge their inseparability' (p. 190). This is a complex but rewarding essay. Peter Holland, in 'Touring Shakespeare' (pp. 194–211), begins with the ingenious assertion that 'All spectators at the theatre are tourists' (p. 194), which allows him to forge an immanence between theatre and travel, with the members of the audience 'taken from their everyday world into the strange other country they visit for the duration of the theatre performance' (p. 194). But, as he goes on to point out, players are also tourists, taking their show to places which may be far removed (geographically or technologically) from their home base. After a brief account of the staggering requirements typical of a touring RSC production (over 50 tonnes of equipment), Holland focuses mainly on the history and varied successes of tours within and beyond Britain; among the companies he considers are the English Shakespeare Company, Cheek by Jowl, and Northern Broadsides. Wilhelm Hortmann's 'Shakespeare on the Political Stage in the Twentieth Century' (pp. 212–29) concentrates, unsurprisingly given his magisterial *Shakespeare on the German Stage: The Twentieth Century* (CUP [1998]; *YWES* 80[2001] 263–4), on the productions in East and West Germany both before and after unification. While the essay demonstrates that politicized Shakespeare is rife, it is less interested in productions characterized by 'out-Kotting Kott in the service of revealing hidden power structures and unmasking their exploiters to effect the ideological transformation of their audiences' (p. 219). Rather, it relishes the 'Unpredictable extraneous events and conditions [which] can suddenly charge plays with contemporary meaning' (p. 216). In fact, Hortmann insists, explicit politicization may be over-egging the pudding: 'In certain political situations some Shakespeare plays only need to be played straight to be politically subversive' (pp. 212–13). While Hortmann rightly acknowledges the impact of Mikhail Bakhtin and Robert Weimann in forging a revolutionary Shakespeare, the consequence—that political Shakespeare is a comparatively recent phenomenon—is inadequately challenged; after all, it is at least as old as the Essex Rebellion with the conspirators' galvanizing performance of *Richard II*.

Three essays on geographically removed Shakespeare complete the book. The book's longest contribution is also its most diffuse, although 'Shakespeare in North America' (pp. 230–59) is not an easy topic to condense. Unfortunately Michael A. Morrison offers lists and descriptions of seminal productions rather than sustained cultural analyses. For instance, while the rapidly expanding railroad is mentioned, a detailed narrative of its impact on touring productions is never attempted. While the first professional productions took place in the States and Canada as early as the mid-eighteenth century, the essay concentrates on those of the twentieth. The usual suspects, John Barrymore, Maurice Evans (whose influence, Morrison insists, remains underestimated), Orson Welles, and Paul Robeson appear, but the recent decline in American Shakespeare is attributed to the better remuneration of television and cinema which draws actors away from the stage, while the theatre has become 'increasingly the province of musicals, comedies, light dramas and foreign imports' (p. 256). Interestingly, Morrison also notes the counterproductive influence of the 'Method' school of acting which is 'ideally suited to modern naturalistic plays and film acting but [is] in many ways antithetical to Shakespeare performance' (p. 256). John Gillies, Ryuta Minami, Ruru Li, and Poonam Trivedi discuss 'Shakespeare on the Stages of Asia' (pp. 259–83), though unsurprisingly the essay breaks into separate sections covering Japan, China, and India. A stridently Saidian post-colonialist beginning asserts that 'Asia' as such 'is a geographic fiction rather than a life world [and that the] very bracketing of these countries bespeaks an implicitly Orientalist standpoint' (p. 259). Yet the sections on Japan and China are at pains to point out how Shakespeare's work is not imported as part of a colonialist enterprise but rather merges with and takes its energies from rich local theatre traditions. For instance, in Ong Ken Sen's *King Lear* [1997] and Rio Kishida's *Desdemona* [2000] (both performed in Japan), 'actors from at least six different traditional performing genres are brought together to play opposite each other in their traditional idioms' (p. 265). The colonial reading seems to cut more ice in the case of India, however. Indeed this part of the essay insists that 'Shakespeare is sponsored into India by the full colonial apparatus: specifically as a mainstay of the entertainment programme for English residents of Bombay and Calcutta from about 1773' (p. 272). Since Indian independence in 1947, however, a 'more self-conscious and thoroughgoing kind of indigenisation has emerged' (p. 276), though the conclusion remains defiant that this should not be seen as an emerging homogenization of Asian Shakespeare.

The book's final essay concerns 'Shakespeare and Africa' (pp. 284–99) and pays specific attention to productions in Tanzania, Sierra Leone, South Africa, Ghana, Ethiopia, Mauritius, and Nigeria. Martin Banham, Roshni Mooneeram, and Jane Plastow assert (perhaps a little surprisingly) that 'Shakespeare's world of princes, kings, warriors, fate, allegory and magic is much less difficult to accept at face value for many African societies than it is today for super-sceptical rationalist Europeans' (p. 288). Having detailed the ways in which Shakespeare can be seen to offer an analogy for the contemporary corruptions of Africa, their conclusion is underwhelming: 'if democracy is to survive, the people must be vigilant' (p. 297). The collection ranges across a wide range of topics both historical and geographical. From the title one might have expected more in terms of the stagecraft and an emphasis on theatrical practicalities. What is here is thorough and detailed, although an editors' conclusion which attempted to draw together the various persistent themes or theorize the whole idea of writing about live performance and the inherent difficulties of rendering the temporary permanent would be a welcome addition.

Robert Shaughnessy's *The Shakespeare Effect: A History of Twentieth-Century Performance* is an elegant and thought-provoking book. It is notable for its accent on the dangers of performance, not simply in terms of its independence from the accumulated inherited weight of literary accounts or previous theatrical incarnations but for what Shaughnessy describes as a wider cultural 'unruliness', that is, the way in which performance can 'evade, exceed or rupture the impression of coherence that is conferred by the presence of Shakespeare, its capacity to work against the text, and against official structures and discourses of legitimation' (p. 7). Moreover, Shaughnessy is right to stress the importance of a 'theatrically-aware approach to the plays at every level of pedagogy, scholarship and performance' (p. 5). Three sections follow. The first deals with the end of the nineteenth and the beginnings and the first third or so of the twentieth century—the pioneering stage experiments of William Poel and the Elizabethan Stage Society, as well as the influence of Terence Gray, founder, patron, and director of the Festival Theatre in Cambridge. Part 2 deals with the emergence and influence of Tyrone Guthrie in the middle years of the century, and the final section examines Edward Bond's *Bingo* and the weirdly radical *Five Day Lear* staged by Forced Entertainment. What binds these apparently disparate sections together is their careful attention to 'the culturally-inscribed historicity which was formally elided in the search for the elusive ideal of essence of

Shakespearean performance' (p. 194). Throughout, performance is implicitly subversive: 'a medium lacking any decisive claims to authority' (p. 25). Read in this light, Poel's revivalist stagings are far from conservative. Indeed, Shaughnessy is especially good on recovering the political implications of Poel's search for authenticity, which is read as an 'attempt to retrieve an unalienated mode of social existence, wherein everyday life, work and culture could become organically integrated' (p. 36). Though this organicism is usually considered reactionary, Shaughnessy is determined to show otherwise: Poel's promotion of 'a medievalised, vibrantly colourful, stylised-realist art' was a way of 'restoring a lost wholeness of life to an increasingly mechanised industrial society' (p. 36). Of course, the discovery of the first quarto of *Hamlet* in 1823 and Poel's staging of it in 1881 provide the sort of assault on textual singularity which Shaughnessy sees at the heart of theatrical production's 'unruliness' (p. 6). Nor should the political implications of this be understated: 'For Poel, to revolutionise the Shakespearean theatre was a step towards changing the world' (p. 36). But Shaughnessy is sensitive to the ways in which, at the same time as voicing this radical approach, Poel was just as much a subject of his own historical situation. His disapproval, for instance, of 'the attention-seeking woman performer' (p. 39) is seen to express a wider cultural anxiety in the decade of the emergence of the New Woman and the dandy.

Terence Gray's production of *Henry VIII* [1931] is considered to be symptomatic of a shift from the extraordinary pageants and elaborate ceremonies typified by the pictorial theatre of the nineteenth century. This production, in which all the characters were dressed as playing-cards, 'generally confirmed Gray's reputation for an irreverence that bordered upon flagrant irresponsibility' (p. 70). Shaughnessy asserts that the influences of Meyerhold and Brecht could be seen in Gray's rejection of 'the dominant theatrical discourse of illusionism [as well as] the humanist consensus that both informs and is sustained by it' (p. 75). Shaughnessy is especially acute in registering the proximity (in both time and location) of such luminaries as F.R. and Q.D. Leavis, Sir Arthur Quiller-Couch, John Dover Wilson, and E.M.W. Tillyard, and he notes that Gray's stagings 'operated within the cultural environment which gave birth to a programme of English literary studies whose effects would be felt way beyond Cambridge university' (pp. 62–3) and, we might add, fold back into what have become the established theatrical centres of the National Theatre and the Royal Shakespeare Company.

The arrival of psychoanalysis is registered in theatre by Guthrie's direction of Olivier's Hamlet [1937]. Funnily enough, while Shaughnessy is sensitive to the tyranny of the theory, he is occasionally its victim, as when, for example, he points out that 'the infant's response to maternal presence and absence is the fundamental key to theatrical experience' (p. 91). When Guthrie recollects his encountering *Peter Pan* in Freudian terms, Shaughnessy is perhaps too ready to go along with him, reading the child's play as a gloss on the later *Hamlet* without necessary critical distance: in Guthrie's account of *Peter Pan*, 'there is the sense of the imminence of death; as in *Hamlet*, there is also the preoccupation with abandonment and maternal betrayal' (p. 86). Interesting in the light of this that Ernest Jones (consulted by director and leading actor) should find fault in Olivier's portrayal of the Prince: 'he quite gets away from the idea of a man *internally* tortured' (p. 104). Shaughnessy gives an excellent account of the Elsinore staging of the production and is especially good on the dodgy political background and the fraught relationship between

Denmark and the Third Reich. Yet for all its diplomatically sensitive and thorough psychoanalytical preparation, the production was thrown into disarray by the elements. A torrential downpour drove it inside, to the ballroom of the Marienlyst Hotel, where it was hastily reblocked and staged with 'a potential for chaos that the performance just managed to keep under control' (p. 117). There follows a brisk account of Guthrie's involvement in the Stratford, Ontario Festival and the way in which it 'has been read as a neo-colonial manoeuvre willingly abetted by the forces of anglophile nostalgia' (p. 124) as well as an attempt to resist creeping Americanization on behalf of a Canadian nationalism.

The final section begins with a detailed and thoroughly contextualized history of Edward Bond's *Bingo* [first staged in 1973]. Read against the crises of the oil shortage, fractious relations between the UK and the European Economic Community, unemployment, inflation, the curbing of union power, the three-day week, and global recession, Bond's bleak vision seems almost understated. Shaughnessy is excellent at catching both the play's and the period's sense of collapse: 'In 1974, to dramatise the death of England's Shakespeare was to draw attention to the fact that England itself was in terminal decline' (p. 164). In comparison with the political significance of Bond's iconoclastic play, Forced Entertainment's *Five Day Lear*, which, in their own words, 'succeeded in turning the play to rubble' (p. 188) seems trivial and insignificant (though the company's *Dirty Work* [1998], in which 'a handsome woman plays a number of popular tunes by farting' (p. 186), at least sounds like fun). Even Shaughnessy is not totally convinced: 'some readers may find [*Five Day Lear*] amusing or intriguing, many others will be dismayed or irritated by such a flagrantly inconsequential and irresponsible venture' (p. 196). The point for Shaughnessy's conclusion is really to illustrate that historical and theatrical change, while it must come, 'will not be a story of progress' (p. 197). Yet this effective and eloquent book illustrates the importance of reading theatrical and cultural meanings as mutually constructive, and for that it deserves high praise.

Shaughnessy's study is rather blandly described as being 'concerned with the cultural and political background of innovative twentieth-century productions' (p. 226) in the whistle-stop tour of recent performance criticism which forms the concluding chapter of *Shakespeare and the Theatrical Event* by John Russell Brown. The first page does not bode well: 'Although its subject is large, this is a short book, offering not an account of any one play but an introduction to phenomena that need to be taken into account if we are to respond to any of the plays in a manner appropriate to the experience they were intended to give' (p. vii)— phew! This verbosely stated aspiration is never really met. Much of the book is startlingly simplistic: 'Shakespeare took great pleasure in the use of words' (pp. 2–3); access to today's theatre may be 'either by public transport or by using convenient and subsidized carparks' (p. 9); the Elizabethans were 'without radio or television' (p. 13); 'In the comedies, some people should look amazingly beautiful [but not in the tragedies?]' (p. 41), while in the tragedies actors 'can enter on stage together and then leave separately, or the other way about [but not in the comedies?]' (p. 117); 'Shakespeare's society was different from ours' (p. 198); 'Reading a Shakespeare play is like swimming' (p. 207), and so on. I am not just sniping at exceptional inanities, rather attempting to show that they make up much of the fabric of the book. Brown is frequently clumsy or just downright ungrammatical: 'a huge hinterland of meanings and sensations lies behind Shakespeare's texts and it contains many paths to explore with different intentions' (p. 27). This, surely, is down to poor editing, as when elsewhere he cites the 'concluding couplet of Sonnet 107' then quotes six lines (p. 33). Occasionally the book offers practical theatrical exercises on voice work and movement etc., though even here the conclusions seem highly questionable. One such odd technique is to represent each person in a scene 'with a coin or small object' (p. 230). These objects are to be moved 'in meaningful relation to each other ... in response to a reading of the text aloud', but even Brown is uncertain of the benefits: 'Nothing very surprising may be discovered.' While Brown insists rightly that our modern conception of character is anachronistic, and while there are thoughtful suggestions for staging individual moments from various Shakespeare plays, even his theatrical know-how is occasionally unreliable; it is simply not true that 'Experience has shown that productions of Shakespeare that do not fill the stage with actors are unlikely to fill theatres with audiences' (p. 170). But the book's most bizarre formulation comes during its account of *King Lear*: 'Lear's talk of sexuality and pain, madness and sanity, age and infancy speaks directly to very ordinary sense-memories derived from watching small creatures copulating' (p. 193), as though the profundity of Shakespearean tragedy could be augmented by a quick visit to the local pet shop!

'Cue for Passion: On the Dynamics of Shakespearean Acting' (*NTQ* 69[2002] 3–7) is typical Charles Marowitz—impetuous and even outrageous. We hear (without a shred of supporting evidence) that the Elizabethan audience assembled amid 'a sexy atmosphere, lots of singles eying [*sic*] the available merchandise and horny young men "making out" or certainly trying to' (p. 5). His description of on-stage activity is no less hyperbolic: 'Marlowe forces the actor to fill his lungs, expand his thorax, quiver his tonsils, and make a godawful noise that probably ricocheted around the perimeter of playhouses like the Theatre and the Rose' (p. 4). Shakespeare, on the other hand, 'moves from cool riffs to mournful blues to swinging up-tempo rhythms' (p. 5). Under all this distortion and exaggerated rhetoric is an interesting argument about the tyranny of prosody represented, for Marowitz, by Peter Hall's productions of *Measure for Measure* and *A Midsummer Night's Dream* staged at the Ahmanson Theatre, Los Angeles, in 1999 with American actors: 'We were so carried away by stress and scansion that motive and meaning fell by the wayside. ... It was a *Dream*-by-numbers' (p. 7). Marowitz goes on to argue that, due to the absolute ascendancy in the States of Lee Strasberg and The Method, 'a technical approach to verse-speaking is precisely what the American actor most lacks. ... Being paralyzed by prosody is one of the great pitfalls of American Shakespeare' (p. 7). Unfortunately no solution is forthcoming other than a call to discover a happy medium which will 'exemplify fastidious attention to original verse structure and fresh insights into the social, psychological, and metaphysical layers' (p. 9), but no clue is proffered as to how to go about this. Perhaps the most eloquent sentence in this bizarre article is its faux-conclusion: 'So rather than sum up, I will simply wrap up'—hear, hear!

Not all theatre directors are as brash as Marowitz, and in 'An Interview with Kent Thompson, Artistic Director of the Alabama Shakespeare Festival' (in Kolin, ed., *Othello: New Critical Essays*, pp. 441–55) Thompson, in conversation with Philip C. Kolin, describes with some delicacy the play's social tensions in the light of his 1994 production with Derrick Lee Weeden in the title role: 'portraying Othello in a pejorative way [is] insulting to today's audiences, especially to African American audiences' (p. 442). At one point he refers to the audience's 'own anxieties about interracial marriages' (p. 445)—one would like to think that these 'anxieties' are confined to the South (or is that just me being 'State-ist'?). Although Thompson's account of specific staging decisions is interesting in its own right, noticeable throughout is an apologetic humility which Kolin would have done well to have interrogated further. When, for instance, Thompson remarks, 'there are several African American actors who don't want to perform Othello, who doubt that we should ever produce *Othello* again. They feel that it's a white man's version of a black man's play' (p. 451), one would have liked some elaboration of the principles at stake—no more *Shrews*, no more *Tituses*, and certainly no more *Merchants*? 'You have to be very careful when you're doing the play. I don't think it is quite as problematic as that other play about Venice—*The Merchant of Venice*' (p. 454).

Mahon and Mahon, eds., *The Merchant of Venice: New Critical Essays* contains three essays of relevance here. Jay L. Halio's 'Singing Chords: Performing Shylock and Other Characters' (pp. 369–73) is brief and not especially profound. Halio addresses himself to the question of 'how to represent fully on stage the inherent contradictions of characters, that is, without risking terrible confusion or blurring of roles' (p. 370) as though that were a problem unique to *The Merchant* rather than virtually *any* play. His concluding sentence is typical and not particularly enlightening: 'The play cries out for complex interpretation, and good actors and directors should be able to render it' (p. 373). Much more rewarding is John O'Connor's long and detailed 'Shylock in Performance' (pp. 387–430), which examines the performances of, among others, Peter O'Toole, Laurence Olivier, Patrick Stewart, Warren Mitchell, David Suchet, Antony Sher, Dustin Hoffman, David Calder, Philip Voss, and Henry Goodman. These portrayals he finds to be more or less sympathetic. Perhaps the most sympathetic and influential of all was Henry Irving. O'Connor cites Irving himself, who (according to Joseph Hatton) remarked, 'I look on Shylock as the type of a persecuted race; almost the only gentleman in the play, and most ill-used' (p. 392). Elsewhere in the same volume, the play's other starring role is examined by Penny Gay in 'Portia Performs: Playing the Role in Twentieth-Century English Theatre' (pp. 431–54). Irving's Shylock may have been sympathetic, but Gay finds Irving himself stifling Ellen Terry's potential: 'What might she have done with the role if she had been allowed to do something other than play second fiddle to Irving's tragic hero?' (p. 437). Other Portias she examines include Peggy Ashcroft, Dorothy Tutin, Janet Suzman, Joan Plowright, Judi Dench, Pennie Downie, and Derbhle Crotty. This is a detailed and eloquent piece, but one wonders about the validity of Gay's rose-tinted claim that 'No other of Shakespeare's plays leaves us with the image of such a powerful and self-determined woman' (p. 431) particularly in the light of Gratiano's misogynist jokes about keeping safe his wife's 'ring'.

While Gay suggests that Shakespeare's Portia is complimentary to female agency, Laurie E. Maguire argues the opposite for Cressida. 'Performing Anger: The Anatomy of Abuse(s) in *Troilus and Cressida*' (*RenD* 31[2002] 153–83) is a passionately written, albeit eccentric, condemnation of Troilus and Diomedes as sexually abusive, while Cressida's submission and infidelity are defended in the light of her identification as a victim of abuse. Of course, it would take a brave critic to dissent from Maguire's dour verdict on *Shrew*: 'in the twenty-first century it is

difficult to find the subjugation of a woman a suitable subject for comic treatment'
(p. 157), but the assumptions underlying this sentiment are that Katherine represents
a real woman and that an audience member who finds Petruchio's perverse
treatment of his wife amusing is going to go home and starve and beat his wife.
There can be no escape from the accusation that in reading Cressida's situation in
the Greek camp as 'a textbook example of abuse' (p. 153), Maguire is out-
Bradleying Bradley: 'My approach is juxtapositional, setting twentieth-century
psychological research about spousal abuse in dialogue with early modern drama'
(p. 155). While this might seem harmlessly idiosyncratic, the explication of
Shakespeare's plays by reference to the rape victims of Yugoslavia is distinctly
unsavoury. Henry V's proposal that he and Princess Katherine produce an heir is *not*
'simply a variant of the Balkan rapes' (p. 163); one happens in a play and the other
is all too horribly real. The essay may have its heart in the right place by drawing
attention, via a dramatic text, to the horrors of domestic or political violence, but its
attempt to explicate that text belongs to the realms of literary scholarship and that,
as we all know in the trade, is an activity impotent to undo the iniquities of political
domination. For all the posturing of the cultural materialists, wars are not solved by
performances of, much less critical essays on, *Twelfth Night*. Of course, in the real
world 'language has agency' (p. 175), but the Grecian camp is, first, an imaginative
and secondly a theatrical *fiction*. Cressida is not 'a woman with little confidence in
her own value' (p. 171); she is a character in a play, and to compare her fictional
sufferings to the 'ongoing Serbian atrocities of genocidal rape' (p. 162) is at best
misguided, and at worst immoral.

Under the general editorship of Robert Smallwood, the Arden Shakespeare, in
association with the Shakespeare Birthplace Trust, has published the first three
volumes of the *Shakespeare at Stratford* series. Gillian Day writes on *King Richard
III*, Miriam Gilbert on *The Merchant of Venice*, and Patricia E. Tatspaugh on *The
Winter's Tale*. Since 1879 the Shakespeare Centre Library has been the repository of
materials (reviews, promptbooks, photographs, stage designs, theatre programmes,
and, more recently, archival video recordings) generated by Royal Shakespeare
Company productions and is thus of world importance to the study of Shakespeare
in performance. As the general editor's preface puts it, 'the aim of the Shakespeare
at Stratford series is to exploit, and indeed revel in, the archive's riches' (p. xi).
These concise studies focus on the performance of Shakespeare in Stratford in the
latter half of the twentieth century. Each is generously illustrated with production
shots, to which the authors frequently refer.

Day's study of *Richard III* considers the play as self-contained as well as a
constituent part of the staging of larger history cycles (such as Peter Hall and John
Barton's *The Wars of the Roses* [1963], or Adrian Noble's *The Plantagenets*
[1988]). Of the latter she rightly asserts that the history cycle has 'featured
significantly in the history of the RSC, as the epitome of its ensemble philosophy,
and the affirmation of its national significance' (p. 7). Her study is thus focused on
the details of specific performances but also displays a sense of the company's role
in re-producing and fashioning the place of Shakespeare in the wider national
culture. Day splits the twelve productions under consideration here into three
groups: 'Political Richards' (William Gaskill [1961]; Peter Hall and John Barton
[1963]; Adrian Noble [1988]); 'Psycho-Social Richards' (Glen Byam Shaw [1953]
and Elijah Moshinsky [1998]; Terry Hands [1970 and 1980]); 'Metatheatrical

Richards' (Barry Kyle [1975] and Sam Mendes [1992]; Michael Boyd [2001]; Bill Alexander [1984], and Steven Pimlott [1995]). The departure from a straight chronological record allows her to make some telling contrasts and parallels, though inevitably the influence of productions on those that come later is less easy to spot (although the tyrannical presence of Olivier is noted at the outset: 'Every production in this volume exists to an extent in Olivier's shadow', p. 5). Day's prose is lively and engaging. There are some acute readings, such as when she describes Ian Holm's 1963 Richard removing his helmet so that, now, 'there are two faces: the fearful Richard, weak and isolated, and the iron mask that Richard has projected as king, the unyielding self-image that he has always aspired to, represented by a hollow shell' (p. 62). Of the shift in connotation between the titles *The Wars of the Roses* and *The Plantagenets*, she suggests that the latter would be read in terms of a family saga (she ingeniously notes its echo of the title of the contemporary television soap-opera, *Dynasty*) rather than the panoramic political history implied by the earlier one. Unusually, Day protests that Hall and Barton's cycle is politically optimistic in contrast with the overwhelming nihilism of Jan Kott's concurrent *Shakespeare Our Contemporary*, though she is neither convincing nor, it would seem, convinced, candidly recording that 'By the time the cycle had reached its finale, some in the audience were sickened and cynical' (p. 21). Perhaps inevitably, Day is forced to conclude that a politically accented reading leads to a diminution of Richard as a Vice-figure 'which stands disruptively outside political ideology and historical account' (p. 93). Her accounts of Simon Russell Beale's and David Troughton's Richards (in Mendes [1992] and Pimlott [1995]) engage fully with this alternative aspect of the play and are probably the book's best sections. Other important Richards are carefully documented: Christopher Plummer [1961]; Antony Sher [1984]; Robert Lindsay [1998], and Aiden McArdle [2001], though the book's Stratford bias means that some major performances, not least Ian McKellen's 1991 National Theatre performance (directed by Richard Eyre and subsequently filmed by Richard Loncraine), are only briefly mentioned.

Whereas Day discusses groups of productions in their entirety, Gilbert's volume on *The Merchant of Venice* works through the play, describing performance choices made along the way. Thirteen productions form the basis of her analysis with directors, as follows: Michael Benthall [1947]; Denis Carey [1953]; Margaret Webster [1956]; Michael Langham [1960]; Clifford Williams [1965]; Terry Hands [1971]; John Barton [1978 and 1981]; John Caird [1984]; Roger Michell [1986]; Bill Alexander [1987]; David Thacker [1993], and Gregory Doran [1997]. Her introduction stresses the popularity of the play (between 1880 and 1944 it appeared in no fewer than thirty-seven seasons) as well as addressing the cultural problems raised by its ubiquity—she cites a truculent Judi Dench, 'I wouldn't ever go to see it again' (p. 6). This popularity, Gilbert suggests, leads to an anxiety of influence on future directors, designers, etc. (paradoxically generated by the very archive from which she is working) so that inspiration may too easily become overwhelming worry about plagiarism: 'Whether one researches past productions or not, the very existence of these [Shakespeare Centre] archives must on some level encourage a director to try something "new"' (p. 9). There follows an excellent discussion of the manner in which audience expectations are influenced by the various designs of theatre programmes, the delicate implications of the ordering of characters (and whether or not they are described in terms of religion, profession, or kinship—if so, how?). In particular she details the changes made to the programme for John Caird's 1984 production in the light of the furore generated by its initial inclusion of anti-Semitic sources, which were subsequently contextualized, toned down, or edited. Despite the appearance of Shylock in only five scenes, Gilbert notes the prevalence of his appearance in photographs of past productions and the way that this inflects audience reaction to his role in the play.

There then follow seven chapters along the lines of 'Shylock'; 'The Venetians'; 'The Trial', and so on. Gilbert makes some telling points: of David Calder's 1993 Shylock, she notes how the similarity of his and the Venetians' costumes suggested the degree to which he had been assimilated by Venetian society. His donning Jewish apparel for the trial scene indicated that he had become 'a Jew by virtue of being persecuted for being a Jew' (p. 35). She is especially good on the sexual politics of the play, pointing out that 'the Venice of the named characters (as contrasted with any extras) seems an exclusively male society' (p. 46), and on the ways in which this facilitates not merely a homosocial reading but a homoerotic one: 'At any rate, from the early 1970s on, hinting at Antonio's repressed homosexual love for Bassanio became a fairly standard reading, both on stage and in critical articles' (p. 55). Indeed, Bill Alexander [1987] 'further emphasized the homosexual relationship between Antonio and Bassanio by mirroring it with the Salerio/Solanio relationship, where again the audience saw a middle-aged man (Michael Cadman's Salerio) in love with a younger man (Gregory Doran's Solanio)' (p. 56). In contrast to this fervent masculinity is the 'female society' (p. 83) of Belmont; moreover, 'the way in which any given production portrays Belmont becomes an interpretation of Portia'. In the light of this balancing out of the gender inequalities, it is interesting to note that the final Belmont scenes were often cut during the nineteenth century. The volume also includes acute discussions of Gobbo, the suitors, and Gratiano— 'the trend in production has been to make him noisy, often irritating, occasionally violent' (p. 59). My single demurral regarding Gilbert's effective study relates to her assertion that, during the trial scene, Shylock 'knows that he doesn't have a chance of winning' (p. 120). The fact that she seems to be asserting this in relation to the play rather than to a single (misguided) production makes the suggestion all the more astounding.

Tatspaugh's *The Winter's Tale* begins with the unpromising assertion that for many years this play was thought 'too complex or too crudely constructed to be staged effectively' (p. 1). Indeed, she goes on, 'No performances in London during the Restoration have been recorded and only sixteen took place in the eighteenth century' (p. 3), though of course these are likely to have been truncated versions or adaptations. But not only is the play a problem, so is the critical enterprise of studying Shakespeare on stage. Tatspaugh's introduction is sensitive to the inherent difficulties of writing a performance history which is, of necessity, heavily reliant on the reviews of others (as inevitably all three of these *Shakespeare at Stratford* volumes must be): 'Reviewers may have blind spots, favour some actors or styles of acting or sounds of voice over others, write for a readership of a particular interest or set of values, and may come to the production with preconceived notions of how the play should—or should not—be presented (or even, in some cases, if it should be presented at all)' (pp. 17–18).

Nine productions form the focus of this study, directed by the following: Anthony Quayle [1948]; Peter Wood [1960]; Trevor Nunn [1969]; John Barton with Trevor

Nunn [1976]; Ronald Eyre [1981]; Adrian Noble [1984]; Terry Hands [1986]; Adrian Noble [1992]; and Gregory Doran [1999]. Unlike Day, who discusses productions of *Richard III* as a whole, or Gilbert, who moves through *The Merchant of Venice* roughly from beginning to end with illustrations of the various staging possibilities, Tatspaugh works incrementally through the play by precise act and scene, detailing how each production staged each moment. Inevitably this makes for a boring read as details from each version are recounted, but without much in the way of interesting cross-comparison or contrast. Too often we simply get an account of 'what happened next'. For instance, Tatspaugh writes of the 1976 Barton and Nunn production (with Ian McKellen as Leontes): 'After Antigonus exited with the infant [Perdita], Mamillius entered and went over to his father. The First Lord entered with news of the imminent arrival of Cleomenes and Dion. Leontes carried Mamillius off' (p. 90). Even when relying on eyewitness accounts, Tatspaugh never really penetrates very deeply; citing the critic of the *Guardian* responding to Nunn's 1969 production, she writes, 'The lighting, [Philip] Hope-Wallace points out, was "curiously effective"' (p. 109); Michael Billington (again of the *Guardian*) described Gemma Jones's 1981 Hermione as 'moving' (p. 113), while Tatspaugh's account of critical responses to Autolycus seems hardly worth formulating: 'As so often seems to be the case with Autolycus, reviewers were either charmed or unamused by his wit, songs and disguises' (p. 151).

The prevailing sense is of a hoovering up of impressions which are, within each scene-by-scene section, randomly arranged; there appears to be no concatenation of ideas or development of argument. Most irritating is the regular reliance on streams of rhetorical questions. These are designed to 'encourage the reader to consider various performance and staging options' (p. 16), but in fact they prove frustratingly banal and prolix. Paragraph-length lists of questions appear at least nine times and they are never particularly searching: 'Is she [Perdita] swaddled in her mother's shawl or some other piece of clothing easily identified as Hermione's? Has she been placed in a Moses basket or some similar object? Does Paulina shield the infant from Leontes' sight until she announces "Here 'tis" (66)? Does she place the baby in his arms? put it on the floor beside him? Does it cry or gurgle? How does Paulina address the lords who would block her entrance? her husband? her monarch? Does she find humour in the scene? How does Leontes respond to his subject's determination?' (p. 84); there are another six questions before the end of this paragraph. At one point Tatspaugh remarks that the language spoken by the three gentlemen in Act V, scene ii, 'demands close attention from the audience and is one of the reasons the scene was not played for many years' (p. 181). Not only does she evince nothing to support this assertion but its implications—that the rest of the play doesn't demand such attention and that apparently 'difficult bits' can be filleted without any damage to the play—are typical of the quirkiness of this book.

In *Rescripting Shakespeare: The Text, the Director, and Modern Productions*, Alan C. Dessen provides one of the most detailed and sensitive accounts of what takes place during that transition we have come trivially to label 'page to stage'. Relying upon nearly thirty years of theatre-going on both sides of the Atlantic, Dessen provides an intelligent, thorough, and above all common-sense account of the reasons why and ways in which printed texts are inflected, cut, and adapted during the course of their theatrical representation. Typical of this refreshing empiricism is his summation of the intrusiveness of interpolated editorial stage directions (both Jonathan Bate and Stanley Wells come under his spotlight): 'I agree with [E.A.J.] Honigmann that "we must ask ourselves whether there is any real need to follow the first Quarto or Folio" ("reason not the need"?), but my own response can be best summed up in the vernacular: "If it ain't broke, don't fix it"' (p. 234).

What Dessen brings to the discussion is an extraordinary wealth of experience as a reader and audience member so that he is able to draw upon 'roughly 280 productions' (p. x) in his illustrations of various forms of adaptation. Moreover, he is refreshingly insistent on the importance of being there: 'I have concentrated on stage productions I was able to see and for which I have reliable notes' (p. 235). The kinds of adaptation he analyses fall into two groups: '*rescripting* denotes the changes made by a director in the received text in response to a perceived problem or to achieve some agenda. For more extensive changes I use the term *rewrighting* to characterize situations where a director or adapter moves closer to the role of the playwright so as to fashion a script with substantial differences from the original' (p. 3). Of course the immediate question arises as to when rescripting becomes rewrighting, a question of which Dessen is fully aware: 'Wherein lies the line between adjustment-improvement and adaptation-translation?' (p. 93). Although it is implicit throughout his book, Dessen does well to avoid this 'How long is a piece of string?' question. Instead he not only defines, explains, and illustrates the various species of rescripting but also demonstrates the need for their having arisen in the first place. Fundamentally, he argues, there has been a shift in sensibility, culture, and ways of seeing: 'Elizabethan and Jacobean dramatists, including Shakespeare, had access to a language of the theatre that included signifiers or ways of signifying that have been screened out by later notions and assumptions linked to psychological realism and narrative credibility' (p. 63). Elsewhere, he describes the tendency of the modern illusionistic theatre to group scenes from single settings together and thus save numerous and elaborate scenery shifts: 'The onstage storytelling of Shakespeare and his contemporaries is often keyed to the rapid alteration of scenes and locales as befits their flexible open stage, but that flexibility or openness can collide with today's sense of "design" or "set" that precludes such alternations' (p. 71). The bottom line is this: 'Shakespeare did not script his plays with us in mind' (p. 238).

The major causes of rescripting include the following: to cut down on running time; to eliminate obscurity; to reduce the number of speaking parts (in order to produce it with a small company and/or save money on actors' salaries); to render the play more acceptable to contemporary sensibilities (especially in relation to politically incorrect or offensive moments); to mould the play to a directorial 'concept'. Such 'streamlining' (p. 24), Dessen notes, is less visible in the Roman and history plays and even less conspicuous in the plays of Shakespeare's contemporary playwrights. As he wryly puts it, 'Beaumont and Fletcher are very much of an age and not for all time, so that many of their effects do not translate well into our idiom and, in fact, often defy our expectations' (p. 57). There are especially good discussions of whether, and if so where, to place an interval, the staging of supernatural elements, and the implications of final scenes. The compression/rewrighting of the three parts of *Henry VI* and the framing of *Taming of the Shrew* justify separate chapters. In the latter case, Dessen carefully details the reasons why 'bolting on' the closure of *A Shrew* is not as easy as it seems. As he puts it, in relation to the 1594 and 1623 versions, 'Playgoers of the period may have seen either or both versions. Playgoers today regularly see neither. And thereby hangs my tale' (p. 185).

While, so often, the theatre demands rescripting for the sake of psychological credibility or realism ('directors must deal with playgoers who have been conditioned by cinema and television', p. 158), this is anathema to academics and scholars of Renaissance theatre. But it is here that Dessen's sensitivity is most discernible as he acknowledges the contribution made by such theatre practitioners: 'From many conversations over the last twenty-five years I have gained a healthy respect for the commitment and expertise of actors and directors, so I will not mount an attack against the director-as-vandal or sing hymns to uncut playscripts' (p. 2). It is this generosity of spirit coupled with a formidable knowledge of these plays which makes *Rescripting Shakespeare* such a profitable volume.

Bettina Boecker examines the fortunes of the Elizabethan audience in a concise and neatly argued essay entitled 'Inventing the Groundling: Shakespeare's Elizabethan Audience and Nineteenth-Century National Identity' (*Folio* 9[2002] 15–21). With the impact of French neoclassicism, Shakespeare is chastised for his failure to observe the unities. He is excused on the grounds that he is 'writing for an uncivilized audience, and therefore cannot be blamed if he does not always transcend these historical conditions' (p. 15). Pushed further, as Boecker ably demonstrates, 'Shakespeare's immense popularity becomes an argument against neoclassicism in its own right' (p. 18) and hence an assertion of an English identity.

English identity and nationhood are also at the heart of Richard Foulkes's *Performing Shakespeare in the Age of Empire*. The general trajectory followed by Shakespeare during this period is, perhaps surprisingly, downward. Foulkes's detailed study begins with Victorian Shakespeare, 'a genuinely popular dramatist amongst all levels of English society' (p. 57), but ends with the depressed status he held on the eve of the First World War: 'In the minds of many Shakespeare had become an unapproachable icon, associated with high culture and erudition rather than the fount of popular entertainment' (p. 206). Foulkes identifies a number of factors in the Bard's decline, including the rise of naturalism 'in the wake of Ibsen' (p. 205), new forms of entertainment such as the music hall and the cinema bringing with them increasing stratification in class terms, and the growing identification of Shakespeare with education. Most significantly though, and running throughout the period under examination, is an indifference at state level towards the founding of a national theatre. Unlike other European nations (notably Germany) there was no government sponsorship in England and, while Victoria and Albert had expressed enthusiasm for the theatre, the 1864 tercentenary unfortunately 'found the royal family not only bereft of the member who would have given the most enthusiastic support, but also in a state of continuing mourning which militated against active involvement by his widow or any of their children' (p. 67). Indeed Herbert Beerbohm Tree's 1911 Coronation Festival resulted in a loss of over £3,000 so that the 'theatre could be said to be subsidising the monarchy' (p. 147).

The picture that emerges is one of a general deterioration in the cultural popularity of Shakespeare despite the intervention of several notable impresarios, and Foulkes's charting of their contributions gives the book a distinctly Victorian air reminiscent of a list of Great Men. The first of these is William Charles Macready, who in 1837 sought the patronage of the newly crowned monarch. Although this was unsuccessful, 'he had succeeded in introducing at the very outset of the new reign a theme—royal patronage—which was to be not only crucial for the theatre, but also significant for the nation in the ensuing decades' (p. 11). While at home he established a norm of 'thorough rehearsals, competent company, restoration of the text, pictorial scenery and appropriate costumes' (pp. 30–1). His visits abroad, to America and France, 'succeeded in extending the appreciation for Shakespeare and his works amongst fellow artistes and the public at large' (p. 31).

Following the abolition, in 1843, of the theatrical monopolies enjoyed since the time of Charles II by Covent Garden and Drury Lane, Sadler's Wells emerged under the management of Samuel Phelps as the first alternative to West End Shakespeare. Foulkes writes, 'In the range of his Shakespearian repertoire, his loyal and talented company, his continuance of Macready's textual restoration, and his harmonious— but restrained—scenery, Phelps made an outstanding and influential contribution to the nineteenth-century Shakespearian theatre' (p. 34). Phelps also took his company to Germany. Appointed director of the Windsor Castle Theatricals in 1848, Charles Kean's principle of theatrical authenticity encouraged the pictorial style of so much Victorian and post-Victorian production. As Foulkes points out, 'The meticulous attention to detail and truth to life, which characterised Kean's productions, was symptomatic of the decade in which the Pre-Raphaelites flourished and photography advanced scientifically and artistically' (p. 47). For all these achievements there follows a sobering chapter on the 1864 tercentenary which accounts for its failure not only in terms of royal indifference but also as stemming from the literary controversies and the in-fighting between vain actors; as Foulkes drily puts it, 'the occasion was singularly lacking in the heroic qualities' (p. 79).

Perhaps most influential was Henry Irving, who managed the Lyceum, 'which he proceeded to make a National in all but name' (p. 108); both at home and abroad, the influence of Shakespeare began to spread. There follow accounts of Beerbohm Tree, Frank Benson, Harley Granville-Barker (who unfortunately appears as 'Baker' in the index and is thus out of sequence), Louis Calvert, and Annie Horniman. Between 1911 and 1914 'British actors toured the empire in unprecedented numbers' (p. 155). Popularity in Germany seemed paradoxically to peak in the run-up to the First World War with the third Annual Shakespeare Lecture in 1913 on the topic 'Shakespeare and Germany' (p. 196). As well as the book's general narrative of the growing marginalization of Shakespeare in England there are some amazing instances of specific misfortunes, such as the spats between Macready and the American actor Edwin Forrest, which exploded in the Astor Place riots in April 1849 with the loss of seventeen lives. Less tragic is the otherwise unidentified American actor, O'Connor, who played Richard III in Chicago 'behind a net which protected him from the avalanche of vegetables, which … O'Connor subsequently sold' (p. 185). Foulkes's study, in its close attention to the problems, serious and less so, experienced by the domestic and international productions of nineteenth-century English actors, gives the lie to the nationalistic rhetoric of those such as S.P.B. Mais who, in 1916, insisted on Shakespearian/English supremacy in the face of Shakespearian/English decline: 'It is the greatest privilege that we enjoy as Englishmen that this man was of our blood, an Englishman for the English. It is by far the greatest achievement that we as a nation have yet wrought that we have produced Shakespeare' (p. 204).

In '"How fine a play was Mrs Lear"': The Case for Gordon Bottomley's *King Lear's Wife*' (*ShS* 55[2002] 128–38), Foulkes describes this prequel to

Shakespeare's play, premiered at the Birmingham Rep on 25 September 1915. He goes on to assert that Bottomley's verse drama justifies the description of him 'as a harbinger of T.S. Eliot, Christopher Fry and their like' (p. 132). Foulkes suggests that, in the context of women's suffrage, the play's accent on the female members of Lear's court 'no doubt struck a chord with many female readers at the time' (p. 132), although Bottomley was working 'in a different tradition from the Ibsenite new woman drama'. The essay reproduces six beautiful designs by Paul Nash which were displayed at the Theatre Exhibition in Amsterdam and subsequently at the Victoria and Albert Museum, but they were never used, and Foulkes concludes his essay with a challenge: 'Uniquely *King Lear's Wife* offers the opportunity of realizing a remarkable partnership between two rare talents: Bottomley's with the poet's pen, Nash's with the artist's brush. Is there a theatre company that will give this distinguished contribution to the afterlife of *King Lear* an afterlife of its own?' (p. 138).

3. Shakespeare on Screen

The year's outstanding monograph is Courtney Lehmann's *Shakespeare Remains: Theater to Film, Early Modern to Postmodern.* Lehmann's main texts are comparatively canonical, but her approach is original and exciting, and although the book is extremely densely argued and at times relentlessly smart, she writes with flair and enthusiasm. Her aim is to go beyond the impasse in current thinking about Shakespearian authorship through the use of film theory. To avoid the seemingly ineradicable oppositions between author and text, between text and performance, and between performance and author, she suggests a change of theoretical scene. Her chosen area is the post-1968 *auteur* theory associated with *Cahiers du Cinema*, which, she argues, differs from post-structuralist literary theory in its refusal to jettison the idea of the author altogether. Instead, authorship is envisaged as a 'montage effect', based on 'constitutive conflict' between an 'author' and the 'apparatus', which is submerged beneath the surface of film. As Lehmann explains, to 'refocus the Shakespearean corpus through the lens of *auteur* theory is to recognise "Shakespeare" as a montage of historically charged collisions between bodies and texts that cannot be reduced to the work of either a solitary "author" or an ever-metamorphosing dramatic and textual "apparatus"'. Adapting the terms of Jacques Derrida's *Spectres of Marx*, she argues that 'the idea of the auteur only appears to be "out in front", coming back in advance—ahead of its time—from the past, indeed, from Shakespeare'. Although *auteur* theory appears to be anachronistic in relation to Shakespeare, the early modern and postmodern are correlative in their attitudes towards authorship, being two periods in which the identity of 'the author' is fragile and contested.

The first three chapters use *auteur* theory to examine Shakespearian authorship in terms of the early modern period. Chapter 1, 'Shakespeare Unauthorized: Tragedy "by the book" in *Romeo and Juliet*', looks at the relationship between Shakespeare's play and its single source or 'auctor', Arthur Brooke's *Tragicall Historye of Romeus and Juliet*. Chapter 2, 'Authors, Players, and the Shakespearean Auteur-Function in *A Midsummer Night's Dream*', situates the play in terms of a 'growing rift' in the 1590s between an 'author's theatre' and a 'player's theatre', while Chapter 3, 'The

Machine in the Ghost: *Hamlet*'s Cinematographic Kingdom', sees Hamlet as a would-be director in a fundamentally cinematic tragedy. The remaining chapters examine postmodern Shakespearian films. Chapter 4, 'Strictly Shakespeare? Dead Letters, Ghostly Fathers, and the Cultural Pathology of Authorship in Baz Luhrmann's *William Shakespeare's Romeo + Juliet*', is reprinted from *Shakespeare Quarterly* (*SQ* 52[2001] 189–221), and was reviewed in *YWES* 82[2003] 84–5. Chapters 5 and 6 examine the 'personal and geopolitical dimensions' of the Shakespearian films of Kenneth Branagh, looking in turn at Branagh as an example of the 'postmodern *auteur*', and at the national politics of *Henry V* as they are exhibited in the portrayal of the Irish captain MacMorris. The final chapter analyses *Shakespeare in Love* as an example of 'Sex, Capitalism and the Authorial Body-in-Pleasure', viewing the 'Shakespearean corpus' as the 'ultimate commodity fetish'. *Shakespeare Remains* is an exhilarating and provocative book, which should be widely read and hotly debated.

Two other monographs, H.R. Coursen's *Shakespeare in Space: Recent Shakespeare Productions on Screen* and Stephen M. Buhler's *Shakespeare in the Cinema: Ocular Proof*, provide an instructive contrast. Coursen sets out to 'to describe and evaluate in conventional terms' Shakespearian film and television of the 1990s. In his introduction, he sets up a tension between a Shakespearian 'script' and the production on which it is based. The script, he writes, 'itself seeks meanings as yet to emerge in society and culture'; the production, on the other hand, 'having illuminated those meanings for a moment, falls back into that moment'. The meaning of a production can be located in the 'spaces' in which it exists: the physical space of the screen itself or the outdoor location; the length of time a film takes to spin its story; the generic 'space' in which a production is situated. This is a promising perspective, and Coursen's breadth of reference is highly impressive. Of particular note are the accounts of television adaptations such as John Caird's *Henry IV* [1995], David Thacker's *Measure for Measure* [1994], the Deborah Warner/ Fiona Shaw *Richard II* [1997], Richard Eyre's *King Lear* [1998], Nicholas Hytner's *Twelfth Night* [1998], and Bonnie Raskin's *Tempest* [1998].

However, Coursen's defensiveness about 'theory', his determined focus on evaluative analysis, and his overt dislike for the majority of avant-garde or period-specific productions, all curtail the scope of his study. Some films are granted measured consideration. For instance, he describes how Branagh's *Love's Labour's Lost* uses anachronistic generic tropes and techniques—'the songs of the 1930s and the wide-screen format of the 1950s'—in a way which avoids squeezing the text's multivalent possibilities into a 'merely contemporary context'. Elsewhere, those less favoured productions are summarily dismissed: Peter Greenaway's *Prospero's Books* is the 'silliest of recent films' and a 'travesty', while the Richard Loncraine/ Ian McKellen *Richard III* 'cannot reach for the script's deeper register' and 'settles for inanity'. *Shakespeare in Space* is thus useful mainly as one critic's response to a series of films and television productions—a series of impressions which seem preliminary to serious analysis—and a reader's response to his insights will probably depend on how far she or he agrees with his particular perspective.

In a review essay, 'Shakespearean Projections' (*Theater* 32[2002] 23–31), Stanley Kaufmann draws a distinction between 'Shakespeare on film', where the plays are filmed 'with cinematic flourish but without converting the plays into film scripts', and those films which are 'a separate art, a melding of Shakespeare with film for which no adequate name has yet been devised'. In Kaufmann's terms, Coursen's interest is in 'Shakespeare on film', a representation of a Shakespearian text which cannot itself be imprisoned in such transitory mediums as film (or, indeed, theatre). On the other hand, Buhler's *Shakespeare in the Cinema: Ocular Proof*, an investigation of 'what the Shakespearean project reveals about individual films and about film in general', perhaps moves closer towards an accommodation of Kaufmann's unnamed genre.

Like Coursen, Buhler ranges widely, covering Anglophone and non-Anglophone films, silent films and talkies, adaptations and documentaries. Unlike Coursen, his approach is not developed in opposition to 'theory', but actively embraces various interpretative paradigms. Chapter 1, for instance, focuses on *Othello* as directed by Dimitri Buchowetzky [1922], Sergei Yutkevich [1955], and Oliver Parker [1995], looking at the interrelation between modes of presentation—in particular the movement between naturalistic and expressionistic techniques—and issues of race. An interesting account of 'Documentary Shakespeare' in chapter 2 examines films which document Shakespearian performances originally created in the theatre, such as Johnston Forbes-Robertson's Hamlet and Laurence Olivier's Othello, in the context of two Shakespearian documentaries, *Master Will Shakespeare*, originally released as a companion to George Cukor's 1936 *Romeo and Juliet*, and *Looking for Richard*.

Particularly useful are two chapters which focus on the agency of the performer. Chapter 3, 'Shakespeare and the Screen Idol', analyses the tension between the Hollywood star system and Shakespearian film. These would-be populist films face the 'unenviable' task of sustaining the general image of stars such as Mary Pickford, James Cagney, Norma Shearer, Elizabeth Taylor, or Mel Gibson while simultaneously 'developing the complex roles that emerge from Shakespeare's language and dramaturgy'. The results are not always those intended: the Reinhardt/ Dieterle *Midsummer Night's Dream*, for instance, 'had its greatest impact in the area of special effects and in dissuading most studio executives from trying anything like it ever again'. Chapter 6, meanwhile, examines the 'revenge of the actor manager' in the careers of Branagh and his 'filmic father-figures', Olivier and Welles. Buhler concludes with an appreciative account of Julie Taymor's *Titus*, suggesting that 'most of the successful adaptations of Shakespeare for the screen have served as interventions in cinema's ongoing relationship with the literary, the dramatic, and other visual arts'.

Another welcome publication is Graham Holderness's *Visual Shakespeare: Essays in Film and Television*, a selection of ground-breaking essays originally published between 1984 and 1998. Sections 1 and 2 provide general essays on television ('Bard on the Box', 'Shakespeare Rescheduled') and film ('Shakespeare and Cinema', 'Shakespeare Rewound'), while section 3 reproduces case-studies of *Henry V*, *The Taming of the Shrew*, and *Romeo and Juliet*. In his introduction, Holderness notes that his work drew its 'theoretical parameters from post-1968 film theory and from the theoretically influenced literary criticism of the same period'. Re-reading his work in 2002 illuminates some of the areas in which the criticism of Shakespeare on film is now succeeding and, sadly, some of those areas in which it is still lacking.

Two valuable collections were edited by Courtney Lehmann and Lisa S. Starks: *Spectacular Shakespeare: Critical Theory and Popular Cinema* and *The Reel*

Shakespeare: Alternative Cinema and Theory. I will make some general comments here, returning to individual essays in the context of the rest of the year's work. The books are complementary: while *Spectacular Shakespeare* focuses on Hollywood films and popular television, *The Reel Shakespeare* takes as its subject films produced outside the mainstream. *Spectacular Shakespeare* explores the 'spectacle' of Shakespeare, the dramatist as the focus of what Lehmann and Starks term 'a new age of Bardolatry in Hollywood' ushered in by *Shakespeare in Love*. The collection breaks down into three sections. Part 1, 'Media Imperialism: Appropriating Culture, Race and Authority', examines the question of Shakespearian appropriation from three national/cultural angles: Marguerite Hailey Rippy examines the racial politics in two American representations of *Othello*, Lisa Hopkins analyses the portrayal of the British royal family in the Loncraine/McKellen *Richard III*, and Alfredo Michel Modenessi looks at Lurhmann's *Romeo + Juliet* from a Mexican perspective. Part 2, 'Reframing Romance: Sex, Love, and Subjectivity', moves from the national to the individual, 'examining the process of early modern identity-formation through the erotic commerce of courtship and marriage' in Nunn's *Twelfth Night* (Laurie E. Osborne), Branagh's *Much Ado About Nothing* (Samuel Crowl), and *Shakespeare in Love* (Lehmann). Part 3, 'The Politics of the Popular: From Class to Classroom', moves to consider the perspective of multiple audiences inside the multiplex and classroom, with essays by Douglas Lanier, Elizabeth A. Dietchman, and Annalisa Castaldo. In his afterword, 'Te(e)n Things I Hate about Girlene Shakesploitation Flicks in the Late 1990s, or Not-So-Fast Times at Shakespeare High' (pp. 205–32), Richard Burt wonders what the next direction might be for the populist Shakespeare craze. Looking at the Shakespearian teen movies *Ten Things I Hate About You* and *Never Been Kissed*, he suggests that Hollywood's current target is a younger generation of potential Bardolators.

Where *Spectacular Shakespeare* aims to explore popular Shakespearian cinema, *The Reel Shakespeare* focuses on 'important, nonmainstream films and the oppositional messages they convey'. In Part 1, 'Art of Film: Shakespeare and Early Cinema', Kenneth Rothwell traces the history of silent films of *Hamlet*. Part 2, 'Film of Art: Shakespeare and Avant-Garde Cinema', explores the 'status of the Shakespearean vanguard', including essays on Peter Hall's *A Midsummer Night's Dream* (Peter S. Donaldson), Jean-Luc Godard's *King Lear* (Alan Walworth), and Greenaway's *Prospero's Books* (Lia M. Hotchkiss). Part 3, 'Film on the Edge: Shakespeare and Countercinema', focuses on 'the violence of the cinematic image' in Taymor's *Titus* (Lisa S. Starks), Polanski's *Macbeth* (Bryan Reynolds), and Welles's *Chimes at Midnight* and Van Sant's *My Own Private Idaho* (Kathy M. Howlett). As in *Spectacular Shakespeare*, a section on Shakespearian pedagogy, 'Film in the Alternative Classroom: Shakespeare and Radical Pedagogy', is included. This comprises essays by Douglas E. Green and John Brett Mischo, which focus on the potential which film has both to 'undermine and to reinforce oppressive ideologies of gender, sexuality, race, and class'. The book concludes with José Ramón Díaz-Fernández's invaluable 'The Reel Shakespeare: A Selective Bibliography of Criticism' (pp. 229–87), an updated compilation of the bibliographies printed in *Post Script* 17:i[1997] and 17:ii[1998].

Most of the year's best general articles can be found in *Shakespeare Quarterly*'s special issue, 'Screen Shakespeare', edited by Barbara Hodgdon, a remarkable collection of essays by some of the most interesting critics currently at work in the field. Richard Burt's stimulating essay, 'Slammin' Shakespeare In Acc(id)ents Yet Unknown: Liveness, Cinem(edi)a, and Racial Dis-integration' (*SQ* 53[2002] 201–26), examines the 'the tensions between Shakespearean and black authenticity' in a variety of productions ranging from *The Cosby Show* and *MTV Celebrity Deathmatch* to the films *Get Over It* [2001], *Renaissance Man* [1994], *True Identity* [1991], and *So Fine* [1981]. 'Theorizing race and Shakespeare as always already mediatized', Burt argues, 'disrupts current discourses about authenticity in studies of Shakespeare and of (black) popular culture as resistant.' Using the concept of 'cinemedia'—the circulation of films between different screens and varying media—he focuses in particular on the use of sound, which, like colour, functions as a racial signifier.

In 'Crouching Tiger, Hidden Agenda: How Shakespeare and the Renaissance Are Taking the Rage Out of Feminism' (*SQ* 53[2002] 260–79), Courtney Lehmann explores the relationship between Shakespeare's popularity in Hollywood in the late 1990s and the film industry's concurrent anti-feminist backlash. Renaissance-period drama—for instance, Shekar Kapur's *Elizabeth* and Michael Herskovitz's *Dangerous Beauty*—shares with Shakespearian spin-offs and adaptations such as *Shakespeare in Love* and Michael Hoffman's *A Midsummer Night's Dream* a tendency to fetishize sex as the only means by which their heroines can advance, trapping them with the imprimatur of History or, 'worse', Shakespeare. These films can be contrasted with female-directed productions such as Agnès Merlet's *Artemisia* or Taymor's *Titus*, which 'resonate as inspiring if ironic exceptions to these antifeminist appropriations of the life, times, or works of William Shakespeare'.

Lehmann's account of *Shakespeare in Love* in *Shakespeare Remains*, which is also available in *Spectacular Shakespeare* (pp. 125–45), is complemented by Jane Kingsley-Smith's 'Shakespearean Authorship in Popular British Cinema' (*LFQ* 30[2002] 158–65), an exploration of the presentation of Shakespeare in three films, *Immortal Gentleman* [1935], *Time Flies* [1944], and *Shakespeare in Love*. *Shakespeare in Love* is illuminated by the earlier films, and all three enact 'a comic ritual in which the death of the Author is threatened'—by writer's block and by doubts about his authorship of the works attributed to him—'but finally averted'.

A group of significant articles focuses on the place of film in Shakespearian pedagogy, moving beyond descriptions of teaching to consider the implications of decisions regarding particular techniques and choices of film. Laurie E. Osborne's 'Clip Art: Theorizing the Shakespeare Film Clip' (*SQ* 53[2002] 227–40) offers a typically cogent critique of the use of extracts from films in the teaching of Shakespeare. We need, she argues, to be more self-aware in our 'too-easy acceptance of pedagogic clipping' and to understand more fully the wider implications which excerpts can have. All too accustomed to presenting Shakespearian film as an adjunct to the text, teachers need also to be aware of their status as film. As noted above, both of the collections edited by Starks and Lehmann include essays on pedagogy. In *Spectacular Shakespeare*, two essays focus on the use of mainstream cinematic Shakespeare, Elizabeth A. Deitchman's 'From the Cinema to the Classroom: Hollywood Teaches *Hamlet*' (in Lehmann and Starks, eds., pp. 172–86) and Annalisa Castaldo's 'The Film's the Thing: Using Film in the Shakespearean Classroom' (in Lehmann and Starks, eds., pp. 187–204). In *The Reel Shakespeare*, two essays consider the extent to which the use of Shakespearian film in teaching can either subvert or maintain oppressive social structures. In 'The Screening of the Shrews: Teaching (Against) Shakespeare's Author Function' (in Starks and Lehmann, eds., pp. 212–28), John Brett Mischo suggests that a 'performance-based pedagogy' can counter students' tendency to assume that Shakespearian authority lies behind particular interpretations and can illuminate dissident perspectives even in Hollywood adaptations of the play. Douglas E. Green's 'Shakespeare, Branagh, and the "Queer Traitor": Close Encounters in the Shakespeare Classroom' (in Starks and Lehmann, eds., pp. 191–211) analyses the way in which three Shakespearian films associated with Branagh, *Henry V*, *Much Ado About Nothing*, and *Othello*, build connections between homoerotics, decadence, misogyny, and treason, and interrogates the ways in which these issues can be developed in undergraduate seminars.

Branagh is also the focus of Mark Thornton Burnett's valuable essay '"We are the makers of manners": The Branagh Phenomenon' (in Burt, ed., *Shakespeare After Mass Media*, pp. 83–105). Burnett examines the development of Branagh's Shakespearian films from *Henry V* to *Love's Labour's Lost*, arguing that Branagh is 'distinctive for having made (or created) the manners (or fashions) that have revitalised "Shakespeare" for a postmodern clientele'. He also looks at the associated question of Branagh's public image as director and as the star of his own films and those of other directors. In Burnett's account, Branagh is both innovator and victim: having enabled a new generation of interventionist directors of Shakespeare, he now has to face their challenge in his own films. Complementary to Burnett's analysis in its focus on Branagh's attempts to produce a populist Shakespeare is Samuel Crowl's illuminating 'The Marriage of Shakespeare and Hollywood: Kenneth Branagh's *Much Ado About Nothing*' (in Lehmann and Starks, eds., pp. 110–24). In another contribution to Branagh studies, Crowl has also published an extended interview with the director, 'Communicating Shakespeare: An Interview with Kenneth Branagh' (*ShakB* 20:iii[2002] 24–8).

Reviewed by Gayle Holst in 'Branagh's Labour's Lost: Too Much, Too Little, Too Late' (*LFQ* 30[2002] 228–30), and found to be 'leaden and labored', Branagh's *Love's Labour's Lost* receives considered scholarly assessment in Ramona Wray's 'Nostalgia for Navarre: The Melancholic Metacinema of Kenneth Branagh's *Love's Labour's Lost*' (*LFQ* 30[2002] 171–8). Wray's focus is on the risky 'generic transformation' of Shakespeare's play in Branagh's adaptation, which melds Elizabethan drama with the generic codes and conventions, and recycled songs, of the 1930s musical. The subject of her analysis is similar to that of Coursen in *Shakespeare in Space*, but her essay's concerns are broader and its conclusions more illuminating. In its fusion, she argues, *Love's Labour's Lost* 'highlights the characteristically postmodern ways in which nostalgia is driven, not from a knowledge of or even a desire for the past, but from a fear or dislike of the present'.

Among other adaptations of Shakespeare's comedies, Nunn's *Twelfth Night* continues to gather criticism. The best of these essays is Laurie E. Osborne's 'Cutting up Characters: The Erotic Politics of Trevor Nunn's *Twelfth Night*' (in Lehmann and Starks, eds., pp. 89–109). Osborne looks at the way in which film editing uneasily reconfigures the early modern text to construct 'fully developed' characters; 'our "natural perspective" on the twins, like that in Shakespeare's play, proves at once fragmented and continuous—and therefore ideological rather than "natural"'. Also worthy of attention is Nicholas Jones's 'Trevor Nunn's *Twelfth*

Night: Contemporary Film and Classic British Theatre' (*EMLS* 8:ii[2002]). Jones focuses on the casting of Ben Kingsley as an 'idiosyncratic and disturbing Feste' and argues that his portrayal 'grounds the film in contemporary issues of feminism, sexuality, and gender identity'. Although on the surface the film has a tasteful period restraint, this critical perspective prevents it from settling into smug complacency.

Kelli Marshall's '"How do you solve a problem like Maria?"': A Problematic (Re)Interpretation of Maria in Trevor Nunn's *Twelfth Night*' (*LFQ* 30[2002] 217–22) argues that Imelda Staunton's 'uncharacteristic' portrayal of Maria as 'somber, introverted, and matronly' works against the film's narrative and the 'typically delightful Shakespearean character'. David G. Hale's 'The End of *Twelfth Night*: Two Recent Performances on Film' (*ShakB* 20:ii[2002] 42–4) also focuses on individual scenes, comparing the conclusion of Nunn's version with that of Hytner's *Twelfth Night*. Meanwhile, in 'Inter-Cutting in Trevor Nunn's *Twelfth Night*' (*LFQ* 30[2002] 179–88), Philippa Sheppard asserts that the 'Shakespearian' inter-cutting of scenes in Nunn's adaptation succeeds in translating Shakespeare's play to the new medium.

In '"Two of Both Kinds": Modernism and Patriarchy in Peter Hall's *A Midsummer Night's Dream*' (in Starks and Lehmann, eds., pp. 43–58), Peter Donaldson develops an argument first advanced by Graham Holderness in 'Radical Potentiality and Institutional Closure: Shakespeare in Film and Television' (in Dollimore and Sinfield, eds., *Political Shakespeare* [1985], pp. 182–201). As Holderness argued, Hall's film moves from 'leftist, avant-garde' techniques associated with Brecht or Godard to a Leavisite emphasis on 'reconstructed community'. Focusing on filmic techniques and the treatment of gender relations in Hall's film, Donaldson concludes that 'the radicalism of Hall's *Dream* does not merely fade away but modulates, carefully, toward the cultural and political mainstream'. A more recent version of *A Midsummer Night's Dream*, radical in its own way, is the focus of Mark Thornton Burnett's '"Fancy's images": Reinventing Shakespeare in Christine Edzard's *The Children's Midsummer Night's Dream*' (*LFQ* 30[2002] 166–70). Unique in contemporary Shakespearian film, Edzard cast children aged between 8 and 12 in all roles. This enables Edzard, Burnett argues, 'to bring back to our understanding of the dramatist a sense of wonder and invention' the effect of which is both affirmative and potentially subversive.

Interested in a different kind of wonder, Neil Forsyth's 'Shakespeare and Méliès: Magic, Dream, and the Supernatural' (*EA* 55[2002] 167–80) looks at the use of special effects in the tradition of Georges Méliès, 'a stage magician turned *cinéaste*' in film versions of *A Midsummer Night's Dream* and *The Tempest*. In these plays, Shakespeare draws parallels between magic and theatre; the films, Forsyth argues, exhibit differing attitudes towards the possibilities of this material in a cinematic environment. Another essay also draws on the relationship between Shakespearian film and theatre. In 'The Incorporation of Word as Image in Peter Greenaway's *Prospero's Books*' (in Starks and Lehmann, eds., pp. 95–117), a revised version of an essay originally published in *Post Script* (17:ii[1998] 8–25; reviewed in *YWES* 79[2000] 267), Lia M. Hotchkiss analyses the film's extravagant textuality. She concludes that, by 'constructing a textual theatrical point of origin as more culturally legitimate than its own cinematic roots, the film consumes itself'.

Two substantial essays on *Hamlet* can be found in the special issue of *Shakespeare Quarterly*. Douglas M. Lanier's 'Shakescorp Noir' (*SQ* 53[2002] 157–

80) examines the Shakespeare film boom of the 1990s in the context of contemporaneous Shakespearian corporate management manuals. Caught up in a fantasy of a newly popularized Shakespeare, academics have been slow to recognize the way in which Shakespeare remains 'an emblem of cultural legitimation for the existing social and economic order'. Deploying film noir codes, Almereyda's *Hamlet* offers a critique, 'albeit halting and incomplete', of this establishment, corporate Shakespeare. In '"Remember me": Psychoanalysis, Cinema, and the Crisis of Modernity' (*SQ* 53[2002] 181–200), Lisa S. Starks traces the associations between the contemporaneous phenomena of cinema and psychoanalysis, focusing on the part played by *Hamlet* in their decentring of subjectivity. Her analysis focuses on the Svend Gade/Asta Nielsen *Hamlet*, which, in its appropriation of *Hamlet*, 'foregrounds the losses of time, the persistence of memory, and the split identity that figure in both psychoanalysis *and* cinema'. The Gade/Nielsen *Hamlet* is also the focus of Monika Seidl's 'Room for Asta: Gender Roles and Melodrama in Asta Nielsen's Filmic Version of *Hamlet* (1920)' (*LFQ* 30[2002] 208–16), which argues that the film not only articulates gender ambiguities prevalent in the 1920s, but also opens up a space for the female audience as well as the female performer. The Gade/Neilsen *Hamlet* is also examined in Kenneth Rothwell's '*Hamlet* in Silence: Reinventing the Prince on Celluloid' (in Starks and Lehmann, eds., pp. 25–40). Rothwell surveys the early production of *Hamlet* on film, including the advertised but untraced Vitagraph *Hamlet*, the Hamlets of Sarah Bernhardt and Johnston Forbes-Robertson, and Eleuterio Rodofi's *Amleto*.

In '"Art thou base, common and popular?": The Cultural Politics of Kenneth Branagh's *Hamlet*' (in Lehmann and Starks, eds., pp. 149–71), Douglas M. Lanier argues that it is no longer possible to sustain a category of high art for Shakespeare, since the old categories have been subsumed in a culture that is increasingly 'mass'. The incorporation of *Hamlet* into mass culture is also examined in two articles that focus on the Indian screen. In '*Hamlet* on the Hindi Screen' (*HSt* 24[2002] 81–93), Rajiva Verma charts the history of adaptations of Shakespeare's tragedy by Raja Athavale [1928], Sohrab Modi [1935], and Kishore Sahu [1954]. He emphasizes the links between all three films and the Parsi stage, in particular two popular Hamlet plays, *Khoone Nahak* ('Unjust Assassination') and *Khoon ka Khoon* ('Blood for Blood'). Esha Niyogi De's 'Modern Shakespeares in Popular Bombay Cinema: Translation, Subjectivity and Community' (*Screen* 43[2002] 19–40) instead places Indian adaptations of Shakespeare in a postcolonial context, focusing on the Modi and Sahu *Hamlet*s. De examines the adaptations as hybrid formations, based on contemporaneous European stage and film productions and relocated in the 'polycultural context of popular commercial Bombay cinema'.

Peter S. Donaldson's '"In fair Verona": Media, Spectacle, and Performance in *William Shakespeare's Romeo + Juliet*' (in Burt, ed., pp. 59–82) offers a nuanced account of Lurhmann's film in the context of 'the present ferment in communications technologies and representational practices'. Drawing on situationist analyses of late capitalism, Donaldson suggests that the film's overwhelming media culture is shown as fuelling the conflict between Montague and Capulet, thus propelling the tragic action. Despite the counter-cultural impulses of the younger generation, lurking on the margins of Verona's metropolis, the film 'concludes as a cruel triumph of the spectacle', as the lovers' bodies are carried away in the glare of the televized epilogue. However, the film's conclusion also uses visual material of different kinds in an attempt 'to give its allegory of life in the age of media spectacle the stature of tragedy'.

Two contrasting articles focus on *Romeo and Juliet* in Mexico. In '(Un)Doing the Book "without Verona walls": A View From the Receiving End of Baz Luhrmann's *William Shakespeare's Romeo + Juliet*' (in Lehmann and Starks, eds., pp. 62–85), Alfredo Michel Modenessi examines the postmodern cultural politics involved in the filming of Luhrmann's film in Mexico City, in particular the film's deployment of Catholic imagery. Where Modenessi studies an American film in the context of Mexican culture, Richard Vela's 'Shakespeare, Hollywood, and Mexico: The Cantinflas *Romeo y Julieta*' (*LFQ* 30[2002] 231–6) examines the appropriation of American Shakespearian film in Mexican cinema. He takes as his subject Miguel M. Delgado's little-known 1943 parody of *Romeo and Juliet*, which starred the comedian Mario Moreno, known as Cantinflas. The film shows, he argues, the intertextual nature of film at this time, weaving in references to American films such as Cukor's *Romeo and Juliet*, which would have been familiar to its Mexican audience.

A number of impressive essays focus on *Titus Andronicus*. Pascale Aebischer's finely argued 'Women Filming Rape in Shakespeare's *Titus Andronicus*: Jane Howell and Julie Taymor' (*EA* 55[2002] 136–47) looks at the problems faced by two female directors in representing the 'unrepresentable' rape of Lavinia. Running the risk of either sanitizing or objectifying the sexual crime, both directors fall into Shakespeare's trap of subsuming Lavinia's suffering within that of Titus himself; the 'representation of Lavinia's individual plight is ultimately not allowed to compete with "the larger event"'. Taymor's *Titus* is also the focus of David McCandless's 'A Tale of Two *Titus*es: Julie Taymor's Vision on Stage and Screen' (*SQ* 53[2002] 487–511). McCandless argues that Taymor, genuinely shocked by the play, sought to 'expose her audience to the contagion of trauma' in her interrelated stage and film productions, hoping to 'startle and goad' her audiences into 'querying their own relation to violent spectacle'. He analyses the way in which audiences experienced violence differently in Taymor's stage and film versions of *Titus*, and argues that the stage production was more successful in 'staging trauma and deconstructing violence'. A different approach to *Titus* can be found in Elsie Walker's '"Now is a time to storm": Julie Taymor's *Titus*' (*LFQ* 30[2002] 194–207). Walker analyses *Titus* as an adaptation in which postmodern form is in tension with the 'Romantic conviction behind its making'. In comparison with the stagy, distancing and eclectic techniques of the film, its final image and the accompanying music form an uneasy, possibly escapist, coda.

Despite strong competition, the year's best article on Taymor's *Titus* is Lisa S. Starks's 'Cinema and Cruelty: Powers of Horror in Julie Taymor's Titus' (in Starks and Lehmann, eds., pp. 121–42), a complex and wide-ranging consideration of the film's deployment of the codes and conventions of horror and, in particular, slasher movies. Starks analyses the film's treatment of genre and gender identity in terms of Julia Kristeva's notion of the abject and its attendant tropes of food-loathing, the decaying or polluted body, the fusion of human and animal, and, above all, what Barbara Creed terms the 'monstrous-feminine'. Starks reads the film's conclusion as 'a note that both refigures the monstrous-feminine and revises the conventions of the horror film in its reinterpretation of Shakespeare's ending'.

Horror is also the subject of Bryan Reynolds's 'Untimely Ripped: Mediating Witchcraft in Polanski and Shakespeare' (in Starks and Lehmann, eds., pp. 143–64), a revised version of 'Untimely Ripped' (*SocSem* 7[1997] 201–18; reviewed in *YWES* 79[2000] 268). Situating Polanski's 1971 film in the context of the Manson family murders of 1969, Reynolds reads it in terms of Gilles Deleuze's concept of the 'crystal image' and Antonin Artaud's 'theatre of cruelty'; it is, he argues a 'cultural-filmic artefact that was ripped from time, just as it rips its viewer from rationality'.

In 'Cinema and the Kingdom of Death: Loncraine's *Richard III*' (*SQ* 53[2002] 241–59) Peter S. Donaldson explores the trope of cinema as necropolis, the 'realm of the absent, the departed, or the dead'. In its use of a range of media, from telegrams to cameras and newsreel, Loncraine's *Richard III* 'extends the metaphor of cinematic representation as death-in-life to a wide range of media', underlying the deadening portrayal of political celebrity in the film. Analysing another kind of celebrity, Lisa Hopkins's '"How very like the home life of our own dear queen": Ian McKellen's *Richard III*' (in Lehmann and Starks, eds., pp. 47–61), explores the film's fascination with the relationship between Britain and America, and with the parallels between Plantagenet and Windsor. Both of these imperatives are highlighted in the casting of Annette Bening as an American Queen Elizabeth, as the film 'takes a very sharp scalpel indeed to its anatomization of English royal identities'.

The year's most interesting essay on *Othello* is Marguerite Hailey Rippy's 'All our *Othello*s: Black Monsters and White Masks on the American Screen' (in Lehmann and Starks, eds., pp. 24–46), which focuses on George Cukor's film *A Double Life* [1947] and a 1983 episode of the sitcom *Cheers*. Rippy argues that the elimination of the Iago figure in both productions shifts the focus onto the psychic fragmentation of their Othellos; both feature a man who plays Othello and as a result of his immersion in the role becomes paranoid about his wife's sexuality. 'American culture', she writes, 'acts as its own Iago, murmuring images of black murderous sexuality and bestiality in all our Othellos' ears and then gasping in titillated wonder when they enact our racial fantasies.' Taking a different perspective on race, James W. Stone's 'Black and White as Technique in Orson Welles's *Othello*' (*LFQ* 30[2002] 189–93) views the film as 'a vehicle for bravura technical achievement', arguing that Welles reduces racial difference to the 'cinematic grid' of 'black and white photography'. The Welles *Othello* also features in Robert F. Wilson Jr., 'Strange New Worlds: Constructions of Venice and Cyprus in the Orson Welles and Oliver Parker Films of Othello' (*ShakB* 20:iii[2002] 37–9).

James Welsh's 'Classic Demolition: Why Shakespeare is not Exactly "Our Contemporary," or, "Dude, where's my hankie?"' (*LFQ* 30[2002] 223–7) reviews Andrew Davies's television adaptation of *Othello* (dir. Geoffrey Sax) and Tim Blake Nelson's *O*. Although he admires some aspects of *Othello*, Welsh ultimately sees both adaptations as devaluing the play in their rejection of its language. Davies's adaptation is also reviewed by H.R. Coursen in 'The PBS *Othello*: A Review Essay' (*ShakB* 20:i[2002] 38–9), who concludes that seeking modern analogues for *Othello* cannot help but diminish the original. In another review (*EMLS* 8:i[2002]), Lisa Hopkins is more sympathetic to the adaptation, but nonetheless concludes that it ultimately packs 'far less emotional punch' than Shakespeare's version.

In 'Cinema Hysterica Passio: Voice and Gaze in Jean-Luc Godard's *King Lear*' (in Starks and Lehmann, eds., pp. 59–94), Alan Walworth uses Lacanian psychoanalytic theory, in particular the work of Slavoj Žižek, to argue that Godard's *King Lear* reflects the early modern construction of hysteria as failure of speech and sight, finally producing a 'hysterical collapse of meaning'. Kristian Levring's *The King is Alive* [2001], a film which incorporates sustained allusions to *King Lear*, is reviewed by Martha P. Nochimson (*FilmQ* 55[2001–2] 48–54), who regrets that the film's 'bold revisioning of cinematic storytelling and of the illusionist nature of human constructs of social and personal reality' may be obscured by its associations with the Dogme 95 movement.

An account of another interventionist reworking of Shakespeare, Kaizaad Kotwal's 'Psychedelic Papas and the Oedipal Mama: Lonesome Trajectories and Psychic Topographies within the Flesh and Psyche in Gus Van Sant's *My Own Private Idaho*' (*FilmJ* 1[2002]) provides a thorough psychoanalytic reading of Van Sant's Shakespearian road movie. In 'Utopian Revisioning of Falstaff's Tavern World: Orson Welles's *Chimes at Midnight* and Gus Van Sant's *My Own Private Idaho*' (in Starks and Lehmann, eds., pp. 165–88) Kathy M. Howlett revises her account of these films from her book *Framing Shakespeare on Film* ([2000]; reviewed in *YWES* 81[2002] 365–6). She concludes that, while Welles 'reads utopia backward against its source', Van Sant 'reads his utopian vision forwards or against performance'. These two adaptations of *Henry IV* are thus exemplars for two different ways of recreating utopia, either as 'the recovery of original meaning or as an exploration of enabling alternatives'.

Finally, a rather different spin on Shakespeare on screen can be found in Craig Dionne's 'The Shatnerification of Shakespeare: *Star Trek* and the Commonplace Tradition' (in Burt, ed., pp. 173–91). Taking *Star Trek*'s frequent allusions to Shakespeare ('All the galaxy's a stage'; 'When you prick me, do I not ... leak?') as his exemplar, Dionne analyses the 'commonplacing' of Shakespeare in popular entertainment. These allusions are part of a non-academic, extratextual tradition of citation, also found in 'famous quotation' handbooks and middle-class conduct manuals, which displays middlebrow anxiety about social status and cultural value. Rather than filtering into the culture from the 'top down' via theatre and high art, Shakespeare is introduced from the 'bottom up' in a progression from a mass-market product to a mass audience, which eventually influences the place of Shakespeare in culture as a whole. As *Eye Weekly* <http://www.eye.net> asked in 1996, 'In the next millennium will *Star Trek* be known for its frequent references to Shakespeare, or will Shakespeare be known for his inclusion on *Star Trek*?'

4. Criticism

(a) General

The Shakespeare International Yearbook provides a convenient starting point for this review; volume 2, 'Where Are We Now in Shakespeare Studies?', focuses on the scholarship and criticism of the 1990s—and sometimes older trends as well—and provides comprehensive and particular assessments of theories and approaches. In the lead essay, 'On Shakespeare and Theory' (*ShIntY* 2[2002] 3–19), Angus Fletcher examines a 'dichotomy in the advanced academic study of Shakespeare and other authors—the split between the text and the poem'. He argues that, since the 1960s, literary theorists have become increasingly obsessed with the 'mechanics of literary power', with the rhetoric of the text's engagement with politics and ideology, and so have abandoned the poem and the poetics of dramatic composition. The poet and author 'has to disappear' for the 'text' to appear, for the theory 'to work', for the play to become a site of contestation in which power relations are negotiated. Fletcher calls for a '*balance*' between criticism and interpretation', an inclusion of the 'poem' as something 'invented in the poet's mind and in the body', as an experience, as a 'paradoxical ephemeral permanence'. He sees in 'much current suspicion of humanist endeavors' a 'disbelief in the poet's own powers of invention; instead, that very smart computer, Society, is treated as the builder and developer forever busy on the cosmic construction site'.

Fletcher's assault on what he sees as the effects of Derridean interpretative scepticism and Benjaminian 'cultural production' offers an analysis dense with emotion, irony, and wit. After all, he says, the targets of the theorists are Shakespeare's (or Chaucer's or Milton's) 'texts' and not Richard Brome's. In contrast, he wants 'to return students to an awareness of artistic and aesthetic values and questions'. In asking for Theory to take on the 'dramatic poem' as its 'source and proper object', Fletcher sketches out some of these values, emphasizing, among other considerations, 'the musical or music-like aspects of the forms involved'.

If Fletcher's attempts to redirect theory away from the obsession with the 'text' and re-establish a 'theory of the poem' seem overdone, one might simply read through the reviews that follow in this and the past few years' *YWES* 'Shakespeare' section. If the musicality of the 'poem' seems an elusive subject for criticism, consider this example, mine not Fletcher's. In Act III, scene i, of *1 Henry IV*, Shakespeare's own stage direction reads: 'The lady sings in Welsh'. Mortimer's wife, Glendower's daughter, provides a static, lyrical moment that follows the rebels' planning for the battle at Shrewsbury and is followed in III.ii by the king's marshalling of his royal forces. The Welsh would have been as unintelligible to the Elizabethan audience as it would be in a performance today—and it would be equally incomprehensible to Fletcher's textualist interpreters. But it forms part of the 'poem' and, in a good production, a striking element in the play's experience.

The remainder of the volume's first part, 'Criticism and Theory', examines recent studies of the sonnets and a few specific plays, and will be reviewed in subsequent sections, as will part 2, 'Text, Textuality and Technology'. Part 3, 'Renaissance Ideas and Conventions', however, offers general assessments of a variety of ways into Shakespeare's dramatic art. Peter M. Daly takes a look at 'Emblematic Studies of Shakespeare since 1990' (*ShIntY* 2[2002] 218–48). Throughout his survey he highlights the importance of the visual culture of the Renaissance yet is judiciously cautious about many of the critical applications of emblem research. Sometimes a dagger is just a dagger. Like dictionaries, emblem books most often catalogued meanings rather than created them, and, like dictionaries, emblem collections are 'repositories of the verbal and visual culture of an earlier period', of the commonplaces, proverbs, and well-worn images that more than likely existed before the vogue for making emblems of them. Many Renaissance emblems interpreted aspects of classical mythology, so John Mulryan's analysis of the 'Italian Mythograpers' (*ShIntY* 2[2002] 305–17) provides a complementary perspective on Shakespeare's visual and verbal imagery. His awareness of the complexity of mythographic approaches helpfully situates Vicenzo Cartari and Natale Conti among older and still surviving traditions of imposing one culture's stories upon another's and of reading *in bono* and *in malo*. He defends the Italian mythographers' 'originality' and their clear superiority to English commentaries, and challenges the contention that Shakespeare went directly to Ovid, concluding that the mythographers offered 'paradigms of Renaissance views of myth that made their way, directly or indirectly, into Shakespeare's conception and instantiation of antiquity'. To accept even such a qualified assertion, one might want a bit more detail from this brief survey of nine pages and perhaps more extensive elaboration of the playfulness which characterizes many of the uses of and allusions to myth in the plays.

Three other surveys assess gender, marriage and property, and scepticism in recent Shakespeare studies. Mario DiGangi's task, 'Shakespeare and Gender' (*ShIntY* 2[2002] 272–89) would definitely appear the most daunting, since critics have addressed gender relations through a very wide variety of approaches. These include considerations of theatrical practice and performance, cross-dressing, homoerotic desire and homosocial relations, marriage and domesticity, and racial and national differences, as well as concepts of masculinity and femininity. The concentration of so much critical interest in these among other gender issues made the 1990s a rich and prolific time for interdisciplinary research and theoretical readjustment of our ways of looking at just about all of the plays and poems; with only a few exceptions, the monographs in his extensive bibliography were all published after 1990. DiGangi sees this outpouring of scholarship as agreeing on the necessity of placing gender within a 'larger web of social and psychic relations' but as differing about the most productive methods of interpreting such an 'intricate cultural web'; but the 'debate currently taking place across so many methodological, disciplinary, and ideological boundaries' is what he believes will keep gender studies of Shakespeare 'vibrant and compelling'. In another survey obviously complementary to DiGangi's, B.J. Sokol and Mary Sokol ask 'Where Are We in Legal-Historical Studies of Shakespeare?' (*ShIntY* 2[2002] 249–71), and limit themselves to questions of marriage and property. They clarify the laws of jointure and dower and the processes by which these applied to the property of widows; 'jointure', usually an agreement made before marriage, is negotiated in *3 Henry VI* and *Merry Wives*, and is relevant to the confusion about Kate's 'dowry' and Petruchio's promises that, in exchange for the dowry, he will leave her well-off after his death, as in 'dower'. Shakespeare himself appears at times to confuse the terms. Open to even more confusion is the question of when two people are 'married', a confusion that the Sokols clearly show was shared by the legal community, which could disagree about when a marriage contract was valid. Such issues form a crucial part of *Measure for Measure* and remain enigmatic even for the legal historian, as they did for the complex litigation the Sokols describe at some length. Further inspired research, rather than any sort of theory, the Sokols conclude, offers the only hope of filling in our understanding the plays' unanswered questions. Lastly, William M. Hamlin's discussion of scepticism in Shakespeare's England, 'Scepticism in Shakespeare's England' (*ShIntY* 2[2002] 190–304), particularly of Sextus Empiricus' Pyrrhonian and Cicero's Academic theories, looks at recent scholarship and points forward to the resources which might be examined to further explore the works of Donne, Shakespeare, and others. He calls for further research into the early modern history of tolerance and open enquiry.

Would Angus Fletcher care for any of this mass of scholarship which his fellow contributors review? Probably not. But he might appreciate David Bevington's simply titled *Shakespeare*, a balanced blend of criticism and interpretation. Bevington starts with Jaques' 'seven ages of man' speech from *As You Like It*, on the face of it not such a promising starting point for a book about Shakespeare's treatment of the life cycle from the cradle to, well, to at least retirement, certainly Prospero's, possibly Shakespeare's, maybe our own, in anticipation of the grave. Jaques' Juvenalian cynicism—the vanity of human wishes and all that—is seldom Shakespeare's and, as Bevington is quick to admit, totally masculine in orientation. The context, of course, undermines the speech, and provides a summary of how Bevington, who has spent a long career teaching, editing, and writing about all the works, sees Shakespeare's humanity: 'The present book, using Jaques's speech as a kind of outline, hopes to explore the ways in which Shakespeare sought to balance ironic and satiric observation with charity and compassion. It is in this balance that we find what is so deeply humane in him.' Very soon, Jaques is forgotten as Bevington stretches the seven ages to include everything relevant to what we might call the developmental stages of life. Youth includes sibling rivalries, education, and friendships; later maturity involves political disillusionment and philosophical scepticism. He brings a great amount of wisdom to an understanding, for example, of Shakespeare's awareness of the emotional necessity of same-sex friendships for both young men and women, and of the need for confidentiality and trust when parental approval or disapproval, competition with brothers and sisters as well as peers, and the stresses of courtship seem overwhelming. Bevington is always reading the poem for what is represented, in the poetry and sometimes in the theatricality. He knows his contexts and his contemporaries' contributions to Shakespearian scholarship, but he wears his learning lightly, seldom participates in Anglo-American theorizing, and writes a book accessible to many levels of readers. Not only are the connections valuable in approaching Shakespeare through various plays which take on one or another moment or stage in the 'seven ages', but Bevington's readings, when he gets into a ten-page or so interpretation, can be very rewarding. He sees the relationship of Othello and Desdemona, for example, as based upon totally masculine-oriented terms, and finally Othello as at the 'mercy' of 'woman', whose power over his self-conception is 'frightening', precisely because he has given her that power through his false views of manliness. If this theme has been reworked often, Bevington's pages nevertheless seem fresh, not an easy achievement for a comprehensive look at much of the canon. On the other hand, he can surprise the reader with some of his readings: one wonders, after his discussion of Hamlet's confrontation of Gertrude in the 'closet scene', if 'Her death is an atonement, and her son is ready now to join her in death'. Bevington openly means the volume as a celebration of Shakespeare's 'genius' (his word), his insight into 'human happiness and unhappiness', his 'negative capability', his engaging our imaginations 'so deeply'. But such moments, even if they seem well earned, are very few among several hundred pages of balancing criticism and interpretation.

Even less academic and theoretical, John Gross's anthology, *After Shakespeare*, collects a rich variety of writings inspired by Shakespeare. The compendium could obviously be many times longer than its 344 pages, so Gross has had to limit his selections. Academic criticism and interpretation is put aside as following a different agenda, and the dramatic criticism of Johnson, Coleridge, Eliot, Bradley, and the like, well known and hence available elsewhere, is only sparingly included. What we have instead are comments on, tributes to, and responses to the man, his legend, and his works and their characters; poems inspired by Shakespeare, speculative vignettes about him, his wife, his friends; reflections and meditations, witty and pithy one-liners; creative fantasies. In one of the entries early in the book, Jorge Luis Borges has the young Shakespeare discover he is 'nobody', set off for London to take up the profession of 'the actor who stands on a stage and pretends to be someone else in front of a group of people who pretend to take him for that other person'. The writing follows, and the nobody exhausts the 'forms of all creatures' until he has imagined everything, filling his emptiness with all those famous lines. Not unexpectedly, Borges's short piece ends with a twist and an unexpected punch-line. Another truly remarkable piece comes from the Nigerian poet Wole Soyinka, whose meditations upon Shakespeare the 'dirge-master' of Antony and Cleopatra's 'unearthly calm at the hour of death' are juxtaposed with passages from Egyptian poets and the Islamic Book of the Dead. Many other selections demonstrate the range of Shakespeare's influence, as Gross includes international poets, dramatists, and novelists who have drawn upon his works for inspiration and sometimes for solace: well-known names such as Pasternak or Heine or Nabokov share space with Miroslav Holub, Zbigniew Herbert, and a host of others. The usual names from our fat two-volume anthologies of British and American literature are of course included: Milton, Dickens, Emerson, Joyce, Auden, Lawrence, and Woolf, for example. I found myself reading *After Shakespeare* front to back, though random sampling will reward readers just as well. Several sections in the latter third of the book provide 'Tales of Shakespeare', 'Tales from Shakespeare', and 'Offshoots and Adaptations', mostly excerpts though sometimes entire short pieces, fictions inspired by Shakespeare and more than what Gross calls the undigested detail of lesser authors whose allusions can be demonstrated in detail. Along with the poems, letters, responses, and opinions, the selections show much Shakespeare's works have shaped global culture. Readers will admire how well-read Gross must be to accomplish such an enormous task, yet at the same time wish he had included more of Henry James or Dickens or Joyce, or more from recent women novelists: Iris Murdoch, for example, is only represented by a few sentences from her essays. Perhaps we may hope for an even fatter second edition.

Other books in this year's work could be characterized as 'after Shakespeare'. The aim of the series International Studies in Shakespeare and his Contemporaries, edited by Jay L. Halio, has been to present historical surveys of Shakespeare's 'global' influence upon the writers, critics, and culture of specific countries or regions, his ability to fire the imaginations, inspire the translations and productions, and shape the critical 'presence' of Shakespeare 'globally'. This year's eighth and ninth collections in the series— Sorelius, ed., *Shakespeare and Scandinavia: A Collection of Nordic Studies*, and Da Cunha Resende and La Borie Burns, eds., *Foreign Accents: Brazilian Readings of Shakespeare*—complement Gross's international collection. The history of Shakespeare is given a rather detailed and fascinating survey in both volumes, and most of the contributions offer fresh perspectives on individual works. Sorelius's new translations of essays by August Strindberg and by the prolific theatre and film director Alf Sjoberg provide illuminating responses, especially in their engagement with Shakespeare's sense of history. These and other contributions mostly concentrate upon specific plays, though quite often the authors' approaches have implications for looking at a larger portion of the canon. Among the Scandinavian and Brazilian contributors, there are academics as well as creative writers and theatre professionals, yet most, especially the Scandinavian professors, stay clear of the Anglo-American trends of recent decades. The Brazilian engagement with Shakespeare's works does not have as long a history, but since the establishment of the Centro Estudios Shakespeareanos in 1991, started by Da Cunha Resende and other university professors, academic scholarship in Brazil has begun to promote the study and performance of Shakespeare more aggressively; unlike their Scandinavian counterparts, the Brazilian are much more interested in gender studies and postcolonial criticism.

If this contrast can be explained by cultural difference, it also demonstrates, as Gross's selections do too, how Shakespeare has long been firing creative and critical imaginations beyond the English-speaking world, as well the truism that anyone can find anything he is looking for in Shakespeare's works. If Shakespeare has been England's most consistently successful export, for Terence Hawkes in *Shakespeare in the Present* his 'Englishness', especially when paired with his 'universality', masks the 'specificity of the present', the lens through which we all see the plays. Hawkes admits the necessity of 'reading Shakespeare historically' but knows that we select the 'facts', the 'history' that we read. Rather than pretend that we are recovering the past conditions of Shakespeare's artistry, he recommends a 'presentist criticism', whose 'project is scrupulously to seek out salient aspects of the present as a crucial trigger for its investigations'. 'Reversing to some degree the stratagems of new historicism', Hawkes writes, 'it deliberately begins with the material present and allows that to set its interrogative agenda'. Why not use what affects our perception anyway, especially when those 'dimensions of the present' clearly connect with 'the events of the past'? The most telling example, and the one which pervades the book's sometimes wildly digressive critical manoeuvres, is Hawkes's take on Britain's 'devolution', a long process culminating in the late 1990s with the commitment to parliaments or assemblies in Wales, Scotland, and Northern Ireland. We can never look at the second tetralogy in the same way again: 'For what confronts us in the plays ... is not the set of permanent, history-transcending truths of whose presence some critics have managed to convince themselves', but the 'now increasingly discernible' outline of 'a matching ideological relationship', the beginnings of what we now experience as the end, a 'close encounter with "modernity"', early modern and postmodern. Along the way other plays and connections across centuries and cultures fall under his often playful 'criticism', a flexible scrutiny that can take in Henry Hunks, the most famous of the bears that Elizabethans loved to torment, as well as other forms of present and past violence, though Hawkes also provides much of what we would call traditional close reading.

Perhaps it is only academics who complain about academic criticism. The year's works reviewed above reveal a wide variety of other ways of engaging Shakespeare's 'presence'. Douglas Lanier's *Shakespeare and Modern Popular Culture* uses a collection of case studies of examples from primarily mass-market culture—films, television, comic books, advertising—to analyse how the 'global reach' of mass media has shaped our perceptions of Shakespeare, his cultural centrality, iconicity, usefulness. Lanier makes a convincing case for studying what are admittedly ephemeral, mostly forgettable appearances, allusions, adaptations, homages, and parodies. His answers for sceptics who would consign Shakespop to oblivion are many: these variations of Shakespeare are the ways in which Shakespeare's cultural significance is extended, challenged, recreated, renewed; in which his 'value' is freed from the 'high' tradition of the school and university classroom, 'high-concept' theatre productions, the annotated editions; in which Shakespeare retains his role, however reluctantly, as an alternative experience for those wearied by postmodern life; in which mass-market culture negotiates its difference from the language and emphases of the 'establishment'. Appropriations of Shakespeare from *Star Trek VI*, Lanier's first example, to the Third Globe, his last, are examined to bring out not only the pervasiveness of Shakespeare in popular culture's vocabulary but also the inventiveness of its creators. Readers may recognize some of the more recent films discussed, but few of the older ones, and perhaps even fewer of the episodes from mostly American television series like *Cosby* and *Star Trek* and *Friends*. But Lanier means to demonstrate the prominent place Shakespeare maintains in mass media which, like Hawkes, is bold in reading Shakespeare through the present.

Lanier's monograph is another in the Oxford Shakespeare Topics series, which has achieved a high level of excellence for its 160-odd page volumes. Another in this series, Ania Loomba's *Shakespeare, Race, and Colonialism*, begins by warning against the dangers of reading the past through the present's assumptions. Shakespeare and his contemporaries did not always use 'race' to refer to skin colour or to ethnic origins; 'race' might at times refer to gender, nationality, a region of a country, even to a family. In 'The Vocabularies of Race' she explores some of the associations of race which are uncommon today: received notions from older literary traditions and more recent experiences from cross-cultural encounters. Here the colonial expansiveness of early modern Europe intersects with varieties of 'otherness' to form a complex sphere in which many national, religious, and linguistic differences emerge, as well as the cultural confrontations, recognitions, and anxieties that result from exploration, trade, and travel to and from England by the English and the 'others'. Loomba's opening chapters especially are dense with scholarship, research that she later employs judiciously in her readings of *Titus*, *Othello*, *Antony and Cleopatra*, *The Merchant*, and *The Tempest*. She stresses in these readings the received assumptions that cling to difference and the necessity of placing our sense of racial and religious differences within the contexts of class, gender, language, and ethnic differences. Throughout her analysis effectively shows how representations of difference mediate 'cultural self-definition'.

Two thoroughly researched academic monographs attempt to recover other aspects of this contemporary redefinition of self, difference, and nationhood. Natasha Korda's *Shakespeare's Domestic Economies: Gender and Property in Early Modern England* explores the 'household stuff' of an increasingly consumerist culture and women's importance in managing it. She looks at objects of the 'material culture' of the family as defining gender relations through the use, market, and status value of these household goods and expanding women's role as 'keepers' of this 'stuff'. Drawing upon many legal documents, economic treatises, household records, and published manuals about marriage and women's roles, she illustrates the disparity between the orthodoxy of the culture and its laws about women and property, and the actual practice of women's growing control over their own economic lives. In readings of *Taming*, *Merry Wives*, *Othello*, and *Measure for Measure*, separate chapters provide persuasive revaluations of representations of domestic property and its social and symbolic presence. Also examining how ideology and practice are often at odds is Karen Cunningham's *Imaginary Betrayals: Subjectivity and the Discourse of Treason in Early Modern England*. The study revolves around three highly visible and controversial sixteenth-century trials for treason, and the rhetorical and social bases for defining the intention and criminality involved. The relevance to plays by Shakespeare and his contemporaries lies in similar imaginings of a 'hidden self' whose motivations were beyond the law's reach, and in methods of interpreting that interiority by creating its stories. Both volumes deepen our understanding of the legal and historical contexts of Shakespeare's culture and confirm the Sokols' contention, noted at the beginning of this section, that English law offers confusions, contradictions, and enigmas that challenge but repay the literary scholar.

(b) Comedies

The largest single contribution to the field in 2002 was Leggatt, ed., *The Cambridge Companion to Shakespearean Comedy*. This collection of original essays is organized into two sections, the first of which introduces the traditions, theories, and sources that shaped Shakespeare's comedies. This section begins with David Galbraith's 'Theories of Comedy', which concentrates for the most part upon classical theories of laughter and comedy, and their reception and appropriation in the early modern period. Galbraith traverses the relevant work of Galen, Aristotle, Cicero, Donatus, and Euanthius, before sketching how Renaissance scholars initially drew upon classical Latin sources; the essay then traces the rise in influence of Aristotle's *Poetics* in the second half of the sixteenth century. Galbraith concludes by suggesting instances where Shakespeare's comedies seem to be embedded within, and resist or transform, these classical traditions. Robert S. Miola's 'Roman Comedy' offers a number of perspectives on Shakespeare's debt to Plautus and Terence. Miola traces contiguities in language and style, in staging, and in plot between the work of early modern playwrights such as Jonson, Heywood, and, of course, Shakespeare, and the comedies of their Latin precursors. Particular emphasis is placed on Shakespeare's development of recognizable character types derived from classical practice, such as the braggart soldier's transformations into Don Armado, Parolles, and Falstaff, and the miser's alteration into Shylock. The argument of Louise George Clubb's 'Italian Stories on the Stage' would suggest that the elements of Plautus and Terence found in Shakespeare's comedies might owe much to the Italian Renaissance stage's ransacking of classical drama. Clubb argues that moving beyond source study to a concern with early modern Italian theatrical practice and repertory offers a wealth of connections. According to Clubb, scenarios, speeches, themes, and characters all made their way from the theatres of early modern Italy to the London stage.

Janette Dillon's contribution, 'Elizabethan Comedy', traces what she sees as the most significant developments in comedy and dramatic form amongst Shakespeare's British precursors. Dillon argues that before the 1580s drama tended towards 'miscellaneity' (p. 49), but, with the work of John Lyly and George Peele in particular, it became more generically classifiable or distinct. The essay identifies the innovations to comedic form introduced by these two writers as well as Robert Greene, before ending with a discussion of another play with a tendency towards miscellaneity, Marlowe's *The Jew of Malta*, which through its use of asides, soliloquies, and comic irony, and its portrayal of a corrupt and amoral world for the audience to revel in, represents 'Perhaps the single most exciting, innovative, and influential play in the sphere of pre-Shakespearean comedy' despite its status as a tragedy (p. 57). In the final essay of the section, 'Popular Festivity', François Laroque places the comedies within a broader context than Shakespeare's precursors on the stage. Opening with a discussion of court activities, Laroque extends his overview to country festivities, the 'green world' of escape from everyday constraints, and other main popular festivals. The essay sketches some of the complex ways in which particular festivals appear in Shakespeare's comedies, but also warns that a generalizing theory of festivity in the plays is dangerous, as 'context, moment and atmosphere' all shape the manner in which references and allusions to festivity function within a work (p. 75).

The second section of the collection turns to the comedies themselves, gathering the plays through themes, principles, and techniques, rather than offering studies on individual works. The result is that some of the essays in this section make interesting connections between plays and draw attention to a number of stimulating points of comparison, yet the same emphasis also means that differences between the plays are on occasions flattened out and some analyses feel rather superficial. The section begins with John Creaser's wide-ranging consideration of the comedies' 'Forms of Confusion' and the terms upon which disarray is resolved. Catherine Bates's contribution on 'Love and Courtship' spans a number of comedies to presents the Shakespearian courtship as an artistic and carnivalesque moment of growth, creativity, illusion, and chaos on the threshold of the ultimate enforcement of societal norms: the regulation of sexuality through marriage. Edward Berry's 'Laughing at "Others"' engages with the plays' laughter at and mockery of social exclusion, whether on the grounds of race, gender, or class. Berry proposes that the Shakespearian comedic form is distinctive in the manner in which differences between those conforming with societal norms and 'others' who resist or cannot adhere to these standards are consistently compromised through (at least invited) final moments of inclusion, the unease with which boundaries between self and other are maintained, and the shifting vantage points of the plays.

Alexander Leggatt's essay on 'Comedy and Sex' draws attention to the embodiment of sexual desire in language and the eroticization of different spheres of activity within the comedies. Characterizing sex as one of the 'low physical realities that demand our attention when we would rather be declaring love or expounding philosophy' (p. 139), Leggatt also sketches how the darker, illicit, or troubling side of sex can be a powerful object of unease. In 'Language and Comedy' Lynne Magnusson attends to early modern theories of rhetoric and logic, as well as the manners in which language becomes associated with a particular gender or becomes unglued from the plot. Through her analysis Magnusson argues that 'the learned arts and the social life of language equally inform Shakespeare's comic discourse and that the plays themselves explore the cultural politics of their own discourse practice' (pp. 175–6). Attending to cross-dressing in the comedies, and responding to many of the received readings of the past twenty years on the erotics of the early modern stage, Barbara Hodgdon's 'Sexual Disguise and the Theatre of

Gender' explores the problematics of theatrical gender performances. In a discussion of the cross-dressed characters of *The Two Gentlemen of Verona*, *The Merchant of Venice*, *Twelfth Night*, and *As You Like It*—which ranges from their performance by early modern boy actors, through the cross-dressing of nineteenth-century actresses, to twentieth-century productions—Hodgdon's suggestive article engages with the manner in which the erotic ambiguity of gender performances always turns on performing bodies in particular theatrical and cultural contexts, placing contingent expectations and responses into *play*.

In a discussion that includes *The Comedy of Errors* and *The Merchant of Venice*, Anthony Miller explains how Shakespeare's comedies touch upon 'Matters of State' in a couple of different ways. According to Miller, the plays frequently show and problematize the workings of law and authority, and also bear the impress of the political anxieties and concerns of early modern England, such as the country's conflict with Spain and contemporary anxieties over the number of 'aliens' in the country. Closing the collection, Michael O'Connell's 'The Experiment of Romance' forms an introduction to this genre and charts some of the features that distinguish the romances from earlier comedies.

Turning from this introductory volume to criticism on individual plays, 2002 saw *The Merchant of Venice* and *The Taming of the Shrew* dominate critical attention. Geoff Baker's Levinas-inspired reading, 'Other Capital: Investment, Return, Alterity and *The Merchant of Venice*' (*UCrow* 22[2002] 21–36), interrogates a number of apparent binaries that appear in the play. According to Baker's argument, all of these binaries—most notably those between Judaism and Christianity, and between justice and mercy—become implicated within the same economy or 'epistemology of return' (p. 33). Gary Rosenshield's 'Deconstructing the Christian Merchant: Antonio and *The Merchant of Venice*' (*Shofar* 20:ii[2002] 28–51) also attends to some of the play's crucial binary oppositions, which, he argues, become 'inviable' in the play's confluence of capital and Christian ideals. Rosenshield's article denies that Antonio may be simultaneously a merchant and a Christian, arguing that the merchant's attempt to distance himself from usury—characterized by his hatred of Shylock—sees him losing his Christian ideals; ultimately, the dichotomy between Christian merchant and Jewish usurer cannot be sustained. In '"Like parrots at a bagpiper": The Polarities of Exchange in *The Merchant of Venice*' (*Parergon* 19:i[2002] 105–20), Lisa Hopkins's exploration of the complex articulations of correspondence and equivalence in the work also questions whether there can be any answer to Portia's questions 'Which is the merchant here? And which the Jew?' (IV.iv.170). Hopkins offers a close reading of the play's systematic and intensive emphasis on exchange, noting that Portia and Shylock represent 'diametrically opposed views on the subject' throughout (p. 105). Crucially, as Shylock moves from language and actions permeated by a sense of exchange and equivalence to an insistence upon the singularity of his bond, Portia turns from the language of differentiation to a view of relative qualities and reciprocity, a sign, according to Hopkins, that she has learned and grown. Jane Freeman also pays close attention to the language of the play, tracing aspects of the classical rhetorical tradition in '"Fair terms and a villain's mind": Rhetorical Patterns in *The Merchant of Venice*' (*Rhetorica* 20:ii[2002] 149–72). Freeman identifies different rhetorical styles with different characters, most notably the theory of status with Portia's forensic strategy and echoes of Sylvain's Declamation 95 from *The Orator* in

Shylock's verbal style—the latter, perhaps, is of particular interest, as in *The Orator* it is the Christian, attacking the Jew, that Shylock's rhetoric follows.

Laurie Shannon's 'Likenings: Rhetorical Husbandries and Portia's "True Conceit" of Friendship' (*RenD* 31[2002] 153–83) reads the relationship between Portia and Bassanio in the light of the antithetical terms of early modern marriage and friendship discourses. Starting from a philological examination of terms such as 'marriage', 'friendship', and, in particular, 'husbandry', the article argues that Portia rewrites the terms of her wedding contract with Bassanio from a hierarchical arrangement based upon gender differentiation to a marriage of likes, *as* one between men. While its primary focus on the German–Jewish relationship perhaps places it beyond the brief of this review, Anat Feinberg's brief history of, and reflection upon, performances and adaptations of the play in post-Holocaust Germany in 'The Janus-Faced Jew: Nathan and Shylock on the Postwar German Stage' (in Morris and Zipes, eds., *Unlikely History: The Changing German–Jewish Symbiosis, 1945–2000*, pp. 233–50) might also be of interest to many readers. Charles Edelman's 'Shakespeare's *The Merchant of Venice*' (*Expl* 60[2002] 124–6) notes the similarity between Antonio's speech 'The Duke cannot deny ... Consisteth of all nations' (III.iii.26–31) and the Venetian Board of Trade's response, *circa* 1597, to the Jewish merchant Daniel Rodriga's petition urging trading rights be given to Levantine and Ponentine Jews. Joel Friedman, in '*The Merchant of Venice*: An Interpretive Note' (*ShN* 52[2002] 79), relates Shylock's remark on first meeting Antonio ('How like a fawning publican he looks', I.iii.36) to the lending practices of innkeepers, and locates this remark at the heart of a reading of Shylock's antipathy to Antonio founded on the latter's threat to Shylock's livelihood.

Drawing on the work of Judith Butler and Elin Diamond on performativity and performance, Amy L. Smith's 'Performing Marriage with a Difference: Wooing, Wedding, and Bedding in *The Taming of the Shrew*' (*CompD* 36[2002] 289–320) urges that we rethink gender and performance in the play. Smith argues that the play's reiterations of marriage and gender, through weddings, banquets, and Kate's final speech see a constant (re)negotiation not just of hierarchies of power, but of sexuality, love, nurture, and money, which opens up for reflection the manner in which each repetition or performance of gender can serve as an occasion for revision. From a very different perspective, appealing to the genre's 'innocent if unsubtle pleasures' (p. 239), Ann Blake's defence of the play as amusing farce in '*The Taming of the Shrew*: Making Fun of Kate' (*CQ* 31[2002] 237–52) also proposes that we rethink much recent criticism. Drawing on comments of women who have played the role of Kate, Blake argues that we must see Kate as a 'woman who has something to learn' at the outset (p. 244), and who has 'found herself' (p. 250) by the end of the play in the final triumph of Petruchio and Kate as a couple. Gary Schneider, in 'The Public, the Private, and the Shaming of the Shrew' (*SEL* 42[2002] 235–58), explores the play's relationship to early modern conceptions of the public and private, arguing that the work's temporal process of taming is also inflected by spatial factors. Schneider traces how the play moves from an emphasis upon publicizing and shaming Kate—through the issuing of banns, the wedding ceremony, and other allusions to public ritual such as carting and dancing barefoot—to a presentation of the private, ascetic processes of teaching civility at Petruchio's house. Finally, Kate re-emerges into the public sphere at the play's end, this time in a metatheatrical performance which consolidates the civilizing process.

Aspinall ed., *The Taming of the Shrew: Critical Essays*, reprints seventeen essays and two reviews from critics as diverse as Sir Arthur Quiller-Couch and Barbara Hodgdon. The collection opens with a section of critical appraisals, which forms the main body of the collection, and concludes with a smaller section of writings on the play on stage, film, and television. Aspinall's introduction identifies and briefly introduces the three key issues which recur in the selections: Katherine's final speech, the relation of the play to *The Taming of a Shrew*, and the Sly framing device. A couple of notes complete the offerings for this play. 'Petruchio's Priest-Beating and Marino Faliero' (*ShN* 52[2002] 11–14), by Rodney Stenning Edgecombe, speculates upon whether Shakespeare might have encountered an anecdote recounting Faliero's assault upon a bishop before creating Petruchio's anti-clerical violence reported in III.ii. Manuel Sánchez-García's 'Shakespeare's *The Taming of the Shrew*' (*Expl* 60[2002] 126–7) draws attention to the alternative meaning of 'wed' to mean wager or stake in Gremio's 'woo her, wed her, bed her' of I.i.138–9, remarking that this alludes to the wager of the final scene.

Cynthia Lewis's 'Soft Touch: On the Renaissance Staging and Meaning of the "Noli me tangere" Icon' (*CompD* 36[2002] 53–73) explores what she identifies as an allusion in *Twelfth Night* to the episode in John 20:11–17 (where Mary Magdalene mistakes the resurrected Christ for the gardener) in Viola's admonition to Sebastian 'Do not embrace me' (V.i.251). Turning to medieval and early modern artistic and theological representations of this biblical episode, Lewis proposes that this allusion resonates with senses of art's legitimacy, mistaken identity, and personal fulfilment. Indira Ghose's 'License to Laugh: Festive Laughter in *Twelfth Night*' (in Pfister, ed., *A History of English Laughter: Laughter from Beowulf to Beckett and Beyond*, pp. 35–46) explores allowed and expected laughter. The essay places the actions of *Twelfth Night*'s subplot within traditions of the fool and carnival, arguing that the gulling of Malvolio 'reflects exactly the motif of Carnival vs. Lent', with Sir Toby acting as a Lord of Misrule to the Lenten Malvolio (p. 38). Ghose then speculates upon why it is that the laughter tends to evaporate in the latter stages of this plot, suggesting that, following the paradigm shift of the Reformation, the history of laughter is one of increasing interiorization and self-control which transformed mirth to the personal, leaving later audiences uneasy at Malvolio's plight.

'Unmasking the Revels: *Love's Labour's Lost*' (*ShIntY* 2[2002] 76–86), by John G. Demaray, argues that the play finds its meanings from 'old pageant' masque form (76), and points out a number of revels elements in the play. Demaray then summarizes some recent criticism which has not made such connections, leaving for the most part implicit, if not unclear, what he believes to be the answer to his own question 'What has this body of criticism revealed?' (p. 80). He concludes the essay with an argument for how the ending of the play sees the intrusion of the real world of social realities at the expense of the pageantry. In 'Charity and Law in *Love's Labour's Lost*: A Calvinist Analogue?' (*N&Q* 49[2002] 224–5), Adrian Streete notes a 'verbal and thematic analogue' (p. 224) between Biron's declaration that 'It is religion to be thus forsworn, | For charity itself fulfils the law, | And who can sever love from charity?' (IV.iii.337–9) and Calvin's *Sermons … on the Epistle of S. Paule to Timothy and Titus* [1579]. Streete suggests that this allusion indicates that early modern literary engagement with Calvin might have been more diffuse, and less religiously polemical, than many scholars claim.

Elizabeth Rivlin's 'Theatrical Literacy in *The Comedy of Errors* and the *Gesta Grayorum*' (*CS* 14[2002] 64–78) traces a number of senses of literacy—spanning various oral competencies, bodily imprinting through violence, and the issuing (and embodying) of bonds—in the comedies. Rivlin argues that both *The Comedy of Errors* and the *Gesta Grayorum*'s description of a production of the play challenge the function of literacy in the grounding of identity and reveal something of how it is implicated in discourses of social hierarchy. In 'The Theatrical Provenance of *The Comedy of Errors*' (*N&Q* 49[2002] 220–2) David Farley-Hills follows the insights of Mariko Ichikawa and Andrew Gurr concerning the number of lines required for exits and entrances, and examines instances of simultaneous staging in the play, to argue that the text does not reflect usual open-air staging, but is more likely to derive from a private performance on a stage with two side entrances.

In 'Touchstone and Kemp in *As You Like It*' (*ShN* 52[2002] 93–4, 106, 110, 126), Juliet Dusinberre argues, against current orthodoxy, that Touchstone was originally played by Will Kemp, and this has significance for our understanding of the fool's interactions with Sir Oliver Mar-text. Dusinberre focuses on Kemp's anti-Martinist history of clowning, jigging, and satire to argue that, in its initial productions, these moments of *As You Like It* offered what would have been familiar comic turns against the Marprelates. William B. Hunter's 'New Readings of *A Midsummer Night's Dream*' (*ANQ* 15:iv[2002] 3–10) builds upon his argument that the play was presented in altered form at the weddings of two families in Queen Elizabeth's court in 1594 and 1596 to explore the differences which he argues must have pertained between the two productions. Contending that the Folio version of *A Midsummer Night's Dream* is closer to the text of the earlier presentation, Hunter argues that John Heminge contributed to the Folio text, emending the quarto version with his own memories of playing Egeus and Puck in the earlier version. Finally, in 'Shakespeare's *The Merry Wives of Windsor*' (*Expl* 61[2002] 11–12), Rodney Stenning Edgcombe suggests that Nim's exclamation 'marry trap with you' in *The Merry Wives of Windsor* (I.i.138–9) does not refer to the game of 'trap-ball' as is often assumed, but derives from a textual corruption of something along the lines of 'may yt rap with you', implying the sense of being hoisted by one's own petard.

(c) Problem Plays

There was a real dearth of material on Shakespeare's problem plays this year, with only four articles in total available for review. Gabriel Egan's 'Leashing in the Dogs of War: The Influence of Lyly's *Campaspe* on Shakespeare's *All's Well That Ends Well*' (*ELN* 40[2002] 29–41) was the only publication for *All's Well*, in which Egan begins by tracing the influence of Lyly's *Campaspe* on both that play and *Timon of Athens*. Egan suggests that, in *All's Well*, Shakespeare is deliberately recalling Lyly's play in which objections to war are positively presented in order to critique the 'social danger of heroic values' (p. 31). The young men of Shakespeare's play involve themselves in a war yet are indifferent to those they fight against, and it is this indifference to specific individuals that, Egan argues, informs 'Bertram's inability to differentiate between the bodies of Diana and Helena' (p. 38).

Measure for Measure fared only slightly better in terms of the number of publications produced this year, with work on the play represented by three articles. In his article, 'Parable, Justice, and the Disguised Ruler in Shakespeare's *Measure for Measure* and Lope de Vega's *El Mejor Alcade, El Rey* (*ShY* 13[2002] 147–58),

Ivan Canadas outlines a series of parallels between the plot structure of the two plays as Shakespeare and de Vega both make use of the motif of the ruler who disguises himself in order to judge his corrupt subjects. Canadas argues that both playwrights utilize this motif in order to offer a critique of the 'discourses of masculine supremacy'. There were two articles I have been unable to see for *Measure for Measure*: 'Of Speaking and Writing in Shakespeare's *Measure for Measure*' (*JCERL* 11[2002] 135–57), by Didi Lonel Cenuser, and 'The Political and Theological Psychology of Shakespeare's *Measure for Measure*' (*IJPP* 29[2002] 153–69), by Nasser Behnegar.

There were only two publications this year on *Troilus and Cressida*, but each indicates the two areas in which the play continues to generate critical interest. The first is Matthew Steggle's note, 'Shakespeare, Jonson, Harington, and *Paper's Complaint*' (*N&Q* 49[2002] 251–53), in which he responds to the debate stimulated by last year's publication of James Bednarz's *Shakespeare and the Poets' War* concerning Shakespeare's involvement in the War of the Theatres. Steggle counters Bednarz's claim that Shakespeare's Ajax is a caricature of Jonson by suggesting that the evidence, based on the reference to Ajax in John Davies of Herford's *Paper's Complaint*, is in fact more likely to be an allusion to Sir John Harington, the author of *The Metamorphosis of Ajax* and as such 'is not valid evidence in the continuing debate over whether or not Shakespeare may personally satirise Jonson in *Troilus and Cressida*' (p. 253).

Laurie E. Maguire's article, 'Performing Anger: The Anatomy of Abuse(s) in *Troilus and Cressida*' (*RenD* 31[2002] 153–83), examines the role of Cressida in the light of twentieth-century psychological research into spousal abuse. Maguire begins by focusing on the linguistic strategies employed by Diomedes and Cressida in Act V, scene iv, to argue that the patterns of verbal and physical techniques of manipulation by Diomedes have been identified as 'standard tactics of abuse'. Cressida's response in yielding, Maguire suggests, is submission as a form of defence: 'Cressida gives in verbally to pacify Diomedes' verbal violence, and she submits sexually to prevent his sexual violence' (p. 163). Maguire indicates that the behaviour of Diomedes is a variation on the behaviour of Troilus earlier in the play, and that verbal abuse of the play's female characters is used to reflect and enact social control.

(d) Poetry

The most substantial scholarly contribution in 2002, covering all the texts in this section, was Burrow, ed., *The Complete Sonnets and Poems*, for the Oxford Shakespeare series. This is a persuasive and eminently readable volume. Burrow's introduction is not interested in 'definitive answers' to the numerous vexed questions surrounding Shakespeare's poetic output, but in providing readers 'with enough information to take up an informed position ... and to feed that information back into the way they read the poems'. This edition is particularly valuable in furnishing the reader with texts attributed to Shakespeare (those attributed more problematically to 'W.S.' are excluded) by his early readers but which he was 'unlikely to have written'. Indeed, the larger emphasis upon early modern responses to the poems is both refreshing and illuminating when offered together within one volume. The 'Shall I die?' lyric is included, but Burrow refuses to countenance the entry of *A Funerall Elegye*. The introductory sections devoted to *Venus and Adonis* and *The Rape of Lucrece* offer the liveliest discussions in the volume, travelling across strategic textual, critical, and cultural areas of interest very economically. Rather than concentrating upon aesthetics or on critical controversies like some recent editions of the sonnets, Burrow maintains his emphasis principally upon historicization. Nevertheless, his often ample footnotes will offer critical reading programmes for those embarking on this area of Shakespeare studies. Throughout the introduction, key areas of scholarly enquiry are mapped out and the reader is constantly asked to consider larger questions in terms of precise textual details. The later discussions of 'Let the bird of loudest lay' and the sonnets prove to be informative throughout but, on the whole, less energetically argued. Here, the stress appears to fall upon establishing the critical *mise à jour* rather than developing avenues for further exploration. The textual apparatus in the main body of the volume is, on the whole, carefully judged, and at no point does it become cumbersome for the reader. In general, this volume will serve as a valuable introduction to the breadth of Shakespeare's poetic output for some time to come.

David Schalkwyk's *Speech and Performance in Shakespeare's Sonnets and Plays* allows poems to rub shoulders with some ten Shakespearian plays in order to investigate textual representations of social action and forms of verbal practice. Wittgenstein and J.L. Austin are quickly enlisted for this journey to consider the performativity of Shakespeare's language. The introductory material is often rather repetitive, but many of the subsequent chapters are more dynamic and successful in their direction and commitment. The discussions of sonnets in relation to *Antony and Cleopatra* (centring on alternating modes of 'theatrical' and 'private' eloquence), *Hamlet* and *King Lear* (centring on discourses of interiority), and *All's Well That Ends Well* (centring on issues of transformation and social action) are the most persuasive, and this volume represents one welcome bid, amongst a growing number, to reclaim Shakespeare's poetry from the margins of the canon.

In 'Good and Bad Loves: Shakespeare, Plato and the Plotting of the Sonnets' (*TLS* [5 July 2002] 13–15), Barbara Everett laments that scholarship devoted to the sonnets has been so taken up with biographical speculation and wrangles, for example, over the presence of Pembroke or Southampton in the poetic narratives. The concern with the Armada, the Essex rebellion or the queen's illness in sonnet 107 is, for Everett, an imposition of 'the wrong kind of historicism' which ignores 'metaphor': 'And to ignore metaphor is to deny the creativity of the human mind.' With the conviction that 'Shakespeare plotted his poems', Everett draws upon the narrative thread of 'friendship' to bind the collection together. How persuasive 'early modern friendship' may be as 'a love unselfish and therefore unsexual in itself' remains a moot point. Nonetheless, dispensing with the markers of 'homoerotic' and 'misogynistic', Everett conjures up a bard ('a married man with children') as a figure receptive to narratives of human relations proposed, for example, in Plato's *Symposium* and *Phaedrus*. In 'Standpoints on the Sexualities of the Sonnets' (*ShIntY* 2[2002] 32–46), Joseph Pequigney returns to the territory of the sexual personae in evidence in the sonnets and the responses to these voiced in recent criticism by such figures as Vendler and Duncan-Jones, as well as 'professors of English who work in the discipline of lesbian and gay studies'. In response to the recurring discussion of ineffability and discursive dilemmas surrounding early modern sexual identities, Pequigney muses, 'how is it that the homosexual practices of ancient Greece and Rome are so much more recoverable than those of early modern England?' He goes on to consider how the 'homoerotic issue' is in some critical quarters being displaced by a focus upon class and race. He recommends in conclusion that 'the obscurations that over the past decade have been imparted to the text under the pretext of "explanatory theory" and cultural contextualising [should be cleared away]. Let "homosexual", ill-advisedly proscribed, speak its name in the commentary, along with "homoerotic" and its other synonyms, perform its regular signifying function and stop being a dismissive weapon wielded by some expositors.' Richard Chamberlain's '"A nothing which counts": Empsonian Ambiguity, the Subject and Shakespeare's Sonnet 1' (*English* 51[2002] 111–25) asks us to turn our attention away (at least for the moment) from the Young Man, the Dark Lady, the Rival Poet, and the Author and to consider 'other kinds of figure which should loom large in any interpretation. The dense and involuted patterning of Shakespeare's figurative images'. Chamberlain's resolve to link rhetoric to modern theoretical considerations of subjectivity takes him on a wide-ranging and tightly argued discussion on the relations between engagements with literature and engagements in identity-formation—all explored through the prism of sonnet 1.

James Schiffer, in '*Othello* Among the Sonnets' (in Kolin, ed., *Othello: New Critical Essays*, pp. 325–45) insists upon the close thematic interests shared by the Jacobean tragedy and the 1609 collection: 'In fact, *Othello* seems to offer a kind of photographic negative of the Sonnets' triangulated relationship between the poet, the fair friend, and the dark lady.' Discussion is organized principally around citation and does not court any particular controversy in probing the community of interests in evidence in both texts. Mark Schwartzenberg's 'Shakespeare's Sonnet 33' (*Expl* 61[2002] 13–14) seeks to recover the death of Shakespeare's son Hamnet as a significant site for the collection as a whole, and in particular for the third quatrain of sonnet 33. In 'Leaf Imagery as a Virgilian Topos in Shakespeare's Sonnet 73' (*ShJE* 138[2002] 128–34), Robert E. Jungman initially examines Vendler's, Booth's, Coldewey's, and Crowe Ransom's responses to the leaf/leave narrative of ageing and departure in sonnet 73, before turning his attentions to book XV of the *Metamorphoses*, book VI of the *Aeneid* and book V of the *Iliad* to compare possible sources. MacD. P. Jackson returns to stylistic considerations of Shakespeare's poetic output with 'The Distribution of Pronouns in Shakespeare's Sonnets' (*AUMLA* 97[2002] 22–38). Concentrating particularly upon 'you' and 'thou', Jackson identifies a systematic sequencing 'too orderly to be accidental, yet not so rigid as to suggest that some meddling re-organizer imposed his own design. The reasonable conclusion is that it originated with Shakespeare himself.' In 'Dating Shakespeare's Sonnets: Some Old Evidence Revisited' (*N&Q* 49[2002] 237–41) Jackson looks back at stylometric analyses by J.A. Fort published in 1933 as well as at studies by Hermann Conrad and Horace Davis to reaffirm that Shakespeare's 'involvement with the sequence must have extended into the seventeenth century, and well beyond the years in which the bulk of the sonnets were probably composed'. In '"I am that I am" in Shakespeare's Sonnet 121 and 1 Corinthians 15:10' (*N&Q* 49[2002] 241–2), Kenji Go proposes that the above phrase may not, as has been the conventional wisdom, necessarily echo Exodus 3:14 but may also relate to the wording of Paul's Epistle. Richard Halpern's *Shakespeare's Perfume: Sodomy and Sublimity in the Sonnets, Wilde, Freud, and Lacan* (UPennP) was not available for review at the time of publication.

Katherine A. Craik draws welcome attention to the close of the 1609 collection with 'Shakespeare's *A Lover's Complaint* and Early Modern Criminal Confession' (*SQ* 53[2002] 437–59) by expanding discussion of the complaint beyond courtly modes to those present in 'popular' 'urban' texts of the period: 'Shakespeare's plays have long been acknowledged to include elements of marginal culture and contemporary social disorder, but his poems have largely resisted such analysis.' In the main body of the article, Craik explores early modern textual and cultural 'performances' of female confession, turning to ballads and legal accounts; in the process, she creates an illuminating and lively angle of vision through which to approach early modern complaint literature. In 'The Transformation of the Earl of Essex: Post-Execution Ballads and "The Phoenix and the Turtle"' (*SP* 99[2002] 57–80), Alzada Tipton reasserts an 'Essex' context for Shakespeare's most cryptic poem. Considering Essex's public personae as related through surviving letters and ballads, she positions him as 'self-sacrificing lover' to Elizabeth as 'demanding lover', and underlines the thematic links of heroic desire and mutual death in evidence in both the poem and the ballads of the period.

Maurice Charney's 'Marlowe's *Hero and Leander* Shows Shakespeare, in *Venus and Adonis*, How To Write an Ovidian Verse Epyllion' (in Deats and Logan, eds., *Marlowe's Empery: Expanding his Critical Contexts*, pp. 85–94) essentially considers Marlowe's earlier epyllion as a model for his successor in terms of their attitudes to Ovid and focus upon immature sexual appetites. At the end of the article, Charney pauses to consider briefly the homoeroticism of the meeting between Adonis and the boar. In 'Shakespeare's Eager Adonis' (*SEL* 42:i[2002] 85–102), Lauren Shohet shapes Adonis as a 'passionate' hunter as a counterweight to the lust-driven Venus. Paying detailed attention to the 'phallic' order of the hunt with its own discourses of desire and representation, Shohet argues that, 'through inclining in both his desires and his semiotics toward deferral, separation, and idiosyncrasy, Adonis emerges as something of a figure for protomodernity, or at least for resistance to the values Venus espouses'. In 'Theatricality in *Venus and Adonis* and its Staging in Germany 1994–1998' (*CahiersE* 61[2002] 31–41), Christa Jansohn initially outlines some of the dramatic devices and conventions in evidence in Shakespeare's narrative poem before considering recent stagings by the Bremer Shakespeare Company [1996], by the Berliner Globe Theatre [1993], and by the Munich National Opera [1997].

In 'Tarquin's Everlasting Banishment: Republicanism and Constitutionalism in *The Rape of Lucrece* and *Titus Andronicus*' (*Parergon* 19:i[2002] 77–104), Andrew Hadfield continues his ongoing investigations into early modern strains of republicanism by turning to two Shakespeare productions which, he submits, stress that 'alternative forms of government, which would either involve dispensing with or curbing the power of the head of state, are possible and desirable for Rome'. The discussion persuasively draws *Lucrece* into a world influenced by Essex's circle and writers with anti-establishment views such as Barnes, Nashe, and Florio. Tarquin's unworthiness as king is articulated in terms of his inadequate self-government, and Hadfield is convincing in his emphasis upon the excessive (and thus flawed) masculinities of the tyrant and upon the poem as a constitutional birthing narrative. In '"To find a face where all distress is stell'd": *Enargeia, Ekphrasis*, and Mourning in *The Rape of Lucrece* and the *Aeneid*' (*CL* 54:ii[2002] 97–126), Marion A. Wells examines the implications for Shakespeare's heroine, poem, and reader of these rhetorical figures in facilitating the transition from the domestic to political foci of interest. Wells's initial submission that the epyllion may be viewed as 'a hybrid genre characterised both by its deployment of vivid description and by its treatment of epic subjects' requires further refining. However, subsequent discussions of classical and early modern responses to enargeia and ekphrasis as forms related to mourning and suffering, as structuring devices, as stimuli to reader engagement, as devices for generating poetic fictions of interiority, and so on are enlightening even if *Lucrece* seems rather to get squeezed out of the frame in the process.

In 2002 attention was returned energetically to the attribution of 'Shall I die?' and *A Funerall Elegye* with Brian Vickers's *'Counterfeiting' Shakespeare*, and his reader is left in no doubt that the stakes are high: 'With a dramatist as universally admired as Shakespeare, the discovery of a so far unknown play or poem would be a cause of great rejoicing. Conversely, the inclusion in his canon of work erroneously attributed to him would be deeply depressing, almost tragic.' Vickers trawls in great detail through narratives of biographical detail, early modern textual production, and stylometric statistics to yield a painstaking insight into methodologies surrounding authorship attribution and to establish that neither of the poems is by Shakespeare (and that the *Elegye* is in fact by John Ford). Along the way, there is more than one spat with Taylor and Foster over the 'rigour' or otherwise with which these minor poems have been attributed to the Bard: 'Most European, and many American scholars would be amazed and disconcerted to be pursued by journalists, interviewers, and TV stations, but Taylor and Foster both seemed to thrive on media attention.' Throughout this carefully planned reading experience, Vickers asks us to attend to the rather heroic figure of a poet ('the mixture of ... genres is so clumsy [in "Shall I die?"] that one cannot imagine Shakespeare perpetrating it at any stage of his career') and to 'the pathetic vulnerability of ordinary readers, including experienced Shakespearians' when confronted with a barrage of numbers and calculations. The enormous forces which Vickers mobilizes to prosecute his case are formidable by any standards and could be thought to bring the controversy to a close. The idea of Ford's authorship of the *Elegye* is also put forward by G.D. Monsarrat in a rather slimmer article entitled '*A Funeral Elegy*: Ford, W.S., and Shakespeare' (*RES* 53[2002] 186–203). Here, Monsarrat engages in some detailed consideration of linguistic echoes of the *Elegye* in Ford's works, most particularly *Fame's Memorial*, *Christ's Bloody Sweat*, and *The Golden Mean*. Nonetheless, Richard Abrams, in 'Meet the Peters' (*EMLS* 8:ii[2002]) fights the corner of the injured parties and finds the attribution to Ford to be 'the latest but not least oddity in the increasingly odd case of WS's Elegy'. Drawing attention to the 'possible' birth of a new genre, the ghostwritten confessional, Abrams turns centrally to the genealogical and cultural contexts of the Peter/Petre family. Here, for example, we learn that 'as an habitué of the Mermaid, Lord Petre may have been on nodding terms with Beaumont and Ben Jonson, if not also Ford and Shakespeare—a possibility with intriguing implications for the Peter elegy'. Must we then think of a W.S. who 'instigates' rather than writes the elegy? Abrams concludes in a beguiling manner: 'If the Elegy's reassignment to Ford may be regarded as secure, that judgment, far from solving the poem's problems, creates new ones'. This does not sound much like a death knell for the controversy as 2002 drew to a close.

(e) Histories

Ronald Knowles's *Shakespeare's Arguments with History* covers both the classical and English histories, seeking to dramatically situate the arguments within them. Knowles argues for a Shakespeare who is 'an empiricist by instinct', pointing out that arguments-in-utterance can often be 'coloured by bias, self-deception and special-pleading'. Even if this is not the case, the dramatic placement of arguments often ironizes them. For example, Knowles posits that, when the Talbots argue in *1 Henry VI*, 'we have the general indefinite thesis, "Should a man flee from the battlefield?" converted to the hypothesis of the particular and definite of place, time and persons'. But, notwithstanding 'immediate audience response', the scene's arguments are ironized, 'given the political manoeuvring which precedes and follows'. More generally, 'argument' in the period often meant 'the "proof" made manifest by an action—by an appearance, happening, incident, occasion, situation, gesture and so on. The physical action of argument has the constant potential of presenting a counter-argument.'

This focus on argument allows a variety of approaches to the plays. Sometimes characters' arguments themselves are assessed. Bolingbroke's argument for his 'rights' in *Richard II* is read using both rhetorical theory and early modern political thought. Falstaff's honour catechism in *1 Henry IV* is an example of 'nominalist scepticism' as well as a rationalization of his own cowardice. The details of Richard III's sophistry are dissected. Sometimes how whole plays treat larger 'arguments' is the topic, such as 'the central paradox of the claims of honour', which is situated in terms of early modern understanding of the medieval in general, and the decline in English feudalism in particular. The chapter on *Henry V* effectively combines a focus on the tendentiousness of Henry's and others' arguments for war with a recognition that the effect of the play as a whole does not stand or fall on such matters. Theatrical modes such as burlesque, parody, and carnival are also recognized for their dualistic relationship to 'argument'—most especially in *2 Henry VI* and the Henry IV plays. The overall picture of the histories is a familiar one—complex in thought and dramaturgy, ambivalent, dualistic—but there are many insightful, theatrically informed readings of scenes and contexts along the way.

James R. Siemon's *Word Against Word: Shakespearean Utterance* develops a Bakhtinian approach to early modern writing analysis, using *Richard II* as a test case. Three long chapters engage with the play. 'Landlord, Not King' reads three Shakespearian garden scenes, including *Richard II*'s, through contemporary discourses of agrarian change. The gardener is a labourer, possessing only his skill in his occupation. This skill as a gardener, however, involves independent discrimination and evaluation that he turns in this scene to political and agricultural critique. He is secure enough to resist the queen's 'degrading attacks'. The gardener's speech here is thus not choric, but rooted in his own competence and knowledge.

In 'Subjected Thus', Siemon seeks to locate Richard's character within language and utterance, beginning and ending with his imprisoned soliloquy at V.v. The situatedness of Richard's contradictory utterance is not, however, a product of his 'character', as through analysis of speeches by Gaunt and others, including Richard himself, the chapter explores how utterances are implicated in dialogicality, 'neither entirely incorrect nor beyond contestation'. 'The Lamentable Tale of Me' situates the play's language within contemporary elegy and lamentation, particularly the self-consciousness of Petrarchan love poetry. Returning to the gardener, Siemon analyses the tonal shifts within his part, and in particular the employment of 'lamentation' as a legitimating mode for critique. Richard speaks as a sonneteering self-ironist. This is a book of great scope, engaging with contemporary discourses of all kinds in its attempt to situate one play, but Siemon convincingly ties in this wealth of Elizabethan context and Bakhtinian theory to close analysis of concrete play-utterances.

Nicholas Grene's *Shakespeare's Serial History Plays* has a double focus, 'the phenomenon of the plays' seriality both in its origins and in its changing theatrical manifestations'. As far as origins go, Grene posits that the first tetralogy was planned as a sequence and the second just growed. The *Henry VI–Richard III* sequence used the 'Schehezerade technique to keep the audience narrative-hungry', functioning commercially rather as two-part plays by other writers did for Henslowe. This then leads him to focus on the narrative rhythms established across the plays seen as 'an incremental series'.

The three chapters on the first tetralogy cover the representation of war, character, and curses and prophecies. There are some interesting points made, but the chapters do not generally bear out Grene's claim that 'serial reading' is a productive approach. So, when considering war, the book distinguishes four kinds—French–English, English–English or Wars of the Roses, Cade's class war, and holy war between good and evil. Grene's promised focus on seriality does not materialize. French–English conflict is discussed entirely in terms of *1 Henry VI* (in fact, in terms of a simple Talbot-versus-Joan binary), class war in terms of *2 Henry VI*, and holy war in terms of *Richard III*. Only the St Albans–Wakefield–Towton civil war series, which Grene rightly but uncontroversially points out features 'escalating violence and degenerating principles', extends over two plays. The chapter's posited 'organic interrelationship' between these different kinds of war turns out to be simply the 'contrast' between them, and the representation of 'a degenerating spiral of violence … over the generations'. The chapter on character supplies five unexceptional character sketches, mostly in long shot, as is the material on actors' interpretations of characters (three different actors playing Henry 'came over rather as idealists with a misplaced belief in the power of principles, gradually ground down by circumstances'—and that's all we hear of *them*).

The chapter on curses asks 'to what extent, and on what scale, is an audience intended to see providential patterns of causality being accomplished through the series of history plays?' and answers, three pages later, that the secularized milieu of the theatre allowed Shakespeare to pick and choose. Curses sometimes work, and sometimes don't. Grene asserts that references to future events bind the plays together, but these events are independent of any drama. Is Henry VI's prophecy of Richmond's future glory in *3 Henry VI* more dramatically effective than Cranmer's about Elizabeth in *Henry VIII* because it is to be dramatized?

The same question pertains to Grene's investigation of the second tetralogy, which begins with a chapter on 'looking back', the ways in which the plays are written 'with a full consciousness of what has gone before … this awareness of previous history shared by the characters and audience becomes a part of the substance of the drama'. The obvious pitfall in this as an argument for 'seriality' rather than historicity as an interpretative principle is that *Richard II* clearly looks backwards not to a Shakespearian precursor, but to historical events. Interestingly, the chapter then goes on to investigate how characters rewrite a history an audience may have already seen. The Percys' accounts in *1 Henry IV* are contrasted with their actual words and behaviour in *Richard II*, so that that the meeting between Hotspur and Bolingbroke in the earlier play is 'satirically recalled' in the later. Grene shows that Percy misremembers or misreports the scene, but over-eggs the pudding by asserting that 'the purpose of the reminiscence must be to remind the audience of what they had watched in *Richard II*', and indeed that these lines 'are significant only for an audience watching *1 Henry IV* after having seen *Richard II*'. The differences are hardly 'striking': Hotspur doesn't mention that he 'initiates the image of maturation' he quotes Bolingbroke as using, and he claims it was addressed to him when it wasn't. This is hardly rewriting history. Similarly, though Henry IV clearly 'rewrites' his own past at the end of *2 Henry IV*, such rewriting does not require a sequence of plays; by definition, *2 Henry IV* includes at least two views of Henry's motives for crusade.

The two final chapters, on 'Hybrid Histories' and 'Change and Identity', investigate generic markers and Hal's metamorphosis into Henry V respectively. The former, focusing particularly on mixed modes, and Hotspur and Falstaff, points out the importance of comedy in establishing a different conception of national history. The latter follows Hal through three plays, without positing a coherent 'development' (and indeed, in the case of the last play, claiming 'no coherently characterised character of the King whose agency can be satisfactorily detected throughout'). It is far from clear how these chapters fit into a book on Shakespeare's 'serial histories'. *Richard II* gets short shrift; the two *Henry IV* plays are, unsurprisingly, read together, and Eastcheap characters and Hal are traced through into *Henry V*.

The scope of the book is its greatest claim to attention: it covers eight plays, and aspects of their performance histories, with a concomitant tendency towards broad-brush descriptive writing. But I am unconvinced that this big picture is worth seeing. Neither the performance materials nor the text-focused discussions of the plays sustainedly support Grene's thesis that they are particularly productively read as part of a larger tetralogical whole. Indeed, the book does not even make that claim for the second tetralogy. Its Shakespearian focus deprives it of one of the most obvious ways of investigating seriality, comparison with non-serial plays on Richard III, or more obviously the Henriad source-play, *The Famous Victories*. The books seeks a general readership, is well written, and engages intelligently and intelligibly with the texts. Readers seeking an engagement with current scholarship and criticism as evidenced in the periodical literature will be disappointed, however. Grene adopts the policy of only referring to 'material that comes directly into the line of my argument'—attention to more than one article from the 1990s, two from the 1980s, two from the 1970s and one from the 1960s would, however, have made this a far more useful book for those other 'general readers', postgraduates and academics.

Tom McAlindon's *Shakespeare's Tudor History: A Study of Henry IV, Parts 1 and 2* begins with a thorough history of pre-1980s criticism of the plays, during which he speculates that the recent lack of readings such as Grene's is because 'the cyclic concept produces critical procedures which distract from the experimental and distinctive nature of each play'. This chapter is part of a combative engagement with the deficiencies of some of the most influential recent accounts of the plays, and in particular their tendency to ignore earlier critical responses. McAlindon argues that contemporary criticism is the poorer through this avoidance of (for example) the 'organicism' of nineteenth-century critics, and those subsequently influenced by them. His own approach might be called historicized thematic criticism. The second chapter provides a history of the sixteenth-century English risings and rebellions as a prelude to suggesting that the two plays address issues that this history raises: 'the past repeating itself in divisiveness and rebellion; a preoccupation with perjury, treachery, and falsehood; and finally a chronicler's exemplary antithesis of a disgraced traitor who could not escape the past, and a ruler who was grace itself'. There follow three long chapters on 'Time', 'Truth', and 'Grace'.

The 'Time' chapter reads Henry, Hal, Falstaff, and the rebels in terms of their relationship and attitude towards time, and demonstrates the implications of such relationships. The impetuousness Hotspur displays is a defect for Calvinists, chroniclers, and Erasmian and Machiavellian humanists alike. Hal, contrariwise, has timing all the above would approve of, so much so that 'most (but not all) critics who have studied the significance of time in *Henry IV* have found that the exercise reinforces a positive view of Hal's character; those whose attitude to him is negative, unsympathetic, or heavily qualified tend to ignore the subject of time and the way in which it directs responses to what he says and does'. Falstaff is more like Hal in this than is commonly recognized, a 'superb opportunist' practising 'a kind of predatory patience'.

The 'truth' chapter looks at the making and breaking of oaths and vows as a symptom of wider cultural trends, with the sixteenth-century experience of swearing and forswearing as a lens through which to read the fifteenth. Shakespeare on this reading is a contra-Machiavel, endorsing 'not only the chivalric ethic of truth but also the classical and humanist doctrine that fidelity or promise-keeping is the foundation of justice and order'. Dramatic irony is a key concept here, with both Henry's duplicity and self-deceptions and John's casuistical treachery at Gaultree implicitly judged against the honesty of Hotspur or Hal. Women's voices, *pace* Rackin and Howard, also function unsubversively, 'as a potential means of saving the man from involvement in a destructive action which concurs neither with patriotic nor with chivalric virtues properly understood'. The central critical question of Hal's fraudulence—insincere with his 'friends', calculating, unloving, acting rather than possessing virtue—here returns. McAlindon argues at some length that Hal's secrecy or deception of his fellows need not imply hypocrisy, that he keeps his promises to his father and the audience, and that his relationship to Falstaff and Poins contains a fair amount of blunt truth-telling (as well as a (truthful?) soliloquy on the 'dead' Falstaff). He lies twice in Part 1, both times on behalf of the fat knight. While allowing that Hal would be a more attractive character if the relationship between his princeliness and his private life was experienced as more problematic, the chapter argues convincingly that such calculation as there is should be balanced by the politic and virtue of his 'hostility to untruth and his fidelity to his sworn word'.

The final chapter, on 'Grace' (to be understood as both courtesy and religious source of political power), argues for its priority over honour in the Tudor period and the plays. The post-medieval world valued nation-centred and civilized chivalry (rather than the rough-and-ready Hotspur variant). Falstaff clearly stands in opposition to these values; Hal just as clearly comes out as their embodiment. The main thrust of the book, in fact, is to provide a sixteenth-century politico-ethical context for a defence of the prince, demonstrated at length and in detail through a close reading of the plays and a range of critical accounts of them. Ditching the 'organicist' assumptions of earlier generations leads, McAlindon convincingly demonstrates, to readings of plays which actually are readings of parts of plays; this book is a reminder of how subversive of some current critical assumptions a return to earlier approaches can be.

Hattaway, ed., *The Cambridge Companion to Shakespeare's History Plays*, is an accessible and helpful collection aimed principally at the undergraduate market. There is an imaginative and stimulating introductory section. Hattaway's introduction is a lucid and thorough consideration of genre, truth and realism, politics, historiography, and 'edification'. Ton Hoenselaars supplies an account of the whole genre, including Continental historical plays. David Bergeron considers pageants, masques, and history, Dominique Goy-Blanquet the issue of sources, and Phyllis Rackin women's roles. The essays on the English histories are of a good standard, with A.J. Piesse on *King John*, Robyn Bolam on *Richard II*, and James Bulman on the *Henry IV* plays particularly worth reading; Janis Lull drew the short straw, having to cover *Edward III* and the first tetralogy in hers. *Henry VIII* gets many mentions but no essay, though the Roman histories do, and there are family trees and notes on principal and recurrent characters as appendices.

Albert H. Tricomi brings a sense of the wider theatrical context to 'Joan la Pucelle and the Inverted Saints Play in *1 Henry VI*' (*Ren&R* 25:ii[2001] 5–31). Beginning from the Dauphin's identification of Joan as 'France's saint', the article investigates how the play re-enacts 'from the safe distance of parody' features of the saints play but is nonetheless dependent upon knowledge (nostalgia?) for a non-Protestant form of worship. After listing the salient features of earlier saints plays, Tricomi goes on to show how Joan is described and shown in terms that invert them. Joan raises devils; she claims divine powers, presenting herself as miraculously transformed; she is worshipped the other side of idolatry by the French; her sexual appeal for the Dauphin links her particularly dangerously to Mary Magdalene; she prophesies. Her desperate death, superficially Foxean, compares unfavourably with the steadfastness of Protestant martyrs. Tricomi convincingly locates the play within its sixteenth-century context as one engaging with 'sainthood, idolatry (especially in respect to female seductiveness) and martyrdom'.

Craig Bernthal investigates 'Jack Cade's Legal Carnival' (*SEL* 42[2002] 259–85), and presents Shakespeare's carnivalizing of the rising as a 'dramaturgic device that allowed him to mix satirical comedy and tragedy in the form of history, criticizing the system and criticizing its critics, all at the same time'. This is a 'commercial device to give everyone in the audience some of what they want, even when those desires are contradictory'. The article focuses on representations of the law and lawyers, but its analysis stops short of engaging with the wider issues the rising raises. For example, the command to emasculate and execute the Sargiant in the quarto 'may have been quite hilarious to the audience and quite gratifying for any unfortunate litigants in the audience'; the Sargiant is 'sycophantic enough to call [Cade] "sir" and treat him as a legitimate judge, a comment on lawyers' willingness to grovel to anyone to get what they want'.

Ramie Targoff raises the issue of '"Dirty" Amens: Devotion, Applause, and Consent in *Richard III*' (*RenD* 31[2002] 61–84). The amens in question—the 'election' of Gloucester, and the crowning of Richmond—are the required resolutions for legitimate royal power, and in the latter case the audience's response also. In terms of amen meaning what it should mean, Richard's 'amen' is clearly 'dirty', compromised by the clear gap between outward and inward assent. But if Richmond is England's legitimate new ruler, why does he ask only God to 'say "Amen" to all'? None of the nobles present adds his own amens to his crowning. The gesture is a refusal of the necessity for popular support. But Targoff convincingly argues for audience applause as, effectively, an amen: 'the decision to close the play with the word "amen" may well have been produced *out* of the impulse, ingrained in Shakespeare as well as his audience, to effect closure through liturgical impulses'.

William O. Scott produces a clear reading of the discourses of property and kingship in *Richard II* in 'Landholding, Leasing and Inheritance in *Richard II*' (*SEL* 42[2002] 275–93). Focusing on 'humbler land transactions', Scott shows that the critique of Richard is articulated through the discourse of property ownership as well as that of royal inheritance. Terms such as 'lease', 'reversion', and, in the deposition, 'convey' and 'seize' are convincingly historicized to destabilize Richard's sense of his kingdom as a possession, rather than a life-grant. His difficulty in finding a language to unequivocally support his claims 'pertains gently to an audience's divided vision of realpolitik'. In contrast to Scott's careful historicization, Derek Cohen's 'History and the Nation in *Richard II* and *Henry IV*' (*SEL* 42[2002] 293–316) breaks no new ground, offering a familiar overview of the second tetralogy in which *Henry V* is 'a celebration of the coherence of the English nation', Richard II is 'a very human character', and 'the energy of the drama of [*1 Henry IV*] whirls about issues of motivation and personal and political morality'.

Jesse M. Lander, '"Crack'd Crowns" and Counterfeit Sovereigns: The Crisis of Value in *1 Henry IV*' (*ShakS* 30[2002] 137–61), investigates the relationship between the monarch and economic value, as figured through images of coinage. Lander reads the Tudor monarchy as guarantor of political and economic value, the latter through its power over coinage. Coin imagery thus leads back to larger questions of royal authority. Lander's close linguistic readings do sometimes illuminate the relationship between royal authority and value, though extravagant claims are also made. I am unconvinced that the image of Hal's coin stretching in his first scene with Falstaff 'suggests a disturbing elasticity that recalls debasement' to anybody not analysing coin images. A similar interpretative stretching appears in the statements that Falstaff's 'very corpulence figures inflation' and that 'the play attempts to manage the crisis of inflation as well as the unsettling history of the Tudor coinage'.

Matthew Greenfield, in '*1 Henry IV*: Metatheatrical Britain' (in Baker and Maley, eds., *British Identities and English Renaissance Literature*, pp. 71–80), ambitiously attempts to read the play's literary features through the new British history. The multiple sites (and references to other sites) in the play are the correlative of the 'failure of communal sentiment' in it. Plotting draws these sites together, but the characters thus connected are rebels as often as loyal citizens. Similarly, the play's shifting generic markers, on the face of it showing an inclusive conception of nation and history, have 'a distinct centrifugal tendency': Glendower's house is generically distinct from the rest of the plot; Falstaff's metatheatricality, and his comic capers with Douglas, similarly point to the impossibility of consolidating the nation-state adumbrated in the play.

Patricia Parker writes on 'Welsh Leeks in *Henry V*' (in Baker and Maley, eds., pp. 81–100). Beginning from the 'Welshness' of the play's climactic scene (IV.vii), Parker uses 'Alexander the Pig' and the 'garden where leeks did grow' as ways into the play's rhetoric. Fluellen's linguistic slip, combining indecorous reference to an animal and a by no means perfect conqueror, compromises his status as loyal borderer; the leek-eating episode suggests the difficulty of incorporating Wales into England, and counters the 'peace and union' theme of the end of the play. Parker's close analysis of the play's rhetoric intervenes in the 'containment' debate over the play, to show that 'multiple (and ultimately unstoppable) contrary voices' subvert the 'heroic voicing of English domination'. William Leahy makes a similar point in '"All would be royal": The Effacement of Disunity in Shakespeare's *Henry V*' (*ShJE* 138[2002] 89–98), though his problematic figure is Williams rather than Fluellen. The encounter between Williams and Henry before Agincourt ends without resolution. An Elizabethan audience is as likely to have identified with Williams's refusal of resolution as with Henry, and Leahy takes issue with a number of critics and editors who have argued otherwise.

Alison Thorne too takes issue with pro-monarchical readings of the play in '"Awake remembrance of these valiant dead": *Henry V* and the Politics of the English History Play' (*ShakS* 30[2002] 162–87). Thorne argues that the play does not support the Chorus's brand of patriotism, but its refusal to do so is more a matter of 'the ironic self-referentiality of its dramatic form' rather than voiced dissent or inadvertent self-exposure. The play thus discourages, rather than invites, uncritical identification of the kind proposed by Nashe and Heywood writing on the genre, by including the anxieties, strains, and contradictions attending the king's imperialist enterprise. Henry's rhetoric before Harfleur attempts to bridge the gap between 'an elitist tradition of martial valour' and a commons army; his implication that anyone can equally participate in this imagined community of brothers is duly contested before Agincourt. After supplying some subtle analysis of Henry's rhetorical strategies, Thorne asks whether we should simply 'assume that the manifold ironies in the exhortations of king and Chorus would have escaped the attention' of plebeian play-goers.

Nina Taunton also explores Henry's image in *1590s Drama and Militarism: Portrayals of War in Marlowe, Chapman and Shakespeare's Henry V* by historicizing him as a general. He is 'a model of manual precept' in justice and severity, with his own men and the enemy, and in his keeping communications open with his soldiers. But there are important ways in which his camp does not display best practice. Henry is initially correctly located at the centre of command, and has chosen his officers (Fluellen, Pistol) wisely. But when he goes walkabout he 'jumps the chain of command', an action Taunton historicizes as 'unprofessional', while recognizing its generic location in the 'disguised king' convention. The French commanders, in contrast, stay put, something Taunton adduces in support of Gary Taylor's editorial use of Q to redistribute military competence more equally between the two sides. Henry's paradoxical character in the camp scenes— sacrificing military competence to fraternize with his men—adds to the debate about his status as ideal monarch by interrogating his status as model general.

Camille Wells Slights, 'The Conscience of the King: *Henry V* and the Reformed Conscience' (*PQ* 80:i[2001] 37–55), explores the tensions between individual judgement and obligations to authority in the representations of conscience in the play. *Henry V* is much more opaque in this regard than a play like *Richard III*. The clergy's narration of his development before he even enters places Henry's acquisition of 'not only a reformed, but a proto-Reformation conscience', moving from 'a true lover of the holy church' to an increasingly independent monarch. Henry thus figures the emergence of a Protestant conscience through an increasing display of interiority, culminating in the pre-Agincourt soliloquies. The combination of abject fear and buoyant certainty here illustrates the 'basic paradox of the emotional workings of the early modern Protestant conscience'. But before the battle Williams challenges Henry as his country's conscience; the 'attenuated ... concept of volition' necessitated by the unquestioning obedience of the common soldier places both Henry and his soldiers in a moral dilemma. Indeed, the Boy's decision to 'seek some better service' than his roguish masters raises the possibility—swiftly curtailed by his presumed death with the luggage—of 'disobedience as a moral duty'. Though conscience and hierarchy are reconciled via the glove trick with Williams, it is still a trick; this plot, this time, moves towards resolution, but the issue does not. David Steinsaltz, in 'The Politics of French Language in Shakespeare's History Plays' (*SEL* 42[2002] 317–35), sees *Henry V* as offering at least one simpler experience, arguing for the play as not merely an English triumph, but as enacting the triumph of English. Positing a shared consciousness of the yoke of Norman, as it were, the article proposes a gleeful enjoyment of the play's presentation of French as 'the language of French poltroons and English thieves, and of all who wish to deceive' ('Le roy'). Katherine's lesson shows, for this audience, 'the inherent vulgarity of the French language'. Henry's rhetoric before Agincourt has few French words; public rhetoric is 'pure Anglo-Saxon'. Steinsaltz contrasts the representation of French with Shakespeare's use of Welsh, which lacks the later play's 'Manichean rancour'.

Dennis Kezar investigates the relationship between law and history in 'Law/Form/History: Shakespeare's Verdict in *All Is True*' (*MLQ* 63:i[2002] 1–30). The play 'challenges the law's normative authority', 'offering an alternate mechanism for negotiating the facts and forms of selfhood', conscience. Buckingham's death shows the law's 'normative incapacity'; Henry's conscience too is beyond the law. But conscience itself is questioned, as we are given the image of his 'capricious and incontinent' conscience. Ultimately, 'the theatregoer becomes the judge'.

(f) Tragedies

Shakespeare's tragedies continue to fascinate readers and critics, and the wealth of material published in the area is astounding. Of all the tragedies, the 'great' tragedies, particularly *Hamlet*, *King Lear*, and *Macbeth*, keep receiving more attention than the rest. The many scholarly contributions reflect a multiplicity of textual approaches and theoretical positions, adding to the richness of the total critical output. In the following survey contributions covering more than one tragedy are placed before those concerned with one specific play. The texts reviewed are ordered according to the particular play they describe, with early tragedies coming before later ones.

John Kerrigan's interesting book *On Shakespeare and Early Modern Literature: Essays* contains one essay of especial relevance to Shakespearian tragedy: 'Shakespeare as Reviser' (pp. 3–22). He considers textual variation, for example in *Hamlet* IV.v.154–64, where he observes that the second edition of the play, a quarto printed from foul papers, has the phrase 'a poore mans life'. Shakespeare later decided that 'poore' was unfocused so, as the Folio reveals, he submitted 'old' for 'poore', but he significantly adds lines to shift the emphasis from age to worth. Kerrigan also comments upon *Othello,* observing that the text has been rethought and recast, depending on the emphasis put on the quarto as opposed to the post-1606 prompt-book-related Folio. As an interesting detail, Kerrigan mentions that 'F regularly removes references to God because an Act of Parliament, passed in 1606, forbade stage blasphemy'. In his discussion he addresses the cluster of variants of great importance in the play—the temptation, fall, and vengeance of Othello. According to Kerrigan, Dr Leavis saw the Moor's behaviour in these scenes as imperceptive and egotistical. In Kerrigan's opinion, critics have remained closer to Leavis than they should: 'For we can deduce from the drift of variants that, after sailing close to the wind in Q, Shakespeare worked to protect Othello'. Shakespeare's willingness to rethink is clearly revealed in Shakespeare's reworking of the play.

Drakakis, ed., *Alternative Shakespeares*, originally published in 1986, has been reissued as a second edition, but with the original text. The volume contains essays from the first edition, including interesting approaches to Shakespeare from a variety of viewpoints, including post-structuralism, deconstruction, gender questions, semiotics, and ideology. Most of the major tragedies are referred to intermittently, with *Hamlet* receiving more attention than other texts in the genre. No apparent effort has been made to update the material.

Harris and Korda, eds., *Staged Properties in Early Modern English Drama*, contains two chapters with special reference to Shakespearian drama. Sasha Roberts's '"Let me the curtains draw": The Dramatic and Symbolic Properties of the Bed in Shakespearean Tragedy' (pp. 153–74) explores the dramatic uses and symbolic meanings of this stage property, and finds the bed one of the most significant of household artifacts in the Shakespearian canon. In his works there are more than 350 allusions to beds, including phrases coined by Shakespeare, such as bed-work, bed-vow, bed-right, and bed-presser. The focus of the chapter is upon the use of this stage property in *Romeo and Juliet* and *Othello*. Roberts considers the bed in the two plays to supply a stage within a stage, an intense visual and symbolic arena where powerful passions and transgressions are acted out. It also becomes a place for mapping the disruptions and collisions of private and public space. In the section of the book devoted to hand properties, Paul Yachnin has written on Othello's handkerchief in 'Wonder-Effects: Othello's Handkerchief' (pp. 316–34). He first considers the handkerchief as a prop, before considering how it speaks about something beyond itself. At this stage he does not regard it as a symbol, but as an object involved in a complex series of exchanges. In this way he hopes to avoid the tendency to read the playhouse as a window onto early modern culture. In his view, localized interpretation helps to shift interpretation from an imaginary, totalized cultural field to one that takes into account the relative autonomy of the stage. It is important first to understand how the handkerchief operated in the playhouse before one can grasp how play and handkerchief worked within the culture at large. A localized interpretation, according to Yachnin, helps to explain the handkerchief as a magical property and an object of wonder. In his opinion, it can also help in seeing the playhouse's strategic representation of the handkerchief as a contribution to the development of the 'wonder-effects' of Shakespeare's works: 'the process by which Shakespeare has come to be for modernity what the handkerchief is for Othello—a possession that possesses the possessor'.

For the student reader *The Cambridge Companion to Shakespearean Tragedy* is probably the most useful single volume in the field from 2002. According to the editor, Claire McEachern, it 'seeks to acquaint the undergraduate reader with the forms, contexts, kinds, and critical and theatrical lives of the ten plays we consider Shakespeare's tragedies'. *In toto* the different essays provide fruitful entries into the world of Shakespearian tragedy. Tom McAlindon, in his carefully argued essay, 'What Is a Shakespearean Tragedy?', comes close to a definition when he describes Shakespearian tragedy as being 'centrally concerned with the destruction of human greatness embodied in individuals endowed with "sovereignty of nature" (*Cor.* IV.vii.35): men who are instinctively referred to as "noble" (in the moral or characterological sense) by those who know them, even their enemies' (p. 8). In his essay on 'The Language of Tragedy', Russ McDonald observes that the burgeoning of Elizabethan tragedy was much indebted to the invention of a poetic language that went well with it, not least blank verse. According to McDonald, there is an exact correspondence between Shakespeare's ambivalent conception of language and the mixed view he takes of his tragic protagonists.

David Bevington, in 'Tragedy in Shakespeare's Career', finds that Shakespeare in one sense wrote tragedies throughout his career, for he definitely pursued tragic themes in his early history plays. But he finds that history, as an ongoing and open-ended endeavour, eclipses tragic form. His essay is a comprehensive account of Shakespeare's employment of the tragic mode throughout his career. Michael Warren's essay deals with Shakespeare's texts as printed and performed, stressing the unstable nature of the texts critics work with. The following four essays deal with the Tudor–Stuart political and social aspects of the tragedies. Huston Diehl sketches the religious picture, while Michael Hattaway considers the political scene. The early modern family is focused on in Catherine Belsey's contribution, 'Gender and Family', while Gail Paster, in 'The Tragic Subject and its Passions', emphasizes the materiality of embodied consciousness in Shakespeare's tragic heroes. The next three essays turn to the traditional sub-genres of Shakespearian tragedy—the plays of revenge and ambition, love, and classical history—but frequently from new perspectives. Robert N. Watson considers 'Tragedies of Revenge and Ambition', naturally paying special attention to *Hamlet* and *Macbeth*. In her discussion of 'Shakespeare's Tragedies of Love', Catherine Bates as a matter of course focuses on *Romeo and Juliet*, *Othello*, and *Antony and Cleopatra*. Coppélia Kahn's essay on 'Shakespeare's Classical Tragedies' discusses how early modern views of classical civilization inform the world of the five Graeco-Roman plays. The final two essays, R.A. Foakes's 'The Critical Reception of Shakespeare's Tragedies' and Barbara Hodgdon's '*Antony and Cleopatra* in the Theatre', consider how reading and playing have formed our experience of these plays. In sum, this is a collection of essays that clearly, concisely, and informatively guides the reader towards a richer experience of Shakespeare's tragedies.

E.A.J. Honigmann's *Shakespeare: Seven Tragedies Revisited*, is partly a reissue of the 1976 edition but contains additional chapters on *Henry V* and *As You Like It*, as well as a survey of some twentieth-century studies of Shakespeare's original audience and of response. The earlier essays on aspects of *Julius Caesar, Hamlet, Othello, King Lear, Macbeth, Antony and Cleopatra,* and *Coriolanus* are preserved.

While acknowledging the fact that, for the violent spectacle of *Titus Andronicus*, Shakespeare drew on Rome's founding myths and the legend of its imperial decadence, Nicholas R. Moschovakis, in '"Irreligious Piety" and Christian History: Persecution as Pagan Anachronism in *Titus Andronicus*' (*SQ* 53[2002] 460–86), reminds us that post-Reformation Christianity contained episodes of bloodshed and persecution that were more recent and closer to home. As Moschovakis observes, critics have recently begun to compare the traumas of *Titus* with those of sixteenth-century religious strife. The main argument of the essay is that 'Shakespeare's glances at contemporary religious conflict in *Titus* question the legitimacy of violence as a means of establishing and preserving Christianity.' While admitting that Shakespeare considered with scepticism the principles of ecclesiastical politics and the invocation of providentialist rhetoric in secular causes, Moschovakis claims that *Titus* evokes troubling parallels among different historically specific instances that were sanctioned by religion. The play does this by implying a resemblance between pious pretexts of Reformation violence and religious justifications of violence in ancient paganism, but also 'in Christianity's own self-authorizing histories of antiquity'.

Richard Levin considers 'The Longleat Manuscript and *Titus Andronicus*' (*SQ* 53[2002] 332–40). The Longleat manuscript is a folio leaf that has at the top a drawing apparently based on the opening scene of *Titus Andronicus*, but with certain references to Act V, and scholars have long argued about the relationship between manuscript and play. The major problem with the drawing, as Levin notes, relates to Aaron's role, because of discrepancies between his part in drawing and play. For example, why is he pictured with a sword when he is himself one of the prisoners? Levin considers some of the recent attempts to approach problems concerning the manuscript and suggests a solution. In Levin's view, the drawing is the artist's reading of Act I, scene i, not a photographic reproduction of the precise details of a specific moment. Several questions relating to the Longleat manuscript remain to be solved, as Levin observes, but, without new evidence, 'these questions remain unanswerable'.

Deborah Willis discusses '"The gnawing vulture": Revenge, Trauma Theory, and *Titus Andronicus*' (*SQ* 53[2002] 21–52). She finds a close parallel between the rise in favour of *Titus Andronicus* among critics and directors and the growth of feminist Shakespeare criticism. Feminist critics have disclosed to what degree the play is informed by gender ideology. In her view, the Rome of *Titus Andronicus* is a male world, and Romanness suggests a male ideology. She interestingly notes that feminist criticism has seldom looked closely at the play's main concern: revenge. Willis finds that *Titus* is special among revenge plays 'for its exposure of revenge as a cross-gender and cross-cultural phenomenon'. Revenge has a levelling aspect in the play, because both women and men, 'others' and Romans, are drawn into its spell. Their acts of revenge are based on honour values and practices that cross national boundaries and have gendered as well as ungendered characteristics. Willis further turns to trauma theory and considers Shakespeare's exploration of the relationship between trauma and revenge, relating this to three traumatic events: the deaths in combat of Titus's sons, the sacrifice of Alarbus, and the rape of Lavinia.

J.J. Tobin's article, 'More Evidence for a 1594 *Titus*' (*N&Q* 49[2002] 222–4), considers the final six paragraphs of the Epistle to the Reader in the second edition of *Christ's Tears Over Jerusalem* [1594]. This material has seemingly provided Shakespeare with a number of words and phrases in *Titus Andronicus*. According to Tobin, two of them are unique in the Shakespeare canon, one occurring for the first time, and a pair occurring in conjunction with one another for the first time in the canon. In context, these parallels suggest borrowings by Shakespeare from Nashe. Tobin argues that *Titus Andronicus* must be the work of early 1594, even if Shakespeare had seen Nashe's manuscript before its publication, since the Epistle in part answers criticism of the early 1594-published *The Unfortunate Traveller*. Tobin concludes that *Titus Andronicus* was composed after Nashe had written the Epistle to the second edition of his pamphlet some time early in 1594.

Romeo and Juliet has appeared in the Shakespeare in Production series, edited by James N. Loehlin. Of Shakespeare's tragedies, *Antony and Cleopatra* and *Hamlet* have already appeared in this series. The Shakespeare in Production publications aim at giving the reader a comprehensive dossier of materials—contemporary criticism, promptbook marginalia, rewritings, additions, stage business, and eyewitness accounts—from which to form an insight into the multiple meanings that a play has carried through time and across the world. These materials are arranged beside the New Cambridge Shakespeare text of the play, edited by G. Blakemore Evans, but Jill L. Levenson's skilful new edition for the Oxford Shakespeare has also been consulted. This edition of *Romeo and Juliet* reflects the view that the text of a play is its starting-point, and that its potential is realized and fully appreciated only in production. The editor's introductory chapter traces the stage history of the play from Shakespeare's stage to our time and also outlines adaptations to film and video. The commentary alongside the play, line by line and scene by scene, is comprehensive and illuminating.

A selection of important essays on *Julius Caesar* by modern critics has appeared in the New Casebook series, edited by Richard Wilson. The editor finds a special necessity for this volume, because *Julius Caesar* has become one of the texts most frequently referred to in debates about critical theory. The striking fact, Wilson observes, is that Shakespeare's tragedy is now less staged than studied, for the play is no longer a favourite of actors. One of the reasons why it has become so influential among theorists, according to Wilson, is that its imaging of the moment 'Between the acting of a dreadful thing | And the first motion' (II.i.63) 'seems to anticipate so much of postmodernism'. Among the many insightful essays, we find Wayne Rebhorn considering 'The Crisis of the Aristocracy' in the play, Richard Wilson dealing with Shakespeare's Roman Carnival, Jonathan Goldberg asking why Brutus conceives of the action of the conspiracy as a theatrical event, John Drakakis studying '*Julius Caesar* and the Politics of Theatrical Representation', and René Girard discussing 'Collective Violence and Sacrifice in *Julius Caesar*'. In her article on 'The Ritual Ground', Naomi Conn Liebler examines the Lupercalian elements in the play, rejects the idea that Shakespeare's detailed attention to Lupercal can be explained by suggesting that all things Roman were of interest to the audience, and finds that the rituals resonate with the semblance of native English rites. Gary Taylor's contribution, 'Bardicide', centres on two oppositions in the play, one between Cinna the poet and the plebeians and one between the poet and 'Cinna the Conspirator' (III.iii.32). Gail Kern Paster examines Shakespeare's use of the bodily signs of blood and bleeding, Cynthia Marshall, in addressing the semiotics of character, rethinks the epistemic relation of body to dramatic character, and ultimately of body to identity, while Richard Halpern tests Jürgen Habermas's narrative of the rise and decline of public culture against the case of *Julius Caesar*. This volume on Shakespeare's first Globe play richly reflects the interchange between modern critical theory and practice and helps to extend the reader's own ideas about the play.

Robert F. Fleissner considers 'The "Brute" Part in Hamlet and *Julius Caesar* Refigured—Regally' (*PLL* 38[2002] 334–6). He discusses Antony's reference to 'the most unkindest cut of all' (*JC* III.ii.183) and speculates whether Shakespeare might have had Brutus sever Caesar's testes for having brought him into the world out of wedlock. Fleissner admits, though, that historically it was just a rumour that Brutus was illegitimate, and such a matter is not specifically alluded to in *Julius Caesar*. He makes the connection to King Arthur, who, according to standard medieval tradition, was likewise killed by his own illegitimate son. Fleissner further comments that, 'at one point in the tales, a removal of sexual organs also happened to occur', even though in this case it was Arthur himself who was responsible. Although these were disparate events, they might half-consciously have been linked by Shakespeare's creative psyche. What Fleissner notes above, he sees in relation to the pun on Brutus as being a 'brute', of having a 'brute part', in *Hamlet* III.ii.101, where the context alludes to a university play, probably *Caesar Interfectus*, performed in Christ Church Hall, Oxford, in 1581–2.

Naseeb Shaheen examines 'Biblical References in *Julius Caesar*' (*N&Q* 49[2002] 226–7). While agreeing with David Daniell in the Arden edition of *Julius Caesar* that II.ii.11–12 may be linked with Exodus 33:20, 23, Shaheen disagrees with Daniell about *Julius Caesar* I.ii.25, where Cassius asks Brutus, 'Will you go see the order of the course?' While Daniell links this passage with Luke 1:8, where the verbal similarity is striking, Shaheen finds a parallel passage in Plutarch, which seems to have been Shakespeare's primary source. The context in Plutarch is exactly the same as in Shakespeare: running the course during the feast, while for Luke 1:8 the context is entirely different.

The question of Caesar's mantle occupies Bill Delaney in his comment on 'Shakespeare's *Julius Caesar*' (*Expl* 60:iii[2002] 122–4). He considers the question of whether the mantle mentioned by Marc Antony in III.ii.175–8 is the same one that Caesar donned in 57 b.c. If it is, Antony is not lying at this point in his funeral oration. The main question for the great dramatist, however, was to use Caesar's mantle for practical purposes. Delaney observes that, in staging the funeral oration, the positioning of the actors was important. While Shakespeare could not display Caesar's mutilated body, he could obtain a much stronger visual effect with the torn and bloody mantle. In another entry on the same play (*Expl* 60:iv[2002] 188–90), Delaney points to Mark Antony's reply to Cassius's flattery in V.i.32–45, which has puzzled scholars. He shows that different editions render the final line 42 of the passage differently. While most editions of *Julius Caesar*, following the First Folio, give Antony's reply to Cassius as 'Not stingless too', with no question mark, the Arden Shakespeare and the Cambridge Shakespeare 'have quite correctly made Antony ask, "Not stingless too?" with a question mark at the end'.

William Poole, in '*Julius Caesar* and *Caesars Revenge* Again' (*N&Q* 49[2002] 227–8), considers the connection between Shakespeare's *Julius Caesar* and the anonymous *The Tragedie of Caesar and Pompey, or Caesars Revenge*. The latter was acted at Trinity College, Oxford, and is thought to have been written in the 1590s because of its echoes of Marlowe, Kyd, Daniel, and Spenser. Poole supports the view that Shakespeare did not only know this obscure work, but echoed it in *Richard II*, *Antony and Cleopatra*, 'and perhaps in the other plays'. Poole further supports a connection between the old play and, specifically, *Julius Caesar*, 'because of one other very obvious verbal parallel perhaps hitherto unnoticed' in the opening scene of the two plays, referring to I.i.32–4 in *Julius Caesar* and sig. A3^V in *Caesars Revenge*.

John V. Robinson, 'Hamlet's Evil Ale: Hamlet I.iv.36–38' (*HSt* 24[2002] 10–25), discusses Hamlet's 'dram of eale' speech. Robinson finds this passage in the 1604 quarto (Q2) of *Hamlet* one of the most puzzling lines in all of Shakespeare. He observes that the most vexing word in this passage is 'eale', which he finds is almost unanimously thought to be a corruption of the word 'evil'. Drawing on supporting evidence from the Shakespearian addition to the manuscript of *Sir Thomas More*, as well as on contemporary warnings against excessive drinking, Robinson suggests that 'eale' is an archaic spelling of 'ale'. See also the earlier and fuller discussion of this article in section 1.

Christopher McDonough focuses on 'Missing Mouse (*Hamlet*, I.i.12)' (*N&Q* 49[2002] 228–9). While crediting Professor R. Chris Hassel Jr. in *Shakespeare Jahrbuch* for a thorough study of the various mouse references in *Hamlet*, McDonough finds it curious that he makes no note of the first mouse mentioned in the play, in the play's opening scene, where Bernardo, replacing Francisco on watch duty, edgily asks his fellow sentinel, 'Have you had quiet guard?', to which the latter responds, 'Not a mouse stirring' (I.i.12). McDonough points out that the mouse's silence had only just achieved proverbial status by the time *Hamlet* was composed.

In 'Bare-Bones Humour in *Hamlet* (V.i) and *Don Quixote* (1,19)' (*HSt* 24[2002] 26–38), Enrique Fernández points out that Hamlet and Don Quixote alike show a strong interest in the decay of flesh after death. He finds that Hamlet's encounter with the gravedigger and Don Quixote's clash with the funeral cortège are 'eerily similar'. In spite of their macabre content, both scenes resort to humour. According to Fernández, this combination of humorous tone and macabre content is 'a way to confront the distressing new conception of death arising in Shakespeare's and Cervantes' days'.

Michael Gooch (*Expl* 60:iv[2002] 186–7) refers to Ophelia' 'remembrances', which she returns to Hamlet in III.i, noting that they were discussed at a workshop session of the Shakespeare Association of America conference [2001], where participants had to explain their choices of remembrances related to how they might be played on the stage. What Gooch proposes, and considers the text supports, is to view Ophelia's prayer book not as a prayer book but as Hamlet's book. After noting the insufficiencies of the most common explanations of Ophelia's remembrances relating to III.i, Gooch suggests that imagining Hamlet seeing Ophelia pondering his book makes us 'anticipate his harsh treatment of her, as well as the rage directed toward Polonius and Claudius, whom he probably knows to be present'. Gooch sees Ophelia as an active participant in the deception that is carried out rather than a pathetic victim of abusive men.

An interesting note on 'Hamlet and Oedipus: A Protest' by John K. Hale is to be found in *Hamlet Studies* (*HamS* 24[2002] 108–15). Hale objects to the idea that Hamlet's character should be understood as an Oedipal case, arguing that the comparison is neither appropriate nor useful, but facile and unfounded, 'and obstructive to more important features of Shakespeare's conception'. On a closing note Hale suggests that a more plausible case for Oedipal analysis than Hamlet would be Coriolanus.

John R. Ford asks the question, how young is 'young Hamlet'? He discusses this in the article 'Finding Young Hamlet' (*POMPA* [2002] 1–7; repr. from *Shakespeare* 6:i[2002]). Ford refers to three recent remarkable but different productions of the play, different in interpretative design, length, and even printed text. But these three *Hamlet*s were all similar in that they had discovered the young, shifty energy of Hamlet as well as of the play. Ford explores the characteristics of each production in some detail, concluding that they were successful because they made their audiences listen and rewarded that attentiveness, making the audience an active participant in the political, religious, and psychological strife that young Hamlet encounters.

In a note on 'Hamlet's Piratical Linkage' (*HSt* 24[2002] 116–22), R.F. Fleissner addresses the topic of whether Hamlet has a secret alliance with the pirates transporting him back to Denmark to be executed. He points out that such a supposition was raised by George Miles as early as 1870, was later resuscitated by Martin Stevens, and was more recently rejuvenated in David Farley-Hill's 'Hamlet's Account of the Pirates' (*RES NS* 50[1999] 320–31). Fleissner's support of this view is partly based on seeing 'two crafts' in III.iv.211 as wordplay in the sense of *two ships*, pointing forward to his getting off his boat and onto the pirate ship while still out at sea, and partly on Hamlet's letter to Horatio with the lines 'they knew what they did: I am to do a good turn for them' (IV.vi.21–2).

Sipiora and Baumlin, eds., *Rhetoric and Kairos: Essays in History, Theory, and Praxis*, contains a chapter on *Hamlet* by James S. Baumlin and Tita French Baumlin, '*Chronos, Kairos, Aion*: Failures of Decorum, Right-Timing, and Revenge in Shakespeare's *Hamlet*' (pp. 165–86). The authors point out that Hamlet, in Rosencrantz's words, is 'most like a gentleman' (III.i.11); his education as a scholar-prince has given him a thorough training in the *studia humanitatis*, which stressed *prudentia* and the necessity of mastering decorum or 'discretion' (III.i.17), as Hamlet terms it. And yet, the authors observe, Hamlet in most respects represents a study in the failure of *prudentia* and thus provides a critical test of humanist educational, ethical, political, and rhetorical theory. The fact that Denmark's 'chiefest courtier' (I.ii.117) fails the test reveals a crisis lying at the play's thematic centre. This crisis is related to the optimism of the age concerning human reason and humanist aspirations to master worldly fortune. The authors focus on Shakespeare's interweaving of three broad themes: the nature of Hamlet's humanist decorum, the Prince's awkward attempts at blood revenge, and 'the play's philosophical exploration of competing temporalities and notions of "right-timing," particularly as reflected in the iconographic symbolisms surrounding Prudence and Fortune, Time and Eternity'.

Ron Rosenbaum considers 'Shakespeare in Rewrite' (*New Yorker* 78[Nov. 2002] 68–77), an informative, but stylistically informal, introduction to the Arden Shakespeare. It recounts Rosenbaum's meeting with Harold Jenkins, the Arden editor, and contains a fair amount of facts about *Hamlet* and its background.

Clinton P.E. Atchley, in 'Reconsidering the Ghost in *Hamlet*: Cohesion or Coercion?' (*Philological Review* 28:ii[2002] 5–20), points out that 'conventional wisdom today subscribes to the proposition that the Ghost is just who he says he is, the ghost of Hamlet's father'. He does not set out to determine the ontological nature of Old Hamlet's ghost to everybody's satisfaction, but he approaches a few puzzling aspects of the Ghost's nature and considers how the Ghost functions in the play. Atchley is interested in the religious orientation of an average Shakespearian audience and what these people would have believed about ghosts. He therefore focuses on Catholics' and Protestants' beliefs concerning ghosts and the supernatural. In Atchley's view, Shakespeare does not solve the problem of the true nature of ghosts for his audience. What he does instead is to incorporate within his play Catholic as well as Protestant perspectives on the Ghost, as well as a third view, one based on folklore.

Hamlet is also part of Eric P. Levy's '"What is a man": *Hamlet* and the Problematics of Man' (*Viator* 33[2002] 377–93). Levy contends that, after four centuries of commentary, *Hamlet* can still be dealt with as 'undiscover'd country', for there are aspects of the play that have not been explored and others whose implications have not been disclosed. Levy first summarizes the dominant theoretical concerns of the last twenty-five years, before dealing with the 'To be' soliloquy, in order to get a view of what has happened to the individual and the whole. This soliloquy opposes two states: the sleep of death and waking consciousness. This opposition, according to Levy, accurately invokes the opposition propounded by Heracleitus of Ephesus, whose view later became the humanist doctrine of the relation between the personal and universal orders. The article further focuses on primacy of reason versus perplexity of reason, where we are reminded that *Hamlet* contains numerous references to the discrepancy between divine and human reason. Another issue Levy raises is a reinterpretation of tragic fault, or *hamartia*. Levi strongly stresses the 'outside controlling perspective' in *Hamlet*. Perplexity bursts the paradigm of certainty stemming from the classical tradition. In *Hamlet* the impulse to discover the cause leads not to certainty about anterior cause but to uncertainty about posterior result.

In *Shakespeare Newsletter* (*ShN* 52:iii[2002] 61, 66, 78, 80, 88, 90), Anthony Burton deals with 'Laertes's Rebellion: Further Aspects of Inheritance Law in *Hamlet*'. In an earlier issue of the journal Burton examined an overlooked pattern of legal references in *Hamlet* relating specifically to inheritance. It showed both Hamlet and Fortinbras to have been defeated in their expectations for inheritance. It is Burton's view that the theme of lost inheritance has a special function within the framework of the play, as inheritance works as a kind of unifying preoccupation. Burton sees an obvious need to extend his study to Laertes for two reasons: first, Hamlet thinks Laertes' cause to be a portraiture of his own, and secondly, according to a long-standing critical view, Hamlet, Fortinbras, and Laertes are literary triplets concerning the motive to achieve justice for their fathers' deaths. Burton emphasizes that Laertes is meant to be part of the same pattern. For Laertes his inheritance matters a great deal, and at the point that the threat of lost inheritance is out of the way for him, he has no further reason to suspect Claudius of the death itself. Legal allusions in *Hamlet* are not purely decorative, neither are they elements of clever legal conundrums. Their purpose is to provide the characters with mutually explanatory purposes.

Jeremy Ehrlich reminds us, in 'The Search for the *Hamlet* "Director's Cut"' (*ES* 5[2002] 399–406), that Shakespeare's *Hamlet* presents an intriguing set of textual problems, since the three surviving printed texts of the play, Q1 from 1603, Q2 from 1604–5, and F from 1623, show important differences. In his paper Ehrlich argues that speculative editing of the Q1 text may disclose useful clues to the state of an early staged version of *Hamlet* which is now lost. The experiment, he notes, suggests that 'an early adapter of the play had a quite different sense of aesthetics than the author of the later, longer texts'.

In '*Hamlet* and the *Odyssey*' (*Literary Imagination* 4[2002] 389–410), Stewart Justman explores intersections between the two works. Pointing out that Shakespeare did not know the *Odyssey* at first hand, but knew the *Iliad*, Justman still finds it profitable to see possible relations between the two texts. He bases his essay on the view that, while the *Odyssey* is not one of Shakespeare's sources in the usual sense of the word, it is what he terms 'an underlying source'. Justman sees Shakespeare as one who injected the comic into tragedy, confounded genre in the problem plays, and 'tapped the richness of a source prior to genre itself'. While *Timon of Athens* generally receives little attention, Robert B. Pierce has written 'Tragedy and *Timon of Athens*' (*CompD* 36:i–ii[2002] 75–90). The paper is primarily a discussion of the term 'tragedy', which Pierce finds 'one of the most vexed terms in literary criticism'. He considers *Timon of Athens* a puzzling play, partly because it seems to be an afterthought in its present location among the tragedies, and partly because the text is unsatisfactory, suggesting that it has not been put into final form for production. On the other hand, Pierce sees *Timon* as a play that in many way is typical of Shakespeare. It focuses on the fall of a major figure, its mood is dark, and it examines issues concerning citizens' duties, friendship, and cynicism. As such *Timon* fits within the limits of early modern tragedy. It has obvious ties to the group of Shakespearian tragedies close to it in time—*Lear*, *Macbeth*—as well as the Roman plays, except *Titus Andronicus*.

Ruth Stevenson refers to Hamlet as a poem in '*Hamlet*'s Mice, Motes, Moles, and Minching Malecho' (*NLH* 33[2002] 435–59), noting that this may strike some readers as anti-dramatic. To disarm such concern, she briefly explains Shakespeare's use of poetry itself and addresses the implications of this use for his audience. According to Stevenson, Shakespeare preserves the distinction between genres; *Hamlet* is a play written in blank verse, but 'he does not tightly constrict his usage to any prescribed generic rule'. While the play opens with a series of staccato questions, blank verse soon becomes its predominant medium. Topics of various sub-genres of poetry emerge, for example, 'in the virtual lyrics of Marcellus's dawn poem (I.i.162–69), Horatio's pastoral (I.i.171–72), Gertrude's elegy for Ophelia (IV.vii. 165–82), Laertes' epitaph for her, and the self-reflexive elegies both of Laertes (V.ii.319–26) and of Hamlet (V.ii.338–63)'. Stevenson also finds 'real lyrics' at crucial stages of the play, such as Hamlet's ballad following the Mousetrap, and Ophelia's ballads and elegies. 'The blank verse accommodates these forms and maintains narrative momentum', just as it did in Marlowe's plays. Stevenson includes prose in her discussion, noting that Shakespeare allotted to Hamlet more prose passages than to any other of his tragic heroes, lines that often seem to be part of the poetry. In responding to Shakespeare's text, the most significant generic issue lies in discriminating between seeing a drama/poem and reading it, rather than questioning the difference between drama and poem. In her essay, Stevenson explores how the poem works within its own linguistic action 'and in particular how its metaphoric language instigates and disseminates correlative metaphors whose interactions shape the consciousness of *Hamlet*'.

In *Shakespeare Bulletin*, Bernice W. Kliman, co-ordinator of the new variorum *Hamlet* project, presents 'Three Notes on Polonius: Position, Resistance, and Name' (*ShakB* 20:ii[2002] 5–6). Kliman observes that the play does not tell us much about Polonius's history. She prefers seeing Polonius as a counsellor who is part of Claudius' court, and she finds support for the notion of royals having their own courts, courtiers, and followers. She finds no good reason, however, for giving Polonius the title of Lord Chamberlain. With regard to Polonius's residence, she finds no proof that he and his family have a residence which is separate from the court. As Kliman notes, 'unit settings usually imply that the Polonius family resides at court—and that seems right both for historical and for dramatic reasons'. Discussing Polonius's name, she observes that this point has been an object of special interest, since Q1 has a different name for the counsellor, and in the play she finds no clues. Shakespeare may have gained from the name of Polonius an allusion to a certain Pole's pedantic style of writing (*De Optimo Senatore*, written by Grimaldus, was translated into English in 1598), but it might also allude to a specific Polish ambassador who paid a visit to the queen in 1597. Shakespeare may have introduced the name of Polonius in part as a compliment to Queen Elizabeth.

Kolin, ed., *Othello: New Critical Essays*, in the Shakespeare Criticism series, is a welcome addition to studies of that particular text. The book contains twenty-one essays on different aspects of the play. The editor has written a substantial and well-researched introductory essay identifying the chief critical problems related to the play. It also evaluates the criticism that has connected the play with various ideological concerns. Its evaluation of significant critical works is a useful guide to the research on the play. Reviewing the critical canon, Kolin refers to the oft-heard question (in Michael Billington's phrasing): 'But who is the central figure? Othello, fatally flawed by his mixture of self-regard and insecurity? Or Iago, the active embodiment of evil?' The fact that Iago speaks almost one-third more lines than Othello raises the question of whether Othello is the subject or object of the tragedy. Kolin's thorough discussion of Othello and Iago approaches this and related issues, and considers *Othello* not only in criticism, but also on stage and on screen. The volume contains essays by critics representing a host of critical positions and methodologies. Approaches range from a focus on interconnections between *The Merchant of Venice* (also known as *The Jew of Venice*) and the later Moor of Venice, Iago's motives and the means by which Othello falls, and the implications of race, performance, and staging, to mention just a few. David Bevington gives a portrait of Othello's marriage, while Scott McMillin considers the mystery of the early *Othello* texts, the *Othello* quarto of 1622, and the First Folio of 1623. All in all, this volume provides significant and varied interpretations of the play.

Millicent Bell's 'Shakespeare's Moor' (*Raritan* 21:iv[2002] 1–14) may serve as an informative introduction to the character of Othello, his uncertain background, his relations to people around him, not least Iago, and his very special and changing relationship with Desdemona. Bell finds that Othello finally gives way to the prison of race he imagined he had escaped. When he turns his dagger towards himself, he re-enacts the killing of an infidel 'in Aleppo once' and again becomes what he was prior to his conversion and career in the Venetian service. He once again kills 'the irreversibly circumcised, unassimilable racial other that he is'.

Christopher Baker (*Expl* 60:ii[2002] 63) refers to *Othello*'s tragic pathos stemming from the fact that 'honest' Iago manages to hide his deceptive nature from Othello. Baker focuses on one example of this deception in II.iii, where Iago is able to manipulate the drunken Cassio into stabbing Montano. Othello arrives, settles the incident, and asks who was responsible for it. Turning to Iago, he says: "Tis monstrous. Iago, who began't?' (II.iii.217). The punctuation here reflects the first quarto's version, while the medial period has been replaced in the First Folio by a colon, suggesting a different interpretation: "Tis monstrous: Iago, who began't?'. In Baker's view 'the colon suggests a revealing linkage of which we are ironically aware but to which Othello remains tragically blind'.

Marguérite Corporaal considers views of the female voice in Jacobean tragedies in her '"Moor, she was chaste. She loved thee, cruel moor": *Othello* as a Starting Point for Alternative Dramatic Representations of the Female Voice' (*Comitatus* 33[2002] 99–111). Corporaal points out that, while woman's silence was considered a mark of feminine chastity and submissiveness, woman's speech might suggest lewd conduct. In the article she shows, however, that the dominant ideology on woman's speech was undermined by Shakespeare in *Othello*. In Corporaal's view, Shakespeare seems to have introduced subversive ideas about the female voice that were further developed by John Webster and Elizabeth Cary. But she emphasizes that, although *Othello* introduces a more positive attitude to woman's speech, the tragic closure confirms the conventional tragic pattern. Desdemona's farewell to the world is marked by self-denial, while Othello's final moments are characterized by self-assertion.

Shoin Literary Review contains an article by Ronald St Pierre: '"Cuckold me": Cuckoldry in Shakespeare's *Othello*' (*ShLR* 35[2002] 1–15). St Pierre remarks that *Othello*, like *The Merry Wives of Windsor* and *Much Ado About Nothing*, depicts cuckoldry to be false and slanderous. *Othello* tries to make a stand against the existence of jealousy in a world where it is unfounded. But the tragedy of *Othello* goes further and demonstrates how cuckoldry, once sown in man's imagination, can lead to tragedy. Shakespeare used what had been a stock comic plot and created tragedy, 'perhaps the first tragedy involving the lore and language of cuckoldry'. Shakespeare achieves this transformation by making use of his scenario to concentrate on the growth, development, and results of unfounded jealousy.

Volume 55 of *Shakespeare Survey*, edited by Peter Holland, is devoted to '*King Lear* and its Afterlife'. Richard Knowles considers 'How Shakespeare Knew *King Leir*' (*ShS* 55[2002] 12–35). He concludes his discussion by suggesting that Shakespeare may have seen old *Leir* in 1594 or before. This may have influenced his handling of a scene or two in *Richard III*, although no proof has been found. Shakespeare may have seen the play after 1594, but that seems unlikely. Furthermore, in spite of occasional similarities, there is little reason to think that the old play exerted a lasting influence on Shakespeare during the next ten to fifteen years. Knowles sees no reason to assume that Shakespeare ever acted in the play, whether with the Queen's men before 1594 or with the Chamberlain's men later on. Nor does he see any reason why the Chamberlain's men should have made him rewrite a version of the old play. 'It is possible, however,' according to Knowles, 'to construct a plausible narrative of how the playbook of the old play was held by the

Queen's Men until 1603 and then sold to Simon Stafford, who arranged with
Edward White and John Wright to publish the play in 1605.' Knowles finds no
reason to think that more than two manuscripts were in circulation, the actors'
playbook and the stationer's alternative copy. In Shakespeare's *Lear* there are nearly
a hundred details revealing a close familiarity with the 1605 edition of the old play.
The fact that Shakespeare possessed this knowledge around the year 1605, when the
old play was first published, and the fact that he did not, as far as we know, write an
earlier version of the Lear story, indicate that he read Stafford and Wright's edition
as soon as it appeared. If it was that edition that gave Shakespeare the idea of writing
his own play, 'then *King Lear* was mainly written in the extremely busy time
between summer 1605 and its first recorded performance, on 26 December 1606, at
court'.

In the same volume, William Scott considers 'Contracts of Love and Affection:
Lear, Old Age, and Kingship' (*ShS* 55[2002] 36–42). He observes that a legal
context for Lear's abdication and division of his kingdom throws one into 'a morass
of power and kingship struggles, and complicates what otherwise seems, perhaps
too readily, a wholly foolish decision by him'. But this way of reading the play,
Scott points out, can help show the dilemma of Lear's situation as well as the ironies
resulting from his choices. Not only family relations of love, but the circumstances
of royal and paternal power may be affected. Lear's announced purpose is 'To shake
all cares and business' either 'of our state' (quarto) or 'from our age' (Folio). While
commoners could reduce the cares of age by giving away property in return for
being provided for in old age, kings are not supposed to dispose of their kingdoms
in such a manner—at least they should not divide the land. Scott notes that it may be
legally problematic to trade property for promises of future service, giving a mixture
of property law and contract law. However, Lear has a family interest, as well as a
dynastic one, in settling his inheritance, remembering his daughters' marriages, with
the objective that 'future strife | May be prevented now' (Folio, I.i.43–4). But, as
Scott points out, the timing of the gift 'is carefully but disastrously planned'.

Andrew Gurr deals with 'Headgear as a Paralinguistic Signifier in *King Lear*'
(*ShS* 55[2002] 43–52). In his opinion, 'the evidence about the wearing and not-
wearing of headgear in the first performances of *King Lear* repays careful study'.
While there is little evidence about what the original players of the tragedy might
have worn, Gurr asserts that the indications about headgear in the text suggest that
they were meant to have a significant function. 'The decline in headgear through the
play was a feature reminding the early audiences of Albion's fall into its old
disunity', according to Gurr. He further points out that in the early production of the
play the headgear changed through the play as authority shifted. Concerning
particulars, there is necessarily much speculation and, as Gurr comments, one is
reminded of the distinct differences between studying Shakespeare on the page and
on stage.

'What Becomes of the Broken-Hearted: *King Lear* and the Dissociation of
Sensibility' is addressed by Drew Milne (*ShS* 55[2002] 53–66). *King Lear*
obviously becomes less of a tragedy if Lear dies from natural causes, 'rather than
from the unbearable weight of the unnatural causes his body and mind have
endured'. It is important to understand the playtext of *King Lear*, Milne maintains,
and this involves carefully considering the implied acting of the tragic body and
Shakespeare's choreography of death. Milne puts it this way: 'The historically

specific condition revealed by analysis is that the play suggests a carefully worked identity between the metaphorical sense of what it means to die of a broken heart and a more literal sense of the breaking of the heart within Elizabethan and Jacobean psychology and medicine.'

In another article in the same volume, John J. Joughin discusses '*Lear*'s Afterlife' (*ShS* 55[2002] 67–81). As he rightly observes, *Lear* is not the type of text that fades away; it retains an enduring significance. Joughin considers *Lear* a text that takes us beyond conventional expectations—'sometimes to the point of incredulity'. The tragedy contains a degree of 'wildness' and formal disintegration that many critics find at once implausible and unactable. Several critics have noted that there is a surplus effect to the play. In his essay Joughin tries to unpack the significance of one after-effect of the play: the '*pietà*-like' image of Lear holding the dead Cordelia in his arms, a scene of 'pity and hope' that has continued to haunt audiences and critics.

Peter Womack deals with 'Secularizing *King Lear*: Shakespeare, Tate, and the Sacred' (*ShS* 55[2002] 96–105). He reminds us that Nahum Tate's *King Lear* was first performed in 1680–1, and the play was performed in his adaptations until Macready went back to a heavily cut Shakespearian text in 1838. Tate's version, with a happy ending, was a success and made the play purposeful, according to Womack. What Tate delivered, and Johnson supported, was a de-Catholicized and empirical Shakespeare, with 'one world' imposed upon the mystery and artifice of *King Lear*, and with the sacred dimension of early modern theatre suppressed.

Janet Bottoms's contribution is '"Look on her, look": The Apotheosis of Cordelia (*ShS* 55[2002] 106–13). Referring to Judith Hawley's argument that the nineteenth century saw a critical division along gendered lines, and that while the male Romantic critics tended to 'aestheticise and psychologise Shakespeare', women showed a persistent concern with and even a 'violent attachment to' morality. This is true up to a point, Bottoms argues, observing that to Hazlitt and Coleridge morality was an issue as well. The essay traces changing views on Cordelia among Romantic and Victorian critics, paralleling views on women generally in the same periods.

In 'Some Lears' (*ShS* 55[2002] 139–52) Richard Proudfoot points to the pursuit of Lear through a number of nineteenth- and twentieth-century rewritings, revisions, appropriations, or adumbrations, and finds that this interest signalled the start of the reappraisal of *King Lear* on its way to becoming the play which most directly spoke to the late twentieth century. Proudfoot exposes some of his own perplexities concerning modern Shakespeare offshoots. Turning to specific appropriations of Shakespeare's play, Proudfoot critically asks: 'How do we know when we are reading an "appropriation"? When is a Lear not a Lear?' His discussion addresses several types of text where an analogy with *King Lear* can be detected, including nineteenth-century novels transposing tragedy into bourgeois or peasant life. Proudfoot finally notes that stage productions and adaptations of Shakespeare are established research areas.

Commending Professor Frances Biscoglio for pursuing the problem of the role of the gods in the lives of humans in *King Lear* (*SNL* 51:iii[2001] 13–18), George Walton Williams contributes to further discussion of the theme in his article 'Invocations to the Gods in *King Lear*: A Second Opinion' (*SNL* 51:iv[2001/2] 89, 106). As Williams observes, the gods in *King Lear* are the pagan deities (when they are named), but he doubts that Shakespeare had any sense of how, historically, the

classical gods would be expected to act in the world that Lear inhabited. Though
Shakespeare creates a non-Christian world, he wrote for an audience that had an
awareness of how the Christian God behaved. While Professor Biscoglio finds that
the gods answer 'some of the prayers', Williams considers this statement
theologically disturbing, pointing out that the Christian audience would have
expected the gods to be consistent, to answer all of the prayers. In Williams's view,
the gods answer all the prayers directed to them, and they answer them positively.
Even Edmund's invocation in I.ii.22, although for his own benefit, results in the
gods accepting his petition seriously and granting him what he wants. Williams also
objects to the view that the gods are inscrutable, suggesting that the difficulty lies in
the inability of man's fallen reason to comprehend their actions, rather than any lack
of clarity in those actions. He fascinatingly notices that the first prayer of the play,
Kent's invocation on behalf of Cordelia in the opening scene (I.i.182), is repeated,
in essence, as the last prayer of the play, the prayer of Edgar for Cordelia (V.iii.357).
Both prayers are by one of the 'good' characters on behalf of another of the 'good'
characters, and in both cases the gods' answer is positive and immediate.

David Webb writes about 'The Interrogation of the Heavens in *King Lear* and
Marlowe's *Dr Faustus*' (*CahiersE* 61[2002] 13–29). Webb notes that *King Lear* has
provoked some critics to argue strongly that the play is Christian, while others see it
as faith-shattering, or firmly agnostic. The play characteristically asks theological
questions but refuses provocatively to give unequivocal answers. In Webb's view,
Dr Faustus works differently but is just as effective. While all Marlowe's plays raise
questions about Christianity, this happens most explicitly in *Dr Faustus*. A key
strategy in the two plays is to hold different theological possibilities in suspension
without allowing any of them to disappear, but the tactics are different. Suffering in
King Lear is part of a structure 'which repeatedly inculcates scepticism and which is
studded with quotable contradictory views about divine justice'. *Dr Faustus* seems
to offer the right answer to questions as to what damns Faustus and when, but each
time that certainty fades, 'and the doubt generated by this process is compounded by
the use of a self-dramatizing hero'.

Lisa Hopkins remarks, in 'Lear's Castle' (*CahiersE* 62[2002] 25–32), that,
according to medieval and Renaissance authors, the historical King Leir was the
founder of the city of Leicester (i.e. Leir's Castle). Using this etymology as a point
of departure, Hopkins explores echoes of Elizabeth I's favourite Robert Dudley, earl
of Leicester in central parts of *King Lear*, and she suggests reasons why Shakespeare
might have considered this texture for some focal ideas in the play. She observes, for
example, that when Edmund, earl of Gloucester, attracts the rival sisters Goneril and
Regan, he finds himself in a situation paralleled by that of Robert, earl of Leicester,
with whom two sisters, Douglas and Frances Howard, were thought to be in love.
Leicester seems to have married Douglas, Hopkins notes, but, despite later
disowning her, the earl acknowledged their son, Robert Dudley, whose legitimate
half-brother was Edmund. That was also the name of Leicester's grandfather, and a
name Shakespeare chose to use in his story of *King Lear*, rather than the name
Plexirtus of his source. Hopkins suggests several other correspondences, including
parallel poison plots. To the question why Shakespeare might have had Leicester in
mind when writing *King Lear*, she answers that Leicester, or events associated with
him, greatly influenced the young Shakespeare. She points out, for example, that
'lines in *A Midsummer Night's Dream* seem to reflect memories of the 1575

Kenilworth entertainments which Leicester had organised for Elizabeth I'. The Leicesters' family affairs were 'topical', and politically Leicester's world assonates with that of *King Lear*. Hopkins argues that Shakespeare wants to evoke the ghost of Leicester in *King Lear* 'because doing so allowed him to make plain the extent to which some of the fundamental mechanisms of Elizabethan courtly power and display are negated and inverted in the world of the play—and, by extension, in the world of the Jacobean court'.

Lisa Hopkins writes about 'Reading Between the Sheets: Letters in Shakespearean Tragedy' (*CS* 14:iii[2002] 5–13). Initially pointing to Bradley's irritation at the fact that Edgar in *King Lear* is assumed to have written Edmund a letter when they were living in the same castle, Hopkins argues that 'we may still miss some of the meanings of the very frequent use of letters in Renaissance plays, and particularly those in Shakespeare's major tragedies'. As Hopkins indicates, letters occur extremely frequently in Shakespearian drama, the word 'letter' occurring thirty-three times in *King Lear* alone. Letters tend to appear at moments of especially heightened significance, frequently serving an important role in plot development, not least in the uncovering of hidden truths. They may in themselves become significant dramatic properties, almost foreshadowing *Pamela* and *Clarissa*. In the article Hopkins does not primarily focus on how the letter functions in the plot, but on 'its role as discourse, and, in particular, its tonal and status relationship to other kinds of discourse in the drama'. The article contains comments on these aspects in *Macbeth*, *Hamlet*, *King Lear*, and *Othello*. According to Hopkins, Shakespeare's use of letter texts within the four major tragedies covers a wide range, including the particular important document revealing more than its sender is aware of, the painstakingly controlled one revealing part of the truth, and the letter characterized by gesture. As Hopkins notes, Shakespeare's use of these written texts 'add to the tonality, indeterminacy and multiplicity of meaning'. The letter within the dramatist's text, exemplifying a ventriloquism inferior to the dramatist's own, increases the audience's perceptions of dramatic speech and thus, ironically, favours the oral rather than the written.

Possible influences on *King Lear* from Greene are focused on in 'The "Part" for Greene's *Orlando Furioso*: A Source for the "Mock Trial" in Shakespeare's *Lear*' (*N&Q* 49[2002] 229–31). Tiffany Stern here remarks that Shakespeare, with his interest in the theatrical presentation of madness, would no doubt have been familiar with both Greene's play *Orlando Furioso* and Ariosto's poem, and asks if Shakespeare refers to Greene's mad hero when writing about his own mad Lear. According to Stern, no other play preceding *Lear* includes a mock trial (present in the complete Greene text), so Shakespeare's use of that piece of staging, dropped in the later Folio text of *King Lear*, might have reminded the audience of popular *Orlando*. The mock trial is only part of a larger relationship existing between the two plays—a relationship based on madness. Stern suggests that Shakespeare may have discovered that 'what was a theatrically weak moment in the Orlando text was a theatrically weak one in his own'.

Neville F. Newman considers 'Shakespeare's *King Lear* (*Expl* 60:iv[2002] 191–3), focusing on the relationship between Cornwall and Edmund, and partly that between Edmund and Gloucester. He maintains that Cornwall's brief relationship is of a significance that extends far beyond a question of the older man's cupidity. It makes us 'contrast his willingness to assume the role of father with the overall

ineptitude of Lear and Gloucester as father figures'. In another short article on
'Shakespeare's *King Lear*' (*Expl* 60:ii[2002] 60–2), Joy Kennedy refers to the use of
pre-Christian imagery in the play. Pointing to IV.vi, where Lear wears his crown of
weeds and flowers, Kennedy states that we may see a startling image of another
pagan figure, the Green Man. A symbol of fertility, the Green Man is one of the most
typical pre-Christian images in British history. Considering IV.vi.114–29, where
Lear enters the scene wearing the crown of weeds and flowers, Kennedy points to
the Lear-as-Green-Man possibilities. She suggests that a pagan image would have
presented itself to the Elizabethan audience during this scene. Yet Kennedy
considers both sides of the pagan versus Christian debate to be strengthened if Lear
is an image of the Green Man in Act IV.

In writing *King Lear*, Frankie Rubinstein posits in 'Speculating on Mysteries:
Religion and Politics in *King Lear*' (*RS* 16[2002] 234–62), Shakespeare created a
surrogate for sixteenth- and seventeenth-century England. Rubinstein explores
relations between the play and Shakespeare's England, pointing to the playwright's
possible despair at the religious and political intrigues in the courts of Queen
Elizabeth and James I, including Essex's rival court from the early 1590s until his
'rebellion', with its band of spies, its machinations and its jealousies. This,
according to Rubinstein, is Shakespeare's world as it is the world of *King Lear*. She
notes that religious issues, and their position in dynastic rivalry, are paramount in the
play, as in history. Specific phrases and metaphors and other 'mysteries' in the play
that can be related to political or religious conditions receive detailed treatment.
Rubinstein sees *King Lear* as 'a sardonic, Jacobean version of the medieval mystery
play'. Its religious irony and apparently irreverent levity 'are in direct proportion to
the falsity it wants to expose and the corrosive nature of the religious and political
bigotry with which it deals'.

Interpretation (29:ii[2002] 171–85) has an article by Zdravko Planinc on '... this
scattered kingdom': A Study of *King Lear*'. Planinc maintains that Shakespeare has
written the play in such a fashion 'that it deliberately subverts any attempt by its
audience to find comfort in the theatrical fallacy'. As spectators we are refused any
distance or sense of escape from the worst, and are compelled to face it. Planinc
finds that many political lessons can be learned from *King Lear*, and the play can be
viewed as being directly relevant to the political and religious conditions in which it
was written. Pointing out that the rudimentary materials for the aesthetic form of the
play are different types of source-texts, including less immediately evident classical
and biblical texts, Planinc notes that it is 'through studying the place and function of
these occulted source-texts in the unique aesthetic form of *King Lear* that the most
difficult aspects of the play's unsettling, and even shocking, depiction of the worst
may be brought to light'. Its deepest insights, according to Planinc, emerge in
approaching the way in which Lear is described 'crawl[ing] toward death' (I.i.40).
The play's aesthetic form is a macrocosmic description of this line. Lear's desire to
master his own end detrimentally affects his soul to such a degree that love is almost
destroyed, and he is changed to a pitiful old fool going mad. In an act of penance he
crawls to Dover, only to have Cordelia hanged before his eyes. The symbolism of
the final episode of Shakespeare's macrocosmic depiction of Lear's dying
(V.iii.268–9), is, in Planinc's view, taken from the crucifixion, but in this case
nothing redeems it.

In 'The Mystery of Walking' (*JMEMS* 32[2002] 571–80) Peter Stallybrass employs Oedipus and the riddle of the Sphinx to say something significant about *King Lear*. Observing that the riddle of the foot has been forgotten in *King Lear* as well as in *Oedipus Tyrannus*, Stallybrass points out that as Lear is dividing up his kingdom, he is presumably booted, recalling that the legs of a monarch are 'appropriated legs: the legs upon the horse on which he rides'. Still, as he uncrowns himself and divides up his kingdom, 'Lear already half grasps the significance of his feet and of walking'. The passage at I.i.36–40 can be seen as Lear rewriting the riddle of the Sphinx, as he will go from two legs, not to three, but to four. The taking off of Lear's boots (in IV.vi.166–9), which, as Stallybrass points out, within early modern aristocratic circles requires the help of another person, is quite suggestive. In doing this, 'Lear both materializes his dependence upon others and unprepares his body for action'. It is paradoxical, therefore, that, at the moment of greatest crisis, Lear will not only walk again but carry the burden of Cordelia's dead body.

David Gervais has written about 'Shakespeare and Night: *The Dream*, *Macbeth* and Racine' (*English* 51[2002] 15–25). His purpose is 'to suggest how "night" figures in some of Shakespeare's poetry rather than to treat it as a sort of abstract category of academic discourse'. The following discussion makes leaps into several texts as well as *Macbeth* and *A Midsummer Night's Dream*, and one sometimes feels the absence of a more concentrated focus on the specific plays. Gervais finds *Macbeth* at its most vivid in the sleep-walking scene, revealing the two Lady Macbeths: one subdued by evil, the other frail and vulnerable. In *Macbeth* we feel haunted by the forces of evil beyond what Macbeth himself does, for in Shakespeare night is there in its own right, enveloping the human world. Racine's *Phèdre*, the tragedy Gervais compares Shakespeare's work with, 'is more exact as to the causes and effects of the tragedy'. In Gervais's view, Racine stresses 'the moral and social status of Phèdre in a way that *Macbeth*, with its storms and witches, is less concerned to foreground'. There is more room for the unexpected and uncertain in Shakespeare than in Racine, Gervais adds, and this may explain the fact that Shakespeare's tragedies contain so much of the unpredictable spirit of comedy.

In 'Shakespeare De-Witched: A Response to Stephen Greenblatt' (*Connotations* 11[2002] 60–77), Inge Leimberg offers a response to Greenblatt's article 'Shakespeare Bewitched' (in *New Historical Literary Study* [1993], 108–35), which focuses on Shakespeare's unique contribution to the problem of witchcraft and witch prosecution. In Leimberg's words, 'according to Greenblatt the leading role the witches play in *Macbeth* makes the historical and the histrionic coalesce and the critic gets a chance to elucidate the dramatist's techniques and purposes by seeing the play in the light of the non-fictional literature on the subject'. Leimberg finds Greenblatt's position convincing in many respects, as he shares the latter's view that the critic should look for facts and texts belonging to the practical as well as intellectual life of a poet's era that may further our understanding of poet and period. But, while largely agreeing with Greenblatt in theory, Leimberg in practice disagrees with him on matters concerned with literal and figurative meaning, with finding the place where theatre and the demonic are constructed, and with exploring the relationship between the Weird Sisters and witchcraft. For example, she refers to Lady Macbeth's pronouncement: 'Hie thee hither, | That I may pour my spirits in thine ear' (I.v.25–6). Greenblatt says that 'The spirits she speaks of here are manifestly figurative', a view Leimberg strongly objects to. She also disagrees with

Greenblatt on the implications of the term 'witchcraft' as applied to *Macbeth*. Furthermore, Leimberg fails to go along with Greenblatt when he sees an etymological rather than a semantic link between the weird sisters and fate in his interpretation of II.iii.117–19 (Greenblatt, p. 125), and she objects to seeing fate, as used here, as an 'abstraction'. To Leimberg fate, in the context of *Macbeth*, denotes 'not an abstraction but a demonic power related to the Weird Sisters in a semantic as well as in a seminal way'.

Albert Rolls writes about '*Macbeth* and the Uncertainties of the Succession Law' (*SNL* 52:ii[202] 43–4, 48). Using Duncan's decision to establish his state upon his 'eldest, Malcolm' (I.iv.35–9) as a point of departure, Rolls thinks some of those watching the play would have found Shakespeare's allusion to the laws of succession quite intriguing in view of the Elizabethan succession controversy. More importantly, Rolls shows that, according to Holinshed, ancient Scottish law denied a minor, which Malcolm was, the right to become king. If Duncan died immediately, Malcolm could not become king without breaking the established law of the realm. Shakespeare's Macbeth might therefore be counting on the legal questions that Malcolm's succession would raise. Rolls sees II.i.25–6 as Macbeth's allusion to a future debate over who should become king. The fact that Macbeth is apparently planning to challenge Malcolm's claim suggests that Shakespeare's Malcolm, like Holinshed's, is a minor. Following Alvin Kernan, Rolls reminds us that, prior to Duncan, the Scottish Crown was not entirely hereditary, so Shakespeare is dramatizing the change in Scottish law that transformed the monarchy into a hereditary one. Rolls discusses to what extent kings had absolute rule. He points out that, prior to the sixteenth century, the king could be regarded as *the* political body or as the head of the political body. This medieval theory of monarchy allowed the lawyers to distinguish between the king who was a subject under the law and the king who was above the law. Following Edward Forset, Rolls finds that Duncan has consulted with his 'choisest advisours' before he changes the law, but this does not necessarily mean that Duncan has gained the consent of these advisers. As the play calls attention to the difficulties that may be caused by Duncan's innovation, it may suggest that he lacks this consent.

Steve Sohmer comments on '"The Moone is downe"': A Note on *Macbeth* and a Query' (*N&Q* 49[2002] 231–4). Referring to *Macbeth* II.i.1–3, particularly Fleance's speech 'The Moone is downe', Sohmer asks whether Shakespeare erroneously ascribed the murder of Duncan to the night of 13–14 August 1046, while the night of 13–14 August 1606 would have been the anniversary of the event which brought the Stuarts to the throne of Scotland and England. Sohmer finds that, thanks to an anomaly in the Julian calendar, the two monarchs, James I and his brother-in-law Christian IV of Denmark, were together on the anniversary of the events described in Act II of *Macbeth*. He finally asks whether anyone can provide evidence that King James and King Christian were together at Greenwich on the afternoon of 9 August, when the King's men might have performed *Macbeth* before them.

'Lady Macbeth and the Daemonologie of Hysteria' is the title of Joanna Levin's article in *ELH* (69:i[2002] 21–55). Levin sees Lady Macbeth in connection with the transformation of the demonic woman into the hysteric, which occurs 'through a rich confluence of political, religious, medical, and legal discourses'. This raises many questions for feminist analysis, such as how this shift affected the position of women in early modern Europe; how these patriarchal categories conceptualize (and manage) female power and agency; and the extent to which we can recuperate such categories for our own feminist politics. According to Levin, the witch, the bewitched, and the hysteric were synchronic categories, 'brought together under the auspices of a complex struggle for religious and political authority at the outset of King James's English reign'. In her article, Levin focuses on the Mary Glover case of 1602, Jorden's etiology, and Lady Macbeth's position of enacting the transformation of the witch into the hysteric. She maintains that Lady Macbeth would have been regarded as a witch according to the Witchcraft Statute of 1604. Levin relates Lady Macbeth to the transformation of the witch into the Mother, and this 'operates within the ideological parameters of a James-centered reading of the play'. In a Jamesian interpretation of *Macbeth*, the witches are part of the 'demonic opposition to godly rule that the rightful monarch must suppress in order to reveal his legitimacy'.

Theatre Journal has an article by Rebecca Lemon on 'Scaffolds of Treason in *Macbeth*' (*TJ* 54:i[2002] 25–43). Referring to the fact that treason plagues *Macbeth* from the opening, with the first Thane of Cawdor having betrayed King Duncan by the second scene of the play, and Malcolm confirming Cawdor's execution for treason by the fourth scene, Lemon has a closer look at the 'scaffold speech', recorded in chapbooks, ballads, and state papers, and delivered by prisoners prior to execution. By analysing Cawdor's execution in the opening scenes as a failure of didacticism, the essay focuses on *Macbeth*'s oppositional potential. For the traitor's speech does not advise Macbeth to avoid treason but virtually offers him a model for his own wicked desires. Cawdor's execution thus fails as an educational spectacle, and 'the staging of this familiar genre of confession before death complicates the articulation of truth in the play'. The result is a mixture of legitimate sovereignty and treasonous deception, producing in Malcolm a leader who combines the values of traitors and sovereigns.

Andrew Hadfield discusses '*Macbeth*, IV.iii.140–158, Edward the Confessor, and Holinshed's *Chronicles*' (*N&Q* 49[2002] 234–6). While the principal source for Shakespeare's history plays was the second edition of Holinshed's *Chronicles of England, Scotland and Ireland* [1587], Hadfield finds that some key passages of that text which were probably used by the dramatist have been under-used by commentators. A case in point is the history of the reign of Edward the Confessor found in volume 1, pp. 186–202. The scene reveals a striking contrast between the cautionary tactics of Malcolm, who, just like Henry V, secretly prepares himself for government and thus discovers who he can trust, and Macduff, who takes no such precautions. There is a pointed contrast between Edward's piety and the way Malcolm must behave in order to rule Scotland. The episode, Hadfield suggests, may well reflect on James's situation. A ruler should be more cunning and artful than a king like Edward, and by implication, Elizabeth, and resemble Malcolm, who having protected himself and his country by being a wise politician, not a saint, can reveal his inherent worth as a king. As Hadfield suggests, *Macbeth* might seem to represent Edward as a type of king that James had better not copy.

Studies in English Literature (*SEL* 42:ii[2002] 335–59) has an article by Alex Garganigo on '*Coriolanus*, the Union Controversy, and Access to the Royal Person'. It is only *Coriolanus*, with its fable of the belly, that explicitly examines the body politic as a theoretical problem, and as a discourse characteristic of the first years of James I's reign, Garganigo observes. In his essay he first considers the place of James's body in discussions of his Union plan and patronage system around the time of the publication of *Coriolanus*, probably in 1607–8. He then examines the relationship of the play in its entirety and the belly fable specifically to these issues by seeing parallels between republican Rome and Jacobean England, as well as between various characters and King James. Thirdly, the essay focuses on the play's exploration of the relationships between the body of the state and the bodies of several characters, particularly Coriolanus. Garganigo then shows that the logic of the royal patronage system influences the play's scenes of supplication, and also the relationship between Coriolanus and Aufidius. Finally, he returns to the belly scene, speculating on the role of such a topic and arguing that in the final analysis the play rejects the body politic metaphor as a means of public discourse.

Clark Lunberry has written an article entitled 'In the Name of *Coriolanus*: The Prompter (Prompted)' (*CL* 54:iii[2002] 229–41). He focuses on the point at which Coriolanus stands accused of mocking the people and is asked to once more seek their approval, whereupon his supporter Cominius simply says, 'Come, come, we'll prompt you' (III.ii.107). The essay turns on the presence of the prompter and the prompted voice in *Coriolanus*. Attributions, distributions, beginnings and endings of the voice are 'repeatedly refined, re-found, and refocused'. Coriolanus, the hero-character, resists and repels all promptings, insisting on speaking only for himself and detesting the thought of having others tell him how and when to speak, and what to say. Reluctantly he is temporarily persuaded to return to the marketplace. When he is required to speak, Coriolanus cannot be prompted, but has to 'speak what's in his heart' (III.iii.28–9). In focusing on Coriolanus, Lunberry finds profitable parallels with Derrida's Artaud: neither of them could abide any notion of a prompter. Lunberry further observes that Coriolanus, of all Shakespeare's major characters, is probably the least loquacious. It is not only prompted language that needs to be resisted, but language in general seems to be suspect. As a matter of fact, the play's neglect, or even dismissal, by critics may in part be due to Coriolanus's relative lack of eloquence. Lunberry further traces the development of the play towards its close, stressing the fact that for Coriolanus there is no world outside Rome, but the price paid for its preservation is Coriolanus's own noble self.

(g) Last Plays

Of all Shakespeare's late plays, *The Tempest* again remains the ground over which most critical battles were fought. Although less work than in previous years was published in this particular field, the work done remains committed to assessing the political and aesthetic qualities of the play and, increasingly, to musing over its own nature as a site of critical conversation. Much of Jonathan Goldberg's work this year centres around *The Tempest*. Continuing a theme found in the criticism of recent years, his *Generation of Caliban*, the 2001 Garnett Sedgewick Memorial Lecture (Ronsdale), gives a consideration of the new historicist interpretations (and misinterpretations) of the play that shows that this issue, and the place of this particular Shakespearean work, is still alive in the consciousness of North American and British critics. Dealing with the representations and readings of Caliban, Sycorax, and discourses of sexuality, Goldberg relates the play to discourses of colonialism through a discussion of the Barbadian novelist and critic George Lamming and his *Pleasures of Exile* [1960], 'in which the relationship of Prospero and Caliban is used throughout as a shorthand for the relationship of colonizer to colonized' (p. 8). Relating Lamming's work to Greenblatt's later well-known essay, 'Learning to Curse', Goldberg points out 'the belatedness of New Historicist interpretations of the play' (p. 8). In fact, in his consideration of the 'place where queer theory and post-colonial interventions may meet' (p. 16), Goldberg is really involved in a critique of later readings of the play.

Goldberg's investigation into this most debated of Shakespeare's late plays continues in 'The Print of Goodness' (in Turner, ed., *The Culture of Capital: Properties, Cities, and Knowledge in Early Modern England*, pp. 231–54). Focusing on Miranda's only speech to Caliban (that beginning 'Abhorrèd slave', I.ii.354–65), Goldberg's article, as described by the editor, anticipates 'Enlightenment discourses of race typical of Kant and Hegel, discourses that postdate early modernity but can be seen to take root in the colonialist encounters of the period' (p. 10). Beginning with the early editorial assignment of this speech to Prospero rather than to Miranda (of which more below), the essay moves to the effects of the speech itself through a careful tracing of the word 'race' and its meanings. Interrogating Miranda's self-scripted position as Caliban's teacher, and what she describes as Caliban's failure to be taught, Goldberg traces the meanings of 'race' through its early modern associations with lineage and animals (bouncing interestingly off Erica Fudge's recent work) to see Miranda's particular use of 'race', in which she categorizes herself as 'human' and Caliban as 'savage', as gesturing towards later Enlightenment interpretations. This Goldberg sees as vastly heightening the impact of Shakespeare's vocabulary, declaring that 'lines like the ones I am examining cannot be cordoned off to some historically remote regime' (p. 234) but rather that their meanings reverberate through and influence contemporary, later, and current readings. The essay concludes with a move through Spivak's recent rereading and problematizing of Kant's oeuvre, and so back to the 'unnameable "it" within Caliban's race that renders him incapable' of learning as Miranda's speech states that he should (p. 240).

This same speech is also the subject of consideration in Sharon O'Dair's *Class, Critics, and Shakespeare: Bottom Lines on the Culture Wars*, which, in common with Goldberg's, is concerned less with Shakespeare's plays themselves than with the ways in which they are deployed, in particular by critics and members of academia. In her reading of Miranda's speech, O'Dair is concerned with the idea of pedagogy and with Shakespeare's position in the discourses surrounding late twentieth-century ideas of education, the academy, and the relationship of those within it to those outside it. In this book, Shakespeare is a tool for argument rather than for sustained critical engagement, but this is a book of lively and committed polemic which lays down a challenge for those of us involved in the academy and its pursuits. In a classic deconstructionist move, O'Dair argues that, despite the ongoing debates over the admission of certain kinds of minorities to higher education and over the kinds of cultures that are studied in such educational institutions, the exclusion of one kind of minority, 'the working class and the poor' (p. 3), is actually intrinsic to the aims of higher education. She writes: 'In the academy, working-class identity is not merely not affirmed, but actually erased' (p. 3).

O'Dair seeks to combine analysis of class in Shakespeare's plays and in early modern England with that of class in the academy and 'in this society' (p. 17). It is here that one criticism can be made of O'Dair's work, in that it is based intensely in the America of its day and, given the powerful focus of its gaze, it finds it hard to look beyond that culture. At certain moments, the book attempts generalizations which try, usually less than successfully, to invoke 'Europe' to back up points about the US. One such moment comes in chapter 2, when the author argues that 'professors' hold an unequivocally high social status, equivalent to that of 'physicians and federal court judges' (p. 25). While probably accurate for North America, this is written with the detachment of someone removed from current crises in the British higher education system where the status of the academic (if not, perhaps, the professor) has been greatly undermined in the wake of successive Conservative and New Labour governments. Further, one benefit of a wider scope would have been the opportunity to discuss one British counterpoint to O'Dair's discussion of the US academy's denigration of the working classes—their romanticization in the face of the particular loathing of many British academics for what O'Dair would call their 'upper-middle-class' backgrounds. For the most part, though, O'Dair doesn't try to range further than the US system, which is clearly a subject quite complex enough to justify her focus. The most obvious criticism, though, is to ask whether O'Dair herself is not replicating the same patterns of the intellectual dictation of cultural programmes to the working class. This criticism itself depends uneasily upon a notion of authenticity but, nevertheless, there are moments in O'Dair's book when it seems as though she has set up a closed system from which she cannot break out.

Her discussion of *The Tempest*, which takes place in chapter 2, '"Burn but his books": Intellectual Domination in *The Tempest*', works with and against recent arguments concerning the academy and the 'culture wars' by John Frow, John Guillory, and Bruce Robbins. Using the discourses of pedagogy and education embedded in Miranda's speech to Caliban, alongside the rebellious figures of Stephano and Trinculo, she considers these characters as emblematic of school students who 'intentionally reproduce themselves as uneducated workers, contemptible in their habits of dissipation, in persisting in doing what they know— or should know—is not in their interests' (pp. 26–7). O'Dair maps the play's embedded discourses of education and rebellion against it onto a reading of *The Tempest*'s status in the wider context of criticism. She sees, with Howard Felperin, that 'colonialist readings of *The Tempest* are not new' (p. 31), but rather that this recent preoccupation is a 'second flowering' of the 'first, pro-imperial set of readings produced in the middle to late nineteenth-century' (p. 31). In examining this second wave, however, she concludes that the convergence of critical interest with 'the moment when the interest of African and Caribbean intellectuals faded' (pp. 31–2) is not coincidental. O'Dair further sees the play as documenting both racial oppression and the class oppression often occluded within post-colonial politics and in particular through the workings of education and intellectuals. She writes that 'mostly white, upper-middle-class American literary critics' (p. 34) will blame Prospero's island hegemony on almost everything—'imperialism, sexism, racism, or capitalism' (p. 34)—except education, knowledge, and learning. Reading Prospero as a tyrannical intellectual who has brought his dukedom low and so lost it to his brother, O'Dair sees Caliban's response to this figure of knowledge and education not, significantly, as a wish to appropriate that learning (figured emblematically in Prospero's books), but to destroy it. 'Seize, possess, burn; it is populism's message, the message of those who distrust and resent both educated and moneyed elites, elites who presume, paternalistically, to determine for the masses what is in [their] best interests' (p. 36). Caliban's famous speech on learning to curse is read as an anatomization of the uses of education for most workers, an outline of 'the costs of book learning ... not just the benefits' (p. 37). And she concludes that Prospero's own acknowledgement of Caliban could be a paradigm for the US academy whose members, she argues, should recognize the 'pain' of the American worker. The book is a polemic which seeks to speak from both within and outside the academy, and which speaks—as such books always do—only to the academy. It does not offer a radical reinvestigation of Shakespeare's plays or the canonical standing of the works, but it is an engaged and committed argument which speaks eloquently of what Russell Jacoby has called the troubling 'gentrification of higher education' (p. 41) and as such deserves attention.

Moving on to articles, but staying with *The Tempest*, the prize for the worst pun in a journal article goes to David Lucking for his essay 'Our Devils [*sic*] Now Are Ended: A Comparative Analysis of *The Tempest* and *Dr. Faustus*' (*DR* 80:ii[2000] 151–67). The content is effectively described by the title: although it takes as its premise the shared examination of 'the problem of knowledge' (p. 151) between the two plays, it attempts nothing like the scope of O'Dair's argument and does little more than move point by point to remark on similarities without drawing many conclusions from those resemblances. Similar in scope though rather more efficient in execution is Lewis Walker's article, 'Chaucer's Contribution to *The Tempest*: A Reappraisal' (*RenP* [2000] 119–35). Again, carrying out the task explained in the title, the author traces the echoes of Chaucer's *Franklin's Tale* in Shakespeare's play, arguing that this is the point at which Shakespeare's 'sensitivity to source appropriation' became more 'spacious' (p. 120). One weak moment, however, comes when Walker suggests that the 'description of Prospero "*on the top*"' parallels the use in the *Franklin's Tale* of theatrical jargon in connection with the creation of an illusion' (p. 124), ignoring the fact that this is a stage direction and that plays, including *The Tempest*, will inevitably be involved in the use of 'theatrical jargon'. More interesting, and certainly pithier, is Bryan Crockett's 'From Pulpit to Stage: Thomas Playfere's Influence on Shakespeare' (*N&Q* 49[2002] 243–5), which similarly seeks out further sources for Shakespeare's play. This time, the potential source identified is the eponymous Jacobean preacher whose sermons make allusion not only to shipwrecks but also to disasters which courtiers stand idly by and watch. From these echoes of the play's first scene, Crockett argues that a further source for *The Tempest* has been found to stand beside the pamphlets on the wreck of the *Sea Venture*.

Attention remained fixed on *The Tempest* and, to some extent, on the assignation of Miranda's speech to Caliban in I.ii (also discussed by Goldberg and O'Dair) in Richard Proudfoot's 'New Conservatism and the Theatrical Text: Editing Shakespeare for the Third Millennium' (*ShIntY* 2[2002] 127–42). This elegant and pithy summary of many of the debates surrounding Shakespearian editing in the twentieth century walks a delicate line between old and new practice with grace and respect for each, a balance summed up in Proudfoot's statement that the twentieth-century publication of Shakespearean facsimiles was 'one real achievement of the New Bibliography and ... the indispensable tool of its opponents' (p. 131). His interest in the late plays becomes clear when he uses passages from *The Tempest* as an extended example of another careful balance, that attempted in the Arden third series between literary and theatrical texts and the complexities of dealing with a literary edition of a theatrical text. The solution to this he sees not as 'archaeology' but rather a 'spirit of attentive questioning' (p. 135). As part of this, Proudfoot discusses the assignation of *The Tempest*'s 'Abhorrèd Slave' speech (I.ii) to Miranda, as in the First Folio. He sees many of the arguments over Miranda speaking the lines as 'circular' (p. 139), while recognizing that those on either side of the debate see the others' arguments as 'rationalization' (p. 139). In the end, though, he decides that the speech should be given to Prospero, but sees gender politics, and in particular the gender politics of theatre, as a reason why this is unlikely to happen, since in the current theatrical climate 'no actress worth her salt is going to put up with the loss of one of her only four speeches of more than ten lines, and a speech in which she can give forceful expression to anger against her would-be rapist' (p. 139). In the absence of definitive answers, and in the knowledge of the contingency of all editorial decisions and their dependency upon the discourses of the moment, Proudfoot concludes that 'The aim of responsible editing thus becomes one of defining the issues with care and indicating the degree of the editor's confidence in any disputed textual decision' (p. 139). I would suggest that Proudfoot perhaps needs to think more widely about the nature of theatre—experimental theatre companies using cross-casting and doubling, for instance, might find themselves under very different pressures than those he describes—but that on the whole his answer is fitting for the kind of market served by Arden. And in the consideration of the late plays it is always salutary to remember that the foundations upon which we build our increasingly complex arguments—the texts—are built on sand.

Editorial investigations into the late plays continued with Elizabeth F. Hart's 'The "Missing" Scene in Act 2 of *Pericles*' (*ELN* 40[2002] 4–12). Hart discusses the problem of a seemingly missing musical scene from the 1609 'bad' quarto of *Pericles*. Noting that the Oxford edition supplies and versifies the equivalent prose passage from George Wilkins's novella, *The Painfull Adventures of Pericles Prince of Tyre* [1608], she argues that this is not necessary since in Shakespeare's *Pericles* language stands in for the literal performance of music in other sources, such as Gower. She therefore concludes that 'the "missing" scene of Pericles' musical performance is not missing at all but has been subsumed into a network of poetic references whose purpose, at least in part, is to transform the rhythms of prose narrative into drama' (p. 10). Thus, Hart sees the example of the "missing" scene as supporting charges against the Oxford editors, Gary Taylor and MacDonald P. Jackson, that they have taken undue liberties with the playtext. One other exploration of *Pericles* is Deanne Williams's 'Papa Don't Preach: The Power of Prolixity in *Pericles*' (*UTQ* 71[2002] 595–622). This sophisticated, wide-ranging, and engaging article also assesses the textual history of the play, dealing with the 1609 'bad' quarto 'on its own terms, as a legitimate artifact' (p. 596), and through this considers the nature of incest in the play, seeing it as more pervasive than authorship debates and the consequent separation of the play into discrete sections had previously allowed. Perhaps Williams's most interesting statement concerns the position of Marina in the play, and in the reconciliation scene in particular. Reading Marina's rhetorical powers as the saving grace of the reunion, she argues that this character's discursive powers offer her the same freedom and protection as that afforded to Shakespeare's earlier heroines by cross-dressing, and that, in contrast, Marina's protection is not stripped from her with her male clothes at the play's conclusion.

There was less work on Shakespeare's other late plays in 2002. Contributions included David Houston Wood's '"He something seems unsettled:" Melancholy, Jealousy, and Subjective Temporality in *The Winter's Tale*' (*RenD* 21[2002] 185–213). Investigating the ever-compelling issue of Leontes' jealousy and extreme actions against his queen and friend, Wood reads the protagonist's actions through the figure of the humoral body and, in particular, through the notion of 'subjective temporality' (p. 186), which he sees as being influenced by the nexus of the psychological and the social within the speaking subject. In addition to Wood's article, *The Winter's Tale* is the subject of two other articles. The first, by Stanford S. Apseloff, is 'Shakespeare's Giulio Romano: *The Winter's Tale*' (*ShN* 52[2002] 87), which focuses on the mention of the eponymous artist in V.ii. Providing a biography and historiography of Romano, and emphasizing his standing as the 'creator of the first famous erotic pictures', he tracks Romano's pictures, their engravings, and Aretino's accompanying sonnets to Shakespeare through, among other sources, Jonson's *Volpone*. He concludes, in a move which does not distance his investigations from work recently carried out by Stephen Orgel, that the reference to Romano is an 'in-joke'. Shakespearean afterlives and appropriation are the subject of the second article, Judith Barbour's 'Garrick's Version: The Production of "Perdita"' (*WW* 9[2002] 125–38). Barbour investigates the resonances of the name 'Perdita' as they were applied to the eighteenth-century actress Mary Robinson, who played the role in David Garrick's 1778 and 1779 productions and who used the name as an authorial signature to her *Memoirs*. Barbour traces what she defines as Robinson's perceived fall from Perdita to Cressida and shows how, through the web of associations between Robinson, Sheridan, and the Prince of Wales, the name 'Perdita' itself became associated with 'general odium' (p. 130).

In contrast, male sexuality is the focus of one of the few articles discussing *Cymbeline*. In '"The city's usuries": Commerce and *Cymbeline*' (*JRMMRA* 19[1998] 229–44), Goran V. Stanivukovic offers a materialist reading of the convergence of early modern masculinity and male sexuality with discourses of commerce in Shakespeare's play, seeing this as confined only to the male characters. He defines his subject as the 'the male anxieties in *Cymbeline* for the stability of masculinity, and the construction of male erotic identity within the public sphere of economy, which conflicts with the imperial and heroic aspects of the play' (p. 280). Although rather heavily dependent upon the work of Bray and Sedgwick, this makes an interesting if rather inconclusive argument.

I conclude with a brief mention of Joe Nutt's *An Introduction to Shakespeare's Late Plays*. Although this is a schematic and often conservative book intended primarily for upper-lever school pupils, Nutt pays enough close attention to the plays to be useful for introductory-level undergraduates who need experience in the close reading of Shakespeare's dramatic works.

Books Reviewed

Anderson, Linda, and Janis Lull, eds. *'A Certain Text': Close Readings and Textual Studies in Shakespeare and Others*. UDelP. [2002] pp. 208. $41.50 ISBN 0 8741 3789 6.

Aspinall, Dana E. ed. *The Taming of the Shrew: Critical Essays*. Routledge. [2002] pp. xii + 388. £70 ($110) ISBN 0 8153 3515 6.

Baker, David J., and Willy Maley, eds. *British Identities and English Renaissance Literature*. CUP. [2002] pp. xvii + 297. £42.50 ISBN 0 5217 8200 7.

Bevington, David. *Shakespeare*. Blackwell. [2002] pp. x + 250. hb £17.77 ISBN 0 6312 2718 0, pb £12.99 ISBN 0 6312 2719 9.

Brown, John Russell. *Shakespeare and the Theatrical Event*. Palgrave. [2002] pp. viii + 237. £14.99 ISBN 0 3338 0132 6.

Buhler, Stephen M. *Shakespeare in the Cinema: Ocular Proof*. SUNYP. [2002] pp. xii + 213. hb £42.50 ($59.50) ISBN 0 7914 5139 9, pb £15.50 ($19.95) ISBN 0 7914 5140 2.

Burrow, Colin, ed. *The Complete Sonnets and Poems*. The Oxford Shakespeare. OUP. [2002] pp. ix + 750. £65 ISBN 0 1981 8431 X.

Burt, Richard, ed. *Shakespeare After Mass Media*. Palgrave. [2002] pp. 336. hb £42.50 ($69.95) ISBN 0 3122 9453 0, pb £16.99 ($26.95) ISBN 0 3122 9454 9.

Coursen, H. R. *Shakespeare in Space: Recent Shakespeare Productions on Screen*. Lang. [2002] pp. 200. $29.95 ISBN 0 8204 5714 0.

Cunningham, Karen. *Imaginary Betrayals: Subjectivity and the Discourses of Treason in Early Modern England*. UPennP. [2002] pp. 213. £30 ISBN 0 8122 3640 8.

Da Cunha Resende, Aimara, and Thomas La Borie Burns, eds. *Foreign Accents: Brazilian Readings of Shakespeare*. UDelP. [2002] pp. 232. £32.95 ISBN 0 8741 3753 5.

Day, Gillian. *King Richard III: Shakespeare at Stratford*. Arden. [2002] pp. xiii + 259. £15.99 ISBN 1 9034 3612 5.

Deats, Sara Munson, and Robert A. Logan, eds. *Marlowe's Empery: Expanding his Critical Contexts*. UDelP. [2002] pp. 209. $40 ISBN 0 8741 3787 X.

Dessen, Alan C. *Rescripting Shakespeare: The Text, the Director, and Modern Productions*. CUP. [2002] pp. xi + 268. £16.95 ISBN 0 5210 0798 4.

Drakakis, John. *Alternative Shakespeares*, 2nd edn. Routledge. [2002] pp. 288. $19.70 ISBN 0 4152 8723 5.

Forker, Charles R., ed. *King Richard II*. ArdenSh. Thomson Learning. [2002] pp. xviii + 593. £7.99 ISBN 1 9034 3633 8.

Foulkes, Richard. *Performing Shakespeare in the Age of Empire*. CUP. [2002] pp. x + 235. £45 ISBN 0 5216 3022 3.

Gilbert, Miriam. *The Merchant of Venice: Shakespeare at Stratford*. Arden. [2002] pp. xv + 183. £15.99 ISBN 1 9034 3613 3.

Goldberg, Jonathan. *Generation of Caliban*. 2001 Garnett Sedgewick Memorial Lecture. Ronsdale. [2002] pp. 36. $8.95 ISBN 0 9218 7093 0.

Grene, Nicholas. *Shakespeare's Serial History Plays*. CUP. [2002] pp. xvii + 278. £45 ISBN 0 5217 7341 5.

Gross, John, ed. *After Shakespeare*. OUP. [2002] pp. xiii + 360 hb £17.99 ISBN 0 1921 4268 2, pb £12.99 ISBN 0 1928 0472 3.

Harris, Jonathan Gil, and Natasha Korda, eds. *Staged Properties in Early Modern English Drama*. CUP. [2002] pp. 358. $70 ISBN 0 5218 1322 0.

Hattaway, Michael, ed. *The Cambridge Companion to Shakespeare's History Plays*. CUP. [2002] pp. xvii + 283. hb £45 ISBN 0 5217 7277 X, pb £15.99 ISBN 0 5217 7539 6.

Hawkes, Terence. *Shakespeare in the Present*. Routledge. [2002] pp. x + 162. hb £60 ISBN 0 4152 6195 3, pb £16.99 ISBN 0 4152 6196 1.

Holderness, Graham. *Visual Shakespeare: Essays in Film and Television*. Hertfordshire UP. [2002] pp. 212. hb £35 ISBN 1 9028 0616 6, pb £14.99 ISBN 1 9028 0613 1.

Honigmann, E. A. J. *Shakespeare: Seven Tragedies Revisited*. Palgrave. [2002] pp. 288. $23.95 ISBN 0 3339 9582 1.

Kastan, David Scott, ed. *King Henry IV Part 1*. ArdenSh. Thomson Learning. [2002] pp. xvii + 398. £7.99 ISBN 1 9042 7135 9.

Kerrigan, John. *On Shakespeare and Early Modern Literature: Essays*. OUP. [2001] pp. 226. £40 ISBN 0 1992 4851 6.

Knowles, Ronald. *Shakespeare's Arguments with History*. Palgrave. [2002] pp. 235. £50 ISBN 0 3339 7021 7.

Kolin, Philip C. ed. *Othello: New Critical Essays*. Routledge/Garland. [2002] pp. 432. £65 ($95) ISBN 0 8153 3574 1.

Korda, Natasha. *Shakespeare's Domestic Economies: Gender and Property in Early Modern England*. UPennP. [2002] pp. 275. £35 ISBN 0 8122 3663 7.

Lanier, Douglas. *Shakespeare and Modern Popular Culture*. OUP. [2002] pp. ix + 187. hb £25 ISBN 0 1981 8703 3, pb £12.99 ISBN 1 1981 8706 8.

Leggatt, Alexander. ed. *The Cambridge Companion to Shakespearean Comedy*. CUP. [2002] pp. xviii + 237. hb £45 ($65) ISBN 0 5217 7044 0, pb £15.99 ($22) ISBN 0 5217 7942 1.

Lehmann, Courtney. *Shakespeare Remains: Theater to Film, Early Modern to Postmodern*. CornUP. [2002] pp. xiv + 267. hb £35.50 ($45) ISBN 0 8014 3974 4, pb £12.99 ($19.95) ISBN 0 8014 8767 6.

Lehmann, Courtney and Lisa S. Starks, eds. *Spectacular Shakespeare: Critical Theory and Popular Cinema*. FDUP. [2002] pp. 248. £39 ($42.50) ISBN 0 8386 3910 0.

Loehlin, James N. *Romeo and Juliet*. CUP. [2002] pp. 286. £47.50 ISBN 0 5216 6769 0.

Loomba, Ania. *Shakespeare, Race, and Colonialism*. OUP. [2002] pp. xi + 192. hb £25 ISBN 0 1987 1175 1, pb £12.99 ISBN 0 1987 1174 3.

McAlindon, Tom. *Shakespeare's Tudor History: A Study of Henry VI, Parts 1 and 2*. Ashgate. [2001] pp. x + 225. £45 ISBN 0 7546 0468 3.

McEachern, Claire. *The Cambridge Companion to Shakespearean Tragedy*. CUP. [2002] pp. 292. hb $65 ISBN 0 5217 9009 3, pb £15.95 ISBN 0 5217 9359 9.

Mahon, John W., and Ellen Macleod Mahon, eds. *The Merchant of Venice: New Critical Essays*. Routledge. [2002] pp. xiv + 456. £65 ISBN 0 4159 2999 7.

Moisan, Thomas, and Douglas Bruster, eds. *In the Company of Shakespeare: Essays on English Renaissance Literature in Honor of G. Blakemore Evans*. FDUP. [2002] pp. 360. $57.50 ISBN 0 8386 3902 X.

Morris, Leslie, and Jack Zipes, eds. *Unlikely History: The Changing German-Jewish Symbiosis, 1945–2000*. Palgrave. [2002] pp. x + 335. hb £45 ($75) ISBN 0 3122 9389 5, pb £14.99 ($24.95) ISBN 0 3122 9390 9.

Nutt, Joe. *An Introduction to Shakespeare's Late Plays*. Palgrave. [2002] pp. 176. £40 ISBN 0 3339 1462 7.

O'Dair, Sharon. *Class, Critics, and Shakespeare: Bottom Lines on the Culture Wars*. UMichP. [2000] pp. 176. $18.95 ISBN 0 4720 6754 0.

Pfister, Manfred. ed. *A History of English Laughter: Laughter from Beowulf to Beckett and Beyond*. Rodopi. [2002] pp. x + 201. pb £22.70 ($35) ISBN 9 0420 1288 9.

Schalkwyk, David. *Speech and Performance in Shakespeare's Sonnets and Plays*. CUP. [2002] pp. x + 262. hb £45 ($60) ISBN 0 5218 1115 5.

Shaughnessy, Robert. *The Shakespeare Effect: A History of Twentieth-Century Performance*. Palgrave. [2002] pp. ix + 221. £45 ISBN 0 3337 7937 1.

Siemon, James. *Word Against Word: Shakespearean Utterance*. UMassP. [2002] pp. xiii + 335. $39.95 ISBN 1 5584 9354 9.

Sipiora, Phillip, and James S. Baumlin, eds. *Rhetoric and Kairos: Essays in History, Theory, and Praxis*. SUNYP. [2002] pp. xii + 258. $23.95 ISBN 0 7914 5233 6.

Sorelius, Gunnar, ed. *Shakespeare and Scandinavia: A Collection of Nordic Studies*. UDelP. [2002] pp. 213. £31.50 ISBN 0 8741 3806 X.

Starks, Lisa S., and Courtney Lehmann, eds. *The Reel Shakespeare: Alternative Cinema and Theory*. FDUP. [2002] pp. 298. £39 ($49.50) ISBN 0 8386 3939 9.

Tatspaugh, Patricia E. *The Winter's Tale: Shakespeare at Stratford*. ArdenSh. [2002] pp. xv + 240. £15.99 ISBN 1 9034 3616 8.

Taunton, Nina. *1590s Drama and Militarism: Portrayals of War in Marlowe, Chapman and Shakespeare's Henry V*. Ashgate. [2001] pp. vii + 239. £47.50 ISBN 0 7546 0274 5.

Turner, Henry S., ed., *The Culture of Capital: Properties, Cities, and Knowledge in Early Modern England*. Routledge. [2002] pp. 256. £17.99 ISBN 0 4159 2925 3.

Vickers, Brian. *'Counterfeiting' Shakespeare: Evidence, Authorship, and John Ford's 'Funerall Elegye'*. CUP [2002] pp. xxvii + 568. hb £55 ($80) ISBN 0 5217 7243 5.

Vickers, Brian. *Shakespeare, Co-Author: A Historical Study of Five Collaborative Plays*. OUP. [2002] pp. xviii + 558. £65 ISBN 0 1992 5653 5.

Warren, Roger, ed. *King Henry VI Part 2*. The Oxford Shakespeare. OUP. [2002] pp. xx + 319. £45 ISBN 0 1981 3000 7.

Wells, Stanley, and Sarah Stanton, eds. *The Cambridge Companion to Shakespeare on Stage*. CUP. [2002] pp. xvi + 322. £15.95 ISBN 0 5217 9711 X.

Whitworth, Charles ed. *The Comedy of Errors*. The Oxford Shakespeare. OUP. [2002] pp. viii + 232. £45 ISBN 0 1981 2933 5.

Wilson, Richard. *Julius Caesar*. Palgrave. [2001] pp. 254. $65 ISBN 0 3337 5466 2.

VII

Renaissance Drama: Excluding Shakespeare

SARAH POYNTING, PETER J. SMITH, MATTHEW STEGGLE AND DARRYLL GRANTLEY

This chapter has three sections: 1. Editions and Textual Scholarship; 2. Theatre History; 3. Criticism. Section 1 is by Sarah Poynting; section 2 is by Peter J. Smith; sections 3(a) and (c) are by Matthew Steggle; and section 3(b) is by Darryll Grantley.

1. Editions and Textual Scholarship

Last year's editorial drought has continued, with only one single edition, one collection aimed at undergraduates, and the Malone Society volume to review this year. The individual edition is particularly welcome, in giving us the first full critical edition of John Ford's play *Love's Sacrifice*, edited by A.T. Moore for the Revels series from ManUP. Moore's edition is based on the only contemporary printing of the play, a quarto publication in 1633 for which, he argues persuasively, Ford himself was responsible. Moore has been conservative in his editing of this text, reinstating readings altered by nineteenth-century editors, and in particular reversing their attempts at regularization of the metre. The italics used for emphasis in Q, which he regards as Ford's own, are, however, not retained, but recorded in the collation together with any of this edition's variants from the copytext, as well as those introduced by earlier editors. The critical footnotes are (as always in this series) very helpful. The introduction focuses on the date, sources, and staging of *Love's Sacrifice*. Moore suggests on the basis of internal textual evidence, the play's likely sources, and its possible influence on Shirley's *Love's Cruelty*, that the most likely period for its writing was 1626–31. Much of this argument is unavoidably speculative, and in an argument about dating I found it distracting that he is repeatedly inaccurate concerning the year of Henrietta Maria's performance of Montagu's *The Shepherd's Paradise*. The discussion of sources is thorough, examining in particular *Othello*, *Romeo and Juliet*, Massinger's *The Duke of Milan* and *The Roman Actor*, works by Sidney, and the 'Gesualdo story', further evidence for which is contained in an appendix which has a translation of the relevant sections of the manuscript version of the story and a detailed comparison between manuscript and play. Other possible allusions to (or borrowings from) plays by Webster, Middleton, and Heywood are also considered. Moore's main interest, however, is in the staging of the play at the Phoenix, and his critical discussion is embedded within an analysis of how it might have been performed there, based on the belief that Inigo Jones's drawings for an unidentified indoor theatre (held at Worcester College) are for that theatre. Again, the evidence for this is looked at in an appendix. This exploration of performance helpfully draws together the play's textual and visual aspects, while also bringing out its ambiguities and interpretative possibilities, including those suggested by other critics, whose views are further examined in a section on responses to it. Disappointingly, though, there is almost no consideration of any context for *Love's Sacrifice* beyond the immediate theatrical one.

English Renaissance Drama: A Norton Anthology, edited by David Bevington, Lars Engle, Katharine Eisaman Maus, and Eric Rasmussen, is so large and so comprehensive as certainly to be worth adding to the increasingly long list of such volumes for recommendation to undergraduates, even if it seems unlikely that many of its intended readers will get through all twenty-seven plays. Most of the works that one would expect to find are here, along with a couple that are slightly less predictable, though the selection clearly (and frustratingly for those of us who would like to be able to persuade students that the Caroline period is worthy of study) reflects the editors' view that 'most of the greatest plays were written between 1585 and 1625' (p. xviii): *The Spanish Tragedy, Endymion, Friar Bacon and Friar Bungay, Tamburlaine Part 1, Doctor Faustus* (A-text), *The Jew of Malta, Edward II, Arden of Faversham, The Shoemaker's Holiday, The Malcontent, The Tragedy of Mariam, Volpone, Epicene, The Alchemist, Bartholomew Fair, The Knight of the Burning Pestle, The Maid's Tragedy, The Woman's Prize, The Revenger's Tragedy, The Roaring Girl, A Chaste Maid in Cheapside, Women Beware Women, The Changeling, The White Devil, The Duchess of Malfi, A New Way to Pay Old Debts, 'Tis Pity She's a Whore*. Each play has been edited from original Folio or quarto copy-texts, with departures from them recorded in notes which also summarize any problematic textual history. Explanatory notes are very brief, single words or phrases being glossed in the margin, while passages requiring a longer paraphrase or explanation are footnoted. These notes, though useful, are not comparable with those found in a full critical edition or even in most cheap student editions such as New Mermaid or the Revels students' series. Individual historical and critical introductions to the plays are also necessarily short (mostly four to five pages in length), and sometimes show a tendency to tell their readers how they ought to respond to, and think about, the work under discussion. However, they do present succinct summaries of key contextual and critical approaches. More substantial is the general introduction by Katharine Maus and David Bevington, who consider significant elements in both the theatrical and socio-historical contexts of early modern drama, linking these to the plays contained in the volume. They look at the position of the theatre and playwrights in relation to material conditions of production and more general social developments; changes in theatrical language; and major themes to be found in drama. These include 'Pushy People' (a heading they might have had second thoughts about), 'Class, Commerce, and Consumption', 'Sex, Marriage, and Gender', 'Religion', and 'Performance and Print'. The discussion of concepts of class is especially useful, but religion deserves a fuller and more nuanced consideration than space allows for here.

The Malone Society volume for this year is a facsimile edition by Leah Scragg of Lyly's *Sapho and Phao*, reproduced very clearly from the quarto now in the Huntington Library, one of only three surviving copies of the first edition of 1584. The introduction has a detailed and scrupulous account of the printing of the play, as well as of the second and third editions and their variants, and of its appearance in a 1632 collection of six of Lyly's plays in which he is named as author for the first time. Scragg also discusses the introduction of one of the prologues from *Sapho and Phao* into the second quarto of *The Knight of the Burning Pestle* (1635), the play's authorship and dating, and the marketing strategy of the publishers in aiming the quarto at an elite readership. She concludes with a brief consideration of critical approaches to the play, particularly in relationship to the Elizabethan court.

The dearth of new editions was only marginally compensated for by the number of articles, most of which were of very specialist interest. Of most general interest was MacD. P. Jackson's 'Determining Authorship: a New Technique' (*RORD* 41[2002] 1–14), in which he outlines a more rigorous method of authorship attribution than could be achieved before the LION (Chadwyck-Healey's Literature Online) database was available. This method is chiefly applicable where there is a small number of candidates for authorship of a play or passage within a play, each of whom was the sole known author of several plays, though ways are suggested of overcoming the distorting effects of canon size. The technique involves searching the database for linguistic minutiae, phrases and collocations, and the method is demonstrated in relation to *A Cure for a Cuckold* and two passages from *Titus Andronicus*. It is further shown in action in Gary Taylor's 'Middleton and Rowley— and Heywood: *The Old Law* and New Attribution Technologies' (*PBSA* 96[2002] 165–217). Taylor considers in detail the evidence for the involvement of Thomas Heywood as the third hand in the play rather than Massinger, who is named on the title-page of the 1656 first quarto. He examines the external evidence of theatre and company before turning to Jackson's technique of LION searching and *OED* comparisons to look at the internal evidence for authorship, and argues on the basis of both of these that Heywood's claim to have written the opening of Act V is stronger than anyone else's. He also considers, more speculatively, whether the evidence points to collaboration or later adaptation. In '*The Old Law* or *An Old Law*?' (*N&Q* 49[2002] 256–8) Taylor examines the evidence for the intended title of the play, named as *The Old Law* in the 1656 edition, but which he suggests should be *An Old Law* on the grounds of a scrap of paper apparently bearing a reference to it as such, found in a manuscript belonging to Sir George Buc, Master of the Revels, who was (unlike Edward Archer, the publisher of the printed edition) generally very reliable in his recording of play titles. This change in title would have further implications for spectators or readers in guiding them in their approach to the questions raised by the play.

Issues of dating arise twice this year. An interesting piece by Matthew Steggle, 'Redating *A Jovial Crew*' (*RES* 53[2002] 365–72), explores the possibility that Richard Brome's play, normally dated to spring 1641, might actually have been written as late as March 1642, since Brome generally dated the year in the English way as beginning on 25 March rather than 1 January. This would solve the particular problem of the play's performance at the Cockpit at a time when it was probably being managed by Brome's enemy, Davenant. More significantly, the action of the play, with aristocrats deserting their centres of power, has much more obvious relevance to the political circumstances of early 1642 than 1641, while the sense of crisis in the prologue is also more appropriate to that period. In 'George Villiers, Duke of Buckingham, and the Dating of Webster and Heywood's *Appius and Virginia*' (*N&Q* 49[2002] 324–7), David Gunby and Hester Lees-Jeffries recognize that there is no evidence by which the play can be exactly dated, but suggest that two passages seem precise in their references. These contain complaints by soldiers about their pay being held back by their leaders, and about the lack of food reaching them, which led F.L. Lucas to suggest that Buckingham was being aimed at in the figure of Appius. Gunby and Lees-Jeffries point out other possible covert allusions to the duke, which imply a likely date of 1626 for the writing of the play. Gunby's thoughts on this play can also be found in 'Webster and Heywood's *Appius and Virginia*: Further Borrowings from Livy' (*N&Q* 49[2002] 258–9), in which he discusses Lucas's footnote references in *The Complete Works of John Webster*, and argues that the playwrights' reliance on Livy was much more extensive than Lucas realized. Footnotes come under consideration as well in Richard Levin's 'Counting Sieve Holes in Jonson and Hobbes' (*N&Q* 49[2002] 249–51), in which he proposes a solution to a problematic reference unexplained by Herford and Simpson in their notes on *The Entertainment at Althorp* (lines 67–70), in which Jonson writes of fairies leading midwives 'With a siue the holes to number'. Levin finds the answer in *Leviathan*, in which Hobbes lists counting holes in a sieve amongst other methods of predicting the future.

In Katherine Rowe's 'Memory and Revision in Chapman's *Bussy* Plays' (*RenD* 31[2002] 125–52), her discussion of the theme of memory and retrospection in *Bussy D'Ambois* is linked to the textual history as well as the dramatic action of the play. She suggests that textual variation illuminates the interplay between 'dramatic convention, audience expectation, and changing social forms'. In considering the variations between the editions of 1607 and 1641, she challenges the idea of memorial reconstruction used by Nicholas Brooke to explain their differences as contrary to what is known about early modern mnemonic practices, and rejects it for its allegiance to biographical memory. This yoking together of theories of memory with textual theory is thought-provoking, but not, for me, entirely persuasive.

Finally, I had no idea what to expect from the title 'Editing: A Can of Worms' (*Library*, 7th series, 3[2002] 199–200), except possibly a piece of rather frightening polemic. I was, then, charmed, to find a witty poem by Ashley Chantler about editorial anxiety, which, being cumulative in its effects, unfortunately does not lend itself to a short quotation; but I recommend it to anyone who has ever struggled with decisions on variant versions, punctuation marks, and life.

2. Theatre History

While the masque has received a good deal of critical attention in recent times thanks to the contributions of Stephen Orgel, David Lindley, John Peacock, and so on, and while this work has concentrated on the ideological effects of this ostentatiously rarefied and obsequious genre, the contribution of women to the staging and interpretation of the masque has remained obscure. This is all the more remarkable given the subsequent and conspicuous arrival of the female player in the theatre after 1660. Clare McManus's *Women on the Renaissance Stage* finds the

Restoration actress's precursor in the Stuart masque and attributes a good deal of agency to 'the powerful expressivity of the Jacobean female masquer' (p. 211), in spite of the fact that she is almost always silent. The volume is subtitled *Anna of Denmark and Female Masquing in the Stuart Court (1590–1619)*, and carefully charts the involvement of the queen (whether performing or commissioning, dancing or spectating) and the importance of the courtly context generally, in terms of aristocratic etiquette for instance, as well as particular historical circumstances which shed further light on specific stagings. Early on McManus rightly and delicately distinguishes between acting, that is, the assumption of another self, which was 'clearly considered detrimental to the status of the courtier' (p. 7), and masquing, which demanded 'neither the effacement of self nor the adoption of an alternative identity' (p. 9). Throughout, the emphasis is on the performance of masque rather than merely its script since, as she firmly asserts, 'critical privileging of its literary text creates a false impression of its form' (p. 19); however, the obvious difficulty arises out of the desire to reconstruct an ephemeral form (and remains unsolved). Moreover the agency attributed to the masquing women always takes place within (and is thus curtailed by) the hierarchical court since, as McManus acknowledges at the outset, 'female performance was possible among the elite of the age only because it was dependent upon the courtly norms and regulations of aristocratic behaviour' (p. 6). Indeed, frequently McManus can be seen to be struggling to attribute much power to female masquing, circumscribed as it is within the patriarchal conventions of Jacobean culture. In her account of Jonson's *Masque of Blackness*, for instance, she emphasizes 'the connection between blackness and femininity as markers of otherness and difference' (p. 77) and asserts that foreign women 'embodied the threat of the other' (p. 90), but this over-reliance on the vague idea of marginality is insufficient to demonstrate that the masque may have aroused such anxieties in its contemporary audience. Indeed some of her performance analyses are simply subjective; for instance, McManus asserts that the bringing together of male transvestite and female body in the masque 'led to a clear distinction being made' (p. 99) between them. But might not the opposite have occurred, that is that the boundaries between male and female might have been confused or blurred? This, after all, is the effect of the gender-bending taking place on the public stage (witness Shakespeare's comedies, for instance). Perhaps not, but certainly this is just as reasonable a hypothesis as McManus's. Elsewhere, the author finds an almost mystical significance in Anna wearing Elizabeth's hand-me-downs during *The Vision of the Twelve Goddesses*: 'The recycling of earlier costumes and the appropriation of a past physical presence could be interpreted as the possession of the dead queen and her corporeal actuality' (p. 108). But what can this mean: that the audience saw Anna as a resurrected Elizabeth? Might they not have seen her as partaking in Elizabeth's regal potency or even merely (though less likely) as a thrifty and practical woman? At such moments, McManus does seem to overplay her hand. Though focused on performance, McManus is too frequently side-tracked by theoretical jargon. There is much on the dynamics of the male gaze (pp. 35–6, 47–8, 51, 53, 55, 104–6, etc.) though nothing at all by way of explanation of the technical dance terms used. What exactly is a 'branle' and how might it compare to a 'pavan'? And while the choreography may require the dancer to figure forth a series of letters, thus spelling out the monarch's name, in what way can it be said that 'the body itself became language' (p. 39) or that such a dance 'textualised the body and made it language' (p. 37)? What can it mean to assert that *Vision* 'after all, is a masque which presented the female body as a readily readable text' (p. 106)? At such moments, McManus seems seduced by her own critical rhetoric.

These flaws aside, there is much original and effective work here. The figuring of James as a questing knight in the aftermath of his mission to Norway to collect his bride in 1589, as well as the mythologizing of Prince Henry as a Protestant hero, are particularly well handled, as is the importance of the masques' various locations— Greenwich, Hampton Court, the Banqueting House, and so on. The gradual marginalization of Anna's influence, signalled by Thomas Campion's *Somerset Masque* [1613]—'unmistakably opposed to the policies and performances of Anna and her court' (p. 178)—is the book's most persuasive section and, despite her eventual marginalization, McManus convincingly demonstrates that Anna's 'loss of power came at the end of a career of oppositional political engagement, cultural agency and dissident performance' (p. 203). Typical of both the book's achievements as well as its tendency to overstate its case is the account of Inigo Jones's design for Anna's funeral catafalque. McManus offers an astute explication of its iconography, reading it as subversive of James's Protestant authority; yet, just as she advances her case for the potency of this symbolic attack, she is forced to acknowledge that 'it is not certain that Jones's design was actually used' (pp. 205–6). Might not its lack of use have resulted from its seditious iconography (in which case McManus's reading is all the more valid), or might its failure to appear render her argument merely academic since subversion, no end of subversion, behind closed doors, amounts to none for us? Unfortunately, McManus doesn't stop to say.

On the same topic is Melissa D. Aaron's 'Tethys Takes Charge: Queen Anne as Theatrical Producer' (*RORD* 41[2002] 62–74). In concentrated form, Aaron's mission is much the same as McManus's inasmuch as both wish to attribute a theatrical role to the queen well in excess of that she is traditionally seen to occupy: 'Anne has been thought of as a patron, but could she not be thought of as a producer, a title that implies a more active role?' (p. 62). Aaron's analysis, while running along the same lines as that of McManus, is a good deal less subtle. She attributes Anne's marginalization to 'perhaps more than a touch of sexism and chauvinism which looks askance at the idea of a queen, and a foreigner at that, producing anything of value' (p. 63), though this sounds unlikely and she offers no specific sources for such prejudice. In the same vein, the idea that Anne has been eclipsed from the creation of *The Masque of Blackness* by 'Ben Jonson's massive ego' (p. 64) is overstating the case. What the essay does have to offer, though, are some intriguing hints as to the level of Anne's involvement in the staging of Samuel Daniel's *The Vision of the Twelve Goddesses*, notably Daniel's own remarks on her contribution which 'gave it so fair an execution as it had' (cited here on p. 66)—though might this not equally be conventional flattery? The description of Anne's character as 'all directing Pallas' is adduced by Aaron as indicating a particularly active part.

The essay also examines Anne's role as official patron of the Queen's Men and the Children of the Queen's Revels. Following a production of Daniel's satirical *Philotas*, the latter troupe ran into trouble with the Privy Council. Nevertheless, they went on to perform the satirical and particularly anti-Jacobean *Eastward Ho!* and *The Isle of Gulls*. Aaron writes, 'Paradoxically, the very freedom that the separate patronage of the Queen had given them probably encouraged them to go too far, until they were totally disbanded and reorganized again under a new management'

(p. 69). The essay continues with an examination of Daniel's *Tethys' Festival* (1610) and the 'collaboration' (p. 70), as Aaron reads it, of Anne and the masque's designer, Inigo Jones. This, she concludes, 'looks forwards to the active theatrical career of Henrietta Maria' (p. 71).

One might have expected to have found a review of Siobhan Keenan's *Travelling Players in Shakespeare's England* in section 2 of Chapter VI above, but in fact the attention paid to specifically Shakespearian matters is so small that it seems better included here—clearly this eponymous mention of Shakespeare is a marketing ploy. While the book's title slightly misleads, in the main it comprises a thorough examination of the variety of venues available to touring players, such as town halls, churches, country houses, inns, the universities, and marketplaces. Unfortunately, as Alan C. Dessen puts it in his *Rescripting Shakespeare* (which *is* reviewed in Chapter VI), 'I am painfully aware of the theatre historian's dirty little secret—how little we actually know about how these plays were first conceived and performed' (p. 237). Keenan is rather more circumspect and understated: 'Generalising about touring theatre in the period is ... difficult' (p. 165). Much of her book is thus hypothetical and necessarily hesitant: 'Predicting what kind and size of audience visiting players might have encountered *if and when* they performed at university colleges is difficult' (p. 126, my emphases); 'Whatever the name and genre of the play performed, it is likely to have been staged in costume and accompanied with props' (p. 142); 'some towns welcomed players, others turned them away' (p. 165); '*If* their platform was set up in a central location, the players *could have performed* completely "in the round", although it is *perhaps more likely* that spectators surrounded the platform on three sides at most' (p. 104, my emphases). The brutal truth is that the REED volumes, upon which so many of Keenan's assertions depend, offer in many places the most tantalizingly incomplete data. While, on the one hand, *Travelling Players* defiantly claims to be 'the first extended published study of provincial English theatre' (p. xv), its vaunted provincialism is also the root of its indeterminacy since unquestionably part of the motivation for touring was the avoidance of the centralized and therefore more efficient metropolitan restrictions on theatre. As Keenan herself puts it, 'players were well known for their canny, opportunistic ability to circumvent restrictions when determined to perform' (p. 34). What the book offers, then, is a glimpse into a shadowy world that is by turns fascinating and frustrating.

It must be said that in places Keenan labours the obvious. Clearly the touring of a troupe of actors named after a patron disseminated and promoted that patron's name in a way not dissimilar nowadays from the corporate sponsorship of artistic events (though the comparison is mine rather than Keenan's). Nor is she particularly earth-shattering when she tells us that 'travelling players' performances proved popular in many regional English communities, often attracting large audiences' (p. 21). However, the book is at its strongest when discussing the variety and details of possible venues, in particular the symbolic import of playing within certain spaces. For instance, Keenan insists on the prestige conferred on the actors by granting them permission to play in town halls: 'they were symbolically performing at the heart of the community' (p. 27). Ecclesiastical prohibitions on playing led to a decline in its frequency in the particularly sensitive spaces of churches and churchyards, although this is part and parcel of a general decline in the number of touring productions which she identifies as taking place throughout the Stuart period. On the other hand,

'Noble patrons and their country houses could play a significant role in provincial dramatic culture' (p. 86) as well as promoting plays seen otherwise only in the capital.

The rarity of purpose-built theatres outside London led to the exploitation of other more common premises, such as drinking places, although the rise of Puritanism and Sabbatarianism, especially in regions such as east Kent, brought about increasing disapproval and 'prohibitive legislation regarding entertainment' (p. 93). In the university towns, opposition to the players intensified from the late sixteenth century onwards. Whether the university authorities were attempting to prevent students being distracted from their studies, the spread of plague, disorder, or damage to university property is not known, but anti-theatricalism was supported by the Earl of Leicester (Chancellor of Oxford), and in 1593 'both universities received a Privy Council letter authorizing a ban on professional public plays within five miles of their institutions' (p. 117). The university practice developed of offering the players money to leave *without* performing. One such troupe bought off in this way was that belonging to Leicester himself!

In Keenan's final chapter, she examines the regional variations in the popularity of this 'gratuity' payment and she notes its correlation with areas of Puritanism such as Devon and Norwich. However, she quite rightly qualifies this by adding, 'In many cases the impetus to regulate or prevent play performances appears to have been pragmatic rather than moral or religious' (p. 177). The tightening of legislation, the establishment of the Stationers' Register and its deployment as a mode of control on new plays, as well as the increasing professionalization of metropolitan theatre, were other contributory factors in the decline of the travelling player outside London throughout the Stuart period. In her eloquent conclusion, Keenan suggests that this decline is 'both a herald of and a contributory factor in the demise of the theatrical culture associated with the Renaissance stage'. Studying this degeneration of regional touring is thus 'a way of enhancing our understanding of the process by which the playing practices and conventions of the Restoration stage emerged from and superseded those of the Shakespearean stage' (p. 185). In its contribution to a greater stage history Keenan's achievement is obvious, but this is a book that is remarkable and important in its own right. (The second edition must eliminate the annoying mixture of imperial and metric measurements, as on pages 110 and 111.)

In a heavyweight essay, Rebecca Rogers and Kathleen E. McLuskie set out to answer the question, 'Who Invested in the Early-Modern Theatre?' (*RORD* 41[2002] 29–61). Their essay is prompted by a dissatisfaction with the state of recent scholarship: 'actual consideration of the economic underpinning of the playing companies has been, at best, ad hoc' (p. 29). Through a number of case studies they establish the 'diversity of investment strategies employed by early modern-playing companies' (p. 54) and document the increasing involvement of non-theatrical investors brought about by the bequeathing of shares to dependants who may have had nothing directly to do with the companies or the theatres. Among such purely commercial investors they note a high proportion of clothing merchants and food vendors. Rogers and McLuskie move on to a consideration of the establishment and maintenance of business networks. Collaboration in a business venture is commonly associated with familial relationships as well as geographical proximity which, in turn, may indicate a shared trade. While the increasing popularity of the theatre demanded the emergence of new economic relations and regulations, the phenomenon of investors sharing trades is reminiscent of the guilds. Thus, they conclude, 'Despite the evident innovation and commercial experimentation undertaken by the theatrical entrepreneurs and companies, it is clear that the older regulatory systems affected the evolution of playing groups' (p. 54). As with so much else in the period, the theatre looked both forwards and backwards.

Robert Reeder, '"You are now out of your text": The Performance of Precocity on the Early Modern Stage' (*RenP* [2001] 35–44), contends that 'the early modern stage was an arena for precocious display' (p. 36), and he examines several instances, including young York in *Richard III*, Cesario in *Twelfth Night*, and the puppets in *Bartholomew Fair*. Of the exchange regarding his uncle's weapons (*Richard III*, III.i) Reeder insists that York 'can grasp mentally, even if he cannot carry physically, the sword that lies before him' (p. 39). While Buckingham and Richard attribute the child's intelligence to coaching by his mother, York's wit 'hovers somewhere between the impressively developed and the externally conferred' (p. 40). Reeder goes on, 'The tension is also present for the child actor: what is his relationship to the words he speaks?' In an effort to answer this question, he turns to the puppets in *Bartholomew Fair*, whose 'display', he contends, 'represents that of a child actor' (p. 41). The proof is not easy to follow, but Reeder is keen to demonstrate an analogy between the puppet master and the puppets on the one hand, and the playwright and the boy actor on the other. This inspiration is part of the theatrical experience itself. Of the willow cabin speech, Reeder asserts, 'If Cesario is a kind of persona for the boy actor, his sudden burst of eloquence celebrates the precocity theater can bestow' (p. 44). Much virtue in that 'if'.

Bartholomew Fair's puppets reappear in 'Boy Actors and the Semiotics of Renaissance Stagecraft' (*RenP* [2001] 45–56) by Thomas L. Martin and Duke Pesta, wherein they take issue with Stephen Orgel, Phyllis Rackin, Lisa Jardine, and others who have suggested that the boy actor constitutes a site of erotic play. Taking the Prologue to *Henry V* as illustration, the authors argue that the theatre foregrounded the artificiality of the dramatic representation as well as the contract between player and audience which relied on the latter's imaginative contribution. Moreover, 'the Elizabethans were quick to parody those incapable of willingly suspending disbelief' (p. 48). Thus the puppet play in *Bartholomew Fair* 'ridicules those who misunderstand or seek to misrepresent the fundamental nature of dramatic art' (p. 49). As he engages the puppets in argument, Zeal-of-the-Land Busy is shown to be participating in the theatricality they represent even as he attempts to reject it. As such he becomes a victim of the theatre's fictionality at the very point at which he denounces it. This, Martin and Pesta contend, is the position of those critics who, 'with an overly theoretical and postmodern cast of mind, insist on seeing through theatrical conventions, not observing them' (pp. 55–6).

3. Criticism

(a) General

This survey begins with a group of book-length studies which range widely across the field of Renaissance drama. Claire Jowitt's *Voyage Drama and Gender Politics, 1589–1642: Real and Imagined Worlds* studies the early modern genre of voyage drama, tracing its interactions with differing concepts of empire and nation and arguing that allegory, in various senses, provides a central component to these plays, particularly when it comes to portrayals of female power. Jowitt considers the impressively numerous travel dramas of the period set out in her title, starting with plays such as Peele's *The Battle of Alcazar* and the anonymous *Famous Historye of the Life and Death of Captaine Thomas Stukley*, and running through works by Fletcher, Heywood, Rowley, Massinger, and others before an excellent concluding examination of Brome's *The Antipodes* in terms of gender politics. Russell West's *Spatial Representations and the Jacobean Stage: From Shakespeare to Webster* shares something of Jowitt's interest in geography, broadly defined, but applies it to spaces of all sorts, not just the long distances of travel drama. Defining Jacobean theatre as an 'ostentatiously spatial art-form', West relates that drama to a social and political context in which many of the central political conflicts, such as enclosure, vagrancy, and social mobility, can be seen in some ways as spatial problems. Informed by a battery of recent work on ideas of theoretical and theatrical space, West applies his approach to Jacobean texts including court masques, city comedies, and travel drama.

Not previously reviewed in *YWES* is Michael Neill's *Putting History to the Question: Power, Politics and Society in English Renaissance Drama*. This collection of essays, many previously published, shows the range and power of Neill's historicist criticism, a criticism remarkable in particular for the respect it pays to the evidence, and for its sensitivity to the sheer complexity of early modern literature. Readers of *YWES* will want to know that, in addition to several essays on Shakespeare, other essays in this collection focus on the language of status in *Arden of Faversham*; the social vision of Massinger's *A New Way to Pay Old Debts*; the treatment of charity in Massinger's *The City-Madam*; bastardy, counterfeiting, and misogyny in *The Revenger's Tragedy*; and fantasies of temperance and empire in Fletcher's *The Island Princess*, a reading interesting to set against that of Jowitt in her book discussed above. But this is to undersell the range of Neill's reference, since the book also includes briefer discussions of many other Renaissance plays, including *The Changeling*, which features at length in an excellent essay on the ways in which servants are imagined on the Renaissance stage. In addition, this is more than a collection of individual essays, since many connections between them are evident.

When it comes to work on specific authors, first and foremost must come the author whom Virginia Woolf identified as one of the most prolific and successful on the early modern stage: namely, Anon. In 'Dramatic Authorship and Publication in Early Modern England' (*MRDE* 15[2002] 77–97), Douglas A. Brooks reviews the statistical evidence concerning attribution of printed drama in this period. He argues that neither the Foucauldian idea that the rise of the author is linked to political transgression, nor Elizabeth Eisenstein's argument that the modern author is a product of the rise of the printing press, is entirely adequate for describing the decline of anonymously printed drama through this period. Incidentally, this forms an interesting pair with an article by Benedict Scott Anderson, 'Thomas Heywood and the Cultural Politics of Play Collections' (*SEL* 42[2002] 361–80), which discusses Heywood's abortive attempts in the 1630s to publish a collection of his plays in the context of changing attitudes to the printing of dramatic texts.

One of Anon.'s many Tudor texts, the 1550s university comedy *Gammer Gurton's Needle*, is analysed by Curtis Perry in 'Commodity and Commonwealth in *Gammer Gurton's Needle*' (*SEL* 42[2002] 217–34). Whereas previous studies have tended to focus on the scatology of this text, Perry relates it to contemporary political thinking, arguing that it engages with the politics associated with the 'commonwealth men' of mid-century Cambridge, and critiques an emerging commodity culture symbolized by the needle itself. Also related to early Tudor drama is an article by Ursula Potter, 'Tales of Patient Griselda and Henry VIII' (*ET* 5:ii[2002] 11–28), which contextualizes John Philip's one known play, *The Commody of Pacient and Meek Grissill*, written at some point between 1558 and 1565. Potter, too, argues for a contemporary political relevance in this play, dramatizing as it does the conflicts between the roles of royal wife and royal mother, and evoking as it seems to do the career of Elizabeth's own mother Anne Boleyn.

Lyly is studied in two articles this year, both of which argue that, in different senses, his works are more subversive than has previously been recognized. While the eponymous central character of his play *Midas* has generally been considered as implicitly representing Philip of Spain, Annaliese Connolly, in '"O unquenchable thirst of gold": Lyly's *Midas* and the English quest for Empire' (*EMLS* 8:ii[2002]), argues that the play is more complicated than this, offering instead 'a complex set of responses to Anglo-Hispanic relations' (p. 1) and to English constructions of self and empire. On the other hand, the sexual politics of *Gallathea* are the focus of an essay by Mark Dooley, 'Inversion, Metamorphosis, and Sexual Difference: Female Same-Sex desire in Ovid and Lyly' (in Stanivukovic, ed., *Ovid and the Renaissance Body*, pp. 59–76). Dooley situates the play relative to Ovid and to Renaissance discourses of female sexuality, arguing that in the end it offers a 'radical alternative to heterosexual marriage' (p. 73).

In the field of Kyd studies, one should start with Lukas Erne's important book *Beyond the Spanish Tragedy: A Study of the Works of Thomas Kyd*, which reviews the extent of the Kyd canon and argues for the importance of lesser-known works by this author. However, the journal literature continues to focus on Kyd's acknowledged masterpiece. Kevin Dunn's '"Action, passion, motion": The Gestural Politics of Counsel in *The Spanish Tragedy*' (*RenD* 31[2002] 27–60), discusses the play relative to contemporary emblematic representations of the ideal counsellor, and the paradox of the 'conciliar myth of self-cancellation' (p. 43). Cinta Zunino Garrido, 'Rhetoric and Truth in *The Spanish Tragedy*' (*SEDERI* 12[2001] 341–8) notes the inconsistency of the various accounts given of Don Andrea's death, relating these accounts to Erasmian ideas of *copia* and to Terence Cave's argument that the idea of *copia* can expose the referential inadequacies of language. Pointing out that Kyd and Spenser were at school together, Frank Ardolino assesses 'The Influence of Spenser's *Faerie Queene* on Kyd's *Spanish Tragedy*' (*EMLS* 7:iii[2002]). Reading Kyd's play through Spenser, Ardolino draws attention to such repeating motifs as the idea of Truth as a daughter of Time, and to the paradoxical treatment of randomness and destiny.

Dekker continues to invite historicist readings of the social world he portrays. Michelle M. Dowd's 'Leaning Too Hard Upon the Pen: Suburb Wenches and City Wives in *Westward Ho*' (*MRDE* 15[2002] 224–42) situates the play within early modern discourses of housewifery in general and urban housewifery in particular. Dowd argues that the play explores anxieties about female household power, with particular reference to female education, financial decision-making, and sexual indiscipline. If the wives within the play do not make full use of this power, then that can be read, in Foucauldian terms, as the emergence of a self-disciplining female subjectivity: but, argues Dowd, the anxieties cannot be put so easily to rest in this play. Ivan Cañadas, 'Class, Gender and Community in Thomas Dekker's *The Shoemaker's Holiday* and Lope de Vega's *Fuente Ovejuna*' (*Parergon* 19[2000] 119–50) compares Dekker's play to Lope de Vega's drama, written 1612–14, concerning a peasant uprising in Andalusia. In particular, both offer sympathetic portrayals of a community of common people: and both plays pit that community against their betters in a conflict inflected by sexual rivalry. Cañadas focuses on the homosocial bonds of the community on display in Dekker's drama, differentiating it from the more heterosocial bonds of the Spanish play.

Gender relations in Dekker do, however, loom large in Barbara Kreps's 'The Paradox of Women: The Legal Position of Early Modern Wives and Thomas Dekker's *The Honest Whore*' (*ELH* 69[2002] 83–102). Kreps's starting point is the perpetual tension inherent in the fact that early modern marriage, like its modern counterpart, creates both a site of licensed sexual activity and an economic unit. Kreps reviews early modern marriage theory and common-law ideas on the economic position of wives, before applying them to *The Honest Whore*, which exposes the contradictions and problems in these ideas of the nature of marriage. Claire Jowitt's 'Political Allegory in Late Elizabethan and Early Jacobean "Turk" Plays: *Lust's Dominion* and *The Turke*' (*CompD* 36[2002] 411–43) discusses a text attributable, based on recent work by Charles Cathcart, to Dekker, Marston, Haughton, and Day. Jowitt's article links it to Mason's play *The Turke* [1607], since both of these plays, she argues, function not merely as representations of Turkishness but also as topical commentaries on the state of British politics: hence the depiction in *Lust's Dominion* of a succession crisis.

Also relating to the Marston canon, James P. Bednarz, 'Writing and Revenge: John Marston's *Histriomastix*' (*CompD* 36[2002] 21–52) is a rejoinder to Roslyn Knutson's article '*Histrio-Mastix*: Not by John Marston' (*SP* 98[2001] 359–77), reviewed last year. In his argument that *Histriomastix* should remain attributed to Marston, Bednarz makes some good points—particularly cogent is his discussion of the 1610 quarto in the context of Thomas Thorpe's other play-printing activities, from which perspective Marston certainly looks like a possible author of the play. And he points out the elusiveness of the evidence, since by common consent the play printed in 1610 could not have been acted as it stands around 1599–1601, when two of the plays associated with the War of the Theatres appear to allude to it. But Knutson's demonstration that the verbal links between *Histriomastix* and Marston are weak and conventional is not fully rebutted by Bednarz's reiterated argument that Chrisoganus is the first in a long line of figurations of Jonson's literary personality.

Meanwhile, Marston's *The Malcontent* is placed alongside Webster's *The Duchess of Malfi* and Middleton and Rowley's *The Changeling* by Katherine A. Armstrong, 'Possets, Pills And Poisons: Physicking the Female Body in Early Seventeenth-Century Drama' (*CahiersE* 61[2002] 43–56), who argues that all three plays share a concern with the unpredictable results of women's use of drugs to alter, in particular, their own bodies in various sexualized ways. According to Armstrong, this cultural anxiety offers 'an insight into Jacobean ideas of the female body' (p.

52), focused most of all in a realization that the most dangerous poison around may be the female body itself.

Two notes consider Webster and Heywood's *Appius and Virginia*, written *c*.1626. David Gunby's 'Webster and Heywood's Appius and Virginia: Further Borrowings from Livy' (*N&Q* 49[2002] 258–9) takes issue with F.L. Lucas on the subject of the play's sources. While Webster and Heywood drew mainly on Dionysius of Halicarnassus' account of the Virginia story, Gunby adduces evidence to show that they also made use of Livy. One moment where Webster and Heywood diverge from all their sources is in the inclusion of lengthy scenes describing famine in the camp. In 'George Villiers, Duke of Buckingham, and the Dating of Webster and Heywood's *Appius and Virginia*' (*N&Q* 49[2002] 324–6), David Gunby and Hester Lees-Jeffries argue that this reflects the disasters that befell English forces sent to help the Elector Palatine in 1624–6, and that the play draws a number of parallels between Appius and Buckingham.

Paulina Kewes, on the other hand, uses *Appius and Virginia* as a touchstone for discussion of another Heywood play set in the semi-mythic Roman past, *The Rape of Lucrece*. In 'Roman History and Early Stuart Drama: Thomas Heywood's *The Rape of Lucrece*' (*ELR* 32[2002] 239–67), Kewes argues that the thirty years of success enjoyed by this play should be read in the light of its depiction of popular resistance to royal tyranny. This politically radical account of the overthrow of an unjust monarchy certainly invites, Kewes argues, parallels between the Tarquins and the Stuarts. Moving from Heywood's history to his domestic tragedy, Michael McClintock writes on 'Grief, Theater and Society in Thomas Heywood's *A Woman Killed with Kindness*' (in Swiss and Kent, eds., *Speaking Grief in English Literary Culture*, pp. 98–118). He argues that both in the *Apology for Actors* and in this play Heywood understands 'theatrical affectivity'—the power of theatre to move spectators—as one of the important forces helping to integrate society, and that the women in the play function as almost iconic images of grief which affect, and reform, those around them. From domestic tragedy, on to Heywood's travel drama: Lisa H. Cooper, 'Chivalry, Commerce, and Conquest: Heywood's *The Four Prentices of London*' (in Perry, ed., *Material Culture and Cultural Materialisms in the Middle Ages and Renaissance*, pp. 159–76), borrows Benedict Anderson's terminology of 'imagined communities' to argue that this play sublimates class ambiguities by making its crusading brothers into 'two sides of a single social coin' (p. 174), at once both gentry and apprentice, as part of a fantasy of social coherence.

Middleton's most studied play this year was *A Chaste Maid in Cheapside*. Alizon Brunning's '"In his gold I shine": Jacobean Comedy and the Art of the Mediating Trickster' (*EMLS* 8:ii[2002]) puts the play alongside *Eastward Ho!* and *The Devil is an Ass*, among other city comedies, in the way that the trickster achieves a productive but illusory metamorphosis that recalls the Ovidian Golden Age. Janelle Day Jenstad, in '"The city cannot hold you": Social Conversion in the Goldsmith's Shop' (*EMLS* 8:ii[2002]), explores these same transformations from the point of view of early modern thinking about commerce, exchange, and the world as mint. In a third article on the play, Robert Irish discusses 'Using Entrances to Affect Audience Response in Middleton's *A Chaste Maid in Cheapside*' (*CahiersE* 61[2002] 57–74). Irish offers a structural analysis of the play in terms of the different types of entrance within it, arguing that such entrances determine who has control of the stage action, and that the audience's position—and therefore their sympathies—are most often aligned with the Touchwood brothers.

Gary Taylor's subject is the tragicomedy by Middleton and Rowley (and perhaps also Heywood) generally known as *The Old Law*. But, as his title asks, should it be '*The Old Law* or *An Old Law*?' (*N&Q* 49[2002] 256–8). Based on the handful of extant early references, and on comparisons to other similar play titles, Taylor smoothly argues the case for the second of these alternatives. Also on the edge of the Middleton canon is that splendidly disturbing celebration of necrophilia, *The Second Maiden's Tragedy*. In 'Animating Matter: The Corpse as Idol in *The Second Maiden's Tragedy*' (*RenD* 31[2002] 215–43), Susan Zimmerman explores this play's approach to 'the ontological status of the corpse' (p. 217), in the context of Renaissance attitudes to death and to idolatry.

George Ruggle's Latin comedy *Ignoramus*, performed in 1615, is an interesting and little-studied text. John Stone's 'Marriage Contracts and Farcical Consideration in *Ignoramus*' (*SEDERI* 12[2001] 331–40), considers the play's presentation of law, concluding that, rather surprisingly for a legal comedy, the concluding twist, in which a marriage contract is rendered invalid because the woman was betrothed to someone else as an infant, is legally nonsensical. Contracts also feature in Katherine Rowe's 'Memory and Revision in Chapman's Bussy Plays' (*RenD* 31[2002] 125–52), which examines 'the shifting connections between memory, emotion, and social debt' (p. 126) in the two *Bussy* texts, using Richard Schechner's terminology of 'restored behaviours' to argue that the differences between the texts are symptomatic of the gradual change from a status-based to a contract-based society.

A John Fletcher play, *The Prophetess*, is the star exhibit in an article by Jeanne Addison Roberts, 'The Crone in English Renaissance Drama' (*MRDE* 15[2002] 116–37). Roberts discusses treatments of old women in Renaissance drama across a wide range of texts from Kyd onwards, generally rudimentary and misogynistic, but culminating in the spectacular and semi-divine Delphia who gives Fletcher's play its title. A similarly pointed Fletcherian play title, *A King and No King*, certainly invites political application, and Zachary Lesser, in 'Mixed Government and Mixed Marriage in *A King and No King*: Sir Henry Neville Reads Beaumont and Fletcher' (*ELH* 69[2002] 947–77), notes that, in the play's later reception history, it was invoked as both a royalist and an anti-royalist text. But his article ultimately deconstructs these binary alternatives: as suggested by the more contemporary record of its approbation by Neville, this is a text which in fact offers a tentative reconciliation of opposites and a vision of mixed government.

Lesser's article goes interestingly with the year's main contribution on Massinger, Thomas C. Fulton's '"The true and naturall constitution of that mixed government": Massinger's *The Bondman* and the Influence of Dutch Republicanism' (*SP* 99[2002] 152–77). Like *A King and No King*, *The Bondman* (first acted around 1623) has a reception history in which it is used as a political tool: indeed, as late as the nineteenth century Coleridge characterized Massinger as a Whig, as against the Tories Beaumont and Fletcher. But Fulton's argument stresses the ways in which *The Bondman* can be seen as reaction to the impact of Dutch political thought in Jacobean England, and the ways in which this play, too, explores ideas of the nature of mixed government.

Government looms large, too, in Margaret Jane Kidnie's '"Enter ... Lorenzo, Disguised like an Amazon": Powerdressing in *Swetnam, the Woman Hater,*

Arraigned by Women' (*CahiersE* 62[2002] 33–46), since she draws attention to this anonymous comedy's interest in state power, in various senses. Kidnie's argument first shows that this play 'neutralizes feminist anger, or rather, mobilizes it as a means to recuperate patriarchal order' (p. 38) by casting Swetnam himself as a scapegoat whose expulsion unites the fictional society of the play: but that the very process by which Prince Lorenzo achieves this neutralization of feminist anger— disguising himself as an Amazon—asks the play's audience deeper questions about the extent to which gender might be performed, rather than essential.

An article by Pilar Cuder-Dominguez, 'The Islamization of Spain in William Rowley and Mary Pix: The Politics of Nation and Gender' (*CompD* 36[2002] 321– 36) considers a near-contemporary of *Swetnam* and of *The Bondman*: Rowley's *All's Lost by Lust*, acted in 1622. Rowley's play dramatizes the loss of Spain to the Moors, and yet, Cuder-Dominguez argues, its main thrust is actually anti-Spanish, with the Moors functioning as 'the long-reaching arm of Justice' (p. 326) punishing the Spanish characters for their sins. The article also compares the play interestingly with Mary Pix's adaptation of it in 1705 as *The Conquest of Spain*.

It has been a good year for Caroline drama as a whole. William Cartwright attracts two articles this year, both of which are concerned, in different ways, to re-establish his credentials as one of Charles's literary champions. Jane Farnsworth sees him as 'Defending the King in Cartwright's *The Lady-Errant* (1636–37)' (*SEL* 42[2002] 381–98), arguing that this drama, usually written off as Neoplatonic fluff, actually addresses 'England's involvement in the war in Europe, the king's personal rule, and the role of women, particularly the queen, in the political life of the kingdom'. On the other hand, Scott Gordon discusses 'The Cultural Politics of William Cartwright's *Royal Slave*' (in Moisan and Bruster, eds., *In the Company of Shakespeare: Essays in Honor of G. Blakemore Evans*, pp. 251–69). In its idealized representation of Cratander, the royal slave of the title, the play 'articulates precisely Charles' commitment to an elitism—both Christian and Platonic—that emphasizes the capacity of extraordinary individuals to transcend all private interests and to desire actively the public good'.

Still on courtly dramatists, broadly defined, Lesel Dawson writes on '"New Sects of Love": Neoplatonism and Constructions of Gender in Davenant's *The Temple of Love* and *The Platonick Lovers*' (*EMLS* 8:i[2002]). Dawson suggests that Davenant's drama actually reacts against Neoplatonic constructions of love, privileging instead a medicalized idea that love is a physiological and sexual condition, and that this in turn implies a defence of the traditional hierarchy of power applied to genders, rather than the more radical possibilities opened up by the Neoplatonism associated with Henrietta Maria.

Ford's *Perkin Warbeck* and Jasper Fisher's *Fuimus Troes* are among the plays considered in Lisa Hopkins's 'We Were the Trojans: British National Identities in 1633' (*RS* 16[2002] 36–51). Hopkins draws attention to the continuing importance of Geoffrey of Monmouth in the construction of Britishness as late as 1633, the year of Charles's Scottish coronation. The same author writes on 'Incest and Class: *'Tis Pity She's a Whore* and the Borgias' (in Barnes, ed., *Incest and the Literary Imagination*, pp. 94–113). She reads the play in the light of its setting in Parma and the lurid reputation of the Borgias, arguing that Giovanni's sexual transgression is juxtaposed with the Cardinal's rigid policing of class borders. Cynthia Marshall's *The Shattering of the Self: Violence, Subjectivity, and Early Modern Texts* includes a chapter on Ford's *The Broken Heart* in the context of a discussion of extreme violence in Renaissance literature including Petrarchanism, Foxe's *Book of Martyrs*, and Shakespeare's *Titus Andronicus*, all of which she relates to a Renaissance tradition of 'textual self-shattering' (p. 141). Marshall's subtle account of the play's use of restraint and self-destruction in various senses is based around the insight that the play works by simulating for the audience the experience of having a heart broken.

James Shirley is discussed in two articles by Julie Sanders. The first, '"Powdered with Golden Rain": The Myth of Danae in Early Modern Drama' (*EMLS* 8:ii[2002]), focuses on Shirley's *The Bird in A Cage*, but also considers other early modern plays that react to the myth of Danae, including Heywood's *The Golden Age* and several Jonson plays, in the context of a contention that the myth is important as an interestingly multivalent parable of female agency. Sanders's other article is 'Beggars' Commonwealths and the Pre-Civil War Stage: Suckling's *The Goblins*, Brome's *A Jovial Crew*, and Shirley's *The Sisters*' (*MLR* 97[2002] 1–14), in which she traces three Caroline portrayals of alternative woodland communities, all of which, she argues, are very much aware of the political resonances of the communities they display.

A Jovial Crew is also the focus of Matthew Steggle's article 'Redating *A Jovial Crew*' (*RES* 53[2002] 365–72), in which it is argued that the play (usually said to have been first performed in April 1641) might well be up to a year later in date than that, a fact which would have implications for the relationship between theatre and civic disorder in the period leading up to the closure of the theatres. Steggle also contributes a note, 'Richard Brome's First Patron' (*N&Q* 49[2002] 259–61) identifying Richard Holford, the dedicatee of Brome's earlier play *The Northern Lass*, as a wealthy west London landowner. The year's other article on Brome is by Athéna Efstathiou-Lavabre, 'Le Théâtre dans le Théâtre: Permanence d'une structure baroque dans *The Antipodes* (1638) de Richard Brome' (*XVII–XVIII* 54[2002] 27–43). In it, Efstathiou-Lavabre considers Brome's use of the play within a play as a curative device, linking it into a Europe-wide Baroque tradition.

Peter Beal prints three previously unknown 'Songs by Aurelian Townshend, in the Hand of Sir Henry Herbert, for an Unrecorded Masque by the Merchant Adventurers' (*MRDE* 15[2002] 243–60). His article transcribes these songs, from a manuscript now in the National Library of Wales; raises, only ultimately to reject, the possibility that they could be connected to Jonson's lost 1616 entertainment for the Merchant Adventurers; and discusses what can be deduced from the songs about what is almost certainly a lost 1630s entertainment presented before Charles I.

Finally, three short notes. Helen Moore, 'Another Link between Anthony Munday and Stephen Gosson' (*N&Q* 49[2002] 254–6), notes that the anti-theatricalist ended up helping the informer and sometime playwright in his continuation of Stow's *Chronicle*. The anonymous *Caesar's Revenge*, acted at Trinity College, Oxford, and printed in 1607, is generally reckoned to have been written in the early 1590s on the basis of its echoes of other texts. William Poole, '*Julius Caesar* and *Caesars Revenge* Again' (*N&Q* 49[2002] 227–8), bolsters these arguments by drawing attention to apparent echoes of *Caesar's Revenge* in Shakespeare. A speech in Beaumont's *The Woman Hater* [1606] alludes to a glover's son who is now a successful social climber at the court of the king. Andrew Gurr argues that this is 'A Jibe at Shakespeare in 1606' (*N&Q* 49[2002] 245–7).

(b) Marlowe

The tide of critical interest in Marlowe continues to swell, with no fewer than four new books on the playwright appearing this year, together with a further volume dividing its focus between Marlowe and Shakespeare, and a host of individual essays that between them take in all the plays, *Hero and Leander*, and aspects of his biography. In a new study examining the relationship between Marlowe's life and work, Constance Brown Kuriyama, *Christopher Marlowe: A Renaissance Life*, points to the problem of writing biography relying on documents that appear to offer objectivity but can be misinterpreted, and also to the difficulties of organizing Marlowe's life in geographical terms. She then proceeds to look at the documentary evidence for the biography afresh, treating it with considerable care and circumspection. Kuriyama challenges several speculations made by earlier biographers, including the idea that he was a spy, and the various conspiracy theories surrounding his death. While being prepared to make deductions from the available data, she is very sparing with these and underlines the conjectural status of many conclusions. She puts the focus on Marlowe's everyday life and relationships, but also looks at possible connections between events in his life and ideas in the plays. There is a discussion of the dramatist's reputation among his contemporaries immediately after his death, and a brief account of his critical reception down to the present day. This valuable and provocative (in the best sense of the word) volume concludes with a useful printing of a large range of documents relevant to the biography.

Ruth Lunney, in *Marlowe and the Popular Tradition: Innovation in the English Drama before 1595*, recognizing that modern critical interests routinely look to Marlowe as an innovator challenging both the theatrical and social values of his time, seeks to view the playwright's work in the context of the popular drama of the sixteenth century in order to assess what is new in what he offers. She discusses first the rhetoric not only of language but of playing, and the ways in which the early drama constructed the expectations of its audience and their ways of seeing, before going on to examine how Marlowe's drama undermines the authority of the dramatic emblem by permitting a diversity of ways for these emblems to create meaning and introduce ironies. This also involves disengaging the 'manifest sign' from its exemplary meaning. Competing voices, especially in *The Jew of Malta*, also shift perspectives from the morality framework that appears to provide a model for the play, and she advances the idea of 'debatable' characters (a pre-Shakespearian example of this phenomenon). Lunney also suggests that Marlowe changes the use of the stage, including adducing potential irony in ceremonial so that theatrical space becomes potentially refractive or deceptive. She concludes that his plays challenge audiences to do more than read visual signs for conventional meanings, emphasizing the playwright's importance as an innovator before Shakespeare.

Deats and Logan, eds., *Marlowe's Empery: Expanding his Critical Contexts*, assembles a range of essays which aim to take the measure of the impact and influence of Marlowe's work in terms of performance and genre, and to take a wider look at its cultural contexts. Roslyn Knutson kicks off with an examination of the reruns of Marlowe's plays on the Elizabethan stage as an indication of his impact in his own time, suggesting the considerable commercial success of his drama on the strength of both this and evidence of other contemporary plays written in imitation (pp. 25–42). David Bevington then explores the implications of the staging of the A-

and B-texts of *Doctor Faustus*, contending that the A-text is closer to Marlowe's original but that the B-text has fuller directions and plays to what is popular in the theatre, thereby sacrificing some of the ambiguities of the possibilities for Faustus's repentance. He points to these changes as illustrating the ways in which the theatre developed new methods, and popular demand determined the shape of plays mounted for its benefit (pp. 43–60). David Fuller concludes the section on performance with a comparative review of three twentieth-century productions of *Tamburlaine*, those of Donald Wolfit, Peter Hall at the National Theatre, and Terry Hands at the RSC, considering such aspects as changes to the text, stage action, tone, and performances of the central character (pp. 61–84). Maurice Charney opens the genre section with a contention that Shakespeare used *Hero and Leander* as a model, though not a source, for *Venus and Adonis*, and supports this by noting not only the erotic games and homoerotic elements in Shakespeare's poem, but also the references to *Hero and Leander* in his other work (pp. 85–94). Rick Bowers then argues for a camp sensibility in *Dido, Queen of Carthage*, which he sees as principally present in the elements of hyperbole, theatricalism, and hysterical characters at the level of both the gods and the humans, and cites the success of modern productions that stress these (pp. 95–106). Sara Deats concludes this section by discussing *Dido*, *Tamburlaine*, *Doctor Faustus*, and *Edward II* as interrogative plays that embody ambivalence, and suggests that Marlowe may have been the first playwright to script dialogic drama (pp. 107–32). Karen Cunningham commences the section on cultural contexts with an examination of treason and its relation to concepts of nationhood in the early modern period, as well as to ideas of friendship and fidelity, and looks at Marlowe's treatment of these issues, arguing that his heroes are alienated by birth, deed, and imagination (pp. 150–63). Randall Nakayama offers a discussion of dress as both a sexual and a social signifier in the *Jew of Malta* and *Edward II*, in the light of sumptuary legislation and social practice and attitudes in the period. Georgia Brown concludes the volume with an essay examining the relationship of *Edward II* to its source, Holinshed's *Chronicles*, and contends that Marlowe's play challenges the chronicle history's promotion of the masculine principle and its marginalization of the private and poetic in its construction of English identity, arguing too that the play asserts the value of authorship in the process (pp. 151–64).

The representation of militarism is the subject of *Marlowe's Soldiers: Rhetorics of Masculinity in the Age of the Armada*, in which Alan Shepard explores the ways in which Marlowe's plays engage with the rhetoric of war in the 1580s and 1590s. He suggests that the plays engage in subtle acts of resistance to martial law (frequently applied at the time), especially in terms of military identity being presented as a 'performance' of masculinity. He examines the seven plays in turn, suggesting first that the Tamburlaine plays exercise anxieties about masculinity, and that in *Dido, Queen of Carthage* Marlowe uses his Trojan material to create an anti-war burlesque in the context of contemporary ideas of epic masculinity. He then discusses the opposition between the martial and pleasure principles in *Edward II*, and that between war and commerce in *The Jew of Malta*, both against the backdrop of Elizabethan politics and evolving trading relationships. The pernicious effects of wars of religion on individual security are seen as being at issue in *The Massacre at Paris*, which is argued to present an even-handed view of the religious conflict and a sophisticated critique of violence. *Doctor Faustus*, in both the A- and B-texts, is, however, presented as working against the impulses identified in the other plays, Faustus operating as a militaristic figure through a form of magical realism. The collective range of plays is argued to expose the contradictions and ambiguities in the rhetoric of war.

In the sole chapter dedicated to Marlowe in Richard Hillman's *Shakespeare, Marlowe and the Politics of France*, a book otherwise largely concerned with Shakespeare's history plays, Hillman focuses on *Edward II* and *The Massacre at Paris*, arguing that in these plays the dramatist manipulated French political discourses. Rather than looking for direct source relationships he prefers an intertextual approach and talks of 'discursive fields', examining principally Marlowe's representations of Henri III and Edward II and their relationships respectively with Épernoun and Gaveston in the context of the ways in which the French king is represented in a range of French texts, dramatic and non-dramatic. *Edward II* is also obliquely the focus of Frank Ardolino's essay 'To Catch a Spy: John le Carré's and Sidney Lumet's Use of Marlowe's *Edward II* in Performance' (*JEP* 22:i–ii[2002] 40–5) which notes that Le Carré's novel *Call for the Dead* [1961] and Lumet's film of it, *The Deadly Affair* [1967], both juxtapose a climactic murder in their plots with a performance of the killing of the king in Marlowe's play. Ardolino argues, however, that the film parallels the play more pointedly, with its stronger emphasis on betrayal, and its epistolatory motif.

Doctor Faustus is the play that enjoys the greatest amount of attention in individual essays, as is often the case. John D. Cox, in '"To obtain his soul": Demonic Desire for the Soul in Marlowe and Others' (*ETREED* 5:ii[2002] 29–46), discusses Mephistophilis's desire for Faustus's soul in relation to medieval representations of the *psychomachia* and the satanic pursuit of the soul of man, especially with reference to earlier drama, seeing *Doctor Faustus* as thus continuing a dramatic tradition. He argues that the play engages with both Calvinist and pre-Reformation conceptions of access to salvation but renders them ambiguous, and is even-handed in its representation of the contestants for Faustus's soul, implying a concealed scepticism. In respect of a question about when in the early modern period 'true' and serious tragedy can be said to appear, David Webb, 'The Interrogation of the Heavens in *King Lear* and Marlowe's *Doctor Faustus*' (*CE* 61[2002] 13–29), reviews the critical discussions on the attitudes to salvation in *Doctor Faustus* and the play's treatment of religion more generally, and goes on to advance the argument that its questioning of religious certainties resides in part in Faustus's self-dramatizing qualities. He explores various instances of this, and the histrionics of the final speech in detail, noting that both this play and *King Lear* hold uncomfortable questions about God before their audiences, the more thinking members of which are not allowed to shelter in traditional theological stances. *Doctor Faustus* in particular persistently seems to offer 'right' answers only to have these eroded and compromised by Faustus's self-dramatization. In 'Contextualizing the Demonic: Marlowe's *Doctor Faustus*' (in Bamford and Leggatt, eds., *Approaches to Teaching English Renaissance Drama*, pp. 186–90) Thomas Akstens gives an account of his focusing on the presence of devils in the play to explore with students differences in the beliefs about the demonic in the early modern and modern periods, as a means of opening up consideration of the cultural contexts of the play. In the same volume Leah Marcus, in 'Texts That Won't Stand Still' (pp. 29–34), considers the problems posed to the teaching of *Doctor Faustus* by the constantly changing versions and treatment of the play in successive modern editions. She proposes the option, especially for more advanced courses, of teaching the A- and B-texts alongside each other, both for the study of the work itself and as a reflection on the ways in which modern editing shapes the texts of plays. A note by Thomas Merriam, 'Faustian Joan' (*N&Q* 49[2002] 218–20), proposes Marlowe's authorship of a passage of 341 lines in Shakespeare's *1 Henry VI*, on the basis of a number of strong verbal parallels with Marlowe's plays, the appearance—unique for Shakespeare—of devils on stage, including a satanic pact, and the frequency of certain common function words in the passage. Finally, Johan Callens, in 'European Textures: Adapting Christopher Marlowe's *Doctor Faustus*' (in Roudané, ed., *The Cambridge Companion to Sam Shepard*, pp. 189–209), gives a detailed account of Sam Shepard's adaptation of *Doctor Faustus* as *Man Fly*, in response to a commission from the Mark Taper Forum in 1974, illustrating how Shepard recast the ideas of the play, relocated it to an American context, and aimed for a 'semi-realistic' interpretation. Callens reflects on the ways in which the adaptation articulates modern cultural experience and embodies preoccupations found elsewhere in Shepard's work, but there is also recurrent reference in his essay back to Marlowe's own work and frames of reference.

The Tamburlaine plays are examined in four essays that bring some very diverse perspectives to bear. Donald Hedrick, in 'Male Surplus Value' (*RenD* 31[2002] 85–124), suggests that a new mode of performative masculinity developed in the Elizabethan theatre, in terms specific to the entertainment industry. He sees Tamburlaine's construction of his style of theatricalized masculinity as consonant with early modern capitalism and points out the debt owed to the extravagant acting of the role by Alleyn, tied to generating monetary profit in the theatre, and connects this with the concept of 'surplus value' in Marxist economics. This is also discussed with respect to certain Shakespeare characters, especially Coriolanus. Roger E. Moore, in 'The Spirit and the Letter: Marlowe's *Tamburlaine* and Elizabethan Religious Radicalism' (*SP* 99:ii[2002] 123–51), presents Tamburlaine as a type of Gnostic, with particular reference to his scorn of religious laws codified in texts. Moore gives some account of Gnosticism and suggests how Marlowe might have been exposed to these ideas, particularly as exemplified in the Family of Love sect. Several other traits of Tamburlaine are also proposed as potentially Gnostic, especially his sense of being above the material world and his violence towards those deemed to be 'earthly', and Moore suggests that the vacuity of these beliefs is exposed by Tamburlaine's final distemper and death. The ending of *Tamburlaine II* is examined by Martin Brunkhorst in '"See, see how the lovers sit in state together": Tragödienschluss und Schlusstableau bei Marlowe, Shakespeare und Dryden' (*LJGG* 43[2002] 331–43), which draws attention to the importance assigned in the early modern period to the emotional impact of the endings of tragedies, and discusses, in the light of this, the problem of the actors who played characters who die on stage having to destroy the illusion by getting up to take their bow. He goes on to discuss a particular style attached to the exit of the dead, especially connected to their social status, through which the solemnity and high style of tragedy may be maintained, and the ways in which both the death of Zenocrate and the final speech of Amyras bring appropriate closure to *Tamburlaine II*, before going on to look at the phenomenon in plays by Shakespeare and Dryden. The final contribution on *Tamburlaine* also focuses on *The Jew of Malta*; this is Anthony Nuttall's admirable and densely argued essay, 'Christopher Marlowe: Iron and Gold' (*CCrit* 24[2002] 37–51). Starting with an argument for the potential of literature to be anti-reductionist, having reviewed the ways in which reductionist thinkers have altered perceptions of the world, Nuttall moves on to consider the Tamburlaine plays, which resist the 'fall of princes' formula to advance the idea of the ascendancy of power over morality. He then compares the alternative sources of power in military might or 'iron' in these plays, and economic might or 'gold' in *The Jew of Malta*, as a challenge to the religious basis of morality that instead becomes a social construct, which makes moral relativism possible. He concludes by contending, with reference to the replacement of old blood feuds with a system of blood money, that Tamburlaine can be seen as embodying a pre-social, and the Jew a social, principle.

Marlowe's poetry also comes in for scrutiny in no fewer than three essays this year, all of which are on *Hero and Leander*. Cindy L. Carlson advances the argument, in 'Clothing Naked Desire in Marlowe's *Hero and Leander*' (in Carlson, Mazzola, and Bernardo, eds., *Gender Reconstructions: Pornography and Perversions in Literature and Culture*, pp. 25–41), that, though Leander is naked when he becomes an object of desire for Neptune, his nakedness is a form of transvestism in that it blazons his androgynous beauty, though the poem withholds full visual satisfaction from the reader by pulling back from explicit revelation. Hero's nakedness is not presented to the reader and stress is laid on her clothing, which presents her in terms of danger and violence, involving the blood of her disappointed lovers and of her priestly sacrifices. The female body is thus rendered inscrutable and unsatisfying as a sexual object, while Leander functions more safely as a focus of desire for both genders. Robert F. Darcy, in '"Under my hands … a double duty": Printing and Pressing Marlowe's *Hero and Leander*' (*JEMCS* 2:ii[2002] 26–56), proposes that Marlowe's poem offers a self-referential representation of how to read it, the confusion of the lovers paralleling the reader's confusion about the vacillation in the poem's adherence to poetic conventions. He discusses the interventions of the printer and modern scholars' attempts to impose meaning, but argues that through its destabilizing tactics the poem invites its readers to bring into play their own epistemological expectations in making sense of it. In the last essay on the poetry, 'Marlowe's Ghost Writing of Ovid's Heroides' (*RenP* [2002] 57–72), Pamela Royston Macfie suggests a much greater use by Marlowe of the *Heroides* in his writing of *Hero and Leander* than hitherto supposed, and that traces of Ovid's work are spread throughout the text, being especially evident in verbal echoes, but also in the tragic and haunted nature of the narrative.

The sole item on Marlowe's biography is Charles Nicholl's short article, 'Scribblers and Assassins: Charles Nicholl Reopens the File on Thomas Drury and the Prosecution of Christopher Marlowe' (*LRB* 24:xxi[2002] 30–3), in which he elaborates on the possible role of the shadowy figure of Thomas Drury in drawing up allegations of atheism against Marlowe, and brings to the fore certain pieces of biographical information about the informer, indicating an involvement with the Elizabethan underworld of spying, an element of criminality, and a tendency towards unscrupulous vindictiveness. On the basis of this, Nicholl calls further into question the reliability of the allegations against the playwright. Another article which I have not been able to see, but which also presumably has some biographical content, is Daniel G. Brayton, 'Christopher Marlowe (1564–1593)' (*British Writers: Retrospective Supplement* I [2001], pp. 199–213).

An essay from 2001 in a volume that appeared too late for inclusion in last year's survey is Nina Taunton's 'Unlawful Presences: The Politics of Military Space and the Problem of Women in *Tamburlaine*' (in Gordon and Klein, eds., *Literature, Mapping and the Politics of Space in Early Modern Britain*, pp. 138–54). Taunton examines the problematic presence of Zenocrate, Zabina, and Olympia as women in the military male environment of the Tamburlaine plays, an environment where they have no designated right of presence and their self-definition needs to be claimed through eroticism and class status. She considers this in the context of contemporary writings on military encampments and representation in the visual arts of juxtapositions of female presence and the military, stressing the extent to which these reveal anxieties about sex, death, and the imperatives of war. Taunton concludes that the Tamburlaine plays explore ways in which women in the military camp could resist obliteration by at once affirming and sidestepping the laws that forbade their presence. Another item from 2001 that I have been unable to track down is Paolo Caponi's 'The Damnation of the Critic: Faustus's Demoniality and Greg's Intentionality' (*ACF* 40:i–ii[2001] 57–77).

(c) Jonson

One should start with James Loxley's *The Complete Critical Guide to Ben Jonson*, the very title of which is, fortunately, belied by the variety of new work on Jonson which has come out this year. Loxley begins with a biography of Jonson in thirty pages of detailed, densely packed prose. A discussion of the works follows, subdivided into ten sections, so that one gets, for example, a ten-page discussion combining *The Alchemist* and *Bartholomew Fair*, thick with references to further critical reading. The third section of the book is a survey of some of the main issues in Jonson criticism, with copious quotation from up-to-date criticism. Loxley's book is a welcome and highly useful guide for undergraduates or for anyone else wanting an overview of the current state of play in Jonson studies.

In addition, two works re-examine the whole question of Jonson's relationship to the category of 'author'. Joseph Loewenstein's monograph *Ben Jonson and Possessive Authorship* offers a wide-ranging and subtle account of the development, through Jonson's works, of the idea of the author. In this account, Martial's fascination with ideas of intellectual property is a major reference point in Jonsonian definitions of what it means to be a writer, and a literary professional at that. On the other hand, an article by Paul D. Cannan, 'Ben Jonson, Authorship, and the Rhetoric of English Dramatic Prefatory Criticism' (*SP* 99[2002] 178–201), argues the importance of the modesty topos, and argues that later Jonson texts actually abandon the habit of making extra-literary assertions of authorial control. A third work one might mention in this context is Douglas A. Brooks, 'Dramatic Authorship and Publication in Early Modern England' (*MRDE* 15[2002] 77–97), discussed in section 3(a) above.

Work on individual plays includes Mario DiGangi, '"Male Deformities": Narcissus and the Reformation of Courtly Manners in *Cynthia's Revels*' (in Stanivukovic, ed., pp. 94–110), which offers a reading of the play informed by queer theory. DiGangi argues that the play is driven by the 'early modern equation between civil manners and civil order' (p. 107), with the absent but persistent Narcissus a symbol of the potential disorder facing the court. Meanwhile, two notes in the *Ben Jonson Journal* address the borders of the War of the Theatres. Charles

Cathcart, 'John Weever and the Jonson–Marston Rivalry' (*BJJ* 9[2002] 235–47), argues that Weever accidentally helped detonate the whole affair by his commendatory poem to Jonson in his *Epigrammes* [1599]. And Stephen Roth, 'How Ben Jonson Berayed his Credit: Parnassus, Shakespeare's "Purge", and the War of the Theaters' (*BJJ* 9[2002] 249–55), suggests that the allusion in *The Return to Parnassus Part II* refers, not to stage attacks on Jonson, but to Jonson's response to those stage attacks: the Apologetical Dialogue to *Poetaster*, which is known to have landed him in hot water with the authorities. Roth also reinvestigates the relative chronology of the texts involved.

City comedies by Jonson—*Eastward Ho!*, *Volpone*, and *The Devil is An Ass*—are discussed by Alizon Brunning in '"In his gold I shine": Jacobean Comedy and the Art of the Mediating Trickster' (*EMLS* 8:ii[2002]), in an article which relates the trickster-figure to the Sidneyan idea that the poet can create a golden world. James Mardock's 'Hermaphroditical Authority in Jonson's City Comedies' (*BJJ* 9[2002] 69–85) focuses mainly on *Epicoene* and *The Devil is An Ass*, arguing that, although these plays associate femininity with artifice, such an equation is complicated by the citizens' use of transvestism as a productive and useful strategy. Also on Jonson's city comedies is Gregory Chaplin's piece, '"Divided amongst themselves": Collaboration and Anxiety in Jonson's *Volpone*' (*ELH* 69[2002] 57–81). For Chaplin, there is a clear parallel between Jonson's depictions of collaborative teams of swindlers and his own experiences of collaborative comedy-writing. This forms the basis for a close reading of the 'tension between collaboration and competition' in *Volpone*, and some interesting discussion of Mosca's almost erotic fascination with the collaborative creation of deceptions. In contrast, taking her cue from the psychoanalytical approaches of Edmund Wilson and William Kerrigan, Lynn S. Meskill writes on 'Jonson and the Alchemical Economy of Desire: Creation, Defacement and Castration in *The Alchemist*' (*CahiersE* 62[2002] 47–63), reading Subtle and Face in terms of a father–son relationship gone psychologically sour. The result is full of interesting observations about the sexual energies within the play— for instance, the acute remark that Hieronimo's cloak, borrowed from *The Spanish Tragedy*, functions as a 'symbol of authorial virility' (p. 51)—and offers yet another way of thinking critically about Jonson. Caroline McManus's study of the play focuses on 'Queen Elizabeth, Dol Common, and the Performance of the Royal Maundy' (*ELR* 32[2002] 189–213). This ritual, in which Queen Elizabeth would wash the feet of the poor on Maundy Thursday, provides McManus with a way in to consideration of how *The Alchemist* approaches the relationship between money and faith, and of how Dol's various disguises offer reflections of the dead queen. One final item that deserves mention here is Robert Shaughnessy, 'Twentieth-Century Fox: Volpone's Metamorphosis' (*TRI* 27[2002] 37–48). Shaughnessy reviews the performance history of *Volpone* since its reintroduction to the stage in 1930, and focuses in particular on the problems presented by its beast fable dimension.

Jonson's late plays, *The Tale of a Tub* and *The Magnetic Lady*, satirize two living, identifiable Laudian vicars. The story is disentangled in Julie Maxwell's fascinating article, 'Ben Jonson Among the Vicars: Cliché, Ecclesiastical Politics, and the Invention of "Parish Comedy"' (*BJJ* 9[2002] 37–68). Maxwell charts the interaction between the plays' geographically unambiguous specificity, the generalized clerical stereotypes that they invoke, and the archival records of the activities of the two particular vicars involved. A similarly political challenge is contained within *The*

New Inn, according to Julie Sanders, '"Wardrobe Stuffe": Clothes, Costume and the Politics of Dress in Ben Jonson's *The New Inn*' (*Renfor* 6:i[2002]). Sanders argues that Jonson's play can be read in the light of Charles's renewed interest in the Office of the Wardrobe, and that it exposes the 'rank-driven operations of costume' (p. 4).

Work on Jonson's masques this year is represented by several articles. Among them, a note by Richard Levin, 'Counting Sieve Holes in Jonson and Hobbes' (*N&Q* 49[2002] 249–51), explores a cryptic allusion to this practice, apparently a form of divination, in the *Entertainment at Althorp* [1603]. Monika Smialowska, in '"Out of the authority of ancient and late writers": Ben Jonson's Use of Textual Sources in *The Masque of Queens*' (*ELR* 32[2002] 268–86) re-examines the extensive erudition lying behind Jonson's *Masque of Queens*, arguing that, although the masque appears to connect fame, virtue, and poetry in an uncomplicated constellation, the sources are handled in a way designed to complicate and undermine this surface effect. Jonson's early Jacobean masques, including *The Masque of Blackness*, are the subject of an article by Philippa Berry and Jayne Elizabeth Archer, 'Reinventing the Matter of Britain: Undermining the State in Jacobean Masques' (in Baker and Maley, eds., *British Identities and English Renaissance Literature*, pp. 119–34). Berry and Archer note the recurring interest in these masques in the ontological nature of union, and the repeated motif of the discovery of an inner, grotto-like, recess or cavity containing the secret centre of Britishness. Jonson's *Oberon* is one of a number of texts from around 1610, including *The Winter's Tale* and the revised version of the anonymous *Mucedorus*, considered by Barbara Ravelhofer in '"Beasts of recreacion": Henslowe's White Bears' (*ELR* 32[2002] 287–323). Ravelhofer presents archival evidence concerning the menagerie kept by Henslowe to support an argument that all three of these texts, featuring bears on stage, may have been responding to the availability of a tame, trained, polar bear kept by Henslowe. Karen Britland's '"All emulation cease, and jars": Political Possibilities in *Chloridia*, Queen Henrietta Maria's Masque of 1631' (*BJJ* 9[2002] 87–108) argues that *Chloridia* chimes interestingly with current political events in Henrietta Maria's home country, offering an implicit commentary on the aftermath of the Day of Dupes even while it also adopts formal features of the French court masque. These parallels offer 'circumstantial evidence that Henrietta Maria or her advisors contributed ideas and motifs to Jonson and Jones during the preparation of the masque' (p. 104).

Finally, Derek Britton reconsiders 'The Dating of Jonson's *English Grammar*' (*N&Q* 49[2002] 330–4), which partly hinges on Jonson's self-description as a *senex*. Britton concludes that there is good evidence to push the date of composition of the text as we have it back to just after the 1623 fire that destroyed Jonson's library, rather than the 1630s date sometimes ascribed to this text.

Books Reviewed

Baker, David J., and Willy Maley, eds. *British Identities and English Renaissance Literature*. CUP. [2002] pp. xvi + 297. £40 ISBN 0 5217 8200 7.

Bamford, Karen, and Alexander Leggatt, eds. *Approaches to Teaching English Renaissance Drama*. MLA. [2002] pp. xv + 230. hb $37.50 ISBN 0 8735 2773 9, pb $18 ISBN 0 8735 2774 7.

Barnes, Elizabeth, ed. *Incest and the Literary Imagination*. UFlorP. [2002] pp. 382. $59.95 ISBN 0 8130 2540 0.

Bevington, David, Lars Engle, Katharine Eisaman Maus, and Eric Rasmussen, eds. *English Renaissance Drama*. Norton. [2002] pp. lx + 1997. £26.50 ISBN 0 3939 7655 6.

British Writers: Retrospective Supplement I. Scribner. [2001] pp. 700. $145 ISBN 0 6843 1227 1.

Carlson Cindy, L., Robert L. Mazzola, and Susan M. Bernardo, eds. *Gender Reconstructions: Pornography and Perversions in Literature and Culture*. Ashgate. [2002] pp. xiv + 208. £67 ISBN 0 7546 0286 9.

Deats, Sara Munson, and Robert Logan, eds. *Marlowe's Empery: Expanding his Critical Contexts*. UDelP. [2002] pp. 210. £32 ISBN 0 8741 3787 X.

Erne, Lukas. *Beyond the Spanish Tragedy: A Study of the Works of Thomas Kyd*. ManUP. [2001] pp. xix + 252. £45 ISBN 0 7190 6093 1.

Gordon, Andrew, and Bernhard Klein, eds. *Literature, Mapping and the Politics of Space in Early Modern Britain*. CUP. [2001] pp. xiii + 276. £42.50 ISBN 0 5218 0377 2.

Hillman, Richard. *Shakespeare, Marlowe and the Politics of France*. Palgrave. [2002] pp. 260. £50 ISBN 0 3336 9454 6.

Jowitt, Claire. *Voyage Drama and Gender Politics 1549–1642: Real and Imagined Worlds*. ManUP. [2002] pp. 368. £45 ISBN 0 7190 5451 6.

Keenan, Siobhan. *Travelling Players in Shakespeare's England*. Palgrave. [2002] pp. xvi + 250. £40 ISBN 0 3339 6820 4.

Kuriyama, Constance B. *Christopher Marlowe: A Renaissance Life*. CornUP. [2002] pp. xxi + 255. $36.95 ISBN 0 8014 3978 7.

Loewenstein, Joseph. *Ben Jonson and Possessive Authorship*. CUP. [2002] pp. 240. £45 ISBN 0 5218 1217 8.

Loxley, James. *The Complete Critical Guide to Ben Jonson*. Routledge. [2002] pp. 223. £11.99 ISBN 0 4152 2228 1.

Lunney, Ruth. *Marlowe and the Popular Tradition: Innovation in the English Drama Before 1595*. ManUP. [2002] pp. x + 24. £40 ISBN 0 7190 6118 0.

Marshall, Cynthia. *The Shattering of the Self: Violence, Subjectivity, and Early Modern Texts*. JHUP. [2002] pp. 232. $44.95 ISBN 0 8018 6778 9.

McManus, Clare. *Women on the Renaissance Stage: Anna of Denmark and Female Masquing in the Stuart Court (1590–1619)*. ManUP. [2002] pp. xi + 276. £14.99 ISBN 0 7190 6250 0.

Moisan, Thomas, and Douglas Bruster, eds. *In the Company of Shakespeare: Essays on English Renaissance Literature in Honor of G. Blakemore Evans*. FDUP. [2002] pp. 357. $57.50 ISBN 0 8386 3902 X.

Moore, A. T., ed. *Love's Sacrifice*, by John Ford. Revels. ManUP. [2002] pp. xxviii + 323. £45 ISBN 0 7190 1557 X.

Neill, Michael. *Putting History to the Question: Power, Politics, and Society in English Renaissance Drama*. ColUP. [2000] pp. 464. $65 ISBN 0 2311 1332 3.

Perry, Curtis, ed. *Material Culture and Cultural Materialisms in the Middle Ages and Renaissance*. Brepols. [2001] pp. 248. $61 ISBN 2 5035 1074 4.

Roudané, Matthew, ed. *The Cambridge Companion to Sam Shepard*. CUP. [2002] pp. xix + 329. hb £45 ISBN 0 5217 7158 7, pb £15 ISBN 0 5217 7766 6.

Scragg, Leah, ed. *Sapho and Phao*, by John Lyly. Malone Society 165. OUP. [2002] pp. xx + 59. £25 ISBN 0 1972 9041 8.

Shepard, Alan. *Marlowe's Soldiers: Rhetorics of Masculinity in the Age of the Armada*. Ashgate. [2002] pp. vii + 248. £40 ISBN 0 7546 0229 X.

Stanivukovic, Goran V., ed. *Ovid and the Renaissance Body*. UTorP. [2001] pp. 281. $65 ISBN 0 8020 3515 9.

Swiss, Margo, and David A. Kent, eds. *Speaking Grief in English Literary Culture*: *Shakespeare to Milton*. Duquesne. [2002] pp. 300. $60 ISBN 0 8207 0330 3.

West, Russell. *Spatial Representations and the Jacobean Stage: From Shakespeare to Webster*. Palgrave. [2002] pp. x + 276. £50 ISBN 0 3339 7373 9.

VIII

The Earlier Seventeenth Century: General, Prose, Women's Writing

JAMES DOELMAN AND LISA WALTERS

This chapter has three sections: 1. General; 2. Prose; 3. Women's Writing. Sections 1 and 2 are by James Doelman; section 3 is by Lisa Walters.

1. General

The most significant publications of 2002 were two major volumes from CUP: Loewenstein and Mueller, eds., *The Cambridge History of Early Modern English Literature* (part of the New Cambridge History of English Literature) and Barnard, McKenzie, and Bell, eds., *The Cambridge History of the Book in Britain*, volume 4: *1557–1695*. Both successfully aspire to a comprehensive overview of their respective fields and will serve as major resources for years to come.

The former offers a great deal of rich historical material: the literature of the time is presented in relation to a variety of contexts (especially political and religious), and the volume summarizes recent work on reading practices, printing, and manuscript circulation. However, like a number of other recent national literary histories, this volume holds back from attempting a narrative, either within the work as a whole or within its individual chapters or sections. In resisting this, *The New Cambridge History* quite deliberately sets itself apart from either the old *Cambridge History* or the *Oxford History of English Literature*, seminal works which served generations of students and scholars, and with which any new publication is bound to be compared. (Inevitable comparisons to the corresponding volumes in the new *Oxford English Literary History* will have to wait until 2005 for Margaret Ezell's volume on the latter half of the century, and 2006 for Katharine Eisaman Maus's one on the first half.)

The volume fairly represents the state of literary studies in the early twenty-first century, reflecting the recent interests in literature as a historical force and site of conflict. Hence, religion and politics are presented not as background, but as areas in which literature was actively engaged. A much wider scope of literature is touched on than in the previous histories, as neglected writings by Scottish, Irish, and female writers are included. Chapters are written by many of the major of literary scholars and historians in the field.

The introduction is to an extent an admission that a new *history* is not really needed and that single-author accounts 'have been rendered masterfully' (p. 7). For those interested in finding out about an individual author they suggest using the index, but two random attempts at this (George Herbert and George Wither) were not satisfactory: the reader is led only to a series of very passing references. The editors' claimed end is to 'achieve freshness': whether such should be the goal of a broad definitive history is open to debate, and ultimately this work is successful less for its freshness than for its careful gathering and synopsis of a wide range of other studies. While not a history in the conventional sense, it provides a very valuable summary of the present state of scholarship in the field, and in a period with so many specialized volumes this plays an important role.

The volume is divided into five sections: one broad overview rather clumsily entitled 'Modes and Means of Literary Production, Circulation and Reception', and then one each for four historical periods ranging from the Reformation to the Restoration. The general overview covers literacy, education, manuscript circulation, print culture, patronage, languages, and habits of reading. Of these, only that by Paula Blank on languages is unexpected: she provides both a history of English and a discussion of the use of other languages in the period. Some of these opening chapters, like Graham Parry's on patronage, provide more of a narrative history than others, which treat the period as one thick slice. Within the latter four sections certain chapter headings ('Literature and the Court') recur: such a structure does lead to occasional repetition, but overall the individual chapters are very strong. That nearly every chapter is entitled 'Literature and ... ' accurately reflects the approach of this work. At no point is literature treated in and of itself: this is all context and very little text. Genre, metre, and form are seldom discussed, and overall the classical tradition and its influence receives less attention than needed.

The volume ends with a series of chronologies (rather oddly organized) and bibliographies of primary and secondary material. These are, by necessity, selective. The primary bibliography identifies modern editions, where these exist. As with most of the volume as a whole, the secondary bibliography is up to date.

The Cambridge History of the Book in Britain, volume 4: *1557–1695* is another significant synthesis of recent scholarship by a gathering of prominent scholars in the field. This one, however, has no real precursor, as it reflects the relatively new field of the 'history of the book'. It traces this history from the granting of the Stationers' Company royal charter in 1557 to the lapsing of the Licensing Act in 1695. This is a long period, and with the coverage of such disparate aspects of the field, it is no surprise that this is such a hefty volume. The introduction provides a concise history of publishing from 1557 to 1695, touching on many factors that are more fully discussed in subsequent chapters. The volume is divided into eight main sections, 'Religion and Politics', 'Oral Traditions and Scribal Culture', 'Literature of the Learned', 'Literary Canons', 'Vernacular Traditions', 'The Business of Print and the Space of Reading', 'Beyond London', and 'The Late Seventeenth-Century Book Trade', and these are further divided into chapters.

The opening chapters on religious publishing masterfully explain this complicated history, and the history of manuscript texts by Harold Love and Peter Beal is lucid. The third section explores the history of the book in a number of special subject areas. Very helpful is the analysis of the exceptional history of map- and atlas-making. At times, the focus on the material book, rather than the subject it presents, is lost: 'Editing the Past' by Nicholas Barker is as much about classical and historical scholarship as it is a history of the book in these areas. Some chapters, for example those on travel and classical scholarship, lapse into annotated lists of books printed with insufficient consideration of readership and the economics of publishing. Most successful are chapters like that by Adrian Johns on 'Science and the Book', which examines the new scientific drive *not* to rely on books as establishing a dynamic different from other fields. Also examined here is the challenge of printing large-scale works with new engravings from specimens. A few authors (Donne, Samuel Hartlib, Hobbes, Milton, Sir Roger L'Estrange) are given chapters of their own as examples of more widespread phenomena. The economic history and material history of the book are not neglected, with chapters on such topics as paper and typography.

The volume largely amounts to a timely and thorough stock-taking, considering what has been accomplished in this relatively new field, and it incorporates even very recent scholarship. As might be expected in a multi-authored work, there is some repetition of material, but few will be reading this work through.

Appended are statistical tables and illustration plates. The referencing system is less than satisfactory: the footnotes only provide author, date, and page number, with further information in the bibliography. This leads to much flipping back and forth, and cryptic references such as 'Raven, below' can be frustrating.

Also relevant to the history of the book is a collection of essays on censorship: Hadfield, ed., *Literature and Censorship in Renaissance England*. Based on a 1999 conference in Newton, Wales, the book opens with a very helpful overview by Hadfield of recent scholarship which does not hesitate to point out the contentions between the contributors to the volume. The essays themselves are divided into three main parts, covering theatrical, religious, and political censorship, and most of the major scholars working in the field are included. Janet Clare's article examines the compromises achieved by dramatists and censors, and also some cases, such as *The Isle of Gulls* and *Eastward Ho*, of failed compromise. Focusing on *Sir John Oldcastle* and *Sir Thomas More*, Stephen Longstaffe examines the limits to the presentation of religious history and controversy on stage in the fraught times of the 1590s. In 'Receiving Offence: *A Game at Chess* Again', Richard Dutton argues that Sir Henry Herbert, the Master of the Revels, understood and accepted the anti-Spanish satire of the play. Richard McCabe re-examines the 1599 Bishops' Ban on histories, satires, and epigrams, and argues that the intent of this edict was to suppress political attacks, not obscenity. Historian David Loades's essay is less concerned with censorship than the publication history and reception of Foxe's *Acts and Monuments*. Purposely moving away from high-profile censorship cases, Arnold Hunt considers the mechanics of licensing religious works, and compellingly argues that in the 1630s this licensing achieved a new role as a type of imprimatur. Hadfield himself offers an essay on the difficulties of discussing Ireland in published works in the 1590s. Cyndia Susan Clegg carefully explores the complex relationship of King James VI and I to publication and censorship. Annabel Patterson, whose *Censorship and Interpretation* [1984] serves as a touchstone for many of the other essays here, argues that Andrew Marvell thrived under the censorship of his time, achieving a position certainly more enviable than that of the censors. The book ends with a broader essay by Richard Burt on the censorship of Elizabeth's image from her own time to the present. Ultimately, this book is a model of what collections of conference papers should be: a cohesive collection of related papers by the leading scholars in the field.

The papers in the broad-ranging if somewhat unfocused van Heijnsbergen and Royan, eds., *Literature, Letters and the Canonical in Early Modern Scotland*, stem from a 1999 conference at St Andrews. Sixteenth-century literature dominates the collection, but the essay by Morna Fleming turns attention to the implications of the English accession of James VI and I for Scottish literature and culture. His post-1603 influence on English literature has been much explored; this essay also looks at the Scottish writers, like Alexander Craig, who were left behind as James moved to his southern kingdom. It helpfully challenges 'the entrenched notion of the Scottish seventeenth century as a barren field' (p. ix), and the collection's concerns with 'decentring' perspective work well in this instance. The loss of the royal court was accompanied by a greater significance for other cultural intermediaries, as Marie-Claude Tucker explores the increasing upper-middle-class audience and the tendency of its members to send their sons to Continental universities, and continue that cultural influence on Scotland. Tucker's more profound argument is that the legal humanism of Scotland produced a very different type of literary mind from that found in seventeenth-century England. The volume as a whole demonstrates some of the continuities of Scottish literature, so often obscured by excessive periodization.

Politics, Religion and Popularity: Early Stuart Essays in Honour of Conrad Russell, edited by the historians Thomas Cogswell, Richard Cust, and Peter Lake, honours the radical influence on Russell on the historiography of the early Stuart period. While Russell himself has made little use of literary sources, many of those who have followed him in the revisionist vein have turned to literary works, and that is reflected in this collection. Russell's continuing attention to the 'British problem' is reflected in a number of essays here. Lori Anne Ferrell, author of two notable works on the English sermon, presents here an essay nicely focused on the sermon and masque of the 1607 wedding of James, Lord Hay, a Scottish favourite, and the wealthy Englishwoman Honora Denny. She follows Stephen Orgel and David Lindley in rejecting the long-standing Whig assumption that the marriage was based largely on the mercenary needs of Honora's father, Sir Edward Denny. She finds the sermon, by Robert Wilkinson, and the masque, by Campion, participating in the broader push for union between England and Scotland. They, more than the event they marked, were a continuing testimony to James's frustrated desire for a union that was both political and religious. This historicist reading works much better than some because of the clear public significance of the event which these two published works addressed. An essay by Thomas Cogswell reconsiders the duke of Buckingham's public image, and shows that the favourite was more inclined to cultivate a positive popular opinion than is usually assumed. While the duke's supporters attempted to use manuscript and print to defend him, they were never successful in convincing the public. Cogswell reads the 1627 conflict with France as Buckingham 'stage-manag[ing] a military campaign with himself cast as the valiant warlord' (p. 224).

In sharp contrast to the Russell Festschrift is James Holstun's *Ehud's Dagger: Class Struggle in the English Revolution*, a work unabashedly Marxist and anti-revisionist in approach, and reflecting strongly the legacy of Christopher Hill. Holstun sees the conflicts of the 1640s as a failed revolution based on class struggle (to which there definitely was a road in the preceding decades). In the first few chapters he takes on revisionism and the new historicism, and through this establishes the theoretical basis of his own approach. In Holstun's argument both revisionism and new historicism have rendered opposition an impossibility in the period, and his quarrel is as much with the one as the other. He is refreshingly straightforward in his approach, puncturing the stances of many academics: 'People don't write revolutions, but fight them.' However, at times the vehemence of his attack distorts his opponents.

The second half of *Ehud's Dagger* consists of five chapters on what Holstun calls 'radical projects' from the 1620s to the 1650s. First discussed is the popular support for John Felton, the assassin of Buckingham, most notably expressed in widely circulating manuscript poems. Holstun argues that 'Felton's intimate and theatrical encounter with Buckingham arose from and opened up into a larger collective and ideological conflict' (p. 144). Chapter 6 turns to the New Model Army, and argues that the Putney Debates were 'the turning point of the English Revolution' (p. xiii), and that the failure of the 1640s and 1650s was the 'failure of land reform'. The prophetess Anna Trapnel is the subject of the next chapter, serving as an example of radical religious opposition to Cromwell. Chapter 8 focuses on Edward Sexby's controversial tyrannicide-affirming pamphlet, *Killing Noe Murder* [1657]. The book concludes with a discussion of Gerard Winstanley and the Diggers, and the hope that 'their lives and words shine out and shout over a gulf of 350 years' (p. 433). While founded on the earlier theoretical chapters (that on Felton begins with a discussion of what revisionists and new historicists might do with the story), these vivid and well-written essays work well on their own. While Holstun may overstate the case that they are ignored figures (certainly his footnotes often point towards far more discussion than his writing itself seems to suggest), his point, that the new historicism has done little to shift attention to non-canonical writers, is evident to any one who flips through recent scholarly journals (or the pages of *YWES*).

In anticipation of the quatercentenary of Elizabeth's death, a number of works on her reputation appeared this year. Nostalgia for Queen Elizabeth in the Stuart period has been something of a commonplace in literary studies for many years, but John Watkins's *Representing Elizabeth in Stuart England: Literature, History, Sovereignty* offers a welcome revisionist corrective to the assumption that later decades looked back to the 'Queen of Famous Memory' with uncomplicated regret. Instead, he shows how different generations and groups within Stuart England used and rewrote Elizabeth's reign in response to local and immediate pressures. Watkins argues that even Whig historiography frequently presented Elizabeth as simultaneously absolutist and the protector of liberties. He traces three main concerns: that nostalgia was constructed rather than inevitable, that there was a perceived continuity between Elizabeth and her Stuart successors, and that Elizabeth's gender was a significant aspect of how she was remembered and her reign compared with the kings and queens of the Stuart period. Parts of this story, such as James's accession, have been told before, but in other chapters Watkins presents less familiar material.

Chapter 1 explores how James's accession was presented by panegyrists as the inheritance of a metaphorical son, pairing him with Elizabeth as bulwarks against papist aggression. This construction of James obliterated the awkward realities of his foreign birth and his mother's execution by Elizabeth. Through a range of literary works (both English and Latin) Watkins traces how the Gunpowder Plot served to reinforce the parallels between the two monarchs. Watkins's main (and very worthwhile) point is that the Armada was not a natural comparison, but that which was, the Babington plot, was unusable given the connection of this with James's mother. While most writers connected James with Elizabeth, Aemilia Lanyer instead presented a range of other female figures as the heirs of Elizabeth in her *Salve Deus Rex Judaeorum*.

Watkins's second chapter presents a welcome discussion of Thomas Heywood's historical drama and verse: he effectively challenges the idea that *If You Know Not Me* is a simple idealization of Elizabeth's reign. Instead, he suggests that Heywood offered a queen who gave up her prerogatives for the sake of the people, a role that challenged the present Stuart reality. In the first part of the play Heywood presents a queen who is humbled, and in the second he shows how a citizen, like Sir Thomas Gresham, might be raised up. Overall, Watkins sees in Heywood's play a celebration of the merchant class and an active and independent citizenry.

Chapter 3 describes the presentation of Elizabeth by three early Stuart historians, Camden, Naunton, and Greville, and suggests that all three emphasized her 'political genius'. An important element here is Watkins's argument that later scholars have selectively misread these historians and overlooked their understanding of the continuities between the two reigns. Naunton presents Elizabeth as ruling through factions rather than favourites in a way that establishes her as an umpire, but firmly in control; this reading provided parliamentarians and royalists with very different ways of celebrating her reign. Greville's Tacitean treatment is of a very different sort: his admiration is for those Elizabethan courtiers (like Sidney) who challenged the queen, rather than Elizabeth herself. At the same time her policies served as a contrast for him to those of James, and Watkins argues that these contradictions 'expose a historiographic moment when Elizabeth ceased to be the Protestant interventionalists' living opponent and became instead a trope that they could deploy against her successors' (p. 78). Both Charles and his parliaments invoked the memory of Elizabeth; the king used her to validate his return to a more closed court, and parliamentarians pointed to her 'Golden Speech' of 1601 as an example of royal deferring. In this reading her gender was important: she deferred appropriately to a male parliament.

The manufactured nostalgia for Elizabeth that inspired the rebels of the 1640s needed to be tempered in the post-monarchical 1650s, where her reign was frequently ignored. Some Commonwealth readings diminished her reign to the point of being proto-republican, linking her with the pre-monarchical judges of the Old Testament. Nostalgia for the time in which she reigned was not always a veneration of the queen herself, but of the administration and parliament of her time. Royalists of the 1640s could use her to argue for the royal prerogative. Watkins argues that, for Restoration writers like Francis Osborne, Elizabeth frequently functioned as a 'fantasy of constitutional equilibrium' (p. 108).

The book's last few chapters examine the increasing exploration of Elizabeth's private life in the Restoration period; some of this gossip extended back to her own time, but now reached print for the first time. With this came the loss of a consensus on her virtue. French romances and the case of a man who claimed to be her great-grandson are among the matters examined here. Watkins concludes that, after the revolution of 1689, while each new monarch was still hailed as a second Elizabeth, her role as a practical political model decreased. William's foreignness got in the way of analogies with Elizabeth, and queens Mary and Anne found that embracing her as an image was fraught with dangers. Her role as powerful Virgin Queen did not fit well with the emphasis *circa* 1700 on female domesticity. From that point, nostalgia for Elizabeth was rendered an innocuous 'vague myth' by the sense that her reign was now irrecoverable.

Michael Dobson and Nicola J. Watson's *England's Elizabeth: An Afterlife in Fame and Fantasy* is much broader in scope, covering the treatment of Elizabeth from her death to films and plays of the last few years. It also differs from Watkins's book in being more concerned with cultural reception than historiography. Its lavish illustrations and at times breathless tone at the range of cultural echoes of Elizabeth seem poised to capture a wider readership than is usual for a university press book. While covering a wide range of paintings, novels, plays, poems, and films on Elizabeth, it uses this material to present a cultural history of nation-building, or national self-consciousness-building. The challenge with this broad sweep is to make sense and a narrative of the four hundred years of material, and not lapse into merely reiterating that each generation remade Elizabeth for its own purposes. Something of this is attempted in the introduction, which is more successful at its end, with an analysis of the treatment of Elizabeth's death, a survey in miniature of what is to come.

In its discussion of treatment of Elizabeth in Stuart literary works, there is little to surprise, and much of the time the book reflects the overly simplified view of nostalgia that Watkins is at pains to counter. Unfortunately, in telling the familiar story of nostalgia for Elizabeth they slip into the contrasting caricature of James I ('a pacifist bisexual ecumenical Scotsman'), and evidence is distorted to fit the assumptions. For example, Cranmer's famous christening speech from *Henry VIII* is presented to illustrate how Jacobeans were 'far more interested in the remembered future of Princess Elizabeth … than in the official agenda of her heir', but this ignores the final twenty lines of that speech, which celebrate her phoenix-heir, James. They focus heavily on the 'costume dramas' depicting Elizabeth by Rowley, Dekker, and Heywood, and worthwhile attention is given to the costumes of these works and to the draping of Elizabeth in visual arts of the period. Overall, the reign of Charles, the Civil War period, and Interregnum are given little attention. Material from the 1650s is collapsed with that from just after James's accession. The 1660s saw the revival of some of these costume dramas, and Dobson and Watson note that, while there was a general turn towards Elizabeth as a private woman, and to 'the representation of apocryphal love plots' in the latter half of the century, the years of the Exclusion Crisis saw a re-emphasis of Elizabeth as a non-Stuart Protestant heroine.

To its credit, the book is up on the recent scholarship; it is only unfortunate that Watkins's book did not appear in time for the authors to draw on it. That the discussion of seventeenth-century productions of Elizabeth is put within a longer tradition, which includes Victorian historical romances and recent films, makes this work worthwhile. Also intriguing is an afterword on Elizabeth in America.

In *Roman Invasions: The British History, Protestant Anti-Romanism, and the Historical Imagination in England, 1530–1660*, John E. Curran, Jr. argues that, despite the 'historical revolution' of Camden and others, English scholars and poets of the early modern period show a continuing strain of anti-Romanism based upon Geoffrey of Monmouth. This 'Galfridian pattern' of resistance to the ancient Roman empire was frequently aligned with militant Protestant attitudes towards the Church of Rome. Yet all who took this view seem to have been conscious of the problems raised by the unreliability of Geoffrey pointed out by humanist scholars. They might wish to take back from Rome the legacy of Troy, but was the story of Brute historical enough to be the basis of a national epic? How should they respond to a Caesar who was both Britain's conqueror and its first historian? How could the claims to British origins coexist with an admittedly preponderant Anglo-Saxon genealogy? Joseph of Arimathea might be claimed as the founder of a British church that pre-existed Roman Christianity, but such an appeal to legendary material was at odds with Protestantism's usual dismissal of appeal to tradition.

The book is divided into six main chapters which typically explore the early modern historiography of the topic (the British Church, the Roman Invasion, Arthur, etc.) before turning to literary treatments. While the book does frequently consider relatively obscure works, such as the 1625 play *Fuimus Troes*, William Rowley's *A Shoomaker, A Gentleman*, and William Warner's *Albion's England*, Spenser, Drayton, Shakespeare, and Milton are the main poets discussed. Curran demonstrates that these four exhibit a typical range of manifestations of the resistance to Rome: Drayton was firmly committed to a Galfridian history, Spenser recognized the problems as well as the usefulness of the tradition, Shakespeare worked through and ultimately rejected Galfridianism, and Milton moved towards an anti-Roman position independent of Geoffrey. This is a clearly written and carefully argued work, solidly based on the historiography of the period.

Rhonda Lemke Sanford's *Maps and Memory in Early Modern England: A Sense of Place* is one of a number of recent studies devoted to mapmaking and other representations of geographical space (including Andrew Gordon, ed., *Literature, Mapping and the Politics of Space in Early Modern Britain*, CUP [2001]). This short book, based on a Ph.D. dissertation, is not concerned only with literal maps, but with mental ones that contributed to the understanding of place. Sanford examines maps as texts, as well as examples of 'cartographic writing', and shows the development of 'map consciousness'. Her opening chapter provides a history of maps in the period and a more extensive explanation of her theoretical framework. Dominant throughout is a concern with shifting centres and margins, with biases and distortions. The book places greater emphasis on literary mappings than on maps as texts, and those looking for the latter will be better served by Bernhard Klein's *Maps and the Writing of Space in Early Modern England and Ireland* (Palgrave [2001]).

Chapter 2 of Sanford's book focuses on the marriage of the Medway and the Thames in Book IV of *The Faerie Queene* to illustrate the making and use of maps in England, particularly in the courtly context to praise and direct the monarch. Through an examination of *Cymbeline*, chapter 3 addresses those maps and cartographic writings that present the mapped landscape as a female body. Chapter 4 considers the emerging science of surveying in the period and the attendant literature of 'surveying', including the 'country house poem'. Sanford suggests that the poet, for example Ben Jonson in 'To Penshurst', is analogous in social position and approach to the estate surveyor, engaged in what she calls a 'shared system of representational practices'. In her final chapter Sanford turns from the rural landscape to the urban, as she explores how accounts of royal progresses, Isabella Whitney's 'Wyll and Testament', city comedies, and other writings reflect a concern with urban districts and the maps that present them. The maps as illustrations are well chosen, if not spectacularly reproduced.

Willy Maley's collection of republished essays, *Nation, State, and Empire in English Renaissance Literature: Shakespeare to Milton*, goes beyond many recent studies of early modern English imperialism by placing discussion within the context of 'the British problem'. This solid study considers the tangled relations of English, Irish, and Scots in literary and political texts of the period 1590 to 1640. The first three chapters concern Shakespeare, both in his own time and in the reception history that has reduced him to an exclusively English playwright. Maley's contention is that Shakespeare is more profitably seen as a 'British' writer. In chapter 4 Maley returns to the subject of his earlier work, *Salvaging Spenser* [1997], arguing here that the complexity of Spenser's *View of the Present State of Ireland* demands a reading that goes beyond simple identification of hostility towards the Irish, and that Spenser shows 'an awareness of the vicissitudes of what historians have come to refer to as the "British Problem", that is, the painstaking process by which the British state was formed' (p. 90). Maley's final three chapters move beyond the well-worn topics of Shakespeare and Spenser as he turns to the little-noted *Certain Considerations touching the Plantation in Ireland* [1609] by Francis Bacon, which he suggests is a subtle examination of the place of Ireland in the attempted Anglo-Scottish union brought about by the English accession of King James. A chapter on John Ford's *Perkin Warbeck* [1633] resumes the focus on the history play, showing that Ford makes explicit use of the 'so-called Celtic fringe' (p. 5) as the main basis of support for Warbeck; in this way the play is more 'British' than narrowly 'English'. Maley concludes with a chapter on Milton's *Observations upon the Articles of Peace with the Irish Rebels* [1649] where he argues that this pamphlet is 'not an anti-Irish treatise in any simple sense' (p. 135), but, like the earlier works, deeply involved in the complexity of Britishness at a time of active strife among England, Ireland, and Scotland.

Another fine historicist study is Ernest Gilman's *Recollecting the Arundel Circle: discovering the Past, Recovering the Future*. Arundel's life has been adequately treated in Mary Hervey's *Life* [1921] and David Howarth's *Lord Arundel and his Circle* [1985], but this study concerns 'the shared local culture' (p. 5) of Arundel and such associates from diverse fields as Robert Cotton, John Selden, Franciscus Junius, Anthony Van Dyck, Henry Peacham, and William Harvey.

He is, quite rightly, attempting to develop a more accurate focus, one that avoids the narrow 'great individual' or the broad 'Caroline England'. Gilman primarily focuses on two overlapping roles of Arundel, those of art connoisseur and would-be developer of a Madagascar colony, and he strives to avoid flattening them into a single narrative or discourse. Arundel supported the work of the scholar Franciscus Junius and his significant *The Painting of the Ancients*, and Gilman reads this history of classical art as 'a work, *of*, as well as *about*, imagination' as Junius describes an art world largely lost to anything but a written record. He approaches Junius's work as a *cento*, both an appropriation of past writers and a setting of them in new contexts. There is rich archival research here, as he draws on Junius's unpublished letters to his uncle Vossius in Holland. These are the two main chapters that have not previously been published. In the chapters on the Madagascar enterprise, Gilman argues that the Arundel 'circle' was more tightly knit than most based on patronage because of the intense interest the earl maintained in his clients' projects. Finally, Gilman argues that Arundel's two main interests, artistic and colonial, pulled in the opposing directions of past and future.

Unfortunately, Gilman's solid work is undermined by numerous editorial lapses. In addition, the parenthetical referencing system is insufficient for the purpose; rich footnotes would have been welcome here, and instead Gilman is forced to stuff the parentheses with additional information. Scholars are referred to who are absent from the list of works cited. As paintings are an important element of the discussion, it is regrettable that the few included here are not better reproduced.

Using an approach that he labels 'transversal theory', Bryan Reynolds's *Becoming Criminal: Transversal Performance and Cultural Dissidence in Early Modern England* examines the culture of rogues and gypsies in the late Tudor and early Stuart period, and affirms that there was such an entity, 'united by its own aesthetic, ideology, language and lifestyle'. The book also fully examines the public and official response to this subculture, and frequently connects this response with our own culture's fascination with the criminal world. Among the works considered are Jonson's *The Gypsies Metamorphos'd*, Brome's *Jovial Crew*, *The Roaring Girl*, and Dekker's pamphlets.

The first chapter is dense with the book's theoretical framework and an incessant barrage of coined terms as Reynolds introduces a new mode of history, what he calls 'the investigative-expansive mode', which 'seeks comprehension of the subject matter's fluid, plural, and evolving relationships to its own parts and to the greater environments of which it is a part' (p. 5). While his insistent coinage of new and awkward terms grates, there is much of substance here. It is unfortunate that the heavy-going theoretical discussions of chapter 1 might obscure these strong and controversial arguments: that 'gypsy' was neither a racial category nor a representation foisted on this group by others, but 'an alternative society and culture that they invented for themselves', and that there were only what he calls 'performative gypsies' at the time in England.

Reynolds is also concerned with the social power of these representations and how they help build up what he calls the 'state machinery' (a corrective to Althusser's 'State apparatus'). Chapter 2 examines the term 'gypsy' and its place in the criminal culture. What makes this analysis compelling is his consideration of the question, 'Why now?' What made the long-standing term 'gypsy' suddenly voguish in the 1620s? However, the rest of the work casts aside this focus on the 1620s, and draws on a range of references from the 1530s to the 1660s. One of his main points is that (*contra* Frank Aydelotte's older, authoritative, study *Elizabethan Rogues and Vagabonds*), gypsies and rogues were not distinguished as two separate groups at the time: they used the same cant. His argumentation here is clear and compelling, and, unlike many recent scholars working in these fields, Russell probes beyond 'representation' to reality. He takes seriously the recurring idea in the statutes that these people 'called themselves Egyptians'.

To explain the 'transversal attraction', Reynolds suggests that gypsies' exoticism attracted the curious who became the victims of their crimes. Using a variety of literary and non-literary sources, Reynolds shows how becoming gypsy appealed not only because of its promised freedom, but also because of its economic advantages. Chapter 3 analyses the prime identifier of criminal culture, its use of cant or an exclusive language or 'antilanguage', which Reynolds sees as an aggressive challenge to the increasing standardization of English in the period. It is not only a challenge to the non-criminal world, but also an 'alluring mystery'. A linguistic analysis of 'cant' follows, which Reynolds sees as both a natural and an artificial language. He notes a consistency in cant terminology from the late sixteenth to the late seventeenth centuries. Chapter 4 examines the mobile aspect of criminal life in the period, another of its distinguishing features, the making of counterfeit passports, and the inability, despite concerted efforts, of the authorities to restrain criminals' movements. The use of St Paul's churchyard and the theatres as sites of activity by the criminal culture is also examined. Consideration of the theatrical connections is extended by exploring the perceived theatrical elements of disguise and deception in criminal behaviour. Criminals were often seen as supreme masters of theatre and rhetoric, and the book's final chapter attempts 'a "transversal poetics" of the public theater' (p. 126). Reynolds sees the theatre itself as 'transversal', and his willingness, unlike other scholars, to see 'the reality of the theatrical threat' is laudable.

Elizabeth Lane Furdell's *Publishing and Medicine in Early Modern England* is like her previous work, *Royal Doctors, 1485–1714* [2001], in being a work of medical history with much to offer the literary scholar. She sets out to consider how medical publishing (which the *Cambridge History of the Book* suggests offered the 'only works of natural knowledge to command a really sizeable readership'; p. 284) contributed to the development of the public sphere in the early modern period. Ultimately, she concludes that medical publishing was chiefly driven by profit, but had the effect of disseminating skills beyond the traditional elites by partaking in the struggles within the medical marketplace itself. Furdell's first chapter provides a clear and succinct overview of the Galenist orthodoxy as it stood in the early sixteenth century, before turning to the published works that challenged it and the struggles between the various groups of practitioners (physicians, surgeons, apothecaries). Chapter 2 places these struggles within the context of the broader history of printing. Furdell then turns in chapter 3 to consider a range of writers and printers of medical works, showing that the frenzied marketplace led printers to be undiscriminating in the range of materials they published. Chapter 4 examines the impetus of Protestantism, especially its more radical forms, on the expanding public exploration and discussion of medicine. 'A Way to Get Wealth' (chapter 5) turns to the little-discussed place of women in early modern medicine and medical publishing, and chapter 6 surveys the major bookshops that sold these works. Medical advertising, which was to become notorious in later centuries, is traced from its beginnings in 1652 (chapter 7): such advertising contributed to the breaking down of the monopoly of elite practitioners. The book's final chapter offers an analysis of the increasingly detailed illustrations of medical works in the period; Furdell suggests that this important dimension has been ignored by medical historians. An epilogue examines the 'Rose case' of 1702–4, which significantly changed the medical marketplace explored in the book by giving apothecaries the right to practise medicine. The attendant controversy included at least a couple of notable literary works: Samuel Garth's *Dispensary* [1699] and Sir Richard Blackmore's *Satyr against Wit* [1700].

While at times the book slides into annotated cataloguing of writers and printers, overall its rich detail will prove a valuable source for historians and literary scholars.

The many studies of the body in early modern literature could certainly benefit from this thorough study of what the medical publishing world was doing with it.

2. Prose

The study of seventeenth-century Utopian literature continued this year with Price, ed., *Francis Bacon's New Atlantis: New Interdisciplinary Essays*. Price's introduction offers a summary of the work, a short thematic analysis, a section on the text and the reader, and a reception history. Paul Salzman examines the generic origins of *The New Atlantis*, showing how it draws upon both the Utopian and the travel narrative traditions, and comparing it to a range of other early seventeenth-century works. The essays by Sarah Hutton and David Colclough are also concerned with form and rhetoric, with both highlighting the reader's engagement with the work. Richard Serjeantson situates Bacon's work in the history of natural science, and shows that his 'scientific interests are not as advanced as they are often thought to be'. Jerry Weinberger's discussion, however, suggests that Bensalem's highly technologized way of life pushes religion and the miraculous to the side. Claire Jowitt examines the text in its immediate context of late Jacobean England and Bacon's tenuous relationship with the court. She finds 'covert criticism' of James I in the work. Like recent articles by William Burns and Peter Pesic, Kate Aughterson challenges the frequent supposition that Bacon's science is highly 'masculinized'. In the final chapter, Simon Wortham re-examines the question of censorship and the production of knowledge in *The New Atlantis*.

Adam H. Kitzes, '*Hydriotaphia*, "The Sensible Rhetorick of the Dead"' (*SEL* 42:i[2002] 137–54), argues that Sir Thomas Browne considers the urns at the centre of that work as rhetorical artefacts, but like such objects the rhetorical function of these is multiple, incomplete and subject to decay. The burial of the dead is a 'defining element of humanity', a material way of communicating to others, in the present and the future, in what is sometimes an orderly, sometimes a random, way. The burials are understood in relation to community, and community-building, as a political act. Finally, he argues that by the time of *Hydriotaphia* Browne was sceptical about an apocalyptic end, and moving away from political engagement.

While the literature of exploration and travel has received much attention in the last decade, few studies on an individual writer have appeared. James Ellison's engaging *George Sandys: Travel, Colonialism and Tolerance in the Seventeenth Century* does this and more: he offers an examination of early seventeenth-century culture through the full life of one individual. While the greatest part of the book considers Sandys's *Relation of a Journey* [1615], chapters are also devoted to his biblical paraphrases (he calls Sandys's *Psalms* 'the most magnificent, ceremonial translations of Scripture which had ever been produced in Protestant England'; p. 30) and translation of Ovid. Ellison argues that Sandys was an early Latitudinarian and champion of tolerant Christian unity, finding analogies with the perspective of the 1630s Great Tew group even in his early writings and action. He traces these roots back to Erasmus and Neoplatonism, and the recent figures of Richard Hooker and George's brother, Sir Edwin Sandys. While Sandys had a position in the Caroline court, Ellison finds in him an opponent of religious persecution and absolutism in both state and church, and hence an example of the variety of opinion in the 1630s. Adopting a largely anti-revisionist reading of the time, he suggests that the official court culture tended to exacerbate the gap between the court and the nation.

Ellison finds in Sandys's poetry reflections of both what he calls 'Hooker the early Laudian' and 'Hooker the ecumenist' (p. 28). A major work of Sir Edwin Sandys, *A Relation of the State of Religion* [1605], based on his journey across Europe in the 1590s, also receives significant attention here: he shows in it an openness to many Catholic customs, and an examination of the potential for reunifying the Church. Ellison suggests that George Sandys's *Relation* is far more directly engaged with political and religious questions than other travel narratives of the time. Sandys saw in the Ottoman empire both a fearsome military power and a model of tyranny that Western princes were too likely to emulate. Unlike Richard Knolles and many others, he did not call for a reunited Christendom to fight against the Turks. Instead, like his brother Edwin, he recognized the role a powerful Ottoman empire played in preventing a Catholic attack on northern European Protestantism. Ultimately, Sandys uses the empire as 'an emblem of unjust government' (p. 61) that is doomed to self-destruction.

Among the fresh editions of primary works is one of 'Overbury's' *Characters*, edited by Donald Beecher as part of the Barnabe Riche Society series. This volume provides an extensive introduction that delineates clearly the complicated publication history of this growing volume, and ably situates it in its social and political context. Especially helpful here is the consideration of the work within the context of contests and games in court and other elite circles. The introduction also steps back to consider the character as a genre, and questions the influence of Theophrastus's writing on the Overburian character. Like the other volumes in this series, this one offers a modern-spelling text with extensive annotations. The edition is based on the 1622 (eleventh) edition of the work, with variants from the first appearance of each character included in an appendix. Short glossing of words appears at the foot of the page, with more extensive commentaries presented as endnotes. Overall, the annotation is generous, befitting a volume geared to students as well as scholars.

A second helpful primary work, *Amazons, Savages, and Machiavels. Travel and Colonial Writing in English, 1550–1630: An Anthology*, by Andrew Hadfield, is a collection of original-spelling excerpts from primary travel accounts of the period. The volume is divided into five sections: general discussion of travel, and then accounts of travel in Europe, Africa, the Near East, the Far East, and the Americas. As Hadfield himself notes, 'otherness' and 'difference' 'have become self-parodic clichés' (p. 1), and his introduction is careful to point out how early modern travel differed from that of the later colonialism and imperialism upon which Said developed his paradigm. Both in the general introduction and the shorter introductions to the five sections and individual writers, he establishes the historical context and functions of the different travel accounts. Some excerpts are well known: Ascham on the 'Italianate Englishman', Smith on Pocahontas, Bacon's 'Of Travel', and Ralegh on Guyana, but also included are some relatively little-known texts: passages from Sir Charles Somerset's diary on Paris and Florence, Giles Fletcher's 'Description of the Country of Russia', and accounts of Japan by Arthur Hatch and John Saris. Hadfield is largely concerned with published works, or at least ones intended for a wide readership. This well-edited volume should work well as a classroom text.

3. Women's Writing

(a) Editions
This year saw an increased interest in editing early modern women's writing, affirmed by the ten editions produced this year. Stephanie Hodgson-Wright addresses the problems of editing anthologies in *Women's Writing of the Early Modern Period, 1588–1688: An Anthology*. The answer to the problems presented by editing her anthology is to explicitly acknowledge that the pieces in the collection have been selected because they share certain characteristics, rather than attempting to provide an authoritative or definitive selection. Consequently, the texts share the characteristics of being published material that revise and challenge master narratives. Although some scholars may find the emphasis on published material anachronistic, this impressive collection aims to demonstrate how women presented themselves to a mass print audience, and the various ways in which they engaged in the dramatic changes that occurred in early modern politics and culture. The anthology covers more canonized material, but contains a wide selection of authors from as early as Jane Anger and Elizabeth I to later seventeenth-century writers such as Bathsua Makin, Anne Bradstreet, and Aphra Behn. A variety of genres is presented, ranging from poetry, drama, speeches, and fiction to polemical prose. Poetic writings from the earlier part of the seventeenth century are represented by Mary Sidney Herbert, Aemilia Lanyer, Lady Mary Wroth, Diana Primrose, and Katherine Philips, while the edition also features drama by Elizabeth Cary and Margaret Cavendish. Prose by Rachel Speght, Anne Stagg, Elizabeth Poole, Anna Trapnel, and Mary Carleton is also included. Hodgson-Wright hopes that the reader will study the pieces in a comparative manner, rather than as individual texts, and has included a useful index of themes to assist teachers in preparing or selecting materials for their courses. The anthology aims to provide a collection of texts that can form the base for a course in early modern women's writing, and full texts or substantial extracts are generally presented to allow for more in-depth study of the pieces. Unfortunately, it does not provide extensive notes or historical background, but the edition does contain a chronological table that places the authors in a literary and historical context while also including a bibliography for further reading and brief biographical information on each author. Containing a wide selection of authors, the edition provides a long-awaited, excellent introduction to early modern women's published texts. Retailing in paperback at £18, and having modernized spellings and punctuation, it is an accessible edition to scholars and students alike, and could make a viable base for a women's writing course.

This year also saw an increasing interest in women's autobiographical writings with the publication of two separate anthologies. In the republished edition of Graham et al., eds., *Her Own Life: Autobiographical Writings by Seventeenth-Century Englishwomen*, it is noted that dozens of seventeenth-century women wrote autobiographical texts. This collection aims to introduce a substantial array of self-writings from women across a range of religious and political ideologies. Consequently, the twelve pieces represent different lifestyles and class backgrounds, with the authors ranging from a shipwright's daughter to a duchess. The various genres also demonstrate the diversity of the edition since literary styles such as diary, romance, defence, memoir, prophecy, conversion narrative, and lyric poetry are represented. All the excerpts, which are substantial in length, are presented with an introduction to the author and the cultural and historical circumstances that influenced the text, along with contextual notes about each written piece. The edition does include already canonized authors such as Margaret Cavendish, Anne Clifford, An Collins, and Anna Trapnel, yet there are also lesser-known writers such as Mary Carleton, Susanna Parr, Katherine Evans, and Sarah Cheevers. The texts portray a wide variety of life experiences and perspectives such as imprisonment under the Spanish Inquisition, legal battles against patriarchal systems of inheritance, religious devotion, spiritual reasons for leaving an abusive husband, and court defences against charges of false prophesying and even bigamy, demonstrating not only the problems that women encountered, but also the diversity of female experiences during the early modern period. Although the retail price may be too high for undergraduates, the opening information about each author, along with modernized spelling, makes this a useful introduction to women's autobiographical writing.

A different approach to autobiography is taken in Booy, ed., *Personal Disclosures An Anthology of Self-Writings from the Seventeenth Century*. The anthology aims not only to contribute to the recovery of women's writing, but also to introduce male self-writings, an area that has received very little scholarly attention. The seventy-two individuals represented include a wide selection of both men and women writers. Though the number of extracts is vast, they provide a good basis for comparison of male and female representations of self. Indeed the collection aims to provoke debate about gendered constructions of identity, and the pieces are organized under six different topic headings to facilitate a comparative study. The categories presented—marriage, parents and children, early adulthood, body and mind, religious experience, and the New World—are individually introduced, and there is an interesting and detailed introduction to the economic, political, and cultural circumstances of each subject. Biographical information about each author is also provided, and the book has modernized spellings; though the extracts may be too brief for those wanting more substantial texts, the volume would provide scholars with a very good basis for beginning research in the field of self-writings, particularly since Booy presents a vast range of genres and styles. He argues that self-writings are not confined to diaries, confessions, and autobiographies, but values and a sense of self-awareness occur in texts where a writer discusses matters outside of the self. Consequently, the edition includes a range of literary forms, from personal diaries and memoirs to narratives of exploration and reports of court proceedings. Most of the pieces are written by members of the middle and upper classes, as there is a lack of self-writings by the plebeian classes, yet ten of the texts are from lower-class origins, portraying diverse experiences and opinions. The edition aims to portray the ways in which people construct, interpret, and create their identity, demonstrating the various understandings of self that were present within the seventeenth century.

Rather than autobiography, letters prove to be a means for portraying politics and culture in Parker, ed., *Dorothy Osborne: Letters to William Temple, 1652–54: Observations on Love, Literature, Politics and Religion*. Compared to his previous

Penguin Classics edition, Kenneth Parker has included more letters addressing issues of family, gender, politics, and literature, and although there have been minor changes, the letters remain largely unchanged. Parker also presents a biography and family histories for both Osborne and William Temple, whose marriage united two important gentry families, in order to emphasize the link between making family fortunes and political power. The introduction discusses Osborne's letters within their political, gender, and literary contexts, including a publication history. Parker suggests that the edition will be of particular interest to scholars engaged in reassessing society during the Civil War.

The series The Early Modern Englishwoman: A Facsimile Library of Essential Works provides 'carefully chosen copies' of texts and has published four editions this year on diverse subjects. Each text has a brief introduction that includes an overview of the life and work of the writer. In *Writings on Medicine*, Lisa Forman Cody states that the four works presented are the only known exclusively medical texts by Restoration women. These pieces dramatically question assumptions regarding female healers and medical practice in early modern England. Although three of the texts are by Jane Sharp, Elizabeth Cellier, and Mary Trye, who were published after 1670, 'The Mid-wives just Petition' was published in 1643. The introduction provides a brief yet interesting overview of women's participation in medicine, contradicting previous understandings of medical history. In the same series, Susan C. Staub's introduction to *Mother's Advice Books* argues that women's advice books offer an alternative to traditional understandings of the family. The collection includes Elizabeth Richardson, Susanna Bell, the anonymous writer of 'The Mothers Blessing: Being Several Godly Admonitions given by a Mother unto her Children upon her Death-bed, a little before her departure', and later male-authored texts about individual mothers such as Mary Pennyman and Elizabeth Walker. The texts included are 'notable for their development of a motherly persona, their emphasis on spiritual and domestic matters and their characterization of the works as legacies'.

The same series also provides two French texts translated by nuns who had moved to Continental Europe. In *Elizabeth Evelinge, I*, Frans Korsten presents the translation of the 'The history of the angelicall virgin glorious S. Clare', a work by the Franciscan priest François Hendricq. Elizabeth Evelinge translated the historical account of St Clare, who was part of a thirteenth-century women's religious order devoted to the ideal of poverty. In *Pudentiana Deacon*, Frans Blom and Jos Blom present 'Delicious entertainments of the soule', Pudentiana Deacon's translation of 'Les vrays entretiens spirituels' ('The Authentic Spiritual Conference') by Francis de Sales. The text is a collection of conferences about religious topics given by St Francis for the order of the Sisters of the Visitation. Unfortunately, the many printing mistakes, owing to the fact that the original publisher did not have an English typesetter, make the work difficult to read.

Churchill, Brown, and Jeffrey, eds., *Early Modern Women Writing Latin*, volume 3 in the series Women Writing Latin, from Roman Antiquity to Early Modern Europe, argue that, although literacy in Latin has been understood as fundamental to institutions of male power and authority, scholars have recently found that women participated in Latin literacy much more than has been recognized. Each section of the collection includes a Latin text, an English translation, a select bibliography, and a biography of each author's life, describing the cultural, religious, and political influences on the texts. Although scholars may find the collection as a whole to be too general as it includes authors from various European countries and ranges from as early as the 1400s, it does include two seventeenth-century British writers. In 'Elizabeth Jane Weston (1581–1612)', Brenda M. Hosington provides nine of Weston's neo-Latin poems, and in 'Bathsua Reginald Makin (1600–1675?)', Anne Leslie Saunders presents part of 'Musa Virginea', a political text written for the king when Makin was only 16 years old.

(b) Books

This year saw quite a few significant and interesting books that explore methods for obtaining literary authority within diverse aspects of early modern culture ranging from silence, violence, and race to death. The rhetoric of silence is discussed in Christina Luckyj's 'A moving Rhetoricke': Gender and Silence in Early Modern England. Luckyj argues that it is misleading to locate power in speech alone since the meaning of silence was an unstable and highly contested site in early modern England. Such competing ideological conflicts had significant implications for gender, particularly since women were supposed to be silent, obedient, and chaste. Challenging the common scholarly assumption that feminine silence was always subjugation, the book situates both males and females within the competing meanings of silence and demonstrates that silence was a powerful rhetoric itself. Initially, Luckyj investigates the complex cultural history of both speech and silence using a multitude of examples from literature, philosophy, and politics and beginning with classical understandings and how they influenced Renaissance thought. In some instances speech was understood as civilizing while silence was anti-social, foolish, or barbarous. Yet silence could also be conceived as a superior form of speech or as a space of resistance that was inscrutable, unfathomable, and potentially very subversive. Many early modern texts demonstrate suspicion over too much feminine silence, investing it with significant power that could threaten masculine authority since it was less tangible or easy to control. Consequently silence was associated with witches, hysteria, and unmanageable female sexuality. Luckyj examines silence in drama by male authors such as Kyd, Marston, Webster, Middleton, and Shakespeare, arguing that a single play might contain a wide range of constructions of silence and gender in complex and overlapping ways and portraying how silence can be both reassuringly submissive and dangerously transgressive. Many women writers, such as Wroth, Cary, and Askew, broaden and complicate the discourse of silence, drawing on its complex history to authorize their texts, and even invoking their own silence as superior to male rhetoric.

Instead of rhetorical silence, Sidney L. Sondergard focuses on how women used or evaded the discourse of rhetorical violence in Sharpening her Pen: Strategies of Rhetorical Violence by Early Modern English Women Writers. Sondergard argues that all language and images of violence used by an author are encoded as methods of persuasion. Although the use of rhetorical violence in early modern women writers is often a response to patriarchy, his intention is not to depict a shared female tradition. Instead he aims to examine how individual women writers employed rhetorical violence in their images, tropes, and arguments while revealing the objectives of using such discourse and the ways in which those objectives were achieved. Six authors in total are discussed in the book; authors from the seventeenth century are represented by Aemilia Lanyer, Lady Mary Wroth, and

Lady Anne Southwell. Sondergard argues that Lanyer uses rhetorical violence to equate cruelty to Christ with cruelty to women, redefining power by creating an opposition to those who practise violence, metaphorical and real, against the innocent. Consequently, she situates her authority as a writer in her suffering as a woman and further urges her readers to become warriors modelled on heroes of feminized myth and Christ. Wroth also uses rhetorical violence to facilitate her entrance into a male-dominated genre while challenging the violence that is implicit in male portrayals of love. Violence is ultimately portrayed as being ineffectual, and although women are depicted as being capable of 'male' aggressiveness, they generally chose to avoid it. Southwell has a different interpretation and use of rhetorical violence as she reveals the cultural traps that await women, particularly those who are married. She constructs a system where she disciplines her own volatile temper, yet concedes that violence is a politically common and effective means of coercion. Lanyer, Wroth, and Southwell demonstrate that although the tactics and reasons for women using rhetorical violence were diverse, it ultimately resulted in attaining autonomy and intellectual authority.

Methods of attaining self-authorization are also found in a very unexpected aspect of early modern life since women found literary authority in the cultural practices and ideologies surrounding death. In *Women, Death and Literature in Post-Reformation England*, Patricia Phillippy discusses the gendered treatment of death in post-Reformation England, demonstrating that women's mourning was condemned as excessive, physical, violent, sexual, and even resistant to the will of God, whereas men's lamentation was perceived approvingly as stoic, internal, and moderate. Since women were believed to focus on the body of the departed rather than the soul, while they were also primarily responsible for performing the physical tasks related to death, this maintained the common cultural association of women with the body. Consequently, gender politics was used to maintain Protestant ideologies since reformers depicted women's grief as resembling Catholic rituals while male lamentation was portrayed as more internal and Protestant. Examining male- and female-authored texts from wide variety of genres such as diaries, poems, plays, plague history, elegies, instructional and consolatory works, and even funerary, liturgical, and lamentational practices, Phillippy explores the ideological functions of images of women's mourning and how they supported masculine polemics, investigating not only the images of feminine lamentation but also the period's treatment of the female body in death. Studying a variety of authors such as Shakespeare, Lady Jane Grey, Phillip Stubbes, Anne Clifford, Elizabeth Russell, Rachel Speght, Alice Sutcliffe, and Aemilia Lanyer, she reconstructs women's lamentation practices, arguing that the same characteristic that opens women's mourning to censure becomes a means of authorizing and empowering women's speech. Death also opened up a sphere of activity where noblewomen could obtain considerable economic and creative licence. Female-authored texts particularly depict how women consistently reinterpret and deploy unorthodox forms of immoderate mourning to support textual expressions of grief that often transgressed patriarchal conventions.

Female literary authorization is also explored in relation to race in Joyce Green MacDonald's *Women and Race in Early Modern Texts*. MacDonald discusses how there was an emerging racial consciousness due to colonization which shaped early modern Englishwomen as well as Englishmen. Since blackness, and black women, are frequently represented as white in the period, African women's bodies had a powerful representational charge. Using critical race theory and investigating texts from the sixteenth century by authors such as Shakespeare and Mary Sidney to later authors such as Aphra Behn and Thomas Southerne, she maps two specifically gendered strategies of empire: the removal of dark-skinned women from representation, and Englishwomen's racial identity being understood in terms of gender. MacDonald portrays how colonialism used gender to naturalize its racial and class hierarchies, yet also investigates how other women's race and sexuality became a powerful instrument for English women writers' own authorial legitimacy. Chapter 6 specifically focuses on Katherine Philips's translation of Corneille's *Pompey*, where the 'good' woman Cornelia is ideologically situated against a demonized dark Cleopatra. Philips uses her own 'whiteness' as well as the race of others for literary self-authorization since female authorship is identified with Cornelia's moral triumph and Cleopatra's political defeat, thus demonstrating MacDonald's argument that 'writing, or refusing to write, racial identity deeply implicates gender'.

Race in relation to gender has also been addressed in two other books this year, both by Lisa Hopkins. In chapter 7 of *Writing Renaissance Queens*, Hopkins draws parallels with Elizabeth Cary's *The Tragedy of Mariam*, not only with the racial discourse surrounding historical rulers but also with the characters portrayed in Shakespeare's texts. In Cary's play, women were constructed as simultaneously black and white, a strategy of comparison and differentiation that acts as a separation which redefines the category of woman. Chapter 1 further provides a very interesting discussion of the various theories of female rule and how Renaissance queens were perceived within their political, religious, and historical context. Hopkins argues that these representations later influenced many early modern texts, consequently affecting the understanding of women's authority in general. Representations of female rulers and race are also explored in chapter 5 of Hopkins's other book, *The Female Hero in English Renaissance Tragedy*, where she examines how representations of women in history and literature are apparent in Elizabeth Cary's *The Tragedy of Mariam* and Jane Cavendish's and Elizabeth Brackley's *The Concealed Fancies*. Both texts depict the figure of Cleopatra, yet Cary's uses her race to create a binary opposition between two women where only 'fair' Mariam is eventually able to transcend her gender and be perceived as fully human. In contrast, Cleopatra is an empowering role model in *The Concealed Fancies*. Both plays contain many theatrical and historical references, demonstrating how women used 'repeated representation and re-presentation' to redefine their role.

The historical representation of women is also discussed in Mary Spongberg's *Writing Women's History Since the Renaissance*. Chapter 2 provides a broad survey of the development of history in relation to gender from the Renaissance to contemporary times. Chapter 3 maps women's historical writing throughout the European and English Renaissance to the late 1700s, analysing British authors such as Ann Fanshawe, Lucy Hutchinson, and Margaret Cavendish. Spongberg demonstrates how these women's commemorative histories of their husbands subverted traditional historical genres and gender expectations. Although interesting, the book may not provide enough focus upon the early modern period, or on Britain, for academics in this field.

The representation of heroism is explored in *Gender and Heroism in Early Modern English Literature*, in which Mary Beth Rose argues that the tradition of heroism is often associated with masculinity. Yet the sixteenth and seventeenth centuries saw heroism in a more passive sense: not as the ability to confront and conquer danger, but as having the capacity to endure and suffer misfortune and malevolence. The book traces the changing cultural meanings and representations of heroism through various texts from male authors, from Shakespeare, Jonson, and Marlowe to later writers such as Milton, Aphra Behn, and Mary Astell. Chapter 2 specifically discusses the heroic identity in Elizabeth I's speeches, which constructed her royal authority through monopolizing all gendered positions without privileging either sex. The representation of her authority and heroism altered during her reign, initially insisting on the absolute privileges of the monarch, then moving to a reciprocity between herself and the subjects. Unlike Queen Elizabeth, other women created themselves as heroes of their own lives in autobiographical writings. In chapter 4, the secular autobiographies of Margaret Cavendish, Anne Halkett, Ann Fanshawe, and Alice Thornton depict women's relations and actions within a social and political world and consequently make their own contribution to the transformations of heroism.

In '"So great a diffrence is there in degree": Amelia Lanyer and the Critique of Aristocratic Privilege' (in Barnaby and Schnell, eds., *Literate Experience: The Work of Knowing in Seventeenth-Century English Writing*), editors Andrew Barnaby and Lisa Schnell argue that Lanyer uses puns and complex word-play to deconstruct the poet–patron relationship which creates the forms of knowing that result from a culture of aristocratic privilege. Rhetorical strategies of self-representation become a point of self-authorization that challenges the boundaries of the patronage system.

In *Poetic Resistance: English Women Writers and the Early Modern Lyric*, Pamela S. Hammons focuses on the poetry of child loss, particularly that of Anne Askew and Katherine Austen, portraying how women placed their poetry into pre-existing poetic traditions and writing practices to alter or reinterpret social conventions. Hammons analyses the work of diverse women from various social stations who held different and opposing values. Yet all of these women employed their poetry as a form of resistance to redefine their position in society while adding their own innovations to lyric traditions. In chapter 2 Hammons argues that both male and female poems mourning other people's children are very similar, using standard conventions of manuscript culture. Yet the frequent demonization and intense blame of mothers requires the mother of a lost child to use a restrictive 'plain style' which suppresses any display of intellectual, creative agency. Some women used the conventions of plain style to resist the cultural pressures that blamed them, simultaneously meeting, surpassing, and redefining the tradition. Rather than mothers, chapter 3 discusses the poetic resistance of a prophet, Anna Trapnel. Hammons demonstrates that, contrary to scholarly criticism, it is crucial to understand Trapnel as a poet since she appropriated poetic practices and biblical subject matter. By analysing specifically how Trapnel appropriates the tropes and themes within the Song of Songs, imitating its repetitive, cyclical construction and the ballad-metre vocabulary common to metrical translations of David's psalms, she justifies both her public speech and her poetic voice. Although she was conservative and concerned with social propriety, chapter 4 discusses widow Katherine Austen's conflict between her status and her gender, provoking complex, discontinuous self-representations. Her strategic self-representations as the assailed widow Penelope, a powerful prophet, and an amateur poet respond to a wide variety of conventional delimitations of her social position. Ultimately, Austen's verse performs the advance in social rank so important to her and so jeopardized by her gender.

Poetry is also the focus of Lynette McGrath's *Subjectivity and Women's Poetry in Early Modern England: 'Why on the ridge should she desire to go?'* Applying post-structural, feminist psychoanalytic theories such as those of Luce Irigaray, Hélène Cixous, Julia Kristeva, and Rosi Braidotti, along with historical scholarship on women's poetry, McGrath's is the first book to apply psychoanalytic theories of linguistic subjectivity exclusively to early modern women's poetry. Using a new historicist approach, McGrath argues that female subjectivity is not a stable position, but can function in a combative dialogue with the patriarchal language which produces it. Early modern women learned to deploy recognizable and discursive strategies to resist and alter the power of male language. In chapter 2, 'The Body', McGrath discusses how women's bodies were perceived as sexual, fragmented, linked with corruption, and reducible, objects of the male gaze. Although the essentializing of women as bodies often repressed their access to language and writing, by deploying various strategies of textual resistance women claimed their bodies in almost every way possible. Chapter 3 discusses cultural views of women's education, arguing that women used conflicting attitudes to find spaces to resist patriarchal dictates. Literacy and learning were a means to subjectivity for women, yet they were also a way for them to become subjects of their own pleasure and choice. Chapter 5 discusses how the language of Elizabeth Cary does not rely on rational consistency, but resembles Irigaray's understanding of female expression and pleasure. The heroine has a fluid subjectivity, often contradictory and inconsistent, yet mobile, and is thus unable to be situated in a solidified, essentialized position. Chapter 7 explores how Aemilia Lanyer depicted a female community which is relational and multi-positioned to construct herself as subject and to rewrite her pleasure. Yet she also used metaphor, particularly through the image of Christ, to authorize and rewrite the female subject and the nature of power itself.

(c) Edited Volumes

Scholars will be pleased to see a number of important edited collections this year. A particularly significant one is Pacheco, ed., *A Companion to Early Modern Women's Writing*. Anita Pacheco claims that the collection aims 'to convey the remarkable extent of women's textual production in early modern England', seeking to situate writings in their historical and cultural contexts. The first section, entitled 'Contexts', provides a broad discussion of early modern life and the gaps between patriarchal decrees and actual practice. Kenneth Charlton's 'Women and Education' discusses how women received education from academies, elementary schools, tutors, church sermons, literature, and other households, including the royal court. Charlton further addresses the extent of their education, which may have included literacy, music, foreign languages, and housewife skills, and examines in what ways women were educators themselves. In 'Religion and the Construction of the Feminine', Diane Willen explores the complicated relationship between women and religion, since religion maintained patriarchy yet was also used to transcend sex inequality. Protestant women developed a dynamic, political relationship with the state that was obscured or hidden by their gender role and the spiritual context in which political issues operated. In 'Women, Property and Law', Tim Stretton discusses women's status in law. Although the legal system severely discriminated against women, particularly their right to own property, the various courts and laws at times applied contradictory legislation. Consequently patriarchal law did not entirely restrict women from controlling land and litigating in courts. In 'Women and Work', Sara Mendelson discusses the various working lives of poor, middle-class, and elite women. Although women were often denied a professional identity, in reality they performed a remarkable range of paid and unpaid work, from manual labour, crafts, service, teaching, running businesses, and estate management to prostitution and theft. In Margaret Ezell's 'Women and Writing', Ezell argues that, although new understandings of authorship have helped in rediscovering women writers, women wrote for a variety of reasons and in a variety of spaces. In privileging the idea of a solitary author who valued publication and payment, scholarship is not considering the larger literary culture and its dynamics of textual production and circulation.

In the same volume, part 2, entitled 'Readings', provides critical introductions to ten major texts, focusing on texts from as early as Isabella Whitney and Mary Sidney to as late as Aphra Behn and Mary Astell. In 'Aemilia Lanyer: "Salve Deus Rex Judaeorum"', Susanne Woods provides biographical information and then argues that Lanyer challenges many of the conventions that she employs, particularly those within the Petrarchan tradition. Woods further compares the text to Jonson's 'To Penshurst', claiming that Jonson celebrates hierarchy, whereas Lanyer does not completely accept class difference. Elaine Beilin's 'Elizabeth Cary: *The Tragedy of Mariam* and History' demonstrates that Cary critiques historiography's attempt to provide a stable historical moment and instead offers a multiplicity of voices and 'truths': 'Cary invites her readers to look at this history play to find wisdom, but implies that only if all its voices are heard will the whole truth emerge'. In Naomi J. Miller's 'Mary Wroth: *The Countess of Montgomery's Urania*', Miller explores the different understandings of female identity, presented particularly in relation to heterosexual desire, maternity, and female friendship, as they transgress and redefine the female role. The variety and diversity of representations of women resist an essentialist interpretation of sex, demonstrating an awareness of the constructed nature of gender. In 'Margaret Cavendish: A True Relation', Gweno Williams claims that, although Cavendish attempts to create a truth/fiction binary along with an idealized portrait of her family intended to support the royalist cause, she nonetheless destabilizes the notion of truth. Williams suggests that perhaps 'A True Relation' was omitted from subsequent publications because her later works transgressed fixed literary genres and notions of truth. Hilary Hinds, 'Anna Trapnel: Anna Trapnel's Report and Plea', examines the ways in which the text functioned as a dialogue with Trapnel's accusers, strategically working to disarm opposition by removing her prophecies and self from problematic signifiers related to body and language, even creating parallels between her condition and that of Christ. In 'Katherine Philips: Poems', Elizabeth H. Hageman suggests that the task of a feminist critic is to understand how an author wrote 'as a woman' and how one would define herself inside patriarchal paradigms. Hageman demonstrates how, in this context, Philips responds to and critiques various male authors and traditions.

Though at times very general, part 3, entitled 'Genres', covers a broad range of literary genres such as autobiography, defences, prophecy, poetry, prose fiction, and drama. Sheila Ottway, in 'Autobiography', traces the development of the potentially transgressive activity of women's self-writing. After examining numerous autobiographical writings in the form of diaries, narrative prose, and poetry, Ottway concludes that there was considerable diversity in the ways in which women understood the self. In 'Defences of Women', Frances Teague and Rebecca de Haas argue that a literary form emerged from misogynist traditions: the defence of women. Teague and de Haas explore the development of the defence in the period 1500–1700, arguing that two literary traditions existed: polemic defences and literary catalogues which praise exemplary women. In 'Prophecy', Elaine Hobby states that prophecy was arguably 'the single most important genre for women in the early modern period'. Hobby examines numerous texts from both ecstatic and visionary prophets and from campaigning Quakers within their historical and political context, demonstrating that most women prophets were concerned with reinterpreting gender. In 'Women's Poetry 1550–1700', Bronwen Price explores the developments and shifts in women's poetry in different historical periods from 1550 to 1700. Analysing numerous poets, Price argues that the period as a whole demonstrates one thematic link: women questioning or redefining gender within a variety of literary shapes and forms. In 'Prose Fiction', Paul Salzman argues that, although prose fiction encompasses a wide variety of genres, few women wrote prose fiction compared to other literary forms. Salzman analyses various texts in their historical context, particularly focusing upon works by Mary Wroth, Margaret Cavendish, and Aphra Behn, who, impressively, wrote in every mode of prose fiction. In 'Drama', Sophie Tomlinson focuses on texts produced for commercial theatre. Discussing numerous dramatists, Tomlinson looks at developments within tragedy and comedy by early modern women, noting that women's tragic drama tends to depict tensions between women and the public sphere while comedy is concerned with social and sexual relations.

Part 4, 'Issues and Debates', is particularly interesting for scholars since it addresses the challenges that face the study of early modern women's writing, such as approaches to the canon and feminist historiography. In 'The Work of Women in the Age of Electronic Reproduction', Melinda Alliker Rabb discusses problems with integrationalist and separatist approaches to the canon, arguing that the field remains marginal because of the conventions of print culture. Yet e-culture not only makes texts accessible outside anthologies, but may also provide new ways of reading and interpreting texts which are more akin to early modern manuscript culture. In 'Feminist Historiography', Margo Hendricks examines the tendency of feminist scholars of history and literature to treat women as if they were a homogenous group regardless of class, race, sexuality, or ethnicity. Evidence suggesting that there were immigrant populations living in England demonstrates the need for more archival research to offer a more representational view of early modern women. The collection as a whole provides an excellent introduction to early modern women's writing and although, sadly, at £75 it is too expensive for undergraduates, it is definitely worth ordering for the library and would be useful for teaching as well as research.

Malcolmson and Suzuki, eds., *Debating Gender in Early Modern England, 1500–1700*, includes articles that address the *querelle des femmes*, the debate regarding the relationship between sexes that took place in early modern England. The collection begins with a section entitled 'Manuscript and Debate' which considers the influence of both earlier and Continental debates as well as the significance of manuscript culture. In 'Christine De Pizan's City of Ladies in Early Modern England', Malcolmson demonstrates that the Tudor courts were, in a limited way, familiar with the idea of 'City of Ladies' and Pizan's works were available in the royal libraries. Consequently, women authors such as Elizabeth I, Aemilia Lanyer, and particularly Margaret Cavendish may have had access to the text. In Elizabeth Clarke's 'Anne Southwell and the Pamphlet Debate: The Politics of Gender, Class, and Manuscript', Clarke argues that, owing to her education and knowledge of coterie society, the unknown Constantia Munda is likely to have been the aristocrat Anne Southwell. Although Southwell had an aversion to print, Clark draws comparisons with middle-class Rachel Speght, who both employed a rhetoric that actively attempted to change misogynist attitudes.

The Swetnam controversy is also addressed in the second section, 'Print, Pedagogy, and the Question of Class', but primarily in regard to middle-class and popular culture. In 'Muzzling the Competition: Rachel Speght and the Economics of Print', Lisa J. Schnell examines the printing histories of the Swetnam controversy, arguing that Sowernam humiliates Speght for her naivety about class decorum and the profit and entertainment motives behind the print industry. Schnell analyses Speght's later work as a response to Sowernam; here she discusses an equality in death which becomes 'her own literary obituary'. In 'Women's Popular Culture? Teaching the Swetnam Controversy', Melinda J. Gough argues that including non-elite authors and genres disrupts the tendency of students to perceive Shakespeare as untouched by popular culture, to read women authors as aesthetically inferior, and to search for essentialized woman's voices. This practice expands definitions of authorship and also demonstrates the literary influence that women had as patrons, investors, and audiences.

The influence of female audiences is also addressed in the third section, 'Women's Subjectivity in Male-Authored Texts'. Sandra Clark's 'The Broadside Ballad and the Woman's Voice' argues that, despite the assumption of male authorship, these texts at times target female consumers since they express women's subject position. Clark demonstrates that, rather than the pamphlet debate being a monolithic patriarchal structure, the broadside ballad challenges patriarchal values regarding marriage. In 'Weele have a Wench Shall Be Our Poet: Samuel Rowlands' Gossip Pamphlets', Susan Gushee O'Malley analyses gossip pamphlets that depict women drinking and talking in taverns, arguing that they were targeted at middle-class and often female audiences. Although Rowlands's work is possibly meant as a satire, O'Malley explores the potential responses from women and suggests that it could have influenced women writers.

The pamphlet debate is further investigated in the context of other genres and literary forms in the fourth section, 'Generic Departures: Figuring the Maternal Body, Constructing Female Culture'. In 'The Mat(t)er of Death: The Defense of Eve and the Female *Ars Moriendi*', Patricia Phillippy argues that Rachel Speght and Alice Sutcliffe use the masculine literary form of *ars moriendi* to enter public discourse and print. Although the ritual of mourning was associated with the private and the feminine, it became a defence of women and a means of literary self-authorization. Rather than death, Naomi J. Miller examines maternity in conduct books, sermons, advice books, and polemical pamphlets in 'Hens Should Be Served First'. Miller traces the competing and contradictory representation of motherhood by men and women writers in order to analyse the strategic uses of the rhetoric of maternity which served to suppress or expand female authority and authorship. In Rachel Trubowitz's insightful essay 'Crossed-Dressed Women and Natural Mothers: "Boundary Panic" in *Hic Mulier*', Trubowitz argues that the period's new construction of a 'natural' motherhood played a role in expansionist myths of England, 'inscribing new cultural roles not only for mothers but also, more implicitly, for whores and transvestites', whose deviance became associated with 'unnatural' and perverse cultures and races.

The final section analyses the effects of the gender debate on political discourse. Katherine Romack's 'Monstrous Births and the Body Politic: Women's Political Writings and the Strange and Wonderful Travails of Mistris Parliament and Mris. Rump' discusses how women's participation in the gender debate stopped during the period 1640–60 when, instead of being bound by the terms of patriarchal dialectic, women discussed citizenship and society. Consequently, allegories linking the female body and childbirth with monstrosity helped ridicule and negate women's political rhetoric. In 'Elizabeth, Gender and the Political Imaginary of Seventeenth-Century England', Mihoko Suzuki traces the various representations of Elizabeth in debates concerning women's participation in politics, beginning with Anne Clifford and Aemilia Lanyer and then examining later writings by both male parliamentarians and Tory women. Suzuki concludes with a discussion of the ongoing debate about Elizabeth in eighteenth-century and twentieth-century historiography.

Manuscript publication is the focus of Justice and Tinker, eds., *Women's Writing and the Circulation of Ideas: Manuscript Publication in England, 1550–1800*. Authors from as early as Mary Sidney to as late as Frances Burney are analysed; though the subject matter is varied, these writers all chose manuscript publication rather than print for the circulation of their works. In 'Creating Female Authorship in the Early Seventeenth Century: Ben Jonson and Lady Mary Wroth', Michael G. Brennan establishes how a small group of writers, including Jonson, had access to Wroth's manuscripts and consequently assisted in the promulgation of her literary reputation. Jonson's public admiration for Wroth's literature may have bolstered his literary career, but it also portrayed her as inheriting the literary genius of Philip Sidney. Another article that discusses literary and political relationships is 'Medium and Meaning in the Manuscripts of Anne, Lady Southwell' by Victoria E. Burke. Although Southwell claimed that she wrote only for herself, analysing how her manuscripts were compiled, bound, and possibly read, Burke examines the political and historical dimensions of how her work came to be scribally published. Margaret Ezell investigates the different reasons for publishing a deceased woman's manuscript, in 'The Posthumous Publication of Women's Manuscripts and the History of Authorship'. Ezell argues that posthumous publications can provide insight into the ways in which manuscript texts were circulated, the circumstances surrounding their preservation, and their mode of presentation, making us reconsider women's participation in literary culture and the contemporary privileging of the printed text over manuscript circulation.

Another interesting area of women's writing has been explored in the confessions of accused witches in Malcolm Gaskill's 'Witchcraft and Power in Early Modern

England' and Louise Jackson's 'Witches, Wives and Mothers', both in Oldridge, ed., *The Witchcraft Reader*. Both articles argue that perhaps some women, because of their disempowered position in society, believed their own confessions. Jackson also explores the idea that witches' supposed crimes were the opposite of the female role. Reviewing various confessions, she argues that the accused may have believed their confessions as a way of dealing with rape, trauma, and fears about not fulfilling their prescribed gender role. Though very interesting, the collection as a whole may be too general for some since the essays cover medieval and early modern witchcraft throughout Britain and Europe.

Self-authorization is explored in John Rogers, 'The Passion of a Female Literary Tradition: Aemilia Lanyer's Salve Deus Rex Judaeorum' (in Mellor, Nussbaum, and Post, eds., *Forging Connections: Women's Poetry from the Renaissance to Romanticism*). Although Lanyer depicts Christ's suffering as feminized, she does not simply use the crucifixion story to authorize herself as a poet; rather, the text is a sacramental method to enact her own poetic incarnation. Appropriating the poetic activity associated with Mary Sidney, Lanyer creates for herself a place as a poet. Chapter 2 of the same book illustrates many of the basic features of women's devotional poetry in Helen Wilcox's '"My hart is full, my Soul dos ouer flow": Women's Devotional Poetry in Seventeenth-Century England'. Wilcox discusses the influences, audiences, and contexts in which women defined themselves in relation to God and patriarchy, and consequently challenges contemporary views of religious women writers.

(d) Journal Articles

This year the journal *Women's Writing* has focused on the theme of dissenting women from 1350 to 1800. In 'Propaganda or Marks of Grace? The Impact of the Reported Ordeals of Sarah Wight in Revolutionary London, 1647–52' (*WW* 9[2002] 215–32), Carola Scott-Luckens examines the account of Sarah Wight, who was tormented by sin and who attempted suicide. The spiritual text not only discusses sin and death, but uses elements of Protestant *ars moriendi* and birth rituals in an attempt to achieve unity between government, parliament, and church leaders. Politics and religion are also examined in 'Elizabeth Poole Writes the Regicide' (*WW* 9[2002] 233–48), in which Marcus Nevitt demonstrates how Elizabeth Poole manipulated biblical tropes and figures to subvert masculinist regicidal discourse, redefining the restrictions on women while commenting on the state of the political nation. Through analysing official reports, he also challenges the recent historiography that dismisses Poole as insignificant. In 'Identities in Quaker Women's Writing, 1652–60' (*WW* 9[2002] 267–84), Catie Gill approaches Quaker conversion narratives as constructions of collective ideals rather than solely as self-writings. Through contextualizing texts within Quaker ideology, writings of the self and of community occur simultaneously. Since Quaker identity was not stable or fixed, women's texts were part of the construction and development of collective identities. In 'A Feminist Critic in the Archives: Reading Anna Walker's A Sweet Savor for Woman (*c.*1606)' (*WW* 9[2002] 199–214), Suzanne Trill questions the model used to edit the growing 'female' canon, arguing that the emphasis on meaning in reference to authorship and the privileging of publication can be limiting. Placing Walker's texts within their literary, historical, and linguistic contexts, Trill demonstrates that Anne Walker's use of the variety of writing styles was a rhetorical strategy, significantly creating possible ways to solve the problem of the devaluation of women's manuscripts.

In 'Shaping a Drama out of a History: Elizabeth Cary and the Story of Edward II' (*CS* 14:i[2002] 79–92), Janet Starner-Wright and Susan M. Fitzmaurice reveal that, although Cary's text is called history, it bears few of the usual markers of a historical account. Through manipulating linguistic and rhetorical features, Cary hides subversive thought which appears as 'truth' within the framework of history and political oratorical discourse. Historical readings are also explored in 'Mary Wroth's Poetics of the Self' (*SEL* 42:i[2002] 121–36), in which Nona Fienberg applies new historicism to feminism, arguing that the more interior the reading of Wroth's poetry, the more her texts reveal a complex negotiation between humanist poetic traditions, such as Petrarchism and the poetry of Anne Cecil, with that of the Jacobean social world. Self-authorization is explored in Colleen Shea's 'Literary Authority as Cultural Criticism in Aemilia Lanyer's *The Authors Dreame*' (*ELR* 32[2002] 386–407). Lanyer's use of the literary form of the dream vision both increases and threatens her authority as a writer. Shea claims that Lanyer does not explicitly reject the patronage system, but tries to rewrite the conventions and rules, criticizing her social superiors while paying them the requisite homage. In 'Ideas in the Mind: Gender and Knowledge in the Seventeenth Century' (*Hypatia* 17:i[2002] 183–96), Paula Findlen explores emerging themes in early modern women's philosophical writings to develop a broader understanding of the relationship between gender and knowledge in the seventeenth century. Although Findlen discusses authors from England, Europe, and the Americas, Anne Conway and Margaret Cavendish's theories are a central focus of the article.

(e) Margaret Cavendish

Scholarly interest in Margaret Cavendish is increasing significantly every year. In this year alone, her work has not only appeared in nearly every anthology, but there have also been numerous article publications and an edition of two of her plays. Scholars of women's drama in particular will be very interested in Alexandra G. Bennett's edition of *Bell in Campo* and *The Sociable Companions*. The plays are presented together since both are satires that 'deal with the circumstances of war, its effects, and its aftermath, particularly in relation to women and their social roles'. *Bell in Campo* portrays women left behind during wartime who form an army that rescues their men, while *The Sociable Companions* explores how women survive the marriage market during the aftermath of the war. Although Bennett claims that it could be argued that the warrior women derived solely from Cavendish's elaborate imagination, women actually did fight during the English Civil War and the appendices provide contemporary eyewitness accounts of such individuals, along with texts that describe the military roles assumed by Queen Henrietta Maria. The appendices are intended to place the plays in their historical and literary context, and include extracts from Cavendish's own autobiography and biography of her husband, while also providing her thoughts regarding the purpose of plays and of marriage. Bennett includes a chronology of Cavendish's life along with some biographical information, making the edition a very useful introduction to her plays. Priced at £8.99 in paperback, it could viably be used for teaching as well as scholarly research.

Critical approaches to Cavendish are questioned in Judith Moore's article 'Twentieth-Century Feminism and Seventeenth-Century Science: Margaret Cavendish in Opposing Contexts' (*Restoration* 26[2002] 1–14). Moore argues that critics focus more on her prefaces and 'tacitly ignore Cavendish's career-long emphasis upon natural science'. Tracing the developments and changes within her prolific scientific and philosophical ideas, Moore challenges critical representations that portray Cavendish's work as uniform throughout. In 'Margaret Cavendish and Cyrano de Bergerac: A Libertine Subtext for Cavendish's Blazing World' (*BSEAA* 54[2002] 165–86), Stephen Clucas examines Cavendish's science fiction, suggesting that Cyrano de Bergerac may have influenced Cavendish's thought. Clucas demonstrates the striking thematic similarities between the libertine de Bergerac's and Cavendish's texts, in terms of their focus on materialism, the plurality of worlds, and atoms, and their scepticism about religion and truth. Sujata Iyengar also examines Cavendish's science fiction in 'Royalist, Romancist, Racialist: Rank, Gender, and Race in the Science and Fiction of Margaret Cavendish' (*ELH* 69[2002] 649–72). Iyengar argues that Cavendish advocates gender and race hierarchy in her science, yet her science fiction contradicts various theories of race and sex difference. Consequently, only in the imagination could people be complete, autonomous beings regardless of race or gender. Guyonne Leduc examines Cavendish's contradictory positions regarding women's education in 'Women's Education in Margaret Cavendish's Plays' (*Cercles* 4[2002] 16–38). Leduc demonstrates that Cavendish questions women's innate intellectual limitations while advocating the importance of education for women, saying that 'the close link she saw between mastering language and successful education [was] illustrated by the educational value of theatre'.

Although Donna Landry discusses poetry as late as 1807, her essay 'Women Poets as Naturalists in 1653–1807' (Mellor, Nussbaum and Post, eds., *Forging Connections: Women's Poetry from the Renaissance to Romanticism*) links Margaret Cavendish with the later Charlotte Smith, who both used 'green language' in their natural history. Landry argues that Cavendish's anti-hunting poetry led not only to ethical statements but to commentary on gender politics. Holly Faith Nelson also links Cavendish's views of animals with gender in '"Worms in the dull earth of ignorance": Zoosemiotics and Sexual Politics in the Works of Margaret Cavendish, Duchess of Newcastle' (*ELN* 39:iv[2002] 12–24). Nelson argues that Cavendish subverts hierarchical binaries as she inverts the definition of man and beast to question the category of woman. Although this may appear to relate to some radical sectaries, Cavendish's egalitarianism often is contradictory and hierarchical.

Books Reviewed

Barnaby, Andrew Thomas, and Lisa Jane Schnell, eds. *Literate Experience: The Work of Knowing in Seventeenth-Century English Writing*. Palgrave. [2002] pp. 296. £37.50 ISBN 0 3122 9351 8.
Barnard, John, D.F. McKenzie, and Maureen Bell, eds. *The Cambridge History of the Book in Britain*, vol. 4: *1557–1695*. CUP. [2002] pp. 922. £95 ISBN 0 5216 6182 X.

Bennett, Alexandra G., ed. *Bell in Campo; The Sociable Companions.* Broadview. [2002] pp. 230. £8.99 ($12.95) ISBN 1 5511 1287 6.

Blom, Frans, and Jos Blom, introd. *Pudentiana Deacon.* The Early Modern Englishwoman: A Facsimile Library of Essential Works. Printed Writings, 1500–1640. Ser. 1, pt. 3, vol. 4. Ashgate. [2002] pp. 364. £45 ($79.95) ISBN 0 7546 0443 8.

Booy, David, ed. *Personal Disclosures: An Anthology of Self-Writings from the Seventeenth Century.* Ashgate. [2002] pp. 456. £52.50 ($94.95) ISBN 0 7546 0121 8.

Churchill, Laurie J., Phyllis Rugg Brown, and Jane Elizabeth Jeffrey, eds. *Early Modern Women Writing Latin.* Women Writing Latin, from Roman Antiquity to Early Modern Europe 3. Routledge. [2002] pp. 368. £85 ($125) ISBN 0 4159 4185 7.

Cody, Lisa Forman, introd. *Writings on Medicine.* The Early Modern Englishwoman: A Facsimile Library of Essential Works. Printed Writings, 1641–1700. Ser. 2, pt. 1, vol. 4. Ashgate. [2002] pp. 638. £67.50 ($114.95) ISBN 0 7546 0214 1.

Cogswell, Thomas, Richard Cust, and Peter Lake, eds. *Politics, Religion and Popularity: Early Stuart Essays in Honour of Conrad Russell.* CUP. [2002] pp. x + 304. £45 ISBN 0 5218 0700 X.

Curran, John E., Jr. *Roman Invasions: The British History, Protestant Anti-Romanism, and the Historical Imagination in England, 1530–1660.* UDelP. [2002] pp. 325. £38.95 ISBN 0 8741 3778 0.

Dobson, Michael, and Nicola J. Watson. *England's Elizabeth: An Afterlife in Fame and Fantasy.* OUP. [2002] pp. xii + 348. £19.99 ISBN 0 1981 8377 1.

Ellison, James. *George Sandys: Travel, Colonialism and Tolerance in the Seventeenth Century.* B&B. [2002] pp. ix + 286. £50 ISBN 0 8599 1750 9.

Furdell, Elizabeth Lane. *Publishing and Medicine in Early Modern England.* URP. [2002] pp. xiii + 282. £50 ISBN 0 5804 6119 0.

Gilman, Ernest. *Recollecting the Arundel Circle: Discovering the Past, Recovering the Future.* Lang. [2002] pp. xi + 182. ISBN 0 8204 6147 4.

Graham, Elspeth, Hilary Hinds, Elaine Hobby, and Helen Wilcox, eds. *Her Own Life: Autobiographical Writings by Seventeenth Century Englishwomen.* Routledge. [2002] pp. 250. pb £18.99 ISBN 0 4150 1700 9.

Hadfield, Andrew, ed. *Amazons, Savages, and Machiavels. Travel and Colonial Writing in English, 1550–1630: An Anthology.* OUP. [2001] pp. 384. hb £50 ISBN 0 1987 1187 5, pb £14.99 ISBN 0 1987 1186 7.

Hadfield, Andrew, ed. *Literature and Censorship in Renaissance England.* Palgrave. [2001] pp. xii + 234. £55 ISBN 0 3337 9410 9.

Hammons, Pamela S. *Poetic Resistance English Women Writers and the Early Modern Lyric.* Ashgate. [2002] pp. 198. £42.50 ($74.95) ISBN 0 7546 0780 1.

Hodgson-Wright, Stephanie, ed. *Women's Writing of the Early Modern Period, 1588–1688: An Anthology.* EdinUP. [2002] pp. 477. hb £53 ISBN 0 7486 1096 0, pb £18 ISBN 0 7486 1097 9.

Holstun, James. *Ehud's Dagger: Class Struggle in the English Revolution.* Verso. [2002] pp. 512. pb £10.35 ISBN 1 8598 4407 3.

Hopkins, Lisa. *The Female Hero in English Renaissance Tragedy.* Palgrave. [2002] pp. 240. £47.50 ISBN 0 3339 8791 8.

Hopkins, Lisa. *Writing Renaissance Queens*. UDelP. [2002] pp. 216. $43.50 ISBN 0 8741 3786 1.

Justice, George, and Tinker, Nathan, eds. *Women's Writing and the Circulation of Ideas: Manuscript Publication in England, 1550–1800*. CUP. [2002] pp. 256. £42.50 ISBN 0 5218 0856 1.

Korsten, Frans, introd. *Elizabeth Evelinge, I*. The Early Modern Englishwoman: A Facsimile Library of Essential Works. Printed Writings, 1500–1640. Ser. 1, pt. 3, vol. 3. Ashgate. [2002] pp. 298. £45 ($79.95) ISBN 0 7546 0442 X.

Loewenstein, David, and Janel Mueller, eds. *The Cambridge History of Early Modern English Literature*. CUP. [2002] pp. xi + 1,038. $140 ISBN 0 5216 3156 4.

Luckyj, Christina. *'A moving Rhetoricke': Gender and Silence in Early Modern England*. ManUP. [2002] pp. 208. £45 ISBN 0 7190 6156 3

MacDonald, Joyce Green. *Women and Race in Early Modern Texts*. CUP. [2002] pp. 198. £42.50 ($60) ISBN 0 5218 1016 7.

Malcolmson, Cristina, and Mihoko Suzuki, eds. *Debating Gender in Early Modern England, 1500–1700*. Palgrave. [2002] pp. 288. £35 ($60) ISBN 0 3122 9457 3.

Maley, Willy. *Nation, State, and Empire in English Renaissance Literature: Shakespeare to Milton*. Palgrave. [2003] pp. xvii + 185. £45 ISBN 0 3336 4077 2.

McGrath, Lynette. *Subjectivity and Women's Poetry in Early Modern England 'Why on the ridge should she desire to go?'*. Ashgate. [2002] pp. 306. £47.50 ($84.95) ISBN 0 7546 0585 X.

Mellor, Anne K., Felicity Nussbaum, and Jonathan F.S. Post, eds. *Forging Connections: Women's Poetry from the Renaissance to Romanticism*. Huntington. [2002] pp. 180. $15 ISBN 0 8732 8197 7.

Oldridge, Darren, ed. *The Witchcraft Reader*. Routledge. [2002] pp. 464. hb £65 ($100) ISBN 0 4152 1492 0, pb £17.99 ($29.95) 0 4152 1493 9.

Overbury, Sir Thomas, et al. *Characters, Together with Poems, News, Edicts and Paradoxes*, ed. Donald Beecher. Dovehouse. [2002] pp. 397. hb ISBN 1 8955 3765 7, pb ISBN 1 8955 3756 8.

Pacheco, Anita, ed. *A Companion to Early Modern Women's Writing*. Blackwell. [2002] pp. 448. £75 ($83.95) ISBN 0 6312 1702 9.

Parker, Kenneth, ed. *Dorothy Osborne: Letters to Sir William Temple, 1652–54. Observations on Love, Literature, Politics and Religion*. Ashgate. [2002] pp. 360. £49.50 ($84.95) ISBN 0 7546 0382 2.

Phillippy, Patricia Berrahou. *Women, Death, and Literature in Post-Reformation England*. CUP. [2002] pp. 324. £45 ($60) ISBN 0 5218 1489 8.

Price, Bronwen, ed. *Francis Bacon's New Atlantis: New Interdisciplinary Essays*. ManUP. [2002] pp. xii + 209. £16.99 ISBN 0 7190 6052 4.

Reynolds, Bryan. *Becoming Criminal: Transversal Performance and Cultural Dissidence in Early Modern England*. JHUP. [2002] pp. xiii + 217. $43 ISBN 0 8018 6808 4.

Rose, Mary Beth. *Gender and Heroism in Early Modern English Literature*. UChicP. [2001] pp. 144. hb $35 ISBN 0 2267 2572 3, pb $15 ISBN 0 2267 2573 1.

Sanford, Rhonda Lemke. *Maps and Memory in Early Modern England: A Sense of Place*. Palgrave. [2002] pp. xiv + 225. £40 ISBN 0 3122 9455 7.

Sondergard, Sidney L. *Sharpening her Pen: Strategies of Rhetorical Violence by Early Modern English Women Writers*. SusquehannaUP. [2002] pp. 192. $36 ISBN 1 5759 1059 4.

Spongberg, Mary. *Writing Women's History since the Renaissance*. Palgrave. [2002] pp. 320. hb £45 ($75) ISBN 0 3337 2667 7, pb £14.99 ($23.95) ISBN 0 3337 2668 5.

Staub, Susan C, introd. *Mother's Advice Books*. The Early Modern Englishwoman: A Facsimile Library of Essential Works. Printed Writings, 1641–1700. Ser. 2, pt. 1, vol. 3. Ashgate. [2002] pp. 340. £49.50 ($84.95) ISBN 0 7546 0210 9.

Van Heijnsbergen, Theo, and Nicola Royan, eds. *Literature, Letters and the Canonical in Early Modern Scotland*. Tuckwell. [2002] pp. 158. £20 ISBN 1 8623 2270 8.

Watkins, John. *Representing Elizabeth in Stuart England: Literature, History, Sovereignty*. CUP. [2002] pp. 264. $60 ISBN 0 5218 1573 8.

IX

Milton and Poetry, 1603–1660

KEN SIMPSON, MARGARET KEAN, P.G. STANWOOD, PAUL DYCK AND JOAD RAYMOND

This chapter has five sections: 1. General; 2. Milton; 3. Donne; 4. Herbert; 5. Marvell. Section 1 is by Ken Simpson; section 2 is by Margaret Kean; section 3 is by Paul Stanwood; section 4 is by Paul Dyck; section 5 is by Joad Raymond.

1. General

Many studies of early seventeenth-century poetry in 2002 continue to unfold the relationship between poetry and power, especially as gender, sexuality, class, and nationality are constructed, while other works engage in more traditional modes of analysis, including the history of ideas, genre studies, and close reading. Perhaps the best metaphor to describe the state of scholarship in this area is the one adopted by the editors Claude J. Summers and Ted-Larry Pebworth in *Fault Lines and Controversies in the Study of Seventeenth-Century English Literature*, an important collection of essays which highlights the fissures and faults that have emerged in the landscape of early modern literary studies. Knowing what the fissures in the discipline are helps to invigorate both sides of the fault lines, encourages a broad range of methods, and leads to new combinations and approaches that best suit the material.

Archival and manuscript studies published this year make significant contributions to our understanding of the period. Foremost among them is H. Neville Davies's outstanding edition, *At Vacant Hours: Poems by Thomas St Nicholas and his Family*, based on the Birmingham Manuscript. It introduces the work of a Puritan activist trained in the law who lived through the chaos of the seventeenth century: born in Kent and educated at Emmanuel and the Inner Temple, he was imprisoned in Yorkshire at Pontefract Castle by royalist forces in 1643, was nominated to the Barebones Parliament in 1653, and was returned as a member for Canterbury in 1656 before being excluded from the first session by Cromwell, an act which turned St Nicholas against the Protector for the rest of his life. In 1659 he was a Clerk of Parliament, an adviser to the Speaker, but by 1660 his political career was over and he returned to Ash, Kent, his birthplace near Sandwich, where he died in 1668. In 'vacant hours', when he wasn't involved in politics or his ironworks business in York, or in managing his family's interests, he turned to poetry. The poetry itself is not exceptional, relying as it does on a not exceptional couplet, primarily in familiar odes or epistles on occasions, people, and virtues, with the occasional venture into common measure for hymns. Scholars will be more interested in the social, political, and religious contexts that the poems illuminate, although literary relationships and parallels between St Nicholas and Joseph Hall, William Spurstow (the Smectymnuuan), Francis Quarles, and Mildmay Fane need to be traced in more detail. Poems on the Conventicle Act, imprisonment during the civil war, advice to family members, spiritual account-taking (metaphors of business and trade appear frequently), providential readings of everyday events, and preparations for death all convey St Nicholas's sincere and engaging personality as he adapts to the unpredictability of seventeenth-century life. This edition, which includes a useful introduction, wonderfully detailed notes and commentary providing cultural background of all kinds, and a CD-ROM of the manuscript itself, is invaluable in the picture it paints, in seventy poems, of the diversity of Puritan culture at mid-century generally, but more importantly of a well-educated Puritan's spiritual and material autobiography in verse.

Several articles also add to our knowledge of the period through their archival or manuscript research. In 'To Entertain a King: Music for James and Henry at the Merchant Taylors Feast of 1607' (*M&L* 83[2002] 525–41), Ross W. Duffin clarifies the nature of 'freemans songs' used at the feast, identifies 'We be three poor mariners' in a collection by Ravenscroft as almost certainly a song mentioned in contemporary accounts, and 'adds to the corpus of songs by Ben Jonson', (p. 540), who was responsible for the entertainment. David Gunby's 'Tourneur's "Of My Lady Anne Cecill"' (*N&Q* 49[June, 2002] 247–9) argues for an early rather than a late date for the poem based on textual and stylistic evidence that reveals Anne Cecil to be the 'last daughter of Thomas Cecil, second Baron Burghley', not Anne, the third daughter of William Cecil, second earl of Exeter. In 'Jonson's Penshurst Reveal'd? A Penshurst Inventory of 1623' (*SidJ* 20[2002] 1–25) Germaine Warkentin examines an inventory for Penshurst Place written in 1623 and explores 'the material culture of Penshurst about the time [Jonson] was writing' 'To Penshurst', finding tension between Sidneyan reality and Jonsonian representation, 'material accumulation and virtue' (pp. 5, 15), a code of aristocratic honour requiring self-display in an increasingly commodified court and Sidney's shrinking base of material wealth. Katherine Duncan-Jones's fascinating study, 'A Feather from the Black Swan's Wing: Hugh Holland's *Owen Tudor* (1601)' (*EMS* 11[2002] 93–108), shows in careful detail how the patronage system and political circumstances alter the materiality of texts. According to Duncan-Jones, *Owen Tudor*, found by the author at Berkeley Castle, is a self-contained fragment prepared by Holland (1563?–1633) and presented to Elizabeth Berkeley for her assessment of the likelihood of its attracting the queen's patronage. Alas, the queen expired before the poem could be presented to her, but that didn't stop the poet: he embeds *Owen Tudor* [1601] in *Pancharis* [1603], claims that he wrote the work with the Stuarts in mind, and dedicates 'a manifestly out-dated poem to the newly acceded King' (p. 98).

Before turning to articles, collections, and books, I should mention two recently published anthologies that reveal very different approaches to the anthology and its uses. Andrew Hadfield's *The English Renaissance, 1500–1620*, part of the

Blackwell Guides to Literature series, is intended for undergraduates. It provides a short chronology of dates and events, an introductory essay on defining the Renaissance, four essays on the history of the Renaissance which underline the role of literature in colonialism and national identity, forty summaries of the important literary figures of the period and their works, excerpts from key texts, and a group of essays on special topics, including humanism, printing, gender, 'attitudes to other nations', and 'current issues in the criticism of Renaissance literature'. Hattaway, ed., *English Renaissance Literature and Culture*, part of the Blackwell Companions to Literature and Culture series, is intended for advanced undergraduate or graduate students and, consequently, is very different in its approach. It includes a wide-ranging collection of essays, many by distinguished scholars in the field, grouped under four rubrics: 'Contexts and Perspectives, *c*.1500–1650', 'Readings', 'Genres and Modes', and 'Issues and Debates'. It is a hefty volume, 747 pages in length, and is a useful reference work, but its length also makes it impractical as a text that teachers can expect students to buy: it might be better to send students to find it in the library or the reference room. Both anthologies, although very different, should be useful as long as they are used for the purposes and audiences for which they were designed. Both anthologies also bear the marks of contemporary scholarly interest in national identity, diverse voices, and cultural construction in literature.

Articles written on works published between 1603 and 1660 reflect the broad critical contours of the discipline: roughly half focus on ideology and politics, while the other half are more literary in emphasis, and include literary history, history of ideas, close reading, and comparative genre approaches. Of the seven articles published on Henry Vaughan, six fall into the latter category, in keeping with the intentions of *Scintilla*, the journal of the Vaughan Society. In 'Henry Vaughan and the Glance of Love: Thoughts on "The Favour"'(*Scintilla* 6[2002] 7–20) Glyn Pursglove argues that 'The Favour' redeploys the language of the *dolce stil nuovo* poets, especially Dante and Cavalcanti, and the courtly love tradition to create a sacred parody. Michael Srigley's 'Thomas Vaughan, the Hartlib Circle and the Rosicrucians' (*Scintilla* 6[2002] 31–54) describes the poet's brother's interest in the revival of Rosicrucianism and the attempt, by Samuel Hartlib and others, to build a Christian scientific community that would include alchemical studies. 'Vaughan and the *Mundus Imaginalis*' (*Scintilla* 6[2002] 110–21) links Vaughan's concept of the spiritual world to Mazdean and Sufi mystic thought concerning the *mundus imaginalis*, a practice of spiritual exegesis, the imaginal faculty which unveils hidden reality, and the intermediary world of the spirit itself, as Alex Cadogan explains. Jonathan Nauman's 'F.E. Hutchinson, Louise Guiney, and Henry Vaughan' (*Scintilla* 6[2002] 135–47) looks at the process of literary biography. Vaughan's 'partisan personality' was toned down by Hutchinson, a 'latitudinarian progressive', when he excised Louise Guiney's royalist, High Church sympathies in the process of transforming her notes into his biography. Roland Mathias also turns to biography in 'A New Language, A New Tradition' (*Scintilla* 6[2002] 161–82). Although he spoke Welsh, Vaughan probably didn't read it, and it is unlikely that he had any serious contact with contemporary Welsh writing or bardic traditions. In a highly personal meditation, Kim Taplin begins with the question underlying Vaughan's 'The Wreath': why write poetry during times of despair and suffering? '"How shall I get a wreath … ?": Some implications of Vaughan's question for contemporary poetry' (*Scintilla* 6[2002] 194–204) examines works by Galway

Kinnel, John Freeman, and Jeremy Hooker, finding in the regenerative process of nature and the celebration of the physicality of human life in these poets a tentative answer to the question. In 'Narrative, Typology and Politics in Henry Vaughan's "Isaac's Marriage"' (*Connotations* 11:i[2001/2] 78–90) Alan Rudrum takes exception to Philip West's description of the poem as 'prim'. Instead, through a careful analysis of the typological connotations of Vaughan's biblical sources, Rudrum uncovers parallels with the Church that exiled royalists and Laudians would have recognized.

Works on Ben Jonson were equally split between literary and political approaches. Bruce Boehrer's 'Horatian Satire in Jonson's "On the Famous Voyage"' (*Criticism* 44:i[2002] 9–26) suggests that critical problems caused by viewing the poem as an imitation of Martial can be solved when we realize that Jonson adapts, and even parodies, Horace's satirical persona in epigrammatic form. In 'The Mixed Genre of Ben Jonson's "To Penshurst" and the Perilous Springs of Netherlandish Landscape' (*BJJ* 9[2002] 1–35) Martin Elsky shows how the complex mix of praise and blame in Netherlandish country house paintings provides an accurate model for understanding Jonson's exploration of the ethics of ownership in his poem. Reuben Sanchez's '"Affairs in tune": The Center and the Circle in Jonson's "Epithalamion"' (*BJJ* 9[2002] 109–28) claims that circle and centre images reveal the politics of patronage. The groom's father, Richard Weston, Lord High Treasurer, and the court are more central than the married couple, indicating how much Jonson has departed from Spenser's example. The role of the literary canon in the construction of nationhood is the subject of 'Pirating Spain: Jonson's Commendatory Poetry and the Translation of Empire' (*MP* 99[2002] 341–56). For Barbara Fuchs, Jonson's appropriations of foreign literary works, particularly in his praise of translators and in the metaphors of trade that he chooses, parallel England's conquests of nations and territories in the early modern period.

Two essays on Thomas Traherne attempt to place his religious and ethical views in broad contexts of intellectual and cultural history and, in doing so, contribute to the venerable history of ideas tradition also seen in Vaughan and Jonson criticism. In 'Thomistic Metaphysics and Ethics in the Poetry and Prose of Thomas Traherne' (*L&T* 16[2002] 248–69) Paul Cefalu continues the reclamation of Traherne from pre-Romantic and Neoplatonic readings. The poet is much more indebted to empirical associationism and Thomistic theories of habit formation than has been previously acknowledged. Felicity, or the state most resembling pure Act in Aristotelian/Thomistic terms, is achieved by instilling the right habits and associations and removing the wrong ones. On the other hand, in 'Heavenly Perspectives, Mirrors of Eternity: Thomas Traherne's Yearning Subject' (*Criticism* 43[2002] 377–405) Carol Ann Johnston discusses Traherne's subjectivity as part of an irreversible trajectory that leads from Petrarchan subjectivity to the subjective idealism of Berkeley and Fichte and the subjectivism of Kant. According to Johnson, Traherne attempts but fails to reverse this trend by adapting mirror images derived from perspectivist painting theory, in which the 'vanishing point' encourages the illusion of an 'objective subjectivity' that resembles God's ability to see all perspectives at the same time, to the construction of religious subjectivity in his poetry.

Subjectivity is also the theme of Laurie Ellinghausen's 'The Individualist Project of John Taylor "the Water Poet"'(*BJJ* 9[2002] 147–69), but this essay assesses the influence of class on Taylor's authorial persona. Constructing himself as a fair, plain, and transparent plebeian individualist while defending stable royalist values at the same time, Taylor, according to Ellinghausen, unwittingly participates in the emergent 'proto-bourgeois' ideology he most loathes. Political turmoil and the declining fortunes of the royalist cause register in Taylor's nonsense verse, according to P.N. Hartle, '"All his workes sir": John Taylor's Nonsense Verse' (*Neophil* 86[2002] 155–69). In Taylor's late nonsense during the civil war, Hartle detects changes in rhetorical strategy as well as a 'radical psychic disturbance' when the role of nonsense—turning the world upside-down—has been appropriated by Taylor's political enemies.

The last four essays also uncover ideological and political nuances in the literature of the period, but they do so in a variety of ways, across a wide variety of texts and genres. 'The Roman Triumph in Purcell's Odes' (*ML* 83[Aug. 2002] 371–82), by Anthony Miller, examines how 'the rhetoric of Rome and its triumphs' (p. 371) is used by Purcell's librettists to give England an imperial status and to perform a variety of political work, from praising James Stuart, Charles II, and William III to prophesying the apocalyptic fall of Rome. According to Miri Tashma-Baum in '*Englands Helicon*: Epideixis, Complaint, and Escapism' (*BJJ* 9[2002] 129–46), this famous collection of pastoral poetry does not merely register the social status of gentlemen poets or the attempt to gain Elizabeth's patronage. A third, more subversive alternative, a 'superior community of mind' (p. 137), is framed by Nicholas Ling, the editor of the volume. The emphasis of Hannibal Hamlin's very fine essay, 'Psalm Culture in the English Renaissance: Readings of Psalm 137 by Shakespeare, Spenser, Milton, and Others' (*RenQ* 55[2002] 224–57), is not really political, even though he does indicate how changes in the interpretation of Psalm 137 reveal contesting political and religious positions throughout the period. He is more interested in explaining how the 'creative interpretation' of the most popular part of the Bible led to the formation of a 'psalm culture', a flexible set of assumptions, motifs, images, and narratives in a variety of genres, from poetry and paraphrases to translations and polemics. In her engaging approach to the politics of culture, Lisa Hopkins examines the year 1633 in 'We Were the Trojans: British National Identities in 1633' (*RS* 16[2002] 36–51). Anxieties about English national identity prompted by events both inside and outside England led to a resurgent, primarily nostalgic interest in the Trojan myth of origins. Others, however, questioned 'the comfort offered by the traditional reliance on Trojanness to mediate the troubling relationship of Englishness, Irishness, Scottishness, and Welshness' (p. 51).

Hopkins also contributes to Herman, ed., *Reading Monarchs Writing: The Poetry of Henry VIII, Mary Stuart, Elizabeth I, and James VI/I*, a collection of eight essays, two previously published, that explores the 'cultural poetics' that are set in motion when 'poetry gets written by the person in power' (p. 6). The collection also includes translations/transcriptions of the important works of each monarch (pp. 215–323), including eight versions of Elizabeth's 'The Doubt of Future Foes', illustrating its transformations in print and manuscript as well as in literary and political contexts. The collection begins with 'Henry VIII and the Poetry of Politics' (pp. 11–34) by Peter C. Herman and Ray G. Siemens, an essay that sets the tone for the volume: they consider not the poetic art of the verse but its role in the cultural production and reproduction of power. Henry's lyrics are shown to enact and intervene in the politics of the court, the king's authorship/authority changing the conventions of the lyric and conflating the public and private spheres. In 'Writing to Control: The Verse of Mary, Queen of Scots' (pp. 35–50) Lisa Hopkins examines Mary's verse as the 'one area where she can exercise queenship and control' (p. 50). Probing the grammar, diction, translation, structure, and tone of the poems, Hopkins uncovers subtle modes of formality in Mary's verse that are often responses to her social and political position. Peter C. Herman contributes a second essay to the volume, '"Mes subjectz, mon ame assubjectie": The Problematic (of) Subjectivity in Mary Stuart's Sonnets' (pp. 51–78). According to Herman, in her sonnets to Bothwell Mary transforms the subject position of the Petrarchan sonnet, but in the process makes herself a subservient subject rather than a monarch by subjecting herself to the power of the beloved. The poetics of monarchy continue in the first of three essays devoted to Elizabeth I, Jennifer Summit's '"The Arte of a Ladies Penne": Elizabeth I and the Poetics of Queenship' (pp. 79–108). For Summit Elizabeth invokes the tropes of secrecy and privacy often expected of women writers in order to construct for herself a more powerful figure of public authority. In 'States of Blindness: Doubt, Justice, and Constancy in Elizabeth I's "Avec l'aveugler si estrange"' (pp. 109–33), Constance Jordan suggests that the queen traces the development of her salvation through four steps, and draws inferences from the body politic and her role in Mary Stuart's execution to reach conclusions about her spiritual future. Leah S. Marcus's 'Queen Elizabeth I as Public and Private Poet: Notes toward a New Edition' (pp. 135–53) destabilizes Elizabeth's authorship, reminding us that 'the most celebrated English Renaissance monarch of all exerted very little control over her poetic materials except by withholding them from circulation' (p. 136). Marcus contrasts the 'marginal locations', 'nearly anonymous' voice, and ephemeral nature of the poems with the carefully constructed presentation of the queen's translations and speeches, showing that, even though Elizabeth's lyrics treated political subjects, she wanted to be seen as a serious author who only trifled with poetry. Two essays on James VI and I's poetry conclude the volume. Sandra J. Bell's 'Kingcraft and Poetry: James VI's Cultural Policy' (pp. 155–77) sees James's *The Essayes of a Prentise, in the Divine Art of Poesie* [1584] as a handbook of cultural policy through which the king hoped to consolidate his power by controlling the style, genre, and content of Scottish verse. In 'War and Peace in *The Lepanto*' (pp. 179–214) Robert Appelbaum considers the rifts between the king and poet, the epic of war and the king's image as a bringer of peace, the allegory of Protestant triumph and the literal triumph of Catholic Europe, the just war and Christian charity in James's epic.

Unlike the previous collection, Cunnar and Johnson, eds., *Discovering and (Re)Covering the Seventeenth Century Religious Lyric* emphasizes literary genre and history. Comprising fifteen essays and a tribute to 'John Roberts, Bibliographer' (pp. 332–9) by Claude J. Summers, the volume is loosely unified by the intention of recovering or discovering the unique contribution to the religious lyric made by women writers and by the 'Anglo-Catholic, High Anglican' tradition, eclipsed over the last two decades by canonical writers discussed in Barbara Lewalski's *Protestant Poetics and the Seventeenth-Century Religious Lyric*. With this twofold focus the editors complicate the construction of the early seventeenth-century literary canon and demonstrate the vital, varied, and contradictory ways in which the religious lyric participates in seventeenth-century culture, especially in the construction of subjectivity, a recurring theme in this collection. In 'Gender and Judaism in Meditations on the Passion: [Elizabeth] Middleton, Southwell, Lanyer, and Fletcher' (pp. 17–40), Kari Boyd McBride argues that the four poets construct divergent identities in their 'poetic meditations on the Passion' (p. 17). By focusing on the 'othering' of the Jew in the passion narratives of the poems, McBride shows how gender, religion, and race are implicated in apparently unrelated discourses. Scott R. Pilarz's '"To Help Souls": Recovering the Purpose of Southwell's Poetry and Prose' (pp. 41–61) explores the poet's identity as a first-generation Jesuit and how his 'pious utilitarianism' or pastoral intention shapes the imagery and structure of his poetry. According to George Klawitter, 'editorial decisions on Alabaster sequencing have contributed to his lack of popularity' (p. 63). 'Alabaster's "Ensigns" Sonnets: Calm Before the Storm' (pp. 62–79) restores the sequence of the poems found in manuscript, revealing Alabaster's use of Ignatian patterns of meditation. Debra Rienstra's 'Dreaming Authorship: Aemelia Lanyer and the Countess of Pembroke' (pp. 80–103) examines Mary Sidney as a model of exegetical and interpretative authority who enabled Lanyer to 'create authorship by connection to a distinguished literary precedent' (p. 83). Patrick Cook's 'Aemelia Lanyer's "Description of Cooke-ham" as Devotional Lyric' (pp. 104–18) outlines the poet's interest in 'salvation history' (p. 105) and her view of Lady Clifford as a model of piety rather than ownership. Robert C. Evans attempts to recover William Drummond of Hawthornden's literary reputation by explaining why his work was more highly regarded in his own day than in ours, not an uncommon predicament in seventeenth-century verse, as Waller and Cowley's careers illustrate. Through close reading of the poetry, Evans makes a strong case in 'Drummond's Artistry in the *Flowres of Sion*' (pp. 119–39) for considering Drummond's work more often. In 'William Austin, Poet of Anglianism' (pp. 140–63) Kate Narveson recovers the work of a writer who does not fit into the handy categories that dominate religious histories of the period. Neither Calvinist nor anti-Calvinist, scripturalist nor sacramentalist, Austin is representative of a 'third alternative', 'Anglianism', a religious practice that values devotion and worship more than 'theological precision' (pp. 140, 141). Sean McDowell returns to the question of religious subjectivity in 'Patrick Cary's Education of the Senses' (pp. 164–84). Despite the small number of Cary's religious poems, McDowell finds in them a mode of consecrating the self through attention to the senses that is unique in English verse. In her densely packed essay, 'Penseroso Triptych: "Eliza", An Collins, Elizabeth Major' (pp. 185–204), Patricia Demers explores the religious melancholy of the three writers, finding them 'unique—though connected—subjectivities' (p. 187) who respond to 'emotional or physiological pain' (p. 191) not with passivity but by 'defying, challenging, transforming *loss*' (p. 204). Michael Rex also turns to 'Eliza's Babes' in 'Eyes on the Prize: The Search for Personal Space and Stability Through Religious Devotion in "Eliza's Babes"' (pp. 205–30). The author hopes to overcome the chaos of the civil war through her 'matrimonial relationship with Christ' (p. 206). In 'An Collins: The Tradition of the Religious Lyric, Modified or Corrected?' (pp. 231–47) Ann Hurley explains that An Collins's work in *Divine Songs and Meditacions* does not fit into traditional categories of seventeenth-century meditative verse, and challenges readers to develop suitable criteria by which to evaluate the didactic aims and style of the genre and the poet. The final essay on women poets of the period, '"It is a lovely bonne I make of thee": Mary Carey's "abortive Birth" as Recuperative Religious Lyric' (pp. 248–72), by Donna J. Long, examines female religious subjectivity and the maternal body in Carey's 'Upon ye Sight of my abortive Birth ye 31th: December 1657'. 'Carey engages a wide range of doctrine and negotiates biblical tropes' (p. 249) in her elegies in order to reclaim 'childbearing as a gift' after her miscarriage. Barry Spurr recovers Thomas Traherne's partisan Anglo-Catholicism, challenging us in 'Felicity Incarnate: Rediscovering Thomas Traherne' (pp. 273–89) to account for the presence of Ignatian devotion, liturgical offices, and the sacramental life more generally in Traherne's works. The last two essays, P.G. Stanwood's 'Revisiting Joseph Beaumont' (pp. 290–307) and Paul A. Parish's 'Ravishing Embraces and Sober Minds: The Poetry of Joseph Beaumont' (pp. 308–31), complement each other. Stanwood argues through close readings that the unity and arrangement of Beaumont's poems reflect his interest in the composition of a 'poetic book' like Herbert's, while Parrish insists that Beaumont's 'exuberant and sensuous' mode is more than an imitation of Crashaw's; many of the poems stand on their own merits. These two essays accomplish the purpose of the collection as a whole: they recover a neglected poet's work and, in the process, revise the canon of the early modern religious lyric.

In *English Lyric Poetry: the Early Seventeenth Century* [1999], published in paperback this year, Jonathan F.S. Post identifies a gaping fault-line in the study of early modern poetry: he admits to 'thoroughly enjoying much of the verse of the period' and contrasts the pleasure of reading poetry with the grand abstractions and narratives of theory that often overshadow the poems (p. xi). The same call for intimate engagement with seventeenth-century poetry informs Post, ed., *Green Thoughts, Green Shades: Essays by Contemporary Poets on the Early Modern Lyric*. Post calls for a 'return to poetry' as an 'alternative to the dominant discourse of political criticism' (p. 4) and hopes to reawaken the 'personal moment of excited discovery' (p. 14) that underlies the experience of literature by gathering essays by contemporary poets who don't abandon theory so much as acknowledge 'the moment of excited discovery' in immediate and personal readings. Heather McHugh's 'Naked Numbers: A Curve from Wyatt to Rochester' (pp. 59–85) traces an idiosyncratic trajectory of the lyric by means of the metaphor of the cover, emphasizing the materiality of the poem and the interdependence of form and content. According to Linda Gregerson in 'Ben Jonson and the Loathed Word' (pp. 86–108) Jonson's search for a plain, transparent style excludes everything distinctive and represents a 'struggle for dominance' (p. 103). Calvin Bedient, in 'Donne's Sovereignty' (pp. 109–35), hopes to recover, like many before him, the 'sovereign playfulness of [Donne's] metaphors' (p. 111) while Stephen Yenser's '"How coy a Figure": Marvelry' (pp. 220–41) reminds us that 'the sexual and the spiritual simply cannot be teased apart' (p. 231) in Marvell's 'On a Drop of Dew'. Carl Phillips's discussion of George Herbert as a confessional poet in 'Anomaly, Conundrum, Thy-Will-Be-Done: On the Poetry of George Herbert' (pp. 136–59) includes brilliant work on Herbert's rhymes, wordplay, stanzas, and typography, while Milton is a different kind of confessional poet in William Logan's 'Milton in the Modern: The Invention of Personality' (pp. 160–75). Milton's colloquial idiom turned the sonnet into a vehicle of personality, paving the way for similar modes in Robert Lowell's *Life Studies*. The idea of this collection is bold and intriguing, and it often succeeds, but there are shortcomings too: isolated from a tradition of critical discourse, the personal and immediate reading can become impressionistic and obscure, and observations can, at times, repeat critical commonplaces. This is a case where the whole is more important than the parts, and the *idea* of the collection is more interesting than the result.

While Jonathan Post highlights one of the fault-lines within early modern literary studies, Summers and Pebworth, eds., *Fault Lines and Controversies in the Study of Seventeenth-Century English Literature*, a collection of thirteen essays presented at the 2000 University of Michigan-Dearborn Renaissance Conference, explores many 'points of friction, vulnerability, and division' (p. 1). Each essay discusses specific texts and many avoid getting bogged down in theory for its own sake. The tone of the collection is moderate as well, which is appropriate for a volume that seeks to contribute to our understanding of the issues rather than to solve them, and, in some cases, to offer further possibilities rather than to limit them.

The first six essays explore theoretical problems arising from a variety of approaches, ranging from pluralism and new historicism to dialogism and exegesis. In '"What is Truth?" Defining and Defending Theoretical Pluralism' (pp. 10–21) Robert C. Evans argues *contra* Ellen Rooney that pluralism is inclusive and multidimensional because it excludes only those theories that exclude others from their reading communities. As Evans notes, 'pluralism is less a theory about literature itself than a method of evaluating competing theoretical claims' that 'emphasizes how each theory can provide insights consistent with the *specific* assumptions the theory entails' (pp. 10, 11). The most polemical essay in a very polite volume, Catherine Gimelli Martin's 'The Ahistoricism of the New Historicism: Knowledge as Power versus Power as Knowledge in Bacon's *New Atlantis*' (pp. 22–49) scrutinizes the assumptions of new historicist critics. Interpretations influenced by Foucault's epistemic categories or the anti-Enlightenment bias of the Frankfurt school have led to misreadings of Bacon's claim that 'knowledge itself is power' and of the potential for *New Atlantis* and other works to contribute to social and political change. Such ahistorical readings impose on the Renaissance a postmodern nightmare of containment from which no one can escape. In 'Conjecture in the Writing of Donne's Biography, with a Modest Proposal' (pp. 50–61) Dennis Flynn invokes Karl Popper's distinction between probability and verisimilitude in conjectures. Improbable conjectures that can be refuted lead to more insight and knowledge in the humanities than probable conjectures based on facts that are irrefutable but lack content. Oppositions exposed along critical fault-lines are also highlighted in Dan Jaeckle's 'Marvell's "Mower against Gardens"' (pp. 62–72) and Tobias Gregory's 'In Defence of Empson: A Reassessment of Milton's God' (pp. 73–87). For Jaeckle, Bakhtinian refraction, rather than reflection or overt commitment, provides the best model of how Marvell's texts relate to ideology, while Gregory cites the debate generated by Empson's critique of Milton's God as an example of the need to include both exegetical and interpretative criticism. The former explains the text and the latter, as in Empson, assesses its contemporary significance or value. In the last essay in this section, 'Milton and Dryden on the Restoration Stage' (pp. 88–110), Elizabeth Sauer sees fissures throughout *Samson Agonistes* in the conflicts between print and performance, elitist republicans and popular tastes, Restoration drama and the Reformation hero in classical form.

The second group of essays address critical issues in the study of early modern religious culture. Kate Narveson's 'Profession or Performance? Religion in Early Modern Literary Study' (pp. 111–29) contrasts two approaches to religious discourse: one clarifies propositional belief and the other situates ideological nuances. Both approaches are important because to appreciate a text's representation of religious experience, including devotional, affective, and corporal dimensions, both propositional and cultural contexts are necessary. Jeffrey Johnson's 'John Donne and the Socinian Heresy' (pp. 130–9) examines propositional belief. The fissures opened by Socinian rationalism in interpretation are closed by Donne's emphasis on Scripture, reason, and tradition. P.G. Stanwood finds gaps rather than fissures in his concise survey of early modern sermon studies. 'Critical Directions in the Study of Early Modern Sermons' (pp. 140–55) urges readers to pay more attention to the 'preeminent literary genre in earlier seventeenth-century England' (p. 141) and identifies the rhetorical tradition, the practical details of sermon composition and revision, including the use of 'distinctiones' in composing sermons, and the works of Mark Frank as areas needing further investigation.

Four essays examining issues of sexuality, race, gender, and/or canon formation conclude the volume. Sharon Cadman Seelig's engaging analysis, 'The Poets of the Renaissance, or the Illusions of My Youth' (pp. 156–69) traces the gradual emergence of women writers in anthologies of early modern literature, from their absence, to their inclusion as 'curiosities' or 'civilizing influence[s]', to their absence again due to the 'professionalization' of literary studies, and finally to their better representation today. Recent studies of women writers have revealed 'a far more complicated web of relationships' (p. 169) in Renaissance literature than existed previously. In 'Donne on Love: Sometimes the End Just Doesn't Justify the Means' (pp. 170–86) Joan Faust discusses Donne's 'fear of sexual love' within the history of sexuality, investigating its possible origins in medical and physiological theories about the nature of semen and orgasm. The 'racialization' of skin colour that would eventually contribute to the colonial enterprise is the subject of Cristina Malcolmson's '"The Explication of Whiteness and Blackness": Skin Color and the Physics of Color in the Works of Robert Boyle and Margaret Cavendish' (pp. 187–203). Margaret Cavendish, argues Malcolmson, avoids the association of race and skin colour implied in Boyle's experiments because, alienated from the Royal Society, she could see more clearly the culturally specific nature of scientific observation. Striding across many fissures and opening others, William Schullenberger's 'Milton's Lady and Lady Milton: Chastity, Prophecy, and Gender in *A Maske Presented at Ludlow Castle*' (pp. 204–26), the last essay in the collection, describes Milton's identification with the female hero of his *Maske* as an important step in the poet's discovery of his own prophetic voice. The *Maske* 'authorizes, rather than appropriates and suppresses, a public speaking site for liberatory female speech' (p. 204). Schullenberger demonstrates that theory and practical criticism can inform each other and lead to insightful appreciations of early modern poetry.

The fissures that appear in our survey of short essays published this year can also be seen in the books. Many of these works take up new historical or cultural materialist concerns, sharing a kind of functional paradigm of critical practice, but, aware of the limitations of these powerful modes of criticism, either extend their thematics in different directions or adapt the methodology to suit their specific projects: Christopher Hodgkins, in *Reforming Empire: Protestant Colonialism and Conscience in British Literature*, adopts a new historicist model of intertextuality but rejects the reduction of religion to a function of ideology, as happens so often in new historicist analysis; David Hawkes practises 'economic criticism' in *Idols of the Marketplace: Idolatry and Commodity Fetishism in English Literature, 1580–1680*; and Robert Appelbaum engages in a Foucauldian analysis of 'utopian mastery' in *Literature and Utopian Politics in Seventeenth-Century England*. On the other hand, even though both are acutely aware of historical context, two other works refer to history in order to illuminate literary texts rather than the other way around: Stella Revard's *Pindar and the Renaissance Hymn-Ode: 1450–1700* is a rich and detailed genre study, while a theoretically informed history of ideas approach which focuses carefully on literature is taken by Joshua Scodel in *Excess and the Mean in Early Modern English Literature*. Revard and Scodel's works are clearly the most impressive in this survey, their erudite scholarship and elegant writing representing the very best our profession has to offer.

The construction of nationality and its role in the ideology of empire is a minor theme in several short essays this year but receives detailed attention in Christopher Hodgkins's *Reforming Empire*. Before empire could become a reality, it first had to be imagined, and it was the 'Protestant imagination that gave the empire its main paradigms for dominion and possession but also, paradoxically, its chief languages of anti-imperial dissent' (p. 2). The scope of this study is ambitious, as it stretches in time from the Renaissance to 1945, but five of its six chapters focus on the early modern period. At times the scope of the thesis and the sheer number of texts under consideration stretch the argument thin: chapter 2, for example, is twenty-three pages long, but it consists of a two-page introduction and ten subtitled subsections, as if changes in font and layout themselves are enough to bear the burden of the argument and make the connections the author wants us to make. More often, however, we are in the grip of a writer whose skill in uncovering the nuances of his theme and making original connections between diverse texts is dazzling. The first chapter looks at the use of the 'matter of Britain' by John Dee, Spenser, Shakespeare, and others to provide a common identity that implied expansion and universalism. The 'lost empire' of Arthur would be the basis of a new 'restored empire', a postcolonial, post-Roman Catholic Britain. Chapter 2 examines the 'Black Legend' of Spanish atrocities in the New World and the importance of a 'shared religious enemy' in shaping Protestant imperialism. Milton's Satan, read alongside narratives of Mexico's colonization by Cortez, is a conquistador, revealing Milton's hatred of evil empire but not empire as such. Chapter 3 is the most insightful and wide-ranging of the early chapters. According to Hodgkins, in rejecting empire, Protestants like Francis Drake demonstrated self-restraint and humility, and thereby staked a deeper and more lasting claim to rule. The account of Drake's rejection of godhead in Hakluyt's *Principal Navigations* [1589], a 'legend of heathen idolatry and protestant humility' (p. 81), is indispensable for the development of the 'imperial imagination' and is traced through several versions from Spenser, Shakespeare, Defoe, and Swift to Kipling and Conrad. Hodgkins then shows in chapter 4 that racism is a function of imperialism by tracing attitudes towards 'blackness' and mixed marriages, especially the marriage of Pocahontas and John Rolfe. At the beginning of the seventeenth century there was 'no such thing as "race"' (p. 114), but within a few decades mixed marriages were illegal and the ground of racism and slavery was prepared and sown. 'Prophets Against Empire: Countertraditions, 1516–1815' brings together many strains of anti-imperial discourse in the humanist tradition from More, Daniel, Herbert, Milton, Swift, and Johnson to Burke, Blake, and Austen. Christian humanist writers such as More insisted that colonization degraded both the colonizer and the colonized, while Protestant 'meliorists' believed in 'trusteeship', 'making the best of a necessary evil' through religious, moral, or, later, economic improvement (p. 192). In the final chapter, the fate of these counter-traditions from 1815 to 1945 is traced. The uneasy relationship between evangelical meliorists and economic imperialists in the colonial enterprise is highlighted, and the variations of the two paths of reaction are subtly conveyed in a wide variety of ways, from Tennyson's elegies for a lost world to Waugh's brutal exposure of Protestant Britain's hollow pretensions to empire. This learned, sweeping study of the early modern Protestant roots of British imperialism combines the best of both literary and historical traditions of scholarship and should be a touchstone for the discourses of colonialism in the early modern period.

The first chapter of Robert Appelbaum's *Literature and Utopian Politics in Seventeenth-Century England* also looks at the conjunction of colonialist discourse and literature, noting the importance of the 'Columbus trope', especially in Bacon's *The Advancement of Learning*, in imagining other worlds but also in the construction of a politics of conquest under the authoritarian gaze of James I. Appelbaum's main concern, however, is in mapping the variations of 'utopian mastery' and ideal politics, the 'symbolic fantasies … through which social and political power was imagined by its subjects' (p. 38). The dominance of James in the discourse of ideal politics is followed by a period of experimentation (1620–38) in which the court is constructed as an ideal world, but a number of writers, including Robert Burton, locate utopian mastery in the self, the 'utopian "I"' (p. 88) duplicating in isolation the political separation of the *Mayflower* voyages in search of an ideal 'city upon a hill'. In the 1640s forms of Puritan millennialism dominate the field, but Hartlibian schemes and the more political hopes of the Levellers are also notable before utopian politics reaches its zenith between 1649 and 1653 when the 'utopian mastery' reached by the 'lonely Columbusoid intellectual' could be achieved 'by a whole public' (p. 141). After a brief burst of utopian energy in the mid-1650s, primarily in the works of Henry Vane and James Harrington, utopian discourse becomes a force of aestheticization and diversion rather than engagement during the Restoration. Appelbaum's historical narrative is well known, and although the style is quirky at times, his analysis of the role played by what Ernst Bloch calls 'anticipatory consciousness' in early modern politics and political discourse is valuable and insightful. He shows that hopes for the future, and the literary forms taken by those hopes, shape the present and sometimes generate the events that become the empirical basis of historical record.

In *Idols of the Marketplace* David Hawkes rewrites Marxist accounts of the emergence of the market economy in seventeenth-century Britain, finding evidence of protest against it in discourses of anti-bullionist economics, anti-theatricalism, usury, divorce, alchemy, religious subjectivity, typology, and teleology in a wide range of early modern literature, from Herbert, Donne, and Shakespeare's lyrics to Milton's divorce tracts, Bunyan's *The Life and Death of Mr. Badman*, and

Traherne's poetry and prose. The 'autonomy of representation' and the commodity fetishism so characteristic of postmodern capitalism have their origins in or are homologous with idolatry, emptied of its religious significance, in each of these diverse areas, turning teleological value into market value, ends into means, nature into custom, spiritual referents into physical signs. In earlier Marxist accounts, which emphasized that feudalism was supplanted as a result of class struggle, a narrative of progress occurs which paradoxically views early modern market capitalism as a positive force, ignoring the anti-market discourse linking market forces with idolatry. Hawkes corrects this view, marshalling the literature of the period to show that idolatry is synonymous with objectification and commodity fetishism.

In *Pindar and the Renaissance Hymn-Ode*, the result of the author's twenty-year commitment to her subject, Stella Revard traces the development of Pindar's odes through Roman, Italian, and French imitations to English Renaissance adaptations, concluding with an excellent discussion of the significance of Cowley's influential philosophical odes. Although she shows how the genre changed in response to historical and ideological pressures, the emphasis throughout is on the poetry and the poet. While Pindaric metrics and triadic verse forms were attempted during the Renaissance—most successfully by Ben Jonson in the ode to Sir Lucius Cary and Sir Henry Morison—they were more often loosely adapted until Cowley abandoned any pretence of imitation, reproducing instead the spirit of Pindar's supposed irregularity. As Revard explains in the first two chapters, Pindar was a model of the inspired poet-priest and of the poet's relationship to the Muses, influencing Christian poets such as Du Bartas, Spenser, and Milton and their celebrations of the divine sources of poetry. He also taught his audience moral and religious lessons through his celebrations of athletes and his use of mythic sources from the past, becoming a model of the Renaissance poet's devotion to advising the monarch and to teaching religious truth, an emphasis Pindar's odes shared with David's psalms. Chapters 3 to 7, however, 'trace the evolution of the hymn-ode on the continent and in England from the hymn or ode to the classical deity to the Christian hymn-ode and finally to the philosophical ode' (p. 339), including a fascinating chapter on the exuberant, 'light, occasional, and song-like ode' (p. 122), of which Ronsard, John Soowthern, Spenser, Drayton, and Milton in *L'Allegro* were all imitators and innovators. Pindar's odes praising athletes and honouring the gods became models for hymns to classical deities during the Italian Renaissance by Marullo and others, and these in turn became the basis of the secular odes of Ronsard, odes to abstract ideas, virtues, and allegorical deities and, finally, hymns to the Christian God by Milton and Crashaw. With Cowley's philosophical ode we enter a different world: it later becomes 'the most popular kind of Pindaric imitation', but it has the least in common with Pindar. Although similar to odes to deities or virtues, Cowley's odes are not religious or moral in purpose but philosophical, even scientific; they are not linked to specific people or occasions, and they deliberately avoid references to divine inspiration.

Like Revard, Joshua Scodel combines meticulous attention to literary detail, rigorous scholarship, historical contextualization, and clear prose in *Excess and the Mean in Early Modern Literature*. He examines how a conventional topos—that virtue consists in a mean or 'middle way' between excess on the one hand and deficiency on the other—is shaped and transformed by literary, philosophical, and political contexts, including the colonial, proto-imperial policies that interested many other writers this year. In part 1, after exploring how the 'vagueness of the mean' (p. 4) even in Aristotle allowed the virtue to be claimed for a variety of often contradictory purposes in Roman and Christian culture, Scodel shows how Donne and Bacon appropriate the mean to validate the sceptical search by free subjects for alternatives in church and state, on the one hand, and the autonomous, Baconian subject's mastery of natural and political orders, on the other. Part 2 turns to the discourse of the mean in the portrayal of national character and climate in the georgics of Virgil, Spenser, Sylvester, Drayton, and Milton before examining the conflict between humble, farmer-soldiers who attain an ideal of temperance while managing the natural world, and the court-centred ethic that often promotes excess in the acquisition of power, property, and luxuries in an era of colonial expansion. John Davies of Hereford's *Microcosmos* [1603] and Denham's *Cooper's Hill* [1642] represent the king and court, not the hearty farmer, as ideals of moderation, but they also register the excess implied in the boundless search for wealth and conquest. The split between personal and domestic temperance and international excess is ignored in Waller's *On St. James Park* [1661] and Cowley's *On the Queen's Repairing Somerset House* [1665], both of which replace 'Virgil's celebration of rural contentment in the middle state with a paean to the blessings of international trade sustained by royal imperial might' (p. 138). In part 3 Scodel analyses the role of excess and the mean in the cultural construction of love, demonstrating that 'extreme passion' becomes identified with an aristocratic nobility above the 'mean' accomplishments of more moderate attachments, sometimes to condemn rank ambition but increasingly to approve of it. Daniel, Lyly, and Sidney negotiate the parallels and contrasts between excess in love and social ambition, while for Caroline writers, especially Davenant and Cowley, negotiations have been called off: erotic excess modified and made docile by Neoplatonism is exclusively aristocratic, and increasingly a sign of superiority. This ideal of erotic excess is then contrasted with the economic discourse of 'interest' and 'rational calculation' (p. 15) in the works of Davenant, Dryden, and Behn. The mean is associated with economic interests and is below the passionate, aristocratic ideal. Part 4 explores the symposiastic lyric in Jonson, Habington, Randolph, Herrick, Lovelace, Brome, Cotton, Milton, and Rochester. Conflicts between the ethical mean and poetic rapture in this genre become polarized as tensions between elite and popular culture, private and public spheres, and Anglican and Puritan ethics intensified throughout the Commonwealth, Protectorate, and Restoration periods. The final section is dedicated to Milton, a steady presence throughout the book, whose view in *Paradise Lost* is that self-respect and self-restraint are the foundations of true pleasure. Indeed, Scodel's Adam and Eve challenge all of the previously discussed permutations of the mean: they challenge the idealization of excess in Restoration and aristocratic erotics and symposiastics; they represent the dignity of labour and personal discipline rather than the acquisition of property and luxuries; they recover pleasure and delight for the ideal of moderated love in marriage; they locate national values in individual choice and self-respect, helping to create the imaginative space where the private sphere eventually emerges in English-speaking culture. In addition to recovering and reinventing the discourse of the mean in early modern culture, however, Scodel stresses the importance of his theme for today in the links he makes to critical theory, the political thought of John

Rawls, Charles Taylor, and Isaiah Berlin, and to the aestheticization of excess in Nietzsche, Blake, and Baudrillard. In every way, this is a deeply satisfying study of a topic that I took for granted but will never see in the same way again.

2. Milton

The work for review this year embraces diverse interests in the reception history of Milton's poetry, as well as a concentration of work on, first, Milton's late poem *Paradise Regained* and, second, his life-long emphasis on liberty.

Heading this year's review are two strong monographs which confidently reassess and critique current critical presumptions within Milton studies. In *Shifting Contexts: Reinterpreting Samson Agonistes*, Joseph Wittreich identifies *Samson Agonistes* as both the climax of Milton's poetic vision and the crux for many of our current critical perspectives upon Milton. Wittreich takes ambiguity to be a core aspect of the dramatic poem's meaning, and he reviews its multiple contexts and traditions in an attempt to get beyond any single reading of either its protagonist, Samson, or the meaning of the text. He is especially good at countering a commonplace Christian redemptive interpretation of Milton's poem based on the New Testament reference to Samson in Hebrews. He points out the widespread theological commentary available on Genesis 49, where the tribe of Dan are excluded as idolaters, and explores the significance of that alternative identification of Samson, who is after all the most famous of the Dananites. Wittreich also enjoys blowing any determined reading of the phoenix simile out of the water, contending that this famous image will function only within its shifting context of a triple simile (i.e. of the dragon, the eagle, and the phoenix). Exploring multiple contexts further allows Wittreich to encourage us to delve deeper into the dramatic influences behind Milton's text, and he discusses both the influence of Euripides and the importance of later biblical drama upon Milton. Overall, Wittreich's approach is both elegant and erudite as he pursues his case for *Samson Agonistes* as a conscious compositional juxtaposition of contradictory frames of interpretation.

Victoria Silver, *Imperfect Sense: The Predicament of Milton's Irony* fits her work on Milton into an extraordinarily rich discussion of Western thought and theology, with, for example, Luther positioned as a major influence on Milton's theology and Wittgenstein as an important theoretical parallel. Silver is interested in what has become known as the problem with Milton's God. She sees theodicy as necessarily involving contradiction, resulting in antithetical presumptions. She has chosen the term 'irony' to cover our abiding experience of frustration in interpretation, arguing that each and any human attempt at comprehension of the divine brings with it difficulties of its own invention. Her remarkably measured and inclusive argument is explored in detail through both the text of *Paradise Lost* and the tradition of Milton commentary. Harold Skulsky, *Milton and the Death of Man: Humanism on Trial in Paradise Lost*, is similarly engaged, viewing the epic theodicy as a conscious trial of God's justice. This monograph is the first of a number of items that were published in 2001 but arrived too late for inclusion in last year's review. Skulsky presents us with the human Advocate within the epic, who is defending (but ultimately fails to acquit) his divine client. The focus this gives to debate and contentious argument within the body of Milton's poem is helpful, particularly as

Skulsky would further argue that the epic stands at a watershed in the history of ideas in Western culture. As his title suggests, he is most interested in the shifting concepts of human nature in the seventeenth century, and he offers a specific take on *Paradise Lost* as a vindication of the 'person' involving a growing sense of the private nature of individual experience. The arguments advanced by both Silver and Skulsky do not seek closure but encourage further discursive exploration and consideration. As Silver puts it, 'there can be no endings in Milton's poetry, where understanding is always imminent' (p. 345).

Anna-Julia Zwierlein, *Majestick Milton: British Imperial Expansion and Transformations of Paradise Lost, 1667–1837*, looks at the appropriation of Miltonic diction and theme by British writers over the course of the long eighteenth century and explores the correlation between Miltonic form and empire-building. This is a mammoth undertaking, particularly as Zwierlein set herself the task of reading numerous minor and mediocre texts in order to obtain a fuller survey of this period's reworking of Milton. She finds that writers in this period are shameless in appropriating Miltonic imagery and style in their endorsement of English patriotism and national imperialism, and that most eighteenth-century adapters of Milton are enthused by their present-day geographical conquests rather than by other-worldly religious concerns. Her research has uncovered numerous quirky texts, and one feels that she must have spent many happy hours browsing through the byways of both history and literature. Certainly her bibliography is extremely full, and it will be an asset to many interested parties. Unfortunately, Zwierlein's own discussion is hampered by the fact that this is a published thesis, with a cripplingly rigid structure. At almost every step one hopes for more detail in the discussion of these less well-known texts. Undoubtedly, Zwierlein will have more to say on this fascinating subject, and indeed one of her essays is included for review below.

Both Catherine Maxwell and Matthew Curr are interested in positioning Milton against the work of later canonical writers. Catherine Maxwell, *The Female Sublime from Milton to Swinburne: Being Blindness*, has produced an excellent discussion of Miltonic inspiration as it was conceived and appropriated by Romantic and Victorian writers. The discussion of the nightingale in chapter 1 is particularly strong, and the provocative argument in chapter 2 on Shelley's indebtedness to Milton is important and convincing. Matthew Curr, *The Consolation of Otherness: The Male Love Elegy in Milton, Gray and Tennyson*, offers a welcome extended reading of Milton's *Epitaphium Damonis* and its use of Theocritus as part of a wider thesis on proscribed love and poetic consolation. Curr traces a movement within Milton's elegy from wild lament to regenerative vision, and later suggests that Tennyson's *In Memoriam* is particularly indebted to this Miltonic work.

A selection of the late D.F. McKenzie's essays have been edited by Peter D. McDonald and Michael F. Suarez, SJ, as *Making Meaning: 'Printers of the Mind' and Other Essays*. This is an excellent volume which will make McKenzie's ground-breaking work in bibliography and book history available to a much wider audience. Miltonists will be especially interested in McKenzie's placement of *Areopagitica* within its immediate economic and social context in 'The London Book Trade in 1644' (pp. 126–43) and in the sensitive discussion of the affinity of Milton's prose to speech in 'Speech–Manuscript–Print' (pp. 237–58).

Dennis Kezar, *Guilty Creatures: Renaissance Poetry and the Ethics of Authorship*, contains a chapter on 'Samson's Death by Theater and Milton's Art of

Dying' (pp. 139–71), a much-revised version of an earlier essay (*ELH* 66[1999] 295–336; reviewed in *YWES* 81[2002] 509). Kezar sees the critical history of *Samson Agonistes* as preoccupied with interpreting the hero's death. However, he also points out that the influence of *Eikon Basilike*, the text published in the wake of Charles I's execution, would have changed the model for the 'art of dying' significantly for Milton and his contemporaries. Kezar therefore suggests that, in his dramatic poem *Samson Agonistes*, Milton intentionally destabilizes the authenticity of any concept of dying well. He also has some interesting points to make about Milton's *The Passion* (pp. 201–5), posing the suggestive question, can Christ be elegized?

Anthony Miller concludes a fascinating discussion of the use of the Roman triumph in early modern England, *Roman Triumphs and Early Modern English Culture*, with a discussion of Milton's awareness of the Roman triumph (pp. 179–89). Aware that Milton repeatedly champions ethical self-mastery over military success, Miller offers an insightful reading of the role of the Son in triumph in *Paradise Lost*, looking at the celebration of the Son's triumph after the War in Heaven, and the prophecies of his future triumph over death and final role as *triumphator* at the Last Judgement. Miller argues that the Son's victories are always presented as seeking the restoration of peace in contrast to the satanic ambition for enslaved captives and a glorification of force. In *Paradise Regained*, the repudiation of military values for a triumph is even stronger, with Book IV including the Son's discourse upon the decline of the Roman triumph into tyrannical spectacle. Miller sees the brief epic as both opening and closing with versions of triumph for the Son's victories and also, in its close, thwarting Satan's expectation of his own triumph.

Two new introductory critical guides are worth noting and comparing in terms of their methodology and house style. Roy Flannagan, *John Milton: A Short Introduction* is part of the Blackwell Introductions to Literature series. Flannagan acts as friend and sponsor to the non-specialist, presenting a personal line of approach for each major text. The approach is broadly biographical and chronological. The Routledge series for which Richard Bradford has produced *The Complete Critical Guide to John Milton* is, on the other hand, a crisp reference volume. Bradford offers a remarkably good overview on the twentieth-century critical approaches to Milton studies, but the series format means that there is little room for more than a brief summary of individual texts and the focus is almost exclusively on Milton's poetry. Alongside these two introductory volumes, it is worth mentioning that the biographical and psychological examination of Milton undertaken by John T. Shawcross in *John Milton: The Self and the World* is now available in paperback.

Also published this year is Osamu Nakayama, *Images of their Glorious Maker: Iconology in Milton's Poetry*. This is a handsomely produced and illustrated volume which reviews aspects of Milton's conceptual indebtedness to the emblem tradition. The similes of *Paradise Lost*, the 'pensive nun' of *Il Penseroso*, the 'two-handed engine' of *Lycidas*, and the phoenix imagery in *Samson Agonistes* all receive attention, and the cultural contextual placement of the whale simile from Book I of *Paradise Lost* is most richly explored.

Other book-length studies which may prove of interest this year include James G. Turner, *Libertines and Radicals in Early Modern London: Sexuality, Politics and*

Literary Culture, 1630–1685. This is a far-ranging textual study of libertinism and sexuality in the Restoration period, including Milton's response in the divorce tracts to the accusations of libertinism made against him in the 1640s and then his own later indictment of Restoration aristocratic licentiousness. Milton is a pervasive presence in Turner's argument and acts as a sounding-board for the wider study. Conversely, Linda C. Mitchell places Milton in a discrete section (pp. 66–72) in her *Grammar Wars: Language as Cultural Battlefield in 17th and 18th Century England.* She divides Milton off from the grammarians because she finds that he is less interested in grammar for its own sake than as a useful tool for the comprehension of literary style. Amusingly enough she reveals that eighteenth-century grammarians, uneasy about the syntactical complexity of Milton's epic, often set the opening lines of *Paradise Lost* as an exercise, tasking the student to apply the rules of grammar in order to straighten out Milton's mistakes. Roy Eriksen, in his *The Building in the Text: Alberti to Shakespeare and Milton,* is intent on exploring more general compositional principles across a range of disciplines. His discussion ranges from Vasari's *Life of Michelangelo* to work by Tasso, Shakespeare, and Philip Sidney. One chapter is dedicated to Milton's formal patterning within *Paradise Lost,* with particular reference to the possible influence of Tasso and Ariosto. Eriksen considers Milton to be indebted to a tradition of structural aesthetics with its roots traceable to classical and Renaissance notions of architecture. Although Eriksen does not have sufficient space here for a full development of the argument as it relates to Milton, there is much that is interesting and important in such compositional enquiry.

We turn now from monographs to this year's clutch of edited collections of essays, then on to the dedicated Milton journals and issues, and finally to the numerous single essays devoted to Miltonic themes. First off we have Parry and Raymond, eds., *Milton and the Terms of Liberty.* This excellent collection of essays themed around Milton's political thought is a selection from the papers given at the Sixth International Milton Symposium held in York in July 1999. It opens with an important and highly resonant essay by Quentin Skinner, 'John Milton and the Politics of Slavery' (pp. 1–22). This focuses on Milton's employment of Roman law, and particularly the importance of Sallust in Milton's understanding of lawful government. Martin Dzelzainis, '"In these western parts of the Empire": Milton and Roman Law' (pp. 57–68), teases out Milton's knowledge of Roman law in the *Judgement of Martin Bucer.* He argues that Milton is clearly in control, willing to award a remarkable status to Bucer's argument but yet happy to elide that argument when convenient. As Dzelzainis shows, the Justinian revocation of the Theodosian law is simply never mentioned by Milton. This is a polished and clear essay which, despite the seemingly esoteric subject matter, has significant implications for our critical understanding of Milton's reading practice, as Dzelzainis is particularly interested in which texts and manuscripts Milton might have seen during his Continental travels. Thomas Corns, 'Milton before "Lycidas"' (pp. 23–36), cautions against over-generalization and presumptions of hindsight when dealing with the decades of the 1620s and 1630s. Corns uses Milton as a case study to trace the failure of policy in Charles's Personal Rule, showing how Milton was at ease in an early Baroque style but later shifted into oppositional radicalism. John Creaser, 'Prosody and Liberty in Milton and Marvell' (pp. 37–55), is a revised, and less technically detailed, version of his article on Milton and Marvell's prosody in *Milton*

Quarterly (*MiltonQ* 34[2000] 1–13, (reviewed in *YWES* 81[2002] 507). Creaser argues that Milton explores asymmetric forms while Marvell seeks formal balance and closure, and applies the respective prosodic methods of the poets within a wider comparative discussion of their approach to political freedom.

Civil war rhetoric is the focus for Joad Raymond, 'The King Is a Thing' (pp. 69–94). This is a tidy and enjoyable discussion of the conscious linguistic play, and the underlying ideological argument over the status of the king, to be found in texts of 1649–51. Christopher Orchard, '"In time of Warre ... our *Language* is all corrupt with military *Tearms*": The Politics of Martial Metaphors in Post-Regicide England' (pp. 95–109) is also interested in the new rhetorical battlefield drawn up after the regicide. Orchard lines up William Davenant and Christopher Wase for the royalists, with Milton's *Eikonoklastes* and his *Defences* on the opposite side. He then considers both the ideology behind their respective methods and their use of martial terms as metaphors. Stephen M. Fallon, 'Alexander More Reads Milton: Self-Representation and Anxiety in Milton's Defences' (pp. 111–24), gives a very helpful consideration of Alexander More's tactics in the famous clash with Milton in the 1650s. Fallon identifies More as a shrewd critic of Milton, capable of really getting under his opponent's skin. Milton is agitated in part because he must admit on some level that More is right to expose the inherent fallibility and egotism of Milton's repeated insistence upon his own personal authorial heroism. John Rumrich, 'Stylometry and the Provenance of *De doctrina christiana*' (pp. 125–36), is deeply sceptical of the utility of statistic proofs or stylometry when dealing with a seventeenth-century theological treatise. The power of his argument is unfortunately diminished by the fact that he becomes unnecessarily overheated in his attack upon those who have recently undertaken the Herculean task of working closely with the *De Doctrina Christiana* manuscript. Michael Lieb's approach (see below) is more measured and, it should be noted, he—unlike Rumrich—seems happy to accept the incompleteness of the manuscript.

Three essays in the collection concentrate on a fuller exploration of the Restoration context for Milton's later work. Janel Mueller, 'The Figure and the Ground: Samson as a Hero of London Nonconformity, 1662–1667' (pp. 137–62), links Milton's *Samson Agonistes* to a number of texts originating in London between 1662 and 1667 which employ the figure of Samson. She is particularly interested in the contrasting perspectives on contemporary events proposed by nonconformist and conforming authors, although she finds a common interest in the Samson figure to be held by authors from opposing political and religious positions. *Samson Agonistes*, she argues, follows a nonconformist view of current affairs in emphasizing imprisonment for true witness, plague, and fire. Mueller finds Samson to be a figure for the experience of the Great Fire of 1666 in a number of contemporary texts, and she uses these as a fascinating backdrop for her exploration of fire imagery in Milton's dramatic poem. Katsuhiro Engetsu, 'The Publication of the King's Privacy: *Paradise Regained* and *Of True Religion* in Restoration England' (pp. 163–74), is also interested in the specific political arguments embedded in imagery and biblical quotation in the Restoration period. He provides a clear and measured examination of the ways in which Milton fuses arguments concerning the public and private sphere in his late texts, *Of True Religion* and *Paradise Regained.* Engetsu argues that the passage on Tiberius in Book IV of *Paradise Regained* is intended as a critique of the decadence of Charles II's private court life. He links this political critique convincingly with Milton's prose text, *Of True Religion*, which he also considers to be a discourse condemning court corruption, specifically court Catholicism. As he points out, the last paragraph of *Of True Religion* identifies popery as the root of all evil. Moreover, a specific reference is made by Milton to a verse from Paul's Letter to the Romans, which in the staunchly Protestant Geneva Bible is footnoted thus, 'The wicked shall be condemned and the faithful delivered'. Barbara K. Lewalski, '"To try, and teach the erring Soul": Milton's Last Seven Years' (pp. 175–90), considers Milton to have maintained an oppositional role as an educator of his readership throughout all his Restoration publications. So for example, *Poems 1671* offers two contrasting models of political response to trial and oppression, with *Paradise Regained* endorsing the radical sectarian principle of the entire sufficiency of the Son's teaching. Lewalski also strengthens the case for Milton's authorship of *De Doctrina Christiana* by indicating the cross-connections between that thesis and both *Artis logicae* and *Of True Religion*.

Completing the volume is Anne-Julia Zwierlein, 'Pandemonic Panoramas: Surveying Milton's "vain empires" in the Long Eighteenth Century' (pp. 191–214). Zwierlein explores the revision and exploitation of Milton's epic by eighteenth-century writers intent on building an English empire. She defines this period's outlook as one that took pride in spatial control, seeking to conquer lands rather than minds. This means that the Miltonic sublime can often be reduced to little more than imperial survey or popular panorama. Zwierlein's description of the instance of 'Hell from *Paradise Lost*' being staged as a spectacle for popular entertainment in 1782 is delightful. *Eidophusikon* was in vogue but Milton's inclusion in Philippe de Loutherbourg's installation is noteworthy, given that this mode was usually reserved for patriotic spectacles.

Three essays in Summers and Pebworth, eds., *Fault Lines*, relate to Milton studies. Tobias Gregory, 'In Defense of Empson: A Reassessment of *Milton's God*' (pp. 73–87), endorses Empson's critical stance as a resonant model for those who wish to remain ethically engaged in their literary criticism. Elizabeth Sauer, 'Milton and Dryden on the Restoration Stage' (pp. 88–110), places *Samson Agonistes* within its Restoration context, concentrating on its place within a commercial marketplace. She argues that after publication Milton could not control how his text was read or received, and she proves her point by examining the appropriation of aspects of *Samson Agonistes* in the work of William Joyner and John Dryden. William Shullenberger, 'Milton's Lady and Lady Milton: Chastity, Prophecy, and Gender in *A Maske Presented at Ludlow Castle*' (pp. 204–26), sees the Lady's voice in *Comus* as the site where Milton discovers his own prophetic voice. The integrity of this active visionary power dissolves gender identification. The masque shows the Lady moving forward to an active life of chaste desire in a manner which allows her role to be compared to the Son in *Paradise Regained* as a model for ethical engagement within the world.

Elsewhere, in Swiss and Kent, eds., *Speaking Grief in English Literary Culture: Shakespeare to Milton*, Margo Swiss tackles an emotive theme in 'Repairing Androgyny: Eve's Tears in *Paradise Lost*' (pp. 261–83). Her focus is on the tears shed by Eve after she has retold her dream in Book V of *Paradise Lost*. Swiss finds Adam to be negligent in his response here, and she views the kissing away of Eve's tears by her husband as amounting to a denial of Eve's need to give expression to her grief. From there Swiss argues for an alienation of both Eve and affective emotion that is not redressed until the reparative tears that close Book X. Although this essay tries to do too much at once, its core identification of grief as both a human and a divine emotion is highly pertinent.

Warren Chernaik, 'Civil Liberty in Milton, the Levellers and Winstanley' (pp. 101–20), is one of the essays first published in a special issue of *Prose Studies* (*PSt* 22:ii[1999]) and now collected in Bradstock, ed., *Winstanley and the Diggers, 1649–1999*. Chernaik compares Milton to Levellers such as Walwyn and Winstanley, arguing that there is a common interest in developing a public sphere for oppositional discourse. He compares Winstanley's *The Law of Freedom* [1652] as a text that distrusts the common people and is the product of bitter experience to Milton's *Readie and Easie Way* [1660] to good effect.

Two new volumes in the *Cambridge Companion* series deserve attention. N.H. Keeble has edited a fine collection, *The Cambridge Companion to Writing of the English Revolution*. Two essays here are of particular relevance. David Loewenstein, 'Milton's Prose and the Revolution' (pp. 87–106), is a sensible introduction to the topic, while Nigel Smith, '*Paradise Lost* from Civil War to Restoration' (pp. 251–67), gives a punchy endorsement of Milton's epic read in the context of contemporary politics. Both essays will be of great assistance as teaching aids. The second volume, *Radicalism in British Literary Culture, 1650–1830: From Revolution to Revolution*, is edited by Timothy Morton and Nigel Smith. This is a diverse and stimulating collection, breaking new ground and encouraging its readers to advance the study of popular radicalism further. Milton *per se* is not a central topic of discussion, but Donald John's 'They Became What They Beheld: Theodicy and Regeneration in Milton, Law and Blake' (pp. 86–100), takes the non-juror William Law as an example of how later readers interpreted the texts of earlier religious radicals. He further considers how radical theology from the mid-seventeenth century was transmitted to, and altered by, the long eighteenth century's view of a Christian theology of redemption.

Finally amongst edited collections, Pfister, ed., *A History of English Laughter: Laughter from Beowulf to Beckett and Beyond* is a collection of essays evolving out of a lecture series at the Free University of Berlin. It includes a chapter by Susanne Rapp on 'Milton's Laughing God' (pp. 47–55) which looks at the anti-episcopal prose, and next at the contrasting positions of God and Satan in *Paradise Lost*, as it considers the power of satirical laughter as an expression of superiority, authority, and self-righteousness.

Milton Studies 41[2002] presents new work on a range of Miltonic texts and themes. Anthony Welch, 'Reconsidering Chronology in *Paradise Lost*' (*MiltonS* 41[2002] 1–17), notes that temporal inconsistencies recur repeatedly at structurally important moments in the epic. He argues that it is high time that critics stopped attempting to regularize the chronology of Milton's epic and instead admitted that temporal gaps and confusions are integral to the reading experience. Stella P. Revard, 'Milton, Homer, and the Anger of Adam' (*MiltonS* 41[2002] 18–37), discovers an emotional debt to Homer in the emotional complexity of Milton's Adam. She compares Adam to the classical heroes of Homeric epic, suggesting that Milton's first man incorporates the great qualities of Achilles (valour), Odysseus (contemplation), and Agamemnon (leadership). She compares Adam and Eve in the final books of *Paradise Lost* to Achilles in some detail, as figures tested by both wrath and pity. As one would expect from Revard, this is a delightful essay full of subtle insights, for example her comparison of Eve clasping Adam's knees to Priam kneeling as a supplicant before Achilles, and her contrast between the final speech by Eve in Book XII and the final female voices of the *Iliad*.

In "'Impregn'd with Reason": Eve's Aural Conception in *Paradise Lost*' (*MiltonS* 41[2002] 38–75), Kent R. Lehnhof offers a detailed, and illustrated, exploration of the artistic and textual tradition of the Virgin Mary's impregnation via the ear as it relates to Eve's temptation in Book IX of *Paradise Lost*. This is a far-ranging essay, and the textual work on the homonyms air/ear/heir is particularly rich. Raymond B. Waddington, 'Murder One: The Death of Abel. Blood, Soul, and Mortalism in *Paradise Lost*' (*MiltonS* 41[2002] 76–93), sees the death of Abel as it is related in Book XI of *Paradise Lost* as representing the death not only of innocence but of the initial commonweal. It is the survivor Cain, after all, who is the builder of cities. Waddington further argues that the actual description of Abel's death ('Groaned out his soul with gushing blood effus'd', XI. 447) makes this another moment in the epic where Milton presents a heretically mortalist argument.

Lauren Shohet, 'Reading History with *Samson Agonistes*' (*MiltonS* 41[2002] 94–116), sees the dramatic poem as a work of historiography, a theory of what it means to read and write history. James Egan, 'Rhetoric, Polemic, Mimetic: The Dialectic of Genres in *Tetrachordon* and *Colasterion*' (*MiltonS* 41[2002] 117–38), finds a development in Milton's prose style from *Tetrachordon* to *Colasterion* as Milton shifts from a discursive perspective to a mimetic argument, and this continues on into the aesthetic production of sonnets relating to the divorce tracts. The argument here links to that in Egan's discussion of the anti-prelatical tracts (see below). John D. Staines, 'Charles's Grandmother, Milton's Spenser, and the Rhetoric of Revolution' (*MiltonS* 41[2002] 139–71), traces the importance of the life and reputation of Mary Queen of Scots to the prehistory of both *Eikon Basilike* and *Eikonoklastes*. He charges Milton with being disingenuous in his own selective use of Book V of Edmund Spenser's *The Faerie Queene*. Milton adopts the figure of Talus as justice from Spenser, but makes no mention of the trial of Duessa or of the moral and political complications embedded in Spenser's text. This manoeuvre is all the more hypocritical, says Staines, given that Milton is, at the same time, accusing Charles of imitating the rhetorical deviousness of his grandmother, Mary Queen of Scots. Finally in this volume comes Michael Lieb, '*De Doctrina Christiana* and the Question of Authorship' (*MiltonS* 41[2002] 172–230). This is a sensible, full, and engaging overview of the critical debacle over the manuscript of *De Doctrina Christiana*. Lieb brings much light to the darkness, explaining the textual issues, and the convolutions of the critical debate in an objective fashion.

Karen O'Brien gave the Warton Lecture on Poetry at the British Academy this year. It is published as 'Poetry against Empire: Milton to Shelley' (*PBA* 117[2002] 269–96). This is a terrific essay which takes *Paradise Regained* seriously. The elevation of Milton's brief epic to a more central position within the critical canon is long overdue, and O'Brien's reading of *Paradise Regained* as the genesis of the Romantic anti-imperial imagination will do much to encourage wider interest in the poem as well as forcing us all to update our general sense of the lines of literary inheritance and the politics of poetry.

Interest in *Paradise Regained* amongst Miltonists is presently increasing incrementally. This is acknowledged in the appearance of a special extra issue of

Milton Studies, devoted to new work on *Paradise Regained*. *Milton Studies* 42[2002] is edited by David Loewenstein and is dedicated to the memory of Louis Martz. In his introduction (*MiltonS* 42[2002] 1–6), Loewenstein rightly identifies that this is an important moment for reconsideration of this late poem. The essays gathered here are particularly historical in outlook, but the questions of genre and theology are also tackled. They are headed by an essay by Louis Martz, '*Paradise Regained*: Georgic Form, Georgic Style' (*MiltonS* 42[2002] 7–25). This lovely essay, which was completed shortly before his death, sees Martz returning to his long-held view that *Paradise Regained* is consciously analogous in style and form to Virgil's *Georgics*. He here takes the time to expand and refine that argument further, assessing the frequent stylistic shifts in both *Paradise Regained* and Virgil's *Georgics* and comparing the Son's rejection of empire to Virgil's lament for the loss of ancient virtue in the Roman people. A more theological bent is taken by Regina M. Schwartz in 'Redemption and *Paradise Regained*' (*MiltonS* 42[2002] 26–49). This is a consideration of Milton's understanding of salvation and redemption as presented in this late poem. Schwartz sees *Paradise Regained* as a text which, in its reliance on obedience rather than doctrinal complications, has pared down the essentials of redemption and, for Schwartz, the text avoids a positive definition of salvation and relies instead on identifying what it is not. Her conclusion is not optimistic. Redemption relies on a refusal of human options and a renunciation of any and all plans for a new paradise on earth. Where Schwarz equates miracles with the satanic, Rumrich positions Christ on the pinnacle as the miraculous arrival of a new world order. The theme in John Rumrich, 'Milton's *Theanthropos*: The Body of Christ in *Paradise Regained*' (*MiltonS* 42[2002] 50–67), is a new exploration of the nature of the Son, as incarnate God-made-man and as Redeemer. Rumrich argues for a hybrid psyche and a hybrid body in this figure, who is both son of God and son of Mary.

Laura Lunger Knoppers, 'Satan and the Papacy in *Paradise Regained*' (*MiltonS* 42[2002] 68–85), takes a more oblique angle of approach to the figuration of the Son within the brief epic. She sees much of the seeming asceticism of the Son as really a Miltonic attack upon the culture of papal Rome and Catholic thought. Working through the poem, Knoppers gives us a surprising amount of material to consider. She has tapped an unexpectedly rich vein of anti-Catholic argument within this late poem, and this essay furthers her work on the embedded political critique in Milton's late poems.

The other contributors to this volume are all, in their own way, focused on the politics of *Paradise Regained* and each provides a significant addition to our current interpretation of this late poem. N.H. Keeble, 'Wilderness Exercises: Adversity, Temptation, and Trial in *Paradise Regained*' (*MiltonS* 42[2002] 86–105), reads the desert setting of the poem as shaped by the cultural landscape of the 1660s, and the contested use of the biblical model of exile by nonconformists and royalists. This is a fine essay, locating Milton's Son in a wilderness shaped by the contemporary Puritan imagination. Thomas N. Corns, '"With unaltered brow": Milton and the Son of God' (*MiltonS* 42[2002] 106–21), explains a curious and conscious ventriloquism within Milton's texts, showing how earlier arguments from the political prose recur and renew themselves within the later poetry. Corns thinks Milton has, both shrewdly and defiantly, adopted the Son as mouthpiece for his own political arguments in a radically inflected *imitatio Christi/imitatio Miltoni*. David Norbrook,

'Republican Occasions in *Paradise Regained* and *Samson Agonistes*' (*MiltonS* 42[2002] 122–48), sees Milton in the 1660s and 1670s as patient in a radical, republican (and Machiavellian) sense, conscious of civic prudence and of the proper way to grasp an opportunity for oppositional comment or seize the occasion for action. Norbrook therefore suggests that we are given two alternative models of how to act appropriately in *Poems 1671*, and he reads these poems against the contemporary atmosphere of political equivocation, and specifically against the choices made by such contemporary figures as Henry Vane, Lucy Hutchinson, George Wither, and Robert Overton. There is much here of interest regarding contemporary adoptions of the Samson figure, but Norbrook also carefully maps out the millenarian context for *Paradise Regained*. Finally, and in ways that complement the work of both Norbrook and Keeble here, John Coffey, 'Pacifist, Quietist, or Patient Militant? John Milton and the Restoration' (*MiltonS* 42[2002] 149–74), gives a historical reassessment of the preoccupation with time and timing in *Paradise Regained*. He suggests that this theme would resonate deeply with republicans and nonconformists, and compares the writings of other radicals, such as Henry Vane, Algernon Sidney, Edmund Ludlow, and John Goodwin. Coffey finally places Milton's argument in a mid-way position between Fifth Monarchist action and Quaker pacifism. The Son is not passive but patient, waiting until the time is right and leaving us a model of how to act in such interim circumstances. Overall, the range and strength of this special issue of *Milton Studies* are admirable, and the political perspectives in particular should mean that *Paradise Regained* will no longer be consigned to the shadows in current Milton studies.

Milton Quarterly 36[2002] is as always catholic in its tastes. Jeanie G. Moore, 'The Two Faces of Eve: Temptation Scenes in *Comus* and *Paradise Lost*' (*MiltonQ* 36:i[2002] 1–19), compares the Lady of *Comus* with Eve in *Paradise Lost* to argue that Milton's Eve is far from being a defective character despite the inherited cultural prejudices. She argues, however, that the Lady has more power of reasoning at her disposal than the unfallen Eve. James D. Fleming, 'Composing 1629' (*MiltonQ* 36:i[2002] 20–33), rethinks our customary dating of the Nativity Ode. He points out that the date is mentioned only in *Poems 1645*, and scrutinizes the possible intention behind this belated marker. He picks apart the possible arguments, wonders whether this is even Milton's dating or whether it might not be that of the publisher, and proves that we really know much less than we would like. Fleming suggests that, if anything, this dating for a Christmas poem may be read as reactionary in intention, and he contends that it is just this kind of problem that should lead us to challenge rather than endorse many of our present critical preconceptions regarding Milton's early politics. Eric C. Brown, 'Underwater Sailors in Milton's "Lycidas" and Virgil's *Aeneid*' (*MiltonQ* 36:i[2002] 34–45), suggests that the presentation of drowned souls in *Lycidas* may have been influenced by *Aeneid* VI. The essay has a commendable lightness of touch, and Brown is, intriguingly enough, the first of two critics this year to have been animated by a specific quotation from Milton's 1639 letter to Lucas Holste (see Hale in *N&Q* 49[2002] 336, reviewed below). Peter Lindenbaum, 'Dispatches from the Archives' (*MiltonQ* 36:i[2002] 46–54), generously gives us a short paper rich in detail. This starts as a summary of biographical and economic information relating to Brabazon Aylmer, publisher of Milton's *Epistolarum Familiarium* and *History of Moscovia*. That leads into some more general revision of our understanding of late seventeenth-

and eighteenth-century publishing house practices, and new research regarding the transfer of publication rights for both *Paradise Lost* and his prose texts.

Ross Leasure's essay, 'Milton's Queer Choice: *Comus* at Castlehaven' (*MiltonQ* 36:ii[2002] 63–86), is a seductive piece on Comus as a subversive and lecherous figure, associated with androgyny and sodomy. The argument linking Comus and Belial is well sustained and important. However, Leasure's main suggestion is that it was the Castlehaven scandal which led to the employment of Comus within a masque themed around the victory of chastity, where the sexual threat should be seen as aimed not just at the Lady but at the two brothers as well. In '"That far be from thee": Divine Evil and Justification in *Paradise Lost*' (*MiltonQ* 36:ii[2002] 87–105), Michael Bryson is thinking about the rigour of the Father's voice in Book III of *Paradise Lost*. He is aware that the Father might be said to be economical with the truth within the text, and explores the paradox of a God who lies. The essay also contains a helpful discussion of the shifting implications of the term 'justify'. Rosa Flotats, 'Translating Milton into Catalan' (*MiltonQ* 36:ii[2002] 106–23), ponders the general issues inherent in any translation process, using examples first from Spanish and Catalan translations of *Paradise Lost* and secondly from her own work translating *Areopagitica* into Catalan.

Milton Quarterly 36:iii is taken up by the publication of a new translation by Alan Fishbone of *Christos Paschon, Christus Patiens or Christ Suffering*. This text is referred to by Milton in the headnote to *Samson Agonistes*, '*Gregory Nazianen*, a Father of the Church, thought it not unbeseeming the sanctity of his person to write a Tragedy, which is entitl'd, *Christ suffering*'. The text presents Euripidean quotations within a Judaeo-Christian context, with little concern for performative needs or dramatic impetus, but it remains an important paradigm for early modern biblical tragedy, and particularly Milton's *Samson Agonistes*. This makes Fishbone's new translation a helpful aid. Joseph Wittreich has an afterword, 'Still Nearly Anonymous: *Christos Paschon*' (*MiltonQ* 36:iii[2002] 193–8), in which he considers the alternative attributions for the text and suggests a link between Milton and Hugo Grotius in their affirmation of Gregory as author. As in his monograph, *Shifting Contexts: Reinterpreting Samson Agonistes* (reviewed above), Wittreich is keen to assert Milton's conscious inheritance of a genre of biblical tragedy.

There were three essays in the final issue of the *Milton Quarterly* for 2002. Nicholas Moschovakis, 'Great Period: Pointing, Syntax, and the Millennium in the Texts of "At a Solemn Musick"' (*MiltonQ* 36:iv[2002] 199–220), is interested in how a Renaissance poem's argument is embedded in its structure and how our reading of a poem might be affected by variants in punctuation. The last manuscript draft for 'At a Solemn Musick' has a full stop at the end of line 16. This is not present in the text printed in *Poems 1645*. Moschovakis shows that the draft variant emphasizes the art of the singer while the printed version places its emphasis on divine omnipotence. He delights in the fact that such a small variance can cause such a shift in emphasis, and wonders whether the change is authorial. Robert Appelbaum, 'Eve's and Adam's "Apple": Horticulture, Taste, and the Flesh of the Forbidden Fruit in *Paradise Lost*' (*MiltonQ* 36:iv[2002] 221–39), has had fun researching the culinary uses and cultural applications of fruit in seventeenth-century England. He comes to the lush conclusion that the exotic description of the forbidden fruit in *Paradise Lost* suggests that Milton may have had in mind the peach, also known as the Persian apple or *Malum persicum*, and not a Granny Smith after all. Lastly, Feisal G. Mohamed, '*Paradise Lost* and the Inversion of Catholic Angelology' (*MiltonQ* 36:iv[2002] 240–52), finds Milton's angelic hierarchy to be an intentional inversion of the Catholic model. He also thinks Raphael holds the subordinate rank of seraph and lacks full first-hand knowledge of God's plans.

Cithara 40:ii[2001] was a commemorative issue dedicated to John M. Steadman. The issue includes an article on Steadman's own poetry (and its Miltonic allusions), John T. Shawcross, '"This illusion of a brighter world": John Steadman's Poetic World' (*Cithara* 40:ii[2001] 8–19), an essay by John Mulryne on how Milton might have thought about the historical figure of Socrates, 'Milton and Socrates' (*Cithara* 40:ii[2001] 20–6), and a useful bibliography of John Steadman's work prepared by Theresa Howe (*Cithara* 40:ii[2001] 50–60). The issue also contains Albert C. Labriola, 'The Annunciation and its Hebraic Analogues' (*Cithara* 40:ii[2001] 27–36) and Jameela Lares, '*Officium concionatoris* (1676) and the Survival of Doctrines-and-Uses Preaching' (*Cithara* 40:ii[2001] 37–49). We might also mention here two short essays by John T. Shawcross himself. In 'The Centrality of Book 8 in *Paradise Lost*' (*ANQ* 14:i[2001] 45–55), Shawcross argues that the birth of Eve as described in Book VIII of *Paradise Lost* is the central act of Milton's epic, and he advances this argument by showing that this episode has been structurally positioned to take place at the golden section within the epic. Secondly, in 'The Temple of *Janus* and Milton Criticism in the New Millennium' (*ANQ* 15:iv[2002] 20–9), Shawcross offers an upbeat review of the current state of Milton studies and the rich diversity of opinion therein. Shawcross both hopes and advises us to retain a courteous republic of letters in the new millennium.

There was a good show of essays on Milton in a range of other journals this year, and there are also a number of essays from previous years to be included here. Charles A. Huttar, 'C.S. Lewis, T.S. Eliot, and the Milton Legacy: The *Nativity Ode* Reconsidered' (*TSLL* 44[2002] 324–48), suggests that C.S. Lewis's poem 'The Turn of the Tide' [1948] is a purposeful reshaping of Milton's Nativity Ode, intended to counter T.S. Eliot's anti-Miltonic arguments in his 1947 British Academy lecture by showing that Milton could be a positive influence upon a modern poet. Julie Sanders, 'Ecocritical Reading and the Seventeenth-Century Woodland: Milton's "Comus" and the Forest of Dean' (*English* 50[2001] 1–18), considers that regional politics are an important factor in reading *Comus* as a provincial masque of the 1630s. She argues convincingly that forest law and the contemporary disputes over common rights versus enclosure within the locality of the Forest of Dean find their way into the text of *Comus*. In a careful and considered argument, Bruce Boehrer, '"Lycidas": The Pastoral Elegy as Same-Sex Epithalamium' (*PMLA* 117:ii[2002] 222–36), finds that *Lycidas* contains an ambivalence over the presence of women and a same-sex erotic charge in the final ecstatic and marital image of the company of the elect in heaven.

Also interested in the development of the younger Milton are Edward Jones and James Egan. Edward Jones, '"Filling in a blank in the canvas": Milton, Horton, and the Kedermister Library' (*RES* 53[2002] 31–60), identifies the Horton years as a period in Milton's life for which critics still have less biographical information than they would ideally like. Jones considers it very likely that Milton would have wished to have access to a remarkable private theological library housed only two miles away from Horton. Jones has made use of a 1638 inventory of the Kedermister library as well as its current holdings to explore the possibility that this is where

Milton did much of his reading during the Horton period and immediately after his return from the Continental tour. He finds that forty writers present in the Kedermister library are referred to in Milton's Commonplace Book. Most are theological, but Holinshed's *Chronicles* was also there, as was Gower's *Confessio Amantis* in the edition used by Milton. Jones cannot prove that Milton used this library, but he has amassed a good deal of circumstantial evidence. James Egan, '"As his own rhetorick shall persuade him": Refutation and Aesthetic Self-Construction in Milton's Anti-Prelatical Tracts' (*PSt* 24:ii[2001] 41–64), traces a developing style of refutation, from analysis and rebuttal in *Of Reformation* towards satiric opposition in *Of Prelatical Episcopy*, and on to a literary contest of wit in *Animadversions*.

James Dougal Fleming, 'Meanwhile, Medusa in *Paradise Lost*' (*ELH* 69[2002] 1009–28), is intrigued by the reference to Medusa as a character (not just an allusion) guarding the ford in *Paradise Lost*, II. 610–14. He explores the implications of this 'cameo' appearance in expert fashion, and is particularly entertained by the possible reference to Renaissance garden statuary, where Medusa statues are petrified by seeing their own reflection in water. Fleming insightfully notes that both the start and the close of Satan's epic quest are linked to the appalling, yet self-cancelling, figure of Medusa. Hannibal Hamlin, 'Psalm Culture in the English Renaissance: Readings of Psalm 137 by Shakespeare, Spenser, Milton, and Others' (*RQ* 55[2002] 224–57), includes a reading of the angelic hymn in *Paradise Lost*, Book III, within a wide-ranging consideration of English Renaissance literary responses to Psalm 137, 'By the rivers of Babylon'. Hamlin sees the usage in Book III as overturning exile in a momentary joining of the narratorial voice to the angelic choir and a rewriting of elegy and lament as a hymn of joy. Donald Cheney, 'The Mysterious Genesis of *Paradise Lost*' (*Connotations* 9:i[1999] 57–70), explores the Ariosto connection in Milton's epic. He would like to see *Paradise Lost* at least considered as the story of a man driven to fatal distraction by love on the model of *Orlando furioso*, although with the understanding that by the close of the later epic we may feel that Milton has overcome some of the limits in Ariosto's argument.

Gregory M. Colón Semenza, '*Samson Agonistes* and the Politics of Restoration Sport' (*SEL* 42[2002] 459–73), further enriches the Restoration context for the dramatic poem by concentrating on its use of the word 'sport'. Semenza sees the struggle in *Samson Agonistes* as in part focused on this term. Samson as *agonist* is a wrestler, an athlete, and he needs to regain a harmony between body and mind. Semenza cleverly balances the spectacles of Restoration culture which are an idolatrous form of sport with Milton's description of a Philistine obsession with 'sport and play' (line 1679), which leads directly to their downfall. Also working on *Samson Agonistes*, Andrew Hiscock, 'Retiring from the Popular Noise: The Nation and its Fugitive Images in Milton's *Samson Agonistes*' (*English* 50[2001] 89–110), takes the dramatic poem to be a meditation upon nationhood as shaped by memory, myths of heroism, and selective forgetting.

John H. Wall, 'The Milton Effect' (*RenP* [2001] 107–25), proposes that readers of Milton are trapped in a mutual appreciation society whereby Milton, having constructed his own ideal audience as classically educated, gives work to the present academic community as we set about explicating Miltonic allusions and thereby displaying our own fitness to be part of his audience. This symbiosis means that critics are often overly accepting of Miltonic allusion and expression as a 'norm', failing to consider the transgressive nature of his texts fully. John T. Shawcross, 'Humor, *Paradise Lost*, the Novel, and its Reader' (*RenP* [2001] 127–49), sees the dialectic nature of Milton's epic, and particularly its use of humour, punning, and parody, as leading towards the new form of the novel. Also engaged by Milton's humour is Roger B. Rollin. In '"And Laughter holding both his sides": Milton as Humorist, Part One' (*SCR* 35:i[2002] 133–48), Rollin notes that the biographical information suggests that Milton was both a cheerful and a social individual, and he therefore suggests that we acknowledge his wit and the humorous asides to be found throughout his poetry. Rollin sees Book VIII of *Paradise Lost* as the most amusing in the epic, and shows that even the Son in *Paradise Regained* has a sense of humour. This critical approach is to be encouraged, but Rollins is surely mistaken when he states categorically that 'From Book X on, no trace of wit, humor, sarcasm, ridicule, mockery, or satire is to be found in *Paradise Lost*' (p. 146).

T. Ross Leasure, 'The Genesis of *Paradise Lost*: What Milton May Have Seen in the Junius Manuscript' (*Cithara* 41:ii[2002] 3–17), looks again at the possibility that Milton's epic composition was influenced by Caedmon's *Genesis* poem. He thinks it probable that Milton would have met the editor of the Caedmonian poem, Franciscus Junius, in London at the start of the 1650s. If such a meeting occurred, he feels sure that the two men would have discussed poetry on the theme of the Fall of Man and that Junius would have offered to show Milton his own manuscript. Leasure further speculates that, if Milton could not himself read Anglo-Saxon, then Junius was on hand to interpret the poetry for him. However, he is equally taken by the alternative argument that language difficulties might have drawn Milton immediately to the illustrations to the manuscript. Leasure finds a number of intriguing correlations between the Junius illustrations and *Paradise Lost*, but fails to deal satisfactorily with the problem of Milton's failing sight.

Christophe Tournu, 'John Milton, the English Revolution (1640–60), and the Dynamics of the French Revolution (1789)' (*PSt* 24:iii[2001] 18–38), explores Mirabeau's publication of adaptations of *Areopagitica* as *Sur la liberté de la presse, imité de l'anglois de Milton* [1788] and Milton's *First Defence* as *Théorie de la royauté, d'àprès de Milton* [1789]. He argues that Mirabeau is importing the concepts of freedom of the press, civil liberty, and regicide into the French political debates from his reading and selective translation of Milton's texts.

Bryan N.S. Gooch, 'Handel, Milton, and Spenser: *The Occasional Oratorio* Revisited' (*SCN* 58:i[2000] 1–15), tells us about Handel's Occasional Oratorio, which was first performed on 14 February 1746. Gooch considers it a more complete and functional piece than has previously been realized, and discusses the remarkable fusion of Milton's psalm translations with Spenserian phrasing in Parts I and II. It is clear to Gooch that the librettist knew Milton's psalms well, but this is a distinctly monarchical appropriation of the texts.

Two textual cruces in Milton's Latin are explored in this year's *Notes and Queries*. Frederick Williams, 'A Textual Problem in One of Milton's Latin Poems' (*N&Q* 49[2002] 334–6), returns to *In obitum Procancellarii medici* and the problem in line 29, 'Tuque o alumno maior Apolline' (Thou who art greater than thy pupil Apollo). Williams thinks there is a printing error here, and suggests that 'Apollineo' would allow both internal rhyme and an elegant means of referencing Aesculapius as Apollo's ward. John K. Hale, in 'Milton's Reading of Virgil's *Aeneid* VI.680 in his Letter to the Vatican Librarian' (*N&Q* 49[2002] 336), is intrigued by Milton's use of *limen* (threshold) as opposed to *lumen* (light) in his letter of 1639 to Lucas Holste. Milton is complimenting Holste on his unpublished commentaries on Greek authors, using *Aeneid* VI. 680 to compare these manuscripts to souls awaiting birth. Hale finds it appropriate, and extremely Miltonic, that the shift from manuscript to print should be described as a form of birth and as the crossing of a threshold. One last note for inclusion comes from the *American Notes and Queries*, where Rodney Stenning Edgecombe, 'Lucretius, Milton, and "L'Allegro"' (*ANQ* 15:iv[2002] 19–20), says that the lines complimenting Shakespeare in *L'Allegro* ('fancy's child | Warble his native Wood-notes wild') are influenced by Lucretius *De rerum natura*, V. 166–8, where Lucretius suggests that people learned the arts of music and poetry from imitating birdsong.

Finally, Peter Harrison, 'Original Sin and Knowledge in Early Modern Europe' (*JHI* 63:ii[2002] 239–59), may be of interest to Miltonists as it offers a helpful overview on the seventeenth-century European debate, including the views of Descartes, concerning Adam's capacity for philosophical thought and the extent to which those faculties were damaged by the Fall.

3. Donne

Several new books devoted principally to Donne have recently appeared. Robert Whalen approaches Donne and also his younger contemporary George Herbert through the lens of 'sacramental poetics' in his important book, *The Poetry of Immanence: Sacrament in Donne and Herbert*, greatly expanding his earlier articles, especially '"How shall I measure out thy bloud?"' (*EMLS* 5:iii[2000]; reviewed in *YWES* 81[2002]). Whalen's book reinforces and extends the approach of Theresa M. DiPasquale, *Literature and Sacrament: The Sacred and the Secular in John Donne* (reviewed in *YWES* 80[2001]). Whalen also treats both the devotional and secular verse of Donne, with an important illustrative chapter on Donne's Christmas sermon of 1626, and adds as well chapters on George Herbert. Whalen invokes a host of recent commentators on Donne (and Herbert), and draws out once more the theological controversies of the early modern period. Calvin's shadow is notably large; his understanding of the doctrine of the eucharist has been transmuted and adapted in the work and thought of Donne and Herbert. Whalen elides the elusive theological positions of these writers with their equally elusive political ideas, concluding that 'both recognized the importance of incorporating ceremonial forms within the framework of prayer, meditation, and homily. Their efforts to establish a *via media* between sacramental and word-based styles of divinity ... were not only spiritual but also political' (p. 168). Whalen writes with conviction and understanding, and his study provides one of the best and most recent contributions to an increasingly popular mode: the uncovering of religious and political contexts for the familiar figures of the earlier seventeenth century.

Peter DeSa Wiggins, in his *Donne, Castiglione, and the Poetry of Courtliness*, travels in a very different direction from Whalen, and one which is likely to prove far more useful. The idea of understanding Donne—however tentatively—through Castiglione's *Courtier* should seem obvious, yet no one before Wiggins has thought to pursue the connection. In this elegantly written and eminently sensible book,

Wiggins convincingly demonstrates that Donne understood very well the life and manners of the courtier, which were clearly set forth in this most popular courtesy book of the time. How surprising, indeed, 'that seekers after the language of social life spoken by Donne and his contemporaries should never have consulted Castiglione', whose book 'was endorsed and promoted by the power elite of Donne's time', and which Donne would obviously have respected (pp. 5–6). Wiggins's readings of a number of Donne's poems show just how the poet's social conventions reflect and implement Castiglione's 'cultural codes'. Donne encountered Castiglione in ways that authorize his satirical art, his aesthetic play, his *sprezzatura*, his 'discerning insincerity'; for Donne 'sincerely respected the cultural codes which he discovered in Castiglione's text' (p. 143), and tried his best to articulate them into his own social reality. One of many striking features of Wiggins's book is his own lively sense of humour, his kindness in rejecting a great deal of current critical comment, and his often unexpected elucidations of 'difficult' poems: 'The Flea', 'A Valediction of the Booke', and 'A Nocturnall upon S. Lucies Day' (with Robert Lowell's fascinating interpretative mirror in 'The Ghost'—the latter poem, in the same stanza form as Donne's poem, also about literary endeavour). Wiggins's work is a splendid addition to Donne criticism, and a very useful corrective to some of its ingenious practitioners.

Another book which seeks to display Donne in terms of the physical world that surrounded him is Clayton MacKenzie's welcome study, *Emblem and Icon in John Donne's Poetry and Prose*. MacKenzie shows how important to Donne were these physical details of his world: the murals, the icons in glass and stone, the emblems and pictures in books. MacKenzie offers a sustained discussion of the iconographic and emblematic influences on Donne's work (both poetry and prose), offering detailed chapters on 'Death', 'Heaven and Hell', 'Love', and 'Fortune', with thirty-eight full-page illustrations. The detailed exposition of these themes is enhanced by reference to the illustrations, which also help to elucidate passages from Donne's own work.

'Dies ist ein weites Feld'—this is a broad field. Indeed, so. And so begins Ulrike Schneider in her careful survey of cosmographical reference, influence, and imagery in early modern poetry. *Kosmographie in der englischen Dichtung, 1600–1660* is an ambitious, systematic (and thoughtfully illustrated) study, with little that is new; but much of the familiar landscape is conveniently organized. The book is divided into three large chapters, on heavenly bodies, world concepts, and geography. Donne appears in them all, generally in the company of his contemporaries or close followers. Schneider's comparison of Donne with Cowley, and with other poets of the seventeenth century, displays the various ways in which new world views were received and transmitted. But Donne was best able to see and appreciate the 'Copernican revolution', and he is the principal figure against whom Schneider portrays other writers and thinkers of his time.

Summers and Pebworth, eds., *Fault Lines*, brings together in revised and expanded form the best of the papers presented at the Dearborn Renaissance Conference of 2000, which marked the last of these biennial gatherings, begun in 1974, and the final volume produced in this excellent series. Four of the thirteen essays in the current volume consider Donne, and are in keeping with the conference theme of 'new' possibilities for literary study. Dennis Flynn writes with his customary lucidity on 'Conjecture in the Writing of Donne's Biography, with a

Modest Proposal' (pp. 50–61). He surveys the several attempts that have been made
in composing Donne's biography, and he concludes that biographers who have left
doubtful gaps and made (sometimes outrageous) guesses (e.g. John Carey) are more
useful than those who leave little room for conjecture (e.g. R.C. Bald). Flynn's
sardonic and slightly perverse 'modest proposal' is 'that we cease privileging the
merely probable conjecture when the more informative, improbable conjecture is
available for refutation' (p. 61). Jeffrey Johnson contributes an essay on 'John
Donne and the Socinian Heresy' (pp. 130–9)—broadly speaking, the doctrine that
denies the Trinity, but also in Donne's time a general term of abuse or of theological
waywardness. Donne rejects Socinianism, but he is most concerned to define the
nature of biblical interpretation and the authority of Scripture, a problem which the
Socinian heresy raised. A clever and very different piece is Joan Faust's 'Donne on
Love' or 'Sometimes the End Just Doesn't Justify the Means' (pp. 170–86). Faust
reviews some of the commentary on Donne's attitude towards physical love, the
most discussed of all issues in his work. What is one to make of Donne's cynicism
about love and also his declarations of true love? Disagreements and controversies
abound amongst Donne scholars; but, according to Faust, these troublesome
problems can only 'be refined and redefined in the context of the history of
sexuality' (p. 186). Finally, P.G. Stanwood, in his 'Critical Directions in the Study
of Early Modern Sermons' (pp. 140–55), urges the expanded study of rhetorical
tradition not only in the sermons of Donne, but also in the sermons of his great
contemporary, Lancelot Andrewes—and as well in many notable but neglected
preachers of the day, such as Richard Hooker, Henry King, William Laud, John
Cosin, Henry Hammond, Jeremy Taylor, Mark Frank, and more. Stanwood
demonstrates one method of rhetorical analysis by a close reading of selections from
Donne's Second Prebend sermon (preached on 29 January 1626). One must give
careful attention not only to the details of language but also to the management of
the entire text, and in a way that recognizes the use of concordances and image
variation.

Another important collection of essays appeared this year, on a theme that has
received increasing attention. Margo Swiss and David A. Kent have edited a lively
and varied work on mourning and consolation, one of the great and most universal
topics of the seventeenth-century experience. *Speaking Grief in English Literary
Culture: Shakespeare to Milton* includes three essays amongst its thirteen
contributions on Donne, although the whole book has a coherence and integrity
whereby each essay speaks to its companions. Robert C. Evans writes powerfully on
'Lyric Grief in Donne and Jonson' (pp. 42–68), pointing especially to Donne's
generally ignored *Epicedes and Obsequies,* representing this work with the 'Elegie'
to commemorate the death in 1609 of Lady Bridget Markham. Evans shows just
how subtle (and 'witty') this poem is, with 'assured craftsmanship' (p. 54) that seeks
'deliberately to master passion by controlling and redirecting thought' (p. 55).
Marjory E. Lange considers religious melancholy, first in Robert Burton, then in
Donne, especially in his sermon of 1627, in commemoration of the Lady Danvers
(George Herbert's mother). In her essay on 'Humorous Grief: Donne and Burton
Read Melancholy', Lange notes that Donne and Burton, though very different in
many respects, have a similar understanding of religious melancholy. We are
reminded that Lady Danvers suffered from melancholy, but, Donne insists, she
remained faithful in her devotion, undeluded, her soul unafflicted. Donne possessed

'compassionate severity'; 'he represents the culmination of the tradition of melancholy as it was expressed in the English Renaissance' (p. 97). P.G. Stanwood discusses the same sermon, as well as Donne's four other funeral sermons in 'Consolatory Grief in the Funeral Sermons of Donne and Taylor' (pp. 197–216). Donne—and Taylor, who followed him—write in measured terms, in artful discourse which may seem distant and cold to us. But both provide 'a channel for grief to discover its own consolation; for great feeling may be contained in the familiarity of common ideas, expressed in conventional forms that generalise universal feelings' (p. 211).

Many journal articles on Donne continue to appear. Of special interest is Mary E. Zimmer's '"In whom love wrought new Alchimie": The Inversion of Christian Spiritual Resurrection in John Donne's "A nocturnall upon S. Lucies day"' (C&L 51:iv[2002] 553–67). Zimmer subtly argues that this difficult poem may be interpreted in accordance with a world view that is common in both Christian and alchemical traditions. The speaker of the poem undergoes a regenerative process wherein alchemical terms are transformed by or subsumed within Christian spiritual resurrection. Thus Zimmer seeks to demonstrate that 'the speaker responds to his beloved's death by spiritually re-creating himself on the basis of this world of non-being and becomes its "Epitaph," in which role he commemorates life amidst death and love amidst loss' (p. 554). A somewhat parallel theme appears in James R. Keller, 'Paracelsian Medicine in Donne's "Hymn to God, my God, in my Sickness"' (SCN 59:i–ii[2001] 154–8). Medicine, alchemy, and cosmology are important allusions in this poem, central to its theme; and Paracelsus's medical theories help to explain Donne's images.

Donne's life, and especially his political and religious attitudes and their connection with his work—particularly his sermons—continues to trouble and fascinate critics. Arthur F. Marotti writes once more with his usual scholarly tact, most recently on 'John Donne's Conflicted Anti-Catholicism' (JEGP 101:iii[2002] 358–79). Mostly through the sermons, Marotti traces Donne's stated feelings towards Roman Catholicism and 'reformed' religion, with the noticeable changes wrought by the different demands of the regimes of James and Charles. Donne is anti-Catholic (or not), with various modulations, according to the demands of the time—yet he remains essentially a moderate conservative, devoted essentially 'to a pastoral, preaching ministry', for his concentration is ultimately 'on spiritual essentials as [in his last sermon] the preacher prepared to face his God' (pp. 378–9). Marotti's concluding remark is to 'Deaths Duell', the subject of an essay by Vanessa Rasmussen, 'Death's Duality: The Dialectics of Donne's Final Sermon' (Schuylkill 4:i[2001] 33–52). Rasmussen writes crudely of the paradoxes inherent in the Christian faith, then urges that Donne's success in his last sermon comes about through the 'dialectical' contradictions that 'a dedication to Christ demanded' (p. 52).

A similarly specialized view, one frequently expressed in contemporary criticism, is well elaborated by Lisa S. Starks in '"Batter my [flaming] heart": Male Masochism in the Religious Lyrics of Donne and Crashaw' (Enculturation 1:ii[1997]). Indebted in part to Richard Rambuss's 'Pleasure and Devotion: The Body of Jesus and Seventeenth-Century Religious Lyric' (in Jonathan Goldberg, ed., Queering the Renaissance [1994]), Starks studies Donne's sonnet, 'Batter my heart', in which she sees a homoerotic poem in which 'strands of identification, erotic desire, masochism, and sadism interact and intertwine'. Starks asserts that the poet 'will be beaten down until he submits to the Holy family, the patriarchy extraordinaire, the Oedipal fantasy on high'. A very general and highly appreciative survey of Donne's poetry and his elusive wittiness is Heather McHugh's 'Naked Numbers: A Curve from Wyatt to Rochester' (*APR* 31:i[2002] 39–48). Her uncritical enthusiasm for Renaissance poetry is a kind of corrective to Starks's deep analysis.

Other articles on particular poems include a major essay by Raymond-Jean Frontain, 'Law, Song and Memory: The Mosaic Voice of Donne's *First Anniversarie*' (*L&B* 19:i–ii[1999] 155–74). Frontain argues that the two *Anniversarie*s are one in the sense that the Christian bible is one, but with two testaments. In his single poetic text, Donne combines 'the dual prophetic operation of "criticizing" and "energizing" … of shattering people's numbness to sin and instilling in them an alternative consciousness' (p. 156): Frontain is paraphrasing Walter Brueggemann, *The Prophetic Imagination* [1978], a powerful work that inspires Frontain's analysis of 'the biblical situation of the *First Anniversarie*' (p. 157); for Donne's purpose in this poem is above all to be prophetic, to act as Moses who warns the people of disasters to come (Deut. 31–2). A very useful note on this poem is Andrew Fleck's 'The Ring of the World: Donne's Appropriation of Petrarch's "Sonnet 338" in *The First Anniversary*' (*N&Q* 49[2002] 327–9). Petrarch's image of the ring of the world to express loss becomes in Donne's adaptation an intensely dark and pessimistic figure. Immediately following this note in the same number of *N&Q*, Andrew Breeze records a further source of Donne, in his Christmas sermon of 1621. Here Donne's reference to 'artillery', by which war may be shortened, is indebted to Camden's *Remains*, where there is a colourful description of contemporary 'life-saving' ordnance. One more note is Bryan Thomas Herek's account of lines 103–10 of Donne's Satyre III (*Expl* 60:iv [2002] 193–6), beginning 'As streames are, Power is', continuing with 'the streames tyrannous rage … Through mills, and rockes, and woods'. Herek ingeniously suggests that the 'tyrannous rage' refers to the torrent of water flowing beneath London Bridge; 'mills' is a reference to a mill on the same bridge, 'rockes' calls attention to various organized religions (all of which may be legitimate), and 'woods' refers to the political sphere, for tree imagery is commonly associated with the ruling class.

Three especially significant bibliographical studies have recently appeared. Dennis Flynn describes 'Donne Manuscripts in Cheshire' (*EMS* 8[2000] 280–92). Flynn reports his finding of three previously unrecorded manuscripts of writings by John Donne in the Cheshire Record Office. One is a copy of Donne's letter to Susan Vere, countess of Montgomery; the second is a copy of 'A Hymne to God the Father'; and the third item is a copy of Donne's elegy 'The Bracelet'. Each of these manuscripts provides certain unique features not occurring in other copies, and they show that these three copies—all of them early—demonstrate Donne's popularity in the seventeenth century, and that important manuscripts may still turn up in well-known record offices. Also in *EMS*, Richard Todd writes of his fascinating work in the holdings of the Koninklije Bibliotheek in The Hague: his study of 'The Manuscript Sources for Constantijn Huygens's Translation of Four Poems by John Donne, 1630' (*EMS* 11[2002] 154–80) describes Huygens's collection of Donne manuscript copies. Since Huygens was the first translator of Donne, his sources are of very special interest. Discussed here are 'The Sunne Rising', 'The Anagram', the 'Recusancy' elegy, and 'A Valediction, Forbidding Mourning'. Huygens made his translations in August 1630 from a variety of scribal manuscript copies, all of them dating probably from the 1620s, or even earlier. Finally, Dayton Haskin continues his study of Donne's reception (and appropriation) in 'No Edition Is an Island: The Place of the Nineteenth-Century American Editions within the History of Editing Donne's Poems' (*Text* 14[2002] 169–207). Haskin examines in particular the 'Boston Edition' [1855] of Donne's poetry, edited by James Russell Lowell, and the 'Grolier Club Edition' [1895]—Lowell's work (with Mabel Lowell Burnett), continued and revised by Charles Eliot Norton. These editors, and others, led the way to Grierson's great edition of 1912, and together they provide insight into editorial procedures, and also into the persistent question that Haskin asks at the conclusion of his study: '[I]n what ways have the Victorians' interests in Donne continued to circumscribe our thinking about him and to infiltrate the questions that occur to us to ask when we come to read his works?' (p. 207). The 'cultural investment' in Donne continues as the great *Variorum Edition of the Poetry of John Donne* proceeds towards its fulfilment.

4. Herbert

In his article 'Show and Tell: George Herbert, Richard Sibbes, and Communings with God' (*C&L* 51:ii[2002] 175–90) Daniel W. Doerksen continues his work on the moderate Calvinist centre of Jacobean doctrine, and particularly on the shared theological thinking of the conforming George Herbert and the Puritan Richard Sibbes. Upon close reading, Doerksen finds striking resemblances of thought and word between the devotional poet and the preacher, noting that the chief difference between the two is literary. While both advocate a personal relationship between the believer and God, Sibbes describes this relationship using the third person, while Herbert exemplifies it in the first person.

The late Louis Martz, in one of his last articles, examines the griefs of Herbert's poetry. 'The Action of Grief in Herbert's "The Church"' (in Swiss and David, eds., pp. 119–35) identifies the many kinds of grief voiced by Herbert's speakers, a range best demonstrated by the fear of damnation, perhaps the worst of human griefs, and the passion of Christ, the most accessible of divine griefs. Martz argues that the power of 'The Church' lies in its continuous striving to comprehend opposite states of mind. Hence, particular doctrinal positions expressed in some of the poetry are contradicted elsewhere. The contest of griefs in 'The Church' comes to its equilibrium in 'Bitter-sweet', the articulation of a faith that does not deny its own trials, but that also comprehends the trials of Christ's passion.

Notes and short articles on Herbert this year include Beatrice Groves's '"Temper'd with a Sinners Tears": Herbert and the Eucharistic Significance of the Word "Temper"' (*N&Q* 49[2002] 329–30). Groves finds a eucharistic pun in the title of the poem 'The Temper' not previously noticed. In addition to its better-established meanings, 'temper' can refer to the mixing of water and wine in the eucharist, suggestive of the word's use also in 'The Sacrifice'. As well, Ceri Sullivan, in 'Herbert's "Artillerie" and Affliction' (*N&Q* 49[2002] 330–1) notes that Herbert's artillery image may not solely refer to militant Christianity, but also to passages in Job 16 and 38 (and in Calvin's gloss on the latter passage) which figure God's archers hemming in the speaker. Rodney Stenning Edgecombe, in 'Some Faint Echoes of *Cymbeline* in Herbert's *Temple*' (*ShN* 52:iv[2002/03] 119, 127), discovers verbal and structural points of comparison between the play and the poetry, speculating on textual evidence alone about Belarius' speeches about court and pastoral retirement as a possible source for Herbert's work. Finally, Roberta Albrecht, in 'Herbert's "Deniall," "Jordan I & II," and "A Wreath"' (*Expl* 60:iii[2002] 127–31), discusses poems about the difficulty of writing poems. Albrecht argues that the first three poems raise the 'sins' of poetry—pride, waywardness, deceit—and that these sins are woven into 'A Wreath', in which the sins become praise via confession.

5. Marvell

In *Nobody's Perfect: A New Whig Interpretation of History*, Annabel Patterson seeks to recover and restore to intellectual respectability a Whig History in the face of conservative attacks, from eighteenth-century Tories to recent revisionists. Chapter 4 (pp. 139–62) places in this context Edward's Thompson's edition of Marvell's works [1776], and by looking at its form, content, and reception, she establishes the ideological charge of the edition. Marvell's reputation as an incorruptible patriot was consolidated in the 1720s by Thomas Cooke's narrative of the poet's refusal of a place at court, despite the king's promise of a rich reward and the poet's poverty. The reality of the latter is confirmed by Art Kavanagh, in 'Andrew Marvell "in want of money": The Evidence in *John Farrington v. Mary Marvell*' (*SCen* 17[2002] 206–12). Kavanagh discusses briefly and concisely the circumstances of this Chancery suit over Marvell's estate, revealing the new evidence of a deposition by the bookseller Nathaniel Ponder that suggests that Marvell was genuinely poor at his death.

Perhaps this year's most interesting interpretative essay on Marvell, Anne Cotterill's 'Marvell's Watery Maze: Digression and Discovery at Nun Appleton' (*ELH* 69[2002] 103–32), suggests that the coherence of the poem lies below its overt, peripatetic narrative in a journey, refracted through the poet's own self-examination and sense of loss, through a psychological landscape in which sexualized and feminized childhood is betrayed by the failures of male guardians. The argument meanders at some length in abundant prose, taking in a number of loose associations, including imagery of the flood and drowning in *The First Anniversary*. Another powerful essay, which unfashionably and informatively addresses formal issues in detail, is John Creaser's 'Prosody and Liberty in Milton and Marvell' (in Parry and Raymond, eds., *Milton and the Terms of Liberty*, pp. 37–55). Creaser contrasts the prosody of the two great 'Puritan' poets: while Milton's liberty commits him to irregularity and experimentalism, Marvell's is a poetry of containment that seeks balance, regularity, symmetry, and closure, and his poetic discipline means that his lyricism and slightest deviations become all the more expressive. This contrast reflects a difference between the two poets' attitudes to liberty: in Marvell's conception it flourishes best against a manifest, stable framework.

Early seventeenth-century Dutch women had an unusually privileged legal status and legal rights, and contemporary Englishmen perceived them as being unattractive in appearance and masculine in conduct, according to D. Christopher Gabbard in 'Sirens without a Song: Gender Stereotyping in Marvell's "The Character of Holland"' (*ELN* 40 [2002] 61–76). Marvell's lampooning of Dutch women conforms to these stereotypes, and reveals a commitment to patriarchal politics that, Gabbard simplistically and erroneously suggests, belies his republican principles. Marvell's critics have gone rather further with his gender politics, as historians of republicanism have developed more complex accounts of its sexual ideologies. Raychel Haugrud Reiff, "Marvell's 'To His Coy Mistress'," (*Expl* 60[2002] 196–8) briefly discusses Marvell's use of the familiar and formal second-person pronouns in order to manipulate his intimate tone.

Finally, there are a handful of notes. David Roberts, in 'Two Shakespearian Allusions and the Date of Marvell's "The Nymph Complaining for the Death of her Faun"' (*N&Q* 49[2002] 338–430), uses the two alleged allusions, to Caesar and Macbeth, to argue, interestingly if at times tenuously, that Marvell's poem refers with non-republican sentiment to the regicide, and was written between early 1649 and early 1651. Emily Wilson's '"Bermudas"' (*N&Q* 49[2002] 343), notes an allusion to Virgil, by which the singers in Marvell's lyric anticipate a destination that will surpass even Rome. Takashi Yoshinaka, 'Another Religio-Political Note on Marvell's "Bermudas"' (*N&Q* 49[2002] 343–4) finds an allusion to Cromwell's projected 'Western Design' in the closing couplet of the same poem. And E.E. Duncan-Jones, in 'Two Notes on Marvell' (*RES* 52[2001] 192–4), glosses the garden fort of 'Upon Appleton House', planted at Nunappleton by the sixteenth-century Sir Thomas Fairfax, with particular reference to Sir Henry Fanshawe's garden at Ware Park in Hertfordshire; and notes a reference by Samuel Johnson to streaky tulips that echoes Marvell but more probably alludes to Matthew Prior.

Books Reviewed

Appelbaum, Robert. *Literature and Utopian Politics in Seventeenth-Century England*. CUP. [2002] pp. xi + 256. $55 ISBN 0 5218 1082 5.

Bradford, Richard. *The Complete Critical Guide to John Milton*. Routledge. [2001] pp. 232. £12.99 ISBN 0 4152 0244 2.

Bradstock, Andrew, ed. *Winstanley and the Diggers, 1649–1999*. Frank Cass. [2000] pp. x + 173. £42.50 ISBN 0 7146 5105 2.

Cunnar, Eugene R., and Jeffrey Johnson, eds. *Discovering and (Re)Covering the Seventeenth Century Religious Lyric*. Duquesne. [2001] pp. viii + 408. $59 ISBN 0 8207 0317 6.

Curr, Matthew. *The Consolation of Otherness: The Male Love Elegy in Milton, Gray and Tennyson*. McFarland. [2002] pp. 184. $32 ISBN 0 7864 1239 9.

Davies, H. Neville, ed. *At Vacant Hours: Poems by Thomas St Nicholas and his Family*. UBirmP. [2002] pp. xlviii + 492. £40 ($60) ISBN 1 9024 5932 6.

Eriksen, Roy. *The Building in the Text: Alberti to Shakespeare and Milton*. PennState [2001] pp. xxi + 194. £26.95 ISBN 0 2710 2022 9.

Flannagan, Roy. *John Milton: A Short Introduction*. Blackwell. [2002] pp. viii + 132. hb £40 ISBN 0 6312 2619 2, pb £9.99 ISBN 0 6312 2620 6.

Hadfield, Andrew. *The English Renaissance, 1500–1620*. Blackwell. [2001] pp. xxiv + 310. £16.99 ($33.95) ISBN 0 6312 2024 0.

Hattaway, Michael, ed. *English Renaissance Literature and Culture*. Blackwell. [2000; repr. 2003] pp. xx + 747. pb $34.95 ISBN 1 4051 0626 3.

Hawkes, David. *Idols of the Marketplace: Idolatry and Commodity Fetishism in English Literature, 1580–1680*. Palgrave. [2002] pp. x + 294. $59.95 ISBN 0 3122 4007 4.

Herman, Peter C., ed. *Reading Monarchs Writing: The Poetry of Henry VIII, Mary Stuart, Elizabeth I, and James VI/I*. ACMRS. [2002] pp. xi + 330. $40 ISBN 0 8669 8276 0.

Hodgkins, Christopher. *Reforming Empire: Protestant Colonialism and Conscience in British Literature*. UMissP. [2002] pp. xii + 290. $37.50 ISBN 0 8262 1431 2.

Keeble, Neil H., ed. *The Cambridge Companion to Writing of the English Revolution*. CUP. [2001] pp. xxii + 296. hb £45 ISBN 0 5216 4252 3, pb £16.95 ISBN 0 5216 4522 0.

Kezar, Dennis. *Guilty Creatures: Renaissance Poetry and the Ethics of Authorship*. OUP. [2001] pp. viii + 268. £32.50 ISBN 0 1951 4295 0.

MacKenzie, Clayton G. *Emblem and Icon in John Donne's Poetry and Prose*. Renaissance and Baroque Studies and Texts 30. Lang. [2001]. pp. x + 209. £38 ISBN 0 8204 5292 0.

Maxwell, Catherine. *The Female Sublime from Milton to Swinburne: Bearing Blindness*. ManUP. [2001] pp. viii + 279. £47.50 ISBN 0 7190 5752 3.

McDonald, Peter D., and Michael F. Suarez, SJ, eds. *Making Meaning: 'Printers of the Mind' and Other Essays*. UMassP. [2002] pp. x + 286. hb $70 ISBN 1 5584 9335 2, pb £17.50 ISBN 1 5584 9336 0.

Miller, Anthony. *Roman Triumphs and Early Modern English Culture*. Palgrave. [2001] pp. vii + 223. £55 ISBN 0 3339 4822 X.

Mitchell, Linda C. *Grammar Wars: Language as Cultural Battlefield in 17th and 18th Century England*. Ashgate. [2001] pp. viii + 218. £45 ISBN 0 7546 0272 9.

Morton, Timothy, and Nigel Smith, eds. *Radicalism in British Literary Culture, 1650–1830: From Revolution to Revolution*. CUP. [2002] pp. x + 284. £40 ISBN 0 5216 4215 9.

Nakayama, Osamu. *Images of their Glorious Maker: Iconology in Milton's Poetry*. Macmillan Languagehouse, Tokyo. [2002] pp. vi + 207. n.p., no ISBN available.

Parry, Graham, and Joad Raymond, eds. *Milton and the Terms of Liberty*. D.S. Brewer. [2002] pp. 240. £35 ($60) ISBN 0 8599 1639 1.

Patterson, Annabel. *Nobody's Perfect: A New Whig Interpretation of History*. YaleUP. [2002] pp. 300. £19.50 ($27.50) ISBN 0 3000 9288 1.

Pfister, Manfred, ed. *A History of English Laughter: Laughter from Beowulf to Beckett and Beyond*. Rodopi. [2002] pp. x + 201. $46 ISBN 9 0420 1288 9.

Post, Jonathan F.S. *English Lyric Poetry: The Early Seventeenth Century*. Routledge. [2002] pp. xviii + 323. pb $25.95 ISBN 0 4152 0858 0.

Post, Jonathan F.S., ed. *Green Thoughts, Green Shades: Essays by Contemporary Poets on the Early Modern Lyric*. UCalP. [2002] pp. xiv + 300. £13.95 ($18.95) ISBN 0 5202 2752 2.

Revard, Stella. *Pindar and the Renaissance Hymn-Ode: 1450–1700*. ACMRS. [2001] pp. xii + 383. £36 ($40) ISBN 0 8669 8263 9.

Schneider, Ulrike. *Kosmographie in der englischen Dichtung, 1600–1660.* Angelsächsische Sprache und Literatur, XIV, 388. Lang. [2002] pp. 360. £34 ISBN 3 6313 8150 6.

Scodel, Joshua. *Excess and the Mean in Early Modern English Literature.* PrincetonUP. [2002] pp. viii + 367. £37.95 ISBN 0 6910 9028 9.

Shawcross, John T., *John Milton: The Self and the World.* UPKentucky. [2001] pp. viii + 358. pb £16.50 ISBN 0 8131 9021 5.

Silver, Victoria. *Imperfect Sense: The Predicament of Milton's Irony.* PrincetonUP. [2001] pp. xiv + 409. £ 39.95 ISBN 0 6910 4487 2.

Skulsky, Harold. *Milton and the Death of Man: Humanism on Trial in Paradise Lost.* AUP. [2001] pp. 262. £35 ISBN 0 8741 3719 5.

Summers, Claude J., and Ted-Larry Pebworth, eds. *Fault Lines and Controversies in the Study of Seventeenth-Century English Literature.* UMissP. [2002] pp. xii + 236. $37.50 ISBN 0 8262 1423 1.

Swiss, Margo, and David A. Kent, eds. *Speaking Grief in English Literary Culture: Shakespeare to Milton.* Duquesne. [2002] pp. xi + 365. $60 ISBN 0 8207 0330 3.

Turner, James G. *Libertines and Radicals in Early Modern London: Sexuality, Politics and Literary Culture, 1630–1685.* CUP. [2002] pp. xxii + 343. $65 ISBN 0 5217 8279 1.

Whalen, Robert. *The Poetry of Immanence: Sacrament in Donne and Herbert.* UTorP. [2002] pp. xxii + 216. $45 ISBN 0 8020 3659 7.

Wiggins, Peter DeSa. *Donne, Castiglione, and the Poetry of Courtliness.* IndUP. [2000] pp. viii + 174. $34.95 ISBN 0 2533 3814 X.

Wittreich, Joseph. *Shifting Contexts: Reinterpreting Samson Agonistes.* DuquesneUP. [2002] pp. 360. $60 ISBN 0 8207 0331 1.

Zwierlein, Anna-Julia. *Majestick Milton: British Imperial Expansion and Transformations of Paradise Lost, 1667–1837.* Lit Verlag/Transaction. [2001] pp. xi + 492. £45 ISBN 3 8258 5432 9.

X

The Later Seventeenth Century

CLAIRE PICKARD, LESLEY COOTE, JANE MILLING AND JAMES OGDEN

This chapter has three sections: 1. Poetry; 2. Prose; 3. Drama. Section 1 is by Claire Pickard; section 2 is by Lesley Coote; section 3(a) is by Jane Milling (with contributions by James Ogden); section 3(b) is by James Ogden.

1. Poetry

James Grantham Turner's 'From Revolution to Restoration in English Literary Culture' (in Loewenstein and Mueller, eds., *The Cambridge History of Early Modern English Literature*, pp. 790–833) arguably provides this year's most concise survey of the writing of the late seventeenth century. While discussing all the main genres, Turner's essay provides broad coverage of the poetry of the period. By placing the major poets of the era in their political, religious, and ideological contexts, Turner produces what will surely be an extremely useful teaching and reference aid.

This year, as last, is dominated by work on Dryden. One of the most wide-ranging considerations of this author is Green and Zwicker, eds., *John Dryden: A Tercentenary Miscellany* (also published as *HLQ* 63:i–ii[2000]). Introduced by Zwicker as a volume intended to demonstrate and celebrate 'the breadth and authority' of Dryden's career, this work presents a comprehensive range of essays on all aspects of his writing, including several which focus specifically on his poetic works.

Alan Roper's 'Who's Who in *Absalom and Achitophel*?' (pp. 99–138) looks at keys to and annotations of this poem. Roper suggests that, 'Just like Dryden's contemporaries, we need to change the names as we read, in order to prevent the characters from slipping into mere types without particular relevance or satiric point.' James A. Winn's wide-ranging 'Past and Present in Dryden's *Fables*' (pp. 157–74) suggests that 'Dryden in his final years took comfort in imagining history moving in grand cycles.' Examining the use of such historical patterns, Winn argues that 'In *Fables*, these patterns include the poet's own life and poetic career, the politically tumultuous century just coming to its end, and the whole of Western literary history.' In '"Our lineal descents and clans": Dryden's *Fables Ancient and*

Modern and Cultural Politics in the 1690s' (pp. 175–200), Sean Walsh also places this text in the context of both Dryden's career and its historical moment. Walsh suggests that '*Fables* is a nuanced examination of the culture that surrounds it and, more broadly, an embodiment of the complexity of cultural contest in a vexed decade.' Anne Cotterill's '"Rebekah's Heir": Dryden's Late Mystery of Genealogy' (pp. 201–26) links an examination of the recusant relations of Dryden's wife with the writer's 'manipulation of gender in fable and miscellany'. Cotterill argues that such links are central to Dryden's 'curious occupying (and then burial) of feminine figures, especially after the loss of public office'. The volume also includes the review essay 'The Text of Dryden's Poetry' (pp. 227–44) by Phillip Harth, which evaluates Paul Hammond's *The Poems of John Dryden* [1995], and David Bywaters' 'Historicism Gone Awry: Recent Work on John Dryden' (pp. 245–55), which considers the quality of much recent historicist criticism of this author.

Despite its focus on a single aspect of Dryden's work, Görtschacher and Klein, eds., *Dryden and the World of Neoclassicism*, has an extremely broad remit. Alongside articles on Dryden's drama and criticism there is a strong focus on the poetic works. Sonja Fielitz's 'John Dryden as Critic and Translator of Ovid: *The Metamorphoses*, or, Neo-classical Standards Put to the Test' (pp. 155–67) argues that Dryden defined Ovid 'as a dramatist who chose the "wrong" genre' and that such an opinion influenced his approach as a translator of Ovid's text. In 'Virgilian Bees in Dryden' (pp. 169–79) Yvonne Noble focuses less on translation than on influence by exploring Dryden's adaptation of bee imagery from the *Aeneid* and the *Georgics* in *Annus Mirabilis*. Tom Mason's 'A Noble Poem of the Epique Kind? *Palamon and Arcite*: Neoclassic Theory and Poetical Experience' (pp. 181–91) considers the reasons behind Dryden's high estimation of Chaucer's *Knight's Tale* and the possibility that the poem provided a solution to the problem of how to construct an epic poem that was neoclassical while also 'embodying Christian morality'. In 'Playfullness and verbal creation in Dryden's *The Medall*' (pp. 193–205) Albert Poyet examines the grammatical, syntactical, and prosodic structures of this text. Poyet outlines the ways in which such features do not always conform to what is seen as 'neoclassicism', and the likely reasons for this.

In the same volume, Simon Edwards's 'Dryden's Baroque: Nature, Power and Utopia' (pp. 207–18) attempts to place Dryden within a context that extends beyond that of English literature. Edwards seeks 'to prise Dryden away from the English Augustan tradition, with its Johnsonian teleology, and to read him as one of the heroic exponents of a pan-European cultural transformation we know as baroque'. Jerome Donnelly, in 'Dryden and the Exoteric Tradition: *Absalom and Achitophel* and the Ages of Man' (pp. 219–29) also argues for the importance of less conventional contexts for Dryden's work. Donnelly situates Dryden in the exoteric tradition and concludes that, although *Absalom and Achitophel* is of its moment, its location within this tradition means that it is 'never confined to that moment'. In 'Shaftesbury, Satan, Persuasion, and Whig Ideology' (pp. 231–41) William Walker focuses on the political context and implications of *Absalom and Achitophel*. Walker argues that the 'Miltonic allusions' in this text seek to undermine Whig ideology 'not just by identifying its main exponent with Satan, but by identifying this ideology itself with a Satanic strategy'. The political connotations of Dryden's poetry also provide the backdrop to Rolf Lessenich's 'Tory versus Whig: John Dryden's Mythical Concept of Kingship' (pp. 243–56). Lessenich presents

Dryden's view of kingship as remaining 'ultimately rooted in time-honoured medieval traditions' of a king who ruled 'by the grace of God' and was neither an absolute monarch 'nor a mere political administrator'. The concluding chapter in this volume, Mark K. Fulk's 'Reading Dryden's Body: Funerary and Neoclassical Poetic Elegy in *The Nine Muses* and *Luctus Britannici*' (pp. 289–99) contrasts the female- and male-authored volumes of elegies on Dryden's death. Fulk concludes that the women writers 'create a community where support and sisterhood instead of pride and exclusion reign', while the men 'all assume a basis for knowledge and exclusion, and a deep seated conservatism that believes they have the answers already'.

In her article 'Temporality, Subjectivity, and Neoclassical Translation Theory: Dryden's "Dedication of the Aeneis"' (*Restoration* 26:ii[2002] 97–118), Julie Candler Hayes also explores Dryden's poetic career within the context of neoclassicism. Hayes argues that the Dedication 'is an exceptionally rich text, in which Dryden works through the complexities of his own role as a translator, a role situated within a network of relations that are simultaneously intersubjective, textual, and temporal'. Robin Sowerby's review essay 'The Augustan *Aeneis*: Virgil Enlightened?' (*T&L* 11[2002] 237–69) also considers Dryden's role as translator of classical texts. This lengthy and detailed essay provides informative summaries and critiques of Richard F. Thomas's *Virgil and The Augustan Reception* and Richard Morton's *John Dryden's Aeneas: A Hero in Enlightenment Mode*.

Two articles by Alan Roper focus on imitations of *Absalom and Achitophel*. In 'Absalom's Issue: Parallel Poems in the Restoration' (*SP* 99[2002] 268–94) Roper seeks to compile a list of poems written in imitation of Dryden's text and discusses the absence of such a list and the 'rewards as well as risks' of trying to create one. Narrowing his focus in this area, Roper concentrates on a single such text in 'The Early Editions and Reception of John Tutchin's *The Tribe of Levi* (1691)' (*PBSA* 96:i[2002] 111–21). In this article, Roper explores the publishing, bibliographical, and reception history of this specific imitation of Dryden's poem.

In 'Endeavouring to Be the King: Dryden's *Astraea Redux* and the Issue of "Character"' (*JEGP* 101[2002] 201–21) Scott Paul Gordon focuses not on Dryden's influence on other writers but on literary influences upon Dryden himself. Drawing attention to the overlooked importance of *Henry V* to *Astraea Redux*, Gordon argues that this Shakespearian influence is significant, 'for to register its presence is to realize that *Astraea Redux* may less depict Charles as "arrived" or "settled" than sketch for him a trajectory he can or must pursue'.

Edward L. Saslow's 'The Rose Alley Ambuscade' (*Restoration* 26:i[2002] 27–49) explores an historical and biographical issue rather than a strictly critical one. Saslow weighs contemporary accounts of the attack upon Dryden in Rose Alley on 18 December 1679, and concludes that the earl of Dorset was the most likely instigator of the assault.

Two articles this year examine the significance, if any, of Roscommon's 'Academy'. Greg Clingham's 'Roscommon's "Academy," Chetwood's Manuscript "Life of Roscommon," and Dryden's Translation Project' (*Restoration* 26:i[2002] 15–26) considers whether 'Dryden's project in translation in the 1680s and '90s took over the cultural and ideological work of Roscommon's formal academy and, in effect, achieved some of its goals by a different route'. Andrew Barclay's 'Dating Roscommon's Academy' (*Restoration* 26:ii[2002] 119–26) concludes 'that the

"Academy," whatever it was, probably existed only during the final months of Roscommon's life'. Barclay therefore views Roscommon's *Essay on Translated Verse* as 'a manifesto of intent' and 'Chetwood's account … as a lament for the potential which Roscommon's death had prevented it from fulfilling'.

James Grantham Turner's 'John Oldham on Obscenity and Libertine Discourse: Unpublished Verses from Bodleian MS Rawlinson Poet. 123' (*N&Q* 49[2002] 346–51) examines some verse fragments omitted from the Brooks and Selden edition of *The Poems of John Oldham* [1987]. Turner argues that these fragments place Oldham 'more firmly in the line that runs from Dryden's *Mac Flecknoe* to Pope's *Dunciad*', and also suggests that Oldham was the author of *Sodom*.

Unsurprisingly, several of this year's considerations of Rochester focus on the poet's eroticism. Jonathan Brody Kramnick's 'Rochester and the History of Sexuality' (*ELH* 69[2002] 277–301) seeks to 'situate Rochester's erotic poetry within its philosophical and literary contexts' and to 'observe how that poetry was read in later decades'. Such discussion is positioned within a broader analysis of the language and 'semantics of desire' and a consideration of the problems of addressing 'the literary history of sexuality'. 'The Meaning of "Scotch Fiddle" in Rochester's "Tunbridge Wells"' by Ashley Chantler (*Restoration* 26:ii[2002] 81–4) considers various glosses on this phrase. Chantler interprets it as meaning the man in the poem 'touching the woman's genitals against her will' and as such sees it as a further aspect of Rochester's 'critique of Restoration manners' and his implication 'that they are constructions adopted to hide the brutal truth of men's nature'. Harold Love's 'Nell Gwyn and Rochester's "By All Love's Soft, Yet Mighty Pow'rs"' (*N&Q* 49[2002] 355–7) seeks 'to propose a court context that would make the lyric a personal address to Nell Gwyn'. Love bases his analysis primarily on a passage in *A Satyr Upon the Mistresses* [1678] by an unknown author.

Two articles consider Rochester manuscripts. Keith Walker's '"Not the Worst part of my wretched life": Three New Letters by Rochester, and How To Read Them' (*EMS* 8[2000] 292–9) discusses letters discovered in the Hamilton papers in the Scottish Record Office in Edinburgh. Walker speculates that the recipient of two of the letters was Anne Hamilton, later Lady Southesk. The third letter, dated six weeks before Rochester's death, is to James Douglas, earl of Arran. In 'A New Dating of Rochester's *Artemiza to Chloë*' (*EMS* 8[2000] 300–19) Nicholas Fisher details the discovery of a manuscript of that poem that suggests it was written five years earlier than previously thought.

Cedric C. Brown's 'The Black Poet of Ashover, Leonard Wheatcroft' (*EMS* 11[2002] 181–202), provides an introduction to the life and writings of the Derbyshire writer and an explanation of why he was known as 'the black poet'. Brown discusses Wheatcroft's manuscripts and also assesses his miscellany *Cum ye gallants looke & buy*. Arthur Sherbo's 'Five More Lines of Swift's Verse?' (*N&Q* 49[2002] 362–3) looks not at manuscripts but at annotations. Sherbo considers the possibility that alterations to Sir William Temple's poem 'Upon the Approach of the Shore at Harwich, in January 1688; Begun under the Mast, At the Desire of My Lady Giffard' in Lady Giffard's copy were by Swift.

This year sees a quantity of work on Marvell, most of which seeks to situate the poet within either an historical or an ideological context. In 'Speaking and Silent Women in "Upon Appleton House"' (*SEL* 42:i[2002] 155–71) Sarah Monette argues that Marvell's text is 'as much a conflict, on its own poetical terms, as the

Civil War itself'. Monette claims that one aspect of such conflict 'is poetic representation, an arena in which the poem's argument with itself plays out most clearly through its use of feminine voices'. Andrew Barnaby's 'Affecting the Metaphysics: Andrew Marvell's Discourse of Love and the Trials of Public Speech at Midcentury' (in Barnaby and Schnell, eds., *Literate Experience: The Work of Knowing in Seventeenth-Century English Writing*, pp. 123–57) is an exceptionally wide-ranging essay that discusses Marvell within the context of Velázquez's art and the writings of Donne, Hobbes, Locke, Bacon, and Johnson. Barnaby concludes that 'Marvell's poetry ... can be read as a particularly self-conscious instance of the English subject's struggle to speak in the wake of the shocking events of the 1640s.'

In 'Marvell's "Mower Against Gardens": Reconsidering Bakhtinian Dialogism' (in Summers and Pebworth, eds., *Fault Lines and Controversies in the Study of Seventeenth-Century English Literature*, pp. 62–72) Dan Jaeckle argues that 'readers are encouraged not to take sides, but to stand outside the struggle between the horticulturalists and the Mower in order to read the poem as a barometer of a conflicted and changing society'. Marvell is therefore seen not as positing a single position but as explaining opposing ones. Anne Cotterill's 'Marvell's Watery Maze: Digression and Discovery at Nun Appleton' (*ELH* 69[2002] 103–32) suggests that *Upon Appleton House* 'slips from the containment of an English country house into a dark landscape which seems at once portraiture of the estate, of the spirit, and of the deepest recesses of the self'. Cotterill argues for a recurrence of 'drowning as an image for chaotic dissolution, whether of the self or state' in other Marvell poems.

In 'Another Religio-Political Note on Marvell's "Bermudas"' (*N&Q* 49[2002] 343–4) Takashi Yoshinaka considers the context of the 1653 Anglo-Dutch war for lines 35–6 of the poem. Concentrating on the same poem, Emily Wilson's 'Bermudas' (*N&Q* 49[2002] 343) argues that 'Marvell implies that the New World of the Bermudas will echo the Golden Age of Rome, but will far surpass it'.

Raychel Haugrud Reiff's 'Marvell's "To His Coy Mistress"' (*Expl* 60:iv[2002] 196–8) contrasts with most of the year's work on Marvell by concentrating on the internal dynamics of the text under consideration rather than its external framework. Reiff explores the use of pronouns in the poem, especially 'thou' and 'you'.

David Roberts's 'Two Shakespearean Allusions and the Date of Marvell's "The Nymph Complaining for the Death of her Faun"' (*N&Q* 49[2002] 338–43) draws attention to references to *Julius Caesar* and *Macbeth* in the poem. Links to the execution of Charles I are also examined as part of a wider debate about the sources and dates of this text. In 'Precious Grief: Mourning and Melancholy in Andrew Marvell's "Nymph"' (in Swiss and Kent, eds., *Speaking Grief in English Literary Culture: Shakespeare to Milton*, pp. 242–60), Phillip McCaffrey identifies this poem as the only one by Marvell to be specifically concerned with grief and mourning. Placing various interpretations of the poem against the background of Freud's essay 'Mourning and Melancholy' [1917], McCaffrey concludes that the text demonstrates 'the way in which mourning can be stalled, can fail altogether and can settle into self-destructive grief'.

Richard Crashaw's approach to grief is the focus of Paul Parrish's 'Moderate Sorrow and Immoderate Tears: Mourning in Crashaw' (in Swiss and Kent, eds., pp. 217–41). Parrish argues that 'The poems written from the perspective of tearful women moved by the life and death of Christ are ... Crashaw's most important contribution to grief expression'. By contrast, Ryan Netzley's 'Oral Devotion:

Eucharistic Theology and Richard Crashaw's Religious Lyrics' (*TSLL* 44:iii[2002] 247–72) explores Crashaw's focus on orifices and the problem of 'how to explain the corporeal devotional consequences of an orally configured communion'. Netzley contends that 'Crashaw takes seriously the fact that, of all the possible orifices and senses, it is the mouth and taste that appear, *de jure*, to have a unique devotional privilege.' A rather different perspective on the relationship between literature and theology is presented in Paul Cefalu's 'Thomistic Metaphysics and Ethics in the Poetry and Prose of Thomas Traherne' (*L&T* 16:iii[2002] 248–69). Cefalu seeks to demonstrate that 'the influence of Scholastic metaphysics on Traherne's poetry and prose' has been overlooked. The article ultimately attempts to 'reconcile Traherne's neo-scholasticism with his non-teleological ethical doctrine'.

One of the most distinctive volumes of the year is Post, ed., *Green Thoughts, Green Shades: Essays by Contemporary Poets on the Early Modern Lyric*. Although much of the volume focuses on writers of the early seventeenth century, some contributions do concentrate on later poets. In 'Naked Numbers: A Curve from Wyatt to Rochester' (pp. 59–85) Heather McHugh plays with the idea that 'A poem's content no less than its form can be a cover: *what* it means may reveal less than *how* it is seen *through*' in relation to the poetry of Vaughan, Wyatt, Donne, Herrick, and Rochester. Stephen Yenser's '"How coy a Figure": Marvelry' (pp. 220–41) is a meditation on the qualities and fascination of Marvell's poetry that offers highly personal readings of 'The Garden', 'The Coronet', 'On a Drop of Dew', 'The Definition of Love', and 'The Gallery'. In his 'Saint John the Rake: Rochester's Poetry' (pp. 242–56) Thom Gunn emphasizes that 'The full Rochester, as we are finally allowed to read him, emerges as a more and more admirable poet.' Gunn stresses the ways in which Rochester manages 'to report on the consistencies and discrepancies between language and experience'. Robert Haas's 'Edward Taylor: What Was He Up To?' (pp. 257–88) concludes the volume with an examination of the Massachusetts poet's poetic practice that explores the style and structure of his poems.

2. Prose

This has been a good year for John Bunyan enthusiasts, with the publication of another issue of the excellent *Bunyan Studies*, and a new biographically based book, Richard Greaves's *Glimpses of Glory: John Bunyan and English Dissent*. This is a painstakingly researched account of Bunyan's life which, although chronologically arranged and presented as biography, is invaluable for students of Bunyan's writings. Throughout the book, Greaves stresses the links between the events and experiences of Bunyan's life and the subjects and method of his writings. Particularly interesting and useful is the examination of Bunyan's mental condition at different periods of his life, most notably his conversion from 'Mr Badman' to charismatic preacher and writer.

At the heart of Greaves's book is the relationship between Bunyan's mental states and the nature of his written work, including major works such as *Grace Abounding* and *Pilgrim's Progress*. Although Greaves admits that this is difficult to prove, his exhaustive investigations are both interesting and plausible. What also emerges from the book is the sheer volume and variety of Bunyan's writings, from his early tracts on infant baptism to his pleas for toleration and his exhortations for Dissenters not to conform to 'established' ideas. Alongside his major works, Bunyan also wrote for children and their parents (noting that 'children' came in a variety of ages), and was very fond of music and poetry, enthusiasms which he shared with colleagues such as Henry Jessey, Benjamin Keach, and Hanserd Knollys.

Greaves makes some very important points about Bunyan's style, noting that, although he pleaded lack of education, Bunyan was in fact very widely read, and one of the strengths of the book is the tracing of influences, personal and literary, on his works. Possible personal influences are fully listed and examined, and a detailed (and large) bibliography encourages further research. The book ends with a chapter on the fate of *Pilgrim's Progress*, its growing popularity, its 'embrace' by the Church of England, and how it was turned into plays, musicals (including an 1870 Welsh-language version), and poems, and was made accessible as a children's book. As well as being a biography of a great writer, *Glimpses of Glory* offers many insights into the world of later seventeenth-century England, its society, its cultural pursuits, and its relationship with the Word, both written and spoken. In short, this book is an extremely valuable addition to Bunyan studies, and to seventeenth-century studies as a whole.

Most of the chapters of Bernaby and Schnell, eds., *Literate Experience*, such as those on Shakespeare, women writers, and Marvell's poetry, concern other sections of this publication, but the central premise of the book, and its first chapter (on seventeenth-century scientific writing) are of such interest and potential usefulness for prose studies that I have decided to mention them here. *Literate Experience* is a book about early modern epistemology, and its place in contemporary natural and social philosophy. The authors begin with the basic premise that questions concerning 'the machinery of knowing' were considered social as well as philosophical, and that the language employed in the investigation and expression of this was vitally important. Bacon, they say, believed that the state of a society was inseparable from the state of its knowing, and natural philosophy formed a basis for social reform. A tool such as epistemology could be used to detach oneself from the faulty past and acquire true knowledge. What was important was the *act* of looking, the *act* of knowing (and how to describe and evaluate it). The subject of each chapter has been chosen as a paradigm, addressing the nature of the relationship between structures of knowledge and structures of power; it seems, however, that what is 'paradigmatic' in this case is a matter of negotiation—one could think of many other, alternative paradigms. One chapter addresses the epistemology of seventeenth-century science, indicating that it was seen to be a fusion of the natural and political worlds, using the example of Rembrandt's *The Anatomy Lesson of Dr Tulp*. The conclusion is that sensory experience and knowledge are complementary, but they exist only in the language by which they are articulated, then subjected to intellectual verification and publicly intelligible discourse. Purely private knowledge is the foundation of tyranny, and all knowledge must be subjected, in discourse, to the criticism of a 'community of knowers'. Most important is the part played by gentlemanly conversation (the 'circle of friends' or Rembrandt's 'guild'), as natural philosophy was seen as part of an exchange between friends. The examples given in the book are extremely interesting and inspiring, illustrating clearly and understandably a subject which can be profitably applied in many other contexts.

Jowitt and Watt, eds., *The Arts of 17th-Century Science: Representations of the Natural World in European and North American Culture*, is a book of essays on this subject, several of which concern prose writings. 'Things Which Are Not: Poetic and Scientific Attitudes to Non-entities in the Seventeenth Century', by Anthony Archdeacon, is an exploration of the use of language to encompass the idea of things which 'are' not, such as the 'nothing' contained in a vacuum, highlighted by the pump experiments of, among others, Robert Boyle. The things of the mind come to possess corporeal reality, and new categories, particularly in the realm of metaphor, are invented using the linguistic and metaphysical inheritance of medieval theology. The journey of mental exploration, Archdeacon explains, becomes a fetish. In another chapter, Jess Edwards highlights the significance of mathematical symbols. To the Neoplatonists this was metaphysical, as Plato believed that the spiritual world was more 'real' than the temporal, and mathematical symbols were both pure and spiritual. Seventeenth-century thinkers preferred this to the ideas of Ramus, which were both more practical and more democratic. In 'Bantering with Scripture' David E. Shuttleton reveals the dangerous world of the dedicated reading circle, obtaining and reading 'experimental' and proscribed books in the interests of knowledge, by examining prosecutions for blasphemy, irreligiosity, and atheism in seventeenth-century Edinburgh, against a background of fear concerning a perceived national decline in faith. There is also an interesting chapter by Peter Mitchell on the use of images of St Sebastian in the art of anatomical illustration.

In the same volume, an insight into the language of seventeenth-century 'science' and its part in the construction of socio-political meanings is provided by Jonathan Sawday in 'The Transparent Man and the King's Heart'. From the outset, Sawday stresses the need to recognize the cultural setting of 'science' or 'natural philosophy' in the seventeenth century, and the opacity of its language. He calls this 'the texture of seventeenth-century science', and seeks to explore this using the example of William Harvey and the circulation of blood. Harvey and Charles I were given a unique opportunity to view the human heart by the presence of Hugh Montgomery, third viscount of the Ards, whose medical condition rendered his beating heart visible through the skin of the left side of his chest. Harvey's observations exploded long-held ideas about the human heart: it was not the seat of sensation, courage, honour, fortitude, generosity, kindliness, love, cruelty, anger, or indifference, but simply a Cartesian mechanism, a pump. The discovery also had profound implications for political ideas, in which the king was seen as the 'heart' of the nation, or commonwealth. Sawday links the embarrassment of learning that the heart was merely a mechanism (the results were published in 1653) with the political theory of the king's two bodies, and with publications such as *Eikon Basilike* and Harvey's own *Exercitatio anatomica de motu cordis et sanguinis in animalibus* [1628], stressing the need to see these in terms of a king whose power has been usurped. Harvey's ideas are taken up in a later article by Ruth Gilbert on 'The Masculine Matrix', in which she cites Harvey's *Exercitationes de generatione animalium* [1651] as an instance of male attempts to usurp the act of creation from the female. She documents the use of language to interpret the birth of science as the penetration of (female) nature, and cites Harvey's musings on whether the male thought actually gave rise to the female act of creation after coitus. She also presents Harvey's frontispiece, an image of Zeus holding the egg from which life is seen to be hatching. The male god thus encompasses the act of creation, effectively usurping it from the female egg.

Andrew Bradstock's 'Restoring All Things from the Curse: Millenarianism, Alchemy, Science and Politics in the Writings of Gerard Winstanley' (in Jowitt and Watt, eds.) examines the question: how 'modern' was Digger leader Gerard Winstanley? Bradstock cites the opinions of Christopher Hill and his followers on Winstanley's communism and his relevance to modern democratic movements, but notes that Winstanley accepted that the universe was divinely ordered and controlled. He differed from most of his contemporaries, however, by believing that it was not contrary to the divine order of the universe to challenge the status quo. The fulfilment of Winstanley's plans did not depend upon divine intervention, although they did ultimately, as they were conceived as part of a millenarian belief that he and his fellows were living in the Sixth of the Seven Ages before the millennium. Bradstock demonstrates evidence of Winstanley's use of new agricultural methods and ideologies, and counters Mulder's view that the Digger leader was a believer in alchemy. He ends with an assertion that it is not possible in Winstanley's work to discern 'scientific' and religious ideas as working in opposition.

Carola Scott-Luckens continues with a similar theme in 'Providence, Earth's Treasury and the Common Weal: Baconianism and Metaphysics in Millenarian Utopian Texts 1641–55' (in Jowitt and Watt, eds.), in which she notes the special importance of the 1640s and 1650s for the mixing of empirical knowledge with a programme of religious, or metaphysical, philosophy. In this connection, she links the Diggers with Samuel Hartlib and his circle, and later with Robert Boyle. She notes the cultural presence of cheap agricultural pamphlets for semi-literate small farmers, making use of proverbs and jingles, and privileging words such as 'order' and 'thrift', and also notes that ideas about the land as a public resource predated Winstanley by about ten years. Scott-Luckens links the ideas and programme of Winstanley with those of Hartlib, and sees many similarities. She also notes the importance of language as a referential source for intricate networks of interlinked knowledge, examining the use of the extended 'beekeeping' metaphor originally derived from Virgil's *Georgics*. In conclusion, she links Hobbes's *Leviathan* with this utopianism.

The Power of the Passive Self in English Literature, 1640–1770, by Scott Paul Gordon, is another example of a book which covers much ground not covered by the criteria of this chapter, but which is worthy of interest on account of the applicability of its general subject—and its chapter on Thomas Hobbes. The object of the book is to trace the presence and function of the disinterested, unselfish hero, operating in pursuit of a good greater than any benefit to himself, in English literature of the period. This renders the subject 'unfree', as is Charles I in *Eikon Basilike*, describing himself as the instrument of God's higher cause in giving himself up to judgment and martyrdom. It is noted that Charles's chief opponent, Oliver Cromwell, also frequently described himself in this self-effacing way, leading to charges of hypocrisy from his enemies. As the author notes, this is a highly convenient way of reapportioning responsibility or blame, but it is also empowering, in the case of female Quaker (and other) prophets, for example. Prophecy, they say, is the expression of complete passivity. One would, however, like to have an assessment of the 'prophecy' of Abiezer Coppe and other Ranters, who used the language of *being* God.

Hobbes maintained, in *Leviathan* and elsewhere, that everyone will ultimately choose what benefits *them*. He aimed to demolish that discourse of the heroic which formed part of the ideology of self-interest, because only the sovereign may exercise the freedom on which this discourse (which ultimately relies on the ability to choose against one's own interest for the good of others, and is termed 'other-directed discourse' by Gordon) depends. Gordon notes the popularity in the early seventeenth century of the herculean hero, independent and self-sufficient, whose virtue is defined by his strength of will, leading to the equivalency of virtue and strength. This was countered by the Carolean rise of the other-directed hero, the passive self. Hobbes had to render this hero 'unreal' in order for all public good to be the function only of the sovereign. In order to achieve this, Gordon charts how Hobbes uses a chain of definitions to demolish the selfless subject, picking out all of his qualities and rendering them imaginary. However, Gordon then raises some problematic questions, including that of subjects who are unaware of their own self-interest. Another question is that of Hobbes himself—what is his self-interest in writing the *Leviathan*? These are philosophical questions with a potentially very long life, but the idea of the 'passive self' is one with considerable application outside the scope of what is covered here. This is a very useful, inspirational book.

Aspects of Hobbes, by Noel Malcolm, is a series of his own published and unpublished essays, some of them expanded and redeveloped specially for this book. Its layout is very carefully thought out, beginning with a short but detailed biography of Hobbes, to place the rest of the book in context. The rest of the book contains essays on various 'aspects of Hobbes', set out in a roughly chronological order, which contextualize him in relation to his works, his publishers, his friends and enemies, his social and 'professional' milieu, and the ideas and opinions of other philosophers of his day. The first chapter investigates Hobbes's relationship with Spinoza, emphasizing in particular their shared ideas about the need for state control of religion, but also notes where they disagree, for example in Spinoza's equation of 'right' with 'power'. An interesting insight into Hobbes's early acquaintance is given in 'Hobbes, Sandys and the Virginia Company', showing how Hobbes came into contact with radical political ideas, and the perceived need to justify colonialism, at an early stage in his life. It also demonstrates, as do many other essays in this collection, the importance of networking in the development of Hobbes's thinking—and in his publishing opportunities and spheres of influence.

Three chapters deal with Hobbesian manuscripts and the attribution of texts: one on Robert Payne, his authorship of the 'Short Tract' and his acquaintance with Hobbes and his ideas; one on Charles Cotton's translation of Hobbes's *De cive*, and their mutual acquaintance with Sir Edward Hyde; and another with the printing of the second edition of *Leviathan*, the so-called 'Bear' edition. These three chapters combine expert manuscript studies with historical investigation. In fact one of the best features of this book is its interdisciplinary nature. Not only is it an example of interdisciplinarity, but it also demonstrates a wide variety of the methodologies involved, in many cases almost seamlessly combining them. As such, it is a marvellous textbook of interdisciplinary skills and how to use them.

Other chapters seek to chart and evaluate Hobbes's friendships with individuals such as the Huguenot merchant Pierre de Cardonnel and Gilles Personne de

Roberval. While comparing Hobbes's philosophical ideas with these and other writers (including those of his great friend, Marin Mersenne), Malcolm highlights many of the chief tenets and developments of Hobbes's own writing, all the more interesting, useful, and insightful in that he is able to use Hobbes's (and, of course, others') Latin works, and to compare the English version of *Leviathan* with the later, Latin edition. There is a lively and intriguing chapter on the 'art history' of the famous title page of *Leviathan*, showing the differences between the manuscript and print versions, and explaining their origin in a particular form of image involving several pictures which, when viewed through a glass tube, make up one figure. The *Leviathan* frontispiece, Malcolm concludes, was very likely based upon an image of fifteen Ottoman sultans which made up an image of Louis XIII, by François Niceron, which Hobbes would certainly have seen in Paris. This was a royal power-image, illustrating the subordination of the many to the one sovereign, the embodiment of Hobbes's theory which would also appeal to his appreciation of optical devices. There are chapters on Hobbes and theological radicalism, and on his theory of international relations, but perhaps one of the most interesting chapters is the last, which seeks to find Hobbes's place in the European 'Republic of Letters'. This reveals the dangers of thinking of Hobbes as belonging to a specifically English sphere of writing, or of thinking of him as the writer of *Leviathan* alone. His most important work on the Continent was, apparently, *De cive*—*Leviathan* was more popular in the United Provinces than anywhere else in Europe. Most vernacular translations (chiefly Dutch and French in the seventeenth century, then German and, in the later eighteenth century, Russian) were taken from Latin versions of his works, as most European translators could not work with English. At first, he was regarded as a metaphysician, but later his political theories were more widely read. It was, however, chiefly his theological ideas which came to be most hotly debated, extrapolated, and used. Interestingly, they were used in pure or adulterated form by a wide variety of polemicists and theologians, from all parts of the theological spectrum. Malcolm notes that they were refuted by both 'sides' of the religious debate in the United Provinces—by the Arminian Grotius and by the Calvinist Voetius. They were even used by underground 'hack-writers' and radicals throughout Europe, such was Hobbes's notoriety.

The book concludes with a large, detailed bibliography, including a very useful list of manuscripts. It also contains a list of the volumes in Pierre de Cardonnel's library, and their present whereabouts (with shelfmarks) if known.

Fashioning Adultery: Gender, Sex and Civility in England, 1660–1740, by David M. Turner, is another interdisciplinary offering, combining literary study with a socio-historical examination of legal records, pamphlet literature, drama, manuals and courtesy books, and other types of documentation to produce a study of the nature of adultery in society during the late seventeenth and early eighteenth centuries. From the outset Turner admits the selective nature of the documents he is using, and intimates that there is a great deal more available. After admitting these limitations (and his method and objectives are very well set out at the beginning), Turner's study is a scholarly one, valuable to historians and literary scholars alike. He is concerned particularly with the language of adultery, and the way in which it both reflects and alters perceptions of this subject. He notes the usefulness of the period for such a study, as the connection between familial and patriarchal authority—and its discourse—had broken down after the death of Charles I. Also important were changes in culture and society: women on the stage (and the advent of movable scenery, enabling previously hidden private assignations to be revealed); the 'invention' of London as a metropolis, with a large, anonymous, and continually shifting population, and large public areas such as parks, squares, and gardens, set aside for the pursuit of pleasure; and the 'social zoning' of larger households and of society in general, creating spaces for intimate meetings between classes. Ideas of what it meant to be 'male' and 'female' are seen to have changed, with women being cast in more passive roles, while masculinity became more negative, consisting increasingly in *not* being an effeminate fop. Turner also discovers ambiguities in the reaction to both adultery and cuckoldry, from condemnation to sympathy for both sides, as the place of marriage in society no longer conditioned these responses entirely. Even jokes about cuckoldry, while mocking, can also be seen to have mitigated the shame of the victim. The useful bibliography includes manuscript sources. There is much in this book which can be related to other areas of research, and inspire further work in many of the areas touched upon by the author, whose style is extremely well informed but clear and easy to read.

Finally, on the subject of books, it would be impossible to ignore Claire Tomalin's Whitbread Prize-winning *Samuel Pepys: The Unequalled Self*, if only because its subject is one of the most famous prose-writers of the later seventeenth century. This is a chronologically arranged biographical narrative, the main part of which is based upon the entries in Pepys's diary, which he kept assiduously from the beginning of 1660 until 1669. Although the background has been researched and other books are cited in the footnotes, these years are mostly taken from the *Diary* itself, without any supplementary material. There are some interesting materials in the notes, and there is an interesting and potentially useful bibliography. Most of the notes are factual, and do not introduce too much in the way of critical or theoretical material.

Tomalin begins with the quarrel between Pepys and his wife Elizabeth, which he recorded in his diary for 1663, during the course of which he tore up their love-letters, among other personal documents. This raises questions about Pepys's nature, his authority and his relationship with his wife and other women, ideas of masculine power, and the links between his private and public life. However, these subjects are immediately dropped in favour of the life narrative (from birth to death), and they arise intermittently throughout the book, where they are not discussed in great detail. Like many biographers, Tomalin appears to have developed an almost personal liking for her subject, which obstructs her criticism somewhat. Although she mentions occasions when Pepys revealed himself to be vain, cruel, unfeeling, selfish, cowardly, peevish, vituperative, bullying, hypocritical, and snobbish, she still admits to great sympathy for him, and tends not to push these arguments to any negative conclusion. She admits to distaste for his use of women, but then mollifies her conclusion with references to his wit, guilt, and self-deprecation; because he felt guilty, he cannot fully be blamed. This is actually a very interesting observation on Pepys's ability as a writer. He understood the power of discourse, and his discourse still has the power to influence those who write about him. Scholars have paid attention to Pepys's language, especially his use of foreign words and phrases for sexual description, but the socio-linguistic workings of his discourse are equally illuminating. What emerges from the book is a portrait of a man whose personal attributes well qualified him for the epithet 'bourgeois', with all its negative, as well as positive, connotations.

Tomalin links Pepys's diary-keeping to his journalistic background (compiling newsletters for his patron and cousin Edward Montagu from 1655 onwards) and his 'office mentality' of tidiness, order, and keeping records, as well as to a desire to justify himself, rather than to the Puritan practice of keeping spiritual diaries (see the review of Oxenham's article, below). She compares this with his attitude to his kidney-stone, which had been surgically removed, and which he kept in a case, boxed and labelled, to show to visitors. He saw his own nature and life in the same way as he and his fellows in the Royal Society viewed natural objects, with objective curiosity, and was subjected to a post-mortem after his death. On the question of public and private, Tomalin argues that Pepys's public and private life cannot, and should not, be separated—and the narrative offers many points of intersection between them. These are interesting observations, which tend to become 'lost' in the narrative, but which can be extracted and applied.

The book is, as might be expected, a mine of factual information, and is valuable as such. Given the popular (but technically good), narrative style, opinion sometimes tends to be presented as fact, and the reader should be aware of this. Having said that, this is a very good introduction to Pepys, the *Diary*, and the social background of his life. It is a book which should be read, but then followed by a reading of the unexpurgated *Diary* itself, so that readers can make up their own minds!

Again on the subject of William Harvey (see review of Jowitt and Watt, eds., *The Arts of 17th-Century Science*, above), I have returned to 1999 for an article in which Stephen Speed examines Harvey's anatomical studies in relation to ideas of 'mapping' the body. In 'Cartographic Arrest: Harvey, Raleigh, Drayton and the Mapping of Sense' (in Fudge, Gilbert, and Wiseman, eds., *At the Borders of the Human: Beasts, Bodies and Natural Philosophy in the Early Modern Period*, pp. 110–27), he maintains that Harvey's observations democratized the use of signs and images, eroding the space between authority and (common) sense, privilege, and 'everyday' society. This was a secularization of knowledge, as the evidence of the senses (i.e. the eyes) has a higher value than that of authority, tradition, or established—often religious—ideologies and iconographies. Harvey revealed the diversity of bodies, so that their inner space could no longer be 'mapped'; sense could be imposed upon the body, but this could no longer be guaranteed. It could not be regarded as permanent or irrefutable knowledge. Speed relates this to Leibniz's idea of multiple folds, folding over and in upon one another (a metaphor for the Baroque), and notes the deep, multiple realities underlying the surface of Harvey's anatomy.

In the same book, Ruth Gilbert's 'Seeing and Knowing: Science, Pornography and Early Modern Hermaphrodites' (pp. 150–70) tackles the subject of scientific writing, pornography, and the hermaphrodite. The hermaphrodite, she notes, sits on the vulnerable threshold between male and female, the human and the monstrous, fact and fantasy. So, in the seventeenth century, did the world of scientific exploration and examination, and Gilbert uses Robert Hooke's *Micrographia* [1655] as an example of the scientist discovering, exploring, and subduing a new world. She then asks what it meant to open up the world of the sexed body, and gives examples of the close relationship between scientific and pornographic writing, in particular French examples (such as the examination of Marguerite/Arnaud Malause, reported in 1686), stressing that the country which produced the best pornographic writing also produced the best scientific examinations of hermaphroditism. The two forms of writing share a culture of 'the naming of parts', and the barrier between the two, if it ever existed, becomes very porous, with the writer increasingly being aware of both readings of the text. Gilbert uses her material to give a lively, readable, and scholarly account of 'the hidden and the revealed'—the shared dialectic of the scientific and pornographic exploration of what lies beneath women's skirts.

P.G. Stanwood, 'Critical Directions in the Study of Early Modern Sermons', (in Summers and Pebworth, eds., pp. 140–55), addresses the difficulty often faced by modern scholars in perceiving the importance of sermons in early modern society, when for members of all classes this was the pre-eminent literary genre. To demonstrate the assertion that sermons were not simply a vehicle for the transmission of religious truths, but were carefully planned works of rhetoric, Stanwood cites several examples, such as Donne's Gunpowder Plot sermon of 1622 and Lancelot Andrewes's Easter Sermon of 1620, carefully citing recent scholarship on these and other sermons. These references in Stanwood's footnotes are potentially very valuable to the researcher. A study of these, together with notes and emendations, enables Stanwood to dissect the texts in order to extract some principles common to many or all of them, and to note that the commendation of religious truths was accompanied by the perfecting of rhetorical style, and a response to contemporary social and political contexts. Stanwood admits that sermon studies are far too few, and that there is still a great deal of work to be done, but there is still much to be 'mined' from this article and its notes for anyone interested in pursuing work on later seventeenth-century sermons.

There has been a new edition of *Bunyan Studies* for 2002, with its commendable interdisciplinary spread of articles, and its variety of interesting subjects. Three articles in particular—on the diverse themes of marginalia, suicide, and 'faith' diaries—fall within the remit of this chapter. In the provocatively entitled 'Bunyan on the Edge' (*BunyanS* 10[2002] 29–45), William Slights examines the page design of Bunyan's works, comparing his use of marginalia with contemporary practice, such as the use of the 'key' to provide access to another 'place' of meaning. In Bunyan's works, this other place is God. Slights tackles difficult problems such as how Bunyan could justify 'glossing' his text in a manner similar to that of Catholic biblical commentators. He also notes the danger of presenting hermeneutical possibilities to a readership which was outside the writer's control. Ideas such as 'the politics of quotation' are very interesting indeed: this article is also a useful study of page design, marginalia, epistemology, and the socio-political hermeneutics of writing.

Galen Johnson's 'Suicide and the Keys of Escape in Bunyan and Donne' (*BunyanS* 10[2002] 46–64) has a more discrete subject, examining Bunyan's beliefs about suicide, and comparing them with those of John Donne, whose study of suicide in *Biathanatos* [1608, but interestingly not published until 1646] concluded that it could be justifiable to kill oneself in impossibly desperate circumstances. Johnson compares this with Bunyan's desperation while imprisoned in Bedford gaol and the episode in *Pilgrim's Progress* which features Christian contemplating suicide in Doubting Castle. Why, Johnson asks, does Christian suddenly find the

Key of Promise? Bunyan's language is strikingly similar to that of Donne, although there is no evidence that Bunyan 'borrowed' from any other writer on this subject. Both men had personal experience of deep despair, but the article concludes that the more mature Bunyan, like the older Donne, came to reject suicide as a viable option for the Christian. This article again raises the question of Bunyan's reading—how far is his treatment of subjects such as these based upon his experience alone, and how much on his reading? There is interesting material in the footnotes for those interested in following this further, or those interested in the more general study of suicide in history and literature.

The third article from *Bunyan Studies* is Sophie Oxenham's "'That I may tye myself under mine own handwriting": Reading and Writing Salvation in the Diaries of Oliver Heywood and Isaac Archer' *(BunyanS* 10[2002] 65–87). Despite the pedantic appearance of its unfortunately long title, this is a lively, well-researched, and well-written article on the very neglected subject of Protestant experiential diary-keeping, which reveals not only the personal lives of two very interesting men, but through them the nature of the society in which they lived. The study is an interdisciplinary one, examining the nature of this type of writing, and relating it to the very different experiences and responses of the two diary-keepers, one who fitted with relative ease into his society and his profession (both were ordained ministers) and one who did not. In this respect, it is also a socio-political study. Given the realization that many historical and literary figures of this period, from Oliver Cromwell to the earl of Rochester, were brought up in this cultural milieu, the insight given by these diary studies into the 'reformed' mind and its impact on society and literature could prove invaluable. This is an exposition of a subject of extreme importance for seventeenth-century studies; it is to be hoped that there is a great deal more to come, from this writer and from others.

'Cain, Abel and Thomas Hobbes' *(HPT* 23[2002] 611–33), by Helen Thornton, examines Hobbes's metaphorical use of the story of Cain's killing of his brother Abel in the Latin version of *Leviathan.* The story does not appear in the earlier, English, version of Hobbes's book, and Thornton concludes that Hobbes included it because he had decided that rhetoric was a necessary aid to understanding his ideas about the state of nature. Hobbes's audience was primarily an educated, Calvinist one; Thornton goes on from this to compare the use of the story in *Leviathan* with its use in Calvinist hermeneutics. She concludes that the story would not have conflicted with Hobbes's ideas on the state of war which exists in 'nature' between those of equal opportunity, the right to act in self-defence, and the need for an overarching authority to punish wrongdoers. Cain failed to recognize God's ability to punish him for his crime, a point which would not disagree with contemporary understandings of the episode in Calvinist theology. As well as addressing this point, the article gives a very well presented and easily understood introduction to Hobbes's theory of the state of nature.

On another aspect of Hobbes's philosophical thinking, 'Wild Ranging: Prudence and Philosophy's Imitation of God in the Works of Thomas Hobbes' *(Inquiry* 45[2002] 81–7), takes up a continuing debate on whether Hobbes envisaged philosophers as imitating God by creating order out of chaos, or whether he envisaged them as *discovering* order in chaos. The writer, Ted Miller, outlined the initial idea in an earlier volume *(Inquiry* 42[1999] 149–76), which was then challenged by Eric Brandon in his subsequent article *(Inquiry* 44[2001] 223–6). In his reply, Miller states that Hobbes creates a barrier between the experience of things outside ourselves and our experience of truth. On one side (experience), prudence helps us to contemplate memories, and on the other (truth), we reason over the meaning of words. Truth can only emerge from words, and philosophy is the means of producing truth by reasoning over words. In this context, Hobbes warns against 'wild ranging', or undisciplined thoughts, which can cause chaos, as does the misuse of speech. Hobbes privileges 'making' over 'discovery', which accounts for, and springs from, his preference for geometry over physics. In geometry (number) philosophers imitate God as Creator.

'Thomas Hobbes and the Blackloist Conspiracy of 1649' (*HistJ* 45[2002] 305–31) is an article by Jeffrey R. Collins, in which he examines Hobbes's apparent sympathy for the Congregationalist cause, as demonstrated in *Leviathan*. This has perplexed historians, who have always regarded Hobbes as committed to the royalist cause. Collins maintains that this is due to his association with a group of Catholics, taking their name from a philosopher-priest, Thomas White, also known as 'Blacklo', who was a friend of Hobbes's great friend, Sir Kenelm Digby. This group split from the other royalists of the so-called 'Louvre' group, and considered a rapprochement with Oliver Cromwell and the Independents (although the 'Louvre' group had urged this course on Charles I after 1647). Cromwell was amenable to this in 1649, as he and the army needed allies, and both sides were prepared to be pragmatic; some Independents had already been conducting covert negotiations with Irish Catholics. This is what earned Hobbes the opprobrium of the 'old royalists', which was instrumental in his ultimately leaving Paris and returning to England during the Protectorate. Collins stresses the fact that the royalists were not a unified force: there was deep division amongst them, and amongst English Catholics. The Blackloists were prepared to consider a departure from papal supremacy in local religion, in return for a general policy of toleration. Collins is careful to stress that Hobbes did not have any personal involvement in the conspiracy, although he knew some of those who did. Some of their ideas, however, did accord with Hobbes's own as expressed in *Leviathan*.

A journal concerned with land economics may be a strange place to find an interesting article on seventeenth-century prose, but 'Restoring the Commons: Toward a New Interpretation of Locke's Theory of Property' (*Land Economics* 78[2002] 331–8) makes extremely interesting reading on the subject of Locke's views on the origins of private property ownership (a 'hot topic' during the earlier civil wars) and their subsequent use and abuse by modern-day Lockean apologists . Rebecca Judge uses Locke's *Second Treatise of Civil Government* as the starting-point for a very clear and readable introduction to Locke's idea that the mixing of labour with natural resources entitles a human to ownership of what, in a state of nature, belongs to all. This derives from the human desire to work coupled with the desire for comfort, which existed before the institution of the state. Locke also states that God forbids waste, and the taking of what denies enough to others. Judge sets up these arguments against modern-day 'Lockean' arguments, which do not allow for these caveats in Locke's theory, and thereby allow for exploitation and waste of natural resources. This is a very interesting exercise in the need to view all works, especially philosophical ones, in their context; indeed, much more which is useful in the twenty-first century may be gained from approaching them in this way.

Another article concerned with the (mis)interpretation of earlier work is 'Isaac Newton and William "Oriental" Jones on Myth, Ancient History and the Relative Prestige of Peoples' (*History of Religions* 42[2002] 1–18) by Bruce Lincoln. Lincoln takes as his starting-point the attempted revaluation of the relative prestige of Oriental and European languages by William 'Oriental' Jones (1746–94). Jones cited Isaac Newton, along with Francis Bacon and James Bryant, as the writer whose work he admired but wished to supersede. Lincoln explains, with diagrams, Newton's attempts to recalculate the chronology of the Old Testament empires, beginning with the Egyptians and Chaldeans, and ending with the Persians. Newton maintained that, historically, false myths are associated with kingship, but not with the Israelites, who adopted kingship from elsewhere. Although he still privileged the Jewish faith and Israelite culture, Newton's views were so radical that they were not published until a year after his death. Jones, on the other hand, believed that oriental vernacular documents were more informative about ancient myths than the Bible, and that kingship was the origin of civilization, not of idolatry. He still privileged Hebrew culture and religion, but less so, and calculated that the peoples of the world derived from three primordial groups: Hindu, Arabian, and Tartarian. Thus, Lincoln notes, was created the racial stemma which led to the twentieth-century doctrine of 'Aryans' and 'Semites'. One of the more interesting features of this article is its demonstration of the seventeenth-century desire to approach the universe through numbers and systems, and seventeenth-century thinkers' acknowledgement of the power of words and of language; the subsequent use of their own theories demonstrates just how far thinkers like Hobbes were justified in their fear of the misuse of words—a subject which seems to recur in many of this year's featured studies.

Next, two articles on Robert Boyle. The first, Michael Ben-Chaim's 'Empowering Lay Belief: Robert Boyle and the Moral Economy of Experiment' (*Science in Context* 15[2002] 51–77), begins by reviewing work on the opinion that Robert Boyle's experimental philosophy marked an intermediate state between medieval natural philosophy and modern 'science'. Ben-Chaim agrees with scholars such as Shapin and Schaffer on the importance of factual knowledge to Boyle, but disagrees on the importance of epistemology, which Ben-Chaim says is too generalized to find a resolution to his own two subjects of enquiry: the extent to which Boyle brought his religious beliefs and views to bear on his experimental philosophy, and the extent to which he departed from existing views on the methods and goals of natural philosophy. Boyle viewed his experimental studies as a form of worship, and set himself against those who believed, like Bacon, that religious faith and the search for knowledge did not go together. Comparing Boyle's views and intentions with earlier, Aristotelian, viewpoints, Ben-Chaim concludes that Boyle did constitute a link between earlier natural philosophy and modern 'science', in that he viewed epistemological principles as of little relevance to the evaluation of factual knowledge; the products of experimental research are no different from the work of an ordinary artisan. By empowering the untutored observer, Boyle thus 'democratized' experimental philosophy, his experiments transforming divinely ordained resources into useful goods. Experimental 'science' was the special discipline of the 'priestly philosopher', with his practical, artisanly experience and technical skill.

Michael Ruse's article, 'Robert Boyle and the Machine Metaphor' (*Zygon* 37[2002] 581–95), focuses on the perceived antagonism between religion (or the Church) and science. He presents a very informative and well-written introduction to Aristotelian thought, and other philosophies, down to seventeenth-century writers. Boyle, he asserts, filled the void created by the 'death' of Aristotelianism, by creating his idea of God as a clockmaker, creating the universe and leaving it to 'tick', although Boyle did believe that God was continually caring for his created universe, and was capable of intervention. Despite this, Ruse notes that Boyle's idea of the universe as machine did open the way for atheist ideas about a purely mechanical universe, without the need for any God at all. Boyle himself believed in Aristotelian final causes, but it could be argued that God, as purely a clockmaker, had none. In the end, Ruse concludes, Boyle did open up new possibilities for science and for natural philosophy, and he could, and should, also open up new possibilities for theology.

Finally, an article on an increasingly popular subject: gardening. Sandra Sherman's 'Replanting Eden: John Evelyn and his Gardens' (*Endeavour* 26[2002] 113–17) looks at the diarist's intellectual, sensual, and spiritual relationship with gardens. For Evelyn, the garden and the gardener are one. The gardener is supposed to own the garden, but he must order his life to fit the needs of his plants, and the rhythms of nature. The garden is a post-lapsarian vision of Paradise, horticultural knowledge enabling a man (not woman in this context, although Milton's Eve might have different views) to approach Adam's prelapsarian purity and control over nature, thus offering an opportunity to participate in Eden. Sherman notes, however, that Evelyn realized that the diversity of nature in the garden precluded any simplistic view of such control. His enthusiasm for preparing sallets (dishes of vegetables) has to be seen in the light of this 'Edenic participation'. He advocated burial in gardens and groves as a return to nature, an ideal interestingly now being put into practice by the ecologically minded. Gardens are a corrective to pride, and to the power of death. Quotations are given from Marvell's garden poems, but no comparison is offered, neither is there any comparison with the views of other seventeenth-century horticulturalists and garden-lovers. This is not the point of the article, but it is to be hoped that further work in these areas will be stimulated.

3. Drama

(a) General

Susan Owen's *Perspectives on Restoration Drama* is a readable and accessible run through the different dramatic genres of the period 1660–1688, in a series of close readings of key texts. Each reading is introduced with a brief overview of current critical response to the play, and each text is elucidated from a central thematic. In dealing with Dryden's *Conquest of Granada* and *Troilus and Cressida*, Wycherley's *Country Wife*, Behn's *Rover*, Lee's *Lucius Junius Brutus*, and Otway's *Venice Preserv'd*, Owen has not chosen strictly 'representative' texts. She acknowledges this within each chapter and briefly and usefully contextualizes her choices in the light of other leading plays of the time. Students will find the compression of debates around libertinism and sexual politics or party rhetoric and the Exclusion crisis a handy reference point. Owen's last chapter explores Dryden's adaptation of

Troilus and tests it against his literary intentions expressed in his prefatory work, and against the politics of its moment of adaptation. This interest in Shakespearian adaptation was echoed in several other pieces during the year.

Barbara A. Murray's *Restoration Shakespeare: Viewing the Voice* usefully surveys what is known and much of what has been thought about Carolean adaptations of Shakespeare. Hence it has seventeen chapters on plays by Davenant, Lacy, Dryden, Shadwell, Duffett, Ravenscroft, Otway, Crowne, Tate, and Durfey, though Duffett's *The Mock-Tempest* is less an adaptation of Shakespeare than a burlesque of Shadwell. Especially interesting chapters deal with relatively neglected plays, such as Davenant's version of *Hamlet*, Lacy's *Sauny the Scot, or, The Taming of the Shrew*, and Durfey's *The Injured Princess* (a version of *Cymbeline*). The book also has a thesis, that new theatrical resources (scenery, machines, actresses) and old literary theory (*ut pictura poesis*) combined to make adapters concentrate on 'the coherently visual in poetic imagery'. Predictably the demands of the theatre are the more convincingly demonstrated, and anyway such influences did not bear exclusively on these adaptations. In 'Performance and Publication of Shakespeare, 1660–1682' (*NM* 102[2001] 435–90) Murray shows that, as only half the plays were performed and published in quarto, usually with extensive and not fully acknowledged changes, only readers of the expensive Folios could properly claim Shakespeare as 'our English Homer'. She concludes her book by reiterating these points and suggesting that much more effort was needed to establish his status; here she could have made more use of Michael Dobson's *The Making of the National Poet* (reviewed in *YWES* 73[1994] 278) and Jean Marsden's *The Re-imagined Text* [1995]. Murray mammocks the work of other scholars in her extended annotations, but does not assimilate it in her main text.

A stronger sense of the impact of the shifting political climate on adaptations of Shakespeare is picked up by Lois Potter, whose article outlines what they reveal about Restoration taste in theatrical and political terms in 'Shakespeare in the Theatre, 1660–1900' (in de Grazia and Wells, eds., *The Cambridge Companion to Shakespeare*, pp. 183–98). Jean Marsden's 'Improving Shakespeare: From the Restoration to Garrick' (in Wells and Stanton, eds., *The Cambridge Companion to Shakespeare on Stage*, pp. 21–36) takes up the theme and gives detailed examples of the ways in which Restoration adapters handled the plays. Her study pays particular attention to the performance context of the works, and to the demands of theatre venues, performers, and audiences.

Misty Anderson offers some detailed study of works from four female playwrights in *Female Playwrights and Eighteenth-Century Comedy: Negotiating Marriage on the London Stage*. Her remit is closely limited, as her subtitle reveals, to discussions of marriage within these playwrights' works, in particular as reflected through female characters within selected comedies. Her readings are based around a central methodology which distinguishes between 'conservative endings and more progressive models of modern marriage ... Comic events establish positions of authority for the negotiating heroines of these plays, while comic closure assures the audience that marriage will survive these negotiations' (p. 2). Her studies of two writers from either end of the long eighteenth century are contextualized within shifting understandings of contract and broader national events. Echoed in Behn and Centlivre, Anderson finds the emergence of a 'modified, libertine individualism' and a sense of the possibilities of contract in the early period. By the time of Cowley and Inchbald, she argues, women's comedy is facing the limitations of female civil authority and a growing disillusionment with contract. Anderson makes some comparison to works from male playwrights and is careful to limit the claims made for proto-feminism in the work.

Someone who has been claimed as a proto-feminist is the philosopher, poet, and dramatist Catherine Trotter. In the first serious biography of Trotter, *An Early Modern Writer in the Vanguard of Feminism*, Anne Kelley offers a carefully contextualized insight in the personal and professional activity of this intriguing Restoration figure. Kelley's biography studies all of Trotter's oeuvre, the philosophical essays, the plays, novella, and poetry in order to chart the development of her thought. Much material about Trotter, including her correspondence, is gathered here for the first time and provides a valuable background to the philosophical and poetic works in particular. Kelley is particularly at pains to examine the different constructions of Catherine Trotter Cockburn and her work over the centuries. Her biography produces a new version of her as a champion of female intellectual development as a mode of female empowerment, and a 'radically feminocentric writer'.

Trotter is also discussed in Marcie Frank's *Gender, Theatre, and the Origins of Criticism: From Dryden to Manley*, which places three women dramatists in an original and illuminating context, studying the critical writing of Aphra Behn, Catherine Trotter, and Delarivier Manley. By focusing on these three writers as 'heirs' of Dryden's attempt to generate a historical literary tradition, Frank offers a clear thesis on the way in which gender inflected and defined the development of literary criticism. Frank's overarching attempt is to recover the place of theatre in the emergence of literary criticism and the 'retention of traces of this dependence even after it comes into its own', and the shifting 'socio-historical coordinates of the critic', who, particularly when female, contributed to the attempt to ignore the performative features of criticism in order to preserve their critical authority (p. 138).

Behn's dramatic work continues to be of interest to scholars. Elliott Visconsi's 'A Degenerate Race: English Barbarism in Aphra Behn's *Oroonoko* and *The Widow Ranter*' (*ELH* 69[2002] 673–702) reads Behn's two late works in the light of a contemporaneous English anxiety about 'a collective genetic predisposition towards violence, greed and restless disobedience'. Visconsi reads the contradictions in the representation of African, American, and English figures within both novel and play as Behn's critique of a putatively Whig ideology which 'threatens not only an appropriate and traditional verticality of class but also denaturalizes the qualities of authority such as moral virtue, mercy, equity, and gentility' (p. 697). Peter Morgan is also intrigued by the cross-dressed figure in Behn's *Widow Ranter* in 'A Subject to Redress: Ideology and the Cross-Dressed Heroine in Aphra Behn's *The Widow Ranter*' (*ECWomen* 2[2002] 23–41). In a detailed close reading of the play she comes to stand for him as Behn's defiant posthumous presence, an active Dionysiac figure.

Kate Loveman offers a new way of reading Otway's study of a paranoid London in 'Imagining London: Thomas Otway's *The Soldiers' Fortune* and the Literature of the Popish Plot' (*Restoration* 26:ii[2002] 85–96). Her detailed reading of the play against the pamphleteers' depictions of London as a hotbed of popish intrigue shows that Otway was offering a calming, loyalist vision of London to its audiences. Kevin

Gardner's 'Patrician Authority and Instability in *The Way of the World*' (*SCRev* 19[2002] 53–75) discusses how the performance of patrician identity is crucial to the success of characters within Congreve's play, and how that is influenced by gender. Lady Wishfort's social performance is too laboured and visible, and Gardner reads her belief in Waitwell's aristocratic disguise as Sir Rowland as antiquated, in contrast to the successful characters of the new patrician order, such as Mirabell. Aparna Dharwadker's 'Authorship, Metatheatre, and Antitheatre in the Restoration' (*TRI* 27:ii[2002] 125–35) charts how the metatheatrical plays within plays of the 1670s share much with anti-theatrical writings of the 1690s, in their concern with the legitimacy of theatrical writing, 'text in performance', and the value of genre.

The Blackwell Essential Literature series produced a truncated version of Womersley, ed., *Restoration Drama: Restoration Comedy*, containing Wycherley's *Country Wife* and Congreve's *Way of the World*. Duncan Wu's brief introduction picks out differences in relationships between characters in a précis of the two texts. Joseph Arrowsmith's comedy *The Reformation* appeared this year in its first critical modern edition, with a thorough, readable, and scholarly introduction by Juan Prieto-Pablos, María José Mora, Manuel Gómez-Lara, and Rafael Portillo, through the University of Barcelona. The editors preface the work with a detailed analysis of the performance possibilities of the play, and its personal satire. They point out the particular delight that a contemporary audience could take in the mockery of Dryden as the stuffy, conceited English Tutor, who pontificates on playwriting.

The same team of editors also produced a new edition of Shadwell's *Epsom Wells*. Some years ago the editorial team gave us *The Virtuoso*, also through the University of Seville, which was welcomed in *YWES* 78[1999] 418. Again we have a comprehensive introduction, a highly readable text, and plenty of annotation. The introduction tells us all we need to know about Shadwell himself, the vogue for spas, and the play in relation to Restoration comedy generally and Dorset Garden theatre particularly. The editors' belief that the play's two young ladies 'of wit, beauty, and fortune' will reform its two young men 'of wit and pleasure' seems to me optimistic; *Epsom Wells* ends with a dance celebrating a divorce, and seems to be a play about a society in which romance is impossible, and even respectful relationships unlikely. The text is based on careful study of all early printed versions, and is conservatively modernized; for today's readers and players, this is a most attractive edition.

Restoration drama remains well represented in the London and provincial theatres. *London Theatre Record* usefully reprints reviews of productions in 2000 of *All for Love* (London), *The Way of the World* (Manchester), *The Provoked Wife* (Colchester), *The Recruiting Officer* (Chichester), and *The Country Wife* (Sheffield); in 2001 of *The Way of the World*, *The Relapse*, and *The Rival Queens* (all London), *Love in a Wood* (Stratford), *The Recruiting Officer* (Colchester), and *The Man of Mode* (Exeter); and in 2002—a lean year—of *The Feigned Courtesans* (London). Sadly the director of *The Feigned Courtesans* did not wholly share the current enthusiasm for Aphra Behn, and supplied 'extra material mocking the script's absurdities'.

(b) Dryden

Studies of plays by Dryden appeared in four of this year's general books. Susan Owen's chapter on *The Conquest of Granada* in her *Perspectives on Restoration*

Drama is an excellent introduction. Owen has read the various interpretations and has settled for a balanced account; Dryden always sees both sides, and 'insight is achieved through dialectic'. Even in the final harmony there are discordant notes, which are amplified in prologues and epilogues. She concludes with the comic relief of *The Rehearsal* and *Sodom*, so I wondered—not for the first time—if the reward for reading heroic drama is appreciation of its parodies. Owen's chapter on *Troilus and Cressida* looks at Shakespeare from Dryden's perspective: Hector's opening speech in the Trojan debate, for example, seemed to Dryden extravagant, but he felt the force of the conclusion, 'let Helen go', and did not alter that. She is less persuasive about his other attempted improvements, which on her own showing are vitiated by the need to point the moral, 'Let subjects learn obedience to their kings.' From our perspective, this is no improvement on Shakespeare's disturbing commentary on politics, war, and human frailty. Even more strikingly, Barbara Murray's chapter on this play in her *Restoration Shakespeare* fails to tell us what she makes of Dryden's complaints that the best things in the original are buried under 'a heap of rubbish', that the ending is hopelessly confused, that the principal characters are left alive, and that 'Cressida is false, and is not punished'. Her chapter on the Dryden–Davenant *Tempest*—a more respectable adaptation—emphasizes the dramatists' reinvention of Prospero as a misguided Puritan, a trouble to himself, his daughters, and his prospective sons-in-law. Susan Shifrin's collection of essays, *Women as Sites of Culture: Women's Roles in Cultural Formation from the Renaissance to the Twentieth Century*, includes Reina Green's 'Eroticising Virtue: The Role of Cleopatra in Early Modern Drama' (pp. 93–103), which explains how the Egyptian queen came to be represented as both erotic and virtuous. Green analyses Mary Sidney's *Tragedie of Antonie* [1592] and Dryden's *All for Love*, to conclude that in neither play can Cleopatra be thought wholly without virtue; in Sidney's she is Antony's wife, and in Dryden's his loving and suffering mistress. This is an admirably succinct essay; quite different is Shankar Raman's chapter on *Amboyna* in his *Framing 'India': The Colonial Theory in Early Modern Culture*. Raman agrees with Robert Markley (*YWES* 79[2000] 366) on some points, but rejects his 'attempt to decouple the play's ideological project from the historical shifts in seventeenth-century economic formations'; rather, its idea of 'fair commerce' became the basis for English colonialism. This is an essay for historians.

I noted only two articles on Dryden's plays in the learned journals. Andrew Fleck's 'Guyomar and Guyon' (*N&Q* 48[2001] 26–8) argues that the grotto scene in *The Indian Emperor* evokes the Bower of Bliss in *The Faerie Queene*. There are parallels between Guyomar's capture of the Spanish chiefs and Guyon's of Verdant and Acrasia, though Dryden's aim may have been to distinguish stout Cortez from his enfeebled underlings. Brian White's 'Grabu's *Albion and Albanius* and the Operas of Lully' (*EMu* 30[2002] 410–27) shows that Louis Grabu and Dryden were above all indebted to Lully and Quinault's *Phaeton*, staged at Paris in 1683. Grabu's music has been underrated, but he sometimes improved on Lully, and deserved Dryden's praise in the preface to the printed version.

Books Reviewed

Anderson, Misty G. *Female Playwrights and Eighteenth-Century Comedy: Negotiating Marriage on the London Stage.* Palgrave. [2002] pp. 262. £37.50 ISBN 0 3122 3938 6.

Barnaby, Andrew, and Lisa J. Schnell, eds. *Literate Experience: The Work of Knowing in Seventeenth-Century English Writing.* Palgrave. [2002] pp. x + 243. £37.50 ($55) ISBN 0 3122 9351 8.

De Grazia, Margreta, and Stanley Wells, eds. *The Cambridge Companion to Shakespeare.* CUP. [2001] pp. 328. £15.95 ($23) ISBN 0 5216 5881 0.

Frank, Marcie. *Gender, Theatre, and the Origins of Criticism: From Dryden to Manley.* CUP. [2002] pp. 175. £40 ($55) ISBN 0 5218 1810 9.

Fudge, Erica, Ruth Gilbert, and Susan J. Wiseman, eds. *At the Borders of the Human: Beasts, Bodies and Natural Philosophy in the Early Modern Period.* Macmillan. [1999] pp. 269. hb £52.50 ISBN 0 3337 2186 1, pb £17.99 ISBN 0 3339 7384 4.

Gordon, Scott Paul. *The Power of the Passive Self in English Literature, 1640–1770.* CUP. [2002] pp. 290. £40 ISBN 0 5218 1005 1.

Görtschacher, Wolfgang, and Holger Klein, ed. *Dryden and the World of Neoclassicism.* Stauffenburg. [2001] pp. 299. ISBN 3 8605 7317 9.

Greaves, Richard L. *Glimpses of Glory: John Bunyan and English Dissent.* StanfordUP. [2002] pp. 693. £ 55.95 ISBN 0 8047 4530 7.

Green, Susan, and Steven N. Zwicker, ed. *John Dryden: A Tercentenary Miscellany.* Huntington. [2001] pp. vii + 255. pb £12.99 ($15) ISBN 0 8732 8194 2; also published as Huntington *Library Quarterly*, 63:i and ii.

Jowitt, Claire, and Diane Watt, eds. *The Arts of 17th-Century Science: Representations of the Natural World in European and North American Culture.* Ashgate. [2002] £45 ISBN 0 7546 0417 9.

Kelley, Anne. *Catherine Trotter: An Early Modern Writer in the Vanguard of Feminism.* Ashgate. [2002] pp. 279. £47.50 ISBN 0 7546 0510 8.

Loewenstein, David, and Janel Mueller, eds. *The Cambridge History of Early Modern English Literature.* CUP. [2002] pp. xi + 1038. £100 ($140) ISBN 0 5216 3156 4.

Malcolm, Noel. *Aspects of Hobbes.* Clarendon. [2002] pp. 644. £ 40 ISBN 0 1991 4714 5.

Murray, Barbara A. *Restoration Shakespeare: Viewing the Voice.* AUP/FDUP. [2001] pp. 306. £35 ISBN 0 8386 3918 6.

Owen, Susan J. *Perspectives on Restoration Drama.* ManUP. [2002] pp. vii + 198. £12.99 ISBN 0 7190 4967 9.

Post, Jonathan F.S., ed. *Green Thoughts, Green Shades: Essays by Contemporary Poets on the Early Modern Lyric.* UCalP. [2002] pp. xiv + 300. hb £32.95 ($50) ISBN 0 5202 1455 2, pb £12.95 ($18.95) ISBN 0 5202 2752 2.

Prieto-Pablos, Juan A., Maria José Mora, Manuel J. Gómez-Lara, and Rafael Portillo, eds. *Epsom Wells,* by Thomas Shadwell. Universidad de Sevilla [2000] pp. lxxiv + 177. ISBN 8 4472 0590 8.

Prieto-Pablos, Juan, María José Mora, Manuel Gómez-Lara, and Rafael Portillo, eds. *Joseph Arrowsmith: The Reformation.* UBarcelona. [2003] pp. 201. ISBN 8 4833 8381 0.

Raman, Shankar. *Framing 'India': The Colonial Imaginary in Early Modern Culture*. StanfordUP [2002] pp. xii + 389. $60 ISBN 0 8047 3970 6.

Shifrin, Susan, ed. *Women as Sites of Culture: Women's Roles in Cultural Formation from the Renaissance to the Twentieth Century*. Ashgate. [2002] pp. xiv + 274. £45 ISBN 0 7546 0311 3.

Summers, Claude J., and Ted-Larry Pebworth, ed. *Fault Lines and Controversies in the Study of Seventeenth-Century English Literature*. UMissP. [2002] pp. ix + 236. £27.95 ($37.50) ISBN 0 8262 1423 1.

Tomalin, Claire. *Samuel Pepys: The Unequalled Self*. Viking/Penguin. [2002] pp. 499. hb £20 ISBN 0 6708 8568 1, pb £ 8.99 ISBN 0 1402 8234 3.

Turner, David M. *Fashioning Adultery: Gender, Sex and Civility in England, 1660– 1740*. CUP. [2002] pp. 236. £ 31.54 ISBN 0 5217 9244 4.

Swiss, Margo, and David A. Kent, eds. *Speaking Grief in English Literary Culture: Shakespeare to Milton*. Duquesne. [2002] pp. viii + 365. £58 ($60) ISBN 0 8207 0330 3.

Wells, Stanley, and Sarah Stanton, eds. *The Cambridge Companion to Shakespeare on Stage*. CUP. [2002] pp. xvi + 322. £15.95 ($23) ISBN 0 5217 9711 X.

Womersley, David, ed. *Restoration Comedy*. Blackwell. [2002] pp. 153. £9.99 ISBN 0 6312 3472 1.

XI

The Eighteenth Century

GAVIN BUDGE, FREYA JOHNSTON, JAMES A.J. WILSON AND
MARJEAN PURINTON

This chapter has four sections: 1. Prose and General; 2. The Novel; 3. Poetry; 4. Drama. Section 1 is by Gavin Budge; section 2 is by Freya Johnston; section 3 is by James Wilson; section 4 is by Marjean Purinton.

1. Prose and General

The long domination of eighteenth-century studies by an authorial canon which was very tightly defined relative to the length of the period has made the advent of postmodern hermeneutic perspectives highly significant for the field, since the change in interpretative paradigm is leading to a shift in disciplinary self-definition for eighteenth-century scholars which is more pronounced than in many other areas of literary study. Johnson studies, so long the defining locus for eighteenth-century prose, is at the faultline in this respect, with liberal humanist celebrations of Johnson's inclusivity and tolerance jostling a new paranoid rhetoric of social alienation and secret Jacobite sympathies.

Predictably, both sides in this debate accuse each other of being 'unhistorical', but what may prove to be of greater and more lasting significance for the field as a whole than the question of whether Johnson was or was not a Jacobite at one time in his life is the disintegration which the dispute marks in the scholarly consensus over how to interpret eighteenth-century culture. If the significance attached to so central a figure as Johnson can vary wildly according to the interpretative frame that is put around his work, then it can no longer be confidently assumed by scholars that there is one self-evidently right approach to the eighteenth century, something which opens the way to an appreciation of the variety of political and religious hermeneutics that were current in the eighteenth century and to explorations of the contested nature of constructions of authority within the period. Some of the most significant scholarship on eighteenth-century prose in the years under review (2001 and 2002) pursued this mapping of eighteenth-century intellectual diversity into areas rarely explored by the literary scholar.

The most explicit airing of this interpretative issue within eighteenth-century studies was Howard D. Weinbrot's 'Johnson and the Jacobite Truffles' (*AgeJ* 12

[2001] 273–90), a response to Niall Mackenzie's "'A Great Affinity in Many Things": Further Evidence for the Jacobite Gloss on "Swedish Charles"' (*AgeJ* 12[2001] 255–72), which, as its title suggests, develops the argument for regarding Johnson's 'The Vanity of Human Wishes' as a poem which hints at Jacobite sympathies by identifying parallels in Johnson's historical milieu for the interpretation of the figure of Charles XII of Sweden, to whom the poem refers, as a coded allusion to the Pretender. One of the most striking features of Weinbrot's article is its refusal to engage in a detailed critique of Mackenzie's historical methodology; Mackenzie's arguments are rejected wholesale as an example of 'the neo-Jacobites' perpetual grasping at straws and aggressively political modes of proceeding' (p. 285), which Weinbrot compares to the interpretative procedures of 'commentators on the ideological left'. Weinbrot prefers instead to appeal to a commonsense understanding of 'Johnson's politics as a generally fluid, practical, and principled construct' (p. 285), a position which he evidently feels excludes the possibility that Johnson's writing could adequately be characterized in terms of an ideological commitment to Jacobitism, or to anything else.

What is at stake in the argument between Weinbrot and Mackenzie is a question not so much of the historical evidence itself as of the hermeneutic assumptions that should inform scholarly interpretation; in effect, Weinbrot is accusing Mackenzie and other scholars who have raised the possibility of a Jacobite Johnson of engaging in a mode of interpretation akin to those employed by contemporary conspiracy theorists, in that they marshal every piece of evidence which could conceivably point to the desired conclusion without taking account of opposing forms of evidence. As is apparent from other articles within the same volume of *The Age of Johnson*, this dispute closely parallels arguments surrounding the interpretative procedures of new historicism, which have been taking place in other areas of literary study over the past fifteen years.

The kind of claims and counter-claims exemplified in the exchange between Weinbrot and Mackenzie are not very productive in scholarly terms, because neither side engages with the other's premises. Interestingly, a number of the essays included in a book edited by two of the main upholders of the Jacobite interpretation of Johnson, Jonathan Clark and Howard Erskine-Hill, eds., *Samuel Johnson in Historical Context*, move away from the narrow interpretative focus condemned by Weinbrot to address broader concerns about the nature of eighteenth-century culture, in a manner which goes a long way to fulfil Erskine-Hill's claim in the introduction that a radical historicism can reveal 'an older and stranger Johnson, reacting to situations and problems not only alien to our own society, but which even modern historical scholarship on the eighteenth century has diminished or occluded' (p. 1). Paul Monod's 'A Voyage out of Staffordshire; or, Samuel Johnson's Jacobite Journey' situates Johnson within the local politics of Staffordshire in a way that makes clear the retrospective nature of political Jacobitism as a reaction against Walpole's machine politics. Richard Sharp, in 'The Religious and Political Character of the Parish of St Clement Danes', explores the High Church religious culture of the parish church Johnson is known to have attended in London, a theme which Eirwen Nicholson continues in an account of the 1726 controversy over the Jacobite visual references of this church's altarpiece. Other essays in the collection explore more narrowly focused issues related to the hypothesis of Johnson's Jacobitism: Niall Mackenzie explores another interpretative crux for a Jacobite reading of 'The Vanity of Human Wishes', and Matthew M. Davis finds Jacobite implications in Johnson's notes to *Richard II*. Some essays also usefully explore more well-trodden ground, with Thomas Kaminski proposing the importance of the Renaissance neo-Latin tradition for an appreciation of Johnson as a stylist, J.C.D. Clark arguing that Johnson's 'authority as a moral critic' results from his 'austere position of internal exile' (p. 79) as a Jacobite, and Murray Pittock re-evaluating Johnson's attitudes towards Scotland by suggesting that Johnson found in Scotland a model for the decay which he feared would overtake English society. The collection also contains essays which locate Johnson's politics within eighteenth-century English society more generally, something which Eveline Cruikshanks seeks to do through offering biographical sketches of Gower and Chesterfield, and Jeremy Black through examining Johnson's involvement in debates about British foreign policy, particularly the Falkland Islands crisis.

In an interesting conclusion to the collection, J.C.D. Clark offers a robust defence against critics such as Weinbrot, who find the kinds of 'alternative readings of … Johnsonian texts' to which the hypothesis of Johnson's Jacobite sympathies has led, overly 'speculative' (p. 296). Clark argues that such views themselves unconsciously reflect the historiographical methodology of Namier and his followers, and makes a case for the Jacobite perspective on Johnson as part of a non-deterministic and counterfactual approach to the historical study of the eighteenth century. Paula McDowell's 'Enlightenment Enthusiasms and the Spectacular Failure of the Philadelphian Society' (*ECS* 35:iv[2002] 515–33) might be cited as an example of this kind of approach, since her aim in drawing attention to the cultural centrality of this group of followers of Böhme during the eighteenth century is to show how 'the late-seventeenth and eighteenth-century reaction against certain kinds of speech, writing, and intellectual inquiry associated with religious "enthusiasm" continues to affect what now counts as the object of English literary study' (p. 517). Although dealing with somewhat similar subject-matter, John D. Morillo's monograph *Uneasy Feelings: Literature, the Passions, and Class from Neoclassicism to Romanticism* is a much more recuperative kind of exercise in which eighteenth-century theories of the passions, and particularly Adam Smith's *Theory of Moral Sentiments*, are interpreted as anticipations of Marx's theory of alienation; as Morillo sees it, the very similarity of human nature implied by eighteenth-century appeals to the passions potentially threatens class distinction, creating a need for the passions to be regulated and policed, an interpretation he supports by discussions of Dennis, Wordsworth, Pope, and Byron.

Another edited collection on Johnson, Philip Smallwood's *Johnson Revisioned: Looking Before and After* engages in a more explicit way with the hermeneutic dilemma between the professionalized interpretative procedures represented by Clark and his fellow contributors and Weinbrot's appeal to a consensual literary understanding. Greg Clingham's essay 'Resisting Johnson' largely sets the tone of the volume, with its call for Johnson scholarship to engage with 'theoretical currents of interest' in other areas of literary studies, noting the way in which 'the work of the great Johnsonians tends to run within the channels of the same liberal-humanist historical understanding of literature and literary history' (p. 23). Several of the following essays engage with popular stereotypes of Johnson and his views, and may be said to have for their aim the creation of a more 'politically correct' Johnson (which, it shouldn't need to be said, might also be a more historically accurate one).

Clement Hawes questions the nationalistic image of Johnson by drawing attention to the cosmopolitan dimension of his thinking and the debunking of literary articulations of nationalism in which he engages. James G. Basker draws attention to Johnson's closeness to late eighteenth-century abolitionist discourse and to the way in which his many enthusiastic female readers, including Mary Shelley, problematize modern assumptions about his anti-feminism, a line of interpretation which is also developed by Jaclyn Geller, who explores the way in which Johnson's 'talent for intimate, Platonic friendship with women' (p. 82) is written out of Boswell's biography, and notes 'a strand of anti-marriage critique in Johnson's literary productions' (p. 90). Other essays explore issues to do with Johnson's relationship to literary history, and to historiography more generally. In 'Ironies of the Historical Past: Historicizing Johnson's Criticism' Philip Smallwood critiques not only new historicist modes of engaging with the criticism of the past, but historicism more generally, arguing that 'the tendency of historians of criticism, like intellectual historians, to conceive their material in terms of *ideas*' (p. 116) (which ultimately descends from late eighteenth-century 'philosophical history') obscures 'Johnson's critical commitment to the world of feeling' (p. 129). This emphasis on the affective dimension of Johnson's writing is continued in the essay by Tom Mason and Adam Rounce, which examines the capacity of his criticism to irritate his contemporaries, and also characterizes Danielle Insalaco's 'Thinking of Italy, Making History: Johnson and Historiography', which makes a case for Johnson as an anticipator of 'microhistory' (p. 99) and 'a precursor of Bourdieu' (p. 104).

Greg Clingham's monograph, *Johnson, Writing, and Memory*, represents a more sustained attempt at defining a 'post-theoretical' Johnson. Clingham's central claim, which he uses to identify common threads in the disparate Johnsonian canon, is that language use for Johnson is always embedded in history. This is most obviously important in literary translation, and Clingham suggests that Johnson in his *Lives of the Poets* characterizes Dryden and Pope 'not incidentally but *fundamentally* as literary and historical translators', understanding 'their respective literary characters as reflecting a *translational* relationship with language, texts, and the world', so that Johnson sees 'their formal translations as constituting their most characteristic work' (p. 122). Clingham argues that translation represents for Johnson a paradigm for literary history, as 'a quintessentially differential mode of discourse located between past and present, partaking of both and yet identified with neither, and turning on the commemorative action of memory' (p. 120). But Johnson, in Clingham's view, also regards translation as emblematic of the intentionality of writing itself, in the necessary discrepancy between aim and achievement which it reveals. The rhetoricity of language, to use Paul de Man's terms, thus for Clingham becomes fundamental to an understanding of Johnson's work, in a way which can serve to defend Johnson's critical authority against the attacks of Marxist historians of literary criticism such as Terry Eagleton: Johnson's cultural authority cannot simply be dismissed as 'rhetorical', because 'the fact that the public sphere is (partly) rhetorical does not necessarily diminish its reality—it *is* always the public sphere—nor does it necessarily undermine a subject's capacity for action, since those are *already* encoded and accepted contextual terms within which meaning is produced' (p. 5). Clingham lays particular emphasis on Johnson's involvement with the discourse of law in his drafting of Chambers's Vinerian lectures: law furnishes the closest analogue to the way in which Clingham envisages the cultural operation of Johnsonian discourse, since it brings to the fore 'the intimate intrinsic relationship between rule-governance and concrete-contextual interpretation' (p. 69) which Johnson, like the hermeneutic philosopher Hans-Georg Gadamer, finds inherent in all language-acts.

Although he doesn't address the issue explicitly, Clingham's hermeneutic approach to Johnson seems to offer some hope of reconciling the opposed positions over Johnson's putative Jacobinism that we have found in MacKenzie and Weinbrot, because it gives full play to Johnson's conservative denial that institutions such as monarchy can be reformed by fiat, whether of parliament or of anyone else, while at the same time suggesting that Johnson might have accepted the need for such institutions to be 'translated' into a form appropriate to the present time. Elsewhere in *The Age of Johnson* can be remarked the same tendency to redefine the traditional image of Johnson which we noted in Smallwood's collection. Thomas M. Curley's substantial article 'Johnson and the Irish: A Postcolonial Survey of the Irish Literary Renaissance in Imperial Great Britain' (*AgeJ* 12[2001] 167–98) reviews Johnson's 'little-known role of intellectual midwife at the birth of the Gaelic revival in Ireland' (p. 69), while Gloria Sybil Gross's catchily titled essay 'In a Fast Coach with a Pretty Woman: Jane Austen and Samuel Johnson' (*AgeJ* 12[2001] 199–253) examines the influence of Johnson's 'radical psychological analyses' (p. 214) on Austen's practice as a novelist, and James G. Basker suggests that Johnson's review of *Oroonoko* in *The Critical Review* for December 1759 testifies to proto-abolitionist sympathies.

In the 2002 volume of *The Age of Johnson*, the editors note a general shift in scholarship on the eighteenth century away from 'interpretations of literary works' towards 'what once seemed to be ancillary topics like economics, the consumption of goods and services, and the emergence of new social classes and new habits of life' (p. xi). This sociological turn is reflected in Nicholas Hudson's 'Discourse of Transition: Johnson, the 1750s and the Rise of the Middle Class' (*AgeJ* 13[2002] 31–51), which makes a case for Johnson as 'a major figure in the promotion and definition of English middle-class ideology' whose rise to prominence is specifically connected with the political events of the 1750s, and in Aaron Stavisky's 'Samuel Johnson and the Market Economy' (*AgeJ* 13[2002] 69–101), who notes 'Johnson's quasi-Ricardian position' (p. 80) in regard to trade. Steven Schewatzky unites these sociological interests with more traditional literary concerns by examining the relationship between Johnson's political attitudes and his theory of the imagination, coming to the conclusion that Johnson emphasized 'the danger of being consumed by politics in the same way he typically warned against complete absorption in any single-minded pursuit' (p. 64), which could perhaps be read as aimed at the crypto-Jacobite interpretation of Johnson.

More traditional modes of studying Johnson, however, are still strongly in evidence. Paul Tankard, in 'That Great Literary Projector: Samuel Johnson's *Designs*, or Projected Works' (*AgeJ* 13[2002] 103–80), produces an impressive and revealing biographical survey of Johnson's various schemes for publications, which makes the important point that such schemes shed light on the literary milieu in which Johnson worked. Betty Rizzo's '"Downing Everybody": Johnson and the Grevilles' (*AgeJ* 12[2001] 17–46) explores the tensions between Johnson and Fulke Greville in a way which makes clear the intersection between personal relationships and the politics of language in Johnson's career. A strong case is made in George

Justice's essay 'Imlac's Pedagogy' (*AgeJ* 13[2002] 1–29) for the continuing relevance of a moral reading of Johnson by treating *Rasselas* as 'a book about the process of education' in which Imlac and his teaching 'function as metonymy for the tale and its circulation through print culture', while Freya Johnston's 'Diminutive Observations in Johnson's *Journey to the Western Islands of Scotland*' (*AgeJ* 12[2001] 1–16) is a close reading of the role of the 'little' in Johnson's work.

Another trend in scholarship of the period is towards a revitalization of intellectual history, a tendency which in part reflects the increased interest shown by academic philosophers in the history of the British empiricist tradition. James Fieser's anthology *Early Responses to Hume's Writing on Religion*, part of his ongoing series on eighteenth- and nineteenth-century Hume reception, is a particularly useful contribution to the understanding of a key topic of debate in the eighteenth century, since, as Fieser notes, 'having the advantage of living during Hume's time, early critics understood Hume's implications better than we might today' (p. xviii). James Gray, in 'From Skeptics to Gullibles: Eighteenth-Century Responses to Miracles' (*AgeJ* 13[2002] 181–206), offers a handy overview of eighteenth-century freethinking and its orthodox opponents, a topic which is also exhaustively explored in David Womersley's magisterial study *Gibbon and the 'Watchmen of the Holy City': The Historian and his Reputation, 1776–1815*. Womersley combines close scrutiny of textual changes in the crucial chapters on the development of Christianity between early editions of the *Decline and Fall of the Roman Empire* with outlines of the responses of Gibbon's early clerical critics and their context in eighteenth-century debates about religion. He argues that Gibbon's development as a historian shows an evolution away from the rather glib deism implied by the language of the first edition of volume 1 of *Decline and Fall* towards an altogether more complex and nuanced stance in volume 2, and that this represents a response to his clerical critics in that Gibbon deliberately sought to wrong-foot them by avoiding 'obvious lines of interpretation' (p. 146). Womersley suggests that 'a complex interplay of expectation and response with readers and critics' (p. 164) thus shapes Gibbon's writings, an argument he extends to the many drafts of Gibbon's *Autobiography*, which he sees as a similarly tactical response to the changed situation after the French Revolution, in which Gibbon 'was in danger of acquiring a spurious, although convincing, radical character as a result of the way the political connotations of the classical past as a subject of study had developed' (p. 230).

A renewal of intellectual history is also apparent in the area of aesthetics, to which a special issue of *Eighteenth-Century Studies* (35:iii[2002]), edited by Peter Fenves, is dedicated. As G. Gabrielle Starr notes in her essay 'Ethics, Meaning and the Work of Beauty' (*ECS* 35[2002] 361–78), the relevance of the aesthetic to critical understanding is currently undergoing re-evaluation within literary studies in a reaction against the suspicion with which the category was regarded by new historicist critics (p. 361); drawing on the work of Elaine Scarry, Starr argues for the significance of Hogarth's aesthetic theories on the basis that, unlike many eighteenth-century theorists of beauty, he did not 'search for an ethical equivalent of beauty' (p. 366). Jonathan Brody Kramnick, in 'Literary Criticism Among the Disciplines' (*ECS* 35[2002] 343–60), is also concerned to relate eighteenth-century arguments about aesthetics to the present-day 'crisis of literary study', which he suggests is endemic 'in the structure of the discipline' (p. 357) as it arose in response to eighteenth-century concern over 'the problem of specialization' (p. 343). David L. Porter (*ECS* 35[2002] 395–411) uses an account of the eighteenth-century vogue for chinoiserie as a basis for examining the relationship between fashion and aesthetics during the period, concluding that the Chinese style was so popular precisely because of its 'cultural illegibility' (p. 405), which put all those who consumed it on a level. David Marshall addresses a similarly ambiguous eighteenth-century cultural phenomenon in his essay 'The Problem of the Picturesque' (*ECS* 35[2002] 413–37), which explores the way in which the picturesque, like certain forms of postmodernism, problematizes the boundary between representation and reality, concluding that 'the picturesque is less a problem *in* aesthetics than a problem *about* aesthetics' (p. 415). More traditional aesthetic problems are examined by Paul Guyer (*ECS* 35[2002] 439–53), who looks at the relationship between beauty and utility in eighteenth-century thought, and Tom Huhn, who in 'Burke's Sympathy for Taste' (*ECS* 35[2002] 379–93) argues for the fundamentally social basis of Burke's conception of mimesis. Dabney Townsend's monograph, *Hume's Aesthetic Theory: Taste and Sentiment*, offers a sustained reading of Hume which emphasizes the centrality of aesthetics to his thinking; refreshingly, Townsend acknowledges the interpretative problems raised by attempts at 're-translation of Hume's concerns into a contemporary philosophical idiom', acknowledging that 'writers such as Hume are rhetoricians with an audience of the educated, not of other professional philosophers' (p. 3) in a way that makes his study very rewarding for the literary scholar.

The increased self-consciousness about the nature of historical evidence and interpretation apparent in much contemporary scholarship has led to some fresh scrutiny of historiographical traditions. Mike Hill's 'The Crowded Text: E.P. Thompson, Adam Smith and the Object of Eighteenth-Century Writing' (*ELH* 69[2002] 749–73) argues that 'an unexamined Smithian legacy' (p. 751) haunts E.P. Thompson's notion of the moral economy of the eighteenth-century English crowd, in that Adam Smith's theorization of capitalism includes the kind of paternalistic assumption of moral responsibility which Thompson assumes is opposed to the nascent capitalism of the eighteenth century, and that this false opposition between morality and political economy leads to a certain circularity in Thompson's historical interpretation which undermines his claim, in his polemic against Althusser, to represent a non-theoretical mode of history which emphasizes the agency of human subjects. Issues of the relationship between rhetoric and evidence also underlie Elizabeth D. Samet's 'A Prosecutor and a Gentleman: Edmund Burke's Idiom of Impeachment' (*ELH* 68[2001] 397–418), which similarly invokes Smith's theory of sympathy in order to examine the forensic problems created for Burke by what he regarded as Warren Hasting's illegitimate blurring of 'the boundaries between private and public' (p. 412). Rosemary Sweet's 'Antiquaries and Antiquities in Eighteenth-Century England' (*ECS* 34[2001] 181–206), meanwhile, aims to dispel the image of Walpolian dilettantism that hangs around late eighteenth-century antiquarianism by examining the productive professional career of Richard Gough.

The recent advances in bibliographical methods made possible by computerization have greatly facilitated work in the history of the book, as Isabel Rivers notes in the preface to her collection *Books and their Readers in Eighteenth-Century England: New Essays*, which revisits the ground of her pioneering 1982 collection. Following James Raven's illuminating survey 'The Book Trades', which stresses the plurality of factors underlying the eighteenth-century expansion of publishing, many of the essays make use of the collection's focus on the material conditions of the printed word to throw an unfamiliar light on the century's intellectual history: thus, Scott Mandelbrote illuminates theological divisions in England by examining the issues of bible translation and distribution, Karen O'Brien suggests that 'the rise of "philosophical" or "Enlightenment" history was a commercial as well as an intellectual phenomenon' (p. 116), and Brian Young draws attention to the substantial overlap between the market for fiction and the market for theological books, in a way that throws into question Ian Watts's characterization of the novel as an inherently secular form. There is also attention to the eighteenth-century origins of modern literary scholarship: Marcus Walsh, for instance, examines the role played by Tonson and other publishers in developing 'the scholarly editorial treatment of the vernacular literary text' (p. 199), Antonia Forster explores the founding of the first review periodicals in the middle of the century, and Isabel Rivers looks at the development of biographical dictionaries in England after Bayle, while Michael F. Suarez SJ argues for the importance of miscellanies for an understanding of the circulation and consumption of eighteenth-century poetry. This more worldly approach to eighteenth-century scholarship is also reflected in George E. Haggerty's 'Walpoliana' (*ECS* 34[2001] 227–49), which provides an entertaining account of the life of Sheldon Lewis, whose collection of Walpole's papers grew into the Lewis Walpole Library, and who was responsible for devising the CIA's information retrieval system.

2. The Novel

It is hard to see the wood for the thickets of jargon obscuring many of this year's publications. Once again, Pickering & Chatto have come up with a handsomely presented set of neglected texts bearing on the history and development of the eighteenth-century novel—but the rationale behind putting them together, and the quality of the editorial apparatus, are not as easy to defend as last year's *Pamela Controversy: Criticisms and Adaptations of Samuel Richardson's Pamela, 1740–1750*. Gary Kelly's six-volume edition of *Varieties of Female Gothic* seeks 'to enable the further development, broadening, diversification and challenging of lines of research and criticism pursued since the 1970s into what has come to be called the "female Gothic"' (vol. i, p. xi). By 'female Gothic' he means 'A species of Gothic fiction from the decades just before and after 1800, written by women, featuring female protagonists ... with distinctively feminine and feminist interests and tendencies, specific to that time, but of continuing interest to women and feminists now' (vol. i, p. xiv). Most of Kelly's fifteen texts, not all of which could be said to endorse 'feminist interests' or to make 'female protagonists' any more of a feature than male characters, have been out of print since their first appearance. The volumes are organized thematically—female Gothic being subdivided into its 'Enlightenment and Terror', 'Street', 'Erotic', 'Historical', and 'Orientalist' manifestations—and chronologically, beginning with Clara Reeve's *Champion of Virtue: A Gothic Story* [1777] and culminating in Sydney Owenson's *The Missionary: An Indian Story* [1811]. Kelly has provided a vast range of prefatory and supporting materials. It seems churlish to raise objections, but his sixty-page general introduction is cumbersome and repetitive; more seriously, it feels very remote from the experience of reading Gothic literature at its best. He appears compelled to reclaim all female varieties of the genre on the grounds of their implicit political radicalism (so implicit that it is frequently hard to discern in the texts themselves), as if it is not enough to defend these works on their literary merits. On the basis of what is included here, in some cases it is clearly not. But it remains hard to believe that 'a strong drive to reform the nation and the state' (vol. i, p. xxii) was what the majority of readers (male and female) discovered or relished in such fantastic publications. It is the restricted definition and organizing principle of 'Gothic' as 'female', however, that causes the real problem, lessening the reader's ability to appreciate the scope and responsiveness of these writers' achievements and the integrated context in which their work was originally produced. Kelly assumes the predominance of a 'gendered discursive hierarchy of the time', which he also claims these novelists successfully 'circumvented' in Gothic fiction (vol. i, p. xxiv). Why, then, should their works be isolated from male practitioners of the genre such as Horace Walpole and Matthew Lewis? Over the past three decades, long-overdue attention has been paid to women novelists of the long eighteenth century, but it has tended to segregate them from their male counterparts—the outcome of such exclusivity being an entrenchment of the same ghettoizing tendencies feminist critics set out to challenge. Thus Kelly's introduction to Reeve's *Champion of Virtue* finds itself in the awkward bind of having to acknowledge the work's genesis as a revision of Walpole's *Castle of Otranto* at the same time as trying to redefine the genre to which it belongs in terms of her gender—which naturally entails Walpole's absence from this volume. Three pages are devoted to summarizing the apparently fruitful intersections between Walpole and Reeve's plots, chivalric trials, supernatural machinery, and so on, yet Kelly denies readers an opportunity to test his introductory claims against two texts that clearly belong together—albeit perhaps not in terms of their political affiliations. On this last point, Kelly ends up weakly asserting: 'The possibility must remain that … Reeve aimed to displace Walpole's work and its aristocratic and elitist Whig ideology with the more bourgeois-democratic politics she promoted in her fiction' (vol. i, p. xxxii). Reeve's 'Address to the Reader', however, asserts her novel's superiority to Walpole's in terms of its ability to suspend disbelief rather than 'destroy the work of imagination', hardly expressing the credo of a politically motivated Gothic: 'I was both surprised and vexed', she writes of *The Castle of Otranto*, 'to find the enchantment dissolved, that I wished might continue to the end of the book' (vol. i, p. 6). She has, at least, a great deal more in common with Walpole than with Mary Butts, teenage author of the mawkish *Traditions: A Legendary Tale*, which occupies the remainder of this volume.

Happily, Joseph F. Bartolomeo, *Matched Pairs: Gender and Intertextual Dialogue in Eighteenth-Century Fiction*, confronts the limitations of Kelly's gender-specific editorial approach; his chapter on 'Confessional Discourse and the (Un)gendering of the Gothic: *The Monk* and *The Italian*', amongst others, demonstrates the rewards of identifying the interactions rather than divisions between male and female authors. That the book does so in terms of gender—seeing feminine ways of writing as not necessarily confined to women, masculine styles as not wholly the province of male authors—is conceived as a direct response to critics whose interpretations of the novel habitually fence off one sex from the other. But its comparative readings have much to say about the subtlety of literary influence in general, regardless of whether the author in question is a man or a woman. Five chapters pair a male and female novelist—Haywood and Defoe, Henry and Sarah Fielding, Richardson and Lennox, Smollett and Burney, Radcliffe and Lewis—in terms of their 'connections and intertextual dialogues' (p. 30). The best of these (they are all well structured and persuasive) is the third, presenting Lennox's *Female Quixote* as 'a rewriting of *Clarissa* in a comic mode' (p. 91), in which episodes and characters that threaten Richardson's heroine are repeatedly translated into 'harmless or benign' equivalents (p. 93). This 'rewriting'—which 'cannot reach the heights but also avoids the pitfalls of Richardson's tragic original' (p. 122)—implies no crude formula, as Bartolomeo is keenly aware, since Lennox's Arabella shares traits not only with Clarissa but with Belford, Lovelace, and Hickman. The Glanville family's project of reforming Arabella after her marriage 'provides a comic analogue to Lovelace's attitude, particularly his belief that he can cure Clarissa of [her] inhibitions' (p. 101); Arabella and Lovelace both suffer from 'fantasies of omnipotence' modelled on 'literary precedents that are as restrictive as they are enabling' (pp. 104, 105). Lennox's original plan may have been to facilitate Arabella's cure by making her read *Clarissa*. Bartolomeo ponders what the heroine might have learnt from Richardson, had she been permitted to recover her sanity in this way. He surmises that the characterization of Clarissa as 'infinitely superior to all other women within the novel makes her fundamentally inimitable for the women who read it'. Lennox, on the other hand, by casting an exceptional woman's tale in a comic setting, 'tempers [Arabella's] rewards and punishments and thus makes her fate and example more appealing than that of her tragic counterpart' (p. 121).

Eleanor Wikborg, *The Lover as Father Figure in Eighteenth-Century Women's Fiction*, is an exploration—again touching on 'female Gothic'—of paternal characters who become the suitors of fictional heroines; it proposes that authors including Haywood, Burney, Edgeworth, and Austen intended their novels to serve as 'conduct books for men' (p. 111). Besides their construction of the father figure as a variety of types—incestuous guardian, princely patriarch, moral guide, ideal lover—Wikborg argues that female novelists attempted to transform him into a character that, after marriage, would freely acknowledge his wife's independence. Their novels accordingly 'seek ways to defend and validate' the 'precariousness of women's self-reliance' (p. 24). In view of her subject, Wikborg's inability to break free of her critical forebears stands out. Reading the book is heavy work—from the outset, it constructs a line of argument simply by restating a whole series of critical commonplaces—and its mode of expression is portentous and ungainly, featuring such jaw-breakers as 'not even the gendered subject is monolithically interpellated' (p. 4). Wikborg's claim to originality is that she is the first to examine the lover as father figure across such a wide range of writers, from familiar suspects such as Behn and Austen to less renowned novelists including Mary Hearne, Mary Collyer, and Elizabeth Griffith. But those who have read Margaret Anne Doody, Carole Pateman, Marilyn Butler, Nancy Miller, Susan Fraiman, and Nancy Armstrong (all cited, amongst others, in the first ten pages of the introduction) will find nothing new in this book, and would do better to go to the primary texts themselves.

Penny Gay, *Jane Austen and the Theatre*, begins with a strenuous denial that Austen abhorred the drama: on the contrary, Gay asserts, her fiction was informed by avid consumption of plays at home and abroad in Bath, Southampton, and London. Even in the *Juvenilia*, Austen employed dramatic techniques as a central element of her literary repertoire. While Fanny Price may have been appalled by private theatricals, Austen contributed enthusiastically to them. Like Fanny, Gay's arguments often sound discordantly solemn and clunky: she asserts that theatrical tropes act as a means for the 'objectified' woman to 'turn her own gaze' back on a 'patriarchal society', thus 'deconstructing the authority it claims to have' (p. 23)—a gloss which reiterates critical cliché without thinking about whether it quite applies to Austen. Of more interest and value is the plentiful evidence Gay has accumulated of the Austen family's staging of sexually charged works, such as Susannah Centlivre's *The Wonder! A Woman Keeps a Secret*. She implies that there may have been biographical grounds for Fanny's trepidation about the consequences of amorous drama: Eliza de Feuillide, who played the lead in *The Wonder!*, subsequently became Henry Austen's wife (although it must have been some performance, since their marriage took place ten years later). Another strength of the book is its practical attention to the design of the theatres Austen attended, and what it felt like to spend an evening in them. It is a shame that more room is not given to this kind of reconstruction. The introduction is marred by an excessively repetitive summary of arguments well in advance of their deployment, but subsequent chapter-by-chapter discussion of the novels in terms of their theatrical devices and scenic construction is illuminating, as is the suggestion that Austen's characters acquire their particular form due to their author's treating, or failing to treat, the reader as audience.

Gloria Sybil Gross, *In a Fast Coach with a Pretty Woman: Jane Austen and Samuel Johnson*, sets out to overthrow 'the stereotype of Johnson's parochialism' and 'the myth of Austen's limitation' by a comparative estimation of their treatments of love, sex, marriage, families, and happiness, revealing 'the dynamic intimacy between one imagination and another' (pp. 6–7, 13). Both authors sought to tackle 'the comfortable hypocrisies of domestic bliss' (p. 15). The subject, as outlined here, is potentially fertile and rewarding, but Gross has unaccountably left some rich sources of influence and interaction untapped. It is not until her conclusion that she registers Johnson's 'alertness to details of the mundane and everyday current of events' (p. 189), although the ethic of attentiveness informing his appetite for concrete particulars fed straight into the allusions to Johnson and his circle that pepper Austen's minutely textured correspondence, and in turn into her fiction. The failure to compare their epistolary arts of writing about nothing misses an opportunity to discuss those rare moments at which Austen directly introduces her favourite prose writer as a model; had Gross included such moments, her broader observations might have held more water. In spite of lengthy quotations from both authors, the book frustratingly eschews every chance to examine the numerous resemblances between Austen and Johnson at the level of style. Instead, Gross presents a chronological series of plot summaries of the juvenilia and completed novels in terms of largely conjectural thematic derivations that are tendentiously elided with assertions of fact: 'Not surprisingly, Johnson's essays on marriage and courtship, and not least the plight of single women, were on Austen's mind when she undertook *Persuasion*' turns out to mean nothing more verifiable than that one of the *Rambler* numbers on marriage 'Perhaps ... sparked the plan of *Persuasion*' (pp. 165, 167). Gross simply provides no firm evidence to support her claims that, for instance, 'Reading Johnson, Austen understood the torrid emotion lurking beneath ostensibly humble facades', that Boswell provided the model for Mr Collins, that Johnson's quarrel with Chesterfield established a precedent for Lady Catherine de Bourgh's insupportable condescension, or that Elizabeth Bennet particularly resembles Floretta, heroine of Johnson's fairy-tale *The Fountains* (pp. 107, 88, 87, 80). Promising that she will seek out 'the *process* rather than product of Johnson's influence on Austen' (p. 13), Gross communicates no precise sense of how one author's writing might have contributed to the shape and development of the other's.

Emily Hipchen, 'Accounting for Fanny: "this curious inventory" in *Mansfield Park* and *The Loiterer*' (in Rivero, ed., *The Eighteenth-Century Novel*, vol. 2, pp. 305–24), marries the fifteenth number of James and Henry Austen's undergraduate periodical with their sister's fiction on the basis of shared concerns about 'the effect of limited or biased perspectives—of any human point of view—on correct judgment, a discussion which the narrator of *Mansfield Park* joins when it inventories Fanny's sitting room' (p. 306). Hipchen examines literary descriptions of domestic interiors as a means of evaluating their owners, arguing that we ought to acknowledge 'Fanny's real engagement in worldly things, in material wealth, in collecting and accounting' rather than her much-vaunted asceticism and piety (p. 315). Such an approach permits us 'to see Fanny's judgment as fallible', since her method of accumulating and counting over her things is marked by a 'fundamental inaccuracy' (p. 321). Although her comparison with the Austen brothers is of limited applicability, and feels slightly forced, Hipchen's irreverent approach to Fanny is welcome. She sees everyone in the novel as preoccupied with the heroine's '"worth", "value", and "moral weight"' (p. 313), characterizing her as 'more invested in pricing, than many might believe' (p. 321)—so it is curious that, in an otherwise alert and dexterous piece of writing, she fails to make anything of the material information that Fanny's surname is Price.

Following on the heels of Irene Collins, *Jane Austen and the Clergy* (Hambledon [1994]), Michael Giffin, *Jane Austen and Religion: Salvation and Society in Georgian England*, surveys Austen's completed novels in terms of their author's grounding in 'canonical scripture as well as in neoclassical philosophy and theology' and her practices as a 'devout' Anglican (p. 2). The key terms in his reading of Austen are 'oikonomia'—employed in the New Testament to describe management of the household, family, and church, and in patristic theology to indicate the external manifestation of God's being and purpose—and 'soteria', or 'wholeness, health, preservation from disease, deliverance from enemies, moral and spiritual deliverance, breadth or enlargement (of vision, or of self-knowledge)' (p. 7). The combination of the two produces what Giffin repeatedly and loosely calls an 'economy of salvation' in Austen's work (p. 30). Thus Catherine and Henry are, at the close of *Northanger Abbey*, 'the focus of Austen's economy of salvation ... in an ordinary but real way' (p. 62); in *Pride and Prejudice*, 'Austen's economy of salvation reveals itself to be a capitalist meritocracy that has distinct feminist overtones' (p. 125); *Mansfield Park* exhibits 'an economy of salvation represented by the three characters of Sir Thomas, Fanny and Edmund, inasmuch as they signify a threefold unity of God, Christ, and the Church' (p. 148); Emma and Knightley 'are fully able to participate in ... the economy of salvation between the Highbury parish and the Donwell Abbey estate' (p. 176). Any attempt to restore Austen to something other than a purely secular context is laudable. Unfortunately, however, Giffin's overbearing analysis shows no awareness of her comic acuity or lightness of touch, even when dealing with matters of religion, and his argument is circular: having defined an 'economy of salvation', he then insists that Austen's works exhibit just that, and fails to be specific about her own use of the words 'economy' or 'salvation'. Anyone reading this book with no prior knowledge of the novels would gain the impression that Austen wrote barely fictionalized religious tracts, with no other design than to reflect the somewhat moribund state of Georgian Anglicanism.

Patricia Michaelson, *Speaking Volumes: Women, Reading, and Speech in the Age of Austen*, is an elegant and original interdisciplinary study of women and linguistic practice in England in the late eighteenth and early nineteenth centuries, highlighting the intersections between speech and reading. The book presents evidence from a wide range of primary sources including elocution manuals, textbooks, private journals, and novels (particularly those of Austen). Without dismissing the experience of the mute and solitary reader, it asserts that reading aloud was a means of rehearsing authoritative speech, and that for women—such as Burney—oral recitals of literature contributed to the formation of middle-class domesticity. Michaelson contrasts the period's treatises on female language with adroitly handled case studies of individual speakers, arguing that eighteenth-century English women deployed the stereotype of linguistic artlessness and ineptitude while also suggesting that gender was not necessarily the most salient feature of their characters. After a valuable survey of writings on eighteenth-century female speech—which emphasizes that women were bracketed together as a single, deficient category of talkers—subsequent chapters each centre on an individual woman. Michaelson describes Quaker language, for instance, as a sociolect with standards different from those of the polite world; she then demonstrates how Amelia Opie employed a highly mediated form of language that identified her alternately as a polished female and a Quaker. Pondering the efforts of the actress Sarah Siddons to reconcile theatrical with ordinary language, Michaelson associates the oral performance of literature with other kinds of conventional female display. Lastly, drawing on Austen, she argues that novels superseded conversation manuals in attempting to model their readers as speakers.

Aileen Douglas, 'Maria Edgeworth's Writing Classes' (*ECF* 15[2002] 371–90), argues that, through her role as family copyist and the primacy attached to forensic and public records in her fiction, Edgeworth 'resisted the notion that literary works were essentially different from other kinds of writing' (p. 372). Unlike Austen—whose characters are, as Michaelson amply demonstrates, assessed predominantly through dialogue—Edgeworth's 'index of social being' remained the written word (p. 373). This, Douglas finds, is due in part to her awareness of increased literacy amongst the labouring classes and the 'permeation of her society by writing' (p. 390). In her novels, social status emerges as precariously dependent on the ownership of appropriate documents such as letters of recommendation or marriage certificates.

Justine Crump, ed., *A Known Scribbler: Frances Burney on Literary Life*, presents a selection of Burney's journals and letters, composed between 1768 and 1839. Focusing on Burney's creative, social, and commercial ambitions and achievements, this user-friendly edition combines her own accounts of the processes of novelistic and dramatic composition with reflections on her unpublished writings as literary productions in their own right. As well as selections from Burney's correspondence, diary entries, *Brief Reflections Relative to the Emigrant French Clergy*, and *Memoirs of Doctor Burney*, Crump includes letters by relations and friends about her literary activities and contemporary reviews of the novels and of *The Diary and Letters of Madame d'Arblay*. The splicing of voices and forms succeeds in locating Burney within a broad social and literary context. Crump wisely makes no attempt to provide a thorough autobiographical account of Burney's life through these extracts, instead choosing those that shed light on her character as author, reader, and active participant in the literary circles of her time. Accordingly, the selections are not evenly distributed across the years; some periods are sparingly represented, while others (such as 1778, the year in which *Evelina* appeared) are extensively covered. Crump's editorial decisions reflect the praiseworthy desire to retain a sense of these writings as messy and incomplete scripts, often bearing the hallmarks of second thoughts and revision.

George Justice, 'Suppression and Censorship in Late Manuscript Culture: Frances Burney's Unperformed *The Witlings*' (in Justice and Tinker, eds., *Women's Writing and the Circulation of Ideas: Manuscript Publication in England, 1550–1800*, pp. 201–22), opens with a moment from *Evelina* in which the heroine is tormented by the tittering public reception of Macartney's verses celebrating her charms. The episode, Justice argues, 'exemplifies Burney's understanding and representation of manuscript circulation' and informs her assertive turn 'toward a skillful manipulation of the possibilities for authorship in the public world of print-publication' (p. 201). Following the triumph of *Evelina*, Burney was pushed towards Johnsonian and Bluestocking coteries that encouraged and ultimately thwarted her dramatic ambitions. The 'still powerful manuscript culture of the late eighteenth century'—associated with the literary salon—is itself presciently dubbed 'anachronistic' in the course of *The Witlings*, as if its author knew that such a culture would strangle its transmission: 'The play's meaning coheres with its own history' (pp. 220, 205). Also arguing for Burney's independent dealings with print culture, Betty A. Schellenberg, 'From Propensity to Profession: Female Authorship and the Early Career of Frances Burney' (*ECF* 14[2001] 345–70), questions the 'critical habit of collapsing Burney's notions of authorship with her portrayals of heroines … whose virtue is partly defined by their horror of publicity, and who inhabit texts peopled primarily by characters whose model of publication is one of epistolary or coterie circulation' (p. 346). In fact, Burney—who benefited from a 'climate of encouragement' of female authors (p. 349)—made conscious decisions about the nature of her authorial identity that, in their turn, influenced future women novelists such as Austen.

Daniel James Ennis's *Enter the Press-Gang: Naval Impressment in Eighteenth-Century British Literature* is a book that should have remained an article. It documents the eighteenth-century practice of naval recruitment by force alongside literary representations of its influence on British society. The author examines scenes that feature press-gangs in novels, plays, ballads, and personal narratives; he argues, with his own kind of coerciveness, that impressment reveals the ways in which genre is related to ideology. Ellis claims that, while eighteenth-century novels always criticize impressment, presenting it as a brutal practice with tragic consequences, eighteenth-century plays invariably defend the state's trumping of habeas corpus both as a necessity and as an opportunity to serve the nation and achieve military glory. The second chapter proposes that the novel, as an emerging genre, is tied to social protest and therefore sets itself against press-gangs, the members of which are invariably represented in fiction as malicious thugs. Yet it muddies the author's claim that novels generically oppose impressment when he observes of *The Adventures of Roderick Random*—'the first English novel to describe the experience of impressment in any detail' (p. 53)—that its hero's capture 'turns out to be an opportunity for class mobility' (p. 54). It is not seen, then, as an unmitigated evil, but rather as a nasty episode issuing in a kind of social enhancement not afforded elsewhere. Other links between impressment and the novel appear similarly forced and reductive. Ellis has (unsurprisingly) discovered few works to exemplify his claims about the centrality of the press-gang to the development of the novel, and is compelled to admit that Defoe's 'interest in the issue does not appear to have carried over directly into his fiction, despite the nautical flavor of works like *Captain Singleton* and *Robinson Crusoe*' (p. 51). He seems unsure whether he is attempting to find literary evidence for the historical facts of impressment, or historical endorsement of the rise of the novel in the activities of the press-gang. In the end, the subject is too narrowly defined for a monograph, and the introductory assertion that 'This book ... is ultimately about literary genres' (p. 16) is never quite realized in the text.

In *Enlightenment Fiction in England, France, and America*, a critical study of why we read novels, William Donoghue contextualizes fiction's rise in popularity against the backdrop of an emerging philosophical scepticism. He stresses a 'rise in popularity of the novel' rather than the standard 'rise of the novel' because he considers novelistic simulations of reality to be 'an antidote to the anxieties and uncertainties of skepticism', palliating the '"epistemological crisis"' of the period (p. 1). The works Donoghue examines—including *Tristram Shandy*, *A Sentimental Journey*, *The Mysteries of Udolpho*, *Caleb Williams*, *The Sorrows of Young Werther*, and *Dangerous Liaisons*—are all said to dramatize the collision of scepticism with realism; his discussion provides new approaches to some familiar texts. Of particular interest is the second chapter's argument that *The Dunciad* foregrounds concerns at the heart of the novel. Donoghue sees Pope, like Richardson, as defending mimetic art against the abuses of the stage; in *The Dunciad*, he presents 'a long-term and powerful polemic on behalf of realism' which implicitly 'contradicts the claim often made, both then and now, that the novel is a skeptical form that cannot support a system of moral beliefs' (p. 22). *Pamela* and *Clarissa* are read in terms of their more direct emphasis on the potential for artifice to be useful, 'enabling and conducive' to knowledge and the morally instructive function of literature (p. 46). Sterne, by contrast, is sceptical of contemporary theories of knowledge and the novel, 'especially of the notion that the two are mutually enabling' (p. 46).

Scott Paul Gordon, *The Power of the Passive Self in English Literature, 1640–1770*, is a wide-ranging literary and historical study which questions recent critical emphasis on a seventeenth-century Protestant discourse of self-sufficiency and autonomy, favouring a counter-tradition that depicts the self as inhabited by another presence: 'By guaranteeing individuals that they do not act self-interestedly, the passivity trope paradoxically enables actions that would otherwise be difficult to conceive' (p. 17). By the eighteenth century, however, such a trope 'disables "active work"' (p. 19). Gordon devotes his final chapter to *Clarissa*, arguing that 'a practice of negativity' (p. 193), rather than the adversarial skill of which the heroine (alongside David Garrick) is often suspected, underlines her sincerity. Mandeville's *Fable of the Bees* had, in the early eighteenth century, transformed all conduct into evidence of self-interest. Its impact on the reception of *Pamela* as the fundamentally rhetorical work of a manipulative author, deploying—like his hypocritical, cunning heroine—the instruments of persuasion to serve his own ends, led Richardson to adopt 'the passivity trope' in order to secure Clarissa from the same misinterpretation. Parting company with recent critics, who read all the letters in *Clarissa* as the suspicious productions of self-motivated advocates, Gordon asserts that 'In this novel everybody but Clarissa is a rhetorical being' (p. 190). Richardson contrives to prevent her from asserting her will, so that she is 'Moved rather than freely moving': 'this figuration protects Clarissa from the Mandevillian charge of self-interest by denying "motivation" altogether' (p. 193). The novel thus endeavours to preserve the heroine's will by denying her the use of it until after her death. From this convincing analysis, Gordon proceeds to argue that *Clarissa* wins over its readers by appealing to their feelings (involved in the story) rather than their judgement (detached from proceedings): 'Deploying a *non-rational* solution to the problem of proof, Richardson counted on his readers' sensibilities, not their intellects, to prove his heroine's sincerity' (p. 196). Yet the distinct categories of '*judging*' and '*feeling*' (p. 197) become elided towards the end of the chapter when Gordon writes that the audience's tears—an index of sensible passivity akin to Clarissa's—'invoke a private *judgment* that obliterates any oppositional argument' (p. 207: my italics). In every other respect, this is a thoughtful and innovative reading of the novel.

Peter Sabor, 'Feasting and Fasting: Nourishment in the Novels of Samuel Richardson' (*ECF* 14[2001] 141–58), revisits a subject discussed by Margaret Anne Doody and (more recently) Donalee Frega, foregrounding *Pamela* and *Sir Charles Grandison*'s attitudes to eating in the light of 'Richardson's own dietetic concerns in the 1730s and early 1740s' (p. 141). He finds a source for the 'consumption and rejection of food so evident in *Pamela*' (p. 153) in the novelist's correspondence with the Bath physician George Cheyne, who combated his obesity with the rigours of a strict vegetarian regime. In the figure of Sir Charles, Sabor argues, 'the antithetical claims of feasting and fasting are finally resolved' (p. 158).

Joe Bray, 'Embedded Quotations in Eighteenth-Century Fiction: Journalism and the Early Novel' (*JLS* 31:i[2002] 61–75), attempts an analytical enquiry into how the language of eighteenth-century fiction is modelled on that of newspaper reporting. Bray focuses on one journalistic technique—indirect speech—that he identifies as a parallel to the submerged quotations in Lovelace's manipulative reports of speech to Clarissa. He is thus stylistically associated both with the eighteenth-century and the modern journalist. Casting her net more widely, Jill Campbell, 'Domestic Intelligence: Newspaper Advertising and the Eighteenth-Century Novel' (*YJC* 15[2002] 251–91), persuasively links the formal realism of Richardson's *Pamela* and *Clarissa*, Behn's *Love-Letters Between a Nobleman and his Sister*, Burney's *Cecilia*, and Edgeworth's *Belinda* with the commercial style and emphases of contemporary notices in publications such as *The Daily Journal* and *The London Gazette*. It may have been in newspaper copy advertising lost goods or items for sale, Campbell suggests, that Richardson honed the 'particularizing description that became the hallmark of his novelistic style' (p. 251). Drawing on Benedict Anderson's *Imagined Communities: Reflections on the Origin and Spread of Nationalism* (Verso [1983]), she sees prose fiction—through its direct references to advertisements and the ubiquity of consumer goods—as affording its readers a means of participating in the experience of an otherwise disparate community of strangers. Novels are themselves marketable products that 'draw on techniques shared by the commercial culture for projecting individual character and evoking the readerly sensation of a common, recognizable physical world' (p. 282).

Even more heavily influenced by Anderson's conception of community, Cohen and Denver, eds., *The Literary Channel: the Inter-National Invention of the Novel*, brings together eleven essays on the interactions between French and British writers and readers of fiction; several contributors focus on the eighteenth century. Cohen and Denver see the novel, which emerged from 'the processes of literary and cultural exchange that occurred across the English Channel', as 'a form constitutively engaged with boundary crossing' (introduction, pp. 1–34: 2, 5). Mary Helen McMurran, 'National or Transnational? The Eighteenth-Century Novel' (pp. 50–72) examines the practice of translation, or rather *translatio*—with its accompanying implications of 'the transfer of power from one empire to another' and 'the transfer of culture through translation, imitation, and adaptation'—as 'central to the eighteenth century's view of the novel' (p. 51). McMurran skilfully deploys three varieties of literary-historical evidence in support of her claim that it is hard to establish the novel as a national or transnational form in this period: first, a bibliographical survey of translations from French into English, and vice versa, establishing a double orientation of the novel market as national and international; second, an examination of eighteenth-century essays on the history of prose fiction, which exhibit opposing conceptions both of *translatio* and nation; third, a study of patriotic language surrounding the exchange of translated British and French novels, which turns out to be inconclusive evidence of the genre's nationalization. The most valuable aspects of this multi-faceted approach include the suggestion that 'transfer' may have been a constitutive feature, even a 'conceptual foundation', of the novel because fictions shared the property of being able to change their form and language without infringing any clear-cut rules (p. 66). To focus on what was being transferred across the Channel might lead us to 'refuse for the moment to define the novel as a form or genre' (p. 57). The pressure of national character exerted on this new kind of writing seems to have had no more lasting or significant impact than any other attempt to categorize it. McMurran underlines throughout her valuable essay the novel's 'fluidity and transmissibility or translatability' (p. 66). Her bibliography should be read alongside two more contributions to the field of novelistic 'transfer': James Raven, 'An Antidote to the French? English Novels in German Translation and German Novels in English Translation' (*ECF* 14[2001] 715–34) and Richard Frautschi and Angus Martin, 'French Prose Fiction Published between 1701 and 1750: A New Profile of Production' (*ECF* 14[2001] 735–56).

Lynn Festa, 'Sentimental Bonds and Revolutionary Characters: Richardson's *Pamela* in England and France' (in Cohen and Denver, eds., pp. 73–105), sees *Pamela* 'as a crux to a set of relationships central to a cross-Channel analysis of the rise of the novel' (p. 73). Like Jill Campbell, she takes her cue from Benedict Anderson in seeking to establish the sentimental novel's contribution to the 'forging

[of] collective identities among readers as consumers in a literary marketplace, as participants in the imagined community of nation' (p. 74). Festa charts Pamela's speedy decline from the original 'model of Virtue' to 'a cheap, mass-produced imitation' on public display in parks and on side-tables, or degraded still further in theatrical adaptations, burlesques, and tawdry paraphernalia (p. 79). The best thing about this essay is its representative selection of French responses to the novel (it should be read as a companion to Thomas Keymer and Peter Sabor's *Pamela Controversy: Criticisms and Adaptations of Samuel Richardson's Pamela, 1740– 1750* (P&C [2001]), which documents British and Irish reactions alone). In August 1793, for instance, the enthusiastic reception of a dramatized *Pamela*, staged in the midst of the Terror, sparked a riot in Paris. Festa derives from this episode a conclusion similar to McMurran's about the novel's resistance to a single line of interpretation—however keenly the revolutionaries may have wished to condemn *Pamela*'s seeming praise of aristocratic English government, what such debates actually reveal is 'the incapacity of sentimental tropes to control what readers identified with in the text' (p. 93). Margaret Cohen, 'Sentimental Communities' (pp. 106–32), again invoking Anderson, covers similar terrain—from *Pamela* to *Uncle Tom's Cabin*—in her endeavour to characterize 'the first modern imagined communities catalyzed by sentimental texts' (p. 107).

Wolfram Schmidgen, 'Illegitimacy and Social Observation: The Bastard in the Eighteenth-Century Novel' (*ELH* 69[2002] 133–66) charts, in political and literary terms, the rise and fall of the illegitimate fictional hero. The structural advantage of such a figure, Schmidgen argues, has only tangentially to do with the author negotiating the claims of blood and merit, inborn and acquired virtue at the level of narrative. The bastard's real use is his or her ability to operate as a mobile commentator on the social scene—he or she may serve not only to criticize the aristocracy, but also to intervene in and contribute to its diversification. This article is largely taken from the third chapter of the author's *Eighteenth-Century Fiction and the Law of Property*, a complex and rewarding investigation of the dynamic relationship elicited in fictional, legal, economic, and aesthetic texts between people and things. Like Cohen and Denver's contributors, Schmidgen interprets the history of the novel in terms of fluidity, transfer, and process. 'Communities of persons and things in eighteenth-century Britain', he argues, 'are on the whole characterized by permeable boundaries, by a sense of open traffic across human and material zones' (p. 1). Informed by the basic Marxist assumption that communal structures arise from the exchange between human and material spheres—but not restricting that interaction to one of economics—he offers readings of the 'textured process of objectification' in Defoe, Fielding, Radcliffe, Walter Scott, Richardson, Mackenzie, and Sterne 'to provide as clear a sense as possible of how exactly these texts intervene in their cultural environment' (pp. 2, 10). This leads to adept consideration of the eighteenth-century novel's 'engagement with "groundedness"', its sense of 'plot' as a piece of land, a series of events and a ground plan, and its consciousness of 'description' as a form of proprietorial enclosure (p. 11). Schmidgen distances himself from Benedict Anderson's view of the novel, which implies that its growth 'coincides with the rise of the modern nation state' (p. 13): where Anderson sees the appearance of modern communal forms and the imaginative procedures that shape them as a sudden crossing of forces, Schmidgen plausibly views their emergence as 'indecisive', 'partial', and 'hardly ... spontaneous' (p. 12) due to the 'obdurate persistence', within and outside fiction, 'of landed property as the ultimate ground of social and political community' in the period (p. 12).

Jonathan H. Grossman, *The Art of Alibi: English Law Courts and the Novel*, is chiefly concerned with nineteenth-century fiction, but devotes one chapter to *Caleb Williams*, in which Godwin is said to have 'produced a newly juridical conception of character and narrative form' (p. 37). Grossman focuses on the concluding volume of the novel, in which the protagonist is haunted by a street-hawker's parasitic 'adventures of Caleb Williams', as a battle of the books between the gallows literature on which Godwin draws and his own fiction: 'Godwin took up the genre of criminal biography in order to repudiate it … After *Caleb Williams* the novel of crime subtly changed from referring itself to criminal biography to distancing itself from it' (p. 48).

Nina Prytula, '"Great-Breasted and Fierce": Fielding's Amazonian Heroines' (*ECS* 35[2002] 173–93), is prone to bursts of enthusiastic overstatement about the importance of its subject: eighteenth-century England 'manifested an unprecedented fascination with the female breast', which was 'an extraordinarily conspicuous feature of eighteenth-century culture and conversation' (p. 173). Fielding, she argues, employs images of the breast as 'a symbolic incarnation of what he considers to be the very best and the very worst aspects of female nature' (p. 175): heroines sport dazzling white bosoms that reinforce their status as paragons, while their physically aggressive counterparts possess an enormous redundancy of décolletage. All this ends up amounting to very little, however, since Prytula concedes that whatever 'mammary symbolism' Fielding may employ to differentiate one woman from another (p. 190), his 'representations of … idealized heroines overlap with those of their Amazonian antitheses in a way that … resolves seemingly crucial distinctions of class, looks, and character into an assertion of the essential sameness of women' (p. 177).

Sara Gadaken, 'Managing and Marketing Virtue in Sarah Fielding's *History of the Countess of Dellwyn*' (*ECF* 15[2002] 19–24), argues that Fielding's penultimate novel 'explores the power that accrues to women in the newly developing commercial culture'; unlike *David Simple* and its sequel, the *History* 'emphasizes women's responses to victimization rather than the suffering occasioned by it' (p. 19). Confronting a paradox of eighteenth-century refinement—which leads, on the one hand, to morally suspect luxury, on the other to an admirable industriousness in the producers and managers of exquisite goods—Fielding combines positive and negative attitudes to consumption. Concentrating on the figure of the superlatively accomplished businesswoman Mrs Bilson, who devises a portable shop to save her family from bankruptcy, Gadaken describes her as blending 'the virtue of the domestic paragon with the power of the marketplace' to produce 'an image of a more vigorous and capable woman than is allowed by the paradigm of virtue-in-distress' (p. 34). Mika Suzuki's 'Sarah Fielding and Reading' (in Rivero, ed., vol. 2, pp. 91–112) is a patient and thought-provoking contribution to studies of this increasingly popular author. Suzuki does not fall into the trap of categorizing Fielding's modesty as the hallmark of a singularly female writer—merely because 'the apologetic tone' of eighteenth-century prefaces 'goes well with the accepted characteristic of women' does not mean that it is, in practice, any less frequently invoked by men (p. 93). Rather, Suzuki sees Fielding's 'awareness of the precariousness of language' as 'related to her perception of authorship' and 'a mass of anonymous and unpredictable readers', not to 'her sense of female victimization by male language' (pp. 92, 109). Fielding is said to conceive of reading as an act of collaboration between author and audience; this collaboration at once encourages the reader's active participation in the text and seeks to curtail the potential range of his or her responses.

Helen Thompson, 'Plotting Materialism: W. Charleton's *The Ephesian Matron*, E. Haywood's *Fantomina*, and Feminine Constancy' (*ECS* 35[2002] 195–214), elicits some connections between the seventeenth-century natural philosopher William Charleton and Eliza Haywood's prose romance. In a densely plotted, inchoate argument that is sometimes difficult to follow, Thompson seeks 'to recover the formal and thematic resources with which Haywood's romance resolves patriarchal contradiction' (p. 196). Haywood's heroine serially transforms herself into a prostitute, a servant, a widow (consciously following the Ephesian matron's example) and a masked woman in order to retain the fickle Beauplaisir's affections. She is thus 'single and many, ruined and unruined: this is the substance of a critique that deploys the materialist conflation of constancy and inconstancy, the particular and the indefinite, to resolve its heroine's contradictory position as object of lust and subject of love' (p. 209).

Alison Conway, 'Defoe's Protestant Whore' (*ECS* 35[2002] 215–33), suggests that Nell Gwyn, the self-proclaimed 'Protestant whore' of the title whom Defoe's Roxana echoes during her adventures in France, holds 'a key to the interpretative locks' of the novel (p. 215). This fascinating, original, and flexible essay—which makes room for analysis of several little-known historical sources—argues that the Restoration setting of *Roxana* allowed Defoe 'to forge powerful links between two apparently opposing discourses: that of the Protestant conversion narrative, and that of the courtesan work and identity eloquently articulated in the figure of Nell Gwyn' (p. 215). During the 1660s, the empty and negative characterization of the Protestant believer intersected with that of the anti-Catholic female libertine. Gwyn defended her own conduct as mere professionalism—the pursuit of an honest livelihood—whereas her Catholic, foreign competitors for the king's affections were cast as treacherous pretenders: 'By emptying out her sexuality of all but its bodily performance, Nell becomes, paradoxically, less dangerously embodied, a suitable cipher of public admiration' (p. 220). *Roxana* confronts the terrors as well as the liberating potential of existing as such a 'cipher'; the heroine 'voices a longing for the release from the pressures imposed by the insistence of Protestantism that individuals take full responsibility for their spiritual well-being' (p. 221).

James Cruise, 'Childhood, Play, and the Contexts of *Robinson Crusoe*' (*AgeJ* 14[2003] 259–80), focuses on the fictional lacuna that is Crusoe's early life 'as constituting a period that is inherently significant with consequences that spur him throughout his adventures' (p. 260). Why then, he asks, 'does Crusoe have no real childhood to report in his narrative life? Were answers as easy as questions' (p. 262). Indeed. Cruise spends the bulk of his article deferring an answer, instead presenting evidence about contemporary developments in child-rearing, even speculating on the contents of a spurious parental 'tea chest' preserving the young Crusoe's toys 'in one of the recesses of the Yorkshire estate' (p. 265). Despite promising us that 'The case I intend to plead' is that Crusoe compensates for his lost childhood 'through play', Cruise is still considering three pages before the end of his essay the conditions that must exist 'Before [Crusoe] can play' (p. 274).

George A. Drake, 'The Dialectics of Inside and Outside: Dominated and Appropriated Space in Defoe's Historical Fictions' (*ECF* 14[2001] 125–40), seeks to renovate critical appreciation of *A Journal of the Plague Year* and *Memoirs of a Cavalier* in terms of the historical developments they register 'in the experience of space' (p. 125). The fictional authors of both narratives 'enact Defoe's ambivalent fascination with spaces dominated by official power and spaces appropriated by individual practices' (p. 125). The Cavalier's desultory, shiftless education as a soldier contributes to the fact that he is 'fully comfortable' only in 'dominated space' (p. 128), while H.F., narrator of the *Journal*, 'plots the chronicle of the mortality schedules in spatial terms' (p. 133). For H.F., the city's shape is determined by, and determines, the nature of collective experience; ultimately, the *Journal* 'explores the hybrid space of the marketplace as it reconfigures strategic domination and individual appropriations of space' (p. 140).

Conceiving literary space in different terms, and relating it to the question of genre, Matthew Wickman, 'Of Probability, Romance, and the Spatial Dimensions of Eighteenth-Century Narrative' (*ECF* 15[2002] 59–80), draws attention to 'the formal parameters of core and periphery' in extracts from *Evelina*, *Tom Jones*, *The Man of Feeling*, and *Love and Freindship* (p. 60). Burney's preface to *Evelina* figures the republic of letters as a core, that of romance as a peripheral region of the marvellous. She thus tries 'to clear a plot for her work somewhere between the normative and the fantastic' (p. 61). Fielding's more enthusiastic endorsements of fiction's probability—also expressed in 'a virtual geography of core and periphery' (p. 70)—aim rather to stimulate his reader's judgement. Wickman's thorough and intelligent textual analysis succeeds in doing the same thing; he is especially sharp on Austen's revisionist attitude to Fielding's 'definition of poetic faith': 'in Austen's narratives, contrary to the ideas espoused in *Tom Jones*, and more in keeping with Burney's secession from the republic of *belles lettres*, even the supposed "bounds of probability" cross into the enchanted fields of literary romance' (p. 78).

Shaun Regan, 'Print Culture in Transition: *Tristram Shandy*, the Reviewers, and the Consumable Text' (*ECF* 14[2001] 289–309), features in an outstandingly rich special issue of the journal (*ECF* 14:iii–iv[2001]), devoted to 'Fiction and Print Culture'. Regan considers Sterne in the light of contemporary satires on review criticism and debates over literary property. He seeks 'to reposition *Tristram*' in two ways: 'textually, by differentiating between local effects which have often been lumped together in previous readings; and culturally, by locating the work more precisely within the print culture of its own day' (p. 290). Regan argues that Sterne's representation of texts as material objects, and his physical manipulation of the novel, reveal an author confronting and negotiating 'the vexed interrelationships between the immaterial creativity of the author, its appearance in manuscript form, and the mechanical reproduction (and mass republication) of the printed artifact' (p. 309). Christopher Flint, 'In Other Words: Eighteenth-Century Authorship and the Ornaments of Print' (*ECF* 14[2001] 627–72), proposes that typographical marks, or printer's ornaments, 'had a peculiar semantic charge, especially as employed in prose fiction, that might very well differentiate them from earlier or later uses' (p. 628). This accomplished investigation of the uses of such ornaments in Swift, Richardson, and Sterne demonstrates how eighteenth-century publishing contributed to the formation of 'an authorial figure that both embodied print culture and often resisted it passionately, producing fame through the mechanics of the print industry while emphatically reserving the imprimatur of the author's name' (p. 632). One of the most welcome aspects of Flint's insightful piece is its relocation of *Shandy* within a prevalent contemporary alertness to paratextual devices. Since criticism has neglected the material conditions of printed text except in the case of *Shandy*, Sterne's work has come to seem more eccentric than it is: 'What makes *Tristram Shandy* "odd," however, is not that Sterne does anything unique to the printed page, but that he compresses in a single work a large number of unusual typographical effects that had already appeared individually in several preceding works' (pp. 633–4). Also examining the multiplicity of eighteenth-century paratexts, Janine Barchas, '*Grandison*'s Grandeur as Printed Book: A Look at the Eighteenth-Century Novel's Quest for Status' (*ECF* 14[2001] 673–714), considers the uses of taxonomy in Richardson's preface as 'a specific set of moral and social axes' designed to assist the reader in navigating the text (p. 674). Elsewhere in the novel, however, his 'penchant for lists risks aligning itself with Lovelace's pseudo-scientific preoccupations' (p. 677). Contrasting his graphic itemizations with Swift and Defoe's catalogues, Barchas locates the eighteenth-century novel's lists amongst other 'collecting, and bundling activities' that reflect the genre's 'endemic materialism' and its proximity to conduct-books, journalism, travel narratives and anthologies (p. 685).

Anne Bandry, '*Tristram Shandy*, the *Public Ledger*, and William Dodd' (*ECF* 14[2001] 311–24), examines one use of the eighteenth-century journalistic convention of employing a fictional character in order to comment on contemporary events and the newspaper itself. The *Public Ledger*'s identity was partially constructed through the persona of Tristram Shandy, whose existence had been made public a few weeks earlier than the paper. Shortly after the first instalment of *Shandy* appeared, the *Ledger* began to print 'Original Letters of Tristram Shandy' and thus initiated 'an alternation between mock-serious and mock-enthusiastic reactions to Sterne' in its pages (p. 313). Bandry's most intriguing discovery is that these letters reveal features in common with episodes of the novel that had yet to be written, suggesting that Sterne tried to hold the attention of the same audience as the hacks who had capitalized on his first instalment.

Maureen Harkin, 'Goldsmith on Authorship in *The Vicar of Wakefield*' (*ECF* 14[2001] 325–44), subtly reconceives the novel in terms of its view of the author as would-be 'arbiter and to some extent regulator' of a vitiated public (p. 336). The opening 'Advertisement' of *The Vicar* places Goldsmith in 'the untenable position of arguing that the writer must supply the absent moral force of the clergy ... but that an attempt to do so is bound to provoke the same sneers, boredom, and indifference which ... greet the sermonizer' (p. 339). This 'untenable position' represents Goldsmith's pessimistic view both of his own authorial plight and the Vicar's, expressed in the risible incapacity of Primrose's written and spoken endeavours at reform to impact on the public (except when he has a captive audience of prisoners) and in his loss of authority at the end of the novel. Harkin concludes that what is, for Goldsmith, the manifest inefficacy of the author's desire to instruct and reclaim his public—a notably less buoyant analysis of the communicative potential of the literary sphere than Jürgen Habermas's—perhaps explains 'why [he] delayed publication of the novel and did not publish another' (p. 344). This is a sophisticated and welcome examination of a novel that—in spite of its renown, and perhaps due to its categorical slipperiness—has yet to gain the widespread critical interest it deserves.

Janet E. Aikins, 'Picturing "Samuel Richardson": Francis Hayman and the Intersections of Word and Image' (*ECF* 14[2001] 465–505), pays fruitful attention to a portrait of the Richardson family, completed while the novelist was engaged in writing, revising, and printing his first novel, and asks whether 'the act of producing the verbal text of *Pamela*' is 'in some way "rendered visible" in Hayman's painted image' (p. 465). The text is itself an inherently visual apparatus that might be said to belong to the same genre of the 'conversation piece' as Hayman's painting (p. 469). Aikins extends the group of Richardson's collaborators to include Hayman, who helped to produce twenty-nine illustrations for the text before the third and fourth volumes were completed: 'Hayman would have us see that there are no "purely" visual and verbal arts, a truth exposed in the iconotexts created by both Richardson and Hayman himself' (p. 505). Robert Folkenflik, 'Tobias Smollett, Anthony Walker, and the First Illustrated Serial Novel in English' (*ECF* 14[2001] 507–32), discusses the achievements of 'the most underrated British book illustrator of the eighteenth century' in order to demonstrate 'how attention to illustrations can help answer questions about the composition of this novel' (p. 507). W. B. Gerrard, 'Benevolent Vision: The Ideology of Sentimentality in Contemporary Illustrations of *A Sentimental Journey* and *The Man of Feeling*' (*ECF* 14[2001] 533–74), looks at illustrators of Sterne's and Mackenzie's fiction in terms of their 'depiction of ethical behaviour that is seemingly recommended by the texts' (p. 534). He finds the visual language of such portrayals 'communicates a type of non-verbal expression similar to what the written text describes': the longing for an inexpressible 'connection' (p. 537). Embodying the 'moral implication' of 'viewing', illustrations could be seen and said to bridge the gap between the author's words and the reader's experience, reinforcing the text's 'words of sentiment' but also expressing 'the physical "connection" lacking in language alone' (pp. 573, 537).

3. Poetry

The year 2002 was a good one for fakers, forgers, counterfeiters, and plagiarists, especially if they wrote poetry during the eighteenth century. Certain tricks and deceptions were thought so appealing that they even graced some of the year's literary criticism, purely for illustrative purposes of course. Jack Lynch opens his article on Samuel Johnson and forgery with some forged quotations from Samuel Johnson (*SEL* 43[2002] 601–18). At least Lynch admits his crime before the reader has time to stretch for an edition of Boswell's *Life*. Nick Groom's *The Forger's Shadow: How Forgery Changed the Course of Literature*, also provides the occasional quotation only to expose it as unreliably sourced, a forgery by another hand. It must be hoped that this year's authors have been as vigilant as Johnson in distinguishing deception from truth (or at least as convincing in their creativity).

Jack Lynch's article examines Johnson's attitudes to forgeries and misrepresentations, in particular those of Thomas Chatterton. His insightful and convincing argument is that the uncertainties of fakes posed an epistemological threat to the realm of moral philosophy, by encouraging a mentality of perpetual doubt. Given that empirical epistemology was based on the truth of experience, misrepresentations (which, it is suggested, Johnson equated with lies) could end up being used as the building blocks for further knowledge, forming dangerously unstable intellectual and moral constructions. Lynch focuses upon Johnson's negative attitude towards forgeries; Nick Groom takes a broader and more theoretical approach to the issue.

Groom interrogates the relationship between writing and authenticity, examining 'how forgeries interpret the rules of representation to create a hybrid realism' (p. 15). He is also keen to encourage the reader to read more Chatterton, although Chatterton is by no means the sole focus of the book. In fact, Groom's subject, and his manner of engaging with it, rather ward against too great a concentration on the life of the forger, deflecting attention on to the status of the forgery and the ghosts seen as incidental to the act of forging. He hopes that by releasing literary forgery from 'intentionalist and biographical criticism' (p. 126), it might be easier to see beyond the myths surrounding the lives of notable forgers. Looking at the case of William Henry Ireland, who forged Shakespeare plays as well as numerous other pieces attributed to various hands, Groom observes that the forger 'dissolves himself as an author-function just at the moment at which the Wordsworthian figure of "the Poet" was beginning to dominate Romantic models of authorship' (p. 252), and this self-effacement is taken in part as justification for such a reversal of critical approach. The profusion of fascinating anecdotes in the book would seem to indicate, however, that it is difficult to keep the author at arm's length from the work, even when this coincides precisely with the author's intention.

The first part of the book is concerned predominantly with establishing a theoretical basis upon which forgeries can be analysed, and their peculiar characteristics and challenges explored. Groom demonstrates a wide knowledge of critical approaches, illustrating his themes with an eclectic selection of commentaries. Beginning by distinguishing the semantic networks surrounding terms such as 'original', 'imitation', 'copy', 'forgery', and 'counterfeit', there seems a danger of the book being distracted by etymology, but Groom works his material well, and what digressions there are, throughout the book, tend to constitute interesting lines of enquiry in their own right. Looking primarily at the productions of James Macpherson, Chatterton, and Ireland, Groom then examines the implications of their works alongside the inspiration afforded by less literary (and more obviously criminal) forgers such as Thomas Griffiths Wainewright.

Unlike Lynch, Groom shies away from firm conclusions as to the perceived menace of forgery, preferring instead to regard reaction in terms of evolving social factors, particularly legal and economic. Given Groom's privileged position of analysing fakes long after they have been exposed as such, he can afford an aloofness not available to the sceptics and dupes he discusses. His decision not to use footnotes—'inappropriate for a book about authenticity' (p. 305)—might also be considered somewhat disingenuous. Despite these mild caveats, this is an exciting and thought-provoking book that is likely to draw forth further debate.

Chatterton, along with his myth, is also the subject of Margaret Russett and Joseph A. Dane's '"Everlasting to Posterytie": Chatterton's Spirited Youth' (*MLQ* 63[2002] 141–65). Like Groom, Russett and Joseph are concerned with Chatterton more to understand the effect he had upon literary culture than to examine his actual productions. They describe their article as being a combination of psychoanalytical and cultural-materialist approaches, and it is indeed a heavily theorized analysis. At points, there is a sense that Chatterton is being unfairly seized upon for Freudian reinterpretation: puns deriving from his Olde Englisshe, for instance, being stretched far into the realm of the subconscious to prove he had misogynistic fantasies. The psychoanalysis does eventually contribute to an interesting diagnosis, however. By creating his 'family romance', Chatterton, it is argued, disrupted the growing counter-myth of the founding fathers of the English tradition, inserting his own creations into history and thus rendering Shakespeare and Spenser 'illegitimate' as originating authors. Chatterton's fictions are regarded as provoking anxiety amongst eighteenth-century critics, but acting as an enabling force for Romantics intent on reinventing the past.

Dianne Dugaw, in her study of social satire and popular culture, *'Deep Play': John Gay and the Invention of Modernity*, applies her knowledge of popular song traditions and period dances to Gay's 'metaleptic' poems and ballad operas in order to examine 'the correspondence of forms of culture with a market-driven, class-shuffling society' (p. 20). Dugaw's Gay is something of a proto-Marxist, his 'mirroring oppositions' reflecting the 'dialectical premises by which social class has subsequently been understood in the Marxist tradition' (p. 21). In order to emphasize Gay's continuing relevance to Western culture, Dugaw, in the opening chapter, traces subsequent reinterpretations of *The Beggar's Opera* through Bertolt Brecht, Václav Havel, and Alan Ayckbourn, seeing each as a demonstration of the powerlessness of Macheaths and Pollys in the face of different centralized institutional structures. These are taken to be bourgeois values, the centralized state, and capitalism respectively. The problem with this (apart from question as to whether each of these qualifies as a 'centralized' system) is that Dugaw establishes a context in which Gay's satires are read backwards through the lens of these later adaptations. This may in some ways be an honest acceptance of the inevitable, the fact that new works modify our ideas of their precursors, but it does seem a little forced when in later chapters Dugaw interrupts her argument for another roll call of Brecht, Havel, and Ayckbourn, or overtly reverses their order of influence, stating, for instance, how Gay's version of the ballad *Three Ravens* produces 'an image reminiscent of Ayckbourn's Guy at BLM' (p. 258). Such passages are intrusive given that for most of the book Gay's sources are located in folk traditions and in contemporary customs and society. And this is clearly where Dugaw's strengths lie.

The chapters on popular culture and oral tradition, mumming, folk songs, and country dances tellingly demonstrate how Gay's satires would have had multiple resonances and associations for his contemporary audiences. Dugaw illustrates how a single ballad tune had often been assigned various different lyrics, with diverse political connotations, before Gay took it up, and she capably draws out the subtle connotations of his allusive technique. Her class awareness, if sometimes anachronistically formalized, also encourages a consideration of the implications of particular popular forms for particular sections of eighteenth-century society. Dugaw's analysis of the satiric bite of Gay's works, as it would have been felt by his contemporaries, is often astute and convincing; rather better than her analysis of Gay as a prophet of the evils of capitalist society.

John Richardson offers a response to one facet of Dugaw's book in his article on John Gay and slavery (*MLR* 98[2002] 15–25). Richardson contends that recent critics have been too generous to Gay, even to the extent of recasting his statements in the 'unironic language of twentieth-century activism' (p. 15). While Richardson excuses Dugaw the worst of these excesses, he does posit a less socially radical Gay than her bold satirist. Gay, it is asserted, knew when he invested in South Sea stock that the company was active in the slave trade, and his attitude to the trade was at best ambivalent. Examining Gay's references to 'slaves' throughout his operas and fables, Richardson concludes that his statements tend to legitimize slavery and that, as the theme is manifested in *Polly*, it is handled with unsophisticated humour that is in poor taste.

Perhaps more radical, then, is Robert Burns, subject of Liam McIlvanney's *Burns the Radical: Poetry and Politics in Late Eighteenth-Century Scotland*. To suggest that Burns adopted politically radical views would be unlikely to cause great consternation in contemporary critical circles. McIlvanney is of the opinion that Burns was a radical throughout his career, seeing his Presbyterian roots, education, and acquaintances as early exposing him to the traditions of radical thought with which his poetry engaged. He also makes the argument that it was the American Revolution, rather than the French, that made the larger and more lasting impression on Burns's politics. After firmly grounding Burns in the intellectual milieux of Scottish Presbyterianism and civic humanism, McIlvanney progresses to a receptive and insightful reading of the political poems, looking at bardic fraternity, the influence of the 'New Light', and anti-clericalism, before turning to examine the later poems composed in response to the events of the French Revolution. The final chapter focuses attention away from Burns himself, instead examining his influence on Ulster Scots poetry.

One of the strengths of McIlvanney's approach is that Burns the radical can be seen very much as a late eighteenth-century radical. Whereas Dugaw sometimes comes uncomfortably close to 'recruiting' Gay, McIlvanney's Burns speaks foremost to his contemporaries, and the lasting influence of his thought is left for the reader to ascertain. While the book is engaging and persuasive throughout, there is perhaps a slight tendency in the early chapters to ascribe ideas and attitudes to particular political or religious factions that were arguably more generally accepted. McIlvanney is also a little too uncritical of Bakhtin's notions of carnival in his chapter on Burn's bawdy poems, although even here he retains the self-restraint to recognize the dangers of overstating 'the political significance of this "alternative state"' (p. 185). Not in the end as radical as its subject, this book should nevertheless be regarded as a useful contribution to Burns studies.

A good accompaniment to Burns was also published in 2002. MacLachlan, ed., *Before Burns : Eighteenth-Century Scottish Poetry*, provides a selection of verse intended to offer a representative sample of poetic voices. In practice, Allan Ramsay and Robert Fergusson dominate the book as might be expected, occupying well over two-thirds of its pages, but room is found nevertheless for poems by twenty-two other authors. MacLachlan's introduction stresses the sense of tradition and community that the featured poets both followed and formed, and tries to direct the reader away from regarding them merely as harbingers of Burns (although the title of the book rather gives the game away). The poets are characterized as modestly writing 'for personal and sometime communal and national expression, not ... for experiment and revolution', and MacLachlan asserts that 'craftsmanship is more evident than change' (p. xvi). Yet there is no lack of robustness in the selections, and Samuel Johnson is not spared the inclusion of Fergusson's Scotch counterblast.

The recent growth of interest in eighteenth-century notions of patriotism was further attested in 2002 by Dustin Griffin's *Patriotism and Poetry in Eighteenth-Century Britain*, a study of various poets, mostly from the middle part of the century. Complaining that, for too long, British poets after Pope have been considered inward-looking and too insecure for major public poetry, Griffin looks for, and finds, writers who 'both professed their love and admiration for their native land, and offered, at least implicitly, to provide some public *service* to the nation' (p. 5). In doing so, he rather gives the lie to Barbara M. Benedict's confident statement in her summary of the year's output (*SEL* 43[2002] 619–74) that 'The separation between the public and private spheres in the long eighteenth century is dead. This is a truth universally acknowledged in Restoration and eighteenth-century studies this year' (p. 619), which in any case sounded rather unlikely, if not reductive.

Situating 'patriotism' within both its conventional sense and its slippery eighteenth-century political discourse, Griffin traces the poetic forms that patriotism could, and did, take. He acknowledges the damage done to genres such as the panegyrical ode by satirical mock-panegyrics, and the difficulties presented to those who would lay claim to the title of patriot after characters such as Gulliver, and various factious politicians, had also made such claims, yet goes on to observe how patriotism was nevertheless adapted and transformed by many of the major poets of the century. Griffin inverts the traditional observations of increasing poetic self-consciousness, arguing that 'it was precisely *because* poets feared that they were losing a public function that they dared to imagine that a poet might serve his nation as a patriot' (p. 71).

Griffin begins his series of individual studies, uncontroversially, with James Thomson. Thomson is seen as redefining the concept of Britain's role in the world through a 'moralized vision of trade' (p. 82) while simultaneously growing uneasy that his model, and his role as poet, were threatened by the evolving political and social structure of the country. Mark Akenside is regarded as significant due to his claims for the political function of poetry, and his odes, in particular, are used to counter the presumption that the genre was essentially 'a meditative-rhapsodical exercise in solipsism' (p. 105). William Collins is considered slightly differently, as an explorer and instigator of the passions that underlie patriotic rhetoric. While it is a good assessment, it is at this point that Griffin's thesis begins to look a little vulnerable, as the patriotic model requires a bit of stretching to incorporate both Collins and then Thomas Gray. We are reminded that Gray was acutely interested in the politics of his day, but Griffin, despite ending on a positive hint from his *Correspondence*, is forced to concede that Gray's outlook for the public poet is not always especially optimistic. John Dyer's positive vision of a socially and economically harmonious Britain puts Griffin back on firmer ground. Dyer's misgivings about both his vision and his role as poet are also nicely observed. Oliver Goldsmith is seen as an ambivalent figure, encouraging an idea of poetry as socially useful while abdicating the role himself. Christopher Smart and William Cowper receive an interesting comparison, which emphasizes the differences in patriotic confidence between two overtly Christian patriots. Smart is regarded, quite reasonably, as more confident than even Akenside in his belief that the poet can serve the state. The book concludes with a chapter on Anne Yearsley, examining the manner in which women could, and were permitted to, raise a poetic voice to address public matters.

Griffin's book ends up as more of a survey than the concentrated thesis it initially suggests, and it is at least as much concerned with the poet's sense of his role as with his patriotism, but this should not be seen as detracting from its value. Griffin's conclusions are realistic. He denies, for instance, that there are distinct trends that can be perceived during the century. The book confirms his suspicion that many poets conceived a greater public role for themselves than has often been assumed, without ignoring the fact that most all of the major writers had misgivings about this role to a lesser or greater extent. This sense of fairness and balance is creditable in a work that sets out intending to shift such a balance.

Patriotism and public poetry, of a kind, also forms the subject of Barbara Olive's article 'A Puritan Subject's Panegyrics to Queen Anne' (*SEL* 43[2002] 475–99). Olive examines the poems of Mary, Lady Chudleigh. Like Yearsley, Chudleigh is revealed as a woman not afraid to engage with the national affairs of her age. Olive argues that, by repeatedly aligning Anne with the policies of William III, Chudleigh's panegyrics were intended to encourage the queen to persist with the former monarch's approach to the toleration of dissenters.

A new biography of Pope entered the market during 2002. Netta Murray Goldsmith's *Alexander Pope: The Evolution of a Poet* covers the entirety of Pope's life in under 300 pages, which may make it more appealing to undergraduates than Maynard Mack's very comprehensive standard. In order to justify the undertaking, Goldsmith adopts what she describes as a 'relatively new approach to literary biography ... a psychobiography' (p. xii). Unfortunately, the book's innovation is also its weakness. Goldsmith utilizes recent research into human creativity, especially research by the psychologist Mihalyi Csikszentmihalyi, to analyse Pope's genius, and explain how he became so successful in his own lifetime. This involves an exploration of the body of knowledge an individual must master before he can contribute to it, the institutions and judges to whom that contribution must appeal, and the innovations that the individual can offer to the field.

In practice, Goldsmith's book does not follow this prescription exactly. In fact, she progresses through Pope's life in a lively and engaging manner, sketching his character and describing his relationships with his contemporaries in a fairly conventional manner. Particular emphasis is given to Pope's Roman Catholicism and its impact on his upbringing and carefully managed image. Goldsmith also ties the poet's career to the fluctuating fortunes of Jacobitism, suggesting that he was sympathetic to the Jacobite cause without necessarily being especially active in his support. The various periods and poses of Pope's life are covered briskly but clearly, and the book offers an entertaining digest of his career and times. It is when the subject of Pope's 'creativity' intrudes that the narrative falters.

First, for all her appeals to modern science, Goldsmith adopts a curiously Romantic attitude to the nature of genius. It seems that one either is, or is not, a genius; there is no sense of a scale of achievement or of questionable cases. Pope clearly *is* a genius. He is witnessed 'in the throes of creation' (p. 10); he is frequently compared to Keats; it is assumed that he would have concurred with a particularly effusive and precious pronouncement by Harold Pinter about the artist feeling banished from himself while not writing (p. 11). Secondly, Goldsmith mostly uses her science to make trite generalizations about how geniuses are created, and how they behave. She makes a sally into genetics to explain how Pope's 'special aptitude almost certainly had a genetic origin' (p. 26); we are informed that 'it has been estimated that three-quarters of the creative individuals who go on to achieve great things experience some kinds of extreme stress in their early family life', so in actual fact the young Pope's misfortunes were 'no bad thing for Pope' (p. 46); Pope's arrogance is a trait often found in 'supremely gifted individuals—in Mozart for instance' (p. 108). Throughout the book, one gets the sense that Pope is being scrutinized for features and patterns of behaviour that correspond with Goldsmith's 'scientific' definition of genius; he must continually be seen to 'fit a recent definition of a prodigy' (p. 39).

Andrew Varney concentrates on Pope's ability to fashion his own public image in his article 'A "Tender Correspondence": Pope and *The Spectator*' (*CS* 14[2002] 42–50). He Contrasts Pope's 1710 epistle to Martha Blount (written to accompany his gift of *The Works of Voiture*) with Steele's *Spectator* 11, containing the story of Yarico and Inkle, which concerns a European selling his Native American lover into slavery for profit. Varney contends (not unreasonably) that Pope's epistle was ultimately intended for publication, and was therefore somewhat duplicitous, conceived as belonging to the public and private realms simultaneously. By linking the 'correspondence' of trade with personal correspondence, Varney reveals the greater subtlety of Pope's duplicity against that of Inkle's, seeing the former as quietly echoing 'the nation's aspiration to move from the asperities of war to a new international harmony' (p. 50). While this is an acceptable reading, the two types of 'correspondence' are linked tenuously at best, and the article is too brief to make its own correspondence of texts meaningful.

A much more significant contribution to Pope studies is provided by Tita Chico's study of *The Rape of the Lock* and *Epistle to a Lady* (*ECLife* 26[2002] 1–23). Chico contrasts Belinda's cosmetic art and Pope's poetic *ekphrasis*, seeing Pope's descriptive power as in rivalry with feminine cosmetics. Chico persuasively argues that Pope is deliberately unforthcoming in the enumeration of his heroine's physical qualities, valuing a 'reader's sense' over a 'gazer's eye' (p. 16) and ultimately denying legitimacy to cosmetic beauty. Pope is demonstrated to use ekphrasis while simultaneously deconstructing it, in order to exercise the moral superiority of the text over the image. Despite this, Chico sees the broader eighteenth-century debate about cosmetics as recognizing their potential to empower women.

Pope's characteristic heroic couplet receives attention from Richard Bradford in his *Augustan Measures: Restoration and Eighteenth-Century Writings on Prosody and Metre*. Bradford admits that prosody, as a subject in its own right, 'enjoys a status somewhere between the arcane and the eccentric' (p. 224), but happily this has not stopped him from producing a surprisingly fascinating and readable book about the subject. Bradford takes issue with earlier studies such as Paul Fussell's *Theory of Prosody in Eighteenth-Century England*, arguing that too much attention has been paid to the wrong aspects of prosody in the period, particularly 'syllabism'. Bradford refocuses attention on theories of rhyme and line integrity, and addresses eighteenth-century concerns as to what precisely differentiated poetry from poetical prose. His study is especially concerned with theoretical responses to Milton's blank verse as contrasted to the paradigmatic rhyming couplet of Dryden and Pope. Throughout the book, Bradford is bracingly frank in his opinions regarding twentieth-century critics and eighteenth-century theorists alike, criticizing his precursors for falsifying or adjusting empirical evidence (p. 51), so it is a relief that his arguments and demonstrations are as convincing as they are.

If there is a hero in this book it is Thomas Sheridan, the elocutionist, whose *Lectures on the Art of Reading* is highly commended for its recognition of the abstract metrical pause. This pause is seen to fix the poetic line as a discrete unit, and it helps justify Milton's use of enjambment. Sheridan's theories are contrasted with the orthodox 'prescriptive' criticism of Bysshe and Kames, seen as a rationalization of the balanced iambic lines of the closed couplet. Being derived from such a rationalisation, this criticism struggles to comprehend the particular characteristics and requirements of blank verse. Sheridan is also differentiated from other elocutionists such as Rice and Walker, who are said to regard the verse line as merely a printing convention, with the rhythmic phrase being interlineal and syntactically defined. When Bradford goes on to analyse Milton's verses, the superiority of Sheridan's prosodic theory becomes evident from the readings afforded by the various approaches. Finally, eighteenth-century practitioners of blank verse such as Thomson and Cowper are examined to demonstrate how prosodic theories influenced actual practice. Bradford is perhaps a little over-insistent about surprising enjambments being the measure of good poetry, and more could have been said about the effects of the syntactical ambiguities that such enjambments entail, but this is nevertheless an excellent study of a neglected aspect of eighteenth-century poetics.

Carson Bergstrom's *The Rise of New Science: Epistemological, Linguistic, and Ethical Ideals and the Lyric Genre in the Eighteenth Century* has a wordy title and an unusual format. Perhaps intending to supplant the need for future reviews, it opens with one of its own, written by Gerald Hammond, praising the work as a 'genuine contribution to the history of ideas' (p. xiii). The device seems almost like a challenge: read the book and try to prove otherwise. Frustratingly, on doing so, one is likely to concur with Hammond's opinion. Bergstrom begins by attacking the Romantic critical paradigms that have, he argues, led to the importance of the lyric to eighteenth-century poetry being overlooked. By defining the lyric according to the terms of Romantic aesthetics, as being a medium for subjective expression, critics have failed to appreciate not only its centrality to the eighteenth century, but also the possibility of it being a 'scientific' form. Bergstrom also re-emphasizes the fact that eighteenth-century poets did not regard the relationship between poetry and science as antipathetic.

Bergstrom's principal contention is that the lyric (including the ode) was seen as an apt genre for the expression of the scientific values that underpinned eighteenth-century attitudes to knowledge. Adopting Raymond Williams's notions of hegemony, Bergstrom establishes the hold that empirical and experimental modes of thinking had on critics and their criticisms of poetry. He argues that this scientific hegemony had an influence on 'identity, concepts of vocation, attitudes to knowledge, use of language, choice of genre' (p. 44). The impact of scientific conceptions of language is observed to be particularly strong. Bergstrom regards the theories of Wilkins, Sprat, and Locke as embodying the ideals of the new science, and constituting a challenge to traditional notions of poetics. Their ideal of linguistic clarity, of using words as directly correspondent to things in an attempt to 'bring *Knowledge* back to our very senses' (p. 72), is seen to lead to a poetry of visualizable phenomena, and to characteristic critical 'rules' as to what is, and what is not, acceptable in verse. Bergstrom interprets certain signs of poetic insecurity as a recognition that poetry needed to adapt to the requirements of the new science, lest the poet lose his traditional role 'as the mediating voice in man's relations with nature and God' (p. 171). James Thomson, in particular, is seen as alert to this new rivalry between science and poetry. Bergstrom's assertions are well supported by quotations from a very wide range of eighteenth-century critics and theorists, and his work displays admirable scholarship. One negative aspect of his approach is that the focus on critical sources is maintained at the expense of practical examples, although when Bergstrom does direct attention towards textual analysis his observations are acute and persuasive. My only other qualm would be that the eighteenth century is regarded as a slightly monolithic entity; more attention to dialectics, and the subtle evolution of attitudes over the period, might have resulted in a more complex consideration of the theme.

Two poets received the honour of being 'reconsidered' in 2002. Robert Dix attempted to resuscitate the reputation of John Gilbert Cooper (*AgeJ* 13[2002] 255–81); and Sandro Jung chose to examine William Shenstone's impact on his contemporaries (*BSEAA* 54[2002] 187–98). Dix's argument for Gilbert Cooper centres on the poet's metrical innovations and his qualities as a translator from French. His reinterpretation of Jean-Baptiste-Louis Gresset's *Ver-Vert* is singled out for praise. Unfortunately, Dix does not allow himself enough space to launch a truly convincing campaign, although he does just enough to suggest that further studies may prove worthwhile. Jung's Shenstone is a sycophantic critic of verses written by his patrons, an encourager and patron himself of promising poets further down the social spectrum, and a man who attempted to construct for himself the persona of a hermit while at the same time occupying the centre of the Birmingham literary scene. The essay does not consider Shenstone's poetry at all, but does offer him as an interesting alternative model of the eighteenth-century patron.

Patronage was also on the mind of Mary Waldron, whose study of Ann Yearsley's later friends provides an explanatory narrative of her relationships (*AgeJ* 13[2002] 283–335). The events and correspondence surveyed provide ample support for Waldron's thesis that Yearsley's angry reaction to Hannah More's patronage (in both senses of the word) had at least as much to do with her personality and aspirations than with any latent class consciousness assigned to her by recent critics.

Samuel Johnson's attitudes and poetry were the focus of two articles in 2002. Nicholas Hudson examined Johnson's attitude to London's urban sprawl, and concluded that he was quite accepting of the 'chaotic spontaneity of the city's postfire evolution' (*SEL* 43[2002] 577–600). Hudson argues that London's largely unplanned expansion during the eighteenth century better reflected the empirical demands of the age, in contrast to the rationalism of seventeenth-century town planners. Hudson also makes the point that Johnson's views about urban environments are 'pre-modern', as he did not assume cities to mould human personality into a distinctively urban mindset. Freya Johnston looks at Johnson's attitude to life and death in her study of his poem 'On the Death of Dr. Robert Levet' (*MLR* 98[2002] 26–35). Johnston claims that the great lexicographer had Watts's poetics in mind when composing the piece, and that, by reflecting on the death of the relatively undistinguished Dr Levet, Johnson could combat his own fears of mortality.

Thomas Gray was afforded good service by Christopher Decker, who compiled and published the records of his library borrowings from Cambridge colleges (*Library* 7th ser. 2[2002] 163–93). Marcus Walsh's similar undertaking for

Christopher Smart (*Library* 6th ser. 12[1990] 34–49) has proved a helpful reference point for scholars, and Decker's article will doubtless prove similarly useful. Gray's *Elegy* received attention from Scott Hess, who re-examined the issue of authorial identity with reference to the expansion of print culture (*AgeJ* 13[2002] 207–37). Hess characterizes Gray as 'unable to establish his authority in terms of a cultural elite and unwilling to appeal to a general public ... writing without a clear sense of audience, public role, or poetic identity'. In this thought-provoking essay, Hess highlights the challenge posed to received ideas of the poet's role by the increasing anonymity of a print audience, seeing the emergence of authorial self-representation as a result.

Language is the focus of Dennis Costa's study of Christopher Smart's *Jubilate Agno* (*EIC* 52[2002] 295–313). In a densely argued essay, Costa summarizes Smart's beliefs about the power of 'right language', and connects these to his metaphysical concepts regarding spiritual forces and processes.

Finally, something completely different, Nicholas D. Smith exercised his scholarship in pursuit of the piscatory (*SP* 99[2002] 432–50). Noting that the volume of eighteenth-century criticism devoted to the piscatory eclogue is of 'modest proportions', Smith sets out to explore the legacy of Jacopo Sannazaro's *Eclogae Piscatoriae* [1528] and its importance to the eighteenth-century pastoral debate. Perhaps surprisingly, he finds an interesting complex of readings and misreadings that reflect on assumptions of what the pastoral should be, and what it should do. Smith's somewhat offbeat study, perhaps paradoxically, typified a year of diverse enquiries and methodologies: 2002 was a year in which a wide variety of apparently authentic, and seemingly original, research was published. Reassuringly, none of the books or articles has yet been exposed as a forgery.

4. Drama

The first part of this section discusses publications from 2001. Nadini Bhattacharya, 'Family Jewels: George Colman's Inkle and Yarico and Connoisseurship' (*ECS* 34[2001] 207–26), considers the play in the context of eighteenth-century racial theory and fascination with antiquity. Both areas involve theatricality as well as marketability, particularly of images. Colman's play reveals the commodification of people, especially women, raising questions about eighteenth-century attitudes about taste, value, and commerce. Yarico functions as a threatening commodity, the racial and sexual 'other' that excites male anxieties, guilt, and power in both familial and commercial venues. In 'James Cobb, Colonial Cacophony, and the Enlightenment' (*SEL* 41:iii[2001] 583–603), Bhattacharya looks at Cobb's plays about 'cross-cultural encounters' as examples of the 'Enlightenment colonial imagination at work on fictions of domestic and colonial reform' (p. 583). An officeholder in the East India Company, Cobb recognized that Britain understood its history through its relations with colonial subjects, and, according to Bhattacharya, Cobb's plays depict two scenarios for conducting British national identity: the first involves women's role as saviour in the romance and marriage myth; the second involves racial others in a public British male identity based on homosociality and aggression. The discourses of slavery and gender are present in the plays and function to destabilize national identity as they revolve around sexual and commodity relations.

Catherine Burroughs, 'British Women Playwrights and the Staging of Female Sexual Initiation: Sophia Lee's *The Chapter of Accidents* (1780)' (*RoN* 23 [August 2001], accessed 23 June 2003 <http://users.ox.ac.uk/~scat0385/23burroughs.html>), draws upon the eighteenth-century erotica of John Cleland's *Memoirs of a Woman of Pleasure* (1749) as a context for examining Lee's play. Burroughs argues that Lee introduces pornographic patterns in the play in order to confront the topic of heterosexual intercourse and sexual fantasies of late eighteenth-century culture. Private theatricals were, claims Burroughs, particularly good sites for the exploration of sexual topics and 'naughtiness', but in social theatres the enactment of sexual topics required the eroticization of defloration to be expressed in more oblique dramaturgy that applies pornography to critique enlightenment ideas. In Burroughs's reading of Lee's play, it makes a feminist statement that asks men and women to share in the consequences of pre-marital sex.

Frank Donoghue, 'Avoiding the "Cooler Tribunal of the Study": Richard Brinsley Sheridan's Writer's Block and Late Eighteenth-Century Print Culture' (*ELH* 68:iv[2001] 831–56), argues that Sheridan's suspicions about the expansion of the reading trade during the eighteenth century, his attitudes towards print culture, and his distrust of the commercial circulation of writing were significant factors in his decision to change careers at the age of 28. Because Sheridan viewed print as a dehumanizing medium he idealized the theatre as a place where unmediated communication between author and audience was possible. He had come to recognize that he could exert considerable influence over the composition of his plays but little over their reception. He came to realize that publication of his plays meant that they were arrested from a living, ongoing process by codification. When the page trumped the stage for drama, Sheridan turned to the oratorical arena of parliament, where he could continue to achieve a theatrical relationship with his audience in an anti-textual environment. Sheridan's parliamentary speeches in the House of Commons were quite moving and performative, for parliamentary reporting was so inchoate that his words and emotions were not at risk for being codified in textual finality.

Robert G. Dryden, 'John Gay's Polly: Unmasking Pirates and Fortune Hunters in the West Indies' (*ECS* 34:iv[2001] 539–57), argues that Gay's banned opera *Polly* [1728] questions 'the presence, motivations, and destructive potential of the English merchant in the colonial setting' because Gay represents and condemns the English merchant as a kind of pirate (p. 539). According to Dryden, *Polly* indicts England's violent acts of colonial appropriation as acts of piracy. Gay's colonial setting reveals how strictly economic the marriage market actually was in the early eighteenth century, how social alliances were rooted in capitalism. Although Gay disturbs and complicates racial and class codes of the colonial setting with his deployment of the noble savage trope, that disruption is silenced at the end of the opera with Morano's death. Morano, the pirate disguised in black face, represents the ambiguous and hybrid identities of the new colonial frontier, an ambiguity that the colonial establishment sought to contain and eliminate.

Andrew Elfenbein, 'Lesbian Aestheticism on the Eighteenth-Century Stage' (*ECLife* 25:i[2001] 1–16), maintains that the lesbian subject position enabled dramatic writers to examine and experiment with forms of agency available to non-heterosexual women, a representation not possible in the novel. His analysis includes Hannah Cowley's *The Town Before You* [1795], Henry Seymour Conway's *False Appearances* [1789], and Mary Berry's *Fashionable Friends* [1802], three comedies of manners that feature what Elfenbein calls the 'lesbian aesthete,' the aristocratic woman of the world whose rebellion against bourgeois norms made her an object of fascination for the eighteenth-century stage (p. 2). In Cowley's play, the heroine is Lady Horatia Horton, a sculptor. Conway's private theatrical features a countess who is an enthusiast for art. Mrs Lovell and Lady Selina Vapour of Berry's play enact a new and different kind of friendship, one that successfully unmasks the destruction wrought by the cult of sentiment. These female representations are reinventions of the aristocratic woman as a respectable lover of art, an alternative to the 'natural' bourgeois normative female.

Keven J. Gardner, 'George Farquhar's *The Recruiting Officer*: Warfare, Conscription, and the Disarming of Anxiety' (*ECLife* 25:iii[2001] 43–61), explains the success of Farquhar's 1706 patriotic comedy in terms of its use of new military technologies, its ironic treatment of British military history, and its promotion of the war effort. The play represents the democratizing shift occurring as swords gave way to guns, their metaphoric connection to a culture that was shifting from aristocracy to bourgeois. New social relations are figured in military metaphors, with recruitment as the play's most important motif. Recruitment is engendered as seduction and enlistment as attractive, for the language of the boudoir is applied to men. Recruitment is imbued with sexual allure, and drill and warfare are naturalized as sex. Therefore, recruitment and conscription function as essential elements in the newly developing social structure of England as individual identity is replaced with regimental identity.

Nicholas Hudson, 'Britons Never Will Be Slaves: National Myth, Conservatism, and the Beginnings of British Antislavery' (*ECS* 34:iv[2001] 559–76), considers Thomas Southerne's *Oroonoko* [1759] and its three rewritings [1759–60] in the anti-slavery debate and argues that they utilize emotional identifications between Britons and Africans. Hudson situates his analysis in the context of slavery and anti-slavery discourses of the period to demonstrate the 'chosen' people posture adopted by Britons that contributed to a nationalist ideology therefore threatened by materialism and commercialism, including the slave trade.

Erith Jaffe-Berg, 'Language, Food and the Hierarchy of Values in the *commedia dell'arte* Performance from the Renaissance to the Eighteenth Century' (*European Studies Journal* 18:i[2001] 115–30), traces the influence of the *commedia dell'arte*'s performing body, the Zanni and Pantalone, on Italian dramatist Carlo Goldoni, and his appropriation of language and food in his Enlightenment plays. Jaffe-Berg's examination of various stagings of speaking and eating demonstrates how eating culture and interiorized scenes were directed to the self-making bourgeois class. These dramas significantly influenced British reworkings of the trope for its staging of new social orders, as well as specific playwrights, notably Elizabeth Griffith.

Anne Kelley, '"In Search of Truths Sublime": Reason and the Body in the Writings of Catharine Trotter' (*WW* 8:ii[2001] 237–52), examines Delarivier Manley's sustained attack on playwright Trotter as a woman of prudery and hypocrisy. Kelley's analysis includes Trotter's correspondence, especially letters written to Thomas Burnet, to her niece Anne Hepburn, and to her husband Patrick

Cockburn before their marriage. Trotter's letters reveal that the emotional and intellectual aspects of woman were inextricably linked in what she considers a balanced life. According to Kelley, Trotter's writings demonstrate her life-long determination to promote the concept of intellectual equality for women and as well as seemingly contradictory female roles of the female intellectual and the private family woman, comfortably integrated, mutually dependent.

Paulina Kewes, "'[A] play, which I presume to call original": Appropriation, Creative Genius, and Eighteenth-Century Playwriting' (*SLI* 34:i[2001] 17–47), looks at the ways in which the emergence of the modern concept of authorship along with the ideal of 'truly original' composition during the eighteenth century diminished the search for new dramatic form and increased the value of old plays, particularly those of Shakespeare. Prompted by the Licensing Act of 1737, the period's theatrical milieu was characterized by a strong demand for script revision and adaptation. Patent House companies relied heavily on revivals, and textual editors and scholars devoted their efforts to Shakespeare. The stage and the page were concerned with profits, and it became generally accepted that earlier drama really could not be improved. Kewes demonstrates the decline in new drama during the eighteenth century by examining the typography of contemporary theatrical playbills and contemporary title pages.

Jayne Lewis, 'The Type of a Kind; or, The Lives of Dryden' (*ECLife* 25:ii[2001] 3–18), argues that it was not until the nineteenth century that Dryden was discovered to have portrayed contradictions, his tragic heroes straddling incompatible domains of value and meaning. Two of Dryden's important nineteenth-century readers were historical novelist Walter Scott and historian T.B. Macaulay, who appropriated and fashioned Dryden to serve symbolic ends for their own projects. Lewis points out the historical distancing needed to realize fully the multiple and even incompatible writers and thinkers Dryden could embody.

Judith Milhous and R.T.C. Hume, 'The Tailor's Shop at the Pantheon Opera, 1790–1792' (*Costume* 35:i[2001] 24–46), recounts evidence from the Bedford Opera Papers, the output of the costume shop, and lists of dressers at the Pantheon on Oxford Street during two seasons at the end of the eighteenth century. Milhous and Hume reconstruct the process of making, deploying, and caring for costumes at the Pantheon under the company tailor Thomas Luppino. According to Milhous and Hume, 'no other comparable range of evidence about the production of costumes exists for any other English theatre of the eighteenth century' (p. 25). Their reconstruction reveals that costuming activities entailed complex interactions among theatrical values, fashion, and star status and that the opera's costumes were elaborate but conceived in terms of production design and adaptation.

Yvonne Noble, 'Light Writing from a Dark Winter: The Scriblerian *Annua Mirabilis*' (*ECLife* 25:ii[2001] 19–31), focuses on the successful production of Richard Steele's *The Conscious Lovers* [1722–3], in which Steele played one of the comic servants, Tom, in a parodic role that denigrated the castrati, whom he deplored. The burlesque of the play created huge, appreciative crowds as well as financial success. Noble examines Steele's play in light of the anonymous comical essay *Annus Mirabilis* and its spin-off *An Epistle To Dr. W—d—d from a Prude*.

Gillian Russell, '"Keeping Place": Servants, Theater and Sociability in Mid-Eighteenth-Century Britain' (*The Eighteenth Century* 42:i[2001] 21–42), looks at the controversy during the 1750s and 1760s surrounding James Townley's farce

High Life Below Stairs [1759] 'to explore the interactions between the idea of the public represented by and in the British theatre of this period and [Habermas's] republic of letters; and to explore the figure of the servant as both historical actor and a focus for anxieties about social difference' (p. 22). In asserting that theatre had an interventionist role in the shaping of public opinion, Russell examines two preoccupations of eighteenth-century society reflected in the play: the reliability of signs, clothing, manners, gestures, and race, as indicators of social rank, and the meaning of rank itself in a culture that was undergoing class destabilization. Demonstrating how performative and theatrical man–servant relations were, Russell analyses the mirror or doubling function of the servant–master relationship as well as the actor's status as 'servant' to the public.

Angela J. Smallwood, 'Introduction to Vol. 6 of *Eighteenth-Century Women Playwrights: Elizabeth Inchbald*' (*British Women Playwrights around 1800* [15 August 2001], accessed 21 July 2003 <http://www-sul.stanford.edu/mirrors/romnet/wp1800/essays/smallwood_introPC.html>) situates Inchbald in an eighteenth-century theatrical milieu but asserts that she achieved a professional style and status not attained by female playwrights who came before her. Smallwood states that her aim in this introductory essay is to free Inchbald's plays from novel-centred criticism in order to situate them in the context of the theatrical culture of the late Georgian stage. It is in this context that she briefly glosses the comedies in the volume: *The Widow's Vow*, *Such Things Are*, *The Child of Nature*, *Next Door Neighbours*, *Wives As They Were and Maids As They Are*. At the heart of all five plays is the conflation of femininity and performance, and Smallwood points out how their female protagonists devise abnormal situations that unmask the illusions associated with the proper performance of femininity.

J. Douglas Canfield, gen. ed., *The Broadview Anthology of Restoration and Early Eighteenth-Century Drama*, offers forty-one plays from 1660 to 1737 from various playwrights, each edited and annotated by respected scholars in the field. In some cases, the editions in this volume are the only modern scholarly editions of the plays. The volume is divided into sub-genres: heroic romance, political tragedy, personal tragedy, tragicomic romance, social comedy, subversive comedy, corrective satire, Menippean satire, and laughing comedy. Students are the primary audience for the anthology, and so its concern is with readability rather than staging or performance. The plays have been modernized, with standardized spelling and punctuation, and information is readily available for students at the foot of the page. At the end of the anthology, students will find a helpful glossary of general terms germane to the period's drama.

The volume's general introduction describes political and theatrical contexts for the period. It delineates theory for the period's shift from aristocratic to bourgeois ethos and an emergent new decorum that blurred generic distinctions between comedy and tragedy. The introduction illustrates changes in the theatre itself, including stage designs and innovations, the inclusion of actresses onstage, and the multi-class audiences. Each play is introduced with brief staging and textual history, political contexts, and a biography of the playwright.

Plays that are not readily available in other editions include John Tatham's *The Rump; or, The Mirror of the Late Times* [1660], edited by Judith Bailey Slagle; Sir Robert Howard's *The Committee* [1662], edited by Cheryl L. Nixon; Roger Boyle's *The History of Henry the Fifth* [1664], edited by Stephan P. Flores; John Lacy's *The*

Old Troop; or, Monsieur Raggou [1664], edited by Maja-Lisa von Sneidern; Thomas Durfey's *A Fond Husband; or, The Plotting Sisters* [1677], edited by Heidi Hunter and Tony Jarrells; John Banks's *The Unhappy Favorite; or, The Earl of Essex* [1681], edited by J. Douglas Canfield; Thomas Southerne's *Sir Anthony Love; or, The Two Sosias* [1690], edited by Kristina Straub; Catharine Trotter's *Love at a Loss; or, Most Votes Carry It* [1700], edited by Roxanne M. Kent-Drury; and Delarivier Manley's *Lusius, the First Christian King of Britain* [1717], edited by Melinda A. Rabb.

Melinda C. Finberg, ed. *Eighteenth-Century Women Dramatists*, includes Mary Pix's *The Innocent Mistress* [1697], Susanna Centlivre's *The Busy Body* [1709], Elizabeth Griffith's *The Times* [1773], and Hannah Cowley's *The Belle's Stratagem* [1780]. In the general introduction, Finberg asserts that these women playwrights and their drama played an important role in eighteenth-century theatre history even though they were not easily accepted in their time. The introduction includes brief biographies of the playwrights and discussions of the characters and plots of their plays, and comments on the staging of the plays. According to the 'Note on the Texts', Finberg relied on the first authorized published editions with modernized and standardized spelling and punctuation. In a segment entitled 'The Restoration and Eighteenth-Century Stages' Finberg traces the evolution of the tripartite Restoration theatre to the bipartite nineteenth-century playhouse. The select bibliography is annotated, and includes studies generally about theatre and specifically about each of the four playwrights in the volume. 'A Chronology of Restoration and Eighteenth-Century Plays By Women' lists first performance dates for plays as well as descriptions of their characters. Both the explanatory notes and the glossary at the end of the volume are extensive and helpful for student readers.

The six-volume *Eighteenth-Century Women Playwrights* (gen. ed. Derek Hughes) includes modernized and annotated editions of drama by eight women playwrights: Delarivier Manley, Eliza Haywood, Mary Pix, Catharine Trotter, Susanna Centlivre, Elizabeth Griffith, Hannah Cowley, and Elizabeth Inchbald, who, according to the general introduction in volume 1, are among the leading eighteenth-century playwrights who have not received critical attention. The introduction addresses some of the large cultural shifts during the long eighteenth century, and the career and contribution of Aphra Behn. Each volume includes an introduction specific to its playwrights and plays, brief biographies, and contextual suggestions for reading the plays. Each volume also includes a chronology of playwrights' careers and lists of performers in their plays. Readers will also find plot and production information before each play and substantive notes and a select bibliography at the end of each volume.

Volume 1 includes Delarivier Manley's *The Lost Lover* [1696] and *The Royal Mischief* [1696], edited by Margarete Rubik; Eliza's Haywood's *The Fair Captive* [1721] and *A Wife to be Lett* [1724], edited by Eva Mueller-Zettelmann. Volume 2 includes Mary Pix's *The Deceiver Deceived* [1698] and *Queen Catharine* [1698] and Catharine Trotter's *Love at a Loss* [1701] and *The Revolution of Sweden* [1706], all edited by Anne Kelley. Volume 3 includes four plays by Susanna Centlivre, edited by Jacqueline Pearson: *The Basset-Table* [1705], *The Busie Body* [1709], *The Wonder: a Woman Keeps a Secret* [1714], and *A Bold Stroke for a Wife* [1718]. Betty Rizzo edits four plays by Elizabeth Griffith in Volume 4: *The Platonic Wife* [1765], *The Double Mistake* [1766], *The School for Rakes* [1769], and *A Wife in the*

Right [1772]. Four plays by Hannah Cowley, edited by Antje Blank, constitute Volume 5: *The Runaway* [1776], *The Belle's Stratagem* [1780], *A Bold Stroke for a Husband* [1783], and *The Town Before You* [1794]. Volume 6 includes five plays by Elizabeth Inchbald, edited by Angela J. Smallwood: *The Widow's Vow* [1786], *Such Things Are* [1787], *The Child of Nature* [1788], *Next Door Neighbours* [1791], and *Wives As They Were, and Maids As They Are* [1797].

Bridget Orr, *Empire on the English Stage 1660–1714*, examines Restoration dramas as reformatory projects to strengthen national identity. Drama, Orr argues, is a genre particularly useful in negotiating issues of empire. In the heroic plays of the 1690s and 1700s, for example, women dramatists figure enslavement of women in exotic despotisms and Tory playwrights criticized the emergent mercantilist colonial state. Although national and class-based manners were featured in comedies, it was the period's serious drama that staged issues of empire, its history and nature, in order to clarify the imperial possibilities for Britain. According to Orr, theatre itself became an instrument of empire: 'theatre provided a space in which previous modes of empire could be explored and criticized as well as celebrated' (p. 60).

Orr's study investigates the roles of Orientalism and racism, their conflation with gender politics, and nationalism. She looks at plays set in Turkey, Morocco, India, China, and Spain for the localized ways in which the familiar tropes of colonial conquest operate. In her analysis of utopian plays, Orr explores the ways in which acting and piracy are staged as potentially subversive activities. Plays set in Rome and ancient Britain betray an ideology from which the British civilizing mission was constructed. Orr concludes with a discussion of John Dennis's *Liberty Asserted* [1704] and Thomas Southerne's *Oroonoko* [1696] as two plays, the first a celebration and the latter a critique, that reflect tensions connected with the development of the newly emergent British empire.

The rest of this section discusses publications from 2002. Paul Goring, '"John Bull, pit, box, and gallery, said No!": Charles Macklin and the Limits of Ethnic Resistance on the Eighteenth-Century London Stage' (*Rep* 29[Summer 2002] 61–81), examines the increasing cultural enfranchisement of the Irish in eighteenth-century London and the ways in which its theatres functioned as sites in which ethnic negotiations occurred. Goring interrogates the dialogue between resistance and counter-resistance to ethnic interaction inspired by theatrical representations. According to Goring, Charles Macklin's career as actor and playwright opened up new possibilities for the representation of the Irish onstage. Macklin's *The True-born Irishman* [1761], for example, overturned stage stereotypes of the Irish, but his two-act farce *A Will and No Will; or, A Bone for the Lawyers* [1746] presents them as humbled. This seeming contradiction is part of Macklin's success as a self-effacing Irishman who was able to critique English perspectives of the Irish with increasing flexibility onstage.

Robert W. Jones, 'Sheridan and the Theatre of Patriotism: Staging Dissent during the War for America' (*ECLife* 26:i[2002] 24–45), contextualizes Sheridan's plays *St Patrick's Day; or the Scheming Lieutenant* [1775], *The Camp: A Musical Entertainment* [1778], and *The Critic; or, a Tragedy Rehearsed* [1778] within the period's political crisis, the moment when a French military invasion seemed inevitable, and the English nation seemed miserably unprepared. Jones argues that Sheridan's plays engaged theatre-goers with patriotic pedagogy. While the dramas criticize the military for its effeminacy, they also satirize as 'mannish' women who frequented the soldiers' camps, the campsite serving as a synecdoche of English culture. The article also impels a revision of our reading of Sheridan's best-known plays *The Rivals* and *The School for Scandal* for their commentary on the circumstances of the invasion crisis and the theatricalization of national politics.

Susan Lamb, 'Applauding Shakespeare's Ophelia in the Eighteenth Century: Sexual Desire, Politics, and the Good Woman' (in Shifrin, ed., *Women as Sites of Culture: Women's Roles in Cultural Formation from the Renaissance to the Twentieth Century*), analyses the Restoration and eighteenth-century adoption of the figure of Ophelia and argues that the figure of the mad Ophelia occurs at the conjunction of the histories of sexuality and of women's political influence so as to emphasize woman's heteronormative sexuality. Lamb asserts that, until the end of the eighteenth century, Ophelia was considered crucial to *Hamlet*, with the most prominent actresses of the day playing the role—fifty-six different actresses had played Ophelia. An icon in the popular imaginary, Ophelia represented ambiguous sexuality as both whore and virgin, but her mental instability gave her permission to express sexual desire in public while simultaneously demonstrating that public display of a woman's sexual desire might cost her her sanity. In the eighteenth century, then, Ophelia's female sexual desire actually served the male-dominated culture at the expense of political, social, and economic improvements in women's lives.

Jean I. Marsden, 'Sex, Politics, and She-Tragedy: Reconfiguring Lady Jane Grey' (*SEL* 42:iii[2002] 510–22), examines the politics of the Hanoverian succession and the aesthetics of a dramatic form founded on passive suffering as enacted by Nicholas Rowe's *The Tragedy of Lady Jane Gray*, a play which was not to become part of the standard eighteenth-century theatrical repertoire despite its being the most successful of the 1714/15 theatre season. Lady Jane Grey was a ready political symbol, but her role on stage created the problem of whether virtue and voyeurism could coexist in tragedy. At the end Jane is a public victim, a theatrical spectacle coded as a sexual object, the suffering object of the male gaze. Rowe's efforts at redefining the heroine as something different from the titillating sexual transgressors of the early she-tragedies were not successful.

Judith Milhous, 'Gravelot and Laguerre: Playing Hob on the Eighteenth-Century English Stage' (*ThS* 43:ii[2002] 148–75), analyses the popular engraved images of Flora and Hob in the eighteenth-century theatre. The country bumpkin or clown Hob was a role Thomas Doggett wrote for himself in 1711, and Milhous compares a selection of plates from Flora with those from Hob to see how they relate to productions. The plates certainly reveal something of the costuming used in the popular afterpieces in which Flora and Hob appeared. Laguerre made Hob's expressions so serious that viewers could hardly tell it was the comic character of farce. Interestingly, Laguerre also figures as subject in Gravelot's work, and so their engravings are satirically interconnected. Flora persisted as a popular subject, highly marketable, but the origin of the Flora songbook is not known.

Peter E. Morgan, 'A Subject to Redress: Ideology and the Cross-Dressed Heroine in Aphra Behn's *The Widow Ranter*' (*ECWomen* 2:i[2002] 23–41), demonstrates how the cross-dressed figure of Behn's play is a symbol of broader cultural struggles and gender politics. The Widow Ranter is a rebel threatening social stability, offering a potential ideological challenge which lower-class women might identify with. Before she cross-dresses, then, the Widow is a disruptive figure, and, even in drag, she refuses to satisfy anyone's definition of 'woman', performing instead self-determination and sexual self-governance.

Daniel O'Quinn, 'Mercantile Deformities: George Colman's *Inkle and Yarico* and the Racialization of Class Relations' (*TJ* 54[2002] 389–409), maintains that *Inkle and Yarico* [1787], George Colman's successful comic opera, functions as a precursor to abolitionist literature in its critique of mercantile ideology and, paradoxically, in its appropriation of late eighteenth-century biomedical discourses of racism. O'Quinn demonstrates how the play mediates and dramatizes concepts that would come to define nineteenth-century imperialism, construct the English bourgeoisie, and stabilize normative heterosexuality, points of departure from William d'Avenant and John Dryden's *The Tempest, Or the Enchanted Isle* [1667], the play Colman recast for the political climate of the late eighteenth century. For spectators, the play's pedagogy fuses morality and economy by staging the cost of interracial desire and miscegenation.

Frances Burney's *The Witlings* and *The Woman-Hater*, edited by Peter Sabor and Geoffrey Sill, gives us teaching texts of Frances Burney's 1779 satire *The Witlings* and her 1800 comedy *The Woman-Hater*, both valuable for classroom and scholarship. The introduction provides biographical and theatrical background important for understanding the plays. Burney's dependence on her father, Dr Charles Burney, the respected musicologist, and her friend Samuel Crisp, the literary critic, for textual approval and theatrical production, for example, reveals how the fate of these playscripts was not of Burney's or her audiences' making. The introductory etymological discussion of the figure of 'Nobody' significantly enriches our reading of the masquerading in *The Woman-Hater*.

Among the appendices to the edition, Sabor and Sill include Burney's Epilogue to John Jackson's tragedy *Gerilda; or the Siege of Harlech* [1777]; comparative scenes from *The Witlings* and Molière's *Les Femmes savantes*, their structural similarities possibly explained by the profusion of translations and adaptations of Molière on the English stage; and Burney's projected cast-list for *The Woman-Hater*, intended for production at Drury Lane. These features are of particular interest to scholars. Students will appreciate the critical essays on 'laughing' and sentimental comedy and the list of literary allusions in the two plays. These editions make the plays accessible and readable. Sabor and Sill's copy-texts rely on Burney's holographic manuscripts of the plays, preserved in the Berg Collection of the New York Public Library. Their in-text notes provide thorough and handy references.

Justine Crump, ed., *A Known Scribbler: Frances Burney on Literary Life*, makes available Frances Burney's journals and correspondence. Crump's introduction situates Burney in the literary marketplace of the eighteenth century as it reviews Burney's life and writings. The brief section on Burney and the eighteenth-century theatre is of particular interest. Crump notes, for example, that Burney was an apt actress, more talented at memorizing her part than in actual performance, however, where she combated stage fright. Her stagecraft experience nonetheless served her well as a playwright. Of course, Burney struggled against cultural and familial expectations of gender that denigrated writing for the public site of the theatre. In an appendix to the edition, Crump includes excerpts from contemporary reviews of Burney's (Madame d'Arblay's) private writings. It is clear that Burney's contemporaries were much more interested in her contributions to the novel than in her work as a dramatist.

Burney was conscious of the potentially public nature of her private letters and journals, as she edited and censored her own writings. Her correspondence with her sister Susanna records conversations with Hester Thrale and Richard Brinsley Sheridan, who urged her to write a play. Her correspondence with her father and Samuel Crisp reveals how she deferred to their masculine sensibility in judging the quality and suitability of her plays. The entries that are relevant to the playwriting Burney are not especially easy to access, however, as Crump's edition includes no index, the journals and correspondence entries being arranged chronologically.

Richard Dircks, ed., *The Memoirs of Richard Cumberland*, emphasizes how Richard Cumberland, during the mid- and late eighteenth century (1732–1811), came into contact with the period's distinguished social and political figures. He contributed to the period's literary and theatrical productions, and he was a player in British politics and policy-making. By 1806, when his *Memoirs* were first published, Cumberland had become a recognized and respected cultural figure. Richard Dircks's modern edition of Cumberland's *Memoirs* makes the life and times of this remarkable writer, politician, and diplomat accessible to us again. It is based on the 1807 second edition, one substantially unchanged from the 1806 version. Dircks's expository footnotes and modern index make Cumberland's *Memoirs* a practical and informative resource. The *Memoirs* include excerpts from his literary writings, including prologues, epilogues, and dialogues from his plays, evidence that Cumberland intended his private writings for public consumption. Dircks's extensive introduction provides us with chronological and cultural contexts for reading Cumberland's life-writings. He points out, for example, how sensitive Cumberland was to criticism about his drama, particularly to allegations of plagiarism at a time when theatrical originality was topical. As Dircks observes, 'An understanding of the plight of the dramatist in the eighteenth century can be gathered from the *Memoirs*, which relate Cumberland's rise from a petitioner whose first play was rejected by Garrick to his great success with comedy during the early phases of his career' (p. xxii). Cumberland's *Memoirs* reveal insights about the production of drama during the period, and also uncover aspects of the age's great theatrical personalities: playwrights Oliver Goldsmith and R.B. Sheridan, and actors John Henderson and David Garrick, for example.

While Cumberland's appointment as Ulster Secretary to Ireland had, as Dircks reflects, little impact on his playwriting career, it significantly influenced his politics and the fashioning of his dramatic characters. Cumberland viewed Ireland as a colonial possession, and his Protestant biases are obvious in his observations. Volume 2, furthermore, details Cumberland's supposedly covert mission to Spain, and his efforts to broker a peace treaty between Spain and England, one that excluded France. Cumberland's recording of his and his family's adventures during his tenure of these political and diplomatic posts contributes to a complex international picture of a period during which England was emerging anew as a colonial power. Cumberland's perceptions of global politics influenced his late dramas and their characters—for example the Jewish moneylender in *The Jew*—that made them so popular with London audiences.

David Womersley, ed., *Restoration Comedy* (with an introduction by Duncan Wu), part of Blackwell's Essential Literature series, is a pocket-sized introduction to

Restoration drama and includes Wycherley's *The Country Wife* [1675] and Congreve's *The Way of the World* [1700]—a shorter version of Blackwell's *Restoration Drama: An Anthology*, edited by Womersley in 2000. Wu's introduction traces theatre history of the period and describes Restoration theatres. He claims that *The Country Wife* exposes a world of infidelity and sexual licence, while *The Way of the World* promotes characters who genuinely care for and love each other even in a satirical play.

Misty G. Anderson, *Female Playwrights and Eighteenth-Century Comedy: Negotiating Marriage on the London Stage*, asserts that eighteenth-century female playwrights sought to reform rather than revolutionize the conditions of marriage through their comic and satiric portrayals of marital relations on the stage. According to Anderson, Aphra Behn, Susanna Centlivre, Hannah Cowley, and Elizabeth Inchbald reflect complicated, contradictory, and changing attitudes about marriage during the long eighteenth century, but they 'did not have a clear proto-feminist agenda' (p. 3) of radical change in their plays.

Situating her analysis within the contexts of the period's marriage laws and social contracts and against a perceptive discussion of gender and genre, Anderson argues that it is in the gap created by the 'narrative struggle between closure and comic event' (p. 7) where eighteenth-century women playwrights created comic pedagogy, a momentary suspension of the status quo and engagement in play-acting, that suggests alternatives, albeit temporary, to marriage determined by patriarchal culture. Behn's Restoration heroines become desiring and desirable women, her comedies giving glimpses of an alternative sexuality to that of objectified woman that was ultimately at odds with 'an emerging economic order' (p. 108). Centlivre exposes her middle-class Whiggish endorsement of free markets by portraying women acting as agents in the making and maintaining of various social and commercial contracts, including that of marriage. Her heroines cross the boundaries between private and public, functional and validated in both spheres.

For Cowley, English nationalism, with its ideal of individual liberty, could grant women control over their lives even as wives and mothers, widows and divorcees. Englishness endowed women with an identity marker of value against which the racialized other of slave or colonized was dehumanized by the mid-eighteenth century. The instability of the 1790s, however, is apparent in Inchbald's comedies, in which nationalism becomes an unstable ground and gender revolutions are seen as dangerous. According to Anderson, Inchbald's plays 'give an account of the messy, imperfect, legally flawed state of marriage at the end of the century' (p. 172). Divorce figures prominently in Inchbald's plays, which explore its social, psychological, and legal implications for women. Anderson successfully demonstrates, through her analysis of representative comedies by these four eighteenth-century female playwrights, how they negotiated publicly, vis-à-vis the stage, the meanings of marriage, setting the stage, as it were, for the revolutionary female playwrights of the Romantic theatre.

Åke Eriksson, *The Tragedy of Liberty: Civic Concern and Disillusionment in James Thomson's Tragic Dramas*, examines three of Thomson's six tragedies— *Agamemnon* [1738], *Sophonisba* [1730], and *Tancred and Sigismunda* [1745]—in the context of their engagement with eighteenth-century political ideology. Eriksson argues that, while Thomson's tragedies incorporate opposition politics, they more importantly explore the complications and contradictions accompanying efforts to establish and maintain civil liberty, a philosophical abstraction and ideal, Eriksson claims, with which Thomson was more engaged in his dramas than in his poetry. The tragedies negotiate the struggles between private and public interests, their denouement problematizing the tragic impossibility of a comfortable or attainable compromise.

After establishing an ideological context that defines liberty in eighteenth-century British terms, cultural and political, Eriksson demonstrates Thomson's unique handling of this stock theme in his tragedies. All three plays displace the issue of British liberty onto classic conflicts in ancient civilizations. *Agamemnon*, Eriksson argues, projects the infeasibility of liberty, even at the cost of personal sacrifice, for the common good. *Sophonisba* depicts irreconcilable struggles between individual liberty and a social system at risk of dissolution. A parallel to Agamemnon, Sophonisba, like Clytemnestra, voices both private grievances and public woes, and she will make sacrifices to save her country. Her tragedy is that of the play: the impossibility of ensuring individual liberty without sacrificing the social structure responsible for that liberty.

Eriksson's analysis gestures towards but does not develop contemporary political events vital to the period's debates about liberty. The study similarly skirts gender and class issues worthy of exploring more thoroughly. The link between death and liberty in Thomson's tragedies is, as Eriksson points out, a precursor to Romanticism's construction of individual freedom from the end of the eighteenth century, but more complicated in the Enlightenment than this study develops. While the Larpent manuscript of Act 1, scenes i and v, included as an appendix, is interesting, the study does not make significant use of it.

Lisa A. Freeman, *Character's Theater: Genre and Identity on the Eighteenth-Century English Stage*, seeks to analyse the construction of identity during the eighteenth century, a preoccupation of the period's novels, and it is the novel that has generally been privileged as the model for the fashioning of the modern subject. Freeman argues, however, that it was in the theatre that the modern subject was made and given meaning. Playwrights overcame cultural critiques of theatrical artificiality and insincerity by deploying a strategy that Freeman terms 'antitheatrical theatricalism' to establish authority and legitimacy. What we find in the drama and on the stage, contends Freeman, is 'a dynamic paradigm for representing identity that derives its force from the concept of "character" as it was elaborated and understood in an eighteenth-century context' (p. 7). Freeman argues that identity is an effect of character, an understanding that the period's playwrights exploited. Furthermore, drama is the genre best suited to manipulate an epistemological frame for various pedagogical purposes, including identity construction. Freeman carefully delineates the cultural contexts of character theory, acting styles, and audience interaction that validate her readings of the plays.

Plays about plays literally stage the strategy of 'antitheatrical theatricalism', at once distancing character as performative with its metadramatics and performing the value of theatricality as everyday occurrences. Character representations, though provisional, are authorized, and mimetic displays are self-reflectively performative and meta-theatrical. Freeman's analysis of Henry Fielding's *The Author's Farce* [1733–4] and George Colman the Younger's *The Female Dramatist* [1781–2] demonstrate comic and serious applications of 'antitheatrical theatricalism' and the ways in which eighteenth-century plays about plays stage bodies as characters and representations as identities.

Tragedies that staged the nation in crisis and the patriotic characters who would come to its rescue comprise the next set of plays that Freeman's study considers. Tragedy fulfilled an important patriotic and moral pedagogy for the emerging middle class in need of character-building and inculcation of English cultural values. At this time the tragic hero emerged as the common man, domestic and individualized, the exemplar of new masculine and English ideologies. Tragedy thus had the potential to expunge the nation of foreign entertainments with their irrational, feminine passions, their morally degenerate spectacles, their threatening influences. Freeman uses Joseph Addison's *Cato* [1746] to illustrate how eighteenth-century tragedy represented this new masculine hero, and she examines George Lillo's *The London Merchant; or, The History of George Barnwell* [1730–1] as a tragedy in which the myths of empire are displaced on to the category of gender. In both plays, female characters are ideologically marginal, neither the embodiment of ideals important to the nation's character nor the representation of notions germane to the imperial imagination. Nicholas Rowe's 'she-tragedies' *The Fair Penitent* [1702–3] and *The Tragedy of Jane Shore* [1713–14] similarly depict women as inherently dangerous to patriarchal order and national stability, the narrative authorities to which they should submit.

Eighteenth-century comedy, Freeman explains, focuses on the private, domestic world that made the English nation possible. Its pedagogical project was to make the audience 'fitter' members of society and reveal that character was, in fact, performative, a parody of historically specific identities. Freeman's 'straight' and sceptical readings of Susanna Centlivre's *A Bold Stroke for a Wife* [1717–18], Hannah Cowley's *A Bold Stroke for a Husband* [1782–3] and *The Belle's Stratagem* [1779–80], George Farquhar's *The Beaux' Stratagem* [1706–7], and Richard Brinsley Sheridan's *The Rivals* [1774–5] expose the ways in which the laughing comedies conflate mimesis and parody and unmask the performative nature of identities, on- and offstage. Proper gender and class hierarchies are temporarily suspended only to restore order in the genre's conventionally happy endings, which reify English culture.

Sentimental comedies, Freeman contends, perform the pedagogic function of importing 'good breeding' to their mercantile and middle-class audiences, codes of conduct and morality intent on maintaining social regulation. Richard Steele's *The Conscious Lovers* [1722–3], Edward Moore's *The Foundling* [1747–8], and Richard Cumberland's *The West Indian* [1770–1] portray exemplars of benevolent patriarchy and mercantile paternity; whether familial, social, or colonial, they enforce a behavioural normativity that ensures a noble character. Freeman's engaging and compelling study illustrates successfully how powerfully the eighteenth-century theatre functioned in English culture as the site where character and identity could be represented and rehearsed, performed and parodied, in public.

Anne Kelley, *Catharine Trotter: An Early Writer in the Vanguard of Feminism*, reads Trotter's drama through her philosophical writings on rationality and responsibility and argues that we should not read Trotter's public persona as a stable one. Kelley reviews the critical reception of Trotter, beginning in the eighteenth century, to reveal how her conformist identity was constructed by critics who sought to level out the complexities of her life and thinking.

Trotter's drama, Kelley asserts, sought to instruct and inspire by example, practical demonstrations of ethical codes that she supported in her intellectual discourse. In fact, writing drama gave Trotter the creative confidence and individuality she needed to enter into public intellectual debate. Kelley situates Trotter's drama in the political context of the Restoration theatre, but asserts that its most important element was its positive staging of the intellectual and rational woman. Her characters struggle with complex moral dilemmas that require for their solution the rational integrity and individual responsibility derived from lived experience. According to Kelley, 'Trotter's depiction of women is unique within drama as a mediating influence within patriarchal structures, representing centers of moral stability which expose the fragility of male codes and practices' (p. 97). Trotter's women are spirited, purposeful, and courageous; not mere foils to male characters. She examines at length *Fatal Friendship* [1698], Trotter's most popular play, *The Unhappy Penitent* [1701], *The Revolution of Sweden* [1706], *Agnes de Castro* [1696], and *Love at a Loss* [1701].

Kelley concludes that Trotter significantly contributed to stage reform and to its restoration to a respected status, despite the fact that her plays were not commercially successful. Her feminocentric drama helped to broaden attitudes about women, to debunk prevailing myths about the female sex, to challenge patriarchy, and to position women at the centre of political, public life.

The appendices to this study are a treasure-trove and include: play plots; performance dates of Trotter's plays, and cast-lists from the playtexts; title pages from *The Adventures of a Young Lady* [1693] and *Olinda's Adventures* [1718]; a photo of a holograph letter [1697] from William Congreve to Trotter; a holograph letter [1703] from William Congreve to Trotter; a holograph letter [1698] from George Farquhar to Trotter; a holograph letter [1739] to her niece; and the holograph Last Will and Testament of Catharine Cockburn and the Last Will and Testament of Reverend Patrick Cockburn.

Matthew J. Kinservik, *Disciplining Satire: The Censorship of Satiric Comedy on the Eighteenth-Century London Stage*, considers the theatrical conditions leading to the 1737 Licensing Act and the effects of the Act on satirical comedy in the eighteenth century. The study is arranged chronologically and examines how the Act affected the production and reception of satirical comedy. Kinservik argues that, in place of punitive satire, the Act encouraged the production and consumption of sympathetic satire; in effect, the Act reformed and disciplined satire.

Kinservik traces this evolutionary disciplining from the experimental and successful satire of Henry Fielding, a playwright whose drama is central to understanding the period's theatrical satire and censorship. Fielding was adept at adapting to the increased policing of satire, turning his own writing to a moral, non-partisan satirical comedy by the 1730s. From 1737 to 1747, the revolution in theatrical taste was reflected by a growing interest in psychological characterization, making the stereotypical mouthpieces of satire undesirable on the stage. During the period 1747–76 there was a resurgence of personal satire, with Samuel Foote as the exemplar who reintroduced mimicry as a performative device into plays. Foote's career tells us that personal satire was not prohibited from the stage by the Licensing Act, but playwrights had to know their limits and choose their targets carefully.

Charles Macklin's serious social satire marks the period 1746–81. Macklin's dramas feature psychologically complex characters engaged in sympathetic and reform-oriented satire. His approach to character revealed how it was possible to write challenging and political satire under the Licensing Act. Kinservik supplies a close reading of Macklin's unfinished seventy-eight-page manuscript *The Spoild Child*; a transcription of the holograph manuscript and commentary appear in the book's appendix. According to Kinservik, *The Spoild Child* is a sympathetic satire that demonstrates the period's shift towards an emphasis on social vices, and exemplifies how censorship under the Licensing Act encouraged playwrights to pursue psychologically developed characterization. In this incomplete play, transgressive satire embraces corrective rather than combative strategies.

Joyce Green Macdonald, *Women and Race in Early Modern Texts*, includes three chapters relevant to eighteenth-century drama. Macdonald examines the white-skinned Imoindas who displaced Aphra Behn's heroine in eighteenth-century dramatizations of *Oroonoko*, for example, in adaptations by Thomas Southerne, John Hawkesworth, Francis Gentleman, John Ferriar, and the anonymous author of *The Royal Captive* [1767], and considers the social functions served by the erasure of Behn's black-skinned Imoinda. Arguing that the writing of, or the refusal to write, racial identity deeply implicates gender; Macdonald emphasizes 'the affectively powerful performance of white women's submission to new inscriptions of their sexually subordinate roles in colonialism's patriarchal culture' (p. 19). According to Macdonald, the *Oroonoko* dramas of pathos and sensibility following Behn required a white heroine in order to affirm socially and culturally white Englishwomen as part of the reading and theatre-going public and in the growing abolitionist movement. The white Imoinda conforms to the interests of a culture that is invested in her chastity and silence. She colludes with the emerging new fictions of race, and she embodies the victimized passivity of a sentimental heroine. Her body is objectified in the economic and sexual exchange of the new mercantile society. She is the character with whom white female spectators identify and patterns the relationship of women and sexual/racial authority in the colonialist matrix.

In looking at Katherine Phillips's *Pompey* [1663] and Behn's *Abdelazar; or The Moor's Revenge* [1676], Macdonald applies feminist and postcolonial theories in her analysis of the ways in which English women writers used race (specifically whiteness and the race of the 'other') in constructing textual characters that enabled them to claim their authorship. Phillips extols female honour based on chastity and self-denial in her characterization of Cornelia, Pompey's widow, while she demonizes Cleopatra, the Egyptian queen who threatened Roman political order. *Pompey*, argues Macdonald, textualizes conservative constructions of gender and femininity by dramatizing the defeat of the 'foreign' alternative female model, the ambitious and powerfully unchaste queen. Behn's only tragedy, *Abdelazar* utilizes race, interrogating the institutional crises of family and politics that it portrays. Monstrous female sexuality reveals the play's royalist and patriarchal agenda, embodied in Isabella, the deviant royal mother who has taken a black lover, Abdelazar. Florella, on the other hand, is faithful and docile, the embodiment of the proper femininity upon which Britain will construct its national sovereignty and white racial purity.

Susan J. Owen, *Perspectives on Restoration Drama*, offers close textual readings of Dryden's *The Conquest of Granada by the Spaniards* (Part I [1670] and Part II [1672]) and *Troilus and Cressida* [1679], Wycherley's *The Country Wife* [1675], Behn's *The Rover; or, The Banish't Cavaliers* [1677], Lee's *Lucius Junius Brutus,*

Father of his Country [1680], and Otway's *Venice Preserv'd; or A Plot Discovered* [1682] in the context of generic and political changes during the Restoration. Owen traces Restoration drama's connections with Shakespeare, offers character analyses, discusses structural and generic elements, compares and contrasts each play with others from the period, and considers the conceptual, thematic, and ideological implications for each play. She pays some attention to staging, theatrics, and dramaturgy.

Owen reads *Granada* as royalist and courtly drama, with its theme that discord destroys a commonwealth. As heroic drama, *Granada* utilizes a providentialist schema and elevated language. Restoration playwrights, claims Owen, altered Shakespeare in order to make him and his plays worthy of elevated and popular status. Adapters of Shakespeare often added music and spectacle, and purified his language. Dryden's alterations might be described as 'masculinist' in his critique of effeminacy, which might be seen as a warning to the libertine Charles and James Stuart. Dryden sought to refine Shakespeare for moral purposes, and his adaptation of *Troilus and Cressida* was important in the development of eighteenth-century adaptation theory.

The Country Wife and *The Rover* might be described as 'sex comedies', plays which endorsed the values of the cavalier class and that functioned as diversions from the increasing political tensions of the 1670s. Appearance and pretence are what *The Country Wife* is about as it exposes instability of meaning, and it is only good nature and civility that prevent the ruin of several female reputations at the end of the play. Similarly, *The Rover* depends on double standards, disguises, dilemmas, and the difficulties women face, but Behn's women are more fully developed than Wycherley's female characters. The focus of Behn's play is how to evade oppressive female destiny, and its dramatic tensions projected from the female perspective work to gain audience support for Florinda, Hellena, and Angellica.

Restoration tragedy had a political impetus, and Owen analyses Lee's *Brutus* and Otway's *Venice* as plays where political meanings are contested. The politics that both plays valorize is that of the Tories. The action of both plays is stimulated by a rape or near-rape, and both plays interrogate the meaning of women's experience. *Brutus* extols the heroic aspects of republicanism, and *Venice* condemns rebellion in its portrayal of a corrupt conspiracy against the senate. Owen contends that Otway's play is more complex as it hints at erotically charged masochism, particularly in the psychologies of Jaffeir and Antonio.

Books Reviewed

Anderson, Misty G. *Female Playwrights and Eighteenth-Century Comedy: Negotiating Marriage on the London Stage*. Palgrave. [2002] pp. x + 262. $65 ISBN 0 3122 3938 6.

Bartolomeo, Joseph F. *Matched Pairs: Gender and Intertextual Dialogue in Eighteenth-Century Fiction*. UDelP and AUP. [2002] pp. 242. $45 ISBN 0 8741 3799 3.

Bergstrom, Carson. *The Rise of New Science: Epistemological, Linguistic, and Ethical Ideals and the Lyric Genre in the Eighteenth Century*. Mellen. [2002] pp. xiii + 334. £74.95 ($119.95) ISBN 0 7734 6909 5.

Bradford, Richard. *Augustan Measures: Restoration and Eighteenth-Century Writings on Prosody and Metre.* Ashgate. [2002] pp. 256. £45 ($79.95) ISBN 0 7546 0711 9.

Canfield, J. Douglas, ed. *The* Broadview *Anthology of Restoration and Early Eighteenth-Century Drama.* Broadview. [2001] pp. 1,977. pb $62.95 ISBN 1 5511 1270 1.

Clark, Jonathan, and Howard Erskine-Hill, eds. *Samuel Johnson in Historical Context.* Palgrave. [2002] pp. 330. £55 ISBN 0 3338 0447 3.

Clingham, Greg. *Johnson, Writing, and Memory.* CUP. [2002] pp. 234. £40 ISBN 0 5218 1611 4.

Cohen, Margaret, and Carolyn Dever, eds. *The Literary Channel: The Inter-National Invention of the Novel.* PrincetonUP. [2002] pp. viii + 319. hb $65 (£42.95) ISBN 0 6910 5002 3, pb $21.95 (£14.95) ISBN 0 6910 5001 5.

Crump, Justine, ed. *A Known Scribbler: Frances Burney on Literary Life.* Broadview. [2002] pp. 380. pb $CAN17.95 (£8.99) ISBN 1 5511 1320 1.

Dircks, Richard, ed. *The Memoirs of Richard Cumberland,* 2 vols. in 1. AMS. [2002] pp. lx + 243. $145 ISBN 0 4046 3532 6.

Donoghue, William. *Enlightenment Fiction in England, France, and America.* UFlorP. [2002] pp. 192. $55 ISBN 0 8130 2481 1.

Dugaw, Dianne. *'Deep Play': John Gay and the Invention of Modernity.* UDelP. [2001] pp. 322. $48.50 ISBN 0 8741 3731 4.

Ennis, Daniel, James. *Enter the Press-Gang: Naval Impressment in Eighteenth-Century British Literature.* UDelP and AUP. [2002] pp. 219. $41.50 ISBN 0 8741 3755 1.

Eriksson, Åke. *The Tragedy of Liberty: Civic Concern and Disillusionment in James Thomson's Tragic Dramas.* Studia Anglistica Upsaliensia 119, ed. Merja Kytö Ludén and Monica Correa Fryckstedt. AUUp. [2002] pp. 144. pb $38 ISBN 9 1554 5253 1.

Fieser, James, ed. *Early Responses to Hume's Writing on Religion,* 2 vols. Thoemmes. [2001] pp. 800. £175 ISBN 1 8550 6797 8.

Finberg, Melinda C., ed. *Eighteenth-Century Women Dramatists.* OUP. [2001] pp. lxi + 380. pb $15.95 ISBN 0 1928 2729 4.

Freeman, Lisa A. *Character's Theater: Genre and Identity on the Eighteenth-Century English Stage.* UPennP. [2002] pp. 298. $47.50 ISBN 0 8122 3639 4.

Gay, Penny. *Jane Austen and the Theatre.* CUP. [2002] pp. xi + 201. £37.50. ISBN 0 5216 5213 8.

Giffin, Michael. *Jane Austen and Religion: Salvation and Society in Georgian England.* Palgrave. [2002] pp. 232. $62 ISBN 0 3339 4808 4.

Goldsmith, Netta Murray. *Alexander Pope: The Evolution of a Poet.* Ashgate. [2002] pp. xiv + 316. £47.50 ($84.95) ISBN 0 7546 0310 5.

Gordon, Scott Paul. *The Power of the Passive Self in English Literature, 1640–1770.* CUP. [2002] pp. xi + 279. £40 ISBN 0 5218 1005 1.

Griffin, Dustin. *Patriotism and Poetry in Eighteenth-Century Britain.* CUP. [2002] pp. 326. £40 ($60) ISBN 0 5218 1118 X.

Groom, Nick. *The Forger's Shadow: How Forgery Changed the Course of Literature.* Picador. [2002] pp. 368. hb £20 ISBN 0 3303 7432 X, pb £8.99 ISBN 0 3303 7433 8.

Gross, Gloria Sybil. *In a Fast Coach with a Pretty Woman: Jane Austen and Samuel Johnson*. Studies in the Eighteenth Century 4. AMS. [2002] pp. 208. $62.50 ISBN 0 4046 3540 7.

Grossman, Jonathan H. *The Art of Alibi: English Law Courts and the Novel*. JHUP. [2002] pp. 216. $41 ISBN 0 8018 6755 X.

Hughes, Derek, gen. ed. *Eighteenth-Century Women Playwrights*. 6 vols. P&C. [2001]. $795 ISBN 1 8519 6616 1.

Justice, George, and Nathan Tinker, eds. *Women's Writing and the Circulation of Ideas: Manuscript Publication in England, 1550–1800*. CUP. [2002] pp. 256. £40 ISBN 0 5218 0856 1.

Kelly, Anne. *Catharine Trotter: An Early Writer in the Vanguard of Feminism*. Ashgate. [2002] pp. ix + 279. $79.95 ISBN 0 7546 0510 8.

Kelly, Gary, ed. *Varieties of Female Gothic*. 6 vols. P&C. [2002] pp. 2,056. £495 ($740) ISBN 1 8519 6717 6.

Kinservik, Matthew J. *Disciplining Satire: The Censorship of Satiric Comedy on the Eighteenth-Century London Stage*. BuckUP. [2002] pp. 301. $48.50 ISBN 0 8387 5512 7.

Macdonald, Joyce Green. *Women and Race in Early Modern Texts*. CUP. [2002] pp. 198. $60 ISBN 0 5218 1016 7.

McIlvanney, Liam. *Burns the Radical: Poetry and Politics in Late Eighteenth-Century Scotland*. Tuckwell. [2002] pp. 272. pb £16.99 ISBN 1 8623 2177 9.

MacLachlan, Christopher, ed. *Before Burns: Eighteenth-Century Scottish Poetry*. Canongate. [2002] pp. xx + 332. pb £9.99 ISBN 1 8419 5253 2.

Michaelson, Patricia Howell. *Speaking Volumes: Women, Reading and Speech in the Age of Austen*. StanfordUP. [2002] pp. 280. $55 ISBN 0 8047 4075 5.

Morillo, John D. *Uneasy Feelings: Literature, the Passions, and Class from Neoclassicism to Romanticism*. AMS. [2001] pp. 313. $69.50 ISBN 0 4046 3537 7.

Orr, Bridget. *Empire on the English Stage, 1660–1714*. CUP. [2001] pp. x + 350. $75 ISBN 0 5217 7350 4.

Owen, Susan J. *Perspectives on Restoration Drama*. ManUP. [2002] pp. vii + 198. pb $27.95 ISBN 0 7190 4967 9.

Rivero, Albert J., ed. *The Eighteenth-Century Novel*, vol. 2. AMS. [2002] pp. 429. $94.50 ISBN 0 4046 4652 2.

Rivers, Isabel, ed. *Books and their Readers in Eighteenth-Century England: New Essays*. LeicUP. [2001] pp. 300. £65 ISBN 0 7185 0189 6.

Sabor, Peter, and Geoffrey Sill, eds. *'The Witlings' and 'The Woman-Hater'*, by Fanny Burney. Broadview. [2002] pp. 329. pb $15.95 ISBN 1 5511 1378 3.

Schmidgen, Wolfram. *Eighteenth-Century Fiction and the Law of Property*. CUP. [2002] pp. 274. £45 ISBN 0 5218 1702 1.

Shifrin, Susan, ed. *Women as Sites of Culture: Women's Roles in Cultural Formation from the Renaissance to the Twentieth Century*. Ashgate. [2002] pp. 292. £47.50 ISBN 0 7546 0311 3.

Smallwood, Philip. *Johnson Revisioned: Looking Before and After*. BuckUP. [2001] pp. 179. $36 ISBN 0 8387 5494 5.

Townsend, Dabney. *Hume's Aesthetic Theory: Taste and Sentiment*. Routledge. [2001] pp. 272. $60 ISBN 0 4152 3396 8.

Wikborg, Eleanor. *The Lover as Father Figure in Eighteenth-Century Women's Fiction*. UFlorP. [2002] pp. xi + 184. £55 ISBN 0 8130 2453 6.

Womersley, David. *Gibbon and the 'Watchmen of the Holy City': The Historian and his Reputation, 1776–1815* . Clarendon. [2002] pp. 464. £65 ISBN 0 1981 8733 5.

Womersley, David, ed. *Restoration Comedy*, introd. Duncan Wu. Malden, MA and Blackwell. [2002] pp. 153. pb $17.95 ISBN 0 6312 3472 1.

XII

The Nineteenth Century: The Romantic Period

CARL THOMPSON, DANIEL SANJIV ROBERTS, ALED GANOBCSIK-WILLIAMS, SARAH WOOTTON, JASON WHITTAKER, EMMA MASON AND AMY MUSE

This chapter has seven sections: 1. General; 2. Non-Fictional Prose; 3. Prose Fiction; 4. Poetry; 5. Blake; 6. Women Romantic Writers; 7. Drama. Section 1 is by Carl Thompson; section 2 is by Daniel Sanjiv Roberts; section 3 is by Aled Ganobcsik-Williams; section 4 is by Sarah Wootton; section 5 is by Jason Whittaker; section 6 is by Emma Mason; section 7 is by Amy Muse.

1. General

Two very useful resources became available to students of the Romantic period this year. *Romanticism and Science, 1773–1833*, edited by Tim Fulford, and *Literature and Science, 1660–1834*, under the general editorship of Judith Hawley, are both large-scale anthologies (running to five volumes and four volumes respectively) that make more easily accessible a mass of primary material relating to scientific discourses in the Romantic period. Consisting of extracts from a very broad range of texts, these two collections not only direct students to specific areas of scientific debate and activity, they also enable an excellent overview of the broader intellectual and cultural developments that transformed 'natural philosophy' into 'science', a far more professionalized and systematic field of enquiry. The two collections approach this huge topic in different ways. In *Romanticism and Science*, the material is organized into twenty-two sections, embracing not only the key scientific disciplines (chemistry, botany, astronomy, and so forth) but also specific topics within those disciplines: heat, electricity and galvanism, theories of life, and so forth. Technology and manufacturing are addressed as well as science, and there are also sections dealing with both the broader social context that enabled the emergence of modern science and the cultural impact of the new scientific discourses and practices: section titles here include 'Women in Science', 'Science and Politics', and 'Science and Social Change'. In *Literature and Science*, meanwhile, each volume is given over to a single theme. Volume 1 addresses 'Science as Polite Culture', and surveys the change in the social and cultural status of science; volume 2 presents 'Sciences of Body and Mind'; volume 3 deals with 'Earthly Powers', by which is meant the sciences of geology, geography, and meteorology; and volume 4 is concerned with natural history, and more specifically botany. As this stands, this is obviously a more limited range of material than that gathered together in *Romanticism and Science*, but the initial volumes of *Literature and Science* are to be supplemented in due course by a further four-volume series embracing 'Fauna', 'Astronomy', 'Natural Philosophy', and 'Chemistry'. Keeping in mind the projected eight volumes of *Literature and Science*, it is not easy to discriminate between the two collections. *Literature and Science* generally has more substantial extracts, and of course takes the longer historical view back to the Royal Society in the seventeenth century; *Romanticism and Science*, meanwhile, probably makes this vast topic more accessible to undergraduates by organizing its material into smaller, more focused units.

The sections in *Romanticism and Science* and *Literature and Science* dealing with botany and natural history complement usefully the three studies that this year returned to that perennial theme in Romantic studies, nature. In this context, some mention must be made of Robert J. Richards's *The Romantic Conception of Life: Science and Philosophy in the Age of Goethe*. Although this study perhaps falls outside the rubric of *YWES*, being chiefly an account of German Romanticism, it will nevertheless be highly useful to students of British Romanticism. It provides an excellent survey of the scientific theories of nature current in the Romantic period, notably the German *Naturphilosophie*, and of the distinctively 'Romantic' contribution to those theories. It also offers an introduction to German Romanticism per se, as Richards's engagingly expansive style interweaves much historical and biographical background in an effort to illuminate the science, and to show how scientific and aesthetic considerations often went hand in hand in this period. The book is organized into three parts. The first surveys the literary, philosophical, and scientific concerns of early German Romanticism, focusing especially on Wilhelm and Friedrich Schlegel, Friedrich Schleiermacher, and Friedrich Schelling. The second part looks in more detail at scientific theories of life, organic form, and nature, and the contributions made in these fields by Kant, Blumenbach, Schelling, Carl Friedrich Kielmeyer, and Johann Christian Reil. The third section then concentrates on Goethe's immense achievement in both art and science, and a final concluding chapter discusses Charles Darwin's debt to his German precursors.

Also addressing the topic of nature, but with one eye on more pressing modern concerns, is Onno Oerlemans's *Romanticism and the Materiality of Nature*. An ecocritical reading of Romanticism, working along lines mapped out by Jonathan Bate and Karl Kroeber although at frequent points usefully qualifying and complicating previous ecocriticism, this study is concerned to rescue the British Romantics from the charge that their interest in nature is merely an evasion of political and social issues, or an obfuscatory, underhand technique by which political ends are covertly pursued. He is concerned equally to contest the view— celebrated by Geoffrey Hartmann, denounced by more recent cultural-materialist critics—that the Romantics, in being interested in nature, are only really being interested in themselves, in the evolution of their minds and ultimately in the seemingly transcendent properties of consciousness. Instead, Oerlemans brings forward evidence for the importance to the Romantics of what he dubs (borrowing from Keats's poem 'Epistle to J.H. Reynolds') the 'material sublime' (p. 4.). In the first place this phrase denotes the insurmountable otherness of the material world: not simply the indifference of non-human species and phenomena to human needs and desires, but more profoundly the resistance of materiality to consciousness and to representation. Secondarily, it denotes the feeling produced in the mind when it is made to register that resistance. Requiring consciousness both to acknowledge its own limits and to confront the paradox that materiality is the ground for its own being, the material sublime for Oerlemans is the necessary starting point for the properly environmental imagination.

To demonstrate how the Romantics initiated, and can continue to contribute to, this environmental awareness, Oerlemans looks for Romantic-era writings which manifest 'a resistance to a sense that we can and should be able to come to a complete and comfortable understanding of nature, [writing] where a sense of [nature's] complexity, intricacy, and otherness is primary and sufficient' (p. 23). It is a resistance that is found chiefly in the poetry of the period (for Oerlemans, as for several recent ecocritics, it is a strong article of faith that lyric is the literary mode most open to otherness and to alienating effects). The first chapter presents a reading of Wordsworth as not so much a 'green' as a 'gray' poet (a distinction borrowed from the critic Paul Fry), attuned to rocks rather than trees, and alert to 'the indifference, hostility, and inimicalness of material reality to an idea of the "one life"' (p. 35). Chapter 2 then deals with the notorious tendency of much Romantic writing to anthropomorphize animals. Refreshingly, Oerlemans does not just trot out the usual objections raised against this rhetorical manoeuvre. In a wide-ranging discussion of the horse paintings of George Stubbs, and the animal poetry of Burns, Clare, Coleridge, and Wordsworth, it is suggested that Romantic anthropomorphisms may (sometimes) be better understood as a recognition of the sentience, emotion, and even consciousness that animals undoubtedly possess, and so in fact repudiate an anthropocentrism that would see these attributes as wholly the preserve of humans (expressed, for example, in the Cartesian understanding that animals are little better than automata). Chapter 3 focuses on Shelley's vegetarianism: the connection here with the 'material sublime' is not entirely clear, but the chapter nevertheless contains many useful insights. Chapters 4 and 5, finally, discuss the many classificatory systems applied to nature in the eighteenth and early nineteenth centuries, and the abundant travel writing of the period (in particular, Dorothy Wordsworth's tour journals), emphasizing in both cases those moments at which natural phenomena seem to surpass and confound the categories that the writer seeks to impose upon them.

Rachel Crawford's *Poetry, Enclosure, and the Vernacular Landscape, 1700– 1830* also offers many illuminating insights into changing attitudes to nature and the rural landscape. Crawford addresses the shifts in taste that took place in the eighteenth century in relation both to landscape and to poetry, and traces the many parallels and interconnections between developments in these two cultural domains. Broadly speaking, her thesis is that the shift witnessed with regard to landscape, from an early eighteenth-century expansionist discourse favouring vast parks and seemingly unbounded views to an early nineteenth-century discourse that celebrates smaller, contained spaces such as the cottage garden and the bower, corresponds with (and possibly even shapes) the course of literary history, as we move from the early eighteenth-century taste for the 'sprawling form' (p. 5) of georgic poetry to a Regency preference for minor lyric forms. In both contexts, Crawford suggests, containment and confined space increasingly become expressive of industry and productivity, as a more middle-class sensibility displaces an aristocratic one. In support of this claim, Crawford offers a series of densely packed, highly nuanced chapters, organized into three sections. The first section explores the complex, and contested, symbolism attaching to agricultural enclosure, and then the changing attitudes to garden and park design evinced in the treatises of Stephen Switzer, Thomas Whateley, and Humphrey Repton. The second section charts the rise and decline of georgic as a poetic genre, from John Philips's *Cyder* [1708] to Richard Jago's *Edge-Hill* [1767], and the third explores the 'trend toward containment' (p. 225) evinced on the one hand in the 'lyric turn' (p. 173) of late eighteenth-century poetry, and especially the revival of interest in the sonnet, and on the other hand in the kitchen-garden manuals of the period. This section concludes with an analysis of the role of the bower in the poetry of Coleridge, Keats, and Felicia Hemans.

Four studies this year approached the Romantic period from a Celtic angle. Ina Ferris's *The Romantic National Tale and the Question of Ireland* took as its starting point the creation in 1801 of the 'United Kingdom of Great Britain and Ireland'—an awkward phrase, and an unstable polity, that left Ireland ambiguously positioned as both part of the British nation yet also outside it. Neither a fully incorporated state within the Union nor straightforwardly a colony, and so somehow simultaneously 'home' and 'abroad', 'domestic' and 'foreign', Ireland after 1801 had a curiously disconcerting, even uncanny aspect to British commentators. This unease produced a flood of writings aimed at assimilating Ireland more completely within Britain, and it is these that form the focus of Ferris's study. Principally she is concerned with the so-called 'national tale' pioneered by Sydney Owenson (later Lady Morgan) in *The Wild Irish Girl* [1806] and developed further by Maria Edgeworth in *Ennui* [1809] and *The Absentee* [1812], and it is accordingly Owenson who is the subject of the two central chapters of this study. But she begins her account with a fascinating survey of the many travel narratives recounting tours of Ireland in the wake of Union. Displaying an admirable awareness of the instabilities and ambiguities inherent in the travel-writing genre, Ferris explores the unease occasioned by Ireland in English travellers and travel texts, even when those travellers evinced considerable sympathy for a nation seemingly let down by an 'incomplete Union' (p. 6). (Catholic emancipation, for example, had been promised as part of the deal, but not delivered.) This unease ensured that Ireland and the Irish remained resolutely 'other', even in texts intended to assimilate them into the British polity, and it was to seek to redress this situation, and 'to gain Ireland a new kind of hearing on the metropolitan stage' (p. 16), that the national tale came into being. Ferris reads the form sympathetically, presenting it as less a dubious packaging of Ireland for English tastes, and more an expression of Irish grievances couched in a style well calculated to win sympathy. 'Displacing its English readers in a way the Irish tour never did, the novelistic genre compelled them to consider Ireland as a habitat (a native and independent place) and not simply as the primitive, ridiculous, or dangerous colony of English imaginings' (pp. 51–2). Chapters 2 and 3 accordingly explore this thesis, chiefly in relation to Sydney Owenson (although reference is also made to Edgeworth and Charles Maturin), looking in the first place principally at *The Wild Irish Girl*, and in the second place at Owenson's later novels *Florence Macarthy* [1818] and *The O'Briens and the O'Flahertys* [1827]. Chapter 4 then addresses the transmutation, at the hands of Charles Maturin, of the Irish national tale into a distinctive form of Irish Gothic. Offering a stimulating analysis of the symbolic function of the ruins in Maturin's *The Milesian Chief* [1812], Ferris reads this genre as the negative, pessimistic counterpart of the optimistic national tale. Expressive of a post-Union sensibility that finds itself at an *impasse*, desiring neither greater incorporation into Britain nor the decisive separation from Britain proposed by Irish nationalism, Maturin's writing for Ferris provides a bleak, sceptical commentary on the possibilities of political and cultural transformation. This political nihilism is in turn contested by the emancipation novels of the 1820s, the subject of the final chapter.

Crossing the Irish Sea, Wales is the principal point of focus in Damien Walford Davies's *Presences That Disturb: Models of Romantic Identity in the Literature and Culture of the 1790s*. This is a diligent and highly nuanced work of historical and literary-historical contextualization that seeks to recover the full contemporary resonance of images and allusions in canonical Romantic texts (most notably Wordsworth's 'Tintern Abbey') so as to contest new historicism's reading of Romanticism as an evasion or transcendence of history and politics. The 'presences' of Walford Davies's title are a series of key figures—drawn variously from history and contemporary world politics—who featured prominently in diverse debates and discourses of the 1790s but are now largely forgotten. Serving as 'instructive exemplars, monitory models and haunting second selves' (p. 1), these celebrated or notorious individuals were often reference-points shared by Romantic writers and readers that did not need to be spelled out explicitly in the literary text; as Walford Davies neatly puts it at one point, there would have been 'an implied presence in absence' (p. 95). The recovery of these ghostly presences, Walford Davies suggests, enables a clearer understanding of the extent to which Romantic texts were 'negotiating rather than euphemizing history' (p. 4), and accordingly leads to the recognition that these texts are often 'more politically aware, more public, and more complex' (p. 6) than recent criticism has allowed.

In pursuance of this contextualizing project, Walford Davies's first chapter identifies antecedents for the hermit in 'Tintern Abbey' in both Tewdrig, a sixth-century Welsh king who became a hermit at Tintern but who left his place of retirement to fight a last battle with the invading Saxons, and David Williams, a contemporary political theorist, adviser to the Girondins, and author of a *History of Monmouthshire* [1796], in which Tewdrig's story features prominently. From both, it is suggested, may have come an understanding that retirement and the turn to nature was not an escape from history but the route back to political involvement. Chapter 2 then examines the associations between the Wye Valley and Vortigern, the British king notorious for betraying his people to the Saxons; again, Walford Davies demonstrates convincingly that these were associations known to Wordsworth as he composed 'Tintern Abbey', establishing a context which inflects the poem with elements of both guilty self-accusation and self-mythologizing. Thereafter, Walford Davies resurrects the careers, and the contemporary iconicity, of the Polish patriot General Kosciusko and the British radical Richard Warner (in chapter 3) and of the Welsh Jacobin bard Edward Williams (in chapter 4), before turning in his final chapter to John Thelwell, whose *Poems, Chiefly Written in Retirement* [1801] are seen as engaged in dialogue with Wordsworth and Coleridge's poetry. (A lengthy appendix also prints for the first time a number of Thelwell's letters to his family.) Throughout, there is a meticulous reconstruction of the tangled web of personal connections, and social, intellectual and literary interactions, that comprised radical culture in the 1790s, with particular emphasis being placed on Welsh contributions to both radicalism and Romanticism. At the same time, Walford Davies offers fascinating insights into the way Wales figured in the Romantic imagination; the Wye Valley especially seems transformed by this study, emerging as a landscape laden with historical and political implications, and not merely a site of picturesque escapism.

Wales is also very much to the fore in Carruthers and Rawes, eds., *English Romanticism and the Celtic World*. Without losing sight of the overarching context whereby Celticism became 'a tool in the construction of the post-1745 British state' (p. 1), the essays gathered here are concerned to trace the complexity, and the dialogic nature, of the cultural exchanges between England and the Celtic regions. Celtic cultural traditions, it is repeatedly suggested, were not merely appropriated by English culture in the construction of 'Britishness', they also made their own contribution to that identity, or worked fruitfully to problematize the identities foisted upon them. Nor are they simply taken up and repackaged for metropolitan tastes by literary Romanticism; rather, as the essays collected here make clear, Celtic culture played a crucial part in the emergence of Romanticism. In this spirit, the collection brings together papers on Macpherson's 'Ossian' poems and on Sir William Jones (by Dafydd R. Moore and Michael J. Franklin respectively), on the Welsh influences underpinning the poetry of Blake, Southey, and Wordsworth (by David Punter, Caroline Franklin, and J.R. Watson), and on Byron's complex relation to Scotland and his own Scottishness (Bernard Beatty and Andrew Nicholson). Arthur Bradley, Malcolm Kelsall, and Michael O'Neill focus on the Irish context: Bradley addresses Shelley's construction of Ireland, Kelsall looks at Charles Lever's melodrama *Luttrell of Arran* [1865], and O'Neill considers the ways in which modern Northern Irish poets have engaged with the legacy of Romanticism. Elsewhere, Murray G.H. Pittock discusses Sir Walter Scott's role in stimulating tourism to Scotland, while William D. Brewer contrasts the versions of cosmopolitanism articulated in Felicia Hemans's and Byron's poetry—the former, it is suggested, looks back to an ancient Welsh tradition of cosmopolitanism that differs significantly from Byron's sense of himself as a citizen of the world.

Finally, Susan Manning's *Fragments of Union: Making Connections in Scottish and American Writing* explores the complex discursive legacy of two moments of political union, that of England and Scotland in 1707 and that of the American states in 1776. In the wake of these two momentous events, Manning convincingly demonstrates, an idiom and imagery of unity and fragmentation, and a preoccupation as to the proper relationship between parts and any whole that they (possibly) make up, came very much to the fore in diverse discourses: not only political theory, but also philosophy, psychology, linguistics and literature. The Scottish negotiation of these concerns, it is suggested, shaped the subsequent American experience, and structured the terms of the transatlantic debate. The interweaving of all these different lines of enquiry can make Manning's overall argument somewhat hard to follow, yet this is undoubtedly a study rich in fruitful juxtapositions and finely nuanced insights. Chapter 1 focuses chiefly on David Hume's *Treatise of Human Nature* [1739–40], and identifies 'an embedded political analogy within the vocabulary of union and fragmentation which structures the expression of Hume's ideas about personal identity' (p. 34). Chapter 2 explores how

Holland functioned in both the Scottish and American contexts as 'a location of resistance against wholesale ingestion by England' (p. 66): the main texts discussed here are William Byrd's mock-epic *The History of the Boundary Line* (unpublished in Byrd's lifetime), James Thomson's *The Castle of Indolence* [1748], George Ogilvie's *Carolina; or, the Planter* [1791], and the novels of Sir Walter Scott. The third chapter then links James Boswell's journals and Benjamin Franklin's autobiography, seeing both as ripostes to the Humean vision of the fundamentally fragmented self, while chapter 4 juxtaposes Macpherson's 'Ossian' poems and various writings by Thomas Jefferson—notably, the Declaration of Independence itself—understanding them as attempts 'to compose (and re-compose) a current national identity from the fragmentary survivals of the past' (p. 148). Chapter 5 turns to the representation of landscape, arguing that Jefferson's *Notes on the State of Virginia*, Hector St John de Crèvecoeur's *Letters from an American Farmer*, and Walt Whitman's *Leaves of Grass* offer different inflections of a 'syntax of space' (p. 197) that is distinctively American but has its roots in Anglo-Scottish structures of thought. Chapter 6, finally, focuses on questions of literary style; it charts the direct and indirect influence of Hugh Blair's *Lectures in Rhetoric and Belle Lettres* on American figures such as Noah Webster, Emerson, William James, and Emily Dickinson. In the American context, Blair's *Lectures* were read somewhat against the grain, in a manner that exposes a tension in his hyphenated, Anglo-Scottish identity. At one level, he praised a 'periodic, clause-determined and hypotactic style' (p. 248) that was the mark of an advanced, fully civilized culture. At another level, however, Blair was nostalgic for an older, 'native' literary style that was 'loose, paratactic and associative'—these attributes being seen as 'reflecting both the nature of political organization and the mental processes of the primitive' (p. 248)—and it was this aspect of his *Lectures* that was to prove a vital stimulus to the forging of a distinctively American literary style.

The Romantic-era perception of the close connection between, on the one hand, language and literary style and, on the other hand, political structures and the state of society, is also central to Richard Marggraf Turley's *The Politics of Language in Romantic Literature*. This is an excellent study that makes vividly clear just what was at stake in Wordsworth's reformation of poetic diction in *Lyrical Ballads*, and in the stylistic experimentation of Keats and Leigh Hunt in the 1810s and 1820s. Marggraf Turley's subject is the extent to which contemporary linguistic theory—the work of Jacob Boehme, Johann Gottfried Herder, Étienne Bonnot de Condillac, and others—was known to, and an influence on, the Romantic poets. In his first chapter, the main eighteenth-century theories relating to the nature and origin of language are surveyed, and the broader cultural and political ramifications of these competing theories are drawn out. Chapter 2 then addresses Wordsworth's application of the more radical elements in contemporary linguistic theory, discussing both the preface to and the poetry of *Lyrical Ballads*. Chapter 3 turns to Leigh Hunt and the 'Cockney School', exploring both Hunt's explicit, theoretical pronouncements on the reform of language, and also the extent to which individual poems—*The Story of Rimini*, Keats's 'On First Looking into Chapman's Homer' and Elgin Marbles sonnets—dramatize contemporary language debates. Chapter 4 then evaluates Keats's debt to two key linguistic theorists, Condillac (possibly the source, it is suggested here, for the enigmatic closing lines of the 'Ode on a Grecian Urn') and the lexicographer Nathaniel Bailey, editor of *The New Universal*

Etymological English Dictionary [1776]. Through all these chapters, Marggraf Turley stresses how contemporary linguistic theory authorized for many Romantics a highly optimistic view of the poetic project: to reform language would be a key step towards reforming society. In his final two chapters, however, Marggraf Turley charts a paradigm shift in linguistics, and in literature a corresponding loss of optimism as to the potentialities inherent in language. The more systematic, scientific study of language inaugurated by Jacob Grimm in Germany seemed to suggest that language developed according to its own evolutionary logic, a logic that bore little relation to the moral and cultural state of any given society. In part, this served to encourage more nationalistic claims on the part of northern languages like English (since Latin and Greek could not now be held up as intrinsically 'better' than the Germanic languages); but it also partly robbed the poet of the earlier conviction that in the very texture of literary style there resided a power to work a significant influence on society. The final chapter shows how Tennyson wrestled with this forlorn possibility, struggling to retain a belief inherited from Boehme and Coleridge that words were in fact invested with a magical life and efficacy. Overall, this is a highly scholarly yet fluently written study that argues persuasively for the 'rigour and sophistication of Romanticism's engagement with philological thought' (p. xii).

Spector, ed., *British Romanticism and the Jews*, aims to fill a gap in literary history by addressing a hitherto little explored topic. Notwithstanding the fact that some of the finest post-war scholars of Romanticism have been Jewish, little work has been done on the contribution of Jews and Jewish culture to Romanticism, nor conversely has the contribution of Romanticism to the British Jewish community, and to the self-image of that community, received much attention. This volume does much to correct this oversight. Chronologically, the collection addresses for the most part the period between 1753, which saw the furore over the so-called 'Jew Bill' (a piece of liberalizing legislation that attempted to remove Jewish legal and economic disadvantages; it was quickly repealed in the face of vehement anti-Semitic protest) and 1858, when Baron de Rothschild was able to take up a seat in Parliament without first swearing an oath as a Christian. This was the period in which British Jews underwent their version of the Enlightenment, the Haskalah, and it was also—as the two landmark events just cited attest—a period in which the British Jewish community became steadily more integrated into British society, its members assimilating themselves while retaining their own ethnic and religious identity. These were developments in part generative of British Romanticism, in part a product of it: the flood of linguistic, theological, and antiquarian texts produced by the scholars of the Haskalah 'provided a significant resource for Romantic intellectual revisionism', while 'British Romanticism provided the cultural basis through which the British-Jewish community was able to negotiate between the competing obligations to ethnicity and nationalism' (p. 8). As a result of the many intellectual and literary exchanges between British Christians and British Jews, the notion of 'the so-called Judeo-Christian tradition' came into being, 'a merger of the two cultures that has provided the basis for post-Romantic Great Britain to today' (p. 2).

In pursuance of these themes, the collection is organized into three sections. The first, on 'Cultural Contexts', explores the historical and philosophical contexts for the interaction between the two cultures. Alan A. Singer addresses the controversy aroused by the 1753 legislation, Mark L. Schoenfield discusses media representations of Jews, Lloyd Davies suggests affinities between Wordsworth and two contemporary rabbis, the Gaon of Vilna and Shneur Zalman of Liady, and Leslie Tannenbaum reads Blake's *Jerusalem* as a response to Moses Mendelssohn's text of the same name. In the 'British Romantics and the Haskalah' section, Christopher Moylan discusses Thomas Lovell Beddoes's adaptation of certain talmudic references in *Death's Jest-Book*, Esther Schor suggests that Jewish debates subtly shaped Scott's analysis of Scottish cultural and religious tensions, Neville Hoad examines Maria Edgeworth's *Harrington* in the light of the controversy caused by the 1753 Jewish Naturalization Bill, and Efraim Sicher examines the shift that takes place in Dickens's representation of Jews, from the notoriously anti-Semitic portrayal of Fagin in *Oliver Twist* to the idealized figure of Riah in *Our Mutual Friend*. Finally, in a section on 'Jewish Writers and British Romanticism', Michael Scrivener, Stuart Peterfreund, Judith W. Page, and Elizabeth Fay discuss, respectively, the theological controversialist David Levi and the writers Isaac D'Israeli, Hyman Hurwitz, and Grace Aguilar. Sheila A. Spector then discusses Benjamin Disraeli's only 'Jewish' novel, *Alroy*, while in a last, especially fascinating piece, David Kaufmann considers how and why modern Jewish critics such as Harold Bloom have made such an important contribution to the study of Romanticism.

Of related interest—and containing also a chapter that usefully complements Ina Ferris's study of the Irish national tale—is Mark Canuel's *Religion, Toleration and British Writing, 1790–1830*. Here Canuel traces the genealogy of British society's much-vaunted reputation for toleration. Focusing in particular on the intersection of religious and political freedoms, and the arguments for and against the removal of restrictions on minority religious groups such as Dissenters, Catholics, and Jews, this finely nuanced, historically rigorous study charts a transformation in the conceptualization of 'Britain'. Previously understood as a community bound together by a common Protestant faith, Britain over the course of the Romantic period was increasingly understood as comprising diverse ethnic and religious communities coexisting within a set of secular political institutions. This is a discursive transformation, Canuel contends, effected not only by the political theorists who explicitly addressed this issue, but also by the literary writers of the period, who in diverse ways brought about a reimagining of British society and its political and religious institutions. They did so in part by dramatizing the failures, and sometimes even the horrors, of enforced religious belief within a community. The Gothic is a principal point of focus in this study, addressed in three chapters that deal chiefly with Ann Radcliffe's novels, with the poetry of Byron and Keats, and with the inquisitorial dramas of Byron, Shelley, and Lord John Russell: on Canuel's reading the enclosed, monastic spaces of Gothic are to be understood as less an attack on Catholicism and more an implicit critique of ecclesiastical authority even as it operates in Britain. Other genres, such as the Irish national tale and the historical novels of Scott (the dual focus of chapter 4 of this study), are more obviously concerned with the way in which local identities and beliefs are negotiated within the political structures that govern Britain as a whole. Chapters 3 and 5, meanwhile, address two figures usually seen as vocal defenders of the established Church, Coleridge and Wordsworth. In the first case tracing continuities in Coleridge's thought from *The Watchman* to *On the Constitution of Church and*

State, and in the second case focusing chiefly on *The Excursion*, Canuel subtly adjusts the conventional image of Coleridge and Wordsworth by exploring the extent to which both were committed to a national Church that embraced dissent and divergent viewpoints, a Church that did not enforce any one form of religious belief so much as provide a framework within which different beliefs could coexist.

Slavery and the Romantic Imagination, by Debbie Lee, is a lively, wide-ranging account of the ways in which Romantic writers grappled with 'the greatest moral question of the age' (p. 29). In a contextualizing study that juxtaposes canonical literary texts with a wealth of background material—pamphlets and prints, travel narratives, medical treatises, melodramas, and much else besides—Lee argues that many Romantic writers engaged with the issue of slavery in an indirect or allusive way. They may have avoided an explicitly moralizing style in their greatest poetry, but these were nevertheless texts that embraced what Lee, drawing on French philosopher Emmanuel Lévinas, terms the poetics of 'alterity' and of the 'distanced imagination' (p. 29): that is to say, they were concerned to make immediate and present to readers scenes and situations that were normally not thought about, because occurring in remote geographical regions. This ethical, and empathetic, aspect of the Romantic imagination is explored in the first place in connection with Coleridge's *Rime of the Ancient Mariner*: the Mariner's agonies are related to contemporary debates about tropical disease, and specifically yellow fever, and to the tendency in abolitionist circles to construe such diseases as products of Britain's participation in slavery. Successive chapters are then given over to Blake's illustrations for John Stedman's *Narrative of a Five Year's Expedition against the Revolted Slaves of Surinam*, which are linked with the scientific theories of race emerging in the period; to Keats's *Lamia* and contemporary images of African religion (specifically, voodoo); and to Shelley's 'The Witch of Atlas', which is viewed in connection with the cartographical ambitions of contemporary African exploration. Mary Shelley's *Frankenstein* is the focus of chapter 7, while the final chapter addresses the mad mothers found in Wordsworth's poetry, relating them to debates about the frequency of infanticide and abortion among slave women: this chapter closes with a discussion of Mary Prince's *History of Mary Prince, A West Indian Slave, Related by Herself* [1831].

In *Waterloo and the Romantic Imagination*, Philip Shaw makes a wide-ranging and insightful survey of contemporary British representations, in both literature and the visual arts, of the climactic battle of the Napoleonic War. As Shaw convincingly demonstrates, Wellington's victory at Waterloo prompted more diverse, and more conflicted, responses in Britain than one might imagine. If from one perspective it was a glorious end to the long hostilities with France, from another perspective it was an awkward beginning to a peace that in some respects was far more problematic than war, a peace in which it was no longer possible to ignore simmering social and political tensions in Britain. And if it was, from one perspective, the high-water mark of British military might, from another, more fraught, perspective it was a moment of such triumph that the only possible future movement seemed to be downwards, towards imperial decline. Such paradoxes and contradictions are adroitly drawn out by Shaw in a study that mixes skilful close reading, and scrupulous attention to questions of genre and narrative form, with subtle theoretical insights gleaned from Hegel and Lacan. The first chapter examines Sir Walter Scott's reaction to the battle, as expressed directly in the minor poem *The Field of Waterloo* [1815], and indirectly in *The Antiquary* [1816], while chapter 2 looks at the tourist industry which sprang up around the battlefield, and the many panoramas that seemingly transported the battlefield back to Britain. Chapter 3 then reviews Southey's argument with the Duke of Wellington over the name of the battle, before looking in more detail at Southey's verse romance *The Poet's Pilgrimage to Waterloo*. Chapter 4 considers Coleridge's war writing, and chapter 5 focuses on Wordsworth, and the notorious 'Thanksgiving Ode' that proclaims carnage to be God's daughter. Chapter 6, finally, discusses Byron's anti-establishment response to the battle, as presented in canto 3 of *Childe Harold's Pilgrimage*. Throughout, Shaw amply demonstrates the unsettling sublimity of Waterloo in its immediate aftermath, and the extent to which it existed for contemporaries as 'a wound or fissure in the text of historical memory' (p. 6).

In *Romantic Medievalism: History and the Romantic Literary Ideal*, Elizabeth Fay contests the notion that Romantic medievalism is invariably a conservative, and conservationist, tendency. Against the strains of conservative medievalism that undoubtedly existed in the period, Fay posits a tradition of radical medievalism that looked not to the knight and to concepts of honour and chivalry—the burden of the conservative tradition—but rather to the troubadour. Understanding the *cansos* of these medieval minstrels as not just love lyrics but also highly charged, politically coded songs, this study presents the troubadour as 'a figure for the combined pursuit of artistic mastery and political resistance that perfectly answered the contingencies of a historically charged moment' (p. 4). The first chapter charts the growth of interest in this figure, paying particular attention to female writers such as Anna Seward, Charlotte Smith, Mary Robinson, and Letitia Elizabeth Landon, to questions of sensibility and gender, and to the topos of the bower in Romantic poetry. A somewhat antagonistic strand of Romantic medievalism, Scott, Wordsworth, and Byron's interest in the conventions of Arthurian romance and in the figure of the knight, is the starting point of the next chapter, but in all three cases, Fay suggests, the knightly persona is to different degrees counterbalanced by the less serious, more subversive persona of the troubadour. Chapters 4 and 5 are then devoted to Keats and the Shelleys respectively. Keats is understood as the 'most troubadorian of the Romantics' (p. 146), a perspective that enables valuable insights into his Spenserianism, his debt to the fake-medieval poetry of Thomas Chatterton, his handling of romance conventions, and, finally, his turn from romance to Shakespearian tragedy in *King Stephen*. The Shelleys, meanwhile, are discussed in relation to the topic of love, with Fay concerned to show how Percy borrows from and adapts courtly love conventions, while Mary critiques those conventions.

The Rhetoric of Romantic Prophecy, by Ian Balfour, is a subtle and illuminating study of the function, form, and diverse modalities of prophecy in both British and German Romantic literature. As a genre or mode of poetry, prophecy flourished in the late eighteenth and early nineteenth centuries, as a consequence not simply of the social and political upheavals of the age but also of a growing tendency to read the Bible in revolutionary new ways, and to emphasize its mythological and poetic aspects. These developments in biblical scholarship are the principal focus of the first part of Balfour's study. After an initial survey of bardic and prophetic figures in the poetry of William Collins, Thomas Gray, and Edward Young, successive chapters describe Robert Lowth's demonstration of the literary sophistication of the Bible (foregrounding its techniques of parallelism and so forth), Richard Hurd's defence of the paradoxical nature of prophetic discourse, and Herder and Johann Gottfried Eichhorn's analyses of the prophetic vocation. All helped to make the role of the prophet, and in some cases also the style of the biblical prophetic books, highly attractive models for literary writers, and in the second part of his study Balfour addresses some of the key figures in the Romantic prophetic tradition. Blake, and specifically *Milton*, is the subject of the first chapter here, followed by chapters on Hölderlin's poetry and Coleridge's *The Statesman's Manual*. Throughout, Balfour convincingly demonstrates that prophecy as a mode of poetry, and the prophet as a persona for the poet, involved much more than just naive claims to predict the future. A 'performative rhetoric beyond the constraints of truth and falsity' (p. 123), prophetic utterance was understood in the period as a speech-act that brought into being certain possibilities and grounds for change, and it is this understanding of the mode's complexities that we need to recover, Balfour suggests, if we are properly to appreciate many key Romantic texts.

For those interested in this area of Romantic studies, Balfour's account of the prophetic mode can be usefully complemented by an excellent collection of essays, Fulford, ed., *Romanticism and Millenarianism*. Here a number of leading practitioners in the field tease out the diverse manifestations and ramifications of millenarian fervour in the period: its potency as a vehicle not only for radical but also for conservative politics (Malthus, for example, employs a decidedly apocalyptic idiom); its connections with mesmerism, mysticism, and popular medicine; its application in colonial and imperial contexts; and lastly, of course, its shaping influence on many Romantic literary texts. As Fulford notes in his introduction, 'what many of the so-called Romantics had in common was less a unique ideology than a shared renegotiation of millenarian belief in the light of historical events' (p. 11). To elucidate these negotiations, the essays collected here bring into fruitful relationship a broad range of famous and forgotten, canonical and non-canonical, figures. Blake and Coleridge are the writers who receive most attention, in essays by John Beer, Michael Simpson, Peter J. Kitson, Anne K. Mellor, G.E. Bently Jr., Martin Butler, and (in a jointly written piece), Morris Eaves, Robert N. Essick, and Joseph Viscomi. Adam Rounce focuses on millennial and apocalyptic anxieties in the poetry of William Cowper's last decade, while Southey is a central figure in articles by Nicholas Roe and Tim Fulford which explore, respectively, the Pantisocracy project and Southey's understanding of millenarian enthusiasm as an Oriental infection. Philip W. Martin discusses Lord Byron's *Heaven and Earth* and Thomas Moore's *The Loves of the Angels* [both 1822]; Gary Harrison addresses the theme of 'ecological apocalypse' (p. 103) in the work of Arthur Young and Thomas Malthus; and David Worrall traces with scrupulous precision the radical circles, deeply informed with millenarian attitudes, in which the printer Robert Hawes lived and worked. The volume as a whole is dedicated to Morton D. Paley, the scholar who has perhaps done most to demonstrate the apocalyptic and millenarian dimensions of the Romantic imagination, and accordingly concludes with a bibliography of Paley's studies of Romanticism.

The contributions to Price and Masson, eds., *Silence, Sublimity and Suppression in the Romantic Period*, all share an original, and fruitful, perspective on Romantic writing. Silence is the central organizing theme here, a topic and trope that opens up some fascinating avenues of enquiry. As Price and Masson point out in their introduction, silence figures prominently in diverse contexts in the period, being a key element in both the discourse of the sublime and the discourse of sentiment. It can also bear a political (and frequently a gendered) inflection, being sometimes the result of the coercive suppression of voice, and sometimes a self-chosen refusal to enter into dialogue on unfair or unequal terms. All of these nuances are teased out in essays that for the most part combine theoretical and philosophical sophistication with diligent close reading. Shelley is the subject of articles by Cian Duffy and Mark Sandy: Duffy advances a materialist reading of 'Mont Blanc', while Sandy explores the fraught self-consciousness of the 'Hymn to Intellectual Beauty', 'To a Skylark', and 'Ode to the West Wind'. Scott Masson, meanwhile, detects an 'existential crisis' (p. 59) in the famous (notorious?) silence of Keats's Grecian urn. Fiona Price, Sue Chaplin, and Rachel Woolley then explore the way in which silence figures as both handicap and enabling device in women's writing of the period. Price addresses Mary Wollstonecraft's insistence on her own originality, which had the effect of silencing influences and rivals; Chaplin draws out the Gothic potentialities of silence in connection with Eliza Fenwick's novel *Secresy, or The Ruin on the Rock* [1796]; Woolley emphasizes Mary Shelley's sophistication as a historical, rather than Gothic, novelist, by focusing on the subtle use made of silence in *Valperga* [1823]. Thereafter, Carol Bolton reflects on certain silences occurring in the context of British imperialism and colonialism, linking Wordsworth's 'Poems on the Naming of Places' with contemporary exploration narratives to consider those native voices and native histories that are necessarily suppressed in such acts of naming. Bharat Tandon then questions the extent to which female reticence is valorized by Jane Austen in *Mansfield Park*. Finally, Amy Billone explores the emotive, sentimental potentialities of silence in the poetry of Charlotte Smith, and Sally Bushell argues in connection with Wordsworth's *Excursion* that silences can be one result of a Romantic self-consciousness and unease with the business of arousing sympathy in readers and listeners.

A more eclectic assortment of essays is found in Peer, ed., *Recent Perspectives on European Romanticism*. The volume is organized into three sections. In the first, 'Romanticism and Emotion', Diane Long Hoeveler writes on late nineteenth-century representations of Salome, Eugene Stelzig identifies an 'aristocracy of consciousness' (p. 33) in Romantic poetry, Marjean D. Purinton discusses hysteria in Joanna Baillie's *Witchcraft* [1836], and Didier Maleuve addresses the theme of patience in Emerson's writing. In 'Romanticism and Individualism', Beth Lau explores how 'self-defining memories' (p. 93) operate in *The Prelude*, Ann R Hawkins reads Byron's *Manfred* as a rewriting of Joanna Baillie's *De Montfort* [1798], Safoi Babana El-Alaoui finds in Jean Rhys's *Wide Sargasso Sea* a critique of Romantic individualism, and Terryl L. Givens considers Byron's distaste for the linguistic mystifications found in many religious discourses. Finally, in 'Romantic Continuities', Eugene Eoyang considers the Chinese poet, painter, and calligrapher Bada Shanren, Lotte Thrane discusses the correspondence between Rainer Maria Rilke and Magda von Hattingberg, and Ray Fleming explores Thomas Mann' interest in Dante.

Linguistic Transformations in Romantic Aesthetics from Coleridge to Emily Dickinson, a collection of essays by Morag Harris edited by Morton D. Paley and Meg Harris Williams, is a more lively and stimulating volume than its rather dry title might suggest. Coleridge, Keats, the Brontës, and Emily Dickinson are the author discussed in papers that combine sensitive close reading with a sophisticated knowledge of German Romantic aesthetic theory. The first essay explores the influence of Coleridge, Schiller, and Goethe on Emily Dickinson; it is followed by two essays on Coleridge, one focusing on the poet's personal and poetic development in 1802, the other addressing his attitude to the key female figures in his life, Sarah Hutchinson and Dorothy Wordsworth. Two essays on Keats discuss, in the first case, the 'Ode to a Nightingale' in relation to the poet's perception of 'the impermanence of particular beauty', and, in the second case, Keats's apprehension of the dangers involved in the perception of beauty. Two final essays explore affinities between the novels of the Brontës and the poetry and letters of Dickinson.

For those with an interest in Romantic-era print culture, publishing, and the history of the book, an excellent collection of essays appeared this year: Clery, Franklin, and Garside, eds., *Authorship, Commerce and the Public: Scenes of Writing, 1750–1850* addresses both the production and the reception of books in an age that witnessed a dramatic expansion, and diversification, of the reading public. The essays are grouped into three sections, 'Authorship', 'Commerce', and 'The Public'. Those in the first section explore the new sense of the 'author', and of authorship as a respectable profession, that emerges in the late eighteenth century. The way in which female writers negotiated the growing professionalization of writing receives much attention here, as Pam Perkins discusses the supposedly artless persona adopted by Anne Grant in her *Letters from the Mountains* [1806], and Paula R. Feldman writes on 'Women Poets and Anonymity in the Romantic Era'. Claire Lamont then explores what was at stake for Sir Walter Scott when he discarded his anonymity as author of the Waverley novels, Douglas S. Mack considers James Hogg's relationship with his publishers, paying particular attention to the book-length poems *The Queen's Wake* [1813] and *Queen Hynde* [1824], and Paul Chirico focuses on how John Clare was presented to readers by his editor and publisher John Taylor. The essays in the second section, 'Commerce', explore the implications and ramifications of the intensifying commercialization of print culture. Robert Jones discusses how Eliza Heywood engaged with the marketplace as editor of *The Female Spectator*, and Sara Salih explores how Frances Burney revised her novel *Camilla* in the light of critical reviews. Christopher Skelton-Foord then considers the role played by circulating libraries in the dissemination and consumption of printing, while Benjamin Colbert probes the Romantic (and specifically Wordsworthian) rejection of popularity and commercial success as the criterion of good poetry. The essays in the final section, 'The Public', reflect on the emergence of the idea of the 'reading public', and on the anxieties increasingly created by the perception of a new, mass audience for books. In this light, Judith Stoddart looks at Charle Knight's *Penny Magazine* [1832], probing the assumptions that contemporary and modern commentators bring to bear on this journal and its mass readership. Michael Franklin addresses the emerging readership in colonial India, focusing on the circle of writers around Warren Hastings; Paul Keen shows how contemporary anxieties regarding an excessively literate, over-educated female readership are reflected in Charles Lloyd's novel *Edmund Oliver* [1798], and specifically in the character of Gertrude Sinclair; and finally William Christie discusses Henry Taylor's abortive attempt in 1835 to introduce state patronage of literature.

Of related interest is Paul Keen's '"The most useful of citizens": Towards a Romantic Literary Professionalism' (*SiR* 41[2002] 627–54), which surveys the shifting cultural terrain and the evolutions in discourse that enabled, and valorized, the persona of the professional 'author'. Also relevant in this context is a special issue of *The Wordsworth Circle* dedicated to the career of bookseller and publisher Joseph Johnson. Here, Marilyn Gaull writes on 'Joseph Johnson's World: Ancestral Voices, Invisible Worms and Roaming Tigers' (*WC* 33:iii[2002] 92–4), Leslie F. Chard on 'Joseph Johnson in the 1790s' (*WC* 33:iii[2002] 95–100), Angela Esterhammer on 'Continental Literature, Translation, and the Johnson Circle' (*WC* 33:iii[2002] 101–3), Beth Lau on 'William Godwin and the Joseph Johnson Circle: The Evidence of the Diaries' (*WC* 33:iii[2002] 104–7), Laura Mandell on 'Johnson's Lessons for Men: Producing the Professional Woman Writer' (*WC* 33:iii[2002] 108–12), Alan Richardson on 'Erasmus Darwin and the Fungus School' (*WC* 33:iii[2002] 113–15), and Debbie Lee on 'Johnson, Stedman, Blake and the Monkeys' (*WC* 33:iii[2002] 116–18). Seamus Perry concludes matters with a piece entitled 'In Praise of Puny Boundaries' (*WC* 33:iii[2002] 119–21) that reflects on the literary-historical usefulness of making groupings such as 'the Johnson circle'.

Finally, as regards book-length studies of Romanticism, two useful introductions to Romantic literature were published this year, *Romantic Literature* by Jennifer Breen and Mary Noble, in the Arnold Contexts series, and *Burke to Byron, Barbauld to Baillie, 1790–1830*, by Jane Stabler, in Palgrave's Transitions series. As one would expect, both engage with a broad range of authors and texts, male and female, canonical and non-canonical, so as to interrogate the nature of Romanticism and the composition of the Romantic canon. That said, Breen and Noble perhaps present a more traditional picture of the period insofar as it is innovations in poetry that receive most discussion in *Romantic Literature*. The three central chapters here offer clear and illuminating accounts on the revival of the ballad form in Scotland and England, and its subsequent influence on lyric poetry generally, and on the revival of the sonnet. These are supplemented by highly informative chapters on the novel in the Romantic period, on satire (focusing on Peacock, Austen, early Blake, Byron, and Burns), on literature and science, and on literary responses to the French Revolution: there is no discussion of Romantic drama. In this regard, however, Breen and Noble's picture of Romanticism can be usefully supplemented by Stabler's. In *Burke to Byron, Barbauld to Baillie* Romantic drama receives a chapter to itself, with Stabler focusing in some detail on Joanna Baillie's *De Montfort*, Byron's *Manfred*, and Elizabeth Inchbald's translation of August von Kotzebue's *Lovers' Vows*, before moving on to consider transitions in audience taste and expectations (in sections which also interweave some fascinating insights into Byron's *Don Juan*). Romantic poetry, and the novel and non-fictional prose of the period, are also allotted a chapter each, and the book as a whole is topped and tailed with chapters exploring the transition into the Romantic period (works by Radcliffe, Burke, and Blake, all published in 1790, are discussed here) and out of it, as Romanticism gave way to Victorian attitudes (works by Hemans, Cobbett, Scott, and Byron, all published or performed in 1830, are discussed here). Throughout, Stabler focuses on fewer texts than Breen and Noble, and presents the period not so much through a broad survey of developments as through a series of hugely insightful close readings. In particular, she concentrates to great effect on moments of transition *within* the literary text: breaches of decorum and sudden changes of tone in poetry, smooth or abrupt shifts in the emotional states of characters on the stage, and so forth. The exhilaration and/or anxiety that these microcosmic transitions could cause are plausibly related back to the macrocosmic political and social developments of the period, and to the contemporary awareness, occasioning both unease and excitement, that this was an age of remarkable, often violent, change. As a result, one gains a wonderful sense of how historical context shapes in the most subtle, intimate ways the writing of literary texts and the development of literary genres.

Turning now to the work published this year in journals, *Nineteenth-Century Contexts* (24:iii[2002]) had two articles falling under the rubric of 'General Romanticism'. In '"The Laureat Hearse Where Lyric Lies": Hunt, Hazlitt and the Making of Romantic Apostasy, 1813' (*NCC* 24:iii[2002] 233–50), Charles Mahoney examined the vigorous, and acrimonious, debate that surrounded the appointment of Robert Southey to the position of Poet Laureate in 1813, while in 'Consuming Egypt: Appropriation and the Cultural Modalities of Romantic Luxury' (*NCC* 24:iii[2002] 317–32), Diego Saglia scrutinizes not only literature but also fashion, furniture, and tableware in connection with the Romantic taste for Egyptian motifs and styles. Elsewhere, Saglia also wrote on 'William Beckford's "Sparks of Orientalism" and the Material-Discursive Orient of British Romanticism' (*TPr* 16[2002] 75–92), using Beckford's career and writings to illustrate how 'Romantic uses of the East are distinguished by an increased representational accuracy and a growing materiality of the orient within an over-arching "consumer orientalism"' (p. 76). Also dealing in questions of the exotic and of travel are Gerald Gillespie's 'In Search of the Noble Savage: Some Romantic Cases' (*Neoh* 29:i[2002] 89–96) and Tim Fulford and Debbie Lee's 'Mental Travellers: Joseph Banks, Mungo Park, and the Romantic Imagination' (*NCC* 24:ii[2002] 117–37). The former is a brisk survey of instances of the noble savage trope from Aphra Behn to Paul Gauguin; the latter traces the influence of exploratory ventures and exploration narratives on writers such as Coleridge and Keats.

Two articles in *Romanticism* this year were of general interest to Romanticists. Colin Winborn discussed 'George Crabbe, Thomas Malthus and the "Bounds of Necessity"' (*Romanticism* 8:i[2002] 75–89), and Fiona Price wrote on 'Democratizing Taste: Scottish Common Sense Philosophy and Elizabeth Hamilton' (*Romanticism* 8:ii[2002] 179–96). In *Romanticism on the Net*, a special issue was given over to the topic of 'Romantic Labor/Romantic Leisure': amongst articles on Blake, Byron, Coleridge, and Wordsworth, one more general paper deserves fuller notice here, Bridget Keegan's 'Lambs to the Slaughter: Leisure and Labouring-Class Poetry' (*RoN* 27[2002]). In earlier editions of *RoN*, Jacqueline Labbe, 'The Romance of Motherhood: Generation and the Literary Text' (*RoN* 26[2002]), surveyed the deployment by female writers of maternal imagery in connection with literary production; Jon Mee, 'Mopping Up Spilt Religion: The Problem of Enthusiasm' (*RoN* 25[2002]), explored the regulatory mechanisms put in place in the period to distinguish legitimate, healing forms of enthusiasm from more dangerous, excessive forms; and Martin Priestman discussed 'Temples and Mysteries in Romantic Infidel Writing' (*RoN* 25[2002]), focusing chiefly on Erasmus Darwin's *The Temple of Nature* [1803].

In addition to the special issue on Joseph Johnson noted earlier, *The Wordsworth Circle* also had an issue dedicated to 'Romanticism and the Physical'. Alongside work on specific named authors, this included a paper by Tim Fulford, 'A Romantic Technologist and Britain's Little Black Boys' (*WC* 33:i[2002] 36–43), on the plight of London chimney-sweeps, and hopes for alleviating their condition raised by advances in chimney-technology; and from Timothy Morton 'Why Ambient Poetics? Outline for a Depthless Ecology' an impassioned claim as to Romantic poetry's ability to enact and produce 'ambience' (p. 52), a 'state of nondual awareness that collapses subject-object division' (*WC* 33:i[2002] 52–6). In its next issue, *The Wordsworth Circle* included an article by Ron Broglio, 'Mapping British Earth and Sky' (*WC* 33:ii[2002] 70–6), exploring the significance of the Ordnance Survey mapping project in Britain.

Finally, in 'Romantic Historicism and the Afterlife' (*PMLA* 117[2002] 237–51), Ted Underwood offers a thought-provoking reading of the Romantic fascination with historical difference, and with the ability of inanimate objects to speak to us of the past, while in '"Back to the Future?": The Narrative of Allegory in Recent Critical Accounts of Romanticism' (*ELH* 69:iv[2002] 1029–46), Karen Hadley offers a theoretical critique of new historicism's tendency to privilege historical narrative over allegory.

2. Non-Fictional Prose

Criticism of non-fictional prose this year comprises a varied and generally excellent crop of articles and book chapters, though the canonical purist—if any such remains—might cavil at the genetically modified nature of a harvest that includes so much interdisciplinary cross-fertilization with political, religious, historical, scientific, and other kinds of discourses with the prose literature of the period. The single book-length work reviewed, apart from collections of essays, is Thomas McFarland's and Nicholas Halmi's edition of *Opus Maximum*, Coleridge's *magnum opus*, which he never completed and which now fittingly though paradoxically brings to a close the commanding Bollingen edition of Coleridge's works.

To commence with the *Opus Maximum*, then, it is appropriate perhaps that the work which Coleridge eternally promised—the 'principal labour' and the 'great object' of his life—but which remained perennially fragmentary during his lifetime, should remain the most resistant to completion, even editorially. The fragments that comprise this master work have appeared all but incomprehensible in any systematic sense, existing as a series of jottings encompassing an omnivorously Coleridgean range of speculations, hints, anecdotes, digressions, and the like, and thus remaining unpublished by Coleridge's nineteenth-century editors such as J.H. Green, despite their devotion to publishing Coleridge's oeuvre. As McFarland argues, however, in the long Prolegomena that prefaces the new edition, post-structuralist thinking has altered our view of the necessity (or indeed the possibility) of achieving theoretical sufficiency in any speculative undertaking of the kind Coleridge envisaged, and we may be more receptive of his work despite its self-evidently fragmentary state at the time of his death. The reality of Coleridge's death, as McFarland argues, presents a textual paradox in relation to his *magnum opus*: what had been incomplete in a tentative and intentional sense for Coleridge was now complete by virtue of this reality. McFarland thus aims to 'present and interpret' Coleridge's text, in the state of completion that death achieved for it, and he expressly avows his intention 'not to transform fragments into a coherent whole' (p. clvii). The massive Prolegomena, covering a range of philosophical topics which McFarland uses to preface the text, seems to serve, then, as a helpful introduction to Coleridge's thinking in the broadest sense, no doubt a vastly speculative arena in itself. However, equally without doubt the fragments themselves, the primary object of the edition, will in time be taken by critical scholarship in different and unanticipated ways. The publication of this meticulous edition, generously annotated and cross-referenced to the other volumes of the Bollingen edition, will thus provide this most fragmentary and elusive of Romantic works a degree of textual authority and 'completeness' paradoxically unachieved in Coleridge's lifetime.

A concern with aesthetics seems to underlie a number of critical essays this year, clearly a wider concern for Romanticists at this time and one that traverses a good deal of non-fictional prose in its ambit. Benjamin Colbert's excellent article, 'Aesthetics of Enclosure: Agricultural Tourism and the Place of the Picturesque' (*ERR* 13[2002] 20–34), argues persuasively against the critical consensus which appears to obtain that the aesthetic of the picturesque was inherently and persistently anti-utilitarian in nature. Turning to Arthur Young's writings of the 1790s, and to a lesser extent to those of his 'literary heir', Morris Birkbeck, in the new sub-genre of the 'agricultural tour', Colbert shows how Young uses picturesque settings to complement his broader concerns for agricultural productivity. That the picturesque itself, the aesthetic focus of materialist and new historicist critiques such as Marjorie Levinson's, could admit a synthetic conception of beauty and utility suggests the ways in which subsequent travel writers would be able to bridge the gap between utility and pleasure in their later imaginings of landscape. Also on the topic of the picturesque, in her article 'Accident or Murder? Intentionality, the Picturesque, and the Body of Thomas De Quincey' (*NCP* 29[2002] 48–68), Alison Byerly focuses on De Quincey's use of the picturesque in his confessional and murder essays, which, she argues, serves to evade the materiality (and pain) of the body through aesthetic distancing. Byerly's suggestion that the picturesque emerges in De Quincey's work as 'a detached, unemotional, culturally specific mode of apprehending the world' (p. 49) usefully contests the identification of his aesthetic as primarily of the sublime mode, but seems to be premised on a fairly rigid reading of the picturesque which disallows the permeability of aesthetic boundaries in De Quincey, the constant parodying and renegotiation of categories that he often achieves so brilliantly. Another essay this year on De Quincey is the present reviewer's 'Not "Forsworn with pink ribbons": Hannah More, Thomas De Quincey, and the Literature of Power' (*RoN* 25[2002]), which attempts to uncover the revisionary nature of De Quincey's later reminiscences of More and to indicate thereby the covert influence of Evangelical thinking on his literary theorizing. Far from absolving literature of politics, however, colonialist and nationalist imperatives typical of Evangelical thinking may be seen to operate within the spiritualized and aesthetic sphere to which literary power is arrogated by De Quincey.

A strenuous consideration of the nexus between medium and message links two articles on Burke and Hazlitt respectively. Siraj Ahmed's essay, 'The Theatre of the Civilized Self: Edmund Burke and the East India Trials' (*Rep* 78[2002] 28–55), examines Burke's speeches and writings on British India, particularly the melodrama implicit in his impeachment of Hastings in 1786. Although Burke's conservative anti-revolutionary writings are sometimes seen as antithetical to his anti-imperialist writings on the American and Indian colonies, Ahmed argues powerfully that both are based on Burke's conception of civil society. Burke's famous indictment of Hastings hinges on his portrayal of him as a degenerate imperial merchant, and of the colonial government in India as one that needed to be restrained by British civil society. Because he saw the British Parliament as complicit in the crimes of colonial government and felt the need to widen his appeal to the very foundations of civil society, the nation itself, Burke transformed his appeal from a merely legal one to the Lords to one of a mass public spectacle, characterized by affective displays of personal involvement. Yet Burke's rhetoric concealed an even deeper anxiety, that imperialism implied the essentially savage nature of civil progress for the ambitious nation-state, although masked by the notion of a civilized self: hence the performative aspect of Burke's indictment of Hastings, based as it is on the conviction of a concealed degeneracy within the civil self. A similar concern with the relations between form and content informs Elizabeth Fay's accomplished essay 'Portrait Galleries, Representative History, and Hazlitt's *Spirit of the Age*' (*NCC* 24[2002] 151–75), which deals with Hazlitt's biographical writings in the context of the conventional eighteenth- and nineteenth-century 'portrait galleries', the popular volumes of plates and essays that enabled middle-class audiences to aspire to consumption of hitherto elitist and expensive society portraits by means of cheap, mechanical modes of reproduction. Hazlitt's *Spirit of the Age*, however, runs counter to the populist direction of this genre, providing a critique of society and the cultural moment through his unadorned and trenchant biographical essays. Hazlitt's quarrel with the genre of the portrait gallery represents his criticisms of Locke's system based, as he saw it, on a mechanical relation between the senses and the intellect, and his criticisms of the zeitgeist are evident in the personalities that he constructs as his indictment of the age.

The bicentenary in 2002 of the foundation of the Romantic period's best-known journal, the *Edinburgh Review*, provides the impetus for a historically minded collection of essays, Demata and Wu, eds., *British Romanticism and the Edinburgh Review*. The opening chapter by Philip Flynn, 'Francis Jeffrey and the Scottish Critical Tradition', delineates Jeffrey as a product of the Scottish Enlightenment especially indebted to Hume's scepticism in his philosophical make-up. Jeffrey's aesthetic, so often slated without understanding on account of his criticisms of Romantic canonical writers, emerges far more comprehensibly from Flynn's account of the complex underpinnings of 'taste' within the Scottish intellectual tradition. Fiona Stafford's article on 'The *Edinburgh Review* and the Representation of Scotland' explores the meaning of the Scottish identity that the journal established for itself during the period when Britain forged a new identity through the war with France, and a new United Kingdom emerged after the Union with Ireland. The formidable talent of the writers as well as the popularity and influence of the magazine led, however, to accusations of 'smartness', a pejorative association that later clung to its image. On a related theme, Timothy Webb's chapter, 'A "great theatre of outrage and disorder": Figuring Ireland in the *Edinburgh Review*, 1802–29', examines the implications of the 'Irish Question' and the issue of Catholic Emancipation during the early years of the journal. Anxieties regarding the rebellious tendencies of the Irish on account of their Catholicism were ambivalently tempered by the *Edinburgh* with sympathetic and wide coverage of Irish history and politics. Reviews of Irish orators and writers such as the Edgeworths, Thomas Moore, and Charles Maturin reveal a tendency to characterize the Irish imagination as eloquent and exuberant, though tending as well to riotousness and a lack of control, reflecting thereby the figurative ambiguity of Ireland itself. Other chapters in this collection covering various generic categories include Massimiliano Demata's 'Unprejudiced Knowledge: Travel Literature in the *Edinburgh Review*', which examines the coverage of travel books during the early years of the magazine, and Susan Manning's 'Walter Scott, Antiquarianism and the Political Discourse of the *Edinburgh Review*, 1802–11', which discusses the discursive possibilities of antiquarianism in the period and indicates interestingly how Scott's departure from the *Edinburgh* and his divergence from Jeffrey involved such concerns. Two other chapters deal with Jeffrey's relationship with canonical poets. Paul Fry's chapter, 'Jeffreyism, Byron's Wordsworth and the Nonhuman in Nature', focuses on Jeffrey's philosophical opposition to idealism and argues for his influence on Byron's criticisms of Wordsworth. Taking a bio-critical approach, Jane Stabler's chapter, 'Against their Better Selves: Byron, Jeffrey and the *Edinburgh*', traces the oscillations in personal and critical relations between these two towering figures of the literary world, sensitively reading their differing approaches to criticism as mutually inflected at various points. In the final chapter, 'Rancour and Rabies: Hazlitt, Coleridge and Jeffrey in Dialogue', Duncan Wu offers a new perspective on Hazlitt's movement from his early admiration for the Lakers to his later, openly and strongly critical, position by focusing on Hazlitt's reviewing, and in particular on two of his reviews of Coleridge. In between Hazlitt's pre-publication review of Coleridge's *Lay Sermons* in 1816 and his later onslaught in the *Edinburgh,* a triangular interchange between them and Jeffrey ensued—a complex transaction involving personalities and ideologies illuminatingly reconstructed by Wu—which underlies Hazlitt's apparently seamless absorption into the *Edinburgh*.

Morton and Smith, eds., *Radicalism in British Literary Culture, 1650–1830: From Revolution to Revolution*, though not necessarily focused on prose, offers one important chapter for our consideration. Peter J. Kitson's '"Not a reforming patriot but an ambitious tyrant": Representations of Cromwell and the English Republic in the Eighteenth and Early Nineteenth Centuries' charts new territory in examining the impact of the English revolution and the figure of Cromwell in particular on a range of eighteenth-century and Romantic writers. While earlier studies of the impact of the English revolution on the Romantics have focused on the canonical writers, Kitson opens the field considerably. Works such as Godwin's magisterial *History of the Commonwealth of England* [1824–8] and Southey's neglected 'Life of Cromwell' for the *Quarterly Review* [1821] could not have come into being without a host of other writers on the commonwealth and the protector as their sources. From such traces, Kitson helpfully excavates a far more ambiguous, and even positively favourable, character for Cromwell than earlier accounts have acknowledged, and one with profound implications for the underground Dissenting traditions of the period. As Kitson suggests, such currents clearly flow into Godwin's sympathetic portrayal of Cromwell as a philanthropist and patriot, though marred by his ambition: an influential depiction that in turn paves the way for Carlyle's *Oliver Cromwell's Letters and Speeches with Elucidations* [1845], usually credited as the earliest major rehabilitation of Cromwell.

3. Prose Fiction

This section discusses publications from 2001, missed last year. Publications from 2002 and 2003 will be reviewed next year.

In their introduction to the special issue of *Novel* on the Romantic-era novel (*Novel* 34:ii[2001] 147–62), Amanda Gilroy and Wil Verhoeven aver that 'the fiction of the Romantic period has remained one of the most underresearched—or unevenly researched—areas of English literature', alluding to the fact that generic studies of the novel have, by and large, ignored the diversity of the fiction of this period, concentrating instead on a very small number of authors, particularly Austen and Scott (pp. 148, 155–6). For, as the co-editors remind us—and it is a point reiterated by Claudia L. Johnson in the issue's first article (*Novel* 34:ii[2001] 163–79)—if the novel can be said to have emerged at any one moment, then the period in which it did so was the Romantic era, and more especially the 1790s (Gilroy, p. 151; Johnson, pp. 165–6). Their aim is not only to assign to the Romantic novel its place in the history of the genre, but also to give the novel, in all its various forms, its due importance in histories of the period in order to provide new perspectives on the 'cultural-historical landscape' (p. 147). 'In this special issue, we attempt to put the Romantic-era novel back into the history of the novel, and histories of the period, and thereby to recover something of the historicity of the Romantic era novel, which is a more expansive concept (plural, fluid, hybrid) than the historical novel as such, to which so much attention has been given, and which has thus managed to eclipse other forms of historical consciousness' ((p. 157; cf. Lukács, *The Historical Novel*). The literary history that most urgently requires reconstitution, Gilroy and Verhoeven suggest, is the prose fiction written from a 'radical' political point of view. They argue, for example, that one reason for the occlusion of the 'hybrid' or generically 'promiscuous' radical novel from histories of the novel is that it was so thoroughly castigated by conservative reviewers and critics, as well as by the counter-action of anti-Jacobin novelists, all of whom associated generic with ideological promiscuity and were keen to reassert generic and ideological discipline (pp. 147, 152–4, 153). As this survey will confirm, a key theme in criticism written in 2001 is the issue limned here by Gilroy and Verhoeven: the recovery of the political and ideological value of Romantic prose fiction.

The most significant study of Romantic prose fiction to appear in 2001, M.O. Grenby's *Anti-Jacobin Novel: British Conservatism and the French Revolution*, takes up the question of occluded history, though not in the way intimated by Gilroy and Verhoeven. In a survey of almost 200 novels Grenby concludes: 'There were in excess of fifty novels published between 1790 and 1805 which were suffused with anti-Jacobinism, with perhaps as many again which were anti-Jacobin in parts or to a limited extent' (pp. xi, 203). Grenby's most important claim is that by far the greatest number of novels produced in the period were conservative rather than radical in their political-ideological outlook, and that this was increasingly the case as the 1790s progressed and as radical confidence waned with the onset of war and with the violent course of the revolution in France. Although only twenty or so 'radical' novels were ever published (most of these appearing before 1796), critical attention has 'understandably' (since literary critics are primarily interested in aesthetic innovation and 'doctrinal originality') focused on the so-called Jacobin novel rather than its conservative counterpart. In the process literary history has produced a one-sided and somewhat distorted view of the ideological orientation of British writers—and of the political consciousness of the population more generally—during the Romantic period (pp. 2, 4–5). The historical landscape Grenby wants to recover for us, then, is 'the emerging hegemony of conservatism in Britain' evinced by the complete ascendancy of anti-Jacobin over Jacobin fiction by 1800 (pp. 169–70).

Grenby's method is to 'see the anti-Jacobin novel as a coherent body of texts rather than as a collection of novels by separately motivated individuals' (p. xii). He is not concerned with 'ideological ambiguity': with discovering unsuspected critical intentions or effects in the writings of conservative authors, for example (p. 3). Grenby assumes, in fact, that the majority of the fictions he looks at are ideologically uncomplicated, and claims, crucially, that it is the very transparency and conventionality of the fictions he investigates that entitles us to see them as representative of the conservative outlook of the wider British public (pp. 1–2). He is finally unconcerned, then, with the question (which has interested critics Claudia Johnson and Eleanor Ty, for instance) of whether or not a profoundly conservative author such as Elizabeth Hamilton wrote anti-Jacobin fiction as a camouflage for her critical analysis of gender propriety, since what he discerns is the more or less complete victory of an anti-Jacobin orthodoxy and the 'co-option of authors by a dominant ideology' (pp. 184–5, 205).

The key to this process of co-option is financial self-interest. Grenby begins with the observation that the anti-Jacobin novel came increasingly to dominate as the threat from Jacobinism receded from about 1798 onwards (pp. 10, 23). This may have been due to the continuing perception of a threat, Grenby concedes, a perception encouraged particularly by those conservative groups, such as the Evangelicals, with an interest in perpetuating the sense of crisis (pp. 7–8). He suggests, however, that it was more the case that authors adjusted themselves to political reality. While the conservative novel initially had an ideological motivation, and while there were a few crusading novelists writing out of genuine ideological fervour, for the most part authors acquiesced in political conservatism by writing to satisfy a demand for a particular kind of fiction (pp. 204–5, 9–10). 'What we can detect in the fictional production of the 1790s and the 1800s is a cyclical relationship between production and reception, a continuum in which authors refined their product according to what their readership demanded' (p. 171). Despite the suggestion, here, of a mutually reinforcing cycle of supply and demand, it is clearly demand which leads in this particular argument. Thus anti-Jacobin fiction was formed by, rather than being formative of, the political conservatism of the nation, more symptom than cause of hegemonic conservatism: it 'reflected the values of the society which commissioned and consumed it' (pp. 9, 169, 12). Anti-Jacobinism, a broad and loosely defined conservatism, 'by the middle of the 1790s, permeated almost the entirety of British society' (p. 8). It is the great strength of the book that Grenby does not lose sight of his deceptively simple overarching argument.

The body of the book is devoted to an analysis of the key strategies of anti-Jacobin novels. Grenby stresses that these are representational strategies and not political principles or ideas as such. He makes clear that anti-Jacobinism, like the Jacobinism against which it was defined, was a rather vague set of political ideas. Indeed, the Jacobinism attacked in the anti-Jacobin novel was the invention of anti-

Jacobinism itself and was invoked to stand 'for all that conservatives found detestable in society' (p. 8). A recurring theme in the book is that the vagueness of the anti-Jacobin ideology was a deliberate strategy and that anti-Jacobins wanted to avoid a rational debate about political principles (pp. 70, 79). Blaming individual ambition and wickedness, for example, was one way in which anti-Jacobinism evaded the discussion of ideas (pp. 114, 124–5). Even if it lacked a coherent ideology, though, literary anti-Jacobinism's fictional strategies gave it a semblance of generic coherence. In chapter 2, for example, Grenby shows how Burkean images were endlessly recycled in anti-Jacobin fiction in order to portray the full horror of the French Revolution. The influence of Burke, in fact, is pervasive, perceptible in all the fictional strategies Grenby analyses. In chapter 5, Grenby shows that the defence of inequality and of subordination was the keystone of conservative ideology, since it was conceived as fundamental to the defence of property. The threat to proper order and gradation of rank came from theories of social and political equality, from social ambition, and from the corrupt manners of the aristocracy (p. 140). Corrupt nobles, as Grenby points out, were perceived to threaten order from the top as surely as did levelling ideas from the bottom (p. 155). Grenby admits that some ideological ambivalence might enter the novels at this point—as it enters Burke's *Letter to a Noble Lord*—since the attack on the behaviour of the elite might be hard to distinguish from the Jacobin attack on the same, but he contends that conservative authors succeeded in upholding a distinction between individuals and the institutions they represented (pp. 160–4, 166, 168).

Grenby's methods and conclusions will not convince every reader. For example, defining the anti-Jacobin novel is something of a problem, and Grenby acknowledges as much when he emphasizes that there were various degrees of conservative ideological commitment in the novel. By treating the novels as if they were 'one text', however, and by not paying attention to the intentions of individual authors, he more or less elides this problem. The lack of 'ideological ambiguity' attributed to the majority of the novels, that is, is assumed as much as proven, and this premise helps to produce the conclusions (p. 3). Moreover, while Grenby's argument that authors acquiesced in anti-Jacobinism out of pecuniary self-interest is convincing, it does not follow that the fears and anxieties and political prejudices of the 'overwhelmingly middle- and upper-class readers' were also those of British society in its 'entirety' (p. 11). In the key sixth chapter Grenby considers in some detail the 'nexus of factors'—publishers, reviewers, critics—'which mediated the demands of audience to authors' (pp. 171, 182, 201). The anti-Jacobin outlook of the majority of critics and reviewers and the publishers' fear of prosecution performed the work of censorship, Grenby argues (pp. 172, 180, 181). Once the influence of critics and reviewers and government legislation is admitted into the equation, it is not so clear that anti-Jacobin novels can be seen as 'an accurate reflection of the society from which they sprang' (p. 202). Nevertheless, this assiduous and readable piece of research will surely lay the ground for more work on this neglected aspect of the period's fictional prose.

In general, it is fair to say, scholarship on the Romantic era continues to be more interested in the 'radical' novel, and particularly in texts which display some ideological complexity. While 2001 was a productive year for female writers of the 1790s, especially for Mary Wollstonecraft, it was a somewhat lean one for the male ones, even for Godwin. All of the articles on Godwin deal with *Things as they are;*

or, Caleb Williams. In an original article, 'Novels and Systems' (*Novel* 34:ii[2001]
202–15), Clifford Siskin looks at the novel's involvement with the eighteenth-
century philosophical 'genre' of system, or systematic explanation. As the term
'system' became politically suspect in the 1790s—because of its associations with
French theory—it became embedded within other genres, such as the novel (pp.
204–5, 209). Godwin's political philosophical system, *Enquiry Concerning
Political Justice*, for instance, informs *Caleb Williams* (pp. 206–7). One result was
that 'system' (in the sense 'of the totalizing of the social') ceased to refer to a textual
strategy for rational explanation and came instead to denote something to which
blame might be attached ('the System' in today's sense) (pp. 211, 213). The
outcome for the novel was a new relationship between individual character and
social system; so, for instance, 'Caleb comes to feel part of the very things that
oppress him' (pp. 211, 213).

More straightforward, though no less illuminating, is Doris Feldmann's
argument, in 'The Detection of the *Homo Politicus*: Textual/Sexual Politics in
William Godwin's *Caleb Williams*' (in Göbel, Schabio, and Windisch, eds.,
Engendering Images of Man in the Long Eighteenth Century, pp. 68–80), that
Godwin's novel is less political allegory than an analysis of the construction of 'the
political' through discourse, especially literary discourse (pp. 69, 78). Monika
Fludernik, 'William Godwin's *Caleb Williams*: The Tarnishing of the Sublime'
(*ELH* 68:vi[2001] 857–96), examines the influence of Edmund Burke's ideas about
the sublime on the novel and claims that, instead of merely rejecting Burke's
aesthetics as the concomitant of his conservative politics, Godwin invests the
sublime with a positive as well as a negative valence, associating it with virtue and
benevolence as well as with power and terror (pp. 861–3, 888). The novel shows
how, in a society founded on the unequal distribution of power and wealth, the 'true'
sublime of virtue is corrupted into the 'tarnished' sublime of terror (pp. 888–9). In a
'companion piece', 'Sympathetic Affect and Artful Deception: Rhetorical
Ambivalence in William Godwin's *Caleb Williams*' (in Göbel et al., eds., pp. 81–
96), Fludernik argues that Godwin's use of Adam Smith's notion of 'sympathy' is
similarly ambivalent (pp. 91, 95). In contrast to other radical writers, Godwin is
suspicious of 'emotionally based processes of oral education' which may
consolidate 'social hierarchy' as much as it might 'enhance human fellowship' (p.
95). Helen M. Buss, 'Memoirs Discourse and William Godwin's *Memoirs of the
Author of A Vindication of the Rights of Woman*' (in Buss, Macdonald, and McWhir,
eds., *Mary Wollstonecraft and Mary Shelley: Writing Lives*, pp. 113–25), argues that
Godwin's 'participatory stance'—which includes elements of self-justification—
makes his posthumous *Memoirs* of his wife a 'paradigmatic text for the study of the
memoir form' (pp. 117, 123).

In his monograph, *The Mental Anatomies of William Godwin and Mary Shelley*,
William D. Brewer takes Godwin and Shelley as case studies for Romantic authors'
predilection for dissecting the mind. Both Godwin and Shelley believed that 'the
workings of the human mind could be dissected, analyzed, and ultimately
understood', and their fictional explorations of the human psyche were shaped by
eighteenth- and early nineteenth-century scientific and philosophical ideas (pp. 15,
16, 18, 27). Each chapter comprises a very detailed discussion of some aspect of
psychic life, through a consideration of several novels by each author. The first
chapter, which is a good example of Brewer's comparative approach, deals with the

influence of Rousseau's *Confessions*, and particularly with the influence of his ideas about 'mental transparency' (p. 30). As deployed by Godwin and Shelley, the confessional narrative allows the reader to see the complex factors determining human motivation and action (p. 24). Godwin's novels typically focus on the protagonist's errors, Brewer argues, while several of Shelley's novels explore the psyche of victims of others' crimes or errors (p. 83). Chapter 2 considers each author's deployment of the notion of ruling passions, the tendency during the eighteenth and early nineteenth centuries to 'defin[e] the mind through the emotions that drive or motivate it' (pp. 93, 86). Chapter 3 considers depictions of madness and argues that, while Godwin has the rationalist's horror of madness, Shelley 'presents a more positive view of madness, linking it to the poetic imagination' (p. 130). Chapter 4 examines the idea that linguistic expression is a kind of therapy for the novels' protagonists, leading to a measure of emotional relief and to increased self-knowledge (pp. 29, 167, 182). Chapter 5 looks at the presentation of dreams in the novels, and contrasts Godwin's scepticism regarding the reliability of dreams with Shelley's exploration of 'the relationship between dreams, the imagination, and prophecy' (p. 184). As Brewer is careful to stress, even in fictional life the mind remains, for both Godwin and Shelley, a puzzle, inaccessible to complete rational analysis; their literary anatomies are, finally, no more than thought experiments (pp. 25, 27). Nevertheless, both believed that insight into the mental processes of fictitious characters could advance human progress by adding to our knowledge of the human species (pp. 211–12).

Three articles testify to the growing interest in transatlantic themes. In '"New Philosophers" in the Backwoods: Romantic Primitivism in the 1790s Novel' (*WC* 32:iii[2001] 130–3), W.M. Verhoeven compares *The Emigrants* to George Walker's anti-Jacobin and 'anti-emigration' novel *The Vagabond* [1799] to show that the changing ideological valence of the idea of 'America' can be a gauge of the changes in the political climate during the 1790s (pp. 130, 132). Lisa M. Steinman, in 'Transatlantic Cultures: Godwin, Brown, and Mary Shelley' (*WC* 32:iii[2001] 126–30) considers the writings of Godwin, Charles Brockden Brown, and Shelley and traces the way in which particular narrative themes and plot lines were 'reinterpreted' and 'recast' as they crossed, via paths of literary influence, from the British cultural context to the American one and back again (pp. 126, 129). Stephen Shapiro's '"I could kiss him one minute and kill him the next!": The Limits of Radical Male Friendship in Holcroft, C.B. Brown, and Wollstonecraft Shelley' (in Göbel et al. eds., pp. 111–32) is similarly promising in its reconstruction of transatlantic literary links in the period. He argues that Charles Brockden Brown's *Jane Talbot* [1801] was an important influence on Mary Shelley's attempt in *Frankenstein* to think through the 'class blindness' of radical novels of the 1790s, such as Thomas Holcroft's *Anna St. Ives* (pp. 117, 126, 130–2).

The novels of Charlotte Smith and Mary Robinson seem to me to warrant more attention than they are awarded. In 2001 there were just three articles on Smith's fiction and two (both by the same author) on Robinson's. Jacqueline M. Labbe, in 'Metaphoricity and the Romance of Property in *The Old Manor House*' (*Novel* 34:ii[2001] 216–31) looks at the way in which Charlotte Smith, in *The Old Manor House* [1793], mixes fiction and fact, the discursive conventions of the romance with those of property law, in order to expose the 'fictionality ... of what her culture considers natural, such things as male primogeniture ... or love' (p. 229). Judith

Davis Miller argues, in 'The Politics of Truth and Deception: Charlotte Smith and the French Revolution' (in Craciun and Lokke, eds., *Rebellious Hearts: British Women Writers and the French Revolution*, pp. 337–63), that Smith's novels in the 1790s elaborate a coherent Godwinian political philosophy in their 'examination of the role of deception as an impediment to the quest for truth so necessary to the personal and public health of the English' (p. 359). Diane E. Boyd, in '"Professing Drudge": Charlotte Smith's Negotiation of a Mother-Writer Author Function' (*SoAR* 66:i[2001] 145–66), examines Smith's nuanced self-representations in her letters and prose prefaces, and contends that she overturns the distinction between professional author and literary drudge, as well as that between the public and private realms (p. 156). In two articles on Mary Robinson's *Walsingham; or, the Pupil of Nature*, Julie Shaffer focuses on the significance of Sidney's successful gender masquerade in the novel: '*Walsingham*: Gender, Pain, Knowledge' (*WW* 9:i[2001] 69–85) and 'Cross-Dressing and the Nature of Gender in Mary Robinson's *Walsingham*' (in Mounsey, ed., *Presenting Gender: Changing Sex in Early-Modern Culture*). Situating the novel within a cultural debate about the nature of sexual identity and gendered behaviour, Shaffer claims that the novel subversively suggests the mutability of gender and questions the idea of innate heterosexuality ('*Walsingham*: Gender, Pain, Knowledge', pp. 70–2; 'Cross-Dressing', pp. 136–8, 160).

In 2001 there was a great deal of critical interest in Maria Edgeworth's fiction, testifying perhaps to the ongoing scholarly disagreement about the political and ideological orientation of her writing. For example, Marilyn Butler focuses on Edgeworth's Irish tales in 'Edgeworth's Ireland: History, Popular Culture, and the Secret Codes' (*Novel* 34:ii[2001] 267–92), and takes issue with 1990s postcolonial readings which tend to read Edgeworth's political motivations from her identity as a member of the Anglo-Irish Ascendancy (pp. 267–9). Close attention to the allusions in Edgeworth's writings, which include references to traditional Irish culture and current Irish politics, show her to be 'much more expressively committed than has hitherto appeared to the history, language, culture, and future of Irish people' (p. 267). Two other essays on Edgeworth's Irish fiction reach a similar conclusion. Michael Neill, in 'Mantles, Quirks, and Irish Bulls: Ironic Guise and Colonial Subjectivity in Maria Edgeworth's *Castle Rackrent*' (*RES* 52[2001] 76–90), suggests that the indeterminacy between narrator Thady Quirk's simplicity/servility and his deceptiveness/subversiveness reveals Edgeworth's familiarity with and understanding of colonized subjectivity (pp. 77, 82, 89). In '"The Plain Round Tale of Faithful Thady": *Castle Rackrent* as Slave Narrative' (*New Hibernia Review* 5:iv[2001] 57–72), Kate Cochran notes structural similarities between *Castle Rackrent* and nineteenth-century American slave narratives and argues that this narrative strategy was an effective way of advocating reform of the way English colonial power was exercised in Ireland (pp. 57–8). The parallel is suggestive, but I am not so convinced by her final claim that it is Edgeworth's 'marginal' status, as a woman within the ruling Ascendancy, that permits her to understand the mentality of its real victims (p. 72).

The question of Edgeworth's political and ideological leanings is pursued by other critics. Nicholas Mason argues, in 'Class, Gender, and Domesticity in Maria Edgeworth's *Belinda*' (*ECN* 1[2001] 271–85), that in her 'domestic' novel *Belinda* Edgeworth adapts the domestic ideology of the middle classes to formulate standards of behaviour for the landowning class to which she belonged (pp. 277, 281). In the novel, domesticity does not mean merely 'proper female behaviour' but suggests 'an obligation to fulfill centuries-old paternalistic duties towards one's tenants or subjects' (pp. 272, 283). There are two articles on the politics of Edgeworth's novel *Harrington* [1817]. In 'Jews, Jubilee, and Harringtonianism in Coleridge and Maria Edgeworth: Republican Conversions' (in Roe, ed., *Samuel Taylor Coleridge and the Sciences of Life*, pp. 69–87), Susan Manly considers the influence of James Harrington's republican political philosophy on Coleridge's ideas about the political organization of the state and on Edgeworth's views on civic liberty as these are expressed in the novel. The novel, Manly claims, is truer to the spirit of Harrington's belief that the English Protestants had something to learn (about religious freedoms, for example) from Jewish history and from the political organization of the ancient Israelites (pp. 71–3, 81, 87). Judith Page argues, in 'Maria Edgeworth's *Harrington*: From Shylock to Shadowy Peddlers' (*WC* 32:i[2001] 9–13), that while *Harrington* critiques British anti-Semitism, this critique is limited by the plot device in which the 'Jewish' heroine, Berenice, turns out to be a Protestant Christian (pp. 12–13).

Finally on Edgeworth, three articles discuss aspects of her formal practice. In 'Maria Edgeworth and the Romance of Real Life' (*Novel* 34:ii[2001] 232–66), an article principally concerned with *Castle Rackrent* and *Ennui*, Michael Gamer makes a case for the 'generic self-consciousness' (p. 261) of Edgeworth's narratives by considering her prose fictions under the genre of 'romance of real life,' a genre that emerged in the 1780s (p. 235). Edgeworth helped to establish a genre that, in her hands, mixed the improbable (romance), the verifiable (factual anecdote), and the instructive (moral fable) (pp. 236–8, 251, 261). Because Edgeworth's prose fictions are not 'novelistic' or realist in the conventional sense (though they clearly 'partake of the "real"'), her representational practice may have helped obscure her place in the novel's history (pp. 235, 261). Francesca Lacaita's 'The Journey of the Encounter: The Politics of the National Tale in Sydney Owensen's *Wild Irish Girl* and Maria Edgeworth's *Ennui*' (in Gillis and Kelly, eds., *Critical Ireland: New Essays in Literature and Culture*, pp. 148–54) contrasts representations of the Irish nation in two national tales, *The Wild Irish Girl* and *Ennui*. She concludes that the ideas of nationhood, allegorized in each, are not only different from each other (the one romantic and multi-cultural, the other modern and cosmopolitan), but are both different from the 'ethno-cultural concept of nationhood which prevailed in the British Isles in opposition to the French Revolution' (pp. 149–50) and from the idea of the nation which was later to prevail in nineteenth- and twentieth-century Irish nationalism (p. 154). Carol Strauss Sotiropoulos argues, in 'Where Words Fail: Rational Education Unravels in Maria Edgeworth's "The Good French Governess"' (*CLE* 32:iv[2001] 305–21), that there is a tension in Edgeworth's fiction between the requisites of a 'good story' and her attempt to inculcate the precepts of a rational education (p. 306).

On the face of it, Hannah More's writings entail rather less ideological complexity than Edgeworth's, but there is a growing body of criticism (including work by feminist critics Anne Mellor and Mitzi Myers) which argues that, read with the same attentiveness to ambiguity, More's texts can be seen as potentially liberatory rather than simply regulatory. Two very fine articles by Jane Nardin continue the re-evaluation of More's politics. In 'Hannah More and the Problem of

Poverty' (*TSLL* 43:iii[2001] 267–84) Nardin looks at a collection of letters written by More to wealthy philanthropic friends, Sir Charles and Lady Middleton and Mrs Bouverie, in which she detailed her charitable work on behalf of the Mendip poor. Nardin argues that, privately, More considered the church and state culpable for the parlous state of the poor (p. 271), but in her public writing she misrepresented these views in order to maintain her reputation with wealthy and powerful donors to her charitable causes (pp. 278–9). In 'Hannah More and the Rhetoric of Educational Reform' (*WoHR* 10:ii[2001] 211–26) Nardin argues that More's Christian scheme of education for the British upper classes amounted to a covert attack on educational theories and practices current in the late eighteenth century (p. 213). Again she makes the point that More had to disguise her reformist ideas in a 'conciliatory rhetoric' (p. 212). Both articles make a convincing case for the re-evaluation of More, although we are left to wonder at what point rhetoric becomes argument.

There were two articles in 2001 on Frances Burney's *The Wanderer; or, Female Difficulties* [1814], which is the only Burney novel I consider here, and they present different views of its politics. Helen Thompson's 'How *The Wanderer* Works: Reading Burney and Bourdieu' (*ELH* 68:iv[2001] 965–89) is a dense article which is difficult to summarize without distorting the subtlety of the argument. Thompson uses Pierre Bourdieu's notion of the *habitus* to suggest the way in which Burney, in her reliance on physical bearing and bodily gestures to represent the central character, the aristocratic Ellis/Juliet, is able to overcome the distinction between internal and external markers of a character's worth (pp. 967, 969). Thompson contends that this new form of distinction is central to Burney's conservative project of 'a postrevolutionary reconstitution of rank' (p. 966). Maria Jerinic's 'Challenging Englishness: Frances Burney's *The Wanderer*' (in Craciun and Lokke, eds., pp. 63–84) argues that Burney's novel refuses to participate in the chauvinistic sentiment in England following the defeat of Napoleon, and, instead, articulates a critique of English society (pp. 63–4).

There are a number of articles which claim on behalf of the works of Walter Scott a radical impulse, or even a 'revolutionary vitality' The phrase is taken from Ian Duncan, Ann Rowland, and Charles Snodgrass's introduction to a special issue of *Studies in Romanticism* (*SiR* 40:i[2001]), 'Scott, Scotland, and Romantic Nationalism', a volume which, the co-editors suggest, might be seen as responding to Trumpener's presentation of Scott, in *Bardic Nationalism: The Romantic Novel and British Empire*, as a purveyor of a repressive, conservative, and aestheticized brand of nationalism (p. 5). In the first essay in the volume, 'Scott's Staging of the Nation'(*SiR* 40[2001] 13–28), for instance, Cairns Craig contends that Scott's theatrical representations of the nation cannot be reduced to aesthetic resolution of conflict. In a reading of the pageant scenes in *Kenilworth* [1821], Craig concludes that 'Scott understood that the dramatization of the nation was not about its fictionality or its truth, but about the values which its imaginings tested and which they projected as the path of action for the future' (p. 27). Stephen Arata, 'Scott's Pageants: The Example of *Kenilworth*' (*SiR* 40[2001] 99–107), like Craig, considers Scott's role in promoting King George IV's 1822 visit to Edinburgh in conjunction with the pageant scenes in *Kenilworth*. Pageants, Arata points out, which are a combination of real/historical and imagined/mythic events quoted into the present, might serve as an emblem for Scott's narrative practice (p. 102). And, in a similar argument to Craig's, Arata finds not that Scott was in the business of mystification but that he had a keen appreciation of pageantry (and of other kinds of spectacle) as 'enabling fictions, structuring narratives for communities to live by' (p. 103).

Other critics, in this volume and elsewhere, attempt to draw out aspects of Scott's 'ideological vitality' (*SiR* 40[2001] 152). In 'Walter Scott and European Union' (*SiR* 40[2001] 137–52), Robert Crawford claims that, especially in the post-Waterloo period, Scott was concerned with Scotland's relationship with Europe (pp. 140, 142–3). In *Quentin Durward* [1823] and *Count Robert of Paris* [1832], for example, while Scott certainly appeals to the anti-French prejudices of his readers, he also complicates these same expectations (p. 45). Again, in the *Life of Napoleon Buonaparte* [completed 1827], Scott uses phrases and concepts ('the general expectations of Europe') that show that he is dealing with the new political reality of a unified Europe. Although Scott presents Napoleon as a tyrant who tried to impose 'one universal European code' on all nations, his altered conceptual framework was partly shaped by Napoleon's career (p. 151). In an elegantly written article, '"The King of England Loved to Look upon a MAN": Melancholy and Masculinity on Scott's *Talisman*', Margaret Bruzelius (*MLQ* 62:i[2001] 19–41) notes that a dominant theme in Scott's fiction is the overcoming of an unruly masculine energy (represented by figures such as Fergus MacIvor, Hugh Redgauntlet, and Rob Roy) by the social and political order of the centre (pp. 26, 30). In this respect, she suggests, Scott's fiction anticipates contemporary theories of masculinity, in which 'adult heterosexual masculinity [is] formed by the rejection of primitive, wild masculinity' (p. 25). What makes *The Talisman* intriguing, in Bruzelius's view, is that Scott creates a different model of masculinity, combining male and female attributes, in Saladin, the leader of the Arab army opposing King Richard's crusading European knights (pp. 27–29, 37). Simon Edwards, in 'The Geography of Violence: Historical Fiction and the National Question' (*Novel* 34:ii[2001] 293–308), argues that a self-reflexive critical reading of a novel like *Quentin Durward* has still the power to betray the reader's own complicity with violence in its many guises (p. 306).

To be sure, some critics continue to see Scott as no more than a staunch Tory. Hence, two articles in the special issue of *Novel* with which I began argue that he was at least partly responsible for the eclipse of the Romantic-era novel from literary history and for neutralizing the radical efficacy of the genre. Claudia L. Johnson, in '"Let me make the novels of a country": Barbauld's *The British Novelists* (1810/1820)' (*Novel* 34:ii[2001] 163–79), accounts for the marginalization of the novel of the Romantic period through a consideration of two collections of the novel, Anna Barbauld's fifty-volume *The British Novelists* [1810] and Scott's ten-volume series of novels *Ballantyne's Novelist's Library* [1821–4]. She notes that, whereas Barbauld's collection of twenty-two novelists includes eight women and gives prominence to the politically charged writings of her contemporaries (pp. 169, 170, 171–2), Scott's narrower selection—more novels by fewer authors, of whom only two were women—was weighted towards the early eighteenth century and was, as a result, less political. 'Particularly considered as a post-Waterloo effort to produce and preserve a national culture, moreover, Scott's *Ballantyne's Novelist's Library* also entails a consolidation and a conjuring of the novel's glorious origins in a remoter and a safer national past' (pp. 173–5). For Johnson, Scott as a historian of the novel helped to erase the highly political works of Romantic-era writers from the literary canon. Robert Miles, in the same journal, attributes a similar reactionary agency to Scott's novels. In 'What is a Romantic Novel?' (*Novel* 34:ii[2001] 180–201), Miles speculates that what characterizes the Romantic novel of ideas—or what Miles calls the 'philosophical romance'—in opposition to the 'Austenian novel of manners' is its critical purchase (p. 198). Hence writers as diverse as Walpole, Lewis, Radcliffe, Godwin, Edgeworth, Dacre, and Maturin, as well as Nathaniel Hawthorne and Herman Melville, are united by the tendency of their writings to 'incorporate a challenge to the standard narratives of national origin', thereby 'creat[ing] the ground for understanding ideology as ideology' (pp. 194, 195–7). This project of ideological demystification was reversed by Scott, Miles argues, whose 'practice is complicit with nationalism, with its predilection for ideological illusion and false consciousness' (p. 196).

Several articles raise the question of Scott's figuring of Scottish nationalism, especially in relation to his project of reconciling Scottish and English national differences. In a very fine essay, Yoon Sun Lee, 'Giants in the North: Douglas, the Scottish Enlightenment, and Scott's *Redgauntlet*' (*SiR* 40[2001] 109–21), looks at Scott's account of the controversy surrounding the 1756 performance of John Home's play *Douglas* in an 1827 review article, and then reads *Redgauntlet* [1824] as Scott's analysis of the rhetorical figures (conjecture and deferral) by which Home—and, by extension, other key members of the Scottish Enlightenment— attempted to marry the discourse of civic virtue with patriotic feeling (pp. 110–11, 114, 118–19). While Scott casts an ironic glance at the nationalist discourse of civic virtue, Lee argues, he appreciated that it was the suspension of political reality that enabled the accommodation of Scottish nationalism within the British state (p. 121). The theme of how to reconcile past and present, Scottish particularity and cosmopolitan Britishness, is taken up by Miranda J. Burgess in 'Scott, History, and the Augustan Public Sphere' (*SiR* 40[2001] 123–35). In a reading of Scott's 1816 novel *The Antiquary*, Burgess contends that for Scott it was the antiquary's 'production' of Scottish tradition for consumption by a nation of 'consumer-citizens' that allowed, tentatively, for the movement towards modernity (pp. 125, 129–30, 133–4). A heavily theorized piece by Zahra A. Hussein Ali, 'Adjusting the Borders of the Self: Sir Walter Scott's *The Two Drovers*' (*PLL* 37:i[2001] 65–84), uses border theory to read Scott's novella *The Two Drovers* as delineating an 'exemplary paradigm of the dynamics and problematics of border crossing' (pp. 66–7). The deaths of the two protagonists, the Scotsman M'Combich and the Englishman Wakefield, occur because they are unwilling or unable to overcome a 'politics of geocultural identity' for 'the values of cultural in-betweenness and self-hybridization' (p. 70), while Scott's 'concept of universal man offers a viable alternative' to both Scottish feudalism and English modernism (p. 77). In 'Roseneath: Scotland or "Scott-land"? A Reappraisal of *The Heart of Midlothian*' (*SSL* 32[2001] 26–36), Julian Meldon D'Arcy sees Scott as much less happy about the loss of political identity. He argues that Scott is pessimistic about the consequences of the 1707 Union for Scotland. Even in *The Heart of Midlothian* [1818], D'Arcy shows, Scott's attitude towards post-Union eighteenth-century Scotland—and implicitly towards the 'modern commercialized, law-abiding society' which the Union was intended to bring about—is one of bleak irony (pp. 28, 33–4).

In 'Walter Scott's Romantic Archaeology: New/Old Abbotsford and *The Antiquary*' (*SiR* 40[2001] 233–51), a wide-ranging essay which includes a detour through nineteenth-century 'scientific' archaeology and postmodern archaeological theory, Shawn Malley reads *The Antiquary* in conjunction with Scott's attempt to secure a genealogy for himself and his family in his construction of Abbotsford (p. 239). In Scott's 'meta-archaeological' historical romance, Malley claims, histories are plural and the past 'malleable' (pp. 237, 230, 258), so that the novel can be seen as an ironic 'counterpoint to the ideological foundation upon which Abbotsford is built' (p. 251). Also treating Scott's treatment of space and architecture, George A. Drake's '"The Ordinary Rules of the Pave": Urban Spaces in Scott's *Fortunes of Nigel*' (*SNNTS* 33:iv[2001] 416–29) considers Scott's representation of Jacobean London in *Fortunes of Nigel* as the space of emergent capitalism in which he anticipates the representation of the city in the nineteenth-century urban novels of Balzac and Dickens (pp. 416, 427). Drawing on the spatial theory of Henri Lefebvre and Michel de Certeau, Drake argues that 'urban spaces are presented phenomenologically' by the quotidian activities of characters whose movements are determined primarily by practices of exchange (pp. 416–17, 418–19, 424).

Finally, there were two ambitious and very good articles dealing with Scott's approach to writing history. Richard Maxwell's 'Inundations of Time: A Definition of Scott's Originality' (*ELH* 68[2001] 418–68) argues that 'Scott's version of historical fiction is the outgrowth ... of the give-and-take between two different kinds of presentness' (p. 420). Maxwell agrees with Nietzsche that Scott's nostalgic, antiquarian perspective creates a sense of national community in his readers through reconstructing the past as something that could be inhabited (pp. 422, 424). He also suggests, following Lukács, that Scott's novels recreate the sense of international crisis in which his contemporary readers had become aware of their simultaneous membership of a national community (pp. 425–6). Scott's originality is that he merges these two points of view. Although the sense of mass involvement in the historical process was a defining feature of the present only for the first time after the French Revolution, Scott projects this sense of 'simultaneity' on to all past eras (p. 458). In his novels it is, paradoxically, the antiquarian investigator of the distant past who is at the same time the 'chronicler of political and social emergency in a present time defined by mass involvement' (pp. 430, 432). Maxwell illustrates his argument by a convincing close reading of each of the first three Waverley novels (pp. 437–58). The curious sense one gets in reading *Waverley*, for example—the sense that the past is both very recent (sixty years ago) and very distant—arises because Scott suggests that mid-eighteenth-century Scotland still existed in a feudal situation a century and a half after England had begun to modernize. As history suddenly accelerates and consigns the period to the past, this period is described as though it were a fitting object for the antiquarian's nostalgia *and* presented as a period of violent upheaval (pp. 444–6). Maxwell's thesis seems to capture the particular mood of Scott's novels: the recovery of the past is both nostalgic and very urgent (pp. 452, 457–8). Ann Rigney's *Imperfect Histories: The Elusive Past and the Legacy of Romantic Historicism* approaches the hybrid form of historical fiction from the perspective of historiography. *Imperfect Histories* is a fascinating book which explores the attempt within the Romantic period to write an alternative 'cultural history' of the customs and mental habits of ordinary folk (p. 8). Each chapter engages with the difficulties attending the project of recovering what was usually overlooked in written history. Only one chapter treats an author with whom we are concerned here: chapter 1, 'Hybridity: The Case of Sir Walter Scott' (pp. 13–

58), looks at Scott's practice of supplementing fact with fiction in *Old Mortality* 'as a response to the inherent difficulties of representing historical reality—and in particular aspects of everyday life—in the form of a narrative' (p. 9). As Rigney points out, Scott's practice of imaginatively adding to the historical evidence does not mean that he 'renege[d] on the claim to have represented Scottish history in such a way as to be true-to-its-meaning', for his method of compressing social groups and cultural ideas into the personalities of a few individuals is what gave him access to the details of quotidian existence (pp. 26, 27–8). Rigney is interested less in the ideological ends served by Scott's narrativizing of the evidence than in the fact that most of Scott's contemporary readers took his novel seriously as history: it elicited 'more accounts of the same events', accounts which purported to corroborate or contest Scott's understanding of events (pp. 33–9, 45–6, 57). The importance of Scott's 'imperfect' history of the Covenanters, then, lay 'as much in the [neglected] history he allowed his readers to imagine as in the fictionalized history he actually wrote' (p. 54).

I turn from Scott to Austen and Shelley, the other novelists of the period who regularly attract the most critical attention. In 2001 there were three excellent articles on Austen's ideas about consciousness and subjectivity which draw out the innovative aspects of Austen's methods of characterization. Margaret Anne Doody's virtuoso performance, "'A good memory is unpardonable": Self, Love, and the Irrational Irritation of Memory' (*ECF* 14:i[2001] 67–94) reads *Pride and Prejudice* in terms of John Locke's philosophical discourse (*An Essay Concerning Human Understanding*), and Friedrich Schiller's treatise on the aesthetic education, to suggest the radical, even 'revolutionary' quality of the novel (p. 94). A manifestation of Schiller's *Spieltrieb* (play drive) and an articulation of his concept of the *lebende Gestalt* (living form) (pp. 88–9), Elizabeth Bennet demonstrates Austen's view that individual and social liberty depend on a 'certain freedom from the bondage of memory' (p. 94). In a strikingly similar take on Austen's notions about memory, Nicholas Dames argues, in 'Austen's Nostalgics' (*Rep* 73[2001] 117–43), that we can see in Austen's novels a 'semantic and conceptual transformation' of the word nostalgia from traumatic to pleasurable remembrance (pp. 121, 127–8). In the late eighteenth century nostalgia denoted a pathological homesickness (p. 118), while in the early nineteenth century it had moved towards our current understanding of the concept as a comfortable (certainly non-traumatic) form of remembrance (p. 120). Most interesting is Dames's argument that Austen's narratives create in the individual—in readers as well as in fictional characters (pp. 127, 130)—the conditions for the physical mobility that is so crucial to modern understandings of the self (pp. 134, 137). Finally, in a very detailed reading of the episode of Louisa's fall from the Cobb at Lyme in *Persuasion*, Alan Richardson argues, in 'Of Heartache and Head Injury: Minds, Brains, and the Subject of *Persuasion*' (in his *British Romanticism and the Science of the Mind*, pp. 93–113), that Austen's last completed novel is informed by 'biological' and 'physiological' notions of character (p. 94). He detects the influence of materialist 'brain-based Romantic psychologies' of scientists such as Erasmus Darwin, and links Austen's new comprehension of subjectivity to her novel method for rendering consciousness in *Persuasion* (pp. 102, 94, 105). Most interestingly, Richardson suggests the potentially subversive implications of Austen's 'affinities' with such unorthodox science (pp. 99–102, 109–12).

Two articles which take opposing views on Austen's authorial stance towards Fanny Price still manage to reach similar conclusions about Austen's social and ethical point of view in *Mansfield Park*. In 'Confusions of Guilt and Complications of Evil: Hysteria and the High Price of Love at *Mansfield Park*' (*SNNTS* 33:iv[2001] 402–15), Anna Mae Duane takes issue with the view of *Mansfield Park* as a 'reassuring endorsement of conservatism' (p. 403). She reconstructs the eighteenth-century's understanding of the links between physical debility and female sexual desire to suggest that Fanny's sickliness might be construed as a covert resistance to the 'genteel coercion' of women under Mansfield Park's 'family system' of values (pp. 404, 412). For Nora Nachumi, 'Seeing Double: Theatrical Spectatorship in *Mansfield Park*' (*PQ* 80:iii[2001] 233–52), the inclusion of Inchbald's play *Lovers' Vows* in *Mansfield Park* evinces Austen's interest in the question of how people, and especially women, respond to fiction (p. 238). Austen is suspicious of the emotional effect of fiction, Nachumi claims, and advocates an attitude of 'critical detachment' (p. 246). She goes on to argue that Austen's narrative technique encourages her readers to judge Fanny with the same detachment and to see her 'love for the social order represented by Mansfield Park' as evidence of her complicity with 'a system of values the novel condemns' (p. 247).

Jung Meier makes an interesting but rather dry excursion into modern theories of emotion in 'Romantic Love as a Narrative Emotion in Jane Austen's *Emma*' (*Prism(s)* 9[2001] 65–86), in order to suggest the 'thoroughness and sophistication' with which Austen treats the emotional life of her characters. He explores Austen's interest in the relationship between emotion and rationality and suggests that, for Austen as for some modern theorists, feelings may have a key role in determining rational behaviour (pp. 66–7). For Shinobu Minma, in 'Self-Deception and Superiority Complex: Derangement of Hierarchy in Jane Austen's *Emma*' (*ECF* 14:i[2001] 49–65), Emma's 'obsession' with the gradations of rank and status in rural society is a sign of what Austen perceives as the 'unhealthy' striving for position among the non-landed *nouveaux riches* and the 'alarming' breakdown of the traditional sense of hierarchy (pp. 53–4, 62–3, 64).

While I have decided not to include the critical work on adaptations of Austen's novels to screen and television—which is becoming an industry in itself—I do want to mention a chapter of John Wiltshire's excellent book in which the original text is partly illuminated by its recent adaptations: '*Pride and Prejudice*, Love and Recognition' (in his *Recreating Jane Austen*, pp. 99–124). Reading the novel though the lens of psychoanalytic theory (Donald Winnicott and Jessica Benjamin) and ethical philosophy (Emmanuel Lévinas), and taking issue with politicized feminist readings of the novel that deprecate Elizabeth's eventual abnegation of herself to Darcy, Wiltshire argues that Elizabeth Bennet and Darcy progress to a model of ethical human relations which we can call 'love' through a psychological 'recognition' of each other's 'otherness' (pp. 103–7, 119–21, 124).

Finally there are several articles on Austen's own readings in eighteenth-century literature. In 'Change and Fixity in *Sense and Sensibility*' (*SEL* 41:iii[2001] 605–22), Rodney S. Edgecombe takes Austen's familiarity with eighteenth-century literature as a point of reference in reconstructing her complex attitude towards the cult for picturesque viewing, a viewing position which is associated above all, Edgecombe claims, with a sentimental resistance to temporal processes (pp. 606–7, 611–13). Elspeth Knights, in '"The library, of course, afforded everything": Jane

Austen's Representations of Women Readers' (*English* 50[2001] 19–38), shows how Austen, attuned to contemporary notions about the effect of reading on women, represented the inner life of her female characters through dramatizing their imaginative engagement with literature (p. 35). Li-Ping Geng, '*The Loiterer* and Jane Austen's Literary Identity' (*ECF* 13:iv[2001] 579–92), claims that James and Henry Austen's Oxford periodical *The Loiterer*, of which sixty weekly issues were published during its brief run from January 1789 to March 1790, was, in 'voice, tone, and sentiment' as well as in 'social, intellectual, and even philosophical' orientation, a strong influence on Jane Austen's development as a writer of fictions (pp. 581–2, 589–90).

Most of the critical writing on Mary Shelley still focuses on *Frankenstein*. Several articles deal with the novel's wider discursive contexts. Anne K. Mellor's '*Frankenstein*, Racial Science, and the Yellow Peril' (*NCC* 23[2001] 1–28) contends that Shelley's description of the creature is similar to the descriptions of the physical characteristics attributed to the 'Mongolian' race by contemporary ethnologists (pp. 2–3, 10). Although Shelley's novel may have initiated a long tradition of pejorative representations of 'yellow-skinned' races in Western culture, representations which were particularly virulent during the Second World War, Mellor claims that the novel itself proposes inter-racial mating as 'a possible solution to racial stereotyping and racial hatred' (pp. 20–2). Like Mellor, Carolyn Williams contextualizes Shelley's novel in terms of contemporary discourses. Williams's fascinating article '"Inhumanly brought back to life and misery": Mary Wollstonecraft, *Frankenstein*, and the Royal Humane Society' (*WW* 8:ii[2001] 213–34) reveals that there is still more to say about Mary Shelley's knowledge of contemporary medical practices and about her relationship to her mother. Resuscitation techniques advocated by the Royal Humane Society may have been used to revive Wollstonecraft after her second suicide attempt in 1795, and Williams uses this link to explore the significance of scenes of revivification in *Frankenstein* (pp. 223, 225). Williams suggests that the novel offers a critique of the resuscitators' rhetoric, which was more about 'self-aggrandisement' than the well-being of the revived (p. 216). Tim Marshall's 'Not Forgotten: Eliza Fenning, *Frankenstein*, and Victorian Chivalry' (*CS* 13:ii[2001] 98–114) provides a fascinating account of some of parallels between the case of Eliza Fenning, a servant wrongly hanged for murder in 1815, and the trial and execution of Justine Moritz in Shelley's novel (pp. 98–101). Whether or not Shelley was consciously alluding to, or even aware of, the Fenning case, the novel is deeply concerned with the question of justice, its miscarriage, and the problem of the 'legitim[acy] of the legal system as perceived by the poor' (pp. 101–2).

In 'Mary Shelley and the Fallacies of Republican Sentiment' (in Göbel et al., eds., pp. 97–110), Saskia Schabio reads *Frankenstein* as a profound engagement with eighteenth-century moral philosophy which anticipates twentieth-century attempts to 'negotiate an ethics based on rational consensus with the demands of the shared life' (pp. 98, 110). Three articles consider literary influences. Michelle Turner Sharp, in '"If it be a monster birth": Reading and Literary Property in Mary Shelley's *Frankenstein*' (*SoAR* 66:iv[2001] 70–93), considers the influence of Milton's *Areopagitica* on Shelley's attempts in her first novel to work through the question of the public responsibility of an author whose books might fall into the hands of immature readers. Robert James LeCussan, in 'Frankenstein: the Modern

Prometheus' (*KSR* 15[2001] 107–17), and Daniel M. Shea, in 'Prometheus the Modern Matricide: Justice and the Furies in Mary Shelley's *Frankenstein*' (*ELN* 39:i[2001] 41–50), argue in different ways for the strong influence on *Frankenstein* of her reading of Greek tragedy. Finally on *Frankenstein*, David Ketterer engages in an apparently arcane and somewhat daunting debate with Charles E. Robinson over the order of composition of the 'Last Draft' of *Frankenstein* (p. 101). In 'The 1817–17 *Frankensteins*: An Alternative Reconstruction of their Composition' (*ESC* 27:i–ii[2001] 99–127), Ketterer himself admits that his discussion of the details of Shelley's manuscript revisions is 'heavy going', but to his credit he does show the significance of the discussion for our understanding of the novel (p. 120). If Ketterer's interpretation of the sequence of composition is correct, we are told, it would suggest that a generic change 'from gothic novel to proto-science fiction' occurred during the process of writing (p. 101).

Three articles treat Shelley's other novels. Sophia Andres, in 'Narrative Challenges to Visual Gendered Boundaries: Mary Shelley and Henry Fuseli' (*JNT* 31:iii[2001] 257–82), explores the intersections between art and literature, and argues that the narrative images in *Matilda* consciously revise the stereotypically passive depiction of female figures in Henry Fuseli's paintings (p. 258). Fuseli, an artist who drew his subjects from literature, was known personally to Shelley, as Andres points out (pp. 259, 261). Lisa Hopkins, in '*The Last Man* and the Language of the Heart' (*RoN* 22[2001]), argues that Shelley's *roman à clef*, *The Last Man*, is a response to the individualist ethos of Romanticism. She notes that not only do the characters in the novel 'experience the landscape around them in terms of their inner lives, they also experience their inner lives in terms of landscape'. The 'interplay' between interiority and exteriority is a 'model for the interaction of the individual and society'. Hence landscape in the novel is a metaphor for the way in which people are formed by their total environment. In a wide-ranging and dense article on the same novel, 'The Limits of Civility: Culture, Nation, and Modernity in Mary Shelley's *The Last Man*' (*CIQ* 37:ii[2001] 164–73), Maria Koundoura opens up an ignored perspective on *The Last Man* by considering its setting in Greece. The novel illustrates the ambivalence of the idea of Greece in the Romantic imagination—celebrated as the beginning of European civilization and condemned as the scene of modern barbarism—and betrays, Koundoura argues, the 'discursive coincidence of philhellenism and orientalism' (pp. 165–7).

There were, finally, two articles on Shelley's short fiction. Marjean D. Purinton's 'Mary Shelley's Science Fiction Short Stories and the Legacy of Wollstonecraft's Feminism' (*WS* 30:ii[2001] 147–74), examines two of Shelley's short stories, 'Transformation' [1830] and 'The Mortal Immortal' [1833], which appear simply to consolidate conventional ideas about femininity, but which, Purinton demonstrates, reveal Wollstonecraft's influence through their covert attack on such views (p. 148). In 'Mary Shelley's "New Gothic": Character Doubling and Social Critique in the Short Fiction' (*Gothic Studies* 3:i[2001] 15–23), A.A. Markley looks at several of Shelley's short stories to examine her deployment of the doppelgänger convention as an indicator of male narcissism and homosocial desire, and argues that Shelley's stories show that women are usually the victims of desire and competition between men (p. 15).

There was not an overwhelming amount of scholarship on the Gothic novel in 2001. There were three articles on Ann Radcliffe. Judith Clark Schaneman, in

'Rewriting *Adèle et Théodore*: Intertextual Connections between Madame de Genlis and Radcliffe' (*CLS* 38:i[2001] 3–45), treats the parallels of plot and character between Madame de Genlis's epistolary novel *Adèle et Théodore* [1782] and Radcliffe's *The Romance of the Forest*. Schaneman is especially interested in the influence of de Genlis on Radcliffe's ideas for the education of women (p. 32). Sue Chaplin, in 'Romance and Sedition in the 1790s: Radcliffe's *The Italian* and the Terrorist Text' (*Romanticism* 7:ii[2001] 177–90), argues for the radicalism of Radcliffe's *The Italian* [1797] on the grounds of both the novel's 'anti-authoritarian' tendency and the literary establishment's response to her writing, which, she shows, is 'strikingly similar' to the language used by the state to condemn radical pamphlets (pp. 183, 177–8). In a rich article, 'Gothic Libraries and National Subjects' (*SiR* 40[2001] 29–48), Deirdre Lynch engages the question of Walter Scott's role in creating a canon and tradition for English literature by recovering his literary debt to female Gothic writers, such as Radcliffe, Eliza Parsons, and Eleanor Sleath (p. 30). Lynch argues that these writers, as women, necessarily had a more 'ambivalent' relationship than Scott to the English cultural nationalism that figures in their novels (p. 47). Though this article appeared in the special issue of *Studies in Romanticism* on Walter Scott, it is more illuminating in what it has to say about the female Gothic than in what it says about Scott.

There are only two articles on the later Gothic novel. Warren Fox, in 'Violence and the Victimization of Women: Engendering Sympathy for Hogg's Justified Sinner' (*SSL* 32[2001] 164–79), attends to a relatively unexplored aspect of Hogg's *Confessions of a Justified Sinner*, the role of female characters, and contends that the reader's sympathy for the novel's protagonist, Robert Wringhim, is produced by his feminization, by the 'morally reprehensible' tactic of first visiting violence on the women characters and then displacing our sympathy for them with sympathy for Robert (pp. 166, 178). Julia M. Wright, 'Devouring the Disinherited: Familial Cannibalism in Maturin's *Melmoth the Wanderer*' (in Guest, ed., *Eating their Words: Cannibalism and the Boundaries of Cultural Identity*, pp. 79–105), looks at the incidence of 'familial cannibalism' in Maturin's 1820 novel within the context of the change from a land-based to a market economy and argues that it serves 'as a metaphor for violence to indigenous lines of inheritance ... through the imposition of a commercial-imperial economy' (pp. 80, 81, 100).

Surprisingly I found no articles on Matthew Lewis's Gothic novel, but in 'Monk Lewis's *Journals* and the Discipline of Discourse' (*NCC* 23[2001] 59–88), Maja-Lisa Von Sneidern offers a Foucauldian reading of Lewis's *Journal of a West India Proprietor* as an attempt to negotiate the incompatibility between institutionalized slavery and a modern, disciplinary mode of social regulation (pp. 60, 66, 71, 74, 79). George Boulukos, in his fine essay 'The Grateful Slave: A History of Slave Plantation Reform in the British Novel, 1750–1780' (*ECN* 1[2001] 161–79), argues that, far from being a key element in the anti-slavery movement, sentimental attacks on the cruelty of the plantation system in the late eighteenth-century English novel served primarily to urge paternalism, a kinder and more efficient form of slave management (pp. 161–2).

It remains for me to wrap up some loose ends by mentioning three interesting articles. In 'Theorising Public Opinion: Elizabeth Hamilton's Model of Self, Sympathy and Society' (in Eger et al., eds., pp. 257–73), Penny Warburton argues that in her philosophical writings Elizabeth Hamilton engages directly with

Enlightenment thinkers such as Adam Smith (pp. 259–64). While Hamilton agrees with Smith's view that the self is primarily motivated by self-interest, she does not believe with him that the self may also have disinterested feelings (p. 269). Deeply conservative, Hamilton rejects the Enlightenment's faith in the possibility of modifying human behaviour via human institutions such as commerce, which she sees as incompatible with virtue, and argues that the 'viciousness of the "selfish principle"' can only be counteracted finally by 'knowledge of God through Divine Revelation' (pp. 269–70). For Ghislaine McDayter, 'Hysterically Speaking: Lady Caroline Lamb's *Glenarvon*' (in McDayter, Batten, and Milligan, eds., *Romantic Generations: Essays in Honor of Robert F. Gleckner*, pp. 155–77), the fact of Lady Caroline Lamb's familiarity with Mary Wollstonecraft's political philosophy helps support an argument for the subtle overlapping of sexual and republican politics in her 1816 novel (pp. 156–7, 162). While Kim Wheatley's article, 'Comedies of Manners: British Romantic-Era Writers on America' (*ECLife* 25[2001] 63–77), belongs in the non-fiction section of this chapter, I include it here as further evidence of the continuing trend for exploring the transatlantic theme. Wheatley asks why accounts of American manners in pro-American British travel literature between 1818 and 1842 have much in common, formally and thematically, with the anti-American rhetoric of Victorian writers such as Dickens and Frances Trollope, and argues that, while the intent of the early-century writers is to entertain their readers, they unwittingly helped to prepare the conventions of anti-American rhetoric (pp. 63–4).

4. Poetry

The most eagerly awaited publication of 2002 was Fiona MacCarthy's biography, *Byron: Life and Legend*. Access to the Murray archive has drawn attention to some relatively neglected areas of Byron's life, such as his relationship with servants and, more sensationally, his bisexuality. Presented as a revelation, MacCarthy's analysis of Byron's homosexual encounters owes much to an ongoing critical debate, particularly in relation to the performative nature of the poet's sexuality. *Life and Legend* does, however, recognize Byron's 'paradoxical nature, his mobility of thinking, the multiplicity of voices in his writing, that connects him to the dislocated attitudes of the present age'. MacCarthy focuses on the legacy of her subject in a section entitled 'The Byron Cult', and ably, if a little disjointedly, demonstrates her subject's 'uncanny capacity to live out the centuries'. The merit of this biography lies not in its depiction of Byron as a poet—in the introduction alone, MacCarthy dismisses his early work as 'wishy-washy love poems' and compares his intellectual capacity to that of a child—but as a portrait of celebrity and sustained cultural relevance. Part biography, part 'imaginary dialogue', David Crane's *The Kindness of Sisters: Annabella Milbanke and the Destruction of the Byrons* attempts to 'dissolve the barriers between past and present' by recreating the meeting between the poet's ex-wife and half-sister. Based on historical accounts and speculation, the dialogue and setting owe much to Victorian melodrama, as does Crane's description of the encounter as the '"High Noon" of Byronic Romanticism'. *The Kindness of Sisters* is entertaining and engaging, yet Crane attempts to make greater demands on his material: this story is presented as indicative of the 'story of the age itself', where

Byronic subversion and alienation confront morality and the conservatism of the community.

A more orthodox approach to reconsidering the poet's legacy is Bachinger, ed., *Byronic Negotiations*. While a number of the essays have previously appeared elsewhere, this volume is testament to the indeterminable qualities of Byron as both a poet and a myth. Essays on Byronic confession by Larry H. Peer, Thomas Moore by Jeffrey Vail, Napoleon by John Clubbe, and the American Revolution by Naji B. Oueijan examine the extent to which Byron was engaged in renegotiations, while essays on Edgar Allen Poe, John Cam Hobhouse, James Hogg, Berlioz, and Macaulay register the impact of subsequent renegotiations of the poet. Of particular interest is an excerpt from Michael Rees's *Lord Byron's Life in Italy*. Also worth noting is 'Writing and Rewriting Byron's Lameness', in which Christine Kenyon Jones reconsiders Byron's perception of his disability as closer to a late eighteenth-century model of subversion and defiance than the sentimental portrait presented by the nineteenth century. In 'Two Landscapes from *Manfred*—A Process of Byron's Healing', Akiko Yamada offers a revisionary reading of the poem as a 'transformation from barrenness into richness' whereby the protagonist's internal landscape is humanized by Nature. The volume concludes with an interesting essay on Byron's appearances in films, which unfortunately evaluates his status as an icon on the basis of historical veracity.

McGann and Soderholm, eds., *Byron and Romanticism*, brings together thirty-five years' work on the poet. Rather than regarding the collection as an achievement (modestly, if misguidedly, evaluating the volume as a failed attempt to discover a 'satisfying form of critical commentary'), McGann traces an invaluable process that concludes with stressing the significance of creative contradictions, performativity, and editing. But the course McGann charts is anything but smooth, with the enigmatic Byron prompting a complete revision—or, as the author states, near-destruction—of his theoretical approach. Although the introduction is sometimes bitty, the informal, almost confessional tone only serves to enhance McGann's continued enthusiasm for, and intellectual engagement with, his subject. McGann also raises a point that is reiterated throughout publications on Byron this year: 'In our day Byron has emerged, has returned, as a demon of great consequence.' The 'vitality of his dark eminence' prompts a consideration of Western civilization that mirrors Bernard Beatty's commentary on the 'destruction and resilience' of cities in Byron's poetry, 'And thus the peopled City grieves' (*ByronJ* 30[2002] 11–20). In addition, McGann's concern with the place or displacement of 'close reading' in historicist readings echoes a wider debate in Byron criticism this year.

In *Byron, Poetics and History*, Jane Stabler ambitiously attempts to combine close formal analysis with an exploration of historical contexts. Stabler is particularly concerned with the reception of Byron's poetry over time, 'the nervous vulnerability of Romantic texts to their readers', and, in contrast to McGann's assertion that Byron's verse 'can't be appreciated in brief quotation', the texture of localized poetic effects. This sensitivity to the particular enables a discussion of poetic digressions that recognizes the indeterminacy of readers' experiences while also appreciating both the 'contemporaneousness and historical difference' of Byron's writing. Discounting previous historical and aesthetic studies on the basis that Byron's 'writing resists the totalising discourse of any one theoretical model',

Stabler develops an approach that values the dynamics of poetry, culture, and a changing audience.

The topical issue of Byron and gender continued to attract critical attention. In 'Byron as Cad' (*P&L* 26[2002] 296–311), Ian Jobling argues the case for applying evolutionary psychology to literature by using Byron as a case study. Jobling identifies the poet's dominant personality traits as those of the cad—aggressive, rebellious, criminal, and promiscuous—and explains his appeal to women, emphasizing heterosexual as opposed to homosexual tendencies, with the 'sexy-son hypothesis'. After critiquing the 'vague, commonsensical, and often empirically unsupported assumptions about human nature' that characterize current scholarship on Byron, Jobling presents a deterministic account of men as either cads or dads that derives from the hunter-gatherer model of primitive gender roles. As Jobling concedes, this is 'basic logic' that cannot conceal the simple-mindedness of such statements, as, 'in many respects, Byron was indeed Byronic'. A more complex exploration of sexuality and gender is evident in 'Bitches, Mollies, and Tommies: Byron, Masculinity, and the History of Sexuality' (*JHSex* 11[2002] 395–438). David Sprague Neff explores Byron's protracted attempts to defend and maintain public and private images of masculinity when negotiating the rival claims of sexual orthodoxy and heterodoxy. On the related issue of seduction and the exotic, Edward Ziter's 'Kean, Byron, and Fantasies of Miscegenation' (*TJ* 54[2002] 607–26) argues that theatre audiences of the early nineteenth century gained vicarious pleasure from exploring and denigrating other races through the safety of Byron's plays and Kean's performances. By contrast, 'deterritorialization' is the subject of Joshua David Gonsalves, 'What Makes Lord Byron Go? Strong Determinations—Public/Private—of Imperial Errancy' (*SiR* 41[2002] 33–64), while Daniela Garofalo's 'Political Seductions: The Show of War in Byron's *Sardanapalus*' (*Criticism* 44[2002] 43–63) examines how Byron's association of violence with seduction is employed to critique, albeit ambivalently, Britain's attraction to 'Napoleonic barbarism' and, more generally, 'martial virility'.

Byron and national identity provide the context for *In Byron's Shadow: Modern Greece in the English and American Imagination*. David Roessel explores Greece's connection with Byron at a time when Byronism faded elsewhere, and the conclusion, entitled 'A New Kind of Byronism', confirms the poet's continued influence on writing about Greece. However, this book is concerned with the wider literary history of Anglo-American fiction based on the country and tracing how writers project their own, and national, concerns on to Greece. Similarly on the poet's cultural durability, Atara Stein's entertaining and informative article on recent incarnations of the Byronic hero, 'Immortals and Vampires and Ghosts, Oh My! Byronic Heroes in Popular Culture' reappeared in February's edition of *Romantic Circles Praxis Series* (*RCPS* [February 2002]). Attempting to be entertaining on the subject of Byron's pervasive influence, Thomas M. Disch's 'My Roommate Lord Byron' (*HudR* 54[2002] 590–4) sees the poet as a 'teenage werewolf' and, somewhat disconcertingly after Jobling's article, 'a perfect cad' whose verse has become a poor version of *Xena: Warrior Princess*. It is hard to know why Disch is so ready to offer his opinions on Byron's 'sheer bad taste' and political incorrectness when they are based on nothing more than superficial misreadings.

A prominent topic this year was the commodification of Byron's poetry. Nicholas Mason's 'Building Brand Byron: Early-Nineteenth-Century Advertising and the Marketing of *Childe Harold's Pilgrimage*' (*MLQ* 63[2002] 411–40) compares the marketing strategies for the first two cantos of *Childe Harold's Pilgrimage* with those of the blacking industry. Mason reads the success of these early cantos as 'a pivotal moment in advertising history' when product branding extended to culture. On a similar theme, Tom Mole's 'The Handling of *Hebrew Melodies*' (*Romanticism* 8[2002] 18–33) attempts to account for the relative critical neglect of this work by arguing that poet and publisher had 'conflicting objectives': Byron needed the stimulation of new forms and styles while Murray needed to sustain his income. In addition, a number of articles dealt with the issue of religion, including Brian Goldberg's 'Byron, Blake, and Heaven' (*RoN* 27[2002] 13) and '*Cain*: Lord Byron's Sincerity' (*SiR* 41[2002] 655–74), in which Ian Dennis explores the various devices Byron employs for questioning religion and the resentment that lies behind them. Also worth noting is the range of essays in *The Byron Journal*, which covers topics from Shakespeare and Berlioz to the Princess of Wales. In addition, Andrew M. Stauffer's 'A New Manuscript of Byron's "The Irish Avatar"' (*N&Q* 49[2002] 38–40) discusses the textually significant, yet unrecorded, manuscript in the New York Public Library, and 'Sorting Byron's "Windsor Poetics"' (*KSJ* 51[2002] 30–4) argues for 'closer attention to the manuscript record of this protean work'.

The perennial topic of Byron's relationship with Shelley did not fail to attract attention this year. Ian Gilmour's *The Making of the Poets: Byron and Shelley in their Time* is a readable and enthusiastic account of the first part of the poets' lives. This is essentially biography interspersed with a rather simplified historical context; to give one example, 'the poets of the age were deeply concerned with such worldly matters as politics and social affairs'. Also worth noting is the immaculate Woodstock facsimile of Edward John Trelawny's *Recollections of the Last Days of Shelley and Byron*.

A number of significant editions of Shelley's work appeared in 2002, not least of which was the extensively revised second edition of *Shelley's Poetry and Prose: Authoritative Texts, Criticism*, edited by Donald H. Reiman and Neil Fraistat. There is little change to the selection of primary texts, with a few minor additions and amendments to the order, but the secondary criticism has received a major overhaul. A new section, entitled 'Shelley's Reputation before 1960: A Sketch', covers some of the older critical debates, so more space can be devoted to recent articles. Surprisingly, two editions of *Zastrozzi* were published this year: an unannotated version with a foreword by Germaine Greer and a scholarly edition. The latter edition, edited by Stephen C. Behrendt, seeks to reinstate Shelley's once popular but now marginalized prose works. The novels, fragments, and reviews collected in this edition aim to reclaim the significance of Gothic literature as inspiration and context for the writings of canonical male poets.

As expected, the subject that dominated Shelley criticism this year was politics. Paul O'Brien's *Shelley and Revolutionary Ireland* is a much-needed study on the poet's experience of Ireland and its impact on his politics. Echoing Behrendt's argument, O'Brien reassesses the divide between Shelley's so-called juvenile and mature phases which has resulted in the poet's politics being censored or 'written off as the passing spasms of a young fanatic' (as Paul Foot comments in his preface). *Shelley and Revolutionary Ireland* brings together Shelley's writing, both prose and poetry, on Ireland, stresses his influence on other Irish writers, such as Yeats, O'Casey, Shaw, and Joyce, and reprioritizes the figures of Harriet Westbrook and Dan Healy. Similarly focusing on Shelley's early work, Michael Ferber's 'Shelley and "the disastrous fame of conquerors"' (*KSJ* 51[2002] 145–73) examines how the poet employs such issues as fame, infamy, and defamation against warriors and tyrants, while J. Andrew Hubbell's '*Laon and Cythna*: A Vision of Regency Romance' (*KSJ* 51[2002] 174–97) sees Shelley attempting to resolve the problematic Wordsworthian binary of public and private by equating private attacks on domestic tyranny with public attacks on political tyranny. In 'Love Against Revenge in Shelley's *Prometheus*' (*P&L* 26[2002] 239–59), David Bromwich reads Shelley's representations of love as advocating with reform. Also exploring the issue of seduction and politics, or how Shelley 'stage[s] the erotic as a device for renegotiating power and privilege', is *Shelley's Textual Seductions: Plotting Utopia in the Erotic and Political Works*. Samuel Gladden draws on various interpretative methodologies to trace Shelley's explorations of the intersections between the sexual, the text, and the political. Continuing the theme of the erotic was A.D. Harvey's 'Shelley and the Seduced Maidens' (*KSR* 16[2002] 56–60), and Peter Sorensen's 'New Light on Shelley's "Ozymandias": Shelley as Prophet of the "New Israel"' also appeared in this year's *Keats–Shelley Review* (*KSR* 16[2002] 74–93). Incidentally, both winners of the Keats–Shelley Memorial Prize wrote on Shelley: Joe Francis, on 'Doubting the Mountain: An Approach to *Mont Blanc*', and Katherine Halsey, on 'Percy Bysshe Shelley and Theories of Language'. Finally, Christopher Goulding's 'Early Detective Drama in Percy Shelley's *The Cenci*' (*N&Q* 49[2002] 40–1) argues that this dramatic work contains the first example of 'ratiocinative forensic detection'.

In terms of editions of Keats's poetry, Woodstock Books reprinted the *Lamia, Isabella, The Eve of St Agnes* volume of 1820, and, most importantly, two editions of the poet's letters were published. Significantly, both editions retain Robert Gittings's transcripts and selection for the 1970 volume. To bring the volume into the Oxford World's Classics series, *John Keats: Selected Letters* has been revised and supplemented with an informative introduction reflecting current critical trends by Jon Mee. Grant F. Scott's *Selected Letters of John Keats* is 'not a rigorously scholarly edition', reducing scholarly annotations and modernizing spelling and punctuation in the interests of readability. This edition also includes letters to Keats and the record of the poet's final months by Joseph Severn. In addition, Scott includes two new letters, including the final leaf of Keats's famous journal-letter to his brother and sister-in-law, and corrects some of Gittings's minor errors (a discussion of which can be found in *KSJ* 51[2002] 21–9). Similarly on the subject of editions was Oskar Wellens's 'Keats in the Netherlands: A Survey of his Dutch Translations and Editions' (*KSR* 16[2002] 61–73), and Phillip Stambovsky's 'Editorial Emendation in Keats's "Ode to Psyche": A Case for Rejecting "Budded Tyrian" (Line 14)' (*RES* 53[2002] 396–8), which argues the case, both stylistically and semantically, for 'syrian'.

One of the most significant publications this year, *Victorian Keats: Manliness, Sexuality, and Desire*, extends recent debates over the poet's gender ambivalence to the now popular topic of masculinity. As James Najarian states, 'My book looks at the ways in which a number of writers find their sexual definition in their relationships to a poet who was depicted as sexually liminal.' Looking at a range of writers, including Tennyson, Arnold, Hopkins, Symonds, Pater, and Owen (Wilde is strangely absent), Najarian explores anxious affinities with Keats over male-male affection and same-sex desires. Najarian questions the practice of identifying nineteenth-century writers with our own gender-specific terms, rather concentrating on the literariness or 'aesthetic necessity' of conveying complex ideas about sexuality. On a similar topic, Argha Banerjee's 'Gaining a Voice: Femininity in *Endymion*' (*KSR* 16[2002] 130–47) traces the growth of the male persona from viewing women narcissistically to valuing their independence and autonomy. This is an interesting article, but it is repetitive, over-reliant on lengthy quotations, and worryingly derivative. Another rather odd article is Richard Marggraf Turley's '"Strange longings": Keats and Feet' (*SiR* 41[2002] 89–106), in which the predominance of foot-related imagery in Keats's poetry is analysed from a psychoanalytical perspective. The reliance on Freudian notions of fetishism can be reductive at times; for example, the poet's avoidance of direct descriptions of female genitalia indicates a problem with the opposite sex, and 'issues' with his dead mother dictate his feelings for women. Yet Turley's concern with the phallic and non-phallic reality of both sexes in Keats's poetry can be insightful and entertaining (the poet's 'unequivocal phallic anxiety' over his height suggests a number of puns regarding the length, or 'shortness', of his poems).

The topic of Keats and science remains popular, with Denise Gigante's 'The Monster in the Rainbow: Keats and the Science of Life' (*PMLA* 117[2002] 433–48) discussing the early nineteenth-century notion of excess as a contemporary counter-theory of life. A Romantic monster that bristles with electric animation, Lamia exceeds the boundaries of material organization and aesthetic description. Equally emphasizing the scientific context of Keats's poetry, Gareth Evans's 'Poison Wine: John Keats and the Botanic Pharmacy' (*KSR* 16[2002] 31–55) discusses botanical literature and focuses in particular on allusions to hemlock and blue monkshood in Keats's poetry. Evans argues that Keats is practising both pharmacy and poetry, an argument reinforced by 'Keats, Hunt, and Soul-Making' (*N&Q* 49[2002] 37–8), in which Rodney Stenning Edgecombe sees medicine and composition combined in the two *Hyperion* poems to form the ideal 'healer' for the ills of mankind. Embracing the position of 'Cockney poet', the figure of the apothecary enables a transformation of the powerful Apollo in 'Hyperion: A Fragment' into the apprentice poet-speaker of 'The Fall of Hyperion'. On the related issue of Keats's social position, Rob Anderson's 'Godwin, Keats, and Productive Labour' (*WC* 33:i[2002] 10–13) discusses the poet's ambivalence over labour and leisure given his own class insecurities and dependence upon the generosity of friends. Other notable essays on the themes of influence, belatedness, and misreading include Charles J. Rzepka's '"Cortez—or Balboa, or Somebody Like That": Form, Fact, and Forgetting in Keats's "Chapman's Homer" Sonnet' (*KSJ* 51[2002] 35–75) and 'Keats against Dante: The Sonnet on Paolo and Francesca' (*KSJ* 51[2002] 76–93). Christopher Harbinson's 'Echoes of Keats's "Lamia" in Hardy's *Tess of the D'Urbervilles*' (*N&Q* 49[2002] 75–6) lists verbal and thematic echoes, while David E. Goldweber's 'Cullen, Keats, and the Privileged Liar' (*PLL* 38[2002] 29–48) identifies Keats as the source of inspiration for Countee Cullen's illusions. Roger Fanning's 'The "Cat with Rabies at the Grave of Keats"' (*KR* 24[2002] 124–5) is a poem that connects the rabid cats in the Protestant cemetery with Keats's feverish state in Rome.

Also worth mentioning were a number of publications intended as an introduction to Keats or aimed at a general readership. As part of the Writers and their Work series, Kelvin Everest's *John Keats* discusses the poems chronologically, interspersing biography and context with close analysis. The most remarkable aspect of this study is the beginning section, entitled 'Why Read Keats?', which argues for the continued relevance of his poetry, social ambiguity, and 'outsider' status, but also, somewhat surprisingly for an introduction of this kind, becomes a commentary on the author's current thinking about theoretical approaches to Keats. Everest 'attempts to develop a way of reading Keats that gives proper countenance to his rootedness in time and history' while also accrediting the poet's imagination and concern with transcendence. Thus, Everest sees Keatsian aesthetics as inseparable from the wider concerns of reality. Strachan, ed., *The Poems of John Keats*, aims to provide the student with an introduction to Keats's writing that includes a selection of letters, extracts from the early reception of his poems, and modern critical positions that range from the 1920s to the late 1990s. Although informative, the lengthy introductions to 'key poems' reduce the space available for poems such as 'Isabella' to appear in their entirety. Aiming for a similar, if slightly younger, student audience, John Blades's *John Keats: The Poems* concentrates on close readings of the major works and includes sections on four prominent scholars (only one of which, however, is current). Stephen Hebron's contribution to the Writers' Lives series, simply entitled *John Keats*, is a beautifully illustrated account. The emphasis is firmly on his tragic end, but Keats is represented as a resilient subject whose time at Guy's Hospital was influential.

A number of publications appeared on John Clare this year, the most significant of which was Roger Sales's *John Clare: A Literary Life*. Observing that the prominence accorded to Romanticism by literary historians has not served Clare well, Sales resituates the poet in a Regency context. Given the constraints of space, he opts for an exploration of culture rather than a detailed analysis of the poems (although there are some sensitive close readings), and gives us an account of how Clare survived mental asylum and the expectations of fame—a problem of social status shared by the other working-class poets Sales introduces—by adopting various literary and social identities. On a related theme, Sam Ward's 'Clare in Fashion' (*JCSJ* 21[2002] 33–51) examines the poet's interest in, and irritation with, poetic trends. Also featured in the *John Clare Society Journal*, Jonathan Bate's 'New Clare Documents' (*JCSJ* 21[2002] 5–18) outlines the scope for the publication of primary material; Misty Beck explores the issue of sensory perception in 'Visual Mimesis in Clare's Open Fields' (*JCSJ* 21[2002] 24–32); Bill Phillips's 'When ploughs destroy'd the green' (*JCSJ* 21[2002] 53–62) examines the poet's ambivalence, tending towards opposition, over the plough and contrasts Clare's approach to Nature with that of his contemporaries; and Kelsey Thornton discusses simplicity and sophistication in 'The Transparency of Clare' (*JCSJ* 21[2002] 65–79). Finally, Robinson and Powell, eds., *John Clare: By Himself*, was republished this year.

With the publication of *Opus Maximum* and the fifth volume of the Notebooks, 2002 was a landmark year for editions of Coleridge's work. *Opus Maximum* gathers together the last major body of Coleridge's prose writings, which aimed to reveal the harmony of all knowledge. Even though such synthesis eluded the writer, this work remains a testament to his intellectual engagement with multiple disciplines. In terms of editing, *OM* poses unique problems with regard to intelligibility. Thomas McFarland's answer has been to provide an extensive commentary, or Prolegomena, in an attempt to create a coherent framework for the fragments. The reader can go directly to one of the thirty-three sections or read *OM* as 'a continuous exposition', McFarland's aim being to 'provide as seamless a flow of elucidation and thought as is possible' while also including an extensive section of fragments and appendices at the end of the volume. Neither 'reading text' nor 'diplomatic text', McFarland arrives at what he describes as a 'compromise between editorial intrusiveness and restraint': there is no attempt to impose sentence structure, but corrections—largely in the form of commas and semi-colons—are imposed upon the text.

Equally impressive, and perhaps more eagerly awaited, was the publication of the final volume of the Notebooks, edited by Kathleen Coburn and Anthony John Harding. Twenty-eight notebooks appear for the first time in their entirety, and entries dated 1827 or later from other notebooks also appear for the first time. Even though the Notebooks were not prepared for publication during Coleridge's lifetime, they remain invaluable for tracing the development of his ideas and situating him in the social context of Reform Bills and religious unrest. As Harding suggests, the Notebooks contain some of Coleridge's most sustained and far-reaching enquiries, alongside insights into the intellectual community that surrounded him and comments on notable contemporaries. The meticulous checking and rechecking of manuscripts and previous transcripts of the notebooks is a tribute to the governing principle of Coleridge's later work—the 'unceasing inquiry after truth'. The Coburn and Harding volume was not the only edition of the Notebooks to appear in 2002, yet, as Seamus Perry states in his introduction, *Coleridge's Notebooks: A Selection* is not intended to be a rival publication. Aimed at the general reader rather than the specialist, the selection of entries from 1794 to 1820 reflects the range of topics covered. Without the exhaustive comprehensiveness and informative, yet equally distracting, companion volume of notes in the Coburn and Harding edition, Perry's selection will introduce this 'unacknowledged prose masterpiece of the age' to a wider audience. On a rather smaller scale, the *Coleridge Bulletin* published six printed versions of 'The Eolian Harp' and the Rugby Manuscript versions of the poem to accompany Paul Cheshire's article (*ColB* 17[2002] 1–26). Overlooked in last year's entry, J.C.C. Mays's edition of Coleridge's plays also appeared, which included different versions (e.g. printed texts) and annotations in an appendix.

One of the most significant studies of the year, Newlyn, ed., *The Cambridge Companion to Coleridge*, focuses on the possibilities and problems of the writer's intellectual interdisciplinarity. Newlyn is keen to move away from the rather dated notion of Coleridge as the author of a few good early works: the first section includes chapters on 'The Later Poems' (in which J.C.C. Mays rejects the idea that Coleridge became a poet concerned with failure), 'The Notebooks', '*Biographia Literaria*' and 'The "Conversation" Poems'. Section 2 moves from the texts to Coleridge's range of talents as a journalist, critic, philosopher, lecturer, and political and religious thinker. The current trend to recover various aspects of Coleridge's talents and contextualize his work is made accessible to the undergraduate students who constitute the target audience for the Companion series. There are, however, difficulties, as Newlyn concedes, with attempting to retrieve some of the writer's 'more inaccessible meanings'; time renders certain political events and theological debates virtually irretrievable for the non-specialist. Given this concern, it is curious to see as much space devoted to these issues as to the student's usual point of contact with Coleridge. Although Tim Fulford's 'Slavery and Superstition in the Supernatural Poems' is a compelling discussion of how the 'inward self is itself shaped by social and political conditions', it remains one reading of some of the most enigmatic poems in English literature. The chapter on 'Coleridge's Life' should also be noted for its lucid account of a most disorderly subject. Yet even Kelvin Everest struggles with Coleridge as both an individual and a subject of his age. The richness of Coleridge's life is the result of personal complexity—resulting in the eclectic nature of this study—and characteristics that 'typify the intellectual destiny of an entire generation'.

Towards the end of the Companion, there is a short section on 'Themes and Topics' which covers 'Symbol', 'Coleridge's Afterlife', and a subject that received a significant amount of coverage this year—'Gender'. Anne K. Mellor sets the terms for this debate in 'Coleridge and the Question of Female Talents' (*Romanticism* 8[2002] 115–30), in which she divides critics into those who argue for the writer as a feminist and those who argue he was a misogynist. Mellor proceeds to separate Coleridge's representations of women into five, somewhat deterministic, categories: the absent mother, the constraining wife, the omnipotent and malignant female, the pure, chaste virgin, and the object of desire. Coleridge therefore omits any portrayal of female talent, except perhaps in 'A Strange Minstrel', because, Mellor argues, he was psychologically immature and felt threatened by women writers. Practically in dialogue with Mellor's article, Anya Taylor's 'Filling the Blanks: Coleridge and the Inscrutable Female Subject' (*WC* 33:ii[2002] 84–8) outlines the complexity of Coleridge's response to women. Taylor comments on how Coleridge lived 'in an unusual flutter of female attention', and traces a shift in his poems from looking to listening. Coleridge depicts the suffocating roles that women were forced to perform as dependants, yet early portraits remain anonymous and bland. By contrast, his poems on Georgiana, Duchess of Devonshire represent a celebration of individual, and particularly maternal, characteristics. Distancing herself even further from Mellor's position, Taylor's article on 'Coleridge's "Christabel" and the Phantom Soul' (*SEL* 42[2002] 707–30) explores psychology to reinforce Coleridge's identification with female suffering. According to Taylor, the passivity and paralysis of young women in this poem suggests the author's sympathy rather than his scorn. Linda L. Reesman's 'Coleridge and the "Learned Ladies"' (*ColB* 20[2002] 122–8) contributes to this issue by arguing that Coleridge's relationships with women were influenced by contemporary debates over female virtues, which, in turn, informed the conception of the Romantic wife.

A number of interesting articles appeared alongside Reesman's in the winter edition of *The Coleridge Bulletin*, including Ronald Wendling's 'Dr. Jekyll, Mr Coleridge, and the Possibilities of Writing' (*ColB* 20[2002] 69–75) and 'Putting Him in His Place: Coleridge in the *Encyclopedia Britannica*' (*ColB* 20[2002] 137–40), in which Alan Gregory traces a process of rewriting the poet for each successive entry of the nineteenth century. A notable article on an individual poem, Leah Richards-Fisher's 'Where There's a Rime, Is There a Reason? Defining the Personae in Coleridge's *The Rime of the Ancient Mariner*' (*ColB* 20[2002] 63–8) discusses the 'three distinct and active personae', focusing in particular on the Scribe as scholar of and commentator on the existing text and the Wedding-Guest as a model for the reader as listener. Richards-Fisher identifies a sequence of different and inadequate interpreters operating within the poem. Other articles on this poem included Michael Murphy's 'John Thelwall, Coleridge, and *The Ancient Mariner*' (*Romanticism* 8[2002] 62–74), which argues that Thelwall was 'a paradigm for the Romantic victim', and Rodney Stenning Edgecombe's 'Otway, Coleridge, and the "Rime of the Ancient Mariner"' (*N&Q* 49[2002] 28). In an attempt to contextualize the poem, Sarah Moss's '"The Bounds of his Great Empire": *The Ancient Mariner* and Coleridge at Christ's Hospital' (*Romanticism* 8[2002] 49–61) draws parallels between Coleridge's schooldays and his attitudes to the sea. Tim May's 'S.T. Coleridge: The 1818 Child Labour Pamphlets' (*N&Q* 49[2002] 30–1) similarly locates the writer in his social context, while two articles in *Romanticism on the Net* explored the politically contentious issue of leisure: Daniel S. Malachuk's 'Labor, Leisure, and the Yeoman in Coleridge's and Wordsworth's 1790s Writings' (*RoN* 27[2002] 9) and Bridget Keegan's 'Lambs to the Slaughter: Leisure and Laboring-Class Poetry' (*RoN* 27[2002] 10–13). Also worth mentioning is the timely republication of Trevor H. Levere's comprehensive and wide-ranging *Poetry Realized in Nature: Samuel Taylor Coleridge and Early Nineteenth-Century Science*.

The spring edition of *The Coleridge Bulletin* was devoted to the significance of place, particularly the city, continuing on from summer 2001's theme of landscape and the mind. Hans Werner Geryon's 'Coleridge, Cologne and the Cathedral; or: Why St. Geryon?' appeared in *The Charles Lamb Bulletin* (*ChLB* 117[2002] 24–5), and Michael Murphy's 'Rereading Coleridge's Pantisocracy' (*ColB* 18[2001] 16–24) reminded us of 'the discursive process of history'. Religious debate was also at the fore of discussion, with the opposing views of 'Coleridge the Unitarian' by Reggie Watters and Phil S. Teacy's 'Coleridge the Anglican' appearing side by side (*ColB* 18[2001] 25–31 and 32–42). Seamus Perry's 'Coleridge, Catholicism, and the Devil in a Strait Waistcoat' (*N&Q* 49[2002] 25–8) explored the doctrinal importance and possible anti-Catholic sentiment of the phrase in *Table Talk*. Two other articles on this issue should also be noted: John Mee's 'Mopping Up Spilt Religion: The Problem of Enthusiasm' (*RoN* 25[2002] 21) and Martin Priestman's 'Temples and Mysteries in Romantic Infidel Writing' (*RoN* 25[2002] 12), which discusses both Shelley and Coleridge. Another article that focused on both these poets and the issue of imaginary punishment was Mark Canuel's 'Coleridge, Shelley and the Aesthetics of Correction' (*WC* 33:i[2002] 7–10), while Phil Cardinale's 'Coleridge's "Nightingale": A Note on the Sublime' (*N&Q* 49[2002] 35–6) notes how Burke's characterizations of the sublime correspond exactly with Coleridge's design in this poem.

A significant publication addressing idealist aesthetics in Coleridge's work was Michael John Kooy's *Coleridge, Schiller and Aesthetic Education*. Through close readings and historical research, Kooy recontextualizes Schiller, assesses the extent to which his theories were available to Coleridge, and stresses the impact they had on his writing. Nicholas Reid's 'Form in Coleridge, and in Perception and Art More Generally' (*RoN* 26[2002] 12) examines the connections between form and aesthetics, while Coleridge's innovative use of form and language is the subject of Paul D. Sheats's 'Young Coleridge and the Idea of Lyric' (*ColB* 20[2002] 14–31) and Christopher Flynn's 'Coleridge's American Dream: Natural Language, National Genius and the Sonnets of 1794–95' (*ERR* 13[2002] 411–25). The themes of language, metamorphosis, and identity run throughout Morag Harris's posthumous collection of essays, *Linguistic Transformations in Romantic Aesthetics from Coleridge to Emily Dickinson*. According to Harris, a poet's idiosyncratic use of language connects them to, but also distinguishes them from, previous poets. Transition is therefore a predominant concern, and a number of essays address Keats's states of being, yet it was Coleridge who remained a constant source of interest for Harris. Also published in 2002 was Nichola Deane's 'Coleridge and J.C. Lavater's "Essays on Physiognomy"' (*N&Q* 49[2002] 29), which discusses Coleridge's employment of Lavater's distinctions and methods, and James Diggle's 'Coleridge's Greek Ode on the Slave Trade' (*N&Q* 49[2002] 31–5), which examines the text, translations, allusions, and critical reception of this poem. Incidentally, both articles featuring new letters this year centred on tensions with family and friends: see Tom Mayberry's 'S.T. Coleridge, Edwin Atherstone and the Grove Conversazione: Some Newly-Discovered Letters' (*ColB* 18[2001] 43–52) and Lynda Pratt's '"Of all men the most undomesticated": Coleridge's Marriage in 1801–1802: An Unpublished Letter by Robert Southey' (*N&Q* 49[2002] 15–18).

As ever, a number of publications explored the relationship between Coleridge and Wordsworth, most notably David D. Joplin's *Coleridge's Idea of Wordsworth as Philosopher Poet*. Joplin connects Coleridge's philosophy to a number of modern metaphysical and psychological comparativists, and proceeds to discuss the ways in which Wordsworth contributes to this 'philosophical effort'. The overall aim is to reveal how 'both philosopher and poet exhibit a mind participating in phenomena'. In addition, John Beer's 'Coleridge's Annotations to a Copy of Wordsworth's *Excursion*' (*N&Q* 49[2002] 460–3) focuses on the relationship during their estrangement, and Gurion Taussig's *Coleridge and the Idea of Friendship, 1789–1804* analyses the poet's most important connections with those around him. Taussig is not, however, concerned with a relationship, but the contextual background to debates on friendship, covering issues of gender and politics, and Blakean, religious, and sympathetic ideals.

Coleridge also features in Duncan Wu's commendable study, *Wordsworth: An Inner Life*, but the emphasis here is on the effect of Wordsworth's childhood on his later poetry. This is neither a biography, although it sometimes reads like one, nor a work of literary criticism, despite close readings of the poems. Wu is primarily concerned with how Wordsworth's 'writing was shaped by the circumstances under which it was composed', attempting to reimagine the moment of writing rather than assessing his works through the filter of subsequent publications. After commencing with the following statement, 'Grief was the making of Wordsworth', Wu proceeds to split his subject's life into 'three pivotal moments': the guilt of his adolescence (with a much-needed emphasis on the poet's juvenilia); the self-fashioning of his collaboration with Coleridge; and, finally, a phase of reassessment that Wu charts until 1813. In tracing the development of Wordsworth criticism, John Williams's *Critical Issues: William Wordsworth* identifies the relationship between the poet as a biographical subject and the interpretation of his verse as a prevailing concern (even though linguistic issues have increasingly come to the fore). In addition, Williams notes the increased interest in Wordsworth and politics, a trend confirmed by this year's contributions, and the number of speculations over the poet's 'oddness', a 'Wordsworth who walked by night'. Overall, however, Wordsworth criticism is dominated by the split or intersections between public and private, a theme that is evident in the next publication.

Following on from her biography of 2000, Juliet Barker's *Wordsworth: a Life in Letters* was published this year. This volume is evidently intended for a general readership as explanatory notes are kept to a minimum, yet the introduction contains an exhaustive list of corrections to previous editions of the letters made from the original manuscripts. Barker includes a selection of contemporary reviews and extracts from a few hundred letters (including correspondence and journal entries from the poet's family and a previously unpublished letter by Dora). There is, however, some confusion as to the purpose of the volume; the poet is not one of the 'most sparkling of letter writers', yet 'few could benefit as much as William Wordsworth from the publication of his letters'. The primary concern of *A Life in Letters* is to reveal the 'real William', a family man, rather than a poet who is interested in creative processes, which raises the ethical issue of Wordsworth's fiercely guarded privacy. Also worth noting are two editions of Wordsworth's poems: the beautifully presented *Lines Addressed to a Noble Lord* by Woodstock Books and the second edition of *William Wordsworth: Poems Selected by Seamus Heaney*.

A prominent theme in Wordsworth criticism this year was politics, particularly in relation to war. Alan G. Hill's 'Wordsworth, Louis Philippe, and *England in 1840!*' (*MLR* 97[2002] 529–38) reads the poet's pamphlet in the light of his interest in French affairs and his preference for conservative rather than radical change. Yet Hill also questions whether *England in 1840!* might have a more urgent message, and concludes that Wordsworth was not as opposed to political change as has previously been thought. In 'Nimrod and Wordsworth's "Simon Lee": Habits of Tyranny' (*Romanticism* 8[2002] 131–60), Arnd Bohm detects Wordsworth's 'hope for fundamental change' and the poet's concern over the general public's acquiescence. On a similar theme, Brian Folker's 'Wordsworth's Visionary Imagination: Democracy and War' (*ELH* 69[2002] 167–97) contends that the poet was an 'astute political thinker, albeit one whose conclusions are essentially pessimistic'. Folker argues that Wordsworth rejected abstract notions of justice in favour of a 'practical equilibrium' to regulate power in society. Echoing Tim Fulford's article of 2001, 'Wordsworth's "The Haunted Tree" and the Sexual Politics of Landscape', Jalal Uddin Khan's 'Wordsworth's "The Haunted Tree": A Political and Dialogical Reading' (*Forum* 38[2002] 241–51) sees the relationship between artistic creation and context as essentially dynamic; the complex historical references of this poem therefore invite dialogical and political readings. Another important publication on this issue was the revised edition of Nicholas Roe's *The Politics of Nature: William Wordsworth and Some Contemporaries*. Roe has updated his study of the Romantic poets and revolution by incorporating new scholarship on history and ecology, thereby raising the problems of recovering '"absent" contexts for Romantic poems' amongst other concerns. Chapters on George Dyer and Charles Lamb have been revisited, the discussion of Southey's Pantisocracy now includes references to Charlotte Smith's *Emigrants*, and the text of John Thelwall's *Essay, Towards a Definition of Animal Vitality* has also been added. Commenting on the historical relationship between science and literature, Nancy Easterlin's 'Voyages in the Verbal Universe: The Role of Speculation in Darwinian Literary Criticism' (*ILS* 2[2001] 59–73) argues for 'interdisciplinary exchange' in an 'ever-expanding verbal universe'.

The contentious political issue of Wordsworth and colonialism is the subject of Mary Persyn's 'The Sublime Turn Away From Empire: Wordsworth's Encounter with Colonial Slavery, 1802' (*RoN* 26[2002] 10) and Ian Smith's 'Misusing Canonical Intertexts: Jamaica Kincaid, Wordsworth and Colonialism's "absent things"' (*Callaloo* 25[2002] 801–20). In the latter, Smith argues that English Romantic poetry, particularly Wordsworth's, has had a profound effect on Kincaid by promising an elusive tranquillity. What Smith is primarily concerned with is the reinvention of 'colonial texts' by postcolonial subjects. In 'Wordsworth Institutionalized: The Shaping of an Educational Ideology' (*HEdQ* 31[2002] 15–37), Ian Reid argues that Wordsworthian assumptions have served as a model for both national and international education. Reid even argues that much of today's curriculum derives from the institutionalization of Romantic ideology (this is fixed rather than discursive), specifically in prioritizing a reader's personal response to the text. Confirming the extent and scope of Wordsworth's influence, Michael Ackland's 'From Wilderness to Landscape: Charles Harpur's Dialogue with Wordsworth and Antipodean Nature' (*VP* 38[2002] 21–32) explores Wordsworth's influence on Australian poetry. Wordsworth's influence on a single poet is the subject of 'Epitaphs, Effusions and Final Memorials: Wordsworth and the Grave of Charles Lamb' (*ChLB* 118[2002] 49–63), in which Samantha Matthews outlines the former's role in constructing the posthumous reputation of the latter and concludes that 'Wordsworth has the last word on Lamb'. From the Romantic period to the present day, in 'Presence and Passage: A Poet's Wordsworth' (*MLQ* 63[2002] 167–95) contemporary poet Heather McHugh recalls her early experiences with Wordsworth and her growing, if somewhat begrudging, appreciation of his poetry. McHugh's style is informal and she can be irreverent—'Wordsworth has his moments'—but her enthusiasm for, and affirmation of, her precursor underpins a discussion of place and presence. Investigating influences on the poet himself, James Mulvihill identifies a possible source for Wordsworth's views on 'natural language' in 'Thomas Sheridan and Wordsworth's "language of men"' (*N&Q* 49[2002] 18–19). As the founder of the Elocutionary Movement and a proponent of the recovery of the spoken work, Sheridan's insistence on the importance of rhetoric and orality may have informed the Preface.

On the subject of language, Michael Turner Sharp's 'Wordsworth's Poetics of Speech and Language Acquisition in Lyrical Ballads' (*WC* 33:i[2002] 14–18) discusses the adoption of language through detachment, while Charles Mahoney's 'Poetic Pains in Formal Pleasures Bound' (*WC* 33:i[2002] 27–32) examines how Wordsworth's poetic pain was conducive to an experimentation with form and language. The issue of form was the topic of an edition of the *European Romantic Review* in 2002, which included a number of articles on Wordsworth and the sonnet. William Richey's 'The Rhetoric of Sympathy in Smith and Wordsworth' (*ERR* 13[2002] 427–43) examines the intersections between the sonnet and the humanitarian poem, focusing on how both poets negotiated the demands of these two seemingly opposed genres. Richey concludes that for Wordsworth the egotism of the sonnet impairs the humanitarian focus. Similarly, Daniel Robinson's '"Still glides the stream": Form and Function in Wordsworth's *River Duddon* Sonnets' (*ERR* 13[2002] 449–64) contends that Wordsworth experienced a creative downturn, yet the River Duddon sonnet sequence of 1820 bucks the trend as one of the poet's last 'truly fine compositions'.

Articles on individual poems include Arnd Bohm's 'An Allusion to Tasso in "The Thorn"' (*WC* 33:ii[2002] 77–9), David Chandler's 'Wordsworth's "Diurnal" Lucy and William Whiston's *New Theory of the Earth*' (*N&Q* 49[2002] 463–65), and Rodney Stenning Edgecombe's discussion of amusement and solitude in 'Wordsworth's "I wandered lonely as a cloud"' (*Explicator* 60[2002] 134–5). Unsurprisingly, a number of articles were devoted to 'Tintern Abbey', including Ted Underwood's attention-grabbing 'How to Save "Tintern Abbey" from New-Critical Pedagogy (in Three Minutes Fifty-Six Seconds)' (*RCPS* February[2002]) and Deborah Kennedy's 'Wordsworth, Turner, and the Power of Tintern Abbey' (*WC* 33:ii[2002] 79–83). Kennedy lists and comments upon the art and literature inspired by Tintern Abbey, focusing in particular on Wordsworth's poem and Turner's paintings, yet few parallels are drawn between the works. In 'The Commodification of Time in Wordsworth's "Tintern Abbey"' (*SEL* 42[2002] 693–706), Karen Hadley brings together historical and literary themes by examining the issue of time through the flux of aesthetic and social concerns. Extending the debate over Wordsworth and memory, Beth Lau's 'Wordsworth and Current Memory Research' (*SEL* 42[2002] 675–92) identifies Wordsworth as an ideal candidate for memory study and urges scholars 'to join the interdisciplinary dialogue'.

Two articles this year addressed the issue of Wordsworth and gender: Philip Shaw's 'Wordsworth's "dread voice": Ovid, Dora, and the Later Poetry' (*Romanticism* 8[2002] 34–48) focuses on Dora, who inhabits a role comparable to that of Milton and Ovid, as a creative source that 'sustains desire' through distance, and Daniel Sanjiv Roberts's 'Wordsworth's Reading of Rachel Lee: De Quincey's Evidence' (*N&Q* 49[2002] 465–7) comments on how De Quincey's useful readings of his contemporary highlight Wordsworth's unusually positive response to this woman writer. Other publications included Robert Anderson's '"Enjoyments of a ... more exquisite nature": Wordsworth and Commodity Culture' (*RoN* 26[2002] 14) and '"Hart-Leap Well": A History of the Site of Wordsworth's Poem' (*N&Q* 49[2002] 19–25), in which David Chandler charts the renovation of this literary place. Landscape and horticulture are the subjects of the beautifully presented *Wordsworth's Gardens*, in which Carol Buchanan describes the poet's interest in plants and their significance to his work. Buchanan provides a brief contextual outline of late eighteenth-century landscape design and the picturesque, but this book is intended as an accessible overview for the general reader with some stunning photographs (a number of which are unfortunately out of focus in places). Finally, William A. Ulmer's *The Christian Wordsworth, 1798–1805* focuses on the poet's changing religious beliefs, detecting Christian sympathies as early as 1798 and arguing for the durability of his faith in a supernatural deity.

5. Blake

The year 2002 was a fairly lean period in terms of book-length studies of Blake, although a considerable number of journal essays appeared, with at least one set of articles, issued as a special edition of *Studies in Romanticism*, offering a major contribution to Blake studies. A comprehensive list of publications for the year is included in G.E. Bentley Jr.'s 'William Blake and his Circle: A Checklist of Publications and Discoveries in 2002' (*Blake* 37:i[2003] 4–31).

The most substantial book of 2002 was Gourlay, ed., *Prophetic Character: Essays on William Blake in Honor of John E. Grant*. The collection as a whole lacks any real focus, with little more than an overall exhortation to consider poetry and pictures in conjunction, but there are some excellent individual essays, such as Michael Ferber's 'In Defense of Clods', which Gourlay himself singles out as closest in attitude to Grant's work. *Prophetic Character* begins with Stephen C. Behrendt's 'The Evolution of Blake's *Pestilence*', indicating some of the ways in which the discovery in 1984 of an intermediate sketch of that painting demonstrated how much Blake modified his compositions. Commenting on Blake's aesthetic stance towards his own art, Behrendt observes that the viewer is not meant to be detached and impartial but committed and engaged; that this art is 'catalytic' rather than representative.

This is followed by J.M.Q. Davies's essay on 'Variations on the Fall in Blake's Designs for Young's *Night Thoughts*', which is accompanied later in the collection by two further essays on Young's poem: Jon Mee's '"As portentous as the written wall": Blake's Illustrations to *Night Thoughts*' and Peter Otto's 'From the Religious to the Psychological Sublime: The Fate of Young's *Night Thoughts* in Blake's *The Four Zoas*'. Davies traces the iconography in the *Night Thoughts* designs, particularly their strong parallels with the later Milton sequences, considering the former as a precursory commentary on the Fall that Blake would return to when illustrating Milton. Mee is more interested in the circulation of *Night Thoughts*, especially as part of a 'cult of poetic enthusiasm' rather than the conventional (even stale) devotional work that most critics have assumed it to be. Blake's designs, then, mix matter and spirit, politics and religion, in a fashion that was judged tasteless and vulgar by Leigh Hunt and others, but which was far more radical than they could accept. Finally, Otto's work draws on his recent book, *Blake's Critique of Transcendence: Love, Jealousy, and the Sublime in 'The Four Zoas'* [2000], suggesting that Blake slowly moved from Young's religious sublime to something more humanist and psychological in *The Four Zoas*.

Ferber's defence of the clod in 'The Clod and the Pebble' is perceptive, witty, and entertaining while making a very serious point about the critical reception of Blake's works. The typical critical consensus, post-Hagstrum, that there is a balanced dialectic between the pebble and the clod is taken apart by Ferber's own 'pebbly stubbornness' that he 'cannot shake the conviction that the poem, or the poem's speaker, endorses the Clod as right' (p. 54), that this is the 'simple Blake' who genuinely believed that self-sacrifice was the key to salvation. The danger is that Ferber's rhetoric, rather than the logic of his argument, leads the reader to support his conclusions, but the notion that Blake's message is simpler and more radically Christian than later critics allow is a timely reminder to anyone who is tempted to make Blake in his or her own less-than-divine image.

Of the other chapters, Everett C. Frost, in 'The Education of the Prophetic Character', reiterates the neglected point that *The Marriage of Heaven and Hell* follows dramatic styles that should not lead us to identify the narrator with Blake, but rather with a character who is slowly being led through a diabolic education. Alexander Gourlay's long essay on Blake's illustration of Chaucer's Canterbury pilgrims demonstrates how Blake's interest in classical antiquity and British mythology was far from simply antiquarian, but concerned with contemporary political satires on Pitt and Fox. Catherine McClenahan concentrates on Blake's unprecedented focus on Ireland in *Jerusalem*, probably in part as a reaction to the repression of the United Irishmen, and Jennifer Davis Michael, in 'Blake's Feet: Towards a Poetics of Incarnation', offers a short but enjoyable reading of Blake's feet as a synecdoche of poetic inspiration. Morton Paley begins his account of 'William Blake and Dr. Thornton's "Tory Translation" of the Lord's Prayer' with an observation on how little scholarly attention has been devoted to Blake's last annotations, showing how these marginal comments were part of a contemporary critique on taxation and the use of religion to sustain an earthly rather than a spiritual kingdom. G.A. Rosso offers an incisive reading of the figure of Rahab in 'The Religion of Empire', returning to the original biblical sources of Rahab and her subsequent development, while Sheila A. Spector continues the themes of her recent marvellous study on Blake and the cabbala, *Wonders Divine* and *Glorious Incomprehensible* [2001], demonstrating how Blake was guided by the principles of gematria and numerological hermeneutics throughout *Jerusalem*. *Prophetic Character* concludes with my second favourite chapter in the collection, Richard J. Squibbs's 'Preventing the Star-Led Wixards: Blake's *Europe* and Popular Astrology', a detailed historicist examination of popular astronomical and astrological discourses on *Europe*, which led Blake to oppose 'star-led' predestination with biblical prophecy.

Tristanne J. Connolly's *William Blake and the Body* begins with the observation that, while there may appear to be little more to say about the body in Blake's works, the tangled symbols he uses to depict the body (corporeal and mortal as well as divine) have never been emphatically extricated. This book, then, is a largely successful attempt to provide a coherent account of the subject, as well as offering a polemical critique that (as with the work of Helen Bruder and Christopher Z. Hobson) combines gender studies with historicism.

Connolly's first comments relate to the textual body and prophetic body of Blake's self-created books. Approaching the subject via Mary Douglas and Julia Kristeva, Connolly is concerned with ritual prohibitions and semiotic chora, how the prophetic text is part of a 'shaken' crossing of boundaries that do not reject but rather transform the body. The author's plan is ambitious at this point though, to be honest, the connection between textual and other bodies often appears forced in this chapter as she jumps from text to text, idea to idea. *William Blake and the Body* settles into its stride from chapter 2 onwards, the moment when Connolly's interests in gender and historicism come to the fore as she considers graphic bodies. Her discussion of the large colour print *Elohim Creating Adam* not only enables Connolly to discuss Blake's evaluation of engravings of Michelangelo's work as a rejection of Reynold's theory of painting, but also to demonstrate how Blake's interest in the anatomy of the human body led him to portray 'figures in situations beyond normal human experience and perception' (p. 31). Blake's bodies, hyper-muscular and yet almost skinless, go beyond mortal capabilities but are also raw and vulnerable: Connolly suggests that Blake's aesthetic theory was affected by anatomists such as William Hunter and contemporaries, concerned as they were to detail the minute particulars of the human body even if they did insist on nature rather than imagination. In contrast to both Reynolds and Hunter, Blake pursues a 'mystical empiricism' that does not seek the ideal abstract, but applies the 'specific, observable thing to the objects of imagination' (p. 40). This is the human form divine rather than concealed, modern man.

The next two chapters deal with the theme of embodiment considered via the motifs of Urizen and Reuben. Particularly intriguing is the fluidity of the physical body in Blake, similar to the metamorphoses of Ovid, and against which Urizen seeks constantly to petrify himself. Connolly evokes very well the body horror of Urizen's transformations, but the chapter on Reuben is more original, using the liminal fugitive from *Jerusalem* to discuss Blake's ambivalent attitude to child-bearing and procreation. Where Tirzah seeks to bind in human form, Reuben is polymorphous, formless, unable to take shape. This leads on to some of the most innovative research in *William Blake and the Body*, centring on the discovery, in records for the Lying-In Hospital at Holborn, of a reference to 'Cath.e Blake', possible evidence of a miscarriage. Such a possibility renders much darker—but also more sympathetic—references in Blake's texts to barrenness and birth as death. The horror that Reuben excites, therefore, arises from his status as an unborn miscarriage, 'a nexus of taboos' (p. 117). If Reuben and Urizen represent two forms of embodiment, so subsequent chapters on sons and daughters and spectres and emanations are also linked as examples of division and commingling. In the proliferations and mutations—Oedipal in the case of Albion's children, examples of gender conflict when dealing with spectres and emanations—Connolly seeks to trace contemporary historicist roots for many of Blake's most striking images, before concluding with a chapter on the Eternal Body as resumption of that paradisiacal body we possessed before the Deluge.

A potentially more controversial reading of Blake is offered in Kevin Hutchings's *Imagining Nature: Blake's Environmental Poetics*, which has its origins in recent studies on 'Green Romanticism', for example the work of Jonathan Bate and Karl Kroeber. Hutchings seeks to challenge the conventional, post-Frye view of Blake as hostile to nature, arguing instead that the poet and artist was opposed to any vision of the world that was hierarchical and anthropocentrically dominant. Of course, considering Blake's fame as *the* Romantic antagonist of nature, to relate his antinomianism to environmental concerns seems difficult, but Hutchings rightly concentrates on precisely which nature is under attack—the 'objective' system of Enlightenment science—as part of a critique that draws on Foucauldian notions of discursive power.

Turning to Blake's writings, Hutchings begins with one of the powerful weapons in the arsenal of those critics who consider Blake to be opposed to nature, his annotations to Wordsworth. These, Hutchings suggests, are hostile less to the natural world than to Wordsworth's passive reaction, part of a wider critique of one particular view of nature which Blake regarded as Deism. Hutchings is very effective in showing how Blake is a writer very much in love with natural productions, especially as these were in danger of disappearing before the encroachments of industrialization and urbanization, but ambivalent about many claims made in the name of nature. Yet, Hutchings claims, Blake continually adapts 'pagan' notions of panvitalism and hylozoism to his own radical hypothesis, an 'environmental ethic' which the author views as close to modern theories of Gaia: 'While pre-modern panvitalism viewed life as the universal norm and death as its anomalous exception, Enlightenment science reversed this formula, positing a vast and lifeless universe in which death became the norm and life the anomaly' (p. 63). Blake's cosmology, by contrast, in texts such as *The Book of Thel*, *Milton*, and *Jerusalem*, animates the entire universe as part of the body of the giant Albion.

The difficulty for Hutchings is that he seeks to negotiate a compromise between Blake's obvious anthropocentric view of the world and an ecological, non-hierarchical viewpoint in which 'everything that lives is holy'. I am not always convinced that he manages to achieve this, but his consideration of Blake's environmental poetic raises many fine points. His reading of *Milton* as a response to 'the legalism inherent in Newton's cosmology' (p. 115) is excellent, and sympathetic to many of the finer nuances of the new physics that were often not appreciated by the supporters of the 'Newtonian Pantocrator'. Likewise, *Imagining Nature* is quite convincing when treating *Jerusalem* as less the culmination of Blake's anti-natural philosophy than a profound meditation on human ecology, rejecting not the natural world but mechanized nature. The human landscape of Albion's cities is not a rejection of nature for culture, but rather the need 'for humans to build civilization in ways that are continuous with, rather than strictly opposed to, processes of biological growth' (p. 160).

Radical Blake: Influence and Afterlife from 1827, by Shirley Dent and Jason Whittaker, is a book that aims to provide the first coherent study of Blake's reception in the nineteenth and twentieth centuries (Deborah Dorfmann's excellent *Blake in the Nineteenth Century* [1967] obviously omits material from the twentieth century, while Robert Bertholf and Annette Levitt's *William Blake and the Moderns* [1982] is a collection of essays that concentrates on Blake's influence in the first part of the twentieth century). Although covering concerns of popular as well as high culture, and Blake's reception in a wide variety of arts and media, such as film, music, and design as well as literature and fine art, both the authors admit that to be truly comprehensive such a book would need to be at least twice the length of *Radical Blake*.

Radical Blake is split into seven chapters that are arranged thematically rather than chronologically, beginning with a discussion of how Blake was interpreted in the field of the fine arts after his death, particularly with regard to artisan or self-taught figures such as William Linton or Paul Nash. 'Metropolitan Blake', the second chapter, is concerned with Blake's influence as a poet of the city, whether the modernist nightmare of James Thomson's *City of Dreadful Night* or the postmodern psychogeography of J.G. Ballard and Iain Sinclair, both this and the preceding chapter arguing that 'there have been, as Sinclair observes, few better guides for the visionary mode than William Blake' (p. 66). Two more explicitly political chapters follow this section, 'Blake and Nationalism' and 'Blake, Emancipation and America'. In the former, Dent and Whittaker demonstrate the effect of Blake's art on the struggle for Irish autonomy, reaction by nineteenth-century radicals to the failure of the Commune, and, in the post-war period, how artists as different as David Jones, Derek Jarman, and Fat Les have invoked Blake's Jerusalem as an alternative national vision in the decades following the decline of Britain's empire. If Blake is appealed to as a poet of non-chauvinist national identity, his influence on American writers and artists such as Walt Whitman, Moncure Conway, the Beats, and Jim Jarmusch is a good example of his international appeal. 'Blake and Women' focuses on the critical and often antagonistic reception of Blake by authors such as Anne Gilchrist, Kathleen Raine, and Angela Carter, while 'Blake and Blasphemy' traces the appeal of Blake's antinomian and heretical thinking to figures such as Swinburne, Aleister Crowley, and Chris Ofili. Finally, 'Hacking Blake' considers the difficulties of pinning down an authoritative Blake by examining some of the ways in which his works have been forged and adapted over the years, often as part of a very self-conscious 'cultural terrorism'. Throughout *Radical Blake*, the authors are at pains to draw upon the insights of new bibliographical studies of Blake, as well as many of the methodologies of new historicism, to provide a scholarly overview of the poet and artist's reception.

Two other books from 2002 deserve mention. Neither deals solely with Blake, but both have a substantial section devoted to him. The first of these, *Pastoral*, published by the Fine Art Society, features a catalogue of Blake's famous woodcuts for Robert John Thornton's translation of Virgil's *Pastorals*, as well as subsequent works by artists influenced by those woodcuts, including Edward Calvert, Samuel Palmer, Paul Nash, and Graham Sutherland. The book is beautifully presented, concentrating on examples of engraved and etched work, and includes a short but perceptive essay on 'Pastoral Vision in England' by Jerrold Northrop Moore. Teachers and students looking for a handsome edition of the Virgil woodcuts and examples of Blake followers could do very much worse than purchase this book.

Although it covers a much wider area, most essays that deal with a single writer in Fulford, ed., *Romanticism and Millenarianism*, focus on Blake. Fulford notes that Blake has been the main subject for most literary considerations of millenarianism, for 'no writer or artist dedicated more genius to restoring sublimity to people, rather than to machines and institutions' (p. 10). The first essay in this collection to deal directly with Blake, however, Anne Mellor's 'Blake, the Apocalypse, and Romantic Women Writers', is an incisive critique of much of Blake's apocalyptic thinking as permeated by masculine epistemological motifs of creation as rupture, ejaculation, and separation. Mellor is primarily concerned with women such as Mary Anne Browne, Mary Shelley, and Joanna Southcott as rare examples of female apocalyptic writers, arguing that they 'opposed Blake's millenarian vision of a future in which "Time was finished!"' (p. 149) in favour of a biological vision of growth and progress.

Blake supplements David Worrall's study of Robert Hawes, a bookseller and printer based in Spitalfields at the end of the eighteenth century, and is a more substantial presence in the final three chapters of *Romanticism and Millenarianism*. G.E. Bentley Jr. discusses the 'perplexing' case of Blake's Visionary Heads, frequently viewed as a curiosity in the twentieth century, but probably the series of works for which the artist was best known immediately following his death. Bentley's essay is divided into two main parts, the former a brief analysis of discourses on Blake's supposed madness that occupied many commentators at the time these drawings were composed, the second a useful catalogue of the Blake–Varley sketchbooks and loose pages containing some of the Visionary Heads. This is followed by a thoughtful chapter by Martin Butlin, 'Word as Image in William Blake', on the visual use of words and texts in religious art and how the illustrated word is developed in Blake's work, not only the pictorial prophetic books but also many of his later paintings which made great use of inscriptions. Morris Eaves, Robert Essick, and Joseph Viscomi have contributed a section on editing copies of the illuminated books for the Blake Archive (to be discussed in more detail at the end of this section), and *Romanticism and Millenarianism* ends with a bibliography of Morton D. Paley's studies of Romanticism, produced by Tim Fulford and D. W. Dörrbecker, which demonstrates at a glance just how important Blake has been to the work of this great Romantic scholar.

Of essays published in *Blake: An Illustrated Quarterly*, the first for 2002 was Robert Essick's round-up of Blakeana in the marketplace for 2001 (*Blake* 35:iv[2002] 108–29), which, he observed, was generally a dull time until the fall and winter, when copy J of *Songs of Innocence* was sold by Christie's for $850,000 to Maurice Sendak, followed by auctions of previously unrecorded prints from *The Book of Urizen* and *Europe: A Prophecy*. Alongside Bentley's checklist of publications for 2001, the first issue of volume 36 for summer 2002 included a 'minute particular' by the late Gert Schiff on *The Night of Enitharmon's Joy* (*Blake* 36:i[2002] 38–9) with a brief introduction by Morton Paley. This was published in Japanese in the catalogue for a 1990 Tokyo exhibition on Blake, and summarizes the painting formerly known as *Hecate* as an allegory of 'Enitharmon's scheme to enslave mankind by way of sexual repression' (p. 39).

The following issue of volume 36 is devoted to Blake's printing methods, with three essays by Michael Phillips, Martin Butlin, and a jointly authored piece by Robert Essick and Joseph Viscomi. Phillips's article, 'Color-Printing *Songs of Experience* and Blake's Method of Registration' (*Blake* 36:ii[2002] 44–5), returns to some of the material discussed in *William Blake: The Creation of the 'Songs' from Manuscript to Illuminated Printing* [2000], noting that he mistook certain marks in photographic slides to be pinholes; in fact both Phillips and Geoffrey Morrow at the National Gallery of Canada now believe that Blake used a simpler method for registration, simply placing a weight to hold prints in place while plates were coloured. This correction is followed by Butlin's rather plaintive '"Is this a private war or can anyone join in?": A Plea for a Broader Look at Blake's Color-Printing Techniques' (*Blake* 36:ii[2002] 39–49). Beginning with a rather acerbic critique of the contexts of Blake's printing techniques offered by Viscomi and Essick in earlier books and essays, Butlin goes on to claim that he lacks their technical experience but points to a number of features that indicate the two experts on Blake's colour printing must have got their facts wrong with regard to whether the artist used an exclusive one-pull or two-pull process. The real point of this debate on printing methods, however, is to remind us that an obsession with one small part of Blake's craft can distract us from 'Blake's development as a whole' (p. 49). Essick and Viscomi, in 'Blake's Method of Color Printing: Some Responses and Further Observations' (*Blake* 36:ii[2002] 49–64), marshal even more technical data to demonstrate how both Butlin and Phillips are wrong in many areas. Their work is detailed, impressive in its scholarly rigour, and also slightly depressing for the more mundane Blake student, who must feel to some degree that, after all, this is a private argument being publicly fought over our heads: some of the issues being raised here are extremely important, but the tone is increasingly bitter.

The final volume of *Blake* for winter 2002 includes two further articles, which one turns to with some relief after the heated discussion of issue 2. Christopher Heppner's 'Bathsheba Revisited' (*Blake* 36:iii[2002] 76–91) returns to Blake's painting of *Bathsheba at the Bath* to correct what Heppner now believes to be an earlier misinterpretation, in *Reading Blake's Designs* [1995], that the woman in the centre of the painting was actually David's previous wife, Maachah. In addition, Heppner uses the art work to explore 'the complex interactions between already existing narratives and Blake's own thoughts and mythology' (p. 76), particularly how Bathsheba is a reinterpretation of Blake's own Vala. G.E. Bentley's delightful 'Richard C. Jackson, Collector of Treasures and Wishes' (*Blake* 36:iii[2002] 92–

105) is an account of an eccentric and extremely wealthy hermit who was not only a patron of Walter Pater and collector of just about everything, but who would also conduct mass wearing gorgeous robes in his own private chapel. The article includes the sort of (equally gorgeous) biographical detail that one expects from Bentley, such as the strangely mundane example from the newspapers in 1923 that Jackson was found dead in his Camberwell mansion 'holding a partly eaten orange in his hand' (p. 92), an image that is at once comic and oddly sad.

The most extensive collection of journal articles on Blake for 2002 was to be found in *Studies in Romanticism*. Entitled 'The Once and Future Blake', the series of six essays was an opportunity to see how the critical reception of Blake had changed since the publication of the last *SiR* special issue on Blake in 1982. As the 1982 issue was conceived as a tribute to David Erdman, at that time perhaps the most important Blake scholar alive, so 'The Once and Future Blake' begins with an interview with three of the most important contemporary Blake scholars, Morris Eaves, Robert N. Essick, and Joseph Viscomi, in 'Once Only Imagined' (*SiR* 41[2002] 143–99). The interview, conducted by Kari Kraus, begins—inevitably—with a discussion of digitization, although it includes a more fascinating reflection on the relationship of Blake to technology than some recent articles on the Blake Archive. It also provides an opportunity to consider recent developments in the Blake industry, as well as other contributions by the three to Blake studies in the areas of bibliography, collecting, and technological history.

This interview is followed by Morton D. Paley's '[Jah] & his two Sons Satan & Adam' (*SiR* 41[2002] 201–35), a discussion of Blake's version of the Laocoön that was presented in preliminary form at the 2000 Tate Britain conference on Blake, Nation and Empire. Working from the genesis of the print, as a rejected commercial illustration to Abraham Rees's *The Cyclopaedia*, Paley reads the later engraving as a critique of the types of classical theories of art (as revived by theorists such as Winckelmann and Goethe) that Blake saw as motivating unimaginative editors such as Rees. What is particularly fascinating about this plate is the textual surround, of which Paley rightly remarks 'there is nothing even in Blake like it' (p. 223). Stephen Vine's 'Blake's Material Sublime' (*SiR* 41[2002] 237–78) offers a reading of the Blakean sublime that, while it finds much in the Romantic's writings and art that corresponds to Kantian notions of the sublime as a valorization of mental powers (even though one prefers reason, the other imagination), is concerned with the corporeal and material transformation of the world, in the line of art and (after Rajan) the encounter with the 'Real' of history. R. Paul Yoder's 'What Happens When: Narrative and the Changing Sequence of Plates in Blake's *Jerusalem*, Chapter 2' (*SiR* 41[2002] 259–78) does what it says on the box, offering a useful summary of critical responses to textual arrangements in *Jerusalem*, and noting that chapter 2 provided particular difficulties.

Of the two remaining chapters, Paul Miner's 'Blake's London: Times and Spaces' (*SiR* 41[2002] 279–316) is an entertaining historicist contextualization of some of the potential sources for Blake's speculations on the geographical locations of his poetry, which if it is somewhat unclear in terms of its overall purpose provides some superb background detail. Finally, David Wagenknecht's 'Mimicry against Mimesis in "Infant Sorrow": Seeing Through Blake's Image with Adorno and Lacan' (*SiR* 41[2002] 317–48) is an interesting contrast to Miner's essay, critiquing the 'antiquarian/archival' tendency in historicist research that contributes to 'the image of a Blake who has little to say to the modern imagination' (p. 319). Wagenknecht attempts to rectify this with reference to the theories of Lacan and Adorno, as well as more recent commentators such as Žižek.

Other occasional pieces from 2002 include a chapter on 'The Mediated Vision: Blake, *Milton*, and the Lines of Prophetic Tradition' in Ian Balfour's *The Rhetoric of Romantic Prophecy*. While Balfour's book is an interesting examination of the role of prophecy in Romantic writing, the chapter on Blake is a little simplistic for serious students of Blake at times, though it firmly makes the point that Blake employed prophecy as a means of 'speaking out' and thus having 'more to do with freedom of expression or sheer speaking out on behalf of God than with prediction of the future' (p. 131). As well as reading Blake's two prophecies proper (*America* and *Europe*), Balfour concentrates on *Milton* as an example of such prophetic freedom of expression: 'No other Romantic poet confronts Milton so directly and so apparently unscathed.'

Morris Eaves's 'Graphicality: Multimedia Fables for "Textual" Critics' is available in Elizabeth Bergmann Loizeaux and Neil Fraistat's *Reimagining Textuality: Textual Studies in the Late Age of Print* ([2002], pp. 99–122). Eaves draws upon the posthumous fate of Blake's illuminated books to explore some of the ways in which interaction between the arts can complicate our reception of texts and the formation of canons. After considering the ways in which picture-making has been extended throughout the twentieth century (from film to X-ray and ultrasound), and with an enjoyable detour via Jim Jarmusch's film, *Dead Man* [1995], Eaves examines ways in which the technological reproduction of Blake's works after his death has helped build up the audience he failed to find during his life. Ironically, however, while digital technologies in particular appear to be drawing renewed attention to the graphicality of Blake's art, for most readers—including the Native American, Nobody, in *Dead Man*—Blake is primarily a verbal artist; even the digital editor and bibliographer may find that 'compared to texts, pictures remain a thorn in the side even in cyberspace' (p. 118), less easy to search and archive and harder to display accurately. At the moment when reproductions of Blake's originals are more widely available than ever before, Eaves seems to warn, the physicality of those originals is in danger of floating away from us on the bitstream.

A delightful paper on *Songs of Innocence*, which displays its scholarly credentials with a light touch, is David Fairer's 'Experience Reading Innocence: Contextualizing Blake's *Holy Thursday*' (*ECS* 35:iv[2002] 535–62). Fairer begins by gently unpicking the innocent reading of 'Holy Thursday' offered by the late Stanley Gardner, where the poem is interpreted almost entirely in representational terms as a documentary depiction of the annual service for charity school children in St Paul's Cathedral, indicating the ways in which Gardner's valuable work all too quickly leads to a celebratory poem immersed in the purity of its young subjects. By contrast, Fairer wishes 'to examine the extent to which charity children were caught up in a system, how they were controlled, exhibited, and interpreted, and how their singing, learning, dress, and behavior were regulated—how, in short, they were contextualized by an anxious society and in the process had their innocence compromised' (p. 538) Working through eighteenth-century debates into the nature and purpose of charity schools—particularly how art (and artfulness) were to be restricted in favour of 'humility, orderliness and uniformity'—Fairer demonstrates how the charity school system was recognized as ambiguous by many of Blake's contemporaries.

Debbie Lee's 'Johnson, Stedman, Blake and the Monkeys' (*WC* 33:ii[2002] 116–18) is a pithy paper that concentrates on two of Blake's engravings for John Gabriel Stedman's *Narrative of a Five Years' Expedition against the Revolted Negroes of Surinam*, 'The Mecoo & Kishee Kishee Monkeys' and 'The Quato & Saccawinkee Monkeys', exploring their significance as emblems of excessive sexuality, sin and, of course, racial anatomy. Lee sees in the engravings a 'mock-mimicry ... where the social order can see itself' (p. 117), visually demanding illustrations that make radical demands on the reader due, in part, to the contradictory personalities of writer and artist. A later issue of *The Wordsworth Circle* includes Nancy Moore Goslee's paper from the 2000 NASSR conference, '"Soul" in Blake's Writing: Redeeming the Word' (*WC* 33:i[2002] 18–23), in which she considers the various permutations of Blake's use of the word 'soul' from the fairly mundane sense of 'passions' in *The French Revolution* to more complex theories of body-soul monism in texts such as *The Marriage of Heaven and Hell* and *The Visions of the Daughters of Albion*.

Robert Rix published two papers on Blake, work developed from his recently completed Ph.D. 'Healing the Spirit: William Blake and Magnetic Religion' (*RoN* 25[2002] http://users.ox.ac.uk/scat0385/25rix.html) delves into the relations between Magnetism and Swedenborgianism, particularly how the mystical spiritualism popularized by Franz Anton Mesmer developed into Swedenborgian faith healing via communication with spirits—a practice that was, however, strongly opposed by the New Jerusalem Church with which the Blakes were briefly affiliated. Rix argues that this conservative opposition was one reason for Blake's sudden quarrel with the Church, and that Blake remained under the influence of 'magnetic spiritism' at least until the publication of *Milton*. Rix's second piece, 'Blake's *A Song of Liberty*' (*Expl* 60:iii[2002] 131–5) offers a brief reading of the song that ends *The Marriage of Heaven and Hell* as a coded clarion call of support for the 'mystico-illuminist branch of Masonry', particularly in response to the arrest of Cagliostro in Rome during 1790.

Sheila A. Spector's fascinating book, *British Romanticism and the Jews*, includes a chapter by Leslie Tannenbaum, '"What are those golden builders doing?"': Mendelssohn, Blake and the (Un)Building of *Jerusalem*' (pp. 79–90). While Tannenbaum recognizes that the Jewish philosopher and Christian poet had both 'squared off on opposite sides of the Enlightenment' (p. 79), he also explores the ways in which both of them invoked Jerusalem as an ideal of a liberated society. Blake's mystical adoption of the cabbala is at odds with Moses Mendelssohn's Enlightenment project to demonstrate the Jewish religion as aligned with natural religion, and Tannenbaum lists the various items over which the two figures would have fought their mental fight, being particularly critical of the ways in which Blake erases Judaism in his appropriation of Jewish culture. Nonetheless, as the chapter concludes, 'Blake's universalised, anthropomorphic, and ultimately humanistic Christianity was a far cry from what most of his contemporaries would be willing to recognize as Christianity' (pp. 86), and represents an attempt to subvert the very dualisms that dominate his thought.

'Digital Facsimiles: Reading the William Blake Archive', by Joseph Viscomi (*Computers and Humanities* 36[2002] 27–48), is a clear exposition of the benefits that digital facsimile reproduction offers to Blake scholars and serves as a convenient introduction to the work done by the Archive in 2002. The first part of 2002 saw the publication of what the editors describe as a 'new wing' of the Archive, a list of references, bibliographies, and collection details intended to aid researchers. By September, three electronic copies of *The [First] Book of Urizen* had also been uploaded, offering facsimiles of copies A, C, and F, with copy A being republished for the first time since 1929. The end of the year also saw the appearance of Blake's illustrations to the book of Job appear on the site, with reproductions made from the first printing of the twenty-two engravings. With each passing year, the Archive becomes an ever more important and valuable resource for Blake scholars, currently holding at least one copy from all of Blake's nineteen illuminated books and, in most cases, multiple facsimiles.

6. Women Romantic Writers

We might start this year's work by turning to several distinguished publications regarding Mary Wollstonecraft, including Barbara Taylor's *Mary Wollstonecraft and the Feminist Imagination*, Saba Bahar's *Mary Wollstonecraft's Social and Aesthetic Philosophy: 'An Eve to Please Me'*, and Claudia L. Johnson's *Cambridge Companion to Mary Wollstonecraft*. Opening this year's work with Taylor's study not only draws attention to the publication of this long-awaited and arguably landmark enquiry but also points to its general discernment regarding what is principally most current in the field, namely, the intersections between aesthetics, philosophy, religion, and politics. Taylor's lively, challenging, and compelling study of Wollstonecraft serves primarily to contextualize her political radicalism within a Christianized imagination. This imagination, Taylor argues, is at once reasoned, creative, and revisionary, able to develop reformist strategies and project utopian ideas, as well as being grounded in unconscious wishes and fantasies that underlie intellectual innovation. An intellectual history and an investigation into the inner sources of Wollstonecraft's radicalism, then, the book shows how religion underscores the *Rights of Woman* [1792] while providing the very utopian thrust behind it, an 'unwavering faith in divine purpose that, suffusing her radicalism, turned anticipations of "world perfected" into a confident political stance'. The very reforms advocated by 1790s radicals were regarded as suspect and fantastical by their deriders because they stood as markers of a radical-democratic utopia of universal freedom and happiness foretold in Scripture. For Wollstonecraft, this biblical promise that a better world awaits became a passionate call for an end to gender hierarchy and the complete eradication, not just of inequality between men and women, but of sexual difference itself. The critical neglect of Wollstonecraft's beliefs, as of so many figures within this period, has led to the misrepresentation of her as a bourgeois liberal, Taylor suggests, ultimately resulting in a deeply flawed vision of her radicalism. The 'displacement of a religiously inspired utopian radicalism by a secular, class-partisan reformism', Taylor powerfully argues, is 'as alien to Wollstonecraft's project as her dream of a divinely promised age of universal happiness is to our own'. Even the secular Godwin gave his wife a Christian funeral out of respect for her piety, and the study pushes readers to recognize the basis of Wollstonecraft's politics in rational Protestant nonconformity as well as in the 1790s philosophies of the revolutionary intelligentsia and commercial world of literary women.

Ripping Wollstonecraft from such a context, warns Taylor, has led some critics to concentrate too much on her intimate history at the expense of considering her role as a Jacobin *philosophe*, a subject addressed in chapter 5's intimate discussion of British Jacobinism and 1790s feminism. The enthusiasm with which she and her fellow radicals greeted the French Revolution, for example, was prompted by metaphysical ideas about human nature evolving through a Christian providentialism that repelled Burkean conservatives. As chapter 2 makes clear, Wollstonecraft's engagement with Burke and Rousseau served to confirm her conviction that the human will, embodying sensibility and reason, bows always to God rather than to an innate moral instinct. 'It was thanks to God', Taylor convincingly declares, 'that Mary Wollstonecraft became a feminist', a statement that ushers in chapter 3's invaluable analysis of religion and feminism. Indeed, Wollstonecraft is unveiled here as a thinker who translated and reviewed theological works in three languages, was fully aware of the major theological debates of her period, and insisted that religion was not a matter of enthusiasm, but one of 'rational opinion respecting the attributes of God'. While the notion of a uniquely feminine sentimentality was abhorrent to Wollstonecraft, she was thoroughly invested in the deep emotions of the true believer, which she unravelled first through Rational Dissent and later within a sacralized sensualism focused on the unity between Self and God. As the heroine of *Mary, a Fiction* [1788] finds, the genderless grace of the soul can offer a counter-ideal to that of fashionable femininity as well as a form of eternal and blissful love unrealizable between mortals. Religious love might partly be a response to the failure of passion on earth, but it nevertheless acts as an agent of human liberation for Wollstonecraft. Believing as she did in a world where all might 'flow with the diffusive soul of mutual philanthropy, and generous, undivided sympathy', it is clear that human relationships will only work when based on the model God demands we forge with him.

Apprehending and identifying with the divine was also fundamental to women's sense of ethical worth, Taylor shows, 'so far-reaching in its egalitarian implications, that it can be properly described as one of the founding impulses of feminism'. Wollstonecraft's leading ambition for women, for example, was that they seek esteem and liberation through the attainment of virtue, reaching a freedom, not to do what one pleased, but to act rightly according to God's design. Only a sense of right-doing founded in an active, self-enlarging virtue rooted in liberated reason would fulfil women's natural potential without regard to their gender, Wollstonecraft thought, all God's children being potentially perfectible. In a free world women would be as good as God intended them to be, rather than falling prey to those 'classic female follies' Wollstonecraft so despised. Taylor explores this question further through the psychoanalytical concepts of wish and fantasy, noting the interplay between unconscious imaginings and utopian aspirations which helped Wollstonecraft render the imagination a sacred faculty designed to direct the soul towards God.

Bahar's study also seeks to cast Wollstonecraft in a new light, here through the relationship between aesthetics and politics rather than through religion. Claiming that most approaches to Wollstonecraft are not attuned to the specific vocabulary and discursive constructs available to her in the 1790s, Bahar strives to uncover the philosopher's creative appropriations of them in her novels, travel writing, and vindications. Instead of focusing on the much-studied framework Rousseau provides for reading these texts, the book works through the relationship between the ethical category of practical virtue and the political one of active citizenship as a foundation for Wollstonecraft's philosophy. Unlike Taylor, Bahar misses the central relevance of religion to the debate, reading Richard Price rather simply as a civic humanist and overlooking the theological implications ethics held for Wollstonecraft. Yet the elevation of Wollstonecraft's construction of the 'public woman' is successful, one that sought to wrench that title away from its sexual connotations and to give it an active and heroic identity rather than one based on passive innocence. Demonstrating how women actively struggle to overcome their wretched condition, Wollstonecraft thus revalorized the public woman role to ensure a space in which women could actively participate in civic life. For Bahar, the aesthetic representation of such a strategy is key, as is the Rousseauian male philosopher figure that appeared in the entire corpus of Wollstonecraft's writings as a vehicle for analysing the problematic relation between women and knowledge. Bahar also argues that Wollstonecraft insisted first on women's moral autonomy and then on their political participation as 'public women', female political subjectivity itself predicated on sentiments of pity and respect. Counter to Adam Smith's *Theory of Moral Sentiments* [1759], for example, Wollstonecraft declares that women cannot be identified with sympathy in an unmediated manner but instead are involved in a self-reflexive working through of relationships. From this standpoint, Wollstonecraft is able to develop an aesthetics of solidarity, Bahar suggests, by developing representations of female suffering in her prose which might then channel sympathy without conflating the sufferer and the spectator in an indiscriminate unit. This attempt is crucial for rendering female suffering visible, a move which renders it an object of public debate and collective political action.

Wollstonecraft, then, is envisaged as a thinker who willed women to reject a model of femininity that positioned them as objects of pity, arguing instead that female subjects can command respect through conscious self-control. This is staged in the study through an examination of Wollstonecraft's dissatisfaction with representations of Eve as they appear in Milton's *Paradise Lost* and Henry Fuseli's projects to illustrate it, as well as through the identification of Catherine Macaulay as an important predecessor of such thought. Bahar moves from this to a discussion of Wollstonecraft's troubled relationship with Rousseau, out of which emerged her independent conception of knowledge and virtue, recalled also in this period in the works of Richard Price. Finally, an excellent reading of *Letters Written during a Short Residence in Sweden, Norway and Denmark* [1796] fashions them as Wollstonecraft's self-conscious attempt to assess her own previous novelistic attempts to configure conventional eighteenth-century scenes of female distress.

Johnson's *Companion* confirms Wollstonecraft's pivotal importance in the field by gathering a number of judicious explorations of this figure in her many brilliant guises. As Johnson suggests in her introduction (pp. 1–6), Wollstonecraft eludes efforts to name her as a novelist, educationalist, political theorist, moral philosopher, historian, memoirist, woman of letters, or even a feminist. Playing all of these roles at once, Wollstonecraft inscribed her own revolutionary mark in the Romantic period as well as fuelling an afterlife that would, through Godwin, be filtered into nineteenth-century politics and philosophy and beyond. For Cora Kaplan, in 'Mary

Wollstonecraft's Reception and Legacies' (pp. 246–70), she even bears the weight of thinking through the 'shaping moment of modernity', caught as it is amidst the conflicting impulses of progressive politics and a market economy. Wollstonecraft seems almost to have controlled her own reception by focusing on the affective ways in which people read and judge, the gendering and moralizing of emotion her most 'insistent' topic, Kaplan writes. Virginia Woolf and Emma Goldman, for example, like many early twentieth-century feminists, found Wollstonecraft's acknowledgement of the significance of emotion key to a political movement focused only on civil and economic rights. Later critics would also use the affective as a way into Wollstonecraft's pedagogical, sexual, and utopian politics, producing readings consistently locked into the shifting terms of feminist debate.

Andrew Elfenbein's 'Mary Wollstonecraft and the Sexuality of Genius' (pp. 228–45) is an engaging example of Kaplan's argument, using current analyses of same-sex desire to look at eighteenth-century conceptions of 'masculinity' and 'femininity'. Wollstonecraft escapes such a binary, Elfenbein suggests, by linking the category of genius to the category of woman. *The Wrongs of Woman, or Maria* [1798], for example, deems Maria more erotically satisfied by nature via the authority her genius grants than by any physical relationship a lover might offer. Johnson's 'Mary Wollstonecraft's Novels' also explores *Maria*, as well as *Mary, A Fiction*, as often disregarded examples of the novel form, unpolished, written 'topically and in haste' and sitting uncomfortably next to Wollstonecraft's own deprecation of trashy fiction (pp. 189–208). Yet as 'the very bookends of her life', Johnson argues, Wollstonecraft's novels might be regarded as canonically pivotal: methodologically innovative, extraordinarily brilliant, intriguingly clumsy, and always in close dialogue with the forms of fiction they attempted to supplant. Susan J. Wolfson's exceptional 'Mary Wollstonecraft and the Poets' (pp. 160–88) carefully traces Wollstonecraft's relationship with poetry, a genre she claimed to be 'the first effervescence of the imagination, and the forerunner of civilisation'. Using and revising poetry to elevate her own voice, Wollstonecraft is shown to be seriously occupied by the form as one which relaxed the control reason had over emotion, as she argued in her 'On Poetry, and Our Relish for the Beauties of Nature' [1797]. While Barbauld, Blake, Polwhele, and George Dyer found good and bad inspiration for their own verse in Wollstonecraft, she in turn was enabled by her reading of figures such as Milton, who offered her, Wolfson suggests, a new way to argue with Scripture. Barbara Taylor also addresses the religion question in her 'The Religious Foundations of Mary Wollstonecraft's Feminism' (pp. 99–118), echoing the sentiments expressed within her book by rendering her a forceful 'religious thinker'.

The remaining essays in the book turn respectively to Wollstonecraft's writing on education, travel, and radical politics. Alan Richardson's 'Mary Wollstonecraft on Education' (pp. 24–41) suggests that education is a concern which runs through all of Wollstonecraft's writing, whether as a pedagogical tool, a foundation for national schooling, or a means by which women might learn how to navigate society. As a liberal reformer who had read Rousseau, Locke, and Macaulay, Wollstonecraft considered childhood the crucial period in which individuals, and hence social groups, were formed, a view which was increasingly coloured by her sustained contact with nonconformist culture. Vivien Jones also explores Wollstonecraft's sense of how readers should be instructed, in 'Mary Wollstonecraft and the

Literature of Advice and Instruction' (pp. 119–40), arguing that both *Thoughts on the Education of Daughters* [1787] and the *Rights of Woman* offer an at once radical and moral model of 'conduct'. Tracts and pamphlets serving to define self-improvement and personal behaviour in the period, Jones suggests, often mirrored educational philosophy and were thus regarded as part of a wider tradition of advice literature. This work, including Wollstonecraft's, ultimately promoted values of self-discipline and regulation from which feminist declarations of independence emerged. Mitzi Myers, in 'Mary Wollstonecraft's Literary Reviews' (pp. 82–98), traces a parallel theme in Wollstonecraft's consistently informative reviews (sometimes signed 'T' for teacher) for Joseph Johnson's *Analytical Review*. Wollstonecraft's journalism, Myers writes, notably clusters around her periods of creative intensity within which she had little time for the period's 'scribbling women', who were treated so gallantly, and perhaps indulgently, by male reviewers. Like Taylor and Kaplan, Myers unveils Wollstonecraft's endorsement of emotion, her reviews consistently contrasting truthful and warm passion with false refinement and affectation.

For Wollstonecraft, travel offered one specific way to counter false feeling, allowing for mental as well as physical exercise that served to address the dangers of inertia. Yet, as Mary A. Favret suggests in her observant *'Letters Written During a Short Residence in Sweden, Norway and Denmark*: Travelling with Mary Wollstonecraft' (pp. 209–27), the spectre of futile locomotion haunted Wollstonecraft, who feared that progression might have no end-point. The misery of wandering and thinking inherent in Wollstonecraft's travel writing, Favret shows, is registered in the *Letters'* images of displaced bodies, geographical upheaval, families torn apart, and rootlessness, each questioning the elevated status of leisurely travel. Janet Todd turns to a different kind of letter in her study of Wollstonecraft's correspondence, 'Mary Wollstonecraft's Letters' (pp. 7–23), 'frequently moving', she argues, 'in their self-centred vulnerability'. The numerous PSs that haunt the letters intimate her longing to reflect her inner reality by adding more and more detail without the knowing glance to the public that writers such as Byron preciously integrated into their post. Owning a diary-like quality, Todd declares, Wollstonecraft's letters are both self-aware and self-absorbed, reiterating her role as an emotional writer particularly within those effusions received by Gilbert Imlay and Godwin. Todd also discusses the politics of Wollstonecraft's lost letters, notably to her childhood sweetheart, Fanny Blood and her antagonistic sisters, Everina and Elizabeth Bishop.

Wollstonecraft's *Vindications* remain central to any discussion of this prolific philosopher and Chris Jones's 'Mary Wollstonecraft's Vindications and their Political Tradition' (pp. 42–58) provides an excellent introduction to their political agenda. As a republican moralist, Wollstonecraft called for the prosperity of each individual, expressed through a Dissenting vision in which feeling and thought were granted equal social expression. Drawing too on a radical sensibility that bonded people through sympathy, Wollstonecraft's political writing is predicated on the idea of natural rights, benevolence, and educated hearts, a philosophy adopted from the Scots rather than from the French. The French Revolution, however, remained central as a force able to establish the rights of men for the first time in history, putting radical theory into practice, as Tom Furniss asserts in 'Mary Wollstonecraft's French Revolution' (pp. 59–81). Attentive to the way in which

Burke had manipulated conventional ideas of gender and class in his *Reflections* [1790], Wollstonecraft looked instead to a new kind of revolution in manners wherein everyone would be educated together regardless of identity. In her *Vindications* and *An Historical and Moral View* [1794] alike, Furniss suggests, Wollstonecraft figures herself as a 'physician of the state' able to respect even the most abhorrent aspects of the revolution in lieu of the advancement of a reformed body politic. Anne K. Mellor's 'Mary Wollstonecraft's *A Vindication of the Rights of Woman* and the Women Writers of her Day' (pp. 141–59) locates this body politic within liberal feminism and contemporary responses to it by Mary Hays, Mary Robinson, Hannah More, Maria Edgeworth, Anna Laetitia Barbauld, and Jane Austen. Her revolution in specifically female manners, designed to produce women as modest, sincere, virtuous, and Christian, was variously adopted by women as a public identity and an emotional stance, rendering their own analyses of religion, politics, and sensibility in increasingly intricate terms.

Turning to further work on Wollstonecraft published this year, sensibility remains a focal point of Beth Dolan Kautz's fascinating 'Mary Wollstonecraft's Salutary Picturesque: Curing Melancholia in the Landscape', read here through medical tracts on the nervous system (*ERR* 13:i[2002] 35–48). Kautz considers the resonances between the culturally rich practice of picturesque tourism and concurrent health theory by making an illuminating comparison between Wollstonecraft's *Letters from Norway* [1796], William Buchan's *Domestic Medicine* [1798], and Thomas Trotter's *A View of the Nervous Temperament* [1807]. For Buchan and Trotter, motion, exercise, and those changes of scenery inherent in travel reorder the jumbled thought patterns of melancholics in a healing and restorative manner; Wollstonecraft, however, draws attention to the problems of a landscape view that might heighten sensibility at the same time as increasing women's vulnerability to nervous illness. Remaining with sensibility, Lori J. Marso's 'Defending the Queen: Wollstonecraft and Staël on the Politics of Sensibility and Feminine Difference' (*ECTI* 43:i[2002] 43–60) uses the term as a way of defining the status of and connections between femininity and class politics in two key events: the October 1789 Women's March to Versailles and the August 1793 trial of Marie Antoinette. For Marso, Wollstonecraft and de Staël offer analyses of the 'twin perils' of reifying a forceful masculine model of sense and essentialized feminine model of sensibility to negotiate a collective-based middle way sensitive to the economic position of women.

Anne Chandler's 'Wollstonecraft's *Original Stories*: Animal Objects and the Subject of Fiction' (*ECN* 2[2002] 325–51) offers a narratological reading of Wollstonecraft's *Original Stories from Real Life* [1788] by suggesting that we might resist the dimension of bourgeois conduct in the stories to focus on the smaller, benevolent incidents that they highlight. In doing so, Chandler shows how the at once affectionate and regulatory narrative voice within the stories overwhelms their more dogmatic pedagogical implications, urging readers to take a controlled pleasure in the education therein offered. A similar argument is forwarded by Lucy Morrison in 'Conduct (Un)Becoming to Ladies of Literature: How-To Guides for Romantic Women Writers' (*SP* 99:ii[2002] 202–28), wherein the proliferation of conduct books at the turn of the nineteenth century is shown to redefine, rather than confirm, the boundaries placed around women in the domestic sphere. Comparing texts such as Gregory's *Father's Legacy* [1774], Edgeworth's *Letters* [1795],

More's *Strictures* [1799], and Ferrier's *Marriage* [1818], Morrison identifies a series of subtexts that run through supposed endorsements of women's conventional positioning in culture and society. In *Thoughts on the Education of Daughters* [1787], Wollstonecraft herself is attributed with affirming marital duty while asserting the imperative of education within such an arrangement.

Scholarship on Hemans continues to build, not least because of the array of first-rate editions of her work that continue to be published. Broadview are again to be praised for issuing both Gary Kelly's *Felicia Hemans: Selected Poems, Prose, and Letters* as well as Susan Wolfson and Elizabeth Fay's *The Siege of Valencia*, both profoundly useful to anyone working in this field. Following Wolfson's pioneering work as Hemans's editor, Kelly's paperback selected poems is a useful teaching volume spanning Hemans's early *Poems* [1808] to the final compositions [1834]. Selections from *The Restoration of the Works of Art to Italy* [1816], *Modern Greece* [1817], *Tales, and Historic Scenes* [1819], and the *Records of Woman* [1828] show the poet to be politically and culturally engaged with her time, and recognized as such by her contemporaries. The inclusion of works from *Songs of the Affections* [1830] and *Scenes and Hymns of Life* [1834] also gives the reader a significant picture of the later Hemans, working in a profound and reciprocal poetic relationship with Wordsworth and Walter Scott and self-consciously constructing herself as a religious but emotive voice to counter the blustering Hannah More.

Kelly's introduction to the volume, in which this scene is set, is worth purchasing the edition for alone, a remarkably comprehensive and smart piece, almost a short book in itself, which stresses the brilliance behind this sometimes maligned poet. Tracing her position within the public sphere and Enlightenment liberal politics, Kelly grants us several extraordinary insights into the career and influence of Hemans: the position of her family in Enlightenment Liverpool; her connections with the radical publisher Joseph Johnson (although some critics would disagree that Hemans's Johnson is the much-commented-on London Johnson); her critiques of global war; the powerful impact she had on William Gladstone and Robert Peel; and the ethical and aesthetic project she engaged her poetry in to feminize, sentimentalize, and Christianize her readers. Her use of the word 'record', for example, is contextualized within the Latin *cor/cordis* ('heart') to highlight Hemans's consistent focus on the humane and social feelings, particularly as they form a shared community based on friendship and love. Unlike many of her female counterparts, however, Hemans was not yoked to any specific belief system, interested in Catholicism and the Quakers as much as in Dissent and Anglicanism, but always seeking to effuse a devotional sentiment that would unite people in a truly open manner. While Kelly's Hemans is sometimes more dogmatic in this respect than we might perhaps understand her to be, she is unmistakably a writer able to manoeuvre past traditions, religious, secular, and aesthetic alike, to make a point about the relevance of feeling to all aspects of life. Her romances, for example, show the knight errant engaged on an internal, subjective, and spiritual journey that underlines his love for God and his people, rather than an external search for an idealized damsel in distress. The addition of two invaluable appendices complete this important edition: the first grants us numerous illuminating letters to her family and such notables as Mary Russell Mitford, William Blackwood, and Maria Jane Jewsbury; the second selects significant views and reviews of the poet from various journals, as well as the reflections of Byron, Letitia Landon, Francis Jeffrey, and William Michael Rossetti.

Wolfson and Fay's parallel-text edition of the manuscript and publication of *The Siege of Valencia* [1823] is further testament to the immeasurable value of Hemans's work, here subjected to a close and scholarly analysis in order to reflect upon modern perceptions of war. In particular, the editors are struck by the poem's relevance in the wake of September 11th, Hemans's imaginative power able to push patriotic rallying of the sort manipulated by George W. Bush to its logical consequence—often the martyrdom of children and women—thereby putting pressure on the whole system of war. Hemans's poem addresses an imaginary thirteenth-century Moorish blockade of Christian Valencia, a city on Spain's Mediterranean coast. As Spain clashes with Africa, Christianity with Islam, maternal love with patriarchal pride, war with peace, martyrdom with surrender, and the ruling classes with the poor, the narrative steadily pulls apart conventional Western notions of how societies work. Moreover, as Wolfson and Fay point out in their incisive introduction to the poem, national myths, codes of honour, masculine patriotism, and governmental and religious authority persist by virtue of the military systems created to defend them at the expense of hearth, home, and affection between people. Such ideological justifications for war were subject to intense debate in the Romantic era, the peninsular campaign against Napoleon, the editors affirm, being 'cheered in England as a chivalric revival untainted by the aristocratic decadence that provoked the French Revolution'. At the heart of such rallying was the figure of El Cid, a national icon for the days of chivalry in Christian Spain, and rendered by Hemans as a warrior-hero through whom the tensions between gallantry and authority might be unravelled. Certainly by the time the poet was at work on *The Siege*, the romance of Spanish resistance had deteriorated, causing Hemans to re-evaluate her narrative. Wolfson and Fay acutely map this re-evaluation by comparing the 1823 publication to a relatively overlooked 191-page manuscript of the poem, held in the archives of the Houghton Library, Harvard. The manuscript is indeed illuminating, evincing Hemans's increased anxiety regarding the suffering caused by war through her more furiously emotive depictions of the poem's players: two of the women, for example, are more deeply impassioned and enraged by their circumstance in the manuscript, as several of the male figures become more bloodthirsty and fatalistic. The editors also track several other key differences between the two texts to grant the poem a depth which demands several sessions on any Romantic-era course as well as centralizing the poem within research on Hemans's early career. With seven detailed appendices including relevant letters, reviews, and reception histories, as well as Hemans's further poems on El Cid and Southey's *Chronicle of the Cid*, this is quite a remarkable edition, and again authenticates Wolfson's extensive and insightful command of the poet.

Hemans's affectionate relationship with Wordsworth is increasingly deemed pivotal to both poets in criticism, and two articles address this issue this year: John M. Anderson's 'Icons of Women in the Religious Sonnets of Wordsworth and Hemans' (in Barth, ed. *Fountain Light*, pp. 90–110) and Ted Underwood's 'Romantic Historicism and the Afterlife' (*PMLA* 117[2002] 237–51). For Anderson, Hemans's rarely examined sonnet sequence, 'Female Characters of Scripture' [1834], neatly illuminates that other neglected series, Wordsworth's *Ecclesiastical Sonnets* [1822], both volumes presenting ideas of religion that attempt to reconcile the personal and the impersonal within faith. Where the national Church provides a way into individual conscience for Wordsworth, it is biblical characters who offer Hemans fellow-sufferers with whom to self-reflect. Both poets focus on powerful female religious figures, Anderson emphasizes, allowing the two sequences to stage a questioning of social conventions, gender relations, and sexuality. Underwood turns to that sense many Romantics claim to own wherein one 'sees or hears historical depth in the inanimate world', apparent in Hemans's 'Voice of the Wind' [1828] as well as in Wordsworth's 'Salisbury Plain' [1793]. The projection of historical difference into this space, Underwood argues, may be regarded as equivalent to the pleasure experienced in seeing, or imagining that one sees, a ghost, a sense of earthly immortality that echoes through Ossian into Keats, Hemans, and Wordsworth.

Nanora Sweet continues to offer readers insightful commentaries on Hemans's poetry, this year in the fascinating 'Felicia Hemans's "A Tale of the Secret Tribunal": Gothic Empire in the Age of Jeremy Bentham and Walter Scott' (*EJES* 6:ii[2002] 159–71). Sweet suggests that, as a Germanic legend of terror and a dramatic property in the 1790s as well as a watchword for both communism and fascism, the Secret Tribunal received a powerful critique in Hemans's suppressed 'Tale'. The poet's associations with literary-judicial reform, shown here to have been forged through Roscoe, Bowring, and Scott, reveal Gothic revenance to be at the centre of British constitutional debate in the 1820s. Richard Cronin's excellent *Romantic Victorians: English Literature, 1824–1840* includes a considerable discussion of Hemans and also Letitia Landon as key figures in the feminization of Romanticism. Noting the devastating effect Byron's death had on Tennyson, Cronin suggests that the event marked 'the beginning of an era of "woman's rule"' in poetry, initiated by Hemans and Landon. Constructing a thoughtful reply to the work of Marlon Ross on masculine desire, Cronin suggests that the two women did not oppose the inner female world to the external masculine world of power and conquest at all, but rather refused the world of money. The opposition, then, as Hemans declared in her essay on Goethe's *Tasso*, was between 'the spirit of poetry and the spirit of the world', their poetry looking back to medieval France or Renaissance Italy as a way of escaping the very commerce and worldliness that so threatened poetic production in the 1830s. One last article on Hemans also deals with Landon, Derek Furr's 'Sentimental Confrontations: Hemans, Landon, and Elizabeth Barrett' (*ELN* 40:ii[2002] 29–47), linking the two in relation to the young Barrett's correspondence with Mary Russell Mitford. By exploring Barrett's desire to distance herself from the supposed sentimentality of the 'female poet', Furr illustrates how she also identified with the role, casting as she did Landon as her immediate precursor and Hemans as a 'spiritual role model'. Arguing that Barrett's Christian faith is at once modelled on Hemans's own belief and essential to her representation of sentimentality, Furr convincingly portrays Landon as an inferior reader of Hemans, too involved in her own self-pity to decipher the more profound feeling Hemans explored.

Landon is treated more favourably in Adriana Craciun's important monograph, *Fatal Women of Romanticism*, which groups the poet alongside Mary Lamb, Wollstonecraft, Mary Robinson, Charlotte Dacre, and Anne Bannerman as women whose work is engaged with the figure of the *femme fatale*. Examining the incarnation of fatal women, seductresses, mermaids, and the image of the queen or muse, Craciun shows how this process did not, as is often thought, emerge simply from the male imagination. Indeed Craciun is much invested in overturning various presumptions regarding the very category of 'women's writing' in this period, especially given her subjects' questioning of the stability and naturalness of sex itself. Her project is thus to emphasize the struggle that takes place over the categories of sex and gender, rather than the struggle's outcome in which femininity is conflated with the 'natural' female body. The unstable slippage between normalization and subversion that underlines this final outcome is particularly clear, Craciun suggests, in the figure of the *femme fatale*, inherently 'double' as both feminine and fatal. Moreover, this double woman allows critics to address women's responses to topics such as aggression, murderousness, sadism, and destructiveness which, the study claims, have no room to surface in current accounts of women and women writers. If these themes creep in at all, it is as responses to masculine injustice and violence which obscures their empowering potential for women writers. Mary Lamb, for example, is a victim of what Craciun calls 'feminism's persistent ideology of the consolation of women's natural non-violence and benevolence', violent and fatal women frequently unsexed by criticism. The unsexed as a way of categorizing identity is connected to the 'undead' and 'inhuman' within the study, each open to be used by Romantic women as a tool for forcibly demystifying the idealized or sacred woman.

While it is unclear which feminisms Craciun is targeting at times, the arguments forwarded around the women writers are engaging, and fall into two sections, the first addressing the politicized and polemic discussions of fatal women by Wollstonecraft, Hays, and Robinson, and the second the explorative work undertaken by Dacre, Bannerman, and Landon amidst an atmosphere of anti-feminist backlash. Wollstonecraft and Robinson are constructed as republican feminists pushing an ideology of physical strength linked directly to the writers' responses to French revolutionary women, notably Marie Antoinette, who herself occupied a double image as a public seductress and private mother. For Craciun, the execution of the queen, and of other prominent public women such as Madame Roland and Charlotte Corday, marks a significant threshold in the history of the sexed body, 'ostensibly eliminating both the feminine body of the aristocratic beauty and mother, and the masculinized body of the republican assassin'. Women writers were thus freed to use these politicized historical figures to make a claim on masculine and feminine spheres of power, revealing French revolutionary debate as a key site in the history of sexual difference. The perhaps darker and supernatural invocations of Dacre and Bannerman also contribute to this debate, both developing an at times depraved, destructive, and degenerate authorial identity. Craciun's excellent examination of Dacre presents her as a sophisticated Gothic writer who regarded subjectivity as a process or struggle in which pornographic, lascivious, or masochistic desire was used to interrogate the 'natural' identity of woman. Bannerman's characters too, in full engagement with Schiller's and Coleridge's supernatural women, fail to embody natural sexual difference, eluding the grasp of readers as ghostly phantasms beyond the realms of the male imagination. Craciun closes her study with Landon's use of mermaids and water within the context of public health debates to unveil the poet's uneasy embodiment of the ideology of the beautiful. Her radical distrust of the natural is rendered as a response to the growing public concern that urban disease, crime, and moral decay emerge from the unhealthy proximity between the living and the dead.

The sustained attention given to Barbauld's work produced some fascinating criticism this year, not least two papers included in Tuite and Russell, eds., *Romantic Sociability*: Anne Janowitz's 'Amiable and Radical Sociability: Anna Barbauld's "free familiar conversation"' (pp. 62–81) and Deirdre Coleman's 'Firebrands, Letters and Flowers: Mrs Barbauld and the Priestleys' (pp. 82–103). For Janowitz, Barbauld's poetic apprenticeship within provincial Dissenting circles led to, and allowed for, her later activist interventions as a poet and polemicist in the print culture of 1790s radical London. Reading Barbauld in this manner enables Janowitz to recognize two eighteenth-century models of sociability: the 'free familiar conversation' of her father, John Aikin; and a more 'urban and militant' sociability wherein benevolence is 'evinced through political activity and analytical perspicacity'. Coleman also discusses Barbauld as a figure able to effortlessly negotiate the domestic and public by focusing on her argumentative relationship with Joseph Priestley. Barbauld's critique of Priestleyan rationalism, opposed to her own investment in sympathy and affection, sociability and taste, anticipates, Coleman argues, Burke's later attack on Dissent as a dry and scientific belief-system. So profound was Priestley's response to this that he charged his friend with popery (and implicitly unregulated feeling), an accusation Barbauld responded to in her privileging of reason in *Civic Sermons to the People* [1792].

Angela Keane's 'The Market, the Public and the Female Author: Anna Laetitia Barbauld's Gift Economy' (*Romanticism* 8:ii[2002] 161–78) turns to the economic, legal, moral, social, and religious aspects of 'giving' in Barbauld's politico-theological writing. Speaking to the poet's position within the arena of professional print culture, Keane argues that Barbauld effaced her physical body to figure herself and her work as part of a gift economy that only functions in relation to the reader, or recipient. Sceptical of a consumerist turn premised on the blinkered quest for individual rights, Keane gives a discerning assessment of Barbauld's alternative pursuit of a communal form of aesthetic pleasure conducive of moral good. Two equally insightful papers highlighted 'The Mouse's Petition' this year: Julia Saunders's '"The Mouse's Petition": Anna Laetitia Barbauld and the Scientific Revolution' (*RES* 53[2002] 500–16) and Amy Weldon's '"The common gifts of heaven": Animal Rights and Moral Education in Anna Laetitia Barbauld's "The Mouse's Petition" and "The Caterpillar"' (*Cardiff Corvey* 8[2002]). Saunders's detailed exposition of the revolution in chemistry depicted in Barbauld's poetry and prose is attentive to both the period's curiosity in natural philosophy as well as the poet's own strategies for addressing the subject. Filtering her scientific rhetoric through a feminine sensibility before using it to energize her political writings, Barbauld was able to promote the ethical and moral dimensions of her research to an often rarefied and usually self-absorbed scientific community. Weldon also explores Barbauld's moral interests, here in relation to a liberal Dissenting philosophy of tolerance and benevolence that countered inhumanity to fellow-humans, as well as to animals. For Dissenters, Weldon writes, anti-slavery and the cause of animal rights were linked via the theological belief in the common subjection of all life before God, an idea Barbauld upheld by rendering simple acts of kindness as the foundation for activism and social change.

Robert Jones's 'What Then Should Britons Feel? Anna Laetitia Barbauld and the Plight of the Corsicans' (*WW* 9:ii[2002] 285–303) turns to issues of nationhood in his focused discussion of the opening title of Barbauld's *Poems* [1773], 'Corsica'. Suggesting that the poem's republican enthusiasm for Corsican liberty emerged from James Boswell's earlier *An Account of Corsica* [1768], Jones reads Barbauld as an activist Dissenter, fully committed to a patriot politics of freedom. Yet her query regarding how the British might feel towards their Corsican comrades is complicated, Jones claims, by Barbauld's abhorrence of war and violence, as well as her fear of establishing virtue and sensibility in a corrupted world. Laura Mandell explores how such virtue was established through Barbauld's transformative role as a children's writer in 'Johnson's Lessons for Men: Producing the Professional Woman Writer' (*WC* 33:iii[2002] 108–12). For Mandell, Barbauld was a key figure for both Johnson's sense of educational material for children and Sarah Trimmer's work, creating as she did a 'professional domesticity' rooted in both liberalism and Dissenting culture. Robin DeRosa's astute paper, 'A Criticism of Contradiction: Anna Laetitia Barbauld and the "Problem" of Nineteenth-Century Women's Writing' (in Shifrin, ed. *Women as Sites of Culture: Women's Roles in Cultural Formations from the Renaissance to the Twentieth Century*, pp. 221–31), attempts to query much current criticism on Barbauld that seeks to explain away her conservatism as a 'failure' or 'limited'. For DeRosa, the self-contradictions inherent in Barbauld's work speak to the poet's own philosophical elaboration of an idea being a combination of moral qualities, questioning the constructedness of things as 'ordered' or commonsensical. An excellent reading of 'Washing Day', for example, highlights the poem's disruption and merging of seemingly opposed subjects such as rational progress and literary dreaming in order to promote a literal, rather than figurative, rethinking of metaphor. Finally, Lisa Zunshine's 'Rhetoric, Cognition, and Ideology in A.L. Barbauld's *Hymns in Prose for Children* (1781)' (*Poetics Today* 23:i[2002] 123–39) offers a cognitive reading of the *Hymns* in order to connect their catechistic mode to the socialization of children in the period. Zunshine argues that, while Barbauld believed she was inscribing a basic Christianized message on the blank slate of the child's mind, she in fact enabled children to conceptualize God as a complex living presence in the world. What Zunshine calls the intuitive 'evolved cognition' Barbauld encouraged in the *Hymns* thus allowed her young readers to separate falsities or absurdities from greater theological concepts.

Charlotte Smith continues to receive sustained attention, notably in Daniel Robinson's special issue of *ERR* addressing 'The Romantic-Period Sonnet', which includes both Anne Myers's 'Charlotte Smith's Androgynous Sonnets' (*ERR* 13:iv[2002] 379–82); and William Richey's 'The Rhetoric of Sympathy in Smith and Wordsworth' (*ERR* 13:iv[2002] 427–43). Myers explores Smith's seemingly 'androgynous' sonnets in which she adopts a masculine persona or speaking voice generally uncommon within the *Elegiac Sonnets* [1784]. What is striking about the sonnets uttered by figures such as Werther is that Smith's usually controlled, stable (female) speaker loses her reason and becomes mentally feeble when male. Where Werther is unable to transform his situation to imagine a state of peace and freedom, Myers contends, her female narrators, however unhappy, are always able to sustain their clear-sightedness and control over their own minds. Richey locates Smith within a fascinating discussion of the relationship between Romantic-era humanitarian poetry, which tended to look outwards in sympathy towards suffering subjects from which narrators were often completely dissociated, and the more self-involved sonnet form, which was assumed by many readers to be egotistical. Smith, like Wordsworth, was able to negotiate the problem of accomplishing the goal of eliciting sympathy by blurring the apparent distinctions between the two genres, urging her readers to sympathize with humanitarian issues they might be distanced from through her personal poetical voice. It also worth noting here a further paper included in this special issue of *ERR*: Harriet Kramer Linkin's 'More than *Psyche*: The Sonnets of Mary Tighe' (*ERR* 13:iv[2002] 365–78), in which four sonnets included in Tighe's *Psyche, with Other Poems* [1811] are analysed. Linkin is eager to rescue Tighe's sonnets from the usual *Psyche*-focused discussions of the poet to illustrate their formal properties in terms of their staging of a complex articulation of the intersection between form and desire. 'Poor, fond deluded heart! wilt thou again', 'For me would Fancy now her chaplet twine', 'As one who late hath lost a friend adored', and 'Written in the Church-Yard at Malvern' are thus read as attempts to contain and control desire and experience, even as desire is the very thing awakened in the language Tighe employs.

A special issue of the *Huntington Library Quarterly* on women's poetry this year, Mellor et al., eds., *Forging Connections: Women's Poetry from the Renaissance to Romanticism*, offered two outstanding papers regarding Smith: Susan J. Wolfson's 'Charlotte Smith's *Emigrants*: Forging Connections at the Borders of a Female Tradition'; and John Anderson's '*Beachy Head*: The Romantic Fragment Poem as Mosaic' (pp. 119–46). Wolfson's reading of Smith's *The Emigrants* [1793] is an exemplary piece of criticism, gracefully unweaving the poem's rewriting of male literary tradition to evince Smith's literary range as well as her complex reception of the situation in France (pp. 81–118). Moving away from Showalter and Mellor's narrow delineation of a female terrain of writing, Wolfson constructs a more finely tuned arena in which to illuminate Smith's frank republicanism, as well as her appeals to the heart through poetic feeling. By comparing *The Emigrants* to More and Burney's examinations of exile, Wolfson subtly demonstrates how Smith's rewriting of James Thompson's tragedy, *Coriolanus* [1749] and Milton's *Paradise Lost* invoke an antipathy towards Continental, monarchical decadence that reflected back on the excesses of British royalty so apparent in the poem's location on Brighton beach, home of the profligate Royal Pavilion. Anderson's paper turns to Smith's *Beachy Head* [1807] to read it as a self-consciously constructed fragment poem that shadows forth the poet's attraction to the ruin as a particular kind of expressive form. 'An elliptical and self-referential collage', writes Anderson, *Beachy Head* appears as a fragment built of fragments, signposting acknowledged and unacknowledged models and sources to rethink them in a new assemblage. Like Blake, but without the hermetic drawbacks, Smith creates a self-referential system of allusions, style, and diction that forges an evolving poetics informed by geological, botanical, historical, and aesthetic contexts. Anne D. Wallace also attends to the specificities of the poem in 'Picturesque Fossils, Sublime Geology? The Crisis of Authority in Charlotte Smith's *Beachy Head*', focusing on Smith's careful use of fossil imagery (*ERR* 13:i[2002] 77–93). Wallace notes that, despite *Beachy Head* being published in the same year as the foundation of the Geological Society of London, fossils remained a puzzle to readers of Smith's poem. Neither the poem's explicit statements about fossils nor its more figurative implications consistently align it with any precise geological theory, yet the poem's speaker refuses to adopt the stance of an amateur collector. For Wallace, the fossils invite readers to infer any reading of the geological record presented, refusing to explain their significance away as Smith does with other scientific topics.

Karen A. Weisman offers further evidence of this year's exceptional work on Smith in 'Form and Loss in Charlotte Smith's *Elegiac Sonnets*' (*WC* 33:i[2002] 23–7), wherein she explores the poet's formalist experimentation with the sonnet. Suggesting that Smith uses the tight structure of the sonnet to cancel the physicality of her female identity, Weisman shows how she reinvigorates the form to produce an anonymity of emotion that comes to characterize Romanticism. The sonnet thus becomes expressive of a sentimentality which is itself directed to flagging up the constraints of expressing sentiment in the period. Elizabeth Kraft's excellent 'Encyclopaedic Libertinism and 1798: Charlotte Smith's *The Young Philosopher*', situates Smith's *The Young Philosopher* [1798] amidst its anti-Jacobin critics, who considered the novel's attack on Burke, the British legal system, aristocratic vice, and implicit revolutionary fervour dangerous and noxious (*ECN* 2[2002] 239–72). Kraft effectively shows how the novel's authorial presence, historicist scope, revisionary bias, and libertine standpoint tie it to the *Encyclopédie*, notably its insistence on reading the world radically. Reflecting such revolutionary encyclopedism, *The Young Philosopher*, Kraft argues, was able to powerfully indict traditional authorities by remapping the period as one of transition and liberty.

While strong work on Wollstonecraft, Hemans, Barbauld, and Smith upholds an at once intellectualized and emotive Romanticism, then, work on Mary Robinson continues to destabilize such a notion by fixating on the coy and performative aspects of the field. Jacqueline M. Labbe's special number of *Women's Writing* (*WW* 9:i[2001]) gathers several papers focused on Robinson as celebrity, deriving from a commemorative conference on the theatrical poet held at the University of Warwick in September 2000. As Labbe confirms in her preface to the volume, 'Mary Robinson's Bicentennial, (pp. 3–8), Robinson was very much a poet of her time, participating in various modes, from Della Cruscanism to the sonnet, sensibility to the lyric. A 'proliferating personality as well as a prolific writer', suggests Labbe, Robinson encapsulates a new kind of pop idol poet, able to transform her guise quickly while representing the consumerist elements of a sometimes superficial literary marketplace. Certainly Tim Fulford illuminates this issue in his entertaining 'The Electrifying Mrs Robinson' (pp. 23–35), a paper which investigates Dr James Graham's notorious 'electrified bed', on which patrons, who included Robinson, could rediscover their sexual inclinations. Fulford shows how Robinson's flirtatiously commanding presence in high society, and over her various famed lovers, rendered her a commodity available to be exploited, and bought, by satirists and caricaturists alike. Judith Barbour also focuses on Robinson's celebrity in her 'Garrick's Version: The Production of "Perdita"' (pp. 125–38), wherein the public popularity of the poet as actress is deemed to be predicated on the physicality of the woman's body as highlighted within contemporary performing traditions in London and regional patent theatres. Her career as a Shakespearian heroine cut short by illness, Robinson was unable to 'make the passage between the wild girl Perdita and the achieved woman Hermione', Barbour writes, confirming the unbreakable connection between body and identity in the period. Indeed, Alix Nathan's 'Mistaken or Misled? Mary Robinson's Birth Date' (pp. 139–42), corrects our presumptions regarding the poet's real age by validating her year of birth as 1758, making her two years older than she suggested throughout her life. Nathan suggests, however, that readers have been misled rather than mistaken in their impressions of Robinson's age, the poet crafting herself as younger than she was to embrace the roles of the victimized child-bride and naive star. Claire Brock concurs, in '"Then smile and know thyself supremely great": Mary Robinson and the "Splendour of a Name"' (pp. 107–24), suggesting that Robinson fully grasped the mechanics of the eighteenth-century 'fame machine' and promoted herself through it in her writing and public existence.

A slightly different image of Robinson emerges in the volume's remaining essays, led by Stuart Curran's 'Mary Robinson and the New Lyric' (pp. 9–22). For Curran, the metrical and sonic surfaces of Robinson's poetry are not superficial but instead might be seen as carefully crafted examples of a flattened blank verse exemplary of a 'populist lyricism unbound from the strictures of formal eighteenth-century decorum'. Forging a technical breakthrough in style via her variations on a repeated balladic refrain, Robinson, Curran shows, sets up a new poetic which foreshadowed the tonal and psychological innovations of Coleridge and Tennyson. Lisa Vargo continues attending to the specifics of Robinson's lyrical voice in her paper, 'Tabitha Bramble and the Lyrical Tales' (pp. 37–52), wherein she explores the poet's exploitation of Smollett's sex-starved old maid, Tabitha Bramble, whose voice she adopted in thirty-nine lyrics written for the *Morning Post*. Robinson's inclusion of six of these rather raucous poems in her *Lyrical Tales* [1800] leads Vargo to posit them as a more gritty interrogation of the same issues Wordsworth responded to in the *Lyrical Ballads*. One might caution against the volume's repeated bullying of Wordsworth as a way of allowing Robinson to triumph, however: Robinson stands, as the papers indeed portray, as an independently fascinating figure who does not need to be celebrated at the expense of her contemporaries. Jane Hodson, for example, in '"The strongest but most undecorated language": Mary Robinson's Rhetorical Strategy in Letter to the Women of England' (pp. 87–105), deftly establishes Robinson's intellectual manifesto in its own right with reference to *A Letter to the Women of England* [1799], arguing for its individual political voice, one that was substantially different from that used by both male politicians and women such as Wollstonecraft and Mary Hays. Employing a greater number of personal pronouns and pre-modifying adjectives than many writers, Robinson developed a personalized rhetorical style designed to more readily communicate her proto-feminist manifesto to other women readers. Ashley J. Cross also focuses on *A Letter* in 'He-She Philosophers and Other Literary Bugbears: Mary Robinson's *A Letter to the Women of England*' (pp. 53–68), promoting its significance as a catalyst for creating a shared intellectual history and community for women writers. Like Robinson's two novels of 1799, *The False Friend* and *The Natural Daughter*, *A Letter*, Cross argues, positions the woman writer as the 'unacknowledged legislator of the world, a project already iterated in her philosophically powerful preface to *Sappho and Phaon*. Finally, Julie Shaffer's '*Walsingham*: Gender, Pain, Knowledge' (pp. 69–85) suggests that Robinson developed a kind of mental androgyny in her famous novel about cross-dressing that went beyond playful acts of gender-blurring. Shaffer shows how Robinson developed an alternative epistemology that rejected the gender binary itself to engage in a narratorial transvestism or masquerade that is more 'genuine' than the false boundary lines of sex.

Also addressing Robinson this year are William D. Brewer, in 'Subverting Individuality: Mary Robinson and Polygraphs' (in Peer, ed., *Inventing the Individual*, pp. 17–26), and Nikki Hessell, in 'Mary Robinson's Poetry and the London Newspapers' (*N&Q* 49[2002] 36–7). Brewer's paper thinks about the manner in which the poet obscured her own individuality, not only through the performance of a number of public roles in society, but also by writing in to her novels several polygraph characters: impersonators who dedicate themselves to imitating others. For Brewer, Robinson's prolific use of the polygraph in her novels was part of a contemporary novelistic commonplace wherein individuality was erased by fluid characters who are able to shift between class and gender positions. Robinson's *Walsingham; or the Pupil of Nature* [1797], for example, explores the consequences of prolonged transvestism for an upper-class woman who performs outside the sphere of acting. Hessell provides Robinson scholars with new information regarding the poet's newspaper publications, confirming her appearance in two tri-weeklies, the *Evening Mail* and the *Whitehall Evening Post*, so adding to debates regarding her place in the literary press.

While consideration of other Romantic women writers was relatively scarce this year, two pioneering volumes should be duly celebrated as contributing new and important material to the field: Gilroy and Hanley, eds., *Joanna Baillie: A Selection of Plays and Poems*; and Anne Stott's *Hannah More: The First Victorian*. Gilroy and Hanley's edition includes the important pre-*Lyrical Ballads* 'Introductory Discourse' to Baillie's *Plays on the Passions*; *De Montfort*; the miscellaneous play *The Family Legend*; and her *Fugitive Verses* and other significant poetry composed after 1790. The additional chronology, select bibliography, and adequate footnotes to the texts render the volume a useful teaching aid, especially for courses wishing to compare her theatrical and poetical compositions. As a dramatist, Gilroy and Hanley point out, Baillie was the most successful woman writer of her time, negotiating a space between the mental imaginings of closet drama and the commercial stage. The latter Baillie found distasteful and slightly frantic, producing, almost as a reaction against this, a new kind of play marked by its emotional control, educative bent, and psycho-social frame. Coming to self-consciously write readable dramatic texts rather than playing-texts, she produced several poetic plays amidst her popular tragedies, *De Montfort* [1798] and *The Family Legend* [1810]. Yet even within these plays Baillie rejected the large-scale visual effects which were becoming the staple of the theatre for a Wordsworthian authentic language of shared feelings which she examined through the category of 'the passions'. Wordsworth, like Scott and Byron, was respectful of Baillie, notably of her conception of 'mental theatre', as well as her investment in cultural identity via her explorations of Scottish history and geography. Her aesthetic of realistic detail ultimately connected her with a tradition of women writers who critique unearthly Romantic ideology, the editors suggest, Baillie, like Barbauld, conceiving of her muse as domestic and social. The volume's poetry illustrates Baillie's communal, domestic consciousness through its celebration of rural life, and her often devotional poems for children also connect her to Barbauld, whose *Hymns in Prose for Children* [1781] are footnoted in her own hymnal pieces. Readers interested in Baillie's religious works may also turn to Christine Colón's 'Christianity and Colonial Discourse in Joanna Baillie's *The*

Bride' (*Renascence* 54:iii[2002] 163–76), an examination of Baillie's most conventional Christian play. For Colón, however, the conservative theories of moral reform put forward in *The Bride* [1828], which was written to convert the natives of Ceylon, insist on a revolutionary and impassioned discourse of equality to redress imperialist endeavour.

Stott's vibrant and exceptionally eloquent *Hannah More* is indispensable to anyone working on this prolific figure. It is the first full-length biography for fifty years and made more significant by its extensive use of unpublished material, such as More's correspondence. Tracing More's life from her beginnings in Bristol, through her friendship with the Garricks, to her conversion to 'vital religion' and her position as an anti-radical but morally driven priestess, the book offers much insight into this often disliked Romantic woman writer. Part of the biography's manifesto seems to be to remedy the damage inflicted by William Roberts's *Memoirs of the Life and Correspondence of Mrs Hannah More* [1834], which, perhaps not intentionally, made her appear to be an authoritarian, pushy, and awkward bigot. Stott privileges the playful More, who, according to her goddaughter, Marianne Thornton, overflowed 'with affection & feeling & generosity' and was spoilt only by 'adulation' and later abuse by her critics. Certainly she was captivated by Bristol's cultural life, especially its strong emphasis on the theatre, which lead to her friendship with David Garrick. His Newtonian revolution on stage, in which he exploited emotion and sentiment to enchant his audience as revivalist lay preachers enchanted theirs, impacted heavily on More, who wrote at length on sensibility and feeling. Stott's reading of More through her relationships with other cultural figures is illuminating, her intimacy with Garrick granting her lodgings at Hampton Court for a while, where she met Samuel Johnson and Elizabeth Montagu. Through Montagu, More was introduced to Barbauld and Hester Chapone, and she was to appear with two of these women in Richard Samuel's *Nine Living Muses of Great Britain* in 1778, establishing her as an educated and cerebral commentator.

More's religious social scene is also treated in lucid detail by Stott, who acknowledges that, even at the height of her worldly success, More considered herself a convinced Christian, infusing her devotional and secular works alike with religious messages. Her spiritual awakening and increased religiosity are dealt with subtly by Stott, who maps out the influence of Dissenters such as Philip Doddridge and William Wilberforce. Eventually, More was unable to reconcile sociability with faith, Stott reporting an incident one Sunday evening at Garrick's in which he kindly excused her before the performance of music began, an inappropriate Sunday activity for an eighteenth-century Christian. Indeed More appears rather dogmatic throughout the study, despite Stott's attempts to render her otherwise. As a young and genial woman, More simply comes across as hypocritical, flirting with Johnson and Walpole but scolding the duchess of Devonshire for her support of the Whig campaign led by Charles James Fox: 'I wish her husband wou'd lock her up or take away her Shoes, or put her in the Corner or bestow on her any other punishment fit for naughty children', More dourly announced. Yet Stott does reveal a less rigid image of More in her correspondence, wherein subjects such as rural life, poverty, and education are regarded in a more subtle and less patronizing manner than that of her many tracts and treatises. More's moralistic agenda too was always entangled with her practical attempts to improve the position of the poor as she attempted to intervene in parliament and to publish nutrition and recipe books for those in need.

Her own sometimes torn agenda—to solve social problems, preach the gospel, and entertain—foreshadows the mixed response of those writing after her: many feminists, George Eliot for example, were unable to accept her prescription of active philanthropy as a solution for women's continuing disadvantages. Her earnestness too proved off-putting for future generations of readers, the indolent prime minister, Lord Melbourne, claiming, almost directly in response to More, that 'Nobody is gay now', they 'are all so religious'. While Stott's More is not exactly 'gay', she is profoundly engaging, and this study, with its mass of references to manuscript sources, contemporary newspapers, journals, and other literature is one of the highlights of this year's work.

Daniel Sanjiv Roberts also addresses More in 'Not "Forsworn with Pink Ribbons": Hannah More, Thomas De Quincey, and the Literature of Power', wherein De Quincey's conception of power is connected back to the Evangelical circles of his mother, a follower of More and a member of the Clapham sect (*RoN* 25[2002]). Repudiating his early Evangelical upbringing, De Quincey revised his position on More, writing scathingly of her literary pretensions in a manner which simply served to highlight his own problems with religion. Roberts even astutely suggests that the colonialist and nationalist imperatives typical of Evangelical thinking shaped and operated within De Quincey's own literary theory. Mary Waldron's 'A Different Kind of Patronage: Ann Yearsley's Later Friends' (*AgeJ* 13[2002] 283–335) turns to that figure most often associated with More, Ann Yearsley. Waldron explores Yearsley's later patrons, who by all accounts were more welcoming of the poet's independent talents, caught as they were in a new moment wherein aristocratic ideals of polite reserve and convention became unfashionable and passé. Taking over from More's reign over Yearsley, the radical publishers G.G.K. and J. Robinson, earl of Bristol and bishop of Derry, Frederick Augustus Hervey, and portraitist Sarah Shiells are just three of the poet's 'later friends' addressed by Waldron in this enjoyable and meticulously researched paper. Frank Felsenstein also provides a thorough examination of questions of patronage in 'Ann Yearsley and the Politics of Patronage: The Thorp Arch Archive: Part I' (*TSWL* 21:ii[2002] 347–92), using the discovery of a new collection of letters between the poet and her later benefactors to re-examine Yearsley's relationship with them. The 'Thorp Archive', Felsenstein reports, comprises twenty-four items dating from January 1788 to November 1789 and includes letters from Yearsley to Eliza Dawson, Wilmer Gossip, Lord Bristol, and Lady Elizabeth Foster.

Stephen C. Behrendt's 'Telling Secrets: The Sonnets of Anna Maria Smallpiece and Mary F. Johnson' (*ERR* 13:iv[2002] 393–410) also branches out into lesser-known aspects of this field, directing our attention to the intellectual and emotional aesthetic forged within the sonnet sequences of two unknown authors. Smallpiece's *Original Sonnets* [1805] and Johnson's *Original Sonnets* [1810] are shown here to share more than a title, both expressing unmediated intense feeling within the sonnet but treading the precarious ground between 'absolute sincerity and shocking insincerity' in the attempt. Inviting readers to think about intertextual and colliding resonances of emotion, such an attempt creates an almost feminist aesthetics of experience, Behrendt eloquently proposes, one that refuses the unified epiphanic mode for a multiple way of telling or narrating.

Two general papers on Romantic women's writing are included in Esterhammer, ed., *Romantic Poetry*, part of John Benjamins's Comparative History of Literatures in European Languages series. Kari Lokke's 'Poetry as Self-Consumption: Women Writers and their Audiences in British and German Romanticism' (pp. 91–111) provides a valuable discussion of why the wealth of material on English Romantic women writers is not reflected in European women's writing. Appealing for more translations of such work, Lokke highlights the poetry of the German Karoline von Günderrode to forward an argument checking the ubiquitous myth of the Romantic poet as abandoned woman. Lokke engagingly overturns the myth by showing how von Günderrode's 'Ariadne auf Naxos' and 'Der Kuß im Traume', as well as Hemans's 'The Last Song of Sappho' and Landon's 'Night at Sea', posit the Sappho-Ariadne figure of the artist as one tormented by her relation to her audience, memory, and poetic tradition, rather than any individual (male) object of desire or passion. Equally significant is Patrick Vincent's engaging 'Elegiac Muses: Romantic Women Poets and the Elegy' (pp. 197–221), a short history of women's elegy, a mode portrayed here as issuing from the feminized cultures of sensibility and sentiment. Examining elegy as a mode or psychological 'mood', Vincent illustrates how the genre's propensity to sublimate erotic passion into tenderness is used in different ways by women writers. Smith and Hemans, for example, turned every poem into a tender last song; Landon, following a French tradition including Adélaïde Dufrénoy and Alphonse de Lamartine, accentuated the erotic and theatrical element of elegy; while the Russian Ekaterina Urusova erased such passion in order to partake of a genre rendered homosocial by her immediate contemporaries. Vincent finally points up women's refusal to substitute poetry for the mourned person and thus assimilate individuals into a generalized immortality.

Paula R. Feldman's 'Women Poets and Anonymity in the Romantic Era' (*NLH* 33:ii[2002] 279–89) offers another characteristically well researched article which overturns the myth of the veiled, private, and secretive Romantic woman poet. Far from being fearful of putting their names before the public, many women poets of this period signed unidentified volumes (as in the case of Mary Tighe), used their real names to ensure the sale of their verse (a tactic exercised by labouring-class women poets), or employed transparent pseudonyms (famously used in Shelley's 'By the Author of Frankenstein'). Feldman suggests that scholars have only thought otherwise due to misunderstandings regarding the practices of periodical print culture, wherein contributions were often anonymous. The article usefully concludes by arguing that women who did remain nameless tended to be associated with controversial or satirical ideas, were published for children rather than adults, or were engaged in collaborative schemes. Stuart Curran also addresses the issue of collaboration in 'Mothers and Daughters: Poetic Generation(s) in the Eighteenth and Nineteenth Centuries' (in Mellor et al., eds., pp. 147–62), recasting the issue in terms of sources of literary inspiration for women. Pitting a 'sincere' and tributorial relationship between women poets and a maternally figured muse against a masculinized invocation of the muse by poets such as Byron, Curran restricts his analysis by casting inspiration in purely familial, rather than familial and sexual, terms. Also disappointing this year was Anne Mellor's contribution to the starkly masculine Fulford, ed., *Romanticism and Millenarianism*, Mellor being both the only female critic included in the collection, and also the only critic to reflect upon women's writing. Naively, perhaps, Mellor's 'Blake, the Apocalypse and Romantic Women Writers' (pp. 139–52) positions Romantic women writers entirely outside apocalyptic thinking, trapped, it is awkwardly asserted, by a biological 'feminine mode' that prevents them from imagining anything outside real time. For Mellor, writers we might assume to be apocalyptic—Mary Ann Browne, Mary Shelley, Joanna Southcott—invoke prophecy only to affirm the evolution of humanity through historical time, endorsing the idea that individual development was a here-and-now process, rather than one to be deferred to a future space.

Greg Kucich offers a rather more engaging paper on the writing of history by Romantic-era women, a task still in its early stages of conceptual and ideological formation: 'Women's Historiography and the (Dis)Embodiment of Law: Ann Yearsley, Mary Hays, Elizabeth Benger' (*WC* 33:i[2002] 3–7). Focusing on the historico-biographical work of Benger, Hays, and Yearsley, Kucich illustrates how the women at once interrogate and sympathize with their female subjects to avoid limiting them within either rational or affective discourses. Jane Stabler too, in 'Taking Liberties: The Italian Picturesque in Women's Travel Writing' (*ERR* 13:i[2002] 11–22), engages in a dynamic discussion of the manner in which a group of women writers, all of whom travelled to Italy, exploited the aesthetic instability inherent in theories of the picturesque to critique models of masculine authority. Hester Piozzi's *Observations and Reflections* [1789], Marianne Baillie's *First Impressions* [1818], Charlotte Eaton's *Rome in the Nineteenth Century* [1820], and Lady Morgan's *Italy* [1821], Stabler shows, are texts that refuse to tidy up the 'unruly' diversity of Italian life to point towards an aesthetic predicated on energy and multiplicity.

Finally, readers' attention might be drawn to two further publications in this field: Pamela Woof's new edition of Dorothy Wordsworth's *The Grasmere and Alfoxden Journals*; and Thomson, Voller, and Frank, eds., *Gothic Writers: A Critical and Bibliographical Guide*. While Dorothy Wordsworth was one of the first women writers to be reclaimed within Romantic studies, scholarship on her work is presently scarce and Woof's fresh edition of her ever-important journals is much to be welcomed. A record of her own experiences with both her brother, and friend Coleridge, the *Journals* grant the reader a number of vibrant and lively insights into the time in which Wordsworth wrote many of his most well-received poetry. Beautifully descriptive, at times domestic, and always emotional, the journals are also important as reminders of the tender and affectionate relationship Dorothy had with William, one only derided by those neglectful of her diary-like testimonies of their shared life. This edition offers all the framing notes, chronologies, maps, and glosses a reader might require, and the meticulous index discloses both the range of Dorothy's allusions and references and Woof's patent expertise as an editor. Thomson, Voller, and Frank's encyclopedic study of Gothic writing is relevant here for its relatively detailed commentaries on several Romantic women writers. Douglass H. Thomson provides entries on Barbauld, Charlotte Dacre, and Sophia Lee; Frederick S. Frank writes on Jane Austen, François Guillaume Ducray-Duminil, and Ann Radcliffe; Jack G. Voller explores Clara Reeve and Charlotte Smith; and Marie Mulvey-Roberts looks at Mary Shelley, in a volume that covers Gothic writers from Walpole to the present day. Offering bibliographical, methodological, and critical information regarding each, the contributors establish these at once market-driven and otherworldly writers in terms of their variously intellectual, religious, expressive, and populist concerns, situating them within an ever-shifting sense of Gothicism.

7. Drama

This year's cause for celebration is the first scholarly biography of Joanna Baillie, Judith Bailey Slagle's *Joanna Baillie: A Literary Life*. Slagle's principal task throughout is to show the ways in which the playwright, poet, and cultural commentator reconciled her ideological identities as nationalist, conservative, and feminist. The meticulous research that has gone into this study is evident; the biography is packed with information that will be mined by scholars and graduate students in search of material on Baillie. Slagle is ever a mindful educator as biographer, and includes extremely thorough notes that incorporate nearly all the contemporary critical studies of Baillie and also identify figures of the era. Some of these latter notes are surprising choices, such as those on Sarah Siddons or Francis Hutcheson, for instance; they lead one to surmise that Slagle presumes her readers are not yet well versed in the history and culture of Baillie's lifetime, yet her academic biography will appeal more to scholars in search of critical information than to the general reader seeking intimate knowledge of Baillie's personality. Given Baillie's current stature in Romantic studies, the biography is also perhaps overly defensive in its tone; Baillie's talent and innovation have been demonstrated many times over in critical analyses and now classroom reading. That said, Slagle's exhaustive research unearthing and cataloguing previously unknown items surely made her protective of her subject's worthiness as a significant literary figure. Throughout the work the emphasis is placed more on intellectual composition than personal life: Slagle works to show us the growth of Baillie's mind and imagination, her contributions to theatre theory, and her sphere of influence. The chapter on Baillie's relationship with Sir Walter Scott is especially engaging; it is here that Slagle reveals more of Baillie's personality and makes her subject come to life.

The penultimate chapter of Slagle's biography addresses Baillie's religious convictions and theological arguments. Baillie's most conventionally Christian play is the subject of Christine Colón's 'Christianity and Colonial Discourse in Joanna Baillie's *The Bride*' (*Renascence* 54:iii[2002] 163–76). This is the only play Baillie wrote for a non-British audience, the natives of Ceylon, with the aim of converting them. Acknowledging the complicated relationship between imperialism and Christianity, Colón argues that Baillie's theory of 'sympathetick curiosity' works to 'transform an admittedly imperialist endeavor into a potentially revolutionary discourse of equality'.

The cultural imperialism of Shakespeare gets its start on the Romantic stage. In Jane Moody's 'Romantic Shakespeare' (in Wells and Stanton, eds., *The Cambridge Companion to Shakespeare on Stage*, pp. 37–57), the political nature of Shakespeare on stage is always at stake. There were institutional battles over who got to interpret him—the legitimate theatres—as well as ideological battles between conservative and radical critics. Actors influenced the rise in character criticism, with stars such as Kemble, Siddons, and Kean changing the way audiences and critics understood characters such as Coriolanus, Lady Macbeth, Shylock, Othello, and Richard III.

Hogle, ed., *The Cambridge Companion to Gothic Fiction*, includes an excellent essay by Jeffrey N. Cox, 'English Gothic Theatre' (pp. 125–44), which points out that, while Northrop Frye was right that there was never one era of Gothic English literature (there was only a 'Gothic impulse' that permeates works from *Beowulf* to the present), there was indeed a specific period of English Gothic drama, with the years 1789–1832 marking its height. Cox shows Gothic drama's debt both to late Elizabethan and Jacobean drama and to eighteenth-century German *Sturm und Drang*, and notes that while it is clearly a 'form of fantasy' it is also an art form that 'represented ideological struggles'.

The Gothic is also under investigation in Horner, ed., *European Gothic: A Spirited Exchange, 1760–1960*. Peter Mortensen, in 'The Robbers and the Police: British Romantic Drama and the Gothic Treacheries of Coleridge's *Remorse*' (pp. 128–46), demonstrates that, while Coleridge was among the critics lambasting the Gothic as 'Jacobinical German drama', he used Gothic mechanisms and spectacle to condemn the coercive power of the police state in his most successful venture, *Remorse*, which Mortensen views as an 'anti-Jacobin rewriting of *Die Räuber*'. Mortensen continues his analysis of Schiller's popular but dangerous play in 'Robbing the Robbers: Schiller, Xenophobia and the Politics of British Translation' (*L&H* 11[2002] 41–61); he looks at translations of *Die Räuber*, particularly Joseph George Holman's *The Red Cross Knights* and Keppel Craven's *The Robbers* (both published in the crisis year of 1797) and observes how the translations 'cleanse' the original radical nature of Schiller's work and make it counter-revolutionary.

Research on Byron continues to reveal the poet as a sophisticated and fascinating dramatic writer. Ian Dennis, in '*Cain*: Lord Byron's Sincerity' (*SiR* 41[2002] 655–74) addresses the ways in which *Cain* has long vexed readers: is Byron's questioning of the story from Genesis simplistically pious and orthodox, or ironic and taunting? Dennis ultimately concerns himself with the expressions of desire in the defiance within Byron's drama, looking at how Byron provokes his audience and its expectations of him. Daniela Garofalo, in 'Political Seductions: The Show of War in Byron's *Sardanapalus*' (*Criticism* 44[2002] 43–63), argues that the image of Byron's weak, passive king in this drama critiques and revises the image of Byronic heroes in his Eastern tales: the seductive, violent, powerful leader. *Sardanapalus* destroys Byron's earlier heroic creation, and in doing so shows the dangerous consequences of worshipping martial heroes (such as Napoleon), yet, pessimistically, fails to offer a viable alternative.

Edward Ziter's 'Kean, Byron, and Fantasies of Miscegenation' (*TJ* 54[2002] 607–26) argues that the fascination with exotic spectacle on the Romantic stage was, in part, a way for British audiences to explore and examine race—to intellectualize their 'fantasies of miscegenation within an emerging ethnographic discourse'. His analysis centres on Kean's exotic performances and the staging of Byron's Turkish tales, in particular *The Bride of Abydos* and parts of *Don Juan*, and concludes that, by the end of the Romantic era, this 'imaginative identification' with the exotic had disintegrated into justification for military intervention in the exotic lands of the eastern Mediterranean.

In another very interesting study of performance, Kathryn Pratt's '"Dark catastrophe of passion": The "Indian" as Human Commodity in Nineteenth-Century British Theatrical Culture' (*SiR* 41[2002] 605–26), argues that the figure of the Native American became a symbol for the British loss of empire. A figure of mourning, the stage Indian became associated with the British, as both lost their land to the new American nation. Pratt uses the 1820 Drury Lane production of Baillie's *De Montfort*, starring Edmund Kean, to demonstrate the importance of the melancholy Indian figure, as both Baillie and Kean were known for their sympathy for 'noble savage' passion. An additional interesting-sounding article, Martin

Prochazka's 'Imaginative Geographies Disrupted? Representing the Other in English Romantic Drama' (*EJES* 6[2002] 207–20) was unfortunately not received in time for review. Finally, Christopher Goulding notes, in 'Early Detective Drama in Percy Shelley's *The Cenci*' (*N&Q* 49[2002] 40–1) that Shelley, working with sources from his father-in-law William Godwin and Dr James Lind MD FRS, created probably 'the first example of ratiocinative forensic detection being presented in a work of drama'.

Books Reviewed

Bachinger, Katrina, ed. *Byronic Negotiations*. Lang. [2002] pp. 245. £23 ISBN 3 6313 9672 4.

Bahar, Saba. *Mary Wollstonecraft's Social and Aesthetic Philosophy: 'An Eve to Please Me'*. Palgrave. [2002] pp. viii + 220. £50 ($65) ISBN 0 3339 7390 9.

Balfour, Ian. *The Rhetoric of Romantic Prophecy*. StanfordUP. [2002] pp. xii + 346. hb $65 ISBN 0 8047 4231 6, pb $24.95 ISBN 0 8047 4506 4.

Barker, Juliet, ed. *Wordsworth: A Life in Letters*. Penguin. [2002] pp. 368. £25 ISBN 0 6708 7214 8.

Barker, Mary, and William Wordsworth. *Lines Addressed to a Noble Lord*, introd. Jonathan Wordsworth. Woodstock. [2001] pp. 34. £30 ($50) ISBN 1 8547 7230 9.

Barth, J. Robert, ed. *The Fountain Light: Studies in Romanticism and Religion—Essays in Honor of John L.Mahoney*. FordUP. [2002] pp. 256. £28.95 ISBN 0 8232 2228 4.

Behrendt, Stephen C., ed. *Zastrozzi and St. Irvyne*. Broadview. [2002] pp. 326. £8.99 ISBN 1 5511 1266 3.

Blades, John, *John Keats: The Poems*. Analysing Texts. Palgrave. [2002] pp. xv + 246. £40 ISBN 0 3339 4894 7.

Breen, Jennifer, and Mary Noble. *Romantic Literature*. Arnold. [2002] pp. ix + 173. hb £35 ISBN 0 3408 0669 9, pb £10.99 ISBN 0 3408 0670 2.

Brewer, William D. *The Mental Anatomies of William Godwin and Mary Shelley*. FDUP. [2001] pp. 246. £35 ISBN 0 8386 3870 8.

Buchanan, Carol, *Wordsworth's Gardens*. TTUP. [2001] pp. xviii + 224. $45 ISBN 0 8967 2445 X.

Buss, Helen M., D.L. Macdonald, and Anne McWhir, eds. *Mary Wollstonecraft and Mary Shelley: Writing Lives*. WLUP. [2001] pp. x + 330. £37.50 ISBN 0 8892 0363 6.

Canuel, Mark. *Religion, Toleration, British Writing, 1790–1830*. CUP. [2002] pp. vi + 317. £45 ISBN 0 5218 1577 0.

Carruthers, Gerard, and Alan Rawes, eds. *English Romanticism and the Celtic World*. CUP. [2002] pp. ix + 265. £40 ISBN 0 5218 1085 X.

Clery, E. J., Caroline Franklin, and Peter Garside, eds. *Authorship, Commerce and the Public: Scenes of Writing, 1750–1850*. Palgrave. [2002] pp. xi + 242. £47.50 ISBN 0 3339 6455 1.

Coburn, Kathleen, and Anthony John Harding, eds. *The Notebooks of Samuel Taylor Coleridge*, vol. 5: *1827–1834*. PrincetonUP. [2002] pp. xxvii + 1104 (text), lv + 817 (notes). $295 ISBN 0 6910 9907 3.

Connolly, Tristanne J. *William Blake and the Body*. Palgrave. [2002] pp. xvii + 249. £45 ISBN 0 3339 6848 4.

Cope, Kevin L. ed. *1650–1850: Ideas, Aesthetics, and Inquiries in the Early Modern Era*, vol. 6. AMS. [2001] pp. xvi + 405. $112.50 ISBN 0 4046 4406 6.

Craciun, Adriana. *Fatal Women of Romanticism*. CUP. [2002] pp. xviii + 328. £45 ($60) ISBN 0 5218 1668 8.

Craciun, Adriana and Kari E. Lokke eds. *Rebellious Hearts: British Women Writers and the French Revolution*. SUNYP. [2001] pp. xiii + 395. hb $62.50 ISBN 0 7914 4969 6, pb $20.95 ISBN 0 7914 4970 X.

Crane, David. *The Kindness of Sisters: Annabella Milbanke and the Destruction of the Byrons*. HC. [2002] pp. x + 293. £19.99 ISBN 0 0025 7052 1.

Crawford, Rachel. *Poetry, Enclosure, and the Vernacular Landscape, 1700–1830*. CUP. [2002] pp. xiii + 318. £45 ISBN 0 5218 1531 2.

Cronin, Richard. *Romantic Victorians: English Literature, 1824–1840*. Palgrave. [2002] pp. viii + 296. £52.50 ($69.95) ISBN 0 3339 6616 3.

Demata, Massimiliano, and Duncan Wu, eds. *British Romanticism and the Edinburgh Review*. Palgrave. [2002] pp. xi + 219. £47.50 ISBN 0 3339 6349 0.

Dent, Shirley, and Jason Whittaker. *Radical Blake: Influence and Afterlife from 1827*. Palgrave. [2002] pp. xi + 237. £45 ISBN 0 3339 8645 8.

Eger, Elizabeth, Charlotte Grant, Cliona Ó Gallchoir and Penny Warburton, eds. *Women Writing and the Public Sphere, 1700–1830*. CUP. [2001] pp. xviii + 320. £37.50 ISBN 0 5217 7106 4.

Esterhammer, Angela, ed. *Romantic Poetry*. Benjamins. [2002] pp. xi + 537. £121 ISBN 9 0272 3450 7 (Europe), $190 ISBN 1 5881 1112 1 (US).

Everest, Kelvin, *John Keats*. WTW. Northcote. [2002] pp. xi + 123. £9.99 ISBN 0 7463 0807 8.

Fay, Elizabeth. *Romantic Medievalism: History and the Romantic Literary Ideal*. Palgrave. [2002] pp. v + 233. £55 ISBN 0 3339 7007 1.

Ferris, Ina. *The Romantic National Tale and the Question of Ireland*. CUP. [2002] pp. x + 205. £40 ISBN 0 5218 1460 X.

Fine Art Society. *Pastoral: An Exhibition of Printmaking in the English Pastoral Tradition from William Blake to Robin Tanner*. [2002] pp. 64. pb £15 ISBN 0 9050 6206 X.

Fulford, Tim, ed. *Romanticism and Millenarianism*. Palgrave. [2002] pp. xvii + 248. £45 ISBN 0 3122 4011 2.

Fulford, Tim, ed. *Romanticism and Science, 1773–1833*. 5 vols. Routledge. [2002] pp. xx + 317 (vol. 1), vii + 264 (vol. 2), ix + 384 (vol. 3), vii + 320 (vol. 4), vi + 310 (vol. 5). £550 ISBN 0 4152 1952 3.

Gillis, Alan A., and Aaron Kelly, eds. *Critical Ireland: New Essays in Literature and Culture*. FCP. [2001] pp. xviii + 221. hb £32.50 ISBN 1 8518 2597 5, pb £19.95 ISBN 1 8518 2598 3.

Gilmour, Ian, *The Making of the Poets: Byron and Shelley in their Time*. RandomH. [2002] pp. xiii + 402. £12.50 ISBN 0 7126 6767 9.

Gilroy, Amanda, and Keith Hanley, eds. *Joanna Baillie: A Selection of Plays and Poems*. P&C. [2002] pp. xlvii + 342. £40 ($60) ISBN 1 8519 6358 8.

Gittings, Robert, ed. *John Keats: Selected Letters*, introd. Jon Mee. rev. edn. OUP. [2002] £8.99 ISBN 0 1928 4053 3.

Gladden, Samuel Lyndon. *Shelley's Textual Seductions: Plotting Utopia in the Erotic and Political Works*. Routledge. [2002] pp. xviii + 351. £65 ISBN 0 4159 3702 7.

Göbel, Walter, Saskia Schabio, and Martin Windisch, eds. *Engendering Images of Man in the Long Eighteenth Century*. Trier: Wissenschaftlicher Verlag. [2001] pp. xiii + 295. pb DM54.50 ISBN 3 8847 6469 1.

Gourlay, Alexander S. *Prophetic Character: Essays on William Blake in Honor of John E. Grant*. Locust Hill. [2002] pp. xxxiii + 396. $60 ISBN 0 9339 5196 5.

Grenby, M. O. *The Anti-Jacobin Novel: British Conservatism and the French Revolution*. CUP. [2001] pp. xiii + 271. £42.50 ($65) ISBN 0 5218 0351 9.

Guest, Kirsten, ed. *Eating their Words: Cannibalism and the Boundaries of Cultural Identity*. SUNYP. [2001] pp. ix + 219. pb £15.50 ISBN 0 7914 5090 2.

Gunther-Canada, Wendy. *Rebel Writer: Mary Wollstonecraft and Enlightenment Politics*. NIUP. [2001] pp. xi + 203. $38 ISBN 0 8758 0280 X.

Harris, Morag, *Linguistic Transformations in Romantic Aesthetics from Coleridge to Emily Dickinson*, ed. Morton D. Paley and Meg Harris Williams. SCL. Mellen. [2002] pp. viii + 236. $109.95 ISBN 0 7734 7029 8.

Hawley, Judith, ed. *Literature and Science, 1660–1834*. Pt. 1, 4 vols. P&C. [2002]. pp. xxxviii + 395 (vol. 1), xxiv + 375 (vol. 2), xviii + 427 (vol. 3), xxiv + 413 (vol. 4). £350 ISBN 1 8519 6737 0.

Heaney, Seamus. *William Wordsworth: Poems Selected by Seamus Heaney*. 2nd edn. Faber. [2001] pp. xii + 140. £4.99 ISBN 0 5712 0699 9.

Hebron, Stephen, *John Keats*. Writers' Lives. BL. [2002] pp. 128. £10.95 ISBN 0 7123 4725 9.

Hogle, Jerrold E., ed. *The Cambridge Companion to Gothic Fiction*. CUP. [2002] pp. 354. $22 ISBN 0 5217 9466 8.

Horner, Avril, ed. *European Gothic: A Spirited Exchange, 1760–1960*. ManUP. [2002] pp. 240. $24.95 ISBN 0 7190 6064 8.

Hutchings, Kevin. *Imagining Nature: Blake's Environmental Poetics*. McG-QUP. [2002] pp. xiv + 256 hb $75 pb $22.95 ISBN 0 7735 2343 X.

Johnson, Claudia L., ed. *The Cambridge Companion to Mary Wollstonecraft*. CUP. [2002] pp. xxi + 284. hb £45.99 ($60) ISBN 0 5217 8343 7, pb £15.99 ($22) ISBN 0 5217 8952 4.

Joplin, David D., *Coleridge's Idea of Wordsworth as Philosopher Poet*. Studies in British Literature. Mellen. [2002] pp. v + 192. $109.95 ISBN 0 7734 7063 8.

Keats, John. *Lamia; Isabella; The Eve of St Agnes*, introd. Jonathan Wordsworth. Woodstock. [2001] pp. 216. £18 ($30) ISBN 1 8547 7252 X.

Kelly, Gary. *Felicia Hemans: Selected Poems, Prose, and Letters*. Broadview. [2002] pp. 493. £12.99 ($18.95) ISBN 1 5511 1137 3.

Kooy, Michael John. *Coleridge, Schiller and Aesthetic Education*. Palgrave. [2002] pp. xii + 241. £47.50 ISBN 0 3337 4936 7.

Lee, Debbie. *Slavery and the Romantic Imagination*. UPennP. [2002] pp. xiii + 296. hb $55 ISBN 0 8122 3636 X, pb $19.95. ISBN 0 8122 1882 5.

Levere, Trevor H., *Poetry Realized in Nature: Samuel Taylor Coleridge and Early Nineteenth-Century Science*. 2nd edn. CUP. [2002] pp. xiii + 271. hb £50 ($75) ISBN 0 5212 3920 6, pb £18.95 ($28) ISBN 0 5215 2490 3.

MacCarthy, Fiona, *Byron: Life and Legend*. Murray. [2002] pp. xiv + 674. £25 ISBN 0 7195 5621 X.

McDayter, Ghislaine, Guinn Batten, and Barry Milligan, eds. *Romantic Generations: Essays in Honor of Robert F. Gleckner*. BuckUP and AUP. [2001] pp. 301. £31.50 ISBN 0 8387 5470 8.

McFarland, Thomas, and Nicholas Halmi, eds. *The Collected Works of Samuel Taylor Coleridge: Opus Maximum*, vol. 15. PrincetonUP. [2002] pp. ccxl + 419. $150 ISBN 0 6910 9882 4.

McGann, Jerome, and James Soderholm, eds. *Byron and Romanticism*. CSR. CUP. [2002] pp. x + 311. £17.95 ISBN 0 5210 0722 4.

Manning, Susan. *Fragments of Union: Making Connections in Scottish and American Writing*. Palgrave. [2002] pp. viii + 339. £55 ISBN 0 3337 6025 5.

Marggraf Turley, Richard. *The Politics of Language in Romantic Literature*. Palgrave. [2002] pp. xxii + 246. £47.50 ISBN 0 3339 6898 0.

Mays, J.C.C., ed. *The Collected Works of Samuel Taylor Coleridge: Poetical Works*, vol. 3: *Plays*, pts. 1 and 2. PrincetonUP [2001]. pp. xliii + 1,652. $195 ISBN 0 6910 9883 2.

Mellor Anne. K., Felicity Nussbaum and Jonathan F.S. Post, eds. *Forging Connections: Women's Poetry from the Renaissance to Romanticism*. Huntington. [2002] pp. 162. pb. £12.99 ISBN 0 8732 8197 7.

Morton, Timothy, and Nigel Smith, eds. *Radicalism in British Literary Culture, 1650–1830: From Revolution to Revolution*. CUP. [2002] pp. x + 284. £40 ISBN 0 5216 4215 9.

Mounsey, Chris, ed. *Presenting Gender: Changing Sex in Early-Modern Culture*. BuckUP/AUP. [2001] pp. 301. £40 ISBN 0 8387 5477 5.

Najarian, James, *Victorian Keats: Manliness, Sexuality, and Desire*. Palgrave. [2002] pp. x + 240. £45 ISBN 0 3339 8583 4.

Newlyn, Lucy, ed. *The Cambridge Companion to Coleridge*. CUP. [2002] pp. xv + 268. hb £45 ($60) ISBN 0 5216 5909 4, pb £15.95 ($22) ISBN 0 5216 5071 2.

O'Brien, Paul. *Shelley and Revolutionary Ireland*, introd. Paul Foot. Redwords. [2002] pp. 327. £11 ISBN 1 8722 0819 3.

Oerlemans, Onno. *Romanticism and the Materiality of Nature*. UTorP. [2002] pp. 253. $45 ISBN 0 8020 4863 3.

Peer, Larry, ed. *Recent Perspectives on European Romanticism*. Mellen. [2002] pp. v + 249. $109.95 (£69.95) ISBN 0 7734 6984 2.

Perry, Seamus, ed. *Coleridge's Notebooks: A Selection*. OUP. [2002] pp. xxiii + 264. £17.99 ISBN 0 1987 1201 4.

Price, Fiona, and Scott Masson, eds. *Silence, Sublimity and Suppression in the Romantic Period*. Mellen. [2002] pp. vi + 229. $109.95 (£69.95) ISBN 0 7734 7244 4.

Rauch, Alan. *Useful Knowledge: The Victorians, Morality, and the March of Intellect*. DukeUP. [2001] pp. x + 292. hb $59.95 ISBN 0 8223 2663 9, pb $19.95 ISBN 0 8223 2668 X.

Reiman, Donald H., and Neil Fraistat, eds. *Shelley's Poetry and Prose: Authoritative Texts, Criticism*. 2nd edn. Norton. [2002] pp. 786. $15 ISBN 0 3939 7752 8.

Richards, Robert J. *The Romantic Conception of Life: Science and Philosophy in the Age of Goethe*. UChicP. [2002] pp. xix + 587. £35 ISBN 0 2267 1210 9.

Richardson, Alan. *British Romanticism and the Science of the Mind*. CUP. [2001] pp. xx + 243. £37.50 ISBN 0 5217 8191 4.

Rigney, Ann. *Imperfect Histories: The Elusive Past and the Legacy of Romantic Historicism*. CornUP. [2001] pp. xii + 209. $39.95 ISBN 0 8014 3861 6.

Robinson, Eric, and David Powell, eds. *John Clare: By Himself*, illustrated by John Lawrence. 2nd edn. Carcanet. [2002] pp. xxiv + 364. £9.95 ISBN 1 8575 4288 6.

Roe, Nicholas. *The Politics of Nature: William Wordsworth and Some Contemporaries*. 2nd edn. Palgrave. [2002] pp. xiii + 244. £50. ISBN 0 3339 6275 3.

Roe, Nicholas, ed. *Samuel Taylor Coleridge and the Sciences of Life*. OUP. [2001] pp. xvi + 364. £62.50 ISBN 0 1981 8723 8.

Roessel, David. *In Byron's Shadow: Modern Greece in the English and American Imagination*. OUP. [2002] pp. xxii + 385. £50. ISBN 0 1951 4386 8.

Sales, Roger. *John Clare: A Literary Life*. Literary Lives. Palgrave. [2002] pp. xviii + 195. £16.99 ISBN 0 3336 5271 1.

Scott, Grant F., ed. *Selected Letters of John Keats*, rev. edn. HarvardUP. [2002] pp. xlv + 526. £26.50 ISBN 0 6740 0749 2.

Shaw, Philip. *Waterloo and the Romantic Imagination*. Palgrave. [2002] pp. xiv + 260. £47.50 ISBN 0 3339 9435 3.

Shelley, Percy Bysshe. *Zastrozzi: A Romance*, introd. Germaine Greer. Hesperus. [2002] pp. 112. £5.99 ISBN 1 8439 1029 2.

Shifrin, Susan, ed. *Women as Sites of Culture: Women's Roles in Cultural Formation from the Renaissance to the Twentieth Century*. Ashgate. [2002] pp. xiv + 274. £45 ($79.95) ISBN 0 7546 0311 3.

Slagle, Judith Bailey. *Joanna Baillie: A Literary Life*. FDUP. [2002] pp. 328. $43.50 ISBN 0 8386 3949 6.

Spector, Sheila A., ed. *British Romanticism and the Jews*. Palgrave. [2002] pp. xii + 294. £40 ISBN 0 3122 9522 7.

Stabler, Jane. *Burke to Byron, Barbauld to Baillie, 1790–1830*. Palgrave. [2002] pp. xiii + 322. hb £45 ISBN 0 3336 9624 7, pb £14.99 ISBN 0 3336 9625 5.

Stabler, Jane. *Byron, Poetics and History*. CSR. CUP. [2002] pp. xiii + 251. £40 ($55) ISBN 0 5218 1241 0.

Stott, Anne. *Hannah More: The First Victorian*. OUP. [2002] pp. xxiii + 384. £25 ($35) ISBN 0 1992 4532 0.

Strachan, John, ed. *The Poems of John Keats*. Routledge Literary Sourcebooks. Routledge. [2003] pp. xi + 198. £50 ISBN 0 4152 3477 8.

Taussig, Gurion, *Coleridge and the Idea of Friendship, 1789–1804*. UDelP. [2002] pp. 376. £50 ISBN 0 8741 3741 1.

Taylor, Barbara. *Mary Wollstonecraft and the Feminist Imagination*. CUP. [2002] pp. xvi + 331. hb £45 ($65) ISBN 0 5216 6144 7, pb £16.95 ($23) ISBN 0 5210 0417 9.

Thomson, Douglas H., Jack G. Voller, and Frederick S. Frank. eds. *Gothic Writers: A Critical and Bibliographical Guide*. Greenwood. [2002] pp. xxv + 516. £64.50 ($99.95). ISBN 0 3133 0500 5.

Trelawny, Edward John. *Recollections of the Last Days of Shelley and Byron*, introd. Jonathan Wordsworth. Woodstock. [2001] pp. 332. £55 ($95) ISBN 1 8547 7245 7.

Tuite, Clara, and Gillian Russell, eds. *Romantic Sociability: Social Networks and Literary Culture in Britain, 1770–184*. CUP. [2002] pp. xii + 267. £40.99 ($60) ISBN 0 5217 7068 8.

Ulmer, William A. *The Christian Wordsworth, 1798–1805*. SUNYP. [2001] pp. xv + 228. hb $62.50 ISBN 0 7914 5153 4, pb $20.95 ISBN 0 7914 5154 2.

Walford Davies, Damien. *Presences That Disturb: Models of Romantic Identity in the Literature and Culture of the 1790s*. UwalesP. [2002] pp. 384. £32.91 ISBN 0 7083 1738 3.

Wells, Stanley W., and Sarah Stanton. *The Cambridge Companion to Shakespeare on Stage*. CUP. [2002] pp. 338. $23 ISBN 0 5217 9711 X.

Williams, John, *Critical Issues: William Wordsworth*. Palgrave. [2002] pp. x + 267. £49.50 ISBN 0 3336 8732 9.

Wiltshire, John. *Recreating Jane Austen*. CUP. [2001] xi + 179. hb £37.50 ($55) ISBN 0 5218 0246 6, pb £13.99 ($20) ISBN 0 5210 0282 6.

Wolfson, Susan, and Elizabeth Fay. *The Siege of Valencia*. Broadview. [2002] pp. 315. £9.99 ($19.95) ISBN 1 5511 1442 9.

Woof, Pamela, ed. *Dorothy Wordsworth: The Grasmere and Alfoxden Journals*. OUP. [2002] pp. 254. £7.99 ($11.95) ISBN 0 1928 4062 2.

Wu, Duncan. *Wordsworth: An Inner Life*. Blackwell. [2002] pp. xviii + 378. £55 ISBN 0 6312 0638 8.

XIII

The Nineteenth Century: The Victorian Period

WILLIAM BAKER, HALIE CROCKER, KIRSTIE BLAIR, JIM DAVIS AND DAVID FINKELSTEIN

This chapter has five sections: 1. Cultural Studies and Prose; 2. The Novel; 3. Poetry; 4. Drama and Theatre; 5. Periodicals and Publishing History. Sections 1 and 2 are by William Baker and Halie Crocker; section 3 is by Kirstie Blair; section 4 is by Jim Davis; section 5 is by David Finkelstein.

1. Cultural Studies and Prose

(a) General

New from the Oxford English Literary History series is *The Victorians*, volume 8: *1830–1880* by Philip Davis, in which the author focuses on, among other subjects, the effects of 'semi-secularization' wrought by industrialization and science. The volume includes the following eleven chapters: 'Rural to Urban, 1830–1850', in which Davis explores the changing economy's effect on urbanization and the resulting transformations and incorporations of old traditions in and into new contexts; 'Nature', in which Darwin and the impact of science are highlighted in a discussion of changes in the 'natural' world order; 'Religion' and 'Mind', which focus on the spiritual and mental implications of a new uncertainty that causes 'belief itself' to be a 'religious phenomenon'; 'Conditions of Literary Production', which highlights the literary profession, book trade, and the rise of prose; 'Debatable Lands: Variety of Form and Genre in the Early Victorian Novel', in which changes in the landscapes of politics and class are explored using writings by Bulwer-Lytton, Disraeli, and Kingsley; and 'Alternative Fictions', which considers sensation novels, fairy-tales, and fantasies. Four chapters ('The Drama', 'High Realism', 'Lives and Thoughts', and 'Poetry') have as a backdrop an important question considered by Carlyle and others as to 'whether this was to be a century of invention rather than creativity, of matter more than spirit, of mechanical rather than dynamic thinking'. The volume is well written and indexed and includes useful author bibliographies.

Krueger, ed., *Functions of Victorian Culture at the Present Time*, is a collection of essays discussing the subject of Victorian principles, world-views, and values as manifested in contemporary culture. Among the subjects discussed are the influence of Jack the Ripper on contemporary police procedures, adaptations of Victorian texts, appropriations of Oscar Wilde in representations of homosexual identity, and the popularity of *Victoria Magazine*. The book consists of the following contributions: 'The Victorians in the Rearview Mirror' by Simon Joyce; 'The Legacy of Victorian Spectacle: The Map of Time and the Architecture of Empty Space' by Ronald R. Thomas; 'The New Victorians' by Miriam Bailin; 'More Stories about Clothing and Furniture: Realism and Bad Commodities' by Ellen Bayuk Rosenman; 'Wilde Americana' by Jesse Matz; 'Victorians on Broadway at the Present Time: John Ruskin's Life on Stage' by Sharon Aronofsky Weltman; 'Rounding up the Usual Suspects: Echoing Jack the Ripper' by Kate Lonsdale; 'Legal Uses of Victorian Fiction: Infant Felons to Juvenile Delinquents' by Christine L. Krueger; '"Nurs'd up amongst the scenes I have describ'd": Political Resonances in the Poetry of Working-Class Women' by Florence Boos; 'Revisiting the Serial Format of Dickens's Novels; or *Little Dorrit* Goes a Long Way' by David Barndollar and Susan Schorn; and 'Disseminating Victorian Culture in the Postmillennial Classroom' by Sue Lonoff.

John Gardiner, *The Victorians: An Age in Retrospect*, looks at changes in attitudes towards the Victorians through the twentieth century, also using four prominent Victorians (Queen Victoria, Charles Dickens, W.E. Gladstone, and Oscar Wilde) to illustrate the degree to which biographical accounts changed over the century. Robert Douglas-Fairhurst's multidisciplinary study *Victorian Afterlives: The Shaping of Influence in Nineteenth-Century Literature* includes discussion of Tennyson and Edward FitzGerald in an exploration of representations and notions of survival, immortality, and influence in Victorian literary criticism, philosophy, and the writings about science.

New from the Victorian Literature and Culture series is Maxwell, ed., *The Victorian Illustrated Book*, an anthology of writings by experts in the field on the role of illustrated books and the use of images in novels and children's books in Victorian culture. The book covers a range of topics, such as the inclusion of maps in fictional works and illustrations in children's books. Also covered are well-known illustrators Aubrey Beardsley, William Morris, and George Cruikshank (more details on contents are given in Section 5 below). Jessica Feldman, *Victorian Modernisms: Pragmatisms and the Varieties of Aesthetic Experience*, examines the works of Dante Gabriel Rossetti, Augusta Evans, John Ruskin (see also the discussion on Ruskin in section (b) Prose below), and William James to illustrate gaps and continuities between modernism and Victorianism, in order to debunk 'truistic notions of Modernism as an art of crisis, rupture, elitism, and loss'.

Lawrence Goldman's comprehensive and carefully researched study, *Science, Reform, and Politics in Victorian Britain; The Social Science Association, 1857–1886*, looks at connections among social thought, policy, and politics during the nineteenth century, focusing specifically on the National Association for the Promotion of Social Science Organization (NAPSS), which was used as a forum to discuss important social issues and monitored almost every major social institution of the time. Examining the history of this influential organization reveals mechanisms by which social policy was developed and implemented in the spheres of public health, crime, education, industry, and women's social and legal emancipation. In part 1 Goldman traces the origins of the association in the 1850s in relation to the political climate; part 2 discusses each of the five divisions which made up the NAPSS's work (the amendment of laws, crime prevention, public health, social economy, and education); part 3 examines the NAPSS's understanding and practice of social science in domestic and international contexts; finally part 4 discusses the decline of the NAPSS's influence from the 1870s.

France and St Clair, eds., *Mapping Lives: The Uses of Biography*, has a chapter on Victorian biography, 'Shaping Victorian Biography: From Anecdote to Bildungsroman' by Elinor S. Shaffer (pp. 115–34), as well as a chapter on Freud, 'Freud and the Art of Biography' by Malcolm Bowie (pp. 177–92). Edward H. Cohen, 'Victorian Bibliography': Seventy Years After' (*VS* 44:iv[2002] 625–38), traces the succession of editors and describes the origins and progress of *Victorian Bibliography*, the first index to Victorian scholarship begun in 1933 by editor William D. Templeman and chair of the Victorian Group, Howard Mumford Jones.

In an entertaining new study, Stephen Van Dulken, *Inventing the 19th Century*, surveys one hundred of the most important, memorable, and quirky inventions of the nineteenth century (from 1837 to 1901), including a diverse range of artefacts, machines, and objects, among them the telephone, dynamite, the safety pin, the machine gun, the light bulb, aspirin, and denim jeans. Including coverage of Britain, the USA, and other countries, Van Dulken also discusses patenting processes and the lives of each inventor.

Peter Hamilton and Roger Hargreaves's fascinating new book *The Beautiful and the Damned: The Creation of Identity in Nineteenth-Century Photography* is a counterpart to the National Portrait Gallery's exhibition in London, having as its subject photography's early development and how the different types of photography (from portrait to celebrity to scientific) illustrate a nineteenth-century interest in classification and ordering, particularly when it comes to identifying images of the 'beautiful' (for example family albums were used as a means of conferring social status) and the 'damned' (in providing 'empirical' evidence of criminality and/or insanity). Placing photography in its cultural and social context, Hamilton and Hargreaves explore the popularity of the 'carte de visite' and the spread of photography into other fields such as evolution, psychology, anthropology, phrenology, and criminology. Illustrated and with over a hundred black and white photos, the study also includes discussion of important figures such as Oscar Rejlander, Bassano, Eugène Atget, and Julia Margaret Cameron.

Luckhurst and McDonagh, eds., *Transactions and Encounters: Science and Culture in the Nineteenth Century*, comprises ten essays devoted to discussing moments when Victorians encountered science in unpredictable ways. They are as follows: 'Introduction: Encountering Science' by Roger Luckhurst and Josephine McDonagh (pp. 1–15); 'Voice, Technology and the Victorian Ear' by Steven Connor (pp. 16–29); 'The Microscope: Mediations of the Sub-Visible World' by Isobel Armstrong (pp. 30–54); '"Thinking Blues": The Memory of Colour in Nineteenth-Century Photography' by Lindsay Smith (pp. 55–74); 'Cross-Cultural Encounters: The Co-Production of Science and Literature in mid-Victorian Periodicals' by Paul White (pp. 75–95); 'Imitation of Life: Science, Literature and the Dissemination of Culture' by David Amigoni (pp. 96–116); 'Passages in the Invention of the Psyche: Mind-Reading in London, 1881–84' by Roger Luckhurst (pp. 117–50); 'Darwin's Barnacles: Mid-Century Victorian Natural History and the Marine Grotesque' by Rebecca Stott (pp. 151–81); *'Woman's Share in Primitive Culture*: Science, Femininity and Anthropological Knowledge' by Lynnette Turner (pp. 182–203); and 'From *The New Werther* to Numbers and Arguments: Karl Pearson's Eugenics' by Carolyn Burdett (pp. 204–33).

Martin Fichman, *Evolutionary Theory and Victorian Culture*, points out that much of the critical scholarship on the development of evolutionary theory focuses on Darwin, while the contributions of other important figures tend to be ignored. Alfred Russel Wallace, for example, arrived at almost identical conclusions about the origin of the species as Darwin, and Herbert Spencer coined the term 'survival of the fittest', a term most people associate with Darwin. Fichman also focuses on Thomas Huxley's prominent role in the debate over evolution, and discusses nineteenth-century debates in the context of twentieth-century debates (for example, the notorious Scopes trial in 1925) and the contemporary debate over 'scientific creationism'.

The subject of an engaging and thoughtful study by Jonah Siegel, *Desire and Excess: The Nineteenth-Century Culture of Art*, is the nineteenth-century emergence of the modern idea of the artist, which Siegel explores in connection with the rise of the museum and the professional art critic (including, for example, Hazlitt, Ruskin, and Wilde). Using visual images as well as text, Siegel argues that the era, though often stereotyped as staid and self-satisfied, actually gave rise to artistic controversies associated with modernism and postmodernism. Siegel examines, for example, the fear that museums would bring about the death of art and the impact on both the viewer and the artist of assembling and displaying art in museum collections. In *Hamlet and the Visual Arts, 1709–1900*, Alan R. Young looks at depictions of Hamlet in the visual media, identifying over 2,000 images and including fifty illustrations.

A special edition of *Studies in the Literary Imagination* is devoted to 'Inauthentic Pleasures: Victorian Fakery and the Limitations of Form' (*SLI* 35:ii[2002]). In the introductory essay, 'These Other Victorians' (*SLI* 35:ii[2002] i–ix), Shelton Waldrep explores 'just what is at stake in the idea of the "real" as defined by the artists and thinkers of the Victorian era'. Included in the issue are the following essays: 'Impostures: Robert Browning and the Poetics of Forgery' by C.D. Blanton (*SLI* 35:ii[2002] 1–25); 'George Eliot and the Fetish of Realism' by Peter Melville Logan (*SLI* 35:ii[2002] 27–51); 'A Fountain, a Spontaneous Combustion, and the *Mona Lisa*: Duchamp's Symbolism in Dickens and Pater' by Jonathan Loesberg (*SLI* 35:ii[2002] 53–78); 'Watching Others Think: Casuistry, Perfectionism, and the Emergence of the Self' by Andrew H. Miller (*SLI* 35:ii[2002] 79–98); 'Affecting Authenticity: *Sonnets from the Portuguese* and *Modern Love*' by Natalie M. Houston (*SLI* 35:ii[2002] 99–122); and 'Authenticity and the Geography of Empire: Reading Gaskell with Emecheta' by Carolyn Lesjak (*SLI* 35:ii[2002] 123–46).

Lynn Zastoupil, 'Defining Christians, Making Britons: Rammohun Roy and the Unitarians' (*VS* 44:ii[2002] 215–44), explores the popularity of civic-minded Rammohun Roy, the Indian reformer and philanthropist from Bengal whose notable involvement in a variety of social, political, and religious reform efforts made him especially well liked by the Unitarians. Rammohun shared common concerns with the Unitarians, and Zastoupil explores how he in turn reflects the Unitarian attempt to reshape and redefine Christian identity to make it more inclusive. In *High Calvinists in Action: Calvinism and the City in Manchester and London, c.1810–1860*, Ian J. Shaw looks at local Calvinist churches and their impact on nineteenth-century urbanization. Drawing on archival manuscripts, printed sources, and sermons, Shaw's work comprises six case studies, each of which examines a particular minister along with his church and congregation, to show how they were responsive to (rather than, as has often been assumed, restrictive of) social urban problems. Shaw also discusses the development of high and evangelical Calvinism.

Spector, ed., *British Romanticism and the Jews: History, Culture, Literature*, brings together a collection of essays demonstrating the pressures exerted by the British Jewish and the British Christian communities on each other from the Enlightenment to the Victorian era and into the late twentieth century. Of special interest to students and scholars of post-Romanticism are essays by Efraim Sicher, Michael Scrivener, Stuart Peterfreund, Elizabeth Fay, and Sheila A. Spector. Sicher's 'Imagining "the Jew": Dickens's Romantic Heritage' reconsiders Dickens's treatment of Jewish characters in *Oliver Twist* and *Our Mutual Friend*. Dickens's revision of his anti-Semitic portrayal of Fagin in *Oliver Twist* is perceived as part of a changing attitude to Jews in nineteenth-century England. Stuart Peterfreund, in 'Not for "Antiquaries," but for "Philosophers": Isaac Disraeli's Talmudic Critique and the Talmudic Way with Literature' examines Disraeli's output for its Jewish framework of 'Talmudic erudition' (p. 190). Elisabeth Fay's 'Grace Aguilar: Rewriting Scott Rewriting History' shows the ways in which Aguilar 'uses her Jewish identity to construct a literary and cultural identity' (p. 12). The essence of Fay's discussion is a 'reading of Grace Aguilar's *Vale of Cedars*; or *The Martyr* (posthumously published in 1850) and Walter Scott's *Ivanhoe* (1819)' (p. 215). Sheila Spector's essay focuses upon one of Disraeli's novels, *The Wondrous Tale of Alroy* [1833]. Her 'Alroy as Disraeli's "Ideal Ambition"' interestingly argues that the novel is 'a Christian apologetic, a fictionalized defense of Disraeli's own apostasy' (p. 12).

New from ABC CLIO is a reissue of W.A. Clouston's *Popular Tales and Fictions: Their Migrations and Transformations*, edited by Christine Goldberg, a classic study of folk- and fairy-tales first published in 1887. Another addition to the ABC CLIO Classic Folk and Fairy Tales series is Joseph Jacobs's *English Fairy Tales; and, More English Fairy Tales*, edited by Donald Haase, which is a reprint of two collections of fairy-tales and oral folk-tales first published in the 1890s. Originally printed in chapbooks, the collection includes the original illustrations and a well-written introduction by Donald Haase on the cultural, social, and political contexts of the tales. Katherine Briggs's *The Fairies in Tradition and Literature* is a history and tradition of fairies, including some discussion of the Victorian era.

In 'Filthy Lucre: Victorian Ideas of Money' (*VS* 44:ii[2002] 185–214), Christopher Herbert discusses the complex, conflicting, and sometimes intersecting relationships of money and filth in Victorian culture and the idea that waste can actually be seen as an enriching force. Focusing on the ideas and writings of Dickens and Freud among others, the essay 'brings into view exactly that conflicted deep structure of thinking about polluting dirt, on the one hand, and "precious ore" and "wealth" on the other, that Dickens, too identifies as central to the imaginary of his moneymaking age, and that Frazer and Freud subsequently reformulate in their own idioms of evolutionary anthropology and psychoanalysis' (p. 211).

A special edition of *Victorian Studies* (*VS* 45:i[2002]) is devoted to the subject of Victorian investments. The essays are as follows: 'Introduction: Victorian Investments' by Cannon Schmitt, Nancy Henry, and Anjali Arondekar (*VS* 45:i[2002] 7–16); 'Writing about Finance in Victorian England: Disclosure and

Secrecy in the Culture of Investment' by Mary Poovey (*VS* 45:i[2002] 17–42); 'Trollope in the Stock Market: Irrational Exuberance and *The Prime Minster*' by Audrey Jaffe (*VS* 45:i[2002] 43–64); 'The First Fund Managers: Life Insurance Bonuses in Victorian Britain' by Timothy Alborn (*VS* 45:i[2002] 65–92); 'Capital and Community: Limited Liability and Attempts to Democratize the Market in Mid-Nineteenth-Century England' by Donna Loftus (*VS* 45:i[2002] 93–120); and 'Fair Enterprise or Extravagant Speculation: Investment, Speculation, and Gambling in Victorian England' by David C. Itzkowitz (*VS* 45:i[2002] 121–48).

Kevin R. Swafford, 'Translating the Slums: The Coding of Criminality and the Grotesque in Arthur Morrison's *A Child of the Jago*' (*JMMLA* 35:ii[2002] 50–64), takes a look at Arthur Morrison's classic but often overlooked 'slum' narrative and its graphic portrayal of London's East End slums. Swafford argues that the novel reflects sociocultural anxieties about criminality and deviancy, and that degeneracy in the slums is depicted as a 'willful act of transgression against normalcy'.

New from Christy Campbell is *The Maharajah's Box: An Exotic Tale of Espionage, Intrigue, and Illicit Love in the Days of the Raj*, an examination of the life of Maharajah Duleep Singh. Forced to give up his throne, Duleep Singh also gave up all his wealth (including the famous Koh-i-noor diamond) when the British annexed the area. Tracing the whereabouts of the lost diamond, Campbell's intriguing examination includes analysis of archives, newspaper articles, personal letters, memoirs, and reports to recount the story of the king of Punjab's early life (he took the throne at the age of five) and his later attempt to overthrow British rule in India.

Margery Sabin brings a fresh voice to post-colonial studies in *Dissenters and Mavericks: Writings About India in English, 1765–2000*, a collection of writings that question or break from traditional imperialist stereotypes. Sabin's study includes excerpts and analysis of writings by Wilkie Collins, along with a variety of well-known and unfamiliar works, including memoirs journals, letters, novels, and travel narratives. There is a new edition of Ketaki Kushari Dyson's *A Various Universe: A Study of the Journals and Memoirs of British Men and Women in the Indian Subcontinent, 1765–1856*, a collection of excerpts from books, journals, and letters on the subject of India, alongside insightful commentary by the author.

The subject of Lara Kriegel's 'The Pudding and the Palace: Labor, Print Culture, and Imperial Britain in 1851' (in Burton, ed., *After the Imperial Turn: Thinking With and Through the Nation*, pp. 230–45) is a short tale about a Christmas pudding published in *Household Words* just six months before the Great Exhibition. In this tale, mercantile commodities of various nations are intended to represent their place of origin, and Kriegel insightfully compares this representation to the Great Exhibition of 1851 with its seeming 'encapsulations of the globe' (p. 231).

Catherine Hall, *Civilising Subjects: Metropole and Colony in the English Imagination, 1830–1867*, discusses how in the mid-nineteenth century the English perceived themselves in relation to the 'other' as a way of understanding their own identities. Peter Cain's thoughtful and carefully researched *Hobson and Imperialism: Radicalism, New Liberalism, and Finance, 1887–1938* marks the 200-year anniversary of J.A. Hobson's influential critique of British imperialism, *Imperialism: A Study*. Cain's study is divided into the following sections: 'Becoming a New Liberal, 1887–1898'; 'Becoming an Anti-Imperialist, 1887–1898'; 'The Economics of Imperialism, 1899–1902'; '*Imperialism: A Study*:

Parasitism and Industry'; 'Dilemmas of a New Liberal: Free Trade, Foreign Investment, and Imperialism, 1903–1914'; 'Late Variations on a Famous Theme, 1914–1938'; and 'Hobson Lives? Finance, Finance Capitalism, and British Imperialism, 1870–1914'.

In '"So help me God, the truth and not the truth": Hyper-Realism and the Taxonomy of Truth-Seeking in the Royal Commission's Inquiry into the 1865 Jamaica Rebellion' (*VIJ* 30[2002] 7–38), Laura Callanan examines the writings produced by the inquiry into and the documentation of the Morant Bay rebellion. Callanan argues that 'the cultural conflict precipitated by this event is in part a rhetorical crisis regarding the transparency of realism—the governmental inquiry's extreme adherence to a visually based empirical taxonomy often lapses into absurdity as it attempts to recreate events' (p. 7).

Susan K. Harris's *The Cultural Work of the Late Nineteenth-Century Hostess: Annie Adams Fields and Mary Gladstone Drew* has as its subject the upper-class female hostess and her influence on art and culture from 1870 to 1920. Focusing on two well-known hostesses—Annie Fields, an American, and Mary Gladstone, an Englishwoman—Harris examines the roles these women played in social and cultural contexts. Of interest to scholars of the Victorian period is the emphasis on Gladstone's reading circle, her epistolary exchanges, and her public influence in the philanthropic sphere. Harris includes excerpts from Gladstone's letters to Lord Acton and her diary entries about John Ruskin. Dorice Williams Elliott, *The Angel Out of the House: Philanthropy and Gender in Nineteenth-Century England*, examines the figure of the philanthropic amateur female heroine in contrast to the later professional philanthropists of the 1870s. Elliott shows how philanthropy in novels helped make charitable work in the private sphere seem 'natural and obvious'. Included in Elliott's study are examinations of writings by, among others, George Eliot, Elizabeth Gaskell, Anna Jameson, and Hannah Moore.

Simon Morgan's 'Seen but not Heard? Women's Platforms, Respectability, and Female Publics in the Mid-Nineteenth Century' (*NCP* 29:i[2002] 50–67) explores acceptable boundaries for women in the context of the nineteenth-century platform culture. Morgan argues that women's participation in public forums was seen as respectable because consensus, rather than controversy, was expressed in the selective reporting of their meetings. In 'Any Questions: The Gendered Dimensions of the Political Platform' (*NCP* 29:i[2002] 118–32), Helen Rogers examines the influence of two female orators, Josephine Butler and Mary Ann Walker, on female public discourse and how they helped bring about changes in the structure of public meetings that allowed for greater acceptance of female oratory. Rogers points out that audiences were reluctant to allow women to participate in public forums mainly because they did not want them to face public interrogation. Eric Gardner, '"A Nobler End": Mary Webb and the Victorian Platform' (*NCP* 29:i[2002] 50–67), takes a look at African American elocutionist Mary Webb and her role in the development of British oratory and transatlantic abolitionism.

Anna Krugovoy Silver, *Victorian Literature and the Anorexic Body*, discusses literary expressions of female characters in terms of their physical state, hunger, fat, and appetite to show how anorexia was the cultural ideal for Victorian middle-class women. Silver covers a wide range of fiction by, among others, Charlotte Brontë, Christina Rossetti, Dickens, Tennyson, Stoker, and Carroll, as well as other types of prose such as medical literature, conduct books, and beauty manuals. Her thoughtful study comprises five chapters: 'Waisted Women: Reading Victorian Slenderness'; 'Appetite in Victorian Children's Literature'; 'Hunger and Repression in *Shirley* and *Villette*'; 'Vampirism and the Anorexic Paradigm'; and 'Conclusion: The Politics of Thinness'.

Valerie Sanders, *The Brother–Sister Culture in Nineteenth-Century Literature: From Austen to Woolf*, looks at novels with 'brother–sister plots' along with the real-life collaborations of brothers and sisters (for example, the Rossettis, the Wordsworths, and the Sitwells) during the Victorian, Romantic, and modern British periods. In particular, Sanders examines common brother–sister literary motifs, such as the figure of the brother as lover, in a variety of canonical and non-canonical works.

An important new reference work is Samson, ed., *The Cambridge History of Nineteenth-Century Music*, which provides an overview of recent criticism about music during the period and its various connections to issues of historical, intellectual, and socio-political importance. Part 1 (covering the years 1800–1850) consists of the following contributions: 'The Musical Work and Nineteenth-Century History' by Jim Samson; 'Music and the Rise of Aesthetics' by Andrew Bowie; 'The Profession of Music' by John Rink; 'The Opera Industry' by Roger Parker; 'The Construction of Beethoven' by K.M. Knittel; 'Music and the Poetic' by Julian Rushton; 'The Invention of Tradition' by John Irving; 'Choral Music' by John Butt; 'The Consumption of Music' by Derek Carew; and 'The Great Composer' by Jim Samson. Part 2 (covering 1850–1900) consists of: 'Progress, Modernity and the Concept of an Avant-Garde' by John Williamson; 'Music as Ideal: The Aesthetics of Autonomy' by Max Paddison; 'The Structures of Musical Life' by Katharine Ellis; 'Opera and Music Drama' by Thomas Grey; 'Beethoven Reception: The Symphonic Tradition' by James Hepokoski; 'Words and Music in Germany and France' by Susan Youens; 'Chamber Music and Piano' by Jonathan Dunsby; 'Choral Culture and the Regeneration of the Organ' by John Butt; 'Music and Social Class' by Derek B. Scott; 'Nations and Nationalism' by Jim Samson; and 'Styles and Languages Around the Turn of the Century' by Anthony Pople. The overview also includes a chronology and a glossary.

Jeffrey Richards's expansive *Imperialism and Music: Britain, 1876–1953* debunks the myth that the British were a people without music. As a cultural historian rather than a professional musicologist, Richards's 'primary focus is not analysis of the music but its cultural impact' and 'to recover the contemporary responses to the music of imperialism' (p. viii). Chapters on 'Sullivan's Empire', 'Music for the Official Occasions: Coronations and Jubilees', and '"Bring on the Girls": Opera, Operetta and Ballet', to name but three, provide a fascinating backdrop for a study of late Victorian and Edwardian British perceptions. Richards writes that his book 'challenges a range of received views: the theory that neither Sullivan nor Elgar was inspired by the Empire; the assumption that the masses were uninterested in the Empire; the idea that Victorian hymns were not imperialistic' (p. ix). Literary critics and scholars can learn much from this informative, well-written, and extremely well-documented book.

Alisa Clapp-Itnyre's *Angelic Airs, Subversive Songs: Music as Social Discourse in the Victorian Novel* is a welcome addition to the growing body of work on the Victorians and music. It is a comprehensive and well-researched assessment of the borders between literature and musical texts, focusing on music as a site of cultural tension. Clapp-Itnyre argues that the Victorian fascination with and idealization of music manifested itself both as a means to advance patriotism, Christianity, and domestic harmony and also to advance politically subversive causes. Idealized constructions of music were also undermined by the sensual 'spectacle' of musical performance. Clapp-Itnyre looks at the domestic ballads in novels by Elizabeth Gaskell, folk music in the novels of Thomas Hardy, and three novels by George Eliot (*Adam Bede*, *The Mill on the Floss*, and *Daniel Deronda*). Pierre Degott, 'The Progress of English Opera in the Nineteenth-Century: Dreams and Reality' (*CVE* 53[2001] 63–84), discusses English opera's failure to gain full recognition from the public as a new artistic form in the nineteenth century.

Two new works this year discuss perceptions of the Irish famine. In *Literature and the Irish Famine, 1845–1919*, Melissa Fegan traces the impact of the famine on fiction, travel narratives, and historiography. In the first chapter, 'Faction: The Historiography of the Great Famine', Fegan looks at writings since the beginning of the Anglo-Irish war up to the present to suggest that the supposed polarity between traditional and revisionist accounts of the famine is 'self-created'. The chapter also examines the role of mythology and oral history in the creation of famine history, noting how historians have used emotive terms such as 'genocide', 'ethnic cleansing', and race memory' as they make connections between the famine and other historical events, such as the Holocaust. Other highlights of this well-researched study include analysis of representations of the famine in *The Times* and *The Nation* (ideologically opposed newspapers), tourist accounts and how they helped overturn the 'determined myopia of those who had no interest in believing in the Famine', and discussion of Anthony Trollope's experience in Ireland and its influence on his work.

Also of interest is Edward G. Lengel's *The Irish through British Eyes: Perceptions of Ireland in the Famine Era*, which treats the following subjects: 'Race, Gender, Class and the Historiography of English Perceptions of the Irish'; 'Public Perception of the Irish Question, 1840–1845'; 'Official Britain and the Condition of the Ireland Question, 1841–1852'; 'The Famine and English Public Opinion, 1845–1850'; and 'Aftermath of Disaster: Public Perceptions of the Irish Question, 1850–1860'. Lengel's study includes a useful bibliography of primary and secondary sources on this subject.

Malcolm Kelsall, *Literary Representations of the Irish Country House: Civilisation and Savagery Under the Union*, is an examination of the dichotomy between the alternative 'savage' culture and the traditional 'civilized' culture as manifested in numerous works (by writers such as Edgeworth, Lever, Trollope, Bowen, and Lady Gregory). Kelsall's study redirects scholarship in Irish studies by placing his subject in a wider European context, rather than a nationalistic one. Christy Campbell, *Fenian Fire: The British Government Plot to Assassinate Queen Victoria*, uses recently declassified secret files to investigate in detail the Irish American Jubilee Plot of the Fenian Brotherhood, arguing that the conspiracy's real target was not the queen, but one of her 'turbulent subjects'. Dominic Rainsford, *Literature, Identity and the English Channel: The Narrow Seas Expanded*, discusses French and British depictions of the English Channel in various genres of literature.

Henry and Mary Ponsonby by William M. Kuhn is a fascinating biography of two of Queen Victoria's high-ranking courtiers in the late nineteenth century. Both from poor families, Henry and Mary met at court, married, and raised their family in

Windsor Castle. Henry, Queen Victoria's private secretary, and Mary, who was his collaborator, advised the queen during difficult times when the monarchy was under political scrutiny by the media and expanding press. Drawing on the royal archives and the almost daily letters written between the two, *Henry and Mary Ponsonby* offers insights into the fascinating inner workings of daily life at Queen Victoria's court.

A very important contribution to the study of Victorian publishing history is David Finkelstein's *The House of Blackwood: Author–Publisher Relations in the Victorian Era*, a full examination of the impact of William Blackwood & Sons on nineteenth- and early twentieth-century literature and culture. Drawing on the archives of the National Library of Scotland, Finkelstein uses a variety of writings (published both in book form and in the monthly *Blackwood's Magazine*) by George Eliot, Thomas de Quincey, Margaret Oliphant, and Anthony Trollope, among others. The study also includes the following helpful appendices: 'Blackwood & Sons Publishing Statistics, 1860–1910', ™Blackwood's Magazine Sales, 1856–1915', and 'Margaret Oliphant Sales, 1860–1897'.

In a new monograph by Paul Delany, *Literature, Money and the Market: From Trollope to Amis*, the author examines the historically hostile division between commercial values and literary aristocratic prestige (which he argues can be traced back to Plato) as seen in representations of money and the literary marketplace in Trollope, Gissing, Woolf, and Conrad. Delany also explores the late nineteenth-century literary marketplace revolution in terms of economic motives for writers, arguing that 'the commodification of literature is unavoidable'. Also included is a useful discussion of women and the marketplace. Included in Finkelstein and McCleery, eds., *The Book History Reader*, is a chapter by John Sutherland, 'The Victorian Novelists: Who Were They?' (pp. 259–68).

Tracey Teets Schwarze, *Joyce and the Victorians*, explores cultural and political currents during the late Victorian period and the influence of literary writings, along with popular and professional documents, on Joyce's writings and his characters, using Lacanian theories of the 'other' to explore ways in which they confront the masculine gaze. Emily Eells, *Proust's Cup of Tea: Homoeroticism and Victorian Culture*, examines Proust's readings of various Victorian writers and their influence on his *Remembrance of Things Past*, focusing on the way in which he aestheticized homosexuality by referring to art and letters of the Victorian period. Robert Dingley, 'Closely Observed Trains: The Railway Compartment as a Locus of Desire in Victorian Culture' (*CVE* 53[2001] 111–40), analyses the role of the railway compartment in erotic Victorian writing. Jonathan Taylor, *Mastery and Slavery in Victorian Writing*, analyses depictions of masters, slaves, and servitude in the works of, among others, Carlyle, Dickens, Collins, Eliot, and Wagner. Representations of figures such as the musician, the slaveholder, the butler, and 'the Jew' are examined in detail. Lynn M. Voskuil, 'Feeling Public: Sensation Theater, Commodity Culture, and the Victorian Public Sphere' (*VS* 44:ii[2002] 243–76), explores the widespread popularity of sensation plays, focusing on the paradox of how the public's intense attraction to their seeming authenticity was located at the very root of the theatrical experience.

Reviews of critical work in cultural studies are as follows: 'Recovering Culture in the Print Media of Nineteenth-Century Britain' by Mary Saunders (*Rev* 24[2002] 111–28); a review of *Serializing Fiction in the Victorian Press*, by Graham Law,

Nineteenth-Century Media and the Construction of Identities, edited by Laurel Brake, Bill Bell, and David Finkelstein; a review of *Trollope and the Magazines: Gendered Issues in Mid-Victorian Britain*, by Mark W. Turner; Timothy L. Carens, 'Dreadful Little People: Victorian Fairies and Fears', a review of *Strange and Secret Places: Fairies and Victorian Consciousness*, by Carole G. Silver (*Rev* 24[2002] 165–73); a review by Laurence Kitzan of M. Daphne Kutzer's *Empire's Children: Empire and Imperialism in Classic British Children's Books* (*VS* 44:iv[2002] 708–11); and a review by Clare A. Simmons of Andrew Wawn's *The Vikings and the Victorians: Inventing the Old North in Nineteenth-Century Britain* (*VS* 44:iv[2002] 721–3).

Other review listings for cultural studies are as follows: *Knowing the Past: Victorian Literature and Culture*, edited by Suzy Anger, reviewed by Kate Flint (*NCL* 57:iv[2002] 549–51); *Science, Technology and Medicine in Colonial India*, by David Arnold, reviewed by Gyan Prakash (*VS* 45:i[2002] 149–50); *Nature's Museums: Victorian Science and the Architecture of Display*, by Carla Yanni, and *On Exhibit: Victorians and their Museums*, by Barbara J. Black, both reviewed by Tim Barringer (*VS* 45:i[2002] 151–3); *English Pasts: Essays in History and Culture*, by Stefan Collini, reviewed by Chris Waters (*VS* 45:i[2002] 153–4); *Useful Knowledge: The Victorians, Morality, and the March of Intellect*, by Alan Rauch, reviewed by Wendell V. Harris (*SNNTS* 34:iv[2002] 476–7); *Men in Wonderland: The Lost Girlhood of the Victorian Gentleman*, by Catherine Robson, reviewed by Carole G. Silver (*NCL* 57:i[2002] 140–3); *The Private Rod: Marital Violence, Sensation, and the Law in Victorian Britain*, by Marlene Tromp, reviewed by Kathleen Lonsdale (*VPR* 35:ii[2002] 191–2); *Women and Literature in Britain, 1800–1900*, edited by Joanne Shattock, reviewed by Deborah A. Logan (*VIJ* 30[2002] 189–94); *Victorian Babylon: People, Streets and Images in Nineteenth-Century London*, by Lynda Nead, reviewed by Roxanne Eberle (*VIJ* 30[2002] 197–202); *Literature, Technology and Magical Thinking, 1880–1920*, by Pamela Thurschwell, reviewed by Patrick Brantlinger (*ELT* 45:iii[2002] 322–4); *The Instability of Human Wants: Economics and Aesthetics in Market Society*, by Regenia Gagnier, reviewed by Sally Ledger (*ELT* 45:iii[2002] 324–7); *Inventing the Victorians*, by Matthew Sweet, reviewed by Anya Clayworth (*ELT* 45:iii[2002] 334–6); and *The English Literary Decadence: An Anthology* and *The Victorians: A Major Authors Anthology*, edited by Christopher S. Nassaar, both reviewed by G.A. Cevasco (*ELT* 45:i[2002] 73–6).

(b) Prose

The year in Victorian prose studies was marked by a continued growing interest in the history and study of books, periodicals, and serialization. James, ed., *Macmillan: A Publishing Tradition*, is a collection of essays examining Macmillan's role in British publishing history, beginning with its founding in 1843. Drawing on a wealth of documents and correspondences in its files along with archival research at the British Library, the essays focus on a range of subjects including Macmillan's business strategies in the nineteenth century, its relations with writers such as Thomas Hardy, Matthew Arnold, and Tennyson, its pioneering monthly magazine, and its expansion into America and India.

Catherine Delyfer, 'Being a Male Artist: Masculine Representations in the Art Magazine *The Studio* (1893–1900)' (*CVE* 53[2001] 85–110), explores the sexual and gender ideologies of *The Studio*, showing how it became less progressive in its willingness to challenge traditional representations of masculinity after the first Wilde trials in 1895. This was owing primarily, according to Delyfer, to the magazine's dependence on its middle-class readership. Simon Cooke, 'George du Maurier's Illustrations for M.E. Braddon's Serialization of *Eleanor's Victory* in *Once a Week*' (*VPR* 35:i[2002] 89–106), points out that, while much criticism has been directed towards du Maurier as a graphic design artist, not much criticism has focused on him as an illustrator—for his pictorial representations in the context of their placement in specific texts. Cooke describes ways in which du Maurier takes the 'dual approach' of alternating between illustrating and interpreting, specifically in Braddon's *Eleanor's Victory*.

Jenny Holt, 'The Textual Formations of Adolescence in Turn-of-the-Century Youth Periodicals: The *Boy's Own Paper* and Eton College Ephemeral Magazines' (*VPR* 35:i[2002] 63–88), explores the ways in which 'adolescence' was constructed by early twentieth-century periodicals and how these periodicals endorsed conservative values in terms of gender and class by attempting to suppress literary creativity.

Aled Jones, 'The *Dart* and the Damning of the Sylvan Stream: Journalism and Political Culture in the Late-Victorian City' (*VPR* 35:i[2002] 2–17), discusses how the *Dart*'s satirical representations of the 'The River' sculpture in Victoria Square were intended as commentary on the notion of urban progressiveness. John Hewitt, '*The Poster* and the Poster in England in the 1890s' (*VPR* 35:i[2002] 37–62), shows how the periodical *The Poster* (which was published in London from 1898 to 1900) helped to create the poster as a specific category. Hewitt also discusses how this category was related to the discourses of art and art magazines.

In a special issue of *Nineteenth-Century Prose* (*NCP* 29:i[2002]), a series of essays is devoted to the platform and lecture culture in the nineteenth century. Martin Hewitt, 'Aspects of Platform Culture in Nineteenth-Century Britain' (*NCP* 29:i[2002] 1–32), contributes the introductory essay, in which he explores the ways in which public speech provided an underpinning for written text. Following this are several more focused essays: 'Finding an Audience: The Political Platform, the Lecture Platform, and the Rhetoric of Self-Help' by Karen Boiko (*NCP* 29:i[2002] 33–49); 'Seen but not Heard? Women's Platforms, Respectability, and Female Publics in the Mid-Nineteenth Century' by Simon Morgan (*NCP* 29:i[2002] 50–67); 'The Egyptian Hall and the Platform of Transatlantic Exchange: Charles Brown, P.T. Barnum, and Albert Smith' by Simon Featherstone (*NCP* 29:i[2002] 68–77); 'The Enslaved as Spectacle: Ellen Craft, Sarah Parker Remond, and American Slavery in England' by Theresa Zackodnik (*NCP* 29:i[2002] 78–102); '"A Nobler End": Mary Webb and the Victorian Platform' by Eric Gardner (*NCP* 29:i[2002] 103–17); 'Any Questions: The Gendered Dimensions of the Political Platform' by Helen Rogers (*NCP* 29:i[2002] 118–32); 'Charles Kingsley Speaking in Public: Empowered or at Risk?' (*NCP* 29:i[2002] 133–50); and 'Working the Room: The Cases of Mary H. Kingsley and H.G. Wells' by Julie English Early (*NCP* 29:i[2002] 151–67).

Susan Hamilton, 'The Practice of Everyday Feminism: Frances Power Cobbe, Divorce, and the London *Echo*, 1868–1875' (*VPR* 35:iii[2002] 227–42), considers Cobbe's use of editorial space, in particular her writings on divorce, to explore the 'non-feminist press's contribution to Victorian feminist practice'. These contributions, argues Hamilton, can enrich our understanding of what constitutes nineteenth-century feminism. In '"Better Arguments": The *English Woman's Journal* and the Game of Public Opinion' (*VPR* 35:iii[2002] 243–71), Janice Schroeder investigates the role of feminist journals in shaping the emerging public feminist identity. Schroeder traces several debates occurring between feminist periodicals (for example, the *English Woman's Journal*) and other, more popular, periodicals, highlighting strategies used by feminist periodicals in defending themselves against attack.

Gates, ed., *In Nature's Name: An Anthology of Women's Writing and Illustrations, 1780–1930*, includes excerpts from non-fiction, fiction, poetry, and drawings of and about nature by Victorian and Edwardian women such as Isabella Bird, Beatrix Potter, Christina Rossetti, and Anna Sewell. Bourke et al., eds., *The Field Day Anthology of Irish Writing*, volumes 4 and 5: *Irish Women's Writing and Traditions*, are part of a five-volume set, the first three volumes of which covered significant Irish writing but excluded many works by Irish women.

In 'The 1899 Anglo-Boer War in Victorian Women's Narrative in South Africa' (*CVE* 53[2001] 211–42), Ludmilla Ommundsen discusses the narratives of Sarah Wilson, Dosia Bagot, and Violet Brooke-Hunt, showing how their writings overlooked the bloodiest battles of the war, a reflection of their refusal 'to see the sexual metropolitan battles that were being waged by a feminist movement which was seemingly threatening the Isle with an apocalyptic sterility. The writing of the turn-of-the-century Anglo-Boer war can be viewed as a weapon used in a war over female territory.' Rosemary O'Brien provides a new introduction for *The Desert and the Sown: The Syrian Adventures of the Female Lawrence of Arabia*, by Gertrude Bell—a first-hand account of the privileged Englishwoman Gertrude Bell's adventures in the Middle East and her trip across the Syrian desert in 1905.

In 'Seeing the Country: Tourism and the Ideology in William Howitt's *Rural Life of England*' (*VIJ* 30[2002] 41–64), Donald Ulin discusses reformer William Howitt's contribution to redefining England's relationship to the countryside and how the national landscape began to be seen as a place for domestic tourism.

A highly useful new anthology edited by Laura Otis, *Literature and Science in the Nineteenth Century*, brings together a wide selection of literary and scientific writing by American and British writers, including excerpts from, among others, Charles Darwin, Sir Humphry Davy, Charles Babbage, Mary Shelley, and George Eliot. The anthology aptly illustrates the complex interactions between science and creative writing and the common imagery and structure used by both to create meaning. A new monograph by George Levine, *Dying to Know: Scientific Epistemology and Narrative in Victorian England*, has as its subject the history of scientific knowledge and moral ideals. Exploring the various ways in which epistemology is affected by narrative, Levine develops his argument around the notion that pursuit of scientific truth has been seen as necessarily involving varying degrees of death and/or self-abnegation. The book includes the following chapters: 'The Narrative of Scientific Epistemology'; 'Dying to Know Descartes'; 'Carlyle, Descartes, and Objectivity: Lessen Thy Denominator'; 'Autobiography as Epistemology: The Effacement of Self'; 'My Life as a Machine: Francis Galton, with Some Reflections on A.R. Wallace'; 'Self-Effacement Revisited: Women and Scientific Autobiography'; The Test of Truth: *Our Mutual Friend*'; '*Daniel Deronda*: A New Epistemology'; 'The Cartesian Hardy: I Think, Therefore I'm

Doomed'; 'Daring to Know: Karl Pearson and the Romance of Science'; 'The Epistemology of Science and Art: Pearson and Pater'; and 'Objectivity and Altruism' (see also the discussions of Carlyle and Pater below in this section, and of Eliot and Hardy in Section 2 below).

In 'Sensationalising Science: Braddon's Marketing of Science in *Belgravia*' (*VPR* 35:ii[2002] 160–77), Barbara Onslow examines sensational depictions of the natural world in the magazine *Belgravia* (of which Mary Elizabeth Braddon was editor) and the ways in which it mediated scientific discovery and controversy to its readers. Virginia Zimmerman, 'The Victorian Geologist: Reading the Relic and Writing Time' (*VIJ* 30[2002] 95–121), discusses the writings of Charles Lyell and Gideon Mantell on the subject of time and geological change to show how changing perceptions of time also redefined notions of authorship.

Hazel Morris's *Hand, Head and Heart: Samuel Carter Hall and The Art Journal* is an interesting study of the nineteenth-century world of art and criticism. *The Art Journal*, founded in 1839, was devoted solely to the arts and had as its editor for over forty years Samuel Carter Hall. Morris discusses the journal's contributors, Hall's achievements as writer and editor, his marriage to Anna Maria Fielding (also a writer), and their collaboration on topographical works. Jamie W. Johnson, 'The Changing Representation of the Art Public in *Punch*, 1841–1896' (*VPR* 35:iii[2002] 272–94), takes a look at the role of the press in the growing enthusiasm for art and art exhibitions. In particular, Johnson focuses on the cartoons of *Punch* and the strain they reveal between 'democracy and aristocracy, education and aesthetics, and the public and the private'. These cartoons reflect subtle changes that indicate their anxiety over keeping art and art exhibits part of an exclusive realm.

Thomas J. Tobin's *Pre-Raphaelitism in the Nineteenth-Century Press: A Bibliography* is a welcome and very useful update of William Fredeman's *Pre-Raphaelitism: A Bibliocritical Study* [1965]. Tobin chronologically catalogues nineteenth-century critical responses to the Pre-Raphaelite movement (specifically, art and poetry) found in books, journal and magazine articles, pamphlets, exhibition catalogues, and other periodical formats. Tobin's bibliography reveals that the critical response to the movement was much more varied and complex than has been demonstrated by other bibliographies (namely Timothy Hilton's *The Pre-Raphaelites* [1970], which only includes reference to twenty sources), and that the Pre-Raphaelites were not as uniformly denounced and ridiculed as has been formerly demonstrated. The subject of Lene Østermark-Johansen's 'The Death of Euphuism and Decadence in Late-Victorian Literature' (*ELT* 45:i[2002] 4–25), is how John Lyly's *Euphues: The Anatomy of Wit* [1578] and *Euphues and His England* [1580] came to be a part of late nineteenth-century discussions about decadence. Deborah Deacon Boyer, 'Picturing the Other: Images of Burmans in Imperial Britain' (*VPR* 35:iii[2002] 214–26), considers the role of the Victorian periodical press in shaping public opinion about Burmans's 'Otherness'.

New in Matthew Arnold studies is Nilli Diengott's 'Arnold's "The Function of Criticism at the Present Time": "Finally, there is the systematic judgment … the most worthless of all"' (*VN* 102[2002] 18–20), which takes a look at Arnold's method of writing in 'The Function of Criticism at the Present Time' to show that it may be 'very unsystematic, but not incoherent or unintelligible'. Anthony Kearney, 'Matthew Arnold and Herbert Spencer: A Neglected Connection in the Victorian Debate about Scientific and Literary Education' (*NCP* 28:i[2002] 63–74), explores the somewhat antagonistic debates between Spencer and Arnold on the subject of literary and scientific education.

In an original new study, *Aubrey Beardsley and British Wagnerism in the 1890s*, Emma Sutton examines in detail the presence of Wagner in the work of Aubrey Beardsley, highlighting references and allusions to Wagner which are often combined with themes associated with the Decadent movement. James Mulvihill, 'Bentham and Elocution' (*N&Q* 49:iv[2002] 471–3), suggests Thomas Sheridan's *A Course of Lectures on Elocution* (1726) as a possible influence for Bentham's distrust of rhetoric in public life.

There are several new works on Carlyle for the year 2002. Vanden Bossche, ed. *Historical Essays: The Norman and Charlotte Strouse Edition of the Writings of Thomas Carlyle*, is the third of eight volumes in the complete and fully annotated Strouse edition of Carlyle's writings. This third edition brings together Carlyle's historical essays, which were originally collected in *Critical and Miscellaneous Essays* [published in 1872] and written throughout his career from 1830 to 1875. This volume includes writings on, among other subjects, Cromwell, Frederick the Great, Marie Antoinette, the kings of medieval Norway, and the French Revolution.

A chapter in George Levine's *Dying to Know* (see also above), entitled 'Carlyle, Descartes, and Objectivity: Lessen Thy Denominator' (pp. 66–84), discusses *Sartor Resartus* and how it illustrates what Levine calls the 'dying-to-know' story, the notion that pursuing scientific truth necessarily entails suffering, and possibly even death. In *Signs of their Times: History, Labor, and the Body in Cobbett, Carlyle, and Disraeli*, John M. Ulrich analyses depictions of the body and the degraded working class in Victorian England. 'The Anatomy of Bigotry: Carlyle, Ruskin, Slavery, and a New Language of Race', a chapter in *Slavery, Empathy and Pornography* by Marcus Wood, discusses and compares Ruskin and Carlyle's racist perspectives on slavery. Manfred Malzahn, 'Thomas Carlyle's Haute Couture of (Self-)Translation' (*Symbolism* 2[2002] 73–88), discusses *Sartor Resartus* as 'an exercise in self-translation' examining how the German Professor and the English Editor 'serve as authorial personae of a Scottish writer bent on "Germanizing" the English reading public'.

A chapter in Hull, ed., *Science and its Conceptual Foundations*, 'Darwin's Romantic Biology' (pp. 514–54), discusses, among other topics, Alexander von Humboldt's influence on Darwin. Hull compares Darwin's archetypal representations of nature to representations of nature by German Romantics and shows how Darwin's perception of the natural world was altruistic in its progressive production of 'higher creatures'.

In a fascinating new study entitled *The Dragon Seekers: How an Extraordinary Circle of Fossilists Discovered the Dinosaurs and Paved the Way for Darwin*, Christopher McGowan chronicles the adventures and discoveries of some of the earliest pre-Victorian fossil collectors (both amateur and professional) and how they helped usher in a new way of thinking about the past. Among the real-life cast of characters are Mary Anning, an uneducated amateur who later became an extremely successful collector, and Dr William Buckland, who discovered one of the world's first dinosaurs, the megalosaurus. The geological and palaeontological findings of these pioneering fossilists ultimately laid the intellectual groundwork for Darwin and helped to initiate a global public interest in the reptile age. Leila S. May, 'Monkeys, Microcephalous Idiots, and the Barbarous Races of Mankind: Darwin's

Dangerous Victorianism' (*VN* 102[2002] 20–7), examines the idea that Darwin's theory was dangerous to traditional belief systems.

The subject of G.A. Cervasco's *The Breviary of the Decadence: J.-K. Huysmans's 'A Rebours' and English Literature* is the influence of Huysmans's novels on George Moore, Oscar Wilde, Arthur Symons, Aubrey Beardsley, and Max Beerbohm. Caroline Roberts, *The Woman and the Hour: Harriet Martineau and Victorian Ideologies*, uses a historical analysis to interpret seven works (including *Illustrations of Political Economy, Letters on the Laws of Man's Nature, and Development*, and *The Hour and the Man*), along with extensive reception histories for each. Roberts discusses a number of Martineau's interests, for example mesmerism, phrenology, atheism, and historiography. A new biography of Harriet Martineau, *The Hour and the Woman: Harriet Martineau's 'Somewhat Remarkable' Life*, by Deborah Anna Logan focuses on Martineau's career as a pioneering feminist and reformer who was active in a variety of causes involving race, gender, and class. Logan also discusses in detail her relationships to other notable female figures of the time, such as Mary Wollstonecraft, Charlotte Brontë, George Eliot, Florence Nightingale, and Queen Victoria. Also of interest are Linda Peterson's '(Re)Inventing Authorship: Harriet Martineau in the Literary Marketplace of the 1820s' (*WW* 9:iii[2002] 337–50) and Ainslie Robinson's 'Playfellows and Propaganda: Harriet Martineau's Children's Writing' (*WW* 9:iii[2002] 395–412).

New in John Stuart Mill studies is Nadia Urbinati's *Mill on Democracy: From the Athenian Polis to Representative Government*, a study of Mill's contributions to modern democratic theory that redirects scholarly attention to Mill as a political thinker, one whose ideas might 'enrich our understanding of the procedures, ethos, and political practice of democracy'. Urbinati also discusses deliberative democracy and its connection to representation and other political processes. Frank Turner, *John Henry Newman: The Challenge to the Evangelical Religion*, provides a re-examination of Newman's involvement with the Tractarian movement and how it shaped nineteenth-century religious life. Turner argues that Newman was a 'disruptive and confused schismatic conducting a radical religious experiment ... Newman's passage to Rome should be understood less in terms of his spiritual development than as an outgrowth of his personal frustrations—including quarrels with his brothers, thwarted university ambitions, inability to control his followers, and his desire to live in a community of celibate males.' In 'The Spirit of the Law in Newman's *Apologia*' (*NCP* 28:i[2001] 46–62), Richard D. Mallen argues that one aspect of Newman's masterful rhetoric in *Apologia Pro Vita Sua* is his use of legal language 'to secularize the contentious issue of whether Catholicism embodies religious truth. In particular, Newman vindicates the Catholic Church and himself on jurisdictional grounds, using a rhetoric of jurisdiction both to assuage Protestant fears that "popery" threatens English sovereignty and to frame his defense against Kingsley in terms of the nonsectarian authority of equity.'

Brake, Higgins, and Williams, eds., *Walter Pater: Transparencies of Desire*, is an interdisciplinary study of Pater, including twenty-one contributions from scholars in five countries. The study includes five sections: 'Considering the Career'; 'Viewing Pater's Reception'; 'Contextualizing the Work: History, Archaeology and Art History'; 'Paterian Genres and Gender'; and 'Current Critical Theory'. A chapter in Levine, *Dying to Know* (see also above), entitled 'The Epistemology of Science and

Art: Pearson and Pater' (pp. 244–67), looks at 'Pater and Pearson as unlikely twins working the same materials into structures only apparently antithetical', in order to 'throw a different light on the way in which cultural criticism, art, and science have so antagonistically divided'. Heidrun-Edda Weikert, 'Pater's 'Pagan and Christian Art and the Identity of European Culture' in *The Renaissance: Studies in Art and Poetry' (Symbolism* 2[2002] 89–132), explores links between art style and religion in Pater's essays, illustrating his appreciation for the two traditions of 'Christian' Gothic and 'pagan' classical heritage in juxtaposition with each other.

In 'The Platonic Eros of Walter Pater and Oscar Wilde: "Love's Reflected Image" in the 1890s' (*ELT* 45:i[2002] 26–45), Gerald Monsman discusses Pater and Wilde's ideas about Platonic aestheticism and their intellectual relationship as they composed their respective works—*Gaston de Latour* [1888–94] and *The Picture of Dorian Gray* [1890–4]. Also new in Pater studies is William Shuter's 'Pater, Overbeck, and Gerhard: Some Emendations and Additions to Billie Andrew Inman's *Pater and his Reading, 1874–1877'* (*PaterN* 45[2002] 11–21).

Fredeman, ed., *The Correspondence of Dante Gabriel Rossetti* is a projected nine-volume set, two volumes of which, *The Formative Years, 1835–1862, from Charlotte Street to Cheyne Walk*, are now in publishable form. Volume 1, covering 1835–1854, and volume 2, covering 1855–1862, completed before William E. Fredeman's demise, are comprehensively annotated and indexed. These volumes will remain as a monument to Fredeman as a great Pre-Raphaelite scholar and critic. We hope that work on the correspondence will continue and find an editor or editors who will build on the excellent foundations laid in the first two volumes. Birch and O'Gorman, eds., *Ruskin and Gender*, is a useful collection of essays reassessing Ruskin's views on gender. Many of the essays challenge interpretations of Ruskin's writings as conventionally patriarchal. Included in the collection is Francis O'Gorman's 'Manliness and the History of Ruskin in Love: Writing Ruskin's Masculinity from W.G. Collingwood to Kate Millett' (pp. 10–28), a description of the long history of biographical interpretation of Ruskin and how these early representations helped shape contemporary interpretations of his views on gender identity. Also, Linda Peterson, 'The Feminist Sources of "Of Queens' Gardens"' (pp. 86–106), argues that Ruskin's 'Of Queens' Gardens' lecture was not antagonistic to the progressive women's movement of the 1850s, but was, in fact, influenced by important leaders of the women's movement such as Anna Jameson and Bessie Parkes. Also included in the collection are the following essays: 'The Stones of Childhood: Ruskin's "Lost Jewels"' by Catherine Robson (pp. 29–46); 'The Foxglove and the Rose: Ruskin's Involute of Childhood' by Lindsay Smith (pp. 47–63); 'Ruskin, Gautier, and the Feminization of Venice' by J.B. Bullen (pp. 64–85); 'Ruskin's "Womanly Mind"' by Dinah Birch (pp. 107–20); '"What Teachers Do you Give Your Girls?" Ruskin and Women's Education' by Dinah Birch (pp. 121–36); '"Any Day That You're a Good Boy": Ruskin's Patronage, Rossetti's Expectations' by Joseph Bristow (pp. 137–58); 'Pantomime Truth and Gender Performance: John Ruskin and Theatre' by Sharon Aronofsky Weltman (pp. 159–76); and 'Images of Proustian Inversion from Ruskin' by Emily Wells (pp. 177–200).

Francis O'Gorman's '"To See the Finger of God in the Dimensions of the Pyramid": A New Context For Ruskin's *The Ethics of the Dust'* (*MLR* 98:iii[2003] 563–73), discusses a collection of lectures on crystallography by Ruskin [1866].

O'Gorman writes that, in *The Ethics*, 'Ruskin asked his respectable mid-nineteenth century middle-class audience to believe in the lessons the ancient Egyptian Neith had taught. He made this audacious statement via a gesture to a scientific discourse that was on the margins of a mainstream public debate in 1864 and 1865' (p. 573). A chapter in Feldman, *Victorian Modernisms* (see also section 1, Cultural Studies, above), discusses Ruskin's friendship with Francesca Alexander, as well as his editorial manipulations of her *Roadside Songs*, a series of sentimental portrayals of Italian peasants in Tuscany. 'The Anatomy of Bigotry: Carlyle, Ruskin, Slavery, and a New Language of Race', a chapter in Wood, *Slavery, Empathy and Pornography*, discusses and compares Ruskin and Carlyle's racist perspectives on slavery. A new edition of *Sesame and Lilies* by Deborah Epstein Nord includes both halves of Ruskin's classic work (first published in 1865) about the nature of men and women: 'Of Kings' Treasuries' and 'Of Queens' Gardens'. Accompanying essays by Elizabeth Helsinger, Seth Koven, and Jan Marsh provide historical and cultural contexts for the work.

A new edition of John Addington Symonds's *The Life of Michelangelo Buonarroti: Based on Studies in the Archives of the Buonarroti Family at Florence* (first published in 1893), is accompanied by an introductory essay by Creighton E. Gilbert explaining the importance of the work and providing a historical context for Symonds's important two-volume biographical study of Michelangelo. A chapter in N. Santilli's *Such Rare Citings: The Prose Poem in English Literature* ('Parallelism: Blake, Wilde, Beckett', pp. 137–60) is devoted to the subject of the British prose poem, which, according to Santilli, is marked by its biblical style and the use of parallelism and the literary technique called 'furtherance'. Among the poems discussed are Wilde's 'The Artist', 'The Doer of Good', and 'The Master'.

Reviews of critical work on Victorian prose are as follows: *The Woman and the Hour: Harriet Martineau and Victorian Ideologies*, by Caroline Roberts, reviewed by Valerie Sanders (*NCL* 57:iv[2002] 552–4); *The Art of the Pre-Raphaelites*, by Elizabeth PretteJohn, reviewed by Beth Harris (*VPR* 35:ii[2002] 185–6); *Nineteenth-Century Media and the Construction of Identities*, edited by Laurel Brake, Bill Bell, and David Finkelstein, reviewed by Mary Elizabeth Leighton (*VPR* 35:ii[2002] 187–8), and by Graham Law (*VS* 44:iv[2002] 690–2); *Serializing Fiction in the Victorian Press*, by Graham Law, reviewed by Dallas Liddle (*VPR* 35:ii[2002] 189–90); *The Rescue of Romanticism: Walter Pater and John Ruskin*, by Kenneth Daley, reviewed by Helen Pike Bauer (*VIJ* 30[2002] 209–15); *Dialogues in the Margin: A Study of the Dublin University Magazine*, by Wayne E. Hall, reviewed by Gordon Bigelow (*VS* 44:iv[2002] 686–8); *Serializing Fiction in the Victorian Press*, by Graham Law, reviewed by Linda K. Hughes (*VS* 44:iv[2002] 688–90); *Late Ruskin: New Contexts*, by Francis O'Gorman, reviewed by Paul Sawyer (*VS* 44:iv[2002] 700–2); and *Solitary Travelers: Nineteenth-Century Women's Travel Narratives and the Scientific Vocation*, by Lila Marz Harper, reviewed by Barbara T. Gates (*VS* 44:iv[2002] 716–18).

2. The Novel

A new contribution to studies in the Victorian novel this year is Baker and Womack, eds., *A Companion to the Victorian Novel*, an overview of the Victorian novel,

which provides contributions from various experts in the field discussing the its
emergence and its precursors, cultural and social contexts, genres, individual
authors, and introductions to critical approaches. Part 1, 'Victorian Contexts',
includes the following: 'The Victorian Novel Emerges, 1800–1840' by Ian Duncan;
'Periodicals and Syndication' by Graham Law; 'Book Publishing and the Victorian
Literary Marketplace' by Peter L. Shillingsburg; and 'Victorian Illustrators and
Illustration' by Lynn Alexander. Part 2, 'Victorian Cultural Contexts', includes:
'The Nineteenth-Century Political Novel' by Julian Wolfreys; 'The Sociological
Contexts of Victorian Fiction' by M. Clare Loughlin-Chow; 'Faith, Religion, and
the Nineteenth-Century Novel' by Nancy Cervetti; 'Philosophy and the Victorian
Literary Aesthetic' by Martin Bidney; 'Science and the Scientist in Victorian
Fiction' by Michael H. Whitworth; 'Law and the Victorian Novel' by Elizabeth F.
Judge; and 'Intoxication and the Victorian Novel' by Kathleen McCormack; Part 3,
'Victorian Genres', includes: 'Ghosts and Hauntings in the Victorian Novel' by
Lucie J. Armitt; 'The Victorian Gothic' by Peter J. Kitson; 'Victorian Detective
Fiction' by Lillian Nayder; 'The Victorian Social Problem Novel' by James G.
Nelson; 'The Victorian Sensation Novel' by Helen Debenham; 'Victorian Juvenilia'
by Christine Alexander; and 'Moving Pictures: Film and the Representation of
Victorian Fictions' by Todd F. Davis. Part 4, 'Major Authors of the Victorian Era',
includes: 'Religion in the Novels of Charlotte and Anne Brontë' by Marianne
Thormählen; 'Victorian Professionalism and Charlotte Brontë's *Villette*' by Russell
Poole; 'Charles Dickens' by K.J. Fielding; 'George Eliot: Critical Responses to
Daniel Deronda' by Nancy Henry; 'George Eliot's Reading Revolution and the
Mythical School of Criticism' by William R. McKelvy; 'Thomas Hardy' by Edward
Neill; 'The Vanities of William Makepeace Thackeray's *Vanity Fair*' by Juliet
McMaster; 'Anthony Trollope and "Classic Realism"' by K.M. Newton; 'George
Meredith at the Crossways' by Margaret Harris; '"Not Burying the One Talent":
Mrs. Gaskell's Life of Duty' by Barbara Quinn Schmidt; and 'Wilkie Collins's
Challenges to Pre-Raphaelite Gender Constructs' by Sophia Andres. Part 5,
'Contemporary Critical Approaches to the Victorian Novel', includes: 'Postcolonial
Readings' by Roslyn Jolly; 'Feminist Criticism and the Nineteenth-Century Novel'
by Eileen Gillooly; and 'Otherness and Identity in the Victorian Novel' by Michael
Galchinsky.

   New from the Blackwell Companions to Literature and Culture series is another
title by the same name, Brantlinger and Thesing, eds., *A Companion to the Victorian
Novel*, which provides a useful overview of Victorian cultural contexts, novelistic
genres, and theories of the novel. Part 1, 'Historical Contexts and Cultural Issues',
provides a general overview of cultural and social contexts, covering such topics as
the publishing world, money and social class, science and psychology, empire and
race, religion, theatre, gender, politics, and law. Part 2, 'Forms of the Victorian
Visual Culture', includes contributions on a variety of forms and genres, such as the
historical novel, the *Bildungsroman*, gothic romance, the detective novel, children's
fiction, science fiction, and 'Condition of England' novels. Part 3, 'Victorian and
Modern Theories of the Novel and the Reception of Novels and Novelists Then and
Now', includes the following contributions: 'The Receptions of Charlotte Brontë,
Charles Dickens, George Eliot, and Thomas Hardy' by Elizabeth Langland;
'Victorian Theories of the Novel' by Joseph W. Childers; 'Modern and Postmodern
Theories of Prose Fiction' by Audrey Jaffe; 'The Afterlife of the Victorian Novel:

Novels about Novels' by Anne Humpherys; and 'The Victorian Novel in Film and on Television' by Josh Marsh and Kamilla Elliott.

Also new from the Blackwell Guides to Criticism series is O'Gorman, ed., *The Victorian Novel*, an overview of critical approaches and responses to the Victorian novel over the past hundred years. Current topics of contemporary critical debate as well as early responses and receptions are covered. Jeffrey Moxham, *Interfering Values in the Nineteenth-Century British Novel: Austen, Dickens, Eliot, Hardy, and the Ethics of Criticism*, discusses imagination and the ethical decision-making process in relation to *Mansfield Park*, *Bleak House*, *Middlemarch*, and *Tess of the D'Urbervilles*. Kate Lawson and Lynn Shakinovsky, *The Marked Body: Domestic Violence in Mid-Nineteenth-Century Literature*, analyses the fiction of American and British writers in terms of 'the violated bodies of middle-class women'. Included are discussions of George Eliot ('Janet's Repentance') Elizabeth Gaskell ('The Poor Clare'), and Wilkie Collins (*Man and Wife*).

Diana C. Archibald, *Domesticity, Imperialism, and Emigration in the Victorian Novel*, provides an interesting reassessment of Victorian imperialist and domestic ideologies, arguing that the two supposedly complementary dogmas are in conflict more than heretofore supposed. Archibald looks at works by Gaskell, Dickens, Thackeray, Trollope, Butler, and Reade to examine encounters in the New World and the unexpected ways in which ideals of womanhood conflict with arguments supporting the demographic imperialist shift to the outskirts of the British empire. Archibald also argues that, according to Victorian constructs of womanhood, the domestic 'angel' and the hearthside had to be firmly rooted on English soil, even during mass geographical shifts to new worlds. Ann Gaylin's critically imaginative study, *Eavesdropping in the Novel: From Austen to Proust*, looks at scenes of curiosity and eavesdropping in nineteenth-century English and French novels to illustrate the 'primal human urge to know' and to examine patterns of information transmission between and amongst characters, narrators, and reader. Analysing the works of Austen, Dickens, Collins, Balzac, and Proust, Gaylin also discusses psychological anxieties surrounding the increased flow of information (due to the rise of information technology), agency in terms of gender and narrative, and individual scenes of narrative resolution and complication.

Hogle, ed., *The Cambridge Companion to Gothic Fiction*, includes the following chapters: 'The Victorian Gothic in English Novels and Stories, 1830–1880' by Alison Milbank, and 'British Gothic Fiction, 1885–1930' by Kelly Hurley.

In *Telling Tales: Gender and Narrative Form in Victorian Literature and Culture*, Elizabeth Langland discusses the impact of gender on narrative in Victorian culture, the 'complex ways in which gender informs the abstract cultural narratives—like space, aesthetic value, and nationality—through which a populace comes to know and position itself'. Included in Langland's study are discussions of, among others, Thackeray, Anne Brontë, Charlotte Brontë, Hardy, Collins, and Braddon. Lisa Sternlieb, *The Female Narrator in the British Novel: Hidden Agendas*, presents a critical reading of female narratives (focusing on Jane Eyre, Nelly Dean, Esther Summerson, Marian Halcombe, and Molly Bloom) to uncover the deceptive and calculating qualities of these supposedly artless and self-effacing narrators. Bill Overton, *Fictions of Female Adultery, 1684–1890: Theories and Circumtexts*, argues that existing theories of the adultery novel are incomplete because they need a more historical foundation. Including discussions of fiction by

Aphra Behn, Mary Wollstonecraft, and Huysmans (as well as works by Flaubert, Maupassant, and Zola), Overton points out that, while earlier adultery novels are written mostly by women, nineteenth-century adultery novels are written mostly by men and are much more concerned with adultery's potential for social disorder. Sally Ledger, 'Chartist Aesthetics in the Mid-Nineteenth Century: Ernest Jones, a Novelist of the People' (*NCL* 57:i[2002] 31–63), focuses on melodrama and the fiction of Ernest Jones to demonstrate how Chartist fiction writers had to compete with the new Sunday newspapers in order to draw readers from commercial presses back to radical presses. Gisela Argyle, *Germany as a Model and Monster: Allusions in English Fiction*, analyses allusions to Germany in English fiction, including a variety of canonical and non-canonical works.

Reviews of critical work on the Victorian novel are as follows: *The Flirt's Tragedy: Desire Without End in Victorian and Edwardian Fiction*, by Richard A. Kaye, reviewed by Ellis Hanson (*NCL* 57:iv[2002] 555–7); *The Sensation Novel and the Victorian Family Magazine*, by Deborah Wynne, reviewed by Mark W. Turner (*NCL* 57:iv[2002] 558–60); *The Anthology and the Rise of the Novel from Richardson to George Eliot*, by Leah Price, reviewed by Eileen M. Curran (*VPR* 35:ii[2002] 178–9); *The Victorian Governess Novel*, by Cecilia Wadsö Lecaros, reviewed by Alison Case (*VIJ* 30[2002]; *Ethics and Narrative in the English Novel, 1880–1914*, by Jil Larson, reviewed by Lesli J. Favor (*ELT* 45:iii[2002] 327–31); and *Ethics and Narrative in the English Novel, 1880–1914*, by Jil Larson, reviewed by Alison Booth (*VS* 44:iv[2002] 731–4).

The first biography of Max Beerbohm in over forty years, John N. Hall's *Max Beerbohm: A Kind of Life*, highlights the celebrated wit's writings and drawings of over sixty years, noting that, even though Beerbohm was a contemporary critic of social issues and art, most of his later works after his retirement in 1910 recall the late Victorian and Edwardian period.

Robert Bearman, 'Mary Braddon in Warwickshire' (*N&Q* 49:iv[2002] 478–85), provides further evidence of how Braddon's impressions of her visits to Warwickshire are reflected in her novel *The Doctor's Wife* [1894]. Simon Cooke, 'George du Maurier's Illustrations for M.E. Braddon's Serialization of *Eleanor's Victory* in *Once a Week*' (*VPR* 35:i[2002] 89–106), points out that more criticism has been directed towards du Maurier as a graphic design artist than as an illustrator. Cooke says that du Maurier takes the 'dual approach' of alternating between illustrating and interpreting, specifically in Braddon's *Eleanor's Victory*. *The Literary Lives of Mary Elizabeth Braddon: A Study of Her Life and Work*, by Jennifer Carnell, is reviewed by Benjamin F. Fisher (*VPR* 35:ii[2002] 180–1).

New in Brontë studies is Glen, ed., *The Cambridge Companion to the Brontës*, a collection of essays providing an introduction to and critical examination of the works of Charlotte, Emily, and Anne. Included in this highly useful reference work are the following original essays: an introduction by Heather Glen (pp. 1–12); 'The Haworth Context' by Juliet Barker (pp. 13–33); '"Our Plays": The Brontë Juvenilia' by Carol Bock (pp. 34–52); 'The Poetry' by Angela Leighton (pp. 53–71); '"Three Distinct and Unconnected Tales": *The Professor*, *Agnes Grey* and *Wuthering Heights*' by Stevie Davies (pp. 72–98); '"Strong Family Likeness": *Jane Eyre* and *The Tenant of Wildfell Hall*' by Jill Matus (pp. 99–122); '*Shirley* and *Villette*' by Heather Glen (pp. 122–47); '"Getting On": Ideology, Personality and the Brontë Characters' by Rick Rylance (pp. 148–69); 'Women Writers, Women's Issues' by

Kate Flint (pp. 170–91); 'The Brontës and Religion' by John Maynard (pp. 192–213); and 'The Brontë Myth' by Patsy Stoneman (pp. 214–41).

Linda Peterson, 'Review of Brontë Studies: The Millennial Decade, 1990–2000' (*DSA* 31[2002] 337–64), is a sustained evaluative survey of a decade's production of work on the Brontës. Peterson's range extends to contemporary rewritings or transformations of the Brontës in popular culture. In '"Hapless Dependants": Women and Animals in Anne Brontë's *Agnes Grey*' (*SEL* 34:ii[2002] 177–97), Maggie Berg makes a convincing argument for the link between attitudes about women's social position in Victorian culture and the treatment of animals. In *Adaptation Revisited: Television and the Classic Novel*, Sarah Caldwell includes a chapter discussing nostalgia and postmodernism in *Wildfell Hall*, the television adaptation of Anne Brontë's novel. Lidan Lin discusses 'Voices of Subversion and Narrative Closure in Anne Brontë's *The Tenant of Wildfell Hall*' (*BST* 27:ii[2002] 131–7). Also of interest is Karen Shaw's '*Wildfell Hall* and the Artist as a Young Woman' (*WVUPP* 48[2001–2002] 9–17).

Heather Glen, *Charlotte Brontë: The Imagination in History*, discusses the ways in which Charlotte's writings engage with the historical and social issues of her time. Chih-Ping Chen, '"Am I a Monster?" *Jane Eyre* among the Shadows of Freaks' (*SNNTS* 34:iv[2002] 367–85), compares the attic scene—when Rochester reveals Bertha's existence to Jane and the wedding party—to a freak show. Chen sees Bertha's 'enfreakment' as a paradigm for Jane's quest for female identity. Maria LaMonaca, 'Jane's Crown of Thorns: Feminism and Christianity in *Jane Eyre*' (*SNNT* 34:iii[2002] 245–63), provides a fresh interpretation of the novel, pointing out that some feminist readings of the ending have tended to ignore Jane's exaltation of St John in the final scene.

In 'Image and Text in *Jane Eyre*'s Avian Vignettes and Bewick's *History of British Birds*' (*VN* 101[2002] 5–12), Susan B. Taylor focuses on Bewick's descriptions of the cormorant and the rook to show how such imagery enhances the complexity of Jane's character. 'Canons to the Right of Them, Canons to the Left of Them: *Mansfield Park*, *Jane Eyre*, and Memorial Subversions of Slavery' is a chapter in Wood, *Slavery, Empathy and Pornography*, which discusses *Jane Eyre* and *Mansfield Park* in terms of slavery and the exploitation of women.

In 'Material Interiority in Charlotte Brontë's *The Professor*' (*NCL* 57:iv[2002] 443–76), William A. Cohen considers images of the body, human interiors, and sensory experience in *The Professor*. Kate E. Brown, 'Catastrophe and the City: Charlotte Brontë as Urban Novelist' (*NCL* 57:iii[2002] 350–80), examines the dispossessed figure of the governess and gothic spaces of urban confinement in *Villette* to explore correlations between catastrophe and mourning. Rajani Sudan, *Fair Exotics: Xenophobic Subjects in English Literature, 1720–1850*, examines the manner in which foreign 'exotics' are both embraced and feared for their 'otherness' during a period of Britain's intense empire-building. Sudan's study includes discussions of Brontë's *Villette* and de Quincey's *Confessions of an English Opium Eater*. Also of interest in Brontë studies are Alison Hoddinott's 'Charlotte Brontë and D.H. Lawrence' (*BST* 27:i[2002] 1–14); Margaret Newbold's 'The Branwell Saga' (*BST* 27:i[2002] 15–26); María Seiji Richart's 'Bruñel's Heights: Abismos de Pasión' (*BST* 27:i[2002] 27–34). In the same issue of *Brontë Society Transactions* Oscar Arnedillo writes on 'Emily Jane Brontë and St. Theresa of Avila: Twin Souls in Different Contexts' (*BST* 27:i[2002] 35–8), and Margaret Smith, in a short notice, writes movingly on the life and achievements of 'Professor Kathleen Tillotson, 1906–2001' (*BST* 27:i[2002] 68–9). The next issue includes Haruko Iwakami's 'The Brontës in Japan: How *Jane Eyre* was Received in the Meiji Period (1868–1912)' (*BST* 27:ii[2002] 91–100); Susan Carlson's 'Fantasies of Death and Violence in the Early Juvenilia of Charlotte Brontë (1829–32)' (*BST* 27:ii[2002] 110–11); and Susan V. Scaff's 'Echoes of Aristotle: Rochester's Rhetorical Ploys in *Jane Eyre*' (*BST* 27:ii[2002] 113–20). The November 2002 issue includes Tom Winnifrith's 'Brontë Biography and Brontë Criticism' (*BST* 27:iii[2002] 181–4); Sarah Fermi's 'Mellaney Hayne: Charlotte Brontë's School Friend' (*BST* 27:iii[2002] 185–99); Jane Nardin's 'A New Look at William Carus Wilson' (*BST* 27:iii[2002] 211–18); John Waddington-Feather on 'The Dialect of Shirley' (*BST* 27:iii[2002] 235–40) and, amongst other articles, James R. Simmons's 'Jane Eyre's Symbolic Paintings' (*BST* 27:iii[2002] 247–50). Humphrey Gawthrop's 'Frances-Mary Richardson Currer and Richard Heber: Two Unwearied Bibliophiles on the Fringe of the Brontë World' (*BST* 27:iii[2002] 225–34) is a fascinating glimpse into minor Victoriana.

Linda M. Austin, 'Emily Brontë's Homesickness' (*VS* 44:iv[2002] 573–96), discusses Emily's and her sisters' depictions of homesickness and nostalgia. Bénédicte Coste, '"Incomparably beyond and above you all": Le Tragique de *Wuthering Heights*' (*CVE* 53[2001] 41–62), focuses on Catherine Earnshaw in terms of Lacanian theories of psychoanalysis. Marilyn Hume, 'Who is Heathcliff? The Shadow Knows' (*VN* 102[2002] 15–18), uses Carl Jung's theory of 'The Shadow' to show how Heathcliff is formed by unconscious projections of characters in the novel, especially the narrators and Catherine. Reviews of critical work in Brontë studies in addition to those covered in the review section of *Brontë Society Transactions* include: *The Brontë Myth*, by Lucasta Miller, reviewed by Anita M. Wyman (*VPR* 35:ii[2002] 195–6) and *The Letters of Charlotte Brontë*, volume 2: *1848–1851*, edited by Margaret Smith, reviewed by Patsy Stoneman (*VS* 44:iv[2002] 692–4). Graeme Tytler discusses 'Animals in *Wuthering Heights*' (*BST* 27:ii[2002] 121–30). Other articles of interest include Sharon Locy's 'Travel and Space in Charlotte Brontë's *Jane Eyre*' (*PCP* 37[2002] 105–21) and Christopher Lane's 'Charlotte Brontë on the Pleasure of Hating' (*ELH* 69:i[2002] 199–222).

David C. MacWilliams, 'The Novelistic Melodramas of Hall Caine: Seventy Years On' (*ELT* 45:iv[2002] 426–39), makes a case for the much-needed reappraisal of Hall Caine's novels and their immense popularity. MacWilliams focuses in particular on how Caine's novels reflect popular literary tastes of the time, as well as attitudes towards conventional morality and the status of women. In a new study of G.K. Chesterton, *G.K. Chesterton as Controversialist, Essayist, Novelist, and Critic*, John D. Coates examines Chesterton's work in its historical context, focusing particularly on problems in the Edwardian age still seen today. Also included are discussions of the many different types of essay Chesterton wrote, the influence of Nietzsche on his work, Chesterton's contributions to the periodical *The Speaker*, and his novel *The Ball and the Cross*.

New in Lewis Carroll studies is Abeles, ed., *The Political Pamphlets and Letters of Charles Lutwidge Dodgson and Related Pieces: A Mathematical Approach*, volume 3. This collection provides a very different perspective on Dodgson, covering the full scope of his theories on voting, from his writings on national politics to his writings on local governance and academic affairs at Christ Church College, Oxford. Among the theories discussed are those about voting anomalies, voting strategies, ranking methods, and objectivity in sport as compared to political elections. Each section is accompanied by an introductory essay with background information and analysis.

Also of interest in Lewis Carroll studies is Taylor and Wakeling, eds., *Lewis Carroll, Photographer: The Princeton University Library Albums*, the most comprehensive collection of his photographs to date, many of which have not heretofore been reproduced. Also included are an introduction by Peter C. Bunnell, a chronology by Edward Wakeling, and a select bibliography by Roger Taylor. The 'Catalogue of the Princeton University Library Albums' and the 'Register of All Known Photographs by Charles Lutwidge Dodgson' are both contributed by Edward Wakeling.

The neglected fiction of Rosa Nouchette Carey (1840–1909) is the subject of Elaine Hartnell's *Gender, Religion, and Domesticity in the Novels of Rosa Nouchette Carey*. Hartnell analyses these almost unknown fictions to demonstrate Carey's treatment of 'all matters concerning women' (p. 200). William Baker provides an important contribution to Collins scholarship in *Wilkie Collins's Library: A Reconstruction*, a useful analysis of the books owned by Collins and his responses to them. Fully indexed, there are 537 entries, each of which includes commentary about the specific book and its significance, along with various dedications, significant quotations, and excerpts from Collins's letters. Also included are tables about imprint dates, place of publication, subject matter, and an appendix entitled 'Paintings and Art Work in Collins's Possession at the Time of his Death'. The subject of Christopher GoGwilt's *The Fiction of Geopolitics: Afterimages of Culture, from Wilkie Collins to Alfred Hitchcock* is 'how the nineteenth-century European hypothesis of culture haunts the twentieth-century fiction of geopolitics'. Part 2 includes an examination of *The Moonstone* in terms of democratic reform and the formalization of empire.

In *Unequal Partners: Charles Dickens, Wilkie Collins, and Victorian Authorship*, Lillian Nayder looks at Dickens's and Collins's collaborative work on the Christmas stories to show how Collins frequently worked against the conservative values of Dickens, especially in terms of gender and imperialism. Tabitha Sparks, 'Surgical Injury and Narrative Cure in Wilkie Collins's *Poor Miss Finch* and *Heart and Science*' (*JNT* 32:i[2002] 1–31), discusses surgery, specifically optical surgery and vivisection, and its representation as a destructive practice in both novels. Also new in Collins studies are 'My Dear Wilkie: The Letters from Dickens to Collins' by Paul Lewis (*WCSJ* 5[2002] 3–23) and 'Collins and Chattos: The Reading Papers' by Graham Law (*WCSJ* 5[2002] 49–56). Eric Levy writes on 'Wilkie Collins' *The Moonstone* and the Problem of Pain in Life' (*VR* 28:i[2002] 66–79). Reviews of critical work on Wilkie Collins are as follows: *Unequal Partners*, by Lillian Nayder, reviewed by Mark Knight (*WCSJ* 5[2002] 57–8), and *Wilkie Collins's Library*, by William Baker reviewed by Steve Dillon (*WCSJ* 5[2002] 63–4).

The year 2002 witnessed the publication of the twelfth and final volume of the expansive British Academy and Pilgrim edition of *The Letters of Charles Dickens*, edited by Graham Storey. This final volume takes us from 1868 to his death in 1870, and includes over a thousand original letters, many of which have been previously unpublished or only published in part. Included in this invaluable collection is an addendum of more than 200 letters found since the publication of volume 7, and a cumulative index of the entire collection. Highlights of the volume are Dickens's very successful final American tour, his renting of Windsor Lodge for Ellen Ternan, his election to the presidency of the Birmingham and Midland Institute, the publication of the first instalments of *Edwin Drood*, and his final British reading tours. The years also saw the death of some close friends: the painter Daniel Maclise, Mark Lemon, with whom Dickens became briefly reconciled, and Chauncy Hare Townshend. This final volume brings the total number of Dickens letters to 14,252. Kathleen Tillotson, who died on 3 June 2002, so intimately connected to the Pilgrim edition, sadly did not live to see the final publication of the project to which she (and many great scholars) devoted so many years. The Pilgrim edition of Dickens's letters represents the summit of monumental British literary scholarship devoted to Victorian literature and life. To use the words of Thomas Carlyle to Foster on Dickens's death: 'I am profoundly sorry for you, and indeed for myself and for us all. It is an event world-wide; a *unique* of talents suddenly extinct; and has "eclipsed" we too may say, "the harmless gaiety of nations".' Carlyle continued 'No death since 1866 [Jane Carlyle's] has fallen on me with such a stroke. No literary man's hitherto ever did' (p. xix). To repeat, all scholars are indebted to those involved in so many years in such a great project as the Pilgrim edition. In addition to Kathleen Tillotson they include Madeline House, Graham Storey, Nina Burgess, Margaret Brown, Douglas Matthews, Ken Fielding, Philip Collins, amongst others, and those who worked on the edition at the Clarendon Press, Oxford.

New from the Critical Issues series is *Charles Dickens* by Lyn Pykett, a study in which each chapter is devoted to a specific period of Dickens's career: 'Introduction: The Dickens Phenomenon and the Dickens Industry'; 'The Making of the Novelist and the Shaping of the Novel, 1835–41'; 'Travails in Hyper-Reality, 1842–8'; 'Mid-Victorian Self-Fashionings, 1846–50'; 'The Novelist as Journalist in *Hard Times*, 1850–7'; 'and 'These Times of Ours, 1858–70'. David Parker's *The Doughty Street Novels: Pickwick Papers, Oliver Twist, Nicholas Nickleby, Barnaby Rudge* focuses on Dickens's experiences at Doughty Street and how they helped shape the four novels he wrote while he lived there. A new biography by Jane Smiley, *Charles Dickens*, provides an overview for general readers of Dickens's publishing career and his work as a novelist. Smiley's biography is very readable, but does not contain footnotes or endnotes, with few sources cited in the text.

Tore Rem, *Dickens, Melodrama, and the Parodic Imagination*, examines Dickens's comic method and his 'double generic use of the melodramatist's emotional excesses and the parodist's detached and ironic stance'. David Lodge includes a chapter of reflection on Dickens, 'Dickens our Contemporary' (pp. 114–35), in his new book entitled *Consciousness and the Novel: Connected Essays*, which has as its subject the ways in which the novel represents consciousness, and 'how this contrasts with the way other narrative media, like film, represent it; how the consciousness, and the unconscious, of a creative writer do their work; how criticism can infer the nature of this process by formal analysis, or the creative writer by self-interrogation'.

Peter Gay, *Savage Reprisals: Bleak House, Madame Bovary, Buddenbrooks*, challenges the idea of the reliable 'realist' narrator to show how the authors of these novels modified and manipulated truths as a kind of distorting mirror for cultural and literary motives. Gay focuses particularly on a characteristic shared by Mann, Dickens, and Flaubert—anger directed towards their bourgeois societies. Along with bibliographical essays for each author, the study includes the following chapters: 'Prologue: Beyond the Reality Principle'; 'The Angry Anarchist: Charles Dickens in *Bleak House*'; 'The Phobic Anatomist: Gustave Flaubert in *Madame Bovary*'; 'The Mutinous Patrician: Thomas Mann in *Buddenbrooks*'; and 'Epilogue: Truths of Fictions'.

Julia F. Saville, 'Eccentricity as Englishness in *David Copperfield*' (*SEL* 42:iv[2002] 781–98), argues that the idea of eccentricity being linked to Englishness has its roots in the eighteenth and nineteenth centuries, and was only consciously recognized and cultivated in the 1830s to 1860s in the works of J.S. Mill and Charles Dickens. Saville shows how the association of eccentricity with Englishness has a double function: 'From within English society it is the mask of oddity that unmasks hypocrisy, constituting earnestness and decency as the bedrock of a moral society. Beyond the borders of England, within the broader empire, it takes the form of a rhetorical and affective excess that parades the Englishman's cultural difference even as it helps to stabilize and disseminate English moral values' (p. 97).

Jerome Meckier, *Dickens's 'Great Expectations': Misnar's Pavilion Versus Cinderella*, convincingly argues that *Great Expectations* is an anti-fairy-tale revision of seven novels modelled on the Cinderella story: Thackeray's *Pendennis*, Shelley's *Frankenstein*, Collins's *The Woman in White*, Emily Brontë's *Wuthering Heights*, Charlotte Brontë's *Jane Eyre*, Charles Lever's *A Day's Ride*, and Dickens's own *David Copperfield*. Central to Meckier's reading is Pip's allusion to Misnar's collapsing pavilion in *The Tales of the Genii*. In 'Dickens, Shelley's *Frankenstein*, and the Importance of *Paradise Lost* to *Great Expectations*' (*Dickensian* 98:i[2002] 29–38), Jerome Meckier considers Dickens's response to the assessment of personal accountability found in Shelley's *Frankenstein* and how it challenges the notions of providence in Milton's *Paradise Lost*. Meckier argues that 'Dickens wants to demolish Shelley in favour of Milton but in ways that promote *Great Expectations* as a better guidebook to human relationships in Victorian England than either *Frankenstein* or *Paradise Lost*' (p. 29).

Francis Ferguson, 'Envy Rising' (*ELH* 69[2002] 889–905), discusses the rise of the recognition of envy and shame as distinct emotions in the works of various writers, and how the two are present in *Our Mutual Friend*. In 'The Trouble with Tartar' (*Dickensian* 98:i[2002] 39–43), Ray Dubberke argues convincingly that the most likely character to play the mysterious part of Dick Datchery is Mr Tartar.

In 'The Psychic Architecture of Urban Domestic Heroines: *North and South* and *Little Dorrit*' (*VIJ* 30[2002] 123–40), Kristina Deffenbacher explores the relationship between self and home in Victorian fiction to show that the 'psyche-as-house model' (in particular in the works of Gaskell and Dickens) is inherently problematic. Jenny Hartley, '*Little Dorrit* in Real Time: The Embedded Text' (*PubH* 52[2002] 5–18), discusses the effects of reading *Little Dorrit* as the original readers did—over an eighteen-month period (from December 1855 to June 1857). In '*The Fall of the House of Usher* and *Little Dorrit*' (*VN* 101[2002] 32–4), Rodney Stenning Edgecombe discusses the possible influence of Poe's collapsing house motif and its possible influence on Dickens's *Little Dorrit*.

The Dickens Studies Annual 31[2002] includes the following articles of interest: Emily Walker Heady, 'The Negative's Capability: Real Images and the Allegory of the Unseen in Dickens' Christmas Books' (*DSA* 31[2002] 1–21); Rachel Ablow, 'Labors of Love: The Sympathetic Subjects of *David Copperfield*' (*DSA* 31[2002] 23–46); S.D. Powell, 'The Subject of David Copperfield's Renaming and the Limits of Fiction' (*DSA* 31[2002] 47–66); Richard Lettis, 'The Names of David Copperfield' (*DSA* 31[2002] 67–86); 'Eric Berlatsky, 'Dickens' Favorite Child: Malthusian Sexual Economy and the Anxiety Over Reproduction in *David Copperfield*' (*DSA* 31[2002] 87–126); Norman Macleod, 'Which Hand? Reading *Great Expectations* as a Guessing Game' (*DSA* 31[2002] 127–57); Rosemary Bodenheimer, 'Dickens and the Identical Man: *Our Mutual Friend* Doubled' (*DSA* 31[2002] 159–74); Grace Moore, 'Swarmery and Bloodbaths: A Reconsideration of Dickens on Class and Race in the 1860s' (*DSA* 31[2002] 175–202); Jan B. Gordon, 'Dickens and the Transformation of Nineteenth-Century Narratives of "Legitimacy"' (*DSA* 31[2002] 203–65); and Catherine Rising, 'The D Case Reopened' (*DSA* 31[2002] 267–79).

David Garlock, 'Recent Dickens Studies, 2000' (*DSA* 31[2002] 305–36), reviews forty-seven articles and books published on Dickens in 2000 to demonstrate 'the unmistakably clear image that emerges from a cacophony of critical postures and styles of a writer and visionary whose legacy continues to fire our imaginations' (p. 305)—which is stating the obvious. *The Dickensian* 98:iii[2002]) includes the following essays of interest: 'The Dickens Fellowship One Hundred Years On' by Tony Williams (*Dickensian* 98:iii[2002] 197–204); 'Stanfield and Dickens at "The Land's End": A Rediscovery in Context' by Pieter Van Der Merwe (*Dickensian* 98:iii[2002] 205–12); 'The Mystery of *John Ackland*' by R.F. Stewart (*Dickensian* 98:iii[2002] 213–24); '"Up the River": Another Mystery in *The Mystery of Edwin Drood*' by Maria K. Bachman (*Dickensian* 98:iii[2002] 225–32); 'Dickens's Villains: A Confession and a Suggestion' by Stephanie Harvey (*Dickensian* 98:iii[2002] 233–5); 'Reappraising Dickens's "Noble Savage"' by Grace Moore (*Dickensian* 98:iii[2002] 236–44); and 'The Letters of Charles Dickens: Supplement I' (*Dickensian* 98:iii[2002] 245–50). Ethical criticism is the subject of Ronald Shusterman's '*Hard Times*: Une éthique de la lecture' (*EA* 55:iii[2002] 286–97). Also of interest to Dickens scholars are the following articles: 'Charles Dickens and his Garden at Gad's Hill Place' by Jean Lear (*Dickensian* 98:i[2002] 5–13); and 'The Short Career of Walter Dickens in India' by Dick Kooiman (*Dickensian* 98:i[2002] 14–28).

In 'Dickens and Poland' (*Dickensian* 98:i[2002] 44–51), Krzysztof Gluchowski considers the anonymous authorship of several articles that are either connected somehow to Poland or sympathetic to the Polish Insurrection and published in the ninth volume of *All The Year Round* [1863]. In 'Dickens' *Pictures from Italy*: The Politics of the New Picturesque' (*NCP* 29:ii[2002] 120–38), Joseph Phelan argues that Dickens's travel narrative is a critique of the Victorian mode of picturesque viewing and its seeming indifference to social inequality and poverty. Dickens calls for a 'new picturesque' based on a sympathetic re-evaluation of the ethics of aestheticizing suffering. Phelan contends, though, that this call for a new picturesque is partially flawed because of its 'mystification of the causes of social inequality and personal division it appears to deprecate'.

A new edition of *Dombey and Son* from Penguin, edited by Andrew Sanders, uses the text of Dickens's single-volume first edition [1848] and includes explanatory notes, original illustrations, chronology, and appendices on serialization and illustrations. Modern Library's *Bleak House* uses as its text the first single-volume edition published in 1853 and includes original illustrations by H.K. Browne. Also included are new notes by Jennifer Mooney and a new introduction by Mary

Gaitskill. A new paperback edition of *Little Dorrit* is set from the 1857 edition of the text and has newly commissioned endnotes and an introduction by David Gates. Modern Library's *Our Mutual Friend* includes new notes by Richard T. Gaughan and notes by Jennifer Mooney. A new edition of *Oliver Twist*, edited by Philip Horne, has as its copy-text the original periodical version, initially published in *Bentley's Miscellany* in instalments between February 1837 and April 1839. This edition includes Dickens's 1841 introduction and 1850 preface, as well as all original illustrations.

Reviews of critical work on Charles Dickens are as follows: *The Cambridge Companion to Charles Dickens*, edited by John O. Jordan, reviewed by Juliet John (*NCL* 57:i[2002] 132–4); *Dickens and Heredity: When Like Begets Like*, by Goldie Morgentaler, reviewed by Catherine Waters (*VIJ* 30[2002] 203–5); *Dickens and the Children of Empire*, edited by Wendy S. Jacobson, reviewed by Laurence Kitzan (*VS* 44:iv[2002] 708–10); and *Dickens Redressed: The Art of 'Bleak House' and 'Hard Times'*, by Alexander Welsh, reviewed by John Bowen (*VS* 44:iii[2002] 491– 2). The subject of Christine Roth's 'Ernest Dowson and the Duality of Late-Victorian Girlhood: "Her Double Perversity"' (*ELT* 45:ii[2002] 158–75), is the 'unstable balance between two paradoxical extremes'. Roth argues that the little girls in Dowson's poems can be characterized by an irreconcilable division between chastity and sexual vice, and that neither can exist without the other because 'if they are isolated, the ideal girl becomes distant and cold, and the "real" or mundane girl becomes fallen, aesthetically flawed, and utterly forgettable'.

Catherine Wynne's *The Colonial Conan Doyle: British Imperialism, Irish Nationalism, and the Gothic* looks at Irish and gothic dimensions of Doyle's fiction to illustrate Doyle's questioning of the fixed nature of racial identity, the interplay of colonizer and colonized, and Doyle's longing for the reconciliation of British imperial identity and Irish nationalism. Among the subjects discussed are colonial topographies and land control, Doyle's interest in spiritualism and mesmerism, the influence of the Belgian Congo abuses on Doyle's snake narrative, the demonstration of irreconcilable political ideologies in the Moriarty figure, and the manifestation of this tension in topographical, sexual, and racial spaces in Doyle's fiction.

Rosamund Dalziell, 'The Curious Case of Sir Everard im Thurn and Sir Arthur Conan Doyle: Exploration and the Imperial Adventure Novel, *The Lost World*' (*ELT* 45:ii[2002] 131–57), presents an examination of two figures central to the characterization of British Guyana in the European imagination: Sir Everard im Thurm, who led an expedition up Mount Roraima in 1884, and Sir Arthur Conan Doyle, whose adventure novel *The Lost World* [1912] provides a depiction of Mount Roraima with which it came to be more closely associated. Jennifer A. Halloran, 'The Ideology Behind the *Sorceress of the Strand*: Gender, Race, and Criminal Witchcraft' (*ELT* 45:ii[2002] 176–94), contrasts the 'masculinist' detective stories of Conan Doyle with *The Sorceress of the Strand*—a volume by L.T. Meade and Robert Eustace, comprising six short stories published in the *Strand* magazine in 1902 and 1903—to show how the latter subverts traditional depictions of the criminal–detective relationship.

John Greenfield, 'Arthur Morrison's Sherlock Clone: Martin Hewitt, Victorian Values, and London Magazine Culture, 1894–1903' (*VPR* 35:i[2002] 18–36), looks at the character of Martin Hewitt, the fictional detective created by Arthur Morrison to take the place of Sherlock Holmes when Arthur Conan Doyle temporarily stopped writing detective stories. Morrison's Martin Hewitt stories were published between 1894 and 1903 in popular magazines such as *The Strand*, *The Windsor*, and *The London Magazine*. Greenfield shows how the two detectives embody many of the same ideological assumptions.

The Modern Library edition of *The Adventures and Memoirs of Sherlock Holmes* brings together all twenty-four Sherlock Holmes stories, the first twelve of which were first published in book form in *The Adventures of Sherlock Holmes* [1891], and eleven of which (not including 'The Cardboard Box') were first published in book form in *The Memoirs of Sherlock Holmes* [1893]. All of the stories in this collection are based on the initial book publication, with the exception of 'The Cardboard Box' and 'The Resident Patient', which are based on their first publication in *Strand Magazine*. This edition includes an introduction by John Berendt and newly commissioned notes by James Danly.

A very important contribution to George Eliot studies is the comprehensive and definitive *George Eliot: A Bibliographical History* by William Baker and John C. Ross, which provides a valuable bibliography of Eliot's publications during her lifetime, including descriptions of all editions, genres, and printings, as well as of her periodical publications. Some posthumous works are also included. For each work Baker and Ross include a publishing, reception, and composition history, descriptions of editions and locations, and, for some entries, facsimiles of covers. Over 145 photographs of bindings and title pages are also included. Extensively indexed, there are appendices in 'Eliotiana' and a partially annotated 'Non-Literary Writings Subsequently Published'. As Carol A. Martin indicates in an extensive review (*GEGHLS* 46–8[2002]), it's a 'work to consult and browse in, to value for the particular details and for the wider vision that it provides. It is a stupendous achievement, the result of many years of research, and a lasting and invaluable contribution to George Eliot studies' (p. 126).

Drawing on essays, journals, reviews, and letters, Nancy Henry, *George Eliot and the British Empire*, takes a look at Eliot's criticism of British colonialism, arguing against Edward Said's assertion that she was a proponent of imperialism. In 'George Eliot's Realism and Adam Smith' (*SEL* 42:iv[2002] 819–36), Imraan Coovadia argues that, in *Felix Holt*, *Middlemarch*, and *Silas Marner*, Eliot echoes the language of Smith's *The Theory of Moral Sentiments* and *The Wealth of Nations*. Smith and Eliot share the idea of modern society being shaped from the 'ground up' by 'its members' intersecting trajectories'. Melissa Valiska Gregory's 'The Unexpected Forms of Nemesis: George Eliot's "Brother Jacob" Victorian Narrative, and the Morality of Imperialism' (*DSA* 31[2002] 281–303) somewhat tendentiously relates George Eliot's short story to the nemesis figure in British colonialism. John B. Lamb, '"To Obey and to Trust": *Adam Bede* and the Politics of Deference' (*SNNTS* 34:iii[2002] 264–81), argues that the ideals of the 'deferential dialectic' are at the novel's ideological centre, and that even though the novel lacks reference to political and reform debates of the day, 'the question of political influence and political rule defines the space of the novel's reception'. Jeff Nunokawa, 'Eros and Isolation: The Antisocial George Eliot' (*ELH* 69[2002] 835–60), explores themes of social alienation and the erotic and in *Adam Bede*. A chapter in Levine, *Dying to Know* (see also Section 1(b) above) entitled '*Daniel Deronda*: A New Epistemology' (pp. 171–99), shows how the novel both supports and struggles against the perception that 'dying to know' was necessarily involved in the pursuit of scientific truth. Damian Walford Davies, 'The Politics of Allusion: *Caleb Williams*, *The Iron Chest*, *Middlemarch*, and the *Armoire de Fer*' (*RES* 53[2002] 526–43), explores the fascination with the horrors of secrecy and disclosure in *Middlemarch* and how the French Revolution's *armoire de fer* (iron chest) episode resonates in pivotal scenes. In 'Eliot's *Middlemarch*' (*Expl* 60:iii[2002] 137–8), Francis O'Gorman explores the meaning and placement of Casaubon's harpsichord (chapter 7), as well as Dorothea's response to it. Thomas Keymer's *Sterne, the Moderns, and the Novel* includes a section on 'Publishing *Middlemarch*, 1871–1872' which discusses how the publication of *Tristram Shandy* at irregular intervals was used as a model for publishing *Middlemarch*, and how this affected sales and readership.

Jeffrey Franklin, 'Memory as the Nexus of Identity, Empire, and Evolution in George Eliot's *Middlemarch* and H. Rider Haggard's *She*' (*CVE* 53[2001] 63–84), discusses the discourses of memory, history, and time in the two texts, arguing that they both 'associate their major characters with competing models of identity, which are defined in reference to competing models of memory. Memory in turn serves as the nexus between competing representations of empire *and* between the competing evolutionary theories, Darwinian and Lamarckian, on which theories of empire drew.' Mark Byron, 'The Question of Aesthetics in George Eliot's *Middlemarch*: "A Study of Provincial Life"' (*L&A* 12[2002] 65–78), analyses the Rome episode and how the characters respond to artwork and aesthetic ideas in those chapters.

Deanna Kreisel, 'Superfluity and Suction: The Problem with Saving in *The Mill on the Floss*' (*Novel* 35:i[2001]) looks at the figure of the hoarder in Ruskin's *Munera Pulveris* and George Eliot's *The Mill on the Floss*, focusing in particular on Maggie's 'confusion of the implications of the narrative of sexual fulfillment with those of the narrative of renunciation and self-denial' (p. 99). Kreisel says this confusion is threatening to the economic views of other characters. Marielle Seichepine, 'L'Eau et le rêve dans *The Mill on the Floss* et *Daniel Deronda*' (*CVE* 53[2001] 243–56), notes that, while critics have often pointed out the significance of water and dream in *The Mill on the Floss*, not much critical attention has been paid to this connection in *Daniel Deronda*. Seichepine explores the function of water and dream in both. Alain Jumeau, '*The Mill on the Floss*: Seuils et limites de la fiction' (*EA* 55:iv[2002] 398–407), examines the novel's title and epigraph. A new edition of *Adam Bede* is taken from her last revision of the work in 1861, and includes an introduction by Joanna Trollope and newly commissioned notes by Hugh Osborne. The text of Modern Library's *Daniel Deronda* is set from the Cabinet edition of 1878, and includes an introduction by Edmund White and newly commissioned notes by Hugh Osborne.

The George Eliot Review (*GER* 33[2002]) contains Daniel Tyler, 'Dorothea and the "Key to All Mythologies"' (*GER* 33[2002] 27–33) and Leonee Ormond, 'Mines of Misinformation. George Eliot and Old Master Paintings: Berlin, Munich, Vienna and Dresden, 1854–5 and 1858' (*GER* 33[2002] 33–50). There are three accompanying illustrations to this most informative article, which is a 'footnote' to Hugh Witemeyer's *George Eliot and the Visual Arts* [1979] and Margaret Harris and Judith Johnston's edition of the *Journals of George Eliot*. Ormond shows that in her journal George Eliot made errors 'of attribution' and 'subject' (p. 48). Beryl Gray explores the topic of 'George Eliot, George Henry Lewes, and Dogs' (*GER*

33[2002] 51–63). In 'Henry James on Digression in George Eliot's Fiction' (*GER* 33[2002] 64–9), Christine Richards re-examines Henry James's response to George Eliot's fiction. A short note, 'George Eliot's Debt to Hardy?' by David McIntosh (*GER* 33[2002] 72–3), considers the issue of whether George Eliot, in *Daniel Deronda*, was influenced by Thomas Hardy's fiction. Barbara Hardy's conference report (*GER* 33[2002] 70–1) provides a succinct account of the conference 'George Eliot: Life and Letters' at the Institute of English Studies, University of London, on 17 and 18 January 2002.

George Eliot–George Henry Lewes Studies (*GEGHLS* 42–3 [2002]) opens with an extensive disquisition by Robert Macfarlane on 'A Small Squealing Black Pig: George Eliot, Originality and Plagiarism' (*GEGHLS* 42–3 [2002] 1–29). In this brilliant and sophisticated article, Macfarlane moves from reflections in the second essay of Eliot's *Impressions of Theophrastus Such* to consider her perception of 'originality' in her fiction and non-fiction prose and writing. Macfarlane relates her opinions of 'the wider debates over the nature and definition of plagiarism, over free circulation versus private property, and over individual versus corporate creation, which had been gaining momentum over the 1860s and 1870s'. It also explores G.H. Lewes's work and shows how it 'influenced and overlapped with Eliot's own attitudes of originality and plagiarism' (p. 7).

'Dinah and the Debate over Vocation in *Adam Bede*' is by Jennifer M. Sholpa (*GEGHLS* 42–3[2002] 30–49). Jessie Wolfe, in 'Iris Murdoch Applied to George Eliot: Prodigal Sons and their Confessions in *Adam Bede, Silas Marner*, and *Middlemarch*' (*GEGHLS* 42–3[2002] 50–68), uses Iris Murdoch's philosophy to illuminate three George Eliot novels. Judaic and specifically mystical ideas are discussed in Brenda McKay's 'Victorian Anthropology and Hebraic Apocalyptic Prophecy: "The Lifted Veil" (*GEGHLS* 42–3[2002] 69–92). 'Two Unpublished George Eliot Letters' now at the Jagiellonian Library, Cracow, are uncovered by Gerlinde Röder-Bolton (*GEGHLS* 42–3[2002] 93–9). The letters are to Ludmilla Assing, niece of the writer Karl August Varnhagen von Ense (1785–1858), dated 3 December [1854], and to von Ense, dated 6 March 1855. In addition to Donald Hawes's 'Articles on George Eliot in 2001: A Selective Survey' (*GEGHLS* 42–3[2002] 100–8), there are reviews by Kenneth Womack on Jill Larson, *Ethics and Narrative in the English Novel, 1880–1914* (*GEGHLS* 42–3[2002] 109–12) and K.M. Newton on Nancy Henry, *George Eliot and the British Empire* (*GEGHLS* 42–3[2002] 112–18).

Recent reviews of critical work in George Eliot studies include: *The Cambridge Companion to George Eliot*, edited by George Levine, reviewed by Kathryn Bond Stockton (*NCL* 57:i[2002] 135–9); *Memory and History in George Eliot: Transfiguring the Past*, by Hao Li, reviewed by George Griffith (*VPR* 35:ii[2002] 183–4); *George Eliot and Victorian Historiography: Imagining the National Past*, by Neil McCaw, reviewed by George Griffith (*VPR* 35:ii[2002] 184–5); *George Eliot and the British Empire*, by Nancy Henry, reviewed by Sophia Andres (*VIJ* 30[2002] 206–8); *The Cambridge Companion to George Eliot*, edited by George Levine, reviewed by Margaret Harris (*GER* 33[2002] 77–9); The Broadview Edition of *Felix Holt*, the Radical, edited by William Baker and Kenneth Womack, reviewed by Mark Turner (*GER* 33[2002] 81–3); and *Theology in the Fiction of George Eliot*, by Peter C. Hodgson, reviewed by Terence R. Wright (*GER* 33[2002] 89–90).

Shirley Foster's *Elizabeth Gaskell: A Literary Life*, a new addition to the Literary Lives series, focuses on sex roles and women's concerns in Gaskell's fiction, her relationship with Dickens (who edited several of her stories), and the publication histories of several of her novels. Josie Billington's *Faithful Realism. Elizabeth Gaskell and Leo Tolstoy: A Comparative Study*, is a textual study comparing portions of Gaskell's novels and their revisions to works by Eliot, Hardy, and Tolstoy. In *Women's Voices in the Fiction of Elizabeth Gaskell (1810–1865)*, Marianne Camus explores cultural contexts for Gaskell's fictions, arguing that Gaskell's particular brand of 'pre-conscious feminism' quietly subverts male authority by including a variety of female voices and discourses. Susan Hamilton's 'Ten Years of Gaskell Criticism' (*DSA* 31[2002] 397–414), in addition to usefully assessing ten years' work in Gaskell scholarship, calls for 'a move away from the preoccupation with Gaskell's canonical status'. Hamilton argues for 'the need to reconceptualize such key paths through her work as feminist and material scholarship if they are to remain productive' (p. 39).

Elizabeth Starr, '"A Great Engine for Good": The Industry of Fiction in Elizabeth Gaskell's *Mary Barton* and *North and South*' (*SNNTS* 34:iv[2002] 385–402), argues that, even though many of Gaskell's social problem novels seem wary about commercialism and urban industry, they also in some ways endorse literary authorship and the business aspects of literature. In 'The Psychic Architecture of Urban Domestic Heroines: *North and South* and *Little Dorrit*' (*VIJ* 30[2002] 123–40), Kristina Deffenbacher explores the relationship between self and home in Victorian fiction to show that the 'psyche-as-house model' (in particular in the works of Gaskell and Dickens) is inherently problematic. Sophia Andres considers 'Elizabeth Gaskell's Re-Presentations of Pre-Raphaelite Gendered Boundaries' (*JPRAS* 11[2002] 39–62). The subject of Natalka Freeland's interesting study 'The Politics of Dirt in *Mary Barton* and *Ruth*' (*SEL* 42:iv[2002] 799–881) is how Gaskell goes beyond the usual outcry against unsanitary living conditions to a more thoughtful depiction of the effects of poverty, urbanization, alcoholism, prostitution, starvation, and murder. While many writers were preoccupied with the dirty conditions themselves, Gaskell goes a step further to examine the underlying cause of dirt—poverty.

'Reinventing Mrs. Gaskell', by Jennifer Mooney, is a review of Linda K. Hughes and Michael Lund, *Victorian Publishing and Mrs. Gaskell's Work* (*Rev* 24[2002] 61–80). *The Gaskell Society Journal* 16[2002] includes the following articles: 'Seen in Passing' by Ian Campbell (*GSJ* 16[2002] 1–13); 'Birds, Bees, and Darwinian Survival Strategies in *Wives and Daughters*' by Mary Debrabant (*GSJ* 16[2002] 14–29); 'The "Condition of England" Debate and the "Natural History of Man": An Important Scientific Context for the Social Problem Fiction of Elizabeth Gaskell' by Louise Henson (*GSJ* 16[2002] 30–47); 'The View from America: Annette Hopkins and Elizabeth Gaskell' by Jo Pryke (*GSJ* 16[2002] 48–63); 'Harriet Martineau and Elizabeth Gaskell' by Valerie Sanders (*GSJ* 16[2002] 64–75); 'Geography and Working-Class Women in *Mary Barton* and *Sylvia's Lovers*' by Shu Chuan Yan (*GSJ* 16[2002] 76–84); and 'Elizabeth Gaskell's Subversive Icon: Motherhood and Childhood in *Ruth*' by Anita C. Wilson (*GSJ* 16[2002] 85–111).

Michael Ainger's extensive and detailed *Gilbert and Sullivan: A Dual Biography* is the first joint biography of Gilbert and Sullivan since Leslie Baily's *The Gilbert and Sullivan Book* [1952] and draws on a more comprehensive collection than ever before of papers, correspondence, and documents from the Dame Bridget D'Oyly Carte collection in the Theatre Museum in London.

Erin Williams, 'Female Celibacy in the Fiction of Gissing and Dixon: The Silent Strike of the Suburbanites' (*ELT* 45:iii[2002] 259–79), takes a look at George Gissing's *The Odd Women* and Ella Hepworth Dixon's *The Story of a Modern Woman* to show how the rhetoric of the rebellious women 'on strike' was aligned with the rhetoric of the dissatisfied industrial worker. Williams shows how the contradictory natures of suburban settings contribute to the tension between elitism and solidarity among female characters in both texts. In 'Mourning, Pleasure and the Aesthetic Ideal in *The Private Papers of Henry Ryecroft*' (*GissingJ* 38:iii[2002] 1–13), Kevin Swafford shows how the title character's experiences of limitation and loss are connected to artistic creation and pleasure.

In '"There's many a true word said in joke": Quixoticism in *The Nether World*' (*GissingJ* 38:ii[2002] 4–20), George Scott Christian considers Gissing as a 'condition of England' novelist and explores the innovations he brought to that genre. More specifically, Scott looks at elements of 'comic consciousness' of *The Nether World* and how these elements are positioned in relation to the realist novel and Britain's economic and social problems. Debbie Harrison, 'The Deadliest Enemy of the Poor?' (*GissingJ* 38:iii[2002] 14–26), considers how Gissing presents a more sympathetic psychological study of alcoholism in *The Netherworld* than is seen in other literature of the period. Constance Harsh, 'Flowers on the Dunghill in *The Nether World*' (*VN* 102[2002] 9–15), discusses how Gissing creates in *The Nether World* a kind of 'ash-can aestheticism in which social stasis guarantees the beautiful effects created by the heroes' nobility. Examining the novel's treatment of systematic thought and the consolations of pessimism reveals how Gissing's form of aestheticism comes into being' (p. 9).

Christine De Vine, 'The Fiction of Class at the *Fin de Siècle*: Walter Besant and George Gissing' (*GissingJ* 38:ii[2002] 21–9), compares the two working-class novelists in terms of artistic and political success, showing that, while Besant depicts the working classes as waiting for the opportunity to emulate the middle classes, Gissing depicts them as having 'a way of being all their own'. In 'George Gissing on Music: Italian Impressions' (*GissingJ* 38:i[2002] 1–24), Allan W. Atlas looks at several diary entries, travelogue, and letters written by Gissing to explore his reactions to the music he heard during his three trips to Italy. *A Garland for Gissing*, edited by Bouwe Postmus, is reviewed by Martin Ryle (*NCL* 57:iv[2002] 561–4).

Jeffrey Franklin, 'Memory as the Nexus of Identity, Empire, and Evolution in George Eliot's *Middlemarch* and H. Rider Haggard's *She*' (*CVE* 53[2001] 63–84), discusses the discourses of memory, history, and time in the two texts, arguing that they both 'associate their major characters with competing models of identity, which are defined in reference to competing models of memory. Memory in turn serves as the nexus between competing representations of empire *and* between the competing evolutionary theories, Darwinian and Lamarckian, on which theories of empire drew.' Broadview Literary Text's edition of *King Solomon's Mines*, edited by Gerald Monsman, uses the first edition for its copy-text and, along with an introduction, footnotes, and endnotes, includes four useful appendices: 'Victorian Critical Reaction', 'Haggard on Africa and Romance', 'Historical Documents: Natives and Imperialists in South Africa', and 'Historical Documents: Spoils of

Imperialism: Gold, Diamonds, and Ivory'. Modern Library's *King Solomon's Mines* includes a new introduction by Alexander Fuller and is illustrated by Walter Paget with notes by James Danly.

Thomas Hardy A to Z: The Essential Reference to his Life and Work, by Sarah Bird Wright, provides a general and comprehensive reference guide to Hardy's major works in all genres along with their critical reception, other aspects of Hardy's life, and suggestions for further reading. Along with alphabetically arranged entries covering individual works and general themes, the following useful appendices are included: 'Topical List of Entries'; 'Media Adaptations of Thomas Hardy's Works'; 'Chronology of Thomas Hardy's Life and Works'; 'Family Trees'; 'Glossary of Place-Names in Thomas Hardy's Works'; 'Translations of Thomas Hardy's Works'; and a bibliography. *Thomas Hardy: A Bibliographical Study*, by Richard L. Purdy, includes a new two-part supplement updating the 1954 first edition, which was edited by Charles P.C. Pettit. The new edition provides annotations and bibliographic references about critical works over the past five decades, updating information included in the Pettit original. The second part of the supplement draws on numerous Hardy scholars to pinpoint errors in the original. Pettit himself provides an interesting introduction to the work, which describes the process of compiling the information for the first edition and its influence on both Hardy scholarship and single-author bibliography.

In *Hardy's Geography: Wessex and the Regional Novel*, Ralph Pite considers Hardy's renderings of locale, focusing in particular on his increasingly complex notion of Wessex and his complicated personal relationship to it. Pite discusses the ways in which Hardy sometimes challenges stereotypical renderings of locales and interactions between reality and dream in his work. He includes a very useful survey of scholarship on Hardy and geography. A chapter in Levine, *Dying to Know* (see also Section 1(b) above) entitled 'The Cartesian Hardy: I Think, Therefore I'm Doomed' (pp. 200–19) shows how, in *Jude the Obscure*, Hardy pushes the 'dying-to-know' narrative of scientific epistemology to its 'logical and merciless conclusion. One literally dies in order to know'. Rose DeAngelis, 'Triangulated Passions: Love, Self-Love, and the Other in Thomas Hardy's *The Well-Beloved*' (*SNNTS* 34:iv[2002] 403–21), offers a Freudian reading of the Jocelyn Pierston character, exploring various manifestations of 'triangulated desire' and Pierston's narcissistic urges when selecting the objects of his desire. Robert Carballo, 'Seeing through a Glass Darkly: Thomas Hardy's Poetic Gothicism' (*CVE* 53[2001] 29–40), looks at a few of Hardy's poems ('Neutral Tones', 'The Souls of the Slain', and 'The Voice', among others) to show their connection to gothic aesthetics and sensibilities. Martin Ray, 'Hardy's "The Dead Man Walking" and Verdi's *Il Trovatore*' (*N&Q* 49:iv[2002] 491), suggests that the 'troubadore-youth' image in Hardy's poem 'Dead Man Walking' is an allusion to the Giuseppe Verdi opera. Martin Ray, 'Hardy's "The Comet at Yell'ham" and Donati's Comet' (*N&Q* 49:iv[2002] 491), identifies the comet in the poem as Donati's comet, not Encke's comet as had previously been thought.

Also of interest in Hardy studies are the following articles: Christopher Harbinson's 'Echoes of Keats's *Lamia* in Hardy's *Tess of the D'Urbervilles*' (*N&Q* 49:i[2002] 74–6); David A. Ifkovic's 'Tess as Innocent' (*THJ* 18:iii[2002] 112–14); Jack R. Bradshaw's 'A Note on *The Mayor of Casterbridge*: The Flaw' (*THJ* 18:i[2002] 81); Helen Carhart's 'Consider Some of the Ways in which Hardy Uses

Place to Shape his Fiction in *The Return of the Native*' (*THJ* 18:iii[2002] 106–11); Andrew Radford's 'The Victorian Dilettante and the Discoveries of Time in *A Pair of Blue Eyes*' (*THY* 33[2002] 5–19); Henry Lock's 'Thomas Hardy and the Locks: A Lock Family Chronicle' (*THJ* 18:i[2002] 66–80); Brigitte Brauch-Velhorn's 'The Reception of Thomas Hardy in Germany (1876–2000)' (*THY* 33[2002] 28–55); Trevor Johnson's 'A Question of Terminology? *Jude the Obscure*, "Midnight on the Great Western" and Hardy's "Churchiness"' (*THJ* 18:ii[2002] 66–76); C.M. Jackson-Houlston's 'Phenology or Dutch Genre Painting? A Case Study of a Hardy Description in *Far From the Madding Crowd*' (*THJ* 18:iii[2002] 60–71); and Andrew Clinton's '"She Stopped Like a Clock": Science and Artificiality in *The Hand of Ethelberta* and the *Cornhill Magazine*' (*THJ* 18:ii[2002] 77–86).

Oxford World's Classics new edition of *Far From the Madding Crowd* is edited and with notes by Suzanne B. Falck-Yi, along with a bibliography, chronology, maps, and explanatory notes. This edition keeps as its basis the critical text that restores passages previously deleted and revised. The Modern Library's reprint of *The Mayor of Casterbridge* uses the 1912 Wessex edition as its text, and includes Hardy's map of Wessex, an introduction by J.I.M. Stewart, and notes by Tess O'Toole. New from Modern Library Classics is a reissue of *The Woodlanders,* with a new introduction by James Wood and notes by Tess O'Toole. Oxford World's Classics new critical edition of *Jude the Obscure* takes into account the revisions Hardy made over twenty-five years. It is edited and with bibliography, revised notes, and new chronology by Patricia Ingham.

Douglas Jerrold: 1803–1857, by Michael Slater, is a new biography of the journalist and dramatist who was once considered part of the famous triad of humorists along with Charles Dickens and W.M. Thackeray. This first full-length biography of Jerrold since Walter Jerrold's *Douglas Jerrold, Dramatist and Wit* [1918], will be of great interest to those interested in the journalistic and theatrical life of the early nineteenth century. Slater draws on a great deal of hitherto unpublished correspondence, along with the private correspondence and writings of contemporaries, to examine Jerrold's life, works, and reputation as 'the wittiest man in London'. Slater writes with learning and is most informative.

The subject of David Gilmour's *The Long Recessional: The Imperial Life of Rudyard Kipling* is Kipling's public role as one who influenced British opinion about the empire. Gilmour's study includes an examination of 'Recessional', a celebration of Queen Victoria's Diamond Jubilee in 1897, as well as his later poems about the dangers of Nazism. Focusing on an episode when Kipling said he saw a vision of his deceased daughter Josephine, William B. Dillingham, 'Kipling: Spiritualism, Bereavement, Self-Revelation, and "They"' (*ELT* 45:iv[2002] 402–25), claims that Kipling may have 'possessed certain psychic senses', but was afraid to acknowledge them. George Kieffer, 'A Contrary Man and Mason' (*KJ* 76:303[2002] 30–40), explores in some detail the influence on Kipling of the Freemasons, of which he was a member. Craig Raine, 'Kipling: Controversial Questions' (*KJ* 76:303[2002] 10–29), reconsiders the extent to which Kipling was really racist, citing several examples from his poetry, travel writings, letters, fiction, and other writings. In a similar vein, Shamsul Islam, 'Imperialism, Racism and "The God of Small Things"' (*KJ* 76:302[2002] 40–7), examines a few of Kipling's Indian stories to argue that Kipling 'is a complex writer who cannot be pigeon-holed in simplistic categories' (p. 40). Peter Havholm, 'Politics and Art in Kipling' (*KJ*

76:304[2002] 22–35), argues that in trying to reconcile Kipling's 'ethically offensive material' one should not attempt to understand his politics separately from his fiction, but that the two can be read together for both 'ethical and aesthetic satisfaction' (p. 22). In 'Did Mary Postgate Leave an Ally to Die?' (*KJ* 76:301[2002] 42–7), Bill Dower challenges readings of the story as being brutal and cruel, arguing that some commentators have failed to see 'the ultimate device which the author has used to tell the story—that of playing on the prejudice of the reader' (p. 43). Sailaja Krishnamurth considers 'Reading Between Lines: Geography and Hybridity in Rudyard Kipling's *Kim*' (*VR* 28:i[2002] 47–65). In 'The Spirit of the Land: *Puck of Pook's Hill*' (*KJ* 76:302 [2002] 20–7), Peter Bramwell writes that 'the edifices of British history and empire ... are flimsy, and are questioned and deconstructed by themselves and by a more inclusive and coherent mythology of the land and spirit' (p. 27). William B. Dillingham, 'Grief, Anger, and Identity: Kipling's "Mary Postgate"' (*KJ* 76:301[2002] 33–42), discusses the psychology of bereavement in 'Mary Postgate'. A chapter on Kipling, 'Three Lives: Joe Orton, Rudyard Kipling, E.M. Forster', is included in Michael Holroyd's *Works on Paper: The Craft of Biography and Autobiography*.

A new edition of William Morris's *News from Nowhere*, edited by Stephen Arata, includes excerpts from Morris's essays, journalism, reviews, and lectures, as well as selections from his writings on art, work, and revolution. An introduction and notes are also provided. A new Oxford World's Classics edition of Samuel Smiles's best-seller *Self-Help; with Illustrations of Character and Conduct* is edited and with introduction and notes by Peter W. Sinnema. The new edition reproduces the 1866 expanded edition in full. Margaret Oliphant's Carlingford series is the subject of Birgit Kamper's monograph focusing on *The Debate on Religion, Class and Gender in the 1860s and 1870s*. Kamper contextualizes Oliphant's fiction, examining debates in periodicals of the 1860s and 1870s. For Kamper, Oliphant's novels are reactions to these debates.

Liz Farr, 'Stevenson's Picturesque Excursions: The Art of Youthful Vagrancy' (*NCP* 29:ii[2002] 197–225), looks at several of Stevenson's travel essays to show how his reformulation of the late eighteenth-century picturesque gives voice to the young middle-class man's desire for aesthetic agency and freedom from a restrictive bourgeois lifestyle.

Brian Gibson, 'One Man Is an Island: Natural Landscape Imagery in Robert Louis Stevenson's *Treasure Island*' (*VN* 101[2002] 12–21), discusses how the landscape in the novel evolves from merely establishing mood to more complex renderings that illustrate facets of Jim's personality. Norton Critical Editions presents a new edition of Stevenson's *The Strange Case of Dr. Jekyll and Mr. Hyde*, edited by Katherine Linehan, which includes annotations, a textual appendix, and critical essays focusing on narrative technique, allegory, and science, and psychology (among other subjects) contributed by experts in the field. The text is based on the 1886 first edition, which was set using Stevenson's manuscript. The Modern Library's *The Master of Ballantrae* is a reproduction of the original edition and includes an introduction by Andrea Barrett. *The Complete Stories of Robert Louis Stevenson: 'The Strange Case of Dr. Jekyll and Mr. Hyde' and Nineteen other Tales* (Modern Library Classics) is edited, with an introduction and notes, by Barry Menikoff, and includes an interesting appendix describing Stevenson's influence on the *Oxford English Dictionary*.

A new addition to the Case Studies in Contemporary Criticism series is *Dracula: Complete, Authoritative Text with Biographical, Historical, and Cultural Contexts, Critical History, and Essays from Contemporary Critical Perspectives*, edited by John Paul Riquelme, which presents, along with the text, an overview of historical and biographical criticism, as well as essays approaching the novel from a variety of critical angles, such as gender and psychoanalytical criticism, deconstruction, and new historicism. Joseph Valente, *Dracula in Dracula's Crypt: Bram Stoker, Irishness, and the Question of Blood*, is an exploration of representations of racial purity in the text using biographical and post-colonial perspectives to offer fresh interpretations of Stoker's views on class and 'ethno-national status'. Valente also cogently argues that Mina Harker represents a powerful healing force of 'social connectivity'.

Judith L. Fisher, *Thackeray's Skeptical Narrative and the 'Perilous Trade' of Authorship*, contributes to our understanding of scepticism in the nineteenth century by describing how Thackeray's narratives progress in such a way as to promote a 'hermeneutic of skepticism', a kind of education for his readers in how to accept a 'world without God' without becoming pessimistic. Christoph Lindner, 'Thackeray's Gourmand: Carnivals of Consumption in *Vanity Fair*' (*MP* 99:iv[2002] 564–81), presents an analysis of the character of Jos Sedley and how he embodies the obsession with commodities and consumer seduction. In 'W.M. Thackeray and his *Cornhill Magazine* in Russia: Nineteenth-Century Attitudes' (*VPR* 35:iii[2002] 295–304), Stella Nuralova examines the reception of Thackeray's works in Russia and perceptions of *Cornhill Magazine*.

A somewhat thin year in Thackeray studies is augmented by Robert A. Colby's 'Thackeray Studies, 1993–2001' (*DSA* 31[2002] 365–96). This is a clearly written retrospective survey of Thackeray scholarship covering the period from 1993 to 2001. He also adds some items omitted from Peter Shillingsburg's previous *DSA* 23[1994] survey, which ended at 1992. Colby uncovers 150 items on Thackeray 'against over a thousand for Dickens', revealing that Thackeray has 'emerged from the shadows, but it seems safe to say by now he will never bask in the limelight that envelops [Dickens]' (p. 365). Also of interest in Thackeray studies are the following articles: Mary Hammond's 'Thackeray's Waterloo: History and War in *Vanity Fair*' (*L&H* 11:ii[2002] 19–38); Donald Hawes's 'Fanny Burney and Thackeray' (*N&Q* 49:i[2002] 63–5); and John McAuliffe's 'Taking the Sting Out of the Traveler's Tale: Thackeray's *Irish Sketchbook*' (*ISR* 9:i[2002] 25–40).

Few publications dealt with Trollope in 2002. Of them, Jill Felicity Durey's *Trollope and the Church of England* provides a detailed account of how his lifelong interest in religion is manifested in his fiction and non-fiction. In 'Who's Who: Land, Money and Identity in Trollope' (chapter 2 of Delany, *Literature, Money and the Market*), Paul Delaney examines identity and reputation as products of the literary marketplace. According to him, Trollope's *The Way We Live Now* recognizes contradictions within the aristocratic myth that 'identity depends on one's rank, lineage, and connection with the land' even while the novel laments the passing away of this prestige order. A new edition of Trollope's *The Last Chronicle of Barset* (the conclusion to Trollope's Barsetshire novels) is edited and with an introduction and notes by Stephen Gill, and also includes a bibliography, chronology, and map. Valentine Cunningham discusses 'Anthony Trollope and Law, Laws, Legalisms and Assorted Legislations' (*REALB* 18[2002] 89–107).

William T. Ross, *Wells's World Reborn: The Outline of History and its Companions*, provides a new and welcome addition to Wells scholarship by focusing solely on Wells's non-fiction. In particular, Ross provides insightful commentary on Wells's views of progress, feminism, and colonialism in *The Outline of History* (which Ross compares to Hendrik Van Loon's *The Story of Mankind* and Will Durant's *The Story of Philosophy*), as well as offering some discussion of Wells's *The Science of Life* and *The Work, Wealth, and Happiness of Mankind*. The colonial imagination of the Other in works by H.G. Wells is discussed in a section of *Poetics of the Hive: The Insect Metaphor in Literature* by Cristopher Hollingsworth.

In 'Working the Room: The Cases of Mary H. Kingsley and H.G. Wells' (*NCP* 29:i[2002] 151–67), Julie English Early discusses the notion of celebrity and compares Wells and Kingsley in terms of how they presented themselves on the lecture platform and in the press. Wells is included, among others, in a discussion of how narratives can be used to give shape to political ideas in Stephen Ingle's *Narratives of British Socialism*.

Trevor Fisher's *Oscar and Bosie: A Fatal Passion* tells the story of 'one of the world's greatest romantic tragedies', focusing in particular on Bosie's desertion of Wilde after Wilde's imprisonment for attempting to sue the marquis of Queensberry for libel.

Richard Halpern's *Shakespeare's Perfume: Sodomy and Sublimity in the Sonnets, Wilde, Freud, and Lacan* challenges the Freudian notion that sexual desire is sublimated into art, arguing instead that art 'gives birth to the sexual'. Included is a discussion of Wilde's *The Portrait of Mr. W.H.* and Freud's essay about Leonardo da Vinci. Colm Tóibín's *Love in a Dark Time: And Other Explorations of Gay Lives and Literature* includes a chapter discussing how Wilde's sexuality informed his work. Ann L. Ardis, *Modernism and Cultural Conflict, 1880–1922*, questions the extent to which turn-of-the-century literary modernists were really radical, demonstrating how writers such as Ezra Pound, T.S. Eliot, and James Joyce supported mainstream views. Of interest to Wilde scholars is a chapter devoted to modernists' conservative responses to the 1895 trials of Oscar Wilde. In chapter 2, 'Inventing Literary Tradition, Ghosting Oscar Wilde and the Victorian *Fin de Siècle*' (pp. 45–77), Ardis considers how the 'London-based modernist avant-garde sought to shore up literature's symbolic capital in the face of the rising authority of the (social) sciences: the invention of a literary tradition in which "classic" works of art are deemed to have universal, transhistorical aesthetic appeal' (p. 8).

Christopher S. Nassaar, 'Wilde's *The Happy Prince and Other Tales* and *A House of Pomegranates*' (*Expl* 60:iii[2002] 142–5), discusses Walter Pater's *Marius the Epicurean* and *The Renaissance* and their influence on Wilde's fairy-tales. Nassaar focuses on instances in the fairy-tales when Wilde echoes (or rejects) Pater's ideas about the blending of aestheticism and Christianity. In 'Wilde's *The Picture of Dorian Gray*' (*Expl* 60:iv[2002] 202–4), Roger Platizky argues that, in chapter 11 of *The Picture of Dorian Gray*, the description of Dorian's collecting of exotic artefacts, which is a parallel of Britain's empire-building, may also reflect a 'veiled critique of the imperial enterprise' (p. 203). Richard Dellamora, 'Bataille/Wilde; an Economic and Aesthetic Genealogy of the Gift' (*Angelaki* 6:ii[2001] 91–9), discusses Wilde in terms of George Bataille's ideas about 'general economy'. Reviews of critical work on Oscar Wilde are as follows: 'The Importance of Being

Decorated: An Exciting New Approach to Reading Oscar Wilde' by James G. Nelson, a review of Nicholas Frankel's *Oscar Wilde's Decorated Books* (*Rev* 24[2002] 199–200); *The Complete Works of Oscar Wilde*, volume 1, edited by Bobby Fong and Karl Beckson, reviewed by Lawrence Danson (*ELT* 45:iii[2002] 331–4); and *Wilde Style: The Plays and Prose of Oscar Wilde*, by Neil Sammells, reviewed by Anya Clayworth (*ELT* 45:iii[2002] 336–7).

3. Poetry

There were few monographs this year specifically devoted to Victorian poetry, yet it seems to be infiltrating a greater number of general studies of Victorian literature and culture: notable this year was the number of essays dealing with poets or poems in wider studies or collections, not to mention journal articles. The status of Victorian poetry as an important constituent of any course on the nineteenth century was also consolidated by the massive Blackwell's *Companion to Victorian Poetry*, reviewed below, a volume which could shape the direction of research in the field for years to come. In terms of the availability of texts, new editions, such as Scott Lewis's edition of Barrett Browning's letters to her sister, or Florence Boos's edition of *The Earthly Paradise*, are doing a great deal to draw Victorian poets and their poetry back into classroom or academic discussions. With regard to this, it is particularly worth remarking the number of editions of Victorian poems published by Fyfield Books, an imprint of Carcanet. Most of these editions are not new, but the fact that they are again available, in paperback and at a low cost, might be read as a hopeful symptom for the rise of Victorian poetry. In 2002 alone, Fyfield printed Malcolm Hicks's edition of *Oscar Wilde: Selected Poems* (first published 1992); Keith Silver's *Lewis Carroll: Selected Poems* [2002], discussed below; and Stevie Davies's *The Brontë Sisters: Selected Poems* (first published 1976). These are attractive scholarly editions, including short introductions, brief notes, and a guide to further reading. Fyfield has also brought out editions of Barrett Browning, Charlotte Mew, Arthur Symons, and Swinburne in the last year, which will be discussed in the 2003 volume.

The widening of the canon which these publications imply is evident throughout this year's work on Victorian poetry, and nowhere more so than in the Blackwell's *Companion*, edited by Richard Cronin, Alison Chapman, and Antony H. Harrison. This book represents a significant achievement, bringing together many of the world's leading scholars in no less than thirty-one essays on the subject, plus a very useful chronology of major events and publications affecting the world of poetry. The editors describe the volume as 'richly and chaotically cluttered' (p. ix), a blend of the well known and the obscure. Unlike other Blackwell Companions, this volume does not deal with individual poets and poems, but is loosely divided into sections on genre ('Epic', 'Hymn', etc.), publication and reception history, and cultural contexts ('Poetry and Science', 'Nationhood and Empire'). The reader seeking information about one particular poem, therefore, would trace it through these various contexts and find it recurring with different emphases in a number of chapters. This gives the *Companion* a sense of expansiveness, and highlights the sheer breadth of Victorian poetry and the multiple possibilities for different readings. It also, valuably, places those authors most likely to be studied in relation to poets whose works would have been familiar in the nineteenth century, but are now neglected. There are inevitably some overlaps: to take one instance, the same passage from Morris's 'The Defence of Guenever' is discussed in 'Pre-Raphaelite Poetry' and 'Arthurian Poetry', but on the whole this occurs surprisingly little. Interesting juxtapositions also occur between chapters—to move from the 'Hymn' to 'Nonsense Poetry', or from 'Working-Class Poetry' to 'The Classical Tradition', is to gain an immediate impression of the disparity of poetic genres in the period. Different readers will undoubtedly find minor objections to the editors' choice of topics for inclusion. For this reader, it seemed a pity that, other than Carol Christ's introductory essay on Victorian poetics, there was no specific discussion of Victorian concepts of poetry and the poet, or of changing ideas about poetic form. Patmore's *Essay on English Metrical Law* is one of few key works missing from the index. Such issues do, however, generally emerge from individual essays.

Given the length of the volume, to provide detailed reviews here of each chapter is impossible. The best essays achieve a good balance between displaying expertise and explaining the topic to an audience who may have no prior knowledge of the field. Few contributors seek to pursue a polemical line of argument, though many aim to change the shape of the field they discuss. Chris Snodgrass on 'The Poetry of the 1890s', for instance, sets out to show that much twentieth-century criticism has misrepresented this decade as one of aestheticism, decadence, and decline, rather than recognizing the true diversity of its poetry. The interplay between canonical and non-canonical in each chapter is also intriguing. Some contributors do focus on Tennyson, Arnold, the Brownings, and Hopkins. Carol Christ's introductory essay on poetics, for instance, neatly surveys a field that mainly consists of the works of these writers. Yet others devote more space to the unusual or intriguing rather than the familiar—Seamus Perry's discussion of humorous elegiacs and poems on the death of animals in 'Elegy' draws the gloom of Wordsworth, Tennyson, and Arnold into negotiation with the black humour of Lear and Housman. Alison Chapman on 'Sonnet and Sonnet Sequence' provides another good example of the shifting of the canon. She starts with Wordsworth, yet ends with an excellent reading of Toru Dutt's 'Sonnet—Baugmaree'. Some surveys are breathtaking in their scope, among which Herbert Tucker's masterly essay on 'Epic' stands out, deftly weaving together the 'ennobling and embarrassing' (p. 29) qualities of religious, national, and subjective epics. Other highlights of the first part, for this reader, included J.R. Watson's sympathetic and comprehensive study of the hymn, Florence Boos on 'Working-Class Poetry', and J.-A. George on 'Poetry in Translation', this last containing an interesting assessment of women poets and their role as translators.

The second part of the volume starts with Lee Erickson's informative account of the gloomy state of the Victorian market for poetry and progresses through Nathalie Houston's study of canon formation, 'Anthologies and the Making of the Poetic Canon', Joanne Shattock on 'Reviewing', and Lorraine Kooistra's illuminating essay on 'Poetry and Illustration', which helpfully includes a number of plates in its accounts of the varying attitudes of poets to their illustrators, from Tennyson's objections to William Allingham's active involvement. Part 3 begins with Margaret Linley on 'Nationhood and Empire': one of the few essays which seemed disappointing in terms of its inclusiveness, as I was expecting some discussion of the poets writing from the margins of empire, as well as a concentration on Tennyson's great British epic, *Idylls of the King*. Matthew Campbell's succeeding 'Poetry in the

Four Nations' also opens with *Idylls*, but then moves outward into a fascinating discussion of Celticism and the cultural connections and disjunctions between English, Irish, Scottish, and Welsh writing. The essay largely focuses on Ireland, though Scotland also features briefly. W. David Shaw comes next with 'Poetry and Religion', a subtle discussion which ranges widely in philosophy. Readers of work such as Cynthia Scheinberg's (see below) might, however, want to question the assumption here that religion was inevitably Christian in emphasis. From religion we move to science, as Alan Rauch summarizes complex scientific and technological debates and their impact on poetry, and to 'Landscape and Cityscape' (an interesting title, rather than 'Nature'), in which Pauline Fletcher nicely reads the transformation of the Romantic Sublime in Victorian poetry. Catherine Maxwell's 'Vision and Visuality' is one of a few essays to discuss previous critical works at any length, and is relatively unusual in presenting a wider argument through an exemplary reading of one poet, Hardy. In the final essays, Julia Saville discusses the great marriage poems of the nineteenth century, and John Maynard gives a theoretically informed and entertaining reading of our response to Victorian sexuality in its many guises.

Blackwell also brought out a student's selection of Victorian poetry in the Essential Literature series, edited by Valentine Cunningham and Duncan Wu. This volume is a condensed version of Cunningham's *The Victorians: An Anthology of Poetry and Poetics*, and is designed as a first introduction to the topic, and to provide students with a small and inexpensive edition of some of the most influential poems of the period. The selection is therefore relatively predictable: the greatest hits of Tennyson and the Brownings account for much of the volume, plus Arnold and Clough, Christina Rossetti's 'Remember' and 'Goblin Market', and a number of poems by Hardy and Hopkins, with Yeats representing the close of the century. There are some more unusual selections. Emily Brontë, for instance, is judged by this collection as equally important as Barrett Browning, Hopkins, Yeats, etc., and Dante Gabriel Rossetti is also elevated to a place in this poetic canon. A volume of this size and scope can naturally not hope to encompass the diversity of Victorian poetry, but it does seem strange, to take the most evident example, to have eighteen poems by Rossetti and none by Swinburne. The concentration on a small number of authors prevents the inclusion of poems which are more quirky, more alien to modern sensibilities, or less easily assessed on our criteria of greatness: nonsense verse, working-class poetry, specifically political poetry, hymns, jingoistic poetry, dialect poetry—in short, popular poetry of all kinds, as considered in the Blackwell *Companion*. This book is a good starting-point for the lay reader, but for the student it should serve as a taster for the larger volume rather than one that should be read alone. In addition, while the pocket size of the book would make it easily portable, the font, similarly condensed, is tricky to read.

Two studies in 2002 dealt with ideas of haunting, the afterlife of texts, and their influences: Robert Douglas-Fairhurst's *Victorian Afterlives: The Shaping of Influence in Nineteenth-Century Literature* and, with less attention to poetry, Julian Wolfreys' *Victorian Hauntings: Spectrality, Gothic, the Uncanny and Literature*. Douglas-Fairhurst's book is wide-ranging and generally concerned with far-reaching relations between texts and contexts. These relations include the textual influence of one work on another, but also take in the personal influence of friends, lovers, and contemporaries, the sense of 'influence' as something in the atmosphere, like a contagion, and the idea of being 'under the influence', in terms of being controlled or moved by something or someone. Nineteenth-century anxieties about the afterlife (or lack of one) are additionally related to interest in how influence might continue after death: the personal afterlife and the afterlife of the text are shared concerns. The writers discussed here—Keats, Hardy, Tennyson, and FitzGerald, among others—were all, Douglas-Fairhurst argues, writing for the future, yet were forced to recognize their engagement with the past. Their texts work as 'mediums' (p. 62), in the sense of something which negotiates between the living and the dead.

Poetry is at the heart of Douglas-Fairhurst's thinking. His first chapters usefully interrogate the work of Harold Bloom and Jerome McGann, and he continues a general discussion of influence, sympathy, and contagion in the next chapters by juxtaposing an immense variety of texts, including poems by Keats, the Brownings, and Hardy. The final two chapters are more focused, simply because they concentrate on two individuals: Tennyson and FitzGerald. Tennyson's poems, Douglas-Fairhurst nicely comments, 'resist their own confines on the pages and reach out to test, unsettle, quarrel with each other' (p. 196). Tennyson's habit of borrowing from his own past work besides that of others, and, in addition, his deep concern with the continuity—or otherwise—of life and afterlife, make him the perfect writer for this study. FitzGerald was equally, Douglas-Fairhurst shows, interested in issues of influence and survival through his work on translation. Critical discussions of Victorian poetry often neglect FitzGerald, and this chapter goes some way towards re-establishing his importance, by indicating how his translations engage with the afterlife of poetry by working with and against the past (the original text which he translates), the present (the work of contemporaries, particularly Tennyson), and the future, which is repeatedly imagined in his verse.

The great strength of *Victorian Afterlives* lies in the brilliance of Douglas-Fairhurst's close readings, and particularly in his attention to the workings of literary form. Conflicts over influence are often revealed through the dynamics of a single word, line, or phrase. This book is full of inspired instances of interpretation. To take only one brief example, he comments on a line from Hardy, 'I play my sweet old airs': 'there is a sudden thickening of the voice on "my sweet" because only now does he hear that she could have been playing *old* airs to recall her husband, "my sweet" to the time when she had first sung for him' (p. 51) The movement between the particularity of such close readings and the more general line of argument can occasionally be hard to follow, though Douglas-Fairhurst's dazzling shifts between disparate authors and ideas are nonetheless impressive.

An important contribution to scholarly work on the early nineteenth century was Richard Cronin's *Romantic Victorians: English Literature, 1824–1840*. Cronin's work is discussed elsewhere in this volume, but it is worth noting that much of his argument about ideas of citizenship in literature of the 1820s and 1830s rests on discussions of Tennyson, Hallam, and the Brownings. Cronin's account of how nationalism becomes a central issue in poetry is compelling. His chapter on Tennyson's and Hallam's shifting political loyalties, including an excellent analysis of Tennyson's poetry in the light of the disastrous Apostolic involvement in Spanish affairs, is very good, as is the material on Browning's *Strafford* and *Sordello*. He also reads Barrett Browning as the poet who, more than any of her contemporaries, succeeded in developing a 'poetic manner that could appeal directly to the reader's sense of social responsibility' (p. 180). These chapters contribute to the ongoing reassessment of nineteenth-century poetry's negotiations with politics. Cronin is also acute on questions of religion and poetry and on Shelleyan free love, 'the most dangerous of Romantic legacies' (p. 237), which he explores from Tennyson's *Lover's Tale* to *Aurora Leigh*. As a whole, *Romantic Victorians* succeeds well in its goal of conveying a sense of the diversity and consequence of literature in the neglected decades between 'Romanticism' and 'Victorianism'.

Missed last year was Catherine Maxwell's significant reassessment of gender and the male poet in *The Female Sublime from Milton to Swinburne: Bearing Blindness* [2001], a book which synthesizes many of the ideas expressed in her earlier articles on Victorian poetry. Three chapters of this book deal with Victorian poets: Tennyson, Browning, and Swinburne. Maxwell sums up her argument in the final chapter in these terms: 'Most signally, male poets beholding the spectacle of the blinded Milton have found themselves in diverse ways duplicating him and the feminized modes he offers ... Male poets mime or identify with Sappho ... or are blinded and feminized by her gaze' (p. 189). *The Female Sublime* thus fits well with work on Sappho and Victorian poets by Yopie Prins and Margaret Reynolds, and also contributes significantly to our understanding of how Milton's influence shaped nineteenth-century writing. In addition, Shelley looms large in the Victorian chapters of this volume, and Maxwell clearly perceives him as the most important presence in the writing of these poets. She shows how, following Shelley, poetry was associated with the sublime through its expression of intense, often painful, emotion. This particular version of the sublime, she argues, was strongly associated with the feminine, and all these male poets therefore enact versions of submission to a female sublime which is frequently figured as aggressive and powerful, able, as she notes of Browning's representations of women, to 'overwhelm the rigidities of "masculine" identity and even reconstruct it' (p. 163).

Maxwell's arguments are subtle and intelligent, and her discussion of how concepts of the sublime can be related to the increasing feminization of male poets and poetry in the Victorian period is a valuable addition to similar arguments in recent years. Each individual chapter here could be read alone, given that they open out the poems under discussion to a variety of readings and reconsider critical interpretations. Tennyson's 'Eleanore', for instance, is reread in the light of Shelley's comments on Sappho, rather than being seen in terms of Sappho's own writing, and a comparison of Ida in *The Princess* to Milton's Satan draws out previously unnoticed aspects of her role. Relatively unfamiliar Browning poems, such as 'Artemis Prologizes' or 'Beatrice Signorini', become highlights of the discussion in chapter 4, while a poem as famous as 'My Last Duchess' still provides an opportunity for an enhanced reading of the relation between the speaker and the 'female sublime' of the portrait. Swinburne is read as the most conspicuous advocate of ideas obliquely expressed by his contemporaries, engaging openly with the male poet's masochistic submission to the feminine. Overall, these three chapters try to demonstrate that Tennyson, Browning, and Swinburne are all more unconventional in their representations of gender than has often been assumed, and largely succeed in doing so.

Arnold, Tennyson, and Wilde are briefly discussed in Emily Haddad's *Orientalist Poetics: The Islamic Middle East in Nineteenth-Century English and French Poetry*. While this book is mainly concerned with earlier nineteenth-century poetry, Haddad does consider Arnold's 'The Sick King in Bokhara' as representative of a tendency to discuss Nature in poetry of the East as limited, compromised, and unforgiving; and she writes interestingly on Tennyson's oriental poems, including the little-discussed early work, 'Written by an Exile of Bassorah'. For detailed accounts of how these writers and Wilde, who is not discussed at any length, dealt with Eastern themes, however, it would be best to look elsewhere. Haddad's conclusion in general is that the Victorian poems she deals with are 'unexceptional' in their use of the Orient, straightforwardly deploying stock poetic tropes.

With regard to minor Victorian poets, an interesting reissue this year was Piers Brendon's *Hawker of Morwenstow: Portrait of a Victorian Eccentric*, first published in 1975 and now available again in paperback. Brendon's account of the strangeness and peculiarities of Robert Stephen Hawker's life in a remote Cornish parish remains lively, highly entertaining, and informative, and his suggestion that Hawker was 'both violently at odds with his age and startlingly representative of it' (p. 23) still rings true. Besides the anecdotes of Hawker's famed practical jokes and accounts of his idiosyncratic mysticism and opium-induced fantasies, the reader of this volume learns a great deal about, for instance, the difficulties of life in an isolated parish, the religious background to the period, contemporary ideas about sexual morality, the hardships endured by the working classes in Cornwall, and the heavy workload of their priests. Hawker's poetry, including his Arthurian legend *The Quest of the Sangraal*, a Victorian poem which deserves to be more widely known, is not the chief focus here, but is discussed with knowledge and insight. Those extracts which are given suggest that it may be worthy of more sustained critical attention than it has received.

Another minor poet who re-emerged this year was Eugene Lee-Hamilton, whose *Selected Poems* were edited by Macdonald Jackson. Lee-Hamilton (1845–1907), Vernon Lee's half-brother, began his career as a diplomat but after a few years became a chronic invalid, more or less confined to his bed in Florence for two decades. His poetry, Jackson notes, is always marked by this experience of (psychosomatic) illness and suffering. Jackson argues that Lee-Hamilton's dramatic monologues, with their 'preoccupation with the macabre, the deviant, and the violent' (p. 7) should be considered in the light of better-known experiments by Tennyson and Browning. In two key volumes of the 1880s, *The New Medusa* and *Apollo and Marsyas*, his characters, like Browning's, reveal themselves both intentionally and unintentionally, confessing their aberrations. From 1885 onwards, Lee-Hamilton turned to sonnets. Jackson describes *Imaginary Sonnets* [1888] as 'among the most innovative, idiosyncratic and imaginative of all English sonnet-sequences' (p. 17). This is characteristic of Jackson's measured yet passionate championship of Lee-Hamilton in his introduction, which certainly serves well to bolster his argument that this poet 'deserves readers'.

The poetry itself does not quite live up to the expectations raised by the introduction. Lee-Hamilton's representation of states of near-insanity and his exploration of temptation and sin are fascinating, but the fascination lies more in the situation than the language, though the simplicity of the latter can certainly add to the horror of the situation. These poems would certainly be worth discussing in relation to Browning and Swinburne, and Lee-Hamilton's frequent representation of nervous or disturbed young men also has its parallels in Victorian fiction. The selections from *Imaginary Sonnets* are in addition formally and generically notable because they explicitly combine the sonnet and the dramatic monologue, representing the thoughts of speakers from Henry I to Napoleon.

A significant addition to our knowledge of the range and scope of Victorian poetry was provided by a *Victorian Poetry* special issue on 'Nineteenth-Century Australian Poetry', edited by Meg Tasker and E. Warwick Slinn. Tasker points out the difficulties of assembling such a collection in her introduction, noting that the existence of the 'Victorian period' in Australia is problematic, and that questions of colonialism mean that only work identified as properly 'Australian' has tended to survive, as part of a national canon. As this volume shows, much Australian verse was also published in short-lived periodicals, and is hence difficult to trace. Yet the contributors here successfully indicate the different voices within Australian poetics, assess their relation to the British canon, and reconstruct the publishing culture of the day. The collection opens with Ian Reid's 'Marking the Unmarked: An Epitaphic Preoccupation in Nineteenth-Century Australian Poetry' (*VP* 40[2002] 7–20). He notes the number of poems dealing with lost or neglected graves in Douglas Sladen's influential collection, *A Century of Australian Song*, and argues persuasively that the image of the forgotten grave in the wilderness signals the Wordsworthian concept of poetry as epigraphy. Michael Ackland's 'From Wilderness to Landscape: Charles Harpur's Dialogue with Wordsworth and Antipodean Nature' (*VP* 40[2002] 21–32) deals more specifically with Wordsworth. Ackland discusses how Harpur, a self-educated republican and nationalist, read radicalism into late Wordsworth and borrowed his ideas to represent the virtues of antipodean nature.

Ann Vickery turns to women's poetry in 'A "Lonely Crossing": Approaching Nineteenth-Century Women's Poetry' (*VP* 40[2002] 33–54). She finds a sense of 'transitoriness' in the poems she studies, which range from Eliza Hamilton Dunlop's sympathetic 'The Aboriginal Mother', in the early decades of the century, to Louisa Lawson's suffragist poems at the close of the period. Her detailed research into these poets has revealed a wealth of material for further study. Barbara Garlick considers engaging problems of canonicity in her essay on James Brunton Stephens, 'Colonial Canons: The Case of James Brunton Stephens' (*VP* 40[2002] 55–70), a poet whose topical humorous verse, published in the popular press, was widely respected in his lifetime but has now become problematic due to the dated and racist sentiments it expresses. In 'Francis Adams and *Songs of the Army of the Night*: Negotiating Difference, Maintaining Commitment' (*VP* 40[2002] 71–86), Meg Tasker studies this volume of radical socialist verse and considers how Adams created an 'implied poet' who is both middle-class sympathizer and oppressed worker. Finally, Christopher Lee, 'An Uncultured Rhymer and his Cultural Critics: Henry Lawson, Class Politics and Colonial Literature' (*VP* 40[2002] 87–104), similarly writes on the neglected political verse of the writer Henry Lawson, which was again published in radical journals and reflected socialist interests of its day. As in many of the articles, this shows Australian poets negotiating with British concepts of culture and poetics, and incidentally demonstrates the popularity of poetry in the nineteenth-century Australian press.

There were several general articles on Pre-Raphaelite or 1890s poets and poetry. Laurence Starzyk contributed a theoretical discussion of ekphrasis in nineteenth-century poetics in '*Ut Pictura Poesis*: The Nineteenth-Century Perspective' (*VN* 102[2002] 1–9), which explores how the verbal and visual come to be seen 'not only as rivals, but as duplicates' (p. 1) in the period, and traces developments in poetic engagement with the image from Wordsworth to Browning and Rossetti. *Journal of Pre-Raphaelite and Aesthetic Studies* has one relevant general article: Thomas J. Tobin's 'The Pre-Raphaelite Craze in Nineteenth-Century Japanese Periodicals', which explores how Japanese admiration for Pre-Raphaelite art and literature mirrored the aesthetic craze for all things Japanese (*JPRAS* 11[2000] 95–113). An excellent article on Ernest Dowson appeared this year: Christine Roth's 'Ernest Dowson and the Duality of Late Victorian Girlhood: "Her Double Perversity"' (*ELT* 45[2000] 158–73). Roth explores Dowson's literary and personal relationships with the figure of the girl, a figure paradoxically seen as both chaste and inviolate, and as containing potential for corruption and sexuality. Her reading suggestively links Dowson's fascination with girlhood to the wider cultural context of the late nineteenth century. Dowson's obsession with the young Adelaide Foltinowicz is also discussed in Thomas Wright's 'The Poet in Hell' (*Wildean* 20[2000] 28–31), in which he suggests that Wilde's anecdote 'The Poet in Hell' was inspired by his knowledge of Dowson's life.

Women's poetry continues to be a source of valuable work. The most important book published in this field in 2002 is likely to be Cynthia Scheinberg's *Women's Poetry and Religion in Victorian England: Jewish Identity and Christian Culture*. Scheinberg argues strongly that women's religious poetry has been neglected and undervalued, perceived as limiting rather than as a 'site in which we find evidence of women's creative and original engagements with religious text and theology' (p. 3). She surveys previous work on women's poetry, and comments that many important feminist analyses have neglected the importance of religious issues. This is a central and recurring point throughout the book, yet even more crucial is her argument that, when religion has been discussed, 'religion' is presumed to mean Christianity, eliding other identities and negotiations with non-Christian texts. Given the clear predominance of Christianity in British Victorian culture and literature, Scheinberg has to work hard to convince the reader that Jewishness is a key issue, and it is a tribute to her book that she generally succeeds. At some points this book does seem to strain to prove its point: Scheinberg has constantly to stress that her discussion of religious identity and female identity can be related to Judaism, even where the relation is not entirely clear. There is hence some disparity between the chapters on Barrett Browning and Christina Rossetti, where the argument about their relation to Jewish identity goes slightly against the grain, and the discussions of Grace Aguilar and Amy Levy, whose Jewishness was inevitably a constituent part of their poetic identity. That said, Scheinberg admirably draws the reader's attention to the 'intersections, collisions, contradictions and elisions between the languages of femaleness and Jewishness' (p. 35). Women poets, she notes, frequently turned to images of the Jewish outsider when figuring their own poetic identity. As poetry became increasingly associated with religious practice, women's lack of access to Christian theological power meant that they identified with the religious other. As a whole, *Women's Poetry and Religion* shows the extent to which Victorian writers alluded to Jewish texts, and suggests many directions for further study in this field.

This year also produced Garlick, ed., *Tradition and the Poetics of Self in Nineteenth-Century Women's Poetry*, which discusses Elizabeth Barrett Browning, Caroline Bowles Southey, Emily Dickinson, and Christina Rossetti as writers who sought to locate themselves within or to form a female tradition. Many of the essays in the volume relate to the vague idea of the 'poetics of self', an idea which could encompass most discussions of women's poetry. Barbara Garlick's introduction identifies the shared feature of that poetry as 'adventurousness' (p. vii), a willingness to challenge convention and to work against as well as in various traditions. The first essay, Virginia Blain's '"*Be* these his daughters?"': Caroline Bowles Southey, Elizabeth Barrett Browning and Disruption in a Patriarchal Poetics of Women's Autobiography' (pp. 1–22) is the most concerned with tradition in the sense of poetic inheritance. Blain traces an anxiety about the father–daughter relationship running from Caroline Southey's *The Birth-Day* to Barrett Browning's *Aurora Leigh*, a line of connection which, she suggests, could be retrospectively read as a tradition. In the next essay, '*Aurora Leigh*: Barrett Browning's Novel Approach to the Woman Poet' (pp. 23–41), Meg Tasker argues that the 'novelistic' qualities of *Aurora Leigh* make it suitable for a Bakhtinian reading, in which it could be seen as part of a novelization of culture, part of a movement to question and subvert conventional genres. The third essay on Barrett Browning, E. Warwick Slinn's 'Elizabeth Barrett Browning and the Problem of Female Agency' (pp. 43–55) is a clever analysis of her presentation of agency and subjectivity. Slinn argues that her poems open up possibilities for 'female subjects whose double utterance constitutes a cultural critique and therefore political action' (p. 45), and demonstrates this through a subtle reading of 'Lord Walter's Wife'.

Turning next to the largest set of essays, those on Christina Rossetti, we start with Susan Conley's 'Burying the Medusa: Romantic Bloodlines in Christina Rossetti's Gothic Epistle' (in Garlick, ed., pp. 97–115). Like Laurence Roussillon on Dante Gabriel and the Medusa myth (see below), Conley links the Medusa to sexuality, but also, more specifically, to a critique of Romanticism and shift towards Christianity in 'The Convent Threshold'. Next, Sharon Bickle's 'A Woman of Women for "A Sonnet of Sonnets": Exploring Female Subjectivity in Christina Rossetti's *Monna Innominata*' (pp. 117–35) discusses Rossetti as a 'translator of and for women' (p. 118), suggesting that she reveals the multiple voices of the suppressed female poetic tradition, chiefly by associating her sonnets with Barrett Browning and the unknown *donne innominate* of the sequence. In '"Thus only in a dream": Appetite in Christina Rossetti's Poetry' (pp. 137–54), C.C. Barfoot argues persuasively, through an excellent reading of 'The Heart Knoweth its Own Bitterness', that Rossetti should be more celebrated as a poet of the physical, giving flesh to the soul's appetites. The succeeding essay, 'Defacing the Self: Christina Rossetti's *The Face of the Deep* as Absolution' (pp. 155–75), turns to prose, as Barbara Garlick assesses how Rossetti reveals the self in her biblical commentary, reconciling the physical face, or surface, with the spiritual self. Garlick concludes by noting that even in death physical images of Rossetti obscured her work. The last essay in the collection, Tomoko Takiguchi's 'Christina Rossetti in Secrecy: Revising the Poetics of Sensibility' (pp. 177–92), investigates points of intersection between Tractarianism and sensibility, and considers sensibility and secrecy (a version of Tractarian reserve) in Hemans, Landon, and Rossetti.

Several essays on women poets appeared in *Victorian Poetry*. In 'Fated Marginalization: Women and Science in the Poetry of Constance Naden' (*VP* 40[2002] 107–30), Patricia Murphy provides an important reading of how Naden's scientific poetry supplies disquieting insights into male scientific preoccupations with female inferiority. Mathilde Blind also emerges as a daring and disturbing poet in James Diedrick's '"My love is a force that will force you to care": Subversive Sexuality in Mathilde Blind's Dramatic Monologues' (*VP* 40[2002] 359–86). This is a wide-ranging and well-researched article which sets Blind's 1891 collection, *Dramas in Miniature*, in her personal, cultural, and intellectual contexts. Another good reading of a late Victorian female poet in context is Jessica Walsh's '"The strangest pain to bear": Corporeality and Fear of Insanity in Charlotte Mew's Poetry' (*VP* 40[2002] 217–40), which considers how Mew's poetry tries to 'conquer and categorize what she saw as a disobedient, unruly body' (p. 218), and relates her sense of isolation and alienation to the powerful strangeness of poems such as 'Saturday Market'. Also in *VP*, Paul Ellis, 'Radical Myths: Eliza Keary's *Little Seal-Skin and Other Poems*' (*VP* 40[2002] 387–408), discusses Yorkshire poet Eliza Keary's volume, *Little Seal-Skin* [1874], attempting, with mixed success, to assess her work in theoretical terms and determine the presence of a feminist consciousness.

Jean Ingelow was the subject of a brief note in *N&Q* (49[2002] 492–3), in which Rosalind Porter identifies the author of *Some Recollections of Jean Ingelow and her Friends* as Eliza Ingelow, Jean's sister. A new letter from Hamilton Aide to Ingelow also provides Robert Dingley with a source for a description of William Barnes's London reading (*N&Q* 49[2002] 73–4).

Only one full-length book was published on Matthew Arnold this year, Alan Grob's *A Longing like Despair: Arnold's Poetry of Pessimism*. Grob laments the decline in new studies of Arnold, and sets out to give a major reassessment of his poetry. He focuses on the philosophy which underlies Arnold's characteristic bleakness, the pessimism which is 'self-evidently most central to his poetry, the malaise that suffuses it, the tragic sense that resides at its very core' (p. 41). He traces the development of this pessimism through Arnold's poetic career, and associates it with European philosophy—primarily Schopenhauer—though less as a direct influence than as a shared sensibility. Arnold's pessimism, he notes, also looks forward to Nietzsche, Freud, and modernism. Grob's individual chapters generally concentrate on one or two poems as they study Arnold's anti-humanistic tendencies, his inability to reconcile individual life with the life of the universe without rejecting human consciousness, his demystification of romantic love, and his troubled sexuality. On the whole, Grob's argument that Arnold's career reverses the general nineteenth-century movement from optimistic historicism to metaphysical pessimism is compelling, and his detailed readings of the poetry support his thesis well. Despite the emphasis on close reading, however, there is a tendency here to read poems as philosophical documents rather than concentrating on the specifics of language, form, etc.—which in many cases could have backed up Grob's readings.

One chapter in Amanda Anderson's *The Powers of Distance: Cosmopolitanism and the Culture of Detachment* is devoted to Arnold, presenting a complex argument which sees him as a thinker who negotiates between subjective, personal understanding and universal, objective standards of judgement. She discusses Arnold's work on cultural and racial heritage as contributing to a sense of 'embodied universality', which to some extent combines these positions. Anderson's arguments, while not always clearly expressed, are certainly worth pursuing.

The Brontës were the subject of several articles focusing on poetry. Linda Austin, in 'Emily Brontë's Homesickness' (*VS* 44[2002] 573–96), discusses scientific discourses on nostalgia, particularly associationist psychology, and attempts to read these into Brontë's poems, considering how poems which seem relatively conventional might reflect on significant scientific debates of their day. In '"Veritable Utterances": Mid-Victorian Interpretations of Emily Brontë's Poems' (*BST* 27[2002] 201–10), Susan Bauman considers how three mid-century reviews constructed Brontë as a female poet, reading her poems in terms of emotional expression, as opposed to earlier reviews in which her gender was uncertain. This volume of *Brontë Society Transactions* also reprints the major review Bauman discusses: *The Christian Remembrancer*'s 'Minor Poets of the Day' (*BST* 27[2002] 219–25). Emma Mason, 'Emily Brontë and the Enthusiastic Tradition' (*RoN* 25[2002]; 19 paras.) explores how Emily Brontë's poems relate to the language of enthusiasm, particularly as found in late eighteenth-century poetics and Methodist religious discourse. She demonstrates well how religious and poetical enthusiasm merge in Brontë's Romantic verse. Alexandra Leach turns to Anne Brontë and religion in 'Escaping the Body's Gaol: The Poetry of Anne Brontë' (*VN* 101[2002] 27–31). She argues that Anne Brontë's work develops from stock Romantic stereotypes into more reflective, Christian works, which reuse Romantic images to argue for the virtues of narrowness and renunciation.

One of the key works to be published in Victorian poetry this year was the two-volume, *The Letters of Elizabeth Barrett Browning to her Sister Arabella*, edited by Scott Lewis. In a review of these letters, 'Viva la trattoria' (*LRB* 25[2002] 28–30) Ruth Bernard Yeazell comments that 'one may even be tempted to conclude that [Barrett Browning's] epistolary art surpasses her achievement as a poet', indicating the degree to which her letters might be valued. These two volumes, reaching over 1,000 pages and containing many unpublished letters from the Berg Library and the Moulton-Barrett collection, will be invaluable for Browning scholars. Arabella was one of Barrett Browning's most faithful and valued correspondents, though her letters have not survived. 'You will set me down as bewitched, Arabel, for sending you all these politics—you would rather hear about Flush perhaps', one of Barrett Browning's letters teasingly suggests (vol. 1, p. 156). The sisters did certainly correspond about their shared interest in Flush—although it is rapidly superseded by interest in Pen—and other domestic and family matters, but Arabel was clearly also keen to hear about Elizabeth's views on politics, art, and religion.

These volumes follow Barrett Browning through her interest in French and Italian politics, her marriage and childbirth, her growing fascination with spiritualism, and the writing of *Aurora Leigh* and *Men and Women*. Of particular note is the number of letters which mention religious issues in Britain, undoubtedly because of Arabella's strong commitment to a Dissenting congregation. As the volumes progress, however, sarcastic references to 'Puseyism' are replaced by a fervent interest in spiritualism, as Barrett Browning's letters pile up evidence to convince her correspondent. These letters also show the Brownings' precarious financial situation: delight at their economy or dismay at their lack of funds are recurring themes. Barrett Browning also makes a number of wry comments on her role as a female writer, such as this revealing statement about the Laureateship: 'The gallantry of England always takes care, thoughtfully taking off its hat, to push a woman against the wall, on principle' (p. 319). As she defies convention to meet

George Sand, and laments missing a meeting with George Eliot, her allegiances to other female writers are also clarified. Lewis's notes to the letters are exemplary: detailed, scholarly, and comprehensive. The volume also includes useful appendices on Barrett Browning's family and friends, plus a copy of the photo album Browning bought her, with its *cartes de visite* of friends and celebrities. All those awaiting the completion of Lewis and Kelley's *The Brownings' Correspondence* will be delighted with these beautifully produced volumes.

Elsewhere, Marjorie Stone provides a stimulating comparison between Barrett Browning and Toni Morrison in 'Between Ethics and Anguish: Feminist Ethics, Feminist Aesthetics, and Representations of Infanticide in "The Runaway Slave at Pilgrim's Point" and *Beloved*' (in Glowacka and Boos, eds., *Between Ethics and Aesthetics: Crossing the Boundaries*, pp. 131–58). Stone questions the ethics of soliciting an aesthetic response to the unspeakable, as both these texts (and Barrett Browning's sonnet on the Greek Slave) strive to do, and by setting Barrett Browning and Morrison in their contemporary contexts she produces excellent readings of their similarities and differences. Barrett Browning's sonnets are, in addition, a key part of Erik Gray's argument in 'Sonnet Kisses: Sidney to Barrett Browning' (*EIC* 52[2002] 56–75), a clever, lively, and original article about how the sonnet tradition embodies the act of kissing. *Sonnets from the Portuguese* are read in terms of their awkward self-awareness, and the uncomfortable reality of their kisses.

A new student guide to Robert Browning came out this year in the Routledge Complete Critical Guide series. Stefan Hawlin's *The Complete Critical Guide to Robert Browning* makes a good job of providing a short yet comprehensive introduction to Browning's life and works. It is divided into sections on 'Life and Contexts', 'Work', and 'Criticism', with detailed cross-references between the three. In the first and shortest part, Hawlin's account of Browning's contexts lays welcome stress on Shelley's influence and on Browning's encounters with the theatre, besides clearly explaining the circumstances of Browning's courtship and marriage and his interest in Italian affairs. The second section, on Browning's works, sees Hawlin with the near-impossible task of discussing all of Browning's poetry in under a hundred pages. From the early poetry, he pays close attention to *Paracelsus* and *Sordello*—though even given his useful summary of *Sordello*'s narrative, most beginning students of Browning will probably skip these and turn straight to the dramatic monologues, where 'My Last Duchess', 'Count Gismond', 'Porphyria's Lover', and 'Pictor Ignotus' are the chief selections for discussion, with 'A Lost Leader' added to show Browning in a more overtly political light. Hawlin is good on Browning's use of irony in dramatic monologues and his explanations are careful and lucid, neatly relating close readings of the poems to critical debates over them. He then reads *Men and Women* in the contexts of art, religion, and love. This last discussion was one of the few points in the book where it seemed that limitations of space were allowing some generalizations: the private intensity of Browning's poetry of relationships is unquestioned, but to state that this means the poems are 'largely unconcerned with marriage or relationships as a public or social fact' (p. 96) seems too bald, particularly given recent readings of marriage in Victorian poetry as an image of political union. Hawlin's short accounts of 'A Woman's Last Word' and 'A Lover's Quarrel', reading these poems as purely about loss, regret, and submission, also ignore alternative readings of the poems as potentially much more forceful and threatening.

Minor quibbles like these also come into Hawlin's study of *The Ring and the Book*, where, surprisingly, there is almost no discussion of Book I, Guido's monologues or that of the Pope, in favour of a concentration on 'Half-Rome', Pompilia, and Caponsacchi. Choices like this are inevitable in such a brief survey, but given that Hawlin's readers are likely to focus on those parts of the poem he seems to recommend, his selections carry considerable weight. With regard to the later poems, he takes a valuable look at *Red-Cotton Night-Cap Country*, 'Ivan Ivanovitch', 'The Parleying with Gerard de Lairesse', and 'Beatrice Signorini'. The closing discussion of criticism seems fairly comprehensive, and his selection of the key works from the last two decades indisputable. Again, Hawlin nicely balances description of critical concerns with a close look at rival readings of particular passages, thus providing helpful illustrations of critical ideas. Overall, this critical guide will be deservedly indispensable for students working on Browning, and should amply serve its purpose of interesting them and guiding them towards further reading.

Several articles also dealt with Browning. Robert Inglesfield, 'Allusion in Robert Browning's "A Death in the Desert"' (*VN* 102[2000] 27–8), briefly discusses how 'A Death in the Desert' relates to contemporary ideas about the progressive, historical concept of revelation. Catherine Ross, in a fascinating if not totally believable reading, gives 'Porphyria's Lover' a surprising twist by suggesting that Porphyria may not die: the 'strangling' might be a game of erotic asphyxiation, rather than straightforward murder (*Expl* 60[2000] 68–72). Michaela Giesenkirchen's '"But Sordello, and My Sordello?": Pound and Browning's Epic' (*M/M* 8[2002] 623–42), is helpful on modernism's deep indebtedness to Browning, focusing on the mixture of irreverence and admiration in Pound's rewriting of Browning's poem. Two further notes appeared on *Sordello*. Britta Martens convincingly suggests that the 'pointing-pole' does not relate to contemporary dioramas but to the puppet-show in *Don Quixote*, where a garrulous boy narrates the action of the puppets (*N&Q* 49[2002] 62–3). In 'Sordello's Story Mis-Told' (*N&Q* 49[2002] 475–6), Stephen Brown points out an inaccuracy in one of Pettigrew's notes to the Penguin edition: Palma is betrothed, rather than married, to Richard of Saint Boniface, a crucial distinction in the plot. *Studies in Browning and his Circle*, which contains further articles on both Brownings, was unavailable for consultation this year and will be discussed in next year's volume.

As mentioned above, Carroll's poems were published in a selected edition, edited by Keith Silver. This is a slim volume, but it does contain the key poems from *Alice in Wonderland* and *Sylvie and Bruno*, all of 'The Hunting of the Snark' with its original Tenniel illustrations, and several of Carroll's other pieces. Silver's introduction gives a brief biographical sketch of Carroll and sets his poems in the context of debates over evolution and science, progress and time. He notes that Carroll's poems, like his fiction, can be far from comfortable in forcing the reader to recognize how their strange logic mimics and mocks a common-sense view of the world. This is a cheap and nicely produced text which will undoubtedly be very useful.

Clough appeared in only two short articles: Gary H. Paterson's 'Lionel Johnson and Arthur Hugh Clough: An Ironic Debt' (*VP* 40[2002] 255–60), in which Paterson finds a source for Johnson's 'A Burden of Easter Vigil' in Clough's 'Easter Day', and Francis O'Gorman's 'An Unnoticed Version of A. H. Clough's "Chrysea kles epi glossa'" (N&Q 49[2002] 48–9), which discusses a version of this poem found in Thomas Arnold's notebook, dated 1841. With the exception of Douglas-Fairhurst's chapter, there was also little work on FitzGerald this year, though Christopher Decker, 'Echoes and Parallels in FitzGerald's Rubaiyat' (N&Q 49[2002] 65–8) did produce a lengthy and helpful list of allusions in the Rubaiyat, demonstrating FitzGerald's familiarity with poets from Spenser to Tennyson.

After last year's strong showing for Hardy's poetry, his poems were the subject of one book and several short notes in 2002. A helpful reissue from Palgrave in 2001, missed last year, was James Gibson's standard edition of Hardy's poems, first published in 1976 and still going strong. It is now again readily available in both hardback and paperback. The Thomas Hardy Yearbook published one article on Hardy's poetry, Trevor Johnson's ' "A Unique Quality of Elegiac Feeling": Hardy's "During Wind and Rain"' (THY 33[2002] 20–7). This expands previous comments made by Johnson on this poem, further analysing the poem's narrative progression, its biographical resonances, and its stylistic qualities. The first volume of THY is of general interest to Hardy scholars, since it consists of the Sotheby's sale catalogue for the Adams collection, which contained many manuscripts, books owned by Hardy (including annotated volumes of Shelley and Browning), and copies of his own works. Martin Ray published four notes on Hardy's poems in Notes and Queries. These remark, in sequence, Hardy's aversion to female reviewers and a new identification of the author of a particularly offensive review; an allusion to Verdi in 'The Dead Man Walking'; the identification of the comet in 'The Comet at Yellham' as Donati's comet; and the change of title in 'Drummer Hodge', caused by the discovery of a poem entitled 'The Dead Drummer' by Richard Barham Harris (N&Q 49[2002] 490–2).

Another addition to work on Hardy this year was Byungwa Joh's Thomas Hardy's Poetry: A Jungian Perspective. Published as part of the Modernist Revolution in World Literature series, it gives a brief assessment of how a psychoanalytical reading of Hardy's poems demonstrates their affinity with Jung's archetypes, particularly that of the mother. The book is more likely to be of interest to Jungians than to Hardy scholars: readings of the poems tend to be basic, historical context is reduced to loose generalizations about the Victorian period, and the focus on reducing Hardy's poems to biographical and psychological documents serves to shut down their ambiguity and complexity. The book is also marred by its English, which is relatively stilted. If Joh's work is seen, as the series title suggests, as an assessment of how modernist ideas might stem from or retrospectively affect our readings of nineteenth-century poetry, then it does hold points of interest, and it certainly provides a good example of how Jung's ideas might be mapped onto literature. But whether this is helpful or not must depend on the reader's willingness to accept the value and truth of Jungian readings.

This has been a very active year in Hopkins studies, and he emerges as the most popular Victorian poet in 2002 by quite a distance. The key work published was probably Bernadette Waterman Ward's World as Word: Gerard Manley Hopkins and Philosophical Theology. Despite the somewhat forbidding title this is a refreshingly lucid account of Hopkins's interest in ideas expressed by Oxford contemporaries, and by mentors such as Ruskin and Newman, plus an interpretation of how these interact with his fascination with Duns Scotus. Ward's reading is strongly against post-structuralist or theoretical interpretations of Hopkins which neglect his intellectual involvement with theological issues. She argues that, for Hopkins, language always involved responsibility towards the world, and the quest for meaning was a quest for something certain, tangible, and even real. Throughout his education at Oxford, the Oratory, and Stonyhurst, Hopkins, Ward suggests, searched for a resolution to his concerns about the subjectivity of religious knowledge by testing various theories—Newman's view that knowledge was based on trust and love, Ruskin's reliance on emotional conviction, and Duns Scotus's philosophy that objects contain within them many different and equally valid perceptions.

Ward is especially good at explaining Duns Scotus, whose theology and philosophy are certainly far from simple, in a comprehensible way. She suggests that Hopkins's inscape corresponds to Scotus's *formalitates*, a concept which serves to 'ground in the reality of a thing each of the many ways of understanding it' (p. 187), as opposed to the critical view that equates inscape with *haecceitas*, a term expressing the uniqueness of each individual thing. This means that for Hopkins 'a thing potentially has as many formalitates as there are truthful ways of looking at it' (p. 190). The word 'truthful' is evidently key here, as Ward wants less to show the multiplicity of interpretation than to suggest how for Hopkins the act of perception had to involve commitment, faith, and love. Faith itself involves a similar act of commitment, and artistic freedom in this faith is found by the ability to resist mastery by anything less than the fullest good. In art, there is no right way of interpretation or seeing, but there are preferable ways, those which are most informed by truth and love. This is an argument which carries great conviction here, not least because Ward's own love for her subject is evident. Her acute close readings of Hopkins's poems also contribute well to her analysis of his theological convictions. A brief review cannot do justice to the detailed material contained in *World as Word*, which should persuade any reader that Hopkins's philosophical theology must be understood if his poems are to be fully appreciated.

A second significant book on Hopkins, Norman White's *Hopkins in Ireland*, adds to White's excellent scholarly biography of Hopkins, now a decade old, by providing greater insight into the years he spent in Dublin. The depression and melancholy Hopkins suffered there, his sense of exile and isolation, have been well documented, but White adds illuminating details to our knowledge of the particular situation of the Englishman in late nineteenth-century Ireland. In tracing the debate which surrounded Hopkins's appointment as professor at University College Dublin, for instance, or even in pointing out how Hopkins's name and accent would immediately have marked him as different, White brings alive the hopelessness of his situation, 'wretchedly out of place ... useless for the students, his religion, and to himself' (p. 46). White is also not afraid of stressing Hopkins's own prejudices against Ireland and the Irish: the lack of sensitivity he showed is helpfully compared to Newman's more sympathetic stance. Yet we do also see how Hopkins became involved in Irish affairs, whether through his contribution of Hiberno-English words to Joseph Wright's *English Dialect Dictionary*, or through his interest in politics— a strong prejudice against Irish nationalism did not, as White comments, prevent Hopkins from appreciating that its success was inevitable.

The poems which Hopkins wrote during his five years in Ireland are largely read as biographical documents giving insight into his despair and mental instability. After the introductory chapters, each chapter focuses on a close reading of a particular poem or poems. The detail in these readings is astonishing: 'Spelt from Sibyl's Leaves', for example, is effectively read word by word. White's immense knowledge is indisputable and he is keenly alert to the sources of Hopkins's vocabulary. The only problem with such nuanced readings is that the poems are not reprinted in full: the reader of this volume needs to have their Hopkins to hand. At points, it is true, White's primary interest in the biographical and psychological implications of the poems, and the clear sense of a hierarchy in which some poems are preferable to others, results in slightly condescending-sounding judgements: this on 'The Soldier', for instance: 'Once the plot is understood the poem seems to have a charm, even though the modern reader still finds it difficult to sympathize with all the soldiering imagery and sentiments of a distant age' (p. 113). The deliberately old-fashioned tinge to comments like this is made clear by the virtual absence of any works published after 1970 in White's bibliography. *Hopkins in Ireland* is a fascinating, well-written, and readable addition to Hopkins studies, and probably the definitive account of Hopkins's years in Ireland, but those seeking more theorized readings of his poems will also want to look elsewhere.

An example of such a reading, very different to White or Ward, can be found in Michael M. Kaylor's queer reading of 'Epithalamion', '"Beautiful dripping fragments": A Whitmanesque Reading of Hopkins' "Epithalamion"' (*VP* 40[2002] 57–87). Kaylor identifies several points of reference between the narrative strategies of Hopkins and Whitman and their eroticized natural worlds. In a playful reading of 'Epithalamion', alert to all possible implications, he suggests that it is a more sensual and disturbing poem than has been appreciated. Tony Harte, 'Imago Christi: Hopkins and Whitman' (*Symbiosis* 6[2002] 1–26), also notes the shared sensuousness of Hopkins and Whitman, but concentrates rather on their shared religious sensibility in this article on 'The Wreck of the Deutschland' and Whitman's 'The Sleepers'.

No less than five further articles on Hopkins appeared in *Victorian Poetry*. Mark Wormald's 'Hopkins, *Hamlet* and the Victorians: Carrion Comfort?' (*VP* 40[2002] 409–31) sets Hopkins in the context of contemporary Shakespearian scholarship. Wormald looks at how Hopkins's notes reveal the influence of Charles Knight's edition of Shakespeare, and gives an excellent reading of how 'Carrion Comfort' is haunted by *Hamlet*. In '"Death blots black out": Thermodynamics and the Poetry of Gerard Manley Hopkins' (*VP* 40[2002] 131–55), Jude Nixon contributes significantly to the growing body of work on Hopkins and science, showing how both Oxford and Stonyhurst provided Hopkins with scientific communities where he could engage with concepts in nineteenth-century energetics—notably heat, waste, and recovery—which then inform his poems. Hilda Hollis contributed a short article on 'The Windhover' (*VP* 40[2002] 433–43), arguing that there are two birds in the poem, and that the poet's heart is stirred for the victim rather than the windhover itself. She sees this as part of a pattern of counterpoint evident in both form and content. Andrew Sean Davidson, in 'Toward a Pragmatic Poetics: The Convergence of Form, Art and Ontology in "The Leaden Echo and the Golden Echo"' (*VP* 40[2002] 189–200), briefly assesses how 'shifts in linguistic or aesthetic form function simultaneously as shifts in action and/or ontology' (p. 195) in this poem. Finally, the first lines of 'God's Grandeur' are re-examined by Elizabeth Villeponteaux (*VP* 40[2002] 201–8), who sees the oil and flame as religious, Trinitarian images.

Critical editions of a recently discovered comic poem and couplet by Hopkins were published by Joseph Feeney in *Hopkins Quarterly*. The first poem, 'Consule Jones', was written as a comic song to entertain Hopkins's fellow Jesuits. Feeney provides a full commentary explaining Hopkins's in-jokes, and even gives the original ballad tune to which it was sung (*HQ* 29[2002] 3–20). The couplet, 'To Jesus on my bed I sue', is dated by Feeney to Hopkins's undergraduate days (*HQ* 29[2002] 21–4). A useful biographical article by Fredric Schlatter, 'Martial Klein: Hopkins' Dublin Colleague' (*HQ* 29[2002] 69–105), adds to White's biography by shedding light on Martial Klein's career in Ireland. Klein was a colleague of Hopkins, though he later left the Roman Catholic Church; he was deeply identified with British interests in Ireland and hence caused minor crises for the Dublin establishment. Two Hopkins critics who were active in publishing elsewhere this year also have articles here. Nathan Cervo, in 'Hopkins' Translation of Horace's "Odi profanum vulgus"' (*HQ* 29[2002] 25–30), shows how many liberties Hopkins took with Horace's original, and argues that, rather than producing a straight translation, Hopkins altered Horace into a 'baroque masterpiece'. Cervo also published a short note on how the word 'buckle' links 'Harry Ploughman' to 'The Windhover' (*HQ* 29[2002] 106–8). Andrew Sean Davidson, 'Reading "the unshapeable shock night"': Symbolic Action and "The Wreck" of Gerard Manley Hopkins' (*HQ* 29[2002] 31–52), provides an analysis of performative language in 'The Wreck of the Deutschland'. He shows how Hopkins uses oxymoron to heighten a sense of devotion, and even provides a lengthy table separating his statements into 'The Order of Hell' and 'The Order of Heaven', dialectical pairings with Davidson sees as crucial. In 'Hopkins at the Bar: The Case of the Missing Will' (*HQ* 29[2002] 53–64), Schlatter examines the legal debate over the right to Hopkins's assets. Finally, Fiona Vance writes on 'Gerard Manley Hopkins: Poetry as Music' (*HQ* 29[2002] 109–25), a relatively straightforward discussion of music theory and poetry, though with interesting comments on sprung rhythm.

Elsewhere, Dennis Sobolev has published two articles on Hopkins in the last two years. In 'Hopkins' Mind: Between Allegory and Madness' (*ES* 82[2001] 34–43) he explores tropes of hell and madness in Hopkins, and suggests that, rather than critical attempts to allegorize 'Spelt from Sibyl's Leaves', it should be read as Hopkins's representation of the hellish state of the mind in its existential reality. Like Ward, he reconsiders inscape in 'Inscape Revisited' (*English* 51[2002] 219–34), similarly rejecting *haecceitas* as a probable explanation, and arguing instead that inscape is best described as 'embodied organized form' (p. 227). Joseph Gardner provided two notes on Hopkins in *ANQ*. In 'Hopkins and the Dragons of Chaos' (*ANQ* 15[2002] 44–7), he argues that the reference to 'endragoned seas' in 'The Wreck of the Deutschland' links the poem to the Hebrew Bible's dragons of chaos. '"But worse": Hopkins and Rossetti' (*ANQ* 15[2002] 21–3) is a brief comparison of Hopkins's view of hell with Dante Gabriel Rossetti's images in sonnet LXXXVI of 'The House of Life'. Hopkins also featured in several collections. In Meyer, ed., *Literature and Musical Adaptation*, Jennifer Stolpa contributed 'Henry Purcell and Gerard Manley Hopkins: Two Explorations of Identity' (pp. 47–59). Both poet and composer, she suggests, focus on 'a complex interaction between individual and group, soloist and chorus' (p. 48), and both thus consider ideas about social and individual identity. She argues convincingly that Hopkins would have known Purcell's sacred music, and that it can be read in relation to his poems. J. Robert Barth, in 'Wordsworth's "Immortality Ode" and Hopkins' "The Leaden Echo and the Golden Echo": In Pursuit of Transcendence' (in Barth, ed., *The Fountain Light: Studies in Romanticism and Religion*, pp. 111–27), suggests that both Hopkins and Wordsworth were writing about the search for lost transcendence. Their poems, he argues, see beyond nature by seeing into nature, and in doing so recognize a link between the earthly world and heaven.

Kevin O'Brien also included a specific chapter on Hopkins in his *Saying Yes at Lightning: Threat and the Provisional Image in Post-Romantic Poetry*, which, as the title suggests, is strongly influenced by Hopkins throughout. In general, O'Brien perceives Hopkins as key to his argument that the nineteenth century saw the poetic image as unstable and provisional, yet used imagery to confront this threat and to attempt to reach a sense of restoration and empowerment. This is an intriguing argument, though his discussion of it sometimes lacks clarity, and the book as a whole contains relatively little engagement with poetic form and structure in relation to imagery, and is uninterested in historical context. O'Brien's second chapter deals exclusively with 'The Wreck of the Deutschland', and he notes that imagistic 'convertibility' or 'reversibility' lies at the heart of the poem, in which disquieting images of force and violence are gradually brought into harmony with God. This line of thought is similar to that of Davidson's article (discussed above), and the two together contribute to an increased awareness of Hopkins's use of language in this poem.

Finally, Joaquin Kuhn and Joseph Feeney edited a tribute to Hopkins's work in the form of a series of highly personal essays from eminent critics, poets, performers, and Hopkins lovers from across the world. *Hopkins Variations: Standing Round a Waterfall* began as a twenty-fifth anniversary project of *Hopkins Quarterly*, the success of which prompted the editors to solicit a wider range of responses. The fifty-five essays here treat Hopkins from a variety of perspectives, many examining their first encounter with the poet, or the reading which prompted them to spend time—in many cases a lifetime—responding to his work. The general tenor of the essays is perhaps best summed up by the opening line of James Finn Cotter's piece, 'Reading Gerard Manley Hopkins has been the best thing to happen to me as a poet, a scholar, and a person' (p. 251). While not all contributors go this far, this is certainly a volume which celebrates a 'life-changing' view of Hopkins's work. As such, it is both fascinating and often touching, reminding the reader of the pleasure of reading and of the existence of a community of readers with shared interests. Hopkins scholars or fans will undoubtedly want to own this collection.

A significant addition was made to editions of Victorian poetry this year with the publication of Florence Boos's two-volume edition of Morris's *The Earthly Paradise*. It is clearly a labour of love, and she is very persuasive on the reasons why Morris's epic deserves to be read and considered more than it has been in the past. She argues that *The Earthly Paradise*: 'shares with other long Victorian poems a preoccupation with transience and incompletion, an excited sense of the beauty of older forms and rhythms, and a paradoxical intermixture of idealized historicism with bitter commentary on the corruptions of the present' (p. 3). The wider themes of the poem, she suggests, are loss and love, with the sense of the former deepening as the poem progresses (and, biographically, as Morris's marriage worsened). Morris emerges from this introduction as a boldly experimental writer, who deploys sophisticated techniques of framing and address throughout. As Boos notes, her edition is the first based on the Kelmscott text and thus undoes many changes made to the standard 1910 edition by May Morris, changes which in some cases (altering Morris's 'god' to 'God' throughout) significantly affected the poem's interpretation. The text here reproduces the typographical details of the Kelmscott edition as much as possible, and provides facsimiles of the title pages, and of Burne-Jones's illustrations, at the start of each volume. At the end of each volume, the collations record the changes made through each major version of the text.

Each pair of classical and medieval tales is helpfully preceded by a short summary of the narrative, comments on the sources used, and a brief critical analysis. These analyses are generally excellent, providing the reader with just enough explanation to engage with the text himself or herself. Boos's notes are also very good, displaying an extensive and detailed knowledge of Morris's alterations to his original sources. There is the odd discrepancy—the introduction to the 'Apology', the first part of the poem, seems to have been misprinted, as it begins its analysis with stanza 5—but this seems the exception rather than the norm. It is also a shame that the volumes are printed on such thin paper. However, we should be glad that they have been printed at all, and that Boos has made *The Earthly Paradise* fully accessible to a wider audience.

Morris was also discussed in Maxwell, ed., *The Victorian Illustrated Book*. Elizabeth K. Helsinger, in 'William Morris Before Kelmscott: Poetry and Design in the 1860s' (pp. 209–38), argues that the mid-1860s saw a new kind of poetry interested in structure, recurrent pattern, and repetition. Poetry hence came to resemble design, and Morris's poems are read as surfaces or structures for decoration and elaboration. Helsinger's comments on the folio edition of *The Earthly Paradise* and its use of Burne-Jones's images are excellent, and fit well with those of Boos.

Christina Rossetti, as noted above, is the subject of five out of ten essays in Garlick, ed., *Tradition and the Poetics of Self*. C.C. Barfoot's piece on Rossetti and appetite in that volume relates neatly to Anna Krugovoy Silver's longer discussion of Rossetti in *Victorian Literature and the Anorexic Body*. Anorexia nervosa was first diagnosed and classified during this period, but Silver is less interested in pursuing the medical angle than in arguing that anorexia provides a symbolic system or paradigm in Victorian texts. She is thus especially interested in tropes of fatness or slenderness, and ideas of consumption and fasting. Her fifth and final chapter, 'Christina Rossetti's Sacred Hunger', argues the standard line that Rossetti saw appetite as dangerously sensual, but attempts to set this in the context of religious fasting and the eucharist. This chapter again highlights the importance of imagery of eating in Rossetti's poems and stories, but Silver's need to relate this to her central thesis about anorexia sometimes seems reductive.

Two more articles dealt broadly with Rossetti's relationship to Christianity. Julie Melnyk's 'The Lyrical "We": Self-Representation in Christina Rossetti's "Later Life"' (*JPRAS* 11[2002] 43–61), studies how Rossetti moves away from lyric subjectivity to incorporate a communal, Christian, 'we' into her sonnets. Another important assessment of Rossetti's use of Christian themes and imagery is Emma Mason's 'Christina Rossetti and the Doctrine of Reserve' (*JVC* 7[2002] 196–219), which examines how both form and content in Rossetti's poetry derive from Tractarian theories of reserve. Mason reads Rossetti's engagement with this tradition as positive, even in some sense liberating. Both articles provide excellent readings of Rossetti, with wider implications for women's poetry in general. *JPRAS* also contains Claire Senior's 'Maiden-Songs: The Role of the Female Child in Christina Rossetti's *Speaking Likenesses*' (*JPRAS* 11[2002] 62–94), a reading of the sexualization of girlhood which would mesh interestingly with Christine Roth's 'Ernest Dowson' (*ELT* 45[2000] 158–73: see above). Elsewhere, in a short note (*Expl* 60[2002] 28–30), Sabine Coelsch-Foisner relates 'Goblin Market' to Herrick's 'Cherry-Ripe', particularly in terms of associations between fruit and carnal love.

One monograph on Dante Gabriel Rossetti appeared this year: Robert N. Keane's *Dante Gabriel Rossetti: The Poet as Craftsman*. Keane sets out to investigate the immense 'paper trail' left by Rossetti, painstakingly examining all the manuscripts and editions in order to identify his processes of revision and the ways in which he reshaped his poems across time. Keane's knowledge of the manuscripts and their contexts is thorough, and he meticulously charts the progress of Rossetti's career through his various volumes of poetry. In order to produce the final version of his 1870 volume, for instance, Rossetti went through six major sets of proofs, which were revised and studied not only by him but by his circle of friends, his family, and his colleagues. While the sheer number of Rossetti's draft versions can easily cause the reader to become lost among the different versions, Keane by and large does a fine job of explaining when, how, and why Rossetti made certain changes. *The Poet as Craftsman* does not in general present an argument which shows Rossetti revising his poems with particular ends in mind; rather, it simply seeks to show that each poem is a meticulously crafted work of art, improved across various versions. Comments on individual poems do indicate a purpose behind the revisions: Keane suggests that the religious implications of Rossetti's early poems, for instance, were deliberately toned down, but questions of why he felt the need to make such changes are dealt with relatively briefly. Keane, on the whole, spends more time describing Rossetti's revisions than analysing their purpose, and there is little focus here on detailed readings of the poems themselves. Critical opinion of Rossetti's poetry is also little discussed: it seems perhaps particularly surprising that Jerome McGann's work on similar subjects is mentioned on page 1 and never again. This volume is primarily factual rather than argumentative, and as such will chiefly be valuable to Rossetti specialists who do not have access to the manuscripts themselves.

In '"Any day that you're a good boy": Ruskin's Patronage, Rossetti's Expectations' (in Birch and O'Gorman, eds., *Ruskin and Gender*, pp. 137–58), Joseph Bristow gives a convincing account of the edgy friendship, relying on patterns of patronage and favours, between Ruskin and Rossetti, and shows how it gradually broke down under the pressure of their different expectations. In a very good article in *Victorian Newsletter*, Ernest Fontana, 'Rossetti's Belated and Disturbed Walk Poems' (*VN* 102[2002] 29–33), assesses the poems from Rossetti's 1853 walking tour, showing how they negotiate with and rewrite Wordsworth by representing Rossetti's encounter with nature as confused and uninspired. *JPRAS* published several pieces on Rossetti. Laurence Roussillon, '*Aspecta Medusa*: The Many Faces of Medusa in the Painting and the Poetry of Dante Gabriel Rossetti' (*JPRAS* 11[2002] 5–18) makes an interesting addition to discussions of the Medusa myth in Victorian culture, arguing that Rossetti's 'Aspecta Medusa' reveals the classic dichotomy between the pure woman and the threatening force of female sexuality. In 'Another Cause for the "Fleshly School" Controversy: Buchanan vs

Ellis' (*JPRAS* 11[2002] 63–7), Andrew Stauffer, as his title suggests, points out that Rossetti and Swinburne's publisher had taken legal action against Robert Buchanan for non-payment of debt, thus giving Buchanan a motive for revenge. *JPRAS* also reprints an 1881 review of Woolner and Rossetti by Alice Meynell, 'The Brush, the Chisel and the Pen' (*JPRAS* 11[2002] 32–8). Missed last year was Beatrice Pardini-Laurent's 'The Dream of a Victorian Quattrocento: Dante Gabriel Rossetti's Answer to the Dilemma of his Anglo-Italian Identity' (in Luyat and Tolron, eds., *Flight From Certainty: The Dilemma of Identity and Exile*, pp. 34–7) is a discussion of how Rossetti was caught between two cultures—the dream-like Italy, which he never visited in reality, and contemporary England. She sees Rossetti as creating a vision of an Anglo-Italian medieval past in order to reconcile these competing claims on his art.

Tennyson, as noted above, was discussed well by Maxwell and Douglas-Fairhurst. Julian Wolfrey's very different *Victorian Hauntings* also discusses *In Memoriam*. Wolfreys' deconstructionist reading examines the endless substitution of tropes in the effort to express faith, meaning that faith itself becomes spectral, uncanny. The poem demonstrates an 'implicit comprehension of the immanence of incarnation everywhere, yet impossible to represent' (p. 55). *In Memoriam*, in this interpretation, lacks any stability or unity. Wolfreys' style is sometimes hard to penetrate, but this is still a challenging and intriguing reading.

A substantial body of articles appeared on Tennyson. Angela Leighton's important 'Touching Forms: Tennyson and Aestheticism', which also appeared in last year's *Tennyson Research Bulletin*, was reprinted in *Essays in Criticism* (*EIC* 52[2002] 56–75). Barri J. Gold, 'The Consolation of Physics: Tennyson's Thermodynamic Solution' (*PMLA* 117[2002] 449–64), provides an excellent interdisciplinary reading of Tennyson's relation to the physical sciences of the day. Although Tennyson could not have known of the laws of thermodynamics, Gold argues that *In Memoriam* is 'saturated with the language of energy physics' (p. 450), and suggests that the poem might have influenced the scientists, as well as vice versa. Catherine Phillips, ' "Charades from the Middle Ages"? Tennyson's *Idylls of the King* and the Chivalric Code' (*VP* 40[2002] 241–53), sets Tennyson in the context of ideals of chivalry in the period, and shows how, in common with other writers and artists of his day, he reworks medievalism into Victorianism. In the same journal, Roger Platizky (*VP* 40[2002] 209–15) notes that Tennyson was often presumed to be an opium addict despite his stated aversion to the drug, a culturally interesting stance given the move towards the regulation and control of opium in the mid-Victorian period. Marylu Hill, in addition, in ' "Shadowing Sense at War with Soul": Julia Margaret Cameron's Photographic Illustrations of Tennyson's *Idylls of the King*' (*VP* 40[2002] 445–62), examines Cameron's photographs for the 1875 volume of *Idylls of the King*, and considers how their blend of romance and realism might have appealed to Tennyson's vision of the poem.

The *Tennyson Research Bulletin* contains three fine essays. Donald Hair, in 'The Voice of Tennyson's Laureate Verse' (*TRB* 8[2002] 2–10), following a path also traced by Matthew Bevis, considers the importance of the 'people's voice' in Tennyson, and reconsiders how the poet's individual voice might participate in a national or universal endeavour. Seamus Perry, 'Two Voices: Tennyson and Wordsworth' (*TRB* 8[2002] 11–27), turns to Tennyson and Wordsworth, and reassesses the ways in which the younger poet saw himself as the inheritor of the older: the article is particularly good on Tennyson's doubts about Wordsworth's 'prosaic aspirations'. In the final essay in this volume, 'Tennyson and the Crisis of the Narrative Voice in *Maud*' (*TRB* 8[2002] 28–43), Saverio Tomaiulo reads *Maud* through the lens of theory as a 'centripetal' poem, fragmenting and dissipating Tennyson's words.

Elsewhere, Marysa Demoor, '"His Way Is thro' Chaos and the Bottomless and Pathless": The Gender of Madness in Alfred Tennyson's Poetry' (*Neophil* 86[2002] 325–35), presents a relatively simple reading of how Tennyson shifts from gendering madness as female—in *The Princess*, 'Boudicca', and 'The Lady of Shalott'—to representing it in masculine terms in *Maud*, a shift that she traces to Tennyson's increased security as a (sane) husband and father. John Talbot enhances our understanding of Tennyson's subtle and intelligent negotiations with the classics by identifying a sly reference to Catullan word-use in 'Hendadecasyllabics' (*N&Q* 49[2002] 474–5). There are also three notes on Tennyson in *Explicator*. Jane Wright (*Expl* 60[2002] 67–8) comments on the ambiguity at the end of *The Princess* and notes that it is critically inaccurate to assume that the couple are united at the end. Nathan Cervo considers some imagery of dissolution (possibly related to onanism) in 'Lucretius' (*Expl* 60[2002] 136–7), and Tim Lovelace (*Expl* 60[2002] 24–5) traces an allusion to the famous meeting between Aeneas and Dido in Book VI of the *Aeneid* in 'The Passing of Arthur', an allusion which has added resonance because of its prior use by Milton and Wordsworth in poems which similarly deal with death and resurrection.

In conclusion, it is worth noting with regard to Tennyson's allusions that Christopher Ricks, in *Allusion to the Poets*, reprints the essay originally published as 'Tennyson Inheriting the Earth' in *Studies in Tennyson* [1981]. Ricks's observations on how Tennyson manages to achieve a 'width of accessibility' by incorporating 'an intimate world of private allusion' (p. 181) remain vivid and acute, and, in the context of this book, show how Tennyson fitted into a poetic tradition, inheriting his words from the past.

4. Drama and Theatre

Despite a relatively small output of publications on nineteenth-century drama and theatre in 2002, new works on burlesque, on performance and evolution, and on melodrama have contributed some interesting fresh perspectives in this field. Richard Schoch's *Not Shakespeare: Bardolatry and Burlesque in the Nineteenth Century* provides a fascinating study of nineteenth-century Shakespearian burlesque as cultural critique. Far from suggesting that such burlesques degraded Shakespeare, Schoch argues that they protected his reputation through their parody of contemporary Shakespearian productions and of the Victorian cultural obsession with Shakespeare. The Shakespeare plays burlesqued tended to be the most popular and/or most recently performed in the canon, while the burlesques themselves posed little threat to Shakespeare, without whose plays they could not have existed anyway. The burlesque's use of slang, topical allusion, and domestication of character also revealed a less rigid perspective on Victorian society. Schoch is less interested in the formal properties of burlesque and more in its attack on cultural practices, together with its implicit nostalgia for what that culture might have been.

In his view burlesque not only criticizes Shakespearian performance, it also corrects it.

Schoch considers the linguistic conventions of burlesque, demonstrating how greatness was made familiar, the familiar absurd. The use of topicality, puns, and revisions during the course of performance forced the spectators into an interpretative act; in their very inaccessibility to the modern reader, as in the tortuous use of puns, the burlesques also drew attention to their problematization of meaning itself. Yet 'the materiality of burlesque language cannot remain detached from its broader cultural significance' (p. 56). Shakespearian burlesque attacked pedantry, bardolatry, poor performances, the heritage industry, the notion of spectacular Shakespeare as 'authentic', implying a restoration of Shakespeare's own authority over his interpreters, and an undermining of such cultural binaries as legitimate/illegitimate, popular/elitist.

Schoch moves on to explore the audience for burlesque and 'investigate how the burlesque critiqued the middle-class cult of respectability from its privileged position within Bohemian "fast" culture' (p. 29). Its audience, he argues, predominantly consisted of 'fast' young men, from middle-class backgrounds, who also possessed a reasonable knowledge of 'legitimate' Shakespeare. Burlesque was dissenting in tone and Bohemian by nature. The study concludes with a close reading of three burlesques—*King John*, *Coriolanus*, and *The Tempest*—demonstrating how burlesque could offer alternative and even fantasized political realities to its spectators. Overall, in treating burlesque not as a literary genre but as a collection of historical documents, Schoch's original and provocative book opens up an exciting new avenue into Victorian cultural and theatrical history.

In her excellent study, *Performance and Evolution in the Age of Darwin: Out of the Natural Order*, Jane R. Goodall considers the ways in which the performing arts engaged with Darwin's theory of evolution in the nineteenth century. Of particular interest for the Victorian period is her discussion of how Darwin's argument for the lowly or bestial origins of the species impacted on the notoriety of certain female performers, especially through their ability to transform licentiousness into profitable theatrical currency. In discussions of Zola's *Nana*, the impact of evolutionary theory on the ideas of Zola, Antoine, and G.H. Lewes, and of 'beast actors' such as Henry Irving, Goodall demonstrates the pervasiveness of Darwin's influence on the theory and practice of nineteenth-century European performance. In the Théâtre du Grand Guignol the 'beast' came home and entered the domestic arena. There is also a fascinating discussion of Wilde's *Salomé* and the challenging way in which 'the apparently contrary directions of symbolism and biologism in [Wilde's] thinking' (p. 210) were brought into conjunction in this play. Goodall sees the fatalism of both *Salomé* and *De Profundis* as influenced by Wilde's own belief that he himself was one of the rejects of natural selection.

New readings of Victorian melodrama continue to appear. In passing, Juliet John's *Dickens's Villains: Melodrama, Character, Popular Culture* [2001] is significant for its discussion of theatrical melodrama. John sees both male and female melodramatic villains as 'products of the dialectical emotional economy governing melodrama, which revolves around the principles of excess and restraint' (p. 11). She locates Dickens's villains within the theatrical and cultural contexts from which they emerged and within an authorial vision, which she sees as both utopian and apocalyptic. However, one misapprehension should be noted: Charles

Mathews the elder, whom John refers to as one of Dickens's favourite actors, is quite distinct from his son, who played the villainous role discussed in her text.

Several articles have contested and reformulated current orthodoxies around nineteenth-century melodrama. In 'Feeling Public: Sensation Theatre, Community Culture, and the Public Sphere' (*VS* 44[2002] 245–74), Lynn M. Voskuil looks at the relationship between the somatic effects of sensation melodrama, particularly with reference to the plays of Boucicault, commodity culture, and the public sphere. The affect and 'authenticity' of sensation melodrama combined with the consumer culture of the post-1850 period to provide a sense of a community at odds with that of the early nineteenth century, when the politically resistant manipulation of theatrical sites by spectators was more common. For Voskuil sensation theatre is 'one of the processes by which Victorians believed themselves to have formed social bonds, a process of mediation and reception enabled by the burgeoning consumer culture of late-Victorian England' (p. 251). The rise of such drama at the time of the Great Exhibition saw a shared and increasing emphasis on spectacle and authenticity in both consumer goods and theatrical performance. But, as the spectators consumed sensation melodrama, authenticity was also sited in their shared physical reaction to the thrills and threats of the genre, even while they shared an awareness that the fantastic rather than the real was at the root of this experience. Audience response to sensation drama, according to Voskuil, enables a reconfiguration of the 'public sphere' by revealing one of the ways in which 'mass subjectivity takes shape in an advanced consumer culture' (p. 269).

Matthew Buckley's 'Sensations of Celebrity: *Jack Sheppard* and the Mass Audience' (*VS* 44[2002] 423–63) also demonstrates new perspectives on melodrama and spectacle. Like Voskuil, Buckley places less emphasis on the political sphere and more on the quotidian experience of those adapting to the urban environment. Within this reconfiguration of modernity Buckley accords an especial significance to Ainsworth's and Cruikshank's *Jack Sheppard* [1839], the craze for which was greatly enhanced by the production of visual media and dramatic adaptations. Indeed the theatrical realization of Cruikshank's illustrations was a significant aspect of the popularization of the novel, although they arguably already borrow from the language of dramatic tableaux to achieve their effects as illustrations. The ways in which J.B. Buckstone's dramatization of the novel adapted Cruikshank's illustrations to the exigencies of the Adelphi theatre are interestingly discussed. 'As a combined pictorial, narrative and theatrical phenomenon' argues Buckley, *Jack Sheppard* 'offered a critique and even a repudiation of the model of community and the associated modes of perception articulated in conventional melodrama. It asserted instead a mode of identity now more accurately suited to the lived experience of its audience—that of the alienated spectator, isolated in practice and perspective, but bonded imaginatively to all fellow enthusiasts' (p. 457). In effect, it articulated 'a transformation of consciousness, from that epistemological community of political modernity to the sensational community of perceptual modernity' (p. 459).

Several other publications are worth noting briefly. A useful footnote to popular melodrama and other forms of entertainment in the nineteenth century is Derek Forbes, *Illustrated Playbills*, which blends copious illustrations with a discussion of the function of woodcuts in advertising popular plays and entertainments. A useful addendum to this is the reprinting of *A Descriptive Catalogue of Theatrical Wood*

Engravings [1865]. In 'Bulwer's Misanthropes and the Limits of Victorian Sympathy' (*VS* 44[2002] 597–624), Christopher Lane briefly touches on the play *Money* [1840] to demonstrate how its satirical potential is tempered by its romantic ending and its softening of the more radical tone apparent in Bulwer's 1830s fiction.

M. Glen Wilson and Daniel Barrett, in 'The End of Charles Kean's Directorship of the Windsor Theatricals' (*TN* 56:ii[2002] 117–25), revisit Charles Kean's resignation from the directorship of the Windsor theatricals, suggesting that the accusation that he was dismissed from the post for short-changing his actors appear untenable. A more likely cause of Kean's departure, they believe, is his disappointment when it became evident that he would not be considered for a knighthood, and his exclusion in 1858 from the theatricals planned to celebrate the marriage of the Princess Royal to Prince Frederick William of Prussia. In 1859 he was invited back to Windsor to direct the royal theatricals planned for 1860, but declined on account of the long-term engagement plans he had already made. It was then that he formally resigned as director of the royal theatrical performances at Windsor, and he subsequently declined any lures to perform there again.

5. Periodicals and Publishing History

In 'Rational Entertainment, Music Hall and the Nineteenth-Century British Periodical Press' (*THStud* 22[2002] 195–213), M. Scott Phillips untangles the discourse of power present in mid- to late nineteenth-century periodical discussions of popular theatre and music-hall traditions. Although tending to sweeping generalizations to make his point, Phillips makes a solid case for claiming that the Victorian periodical press was on the whole used to create and bolster the image of stage and theatre as a respectable and legitimate art form at the expense of more popular entertainment. Distinctions were drawn in contemporary press accounts between the theatre and the music hall, one representing morally sound art and middle-class respectability, the other representing unruly, disreputable, and distinctly lower-class tendencies. Phillips analyses the language in press pieces to illustrate how the 'vocabulary of rational recreation' (p. 210), reminiscent of the rhetoric of colonialism, was utilized to establish a social hierarchy of performance, with the West End at the highest level, and the music halls of Leicester Square on the bottom rung.

Art could be just as highly structured within periodical discourse, as Jamie W. Johnson demonstrates in a carefully delineated study of *Punch*'s shifting presentation of the art-loving public, 'The Changing Representation of the Art Public in *Punch*, 1841–1896' (*VPR* 35:iii[2002] 272–94). Through satirical illustrations, articles, and verse, *Punch* could be equally scathing and supportive of the art mania that accompanied major exhibitions and annual art reviews at London galleries. But initial presentations of art-viewing as an activity accessible to all classes would shift as the century progressed, to endorse a view of art as an exclusive world for privileged, knowledgeable insiders. The piece demonstrates quite well how such views were communicated visually and textually, and what the end results were.

Visual culture and the economics of publishing and literary production coincide nicely in the excellent collection *The Victorian Illustrated Book*, edited by Richard

Maxwell. A short but useful introduction contextualizes Victorian productions of illustrated works. Such textual and visual collaborations can be seen to have started with the explosion of visual production in the 1830s and 1840s pioneered by Dickens and his artist collaborators (pre-eminently George Cruikshank, Hablot Browne, and George Cattermole). The essays in this collection trace the shift in visual material from initial caricature and satirically influenced work to 'poetic naturalism' of the 1860s and into the complex visual expression of William Morris, and then to the illustrations of the turn of the century, influenced by photography. All engage with the issue of how Victorian illustrations emanated from, or resisted, particular commercial imperatives present in the publishing process, as well as the links between texts and contexts, formats and literary intonations. Richard Maxwell leads off with 'Walter Scott, Historical Fiction, and the Genesis of the Victorian Illustrated Book', an analysis of the visual material accompanying the publication of Walter Scott's historical fiction between 1820 and 1840. Subsequent pieces work chronologically in sequence, and include: Steven Dillon, 'Illustrations of Time: Watches, Dials and Clocks in Victorian Pictures'; Robert L. Patten, 'Serial Illustration and Storytelling in David Copperfield'; Simon Joyce, 'Maps and Metaphors: Topographical Representation and the Sense of Place in Late-Victorian Fiction'; Herbert F. Tucker, 'Literal Illustration in Victorian Print'; Elizabeth K. Helsinger, 'William Morris before Kelmscott: Poetry and Design in the 1860s'; Jeffrey Skoblow, 'Beyond Reading: Kelmscott and the Modern'; Nicholas Frankel, 'Aubrey Beardsley "Embroiders" the Literary Text'; Charles Harmon, 'Alvin Langdon Coburn's Frontispieces to Henry James's New York Edition: Pictures of an Institutional Imaginary'; and Katie Trumpener, 'City Scenes: Commerce, Utopia and the Birth of the Picture Book'. The collection as a whole is a very significant and vivid addition to an understanding of the interweaving of text and illustration throughout significant periods in Victorian illustration history.

Equally vivid is 'Sympathy as Subversion? Reading Lady Audley's Secret in the Kitchen' (Journal of Victorian Culture 7:i[2002] 60–85), Andrew King's analysis of Mary Elizabeth Braddon's Lady Audley's Secret in its 1864 serialized form in the popular weekly fiction magazine London Journal. King reads Braddon's work in the context of its publishing history and the serial's accompanying visual illustrations. He demonstrates how contemporary middle-class critical judgement of Braddon's text failed to account for the novel's appropriation of themes, tropes, and literary traditions familiar to readers of similar material in mass-readership periodicals such as the London Journal. Equally interesting is the inconsistency in the visual treatment of the novel's characters in the illustrations accompanying each serialized section: the changing depiction of the main personalities from issue to issue reflected the difficulty the Journal artists had in representing the 'moral nature' of the characters.

King is not the only one to focus on the links between visual and textual material in Braddon's serialized novels. In 'George du Maurier's Illustrations for M.E. Braddon's Serialization of Eleanor's Victory in Once a Week' (VPR 35:i[2002] 89–106), Simon Cooke ably dissects the dissonances between picture and text found in Braddon's serial featured in Once a Week between March and October 1863. While du Maurier's images have frequently been commented on and reproduced as examples of his art, they have never been discussed in their periodical and serialized context. Cooke uses this opportunity to skilfully demonstrate du Maurier's nuanced response to the text, which highlighted Braddon's interesting character development and unusual realist themes.

Braddon is also the subject of Barbara Onslow's 'Sensationalising Science: Braddon's Marketing of Science in *Belgravia*' (*VPR* 35:ii[2002] 160–77). In this case, though, Onslow vigorously examines Braddon's successful editorial attempts in the 1860s to weave scientific discovery and the sensational within the literary journal she edited for over a decade from 1866. Onslow argues convincingly that Braddon's marketing strategies for the *Belgravia* balanced lurid fiction with topical essays aimed at drawing on contemporary readership interests in science-based material and discoveries, a formula that sold well and established the journal in an extremely competitive literary market.

Frances Power Cobbe navigated her role as leader writer for the London *Echo* between 1868 and 1875 with a strategic goal of applying feminist logic to the interpretation of the day's news, claims Susan Hamilton in 'The Practice of Everyday Feminism: Frances Power Cobbe, Divorce, and the London *Echo*, 1868–1875' (*VPR* 35:iii[2002] 227–42). Hamilton takes Cobbe's published comments on contemporary divorce cases to suggest that Cobbe's work resisted traditional interpretations of such issues. The result was an unusually direct evaluation of world events that offered alternative visions of women's lives and values within the context of a mainstream media source.

Whereas Cobbe was able to successfully resist dominant social formations in periodical and media sources, other women faced difficulties in the arena of the nineteenth-century periodical press. In '"Better Arguments": The *English Woman's Journal* and the Game of Public Opinion' (*VPR* 35:iii[2002] 242–71), Janice Schroder discusses how this journal faced criticism of its aims following its founding in 1859, and analyses the strategies its editors undertook to combat and deflect the antagonistic reception it received. The analysis is revealing of how newcomers such as Bessie Rayner Parkes could successfully engage and survive in the male-dominated world of nineteenth-century periodical journalism.

Realism features in Silvana Colella's 'Intimations of Mortality: The Malthusian Plot in Early Nineteenth-Century Popular Fiction' (*NCC* 24:i[2002] 17–32). In this case, the reality and morality of marriage and relationships is reflected in popular work produced in the 1820s and 1830s for twopenny British magazines such as the *Mirror*, the *Portfolio*, the *Freebooter* and the *Olio*. Colella argues that, counter to developments in contemporary early century novels, where marriage tended to complete and resolve most domestic plot complications, shorter fiction published in the ephemeral pages of contemporary journals tended towards the melodramatic and tragic. Of 372 tales published in the four case-study periodicals between 1823 and 1832, over 80 per cent of those featuring love plots concluded tragically. Colella argues rather tenuously that such themes link into contemporary discussions and adoption of Malthusian principles of population control and social formations.

Local politics and the place of periodical journalism in agenda-setting as conceived through Habermas's concept of the public sphere are the concerns of Aled Jones's 'The *Dart* and the Damming of the Sylvan Stream: Journalism and Political Culture in the Late Victorian City' (*VPR* 35:i[2002] 2–17). Jones draws on a particular event in the history of the development of the English city of Birmingham, the 1892 scheme to supply it with water diverted from the Welsh countryside, and juxtaposes the discourse of progress used by Birmingham officials in their locally controlled press to justify the scheme with that of the obscure local opposition paper *The Dart*. Jones provides a perceptive example of how those for and against the scheme utilized periodical space to construct differing images of the same Welsh landscape: in this case, either as a resource and utility that required public development, or as an area of private consumption requiring development through commercial tourist activity. Jones's analysis of the *Dart* coverage is a useful example of the use of a micro-study to illuminate more general points about the periodical press.

A sophisticated analysis of similar agenda-setting is to be found in Rebecca Edwards Newman's '"Prosecuting the Onus Criminus": Early Criticism of the Novel in Fraser's Magazine' (*VPR* 35:iv[2002] 401–19). This award-winning essay takes as its thesis critical debates on the novel instituted in the 1830s and 1840s in *Fraser's Magazine*. Newman argues persuasively that *Fraser's* hierarchizing and categorizing of the form of the novel in the strongly worded reviews that appeared in its pages did much to reconfigure, reformulate, and determine contemporary reception of the novel as a recognized mode of literature. Its attacks on what were to become known as 'Newgate novels' are cited as examples of the magazine's place in shaping literary discourse.

Intertextual and contextual analysis is strongly in evidence in Gowan Dawson's 'Stranger than Fiction: Spiritualism, Intertextuality, and William Makepeace Thackeray's Editorship of the *Cornhill Magazine*, 1860–62' (*Journal of Victorian Culture* 7:ii[2002] 220–38). Dawson writes well on an aspect of Thackeray's short-lived editorship of the *Cornhill Magazine* that few commentators have remarked on—namely, his interest in spiritualism, and its subsequent featuring in the *Cornhill*. Dawson convincingly demonstrates how Thackeray used astute commercial tactics to generate reaction to and sales for his new enterprise, tapping into contemporary phenomena much in discussion in Victorian society. The article makes good use of close reading and contemporary media sources to support the themes investigated. In similar vein, Stella Nuralova, in 'W.M. Thackeray and his *Cornhill Magazine* in Russia: Nineteenth-Century Attitudes' (*VPR* 35:iii[2002] 295–304), examines the contemporary Russian reception of Thackeray's tenure as editor of the *Cornhill*. She concludes that favourable readings of the *Cornhill* greatly influenced the development, format, and content of Russian literary journals in subsequent years.

Representations of Burma and the Burmese in the Victorian periodical press were few until British annexation of the country in 1885. In 'Picturing the Other: Images of Burmans in Imperial Britain' (*VPR* 35:iii[2002] 214–26), Deborah Deacon Boyer traces some of the tropes of otherness and orientalized imagery evident in journals such as *Punch*, *Illustrated London News*, and *The Pall Mall Gazette*. Invariably, views of Burma fluctuated according to the level of threat it presented to British interests: during periods of conflict, negative portrayals of its leaders and people prevailed, to be followed by depictions of Burma as a paradisical state once pacification was complete.

Locating mass culture within the framework of both mass journalism and periodical studies lies at the core of Martin Conboy's *The Press and Popular Culture*. Conboy reflects on the links between theorized definitions of popular culture within both cultural and journalism studies debates, and brings a range of critical discourses to bear on an analysis of a series of periodical and newspaper case studies from both the US and the UK, covering 1650 to the present. He admits that the survey he undertakes does no more than scratch the surface of the critically informed and historically inflected study possible in the area, but the short volume he has produced provides useful material for further consideration and implementation.

Similar historically inflected case studies are in evidence in Brügger and Kolstrup, eds., *Media History: Theory, Methods, Analysis*. Their concern is to situate more conventional media sources (television, radio, newspapers) within a theoretical framework that draws on political, cultural, and social modes of discourse. The case studies are for the most part contemporary in nature, although comparative periodical studies interests can be found in Søren Kolstrup's analysis of Danish periodical history, 'The Change of News Structure: Danish Newspapers 1873–1914'.

John Greenfield, 'Arthur Morrison's Sherlock Clone: Martin Hewitt, Victorian Values, and London Magazine Culture, 1894–1903' (*VPR* 35:i[2002] 18–36), plunders the *Strand Magazine* to discuss Arthur Morrison's serialized imitations of Arthur Conan Doyle's detective fiction. Between 1894 and 1903 Morrison, better known for realist works centred on life in the slums of London's East End such as *Tales of Mean Streets* and *A Child of the Jago*, produced twenty-five tales of detection featuring the plump Martin Hewitt and his journalist sidekick Brett. Greenfield competently if rather flatly analyses the plots of several of these to demonstrate how Morrison, like Doyle, produced work that played to the prejudices and ideological assumptions of the *Strand Magazine*'s main readership—a conservative, urban, and professional middle class. As Greenfield concludes, 'fictional detectives such as Holmes and Hewitt provided a safe haven against the perceived onslaught of not only domestic crime and foreign threats but also, in their predictable restoration of property, inheritance, reputation, and order, against change itself' (p. 35).

A journal produced between 1897 and 1900 in Belfast in support of the turn-of-the-century nationalist-based Irish literary revival is the subject of Karen Steele's competent and able 'Editing Out Factionalism: The Political and Literary Consequences in Ireland's *Shan Van Vocht*' (*VPR* 35:ii[2002] 113–32). Issued between 1897 and 1900 as a twopenny, sixteen-page monthly edited by two nationalist supporters (Alice Milligan and Anna Johnston), the journal has been credited with inaugurating what has been called 'the advanced-nationalist press', media sources dedicated to the social, political, and economic revival of Ireland during a crucial period of its history. Steele outlines its history and the authors who wrote for it, and argues that the editorial and literary content of the journal proved equally subversive in its politics and in its fiction, particularly in the context of its depiction of women's roles in Irish society. Its successes, and failures, would influence subsequent female journalists engaged in the Irish movement in the early twentieth century.

How women fared in a different periodical context informs Cheryl M. Cassidy's discursive and short piece 'Dying in the Light: The Rhetoric of Nineteenth-Century Female Evangelical Obituaries' (*VPR* 35:iii[2002] 206–13). Her analysis of obituaries of women missionaries in a series of Presbyterian and foreign missionary publications issued between 1880 and 1900 yields the unsurprising conclusion that the eulogistic rhetoric underpinning these reports varied according to the social status of the individual: young, single women and indigenous converts were presented differently from those further up the social scale, such as married and home-based missionary women.

The aesthetic qualities of *fin-de-siècle* ephemeral commercial poster productions, celebrated in the short-lived London monthly periodical *The Poster* issued between 1898 and 1900, are interestingly dissected by John Hewitt in 'The Poster and the Poster in England in the 1890s' (*VPR* 35:i[2002] 37–62). *The Poster* featured mainly black and white reproductions of posters, poster designs, and related art work, and sought to reach two very different audiences: on the one hand art connoisseurs and collectors, and on the other printers and advertisers. Hewitt very ably uses internal evidence to explicate how the tensions between competing readership agendas, and the changing needs of the journal's initial main advertisers, ultimately led to its collapse.

Adolescent responses to the periodical press are more difficult to gauge. In 'The Textual Formation of Adolescence in Turn-of-the-Century Youth Periodicals: The *Boy's Own Paper* and Eton College Ephemeral Magazines' (*VPR* 35:i[2002] 63–88), Jenny Holt deconstructs the ephemeral journals produced by Eton College secondary school students between 1901 and 1915, comparing their language and tropes of meaning with that of the formal rigours of the popular periodical the *Boy's Own Paper*. Responses to issues raised in the *BOP* are evident throughout the student journals scanned by Holt, and she uses sophisticated theoretical interpretation to suggest that, while periodicals produced for adolescents by adults such as the *Boy's Own Paper* attempted to foster rigid norms of class, gender, and educational achievement as well as to suppress literary creativity as a positive activity amongst its readers, evidence from productions such as those found at Eton College show some adolescent readers resisting and subverting such dominant discourses for their own consumption. Holt suggests more work on the subject might reveal more about adolescent resistance to contemporary Edwardian assumptions about such readers.

Rosie Findlay turns to a broader canvas in 'Small Print: The Golden Age of Children's Periodicals in Great Britain' (*CVE* 55[2002] 53–69). Her theme, shaped from a conference paper given in 2000, is that the Victorian and Edwardian period saw a flowing stream of publications dedicated to children that matched the golden stream of periodicals produced for the adult market. She argues erroneously that little has been done to study the children's periodical press, but notes astutely that the sheer volume of children's press material from this period reflects an interesting shift in the nature of general content, from religious to secular, instructional to entertainment. More, indeed, needs to be done to review the impact of such material on contemporary society.

Children's access to early nineteenth-century circulating libraries is the subject of M.O. Grenby's exploratory study 'Adults Only? Children and Children's Books in British Circulating Libraries, 1748–1848' (*BoH* 5[2002] 19–38). Most library and book historians assert that, prior to the passing of the British Public Libraries Act in 1850 and the establishment of a network of local public libraries servicing large communities, none of their predecessors (the circulating libraries) catered for children. Closer examination of records from British sources, however, suggests otherwise. Use was sporadic, but cultural and social issues concerning children's reading accounted for this. Grenby notes usefully that the incompatibility of contemporary views on children's access to literature (emphasizing the value of supervised and directed reading) with the general philosophy of the circulating libraries (emphasizing open access to all general stock for a fee) prevented many from openly catering to children. Nevertheless, material from English and Scottish circulating libraries offers tantalizing evidence that children did indeed find their way into these closed spaces, thus modifying our understanding of the place of circulating libraries in the reading lives of early nineteenth-century British youth.

Andrew Leng turns our attention to Ruskin's famous attack on Whistler in 1877 in Ruskin's personally funded epistolary periodical *Fors Clavigera*. In 'Letters to Workmen? *Fors Clavigera*, Whistler vs. Ruskin and Sage Criticism in Crisis' (*PSt* 24:i[2002] 63–92), Leng links Ruskin's attack to the style of Tory conservative, *ad hominem* criticism of earlier journals such as *Blackwood's Magazine*, and in particular to *Blackwood's* critical assaults on the Cockney school of poetry. Ruskin's view that his highly controlled, limited-circulation journal would be safe from the legal standards of libel imposed on other, more widely distributed, mass-market productions was to backfire when Whistler sued him. Leng suggests that Ruskin's failure to adjust his critical perceptions to the realities of the literary marketplace is an issue long overlooked in studies on the matter.

Of the same period but working in a different arena was the naturalist George John Romanes, a disciple of Charles Darwin whose efforts to engage the general reading audience in matters scientific form the subject of Joel S. Schwartz's solid survey 'Out from Darwin's Shadow: George John Romanes's Efforts to Popularize Science in *Nineteenth Century* and other Victorian Periodicals' (*VPR* 35:ii[2002] 133–59). Schwartz examines Romanes's output between the 1870s and 1890s in the *Contemporary Review*, the *Nineteenth Century* and the *Fortnightly Review*, and in particular focuses on his efforts to further interest in and knowledge of Darwin's concepts of evolution through these general periodical outlets. The results were mixed: Romanes's academic style of writing proved less popular than the writing of contemporaries such as Robert Chambers and Thomas Henry Huxley, but his strong defence of Darwinian concepts established and consolidated his professional reputation as a naturalist. Schwartz usefully draws out these distinctions in his analysis of Romanes's material and the subsequent move into the public sphere.

The art of the early nineteenth-century literary reviewer came under fire in the 1850s, when influential editors such as Leslie Stephens began reappraising the contributions of an earlier generation of writers to such journals as the *Edinburgh Review*. Much of this reappraisal was accompanied by self-congratulatory statements about the general rise in scope and ambitions to be found in contemporary literary productions. Recent criticism has suggested that such discussions marked a turning point in literary criticism, and in particular in the area of poetry reviews. Thus academic work by John Woolford and Isobel Armstrong, among others, has suggested that a reorientation in British review work occurred in the 1850s and 1860s, marking a move from 'adjectival' criticism to more analytical interpretations. In 'Reviewing Generations: Professionalism and the Mid-Victorian Reviewer' (*VPR* 35:iv[2002] 384–400), Joanne Shattock challenges this view, suggesting instead that a decisive change in poetry reviewing practice would more appropriately be sited in the 1880s and 1890s, coinciding in particular with the development of an expanded presence of women reviewers working for the influential *Athenaeum*.

Nineteenth-century publishing strategies aimed at keeping in circulation a now classic work in the history of science are central to Aileen Fyfe's well-argued 'Publishing and the Classics: Payley's *Natural Theology* and the Nineteenth-Century Scientific Canon' (*Studies in the History and Philosophy of Science* 33[2002] 729–51). First published in 1802, William Paley's book was initially interpreted as a work of natural theology. Over the century, interpretations of its significance changed, and it was seen first as a work for use in formal or informal education in science, and then latterly (after the impact of the anonymous *Vestiges of the Natural History of Creation* and Darwin's *Origins of Species*) as a work of Christian apologetics. Fyfe carefully traces the manner in which cheap reprints of the work by various publishers each contributed to the layering and altering of the text's reception, ultimately providing an instructive lesson on the importance of such hidden cultural agents in the formation of social and cultural activity.

Contextual studies of publishing houses dominant in the Victorian era have been published with greater frequency over the past few years, particularly as scholars begin revealing details gathered from long hours spent in extant publishing archives. One such example of archival results is David Finkelstein's *The House of Blackwood: Author-Publisher Relations in the Victorian Era*, a compact study of the Edinburgh firm William Blackwood & Sons, best known as the publishers of George Eliot and Joseph Conrad. Finkelstein intersperses chapters contextualizing the firm's activities between 1860 and 1910 with case studies on the production of work by Charles Reade, the ghostwriting of the African exploration diaries of John Hanning Speke, the tangled background to Margaret Oliphant's final work for the firm (its three-volume house history), and the changing nature of literary agency during the period. The work also contains appendices detailing general publishing statistics, sales of *Blackwood's Magazine*, and sales of Margaret Oliphant's work for the years covered by the book.

Following on from his biography of George Palmer Putnam issued last year, Ezra Greenspan has come forward with *The House of Putnam, 1837–1872: A Documentary Volume*, an extremely valuable edited volume of original material related to this New York-based publisher. Part of the *Dictionary of Literary Biography* series, the volume includes letters culled from extant archives, excerpts from and material related to contemporary authors and business members associated with the firm, and valuable extracts from George Putnam's writings on the profession of publishing. Most relevant are the sections dealing with Putnam's sojourns in Britain and Europe in the 1830s–1850s, along with his recollections of significant contemporary British publishers. The work is well illustrated and an important publishing history resource; its prohibitive price, however, will most likely mean that few will enjoy access to it.

An area of book history and print culture studies that has begun to take on increasing critical significance is that of readership and reading experiences. Recent examples of this include two overlapping articles covering the peculiar history and place in late nineteenth-century print culture of the National Home Reading Union. Founded in 1889 by the London School Board to encourage 'home reading' in Britain amongst young people, manual workers, and those without advanced educational qualifications, the organization was to enrol several hundred thousand members throughout its forty-one-year existence. Felicity Stimpson, in 'Reading in Circles: The National Home Reading Union' (*PubH* 52[2002] 19–82), focuses on the first eleven years of the NHRU's existence (1889–1900), highlighting in particular points to be learned of the reading patterns and habits of the movement's main constituents, young people and middle-class British women with little access to formal higher education. In contrast, Robert Snape's 'The National Home Reading Union' (*JVC* 7:i[2002] 86–110) looks more generally at reading circles and the underlying attitudes to popular reading that motivated the NHRU in Britain and similar organizations in the US), suggesting that the rise and fall of the NHRU can be linked to the development of a professionalized educational system that propounded a vision of culture as the preserve of an educated elite (as per F.R. Leavis and T.S. Eliot).

The increasing sophistication with which authors engaged in securing a livelihood for themselves following the enshrinement of literary property copyright law at the end of the eighteenth century has been much commented on in recent years. A special issue of *Women's Writing*, dedicated to the career and work of the extraordinary Harriet Martineau, includes several articles that focus on her development of a profitable authorial presence both in her fiction and in her journalism. Linda Petersen, in '(Re)inventing Authorship: Harriet Martineau in the Literary Marketplace of the 1820s' (*WW* 9:iii[2002] 337–50), argues tellingly that Martineau's early career was modelled less on Romantic notions of originality and genius than on a Victorian engagement with authorship as a vocation attuned to the wishes of the marketplace. Maria Frawley, on the other hand, focuses on Martineau's later years to suggest a deliberate use of her invalid status to add weight to her periodical output in the 1850s and 1860s for the popular journal *Once a Week*. Her work on a series of articles on workers' health for the journal, drawing on external material provided by fellow invalid and friend Florence Nightingale, was actively linked to her own physical situation as a means of personally challenging and attempting to define government policy on health matters.

For every author that benefited from literary property rights, there were others for whom the lack of an international copyright agreement caused great consternation. Nowhere was this more true than in the United States, where throughout the nineteenth century (until the passing of the Chase Act in 1891), British works were consistently reissued in cheap editions with little if any recompense for the authors and British publishers who had published the originals. David Alan Richards competently explores how this situation affected Rudyard Kipling's career in 'Kipling and the Pirates' (*PBSA* 96:i[2002] 59–109). Early popular works such as his *Plain Tales from the Hills* were issued in the US within a year of British and Indian publication. From 1890 onwards, Kipling and his literary agent A.P. Watt sought to stem such illicit incursions through careful monitoring of newspaper syndication agreements, and by issuing authorized American editions that enabled the active pursuit and suppression of unauthorized re-publications.

Changes in *fin-de-siècle* British publishing practices could also drastically alter an author's fortunes, the subject of Andrew Nash's 'Life in Gissing's New Grub Street: David Christie Murray and the Practice of Authorship, 1880–1900' (*PuHy* 51[2002] 21–60). Nash skilfully analyses data from the Chatto & Windus publishing archives to track the rise and fall of the literary career of the obscure David Christie Murray, London-based novelist, bellettrist, and journalist. In doing so he offers a useful object lesson in the effect of literary property copyright handling on the changing fortunes of writers of the period. Murray, best known for his 1881 novel

Joseph's Coat, reaped significant rewards at the start of his career through serialization rights of his novels. Chatto & Windus's assiduous acquisition of the copyright to his novels through outright purchase from the author, however, and the firm's subsequent exploitation of them through cheap editions and sales of subsidiary and overseas rights, placed Murray at a financial disadvantage towards the waning end of his career. His inability to manage his literary property in the face of changing business practices was not a unique experience in the 'Grub Street' of *fin-de-siècle* London.

Similar themes are present in John R. Turner's 'Joint Publishing Agreements, 1850–1919' (*PubH* 51[2002] 5–19). The focus here shifts to English provincial book publishers, who throughout the second half of the nineteenth century increasingly sought joint publication agreements with London publishers so as to assure themselves of representation in the main British markets. Turner studies the details of co-publication agreements between Exeter publisher James G. Commin and Chatto & Windus, Sidgwick & Jackson, Simpkin & Marshall and Longmans between 1850 and 1919, concluding that in most cases the agreements worked to the distinct disadvantage of the provincial representatives. Although the provincial book publisher gained access to the London market through such co-publication deals, it was usually to the greater profit and benefit of well-positioned London firms such as Simpkin & Marshall.

But even London-based firms could face rocky times trying to access British mass markets. Witness the attempts to popularize Shakespeare for a nineteenth-century mass market, a history recounted by Marvin Spevack in 'What Price Shakespeare? James Orchard Halliwell-Phillipps and the Shilling Shakespeares of the 1860s' (*PBSA* 96:i[2002] 23–47). In the mid-1860s, the Shakespeare enthusiast and entrepreneur James Orchard Halliwell, in conjunction with the London publisher John Camden Hotten, sought to issue editions of Shakespeare's plays in shilling editions. Routledge, Warne & Co. and John Dicks quickly launched three other competing series. The results, as analysed by Spevack, are important links in the study of the reception of Shakespeare's work that repay examination and interpretation.

Publishers have recently woken up to the fact that book history is a growing field in need of teaching- and research-based material. Some have approached the matter by commissioning new texts that inform as well as provide supporting material, while others have drawn together collections providing new material for thought, and reprints of classic texts that flesh out the book history perspective. Those who work in this area may feel justifiably smug now that the academic publishing world has woken up to the value of what is being done in this field. But understanding the value of book history and print culture studies has until recently been hampered by a lack of readily available teaching and research tools for those who wish to engage students in the area. A recent entry seeking to remedy this is Casper, Chaison, and Groves, eds., *Perspectives on American Book History: Artifacts and Commentary*, useful as a general resource for teachers and students of book history, but written with a particular US perspective on the subject. The work is divided into seventeen chronological sections covering a range of topics, from the seventeenth century through to a speculative chapter on the future of the book. The sections are a mix of historically based and thematically focused material—while some focus on 'flashpoints' in US history, others focus on more general themes, such as print culture and the labouring classes, debates on 'middlebrow' culture, and non-mainstream textual production. Each section includes short introductions, extracts from primary texts, and extensive concluding commentary placing these extracts in appropriate historical contexts. The editors have brought together a range of contributors, mainly new and emerging scholars in the field, who present material they use in classroom settings in strongly crafted and illuminating fashion. One of the aims of this text is to highlight 'the new history of the book: a medium for teaching and scholarship well suited to the needs of a "media age"' (p. 3), and it does this in practice by attaching to the back cover a CD-ROM that provides over 200 printable images with supporting commentary, linked to the areas covered in the text. The images can be downloaded for projection via a computer, or printed off as transparencies, and the range of illustrations (from early British newspaper covers and linotype and composition machines to an advertisement advising readers on how to negotiate their way through Joyce's *Ulysses*) is worth the price of the book alone, even for those teaching courses in European or non-US print culture and book history studies. What is particularly welcome about this collection of artefacts is that it offers a broad mixture of original texts supplemented by visual images both in the text and on accessible CD-ROM. The commentary that frames these sources allows readers to understand the overall historical and social context of the material while at the same time leaving them free to dip in and make their own use and judgement of relevant items.

The University of Massachusetts Press has just issued a welcome paperback collection of the late Don McKenzie's best work on book history: McDonald and Suarez, eds., *Making Meaning: 'Printers of the Mind' and Other Essays*. While most of the collection focuses on McKenzie's area of expertise (the seventeenth century), also represented are significant essays on the history of the book and textual editing that repay rereading from a Victorian studies perspective, including '"What's Past is Prologue": The Bibliographical Society and History of the Book'.

McKenzie is also the focus of Thomson, ed., *Books and Bibliography: Essays in Commemoration of Don McKenzie*, a collection arising from an international symposium held at the National Library of New Zealand in 2001. In this case, fourteen contributors present work that utilizes, debates, or challenges McKenzie's theoretical perspectives on book history and literary culture. The topics range from a study of the role of Victorian settlers in establishing print culture in New Zealand's Wellington community (Kathleen Coleridge, 'Artisan Radicals in Wellington, 1840–1860'), to the trans-Tasmanian links between New Zealand and Australia fostered by British emigrant printers and artists in the second half of the nineteenth century (Ian Morrison, 'Cook's Choice: Reflections on Trans-Tasman Literary Culture'), and the place of oral culture and material contexts in the promotion of a nineteenth-century British bestseller, in this case George Chesney's 1871 invasion scare novella 'The Battle of Dorking' (David Finkelstein, 'From Textuality to Orality: The Reception of *The Battle of Dorking*'). While other essays in this collection may prove irrelevant to nineteenth-century research interests, the work on the whole shows the range of subjects influenced by Don McKenzie during a long and illustrious career.

Maori newspapers have recently been investigated by researchers across New Zealand, and the results both placed on the web and expatiated in a compact and valuable essay collection, Curnow, Hopa, and McRae, eds., *Rere atu, taku manu!*

Discovering History, Language and Politics in the Maori-Language Newspapers. What is especially valuable from a print culture perspective are the details that emerge of the collaboration and cross-cultural links between emigrant printers and Maori cultural agents. While initial expertise in the setting up and running of print media outlets was provided by nineteenth-century British settlers, missionaries, and government agents, the progress of an indigenous press reflected an adaptation of format, convention, and activity to match Maori expectations and cultural concerns. Thus interesting themes emerge in this collection: the role of oral culture in shaping textual presentation; the adaptation of Methodist missionary publications in the face of reader responses; and the refraction of the dynamics of colonial politics in Maori newspaper reports and dialogues. The book provides an intensely valuable insight into transnational print culture activity which will be equally useful in Victorian and twentieth-century literary studies.

Other colonial encounters in book history terms come through in *In Another Country: Colonialism, Culture, and the English Novel in India*, Priya Joshi's complexly articulated study of Indian readership, consumption, and reception across the nineteenth and twentieth centuries. A mix of archival work and theoretical enquiry blend into a work of two halves: the first concerned with the circulation of Victorian popular novelists in India in the second half of the nineteenth century, and the development of British publishing material targeted specifically at an identified indigenous and colonial Indian audience, and the second half examining Indian fiction in the twentieth century produced in reaction to such colonial imports. Readers of the annual *Book History* will recognize material from the first section, which featured recently in its pages. Much valuable empirical and *Annales*-influenced work is in evidence, with a wealth of material culled from the Macmillan archives in London and from original documentation in Indian institutions. This said, the two halves of the work meld with difficulty, reflecting a tension between the author's desire to mesh empirically grounded book history techniques with literary-critical discourse derived from postmodernist and postcolonial theoretical concerns.

Books Reviewed

Abeles, Francine F., ed. *The Political Pamphlets and Letters of Charles Lutwidge Dodgson and Related Pieces: A Mathematical Approach*, vol. 3. UPVirginia. [2002] pp. 280. $51.95 ISBN 0 9303 2614 8.

Ainger, Michael. *Gilbert and Sullivan: A Dual Biography*. OUPAm. [2002] pp. 528. £25 ISBN 0 1951 4769 3.

Anderson, Amanda. *The Powers of Distance: Cosmopolitanism and the Culture of Detachment*. PrincetonUP. [2001] pp. 196. £39.95 ($55) ISBN 0 6910 7496 8.

Arata, Stephen, ed. *News from Nowhere*, by William Morris. Broadview. [2002] pp. 356. $12.95 ISBN 1 5511 1267 1.

Archibald, Diana C. *Domesticity, Imperialism, and Emigration in the Victorian Novel*. UMissP. [2002] pp. 232. $39.95 ISBN 0 8262 1400 2.

Ardis, Ann L. *Modernism and Cultural Conflict, 1880–1922*. CUP. [2002] pp. 198. $55 ISBN 0 5218 1206 2.

Argyle, Gisela. *Germany as a Model and Monster: Allusions in English Fiction.* McG-QUP. [2002] pp. 257. $70 ISBN 0 7735 2351 0.

Baker, William. *Wilkie Collins's Library: A Reconstruction.* Greenwood. [2002] pp. xv + 192 $74.95 ISBN 0 3133 1394 6.

Baker, William and John C. Ross. *George Eliot: A Bibliographical History.* OakK. [2002] pp. 715. $79 ISBN 1 5845 6069 X.

Baker, William and Kenneth Womack, eds. *A Companion to the Victorian Novel.* Greenwood. [2002] pp. xii + 445. $94.95 ISBN 0 3133 1407 1.

Barth, J. Robert, ed. *The Fountain Light: Studies in Romanticism and Religion—In Honour of John L. Maloney.* FordUP. [2002] pp. xv + 289. hb £32.50 ($40) ISBN 0 8232 2228 4, pb £16.50 ($20) ISBN 0 8232 2229 2.

Billington, Josie. *Faithful Realism: Elizabeth Gaskell and Leo Tolstoy—A Comparative Study.* BuckUP. [2002] pp. 227. $43.50 ISBN 0 8387 5458 9.

Birch, Dinah, and Francis O'Gorman, eds. *Ruskin and Gender.* Palgrave. [2002] pp. 227. $62 ISBN 0 3339 6897 2.

Boehmer, Elleke. *Empire, the National, and the Postcolonial, 1890–1920.* OUP. [2002] pp. viii + 239. £40 ISBN 0 1981 8446 8.

Boos, Florence S., ed. *The Earthly Paradise*, by William Morris. 2 vols. Routledge. [2002] pp. lii + 687 (vol. 1), pp. lxxii + 779 (vol. 2). £195 ($275) ISBN 0 4159 4150 4 (vol. 1), ISBN 0 4159 4151 2 (vol. 2), ISBN 0 8153 2104 X (set).

Bourke, Angela, et al., eds. *The Field Day Anthology of Irish Writing*, vols. 4 and 5: *Irish Women's Writing and Traditions.* NYUP. [2002] pp. 3,200. £162.50 ISBN 1 8591 8280 1.

Brake, Laurel, Lesley Higgins, and Carolyn Williams, eds. *Walter Pater: Transparencies of Desire.* UNCP/Greensboro. [2002] pp. 400. $40 ISBN 0 9443 1816 9.

Brantlinger, Patrick, and William B. Thesing, eds. *A Companion to the Victorian Novel.* Blackwell. [2002] pp. 528. £85 ISBN 0 6312 2064 X.

Brendon, Piers. *Hawker of Morwenstow: Portrait of a Victorian Eccentric.* Pimlico. [2002] pp. 270. £12.50 ISBN 0 7126 6772 5.

Briggs, Katherine. *The Fairies in Tradition and Literature.* Routledge. [2002] pp. xiii + 324. $14.95 ISBN 0 4152 8601 8.

Brügger, Niel, and Søren Kolstrup. *Media History: Theories, Methods, Analysis.* AarhusUP. [2002] pp. 196. £14.95 ISBN 8 7728 8839 3.

Burton, Antoinette, ed. *After the Imperial Turn: Thinking With and Through the Nation.* DukeUP. [2003] pp. 369. hb $79.95 ISBN 0 8223 3106 3, pb $23.95 ISBN 0 8223 3142 X.

Cain, Peter. *Hobson and Imperialism; Radicalism, New Liberalism, and Finance, 1887–1938.* OUP. [2002] pp. 400. $70 ISBN 0 1982 0390 X.

Caldwell, Sarah. *Adaptation Revisited: Television and the Classic Novel.* ManUP. [2002] pp. 224. $74.95 ISBN 0 7190 6045 1.

Campbell, Christy. *Fenian Fire: The British Government Plot to Assassinate Queen Victoria.* HC. [2002] pp. 320. £18.99 ISBN 0 0071 0483 9.

Campbell, Christy. *The Maharajah's Box: An Exotic Tale of Espionage, Intrigue, and Illicit Love in the Days of the Raj.* Overlook. [2002] pp. 474. $29.95 ISBN 1 5856 7293 9.

Camus, Marianne. *Women's Voices in the Fiction of Elizabeth Gaskell (1810–1865).* Mellen. [2002] pp. 292. $119.95 ISBN 0 7734 6927 3.

Carpenter, Kenneth E. *The Dissemination of 'The Wealth of Nations' in French and in France, 1776–1843*. OakK. [2002] pp. 336. $45 ISBN 0 9149 3017 6.

Casper, Scott E., Joanne D. Chaison, and Jeffrey D. Groves, eds. *Perspectives on American Book History: Artifacts and Commentary*. UMassP. [2002] pp. ix + 461. pb £20.95 ISBN 1 5584 9317 4.

Cervasco, G.A. *The Breviary of the Decadence: J.-K. Huysmans's 'A Rebours' and English Literature*. AMS. [2002] pp. 227. $64.50 ISBN 0 4046 4455 4.

Clapp-Itnyre, Alisa. *Angelic Airs, Subversive Songs: Music as Social Discourse in the Victorian Novel*. OhioUP. [2002] pp. 226. $49.95 ISBN 0 8214 1431 3.

Coates, John D. *G.K. Chesterton as Controversialist, Essayist, Novelist, and Critic*. Mellen. [2002] pp. 200. $109.95 ISBN 0 7734 7096 4.

Conboy, Martin. *The Press and Popular Culture*. Sage. [2002] pp. xi + 194. £16.99 ISBN 0 7619 6661 7.

Cox, Michael, and R.A. Gilbert, eds. *The Oxford Book of English Ghost Stories*. OUP. [2002] pp. 525. £9.99 ISBN 0 1928 4085 1.

Cronin, Richard. *Romantic Victorians: English Literature, 1824–1840*. Palgrave. [2002] pp. viii + 296. £55 ($69.95) ISBN 0 3339 6616 3.

Cronin, Richard. Alison Chapman, and Antony H. Harrison, eds. *A Companion to Victorian Poetry*. Blackwell Companions to Literature and Culture. [2002] pp. xv + 602. £85 ($124.95) ISBN 0 6312 2207 3.

Cunningham, Valentine, and Duncan Wu, eds. *Victorian Poetry*. Blackwell Essential Literature. [2002] pp. 185. hb £49.95 ($60) ISBN 0 6312 3075 0, pb £9.99 ($17.95) ISBN 0 6312 3076 9.

Curnow, Jennifer, Ngapare Hopa, and Jane McRae, eds. *Rere atu, taku manu! Discovering History, Language and Politics in the Maori-Language Newspapers*. Auckland University Press. [2002] pp. xv + 241. £13.50 ISBN 1 8694 0279 0.

Davies, Stevie, ed. *The Brontë Sisters: Selected Poems*. Carcanet. [2002] pp.123. £6.95 ISBN 0 8563 5131 8.

Davis, Philip. *The Victorians*, vol. 8: *1830–1880*. OUP. [2002] pp. 264. $45 ISBN 0 1981 8447 6.

Delany, Paul. *Literature, Money and the Market: From Trollope to Amis*. Palgrave. [2002] pp. 251. $45 ISBN 0 3339 7135 3.

Demata, Massimiliano, and Duncan Wu, eds. *British Romanticism and the Edinburgh Review: Bicentenary Essays*. Palgrave Macmillan. [2002] pp. xii + 219. £47.50 ISBN 0 3339 6349 0.

Dickens, Charles. *Bleak House*. Modern Library. [2002] pp. xxxv + 880. $10.95 ISBN 0 3757 6005 9.

Dickens, Charles. *The Haunted House*. Hesperus Press. [2002] pp. 100. $12 ISBN 1 8439 1021 7.

Dickens, Charles. *Little Dorrit*. Modern Library. [2002] pp. 912. $8.95 ISBN 0 3757 5914 X.

Dickens, Charles. *Our Mutual Friend*. Modern Library. [2002] pp. xxx + 834. $10.95 ISBN 0 3757 6114 4.

Douglas-Fairhurst, Robert. *Victorian Afterlives: The Shaping of Influence in Nineteenth-Century Literature*. OUP. [2002] pp. xi + 372. £45 ($74) ISBN 0 1981 8727 0.

Doyle, Arthur Conan. *The Adventures and Memoirs of Sherlock Holmes*. Modern Library. [2002] pp. 501. $12.95 ISBN 0 3757 6002 4.

Durey, Jill Felicity. *Trollope and the Church of England*. Palgrave. [2002] pp. 256. $62 ISBN 0 3339 8790 X.

Dyson, Ketaki Kushari. *A Various Universe: A Study of the Journals and Memoirs of British Men and Women in the Indian Subcontinent, 1765–1856*. OUP. [2002] pp. 428. £20 ISBN 0 1956 6114 1.

Eells, Emily. *Proust's Cup of Tea: Homoeroticism and Victorian Culture*. Ashgate. [2002] pp. 231. $79.95 ISBN 0 7546 0518 3.

Eliot, George. *Adam Bede*. Modern Library. [2002] pp. xvii + 592. $8.95 ISBN 0 3757 5901 8.

Eliot, George. *Daniel Deronda*. Modern Library. [2002] pp. xxv + 796. $9.95 ISBN 0 3757 6013 X.

Elliott, Dorice Williams. *The Angel Out of the House: Philanthropy and Gender in Nineteenth-Century England*. UPVirginia. [2002] pp. 264. $35 ISBN 0 8139 2088 4.

Falck-Yi, Suzanne B., ed. *Far From the Madding Crowd*, by Thomas Hardy. OUP. [2002] pp. 490. £3.50 ISBN 0 1928 0149 X.

Fegan, Melissa. *Literature and the Irish Famine, 1845–1919*. OUP. [2002] pp. 281. £30 ISBN 0 1992 5464 8.

Feldman, Jessica. *Victorian Modernism: Pragmatisms and the Varieties of Aesthetic Experience*. CUP. [2002] pp. 276. $60 ISBN 0 5218 1581 9.

Fichman, Martin. *Evolutionary Theory and Victorian Culture*. Prometheus. [2002] pp. 150. £17 ISBN 1 5910 2003 4.

Finkelstein, David. *The House of Blackwood: Author–Publisher Relations in the Victorian Era*. PSUP. [2002] pp. viii + 198. £44.95 ISBN 0 2710 2179 9.

Finkelstein, David and Alistair McCleery, eds. *The Book History Reader*. Routledge. [2002] pp. 368. $90 ISBN 0 4152 2657 0.

Fisher, Judith L. *Thackeray's Skeptical Narrative and the 'Perilous Trade' of Authorship*. Ashgate. [2002] pp. 310. $79.95 ISBN 0 7546 0651 1.

Fisher, Trevor. *Oscar and Bosie: A Fatal Passion*. Sutton. [2002] pp. 267. $29.98 ISBN 0 7509 2459 4.

Forbes, Derek. *Illustrated Playbills*. STR. [2002] pp. xi + 132. £14.99 ISBN 0 8543 0072 4

Foster, Shirley. *Elizabeth Gaskell: A Literary Life*. Palgrave. [2002] pp. 215. $49.95 ISBN 0 3336 9581 X.

France, Peter, and William St. Clair, eds. *Mapping Lives: The Uses of Biography*. OUP. [2002] pp. 358. £35 ISBN 0 1972 6269 4.

Fredeman, William E., ed. *The Correspondence of Dante Gabriel Rossetti*, vol. 1: *1835–1854*. Brewer. [2002] pp. 442. £95 ISBN 0 8599 1528 X.

Fredeman, William E., ed. *The Correspondence of Dante Gabriel Rossetti*, vol. 2: *1855–1862*. Brewer. [2002] pp. 640. $165 ISBN 0 8599 1637 5.

Gardiner, John. *The Victorians: An Age in Retrospect*. Hambledon. [2002] pp. xii + 292. $29.84 ISBN 1 8528 5385 9.

Garlick, Barbara, ed. *Tradition and the Poetics of Self in Nineteenth-Century Women's Poetry*. Costerus new series. Rodopi. [2002] pp. xi + 199. £40 ($48) ISBN 9 0420 1300 1.

Gates, Barbara T., ed. *In Nature's Name: An Anthology of Women's Writing and Illustrations, 1780–1930*. UChicP. [2002] pp. 673. $27.50 ISBN 0 2262 8444 1.

Gay, Peter. *Savage Reprisals: Bleak House, Madame Bovary, Buddenbrooks.* Norton. [2002] pp. 192. $24.95 ISBN 0 3930 5118 8.

Gaylin, Ann. *Eavesdropping in the Novel from Austen to Proust.* CUP. [2002] pp. 256. $55 ISBN 0 5218 1585 1.

Gibson, James, ed. *Thomas Hardy: The Complete Poems.* Palgrave. [2001] pp. 256. hb £40 ($55) ISBN 0 3339 4928 5, pb £13.99 ($21.95) ISBN 0 3339 4929 3.

Gill, Stephen, ed. *The Last Chronicle of Barset,* by Anthony Trollope. OUP. [2002] pp. xxiv + 904. £5.99 ISBN 0 1928 3534 3.

Gilmour, David. *The Long Recessional: The Imperial Life of Rudyard Kipling.* Murray. [2002] pp. 362. £22.50 ISBN 0 7195 5539 6.

Glen, Heather, ed. *The Cambridge Companion to the Brontës.* CUP. [2002] pp. 270. $60 ISBN 0 5217 7027 0.

Glen, Heather, ed. *Charlotte Brontë: The Imagination in History.* OUP. [2002] pp. 314. £50 ISBN 0 1981 8761 0.

Glowacka, Dorota, and Stephen Boos, eds. *Between Ethics and Aesthetics: Crossing the Boundaries.* SUNY. [2002] pp. 286. hb $81.50 ISBN 0 7914 5195 X, pb $27.95 ISBN 0 7914 5196 8.

GoGwilt, Christopher. *The Fiction of Geopolitics: Afterimages of Culture, from Wilkie Collins to Alfred Hitchcock.* StanfordUP. [2002] pp. 248. £42.95 ISBN 0 8047 3726 6.

Goldberg, Christine, ed. *Popular Tales and Fictions. Their Migrations and Transformations: 'W.A.' by Clouston.* ABC CLIO. [2002] pp. 700. $55 ISBN 1 5760 7616 4.

Goldman, Lawrence. *Science, Reform, and Politics in Victorian Britain: The Social Science Association, 1857–1886.* CUP. [2002] pp. 446. £50 ISBN 0 5213 3053 X.

Goodall, Jane. R. *Performance and Evolution in the Age of Darwin: Out of the Natural Order.* Routledge. [2002] pp. xi + 266. hb £60 ISBN 0 4152 4377 7, pb £18.99 ISBN 0 4152 4378 5.

Greenspan, Ezra. *The House of Putnam, 1837–1872: A Documentary Volume.* The Gale Group. [2002] pp. xxvii + 420. $190 ISBN 0 7876 5248 2.

Grob, Alan. *A Longing Like Despair: Matthew Arnold and the Poetry of Pessimism.* UDelP. [2002] pp. 249. £35 ($43.50) ISBN 0 87413 7527.

Grossman, Jonathan H. *The Art of Alibi: English Law Courts and the Novel.* JHUP. [2002] pp. 202 + xii. $39.95 ISBN 0 8018 6755 X.

Haase, Donald, ed. *English Fairy Tales; and, More English Fairy Tales,* by Joseph Jacobs. ABC CLIO. [2002] pp. 369. $45 ISBN 1 5760 7426 9.

Haddad, Emily. *Orientalist Poetics: The Islamic Middle East in Nineteenth-Century English and French Poetry.* Ashgate. [2002] pp. vii + 220. £40 ($69.95) ISBN 0 7546 0304 0.

Haggard, H. Rider. *King Solomon's Mines.* Modern Library. [2002] pp. 304. $8.95 ISBN 0 8129 6629 5.

Hall, Catherine. *Civilising Subjects; Metropole and Colony in the English Imagination, 1830–1867.* Polity. [2002] pp. 576. £19.99 ISBN 0 7456 1821 9.

Hall, John N. *Max Beerbohm: A Kind of Life.* YaleUP. [2002] pp. 224. $24.95 ISBN 0 3000 9705 0.

Halpern, Richard. *Shakespeare's Perfume: Sodomy and Sublimity in the Sonnets, Wilde, Freud, and Lacan.* UPennP. [2002] pp. 125. $29.95 ISBN 0 8122 3661 0.

Hamilton, Peter, and Roger Hargreaves. *The Beautiful and the Damned: The Creation of Identity in Nineteenth-Century Photography*. LH. [2002] pp. 126. $60 ISBN 0 8533 1821 2.

Hardy, Thomas. *The Mayor of Casterbridge*. Modern Library. [2002] pp. xl + 366. $7.95 ISBN 0 3757 6006 7.

Hardy, Thomas. *The Woodlanders*. Modern Library. [2002] pp. xxx + 407. $7.95 ISBN 0 3757 6120 9.

Harris, Susan K. *The Cultural Work of the Late Nineteenth-Century Hostess: Annie Adams Fields and Mary Gladstone Drew*. Palgrave. [2002] pp. 212. $49.95 ISBN 0 3122 9529 4.

Hartnell, Elaine. *Gender, Religion and Domesticity in the Novels of Rosa Nouchette Carey*. Ashgate. [2002] pp. 256. $79.95 ISBN 0 7546 0283 4.

Hawlin, Stefan. *The Complete Critical Guide to Robert Browning*. Routledge. [2002] pp. xiii + 222. hb £50 ($75) ISBN 0 4152 2231 1, pb £12.99 ($19.95) ISBN 0 4152 2232 X.

Henry, Nancy. *George Eliot and the British Empire*. CUP. [2002] pp. 198. $50 ISBN 0 5218 0845 6.

Hicks, Malcolm, ed. *Oscar Wilde: Selected Poems*. Carcanet. [2002] pp. 128. £6.95 ISBN 0 8563 5984 X.

Hogle, Jerrold E., ed. *The Cambridge Companion to Gothic Fiction*. CUP. [2002] pp. 354. $60 ISBN 0 5217 9124 3.

Hollingsworth, Cristopher. *Poetics of the Hive: The Insect Metaphor in Literature*. UIowaP. [2002] pp. 334. $47.95 ISBN 0 8774 5786 7.

Holroyd, Michael. *Works on Paper: The Craft of Biography and Autobiography*. Counterpoint. [2002] pp. 336. $27 ISBN 1 5824 3150 7.

Horne, Philip, ed. *Oliver Twist*, by Charles Dickens. Penguin. [2002] pp. liii + 553. £3.50 ISBN 0 1404 6522 0.

Hull, David L., ed. *Science and its Conceptual Foundations*. UChicP. [2002] pp. 488. $35 ISBN 0 2267 1210 9.

Ingham, Patricia, ed. *Jude the Obscure*, by Thomas Hardy. OUP. [2002] pp. lvi + 416. £3.50 ISBN 0 1928 0261 5.

Ingle, Stephen. *Narratives of British Socialism*. Palgrave. [2002] pp. 208. $68 ISBN 0 3335 1083 6.

Jackson, Macdonald P., ed. *Selected Poems of Eugene Lee-Hamilton: A Victorian Craftsman Rediscovered*. Studies in British Literature. Mellen. [2002] pp. v + 208. £34.95 ($89.95) ISBN 0 7734 7305 X.

James, Elizabeth, ed. *Macmillan: A Publishing Tradition*. Macmillan. [2001] pp. 301. $69.95 ISBN 0 3337 3517 X.

Joh, Byunghwa. *Thomas Hardy's Poetry: A Jungian Perspective*. Modernist Revolution in World Literature. Lang. [2002] pp. 131. £32 ($46.95) ISBN 0 8204 5167 3.

John, Juliet. *Dickens's Villains: Melodrama, Character, Popular Culture*. OUP. [2001] pp. xiii + 258. hb £50 ISBN 0 1981 8461 1, pb £16.99 ISBN 0 1992 6137 7.

Joshi, Priya. *In Another Country: Colonialism, Culture, and the English Novel in India*. ColUP. [2002] pp. xix + 363. £36.50 ISBN 0 2311 2584 4.

Kamper, Birgit. *Margaret Oliphant's Carlingford Series: An Original Contribution to the Debate on Religion, Class and Gender in the 1860s and 70s*. Lang. [2001] pp. 329. $52.95 ISBN 3 6313 7558 1.

Keane, Robert. *Dante Gabriel Rossetti: The Poet as Craftsman*. Studies in Nineteenth-Century British Literature. Lang. [2002] pp. x + 219. £38 ($55.95) ISBN 0 8204 5114 2.

Kelsall, Malcolm. *Literary Representations of the Irish Country House: Civilisation and Savagery Under the Union*. Palgrave. [2002] pp. 224. $62 ISBN 0 3337 7936 3.

Kemp, Sandra, Charlotte Mitchell, and David Trotter, eds. *Edwardian Fiction: An Oxford Companion*. OUP. [2002] pp. 464. £14.99 ISBN 0 1986 0534 X.

Keymer, Thomas. *Sterne, the Moderns, and the Novel*. OUP. [2002] pp. 236. £45 ISBN 0 1992 4592 4.

Krueger, Christine L., ed. *Functions of Victorian Culture at the Present Time*. OhioUP. [2002] pp. xx + 195. hb $44.95 ISBN 0 8214 1460 7, pb $19.95 ISBN 0 8214 1461 5.

Kuhn, Joaquin, and Joseph J. Feeney, SJ, eds. *Hopkins Variations: Standing Round a Waterfall*. St Joseph's UP/FordUP. [2002] pp. xxi + 315. £29.95 ($37) ISBN 0 9161 9139 8.

Kuhn, William M. *Henry and Mary Ponsonby*. Duckworth. [2002] pp. 302. £20 ISBN 0 7156 3065 2.

Langland, Elizabeth. *Telling Tales: Gender and Narrative Form in Victorian Literature and Culture*. OhioUP. [2002] pp. 163. $44.95 ISBN 0 8142 0905 X.

Lawson, Kate, and Lynn Shakinovsky. *The Marked Body: Domestic Violence in Mid-Nineteenth-Century Literature*. SUNYP. [2002] pp. 204. hb $59.50 ISBN 0 7914 5375 8, pb $19.95 ISBN 0 7914 5376 6.

Lengel, Edward G. *The Irish through British Eyes: Perceptions of Ireland in the Famine Era*. Praeger. [2002] pp. 264. $64.95 ISBN 0 2759 7634 3.

Levine, George. *Dying to Know: Scientific Epistemology and Narrative in Victorian England*. UChicP. [2002] pp. 320. $45 ISBN 0 2264 7536 0.

Lewis, Scott, ed. *The Letters of Elizabeth Barrett Browning to her Sister Arabella*. 2 vols. Wedgestone. [2002] pp. xlvii + 590 (vol. 1), pp. xiv + 624 (vol. 2). $300 ISBN 0 9114 5929 4.

Linehan, Katherine, ed. *The Strange Case of Dr. Jekyll and Mr. Hyde*, by Robert Louis Stevenson. Norton. [2002] pp. 222. $9.25 ISBN 0 3939 7465 0.

Lodge, David. *Consciousness and the Novel: Connected Essays*. HarvardUP. [2002] pp. 272. $24.95 ISBN 0 6740 0949 5.

Logan, Deborah Anna. *The Hour and the Woman: Harriet Martineau's 'Somewhat Remarkable' Life*. NIUP. [2002] pp. 343. $42 ISBN 0 8758 0297 4.

Loizeaux, Elizabeth Bergmann, and Neil Fraistat, eds. *Reimagining Textuality: Textual Studies in the Late Age of Print*. UWiscP. [2002] pp. vii + 262. £19.50 ISBN 0 2991 7384 4.

Luckhurst, Roger, and Josephine McDonagh, eds. *Transactions and Encounters: Science and Culture in the Nineteenth Century*. ManUP. [2002] pp. 256. £15.99 ISBN 0 7190 5911 9.

Luyat, Anne, and Francine Tolron, eds. *Flight from Certainty: The Dilemma of Identity and Exile*. Rodopi. [2001] pp. 254. £38.50 ($53) ISBN 9 0420 1595 0.

Maxwell, Catherine. *The Female Sublime from Milton to Swinburne: Bearing Blindness*. ManUP. [2001] pp. viii + 279. £47.50 ($74.95) ISBN 0 7190 5752 3.

Maxwell, Richard, ed. *The Victorian Illustrated Book*. Victorian Literature and Culture. UPVirginia. [2002] pp. xxx + 440. £33.50 ($45) ISBN 0 8139 2097 3.

McDonald, Peter D., and Michael F. Suarez, SJ, eds. *Making Meaning: 'Printers of the Mind' and Other Essays*. UMassP. [2002] pp. x + 286. £19.50 ISBN 1 5584 9336 0.

McGowan, Christopher. *The Dragon Seekers: How an Extraordinary Circle of Fossilists Discovered the Dinosaurs and Paved the Way for Darwin*. Little Brown. [2001] pp. 281. £18.99 ISBN 0 3168 5783 1.

Meckier, Jerome. *Dickens's 'Great Expectations': Misnar's 'Pavilion Versus Cinderella'*. UPKen. [2002] pp. 296. $38 ISBN 0 8131 2228 7.

Menikoff, Barry, ed. *The Complete Stories of Robert Louis Stevenson: 'The Strange Case of Dr. Jekyll and Mr. Hyde' and Nineteen other Tales*. Modern Library. [2002] pp. 880. $14.95 ISBN 0 3757 6135 7.

Meyer, Michael, ed. *Literature and Musical Adaptation*. Rodopi Perspectives on Modern Literature. Rodopi. [2002] pp. 221. £38.95 ($52) ISBN 9 0420 0812 1.

Monsman, Gerald, ed. *King Solomon's Mines*, by H. Rider Haggard. Broadview. [2002] pp. 306. $9.95 ISBN 1 5511 1439 9.

Morris, Hazel. *Hand, Head and Heart: Samuel Carter Hall and The Art Journal*. Russell. [2002] pp. 224. £24 ISBN 0 8595 5273 X.

Moxham, Jeffrey. *Interfering Values in the Nineteenth-Century British Novel: Austen, Dickens, Eliot, Hardy, and the Ethics of Criticism*. Greenwood. [2002] pp. 248. $64.95 ISBN 0 3133 2283 X.

Nayder, Lillian. *Unequal Partners: Charles Dickens, Wilkie Collins, and Victorian Authorship*. CornUP. [2002] pp. 248. $35 ISBN 0 8014 3925 6.

Nord, Deborah Epstein, ed. *Sesame and Lilies*, by John Ruskin. YaleUP. [2002] pp. xxiv + 207. $35 ISBN 0 3000 9259 8.

O'Brien, Kevin. *Saying Yes at Lightning: Threat and the Provisional Image in Post-Romantic Poetry*. Lang. [2002] pp. 295. $62.95 ISBN 0 8204 3957 6.

O'Brien, Rosemary, ed. *The Desert and the Sown: The Syrian Adventures of the Female Lawrence of Arabia*, by Gertrude Bell. Cooper. [2001] pp. 368. $19.95 ISBN 0 8154 1135 9.

O'Gorman, Francis, ed. *The Victorian Novel*. Blackwell. [2002] pp. 368. $27.95 ISBN 0 6312 2704 0.

Otis, Laura, ed. *Literature and Science in the Nineteenth Century*. OUP. [2002] pp. lii + 575. £9.99 ISBN 0 1928 3979 9.

Overton, Bill. *Fictions of Female Adultery, 1684–1890: Theories and Circumtexts*. Palgrave. [2002] pp. 304. £45 ISBN 0 3337 7080 3.

Parker, David. *The Doughty Street Novels: Pickwick Papers, Oliver Twist, Nicholas Nickleby, Barnaby Rudge*. AMS. [2002] pp. xiv + 240. $64.50 ISBN 0 4046 4453 8.

Pite, Ralph. *Hardy's Geography: Wessex and the Regional Novel*. Palgrave. [2002] pp. 264. $65 ISBN 0 3339 8774 8.

Purdy, Richard L. *Thomas Hardy: A Bibliographical Study*. OakK. [2002] pp. 432. $65 ISBN 7 5845 6070 3.

Pykett, Lyn. *Charles Dickens*. Palgrave. [2002] pp. 224. £16.50 ISBN 0 3337 2803 3.

Rainsford, Dominic. *Literature, Identity and the English Channel: The Narrow Seas Expanded*. Palgrave. [2002] pp. 201. $62 ISBN 0 3337 7389 6.

Rem, Tore. *Dickens, Melodrama, and the Parodic Imagination*. AMS. [2002] pp. xii + 239. $72.50 ISBN 0 4046 4451 1.

Richards, Jeffrey. *Imperialism and Music: Britain 1876–1953*. ManUP. [2001] pp. x + 534. £19.99 ISBN 0 7190 6143 1.

Ricks, Christopher. *Allusion to the Poets*. OUP. [2002] pp. 345. pb £12.99 ($18.95) ISBN 0 1992 5032 4.

Riquelme, John Paul, ed. *'Dracula' by Bram Stoker: Complete, Authoritative Text with Biographical, Historical, and Cultural Contexts, Critical History, and Essays from Contemporary Critical Perspectives*. Palgrave. [2002] pp. 622. $45 ISBN 0 3122 3710 3.

Roberts, Caroline. *The Woman and the Hour: Harriet Martineau and Victorian Ideologies*. UTorP. [2002] pp. 253. $50 ISBN 0 8020 3596 5.

Ross, William T.H.G. *Wells's World Reborn: The Outline of History and its Companions*. SusquehannaUP. [2002] pp. 136. $33.50 ISBN 1 5759 1057 8.

Sabin, Margery. *Dissenters and Mavericks; Writings about India in English, 1765–2000*. OUP. [2002] pp. 250. £25 ISBN 0 1951 5017 1.

Samson, Jim, ed. *The Cambridge History of Nineteenth-Century Music*. CUP. [2002] pp. 788. £80 ISBN 0 5215 9017 5.

Sanders, Andrew, ed. *Dombey and Son*, by Charles Dickens. Penguin. [2002] pp. xxxii + 996. £7.99 ISBN 0 1404 3546 8.

Sanders, Valerie. *The Brother–Sister Culture in Nineteenth-Century Literature: From Austen to Woolf*. Palgrave. [2002] pp. 236. $62 ISBN 0 3337 4930 8.

Santilli, N. *Such Rare Citings: The Prose Poem in English Literature*. AUP. [2002] pp. 288. $47.50 ISBN 0 8386 3951 8.

Scheinberg, Cynthia. *Women's Poetry and Religion in Victorian England: Jewish Identity and Christian Culture*. CUP. [2002] pp. xi + 275. £40 ($55) ISBN 0 5218 1112 0.

Schoch, Richard W. *Not Shakespeare: Bardolatry and Burlesque in the Nineteenth Century*. CUP. [200] pp. xiii + 209. $55 ISBN 0 5218 0015 3.

Schwarze, Tracey Teets. *Joyce and the Victorians*. UFlorP. [2002] pp. 272. $55 ISBN 0 8130 2437 4.

Shaw, Ian J. *High Calvinists in Action: Calvinism and the City in Manchester and London, c.1810–1860*. OUP. [2002] pp. 426. £55 ISBN 0 1992 5077 4.

Siegel, Jonah. *Desire and Excess: The Nineteenth-Century Culture of Art*. PrincetonUP. [2002] pp. 328. $75 ISBN 0 6910 4913 0.

Silver, Anna Krugovoy. *Victorian Literature and the Anorexic Body*. CUP. [2002] pp. 220. £40 ($55) ISBN 0 5218 1602 5.

Silver, Keith, ed. *Lewis Carroll: Selected Poems*. Carcanet. [2002] pp. xxii + 122. £6.95 ISBN 1 8575 4147 2.

Sinnema, Peter W., ed. *Self-Help*, by Samuel Smiles. OUP. [2002] pp. 512. £7.99 ISBN 0 1928 0176 7.

Slater, Michael. *Douglas Jerrold: 1803–1857*. Duckworth. [2002] pp. 272. $35 ISBN 0 7156 2824 0.

Smiley, Jane. *Charles Dickens*. Viking. [2002] pp. 212. $19.95 ISBN 0 6700 3077 5.

Spector, Sheila A., ed. *British Romanticism and the Jews: History, Culture, Literature*. Palgrave. [2002] pp. 308. $59.95 ISBN 0 3122 9522 7.

Sternlieb, Lisa. *The Female Narrator in the British Novel: Hidden Agendas.* Palgrave. [2002] pp. 189. £42.50 ISBN 0 3339 7372 0.

Stevenson, Robert Louis. *The Master of Ballantrae.* Modern Library. [2002] pp. xxvi + 246. $9.95 ISBN 0 3757 5930 1.

Storey, Graham, ed. *The Letters of Charles Dickens,* vol. 12: *1868–1870.* OUP. [2002] pp. 842. $125 ISBN 0 1992 4596 7.

Sudan, Rajani. *Fair Exotics: Xenophobic Subjects in English Literature, 1720– 1850.* UPennP. [2002] pp. 200. $45 ISBN 0 8122 3656 4.

Sutton, Emma. *Aubrey Beardsley and British Wagnerism in the 1890s.* OUP. [2002] pp. viii + 225. £40 ISBN 0 1981 8732 7.

Symonds, John Addington. *The Life of Michelangelo Buonarroti: Based on Studies in the Archives of the Buonarroti Family at Florence.* UPennP. [2002] pp. 992. $45 ISBN 0 8122 1761 6.

Taylor, Jonathan. *Mastery and Slavery in Victorian Writing.* Palgrave. [2002] pp. 240. $62 ISBN 0 3339 9312 8.

Taylor, Roger, and Edward Wakeling, eds. *Lewis Carroll, Photographer: The Princeton University Library Albums.* PrincetonUP. [2002] pp. 304. $49.95 ISBN 0 6910 7443 7.

Thomson, Douglass H., Jack G. Voller, and Frederick S. Frank, eds. *Gothic Writers: A Critical and Bibliographical Guide.* Greenwood. [2002] pp. 544. $99.95 ISBN 0 3133 0500 5.

Thomson, John, ed. *Books and Bibliography: Essays in Commemoration of Don McKenzie.* Victoria University Press. [2002] pp. 216. $NZ39.95 ISBN 0 8647 3429 8.

Tobin, Thomas J. *Pre-Raphaelitism in the Nineteenth-Century Press: A Bibliography.* ELS. [2002] $25 ISBN 0 9206 0481 1.

Tóibín, Colm. *Love in a Dark Time and Other Explorations of Gay Lives and Literature.* Scribner. [2002] pp. 272. $24 ISBN 0 7432 2944 4.

Turner, Frank. *John Henry Newman: The Challenge to the Evangelical Religion.* YaleUP. [2002] pp. 752. $35 ISBN 0 3000 9251 2.

Ulrich, John M. *Signs of their Times: History, Labor, and the Body in Cobbett, Carlyle, and Disraeli.* OhioUP. [2002] pp. 221. $44.95 ISBN 0 8214 1401 1.

Urbinati, Nadia. *Mill on Democracy: From the Athenian Polis to Representative Government.* UChicP. [2002] pp. 256. $37.50 ISBN 0 2268 4277 0.

Valente, Joseph. *Dracula's Crypt: Bram Stoker, Irishness, and the Question of Blood.* UIllP. [2002] pp. 192. $29.95 ISBN 0 2520 2696 9.

Vanden Bossche, Chris R., ed. *Historical Essays: The Norman and Charlotte Strouse Edition of the Writings of Thomas Carlyle,* vol. 3. UCalP. [2002] £63 ISBN 0 5202 2061 7.

Van Dulken, Stephen. *Inventing the 19th Century.* BL. [2001] pp. 224. £16.95 ISBN 0 7123 0881 4.

Ward, Bernadette Waterman. *World as Word: Gerard Manley Hopkins and Philosophical Theology.* CUAP. [2002] pp. x + 292. £48.50 ($59.95) ISBN 0 8132 1016 X.

White, Norman. *Hopkins in Ireland.* UCD. [2002] pp. xviii + 217. hb £39.95 ($59.95) ISBN 1 9006 2171 1, ISBN 1 9006 2172 X.

Wolfreys, Julian. *Victorian Hauntings: Spectrality, Gothic, the Uncanny and Literature*. Palgrave. [2002] pp. xiv + 175. hb £46.50 ($69.95) ISBN 0 3339 2251 4, ISBN 0 3339 2252 2.

Wood, Marcus. *Slavery, Empathy and Pornography*. OUP. [2002] pp. 478. £35 ISBN 0 1981 8720 3.

Wright, Sarah Bird. *Thomas Hardy A to Z: The Essential Reference to his Life and Work*. FOF. [2002] pp. xvii + 430. $65 ISBN 0 8160 4289 6.

Wynne, Catherine. *The Colonial Conan Doyle: British Imperialism, Irish Nationalism, and the Gothic*. Greenwood. [2002] pp. 224. $61.95 ISBN 0 3133 2005 5.

Young, Alan R. *Hamlet and the Visual Arts, 1709–1900*. AUP. [2002] pp. 408. $65 ISBN 0 8741 3794 2.

XIV

Modern Literature

JULIAN COWLEY, COLIN GRAHAM, LYNNE HAPGOOD, CHRIS HOPKINS, DANIEL LEA, BETHAN JONES, JOHN NASH, NANCY PAXTON, JOHN BRANNIGAN, ALEKS SIERZ, JO GILL AND FRAN BREARTON

This chapter has seven sections: 1. General; 2. Pre-1945 Fiction; 3. Post-1945 Fiction; 4. Post-1950 Drama; 5. Pre-1950 Poetry; 6. Post-1950 Poetry; 7. Irish Poetry. Section 1(a) is by Julian Cowley; section 1(b) is by Colin Graham; section 2(a) is by Lynne Hapgood; section 2(b) is by Chris Hopkins; section 2(c) is by Daniel Lea; section 2(d) is by John Nash; section 2(e) is by Bethan Jones; section 2(f) is by Daniel Lea; section 2(g) is by Nancy Paxton; section 3 is by John Brannigan; section 4 is by Aleks Sierz; section 5 is by Jo Gill; section 6 is by John Brannigan; section 7 is by Fran Brearton. The section on Pre-1950 Drama has been omitted this year, but will cover 2002–3 publications in *YWES* 84.

1. General

(a) British
Walton Litz, Menand, and Rainey, eds., *The Cambridge History of Literary Criticism*, volume 7: *Modernism and the New Criticism*, interrogates T.S. Eliot's pivotal position in familiar alignments of modernism with New Critical practices. Menand argues that Eliot's crucial contribution, for a long time the key to his institutional centrality, was to sever literary criticism from other forms of intellectual activity, establishing an autonomous discipline. Vincent Sherry, on the other hand, points to Wyndham Lewis's insistent provision of context for literary study as a basis for increased interest in his work with the growth of cultural studies. Walton Litz and Rainey trace acceleration and decline of critical momentum in Pound's prose and poetry. Steven Meyer indicates a challenge to idealist assumptions posed by Stein's 'multiple accounts of herself writing, and of her writing self' (p. 93). Maria DiBattista presents Virginia Woolf as a sophisticated if unmethodical pioneer of reader-response criticism. Lucy McDiarmid looks at Yeats's oppositional criticism. Michael North examines issues of art and politics in the Harlem Renaissance. A section of the book is given over to essays addressing the

work of I.A. Richards, the Southern New Critics, William Empson, R.P. Blackmur, Kenneth Burke, and Yvor Winters. Wallace Martin examines the emergence and divergent development of English literary study in British and American universities; Morris Dickstein investigates the critical practitioner's sense of criticism's relationship with society, politics, and history in the span from James to Orwell; Josephine Guy and Ian Small sketch the rise of the professional in British letters. Michael Bell presents F.R. Leavis as 'the English analogue of Nietzsche and Heidegger' (p. 400); Harvey Teres casts Lionel Trilling as 'a visionary' (p. 438). The volume closes with Lawrence Lipking's account of the rise and passing of poet-critics, and Michael Levenson's concentrated survey of criticism of fiction from James to Wayne Booth.

Verdicchio and Burch, eds., *Between Poetry and Philosophy: Writing, Rhythm, History*, brings together essays that engage with 'a discourse bounded by the interplay of meaning and truth' (p. 3). The term 'poetry', separated from concerns of metre and verse, here signifies all creative production of meaning, while 'philosophy' is construed, in accordance with its etymology, as love of wisdom manifested in quests for truth. In the book's first section, Italian philosopher Carlo Sini considers these terms, plus 'history' and 'philosophy', as genres of the written word. Forrest Williams, looking into Sini's work on the ethics of writing, makes use of poems by W.E. Henley and Dylan Thomas. The second section addresses post-Hegelian conceptions of identity in relation to difference. In part 3 readings of Beckett's radio play *Cascando* and texts by Heidegger, Hölderlin, Rilke, and Nietzsche 'problematize their referential character, within the determining context of meaning' (p. 6). The concluding section returns to an ancient sense of 'rhythm' as form or shape of things to make evident the importance of rhythm to 'the relation of our language and body, the fundamental character of our thinking, and the very tenor and tone of our lives' (p. 7). In this context, David Halliburton considers Proust as a connoisseur of speed.

Hutcheon and Valdés, eds., *Rethinking Literary History: A Dialogue on Theory*, is a forum for a distinguished panel of theorists. It opens with Hutcheon's argument for the desirability of rethinking the dominant national model of literary history in our 'globalized, multinational, and diasporic world' (p. 3). Stephen Greenblatt responds, disputing Hutcheon's explanation for the persistence of that model. He suggests it is 'disruptive forces that principally shape the history and diffusion of languages' rather than 'a rooted sense of cultural legitimacy' (p. 61). Valdés considers possibilities for opening out practices of literary historiography and the identities they produce. Marshall Brown rethinks the scale of literature's history by means of suggestive musical allusion, positing 'a sounding together in temporally ordered form of the disparate voices and strands of utterance claiming our attention from the past' (p. 143). Walter D. Mignolo addresses the colonial model and, drawing insights from Emmanuel Lévinas, arrives at the view that 'literary cultures in history should go together with a diversification of Being' (p. 186). In an Afterword, Homi K. Bhabha gives a personal response to the five preceding essays.

Valentine Cunningham's *Reading After Theory* is a polemical riposte to slack and indulgent habits of reading that, in his view, entered literary critical practice with the advent of Theory during the 1960s. Cunningham acknowledges that theorizing of some kind precedes all reading. He appreciates the virtuosity of some post-structuralist reading and welcomes its recuperation of 'marginal interests' (p. 53).

but is uncomfortable with Theory's current ubiquity, and is keen to know what might follow in the wake of 'the linguistic turn and its afterquakes' (p. 54). He identifies a debilitating lack of tact in Theory's stock responses and grandiose aspirations, and advocates instead a hands-on experience of texts, 'proper tactility' (p. 156). The Theorists, he insists, have mishandled; 'all good and true reading is close reading' (p. 167), of the kind practised with subtlety and expertise by Christopher Ricks. Cunningham's upbeat conclusion is that even in the work of evangelical Theorists, such as Julian Wolfreys, there has recently been a discernible return to 'sound sense' (p. 168) and 'readerly tact' (p. 169).

In his timely book *Digital Poetics: The Making of E-Poetries*, Loss Pequeño Glazier stresses that not only does computer technology offer new and expanded means for producing, archiving, distributing, and promoting poetry texts, 'but the most important aspect of electronic space is that it is a space of poeisis' (p. 3). Anticipations of digital practice are found in writing by Pound, Stein, Apollinaire, Zukofsky, Olson, Creeley, Burroughs, John Cage, Jackson Mac Low, Charles Bernstein and various contributors to Oulipo, 'the Mimeo Revolution', concrete poetry and Fluxus. Glazier asserts that the programmer's code is 'as real as ink or an awl' (p. 113), insists upon the materiality of electronic writing, and indicates continuities between innovative practice in print and opportunities opened by refinement of digital media. Web-based electronic writing is looked at through the lens of poetic procedures with the aim of casting light on the scope of digital practice. *Digital Poetics* is offered as, successively, a manifesto, treatise, lab book, and prospectus.

Clive Bloom's *Bestsellers: Popular Fiction Since 1900* aims to be 'the most complete record so far of best-selling fiction in Britain' while also offering 'the sense of a cultural, sociological and cultural context' (p. xii). Supporting evidence, Bloom stresses, is incomplete, not least because documentation for statistical and comparative purposes was not collated until the late 1970s. A preliminary overview of issues refers to Marie Corelli and Thomas Hall Caine, who effectively laid foundations for later best-selling adult fiction. Bloom contends that 'narrative does not need style, it needs panache' (p. 20) and argues that 'popular fiction when it reaches best-seller level tells us about a condition of reading which has been *proletarianised*', adding that it nonetheless 'includes imagination, negotiation and *refusal*' (p. 28). A brief survey of British reading habits is followed by consideration of genre, especially the enduring popularity of crime fiction and women's romance. The bulk of the second half of the book is given over to a selective survey of best-selling authors, registering in brief summaries both their specific achievement and their typicality, where appropriate. The survey is divided into chronological periods within which novelists are arranged alphabetically. There are familiar names such as Arnold Bennett, Agatha Christie, Hammond Innes, Barbara Cartland, and Ruth Rendell, and less well-known figures such as Nat Gould and Berta Ruck, whose fame has waned despite former commercial success.

Karin Molander Danielsson's dissertation *The Dynamic Detective* is a study of special interest and seriality in contemporary detective fiction. Danielsson generously defines special interest as 'a political, ethnic, regional, professional or hobby-related agenda' (p. 13), usually implicating writers, readers, and protagonists. Community-building is acknowledged as a function of current detective writing in all its diversity, popular fiction being 'no longer aimed at an indiscriminately large readership, but at many smaller readerships' (p. 83) clustered in subcultures or configured by a particular interest. Danielsson's sampling of this pool results in examination of the political implications of fiction by American authors Tony Hillerman, Walter Mosley, Barbara Neely, and Amanda Cross, while novels involved with equestrian sports provide matter for discussion of the practices of Dick Francis, Jody Jaffe, and Carolyn Banks. Danielsson argues that the intensified and extended seriality of contemporary detective fiction orientates the genre towards its origins in 'the character-driven novel of manners' (p. 181), separate volumes forming cumulatively a kind of chronicle, with significant implications for suspense and closure.

Dani Cavallaro's *The Gothic Vision* is subtitled 'Three Centuries of Horror, Terror and Fear'. The book argues that terror and horror are complementary and colluding responses to 'narratives of darkness' (p. vii), and that fear is a function of consciousness, interweaving repulsion and attraction and illuminating the fractured and chaotic nature of human experience. Gothic, a ubiquitous cultural discourse using 'images of disorder, obsession, psychological disarray and physical distortion for the purposes of both entertainment and ideological speculation' (p. vii), is identified as the representational field in which these propositions receive patent corroboration. An overview of theoretical debates opens the discussion. Subsequent section headings indicate this study's broad areas of concern: 'Darkness', 'Haunting', 'Narrative and the Self', 'Child and Adult', and 'Monstrosity'. Cavallaro stresses that particular structures of fear arise in accordance with prevailing political, ideological, and historical circumstances. The Gothic text is taken to be 'a composite entity wherein disparate narrative strands parallel the split subjectivities of both characters and readers' (p. 115). Organization is not chronological, but the analysis touches on major and less prominent instances in literature, from William Beckford, Horace Walpole, and Mary Shelley, through Henry James, Bram Stoker, and M.R. James, to Stephen King, Clive Barker, and Anne Rice.

In *The Work of Ian McEwan*, C. Byrnes offers analysis along psychodynamic lines, drawing eclectically upon the work of several theorists, including Melanie Klein, John Bowlby, and Donald Winnicott. McEwan is taken as a case study, biographical details and quotations from interviews being subjected to analysis, along with unconscious and conscious designs within his fiction, from controversial early short stories to the Booker Prize-winning novel *Amsterdam* [1998]. Byrnes traces development and change, arguing that McEwan's increasingly conscious manipulation of the images and ideas that might arise from the unconscious not only indicates his personal growth and strengthening as a writer but places him in the vanguard of a search for new collective values. The study's conclusion is that McEwan 'can be said to articulate the spirit of his time' (p. 300).

Laura Frost's *Sex Drives* investigates representations of sexualized fascism in literary modernism, asking where such images come from and why they arise, what meaning they acquire in their immediate historical context, and to what ends they have been consciously directed by British, French, and American writers. An appropriate analytical focus for this project is established by linking national identity with constructions of respectability and standards of sexual normality. The opening chapter discloses continuities between anti-German propaganda issued in the First and Second World Wars, a libidinal trope of Germanic authoritarianism establishing terms for subsequent representations of Nazism. *Aaron's Rod*, *Kangaroo*, and *The Plumed Serpent*, D.H. Lawrence's leadership novels, are then read as explorations of the attraction of proto-fascist ideology. Frost teases apart knots of erotics and politics in works by Georges Bataille and visual artist Hans Bellmer. She scrutinizes radically differing rehearsal and revision of standard representations of Nazi soldiers in the novella *The Silence of the Sea* by Vercors (Jean Bruller) and Jean Genet's novel *Funeral Rites*. The provocative assertion that every woman adores a fascist kick-starts a chapter that looks at feminist visions of fascism in Katherine Burdekin's *Swastika Night*, Virginia Woolf's *Three Guineas*, Marguerite Duras's *Hiroshima mon amour*, and Sylvia Plath's poetry. Frost's conclusion alludes to pornography to clarify ways in which the distance between mainstream culture and deviation has been represented as the distance between mainstream culture and fascism.

Thomas Foster's *Transformations of Domesticity in Modern Women's Writing: Homelessness at Home* examines ways in which feminist modernism tackles the nineteenth century's legacy of domestic womanhood represented graphically in the ideology of separate spheres. Marianne Moore, H.D., Woolf, Stein, Sylvia Townsend Warner, and Emily Holmes Coleman are shown to problematize that inheritance through forms of self-critique, and Zora Neale Hurston provides a different class and race perspective on domesticity that both extends and sheds critical light on positions assumed by those middle-class writers. Emily Dickinson is taken as a significant precursor, writing out of the condition of being 'homeless at home', a phrase lifted from her poetry to serve as the book's subtitle. *The Years* is selected for use as Woolf's 'most explicit intervention in the traditions of domestic fiction and social realism' (p. 98). Theoretical apparatus is derived from a variety of sources, including Donna Haraway, Henri Lefebvre, and Julia Kristeva. Literary strategies for reassessing, redefining, and relocating feminine spaces are of primary concern.

Colin Duriez compiled *The C.S. Lewis Encyclopedia* to assist general readers with limited awareness of Lewis's varied oeuvre, who might wish to extend their knowledge of his writing and draw together its disparate threads. In his preface, Duriez registers admiration for one of the greatest popularizers of the Christian faith, and his appraisal of Lewis's achievement in the entries that follow is wholeheartedly supportive. Organization of materials is alphabetical, without further subdivision, so names of characters from the fiction nestle alongside titles of theological essays, thematic issues, contextual information, and names of colleagues, friends, relatives, and places. Kenneth Tynan is found in close proximity to both 'Trumpkin the dwarf' and *Transposition and Other Addresses*; John Wain precedes War; Charles Williams falls between the White Witch and the Narnian giant Wimbleweather. A concluding 'Reference Guide' suggests groupings of entries (such as 'Life', 'The Literary Criticism', 'The Thought and Context') that may serve as paths through the alphabetical thicket. More scholarly and rigorous guides exist; this is a book designed for the enthusiastic non-specialist.

Peter J. Schakel, in *Imagination and the Arts in C.S. Lewis: Journeying to Narnia and Other Worlds*, affirms that for Lewis imagination was a faculty that established meaningful relationships among things, with a key role in the formation of unified wholes assigned to intuition or inspiration. Schakel indicates how this conception fuelled Lewis's insistence on the need for receptivity to literature and the arts, and his antipathy to 'Cambridge English'. The bulk of Schakel's study is given over to consideration of Lewis's imaginative writing, which often reflects Lewis's love of books and commitment to a holistic experience of reading. Schakel ponders the best order for reading volumes of the Narnia chronicles, muses on the various elements that form the imaginative appeal of a story, and considers the presence of the storyteller in Lewis's fiction for adults and children. He disputes Lewis's alleged distaste for music, examines the recurrence of the motif of dance in his fiction, and groups visual art, architecture, and clothing together in a single chapter for consideration as celebrations of human nobility and value. Schakel's concluding chapter, which includes observations on J.K. Rowling's Harry Potter books, argues that fundamentally Lewis's interest in the arts served his goal of nurturing 'the moral imagination'.

Julia Eccleshare has written *A Guide to the Harry Potter Novels*, an attempt to shed light upon the appeal of J.K. Rowling's extraordinarily popular stories of a boy wizard. After briefly sketching the planning of the series and the role of agent, publisher, and reviewers in promoting the initial volume, *Harry Potter and the Philosopher's Stone*, Eccleshare suggests ways in which these fundamentally simple tales of good triumphing over evil manage to capture the imagination of children and adult readers. She identifies effective qualities of plot, characterization, and description and indicates Rowling's skill in deploying storytelling tropes and devices familiar from myths, folk tales, and other literary works. Critical assessment is made of each of the first four Harry Potter novels, considered as parts of a developing series, with Potter increasingly cast as romantic hero, and in terms of Rowling's growth as an author. Comparison is made between her achievement to date and that of her highly successful precursors Enid Blyton and Roald Dahl. The Potter fiction is also placed in relation to traditions of school stories and fictional fantasy worlds. Eccleshare addresses pertinent race and gender issues, examines Rowling's handling of education and the family, and touches on some broad social implications of current widespread enthusiasm for Harry Potter.

In his foreword to James, ed., *Macmillan: A Publishing Tradition*, John Sutherland muses on the discipline of publishing history and praises the British Library's careful work ordering the extensive Macmillan archive, now in that institution's possession. Elizabeth James, the British Library's Curator of British Collections, 1801–1914, has drawn together contributions that illustrate the range encompassed by the Macmillan 'tradition' and demonstrate some of the methodological options available to the historian of publication. Simon Eliot presents a meticulous quantitative account of the company's rise to prominence during the latter half of the nineteenth century. Bill Bell shows how Matthew Arnold's alliance with Macmillan recast him as an author in the marketplace. Michael Millgate charts the vicissitudes of Hardy's involvement with the publishing house and, in another essay, looks into Tennyson's late engagement with it. Warwick Gould casts an expert's eye across the tribulations and triumphs of Yeats's publishing career leading to his accession to the status of a Macmillan London author in 1916. Michael Bott adds his own postscript to a substantial collation of letters to Macmillan written between 1875 and 1890 by explorer and author Samuel White Baker. D.E. Moggridge looks into the terms under which John Maynard Keynes wrote for the company. George Worth takes Margaret Oliphant as focal point for his account of *Macmillan's Magazine*. Rimi Chatterjee examines aspects of the company's trade with India; Elizabeth James investigates its participation in the American market. Frances Spalding discusses Gwen Raverat's eagerness to provide wood-engraved illustrations for a reprint of the Victorian novel *The Runaway*, and recently retired editor Michael Wace offers an informed overview of issues relating to Macmillan's provision of other books for children, from Carroll's Alice stories to Richmal Crompton's William series. The collection concludes with a personal reminiscence by bibliographer and historian of books Nicolas Barker.

Randall W. Scott's *European Comics in English Translation: A Descriptive Sourcebook* is a helpful bibliographical tool for researchers into the comic-book's coupling of text and pictures. Scott, wary of pretentiousness, avoids the term 'graphic novel', deeming it generally too weighty for those productions to which it might be applied. He prefers to use 'comic albums'. The majority of those listed and described date from the period following the foundation in 1975 of the influential French magazine *Métal hurlant*. Notable exceptions to this are the Belgian comic series 'Tintin' by Hergé (Georges Remi) and 'Willy and Wanda' by Willy Vandersteen. The volume is a sourcebook designed to stimulate interest amongst English-language readers. Entries are arranged alphabetically by author (Philippe Adamov to Bernard Yslaire) and numbered serially (1 to 543). Each entry comprises citation of a specific text, in the manner of a library catalogue, and a summary of the main features of its story. A supplementary section offers concise notes concerning each author and translator. A brief list of sources consulted and further reading is included.

In *Literature, Identity and the English Channel: Narrow Seas Expanded*, Dominic Rainsford considers how the varied existence of that stretch of water as a space in literature has contributed to recognition of it as 'a charged locality with a powerful history' (p. 2). He takes the French Revolution as convenient starting point and, after a brief account of a balloon crossing in 1785, discusses the Romantic poem 'Beachy Head' by Charlotte Smith, making excursions into writings by Dorothy and William Wordsworth and Chateaubriand. The ensuing study of varied travellers' responses, historical moments, and perceived identities, of 'a real formation that functions metaphorically' (p. 159), touches on numerous written documents and literary works, with prominence assigned to Dickens, Michelet, Arnold, Gautier, Symons, Swinburne, Hugo, Jonathan Raban, Paul Theroux, and Julian Barnes.

Raphaël Ingelbien's *Misreading England* (also reviewed in *YWES* 82[2003]) is subtitled 'Poetry and Nationhood Since the Second World War'. Ingelbien's method adapts Harold Bloom's theory of poems as productive distortions of other texts, or reactions to them. Philip Larkin's verse is read as subversive of the symbolic props to religious patriotism in Eliot's *Four Quartets*. Geoffrey Hill's poetry is analysed in the light of his opposition to the vision of England found in Larkin and in Eliot's later work. Hopkins, in his 'propensity towards baroque excess' (p. 85) and in his expansive awareness of the national language, is identified as an important aesthetic precedent for both Hill and Ted Hughes. Hughes is shown questing for traces of primitive England while developing an idiosyncratic, self-deconstructing mythology of English nationhood. Creative misreading of Hughes's excursions into national myth is seen at work in Seamus Heaney's pursuit of an Irish neo-nationalist agenda with links to an ancestral England. Heaney's attention to Larkin is traced from initial antipathy to eventual alliance. The broad sweep of the book is to insist upon the continued, sometimes unpredictable meshing of English and Irish poetics of nationhood.

Murray, ed., *Scottish Writers Talking 2*, sequel to a volume that appeared in 1996, presents substantial transcribed dialogues between the editor Isobel Murray, sometimes with Bob Tait's assistance, and Iain Banks, Bernard MacLaverty, Naomi Mitchison, Iain Crichton Smith, and Alan Spence. The earliest interview, with MacLaverty, dates from April 1984; the most recent, with Spence, is from 1999. The conversation with Mitchison is firmly centred on her fiction. That focus on the writing is less steady elsewhere, but in each case biographical detail and personal perceptions are shared, with Murray's encouragement, and readers may find these disclosures cast some light on aspects of the literary work.

Iain Banks is one of six writers addressed by Cristie L. March in *Rewriting Scotland*. Irvine Welsh, Duncan McLean, Alan Warner, Janice Galloway, and A.L. Kennedy are also read in terms of their negotiations through fiction with currently available Scottish identities. March considers Welsh as an international icon of 'youth culture' (predominantly comprising drug abuse and sexual opportunism) and looks at Warner's handling of 'youth culture' issues in Scottish Highlands and Islands settings. McLean's fiction is shown to reconstruct rural Scotland in ways that register social fragmentation. Narrative and linguistic manipulations performed by Banks in his science fiction output are seen to be continuous with the composition of his other novels. In each case March is alert to gender issues that are addressed more concertedly in her chapters on Galloway, making visible the marginalized lives of Scottish women, and on Kennedy, tracing damaging disruptions of relationships. A brief concluding chapter surveys related and divergent strands in contemporary Scottish writing.

Patrick Ward begins *Exile, Emigration and Irish Writing* with a selective survey of critical concepts of exile, some referring specifically to Ireland's history, others more generalized and theoretical. He then looks into 'the ideological formulations and leitmotifs of exile in pre-Famine culture' (p. 28). The term 'exile' is shown to resist monologic reading, even when caught up in interplay with the consolidation of nationalist attitudes. The cultural dynamics of a mythicized 'Holy Ireland', in popular and literary traditions, are subjected to critical analysis. Individual authors such as James Clarence Mangan and Charles Kickham are singled out for special attention, and a chapter is devoted to George Moore's Irish writings, but the study as a whole sustains a broadly based reading of historical events and documents. Ward's final chapter draws a line of connection between three 'texts' of 1916: *The Proclamation of the Republic*, Joyce's *A Portrait of the Artist as a Young Man*, and the battle of the Somme.

Kenneth Rexroth, in 1956, suggested that Samuel Beckett's mind resembled that of an eighteenth-century Englishman in its toughness and stability. Frederik N. Smith, in *Beckett's Eighteenth Century* finds that Beckett's fiction regularly enters into dialogue with authors such as Swift, Defoe, Sterne, Fielding, and Johnson. Smith draws evidence from various documents, including examination papers, to affirm that as an undergraduate Beckett read extensively in English as well as French and Italian literature. Examples and allusions are piled up to suggest the meshed horizons of Beckett's writing and eighteenth-century antecedents. A chapter investigates his fictional characterization of 'the reader' and identifies lessons in giving point to this device learned from Sterne and Fielding. *A Voyage to Lisbon* and

Tristram Shandy are invoked during discussion of Beckett's literary interest in old men. Other chapters address his fascination with the valetudinarian Dr Johnson and the aesthetics of decay that, Smith suggests, Beckett shared with Pope.

Buning, Engelberts, and Houppermans, eds., *Pastiches, Parodies and Other Imitations*, the twelfth edition of the annual bilingual review *Samuel Beckett Today/ Aujourd'hui*, collects twenty-two essays that probe Beckett's attitudes towards inherited forms and literary antecedents. Essays adopt disparate methods, raise diverse concerns, and regularly shift the book's focus. The collection encompasses indebtedness to Robert Burton; travesty of Carlyle; allusion to Browning and to Beethoven; comparison with Heidegger, with Marinetti, and with John Cage's angle on silence; Beckett's contention in *Proust* of music's transcendent status; self-translation; and theoretical issues of intertextuality.

(b) Irish

Divining the current critical consensus in Irish studies, or even its prevailing trend, has become increasingly difficult. While Irish critical discourse was going through the polarization of the nationalism versus revisionism debate, and the contortions of nationalism were transforming through varieties of postcolonial theory, criticism looked to have its finger on the pulse of Northern politics as they hung over the entire island's culture. Yet while those politics changed, with a certain subterfuge, below the surface, and while the Republic was being dubiously transformed by the Celtic Tiger economy, Irish criticism perhaps got caught up in its own affairs for too long. That time lag still shows occasionally, and is exacerbated by the ways in which postcolonialism is still playing itself out through studies of individual authors or restatements of already rehearsed debates.

Carroll and King, eds., *Ireland and Postcolonial Theory*, looks like it should be the definitive word on the subject, given its impressive list of contributors (Joe Cleary, David Lloyd, Clare Carroll, Luke Gibbons, Kevin Whelan, Seamus Deane, Amitav Ghosh, Joseph Lennon, Gauri Viswananthan, and an Afterword by Edward Said). Through its various contributions a strong sense of an agreed and shared theoretical and political ground emerges, and it is particularly worth noting that this commonality is now so solidly known and understood that it is only in Clare Carroll's introduction, 'The Nation and Postcolonial Theory', that a truly combative form of historicized criticism feels the need to assert itself. Carroll's suggestion that Ireland is, for example, one of the 'ravaged sites' (p. 1) of colonial and postcolonial history signals a lack of nuance which is further apparent in her notion that it is a shame that Northern unionists feel 'unable to identify with the inclusive politics of the United Irishmen' (p. 4)—this is either genuine naivety or, worse, strategic naivety, and gives an unfortunately trenchant backward look to her later explanation that: '[the] question of how the Republic of Ireland will relate to Northern Ireland and how and what it will mean to be Irish in the future are beyond the scope of this volume' (p. 6). Awkward and inadvertent as it is, this inability to look forward does point to a major critical and political blockage in current movements in Irish postcolonialism, in which the genuinely radical thinkers in the discipline find their utopian moments in the 'ravaged' past but struggle to connect that with Ireland's unpalatable present(s), and are even less able to offer a hint of a different future. In this context, for example, Luke Gibbons's excellent essay on the United Irishmen seems to end with a wishfully fulfilled moment in which the United Irishmen are the (perhaps only) true inheritors of the radical mantle of the French Revolution, a point made by setting them against the fate of the same revolutionary ideals in Scotland. Irish criticism's investment in the United Irishmen has increased in recent years, particularly since the bicentenary, and Gibbons's own evidence, used to make his point, might suggest that the leaders of 1798 were not as unlike their fellow bourgeois radical revolutionaries across Europe as Gibbons may like to believe, in that their radicalism was still ineffably bourgeois, mercantilist, and, in that sense, limited.

Elsewhere in *Ireland and Postcolonial Theory* Joe Cleary attempts to show how the postcolonial controversy in Irish studies is in fact an argument about the mediation 'by colonial capitalism' of 'Irish social and cultural development', and Cleary insists that, whatever comparative arguments can be made, or apparently refuted, Ireland must be seen as having taken part in 'an international process through which different parts of the globe were differentially integrated into an emergent world capitalist system' (p. 43). As Cleary patiently notes, if this is accepted, then Irish nationalism itself is 'a product of the global' (p. 44). If Cleary's sharp-sighted criticism is welcome here, it is even more evident in his monograph *Literature, Partition and the Nation-State: Culture and Conflict in Ireland, Israel and Palestine*, in which he balances the possibility of post-imperial partition being a shared experience in Ireland, Israel, and Palestine. Partition is imagined by Cleary in its broadest senses, as a long-standing cultural binary of north and south, and more specifically as a response typical of the aftershocks of colonialism, in which the excessive reliance on the dichotomy of tradition and modernity, which underlies colonial ideology, is made manifest in geopolitics, cultural definition, and literary production. *Literature, Partition and the Nation-State* examines the anti-colonial, and statehood-directed, political energies of Irish nationalism and Palestinian resistance in terms of their relationship to modernity, and in turn modernity's relationship to colonial nationalism, before extending this theoretical reading into the experience of partition in both, necessarily 'incomplete', states. The second part of Cleary's book has an admirably acute reading of how partition is not only represented in, but structurally determines, narrative in (Northern) Irish culture and discusses in particular the novels for teenagers, beginning with *Across the Barricades*, written by Joan Lingard, Bernard McLaverty's novel *Cal*, and Neil Jordan's *The Crying Game*. Cleary concludes this chapter with a brief but illuminating move into discussing the peace process and its effect on literary fiction, suggesting that the politics of the process are such that the 'tentative climate' (p. 140) which currently persists has not changed the perception that the 'zero-sum struggles' of the past continue, and thus '[plot] endings remain stalled in an unredeemed now' (p. 140). *Literature, Partition and the Nation-State* is one of the most significant books in Irish studies in recent years; significant for its critical and conceptual intelligence, but also for its willingness to shift the agenda of Irish postcolonial critique into truly challenging arenas, where the curiously under-researched phenomenon of partition means that Neil Jordan can be read in the same matrix as Amos Oz.

Northern Irish culture is also under the microscope in Richard Kirkland's I*dentity Parades: Northern Irish Culture and Dissident Subjects*, a book which follows on from his *Literature and Culture in Northern Ireland Since 1965: Moments of Danger* [1996]. As with this previous book, Kirkland here shows himself to be one of the most sensitive, sophisticated, and intelligent critics of Northern Irish culture writing today, and *Identity Parades* displays the same wit and acuity which characterized his first book. It begins with an acknowledgement of the prominence of notions of identity, not only in contemporary cultural criticism but in contemporary culture, and Kirkland's method is both to see the necessity of identity for lived culture and cultural identity and to note the inherent incapacity, written into the structure of identity politics, which means that it can never entirely explain or cope with the complexities which the world confronts it with. Identity thus becomes a failed promise to articulate a position it forces a speaker into, and it is in the process of articulation that Kirkland begins to unfold his readings, 'with the object of tracing their inner contradictions' (p. 3). This Kirkland does through readings of critics such as Joe Cleary, David Lloyd, and Seamus Deane, a chapter on film (including a weary sense that *The Crying Game* is an exhausted critical resource), and a chapter on 'Violence, History and Bourgeois Fiction'. *Identity Parades* ends with one of the best pieces of critical writing in Irish studies in recent years, one which designates three types of 'camp' as characteristic of Northern culture, characteristics which arise because of the very inadequacies of identity politics which Kirkland begins with. 'Dissenting Camp', 'Unionist Camp', and 'Nationalist Camp' are the three categories Kirkland playfully discerns, and the result is a wonderful overturning of the pieties of liberal discourse on the North so that for once its complexities are rendered with a truly varied critical palette.

Gerry Smyth's *Space and the Irish Cultural Imagination* takes a different turn in trying to find a way out of the cul-de-sac which many critics either implicitly or explicitly recognize as a danger in contemporary Irish criticism. While Kirkland argues that identity politics can be turned inside out and made to look to the future through showing the faultlines within, Smyth takes 'space' as a starting point for an examination of Irish culture because 'modern Ireland is obsessed with issues of space' (p. xiv). Smyth particularizes this potentially amorphous final frontier through the macro-politics of Europe and partition (though the split nature of the national space is not a focus of his book, and thus sits interestingly against Cleary's view that the experience of partition is formulative of post-independence Ireland), an urban/rural split, and the development of interest in the local, whether it be through local or parish history, or a feeling of disenchantment with the national body politic. Smyth's argument is broadly that a move should be made from a historical focus on 'identity' in Irish studies to one which takes account of spatial conceptualizations of 'identity'. Smyth of course thus bolsters the place of identity at the centre of Irish studies, so that centre becomes more resonantly geographical as well as figurative, and in this he slightly runs the risk of an essentialism which he himself sees as a danger (p. 13), even though he does summarize the arguments of 'postmodern geography' which emphasize the contingency of identity. Smyth's introductory chapters are lucid, and constitute a broadly persuasive argument about the historical obsessions of Irish criticism; they do rather frustratingly tend to summarize a series of other positions (ecocriticism, for example, or Marxism) without entirely providing a unique assimilation of these into a coherent agenda. The rest of the book occasionally suffers from this lack at the beginning, since its chapters are on topics such as Seamus Deane's *Reading in the Dark* (in which the issue of the border is addressed), the music of U2, and the area of Tallaght where Smyth grew up, which could only be held together by a strong theoretical matrix. It remains to be seen whether Smyth's clarion call to a spatial politics is exact and enticing enough to be answered.

If Cleary, Kirkland, and Smyth are what is, in clichéd terms, described as the cutting edge of Irish studies, its blunter instruments are all altogether less edifying. Patsy J. Daniels's *The Voice of the Oppressed in the Language of the Oppressor: A Discussion of Selected Postcolonial Literature from Ireland, Africa and America* offers little beyond the by-rote truisms of postcolonial assumptions rather than postcolonial criticism. Apart from its crude belief that the experience of oppression is 'common' in all three circumstances, and all the objectionable politics which flow from that, Daniels's book is disappointingly unoriginal in its reading of Yeats (following Said, who has barely written on Yeats at all, and Kiberd), and then finding herself in the tangle of describing Yeats's doubled 'other' status as Irish (against Englishness) and Anglo-Irish (other to Catholic Ireland). To at once claim that this is otherness and that one is privileged and one not makes a nonsense of the notion of 'otherness' as akin to oppression and questions the very terms being deployed here. But equally importantly it shows a lack of historical and critical nuance, of the kind which leads to a reading of 'Leda and the Swan' as showing that 'Ireland has been raped by England in a similar way to Leda's rape by Zeus' (p. 38). This un-Yeatsian allegorical reading of Yeats is made worse by a series of questions which include 'Was she [Ireland] *asking for it*? Did she *enjoy it*?' in which twenty or so years of Irish feminist theory are temporarily in danger of drowning.

The political and cultural constitution of Irish nationalism is the subject of Eugene O'Brien's *Examining Irish Nationalism in the Context of Literature, Culture and Religion: A Study of the Epistemological Structure of Nationalism*. O'Brien takes his cue from an essay by Willy Maley, part of a debate over several issues of *Irish Studies Review* in the mid-1990s, and attempts to interrogate Irish nationalist ideology for its potential pluralities. O'Brien's work is primarily descriptive rather than polemical—his aim is to 'allow for a more reasoned discussion of [the] modalities' (p. 7) of nationalism, and this in turn comes from his not entirely convincing belief that nationalism in Ireland is much discussed but little understood. The book variously examines nationalist ideology in relation to religion, cultural nationalism, and the self, and in this its desire to carry out a forensic investigation of nationalism in Ireland is laudable. Occasionally, though, O'Brien's positions are led more by the desire to fit his discussion to a particular terminology than to provide conceptual clarity: so he argues, for example, that 'both the nationalist and unionist positions are, essentially, *nationalist* in ideological formation' (p. 3), an idea with some logic, though one which, whether insensitively phrased or not, might call into question the extent to which nationalism as a term of political ideology can be extracted from its various contexts as a lived ideological practice—the very question which is at the heart of the book.

Criticism of Irish drama has been healthily prosperous in recent years. Colm Tóibín's marvellously and enjoyably eccentric book *Lady Gregory's Toothbrush* is something of a prelude to his first stage play [2004] based on the early years of the Abbey. The book explores Gregory's life from Tóibín's novelistic viewpoint, weaving the playwrighting side of her life with her role as theatre manager, and in turn making this intertwine with the politics of landowning in early twentieth-century Ireland. Tóibín thus manages to suggest an intriguingly complex foundation for the Abbey theatre and all it has engendered, a story which Tóibín will hopefully go on to imagine again in his writing.

More typical of criticism of Irish drama is Ronan McDonald's *Tragedy and Irish Literature: Synge, O'Casey, Beckett*, a fine book which brings a seriousness about literary form to the plays of the three writers and convincingly demonstrates a tradition of tragedy emerging over the century, while allowing for the individuality of these major writers to jostle against the confines of an Irish dramatic heritage. McDonald achieves this through an understanding that tragedy itself is incapable of holding together the elements which make it what it is. His readings accept the distance between 'language and reality' so that, adopting Synge, McDonald argues that 'the gallous story never manages to transform the dirty deed' (p. 7)—and in this gap 'the omissions often speak louder than the language, whose every eloquence distances it from the pressing drudgery of day-to-day life' (p. 7).

Other books published in 2002 on Irish drama include Susan Cannon Harris, *Gender and Modern Irish Drama*, which concentrates largely on male playwrights at the beginning of the century (Yeats and O'Casey, but also Pearse) and Margaret Llewellyn-Jones, *Contemporary Irish Drama and Cultural Identity*, which discusses Friel, McGuinness, and Tom Murphy and then moves into the under-explored areas of the politics of globalization on the one hand and dramaturgy and performance on the other. Nelson O'Ceallaigh Ritschel, *Synge and Irish Nationalism: The Precursor to Revolution*, reads Synge's Irishness in line with a Revival nationalism which is being revised by other critics, and the difference in approach here may well be one of the debates to come. In contemporary theatre studies, Helen Lojek has edited *The Theatre of Frank McGuinness: Stages of Mutability*, which includes essays by Bernice Schrank, Margot Gayle Backus, Eamonn Jordan, Christopher Murray, and others, covering most of McGuinness's output and paying particular attention to the politics of gender which he has brought to the Irish stage.

Jennifer M. Jeffers's *The Irish Novel at the End of the Twentieth Century: Gender, Bodies, and Power* is an engaged and theoretically challenging work which uses Deleuzian theory to discuss the ways in which regulation of the (usually female) body is manifested in contemporary novels. Jeffers discusses work by John Banville, Seamus Deane, Deirdre Madden, Patrick McCabe, and Emma Donoghue in the belief that the 'body blurs the power grid' (p. 8) of Irish culture. Taura Napier, in *Seeking a Country: Literary Autobiographies of Twentieth-Century Irishwomen*, opens up a new field of study, discussing the autobiographical writings of Lady Gregory, Katharine Tynan, Mary Colum, Elizabeth Bowen, Kate O'Brien, and Eavan Boland. In her readings Napier shows a good understanding of the quest for self and that continual nag for national identity with which we began, and sees that women's autobiography provides an arena for the testing of the gendered self against the nation. Napier's work here feels like the beginning of another project on contemporary women's self-narration, and certainly Boland seems like a less than satisfactory contemporary example with which to update the genre.

Finally, the new does continue to emerge, despite the sometimes discouraging uniformity of Irish criticism. Crossing the boundaries of literature and history in a rarely genuine way is the special issue of *Textual Practice* (*TPr* 16:ii[2002]), edited by Lucy McDiarmid, on 'Irish Secular Relics'. This includes excellent essays by Margaret Kelleher on 'Hunger and History: Monuments to the Great Irish Famine', Siobhán Kilfeather on 'Oliver Plunkett's Head', Hugh Haughton on Derek Mahon,

and McDiarmid on Casement. All the essays in the issue take the materialism of
Irish culture as their starting point and treat the topic with a fascinated scrutiny that
is typical of McDiarmid's own approach. Perhaps this sometimes quirky close
reading of material objects is the place where new agendas in Irish criticism will be
found.

2. Pre-1945 Fiction

(a) The English Novel, 1900–1930
The important critical concerns in discussions of the novel of this period continue to
be the vexed question of its relation to modernism, an emphasis on increasingly
inclusive approaches, and the recovery of women's writing.

Michael Steinman's edition of the selected letters of Sylvia Townsend Warner
and William Maxwell, *The Element of Lavishness: Letters of Sylvia Townsend
Warner and William Maxwell, 1938–1978*, is a remarkable testament to their
friendship. There are few writers whose letters merit as much attention as their
fiction, but these letters to Warner's American editor, William Maxwell, are works
of art in themselves, and Steinman's selection creates a satisfying coherence out of
a sample of a correspondence that lasted for forty years. The letters never seem self-
conscious, for each of the correspondents is so deeply absorbed in the business of
writing, of sharing literary insights, of discussing editorial changes and future
projects that being a writer becomes the stuff of daily conversation and the building-
blocks of a steadily maturing friendship. In later letters, they also exchange details
about their lives and dilemmas, and share moments of personal joy or sadness. In
one of her last letters to Maxwell, Warner describes how her father-in-law's letters
took on 'a kind of radiance' as he grew older. The phrase applies equally to her own
letters: the exquisite precision of expression is energized by a zest for living that
communicates itself to the reader and for which Maxwell's replies provide a
satisfying context. This is a striking narrative of a working writer, a devoted
friendship and an observing eye, which is appropriately complemented by the
simultaneous publication of a collection of Warner's short stories, *The Music at
Long Verney: Twenty Stories*.

Sylvia Townsend Warner is the focus of Gay Wachman's *Lesbian Empire:
Radical Crosswriting in the Twenties*, both for her oppositional feminist politics and
what Wachman calls her 'literary crosswriting': that is, co-opting male (usually gay)
narratives to liberate the lesbian voice. The frame for Wachman's perspective on the
sexually radical fiction of lesbian writers in the 1920s is what she calls an
'alternative modernism' which is not concerned with disrupting traditional
aesthetics but rather with disrupting the gender practices of an imperialist ideology.
As the discussion unfolds, Warner is linked with other lesbian or bisexual writers,
Radclyffe Hall, Evadne Price, Clemence Dane, Rose Allatini, and, more briefly,
Virginia Woolf. This is not primarily a literary or a historical discussion: at times it
appears divided in its objectives, despite the attempt to provide an inclusive reading.
Novels tend to be seen almost exclusively as manifestations of national and personal
histories, while history is largely viewed through a case-study approach, such as
Radclyffe Hall's and Townsend Warner's legal challenges or other conflicts
generated by the turbulent nature of post-war society. However, Wachman deals

with an important topic, bringing a number of forgotten writers and novels back into critical discourse via queer theory.

Biography is an important tool for recovering the profiles of neglected women writers whose work may not be currently in print. Both Selina Hastings's biography, *Rosamond Lehmann*, and Vineta Colby's *Vernon Lee: A Literary Biography* pursue this objective. Rosamond Lehmann's life provides telling examples of a number of aspects of women's social and literary history in Selina Hasting's interesting biography. Hastings's readings of the novels are largely biographical as she seeks to trace Lehmann's personal desire for passion and romance and her search for the fulfilment of a desired feminine persona by linking the heroes in her novels with her succession of lovers and husbands. Hastings not only exposes the gap between life and fiction, but the unresolved contradictions of a woman whose beauty and social position promised a passive social success, but whose intelligence and energy drove her to take advantage of the (relatively) greater opportunities for women in a post-war society. Indeed, although she lived on to be rediscovered by the feminist critics of the 1980s, her fiction and her identity were shaped, as Hastings explores, by the extraordinary milieu of the inter-war period. This biography provides a valuable context for Lehmann studies, while also offering a broader view of the long trajectory of women's writing.

In contrast, Vineta Colby focuses on the idea of 'a writing life' as she charts the prodigious range of Vernon Lee's output—her fiction, essays on Italian history and art, aesthetics and travel. In this study, Lee (the pseudonym of Violet Paget) emerges as a victim of history, missing the tide of change as surely as Lehmann caught it. Colby studies the impact on Lee's reputation of the shift in literary taste and fashion at the turn of the century, which seemed to draw a line under the work she did in the 1880s and 1890s even though she continued to inhabit the margins of Bloomsbury in the first decade of the new century. Colby makes a balanced and fair assessment of a women working in a society charged with social and sexual controversies, and offers an empathetic ('empathy' was a word to which Vernon Lee gave currency) perspective on Lee's position within it and her contribution to it.

Caws, ed., *Vita Sackville-West: Selected Writings*, includes samples of poetry, and extracts from novels, journalism, letters, and diaries—and makes interesting reading. Collections such as this help to redefine literary boundaries and to highlight women's particular contribution to challenging the canon. Rebecca West, *The Sentinel: An Incomplete Early Novel*, edited with excellent notes by Kathryn Laing, is essential reading within the more traditional critical framework of a novelist's development. *The Sentinel* is interesting in itself for the picture it gives of contemporary issues, such as women and education, sexual morality, and the campaigns for women's suffrage. However, seven years intervened between this unpublished first attempt and the publication of the accomplished *The Return of the Soldier* in 1918, which inevitably means that its greatest interest lies in seeing how remarkably West's skill in representing the impact of social and political questions on individuals matured during this time.

It is a rare occurrence for an unknown manuscript of an established writer to emerge, but that is the case with G.K. Chesterton, *Basil Howe: A Story of Young Love*. The notebooks in which Chesterton wrote *Basil Howe* (a title conferred by the editor, Denis J. Conlon) when he was only 19 or 20, were found among other papers nearly fifty years after his death. *Basil Howe* is a two-part novella, telling the story of the meeting of Basil Howe and Gertrude Grey and their re-encounter five years later, when they confess their love for one another. Although the plot is conventional and the characterization rather static, it is written with Chesterton's characteristic assurance and vigour, while the dialogue rivals Oscar Wilde at his best for the sheer cleverness of its humour and the capacity to make the apparently meaningless and nonsensical meaningful. The publication of *Basil Howe* will also be interesting for Chesterton scholars in its anticipation of themes and modes of thought that resonate through his writing. The denunciation of *fin-de-siècle* superficiality; the oblique and the contradictory as a means to truth; the nature of the extraordinary—all important tropes in Chesterton's later work—appeared first, as we now know, in this early novella. Conlon's introduction and the inclusion of an unfinished novel, *Our Future Prospects*, which was intended to be completed by members of Chesterton's school debating society, suggest a strongly autobiographical context for Basil Howe.

The publication of *G.K. Chesterton, The British Library Catalogue of Additions to the Manuscripts. The G.K. Chesterton Papers: Additional Manuscripts 73186–73484* completes the archival arrangement of the papers made available after the death of Chesterton's secretary and friend Dorothy Collins in 1988. The chequered history of Chesterton's papers is outlined in R.A. Christopher's introduction. The archive includes the manuscript of *Basil Howe* among a range of personal and working papers from 1870 to 1930. It is incomplete and occasionally fragmentary since, despite several attempts to order and catalogue material during his lifetime, various events and Chesterton's own sporadic lack of attention undermined its coherence. It seems in character that Chesterton would be so little concerned with creating an archive for posterity that he would, for instance, tear pages out of old notebooks and write on the back of them. As with all catalogues, it imposes admirable order on confusion but also opens up further scholarly opportunities.

This year also saw the re-issue of Chesterton's *The Victorian Age in Literature*. A copy of this short history can be found in most pre-1960 university libraries, but it has long since lost its currency in literary-critical thought today. Adopting the stance of an amateur, in a period when literature as an academic subject hardly existed, Chesterton engages the reader in a journey of ideas. As we might expect, he has no problem with the word 'genius', but he is more interested in the responses of writers to the specific debates that shaped and informed their literary development than in examining individual brilliance. He was an early advocate of 'the strength and subtlety' of women's writing in the early part of the century, and argues persuasively that socialism and imperialism were the twin influences between which the spirit of Victorianism was squeezed at the end of the century. It is tempting to heap quotation on quotation to capture his assessments of, for instance, George Eliot, R.L. Stevenson, Bernard Shaw, and Jane Austen, among many others, for his success depends on the sparkle and zest of his language, and the power his statements have to trigger instant agreement or controversy.

Tim Robinson, in 'G.K. Chesterton and the Classic Detective Story' (*LMag* 41:i–ii[2001] 55–64), takes us back to familiar fictional territory arguing that the enduring popularity of the Father Brown stories is no coincidence. The detective genre provided Chesterton with the necessary structure for his 'over-riotous imagination', which some critics claim mars the achievement of his novels, and invests his familiar emphasis on the extraordinariness of the ordinary with a distinctive vividness. In addition, Chesterton's Catholic sympathies provide an interesting dimension to the detective persona since Father Brown understands the depths of evil from a position of unworldly innocence.

Rudyard Kipling's life continues to fascinate biographers as much as his writing does the literary critics. David Gilmour's *The Long Recessional: The Imperial Life of Rudyard Kipling* is the third major biography in three years. Gilmour's focus, as the title suggests, is on Kipling's relationship to the imperial ideal and its practice, and its role in taking him from being the spokesman of the nation at the height of his fame to the sidelines of history at his death in 1936. For an important period, the strength of his beliefs and his energy of action coincided with and articulated the national mood. Gilmour explores this process of the personal becoming political in his discussion of the importance of Kipling's post-war contribution to the Imperial War Graves Commission, when his desire for a national identity in which everyone played a vital part, his grief at the loss of life, and his unerring choice of appropriate words to link event with public memory are seen at their most powerful. Any study of Kipling, whether its emphasis is literary or historical, returns to the complexity of his work and his identity, and Gilmour's is no exception. However, he is less inclined than some biographers to try and reconcile the apparently contradictory sides of Kipling's identity. Instead he allows the reader to understand that the contradictions were indeed the man, rejecting the crude stereotype of the jingoistic imperialist and resisting temptations to be Kipling's apologist.

A desire to crack Kipling's personal and literary 'code' is behind William B. Dillingham's 'Kipling: Spiritualism, Bereavement, Self-Revelation, and "They"' (*ELT* 45:iv[2002] 402–25). Dillingham agrees with the critical consensus on the autobiographical provenance of the short story 'They', but argues further for its self-revelatory nature. In a well-worked and intriguing argument, he brings together information about Kipling's sister's well-known involvement with automatic writing, his own claim that his best writing seemed to be dictated to him, his deep grief at the recent death of his daughter, and even his fascination with driving to suggest that 'They' is a self-revelatory acknowledgement of the existence of psychic powers, of his bond with his sister (fictionalized as Miss Florence), and of the power of love. The Egg, the catalyst for much critical discussion, is understood as the third eye of spiritualist discourse. Perhaps the argument is a little too neat, but it is certainly interesting.

Stephen Benson, in 'Kipling's Singing Voices: Setting the *Jungle Books*' (*CS* 13:iii[2001] 40–60), demonstrates from a new perspective the remarkable versatility of Kipling's creative range. Benson considers the *Jungle Books* in the light of Berkeley's and Maloufé's 1993 opera, exploring the textual 'vocal spaces' (p. 41) and the interaction of voice and narrative that a musical rendition makes explicit. Without subordinating the pleasurable elements of storytelling, Benson uses the language of music to extend the reach of literary criticism to include Kipling's modal diversity—the songs, verbal rhythms, jungle sounds, and multiphonic levels—as an integral part of his achievement. It is difficult to merge two critical discourses without strain, but Benson's argument for Kipling's 'melopoetic engagement' (p. 56) is convincing and refreshing.

Ann L. Ardis, in *Modernism and Cultural Conflict, 1880–1922*, mounts a vigorous interrogation of modernism and its location in the literary scene. The title of her book sets the totemic date 1922 as her chronological boundary, but her aim is not to validate such embedded assumptions. She sets out to extricate the modernists from their construction of their own distinctiveness and to attempt a more objective assessment of their contribution to literary innovation and the continuing influence of their ideas. She integrates the history of literary criticism and of university English departments into this argument, claiming that a significant aspect of the modernists' influence has been critics' tendency to accept modernists' judgement of their own and their contemporaries' work. This book marks a significant step forward in recent attempts to resituate the turn-of-the-century literary world. The opening chapter, which examines Beatrice Webb's writings as a source of literary achievement and judgement, sets the trajectory for an invigorating and often surprising survey. Oscar Wilde, D.H. Lawrence, Wyndham Lewis, 'middlebrow Edwardian' novelists, and the self-styled iconoclastic journal *The New Age* are the focal points of chapters that offer well-argued and challenging perspectives on the cultural power of modernism.

I wonder, however, why David Medalie, in *E.M. Forster's Modernism*, chose modernism for the keyword in his title, since his discussion ranges far more widely and with greater complexity than this suggests. Medalie sees Forster's artistic position as a synthesis of literary modes, and discusses the novels from a number of different perspectives: liberal humanism, romantic realism, formal issues, and, finally, modernism. Although the argument concludes with a discussion of modernism, it is only offered as one literary mode among others. Medalie's particular strength lies in close analysis of the novels: these discussions make for engaging reading. He is less secure in building up his argument. The chapters are very unequal in length, which seems to imply (although I assume this is unintended) some indication of their relative importance. Perhaps it simply reveals uncertainty about an appropriate structure. For instance, his decision to discuss each novel from the different perspective of each chapter ensures a multi-layered interpretation but requires considerable work on the reader's part to bring the information together. However, this book is full of useful contextual information—the liberal humanism chapter, in particular, took the time to interrogate and complicate a term that has become something of a cliché in Forster studies—and Medalie demonstrates a scrupulous concern to allow Forster's novels the fullest range of interpretative possibilities.

A.A. Markley contributes to queer readings of Forster's novels in 'E.M. Forster's Reconfigured Gaze and the Creation of a Homoerotic Subjectivity' (*TCL* 47:ix[2001] 268–92). He explores the way in which Forster sexualizes the male body in a series of tableaux that invite an erotic response and act as a disruption to the mainstream narrative. Drawing on the notion of a reconfigured Lacanian male gaze transposed to the female gaze, Markley argues that Forster wrote dual narratives that both satisfied a conventional Edwardian readership and simultaneously appealed to a gay male readership. Through discussion of selected passages from *Where Angels Fear To Tread*, *The Longest Journey*, and *Room with a View*, Markley shows how the reader's gaze is diverted from the female figure to linger on masculine physical possibilities but is made safe (in an Edwardian context) by being directed through the observing, but unsuspecting, female eye.

The First World War provides an apparently inexhaustible source of literary interest. The fifteen essays in Quinn and Trout, eds., *The Literature of the Great War Reconsidered: Beyond Modern Memory* (see also *YWES* 82[2003]) comment on the writings of the Great War in a way that is coherent, challenging, and often surprising. The editors generously acknowledge the inspiration of recent scholarship, but even so they considerably increase our awareness of the hinterland of writings that are available to scholars, and how partial even the revised work of Paul Fussell (to whose *The Great War and Modern Memory* the title, of course, refers) has begun to seem. Each of the first nine essays addresses how to discuss and make 'criticizable' (p. 23) disparate writings that expand previous Great War literary categories, such as narrative-style autobiography, pre-war journalism, pro-war fictions, translations, and Commonwealth and American fiction. The first of the two essays on modernist responses explores how the rupture represented by war, which the modernists theoretically welcomed, radically changed their project. An appendix to Milton A. Cohen's 'Fatal Symbiosis: Modernism and the First World War' (pp. 159–71) is a modernist war memorial, and, although the critic in me quibbles at categorizing Edward Thomas, Rupert Brooke, and some others as modernist, the simple list of fatalities balanced against the pre-war intellectual bravado Cohen describes brings the emotional and intellectual arenas movingly together. The last section revisits Wilfred Owen and Siegfried Sassoon, although there is no claim to revaluate them. Instead, with an integrity that is the hallmark of this collection, Owen's poetry is reconsidered through his letters, and through issues of class, while Sassoon is read through *The Instinct and the Unconscious*, published by the psychoanalyst W.H.R. River's in 1920. The final essay considers Sassoon's later poems and concludes with a discussion of 'Thoughts in 1938' as the Second World War moved inexorably closer. The reader is again made aware of the contingent intersection of history, artistry, and subjectivity.

Len Platt rightly claims, in *Aristocracies of Fiction: The Idea of Aristocracy in Late-Nineteenth-Century and Early-Twentieth-Century Literary Culture*, that the aristocracy, both as a theme and as an idea, is a neglected dimension of the literary studies of this period. More interested in literary responses than in 'fixing historical realities' (p. xiii), Platt cuts across aesthetic hierarchies to show that the aristocracy was 'common currency that travelled across diverse and often antagonistic literary cultures with some degree of consistency' (p. xvi). The introduction contextualizes this literary trope with a brief discussion of the political and economic decline of the aristocracy (although its power continued to be far more considerable than Platt acknowledges), and explores the way in which writers co-opted ideas of the aristocracy in diverse ways. Popular genres, such as romance and detective and comic fiction, and writers such as Jeffery Farnol, Robert Hichens, and Baroness Orczy are considered alongside Henry James, Ezra Pound, and Virginia Woolf. There is some hesitancy on Platt's part to pursue this approach. Certainly, the familiar canonical names of the period—James, Pound, Wyndham Lewis, Woolf— are given the fullest consideration, and the coda chapter over-extends the argument by considering Joyce's 'aristocracy of form' (p. 135). A late chapter on Shaw's dramas provides a useful balance and a welcome investigation of both aristocratic and socialist ideas in his life and his work. Overall this is an uneven book; even so, it brings an interesting topic into the critical arena and, hopefully, will provoke more detailed examination of the issues it raises.

Both Andrzej Gasiorek, in 'Ford Madox Ford's Modernism and the Question of Tradition' (*ELT* 44:i[2001] 3–27), and Andrew Radford, in 'The Gentleman's Estate in Ford's *Parade's End*' (*EIC* 52[2002] 314–32), consider Ford's relation to tradition, the modern, and modernism. Gasiorek sees Ford as a modernist writer, although he is careful to tease out a definition of modernism as a transformation, rather than a disruption, of literary tradition. The first half of the article considers some of Ford's own arguments about literature, and the second half focuses on *The Good Soldier* [1915] in an attempt to situate his work between 'tradition-making' and 'modernist aesthetics' (p. 11). In conclusion, Gasiorek considers the question of obscurity and elitism, terms which have been used to characterize modernists but which, he argues, were not applicable to Ford, who preferred his work to reach a wide audience.

Radford addresses notions of the rural in *Parade's End*, but presents a counter-argument to frequent criticisms of Ford's nostalgic and escapist gentleman's view of landscape. The view of the countryside taken by Christopher Tietjens, the central character, at the beginning of the novel is both confirmed and reconfigured by his wartime experiences. What Radford calls a 'linguistic ordering', where the image of a settled, productive, and harmonious landscape comes appropriately together in pleasing descriptions, is inadequate for imposing order on the chaos of wartime landscapes. He argues that the return to the English countryside after the war, in *Last Post* [1928], is not Ford writing in escapist mode, but an attempt to draw on 'the only coherent force' that remains in order to provide a counterpointing vision to the emptiness and despair of Great War landscapes, and to sustain hope for the future.

In '"X2": The Final Chapter of *Tono-Bungay*' (*CS* 13:iii[2001] 78–88), Philip Griffin focuses on the final chapter of H.G. Wells's novel, beginning with a brief survey of the critical differences over its function and its success as a conclusion to the novel. George Ponderevo's unexpected change of career to ship designer and the descriptions of the sea-trials of the experimental destroyer, the *X2*, are contextualized by a discussion of the contemporary military situation. Griffin argues that Wells interweaves the possibilities of both a negative and a positive future for Europe in this episode. The negative is framed by the historical reality of Germany's naval supremacy (an interesting link with Kipling is made at this point), and the positive by the location at the mouth of the Thames, which, in leading out to sea confronts the future, in contrast to writers such as William Morris and Jerome K. Jerome, whose earlier utopian fictions follow the Thames upstream and away from the challenge of modernity.

Judith Scherer Herz, in 'To Glide Silently Out of One's Own Text: Leonard Woolf and "The Village in the Jungle"' (*ArielE* 32:iv[2001] 69–88), identifies the continuing significance of Leonard Woolf's novel *The Village in the Jungle* to Sri Lankan culture and its influence on writers such as Michael Ondaatje. She makes it her declared intention to resituate Leonard Woolf in English literary-critical history. A brief biographical account of Woolf's arrival in the former British colony of Ceylon and his involvement with colonial administration traces his growing disillusionment with colonial governance but his growing love for the landscape and people. *The Village in the Jungle* was written on his return to England, and through a close analysis of the novel Herz traces the evolution of his pro-imperialist stance to his later strongly anti-imperialist position.

Michael Maiwald's 'Race, Capitalism and the Third-Sex Ideal: Claude McKay's *Home to Harlem* and the Legacy of Edward Carpenter' (*MFS* 48:iv[2002] 825–57) stretches the remit of this section, but the queer connection that Maiwald explores between the work of the white, middle-class Edward Carpenter in the late nineteenth and early twentieth centuries and the African American writer Claude McKay provides an interesting insight into how marginalized positions can find common ground despite obvious cultural differences. *Home to Harlem* [1928], with its portrayal of black vernacular and black folk culture, became an immediate bestseller and was popular with the younger generation of Harlem Renaissance participants. McKay appears to have shared Carpenter's fundamentally utopian position, and Carpenter's theories helped him by linking working-class life and queer subjectivity to give homosexuality a non-political, progressive role in shaping the future.

(b) The English Novel, 1930–1945

In 1981 the critic Hermione Lee opened her book-length study of Elizabeth Bowen by remarking that she had been 'peculiarly neglected' (p. 11). Several essays published on Bowen since 2000 suggest that this is much less the case now. Yoriko Kitagawa's 'Anticipating the Postmodern Self: Elizabeth Bowen's *The Death of the Heart*' (*ES* 81[2002] 484–96) argues that the novel mirrors 'an epistemological shift' in the 1930s away from 'modernist thinking' (p. 484): 'the novel's peculiarity lies in its astute response to modernism as well as to traditional realism ... [it] both inherits and disowns these two types' (p. 484). The article's claim that Bowen's fiction 'resists easy classification' is not wholly new; nor does the statement that her work has been 'confined' within the 'mold of conventional criticism' seem very accurately to characterize the critical attention paid to Bowen. Her debts and disputes with realism and modernism have been discussed before (see, most notably, Bennett and Royle, *Elizabeth Bowen and the Dissolution of the Novel* [1995], or Chris Hopkins, 'Realism, Modernism and Gendered Identity in Elizabeth Bowen's Novels of the Nineteen Thirties', *JGenS* 4:v[1995]). However, the article identifies some interesting examples in the novel of what can be argued to be postmodern forms of representation of identity, perhaps most strikingly in an aside on the observation that Eva Trout, in Bowen's last novel, herself discusses identity as 'a slippery fish' (p. 494). A more striking development of Royle and Bennett's insights, as well as of recent scholarship about the Anglo-Irish and Ireland, is provided in Neil Corcoran's fine essay on Bowen's second novel: 'Discovery of a Lack: History and Ellipsis in Elizabeth Bowen's *The Last September*' (*IUR* 31:ii[2001] 315–33). Corcoran starts with the observation that the novel is full of 'ellipses, lacunae [and] irresoluble aporia' (p. 315). He develops this idea into an illuminating, detailed, and nuanced historicization of the novel and the position of the Anglo-Irish. That which cannot be mentioned, discussed, even noticed—including perhaps their dependence on 'the paramilitary terror of the State' (p. 318)—is, according to the article's argument, central to the situation of the Anglo-Irish. Hence, 'there is a real, if paradoxical sense ... in which history is most present in *The Last September* when it is most absent' (p. 321). Chris Hopkins gives an overview of Bowen's writing career (as both novelist and short storywriter) in 'Elizabeth Bowen' (*RCF* 21:ii[2001] 114–49). He argues that her utilization of a range of traditions not only across her career, but within a single work is 'an essential part of her method' (p. 114). Her texts do not try to present a single surface or style, but prefer a 'jerkiness' with which the reader must cope as best they can: 'She does not even attempt to combine all her varying influences into a smooth, homogenous text, but allows them ... to work with or against each other' (p. 114).

The year saw two essays on Sylvia Townsend Warner. Jennifer Poulos Nesbitt, in 'Sharing "A Worldliness of Austerity": Sylvia Townsend Warner and Jane Austen'

(*JSTWS* [2002] 27–38) discusses the relationship which Townsend Warner herself acknowledged with Austen's work. The essay starts from Townsend Warner's own critical comments on Austen's achievement of an 'untrammelled technical amiability by an underlying austerity of choice' (p. 28). It then goes on to discuss the differences and similarities between Austen's and Townsend Warner's uses of irony and circumscribed content, as well as the problems of their reception at times as principally 'stylists'. Brooke Allen, in 'Sylvia Townsend Warner's Very Cultured Voice' (*NewC* 19:vii[2001] 20–7), discusses the writer's oeuvre, arguing unusually that her short stories represent the best of her work. Allen's view of the novels differs from the general critical consensus: he regards *Summer Will Show* as Townsend Warner's 'only really bad novel' (p. 24) and says (oddly) that '*Lolly Willowes*, Warner's first book, is the only one that could be described as explicitly feminist' (p. 21).

If Elizabeth Bowen and Sylvia Townsend Warner have suffered periods of critical neglect from which they have emerged over the last two decades, the same cannot be said of another writer of the period, Pamela Hansford Johnson, who was once regarded as a firmly established serious novelist in both Britain and the US, but whose work has faded almost utterly from view since the 1980s. It is good therefore to see an interesting essay, 'Glancing Down the Cliff of Time: Pamela Hansford Johnson and Dylan Thomas' (*NWRev* 58[2002] 35–42), by James A. Davies, about the mutual influence of the two writers. Davies traces the impact of their relationship on their writing between 1933 and 1936. For Hansford Johnson the main manifestations of her personal and intellectual engagement with Thomas occur in her first novel, the once notoriously shocking (or pioneering), *This Bed Thy Centre* [1935]. It is well known that Thomas suggested the title, but Davies teases out the ways in which language, plot, characterization, and representations of sexuality also draw on—and demur from—Thomas's ideas and poetry of the period. The essay suggests too that Hansford Johnson's later novel, *The Survival of the Fittest* [1965], returns to re-examine her relationship with the by then deceased Thomas.

A number of productive essays on travel writing by novelists of the period have been published. All of these essays share a sense that travel writing is not a marginal genre but central to writing of the period, and, indeed, very much connected to centrally literary prose genres. Adam Piette thus opens his essay, 'Travel Writing and the Imperial Subject in 1930s Prose: Waugh, Bowen Smith and Orwell' (in Siegel, ed., *Issues in Travel Writing: Empire, Spectacle, Displacement*) by quoting—and expanding—Andrew Gurr's view that 'exilic travel really defines the role of the writer in the twentieth century (p. 53). Piette adds to Gurr's insight by stressing the inherent politicization of all acts of travel in the 1930s: 'Travel writing in the thirties sets out to demonstrate the close ideological parallels between the ways the private self relates to its environments and the ways a nation relates to supposedly alien cultural forces' (p. 53). Piette shows how the politics of travel are central not only to travel narratives but also to fictions of the period, discussing (in a rather concentrated form) Elizabeth Bowen's *To The North* [1932], Stevie Smith's *Over the Frontier* [1938], Orwell's *Road to Wigan Pier* [1937], and Evelyn Waugh's *When the Going Was Good* [1946]. Piette argues that, as the decade wore on, 'travel writing became a distorted vision of war reportage written at the shifting borders between the political unconscious and a culture gearing itself up for war' (p. 63). Andrew Thacker's 'Journey With Maps: Travel Theory, Geography and the

Syntax of Space' (in Burdett and Derek, eds., *Cultural Encounters: European Travel Writing in the 1930s*) uses Graham Greene's *Journey Without Maps* to illustrate how we might read the texts of travel writings and the maps which invariably accompany—or are part of?—those texts. The essay draws on the work of theorists of geographical representation such as J.B. Harley and Michel de Certeau to discuss how narrative movement in the written text interacts with the kinds of representation (partly written, partly pictorial, partly more technically cartographical) made in associated maps. Noting the paradox that a central part of Greene's travel book is a claim to be an account of a place beyond mapping, metaphorically and literally, but that maps of those areas are nevertheless included in the text, the essay argues that *Journey Without Maps* is characteristic of much travel writing in undermining the fixed certainty of the knowledge that maps seem to offer: 'Travel writing is perhaps always a form of mapping, of offering an alternative vision to that endorsed by various cartographic regimes ... often at odds with official representations of space' (p. 24). The same volume also includes an essay on Robert Byron by Howard J. Booth: 'Making the Case for Cross-Cultural Exchange: Robert Byron's *The Road to Oxiana* (1937)'. Booth argues that an understanding of the relationship between literary modernism and imperialism provides an essential context for writing, including travel writing, of the 1930s. He suggests that there has not yet been a satisfactory account of the relations between modernist writing—including the responses of writers of the 1930s to modernism—and imperialism. He thinks that many critical accounts are monolithic; there is a 'tendency to demand a single narrative of the period—either colonialism was strongly sustained or collapsing ... the writing of the period [either] questioned or supported colonialism' (p. 161). Booth writes about how Robert Byron shows the more complex ways in which empire could engage writers in the 1930s. Byron's writing draws on some hegemonic British cultural assumptions, but is simultaneously critical of Eurocentric superiority. Far from supporting any conventional subject position for the reader, Byron's travel writing, for example, in its championing of Byzantine art, challenged unthinking positions and suggested ways in which other cultures could offer critiques of what to modern European thought seemed self-evident. Thus *The Road to Oxiana*'s 'deliberate use of ambivalence forces the reader to engage with difficulties of interpretation ... Byron's aim was to question the dominance and univocal deployment of Western and colonialist narratives' (pp. 163–4).

There is, as usual, a good deal of criticism on Graham Greene's work, much of it from a Catholic or other Christian viewpoint. An essay by Bates Hoffer entitled 'Greeneland's *Brighton Rock*' (*L&L* 27[2002] 87–111) argues that Greene's texts are 'psychologically unitary' (p. 87) and that one of the many 'advantages of the cultural matrix is that many of the lingering critical problems are resolved without residue' (p. 89). The fundamental idea of the cultural matrix is not entirely clarified in the essay (we are told that 'philosophers' have worked on the matrix, but no names or references are given to allow the philosophical underpinnings of the idea to be traced, and the essay comments that the system is 'here ... very sketchily conveyed', p. 92). The central idea seems to be that Greene's novels demonstrate the eternal consequences of any imbalance between three different kinds of love: *eros*, *philia*, and *agape*.

An issue of *Renascence* (55:i[2002]) is devoted to 'Recent Critical Perspectives on Graham Greene'. This includes essays on 'Graham Greene, Evelyn Waugh And Mexico' (Michael G. Brennan), on travel and the primitive (Adam Schwartz), on genre in *The Confidential Agent* (John Coates), on Scobie and conscience (Lisa Crumley Bierman), on realism and fantasy in Greene and Tolkien (Thomas A. Wendorf) and a note on *Brighton Rock* called 'How Did Hale Die? (Bernard Bergonzi). Michael Brennan's essay is particularly illuminating—reconstructing the ways in which both Waugh and Greene associated the persecution—and survival—of faith in 1930s Mexico with the martyrs of Reformation England. Brennan persuasively makes the case that Greene was especially influenced by Waugh's biography of the English martyr Edmund Campion (published in 1935). The essay traces the links both writers made between the persecution of priests, not only in Mexico but in other parts of the world in the 1930s and during the Second World War: 'the haunted, trapped, murdered priest is our contemporary' (Evelyn Waugh) (*Renascence* 55:i[2002] 10).

Hill, ed., *Perceptions of Religious Faith in the Work of Graham Greene*, is a substantial collection of twenty-four essays, including, among others, articles by Bernard Bergonzi, on *Brighton Rock* and Greene's career as 'Catholic novelist', Michael Brennan, on Greene and Waugh's sense of divine consolation, R.H. Miller, on Scobie's faith, and Kenneth R. Morefield, on the impact of Greene's 'epitexts' (essays, autobiographies, letters) on the interpretation of his fiction.

Avril Horner and Sue Zlosnik published two related essays about the unsuspected survival of popular forms of American Gothic within modernism. Horner's 'Strolling in the Dark: Gothic Flanerie in Djuna Barnes's *Nightwood*' (in Smith and Wallace, eds., *Gothic Modernisms*) suggests that, 'in spite of its Parisian setting, *Nightwood* owes much to American Gothic ... the Paris of *Nightwood* is represented as dark and labyrinthine: a Gothic space in which the boundaries of an everyday reality threaten to dissolve' (pp. 78–9). The essay argues that the continuing unease with which readers and critics respond to the novel is itself derived from the ways in which the text's protagonist and *flâneur*, Robin Vote, crosses generic and modal boundaries between popular and high, sensational and intellectual: 'the uncanny meeting of the atavistic and the modern in the novel's final scene is the ultimate destination of Robin's "strolling in the dark"' (p. 91). Zlosnik's essay, 'Unreal Cities and Undead Legacies: T.S. Eliot and Gothic Hauntings in Waugh's *A Handful of Dust* and Barnes's *Nightwood*' (in Beer and Bennett, eds., *Special Relationships: Anglo-American Affinities and Antagonisms, 1854–1936*) draws on similar ideas, deriving both Waugh's and Barnes's rather different uses of the Gothic from Eliot's own (suppressed) use of this American popular form. In both texts the 'scene of horror is both the "unreal city" and the wilderness; they are ultimately interchangeable' (p. 238).

Mengham and Reeve, eds., *The Fiction of the 1940s*, is an excellent collection of essays devoted to a period which is still widely ignored or skipped over by literary-historical periodization and valuation. As the editors quite rightly observe, 'The 1940s as a literary period is only now beginning to receive the kind of attention regularly afforded to decades such as the 1910s and 1930s, and to movements or phenomena such as Modernism' (p. xi). The collection includes essays by Maud Ellmann (on Elizabeth Bowen), Geoff Ward (on addiction in the writings of Malcolm Lowry, Patrick Hamilton, and Anna Kavan), Lyndsey Stonebridge (on psychoanalysis and Henry Green's Caught), Phyllis Lassner (on Rosamond Lehmann and Kate O'Brien), Howard Erskine-Hill (on the novel sequences of Joyce Cary), Mark Rawlinson (on Jocelyn Brooke and the militarization of the English landscape), Rod Mengham (on the meanings of 'broken glass' in the fiction of the period), Barbara Hardy (on Ivy Compton Burnett's Elders and Betters), N.H. Reeve (on William Sansom and Elizabeth Taylor), Gerard Barrett (on Henry Green's Back), and Peter Mudford (on Waugh's and Greene's post-war sense of defeat in the jaws of victory). All of these essays are very much original and worth reading. Most take a strongly and productively historicizing approach, though a few draw attention in more straightforward ways to neglected authors of the period.

(c) Joseph Conrad

Conrad studies continue to be a particularly fertile area for academic research, and this year's crop of monographs and scholarly articles maintains a high standard both in terms of innovative thinking and academic rigour. Though published monographs still focus discussion heavily on the main fictions, work in the journals has been far more eclectic in focus and expansive in conception. Conrad's problematic dramatic career has become a consistent location of critical attention this year, as has his engagement with issues surrounding linguistic authenticity. At the same time much painstaking work has enlivened bibliographical studies of the man and his work.

Con Coroneos's *Space, Conrad, and Modernity* seeks to contextualize Conrad within a significant cultural and ideational shift between the nineteenth and twentieth centuries. It is a shift that is reproduced for Coroneos through contested articulations of space, for it is the utilization of space (open and closed, liberational and cramped) that is most closely associated with the experience of modernity and the most telling epistemic shift from post-Enlightenment rationalism. This book concerns itself only in part with Conrad's writing; its ambitions are more expansive and its argument draws eclectically from cultural and philosophical theory, to form a challenging framework for the reinterpretation of the spatial concerns of modernity. Conrad is employed as a principal illustrative vehicle because he seems most effectively to conceptualize the symbolic transformations of space that Coroneos proposes. Conrad's abiding fascination with geographies and topographies, with the open spaces of the sea and the enclosed claustrophobia of the cabin, provides Coroneos with persuasive material for his argument. The volume engages primarily with the main fictions—*The Secret Agent, Nostromo, Heart of Darkness*, and *Lord Jim*—and all receive extensive consideration, but, as previously stated, Coroneos's focus is broad, and incorporates Saussurian linguistics and Foucauldian epistemology. *Space, Conrad, and Modernity* is divided into two sections, the first of which engages with some versions of closed space, the second with the potential of language for opening up and liberating those closed spaces. While the first section addresses instances of enclosure and confinement in Conrad's writing the second introduces a more freewheeling discussion of topics such as spiritualism's impact on early modernism. As may be inferred from this rather abrupt shift in focus, the book tends to lurch rather playfully between ideas, and this lack of critical consistency is a disappointing feature of an otherwise provocative and insightful study.

Taking up the theme of language as an inherently limited and frustratingly imprecise means of communication is Michael Greaney's *Conrad, Language, and*

Narrative, a confident and assured contribution from a young Conrad scholar. Greaney focuses on Conrad's struggle for an authentic relationship between language and the world, one in which referential solidity could be established and where transparent meaning could be the basis of interaction between speech communities. For Greaney, Conrad's writing returns obsessively to the themes of orality, story-telling, silence, and inarticulacy evidencing a deep-seated discomfort with the slipperiness and protean qualities of language. While he dreams of 'a community of speakers sharing a language of transparent referentiality and self-present meaning', a form of 'linguistic utopia' (p. 2), he is deeply suspicious of the propensity of language to deviate from meaning into artificiality and inauthenticity. Greaney, in the first of three main sections, explores Conrad's sea stories, intimating that the company of the ship represents a tightly bonded, self-validating linguistic community that dispels indeterminacy, thereby authenticating its own experience. Much of his later work is a nostalgic paean for this form of referential simplicity. It is the voice that Greaney identifies with this authenticity, and the second section of the book focuses on the most celebrated voice in Conrad's fiction—Marlow. It is in the Marlovian narratives that the frailty of discursive practice becomes enmeshed with an increasingly modernist sense of the self-reflexivity and self-negations of language. The final section deals with the 'political' novels—*Nostromo*, *The Secret Agent*, and *Under Western Eyes*—in which Greaney raises the importance of silence as an evasion of ambiguity. This is a well-argued and detailed reading of Conrad that offers much to the current language-centred debates of his work.

Cesare Casarino's study, *Modernity at Sea: Melville, Marx, Conrad in Crisis*, engages with Conrad's writing only in parts and focuses most specifically on *The Nigger of the 'Narcissus'* and *The Secret Sharer*. Casarino's rather unwieldy analysis takes as its central investigative point the impact of the nineteenth-century sea narrative on the emergence of modernism, and more particularly on what he calls 'the spatio-temporal matrix of the crisis of modernity' (p. 1). The sea narrative stands as a curiously resilient genre throughout the nineteenth century, it is argued, and plays an important role in the transition from a mercantile to an industrialized capitalism. In this exchange the sea (and perhaps more significantly the ship) performs a symbolically resonant function, for it articulates a spatial nexus of exchange between modes of capital production and increasingly globalized political economies. For Casarino the pulsating heart of ship life reflects the emergent form of the modernist narrative but also indicates the competing dialectics of power, labour, and capital.

In a different register, also published this year was Hawkins and Shaffer, eds., *Approaches to Teaching Conrad's 'Heart of Darkness' and 'The Secret Sharer'*. The text forms part of the MLA's Approaches to Teaching World Literature series that now numbers over seventy volumes. I have a long-standing regard for this series, providing as it does a number of pedagogically innovative approaches to textual study as well as a significant body of bibliographical and extra-textual resource material. The volume on Conrad is divided into two main sections, the first being devoted to editions, critical commentaries, and audio-visual aids. The second section covers approaches to teaching the texts, and numbers some twenty essays divided into the broad categories 'Teaching Social Contexts and Literary Issues', 'Teaching the Controversies', and 'Specific Courses'; the last of these offers a context-specific selection of insights into areas such as 'Teaching *The Secret Sharer* at the United States Naval Academy and 'Teaching *Heart of Darkness* in a Western Civilization or Humanities Core Course'. As may be inferred from such titles, the audience for this volume is primarily North American, and the applicability of some of the pedagogical approaches to a non-US teaching system could be debatable. However, the material contained in the essays is thought-provoking and provides a consistently stimulating, student-centred methodology that addresses important textual questions with energy and conviction.

The journals contain the customary mélange of bibliographical research, critical opinion, and the occasional off-beam but entertaining diatribe. On balance *The Conradian* probably collects the most provocative array of articles. The most striking piece in the first number is Robert McGill's '"The Germs of Empire": Decivilization and Conrad's Discontent' (*Conradian* 27:i[2002] 51–64). McGill explores Conrad's writing within the context of *fin-de-siècle* anxieties over contamination and infectious disease. As an outsider to the British empire Conrad stands, it is argued, as a potential harbinger of infection, and his fiction returns insistently to the themes of degeneracy and contamination. Yet for McGill Conrad's concern is not with stifling the fear of infection but with opening up a limited imperial mindset to the abundance and excess of the colonial panoply. In a largely expository article, 'Bruno Winawer's *The Book of Job*: Conrad's Translation' (*Conradian* 27:i[2002] 1–23) Gra_yna Branny details the literary relationship between Conrad and the Polish dramatist Bruno Winawer, whose play *The Book of Job* Conrad translated for the English stage. Branny's article carefully explores the background to the project and analyses some of Conrad's textual alterations.

Nathalie Martinière's 'Symbolic Space and Narrative Focus: The Cabin in Conrad's Sea Stories' (*Conradian* 27:i[2002] 24–38) is an interesting but oddly flat consideration of the symbolic connotations of the cabin in Conrad's sea narratives. She argues that the cabin is at once a place of 'revelation of one's hidden and dangerous impulses' and a place of 'creative potential, born from one's temptations' (p. 37). In '*Le Dernier des Trémolins*: A Source for *The Inheritors* and *The Mirror of the Sea*' (*Conradian* 27:i[2002] 39–43) Mario Curelli identifies Édouard Drumont's 1879 novel as a potential precursor of Conrad's texts. In the same volume J.H. Stape and Gene M. Moore, in '"The Stone of the Sultan of Succadana: Another Source for *Lord Jim*' (*Conradian* 27:i[2002] 44–50), offer factual records detailing accounts of a legendary jewel, which Conrad may have rewritten and included in *Lord Jim*. Raymond Brebach's 'Ford Madox Ford's "A Note on Romance": Reconsidering the Ford–Conrad Collaboration' (*Conradian* 27:i[2002] 65–71) offers some useful insights into the collaborative and competitive nature of Ford and Conrad's working relationship. Finally in the first number, J.H. Stape and Ernest W. Sullivan II examine the case against the Heinemann Collected Edition of *Lord Jim* as the authoritative text of the novel. 'The Heinemann Collected Edition of *Lord Jim*: An Unauthoritative Text' (*Conradian* 27:i[2002] 72–87) presents a detailed analysis of the proofs of the edition, and concludes that in all probability many of the alterations made to the manuscript were by a hand other than Conrad's.

The second number of this year's *Conradian* is given over to Gene M. Moore's 'A Descriptive Location Register of Joseph Conrad's Literary Manuscripts' (*Conradian* 27:ii[2002] 1–93). Moore's overview of the extant manuscripts builds on Gordon Lindstrand's earlier 'Bibliographical Survey of the Literary Manuscripts of Joseph Conrad' and provides an invaluable reference point for Conrad scholars.

Moore not only furnishes the current locations of 330 manuscripts but also details (where appropriate) the provenance and bibliographical history of each work. In updating Lindstrand's register Moore has also substantially increased the number of manuscripts (from 203) and reduced the percentage of uncertain locations from 29 to 11 per cent. This painstaking scholarship will prove an important resource for Conrad researchers for many years to come.

The first two numbers of *Conradiana* are combined to include a representative selection of papers presented to the International Joseph Conrad Conference at Texas Tech University. Zdzislaw Najder's 'My Half Century with Conrad' (*Conradiana* 34:i–ii[2002] 1–14) begins the collection, and is both a poignant reminiscence of an academic career immersed in Conrad studies and an eloquent overview of the state of play of those studies. Most moving in Najder's paper is his insistence on the concrete ethical touchstones of Conrad's world: honour, fidelity, and solidarity. In 'Transactions and Transtextualities: "The Lagoon", "Because of the Dollars", "The Warrior's Soul" and "Christmas Day at Sea"' (*Conradiana* 34:i–ii[2002] 15–30) Cedric Watts expounds his notion of transtextualities—that significant narrative elements can extend across several works by a writer—and illustrates his argument through analysis of some of Conrad's less celebrated writings. Such transtextualities, it is argued, offer networks of interpretative resonance that are often overlooked in the appreciation of works as separate textual artefacts. Transtextuality also emerges as the theme of Robert Hampson's '"Because of the Dollars" and the Already Written' (*Conradiana* 34:i–ii[2002] 95–105), where the relationship between "Because of the Dollars" (strangely ubiquitous this year) and *Victory* (amongst others) is traced. Hampson employs Watts's idea of transtextual resonances to explore the representation of south-east Asian pirates in Conrad's writing.

The multiplicity of Conradian intertextual echoes within contemporary writing concerns David Leon Higdon in 'Reinscribing *Heart of Darkness*: Margaret Drabble Confronts Joseph Conrad' (*Conradiana* 34:i–ii[2002] 31–42). Higdon explores the consonances between Conrad's novella and Drabble's south-east Asian novel *The Gates of Ivory*. His conclusions are ultimately disappointing, but the comparison throws interesting light on a literary debt. Susan Jones's '"Creatures of our light literature": The Problem of Genre in *The Inheritors* and Marie Corelli's *A Romance of Two Worlds*' (*Conradiana* 34:i–ii[2002] 107–22) explores the relationship between Conrad's writing and the popular novel. Jones argues that the two texts evidence generic experimentation with forms of romance while also trying to encompass contemporary concerns about scientific developments and *fin-de-siècle* gender politics.

This number also contains three articles on Conrad's play *Laughing Anne*. Richard J. Hand's 'Producing *Laughing Anne*' (*Conradiana* 34:i–ii[2002] 43–62) details the provenance of the play and some critical responses to it before outlining some of the production decisions involved in its premiere in 2000 for the International Joseph Conrad Conference. Alison Wheatley also addresses the play and covers similar ground to Hands in '*Laughing Anne*: "An Almost Unbearable Spectacle"' (*Conradiana* 34:i–ii[2002] 63–76). The third article on the play is Marjean D. Purinton's '"The Laugh of the Medusa" and *Laughing Anne*: A Feminist Reading of Joseph Conrad's Play' (*Conradiana* 34:i–ii[2002] 77–94). Through the focus of Cixous's essay Purinton examines potential readings of the play that disrupt the pervasive phallocentric and imperialistic norms of Conrad's writing. The argument is provocative without ever being convincing, but Purinton's discussion of Conrad's challenge to dramatic conventions is useful. Also included in this number are Adam Gillon's 'Words Beyond the Life of Ships: Joseph Conrad's Impact on Polish Poetry' (*Conradiana* 34:i–ii[2002] 123–34) and Yannick Le Boulicaut's 'Is There Therapy in Speech in Conrad's Works?' (*Conradiana* 34:i–ii[2002] 135–44).

To the third number of *Conradiana* Linda J. Dryden contributes her essay '"To boldly go": Conrad's *Heart of Darkness* and Popular Culture' (*Conradiana* 34:iii[2002] 149–70) an engaging, eclectic, and entertaining overview of the impact of Conrad's novella on twentieth-century culture. Dryden devotes space to the synergies between Conrad's work and Francis Ford Coppola's *Apocalypse Now* and to media creations as diverse as *The Simpsons* and *Star Trek*. Her framing argument concerns popular culture's appropriation of 'high' culture as a means of self-validation, and this article makes a good case for *Heart of Darkness*'s place as a nexus of cultural transaction. Remaining on a popular cultural theme, Ted Billy's '"So little more than voices": Orson Welles's 1945 Radio Dramatization of *Heart of Darkness*' (*Conradiana* 34:iii[2002] 171–80) examines Welles's celebrated fascination with Conrad's novella and focuses on one of the three adaptations that he attempted. Interestingly Billy suggests that for Welles the tyranny of Kurtz's rule found a parallel in Hitler's dictatorship, and Kurtz's own megalomania is expressed as a brutal fascism. Barbara Kingsolver's *The Poisonwood Bible* is the intertextual descendant of *Heart of Darkness* that Pamela H. Demory focuses on in 'Into the Heart of Light: Barbara Kingsolver Rereads *Heart of Darkness*' (*Conradiana* 34:iii[2002] 181–94). Not only does Kingsolver update Conrad's tale to a satire of American exploitation of the Congo in the mid-twentieth century, but the novel also critiques Conrad's implicit masculinism.

In 'The Gibberish Threat: Unrestrained Narrative in *Heart of Darkness*' (*Conradiana* 34:iii[2002] 195–210), Lee Rumbarger argues that language in the novella is continually threatened with a descent into meaninglessness, disconnection, and silence. In a work obsessed with the telling of stories, words offer only lies and imprecision. The definitive relationship between world and word is, for Rumbarger, represented by the elusiveness of Kurtz's voice and ultimately by his silence. Diana Arbin Ben-Merre's 'Conrad's Marlow and Britain's Franklin: Redoubling the Narrative in *Heart of Darkness*' (*Conradiana* 34:iii[2002] 211–26) engages with the figure of Sir John Franklin, a celebrated mid-nineteenth-century arctic explorer who met his end on expedition amidst stories of cannibalism. Ben-Merre's article argues that the popular horror of anthropophagy by white men becomes ironically inverted in *Heart of Darkness* into black cannibalism in Africa. The final article in this year's volume is Mary Morzinski's '*Heart of Darkness* and Plato's Myth of the Cave' (*Conradiana* 34:iii[2002] 227–34) which draws comparisons between Conrad's fiction and *The Republic*. The concept is intriguing but Morzinski's exposition is too underdeveloped to persuade completely.

One article of note outside the principal Conradian journals is M. Kellen Williams's '"Where all things sacred and profane are turned into copy": Flesh, Fact and Fiction in Joseph Conrad's *The Secret Agent*' (*JNT* 21:i[2002] 32–51). Williams's article addresses (amongst other things) the image of the fragmented body in Conrad's novel. The body as a space of fetishized reinscription pervades the narrative and is tied, in Williams's view, to the transformation of the authentic (be that in terms of ideas or language) into the artificial and ready-made.

(d) James Joyce
There seems to be no slackening in the production of work on Joyce, with the trend towards historical and contextual readings of one form or another increasingly dominant. Among these, a new book by Andrew Gibson stands out, but first mention goes to the continued publication of the *Finnegans Wake* notebooks, an archival project that allows for the sort of critical historicizing undertaken by Gibson and others. This year saw the release of three further notebooks in the Brepols series: VI.B.6, VI.B.14, and VI.B.25, edited by Vincent Deane, Daniel Ferrer, and Geert Lernout. I won't add much to the discussion of the first releases (see *YWES* 82[2003]) other than to say that both scholarship and production values continue to be excellent. These volumes are a testament to the archival work of many researchers. Lernout puts some of the new information detailed in this series to good use in his essay on Wagner's *Tristan und Isolde* in the early composition of Joyce's last work (*JJQ* 38[2002] 1–2). It is perhaps not surprising that critical reflections on the cataloguing process have begun to appear, among them Wim van Mierlo's strong defence of the kind of archival digging best exemplified by these notebooks, 'Reading Joyce In and Out of the Archive' (*JoyceSA* 13[2002] 32–63).

Joyce's Revenge: History, Politics and Aesthetics in 'Ulysses', by Andrew Gibson, is an important contribution to recent debates on the political contexts of Joyce and, for this reviewer, the highlight of the year's work. Gibson persuasively sets out the extent to which 'Joyce's revenge' was not merely a personal question but was also embedded in a range of specific cultural discourses operative in England in the decades immediately prior to *Ulysses*. Two brief chapters on the initial episodes of the novel set out the ways in which Stephen Dedalus and Leopold Bloom in turn react against their surroundings and offer a glimpse of cultural difference. The broader argument, at this stage, has become familiar enough, though Gibson enlivens it with specific vignettes, notably on Haines and Deasy in relation to constructive Unionism, and on Bloom's complex cultural belonging. The real distinction of this work lies in the following chapters, as they relate the last ten episodes of *Ulysses* to particular discourses. In formulating the book's variety of styles, Joyce was also, argues Gibson, rewriting a set of historically particular English and Anglo-Irish discourses of cultural nationalism that were operative in the period 1880–1920. By so doing Joyce took his 'revenge' on the oppressive and disabling forces of the colonial power. To put the case so starkly, however, implies a restrictive replication of the very structure of that power, as Gibson's Joyce is well aware. Instead, a subtle and liberating revenge is precisely what Joyce achieves through his scepticism towards an oppositional stance. Revenge, then, comes not only in borrowing and undermining those discourses but also in Joyce's refusal of the premises of the discourses he plays with. 'Scylla and Charybdis' provides a notable example. The Shakespeare controversies and bardolatry of Victorian-Edwardian England provide the context in which to read the debate in the National Library. Gibson shows how Stephen here has ousted his own earlier imagining of history as narratives of possibilities and instead resorts to a factuality and mastery of his sources that rebuts Arnold's notion of the fanciful Celt. Unionist activists and Shakespearians like Edward Dowden and A.S. Canning are rightly brought to the fore by Gibson to illuminate the context for Stephen's argument; furthermore, Joyce finds an accomplice in Shakespeare, working his language and inventing a Shakespearian language so that the local discursive context is not overburdening. This 'one strict principle' of simultaneous 'fidelity to and betrayal of' the relevant discourse in question is the methodological basis of the book. After only a brief mention of 'Sirens', Gibson unpicks the revivalist historiography of O'Grady and others, demonstrating how its gigantism informs 'Cyclops'. An excellent chapter on 'Nausicaa' provides some convincing new explanations of particular allusions, clearly setting out the extent to which Joyce had culled material from a range of women's magazines. Joyce's knowing disclosure of these details shows the ideological forces at work in Gerty's world; moreover, Gerty's own knowing disclosure is itself a resistance to contemporary notions of sexual purity and its policing. She stands at the edge of coming to 'modern consciousness' characterized by literacy, the circulation of texts, and a political awareness that especially concerned Irish women in this period. Another excellent chapter, on 'Oxen', demonstrates the particular relevance to Ireland of the discourses of Malthusianism and of the anthology. Joyce provides an additional challenge to the Malthusian argument, citing the specificity of a Catholic and colonized nation, and in hand with this Gibson shows how Ireland became a key case for economists' debates in the late nineteenth century. At the same time, 'Oxen' expands on traditional Irish fertility rites and charts the rise to prominence of a new, young Catholic middle-class whose presence betokens the shifting of power within the medical profession. The final, remarkable, chapter reads 'Penelope' alongside accounts of the narratives of Gibraltar, dominated by the defensive rhetoric of military historians. Counter to this, Gibson argues, is Joyce's rendition of an 'ordinary' Gibraltar, where flora rather than guns are worth describing. Against the grain of this opposition runs the voice of Molly, seductively urging not resistance but reconciliation. In citing Joyce's famous line that Molly's 'yes' signifies the 'end of all resistance', Gibson argues that 'Penelope' signals the possibility opened up by the truce that ended the War of Independence, a truce signed at the same time as Joyce was planning 'Penelope', a possibility decidedly not taken in the early years of the Free State. An important theme gradually develops in Gibson's argument, that is, an exposition of the ways in which Dublin stood on the cusp of modernity at the turn of the twentieth century while still being restrained by a variety of cultural and political forces. This notion stands behind most of the later chapters, though if space could have been found for more historical and theoretical detail on the book's engagement with the meanings of modernity it would have been welcomed by this reviewer. Nonetheless, this book is clearly a significant addition to contemporary debates in historicizing Joyce. Gibson has also co-edited a volume that is discussed below; his chapter on Bloom's cultural identity might be complemented by Neil Levi, '"See that straw? That's a straw": Anti-Semitism and Narrative Form in *Ulysses*' (*MoMo* 9:iii[2002] 375–88).

The prolific Florida series has produced several more books this year, two of which dovetail nicely with Gibson's study. *Joyce's 'Ulysses' as National Epic*, by Andras Ungar, is notable for its detailed reappraisal of the historical and political parallels of the epic genre in Joyce's novel. *Ulysses* emerges as a book that recovers the epic's sense of collectivism and community, a book that looks ahead to future national self-definition while reading backwards into turn-of-the-century Dublin. As such, Ungar argues, it shapes the epic to historiography while maintaining its textual self-reflexivity. The argument can be seen as a nuanced follow-up to the work of Enda Duffy, tracing the coincidence of *Ulysses*' publication with Irish independence. Ungar describes *Ulysses* as 'epic fable': it is epic in that it carries 'the aura of epic foundational moments' such as Virgil's paean to imperial Rome, while its fable—defined as the part of narrative corresponding to Chatman's sense of 'story'—'performs' the political development of the nation-state through the relationship between Stephen and Bloom. Ungar suggests that *Ulysses* sees itself as implicated in the construction of Irish nationhood, an identity which would have 'self-evident coherence' (p. 8) for future generations (Ungar is not explicit, but I think he must mean generations that are still to come). This is a highly ambitious book that carries its argument rather heavily: the going is tough, sometimes unnecessarily so, and, at nearly a hundred notes just for the introduction, the author's voice is occasionally crowded out by the range of sources. The book is too brief (150 pages) for its topic and lacks crucial historical detail. In an argument for which the 1921–2 Treaty is surely significant, it is perhaps odd not to find a single reference to de Valera's 'document no. 2', but what is surely remiss is the absence of any mention of de Valera himself. The strength of the book lies in its extensive development of the historical and textual significance of Arthur Griffith's *Resurrection of Hungary*.

A more localized argument for the importance of Victorian and Edwardian cultural discourses in Joyce's work comes from Tracey Teets Schwarze. Developing the earlier work of Kershner, Herr, and others on the significance of popular cultural practices and ideologies in Joyce, her *Joyce and the Victorians* considers constructions of Irishness, Catholic orthodoxy and dissent, masculinity, vice, domesticity, female 'sickness', and New Women. The various inflections of gender are, then, the main concern of the book. Schwarze steers away from an optimistic, 'liberationist' reading of Joyce's wordplay, arguing instead for its groundedness in everyday experience. Joyce's work thus grants '"dissidence" rather than revolution' (p. 12) to its characters. For a work informed by cultural studies, this book is oddly dependent still on the elucidation of characters' motivations and energies (to the extent of reading *Finnegans Wake* along these lines). The specific cultural constructions analysed by Schwarze usually form short introductions to a chapter which is then steeped in close textual detail, whereas work of this kind, which emphasizes the ways in which literary texts are meshed within other forms of cultural signification, is often more closely interwoven with its contextual sources. These readings do offer a further picture of the 'emergent' in Joyce, reviewing aspects of one social milieu into which his work inserts itself, although their benefit is ultimately less in the historical research (much of which seems already slightly dated) and more in the textual readings. The Victorian-Edwardian sensibilities that inflect Joyce's characters are brought out here in a thorough and often persuasive way.

On a different methodological note, two further studies also extensively concerned with gender—by Marian Eide and Kimberly J. Devlin—have shown the continued strengths of conceptual readings of Joyce. Drawing on the body of post-structuralist criticism, but especially Derrida's readings of Lévinas, Eide's *Ethical Joyce* adds the recently popular notion of an 'ethics of interpretation' (p. 33) to the familiar figure of interpretative aporia which she finds implicit in Joyce's characteristic open-endedness. Such an ethics implicates the reader, not by instruction but by calling for response, not by judgement but by placing readers in an 'undecidable' position. Eide's primary location for ethical issues, as it is for Lévinas, is in daily face-to-face interactions, notably in the home. Eide's first chapter defines the implied ethical subject as incomplete, in need of a community of others to whom in turn the subject is responsible. A notable reading of the figure of the gnomon in *Dubliners* exemplifies this by virtue of its appeal to an other as interpreter, but an other to whom the gnomon nonetheless 'belongs'. Similarly, in *Exiles*, the figure of aporia places readers in the impossible position of suspending decisions. In the following chapter, Eide's analysis of *A Portrait* and *Ulysses* focuses on pedagogical issues. She argues that Joyce resisted the manner of his own education and in his writing proposes a different epistemology. The distance of his alter ego, Stephen Dedalus, from authority figures is thus a mark of ethical difference. Yet Stephen is unable to mature in relation to others, including his friends, because he has not come to terms with 'the ethical habitat provided by his mother' (p. 81). Eide reads Stephen's poem—composed on a 'gnomon' made from Deasy's torn letter—as an example of his 'emerging ethic' (p. 82). The crux of ethical responsibility in these books, however, is not with Stephen but with May Dedalus. Eide confidently proclaims *amor matris* as the word known to all 'humans' (p. 82). The second half of Eide's book is concerned with a mother and a daughter: a chapter on ALP's language as it 'performs Joyce's ethics' by deconstructing the 'political and moral certainties' (p. 85) of her sons, and a good chapter about Joyce's anxious identification with his daughter, Lucia, during her mental illness in the 1920s and 1930s. In providing a theoretical introduction to post-structural ethics, Eide does open an interesting space for examination of the roles of, particularly, mothers and daughters in Joyce's work and life. Yet the cost of this notion of ethics is, all too often, a reduced awareness of the political and historical situations within which Joyce's work was rooted.

Kimberly J. Devlin, one of the leading American Joyce scholars, has released *James Joyce's 'Fraudstuff'* in the Florida series, reworking a number of previously published essays. Her initial argument is that Joyce increasingly moved away from an authentic sense of representation typified by the epiphany and towards a more deceptive writing which is self-consciously a sham. In doing so, she compares the different portraits of Dedalus, noting the shift from fraudulence in others to the construction of various self-delusions. So far this might not seem especially groundbreaking, but, as always, it is in Devlin's detail that her work's strength emerges. In separate chapters, Devlin draws heavily on the work of Lacan, and, to a lesser degree, that of Judith Butler, to show how gender is performative. With Lacan, she takes the notion that in a scopic relationship the subject depends upon the gaze as a type of phallus. This 'privileged object' promises to remedy the lack (for Lacan, castration fear) that characterizes an imaginary perception. This notion offers Devlin plenty of scope for reading the peregrinations of Bloom in 'Nausicaa' and 'Sirens'. One chapter offers a lengthy analysis of Gerty MacDowell and Molly Bloom, returning to Joyce's source-texts for 'Nausicaa' (Gibson, discussed above, has identified more) in order to show how 'femininity' is a kind of 'fraudstuff' (the word is from the *Wake*). Turning to Molly, Devlin adds textual close reading to the theoretical difference between female masquerade and female mimicry, asserting the potentially subversive quality of the latter as an impersonation of female gender roles. Such mimicry is associated with Molly, and the more restrictive and disabling masquerade is likened to Gerty. Two more chapters deal significantly with Leopold Bloom and 'Circe': the first reads *Ulysses* as a form of 'police novel' in which Bloom's identity collapses under the gaze of surveillance; the second analyses an intriguing detail in Bloom's day—his internalization of the picture of Christ and the sisters of Lazarus. Bloom appears here as a fraudulent Christ-figure, a perception which he attempts to repress but which manifests itself in 'Circe'. The final chapter looks at forms of clothing—which don't so much disguise as constitute the body— in the hallucination of 'Circe' and in *Finnegans Wake* II.3. Many, though not all, of the passages under scrutiny in this volume are fairly standard loci for critical comment, but they are again enriched here by Devlin's arrangement, her keen eye, and her readable, engaging sense of narrative. Further reflections on the state of gender analysis are contained in Richard Brown's essay '"When in doubt do gender": Constructing Masculinities in "Penelope", "they're all Buttons men"' (*JoyceSA* 13[2002] 147–59).

Also in the Florida series, David Spurr's *Joyce and the Scene of Modernity* has a promising title, and offers much—including a synthesis of historical and theoretical readings—although its collection of essays might have been more strictly focused on the meanings of modernity in order to posit an individual thesis. This is another volume from Florida that is too short for its topic. The objects of Spurr's analyses range from the disruptions of colonial hegemony within the urban spaces of Dublin to modernist anthropologies exemplified by Joyce, Eliot, and Lévy-Bruhl. Another writer who figures significantly in this book is Proust, who is compared with Joyce in two chapters. On the one hand, both authors express a 'comedy of intolerance' in which the exclusion of Jewish characters is treated with 'comic equivocation' (p. 37). On the other hand, the two writers differ in their representation of 'the scene of reading': Proust is elegiac in his recovery of subjective unity through the privacy of reading whereas Joyce 'effaces the boundaries dividing ... reading from the rest of life' (p. 97). For such potentially rich material, the subtleties of Joyce's near-obsession with reading and readers might have been worked out at greater length. In another chapter, Spurr takes a further look at Joyce's reading of *Hamlet* though the reading of that play by Mallarmé, and finds in its excessive morbidity an identification with spectrality that lies at the heart of writing. Spurr's method, as these examples suggest, is a blend of almost deconstructive close reading with historical and political argument. Notably, this latter component of the work seems to come out when the topic is Ireland or colonialism, but is rather reserved at other times and sits somewhat oddly with the implicit insistence on canonical European modernist contexts in many chapters. However, having said that, Spurr can be commended for his willingness to engage Joyce with other writers—a feature often lacking in current Joyce studies.

Another work in part informed by deconstruction, in both rhetoric and logic is *Joycean Temporalities: Debts, Promises and Countersignatures* by Tony Thwaites, the premise of which is a convincing elucidation of Kant's art as 'purposiveness without purpose'. For Thwaites, Joyce's work exemplifies the 'empty space of intentionality'—it is like Dedalus's God, indifferently paring his fingernails— which means that it is a 'writing whose intention ... is to be without intention' (p. 25). (Not surprisingly, *Finnegans Wake* figures large in the following analysis.) The upshot of this seeming paradox is that Joyce's texts are self-consciously left open for readers to 'conclude' in whatever manner seems appropriate (compare Eide, above).

Their many seemingly marginal mysteries, such as those old chestnuts Mc'Intosh and UP:up, are actually central to the logic of the work. Relatively little has been written recently on *A Portrait*, and Thwaites's reading of this novel offers a lively rejoinder to some older debates. The point is less that the book may enact Dedalus's aesthetics, Thwaites argues, and more that it displays '*aestheticizing*' (p. 112). By self-reflexively staging the *Bildungsroman* in its 'concluding' chapter, *A Portrait* draws attention not only to the developing promise of its main character, but also to it own frustrated textual promises. This might be called an aesthetics of aestheticizing, and Thwaites shows how it undermines the distinction between art and the marketplace upon which Dedalus's theory rests. Heavily deconstructive in thought, the argument also includes sharp readings of other crucial thinkers, such as Walter Benjamin. Thwaites posits an 'arrest' in Joyce that is akin to Benjamin's 'shock': the coming of the new which is a disturbing arrival, promising a definitive point of departure to an unknowable future. Rather like Dedalus's sense of history in *Ulysses*, one can see 'from the rupture of the arrest, other times and other possibilities open out. Or perhaps simply possibility itself' (p. 66). *Joycean Temporalities* is an unashamedly theoretical exploration in the best sense of that term: not an 'application' of a set of ideas but a working through of immanent ideas. Without pretence to a politics or a contextual history, this book instead exhibits the resourcefulness, and serendipity, of Joyce's language. Derrida's own readings of Joyce have been discussed by Jean-Michel Rabaté in 'Des Lectures de Joyce, oui' (*EF* 38:i–ii[2002] 179–88).

A collection of essays specifically devoted to Joyce's engagement with languages and philological issues has been edited by Dirk van Hulle under the rather prosaic title *James Joyce: The Study of Languages* (also one of Joyce's school essay titles). All but one of the essays arranged here deal principally with *Finnegans Wake*. The exception is the long final contribution by Gregory M. Downing, which considers some of the pioneers of nineteenth-century popular and applied philology before going on to show how Joyce appropriated a number of their ideas in *Ulysses*. The other contributors and topics are: Sam Slote on Raymond Queneau and the *Wake*; Finn Fordham on Joyce's corrections to *Finnegans Wake*(!); Erika Rosiers and Wim van Mierlo on the *Wake*'s allusions to contemporary linguist Otto Jespersen; Ingeborg Landuyt on Joyce's notes from *Cymbeline* in notebook VI.B.4; Laurent Milesi on Joyce's notes from Sir Richard Paget in VI.B.32; and Dirk van Hulle on Fritz Mauthner, I.A. Richards, and the development of 'Wakese'.

Three further collections of essays have been released in the European Joyce Studies series. Gibson and Morrison, eds., *Joyce's 'Wandering Rocks'*, contains eight essays and an introduction on the pivotal chapter of *Ulysses*. Morrison's excellent introduction dwells on the different senses of the chapter's possible centrality and the various ramifications for the book as a whole that these senses imply. Clive Hart writes on chiastic patterns in the chapter and discusses the relationship between determinate textual elements and the apparently indeterminable (he even provides another of his handy charts). Gibson's essay looks at the chapter's 'macropolitical and micropolitical' aspects, providing further historical substance to read it as a revisitation of 1880s Parnellite Dublin and the political drudgery of the following period. Richard Brown's characteristically deft argument that the urban and the textual merge in *Ulysses* follows some of the conceptual pathways of Michel de Certeau, noting the familiar landmarks and destabilizing shocks that both text and city provide. A thorough account and analysis of the reading material in the episode is provided by David Pierce, who argues that it is saturated in intertextuality. Stefan Haag reads 'Wandering Rocks' as a 'soundscape' or 'acoustic space' (p. 107) in which noise frequently interrupts in unexpected ways that undermine determinate readings of the chapter's mechanics. The potential for this essay to be read alongside Hart's is minimized by their distant placement. William Stephenson regards the contrasting qualities of eroticism and 'lightness' (p. 121) in the chapter; Len Platt places the episode within the colonial context of 1904 Dublin; and Fritz Senn sees the chapter's characteristic 'interlocations' as providing 'a continual sense of "elsewhereness"' (p. 155). On the whole this volume achieves a successful balance of the historical, conceptual, and textual and is a worthy addition to the studies of 'Circe' and 'Ithaca' already edited by Gibson in the European Joyce Studies series. A pertinent article on 'Joyce's Geodesy' (*JML* 25:ii[2002] 80–96), by Eric Bulson, considers Joyce's treatment of the geography of Dublin in relation to the Ordnance Survey.

Boldrini, ed., *Medieval Joyce*, in the same series, brings together Joyce specialists with medievalists. Among the former, Sam Slote writes on the medieval irony of *A Portrait* and among the latter Helen Cooper argues the case for Chaucer as 'Joyce's Other Father'. As possible follow-ups to Boldrini's own book on Dante in *Finnegans Wake* (see *YWES* 82[2003]), there are essays by Jennifer Fraser on the *Commedia* and ALP; Reed Way Dasenbrock and Ray Mines on Dante, mathematics, and the ending of *Ulysses*; and Jeremy Tambling on Dante's modernism. There are also pieces by Jed Deppman on Joyce in 1923 and Guillemette Bolens on medieval interlacing as it pertains to Milly's dream and Bloom's body.

Nash, ed., *Joyce's Audiences*, edited by this reviewer, assembles an international range of commentators to address the various means by which audiences in/of Joyce might be understood. The collective purpose of the volume is to show some of the complexities of a writer's reception: how it is a complex form of cultural history; how Joyce's work anticipates issues of reception in its frequent scenes of reading; how influential individuals or social movements affect readings of the work in diverse cultural situations. Barbara Leckie and Jean-Michel Rabaté each separately consider aspects of the audience implied in the construction of 'modernism', with Leckie focusing on censorship and Rabaté looking at the notion of a 'plain reader'. One distinctly non-plain reader, Richard Ellmann, is the topic of John McCourt's assessment of the monumental, but flawed, biography. Roy Gottfried reconsiders *Stephen Hero* and *A Portrait* as autobiographies with quite different implied audiences. The history, and future, of Joyce studies in Taiwan is discussed by Yu-chen Lin, while Craig Monk looks back to the reception accorded to 'Work in Progress' in the United States. An essay by the editor focuses on the depiction of scenes of reading in *Finnegans Wake* and relates them to contemporary complaints about the lack of time for reading. Meanwhile, a complementary essay by Ingeborg Landuyt brings to light a number of previously unnoticed allusions in the *Wake* to critics of *Ulysses*. Brian G. Caraher suggests a number of 'protocols' for reading *Ulysses* in his comparison of the interpretative strategies of Edmund Wilson and Terry Eagleton. An overview of the dovetailing between feminist theory and feminist Joyce studies is given by Catherine Driscoll, while Joe Brooker rounds off by observing the 'belatedness' that affects post-structuralist accounts of Joyce.

The premier journal of Joyce studies, *James Joyce Quarterly*, this year produced two special double issues. 'Joyce and Opera', guest-edited by Timothy Martin (*JJQ* 38:i–ii[2002] 431–52), collects a number of excellent articles and notes on the theme, including Lernout's essay mentioned above and Allan Hepburn's '*Ulysses*, Opera, Loss'. The other collection, themed around 'Joyce and Trieste' and guest-edited by John McCourt, contains several pieces analysing the history and literary implications of Joyce's time in the city and his encounter with a range of peoples and languages. Among these, an essay by Erik Schneider discusses that old chestnut for Joyce biographers, the possibility of his contracting syphilis (*JJQ* 38:iii–iv[2002]). It was a thin year for articles on Joyce among journals devoted to a broader range of material than the specialist *JJQ*, which appears now to be picking up in speed and quality after a temporary loss of form.

Finally, a special edition of the *Yale Journal of Criticism* (*YJC* 15:i[2002]) has been released under the heading 'The Theater of Irish Cinema', guest-edited by Dudley Andrew and Luke Gibbons, and dealing in large part with 'The Dead' and John Huston's film version. Two essays of particular note, each concerned with both story and film, are those by Gibbons, on the depiction of spectacle, and by Marjorie Howes, on the relationship between migration, gender, and cultural nationalism.

(e) D.H. Lawrence

In two studies considered below, Gary Adelman bemoans Lawrence's waning reputation among scholars over the past fifteen years. Yet the sheer breadth and diversity of material reviewed here appears to belie such pessimism. These books and articles adopt a range of approaches, engaging with Lawrence through biographical, interdisciplinary, theoretical, and socio-historical contextualization while also employing more traditional close-reading techniques. The texts are grouped appropriately, according to method or content.

It seems appropriate to begin with a scholarly, biographical work, namely *Living at the Edge: A Biography of D.H. Lawrence and Frieda von Richthofen* by Michael Squires and Lynn K. Talbot. This book offers an original, 'double' approach both in relation to its subjects (Lawrence and Frieda), and through its engagement with the implications of joint authorship. Squires and Talbot have been collecting the letters of Frieda Lawrence for several years, and now have around 1,600. They claim that their biography 'takes its direction from [this] rich material', also proceeding from the belief that the 'emotional dynamics' of the Lawrence–Frieda relationship can best be probed by a couple, from within a marriage. Overall, the authors contend that, through a modification of previous approaches, their book 'reshapes the space between Lawrence's life and art'.

While some of the authors' claims for uniqueness seem questionable, they have produced a book which provides a comprehensive account of the marriage of Lawrence and Frieda and a valuable report of Frieda's life after Lawrence's death. Brenda Maddox and Richard Lucas have, of course, covered the same ground, but it is almost thirty years since the Lucas biography, and the new material in Frieda's letters does provide some fresh insights into her life after 1930 (the accounts of her visits to Hollywood and the fate of the manuscripts in her possession are of particular significance).

There are a number of minor inaccuracies arising from an insecure knowledge of British geography, and two errors relating to the Chambers family: Alan is included among Lawrence's fellow apprentice teachers (p. 14), while Jessie's husband, Jack Wood, is described as a farmer (p. 75), when he was actually a teacher at the time of (and subsequent to) meeting Jessie. Occasionally the writing is a little awkward or over-elaborate, and the interpretations far-fetched, such as the claim that Ravagli's name pronounced backwards converts to Oliver (Parkin/Mellors) and thus covertly alludes to the 'emotional realignment' to which the Lawrences allegedly progressed. Yet these minor caveats do not detract from the general impact of a book that contains much new and interesting material—including a number of well-judged illustrations, several of which are relatively unfamiliar—and is a welcome addition to the Lawrence biographies.

The first predominantly critical work considered here is *The Complete Critical Guide to English Literature: D.H. Lawrence*. Fiona Becket admirably fulfils the general aim of the series—to give a readily accessible and full account of an author's life and work, and of apposite literary criticism—writing on D.H. Lawrence with great clarity but without over-simplification. The first part of the book deals with Lawrence's life, while in the substantial central part devoted to Lawrence's work, Becket selects from his vast output using the criteria of acknowledged cultural significance and the illustration of key developing or recurrent themes. Of particular interest is her perceptive analysis of the relationship between Lawrence's philosophical writing as conveyed in his essays, and their fictional embodiment.

A striking feature of the book is the way all three parts interrelate, so that the final section on critical responses has been clearly signalled. Becket discusses criticism, from that of Lawrence's contemporaries right to the present, bringing out the full range of response from the highly positive to the equally scathing. Beginning with the oft-cited rejection of Lawrence by T.S. Eliot alongside F.R. Leavis's refutation of this negative view, she proceeds to discuss, for example, critiques of Lawrence's views on his contemporary society, feminist criticism (particularly that of Kate Millett), and the writings of post-structuralist critics. The effectiveness of this excellent guide to Lawrence is enhanced by a chronological table, an extensive bibliography, and a number of suggestions for further reading interspersed throughout the text.

Stefania Michelucci's *Space and Place in the Works of D.H. Lawrence* takes an original approach to a fascinating theme in Lawrence's work: the evocation of space as created and imagined, of areas and arenas within which characters are situated and interact. The author is clearly attuned to Lawrence's way of perceiving and portraying characters according to the places inhabited and the spaces around them. She argues perceptively that Lawrence is not merely a 'psychological' author: rather, he is concerned with the external as much as the internal, as chapter titles such as 'Breadalby' and 'Shortlands' in *Women in Love* suggest. There are occasions in this book where the writing is a little lacking in clarity, not as a result of the English translation, which is excellent, but because the slightest hints of imprecision in the Italian are magnified when rendered in English. Yet this minor stylistic issue does not compromise the overall effectiveness of a book that offers an extremely insightful perspective on an important aspect of Lawrence's writing and thinking.

The next three books have been grouped together as they are predominantly theoretical and interdisciplinary, employing psychoanalysis, philosophy, and stylistics respectively in their approach to a range of Lawrence texts. James Cowan's

D.H. Lawrence: Self and Sexuality spans the related fields of literature and psychology, proceeding from the assumption that, 'If literature can give to medicine a humanities perspective, medicine can contribute to literary criticism a view of health and informed medical criteria in an attempt to enlarge our understanding of the human condition' (p. xiii). Cowan possesses unique attributes for this task: he is a professor and scholar of modern English literature with a specialism in D.H. Lawrence, and is also qualified as an Academic Associate in Psychoanalysis. By means of a form of applied psychoanalysis (and Cowan stresses that literary subjects cannot merely be classed as 'patients' or 'analysands'), the author examines a number of Lawrence texts, attempting to 'construct interpretations of meanings that ordinarily remain unconscious or preconscious but are substantiated by thematic and formal elements in the work itself that are conscious' (Charles M.T. Hanly, quoted on page xiv). In the absence of the free associations or dreams of the author to employ in the interpretative process, Cowan uses letters and other biographical materials (alongside the key fictional texts) to shed light on Lawrence's 'personal psychological issues' and views on human sexuality.

In spite of the inherently challenging and complex nature of its subject, this book remains lucid, coherent, and unintimidating throughout. The introduction sets forth the premise of the study and provides a clear chapter summary, indicating the place of each topic within the trajectory of the general argument. Cowan also outlines his credentials for the task and explains the project's origin, as well as indicating the ways in which it will engage with and develop previous scholarship in this area.

An extremely useful glossary is provided in which all key terms derived from the work of psychologists are explained and attributed. Full and informative notes, an extensive index, and a comprehensive bibliography all contribute to the overall accessibility of this work: it remains compelling throughout, despite moments in which the juxtapositions and the conclusions drawn seem rather unconvincing. Overall, this text both serves as a useful survey of previous psychological approaches to Lawrence and provides new insights, particularly through reference to the pre-Oedipal theories developed within the 'widening scope of mainstream psychoanalysis today' (p. x).

Paul Sheehan's *Modernism, Narrative and Humanism* analogously spans two related disciplines—literature and philosophy—exploring humanism in relation to literary modernism through focusing on four writers: Conrad, Lawrence, Woolf, and Beckett. Sheehan acknowledges the significance and extent of this post-war process of redefinition, in which the human being became a 'site of contention' (p. ix). Yet his argument derives from a perception that the critical engagement with the human is not merely a 'post-war skirmish' (p. x) but has its roots in a century-long project spanning the nineteenth and early twentieth centuries. The chosen writers are examined in relation to the humanist/counter-humanist dichotomy, with a view to establishing both contrast and affinity: the author interrogates their 'reflection on human being within the constellation of their narrative poetics' (p. xii). The chapter entitled 'The Lawrentian Transcendent: After the Fall' juxtaposes D.H. Lawrence and Martin Heidegger, identifying parallels which are 'cursory and indirect' yet 'undeniable' (p. 91). Sheehan discusses both in relation to the concept of a fall, suggesting that they analogously identify man as a 'degraded entity' which has lost either its relationship with being (Heidegger) or its sense of connection to all things (Lawrence). The chapter establishes its philosophical premise through situating

Heidegger within the 'anthropometric' context, before focusing more specifically on *Sons and Lovers*, *The Rainbow*, and *Women in Love*. The writing here is dense, intricate, and laden with elevated philosophical discourse; it is challenging, and not for the faint-hearted. The book is a genuine literary/philosophical hybrid offering new perspectives on literary modernism and, from a Lawrentian point of view, extending the scope of research in this area, supplementing the work of such critics as Michael Bell and Fiona Becket.

D.H. Lawrence's Novels: A Stylistic Approach, by Prakash Pradhan, consists of twelve papers written while the author studied for a Ph.D., and later revised for publication. Throughout, Pradhan repeatedly asserts the necessity for a stylistic analysis of literary works: an approach which is allegedly contrary to the traditional methods employed in most Indian universities—methods he considers to be partial and imprecise. Analysis, he argues, should move beyond patterns of language to include 'extra-linguistic' elements of discourse which have significance in society's value systems. Thus, he describes his theories of the stylistics of fiction, which he outlines in the first section of the book, as 'inclusive, multi-functional and socio-linguistic'. The extensive middle section shows his analytical techniques being employed in the study of *Sons and Lovers*, *The Rainbow*, and *Women in Love*. He concentrates on lexis, syntax, metaphor, textual organization, and modes of discourse. These are perceived not simply as surface structures but as generated within a socio-cultural context, and conflicting world-views are evident in the contrasting voices of the characters. The author admits to being 'disturbed' by the discovery that Lawrence does not give his support to one particular view. Yet he does allude to Lawrence's belief that literature has a crucial role to play in the act of living, referring to his 'intuitive experience, psychological insight and vision of life' (p. 227), while suggesting that this unique quality in Lawrence's fiction is only to be unearthed and comprehended through stylistic analysis. This is not an easy book to read. Sometimes difficult concepts and arguments are presented too briefly and the organization could have been improved. Nevertheless, it is in general an interesting and scholarly text which may well prove to be of significance in developing the teaching of English literature in India.

By contrast with the texts discussed above, the following three books adopt relatively conventional reading strategies in their analysis of Lawrence's fiction, poetry, essays, and paintings. J.C.F. Littlewood's *D.H. Lawrence: The Major Phase. Studies in Tradition and Renewal* has unusual status in that the author died in 1984, with the book unfinished. He left a title, a contents page, and a completed introduction. The remaining chapters incorporate published and unpublished material, including lecture notes, ranging in date from the 1960s to the time of his death. Problems of provenance are discussed in an introduction and appendices by the editor, William Shearman, who has carefully organized the material and supplied footnotes. Littlewood argues that Lawrence's 'whole undertaking as a writer was an attempt to make amends to life itself by bringing what his father represented in his imagination into fruitful relation with what his mother represented there—body with soul, female with male' (p. 48). The book seeks to clarify this 'fruitful relation', arguing that, after the composition of the inherently flawed *Sons and Lovers*, there are two breakthroughs in the development of Lawrence as a writer, the first resulting in *The Rainbow*, the second in *Women in Love*. It also traces Lawrence's development in relation to major literary figures including Shakespeare,

Blake, Dickens, and Emily Brontë. Historical, cultural, and religious circumstances are shown to have had a formative influence.

Littlewood's book reveals his central concern with defining what a study of literature should be, and his trenchant criticism of so many scholars cannot be ignored. He argues that Lawrentian scholarship, 'for over a quarter of a century has busied itself with every aspect of Lawrence except ... his genius' (p. 253). More specifically, he makes the odd allegation that, in the Cambridge University Press edition of Lawrence's letters (and he is referring here specifically to the first two volumes), the 'genius has been eliminated altogether' (p. 253), accusing the authors of erroneous value-judgements (p. 257). Clearly the book is controversial and at times wrong-headed, and there have been vast changes in literary criticism in the twenty years since the author's death. It is essentially a work of traditional literary criticism, as might be expected from a pupil and admirer of F.R. Leavis—yet, as such, it remains a searching and compelling study.

Cornelia Schulze, in her published doctoral thesis entitled *The Battle of the Sexes in D.H. Lawrence's Prose, Poetry and Painting*, also challenges accepted views and aims to articulate a ground-breaking approach within Lawrence studies. Dismissing existing biographical accounts as either one-dimensional or lacking in coherence, she seeks a vision of a 'whole' Lawrence which will reconcile the often contradictory facets of his nature and writing. Interestingly, she points out that his own deconstruction of the concept of a stable personality underlines the biographer's difficulties. So, 'only when seeking for his most fundamental issue that unifies his life and work can a less fragmentary Lawrence be presented' (p. 12). She claims to have achieved this, arguing that the 'battle of the sexes' is the 'dominant narrative' both in his writing and in his life. The 'whole' Lawrence will be revealed in his evolving views of this 'battle'.

Schulze identifies a 'crisis of manhood' in Lawrence's social background and argues that this must have influenced his perception of sexual roles. She also provides 'biographical sketches', selecting those experiences which impinged upon Lawrence's sense of a 'male self' and his view of women. Both the socio-historical context provided and the biographical material are clearly orientated towards justifying and excusing Lawrence's alleged misogyny so often reviled by feminist critics. The author does not attempt to deny that there is such an element in his earlier works, but the whole thrust of her extended analysis of his 'battle of the sexes' is that he gradually moves from this to a much more sympathetic portrayal of women. Schulze divides Lawrence's prose and poetry into sections, each said to illustrate a different stage in the movement from seeing the male–female relationship as 'sheer opposition' to what she argues is a 'solution' in the late fiction, through the attainment of 'tender love'. She also argues that Lawrence's view of 'tender love' is expressed in his paintings, seven of which are included in her book. She discusses these paintings as celebrations of human sexuality, interrogating the distinction between prose and 'fixed' visual art in portraying living relationships.

Finally Schulze includes Garry Shead's essay on Lawrence and three of his paintings from the *Kangaroo* series in order to provide an example of a modern artist responding to the 1923 novel. Yet, while the material included is interesting, she is rather unconvincing in alleging that Shead 'anticipates the sense of reconciliation between the sexes Lawrence himself only discovered shortly before his death' (p. 303). Generally, however, Schulze's individual analyses are perceptive, and she presents sound evidence for the progression of Lawrence's views in relation to her central thesis. It is, of course, questionable to refer to a 'solution', and to chart a progression through Lawrence's life and art according to clearly definable stages. Yet this is indeed a fresh and lively approach to Lawrence, in which ostensibly familiar material is presented from a different standpoint, while the inclusion of visual art is an enriching addition to the book.

Kumar Mukhopadhay begins *The Poetry of D.H. Lawrence: Modernism Without Artifice* by emphasizing the previous neglect or dismissal of Lawrence's poetry by notable critics (such as R.P. Blackmuir), and states his intention of attempting to redress this balance through a revaluation of Lawrence's entire poetic output and his 'poetics'. He desires to establish Lawrence as a crucial poet in the modernist period: a truly 'modern' figure breaking new ground through his poetry of intimate sexual experience and the natural world; through poetry articulating a new perspective on the war and 'unlovely actualities' (p. 3); through his 'stark' new poetry of the present; and through the flexible control of his free verse. However, in addressing (or redressing) extreme views, the author sometimes pushes to the opposite extreme, making some over-effusive assertions and questionable judgements.

After progressing through the trajectory of Lawrence's entire poetic oeuvre, Mukhopadhay devotes the penultimate chapter to a general (and illuminating) discussion of Lawrence's free verse, also discussing the poetry of Pound, Eliot, and Whitman, while the final chapter charts lines of influence between Lawrence and his contemporaries, as well as his impact on the writing of later poets. The book refers to the work of numerous scholars, also providing relevant intertextual perspectives through alluding to Nietzsche, James Frazer, Jane Harrison, John Burnet, and Charles Darwin. It is refreshing, too, that the early poetry and *Bay*—poems that rarely feature in Lawrence criticism—are given due weight and prominence. The final chapter is of particular interest, making some fascinating juxtapositions of texts and authors. Placed alongside Gary Adelman's book, *Reclaiming D.H. Lawrence: Contemporary Writers Speak Out*, and his article 'D.H. Lawrence, Working Poets, and Political Correctness' (*SoR* 38:ii[2002] 334–57), this final chapter effectively demonstrates the degree to which Lawrence-as-poet has been, and continues to be, influential in a way that belies and challenges critical neglect.

My discussion of the two Gary Adelman works mentioned above—works employing analogous strategies, and thus considered together—will effect the transition between the previous book review section, and the following review of articles. As Adelman points out, a good deal has been, and continues to be, written about Lawrence's waning reputation among scholars, particularly during the last fifteen years. Drawing on his experience of teaching Lawrence to undergraduates, he juxtaposes the critical sidelining of Lawrence with a sense of predominant student hostility to Lawrentian ideology.

Adelman describes the process of contacting numerous contemporary writers of fiction and poetry, in order to ascertain the extent to which they have been influenced by Lawrence. The book and article contain the fascinating results of these surveys, with lengthy passages quoted in which significant (predominantly American) novelists and poets talk openly about the way in which Lawrence has impacted on their lives and art. The book (though containing a rather oddly personal afterword) is fascinating through being 'full of voices' (p. 17): it contains quotations from students, writers, academics, teaching assistants, and even the caretaker at the

Lawrence Ranch near Taos. The article focuses specifically on the responses of poets, and Adelman concretizes the accounts given through a lively discussion of poem excerpts: notably the Tortoise sequence, 'The Ship of Death' with its adjacent clusters, and finally 'Snake'. He also touches on the dynamics of the poet–audience relationship (to the detriment of the latter), and the way in which the prioritization of theory impinges on the creative, living response to texts.

Virginia Hyde's wide-ranging article, 'D.H. Lawrence, W.B. Yeats, and the *Rosa Mundi*' (*SCR* 35:i[2002] 68–82), juxtaposes Lawrence's and Yeats's use of 'rose' symbolism in poetry, fiction, and visual art. She considers Lawrence's (unused) jacket design for *Birds, Beasts and Flowers* and his illustration of the priestess of Isis for 'The Escaped Cock', in conjunction with the dustjacket of Yeats's *The Secret Rose*, commissioned by the poet and designed by Althea Gyles. Through reference to these designs, in addition to a range of poems, novels, and essays by both authors, Hyde discusses diverse manifestations of the rose in relation to its Edenic implications; the spirituality/sensuality paradox; love, connection, opposition and selfhood; Blakean contraries; tree cosmology; the 'world-soul'; and Rosicrucian/cabbalistic imagery.

From the rose to 'appleyness'—the apple being, as Virginia Hyde points out, one representative of *Rosaceae*. In his article 'Pan and the Appleyness of Landscape: Death of the Procreative Body in "The Princess"' (*SNNTS* 34:iii[2002] 282–302), Peter Balbert offers a rich and perceptive analysis of Lawrence's story 'The Princess' in conjunction with related essays: namely, 'Introduction to these Paintings' and 'Pan in America'. He explores the notion of 'appleyness' as conveyed in the former, drawing on Lawrence's identification of this quality in Cézanne's best still lifes, and interrogating the paradox of mobility within stasis that it entails. He proceeds to relate this concept to the prose style, character interactions, and portrayal of landscape in 'The Princess'. Alluding to 'Pan in America' he offers another perspective on the natural landscapes of the story, seeing it as infused with pagan vitalism: a quality which is absent from the static, immature, narcissistic Dollie, and waning in the 'morbidity and defeatism' of Romero. Balbert interestingly links the above elements to biographical contexts (the death of Arthur Lawrence immediately before the writing of this tale, and his son's revised opinion of the dynamic within his parents' relationship); as well as the socio-historical impact of syphilis on the proliferation of increasingly negative attitudes to the procreative body during this period.

The next two articles discuss the concept of desire in Lawrence, the first in relation to homosexuality, and the second in relation to human–animal interaction. In the article 'D.H. Lawrence and Homosexual Desire' (*RES* 53[2002] 86–107), Howard Booth both celebrates and challenges the perspective on Lawrence and homosexuality conveyed in Mark Kinkead-Weekes's masterly biography of Lawrence's middle period, *Triumph to Exile*. Booth alleges that Lawrence remained unsettled, deeply disturbed, by the subject of same-sex desire, and adopted a number of fictional strategies in order to 'act on' his own sexuality, as well as attempting to influence others. The 1917–18 period does contain Lawrence's most positive assertions on the subject, but (according to the author) this interest continued into the 1920s—though becoming increasingly condemnatory and with a gradual dwindling.

In 'Beastly Desire: Human/Animal Interactions in Lawrence's *Women in Love*' (*PLL* 38:iv[2002] 429–41), Andrew Howe explores Lawrence's portrayal of sado-masochism in this novel, suggesting that the violent and brutal impulses within human relationships are displaced onto animal doubles. There are some errors and inadequacies in this article, such as the assertion that Hermione is Birkin's ex-wife, while Gerald is seen exclusively as the controlling figure in his relationship with Gudrun. At times, too, the interpretations are forced, exaggerated, or far-fetched. Yet there are interesting ideas here relating to the evolving relationship of Gerald and Gudrun in which Gudrun reveals an increasing acceptance of Gerald's violence, some perceptive close analysis of key scenes, and interesting incorporation of Freud at the close.

Each of the following two articles engages predominantly with a single Lawrence text, the first discussing the portrayal of human and beast within the story 'The Fox'. Doris Lessing's piece, simply entitled '"The Fox" of D.H. Lawrence' (*NYRB* 49:xix[2002] 18–19), situates her discussion of Lawrence's story in the context of both the shifting, conflictual critical attitudes towards Lawrence generally, and her own response to him, spanning a period of sixty years. She interrogates the implications of the female–female relationship of the tale and the intrusion of the human 'fox'—the young soldier—into their world. She also considers the portrayal of the actual fox, in relation to the habits of tamed and wild animals as observed in the world today, and in relation to the beasts portrayed by the old shamans or storytellers. At its close, the discussion offers an interesting perspective on Lawrence's astonishing 'supranormal sensitivity' (p. 19), attributing this to the impact of tuberculosis, which over-sensitizes, unbalances, provokes heightened sexual response, and then renders impotent. Lessing's analysis of this text, and of Lawrence in general, is both insightful and energizing. She offers a range of perspectives, affirming Lawrence's significance with appropriate vigour but never idealizing him, or dismissing alternative views. Admiration, here, is never at the expense of judgement.

Nader Elhefnawy's two-page article 'Lawrence's *The Rainbow*' (*Expl* 61:i[2002] 41–3), offers a pertinent reading of the text as an attack not directly on war, but on nationalism and the idea of the nation-state, through the portrayal of Paul and Lydia Lensky, as well as Anton Skrebensky. This account provides a convincing, if not entirely new, perspective on the novel's notoriety at the time of its initial publication.

The *D.H. Lawrence Review* furnishes a significant body of Lawrence criticism each year, and the articles discussed below derive from volume 30:i–iii[2002]. The first of these issues incorporates three related essays discussing the same novel: 'Losing the Old National Hat: Lawrence's *The Lost Girl*' by Michael L. Ross; 'The Encoding of *The Lost Girl*' by H.M. Daleski; and 'Myth and Biography in *Where Angels Fear to Tread* and *The Lost Girl*'. The succeeding article, 'The Peasants of the Villa Mirenda' (*DHLR* 30:i[2002] 43–54) by Stefania Michelucci, displays the results of meticulous and original scholarship in which the author provides an account of the families living near to the Villa Mirenda (Scandicci), during the Lawrences' occupation of the house in the late 1920s. Lawrence grew closer to the Italian peasant families working on the estate than was habitual: Julia Pini, who was entrusted with the upkeep of the house when the Lawrences were absent, provides one specific example. It is an impressive achievement to have conducted such extensive and successful research eighty years after the event, providing pictures of these families as well as interesting and relevant documentation.

The next issue (*DHLR* 30:ii[2002] 5–79), a special issue, and the second dedicated entirely to John Turner's research, forms an apposite sequel to the previous number in offering further scholarly material that sheds light on the Lawrences' life at the Villa Mirenda from 1926 to early 1928. Turner prints material derived from diaries composed by the Wilkinsons—artist friends of the Lawrences—who lived only five minutes away during this period. The diaries were previously thought lost, but Turner, having discovered them in the possession of the Wilkinsons' relatives, prints them here with an excellent introduction and scholarly annotation.

The next issue opens with Jad Smith's article, 'Völkisch Organicism and the Use of Primitivism in Lawrence's *The Plumed Serpent*' (*DHLR* 30:iii[2002] 7–24). The author counters simplistic assumptions in which this novel is seen as an unequivocally proto-fascist work, highlighting the vacillations in Lawrence's political thinking subsequent to its composition. The second key strand of the article focuses on racial ideologies, principally racism conveyed in ethnocentric primitivism and a proto-fascistic politics of 'the people'. Smith draws on the work of contemporary postcolonial critics, indicating finally that, rather than adhering to a discernible and limited doctrine, the novel divides *völkisch* organicism 'against itself'.

Robert Burden analogously focuses on a novel of the 1920s in 'Parody, Stylization, and Dialogics: A Bakhtinian Reading of *The Lost Girl*' (*DHLR* 30:iii[2002] 25–42), supplementing the approaches to this novel provided in 30:i. Here, Burden argues for the fruitfulness of a genuinely Bakhtinian reading of Lawrence, one that moves beyond an emphasis on polyphony or focalization. He examines *The Lost Girl* as a work characterized by self-questioning, parody, and stylistic play, carnivalizing other texts of the period, such as Arnold Bennett's *Anna of the Five Towns*, through its satire on English class-related speech mannerisms. He sees the text as indicating a new direction in Lawrence's writing.

The last article in this issue is 'Lawrence or Not: The Letter Fragments of H.D. and E.T.' (*DHLR* 30:iii[2002] 43–53), by John Worthen. The author argues for the existence of Lawrence texts within Hilda Doolittle's autobiographical novel *Bid Me To Live*. According to Worthen, either one or two letters from Lawrence to H.D. are incorporated: letters whose status remains slightly unreliable, but which are as trustworthy, for example, as Jessie Chambers's recreation of Lawrence's correspondence to her. Worthen's characteristically powerful argument was sufficient to convince James T. Boulton to incorporate this newly discovered Lawrence material in volume 8 of the CUP *Letters*.

Finally, two articles are considered which derive insight from their consideration of Lawrence as correspondent. In '"Reducing Down": D.H. Lawrence and Captain Scott' (*CS* 14:iii[2002] 14–27), John Turner's argument is based on a letter written by Lawrence to Edward Garnett, in which he responds feelingly to the demise of Captain Scott and his fellow explorers in 1913. Turner examines the implications of outer and inner modes of exploration, identifying the point at which Lawrence moved beyond his early association of the artistic thought-adventure with degeneracy or degradation, to a position where he could recognize Scott, the man of action, as a double. Turner examines *Sons and Lovers* and *Women in Love* as texts which explore the process of reducing down, the death of Gerald in the snow constituting an obvious parallel with Scott's fate. Turner brings in psychoanalytical perspectives, alluding to Winnicott and Freud, before finally discussing 'The Man Who Loved Islands', considering Lawrence's portrayal of 'reducing down' as the islands literally reduce in size and the protagonist becomes increasingly misanthropic.

In 'Letters, Lawrence, Shakespeare and Biography' (*JES* 32:ii–iii[2002] 121–34), David Ellis discusses the implications for the biographical process of possessing authorial letters. Starting with Shakespeare, he examines the process by which a dearth of autobiographical resources has provoked a number of extravagantly speculative biographies. Ellis proceeds to consider the entirely different case of D.H. Lawrence, whose copious letters exist in eight thick volumes, providing a wealth of material. Yet even then, he argues, the process is problematic, as indicated by the dichotomous interpretations of selfhood deriving from the Romantic and sociological perceptions. Is the 'self' a centre or core from which everything emanates, or is it constructed according to one's relationship to others? In the light of this question, Ellis discusses the status of the letters, and other autobiographical materials, as correspondence between author and (real, imagined, or implicit) addressee. He leaves us pondering on the role and status of biography in a postmodern age, in which letter-writing is dwindling and may no longer function as a key biographical resource. This is an important, varied article, tackling a fundamental issue and written with Ellis's characteristic wit, precision, and incisiveness.

(f) George Orwell

This has certainly been a thin year for Orwell studies, and this reviewer has received no monographs and has been able to track down very few articles. With the centenary of Orwell's birth in 2003 it can only be assumed that authors and publishers have delayed publication to coincide. I regret being unable to obtain copies of several articles which look very interesting and offer fresh perspectives on Orwell as writer and critic. These include Rob Breton's 'Crisis? Whose Crisis? George Orwell and Liberal Guilt' (*CollL* 29:iv[2002] 47–66), Douglas Kerr's 'Orwell's BBC Broadcasts: Colonial Discourse and the Rhetoric of Propaganda' (*TPr* 16:iii[2002] 473–90), and Melinda Spencer Kingsbury's 'Orwell's Ideology of Style: From "Politics and the English Language" to *1984* [*sic*]' (*JKS* 19[2002] 108–13). William Dow's lengthy article, 'Down and Out in London and Orwell' (*Symbiosis* 6:i[2002] 69–94) is a dense and unwieldy exploration of the tramp's psychosomatic identity as present in Jack London's *The People of the Abyss* and Orwell's *Down and Out in Paris and London*. Dow's argument is insufficiently clear to summarize, but involves the relationship between the body of the tramp as an ontological site of social inscription and the psychological performance of the role by London and Orwell.

(g) Virginia Woolf

Haule and Stape, eds., *Editing Virginia Woolf: Interpreting the Modernist Text*, ranks as one of the most important, if controversial, publications on Woolf scholarship published this year. This volume variously summarizes the editorial activity surrounding the publication of 'reliable texts' of Woolf's writing, but it should be read in conjunction with George Bornstein's *Representing Modernist Texts: Editing as Interpretation* [1991] and Julia Briggs's earlier review essay, 'Editing Woolf for the Nineties' (*SCR* 29:i[1996] 67–77) for a more complete perspective on the textual controversies concerning Woolf's writing in the last two decades. With the exception of Anne Olivier Bell's 'Editing Virginia Woolf's *Diary*', all the essays in this volume were written by scholars who have either served on the editorial board for the Shakespeare Head Press editions of Virginia Woolf's writing or who were selected by them to produce 'a reliable reading text, informed by historical and archival research' for this series published by Blackwell (p. 4). In their introduction Stape and Haule assert the importance of establishing 'reliable texts' of Woolf's writing 'through the analysis of variants', though they acknowledge that electronic technologies have now made it possible for many more scholars to consult Woolf's earlier manuscripts and typescripts, making her drafting process and the work of her textual editors much more transparent. Recognizing critical trends that have raised questions about the 'prestige, status, and authority' of editors, they assert, nonetheless, that 'facts can be established, that evidence is not merely or solely a matter of interpretation, and that the work of the author takes precedence over an ideally self-effacing editor-critic' (p. 8). They also rather defensively criticize the editors of competing 'feminist' editions of Woolf's novels, and the scholars who cite them, but they fail to admit the price differential that prevents most students and faculty from being able to purchase Shakespeare Head Press editions. In fact, several of the essays in this volume show how the explicit and implicit practices and philosophies of Woolf's recent editors have amplified some of the differences that have determined how and why Woolf's texts have been received and read so differently on either side of the Atlantic, or on either side of the gender gap.

Several of the essays in *Editing Virginia Woolf* describe the editorial decisions made in preparing more accurate texts of Woolf's best-known novels and essays. J.H. Stape's 'The Changing Shape(s) of *Orlando* and the Myth of Authorial Control', for example, recounts his painstaking efforts to establish the best and most 'reliable' copy-text for this novel, though he doesn't acknowledge why so many recent commentators have preferred a more 'composite' approach to *Orlando* or identify the cultural and personal pressures to censor this text that Woolf resisted in revising this manuscript for publication. Edward Bishop's 'The Alfa and the *Avant-texte*: Transcribing Virginia Woolf's Manuscripts' contrasts Louise De Salvo's editorial decision to produce an easily readable 'clean text' of Woolf's *Melymbrosia* with his own decision to produce a facsimile transcription of the holograph of *Jacob's Room* that preserves the 'sense of textual life and activity that conventional printed documents deny' (p. 151). James M. Haule, by contrast, in his 'Version and Intention in the Novels of Virginia Woolf', observes that the vast majority of the textual discrepancies between the Brace Harcourt's American editions and Hogarth Press's English editions of Woolf's best-known novels 'originated with Woolf herself' (p. 172), and notes that her inconsistencies in correcting proofs, often coupled with the loss of corrected page proofs, have made it nearly impossible to determine her final 'intentions'. He then outlines his analysis of corrections that prompted him to select the English edition as the copy-text for *The Waves* (p. 187), and argues that, in a case like *To the Lighthouse*, where 'more than one edition is authoritative', editors should show greater openness about their 'negotiations' in determining the text to be used. Morris Beja, in his genial and disarming 'Text and Counter-Text: Trying to Recover *Mrs Dalloway*', surveys the extant copies of page proofs for this novel and explains why he has preferred the American edition as the 'most reliable' copy text. In closing, he counters Bishop's defence of holographic texts by asserting that the 'common reader', in contrast to the 'textual critic', typically 'does not want to put a book together but to read one' (p. 128). S.P. Rosenbaum, in 'The Writing of *A Room of One's Own*', details Woolf's process in transforming her manuscript, 'Women in Fiction', into the subsequent book and briefly summarizes the substantive differences between these two texts. Naomi Black's '"Women Must Weep": The Serialization of *Three Guineas*', offers a perceptive close reading of the textual differences between the Hogarth Press's first edition of *Three Guineas* and the much shorter version of this essay that Virginia Woolf serialized for *The Atlantic Monthly*, indicating how and why she adjusted it for an American audience.

Other essays in *Editing Virginia Woolf* provide valuable information about how the final texts and interpretative apparatus were assembled for Woolf's unpublished writing. It is useful to compare Anne Olivier Bell's essay, 'Editing Virginia Woolf's Diary', with Joanne Trautman Banks's 'The Editor as Ethicist'. Olivier Bell describes her efforts in producing notes for Woolf's diaries that were as accurate, complete, and succinct as possible. While Bell says almost nothing about how she resolved chronological discrepancies in Woolf's often undated, unnumbered, and sometimes chaotically organized notebooks, how she decoded Woolf's difficult handwriting, or decided which of two or more conflicting 'factual accounts' she recorded, she explains how she developed a comprehensive chronology of Woolf's life and a complete index of her acquaintances, which Quentin Bell also used in writing his landmark 1972 biography of Woolf. Trautman Banks, having already provided an account of how she and her co-editor Nigel Nicholson collected, dated, transcribed, and annotated over 4,000 letters written by Woolf, offers here a 'narrative about why the Woolf *Letters* exist in their present form' (p. 26). Frankly identifying differences of opinion between herself and Nigel Nicholson, Trautman Banks defends their decision to arrange Woolf's letters in chronological order, despite the challenges posed by many undated letters, and to convert her ampersands into 'ands' and similar textual details. Trautman Banks also qualifies Woolf's claim that she 'never' redrafted her letters (iii.247) by noting that they found evidence that she revised her early letters, especially those written to Clive Bell and Lytton Strachey. In discussing the ethical concerns she faced in editing Woolf's letters, Trautman Banks acknowledges Quentin Bell's 'influence', notes the 'special obligation thrust upon the biographer or editor who is a family member or close friend' (p. 48), and describes her concessions to English libel laws, in the case, for example, of thirteen potentially scandalous words describing Lydia Lopokova's sexual history. She concludes by recognizing the wisdom of Nicholson's practice of 'sending Woolf's potentially hurtful lines to people still alive for their information and vetting' (p. 46) before their publication in Woolf's *Letters*, indicating the care and thoroughness that has made this edition of the letters so widely cited and praised. Susan Dick, in 'A Book She Never Made: The Complete Shorter Fiction of Virginia Woolf', explains how she selected, organized, and edited Woolf's previously published and unpublished short stories, expresses some of her reservations about publishing texts that Woolf would 'undoubtedly have revised' (p. 125), and details how she annotated them.

The most eloquent and illuminating essay in this volume is Diane Gillespie's 'The Texture of the Text: Editing *Roger Fry: A Biography*', which illustrates her responsiveness to the most important trends in textual editing over the last decade as well as her knowledge of how they have contributed to recent themes in Woolf scholarship. Gillespie explains that, in writing her biography of Fry, Woolf not only conducted an 'admirable experiment in re-animating a complex man both for the people who knew him and for his time' (p. 94), she was also prompted to reconsider the 'fine line' between 'self-editing and self-censorship'. Using Woolf's thoughtful reconciling of the conflicting demands of truth and tact, or what Woolf regarded as concessions to the 'spirit of the times', as a model for her own practice as editor of this text, Gillespie shows what can be gleaned from a careful consideration of Woolf's 'composite' text by describing the results of her comparison of an extant typescript with the English first edition of the biography. Gillespie also argues that annotations that recognize the 'dialogic' and collaborative relationships between a writer and her readers can enhance an appreciation for Woolf's choices and subtle artistry. Thus, Gillespie shows that by this point in her career, at least, Woolf was not a 'passive victim of censorship or self-censorship' but rather 'an active, thoughtful editor, writer, and biographical theorist, aware of her audience, aware of her options, and capable of making careful choices among them' (p. 100). The same can certainly be said of Gillespie's fine work as editor of this text.

While James M. Haule and J.H. Stape describe their collection as 'a partial survey' of the ongoing trends in the editing of Woolf's writing, they do not comment on the odd organization of the volume or explain the absence of essays on the novels that have been most central to current feminist debates: *The Voyage Out*, *The Years*, and *Between the Acts*. Commentators who have taken more 'composite' textual approaches to these novels have shown how Woolf's revisions illuminate her experiences of censorship and self-censorship, her reaction to sexual abuse, her 'Sapphist' inclinations, her response to serious mental illness, and her ambivalence about her marriage.

In calling for a greater recognition of the 'ongoing dialogue' that shapes how we now read Woolf's writing and why we prefer the texts we do, Diane Gillespie suggests a more constructive approach to the enormous range, differing purposes, and critical backgrounds of the scholars and writers who have published studies of Virginia Woolf in English this year. Some of the most obvious differences are evident in studies that take a partly or wholly biographical approach to Woolf's writing. Katherine Dalsimer, in her creative and deftly organized *Virginia Woolf: Becoming a Writer*, presents a study of Woolf's early diaries and best-known novels, from *The Voyage Out* to *To the Lighthouse*, in an analysis that is elegantly informed by her training and experience as a practising psychotherapist. Very sensitive to the nuances of Woolf's language, Dalsimer is especially astute in her assessment of the effects of Woolf's childhood losses, her experiences of mental illness, and her responses to repressed grief. Beginning with Woolf's often-cited comment from 'A Sketch of the Past' that she ceased to be 'obsessed' with her mother after she finished writing *To the Lighthouse*, Dalsimer confirms the truth of Woolf's observation, 'I suppose I did for myself what psychoanalysts do for their patients' (pp. 2–3). Avoiding almost entirely the arcane technical language that characterizes many of the most influential psychoanalytic studies of Woolf's writing, as well as the critical wrangling that often preoccupies more academic studies, Dalsimer offers beautifully observed close readings of Woolf's novels, substantiated by more or less familiar passages from her early diaries and essays, to show Woolf's courage in writing about the 'things it was impossible to say aloud' (p. 22). Dalsimer's most original contribution to Woolf scholarship is her claim that the fragments and random lines that interrupt the narratives of her early diaries are not exercises in penmanship, as some critics have assumed, but rather a 'subtext' that reveals Woolf's subconscious preoccupation with 'guilt and judgment, wrath and blame' (p. 65). I would recommend this clearly written, accessible, and luminous study to any reader who wants to know more about how Woolf's modernist techniques express her complex personal responses to trauma, loss, and repressed grief in her great innovative novels of the 1920s.

Vanessa Curtis's biographical study, *Virginia Woolf's Women*, like Dalsimer's, describes Woolf's early relationships with her powerful mother and sisters, but she also attempts to capitalize on the widespread interest in Woolf's friendships with several other famous, and infamous, women, by devoting separate chapters to summarizing Woolf's relationships with Violet Dickinson, Ottoline Morrell and Katherine Mansfield, Dora Carrington, Vita Sackville-West, and Ethel Smyth. In detailing Woolf's complex, intimate, ambivalent, and often erotic relationships with so many women, Curtis understandably economizes by citing only very sparingly from Woolf's diaries and novels, and hardly at all from other biographies or more focused scholarly studies. Readers familiar with Hermione Lee's *Virginia Woolf* [1998] or Jane Lilienfeld's *Reading Alcoholisms: Theorizing Character and Narrative in Selected Novels of Thomas Hardy, James Joyce, and Virginia Woolf* [1999], for example, may be dubious about Curtis's conclusion that Virginia Stephen did not show the expected 'behaviour from the victims of any serious sexual abuse' (p. 60), or that she learned to be more comfortable with her sexuality by 'flirting' with Clive Bell in the years before her marriage. Likewise, readers who know Angela Smith's, Sydney Janet Kaplan's, Patricia Moran's, or Janet Winston's studies of Woolf's edgy relations with Katherine Mansfield may find that Curtis's inclusion of Mansfield in the same chapter as Lady Ottoline Morrell underestimates, among other things, the class differences that separated all three women. Finally, Curtis's chapters on Woolf's relationships with Vita Sackville-West and Ethel Smyth are most impoverished by her omission of any of the insights of scholars such as Jane Marcus, Patricia Juliana Smith, Eileen Barrett, Patricia Cramer, Gaye Wachman, Laura Doan, and Judith Roof, among many others who have analysed Woolf's complex sexual and gender identity. Curtis makes perhaps her most original contribution to Woolf scholarship in her use of and comments about the 'unpublished archive photographs' she includes and describes in this volume.

Two other recently published studies of Woolf's marriage also invite comparison in this context, Irene Coates's *Who's Afraid of Leonard Woolf? A Case for the Sanity of Virginia Woolf*, first published in Australia in 1998, and Natania Rosenfeld's *Outsiders Together: Virginia and Leonard Woolf*. Coates's biography is a deliberately iconoclastic one, as she frankly avows in describing her trespassing at Asheham House and her intention to 'cut through the barbed wire; tear down the wallpaper of later generations, and remove the partitions within' (p. 22) in order to reveal a more complete picture of Virginia Stephen's relationship with Leonard

Woolf before and after their marriage. Coates's dramatically imagined and relentlessly polemical narrative challenges Leonard's status as 'saint' by arguing that Virginia was in many respects his victim in their marriage. In questioning whether Woolf was really 'mad' at all, Coates explores ground already well surveyed, for example, by Roger Poole, who, in *The Unknown Virginia Woolf* [1978], pointed out the 'crassness' of the labels that her family used to describe her as 'insane' and 'mad' at a time when psychoanalytic discourse began to offer much more precise terms and diagnoses. While Poole characterizes Leonard as distrustful of his wife's irrationality, he nonetheless describes him as a 'good' and loyal man, the 'very fine flower of Bloomsbury rationalist-reductive consciousness' (p. 63). Coates hardly considers the effects of his upward mobility, or his Cambridge education, characterizing Leonard instead as dishonest, insensitive, insecure, controlling, and covetous of his wife's money. Apparently deaf to his self-deprecating irony, she cites Leonard Woolf's comment in his autobiography that at 10 he was 'a fully developed human being, mean, cowardly, untruthful, nasty, and cruel' (p. 11) and attempts to prove he remained so throughout his life. Coates dismisses much of the evidence of Virginia's love and appreciation for Leonard evident in her diaries by claiming, for example, that, shortly after her major breakdown in 1914, he 'laid down certain rules and restrictions concerning what Virginia could and couldn't write in her diary' (p. 173). She also diminishes Leonard's political commitment to the Labour Party by suggesting that he was less motivated by egalitarian sympathies than by sexual desire when he 'flirted' with Margaret Llewelyn Davies in 1915, prompting Virginia to worry that he was 'transferring' his affections and admiration to her (p. 191). Sibyl Oldfield offers a much more plausible description of this friendship in her essay, 'Margaret Llewelyn Davies and Leonard Woolf' (in Chapman and Manson, eds., *Women in the Milieu of Leonard and Virginia Woolf: Peace, Politics, and Education* [1998], pp. 3–32). Despite its excesses, Coates's biography does offer a detailed, though idealized, description of Woolf's relationship with Vita Sackville-West, an original reading of Woolf's manuscript for *Between the Acts* (pp. 336–7), and a chilling demonstration of how the rhetoric of Woolf's suicide note echoes Rachel Vinrace's hollowly conventional language after her engagement to Terence Hewet in *The Voyage Out*.

Natania Rosenfeld's *Outsiders Together* presents an argument that is diametrically opposed to Coates's in nearly every respect. Offering a textually rather than biographically focused argument, Rosenfeld does not directly counter arguments like Coates's and only mentions Laura Moss Gottlieb's 'The War Between the Woolfs' (in Jane Marcus, ed., *Virginia Woolf and Bloomsbury: A Centenary Celebration* [1987]) later in her analysis, but her book offers a defence of Leonard and Virginia's partnership. Rosenfeld 'reads' Virginia's changing relationship with Leonard by considering how marriage in their writings 'always' appears as 'a metaphor' for 'a dialogue, in which neither subjectivity drowns out the other and both partners thrive' (p. 3). Drawing on important biographies, recent studies of Woolf and other modernists, and on postcolonial, psychoanalytic, and Derridean theory, Rosenfeld demonstrates the outsider status of both Leonard and Virginia by comparing his Jewishness with her somewhat more paradoxical status as an 'outsider' in British culture because of her gender. Rosenfeld contends that 'prejudice and empathy' complicated their relationship 'in the same ways that it does Virginia Woolf's work' (p. 6), and illustrates this premise by comparing

Virginia's representation of colonial life in *The Voyage Out* with Leonard's in *The Village in the Jungle*, offering a sensitive interpretation that demonstrates Leonard's criticism of the exploitation of Ceylonese women by the colonizing men described in this novel. While Rosenfeld subsequently offers a fairly persuasive reading of *The Wise Virgins* and *Night and Day* as 'escape novels', she sidesteps much of the evidence of Woolf's anguish in her diaries from this period, barely acknowledging her reaction to what she calls Leonard's 'management' of her mental health and documenting, instead, his efforts to find an outlet for his 'deeply principled egalitarianism' through his work with the Women's Cooperative Guild and the Labour Party in these years. Leonard's voluminous writing fades from view when Rosenfeld analyses Virginia's great novels of the 1920s and early 1930s. Her reading of *Orlando* as an entirely affirmative statement about heterosexual marriage is the least convincing chapter in this book. Space is given in the final chapter to Leonard's curtain call, as Rosenfeld compares his essay 'Quack, Quack' with Virginia's *Three Guineas* and *Between the Acts*, but Rosenfeld's study reveals some of the limitations of a selective, text-based approach.

Anna Snaith presents a more balanced and materialist approach to many of these same questions in her theoretically sophisticated study, *Virginia Woolf: Public and Private Negotiations*. Snaith charts Woolf's changing view of the 'conceptual dichotomy between public and private spaces, spheres, languages, voices, issues and discourses' and illustrates how and why this concept is so central to a more complete understanding of Woolf's feminism, socialism, and pacifism. Snaith documents Woolf's political engagement with the 'real world' by describing her work for women's suffrage in 1910, for the Richmond Women's Cooperative Guild, and for the Rodmell Labour Party, but she also convincingly shows how Woolf's need for privacy prompted her to explore the 'philosophical and political advantages' it offered. Snaith's study presents an original and thought-provoking analysis of the consequences of Woolf's famous move from the 'muffled silences' and sequestered spaces of Leslie Stephen's household to the 'psychological and intellectual space' and politically bracing neighbourhood of Bloomsbury. In her subsequent analysis, Snaith shows how Woolf's perspectives on the public and private realms structure all her major works and prompt her greatest formal experiments. Snaith offers brilliant analyses of Woolf's narrative experiments in *Mrs Dalloway*, *To the Lighthouse*, and *The Waves*, showing how these texts express her efforts to 'negotiate' a more aesthetically satisfying balance between the public and private. Her study concludes with a poignant description of how the approach of the Second World War forced Woolf to recognize how the public could invade the private, prompting her to invent more postmodern techniques in her final works. Readers interested in comparing Woolf's lifelong pacifism with the positions taken by other members of the Bloomsbury group will also be interested in Jonathan Atkin's detailed historical study, *A War of Individuals: Bloomsbury Attitudes toward the Great War*.

Smith and Wallace, eds., *Gothic Modernisms*, includes two essays that consider Woolf's writing in more philosophical and intertextual contexts. Judith Wilt's stunning and poetic 'The Ghost and the Omnibus: The Gothic Virginia Woolf' reminds her readers of the many ghosts that haunt her fiction. Rather than describe Woolf's childhood losses once again, Wilt recounts instead how, for Woolf, ghosts figure forth 'the terror of death and of the burden of the finished past' (p. 65). She powerfully demonstrates how the 'ghost as privilege and punishment, exorcised and incarnate, single and "omnibus"' (p. 65) reveals Woolf's ultimate vision in *Mrs Dalloway*. Describing Mrs Dalloway's 'ghost story plot' as encircling Septimus's sighting and recovery of a reincarnated Evans, Wilt explains how Clarissa 'feels her way toward fearlessness' by accepting Septimus's 'ghost' at her party and so embracing 'life in its ecstatic aspect, life as unforced souls, life as streaming mist, life holding but not held by death' (p. 71). David Seed, in his essay '"Psychical" Cases: Transformations of the Supernatural in Virginia Woolf and May Sinclair', reads Woolf's 'The Haunted House' and *Night and Day* to show how she 'assimilates the non-rational into the workings of the mind' (p. 45) and compares these texts with Sinclair's representations of the 'paranormal' in 'The Intercessor' and several stories from her collection, *Uncanny Stories*. Seed's essay, however, would be significantly enhanced by the inclusion of studies such as Terry Castle's *The Apparitional Lesbian: Female Homosexuality and Modern Culture* [1993] and Robert Caserio's discussion of the supernatural in *The Novel in England, 1900–1950: History and Theory* [1999].

Readers interested in the reception of Virginia Woolf's novels and essays will find much of interest in Caws and Luckhurst, eds., *The Reception of Virginia Woolf in Europe*, the first volume in the Athlone Critical Traditions series, edited by Elinor Shaffer, dedicated to documenting the reception of British authors in Europe. It is a shame that the high price of this book virtually guarantees that it will be purchased primarily by research libraries since this collection provides many fascinating 'worlded' perspectives on Virginia Woolf's writing. The goal of the collection, as Mary Ann Caws explains, is 'to address both the general question of how Virginia Woolf is received, translated and evaluated in the various parts of Europe, and the differing local questions, problems and solutions' that variously shape this reception (p. xix). Nicola Luckhurst outlines the intellectual territory mapped by her contributors, who consider Woolf's reception not only in France, Germany, and Spain but also in Catalonia, Denmark, Galicia, Greece, Italy, Poland, Portugal, and Sweden. Luckhurst briefly summarizes Woolf's initial reception, and presents a fascinating discussion of the response to Woolf's writing in the 1930s and 1940s in her wide-ranging analysis of the various fortunes of modernism, its literal censorship by Hitler and Franco, and its subsequent de facto censorship by editorial and market forces throughout post-war Europe. The introductory matter also includes a useful chart that will allow the reader to compare the dates of various translations of Woolf's novels and essays in the countries represented in this collection.

Several essays in *The Reception of Virginia Woolf in Europe* demonstrate how particular individuals shaped Woolf's reception in a particular country or region. Mary Ann Caws, for example, in 'A Virginia Woolf with a French Twist', explains how Woolf arranged for Charles Mauron to translate into French a 'story' that later became the 'Time Passes' section of *To the Lighthouse*, and she concludes by demonstrating the wit and subtlety of Mauron's subsequent translation of Woolf's *Orlando*. Laura Maria Lojo Rodriguez, in 'A Gaping Mouth, But No Words: Virginia Woolf Enters the Land of the Butterflies', recounts Victoria Ocampo's meeting with Woolf in 1934 and how she helped to cultivate interest in Woolf's writing in Latin America and Spain when she arranged for Borges's Spanish translation of *A Room of One's Own* (published in Ocampo's *Sur* [1935–6]), and describes the popularity of Woolf's *Orlando* in Latin America following its Spanish translation [1937]. Perhaps the most memorable essays in this collection not only offer similar chronologies but also provide miniature cultural studies that explore how larger artistic and political trends, as well as the emergence and dynamics of local feminist movements, facilitated and shaped Woolf's reception. France is given pride of place in this collection, for, as Luckhurst notes, 'Proust haunted Woolf, and haunts this volume', but she admits 'often the trinity of Joyce, Proust and Woolf is rearranged in a pecking order that is invariably to Woolf's disadvantage' (p. 3). Pierre-Eric Villeneuve, in 'Virginia Woolf among Writers and Critics: The French Intellectual Scene', persuasively explains why so many French writers continue to 'refer (or defer) to Joyce' (p. 19) and to consider Woolf as a rather one-dimensional 'psychological' writer. Ansgar and Vera Nünning, in their illuminating and superbly detailed survey, 'The German Reception and Criticism of Virginia Woolf: A Survey of Phases and Trends in the Twentieth Century', explain that the first German translations of *Mrs Dalloway*, *Orlando*, *To the Lighthouse*, and *The Waves* began to appear between 1928 and 1934, but interest in her work came to an 'abrupt and untimely end' when her name appeared on the Nazi's list of 'enemy' authors in 1942. They note that Auerbach's *Mimesis*, with its famous chapter on *To the Lighthouse*, 'ushered in a renaissance of Woolf studies' (p. 73), prompting interest especially in the influence of post-impressionist painting on Woolf's aesthetics, and they subsequently describe how German feminism has created a 'tidal wave of interest in her life and work since the end of the 1970s' (p. 81). Laura Marcus's 'The European Dimensions of the Hogarth Press' rounds out this volume by documenting the role that Virginia and Leonard's Hogarth Press played in disseminating the work of important European authors, particularly by publishing the English translations of Freud and other psychoanalytical texts, as well as more than a dozen works by Russian authors.

While it is impossible to notice all the important Woolf scholarship that has appeared in periodicals this year, several essays should be particularly mentioned in this review. Given the flurry of interest in *Mrs Dalloway* prompted by Stephen Daldry's film *The Hours*, Christine Froula's splendid and ambitious essay, '*Mrs Dalloway*'s Postwar Elegy: Women, War, and the Art of Mourning' (*Mo/Mo* 9:i[2002] 125–63), could hardly be more timely. Froula presents a comprehensive, eloquent, and provocative reading of this novel as a new type of 'elegy'. She shows that, 'in modernizing the elegy by adapting its poetics to prose fiction and its work of mourning to postwar London's post-theological cosmos', Woolf in *Mrs Dalloway* reveals the genre's 'full profundity, complexity, and power' (p. 125). While Froula acknowledges that the 'tinselly' Clarissa Dalloway, who has not suffered any immediately personal losses in the Great War (p. 128), might seem an unlikely subject for an elegy, she argues that Woolf made Clarissa the central 'consciousness' of this novel so that she could 'transpose certain gender-inflected registers' of the elegy into a more female mode, and better display the 'terrible losses' suffered by both men and women during this devastating war. Froula cites from a full range of primary sources that contributed to Woolf's final text for this novel, including her earlier characterization of Clarissa Dalloway in *The Voyage Out*, her 1922 short story, 'Mrs Dalloway in Bond Street', and her draft manuscript initially called *The Hours*, as well as noting the biographical details that link Clarissa Dalloway with Woolf's friend, Kitty Lushington Maxse, who died in a mysterious accidental fall in 1922. Froula argues that Clarissa 'bodies forth the "divine vitality" that the elegy seeks to recover, while her double the (partly autobiographical) war veteran Septimus Smith, suffers a death that enacts a potentially redemptive "message" in his witness to social violence' (p. 126). Froula's analysis is particularly impressive because it is informed by nearly all the major critical studies of *Mrs Dalloway* published in the last decade, work she scrupulously acknowledges. Her argument is perhaps most original in her revisionary readings of how Septimus Smith illustrates the 'insane' logic of war which transforms murder into a heroic act, and how the infamous Miss Killman 'reflects how wartime nationalist paranoia has blighted her life' while Clarissa's jealous response to her reveals how 'enemies, dominators, and war' are produced 'by an unacknowledged violence within' (p. 140). Whether Froula's reading of this novel finally remains too tightly constrained by the Freudian paradigm of trauma and loss that frames it will depend upon one's own theoretical presumptions, but perhaps because of it she does understate the 'female sacrifice' of desire that Clarissa enacts when she turns away from the satisfactions promised by Sally Seton's kiss.

Drawing similarly on histories of the elegy as well as on a sophisticated selection of narrative and aesthetic theories, Kathleen Wall, in 'Significant Form in *Jacob's Room*: Ekphrasis and the Elegy' (*TSLL* 44:iii[2002] 302–23), shows how the narrator's 'uneven authority' and the text's frequent references to visual images express Woolf's 'elegiac' purpose in *Jacob's Room*. Beginning with the well-established premise that Woolf's brother Thoby was the model for Jacob Flanders, Wall points out that, in fictionalizing his death in 1906, Woolf also changed the time-frame so that Jacob dies in the Great War, making the novel 'into an elegy for a generation of young men, for an age, and for its worldview' (p. 305). What is perhaps less persuasively developed is Wall's contention that *Jacob's Room* reflects Woolf's persistent questioning of a modernist aesthetic, such as Clive Bell's in *Art* [1914], which asserts that the private experience of art can be 'disconnected' from its public meaning. Hsiu-Chuang Deppman, in 'Rereading the Mirror Image: Looking-Glasses, Gender, and Mimeticism in Virginia Woolf's Writing' (*JNT* 31:i[2001] 31–64), arrives at similar conclusions about Woolf's modernist aesthetics but through a very different route, in this analysis of Woolf's treatment of women's relation to mirrors in her fiction and essays (p. 33). Deppman is most interesting in illustrating how Luce Irigaray's theory of the 'speculum' applies to Woolf's short story 'The Lady in the Looking-Glass', revealing how for the female protagonist in this story 'the physical space of the body, ruled by vision, reason, and convention, collides with the disembodied space of the mind, governed by the invisible, the convolvulus and the imaginary' (p. 53).

Finally, Maren Linett's important '"The Jew in the Bath": Imperiled Imagination in Woolf's *The Years*' (*MFS* 48:ii[2002] 341–61) offers another 'composite' textual approach to Woolf's writing, in one of several essays published this year which indicate a general shift of attention among Woolf scholars from her early novels to texts published after *The Waves*. Linett analyses Woolf's problematic representation of the Jew 'who shares a bath' with Sara Pargiter in *The Years*. Drawing on work, for example, by Phyllis Lassner and Bryan Cheyette in *Between 'Race' and Culture: Representations of 'the Jew'* [1993], Linett challenges arguments, such as Jean Moorcroft Wilson's in *Virginia Woolf and Anti-Semitism* [1995], which downplay

Woolf's anti-Semitism, arguing instead that her progressive editing shows how this Jewish figure acts as 'a sort of metatextual scapegoat' who expresses the 'political and artistic pressures' that Woolf resisted, and which urged her to abandon her pacifism and to sacrifice her emphasis on interiority and 'vision' (p. 349) in the last decade of her life. Linett provides excerpts from her own transcription of unpublished portions of the manuscript of *The Pargiters* as well as from *Three Guineas*, and current scholarship on it, to illustrate the 'ideological bind' that this figure reveals in Woolf's later writing, suggesting how what Linett calls her 'resilient anti-Semitism' continued to coexist with the 'fervent antifascist commitments that animate *The Years*' (p. 357). What neither Linett nor Rosenfeld seems to consider is how Leonard Woolf's education and class mobility, confirmed by his marriage to Virginia, allowed him to share many of the attitudes they identify as 'anti-Semitic'.

3. Post-1945 Fiction

A new survey of post-war British fiction has been published this year. Dominic Head compares his study, *The Cambridge Introduction to Modern British Fiction, 1950–2000*, to Steven Connor's *The English Novel in History, 1950–1995* [1996] and Andrzej Gasiorek's *Post-War British Fiction* [1995], but Head's survey is not quite from the same mould. Head begins by claiming that in his volume 'reference is made to more than a hundred novelists, and to some two hundred fictional works' (p. 1). This claim reflects the true leanings of the study, which is really a work of reference for undergraduates, in which the discussion of each novel tends to be confined to a page or two of summary, and the choices of texts and themes tend to be predictable, with just a few exceptions. For example, the chapter on class and social change surveys a fairly well-established canon of social realist novelists, including John Braine, John Wain, David Storey, Stan Barstow, and Alan Sillitoe. B.S. Johnson is considered briefly towards the end of the volume, but he might have made an interesting contrast to social realism in the chapter on class. Likewise, Sam Selvon's *The Lonely Londoners* is considered in the chapter on multiculturalism, but could have equally well have been used to develop the discussion of working-class identities. Throughout the book, for the most part, Head sorts the feminist novels into the chapter on gender, the social realist novels into the chapter on class, the novels by Rushdie, Ishiguro, Lamming, and Selvon into the chapter on multiculturalism, and so on. The focus is on fictional works which are set in post-war Britain, and hence Pat Barker's *Regeneration* trilogy and Evelyn Waugh's *Sword of Honour* trilogy are justifiably omitted (although this is contradicted by the inclusion of J.G. Farrell's *The Siege of Krishnapur* and *Troubles*, for example). The design of the book reflects, of course, how Head imagines the undergraduate will want to use it, and its virtue is that it organizes modern British fiction into such neat, digestible bites. One can't help reading a book which claims representativeness as its strength for its eccentricities, however. Student readers will emerge from this volume with an inflated sense of the significance of Raymond Williams's novels, for example, and the influence of D.H. Lawrence's *The Rainbow* seems pervasive. John Fowles's *Daniel Martin* seems able to illustrate many of Head's themes on its own, while the touchstones of modern British fiction for Head are, alongside Raymond

Williams, Margaret Drabble, Angus Wilson, and Iris Murdoch. The attention devoted by other critics to Angela Carter or Salman Rushdie is almost dismissed as an effect of the preponderance of 'theory'. There are some curious omissions from the book, too. Iain Sinclair should figure in the discussion of place. A.S. Byatt's *Possession* has fallen between the cracks of Head's thematic structure. Colin MacInnes surely deserves a mention in the section on youth culture, while Doris Lessing is missing from the chapter on gender, or class, or multiculturalism (and neither can be omitted for not being British, given the inclusion of Roddy Doyle, to take one example). The larger argument—that the post-war novel embodies some form of social and moral awareness—is sketched and illustrated at various points, but the attempt to 'cover' a representative range of fictional texts hampers the development of the argument.

There have been just a few studies of academic fiction, surprisingly few given how richly endowed with ethical and critical issues Kenneth Womack shows the genre to be in his study, *Postwar Academic Fiction: Satire, Ethics, Community*. Womack establishes two key contexts in which academic fiction might be read productively and critically. The rise of ethical criticism as a distinct area of literary studies provides one possible approach to the ways in which academic fictions satirize the professional and institutional dogmas of higher education. Womack begins his study with a chapter which traces the emergence of ethical criticism and surveys the arguments of its key exponents, and each of his chapters finds academic novels taking up serious ethical issues. The other context in which Womack reads these novels is the 'culture wars' which have dominated literary theory and literary studies for the past few decades. This is particularly apparent in the chapter on Gilbert and Gubar's *Masterpiece Theatre*, in which Womack finds Gilbert and Gubar satirizing the academy, particularly for its often contradictory entanglement of commercial and humanistic impulses. The 'culture wars', broadly characterized as a conflict between right-wing monoculturalists and left-wing pluralists, are centrally concerned with the future of the humanist mission of the academy. Womack argues in his conclusion that ethical criticism may yet prove 'a progressive and pluralistic means of direction for the future of literary study in a cynical era of institutional budget restrictions and shrinking employment opportunities in higher education' (p. 162). Too often, however, ethical criticism is understood as a throwback to the concerns and methods of humanist criticism, and therefore too easily allied with conservatism in the academy. Womack identifies this as the central problem faced by ethical critics in attempting to shape the direction of literary study in the twenty-first century. The urgency and significance of Womack's assessment of ethical criticism is reason enough to read this study, and the chapters on academic fictions seem at times like asides to the general tendency of the book. Womack begins with *Lucky Jim*, and proceeds through studies of Nabokov, Joyce Carol Oates's *The Hungry Ghosts*, David's Lodge's trilogy of academic novels, Mamet's *Oleanna*, Reed's *Japanese by Spring*, Gilbert and Gubar's melodrama, and finally Jane Smiley's *Moo*. Each of these chapters examines what Womack calls the 'pejorative poetics' of the genre, chiefly the satirical mode in which academic fiction critiques the ethical inequalities, self-indulgence, elitism, ideological obduracy, and growing consumerist tendencies of the academy. The university proves a dynamic and rich setting for fiction, just as Womack argues that university fiction proves a dynamic and rich field of study for ethical criticism, but Womack shows that academic fiction works principally by deflating and satirizing the role of universities as 'social and educational leaders of an expanding global culture' (p. 26).

B.S. Johnson has almost been forgotten since his suicide in 1973, and when he has been remembered he has often merited merely a mention in footnotes about Beckett's influence on experimental fiction, or about precursors to the postmodern fiction of later decades. A handful of critical essays is all the academic attention Johnson has received prior to Philip Tew's ambitious and persuasive *B.S. Johnson: A Critical Reading*. Tew understands that he has a daunting task not only in resurrecting the fortunes of Johnson's novels (his book coincides with the reissue of some of these, and the anticipation of a biography of Johnson by Jonathan Coe), but also in arguing that Johnson deserves serious consideration on his own merits rather than as a mere afterthought or precursor. The latter task is one Tew handles with authority and dexterity. Johnson is shown to have forged his early novels from the shadows of Laurence Sterne, not Beckett, and to make sense in relation to situationists and the 'Independent' group of artists of the 1950s and early 1960s, not postmodernism. Where Tew finds that Johnson has been written off as a kind of impresario of formal tricks, he counters with a detailed and sagacious reading of his novels in relation to the modalities of philosophical realism. The writings of Merleau-Ponty, Habermas, Bhaskar, Bourdieu, Pols, and Lefebvre are marshalled in support of the argument that Johnson is a writer seriously concerned with the novel as a mode of searching for truth. Tew recovers Johnson's novels as a more or less coherent philosophical-literary project, which places him as a more significant writer in post-war literary history than has hitherto been appreciated. The touchstones of Johnson's childhood experiences—his working-class roots, the divided consciousness of the scholarship boy, London and his evacuation from it—form part of Tew's analysis too, but what he recovers more precisely and fully is the texture of Johnson's writings: 'a series of apparently reflexively interrogative discurses in experimental mode' (p. 73). Johnson's experiments—the loose, randomly readable chapters of *The Unfortunates*, the ledger columns of *Christy Malry's Own Double Entry*, or the cut-out holes of *Albert Angelo*—make sense, in Tew's account, only when seen as part of a carefully elaborated dialectical philosophy, and are part of his working out of a belief in the radical potential for communicative interaction, constrained by the dogmas and delusions of ideology. The hope that Johnson will be read more widely after Tew's book is probably beyond the legitimate expectations of an academic study, but what Tew has ensured is that he will certainly be read better.

In a similar spirit to Tew's study of Johnson, John Fordham has published a critical study of the life and work of James Hanley: *James Hanley: Modernism and the Working Class*. Fordham refutes the early and reductive reputation Hanley acquired in the 1930s as a proletarian realist, and instead situates his copious output of novels, short stories, and drama in relation to an affinity between certain forms of working-class experience and non-realist techniques of representation. Fordham extends and develops Ken Worpole's celebrated essay on Hanley, George Garrett, and Jim Phelan, 'Expressionism and Working-Class Fiction', arguing that Hanley's experiences of urban modernity in his Liverpool Irish upbringing, of the disaster at Gallipoli and trench warfare in France, and of the rootless, complex life of the working seaman shaped his early forays into literary expressionism. Worpole did much to correct the erroneous perception of working-class writing as documentary realism, and Fordham probes even deeper, showing Hanley to have engaged widely with working-class and bourgeois literary traditions, with English, Welsh, Irish, European, and American writers, and with an eclectic range of styles and media, and to have explored the rich layers of meaning, communication, and feeling in working-class experience. Hanley emerges as a representative figure for a complex and fascinating relationship between social class and modernism, and it is the great strength of Fordham's study that he complicates and enriches understandings of the three terms of his title—Hanley, the working class, and modernism—throughout his study. Modernism, in particular, is shown to have emerged through particular kinds of social and cultural conflict, and Hanley's significance is that he 'returns us to those historical periods of modernism in which cultural matters were precisely about struggle between competing meanings of tradition, reality, art and history' (p. 236). Fordham also leaves no stone unturned in situating Hanley's writings more precisely in relation to his precursors and contemporaries. Conrad and Melville are dominant influences on his 'sea' writings. Balzac and Dostoevsky inform his narrative techniques. Fordham is instructive about a wide range of working-class writing throughout Hanley's career, and is persuasive in his brief rereading of 1950s 'realism' as in fact a form of late modernism. Hanley's association with a wide range of writers through the German anarchists Charley and Esther Lahr is charted, and his wartime writings compared to those of Henry Green. The comparisons with Beckett and Elizabeth Bowen are insightful, and these help in particular to pinpoint Hanley's shift away from the roots of his working-class experiences to the more scattered intersections of home and exile, metropolitan and provincial, proletarian and bourgeois, which shaped his life in Wales after the war. His involvement in radio drama and television in the 1950s and 1960s is also a useful indicator of his continuing search for new forms and techniques of representation. If Fordham's book has a weakness, it is merely that of brevity, for he encompasses the wide range of Hanley's writings and his social and cultural contexts in a compact, allusive style. Hanley emerges not only as a writer deserving of re-publication and rereading, but as a figure of some considerable significance for the wider study of modernism, writing, and social class.

Tew and Fordham are contributing in their studies to a growing and much-needed effort to revisit and redefine the literature of mid-twentieth-century England. This reviewer (John Brannigan) has also contributed to this effort in his *Literature, Culture and Society in Postwar England, 1945–1965*. The main argument of the study is that the period after the war has been too often defined as anti-modernist and conservative, and identified with the Movement poets and the Angry Young Men. The first chapter of the book re-examines the conservatism of writers such as Amis, Osborne, Larkin, and Braine, but the next five chapters explore a much wider range of writers in England in the post-war decades, and situate post-war writing in relation to a series of socio-historical discourses. Working-class writers are explored for how they engaged with the myths of the affluent society; women writers for how they engaged with the apparent consensus on post-war feminism; a number of writers for how homosexuality was represented; and two final chapters examine the output of postcolonial writers in England, especially the writings of the Caribbean authors who came to England in the early 1950s.

Ruvani Ranasinha has published a short study of the work of Hanif Kureishi in the Writers and their Work series published by Northcote House. This series continues to offer impressive and authoritative critical overviews of its subjects, and Ranasinha's *Hanif Kureishi* is another fine example of its merits. She surveys Kureishi's oeuvre from his early stage plays on London's white underclass, through his celebrated explorations of multicultural London in *My Beautiful Launderette* and *The Buddha of Suburbia*, to the more recent writings which centre on mid-life crises, love and sexuality, and, according to Kureishi, 'what it is like to be a human being' (p. 102). In Ranasinha's view, Kureishi has never perceived himself as an Asian or even British Asian writer, and has struggled against the misperception of early reviewers that he spoke for Pakistanis in Britain. She shows Kureishi to be a more complex and diversely oriented writer than his critical reputation has conventionally allowed, although she is also canny in observing that his success as a writer came not simply from a minority-based opposition to the right-wing racism of the 1980s, but also from the fact that his writings espoused a liberal multiculturalism which itself had become part of mainstream culture. Kureishi has always had a larger agenda than the racialized contexts in which his work has habitually been situated, and this is particularly evident for Ranasinha in his writings since 1997. She argues in fact that Kureishi's oeuvre can be divided into two phases. In the first phase, he explored the ambivalence of individual protagonists towards communal forms of solidarity, particularly focused around forms of ethnic belonging. Since 1997, however, Ranasinha believes Kureishi has abandoned race as a focus, while continuing his interest in representing sexual relationships, and that his more recent writings are more broadly concerned with how individuals define themselves within groups, and struggle with competing demands between the self and others. On the whole Ranasinha explores Kureishi's oeuvre sympathetically, often quoting with approval Kureishi's own opinions of his work, but she does not shirk from identifying its weaknesses or flaws.

Bénédicte Ledent has published the first book-length study of the writings of Caryl Phillips in Manchester's impressive Contemporary World Writers series. Ledent shows that Phillips has always been motivated to write about experiences of displacement and exile, from his earliest plays and novels centred on migration between the Caribbean and Britain, to his later fictionalizations of diasporic relations and identities more generally, particularly in *Crossing the River* and *The Nature of Blood*. Phillips began his writing career as a dramatist, and Ledent argues that his strengths as a dramatist, and indeed the themes which he explores in his dramas, are evident in the textual voices and strong dialogues of the novels. It is as a novelist that Phillips came to prominence, however, and Ledent rightly concentrates on the expanding range and challenging forms of Phillips's novels. There are a number of fascinating arguments developed in Ledent's study: that the Caribbean serves not just as a literary and historical resource for Phillips, but is a metaphor for the multiculturalism, diasporic postcolonialism, and historical complexity which he has been charting throughout his oeuvre; that Phillips is heavily influenced by musical motifs and structures, particularly in the contrapuntal and symphonic arrangements of his novels; and that Phillips's novels have always been concerned with the urgent issues of Caribbean communities and identities in England, but that such issues are represented at 'a temporal and spatial remove' (p. 18). Ledent is informative and thorough on almost every aspect of Phillips's fiction, tracing his debt to and differences from the earlier generation of Caribbean migrants writing in Britain, such as Sam Selvon, George Lamming, and V.S. Naipaul, charting Phillips's increasing sense of historical responsibility, explaining his diversification into the history of the Jewish diaspora in *Higher Ground* and *The Nature of Blood*, analysing the linguistic and technical sophistication of his texts, and situating his novels in a dense web of literary and cultural interchanges. Ledent is too brief in some allusions—the influence of T.S. Eliot, Shûsaku Endô, and Brian Friel are too intriguing to leave unexplored—and she acknowledges that lack of space prevents her from analysing the stylistic sophistication of *The Nature of Blood* as fully as is necessary. In a wide-ranging conclusion, Ledent tackles the relationship between Phillips's novels, postcolonialism, and postmodernism, and this yields some of her most perceptive insights. *The Nature of Blood* is compared to Martin Amis's *Time's Arrow*, for example, and Ledent finds that, unlike Amis, Phillips 'envisages the past neither as a site of playful experimentation nor as a source of apocalyptic vision, but as an often painful reality that has to be reworked and whose present ramifications need to be assessed honestly' (p. 167). Similarly, Ledent finds a critical difference between Homi Bhabha's theorization of postcolonial migrancy, which is in danger of metaphorizing diaspora and exile away from their historical actualities, and Phillips's fictions, which, for Ledent, are always rooted in 'complex historical reality' (p. 175). Ledent champions Phillips for remaining committed to the historical and political realities of specific places, Britain or the Caribbean, even as his fiction shows him to be an exilic writer, comfortable exploring the ambivalence of belonging in post-migratory and postcolonial contexts.

4. Post-1950 Drama

Six books on individual playwrights tackle important figures such as Samuel Beckett, John Osborne, and Tom Stoppard as well as more recent writers such as Sarah Kane. There's also a book by Alan Ayckbourn which examines his craft as writer and director, and a collection of the writings of John McGrath. Five more books examine diverse aspects of recent theatre history.

Some narratives never die. Despite the attempts of revisionist historians to downgrade the mythical press night of John Osborne's *Look Back in Anger* in May 1956, it remains the central turning-point in any history of post-war drama. After all, it not only marks the emergence of a distinctive new dramatic sensibility, but it also represents the foundation myth of a theatre, the Royal Court in London, which has done more than any other to promote the central tradition of British naturalistic and social realist drama. The rival turning-points advocated by revisionists—from the London opening of Samuel Beckett's *Waiting for Godot* in 1955 to the exaggerated claims made for one-hit wonders such as Shelagh Delaney at Joan Littlewood's Theatre Royal Stratford East—are all deeply unconvincing. Beckett's work, for example, has always had the anomaly of genius, and his later plays were put on by the Royal Court anyway. In fact, the history of British post-war new wave drama, with a handful of exceptions such as Tom Stoppard, is the history of the Royal Court.

Although Luc Gilleman refrains from making such exaggerated claims for the importance of the Royal Court, his *John Osborne: Vituperative Artist* thoroughly appraises the writer who was there at the start of this great adventure. He charts Osborne's career from *Look Back in Anger* right up to his final play in 1992, the aptly named *Déjà vu*, which also features a character with the initials JP and a woman at an ironing board. Showing how his writing emerged from specific theatrical contexts—the Royal Court's proscenium arch, the restrictions imposed by the Lord Chamberlain, or the expectations created by the naturalistic well-made play—Gilleman emphasizes how Osborne reacted against such restrictions, trying to expand the language of drama. In what is a refreshingly traditional book, readable, reasonably jargon-free and to the point, the focus is on the work, which is analysed in depth, in a way that mixes interesting insights with provocative ideas. Unlike many books on writers, facile links between biographical information and the plays are generally avoided, and instead the major plays are considered in three sections, which cover 'Rise to the Top, 1956–1963', 'At the Top, 1964–1971', and 'The Long Descent, 1972–1994', each including a glimpse of the cultural context. Although, in the introduction, Gilleman makes some banal assertions about Osborne being initially a left-wing dramatist—albeit one who 'thought of socialism mainly in terms of outrage and scandal' (p. 2)—and a true artist, he's on profounder ground with his account of the writer's main characters, Jimmy Porter, Archie Rice, Bill Maitland, Luther, Alfred Redl, and Laurie. In his close reading of each work, Gilleman shows in detail how the artist worked and how the sensibility that he calls 'vituperative' (p. 22) at first energized the writing and finally all but overwhelmed it as the angry young man turned into the snarling old codger. Using Osborne's archive in Austin, Texas, as well as referring to his occasional journalism, Gilleman often falls back on psychoanalysis as his preferred theoretical model. Thus Osborne's fabled verbal extravaganzas are seen as compensations for fears about masculinity in what is characterized as his 'phallic art' (pp. 20–5). 'For Osborne, anger is the courage of weakness. Turning out well-honed yet sharply abrasive phrases became his way of constructing masculinity' (p. 21). Whatever you might think of such suggestions, it is clear that Gilleman's book is a welcome addition to the pile of monographs on this perennially exasperating and exhilarating dramatist.

Aptly enough, the spirit of Osborne lives on: a black cat at the Royal Court is named after him and, in the first John Osborne Memorial Lecture in June 2002, playwright David Hare passionately defended his subject's idiosyncratic dramatic style. Osborne also has a firm place in the field of literary entertainment: Humphrey Carpenter's *The Angry Young Men: A Literary Comedy of the 1950s* is a swift jaunt through the late 1950s which places him firmly in his literary and social context. Although this relies heavily on previous work, notably Harry Ritchie's well-researched *Success Stories: Literature and the Media in England, 1950–59* [1988], it retells the story of Osborne's career up to the early 1960s with clarity and vigour.

Not all writers are such good subjects. Some refuse to sanction biographies. With a gesture that feels like a pre-emptive strike, Tom Stoppard is quoted as saying of the first full-length account of his career, *Double Act: A Life of Tom Stoppard*: 'I want it to be as inaccurate as possible' (p. xi). But if there's no evidence that Ira Nadel has obliged Sir Tom with deliberate mistakes, his thesis biography at times conceals as much as it reveals. Nadel's theory is that Stoppard has lived a double life (both English and Czech, gentile and Jew, insider and outsider), and that 'the personal and theatrical contradictions' fuel each other as the playwright 'incorporates the strategies that address displacements he has encountered' (p. xiii). Certainly it's true that displacement made Stoppard, who was born Tomas Straüssler in Bohemia to Czech Jewish parents. The family left in 1939, and ended up in Singapore. After the 1942 Japanese invasion, the Straüsslers went to India, Tom's father was killed in the evacuation, and three years later his mother married an Englishman called Kenneth Stoppard. Plenty of dislocations here, but when Nadel, talking of Stoppard's early life in England, says that nearby Chatsworth House taught him 'how to adapt the antithetical' (p. 44), you simply have to point out that, at the time, the boy wasn't even 10 years old.

What the thesis biography misses is the roughness and loose ends of a person's life. Thankfully, Nadel soon stops underlining the contradictions, antitheses, and oppositions of Stoppard's 'double life', and concentrates on a straightforward account of his career, from its beginnings in journalism to the award-laden life of the writer of such classics as *Rosencrantz and Guildenstern Are Dead* [1966] and *Arcadia* [1993], as well as of films such as *Shakespeare in Love* [1998]. The book's main strength is that its accounts of Stoppard's plays, with simple and brief plot summaries, concentrate on the practicalities of how they were conceived, produced, and received. Clearly written, full of information, often engaging, and thoroughly researched, the account goes up to 2001, ending before the première of his trilogy, *The Coast of Utopia*. Nadel argues that Stoppard's plays, with their revisiting of Shakespeare and Wilde, 'taught the English something about England' (p. 465). If his views have been condemned as reactionary, and his politics as conservative, it is apt that his theatre sees England not only as a traditional land, but also as one that can be subject to dramatic subversions.

A much darker vision of Britain was staged in the mid-1990s, when a dramatic upsurge in new writing for British theatre was exemplified by controversial in-yer-face plays such as Sarah Kane's *Blasted* [1995] and Mark Ravenhill's *Shopping and Fucking* [1996]. But although at first it seemed that this phenomenon would attract a clutch of studies, there have actually been very few. So far, for example, Sarah Kane has been the only young writer to receive special attention, with the publication of the first full study of her work, Graham Saunders's *'Love Me or Kill Me': Sarah Kane and the Theatre of Extremes*. This gives a sound account of the radically innovative playwright who committed suicide at the age of 28 in 1999, leaving behind a small but powerful body of work. She saw nihilism as an extreme form of Romanticism, and the tension between self-destruction and self-affirmation seems to pervade her creativity. Although her five plays and one screenplay are mainly about love, they all feature a character who attempts, with or without success, to commit suicide.

In January 1995 *Blasted*, Kane's debut at the Royal Court, set the tone for the reception of her work. Written with a mix of raw sensibility and a mature theatrical intelligence, it startled critics and audiences with its blatant aggression and violent stage images. Denounced by the *Daily Mail* as 'This disgusting feast of filth', *Blasted* became a *cause célèbre*. Her later plays did much to change this image of a provocative antagonist, and subsequent revivals of her work in Britain and its widespread appreciation on mainland Europe have secured her a place in the canon of 1990s drama. Saunders places her work within the context of new writing, while emphasizing its continuity with previous playwrights such as Samuel Beckett and

John Webster. In chapters on each of her main plays—*Blasted* [1995], *Phaedra's Love* [1996], *Cleansed* [1998], *Crave* [1998], and *4.48 Psychosis* [2000]—Saunders succinctly analyses the texts, and comments on the problems of staging an author who specified acts of explicit sex and violence, as well as challenging directors by giving stage directions such as 'the rats carry Carl's feet away'. He rightly stresses that, for all its confrontation, *Blasted* is finally an optimistic play, and one whose horrific blinding scene was influenced as much by the fate of Shakespeare's Gloucester as by a lurid, if improbable, story, told by Bill Buford in *Among the Thugs*, of a football hooligan who sucked out the eye of his victim. With *Cleansed*, Saunders shows the influence of Georg Büchner's *Woyzeck* as well as that of Kafka and Orwell. By the time of *Crave* and *4.48 Psychosis*, Kane's radical innovations in form had led to the abandonment of plot and traditional characterization, and Saunders steers us through the problems of how to construct meaning from such complex texts. The book includes revealing interviews with theatre-makers—directors, actors, writers, and an agent—who worked with Kane, plus a rather inaccurate afterword by playwright Edward Bond. By stressing her links with theatre traditions Saunders underplays the influence of pop culture on her work, and he is rather uncritical of its shortcomings. The book has been badly proof-read, and has a sloppy attitude to basic facts, such as dates of the work of other playwrights. So although Saunders makes the case for Kane's genius, it is now up to others to produce a more rounded account of her achievements.

Saunders reminds us that one of Kane's influences was Beckett, long the subject of increasingly specialized studies. For instance, John Robert Keller's *Samuel Beckett and the Primacy of Love* is an example of the psychoanalytical approach to the playwright and his descriptions of the emotions, arguing that his work is the site of a struggle to remain in contact with a primal sense of inner goodness based on early experiences with his mother and exemplified in a tension between the narrative self and the maternal mind. In the main chapter on drama, an interpretation of *Waiting for Godot*, Keller says that 'Lucky's monologue, delivered towards the end of the first act, expresses the emotional heart of the play, and of the oeuvre, by demonstrating the intrapsychic consequences of ruptures and the early mother-infant dyad' (p. 134). Most theatregoers, however, will stubbornly insist that it's just an enjoyable and inspired tour de force of linguistic imagination.

By contrast, Lois Gordon belongs to the camp that emphasizes the religious side of Beckett's work. But *Reading 'Godot'* ambitiously puts the play in its historical, philosophical, biographical, and literary contexts, stressing the writer's relationship to Freud, French literature, and the culture of the 1930s and 1940s. Her exploration of his relationship to the artistic milieu of the 1930s is detailed, and contains much new research. Gordon shows how Beckett's existential questioning is echoed by Estragon and Vladimir, and reminds us of the importance of the parable of the two thieves at the centre of the play. As you'd expect from the author of the excellent *The World of Samuel Beckett* [1996], she approaches the play scene by scene, exploring the text linguistically, philosophically, critically, and biographically. She argues that the play portrays more than the rational mind's search for self and worldly definition—it also dramatizes Beckett's insights into human nature, into the emotional life that frequently invades rationality and liberates, victimizes, or paralyses the individual. She carefully and clearly outlines the artistic composition, visual impact, and philosophical meaning of *Waiting for Godot*, showing how

Beckett—an artist of the psychic distress born of relativism—portrays humanity in conflict with mysterious forces both within and outside the self.

Less successfully, Shimon Levy's *Samuel Beckett's Self-Referential Drama: The Sensitive Chaos* mixes theoretical perspectives with accounts of actual productions, while giving an Israeli slant on the playwright. Starting with a chapter that asks whether Chaos Theory can be useful in analysing either Beckett or theatre in general, the book broadens into substantial chapters on the traditional philosophical approaches to the canon, a close reading of Beckett's stage directions, and an original account of 'offstage'—which is described 'as a unique theatrical device that Beckett employed with amazing ingenuity' (p. vii). Added to this are chapters on his radio plays, and spirituality in his film and television scripts. But the most interesting chapters deal with actual productions. In 'Godot: Resolution or Revolution', Levy gives a fascinating account of some stagings of Beckett's most famous play in Israel. As always in theatre, meaning comes from cultural context. As in Europe, early productions of *Waiting for Godot* in the 1950s ran into a mixture of incomprehension and hostility, but with a very specific local tinge: '"Lack of purpose" was certainly the most abusive term. Vladimir and Estragon did not, for example, reinforce a simple notion such as active engagement to build a new kibbutz. However they did import a whiff of European elegance, subtlety, morbid humour and other cultural phenomena which some Israelis, as ex-Europeans, knew and appreciated' (p. 120). It is also remarkable that early productions featured actresses playing Lucky. As late as 1968, 'Beckett's stage directions were largely ignored and a number of cuts were made' (p. 123), surely something no European production could have got away with. In the final chapter, which quotes from several of the actresses with whom Levy worked to stage *Not I* over twenty-five years, he rightly stresses how the piece touched the 'profound mental recesses' of his performers (p. 159) and details incidents such as the time when a fly flew into the mouth of one of the actors during a performance (p. 161). Finally, this year's volume of *Samuel Beckett Today/Aujourd'hui*, edited by Marius Buning, Matthijs Engelberts and Sjef Houppermans, is called *Pastiches, Parodies and Other Imitations*, while the most recent Harold Pinter bibliography, compiled by Susan Hollis Merritt, is published in Gillen and Gale, eds., *The Pinter Review: Collected Essays 2001 and 2002*. The same publication also has Merritt's account of the Lincoln Center symposium held during the July 2001 Harold Pinter Festival (pp. 144–67) and Mel Gussow's interview with Pinter at the same event (pp. 14–37).

When someone of the status of Sir Alan Ayckbourn writes a book about the art of theatre-making—based on his forty years' experience of writing more than sixty plays and directing more than 200—your reaction is likely to be based on what you think about his work. Is he a trivial boulevardier, peddling light comedies to the suburban masses, or is he a master of darkness, an experimenter with form and an explorer of a particularly English form of angst? Unsurprisingly, this slim volume, *The Crafty Art of Playmaking* is a light, entertaining, and practical guide to the rough and tumble of writing and directing, which both 'rely ultimately on a spontaneity and instinct that defies theory' (p. ix). At the same time, his take on these activities is spiced with a dash of provocation: literal facts 'often get in the way of a good story', and the only essential truth in theatre is 'truth of character', so, 'by all means believe some of this book, but never all of it' (p. x).

Divided into two parts, the first about writing and the second about directing, the book is notably sympathetic to actors, but rather waspish about other theatre technicians, such as designers. In the opening pages, Ayckbourn shares his sound if simple ideas about comedy and tragedy, gives some valuable advice about construction, time, and location, before exploring dialogue by using several examples from his own plays. Perhaps inevitably, the book tells you more about his own style of writing, with its subtext and experiments with genres such as farce, than about new writing in general. You look in vain for advice on individual tone of voice, or exercises to improve specificity of setting, never mind on writing a large political drama or even a history play. As a collection of anecdotes, the book takes off in the second half, with Ayckbourn's amusing accounts of directing in the teeth of vain authors, sulky stars, and pushy producers during the typical roller-coaster ride of rehearsals. Beginners will find it a simple introduction: humane, modest, and occasionally inspiring. For old hands, it will be familiar enough to raise a weary smile. His detractors, however, will be infuriated by his superficiality and will see this book as evidence that English theatre is in terminal decline.

The same opinion might also be held by admirers of John McGrath, who by the time of his death in January 2002 was already a theatre legend. As a doughty campaigner for a popular theatre that was both entertaining and politically committed, and reached a large working-class audience, he toured his 7:84 theatre group—which he founded in 1971 with his partner Elizabeth MacLennan—around Scotland, playing in church halls and working-men's clubs. Named after an *Economist* magazine statistic—7 per cent of Britain's population owned 84 per cent of national wealth—the company staged works, such as *The Cheviot, the Stag and the Black, Black Oil*, which are now modern classics. As a writer, director, and producer, McGrath worked on more than sixty plays, and his 1981 book, *A Good Night Out*, is a sharp criticism of much of what passes for political theatre, as well as being a passionate defence of his own practice. His ideas have been hugely influential on community theatres all over the world. But the main problem with his legendary reputation is that it raises expectations that are difficult to meet. In *Naked Thoughts That Roam About: Reflections on Theatre*, a comprehensive collection of essays, lectures, reviews, poems, and letters from a career spanning forty years, both the inspiring and the frustrating aspects of his project are exposed.

McGrath's writing life started full of fire and fury. His 1959 contributions to *Isis*, the Oxford undergraduate magazine, attacked icons such as John Osborne—'the most grossly over-rated phenomenon since Ezra Pound' (p. 9)—and Arthur Miller—'pale, thin, dry and dull' (p. 8)—and argued passionately in favour of 'precision, vigour, theatrical skill and the sheer ability to entertain' (p. 8). As the 1960s unfolded, the excitement of the times—utopian dreams, irrepressible optimism, and the heavy hand of Marxist ideology—all got a grip on McGrath. Inspired by the events of May 1968 in Paris, which he witnessed, he lashed out at bourgeois theatre, sell-outs, and anything that smacked of lethargy and complacency. Sadly, like so many lefties, he reserved his most bitter bile for allies rather than enemies. His hysterical attack on Arnold Wesker in 1970, with its trite evocations of 'the working class' and scorn for 'bourgeois cultural elitist ideas' (pp. 34–5, 39), was embarrassingly awful, but McGrath knew that and was brave enough to include Wesker's reply, a model of eloquent humanism, in this anthology (pp. 36–8).

Ten years after having started work at the BBC, on the first [1962] episode of the memorable *Z-Cars*, McGrath turned his back on mainstream success in order to search for a genuine working-class audience. Setting up 7:84, he attempted to create an alternative popular theatre culture, and the best pieces in this anthology are the detailed accounts of touring shows around Scotland: in Aberdeen, the locals cheered them to the rafters; in Golspie the countess of Sutherland attended a play that attacked her and took the criticism 'on the chin' (p. 65). Tensions within the group resulted in earnest discussion but never degenerated into the crazy political correctness that destroyed the English branch of 7:84. By the 1980s, the Thatcherite attack on radical touring companies led to cuts in 7:84's subsidy and forced McGrath into a freelance career. He collaborated on the staging of the 'Arms to Iraq' inquiry at London's Tricycle Theatre, produced films such as *Carrington*, and wrote about subjects such as Rigoberta Menchu, the Guatemalan human rights activist. Although by now McGrath had abandoned the painfully crude rhetoric of his youth, you can't help feeling that he didn't get a grip on post-Thatcherite realities. He never really confronted the issue of why the state should fund radical theatre groups that want to destroy it, nor the clear preference of working-class audiences for sentimental musicals rather than subversive plays. Still, anyone who has been appalled by the 1980s slide of culture into commerce will certainly find much to sympathize with here. There's a lot of material which is thought-provoking, and McGrath's style is engaging and warm-hearted. At its best, his mix of dry wit and linguistic clarity reflects the influence of Orwell. With a clear and thorough introduction by Nadine Holdsworth, who worked closely with McGrath right up to his death, the book is a must for anyone interested in political theatre, and a reminder that to make changes in society requires both pessimism of the intellect and optimism of the will. McGrath had both.

You could say the same about Christopher Innes, whose extensively revised version of *Modern British Drama*, which was originally published in 1992, is the most comprehensive recent account of British playwrights. Now extended to cover the whole of the twentieth century, it is a superb introduction to the development of modernist writers from George Bernard Shaw to Patrick Marber and Sarah Kane. Instead of taking a chronological approach, Innes groups the writers in 'three major types of theatre, defined equally by stylistic approach and thematic focus: Realism; Comedy; and Poetic Drama' (p. 8). Whatever the problems of squeezing authors into these tight categories, Innes's reading of the work of individual playwrights is always stimulating, often provocative, and usually rewarding. The book has a comprehensive feel, and comes complete with a useful chronology, illustrations, and reasonably up-to-date bibliography. Of 1990s writers, his account of Patrick Marber (pp. 427–35) is better than the new section on Sarah Kane (pp. 528–37), which is marred by various inaccuracies. Although Innes's comparison of her work with that of Antonin Artaud and David Rudkin is telling and accurate, I'm not convinced that she fits easily into the category of 'feminist drama' (p. 529), although I do see the connection between her imagination and that of Caryl Churchill. As regards Innes's reading of *Blasted*, it doesn't emphasize enough the radical break in structure at the heart of the play. Furthermore, Kane's problem was not—as Innes states—that she has no moral framework or perspective, but that her morality was absolute rather than relative or contingent. In other words, in *Blasted* she equates a domestic rape with the use of rape as a weapon of war, which is an absolutist moral idea quite useless for our understanding of either a domestic rape or a war crime. In *Cleansed*, her ideas of absolute love have a similar character. On a more detailed level, Innes is wrong to think of *Blasted*'s Cate as either retarded or a prostitute. As the dialogue makes clear, she used to be Ian's girlfriend, but is no longer in love with him. Likewise, the final stage picture of Cate returning with blood running down her legs is not the result of rape but rather of her selling herself to the soldiers for food, which in a final act of redemptive mercy she offers to an already dead—but still talkative—Ian. It's difficult to agree that plot or characterization are non-existent here (p. 530), but it is true that Kane avoided a lot of the social realist markers that are commonly associated with political drama. Still, despite such objections, Innes's book remains an important text which proves that you don't need abstract theory to discuss the meaning of a play in a thoroughly satisfying way.

Innes belongs to a German group, Contemporary Drama in English (CDE), whose members have done much to advance the study of both new writers and old hands. A collection of essays, edited by two CDE members—Bernhard Reitz and Mark Berninger—comprehensively explores British drama in the 1990s. After a brief introduction by the editors, Klaus-Peter Müller surveys political drama in 1990s Britain, offering a typology whose categories range from traditional playwrights such as David Hare and David Edgar through political ethnicity and oblique forms of politics—Caryl Churchill, April de Angelis, and Judy Upton—to new male writers such as Nick Grosso, Anthony Neilson, and Nick Stafford. Berninger himself contributes a stimulating piece on the under-researched topic of historical drama, which is followed by a bad-tempered article by Mary Luckhurst, who proclaims 'I am not of the view that Kane was a great writer nor that her plays represented a defining moment' (p. 72, but see also p. 73). Bizarrely, she follows this up by stating what an excellent writer Kane was in terms of theatrical vision, and as regards her stagecraft. Luckhurst can only fault Kane's dialogue and her right-wing politics: since she produces not a shred of evidence to support this latter accusation, it seems frankly irresponsible to calumniate a dead writer in such a way. More interesting are the chapters by Heiko Stahl on black women playwrights, Christopher Innes on the now popular theme of science on stage, Aleks Sierz on Mark Ravenhill, Graham Saunders on Sarah Kane, Michael Raab on Patrick Marber's *Closer*, Raimund Borgmeier on Stoppard's *The Invention of Love*, Bernhard Reitz on Pinter's political drama, and Heiner Zimmermann on Howard Barker. All in all, this is a satisfying collection. In another volume, its annual publication for 2002, CDE takes a global perspective. Although the majority of articles focus on the United States, and especially on Sam Shepard, there is a handful of contributions to the study of British drama: Cordula Quint on 'Terror of the Contemporary Sublime: Regional Responses to the Challenges of Internationalism and Globalization in the Drama of Caryl Churchill and David Edgar', Kara McKechnie on 'Homely Northern Women in Sensible Shoes: Alan Bennett and the Pleasures of Provincialism', and Jürgen Wehrmann on 'Revising the Nation: Globalization and Fragmentation of Irish History in Sebastian Barry's Plays'.

In journals which deal with drama, the subject of post-war British writers remains under-explored, often edged out by the more fashionable concerns of high theory or obscure accounts of the performative. In *New Theatre Quarterly*, notable exceptions include this reviewer's (Aleks Sierz) 'Still In-Yer-Face? Towards a Critique and a Summation' (*NTQ* 69[2002] 17–24), an attempt to move beyond the categorization of 1990s British drama as raw provocation—popularized in my *In-Yer-Face Theatre: British Drama Today* [2001]—and Catherine Prentice and Helena Leongamornlert's study (*NTQ* 69[2002] 47–58) of an experiment in documentary drama, the Royal Shakespeare Company's *The Dillen* [1983]. Recent deaths have inspired several tributes in the same publication. John McGrath elicits a moving piece from Simon Trussler, 'In Memoriam: Jan Kott and John McGrath' (*NTQ* 70[2002] 90–102), and the issue also features McGrath's own 'Theatre and Democracy' (*NTQ* 70[2002] 133–9; also included in *Naked Thoughts That Roam About*). Similarly, Spike Milligan receives an appreciation from Peter Barnes, '"An Uncooked Army Boot": Spike Milligan, 1918–2002' (*NTQ* 71[2002] 205–10), an issue which also has Trussler's tribute to Martin Esslin, 'Remembering Martin Esslen, 1918–2002' (*NTQ* 71[2002] 203–4), whose radio work nurtured new drama in Britain. *NTQ* 72[2002] contains a collection of essays on various aspects of McGrath's work, including contributions from Adrian Mitchell, Michael Kustow, David Edgar, Pamela Howard, and Drew Milne. There is an article by Stephen Lacey on McGrath and Lukácsian realism (*NTQ* 72[2002] 325–32), plus an account by David Bradby and Susan Capon of 'Plugged into History', the conference about his work held at Royal Holloway, University of London, in April 2002 (*NTQ* 71[2002] 392–3). Finally, *Modern Drama* contains articles which may be of interest, including, in the spring issue, Caryl Churchill's '*The Hospital at the Time of the Revolution*: Algerian Decolonization in a Protean Contemporary Context' by Iris Lavell (*MD* [2002] 76–94), and, in the winter issue, 'Life Goes On: *Endgame* as Anti-Pastoral Elegy' by Geoff Hamilton (*MD* [2002] 611–27), 'The Aesthetics of Refusal: Pinter Among the Radicals' by Varun Begley (*MD* [2002] 628–45), and 'Adaptation After Darwin: Timberlake Wertenbaker's Evolving Texts' by Sara Freeman (*MD* [2002] 646–62).

But although it's good to focus on individual writers, it's important to remember that the context of their work involves theatres. The Donmar Warehouse, in central London, celebrates its tenth anniversary with a book by *Variety*'s theatre critic Matt Wolf, *Sam Mendes at the Donmar: Stepping into Freedom*. At the age of 24, Mendes took the closed-down venue, which had been the Royal Shakespeare Company's studio theatre between 1977 and 1981, and turned it into one of the capital's trendiest venues, attracting Hollywood stars such as Nicole Kidman (in David Hare's *The Blue Room*) and Gwyneth Paltrow to tread its newly polished boards. This account, based on interviews with a range of theatre-makers and lavishly illustrated with production photographs, concentrates on Mendes's hallmark, modern American classics and chamber musicals. However, there is also some material on important revivals of British plays, such as Samuel Beckett's *Endgame* [1996], Tom Stoppard's *The Real Thing* [1999], Christopher Hampton's *Tales from Hollywood* [2001], C.P. Taylor's *Good* [1999], and Peter Nichols's *Passion Play* [2000] and *Privates on Parade* [2001]. But readers looking for information about younger British writers, such as Mark Ravenhill, David Greig, Joe Penhall, or David Eldridge—all of whom have worked at this venue—will be disappointed.

Theatre critics have always been vital as reporters of what playscripts actually looked or felt like when they were staged, but they have rarely been great writers or worth rereading. So it is no surprise that Sheridan Morley's *Spectator at the Theatre*, his collection of reviews of selected 1990s shows, fails to set the pulses racing. But, despite the leaden prose and his tendency to state the obvious in the most pompous way, here are reviews—which first appeared in *The Spectator* magazine—of the first productions of important plays by Tom Stoppard (*Arcadia*, *The Invention of Love*), David Hare (the trilogy, *Skylight*, *Amy's View*), and even Alan Bennett (*The Madness of George III* if not *The Wind in the Willows*). Similarly, it is good to see accounts of revivals of classics by Beckett (*Waiting for Godot*) and Pinter (*The Birthday Party*, *No Man's Land*). And although Morley doesn't appreciate the talent of Sarah Kane (whose *Cleansed* he trashes), he is vaguely aware of the stirrings of a renaissance in British new writing, and covers talents as varied as Patrick Marber (*Dealer's Choice*, *Closer*), Conor McPherson (*The Weir*, *Dublin Carol*), and Joe Penhall (*Blue/Orange*). Scandalously, he omits entirely the advent of Mark Ravenhill, who is now an associate at the National Theatre. Most usefully, Morley includes a comprehensive appendix of the Olivier and *Evening Standard* awards. This collection gives a conservative impression of London and Broadway stages, but is unable to grasp the sheer innovation and invention of many younger playwrights.

By contrast, maverick director Dominic Dromgoole has always been an intelligent advocate of the new. But, when his *The Full Room: An A–Z of Contemporary Playwriting* came out in 2000, its 112 short essays on writers such as Sebastian Barry, Caryl Churchill, David Hare, Sarah Kane, Mark Ravenhill, Harold Pinter, and Tom Stoppard—arranged alphabetically, from Samuel Adamson to Richard Zajdlic—were distinguished not only by their author's idiosyncratic and flamboyant judgements but by a long list of inaccuracies. For example, the names of Conor McPherson and Anthony Neilson were misspelt, Aphra Behn was placed in the wrong century, Chinua Achebe's evocative *Things Fall Apart* became the banal *Things Change*, and Howard Barker's *Scenes from an Execution* appeared as *Scenes Before an Execution*. In the paperback edition, these howlers have been corrected and Dromgoole adds a seven-page afterword which begins with the effect of 11 September, 'the great shudder that wobbled the world' (p. 300), on contemporary British drama and ends in a series of self-justifications for his work and random attacks on critics. The book, however, still omits significant talent such as David Greig, David Lan, and Judy Upton, and international stars such as Brian Friel and Yasmina Reza merit only a sentence each. In general, the book lacks factual content: there are few dates, production details or directors' credits. It has no index. As a source for understanding Dromgoole's enthusiasms, it is priceless; as a guide to new writing, it is still extremely disappointing.

Finally, although most of Bradby and Delgado, eds., *The Paris Jigsaw*, is about that city's magnetic effect on artists from across the world, from those fleeing the Russian Revolution to more recent African migrants, it ends with a short afterword (pp. 277–86) by Peter Lichtenfels which outlines some of the creative connections between Paris and Britain. He concentrates his account on John McGrath and Royal Court director James Macdonald (who staged the premieres of Sarah Kane's work). It's somehow comforting to be reminded that, whenever it seems that things are not going too well in Britain, Paris continues to be a 'beacon of hope' (p. 286).

5. Pre-1950 Poetry

2002 may be regarded as the year of the poetry biography. This impression is consistent with a tendency in many of the books and articles discussed below to eschew discussion of modern poems in favour of analysis of all manner of other things: Dylan Thomas's fans, or T.S. Eliot's journalism, or Charlotte Mew's sexuality. This is not necessarily to be regretted, and it would be a narrow view of poetry which saw it as something which could or should be divorced from its culture. Indeed, some of the best articles this year have been those which have struck out in new directions, either by examining new material (Thomas Dilworth on David Jones, for example) or by bringing early twentieth-century poetry into productive contact with late twentieth-century theory (Gyllian Phillips on Edith Sitwell). However, it is also the case that the most interesting and academically valuable essays are those which have kept their roots in a full and informed reading of the poetry.

Turning first to some recent biographies of poets, Bevis Hillier's *John Betjeman: New Fame, New Love*, the second of three volumes, covers the period from Betjeman's marriage in 1933 to the successful publication in 1958 of his *Collected Poems*. It is also, inescapably, the biography of a lost age and a dissolved coterie—of tangled networks of friends who were also writers, critics, potential lovers, alleged spies. And it is arguable that rather too many of these tangential figures, relationships, and sub-relationships are delineated here, such that Betjeman himself sometimes disappears from view. Hillier's decision to structure the book according to discrete and clearly signposted chapters ('Film Critic', 'The Diarist', 'Ireland', 'Television Personality') does, however, help to extricate the subject from the morass of background detail and affirms him as a man of many—and intriguing—parts.

Covering the same period as each other, but telling very different stories, are Robert Ferguson's aptly entitled *The Short Sharp Life of T.E. Hulme* and Dominic Hibberd's *Wilfred Owen: A New Biography*. It is a measure, perhaps, of how distinct are the personal experiences and aesthetic concerns of the two poets that Hulme is mentioned only once in Hibberd's book, and Owen not at all in Ferguson's. Ferguson tells the hitherto undocumented story of one of modernism's posthumously proclaimed fathers. It is a tale of precocious talent, iconoclasm, and volatility. Slowly emerging from the pell-mell of egotism and disgrace which marked Hulme's adolescent years are signs of his potential as a philosopher and critic and, in particular, as a sympathetic commentator on contemporary art—he was drafting a book (now lost) on Jacob Epstein at the time of his death in the trenches in 1917. Hulme the nascent poet, however, remains a more shadowy figure.

Hibberd's life of Owen adds much to our understanding of the young man and his work, and offers valuable information about the specific wartime conditions and strategies against which he struggled. A regrettable preoccupation, though, is with Harold Owen, Wilfred's brother and one-time 'keeper of the flame', whose actions in seeking to restrict or influence critical interpretation are the source of persistent and finally peevish speculation and complaint on the part of Hibberd.

The late Ian Hamilton's *Against Oblivion: Some Lives of the Twentieth-Century Poets* offers a series of potted biographies of marginalized figures of the period. Its publishers claim that it is an 'unorthodox' book, although its obvious model, Samuel

Johnson's *The Lives of the English Poets*, and the example of Michael Schmidt's *Lives of the Poets* [1998], rather confound such a view. Nevertheless, Hamilton's emphasis on hitherto neglected writers makes this a valuable read. *Against Oblivion* adopts a Bloomian perspective, focusing on the ways in which emerging modern poets have struggled with their forebears. There may well be an argument here, but its potential is rather obscured by the succession of swift and equitable thumbnail sketches which makes up the bulk of the book. Given Hamilton's enormous contribution to the understanding of modern poetry, there is surprisingly little attention paid here to poetics: to the structure, strategies, and language of the poetry (a fleeting reference to Wilfred Owen's 'pararhymes' marks the exception to this rule).

In contrast, and moving on to recent overviews of the poetry of the period, James Fenton's *An Introduction to English Poetry* is a companion to his *The Strength of Poetry* [2001] and offers a basic practical guide to poetic practice. It draws its examples from a range of poets, periods, and forms (the first chapter alone ranges from *Gawain* to Shakespeare to Auden to the oral traditions of the American slave states). Kipling, Lawrence, Eliot, Dylan Thomas, and T.E. Hulme figure subsequently.

Davis and Jenkins, eds., *Locations of Literary Modernism: Region and Nation in British and American Modernist Poetry*, offers a useful riposte to the tendency to view modernism as a transnational movement. Davis and Jenkins see it instead as rooted in, and responsive to, numerous local, regional, and discretely national variables. Robert Crawford is on his usual knowledgeable and impassioned form in 'MacDiarmid in Montrose', a provocative opening chapter which focuses on the small-town location and international resonance of MacDiarmid's writing. John Goodby and Chris Wigginton, editors of *Dylan Thomas* in the New Casebooks series (see *YWES* 82[2003]), propose a defiant reading of Thomas's poetics and of his contestatory relationship with modernist and metropolitan elites. They argue for a recuperation of Thomas as a key modernist figure, rather than a late-Romantic icon. Edward Thomas, who has been unjustly overlooked of late, is a central figure in Stan Smith's chapter '"Literally, for this": Metonymies of National Identity in Edward Thomas, Yeats, and Auden'. Smith sensitively details Thomas's affinity with his (literal) homeland (that is, his awareness and evocation of the materiality of his native earth) and suggests that this is fundamental to his larger sense of identity and nationality. Thomas Dilworth's 'Antithesis of Place in the Poetry and Life of David Jones' explores the tension between rural and regional isolation and metropolitan pressure.

This is a tension which also tacitly underpins Dilworth's reading of Jones's *Wedding Poems* in his exquisite edition of the same. *Wedding Poems* publishes for the first time Jones's 'Prothalamion' and 'Epithalamion', and appends valuable supplementary material including facsimiles and drafts of a third poem 'The Brenner'. The work is knowledgeably introduced, explicated, and annotated, and is beautifully designed and produced, thereby honouring the artist-poet's own aesthetic values. The two complete poems were written in London in 1940 to honour the marriage of two of Jones's close friends, and Dilworth shows how the specific historical and biographical circumstances (Jones's own nervous stress, persisting since his own experience in the First World War) have shaped the texts. The 'Prothalamion' in particular seems to offer a form of respite, or source of optimism;

Jones sees the union of his two friends as a fragment to shore against the ruins of civilization—a chance to 'mock | the unmaking'. *Wedding Poems* brings the last of David Jones's complete poems into print; modest and unassuming, it is a true addition to our understanding of the literature and culture of the period.

Two essays in the wide-ranging Korte and Schneider, eds., *War and the Cultural Construction of Identities in Britain*, are worthy of note. Paul Goetsch writes on 'The Fantastic in Poetry of the First World War'. The term 'fantastic' denotes a mélange of mythological and archetypal tropes which, Goetsch suggests, were drawn on by British writers in their attempts to represent the inconceivable and incomprehensible—'the strange, uncanny world of the front' (p. 127). Poems by Richard Aldington, Edgell Rickword, and Herbert Read are discussed alongside those of better-known figures: Rosenberg, Owen, and Sassoon. Briefly mentioned in Jenni Calder's 'World War and Women—Advance and Retreat' are poems by Jessie Pope and Nina Macdonald which reflect on the representation of women's employment in the period.

Deen, ed., *Challenging Modernism: New Readings in Literature and Culture*, contains just a couple of essays on early twentieth-century poets. Diana Austin's '*Over the Frontier* and into the Darkness with Stevie Smith: War, Gender, and Identity' largely discusses Smith's fiction, but also proposes a broader argument about her negotiation of gender ideologies during the inter-war years. In 'T.S. Eliot and the "Journalistic Struggle"' Patrick Collier offers a critical reading of Eliot's relationship with the media and of his 'conflicted, ambivalent, and at times contradictory' (p. 188) attitudes towards the popular press. Collier looks in particular at Eliot's aspirations for *The Criterion*—aspirations which he perceives to have been motivated partly by pecuniary need, and partly by his larger ambition to produce an organ of sufficient depth and quality to match the great quarterly reviews of an earlier golden age.

The 'ill-tempered spat' over poetry of the 1930s which my predecessor noted (*YWES* 79[2000] 661) is recapitulated in Jan Montefiore's *Arguments of Heart and Mind: Selected Essays, 1977–2000*. This is a rich and polemical collection which evidences the breadth and commitment of Montefiore's scholarship. In the chapter 'Edgell Rickword: An Exchange with Alan Munton', Montefiore sportingly reprints Munton's defensive critique of her 1996 book *Men and Women Writers of the 1930s*. In equally defensive riposte, she also reproduces her 1998 response to that review. The exchange, although fairly tiresome to outsiders, does sit at the literal heart of her book, and its themes (politics, gender, biography, criticism, engagement) permeate the whole.

Looking back to the early years of the twentieth century, Suzanne Raitt's 'Queer Moods: The Life and Death of Charlotte Mew' (in Chedgzoy, Francis, and Pratt, eds., *In a Queer Place: Sexuality and Belonging in British and European Contexts*) delineates the circumstances of Mew's life, writing, and death by suicide. Raitt reads Mew's death from the perspective of recent queer theory and in terms of its 'negotiation of locutionary position and verbal mood' (p. 26); however, she is alert to the potential dangers of asserting a contiguity between sexuality and suicide, particularly when 'queer politics and poetics ... mobilizes exactly *against* death' (p. 31). She is refreshingly attuned to the peculiarly redeeming aesthetic of Mew's work, even when it seems motivated and shaped by loss, and offers a series of fine close readings (one of few in the works surveyed this year) in order to illustrate this.

W.H. Auden, who figured only in passing in last year's round-up, has received significantly more critical attention this year. Izzo, ed., *W.H. Auden: A Legacy*, proposes a timely survey of his influence on twenty-first-century culture. Largely the work of appreciative enthusiasts ('both the world at large and the academy need to be reminded of who he *is*!', p. xxxv, emphasis in the original), the twenty-five essays in the volume vary enormously in quality and interest—some are too anecdotal, or 'impressionistic', as the editor concedes (p. 47) to be of any real value; others have more to offer. 'Auden on Tolkien: The Book That Isn't, and the House That Brought It Down' by Rod Jellama, Auden's prospective editor for a short book on Tolkien, untangles the tale of inadvertent offence and umbrage which lies behind the project's abandonment. Other essays address Auden's sexuality, his Icelandic poems, his relationship with other writers (D.H. Lawrence, Naomi Mitchison), and his plays and libretti. This is an eclectic collection which, regrettably, promises rather more than it delivers. It is too discursive, and covers too much familiar ground, to be of value to the Auden scholar. This is a pity because, as the wealth of other new writing on Auden suggests, there is much to be said about his persistent importance.

Regrettably omitted last year is Richard Bozorth's *Auden's Games of Knowledge: Poetry and the Meanings of Homosexuality*. Bozorth writes cogently and with an affinity with Auden's writing and its historical and cultural contexts. His book explores how Auden's work 'provokes a dynamic of knowledge bound up with homosexual desire and identity' (p. 3), and his concern throughout is to examine Auden's negotiation of the boundaries between private and public experience and knowledge. Amongst other things, he addresses the pathologization of Auden's sexuality and his representation of religious faith, and offers a radical reading of *Paid on Both Sides* and *The Orators*. Of particular interest is his chapter '"Tell me the truth about love": Confessional Lyric and Lovers' Discourse', which explores the implications for the reception of Auden's writing of his valorization in the film *Four Weddings and a Funeral* [1994]. Bozorth peels back the bibliographical and epistemological layers of this and other poems, and offers a persuasive reading of . Auden's poetry as a form of (Foucauldian—although Bozorth does not label it as such) discourse—as the self-conscious 'site of intimate relation between poet and reader' (p. 175).

Edward Mendelson's devotions to the work of Auden are gratefully acknowledged in Bozorth's book, as elsewhere. The most recent fruit of his scholarship is volume 2 of *The Complete Works of W.H. Auden: Prose* which covers material (often book and theatre reviews) written from the time of the poet's arrival in America in January 1930 through to late 1948. Essays are published in chronological order, producing some provocative juxtapositions, and there are a hundred pages of appendices, including syllabuses and examination papers devised by Auden while teaching in the United States, and—tantalizingly—a list of 'Lost and Unwritten Work'.

In 'W.H. Auden and "The 'Barbaric' Poetry of the North": Unchaining One's Daimon' (*RES* 53[2002] 167–85), Chris Jones examines the roots and sustained significance to Auden of the Old English tradition. For Auden, he argues, it was both the metrical and the rhetorical qualities of the verse which appealed. Based on a sensitive and enthusiastic reading of Auden, and thorough and original research, Jones convincingly delineates a real communion across the centuries between

Auden and his ancestor-poets, with Tolkien serendipitously—although as Rod Jellama's essay, cited above, suggests, not always harmoniously—functioning as a kind of mediator. Also on Auden, William Ruleman's 'Form, Meaning and Reader Implication in W.H. Auden's "The Shield of Achilles"' (*NCL* 32:iii[2002] 10–13) argues that Auden's use of ballad form and rhyme-royal represents an attempt to yoke an oral tradition with an anti-heroic impetus. The effect of this, Ruleman suggests, is to implicate a broad and contemporary readership in ostensibly historical circumstances, teaching us about 'our common complicity, if not in evil, then at least in human frailty' (p. 12).

In John Smart's 'An Unpublished Letter' the *W.H. Auden Society Newsletter* (*WHASN* 23[2002] 8–11) reproduces a hitherto unseen letter from Auden to a pupil of his old school. The letter, 'written in a vivid green ink' (p. 8), dates from July 1951 and offers a critique of the schoolboy's poetry, and advice on the importance of attentiveness—in poetry as in life. Also in the *Newsletter* is 'Wallace and Wystan: Antimythological Meetings' (*WHASN* 23[2002] 12–23). Here Liesl M. Olson delicately traces the wary literary relationship between Auden and Wallace Stevens. It argues that the former's manuscript poem 'Miss God on Mr Stevens'—drafted in response to the latter's 'Notes Towards a Supreme Fiction'—embodies a provocative, and finally dominant, stance on debates about sexuality, politics, representation, and imagination. Two further essays, Paola Marchetti Rognoni's 'Auden and Italy' (pp. 25–32) and Rainer Emig's 'Teaching Auden in Britain' (pp. 32–7) bring Auden into the present day, assessing his profile in academia and popular culture.

T.S. Eliot continued to stimulate debate in academic journals in 2002 although, after last year's bumper crop, this has been a quieter year for monographs. The best of the Eliot essays (and indeed the most impressive of all of the works under review this year) is Elisabeth Cardonne-Arlyck's 'Mind Your Tongue: Autobiography and New French Lyric Poetry' (*NLH* 33[2002] 581–601), which proposes an exciting reading of Eliot's 'The Love Song of J. Alfred Prufrock'. Cardonne-Arlyck attends to the voice of the poem (the 'feigned lyric I', as she terms it, borrowing from Käte Hamburger's *The Logic of Literature* [1973]) and suggests that this represents something more than a hermetic (limited and limiting) utterance. Instead, like the autobiographical 'I', it offers the possibility of presence and action—a possibility which is realized in the process of reading. There is a fine and nuanced argument here, one which sets its reading of the voices and masks of the poem within a cogent context of current autobiographical theory.

Prufrock re-emerges in Patrick Query's '"They called me the hyacinth girl": T.S. Eliot and the Revision of Masculinity' (*YER* 18:iii[2002] 10–21), which examines 'The Love Song of J. Alfred Prufrock' and *The Waste Land* in order to reassess the question of Eliot's (latent homo?)sexuality. Query reads both poems against the background of shifting attitudes towards masculinity and nationality in the period and traces the resonance of the American Eliot's friendship with the young Frenchman, Verdenal. He also speculates—not entirely convincingly—on the synchronicity which saw Eliot suddenly marrying Vivien Haigh-Wood within weeks of Verdenal's death. The same journal contains Robert Fleissner's '"Time to turn back and descend the stair": Prufrock as Modernist in Juxtaposition to Duchamp's "Nude" (An Interart Study)' (*YER* 18:iii[2002] 2–9). The convoluted title is in keeping with the curiously circumlocutory tone of the essay. Fleissner is actually on to something quite interesting and helpful (his premise being that Prufrock's descent of the stairs in 'The Love Song' owes as much to Duchamp's painting on this theme as to, as is commonly argued, Dante's *Inferno*). Quite why he feels it necessary to be so hesitant—the article opens with a defensive and rhetorical 'Should not the … ?' and proceeds with a succession of qualifications, passives, and negatives—is not clear.

Also looking to fine art for Eliot's sources is Derek Roper's 'T.S. Eliot's "La Figlia Che Piange": A Picture without a Frame' (*EIC* 52[2002] 222–34). Roper reads Eliot's text as a picture poem, one which derives from the poet's contemplation of one or several contemporary portraits of women posed in a garden. In 'La Figlia Che Piange', as in such portraits, the chief focus is the emotional turmoil of the subject. Roper rightly concedes that the precise visual inspiration for the poem may never be known. He also contends that the real strengths of the poem—its 'aesthetic effect' (p. 230) and its self-conscious exemplification of the relationship between art and audience—owe a great deal to these putative sources.

Stefan Collini's F.W. Bateson Memorial Lecture, 'Eliot Among the Intellectuals' (*EIC* 52[2002] 101–25), concentrates on Eliot's late prose and 'social criticism'. What characterizes this work of the 1930s and 1940s, he suggests, is a preoccupation with questions of 'cultural authority' (p. 102) and an interest in the relationship between the intellectual and the man of letters, the expert and the amateur—concerns widely shared in his milieu. Eliot's essays seek, some more successfully than others, to find a voice which recognizes, while also reconciling the differences between, the two standpoints. In '*East Coker* III, Again' (*N&Q* 49[2002] 498–9) James T. Bratcher suggests as a source for Eliot's 'East Coker': James Thomson's *City of Dreadful Night*. In defence of this hypothesis he argues that 'Eliot had a re-shaping, or one might even say manipulative, imagination' (p. 498).

The poetry of D.H. Lawrence continues to gain sporadic attention. In a fascinating, engaged, and engaging article, 'D.H. Lawrence, Working Poets, and Political Correctness' (*SoR* 38:ii[2002] 334–57), Gary Adelman asks why Lawrence's work has ceased to be taught in English and American universities. He recounts his experience of inviting the views of 133 living poets on the influence of Lawrence on their own writing, and reproduces excerpts from some of their replies, including Robert Creeley: 'He was my model, both in prose and poetry—and now in age I probably think of his own late poems daily' (p. 337), Carolyn Kizer: 'My belief in his genius never wavered' (p. 341), Li-Young Lee: 'I have to admit that I *love* Lawrence's novels and only sometimes enjoy his poetry' (p. 344), and Thom Gunn: 'The poetry seem[s] to me more important than ever' (p. 342). Through his survey of contemporary poets and his close reading across and between Lawrence's writing and the work of his successors, Adelman provides compelling evidence for the lasting influence of Lawrence's poetry on modern American verse. Where his argument seems less convincing is in his attempt to apportion blame for Lawrence's fall from grace, citing (although to be fair, sometimes here merely reporting the views of his correspondents) the rise of 'theory' or 'political correctness' or a non-specific distaste for sexual explicitness. Adelman's own solution to this decline lies, optimistically—if not self-defeatingly—in a return to what he regards as the 'life-affirming spirit' (p. 356) of the work.

Howard J. Booth's 'D.H. Lawrence and Male Homosexual Desire' (*RES* 53[2002] 86–107) revisits recent scholarship (for example, by Mark Kinkead-

Weekes) about Lawrence and homosexuality and argues for a more persistent ambivalence on Lawrence's part than is typically perceived. Regrettably—given the fruitfulness of the poetry in this respect—Booth confines most of his discussion to the fiction.

Dylan Thomas, too, features sporadically this year. In *New Welsh Review*, Gilbert Bennett and Donna Jones Paananen's 'Dylan Thomas: The Celebration' (*NWRev* 55[2002] 25–30) offers a rather casual overview (Professor Barbara Hardy is described as a 'Swansea girl', p. 26) of 2001's Dylan Thomas 'Celebrations' and publications. James A. Davies's 'Glancing Down the Cliff of Time: Pamela Hansford Johnson and Dylan Thomas' (*NWRev* 58[2002] 35–42) is more useful. It discusses the relationship between the novelist and poet and detects Thomas's hand in some of the ideas and images in Hansford Johnson's *This Bed Thy Centre* [1935].

Poetry and Nation Review continues its sterling work in recuperating the reputations of lost poets and reappraising the stock of others. Their ninetieth birthday tribute to F.T. Prince opens with Anthony Rudolf's 'I *have* written other poems, you know' (*PNR* 29:i[2002] 26–8). Rudolf reproduces a letter from T.S. Eliot to the younger poet, dated 10 September 1935, in which Eliot comments on a number of Prince manuscripts which he was about to publish in *The Criterion*. In the same issue Mark Ford, in 'A Wide and Wingless Path to the Impossible: The Poetry of F.T. Prince' (*PNR* 29:i[2002] 31–3), discusses the relationship between Prince's work and the early poetry of W.H. Auden. An earlier volume of *PNR* includes Charles Mundye and Patrick McGuinness's 'Revisiting A Collaboration' (*PNR* 28:vi[2002] 46–9), which takes a new look at Laura Riding and Robert Graves's *A Survey of Modernist Poetry* and *A Pamphlet Against Anthologies*. Amongst other things, Mundye and McGuinness identify areas where the two poets' perceptions of modernism deviate from the contemporary 'orthodoxy' (p. 47). Their essay points to the importance, in the *Survey* in particular, of Riding and Graves's recognition of the responsibilities and rights of poet and reader respectively.

Notes and Queries, too, continues to publish rewarding snippets which cast new light on familiar poems (see, for example, James Bratcher's article, above, on Eliot's 'East Coker'). Archie Burnett suggests 'Two Sources for A. E. Housman' (*N&Q* 49[2002] 493)—specifically for 'I shall not die for you' and *The Eleventh Eclogue*. In '*Things to Come* and "Newsreel": Versions of Cinematic Influence' (*N&Q* 49[2002] 91–3), Stuart Sillars revisits Cecil Day Lewis's poem 'Newsreel' [1938] and persuasively demonstrates its debt to William Cameron Menzies's film, *Things to Come* [1936], which, in turn, draws on H.G. Wells's novel *The Shape of Things To Come*. Sillars argues that this borrowing is evidence of the conflation of generic boundaries during the period. Of interest to scholars of Vorticism and of the little magazines of the period is Michael E. Leveridge's 'The Printing of Blast' (*WLA* 7[2001] 20–31). Leveridge is the grandson of the proprietor of the printer who produced the 1914 and 1915 issues of *Blast*, and provides a detailed account of the somewhat chaotic printing history of the magazine.

The aural dimension of poetry is the theme of the final two essays discussed here. In Meyer, ed., *Literature and Musical Adaptation*, Gyllian Phillips's 'Something Lies Beyond the Scene [seen] of *Façade*: Sitwell, Walton and Kristeva's Semiotic' is cogently written, argued, and annotated. Phillips directs attention to Sitwell's often overlooked *Façade*—a series of poems which she set to music in collaboration with William Walton and which Phillips regards as 'one of the most important events in the history of modernist poetics' (p. 61). In the poems, it is suggested, visual representation (the scene/seen) is displaced by a new economy of sound, one which is attuned to unconscious processes, disruptive of 'the discipline of meaningful language' (p. 64) and thus amenable to being read from the perspective of Kristeva's theory of the semiotic. Phillips's is an original and ambitious argument, convincingly presented. Finally, and also impressively alert to the sound of poetry, is Sarah Parry's 'The Inaudibility of "Good" Sound Editing: The Case of Caedmon Records' (*Performance Research* 7:i[2002] 24–33). Parry argues for a new awareness of the complex and mediated nature of recorded poetry. The poet's voice, when thus captured, is not direct, authentic, or real; rather, it is constructed, artful, performed. Parry takes Caedmon Records—instrumental, as all scholars in the field would acknowledge, in recording and making available the voices of modern poetry—as her example, and analyses a number of variables, from the differences between rehearsed studio recordings and live recordings of public readings to the impact of developing technologies on the kind, scale, quality, and availability of recordings. Crucially, she draws attention to the editorial decisions and processes which have led, in Caedmon in particular, to the construction of a particular kind of sound. Parry looks to current performance theory (to Bourdieu and others) to theorize the meaning, or rather meanings, of recorded poetry and offers close analyses of the sounds of a number of early Caedmon contributors, including T.S. Eliot, Dylan Thomas, and Edith Sitwell.

6. Post-1950 Poetry

This has been a thin year for publications about post-war poetry, made even thinner as some books were not received in time for review. Just three books have been received, all of which concern perhaps the most significant poet of the period, Philip Larkin.

B.C. Bloomfield has published the revised and expanded edition of his *Philip Larkin: A Bibliography, 1933–1994*, the original edition of which was published in 1979 and covered up to 1976. The new edition covers entries up to December 1994, which already seems a long time ago in Larkin criticism. Nevertheless, Bloomfield's revised edition is an essential tool for Larkin scholars, and there are obvious developments in Larkin scholarship between 1976 and 1994 to necessitate the new volume. Larkin's death in 1985 is reflected in the addition of obituaries and commemorative poems, for example, as well as the completion of lists of the poet's publications, appearances, and interviews. The publication of Faber's *Collected Poems* [1988], Anthony Thwaite's *Selected Letters* [1992], Andrew Motion's biography [1993], as well as a number of important critical books and articles, all listed and detailed in this revised bibliography, reflect the fact that Larkin studies grew significantly during this period. Budding Larkin students will have to add their own bibliographical searches to cover the developments in Larkin critical studies since 1994, but Bloomfield's bibliography is invaluable not for its listing of critical studies, but for its extensive documentation of Larkin's publications. Bloomfield provides details of the original format, binding, paper, contents, print runs, prices, and significant reviews for each edition. The contents listing for each of Larkin's poetry books also gives full details of if and where any of the poems were published previously or reprinted. His notes for each publication include some intriguing items of interest. The aspiring poet of *XX Poems*, who privately printed a hundred copies and sent them to prominent literary figures, solicited little response, 'insufficient stamps having been put on the envelopes because postage rates had just been raised' (p. 17). The print runs of the Faber paperback editions of *The North Ship*, *The Whitsun Weddings*, and *High Windows* reached five-figure peaks in the mid- to late 1980s, no doubt stirred by Larkin's death, but dwindled to low four-figure numbers in the early 1990s, evidently because of the more than 80,000 paperback copies of the *Collected Poems* then available. Bloomfield's foreword charts his friendship with Larkin and the circumstances of their working together on library committees, and also provides some insights into Larkin's personality and his achievements as a librarian at Hull. It is chiefly as a bibliographical resource rather than a biographical source that Bloomfield's book will be used, of course, and it is an indispensable addition to the resources available to Larkin scholars.

Following the publication of Motion's biography of Larkin and Thwaite's edition of his letters in the early 1990s, Larkin seemed to become known for his racist and misogynist views, for being abusive about his friends, and narrow-minded about strangers. The disclosure of his right-wing prejudices led to a revaluation, not just of Larkin the man, but also of Larkin the poet. Maeve Brennan's *The Philip Larkin I Knew* is an attempt to counter this reputation with an account of her close friendship with Larkin, whom she depicts as courteous, honest, loving, generous, witty, and compassionate. She also quotes liberally and approvingly from Larkin's poetry, prose, and letters to illustrate her account, and celebrates his literary talents. Brennan was a senior member of the library staff at the University of Hull throughout the time that Larkin was librarian there, and they developed an intimate relationship between 1960 and 1978, and remained friends until his death in 1985. Brennan reveals only enough of their relationship to show Larkin as a loving although guardedly private man, capable of much warmth and fun, even though self-absorbed and unable to commit himself to marriage. She shows no signs of difficulty with his simultaneous pursuit of a relationship with Monica Jones, although she does make mention on a couple of occasions that Larkin voiced the opinion that he might better be able to marry Brennan than Jones. She was hurt, however, when she discovered after his death that Larkin was duplicitous with another woman, Betty Mackereth, although she eventually decided to find charming the fact that Larkin protected her from this knowledge. Brennan confesses to being somewhat prudish and naive, and this is evident in the way in which she shies away from Larkin's use of 'foul language' in letters which she only read after his death, in the way in which she circumvents discussion of sexual relations and intimacy, and also, more broadly, in the way in which she defends Larkin's right-wing prejudices as the conventional views of her generation. The book abounds with compliments to Larkin, and Larkin's compliments to Brennan. Brennan's account is not unalloyed romantic myth, however, as she acknowledges that reading Larkin's youthful letters to James Sutton compelled her to admit that there were two sides to Larkin's personality. She gives some consideration to how she might figure in some of Larkin's poems, which may be useful to Larkin scholars. She had much influence, it seems, on *The Whitsun Weddings*, and she prefers the warmth of this volume to the cold and more cynical views of *High Windows*. She is informative about Larkin's literary and cultural tastes, including his fascination with James Bond films, his admiration for Waugh's

Sword of Honour trilogy, and their shared enthusiasm for Margery Sharp's children's stories, beginning with *The Rescuers*. Sharp's stories centred on the adventures of a white mouse called Miss Bianca, which Larkin identified with Brennan, and embodied a fantasy element in their relationship. She greatly admires Larkin's abilities as a librarian, and celebrates him as the author of the first post-war academic library. She includes as an appendix eighty pages of letters between her and Larkin, which reveal their affection for each other, and show a romantic, warm side to Larkin which his reputation in the 1990s began to belie. Brennan's wish for her book is that it helps to fulfil Larkin's hope that 'what will survive of us is love', which forms the title of her final chapter.

Philip Larkin's *Further Requirements*, edited by Anthony Thwaite, is, as its title suggests, a sequel volume to *Required Writing*, the collection of prose writings which Larkin published in 1983. *Further Requirements* comprises pieces omitted from the first volume, and those written between 1982 and 1985. It is organized into four sections: 'Statements and Interviews', 'Broadcasts', 'Forewords', and, by far the largest section, 'Reviews'. Far from the diffidence and awkwardness sometimes associated with Larkin, the volume and breadth of these assembled pieces seems to testify instead to a garrulous, sociable man, and a more prolific reviewer and generous interviewee than I had realized. Above all, it is the quality of Larkin's writings and his fine sense of judgement which come across, and it is hard to disagree with John Carey's assessment printed on the back cover, to the effect that if this volume constitutes Larkin's 'second best', it 'excels almost anyone else's best'. The interviews with Ian Hamilton, Neil Powell, and John Haffenden are informative and engaging. Larkin's autobiographical essay about growing up in Coventry, 'Not the Place's Fault', first published in 1959, is good to have in such an accessible collection. His lament about the sale of English literary manuscripts to US libraries in 1967 is both prescient and constructive. Many of the pieces included in the volume are short—there are sleeve-notes to recorded readings, published statements made in answer to questionnaires or journal editors, and brief contributions to anthologies. The forewords which he wrote for other people's books, and the many reviews he wrote of other people's work, are often fascinating. They chart in particular his enormous enthusiasm for the work of Barbara Pym, Anthony Powell, John Betjeman, W.H. Auden, and Thomas Hardy. Dick Francis and Ian Fleming are also celebrated. Kingsley Amis's *New Oxford Book of Light Verse* found a rather more tepid response from Larkin, however. Anthony Thwaite comments in his introduction that the publication of Larkin's non-fiction prose is not yet complete with this volume, but that it 'goes as far as the literary executors (Thwaite and Motion) feel it useful or appropriate to go at the present time' (p. xvi).

7. Irish Poetry

It's tempting to describe Kennedy-Andrews, ed., *The Poetry of Derek Mahon*, the eleventh offering from the Ulster Editions and Monographs series, as a round-up of the usual suspects. And, with the exception of Edna Longley, they're once again fielding an all-male side. But sometimes the usual suspects are rounded up for good reasons. Many of the contributors to this book have written seminal criticism of Derek Mahon's work, as illustrated in Kennedy-Andrews's introduction, which provides a useful overview of the critical reception of Mahon's work to date. Inevitably with this kind of book—the first collection of essays devoted solely to the poet and written for the occasion—it is the case that some of the most significant criticism of Mahon's work predates it. The very considerable extent to which, for example, Longley's earlier work on Mahon and religion, or Haughton's on Mahon and place, or Stan Smith's 1980s Marxist anxieties about Mahon's lack of commitment, set either the terms or the standard for much of what is included here, and condition—even if by providing something to react against—more recent critical responses is more than usually noticeable throughout. One thing *The Poetry of Derek Mahon* thus highlights is that it is a pity that some of the work on Mahon published through the 1980s and early 1990s has not itself been made available in a collection of essays: if ever a body of criticism on a contemporary poet warranted a critical casebook or equivalent, this is surely it. Nevertheless, *The Poetry of Derek Mahon*, as with last year's *The Poetry of Michael Longley*, is an important and necessary validation of the poet's international reputation, and one which for this poet, too, was overdue.

The papers included here were given at the Derek Mahon symposium held in Coleraine in 1998. That has a few consequences for the book. First, while there are some excellent essays here, essays which ensure the critical significance of the book, it appears that all the symposium papers have been included. The result is a noticeable unevenness in style and quality. Some contributions are only brief forays into their subject (as in Gerald Dawe's discussion of Mahon's influence); it's difficult to see how much is added by others to the existing debate—Richard York on Mahon and painting for example—even though they may have worked well as visual/oral presentations. And a cover-to-cover read is conducive to feelings of *déjà vu*: often quoted is the phrase 'the forest of intertextuality', which takes on a pertinence in relation to these essays that might not have been anticipated; nor is there much chance of missing the dirty dog or the fiery gin. A more ruthless selectivity, and a heavier editorial hand, might have served both poet and critics better overall. Second, the controversial reviews of the then recently published *The Yellow Book* (Peter McDonald, in *Poetry Ireland Review*, is the usual villain of the piece here), and ambiguous responses to *The Yellow Book* itself, seem to operate as a subtext to the proceedings. Edna Longley's integration of *The Yellow Book* into a reading of Mahon's oeuvre, and Patrick Crotty's balanced and thoughtful analysis of the collection, are the contributions that speak clearly beyond the debate as it existed at that particular moment in time. Other essays that have an important and original contribution to make include Michael Allen's seminal study of Mahon's rhythms and revisions, Neil Corcoran's consideration of place and America in Mahon's poetry, Jarniewicz's insights into the vexed question of Mahon and history, and Hugh Haughton's examination of Mahon and translation. Perhaps the idea of this book is better, on balance, than the finished product itself: nevertheless, there's enough here to make it necessary—and often compelling—reading, and its appearance should go some way towards redressing an imbalance in Northern Irish poetry criticism that has sometimes compounded Mahon's own elusiveness.

Self-promotion, and the cult of personality have, it seems, become important factors in the development of a poet's profile. Fortunately for the shy and retiring Mahon, and others like him who shun headlines, Peter McDonald's *Serious Poetry: Form and Authority from Yeats to Hill* provides a much-needed counterblast to what he sees as some alarming trends in contemporary attitudes towards poetry, where 'Top poets and poems (if less good than top films or pop stars) still make good copy', where 'poetry is replaced with poetries' and where '"the democratic voice" calls the tune'. Where, he asks, would 'the promotion of contemporary poetry be without personalities to push'? Perhaps, *Serious Poetry* suggests, in a better place than it is now. Given the recent *fin-de-siècle* interest in poets (if not in poetry) of the Millennium Dome, Late Show, and Laureate variety, *Serious Poetry* is a timely reminder of what should be taken seriously. McDonald runs against the critical tide in putting 'poetic form' in the place of 'personality', arguing persuasively that 'form is the serious heart of a poem ... where such "authority" as poetry bears must reside'. The focus here is not Irish poetry in particular: McDonald's subjects include Auden, Eliot, and Hill as well as Yeats, MacNeice, and Heaney—and although two-thirds of the book is focused on Yeats, it is Geoffrey Hill who serves, ultimately, as McDonald's test case. But the study reverberates in an understanding of both English and Irish poetry. McDonald is a meticulous and insightful critic of modern poetry, who can remind his reader that even the most familiar texts may yet yield some surprises: his chapters here on Yeats and remorse, and on Yeats's poetic structures, have a claim to be considered some of the most important work on that poet in recent times. In 'Yeats, Form and Northern Irish Poetry', the clear distinction drawn between form and formalism which critics have sometimes chosen, in the interests of ideological positioning, to collapse, has important implications for understanding the formal structures of contemporary poetry: Yeats's 'sense of closure, of formal completeness' which critics 'sometimes deplore' is, as McDonald shows, 'always a battle won rather than an accommodation easily engineered'. To understand this is to rethink what some critics see as the 'problem' of Yeats and/or the supposed 'problem' (in political terms) of much Northern Irish poetry's adherence to traditional forms. To run against the zeitgeist is, of course, always problematical; in criticism of Irish poetry, a willingness to give form the kind of attention—and critical work—that McDonald demonstrates it deserves may not sit easily with other preoccupations in the current cultural climate. But for any serious reader of *Serious Poetry*, his arguments are likely to prove impossible to ignore.

In Roberts and Allison, eds., *Poetry and Contemporary Culture; The Question of Value*, some of McDonald's concerns are echoed. Roberts too, for example, notes that a case could be made that 'in the contemporary literary marketplace, "personality" is the equivalent of money'. But the comparison really ends there. *Poetry and Contemporary Culture*'s concern (formulated here in rather stodgy and uninspiring terms) is with the 'cultural institutions, media and literary practices through which and by which poetic value is constructed, mediated or represented'. It has no particular claim to be reviewed under the heading 'Irish Poetry', though Jonathan Allison and Cairns Craig both deal with recent Irish poetry in their excellent essays; but, more than that, one senses that it is a book which hasn't quite found its niche or its audience anywhere in particular. This is partly because its remit is potentially vast: the essays collected here include Marjorie Perloff flying the flag of the American experimentalists and Language poets again; Andrew Michael Roberts on 'Recent British Anthologies' (by which he means British and Irish— although the existing debate in Irish Studies about the politics of anthologizing has largely passed him by); Romana Huk on 'Reading/Writing Race and Culture According to Universal Systems of Value'; Jonathan Allison on 'Contemporary

Poetry and the First World War'; Robert Crawford on 'Poetry and Academia'. There are also essays on poetry and radio, and poetry and film. It is also therefore a book that could slip through the net partly because it steps beyond the boundaries of categories easily catalogued, exploring as it does so many different media, and poetry from the US, Ireland, Scotland, and England. But, beyond the interest of Allison's, Craig's, and Crawford's contributions, the book has another particular, if oblique, relevance to Irish poetry criticism. Since the 1960s, many of the best-known Irish poets—Longley, Muldoon, Carson, Heaney, to name some—have been directly involved with the work of cultural institutions—the Arts Councils, the BBC, the universities—work which is seldom discussed in criticism. *Poetry and Contemporary Culture*, even though Ireland is not its subject, does suggest some ways in which the relation of poetry to institutions in Ireland might be rethought.

Robert Crawford, like Peter McDonald, is concerned, in *Poetry and Contemporary Culture* with the poet as critic, and with the terms on which 'authority' is granted to the poet's critical voice. Auden professed an interest in 'hearing what a poet has to say about the nature of poetry, though I do not take it too seriously'. McDonald also quotes Auden's caustic comment that 'In unkind moments one is almost tempted to think that all they are really saying is: "Read me. Don't read the other fellows."' It would be more than unkind to respond to Haberstroh, ed., *My Self, My Muse: Irish Women Poets reflect on Life and Art*, in such terms; although, given the debates which emerged this year about authority, value, and 'impersonality' (or otherwise), the book, by its nature, is implicated in these questions too. Patricia Boyle Haberstroh's introduction acknowledges that fact directly; she also stakes out her own position by example. On the one hand, she acknowledges that Sylvia Plath is not well served by being seen as 'a character in an American melodrama'; on the other, she argues that 'One certainly cannot appreciate the full value of the very successful poems of Plath's final year outside the context of her life.' Awareness of a 'gendered cultural context ... enhances our understanding of a poem'; the whole purpose of this book is 'to illustrate the relationship between autobiography and poetry'. The introduction also provides a critical context for what follows, one which draws on and develops from Haberstroh's earlier study, *Women Creating Women: Contemporary Irish Women Poets*. It's hard to imagine Irish Men Poets reflecting on life and art in quite this way; then again, since the poet-critic seems to be a predominantly male phenomenon, there may be different strategies required for female poets. Fortunately these are not of the 'read me rather than her' variety. The contributions to this book—by nine poets including McGuckian, Boland, and Ní Chuilleanáin—all have some interest as autobiography and cultural history whether or not they illuminate the poems, although the degree of interest, for this reader at least, is related to perceptions of their respective merits as poets.

Interest in the poet-critic this year seems particularly apt since 2002 also saw the publication of Seamus Heaney's monumental *Finders Keepers: Selected Prose, 1971–2001*. Most of the material has been readily available in book form: this gathers together criticism from *Preoccupations, The Government of the Tongue, The Redress of Poetry*, and *The Place of Writing*. Heaney's criticism sits very obviously in the new-critical school in which he was educated, and he is a stylish and eloquent advocate and close reader of nineteenth- and twentieth-century poetry. But Auden perhaps has more pertinence here: Heaney's authority as critic does derive in part from his status as poet (for McDonald, only Geoffrey Hill's criticism stands up entirely on its own merits in this regard), and if *Finders Keepers* isn't concerned with encouraging the reader to read Heaney's poetry, his criticism has always implicitly suggested ways in which that poetry might be read. Occasionally, the poet can lead the critic astray—Larkin, for instance, becomes distorted in the refracting prism of Heaney's own aesthetic preoccupations—but Heaney's usual sensitivity as a reader of poetry makes his criticism invaluable in terms of understanding poetry as well as understanding Heaney.

Finders Keepers, in style and subject, makes evident Heaney's academic background and credentials as well as his poetic ones. In a different style is the work of another poet-critic, Dennis O'Driscoll, whose *Troubled Thoughts, Majestic Dreams: Selected Prose Writings* appeared in 2001. It is, O'Driscoll points out, 'an unscholarly book', a collection of essays, reviews, and autobiographical pieces written 'in the spare half hours of life' (O'Driscoll works for the Irish Civil Service), more reminiscent of such collections as Mahon's *Journalism* or Larkin's *Required Writing* than of the work of poet-critics like Heaney or Jarrell. But, as a literary journalist, O'Driscoll is also attuned to issues which concern McDonald and Crawford: the over-production of mediocre poetry; the cult of 'personality'; the cultivation of academics who can make all the difference to a poetic career—the benefits of having one's own equivalent of a Helen Vendler may be considerable for the poet looking for a 'market' outside Ireland. In some ways, O'Driscoll is both less scholarly and more cynical than McDonald in his exposé of such things; some of his more uncomfortable judgements ('A national reputation is not all that hard to achieve when the nation is a small one'; 'the approbation of American academics is feverishly sought') should nonetheless be heard—and heeded. But his most troubled 'troubled thoughts', one senses, relate to Northern Ireland, and Northern Irish poetry. O'Driscoll provides a 'Map of Contemporary Irish Poetry' in a 1995 essay, revised for this edition, in which Muldoon's *Faber Book of Contemporary Irish Poetry* [1986] still rankles. Here, and elsewhere, O'Driscoll objects to the depiction of 'the corpus of Irish poetry with a bloated Northern head on a spindly Southern body'. Northern writers are culpable in two ways for O'Driscoll: first, by their 'depth of assurance' that the Northern province has a monopoly of talent; second, by their lack of proper appreciation of one of their own—Seamus Heaney. O'Driscoll's criticism thus provides a useful reminder that things can look very different depending where you're standing, and that mapping is fraught with problems. Much of *Troubled Thoughts* is not concerned directly with Irish poetry, but his essays here on contemporary writing, Irish language poetry, and his graceful insights into Thomas Kinsella's often difficult poetry, offer a perspective on Irish poetry—particularly poetry written in the Republic—that sometimes gets missed.

Fleming, ed., *W.B. Yeats and Postcolonialism*, suffers from a degree of compulsive definition syndrome in relation to one of the most complex and indefinable figures of Irish literary history. There are some more established names in this collection of essays; but, for the most part, the book comprises a kind of US equivalent of the 'new voices in Irish criticism' series. Its virtue is that a range of specialisms and enthusiasms are brought to bear on the subject: there are essays here comparing Yeats with Rushdie, Walcott, and Okigbo, for example. At the same time, given the probability that this book's appeal will be to a fairly specialized audience, it's also the case that, in some of the essays, the background or contextual material brought to bear could be considered excessive or predictable. The reader could also suffer from label fatigue—'As Yeats is colonial/nationalist/modern, he also becomes postcolonial/liberationist/postmodern' is one conclusion reached here that, in effect, restates all the problems. With only a couple of exceptions (Eugene O'Brien, for example), the essays don't engage with more recent theorizing (by Willy Maley and Colin Graham among others) on the subject of Ireland and postcoloniality, preferring to concentrate on the writings of Said and Deane from the 1980s. And the picture of Irish poetry that emerges from the pages of this book might make many critics uneasy, not least because it suggests that the lines of communication between Irish Studies in the US and in Ireland and the UK have some problems. There are some complex, scholarly, and thoughtful essays here; but the weaknesses of other contributions—and of the introduction, which comprises rather laboured summaries of each essay—mean that it is unlikely overall to make much of a mark on the field.

If there's one thing Ann Saddlemyer's superb *Becoming George: The Life of Mrs W.B. Yeats* makes clear, it is Georgie Hyde Lees's willingness to subordinate her own talents to the needs—practical, emotional, and aesthetic—of her husband. That being the case, one can't help feeling pleased that the biography of George Yeats predates by a year volume 2 of R.F. Foster's biography of W.B. himself. Saddlemyer grapples with two difficulties. The first is George Yeats's self-effacement: she did not keep many papers and letters relating to her private life. Yeats himself observed of her and to her, soon after their engagement, 'You are only confident I think in the service of others'. The second is the automatic writing: a marriage in which the spirits are asked for guidance on a regular basis brings certain problems for the biographer. It is a testament to Saddlemyer's style and sensitivity that the life lived by the Yeatses has a credibility within the pages of this biography, without either the reader or the subject, George Yeats, forced into belief or disbelief as regards their more esoteric preoccupations. What does emerge is the portrait of a woman who was, in Lily Yeats's words, 'delightfully sane' ('Willy', she concluded, 'is in luck') and whose importance for Yeats's poetic development in his middle and later periods can only now be properly understood. Robert Graves's jibe notwithstanding ('Undergraduate: Have you written any poems recently, sir? Yeats: No, my wife has been feeling poorly and disinclined'), *Becoming George* establishes for the first time a full understanding of the nature of their literary partnership, one in which, against the odds, George Yeats supplants Maud, Iseult, and Lady Gregory to become Yeats's centre.

Yeats famously wrote: '*Accursed who brings to light of day | The writings I have cast away!*' Undeterred, George Yeats, even in the very early days of the marriage, began fishing manuscripts out of the wastepaper basket for posterity. The Cornell general editors have also taken their chances and disregarded the curse. This year three more volumes in the Cornell Yeats series, which presents all available manuscripts, revised typescripts, and proof-sheets of Yeats's poems and plays, have seen the light of day: Curtis, ed., *The Land of Heart's Desire*; Fitzgerald, ed., *The Words Upon the Window Pane*; and Holdeman, ed., *'In the Seven Woods' and 'The Green Helmet and Other Poems'*. Yeats might have disapproved, but the volumes are a treasure for the Yeats scholar. Yeats's handwriting, with its erratic spelling and idiosyncratic shorthand, is notoriously difficult: the quality of both the photographic reproductions of the manuscripts and the transcriptions is impressive. The volumes are also critically illuminating. In the case of *The Land of Heart's Desire*, the first Yeats play produced in the commercial theatre, the revisions show how Yeats responded to practical theatrical needs, aiming for, in Curtis's phrase, a more 'playable script'. Where *Land of Heart's Desire* was inspired, in part, by Florence Farr and Maud Gonne, the writing of the more 'tightly constructed' *Words Upon the Window Pane* was, Fitzgerald notes, urged on Yeats by George Yeats, and it is, she argues, a 'masterpiece' of his later period. Fitzgerald's introduction also makes a convincing case for a hitherto unnoticed source for Yeats's *Words Upon the Window Pane*, a 'deservedly unknown' play by Charles Edward Lawrence, one which helps to explain the speed and fluency with which Yeats produced his first draft. Unfortunately, few of the manuscripts from the period in which Yeats wrote *In the Seven Woods* and *The Green Helmet* have survived (George Yeats not yet being at hand); but from those that have, and from typescript and proof revisions, David Holdeman's edition gives an extraordinary insight into Yeats's development in what was both a fallow period (during which he was much occupied with the Abbey theatre) and a period in which the poet's style was undergoing significant changes: Holdeman traces the alterations to *In the Seven Woods* through three subsequent versions of his collected poems published between 1906 and 1908, a process which transformed the volume, and which anticipates the lyrics eventually collected in *The Green Helmet and Other Poems*. He also brings to light the handful of uncollected (and sometimes unpublished) poems Yeats wrote between 1899 and 1912. Yeats's 'curse' about his discarded manuscripts concludes: '*But blessed he that stirs them not | And lets the kind worm take the lot*'. Given the insights and possibilities yielded up by the Cornell Series, one can only disagree with him.

Books Reviewed

Achilles, Jochen, Ina Bergmann, and Birgit Däwes, eds. *Global Challenges and Regional Responses in Contemporary Drama in English*. Contemporary Drama in English 10. Trier: Wissenschaftlicher Verlag. [2003] pp. 280. pb. _24.50 ISBN 3 8847 6590 6.

Adelman, Gary. *Reclaiming D.H. Lawrence: Contemporary Writers Speak Out*. BuckUP. [2002] pp. 174. £19.78 ISBN 0 8387 5528 3.

Ardis, Ann L. *Modernism and Cultural Conflict, 1880–1922*. CUP. [2002] pp. ix + 187. £40 ISBN 0 5218 1206 2.

Atkin, Jonathan. *A War of Individuals: Bloomsbury and Attitudes toward the Great War*. ManUP. [2002] pp. 250. hb. £45 ISBN 0 7190 6070 2, pb. £15.99 ISBN 0 7190 6071 0.

Ayckbourn, Alan. *The Crafty Art of Playmaking*. Faber. [2002] pp. xii + 173. £14.99 ISBN 0 5712 1509 2.

Becket, Fiona. *The Complete Critical Guide to English Literature: D.H. Lawrence*. Routledge. [2002] pp. xv + 186. hb. £50 ISBN 0 4152 0251 5, pb. £12.99 ISBN 0 4152 0252 3.

Beer, Janet, and Bridget Bennett, eds. *Special Relationships: Anglo-American Affinities and Antagonisms 1854–1936*. ManUP. [2002] pp. xi + 266. £15.99 ISBN 0 7190 5818 X.

Bloom, Clive. *Bestsellers: Popular Fiction Since 1900*. Palgrave. [2002] pp. xiii + 292. hb. £45 ISBN 0 3336 87426, pb. £9.99 ISBN 0 3336 8743 4.

Bloomfield, B.C. *Philip Larkin: A Bibliography, 1933–1994*, rev. edn. BL/OakK. [2002] pp. xix + 226. £45 ISBN 0 7123 4747 X.

Boldrini, Lucia, ed. *Medieval Joyce*. European Joyce Studies 13. Rodopi. [2002] pp. 235. _55 ISBN 9 0420 1409 1.

Bozorth, Richard. *Auden's Games of Knowledge: Poetry and the Meanings of Homosexuality*. ColUP. [2001] pp. xiv + 340. $20.50 ISBN 0 2311 1353 6.

Bradby, David, and Maria M Delgado, eds. *The Paris Jigsaw: Internationalism and the City's Stages*. ManUP. [2002] pp. xvi + 286. pb. £14.99 ISBN 0 7190 6184 9.

Brannigan, John. *Literature, Culture and Society in Postwar England, 1945–1965*. Studies in British Literature 57. Mellen. [2002] pp. vi + 301. £74.95 ISBN 0 7734 7169 3.

Brennan, Maeve. *The Philip Larkin I Knew*. ManUP. [2002] pp. xii + 240. £14.99 ISBN 0 7190 6276 4.

Buning, Marius, Matthijs Engelberts, and Sjef Houppermans, eds. *Pastiches, Parodies and Other Imitations / Pastiches, Parodies et Autres Imitations*. Samuel Beckett Today/Aujourd'hui. Rodopi. [2002] pp. 325. hb. ISBN 9 0420 1094 0, pb. _35 ISBN 9 0420 1084 3.

Burdett, Charles, and Duncan, Derek, eds. *Cultural Encounters: European Travel Writing in the 1930s*. Berghahn. [2002] pp. ix + 211. £17 ISBN 1 5718 1501 5.

Byrnes, C. *The Work of Ian McEwan: A Psychodynamic Approach*. Paupers. [2002] pp. vii + 318. pb. £16.95 ISBN 0 9466 5075 6.

Carpenter, Humphrey. *The Angry Young Men: A Literary Comedy of the 1950s*. Penguin. [2002] pp. 229. pb. £8.99 ISBN 0 1410 0004 X.

Carroll, Clare, and Patricia King. *Ireland and Postcolonial Theory*. CorkUP. [2003] pp. x + 246. £35 ISBN 1 8591 8350 6.

Casarino, Cesare. *Modernity at Sea: Melville, Marx, Conrad in Crisis*. UMinnP. [2002] pp. xli + 271. hb. £52.50 ISBN 0 8166 3926 4, pb. £16 ISBN 0 8166 3927 2.

Cavallaro, Dani. *The Gothic Vision: Three Centuries of Horror, Terror and Fear*. Continuum. [2002] pp. ix + 230. hb. £55 ISBN 0 8264 5601 4, pb. £19.99 ISBN 0 8264 5602 2.

Caws, Mary Ann, ed. *Vita Sackville-West: Selected Writings*. Palgrave [2002] pp. xiv + 370. £19.95 ISBN 0 3122 3760 X.

Caws, Mary Ann and Nicola Luckhurst, eds. *The Reception of Virginia Woolf in Europe*. Continuum. [2002] pp. 480. £125 ISBN 0 8264 5588 3.

Chedgzoy, Kate, Emma Francis, and Murray Pratt, eds. *In a Queer Place: Sexuality and Belonging in British and European Contexts*. Ashgate. [2002] pp. 229. £40 ISBN 0 7546 0147 1.

Chesterton, G.K. *The* British Library *Catalogue of Additions to the Manuscripts. The G.K. Chesterton Papers: Additional Manuscripts 73186–73484*. BL. [2001] pp. xvii + 283. £50 ISBN 0 7123 4677 5.

Chesterton, G.K. *The Victorian Age in Literature*. Edgeways Books. [2001] pp. 159. £6 ISBN 0 9078 3965 7.

Cleary, Joe. *Literature, Partition and the Nation-State: Culture and Conflict in Ireland, Israel and Palestine*. CUP. [2002] pp. xii + 259. £16.99 ISBN 0 5216 5732 6.

Coates, Irene. *Who's Afraid of Leonard Woolf? A Case for the Sanity of Virginia Woolf*. Soho. [2002] pp. 456. pb. £8.60 ISBN 1 5694 7294 7.

Colby, Vineta. *Vernon Lee: A Literary Biography*. UPVirginia. [2003] pp. xiv + 387. £32.50 ISBN 0 8139 2158 9.

Conlon, Denis, ed. *Basil Howe: A Story of Young Love* by G.K. Chesterton. New City. [2001] pp. 189. £12.95 ISBN 0 9042 8774 2.

Coroneos, Con. *Space, Conrad, and Modernity*. OUP. [2002] pp. viii + 199. £40 ISBN 0 1981 8736 X.

Cowan, James. *D.H. Lawrence: Self and Sexuality*. OSUP. [2002] pp. xv + 225. £33.40 ISBN 0 8142 0914 9.

Cunningham, Valentine. *Reading After Theory*. Blackwell Manifestos. Blackwell. [2002] pp. 194. hb. £45 ISBN 0 6312 2167 0, pb. £12.99 ISBN 0 6312 2168 9.

Curtis, Jared, ed. *W.B. Yeats: The Land of Heart's Desire Manuscript Materials*. CornUP. [2002] pp. xxxiv + 273. £48.95 ISBN 0 8014 4048 3.

Curtis, Vanessa. *Virginia Woolf's Women*. Hale. [2002] pp. 220. £20 ISBN 0 7090 6946 4.

Dalsimer, Katherine. *Virginia Woolf: Becoming a Writer*. YaleUP. [2001] pp. 224. $24.95 ISBN 0 3000 9208 3.

Daniels, Patsy J. *The Voice of the Oppressed in the Language of the Oppressor: A Discussion of Selected Postcolonial Literature from Ireland, Africa and America*. Routledge. [2001] pp. ix + 190. £55 ISBN 0 4159 3691 8.

Danielsson, Karin Molander. *The Dynamic Detective: Special Interest and Seriality in Contemporary Detective Series*. Uppsala. [2002] pp. 193. ISBN 9 1554 5332 5.

Davis, Alex, and Lee Jenkins, eds. *Locations of Literary Modernism: Region and Nation in British and American Modernist Poetry*. CUP. [2000] pp. xi + 296. £43.50 ISBN 0 5217 8032 2.

Deane, Vincent, Daniel Ferrer, and Geert Lernout. *The Finnegans Wake Notebooks at Buffalo* Brepols. *Notebook VI.B.6*. pp. 250. €85 ISBN 2 5035 1350 6. *Notebook VI.B.14*. pp. 312. €85 ISBN 2 5035 1351 4. *Notebook VI.B.25*. pp. 64. €85 ISBN 2 5035 1352 2.

Deen, Stella, ed. *Challenging Modernism: New Readings in Literature and Culture, 1914–45*. Ashgate. [2002] pp. x + 223. £40 ISBN 0 7546 0670 8.

Devlin, Kimberley. *James Joyce's 'Fraudstuff'*. Florida James Joyce Series. UPFlor. [2002] pp. xviii + 201. £44.50 ISBN 0 8130 2452 8.

Dilworth, Thomas, ed. *Wedding Poems* by David Jones. Enitharmon. [2002] pp. 83. £12 ISBN 1 9005 6487 4.

Dromgoole, Dominic. *The Full Room: An A–Z of Contemporary Playwriting*. Methuen. [2002] pp. 306. pb. £8.99 ISBN 0 4137 7134 2.

Duriez, Colin. *The C.S. Lewis Encyclopedia*. Azure. [2002] pp. 240 pb. £14.99 ISBN 1 9026 9426 0.

Eccleshare, Julia. *A Guide to the Harry Potter Novels*. Contemporary Classics of Children's Literature. Continuum. [2002] pp. 114. hb. £45 ISBN 0 8264 5316 3, pb. £12.99 ISBN 0 8264 5317 ?.

Eide, Marian. *Ethical Joyce*. CUP. [2002] pp. x + 199. £40 ISBN 0 5218 1498 7.

Fenton, James. *An Introduction to English Poetry*. Penguin. [2002] pp. 137. £14.99 ISBN 0 6709 1100 3.

Ferguson, Robert. *The Short Sharp Life of T.E. Hulme*. Lane. [2002] pp. xix + 314. £20 ISBN 0 7139 9490 8.

Fitzgerald, Mary, ed. *W.B. Yeats: The Words Upon the Window Pane Manuscript Materials.* CornUP. [2002] pp. xxx + 237. £44.95 ISBN 0 8014 4047 5.

Fleming, Deborah, ed. *W.B. Yeats and Postcolonialism.* Locust Hill. [2001] pp. xxxii + 338. $45 ISBN 0 9339 5188 4.

Fordham, John. *James Hanley: Modernism and the Working Class.* UWalesP. [2002] pp. xii + 315. £27.50 ISBN 0 7083 1755 3.

Foster, Thomas. *Transformations of Domesticity in Modern Women's Writing: Homelessness at Home.* Palgrave. [2002] pp. vi + 213. £42.50 ISBN 0 3337 7347 0.

Frost, Laura. *Sex Drives: Fantasies of Fascism in Literary Modernism.* CornUP. [2002] pp. viii + 197. pb. £11.95 ISBN 0 8014 8764 1.

Gibson, Andrew. *Joyce's Revenge: History, Politics and Aesthetics in 'Ulysses'.* OUP. [2002] pp. 318. £50 ISBN 0 1981 8495 6.

Gibson, Andrew and Steven Morrison, eds. *Joyce's 'Wandering Rocks'.* European Joyce Studies 12. Rodopi. [2002] pp. 188. _55 ISBN 9 0420 1547 0.

Gilleman, Luc. *John Osborne: Vituperative Artist.* Routledge. [2002] pp. xii + 300. £55 ISBN 0 8153 2201 1.

Gillen, Francis, and Steven H. Gale, eds. *The Pinter Review: Collected Essays 2001 and 2002.* UTampaP. [2002] pb. $15 ISBN 1 8798 5216 0.

Gilmour, David. *The Long Recessional: The Imperial Life of Rudyard Kipling.* Murray. [2002] pp. xii + 351. £22.50 ISBN 0 7195 5539 6.

Glazier, Loss Pequeño. *Digital Poetics: The Making of E-Poetries.* UAlaP. [2002] pp. xii + 213. hb. £46.50 ISBN 0 8173 1074 6, pb. £21.50 ISBN 0 8173 1075 4.

Gordon, Lois. *Reading 'Godot'.* YaleUP. [2002] pp. 224. pb. £18.50 ISBN 0 3000 9286 5.

Greaney, Michael. *Conrad, Language, and Narrative.* CUP. [2002] pp. ix + 194. £40 ISBN 0 5218 0754 9.

Haberstroh, Patricia Boyle, ed. *My Self, My Muse: Irish Women Poets Reflect on Life and Art.* SyracuseUP. [2001] pp. xiii + 167. £16.95 ISBN 0 8156 2910 9.

Hamilton, Ian. *Against Oblivion: Some Lives of the Twentieth-Century Poets.* Viking. [2002] pp. 352. £20 ISBN 0 6708 4909 X.

Harris, Susan Cannon. *Gender and Modern Irish Drama.* IndUP. [2002] pp. x + 307. £43 ISBN 0 2533 4117 5.

Hastings, Selina. *Rosamond Lehmann.* Chatto. [2002] pp. xiii + 476. £25 ISBN 0 7011 6542 1.

Haule, James M., and J.H. Stape, eds. *Editing Virginia Woolf: Interpreting the Modernist Text.* Palgrave. [2002] pp. 198. £45 ISBN 0 3337 7045 5.

Hawkins, Hunt, and Brain W. Shaffer, eds. *Approaches to Teaching Conrad's 'Heart of Darkness' and 'The Secret Sharer'.* MLA. [2002] pp. xiii + 195. £12 ISBN 0 8735 2903 0.

Head, Dominic. *The Cambridge Introduction to Modern British Fiction, 1950–2000.* CUP. [2002] pp. viii + 307. hb. £40 ISBN 0 5216 6014 9, pb. £14.95 ISBN 0 5216 6966 9.

Heaney, Seamus. *Finders Keepers: Selected Prose 1971–2001.* Faber. [2002] pp. x + 416. £20 ISBN 0 5712 1080 5.

Hibberd, Dominic. *Wilfred Owen: A New Biography.* W&N. [2002] pp. xix + 424. £25 ISBN 0 2978 2945 9.

Hill, William Thomas, ed. *Perceptions of Religious Faith in the Work of Graham Greene*. Lang. [2002] pp. ix + 691. £47 ISBN 3 9067 6788 4.

Hillier, Bevis. *John Betjeman: New Fame, New Love*. Murray. [2002] pp. xv + 736. £25 ISBN 0 7195 5002 5.

Holdeman, David, ed. *W.B. Yeats: 'In the Seven Woods' and 'The Green Helmet and Other Poems' Manuscript Materials*. CornUP. [2002] pp. lix + 281. £51.50 ISBN 0 8014 4034 3.

Hutcheon, Linda, and Mario J. Valdés. *Rethinking Literary History: A Dialogue on Theory*. OUP. [2002] pp. xiii +215. £25 ISBN 0 1951 5254 9.

Ingelbien, Raphaël. *Misreading England: Poetry and Nationhood Since the Second World War*. Rodopi. [2002] pp. 252. pb. _50 ($55) ISBN 9 0420 1123 8.

Innes, Christopher. *Modern British Drama: The Twentieth Century*. CUP. [2002] pp. xxvii + 552. pb. £23 ISBN 0 5210 1675 4.

Izzo, David Garrett, ed. *W.H. Auden: A Legacy*. Locust Hill. [2002] pp. xxvi + 510. $56.50 ISBN 0 9339 5194 9.

James, Elizabeth, ed. *Macmillan: A Publishing Tradition*. Palgrave. [2002] pp. xxvii + 273. £45 ISBN 0 3337 3517 X.

Jeffers, Jennifer M. *The Irish Novel at the End of the Twentieth Century: Gender, Bodies, and Power*. Palgrave. [2002] pp. 207. £32.50 ISBN 0 3122 3839 8.

Keller, John Robert. *Samuel Beckett and the Primacy of Love*. ManUP. [2002] pp. 240. pb. £15.99 ISBN 0 7190 6313 2.

Kennedy-Andrews, Elmer, ed. *The Poetry of Derek Mahon*. Smythe. [2002] pp. viii + 361. £35 ISBN 0 8614 0425 4.

Kirkland, Richard. *Identity Parades: Northern Irish Culture and Dissident Subjects*. LiverUP. [2002] pp. x + 198. £18.50 ISBN 0 8532 3636 4.

Korte, Barbara, and Ralf Schneider, eds. *War and the Cultural Construction of Identities in Britain*. Rodopi. [2002] pp. 300. £42.15 ISBN 9 0420 1259 5.

Laing, Kathryn, ed. *The Sentinel: An Incomplete Early Novel* by Rebecca West. Legends/European Humanities Research Centre. [2002] pp. lxxiv + 227. £35 ISBN 1 9007 5551 3.

Ledent, Bénédicte. *Caryl Phillips*. ManUP. [2002] pp. xii + 212. £11.99 ISBN 0 7190 5556 3.

Levy, Shimon. *Samuel Beckett's Self-Referential Drama: The Sensitive Chaos*. SussexAP. [2002] pp. viii + 181. pb. £16.95 ISBN 1 9022 1046 8.

Littlewood, J.C.F. *D.H. Lawrence: The Major Phase. Studies in Tradition and Renewal*, ed. William Shearman. Brynmill. [2002] pp. xxvi + 299. £25 ISBN 0 9078 3961 4.

Llewellyn-Jones, Margaret. *Contemporary Irish Drama and Cultural Identity*. Intellect. [2002] pp. vi + 182. £19.95 ISBN 1 8415 0054 2.

Lojek, Helen, ed. *The Theatre of Frank McGuinness: Stages of Mutability*. Carysfort. [2002] pp. ix + 197. £9.60 ISBN 1 9045 0501 5.

McDonald, Peter. *Serious Poetry: Form and Authority from Yeats to Hill*. Clarendon. [2002] pp. 225. £40 ISBN 0 1992 4747 1.

McDonald, Ronan. *Tragedy and Irish Literature: Synge, O'Casey, Beckett*. Palgrave. [2002] pp. x + 201. £60 ISBN 0 3339 2393 6.

McGrath, John. *Naked Thoughts That Roam About: Reflections on Theatre*, ed. Nadine Holdsworth. Hern. [2002] pp. xxii + 252. pb. £14.99 ISBN 1 8545 9239 4.

March, Cristie L. *Rewriting Scotland: Welsh, McLean, Warner, Banks, Galloway and Kennedy.* ManUP. [2002] pp. xi + 179. pb. £14.99 ISBN 0 7190 6033 8.

Medalie, David. *E.M. Forster's Modernism.* Palgrave. [2002] pp. ix + 213. £11.99 ISBN 0 3339 8782 9.

Mendelson, Edward, ed. *The Complete Works of W.H. Auden,* vol. 2: *Prose: 1939–1948.* PrincetonUP. [2002] pp. xxxiv + 556. $69 ISBN 0 6910 8935 3.

Mengham, Rod, and N.H. Reeve, eds. *The Fiction of the 1940s.* Palgrave. [2001] pp. xiii + 207. £55 ISBN 0 3339 1885 1.

Meyer, Michael J., ed. *Literature and Musical Adaptation.* Rodopi. [2002] pp. 227. £19.45 ISBN 9 0420 0812 1.

Michelucci, Stefania. *Space and Place in the Works of D.H. Lawrence,* trans. Jill Franks. McFarland. [2002] pp. xii + 178. £22.50 ISBN 0 7864 1152 X.

Montefiore, Jan. *Arguments of Heart and Mind: Selected Essays 1977–2000.* ManUP. [2002] pp. xvi + 270. £45 ISBN 0 7190 5347 1.

Morley, Sheridan. *Spectator at the Theatre.* Oberon. [2002] pp. 217. pb. £16.99 ISBN 1 8400 2247 7.

Mukhopadhay, Samir Kumar. *The Poetry of D.H. Lawrence: Modernism without Artifice.* Progressive Publishers (Calcutta). [2002] pp. 255. 250 rs B0000CPM7F.

Murray, Isobel. *Scottish Writers Talking 2.* Tuckwell. [2002] pp. 207. pb. £9.99 ISBN 1 8623 2280 5.

Nadel, Ira. *Double Act: A Life of Tom Stoppard.* Methuen. [2002] pp. xviii + 598. £25 ISBN 0 4137 3050 6.

Napier, Taura S. *Seeking a Country: Literary Autobiographies of Twentieth-Century Irishwomen.* UPA. [2002] pp. 234. £26.50 ISBN 0 7618 1934 7.

Nash, John, ed. *Joyce's Audiences.* European Joyce Studies 14. Rodopi. [2002] pp. 225. _55 ISBN 9 0420 1113 0.

O'Brien, Eugene. *Examining Irish Nationalism in the Context of Literature, Culture and Religion: A Study of the Epistemological Structure of Nationalism.* Mellen. [2002] pp. xii + 171. £69.31 ISBN 0 7734 7238 X.

O'Driscoll, Dennis. *Troubled Thoughts, Majestic Dreams: Selected Prose Writings.* Gallery. [2001] pp. 360. £13.78 ISBN 1 8523 5289 2.

Platt, Len. *Aristocracies of Fiction: The Idea of Aristocracy in Late-Nineteenth-Century and Early-Twentieth-Century Literary Culture.* Greenwood. [2001] pp. xix + 161. £50.50 ISBN 0 3133 1673 2.

Pradhan, Prakash Chandra. *D.H. Lawrence's Novels: A Stylistic Approach.* B. K. Taneja (New Delhi). [2002] pp. ix + 230. $20 ISBN 8 1705 4317 7.

Quinn, Patrick J., and Steven Trout, eds. *The Literature of the Great War Reconsidered: Beyond Modern Memory.* Palgrave. [2001] pp. xiv + 245. £55 ISBN 0 3337 6459 5.

Rainsford, Dominic. *Literature, Identity and the English Channel: Narrow Seas Expanded.* Palgrave. [2002] pp. vii + 191. £42.50 ISBN 0 3337 7389 6.

Ranasinha, Ruvani. *Hanif Kureishi.* Northcote. [2002] pp. xii + 147. £9.99 ISBN 0 7463 0951 1.

Reitz, Bernhard, and Mark Berninger, eds. *British Drama of the 1990s.* Winter. [2002] pp. 203. pb. _22 ISBN 3 8253 1375 1.

Ritschel, Nelson O'Ceallaigh. *Synge and Irish Nationalism: The Precursor to Revolution.* Greenwood. [2002] pp. xvi + 113. £38.75 ISBN 0 3133 2424 7.

Roberts, Andrew Michael, and Jonathan Allison, eds. *Poetry and Contemporary Culture: The Question of Value*. EdinUP. [2002] pp. x + 236. £48 ISBN 0 7486 1137 1.

Rosenfeld, Natania. *Outsiders Together: Virginia and Leonard Woolf*. PrincetonUP. [2000] pp. 215. hb. $45 ISBN 0 6910 5884 9, pb. $16.95 ISBN 0 6910 8960 4.

Saddlemyer, Ann. *Becoming George: The Life of Mrs W.B. Yeats*. OUP. [2002] pp. xi + 808. £25 ISBN 0 1981 1232 7.

Saunders, Graham. *'Love Me or Kill Me': Sarah Kane and the Theatre of Extremes*. ManUP. [2002] pp. xi + 198. pb. £14.99 ISBN 0 7190 5956 9.

Schakel, Peter J. *Imagination and the Arts in C.S. Lewis: Journeying to Narnia and Other Worlds*. UMissP. [2002] pp. xv + 214. $39.95 ISBN 0 8262 1407 X.

Schulze, Cornelia. *The Battle of the Sexes in D.H. Lawrence's Prose, Poetry and Painting*. Winter. [2002] pp. 307. _50 ISBN 3 8253 1359 X.

Schwarze, Tracey Teets. *Joyce and the Victorians*. Florida James Joyce Series. UPFlor. [2002] pp. xiv + 246. £45.50 ISBN 0 8130 2437 4.

Scott, Randall. *European Comics in English Translation: A Descriptive Sourcebook*. McFarland. [2002] pp. v + 395. pb. $75 ISBN 0 7864 1205 4.

Sheehan, Paul. *Modernism, Narrative and Humanism*. CUP [2002] pp. xii + 234. £35 ISBN 0 5218 1457 X.

Siegel, Kristi, ed. *Issues in Travel Writing: Empire, Spectacle, Displacement*. Lang. [2002] pp. viii + 303. £18.90 ISBN 0 8204 4580 0.

Smith, Andrew, and Jeff Wallace, eds. *Gothic Modernisms*. Palgrave. [2001] pp. x + 232. £47.50 ISBN 0 3339 1873 8.

Smith, Frederik N. *Beckett's Eighteenth Century*. Palgrave [2002] pp. x + 219. £40 ISBN 0 3339 2539 4.

Smyth, Gerry. *Space and the Irish Cultural Imagination*. Palgrave. [2001] pp. xviii + 228. £55 ISBN 0 3337 9407 9.

Snaith, Anna. *Virginia Woolf: Public and Private Negotiations*. Palgrave [2000] pp. 194. hb. £50 ISBN 0 3337 6027 1, pb. £15.99 ISBN 1 4039 1178 9.

Spurr, David. *Joyce and the Scene of Modernity*. Florida James Joyce Series. UPFlor. [2002] pp. xiv + 151. £45.50 ISBN 0 8130 2550 8.

Squires, Michael, and Lynn K. Talbot. *Living at the Edge: A Biography of D.H. Lawrence and Frieda von Richthofen*. Robert Hale. [2002] pp. xv + 501. £35 ISBN 0 7090 5725 3.

Steinman, Michael, ed. *The Element of Lavishness: Letters of Sylvia Townsend Warner and William Maxwell, 1938–1978*. Counterpoint. [2001] pp. xxvii + 356. $27.50 ISBN 1 5824 3118 3.

Tew, Philip. *B.S. Johnson: A Critical Reading*. ManUP. [2001] pp. xiii + 274. £45 ISBN 0 7190 5626 8.

Thwaite, Anthony, ed. *Further Requirements: Interviews, Broadcasts, Statements and Book Reviews* by Philip Larkin. Faber. [2002] pp. xvii + 391. £12.99 ISBN 0 5712 1614 5.

Thwaites, Tony. *Joycean Temporalities: Debts, Promises, and Countersignatures*. Florida James Joyce Series. UPFlor. [2001] pp. xviii + 225. £44.50 ISBN 0 8130 2114 6.

Tóibín, Colm. *Lady Gregory's Toothbrush*. Lilliput. [2002] pp. 127. £12.99 ISBN 1 9018 6682 3.

Ungar, Andras. *Joyce's 'Ulysses' as National Epic: Epic Mimesis and the Political History of the Nation State*. Florida James Joyce Series. UPFlor. [2002] pp. xii + 154. £44.50 ISBN 0 8130 2445 5.

van Hulle, Dirk, ed. *James Joyce: The Study of Languages*. New Comparative Poetics. Lang. [2002] pp. 168. £16 pb. ISBN 9 0520 1977 0.

Verdicchio, Massimo, and Robert Burch, eds. *Between Philosophy and Poetry: Writing, Rhythm, History*. Continuum. [2002] pp. vi + 222. hb. £65 ISBN 0 8264 6005 4, pb. £19.99 ISBN 0 8264 6006 2.

Wachman, Gay. *Lesbian Empire: Radical Crosswriting in the Twenties*. RutgersUP. [2001] pp. xii + 236. $24 ISBN 0 8135 2941 7.

Walton Litz, A., Louis Menand, and Lawrence Rainey, eds. *The Cambridge History of Literary Criticism*, vol. 7: *Modernism and the New Criticism*. CUP. [2000] pp. x + 565. £75 ISBN 0 5213 0012 6.

Ward, Patrick. *Exile, Emigration and Irish Writing*. IrishAP. [2002] pp. xii + 298. £35 ISBN 0 7165 2658 1.

Warner, Sylvia Townsend. *The Music at Long Verney: Twenty Stories*. Harvill. [2001] pp. xiv + 193. $17.95 ISBN 1 5824 3112 4.

Wolf, Matt. *Sam Mendes at the Donmar: Stepping into Freedom*. Hern. [2002] pp. 181. pb. £14.99 ISBN 1 8545 9705 1.

Womack, Kenneth. *Postwar Academic Fiction: Satire, Ethics, Community*. Palgrave. [2002] pp. viii + 207. £47.50 ISBN 0 3339 1882 7.

XV

American Literature to 1900

HENRY CLARIDGE, ANNE-MARIE FORD AND THERESA SAXON

This chapter has three sections: 1. General; 2. American Literature to 1830; 3. American Literature, 1830–1900. Sections 1 and 2 are by Henry Claridge; section 3 is by Anne-Marie Ford and Theresa Saxon.

1. General

Current bibliographical listings for books in the field and period continue to be available quarterly in the 'Book Reviews' and 'Brief Mentions' sections of *American Literature* (*AL*). Annually the *Modern Language Association International Bibliography* (*MLAIB*) provides an exhaustive bibliography of books, articles, review essays, notes, and dissertations that is an indispensable resource for scholars. *American Literary Scholarship: An Annual, 2000* (*AmLS*), a narrative bibliography under the editorship of David J. Nordloh, casts its informed and attentive eye over the year's critical and scholarly writings: the editor and his contributors have an increasingly difficult job to do, given the sheer magnitude of the scholarship they are expected to review, yet *ALS* remains the best and most thorough narrative bibliography in the field.

All students and scholars of American literature will find something of interest and value in Martha Nell Smith's 'Computing: What's American Literary Study Got To Do with IT?' (*AL* 74[2002] 833–57). She considers the enormous implications that developments in computer technology, IT, and digital imaging have (and will continue to have, although not necessarily in ways that are immediately predictable) for scholarship and study. Her primary focus is on the Dickinson Electronic Archives, and her work at the Institute for Advanced Technology (IATH) in the Humanities at the University of Virginia, and similar work at the Maryland Institute for Technology in the Humanities (MITH), resulted in the production of a 'critical digital edition' of Emily Dickinson's correspondence. Part of her essay is concerned with the ways in which digital imaging on the computer can optimize the reader's understanding of the poetry by reproducing 'images as well as print translations of Dickinson's holographic and handmade literary works', thus creating 'opportunities for far more members of her audience to take into account elements of writing practices not seen in print'. She is responding here, specifically, to R.W. Franklin's edition of *The Poems of Emily Dickinson* [1998], which 'depends almost entirely on description and print translation to help readers visualize Dickinson's poetry'. Thus, she argues, access to the physical image of a Dickinson poem can overcome the errors of those critics who 'have characteristically imagined her poems as print objects, assuming that any variable in the handwriting that does not cohere with the regularizations of print is due to her personal writing utensils and that such accidents need not be conveyed to readers'. This is fair enough, but it meets with the obvious objection that Dickinson sought, through her use of the English language, to communicate with her readers and that the words of a poem (which we both see *and* hear), should, if the poems are to survive, be able to bear the ultimately minor misrepresentation that comes with conventional transcription. We can 'fetishize' scholarly accuracy too readily. So much so that we might end up thinking that a 'performative' poet like Robert Frost, who read his poetry aloud frequently (and was rather good at it), should only be studied by *listening* to him. Smith's essay, however, is not exclusively concerned with matters of scholarly transcription of the kind I have described in her work on Dickinson, and she offers some valuable thoughts on digital surrogates, electronic publication incorporating audio and video, collaborative scholarship by email and the internet, and the need to rethink the basic premises of research and its rewards that few scholars in the field will not, in some way, benefit from.

Three volumes have appeared this year in the Facts on File Library of American Literature that will be useful additions to library holdings. *The Encyclopedia of American Literature* is divided into *The Colonial and Revolutionary Era, 1607–1814*, edited by Carol Berkin, *The Age of Romanticism and Realism, 1815–1914*, edited by Lisa Paddock, and *The Modern and Postmodern Period From 1915*, edited by Carl Rollyson. Each of these large-format books runs to between, roughly, 260 and 300 double-column pages. Entries are by authors, texts, characters, institutions (for example, newspapers, periodicals, and societies), and movements. Most of the entries are relatively brief, but those I randomly consulted in each edition are clear, informed, and (as far as I can determine) accurate. Author entries come with bibliographies, but these are not particularly fulsome: that for Herman Melville in volume 2 lists only five works (though Ahab and Queequeg gets their entries as characters elsewhere in the volume), and that for William Faulkner in volume 3 lists only seven works. Each volume comes with a brief introductory essay, a chronology (which is particularly useful for publication dates), and a good index. The price for the set, however, is rather high, and the volumes, as I indicated above, are aimed at libraries rather than the private reader.

2. American Literature to 1830

Richard Middleton's *Colonial America: A History, 1565–1776*, first published in 1992, is reissued this year in a third edition. Middleton has added a new chapter on the colonies of Spain and France, and has extensively revised the bibliography. This is a 'textbook' history, of particular value to undergraduate students, but it is also an excellent resource for literary scholars who seek an overview of historical events and their likely impact on the shaping of colonial thought and colonial writings. The edition comes with chronologies, which head each section (of which there are twenty-one), numerous black and white illustrations, eighteen maps, thirty-five documents (among them the Mayflower Compact, the 'examination' (trial) of Mrs Hutchinson, and the Albany plan of union of 1754), and a very comprehensive bibliography. A pity, however, that this paperback edition is somewhat expensive.

Elliott, ed., *The Cambridge Introduction to Early American Literature*, appeared in an earlier version as part of the first volume of *The Cambridge History of American Literature, 1590–1820* [*YWES* 75[1996] 554–5], under the general editorship of Sacvan Bercovitch. In the earlier work Elliott contributed the chapter on 'New England Puritan Literature' and here essentially the same account (with, broadly speaking, the same range of materials) is amplified to monograph scale. Elliott's first chapter ('Brave New World') establishes the larger context of New World exploration and conquest, but from this point on his concerns lie squarely with New England, especially Puritan, literature and culture. His chapters on literary forms, notably those of personal narrative and history, poetry, and the Jeremiad, offer lucid, informed, and intelligent accounts of the most enduring contributions to English literature written in the American colonies. His concluding chapter, however, 'Toward the Formation of a United States', enlarges the discussion to matters of political culture, Elliott arguing that attention to 'this literary foreground deepens our appreciation of the American democratic literary heritage'. Readers who are familiar with the scholarly and critical writing on Puritan America will find little here that is new or particularly provocative, but Elliott's book is aimed (one assumes) at the undergraduate, rather than the specialist, reader, and in its general clarity and good sense it has much to recommend it.

Interest in the late eighteenth and early nineteenth centuries has tended, in recent years, to focus on the sentimental novel and what might be called the 'emotional history' of the early American republic, and I have had occasion to remark on the difficulties critics face trying to turn essentially second-rate works into important commentaries on the national character. Happily, Paul Downes's *Democracy, Revolution, and Monarchism in Early American Literature* marks a return to more mainstream concerns. Downes attempts to 'deconstruct the revolutionary opposition between democracy and monarchism by considering some of the ways in which the democratic state and the democratic subject inherit the *arcana imperii* of the absolute monarch'. His interests lie, in part, in the persistence of monarchical imagery, and with it the residue of monarchical political structures, and how these lead to the paradox that, while determined 'to defend its purity through an absolute rejection (or exorcism) of all traces of monarchic obfuscation, democratic idealism proceeded to abandon some of the ways in which its own mysteries (mysteries which I have gathered together under the *spell* of democracy) might contribute to expanded political participation and opportunity'. A lexicographical essay on the various meanings of the word 'spell' provides Downes's starting point, but from this point on his itinerary follows a more predictable course through the mock 'executions' of George III in 1776, Crevecoeur's 'tormented' attachment to the King of England, the memoirs of Stephen Burroughs and Benjamin Franklin, which are read as differing models of 'revolutionary subjectivity', and the fiction of Charles Brockden Brown, where Downes addresses the ways in which Brown's characters 'experience independence'. The concluding chapters deal with Washington Irving and James Fenimore Cooper; I shall return to these writers individually later. Downes's is a very learned, informed and, in many ways, provocative book. Some readers may find the 'theorizing' occasionally a little heavy-handed, but, as I have said above, the 'mainstream' preoccupations of this study keep Downes grounded in substantive and important matters. This is an interdisciplinary work, a contribution as much to American Studies as it is to the study of American literature, and one in which few scholars of the period will not find something of value.

Brooks and Saillant, eds., *'Face Zion Forward': First Writers of the Black Atlantic, 1785–1798* is an anthology of writings of considerable intrinsic importance. In 1783, towards the end of the war between Great Britain and her American colonies, some 3,000 African American loyalists, many of whom had been liberated from slavery by enlistment in the British army, left New York for Nova Scotia and established an independent black community at Birchtown in Canada. The broadly anti-slavery stance taken by British courts, notably Lord Mansfield's ruling in the Somerset case of 1772, caused some African Americans to think that their 'salvation' lay with the Crown rather than the newly democratic United States. In 1791 a considerable number of this black community removed to Sierra Leone with plans to establish a free black nation on the West African coast. Out of these enforced migrations emerged what the editors of this collection, Joanna Brooks and John Saillant, call a 'black Zionist impulse to transcend this imperfect liberty and enjoy a secure freedom'. The collection draws together memoirs, sermons, and speeches, some directly based on the Birchtown experience, others responding to it, that offer important insights into the shaping of 'black political and religious thought at the end of the eighteenth century'. The editors provide an informative introduction that contextualizes these black 'Atlanticist' writings in contemporary political and theological debates, and the volume comes with a very useful body of explanatory and bibliographical notes. J.R. Oldfield's 'Transatlanticism, Slavery, and Race' (*AmLH* 14[2002] 131–40) usefully reviews recent work on 'transatlanticism' and the African diaspora, among them Roxann Wheeler's *The Complexion of Race: Categories of Difference in Eighteenth-Century British Culture* [2000] and Helen Thomas's *Romanticism and Slave Narratives: Transatlantic Testimonies* [2000]. Another review essay worthy of note is Robert S. Levine's 'Slavery, Race, and American Literary Genealogies' (*EAL* 36[2001] 89–113), which covers seven recent studies, among them Jared Gardner's *Master Plots: Race and the Founding of an American Literature, 1787–1845* [1998] and Dana D. Nelson's *National Manhood: Capitalist Citizenship and the Imagined Fraternity of White Men* [1998].

Mulford, ed., *Early American Writings*, is a new anthology of writings of the period that competes squarely with other anthologies currently in print, perhaps above all with Myra Jehlen's and Michael Warner's *The English Literatures of America, 1500–1800* (*YWES* 78[1999] 715–16). Mulford extends her range of materials beyond the European boundaries of the Jehlen and Warner anthology, and thus her first section contains a number of written (usually modern) versions of Penobscot, Algonquian, Iroquois, and other Native American myths. Sections 2 and 3 gather together European responses to the New World from the fifteenth, sixteenth, and seventeenth centuries alongside Mayan, Aztec, Hopi, and Yuchi materials (again, largely mythological), but the seventeenth- and eighteenth-century writings anthologized here are predominantly, but not exclusively, English. Indeed, one of the particular benefits of Mulford's anthology is that she includes a considerable amount of French, Spanish, Dutch, German, and Swedish writings about the New World (all in English translation), and those who dip into this collection at random will find their understanding of the Atlantic world in the colonial period greatly amplified by the capaciousness of her selections. Whether this collection, however, is suited to the undergraduate reader (who, in this country at least, is largely preoccupied with English materials) is another matter; and at £55 for the hardback edition the cost is rather forbidding.

Early American Literature devotes the whole of its first issue of the year (*EAL* 1[2002]) to issues of 'Interiority in Early American Literature'. This special issue, edited by Christopher Castiglia and Julia Stern, gathers together five essays, by Kathleen Donegan, Janice Knight, Michael Meranze, Max Cavitch, and Bruce Burgett. The introductory essay, by Castiglia and Stern, addresses what they call 'the history of the human interior' as a means by which we might explore 'the inner life of early America' without the guidance of the '"main actors" of early American history: those who listened to John Winthrop preach aboard the *Arbella* but themselves gave no sermons ... '. To this end the essays by Donegan, Knight, and Meranze 'focus on the role played by the suffering body in the forging of post-emigration consciousness, post-possession coherence, and the evacuated will, describing the phenomenology of such altered states in the language of trauma'. Indeed, Janice Knight's essay, 'Telling It Slant: The Testimony of Mercy Short' (*EAL* 37[2002] 39–69), in particular, is an attempt to give voice to 'the unnarrated captivity' of Mercy Short, whose mother, father, and three siblings were murdered by French soldiers and Sokoki braves in Salmon Falls, Massachusetts (now Maine) in March 1690. Short left no record of her captivity, but after a return to a life of domestic servitude 'she suddenly fell victim to the extraordinary physical and mental suffering that Puritans diagnosed as demonic possession'. Knight's essay seeks to 'recreate' Short's experiences, both by an appeal to what we know of the Salmon Falls massacre and to contemporary feminist and psychoanalytical theory. This is a fascinating essay, but its interpretative conclusions are entirely at the level of the hypothetical. Bruce Burgett, whose *Sentimental Bodies: Sex, Gender, and Citizenship in the Early Republic* [*YWES* 79[2000] 681–2] addresses issues that arise out of what he sees as the complex relationship between democratic liberalism and the public sphere in early American fiction (particularly the writings of Hannah Foster and Charles Brockden Brown), furthers 'a queer history of sexuality' in his essay 'Between Speculation and Population: The Problem of "Sex" in Our Long Eighteenth Century' (*EAL* 37[2002] 119–53) The essay starts with an intriguing account of the uncanny resemblances between President Clinton's 'misdemeanours' with Monica Lewinsky and Alexander Hamilton's adulterous affair with the wife of James Reynolds, a convicted swindler, but quickly becomes a rather more densely theoretical account of the ways in which a 'queer history' might help us understand better what the editors call 'the heavily mediated and contested terrain between the state and the body, institutional and private life, and finally between inner desires and outer senses'. Discussion of the whole issue will be of value to those with an interest in how contemporary critical theory is reconfiguring our understanding of early American writings, but the essays herein often make for difficult, and demanding, reading. Relatedly, Marion Rust's "Into the House of an Entire Stranger": Why Sentimental Doesn't Equal Domestic in Early American Fiction'

(*EAL* 37[2002] 281–309) looks at the fiction of Catharine Maria Sedgwick and Susanna Rowson to challenge the facile critical use of interchangeable terms such as 'the sentimental novel' or 'the domestic novel', and seeks to refine our use, and understanding, of these terms in the light of the 'coerciveness' of the domestic ideology that informed early American sentimentalism.

I have seen little on seventeenth- and eighteenth-century poetry this year that is worthy of note, but Chris Beyers's 'Maryland's "FIRST ESSAY of *Latin* Poetry in *English* Dress"' (*EAL* 37[2002] 247–80) explores the writings of Richard Lewis, the Latin master at King Williams School in Annapolis, who had migrated to Maryland in 1725. Lewis is an obscure figure, known only for his translation of Edward Holdsworth's *Muscipula* [1728], a rather leaden mock-heroic satire that was popular in the early eighteenth century. Beyers's starting point is the question: ' ... why begin Maryland's colonial *belles lettres* with a translation?' Beyers argues that Lewis was driven by considerations of politeness and the tastes of the age, but that, despite these constrictions, *Muscipula* 'discloses the tensions of a Chesapeake society in the midst of social transformation and shows how that transformation was conceptualized'. This is an essay of both literary and historical interest that throws some new light on a rather neglected corner of early eighteenth-century American writing.

Four years of Jonathan Edwards's sermons and lectures are collected in the latest volume of Yale University Press's edition of his works. M.X. Lesser, the editor of *The Works of Jonathan Edwards*, volume 19: *Sermons and Discourses, 1734–1738*, notes that fewer than half of Edwards's writings from this period have survived, but the present volume contains his account of the Northampton revival, 'A Faithful Narrative of the Surprising Work of God', and the 'Discourses on Various Important Subjects', largely sermons about the Great Awakening. The standard of scholarly editing of this volume, as with its predecessors, is exemplary.

Washington Irving remains a major author too little studied, perhaps because of the clarity, directness, and sheer 'uncomplicatedness' of his style. Most contemporary commentary on his work inclines either to the historical (and there are many historical contexts against which his works can be understood) or seeks to enlarge our understanding of him through the vocabularies of recent developments in critical theory. To some extent Paul Downes has the best of both worlds in his chapter 'Luxury, Effeminacy, Corruption: Irving and the Gender of Democracy' (in his *Democracy, Revolution, and Monarchism in Early American Literature*, also discussed above). He deals with a very familiar tale, 'Rip Van Winkle', which, he argues, gives us 'insight into the anxiety generated by an expanded body politic'. He places Irving's story in the context provided by late eighteenth-century American debates about the extent of the franchise, and, more particularly, the evidence of the extension of suffrage to women and African Americans in New Jersey in the 1790s. Downes seeks to understand what Irving's famous story says about the relationship between gender and the democratic revolution. This he calls the story's 'theory', though whether Irving would have deemed his comic tale 'theoretical' is to be doubted. But he 'weaves' feminist readings into the more conventional historical accounts (the story as an allegory of the American revolution, the Dame representing Great Britain and the Crown, Rip her refractory children, the colonies) in cogent and consistently provocative ways. Thus the revolution has 'simply allowed democratic politicians to take over the tyrannical position vacated by Dame

Van Winkle', and while the Dame's 'self-destruction is coded as an end to despotism in the story, Rip's peaceful retirement from unemployment is rendered as a happy ending'. He concludes by saying that to be 'nostalgic for Rip Van Winkle is to participate in the curious double logic of a revolutionary monarchophobia that misses the revolution in the very act of revolting; it is also to participate in an American literary imagination that is more at home with outlaws of "majestic" nature than with the revolutionary founders of the structures and institutions of an emasculating democracy'. This is a major contribution to Irving criticism and scholarship. Bryce Traister's 'The Wandering Bachelor: Irving, Masculinity, and Authorship' (*AL* 74[2002] 111–37) reads Irving as a 'man without': unemployed, unmarried, and expatriated. He argues that 'Irving's literary mobilization of the American bachelor figure serves to domesticate the threat by rendering him simultaneously harmless and authoritative: a voice of genteel charm whose ironic detachment both aggressively and defensively asserts what "true" national character looks like'. This is pursued through readings of Irving's journalism, *The Sketch Book*, *A Tour of the Prairies*, and *Bracebridge Hall*. Traister also contributes an essay on Hector St John de Crèvecoeur to *EAL*. In 'Criminal Correspondence: Loyalism, Espionage and Crèvecoeur' (*EAL* 37[2000] 469–96) he pursues the evidence of Crèvecoeur's acting as a revolutionary spy (despite the 'enduringly loyalist' sentiments of *Letters from an American Farmer*), and concludes (somewhat unconvincingly) that in the *Letters* we find 'an enigmatic author producing a series of layered textual masks which, taken together, begin to find explanation as part of a loyalist attempt to communicate the secrets of America to the British'. The Crèvecoeur that emerges here is a long way removed from the '*intellectual* savage' of D.H. Lawrence's essay in *Studies in Classic American Literature*.

Two valuable editions, at rather extreme ends of the price spectrum, of James Fenimore Cooper's fiction have appeared this year. Elliott and Pickering, eds., *The Spy: A Tale of the Neutral Ground*, in the AMS series The Writings of James Fenimore Cooper, comes armed with all the apparatus of modern scholarly editions (this one, of course, an MLA-approved edition): an historical introduction, Cooper's letter to James Aitchinson of 1821 in which he addresses the issue of 'national partiality', the preface of 1821 to the first edition, the preface of 1822 to the second edition, the preface of 1822 to the third edition, the introduction to the edition of 1831, written in Paris, the introduction of 1849, written in effect from retirement in Cooperstown, explanatory notes, textual commentary, textual notes, a list of emendations, a list of rejected readings, and, finally, a list of word divisions, that is, hyphenated compounds. The introduction is largely factual, but useful, and the explanatory notes are, again, helpful but fairly sparing. The actual text of the novel, however, is presented in a clear and readable face, though whether this alone will induce anyone to spend $115 on the edition is another matter. This is a text we will consult in an academic library. But, David Blair's excellent edition of *The Last of the Mohicans* comes in at only £1.50 for this paperback from Wordsworth Classics. Blair reprints, as an appendix, Cooper's important preface to the first edition of 1826, but not the introduction of 1831, which, arguably, has less importance but should still be read by most students of the novel. Blair's introduction, informed as it is by his extensive knowledge of Sir Walter Scott's fiction, lucidly explains Cooper's indebtedness to *Waverley*, and the notes helpfully clarify matters of fact and interpretation without intruding too much on the experience of reading the novel. This edition is highly recommended, especially for undergraduate use. In *Democracy, Revolution, and Monarchism in Early American Literature* Paul Downes reads *The Spy* as an expression of how 'Cooper found in the figure of the spy an ideal revolutionary whose exemplarity paradoxically demanded that his commitment to the revolution remain a secret'. The novel, he argues, 'dramatizes both the appeal and the threat of democracy's relationship to monarchism: Cooper's post-revolutionary America finds itself in debt to a figure of radical independence whose sovereign obscurity can only be claimed for democracy via the perpetual reassurance of its dissolution'. Arguably this 'over-theorizes' Cooper's essentially melodramatic use of the conventions of masks, confused identities, and divided loyalties, but, as with so much of Downes's analysis in this book, one finds familiar works cast in a new and often intriguing light.

3. American Literature, 1830–1900

In *Romantic Cyborgs: Authorship and Technology in the American Renaissance*, Klaus Benesch investigates the attitude of antebellum writers towards the developing machine age by examining the works of major writers of the Renaissance period. As writers sought to redefine their place within a culture in which technology was growing in power and importance, Benesch argues that they conjured up 'cybernetic' self-representations. Such images helped writers to construct a hybrid identity that sought to reconcile new modes of technological production with established models of professional writing. In 'Contested Ideologies of Authorship and Technology' Benesch examines texts by Benjamin Franklin, Herman Melville, Ralph Waldo Emerson, and Walt Whitman, progressing to a study of Nathaniel Hawthorne's 'Artist(s) of the Beautiful' and Edgar Allan Poe's 'Technology of Discourse'. In 'Figuring Modern Authorship', Benesch discusses Melville's narratives and his representations of technological encroachment. The tension between creativity and technology is most powerfully discussed, however, in the concluding chapter, 'The Author in Pain: Technology and Fragmentation in Rebecca Harding Davis'. What Benesch offers is a fresh perspective on antebellum literary discourse in tension with technological development, presenting the implications of what it meant to write under the conflicting conditions of modernity.

Charting the role of sympathy in American literature from the colonial era to the Gilded Age, Kristin Boudreau, in *Sympathy in American Literature: American Sentiments from Jefferson to the Jameses*, illustrates the relationship between national and personal crises and the recruitment of the sentiment of fellow feeling. Avoiding radical or conservative explanations of sympathy, Boudreau focuses on a range of texts, from John Winthrop's *Model of Christian Charity* [1630] to William James's *Varieties of Religious Experience* [1902], incorporating studies of works by Thomas Jefferson, Ralph Waldo Emerson, Frederick Douglass, Nathaniel Hawthorne, Alice James, Henry James, and William Dean Howells along the way, exploring the complex inheritance of sympathy in America, a sympathy that did not end with the onset of the civil war. Examining texts from both inside and outside the canon, as well as a variety of theorists, notably Sigmund Freud, Jürgen Habermas, and Adam Smith, Boudreau considers the 'cultural fiction' of consanguinity—shared blood—in American sentimentality, as an integral feature of social and political concord as well as conflict, in a broad, detailed account that will be of interest to the student of American studies as well as the more general reader.

In Justin D. Edwards's *Gothic Passages: Racial Ambiguity and the American Gothic* photographic images of twisted tree trunks lead the reader into an in-depth discussion of grotesque bodies, unstable identity, race, gender, and family bloodlines. All these anxieties are woven into, and find expression in, nineteenth-century American literature. Issues of identity are examined in part 1, 'Creating a Self in the Antebellum Gothic Narrative'. A discussion of Edgar Allan Poe's *The Narrative of Arthur Gordon Pym of Nantucket* [1838], entitled 'Hybrid Bodies and Gothic Narratives', probes Gothic realizations of the body through the dichotomy of black and white. The conflict between defenceless victims and abusive tyrants within a racialized framework expresses American recognition and response to the ongoing instability of the master/slave dynamic. 'Gothic Travels in Melville's *Benito Cereno*', Herman Melville's novel of 1855, investigates similar themes of racial ambivalence through the conventions of travel writing. In contrast, 'Passing and Abjection in William and Ellen Craft's 1848 *Running a Thousand Miles for Freedom*' offers an African American intervention into the discourses of racial ambiguity. Shifting images of identity are discussed through themes of the wildly romantic, as Ellen Craft and her husband, William, adopt roles of white master and slave in their bid for freedom. Complications of gender difference are thus embedded in unstable racial (and gender) identities. Part 2 of this study discusses 'Exploring Identity in Postbellum Gothic Discourse' through a close reading of Frances E.W. Harper's *Iola Leroy* [1892]. She uses the Gothic and the terrors of slavery as a method of revealing and interrogating the oppression of black Americans. Harper plays on ideas of slavery, gender, and passing, and this negotiation of boundaries of difference embraces a Gothic trope of white slavery. This is vital, since it challenges anxieties which problematize the conventions of narrative patterns written on the body. 'Genetic Atavism and the Return of the Repressed in William Dean Howells' *An Imperative Duty*', a novella published in 1892, asks what it means to be American in a country of immigrants. The breakdown of ethnic and racial categories is at the core of Howells's narrative, a discussion continued in 'The Haunted House behind the Cedars', which investigates Charles W. Chesnutt's portrayal of the 'white Negro'. Chesnutt's destabilization of racial identity is realized through the force of his Gothic imagination. This Gothic element is fused within social, political, and material discourses to produce fluid images of identity, which reveal human beings' irrational perspective—a revelation that is suggestive of the Gothic nightmare. Notes and bibliography offer useful tools for further study.

Michael, A. Elliott's *The Culture Concept: Writing and Difference in the Age of Realism* is a carefully researched text which begins with an examination of 'Culture, Race, and Narrative', through a close reading of Franz Boas. In the 'letters' section of *Science*, published in May 1887, Boas was to launch a bitter battle against the American anthropological establishment. Elliott devotes this initial chapter to Boas's articulation, both in the article and subsequently, of what culture is and how it is represented. In his campaign, Boas offered a model for the kind of narrative structure anthropology should employ to organize its knowledge, and brought it into the public arena. Elliott continues to explore concepts of culture in the second chapter, 'American Literary Realism and the Documentation of Difference', in which he examines the narratives of writers who produced regional fiction. He explores the cultural world evoked in the writings of Sarah Orne Jewett, Hamlin Garland, George Washington Cable, and Kate Chopin. The work of writers Paul Laurence Dunbar and Charles W. Chesnutt are also investigated, and form the basis for a discussion entitled 'Between Race and Culture'. Elliott then moves seamlessly into an exploration of ethnicity in 'Searching for the "Real" Indian: Ethnographic Realism and James Mooney's *Ghost-Dance Religion*'. Mooney's text of 1896, divided into two separate sections, the narrative and the songs, was determinedly (and unusually) anti-sentimental, and remains a powerful expression of an ethnic culture. A range of fascinating texts is then explored by Elliott, in 'Culture and the Making of Native American Literature', including Zitkala-Sa's *Old Indian Legends* [1901]. The study concludes with a reflection on realism, in 'Beyond Boas', together with detailed notes and a bibliography; fascinating black and white prints further enhance the text.

Susan K. Harris's *The Cultural Work of the Late Nineteenth-Century Hostess: Annie Adams Fields and Mary Gladstone Drew* is a fascinating exploration of the influence of these women on contemporary literary and political culture. Harris has made use of both personal journals and correspondence in order to more fully examine the power wielded by American Annie Adams Fields and British Mary Gladstone Drew as they became leading society hostesses, entertaining the important figures of the day. Fields was married to the influential Boston publisher James T. Fields, through whom she was to meet the most prominent literary exponents of the time. Drew was a daughter of the British prime minister William Gladstone, a position which also gave her access to leading public figures. The book begins by sketching the lives of these two powerful women, and their roles within society. Harris then offers close readings of their diaries and personal correspondence in order to reflect upon the women's participation in wider social and cultural contexts. A detailed study of their reading communities, including personal commentaries on a range of books and articles, offers a rich area for exploration of social dynamics 'up close and personal'. Both Fields and Drew were members of a social elite and, as such, were well placed to transfer their skills as hostesses into the public arena. In this space they fought to develop major cultural institutions, as wide-ranging as the Organization of Boston Charities and London's Royal College of Music. Harris debates the possibilities and the limitations of their public personas, as well as their personal longings and artistic endeavours, in a compelling body of research. Detailed notes and bibliography encourage further study and investigation.

The American Vision: Actual and Ideal Society in Nineteenth-Century Fiction, by A.N. Kaul, reflects on the social and cultural world of novelists James Fenimore Cooper, Nathaniel Hawthorne, Herman Melville, and Mark Twain. The experiences that forged the literary creativity of these men are examined in the opening chapter, which considers the way in which they created reality out of myth. An absorbing essay on the themes and patterns of nineteenth-century fiction succeeds this introduction, in which Kaul discusses the power of American heritage upon the imaginations of these writers. Kaul focuses on Cooper's writings in chapter 3, 'The History and the Myth of American Civilisation', where he uses the Leatherstocking tales as a frame of reference. He elaborates on Cooper's method of rooting his narrative in the reality he knew, while reflecting on his vision of what might be. The mythic possibilities of American civilization are celebrated, therefore, even as a different reality is acknowledged. Kaul's discussion of Nathaniel Hawthorne, in chapter 4, as 'Heir and Critic of the Puritan Tradition', reflects on the opposing forces found in his fiction. *The Scarlet Letter*, *The House of the Seven Gables*, and *The Blithedale Romance*, as well as some of Hawthorne's short stories, form the basis of this enquiry into the tensions inherent in the ethical values of America's past. The religious preoccupations of their founders naturally led Americans to experience good and evil through symbolic representations of Eden and the fall of man, symbols that are evident in Hawthorne's finest work. Kaul's 'New-World Voyageur' explores similar ideas, as he traces Melville's literary vision of community, a return to nature, and experiences of the exotic ideal. Melville's visionary glimpses of Edenic bliss, at odds with the limitations of humanity, speak of disillusionment, itself a symbol of the age. The study concludes with an essay on Mark Twain's *The Adventures of Huckleberry Finn*, entitled 'A Southwestern Statement'. Returning to the theme of frontier life with which Kaul began his study in his exploration of Cooper's myth-making, this chapter recognizes a new vitality in an old theme. In fact, Huck's rejection of civilization and its imperatives echoes both Cooper and Melville, balancing ideas about human fellowship against a world perverted by greed, hypocrisy, and violence. Kaul recognizes a powerful expression of social reality and aspirational ideals as they are documented in the literary output of Cooper, Hawthorne, Melville, and Twain. His study makes an important and valuable contribution in the field of American studies.

Kate Lawson and Lynn Shakinovsky are the editors of *The Marked Body: Domestic Violence in Mid-Nineteenth Century Literature*, a study of fiction and poetry inhabited by rejected and violated bodies. The opening section concerns itself with a nineteenth-century New Englander, Nathaniel Hawthorne, 'A Frightful Object' reflecting images of romance, obsession, and death in Hawthorne's 'The Birth Mark'. This story of male obsession with female perfection dwells on a body that is blemished, and which reaches perfection only through death. It is the reverse of the idea of domestic violence brutalizing and marking the body, yet its psychological depths allow the reader to reflect on the power of the male to destroy. In a chapter divided into three sections, the editors discuss 'Significators and the Female Body' by offering readings of the mark on Georgiana's face. The way in which it is read is, after all, fundamental to any interpretation of the story itself. 'The Object, the Narrator, and the Gaze' considers the act of looking. Aylmer's gaze indicates his social, sexual, and scientific power. Yet the mark also appears to defy his power, which he needs to test, in a determination to create female perfection. 'The Home as Domestic Laboratory' is the concluding section of this chapter. Tracing the movement of Georgiana and Aylmer from their first home to a new domestic space within his laboratory, the editors examine this residence as an experimental area, in which the female is to be victimized by the perverted male presence. Detailed discussion of this text is followed by a comparison of Hawthorne's narrative with that of contemporary British writers.

Realist writers William Dean Howells, Henry James, Mark Twain, and Charles Chesnutt take a prominent position in Sämi Ludwig's *Pragmatist Realism: The Cognitive Paradigm in American Realist Texts*. Arguing that literary realists have regularly been rebuffed by modernist and post-structuralist critical writers for their etymological naivety and non-sophisticated aestheticism, Ludwig proposes that realist texts can be appreciated more appropriately by considering them from a cognitive perspective, which, in its pragmatic origins, is closely associated with the culture of American realist writers. Forging links between realist writing and the pragmatic philosophy of William James and Charles Sanders Pierce, Ludwig contends that the purpose of realism, corresponding to that of cognitive science, charts a learning curve of experience, an approach that according to Ludwig should enhance our comprehension of literary representation more generally, in an examination of literature and pragmatism that will be of value to the theoretically minded scholar.

Laura Otis is the editor of *Literature and Science in the Nineteenth Century*, a collection of wide-ranging materials exploring the development and understanding of science and its expression through the literary in the nineteenth century. American works examined in this study are Nathaniel Hawthorne's *The Birthmark* [1846], and an extract from Herman Melville's *Bartleby the Scrivener* [1856], both of which are used to explore 'The Relationship between Mind and Body'. Texts which focus on 'Nervous Exhaustion' include Charlotte Perkins Gilman's *The Yellow Wall-Paper* [1892], while Edgar Allan Poe's *Mesmeric Revelation* [1844] makes an important appearance in the section on 'Mesmerism and Magnetism'. Poe's work can also be found in 'Hygiene, Germ Theory, and Infectious Diseases', where *The Mask of the Red Death* [1842] is discussed alongside Oliver Wendell Holmes's *The Contagiousness of Puerperal Fever* [1843]. 'Animal Electricity' includes consideration of Walt Whitman's 'I Sing the Body Electric' [1855; 1867] and his 'To a Locomotive in Winter' [1876] can be found in the section devoted to 'Bodies and Machines'. Otis has begun her study with a poem by Poe, 'Sonnet—To Science' [1829], one which is suggestive of the complex relationship between the literary and the scientific which she sets out to explore. A select bibliography is included, as well as a helpful chronology and explanatory notes.

John Peck's investigation of seafaring writers, *Maritime Fiction: Sailors and the Sea in British and American Novels, 1719–1917*, contains two significant chapters for students of nineteenth-century American literature, one that focuses on the works of James Fenimore Cooper, Edgar Allan Poe, and Richard Henry Dana, and another devoted to an extended evaluation of America's most notable sailor-writer, Herman Melville. Throughout this study, Peck explores the relationship between the sea, fiction, and national identity, taking into consideration the impact of social, economic, and historical forces on the sea novel; the chapters that discuss American sea writers follow this pattern. Examining Cooper's sea fiction, from *The Pilot* to *Afloat and Ashore*, Poe's *The Narrative of Arthur Gordon Pym* and Dana's *Two Years Before the Mast*, Peck contends that a national identity, influenced by the economic activity of the emerging American nation, was primarily focused on its ports (with whaling as the largest industry), and was increasingly problematized by American maritime writers, who were aware of the disparity between the social codes that appeared to be accepted on land and the extreme brutalities of the overtly masculine life of the sailor. Contending that Melville, like Joseph Conrad, was writing at a time when the maritime-based economic order was disintegrating, Peck points out that *Moby-Dick* consolidates the themes of Melville's earlier sea narratives, such as *Typee* and *White-Jacket*, constituting a valediction to the significance of the sea in constructions of American identity, as the national focus shifted from the frontier of the sea to that of the land, while *Billy Budd*, written towards the end of the nineteenth century, anticipates twentieth-century sea novels in which maritime references become less associated with maritime economies and activities, forming instead a set of metaphorical resources, creating a private, psychological journey of self-exploration and discovery.

In *Edgar Allan Poe, Wallace Stevens and the Poetics of American Privacy*, Louis A. Renza contends that American literary texts, most notably illustrated by the work of Poe and Stevens, engage with the social, cultural, and political anxieties instigated by perceptions of privacy, thus extending the definition of privacy beyond current psychological and postmodern theoretical stances. Renza takes issue with the paradigm of privacy in cultural studies which locates the 'private' imaginative space as socially constructed and therefore inherently political, arguing that there is a 'radical' privacy in the works of Poe and Stevens that continually resists appropriation, through close textual readings of Poe's essay *Eureka* and Stevens's *Harmonium* poems. Contending that Poe and Stevens jointly ground the concept of privacy in an incorporation of multiple interpretative possibilities, Renza argues for a 'radical' autonomy of authorship that resists elitist claims of individual genius. Renza's investigation constitutes a significant volume in studies of Poe and Stevens, as well as in American cultural criticism.

Daneen Wardrop's *Word, Birth, and Culture: The Poetry of Poe, Whitman, and Dickinson* discusses language, for both Whitman and Dickinson, as an interrogatory, unstable, and disruptive medium. Moreover, she connects these elements to the writings of Poe, demonstrating that all three explore and resist conventional patriarchal notions of gender and sexuality. Wardrop begins her study by focusing on Poe, and specifically 'The Raven' [1845], in which she discusses the fragmentation of the self. The subsequent chapters explore Whitman's 'Song of Myself' and Dickinson's Fascicle Twenty-Eight, before turning to a detailed, although narrow, examination of cultural influences on the use of language. These influences are very specific—alchemy, hydrotherapy, and botany—as they concern, respectively, Poe, Whitman, and Dickinson. A fascinating discussion on the process of death, dying, and resurrection as represented in Poe's poetry and prose follows; the way in which he buries names in acrostics, for example, is reminiscent, Wardrop argues, of alchemists' attraction to secret writing. The alternative medical therapy of water cures is then discussed in relation to the water imagery in Whitman's poetry. While this fashion was one to which Whitman seems to have been drawn, the linking of this interest to that of images of the maternal sea in his writing fails to convince as a poetic strategy influenced by hydrotherapy. The symbolism of the sea as a maternal, mystical force was a common conceit, and can be traced in the writings of a number of Whitman's contemporaries. More convincing, perhaps, is the chapter reflecting on Dickinson's interest in botany. The poet's engagement with Nature, and especially plant life, is indeed powerfully realized in many of her poems, yet, somewhat disappointingly, few of these appear here. Instead, Wardrop focuses on maternal, female, and father images, before concluding with a discussion on the timelessness of the poetry of all three writers. Detailed notes and bibliography provide helpful additional material.

Russell Duncan and David J. Klooster are the editors of *Phantoms of a Blood-Stained Period: The Complete Civil War Writings of Ambrose Bierce*, which explores Bierce's literary responses to his war experience. His writings were explicit, ironic, and truthful accounts and, as such, were doomed to be unpopular. Renderings of the civil war were required to be honourable, patriotic, and glorious in order to sustain the national myth. Bierce's writings about this conflict reflect an uncompromising view that forms a unique impression of those war years demonstrating the writer as essentially destroyed by war, both exhilarated and horrified by the experience. This collection of fiction, battlefield maps, letters, and articles traces the ghosts and visions that haunted Bierce for the rest of his life. Organized chronologically, the study provides a clear and compelling record of the battlefield, the personal and horrifying experiences of the soldiers, and the mental anguish of those who survived. Bierce dwells on the brutal realities of war in a determined effort to confront the truth. 'Patricide in the House Divided, 1861' opens with several non-fiction pieces, written when Bierce revisited the sites of his early battles of the civil war. This section is followed by a collection of materials under the title, 'What War Really Is, 1862'. Here, he explores the harsh reality of winter camp and, in battle, describes mutilated men, the mass of deserters, and the execution of captured spies. Chapter 3 reflects Bierce's own belief that 'A True War Story is Never Moral, 1863'. Most narratives of battle draw a picture of men charging and winning, or retreating and losing, but war happened in towns and villages, it involved the local population, women and children, and this was the kind of war Bierce knew, and wrote about. The subsequent section, 'War is Hell, 1864', records a view shared by many, while the concluding chapter is a testament to the effects of war on its survivors. In 'Phantoms of a Blood-Stained Period, 1865 and Later', Bierce's final years are explored through an examination of his fiction and personal letters, before he chose to finally disappear into the Mexican civil war, in 1913.

Clarke, ed., *Emily Dickinson: Critical Assessments*, volumes 1–4, is a fascinating collection of materials on the writings of Emily Dickinson, one which makes an important contribution to scholarly debate in this field. Bound into four separate volumes, volume 1 offers a detailed biography and examples of early studies of this remarkable woman's poetry. Copies of original materials, such as Genevieve Taggard's *The Life and Mind of Emily Dickinson* and Josephine Pollitt's *Emily Dickinson: The Human Background to her Poetry*, date back to 1930. Two contributions by Millicent Todd Bingham, *Ancestors' Brocades: The Literary Discovery of Emily Dickinson* [1945] and *Emily Dickinson: A Revelation* [1954], are also included. This exceptional material, reflecting the growing twentieth-century awareness of Dickinson's importance, is introduced by an essay, 'Emily Dickinson', written by Denis Donoghue in 1969. Volume 2 considers the early responses of, among others, Thomas Wentworth Higginson, to Dickinson's artistic endeavours, and also includes some fascinating articles about Dickinson's poetry written by poets from different times and different places, including Edmund Blunden, Hart Crane, Ted Hughes, Amy Lowell, Adrienne Rich, and Richard Wilbur. Early reviews of Dickinson's work are taken from such important journals as the *Boston Courier*, *The Nation*, *The Critic*, *Harper's Magazine*, *Scribner's Magazine*, and the *Saturday Review*. All these reviews were published during the last decade of the nineteenth century, many anonymously, and are a veritable treasure trove. Volume 3 is organized chronologically, and considers writings on both Emily Dickinson and her poetry from 1900 to the 1970s, which enable the reader to trace her critical reclamation. Materials both familiar and obscure make this a fascinating section for researching twentieth-century responses to Dickinson's unique style of writing, as she slowly came to pre-eminence. The fourth volume continues to employ a chronological method for discussing this singular poet and her creative genius, as well as the responses her writings evoked. These volumes seek to remain faithful to Dickinson both as a subject and as an influence. Chronologies of both Dickinson's life and critical materials examined, together with a selected bibliography, offer a powerful tool for research and debate on the writings of one of America's foremost poets.

In *Emerson, Thoreau and the Role of the Cultural Critic*, Sam McGuire Worley argues that the most significant social criticisms produced by Emerson and Thoreau were deeply embedded in issues of community and should therefore be regarded as immanent rather than transcendent. Historicizing works such as Emerson's 'Politics', *Representative Men*, and 'The Fugitive Slave Law', and Thoreau's *Walden*, in relation to issues of community—with specific reference to the encounters with contemporary figures such as Theodore Parker, John Brown, and Daniel Webster—McGuire Worley contends that Emerson and Thoreau jointly exhibit an ironic and complex image of self and community. Focusing on work done by key contemporary critics, including Michael Walzer, Alasdair MacIntyre, Charles Taylor, and Stanley Cavell, McGuire Worley's analysis will also be of interest to readers more generally concerned with the social and cultural anxieties of antebellum America.

Rita K. Gollin's *Annie Adams Fields: Woman of Letters* celebrates Fields as a leading figure in nineteenth-century Boston's cultural life. New England authors, including Ralph Waldo Emerson, Nathaniel Hawthorne, Oliver Wendell Holmes, Henry Wadsworth Longfellow, and John Greenleaf Whittier were well known to Annie Fields. She also maintained close friendships with a range of eminent women writers, among them Lydia Maria Child, Rose Terry Cooke, Harriet Prescott Spofford, Harriet Beecher Stowe, and Sarah Orne Jewett. Gollin develops her study in two separate sections. Part 1, 'Mrs James T. Fields (1854–1881)', divided into three sections, focuses on Annie Fields's marriage, followed by the grand tour, and her return home. Here she was to establish herself as a 'conservative feminist', placing her husband's career and ambitions before her own. Forming relationships with Nathaniel Hawthorne and Charles Dickens, Annie Fields also developed a role as a literary historian, helping her husband to write 'Some Memories of Charles Dickens', following Dickens's death. The second section, 'Befriending Women', dwells on friendships with Sophia Hawthorne, Harriet Beecher Stowe, and Laura Winthrop Johnson, and the third section concludes with reflections on the life Annie and James T. Fields led following his retirement. Part 2, 'Mrs Annie Fields (1881–1915)', examines the way in which her life changed dramatically following the death of her husband. Section 4 dwells on widowhood, her close friendship with the writer Sarah Orne Jewett, and the trips they took together. Gollin traces Annie Fields's life as she travelled abroad, and her return to enjoy the social and cultural experiences Boston had to offer her during the 1890s. Her own literary aspirations appear to have been less important to her than those close to her. Her last work was to collect, edit, and write an introduction to *The Letters of Sarah Orne Jewett*, published in 1911. Investigating Fields's life, Gollin reveals an extraordinary woman who chose to dedicate herself to her husband and his career, even while she challenged the conflicting values of her time and place. The impressively researched study makes for lively and fascinating reading and includes detailed notes, as well as illustrations to augment the text.

Darlis A. Miller's *Mary Hallock Foote: Author-Illustrator of the American West* is a compelling record of a woman who achieved popularity and fame as a novelist and illustrator. Hallock Foote published twelve novels, four short-story collections, and almost two dozen stories and essays; in addition, she worked as an illustrator for eminent writers of the day, including Henry Wadsworth Longfellow, John Greenleaf Whittier, Nathaniel Hawthorne, and Alfred, Lord Tennyson. Her images, reflecting a domestic world of families and settlements, were unusual, in that they were considerably more sensitive than those depicted by male artists of the period. Miller's study elaborates on this by using one of Hallock Foote's illustrations as the artwork for the cover of this fascinating study. Miller explores her early childhood, her Quaker upbringing, and her education at the School of Design for Women in New York, prior to her marriage to Arthur De Winte Foote. The experiences Hallock Foote both endured and enjoyed form part of the narrative, and Miller's access to personal family documents enables her to discuss the previously unexplored last two decades of her life. Hallock Foote, as a wife and mother, created homes and raised her family in key western areas of development. Miller examines the opportunities and restrictions of her existence and the east–west tensions in her life and work, as well as her development as an artist, writer, and businesswoman. It is the tension created by combining the roles of wife and mother with that of professional writer and artist that is at the heart of Miller's study, a remarkable story of a gifted and spirited woman who moved west with her husband, and whose work reflected her experiences. Miller makes extensive use of Hallock Foote's personal letters and documents, as well as examples of her literary output, drawings, and black and white photographs to create an inspiring story of a woman pioneer.

Cecile Mazzucco-Than's *'A Form Foredoomed to Looseness': Henry James's Preoccupation with the Gender of Fiction*, volume 3 in The Modernist Revolution in World Literature series, sets out to examine James's critical prose alongside that of a variety of British and American writers to establish that a pattern emerges in relation to a subtextual debate about the gender of fiction. Mazzucco-Than's close textual assessment of the metaphors that describe the writing of fiction exposes an inherent socio-cultural evaluation of the relative worth of women's work versus men's. While the strongest evidence, Mazzucco-Than argues, assessing the production of a specifically gendered language, can be found in James's critical writing, this pattern is also discernible in the work of American writers such as W.D. Howells and British author Robert Louis Stevenson. Mazzucco-Than examines James's non-fiction alongside the work of Margaret Fuller and Henry Adams, as well as of Howells and Stevenson, arguing that James struggled with the gender and art of fiction, yet managed to transcend the social forces of his own era, to anticipate a new era of the modern novel form.

Guert Buelens's *Henry James and the Aliens: In Possession of the American Scene* (volume 10 in the Amsterdam Monographs in American Studies series, general editor, Rob Kroes) substantially locates itself as a part of a key debate in James studies, contributing significantly to work done in areas of cultural, ethnic, and queer studies. Focusing predominantly on the question of identity, particularly as it is shaped in the later style exemplified by *The American Scene*, Buelens argues that James's response to the ethnic other cannot be grasped as an attempt to police, supervise, or master the other, or as the politics of non-identical surrender to that other; rather, he argues that there is a continuum of identity in which positions of control and submission are alternately adopted by self and other, native and alien, at times in possession of the American scene, and at times possessed by that scene. Although Buelens contends that the appropriate term for sexual identity in James's narrative is 'queer', he does point out that the term should be disengaged from any automatic link to the homoerotic, arguing instead that the eroticism of the late Jamesian style takes little or no interest in the sexual identity of the object by which it is inspired, whether male or female, but is instead focused on an object that is itself masterful enough to resist the Jamesian analytical and erotic mastery. An intensely analytical study, this text provides a valuable asset for the James scholar, as well as for cultural theorists in the area of queer studies.

In 'The Funny Side of James: Gendered Humour in and Against Henry James' (in Pfister, ed., *A History of English Laughter: Laughter from Beowulf to Beckett and Beyond*, pp. 153–74), Renate Brosch traces the history of criticism and witticism that James has provoked in order to assess how the attitude of mockery has interacted with the formation of the canon, James being both institutionalized in the tradition of 'great' literature, yet mocked and parodied by certain critics. Arguing that the disparaging criticism that has questioned James's continuation in the canon ironically serves to provide impulses for favourable reappraisals and has therefore contributed to his lasting reputation, Brosch locates those humorous disparagers as more conservative than James in their attitude towards gender, adhering as they do to the modernist assumptions concerning superiority and sexuality. Brosch suggests that, ultimately, the most playful, endearing, and self-ironical features of the Master's writing have been uncovered through such originally negative responses, in an essay that constitutes a useful resource for the Jamesian scholar.

Alfred Habegger's *The Father: A Life of Henry James, Senior*, originally published in 1994, has been reissued in paperback. Habegger traces the life of Henry James Sr. in terms of the cultural context of his era, foregrounding the intellectual context of the day, particularly with regard to education and religious aspirations in the nineteenth century, but also charts the development of James Sr.'s convoluted personal philosophy, which attempted to account for feelings of guilt, sin, and evil, in an extensive account that has much to offer the general student of American studies as well as dedicated Jamesians. Andrew Taylor focuses specifically on the relationship between Henry James and his father, in *Henry James and the Father Question*, the latest publication in the Cambridge Studies in American Literature and Culture series (editor, Ross Posnock), exploring how James's writing responds to his father's epistemological, thematic, and narrative concerns, and how he reworked them in his own more secularized and cosmopolitan world. Taylor examines the autobiographical strategies of father and son and investigates the impact of Emersonian transcendentalism on their work, arguing for a reading of Henry James that is structured by an awareness of the paternal inheritance. Revealing a complex and sometimes antagonistic relationship, Taylor also refers to the works of Walt Whitman alongside consideration of the implications of nineteenth-century Romanticism, reading in detail a variety of texts, particularly the fiction of Henry James Jr., in an assessment that will be of considerable use to the James scholar.

In *Literature and Moral Reform: Melville and the Discipline of Reading*, Carol Colatrella sets out to explore how literature reflects and refracts nineteenth-century ideas regarding moral rehabilitation and penitentiary reforms, through an examination of Melville's narratives from *Typee* to *Billy Budd*. Colatrella's analysis of Melville and reform issues builds on the investigations carried out by social historians into procedures used in European and American penitentiaries, appropriating Michel Foucault's penitentiary paradigm and Erving Goffman's claims regarding the disciplinary power of institutions. Connecting thematic and cultural analyses, Colatrella argues that Melville's narrative strategies challenge nineteenth-century ideas about social injustice, specifically focusing on stereotypical representations of class and ethnicity, and structures of deviance. Investigating nineteenth-century socio-political forces, Colatrella also assesses representations of readers and the reading process in Melville's narratives, evaluating how they illustrate his ideas about literacy and moral character. Arguing that Melville's work promotes ambiguity, political moderation, and a celebration of diversity, Colatrella's text will be of significant import for the dedicated Melville scholar as well as students of nineteenth-century American culture.

The American Novel series, which aims to provide students of American literature and culture with introductory critical guides to American novels, has this year published Yanella, ed., *New Essays on Billy Budd*, a collection of essays which variously investigate Melville's last novel, published posthumously in 1924. In 'Billy Budd and American Labor Unrest: The Case for Striking Back', Larry J. Reynolds focuses on the context of the political and social dynamics of the late 1880s, particularly referring to Melville's long-time concerns with issues of democracy and authority. In 'Religion, Myth and Meaning in the Art of *Billy Budd, Sailor*', Gail Coffler examines the novel as it draws on the mythology and histories of the classical world and Judaeo-Christian civilization. Robert Milder, in 'Old Man Melville: The Rose and the Cross', looks at *Billy Budd* in relation to Melville's late poetry, while John Wenke constructs a close textual analysis of the Merton and Sealts 1962 edition of the novel, in 'Melville's Indirection: *Billy Budd*, the Genetic Text, and "the deadly space between"'. Including a useful introductory essay by editor Donald Yanella, which places *Billy Budd* in relation to the Melville canon, this edition constitutes an informative and accessible critical guide for the Melville scholar. Herman Melville's *The Encantadas, or Enchanted Isles*, first published in 1854, has been republished this year by Hesperus Press, in an edition with an entertaining foreword by Margaret Drabble, assessing the inherent paradox between the bleakness of the scene which yet appears to inspire, in Melville, a sense of exhilaration.

The four volumes of Lee, ed., *Herman Melville: Critical Assessments*, the latest in the Critical Assessments of Writers in English series, set out to chart the expanding response to one of America's most challenging writers. From his initial early success with *Typee*, Melville became almost invisible on the literary scene, but has now taken his place as one of the most significant American writers. Volume 1 of the *Assessments* begins with a series of overviews of Melville's life and works, tracking his shifting reputation, and ends with a sequence of valuations dating from the 1920s Revival period, incorporating Carl van Doren's 1917 entry in the *Cambridge History of American Literature*. Volume 2 concentrates on critical evaluation of Melville's first six narratives, *Typee, Omoo, Mardi, Redburn, White-*

Jacket and most significantly *Moby-Dick*, charting the movement of critical focus from thematic readings to a more subtle consideration of the Melvillean strategy, notably in the narratological studies of Walter E. Bezanson and Harrison Hayford. Volume 3 continues the task of assessment, looking at *Pierre, Israel Potter*, and *The Confidence Man*, in addition to the short stories published between 1853 and 1856. Volume 4 consists of considerations of Melville's poetry as well as *Billy Budd*, with brief accounts of Melville as a journal writer and a concluding section which analyses him from a variety of perspectives. An epilogue featuring pieces by Hart Crane, W.H. Auden, and Robert Lowell completes this very fine collection of the critical heritage on Melville.

Dean Grodzins's *American Heretic: Theodore Parker and Transcendentalism* is a study of Theodore Parker as both heretic and prophet and is a well-researched and compelling account of the man and his time. A scholar and preacher, Parker was a controversial figure who spoke powerfully on the abolition of slavery, women's rights, and the Transcendentalist movement. Grodzins's historically detailed picture of Boston Unitarianism informs the religious and cultural base from which Parker was to develop his own iconoclastic philosophy and theological values. A brilliant scholar and political theorist, Parker's life was one of passionate rebellion. A fascinating and interwoven thread in this study is Grodzins's exploration of Parker's personal life, which he undertakes in order to better understand what moved Parker from poverty and obscurity to fame and notoriety. A generation of New England-born intellectuals, including Thomas Wentworth Higginson and Caroline Healy Dall, regarded Parker as a mentor. Notable men and women, many of whom were controversial figures themselves, counted him their friend and, in many cases, their pastor as well. Elizabeth Cady Stanton was for a time part of his congregation, as was Julia Ward Howe. Parker's effect on others seems to have been the result of a combination of a forceful personality, the exciting power of his prose, and the strength of his ideas. The profound religious, intellectual, and political issues with which Parker struggled, and which drew him into the Transcendentalist movement, form an interesting part of the whole. Naturally, leading members of the Transcendentalists, including Ralph Waldo Emerson, Margaret Fuller, and Bronson Alcott, also appear in these pages, and Parker's relationship with such colleagues is discussed in detail, offering fresh insights. Parker's ideas upset conventional thinking: he challenged the way in which people thought about religious truth. Many writings that Parker had originally published anonymously are used by Grodzins in this study in order to elaborate on Parker's movement from prophet to heretic. These, together with extensive notes, provide a fascinating exploration of a powerful preacher whose iconoclasm was shaped by his passionate responses to the concerns of his age.

William Freedman, in *The Porous Sanctuary: Art and Anxiety in Poe's Short Fiction* (volume 10 in the Sexuality and Literature series, general editor, John Maynard), argues that the indeterminacy discernible in Poe's short fiction, which has been established by frequent deconstructive readings, can be helpfully interpreted psychologically as constituting a series of self-reflexive narratives, incorporating strategies of obfuscation and evasion, which serve to obscure intimidating realities of carnality, decay, and death, most particularly in association with the female body. In an examination of such shorter fiction as 'The Premature Burial', 'The Imp of the Perverse', 'Berenice', 'The Purloined Letter', 'The Tell-

Tale Heart', and 'The Masque of the Red Death', amongst others, Freedman further contends that, although Poe regarded art as a sanctuary from such grim realities, it was inevitably a 'porous' one, which permanently incorporated those threatening realities that it intended to exclude.

Hayes, ed., *The Cambridge Companion to Edgar Allan Poe*, the latest publication from the Cambridge Companions to Literature series, consists of a collection of essays focusing on various aspects of Poe's life and times. The first three chapters look at Poe's life and critical writings. Kent Ljungquist's 'The Poet as Critic' provides an overview of Poe's criticism as well as his life and literary profession. The second chapter, 'Poe and his Circle' by Sandra Tomc, also examines Poe's life and critical writings, arguing that, like his contemporaries, notably N.P. Willis and Rufus Wilmot Griswold, Poe incorporated sensationalism in his literary writing in order to gain notoriety and establish a literary career. 'The Literary Life of Thingum Bob' is the subject of Rachel Polonsky's 'Poe's Aesthetic Theory', which is considered alongside an account of Poe's connections with European aesthetic theory. The next seven chapters examine Poe's generic strategies. In 'Poe's Humor', Daniel Royot positions Poe's humour in a tradition of American literary and folk humour. Benjamin Franklin Fisher, in 'Poe and the Gothic Tradition', assesses Poe in the Gothic tradition of Anglo-American writers, providing close readings of several tales, illustrating Poe's manipulation of the conventions of the Gothic mode. In 'Poe, Sensationalism and Slavery', Teresa Goddu examines Poe's uses of horror as complicated by his indebtedness to anti-slavery discourse, which itself recognized the value of horror as a rhetorical strategy, as much as Poe found literary values in abolitionist depictions of slavery. John Tresch evaluates claims that Poe can be recognized as the inventor of science fiction, in 'Extra! Extra! Poe Invents Science Fiction!', charting Poe's contribution to the genre and how this contribution is reflected in ensuing science fiction productions. The origins of the detective genre form the subject of Peter Thom's 'Poe's Dupin and the Power of Detection', noting that detective fiction was an unknown quantity prior to Poe's invention of master-sleuth C. Auguste Dupin. Karen Weekes investigates Poe's delineation of women in prose and poetry, in 'Poe's Feminine Ideal', locating Poe's fictional women as intellectual manifestations of his own ideas, rather than embodying any notion of an ideal femininity. The following two chapters focus closely on individual works. Geoffrey Sanborn, in 'A Confused Beginning: *The Narrative of Arthur Gordon Pym, of Nantucket*', argues that the only book-length Poe publication constitutes a search for identity, a common experience for young men in 1830s America. Scott Peeples provides what Kevin Hayes refers to as a 'Neo-Structuralist' reading of 'The Fall of the House of Usher', in 'Poe's "Constructiveness" and "The Fall of the House of Usher"', arguing that Poe's ability as a craftsman is reflected in the story of the House of Usher. Richard Kopely and Kevin J. Hayes examine two of Poe's most famous poems, in 'Two Verse Masterworks: "The Raven," and "Ulalume"'. Kopely's close reading of 'The Raven' analyses the themes of the poem in relation to the popular culture of our own time, while Hayes examines the topical references of 'Ulalume' in connection with the formal and thematic devices Poe incorporates. The final two chapters focus on Poe's cultural influence through to the present day. In 'Poe and Popular Culture', Mark Neimeyer considers a wide range of popular culture, including cinema and comics, illustrating how Poe's life and works have become integral to the mass culture of the United States and beyond. Editor Kevin

J. Hayes contributes the final essay of the collection, 'One-Man Modernist', which establishes Poe's influence on avant-garde art movements from the mid-nineteenth century onwards. Covering a wide range of material and critical approaches, the Poe *Cambridge Companion* constitutes an invaluable source guide for all students of American literature and culture.

Henry David Thoreau kept a journal from 1837 until 1861, initially as a conventional record of ideas, which became the source of much of his writing as well as a record of his interior life and his studies into the natural history of Concord. This year sees the publication by Princeton University Press of *Henry D. Thoreau, Journal*, volume 8: *1854*, edited by Sandra Harbert Petrulionis, which covers the period from 13 February to 3 September. This volume reveals Thoreau to be an increasingly competent taxonomist, and also charts the impact of two significant public events, the anti-slavery rally he attended that took place in Framingham, Massachusetts, and the publication by Ticknor and Fields of *Walden*. Including annotations, maps, and a useful and extensive historical introduction, as well as cross-references to previous published editions, this journal will be an asset for dedicated scholars of Thoreau, as well as those readers with an interest in antebellum America.

Christopher Krentz's 'Exploring the "Hearing Line": Deafness, Laughter, and Mark Twain' appears in Snyder, Brueggemann, and Garland-Thomson, eds., *Disability Studies: Enabling the Humanities*, pp. 234–47, a collection that aims to address the exclusion of disability and disabled people from scholarly intercourse, seeking an enabling of language and literature that positions disability as a critical experimental and pedagogical discourse. Krentz explores the comical send-ups of deaf and hearing people interacting with or mimicking each other in Twain's fiction, as emblematic of how Twain and other nineteenth-century Americans grappled with concepts of difference. Appropriating W.E.B. Dubois's theory of the colour line, Krentz suggests that Twain explores what could be termed the hearing line, an invisible boundary that separates deaf and hearing human beings, and in the process expresses both fear and sympathetic understanding, challenging, while problematically reinforcing, stereotypical ideas about deaf people. Focusing specifically on incidents in *Huckleberry Finn*, Krentz argues that Twain uses humour to bridge the hearing line, bringing deaf and hearing people closer together, achieving connection through empathy and laughter.

Jeffrey Alan Melton, in *Mark Twain, Travel Books and Tourism: The Tide of a Great Popular Movement*, the latest volume in the Studies in American Literary Realism and Naturalism series (editor, Gary Scharnhorst), argues that Twain's five travel books are linked not only by the writer's awareness of generic conventions, but by his recognition and manipulation of an emerging touristic sensibility. Rather than aiming for a biographical examination of Samuel L. Clemens, Melton chooses instead to focus on Mark Twain as tourist/narrator, locating the dual perspective of the travel writer and the tourist in Twain's narratives of travel, and proposing a 'tourist theory' as a controlling critical perspective through which to read the travellers' tales of Old World and New. Exploring *The Innocents Abroad* and *A Tramp Abroad* as confronting the limitations of the tourist experience, and as exploration of imagination and self-delusion, *Roughing It* and *Life on the Mississippi* as an attempt to reconcile Twain's tourist as outsider with the symbolic quest for home, and *Following the Equator* as a search for escape from the reality of imperialism, Melton's analysis constitutes a useful tool for the Twain scholar, as well as providing an important guide through the narrative conventions of the travel book.

The latest volume in the Iowa Whitman series (general editor, Ed Folsom), Stephen John Mack's *The Pragmatic Whitman: Reimagining American Democracy*, argues that Whitman's own brand of patriotism can be intrinsically linked to his far-reaching vision of democracy. Whitman, according to Mack, located loyalty to the nation as loyalty to democracy. Mack further contends that Whitman recognized that democracy was more than a political system, being a social and cultural process as well, an idea that is often associated with American pragmatic thinking. He therefore establishes links between Whitman and the philosophical tradition of American pragmatism, particularly its key participants: Ralph Waldo Emerson, William James, John Dewey, George Herbert Mead, and Richard Rorty. Examining Whitman's democratic vision both in its parts and as a whole, Mack also considers the processes shaping and reshaping that vision throughout the poet's career. In an evaluation of Whitman's early and late works, Mack contends that the term 'democracy' is applied to a number of different and at times contradictory ideas, from Whitman's initial conception of democracy as aligned with individual liberty to his later belief in a more prescriptive form of self-government. Mack focuses initially on the 1855 and 1856 versions of *Leaves of Grass* before moving on to consider the impact of the civil war and Whitman's own sexual crisis on later productions, such as 'Sea-Drift', 'Calamus', *Drum-Taps*, and *Democratic Vistas*.

Brehm, ed., *Constance Fenimore Woolson's Nineteenth Century: Essays*, gathers together a series of essays from a variety of comparative and critical perspectives on one of America's lesser-known writers, aiming to reclaim Woolson from the margins of the scholarship of nineteenth-century literature. The first section in this collection, 'Precursors and Contemporaries: The Context of Woolson's Art', establishes the cultural and historical context of her work. In 'Revising the Legacy of 1970s Feminism', Nina Baym argues for formal analysis and aesthetic criteria in her examination of political and social themes in women's writing, locating Woolson as a writer of ironic social commentary immersed in and cognizant of national debates. In a comparative account of Elizabeth Stoddard and Constance Fenimore Woolson, Lisa Radinovsky's 'Negotiating Models of Authorship: Elizabeth Stoddard's Conflicts and her Story of Complaint' contends that Stoddard's real and fictional complaints, relating to domestic duties and the writer's problem of editorial policing is linked to the incompatibility in mid-nineteenth-century American culture of the terms 'genius', 'woman', and 'author'. In 'Constance Fenimore Woolson's Critique of Emersonian Aesthetics', John H. Pearson argues that Woolson inherited the ambivalence of Emerson's concept of ideal beauty, and was thus able to revise that concept, relocating beauty as the product of human experience rather than an escape from it, therefore freeing women from the restrictions imposed by notions of the ideal. Richard Adams's 'Heir Apparent: Inheriting the Epitome in Sarah Orne Jewett's *A Country Doctor*' examines the uneasiness expressed by Woolson's contemporaries, notably Sarah Orne Jewett, as a product of the burgeoning industrial economy. Representations of domestic violence form the subject of Caroline Gebhard's 'Romantic Love and Wife-Battering in Constance Fenimore Woolson's *Jupiter Lights*', arguing that, unlike the temperance tracts and Gothic tales that abounded at that time, Woolson's investment in erotic domination places domestic violence at the centre of the tale, in an examination of the relationship between the protagonist and her battered sister-in-law. The second section of the collection, 'Fractured Landscapes, Mordant Travellers: Woolson's Regionalism', deals with Woolson's classification as a regional writer. In 'Castle Somewhere: Constance Fenimore Woolson's Reconstructed Great Lakes', Victoria Brehm argues that Woolson's Great Lakes texts suggest that the scenes and cultures depicted had vanished for ever, leading to mordant satire or mourning for that loss. Dennis Berthold contends, in 'Miss Martha and Ms Woolson: Persona in the Travel Sketches', that Woolson's travel sketches, produced for *Harper's* and other magazines, enabled her entry into the 'masculine preserve' of travel writing, producing a satire on the conventions of the travel sketch. In '"Clean Forgotten": Woolson's Great Lakes Illustrated', Kathleen Diffley examines the early illustrations of Woolson's stories, revealing the cosmopolitan nostalgia of the nineteenth-century audience for the picturesque, which was at odds with the remote and charmless scenes of isolation experienced by many of her women characters. Sharon Kennedy-Nolle's essay, '"We are most of us dead down here": Constance Fenimore Woolson's Travel Writing and the Reconstruction of Florida', argues that Woolson's travel narratives reflect the complex attitude expressed by northerners towards the acknowledgement of ex-slaves as citizens, reading Woolson against other travel writers in addition to a consideration of the archival records of the Freedmen's Bureau. In 'Corinne Silenced: Improper Places in the Narrative Form of Constance Fenimore Woolson's *East Angels*', Katharine Swett looks at the aesthetic debate concerning plot and description that was conducted by Howells and James, contending that Woolson provides a key to the gender issues that lie behind this debate, as elements of fiction are associated with male and female characters. The final section of this collection, 'The Figure of the Artist: Woolson, James and Wharton', examine the significance of gender and writing. In 'Anticipating James, Anticipating Grief: Constance Fenimore Woolson's "Miss Grief"', Anne Boyd suggests that, while Woolson admired James's writings, she also rewrote and revised his views of women and women writers in response to what she could only have perceived as the patronizing tone of the Master. Kristin M. Comment also focuses on 'Miss Grief', in 'The Lesbian Impossibilities of Miss Grief's "Armor"', suggesting that Woolson encoded homoerotic elements into the story, while maintaining awareness that same-sex 'friendships' were becoming perceived as sexual perversion. Sharon Dean examines the relationship between Woolson and Wharton, in 'Edith Wharton's Early Artist Stories and Constance Fenimore Woolson', suggesting that, where Woolson focused on the nature of art and the difficulties faced by women who defied convention, Wharton de-emphasized the artist in favour of exploring women. A diverse and yet integrated study, this collection will be of considerable value to students of nineteenth-century American writers and their culture.

Books Reviewed

Benesch, Klaus. *Romantic Cyborgs: Authorship and Technology in the American Renaissance*. UMassP. [2002] pp. 246. £25.95 ISBN 1 5584 9323 9.

Berkin, Carol, Lisa Paddock, and Carl Rollyson, eds. *Encyclopedia of American Literature*, vol. 1: *The Colonial and Revolutionary Era, 1607–1814*; vol. 2: *The Age of Romanticism and Realism, 1815–1914*; vol. 3: *The Modern and Postmodern Period from 1915*. FOF. [2002] pp. xxi + 262 (vol. 1), xvii + 262 (vol. 2), xxi + 330 (vol. 3). £175.95 ISBN 0 8160 4121 0.

Blair, David, ed. *The Last of the Mohicans* by James Fenimore Cooper. Wordsworth. [2002] pp. xxiv + 350. pb. £1.50 ISBN 1 8532 6049 5.

Boudreau, Kristin. *Sympathy in American Literature: American Sentiments from Jefferson to the Jameses*. UFlorP. [2002] pp. xvi + 248. £44.50 ISBN 0 8130 2433 1.

Brehm, Victoria, ed. *Constance Fenimore Woolson's Nineteenth Century: Essays*. WSUP. [2001] pp. 256. £29.95 ISBN 0 8143 2933 0.

Brooks, Joanna, and John Saillant, eds. *'Face Zion Forward': First Writers of the Black Atlantic, 1785–1798*. NortheasternU. [2002] pp. x + 242. pb. £13.95 ISBN 1 5555 3539 9.

Buelens, Gert. *Henry James and the Aliens: In Possession of the American Scene*. Rodopi. [2002] pp. vi +164. pb. £22.70 ISBN 9 0420 1280 3.

Clarke, Graham, ed. *Emily Dickinson: Critical Assessments*, vols. 1–4. Helm. [2002] pp. 3,016. £375 ISBN 1 8734 0338 0.

Colatrella, Carol. *Literature and Moral Reform: Melville and the Discipline of Reading*. UFlorP. [2002] pp. x + 340. £44.50 ISBN 0 8130 2568 0.

Downes, Paul. *Democracy, Revolution, and Monarchism in Early American Literature*. CUP. [2002] pp. xii + 239. £40 ISBN 0 5218 1339 5.

Duncan, Russell, and David J. Klooster, eds. *Phantoms of a Blood-Stained Period: The Complete Civil War Writings of Ambrose Bierce*. UMassP. [2002] pp. 352. pb. £17.50 ISBN 1 5584 9328 X.

Edwards, Justin D. *Gothic Passages: Racial Ambiguity and the American Gothic*. UIowaP. [2002] pp. xxxiii + 146. £25.95 ISBN 0 8774 5824 3.

Elliott, Emory. *The Cambridge Introduction to Early American Literature*. CUP. [2002] pp. viii + 198. £14.99 ISBN 1 5555 3539 9.

Elliott, James P., and James H. Pickering, eds. *The Spy: A Tale of the Neutral Ground* by James Fenimore Cooper. AMS. [2002] pp. xxxv + 551. $115 ISBN 0 4046 4454 6.

Elliott, Michael, A. *The Culture Concept: Writing and Difference in the Age of Realism*. UMinnP. [2002] pp. xxviii + 240. £46 ISBN 0 8166 3971 X.

Freedman, William. *The Porous Sanctuary: Art and Anxiety in Poe's Short Fiction*. Lang. [2002] pp. 158. £48.95 ISBN 0 8204 5181 9.

Gollin, Rita K. *Annie Adams Fields: Woman of Letters*. UMassP. [2002] pp. 374. £33.50 ISBN 1 5584 9313 1.

Grodzins, Dean. *American Heretic: Theodore Parker and Transcendentalism*. UNCP. [2002] pp. 632. £23.50 ($39.95) ISBN 0 8078 2710 X.

Habegger, Alfred. *The Father: A Life of Henry James, Senior*. UMassP. [2001] pp. 578. pb. £16.50 ISBN 1 5584 9331 X.

Harris, Susan K. *The Cultural Work of the Late Nineteenth-Century Hostess: Annie Adams Fields and Mary Gladstone Drew*. Palgrave. [2002] pp. 192. £37.50 ISBN 0 3122 9529 4.

Hayes Kevin J., ed. *The Cambridge Companion to Edgar Allan Poe*. CUP. [2002] pp. xx + 266. pb. £15.95 ISBN 0 5217 9727 6.

Kaul, A. N. *The American Vision: Actual and Ideal Society in Nineteenth-Century Fiction*. OUP. [2002] pp. 340. £25.00 ISBN 0 1956 6107 9.

Lawson, Kate, and Lynn Shakinovsky, eds. *The Marked Body: Domestic Violence in Mid-Nineteenth Century Literature*. SUNYP. [2002] pp. 203. pb. £14.25 ISBN 0 7914 5376 6.

Lee, Robert A., ed. *Herman Melville: Critical Assessments*, 4 vols. HelmI. [2001] pp. 265. £375 ISBN 1 873403 50 X.

Lesser, M. X., ed. *The Works of Jonathan Edwards*, vol. 19: *Sermons and Discourses, 1734–1738*. YaleUP [2001] pp. xiv + 849. £60 ISBN 0 3000 8714 4.

Ludwig, Sämi. *Pragmatist Realism: The Cognitive Paradigm in American Realist Texts*. UWiscP. [2002] pp. x + 304. pb. £17.50 ISBN 0 2991 7664 9.

Mack, Stephen John. *The Pragmatic Whitman: Reimagining American Democracy*. UIowaP. [2002] pp. xxiv + 184. £29.95 ISBN 0 8774 5822 7.

Mazzucco-Than, Cecile. *'A Form Foredoomed to Looseness': Henry James's Preoccupation with the Gender of Fiction*. Lang. [2002] pp. xvi + 244. £57.95 ISBN 0 8204 6166 0.

Melton, Jeffrey Alan. *Mark Twain, Travel Books and Tourism: The Tide of a Great Popular Movement*. UAlaP. [2002] pp. xviii + 207. £34.95 ISBN 0 8173 1160 2.

Melville, Herman. *The Enchanted Isles*. Foreword by Margaret Drabble. Hesperus. [2002] pp. x + 102. pb. £5 ISBN 1 8439 1015 2.

Middleton, Richard. *Colonial America: A History, 1565–1776*. 3rd edn. Blackwell. [2002] pp. xiii + 558. £17.99 pb. ISBN 0 6312 2141 7.

Miller, Darlis, A. *Mary Hallock Foote: Author-Illustrator of the American West*. UOklaP. [2002] pp. 298. £29.95 ISBN 0 8061 3397 X.

Mulford, Carla, ed. *Early American Writings*. OUP. [2002] pp. xxii + 1,127. £55 ISBN 0 1951 1840 5.

Nordloh, David J. ed. *American Literary Scholarship: An Annual, 2000*. DukeUP. [2002] pp. xxii + 558. £59 ISSN 0065 9142.

Otis, Laura, ed. *Literature and Science in the Nineteenth Century*. OUP. [2002] pp. xlii + 576. pb. £9.99 ISBN 0 1928 3979 9.

Peck, John. *Maritime Fiction: Sailors and the Sea in British and American Novels, 1719–1917*. Palgrave. [2001] pp. x + 214. £55 ISBN 0 3337 9357 9.

Petrulionis, Sandra Harbert, ed. *Henry D. Thoreau, Journal*, vol. 8: *1854*. PrincetonUP. [2002] pp. 508. £46.95 ISBN 0 6910 6541 1.

Pfister, Manfred. *A History of English Laughter: Laughter from Beowulf to Beckett and Beyond*. Rodopi. [2002] x + 202. pb. $42 ISBN 9 0420 1299 9.

Renza, Louis A. *Edgar Allan Poe, Wallace Stevens and the Poetics of American Privacy*. LSUP. [2002] pp. xxiv +278. £33.50 ISBN 0 8071 2755 8.

Snyder, Sharon L., Brenda Jo Brueggemann, and Rosemarie Garland-Thomson, eds. *Disability Studies: Enabling the Humanities*. MLA. [2002] pp. 400. pb. £28.50 ISBN 0 8735 2980 4.

Taylor, Andrew. *Henry James and the Father Question*. CUP. [2002] pp. x + 236. £40 ISBN 0 5218 0722 0.

Wardrop, Daneen. *Word, Birth, and Culture: the Poetry of Poe, Whitman, and Dickinson*. Greenwood. [2002] pp. 172. £38.25 ISBN 0 3133 2234 1.

Worley, Sam McGuire. *Emerson, Thoreau and the Role of the Cultural Critic*. SUNYP. [2002] pp. xviii + 174. pb. £15.50 ISBN 0 7914 4826 6.

Yanella, Donald, ed. *New Essays on Billy Budd*. CUP. [2002] pp. xiii + 152. pb. £15.95 ISBN 0 5214 2829 7.

XVI

American Literature: The Twentieth Century

VICTORIA BAZIN, STEPHEN MCVEIGH, ELIZABETH NOLAN,
SARAH MACLACHLAN, NERYS WILLIAMS, STEVEN PRICE,
ALAN RICE AND A. ROBERT LEE

This chapter has six sections: 1. Poetry; 2. Fiction 1900–1945; 3. Fiction since 1945; 4. Drama; 5. Native, Asian American, Latino/a, and General Ethnic Writing; 6. African American Literature. Section 1 is by Victoria Bazin; section 2 is by Stephen McVeigh and Elizabeth Nolan; section 3 is by Sarah MacLachlan and Nerys Williams; section 4 is by Steven Price; section 5 is by A. Robert Lee; section 6 is by Alan Rice.

1. Poetry

This year there is a perceptible shift away from monographs and towards thematic studies of poetry that engage with the work of at least four or five individual poets. While there are monographs on Robert Frost, Wallace Stevens, Ezra Pound, William Carlos Williams, Sylvia Plath, Robert Duncan, and Gregory Corso, there are also important studies of visual media in poetry, the queer lyric, nature, modernist museum cultures, and the occult, as well as the gendered poetics of 'self-restraint' and 'enclosure'. As a result, criticism crosses the modern/postmodern divide, tracing poetic continuities as well as identifying aesthetic difference.

It seems appropriate to begin with critical studies of Robert Frost in a year which saw the publication of two monographs on this poet. Recently, Frost's reputation as a nature poet has been re-evaluated by critics who have uncovered the poet's extensive engagement with modern scientific theory. Robert Bernard Hass's *Going by Contraries: Robert Frost's Conflict with Science* argues that Frost's familiarity with theoretical physics provided him with a way of understanding scientific models as metaphors rather than 'facts'. This scepticism combines with a desire to see a 'design' or a shape to the world that is divine or has a spiritual dimension. In this respect, Frost's position as a first-generation modernist put him in a different cultural place to the later modernists such as Pound and Hemingway, who had more emphatically broken with the old order. Yet, as Hass argues, this afforded Frost an interesting and unique perspective on modernity.

Year's Work in English Studies, Volume 83 (2004) © *The English Association; all rights reserved*

John H. Timmerman also contributes to the re-evaluation of Frost in *Robert Frost: The Ethics of Ambiguity*, a study that returns to the aesthetic theory of George Santayana in order to understand how Frost's formal technique is ethically charged. Through close analysis Timmerman demonstrates how Frost builds ambiguity into poems such as 'Design' in order to raise ethical questions for his readers. After making his point with a series of interpretations of some of Frost's most well-known poems, Timmerman introduces other philosophical frames and tests Frost's poetry against the ethical imperatives of rationalism, theology, existentialism, deontological philosophy, and social ethics. The central thesis is convincing, and the lengthy critical discussions of poems such as 'Stopping By Woods', 'Mowing', and 'To a Thinker' are accessible without being simplistic. Timmerman draws on the philosophical contexts within which Frost was working, as well as biographical material, to reinforce his analysis, but then expands the discussion to include a consideration of ethical questions that dominated late nineteenth- and twentieth-century thinking. In doing so, he makes a case for Frost's significance to modernism as well as his significance as a poet in the twenty-first century.

However, Timmerman's thesis is roundly challenged by an article published this year by the Frostian scholar Peter J. Stanlis, who argues that Frost rejected Santayana's aesthetic philosophy. In 'Robert Frost and Creative Evolution' (*ModA* 44[2002] 107–28) Stanlis provides ample evidence supporting his claim that Frost's aesthetic theory was grounded in Puritanism and a poetics of self-restraint. He then goes on to link Frost's poetry to the concept of evolution in biological and aesthetic terms. Martin Bidney's 'The Secretive-Playful Epiphanies of Robert Frost: Solitude, Companionship, and the Ambivalent Imagination' (*PLL* 38[2002] 270–94) takes a very different approach to Frost by focusing on a pattern of epiphanic moments in Frost's poetry. According to Bidney, these epiphanies not only have a powerful impact on the reader but can also be analysed using objective phenomenological criteria. These criteria, taken from the thinking of Gaston Bachelard, identify five key component features of the epiphany which are then examined in relation to several well-known poems by Frost. Bidney's approach illustrates both the strengths and weaknesses of a formalist critical approach.

Robert Frost is one of the three poets Richard Hoffpauir considers in *The Contemplative Poetry of Edwin Arlington Robinson, Robert Frost and Yvor Winters*. Hoffpauir is concerned with a neglected tradition of American poetry that emerged alongside modernism at the beginning of the twentieth century. This tradition is defined by Hoffpauir largely in opposition to an Emersonian pragmatism, and deliberately resists the influence of pragmatist philosophers such as William James and John Dewey. Thus Hoffpauir's study clearly offers a radically different reading of Frost to the critical construction of the poet that has emerged in the work of Richard Poirier and Frank Lentricchia. Clearly this study is written, in part, to recover the work of two marginal poetic figures: Robinson and Winters. While the discussion of Robinson raises some interesting questions, the chapter on Winters is less convincing, largely because his poetry is not nearly as good as his critical work.

The other modernist poet who continues to be a popular subject of critical debate is Wallace Stevens. This year sees the publication of an important monograph on Stevens that contributes to the debate concerning the relation between Stevens's poetics and what Alan Filreis calls 'the actual world'. Justin Quinn's *Gathered Beneath the Storm: Wallace Stevens, Nature and Community* refuses to oppose nature to culture and/or society; instead, the poet's figurative use of landscapes is a space within which to meditate 'on the way that human societies produce cultural and political meaning'. While Quinn acknowledges his debt to critics such as Filreis and James Logenbach, at the same time he raises objections to the historicist approach adopted by both. His own analysis maintains the 'supreme fiction' of an imaginative poetic site that is not separate from ideology but nevertheless distinct from it. To put this in slightly different terms, for Stevens ideology is 'readable'. This study is aware of the ideological pressures upon poetry but doesn't allow that awareness to disrupt the notion that poetic language is a discourse distinct from the political and ideological. Another reconfiguration of Stevens within a historical frame is offered by Eric Keenaghan in 'A Virile Poet in the Borderlands: Wallace Stevens's Reimagining of Race and Masculinity' (*Mo/Mo* 9[2002] 439–62). Here Keenaghan offers a corrective to Frank Lentricchia's *Ariel and the Police* (UWiscP [1988]) by suggesting that Stevens's 'gender trouble' is not an individual psychological struggle but a more public and social struggle to conceive of poetry as an 'erotic engagement' with 'the real'.

While Sara J. Ford's *Gertrude Stein and Wallace Stevens: The Performance of Modern Consciousness* does not devote many pages to poetry, it does begin with a very useful chapter on the modernist interrogation of the sovereign subject, offering a clear and concise account of the most significant ideas shaping modernist writing. Her central argument is that both Stein and Stevens 'stage the modern self' in their work, particularly in their plays and when they deployed theatrical metaphors in their poetry. Stein's plays are rarely considered, so it is interesting to read discussions of *Listen to Me*, *What Happened*, and *A Play Called Not Now*, as well as the better-known *Four Saints in Three Acts*. Stevens's early experiments in verse drama have been given even less critical attention, so Ford's examination of *Three Travellers Watch a Sunrise*, *Carlos Among the Candles*, and *Bowl, Cat and Broomstick* provides an insight not only into neglected work but also into how the dramatic work relates to Stevens's poetry.

In *Edgar Allan Poe, Wallace Stevens and the Poetics of American Privacy*, Louis A. Renza defines privacy in terms of an otherness which can exist beyond or outside public constellations. Beginning with Hannah Arendt's assertion that the 'intimate life' is a shadowy, troubling realm that can only be known once 'deprivatized and deindividualized', Senza's reading of both Poe and Stevens concerns their attempts to resist deprivatization. The three chapters on Stevens focus on *Harmonium*, the poet's first collection, allowing space for full and lengthy exegeses. For instance, Renza's rereading of 'Anecdote of the Jar' is subtle and persuasive, identifying this familiar poem as having a political charge but yet insisting upon its unwillingness to engage directly with its public. This tension at the heart of Stevens's poetry, the problem of including a public 'he instinctively wishes to occlude', offers an alternative perspective on Stevens that falls awkwardly and interestingly between historicist and formalist readings of his work. While acknowledging that Stevens adopts a 'radically private position in writing', Renza also provides an account of what privacy might mean in different socio-historical contexts.

Stevens is also prominent in Sarah Riggs's *Word Sightings: Poetry and Visual Media in Stevens, Bishop, and O'Hara*, which draws on recent work that examines the intersection between visual art and textual theory by critics such as Naomi Schor, Johanna Drucker, and W.J.T. Mitchell. Riggs spends time with individual poems: for instance, Stevens's 'An Ordinary Evening in New Haven' is given a lengthy exegesis, as is Bishop's 'The Fish'. The focus on Stevens's interest in postcards and vicarious forms of travel develops into a convincing argument that his poetry is non-mimetic and rejects the ekphrastic tradition that he is sometimes associated with. Bishop's desire for developing an enhanced way of seeing is described in terms of a form of writing inscribed over the image side of a postcard. O'Hara's poetry seems much more comfortable with the new technologies of his age, particularly the cinema, resulting in what Riggs describes as a 'collapse of the technology-poetry paradox'. The discussion of the work of all three poets is insightful and suggestive, offering new ways of thinking about modernist and postmodernist poetics.

The consistently excellent *Wallace Stevens Journal* continues to publish important criticism not only on Stevens but on his contemporaries as well. There is a nautical theme to the first number of the journal (*WSJour* 26:i[2002]) where oceans, shores and the sea are poetic motifs that recur. Kay Harel's 'Again Is an Oxymoron: William James's Ideas on Repetition and Wallace Stevens' "Sea Surface Full of Clouds"' (*WSJour* 26[2002] 3–14) uses William James's *Principles of Psychology* to make some sense of Stevens's unfathomable poem. B.J. Leggett's 'Anecdotes of Stevens' Drunken Sailor' (*WSJour* 26[2002] 15–21) examines 'Disillusionment of Ten O'Clock', claiming that this seemingly simple poem has been widely misunderstood. '"Receding shores that never touch with inarticulate pang": Stevens and the Language of Touch' (*WSJour* 26[2002] 22–40) is Carolyn Masel's consideration of the metaphorical weight of touch in Stevens's poetry. In a survey of the philosophical scene of modernism, Temenuga Trifonova's 'The Poetry of Matter: Stevens and Bergson' (*WSJour* 26[2002] 41–69) attempts to clarify Stevens's aesthetic theory. There are two essays that discuss the same poem and offer contrasting perspectives on a familiar subject: Wallace Martin's 'She and/or Sea in "The Idea of Order at Key West"' (*WSJour* 26[2002] 88–98) and Aaron McCollough's '"Desiring Production" in Stevens' "The Idea of Order at Key West"' (*WSJour* 26[2002] 99–110). Finally, in John Beckman's 'Good, Bad, and Supreme Risks: Wallace Stevens' Surety Claim On/Against the Death of the Father' (*WSJour* 26[2002] 70–87), 'Notes Toward a Supreme Fiction' is read alongside Stevens's insurance essays in an attempt to show the tensions between the poet's work and his poetic play with the sign.

A special issue of this journal (*WSJour* 26:ii[2002]) publishes an important group of essays circulating around Marjorie Perloff's influential essay 'Pound/Stevens: Whose Era?' [1982]. Perloff herself begins by contextualizing her own essay in '"Pound/Stevens: Whose Era?" Revisited' (*WSJour* 26[2002] 135–42), describing the marginal status of Pound and the way in which Harold Bloom canonized Stevens as the great poet of the twentieth century. She then goes on to suggest how the critical construction of modernism has shifted in the twenty years since the publication of her seminal essay. In 'Bloody Battle-Flags and Cloudy Days: Metaphor in Pound and Stevens' (*WSJour* 26[2002] 143–59) and 'The Pound/ Stevens Era' (*WSJour* 26[2002] 228–50) Patricia Rae and Charles Altieri, respectively, focus on the similarities between these poets rather than their differences. Likewise, Leon Surette's 'Pound vs. Stevens: Old Wine in New Bottles or New Bottles for Old Wine' (*WSJour* 26[2002] 251–66) is not at all convinced by Perloff's argument, finding that there is a case to be made for putting Stevens where

Perloff places Pound, as a modernist rather than a Romantic. Douglas Mao's 'How To Do Things with Modernism' (*WSJour* 26[2002] 160–80) mulls over the implications of Perloff's essay and then suggests that the central questions raised by modernism are now being returned to. Alan Filreis's essay, 'Stevens/Pound in the Cold War' (*WSJour* 26[2002] 181–93) returns to the post-war critical response to Stevens and Pound and finds little consensus, little sense that the poetry stood for any one thing. The polarization of modernism, the splitting between Pound and Stevens, came much later but, Filreis argues, has since been abandoned. In 'Genius For Sale' (*WSJour* 26[2002] 194–210) Rachel Blau DuPlessis is also troubled by the business of setting two 'great' poets up against each other, but her objections are concerned not with what this opposition does to our understanding of modernism but with the underlying assumptions such a question is based upon. These assumptions, argues DuPlessis, tend to reinforce the notion that genius is more likely to manifest itself in the form of a white man than in that of a woman or person of colour. Rather than relying upon two towering poetic figures as modernism's goalposts, DuPlessis suggests that we see that 'poems are made in affiliative networks'. 'Poets/Readers: Whose Era?' (*WSJour* 26[2002] 211–27) is Vincent N. Lolordo's discussion of Perloff's essay in relation to contemporary American poetry. Focusing on John Ashbery's book-length poem *Flow Chart*, Lolordo finds that constructing poetic polarities tends to miss the point about the most interesting and ambivalent poetry being written.

This leads us on to a consideration of criticism on Pound who, judging by this year's criticism, is still very much at the centre of debates on modernism. In *The Poetics of the Ideogram*, Songpin Jin examines Pound's ideogrammatic method from his early imagist phase through to *The Cantos*. The work of Ernest Fenollosa figures prominently in the opening chapter, but Jin goes on to argue that Pound moved away from Fenollosa's interpretations of the Chinese written character in order to develop his own distinct poetic method. In fact, Pound's technique is based on a variety of different poetic methods which are intertextually bound together in a similar manner to the ideogram itself. Jin also examines Pound's translations of Noh plays as well as the influence of Confucian canons and metaphors on Pound's aesthetic theory and practice. Most importantly, Jin regards Pound's translation work as a means of engaging creatively with ideas, and does not find the poet's inaccuracies problematic when read in this way. This is a dense and highly specialized study of Pound that provides a detailed analysis of the cultural traditions of the ideogram.

Pound is also the subject of Pratt, ed., *Ezra Pound: Nature and Myth*, based on papers presented at the fifteenth Ezra Pound International Conference in Rapallo in 1993. As such, this volume contains a series of brief and rather quirky essays that engage with a wide variety of intertexts and influences at work in Pound's poetry. The collection begins with an essay by Pound himself, entitled 'European Paideuma', never before published in its entirety. This is followed by an account by Massimo Bacigalupo of the essay's publication history. Anne Conover Carson's biographical account of Olga Rudge's relationship with Pound, 'Her Name Was Courage: Olga Rudge, Pound's Muse and the "Circe/Aphrodite" of *The Cantos*' offers a fascinating insight into the presence of Olga in Pound's poetry as well as her presence in his life. Other essays deal more explicitly with myth, such as Massimo Pesaresi's 'Ezra Pound, A Poet from Hellas: The Dionysian Persona', Alan

Peacock's 'Pound, Catullus and Imagism', and Peter Makin's 'Myth and *Hagoromo*'. Michael Faherty's 'The Myth of the Mad Celtic King: Another Voice in the *Pisan Cantos*?' examines the influence of Yeats on Pound's later work, while William Pratt considers Pound's representation of hell in 'Pound's Hells, Real and Imaginary'. Richard Caddel's contribution, 'Secretaries of Nature: Towards a Theory of Modernist Ecology', is a rather rough and ready essay that offers some suggestions for an ethical understanding of 'nature' in poetry. Peter Nicholls's 'Against Nature: Time and Artifice in Pound's Early Work' suggests that Pound treats history as a textual object to be worked upon in order to free the poet from a debilitating nostalgia for the past.

Another essay on Pound by Peter Nicholls, '"Arid Clarity": Ezra Pound, Mina Loy, and Jules Laforgue' (*YES* 32[2002] 52–64), suggests that reading Loy helped Pound to formulate a critical theory for his own poetry. Much of Nicholls's argument is based on Pound's 1918 review of Mina Loy and Marianne Moore, though he seems reluctant to consider Moore's influence on Pound. While Nicholls complains that there is little information concerning the Pound–Loy relationship, there is ample evidence indicating that Pound was indebted to Moore. Peter Wilson's essay, 'Prefiguring Cantonic Time: Temporal Categories in the *Collected Shorter Poems* of Ezra Pound' (*YES* 32[2002] 65–76), suggests that it is not only in *The Cantos* that Pound develops what is described as 'cantonic time'. A rather different approach to Pound is offered by Rebecca Beasley, who considers the influence of Whistler on Pound's poetics. 'Ezra Pound's Whistler' (*AL* 74[2002] 485–516) examines in detail the poet's writing on Whistler and other visual artists, thereby showing modernism's relation to *fin-de-siècle* aestheticism. In 'Propounding Modernist Maleness: How Pound Managed a Muse' (*Mo/Mo* 9[2002] 489–505), Rachel Blau DuPlessis deals specifically with 'Portrait d'une Femme' in relation to Florence Farr, the original 'muse' of the poem. As usual, DuPlessis's argument is very convincing, combining as it does a sensitivity to textuality as well as a sense of the text's social and ideological embeddedness. Finally, Matther Hofer's 'Modernist Polemic: Ezra Pound v. "the perverters of language"' (*Mo/Mo* 9[2002] 581–604) provides an insight into the trajectory of Pound's career from the early 1920s to his radio diatribes of the 1930s. Particularly useful is the account of Pound's Hell Cantos, providing as it does the names of those public figures Pound caricatured in these poems.

William Carlos Williams and Sylvia Plath have little in common as poets, but this year the work of both is re-evaluated in historicist terms. Paul R. Cappucci, *William Carlos Williams' Poetic Response to the 1913 Paterson Silk Strike* uncovers a radical and politicized moment in American poetic history. In this respect, it has much in common with several other recent accounts of left poetry, such as Cary Nelson's *Repression and Recovery* (UWiscP [1989]). However, while Cappucci provides a considerable amount of historical detail concerning the strike itself and the history of the industrialization of Paterson, he seems unaware of, or unwilling to acknowledge how his approach is part of, a larger critical project concerned with revitalizing the relation between poetry and politics. The involvement of the Industrial Workers of the World, particularly their charismatic leader, 'Big' Bill Haywood, as well as the presence of John Reed and other left intellectuals provides a fascinating insight into pre-First World War cultural politics in America. However, the analysis of 'The Wanderer: A Rococo Study', the poem Williams wrote in response to the strike, seems unable to engage with its formal complexities. While this poem is described by Williams himself as 'the genesis of *Paterson*', there is little sense here of how the poet moved from the local accounts of Paterson's history to the large-scale epic poem of his later years.

Robin Peel's *Writing Back: Sylvia Plath and Cold War Politics* describes itself as a materialist reading of Plath's later poetry and prose. The problem here is that, while Peel convincingly demonstrates the limitations of the biographical approach to Plath, there is little new evidence of Plath's poetic engagement with contemporary political issues. It is only in chapter 8 that Peel begins to examine the *Ariel* poems, and even here there is little detailed analysis of individual poems, but rather recourse to journal entries and newspaper articles Plath might have been reading at the time she was composing her poetry. The use of Holocaust imagery in Plath's work is related to contemporary events such as the Cuban missile crisis and, more widely, to the prevailing sense of a nuclear threat during the late 1950s and early 1960s, though Peel finds it difficult to make explicit links between these wider cultural contexts and the poetic texts she is reading. Peel's study of Plath is ambitious, but it lacks the detailed textual analysis needed to clearly demonstrate the ways in which the poet was responding to her political and social environment. Having said that, what makes this book worth reading is Peel's use of archival material which offers the reader an insight into Plath's method of composition, suggesting some interesting textual relationships between the poetry and prose.

While Peel's book-length study lacks critical depth, it has good intentions. As Peel rightly points out, many studies of Plath's poetry read her work as an expression of her interior life rather than as an engagement with public life. We can find an example of this kind of critical approach in Jooyoung Park's '"I could kill a woman or wound a man": Melancholic Rage in the Poems of Sylvia Plath' (*WS* 34[2002] 467–98). Park adopts a psychoanalytical approach to Plath, drawing on the work of Freud as well as feminist psychoanalytical theory. The focus is primarily on Plath's feelings of rage towards her mother and her expression of that rage in her poetry. While critics such as Jacqueline Rose, in *The Haunting of Sylvia Plath*, are able to use psychoanalytical theory to suggest the political tensions in Plath's work, Park's readings don't seem to be able to move beyond an examination of Plath's psychic life, and thus fail to engage in a significant way with her poetry.

In contrast to this rather limited approach is Emma Jones's '"Silence of another order": Negativity and Trope in the Late Poems of Sylvia Plath' (*SSEng* 28[2002] 87–102), which examines the playful, excessive, and textual nature of Plath's poetry by attending to certain frequently used tropes. Jones's readings of individual poems are perceptive encounters with Plath's poetic language, identifying, for instance, the use of whiteness as it reappears in poems such as 'Insomniac', 'The Rival', 'A Life', and 'Whitsun'. Whiteness here is a sign of a lack, a 'landscape of empty surfaces' that establishes an absence as presence is simultaneously figured. Also resisting the biographical reading is Ellen Miller's 'Philosophizing with Sylvia Plath: An Embodied Hermeneutic of Color in "Ariel"' (*PhT* 46[2002] 91–101). Here Miller focuses on that elusive late poem by Plath, using a phenomenological approach that owes much to the work of Merleau-Ponty but that also draws on the feminist philosophy of Luce Irigaray, showing how philosophical approaches are capable of offering original insights into Plath's poetry. Finally, Andrea Gerbig and Anja Muller-Wood use linguistic theory as a way of breaking free from the pathological reading of Plath's poetry that has become so popular in recent years. In 'Trapped in Language: Aspects of Ambiguity and Intertextuality in Selected Poetry and Prose by Sylvia Plath' (*Style* 36[2002] 76–92), they argue that the essential ambiguity of language itself and the intertextual nature of the literary text suggest that Plath's poems are much more complex than biographical readings would suggest. Finally, Gillian Banner returns to the controversy surrounding Plath's use of Holocaust imagery in 'Sylvia Plath and Holocaust Poetry' (*Immigrants and Minorities* 21[2002] 231–48). Banner relies heavily on Jacqueline Rose, though she supplements these psychoanalytical insights with the work of James Young, who writes on memory and the Holocaust. Her close readings of both 'The Thin People' and 'Little Fugue' help readers to see how Plath's imagery operates at a psychic and social level.

Plath's fellow 'confessional', Robert Lowell, receives scant attention this year, inspiring just one journal article. Wai Chee Dimock's 'Non-Newtonian Time: Robert Lowell, Roman History, Vietnam War' (*AL* 74[2002] 911–31) offers a highly original postcolonial perspective on this poet. In the 1960s, argues Dimock, Lowell's poetry disrupts the progressive, linear conception of time that reinforces imperialism; more specifically, Lowell's poetry offers a critique of US imperialism in Vietnam as the poet publicly declared his opposition to the war.

Staying with post-war poetry, it seems that the work of Robert Duncan is beginning to be more widely recognized and valued. This year sees the publication of Peter O'Leary's *Gnostic Contagion: Robert Duncan and the Poetry of Illness*, which begins with an important chapter on the relation between H.D. and Duncan and their common fascination with forms of mysticism, psychoanalysis, and illness. O'Leary also offers readings of some of Duncan's most important work. For instance, 'Often I Am Permitted to Return to a Meadow' is lucidly discussed in relation to a recurring dream of Duncan's where he finds himself at the centre of a circle of children playing, somehow both chosen and excluded. It is the poetic interpretation of this dream that is at the centre of Duncan's most important work, with its repeated return to meadows and fields, places of order that are bounded by chaos. Illness, for O'Leary, is a way of allowing that chaos to enter the psyche in both creative and destructive ways; this thesis is supported by a range of references to gnosticism, spiritualism, and non-Western religious beliefs. O'Leary doesn't attempt to provide any sort of coverage of the full range of Duncan's poetry, but he does examine Duncan's influence on the poetry of Nathaniel Mackey and John Taggart. This is a significant publication on the work of a poet who has received relatively little critical attention.

Devin Johnston also considers the work of Duncan in *Precipitations: Contemporary American Poetry as Occult Practice*, a study that considers the Romantic critique of rationalism in the work of H.D., Robert Duncan, James Merrill, Nathaniel Mackey, and Susan Howe. In the introduction Johnston provides a useful overview of the historical and conceptual meanings of occultism in poetry, describing this strain as a 'modern pastiche of religious practices from diverse cultures and historical periods'. For these poets the occult provides a means of resisting a form of teleological unity, offering instead the possibility of multiplicity and textual pleasure; yet at the same time there is a darker side to this desire to resist closure. In some of Duncan's poetry, for instance, pleasure gives way to an experience that is overwhelming and might be described in terms of the sublime.

Nathaniel Mackey's 'The Phantom Light of All Our Day' is read as a response to Duncan's apocalypticism, and Susan Howe's poetry takes the Romantic sublime as her point of departure. *Precipitations* identifies an important impulse in American poetry which can be traced back to Romanticism but which still seems relevant in this sceptical, 'secular' age.

Robert Duncan's poetry is also central to Steven Collis, '"The Frayed Trope of Rome": Poetic Architecture in Robert Duncan, Ronald Johnson, and Lisa Robertson' (*Mosaic* 35[2002] 143–62). Here Collis uses postmodern architectural theory, particularly the work of Charles Jencks and Robert Venturi, as a way of understanding the work of Duncan and the more recent Language poetry of Johnson and Robertson. The thrust of Collis's argument is that the continuities and connections between the modern and the postmodern are revealed, in part, in and through the discursive architectures of the cityscape.

Gregory Corso has also been a marginal figure in American poetry, frequently dismissed as the least significant of the Beat poets and known only for one poem, 'Marriage'. It is not surprising, then, that there have been few book-length studies of his work, but Kirby Olson's *Gregory Corso: Doubting Thomist* is an attempt to fill this critical void. The central argument is that, during Corso's unsettled and troubled early life, his one stable reference point was Catholicism; as a result, one of the central and recurring themes of his work is the possibility of faith in God. It is not that Corso remains faithful, but that his poetry keeps religious belief alive through its sceptical stance. However, though Olson declares this to be the critical framework for understanding Corso, the poetry itself seems to tell a very different story. There is a restless, impatient quality to Corso's work which resists conventional critical analysis and makes it difficult to produce a coherent account of it. As a result, this is a rather fractured and inconsistent study of a poet whose work could already be described as uneven.

There are several studies that trouble the distinction between modernism and postmodernism. The most important of these is Tim Woods's *The Poetics of the Limit: Ethics and Politics in Modern and Contemporary American Poetry*, which focuses on Louis Zukofsky. Quite correctly, Woods identifies several 'missing links' in the narratives that account for the development of twentieth-century American poetry, suggesting that the ethico-political poetics of Zukofsky can explain how we get from Pound and Williams to the Language poets. Drawing on the work of Frankfurt school cultural theorist Theodor Adorno, as well as the Jewish philosopher of ethics, Emmanuel Lévinas, Woods argues that Zukofsky is engaged in formal experiments in language that attempt to find ways of seeing 'things' without colonizing them. Understandably, Zukofsky's labyrinthine life's work '*A*' is given a great deal of deserved attention, but so too is his other work, such as *Bottom: On Shakespeare* and *Catallus*. There is also an important chapter on George Oppen, a fellow objectivist whose work is also preoccupied with forging an ethical relation to the object world. The final chapter is dedicated to the work of a number of Language poets such as Charles Bernstein, Lyn Hejinian, and Ron Silliman who are all, in different ways, rethinking 'the direction of subjectivity and its ethical action'. *The Poetics of the Limit* is a major contribution to the understanding of American poetry and poetics and offers new ways of thinking about the political implications of formal experimentation in language.

George Oppen is also considered in Rocco Marinaccio's 'George Oppen's "I've Seen America" Book: *Discrete Series* and the Thirties Road Narrative' (*AL* 74[2002] 539–69), but the focus on Oppen's first published book is an unusual one. As Marinaccio points out, *Discrete Series* is often dismissed as flawed and less accomplished than Oppen's later work, thereby marginalizing the more overtly politicized poetry produced in the early 1930s.

Another thematic study that traces the links between modernist and postmodernist poetry is John Emil Vincent, *Queer Lyrics: (Difficulty and Closure in American Poetry)*. Vincent's study of Walt Whitman, Hart Crane, Marianne Moore, John Ashbery, and Jack Spicer focuses on the ways in which each of these poets challenges heteronormative meaning by resisting or refusing forms of closure. For me, the most insightful moment of the book comes when Vincent is dealing with the controversy surrounding Marianne Moore's revision of Hart Crane's 'The Wine Menagerie' when she was editor of *The Dial*. Rather than reading this encounter as evidence of each poet's eccentricities, Vincent suggests that Moore revises the original poem's theory of desire. Moore's revision is interpreted as not so much an act of editorial violence as a creative contribution to Crane's original poem. Vincent also points to the influence of Moore on Crane and the subsequent influence of Crane on Moore, a textual dynamic that has not previously been considered. Vincent's careful readings of poets as they interpret and comment upon each other produces the most revealing insights into the nature of the queer lyric.

Nature continues to be a significant theme in critical accounts of twentieth-century poetry. There are two studies this year that make a case for the centrality of ecological issues to the American poetic tradition. In *Greening the Lyre: Environmental Poetics and Ethics*, David W. Gilcrest develops what might be described as an ecopoetics in order to understand one particular strand of contemporary American poetry. Gilcrest is looking at poetry that aligns itself with the politics of environmentalism; the poems he considers are engaged in finding ethical ways of writing about nature. Perhaps not surprisingly, the poet most central to this discussion is Frost, though Gilcrest offers other examples of poets working within this tradition, such as Charles Wright, Adrienne Rich, and A.R. Ammons. Particularly convincing is the analysis of Ammons's 'Corsons Inlet', which Gilcrest reads as an example of 'pragmatic environmental poetics'. This study is clearly in dialogue with Guy Rotella's *Reading and Writing Nature: The Poetry of Robert Frost, Wallace Stevens, Marianne Moore, and Elizabeth Bishop* [1991], although, rather than arguing for what Rotella calls an 'epistemological nature poetry', Gilcrest prefers to describe this tradition as 'hermeneutical environmental poetry'. This shifts the terms of the argument in order to more adequately account for poetry written in the wake of modernism and allows Gilcrest to develop a poetics capable of responding to a range of poetry written in the twentieth century.

Jed Rasula's *This Compost: Ecological Imperatives in American Poetry* is difficult to categorize, falling as it does somewhere between prose, poetry, and criticism. Rasula's study focuses on what might be described as a postmodern form of organicism, a Romantic hybrid cultivated in the twentieth century. In order to create a sense of a poetic field rather than a linear genealogy, Rasula uses quotations without naming the author in the main body of the text (though he provides references at the end of the book). Thus poetic signatures are temporarily concealed, suggesting an intertextual network of references and allusions that fuse and combine to produce a fertile poetic compost site. Looming large in this study is Charles Olson's *Maximus Poems*, though Rasula moves backwards to take account of Whitman and Dickinson and forwards to Ron Silliman and Adrienne Rich, suggesting that there is a political dimension to the poetics of the 'open field'. Rasula's approach is unconventional but effective, mimicking the poetic desire to produce a textual terrain that is no one poet's property but rather a communal site of creative energy.

Though strictly speaking Louise Blakeney Williams's *Modernism and the Ideology of History: Literature, Politics, and the Past* does not engage directly with American poetry, it does examine the influence of Ezra Pound in the years immediately preceding the First World War. This intellectual biography examines a group of modernist writers and thinkers—W.B. Yeats, Ford Madox Ford, T.E. Hulme, D.H. Lawrence, and Pound—who were all engaged in interrogating the idea of history as a progressive and linear narrative. Williams provides a detailed description of the cultural climate in Britain in the pre-war years, as well as an account of how these writers developed their own aesthetic principles. This neglected period of modernism is clearly an important one, providing as it does a sense of why poets like Pound were engaged in formal experimentation in the first place. Particularly interesting is the chapter dedicated to the modernist interest in Asian art, which identifies the ways in which the aesthetic and political dimensions of certain Asian art forms appealed to the anti-humanism of these modernists. The only objection one might have to Williams's account of the incipient stages of modernism is that it reinforces a rather masculinist and Anglocentric view of modernism.

Remaining with modernism, Catherine Paul's *Poetry in the Museums of Modernism: Yeats, Pound, Moore, Stein* is part of a growing body of work on the sociopolitical frames circumscribing literary modernism. As its title indicates, the relation between museum culture and modernist writing is examined in relation to the work of four canonical writers whose poetry might in some respects be described in curatorial terms. Paul's basic thesis, that books of poems are rather like museums in that they display objects for the reader to observe and scrutinize, is reinforced by a great deal of evidence from archives and correspondence showing how each of these writers thought of him or herself as cultural curators or collectors. Each chapter describes a pairing between writer and museum: Yeats and the Municipal Gallery in Dublin, Pound and the British Museum in London, Moore and the American Museum of Natural History in New York and Stein and her own collection of art displayed in her home. There is a considerable amount of discussion here concerning the ways in which museums reinvented the art of display at the beginning of the twentieth century but, at the same time, Paul gives an account of the distinctiveness of each of these museums and likewise the distinctiveness of each writer's approach to the art of collecting. This argument certainly opens up aspects of these writers' work that have not been adequately considered, though the range of texts discussed is, by necessity perhaps, quite limited.

Marianne Moore is also prominent in Kirstin Zona Hotelling's *Marianne Moore, Elizabeth Bishop, and May Swenson: The Feminist Poetics of Self-Restraint*, which argues that all three women poets deploy the subtly subversive strategy of 'self-restraint' interrogating the Romantic lyric 'I' that so often tacitly underpins feminist readings of poetry. It is because of this resistance to 'self' expression that the work of Moore, Bishop, and Swenson has either been neglected by feminist criticism or misread. Hotelling tries to redress the balance with this study of the poetic and critical exchanges between Moore and Bishop and Bishop and Swenson, using post-structuralist feminist theory to bolster her argument. While Swenson's poetry might not initially seem allied in any way to the work of Moore and Bishop, Hotelling uses the work of Judith Butler to argue convincingly that Swenson uses a performative language in many of her poems and resists a 'heterosexual matrix'. Thus the 'fleshy' lush and sensual language of her poems might be read as a form of self-restraint, thereby linking her work to the more detached and cerebral poetry of both Moore and Bishop. The use of post-structuralist feminist theory seems incongruous at times, particularly in relation to Moore, yet the final chapter on Swenson's poetry does a good job of rescuing her from essentialist and reductive readings of her work.

Lesley Wheeler's *The Poetics of Enclosure: American Women Poets from Dickinson to Dove* begins by engaging with the critical history and form of the lyric in the twentieth century, though a definition is wisely avoided. Instead, Wheeler's emphasis is upon the ideological nature of the lyric, in particular its gendered aspects. The focus of this study is on the ways in which six women poets (Emily Dickinson, Marianne Moore, H.D., Gwendolyn Brooks, Elizabeth Bishop, and Rita Dove) all practise a form of resistance to the lyric mode while remaining, inevitably, indebted to its traditions. This resistance is described in terms of 'enclosure', which Wheeler conceives of as a formal strategy, a recurring subject of interest for all these poets as well as a dominant trope. Clearly, this is an attempt to redefine the American poetic canon by identifying the figurative use of interior space in poetry by women. This attempt to shift the critical ground by developing a 'poetics of enclosure' reveals the extent to which the lyric form itself is both enabling and constraining.

Two other post-war poets receive critical attention in journal articles. Daniel Mark Epstein, 'Merrill's Progress' (*NewC* 20[2002] 24–32) is an overview of James Merrill's career from his early Stevensian imitations to the later and, in Epstein's opinion, more intimate lyrics of *The Fire Screen* [1969], *Braving the Elements* [1972], and *Divine Comedies* [1976]. Merrill's elegant formalism made him deeply unfashionable in the 1960s, but his work is now being rediscovered by critics such as Epstein who make a convincing case for his value as a poet. Stephen Burt's essay, 'Randall Jarrell: Time, Verse, and the Sense of the Self' (*PNR* 29[2002] 40–6) considers poems such as 'The Player Piano' and 'Well Water' in terms of the relation between time and identity. A strong and recurring theme in Jarrell's poetry is the sense of exile felt as the passage of time severs past selves from the present self. Jarrell considered Proust to be the greatest writer of the twentieth century, and Burt convincingly argues that Jarrell appropriated and adapted a Proustian conception of time and memory in his poetry.

Finally, Stephen Yenser's *A Boundless Field: American Poetry at Large* is a vigorous defence of contemporary poetry against its detractors. This is a collection of reviews by the author, a poet himself, who has clearly become impatient with recent criticism on poetry. Consisting of previously published reviews (mainly in *The Yale Review*), this collection offers a useful overview not only of Yenser's own taste in poetry but the recent trends dominating the American poetic scene. It's helpful, for instance, to read essays that characterize certain poetic styles in a critical language that is suggestive, subjective, and gestural. Even if one doesn't agree with

Yenser's opinions, he clearly has plenty of them, and they provide readers who are unfamiliar with contemporary American poetry with a brief but enthusiastic introduction to some interesting poets. Though the opening chapter is largely negative in tone, Yenser goes on to provide thoughtful discussions of a wide variety of contemporary poets such as Philip Levine, Robert Pinsky, Susan Mitchell, Michael Palmer, Harryette Mullen, and Jorie Graham.

2. Fiction 1900–1945

William Faulkner, Ernest Hemingway, and F. Scott Fitzgerald, whether taken alone or in relation to other writers, once again make up the main focus of critical attention, in terms of conference proceedings, monographs, and essays. Of the three, Faulkner is by far the most popular subject. Evelyn Jaffe Schreiber's *Subversive Voices: Eroticizing the Other in the William Faulkner and Toni Morrison*, while spending more time on the latter writer, offers an analysis of the patriarchal structures in Faulkner's work and the ways in which the voices of the other, the subversive voices of the title, and their articulation of difference produce societal change despite the dominant cultural, social, and psychological structures that typically create and maintain identity. Schreiber uses Lacanian theory, specifically his notion of the human desire for an imagined wholeness, the search for the imaginary object that will overcome the 'lack'. In so doing, she illuminates Faulkner's use of nostalgia as a 'screen' which preserves the power of patriarchal structures and serves to eroticize the other for the dominant culture by using marginalized others to fulfil the desire for an imagined wholeness. From this analysis, Schreiber describes how it is, in the light of these southern patriarchal structures and the sense of nostalgia with which Faulkner presents their passing, that marginalized voices in Faulkner's work are empowered and able to achieve agency. Schreiber argues that such voices lead to cultural transformation in Faulkner's work because the subversive voice arises to expose the reality of the nothingness that lies at the core of identity, and the recognition of this nothingness allows the reality of the other to manifest itself and have agency in the social world. This is a challenging and rewarding analysis.

Dana Medoro's *The Bleeding of America: Menstruation as Symbolic Economy in Pynchon, Faulkner, and Morrison* also takes Faulkner and Morrison together and adds Thomas Pynchon to the mix. Medoro argues that the Puritan construction of America as a new Eden continued to be fundamental to the construction of American literature in the twentieth century, and further that this Edenic myth is a feminine one: a place where a new, American culture and society was given birth. From this perspective she analyses the rhetoric and symbolism of blood, its ability to function as a 'symbol of defilement and purification'. She argues that menstruation as a system of recurring images fundamentally informs the articulation of a feminine America in the nation's literary tradition: in this conception, America, as a New World Eden, is haunted not only by the Fall, but also by the 'curse of Eve'. Placing Thomas Pynchon, William Faulkner, and Toni Morrison within this tradition, the author demonstrates that their novels link variations on the figure of the menstruating woman both to the bloody history of the United States and to a vision of the nation's redemptive promise. Medoro makes detailed readings of nine novels (three by each author, the Faulkner novels being *The Sound and the Fury*, *Light in August*, and *Absalom, Absalom!*), which exhaustively identify and interpret recurrent images and references to menstruation. Medoro's analysis then seeks to place this 'other' blood within the complex semiotics of blood as an American symbol: '[blood] signifies in several circuitous and metaphoric directions, toward and away from life and death, waste and regeneration, violence and passion'. Medoro's approach is significantly multidisciplinary, employing methods, models, and contexts including religion, medical history, mythography, anthropology, and psychoanalysis. This is wide-ranging but focused analysis, passionately and cogently presented.

A quite different connection between Faulkner and Pynchon, as well as many others, is drawn in the proceedings from the 1999 Faulkner and Yoknapatawpha conference, held at the University of Mississippi. In Duvall and Abadie, eds., *Faulkner and Postmodernism*, Faulkner and his fiction are explored in relation to an array of postmodern approaches. Building upon the accepted foundation that Faulkner is a central figure of international modernism, the eleven essays collected here explore how he and his fiction can be as fruitfully explored in relation to postmodernism in the light of postmodern literature, culture, and theory. The volume explores the variety of ways in which Faulkner's art can be used to measure similarities and differences between modernism and postmodernism. Essays in the collection approach Faulkner in a number of differing ways: those that use his novels as a way to elaborate on the shifts between modernism and postmodernism, those that see postmodern tendencies in Faulkner's fiction, and those that read Faulkner through the lens of cultural studies. In their endeavours to explicate the connections between Faulkner and postmodernism, the essays compare him to a slew of contemporary novelists such as Ralph Ellison, Vladimir Nabokov, Thomas Pynchon, Richard Ford, and, of course, Toni Morrison. In one entertaining essay, Cheryl Lester uses Elvis Presley as a parallel southern life to uncover some wonderful resonances. There is not only variety in terms of connection to literary figures or styles; the essays are also framed by a raft of theoretical perspectives, with varying degrees of sympathy for the usefulness of postmodernism as an approach to Faulkner. The strength here is the variety offered, but the conclusion that can be drawn is more unified: regardless of differences of approach, Faulkner remains at the forefront of literary debate into the twenty-first century.

The literary comparisons between aspects of the work of William Faulkner and Toni Morrison that are apparent in the books continue in two essays published in 2002. Jill C. Jones, 'The Eye of a Needle: Morrison's *Paradise*, Faulkner's *Absalom, Absalom!*, and the American Jeremiad' (*Faulkner Journal* 17:ii[2002] 3–23), argues that *Paradise* can be read as a reworking of *Absalom, Absalom!*. She specifically highlights two major issues to illustrate her comparison: the theme of empire-building, or 'how people come to become exactly what they hate and fear', and written style, a concern with form and language. She argues that, by reading the novels in this way, it is possible to discern Morrison reworking Faulkner's 'white, male southern lens', allowing the similar themes in Morrison's novel to be viewed from an entirely different perspective. This reframing or repositioning is illustrated by taking scenes that Jones considers to have been revised in Morrison's novel, scenes which present an inner black self rather than a view of black character's exteriors. This is a nuanced and valuable analysis that identifies a great many solid connections.

Taylor Hagood looks in an entirely different direction for a literary comparison to Faulkner in 'Faulkner's "fabulous immeasurable camelots": *Absalom, Absalom!* and *Le Morte Darthur*' (*SLJ* 34:ii[2002] 45–63), which sees in Faulkner's novel an exemplary illustration of the author's use of Arthurian mythology and, more generally, offers a frame of reference for similar analysis of other Faulkner works. The story of Thomas Sutpen's rise and fall is for Hagood an embodiment of the Arthur myth, Faulkner's representation of the mythic Old South interpreted as a version of Sir Thomas Malory's Camelot. And, just as Camelot's demise secured its immortality, so too with the Old South. Hagood argues that, by using such mythological underpinnings 'as a model and foundation' to this Old South narrative, Faulkner is able to 'construct a mythic [location] full of the tensions created by juxtaposing elements of glory and corruption. In so doing, he packs the Old South myth full of excruciating tragedy that permeates Malory's Camelot.' This is an entertaining essay that illuminates an interesting aspect of the construction Faulkner's world, even if it is heavy on the detail of the Arthurian literary context.

In 'Crowd and Self: William Faulkner's Sources of Agency in *The Sound and the Fury*' (*SLJ* 34:ii[2002] 30–44), Jeffrey J. Folks discusses the novel in relation to its emergence at a specific point in Faulkner's life. The autobiographical impetus for *The Sound and the Fury*, and specifically its theme of victimization, can be traced, according to Folks, to Faulkner's perceived mistreatment by his publishers, in the wake of the rejection of *Sartoris*, the work Faulkner believed would make his name: 'I have written THE book of which the other things were but foals.' After rejection, Faulkner suggested he would never write again. His feeling, as Folks describes it, pitches him as the isolated individual who is the victim of a crowd of New York publishers. At the same time, Folks presents Faulkner as becoming increasingly anxious about mounting family responsibilities. Folks argues that it was this mix of circumstances that 'accompanied and nourished the composition of *The Sound and the Fury*'. In this analysis the novel comes to represent a Faulkner who finds agency in his own demise, and who subsequently imbues each of his characters with a sense of loss. *The Sound and the Fury* intriguingly comes to represent a 'disburdening', and becomes a novel that 'memorialize[s] his own metaphorical descent into death'.

Also of note is Fant and Ashley, eds., *Faulkner at West Point*, a commemoration of the writer's visit to West Point forty years ago and of the academy's bicentennial. This is a new edition of a book first published in 1964, and includes a new preface, an introduction, and reflections on the historic visit written by two graduates who were present as cadets during the Nobel writer's appearance. Faulkner visited the United States Military Academy at West Point less than three months before his death in 1962. The book offers a series of 'moments', such as the night of 19 April, when Faulkner read episodes from his forthcoming novel *The Reivers* before an audience of cadets, faculty, and staff; the session after the reading in which he answered questions about his works and the art of writing; and the following day, when he met students on two literature courses and discussed a wide range of subjects, including his philosophy of life, his writings, and his views on America. This fascinating book gives an insight into Faulkner—the man himself and his conception of the art of writing—and collects his thoughts and opinions shortly before his death.

Although several of the essays in Wagner-Martin Smith, eds., *William Faulkner: Six Decades of Criticism* have been discussed in previous editions of *YWES*, the book represents a superlative collection of Faulkner criticism which addresses the range of issues, themes, and theories over the full body of his work. It brings together diverse responses to his oeuvre, a collection of material that is still vigorously debated. Given its sixty-year scope, this invaluable volume reveals ways in which literary criticism has changed in that period, while simultaneously offering a record of how these new directions (structuralism, feminism, post-structuralism, psychoanalysis) have impacted upon the understanding of Faulkner's work.

Ernest Hemingway is treated to a single-author collection of essays in Robert E. Gajdusek's *Hemingway in his own Country*. Gajdusek, one of the leading Hemingway interpreters, offers here twenty-six essays, spanning fifteen years and covering all of Hemingway's writings. The order is not chronological, which lends itself to an accessible, rich, and multifaceted approach to Hemingway and his works. Gajdusek is not coy about his admiration for his subject: 'He is a great, great artist ... probably our best and most studied craftsman.' However, this conventional, recognizable version of Hemingway is precisely what Gajdusek is challenging. He goes on, 'but we as a culture still often read him as though he had but offered us portraits and accounts of hunting and fishing, of wars and travels in diverse countries, and of careless sequential loves'. His aim, then, is to move beyond the accepted clichés of Hemingway's public persona and attempt to address what made him so different, so unusual. As he states, the book's chapters represent 'waystations on [Gajdusek's] journey toward a new understanding of Hemingway'. They offer insights into Hemingway's life as well as his writings, and this means that the collection presents a sophisticated and accessible synthesis of biographical material with academic enquiry. To achieve all of this, Hemingway is explored on many levels and from a variety of angles. So Gajdusek offers examinations of influences upon him (specifically in two essays the influence of James Joyce); focused analyses of passages or sections of larger works; explorations of themes within a single work and sustained across a wider range of Hemingway's writings; and investigations into Hemingway the man and the writer. This is a book of immense riches and does a fine job of presenting the reader with an unusual Hemingway, 'in his own country', on his own terms.

Deirdre Anne Pettipiece, *Sex Theories and the Shaping of Two Moderns: Hemingway and H.D.*, presents another unusual literary comparison. The book takes the sexological theories of Charles Darwin, Sigmund Freud, and Havelock Ellis and their profound impact upon the modern world as a springboard into the work of Hemingway and H.D., exploring the ways in which Hemingway and H.D. explain human behaviour through the sexual complexity of their characters and how this complexity resonates with contemporary sexual theories. The connection she draws between the two authors lies in the way in which they negotiate what it means to be a man or a woman in the modern era, an era in which the ideas of Darwin, Freud, and Ellis have become pervasive. Pettipiece presents the two writers as taking such theories, incorporating them into their fiction, and thus demonstrating the complexities of human social and psychological motivation. For Pettipiece, Hemingway and H.D. exemplify the 'evolutionary and psychological examination [that] seemed to be in the air in the 20s'. The authors, she argues, attempt to define and describe human motivation and behaviour, but she also notes that both writers present characters whose sexuality is not in keeping with expected gender traits. She sees this 'blurring and shifting of gender [as] nearly constant in the texts of both Hemingway and H.D.'. This pattern, she suggests, is evidence of the authors' close examination of sexological theories. Such engagement in Hemingway's works sees him privileging biological forces in the construction of human behaviour such that he creates characters who illustrate the Darwinian conflict, the survival of the fittest. To illustrate Hemingway's use of such theories, she offers reference to the range of his works, but it is *The Garden of Eden* which receives the most sustained scrutiny. This is an insightful and sometimes surprising analysis which makes a useful and enlightening connection between these 'strange bedfellows' (as she terms them in her introduction) and aspects of the era in which they are writing.

Broer and Holland, eds., *Hemingway and Women: Female Critics and the Female Voice*, comprises seventeen essays, original to this volume, which seek to emphasize the centrality of women and the feminine voice in the author's works. This study of women in Hemingway's life and art is undertaken here by female scholars. The collection takes as an important locus, again, the posthumously published novel, *The Garden of Eden*, and the manner in which it refreshed and reinvigorated the nature of and debate surrounding Hemingway's construction of gender. Although *The Garden of Eden* receives much significant attention (specifically in essays by Nancy Comely and Amy Strong), Hemingway's earlier female characters (Catherine Barkley and Brett Ashley, for example), his short stories, and the real women in his life are also fruitfully explored, providing a full and rich collection of material that moves fluidly between Hemingway's fiction and his biography. This is a volume that offers a range of excellent insights into Hemingway's personal complexity and that of his female companions and characters.

The trends apparent in this year's book-length studies of Hemingway emerge also in a number of notable essays. Gajdusek's call to locate Hemingway 'in his own country', and Broer and Holland's focus on gender, connect three essays published in 2002. In 'Fathers, Lovers, and Friend Killers: Rearticulating Gender and Race via Species in Hemingway' (*Boundary* 29:i[2002] 223–57), Cary Wolfe begins by suggesting, like Gajdusek, that 'no writer is more overdue for a critical facelift' than Hemingway. What Wolfe wants is a movement away from the 'hairy chested persona', the parodic version of Hemingway that dominates popular perceptions. The perspective from which Wolfe launches this re-evaluation originates in what, he believes, Hemingway 'was interested in all along': 'the transgressive possibilities of gender performativity'. The catalyst for this shift, suggests Wolfe, is once again the posthumously published novel, *The Garden of Eden*. He articulates the novel's importance in this way: 'this assessment hangs in no small part on Hemingway's fascination with themes of androgyny, gender experimentation, and their relation to creativity'. But Wolfe explores themes of gender and race by foregrounding the discourse and implications of species, reflecting on the author's use of animals (elephant, dog). Wolfe interrogates this discourse to uncover its purpose, to find out whether such depictions are always 'counter or cover for some other discourse' (gender, race, class). By exploring the matrices of connections in the novel between the protagonists and non-human others, Wolfe convincingly illuminates a rich, unusual dimension to Hemingway's portrayal of gender and race issues. This sophisticated and probing study speaks strongly for a reassessment of the author that looks beyond the conventional caricatures.

In 'War, Gender and Ernest Hemingway' (*Hemingway Review* 22:i[2002] 34–55), Alex Vernon examines a number of Hemingway texts (with an emphasis on *A Farewell to Arms*, 'Cross-Country Snow', 'An Alpine Idyll', and 'The Short Happy Life of Francis Macomber') in relation to two pre-existing, differing readings of 'Big Two-Hearted River': one reading grounded in a reaction to the his war experience, the other in the 'open warfare' Hemingway had engaged in against his mother, Grace. Where previous criticism has dealt with either war or gender in its interpretation of Nick's behaviour and persona, Vernon asks, 'Why must the story … be about either war or Nick–Ernest's mother? Why can't it be about both?' Vernon puts forward a useful, synthesized approach to the characters and themes in these texts, offering a reading of Hemingway's service in the First World War which emphasizes a 'femininity'. Citing war posters that depicted Red Cross work as a 'feminine endeavour', he posits that 'Hemingway could only be acutely sensitive the implications of his Red Cross days'. Such sensitivity, he argues, lies behind Hemingway's exaggerations of his war exploits. He connects a further war/gender component by referring to a letter sent by Hemingway's mother while he was recuperating from his wounds in a Milan hospital, in which she says, 'it's great to be the mother of a hero'. He suggests that, given Hemingway's sensitivity to the nature of his service and the context of his wounding (delivering candy and tea to 'real' soldiers), such a letter fed unmanly and unheroic anxieties. From this basis, Vernon charts a variety of shifting sexual and gender associations in the texts (exposure to European notions of sexuality; emasculating effects of modern technological warfare; images of pregnancy and childbirth). As such, he traces a fascinating outline of the ways in which the perspectives can not only be read together but should also be synthesized, and he argues cogently that to try and understand Hemingway and his writing excluding one of these approaches is 'a serious critical oversight'.

In 'Nick at Night: Nocturnal Metafictions in Three Hemingway Short Stories' (*Hemingway Review* 22:i[2002] 19–33), Margot Sempreora offers another exploration of the importance of Nick's experience as a soldier in relation to the mother-figure and childhood trauma in analysing 'Now I Lay Me', 'A Way You'll Never Be', and, once again, 'Big Two-Hearted River' (the first acting as a subtext for the following two). Rather than believing Nick to be suffering from some kind of shellshock or psychic trauma as a result of his wartime service, she argues that he attempts to keep his soul in his body by revisiting intense childhood moments. Sempreora, using Kenneth Lynn's notion that Nick is Hemingway's 'talking horse', charts the interconnections between Hemingway's biography and the stories, and interprets Nick's obsessive style as Hemingway's own meditations on the nature of composition. In essence she argues that the three stories are metafictions, and that Nick is a 'stand-in psyche—an experimental, remembering, reacting consciousness for Hemingway'. Sempreora identifies chronological, thematic, and biographical links between the three stories, and labels them 'brother stories' that represent an insight into a particular period of Hemingway's thinking. Echoing Vernon, Sempreora argues that the central motivation for Nick's work 'is not a war trauma, but a parental battle'. This analysis also offers a terrific insight into the connections between Hemingway's own remembrances and his beliefs and attitudes towards writing. By highlighting symbolic and stylistic similarities across the stories, Sempreora presents a wide-ranging and effective argument.

The relationship between Hemingway and Fitzgerald and the historical moment in which they produced their works is explored in Ronald Berman's *Fitzgerald, Hemingway and the Twenties*. In the first instance, the book takes stock of the psychological, philosophical, literary, and cultural terrain of the 1920s before locating the two writers in relation to these contexts. Given the familiarity of much of this material, the history as well as the texts, it is no small feat that Berman is able to present a full and lively collection of fascinating insights about the writers themselves, their texts, and the era surrounding them. The book does not present itself as a unified analysis—he openly admits that 'no absolute connection exists between all the subjects or texts I cover'—yet the whole does not ever feel dislocated, due in large part to the connecting focus on the philosophical issues of the decade. Berman identifies the two authors as great readers, suggesting that they would be amply aware of the direction of contemporary American thought and that, further, both Hemingway and Fitzgerald find their voices in the 1920s amidst such an atmosphere. He locates the two in a version of the 1920s that sees notions of the American self in crisis and the nation itself drifting, having lost a sense of shared values such as religion, community, and family in a society affected by the Great War and experiencing the onset of rapid technological and scientific development. Berman interrogates an authoritative selection of the authors' texts in an effort to uncover their relationship with the era's philosophical debates. His material is largely grounded in insightful and sometimes refreshingly original analyses of Fitzgerald's *The Great Gatsby*, 'Bernice Bobs her Hair', and 'The Diamond as Big as the Ritz', and Hemingway's 'The Killers', *A Farewell to Arms*, and *The Sun Also Rises*, but he deftly connects his themes and ideas to a wider American literature, reinforcing the strength of his argument. This is a learned yet accessible study that not only demonstrates Hemingway's and Fitzgerald's works as reactions to philosophical discourse and the direction American society was taking, but also shows how the writers themselves were key voices within this discourse, while simultaneously presenting an image of the 1920s that is far removed from the Jazz Age clichés.

The interconnection between Fitzgerald's life and work is treated in Andrew Hook's *F. Scott Fitzgerald: A Literary Life*. Hook's angle is to explore Fitzgerald's chaotic life in relation to his needs as a man as well as a writer, such that Hook sees the need in Fitzgerald to live life unreservedly and the extent of his commitment to experience, but at the same time his commitment to his art and the discipline of writing. Hook thus presents an intriguing and insightful account of Fitzgerald's life and work as a balancing act between two almost contradictory demands. His book sets out to 'trace the professional, publishing and social contexts which shaped [the writer's] writing'. Although concise, it offers some wonderful insight into Fitzgerald's life. However, as fascinating and as insightful as this glimpse into the author's biography is, Hook does not provide much fresh material in relation to the works themselves. He has mined a broad spectrum of sources, although he leans heavily on Fitzgerald scholar Matthew Bruccolli. To those well read in the life and works of Fitzgerald, a good deal of the ground covered will be familiar. But Hook's thesis is an interesting one: according to him, Fitzgerald recognized early in his writing career that a novelist is caught between his 'tender-minded' impulses to be a good person and his 'tough-minded' impulses to be a good writer, no matter what the cost to others. Hook claims that by the 1930s Fitzgerald seemed stymied as a novelist because of his inability to choose between these two impulses. His short book ultimately adds an interesting perspective to the study of Fitzgerald.

Also of note is West, ed. *Tales of the Jazz Age*, the latest volume in *The Cambridge Edition of the Works of F. Scott Fitzgerald*. This is Fitzgerald's second collection of short stories, and includes the recognized masterpieces 'May Day' and 'The Diamond as Big as the Ritz'. Alongside such renowned stories are some that Fitzgerald chose not to collect from the early 1920s, perhaps the most illuminating of which is 'Dice, Brass Knuckles and Guitar', a story from 1923 that resonates interestingly with the themes and characters in *The Great Gatsby*. The strength here, as with the other volumes in the series, is the rich, vivid insight into Fitzgerald's craft. The book offers an account of the history and development of the stories, his editorial decisions, and his variations, as well as reproductions of surviving manuscripts that are indispensable for the Fitzgerald scholar and those interested in American literature generally.

Away from the dominance of Faulkner, Hemingway, and Fitzgerald there are some works of significant merit. Richard Lingeman, *Sinclair Lewis: Rebel from Main Street* attempts to rehabilitate the work and legacy of the Nobel Prize-winning novelist. Lingeman's extensive biography of Lewis is written very much in relation to the weighty biography by Mark Schorer, *Sinclair Lewis: An American Life* (McGraw-Hill [1961]). Where Schorer presented Lewis as an unlikeable figure with a destructive alcohol problem, and consequently discusses the production of such novels as *Babbit*, *Main Street*, and *Elmer Gantry* as 'miraculous' (Schorer had a very low opinion of Lewis's work altogether, calling him 'one of the worst writers in modern American literature'), Lingeman offers a very different assessment. He wants to exhume Lewis, to reinterpret his life and works, and to present him as one of the most important writers in modern American literature. To do this, he reinterprets the mass of material assembled by Schorer and proceeds to offer Lewis as a writer who interrogates the values of his era. In this sense, Lingeman uses Schorer's encyclopedic research to create a Lewis of his own, a professional writer and craftsman who churned out popular stories to support the production of the serious novels. Lingeman argues that Schorer's dislike of Lewis's persona and prose style led him to underrate his achievements and subsequently gave readers reasons to dismiss him. He also argues convincingly for more favourable reappraisals of Lewis's less respected novels, specifically *Kingsblood Royal*. Lingeman has produced a convincing reassessment of Lewis's literary reputation, as well as a vivid and enthralling biography of an interesting, contradictory figure. Lewis is also the subject of Andrea Newlyn, 'Undergoing Racial "Reassessment": The Politics of Transracial Crossing in Sinclair Lewis's *Kingsblood Royal*' (*MFS* 48[2002] 1041– 74). Like Lingeman, Newlyn finds herself rescuing Lewis from Schorer, who labelled this novel a failure, 'one of those good bad books that, for the wrong reasons, continue to have a certain fascination', and who noted the critical consensus that Lewis's work had taken a permanent downward turn. Newlyn contends convincingly that *Kingsblood Royal* is every bit as important as the more accepted works, that it fits into Lewis's overall thematic landscape, and that it offers some excellent insights into race in the contemporary United States. Newlyn also goes some way towards signalling the beginning of a reassessment of Lewis and his place in American literary tradition. She examines the narrative logic of *Kingsblood Royal*, in which a banker discovers in mid-life that he has 3.125 per cent African

American ancestry. By focusing on the slippage between identification and desire that results from Kingsblood's movement across racial lines, Newlyn demonstrates how such 'transracial' narratives 'form a productive counter-logic to a narrative dynamic that weds racial ideology to narrative form'.

Hodson and Reesman, eds., *Jack London: One Hundred Years a Writer*, is an attempt on his centennial to present a new London, away from the clichés and myths. The book is published by the Huntington Library, which since shortly after his death in 1916 has been acquiring London's papers and is today the premier archive for such material. There is a sense of new and old underpinning the stated intentions of the book, a wish to address the tension between the image of London as a hack writer churning out adventure stories, and the version of him as a serious and significant figure in American letters: 'Modern scholars who now come to London's works free of earlier dismissive attitudes have emphatically placed London among the best American authors.' The eight essays here offer analyses and insight into both the works themselves and the man behind them. The book positions itself as an assessment of the state of London criticism today, as well as highlighting where it can go in the future. A dominant idea in it is to arrive at some kind of balance between the versions of London as an author that emerge, on the one hand, from his writing and, on the other, from the stories he told about himself and his approach to the craft of writing. This is a valuable and illuminating collection that makes a suitably passionate claim for London's importance a hundred years after his first literary successes.

Mark Whalan, 'Dreams of Manhood: Narrative, Gender, and History in *Winesburg, Ohio*' (*SAF* 30[2002] 229–48), takes to task the conventional gender critique of Sherwood Anderson's text as a book that represents women in binary terms—activity/passivity, culture/nature—and has led to Anderson's identification with patriarchal culture. Whalan points out that this text was written during the First World War (although published in 1919, the stories were written consecutively between late 1915 and early 1916), and so represents Anderson as a figure writing at precisely the same time as he (and the wider American culture) was trying to comprehend the implications of the war in Europe. In Whalan's conception, the Great War represents 'a crucial, but often overlooked, historical context for Anderson's most famous work'. Whalan frames this context in terms of a 'historical trauma', a trauma that 'problematised the "dominant fictions" of personal (and specifically gender) identity'. Whalan uses this notion of trauma as a starting point for his analysis. In a similar manner to Vernon, Whalan convincingly discusses, via Anderson's stories, the effects of the First World War on white American masculinity.

It is pleasing to see Nathanael West receive some cutting-edge treatment in Lee Rozelle's 'Ecocritical City: Modernist Reactions to Urban Environments in *Miss Lonelyhearts* and *Paterson*' (*TCL* 48:i[2002] 100–15). In demonstrating the validity of ecocriticism, Rozelle discusses the texts as works which 'suggest the foreboding notion that technological and urban developments might well erode both nature and community in an unending push for unregulated replication'. Rozelle finds in *Miss Lonelyhearts* a modernist representation of urban space that resonates with contemporary ecocritical ideas in some interesting ways. The novel simultaneously reflects and offers itself as a critique of contemporary environmental problems, depicting images of 'stoniness and aridity', lamenting the American drive to build and consume, to break stones, and demonstrating a concern with the 'spiritual deficiencies of urban space'. In so doing Rozelle uses *Miss Lonelyhearts* to illustrate the value of the ecocritical perspective, while at the same time demonstrating West to be an important writer, actively engaged with such issues, long before the vocabulary of environmental awareness was fully available.

Willa Cather attracts significant critical interest this year. In *Memorial Fictions: Willa Cather and the First World War*, Steven Trout offers a reconsideration of Cather's war fictions, focusing on the Pulitzer Prize-winning *One of Ours* [1922] and *The Professor's House* [1925]. Seeking to counter the largely negative criticism that the earlier work has consistently attracted, he puts forward a persuasive argument to suggest that the novel has a greater complexity than has previously been acknowledged. Highlighting the minimal authorial commentary, and the unreliable narration suggested by multiple, contradictory perspectives, Trout re-examines the text's relation to literary modernism and attempts to secure a place for the author in the canon of war literature, from which she has been excluded. In what is an original approach to Cather's work, this study situates *One of Ours* within the context of American military commemorations through a discussion of various public monuments and shrines, including the Liberty Memorial in Kansas City. Trout considers the possibility of the text as a 'war memorial in prose', as a part of the nation's attempt to assimilate and interpret the conflict experience, which draws much of its imagery from the 'iconography of remembrance'. He goes on, however, to evoke the sense of 'modernist ambiguity' he has identified in the writing to figure Cather's response as a collapsing of such 'iconography', an exploration of the instability of the meaning of war. A slight imbalance in this volume arises from the comprehensive, three-chapter analysis of *One of Ours*, leaving only a single section for consideration of *The Professor's House*. Commentary on the later novel examines its concentration on the aftermath of war and the implications for Western civilization, intellectualism, and scientific enquiry. Trout discusses the way in which the novel interrogates historical narratives and highlights the significance of Cather's use of silence, suggesting that 'the thing not named' in *The Professor's House* is, in fact, the First World War. The little attention the second novel does receive suggests an insightful reading which would bear greater development.

The Professor's House, together with another of Cather's novels of the 1920s, *Death Comes for the Archbishop*, is also the focus of Swift and Urgo, eds., *Willa Cather and the American Southwest*, a collection of essays drawn from the 'Willa Cather on Mesa Verde' symposium of October 1999. This volume takes as its unifying theme Cather the traveller and the tourist, and evaluates the importance of landscapes, both geographical and cultural, in her fictions. As the title suggests, particular emphasis is placed on her 'complicated relationship with the American Southwest', a 'place of intersecting cultures and histories', and its influence on her literary imagination. Divided into three sections, 'On Mesa Verde', '*The Professor's House*', and '*Death Comes for the Archbishop*', the essays explore Cather's interest in cultures specific to the region, and discuss the appearance of the markers and symbols of such cultures, including Native American artefacts, Mexican folk art, and religious iconography, in her writings. Several of the contributors read these engagements with the histories and traditions of the ancient civilizations of the American Southwest as Cather's literary response to the absence of culture she often identified in her native land. Her elevation of the folk art of the region to the level of high art is interpreted by some as the attempt to establish a sense of a distinctly American culture comparable with that of European models she had encountered and appreciated on her wider travels. Contributions to this compilation are rather diverse, ranging broadly from an examination of Cather's fascination with indigenous cliff-dwellers to a consideration of the appropriation of Native American artefacts by nineteenth-century European collectors. There are structural analyses of the novels, and, in one essay, the discussion of a possible dialogue between Cather and Mark Twain. A further piece aligns Cather's literary strategies with those of Latin American magical realism. Whilst varied in theme, however, the essays in this collection provide fascinating background information on the history and culture of the American Southwest and useful and thought-provoking insights into Cather's work.

Marion Fay, 'Making her Work her Life: Music in Willa Cather's Fiction' (in Meyer, ed., *Literature and Music*), focuses on Cather's lifelong interest in music, particularly Western music. Fay contends that Cather's passion for music 'found expression in the lives of many of her fictional characters'. She notes that at least twenty of the author's short stories and 'all twelve of her novels involve musicians and/or music'. In 'Who Stole Willa Cather?' (*Sal* 135–6[2002] 90–102), Susan Kress enters into dialogue with critic Joan Acocella, taking issue with her attack on 'feminists, queer theorists, and multicultural critics', who, Acocella believes, have 'seized upon Cather, distorted her life and her record' in order to suit their various critical agendas. Kress defends her fellow Cather scholars by dismissing Acocella's readings of the author's work, which urge taking the text at 'face value', as sentimental, naïve, and reductive. She argues that the more interrogative criticism of recent years has 'propelled new readings of old texts, testing the conventions of character, plot, and landscape'. Karen A. Hoffmann, 'Identity Crossings and the Autobiographical Act in Willa Cather's *My Ántonia*' (*ArQ* 58:iv[2002] 25–50), discusses the narrative strategies at work in Cather's 1918 novel. Jim Burden's autobiographical narration, his identification and alignment of himself with female and immigrant characters, is figured in terms of the possibilities it affords for the crossing of social and gender identity boundaries.

Cather shares space with Edith Wharton and the lesser-known Fannie Hurst in Stephanie Lewis Thompson's *Influencing America's Tastes: Realism in the Works of Wharton, Cather and Hurst*, which aims to introduce 'a new way of understanding the development of early twentieth-century American literature', in particular the relationship to literary modernism of women writers who demonstrate 'hostility' towards the movement and who have positioned themselves outside it. Seeking to broaden definitions of modernism, Thompson figures the writings of these women as a rejection of traditional conventions, discussing especially the perception of their work as aesthetically inferior, and the notion that it functions merely as a guiding 'moral influence' on an emerging 'middlebrow' culture. In a consideration of 'modernist' elements in Cather's work, Thompson notes the 'montage of sensations, impressions, and stories' presented in *My Ántonia*, but makes distinctions between the 'egotism' and 'alienation' inherent in the aesthetics of 'high' modernism and the focus on oral storytelling, folk art, and community which is characteristic of Cather's writings. Edith Wharton is discussed here in terms of her attempts to create a 'modern fiction in a changing world' that remained true to her sense of order and balance. A thoughtful reading of *Summer* suggests that

Wharton effects a subtle critique of Victorian expectations of gender by creating a language of sexual desire for women. Considerations of *Hudson River Bracketed* and *The Gods Arrive* discuss the author's interest in the 'problem of creative expression for women', and, while suggesting their modernist concern with alienation in contemporary culture, examine the novels' critique of overt literary experimentation.

Janet Beer's *Edith Wharton* is a valuable addition to the Writers and their Work series. Providing biographical, social, and literary contexts, together with an overview of recent critical responses to the author's work, this volume offers an accessible introduction to Wharton studies. The text is divided into six sections, which focus on Wharton's travel writings, her New York society novels, the short stories and novellas, her literary engagement with European culture and issues of 'morality' in twentieth-century America, and a final chapter considering Wharton as a 'reader' as well as a writer. In an original piece of scholarship, Beer considers the contents of Wharton's own recently reassembled library, many of the books complete with handwritten annotations, to evaluate the author's literary influences, and her 'affinity' and 'interaction' with other artists. In a departure from the familiar concentration on 'Wharton's long and loving relationship with the classics—old and new—of European literature', Beer 'direct[s] attention back to the American Wharton' by focusing on her relationship with Walt Whitman. An informative and authoritative introductory guide to Edith Wharton's repertoire, this study identifies thematic strains across the body of her work, considers the importance of her friendships with fellow artists, and examines the influence of the First World War on her writing. The text is completed by a useful bibliography which directs interested readers towards landmarks in Wharton criticism.

An essay worthy of note is Judith P. Saunders's 'Portrait of the Artist as Anthropologist: Edith Wharton and *The Age of Innocence* (*ISL* 4:i[2002] 86–101), which explores the way in which Wharton's keen interest in anthropology makes itself evident in the 1920 novel *The Age of Innocence*, which, Saunders argues, 'bears glowing witness to the powerful influence of emerging ethnographic research and theory on her interpretation of her own social environment and, indeed, on her understanding of the human condition in the largest sense'. Edith Wharton's personal and professional relationships and literary influences are the subject of several articles published this year. In his substantial essay 'Edith Wharton and Ronald Simmons: Documenting a Pivotal Wartime Friendship' (*YULG* 77[2002] 51–85), Frederick Wegener gives a comprehensive account of the author's friendship with the young Yale graduate and artist, arguing that the relationship was 'more estimable and multifaceted, and its legacy in Wharton's life and writing a good deal more substantial, than heretofore appreciated'. Wegener considers the 'shattering effect' on Edith Wharton of Simmons's premature death while serving as a wartime intelligence officer, and the way in which she memorialized him in her fictions. In 'The Custom of the Country: George Sand's *Indiana* and Edith Wharton's Indiana/Undine' (*EWhR* 18[2002] 1–7), Abby Werlock discusses Wharton's affinity with, and admiration for, Sand and identifies similarities between Sand's novel *Indiana* [1832] and Wharton's *The Custom of the Country* [1913], claiming that the 'central theme in both novels is that the custom of the countries [Sand's France and Wharton's America] is to treat marriage as a business affair in which women have no real stake'. Katherine Joslin's 'Embattled Tendencies:

Wharton, Woolf and the Nature of Modernism' (in Beer and Bennett, eds., *Special Relationships: Anglo-American Affinities and Antagonisms, 1854–1936*), places in 'transatlantic dialogue ... the two most articulate and influential literary women of the modern period' who 'apparently never met' but who read and offered vigorous critiques of each other's aesthetic practices. Through incisive readings of key texts, and a consideration of critical responses to their work, Joslin considers the diverse literary strategies of the two writers, their widely divergent relationships to literary modernism, and the centrality of these 'two dissonant yet overlapping voices' to the development of transatlantic literary movements.

In the same collection, the contribution of Janet Beer and Ann Heilmann, '"If I were a man": Charlotte Perkins Gilman, Sarah Grand and the Sexual Education of Girls', again considers the work of two women who probably never met. In this case, the cross-cultural connections are established through a shared involvement in 'social purity feminisms', a mutual concern with the 'ignorance of women and girls in matters of sexual hygiene', and a common didactic intent in writings which were 'designed to make up for the (sex) education that women were denied by society and the state'. Attention is also paid here to the often unsettling eugenicist policies which permeate the writings, and the authors' unproblematic advocacy of ensuring 'hygiene' through a 'state-controlled system of eugenic sexual selection'. Elsewhere, two essays treat what is probably Gilman's best-known work, the short story 'The Yellow Wallpaper'. Barbara Hochman, 'The Reading Habit and the "Yellow Wallpaper"' (*AL* 74:i[2002] 89–110), concentrates on the act of reading, on Gilman's own reading practices and those of her story's protagonist who, Hochman claims, analyses, or 'reads' the wallpaper as text. 'The Yellow Wallpaper', this essay suggests, explores the 'transformative power of reading' and the 'destructive consequences' of solitary reading for the purposes of escape. In 'Managing Madness in Gilman's "The Yellow Wallpaper"' (*SAF* 30:i[2002] 3–20), Beverly A. Hume also makes reference to Gilman's reading habits, citing the influence of Poe's 'The Black Cat' in a Gothic interpretation of the text.

Some interesting engagements with the work of Jewish American writer Anzia Yezierska have been published this year. In Delia Caparoso Konzett's *Ethnic Modernisms: Anzia Yezierska, Zora Neale Hurston, Jean Rhys, and the Aesthetics of Dislocation*, Yezierska's work is considered within the framework of 'new definitions of modernism' which move away from 'elitism' and offer 'alternatives to male Eurocentric versions'. The study suggests that, in this 'era of transformation and displacement', the experience of immigration, with its inherent traversing of national and cultural boundaries and the consequent destabilization of ethnic identities and categories, engenders new forms of artistic expression. New York's Lower East Side, the childhood home of Anzia Yezierska and the setting for much of her fiction, is figured as a site of 'transition', while her work is considered part of the 'modernist ethnic avant-garde'. Konzett identifies an ambiguity in the writings of Yezierska, who, she argues, has been variously perceived as an 'ardent assimilationist' and an 'ethnic protest writer', and situates her work within the context of 'an emerging modernism of cultural transformation'. Ruth Beinstock Anolik's essay, '"All words, words, about words": Linguistic Journey and Transformation in Anzia Yezierska's *The Bread Givers*' (*SAJL* 21[2002] 12–23), discusses Yezierska's novel as an expression of the lack of communication between the sexes in a Jewish American culture where the men and women literally speak different languages, the former scholarly Hebrew, the latter Yiddish English. Anolik also discusses the centrality of language acquisition to the immigrant's assimilation into mainstream culture, identifying women as the primary cross-cultural mediators whose gradual mastery of English affords opportunities for advancement, while simultaneously erasing the 'richness' of speech patterns which are markers of ethnic culture. In the same issue, Ellyn Lem also takes Anzia Yezierska as a subject, comparing her humble east European immigrant background with that of the middle-class, San Franciscan origins of Alice B. Toklas. In common with Anolik's essay, 'You say "Canapé," and I say "Kreplach": Reading the Cultural Culinary Conflicts in Jewish American Writers' (*SAJL* 21[2002] 94–107) is concerned with assimilation and the merging of cultures, but in this case the focus is placed on how this is variously expressed in terms of food imagery.

As one would expect, Alice B. Toklas also features in Seymour I. Toll's consideration of Gertrude Stein's 1934–5 lecture tour of the United States. 'Gertrude Stein Comes Home' (*SR* 110:ii[2002] 242–66) considers the paradox of Stein's celebrity and enduring appeal despite the fact that her challenging literary style remains 'unintelligible' to many. A chapter-length discussion of Stein is included in Zofia P. Lesinska's *Perspectives of Four Women Writers on the Second World War*, where she shares space with Janet Flanner, Kay Boyle, and Rebecca West. This is a meticulously researched study which effectively situates itself in relation to the burgeoning field of scholarship on women's war writings. Under discussion here are Stein's autobiographical writings, Flanner's political journalism, Boyle's fictions, and West's account of her travels through Yugoslavia in the 1930s. Although treating a wide range of genres and approaches to the war narrative, Lesinska makes connections between her chosen authors through their shared interest in, and engagement with, the turbulent European political climate of the 1930s and 1940s. Particularly concerned with issues of gender, she positions the authors as 'chroniclers, historians and important figures in literary history', noting that in foregrounding the experience of the civilian and the conquered rather than that of the combat soldier, these female perspectives pose a challenge to the exclusively male canon of war literature, and 'unsettle mainstream constructions of the history of the 1930s and the Second World War'. In her consideration of Stein, Lesinska negotiates the author's controversial 'pro-Vichy political stance' and 'reticen[ce] about the situation of Jews' in Europe, to establish her wartime compositions, *Paris, France*, 'The Winner Loses', and *Wars I Have Seen* as valuable 'creative accomplishments' and 'historical records'. With its focus on the 'continuous present moment', *Wars I Have Seen* is identified as a complex, innovative narrative, a 'polyphonic text [which] attempts to engage its future audiences in a dialogue about the history of the Second World War'.

3. Fiction since 1945

(a) General

Published in 2001 but not reviewed last year, Cyrus R.K. Patell in *Negative Liberties: Morrison, Pynchon and the Problem of Liberal Ideology* argues that the problem with contemporary US liberal ideology is its dependence upon Emersonian models of thought. He suggests that an overt dependence on a philosophy of individualism as a grounding for liberal ideology creates difficulties in addressing social issues. The ambition of *Negative Liberties* is twofold. Initially it attempts to revise the traditional view of mainstream liberal political theory by arguing that the work of twentieth-century thinker John Rawls must be considered in tandem with Emersonian thought. Secondly, Patell argues that elements of the most important philosophizing within twentieth-century US culture can be found in works of fiction. Concentrating on novels by Thomas Pynchon and Toni Morrison enables the author to examine the complex cultural dynamics both embodied in and effaced by dominant narratives generated by Emersonian liberalism. Patell argues that both Morrison and Pynchon are simultaneously drawn to Emersonian ideals of freedom but suspicious of flaws that arise from liberalism's Enlightenment inheritance. Attention is given to Morrison's *Playing in the Dark, The Bluest Eye, Beloved, Jazz, Song of Solomon*, and *Sula*. Readings of Pynchon's novels include *V, Crying of Lot 49, Gravity's Rainbow, Mason & Dixie, Vineland*, and *Slow Learner*. Effectively *Negative Liberties* discusses both Pynchon and Morrison's scepticism regarding idealizations of community. In concluding, Patell proposes that their work gestures towards the necessity of conceiving individual, communal, and national identities in terms that both respect the differences between individuals and respond to the links that connect them.

Also not reviewed last year, Paul Jahshan in *Henry Miller and the Surrealist Discourse of Excess: Post-Structuralist Reading* tackles what he suggests is a deficit in the study of the novelist's work. Too often, he argues, discussions of Miller's novels have relied on biographical exegesis. Instead Jahshan proposes to examine the textual 'excess' of the writer's style through a comparative reading of the tenets of surrealism. Jahshan suggests that, although surrealism is a key word associated with Miller's writing, a full account of this tendency has yet to be navigated. Usefully this investigation links surrealism with concepts of literary deviation. Initially through gesturing towards ideas of 'strangeness' in Russian formalism, Jahshan maps out successive theoretical ideas of literary deviation which include references to the writings of Michael Riffaterre, Jacques Derrida, Roland Barthes, and Umberto Eco. Jahshan links the literary 'deviancy' or excesses of Miller's writing style with arguments regarding sexual politics in his work. Part 1 of the discussion provides a stylistic study of French surrealism through the ideas and writing of André Breton and George Bataille. The second section focuses on deconstructing the surrealist texture of the writing in Miller's novels such as *Tropic of Cancer, Tropic of Capricorn*, and *Plexus*. Jahshan identifies key surrealist 'Millerian' traits, which include his use of metaphor, quest for voice, deviation, automatism, and the relationship between textual pleasure and duplicity.

In *Uncontained: Urban Fiction in Postwar America* Elizabeth Wheeler focuses on the imagery of containment in urban U.S. fiction in the era between the Second World War and the mid-1960s as a response to historical shock. Wheeler's insightful and exhaustive treatment of the theme of containment seeks to re-route critical attention from abstract ideology to material history and lived experience. Interested in the ways in which a sense of place changed in US cities after the Second World War, Wheeler connects urban segregation with repressed trauma in a combined study of geographical and emotional containment. She outlines and moves beyond fictions of containment (representations of the lone man) to consider those which contest its logic (fictions of diversity). She summarizes her project as the placement of the discourse of straight white men in the context of gay, African American, Asian American, and women's discourses to oppose urban solitude with visions of urban community. The study begins with a consideration of 'hipster' fictions alongside 'housewife' fictions to expose the ways in which women's writing challenges containment via a critique of gender roles. This model is extended in relation to fictions of racial segregation and coming-of-age or cult novels, which similarly project new versions of community, liberation, and openness. Writers discussed include Ann Bannon, Gwendolyn Brooks, William Burroughs, Truman Capote, John Cheever, Ralph Ellison, Allen Ginsberg, Chester Himes, Jack Kerouac, Paule Marshall, Tillie Olsen, Grace Paley, Walker Percy, Sylvia Plath, Philip Roth, J.D. Salinger, Hubert Selby Jr., Jo Sinclair, Gore Vidal, and Hisaye Yamamoto.

Alan M. Wald's *Exiles from a Future Time: The Forging of the Mid-Twentieth Century Literary Left* is an impressive major new study of the often turbulent relationship between politics and literature in America. Wald traces the literary left in the United States from the inception of a communist-led tradition established in the early 1930s to the New Left cultural upheaval in the 1960s. *Exiles* is a thorough and investigative survey of this much-overlooked transition period in leftist American literature. Wald draws on original research from archive material, interviews with writers and their families, and unpublished memoirs, fiction, and poetry. There are familiar names here, such as Mike Gold, Langston Hughes, Meridel LeSueur, and Muriel Rukeyser, coupled with less familiar ones: William Attaway, John Malcolm Brinnin, Stanley Burnshaw, Joy Davidman, Sol Funaroff, Joseph Freeman, Alfred Hayes, Eugene Clay Holmes, V.J. Jerome, Ruth Lechlitner, and Frances Winwar. The range of Wald's project is immense: he successfully chronicles the cultural communist movement from its initial founding ambitions to its development and dispersal over four decades. In this, the first volume of a trilogy, Wald examines the relationship between a cultural communist movement and avant-garde poets, the fashioning of a Black radical literary movement, and the unease between feminist concerns and class identity and the personalities involved in party-led publications and institutions. He states that the sheer expansiveness of this study required him to write not a literary study *per se* but 'a collective biography', an ambition which he names as a 'humanscape'. The result is an intricate patterning of intersecting personal histories, historical accounts, and cultural ambitions.

In a similar vein M. Keith Booker's study *The Post-Utopian Imagination: American Culture in the Long 1950s* scrutinizes the relationship between cultural production and American politics. Interestingly Booker seeks to extend a definition of the 1950s as a neatly ringfenced decade, arguing instead for a consideration of what he terms 'the long fifties'. In doing so he seeks to encompass a sense of continuity between post-war fiction and American Cold War hysteria. His key argument is that a close interrelationship exists between the Cold War and the rise of postmodernism. The first chapter makes considered reflections upon a 'bleak vision' in American fiction of the period which includes Joseph Heller's *Catch-22*, J.D. Salinger's *The Catcher in the Rye*, and E.L. Doctorow's *Welcome to Hard Times*. The chapter's main focus is Nabokov's novels, especially *Invitation to a Beheading*, *Bend Sinister*, *Lolita*, and *Pale Fire*. Booker's second chapter examines the relationship between American realism and leftist fiction of the 'long fifties'. Initially he contextualizes this discussion by addressing the proletarian fiction of the

1930s and 1940s. Major attention is paid to African American writers W.E.B. Du Bois, Richard Wright, Chester Himes, and Ralph Ellison, while of particular relevance to this section is the overview offered on the work of John Dos Passos, Norman Mailer, Upton Sinclair, Mary McCarthy, Budd Schulberg, and Alvah Bessie. The third chapter considers the explosion in the production and consumption of popular literature. Booker suggests that the popular fiction of the post-war period lacks a utopian energy, and provides readings of crime fiction ranging from Mickey Spillane's novels to Jim Thompson's pulp fiction. Individual works by Thompson examined in detail include *Now on Earth*, *Heed the Thunder*, *Nothing More Than Murder*, *Savage Night*, *The Killer Inside Me*, *Pop. 1280*, *The Kill-Off*, and *The Getaway*. Booker suggests that Thompson's pulp fiction can be read as an incisive denouncement of American capitalism. The final chapter offers a cultural reading of American film through focusing on the anti-utopian orientation of the films of Alfred Hitchcock. Booker's chronicling of the Hitchcock oeuvre is remarkably placed in juxtaposition to the Walt Disney films of the same period.

An extensive survey of post-war American fiction is mapped out in Morris Dickstein's *Leopards in the Temple: The Transformation of American Fiction, 1945–70*. Dickstein reflects upon the relationship between the individual and culture, suggesting that literary representations of alienation and psychic disintegration reflect the anxieties of the Cold War and the atomic age. Importantly, he demonstrates how writing challenges the official values of a repressive post-war culture. His key thesis is that the changes in American fiction during this period reflect the transformation of society as a whole. In surveying novelists of the 1950s he suggests that, 'where Marx had once been their guide to class conflict they turned to Freud, to existentialism or even theology as tutors in the shadowy recesses of the psyche'. Persuasively *Leopards in the Temple* examines how the writing of the 1960s emerged from the cultural phenomena of the preceding decades, including road novels, avant garde painting, bebop, film, and psychoanalysis. As mentioned, the range of this survey is impressive, and the multiple references to different novels are encyclopedic. The study is divided into four key chapters. Dickstein's first chapter examines war novels from the Second World War to Vietnam, with detailed examination of Kurt Vonnegut, Norman Mailer, James Jones, Joseph Heller, Thomas Pynchon, and Tim O'Brien. The second chapter examines the 'New Fiction' of the 1950s, including Saul Bellow, Gore Vidal, and Truman Capote. The spontaneity and vitality of 1950s and 1960s counter-culture is scrutinized in the third chapter. Dickstein proposes that the emergence of Beat writing must be analysed in relation to the economic expansion and social mobility of the post-war decades, and considers the work of Jack Kerouac, J.D. Salinger, John Updike, John Cheever, Vladimir Nabokov, John Barth, and Richard Yates. The final chapter, entitled 'Apocalypse Now', considers a literature of extremity, and charts the development of both Mailer's and Bellow's writing into the 1960s and 1970s, as well as giving detailed attention to the Bildungsromans of African American authors Ralph Ellison and Richard Wright. *Leopards in the Temple* provides a detailed chronology of this period in American fiction, indicating how material consumption in post-war society 'soon translated into cultural consumption, into changes in morality, values and style'.

The enthusiasm for a critical mapping out of Beat literary communities continues this year. A major collection of fourteen essays, Myrsiades, ed., *The Beat*

Generation: Critical Essays, examines the range of writing that can be categorized as Beat and the influence it still exerts on contemporary fiction. The discussions range from the work of key Beat figures Jack Kerouac, William Burroughs, and Allen Ginsberg to lesser-known writers such as Oscar Zeta Acosta and William Kotzwinkle. In his introduction Robert Bennett argues for a more critical contextualization of Beat literature. He states that 'a central pedagogical objective of teaching Beat literature is to complicate a commonly held oversimplified understanding of the 1950s as a cultural war between the Beats and the Squares'. The first essay, by Ann Douglas, examines Kerouac's poetics, making reference to the author's key novels *On the Road, Visions of Cody, Big Sur*, and *Dr. Sax*. Ronna C. Johnson reads Kerouac's work within a postmodern context, while a configuration of temporality in *On the Road* is offered by Erik M. Mortenson's essay. Steve Wilson examines both *On the Road* and *The Subterraneans* as a writer's quest for spiritual pilgrimage. Nancy McCampbell Grace provides a study of race, gender, and class in Kerouac's *Maggie Cassady, The Subterraneans*, and *Tristessa*. Fiona Paton concentrates her reading on the stylistic achievements of *Dr. Sax*. Two essays are dedicated to the work and reception of Burroughs's writing: Douglas G. Baldwin concentrates upon the complex relationship between textual experimentation and the language of film in the author's novels, while Timothy S. Murphy investigates the problems of teaching Burroughs's *Naked Lunch*. Terence Diggory and Robert Kern provide readings of Ginsberg's and Gary Snyder's poetry. Of further relevance to this section are the three final essays of the collection, which seek to extend an understanding of the category Beat writing and also its influence. A. Robert Lee provides a reading of an ethnic Beat culture by focusing on the writing of Oscar Zeta Acosta. Robert E. Kohn draws critical attention to the largely neglected novel *The Fan Man* by William Kotzwinkle. The final essay of the collection by Anthony Waine and John Wooley considers the impact and influence of Beat writing upon German writers Wolf Wondratscheck, Rolf Dieter Brinkmann, and Jörg Fauser.

A further groundbreaking contribution to this field has been published this year. Johnson and Grace, eds., *Girls Who Wore Black*, is a collection of eleven essays devoted to the poetry and prose of three generations of women associated with Beat writing. In a revisionary evaluation the editors state that, in spite of their exclusion from discourses of Beat art and creativity, 'women were integral to Beat's development and culture and conventions'. The collection focuses much-overdue critical attention on the work of writers Helen Adam, Diane di Prima, Joyce Johnson, Hettie Jones, Elise Cowen, Brenda Frazer, Joanne Kyger, and Ann Waldman. Pertinent to this section are the following essays on prose and memoirs from a second generation of Beat writers. Ronna Johnson examines the first Beat novel written by and about a Beat woman, Joyce Johnson's *Come Join the Dance*; Barrett Watten investigates Hettie Jones's poetics and memoir-writing; and Nancy Grace draws from memoir-writing by Hettie Jones, Diane di Prima, and Brenda Frazer, arguing that women Beats' experimentation with the genre of life-writing expands the limits of Beat literary discourse. The closing essay of the volume, by Tim Hunt, reflects on the impact on Beat studies of the emergence of Beat women writers as a viable locus of critical enquiry. The expansiveness and range of this collection, moving from detailed examination of poetry and poetics to novel and memoir, force one to reconsider the established paradigm of Beat writing as exclusively male territory. Furthermore, *Girls Who Wore Black* makes important assertions on the relationship between the textual representation of female subjectivity and literary and cultural transgression.

In *The Holocaust of Texts: Genocide, Literature and Personification* Amy Hungerford proposes that 'an understanding of literature and understanding of holocaust are connected by certain beliefs about the nature of representation and its relation to persons in the second half of the twentieth century'. Although the volume does not propose to be an overall survey, Hungerford's study situates elements of post-war American literature and culture in relation to a theoretical understanding of Holocaust Studies. She challenges what she calls the 'personification' of texts. Chapter 1 examines the Holocaust imagery of Sylvia Plath's poetry. Chapter 2 considers Ray Bradbury's *Fahrenheit 451* as a text examining nuclear holocaust and political and literary commentary. The third chapter focuses on the memorialization of the Holocaust through a discussion of the United States Holocaust Memorial Museum, Art Spiegelman's *Maus*, and Steven Spielberg's *Schindler's List*. Hungerford also considers the impact of trauma theory upon the reading of Holocaust survivor narratives. The final chapter provides a sustained analysis of the works of Saul Bellow, including *The Adventures of Augie March* and *Mr Sammler's Planet*, and Philip Roth's *The Ghost Writer* and *The Human Stain*. With both novelists Hungerford attempts to indicate how the legacy of the Holocaust determines the mapping out of family history.

Kenneth Womack's *Postwar Academic Fiction: Satire, Ethics, Community* traces the emergence and changing form of the academic novel from the 1950s to the present day. Womack examines what exactly an 'ethics' of reading might be by focusing on the reflexive process that occurs between the text and the reader. He interestingly proposes that the challenge faced by critics is how to construct an 'ethical criticism'. This term he suggests can be understood as a form of analysis which combines a responsiveness both to theorization and important social and cultural concerns. Individual chapters address the potential role of ethical criticism in relation to the Anglo-American novel. Detailed discussions which are of relevance to this section include chapters on Vladimir Nabokov, Joyce Carol Oates, and Jane Smiley.

Critical awareness of the dialogue between contemporary American anxieties and nineteenth-century culture informs a wide-ranging and imaginative collection of essays, Kucich and Sadoff, eds., *Victorian Afterlife: Postmodern Culture Rewrites the Nineteenth Century*. The essays attempt to historicize contemporary rewritings of Victorian culture by focusing attention on a postmodern fixation on the nineteenth century as site of the specific break between past and present. Drawing attention to 'postmodernism's privileging of the Victorian as its historical "other"', the editors suggest that contemporary Victoriana flourishes because of postmodernism's interest in 'the emergent', as it relates to economic, sexual, and political practices, in which the nineteenth century functions as a site of multiple possibilities for rupture through which postmodernism constructs its own cultural identity. Opening with a discussion of Amy Heckerling's film *Clueless* ([1995], based on Jane Austen's *Emma*) the editors discuss the crisis of postmodern historiography, or the loss of history, by pointing to the film's tongue-in-cheek substitution of contemporary icons for a range of textual 'originals', a process which 'foregrounds the dysfunctions of cultural memory in the construction of postmodern identity'. Postmodern Victoriana looks back on a lost era of high culture and popularizes its imitations. Discussion of this kind of appropriation is extended throughout the collection in relation to British and American fiction, film, and popular cultural discourses, the essays variously engaging with the suggestions that this is a manifestation of the failure to think historically or a more positive, dialogic understanding of historicity. The collection provides a theoretically informed cultural and critical guide to contemporary culture, but of particular interest in this section are references to the fiction of Caleb Carr, Michael Crichton, Philip K. Dick, E.L. Doctorow, William Gibson, Bruce Sterling, Vladimir Nabokov, Thomas Pynchon, Leslie Marmon Silko, and Neal Stephenson. Although more generally focused on the Gothic of the eighteenth and nineteenth centuries, including a chapter on the rise of American Gothic, Hogle, ed., *The Cambridge Companion to Gothic Fiction*, points to the centrality of American writers and film-makers in the evolution and popularization of contemporary Gothic. Writers discussed include William Peter Blatty, Poppy Z. Brite, Stephen King, and Anne Rice.

Specifically focused on the contemporary US, Rob Latham's *Consuming Youth: Vampires, Cyborgs, and the Culture of Consumption* addresses the convergence of the vampire and cyborg in popular culture as a manifestation and critique of the forces of consumer culture. A theoretically informed and economically focused approach to postmodern culture frames readings of cyber culture, youth fetishism, the yuppie–slacker dialectic, androgyny and MTV, information technology, and hacking. Latham points to the rise of vampires (as insatiable consumers) and cyborgs (as embodiments of the machineries of consumption) in contemporary American popular culture alongside an increasing critical awareness of their significance for understandings of postmodern subjectivity. The vampire and the cyborg 'provide fruitful models for apprehending the forms of cultural activity—of labor and of leisure—that contemporary capitalist society has staked out for American youth, offering a potent meditation on the promises and perils inherent in youth consumption'. Again, the vampire–cyborg continuum is related to an interest in the connection between contemporary culture and a past which gave rise to the development of consumer culture. Writers discussed (alongside a range of prominent film-makers) include S.P. Somtow, Anne Rice, Poppy Z. Brite, Douglas Coupland, and Pat Cadigan.

Bertens and Natoli, eds., *Postmodernism: The Key Figures*, provides an accessible and indispensable survey of postmodern critical and creative thought. Chapters covering the works of Paul Auster, John Barth, Robert Coover, Don DeLillo, William H. Gass, Toni Morrison, Thomas Pynchon, and Kurt Vonnegut are collected alongside discussions of major theorists and film-makers. The diversity of the collection is discussed by the editors as a means of addressing the difficulties in selecting a representative sample of postmodern texts, although the editors suggest that the selection provides a shortcut to some fundamental tropes. Advancing the discussion of selection in relation to the presentation of a sample of postmodern work, Joseph M. Conte, in *Design and Debris: A Chaotics of Postmodern American Fiction*, views a range of postmodern authors through the frame of chaos theory, discussing the relationship between order and disorder in the writing of John Hawkes, Harry Mathews, John Barth, Gilbert Sorrentino, Robert Coover, Thomas Pynchon, Kathy Acker, and Don DeLillo. Conte distinguishes 'proceduralists' (those whose works are based on narrative structures which locate order hidden in disorder) and 'disruptors' (those whose works discern disorder emerging from conditions of order). Concerned with the shift from modernism to postmodernism, Conte's discussion of 'proceduralists' corresponds to his understanding of the former, while his attention to 'orderly disorder' is equated with the disruptive practices of postmodern fiction which converge with contemporary scientific theories of chaos. However, 'just as order and disorder are discovered to be closely interrelated, so the methodologies of the proceduralists and the disruptors may appear to be in continual exchange and express themselves simultaneously in any given work ... so postmodern fictions perform an ... ongoing metamorphosis between figures of design and debris'.

In *Hicks, Tribes, and Dirty Realists: American Fiction after Postmodernism* Robert Rebein discusses a dominant critical attention to postmodern theories and fictions in the 1980s and early 1990s as a refusal of the writer's creative future. Rebein focuses on the postmodern suspicion of conventional narratives, on theories heralding the 'end of innocence with regard to language and mimesis' as leading to a problematic disregard for fiction that returns to realism in its evocation of a coherent sense of place and identity. For Rebein, that return, viewed as regression by postmodern orthodoxy, is often motivated by the desire to express marginal experiences for the first time. Rebein outlines two critical positions in relation to the rise of the postmodern: on the one hand the lamentation that it represents a break with modernism, and on the other the celebration of that break. Rebein, in line with recent critical attention to the relationship between modernism and postmodernism, is interested in a third possibility, that no definitive break has occurred, although this suggestion is viewed as a further challenge to the exploration of contemporary fiction through the lens of postmodernism. Rather, Rebein is interested in writers who move 'beyond' postmodern critiques of the construction of meaning to revitalize realism in the early 1990s: Tom Wolfe, Robert Stone, Alice Munro, Rick Bass, Robert Olen Butler, Denis Johnson, Thom Jones, Lorrie Moore, David Foster Wallace, Joyce Carol Oates, and Tobias Wolff, writers who accept the mimetic limitations of realism, absorbing the gains of postmodern fiction as 'experiments' to produce adaptations and evolutions of the realist mode. Interestingly, and in common with other considerations of Don DeLillo's recent work as a 'return' to the forms and thematics of 'stability' (see below), Rebein concludes his study with a consideration of DeLillo's *Underworld* as a text which 'consciously takes up ... millennial themes ... with an authority over detail borrowed from the broad tradition of realism, and an uncommon artistry born ... of the formal innovations of literary postmodernism'. Rebein's study is split into chapters on minimalism, dirty realism, hick chic or the 'white trash aesthetic', the return of the native, the 'New West' or the borderlands, tribes and breeds, coyotes and *Curanderas*, and the white prison novel. Writers considered in these categories include Raymond Carver, Frederick Barthelme, Anne Beattie, Bobbie Ann Mason, Richard Ford, Jayne Anne Phillips, William T. Vollman, Dorothy Allison, Cormac McCarthy, E. Annie Proulx, Leslie Marmon Silko, Madison Smartt Bell, Charles Frazier, Jane Smiley, Barbara Kingsolver, Thomas McGuane, Louise Erdrich, Larry McMurtry, James Welch, N. Scott Momaday, Sherman Alexie, Sandra Cisneros, Seth Morgan, Edward Bunker, and Malcolm Braly.

In 'The Exhaustion of Literature: Novels, Computers, and the Threat of Obsolescence' (*ConL* 43[2002] 518–59), Kathleen Fitzpatrick explores the impact of computer technologies on the status of the novel, outlining a range of conflicting responses to the possibilities for an electronic literary future. Fitzpatrick's concern is not so much in answering the questions she raises about the positive and negative effects of technology on literary culture, but in understanding the anxieties that underpin them through an attention to representations of computers and writers in conflict. A range of texts concerned with cyberculture are referred to, but John Barth's *LETTERS* and Richard Powers's *Galatea 2.2* are discussed at length. Fitzpatrick points out that, in the texts she considers, anxieties about the death of print lead to the production and distribution of more print, a process aimed at addressing fears about the move from humanism to post-humanism. Fitzpatrick connects these fears to the loss of white male privilege that a dismantling of hierarchical (Enlightenment) notions of the 'human' supports. The threat of obsolescence (of print) is thus translated into the framework of anxieties about cultural diversity. Another article which considers the implications of the convergence of literary and electronic culture is Jay Clayton's 'Convergence of the Two Cultures: A Geek's Guide to Contemporary Literature' (*AL* 74[2002] 807–31). Clayton explores the shifting relations between science, technology, and literature as represented in a range of contemporary fiction, discussing Neal Stephenson's *Cryptonomicon* at length, to suggest ways in which this convergence not only challenges but is also able to support humanist values. See also Marjorie Worthington's 'Bodies That Matter: Virtual Translations and Transmissions of the Physical' (*Crit* 43:ii[2002] 192–207) for a discussion of the translation of the physical body into cyberspace and its implications for understandings of subjectivity in Maureen McHugh's short story 'Virtual Love' and Caitlin Sullivan and Kate Bornstein's *Nearly Roadkill: An Infobahn Erotic Adventure*.

In *Trauma and Survival in Contemporary Fiction*, Laurie Vickroy applies the gains of the burgeoning field of trauma theory to contemporary fictions of trauma out of a concern with the ways in which questions of ethics, identity, relationality, and intentionality are explored in the intersection between private and public. In its attention to the ways in which the past is understood in the present, Vickroy's study shares some of the theoretical concerns outlined above concerning the renewed interest in the nineteenth century as part of a potentially radical historiographical project, as well as the relationship between modernism and postmodernism in changing conceptions of subjectivity and the construction of meaning. Like Rebein, Vickroy is interested in how new narrative forms are generated as a response to the legacy of postmodernism (while moving beyond it) to express marginal experiences. Attending to the thematics and stylistics of survival narratives, the concern with the oppressive nature of silences, Vickroy traces the ways in which contemporary fictions of trauma negotiate individual and collective memory in attempting to widen understandings of traumatic historical events. Of interest in this section is Vickroy's discussion of Toni Morrison's *Beloved* and *The Bluest Eye* alongside Dorothy Allison's *Bastard Out of Carolina* and Larry Heinemann's *Paco's Story*.

(b) Individual Authors

Critical interest in Flannery O'Connor's short stories and novels shows no sign of abating. In *Return to Good and Evil: Flannery O'Connor's Response to Nihilism*, Henry T. Edmondson considers the author's fascination with nihilism. He suggests that O'Connor's writing creates a modern landscape inhabited by individuals without faith, vision, or purpose. Initially he briefly draws attention to Nietzschean thought, but proposes that O'Connor's nihilistic strain is indicative of a larger cultural preoccupation. The first two chapters examine O'Connor's Catholicism and her interest in theological and philosophical treatises. The second chapter introduces two of O'Connor's academic sources: her college philosophy textbook and an article by the Jesuit philosopher Frederick Copleston on Nietzsche and Thomas Aquinas. These elements of 'nihilistic thought' are then related to the literary style, with particular reference the consideration of a Southern grotesque. The main chapters are dedicated to individual works by O'Connor. Edmondson suggests that *Wise Blood* can be read as a modern religious allegory. 'Good Country People' is considered in tandem with the philosophy of René Descartes. A philosophical reading of evil is proposed for 'The Lame Shall Enter First', while 'The Enduring Chill' is examined in the context of social philosophy. The theological works of Jacques Martin are read in conjunction with O'Connor's fascination with religious mystery in 'A View of the Woods' and the theme of redemption is considered in relation to 'The Artificial Nigger'. Edmondson's concluding chapter closes with a final examination of 'nihilism' coupled with the concepts of religious grace and prophecy as they are configured in O'Connor's writing.

The influence of Russian writer Nikolai Gogol on O'Connor is examined by Derek Maus in 'Another Roadside Epiphany: Flannery O'Connor's *Wise Blood* and Nikolai Gogol's *Dead Souls* as Religious Satires' (*SoQ* 40:iv[2002] 53–67). Maus contends that O'Connor and Gogol share similar concerns about the critical reception of their work. Maus's close textual analysis of *Wise Blood* reveals how O'Connor adopts many of the tropes, symbols, and satirical devices found in *Dead Souls*, while providing evidence that aspects of O'Connor's philosophical thought in her important essay, 'Some Aspects of the Grotesque in Southern Fiction', are directly influenced by Gogol's text. In the same journal Carey Wall, 'Ritual Technique and Renewal in "Kin"' (*SoQ* 40:iv[2002] 39–52) examines two short stories by Eudora Welty, 'The Wanderers' and 'Kin'. Wall proposes that the patterning of Welty's short stories highlights the passage from traditional storytelling techniques to a modernist aesthetic.

An extensive two-volume study of Nabokov's writing, Grayson, McMillin, and Meyer, eds., *Nabokov's World* appears this year. The first volume, *The Shape of Nabokov's World*, makes considerable reference to Nabokov's cross-cultural and linguistic situation as an immigrant in the United States. This cultural mapping is investigated through individual essays on Nabokov's *Bend Sinister*, *Glory*, *Lolita*, and *Pale Fire*. Two essays directly address Nabokov's status an immigrant and exile in the United States. D. Barton Johnson considers Nabokov's engagement with 1960s culture and Suellen Stringer-Hye investigates Nabokov's representation of popular culture in his novels. The second volume, *Reading Nabokov*, addresses influences on the author's work. Individual chapters examine his early writing, including his poetry and short stories, and his indebtedness to Alexander Pushkin and Fyodor Dostoevsky. Neil Cornwell considers the influence of Henry James on his novels, while John Burt Foster Jr. draws parallels between his works and the modernism of W.B. Yeats. *Lolita* is considered by Ellen Pifer in relation to Edith Wharton's *The Children*.

As already mentioned, critical interest in Beat literature is evident in this year's review. An additional response to Kerouac's poetics is provided by John Shapcott in

"'I didn't punctuate it": Locating the Tape of Jack Kerouac's *Visions of Cody* and *Doctor Sax* in a Culture of Spontaneous Improvisation' (*JAmS* 36:ii[2002] 231–48). Shapcott examines the relationship between recorded or taped material and Kerouac's written text and considers the intersection between the spontaneity of Kerouac's performance and its transcription on the page in terms of contingency. He also provides an illuminating discussion of the problems of defining performance genres.

In *Colonial Affairs: Bowles, Burroughs and Chester Write Tangier*, Greg A. Mullins investigates the relationship between homosexuality and colonialism in the novels of Paul Bowles, William Burroughs, and Alfred Chester. Drawing on elements of psychoanalytic, queer, and colonial theory, he examines each novelist's attempt to construct an individual response to race and colonialism. Mullins integrates biographical study with textual analysis to illustrate how Tangiers for these three writers becomes an 'interzone' for intersecting dualities. Furthermore he provocatively suggests that Tangiers is an expedient location which enabled the novelists to address the multiple crises of identity, desire, and loss that motivated their writing. The chapters on Bowles pay close attention to his novels *The Sheltering Sky*, *The Spiders House*, and *The Time of Friendship*, and the early short story 'Tea on the Mountain'. The concluding chapter examines Bowles's collaboration with and translations of Moroccan writers Larbi Layachi, Mohammed Mrabet, and Mohamed Choukri. Mullins suggests that these translations provide a space to interrogate narratives of identity that dissect the distinction between 'author' and 'translator'. Through examining Burroughs's novels *Junky*, *Queer*, and *Naked Lunch* Mullins charts the novelist's relationship to opiates, sexuality, writing, and repatriation, arguing that for Burroughs the promiscuous mixing occasioned by Tangiers' sexual tourism establishes a space where national, religious, and cultural interests become blurred. Framed in this way, in Burroughs's novels desire supplants rigorous boundaries and ideologies. In exploring Chester's writing Mullins also makes reference to his periods of exile in Morocco, reading his work as reflective of issues of importance to post-war American culture. Chester's short stories, the novel *The Exquisite Corpse*, and the fragment of a book-length project entitled *The Foot* all represent a subjectivity that is fractured and violently dispersed. Mullins also suggests that Chester's writing challenges the violence enforced through the categorization of identity along lines of gender, sexuality, race, and religion. *Colonial Affairs* contends that in Morocco Chester imagined a surreal world in which sexual, cultural, and racial difference did not matter.

In 'A Place Both Imaginary and Realistic: Paul Auster's *The Music of Chance*' (*ConL* 43[2002] 488–517), Ilana Shiloh draws on theories of chance outlined by Jacques Derrida and Mikhail Bakhtin to consider affinities between the picaresque tradition and the American road narrative, as they each present models of freedom based on the experience of wandering outsiders. Attending to the ways in which the picaresque elements of Auster's road narrative shift towards tragedy, Shiloh charts the movement by which the two conflicting modes implode, the tragic subverting the carnivalesque elements of the picaresque, the picaresque stripping the tragic elements of their gravity. For Shiloh, this collision of genres results in a destabilization of the ontology of the fictional world which critiques an American ethos formed in relation to notions of paternity and the conditions of late capitalism. Joseph S. Walker, in 'Criminality and (Self) Discipline: The Case of Paul Auster'

(*MFS* 48[2002] 389–421), discusses the interplay of two opposed forms of disciplinary power in Auster's fiction: a dominant, patriarchal social structure, and a self-discipline that contains the hope for freedom. Walker traces the ways in which crime is represented as a point of crisis at the interface between these conflictual models of power, extending the discussion with reference to a Foucauldian frame to suggest that Auster's fiction demands that the reader inhabit a middle ground of textual criminality. Also published this year but not received was Ilana Shiloh, *Paul Auster and Postmodern Quest: On the Road to Nowhere* (Lang).

In 'Don DeLillo's Return to Form: The Modernist Poetics of *The Body Artist*' (*ConL* 43[2002] 736–59), Philip Nel attends to DeLillo's use of language in the construction of a text which moves away from the postmodern social concerns of his earlier works towards a modernism of form, focused on the relationship between language and meaning. Although Nel acknowledges the political dimension of modernism, his emphasis on DeLillo's attention to language as removed from social issues conforms to a universalizing tendency often inherent in literary and critical 'returns'. Leonard Wilcox, in 'Don DeLillo's *Underworld* and the Return of the Real' (*Con L* 43[2002] 120–70), discusses the return of the 'real' as the belated traumatic effects of the bomb in post-war America. For Wilcox 'in its exploration of traumatic alterity, the novel explores the residue of the real harbored in the cultural unconscious', a position which leads to a focus on language which contrasts with that of Nel (above) in its politically engaged assertion that 'writing the unsayable alterity of the real is always an act of hopeful excess and desire which is implicated in the traces, metonymic displacements and relays of language'.

Lilley, ed., *Cormac McCarthy: New Directions*, collects new readings of McCarthy's work as they contribute to an understanding of his treatment of race and gender, an area of enquiry surprisingly neglected in previous years. Essays in the collection employ a variety of critical frames: in those by Dana Phillips, K. Wesley Berry, and Sara Spurgeon, McCarthy's attention to the timeless, the inhuman, and the failure of myth is considered as the foundation of an ecocritical approach; McCarthy's revisionist history of the Southwest is understood by Adam Parkes as an emphasis on the performativity of American selfhood; Ann Fisher-Wirth celebrates McCarthy's exploration of femininity and abjection in *Outer Dark*; Daniel Cooper Alarcón considers McCarthy's validation of the chivalric code of the American West alongside a self-conscious treatment of stereotypical representations of Mexico; Timothy P. Caron discusses the possibilities for pedagogy and multiculturalism in the teaching of McCarthy's *All the Pretty Horses*; Dianne C. Luce assesses McCarthy's engagement with Platonic philosophy in *Child of God*; Rick Wallach traces connections between *Blood Meridian* and Old English epic; and Edwin T. Arnold (*The Crossing*), George Guillemin (*Blood Meridian*), Linda Townley Woodson (*The Border Trilogy*), Matthew R. Horton (*The Orchard Keeper*), and Robert L. Jarrett (*Cities of the Plain*) explore the possibilities for theological, psychoanalytic, semiotic, historiographical, and postmodern readings respectively. Like several of the essays above, Robert C. Sickels and Marc Oxoby's 'In Search of a Further Frontier: Cormac McCarthy's Border Trilogy' (*Crit* 43:iv[2002] 347–59) explores conflictual strands in McCarthy's work—in *The Border Trilogy*, the movement from a celebration of pastoral vision to a recognition that its realization is permanently impossible is understood as a chronicle of the death of American pastoralism, as well as its defining work, 'in which a nostalgia for what can never again be attained replaces dreams of a pastoral future'. In *The Late Modernism of Cormac McCarthy*, David Holloway historicizes McCarthy's fiction as a response to the conditions of late capitalism, suggesting that it dramatizes a dialectic between modernism and postmodernism. In Holloway's schema modernism is conceptualized as an attempt to 'recover or reinvent some sense of a critical distance between culture and the world upon which culture reports' and postmodernism as 'a logic of paralysis and closure [in which] ... the chain of signification that words form now defers the capacity of language to say anything determinate or meaningful about the concrete objects ... that language was once thought to interrogate or name'. Holloway's study represents a theoretically informed and innovative integration of opposing schools of McCarthy criticism.

In *Lines of Flight: Discursive Time and Countercultural Desire in the Work of Thomas Pynchon*, Stefan Mattessich presents a theoretically dense and specifically focused study of Pynchon's concern with the features of late capitalism (namely the rise of the military-industrial complex, consumerism, bureaucratization, specialization in the workplace, standardization of social activity, and the influence of the mass media) to suggest that Pynchon's use of parody, satire, and farce dramatizes the transformation of experiences of time in the post-war period. Mattessich connects Pynchon's attention to temporal transformation with the more general counter-cultural impulse of the 1960s and 1970s towards escape, suggesting that flight from the dominant culture becomes an act of self-negation; the inherent problem with this movement is that such opposition is defined by the very order it seeks to reject. Mattessich's reading of Pynchon centres on the ethical necessity of recognizing one's own susceptibility to discursive forms of determination. Samuel Cohen, in '*Mason & Dixon* & the Ampersand' (*TCL* 48[2002] 264–91), presents a more optimistic reading of Pynchon's 1997 novel. He discusses Pynchon's involvement in the graphic design of the text, particularly in relation to the centrality and magnification of the ampersand, as connected to his central concern in the novel—the emphasis on relation, connection, and possibility in America, an emphasis which represents a departure from the concerns with detachment and isolation of his earlier works.

In 'Postmodern Jewish Identity in Philip Roth's *The Counterlife*' (*MFS* 48[2002] 422–43), Derek Parker Royal cites *The Counterlife* as marking a turning-point in Roth's career, in its 'use of narrative labyrinths in articulating the construction of a postmodern Jewish-American identity'. For Royal, this text is the first in which Roth marries a concern with finding a place within the larger Jewish community with a narrative instability and non-linearity which problematize ethnic identity—an endeavour which seeks to negotiate between choice (identity as indeterminate) and responsibility (Jewish history as materiality). In 'Tragedy and Farce in Roth's *The Human Stain*' (*Crit* 43[2002] 211–27) Elaine B. Safer presents a detailed close reading of the novel which attends to the ways in which Roth's exaggeration and distortion work to evoke a comic response to tragic events. Safer suggests that Roth uses 'extremely farcical black-humor ... to disorient readers and make them vulnerable to ... tragic irony'.

4. Drama

(a) General

With each passing year it becomes harder to maintain the fiction that the boundaries of twentieth-century American drama are remotely stable. The old view that American dramatic literature only came of age with Eugene O'Neill, who conveniently began serious work as a playwright as the First World War loomed, has recently been undermined by heavyweight studies, including several chapters in the three-volume *Cambridge History of American Theatre*, edited by Don B. Wilmeth and Christopher Bigsby [1998–2000]. Recent critical work confirms the obvious point that O'Neill is a decidedly melodramatic playwright with significant roots in nineteenth-century American theatre, but more importantly indicates the erosion of a previously confident general distinction between Victorian melodrama and twentieth-century realism and modernism. Consequently, a study like Alan L. Ackerman, *The Portable Theatre: American Literature and the Nineteenth-Century Stage*, which is primarily concerned with the influence of theatre on writers like Herman Melville, William Dean Howells, Louisa May Alcott, and Henry James, is of potential interest to scholars of twentieth-century drama, who are increasingly obliged to familiarize themselves with the preceding period.

Still more unavoidable is the welter of studies dedicated to theatre and performance, as opposed to drama. Such work makes problematic, even suspect, the attempt to restrict discussion to playwrights whose work can be studied as written texts. So, too, does much of the primary material itself. What, for example, is one to make of a figure like Anna Deavere Smith, whose work can exist as text yet is conceptually inextricable from her own performance? Such questions are prompted by the proliferation of books on performance, such as Mason and Gainor, eds., *Performing America: Cultural Nationalism in American Theatre*. This contains useful essays on figures such as Suzan-Lori Parks, alongside David Savran's essay 'Queering the Nation', on the already canonical Tony Kushner; yet the general orientation towards performativity and various modes that are inflected by a sense of theatricality, and away from prioritizing the written text, places much of the book outside the present discussion.

I mention *The Portable Theatre* and *Performing America* this year, however, because although they passed under the radar when they were published in 1999 they are the occasion of an important short essay by Bruce McConachie, 'American Theater History Coming of Age' (*AmLH* 14:i[2002] 141–8), which raises issues that are absolutely central to the current state of American theatre history. McConachie argues that the 'linguistic turn' in the humanities, whereby distinct practices have been recast as discourse, 'ha[s] difficulty articulating the theater's relations with other fields of practice and hence in explaining historical change'. Moreover, criticism in this area has failed to establish its own 'good set terms', a charge McConachie levels with devastating accuracy at both of the above-mentioned books. Ackerman is guilty of maintaining too rigidly his structuring dualism of melodrama and realism; conversely, most of the contributors to *Performing America* 'muddy significant distinctions among nationalism, community cohesiveness, and racial solidarity, and this conflation obscures the meaning and coherence of their essays'. Despite its brevity, McConachie's trenchant analysis raises important supplementary questions to those covered at greater length in Susan Harris Smith's

American Drama: The Bastard Art (CUP [1997]), and although technically it is little more than a review article, anything by this critic is worth reading. I was reminded of his critique of discourse, for example, in reading Greg Miller, 'The Bottom of Desire in Suzan-Lori Parks's *Venus*' (*MD* 45:i[2002] 125–37). This takes 'a Deleuzian perspective' on this little-studied play, and 'see[s] Parks not as restaging or reinterpreting history, but as producing narratives that are defiantly antihistorical, narratives that elude the inevitably commodified representations of conflict and instead present audiences with the production of sense, the production of desire'. Although Miller's article is not a work of theatre history, one can see here both the strengths and weaknesses of some post-structuralist and postmodern theory in its simultaneous engagement with, and erasure of, history.

Slippage in the use of geographical terminology, which as McConachie shows is a central problem in several of the discussions of nationalism in *Performing America*, is addressed directly as an issue in two other recent publications. Gerri Reaves, *Mapping the Private Geography: Autobiography, Identity, and America*, notes that America may be viewed as 'an ideology, a set of cultural codes, a geographical place, a metaphorical space, a myth, a fiction, or even a state of mind'. She advances the general structural principle that in addition to the two obviously dominant properties of autobiography—genre or text, and identity or self—we 'need to add *place* as a third term'. This is partly because geographical metaphors, according to Reaves, are inescapable in studies of the self, since it is necessary 'to define the emotional, cultural, and psychic landscape in which one conceives that self to exist'. Broadly, she argues that these metaphors are self-deconstructive, and contribute to 'the crisis in autobiography studies, which focuses on authority, truth, and the stability and coherence of the subject/author'. This 'crisis', however, is nothing new: one need only consider Benjamin Franklin to be aware that self-fashioning as a construct has been refreshingly conspicuous and transparent in American autobiography for centuries. Reaves is in danger of constructing a straw man, a problem compounded by the fact that her three primary examples—Gertrude Stein's *Everybody's Autobiography* [1937], Lillian Hellman's *Scoundrel Time* [1976], and Sam Shepard's *Motel Chronicles* [1982]—are all the work of playwrights used to constructing texts from polyphonic and competing voices, with the inevitable result that any monologic, autobiographical voice in these texts appears to issue from within an ironic frame. Reaves's approach is not unconvincing, merely less radical than the theoretical platform would have us believe. The chapters on the texts themselves are detailed and persuasively argued.

The familiar problems occasioned by the use of the word 'Southern' in relation to writers hailing from that part of the United States are widely rehearsed in McDonald and Paige, eds., *Southern Women Playwrights: New Essays in Literary History and Criticism*. This brings together sixteen articles on writers as diverse as Zora Neale Hurston, Lillian Hellman, Carson McCullers, Alice Childress, Beth Henley, Marsha Norman, and Suzan-Lori Parks, as well as less widely known figures such as Rebecca Gilman, Naomi Wallace, Amparo Garcia, and Regina Porter. Some of the contributions focus on the influence of place on writer: Theresa R. Mooney's 'These Four: Hellman's Roots Are Showing', for example, uses original research productively to demonstrate the Southern contexts of Hellman's writing, while Linda Rohrer Paige identifies Atlanta as a 'hub' from which a succession of promising playwrights has recently emerged. Several critics note the benign influence of the Actors Theatre of Louisville, which is the subject of a helpful piece by Elizabeth S. Bell. The inclusion of an essay on the Maryland writer Paula Vogel (by Alan Shepard and Mary Lamb), as well as, arguably, J. Ellen Gainor's entertaining contribution on the pseudonymous and as yet unidentified 'Jane Martin', brings into play the equally familiar argument that 'the South' is less a region than an idea or state of mind. None of the pieces collected here introduces any startlingly new view on these well-worn topics, but the editors are acutely aware of the issues, and have compiled a volume of solid studies of a range of important writers. Those focusing on the issue of Southernness itself will already know to look elsewhere first, particularly to the work of Richard Gray.

King, ed., *Hollywood on Stage: Playwrights Evaluate the Culture Industry*, brings together a range of new essays devoted to plays written about Hollywood. Interestingly, if somewhat misleadingly, the earliest plays considered in detail in the book—George S. Kaufman and Marc Connelly's *Merton of the Movies* (discussed in an essay by William Hutchings), and plays by S.N. Behrman (Robert Gross)— suggest that Broadway playwrights' views of Hollywood in the 1920s were ambivalent, and that it was only with Clifford Odets's *The Big Knife* (discussed by Albert Wertheim) that, in the editor's words, 'Broadway's demonization of Hollywood begins full scale'. Thereafter there is something of a chronological gap in the collection, with the majority of the contributions being devoted to more recent and contemporary writers like Brad Fraser, Arthur Kopit, Adrienne Kennedy, Sam Shepard, and especially David Mamet, the subject of no fewer than three essays. Leslie Kane provides a detailed reading of *Speed-the-Plow* that teases out its Jewish inflections and significations, and Katherine H. Burkman discusses this play and Sam Shepard's *True West*, in both of which she finds misogyny and 'a kind of duplicity ... the playwrights, who purport to offer a critique of Hollywood, offer instead a celebration'. More sympathetic, and richer and more suggestive, is Toby Silverman Zinman's splendid 'So Dis Is Hollywood: Mamet in Hell', in which she compares Mamet's recurrent protagonist Bobby Gould to that of Dante's *Inferno*. King's collection also contains a few pieces on broader Hollywood-related topics, of which Stephen Watt's discussion of the contestable territory of low and high art, and Leslie Frost's essay on pornography, are particularly noteworthy.

Sanford Sternicht's *A Reader's Guide to Modern American Drama* is the kind of book that gives shoddiness a bad name. After a breezy overview of the 'backgrounds' and dreaded 'themes in modern American drama', Sternicht divides the century into four chronological sections, some with strange sub-headings (the last is 'August Wilson and the New Dramatists: Post-World War II Generations Sure of Themselves'), and in each section gives one playwright pride of place (O'Neill, Williams, Albee, and Wilson). With the exception of O'Neill, who gets over thirty pages, each playwright is given no more than thumbnail sketch followed by summaries of the plays that are often useless even as synopses, and sometimes barely literate: 'In *The House of Blue Leaves*, contemporary American family life is depicted in a zany situation'; 'In *American Buffalo* Mamet presents a bleak vision of American life as it satirizes capitalism'. Perhaps the book is aimed at children, but your children won't thank you if you make them read it.

American Drama (11:ii [2002]) is a special issue on gender. Once again, Suzan Lori-Parks emerges as a key figure on the contemporary American stage. Haike Frank, 'The Instability of Meaning in Suzan-Lori Parks's *The America Play*'

(*AmDram* 11:ii[2002] 4–20), serves very well not only as an introduction to this play but to Parks's work more generally. Frank makes productive use of Henry Louis Gates's seminal *The Signifying Monkey: A Theory of Afro-American Literary Criticism* (OUP [1988]), and although this approach is familiar, the discussion of Parks's work in terms of 'signifyin(g)' and what Parks terms 'Rep & Rev', or repetition and revision, is convincing. Deborah R. Geis, 'Deconstructing (A Streetcar Named) Desire: Gender Re-citation in *Belle Reprieve*' (*AmDram* 11:ii[2002] 21–31) briefly considers intertextual connections between Williams's play and three other works, including Tony Kushner's *Angels in America*, before analysing *Belle Reprieve*, a collaboration between Bloolips and Split Britches that Geis describes as 'an explicitly queer, decidedly deconstructive re-vision of *Streetcar*'. Similarly, Catherine Wiley's 'Cherríe Moraga's Radical Revision of *Death of a Salesman*' (*AmDram* 11:ii[2002] 32–46) argues that Moraga's *Shadow of a Man* 'takes the subtext of Miller's play for its subject'. Less clearly focused on the ostensible theme of this issue of *American Drama*, but absolutely in keeping with its series of essays on the almost Bloomian intertextual struggle between a contemporary text and a canonical antecedent, is Robert J. Andreach's '*The Maiden's Prayer*: Nicky Silver's Chekhovian Play' (*AmDram* 11:ii[2002] 47–66), which seeks to rescue this 1998 play from its 'tepid' reviews by exploring its connections to *The Three Sisters*. Mara Reisman takes a somewhat different, broader, and fascinating approach to intertextuality in 'Quenching the Flames of History: Joan Schenkar's *Burning Desires*' (*AmDram* 11:ii[2002] 67–85), a play Reisman sees as participating in the 'cultural bricolage' surrounding Joan of Arc in history and in stage representations.

American Drama published two further essays on writers not considered elsewhere in this year's review. Mauricio D. Aguilera Linde, 'Saroyan and the Dream of Success: The American Vaudeville as a Political Weapon' (*AmDram* 11:i[2002] 18–31), persuasively argues that in appropriating the vaudeville form for his play *Subway Circus* Saroyan subverts its usually optimistic, Horatio Alger-ish ideology, although Linde's argument that by 1930 the form 'had been absorbed by the radio and the sound films' perhaps takes insufficient account of its transformation into the grotesque and into the kinds of Brechtian political theatre that became important in the 1930s. Christopher Wixson, '"A Very Carefully Orchestrated Life": Dramatic Representations of and by Zelda Fitzgerald' (*AmDram* 11:i[2002] 32–57) concentrates on Zelda's play *Scandalabra*, but also examines her appearance in works by other writers while considering hers to be a life characterized more generally by theatrical and performative self-representations.

(b) Individual Playwrights

Madeline Smith and Richard C. Eaton, *Eugene O'Neill: An Annotated International Bibliography, 1973 through 1999*, is an extremely useful and compendious volume. The rationale for the starting date is that this is where Jordan Y. Miller's bibliographical work paused in the 1973 edition of his *Eugene O'Neill and the American Critic* (Archon). Recognizing that to continue with Miller's restriction of the terrain to America only would distort the recent history of production and publication, Smith and Eaton have included sections on foreign-language scholarship and criticism, foreign-language productions, and translations within the section on primary works. In their evaluative remarks the authors have generally accentuated the positive, and there are occasions on which one would have welcomed a more sensitive filtering mechanism. In all other respects this is an invaluable reference source that should be a compulsory library purchase for university courses on American drama. Smith and Eaton comment rather anecdotally on their experiences working on the book in 'IT HATH MADE US MAD: Two O'Neillians' Adventures in Bibliography' (*EONR* 25:i–ii[2001] 54–9).

Zander Brietzke, *The Aesthetics of Failure: Dynamic Structure in the Plays of Eugene O'Neill*, takes a potentially combative tack for a book-length study: he largely accepts the most negative critical views regarding O'Neill's work, and then considers how what might be seen as the playwright's potentially anti-theatrical formal predilections work, or fail to work, in the plays themselves by examining them from a different formal perspective in each chapter. In the first, he argues that O'Neill's was a novelistic imagination, at least to the extent that his 'narrative impulse' sprang from a 'profound antitheatrical prejudice'. The second looks at literal and metaphorical masking and unmasking of characters, a rather traditional approach that might have benefited from a more rigorous semiotic analysis. In the third, Brietzke examines the tension between onstage action and the framing of that action by the offstage world, for which the characters generally long and which therefore has an unseen but always keenly sensed structuring effect on character and action. In the final chapter he discusses the tension between tragedy and melodrama. While the discussion of the plays is solid enough, and there are useful local insights throughout the book, it is only in the penultimate chapter, on repetition and closure, that Brietzke approaches a real contribution to an understanding of O'Neill. As he explains, 'Tension always exists between the narrative drive of the plot to end in closure (e.g., suicide) and the competing desire for the play to repeat itself and form part of what O'Neill might call, with echoes of Nietzsche, the recurring life force.' That goes beyond the familiar recognition of the influence of Nietzsche towards discovering a range of possible explanations for the repetition, prolixity, and sheer length that characterize much of the playwright's work. Elsewhere, however, Brietzke too often does little more than restate well-worn, often crude or dull, views of the plays, and there are some unsophisticated passages: the blurb even suggests that Brietzke believes not only that the plays are bad, but that this 'failure' is of a similar order to the failures dramatized in tragedy. There's a certain lack of self-confidence, too, in the strange decision to give up thirty of the 258 pages to an unnecessary compilation of 'play abstracts'—although this does double as an index to Brietzke's commentary on the plays elsewhere in the book—and in the truly bizarre acts of self-flagellation in the acknowledgements, including the revelation that Charles Lyons 'advised me once never to publish anything'. Had he but thought, Lyons would presumably have advised him above all never to publish that particular remark.

In 'O'Neill' (*SoR* 38[2002] 842–8), fellow playwright Romulus Linney recalls that during his college days (1949–53) his instructors disparaged O'Neill in terms that recall those surveyed by Brietzke. Linney recalls how the experience of watching Fredric March and Jason Robards in the seminal performances of the late O'Neill's work persuaded him to become a writer. Another piece by Zander Brietzke, 'Too Close for Comfort: Biographical Truth in *Long Day's Journey into Night*' (*EONR* 25:i–ii[2001] 24–36), takes a pedagogical approach that is supplemented by three other pieces, drawn from a round-table discussion, that are also published in the latest *Eugene O'Neill Review* (25; nominally 2001, although not published until 2003). These are Thomas F. Connolly, 'The Hairy Ape in the Context of Early 20th Century American Modernism' (*EONR* 25:i–ii[2001] 77–9); Laurin Porter, 'Teaching *Long Day's Journey into Night* and Shepard's *Buried Child*' (*EONR* 25:i–ii[2001] 80–4), which not surprisingly argues that the former is modern and the latter postmodern; and Glenda Frank, 'Using O'Neill on the Immigrant Experience in the American Literature Classroom' (*EONR* 25:i–ii[2001] 85–8), which concentrates on *A Touch of the Poet*. More substantial is Richard Hayes, '"The Scope of the Movies": Three Films and their Influence on Eugene O'Neill' (*EONR* 25:i–ii[2001] 37–53), which importantly revisits O'Neill's relationship with cinema, noting that—like so many playwrights—his denunciation of the medium was accompanied by a fascination with its financial rewards, and by occasional participation in adaptations of his own plays. The three films Hayes examines are *Cabiria* [1914], *The Cabinet of Dr Caligari* [1919], and *Broadway Melody* [1929], all of which the playwright admired and which, Hayes suggests, 'had a shaping influence on O'Neill's art'. William Davies King, '"A Home! Our Home!": Eugene O'Neill and Agnes Boulton at Spithead' (*EONR* 25:i–ii[2001] 60–9), and Eileen Herrmann-Miller, 'Staging O'Neill: Staging Greek Tragedy' (*EONR* 25:i–ii[2001] 70–5), are the kind of biographical and performance pieces, respectively, that have long formed the core of the *Review*'s appeal. To my mind, the inclusion of O'Neill-oriented poetry and pastiche elsewhere in this year's issue has regrettable shades of the fanzine.

J. Chris Westgate, 'Stumbling Amid the Ruins: Yank's Absurd Inheritance in *The Hairy Ape*' (*EONR* 25:i–ii[2001] 5–11) discusses, in the context of Yank's failed ideology, the play's explicit references to the Industrial Workers of the World. According to Lawrence Dugan in 'O'Neill and the Wobblies: The IWW as a Model for Failure in *The Iceman Cometh*' (*CompD* 36:i–ii[2002] 109–24), the same organization is alluded to as the 'Movement' in O'Neill's play. Dugan uses this connection to explore the class divisions and theme of failure in *Iceman*. Brenda Murphy, 'The "Genius" as Iceman: Eugene O'Neill's Portrayal of Theodore Dreiser' (*ALR* 34:ii[2002] 135–45), suggests the Dreiser of 1915 as a model for the character of Hickey in the same play, and draws parallels with Dreiser's novel *The 'Genius'*. Christopher S. Glover, 'Female Characters in (and not in) Eugene O'Neill's *The Iceman Cometh*: Tracing Twentieth-Century Feminist Response into a New Era' (*EONR* 25:i–ii[2001] 12–23), takes a curiously bifurcated approach by simply dividing his essay into two parts. The first looks at the play in the light of Simone de Beauvoir's ideas, while the second attempts 'a more (post)modern feminist reading' that rather schematically borrows from Alice Jardine a set of binary oppositions conventionally used to identify the characteristics of the sexes, and suggests that the play inverts them.

Marcia Noe, 'Intertextuality in the Early Plays of Susan Glaspell and Eugene O'Neill' (*AmDram* 11:i[2002] 1–17), indicates the difficulties presented by criticism's failure to establish its 'good set terms' (see the article by Bruce McConachie discussed in section 4(*a*) above). Here the problem surrounds the notoriously indeterminate word 'intertextuality'. Noe begins excitingly: 'Susan Glaspell and Eugene O'Neill: exactly what was the nature of their professional relationship? Did they ever attempt to collaborate on a play or read their works in progress to each other? Did they consult one another when stuck or blocked? Did they try out on each other ideas for plays?' Despite an equally arresting conclusion that sees them 'echoing and rewriting each other', however, the essay fails to unearth substantial primary material that would answer these questions directly, and instead examines the more loosely 'intertextual' resemblances between O'Neill's *In the Zone* and Glaspell's *Trifles*, though Noe does have important observations about the contemporary historical and cultural contexts. Anna Siomopoulos, 'The "Eighth o'Style": Black Nationalism, the New Deal, and *The Emperor Jones*' (*ArQ* 58:iii[2002] 57–81), argues against the view that Dudley Murphy's 1933 film version of O'Neill's work is more racist than the stage play. On the contrary, Siomopoulos provocatively argues that the title character should be seen not as a portrait of Marcus Garvey or, indeed, 'any other historically significant black nationalist ... but rather [of] Franklin Delano Roosevelt, insofar as FDR represented a new kind of imperialist president, and the welfare state represented a new kind of feudalism to millions of African Americans'. Siomopoulos further argues that the film transfers the emphasis away from Jones and towards the natives, who take on some of the qualities of the grass-roots nationalism associated with W.E.B. Du Bois. This is a stimulating and well-researched contribution to the discussion of one version of O'Neill's most controversial play. Paul Rosefeldt, 'From *Strange Interlude* to *Strange Snow*: A Study of the Absent Character in Drama' (*JEP* 23:ii–iii[2002] 117–30), investigates 'the relationship between the absent character, the concept of mourning, and the conflictual nature of war' in O'Neill's *Strange Interlude*, Arthur Miller's *All My Sons*, and Steve Metcalfe's *Strange Snow*. The figure of the absent character is relevant to drama in general, and although Rosefeldt's comments are sound enough, the selection of just three plays looks inadequate and arbitrary, the conclusions so broad as to be useless for the purposes of discrimination: 'behind every drama is a timeless pattern which unfolds the inner workings of drama itself'.

The structuralist privileging of similarity over difference also informs Judith J. Thompson, *Tennessee Williams' Plays: Memory, Myth, and Symbol*. The book focuses primarily though not exclusively on eight major plays in which Thompson discerns 'a single structural pattern', her description of which is so impressive as to be worth quoting at length. It is:

> a pattern based on the narration of a past event in the memory of a play's protagonist that invests both tale and teller with mythic significance, followed by the memory's dramatization, or reenactment, in a demythicized and consequently ironic version. The nature and content of the mythicized memory-story determine the play's symbolic characterization, mythical allusions, and archetypal images, whereas the memory's demythicized reenactment decides the play's outcome, theme, and mode. This pattern of recollection and reenactment is fundamental to the dual vision of Williams' drama: its evocation of past and present, romanticism and realism, the mythic and the mundane.

That seems to me precisely right, and Thompson's introduction, in which she adds flesh to this wonderfully healthy bone structure, is as illuminating a piece of criticism on Williams as I have seen. The problem is that it is *too* good: armed with this heuristic critical model, the attentive reader could be left to reconsider the plays alone. Expanded to book length via detailed, persuasive, but ultimately somewhat repetitive analyses of the plays, the force of Thompson's initial insight becomes dissipated, and one is left with the old problem that the mythic, structural, or Jungian model will always tend to produce sameness, with contrary details and interpretations unavoidably sidelined.

Roessel and Moschovakis, eds., *The Collected Poems of Tennessee Williams*, concentrates on published verse, and does not include any of the vast quantity of unpublished work. Although this may disappoint, the published poems are sufficiently variable in quality to suggest that this may not be an opportunity missed. As others have noted, in the best of his poetry Williams works through the dramatization of memory that finds fuller expression in his plays. The editors have included an informative introduction and helpful explanatory notes, publication histories, and textual variants. Kenneth Holditch and Richard Freeman Leavitt, *Tennessee Williams and the South*, provides an illustrated biographical account of the subject. Like McDonald and Paige's *Southern Women Playwrights* collection, reviewed above, it situates the writer within a Southern context while often making one equally aware of the South as an absence, of something consciously or unconsciously left behind in the creation of the plays. The most valuable feature of the book is the extensive photographic record, presented in a format that gives this the feel of a coffee-table book, but there is much of interest too in the sound, straightforward textual narrative.

Essay collections on Williams continue to proliferate. I have not yet seen Philip C. Kolin, *The Undiscovered Country: The Later Plays of Tennessee Williams*, which given the subject promises to be an important volume. Of those I have been able to review this year, the most useful is Gross, ed., *Tennessee Williams: A Casebook*, which benefits from the relatively high percentage of essays that consider lesser-known plays, or place Williams in less familiar contexts. There are discussions here of recently unearthed, late, and little-known pieces including *Not About Nightingales*, *Spring Storm*, *The Notebook of Trigorin*, *Out Cry*, and *Clothes for a Summer Hotel*, although there is also no shortage of articles on the most familiar work. Several comparative pieces consider Williams's work alongside that of other writers. One would have thought the comparisons to Chekhov and D.H. Lawrence were too familiar to need restating, although even here the contributors generally find something fresh to say, while some of the studies here are more ambitious, such as those by Frank Bradley and Stephanie B. Hammer that place Williams in an Enlightenment tradition. Similarly, Williams's dramatization of sexual desire has been considered countless times before, but Michael R. Schiavi still manages to take a different tack by looking at the representation of physically large women in the fiction. Gross has produced a book that will serve as a useful point of departure both for those wishing to refresh their knowledge of the major strands of Williams criticism and for those looking for something a little different.

Voss, ed., *Magical Muse: Millennial Essays on Tennessee Williams*, is derived mainly from the proceedings of a 1999 conference. Anthologies drawn from such sources tend to be of inconsistent quality, and although Voss has assembled an impressive team of scholars, some pieces are too occasional to be of particular value, and critics in general rarely keep their best critical analyses for collections of this kind. An unhelpfully hagiographic note also creeps in on occasion. Still, the interested reader will find many worthwhile pieces, such as Allean Hale and Jackson Bryer's discussions of late plays (*In the Bar of a Tokyo Hotel* and *Clothes for a Summer Hotel*, respectively), and Nancy M. Tischler's take on the filming of *A Streetcar Named Desire*. There is also some solid research here, including Albert J. Devlin's discussion of some of Williams's correspondence, and Jeff Loomis's study of manuscript variants of *Cat on a Hot Tin Roof*.

The least impressive anthologies are those published by Chelsea House in their Modern Critical Interpretations series under the editorship of Harold Bloom. The longer this series has gone on, the more it has seemed as if Bloom must be engaged in some sort of competition with himself to see who can put together a critical anthology in the shortest time. All the essays are previously published, with Bloom's 'Editor's Note' contributing at best a mere introductory sentence to each, and none to accounting for their selection. Some are good, some indifferent, and most have been culled from the most obvious sources such as standard monographs and leading journals. Bloom's critical introductions to the texts are almost equally perfunctory and in some cases as likely to say nearly as much about the bisexual human condition as about the ostensible subject of the book. Although his judgements can seem bizarre, however, it is always worth reading them on the off-chance that some gem will be concealed in a seemingly throwaway remark. The volume on *Cat on a Hot Tin Roof* is a case in point. Most of the essays are of fairly recent vintage, and certainly the reader unfamiliar with the essays by John M. Clum and David Savran, for example, will benefit from consulting them. Bloom himself, with seemingly wilful perversity, asserts that Williams 'cannot represent inwardness', and this accounts for his contention that Brick's problem is less to do with sexuality than with an unexplored and unexplained nihilism, and that therefore the play fails. Related ground is covered in more detail in Michael P. Bibler, '"A tenderness which was uncommon": Homosexuality, Narrative, and the Southern Plantation in Tennessee Williams's *Cat on a Hot Tin Roof*' (*MissQ* 55[2002] 381–400). Bibler similarly notes that the audience's experience of the play revolves around the knowledge that, if only we could understand Brick, everything would fall into place. Unlike Bloom, Bibler maintains the more familiar focus on the question of Brick's sexuality. Accepting that this is ultimately unknowable, Bibler explores instead the imbrication of white male homosexuality and the plantation setting as the cause of this undecidability. Although homosexuality is 'ideologically inconsistent' with the socio-economic context of the plantation, not least because it constructs a barrier to succession, it remains 'a viable option for men of the planter class' as long as it does not contradict 'the patriarchal hyper-valuation of white masculinity', a line of sameness and repetitive relations between patriarchs that can 'leave the hierarchies of race, class, and gender intact'.

Philip C. Kolin continues to publish prolifically on Williams, often in the genre of the very short essay. 'Vulnerable Intimacies in Tennessee Williams's "Happy August the Tenth"' (*NConL* 32:v[2002] 4–6) looks at the exploration of sexuality in this short story, while 'Tennessee Williams, "Mother Yaws," and AIDS' (*PCRev* 13:i[2002] 63–7) is another brief account of a relatively little-known story. In other pieces Kolin considers some of the plays, as in 'Eyewitnessing in Tennessee Williams's *Small Craft Warnings*' (*NConL* 32:ii[2002] 9–11). In 'Williams's *Will Mr. Merriwether Return from Memphis?*' (*Expl* 60:ii[2002] 97–9) Kolin calls for greater appreciation of this rarely produced two-act comedy. In the same journal, he considers the implications of Skipper's name in 'Williams's *Cat on a Hot Tin Roof*' (*Expl* 60:iv[2002] 215–16). *Explicator* published a third short piece on Williams: Elizabeth C. Kobbe, 'Williams's *The Glass Menagerie*' (*Expl* 61:i[2002] 49–51), which briefly considers the differences between three versions of the play published between 1945 and 1948. Leonard J. Leff, 'And Transfer to Cemetery: The Streetcars Named Desire' (*FilmQ* 55:iii[2002] 29–37), is an important essay tracing the implications of the 1993 're-release' of Elia Kazan's 1951 film. Leff notes the alterations made in restoring four minutes of footage cut due to the demands of censorship, explores the several resulting versions of the text (including the stage version), and highlights the editorial problems posed by such restorations. JoAllen Bradham, 'Reprising *The Glass Menagerie*: William Inge's *My Son Is a Splendid Driver*' (*AmDram* 11:i[2002] 58–72) explores the intertextual connections between Williams's play and Inge's novel.

Mel Gussow, *Conversations with Miller*, appears in a now well-established series in which Gussow compiles substantial interviews he has conducted with major playwrights, and of course provides an indispensable, as well as engaging and entertaining, resource. Recent articles on Arthur Miller often mention a 1999 poll conducted by London's National Theatre that voted him the most important English-language playwright of the twentieth century, and placed *Death of a Salesman* and *The Crucible* at numbers 2 and 6 in the charts, respectively. Certainly there is no shortage of commentary on him at the moment, with essay collections on both of the aforementioned texts appearing recently, alongside a third on Miller's first major play: *Readings on 'All My Sons'*, edited by Christopher J. Smith, which is aimed squarely at the high-school market. It consists of excerpts from previously published criticism, some but not all of it from the best sources, and concentrates on the predictable elements of plot, character, and theme. In boxes offset from the text there is some useful additional material that is often more interesting than the essay extract alongside which it appears, but overall there is little here to command the attention of those outside its target audience.

Marino, ed., *'The "Salesman" Has a Birthday': Essays Celebrating the Fiftieth Anniversary of Arthur Miller's 'Death of a Salesman'*, is more substantial, containing ten essays on the dramatist's best-known play. It has been apparent for many years that critics have had trouble coming up with anything new and substantial to say on *Salesman*, and several of the essays in this book are relatively lightweight, even a bit folksy, perhaps unsurprisingly given the book's origins in the Fifth International Arthur Miller Conference at New York in 1999. The most effective contribution is Christopher Bigsby's keynote 'Arthur Miller: Time Traveller', which utilizes John Fowles's idea of 'wormholes' to examine Miller's conception of space-time throughout his career. Other essays that connect the title play to others in Miller's oeuvre are also quite revealing, including Susan C. Abbotson's treatment of *The Ride Down Mount Morgan* as a kind of sequel, and Marino's account of the play's rural, even pastoral, Brooklyn and the tension between city and country. That use of binary opposition characterizes many of the pieces that restrict themselves to the title play: Heather Cook Callow suggests that Willy's masculine and feminine sides undergo a reversal, George P. Castellito suggests that the play explores 'the tension between Marxism and Capitalism', and Matthew Roudané and Steven R. Centola also use binary oppositions in more general studies of the play. Elsewhere there are solid contributions from Brenda

Murphy and Jane K. Dominik, but the overall impression, given the pedigree of the contributors, is one of disappointment.

Bloom, ed., *The Crucible*, is yet another volume in Bloom's interminable Modern Critical Interpretations series. The previously published essays present a better-selected and more stimulating range of approaches than is sometimes the case with this series, and *The Crucible* does lend itself to critical revisitation in ways that *Salesman* does not. On the other hand, it is disappointing that the large majority of these pieces were published before 1990. The best critical work on Miller is not always the most sympathetic, and this play has occasioned a number of powerful feminist critiques, well represented here in the essays by Iska Alter and Wendy Schissel. Elsewhere there is a range of critical perspectives, many of them largely concerned with John Proctor, alongside Robert A. Martin's helpful discussion of the sources. Bloom himself doesn't like the play, which he considers dreary and inferior both to Ibsen and to Shaw's *St. Joan*. 'Miller has no imaginative understanding' of the religious sensibility of Danforth and Hathorne, but, still, the play has done some social good. Given that his introductions in this series occupy a mere page or two, it is hard not to find the self-indulgence irritating. 'I am aware that I tend to be an uncompromising aesthete', he writes. We're all aware of that, Harold.

Terry Otten, *The Temptation of Innocence in the Dramas of Arthur Miller*, is similar in many respects to Judith J. Thompson's book on Williams, reviewed above. Like Thompson, Otten begins by arguing for the presence of a dominant structuring idea in most of the playwright's work, which is then used to inform a survey of the career in the rest of the book. For Otten, 'The central threat underlying most of his plays is not the destruction *of* innocence but destruction *by* innocence and the subsequent evil it can generate.' Virtually every Miller protagonist is in pursuit of an innocence that he or she knows, consciously or unconsciously, does not exist and cannot be earned. Miller explores a post-Nietzschean world 'after the fall', while retaining an essentially religious sensibility in some respects, not least in his continuing commitment to the possibility of modern tragedy. Again, it seems to me that these arguments are right, but determine too greatly the aspects of the plays that Otten considers in the analyses of the plays that follow. Undoubtedly useful is Stefani Koorey's mammoth, 888-page *Arthur Miller's Life and Literature: An Annotated and Comprehensive Guide*, which contains an invaluable annotated survey of the criticism, as well as a chronology, a 161-page section on the primary material, and entries on doctoral dissertations and media resources, while in the survey of biographical studies there are over a hundred pages on articles alone. One can quibble—in particular, the enormous survey of play reviews would have been far more user-friendly had it been arranged by production—but anyone conducting research on Miller would be well advised to make this one of the first ports of call.

Brenda Murphy, 'Arendt, Kristeva, and Arthur Miller: Forgiveness and Promise in *After the Fall*' (*PMLA* 117:ii[2002] 314–16) uses a sophisticated framework in restating a familiar argument: that this play 'is not only a striking instance of th[e] therapeutic use of writing but also a dramatization of the operation of forgiveness and promise'. Cheryll Glotfelty, 'Old Folks in the New West: Surviving Change and Staying Fit in *The Misfits*' (*WAL* 37:i[2002] 26–49), has some interesting observations about the Nevada setting, and attempts to place Miller's characters within a framework that examines the ageing process in relation to this social and environmental context, but in general the essay is a little whimsical and even banal:

'the film suggests that change—all kinds of change—is inevitable, an ineluctable reality, and that in the face of change the best response is to adapt and become new rather than to be inflexible and get old'. Terry W. Thompson, 'Miller's *Death of a Salesman*' (*Expl* 60:iii[2002] 162–3), notes the irony of Willy's comparison of his sons to 'Adonises', since the allusion hints at their ultimate waste of their youth. Frank Ardolino, '"I'm not a dime a dozen! I am Willy Loman!"': The Significance of Names and Numbers in *Death of a Salesman*' (*JEP* 23:ii–iii[2002] 174–84), addresses an old question: are the scenes from Willy's past memories or hallucinations? Ardolino concedes that this may be impossible to resolve, but aims 'to determine the psychological associative processes which dictate why and how Willy experiences these events' by examining the repetition of verbal, visual, and numerical references. In practice, this approach adds little to other studies of the expressionistic devices in the play, and there are times when Ardolino strains for effect: 'Bangor, the name of the last city on Willy's route, onomatopoetically explodes—bang!—recalling imagery of emotional inflation and collapse associated with Willy's dreams.' As one who has inhabited a different Bangor for many years I remain convinced that these places rarely explode, onomatopoetically or otherwise.

Gregory J. Hampton, 'Black Men Fenced In and a Plausible Black Masculinity' (*CLAJ* 46:ii[2002] 194–206) explores some of the connections between August Wilson's *Fences* and *Death of a Salesman*, which is unmistakably one of its major sources. Wilson's plays are usually and inevitably considered primarily in the context of African American history, but John J. Hanlon's '"Niggers got a right to be dissatisfied": Postmodernism, Race, and Class in *Ma Rainey's Black Bottom*' (*MD* 45:i[2002] 95–124), despite the unpromising list of abstract nouns in the title, fascinatingly reads the play in terms of postmodern economics. Hanlon finds a tension between the Fordist model of production that operates in the 1927 world of the play, and the post-Fordist, postmodern 'flexible accumulation' that actually characterizes the practices in which the characters are involved, notably the recording and marketing of music. Although this tension between the blues and market consumption has been noted before, and might easily be read in terms of specifically African American history, Hanlon convincingly argues that it expresses a more general shift in Western society and economics.

Roudané, ed., *The Cambridge Companion to Sam Shepard*, appears in a well-established series that presents all-new collections of essays by major critics. Some of the volumes in this series have been a little dull and repetitive, because not all writers have the complexity or range of material to repay repeated re-examination. This is not the case with Shepard, who for some inexplicable reason has received less attention of late than his work merits, and Roudané's volume is outstanding. The editor himself contributes a brief introductory overview, a substantial new interview with the playwright, and the first major critical discussion of *The Late Henry Moss*, his most recent play at time of publication. Christopher Bigsby's contribution, 'Born Injured: The Theatre of Sam Shepard', is a more substantial, poetically charged introductory piece that identifies familiar Shepardian themes of impermanence of place and identity while more unusually suggesting continuities with the work of Federico García Lorca and, provocatively, Georgei Gurdjieff. Other contributors provide detailed accounts of the major plays, including Thomas P. Adler on *Curse of the Starving Class* and *Buried Child*, Leslie Kane on *True West* and *A Lie of the Mind*, and Leslie A. Wade on the plays of the 1990s. Other writers look at Shepard through a range of interpretative lenses: Carla J. McDonough writes on 'patriarchal pathology from *The Holy Ghostly* to *Silent Tongue*', while John M. Clum gives a fascinating take on the 'Western' quality of Shepard's work by exploring in detail its intertextual relations with the Western film genre. The remarkable scope and inventiveness of Shepard's career is well brought out in a range of more specialized discussions: Kimball King writes on cinema, David J. DeRose on music, Ann C. Hall on non-dramatic works, and Brenda Murphy on postmodern self-reflexivity in Shepard's writing. Similarly, the essays on performance, including Stephen J. Bottoms on Theatre Genesis, pieces by and about Joseph Chaikin, and Johan Callens's account of the unproduced and unpublished *Man Fly* (Shepard's adaptation of Marlowe's *Doctor Faustus*) bring out his experimentation and potential for theatrical reinterpretation. In this way the collection establishes Shepard's synaesthetic quality, his fascination with all aspects of visual and aural presentation that allows a volume of this kind to give a multivalent, cubist set of perspectives on the subject and prevents it from becoming a mere introductory trawl through the texts.

Philip Hanson, 'Against Tribalism: The Perils of Ethnic Identity in Mamet's *Homicide*' (*Clio1* 31:iii[2002] 257–77), provides a solid account of the various national, ethnic, and familial identities competing for the allegiance of Bobby Gold, the protagonist of Mamet's film, and deftly integrates his analysis with a lucid and well-informed understanding of some of the major theories of nationalism and ethnicity. As such, it is another contribution to the currently dominant focus on these issues (see McConachie, above). Michele Ronnick, 'David Mamet at Play: Paronomasia, the Berlin Soldier Conrad Schumann (1942–1998) and *Wag the Dog*' (*Germanic Notes and Reviews* 33:i[2002] 26–8), suggests a connection between the character of Schumann, who is not present in the source novel, and Conrad Schuman, who escaped from East Berlin in 1961 in what Ronnick describes as 'a "media-enhanced" event'. There is inconsistency in the spellings of each Schumann's name in the original. Douglas Stenberg, 'Chekhov's *Uncle Vanya* Translated on 42nd Street' (*LFQ* 30:i[2002] 24–8), briefly indicates some of the differences between the film, derived from Mamet's stage adaptation, and Chekhov's play, specifically with regard to the language.

Boris Trbic, 'Mamet's Business as Usual: Moviemaking and the "Quest for Purity" in Mamet's *State and Main*' (*Senses of Cinema* 14[2001]) is published in an Australian electronic journal I have not yet seen. Three pieces on Mamet not reviewed in *YWES* in their year of publication should also be mentioned. Andrea Greenbaum, 'Brass Balls: Masculine Communication and the Discourse of Capitalism in David Mamet's *Glengarry Glen Ross*' (*JMS* 8:i[1999] 33–43) gets onto the wrong tack immediately in stating that 'there has been scant critical examination of the purely masculine elements that permeate the play', and with few exceptions 'no direct extensive criticism addressing the overt parallel between masculinity and capitalism, and the means by which Mamet's characters, who are constituted by the demands of capitalism, use language as a source for domination and manipulation'. On the contrary, this is a precise description of the very topics that inform virtually everything that has ever been written about the play, and Greenbaum's discussion, while perfectly competent, says nothing that has not been said before. Similarly, Richard Badenhausen, 'The Modern Academy Raging in the

Dark: Misreading Mamet's Political Incorrectness in *Oleanna*' (*CollL* 25:iii[1998] 1–19), contends that the play is less about political correctness than about 'the difficulties of acquiring and controlling language, especially in the specialized environment of the academy. ... *Oleanna* ultimately explores the perils of inferior teaching'. This really is not news, and although Badenhausen presents his arguments cogently, it is impossible any longer to muster enthusiasm for essays that treat this over-exposed play thematically, or as a serious debate. As Mamet himself says, 'thematic considerations are not that important to me. It's poetical considerations.' That observation comes from an interview conducted by his former college tutor, Barry Goldensohn, who in 'David Mamet and Poetic Language in Drama' (*Agni* 49[1999] 139–49) gives a lively and entertaining reading of several passages, focusing on connections with Beckett and Pinter.

Gene A. Plunka, *The Black Comedy of John Guare*, is the first book-length critical study of this playwright. The introductory chapter provides a career overview and a summary of Plunka's general view of Guare. Some of this is uninspiring: 'there is no human or spiritual connection; American society has turned individuals into neurotic individuals out of tune with self and others. Guare laments that the hype to be rich and famous, the need to rely on pop fantasies, has become synonymous with the American dream'. There is little here to distinguish Guare from a lot of other playwrights, and the thematic approach, which rarely helps to identify the distinguishing characteristics of a playwright, is sometimes married unhappily, as here, to an enervating clunkiness of expression. The rest of the book, a chronological survey of the career, is better written and brings out well Plunka's central argument that the human imagination, which is seen as escape, is expressed in the comic and farcical forms and the bizarre transitions and juxtapositions that escape the bounds of the naturalistic straitjacket. A related view of what is probably Guare's best-known play is given in Gordon E. Slethaug, 'Chaotics and Many Degrees of Freedom in John Guare's *Six Degrees of Separation*' (*AmDram* 11:i[2002] 73–93), which provides a thorough, if slightly schematic, reading of the play in terms of chaos theory. This approach has been applied to contemporary drama many times (notably in William W. Demastes, *Theatre of Chaos: Beyond Absurdism, into Orderly Disorder*, CUP [1998]) without supplying the discriminatory potential of a truly productive theory, and Slethaug's disappointingly bland conclusions are a case in point: 'Disorder and order, randomness and pattern, inside and outside, center and margins, black and white, male and female (or male and male), experience and narrative—these are inextricably intertwined. One without the other makes life unbearable, either totally dull or utterly random and uncontrollable.'

Plunka's book is usefully supplemented by Jane Kathleen Curry, *John Guare: A Research and Production Sourcebook*. This contains a chronology and a short chapter on the life and career, as well as surveys of the primary and secondary material. The plot summaries of some of the harder-to-obtain items are helpful, and overall I found this volume more useful than Barbara Lee Horn, *Lillian Hellman: A Research and Production Sourcebook*, also from Greenwood. The format of each volume is the same, with entries on each play providing a synopsis, critical overview, and cross-references to production reviews elsewhere in the book; but Curry's survey of Guare provides more detail, and the Hellman study suffers more from the restriction to plays.

Gail Ciociola, *Wendy Wasserstein: Dramatizing Women, their Choices and their Boundaries*, begins with an overview of Wasserstein's relationships to liberal, cultural, and materialist feminisms. Although Ciociola's is the first book-length study of Wasserstein, this approach to women's writing in general is terribly familiar; and most of us by now, surely, are bored to tears with the construction of neologisms such as 'fem-en(act)ment' to describe ideas that might have been better expressed without resort to the off-the-shelf hyphens and parentheses. Moreover, drama by American women has been receiving overdue but extensive critical attention for many years now, with writers like Susan Glaspell, Lorraine Hansberry, and Adrienne Kennedy, to name but a few, now accepted as major figures in their own right; so to suggest, by way of conclusion, that one of the reasons for Wasserstein's failure to attain canonical status to date is patriarchal oppression looks crude and opportunistic. The analyses of the plays themselves are substantial, however, and ironically do much to bring out the importance of Wasserstein's humour, although there is no corresponding lightness of touch in Ciociola's style.

5. Native, Asian American, Latino/a, and General Ethnic Writing

Ron Welburn's *Roanoke and Wampum: Topics in American Heritage and Literatures*, a 2001 publication in Lang's American Indian Studies series which draws on his own mixed Cherokee/Assateague-Gingaskin and African American lineage, pursues a number of interlinking lines of enquiry. The span includes the 'Other Middle Passage' of Native alongside African slavery; a sharp diagnosis of Jeffery, Lord Amherst, as both founder of Emily Dickinson's New England liberal township and yet the man who introduced germ warfare in the form of smallpox blankets against Native populations; 'spiritual stability and cultural displacement' in the mixedblood Pequot life and writings of William Apess as early nineteenth-century Massachusetts convert and missionary; a critique of the popular fiction of Robert Conley as prolific contemporary Cherokee author and of Joseph Bruchac as Abenaki poet, storyteller, and anthologist; and an appreciation of the Chippewa figure of Thomas Whitecloud (1914–72), a Yale graduate and medical doctor, whose only published work, 'Blue Winds Dancing', has deservedly become a minor Native literary classic. Welburn displays a canny knack for probing under-attended corners.

A deserved front-runner in the literary scholarship of Native America, Arnold Krupat writes with all his usual intellectual scruple and self-positioning throughout the five essays, several of them reprints, which make up *Red Matters: Native American Studies*. The opening chapter posits that three avenues into Native writing have emerged: nationalist, as in voices like Elizabeth Cook-Lynn or Craig Womack; indigenist, in which the earth serves as the source of values, as in Winona Stevenson or Linda Hogan; and a 'cosmopolitan ethnocriticism', in whose ranks he lists Louis Owens, Gerald Vizenor, Diane Glancy, and himself. Whatever the risk of sounding too regulatory, it makes for a challenging taxonomy. Subsequent chapters explore the contextual tribal and related criteria for best translation of song or story 'from oral performance to page of text'; the gaps, and their implications, between Native cultures as customarily offered in the US national narrative and Native-conceived and written history; the vexed issues of blood quanta, or as Krupat calls it 'half-blood to mixedblood', in writings from Mourning Dove's *Cogewea: The Half-Blood* [1927] to contemporary Native authorship; and the historical and literary impetus behind the revenging violence (Krupat's term is 'rage stage') in Sherman Alexie's *Indian Killer* [1996].

Given Louis Owens's premature death in 2002, a first full-length appraisal of his fiction could not have been timelier. Chris Lalonde's *Grave Concerns, Trickster Turns: The Novels of Louis Owens* does excellent explicatory service, a convincingly well-supported overview of the five novels inaugurated with *Wolfsong* [1991] and which makes good use of the discursive and autobiographical essays gathered in *Mixedblood Messages: Literature, Film, Family, Place* [1998]. Owens's subsequent collection, *I Hear the Train: Reflections, Inventions, Refractions* [2001], came out too late to be brought into play, but not so his landmark literary-critical study, *Other Destinies: Understanding the American Indian Novel* [1992]. In a chronological working-through of the oeuvre, Lalonde takes up a number of interacting motifs: William Bevis's celebrated notion of 'homing in'; the fiction's trickster fashioning and figures, among them Jake Nashoka in *Dark River* [1999]; Owens's repudiation of the Native as Vanishing American—a keen reading of tribal and topographical semiotics in *Wolfsong*; and mixedblood family identity and the meanings of place, not least as reflected in the Choctaw-Cherokee play of heritage in *Nightland* [1996]. Owens's intertextual flair, from Herman Melville to Gerald Vizenor, is given full recognition, as are his turns of irony. Lalonde deserves congratulation. His study helps establish yet further the grounds for Owens's claim to be a leading Native literary contemporary.

In '"Stranded in *The Wasteland*": Literary Allusion in *The Sharpest Sight*' (*SAIL* 14:i[2002] 2–25), Carolyn Herbert pursues the intertextual and greatly mythopoeic fashioning within Owens's 1992 novel. She explores Diana Nemi as catwoman-villain folkloric figure. With due reference to Frazier's *Golden Bough* and T.S. Eliot's *The Waste Land* and 'The Hollow Men', she moves into how the Native main plot of murder and rape unravels a connecting seam of allusion to Jonathan Edwards, Tennyson, and Edward Lear. The upshot reads persuasively, the story of Diana, Deal, and Hoey Mountain to be understood as having been connected by Owens into both Native and non-Native mythic frames. *SAIL* (14:ii–iii[2002] 67–102) offers an album of short remembrances of Owens as writer, friend, professor, and critic from such figures as Gerald Vizenor, Arnold Krupat, John Purdy, James Thomas Stevens, Linda Helstern, and Kimberley Blaeser.

The Depression-era Osage novelist John Joseph Matthews has been principally remembered for his novel *Sundown* [1934]. The effect, as Susan Kalter shows in her 'John Joseph Matthews, Reverse Ethnography: The Literary Dimensions of *Wah'Kon-Tah*' (*SAIL* 14:i[2002] 26–50), has been to eclipse *Wah'Kon-Tah* as Matthews's first work of fiction or, at least, to see it relegated to the status of some lightly fictionalized work of history. Interpreted, usually, as a chronicle given over to the life of Major Leban Miles, Indian Agent, for Kalter this emphasis does considerable injustice to Matthews's narrative subtlety. The novel, she suggests, deserves to be better understood through its creation of ironic distance, the operative prism of Osage 'tribal consciousness'. Far from giving the limelight only to the figure of Leban Miles, *Wah'Kon-Tah* actually situates him within the Native gaze, as much object as subject, a well-taken argument for radical alteration of the usually assumed perspective.

MELUS 27:iii[2002] dedicates its entire issue to Native writing. The highlights are several. Roumiana Velikova looks at how the video *Running on The Edge of The Rainbow* [1978], in which Leslie Marmon Silko offers commentary, can be used to gloss the oral-scriptural transitions and appeal to the reader-as-listener in the poetry of *Storyteller* [1981] and Silko's other writings (*MELUS* 27:iii[2002] 9–42). Margo Lukens revisits the issue of Pauline Johnson's Mohawk-British and Canadian mixedblood legacy using the story 'My Mother', originally published in her collection *The Moccasin Maker* [1913], as focus (*MELUS* 27:iii[2002] 43–56). Brewster E. Fritz offers a helpful reprise of Silko's celebrated story 'Coyote Holds a Full House in his Hand' as the interplay of oral-trickster interior monologue and the larger story-frame within *Storyteller* (*MELUS* 27:iii[2002] 75–92). Nora Baker Barry annotates the bear figurations in Gerald Vizenor's texts, especially their role as agents of transformation and renewal. She covers his retelling of early Anishinaabe narratives along with *Bearheart* [1978, 1990], *Griever* [1987], *Heirs of Columbus* [1991], and, centrally, *Dead Voices* [1992], with its presiding figure of Bagese as bear-woman shaman (*MELUS* 27:iii[2002] 93–113). Roberta Rosenberg tackles Louise Erdrich's *Tales of Burning Love* as a story-cycle whose 'creative blending', if it can summon a tradition from Chaucer onwards, equally acts in the tradition of Anishinaabe multiple-story healing of human fissure (*MELUS* 27:iii[2002] 114–32). Bryson J. Scott examines the dialectic of place and time in Joy Harjo's poetry, notably *In Mad Love and War* [1990], *The Woman Who Fell From The Sky* [1994], and *She Had Some Horses* [1997], a well-turned anatomy of how Harjo finds a countering local humanity against a timeline of historic dispossession. Meanwhile, *MELUS* 27:ii[2002] gives over a whole issue to ethnic writing for children, an important reference and bibliographic resource.

For Joseph L. Coulombe in 'The Approximate Size of his Favorite Humor: Sherman Alexie's Comic Connections and Disconnections in *The Lone Ranger and Tonto Fistfight in Heaven*' (*AIQ* 26:i[2002] 94–115), much of the disquiet at Alexie's sometimes alleged 'harmful pandering to white expectations', or his humour as mere extraneous throwaway, has been seriously misplaced. It is too easy, he suggests, to miss the always humanizing purposes of his cascades of invention and wit. In a keen, conscientious diagnosis of the stories in *The Lone Ranger and Tonto Fistfight in Heaven*, and above all 'The Approximate Size of his Favorite Tumor', from which the article's title is adapted, Coulombe demonstrates how the jokery underscores, precisely, a 'common humanity' in all its shared capacity for pratfall. Coulombe's account supplies not only the linkage of motif within Alexie's story-cycle but a timely rebuttal to those who chastise him for seeming self-indulgence.

To Michelle Burnham in 'Pomo Basketweaving, Poison and the Politics of Restoration in Greg Sarris's *Grand Avenue*' (*SAIL* 14:iv[2002] 18–36), the key organizing trope in Sarris's California-set 'complex genealogical narrative' indeed lies in its use of the Pomo art of basketweaving. This trope, she engagingly demonstrates, works in a twofold manner. It supplies a pathway into the intimate human overlap of tribal family (figures such as Alice, Nellie, Steven, and the like), and it gives a reflexive quality to the novel's own storytelling. Sarris is well served by this account, an enlightening argument as to *Grand Avenue*'s compositional density as narrative.

Winona LaDuke, California-raised and a long-time Native activist, won minor headlines as Ralph Nader's Green Party running-mate in the 2000 presidential election. In 'Digging Up the Bones of the Past: Colonial and Indigenous Interplay in Winona LaDuke's *Last Standing Woman* (*AICRJ* 26:iv[2002] 21–43), Steven Salaita issues a well-chosen reminder of her claims as novelist. He reads LaDuke's *Last Standing Woman* through a series of positioning frames: its use of an Anishinaabe (Chippewa-Ojibway) setting like White Earth; the manner in which its activist cast shadows AIM figures like Dennis Banks; its use of Ishkewegaabawiikwe as woman-narrator in remembering the colonialist underpinning to historic Anishinaabe–white settler interaction; and insider–outsider issues of 'authenticity', especially as embodied in the novel's unflatteringly named anthropologist figure of Ales Hrdlicka.

Kanellos, ed., *Herencia: The Anthology of Hispanic Literature of the United States* signifies a genuine landmark, its timeline one of literary voice from Spanish first discovery through to Latino/a American modernity and the postmodern. The editorial helm is taken by Nicolás Kanellos, founder of Arte Público Press, and whose directorship of the Recovery of US Hispanic Literature project, from the outset, has deserved plaudits. The span of his anthology, much of it given in both Spanish and English and suitably annotated with scholarly headnotes and prefaced by Kanellos's own sharp, informative overview, begins from founder-generation names such as Cabeza de Vaca and Gaspar Pérez de Villagrá, author of the thirty-four-canto epic poem *The History of New Mexico*. The subsequent extracts he gathers into twenty or so sections, each reflective not only of Mexican, Chicano, Nuyorican, and Cuban American literary tradition but also of the multiple other Latin Americas which have fed into the north. The collection runs from early *mestizo* writing and early *corridos* such as 'The Ballad of Gregorio Cortez', through to a rich spectrum of moderns and contemporaries. The latter include 'Corky' Gonzalez, Alurista, Piri Thomas, Miguel Algarín, Nicholasa Mohr, Gloria Anzaldúa, Helena María Viramontes, and Judith Ortiz Cofer. Other writing enters under headings such as 'Encounters with the Modern City', 'The Literature of Exile', and 'Sin Fronteras', the latter, aptly, illustrated in an extract from Guillermo Gómez-Peña as leading border performance-artist. In reflecting the eclectic literary proliferation of Hispanic North America *Herencia* does excellent service. It also offers the further, and always timely, reminder that throughout all its formation American literature has been multicultural, as genuinely plural in language and story as in history.

In *Disrupting Savagism: Intersecting Chicano/a, Mexican Immigrant, and Native American Struggles for Self-Representation*, which arrived too late for inclusion last year, Arturo J. Aldama makes his departure-point a linked pair of questions: 'What aspects of our hybrid (mestiza/o) identities are celebrated and suppressed? How do we decolonize ourselves without returning to a static and utopic precolonial past?' The answering account, busily theory-referenced, availing itself of ethnology, literary texts, and cinema, and whose 'we' includes the author himself as Californian of Mexican birth, amounts to a deconstruction of the historical workings of savagism as mystique since Columbus's landfall. Aldama tackles a broad span: literary and other indigenous 'talking back' from the era of Nueva España through to NAFTA (his sources include Chandra Mohanty, Norma Alarcón, and Louis Owens); the US–Mexico border as at once historic and figurative in shaping 'otherness'; Leslie Marmon Silko's *Ceremony* [1977] as a Laguna-centred novel which serves as a 'model of decolonization'; the role and counter-hegemony represented by *mestizaje*; and a film like Miguel Arteta's *Star Maps* [1997] as a refraction of how the Latino/a body has been sexually and economically fetishized. The upshot amounts to a carefully marshalled cultural-studies anatomy, bracing in its challenge to pre-emptive stereotypes of immigrant Mexican, Chicano/a, and Native American.

The twenty essays brought together in Aldama and Quiñonez, eds., *Decolonial Voices: Chicana and Chicano Cultural Studies in the 21st Century*, do related deconstructive good service. Under a three-part layout of 'Dangerous Bodies', 'Dismantling Colonial/Patriarchal Legacies', and 'Mapping Space and Reclaiming Place', *chicanismo* in its ready cultural variety, high and popular, is given deserved attention. The 'bodies' section, for instance, offers sharp essays on new Chicana art (Laura E. Pérez), New Wave Chicano/a cinema (Ramón Garcia), and Edward J. Olmos's landmark film, *American Me*, as taken up with the imprisoned Chicano body and the machismo-rape syndrome (Frederick Luis Aldama). 'Legacies' includes a reinvestigation of the politics and literature of La Malinche (Naomi H. Quiñonez), of the cultural semiotics of the US–Mexico border as but one of many borders— be they territorial, sexual, or class-based—within America's making (Patricia Penn-Hilden), and of the informing feminism behind the fiction of Estela Portillo Trambley—most notably her *Rain of Scorpions and Other Stories* (Cordelia Candelaria). 'Space and Time', among other essays, yields José David Saldivar's composite, and fine-tuned, analysis of different kinds of borderland in the scripts of Guillermo Gómez-Peña, a key story like Helena María Viramontes's 'The Cariboo Café', and the early and Hollywood fiction of John Rechy. This collection speaks convincingly from, and to, the cultural nuance of *chicanismo*, not least because of the contributors' well-taken cross-referencing of history, gender, and genre studies.

Cantú and Nájera-Ramirez, eds., *Chicana Traditions: Continuity and Change*, sets itself to explore the 'expressive culture', by which is meant the gender and related folklore, of Chicana tradition. The thirteen essays cover a broad range, if not explicitly angled to elucidate literary fiction then a useful arena of popular allusion and reference. 'Enduring Traditions' looks, among other features, to *quinceañera* as female coming-of-age (Norma E. Cantú), the religious iconography of *santero* (Helen R. Lucero), and the multiple legends of La Llorona, or the weeping woman (Domino Renee Pérez). 'Practicing Traditions' alights on 'Indianizing Catholicism', the hybridity of Spanish-bequeathed Christianity and indigeneity (Yolanda Broyles-González), and a carefully documented account of women performers' entry into mariachi music and the gender transgressions this has involved (Leonor Xóchitl Pérez). 'Transforming Traditions' offers analysis of musical figurations of women in mariachi tradition (Cándida F. Jáquez), portraits of Lydia Mendoza as transnational 'ranchera' singer (Yolanda Broyles-González) and Selena as Texan/ *tejana* vocalist (Deborah R. Vegas), and an essay on the New Mexico vernacular performance and installation art of Goldie Garcia (Tey Marianna Nunn). The upshot is a collection full of contextual illumination, the sediments and recreations of popular belief, word, art, and sound within chicana culture at large.

In 'Nature's Voice: Ecological Consciousness in Rudolfo Anaya's Albuquerque Quartet' (*Aztlán* 27:ii[2002] 119–38), Carmen Flys-Junquera tackles the landscape, *la tierra*, of the southwest as not merely physical frame but a kind of moral ecology in Anaya's later novels. *Alburquerque* [1994], a narrative of family genealogy, she reads through its situating imagery of earth, river, and mountain. The three Sonny Baca sleuth-novels, *Zia Summer* [1995], *Rio Grande Fall* [1996], and *Shaman Winter* [1999], their respective plots taken up with cult murder, drug dealing, and the conspiracy-theft of a nuclear bomb, likewise centre in the powers of New Mexico as redemptive landscape. This same landscape has been host to a 'diverse, but harmonious Chicano heritage ... the beliefs of Catholicism, Pueblo Indian cosmology, and Aztec beliefs'. It makes for an illuminating gloss.

Charlotte Rich's 'Talking Back to El Jefe: Genre, Polyphony and Dialogic Resistance in Julia Alvarez's *In the Time of the Butterflies*' (*MELUS* 27:iv[2002] 165–82) subjects Alvarez's justly celebrated novel of Trujillo dictatorship in the Dominican Republic, and the historic murder of three sisters in the resistance movement, to a Bakhtinian treatment. In Alvarez's polyphonic use of time present as an overlay to the time past of the 1960s, and its multiple tiers of narration as given, respectively, in Minerva, Patria, and María Theresa, along with the resorts to *campesino*, Taino, and African-Dominican voice, the novel uses its refusal of any one totalizing narrative authority to enact a 'resistant response to Trujillo'. Rich's reading pays intelligent, and persuasive, tribute to Alvarez's text.

Marta Caminero-Santangelo's 'Margarita Engle, Cuban American Conservativism, and the Construction of (Left) US Latino/a Ethnicity' (*LIT* 13:iv[2002] 249–67) explores the implications of Engle's rightist, fervidly anti-Castro fiction. Using *Singing To Cuba* [1993] and *Skywriting: A Novel of Cuba* [1995] as illustrative texts, she highlights the irony of Engle's embrace of Afro-Cuban hybridity while perpetuating a one-note anti-Castroism: 'Engle's writing ... obscures the complexity of Castro's regimes, in which human rights abuses exist side-by-side with ... increased education, health care, affordable housing, and other opportunities for Cuba's poor'. The analysis on offer reads judiciously, a due airing of Engle's strengths and defects as ideological novelist.

Elizabeth Coonrod Martinez's 'Crossing Gender Borders: Sexual Relations and Chicana Artistic Identity' (*MELUS* 27:i[2002] 131–49) unfolds a lively taxonomy of how sexual passion has been depicted in Chicana fiction, beginning from Sandra Cisneros's *The House on Mango Street* [1984] and to include as four further texts Estela Portillo-Trembley's *Trini* [1986], Alma Villanueva's 'Ripening' [1984], Erlinda Gonzalez-Berry's *Paletitas de guayaba/Guava Popsicles* [1991], and Ana Castillo's *So Far From God* [1993]. Martinez's lively account looks to how each rewrites gender roles with an eye to women's control of sexual experience or as upsetting long-ingrained touchstones of (especially Latino/a) masculinity and femininity.

In her spirited feminist account, and with the warmest recognition of the landmark voice of Nicholasa Mohr, Carmen S. Rivera, in *Kissing The Mango Tree: Puerto Rican Women Rewriting American Literature*, alights upon names including Judith Ortiz Cofer, Sandra María Esteves, Rosario Morales, Aurora Levins Morales, Esmeralda Santiago, and Luz María Umpierre-Herrera. Rivera conscientiously looks to the historic transition from island to mainland, the place of Piri Thomas's *Down These Mean Streets* [1967], and, of most consequence for her account, both the linkage and gaps between island life as *jíbara* (or indigenous *puertorriqueña*) on the one hand, and Manhattan and other city or barrio life as Americana on the other. The account, throughout, read assiduously, whether island-to-mainland autobiographical fictions such as Esmeralda Santiago's *When I Was Puerto Rican* [1993]; Manhattan and Bronx mother–daughter fictions such as Mohr's *Nilda* [1973], *In Nueva York* [1993], and *Felita* [1997]; Jewish-*riqueña* intergenerational collaboration such as *Getting Home Alive* [1987] by Rosario and Aurora Morales; the ideological freedom poetry of Esteves and Umpierre-Herrera; or the multi-genred stories and poetry of Judith Ortiz Cofer, of which *The Latin Deli* [1993] can be thought symptomatic. Rivera manages a nice balance throughout, with evident commitment to so burgeoning an archive of woman-authored writings and yet always a right measure of critical distance.

Helena Grice's *Negotiating Identities: An Introduction to Asian American Women's Writing* winningly combines an engaging sweep of reference, including a helpful primary and secondary bibliography, with exact local readings. Hers is very much the project of critical mapping, clear, bold explicatory accounts of literary names from Edith Eaton/Sui Sin Far and Diana Chang through to Gish Jen and Bharati Mukherjee, and with necessary consideration of Maxine Hong Kingston and Amy Tan. If the occasional footfall of the doctoral thesis from which the book derives still shows, that is not to underestimate its overall contribution. Grice also gives a liberal, and comparative, take on these Asian American texts by her use of analogous writings from Canada and Britain. Her account proceeds through a series of paradigms: different kinds of mother–daughter dynamic from Kingston's *The Woman Warrior* [1976] to Joy Kogawa's *Obasan* [1981]; mixed or hybrid genre and its interaction with gender, of which Jessica Hagedorn's *Dogeaters* [1991] is taken to be symptomatic; 'Red China' novels of a kind readily seized upon in the West, such as Jung Chang's *Wild Swans: Three Daughters of China* [1991] and Hong Ying's *Daughter of The River* [1997]; Eurasian texts from those of the Eaton sisters (Sui Sin Far and Onoto Watanna) onward through to Aimee Liu's remarkable novel *Face* [1994]; identity narratives given over to Japanese America, and its experience of Second World War camp internment under Executive Order 9066, by Miné Okubo, Monica Sone, Yoshiko Uchida, and Jeanne Wakatsuki Houston; and narratives of US homecoming in all its contraflows and ironies, from Bharati Mukherjee's *Wife* [1975] to Meena Alexander's *Fault Lines: A Memoir* [1993]. The scholarship to hand reads with great flair: this is accessible, informed, and a prompt to ongoing study.

For Viet Thanh Nguyen in *Race and Resistance: Literature and Politics in Asian America*, time needs to be called on any over-homogenous view of what Asian American literature has been and should be. He argues for more rigorous cognizance of ideological diversity, the complicity of many Asian Americans in US capitalist practice and the 'marketing' of racial identity. Taking his cue from fellow recent Asian Americanists such as David Leiwei Li, Jinqi Ling, and Patricia Chu, he urges a more problematic (or 'Bad Subjects') approach. His own examples include fiction by the Eaton sisters, a line of literary-ideological dissidence from John Okada to Frank Chin, Carlos Bulosan to Le Ly Hayslip, Theresa Hak Kyung Cha's *DICTEE* [1982] to Lois-Ann Yamanaka's *Blu's Hanging* [1997], and texts such as Ninotchka Rosca's *State of War* [1988] and Jessica Hagedorn's *Dogeaters* [1990] as evidence of contestatory national and sexual politics. Nguyen's point is to warn against mere multicultural good feeling yet to show his own wariness about Asian American separatism. The 'space of racial identity', he argues, needs to get beyond present terms of debate into 'a future after multiculturalism'. His argument can at times read knottedly. But he offers a worthy prospectus, the call to new terms of reference for 'Asian American' as literary and political category.

Davis and Ludwig, eds., *Asian American Literature in the International Context: Readings on Fiction, Poetry, and Performance*, under Spanish-Swiss co-editorship and the outcome of a conference panel of EAAS in Lisbon, inaugurates a new Asian American literary series from Lit Verlag. Its sixteen essays give a fair coverage of the waterfront: from the turn-of-the-century bicultural authorship of Edith and Winnifred Eaton (Carol Roh-Spaulding) to the US–South Asian contemporary writings of Bharati Mukherjee and Bapsi Sidhwa (Carmen Faymonville). Gordon Taylor explores the languages of identity in Frank Chin's *Donald Duk* [1991] as a rite of passage into usable Chinese American selfhood, whether the historical role of kites, lanterns, dance, food, or railways. Zhou Xiaojing maps the interaction of self and history in the poetry of Marilyn Chin, a well-turned close inspection of intertextual Chinese and US cultural reference. Dorothy J. Wang does a first-class exegesis of John Yau as 'Undercover Asian' and the oblique authorial masks he uses throughout his poetry (especially in his 'Genghis Chan' series). Johnny Lorenz looks to Li-young Lee's use of historical calendar, and time-zones within, in the poetry of *Rose* [1986] and *The City in which I Love You* [1990], along with his important family memoir, *The Winged Seed: A Remembrance* [1995]. Kirsten Twelbeck tackles 'otherness' in Theresa Hak Kyung Cha's *DICTEE*, a genuinely well-considered focus on notions of home, language, and gender in this key postmodern script. The late Amy Ling, a seminal scholar of Asian American literature, contributes a typically alert essay on Gish Jen's *Mona in the Promised Land* [1996] with its Chinese–Jewish 'cultural cross-dressing' as the figuration of an ever more open and hybrid US multicultural order.

Fenkl and Lew, eds., *Kori: The Beacon Anthology of Korean American Fiction*, confirms the impressive and continuing textures of story voice within the line of Korea-heritaged US writing. The sixteen extracts represent a considerable literary span, whether Younghill Kang's *The Grass Roof* [1931] as the portrait of Korean struggles for liberation from Japanese occupancy and migrant entry into a far from welcoming America, or Kim Ronyoung's *Clay Walls* [1986] as immigrant first-generation marriage and family in Second World War Los Angeles, with Korea as a war-contested terrain of dynastic origins; or, latterly, Chang-rae Lee's *Native Speaker* [1995] as the reflexive anatomy of Korean American and other ethnicity in the form of a domestic spy story set busily, and stylishly, inside New York borough politics. Other inclusions look to the 'Choral Dance' sequence in Theresa Hak Kyung Cha's *DICTEE*, the Hawaii-centred storytelling of Gary Pak (his subtly atmospheric and political 'The Valley of the Dead Air'), Nora Okja Keller's harrowing dynastic novel *Comfort Woman* [1997], and Sukhee Ryu's 'Severance', a story inventively, not to say erotically, pitched as the subversion of Korean American ethno-piety and patriarchy.

Custom has long held that Edith Eaton, as Sui Sin Far, somehow created a legitimate Chinese imaginative terrain, whereas Winnifred Eaton, as Onoto Watanna, somehow gave a betraying fantasy of its Japanese equivalent. In *Edith and Winnifred Eaton: Chinatown and Japanese Romances*, Dominika Ferens intelligently dismantles this authentic/inauthentic dichotomy, and argues that both sisters were working within, and yet subtly against, the ethnographic constructions of 'the East' within their own turn-of-the-century era. Invoking a complex body of orientalist versions of the Chinatowns and Japans in play, she maps, precisely, the popular-cultural hinterland behind best-known key texts like Edith Eaton's China-focused *Mrs. Spring Fragrance* [1913] and Winnifred Eaton's *Miss Numè of Japan: A Japanese-American Romance* [1899], with its parallel cross-ethnic couples. Both literary careers are given in scrupulous detail, with emphasis on issues of US and Canadian assimilation and race, on the calculations behind the respective personae, and on how Eurasianism, in all its historic ambiguity of mask, and explicitly or obliquely, determines their writing.

In 'The Enunciation of the Tenth Muse in Theresa Hak Kyung Cha's *DICTEE*' (*LIT* 13:i[2002] 1–20) Stella Oh engages with the structure of Cha's now almost canonical Korean American text, and especially its rubric of the nine muses. Glossing Cha's use of *diseuse* as 'skilled female reciter', she suggests that *DICTEE* offers its own feminist and postcolonial counter-trinity to Christianity's Father, Son, and Holy Ghost in the persons of Yu Guan Soon as Korean mother of the nation in the face of the Japanese occupation, Joan of Arc, and Santa Teresa. The tenth muse is Cha's own not a little utopian 'autonomous and absolute *I*', a self-authoring beyond patriarchy and all other 'dictated' identity. Oh writes shrewdly, and challengingly, and her account is a skilled piece of exposition.

In 'Blurring the Borders Between Formal and Social Aesthetics: An Interview with Mei-mei Berssenbrugge' (*MELUS* 27:i[2002] 199–213) Zhou Xiaojing usefully, if briefly, explores issues of Berssenbrugge's identity as poet of mixed Chinese, Dutch, and Asian American identity, her role in the 1970s multicultural movement, and the genesis of collections from *Random Possessions* [1979] to *Four Year Old Girl* [1998]. Leslie Bow's 'Beyond Ragoon: An Interview with Wendy Law-Yone' (*MELUS* 27:iv[2002] 184–200) addresses the Myanmar life behind the author who established her American literary credentials in *The Coffin Tree* [1983], with its affecting story of migrant sibling defeat in the USA, and *Irawaddy Tango* [1993], with its complex interplay of exile and sexuality. Bow revisits with Law-Yone the figure of her father, Edward Law-Yone, as publisher-journalist and activist in the fight for Burmese independence from the British in 1948; the family's Catholicism and Burmese-Chinese roots; the politics of Myanmar's present-day dictatorship; the oppressive 'myth of success' in the USA; and Wendy Law-Yone's own call to authorship and the writing of her novel, *Wanting* (still in progress), and first-person memoir, *The Old Burma Road*.

Amerasian Journal 28:iii[2002], an issue devoted to 'The Politics of Remembering', centres on the case of Vincent Chin, the Chinese American murdered in 1982 in Detroit, the car-manufacturing hub at the time of the anti-Japanese and protectionist 'Buy American' fever. Chin has long passed into being an iconic figure, a martyr to anti-Asianism. The issue, accordingly, looks to reminiscences by his family and others, to Renee Tajima-Peña's film *Who Killed Vincent Chin?*, and to the ways in which Chin has featured in a range of storytelling and case studies.

In 'Performing Tricksters: Karen Tei Yamashita and Guillermo Gómez-Peña' (*AmasJ* 28:ii[2002] 217–25) Alvina E. Quintana offers a lively comparison of Gómez-Peña's *Border Brujo* [1988] with Yamashita's *Tropic of Orange* [1997] as literary-cultural explorations of US–Mexico 'multiple borders'. Both, she suggests, operate as trickster performance texts whose shared critiques of 'unicultural' America 'emerge from within as well as outside the text itself'. Quintana sees a play of rhetorical strategies in *Border Brujo* and *Tropic of Orange* by which the USA and Mexico in fact overlap and culturally hybridize each other even as they persist with formal north–south divides of territory.

Marçais, Niemayer, and Waegner, eds., *Literature on The Move: Comparing Diasporic Ethnicities in Europe and the Americas*, thirty or so papers from the second *MELUS* Europe conference held at the University of Orléans in 2000, underscores the genuine width of international interest in America's ethnic-literary spectrum. Any number repay attention. Lisa Lowe opens with a sharp enquiry into ethnicity and modernism with Jessica Hagedorn's *Dogeaters* as illustrative text. Rocío Davis tracks girl-characters as narrators who embark upon their own home-leaving in Sandra Cisneros's *The House on Mango Street* and Lois-Ann Yamanaka's *Blu's Hanging*. Wolfgang Binder offers an exhilarating sweep focused upon the turns and play of memory in Caribbean and US Latino poetry. Cathy Waegner writes a bold, engaging comparison of African American and German Jewish cemeteries as comparative cultural texts. Sterling Stuckey does a brilliant piece of literary-historical excavation on the way in which African American slave art and language enters the work of Melville, Paul Robeson, and Richard Wright. A. Robert Lee annotates 'Ethnics Behaving Badly' in US narrative, multicultural writings fashioned against the grain with principal examples in the texts of Zora Neale Hurston, Gerald Vizenor, Oscar Zeta Acosta, and Jessica Hagedorn. Karla F.C. Holloway, paying a warm tribute to the contribution of the late Barbara Christian, revisits the issue of theory, a call for its grounding as much in 'literatures of color' as in the standard US and Western canon. These, and their companion essays, offer a genuine plenty.

Elise Lemire's *'Miscegenation': Making Race in America* takes as its focus the antebellum legacy of US slave-ownership, interracial sex, and the hysteria it has long enjoined. Her study tidily works its way through nineteenth-century texts to include the *Three Folio* poems given over to racial scurrility about Jefferson and Sally Hemings, James Fenimore Cooper's *The Last of the Mohicans* and its race-determinist categories of white and Native 'blood', and a run of anti-miscegenation texts in Poe and Louisa May Alcott, together with a wide folder of race-loaded visual work and popular writing, including the 1863 pamphlet in which the word miscegenation first appears. This historically well-grounded study concludes that, whatever the colour-line alarmism or resort to a rhetoric of eugenics and mongrelization, sexual life, in truth, is actually neither interracial nor even racial. A better understanding of this, as Lemire rightly argues, might have spared much of the phobia which, from European settlement through to Dixie slaveholding and beyond, has so fatally underwritten not only American but virtually all Western constructions of race.

Epifanio San Juan Jr. has long established himself a doyen of neo-Marxist dissent. His *Racism and Cultural Studies: Critiques of Multiculturalist Ideology and the Politics of Difference* adds a latest critique to the roster: a compendious assault on historic and 'institutional' US and Western hierarchies of power. He works his way through the cultural politics of hegemony, race, class, gender, capital, nationalism, ethnicity, postcoloniality, and globalization like the dissident true believer. Liberal multiculturalism, he alleges, is to be decried as for the most part no more than gestural, an evasion of genuine strategies towards communitarian-socialist renewal and change. This is fiery enough polemic, a credo of commitment with due names busily invoked from Marx to Fredric Jameson, Raymond Williams to Pierre Bourdieu, and with his own Philippines as cultural paradigm. Literary work does make its entry, as do accounts of the rise in the US of academic departments of ethnic studies. But the literary issues, for the most part, assume a secondary role and, to good or bad purpose, receive judgement according San Juan's ideological litmus test.

Shell, ed., *American Babel: Literatures of the United States from Abanaki to Zuni*, acts enlighteningly on the proposition that from the outset American literature has looked as much to a multilingual as to an English-language literary record. To recover and publish these texts Shell, along with Werner Sollors, co-founded in 1994 Harvard's Longfellow Institute, no inappropriate title given Longfellow's own polyglot abilities as holder of the university's Smith Chair of Languages. The twenty-five essays which make up the collection confirm a genuine variety of voice, from the late nineteenth-century statesman Alexander del Mar on the Emerigo Vespucci controversy over America's very naming through to the Canadian-born Shell himself on Mark Twain's 'The Jumping Frog of Calaveras County'. The latter, he argues, offers both vintage frontier humour and, given the story's vexed history in French and other translations and Twain's own bemused reaction to them, a case study in what he terms 'linguistic leap-frogging'. Under these shared American auspices yet other considerations look to Arab-language slave narrative (Ala Alryyes); Greek self-representation and deliberate self-misrepresentation in the First World War (Yota Batsaki); 1930s German Jewish women's poetry (Elisabeth Lenckos); the Welsh Eisteddfod Bible epic *Mordecai and Haman*, first performed in Pennsylvania in 1869 (Esther Whitfield); Yiddish, or rather 'Yinglish', writing (James Loeffler); Hawai'i's various styles of pidgin storytelling (Susannah Young-Ah Gottlieb); Irish Gaelic literature as evolved across the Atlantic (Kenneth Wilson); Zuni oral-into-written tribal storytelling (Dennis Tedlock); Spanish language code-switching and counterpoint, whether of the street or law or literature (Doris Sommer); Thuong Vuong-Riddick's *Two Shores/Deux Rives* [1995], a Vietnamese-authored yet 'American' novel first published in English and French in Vancouver (Dan Duffy); the engraved Chinese wall-poems of Angel Island as migrant histories-in-miniature (Te-Hsing Shan); and the evolution of Haitian US writing replete with a helpful bibliography (Jean Jonassaint). These, and accompanying contributions, should help deliver a provocative and timely reminder of what historically have always been the more inclusive languages of America's literary-cultural voice.

6. African American Literature

African American literary criticism is increasingly intercultural and transnational, and this is shown over a wide range of the material reviewed here. Two suggestive studies of the relations of African American literature to modernism were published in 2002. Edward M. Pavlic, *Crossroads Modernism: Descent and Emergence in African-American Literary Culture*, places African American culture at the crucial crossroads of modernist aesthetics. It is a little disappointing that a study staking such a claim for dynamic new readings is rather over-reliant on the binary critiques of Robert Stepto's *From Behind the Veil* (UIllP [1979]). This unfortunately often leads to over-reductive readings of writers such as Zora Neale Hurston and Richard Wright through a development of the Stepto paradigm of 'ascent' and 'descent'. Despite this there are rich readings of canonical writers such as Ralph Ellison and Toni Morrison, and more marginal figures such as Yusef Komunyakaa and David Bradley. The study claims to be multi-disciplinary, with work on film, music, and visual arts; however, with the exception of an excellent, nuanced reading of Julie Dash's *Daughters of the Dust* that dynamically emphasizes its diasporic modernism rather than its womanist Afrocentrism, other artistic forms are generally approached through readings of the literary text and hence marginal to the argument. In commenting on Jean Toomer, Pavlic highlights how he 'subvert(s) the binary structures of American modernity'. This paradigm of African American writers enriching modernism because of their diasporan roots is developed by Pavlic to create a tapestry of readings that make this a valuable addition to the critical canon of modernism and African American literature. An alternative version of the groundbreaking work on Robert Hayden (a poet noted as having 'the best underground reputation of any poet in America') comes in Pavlic's essay '"Something patterned, wild, and free": Robert Hayden's Angles of Descent and the Democratic Unconscious' (*AAR* 36[2002] 533–55).

Delia Caporoso Konzett, *Ethnic Modernisms: Anzia Yezierska, Zora Neale Hurston, Jean Rhys, and the Aesthetics of Dislocation*, like Pavlic's study, interrogates monocultural readings of modernism, but stretches wider than African American texts while raising 'the combined question of dislocation and ethnicity as key features of modernism'. Her work on Hurston is rich, revealing, and original, critiquing Hazel Carby's 'ahistorical representation of Hurston as a traditionalist' which 'cannot be sustained if one carefully considers her urban folklore and its impact upon her subsequent work' such as *Tell My Horse* [1938], *Moses Man of the Mountain* [1939], and *Seraph on the Suwanee* [1948]. Her argument is that critics have been too constrictive of Hurston, seeking to compartmentalize her too 'narrowly within African American or feminist canons', and by doing this they have 'closed the door to other aspects of her work, particularly her transnational treatment of African diasporan culture in the various regions of the Americas'. The combination of Yezierska, Rhys, and Hurston leads to a transnational, intercultural reading of modernism which, like Pavlic's study, complicates narrow national or racial conceptions of the period.

Carla Kaplan's *Zora Neale Hurston: A Life in Letters* is an interesting addition to the Hurston oeuvre. It is unfortunate but not unexpected that most of Hurston's letters that have survived are those sent to her patrons, employers, teachers, and publishers, and to the foundations that funded her research. In only a very few letters—mainly those to close friend and fellow author Langston Hughes—do we get more than a glimpse of a more genuine, heartfelt expression. It's a pity that more letters to other contemporary black writers have not yet turned up. Kaplan makes a few editorial slips: one letter from Honduras is printed out of sequence, giving the impression Hurston went there in 1930 as well as the late 1940s, and her notes occasionally and misleadingly misidentify the books in progress Hurston refers to. But otherwise the volume is carefully annotated and usefully supplemented by notes on key individuals, a chronology of Hurston's life, and a good index.

Hurston is becoming nearly as popular a subject in journals as Toni Morrison. Leigh Ann Duck's thoughtful and non-judgemental essay '"Go there tuh *know* there": Zora Neale Hurston and the Chronotope of the Folk' (*AmLH* 13[2001] 265–94) discusses Hurston's positioning in the folk-against-modernity debate. The essay discusses the critiques of Hurston's naive politics by contemporaries such as Richard Wright and critics such as Hazel Carby. Using *Mules and Men* and *Their Eyes Were Watching God* as exemplar texts, Duck shows that Hurston, '[d]espite her talent for negotiating cultural differences ... found it difficult to reconcile the conflicting claims of cultural maintenance and social change'. A more dynamic and subtle argument is found in Brian Carr and Tova Cooper, 'Zora Neale Hurston and Modernism at the Critical Limit' (*MFS* 48[2002] 285–313), where *Mules and Men* is used to show Hurston's complexity within debates around modernism and modernity. Carr and Cooper finally 'offer Hurston as a figure who might be understood as defamiliarizing the dominant cultural rubrics through which she is so frequently read: modernism, the Harlem Renaissance, ethnography and postmodernism'. This essay delights in overturning the critical orthodoxies about Hurston, including some excellent and incisive commentary on the subtle ambivalence of her essay 'How Does It Feel To Be Colored Me', which has far too often been read with a straight face.

Other work on Hurston includes Ryan Simmons, '"The Hierarchy Itself": Hurston's *Their Eyes Were Watching God* and the Sacrifice of Narrative Authority' (*AAR* 36[2002] 181–93), which discusses Joe Starks as a key authority figure and Janie's two early marriages as re-enactments of the struggle between Booker T. Washington and W.E.B. Du Bois's ideas. There is much interesting discussion of the novel here, especially in terms of the dialogic and the monologic and of Janie's power of voice and the limitations on it. Philip Joseph, 'The Verdict from the Porch: Zora Neale Hurston and Reparative Justice' (*AL* 74[2002] 455–83) discusses Hurston's work in the light of the contemporary reparations movement. He makes this move by citing the importance of justice as a theme in her work. This presentism (who actually cares whether Hurston would have supported a reparations movement?) undermines what is a solid argument about the rhetoric of the folk. Of most interest is the discussion of Hurston as Southern sceptic. Joseph interestingly contends that 'Zora the celebrant of folk and Zora the skeptic toward race consciousness can thus begin to look like one and the same writer'. Hurston inspires not only academics but also other writers, and Patricia R. Schroeder describes the importance of the Harlem Renaissance figure to the contemporary writer Arthur Flowers, in 'Rootwork: Arthur Flowers, Zora Neale Hurston and the "Literary Hoodoo" Tradition' (*AAR* 36[2002] 263–72). Hurston makes a cameo appearance in Flowers's novel *Another Good Loving Blues* [1993], and Schroeder shows how Flowers signifies on both Hurston's life and *Their Eyes Were Watching God*, foregrounding through these his 'central theme: that connections to African-derived cultural traditions are essential to the spiritual health of African Americans'. Schroeder illustrates Flowers's debt to Ishmael Reed and to his concepts of hoodoo and 'borrowing' that make the novel a postmodern *tour de force*. Deborah Clarke's essay '"The porch couldn't talk for looking": Voice and Vision in *Their Eyes Were Watching God*' (*AAR* 35[2001] 599–613) illuminates Hurston's text as combining oral and visual modes that would complicate a trajectory of African American poetics attuned merely to the oral. She describes how the text, 'with its privileging of "mind pictures" over words ... goes beyond a narrative authority based solely on voice'. There is much excellent feminist critique here, particularly on the phallocentric discourse of Joe Starks and Hurston's critique of it through debilitating pictorial language. Clarke shows how Hurston 'provides a model for reconciling voice and vision, for transforming black bodies from museum pieces or ethnographic objects into embodied voices'. Stuart Burrows elaborates on Clarke's arguments in his essay '"You heard her; you ain't blind": Seeing What's Said in *Their Eyes Were Watching God*' (*Novel* [2001] 434–52). He discusses how the legacy of vernacular criticism from critics such as Henry Louis Gates, Jr. privileges 'Blackness [as] ... a matter of sound rather than sight, a discursive reconstruction of an all too visible image'. Such critical orthodoxy undermines the signal importance of vision in a text like Hurston's, where photography and Janie's image are key to understanding. Burrows provides an excellent discussion of race and class as visualized in the 1930s South and mediated by Hurston. The essays by Clarke and Burrows feed off each other wonderfully and show the importance of taking on the critical shibboleths in the Academy.

A contemporary and combatant of Hurston's was Richard Wright, whose transnational trajectory is examined anew in the first book-length study devoted exclusively to his travel writings. Whatley Smith, ed., *Richard Wright's Travel Writings: New Reflections*, is an interesting collection of essays written by a multinational collection of scholars, which discusses writings from *Black Power* [1954] through *Pagan Spain* [1956] to an unfinished draft on French West Africa. This volume prints photographs taken by Wright and others collected by him, which he had intended to use in *Pagan Spain*. Their reprinting here is an excellent contribution to Wright scholarship. These fascinating pictures excised from the text show the richness of Wright's vision and would, if used, have made the book resemble his earlier *12 Million Black Voices*. His great empathy for the plight of Spanish women is discussed in Dennis F. Evans's 'The Good Women, Bad Women, Prostitutes and Slaves of *Pagan Spain*: Richard Wright Looks Beyond the Phallocentric Self'. Evans argues that such empathy comes from his own subject position growing up in the Jim Crow Southern American states. Evans describes this as an important moment in Wright's career that in some small way compensates for the misogyny of other texts such as *Native Son*. Nagwarsungu Chiwengo's 'Gazing Through the Screen: Richard Wright's Africa' indicts Wright for using Africa as 'merely a background against which African American subjectivity is construed and negotiated', writing in effect an 'eclectic neo-slave travelogue'. This ethnocentrism is closely argued by Chiwengo using postcolonial theory to critique Wright's First World positionality. Though more sympathetic to Wright's position, S. Shankar's 'Richard Wright's Black Power: Colonial Politics and the Travel Narrative' also notes that the text is both an 'anti-colonial and a colonial travel narrative'. More sympathetically, Virginia Whatley Smith, in 'Richard Wright's Passage to Indonesia: The Travel Writer/Narrator as Participant/Observer of Anti-Colonial Imperatives in *The Color Curtain*', discusses how Wright's travel writing foreshadows postcolonial theories and concepts of ethnography and travel writing which were going to come into vogue in the 1990s. Whatley Smith meticulously delineates discussions with Wright's British and American publishers as to whether the books were mere travel books or something more rigorous, philosophical, and sociological altogether. In arguing for the latter, Whatley Smith does Wright's travel writing a great service. However, the collection as a whole could have debated with postcolonialism and the paradigm of the transnational even more, and it is telling that Frantz Fanon and Paul Gilroy hardly merit a mention.

A text that tries to negotiate between postcolonial and African American literary criticism is S. Shankar, *Textual Traffic: Colonialism, Modernity and the Economy of the Text*. This wide-ranging study consists of a number of case studies including two essays on Richard Wright and Zora Neale Hurston, using Conrad's *Heart of Darkness* as a foil, a work which Shankar claims reproduces the 'textual economy of the colonialist travel narrative'. He finds that Hurston's *Mules and Men* [1935]—another account of a voyage to the 'colonial world' (in this case, impoverished communities in the US South)—challenges this textual economy, not least because 'going native' here, rather than inspiring horror on the part of the narrator, is actually part of 'going home'. Although Hurston does not escape colonial paradigms entirely, there is an instructive difference in the way in which Chinua Achebe's attempt to de-canonize Conrad's novel has not been as successful as Alice Walker's attempt to canonize Hurston's work. Shankar's assessment of Wright's *Black Power* [1954] is more cautious. This account of a visit to the Gold Coast on the eve of independence owes much to the colonial travel-writing tradition represented by Conrad. While the author expresses a sense of ancestral identification with Africans, and endorses the project of national liberation, his conception of Gold Coast culture and politics (irrational, primitive) is generally structured round an evolutionary contrast with the West (rational, civilized). Shankar thus insists on the ambivalence of the text and its subsequent loss of radical edge. Such intercultural criticism of African American literature and culture contributes to a healthy cosmopolitanism that can defy the narrow nationalism of the worst excesses of the American critical academy.

In the journals there have been many excellent contributions on Wright. For instance, James Smethurst's illuminating 'Invented by Horror: The Gothic and African American Literary Ideology in *Native Son*' (*AAR* 35[2001] 29–40) situates the novel in a Gothic paradigm whereby its Marxist legacy is enhanced through the idea that the 'dead generations weigh like a nightmare on the brain of the living'. According to Smethurst, a close reading of the novel shows the Gothic as 'crucial to Wright's project because it is the perfect literary analogue to what Wright sees as the ideology and psychology guiding the relations between black and white Americans ... under late capitalism'. Violence, class, and gender are the concerns in Sondra Goltman's 'What Bigger Killed For: Rereading Violence Against Women in Native Son' (*TexasSLL* 43[2001] 169–93), which investigates the 'significance of the relationship the novel establishes between violence against women and a class analysis'. There is much to commend here in an essay that negotiates the thorny ground of rape and lynching through close analysis of Bigger Thomas's sexual contacts with white and black women.

In a more regionalist approach, the Manichean vision promulgated by Southern racial thought is seen as a key precursor of *Native Son* in Clare Eby's closely argued and convincing 'Slouching Toward Beastliness: Richard Wright's Anatomy of Thomas Dixon' (*AAR* 35[2001] 439–58), in which the racist logic of Dixon's *The Clansman* [1905] is shown to help create the character of Bigger Thomas. Eby concludes that '*Native Son* shows white America locked into a deadly battle with a stereotype it had created and that Wright's triumph lies in his anatomy of the reasons for Bigger's truncated humanity'. In a similar vein, Vincent Perez, in his convincing

'Movies, Marxism and Jim Crow: Richard Wright's Cultural Criticism' (*TexasSLL* 43[2001] 142–68), eschews over-reductive views of Bigger Thomas that earlier mass-cultural perspectives have taken. He describes how Wright shows Thomas as a critical interpreter of mass culture, indicating that 'not only does Bigger negotiate media culture, he also reads his own utopian hopes and desires into its narratives and imagery'. Wright is shown to believe that 'subordinated groups have the capacity to resist their ideology-saturated environment', and that this view tempers what past critics have called his 'cultural pessimism'.

The publishing history of *Black Boy/American Hunger* is shown to have regional implications in Jeff Karem's incisive '"I could never really leave the South": Regionalism and the Transformation of Richard Wright's *American Hunger*' (*AmLH* 13[2001] 694–715), where the Book of the Month Club's decision to excise the latter, Northern section of the autobiography is shown to have major implications for the reception of the text and to make its impact more narrowly focused as a Southern text telling a national story of triumph, undermining somewhat the original intention of the book. Wright's literary influences interest Frederick D. Griffiths, whose 'Ralph Ellison, Richard Wright and the Case of Angelo Herndon' (*AAR* 35[2001] 615–36) posits the black communist Angelo Herndon's autobiography *Let Me Live* [1937] as a key precursor of both Ellison's and Wright's works. He traces plot developments and characters in *Invisible Man* that borrow prodigiously from Herndon, albeit Ellison often develops them in different directions. Alternatively, he shows that Wright's autobiographical writing is indebted to Herndon's text as a model rejected. As Griffiths contends, 'Herndon's sentimental and often cliché-ridden Marxist autobiography was at many points a closely observed and vigorously rejected model' for Wright.

Angelo Herndon is seen as a crucial influence on Ellison in Lawrence Jackson, *Ralph Ellison: Emergence of Genius*, probably the richest biographical study of 2002. This weighty tome, the first major Ellison biography, takes Ellison from birth to 1953—just after the publication of *Invisible Man* [1952]. It is excellent on the early years, detailing his close and complicated relationship to his mother and the absent and surrogate fathers who influenced the psychological trajectory of his writings. It is painstakingly researched, and the early Oklahoma years are brought to vivid life and shown to effect the later writings. Ellison's complicated relationships with Langston Hughes and Richard Wright are detailed, and their varied influences delineated. Jackson shows how both act as surrogate father-figures that he must move beyond. The sections on writing process as Ellison begins the long road to writing his first novel do not have the verve of the rest of the study. However, Jackson communicates excellently the intensely solitary nature of the writer's craft according to Ellison. This is a study that will be the standard work for years to come.

It is complemented by Robert O'Meally, ed., *Living with Music: Ralph Ellison's Jazz Writings*, which collects for the first time fictional and non-fictional writings about jazz, including key letters and interviews. It is an invaluable resource for those working in the fields of literary and music criticism. Of particular interest is a previously unpublished 1971 letter to Charlie Davidson about the musician Bobby Short, which berates 'the dreary, reductive, paper-thin images of Negro American life-style and personality that are now so fashionable'. The introduction by O'Meally delineates the centrality of black music to Ellison's world-view, although there could have been more material on jazz as an organizing structure of his prose style. His comment that, 'Most emphatically, he [Ellison] detects a blues-based jazz element at the core of twentieth century American culture, in which styles of dancing, speaking, dressing and playing sports may be termed, in Ellison's phrase, "jazz-shaped"', could stand as an explicator of Ellison's debt to jazz in his complex reaction to American realities.

Jim Neighbours's Derrida-influenced, deconstructive 'Plunging Outside of History: Naming and Self-Possession in *Invisible Man*' (*AAR* 36[2002] 227–42) begins poorly with a meditation on the self that would be more at home in an undergraduate seminar. His aim to show that 'the relation between Invisible Man and his name is not dialectical but aporetic' leads him into linguistic dead-ends that undermine what could have been an interesting thesis, and lead to confusion rather than a clear argument. Much more successful is Christopher A. Shinn's engaging meditation on 'Masquerade, Magic and Carnival in Ralph Ellison's *Invisible Man*' (*AAR* 36[2002] 243–61), which talks of a 'distinct carnival poetics' in the novel. Having traced the lineage of such a poetics through Mikhail Bakhtin and Wilson Harris, Shinn moves to some excellent close reading, showing how the carnivalesque allowed Ellison a 'celebration ... a clear protest against black nihilism and white supremacist rituals of annihilation ... [hence] affirming the essence of a carnival life-principle'.

If Ellison's Oklahoman roots had a decided influence on his later writing trajectory, then Ernest J. Gaines's upbringing in the bayou country of Louisiana is even more foundational for his oeuvre. Mary Ellen Doyle, *Voices from the Quarters: The Fiction of Ernest J. Gaines*, outlines how Gaines felt a sense of vocation 'to be the last witness to his people's way of life before it passes'. Doyle's account is a rather old-fashioned, almost pre-theory, formalist and decidedly biographical approach to its subject, and on these sometimes rather proscriptive terms it provides an excellent introduction to all of Gaines's fiction. There are illuminating primary resources used here, including interviews with Gaines and his close family and friends and evocative photographs of the writer and the River Lake Plantation in Point Coupee parish, where he grew up in an extremely stratified community divided between Cajuns, blacks, and rich plantation whites. As Doyle attests, it is this area that 'he has re-created, book after book, in all its phases of life'. Doyle makes the case for the importance of this very local fiction for the telling of a national story of class, inter-ethnic, and race relations. Gaines only turns up occasionally in journals, but an interesting essay comparing him to Toni Morrison appeared in 2002. Anissa J. Wardi's 'Inscriptions in the Dust: *A Gathering of Old Men* and *Beloved* as Ancestral Requiems' (*AAR* 36[2002] 35–53) argues for the importance of graves and burial practices in these two novels. This closely argued and well-researched essay discusses the history of African American burial practices, opposition to them from slave-masters and white authorities, and how these are mediated in Gaines's and Morrison's texts. Wardi's essay concludes that these texts highlight that 'cemeteries and other interment sites are complicated ancestral spaces of mourning and remembrance in the African American pastoral tradition'.

A more extended and multivarious discussion of Gaines's fiction comes in Jeffrey J. Folks, *From Richard Wright to Toni Morrison: Ethics in Modern and Postmodern American Narrative*. However, discussions of *A Gathering of Old Men* and *A Lesson Before Dying* are disappointingly little more than extended plot summaries. This is typical of a rather pedestrian monograph which contains somewhat one-dimensional and underdeveloped readings of works by both Anglo and African American writers. There is a more sophisticated reading of Toni Morrison's *Jazz* that interestingly uses Ngugi wa Thiong'o's *Decolonising the Mind* (Heinemann [1986]) to emphasize Morrison's concern to reclaim language 'as a first step toward cultural assertion'. Apart from this interesting use of postcolonial criticism, the book shows the limitations of an ethical approach in a brief study where there is not enough room to fully contextualize the works.

If an over-generalized approach is the fault in Folks's study, Devon Boan's *The Black 'I': Author and Audience in African American Literature* has a different problem, an over-schematic and reductive theoretical model that differentiates between black and white readers for texts in ways that make gross and unfounded generalizations about oppositional black and white readers. Furthermore, it separates out four literary types—Literatures of Inversion, Vivification, Subversion and Mythification—that seem to this reader hardly helpful for understanding the African American literary canon. For instance, the description of Morrison as engaged in constructing a literature of mythification in her later fiction leads to a rather grumpy, literalist reading of *Beloved*. This is nowhere more evident than in Boan's discussion of the passage where the ghost, Beloved, Sethe, and Denver 'harmonize in a series of parallel internal monologues'. Boan delineates this as 'monologic' and as 'something between a soliloquy and a sermon, but nothing that seems designed to engage a reader of either race in dialogue' thus 'eliminat(ing) the dialogue between author and reader (black and white)'. But the very openness of this poetic passage allows for multiple readerly interpretations that make it dynamically dialogic and serves up the book for multiple dialogues between readers, and between readers and the author. Despite the limitations of his model Boan's text is useful for containing work on less canonical writers such as Henry Dumas and Daryll Pinckney.

A more successful structuralist reading of African American fiction comes in Bertram D. Ashe's *From Within the Frame: Storytelling in African-American Fiction*, wherein Ashe 'suggests a way to read significant texts in African American literature—texts which use the spoken-voice storytelling format in some manner— in the context of the frame'. He delineates how contemporary black writers use various kinds of framing technique, and this approach is used to critique a wide range of writers, from Charles W. Chesnutt through to more modern writers such as James Alan McPherson, Toni Cade Bambara, and John Edgar Wideman. The most satisfying readings, though, are of Zora Neale Hurston's *Their Eyes Were Watching God* and Ralph Ellison's *Invisible Man*. In the former Ashe shows, in a complex, multi-layered reading, how 'Hurston critiques her audiences, both inside and outside the text, as she displays, in the close frame (the final two pages), a telling ambivalence towards audience that spreads a layer of complexity over the storytelling aesthetic itself'. Thus, Ashe shows how simplistic readings of the novel that promote its storytelling aesthetic as unambiguously positive must be tempered by acknowledgement that the novel 'becomes a treatise on audience as much as a text about voice'. The reading of Ellison's novel is also a dynamic foregrounding of the importance of the Trueblood storytelling frame for the rest of the book. Ashe asserts, '*Invisible Man* provides a storytelling event in the second chapter and then allows its readers the rest of the book to view its results'.

Yemisi Jimoh's comprehensive survey of music as theme, *Spiritual, Blues and Jazz People in African American Fiction: Living in Paradox*, has a dynamic reading of *Invisible Man*, including much useful explication of the different musical allegiances of the characters. Her study also has extensive and incisive discussion of Albert Murray's *Train Whistle Guitar*, Ann Petry's *The Street*, Toni Morrison's *Sula*, James Baldwin's short story 'Sonny's Blues', and Wallace Thurman's *The Blacker the Berry*. The concentration here is on characterization rather than the musical structures underpinning the works, but there is much useful commentary on the sustained musicality of African American fiction and on the different valencies of spiritual, blues, and jazz characters. At times it is rather over-schematic and reductive in its discussion of these three types, but overall this is a stimulating and exciting development of the musical aesthetic applied to African American literature.

Dana Williams's foregrounding of the importance of the novels of Leon Forrest is most timely, and she, like Jimoh, uses a musical approach. Her article 'Preachin' and Singin' Just To Make It Over: The Gospel Impulse as Survival Strategy in Leon Forrest's *Bloodworth Trilogy*' (*AAR* 36[2002] 475–85) is an excellent and astute discussion of Forrest's musical structures. It uses earlier evaluations of vocalized music by Forrest which underlines his debt to gospel and jazz vocalists. As Williams exhibits through some excellent close reading of the novels, 'Forrest uses the gospel impulse and its magical use of reinvention as an art form to address the theme that permeates his novels: the transformation of the self as an act essential to survival during spiritual agony.' One hopes that such inspiring criticism will persuade more of us to use Forrest in our survey courses of African American writers. Of allied interest is Richard Swope's comprehensive and articulate 'Crossing Western Space, or the HooDoo Detective on the Boundary in Ishmael Reed's *Mumbo Jumbo*' (*AAR* 36[2002] 611–28), which discusses the novel in terms of Reed's own ironic description of it as 'the best mystery novel of the year'. After describing how it resembles yet signifies the detective novel tradition, Swope moves to a complex discussion of the working of voodoo, jazz, Egyptian philosophy and biblical exegesis that illuminates the novel's status as a prime postmodern black text.

Another key black male writer who is sometimes neglected in critical writings is John Edgar Wideman. Lisa Lynch's 'The Fever Next Time: The Race of Disease and the Disease of Racism in John Edgar Wideman' (*AmLH* 14[2002] 776–804) looks at Wideman's historical writing in his short story 'Fever' and novel *The Cattle Killing*. The essay shows how the novel develops out of the short story and is concerned with the 1793 Philadelphia yellow fever epidemic. Lynch's varied discussion of the black Atlantic valencies of the tale includes attention to Xhosa culture and folk explanations of the spread of yellow fever based on a critique of transatlantic slavery. Lynch astutely uses Soshona Feldman's and Cathy Carruth's work on trauma and narrative to fully flesh out the meaning of the texts.

Monographs that foreground such contextual rather than structural approaches to African American literature are represented by Robert E. Washington, *The Ideologies of African American Literature: From the Harlem Renaissance to the Black Nationalist Revolt*. This is a deeply troubling study, as its vulgar Marxist approach allows no room for the complexity of writers' ideological positions. This leads to numerous over-simplifications that include the depiction of Paul Laurence Dunbar as thoroughly in the plantation tradition when his work, at least in part, attempted to use its forms to critique it; of Claude McKay as 'more a Bohemian adventurer than a race man or political rebel', when his complex subject position as a Caribbean and global intellectual allowed him a unique perspective on the narrowness of American political posturing; of Zora Neale Hurston as 'collecting black folk material in Florida that fit into [her patron Charlotte Osgood Mason's] conception of primitive black culture', when she was deliberately showing Osgood only some of her findings; and of Ralph Ellison as promoting 'a deracinated and rootless individualism', when his works articulate a multi-layered African American community undermined by a racist, atomizing American Cold War culture. Moreover, the Harlem Renaissance is seen as consisting of undifferentiated, like-minded hedonists, when there is a great variety of ideological positions in a multivarious grouping. Worse, Washington portrays African American writers as the dupes of their white patrons, and as being 'dragged into the swirling vortex' of primitivism. There are also many critical omissions in the book that point to an over-reliance on pre-1990 criticism, so that the discussion of minstrelsy does not engage with important critics like Eric Lott and Michael Rogin and thus appears very outdated and narrow, while Robert Bone's 1958 study of the black American novel is treated as though it were the height of modern critical orthodoxy. Throughout his critique of *Invisible Man*, Washington equates Ellison with his character and indicts the book for being 'a virtual hymn celebrating the ethos of the assimilationist black bourgeois'. This is a serious charge, and Washington's need to commit the intentionalist fallacy to make it stick shows its absurdity.

A more illuminating, though still problematic, contextual study is Maurice O. Wallace, *Constructing the Black Masculine: Identity and Ideality in African American Men's Literature and Culture, 1775–1995*. Wallace uses seven case studies to investigate black masculine identity in the context of slavery, post-civil war Jim Crow society, and late twentieth-century manifestations. As well as canonical figures such as Frederick Douglass, W.E.B. Du Bois, Booker T. Washington, Richard Wright, and James Baldwin, Wallace usefully interrogates figures not usually foregrounded such as Martin Delaney, Prince Hall, and Melvin Dixon. Moreover, a final chapter uses Frantz Fanon's theories to move the argument beyond American shores; unfortunately there is no mention of diasporan theorists Edouard Glissant, Paul Gilroy, or Stuart Hall to further nuance his argument here. Despite such narrowness there is much interesting and provocative work throughout the study, although a tendency to over-elaborate theorizing and the construction of unnecessary neologisms (e.g. 'frame(-up)' and 'b(l)ackside') undermines the solid work of the book in such sections as the discussion of James Baldwin's FBI files. Sometimes Wallace promulgates rather overdetermined, narrow views, such as in a close reading of Wright's *Native Son* where Freud, Derrida, the black phallus, theories of blindness, and the history of lynching combine to create a reading that ultimately loses the reader in the maze of dense argument and obfuscatory language. Nevertheless, this is a promising study that shows how the black male, simultaneously facing 'hypervisibility' and perpetual surveillance, devises textual and other strategies to negotiate his way through the racial maze.

Article-length studies of masculinity include Marilyn C. Wesley's 'Power and Knowledge in Walter Mosley's *Devil in a Blue Dress*' (*AAR* 35[2001] 103–16), which uses a Foucauldian paradigm to discuss Mosley's construction of race relations. She shows how Mosley promotes no simplistic leftist solution but is more interested in 'articulating the full, complex power relations which Easy uncovers as issues of black and white violence'. More critical of its subject and his critics, David Ikard's 'Love Jones: A Black Male Feminist Critique of Chester Himes's *If He Hollers Let Him Go*' (*AAR* 36[2002] 299–310) is an incisive critique of past phallocentric readings of the novel, principally by black nationalist critics such as Addison Gayle. Ikard calls attention to the 'erasure of the black female social perspective in the novel' and shows how the protagonist Bob Jones's 'project of black resistance to white racism is gendered in ways that reify rather than subvert white patriarchy'. The essay pays close attention to Jones's relations to white and black women while showing the importance of Himes's own misogyny to his construction of Jones's character. The bald conclusion that 'Bob Jones, and to a disturbing extent, Chester Himes could not imagine subverting white supremacy without domination of the white female body' is backed up by an excellent sustained argument.

Linda Williams's excellent *Playing the Race Card: Melodramas of Black and White from Uncle Tom to O.J. Simpson* delves in similar deeply contested waters. It is a decidedly cultural studies take on a wide variety of mainly non-literary melodramatic texts, and is wonderfully contextualized. There is much here about the popular literature of slavery, and excellent, historically informed discussions of key films of importance to African American culture such as *The Jazz Singer*, *Show Boat*, and *Gone With the Wind*. The African American writer dealt with at greatest length here is Alex Haley, and the closeness of his text *Roots* to the plantation legend is elucidated, Williams citing it as an Afrocentric version of the mode: 'the accomplishment of *Roots* is to have exalted the impossibly singular root of the past African heritage over the multiple roots of American hybridity, even as it accommodates to a future hybridity and assimilation'.

As with Haley, scholarship on Wallace Thurman is thin on the ground. That he deserves more attention is suggested by Terrell Scott Herring's illuminating 'The Negro Artist and the Racial Manor: *Infants of the Spring* and the Conundrum of Publicity' (*AAR* 35[2001] 581–97), which contextualizes him through his description of the public face of the black writer. Herring describes the debilitating nature of public expectations of the so-called 'New Negro' in the Harlem Renaissance, and the dangers attendant on their policing by white and bourgeois cultural commentators. Jean Toomer is more thoroughly represented in work on the Harlem Renaissance. Charles Scruggs, in his excellent and groundbreaking 'Jean Toomer and Kenneth Burke and the Persistence of the Past' (*AmLH* 13[2001] 41–66), highlights the importance of Burke to Toomer's maturation, showing how Burke's ideas heavily influenced Toomer in the 1920s. He makes the case for Burke's influence superseding that of Waldo Frank in this period, and shows how Toomer's decision to renounce his race can be traced to Burkean ideas. The development of the argument through close reading of *Cane* and other texts is exemplary, and proves that Burke's influences on African American literary tradition were earlier and more widespread than has hitherto been allowed for. Mark Whalan's excellent 'Jean Toomer, Technology and Race' (*JAmS* 36[2002] 459–72) discusses the importance of technology to his thought, showing how he engaged with such European art movements as 'Dadaism and Futurism and their proposals for new relations between machine design and literary aesthetics'. Looking at machines as theme and symbol in *Cane*, Whalan outlines Toomer's fascination with generators, dynamos, and the mechanized city. Toomer is described as seeing 'technology as offering a way out of this closed circuit of aesthetics, oppression and violence within the rural South'. Mary Battenfeld's '"Been shapin words t fit m soul": Cane, Language, and Social Change' (*Callaloo* 25[2002] 1238–49) also concentrates on the social context of *Cane*. She insists that 'In form *Cane* is not a work of social realism. Yet we do Toomer a disservice when we ignore the ways his masterpiece confronts the material conditions of black life.' Her essay illuminates the novel as a clash between the Northern black intellectual and the Southern black folk, wherein inspired language fails to undermine societal violence and inequality. Less inspired is Jennifer L. Shulz's rather pedestrian 'Restaging the Racial Contract: James Weldon Johnson's Signatory Strategies' (*AL* 74[2002] 30–58), which discusses Johnson's work in terms of social contract theory using 'the notion of a racial contract to examine the ways that nonideal contracts involving race … both reiterate and repudiate the ideal social contract'. Using examples from *Along This Way* and *Autobiography of an Ex-Colored Man*, Shulz analyses Johnson's acute understanding of early twentieth-century race relations.

Scholarship on African American women's writing, feminism, and gender issues is represented strongly in 2001 and 2002. Trudier Harris's *Saints, Sinners, Saviors: Strong Black Women in African American Literature* has the interesting premise that black women's strength is deployed by writers in ways that show its negative as well as its positive characteristics. She discusses the 'problematic pause—when the virtue of strength metamorphoses into the virus of disease—that has informed the creation of black female character almost from the moment of its inception in African American literature'. In a series of readings of canonical writers, such as Lorraine Hansberry, Ishmael Reed, Toni Morrison, Toni Cade Bambara, and Ernest Gaines, as well as lesser-known writers such as Octavia Butler, Dorothy West, and Pearl Cleage, she undertakes character studies of strong black women that delineate their ambivalence. Although there is much useful commentary on the way, these discussions too often lapse into extended plot synopses. Strangely there is no sustained discussion of Michele Wallace's seminal *Black Macho and the Myth of the Superwoman* (Dial [1979]), which one would have thought could have made an excellent starting point for Harris's discussion. Nor, indeed, is there a comparative dimension: Caribbean or African or indeed Black British literatures could have been studied to show whether there is a specifically diasporan archetype of the strong black woman. This American-centred approach leads to an unfortunately narrow focus.

An excellent new anthology, Bobo, ed., *Black Feminist Cultural Criticism*, includes many of the foundational essays in the field, including contributions from Barbara Smith, Audre Lorde, Angela Davis, Barbara Christian, and Deborah Macdowell. The criticism emanates from 'the notion … that ordinary, everyday women are the unheralded bedrock of Black feminist social, political, and cultural activism'. It is a timely gathering together of such 'drylongso' criticism. An interesting special issue in a related field is the *Modern Fiction Studies* 'Queer Fictions of Race' (*MFS* 48:iv[2002]), which includes three essays that offer significantly new takes on the Harlem Renaissance: 'The Russian Connection: Interracialism as Queer Alliance in Langston Hughes's *The Ways of White Folk*' (*MFS* 48[2002] 795–824), by Kate A. Baldwin; 'Race, Capitalism and the Third Sex Ideal: Claude McKay's *Home to Harlem* and the Legacy of Edward Carpenter'

(*MFS* 48[2002] 825–57), by Michael Maiwald; and 'Sweetback Style: Wallace Thurman and a Queer Harlem Renaissance' (*MFS* 48[2002] 899–936), by Stephen Knadler. Elsewhere in the issue Alice Walker's deconstruction of the black family romance in *The Color Purple* is dynamically treated in Candice M. Jenkins, 'Queering Black Patriarchy: The Salvific Wish and Masculine Possibility in Alice Walker's *The Color Purple*' (*MFS* 48[2002] 969–1000). These essays address 'transnational exchanges of desire and identification' and are 'indebted to the insights of both queer theory and critical approaches to race and ethnicity'. Jeremy Braddock, 'The Poetics of Conjecture: Countee Cullen's Subversive Exemplarity' (*Callaloo* 25[2002] 1250–71) similarly interrogates homoerotic and same-sex desire. In a closely argued, astute, textual analysis, Braddock shows how Cullen's poetry, even when it seems to be far from any homoerotic subtext, 'speaks to the politics of sexuality in Harlem in the early 1920s'.

Feminist approaches to African American women writers engage with a variety of authors. James D. Sullivan's incisive article, 'Killing John Cabot and Publishing Black: Gwendolyn Brooks's *Riot*' (*AAR* 36[2002] 557–69), delineates the importance of Brooks's decision to change her publishers from a white mainstream press, Harper & Row, to the Dudley Randall-run black imprint, Broadside Press. He describes how the move made it harder for critics to discuss her poetry in universalist terms and meant that they had to take on board her nationalist position. Sullivan's insistence on the importance of publishing contexts is well made here. Eisa Davis, 'Lucille Clifton and Sonia Sanchez: A Conversation' (*Callaloo* 25[2000] 1038–74), is the transcription of an evening of poetry reading and discussion about the tradition of black women's poetry, and includes some dynamic and incisive dialogue between these radical poets. Elizabeth Muther's 'Bambara's Feisty Girls: Resistance Narratives in *Gorilla My Love*' (*AAR* 36[2002] 447–59) usefully engages with Toni Cade Bambara's often neglected short stories. It engages with critics such as Keith Byerman and Susan Willis and contextualizes the stories in terms of Bambara's political engagement and her important anthology publication *The Black Woman* [1970], but otherwise is little more than a character analysis of the child narrators and characters.

A rather more interesting perspective on an African American author not covered much in 2001–2 is provided by Anna Brickhouse in 'Nella Larsen and the Intertextual Geography of *Quicksand*' (*AAR* 35[2001] 533–60), which thoroughly delineates the author's varied literary influences through an intricate reading of a novella that for Brickhouse is 'a veritable patchwork of prior texts—above all else, a book about books'. She shows the myriad of influences, including Theodore Dreiser, Gertrude Stein, Jean Toomer, and Carl Van Vechten, and describes how the novella 'functions as a kind of geographical theory of intertextuality in itself, one that speaks productively to recent critical interest in spatiality and the relation between place and narration'. Set in the context of the accusations of plagiarism that dogged Larsen's literary career, the essay points to new intercultural and theoretical contexts in which the author should be situated. Biman Basu's highly theorized 'Hybrid Embodiment and an Ethics of Masochism: Nella Larsen's *Passing* and Sherley Anne Williams *Dessa Rose*' (*AAR* 36[2002] 383–401) uses Gilles Deleuze's work on masochism to interrogate the political and racial economy described in these texts, which have rarely been compared. The essay fails to convince, however, particularly as it eschews some key work by critics such as

Hortense Spillers and Anne E. Goldman that might have grounded the essay and helped to avoid the excesses of obfuscatory language that sometimes render it virtually unreadable. Less ambitiously, Pamela Peden Saunders's rather pedestrian 'The Feminism of Dorothy West's *The Living Is Easy*: A Critique of the Limitations of the Female Sphere through Performative Gender Roles' (*AAR* 36[2002] 435–46) convincingly foregrounds the feminism of the novel, which she hopes will 'help raise awareness of the richness of her work and consequently raise this text to the level of recognition that it very much deserves'. A decidedly unfeminist approach comes in Pat Righelato, 'Geometry and Music: Rita Dove's *Fifth Sunday*' (*YES* 31[2001] 62–73), a formalist critique of Dove's short story sequence that compares it to Joyce's *Dubliners*. This is a strangely abstract, Eurocentric, and aestheticized reading that makes little reference in its discussion of music to the welter of criticism from African Americanists over the last ten years.

Therese E. Higgins' study, *Religiosity, Cosmology and Folklore: The African Influence in the Novels of Toni Morrison*, spreads its wings further, investigating the African roots of Morrison's oeuvre. She describes how African cosmology suffuses the work, and argues that the 'basic underlying material is pure African'. The study is at its most convincing in describing the working of the flying myth in *Song of Solomon* and the African myths that feed into the novel from various geographical points in Africa. There is also excellent criticism in the chapter on *Beloved* which disrupts the perfunctory use of the Gothic by Anglo-American critics through close attention to Mende ancestral spirits whose manifestations are paralleled in the plot development of the novel. Despite these promising uses of African belief systems to explicate the diasporan roots of Morrison's work, Higgins's Afrocentric predilections mean that the text sometimes strays into an essentialism that undermines the argument. This is seen at its worse in her discussion of *Jazz*, where Higgins asserts that 'African cosmology, especially the quest for the ancestors, permeates the novel's interior—all other things become subordinate in light of this one overall theme'. (Hardly: this omits, for a start, modernity, migration, and music.) Despite Higgins's over-enthusiastic promotion of the African cosmological approach, there are some valuable insights here.

A feminist interpretation of African American literature in terms of the history of violence could, again, have benefited from a more comparative approach. Carol E. Henderson's *Scarring the Black Body: Race and Representation in African American Literature* disappointingly fails to engage with European critics such as Marcus Wood, whose *Blind Memory* (ManUP [2000]) discusses whipping, scarring, and violence in a transatlantic context. Henderson states that 'African American writers recoup the African American body through a literary evocation of its physical trauma, thus reclaiming the essence of a selfhood fragmented under the weight of a dominant culture's gaze'. She talks of a 'body woundedness' that infects African American literature. Much of the ground she traverses to investigate these ideas will be familiar to academics who know the historiography of slavery. However, she often has a neat turn of phrase: for example, in discussing attempts by abolitionists to manipulate Frederick Douglass's discourse, she notes that his body is as crucial as anything he might say to their reading of him, and hence they attempt 'to bind the speech of "the slave" to the social predicament of his body'. There are rather gratuitous personalized introductions and codas here that add little to the text, but nevertheless the monograph is a useful summary of the importance of violence to the representation of African Americans in the literary tradition.

A more dynamic intervention is provided by M. Giulia Fabi's excellent *Passing and the Rise of the African American Novel*, which traces a dynamic tradition of the 'passing novel' stretching back to the beginning of the African American literary tradition in the mid-nineteenth century. Her belief that early African American fiction has been unfairly traduced is developed through excellent close readings of a wide range of passing and other texts by authors as varied as William Wells Brown, Frank J. Webb, Frances E.W. Harper, Pauline E. Hopkins, Sutton E. Griggs, Charles W. Chesnutt, and James Weldon Johnson. These authors have often been talked about as speaking mainly to a white audience, but Fabi insists on the dual black and white audiences for their books, which she sees as more radical than they might at first seem as they move into the 'extravagant, aggressive territories of irony, sarcasm and parody'. Fabi argues for 'the distinctiveness of the poetics of passing in pre-Harlem Renaissance fiction, demonstrating its centrality to the rise and development of the African American novelistic tradition'. She also foregrounds the Utopian novels of the late nineteenth century and how they have been ignored by mainstream critics in this field. She maintains that the recovery of these texts 'alters profoundly the literary critical approach to late-nineteenth century Utopias as a whole'. A final chapter intervenes in the canon-making work of the last two decades to critique Houston Baker Jr. for misreading African American literary foremothers, and to criticize the new anthologies of African American literature for downplaying the importance of these neglected nineteenth-century novels.

Caroline Rody's fine monograph, *The Daughter's Return: African-American and Caribbean Women's Fictions of History*, explores the daughterly quest for maternal origins in African American and Caribbean women's fiction. The writers whom Rody discusses—Toni Morrison, Jean Rhys, and Michelle Cliff among others—make imaginative returns to their ancestral pasts in the persona of the allegorical magic black daughter, who, transcending time, revisits the past to contact her foremothers. The bipartite structure of her book demonstrates Rody's respect for cultural and historical difference, while enabling productive dialogue between her African American and Caribbean writers. Meticulously researched and admirably lucid in style and argument, *The Daughter's Return* is an immensely readable as well as an intellectually robust addition to and intervention in the critical response to African American and Caribbean women's writing.

Nada Elia's *Trances, Dances and Vociferations: Agency and Resistance in Africana Women's Narratives* is an engaged and stimulating study of four women writers of the African diaspora: the Algerian Assia Djebar, the Antiguan Michelle Cliff, the Bajan-African American Paule Marshall, and the Ohioan Toni Morrison. The study foregrounds the importance of the vernacular and folklore to all the writers, but always remains committed to a materialist critique of the worst excesses of feminist or Afrocentric essentialism. Especially valuable is the commentary on 'colour blind' French feminists such as Hélène Cixous, who regard themselves as 'symbolically black' and 'discuss "blackness" and Africa strictly in symbolic terms, co-opting these to represent European women's experiences, and thus usurping the space that would rightly be occupied by women of color'. There is excellent work here on the legacy of middle passage for all these authors, and some interesting new scholarship to further cross-cultural links, including the uncovering of flying myths in harems in North Africa of remarkable similarity to those found in African American folklore. Elia shows how all her authors underline the 'insularity' of Anglo-American culture through their texts' use of the vernacular to show up difference, and also to highlight the stereotyping praxis which sees such difference as exoticism. Concluding pithily by following Djebar, she describes how they 'juxtapose official and unofficial histories, with nomad memory and intermittent voice, thus significantly undermining the hegemonic discourse's claim to truth'. Commitment to the vernacular is also shown to be central to the poetics of Jayne Cortez in Tony Bolden's foundational 'All the Birds Sing Bass: The Revolutionary Blues of Jayne Cortez' (*AAR* 35[2001] 61–71). His discussion of her poetry as exhibiting a blues aesthetic, and of the importance of its performative aspect, is made through a discussion of African American vernacular aesthetics and by close reading of a number of the poems as performed and recorded. Bolden describes how Cortez's version of blues poetry 'constitutes a profound challenge to literary conventions and demonstrates the eloquence of contemporary blues poetics'.

The veritable Toni Morrison industry is represented by numerous articles across a range of journals. For instance, John Young's 'Toni Morrison, Oprah Winfrey and Postmodern Popular Audiences' (*AAR* 35[2001 181–204) directly addresses the public Morrison through a discussion of the adoption of her books by Oprah's Book Club. The article describes the marketing of Morrison and shows how her textual authority has been enhanced by her superstar status, so that the early novels as repackaged have moved from a 'conflicted presence within the mainstream, white publishing structure' to a privileged position in the mainstream itself. Juda Bennett's 'Toni Morrison and the Burden of the Passing Narrative' (*AAR* 35[2001] 205–17) discusses Morrison's oeuvre in the context of the passing genre that had been so foundational in earlier African American literature. Her comprehensive essay is at its most interesting in discussing the short story 'Recitatif', where Bennett speculates that such modern passing narratives have moved to foregrounding the relationship between character and reader rather than, as traditionally, the dynamic between characters in the text. An excellent contextual essay on Morrison is Jennifer Gillan's 'Focusing on the Wrong Front: Historical Displacement, the Maginot Line and *The Bluest Eye*' (*AAR* 36[2002] 283–98), which discusses the way in which Morrison tries to tell alternate histories through *The Bluest Eye* so that it can be read as a commentary on the artificial boundaries of citizenship, gender, race, and history. Laura Berlant's theory that citizenship is embodied in whites is used dynamically as the starting point for a discussion of how 'Morrison eschews the dramatic foreground of national history for the undramatized background'. By foregrounding the usually peripheral, Morrison is shown to be engaged in a reconceptualization of American realities whereby 'a little girl's identity crisis' is linked to 'America's national identity crisis'.

Naomi Mandel's '"I made the ink": Identity, Complicity, 60 Million and More' (*MFS* 48[2002] 581–613) interestingly revisits the controversy over *Beloved*'s epigraph to the 'Sixty Million and More' victims of slavery. Mandel discusses both the historical controversy over slavery's victims and the suggestion, implicit in the title quotation from Morrison, of a form of competition between them and the victims of the Holocaust. This is an informed discussion of the text that is illuminating and often original. In comparison, Jeanna Fuston-White's wholly derivative '"From the seen to the told": The Construction of Subjectivity in Toni

Morrison's *Beloved*' (*AAR* 36[2002] 461–73) describes how Morrison's novel 'poses a strong challenge to the Modernist tradition of knowledge, reason, language, history and identity' before 'reconstruct(ing) knowledges, histories and identities'. This critical commonplace has been reworked for the last twenty years, and although the criticism of the text is adequately argued, unfortunately there is little new here. Chikwenye Okonjo Ogunyemi's Afrocentric 'An Abiku-Ogbanje Atlas: A Pre-Text for Rereading Soyinka's Ake and Morrison's *Beloved*' (*AAR* 36[2002] 663–76) delineates the Igbo *ogbanje* condition and the Yoruba concept of *abiku* as key precursors of both novels. The idea of reincarnation obviously works well for both novels, but the essay is undermined by a romanticized, mystical tone. Some of this hardly merits discussion as criticism, for example: 'Are Americans ready for her [Beloved]? The cold reception of Jonathan Demme's movie *Beloved* indicates that the American public is not ready to play their part in tackling the painful drama. The ogbanje is free to roam at large, still vexed, still vexatious.' Such emotive (and wrong-headed) commentaries exemplify the worst of Morrison criticism.

Critiques of *Jazz* are, by contrast, often much more interesting. For instance, *The Story of Jazz: Toni Morrison's Dialogic Imagination*, the second volume of Justine Tally's trilogy on Toni Morrison's own monumental late twentieth-century trilogy, is a useful critical intervention. Tally conscientiously navigates much previous criticism of *Jazz* before moving to a forthright negotiation of the novel in relation to an admirably clear exposition of Mikhail Bakhtin's theories of storytelling and the dialogic. On storytelling she notes that the 'whole process ... becomes part and parcel of the significance of the novel', and that the novel itself is 'about the ways and means of storytelling itself and the language of narrative process'. There is also an excellent close reading of the novel in relation to detective fiction. Less assured is Tally's exposition of the limitations of the so-called 'jazz critics' of Morrison. Following Alan Munton, she considers that 'jazz is a rather over-worked metaphor' and that reading the novel in terms of jazz is a 'distraction'. I would be the first to admit that such critics sometimes allowed their enthusiasm to overcome their critical acumen (*mea culpa*), but Tally's dismissal undermines a more integrative reading that could have used Bakhtinian theory to negotiate between the jazz in the novel and the jazz it seeks to honour. Jazz critics such as Paul Berliner (on improvisation) and Ingrid Monson (on antiphony) would have been useful here, and their absence means that the book's value as a commentary on the cultural context of Morrison's work as promulgating the importance of jazz is rather undermined. As literary criticism, Tally's work is exemplary, explicating difficult theoretical ideas and applying them most appositely. Her historical context for the novel is also assured and comprehensive, giving a context to the work that supports the close criticism. Ann-Marie Paquet Deyris's 'Toni Morrison's *Jazz* and the City' (*AAR* 35[2001] 219–31) revisits old ground about Morrison and musicality, but is most interesting in its discussion of the novel as playing with an 'aesthetic of displacement' whereby the city 'becomes an enacting site of reconstruction, of potential and actual articulation of some traumatic traces of the past'. Caroline Brown, 'Golden Gray and the Talking Book: Identity as a Site of Artful Construction in Toni Morrison's *Jazz*' (*AAR* 36[2002] 629–42), manages to say something new about music in Morrison's fiction, illustrating how '*Jazz* is, quite literally, the textual negotiation of freedom through the grammar of the erotic'. The close attention to Golden Gray takes the discussion of jazz as aesthetic form in the novel into new areas that contribute to a dynamic new reading.

There is an increasing number of essays on Morrison's final twentieth-century novel. Probably the best is Peter Widdowson's 'The American Dream Refashioned: History, Politics and Gender in Toni Morrison's *Paradise*' (*JAmS* 35[2001] 313–35). Widdowson exhaustively follows up the many historical references in the text as he demonstrates that the novel 'is an attempt to write several concentric histories of the American experience from a distinctively African American experience'. The novel, 'a fictional intervention into American historiography', is an African American feminist reworking of many of the foundational myths of the American nation. The critique of the text is astute throughout. Philip Page's 'Furrowing All the Brows: Interpretation and the Transcendent in Toni Morrison's *Paradise*' (*AAR* 35[2001] 637–49) describes how the novel develops Morrison's complex relations with her readers so that they are encouraged to become 'co-creators rather than merely passive respondents'. He describes the difficulties associated with the novel as coming from this open-endedness, which leaves even the race of crucial characters open to interpretation. By being encouraged to eschew authoritarian (and authorial) viewpoints readers are interpellated as co-creators, and Page rightly sees this as a key part of Morrison's political agenda. This stimulating short essay highlights the importance of reader-response criticism to Morrison's work. Linda J. Krumholz, 'Reading and Insight in Toni Morrison's Paradise' (*AAR* 36[2002] 21–34) also emphasizes the importance of readerly response and racial marking (or rather the lack of it) in the novel, contextualizing it through Morrison's own avowed interest in key racial struggles of the 1990s such as the Clarence Thomas hearings and the O.J. Simpson trial. She describes how Morrison makes whiteness lose its potency in the novel as she 'opens up the bounds of the racial imaginary without substituting one fixed system for another, without reproducing the "white man's law" of the racial house'. Katrine Dalsgard's interesting and well-argued 'The One All-Black Town Worth the Pain: African American Exceptionalism, Historical Narration and the Critique of Nationalism in Toni Morrison's *Paradise*' (*AAR* 35[2001] 233–48) debates with Deborah Madsen's use of Morrison as paradigmatic of an anti-exceptionalist tendency in African American thinking. She describes how African American culture is replete with exceptionalist rhetoric, and shows how Morrison critiques it throughout her novel. On the other hand, Magall Cornier Michael's 'Re-imagining Agency: Toni Morrison's *Paradise*' (*AAR* 36[2002] 643–61), while usefully contextualizing *Paradise* through the civil rights movement, is rather dogmatic. Michael describes Morrison's feminist intent in the novel by outlining how it 'engages in a critique of the patriarchal aspects of the Movement and the limitations that result as a consequence of these aspects'. This is true, but hardly an earth-shattering revelation.

The most useful reference guide to African American literature has now been published in an inexpensive, paperback, concise version. Andrews, Smith Foster, and Harris, eds., *The Concise Oxford Companion to African American Literature*, is a wonderful reference guide. As the editors attest, 'it is an effort to update the original ... while at the same time distilling the former volume's contents to its biographical and textual essentials'. It is a testament to the distillation that in using the concise edition this reviewer rarely needs to rush to his library to chase up the original volume. Another valuable reprint published in 2002 was Arnold

Rampersad's magisterial *The Life of Langston Hughes*, volume 2: *1941–1967: I Dream a World*. Most interestingly for Hughes scholarship, Rampersad, in a new afterword, replies to critics who have accused him of homophobia for describing Hughes as asexual rather than homosexual, and discusses the controversy over Isaac Julien's film *Looking for Langston*, with its overt references to Hughes's homosexuality. Rampersad trenchantly defends Hughes's ambivalent sexuality, describing how 'Clearly Hughes never wanted to be known publicly as gay'. The controversy will continue, but Rampersad's comments are a crucial update from Hughes's major biographer and a co-trustee of his estate.

An excellent centennial celebration of Hughes was published in *Callaloo* (*Callaloo* 25:iv[2002]). Complete with a variety of wonderful photographs, memoirs, and excellent academic essays, it is worthy of separate publication as a tribute volume. A gem for Hughes collectors is the series of poems he wrote during his visit to central Asia which have only ever been available in Uzbeki before. David Chioni Moore, 'Colored Dispatches from the Uzbek Border: Langston Hughes' Relevance 1933–2002' (*Callaloo* 25[2002] 1115–35), details the publishing history of these poems and the importance of Hughes's visit for the development of his political and cultural ideas. Hughes was the first American writer translated into any central Asian language, and his relations with Uzbeki writers showed him an aspect of Soviet culture away from the mainstream that nuanced his feelings about communism. There are remarkable photographs here of Hughes in the company of Uzbeki writers and intellectuals. Most poignantly Hughes and Arthur Koestler are pictured picking cotton, as Hughes contends, 'for the fun of it'. Meta Duewa Jones's excellent 'Listening to What the Ear Demands: Langston Hughes and his Critics' (*Callaloo* 25[2002] 1145–75) makes the case for the importance of the later jazz poetry such as *Montage of a Dream Deferred* [1951], *Ask Your Mama: 12 Moods for Jazz* [1961], and the recording of *The Weary Blues* [1958]. She describes how 'Langston Hughes was a jazz musician in a poet's body', and concludes that these key jazz poems combine 'formal innovation and social critique' and are 'essential to the development of a modernist American poetry in general and to jazz-influenced poetry in particular'.

Less innovative is Elizabeth Schultz's pedestrian analysis of Hughes's fiction in 'Natural and Unnatural Circumstances in Langston Hughes' *Not Without Laughter*' (*Callaloo* 25[2002] 1177–87). She describes how 'natural metaphors become the means for both conveying and mitigating the powerful sexual subtexts of the blues and dance'. More dynamically, Jeff Westover, in 'Africa/America: Fragmentation and Diaspora in the Work of Langston Hughes' (*Callaloo* 25[2002] 1207–23), follows Paul Gilroy in discussing the meaning of modernity and diaspora to Hughes. Westover shows how 'representations of Africa inform, and even constitute, his conceptions of the United States and his place within it'. James Smethurst's "'Don't say goodbye to the porkpie hat": Langston Hughes, the Left, and the Black Arts Movement' (*Callaloo* 25[2002] 1225–36) valuably discusses the influence of Hughes on the leftist and nationalist poets who followed him, and shows that his radicalism continued into the later decades of his life. He shows how Hughes 'promoted young radicals even as he engaged in a critical dialogue with them'. By far the best essay in the special issue, and probably the most astute of those reviewed in this section, is Seth Moglen's 'Modernism in the Black Diaspora: Langston Hughes and the Broken Cubes of Modernism' (*Callaloo* 25[2002] 1189–1205). He analyses the neglected poem 'Cubes' [1934], 'a powerful critique of modernism from a black perspective', showing how it foregrounds Hughes as espousing a 'distinctive, populist and revolutionary version of modernism'. Hughes uses the twin forms of cubism and jazz to create what Moglen calls a 'black vernacular literary cubism that critiques modernism whilst engaging with its forms'. The essay fully engages with a postcolonial critique of modernism from the 'margins', showing how 'modernism can perhaps alone reveal to us the "disease" that brought it into being', and that Hughes's poem reveals him to be a modernist *par excellence*. Such attendance to the transnational and the intercultural throughout the special issue makes it symptomatic of cutting-edge criticism that marks the best of the work in African American literary criticism reviewed here.

Books Reviewed

Ackerman, Alan L. *The Portable Theatre: American Literature and the Nineteenth-Century Stage.* JHUP. [1999] pp. 304. $52 ISBN 0 8018 6161 6.

Aldama, Arturo J. *Disrupting Savagism: Intersecting Chicano/a, Mexican Immigrant, and Native American Struggles for Self-Representation.* DukeUP. [2001] pp. 186. pb $19.95 ISBN 0 8223 2748 1.

Aldama, Arturo J. and Naomi H. Quiñonez, eds. *Decolonial Voices: Chicana and Chicano Studies in the 21st Century.* IndUP. [2002] pp. 413. pb $24.95 ISBN 0 2533 4014 4.

Andrews, William L., Frances Smith Foster, and Trudier Harris, eds. *The Concise Oxford Companion to African American Literature.* OUPAm. [2001] pp. xxii + 488. pb $24.95 ISBN 0 1951 3883 X.

Ashe, Bertram D. *From Within the Frame: Storytelling in African-American Fiction.* Routledge. [2002] pp. ix + 147. £45 ISBN 0 4159 3954 2.

Beer, Janet. *Edith Wharton.* WTW. Northcote. [2002] pp. xi + 99. pb £9.99 ISBN 0 7463 0898 1.

Beer, Janet and Bridget Bennett, eds. *Special Relationships: Anglo-American Affinities and Antagonisms, 1854–1936.* ManUP. [2002] pp. x + 266. hb. £47.50 ISBN 0 7190 5817 1, pb. £16.99, ISBN 0 7190 5818 X.

Berman, Ronald. *Fitzgerald, Hemingway and the Twenties.* UAlaP. [2002] pp. 176. pb $19.95 ISBN 0 8173 1057 6.

Bertens, Hans, and Joseph Natoli, eds. *Postmodernism: The Key Figures.* Blackwell. [2001] pp. xvi + 384. pb £16.99 ISBN 0 6312 1797 5.

Bloom, Harold, ed. *Cat on a Hot Tin Roof.* MCI. ChelseaH. [2002] pp. 155. $37.95 ISBN 0 7910 6342 9.

Bloom, Harold, ed. *The Crucible.* MCI. ChelseaH. [1999] pp. 205. £29.95 ($34.95) ISBN 0 7910 4775 X.

Bloom, Harold, ed. *Long Day's Journey into Night.* YaleUP. [2002] pp. 179. hb. $22.95 ISBN 0 3000 9410 8, pb. $12.95 ISBN 0 3000 9305 5.

Boan, Devon. *The Black 'I': Author and Audience in African American Literature.* Lang. [2002] pp. x + 131. pb $22.95 ISBN 0 8204 5737 X.

Bobo, Jacqueline, ed. *Black Feminist Cultural Criticism.* Blackwell. [2001] pp. xxv + 337. hb. £55 ISBN 0 6312 2239 1, pb. £19.99 ISBN 0 6312 2240 5.

Booker, M. Keith. *The Post-Utopian Imagination: American Culture in the Long 1950s*. Greenwood. [2002] pp. 226. £38.75 ISBN 0 3133 2165 5.

Brietzke, Zander. *The Aesthetics of Failure: Dynamic Structure in the Plays of Eugene O'Neill*. McFarland. [2001] pp. 258. £25.95 ($35) ISBN 0 7864 0946 0.

Broer, Lawrence R., and Gloria Holland, eds. *Hemingway and Women: Female Critics and the Female Voice*. UAlaP. [2002] pp. 296. $39.95 ISBN 0 8173 1136 X.

Cantú, Norma E., and Olga Nájera-Ramírez, eds. *Chicana Traditions: Continuity and Change*. UIllP. [2002] pp. 269. pb $18.95 ISBN 0 2520 7012 7.

Cappucci, Paul R. *William Carlos Williams' Poetic Response to the 1913 Paterson Silk Strike*. Mellen. [2002] pp. 206. £60 ISBN 0 7734 6912 5.

Ciociola, Gail. *Wendy Wasserstein: Dramatizing Women, their Choices and their Boundaries*. McFarland. [1998] pp. 168. $35 ISBN 0 7864 0523 6.

Conte, Joseph M. *Design and Debris: A Chaotics of Postmodern American Fiction*. UAlaP. [2002] pp. xi + 271. pb £19.50 ISBN 0 8173 1115 7.

Curry, Jane Kathleen. *John Guare: A Research and Production Sourcebook*. Greenwood. [2002] pp. 296. £48.50 ($74.95) ISBN 0 3133 1252 4.

Davis, Rocío G., and Ludwig, Sämi, eds. *Asian American Literature in the International Context: Readings on Fiction, Poetry, and Performance*. Lit Verlag/Transaction [2002] pp. 265. _25.90 ISBN 3 8258 5710 7.

Dickstein, Morris. *Leopards in the Temple: The Transformation of American Fiction 1945–70*. HarvardUP. [2002] pp. xii + 242. pb £10.95 ISBN 0 6740 0604 6.

Doyle, Mary Ellen. *Voices from the Quarters: The Fiction of Ernest J. Gaines*. LSUP. [2003] pp. xiv + 245. pb $14.95 ISBN 0 8071 2910 0.

Duvall, John N., and Ann J. Abadie, eds. *Faulkner and Postmodernism*. UMP. [2002] pp. 203. $45 ISBN 1 5780 6459 7.

Edmondson, Henry T. *Return to Good and Evil: Flannery O'Connor's Response to Nihilism*. Lexington. [2002] pp. 202. £18.95 ISBN 0 7391 0421 7.

Elia, Nadia. *Trances, Dances and Vociferations: Agency and Resistance in Africana Women's Narratives*. Garland. [2001] pp. xi + 169. pb $16.99 ISBN 0 8153 3843 0.

Fabi, M. Giulia. *Passing and the Rise of the African American Novel*. UIllP. [2002] pp. xi + 187. pb $32.50 ISBN 0 2520 2667 5.

Fant, Joseph L., and Robert Ashley, eds. *Faulkner at West Point*. UMP. [2002] pp. 125. $22 ISBN 1 5780 6445 7.

Fenkl, Heinz Insu, and Walter K. Lew, eds. *Kori: The Beacon Anthology of Korean American Fiction*. Beacon. [2001] pp. 263. $16 ISBN 0 8070 5917 X.

Ferens, Dominika. *Edith and Winnifred Eaton: Chinatown Missions and Japanese Romances*. UIllP. [2002] pp. 221. $34.95 ISBN 0 2520 2721 3.

Folks, Jeffrey J. *From Richard Wright to Toni Morrison: Ethics in Modern and Postmodern American Narrative*. Lang. [2001] pp. x + 199. pb $29.95 ISBN 0 8204 5105 3.

Ford, Sara J. *Gertrude Stein and Wallace Stevens: The Performance of Modern Consciousness*. Routledge. [2002] pp. 144. £45 ISBN 0 4159 3944 5.

Gajdusek, Robert E. *Hemingway in his own Country*. UNDP. [2002] pp. 440. pb $32 ISBN 0 2680 3059 6.

Gilcrest, David W. *Greening the Lyre: Environmental Poetics and Ethics.* UNevP. [2002] pp. xii + 169. £19.95 ISBN 0 8741 7494 5.

Grayson, Jane, Arnold McMillin, and Priscilla Meyer, eds. *Nabokov's World*, vol. 1: *The Shape of Nabokov's World.* Palgrave. [2002] pp. 208. £55 ISBN 0 3339 6415 2.

Grayson, Jane, Arnold McMillin, and Priscilla Meyer, eds. *Nabokov's World*, vol. 2: *Reading Nabokov.* Palgrave. [2002] pp. 208. £55 ISBN 0 3339 6417 9.

Grice, Helena. *Negotiating Identities: An Introduction to Asian American Women's Writing.* ManUP. [2002] pp. 257. pb £11.24 ISBN 0 7190 6031 1.

Gross, Robert F. *Tennessee Williams: A Casebook.* Routledge. [2002] pp. 214. £55 ($55) ISBN 0 8153 3174 6.

Gussow, Mel. *Conversations with Miller.* Applause. [2002] pp. 224. $22.95 ISBN 1 5578 3596 9.

Harris, Trudier. *Saints, Sinners, Saviors: Strong Black Women in African American Literature.* Palgrave. [2001] pp. vi + 218. pb $16.99 ISBN 0 3122 9303 8.

Hass, Robert Bernard. *Going by Contraries: Robert Frost's Conflict with Science.* UPVirginia. [2002] pp. xiii + 220. £34.50 ISBN 0 8139 2111 2.

Henderson, Carol E. *Scarring the Black Body: Race and Representation in African American Literature.* UMissP. [2002] pp. xiii + 183. $39.95 ISBN 0 8262 1421 5.

Higgins, Therese E. *Religiosity, Cosmology, and Folklore: The African Influence in the Novels of Toni Morrison.* Routledge. [2001] pp. xiv + 149. $50 ISBN 0 4159 3565 2.

Hodson, Sara S., and Jeanne Campbell Reesman, eds. *Jack London: One Hundred Years a Writer.* Huntington. [2002] pp. 223. $37.95 ISBN 0 8732 8195 0.

Hoffpauir, Richard. *The Contemplative Poetry of Edwin Arlington Robinson, Robert Frost and Yvor Winters.* Mellen. [2002] pp. vi + 263. £60. ISBN 0 7734 7198 7.

Hogle, Jerrold E., ed. *The Cambridge Companion to Gothic Fiction.* CUP. [2002] pp. xxv + 327. pb £16.99 ISBN 0 5217 9466 8.

Holditch, Kenneth, and Richard Freeman Leavitt. *Tennessee Williams and the South.* UMP. [2002] pp. 111. £29.95 ($30) ISBN 1 5780 6410 4.

Holloway, David. *The Late Modernism of Cormac McCarthy.* Greenwood. [2002] pp. xiv + 198. £42 ISBN 0 3133 2227 9.

Hook, Andrew. *F. Scott Fitzgerald: A Literary Life.* Palgrave. [2002] pp. 192. pb £16.99 ISBN 0 3338 0334 5.

Horn, Barbara Lee. *Lillian Hellman: A Research and Production Sourcebook.* Greenwood. [1998] pp. 170. £42.75 ($62.95) ISBN 0 3133 0264 2.

Hotelling, Kirstin Zona. *Marianne Moore, Elizabeth Bishop, and May Swenson: The Feminist Poetics of Self-Restraint.* UMichP. [2002] pp. 76. 24.50 ISBN 0 4721 1304 6.

Hungerford, Amy. *The Holocaust of Texts: Genocide, Literature and Personification.* UChicP. [2002] pp. 296. £28 ISBN 0 2263 6076 8.

Jackson, Lawrence. *Ralph Ellison: Emergence of Genius.* Wiley. [2002] pp. xiii + 498. £19.50 ($30) ISBN 0 4713 5414 7.

Jahshan, Paul. *Henry Miller and the Surrealist Discourse of Excess: A Post-Structuralist Reading.* Lang. [2001] pp. viii + 214. £39.97 ISBN 0 8204 5284 X.

Jimoh, A. Yemisi. *Spiritual, Blues, and Jazz People in African American Fiction: Living in Paradox.* UTennP. [2002] pp. viii + 284. $30 ISBN 1 5723 3172 0.

Jin, Songpin. *The Poetics of the Ideogram*. Lang. [2002] pp. ix + 221. pb £26 ISBN 3 6313 7979 X.

Johnson, Ronna C., and Nancy M. Grace, eds. *Girls Who Wore Black: Women Writing the Beat Generation*. RutgersUP. [2002] pp. 295. pb £15.50 ISBN 0 8135 3065 2.

Johnston, Devin. *Precipitations: Contemporary American Poetry as Occult Practice*. WesleyanUP. [2002] pp. xii + 200. hb. £27.50 ISBN 0 8195 6561 X, pb. £13.95 ISBN 0 8195 6562 8.

Kanellos, Nicolás, ed. *Herencia: The Anthology of Hispanic Literature of the United States*. OUP. [2002] pp. 644. $19.95 ISBN 0 1951 3825 2.

Kaplan, Carla. *Zora Neale Hurston: A Life in Letters*. Doubleday. [2002] pp. ix + 880. $40 ISBN 0 3854 9035 6.

King, Kimball, ed. *Hollywood on Stage: Playwrights Evaluate the Culture Industry*. Garland. [1997] £50 ($80) ISBN 0 8153 2823 0.

Konzett, Delia Caparoso. *Ethnic Modernisms: Anzia Yezierska, Zora Neale Hurston, Jean Rhys, and the Aesthetics of Dislocation*. Palgrave. [2002] pp. xiv + 202. £37.50 ISBN 0 3122 9345 3.

Koorey, Stefani. *Arthur Miller's Life and Literature: An Annotated and Comprehensive Guide*. Greenwood. [2000] pp. 888. £76 ($95) ISBN 0 8108 3869 9.

Krupat, Arnold. *Red Matters: Native American Studies*. UPennP. [2002] pp. 167. $33.50 ISBN 0 8122 3649 1.

Kucich, John, and Dianne F. Sadoff, eds. *Victorian Afterlife: Postmodern Culture Rewrites the Nineteenth Century*. UMinnP. [2000] pp. xxx + 344. pb £14 ISBN 0 8166 3324 X.

Lalonde, Chris. *Grave Concerns, Trickster Turns: The Novels of Louis Owens*. UOklaP. [2002] pp. 220. $34.95 ISBN 0 8061 3408 9.

Latham, Rob. *Consuming Youth: Vampires, Cyborgs, and the Culture of Consumption*. UChicP. [2002] pp. x + 321. pb £15.50 ISBN 0 2264 6892 5.

Lemire, Elise. *'Miscegenation': Making Race in America*. UPennP. [2002] pp. 204. $35 ISBN 0 8122 3664 5.

Lesinska, Zofia P. *Perspectives of Four Women Writers on the Second World War: Gertrude Stein, Janet Flanner, Kay Boyle, and Rebecca West*. Lang. [2002] pp. vi + 189. £39 ISBN 0 8204 6103 2.

Lilley, James D., ed. *Cormac McCarthy: New Directions*. UNMP. [2002] pp. x + 350. £24.50 ISBN 0 8263 2766 4.

Lingeman, Richard. *Sinclair Lewis: Rebel from Main Street*. RandomH. [2002] pp. 688. $35 ISBN 0 6794 3823 8.

McDonald, Robert L., and Linda Rohrer Paige, eds. *Southern Women Playwrights: New Essays in Literary History and Criticism*. UAlaP. [2002] pp. 257. hb. £44.50 ($55) ISBN 0 8173 1079 7, pb. £20.50 ($24.95) ISBN 0 8173 1080 0.

Marçais, Dominique, Mark Niemeyer, and Cathy Waegner, eds. *Literature on the Move: Comparing Diasporic Ethnicities in Europe and the Americas*. CWU. [2002] pp. 360. _50 ISBN 3 8253 1405 7.

Marino, Stephen A. *'The Salesman Has a Birthday': Essays Celebrating the Fiftieth Anniversary of Arthur Miller's 'Death of a Salesman'*. UPA. [2000] pp. 143. hb. $52 ISBN 0 7618 1653 4, pb. $27.50 ISBN 0 7618 1654 2.

Mason, Jeffrey D., and J. Ellen Gainor, eds. *Performing America: Cultural Nationalism in American Theatre*. UMichP. [1999] pp. 288. $50 ISBN 0 4721 0985 5.

Mattessich, Stefan. *Lines of Flight: Discursive Time and Countercultural Desire in the Work of Thomas Pynchon*. DukeUP. [2002] pp. 291. pb £16.95 ISBN 0 8223 2994 8.

Medoro, Dana. *The Bleeding of America: Menstruation as Symbolic Economy in Pynchon, Faulkner, and Morrison*. Greenwood. [2002] pp. 240. $61.95 ISBN 0 3133 2059 4.

Meyer, Michael J., ed. *Literature and Music*. Rodopi. [2002] pp. 238. pb £15.50 ISBN 9 0420 1191 2.

Mullins, Greg A. *Colonial Affairs: Bowles, Burroughs and Chester Write Tangier*. UWiscP. [2002] pp. 192. pb £14.50 ISBN 0 2991 7960 5.

Myrsiades, Kostas, ed. *The Beat Generation: Critical Essays*. Lang. [2002] pp. x + 352. pb £22.63 ISBN 0 8204 5778 7.

Nguyen, Viet Thanh. *Race and Resistance: Literature and Politics in Asian America*. OUP. [2002] pp. 228. pb $19.95 ISBN 0 1951 4700 6.

O'Leary, Peter. *Gnostic Contagion: Robert Duncan and the Poetry of Illness*. WesleyanUP. [2002] pp. 286. hb. £27.50 ISBN 0 8195 6563 6, pb. £13.95 ISBN 0 8195 6564 4.

Olson, Kirby. *Gregory Corso: Doubting Thomist*. SIUP. [2002] pp. viii + 183. £30.50 ISBN 0 8093 2447 4.

O'Meally, Robert G., ed. *Living with Music: Ralph Ellison's Jazz Writings*. Modern Library. [2001] pp. xxxv + 290. pb $13.95 ISBN 0 3757 6023 7.

Otten, Terry. *The Temptation of Innocence in the Dramas of Arthur Miller*. UMissP. [2002] pp. 280. £29.95 ($39.95) ISBN 0 8262 1406 1.

Patell, Cyrus R.K. *Negative Liberties: Morrison, Pynchon and the Problem of Liberal Ideology*. DukeUP. [2002] pp. 288. pb £13.50 ISBN 0 8223 2669 8.

Paul, Catherine. *Poetry in the Museums of Modernism: Yeats, Pound, Moore, Stein*. UMichP. [2002] pp. 280. £30.50 ISBN 0 4721 1264 3.

Pavlic, Edward M. *Crossroads Modernism: Descent and Emergence in African-American Literary Culture*. UMinnP. [2002] pp. xxi + 314. pb $19.95 ISBN 0 8166 3892 6.

Peel, Robin. *Writing Back: Sylvia Plath and Cold War Politics*. AUP. [2002] pp. 289. £35 ISBN 0 8386 3868 6.

Pettipiece, Deirdre Anne. *Sex Theories and the Shaping of Two Moderns: Hemingway and H.D.* Routledge. [2002] pp. 140. $60 ISBN 0 4159 3786 8.

Plunka, Gene A. *The Black Comedy of John Guare*. AUP. [2002] pp. 289. £35 ($43.50) ISBN 0 8741 3763 2.

Pratt, William. *Ezra Pound: Nature and Myth*. AMS. [2002] pp. vii + 158. £55.95 ISBN 0 4046 1593 7.

Quinn, Justin. *Gathered Beneath the Storm: Wallace Stevens, Nature and Community*. UCDubP. [2002] pp. ix + 157. hb. £39.95 ISBN 1 9006 2166 5, pb. £17.95 ISBN 1 9006 2167 3.

Rampersad, Arnold. *The Life of Langston Hughes*, vol. 2: *1941–1967: I Dream a World*. OUPAm. [2002] pp. viii + 522. pb 16.99 ($21.50) ISBN 0 1951 4643 3.

Rasula, Jed. *This Compost: Ecological Imperatives in American Poetry*. UGeoP. [2002] pp. xv + 259. £32.95 ISBN 0 8203 2366 7.

Reaves, Gerri. *Mapping the Private Geography: Autobiography, Identity, and America*. McFarland. [2001] pp. 162. £29.95 ($32) ISBN 0 7864 0877 4.

Rebein, Robert. *Hicks, Tribes, and Dirty Realists: American Fiction after Postmodernism*. UPKen. [2001] pp. 207. £16.95 ISBN 0 8131 2176 0.

Renza, Louis A. *Edgar Allan Poe, Wallace Stevens and the Poetics of American Privacy*. LSUP. [2002] pp. xix + 277. £34.50 ISBN 0 8071 2755 8.

Riggs, Sarah. *Word Sightings: Poetry and Visual Media in Stevens, Bishop, and O'Hara*. Routledge. [2002] pp. xxiv + 134. £45 ISBN 0 4159 3859 7.

Rivera, Carmen S. *Kissing the Mango Tree: Puerto Rican Women Rewriting American Literature*. Arte Público Press. [2002] pp. 188. pb $19.95 ISBN 1 5588 5377 4.

Rody, Caroline. *The Daughter's Return: African-American and Caribbean Women's Fictions of History*. OUPAm. [2002] pp. x + 267. $52 ISBN 0 1951 3888 0.

Roessel, David, and Nicholas Moschovakis, eds. *The Collected Poems of Tennessee Williams*. ND. [2002] pp. 304. £23.95 ($34.95) ISBN 0 8112 1508 3.

Roudané, Matthew, ed. *The Cambridge Companion to Sam Shepard*. CUP. [2002] pp. 329. hb. £45 ($65) ISBN 0 5217 7158 7, pb. £15.95 ($23) ISBN 0 5217 7766 6.

San Juan, Epifanio Jr. *Racism and Cultural Studies: Critiques of Multiculturalist Ideology and the Politics of Difference*. DukeUP. [2002] pp. 428. pb $24.95 ISBN 0 8223 2866 6.

Schreiber, Evelyn Jaffe. *Subversive Voices: Eroticizing the Other in William Faulkner and Toni Morrison*. UTennP. [2002] pp. 200. $25 ISBN 1 5723 3151 8.

Shankar, S. *Textual Traffic: Colonialism, Modernity and the Economy of the Text*. SUNYP. [2002] pp. xvii + 224. hb. $58.50 ISBN 0 7914 4991 2, pb. $21.95 ISBN 0 7914 4992 0.

Shell, Marc, ed. *American Babel: Literatures of the United States from Abanaki to Zuni*. HarvardUP. [2002] pp. 522. pb _16.50 ISBN 0 6740 0661 5.

Smith, Christopher J., ed. *Readings on 'All My Sons'*. Greenhaven. [2001] hb. $33.70 ISBN 0 7377 06899, pb. $22.45 ISBN 0 7377 0688 0.

Smith, Madeline, and Richard C. Eaton. *Eugene O'Neill: An Annotated International Bibliography, 1973 through 1999*. McFarland. [2001] pp. 242. £40.95 ($55) ISBN 0 7864 1036 1.

Sternicht, Sanford. *A Reader's Guide to Modern American Drama*. SyracuseUP. [2002] pp. 260. pb £16.50 ($19.95) ISBN 0 8156 2939 7.

Swift, John N., and Joseph R. Urgo, eds. *Willa Cather and the American Southwest*. UNebP. [2002] pp. vi + 172. £30.50 ISBN 0 8032 4557 2.

Tally, Justine. *The Story of Jazz: Toni Morrison's Dialogic Imagination*. Lit Verlag. [2001] pp. ii + 150. pb $22.95 ISBN 3 8258 5364 0.

Thompson, Judith J. *Tennessee Williams' Plays: Memory, Myth, and Symbol*. Lang. [2002] pp. 261. $29.95 ISBN 0 8204 5744 2.

Thompson, Stephanie Lewis. *Influencing America's Tastes: Realism in the Works of Wharton, Cather and Hurst*. UFlorP. [2002] pp. xii + 234. £44.50 ISBN 0 8130 2480 3.

Timmerman, John H. *Robert Frost: The Ethics of Ambiguity*. BuckUP. [2002] pp. 198. £32 ISBN 0 8387 5532 1.

Trout, Steven. *Memorial Fictions: Willa Cather and the First World War*. UNebP. [2002] pp. ix + 225. £30.50 ISBN 0 8032 4442 8.

Vickroy, Laurie. *Trauma and Survival in Contemporary Fiction*. UPVirginia. [2002] pp. xvi + 266. pb £12.95 ISBN 0 8139 2128 7.

Vincent, John Emil. *Queer Lyrics: (Difficulty and Closure in American Poetry)*. Palgrave. [2002] pp. xix + 215. £35 ISBN 0 3122 9497 2.

Voss, Ralph F., ed. *Magical Muse: Millennial Essays on Tennessee Williams*. UAlaP. [2002] pp. 251. $39.95 ISBN 0 8173 1127 0.

Wagner-Martin, Linda, and Patrick A. Smith, eds. *William Faulkner: Six Decades of Criticism*. MichSUP. [2002] pp. 352. pb $29.95 ISBN 0 8701 3612 7.

Wald, Alan M. *Exiles from a Future Time: The Forging of the Mid-Twentieth Century Literary Left*. UNCP. [2002] pp. 412. £35.50 ISBN 0 8078 2683 9.

Wallace, Maurice O. *Constructing the Black Masculine: Identity and Ideality in African American Men's Literature and Culture, 1775–1995*. DukeUP. [2002] pp. xiii + 236. pb $19.95 ISBN 0 8223 2869 0.

Washington, Robert E. *The Ideologies of African American Literature. From the Harlem Renaissance to the Black Nationalist Revolt*. R&L. [2001] pp. ix + 361. $29.95 ISBN 0 7425 0950 8.

Welburn, Ron. *Roanoke and Wampum: Topics in Native American Heritage and Literatures*. Lang. [2001] pp. 255. pb $29.95 ISBN 0 8204 3901 0.

West, James L.W. III, ed. *The Cambridge Edition of the Works of F. Scott Fitzgerald: Tales of the Jazz Age*. CUP. [2002] pp. 539. £47.50 ISBN 0 5214 0238 7.

Whatley Smith, Virginia, ed. *Richard Wright's Travel Writings: New Reflections*. UMP. [2001] pp. xv + 237. $42 ISBN 1 5780 6347 7.

Wheeler, Elizabeth A. *Uncontained: Urban Fiction in Postwar America*. RutgersUP. [2001] pp. x + 301. pb £15.50 ISBN 0 8135 2973 5.

Wheeler, Lesley. *The Poetics of Enclosure: American Women Poets from Dickinson to Dove*. UTennP. [2002] pp. x + 201. £14.95 ISBN 1 5723 3197 6.

Williams, Linda. *Playing the Race Card: Melodramas of Black and White from Uncle Tom to O.J. Simpson*. PrincetonUP. [2001] pp. xviii + 401. pb 11.95 ISBN 0 6911 0283 X.

Williams, Louise Blakeney. *Modernism and the Ideology of History: Literature, Politics, and the Past*. CUP. [2002] pp. ix + 265. £42.50 ISBN 0 5218 1499 5.

Womack, Kenneth. *Postwar Academic Fiction: Satire, Ethics, Community*. Palgrave. [2002] pp. 192. £55 ISBN 0 3339 1882 7.

Woods, Tim. *The Poetics of the Limit: Ethics and Politics in Modern and Contemporary American Poetry*. Palgrave. [2002] pp. xvi + 287. £35 ISBN 0 3122 9322 4.

Yenser, Stephen. *A Boundless Field: American Poetry at Large*. UMichP. [2002] pp. 241. £27.50 ISBN 0 4721 1278 3.

XVII

New Literatures

FEMI ABODUNRIN, ELIZABETH WEBBY, JULIEANNE LAMOND, RICHARD LANE, ASHOK BERY AND NELSON WATTIE

This chapter has five sections: 1. Africa; 2. Australia; 3. Canada; 4. India; 5. New Zealand and the South Pacific. Section 1 is by Femi Abodunrin; section 2 is by Elizabeth Webby and Julieanne Lamond; section 3 is by Richard Lane; section 4 is by Ashok Bery; section 5 is by Nelson Wattie.

1. Africa

(a) General

Reif-Hulser, ed., *Borderlands: Negotiating Boundaries in Postcolonial Writing*, is a collection of essays that accrued from the ASNEL (Association for the Study of the New Literatures in English) conference held at the University of Constance, Germany, in September 1996. Negotiating with the questions proceeding from the epistemic issues of border-crossing and transgression of boundaries, as well as those relating to the formation of cultural and personal identities preoccupying literary and cultural studies, the aim of *Borderlands*, according to Reif-Hulser, 'is to represent a variety of approaches to these questions—approaches from different angles and different disciplines but concentrating on the post-colonial paradigm'. The book is divided into five sections, each of which concentrates on a thematic focus, and ends with the solitary 'Coda', entitled 'Cross-Cuts: In Lieu of a Resumé' (pp. 273–89), intended as a broad summation of the major arguments of the book. The revisioning of discourses of fiction, philosophy, sociology, and cultural criticism that the 'Coda' carries out typifies the practical and theoretical aims and orientation of the book, to traverse 'the two interpretative categories of "boundary" and "in-between space"' through selected instances of theory and interpretation. Part 1, 'Boundaries of Theory', comprises Frank Schulze-Engler's 'Globalization, Migration, and the Post-Colonial Transition' (pp. 3–15), Zbigniew Bialas's 'Ambition and Distortion: An Ontological Dimension in Colonial Cartography' (pp. 17–28), Martina Ghosh-Schellhorn's 'Spaced In-Between: Transitional Identity' (pp. 29–42), and J.E. Elliott's rhetorical 'What's "Post" in Post-Colonial Theory?' (pp. 43–53).

Beginning with Schulze-Engler's demarcation of the need to address 'the spatial imagery with which "modernity," "post-modernity," and "post-colonialism" are linked', it is apparent that each of these theoretical positions takes it as a given that 'it is in post-colonial writing more than anywhere else that the dialectical relationship between sameness and difference is acted out, trans-national interpenetrations replace inter-national dialogue, economic and political connections condition the framework of cultures'. However, since there seems to be no easy way around the vexed term 'post-colonial', it is between Schulze-Engler's demarcation of a postcolonial transition and Ghosh-Schellhorn's identification of 'transitional identity' in the postcolonial paradigm that the engagement with a secular 'long term process which effectively entails the withering away of the "post-colonial" and a growing concern with specific, local modernities' can be located. 'Transitionality', a term that incorporates 'exile, emigration, immigration and displacement', is, according to Ghosh-Schellhorn, 'political in its origins', and the collapse of empires in the past has been responsible for the global dimensions of this phenomenon:

> In the case of the British Empire, we could say that imperial caprice, implementing as it did the strategy of 'divide and rule', split up its colonies into strategic units in benign defiance of traditional allegiances to feudal chiefs or local government. This process had begun with the East India Company's 'conquest and patchy exploitation of India', which historians regard as 'one of the first and most striking examples of the forging of dependent economic relations between the north European world economy and non-European societies', a prototypical process which 'later engulfed much of the rest of Asia, Africa, Latin America and the Far East'.

Thus, in positing her theory of 'Transitionality', like Schulze-Engler, Ghosh-Schellhorn advocates an understanding of the ways in which 'transitional identity', when set against the traditional societies that it is modelled on, which should not be envisaged as unchangingly monolithic, 'strives to reflect the chaos of states always in a state of flux, incessantly open to the influence of motion, hence constantly modified by the experiences which act on them'. Thus, whether it entails an uprooting of the 'Self' or not, the state of transitionality is always quotidian; her uprootedness, for example, enables the critic Gayatri Spivak to state, 'I am bicultural, but my biculturality is that I'm not at home in either of the places (Calcutta or the USA)'. For writers like Chinua Achebe, Nayantara Sahgal, and Anita Desai, according to Ghosh-Schellhorn, 'there can be no reverting to some unchanging monolithic tradition. ... Their egocentres nonetheless have to react to interpellation as the legitimate heirs of the former masters, the descendants of that "class," to quote Thomas Babington Macaulay, created by the British to be the "interpreters between us and the millions whom we govern; a class of persons, Indians in blood and colour, but English in taste, in opinions, in morals, in intellect".' Again, while, in her exploration of the concomitant effects of the development of 'transitional identity', Ghosh-Schellhorn employs the consequences of Althusser's development of Gramsci's theory of hegemony as regards ideology, 'in conjunction with a Lacanian conceptualization of the Imaginary and Symbolic as constituents of the self', Elliot's rhetorical 'What's "Post" in Postcolonial Theory?' dwells on the major differences between postcolonial theory and the other major theoretical foci of the twentieth century: 'What distinguishes post-colonial theory, therefore, from deconstruction, New Historicism, Cultural Studies, and the like is, clearly enough, its milieu of colonial appropriation and the responses, largely textual, that this has inspired.' However, while, according to Schulze-Engler, Raja Rao's *Kanthapura* remains a classic case of anti-colonial 'writing back' to British rule in India, and another such textual response from the African experience is 'the sudden shift towards a half-satirical, half-fictional engagement with the political realities of independent Nigeria in Chinua Achebe's fourth novel, *A Man of the People*', Elliot argues that the 'colonial'—associated with the colonial component of postcolonial theory—'designates a historico-ethnic phenomenon that can neither be denied nor ignored without abandoning a specifically post-colonial investigation'. Zbigniew Bialas's study of the ontological ambition of colonial cartography perhaps answers some of Elliot's critical disquiet about postcolonial theory's hypersensitivity and tendency to assert that the field's 'real world referent is "first and last ... colonialism"'. According to Bialas, colonial maps, a minute aspect of the colonial enterprise, which '[relate] to issues of being, at the same time assume functions of creation and annihilation; they reveal a tendency to minimize the assumed "entropy principle" of land reality by hierarchizing space and superimposing a cartographically stylised order'.

Flora Veit-Wild's 'Borderlines of the Body in African Women's Writing' (pp. 123–34) and Norbert Platz's 'Rediscovering the Forgotten Space of Nature: A Plea for Ecocriticism in the New Literatures in English' (pp. 175–88) are two essays belonging to sections 3 and 4 of *Borderlands*, entitled, respectively, 'Repossessing Gender' and 'Imaginary Spaces'. For the African woman on the way to authoring her own life, according to Veit-Wild, a whole range of theoretical, practical, and creative options is available; 'killing one's offspring, hating oneself, starving one's body, enduring pains: all such experiences of the precarious borderline between physical and mental, sanity and insanity, appear as important conditions' for the African woman writer. Drawing on contexts ranging from Fanon's identification of the skin 'as the primary medium of sensuous contact with the world—whereby the skin at the same time becomes a metonymic marker of racial/racist borderlines'—to creation myths and the ways in which pre-colonial African societies apprehended gender in/equality, African women writers have articulated not just the protection provided by the traditional community that the African woman lost in the process of colonization and urbanization, but also 'the extent to which the colonial or post-colonial situation in which they are living has enforced this "nervous condition"'. From Bessie Head's borderline novel, which blurs the boundaries between sanity and insanity, to the Kenyan Rebeka Njau's intertextual response to the seminal *Song of Lawino*, a prototypical example of the projection of male fears on to the female body, or to the 'nervous condition of the colonized woman' depicted by the Zimbabwean writer Dangarembga, and by her compatriot Yvonne Vera, who re-establishes the link back to the creation myth, the writing woman, according to Veit-Wild, 'recognises herself as the one with the wound: she is and she remains vulnerable, exposed'. Finally, in his plea for ecocriticism in the new literatures in English, Platz argues for an exploration of a new semantic space between natural and cultural processes, 'whose study might be fruitful in the long run, not least because of its practical implications, as far as the struggle for human survival is concerned'. Although concentrating most of his critical attention on Australian and New Zealand texts and writers, Platz makes a compelling case for an extension of an ecocritical dimension to the 'literatures of Canada, Africa, India and the Caribbean'.

David Chioni Moore's 'Where Are All the African and Caribbean *Critics*?—The MLA, Honorary Members and Honorary Fellows' (*RAL* 32:i[2001] 110–21) addresses the preponderance of what it calls African literary scholarship's focus more on textual and cultural analyses at the expense of institutional critique. Moore offers one such institutional critique, 'by addressing the [minimal] Africanity of the Modern Language Association's lists of Honorary Members and Fellows, twin lists that anoint or recognize, respectively, the non-North-American world's most distinguished writers'. Moore's sustained analyses address the Eurocentrism of the MLA's two honorary lists, and particularly its honorary scholars list: 'Its scholars list, in particular, has systematically (or rather institutionally) excluded African and Caribbean critics, and it is time for that to change. In order to understand how this situation came to be, and what might be done about it, it will first be necessary to review the history of the honorary lists—those two pages many MLA members scan each year in each September's much-thumbed PMLA "directory" edition'. Moore's review reveals a situation in which 85 per cent of the present scholars honoured by the MLA come from ten European nations that together account for under 8 per cent of global population, and only nine out of the sixty-two honoured writers are from Africa and the Caribbean: 'This is even more interesting stated comparatively: nine of the sixty-one honoured writers, but zero of the fifty-two honoured scholars, is African or Caribbean.'

(b) West Africa

Omar Sougou's *Writing across Cultures: Gender Politics and Difference in the Fiction of Buchi Emecheta* is a book-length study of the compulsive oeuvre of this Nigerian-born novelist, resident mainly in London. Emecheta, according to Sougou, is a cross-cultural figure, and one who 'writes in the African tradition, drawing on African materials and experience'. Described variously as the 'most sustained and vigorous voice of direct feminist protest' in African literature, Emecheta has produced a wide range of fiction that fits into categories and typology as diverse as the 'belles-lettres' tradition and 'popular' and children's literature. In six lengthy chapters, Sougou has focused on ten of Emecheta's novels in order to offer various perspectives on her works, in an investigation that 'is set against the broad basis of literature and society in Africa, in the context of both the writing of established male novelists and of women writers'. Often described as documentary novels, semi-autobiography, or even semi-documentary proto-novels, *In the Ditch* [1972] and *Second-Class Citizen* [1974] are Emecheta's novels of self-definition, and read together with the later, more pointedly autobiographical, *Head Above Water* [1986], they reveal, according to Sougou, 'Emecheta, taking the power of the word into her own hands, represent[ing] and project[ing] a presence, an identity, that is neither purely individualistic nor purely collective; it "merges the shared and the unique"'. Focusing on the implications of such societal factors as tradition, Christianity, and colonialism on the lives of girls and women, *The Bride Price* [1976] and *The Slave Girl* [1977] are the objects of critical focus in chapter 3, entitled 'Articulating Protest'. Sougou observes, 'The novels retrospectively chart how these phenomena individually operate or collude to entrench the oppression of the female gender. Emecheta goes as far back as the nineteenth century in order to probe into womanhood in traditional, precolonial, colonial and urbanized Nigerian society, which might stand for Africa in general.' Chapter 4, 'Towards Consciousness', focuses on Emecheta's *The Joys of Motherhood* [1979] and *Destination Biafra* [1982]. While the former presents a radical questioning of the myth of motherhood as it has crystallized in African societies and writing, the latter constitutes another stage in Emecheta's writing—'here, a woman is at the centre of political events'. *Naira Power* and *Double Yoke*, both published in 1982, are treated in chapter 5, 'African Popular Novels'. Finally, in chapter 6, entitled 'Homecoming', *The Rape of Shavi* [1983] and *Gwendolen* [1989] are discussed. The former 'furthers the homecoming initiative pointed out in *The Joys of Motherhood*', whereas the latter, though published five years later, was begun in 1984, when Emecheta announced that she was 'sketching out a new book to be called *Gwendolen*—stories of black girls in Britain who have been sexually harassed by their fathers'. From the early works to *Gwendolen*, from the autobiographical orientation of the early novels to the later fictions that 'offer a relative degree of representational verisimilitude in terms of gender and social issues', Sougou has established a pattern of creative articulation in Emecheta's writing that 'stands at the crossroads of African "high" and popular literature'. Furthermore, Sougou offers a critical reading in which the basic concern has been 'culture, race and gender, questions of readership, and the strategies involved in writing back, but Emecheta's work remains fruitful ground for further inquiry into the condition of women, feminist concerns generally, and the critical theory of African literature'.

Wendy Griswold's *Bearing Witness: Readers, Writers, and the Novel in Nigeria* is, perhaps, the most comprehensive study to date of the various socio-cultural and political factors that constitute what it calls 'the contemporary analogue to telling tales in the moonlit village'. Nigerian novelists, according to Griswold, certainly see themselves as storytellers. Griswold's study attempts to understand the Nigerian novel by addressing two sets of questions: 'What is the Nigerian literary complex like, and how does it relate to postcolonial Nigerian society?' In three lengthy chapters, and, in lieu of a conclusion, a fourth chapter of merely five pages (pp. 269–73), entitled 'Capturing the Past and Inventing the Future', Griswold employs procedures that involve productive readings of texts and the performing of comparative operations on them, in a determined, if imperfect, effort to understand the novel in Nigeria. At the beginning of the book is a list of key dates and events, both political and cultural, which constitute what most people would accept as 'Nigerian history'. Among the most persistent chroniclers of the contemporary political, economic, and moral problems, Nigerian novelists continue to express vast ambivalence towards their country, and the 'bearing witness' in the title of the book emanates from the quintessential role of the novelist: 'They used the expression "bearing witness" repeatedly when they were talking with me about the role of the novelist—in order to help bring about the transition to a better future.' Like the novel, Nigeria is an artificial but operationally useful designation, and just as the novel could be assumed to be fictitious, so is Nigeria: 'Nigeria's first fiction is its name. "Nigeria" is a Latinate evocation of the Niger River, which makes a curving T shape that divides the country into three regions, as shown on the map.' The Nigerian novel, therefore, is as tenuous as the people's identity as Nigerians:

Griswold employs the term 'Nigerian' to demarcate the cultural object of this study, and offers one of many justifications 'for taking the country as defining the analytic unit. The first is temporal. Nigeria has been an independent state only since 1960, and the Nigerian novel is not much older. The first novel appeared in 1952, and the overwhelming majority have been published since Nigerian independence. So it happens that the "Nigerian novel" has developed in conjunction with the country itself.' Griswold identifies three schools of thought that rely on somewhat different theories of cultural transformation regarding the African novel in general, and two types of readers of the Nigerian novel in particular. The various sources and data garnered from Griswold's meticulous research have been used to put together a picture of the Nigerian literary complex: 'It is a complex, consisting of multiple parts that do not fit together very well. It is a complex that is global as well as local ... In this complex, Nigerians have been reconstructing the novel, using both Nigerian and Western blueprints, to make money, to entertain, to instruct, to influence, to celebrate their country's cultural diversity and potential, and to bear witness to its problems.'

In a similar vein, Walter Gobel's 'Teaching Nigerian Novels: Hermeneutic and Didactic Aspects' (in Reif-Hulser, ed., pp. 255–69) examines what it calls the contextual, the productive, and the receptive impasses and the roles they play in the teaching and reception of Nigerian novels in English. It focuses pre-eminently on the productive impasse, or a process in which the literary works privileged in humanities courses offer mediated versions of the culture of origin, partly 'because (a) every work of art selects and/or models a vision of articulating some form of intervention, and (b) the author is, especially in largely non-literate cultures, more or less estranged from his own culture by education and the conventions of literacy'. Concerning aesthetic selections and cultural mediations in teaching the Nigerian novel, from Chinua Achebe's *Things Fall Apart* through Amos Tutuola's *The Palmwine Drinkard* to 'the innumerable mythic intertexts—prophecies, mysteries, wonders, proverbs, fables'—contained in Ben Okri's *The Famished Road*, according to Gobel, there is some space for traditional hermeneutics. He notes, in this connection, 'The difficulty for the Western teacher is that he has to undertake a leap beyond his cultural traditions in order to foreground the necessary African intertexts, an epistemic leap beyond Gadamer's model of hermeneutics towards a model like that presented by Clifford Geertz, which allows for the limited autonomy of cultural islands.' Finally, Bill Hemminger's 'The Way of the Spirit' (*RAL* 32:i[2001] 66–82), about Ben Okri's 'highly suggestive and constructive portrait of being-in-the-world' in his 1991 novel *The Famished Road*, completes this coverage of critical interest in the Nigerian novel. Okri's novel and its sequel *Songs of Enchantment*, according to Hemminger, 'redefine the world human beings inhabit and argue for increased interplay between physical and spiritual in a modern technologized world'.

Oni and Ododo, eds., *Larger than his Frame: Critical Studies and Reflections on Olu Obafemi*, is a collection of twenty critical essays and thirteen reflections on the Nigerian playwright and academic of the immediate post-Soyinka generation, Olu Obafemi. Obafemi has published five full-length plays, a novel, a collection of poems, and several volumes of critical writing, and 'all these works have constituted the focus of attention of the critical essays while the impact and person of Professor Olu Obafemi has been adequately addressed in the Reflections section of this book'.

In the mould of the growing corpus of African biocritical literature, such as *Eagle on Iroko* (on Achebe) and *Before Our Eyes* (on Soyinka), *Larger than his Frame* commemorates Obafemi's attainment of the golden age of 50, and his numerous contributions to the development of theatre and the arts in Nigeria. In his critical introduction to the volume, Duro Oni's 'Olu Obafemi: An Eclectic Artiste and Scholar' (pp. 1–8) places Obafemi in his historical context as a member of that second generation of Nigerian playwrights whose 'works have shown sharp departures from the well-made plays of the first generation to a more socially committed and in some cases radical theatre'. Ostensibly, twelve out of the twenty essays in this volume concentrate on various aspects of Obafemi's dramaturgy in ways that echo Oni's observation that 'the work presented here not only examines the works of Olu Obafemi, but provides a significant insight into contemporary Nigerian theatre and playwriting cast in the mode of the now commonly referred to "second generation of playwrights" prominently featuring Femi Osofisan, Kole Omotoso, Tunde Fatunde, Segun Oyekunle and Bode Sowande'. Sunday E. Ododo's 'Documenting Theatre Practice in Nigeria: Ajon Players in Perspective' (pp. 82–102), Aderemi Bamikunle's 'The Revolutionary Vision of Olu Obafemi's Theatre' (pp. 103–14), Demola Jolayemi's 'Language and Style: A Systemic Textlinguistic Study of Olu Obafemi's Plays' (pp. 115–33), Victoria Alabi's 'The Seven-Shaped Beasts of Prey: A Logico-Semiotic Reading of Olu Obafemi's Plays' (pp. 134–46), and Sola T. Babatunde's 'The Rhetoric of Mass Protest: Persuasive Strategies in Olu Obafemi's Plays' (pp. 147–64) are some of the prominent essays focusing on various aspects of what one of the leading critics, Bamikunle, describes as Obafemi's theatrical aims and objectives and of the bid 'to determine the broad dramatic forms, techniques, aesthetics and strategies'. The most distinguishing form of Obafemi's drama is coterminous with that of the new generation of practitioners whose works contrast sharply with those of J.P. Clark, Wole Soyinka, and Ola Rotimi. Premised on a radical view of history, which becomes very important in their work in all its phases, their productions elicit the following comment from Bamikunle: 'To better understand Olu Obafemi's revolutionary vision it is good to place his works in the broad context of the generation of writers in the 80s, who referred to themselves as "revolutionaries", who proffered a "radical social vision" for the Nigerian society. The economic woes ... which first manifested in the 80s and have plagued Nigerians since then led to a focus on social and politico-economic realities and the deprivations they visited on Nigerians.' In this revolutionary context, according to Babatunde, the play-text becomes nothing but 'one long assertive act in which the playwright utilises the whole gamut of the linguistic, communicative and literary presuppositions he shares with the audience to give a capsular message with the aim of persuading the audience to take an intended line of action'. Olu Obafemi's 'programme note' to the premier production of his 1993 play, *Nights of the Mystical Beasts*, alone 'sums up the size of the societal structures which ceaselessly impose itself [*sic*] on the patriotic and ideological sensibility of the playwright'. However, again, according to Bamikunle, a clear definition of the nature of their art and their objectives is carried out by the new generation of artists 'without belittling the pleasure aspect of art'.

The next crop of essays, ranging from Abimbola Shittu's 'The Aesthetics of Olu Obafemi's Drama' (pp. 180–5) to Taiye S. Adeola's 'Music in Olu Obafemi's Plays' (pp. 186–96) and Felix A. Akinsipe's 'The Communicative Indices of Dance in Drama Production: A Choreographic Approach to Olu Obafemi's Plays' (pp. 197–205), to name just a few, focus on the various theoretical, practical, and creative strategies that Obafemi employs to realize these pleasurable aspects. Meanwhile, Tale M. Olujide's 'A Stylistic Analysis of Olu Obafemi's *Wheels*' (pp. 238–50) and Josephine I. Oyebanji's 'African Feminist Concepts in *Wheels*' (pp. 251–66) concentrate on Obafemi's solitary but compelling contribution to the novelistic genre, a story in which, according to Oyebanji, Obafemi 'aptly demonstrates a sense of deep regard for feminist ideas and ideals as conceived by African feminist theorists'. Olu Obafemi's volume of poetry and his foray into journalistic writing are the subjects of Aderemi Bamikule's 'Olu Obafemi's *Songs of Hope*: A Review Essay' (pp. 270–85), Olufemi I. Dunmade's 'The Landscape within Olu Obafemi's *Songs of Hope*: A Bird's Eye View' (pp. 286–301), Joseph O. Omoniyi's 'The Problems of our Time: Olu Obafemi's Ideological War of Rebirth and Regeneration in Selected Newspapers' (pp. 302–11) and 'Language and Style in Olu Obafemi's Essays: An Examination of *The Post Express* Opinion Column' (pp. 312–23). But Obafemi is also a literary critic and a leading theorist of the postcolonial situation in Nigeria and the rest of Africa, and Charles Bodunde's 'Olu Obafemi as a Literary Theorist: The Transposition of Cultural Materialism' (pp. 69–81) focuses on Obafemi's dual position as critic and writer. According to Bodunde, Obafemi's work, which draws on an intellectual tradition that was itself shaped by a renewed interpretation of the idea of culture, demonstrates 'a theoretical pattern which is derivative … following Raymond Williams' materialist theory of culture'. Finally, the thirteen 'Reflections' on Olu Obafemi's evolution as a writer, scholar, and critic range from David Ker's 'Reflections and Reminiscences on Olu Obafemi' (pp. 17–20), through Sam A. Adewoye's 'Olu Obafemi—A Trainee Becomes a Trainer" (pp. 21–4), to Martin Banham's 'The Leeds–Ilorin Connection' (pp. 25–7) and Femi Osofisan's 'For Olu Obafemi, at Fifty' (pp. 35–7), to name just a few. Martin Banham, for example, focuses on the heady days of the early 1980s, when Olu Obafemi pursued doctoral work at the University of Leeds, to their culmination in the première of his seminal play *Naira Has No Gender* in the Workshop Theatre at Leeds in 1990, when Obafemi was Visiting Fellow: 'For many of us this was an introduction to the new phase of radical Nigerian playwriting being undertaken by that generation influenced by, but determined to be independent from, the established "literary" giants of the 1960s and 1970s.' Fittingly, the book ends with Sunday E. Ododo's 'Collectivist Approach to Theatre Production: The Theatre of Olu Obafemi' (pp. 324–43), which consists of excerpts from his interview session with the writer and critic in which the diverse sources of Obafemi's creative inspiration, artistic vision, and collectivist approach to theatre production are broached. Concerning his creative vision as a playwright, Obafemi's response could not be more categorical: 'So my preference is for a creative vision that is collective, a creative vision that is committed to the upliftment of the living condition of the ordinary man. My preference for the uprootment of injustice and inequality of society arose from that original sense of a search for a just society. Whether I have achieved that is a different matter.'

Victor Samson Dugga's *Creolisations in Nigerian Theatre* is number 61 in the eclectic Bayreuth African Studies series. In five lengthy chapters, Dugga examines three theatre traditions that constitute and give room for a progressive, historical, theoretical, and practical descriptive analysis of social change and transitions in culture and performance in Nigeria: 'These are traditional Eggon theatre from Central Nigeria, the literary theatre of Wole Soyinka and Femi Osofisan which draws upon Yoruba traditions of Western Nigeria, and the emerging functionality of performance-based modern theatres for specific purposes in contemporary society.' Within the particular postcolonial (nation) context of Nigeria, and in the particular instance of the Eggon, which is representative of the Central Nigerian region, populated by a cluster of not less than 150 ethnic groups, cultural specificity leads to developments that reiterate those conditions often ignored by postcolonial theorists, but which are central to the minority angle that perceives colonialism as having 'replicated and conjugated the power structure and relations in the post-colony'. Dugga's study relies on the concept of creolization, 'used in this study to describe the condition of hybridity of theatre performances in Nigeria', for theoretical grounding. 'Creolization', a term often frowned upon as a result of its controversial application to language development, is, according to Dugga, adopted here 'primarily to emphasise the process of transformation, to acknowledge the interactive forces in the process, and account for the present state of theatre practice in Nigeria'. Groups like the Eggon, whose existence was marked by pacification, forceful incorporation, and now membership of a larger society of the nation-state, were involved in processes upon which they exerted no influence or control. Ostensibly, if the history of the Eggon is an obscure one in the footnote of Nigerian history, its theatre is even less known, and 'the desire is to present a slice of social reality from Eggon as an ethnic minority culture and the dynamics of survival in contemporary Nigerian post colonial history. ... Their story could well be that of any of the over one hundred and fifty ethnic groups that cluster the central region of Nigeria.' The literary theatre of Wole Soyinka and Femi Osofisan is the object of critical focus in chapter 3 of the book, whereas 'Theatre for Specific Purposes: Women's (Human) Rights Campaign and Corporate Image Making' is discussed in chapter 4. Chapter 5, 'Shades and Patterns in the Creoles', summarizes the major arguments of the book, most especially the ways in which the three theatre practices discussed are living concurrently in post-independence Nigeria: 'The study unveils the diversities and directions of theatre within one post-colonial cultural space and how these have been unfettered to live in new ways. They have shown that there are different dynamics to theatre as a cultural construct, determined by its form, location and practitioners.'

Abodunrin, Obafemi, and Ogundele, eds., *Character Is Beauty: Redefining Yoruba Culture and Identity, Iwalewa-Haus, 1981–1996*, is a collection of essays, interviews, and monographs on Yoruba music, art, philosophy, religion, and literature accruing from the in-house publication outfit of the ubiquitous Iwalewa-Haus of the University of Bayreuth in Germany, and the activities as well as cultural practices of the founding director of Iwalewa-Haus, Ulli Beier. According to the editors, the house publishes on almost all aspects of Third World culture and society but, precisely because of Ulli Beier's special connection with Yoruba society and people, its publications on that society are unique, in addition to which there is the fact that 'the house has been actively promoting all aspects of Yoruba theatrical performances and artistic practices or reviving and supporting them where they have been in danger of dying'. The publications include interviews with Wole Soyinka and other Yoruba scholars, autobiographical documents and interviews with virtually all members of the Osogbo Art Movement, books, memoirs, and interviews on the Duro Ladipo theatre by other members of the company, as well as Ulli and Georgina Beier's own memoirs and reflections on that theatre and the Art Movement. It is from this rich and unrivalled collection that the editors have selected the papers, interviews, and monographs in the present book for publication, partly because 'we think that as most of the papers deal with the past and present states of Yoruba society and culture, the connected themes of past glory, (brief) renaissance, and present crises can be coherently put together. This third reason means that the motivation to assemble the papers which make up this book is more than the merely academic.' The preface to the book is Olu Obafemi's 'Forty Years in African Art and Life: Reflections on Ulli Beier' (pp. xii–xvii), which chronicles Ulli Beier's ubiquitous roles in Francophone and Anglophone African writing in general and Yoruba society in particular, and the ways in which Beier's enduring artistic and cultural creations brought 'to the limelight great African writers like Gabriel Okara, Wole Soyinka, Christopher Okigbo, J.P. Clark, Dennis Brutus, Alex la Guma, Ama Ata Aidoo and Kofi Awoonor, all of whose works he first published'.

'The Crisis of Yoruba Culture: Wole Soyinka and Ulli Beier' (pp. 3–25) is the leading discussion that chronicles a dialogic, reflexive debate, which is nostalgic and passionate, and one which collectively addresses the issue of the crisis of Yoruba culture in contemporary times. Again, according to the editors, 'the leading discussion between Ulli Beier and Wole Soyinka recalls the serenity, the integrity and the dynamism of the cultural and theatrical praxis in Ibadan a decade before and shortly after independence'. Ulli Beier's 'The Return of Shango: The Theatre of Duro Ladipo' (pp. 59–74), Olu Obafemi's 'The Yoruba Operatic Theatre: A World in Search of Harmony and Social Order: Ladipo, Ogunde and Olaiya' (pp. 75–102), and Femi Abodunrin's 'Esu-Elegbara and the Carnivalesque' (pp. 103–48) examine the varied provenances of this cultural and theatrical praxis in Ibadan and across Yorubaland: 'This section therefore concerns the history, development and character of contemporary Yoruba theatre from its beginnings through the triumphant phase of the Yoruba Travelling Theatre, to the present phase of "decline" into cheap, cash-driven video productions.' Finally, permanence of value, as derived from both the physical state and the spiritual/metaphysical significance that constitute the basis of 'Yoruba Religion, Arts and Aesthetics', underlines the pre-eminent focus of a whole range of other essays and discussions in the book: Susanne Wenger and Ulli Beier's 'The Osun Grove of Osogbo: Symbol of the Crisis of Yoruba Culture' (pp. 27–36), Wole Ogundele and Ulli Beier's 'The Age of Miracles: Crises in Contemporary Yoruba Society' (pp. 37–55), Sophie B. Oluwole's 'Womanhood in Yoruba Traditional Thought' (pp. 223–34), Georgina Beier's 'To Organise Is To Destroy: The Osogbo Art School' (pp. 203–19), and Roland Abiodun and Ulli Beier's 'Yoruba Aesthetics' (pp. 191–202), to mention just a few. The paradigmatic *Death and the King's Horseman*, Wole Soyinka's Nobel Prize-winning play, forms the basis of the conversation between Soyinka and Ulli Beier (pp. 175–88). Soyinka's response to Beier's summation that, in *Death and King's Horseman*, 'once the ancient ritual cycle is broken, it can never be revived again', encapsulates the essence of the crises that the book pursues: 'Yes, it is often the trivial incident that has the most profound and far reaching consequences! And that's why for me the play is not just a thing in itself; it's a parable. A parable for the many things that have happened to Yoruba society. A parable of history.'

Wumi Raji's 'Blurred Boundaries: Femi Abodunrin's *It Would Take Time: Conversation with Living Ancestors*' (*JHu* 16[2001] 104–9) is a review essay examining what it calls 'this search for a cultural back-up' that Abodunrin carries out in *It Would Take Time*: 'To be sure, even as a scholar, Abodunrin has always been concerned with the possibility of negotiating a path through the past to the future of the black race. In *Blackness: Culture, Ideology and Discourse* [1996] ... Abodunrin proposes a theory of black criticism derived from the carnivalesque perspective of Esu, the Yoruba god of fate and of the crossroad.' Transgression of boundaries, 'at formal, stylistic, generic, contextual and thematic levels', is, according to Raji, part of the essence of *It Would Take Time*, in which the immediate point of reference is the author's contemporary Nigerian society: 'The country came into existence following a decision by the British colonizers to amalgamate the Northern and Southern protectorates in 1914. Since this arbitrary act, the country has continued to totter at the edge of the precipice, transiting as it were, from one crisis to the other. *It Would Take Time* represents therefore a kind of quest, a search actually for an alternative to the current obsolescence.'

Jan Jensen's 'The Sunjata Epic—The Ultimate Version' (*RAL* 32:i[2001], 14–46) is a comprehensive account of the famous Sunjata epic that has enjoyed much attention as a masterpiece of African oral literature in the past few decades. It is the only epic in the world that is entirely orally transmitted as well as performed in a ceremonial context, namely, in the famous septennial Kamabolon ceremony in Kangaba, Mali. There is a paucity of data and information about the ceremony for a number of reasons:

> First, the people responsible for reciting the 'ultimate version' of the Sunjata epic, the Diabete griots from Kela, are reputedly difficult to work with. Second, the recording of rehearsals is prohibited. Third, rehearsals are rare. Finally, the authoritative recitation takes place in the Kamabolon sanctuary and is not accessible for outsiders and thus cannot be heard. Quite discouraging factors for researchers!

For a researcher whose entire academic career 'has been a preparation to study the Kamabolon ceremony and the role of the griots in the ceremony', Jansen's essay aims to make a twofold contribution to the studies of African oral literature: 'First, it will answer several questions about the kind of texts recited during rehearsals and the performance of the Kamabolon ceremony ... Second, it will illustrate that the recitation of the Sunjata epic is not necessarily in the first place the product of the griots' imagination and literary creativity, but a highly standardized oral text that is carefully reproduced by its "owners".'

(c) East and Central Africa

Felicity Hand's 'Negotiating Boundaries in the Horn of Africa: Women in the Fiction of Nuruddin Farah' (in Reif-Hulser, ed., pp. 115–22) is a critical exploration of the ways in which some of Farah's female characters 'illustrate, on the one hand, how East African women are retained in the "space-between," neither chattel nor complete human being, and on the other, how they can trace a new boundary for the female self despite the constraints of a patriarchal Islamic environment, bearing in mind that virtually the whole populations of Somalia are Muslim'. Examined against the backdrop of the boundaries of the nations that make up the Horn of Africa, Nuruddin Farah, according to Hand, 'uses the metaphor of the Somali family as a basis for his harsh critique of the rigidity of political spaces in the Horn of Africa'. The portrayal of women as objects rather than subjects of national aspiration, which leads to the 'Mother Africa/Whore dichotomy', is one of the stereotyped conceptions of women that Farah's fiction avoids: 'He traces a kind of family saga in his novels, which echoes the colonial or even post-colonial power structure underlying the work of many African writers; but Farah's novels depict much more than the post-colonial mess Somalia finds itself in.' The feminization of colonial territory, a familiar trope in imperialist discourse, and one which has been carried over to the postcolonial period, is responsible for what Hand has described as the tendency in contemporary African writing to use 'the oppression of women as a convenient metaphor for the degradation of their societies, without really posing serious questions about the role of women in private and public life'. However, from his earlier *From a Crooked Rib*, through the trilogy *Sweet and Sour Milk*, *Sardines*, and *Close Sesame*, to the later novel *Gifts*, what is relevant is that Farah, according to Hand, 'offers choices, alternative spaces for Somali women that are not determined by fathers, brothers or husbands'.

Alison McFarlane's 'Changing Metaphorical Constructs in the Writing of Jack Mapanje' (*JHu* 16[2001] 1–24) explores what it calls the Malawian poet Jack Mapanje's 'nostalgic yearning for the immutability of traditional myths and metaphors'. Mapanje's first volume of poetry, *Of Chameleon and Gods* [1981], a summary of all the implied paradoxes of cultural cross-pollination, initiates his contribution to the perceived role of African writers today, 'to preserve through metaphor their cultural heritage which must be a fusion of their ancestral culture and that of the rest of the world to which they have been exposed by their British education'. Ostensibly, the question arises whether, 'by writing in English ... Mapanje [is] contributing to the demise of his own culture', or whether 'his changing metaphorical structure reflect[s] the demands that social history and politics impose on any poet'. The language issue, however, remains an emotive and controversial one in African literature, and one of McFarlane's primary conclusions is that 'Mapanje's three volumes approximate three stages in the conversion of the oral, indigenous language to the written English language form of poetry. ... The very act of striving to synthesise a newly acquired "writerly" practice with an inherited oral tradition is what succeeds in ushering the reader into Mapanje's "fourth world": African writing in English.'

Said A.M. Khamis's 'Classicism in Shaaban Robert's Utopian Novel, *Kusadikika*' (*RAL* 32:i[2001] 47–65) examines the Tanzanian writer Shaaban Robert's 1951 novel of grand style, which has an ambivalent theme that bears some relevance today, as it did when it was first written. Khamis's essay aims 'to show the classical nature of *Kusadikika* and how it transfuses its relevance to the contemporary situation'. *Kusadikika*, according to Khamis, cannot be restricted to the Tanzanian situation and the colonial period in which the novel was written: '*Kusadikika* deals with universal and contemporary themes that give the novel a sense of immortality and timelessness and make it one of the most important novels to be written in African literatures'. Evolving from the author's colonial past, in the Kiswahili language in which the novel was originally written, the name *Kusadikika*, meaning '"The Believable," or perhaps "The Unbelievable"', is in the mould of other existentialist or utopian works of its kind: 'This name is comparable to More's *Utopia* (Nowhere), Butler's *Erewhon* (also Nowhere), and Swift's *Gulliver's Travels* (especially the land of the Houyhnhnm—Perfection of Nature).' Khamis's examination of the utopian nature of the novel and other artistic aspects, such as '*Kusadikika* as a satirical tale; characterization; plot, story, language, and narrative style; and axiomatic endings', yields a pattern of depiction, which, as in all classical works, 'shows openendedness and a certain flexibility that allows for an analysis oscillating between the past and the present'.

(d) Southern Africa

Brown, ed., *Oral Literature and Performance in Southern Africa*, is a collection of essays that seeks to contribute to current efforts to grant oral forms and research about their greater visibility and stature. Despite the brutal political history of the Southern African region, and a cultural history which has been suppressed by colonialism and apartheid, oral forms, according to Duncan Brown, have remained 'important means of social articulation throughout the history of South Africa, and continue to adapt to new contexts'. Brown's lucid introduction to the volume contextualizes further all the critical issues involved in what it calls 'the remarkable resilience of many oral forms to the colonising forms of print, and the transformative power of orality on literate discourses'. While concerned specifically with orality and performance studies, the thirteen essays in this volume 'open constantly towards the broader questions which engage Southern African studies'. While the orality-literacy question epitomizes the conceptual and historical themes of Southern African life, there is the need to challenge the rigid boundaries of disciplinary research, and the volume seeks to 'contribute to understandings of cultural interchange and difference, and increase our respect for the human creativities of the Southern African region'. Isabel Hofmeyr's 'Making Symmetrical Knowledge Possible: Recent Trends in the Field of Southern African Oral Performance Studies' (pp. 18–26), Karin Barber's 'Obscurity and Exegesis in African Oral Praise Poetry' (pp. 27–49), and Liz Gunner's 'The Role of Orality in the Liberation Struggle and in Post-Apartheid South Africa' (pp. 50–60) begin this process of making symmetrical what Hofmeyr has termed the unequal relationship between local and global knowledge, between 'written and oral literatures in southern Africa, where oral forms are only infrequently brought into the purview of academic institutions'. The preponderance of written forms at the expense of their oral counterparts, even when works which explore the latter have undergone a quite spectacular growth, is all too evident. According to Hofmeyr, 'the claim of marginality is of course true, and the study of oral forms both here and internationally does not begin to approach in either glamour or volume studies on written forms'. However, in order for symmetrical knowledge to emerge, Hofmeyr examines two recent paradigms: David Coplan's *In the Time of Cannibals* [1994], which exemplifies more recent historico-poetic approaches, and Megan Biesele's *Women Like Meat* [1993], which returns to questions of evolutionism. One of Hofmeyr's primary conclusions is that, 'whether in the Biesele or Coplan mould, however, Southern African oral performance scholarship has built up a considerable bank of knowledge regarding "subaltern" literary and intellectual traditions which it is now difficult to ignore'. Looking at the African situation in general, Karin Barber examines African genres of praise poetry, and why so many genres of African oral praise poetry are often described as 'obscure'. Barber employs a comparative approach to illustrate the fact that 'an investigation of the differences between modes of meaning assignment in two parallel genres from different culture areas may serve to support the claim that such modes are culture—or genre—specific and must be learnt, rather than being transparently and self-evidently open to interpretation by anyone who speaks the language or has a translator at hand'. The Yoruba *oriki* and Sotho *lithoko*, like most genres of sub-Saharan 'praise poetry', according to Barber, share certain fundamental features with one another: 'The differences between *oriki* and *lithoko*, however, also need to be borne in mind in an investigation of the operations of generic conventions'. Concerning conventions of exegesis, however, Barber observes further that generic conventions are not reducible to a short list of clear rules: 'One direction future comparative work on African oral genres might take, then, is the investigation of the conventions of exegesis, as embodied in the actual practice of interpretation of texts'. Liz Gunner's contribution examines one such exegetical convention vis-à-vis the ubiquitous role orality has played in the liberation struggle and in post-apartheid South Africa. Gunner's major concern is 'the way in which the poetry of remembering—for that is what a lot of South Africa's oral poetry is—until very recently has been excluded from serious political discourse and, more than that, from any real sense of nation and culture'. That the oral tradition is malleable and volatile, and the written one is 'fixed', is one perception upon which the exclusion of oral forms is built, but while agreeing that, 'in a sense, certainly, praise poetry is atavistic', Gunner proffers further that 'it can at the same time make itself part of the present and the "modernity" of national culture. And it is precisely the regenerative power of memory, which is harnessed as the key literary feature of praise poetry, that enables this to happen'. The post-apartheid situation in which the praise poet is being, paradoxically, both marginalized and canonized, is, according to Gunner, coterminous with the present position of national security in which culture is more marginalized: 'The "war" in one sense is over, the "struggle" is over.' However, any attempt to predict the praise poet's or praise poetry's last word may simply overlook the enormous subversive power of oral genres in a modern situation: 'The warrior image may surface again in search of a different agenda and a different home for that slippery and resilient genre, full of intellectual gristle, the praise poem.'

The other choice essays in the volume include Judith Lutge Coullie's '(Dis)Locating Selves: *Izibongo* and Narrative Autobiography in South Africa' (pp. 61–89), Jeff Opland's 'The Image of the Book in Xhosa Oral Poetry' (pp. 90–110), Thengani H. Ngwenya's 'Orality and Modernity in Autobiographical Representation: The Case of Naboth Mokgatle's Life Story' (pp. 111–31), and Megan Biesele's '"Different People Just Have Different Minds": A Personal Attempt to Understand Ju/'hoan Storytelling Aesthetics' (pp. 161–75), to mention just a few. In addition, Michael Chapman's 'Mandela, Africanism and Modernity: A Consideration of *Long Walk to Freedom*' (pp. 132–7), Craig Mackenzie's 'The Emergence of the South African Oral-Style Short Story: A.W. Drayson's *Tales at the Outspan*' (pp. 148–60), and Duncan Brown's 'Orality and Christianity: The Hymns of Isaiah Shembe and the Church of the Nazarites' (pp. 195–219) contextualize further what Duncan Brown describes as Southern Africa's complex intersections of orality and literacy, 'the fact that almost all oral cultures on the subcontinent have been influenced by their contact with the literate cultures of the colonial settler'. Nelson Mandela's *Long Walk to Freedom* [1994] is, according to Chapman, a tale that 'refuses separation of the private and the public figure and, as a result, assumes proportions of national epic'. By marrying form and content, and in reiterating the central trope of South African narrative, 'the trope continues to be an experiential reality—*Long Walk to Freedom*, which was awarded the 1995 Alan Paton Literary Prize, follows the Jim (Nelson) who comes to Joburg and, like the hero of folktale (or like Paton's Rev. Stephen Kumalo), is guided by the wise man (Msimangu or, in Mandela's case, Walter Sisulu) into the trials of modern, industrial South Africa'. Meanwhile, Craig MacKenzie's concern with a certain tradition or sub-genre of South African short story, which he has defined as the 'oral-style story' from A.W. Drayson's fireside tales in 1862 to Bosman's bushveld stories of the 1930s, 1940s, and 1950s, explored in his seminal *The Oral-Style: South African Short Story in English: A.W. Drayson to H.C. Bosman*, was given extensive coverage in this section last year. Duncan Brown's contribution, on the other hand, examines the ways in which the syncretization of the belief systems of Zulu tradition with those of Christianity, and the hybridization of Christian hymns with Zulu poetry and song, are used by the messianic Zulu evangelist Isaiah Shembe to create forms that express religious and political resistance to colonial oppression. Shembe stands as an important transitional figure for South African literary history: 'His hymns look back to the Zulu nationalism of Shaka, though they draw this nationalism into a context of colonial subjugation; and they look forward, through the doctrine of the Black Christ, to the political concerns of Black Consciousness and Black Theology.' The volume ends with Carol Muller's 'Chakide—The Teller of Stories: Space, Song and Story in Zulu *Maskanda* Performance' (pp. 220–34), an exploration of the 'Zulu guitar performance' or *Maskanda* style, which has developed over the last century amongst male migrants, many of whom have been employed as domestic workers in what is now KwaZulu Natal. Like Isaiah Shembe before him, Thami Vilakazi, whose *Maskanda* performances Muller's essay focuses on, composes song texts that are remarkable for the series of embedded conflicts which they reveal; like a modern *imbongi*, Vilakazi's songs deal with the 'contest over belief systems—those of Christianity and Zulu traditional religious practices'.

Muponde and Taruvinga, eds., *Sign and Taboo: Perspectives on the Poetic Fiction of Yvonne Vera*, is a collection of essays examining the dense poetic prose of Yvonne Vera. Vera's allusive style, and her ability to handle the most difficult subjects and confront taboos, 'often evokes strong and diverse responses in the reader and has fostered intense discussion about her writing'. Vera's compulsive oeuvre paints powerful and unique facets of Zimbabwe as a post-colony, and, according to the editors of the volume, from *Nehanda* [1993] to *The Stone Virgins* [2002], Vera gives us an emerging chain of female voices, and a new spiritual and psychological cartography of female consciousness: 'The fact that her fiction is rooted in critical and decisive moments of Zimbabwean history reveals the value of an alternative psycho-social signage by which herstory of the nation may be told.' The book is divided into five parts, each containing essays with allied, but not necessarily similar, approaches. Part 1, entitled 'Language, Voice and Presence', comprises Kizito Z. Muchemwa's 'Language, Voice, and Presence in *Under the Tongue* and *Without a Name*' (pp. 3–14), Meg Samuelson's '"A River in My Mouth": Writing the Voice in *Under the Tongue*' (pp. 15–24), and Carolyn Martin Shaw's 'The Habit of Assigning Meaning: Signs of Yvonne Vera's World' (pp. 25–

36). Comparing Vera's postmodernist thrust to the style of Zimbabwe's other iconoclastic writer, the late Dambudzo Marachera, Muchemwa describes Vera's fictional style as 'an amalgam of "lyrical method", post-modern narrative techniques, and reconstructed orature'. As a recovery of the repressed discourse of women, Samuelson discusses the loss of speech that arises out of patriarchal prescriptions in *Under the Tongue*: 'This silencing operates most fully under the restrictions of taboo, which mute the cry of pain from the female body.' However, in her examination of Vera's habit of assigning meaning, Shaw describes Vera's female protagonists as 'introverted, inarticulate, desperate, but it is only through identification with them that the novel moves'. While each novel presents alternative world-views, the consistency of Vera's sign system, according to Shaw, 'produces one, complex, reality. She imbues nature with meanings that carry over from one novel to the next'. In part 2, 'Language, Technique and Imagery', Jane Bryce's 'Imaginary Snapshots: Cinematic Technique in the Writing of Yvonne Vera' (pp. 39–56), Jessica Hemmings's 'The Voice of Cloth: Interior Dialogues and Exterior Skins' (pp. 57–62), and Lizzy Attree's 'Language, Kwela Music and Modernity in *Butterfly Burning*' (pp. 63–80) examine from different critical viewpoints what Bryce describes as 'the key to Vera's hermeneutics, the method by which she constructs meaning in her fiction'. Born out of what the Nigerian novelist Ben Okri has described as 'a growing disenchantment with naturalism as a way of describing African life', Vera's narrative style, like that of her generation of writers, who have been 'shaped by the post-independence era', stands in sharp contrast to the narrative modes used by writers of the colonial era 'for whom [colonialism] constituted an overarching fact of existence'. Lizzy Attree, on the other hand, remonstrates with the preponderance of critical attention on Vera's choice of taboo-breaking subject matter and the use of a female perspective, at the expense of what she calls 'the way in which her language and imagery are constructed to provide an alternative, fluid and often ambiguous perspective on life, language and conflict'. Part 3 is on 'Body Politics, Memory and Belonging', and Carolyn Martin Shaw's 'A Woman Speaks of Rivers: Generation and Sexuality in Yvonne Vera's Novels' (pp. 83–92), Meg Samuelson's 'Remembering the Body: Rape and Recovery in *Without a Name* and *Under the Tongue*' (pp. 93–100), Ranka Primorac's 'Iron Butterflies: Note on Yvonne Vera's *Butterfly Burning*' (pp. 101–8), and Ruth Lavalle's 'Yvonne Vera's *Without a Name*: Reclaiming That Which Has Been Taken' (pp. 109–14) focus on what Samuelson describes as the ways in which 'the violated, dismembered female body moves to the centre of the narratives as Vera's novels envisage the means by which the raped body can find recovery'. The penultimate section, 'Spirit Possession and Resistance', comprises the duo of Robert Muponde's 'The Sight of the Dead Body: Dystopia as Resistance in Vera's *Without a Name*' (pp. 117–26) and Maurice T. Vambe's 'Spirit Possession and the Paradox of Post-colonial Resistance in Yvonne Vera's *Nehanda*' (pp. 127–38). While Muponde situates the deployment of dystopian tropes in *Without a Name* 'within the various socio-historical contexts out of which the narrative secretes its multiple meanings', Vambe argues that, in *Nehanda*, 'Vera's failure to adequately differentiate the contradictory identities of black women that have formed/evolved within the post-colonial space they inhabit traps the novel's discourse in the very nationalist ideology that it implicitly challenges whilst retaining and endorsing a nationalist romance.' Part 5, entitled 'History, Fiction and the Colonial Space', comprises Khombe Mangwanda's 'Remapping the Colonial Space: Yvonne Vera's *Nehanda*' (pp. 141–54), Nana Wilson-Tagoe's 'History, Gender and the Problem of Representation in the Novels of Yvonne Vera' (pp. 155–78), Emmanuel Chiwome's 'A Comparative Analysis of Solomon Mutswairo's and Yvonne Vera's Handling of the Legend of Nehanda' (pp. 179–90), Violet Bridget Lunga's 'Between the Pause and the Waiting: The Struggle against Time in Yvonne Vera's *Butterfly Burning*' (pp. 191–202), and Terence Ranger's 'History has its Ceiling: The Pressure of the Past in *The Stone Virgins*' (pp. 203–16). Wilson-Tagoe explores the problematic relationship between history and fiction in African literature vis-à-vis Vera's engagement with history, particularly 'with cultural assumptions that have traditionally regulated gender relations', and reaches the primary conclusion that 'a combined focus on history and gender in exploring her work reveals gender itself as a historical category that may be re-imagined and transformed'. The historian Terence Ranger observes how, in the novels before *The Stone Virgins*, Vera discards the techniques of male historiography, and he examines the ways in which the later novel 'represents a development, or at least a change, in Vera's engagement with history'. The book ends with Jane Bryce's August 2000 interview with Vera, entitled 'Survival in the Mouth' (pp. 217–26), and, as Bryce observes, if Vera's 'writing is spare to the point of minimalism, in speech she has the eloquence of a traditional storyteller like her grandmother, themes and stories weaving together with almost unconscious artistry, producing patterns which are part of a larger design'.

Albert Wertheim's *The Dramatic Art of Athol Fugard: From South Africa to the World* is a book-length study of the creative output of the prolific Athol Fugard, one of 'the six or seven most significant English-language playwrights alive in the last decade of the twentieth century'. From August 1958, ten years after the 1948 initiation of apartheid, when his first extant play, *No-Good Friday*, was performed, 'Fugard's plays have been milestones and signposts of apartheid's devastating progress, its demise, and the future that is unfolding in its wake'. Despite chronicling Fugards' reaction to the vexed questions of art, politics, and race in his country and more universally, Wertheim maintains that Fugard's 'plays and the ideas expressed in his work are the major concern of the study'. His detailed account of Fugard's artistic growth and development is divided into eight topical sections or chapters, which include 'Early Work and Early Themes', before journeying through 'The Port Elizabeth Plays: The Voice with which we Speak from the Heart', to the quintessential question 'Where Do We, Where Do I, Go From Here?: Performing a New South Africa'. Informed by and benefiting from Beckett's minimalist dramaturgy as well as from Beckett's ideas, Fugard's *No-Good Friday*, which was produced by the newly formed African Theatre Workshop in 1958 with a racially mixed cast, a daring move then, is ostensibly the starting point of an awareness of both the advantages and the limitations his skin affords. Wertheim argues that '*No-Good Friday* and *Nongogo*, Fugard's first plays, both of which are set among Sophia Town blacks, are much more than the "thin slice of township life" that Vandenbrouke, for example, claims *Nongogo* to be'. The plays effectively weave together the realism or naturalistic setting of a township clothesline with its symbolic meaning, and according to Wertheim, it is that mixture, 'that interweaving of real and symbolic, [which] distinguishes *No-Good Friday* and *Nongogo*, and [which], when perfected and burnished by Fugard, will be the source of dramatic power in his later works'. Those later works include *The Blood Knot* [1961], which

Fugard himself has described as a 'watershed play' and which other critics have recognized 'as the gateway to a range of later Fugard plays'. This, along with the other so-called Port Elizabeth plays *Hello and Goodbye* and *Boesman and Lena*, launched his career. Fugard did not just create voices that are able to articulate the realities of South African life, but he also found 'an appropriate channel for evoking "the voice with which we speak from the heart"'. According to Wertheim, 'with this in mind, it is easy to see how Fugard very naturally moved on to create with John Kani and Winston Ntshona *Sizwe Bansi Is Dead* and *The Island*, performance pieces that grew out of remembered images, mimes, and acting exercises'. Along with what it describes as the first of Fugard's 'witness to apartheid plays', *Statements after an Arrest under the Immorality Act* [1974], *Sizwe Bansi* and *Island* are discussed in chapter 3, entitled '"Acting" Against Apartheid'. Chapter 4 is a critical examination of *Dimetos*, entitled '*Dimetos*: Fugard's First Problem Play'. Wertheim gives the background to Fugard's composition of this play: 'Appropriately, the idea for *Dimetos* came to Fugard through his instinctive feelings as he read a short disembodied passage in the first volume of Albert Camus's *Carnets*.' Its obscurity and its highly poetic and parabolic nature notwithstanding, Wertheim argues that, even though it stands as an anomaly among Fugard's works, *Dimetos* 'is, nevertheless, a stunning exploration of the problem of art that Fugard ponders and of his Blakean vision of life'. *The Road to Mecca* and *A Lesson from Aloes* are explored in chapter 6, under the title, 'The Other Problem Plays'. Fugard, according to Wertheim, simply returns to the theme of the reclusive artist that he began to examine in *Dimetos*, 'and to the portrait of the persistent, indefatigable Afrikaner he outlined in his portrait of Piet Bezuidenhout in *A Lesson*'. Chapter 7, 'Writing to Right: Scripting Apartheid's Demise', and chapter 8, 'Where Do We, Where Do I, Go from Here?: Performing a New South Africa', focus pre-eminently on Fugard's post-apartheid plays and the plays that prompted the recognition that apartheid's days were numbered, beginning with the paradigmatic *My Children! My Africa!* [1989]. The 1990s plays, especially *My Life* [1994] and *Valley Song* [1995], staged in and for the 'new' post-apartheid South Africa, constitute 'an eloquent record of Fugard's adjustment to the changes in South Africa and to his role as an artist'. Whereas to the vast majority of readers and theatre-goers, Fugard is and will remain a political playwright, race and apartheid constitute 'just one aspect of Fugard's works'. In this very readable account, one of Wertheim's primary conclusions is that Fugard's 'great achievement is to see into the depths of the human soul, portraying the force of human interactions in their often tragic dimensions'.

2. Australia

(a) Land, Place and Politics: Writing Australia's Cultural History

Barry Hill's *Broken Song: T.G.H. Strehlow and Aboriginal Possession* is a remarkable book which brings together several of the themes pervading this year's scholarship in Australian literature. Not least of these is the role of literature in relationships between Aboriginal and settler Australians, and the position of non-Aboriginal Australians in the production, reception, and criticism of Aboriginal literature. *Broken Song* is a biography of Strehlow, son of a Lutheran missionary who grew up speaking German, English, and Aranda, a Central Australian

Aboriginal language. Trained in English literature, Strehlow's life's work was the collection of Aranda sacred objects, ceremonies, and songs, and the translation of a large body of Aranda song or poetry into English. This was, as Hill argues, a literary engagement with Aboriginal culture, and as such his story raises many questions relating to how white Australia positions itself in relation to Aboriginal cultures, which may, in some cases, be 'broken' due to European settlement, and the work of missionaries, with whom Strehlow felt a strong affinity.

With *Broken Song*, Hill provides not only a biography of Strehlow, but a deeply engaged criticism of his work in collecting and translating the Aranda songs, and also, almost incidentally, a particularly well-written history of black–white relations in Australia from the 1890s to the late 1970s. Strehlow's conflict was in many ways emblematic of that facing many non-Aboriginal scholars (and policy-makers) in the field of Aboriginal culture and politics: his deep respect for Aranda culture was tempered by the assumption in much ethnographic work of the time that Aboriginal culture was dead or dying. Like many of this year's literary critics, Strehlow's literary work continually returned to the question of how Aboriginal culture could best survive settler society, and how to steer a path that avoided the worst excesses of either assimilation or self-determination.

Hill presents the history of the mission at Hermannsburg, and the conflicted position of missionaries who were also, through their ethnographic work, preserving and translating aspects of what they considered to be 'heathen' spirituality. His book is also a history of how Aboriginal spirituality—sacred stories, objects, ceremonies and songs—was taken and used by white people, especially ethnographers and anthropologists, and shows a good understanding of the implications of translating from an oral culture into written texts. Relying heavily on Strehlow's extensive diaries, Hill's discussion of Strehlow's time as patrol officer for the Chief Protector of Aborigines provides a particularly complex and illuminating account of the 'frontier' between Aboriginal and settler Australians, especially with regard to sexuality. Of particular interest to literary scholars are Hill's insightful readings of Strehlow's reports as patrol officer, which often strayed so far into the realm of the literary that he was rebuked by his superiors. Hill's careful reading of Strehlow's writing in its many forms is revealing as to the man's beliefs about language, religion, place, and the body. Hill asks the important question: 'What did Strehlow do to the Aranda songs by writing them down?' (p. 454). He also considers Strehlow's involvement in the trial of Rupert Max Stuart in 1959, the meanings of collecting sacred objects or *tjurunga* for Strehlow, the writing of *Journey to Horseshoe Bend* and its connection of topography and Aboriginal myth, and the scandals relating to his collections that dogged the latter part of Strehlow's life.

Bonyhady and Griffiths, eds., *Words for Country: Landscape and Language in Australia*, is enlightening for literary scholars, although most of the texts considered within it are not literary. This collection of essays, mainly by social or environmental historians with an interdisciplinary bent, examines ways in which narratives about, and names for, landscape inform our understandings of it. It is particularly useful for its broad perspectives on the intersection (or conflict) between Aboriginal and settler ways of knowing, owning, and describing places. Its juxtaposition of some literary with non-literary texts, such as those of oral history, science, and government, helps to place Australia's literature within a wider body of writing and speaking about Australians' relationships to the land.

Heather Goodall, in 'The River Runs Backwards', investigates the cultural impacts of irrigation on the Darling floodplain. P.R. Hay assesses 'insider' and 'outsider' views of Queenstown, on Tasmania's west coast, in 'These Blarsted Hills'. Alongside recent community consultation regarding revegetation of a landscape that has been vastly changed by mining, Hay looks at the poetry of Graeme Hetherington and David Owen's *The Devil Taker* in considering a 'heroic' construction of Queenstown and its relation to ideas of wilderness.

In 'Scarcely Any Water on its Surface', Kirsty Douglas notes a correlation between colonial accounts of landscape formation (including the writings of Charles Sturt, Thomas Mitchell, and Barron Field) and twentieth-century scientific accounts of the same places. Nicholas Brown ('Everyone who has ever done a tree sit always says that the tree talks to you') raises questions relating to 'speaking about place and identity in Australia' (p. 86) in his look at the south coast of New South Wales. Juxtaposing texts of history, government, and activism with David Foster's *The Glade within the Grove*, Francis Webb's *A Drum for Ben Boyd*, and the poetry of R.F. Brissenden and David Campbell, Brown aims 'to understand what has informed the language in which [people of the South Coast] recognize themselves' (p. 101).

Howard Morphy and Frances Morphy, in 'The Spirit of the Plains Kangaroo', are concerned with 'the interweaving of European and Aboriginal histories of place in the Roper Valley, and with the historical processes that have resulted in present attachments to land and patterns of land use' (p. 122). Brigid Hains, in 'The Graveyard of a Century', approaches the question of landscape and language from another direction, thinking about how the books read by members of Mawson's Australasian Antarctic expedition influenced their understandings of the Antarctic landscape.

Pertinent questions about the politics of naming places are raised by Tim Bonyhady in his discussion of the history of Kutikina (once Fraser) Cave on the Franklin River in 'So Much for a Name'. Paul Sinclair cites the poetry of P.R. Hay and Philip Hodgins in his consideration of the reconciliation process, focusing on the use of and attitudes towards shell middens along the Murray River in northern Victoria, in 'Blackfellow Oven Roads'. In 'Uluru', Michael Cathcart considers the white 'discovery' of Uluru, and its representation in the writings of explorers, journalists, bureaucrats, and anthropologists, as he surveys the 'shifting meanings of the Rock in the dominant white ideology' (p. 220).

Of related interest is Amanda Laugesen's *Convict Words: Language in Early Colonial Australia*, which considers the influence of the convict system on the development of the English language in Australia between 1788 and 1860. While many of the terms discussed are meaningful mainly in relation to the convict period, it is fascinating to discover that 'public servant' was first used in 1797 as a euphemism for 'convict', initially with reference to a convict assigned to work for the government instead of for a private person.

Literary responses to landscape as a way of considering Aboriginal and settler relations are also the subject of Belinda McKay and Patrick Buckridge's 'Literary Imaginings of the Bunya' (*QR* 9:ii[2002] 65–79). They analyse the range of meanings associated with the bunya tree in Australian literature, with a particular focus on the work of Rosa Praed, Cornelius Moynihan, and Roy Connolly. Early accounts of the bunya, particularly those of Praed, associate the tree with Aboriginal gatherings and 'bunya feasts', at which, according to unproven accounts, cannibalism occurred. They argue that this association with cannibalism enabled the bunya to act 'as a lightning rod for such colonial anxiety' (p. 68). They also posit the bunya as a key component in Praed's 'sublime landscapes' as presented in her novels *Policy and Passion* and *Outlaw and Lawmaker*. Moynihan's representation in *The Feast of the Bunya* is of particular interest, since he was unwilling to write an epic poem on the subject because of his inability to imaginatively enter the minds of Aboriginal characters—indeed, he believed that such a poem could not be written 'in the absence of an aboriginal genius' (p. 74). In both Moynihan's poem and Connolly's *Southern Saga,* Buckridge and McKay see an important role for the bunya in structuring white perceptions of their relationship to Aboriginal culture and history in Queensland.

In 'The Queensland Shearers' Strikes in Rosa Praed's Fiction' (*QR* 9:i[2002] 67–87), Patricia Clarke investigates the depiction of the 1891 and 1894 strikes in Praed's novels *Mrs Tregaskiss: A Novel of Anglo-Australian Life* and *Lady Bridget in the Never-Never Land*. She examines the sources of information available to Praed about the strikes (as she was writing from London); these were provided primarily by Praed's sister, and mainly presented the squatters' side of the affair. Clarke expresses surprise at Praed's lack of understanding of the aims of the unionists as demonstrated in her novels.

Sheahan-Bright and Glover, eds., *Hot Iron Corrugated Sky: 100 Years of Queensland Writing*, is an anthology of Queensland prose, poetry and drama from 1901 to 2001, interspersed with eleven essays on the state and development of Queensland writing by contemporary Queensland writers. These are not, as the introduction points out, scholarly accounts, but are for the most part valuable for their personal observations. Editors' notes relate these personal experiences to more general features of Queensland writing over the period. John Birmingham discusses the effect of changes to Queensland architecture on the kinds of stories that can be told about Brisbane in 'The Lost City of Vegas: David Malouf's Old Brisbane'. Mary-Rose MacColl suggests the importance of the David Unaipon Award, UQP's related increase in publishing of Indigenous writing, and the Goss government's commitment to arts funding, to the relative 'boom' of Queensland writing in the 1990s, in 'A Room of One's Own, a Pay Packet and a Few Friends: Queensland Writers in the 1990s'. Andrew McGahan thinks about why local film production is important, and why the film based on his novel *Praise* was shot in Sydney, in 'Not Made in Queensland'. In 'Sport, Plovers and Miss Wonderful', Steven Herrick seeks connections between the success of Queensland's writers for young people and the vagaries of the Queensland education system. Jay Verney writes of her appreciation of Thea Astley's work in 'The Multiple Effects of Thea Astley's Fiction'. Similarly, Melissa Lucashenko considers Oodgeroo's achievements in 'Oodgeroo: Island Poet'. She looks at the reception of Oodgeroo's work and its influence on her generation of Aboriginal writers. Martin Duwell, in 'Pelicans, Cycads and Ghost Crabs: Judith Wright and the Poetry of Queensland', relates his overview of Queensland poetry to the life and work of Wright. Nigel Krauth considers Queensland the home (temporary haven or otherwise) of literary 'Mavericks and Misfits', such as Banjo Paterson, Xavier Herbert, David Malouf, Thea Astley, and Andrew McGahan. Steele Rudd's contribution to Australian literary stereotypes get a look-in with Mark Svendson's 'The Real Stud: Arthur

Hoey Davis and Queensland's Literary Stereotypes'. Svendson considers how his 'Victorian caricatures—such as the innocents and scoundrels of popular melodrama—were mistakenly placed at the heart of populist sentiment' in Australia (p. 182).

Paul Galloway holds popular melodrama in higher esteem in his valuable contribution, 'Lively Art, Dismal Science: A Century of Queensland Playwrighting'. Of the success of Australian popular theatre in the thirty years around federation (despite the resistance of theatre management), Galloway notes: 'There was no Cultural Cringe—there never has been in popular entertainment. The Cringe came later and was largely the product of an aspiring middle-class' (p. 205). He includes in his survey more ephemeral forms of drama (such as vaudeville, sketch and radio plays), moving through the New Theatre, Little and Repertory theatres, and the more recent La Boite, TN!, and the Queensland Theatre Company. He expresses reservations regarding the effect of tight government funding on the size and scope of plays that are produced, repeating the joke that La Boite 'is looking for a brilliantly-written no-hander' (p. 212), and also the effect on the ideological nature of plays that are funded, which he suggests is a form of 'agitprop-lite' (p. 212).

Chittleborough, Dooley, Glover, and Hosking, eds., *Alas, for the Pelicans! Flinders, Baudin and Beyond*, celebrates the 200th anniversary of the encounter of Nicholas Baudin and Matthew Flinders off the coast of South Australia. Essays on the cultural contexts and ramifications of the encounter are placed alongside a selection of poetry from 1828 to 2002, with this area and period of history as its theme. Gillian Dooley considers the literary merits of Matthew Flinders's writing while he was imprisoned on Mauritius. Elizabeth Gertsakis examines the extant letters of Ann Chapelle Flinders with an eye to suggesting why she may have destroyed those to her husband, taking into account contemporary attitudes towards women, writing, and genre. Rick Hosking looks at William Cawthorne's novella *The Kangaroo Islanders*, one of the few novels concerning this period of Kangaroo Island's history, and at the lives of the sealers and the Indigenous women living with them, and Keryn James uses archaeological sources to question the status of these women as slaves.

Paul Miller examines the role of popular travel narratives in debates surrounding Aboriginal Australians in 'Metamorphosis: Travel Narratives and Aboriginal/Non-Aboriginal Relations in the 1930s' (*JAS* 75[2002] 85–92). Miller looks at the popularity of writers including Robert Plowman, George McIver, and Ernestine Hill.

In 'Australia's Sublime Desert: John McDougall Stuart and Bruce Chatwin' (in Gilbert and Johnston, eds., *In Transit: Travel, Text, Empire*, pp. 149–72), Robert Clark considers Stuart's journals and Chatwin's *The Songlines* as allegory, marked by their use of the language and ideology of the sublime. Arguing that 'the primitivism of *The Songlines* ... recuperates the doomed race rhetoric of the past' (p. 158), Clarke suggests that 'readers of *The Songlines* re-produce the contemporary traveler, like his nineteenth-century predecessor, as a metonymy in his culture's grand and sublime narratives of progress'. Of related interest is Clare Johnson's discussion of the re-enforcement of colonial and racial boundaries in 'Crossing the Border: Bruce Chatwin and Paul Theroux' (*Antipodes* 16:i[2002] 59–62). Johnson echoes Clark's concerns regarding the 'primitivism' evident in Chatwin's *Songlines* in her examination of the ways in which 'Chatwin and Theroux reduce their anxieties about the dissolution of boundaries between self and other by constantly creating new ones' (p. 59).

Also in the Gilbert and Johnston volume is Robert Dixon's 'Frank Hurley's *Pearls and Savages*: Travel, Representation and Colonial Governance'. Dixon examines the production and reception of Hurley's films and books on Papua in order to interrogate the relation between 'culture, particularly commercial mass entertainment associated with travel and tourism, and governance' (p. 213). The piece is revealing as to the ambivalent and often contradictory relations between Hurley's commercial enterprise in Papua and the Australian bureaucracy there. Of related interest is Juniper Ellis's questioning of Australia's place in its region in terms of its literature, in 'Australia in Oceania' (in Callahan, ed., *Contemporary Issues in Australian Literature*, pp. 153–72).

Katy Nebhan looks at accounts of pilgrimage by Australian Muslims in 'Australian Muslim Experiences of the Meccan Pilgrimage or Hajj' (in Siegel, ed., *Issues in Travel Writing: Empire, Spectacle, and Displacement*, pp. 253–67). Mudrooroo Nyoongah questions the idea of 'homeland' as it relates to processes of mourning and to displaced people, and the role of Tibet as a spectral homeland apparently available to people in Western nations, in 'The Spectral Homeland' (*Southerly* 61:i[2002] 25–36). In the same issue, Uli Krahn provides an engaging piece on the many and various ways of thinking about the antipodes from the ancients onwards, in 'Falling into the Sky, or, the Myth of the Antipodes as a Generative Force' (*Southerly* 61:i[2002] 78–90). Krahn tells her grumpy interlocutor Harry: 'The empty space between misery and promise, that's the home of the antipodean imagination, see? Imagination abhors a vacuum, remember, filling gaps with its monstrous children ... ' (p. 87): perhaps the most delightfully written piece of scholarship for the year.

In 'Future Fusions and a Taste for the Past: Literature, History and the Imagination of Australianness' (*AHS* 33:cxviii[2002] 126–39), Hsu-Ming Teo argues that history and literature in Australia are mutually dependent activities. She suggests that 'history in Australia has got to be reconceptualised not simply to make visible the lives of ethnic minorities of the last two hundred years but to integrate these lives, cultures and histories into larger national narratives which then interlock at various points with the histories of other nations and regions, producing Australian histories which are also crucial components of more globalized histories' (p. 138).

Graham Huggan, in 'Cultural Memory in Postcolonial Fiction: The Uses and Abuses of Ned Kelly' (*ALS* 20:iii[2002] 142–54), looks at the process of creating and transforming 'cultural memory', arguing that Peter Carey's *True History of the Kelly Gang* and Robert Drewe's *Our Sunshine* 'illustrate the importance of the literary text in structuring the individual/collective memory process' (p. 143). Carey's use of the letter in perhaps just such a process in his rewriting of the Kelly story is briefly considered by Alan Atkinson in his discussion of the engagement of novelists (including Carey, Wilkie Collins, and Marcel Proust) with technological changes to the speed and efficiency of communication. In 'The World Laid Open: Writing and Technological Change' (*AuBR* 241[2002] 41–4), Atkinson suggests that 'historical novels may have a special usefulness because they allow both writer and reader to pretend that the world is not laid open, that we still live either alone or face-to-face' (p. 44).

Robert Drewe, in 'Where the Yellow Sand Stops' (*Westerly* 47[2002] 25–33), also wonders why, in Australian literature, 'the Good Old Past is always being trotted out for one more waltz'. He suggests that, 'when we think of Outback we really mean the Past' (p. 27), and in questioning why Australian writers have been loath to document Australia's shift to suburban and urban life posits that it is 'mostly to do with our cultural cringe and our over-enthusiastic aping of the established romantic English tradition' (p. 28), noting the perseverance of the 'romantic/ political notion that moral stamina was sapped by the city and nurtured by the country' (p. 29). (See also John Rickard's discussion of the 'cringe' below).

Drusilla Modjeska was another to question our novelists' unwillingness to engage with contemporary Australian life. In 'The Present in Fiction' (in her *Timepieces*, pp. 201–20), she suggests that the gap has been filled, to an extent, by non-fiction, which has become increasingly popular with Australian readers. Novelists may be influenced, she argues, by the need to sell books to an overseas audience likely only to be interested in the more 'exotic' aspects of Australian life: its past, its 'Outback'—or Tasmania.

Along with concern about Australia's history comes an anxiety about our place in the world, a worry that has been exacerbated by Australians becoming, possibly for the first time, a terrorist target in the bombings in Bali in October 2002. Australia's treatment of asylum-seekers remained in the news throughout 2002, a continual reminder that Australia is no longer so isolated from the rest of the world, and that it might have obligations towards those who face persecution in their own countries. Australia's flaunting of international human rights instruments in this respect has raised serious, and in most cases, unanswered, questions about its relations with its neighbours and with the international community. It has also led to increasing polarization in public debate.

David Walker, in 'Survivalist Anxieties: Australian Responses to Asia, 1890s to the Present' (*AHS* 33[2002] 319–30), argues that the idea of 'Asia' has been an essential element in the formation of Australian nationhood, and that the role Asia plays in this respect has not changed dramatically over time. Walker analyses how narratives involving Asia (particularly invasion stories) have helped delimit Australian national identity. He writes:

> In Australia's post-Tampa world we have seen a return of survivalist anxieties in which human rights and citizenship, categories that the west sought to universalize and institutionalize after the Second World War, are weighed against the rights of a supposedly embattled nation to secure its borders. When the survival of the nation is said to be at risk, upholding the rights of refugees and minorities can be represented as a luxury the nation can no longer afford. The logic of this kind of survivalism is to reduce the world to a battle between them and us where 'their' role is to subvert, undermine and weaken 'our' will to survive as a nation. (p. 329)

Lars Jensen 'reverses the gaze' in considering how Australia looks from a comparative Asian perspective in 'From European Satellite to Asian Backwater?' (in Callahan, ed., pp. 133–52).

A varied collection of conference papers can be found in Pons, ed., *Departures: How Australia Reinvents Itself.* Including ruminations on change and tradition, identity, migration, travel, and death, from historians and literary and cultural critics, these papers are reviewed throughout this section, as befits the thematic breadth of the collection.

In 'From "Hello Freedom" to "Fuck You Australia"': Recent Chinese-Australian Writing' (in Pons, ed., pp. 61–9), Wenche Ommundsen explores the tropes of arrival, departure, and return in Chinese Australian writing, suggesting that the re-creation of such moments of arrival or departure is a fraught activity for writers including Ouyang Yu, Lillian Ng, and Fang Xiangshu. Of related interest are Lyn Jacobs's 'About Face: Asian-Australians at Home' (*ALS* 20:iii[2002] 201–14), and Tim Kendall's 'Looking for New Opportunities: Sang Ye and the Discourse of Multiculturalism' (*JAS* 72[2002] 69–78), which questions the authority and control of the mediated texts of oral history.

In 'No More "National Identity"': Ethnicity and Alternative Sexual Orientation in Australian Movies of the 1990s' (in Pons, ed., pp. 79–90), Adi Wimmer looks at some of the implications of globalization for the Australian film industry, arguing that national identity 'no longer mattered' (p. 80) to Australian film-makers of the 1990s. He defends the 'normalization' of diverse ethnic and sexual identities in recent Australian films while neglecting to take into account the intersection between the two.

Sonia Mycak, in 'Australian Multicultural Literature: Dynamics and Dilemmas of the Self' (*L&A* 12[2002] 79–104), argues that multicultural writing in Australia has an important place within contemporary philosophical debate about the nature of subjectivity. Reading multicultural writing as 'a body of writing in which radical notions of the subject are made manifest in the text' (p. 80), Mycak examines the representation of the 'split subject' in the work of several Australian poets and novelists.

Benjamin, Davies, and Goh, eds., *Postcolonial Cultures and Literatures: Modernity and the (Un)Commonwealth*, is a collection of papers 'on the varieties and vagaries of post-imperial identity' (p. xvii). James N. Brown and Patricia M. Sant, 'Settling Identities: Britishness Abroad', trace 'the history of Britishness in Australia and Asia in order to conceptualize present debates on race and nation in Australia' (p. 12). They take as their case studies Henry Stuart Russell's *The Genesis of Queensland*, Conrad's 'Karain: A Memory', and the writing and artwork of Donald Friend.

In another forum, David Carter queries the notion that elite culture in Australia is Anglophile and working-class culture the seat of authentic Australianness. In 'Going, going, gone? Britishness and Englishness in Contemporary Australian Culture' (*Overland* 169[2002] 81–6), Carter suggests that Britishness no longer rates particularly highly on the radar of Australian 'high' culture, relating this to the decreased centralization of the production and consumption of cultural products. In this sense, 'London can no longer stand in for the world' (p. 82).

Australia's attitude towards the rest of the world and its cultural products is also questioned by John Rickard in 'Keeping Up with the Cringe' (*AuBR* 245[2002] 43–

6), a valuably balanced analysis of the changing notion of Australia's 'cultural cringe'. Judging by this year's criticism, the term is still alive and well.

One topic that our literary critics are doing anything but cringe from this year is politics. In 'Globalization and its Discontents' (in Pons, ed., pp. 258–68), Paul Gillen compares responses to globalization in the genres of fiction and of social commentary, and finds an (unsurprising) variance in tone. Analysing social commentaries by John Wiseman and McKenzie Wark alongside novels by Elliott Perlman, Bernard Cohen, and Anthony Macris, Gillen finds the emotional responses to the effects of globalization in the novels a great deal bleaker than the solution-finding responses of 'optimists of the will', the social commentators.

Perhaps the most important book published this year on literature and politics is Adams and Lee, eds., *Frank Hardy and the Literature of Commitment*. This collection of essays reproduces some earlier work by John Frow and Peter Williams along with recent essays on Hardy and the broader project of communist or socialist realist writing in Australia. The volume includes an interview with Hardy, his last (posthumously published) piece, and Dave Nadel's key to *Power without Glory*. The essays approach a fraught period in Australia's literary and political life from a range of perspectives, though all consider the tensions involved in combining the project of communist activism with that of literature, and the relationship of socialist realism to the Australian literary tradition.

The two reprinted pieces mark important points in the debate surrounding Hardy. Peter Williams takes issue with Jack Beasley's portrayal of Hardy in his *Red Letter Days*, arguing that he 'parallels and complements a backlog of bitter attacks on that writer and on other people associated with the Australian Left' (p. 130). John Frow agrees with Williams as to the conservatism of contemporary literary orthodoxy, arguing that 'its typical strategies are those of decontextualisation and depoliticisation' (p. 137). He looks at the primacy of intertextuality in Hardy's writing and the implications of this for critical interpretation. Paul Adams argues that Frow overstates this point, failing to take into account the intertextuality that marks the yarn, a genre that Hardy draws on heavily.

Allan Gardiner considers Hardy's relationship to communist cultural institutions in the light of the recent increase in commentary on Hardy. He discusses the formation and competing aims of the Australasian Book Society and the Realist Writers Group, focusing on tensions between socialist and nationalist objectives. This becomes a recurrent theme across these essays. John McLaren outlines the debates over the 'Australian Literary Tradition' played out in *Overland*, *Meanjin*, and other periodicals. Carole Ferrier compares the experiences of Hardy, Dorothy Hewett, and Jean Devanny, arguing that, while each of them encountered difficulties within the party due to their 'dynamic' personalities and 'innovatively radical' writing, consideration of Hewett's and Devanny's writing had a significant (and pejorative) gender inflection. Of related interest is Susan Pfisterer's 'Brave Red Witches: Communist Women Playwrights and the Sydney New Theatre' (in Pons, ed., pp. 167–74), a discussion of the opportunities membership of the CPA, as well as of the New Theatre movement, opened up for women dramatists in this period. Pfisterer focuses on the work and lives of Oriel Gray and Mona Brand.

Still in Adams and Lee, eds., David Carter rigorously considers the Australian literary tradition as it related to communist writers. He looks at tensions within the CPA regarding the role of literature, and also at changes in Australian literary institutions during the mid-1950s. Several essays in the collection note the increasing influence of conservative academic literary criticism in this period, exemplified for some by the lauding of Patrick White and other non-realist writers. Carter also discusses the alignment of radical nationalism with the Australian democratic tradition that enabled communist writers 'to position themselves at the centre of a progressive tradition rather than at the radical margins' (p. 97). He considers Judah Waten's *Time of Conflict* in the light of these tensions.

Cath Ellis takes a similar approach with the Goldfields Trilogy of Katharine Susannah Prichard, looking at the impact of socialist realism on her narrative style. She suggests that, 'by offering a single, assured and determined political position, these novels lose the narrative tension that characterizes her earlier, more dialectically energetic novels' (p. 201). Prichard is also the focus of Delys Bird's piece, which looks at the politics of race in her work, and how they are played out in her crossing of generic boundaries. She suggests that 'Prichard's race politics are inscribed, as her socialist politics are, in the tensions between romanticism and realism' (p. 195). Of related interest is Cynthia Vanden Driesen's 'The (Ad)Missions of the Colonizer: Australian Paradigms in Selected Works of Prichard, Malouf and White' (in Stilz, ed., *Missions of Interdependence: A Literary Directory*, pp. 310–19). Vanden Driesen looks at *Coonardoo* alongside Malouf's *Remembering Babylon* and White's *A Fringe of Leaves* and *Voss* to briefly consider the revealed attitudes to Indigenous Australians.

Cathy Greenfield and Peter Williams take a brief look at some of the political effects of Hardy's writing, focusing on the trope of the stranger. Paul Genoni examines the tension between, and coexistence of, realism and Catholicism in the work of Hardy and Ruth Park. Nathan Hollier takes an interesting view of the way in which Hardy came to represent an Australian working-class masculinity that became particularly popular in the 1970s. Of related interest is Rebecca Johinke's 'Misogyny, Muscles and Machines: Cars and Masculinity in Australian Literature' (in Callahan, ed., pp. 95–111), a discussion of representations of working-class masculinity in Peter Carey's 'Crabs'.

David Carter again deals with the question of what might make a novel communist or, for that matter, Australian, in 'Communism and Carnival: Ralph de Boissiere's *Crown Jewel* and its Australian Context' (*ACH* 21[2002] 91–106). Laurie Duggan, 'On Working Class Poetry' (*Overland* 166[2002] 101–2), continues the contemporary debate on the intersection of class politics and literature in a response to the 'Working Class Poetry' edition of *Overland* (165[2001] 1–128). Of related interest is John McLaren's discussion of 'The British Tradition in John Morrison's Radical Nationalism' (*ALS* 20[2002] 215–24). McLaren claims that Morrison, alone of all the writers of his era, 'derives his politics—as well as his vocabulary—from the centrality of work in defining and fulfilling the worker', and that this 'has its origins in a British, specifically Scottish, Presbyterian tradition that saw work as itself redemptive within a general framework of personal discipline and service to the community' (p. 219).

Interest in the relationship between politics and the Australian literary canon continues in Christopher Lee's 'An Uncultured Rhymer and his Cultural Critics: Henry Lawson, Class Politics, and Colonial Literature' (*VP* 6.26.26.240[2002] 87–104). Lee looks at the influence Lawson's politics has had on his critical reception, suggesting that the academy has embraced a depoliticized Lawson, which has led to an under-acknowledgement of Lawson's role as a verse writer and as a popular writer. Lee would be pleased by a new edition, *Henry Lawson*, edited and introduced by historian Geoffrey Blainey, which includes a selection of his verse as well as stories. Les Carolyn mentions this edition in his piece on the connections between Lawson and Mark Twain, 'The Lore Makers' (*Bul* 120:6314[2002] 32–6).

Michael Leach notes that Lawson's influence extends to unexpected places in 'Don Eduardo Is Sleeping: A Return to New Australia, Paraguay' (*Overland* 169[2002] 90–7). He finds in the descendants of William Lane's utopian 'New Australia' settlement particularly strong remnants of 1890s Australian culture.

(b) Canons: Reference Works, Oz Lit and the History of the Book
Bibliographies, biographies, indexes, and finding lists are essential tools for the literary scholar and cultural historian, but ones often lacking for Australian material. Recently, however, a number of very useful reference works have been published, while increasing attention is being paid to the history of authorship, publishing and reading in Australia.

The Bibliography of Australian Literature project has been under way at the Centre for Australian Studies at Monash University since 1990. It has now combined forces with another major Australian literature bibliographical database, AUSTLIT, to form the electronic Australian Literature Gateway, based at the University of Queensland. While electronic databases have revolutionized access to information about Australian literature, there are still advantages in having such information available in volume form, so the arrival of the first volume, *The Bibliography of Australian Literature A–E*, edited by John Arnold and John Hay, is most welcome. Thanks to the inclusion of popular as well as literary authors it is possible for the first time to begin to get a true overview of the publishing of Australian fiction. The star, at least for the first section of the alphabet, was clearly the detective writer 'Carter Brown', otherwise A.G. Yates, whose list of publications runs to fifteen pages. As well as all the standard details about an author's publications, there is much information about reception, including translations, adaptations, and prizes. There is also information about an author's work in other genres, where manuscripts are held, and where a reader can turn for further information. Finally, there is an index of titles and of pseudonyms and variant names.

It has become increasingly apparent that one cannot seriously study the writing or the reading done by Australians during the nineteenth century without paying attention to what was being published in the major newspapers and periodicals. Toni Johnson-Woods's *Index to Serials in Australian Periodicals and Newspapers* will be especially useful for those interested in investigating what Australians were reading during this period, since she does not confine herself to works by Australian authors. As she demonstrates, the bulk of the serials published were by overseas authors, especially those she calls 'second-string' English writers, such as Mary Elizabeth Braddon, William Black, Walter Besant, and Wilkie Collins. Some periodicals did, however, feature serials by American writers; this was especially true of Melbourne's *Australian Journal* and its cheaper stablemate *Once a Week*, which concentrated on American work. It is therefore clear that American popular culture was having an impact in Australia a good deal earlier than is generally supposed, and via fiction as well as the stage, a topic crying out for detailed research.

While Toni Johnson-Woods's index is confined to fifteen publications, all from Victoria, Queensland, and New South Wales, and mainly published between the 1860s and 1899, it includes those with the largest and widest circulation within Australia during this time. As well as details of the works it serialized, Johnson-Woods gives a useful overview of the history of each publication, and provides an author and title index.

The significance of periodicals in the publication of Australian poetry during the nineteenth century is also obvious from the *Analytical Finding List* of Charles Harpur's poems prepared by Elizabeth Holt and Elizabeth Perkins. This lists all the different versions of poems included in the Harpur manuscripts in the Mitchell Library as well as those published during the nineteenth century. In most cases, each poem appears many times, since Harpur was an inveterate reviser and rewriter. There is also a valuable chronology of Harpur's life, and detailed descriptions of his manuscripts.

The first two of a projected four volumes on Australian literature have been published in the American series, *Dictionary of Literary Biography*, edited by Selina Samuels and covering the periods 1788–1914 and 1915–1950. As those familiar with this series will know, the standard entry here is not confined to a few hundred words but ranges across many pages. Each begins with a list of the author's publications, including in many cases uncollected ones from periodicals; each ends with a list of references and information on manuscript holdings. In between one gets, in the best examples, an informative and entertaining account of the life and work, and of the ways in which these have interacted. And, unlike most reference works of this kind, there are also many illustrations: not just portraits of the authors but images of book covers, of manuscripts, of houses, and of family and friends. The 1788–1914 volume clearly demonstrates the results of recent feminist rereadings and research in this period, with entries on nineteen women authors as against twenty-two men. There are, however, very few convict authors included, no dramatists, and hardly any of the many non-fiction writers of the period. The volume for 1915–1950 has the more usual ratio of twice as many men to women, the only real surprise being the inclusion of Mary Durack, especially when a number of other significant women, such as Kylie Tennant, Lesbia Harford, and Eve Langley, are left out. One might also have expected to find Charles Bean, even if no other non-fiction writers.

Despite a higher percentage of errors than is acceptable in a major reference work—my favourite is the name of William Charles Wentworth's Cambridge college, which appears twice as 'Porterhouse'—these two volumes of the *Dictionary of Literary Biography* provide readers of Australian literature, whether at home or abroad, with comprehensive accounts of the lives and work of eighty-six significant authors. In some cases, as with Rosalind Smith's essay on the nineteenth-century poet 'Australie' (Emily Manning) or Don Grant's on the Western Australian short story writer and novelist Gavin Casey, these are the most comprehensive accounts currently available. Even where a recent biography of an author does exist, it is still extremely useful to have a condensed version of it, often written by the same person. For the specialist, there is the added interest of seeing obvious gaps in the critical record, especially in relation to authors writing in the first half of the twentieth century. Many male authors included in the volume for 1915–1950 have been largely neglected since their deaths, though all were leading players on the

Australian literary scene during their lives. David Campbell, Douglas Stewart, R.D. FitzGerald, David Martin, Kenneth Mackenzie, and Frank Dalby Davison all deserve the detailed biographical and critical attention that has recently been given to many of their female contemporaries.

Laurie Hergenhan reviews the implications for the study and readership of Australian literature of some recent bibliographical projects in 'Containing the Mass: New Maps of Australian Literature.' (*Quadrant* 36:xii[2002] 59–63). Marie-Louise Ayres joins Hergenhan in discussing the advent of the Australian Literature Gateway online database in 'National News' (*AuBR* 243[2002] 46).

Paul Eggert responds rather forcefully to reviews by both Hergenhan and Brian Kiernan of the first three titles in the Academy Editions of Australian Literature, in 'Why Critical Editing Matters: Responsible Texts and Australian Reviewers' (*ESC* 27[2001] 179–204), arguing for the importance of dedicating time and resources to researching the reliability of the texts upon which Australian literary studies relies, noting that what 'are often reproduced as "Australian" texts have, in many cases, been massaged by publishers' editors in London or abridged by the author, or author and publisher, for imperial distribution' (p. 194). He points out that Hergenhan and Kiernan's call for cheap reliable student editions cannot be met until the task of critical editing has been undertaken.

Literary awards provide Australia's media and cultural community with a dependable measure of annual scandal and controversy. Tess Brady wades into the fray with a quantitative approach, presenting some of the results of her collation and assessment of data regarding the Australian/Vogel Literary Award, including the backgrounds and subsequent careers of winners and shortlisted writers. In 'The Australian/Vogel Literary Award: A Preliminary Investigation into Three Myths' (*TJAAWP* 6:ii[2002] 82 paras.), she addresses some commonly held beliefs regarding the award: that winners are always 'one-book wonders', that only winners gain benefits from the award, and that winners come from a wide range of backgrounds (as opposed to from the university sector). Suneeta Peres Da Costa revisits the debates surrounding Miles Franklin winner Helen Darville/Demidenko's *The Hand That Signed the Paper* in 'Tautological Modernity, Democracy, Magic and Racism in the Demidenko-Darville Affair' (*CulSR* 8:i[2002] 72–92).

Unsurprisingly, this year also saw continued debate over the place of Australian literary studies in relation to disciplinary approaches that can be broadly categorized as 'cultural studies'. Carole Ferrier, in '"A whole other story vibrating within it": Some Approaches to the "New Literatures"' (in Collier and Schulze-Engler, eds., *Crabtracks: Progress and Process in Teaching the New Literatures in English*, pp. 111–40), makes a thoughtful tour of approaches to reading 'New Literatures', engaging with literary and theoretical texts in a well-considered potted history of developments in some aspects of literary theory over the past fifty years or so. She considers difficulties of, and possibilities for, new approaches relating to cultural studies, multiculturalism, the theorizing of whiteness, debates over political correctness, 'black armband' and 'white blindfold' views of history, postcoloniality, and cultural crossings.

David Callahan considers the role and value of Australian literary studies under 'the shadow cast by cultural studies' (p. 2) in 'Australian Literary Studies Bushwhacked?' (in Callahan, ed., pp. 1–16). In the same volume, Ruth Brown, 'Cyberspace and Oz Lit: Mark Davis, McKenzie Wark and the Re-Alignment of

Australian Literature' (pp. 17–36), argues for a 'complete re-think of what constitutes a "national" literature' (p. 18).

Scott Brook and Paul Dawson both review the debate surrounding fictocriticism and its place in academia. Despite differences in their approaches and attitudes, their conclusions are similar. In 'Does Anybody Know What Happened to "Fictocriticism"? Towards a Fractal Genealogy of Australian Fictocriticism' (*CulSR* 8:ii[2002] 104–18), Brook suggests that the term 'fictocriticism' 'is not only redundant, but that it also obscures the fact that genres are never as stable as they seem. One of the ironic effects of thinking about fictocriticism as a transgressive, hybrid form of writing might be to shore up the differences between its constitutive parts' (p. 113). Dawson, in 'A Place for the Space Between: Fictocriticism and the University' (*Westerly* 47[2002] 139–51), takes a somewhat broader perspective, agreeing with Brook as to the importance of maintaining the 'conceptual differences of genres', but arguing that the 'practical possibilities of permeability (rather than contamination)' can still be explored (p. 149). Essentially, both suggest that the term 'fictocriticism' may have been overdetermined, but that as a practice it might be possible without dissolving existing categories. Dawson's piece is particularly interesting in its examination of fictocriticism as a product of institutional forces, especially the teaching of women's studies and creative writing alongside theory in universities.

Fictocriticism is one of the genres covered in Walker, ed., *The Writer's Reader: A Guide to Writing Fiction and Poetry*, in which novelist and academic Brenda Walker brings together helpful advice for would-be authors from twenty-seven writers, most of whom are also well-known novelists and poets. Many address issues of fictional techniques, with Marion Halligan, for example, discussing structure, Glenda Adams, voice, and Marele Day, characterization. Others write on different fictional genres, including autobiographical as well as popular, historical, and science fiction. The poets address questions of metaphor and rhythm as well as the necessary 'hell' of drafting and redrafting. There are also essays on more general issues, one on the need for writers to read as well as write being especially pertinent, as well as hints on what to do and not to do from publishers and editors of literary magazines.

David Brooks discusses his writing process and its relation to his theoretical interests with Marty Wechselblatt in 'No End to Motivations: A Conversation with David Brooks' (*Antipodes* 16:i[2002] 34–9).

Patrick Buckridge, in '"Good Reading" in the *Australian Women's Weekly*, 1933–1970' (*JASAL* 1[2002] 32–43), looks at the circulation and promotion of ideas about the practice of 'good reading' in the magazine, through its letters, editorials, and features. Buckridge notes significant changes in the 'way reading was valued and practiced' (p. 32) over this period, from the letters in the 1930s suggesting 'a collection of keen women readers of varied education levels, who have never been part of the public literary culture' (p. 36), to a social-democratic emphasis of 'writer as social intellectual' from the 1940s, which seems to have alienated many readers of the *Weekly*.

Editor Craig Munro lends his expertise to review the careers of some of Australia's most (in)famous book editors, including both George Robertsons, A.G. Stephens, P.R. Stephenson, Beatrice Davis, and Hilary McPhee, in 'Editors at Large' (*Meanjin* 61:iii[2002] 53–61). The aims and risks of feminist publishing are examined by Louise Poland in 'Setting the Agenda: The Politics of Feminist Publishing in Australia' (*AuWBR* 14:ii[2002] 23 paras.).

A special edition of the *La Trobe Journal* (*LTJ* 70[2002]) focuses on Henry Lawson, with particular consideration of the papers of one of his publishers, Thomas Lothian. Cecily Close provides a history of the publisher from 1905 to 1917, including details of business arrangements with printers, authors, and booksellers. John Lawson outlines the stormy relationship between Lawson and Thomas Lothian, epitomized in the tortuous circumstances of the publishing of Lawson's *For Australia* and *Triangles of Life*. John Barnes presents a biographical piece, concentrating on Lawson's relationship with his father and sense of himself as 'Norse' or of 'foreign' lineage.

Richard Nile's *The Making of the Australian Literary Imagination* is a broad though uneven narrative history of the conditions under which Australian literature was produced in the twentieth century. Nile provides an overview of the development of the Australian publishing industry, including conditions for the publishing of Australian literature in Britain. The second section covers the development of 'creative industries' in Australia, including the rise of the mass-market paperback. There is a cursory glance at the publishing of poetry, short stories, and drama, but Nile's primary concern is the novel, which he claims 'became Australia's essential literary form' (p. 97) in this period. He compares the Australian film and publishing industries over the twentieth century, arguing that the monopolization by American studios of the distribution of films in Australia ensured that 'Australian literature had the field of national expression to itself for a very large part of the twentieth century' (p. 130). Citing Graeme Turner, Nile posits that, thanks to the unpopularity at the end of the century of nationalism as an ideology in the humanities, 'the critical apparatus so important to the justification of the category "Australian Literature" was turning on one of its fundamental justifications' (p. 131).

As his title suggests, Nile is keen to emphasize that the 'Australian literary imagination' did not spring into the twentieth century fully formed, but was consciously developed, in some cases by a limited few. Vance and Nettie Palmer's project of literary nationalism or 'nation-building' is singled out as the clearest example of this. Nile suggests that the Palmers had a very clear idea of what the national literature should be like, and set about encouraging writing that conformed. Their actions, he argues, had a powerful influence on the shape and reputation of Australia's national literature. Nile notes that their notion of the public as 'promiscuous' in their reading and having 'false bourgeois values' left little room in the emerging tradition for more commercial writers less concerned with liberal humanism or with nation-building, and also failed to take into account the emergence of a highly literate working class. He suggests that this division between socially conscious and popular writing may have done more harm than good in the attempt to establish literary democracy.

Nile examines the development of patronage (government and otherwise) of writers throughout the century, noting changes in emphasis from state-sponsored welfare, to nation-building, to a concentration on the 'distinctive Australianness invested in high profile sponsored authors' (p. 243). He also outlines early discussions over whether and at what point the subject of Australian literature was fit to become an academic discipline. Nile also devotes space to the effects of

censorship on the production of Australian literature, noting that, although the
censorship of political material received more attention at the time, censorship of
obscenity or indecency may have had an equal impact on what kinds of books
writers felt they could publish. Nicole Moore takes up this matter in her discussion
of Robert Close and the *Love Me Sailor* obscenity case (*ALS* 20[2002] 316–29).
Moore also looks at censorship of women's writing involving contraception or
abortion in 'Interrupting Maternal Citizenship: Birth Control and Mid-Wave
Women's Writing' (*AuFS* 17[2002] 151–64). Moore suggests that, by 'interrupting
maternal destinies for their characters, birth control plots also interrupt historical
accounts of Australian feminism that offer maternal citizenship as its best model'.

Similar questions are raised by Donna Coates in 'Sleeping with the Enemy:
Patriot Games in Fictions by Lesbia Harford, Gwen Kelly, and Joan Dugdale' (*JCL*
37ii[2002] 157–73). In considering the publishing history of Harford's *The
Invaluable Mystery*, Kelly's *Always Afternoon*, and Dugdale's *Struggle of Memory*,
Coates makes a convincing case for the suppression of stories that ran counter to the
Anzac myth in portraying Australia during the First World War, particularly those
written by women. Coates questions the effect such suppression may have had on a
female participation in the genre of war writing.

The effect of war on women's cultural and political opportunities is also reflected
on in Susan Sheridan's 'Cold War, Home Front: Australian Women Writers and
Artists in the 1950s' (*ALS* 20[2002] 155–66). Focusing on the life and work of
Dorothy Green, Sheridan notes that, owing to political polarization in this period,
concerns in the work of women artists were not recognized as political unless they
were explicitly socialist.

(c) Writing Lives/Writing About and By Indigenous Australians
Questions of life-writing, particularly as it relates to the project of reconciliation,
were raised repeatedly in 2002. There was much interest in perennial questions
about the relationship of lived experience to writing fiction, autobiography, and
biography.

In *The Boyds: A Family Biography*, Brenda Niall, author of an earlier biography
of novelist Martin Boyd, provides an account of the lives of several generations of a
family which has contributed more than any other to Australian artistic culture.
While the painter Arthur Boyd and his cousin the architect Robin Boyd are, with
Martin Boyd, the best-known members of the family, many others have done
significant work as painters, sculptors, and potters, a tradition being carried on by
several from the present generation. All of this began from the highly unlikely
conjunction of the son of the teetotal Chief Justice of Victoria and the daughter of a
convict who had made good as a brewer. Since Martin Boyd drew on family history
for many of his novels, especially those known as the Langton Quartet, the interest
of this work for literary scholars extends beyond the sections specifically devoted to
him. In organizing her study around the houses owned by members of the extended
Boyd family, Niall echoes Martin Boyd's own preoccupation with place, and
provides a fascinating account of changes and continuities across the generations.

At just over 500 pages, Frances de Groen's and Laurie Hergenhan's edition of
selected correspondence of the novelist Xavier Herbert, *Xavier Herbert: Letters*,
gives some indication of just how prolific a letter-writer he was. Unlike some more
recent editions of Australian literary letters, too, this one only includes those by

Herbert, not those to him. The letters have been divided into six sections, corresponding to various periods in Herbert's life, with a particular concentration on letters from those in which he was producing his two epic works on life in Northern Australia, *Capricornia* [1938] and *Poor Fellow My Country* [1974]. Although letters to over forty individuals or institutions are included, the majority are to a handful of correspondents: many of the earlier letters are to his friend Arthur Dibley, many from the 1960s are to his wife Sadie, and many of the later ones are to Laurie Hergenhan himself, as he helped Herbert with the manuscript of *Poor Fellow*. There are also many to editors, literary agents, and publishers, especially Walter Cousins and Beatrice Davis of Angus & Robertson, as well as letters to a wide range of other literary figures. Hence, as well as extensive insights into Herbert's ideas and obsessions, we are given many intriguing glimpses of Australian literary life and of its institutional underpinnings at a time of growing confidence. As well as extensive explanatory footnotes and information about the recipients of the letters, the editors have included useful notes on individuals mentioned by Herbert. Several of his letters (not published in the de Groen and Hergenhan volume) are printed in *Overland* (169[2002] 59–63). These relate to his hitchhiking journey from Sydney to Darwin in 1935.

Days Never Done: The Life and Work of Hesba Fay Brinsmead, Michael Pollak and Margaret McNabb's biography of the children's author and environmentalist, provides some insight into the often difficult position of a woman who was deeply committed to both her writing and her environmentalism, but was in many ways constrained by her duties as wife and mother in the 1940s and 1950s. Despite these restrictions (at one stage working in a spare room in the local branch of her bank!), Brinsmead managed a successful career in professional writing, publishing many stories and pieces of journalism in magazines, and writing for radio, as well as producing her well-known novels for young adults and children. Pollak and McNabb suggest that Brinsmead was ahead of her time in her novels' engagement with questions of environmental degradation wrought by development, industry, and mining. They also outline the difficulties Brinsmead experienced in publishing work for adults (either fiction or non-fiction) after the success of her children's books.

Nadia Wheatley discusses the process of writing her biography of Charmaine Clift in 'Lies and Silences' (*Meanjin* 61:i[2002] 60–9), focusing on how a biographer might deal with her subject's prior representation of her own life story— particularly when the biographer encounters 'lies and silences' within that story. In the same issue, in 'Getting a Life' (*Meanjin* 61:i[2002] 94–7), John Ritchie, general editor of the *Australian Dictionary of Biography*, offers some insight into the art of biography, and David McCooey, 'Lives of the Poets' (*Meanjin* 61:i[2002] 104–13), considers the often overlooked form of biographical poetry. Richard Freadman, 'Sister Pacts' (*Meanjin* 61:i[2002] 186–95), thinks about what the disagreement between sisters Doris and Lily Brett over their family's story might reveal about the 'narrative pact' involved in autobiographical writing, and about 'the part that such narrative pacts play—or might play—in our ethical lives'.

Helen Garner's 'I' (*Meanjin* 61:i[2002] 40–3) discusses the implications of writing from experience: 'Writing, it seems, like the bringing up of children, can't be done without causing damage' (p. 43). Of related interest is Eden Liddelow's 'Helen Garner: Honour and the Recording Angel' (in her *After Electra: Rage, Grief and Hope in Twentieth-Century Fiction*, pp. 79–92), a wide-ranging analysis of the workings of rage and grief in Garner's writing, suggesting an interest in the self's 'capacity for duality' in the face of 'fallenness' and hopes for redemption, and also offering reflections, in Garner's recurring pairs of women split between rage and grief, of aspects of the writing self.

The question of who is an acceptable subject of biography is raised by Heather Wearne in 'Risky Business: Writing the Personal' (*LiNQ* 29:ii[2002] 11–18). Discussing her motivations for writing a biography of her 'working-class, fully domesticated' mother, Wearne argues that it is about time that such people became 'authorized subjects' of biography (p. 12), joining the ranks of 'hero' biographies which 'interpellate very particular subjects into the making of the meanings of nation' (p. 17).

Similar questions are raised throughout the essays in Drusilla Modjeska's characteristically candid and meditative collection, *Timepieces*. In 'The Englishness Problem: Two Anecdotes and a Review', Modjeska, like Wearne, thinks about writing biographies of 'ordinary' people—and, like Wearne, she refers to her writing about her own mother in *Poppy*. She raises the possibility that Australian writers began to cross boundaries between biography, autobiography, and fiction earlier and more easily than English writers. The collection centres on questions of auto/biography, genre-crossing, and Modjeska's own writing practice. 'Writing *Poppy*' and 'On Not Owning a Grace Cossington Smith' shed some light on Modjeska's writing process—particularly interesting in the former is the recounting of her negotiations between genres in order to write the story of her mother's life. 'Memoir Australia' is an extended discussion of the development and state of Australian memoir, looking at the effect of changes in generations, politics, and public opinion on the movement between fiction and autobiography. She compares Kerryn Higg's *All That False Instruction* with Robert Dessaix's *A Mother's Disgrace* to suggest that topics that, thirty years ago, could only be broached in fiction, can now confidently be the subject of memoir. Regarding the autobiographies of successful feminists of her own generation, who are 'writing accounts of their lives because they recognize their public significance' (p. 167), Modjeska joins Henderson (see below) in noting their lack of interiority, and also looks forward to the memoirs of their daughters' generation. She lauds men's responses to 'thirty years of upheaval in gender relations' (p. 173), including memoirs by Robert Drewe, Michael McGirr, Brian Matthews, and Louis Nowra. In her consideration of questions of trust, memory and truth in memoir, Modjeska also looks at Raimond Gaita's *Romulus, My Father*, Peter Read's *Belonging*, Kim Mahood's *Craft for a Dry Lake*, Rita and Jackie Huggins's *Auntie Rita*, Lynette Russell's *A Little Bird Told Me*, Inga Clendinnen's *Tiger's Eye*, and Kim Scott's *Benang*.

In 'Apprentice Piece', Modjeska recounts her conversations and relationships with writers and editors, including Dora Russell, Marjorie Barnard, Eleanor Dark, Christina Stead, George Munster, Hilary McPhee, and Dorothy Green. It is an extended acknowledgement of their generosity towards her and also a discussion of her experiences in writing and publishing.

Margaret Henderson examines autobiographies by 'successful' feminists Anne Summers, Susan Ryan, and Wendy McCarthy in 'The Tidiest Revolution: Regulative Feminist Autobiography and the De-Facement of the Australian

Women's Movement' (*ALS* 20:iii[2002] 178–91). She suggests that 'these feminist texts have been attracted by the lure of power and authority that the regulative codes of conventional autobiography promise, and have in many ways been textually tamed' (p. 179). Henderson suspects that these women's consciousness of writing for the historical record entails a shoring up of 'a specifically masculine type of sensibility' (p. 185). Of related interest is Ken Stewart's reading of autobiographies that engage with both feminism and academia in 'The Roundabout and the Road: Shirley Walker, Jill Ker Conway and Female Autobiography' (in Stewart and Walker, eds., *'Unemployed at Last!' Essays on Australian Literature to 2002 for Julian Croft*, pp. 119–23). Gillian Whitlock also discusses the development of the 'academic self' in autobiographical writing in 'Leaving "ME"' (*AuHR* 26[2002] 12 paras.). In this response to an autobiographical piece by writer and academic Kerryn Goldsworthy, 'After the Academy' (*AuBR* 242[2002] 24–8), Whitlock considers the effects of different kinds of institutions on academic selfhood, and suggests that the 'readily available script' repeated by many Australian academics regarding the degeneration of academic life in this country might be overstated. This prompted responses in the *Australian Humanities Review* from Kerryn Goldsworthy (*AuHR* 28[2003] 6 paras.), Adi Wimmer (*AuHR* 28[2002] 6 paras.), Philip Neilsen (*AuHR* 26[2002] 2 paras.), and Nicholas Birns (*AuHR* 26[2002] 4 paras.). Questions of truth and authority as they apply to autobiography are also raised by Donna Lee Brien in 'Being Honest About Lying: Defining the Limits of Auto/biographical Writing' (*TJAAWP* 6:i[2002] 29 paras.).

Craven, ed., *The Best Australian Essays 2002* includes autobiographical pieces by Kerryn Goldsworthy and Peter Foster (who admits that he was once a drummer), a piece by Ihab Hassan on the role of rootlessness in our literary culture and spiritual lives, and some explorations into European and translated literature from Murray Bail, Brian Castro, and Peter Porter.

The role of place and family in semi-autobiographical writing is again raised in Emma Sorensen's interview with Gillian Mears, 'A Map of Mears' (*Meanjin* 61:iii[2002] 72–80). Similar issues arise in Hazel Rowley's essay on Christina Stead in Peter Craven's collection. Rowley discusses Stead's use of letters from friends and family as material for her novels, and the implications of her inclusion of vividly recognizable portraits of people she knew in her novels. Rowley also takes up some of the problems faced by Stead and other expatriate Australian writers. Further light on Stead's writing process is shed by Margaret Harris in her essay, 'Dearest Munx: The Love Letters of Christina Stead' (*AuBR* 243[2002] 30–7), in which she discusses a series of letters between Stead and her partner, Bill Blake, that have recently come out from under embargo.

Rosamund Dalziell, in 'Shame and Slaughter' (*Meanjin* 61:iii[2002] 97–105), considers the role of shame in driving the autobiographical act in Robert Drewe's *The Shark Net*. Dalziell also edited *Selves Crossing Cultures: Autobiography and Globalisation*, a collection of papers addressing the intersection of life-writing, culture, place, and identity. David Parker, in 'Locating the Self in Moral Space: Globalization and Autobiography', looks at Andrew Riemer's *Inside Outside* and Ien Ang's 'On Not Speaking Chinese: Postmodern Ethnicity and the Politics of Diaspora', alongside autobiographies by American writers Eric Liu and James McBride in the light of the changes globalization may have brought to the contexts and processes of identity-formation. Riemer is also the focus of Mary Besmeres's consideration of the effects of taking on another culture: she looks at the role of embarrassment—as a concept structured by particular cultural values—in 'Immigrant Embarrassment and Self-Translation in Andrew Riemer's *The Hapsburg Café*'. Joy Hooton discusses how the experience of war may have affected Boyd's sense of home and belonging in 'The Self as Homeless: The Case of Martin Boyd'. Hal Porter's representations of Japan are read as 'an index of subjectivity, in terms of its relation to memory, nationalism and alterity' (p. 92) in David McCooey's 'Orientalism and Nostalgia: Hal Porter and Japan'. Adrian Carton uses autobiography to 'recover' the hybrid voice from the totalizing and sometimes appropriative effects of globalization; his account of growing up without a singular claim to national or ethnic identity illuminates his theoretical considerations in 'Hybridity and Autobiography: Eurasian Selves in Transnational Transit'. Gillian Whitlock, in 'Strategic Remembering: Fabricating Local Subjects', sees recent memoirs by Australian intellectuals as an effect of, and response to, intensely conflicting notions of nationhood, the role of the intellectual, and particularly the testimonies of the 'Bringing Them Home' Report. She notes that reconciliation drives and is being driven by memoir, both Indigenous and non-Indigenous. Christine Watson relates her experiences as a non-Aboriginal fieldworker living and working closely with an Aboriginal community, and the effects of her involvement in the social practices and cosmology of the community on her sense of selfhood, in 'Experiences in the Field: Negotiating between Selves'.

Tanya Dalziell considers the contradictory role of ethnography in constructing the figure of the 'sympathetic woman' in '"We should try, while there is yet time, to gather all the information possible of a race fast dying out": Unsettling Sympathetic Women' (*AuFS* 17[2002] 325–42). Dalziell looks at Katherine Langloh Parker's *Australian Legendary Tales* and Catherine Martin's *An Australian Girl* to examine the figure of the sympathetic white woman in colonial Australia with an eye to the implications of such representations in contemporary feminist and postcolonial work.

Also considering the role of the white woman writer as ethnographer is Gillian Whitlock, in 'Instant Infamy: A Short History of *Broometime*' (in Gilbert and Johnston, eds., pp. 235–53). Among the many questions raised by the writing and reception of Varga and Coombs's text are those of the relationship between writer and subject in travel writing, the recent emergence of the memoir or travelogue as a means for non-Aboriginal writers to reassess their relationship to Aboriginal Australia, the positioning of immigrant Australians in debates about reconciliation, and collaborative forms of writing within a lesbian relationship. Of related interest is Judy Skene's 'Pulped Fiction: *Broometime* and the Ethics of Oral History' (*JAS* 72[2002] 181–9). Skene's consideration of the controversy over the use of oral history and testimonies in the text raises a question that has been ubiquitous in work on Indigenous literature this year, that of the position of non-Indigenous writers and academics in speaking for or about Indigenous Australians. Skene suggests some ethical guidelines for oral history, as does Anita Heiss in 'Writing about Indigenous Australia: Some Issues to Consider and Protocols to Follow—A Discussion Paper' (*Southerly* 62:ii[2002] 197–205). In this balanced overview of arguments about 'writing about Indigenous Australia', she cites Indigenous and non-Indigenous writers and academics regarding the importance of consultation and respect.

This special edition of *Southerly*, 'Stories Without End' (62:ii[2002]), is a wide-ranging collection of Indigenous and non-Indigenous stories, essays, poems, and drama. Sabina Paula Hopfer examines the work of Lionel Fogarty in 'Re-reading Lionel Fogarty: An Attempt to Feel into Texts Speaking of Decolonisation' (*Southerly* 62:ii[2002] 45–64), and Anne Brewster looks at the interventions of Aboriginal writing (particularly life-writing) in the public sphere in 'Aboriginal Life Writing and Globalisation: Doris Pilkington's *Follow the Rabbit-Proof Fence*' (*Southerly* 62:ii[2002] 153–61). The release in 2002 of the film adaptation of Pilkington's book, directed by Phillip Noyce and with screenplay by Christine Olsen, followed by two reprints of the book, have sparked a renewed interest in it, both in academic journals and in the media more generally. Tony Hughes D'Aeth looks at the marketing and reception of the film in 'Which Rabbit-Proof Fence? Empathy, Assimilation, Hollywood' (*AuHR* 27[2002] 30 paras.), positioning the film within an emerging history of the stolen generations. He writes that 'well-established (and well-founded) critiques of universalism are bypassed by the language of empathy, but also by an implicit understanding that Hollywood film acts as a *de facto* forum for final justice, for "global" justice'. Monique Rooney looks at the forms of storytelling used by Phillip Noyce, particularly as they relate to fairy tale, in '"Echoes Across the Flats": Storytelling and Phillip Noyce's *Rabbit Proof Fence*' (*Southerly* 62:iii[2002] 107–17). Tony Birch, in '"This is a true story": Rabbit-Proof Fence, "Mr Devil" and the Desire to Forget' (*CulSR* 8:i[2002] 117–29), considers the marketing of the film, and notes some personal reactions and observations.

Kate Douglas raises some pertinent questions as to the role of life-writing in normalizing certain beliefs and experiences in the light of the current popularity of the genre, in 'The Universal Autobiographer: The Politics of Normative Readings' (*JAS* 72[2002] 173–9). Examining in detail the marketing and reception of Donna Meehan's *It's No Secret* and Rosalie Fraser's *Shadow Child*, Douglas argues that 'dominant social values relating to universal subjects and narratives of social success or the overcoming of adversity permeate the production and reception of autobiographies' (p. 3), also noting that life stories about race and dispossession are often received in such a way as to place emphasis on personal, and not national or institutional, responsibility. Of related interest are Dolors Collellmir's 'Australian Aboriginal Women Writers and the Process of Defining and Articulating Aboriginality' (in Russell, ed., *Caught Between Cultures: Women, Writing and Subjectivities*, pp. 53–75) and Graham Huggan's 'Ethnic Autobiography and the Cult of Authenticity' (in Callahan, ed., pp. 37–62).

Kay Schaffer, in 'Stolen Generation Narratives in Local and Global Contexts' (*Antipodes* 16:i[2002] 5–10), explores the effects of stolen generation narratives (and particularly the 'Bringing Them Home' Report) on public life in Australia and overseas. She suggests that these stories had been told before, in various forms, but that the 'translation' they had undergone, into fiction or autobiography, had rendered them much less shocking to white readers than those found in the report. She argues that the 'Bringing Them Home' narratives sometimes show damage that is irreparable—telling the stories of people who have not necessarily had happy endings and speaking not only of past injustices, but of their ongoing effects. Of related interest is Alisoun Neville's discussion of the role Indigenous life-writing might play in challenging institutional discourse in '"The killing times are still with us": Readings of Truth in Ginibi's *Haunted by the Past*' (*R&C* 44:i[2002] 124–9).

Some recent books about the effect of mission life on Aboriginal identities are reviewed by Kim Scott in 'Between Black and White' (*Bul* 120:6326[2002] 74–5), including those by Edie Wright, Lynette Russell, Albert Holt, Fabienne Bayet-Charlton, Doris Pilkington, and Ambrose Mungala Chalarimeri.

Fiona Probyn considers the ways in which Muecke and Somerville negotiate writing about Indigenous Australians in 'A Poetics of Failure Is No Bad Thing: Stephen Muecke and Margaret Somerville's White Writing' (*JAS* 75[2002] 17–26). Probyn suggests that the work of Somerville and Muecke is marked by 'a poetics of failure that foregrounds the limitations of the project to speak with/on behalf of, to write with/on behalf of, Indigenous people and Indigenous knowledge' (p. 25). Probyn extends this argument in 'How Does the Settler Belong?' (*Westerly* 47[2002] 75–95), comparing the approaches to settler belonging made by Somerville and by Peter Read in *Belonging: Australians, Place and Aboriginal Ownership*, emphasizing again the need to take into account the 'epistemic violence' through which settler culture lays claim to belonging. Probyn argues that Read's insistence that Aboriginality be supplementary to settler belonging is contradicted by the consistent focus on Aboriginality in his own work.

Lisa Slater thinks of Somerville's work as 'an important intervention in the uneasy relationship between feminism and postcolonialism' (p. 182) in 'Is Any Body Home? Rewriting the Crisis of Belonging in Margaret Somerville's *Body/Landscape Journals*' (*Southerly* 62:i[2002] 181–92). Slater considers Somerville's strategies for recognizing different ways of belonging, in an embodied sense, to the land. Michael Jacklin examines the other side of Indigenous–non-Indigenous collaborations in 'Collaboration and Resistance in Indigenous Life Writing' (*ACS* 20:i[2002] 27–45) by looking at *The Two Worlds of Jimmie Barker* and *Goodbye Riverbank*. Of related interest is Wenche Ommundsen's consideration of the implications of collaboration in Chinese Australian life-writing in 'Of Dragons and Devils: Chinese-Australian Life Stories' (*JASAL* 1[2002] 67–80).

Ceridwen Spark looks at the limitations of Native Title Law in expressing the complexities of Aboriginal Australians' relationships with land in 'Rethinking Emplacement, Displacement and Indigeneity: *Radiance*, *Auntie Rita* and *Don't Take Your Love To Town*' (*JAS* 75[2002] 95–103). She writes that these texts 'acknowledge person–place relations that would be negated and excluded by the Native Title framework as it currently exists' (pp. 96–7). Frances Devlin-Glass considers the role of the internet and audio-visual technologies in the revival and protection of Indigenous (particularly Yanyuwa) culture, comparing this process to the Irish Literary Revival, in 'Reviving Cultures: Irish Culture in the Nineteenth Century and Aboriginal Culture in Cyberspace in the Early Twenty-First Century' (in Stewart and Walker, eds., pp. 18–34.)

Sue Ryan-Fazilleau, in 'Thomas Keneally's *The Chant of Jimmie Blacksmith* and the Palimpsest of Jimmy Governor' (*CE&S* 25:i[2002] 27–39) argues that Keneally's retelling of the story of Jimmy Governor attempts to 'erase the colonialist attitudes' underpinning contemporary representations of his life but only succeeds in reinscribing traces of his own, 1970s-inflected, ideology. Of related interest is Sheila Collingwood-Whittock's 'Sally Morgan's *My Place*: Exposing the (Ab)original "Text" Behind Whitefella's History' (*CE&S* 25:i[2002] 41–58). Also in this volume is Françoise Kral's 'Resurfacing through Palimpsests: A (False) Quest for Repossession in the Works of Mudrooroo and Alexis Wright' (*CE&S* 25:i[2002] 7–14). Kral looks at the use of the palimpsest in the landscapes and intertextual devices of both novelists. Of related interest is Anne Maxwell's 'Melancholy in Mudrooroo's *Dr Wooreddy's Prescription*' (in Callahan, ed., pp. 63–83).

Eva Rask Knudsen, in 'Mission Completed? On Mudrooroo's Contribution to the Politics of Aboriginal Literature in Australia' (in Stilz, ed., pp. 321–32), makes an illuminating critical reading of both *Dr Wooreddy's Prescription for Enduring the End of the World* and *Master of the Ghost Dreaming*, taking the mission as emblematic of Aboriginal experience in Australia. She reads Mudrooroo's novels as working against a politics of identity 'that focuses on essential notions of being at the expense of cross-cultural processes of becoming' (p. 329), and in doing so makes a forceful argument against the 'cultural essentialism' she sees as fuelling the 'critical preoccupation' with Mudrooroo's identity. Knudsen also notes that, while both character and writer in *Dr Wooreddy* are constrained by white forms and customs (in the case of the latter, the genre of the historical realist novel), both the protagonist and writer of *Master of the Ghost Dreaming* are much more successful in breaking free of white customs, generic and otherwise.

Gerry Turcotte also takes up Mudrooroo's rewriting or 'making uncanny' of generic markers in 'Mission Impossible: Mudrooroo's Gothic Inter/Mission Statement' (in Stilz, ed., pp. 333–46). In this discussion of Mudrooroo's use of the Gothic in *Dr Wooreddy*, *Master of the Ghost Dreaming*, and, particularly, *The Undying*, Turcotte looks at narratives of contamination and contagion as appropriate metaphors for the effect of colonization on Aboriginal culture, and at the play with the fear of 'reverse colonization' implicit in vampire narratives. Turcotte argues that, in *The Undying*, Mudrooroo 'specifically invokes a range of master narratives in order to expose their hidden agendas' (p. 343).

(d) Drama

In his *The Convict Theatres of Early Australia, 1788–1840*, Robert Jordan replaces earlier speculative and fragmentary accounts of Australian convict theatre with a coherent narrative based on an exhaustive search for documentary evidence. While gaps remain in the story, some of which may eventually be filled, it is hard to imagine any future scholar changing Jordan's outline in any radical way. Besides raising the possibility of a theatre in Sydney as early as 1794, Jordan suggests that the theatre associated with the convict baker Robert Sidaway may have been in fairly continuous operation from 1796 until 1804 or even 1807. His chapters on this theatre, its actors and audiences, are based on extensive biographical research into convicts associated with it, which is presented in a seventy-page appendix. The remaining chapters provide briefer but equally compelling accounts of the convict theatres operating for various shorter periods at penal stations at Norfolk Island, Emu Plains, and Port Macquarie, as well as an overview of theatrical events in Sydney up to 1830. As Jordan notes, the most striking features of these early attempts to establish theatres are their number and persistence, now fully revealed to us for the first time.

Nathan Garvey surveys the evidence, in 'Reviewing Australia's First Performance: *The Recruiting Officer* in Sydney 1789' (*ADS* 40[2002] 26–57), putting forward some well-supported speculations as to the circumstances of this production: its instigation, cast, text, venue, staging, and actors. 'The Hard Road to Stardom: The Early Career of Essie Jenyns' (*ADS* 40[2002] 74–89) is Janette Gordon-Clarke's account of the state of stardom in colonial Australia.

In 'Young Colonists on the Stage: Adaptations of *Paul et Virginie* by James Cobb and Marcus Clarke' (*ADS* 40[2002] 90–105), Ian Henderson looks at the implications of changes made to the narrative of Saint-Pierre's novel in its Australian adaptation for the stage by James Cobb, particularly of its arguments regarding the New World, innocence, and sexuality. Henderson relates these changes to a burgeoning and increasingly respectable female audience for the Australian theatre of the 1840s, and to anti-transportation campaigns, while also bearing in mind the possibility of radically different responses from ex-convict audiences, particularly with regard to the play's treatment of slavery. He also looks briefly at a manuscript sketch made by Marcus Clarke for an adaptation of the story, clearly owing a debt to Cobb's adaptation, and also reflective of Clarke's interest in Saint-Pierre's novel as evidenced by its repeated mention in *His Natural Life*. Also on adaptation, Elizabeth Webby examines the differences in perceived audience expectations revealed in earlier and later Australian stage and film versions as compared with the 1957 British film adaptation of Boldrewood's novel, in 'Killing the Narrator: National Differences in Adaptations of *Robbery Under Arms*' (*JASAL* 1[2002] 44–50).

Michelle Arrow, in *Upstaged: Australian Women Dramatists in the Limelight at Last*, sets the record straight as to the role of women dramatists in Australian theatre from the 1920s through to the 1960s. In the process she effectively rewrites this period of Australia's theatre history, arguing for a complete revision of the common perception that such history began with Ray Lawler and was continued only by the New Wave of the 1970s. Arrow provides a detailed examination of the working lives and conditions of playwrights, including Oriel Gray, Mona Brand, Gwen Meredith, and Betty Roland, all of whom were prominent throughout the 1940s and 1950s but who 'had all but disappeared from public view' by the late 1960s (p. 191). Her insightful readings of autobiographical writing by these playwrights explores the conflicts they faced as 'professional' (as opposed to 'literary') writers and as women, conflicts illuminated by their representation in the media as 'prize-winning housewives'.

Most impressive perhaps is Arrow's work on the substantial involvement of women in the 'golden years' of radio and radio drama, during which it became increasingly feasible to make a living as a playwright. She investigates the cultural, social, and material conditions under which women such as Mary Wilton and Kay Keavney worked, as well as the decline of both radio drama and opportunities for Australian playwrights with the coming of television.

Arrow also looks at the politics of the production and support of local drama during the period, including that from theatres, writers' organizations, publications, reviewers, and competitions. Chapters are devoted to the political commitment of women playwrights, with an astute focus on the retrospective reconstruction of political belief in their autobiographies, and also to the key role of women playwrights in the New Theatre movement. Arrow suggests that Mark Davis's argument (in *Gangland*) 'neglects another, important area of [baby] boomer dominance—their control over the stories of Australia's cultural past' (p. 195). She argues that the New Left and New Wave theatre movements effectively shouldered the New Theatres out of history, failing to acknowledge their debts to the earlier movement: 'They have often neglected the role played by the pre-60s pioneers in theatre and radio, and hence (unwittingly?) rewritten the story to place themselves at the centre of it' (p. 194). In attempting to write the history of Australian women playwrights from the 1920s to the 1960s, Arrow has ended up writing a comprehensive history of this period of Australian theatre as a whole.

John McCallum argues for a similar redress in 'Rattling the Manacles: Genre and Nationalism in the Neglected Plays of the Campbell Howard Collection, 1920–1955' (in Stewart and Walker, eds., pp. 86–104). Surveying what he suggests are the best works in the collection, McCallum looks at the 'genre' plays written for commercial theatre: bush realist melodramas, station dramas, and family sagas, amongst others, suggesting that these are 'the truly neglected plays of the 1920s–1950s' (p. 87), which have been overlooked in discussions of nationalism in Australian theatre.

The role of government in defining 'national' culture is examined by Donald Batchelor in 'Political Maneuvering behind the Scenes: The Development of the National Theatre Idea in Australia during the 1940s' (*ADS* 40[2002] 58–73).

John Rickard, in 'Culture for the Colonials' (*Meanjin* 61:iii[2002] 128–38), gives a lively account of the post-war Australian tours by the Old Vic and Stratford theatre companies, and the impact they had on the local theatrical scene. Rickard suggests that the embrace of Britishness exemplified in the reception of these tours was perhaps an expression of worry about post-war migration: 'this was the time when Australians were adjusting to the realities of the postwar immigration program, and when migrants were being told to assimilate to "the Australian way of life". But what was "the Australian way of life"? The need to articulate just what migrants were being expected to conform to encouraged a reaffirmation of the Anglo-Saxon—and by extension Anglo-Celtic—heritage' (p. 137).

In '*Summer of the Seventeenth Doll* and *Summer of the Aliens*: Arcadia, Dystopia and the Australian Ethos' (in Stewart and Walker, eds., pp. 105–18), T.G.A. Nelson compares representations of Australian life and ethos in the plays by Ray Lawler and Louis Nowra.

Donald Pulford, in 'Two Plays, One Nation' (*Meanjin* 61:iii[2002] 121–7), looks at racism and xenophobia in Australian culture in the light of the 'Children Overboard' affair and public acceptance of the mandatory detention of asylum-seekers, relating this to the rise of Pauline Hanson's One Nation party in 1997. He reads Alex Buzo's plays *Norm and Ahmed* and *Normie and Tuan* as explorations of the persistent anxieties underlying both the current attitudes towards asylum-seekers and the popularity of One Nation.

In 'Immigrant Voices in Recent Australian Theatre' (in Pons, ed., pp. 70–5), Pulford traces a progression in the aspects of immigrant experience represented in Australian drama. Asserting the role of theatre in developing and reinforcing 'hybrid' identities, Pulford also notes the emergence of migrant theatre into the Australian theatrical mainstream, suggesting that the commercial success of productions such as the *Wogs out of Work* series may stem from their 'celebratory' aspects. He then considers the sell-out Melbourne season of Tess Lyssiotis's trilogy, seeing it as evidence of a new place for migrant experiences within general representations of human experience.

Ulrike Garde, 'Drama by German-Speaking Playwrights in the Australian Theatrical Landscape: Changing Attitudes and Expectations' (*AUMLA* 98[2002] 99–115), raises some fruitful questions about the role of cultural products from 'elsewhere' in the development of Australian national identity in her discussion of the Australian reception of Austrian, German, and Swiss plays.

Theatre with active links to overseas political events, and Australia's implication in them, is examined by Lesley Delmenico in 'Historiography and Rewriting: Performing on/as East Timorese Bodies in *Death at Balibo* and *Diablo!*' (*ADS* 40[2002] 8–25). Delmenico looks at two productions in Darwin which involved the local Timorese community, considering them 'as a cycle of representation and resistance' (p. 8).

Contemporary theatre is also under the microscope in Russell Fewster's 'A Director in Rehearsal: Neil Armfield and the Company B Production of *The Blind Giant is Dancing* by Stephen Sewell' (*ADS* 40[2002] 106–18). Analysing Armfield's directing practice, Fewster notes that, while it is 'more democratic than much of standard Australian mainstream practice' (p. 114), Armfield still offers prescriptive direction.

(e) Poetry

Australia lost one of its most prolific and significant literary figures when poet, playwright, autobiographer, and novelist Dorothy Hewett died on 25 August 2002. Tributes and obituaries appeared in all major Australian newspapers and literary journals. *Overland* 169[2002] included a memoir from Hewett's husband, Merv Lilley ('My Life with Dorothy Hewett'), Nicole Moore's 'Dorothy Hewett: Twentieth-Century Writer', and Jasna Novakovic's review of Hewett's impact on Australian theatre, 'Fictional Characters Take Over'.

Hewett was never afraid to talk politics, and another poet, Peter Porter, takes up the theme of poetry's continuing relevance to public life in 'The Survival of Poetry' (*AuBR* 245[2002] 30–6). Subtitling his piece 'Postponing the Apocalypse', Porter argues for the steadfastness of poetry as commentator in the face of ongoing 'states of emergency', such as that heralded by the attacks in New York in 2001. Of related interest is Peter Steele's discussion of Porter's poetry, focusing on its attention to the tropes of love and vigilance, 'Swerving to Happiness, A Letter to the World: Love and Peter Porter' (*EST* 12:vi[2002] 34–41).

Porter is among those paying tribute in Bolton, ed., *Homage to John Forbes*. Poets and critics, many of whom were Forbes's friends and contemporaries, recall his life and work. The collection includes remembrances from Bolton, Porter, Carl Harrison-Ford, Laurie Duggan, John Kinsella, Tracy Ryan, and Pam Brown, and an interview with Forbes and Catherine Keneally. Ivor Indyk contributes a thoughtful piece of criticism on the 'awkward grace' of Forbes's poetry; Rosemary Hunter writes about his relationships with women and his understanding of feminism, and Alan Wearne provides a spirited account of his literary loves and influences. Forbes's entertaining account of his own working life is also reprinted here.

In an introduction to his impressive collection, *In Your Face: Contemporary Chinese Poetry in English Translation* (*Otherland* 8[2002] 1–4), Ouyang Yu writes:

> When I looked at these poems, I had a feeling that I was smuggling them into Australia as if they were illegal immigrants that this country

never likes ... and yet by their very existence they insist on coming in, much the same way the recent boatloads of people did whether you like it or not ... they won't help anyone win an election, although they may convert one or two by opening up a new world for us to see. They invite entry, with love, with hatred, with nonchalance, or a mixture of the three ... Hence this anthology, to give back what has been rejected, in your face. (pp. 1–4)

The collection includes translations of work by Melbourne-based poets Shi Xiaojun, Ma Shiju, and Zhang Yougong.

Les Murray might share Ouyang Yu's perception of banging on the door of literary orthodoxy, sometimes to no avail. Indeed, there are similarities in these poets' defiant (and sometimes belligerent) flouting of such orthodoxy. Murray, however, does not seem to have been able to put anyone offside this year. Smith, ed., *Les Murray and Australian Poetry*, is a varied collection of essays on Australia's most internationally successful poet. John Lucas, in 'How It Strikes an Outsider', suggests that Australian poetry has a heterogeneity not always recognized by anthologies and special editions of overseas poetry magazines. He also considers the anxiety of national identity evident in much Australian criticism. Steven Matthews, in 'Murray and a Music of Indirection', questions the sufficiency of critical approaches to Murray's poetry that read his take on the pastoral as 'a direct and uncomplicated relation with locale' (p. 24). Matthews emphasizes the 'oblique, dynamic and unsettled' (p. 28), as well as the performative, elements of Murray's work.

In his detailed look at Murray's use of 'centering' as a meditative process, '"Only the centre holds": The Meditative Landscapes of Les Murray', Martin Leer thinks about the trope of centre in Murray's Australian landscapes. Les Murray, in 'How Fred and I wrote *Fredy Neptune*', comments on his use of vernacular and bilingual voices, and the reception of the book, among other things. Bruce Clunies Ross, in '*Fredy Neptune*: The Art of "Cracking Normal"', reads Murray's poem within the tradition of the verse novel in English in which, he argues, the margins 'are more prominent than the centre, which is mainly vacant' (p. 83). He lauds Murray's use of novelistic and poetic techniques, particularly in creating a vernacular, retrospective, narrating voice, and argues that '*Fredy Neptune* is a move towards stabilizing the genre of the verse novel' (p. 88).

Ian J. Bickerton also lauds Murray's verse novel in 'Fredy Neptune Goes to War' (*JAS* 73[2002] 67–77), reading it as 'history from below'. Gary Clark presents a 'predominantly authorial' reading in 'Transmuting the Black Dog: The Mob and the Body in the Poetry of Les Murray' (*Antipodes* 16:i[2002] 19–24). Clark suggests that Murray's poetry is an effect of, and an escape from, disembodiment. Of related interest is Martin Duwell's insightful reading of Peter Alexander's biography of Murray in 'One of Them Kinds of Kids: The Lives of Les Murray' (*ALS* 20:iii[2002] 192–200).

Marian Devitt surveys a group of poets with a sustained engagement with a particular place in her 'Northern Territory Poetry: Ten Degrees of Separation' (*Thylazine* 5[2002] 32 paras.) The state of Queensland poetry is discussed by Paul Hardacre and poet and event-organizer Brett Dionysius in 'Dionysius Unbound: An Interview with Brett Dionysius' (*LiNQ* 29:i[2002] 9–16).

Anderson, ed., *Australian Divagations: Mallarmé and the 20th Century*, is a collection of essays from a conference held in Melbourne in 1998 to commemorate the centenary of Mallarmé's death, covering a good range of recent scholarship on the connections between Mallarmé and Australia. Rosemary Lloyd looks at Christopher Brennan's reading and criticism of Mallarmé, and at Mallarmé's perhaps less critically engaged than contemplative responses to Brennan's work. Chris Wallace-Crabbe presents a delightfully engaging reading of the relation between Mallarmé and Australian poet John Forbes. For all that Forbes's poetry is heavily invested in popular culture, Wallace-Crabbe argues, 'both were practitioners of a non-mimetic poetry ... of a linguistically aware, oddly pure, self-dismantling art' (p. 31). David Brooks traces the influence of the Symbolist movement on another Australian poet, A.D. Hope, arguing for a more enduring connection than has previously been assumed. In 'The Politics of Symbolism: The Correspondence of Randolph Hughes and Jack Lindsay', John Hawke provides a detailed account of the correspondence between Hughes, whose stout adherence to Symbolist philosophy coincided with fascist and anti-Semitic beliefs, and Lindsay, who had recently converted to Marxism. Their arguments about politics, and about the nature and role of art, are illuminating as to the political implications of Symbolist aesthetics. This piece also provides an interesting context for the Adams and Lee volume (see Section 2(*a*) above).

Michael Brennan, in 'Becoming "Absolutely Modern": Adamson and Tranter's Abandonment' (in Pons, ed., pp. 225–35), reads the development of Robert Adamson's and John Tranter's poetry in the light of Rimbaud's injunction to be 'absolutely modern', and his 'subsequent (or arguably consequent) abandonment of poetry' (p. 234). Brennan's discussion of these Australian poets' transformation of the Symbolist influence is revealing, particularly regarding Adamson's ironic play with the idea of modernity and Tranter's struggles with the possible defeat of meaning inherent in the poem as artefact.

Australia's most famous non-existent poet was the subject of two articles this year: Cassandra Pybus, in 'The Black Swan of Trespass: James McAuley and the Ern Malley Hoax' (*Brick* 70[2002] 140–9), gives a biographical sketch of the friendship between McAuley and Harold Stewart, along with an account of the hoax. Cassandra Atherton provides an overview of both the Ern Malley hoax and Gwen Harwood's hoaxes of the *Bulletin* editors in '"Fuck all editors": The Ern Malley Affair and Gwen Harwood's *Bulletin* Scandal' (*JAS* 72[2002] 151–7).

Olga Sudlenkova offers a reading of eighteenth- and nineteenth-century British attitudes and poetic responses to emigration, particularly emigration to Australia. In 'Fair Australasia: A Poet's Farewell to Emigrants' (in Stilz, ed., pp. 267–74), Sudlenkova focuses on Thomas Campbell's poem 'Lines on the Departure of Emigrants to New South Wales' [1828], revealing its understandings of, and hopes for, Australia, and use of America as a model for utopian pictures of Australia. Frank Molloy considers the influence of Ireland on colonial Australian poetry, including that of Eliza Hamilton Dunlop, Charles Harpur, and Victor Daley, in '"Affection's broken chain": The Irish and Colonial Poetry' (*AJIS* 2[2002] 122–34).

Of particular interest this year was a special edition of *Victorian Poetry* (*VP* 40:i[2002]) on nineteenth-century Australian poetry. In her introduction, Meg Tasker notes that 'there are now more "cross-over" Australianists/Victorianists ... who are well equipped to read nineteenth-century Australian writing in its Anglo-

Australian cultural, political and social context—that is, with an intimate knowledge of the literary and cultural "norms" against which many of the colonial writers and readers still defined themselves' (p. 1), something certainly in evidence in this broad and impressive collection.

The relationship between politics and poetry is questioned in several of these essays. Meg Tasker, in 'Francis Adams and *Songs of the Army of the Night*: Negotiating Difference, Maintaining Commitment' (*VP* 40[2002] 71–85), makes a similar point to Christopher Lee in a piece on Henry Lawson mentioned in Section 2(*a*) above (*VP* 40[2002] 87–104): for both Lawson and Adams, the expression of political commitment in their poetry made it particularly difficult to sell. Francis Adams faced the issue raised again and again in the work surveyed this year—'the need to identify and develop valid roles and valid voices for social protest by those whose class and cultural affiliations would not obviously qualify them to make such a protest' (p. 85). Barbara Garlick's 'Colonial Canons: The Case of James Brunton Stephens' (*VP* 40[2002] 55–69) illustrates the ways in which the demands of local print media for topicality can later work against a poet's inclusion in literary canons. Garlick points out the high regard for Stephens's poetry in the late nineteenth century, and his subsequent disappearance from accounts of Australian literature, relating this to the 'public', topical, and thus political nature of much of his work.

Ann Vickery surveys the work of Eliza Hamilton Dunlop, Caroline Leakey, Emma Anderson, Ada Cambridge, Grace Jennings Carmichael, and Louisa Lawson in 'A "Lonely Crossing": Approaching Nineteenth-Century Australian Women's Poetry' (*VP* 40[2002] 33–53). She suggests that women poets were in a similar bind to the one described by Garlick: the marketplace would only accept certain genres and subjects from women poets, which in turn led to them being 'elided in the construction of an Australian literary heritage' (p. 33).

Ian Reid traces a fascinating recurrent trope in 'Marking the Unmarked: An Epitaphic Preoccupation in Nineteenth-Century Australian Poetry' (*VP* 40[2002] 7–20). Exploring the function of images of unmarked graves in Australian poetry of the period, Reid suggests 'the act of inscription itself as a testimony to, and surrogate for, lost meanings' (p. 9). He posits that 'what makes such lonely graves an emblem, then, of a specifically colonial bereavement in a still inchoate society is not only the absence of the one being mourned, but an absence of mourners, too, and of all that the collective observance of mourning would imply about shared meanings' (p. 18). Both Reid and Michael Ackland consider the influence of Wordsworth on Australian poets, particularly Charles Harpur. Ackland's 'From Wilderness to Landscape: Charles Harpur's Dialogue with Wordsworth and Antipodean Nature' (*VP* 40[2002] 21–32) seeks 'to clarify the precise nature of Harpur's debt to Wordsworth, especially as it bears on the relation of thought to landscape depiction in his work, and to show how the Australian, not content with simple emulation, extended Wordsworth's concerns in conformity with his own radical program' (pp. 21–2).

More recent Australian engagements with the elegy are considered in '"To fresh woods and pastures new"? Modern Australian Elegy and Literary Tradition' (in Pons, ed., pp. 127–36). Werner Senn focuses on Australian instances of the 'tombeau', or elegy on the death of a poet, in his discussion of the way in which poets, including David Campbell, Gwen Harwood, and Robert Adamson, work within and depart from the conventions of the elegy. Dennis Haskell, in the same volume, also notes the strength of the elegiac tradition in Australian poetry, pointing to its propensity towards the cynical or 'anti-elegy'. In his study of Bruce Dawe's use of the elegy, Haskell points to a transformation of 'the necessity of death into statements of care, awareness and human value' (p. 144).

In 'Minding your "Ps and Qs": Poetry, Propaganda, Politics and Pictures' (*Papers* 12:ii[2002] 38–49), Alison Halliday examines the illustrations that have accompanied Henry Kendall's 'The Last of his Tribe' when it has been (often) anthologized, and also in its production as a picture book in 1989, illustrated by Percy Trezise and Mary Haginikitas, comparing this with the picture book based on Ted Egan's song 'The Drover's Boy', illustrated by Robert Ingpen. Ken Goodwin, in 'Henry Kendall's Religion' (*ALS* 20:iii[2002] 225–30), takes up Douglas B.W. Sladen's assertion that Kendall 'was something of an outsider in social and literary circles in so far as he was a Roman Catholic' (p. 225). Goodwin concludes that Kendall was not, in fact, Catholic, nor were Catholics subject to any particular censure in Sydney in the period. Of related interest is Doug Jesberg's reading of Kendall's 'Orara' and 'Euterpe: An Ode to Music' in 'Henry Kendall and his Fictions' (*Antithesis* 13[2002] 117–30). Also of related interest is Jennifer Strauss's examination of the nature of Mary Gilmore's faith and beliefs in '"Mary Gilmore, she died in the faith"' (in Stewart and Walker, eds., pp. 59–71).

In 'Deviation and Devotion: Francis Webb's "Homosexual"' (in Pons, ed., pp. 184–91), Noel Rowe offers an enlightening reading, looking at the tensions between deviation and devotion in the poem, and also considering Webb's use of images of innocence and threatening sexuality. His reading of 'Homosexual', in terms of the transfer of power or unsettling of subjectivity that the poem effects, challenges the unproblematic distinction between sin and sinner emphasized in the pastoral care of homosexuals at the time Webb was writing. Rowe suggests that 'There is a difference between seeing oneself as loving Christ in the least and seeing the least as Christ loving; the politicians of morality favour the former as it keeps them in power, but the poem is making the latter happen' (p. 184). Lyn Jacobs also supplies useful critical readings of Webb's poetry in 'Webb's "Socrates"' (*Southerly* 62:iii[2002] 40–6).

Bernadette Brennan raises the ubiquitous question about the nature of the relationship between poetry and politics in 'Poetry and Politics: In Conflict or Conversation? Aboriginal Poetry, Peter Skrzynecki and Bruce Dawe' (*SSEng* 28[2002] 103–23). Brennan asserts poetry's 'capacity to engender empathetic imagination' (p. 104) as a way of informing people's beliefs and understandings. She also relates Noel Rowe's 'fantasy (or was it a dream?)' that Eva Johnson read her poem 'A Letter to My Mother' to the Federal Parliament so that politicians could 'enter into a more companionable way of knowing' (p. 109).

Dennis McDermott, in 'Bare Feet, Broken Glass: Aboriginal Poetry and the Leaving of Trauma' (in Pons, ed., pp. 271–81), writes as both psychologist and poet in thinking about Aboriginal poetry as a 'poetry of witness'. After Natalia Kariaeva, he looks at the process of moving pain 'from the unknowable private sphere to the accessibility of the public' (p. 272), as necessary in recovery from trauma, and also as a role for Aboriginal poetry. He writes of the need to 'spark fresh patterns of neural connection' in order for Aboriginal poetry to 'bridge the gap' between private and communicable experience. McDermott also takes up the overdetermination of authenticity in much discussion of Aboriginal poetry in relation to the damage to identity and self-regard that can be a continuing result of trauma. He warns of the dangers of devaluing the hybridized: 'There is no one Aboriginal voice. The notion of "the" Aboriginal voice denies multiplicity, denies the reality of Aboriginal politics and may, indeed, have little relevance outside broad-brush politicking' (p. 280).

Robert Savage, in 'The Politics of Influence: Bruce Beaver's "Letters to Live Poets"' (*Colloquy* 6[2002] 25 paras.), reads Beaver's sequence in conversation with Rilke, arguing that this opens up a space for 'social concern' apparently absent elsewhere in Beaver's work. Patrick McCauley makes a case for further funding and support for performance poetry, as against 'academic' or 'elitist' poetry, in 'The Dreadful Orthodoxy' (*Quadrant* 46:ix[2002] 62–5). Peter Denney takes an interdisciplinary view of Slessor in 'Botanising on the Asphalt: Australian Modernity and the Street Poetics of Kenneth Slessor' (*JAS* 72[2002] 159–65). Reading Slessor 'in the context of Australian urban modernity and the cultural criticism of Walter Benjamin', Denney explores the poet's 'tendency to relocate meaning away from the metaphysical and direct it towards the everyday life of the multitude, of modernity and mass culture'. He relates this to developments in modern architecture.

Peter Coleman looks at *Quadrant*'s years under the editorship of James McAuley in 'At the Height of our Time? James McAuley's Twenty *Quadrants*' (*Quadrant* 46:ix[2002] 18–21). Of related interest is Geoffrey Lehmann's 'James McAuley: Literary Criticism in the Form of a Memoir' (*Quadrant* 46:xii[2002] 54–8). Also in *Quadrant*, Gary Catalano considers the aural qualities of John Shaw Neilson's poetry, alongside his responses to the landscape of the Mallee and the comparisons often made between the Australian poet and William Blake, in 'Poet in a Landscape: Some Reflections on Shaw Neilson' (*Quadrant* 46:x[2002] 61–5).

In 'Olive Hopegood: "Not every piglet makes a Hamlet"' (*Southerly* 62:i[2002] 115–29), Elizabeth Parsons traces Olive Hopegood through Australian literary history, suggesting some reasons for her poetry manuscript never getting published, and for it subsequently being lost.

John Jenkins, in 'Provincial to Post-Modern: The Poetry of Philip Salom' (*HEAT* 2[2002] 219–30), provides an overview of Salom's work, with some biographical commentary, noting a correspondence between the poet's '"re-making of the self" and the re-invention of cultural forms in a time of rapid, post-industrial change' (p. 225).

Emily Apter reads John Kinsella and Lionel Fogarty in conversation with works by visual artists William Kentridge, Andreas Gursky, and John Klima, in 'The Aesthetics of Critical Habitats' (*October* 99[2002] 21–44). As a frame for her reading, she considers the idea of 'critical habitat', 'as a concept that explores the links between territorial habitat and intellectual habitus; between physical place and ideological forcefield, between economy and ecology' (p. 23). Kinsella himself examines the relationship between city and bush in 'The Shifting City and the Shifting Bush: From Paranoia to Celebration' (*Overland* 169[2002] 23–34). In discussing Dorothy Hewett's writing, Kinsella posits that 'the city and the bush require one another—both are constantly shifting in their relationship. They tend to create paranoid mythologies of one another—both are vulnerable while claiming strength, indifference, and distance' (p. 34). Elsewhere, in 'Distortions: On Questioning the Primacy of the Accented Syllable: Notes on Alternative Spatialities for Poetic Rhythm' (*JCL* 37:i[2002] 133–47), Kinsella draws on his experiences of teaching Australian poetry to British students in discussing the implications, in terms of distortions in rhythm and accented syllables, resulting from reading poetry in different accents.

Eden Liddelow explores the relation of selfhood to syntax in her detailed and insightful discussion of Ania Walwicz's work in 'On a Dark Stage Struck: The Prose Poetry of Ania Walwicz' (in *After Electra*, pp. 172–82). Felicity Plunkett looks at the reception of Dorothy Porter's work in '*The Monkey's Mask* and the Poetics of Excision' (in Stewart and Walker, eds., pp. 72–85). In response to a review by Finola Moorhead, Plunkett considers *The Monkey's Mask* in terms of what has been perceived to have been excised from the text, tracing the workings of loss, mourning, and elegy within it, as well as the metaphors of cutting and excision that pervade both the text and critical responses to it.

(f) The Novel

With "'There are French novels and there are French novels": Charles Reade and the "Other" Sources of Marcus Clarke's *His Natural Life*' (*JASAL* 1[2002] 51–66), Ian Henderson aptly illustrates Meg Tasker's point regarding the abilities of our cross-over Australianists/Victorianists. Elucidating Clarke's debt to the popular romances and melodramas of Charles Reade, Henderson reconstitutes *His Natural Life* 'as a work of Victorian modernity, interested as much in contemporary issues of international significance—issues like the "marriage" question and the place of spirituality in modern life—as it is in reconstructing Australia's convict past' (p. 51). This enables a reading of the novel 'as a response to modern French literature and all it asserted about the composition of "natural life"' (p. 51), a far cry from the previous critical focus on historical sources and the thematics of convictism.

Andrew McCann takes a rather fabulous view of Marcus Clarke's journalism in 'Bohemia and the Dream-life of the Colonial City' (*JASAL* 1[2002] 4–18). He looks at the function of images of Bohemia for nineteenth-century Australian writers, seeing them as a claim to cultural distinction from the middle-class profession of journalism in which most such writers were involved. He considers Clarke's writing of the city as 'phantasmagoric', in Walter Benjamin's sense of the term, arguing that his use of panoramic stylistic devices—mobility of narrative perspective, shifting of scenes, and his depiction of crowds—enabled representations of the city that appeared desirable for their radical otherness from the everyday. He posits that, in Clarke's journalism, 'a city that was barely thirty years old emerges as one capable of producing the same sorts of aesthetic effects as Hugo's Paris or Mayhew's London' (p. 16). Of related interest is Peter Christiansen's account of 'Bohemia's Godfather: George William Louis Marshall-Hall' (*Heat* 3[2002] 91–107), the eccentric music professor and poet who sparked much debate in 1890s Melbourne on bohemianism and associated ideas about manhood and virility.

Helen Thomson's examination of the writing of Catherine Helen Spence is revealing about the implications of Enlightenment philosophy for the colonial project and its literature. In 'Catherine Helen Spence: Enlightenment Woman' (in Pons, ed., pp. 236–44), Thomson suggests that Spence is 'both complicit in the colonial process and part of the counter-discourse to it' (p. 238). Spence's attitude towards (and effective dismissal of) Aboriginal Australians is representative of an

Enlightenment view of 'universal humanity' (informed by Adam Smith's theories of human development) that has no place for the racialized other.

In 'Debatable Ground: Anthony Trollope and the Anxiety of Colonial Space' (in Stewart and Walker, eds., pp. 35–43), Robert Dingley finds a 'semantic diffusion' of the categories of gentleman, squatter, and land-owner in Trollope's *Harry Heathcoate of Gangoil*, suggesting that colonial experience renders these previously fixed concepts unstable. Dingley argues that Harry Heathcoate's experience points to the fact that 'settlement is always provisional and always vulnerable to reverse' (p. 42).

Patrick Morgan considers the nineteenth-century Australian preoccupation with the narrative trope of 'the lost aristocrat down under' (p. 9) in 'Tichborne Fictions' (*Margin* 57[2002] 5–9). He argues that 'The lost aristocratic fable was perhaps the main organizing principle of the Australian colonial novel, but it has not come down to us in any clarity because it was overtaken and suppressed by the late nineteenth-century vogue for exclusive nationalism' (p. 9), suggesting that this trope celebrated aspects of social mobility and ambiguity in Australian national identity that are now elided by a more restrictive sense of what is Australian.

Morgan's argument is reinforced by Toby R. Benis's examination of an early convict text in 'Criminal Transport: George Barrington and the Colonial Cure' (*ALS* 20:iii[2002] 167–77). Benis looks at the way in which Barrington's text speaks to some of the 'galvanizing fears of its era', regarding convicts as carriers of physical diseases and social contamination in their mobility between criminal and 'respectable' society. Barrington's *Voyage to Botany Bay* presents a different view of transportation as a redemptive opportunity for the reinstatement of social and economic distinctions. Of related interest is Suzanne Rickard's 'Whose Voice Is It Anyway? The Eighteenth-Century Colonial Experience of George Barrington' (in Dalziell, ed., pp. 41–52). Rickard reviews the 'publishing scam', which resulted in the works attributed to Barrington, and their popularity in England and elsewhere.

J.S. Ryan traces Rolf Boldrewood's observations and insights into the social history of Australian gold-mining in 'From a Mining Warden's Verandah: Thomas Browne as "Nation" Watcher-Ethnographer' (in Stewart and Walker, eds., pp. 44–58), focusing on the contribution of miners from overseas to 'the evolving Australian character and stock' (p. 57) as represented in Boldrewood's fiction. Brenda McAvoy surveys the work of Jessie Lloyd, in 'The Life and Writings of Silverleaf' (*Margin* 56[2002] 8–27), noting her interest in the implications of gold-mining for the natural environment, and her sustained focus on Australian subject matter.

For the copy-text of her scholarly edition of Tasma's (Jessie Couvreur's) best-known novel, *Uncle Piper of Piper's Hill*, Margaret Bradstock returned to the version serialized in the *Australasian* between January and May 1888 under the title *The Pipers of Piper's Hill*. This, as she demonstrates in her detailed introduction, was the only one of many later editions and reprintings over which Tasma had any control. As is usual with titles in the Colonial Texts series produced by the Australian Scholarly Editions Centre at ADFA, this work has been meticulously edited, with extensive explanatory notes, a list of editor's emendations, and a sample collation. Bradstock also provides a succinct account of Tasma's life and work, along with much valuable information on the reception of this novel, hailed by the

Spectator in 1889 as worthy of a place alongside Clarke's *His Natural Life* and Boldrewood's *Robbery under Arms*.

Another very welcome scholarly edition of a novel by a nineteenth-century Australian woman has appeared in the Academy Editions of Australian Literature series. Rosemary Campbell's edition of Catherine Martin's *An Australian Girl* makes available for the first time since the first edition of 1890 the full text of the novel. It was later abridged at the request of the publisher, Richard Bentley, to remove much of the material relating to such contemporary debates as euthanasia, eugenics, religious doubt, and German socialism, in favour of a greater focus on the central story of love and betrayal. Rosemary Campbell's introduction provides a fascinating account of the novel's production and reception, showing once again how influential English publishers could be in determining the Australian literary tradition. Her detailed explanatory notes also provide excellent background information about Martin's many political, religious, intellectual, and literary references, enabling contemporary readers to appreciate the range and depth of this remarkable novel.

Australian Literary Studies (20:iv[2002]) celebrates the centenary of publication of Miles Franklin's *My Brilliant Career*, another text which suffered at the hands of British publishers. Susan Sheridan looks at the publication history and critical reception of the novel as it has been swept up in varying critical and ideological tides in 'The Career of the *Career*' (*ALS* 20:iv[2002] 330–5). Stephen Garton, in 'Contesting Enslavement: Marriage, Manhood and *My Brilliant Career*' (*ALS* 20:iv[2002] 336–49), provides an analysis of the confusions and insights into the erotic, political, and cultural implications of 'manhood' within the novel. He suggests that the portrayal of Harold as the 'ideal bushman' type of the 1890s reveals a deep uneasiness about colonial masculinity.

Elizabeth Webby notices similarities between the narrative modes of *My Brilliant Career* and Joseph Furphy's *Such is Life*, pointing out that, while critical approaches to the latter have changed dramatically over time, critics still often fail to distinguish author from narrator in Franklin's novel. Jill Roe, on the other hand, makes a biographical reading in thinking about the influence of Goulburn as a location in the writing of the novel, in '*My Brilliant Career* and 1890s Goulburn' (*ALS* 20:iv[2002] 359–69). Bruce Scates also discusses the novel within its historical context in '*My Brilliant Career* and Radicalism' (*ALS* 20:iv[2002] 370–8), arguing that 'the radical disquiet of *My Brilliant Career*, its forceful egalitarianism, its endless parody of class distinction, its strident sympathy for the dispossessed, drew much of its inspiration from the Georgist critique of land monopoly' (p. 373), placing the novel within the nineteenth-century radical tradition.

Jane Hunt questions the assumption that Sybilla's mother was based on Susannah Franklin in 'Unrelaxing Fortitude: Susannah Franklin' (*ALS* 20:iv[2002] 379–88). Hunt's examination of the relationship between Miles Franklin and her mother supports Franklin's assertion that the portrait in the novel is fictional. Susan Magarey considers '*My Brilliant Career* and Feminism' (*ALS* 20:iv[2002] 389–98), looking at feminist readings and reception of the novel, and also at Franklin's attempts to balance work for 'causes' with her writing.

Mimi Colligan follows up references in Furphy's *Such is Life* to women who lived as men in 'The Mysterious Edward/Ellen de Lacy Evans: The Picaresque in Real Life' (*LTJ* 69[2002] 59–68). Furphy also rates a mention in Marion Halligan's 'Such is Gossip' (*Meanjin* 61:iii[2002] 62–9), a discussion of the relationship between novels and gossip. Robert Wilson provides a biographical sketch of convict author James Hardy Vaux in 'Adventures of a Literary Lag' (*Margin* 57[2002] 10–14). Caroline Innet, in 'Our First Bushranger Book' (*Margin* 57[2002] 14–18), considers *Michael Howe, the Last and Worst of the Bush Rangers of Van Diemen's Land*, and looks at early tussles over control of the colonial press.

Eve Langley's work, according to Joanne Winning, in 'Wilde Identifications: Queering the Sexual and the National in the Work of Eve Langley' (*ALS* 20:iv[2002] 301–16), has been perceived to have the '"taint" of auto/biographical "excess"' (p. 301) for which female novelists are often marginalized. In her wide-ranging reading of Langley's unpublished novel 'Wild Australia', Winning argues that Langley's identification with Wilde can be read as a strategy for articulating marginalized sexual and national identities. She relates Langley's use of Wilde to that of Anglo-American lesbian modernists (particularly Dorothy Richardson). She also questions the position of Wilde in the novel as colonial revenant, rendering Langley's 'unreconstructed' nationalism problematic. Of related interest is Rhonda Ellis's analysis of Joy L. Thwaite's *The Importance of Being Eve Langley* and Lucy Frost's *Wilde Eve: Eve Langley's Story*, in 'Who Was Eve Langley?' (*Colloquy* 6[2002] 34 paras.).

Ian Saunders, in 'On Appropriation: Two Novels of Dark and Barnard Eldershaw' (*ALS* 20:iv[2002] 287–300), points to some significant similarities in the structures and plots of *Tomorrow and Tomorrow and Tomorrow* and *The Little Company*. He makes a case for a 'borrowing' relationship between the two novels, suggesting that the structure of *Tomorrow* provided Dark with a way to bring together the 'scraps' that she had been writing into the form of a novel. Of related interest is Robert Darby's 'Dampening the Incendiary Ardour: The Roots of Marjorie Barnard's *The Dry Spell*' (*Quadrant* 46:vi[2002] 62–8), which reads the story in the light of Barnard's other work and her political engagements.

Robert L. Ross compares two novels written during the Depression in 'Departures to the Promised Land: Kylie Tennant's *The Battlers* and John Steinbeck's *The Grapes of Wrath*' (in Pons, ed., pp. 37–43). Ross notes that the two novels have often been compared, in that both subvert certain national literary traditions and explore utopian possibilities. Of related interest is Jane Grant's study, in 'Rehearsing the Novel' (*NLAN* 8:i[2002] 14–17), of 'the extreme and unusual lengths' Tennant went to 'to ensure the veracity of her copy'.

Anne Pender takes issue with 'psychoanalytical' readings of Christina Stead's work made by Hazel Rowley and others in her *Christina Stead: Satirist*. She argues there has been an under-recognition of Stead's work as satire, and that many of the criticisms often levelled at her novels—such as excess, exaggeration, and use and distortion of real people in her characterization—are in fact markers of satire. She suggests that critics often read Stead's portraits as evidence of some pathology or anger directed at the 'models' for her characters, overlooking their role as allegorical or 'highly representative figures—and satiric targets' (p. 8). Pender argues that Stead's project was 'to present a satirical history of her times' (p. 127). She reads eight of Stead's novels and several of her stories with an eye to her development as a satirist, her use and transformation of the techniques of Horace and Juvenal, and also her consistent engagement with history. Stead uses irony, allegory, sardonic commentary and often savage attack to dissect 'folly and vice', and to analyse moral ambiguity, in matters as varied as sex under capitalism, wartime profiteering, the failure of radical politics in England, and the Cold War in Hollywood. Read as a whole and as satire, Stead's novels appear as a radical commentary on Western society from the 1930s through to the Cold War. Despite some overstating of her case, Pender's reading of Stead's work in terms of its satirical and historical engagements is certainly warranted.

Also relating to the use of autobiographical material in fiction is Sally Newman's discussion of the difficulties of working with the papers of one of Australia's most self-consciously literary families, in 'Silent Witness? Aileen Palmer and the Problem of Evidence in Lesbian History' (*WoHR* 11[2002] 505–30). Newman raises the possibility that Aileen Palmer's genre-crossing and fictionalizing of autobiographical material might have been an effect of, and an act of resistance against, belonging to a family with such a consciousness of the literary, and of the use of personal history in literary work.

Axel Kruse reads Patrick White's 'The Twitching Colonel' and *Happy Valley* in 'Patrick White's Early Work: An Introduction to a Literary Puzzle' (in Benjamin, Davies, and Goh, eds., pp. 275–90). Keeping in mind the influence of surrealism and abstract painting on White's work, Kruse focuses on White's wordplay, reading into the 'conventional narrative' of *Happy Valley* a 'trick of perspective like an exercise in literary anamorphosis' (p. 287). He suggests a reading of *Happy Valley* that 'turns into a portrait of the artist as a young queen involved in a queer literary revolution which includes a great deal of absurd camping around under the cover of conventional English literature' (p. 289). Juliana De Nooy, 'Reconfiguring the Gemini: Surviving Sameness in Twin Stories' (*AUMLA* 97[2002] 74–95), discusses White's *The Solid Mandala*, considering the effects of current theories about the split subject on representations of sameness and coupledom in narratives about twins. Also on the subject of White, Briar Wood considers 'Abjection and Nationality in Patrick White's *A Fringe of Leaves*' (in Callahan, ed., pp. 84–94).

The major critical work on Patrick White this year is Helen Verity Hewitt's *Patrick White, Painter Manqué*. This well-presented volume investigates the depth of White's engagement with painters and their work, and the ways in which this affected his writing. Hewitt looks at White's friendships with artists such as Roy de Maistre, Tom Gleghorn, William Dobell, Stanislaus Rapotec, Lawrence Daws, Sidney Nolan, Brett Whitely, and Francis Bacon, reading several of White's novels as consciously part of the same (Romantic) modernist project in which some of these painters were involved. She also looks at the influence of earlier painters, including Walter Sickert, Paul Klee, Vincent Van Gogh, William Blake, and Eugène Delacroix. White's writing emerges from this analysis as 'painterly', and particularly influenced by the abstract expressionism of Australian painters during the late 1960s. Hewitt argues that the visual arts were primary in White's imagination, and that he tried to achieve, though prose, equivalent effects to those that moved him in the paintings he admired. It appears that White's oeuvre can be read as a continual interpretation and recreation of particular artworks. In effect, Hewitt suggests that his engagement with the visual arts enabled the development of White's particular prose style. As well as examining the influence of artists and particular paintings on each of White's novels, she also considers his activities as a collector and patron of artists. The volume includes full-colour plates and a list of White's many gifts and bequests to the Art Gallery of New South Wales.

Of related interest is Roberta Buffi's *Between Literature and Painting: Three Australian Women Writers*. Buffi looks at the prevalence of visual strategies and tropes in the work of Janine Burke, Beverly Farmer, and Drusilla Modjeska with an eye to how they form 'underlying motifs and structuring devices that shape, voice and negotiate women's forms of subjectivity' (p. 2). Buffi also explores the ways in which these writers challenge discourses and representations that are traditionally framed by masculinity.

Patrick Buckridge gives an overview of the novels of Godfrey Blunden in 'A Kind of Exile: Godfrey Blunden—An Australian in Paris' (*JAS* 73[2002] 111–18). Buckridge observes that 'the myth of voluntary exile has long been absorbed into the vocabulary of Australian cultural nationalism' (p. 111), and notes the absence of exile as a prominent theme in Blunden's novels, which principally draw on his experiences as a journalist in Russia and Geneva. Alan Gould, in 'The Sea' (*HEAT* 3[2002] 161–8), explores 'the complex attraction of maritime histories' (p. 162) for himself as a writer, and for readers more generally.

The relation of religion and sexuality to beauty is explored in Jenny Blain's discussion of Martin Boyd's conversion to Roman Catholicism in 'Martin Boyd: Complicating the Deity with Erotic Impulses' (*Southerly* 62:iii[2002] 82–92). In the same volume, Katherine Crawford examines the reconstitution of the masculine body in the writing of Morris West, in 'Body Building and Body Scarring: Transforming the Male Body in Morris West' (*Southerly* 62:iii[2002] 123–36).

Anthony Hassall considers the disjunction between Thea Astley's (largely positive) extra-fictional comments about country towns and her (overwhelmingly negative) representations of them in her novels in 'The Deserted Village? Thea Astley's *Drylands*' (in Stewart and Walker, eds., pp. 133–46). Hassall suggests that this disjunction might 'constitute yet another paradoxical version of the "Sydney or the bush" topos in Australian literature and culture' (p. 150). Also in this volume, Shirley Walker suggests ways in which novels by Carmel Bird, Drusilla Modjeska, and Marion Halligan might give different meaning to the concept of intertextuality in 'Intertextuality: *The White Garden*, *The Orchard* and *The Fog Garden*' (pp. 161–74), focusing on images of gardens and instances of genre-crossing. Of related interest is María Socorro Suárez Lafuente's discussion of the part played by writing in the development of Australian women's subjectivity, focusing on the spaces of verandah and garden, in 'Creating Women's Identity in Australian Civilization' (in Russell, ed., pp. 35–52). The literary uses of the verandah are also at issue in Alistair Rolls and Vanessa Alayrac's reading of Robert Drewe's novel in 'Changing the Tide and the Tidings of Change: Robert Drewe's *The Drowner*' (*Southerly* 62:iii[2002] 154–67).

Alan Sandison thinks about the effect of a political and social issue on the genre of tragedy in 'Holding the Man: Tragedy and the Literature of AIDS' (in Stewart and Walker, eds., pp. 187–209). Discussing the relationship of tragedy to humanism, Sandison uses Timothy Conigrave's *Holding the Man* to consider 'the conditions for and of tragedy in our own time' (p. 190). Dennis Haskell makes a considered and insightful reading of the notion of wholeness, and its relation to Australia and art, in the writing of David Malouf (focusing on his *Conversations at Curlew Creek*) in 'Australia and Wholeness of Meaning: Reasoning and Art at Curlew Creek' (in Stewart and Walker, eds., pp. 133–46). Of related interest is James Bulman-May's

'Alchemical Tropes of Irish Diaspora in David Malouf's *Conversations at Curlew Creek* and *Remembering Babylon*' (*NIS* 1[2002] 63–76).

In 'David Malouf's *Fly Away Peter*: A European View' (in Stilz, ed., pp. 275–84), Marc Delrez reads David Malouf's work in the light of some questions raised by Stephen Slemon regarding the extent to which white settler literatures 'can be seen to further native dispossession, insofar as the authors aim to secure for themselves and for their readership a sense of cultural rootedness which effectively displaces prior claims' (p. 276). Delrez suggests that Malouf's novels are an example of an Australian propensity towards a cultural 'binge' or inverted cringe, suggesting that 'the postcolonial desire to oppose, and indeed to reiterate one's opposition to, the traditional bugbear of European imperialism, in fact springs from a perception of embarrassing proximity to that very same Europe' (p. 277). He sees in Nicholas José's *The Custodians* an alternative means by which Australia might claim postcoloniality—not through ownership, but through shared custodianship of, and responsibility for, the land. David Malouf briefly takes up the question of reconciliation alongside a general discussion of his work in an interview with Jennifer Levasseur and Kevin Rabalais, 'Public Dreaming' (*KR* 24:iii–iv[2002] 164–73).

In 'The Westering of Quasimodo: The Legacy of the Grotesque in the New World' (in Pons, ed., pp. 211–21), Michael Ackland notes both the particular valence of the grotesque for Australian settler culture, and the transformation of the form of the grotesque in Australian literature. He argues that Marcus Clarke, heavily influenced by Victor Hugo's grotesque, was able to sever it from its 'uneasy association with a Christian metaphysic' (p. 215), and adapt it to the particular fears and tensions of colonial Australia. Reading David Malouf's *Remembering Babylon* as a modern reworking of the Australian grotesque, Ackland cites Gemmy as 'an amplified version of obsessive white fears' (p. 219).

Malouf's novel is also the focus of Alice Brittan's argument as to the role of possession, naming, and material transaction in Australia's colonial history, in 'B-b-british Objects: Possession, Naming and Translation and David Malouf's *Remembering Babylon*' (*PMLA* 117[2002] 1158–71). Brittan characterizes the convict and settler society of early New South Wales as one of 'acute and sustained material anxiety' (p. 1159), a response in part to the dispossession of Aboriginal people, and suggests that 'Malouf's settlers use naming as a palliative against disturbances of material value and social meaning' (p. 1166).

Julie K. Eberly, in 'Reading the Motif of Captivity: Fragmentation or Unity in *Remembering Babylon*' (in Benjamin, Davies, and Goh, eds., pp. 261–74), reads Malouf's novel in the context of other postcolonial narratives of captivity. She examines the use of the motif of captivity in the novel to explore the development of individual and national identities. Of related interest is Karen Barker's consideration of 'Vitalist Nationalism, the White Aborigine and Evolving National Identity' (in Pons, ed., pp. 105–11). Reading recent Australian novels that have taken the 'white Aborigine' as their theme (including *Remembering Babylon*, Richard Flanagan's *Death of a River Guide*, Liam Davison's *The White Woman*, Kim Scott's *True Country*, and Brian Castro's *Drift*) in the light of the 'vitalist nationalism' of P.R. Stephensen and William Baylebridge, Barker raises some pertinent questions as to what this trope may reveal about the quest for reconciliation in Australian writing.

In reply to critics who have claimed Brian Castro as either proponent or detractor of theory, Karen Barker sets out to examine the role of theory in Castro's novels, focusing on *Double-Wolf*, in 'The Artful Man: Theory and Authority in Brian Castro's Fiction' (*ALS* 20:iii[2002] 231–40). The result is a clear account of the opportunities and pitfalls of the use of theory in fiction; Barker concludes that *Double-Wolf* makes an argument against 'discursive totalitarianism' of any kind. These themes are continued and extrapolated in Barker's interview with Castro, 'Theory as Fireworks' (*ALS* 20:iii[2002] 241–8), in which Castro talks at length on the nature of theory, history and fiction, hybridity, death and writing, and the idea of a 'morality of style'.

Bernadette Brennan wades into the 'labyrinth of mirrors' that is Castro's work in 'Writing of Death and Death of Writing in Brian Castro's *Stepper*' (in Pons, ed., pp. 145–52). Reading *Stepper* as an investigation of the relationship between writing and death, Brennan unravels one of Castro's many puzzles in relating the figure of Stepper to Heidegger's concept of *sorge* (signifying 'care' or 'concern') and of 'being-free'. She argues, 'It is this radical nihilism, this resounding "yes" to the acceptance of death, that Stepper applauds' (p. 151). In another investigation of an author who writes himself out of the story, Karin Hansson makes a good-humoured 'postmodern and poststructuralist reading' of Gerald Murnane's work, in 'The Departure of the Author: Gerald Murnane's *Landscape with Landscape*' (in Pons, ed., pp. 153–63). She suggests that the book be read 'as a commentary on modern literary theory, a book of metacriticism, a piece of writing constituting at the same time a deconstructive instrument and the outcome of the deconstruction' (p. 154). Hansson also notes Murnane's disruption of the traditional Australian narrative, 'as the solitary figure is not a brave explorer in the outback but a conceited and unreliable writer in a Melbourne suburb' (p. 155). Of related interest is Gerald Murnane's account of his personality, habits, and thoughts about writing in 'The Breathing Author' (*HEAT* 3[2002] 19–31). Murnane is given particular attention in Nicholas Birns's argument, in 'May in September: Australian Literature as Anglophone Literature' (in Callahan, ed., pp. 112–32), for the way in which 'the very presence of Australian literature in the Anglophone text-milieu has a revolutionizing effect on the idea of literature in English' (p. 114).

Sigrun Meinig, in 'Framing History: Photography in Rodney Hall's *Yandilli Trilogy*' (*Antipodes* 16:i[2002] 29–33), looks at representations of photography in Hall's novels, in the light of Paul Valéry's notion of photography as allowing for the verification of objectivity in history in order 'to pinpoint the novels' presentation of historical consciousness and knowledge' (p. 29).

Tony Hughes D'Aeth presents a fascinating piece of criticism in 'Australian Writing, Deep Ecology and Julia Leigh's *The Hunter*' (*JASAL* 1[2002] 19–31). He suggests that some previous critics, reading within the traditions of the Australian environmental novel, have failed to take into account the possibility that the novel is addressing 'the limits of liberal ecology' (p. 25). He reads the novel as a subversion of a genre that usually takes the form of melodrama, with unproblematic moral structure, and a critique of the 'eco-fantasy', which often revolves around 'the rather paradoxical idea that as humans become more natural they also become more humane' (p. 22). He also reads the novel as an examination of the trope of the 'natural man', one heavily invested in throughout Australian literature in the figure of the bushman. Considering the novel in terms of the relativization of human values argued for in theories of 'deep ecology', D'Aeth notes that 'what makes *The Hunter* intriguing is that it uses the humanist machinery of the novel to expose the limits of human-centred values' (p. 28).

Of related interest is Narelle Shaw's discussion of David Foster's 'deep-ecological inclination' in 'Experiencing a Wilderness and Cultivating a Garden: The Literary Environmentalism of David Foster and David Malouf' (*Antipodes* 16:i[2002] 46–52). Shaw explores the relationship between consciousness, imagination, and land in the novels and non-fiction of both writers, suggesting that the two bodies of work evidence radically different experiences of the land.

Sue Lovell gives a reading in a similar spirit to that of D'Aeth in 'Janette Turner Hospital's *The Last Magician*: "A feminist's nightmare"?' (*Hecate* 28:ii[2002] 46–63). Taking up Kate Temby's claim that Turner Hospital's novel is 'a feminist's nightmare', Lovell argues that 'Temby's response is a result of thwarted desire: she wants to see the marginalized admitted into the realms of meaning-making, she wants evidence that the voice of the other makes a difference. The desire for change is intense because it has been stimulated but not consummated' (p. 46). She suggests that Turner Hospital's novel works towards a 'posthumanist' subjectivity, in which the role of desire in 'creating reality' is revealed and interrogated.

Eden Liddelow, 'Babies Eat their Lace: Elizabeth Jolley and the Slaughter of Decorum' (in her *After Electra*, pp. 118–36), looks at the doubling of the subject as defined by need and loss. Liddelow considers the tropes of the natural, the figure of the mother, and the abject throughout Jolley's novels. Alistair Thomson, 'Landscapes of Memory' (*Meanjin* 61:iii[2002] 81–96), uses Jolley's autobiographical writing to think about the effect of migration on the perception and representation of landscapes in her novels.

Sue Thomas, in 'White Gothic in *Jane Eyre*, *Wide Sargasso Sea* and *The Albatross Muff*' (*ACH* 21[2002] 89–96), examines the workings of class and race through generic conventions of the Gothic in the novels of Charlotte Brontë, Jean Rhys, and Barbara Hanrahan. She argues that, in these novels, 'the endings of the Gothic plots involving white female protagonists and their nurses as surrogate mothers resolve anxieties surrounding middle-class feminine sensibility' (p. 96).

Lyn Jacobs, 'Remembering Forgetting: Love Stories by Nicholas José, Simone Lazaroo and Hsu-ming Teo' (*Intersections* 8[2002] 33 paras.), uses Moira Gatens's examination of difference through the concept of 'imaginary bodies' to read *The Red Thread*, *The Australian Fiancé*, and *Love and Vertigo*. Arguing for a view of fiction as performative, Jacobs suggests that these novels are examples of 'fictions which interrogate imaginaries and offer alternative perspectives to challenge populist assumptions', particularly in regard to Australian responses to Asia.

In 'Ahasverus on the Walkabout: The Motif of the Wandering Jew in Contemporary Australian Fiction' (*Antipodes* 16:i[2002] 11–16), Gloria Gebhardt considers the figure of the 'wandering Jew' as recurrent in Australian literature, focusing on Tim Winton's *The Riders*, Peter Carey's *Illywacker*, and David Malouf's *Harland's Half-Acre*. Barbara Aritzi Martin gives another reading of Winton's novel in 'The Crisis of Masculinity in Tim Winton's *The Riders*' (*Com* 24:ii[2002] 29–45).

Ralph Pordzic examines Peter Carey's engagement with the generic conventions of dystopia in 'Reinventing the Future(s): Peter Carey and the Dystopian Tradition in Australian Fiction' (in Stilz, ed., pp. 285–98). Pordzic argues that Carey extends the possibilities of the genre as it has been written in Australia, moving away from the 'dispirited cultural self-image' (p. 285) figured in other Australian dystopian works towards a reimagining of concerns about postcolonialism and Australian identity. In the same volume, Sigrun Meinig, in 'Literary Lessons from the Past: Stereotypes and Intertextuality in Peter Carey's *Jack Maggs*' (pp. 299–307), looks at the portrayal of convict characters in both Carey's novel and its 'intertext', Dickens's *Great Expectations*.

Continuing the themes of travel and of place is Shirley Walker's overview of recent fiction, 'Coming and Going: A Literature of Place: Australian Literature, 2001–2002' (*Westerly* 47[2002] 38–51). Walker reviews Richard Flanagan's *Gould's Book of Fish*, Tim Winton's *Dirt Music*, Chloe Hooper's *A Child's Book of True Crime*, Joan London's *Gilgamesh*, Eva Sallis's *City of Sealions*, and Arnold Zable's *Café Scheherazade*, among others. In 'The Traveling Heroine in Recent Australian Fiction' (in Stewart and Walker, eds., pp. 175–86), Elizabeth Webby discusses some of the same texts, focusing on the figure of the travelling heroine. In looking at novels by Rodney Hall, Joan London, Tim Winton, Nicki Gemmel, Alex Miller, and Tom Keneally, Webby considers an apparent avoidance of contemporary political and social issues and a new interest in historical fiction set in the twentieth century. Joan London thinks about the extent to which her writing, particularly her recent novel *Gilgamesh*, evidences a 'Western Australian' sensibility in 'How Deep Does the Yellow Sand Go?' (*Westerly* 47[2002] 20–4).

Toni Johnson-Woods gives an overview of 'hard-boiled' pulp crime writing in Australia through its heyday in the 1940s and 1950s in 'Hardboiled Pulp Australian Style' (*CF* 5[2002] 42–6). She looks at the work of Carter Brown (Alan Geoffrey Yates, whose innovative titles included *The Flagellator* and *A Good Year for Dwarfs*), Gordon Clive Bleeck, Marc Brody (W.H. Williams), Larry Kent (Don Haring and Des R. Dunn), and K.T. McCall (Audrey Armitage and Muriel Watkins).

Such 'hard-boiled' crime writing seems to be outside the focus of Michael Pollak and Margaret McNabb in their survey of Australian crime writing, *Gothic Matilda: The Amazing Visions of Australian Crime Fiction*. This is not so much a work of criticism as a useful overview of the biography, plots, and concerns of major Australian crime writers. Pollak and McNabb consider the available biographical detail of each of their surveyed writers, look at each of their novels or stories, outlining plots, relation to generic conventions, and (very briefly) their critical reception. The authors' own critical comments on these novels are largely biographical in focus. Starting with Fergus Hume and Francis Adams (who wrote one mystery novel), Pollak and McNabb leap straight to the 1960s novels of Patricia Carlon, whose novels have not received much attention in Australia but have recently been reprinted in the United States. They note the unusual complexity of her portrayals of children and their relationships with adults. Peter Corris receives attention for his sense of social justice, his vivid portrayal of Sydney's corrupt institutions, and his battles with alcohol abuse and diabetes. The review of Gabrielle Lord also focuses on her portrayals of children, child abuse, and 'dysfunctional' families, relating this to her own experiences in childhood, and of alcohol abuse as an adult. J.R. Carroll is noted for his insight into the effects of the Vietnam War on violence within Australian society, Peter Temple for his cynical view of wealth and politics, and his close observations of Melbourne and its inhabitants, and John Dale for a similar attention to detail about Sydney and police corruption within it. Finally, they look at comic thriller writers Shane Maloney (who they suggest extends the possibilities of the genre in terms of comedy and a most unusual Australian Labor Party-affiliated 'hero'), Richard Hall, and Paul Thomas. The last two are acclaimed for their spoofing of Australian intelligence agencies and foreign affairs.

Several readings of young adult literature this year focus on issues of gender representation. Anna Beth McCormack takes up the controversial question of young adult literature about sexual abuse and incest in '"A song in search of a voice that is silent": Feminist Readings of *When She Hollers* and *Touching Earth Lightly*' (*Papers* 12:iii[2002] 28–33). In her feminist readings of novels by Cynthia Voigt and Margo Lanagan, McCormack suggests that the relative dearth of writing for young people on this important subject may be due to the difficulty of presenting positive gender representations in these kinds of stories. Wendy Michaels and Donna Gibbs, in 'Fictional Fathers: Gender Representation in Children's Fiction' (*Papers* 12:iii[2002] 35–45), focus on the shortlist for the CBCA in 2001 to analyse the characters, roles and relationships, and moral behaviour of father-figures in Judith Clarke's *Wolf on the Fold*, Bill Condon's *Dogs*, Sonya Hartnett's *Thursday's Child*, Steven Herrick's *The Simple Gift*, James Maloney's *Touch Me*, and Markus Zusak's *Fighting Ruben Wolfe*.

3. Canada

(a) General

Major contributions to critical and reference work are Ivison, ed., *Dictionary of Literary Biography*, volume 251: *Canadian Fantasy and Science-Fiction Writers*, and New, ed., *Encyclopedia of Literature in Canada*. *DLB* 251 contains thirty-eight entries on individual authors, a checklist of further readings, notes on contributors, and a standard *DLB* cumulative index. The introduction offers a comprehensive survey of science fiction and fantasy writing in Canada (both known as speculative fiction, or SF), and defines the parameters of the volume as a whole, tracing the roots of SF in this context to oral Native storytelling. The colonial period is covered, and then twentieth-century SF writing is analysed and surveyed in some detail, including the cultural crossovers that were generated by the explosion of SF publications in the USA starting in the 1920s. Contemporary Canadian authors known outside the SF field get good coverage, for example the entry on William Gibson, written by Douglas Ivison, which begins with a bibliography of primary texts including scripts and other materials, and ends with an extensive bibliography of criticism, including interviews; the entry also reproduces three covers of early Gibson works and a photograph of him. The coverage of Gibson's works is exhaustive, noting the impact he has had on 'late-twentieth-century culture', especially with the publication of his novel *Neuromancer* [1984], and the fact that Gibson coined the term 'cyberspace'. The entry gives biographical information, covers Gibson's short stories, examines his collaborative work with other leading SF writers, and moves on to the award-winning *Neuromancer* before examining his turn towards a more mainstream fiction writing style. Production values throughout the *DLB* volume are high, including an excerpt from the manuscript of Margaret Atwood's *The Handmaid's Tale* [1985], a plot outline from Dave Duncan's working notes for the third volume of his *The King's Blades* trilogy [2000], Daniel Sernine's earliest map of the fictional

Paskédiac Valley, and a corrected typescript page by Jean-Louis Trudel, among many other interesting visual materials. The entry on Margaret Atwood, written by Lee Briscoe Thompson, will be of particular interest to scholars of Canadian literature. After a standard biographical introduction, Thompson situates Atwood's *The Handmaid's Tale* within Canadian SF writing as a whole, noting the novel's international appeal (winning, among other awards, the UK's Arthur C. Clarke Award in 1987). Thompson groups together some of Atwood's poems, short stories, and *The Blind Assassin* [2000] to reveal a strong interest in fabulation and the fantastic. Critical terms are compared, with Atwood favouring 'speculative fiction', and Thompson suggesting as potentially more appropriate the term 'social science fiction', defined as the 'pushing of familiar social structures into new configurations, usually dire ones' (p. 13). The in-depth analyses of *The Handmaid's Tale*, and Atwood's following related SF texts, dominate the entry, including comparative reference to other dystopian classics, and a critical survey. *DLB* 251 is more than just a reference work: it provides a range of critical, biographical, and bibliographical materials that make it a very useful pedagogic tool for the study of Canadian SF.

'Science Fiction and Fantasy' (Robert Runté) is just one of over 2,000 entries in New's *Encyclopedia of Literature in Canada*. Entries cover specific topics—for example, 'Comic Books and Graphic Novels' (Bart Beaty), 'Gay and Lesbian Writing' (Tom Hastings), 'Inuit Literature' (Dale Blake)—and individual writers such as 'Atwood, Margaret Eleanor' (Shannon Hengen/WN) and 'King, Thomas' (N.E. Currie). Topic entries provide information, and often take interdisciplinary approaches or provide pedagogical material. The entries vary in length, with the many unsigned entries being written by New. The encyclopedia also provides a chronology, compiled by Gerald Friesen, an index by contributor, an index of authors, and a supplementary index. This last reveals the massive overall scope of the volume and the vast range of critical and creative subjects covered: there are entries that will be useful to all scholars and students of Canadian literature. Selected notable entries include: 'Archives, Manuscripts, and Special Collections' (Joann McCaig); 'Asia and Canadian Literature' (Chelva Kanaganayakam); 'Awards and Literary Prizes' (R.G. Siemens); 'Biography' (Ira B. Nadel); 'Caribbean and Canadian Literature' (Michael A. Bucknor); 'Cree Literature' (H.C. Wolfart); 'Criticism and Theory' (Michael Grove); 'Cultural Plurality and Canadian Literature' (Winfried Siemerling); 'Drama in English' (Ric Knowles); 'Drama in French' (André Loiselle); 'Exploration Literature' (Bill Moreau); 'Film, Television, and Literature' (Richard Bruce Kirkley); 'First Nations Literature' (Lally Grauer); 'Gender and Gender Relations' (Donna Palmateer Pennee); 'Jewish Canadian Writing' (Michael Greenstein); 'Language: Aboriginal and Trade Languages in Canada' (M. Dale Kinkade); 'Language: Canadian English' (Margery Fee); 'Language: Canadian French' (Douglas Walker); 'Race and Racism in Canadian Literature' (George Elliott Clarke); 'Reference Guides to Canadian Writing' (Catherine Sheldrick Ross); 'Religion and Literature' (Barbara Pell); 'Teaching Canadian Literature' (Margery Fee/Leslie Monkman); 'Technology, Communications, and Canadian Literature' (Mark Libin); 'Translation' (Jane Koustas); and 'United States and Canadian Literature' (Susie O'Brien). Individual authors can be found in author entries, or cross-referenced in topic entries: for example, there is an entry for the infamous impostor 'Grey Owl' (unsigned) and

Grey Owl also appears in the topic entry 'Hoaxes, Forgeries, Impostors' (Andreas
Schroeder). 'Literature' in Canada is used as a flexible term, and includes significant
canonical and numerous lesser-known writers. Many crossovers are inevitable and
necessarily occur; for example, there is an entry for the talented artist and writer
'Emily Carr' (Misao Dean), and Carr appears in the topic entry 'Group of Seven'
(unsigned). 'Literature' includes oral and other modes of expression, including
'Oral Literature and History' (Robin Ridington) and 'Radio Drama' (Howard Fink).
New's monumental *Encyclopedia of Literature in Canada* is a reference text
(currently accurate up to the year 2000) that gathers together descriptive data and
wide-ranging critical essays on key topics; the encyclopedia reflects New's lifelong
generous commitment to the analysis, explication, and dissemination of writing in
Canada.

George Elliott Clarke, *Odysseys Home: Mapping African-Canadian Literature*,
argues that 'a primary ontological conundrum to confront the analyst of African-
Canadian literature is as obvious as it is invidious: How Canadian is it?' (p. 71). In
many respects, Clarke's landmark book attempts to answer this question from a
multitude of perspectives, utilizing diverse theoretical approaches. The essays are
divided into three main sections preceded by an introduction: 'Sorties' (twelve
essays), 'Incursions' (scholarly reviews), and 'Surveys' (in two parts—'A Primer of
African-Canadian Literature' and the bibliography, 'Africana Canadiana'). The
autobiographically situated introduction, 'Embarkation: Discovering African-
Canadian Literature', charts Clarke's own progression from identifying himself as a
'Black (American) Novia Scotian' to his own attempt to understand the term
'African Canadian', in the process undertaking a responsibility for the contestation
of the ongoing effacement of black Canadian culture and history. Clarke critiques
the 'Black Atlantic' theories that virtually ignore the Canadian experience, arguing
that 'Canadacentric research is necessary because the expansive cosmopolitanism of
the African Diaspora cannot be understood without taking into account the creative
ways in which *blackness* has managed to thrive in this predominantly white settler-
state' (p. 10). The first four main essays in the book—'Contesting a Model
Blackness: A Meditation on African-Canadian African-Americanism, or the
Structures of African-Canadianité', 'Must All Blackness Be American? Locating
Canada in Borden's "Tightrope Time," or Nationalizing Gilroy's *The Black
Atlantic*', 'The Career of Black English in Nova Scotia: A Literary Sketch', and
'The Birth and Rebirth of Africadian Literature'—provide sustained exploration and
mapping of Clarke's neologism 'Africadian'; the essays that follow perform close
readings of authors and movements. Useful pedagogical tools include the glossary
of 'Africadian' English, the selected reviews, and the bibliographical research—'A
Primer of African-Canadian Literature', 'Africana Canadiana: A Select
Bibliography of Literature by African-Canadian Authors, 1785–2001, in English,
French, and Translation' and the additional references to primary 'Africadian' texts
in the 'Works Cited'. Clarke's book dovetails critical appreciation with reference-
quality research and tools.

Laurie Ricou similarly dovetails criticism and bibliographical research in another
major publication: *The Arbutus/Madrone Files: Reading the Pacific Northwest*.
Richly illustrated, the book is split into two main sections—'Files' and 'Afterfiles'.
The 'Files' are literary-critical close readings, while the 'Afterfiles' partly mirror the
former in their titles, giving detailed annotated bibliographical information; thus, for

example, the 'Raven File' is mirrored by the bibliographical 'Afterfile' called simply 'Raven'. Ricou chooses as his starting point and overall metaphor the doubled name for a single species of tree, the 'arbutus' (in Canada) or 'madrone' (in America), to map the literatures of the Pacific Northwest, arguing that the latter description gets one beyond the borders of conventional studies of British Columbian/Canadian literature. The region's writing is thus deeply informed, in Ricou's interpretation, by ecological tropes, and the word 'files' evokes the gathering and collecting of discursive formations as with the gathering and collecting of plant species. These eco-formations are reflected in the chapter titles: 'Mistory File', 'Island File', 'Raven File', 'Rain File', 'Kuroshio File', 'Salal File', 'Sasquatch File', 'Salmon File', 'Woodswords File', 'Great Blue Heron File', 'Intertidal File', 'Anasayú File'. Ricou reads Pacific Northwest literatures not just through ecological tropes, but as part of a textual ecosystem; this calls for a new mode of doing literary criticism, which the book makes an admirable attempt to develop: canonical literature, popular writing, history, ecology, myth, and mystery are creatively woven together. Ricou's original approach and useful annotated bibliography of the region are well combined, resulting in a book which is critically groundbreaking and of lasting value in the classroom. Wayde Compton, editor of *Bluesprint: Black British Columbian Literature and Orature* [2001], brings the Pacific Northwest focus back to Canada with his timely anthology, with extracts which range from Sir James Douglas's *Journal* [1843] to Sara Singh Parker-Toulson's *On Being a Black Woman in Canada (and Indian and English too) ...* [2001]. Compton's introduction covers the history of British Columbia's black population, including travel narratives, the first British Columbian black poetry, correspondence, slave narratives, and orature. Self-publishing necessarily played a major part in this history, and Compton thus examines the self-published works of Christopher James, Truman Green, and Fred Booker. Compton ends his critical survey by turning to other media for the dissemination of black writing, including the San Francisco-based *The Elevator*, and other journals and magazines, as well as performance spaces and writers' networks.

Women's writing and post-structuralist theory are the focus of both Lorraine York's *Rethinking Women's Collaborative Writing: Power, Difference, Property* and Marie Carrière's *Writing in the Feminine in French and English Canada: A Question of Ethics*. York concentrates on contemporary collaborative writing because of the theoretical, and in particular post-structuralist, reconfigurings of the author which reinvigorated theoretical notions of authorship *per se*; she resists the idea that women's collaborative writing is specifically feminist, arguing rather that such writing harbours a variety of ideological positions and radical potentials. There are six main chapters and an epilogue: 'Theorizing Contemporary Women's Collaborative Writing'; '"We have horrible disagreements about 'moreovers'": Collaborative Theory and Criticism'; 'Collaborative Predecessors'; '"The High Wire of Self and Other": Prose Collaborations'; 'Being Alone Together: Collaborative Poetry'; and '"It ... shook up my easy theories": Theatrical Collaboration'. The historical range covered by York is impressive: all manner of literary and critical collaborations are discussed, going well beyond the most famous, such as Sandra Gilbert and Susan Gubar, although they also receive excellent coverage. Canadian collaborators and texts covered include the theatrical productions and self-reflections of Maria Campbell and Linda Griffiths, *The Book of*

Jessica: A Theatrical Transformation [1989], a novel by Blanche Howard and Carol Shields, *A Celibate Season* [1991], and a collection of poetry by Daphne Marlatt and Betsy Warland, *Two Women in a Birth* [1994]. The book ends with a short but insightful meditation upon the contradictions in Canadian academia between state-funded collaborative work and the demand for individualist-focused academic achievement and concomitant success. Carrière opens her study with a survey of critical and creative feminist collaborations in French- and English-speaking Canadian writing, arguing that, since the 1970s, there has been an intentional forging of a distinctive, highly theoretical feminist aesthetics. The authors focused on are Di Brandt, Nicole Brossard, Erin Mouré, France Théoret, and Lola Lemire Tostevin; Carrière argues that these authors not only develop a trans-disciplinary feminist poetics but also a feminist ethics. Carrière braids literature and theory in complex ways: her book has nine main chapters and a conclusion, arranged in four main parts: 'Poetics, Ethics, and Writing in the Feminine'; 'Mothers and Daughters'; 'Mothertongues'; and 'Beyond Ethics'. The first part provides the theoretical underpinnings, with a detailed discussion of major Canadian feminist critical publications and then the philosophical-ethical works of Levinas and Ricoeur among others; the second part consists of three close readings of Brossard, Brandt, and Théoret; the third part covers Mouré and Tostevin; and part 4 goes 'beyond ethics' with an even more theoretical analysis of the authors, mainly via ethics of 'selfhood' and love.

The international 'stature' of Canadian literature is affirmed in Steenman-Marcuse, ed., *The Rhetoric of Canadian Writing*, a significant collection of sixteen essays from the fourteenth Leiden October Conference in 2000, which are reviewed below in my own thematic and critical groupings. Steenman-Marcuse, in 'The Rhetoric of Canadian Writing: Introduction', shifts the critical agenda from identity and Canadian literature to one of rhetorical strategies. The opening 'keynote' addresses/essays are Susan Swan, 'The Writer's Conscience and the Rhetoric of Canadian Writing', and Louise Dupré, 'Women's Writing in Quebec: From Rhetoric to New Social Propositions' (trans. Michelle Carolyn Tracy). Swan writes a reflective piece on her own creative work, showing how she has tried to put into practice her notion that literary imagination is essentially a manifestation of the author's conscience. Dupré maps the history of Quebecois women's writing, showing how a real creative upsurge occurred in the early 1960s with the Quiet Revolution signifying an epistemic shift; Dupré explains *l'écriture féminine* as an ongoing desire and project to dismantle generic boundaries, also arguing that *l'écriture féminine* is grounded in the concrete world, demystifying Romantic notions of the writer. The essay is a clear, if at times rather general, introductory tracing of important changes in society for Canadian women writers. Complementing Dupré's chapter is an examination by Jaap Lintvelt, 'Quebec: City and Identity' (trans. Paula Roberts), of the ways in which literary spaces are 'imbued with ideological values'. The essay is in two main parts: 'Space as Expression of Social and Cultural Identity' and 'Male and Female Perceptions of Space: Gender Identity'; the first part analyses, a decade at a time (starting with the 1930s), the literary representations of Quebec city. Spatial metaphors continue with a largely descriptive essay by Graciela Martínez-Zalce, 'Montreal: Several Versions of a City', which looks at the film *Montréal vu par... Six variations sur un thème* [1992], directed by Patricia Rozema et al. A long historical reach to the late eighteenth century is Eric Miller, 'Elizabeth Simcoe and the Fate of the Picturesque'. Elizabeth Simcoe, a writer and artist, was married to the Lieutenant-Governor of Canada, John Graves Simcoe (1752–1806), and lived in Upper Canada during his tenure of 1791–6. Miller does a fine job of reconstructing the aesthetic and interpretative codes and conventions of the English picturesque mode as seen through Simcoe's works. Related work on travel narratives as generic templates is found in Suzanne James, 'The "Indians" of Catherine Parr Traill's *The Backwoods of Canada*', which also examines Traill's depictions of indigenous people. James takes a refreshing approach to a much-examined text, reading it not just as a hybrid text, but one that generates a 'cacophonic blend of voices' that become encoded and filtered by ideological factors. Two novels of historical significance for American and Canadian studies are compared in Monique W. Dull, 'Kinship and Nation in *Amelia* (1848) and *Anne of Green Gables* (1908)'. Both novels are playful and intertextual, especially concerning Gray's *Elegy Written in a Country Churchyard* [1751]. Dull notes that the American novel interprets kinship and citizenship via the sublime, whereas the Canadian novel constructs kinship via a far more heterogeneous notion of identity. Historical perspectives are also provided by E.F. Dyck, 'The Places of Aboriginal Writing 2000 [*sic*] in Canada: The Novel'. In placing Native writing, Dyck argues that there was a 'full appropriation of native culture' in Canada, a statement which appears to ignore the acts of cultural and/or ideological resistance among Canada's First Nations to the implementation of the Indian Act of 1876, such as the continuation of potlatches after they had been made illegal. However, Dyck does explore well the implications of intra-cultural appropriation within First Nations writing itself, before he moves on to an interesting discussion of 'the topos orality/literacy': texts covered include Thomas King's *Green Grass, Running Water* [1993], Tomson Highway's *Kiss of the Fur Queen* [1998], and Jeannette Armstrong's *Slash* [1985]. The concept of rhetoric is returned to as the main subject with Martin Reinink, 'The Rhetoric of Emerging Literatures', which analyses the spatial and racial structuring and organization of rhetorical strategies in key Canadian anthologies and works of criticism, such as Smaro Kamboureli, ed., *Making a Difference: An Anthology of Canadian Multicultural Literature* [1996], Thomas King, ed., *All My Relations: An Anthology of Contemporary Canadian Native Fiction* [1990], and Penny Petrone, *Native Literatures in Canada: From the Oral Tradition to the Present* [1990]. Kathleen Venema, 'Shifting Rhetorics of Space in English-Canadian Exploration Literature', takes as her main text Rudy Wiebe's *A Discovery of Strangers* [1994], which focuses on the Canadian fascination with the mythological figure and concomitant narratives of John Franklin. Wiebe's novel reconstitutes and reconceives the first of Franklin's three expeditions. Three essays which take diverse but related approaches to women's literature are Conny Steenman-Marcuse, 'The Rhetoric of Autobiography in Susan Swan's *The Biggest Modern Woman of the World*', Anna Branach-Kallas, 'Lovers and/or Enemies: Love and Nationality in Nancy Huston's *The Mark of the Angel*', and Coral Ann Howells, 'Margaret Atwood's Discourse of Nation and National Identity in the 1990s'. Steenman-Marcuse describes Swan's novel within a feminist context as well as explicating the links between the female body, desire, and nationalism; Branach-Kallas introduces Huston's novel, which was first published in French as *L'Empreinte de l'ange* [1998]; Howells traces evolving discourses of nationalism via official Canadian discourses of multiculturalism and Atwood's ongoing interrogation of Canadian history. Howells mainly reads closely Atwood's *Wilderness Tips* [1991], *The Robber Bride* [1994], *Alias Grace* [1997], and *The Blind Assassin* [2000]; the essay serves as a useful introduction to this period in Atwood's writing, including her essays and poetry. Robert Druce, 'A Visiting Distance: Patrick Anderson, Poet, Autobiographer, and Exile', combines biographical description with critical appreciation of the poems and other writings of this peripatetic Canadian/English writer who co-founded in 1942 the literary journal *Preview*; the essay is highly readable and a useful resource for introducing Anderson's work. Two essays on regional writings are also of use for introductory materials: Hans Bak, 'Writing Newfoundland, Writing Canada: Wayne Johnston's *The Colony of Unrequited Dreams*', and J.M. MacLennan and John Moffat, 'An Island View of the World: Insularity in the Popular Writing of Stompin' Tom Connors'. Bak takes a by now overly familiar notion of postmodernism and the 'fictionality of history' but applies such concepts to new territory, while MacLennan and Moffat take an off-the-wall look at the island perspective in the folk lyrics of Connors, as well as in his autobiography *Stompin' Tom: Before the Fame* [1995], arguing that key folk elements—heroism and eccentricity, community and singularity, and survival against the odds—are typical of Connors's work. *The Rhetoric of Canadian Writing*, while exhibiting some of the deficiencies of the symposium collection, such as very short essays that need expansion, offers genuinely new research and some clearly written introductions to contemporary issues in Canadian literary studies.

Another international examination of Canadian literature is Schaub and Verduyn, eds., *Identity, Community, Nation: Essays on Canadian Writing*, which examines the ways in which 'Canadian writers have interrogated identity, explored community attachments and articulated desires of belonging, thereby highlighting hybridity and diversity' (introduction, p. xii). Significant essays in the collection include Danielle Schaub, 'Reflections on Identity and Language in the New Hybrid Culture of Postmodern Canada', which is a linguistic analysis of the construction of hybrid identities in critical and literary texts, and two challenging studies of autobiography—Bina Toldeo Freiwald, 'Identity, Community, and Nation in Black Canadian Women's Autobiography', and Patricia Smart, 'Sons on their Fathers: Identity and Community in Some Recent Canadian Men's Autobiographical Writing'. For Freiwald, 'thinking Canadian blackness' is a project that involves 'collective identity in Canada' and the problematics therein; the four autobiographies explored are Carrie Best, *That Lonesome Road* [1977], Carol Talbot, *Growing Up Black in Canada* [1984], Cheryl Foggo, *Pourin' Down Rain* [1990], and Karen Shadd-Evelyn, *I'd Rather Live in Buxton* [1993]. These texts are seen as challenging binary nationalist narratives. For Smart, the contemporary immense popularity of the 'memoir form' is of interest, and is 'indissociable' from the current obsession with local identity politics in an era of internationalism and globalization. The three autobiographies studied are Wayne Johnston, *Baltimore's Mansion* [1999], Joe Fiorito, *The Closer We Are To Dying* [1999], and Roy MacGregor, *A Life in the Bush: Lessons from my Father* [1999]. Other essays in the collection are as follows: Christl Verduyn, '"Breath on a window pane": Identity, Community and Nation in André Alexis' *Childhood*'; Susan Billingham, 'Migratory Subjects in Shani Mootoo's *Out on Main Street*'; Radha Chakravarty, '"Go, be brave": Changing Subjectivities in Bharati Mukherjee's Fiction'; Lalitha

Ramamurthi, 'Indo-Canadian Symbiosis: A Dialogic Review of Uma Parameswaran's *The Door is Shut Behind Me*'; Jade Bar-Shalom, 'Multicultural Critics-at-Large: Dis-Identification in Beatrice Culleton's *In Search of April Raintree*'; Jane Koustas, 'Shifting Identities in the Theatre of Robert Lepage: *The Seven Streams of the River Ota*'; Yehudi Lindeman, 'Old for New: Narratives of Changing Identity in Three "New" Canadian Authors'; and Peggy Devaux, 'The Return Journey: Necessary Displacement in the Immigrant/Ethnic Writers' Quest for Identity'. The collection ends with a selection of photographic portraits of Canadian authors, in Danielle Schaub, 'Seeing Canadian Voices: Writers in Light and Shadow'. The collection is particularly useful for its introductory essays on ethnicity and cultural diversity within Canada.

Three theme issues approach diverse but contemporary obsessions or subjects in Canadian writing: *Canadian Literature* explores 'Auto/biography' (*CanL* 172[2002]), while *Essays on Canadian Writing* surveys 'Literatures, Cinemas, Cultures' (*ECW* 76[2002]) and 'Food, Cooking and Eating' (*ECW* 78[2002]). Susanna Egan and Gabriele Helms situate multi-media interest in auto/biography in Canada (where the slash indicates contemporary theoretical approaches to life-writing covering both biography and autobiography) in their editorial introduction, 'Auto/biography? Yes. But Canadian?' (*CanL* 172[2002] 5–16). They also place the theme issue as an updating of previous work done by Shirley Neuman, who had argued that this subject was not receiving adequate critical coverage in Canada; Egan and Helms note that contemporary auto/biographical productions are far more critically aware and self-reflexive as well as being generically hybrid and produced via a range of media. Bina Toledo Freiwald, 'Nation and Self-Narration: A View from Québec/Quebec' (*CanL* 172[2002] 17–38), begins with the linguistic theories of Benveniste to argue that the subject is both interpellated by national identities and by auto/biographical acts which can become both model and medium for new ideals of nationhood. Freiwald elucidates this argument through a reading of Quebecois politics and autobiographical narratives. The subject of collaboration—in this case denied by one of the authors—returns in Neil ten Kortenaar, 'Nega Mezlekia Outside the Hyena's Belly' (*CanL* 172[2002] 41–68), where Mezlekia refused to acknowledge Anne Stone's part in writing *Notes from the Hyena's Belly* [2000]. Kortenaar suggests that notions of authorship involve the contestation of ownership and self-expression, thus leading to a double bind for Mezlekia and Stone. Cultural issues thereby come into play, such as the problematic 'collaborative' relationship between informant/subject and ethnographer; Kortenaar deals with these issues by multiplying the narrative voices involved, revealing the 'refracted' and 'compounded' nature of auto/biographical expression. Problematic collaboration issues are also explored by Sophie McCall, '"A life has only one author": Twice-Told Aboriginal Life Narratives' (*CanL* 172[2002] 70–90), where Lee Maracle's revised edition of *Bobbi Lee, Indian Rebel* [1990] is the life story allegedly editorially compromised by Don Barnett. McCall examines twice- and even thrice-told life stories to clarify the 'multiple forms of mediation' involved in any life story. Sherrill Grace, 'Creating the Girl from God's Country: From Nell Shipman to Sharon Pollock' (*CanL* 172[2002] 92–111), asks a deceptively simple question: 'How does one take an autobiography from the page to the stage, and what happens to the life story and its meaning when it is performed?' Grace answers via a comparative analysis of Nell Shipman's *The Silent Screen & My Talking Heart*

[1987] and the play based on Shipman's life stories by Sharon Pollock, *Moving Pictures* [1999]. Grace argues that Pollock reframes and retells Shipman's life stories from a more radically articulated feminist perspective, drawing in the process upon her own life experiences. The special issue of *CanL* ends with an interview that forms part of a larger Social Sciences and Humanities Research Council of Canada project called 'Diaspora, Indigeneity, Ethnicity': Margery Fee, Sneja Gunew, and Lisa Grekul, in 'Myrna Kostash: Ukrainian Canadian Non-Fiction Prairie New Leftist Feminist Canadian Nationalist' (*CanL* 172[2002] 114–43), discuss with Myrna Kostash work that reflects a sense of belonging to ethnic/indigenous communities.

The question of film adaptations of literary texts is now a key aspect of many literature and media studies courses; Peter Dickinson, 'Introduction: Reading Movies' (*ECW* 76[2002] 1–45), traces Canadian literary adaptations back to the silent movie era of the 1910s and 1920s, including the extensive Hollywood productions about Canada (i.e., not always texts by Canadians), and the extensive *Anne of Green Gables* [1908] production industry. Dickinson situates important historical events in the Canadian media industry, such as the formation in 1939 of the National Film Board of Canada/Office National du Film de Canada, in relation to a more subversive history of gender and genre where film adaptations have given rise to the sub-category of the iconographic figure of the drag queen. Susan Swan, 'A Novel's Journey into Film' (*ECW* 76[2002] 46–50), discusses the 'translation' process that occurred during the film production of her novel *The Wives of Bath* [1993], concluding that faithfulness to the literary text should not be the final criterion of success. The transferral or transcoding of meaning 'between different verbal and visual registers' is also the subject of Lee Parpart, 'Adapting Emotions: Notes on the Transformation of Affect and Ideology from "We So Seldom Look on Love" to *Kissed*' (*ECW* 76[2002] 51–82). Parpart attempts an in-depth reading which encounters productive aspects of 'fidelity criticism' and combines them with narratological approaches to verbal and visual processes, thereby leading to an understanding of how reorienting affective cues in the viewer can also involve ideological transformations. Elspeth Tulloch, 'Yves Simoneau's Rewriting of the Troubled Manhood Script in Anne Hébert's *Les Fous de Bassan*' (*ECW* 76[2002] 83–116), examines the rewriting and revision of a complex feminist text into a film that is largely produced from the perspective of a male focalizer, and the concomitant problems. Death is the metaphor to explore the relationships between centrifugal cinema and centripetal drama in André Loiselle, 'The Corpse Lies in *Lillies*: The Stage, the Screen, and the Dead Body' (*ECW* 76[2002] 117–38). Two essays examine visual media versions of L.M. Montgomery's fiction: Benjamin Lefebvre, 'Stand by Your Man: Adapting L.M. Montgomery's *Anne of Green Gables*' (*ECW* 76[2002] 149–69), and Patsy Aspasia Kotsopoulos, 'Avonlea as Main Street USA? Genre, Adaptation, and the Making of a Borderless Romance' (*ECW* 76[2002] 170–94). Lefebvre looks at the interesting situation that has arisen in the popular reception of Montgomery: that film and television adaptations are better known than the texts they purport to be based on, with a concomitant downgrading of satire. Kotsopoulos regards co-production as a move towards borderless representation which 'flattens the historical past'—in particular the Canadian content, which is sacrificed for American consumers. Two essays will be particularly useful for study of the novel and film versions of Michael Ondaatje's

The English Patient [novel 1992; film 1996]. Ondaatje's 'authorization' of the film version is central for Gillian Roberts, "'Sins of Omission": *The English Patient*, THE ENGLISH PATIENT, and the Critics' (*ECW* 76[2002] 195–215), where she looks at the processes that lead to critics ignoring the important changes and omissions in the film version because of this authorization. The postcolonial focus is sharpened even more with Glen Lowry, 'Between *The English Patients*: "Race" and the Cultural Politics of Adapting CanLit' (*ECW* 76[2002] 216–46); Lowry argues that the film's effacement of Canadian content has been largely overlooked because of box-office success. Finally, issues such as morphing and shape-shifting, especially where the latter is foregrounded, are explored by John Greyson in 'The Coconut Strategy' (*ECW* 76[2002] 263–6).

The rise of 'food' as a cultural commodity is the subject of Kathleen Batstone's introduction (*ECW* 78[2002] 1–15), with the concomitant shift 'from food as material object to food as artistic spectacle'. S. Leigh Matthews, '(Nearly) Sacred Achievements: Culinary Place in Women's Prairie Memoirs' (*ECW* 78[2002] 16–41), takes another look at women's memoirs as a mode of 'sensory remembrance' that interrogates normative metanarratives of western settlement. From a Rabelaisian perspective, Marta Dvorak, 'Books and Bread: Carnivalesque Patterns of Alimentary Discourse in *Beautiful Losers*' (*ECW* 78[2002] 42–60), enjoys Cohen's scatological approach to 'alimentary dynamics'. Dvorak's essay neatly conjoins a number of theoretical issues in Canadian writing, such as postmodern metafiction, the carnivalesque, and postcolonialism. Postcolonial hybridity is read as 'hyphenated' in Michelle Hartlet, 'Does Shirley Temple Eat Chicken Feet? Consuming Ambivalence in Wayson Choy's *The Jade Peony*' (*ECW* 78[2002] 61–85), while ethnic and regional identity are also examined from a culinary perspective in Tanya Lewis, 'Eating Identity: Food and the Construction of Region in *The Cure for Death by Lightning* and *Fall on Your Knees*' (*ECW* 78[2002] 86–109). Lewis notes that culinary tropes should not simply be seen as an expression of individual identity since they also establish regional identity. Bakhtin is returned to with the 'distinction between the classical and the grotesque body' in Susan Kevra, 'Indigestible Stew and Holy Piss: The Politics of Food in Rodolphe Girard's *Marie Calumet*' (*ECW* 78[2002] 110–36): food management is regarded 'as a subversive tool' that constructs the 'grotesque realism that infuses Girard's novel'. Candida Rifkind, 'The Hungry Thirties: Writing Food and Gender during the Depression' (*ECW* 78[2002] 163–91), reveals the way in which paying attention to the representation of food involves widening the discursive registers of an encroaching Canadian modernity. Nathalie Cook's 'Getting the Mix Just Right for the Canadian Home Baker' (*ECW* 78[2002] 192–219) is a study that critically examines the claims of well-known 'fictional food figures' in Canada who were a central iconic component in the rise of consumer culture. Mervyn Nicholson, 'Lowther, Neruda, and the Secret Wisdom of Food' (*ECW* 78[2002] 220–42), critiques the commonly held notion of the consumption of food as a manifestation of power.

A late arrival, *The Christie Harris Papers*, an inventory of the archive at the University of Calgary Library, is compiled by Mary Chevrefils, edited by Apollonia Steele, with a 'biocritical essay' by Alexandra West. The essay is a clearly written introduction to the wide range of materials published by Harris (perhaps most famous for her novels *Once Upon a Totem* [1963], *Raven's Cry* [1966], and *Mouse Woman and the Vanished Princesses* [1976]), ranging from children's literature, radio programmes, and radio dramas to historical and auto/biographical books. The issue of appropriating First Nations stories, i.e., cultural property, is touched upon and given some critical attention, but there are also problematic references to 'the preservation of disappearing Canadian native culture' (p. xxix), a subject which is not adequately addressed even given the extensive quotation of postcolonial critic Penny Petrone; an uninformed reader of the essay could be left with the impression that First Nations culture only survived with the aid of Western anthropologists and writers. The essay does serve, however, as an excellent starting-point for the discussion and deeper exploration of the complex issues of Western appropriation of First Nations stories. The 'Archival Introduction' by Jean F. Tener and Mary Chevrefils discusses the importance of finding aids for researchers who sometimes see archives as sources not of information but, instead, of frustration. The essay also describes the Harris archive's organization, along with its acquisition history, and gives an overview of content. As an aid to research, the inventory is very useful: there are many interesting entries, such as a file with letters from the acclaimed Haida artist and writer Bill Reid (1920–98), alongside related materials and many files concerning Harris's interaction with leading Canadian critics, publishers, and universities.

(b) Fiction

Many of the essays that cover fiction are published in theme collections, reviewed above. Two novels by Margaret Atwood receive excellent coverage in Gina Wisker's *Margaret Atwood's 'Alias Grace': A Reader's Guide* and Jennifer Murray's 'Questioning the Triple Goddess: Myth and Meaning in Margaret Atwood's *The Robber Bride*' (*CanL* 173[2002] 72–90). Wisker writes in the Continuum Contemporaries series, following a standard format which includes bibliographical information, close reading of the novel, summaries of initial—and contemporary—receptions to the novel, discussion questions, and bibliographical information, including web-based materials. Reading *Alias Grace* [1996], Wisker does a good job of situating the novel as a postmodernist text and with regard to literary traditions, for example, comparing Grace's first-person narrative with Joyce's *A Portrait of the Artist as a Young Man* [1914–15]. 'Women's Lives and Roles' is a section which contextualizes Atwood's work, showing how the novel reveals the enabling and disabling social roles of women in nineteenth-century Canada. Wisker analyses language and genre, especially Atwood's use of the Canadian Gothic; the discussion questions are simple but effective. The book is very useful for introductory, but also wide-ranging, study of Atwood in context. Jennifer Murray examines mythical intertextuality in Atwood's Gothic novel *The Robber Bride* [1993], arguing that there are two modes of intertextuality at work: the 'open-ended mode ... whereby familiar [mythical] content is reworked into a later moment of textual production' and the framing mode, whereby intertextuality 'takes over not so much the content as the structure of the work to which it refers' (pp. 72–3). Murray argues that Atwood's use of myth can be seen as restrictive, especially with outmoded notions of gender and sexuality at work in the myths of the Triple Goddess and the Three Little Pigs, where, in particular, the 'three-in-oneness' of the former is transposed via character development and narrative organization. Murray thus critiques Atwood's use of myth and argues for a more realist and critically complex mode of engaging with women's identities.

Short stories are the focus of Richard Dellamore, 'Isabella Valency Crawford and an English-Canadian Sodom' (*CanL* 173[2002] 16–32), and Ildikó de Papp Carrington, 'Where Are You, Mother? Alice Munro's "Save the Reaper"' (*CanL* 173[2002] 34–51). Dellamore analyses the short story that opens Atwood's selection in *The Oxford Book of Canadian Short Stories in English* [1986], that is, Crawford's 'Extradited' [1886], which in turn draws upon Genesis 18–19; Atwood's choice is of importance because of the ways in which 'Extradited' has an ambivalent relationship with 'emergent' English Canadian nationalism. Carrington observes that Munro introduces a new perspective to the representation of the mother–daughter relationship in her fiction in her short story 'Save the Reaper': that of a mother's/grandmother's point of view with the protagonist called Eve; through narrational anachronisms, Munro explores ongoing transformational roles in four generations of mothers and daughters.

Margaret Morriss, '"No Short Cuts": The Evolution of *The Double Hook*' (*CanL* 173[2002] 54–70), performs a fascinating close analysis of the draft and published versions of Sheila Watson's canonical Canadian novel *The Double Hook* [1959], noting how the two major revisions are 'emendations' rather than simply narrative or structural changes. While paying close attention to suggested, and actual, emendations in the draft versions, Morriss notes that the most drastic revisions occur between the second draft and the published version; Morriss provides description, commentary, and deeper analysis of the versions, concluding in part that the revisions enhance the situational sense of drama, terrain, and character. A significant addition to Sara Jeannette Duncan studies is Kathryn Ready, 'Sara Jeannette Duncan's *A Daughter of Today*: Nineteenth-Century Canadian Literary Feminism and the Fin-de-siècle Magic-Picture Story' (*CanL* 173[2002] 95–112), which situates *A Daughter of Today* [1894] in relation to Oscar Wilde's *The Picture of Dorian Gray* [1891] and the genre of the magic-picture story. Ready suggests that, in the adaptation of this genre, Duncan explores and dramatizes major challenges for women artists of the 1890s in particular, in wresting the woman's role away from the Victorian ideal of the Angel in the House. Ready's close reading of Duncan's novel and comparative analyses of Duncan and Wilde (and other key texts) are in-depth and extensive. Winner of the 2001 George Wicken Prize in Canadian Literature is an essay by Lindsey McMaster, 'The Urban Working Girl in Turn-of-the-Century Canadian Fiction' (*ECW* 77[2002] 1–25), which is also a close reading of four key texts with working-class female characters, Agnes Maule Machar's *Roland Graeme* [1892], Isabel Ecclestone Mackay's *The House of Windows* [1912], Bertrand William Sinclair's *North of Fifty-Three* [1914], and Jessie Georgina Sime's *Sister Woman* [1919]. McMaster compares and contrasts the American and Canadian literary treatment of working women, and has sections on 'Social Realism and Working Women in Canadian Literature', 'Class Cross-Dressing in *The House of Windows*' and 'Sex and the City'. Her argument is wide-ranging, and she suggests that the engagement with, and representation of, 'the working girl' leads to an insistence on 'new distributions of social respect' and validates 'the cultural innovations of independent women'. The essay also expands and updates from a feminist perspective the emerging body of work on the popular fiction writer Bertrand William Sinclair.

The work of Dionne Brand continues to receive in-depth analysis, with Joanna Luft, 'Elizete and Verlia Go To Toronto: Caribbean Immigrant Sensibilities at

"Home" and Overseas in Dionne Brand's *In Another Place, Not Here*' (*ECW* 77[2002] 26–49). The essay explores the double bind for the Caribbean immigrant, where Toronto and the homeland are both 'impossible' spaces to inhabit: the new country offers meagre opportunities to Caribbean immigrants, a situation which, Luft argues, is expressed in Brand's novel by the 'heightened marginalization' of the protagonists. Doubling is the main feature of Li-Ping Geng's 'The Rival Editions of Ethel Wilson's *Swamp Angel*' (*ECW* 77[2002] 63–89), a study of the two separate versions, with different endings, of this Canadian classic published in 1954. Geng's analysis and comparison of editions is meticulous, and a new third edition is argued for, one that is editorially authoritative. Alison Calder, 'The Wilderness Plot, the Deep Map, and Sharon Butala's Changing Prairie' (*ECW* 77[2002] 164–85), traces the changing representation of wilderness in Butala's *The Perfection of the Morning* [1994] and *Wild Stone Heart* [2000].

(c) Poetry and Drama
The disjunction between commonly held post-structuralist views and those of ecocriticism is the subject of Sophia Forster, 'Don McKay's Comic Anthropocentrism: Ecocriticism Meets "Mr. Nature Poet"' (*ECW* 77[2002] 107–35); where post-structuralism regards all worlds as textual or representational constructs, ecocriticism often posits the natural world as preceding human intervention. Forster compares comic and tragic modes of poetic representation, where the former deflates or decentres the technological subject in favour of ecocritical ideology; there is also an interesting analysis of the concept of *matériel* in the poetry of McKay. Turning again to post-structuralist problematization, this time of the traditionally held differences between oral and written traditions, First Nations written storytelling is situated as a trans-genre mode in Blanca Schorcht, 'The Storied World Of Harry Robinson: *Emerging Dialogues*' (*BCS* 135[2002] 145–62), where it is argued that Robinson's readers engage with multiple layers of stories, voices, and intersubjective worlds, an engagement that is mimetic of the processes of First Nations orality.

'The body' is the theme of *Canadian Theatre Review* 109[2002], edited by Catherine Graham; it is contextualized as a rejection of Cartesian thought in her opening piece, 'Theatrical Bodies and Everyday Life' (*CTR* 109[2002] 3–4). Such a rejection is embodied by the holistic approach advocated by Judith Koltai, 'Making Sense, Getting Through—"The Word's Body"' (*CTR* 109[2002] 5–7), where a mode of bodily expression and practice in performance is regarded as resonating with the 'lived experience' that gave birth to the theatrical text. Kathleen Gallagher, 'Gendered Bodies and High School Girls: Devising Theatre' (*CTR* 109[2002] 8–11), utilizes performance in schools as a way of creatively expressing a 'way out' of oppressive situations. The group discussion format is used by Erika Batdorf, Leslie French, Sallie Lyons, and Catherine Marrion, 'Sitting and Talking ... about Movement?!' (*CTR* 109[2002] 12–17)—a conversation in progress on the role of the movement teacher and of movement in theatre. It also contains a useful section on influences and suggested reading. Theories of symptoms and their embodiment are explored by Michelle Newman, 'Body/absence/body: Symptomatologies' (*CTR* 109[2002] 18–21), which also asks how, after the deconstruction of the subject, the unified body can still be considered a theatrical aim. W.A. Hamilton describes the process of writing and producing a play that went through a number of formats, in

'Making *Mindlands*' (*CTR* 109[2002] 22–3), followed by a discussion of the restaging of the play as a one-man multimedia production, in Paul Rivers, 'Making *Mindlands*: The Multimedia Production' (*CTR* 109[2002] 24–5). The script of *Mindlands* is published in this issue (*CTR* 109[2002] 46–69). Hybrid performance via 'image theatre' is the subject of Erin Hurley, 'Carbone 14's Intelligent and Responsive Body' (*CTR* 109[2002] 26–31), where Carbone 14's choice of the dancing body as 'the primary signifier of meaning in performance' is predicated upon the body as 'communicative vessel' not in need of supplementary textual interpretation. The gap between ethnic visibility and cultural identity is an issue for many first- and second-generation immigrants to Canada; Rosalind Kerr, 'Re-Surfacing the Chinese-Canadian Body in Performance: Elyne Quan's "Surface Tension" and "What?"' (*CTR* 109[2002] 31–7), looks at the journeys involved in comprehending this 'gap' performed in two plays. The citational nature of the gendered body in a theatrical 'emotional landscape' is the subject of David Bateman, '"Performing Femininity" On Stage and Off' (*CTR* 109[2002] 38–41). Study of the acrobatic body completes the theme issue, in Bernard Lavoie, 'DynamO Théâtre: Moving Images of Teenage Life' (*CTR* 109[2002] 42–5). The risk-taking and constant pushing of physical limits by teenagers find expression on the acrobatic stage. The theme issue as a whole, rich with visual images, will provide plenty of ideas for the criticism and production of theatre that pays close attention to the body in performance; the issue should also appeal to a wide range of critics, not just those who study Canadian theatre, since literary-critical theories of 'the body' sometimes lack practical applications and/or examples, both of which are admirably provided by this text.

Chinese Canadian theatre is the subject of *CTR* 110[2002], edited by Jennifer Kay Chan, who asks in her editorial (*CTR* 110[2002] 3–4), 'Does race stereotype or classify a playwright?' She answers that the theme issue on Chinese Canadian theatre should be read as a celebration of an increasingly large and visible body of work that encounters ethnicity in all of its complexities. Reacting to the label 'Chinese', however, Jean Yoon, 'Chinese Theatre in Canada: The Bigger Picture' (*CTR* 110[2002] 5–11), argues that the Asian Canadian theatre scene is far more diverse than this term signifies, and she backs this statement up with a historical overview of Asian Canadian immigration and performance. Marty Chan, author of 'The Ethnic Playwright's Challenge' (*CTR* 110[2002] 12–15), who is mainly known for his play *Mom, Dad, I'm Living with a White Girl* [1995], problematizes the notion that Chinese Canadian playwrights are different from Caucasians, and worries that he will become ghettoized as a 'resident expert' on anything to do with Chinese culture. Three separate 2001 shows from Toronto—*Ghost Train*, *Iron Road*, and *Mother Tongue*—are critically reviewed by Derrick Chua in 'The Spirit of China Lives in Canadian Theatre' (*CTR* 110[2002] 16–19), and by John Karastamatis in 'Missed Stories' (*CTR* 110[2002] 21–3), while the focus on production is the essence of Jennifer Kay Chan, 'Hey, Mr. Producer' (*CTR* 110[2002] 20). The transition from China to Canada is explored by Bernard Nguyen in 'Theatre in Québec: A Test Of Perseverance' (*CTR* 110[2002] 23–5), focusing on the career of Chinese-born actor Aimee Lee, while the energies both personal and professional of actor Marjorie Chan are explored in discussion with Gloria Kim, 'Marjorie Chan' (*CTR* 110[2002] 26–30). Two aspects of the play by Simon Johnston, *Running Dog, Paper Tiger* [1997], get coverage: first, through an auto/

biographical survey of Johnston's theatre career in Doretta Lau and Jim Wong-Chu, 'Simon Johnston: Two Cultures, One Vision' (*CTR* 110[2002] 31–4), and, second, from the perspective of a person who had acted in and directed the play, John James Hong, '*Gold Mountain Guest*: A Director's Diary' (*CTR* 110[2002] 35–7). The collaborative processes in theatre and opera, so well explored in the theme issue, continue with Chan Ka Nin, 'My First Opera' (*CTR* 110[2002] 38–40), which charts the difficulties and the long process of creating an opera from beginning to end. Catherine Hernandez, 'Beijing Opera in Canada' (*CTR* 110[2002] 41–3), looks at not only the survival but also the development of a living art form in Canada, and this is complemented by Heidi Specht, 'Into the Heart of Beijing Opera' (*CTR* 110[2002] 44–6), which opens up the art form further to young Canadians. Specht's essay is useful in that it describes in clear terms the various components and categories of Chinese opera, especially given her argument that the Western word 'opera' is confusing and misleading in a Chinese artistic context. Keira Loughran, 'One Side of the River: A Chinese Odyssey' (*CTR* 110[2002] 47–8), writes a journal from the perspective of a third-generation Chinese Canadian theatre artist returning to her homeland. Jennifer Yap, '*I* as Collage: Playwright John Ng on the Modern Immigrant Experience' (*CTR* 110[2002] 49–52), explores the ways in which Asian Canadian theatre constantly returns to originary accounts, especially that of the immigrant experience. There are four scripts, Marty Chan, 'The Meeting' (*CTR* 110[2002] 53–7), Bobby Del Rio, 'Half-Chinx Taking Over the World' (*CTR* 110[2002] 58–62), John Ng, 'I' (*CTR* 110[2002] 63–82), and Yung Luu, 'I Chink' (*CTR* 110[2002] 83–7). While the issue presents diverse Asian Canadian theatre experiences from a multitude of perspectives such as those of actors, writers, directors, and so on, it does at times feel overly descriptive; however, as Jennifer Kay Chan writes, the Chinese Canadian 'artists today would not be here were it not for the hard work of the mentors, writers and artists that paved the way and set the standards' (p. 4). It is presumably now the responsibility of the critics of Canadian theatre to follow up on this issue with more analytical work.

Adapting Shakespeare in Canada is the theme of *CTR* 111[2002], edited by Daniel Fischlin and Ric Knowles, who suggest in their editorial (*CTR* 111[2002] 3–4) that Canadian adaptations go far beyond the purely dramatic to perform a variety of cultural and political roles. The opening essay by Linda Burnett, '"Redescribing a World": Towards a Theory of Shakespearean Adaptation in Canada' (*CTR* 111[2002] 5–9), examines four dramatic adaptations: Ann-Marie MacDonald's *Goodnight Desdemona (Good Morning Juliet)*, Margaret Clarke's *Gertrude & Ophelia*, Ken Gass's *Claudius*, and Djanet Sear's *Harlem Duet*. Arguing that postmodern parody is at play, Burnett also distinguishes the differences between what she categorizes as a 'deconstructive postmodernism' and 'constructive postcolonialism', where the latter is an affirmative way of adding to cultural and political texts, in the process performing what Salman Rushdie calls 'redescribing a world'. Ellen Mackay, 'The Spectre of Straight Shakespeare' (*CTR* 111[2002] 10–14), criticizes the overriding promotion of straight gender roles in Canadian productions, which he calls 'heteronormative'. The interrogation of this heteronormativity in Ann Marie MacDonald's *Goodnight Desdemona (Good Morning Juliet)* and Michael O'Brien's *Mad Boy Chronicle* is the basis of Mackay's analysis of performing gender. The exploration of cultural difference and resistance via performance is the subject of Leanore Lieblein, '*Dave veut jouer* Richard III'

(*CTR* 111[2002] 15–21), where 'disability' and the body are brought centre stage in a Nouveau Théâtre Expérimental 2001 production. Lieblein argues that one of the central processes involved is that of cannibalizing the Shakespearian text to explore issues of performing otherness, especially where the latter involves asserting the participatory rights of the 'handicapped' body. Susan Bennett, 'Virtually Canadian' (*CTR* 111[2002] 22–7) looks at the 'Canadian-sourced cyber-Shakespeares' that are available from a variety of providers, such as the CBC (Canadian Broadcasting Corporation), the online *Canadian Theatre Encyclopedia*, the website for the Stratford Festival, and various other electronic offerings from theatre companies doing performances. Bennett doesn't just review these sites; rather, she examines how Shakespearian adaptations 'for the virtual domain' are tied in with the ways in which such web-based productions exemplify reworkings of Canadian cultural identity; Bennett's 'Works Cited' is a rich resource of website addresses. The following essay by Jennifer Ailles, 'Adapting the Bard: A Virtual Guide' (*CTR* 111[2002] 28–32), is a companion piece, which systematically reviews Shakespeare festival websites including the Victoria Shakespeare Festival, Bard on the Beach (Vancouver), Shakespeare on the Saskatchewan Festival, York Shakespeare Festival, A Company of Fools (Ottawa), Shakespeare by the Sea Festival (St Johns) and the Stratford Festival of Canada. Ailles argues that the essentially transient nature of web-based materials is problematic but also analogous to the ephemeral nature of theatrical performance itself. Mark McCutcheon, 'A Midsummer Night's Mash-Up' (*CTR* 111[2002] 33–42), looks at a 'rave' adaptation by Serenity Industries [2000] of *A Midsummer Night's Dream*; McCutcheon contextualizes the rave scene and how it functions as a site of cultural reworking and production. Mark Fortier, 'Dancing with Shakespeare' (*CTR* 111[2002] 43–5), looks at the ways in which Shakespeare was drawn on by artistic director Tom Stroud, specifically *Romeo and Juliet* for *R & J ... 21 Scenes for Romeo and Juliet* [1994] and *Hamlet* for *The Garden* [2001]. Fortier notes how Stroud finds components of the Shakespearian text that correspond with dance structures. Jessica Schagerl, 'Shakespeare in a Blender' (*CTR* 111[2002] 46–9), intriguingly links the street-theatre context with the Company of Fools adaptations of Shakespeare to reveal both site-specific performance needs and inherent possibilities in Shakespeare's texts. Tanner Mirrlees's 'Kate Lynch's All-Woman *Dream*' (*CTR* 111[2002] 50–9) is an interview with the director of Theatre Pass Muraille concerning an all-woman production of *A Midsummer Night's Dream*. Another interview follows, by Judy Van Rhijn, 'Loreena McKennitt, Merchant of Song' (*CTR* 111[2002] 60–2), which explores the ways in which the musical score can help reinterpret a play in relation to contemporary issues. Stephen Heatley, 'Adapting Shakespeare to an Outdoor Canadian Prairie Reality' (*CTR* 111[2002] 63–6), argues that the resurgent interest in this British playwright is caused by the essentially Canadian processes of social and aesthetic adaptation. Daniel Fischlin, 'Theatrical Adaptations of Shakespeare in Canada: A Working Bibliography' (*CTR* 111[2002] 67–73), provides an important and significant resource in Canadian Shakespeare studies. The bibliography, a major project in process, lists 161 adaptations. Daniel Fischlin, 'Adaptation as Rite of Passage: *A Shakespeare Pageant*' (*CTR* 111[2002] 74–5), introduces the first play published in the theme issue, and describes its Roman Catholic school contexts, besides discussing how the play itself was recovered by the Canadian Adaptations of Shakespeare project. The title pages of 'A Shakespeare Pageant' (*CTR* 111[2002]

76–7) are reproduced, as well as the play itself, in S.M.A. (Sister Mary Agnes), 'A Shakespeare Pageant: Dialogue for Commencement Day' (*CTR* 111[2002] 78–86). Ric Knowles introduces the second play in the theme issue, 'Reading *Elsinore*: The Ghost and the Machine' (*CTR* 111[2002] 87–8), by meditating on the question of whether *Hamlet* is in many ways formative for contemporary culture, for example in relation to how the canonical Victor Hugo translation impacted on Francophone discursive fields. The script of 'Elsinore', adapted by Robert Lepage, follows (*CTR* 111[2002] 89–99). *CTR* 111 is a particularly rich issue, providing a wealth of insightful, well-written critical essays and bibliographical and dramatic materials.

The final issue of the year, *CTR* 112[2002], is on 'Jazz, Blues and Theatre' and is edited by Allan Watts, who provides a clearly written editorial on the subject of jazz and blues, linking them with theatre via the shared practice of improvisation. Jesse Stewart's 'Passages on *Passages*: Some Reflections on the Creation of a Multimedia, Improvised, Jazz Opera' (*CTR* 112[2002] 5–10) is an account of the creative processes involved and the essential impetus to conceive a work that meditates upon the ephemeral nature and temporality of improvisatory performance; the piece segues directly into the '*Passages* Libretto' by Paul Haines (*CTR* 112[2002] 10–12). Ric Knowles's 'Impro' (*CTR* 112[2002] 13–15) is a short critical commentary on 'freedom versus structure' in improvisation, especially the 'process-versus-product issue' which includes the question of audience. Allan Watts, 'Directing *Red Mango*: A Blues Conversation with John Cooper' (*CTR* 112[2002] 16–20), explores the interactions between musical and theatrical form in an interview. The crossing of boundaries by jazz musicians is the subject of Frédérique Arroyas, '«Dis, Blaise …»: The *Poème simultané* According to Cartier' (*CTR* 112[2002] 21–4), which is a fascinating examination of the relations between text and performance. A key bibliography is compiled by Bart Vautour, Tanner Mirrlees, and Allan Watts, 'Jazz and Blues Dramatic Literature and Performance Bibliography' (*CTR* 112[2002] 25–6). Three innovative scripts are published: George Elliott Clarke, 'Québécité: A Libretto in Three Cantos (First Draft)' (*CTR* 112[2002] 27–45); Audrei-Kairen, 'Big Mama!—The Willie Mae Thornton Story' (*CTR* 112[2002] 46–56); and David King, 'Issues of the Night Time: A Play with Blues Music' (*CTR* 112[2002] 57–69). *CTR* 112 provides a rare glimpse into the creative and critical processes of an otherwise ephemeral performance form; it is another example of the wide-ranging and innovative exploration of theatre in Canada published by this outstanding journal.

4. India

(a) General

Shyamala A. Narayan's annual bibliography 'India' (*JCL* 37:iii[2002] 61–100) is, as ever, a helpful and informative guide to creative and critical writing published during the previous year. Narayan has also collaborated with M.K. Naik to produce *Indian English Literature, 1980–2000: A Critical Survey*, which is a sequel to Naik's *A History of Indian Literature in English* [1982]. Although the survey approach of the book has obvious limitations, this is a useful and helpful volume.

A number of essays discuss the role of the English language in India. Amit Chaudhuri's 'Poles of Recovery: From Dutt to Chaudhuri' (*Interventions* 4[2002]

89–105) is an offshoot of his anthology *The Picador Book of Modern Indian Literature* [2001]. Focusing particularly on Michael Madhusudan Dutt and Nirad Chaudhuri, the essay explores the Indian writer's attitude to the relationship between the mother tongue and English, arguing that Dutt's and Chaudhuri's attitudes towards the vernacular language and towards 'Indianness' were formed by the dual impulses of 'disowning' and 'recovery', and that these impulses in turn were 'inextricably linked ... to the English language'. The relationship between English and other languages also forms the subject of K.C. Belliappa's 'Problematising Indian Writing in English' (*JIWE* 30:ii[2002] 1–9). Belliappa surveys some of the difficulties in the relationship and calls for a complementary rather than adversarial attitude. Vinay Dharwadker's article, 'English in India and Indian Literature in English: The Early History, 1579–1834' (*CLS* 39:ii[2002] 93–119), sees the process of diffusion of English in India as being rooted in the Indian participants' prior existence in a multilingual, multicultural, literate world. This, he suggests, 'introduced powerful *pre*colonial and *non*colonial elements' into the construction of Indian discourse in the English language. Specific writers discussed include Din Mohammed, Cavelli Venkata Boriah, and Rammohun Roy. Dharwadker discusses the history of English in India as a story of two competing discourses: British discourse about India and an Indian counter-discourse, which seeks to contest British representations, and which begins with *The Travels of Dean Mahomet* [1794].

Two significant and welcome features seem to stand out in the year under review: a movement towards pushing back the temporal boundaries of the study of Indian literature in the English language, and an increasing emphasis on literary, cultural, and historical contextualization. These tendencies are exemplified in a number of books and articles. Lynn Zastoupil's 'Defining Christians, Making Britons: Rammohun Roy and the Unitarians' (*VS* 44[2001–2] 214–43) discusses Roy's popularity during his visit to Britain in the early 1830s as an indication of the fact that 'colonial encounters were not always about the construction of difference'. His point of entry into British society, she suggests, was Unitarianism, which was engaged in redefining Christian and British identity. In Roy, consequently, Britons could see what the 'dismantling of the established order held in store for themselves'.

C.L. Innes's *A History of Black and Asian Writing in Britain, 1700–2000* discusses a number of writers who are often claimed for Indian literature, although, as she notes, problems of labelling arise with such writers. Authors included in her book lived in Britain for at least five years, and the works discussed were published in Britain and/or addressed mainly to a British audience. Innes moves easily and confidently between accounts of the historical and ideological contexts and analyses of individual writers. The most valuable feature of her book, as far as India is concerned, is its discussion of writing before the generation of Mulk Raj Anand, Raja Rao, and R.K. Narayan. A succinct account of Dean Mahomed emphasizes the duality of his position as someone who identified with the English and English culture but was also eager to assert himself as an Indian who could speak with authority on the country and its people. A brief discussion of the Parsi Behramji Malabari focuses on his writing on behalf of Indian women and his account of London (*An Indian Eye on English Life*), which is seen as a counter-discourse to European travel writings on India. A chapter on the sisters Cornelia and Alice

Sorabji discusses their life and writing (both fiction and non-fiction), suggesting that Alice tended to reproduce English stereotypes of manliness and Indian nationalism, while Cornelia presented 'a more complex, ambivalent, and hybrid picture' of both Indians and the English. Writers of later generations are dealt with more briefly. There are short accounts of novelists such as Mulk Raj Anand, Aubrey Menen, and G.V. Desani. An epilogue surveying trends from the 1950s onwards includes some pages on Salman Rushdie and hybridity.

Elleke Boehmer's *Empire, the National and the Postcolonial, 1890–1920: Resistance in Interaction* aims to avoid concentration on the 'conventional axis of interaction' between colonizer and colonized by examining processes of solidarity and influence between nationalist and anti-colonial movements, writers, and thinkers from different regions, in particular South Africa, Ireland, and India. Two chapters explore the relationship between the Irish-born devotee of Kali, Margaret Noble (Sister Nivedita) and the Bengali radical turned sage and poet, Aurobindo Ghose, as well as Nivedita's relationship with her 'Master', the charismatic Swami Vivekananda. Boehmer draws attention to, amongst other things, the 'spiritual nationalism' to which they subscribed and to the ways in which religious symbols such as Kali served as channels for anti-colonial interchanges. A chapter on the South African nationalist Solomon Plaatje includes an account of similarities between Plaatje and Gandhi (although the two never seem to have made direct connections, and indeed were concerned in exclusivist ways with their own communities). The final chapter explores the intersections between metropolitan modernism and the cross-cultural contacts engendered by empire. The experience of otherness, it is argued here, allowed Yeats to discover a 'spiritual intersubjectivity' in the work of Tagore; Leonard Woolf, who internalized 'native' perspectives in his novel *The Village in the Jungle*, later showed the impact of cultural otherness in more mediated forms through his journalism and through his contribution to the anti-imperialism embedded in his wife Virginia's fiction.

The autobiography of one of the writers discussed by both Innes and Boehmer, Cornelia Sorabji, has been republished with a slightly altered subtitle as *India Calling: The Memories of Cornelia Sorabji, India's First Woman Barrister*. The book is edited by Chandani Lokugé, whose introduction explores the different cultural elements which shaped Sorabji: the Parsi, the Indian, and the British. Like other Parsis, Sorabji supported the British and opposed Indian nationalism. There is also a useful account of the complexities of her feminism and her Orientalist attitudes to the institution of the *zenana*.

Sorabji is just one of the many women writers—others include Pandita Ramabai, Toru Dutt, and Sarojini Naidu—represented in de Souza and Pereira, eds., *Women's Voices: Selections from Nineteenth- and Early Twentieth-Century Indian Writing in English*. The title is a little misleading, since work published as late as the 1950s finds its way into the anthology. This volume contains work in a variety of forms: fiction, letters, memoirs, essays, reformist tracts, and a number of other modes. As Eunice de Souza points out in her brief introduction, nationalism and the women's movement figure extensively in these writings. Lindsay Pereira provides helpful biographical and contextual notes for each author.

Devy, ed., *Indian Literary Criticism: Theory and Interpretation*, is an ambitious anthology of criticism ranging over nearly two millennia from Bharatmuni (third century or earlier) to A.K. Ramanujan, Aijaz Ahmad, and Gayatri Spivak in the closing decades of the twentieth century. One of the major aims of the volume is to provide easier access to India's relatively neglected critical tradition. As Devy notes in his preface, this should in reality be a multi-volume project. For reasons of space, however, many of the major critical thinkers can only be represented here by brief excerpts from their writing. The longer first section of the book, 'Theory', includes extracts from such classics as Bharatmuni's account of the *rasa* theory and Anandavardhana's analysis of *dhvani* (the suggestive quality of poetic language). Nearer our own time, a valuable feature of the book is the essays from writers such as Tagore, Aurobindo, B.S. Mardhekar, and Bhalcandra Nemade. Some incisive letters from the Urdu/Persian poet Ghalib, written in the aftermath of the revolt of 1857, shed light on his state of mind at the time, but have little to say about either the qualities of his own writing or poetry in general. The shorter second section, 'Interpretation', contains a number of commentaries on Indian criticism, including K. Krishnamoorthy's helpful overview of Sanskrit poetics and Ramanujan's account of Tamil poetics. In bringing this material together Devy has performed a valuable service for students of Indian literatures.

Margery Sabin's *Dissenters and Mavericks: Writings about India in English, 1765–2000* considers work from the colonial period and after. One of the chief aims of her book, she states in a polemical introduction which takes issue with Ranajit Guha, Homi Bhabha, and Edward Said, is to focus on the individual literary qualities of her chosen authors rather than submerge them in wider discourses of colonialism and postcolonialism. *Dissenters and Mavericks* looks at work by a variety of 'dissenters' in a number of forms and genres, including fiction, letters, autobiography, travel narratives, and journalism. The first part of the book discusses Horace Walpole's letters, Burke's speeches and writings, an account of *sati* in Sleeman's memoirs, and Wilkie Collins's *The Moonstone*. In the second section, which turns to the postcolonial period, Sabin begins with Nirad Chaudhuri's *Autobiography of an Unknown Indian*, noting Chaudhuri's reliance on Victorian and Romantic models, but also drawing attention to the fragmentariness and 'latent modernism' in his work. These formal characteristics, she suggests, bear witness to the tensions of fashioning a Bengali identity. A subsequent chapter on Indian cultural politics during the 1950s focuses on the way in which writers for the journal *Quest* attempted to articulate independent attitudes in the face of foreign and indigenous pressures. Naipaul's Indian writings are discussed in relation to his 'troubled self-consciousness about the meaning of postcolonial individuality', his 'vacillation between self-effacement and self-assertion'. The epilogue to the book offers the writings of Pankaj Mishra as examples of 'a new cosmopolitanism oriented specifically to Indian conditions'.

Rukmini Bhaya Nair's *Lying on the Postcolonial Couch: The Idea of Indifference* collects some of her essays and lectures. The introduction argues that the theme uniting the essays is colonial and postcolonial indifference, 'a cold life-denying apparatus of print, of meaningless reductionism and arcane formalisms'. One of the chapters, 'The Testament of the Tenth Muse: Toward a Feminist Sensibility', is a discussion of Indian women's poetry which appeared in much the same form in K. Satchidanandan, ed., *Indian Poetry: Modernism and After* (reviewed in *YWES* 82[2003]). Other essays deal with teaching Poe and English literature in Indian universities. Essays on fiction are reviewed below in Section 4(*b*).

Nair has also edited *Translation, Text and Theory: The Paradigm of India*, a volume of essays exploring aspects of translation and translation theory in the multilingual context of the Indian subcontinent. The volume contains a wide range of material, but some of the essays will be of more immediate interest than others to those whose main interests lie in Indian writing in English. Jhumpa Lahiri's 'Intimate Alienation: Immigrant Fiction and Translation' reflects on her own bicultural situation, discussing both her connections with and her distance from India and from the Bengali language of her parents. 'Authorial Submissions: Publishing and Translation' by Ritu Menon, one of the founders of the feminist publishing house Kali for Women, provides a succinct account of the present situation in translations from regional languages into English. Krishna Rayan's 'Classical Idiom: Translating Sanskrit Critical Terms' sheds light on the meaning of concepts such as *rasa* and *dhvani*. The volume also contains Tejaswani Niranajana's 'Post-Colonial Representation: Translation as Disruption', which has been published in various forms and places, including in her book *Siting Translation*.

Basu, ed., *Translating Caste: Stories, Essays, Criticism*, and Bose, ed., *Translating Desire: The Politics of Gender and Culture in India*, are two new additions to Katha's Studies in Culture and Translation series, which was inaugurated by *Translating Partition* [2001] (see *YWES* 82[2003]). Both of these are wide-ranging in scope, dealing with contexts, film, and history, amongst other aspects of their subjects. Parts of these books dealing with fiction are dealt with in Section 4(*b*) below. *Translating Caste* contains a helpful annotated bibliography and a number of contextual and general critical essays. Tapan Basu's introduction outlines the theory, practice, history, and politics of caste, and he also contributes an essay surveying the development of Dalit literature. Sisir Kumar Das's 'The Narrative of Suffering: Caste and the Underprivileged' is more or less a reprint of a chapter with the same title, which was first published in his *History of Indian Literature, 1911–1956* [1995]. G. Arunima's essay on caste and gender explores the ways in which a focus on caste solidarity leads to a marginalization of gender issues. Gender is also one of the subjects discussed in the book's concluding chapter, an interview with the Marathi Dalit writer Urmila Pawar.

Gender is the principal theme of *Translating Desire*, a collection of twelve essays (and one short story) dealing with various aspects of the subject, including mythology and cinema as well as literature. Brinda Bose's introduction explores the connections between sexuality, nationalism, and culture, with the controversial film *Fire* (also the subject of another essay in the volume) forming one of her chief examples. Ruth Vanita's 'Same-Sex Love in India: An Overview' deals briefly with representations of her subject in ancient, secular, and religious texts, modern cinema, and contemporary gay culture in India. The book also contains essays on mainstream Bombay cinema and on *Bandit Queen*.

Vanita has also edited *Queering India: Same-Sex Love and Eroticism in Indian Culture and Society*, a kind of companion piece to the anthology *Same-Sex Love in India: Readings from Literature and History* [2000], which she brought out with Saleem Kidwai. The essays included in this volume discuss law, the cinema (Deepa Mehta's *Fire* in particular), television, and advertising, as well as literature. Two of the essays explore the Urdu and Persian traditions, while another examines female impersonation in the Parsi, Marathi, and Gujarati theatres. Leela Gandhi's 'Loving Well: Homosexuality and Utopian Thought in Post/Colonial India' argues that

Edward Carpenter's anti-colonial and utopian homosexual dissidence finds later echoes in the poetry and fiction of Vikram Seth and Aubrey Menen. In '"Do I Remove My Skin?" Interrogating Identity in Suniti Namjoshi's Fables', Anannya Dasgupta finds that Namjoshi's work 'traces the homoerotic in the cultural unconscious of a consciously heterosexist world and the East in a consciously Westcentric world'. Rosemary Marangoly George argues that same-sex desire in Kamala Das's poetry and fiction has often been misread in heterosexual terms. Ruth Vanita's own essay contrasts the homophobia evident in controversies generated by a number of literary representations of homosexuality earlier in the twentieth century with an apparently greater tolerance of homoeroticism in advertisements during the 1980s and 1990s. The modern Indian middle class, she suggests, has the confidence to deal with a blurring of sexual categories.

Jain and Singh, eds., *Indian Feminisms*, is a collection of essays, fiction, poetry, and memoirs. Meenakshi Mukherjee analyses narratives of conversion to Christianity by two nineteenth-century Indian women, one of whom is Krupa Satthianadhan. Other essays in the volume include studies of Gujarati and Hindi fiction, Marathi women's autobiographies, early Bengali women writers in English, and Dalit women poets writing in Telugu. Sudha Rai explores the process of recovering a tie with India through matrilineage in the poetry of Sujata Bhatt, Meena Alexander, and Chitra Divakaruni Banerjee. The volume also contains a number of essays on fiction in English which are discussed in Section 4(*b*) below.

Monti and Dhawan, eds., *Discussing Indian Women Writers: Some Feminist Issues*, includes a number of essays on autobiography, poetry, and drama by women. Bhagyashree Varma compares the autobiographies of Amrita Pritam, Kamala Das, and Jean Rhys. Silvia Albertazzi discusses representations of the female body in the poetry of Eunice de Souza, Kamala Das, and Sujata Bhatt. A rather uncritical essay by Alka Saxena looks at Arlene Zide's anthology of poetry by Indian women, *In Their Own Voice* [1993]. Mahasweta Devi's play *Mother of 1084* is the subject of a brief essay by A. Ramadevi. A more substantial piece by Sivamohan Sumathy considers questions of postcolonial female identity in the poetry of the Sri Lankan writer Jean Arasanayagam, Suniti Namjoshi's *Mothers of Maya Diip*, and Arundhati Roy's *The God of Small Things*. Essays from this volume dealing primarily with fiction are discussed in Section 4(*b*) below. Joel Kuortti's *Indian Women's Writing in English: A Bibliography* is a useful reference work covering both primary and secondary sources.

Poetry and drama are, as usual, critically neglected in comparison to prose fiction and non-fiction. There are, however, several items on the poet Agha Shahid Ali, most of them unfortunately occasioned by his tragically early death in 2001. A special section in his memory in *Massachusetts Review* (*MR* 43[2002] 260–76) contains a translation by Ali, along with early drafts and the final printed version of his poem 'The Floating Post Office'. Christine Benvenuto contributes an account of a conversation with him about his background, working methods, and poetic form. Amitav Ghosh's '"The Ghat of the Only World": Agha Shahid Ali in Brooklyn' (*Postcolonial Studies* 5[2002] 311–23), an affectionate personal memoir of Ali, also briefly discusses his views about Kashmir and suggests that poetically he was 'more the heir of Rumi and Kabir than Eliot and Merrill'.

An interview with Ali forms part of a special feature on Indian poetry in *Verse* (17:ii–iii/18:i[2001] 213–87). Ali discusses a range of subjects, including his own work, verse form, and translation. The feature also contains a selection of poetry and translations by a number of poets, including Jayanta Mahapatra and Ali himself. A brief piece by Randall Mann examines the darkness of Mahapatra's poetry. The feature concludes with a peculiar essay by Prema Nandakumar, 'One Hundred Years of Indian Poetry in English', which sees Aurobindo as the main figure in the tradition and looks nostalgically towards a revival of the epic tradition.

Too much of Rama Nair's brief study, *'Of Variegated Hues': The Poetry and Translations of A.K. Ramanujan*, is taken up with discussing well-worn themes concerning the development of Indian English poetry, the validity of writing in the English language, and ideas of 'Indianness'. There is, however, a useful chapter looking at Ramanujan's translations in conjunction with his original poetry in English.

Social Text (*SocT* 72[2002]), a special issue on September 11, contains 'Lyric in a Time of Violence', a sequence of poems by Meena Alexander responding to the events of that day (*SocT* 72[2002] 21–9), and 'The Poet in the Public Sphere: A Conversation with Meena Alexander' (*SocT* 72[2002] 31–8), in which Lopamudra Basu questions Alexander about her reaction to the events and about a variety of other issues, including her Indian/African childhood, responses to violence in India and migrancy. Sudeep Sen is interviewed about his poetry in *JCL* 37:i[2002] 149–62.

A talk by the playwright Mahesh Dattani, 'Contemporary Indian Theatre and its Relevance' (reproduced in *JIWE* 30:i[2002] 1–4), discusses Indian theatre in relation to three 'ideological spaces': the traditional, the 'continual' (contemporary work drawing on older traditions), and the radical. Dattani's own work is the subject of Susan Oommen's essay 'Inventing Narratives, Arousing Audiences: The Plays of Mahesh Dattani' (*NTQ* 17[2001] 347–56). Oommen looks at Dattani's plays as conversations with the audience in which there is a queering of 'audience sensibility and identity'. John Russell Brown's 'Voices for Reform in South Asian Theatre' (*NTQ* 17[2001] 45–53) reports on a symposium held in Dhaka in 1999 where it was argued that a return to the first principles laid out in the ancient Sanskrit manual, Bharata's *Natyasastra,* would facilitate the development of styles which could be Asian and modern at the same time.

Interventions 4[2002] 159–211 is a special section on Gayatri Chakravorty Spivak's *Critique of Postcolonial Reason*, gathering together papers originally presented at the annual meeting of the International Association for Philosophy and Literature. Spivak's work is approached by a number of writers from a variety of angles. Although there is nothing specific on Indian literature, Spivak's writings on India are used as a regular reference point, and Spivak herself, in responding to the papers, touches on subjects such as *sati*, Hinduism, and Bengali culture.

(b) Fiction

This section reviews criticism that focuses on prose fiction, but readers should also refer to Section 4(*a*) above for work that considers fiction along with other forms.

The historicization and contextualization referred to in Section 4(*a*) are also features of writing on fiction during the year under review. Mukherjee, ed., *Early Novels in India*, is a collection of essays dealing with work in a number of different Indian languages. One of the aims of the book, Mukherjee points out in her introduction—and the point is reiterated by Namwar Singh in the first essay—is to re-examine the widely held idea that the novel in India was essentially an imported and derivative form. This view, Namwar Singh argues, comes from the assumption that 'realism is the only touchstone for the novel'. The essays in the first part of the book look at the emergence of the novel in a variety of Indian languages, while the second part focuses on individual texts. While many of the essays provide useful contexts and backgrounds for those whose primary interest is in the Indian English novel, the only essay which deals centrally with writing in English is Makarand Paranjape's 'The Allegory of *Rajmohan's Wife* (1864): National Culture and Colonialism in Asia's First English Novel', which argues that Bankim Chandra Chatterjee's first novel is an allegory, 'an imagined history of modern India'.

Priya Joshi's *In Another Country: Colonialism, Culture and the English Novel in India* explores the development of the novel in India by looking, first, at how the English novel was read in India during the nineteenth century, and then at a selection of nineteenth- and twentieth-century writers. The two parts are linked by 'narrative indigenization, a process by which first Indian readers and then writers transmuted an imported and alien form into local needs'. In the first part of the book, Joshi delves into library records, publishing history, and contemporary reviews, concluding that Indian readers displayed a preference for melodramatic and didactic British popular fiction and made connections between such work and prior Indian narrative forms. Part 2 looks at a number of different novelists. Bankim Chandra Chatterjee's work is treated as a case history both of the obstacles to the indigenization of the novel and of its eventual successful adaptation in his Bengali writing. The remaining chapters turn to the English-language novel. Krupa Satthianadhan's fiction, it is argued, reshapes the novel form to depict a complex set of negotiations between tradition and modernity in regard to gender, negotiations in which reform does not simply occur at the expense of the past. Ahmed Ali's *Twilight in Delhi* is analysed as a hybrid of an Urdu verse form, the *shehrashob* (a lament on a declining city) and the English novel. The pessimism of the novel, it is suggested, is countered by 'an alternate way of apprehending historical rhythms'. The final chapter considers *Midnight's Children* in relation to both its indigenization of form (the use of techniques from the oral epic) and Rushdie's claims for English as an Indian language. This and succeeding novels by other writers are seen as versions of the family romance. Despite labouring its points somewhat, part 1 is rather more original than the later analyses of specific writers, which tread routes others have trodden before. The discussion of the English-language texts in part 2 does not connect very clearly with the analysis of the patterns of reading discussed in the book's early chapters. Nevertheless, Joshi's study of reading patterns is an illuminating approach to the novel in India.

A welcome reissue of Meenakshi Mukherjee's classic study *The Twice-Born Fiction: Themes and Techniques of the Indian Novel in English* [2001; originally published in 1971], contains a new preface which reflects briefly on changes in the status of Indian writing in English since the book was first published, and on themes such as gender, subalternity, and the nation which have become prominent in readings of Indian fiction during the past thirty years.

In her essay 'India in the Mirror of World Fiction' (*NLR* 13[2002] 75–88), Francesca Orsini explores the relationship between Indian fiction in the vernaculars and Indian fiction in English. Proceeding largely by way of an assessment of Amit Chaudhuri's *Picador Book of Modern Indian Literature*, but also responding to

recent accounts of world literature by Franco Moretti and Pascale Casanova, the essay concludes that in the 'post-Rushdie, postcolonial novel', the West contemplates 'its latest reinterpretation of itself'. Hindu and Urdu writing, by contrast, present an India which the West 'does not like to think about for too long'.

Translating Caste (see also Section 4(*a*)) contains eight short stories translated from seven Indian languages. For many readers, the best known of the writers will be Mahasweta Devi, whose story 'Bayen' is included here. Amongst the others are the Kannada writer Mogalli Ganesh, and the Malayalam writer M.T. Vasudevan Nair. Four of the stories are accompanied by critical commentaries, and Uma Chakravarti's essay, 'Through Another Lens: Men, Women and Caste', reads a number of the stories in the light of issues concerning caste, class, gender, and sexuality.

Bose, ed., *Translating Desire*, also discussed in Section 4(*a*), includes a number of essays on fiction. Dolores Chew's account of the representation of Anglo-Asian women in colonial and postcolonial writing contains a brief discussion of I. Allan Sealy's *The Trotter Nama*, which, Chew argues, is one of the few works to represent the Anglo-Indian community without falling into the trap of gender and racial stereotyping. Chew also offers a helpful account of the development of the community. Udaya Kumar contributes an essay on discourses of the body in Malayalam literature, while Anjana Sharma discusses how sexuality is figured through food in a number of novels by women, including Anita Desai's *Fasting, Feasting*. The editor, Brinda Bose, also contributes a piece on the politics of translation, with a specific and cautionary focus on Spivak's translation and discussion of Mahasweta Devi's story 'Draupadi'. There is a danger, Bose argues, in Spivak's 'critical/theoretical formulations and explications that insidiously direct the reader to certain foci'.

Settar and Gupta, eds., *Pangs of Partition*, volume 2: *The Human Dimension*, is part of a two-volume set sponsored by the Indian Council for Historical Research (volume 1 focuses on historical accounts). This second volume contains twenty-three essays discussing representations of partition in a variety of media, including film, painting, oral history, and popular culture, as well as literature. The essays on literature, which are of varying quality and incisiveness, cover a number of languages. An interview with the Hindi writer Bhisham Sahni concentrates on his novel *Tamas*. *Tamas*, Bapsi Sidhwa's *Cracking India*, and oral histories are discussed by Nandi Bhatia as critiques of official history. The historian Mushirul Hasan also argues that literary works can lead to new approaches to partition. Alok Bhalla finds deficiencies in translations of Saadat Hasan Manto's work. Bhalla's own anthology, *Stories about the Partition of India*, is analysed by M. Asaduddin. The Punjabi writer K.S. Duggal discusses his own and others' writing about partition. Sukrita Paul Kumar's 'On Narrativizing Partition' surveys writing in a number of languages, and Bengali writing is the subject of a number of essays. Two essays concentrate specifically on work in English. Naresh Jain's 'The Muslim Polyphony in Attia Hosain's *Sunlight on a Broken Column*' argues that Hosain gives voice to a variety of Muslim attitudes while avoiding the apportionment of blame. Shikoh Mohsin Mirza's essay on *Train to Pakistan* offers a brief survey of Khushwant Singh's novel.

Collier and Schulze-Engler, eds., *Crabtracks: Progress and Process in Teaching the New Literatures in English*, a volume of essays in honour of Dieter

Riemenschneider, contains several essays on Indian fiction. Riemenschneider himself contributes an essay, 'The Function of Labour in M.R. Anand's Novels', which applies Marxist categories to a number of Anand's novels and concludes that Anand shows an understanding of the alienation of labour, while also representing the theme in an 'aesthetically convincing' manner. Devindra Kohli's 'The Embrace of Recognition: Landscape, Memory and Identity in Anita Desai' discusses a number of Desai's novels in terms of the disharmony between internal and external landscapes, and the depiction of consciousnesses engaged in reconciling the two. 'A Note on Painting in *The Moor's Last Sigh*' by Hena Maes-Jelinek explores Rushdie's use in the novel of 'painting as a metaphor for the art of writing in general and his own in particular'. An open letter to Riemenschneider by Viney Kirpal addresses the problems of teaching new literatures in India, and argues that texts should precede theory rather than the other way round.

Gyssels, Hoving, and Bowers, eds., *Convergences and Interferences: Newness in Intercultural Practices / Écritures d'une nouvelle ère/aire*, contains a number of essays on Indian authors. Chandra Chatterjee's 'The "Unfettered Vacuum": A Postcolonial Reading of Anita Desai's *Journey to Ithaca* and *Fasting, Feasting*' asserts that these two novels move away from binarisms and from categories such as race, religion, and country. Resistance is represented as individual. In 'Geographical and Generic Traversings in the Writings of Amitav Ghosh', Kanika Batra sees Ghosh's fiction and non-fiction as being allied to postmodernist theory and suggests that Ghosh's 'traversings' are 'symptomatic of his privileged diasporic status as an intellectual in the first world academy'. Nandini Bhattacharya's 'A City Visible but Unseen' discusses Rushdie's representation of the hybrid postcolonial city (Bombay in particular) and concludes that it must inevitably be an imaginary site.

Mittapalli and Monti, eds., *Commonwealth Fictions: Twenty-First Century Readings*, a selection of articles from *The Atlantic Literary Review*, contains a number of essays on Rushdie and other Indian writers. In 'A Post-Modern, Provocative, Metropolitan Mother India: Aurora Zogoiby of Rushdie's *The Moor's Last Sigh*', P. Balaswamy examines Rushdie's revisioning of the traditional Mother India figure, as embodied in the famous Hindi film of the 1950s, and sees the novel as a warning to modern India. Drawing on Rushdie's own reworking of the myth of Orestes and the Furies in *Fury*, Celia M. Wallhead, in 'A Myth for Anger, Migration and Creativity in Salman Rushdie's *Fury*', argues that the protagonist of this novel, Malik Solanka, comes to see fury all round him but also discovers a positive, creative energy in anger. Stuti Khanna's essay, 'The Novels of Migration: Naipaul, Rushdie, Selvadurai and Mistry', explores responses to the migrant condition in the four writers named in her title, suggesting that, despite the differences between them, they all seem to avoid political engagement. K. Jeevan Kumar's reading of Raj Kamal Jha, in 'Transmuted Reality in Raj Kamal Jha's *The Blue Bedspread*', proposes that this novel highlights the arbitrariness of the word and the indeterminacy of its fictional world. Mary Condé's 'A Feminist View of Partition: Shauna Singh Baldwin's *What the Body Remembers*' sees Baldwin's novel as one that looks at partition 'more in terms of a male-female division than in terms of ethnicity or religion', and does so by focusing on 'women's bodies and memory'. Mala Pandurang, 'Rani Dharker's *The Virgin Syndrome*: Challenging Constructs of Female Sexuality', looks at Dharker's novel as a challenge to the way in which middle-class Hindu society constructs female sexuality through the use of myth.

Chandra Holm, 'Potent Remedies: Themes and Techniques in Shashi Deshpande's *Small Remedies*', offers a rather general account of Deshpande's novel. In 'Failed Householders: Renouncement and Distributive Strategies in *Fasting, Feasting*', Alessandro Monti draws on myth and anthropology to analyse Anita Desai's novel in relation to the motifs of asceticism and eroticism, the 'two sides of the Hindu frame of identity'. Rama Kundu's '*The Shadow Lines*: A New(er) Historicism' analyses the fluidity of time, space, and history in Ghosh's novel.

Another collection of essays is Hale and Khair, eds., *Angles on the English-Speaking World*, volume 1: *Unhinging Hinglish: The Languages and Politics of Fiction in English from the Indian Subcontinent*. Meenakshi Mukherjee's opening essay, a keynote address at the conference where these papers were originally delivered, looks at the bi- or multi-lingual location of the Indian reader of fiction from the subcontinent written in English. Maryam Khozan and Charles Lock discuss the reception of Anand's *Untouchable* in England in the 1930s in relation to Bakhtin's theory of the dialogic nature of the novel. Martin Leer examines the significance of railways in English fiction about India as well as in Indian English fiction. Peter Morey discusses Rohinton Mistry's *A Fine Balance* as a national allegory, but one in which the 'stories that go to make up India' proliferate. Tobias Wachinger takes issue with the use of Rushdie's and Kureishi's fictions as paradigms of the celebration of hybridity, suggesting that the implications of infertility bound up with the term 'hybridity' return to 'haunt the texts'. Tabish Khair compares a writer located in the West (Jhumpa Lahiri) with two located in India (Mahasweta Devi and Shashi Deshpande) to suggest that in the former 'knowledge is loss', while in the latter two the relationship between knowledge and loss is not so simple. These two different positions are linked with the respective authors' discursive and geographical locations. Other essays look at Paul Scott's *Raj Quartet*, Michael Ondaatje, and Shyam Selvadurai's *Cinnamon Gardens*.

Rukmini Bhaya Nair's *Lying on the Postcolonial Couch*, also discussed in Section 4(*a*), includes two chapters on fiction. The first of these, 'The Pedigree of the White Stallion: Postcoloniality and Literary History', explores the connections between Kipling's *Kim*, Tagore's *Gora*, and, more briefly, I. Allan Sealey's *Trotter-Nama*. While *Kim* attempts to counter anxieties about the permanence of British rule, Nair argues, Tagore 'absorbs the motifs of *Kim* into a larger counternarrative', a 'vision of an India whose independent status comes from a mature ability to contain its antagonisms'. Sealey's novel is discussed in terms of its attempt to rescue the Anglo-Indian community from the marginalization and contempt to which it is usually subjected. The last chapter of the book is a somewhat circuitous journey round Rushdie's work, dealing with themes of censorship and free speech.

As usual, Rushdie is the individual writer most widely written about. In *Stranger Worlds: Salman Rushdie's Other Worlds*, Roger Clark investigates Rushdie's allusions to cosmology, mythology, and mysticism and their role in shaping his first five novels. Rushdie's reference points in these areas are, as one would expect, largely Islamic, although Hindu and other myths also play a role. Clark argues that the first five novels are more interesting than the later work because they play off other worlds and the epistemologies associated with them against this world and realist epistemology. Rushdie's iconoclasm, Clark suggests, is 'mitigated ... by his secular idealism and by his ... homage to mystical ideals of the past'. The fragmentation of self and universe in Rushdie's work is counterpointed with a 'mystical ideal of unity, a secular salvation'. In Clark's view, *The Moor's Last Sigh* and *The Ground Beneath her Feet* disappoint partly because, while they continue to use mythological motifs, these remain on the level of metaphor; there is little sense of tension between other worlds and this world. This is a thorough exploration of Rushdie's use of myth, but the accounts of the novels often tend to drown in detail, both of their plots and their mythological connections.

Another book-length study is Sabrina Hassumani's *Salman Rushdie: A Postmodern Reading of his Major Works*, which argues that Rushdie makes use of post-structuralist strategies to question binary myths of identity and to construct a postmodern space, which 'rewrites the center' as 'impurity, hodgepodge, melange, hybridity'. While the book generally goes over well-trodden ground, it offers a lucid argument and does a useful service in again drawing attention to some of the silences both in Rushdie's own work and in the reception of that work: his neglect of the subaltern, for instance, the 'lack of flexibility' in *Shame*'s representation of Pakistan, and self-congratulatory readings of *Haroun and the Sea of Stories* as a book which celebrates Western values of 'free speech, individualism, creativity'.

Rushdie is juxtaposed with Anita Desai in Joyce Wexler's 'What is a Nation? Magic Realism and National Identity in *Midnight's Children* and *Clear Light of Day*' (*JCL* 37:ii[2002] 137–55), which suggests that in Desai's novel elegy and a concern with domestic issues ultimately displace politics, while Rushdie's magic realism is effective in engaging with politics and fostering collective national identity.

In 'Salman Rushdie's Magic Realism and the Return of Inescapable Romance' (*UTQ* 71[2002] 765–85), Neil Ten Kortenaar sees magic realism as a return of the romance mode, which was displaced by realism. Analysing romance motifs in *Midnight's Children*, he suggests that romance and realism exist in a dialectic between meaning and authority. Magic realism is suited to describing Indian reality because 'postcolonial identity is a matter of conflicting desires and anxieties'.

Twentieth Century Literature 47:iv[2001] is a special issue on Rushdie. In an introductory piece entitled 'Reading Rushdie after September 11, 2001' (pp. 431–43), the editors of the issue, Sabina and Simona Sawhney, note that Rushdie's journalistic writings after September 11 seem to reiterate 'prevalent stereotypes about Islam', but point out that these writings are 'incongruent with the general trajectory of his [fictional] work'. Andrew S. Teverson's 'Fairy Tale Politics: Free Speech and Multiculturalism in *Haroun and the Sea of Stories*' (*TCL* 47:iv[2001] 444–66) relates Rushdie's text to Bhabha's ideas of the nation, and to *The Conference of the Birds* by the thirteenth-century Sufi Farid ud-Din Attar, who also fell foul of the Islamic authorities. In *Haroun*, Teverson concludes, Rushdie represents the nation as 'a complex and multiform body of competing discourses', analogous to Bhabha's 'performative' conception of the nation. In 'Bouncing Down to the Underworld: Classical *Katabasis* in *The Ground Beneath her Feet*' (*TCL* 47:iv[2001] 467–509), an essay which overwhelms the novel (hardly one of Rushdie's best) with the weight of its critical terminology and conceptual scheme, Rachel Falconer suggests that the book has the shape of classical and medieval *katabatic* narratives (descent to, and return from, the underworld), and that such narratives have parallels with migrant experience. Falconer's essay is followed by two on *Midnight's Children*. In '*Midnight's Children*: Kashmir and the Politics of Identity' (*TCL* 47:iv[2001] 501–44), Patrick Hogan draws attention to the Kashmir chapters at the beginning of the novel, and to the apparent marginalization of Mahatma Gandhi, suggesting that Rushdie's imagination is in fact far more marked by Gandhi than the common view suggests. Drawing on the work of the contemporary neo-Gandhian Ashis Nandy, Hogan argues that *Midnight's Children* constitutes a critique of modern 'categorical identity' (rigid, often antagonistic forms such as religion and nation) and an endorsement of the more fluid 'practical identity' ('the entire complex of habits, expectations, abilities, routines that integrate one's daily activities with those of a community'). In 'Epic of Failure: Disappointment as Utopian Fantasy in *Midnight's Children*' (*TCL* 47:iv[2001] 545–68), John J. Su claims that the novel 'answers the national longing for form ... by creating an *epic of failure*, that it 'can be read as an effort to imagine a more egalitarian India through depicting the personal tragedy of Saleem Sinai'. Readers 'experience the "multitudinous" nature of India by perceiving how the efforts to unify its history in an epic form fall apart'. Regeneration out of failure is also the leitmotif of Alexandra Schultheis's 'Postcolonial Lack and Aesthetic Promise in *The Moor's Last Sigh*' (*TCL* 47:iv[2001] 569–95), which suggests that this novel's pessimism is tempered with the 'regenerative potential of the aesthetic', which can 'heal historical wounds *enough* to make renewed faith in the nation possible'. In the concluding essay, 'Salman Rushdie: The Ambivalence of Migrancy' (*TCL* 47:iv[2001] 596–618), Shailja Sharma explores the intersection of the politics of class and migrancy as evidenced by the *Satanic Verses* affair. Rushdie's affiliations, she argues, have been more with the 'mainstream Left ... than with the South Asian community', and as a consequence most Muslims see him as 'aligned with the enemy'. The novel and the ensuing controversy have highlighted class differences in the 'immigrant experience'.

Some of these themes are also dealt with in Gillian Gane's 'Migrancy, The Cosmopolitan Intellectual, and the Global City in *The Satanic Verses*' (*MFS* 48[2002] 18–49). According to Gane, Rushdie celebrates migrancy and mutability, but also 'raises fundamental questions about the danger of discontinuity'. In its depiction of London, the novel is, in part, the source of a new kind of transnational politics, but—through its representations and omissions of various social groups— it also reproduces the inequities of the outside world. The same issue of *Modern Fiction Studies*—a special issue on 'Postmodernism and the Globalization of English'—contains two other essays on Rushdie. Peter Kalliney's 'Globalization, Postcoloniality, and the Problem of Literary Studies in *The Satanic Verses*' (*MFS* 48[2002] 50–82) sees Rushdie's novel as 'rejecting the sovereignty of the nation-state and embracing hybridity and international mobility' but also leaving important questions unanswered in its ending, which escapes from the 'production of localized social inequality'. Ayelet Ben-Yishai's 'The Dialectic of Shame: Representation in the Metanarrative of Salman Rushdie's *Shame*' (*MFS* 48[2002] 194–215) takes up the question of gender, arguing that, while the women in the novel are silent and unemancipated, the *way* in which they are represented constitutes a critique of domination.

The Satanic Verses is one of the novels discussed by Daniel Punday in 'Narrative Performance in the Contemporary Monster Story' (*MLR* 97[2002] 803–20), which argues that late twentieth-century monster novels give writers the opportunity to look at the nature of narrative. Ananya Jahanara Kabir's essay 'Subjectivities, Memories, Loss: Of Pigskin Bags, Silver Spittoons and the Partition of India'

(*Interventions* 4[2002] 245–64) draws on scholarship about the Holocaust to discuss representations of the partition of India in general and, more specifically, Book I of *Midnight's Children*, which is read as being marked by 'unresolved conflicts within the minority subjectivity of the Indian Muslim'.

Mark Mossman's 'W.B. Yeats and Salman Rushdie: Political Advocacy and an International Modernism', in Fleming, ed., *W.B. Yeats and Postcolonialism*, argues that, although both writers understand the world through postcolonial discourses, Yeats's project is a national one, while Rushdie explodes the idea of nationalism and constructs international models of community.

Elisabeth Bronfen's 'Celebrating Catastrophe' (*Angelaki* 7:ii[2002] 175–86) links modern society's fascination with celebrities who die in catastrophic circumstances (Gianni Versace and Princess Diana) to Rushdie's *The Ground Beneath her Feet*. Our obsession with celebrity, Bronfen suggests, occludes ordinary human realities and pain. Rushdie's novel 'deconstructs the fatality, if not the futile vanity, underlying our obsession with celebrity'. Bronfen's essay appeared in more or less the same form under the title 'Fault Lines: Catastrophe and Celebrity Culture' in *European Studies* 16[2001] 117–39.

In 'Writing as Translation in *The Ground Beneath her Feet*' (*CE&S* 24:ii[2002] 47–57), Florence Cabaret examines Rushdie's 'playing with etymologies and long-forgotten meanings' to argue that he writes as if he were 'translating a source text', thus reshaping the English language and 'questioning the notion of origin'. Another essay on this novel, Geetha Ganapathy-Dore's 'An Orphic Journey to the Disorient: Salman Rushdie's *The Ground Beneath her Feet*' (*WLWE* 38:ii[2000] 17–27), looks at the use of the concept of metamorphosis and the theme of disorientation. Mini Chandran's 'Fabulation as Narrative in *Haroun and the Sea of Stories*' (*Jouvert* 7:i[2002] 23 paras.) points out different levels of meaning in this text, ranging from Aesopian fable to political resistance.

In 'Mixed-Up, Jumble-Aya and English: "How Newness Enters the World" in Salman Rushdie's "The Courter"' (*ArielE* 32:iv[2001] 47–68), Gillian Gane argues that, in 'The Courter' from Rushdie's short story collection *East, West*, the 'broken English' of the main characters is what allows for the possibility of newness and the crossing of national barriers. A broader range of Rushdie's work is dealt with in Stéphanie Ravillon's article 'The Abdication of Chronos: The Representation of Time in Salman Rushdie's Novels' (*CE&S* 24:ii[2002] 59–68), which argues that, for Rushdie, the migrant's desire to reclaim a lost past takes the form of a critique of the idea of linear time. Among the alternatives which Rushdie uses to shape his narratives are the idea of the spiral, the prism, and the palimpsest.

The palimpsest also figures in Aïda Balvannanadhan's 'Re-Membering Personal History in *The God of Small Things*' (*CE&S* 25:i[2002] 97–106), in which Arundhati Roy's novel is seen as a 'palimpsestic narrative', moving back and forth in time, and thereby 'inscribing the silenced truth on the official version of the tragedy'. Roy is also the subject of Madhu Benoit's 'Circular Time: A Study of Narrative Techniques in Arundhati Roy's *The God of Small Things*' (*WLWE* 38:i[1999] 98–106; this issue of *WLWE* was published in 2002). Benoit connects the fragmented time structure of the novel to Roy's political purposes; the narrative method, she suggests, forces the reader to take an actively critical stance towards orthodoxy.

Amitav Ghosh is probably becoming the most widely discussed Indian writer after Rushdie. Chowdhary, ed., *Amitav Ghosh's 'The Shadow Lines': Critical Essays*, is designed mainly to elucidate Ghosh's novel to the student. The essays, by a variety of critics based at Delhi University, address such topics as memory, the narrator, the nation, imagery, gender, and identity. Though the essays rarely break new ground, a number of them provide useful accounts of different themes and approaches.

Ghosh's first novel is the subject of Yumna Siddiqi's 'Police and Postcolonial Rationality in Amitav Ghosh's *The Circle of Reason*' (*CulC* 50[2002] 175–211). Siddiqi argues that, in this novel, the postcolonial state is depicted as inheriting the 'repressive aspects of colonial rationality', but that, in addition, Ghosh suggests an emancipatory role for postcolonial reason. Karen Piper's *Cartographic Fictions: Maps, Race and Identity* contains a chapter, 'Postcolonial Occupations of Cyberspace', discussing Ghosh's *The Calcutta Chromosome* as an example of postcolonial science fiction, a novel which takes over cyberspace while also allegorizing colonialism's failures. Tuomas Huttunen's 'Narration and Silence in the Works of Amitav Ghosh' (*WLWE* 38:ii[2000] 28–43) discusses Ghosh's first four novels in the context of questions about whether the encounter between different cultures should be represented in terms of difference or a universalism that might turn out to be a mask for Western hegemony. Ghosh, Huttunen suggests, uses silence as a way of resisting hegemonic narration.

In an interview published in *World Literature Today* 76:ii[2002] 84–90, Ghosh talks to Frederick Luis Aldana about a variety of issues: his beginnings as a writer, the forms and details of his novels and non-fiction, particularly *The Glass Palace*, and the different reception he receives in India and in the West. He contests the stereotyping of magical realism as something that comes out of the Third World, and argues that much Indian fiction is structured round the family rather than the nation. An interview with Vikram Chandra can be found in *Wasafiri* 37[2002] 5–7.

Bart-Moore Gilbert takes up a complex subject, the relationship between Kipling and South Asian literature, in his essay, '"I am going to rewrite Kipling's *Kim*": Kipling and Postcolonialism' (*JCL* 37:ii[2002] 39–58). While noting the hostility or indifference towards Kipling displayed by a number of South Asian writers, Moore-Gilbert also sees Kipling as a productive influence on several writers, including I. Allan Sealy, Salman Rushdie, G.V. Desani, Hari Kunzru, and Hanif Kureishi. Tabish Khair's 'Can the Subaltern Shout (and Smash)?' (*WLWE* 38:ii[2000] 7–16) reads *Kim* alongside Forster's *A Passage to India* and Spivak's essay 'Can the Subaltern Speak?' to argue that the subaltern's body 'exceeds subalternity' and that the subaltern can speak in ways other than language: 'action and noise—shouting, smashing'.

The diaspora has become the area of most rapid growth in critical writing on India. Luyat and Tolron, eds., *Flight from Certainty: The Dilemma of Identity and Exile*, includes an opening section, 'The Eighth Continent', which explores dilemmas of home and identity in general terms, as well as more specific sections on Australia, New Zealand, Africa, North America, and the Indian subcontinent. The essays on Indian diasporic writing offer few new insights or approaches. Nilufer Bharucha's 'Real and Imagined Worlds: Salman Rushdie as a Writer of the Indian Diaspora' examines Rushdie's novels up to *The Ground Beneath her Feet*, concludes that his fiction is not simply about being 'unhomed', and that it is an 'expansive discourse'. Sooyoung Chon's essay on *The Satanic Verses* offers a juxtaposition of Bhabha and Rushdie. In an essay discussing *The Moor's Last Sigh*, Madelena Gonzalez argues that, for Rushdie, 'exile *is* identity'—a creative 'exile from fixed truths'. Corinne Liotard's account of Anita Desai's novel *Baumgartner's Bombay* examines the protagonist's relationship to language and place and suggests that the novel is constructed round a void. Florence D'Souza discusses Amit Chaudhuri's novels in relation to both their continuities with the past and their 'interrogations of the future'.

Unlike the essays just mentioned, Amitava Kumar's *Bombay–London–New York* at least attempts a novel approach to the subject of the diaspora. Although it advertises itself on its first page as a book 'about recent Indian fiction in English', it is in fact a hybrid work, using photographs, autobiography, literary criticism, discussions of Bollywood films, and what I presume are the author's own poems to sketch a portrait of the diasporic cultures of Britain and the US. The book explores the kinds of relationships different segments of these diasporas have towards India and towards their new (sometimes temporary) homelands. There are comments on a range of writers, including Naipaul, Rushdie, A.K. Ramanujan, and Hanif Kureishi. The book is rather uneven in quality: the autobiographical element generally works well, but the author's poems are not especially distinguished (although there is an interesting translation from the Hindi poet Alokdhanwa), and other parts of the book often read like extended pieces of journalistic feature writing, offering few original insights into the condition of diasporic Indians.

Susheila Nasta's *Home Truths: Fictions of the South Asian Diaspora in Britain* aims, among other things, to broaden the historical and cultural framework within which the literature of this diaspora is discussed. Her first chapter, accordingly, looks at representations of 'home' and 'abroad' in a range of figures, including Dean Mahomed, Behramji Malabari, Aubrey Menen, Attia Hosain, Mulk Raj Anand, and G.V. Desani. The next chapter explores Sam Selvon's creolization of London, locating his work in the context of other Caribbean representation. Subsequent chapters contrast the colonial anxieties of V.S. Naipaul with Rushdie's apparently more celebratory outlook, while also detecting convergences in a sense of exile. The final section of the book examines the work of writers who emerged in the later 1980s and the 1990s, such as Kureishi, Ravinder Randhawa, Sunetra Gupta, Aamer Hussein, and Romesh Gunesekera. *Home Truths* covers a wide range of ground, both historically and culturally, and moves easily between accounts of the discursive context and how complexities at this level manifest themselves in terms of form. The book is a welcome addition to the burgeoning work on the literature of the diaspora.

One of the diasporic writers discussed by Nasta is the subject of *Attia Hosain: A Diptych Volume* by R.K. Kaul and Jasbir Jain. Kaul's section, 'Attia Hosain and her Milieu', focuses largely on Hosain's depiction of Muslim society, using a number of other works—in particular, Ahmed Ali's *Twilight in Delhi*, Zeenuth Futehally's *Zohra* and Ismat Chughtai's *Terhi Lakir (The Crooked Line)* and *Masooma*—as recurrent points of reference. There is useful contextual and comparative material here, particularly in relation to the Urdu tradition, but Kaul can be a little reductive, moralistic, and prone to abrupt judgement. Jasbir Jain's section, 'Attia Hosain: The Writer as Exile', is a more suggestive account, opening up different avenues of exploration, particularly in relation to Hosain's novel *Sunlight on a Broken Column*.

Amongst the aspects of the book Jain explores are loneliness and belonging, narrative polyphony and its dismantling of polarities. As the title indicates, exile is seen as the key to Hosain's writing: 'both her articulation and silence', Jain says, are 'located in this sense of exile'.

Jasbir Jain and Avadhesh Kumar Singh are the editors of *Indian Feminisms* (also discussed in section 4(*a*)), which contains a number of essays on women's fiction in English and other languages. Anu Celly discusses Chughtai's *Tehri Lakir* as not only a critique of imperialism but also a repudiation of nationalist male paradigms. The Hindi writer Krishna Sobti's *Zindaginama* is seen by Tripti Jain as providing insights into 'aspects of history which ordinarily do not find expression in masculine visions'. Mohini Khot's 'The Feminist Voice in Arundhati Roy's *The God of Small Things*' discusses the novel as a protest against gender and caste oppression. The concluding essay, by Rajul Bhargava, looks at Githa Hariharan's short story collection *The Art of Dying* in relation to its 'empty spaces' and to the 'post-feminist ethos'.

Representations of gender are discussed in a number of other books and essays. In 'The Emblematics of Gender and Sexuality in Indian Nationalist Discourse' (*MAS* 36[2002] 913–36), Anshuman Mondal locates Raja Rao's novel *Kanthapura* within the 'genealogy of gender representations' that the discourses of Indian nationalism had evolved. Nalini Natarajan's *Woman and Indian Modernity: Readings of Colonial and Postcolonial Novels* explores the ways in which 'gender is reconstructed in the literary representation of modernity'. The opening chapter juxtaposes Jane Austen's novels with Saratchandra Chaterjee's *Swami* [1915] in order to argue that, both in Austen and in debates about gender in late colonial India, daughters can represent 'a way for the changes of modernity to enter, then be contained to suit the contradictions in patriarchal ideology'. A reading of Anantha Murthy's classic Kannada novel *Samskara* examines the intersections of gender, caste, and modernity and concludes that the book's 'resolve to modernity' is 'flawed' because of its binary representation of women as either lower-caste temptresses or upper-caste inhibitors of sexuality. A chapter on *Midnight's Children* reads it against Bombay cinema, concluding that the novel parodies the cinema's representation of the female body and its 'engendering of [the] nation as male', while also being complicit in the cinema's representations. In the penultimate chapter, Arundhati Roy's *The God of Small Things* is read in the context of legal struggles over women's rights of inheritance in the 1980s. The book concludes with an analysis of Rohinton Mistry's *A Fine Balance*, in which the character Dina Shroff's story is seen as an expansion of 'female subjectivity outside the middle-class home' and a stage in the 'indigenization of the Parsi'. The book contains interesting but sometimes convoluted readings of its chosen texts, the discussions of the contexts occasionally overwhelming the novels they are meant to illuminate.

The interaction between gender and modernity is also the subject of Priyamvada Gopal's essay, 'Sex, Space, and Modernity in the Work of Rashida Jahan, "Angareywali"', in Bartolovich and Lazarus, eds., *Marxism, Modernity and Postcolonial Studies*. Gopal concentrates on the Urdu short story 'Voh' ('That One') by Rashida Jahan, whose writing aroused controversy when it was published in the 1930s. The story, which concerns the relationship between a prostitute disfigured by venereal disease and a middle-class woman teacher, is used by Gopal to explore issues concerning the relationship between subaltern and hegemonic perspectives.

By charting the encounter between a gendered subaltern and modernity, Gopal concludes, Jahan prompts a rethinking of our views on modernity and progress.

Monti and Dhawan, eds., *Discussing Indian Women Writers*, also discussed in Section 4(*a*), includes essays on a variety of authors and topics. Monti himself contributes two essays, one on the representation of Hindu widows in fiction (particularly by Anita Desai), and one on *purdah* in Rama Mehta's relatively neglected novel *Inside the Haveli*. Mrinalini Sebastian explores the cultural history of the *devadasis* (temple dancers) and discusses R.K. Narayan's use of this figure in *The Guide*. Jyoti Nandan examines culturally specific forms of gender oppression in Anita Desai's *Fasting, Feasting*. Shauna Singh Baldwin's *What the Body Remembers* figures in essays on partition by Seema Malik and Mary Condé (the former also discusses other works, including Anita Kumar's *The Night of the Seven Dawns* and Mehr Nigar Masroor's *Shadows of Time*). Rebecca Sultana's discussion of Meena Alexander's fiction contrasts Alexander's 'resistant ideology' with Bharati Mukherjee's 'assimilative' one. There are some rather descriptive essays on other writers and texts: Kamala Markandaya's *Nectar in a Sieve*, Jhumpa Lahiri's *The Interpreter of Maladies*, and Manju Kapur's *Difficult Daughters*.

5. New Zealand and the South Pacific

John Thomson's annual review of the literature introducing his comprehensive bibliography in *The Journal of Commonwealth Literature* has amounted, in the course of time, to an unusual kind of literary history. Although he draws attention to earlier developments and works, it is an essentially year-by-year account of the literature as it evolves. It is continued for the year 2001 in *JCL* 37:iii[2002]. Thomson notes the ongoing trend, already recorded in the previous year, for New Zealand writers to set their fiction outside New Zealand. In some cases the setting is exotic, in others imaginary. In the case of Barbara Anderson and C.K. Stead, a link with their native country is preserved by the fact that their central characters are New Zealanders living abroad. More conventional in setting but less so in character and plot is Maurice Gee's novel, *Ellie and the Shadow Man* [2001]. Other familiar novelists who published new work in that year are Chris Else, Patricia Grace, and Shonagh Koea, while the most remarkable new novelists are Craig Marriner and Tim Corballis. Of the poetry, the most outstanding is, inevitably, the posthumously published work of Allen Curnow, *The Bells of St. Babel's*. Thomson discusses the stricter poetic forms in work by Vincent O'Sullivan, Brian Turner, and Ian Wedde and remarks that the Polynesian and women poets depend less on form for their effects. Large retrospective collections were published of Bill Manhire and the late Lauris Edmond.

In 2000 Auckland University Press published a substantial book of literary essays by C.K. Stead under the title *The Writer at Work*. This has now been followed in 2002 by an even larger collection, *Kin of Place: Essays on 20 New Zealand Writers*, a reminder that Stead is not simply the polemicist he is often dismissed as, but is in fact a scholar of wide-ranging and prolific interests. The new book is certainly provocative, but it is also based on a generous selection of carefully read texts. The tone of self-congratulation that irritates many readers is more restrained in this latest collection. Most of the thirty essays have been published before, but they include nine published here for the first time. One of these is a study of Frank Sargeson's relatively neglected novel *Memoirs of a Peon* [1964]. This novel seemed liberating to Stead when it first appeared but now he finds it 'stuffy and constricting'. Alongside two older essays there is a new one on Allen Curnow, a survey of his work, emphasizing the painstaking care with which the poems were written—and sometimes ultimately failed to be written. In another new essay, this quality of Curnow is contrasted with the constant flow of words proceeding from the prolific, yet difficult, Kendrick Smithyman. Stead is ambivalent about Smithyman's most notable quality—his obscurity—but concludes with a generous statement that Smithyman's life-work was 'an heroic enterprise'. Stead has two new pieces on Janet Frame. One is a brief account of her poetry, finding a certain roughness, which, however, invites the reader in, to reconcile its terms. The other is a review of Michael King's biography of Frame, *Wrestling with the Angel* [1996]. There is also a provocative study of Lauris Edmond's poetry, suggesting that its nearness to solipsism defeats its own claim to generosity of spirit. A review of Maurice Gee's *Ellie and the Shadow Man* praises its powerful 'realism', but finds that it is often compromised by a tendency to moralism. In two other new essays, Ian Wedde and Elizabeth Knox come in for warm praise. In general, the warmth of these new essays gives the lie to the image of Stead as cold and sarcastic. He is a more complex and interesting figure than his critics have yet perceived.

Chadwick Allen's book on Maori and 'American Indian' literary and activist writing, *Blood Narrative: Indigenous Identity in American Indian and Maori Literary and Activist Texts*, is at its best in individual analyses of texts, where the specifics of the text are shown to illuminate much broader contexts. Readers of Patricia Grace, Witi Ihimaera, and Keri Hulme will benefit from referring to Chadwick's accounts. The theoretical framework of the book, however, is more problematic. No doubt its cloudiness and contradictions reflect the existence of yet to be resolved dilemmas in the relationships between 'indigenous' and 'settler' populations. It would be unreasonable to expect one author to solve problems so complex and so thorny. However, beyond this, two aspects of Allen's approach seem problematic in themselves. One is his tendency to view the two populations as separate, self-contained units; this inevitably supports a 'culture clash' view of the relationship, underestimating the even more complex, yet realistic, intermingling of the two populations and the dilemmas and problems they share. The other is Allen's terminology. Certainly, there is practically no term used in this debate that does not carry a burden of past misuse and internal conflict. But the use of 'blood' in the very title of the book, a word that is inseparable from D.H. Lawrence's views of sexuality and instinct and, even more problematically, the eruptive 'blood and soil' emotionality of Nazi race theories, is unfortunate (to put it mildly). It partly defeats the author's purpose of introducing clarity to much-muddied waters. Metaphors of this jaded kind should have no place in academic discourse. Similarly his locution '(post)colonial', which he claims is ironic, suggests that there is no distinction between the attitudes of early settlers and those of citizens in much more complex societies, in this way, again, obscuring rather than clarifying the issues under discussion. For all this, Chadwick's book deserves to be read closely and widely, as well as critically, for its contribution to an important debate.

A view of New Zealand literature from the perspective of writers who feel disadvantaged by the commercial and conservative literary 'establishment' in New

Zealand is provided by Michael O'Leary in his *Alternative Small Press Publishing in New Zealand: An Introduction with Particular Reference to the Years, 1969–1999.* Beginning with missionaries who struggled to carry heavy printing presses and type from boat to shore in the 1820s, and who published tiny tracts, much New Zealand writing, including much in the conventional literary genres, has been brought to the reader by immense personal effort and for little material gain. To this very day, hand-setting is still a feature of New Zealand 'alternative' publishing, partly for financial reasons but also for aesthetic ones. O'Leary names a wide range of writers, mainly poets, whose work was first published in minimalist ways and is now carried by major 'large' presses and publishers. There is the inevitable tension between 'alternative' and 'establishment' literature, and O'Leary provides a service by suggesting a variety of ways in which to distinguish these two terms. Doing so is made difficult by the way they overlap. One measure of the 'established' is inclusion in standard reference works and surveys, and although such volumes tend to be generous in New Zealand, O'Leary is able to make a strong case for the inclusion of hitherto neglected works and publisher's lists (notably the Caveman Press) in the literary canon. Any informed reader will feel provoked to thought by O'Leary's account, even while disagreeing, perhaps, with some of his individual judgements.

In her essay, 'Translation in New Zealand: Texts, Issues, Ideologies' (*BRONZS* 13[2001/2] 59–82), Janet Wilson first covers some of the familiar problems revolving around Maori and English versions of the *Treaty of Waitangi*, but then widens her notion of 'translation' to include the difficulties of presenting Maori realities in the English language. In such cases the translation is more implicit and may be called cultural translation rather than linguistic translation. However, it remains true that the Maori language contains resources for presenting the cultural material that are not available to the user of English, who must find creative ways to bridge the gap. Wilson concentrates on short fiction by Patricia Grace to illustrate these points. In a final section, she examines Janet Frame's use of local English to express local realities, a necessary step to authenticity but a problem to readers even when the texts are shifted to another part of the English-speaking world: American publishers, for example, changed Frame's 'kerosene box' into 'gasoline shed', rendering her sentence 'meaningless', as Frame herself remarked.

Recent years have seen a flurry of intellectual and literary biographies and autobiographies in New Zealand. This continued to be true in 2002. Michael King's richly illustrated *An Inward Sun: The World of Janet Frame* is a much briefer successor to his major biography of the writer, *Wrestling with the Angel* [2000]. It follows the life of its subject but emphasizes the intricate relationship between what is 'real' and what is 'imagined' in her life and writing. The title is Frame's own metaphor for the imagination: 'I don't know what these things are until I see them in an imaginative light, which is a bright light, without shade—a kind of inward sun.' Theoretically, it might seem risky to move from that imaginative vision to some relatively naive concept of 'reality', but in practice the generous provision of photographs does create a lively world of its own that might stimulate the viewer's imagination in a different way to that of Frame's writing. There are more than a hundred photographs in the book, many of them from Frame's private collection and never before published. King's narrative biography provides a context for the photographs rather than the other way around. In any case the material is of great interest not only to Frame specialists but also to students wishing to test the sources of fiction in the 'reality' of a different medium, bearing in mind, of course, that the photographs are also carefully composed.

The most substantial of the biographical studies, indeed the longest literary biography in New Zealand's history, is Derek Challis's long-awaited book on his mother, Iris Wilkinson, better known under her pseudonym, Robin Hyde. *The Book of Iris: A Life of Robin Hyde* is based on notes and a partial biography by the late Gloria Rawlinson, who is acknowledged as co-author, but it is mainly the result of Challis's own research, initiated by a letter from him to Rawlinson in 1947. The fifty-year history of the book's gestation is told in Challis's introduction. Of even greater interest are the accounts of the origins of Hyde's own novels and poems. In a life of thirty-three years (1906–39) she published five long and complex novels, still awaiting detailed interpretation and debate, three volumes of non-fiction, and three volumes of poetry, which have been supplemented since her death by further volumes from her extensive unpublished work. This achievement, considerable in itself, is remarkable considering the pain of physical and mental illness she endured, the hidden pregnancies, the life of a solo mother in an age when that meant social disgrace, the hindrances created by sexist editors and publishers, and the courageous journey into China during wartime. Challis and Rawlinson present these events and situations in a restrained tone, with extensive (too extensive?) quotations from letters, book reviews, and other documents. It is not always easy to discern the authors' attitude to what is told through the mosaic of other people's quoted views, and at times the narrative wood is obscured by the trees, but this book provides unusual insights into the nature of journalism, publishing, literary endeavour, and family life, especially in the 1930s, and tantalizing glimpses of other people who are figures in the story of New Zealand's literary and political history.

Although more notable as a historian, W.H. Oliver is also a recognized poet, and in his memoir *Looking for the Phoenix* he focuses especially on his relationship with language, from a fascination with word-games in childhood, through a growing awareness of the power of poetry, to his own attempts, presented modestly, to establish himself by publishing poems in local Wellington journals, *Hilltop* and *Arachne*, before reaching out to a wider audience in *Landfall*, edited by his friend Charles Brasch, and ultimately publishing a volume of verse. Although Oliver expresses mild and ironic surprise at the way he and his friends became known to literary history as the Wellington Group (he prefers 'Wellington school', including the lower case), in fact he brings a decade of that history into interesting life by exploring his friendships with James K. Baxter, Alistair Campbell, Louis Johnson, and others. The emergence of this movement in the late 1940s from a student hostel, Weir House, to the place it now occupies in literary histories is an interesting story, here told in a low key but with a sensitive awareness of its potential to fascinate. Later, Oliver turned his attention to intellectual and historical debate, but the memoir at no point ceases to demonstrate that the love of fine language guided him through those endeavours as well as his more obviously literary ones.

For many decades Allen Curnow has stood as a mighty stone image at the door of New Zealand poetry. His gift was clearly outstanding, but, it must be said, his awareness of it tended to lower its status. His care and attention to maintaining an image of grandeur and distance actually diminished him and brought his stature down to that of seemingly lesser beings. After his death a series of tributes celebrated his gift, but his own undermining of it has been explored primarily by

Patrick Evans. In his essay, '"A Very Emotional Person As Well": Allen Curnow, 1911–2001', published in *Landfall* 203[2002] 9–21, Evans claims that the prevailing image of Curnow's mastery, according to which he wrote only what was already resolved in his own fine mind, 'leaves out those aspects of his poetry that are so manifestly strange, so obviously unhealthy, so clearly written out of unhappiness, unease, anger, fear or something else we will never know about'. Perhaps it is not surprising to see a great man pulled from his pedestal after his death, but Evans does much more than that: he actually reveals a poet more interesting, because more full of the tensions of human life, than the stone image Curnow tried to turn himself into.

Ian Gaskell's essay, 'Whole Fragments: Mapping Discourse in Toa Fraser's Plays' (*SPAN* 52[2002] 66–87), is the first extended attempt to analyse Fraser's work, and some allowances must be made for the need to introduce it to a wider audience than their brilliant stage presentations have drawn in. Consequently, much of Gaskell's essay is descriptive, narrating the way in which Fraser paradoxically uses a single actor to create a truly theatrical rather than narrative text. From another point of view Gaskell translates the dramatic texts into academic discourse. The level of commentary remains thin and there is still much work to be done on this young Fijian writer, relating him to other dramatic monologue writers, of whom there are many in New Zealand, and comparing him with British models, exploring the thematic imagery, tying him in with Pacific novelists, and so on. Gaskell leaves these tasks to future commentators.

In 'Fashioned Intimacies: Maoriland and Colonial Modernity' (*JCL* 37:i[2002] 31–48), Jane Stafford and Mark Williams locate Katherine Mansfield's modernist writing in a pre-modernist New Zealand context they call 'Maoriland writing'. Maoriland suggested, in the late colonial period, a nostalgia for the 'dying race' and an image of New Zealand as a country filled with Maori ghosts while growing in 'white' civilization. Stafford and Williams focus attention on two practitioners of Maoriland writing: Jessie Mackay and Blanche Baughan. To a degree they rehabilitate them, by showing that their project was more complex and more courageously sincere than they have been given credit for since Curnow's patronizing view of his predecessors when he wrote in the 1940s. By the time Patrick Evans came to write his history of New Zealand literature, in 1990, this critical air of superiority had developed into a mocking, jocular tone. Mackay and Baughan, the authors argue, were not merely confronting New Zealand realities with Victorian language but were quite consciously and conscientiously forging a language of their own to create a new country in poetry. Although they were not entirely successful, their attitude to the task has shown more continuities with later writing than Curnovians have been willing to acknowledge. Paradoxically, Maoriland writing diminishes the Maori presence and reinforces non-living traditional crafts as a source of nostalgia; it is a path of escape from difficult realities. Mansfield's modernism, which constructs an aesthetic alternative to those same realities, is a different form of escape. What she shares with Mackay and Baughan is their urge to 'transcend' the world they discover around themselves.

In 'Postmodern Ethnicity or Utopian Di-Ethnia? Women's Multilingual/ Multicultural Writing in Aotearoa/New Zealand' (*JCL* 37:i[2002] 101–20), Livia Käthe Wittmann explores the space between cultures and languages occupied, on the one hand, by Maori women who have been separated from their cultural identities by the acts of colonialism, and, on the other, by first-generation immigrant women from non-English-speaking countries who must learn to use the local language effectively. Although this is material often explored, Wittmann focuses on particular writers (why only women?) and attempts to introduce certain terms to describe their dilemmas.

W.E. Maning (1811–83) is not always recognized by critics as one of New Zealand's most fascinating writers, although his two books, especially *Old New Zealand* [1863], have been reprinted and republished again and again. Alex Calder has written before of the curious blend of objectivity and satire in Maning's style, and he has now provided a scholarly edition of the two books (the second is the *War in the North* [1867]), adding a selection of previously unpublished letters. Calder's short introduction and a chronology of Maning's life provide a useful context, and a large number of obscurities and references are clarified in the excellent notes. It would be sensible to let the popular editions of *Old New Zealand* fade away, since this new presentation of Maning's work will provide a sounder, clearer version for future readers.

John O'Carroll's essay 'Envisioning the Real: Two Mishras on a Girmit World' (*SPAN* 52[2002] 101–26) provides a useful overview of the work of two Indo-Fijian writers who happen to share a family name: Vijay Mishra and Sudesh Mishra. Evaluating his comments on the first of these is difficult because he focuses on a set of essays that are as yet unpublished. It would seem that Vijay Mishra is highly critical of other Indo-Fijian writers for their incapacity to deal with the realities that followed the traumatic 'Pacific coup' of 1987. Of writers from the Indian diaspora, he favours V.S. Naipaul and wishes that Naipaul could visit Fiji to provide 'a much sharper conceptual framework to work with'. Vijay Mishra's approach to literature is highly political, based on the ideas of certain Marxist writers, and he tends, it would seem, to scorn aesthetic evaluations. However, the more O'Carroll examines this approach the more problematic he finds it. In spite of the 'materialist' basis of his own theory, Mishra accuses Fijian society of 'materialism' in a negative sense, and O'Carroll finds this unfair, since every modern society could be arraigned in the same way. Sudesh Mishra is presented as a contrast to Vijay Mishra, and particularly as a writer able to incorporate the changed visions of new Fiji into verse. In a reading of Sudesh Mishra's poems and plays, O'Carroll draws out this power of literary vision, concluding that 'the work of Sudesh Mishra presents a complex and more-than-adequate analysis of the situation in Fiji'. In a conciliatory epilogue he concedes that both Mishras—the one he favours and the one who troubles him—provide ways to advance in an understanding of modern Fiji.

It is helpful to read Sudesh Mishra's essay, 'The Time Is Out of Joint' (*SPAN* 52[2002] 136–45), in conjunction with O'Carroll's. Mishra provides a kind of metaphysical account of the pain of 'girmit' and then a historical account of it in relation to literature. The word 'girmitya' was coined by labourers brought from India to Fiji by British colonists and subjected to cruel oppression. It is derived from the English 'agreement', but implies physical and mental suffering.

An important essay for postcolonial literatures is Subramani's account of his own shift from writing English fiction to writing a long novel in the language of certain Indo-Fijians. In 'Altering Fictional Maps: Inscribing Childhood Vernacular' (*SPAN* 52[2002] 88–94), he describes how his New Delhi publisher was astonished to read 'a novel in a language that sounded like a mixture of Awadhi, Bhojpuri, Hindustani' and Fiji Hindi, which has borrowed widely from the local Fijian language and

English. What seemed like a linguistic mishmash even to an experienced Indian reader was the language Subramani had grown up with as his 'lingual intermediate world' (Weissgerber). Like Ngugi wa Thiong'o in Kenya many years before him, Subramani was hoping to appeal much more immediately to his own community of readers. In fact, as Sudesh Mishra points out in his introduction to *SPAN* 52, that community has already been decimated and barely exists. Subramani cares nothing about that, but writes for a community vivid in his mind. In the essay, he asserts that his earlier work in English had always been a translation from his inner language, and his direct use of the latter comes as an immense relief to him. This is clearly of significance not only to writing in such vernaculars but also to the writing of English fiction and poetry by people who, sometimes secretly, experience English as a second language (see the discussion of Janet Wilson's essay above). Subramani's autobiographical account of this experience is moving and revealing. He has discovered that writing in his childhood language enables him to do many things, such as using humour, with a new 'depth and sincerity': 'All that had eluded the writer in English—all that was "not said", the repressed histories, secrets, silences, and certain social experiences—become available through the bilingual writer's other tongue' (p. 89). Compassionate readers will be aware of such unspoken texts, however dimly, when they read the work of second-language writers in English.

Throughout his writing career, Albert Wendt has acknowledged his debt to existentialism, and especially to Albert Camus. The view of European man as living in a world where traditional values no longer have their old force melds with the view of postcolonial man living in a world where 'native' values have been destroyed and have not been credibly replaced with those of the colonist. This is familiar territory to Wendt's readers, but it is explored systematically in relation to a particular text in Michelle Keown's essay on Wendt's novel *Leaves of the Banyan Tree* [1979]: 'The Samoan Sisyphus: Camus and Colonialism in Albert Wendt's *Leaves of the Banyan Tree*' (*JCL* 37:i[2002] 49–64). Direct parallels are drawn between Mersault in Camus's *L'Étranger* and Pepe in Wendt's book.

In 'Selling the House' (*Landfall* 204[2002] 186–8), an essay-review of Damien Wilkins's novel *Chemistry*, Michael Gifkins attempts to trace a line of development through the output of a peculiarly protean writer. He takes Wilkins's cavalier treatment of the reader as a common characteristic that undergoes variations in a small string of novels and stories. He also sees in Wilkins a 'nascent humanism, offering his characters the beneficence of his tenderness while declining to bend them to his authorial will'. This is a paradoxical concept, born from quite cleverly trying to manage the incoherencies that most readers find in Wilkins's work. Like the fluid characters, the sense of place in these novels is distinctly odd. Whether the setting is the English home counties (*Little Masters* [1966]), America's Pacific Northwest (*Nineteen Widows Under Ash* [2000]), or a small New Zealand town (Timaru in *Chemistry* [2002]), Wilkins contrives to make it seem highly specific yet vaguely general and universal at the same time. This sense of the nebulous in the midst of the apparently grounded is confusing, and Gifkins fails, despite his best efforts, to solve the conundrum.

Books Reviewed

Abodunrin, Femi, Olu Obafemi, and Wole Ogundele, eds. *Character Is Beauty: Redefining Yoruba Culture and Identity, Iwalewa-Haus, 1981–1996.* AWP. [2001] pp. 372. hb. $84.95 ISBN 0 8654 3623 1, pb. $29.90 ISBN 0 8654 3624 X.

Adams, Paul, and Christopher Lee, eds. *Frank Hardy and the Literature of Commitment.* VP. [2003] pp. 296. pb. $A39.95 ISBN 0 9580 7941 2.

Allen, Chadwick. *Blood Narrative: Indigenous Identity in American Indian and Maori Literary and Activist Texts.* DukeUP. [2002] pp. 308. hb. $59.95 ISBN 0 8223 2929 9, pb. $19.95 ISBN 0 8223 2947 6.

Anderson, Jill, ed. *Australian Divagations: Mallarmé and the 20th Century.* Lang. [2002] pp. ix + 335. £45 ISBN 0 8204 5297 1.

Arnold, John, and John Hay, eds. *The Bibliography of Australian Literature, A–E.* ASP. [2001] pp. 808. $A220 ISBN 1 8756 0690 4.

Arrow, Michelle. *Upstaged: Australian Women Dramatists in the Limelight at Last.* Currency. [2002] pp. 272. pb. $A29.95 ISBN 0 8681 9690 8.

Bartolovich, Crystal, and Neil Lazarus, eds. *Marxism, Modernity and Postcolonial Studies.* CUP. [2002] pp. 290. hb. £45 ISBN 0 5218 1367 0, pb. £16.95 ISBN 0 5218 9059 4.

Basu, Tapan, ed. *Translating Caste: Stories, Essays, Criticism.* Katha. [2002] pp. xxxv + 262. pb. $24.95 (Rs295) ISBN 8 1876 4905 4.

Benjamin, Andrew, Tony Davies, and Robbie B.H. Goh, eds. *Postcolonial Cultures and Literatures: Modernity and the (Un)Commonwealth.* Lang. [2002] pp. 376. £44 ISBN 0 8204 5140 1.

Blainey, Geoffrey, ed. *Henry Lawson.* Text. [2002] pp. xxxii + 283. pb. $A27.50 ISBN 1 8770 0811 7.

Boehmer, Elleke. *Empire, the National and the Postcolonial, 1890–1920: Resistance in Interaction.* OUP. [2002] pp. ix + 239. £40 ISBN 0 1981 8446 8.

Bolton, Ken, ed. *Homage to John Forbes.* Br&S. [2002] pp. 200. pb. $A28.95 ISBN 1 8760 4038 6.

Bonyhady, Tim, and Tom Griffiths, eds. *Words for Country: Landscape and Language in Australia.* UNSW. [2002] pp. 288. pb. $A39.95 ISBN 0 8684 0628 7.

Bose, Brinda, ed. *Translating Desire: The Politics of Gender and Culture in India.* Katha. [2002] pp. xxx + 311. pb. $24.95 (Rs295) ISBN 8 1876 4933 X.

Bradstock, Margaret, ed. *Tasma's The Pipers of Piper's Hill.* ADFA. [2002] pp. xxxviii + 329. pb. $A39.95 ISBN 0 7317 0521 1.

Brown, Duncan. *Oral Literature and Performance in Southern Africa.* Currey. [2001] pp. 241. hb. £40 ISBN 0 8525 5559 8, pb. £14.95 ISBN 0 8525 5554 7.

Buffi, Roberta. *Between Literature and Painting: Three Australian Women Writers.* Studies of World Literature in English. Lang. [2002] pp. 213. £38 ISBN 0 8204 5257 2.

Calder, Alex, ed. *Old New Zealand and Other Writings. The Literature of Travel, Exploration and Empire,* by F.E. Maning. LeicUP. [2002] pp. 232. hb. $125 ISBN 0 7185 0196 9, pb. $49.95 ISBN 0 7165 0196 5.

Callahan, David, ed. *Contemporary Issues in Australian Literature.* Cass. [2002] pp. 183. pb. £16.50 ISBN 0 7146 8219 5.

Campbell, Rosemary, ed. *An Australian Girl*, by Catherine Martin. UQP. [2002] pp. lx +727. $A175 ISBN 0 7022 3368 4.

Carrière, Marie. *Writing in the Feminine in French and English Canada: A Question of Ethics*. UTorP. [2002] pp. 243. £35 ($55) ISBN 0 8020 3620 1.

Challis, Derek, and Gloria Rawlinson. *The Book of Iris: A Life of Robin Hyde*. AucklandUP. [2002] pp. 778. $NZ 69.95 ISBN 1 8694 0267 7.

Chevrefils, Marlys (comp.). *The Christie Harris Papers*, ed. Apollonia Steele. UCalgaryP. [2000] pp. 270. $24.95 ISBN 1 5523 8023 8.

Chittleborough, Anne, Gillian Dooley, Brenda Glover, and Rick Hosking, eds. *Alas, for the Pelicans! Flinders, Baudin and Beyond*. Wakefield. [2002] pp. 221. pb. $A29.95 ISBN 1 8625 4603 7.

Chowdhary, Arvind, ed. *Amitav Ghosh's 'The Shadow Lines': Critical Essays*. Atlantic. [2002] pp. xiv + 225. Rs450 ISBN 8 1269 0195 0.

Clark, Roger Y. *Stranger Worlds: Salman Rushdie's Other Worlds*. McG-QUP. [2001] pp. xxii + 226. hb. £40 ($CAN70) ISBN 0 7735 2107 0, pb. £19.95 ($CAN27.95) 0 7735 2193 3.

Clarke, George Elliott. *Odysseys Home: Mapping African-Canadian Literature*. UTorP. [2002] pp. 491. hb. £60 ($85) ISBN 0 8020 4376 3, pb. £22.50 ($35.95) ISBN 0 8020 8191 6.

Collier, Gordon, and Frank Schulze-Engler, eds. *Crabtracks: Progress and Process in Teaching the New Literatures in English, Essays in Honour of Dieter Riemenschneider*. Cross Cultures 59. Rodopi. [2002] pp. xviii + 409. hb. $100 (€80) 9 0420 1549 7, pb. $50 (€40) ISBN 9 0420 1539 X.

Compton, Wayde, ed. *Bluesprint: Black British Columbian Literature and Orature*. Arsenal. [2001] pp. 315. $CAN24.95 ($19.95) ISBN 1 5515 2118 0.

Craven, Peter, ed. *The Best Australian Essays 2002*. Black. [2002] pp. 400. pb. $A29.95 ISBN 1 8639 5187 3.

Dalziell, Rosamund, ed. *Selves Crossing Cultures: Autobiography and Globalisation*. ASP. [2002] pp. xx + 217. pb. $A34.95 ISBN 1 7409 7009 8.

de Groen, Frances, and Laurie Hergenhan, eds. *Xavier Herbert: Letters*. UQP. [2002] pp. xviii + 490. pb. $40 ISBN 0 7022 3309 9.

de Souza, Eunice, and Lindsay Pereira, eds. *Women's Voices: Selections from Nineteenth- and Early Twentieth-Century Indian Writing in English*. OUPI. [2002] pp. xxii + 451. £25 ISBN 0 1956 5915 5.

Devy, G.N., ed. *Indian Literary Criticism: Theory and Interpretation*. Orient Longman. [2002] pp. xvi + 430. pb. £19.95 ISBN 8 1250 2022 5.

Dugga, Victor Samson. *Creolisation in Nigerian Theatre*. African Studies 61. Bayreuth. [2002] pp. 197. pb. €20.95 ISBN 3 9275 1072 6.

Fleming, Deborah, ed. *W.B. Yeats and Postcolonialism*. Locust Hill. [2001] pp. xxxii + 338. $45 ISBN 0 9339 5188 4.

Gilbert, Helen, and Anna Johnston, eds. *In Transit: Travel, Text, Empire*. Lang. [2002] pp. 286. pb. £21 ISBN 0 8204 5699 3.

Griswold, Wendy. *Bearing Witness: Readers, Writers, and the Novel in Nigeria*. PrincetonUP. [2000] pp. 340. hb. $52.50 ISBN 0 6910 5828 8, pb. $27.95 ISBN 0 6910 5829 6.

Gyssels, Kathleen, Isabel Hoving, and Maggie Ann Bowers, eds. *Convergences and Interferences: Newness in Intercultural Practices/Écritures d'une nouvelle ère/*

aire. Rodopi. [2001] pp. 293. pb. $88 (€70) ISBN 9 0420 1538 1, ISSN 1381 1312.

Hale, Ninette, and Tabish Khair, eds. *Angles on the English-Speaking World,* vol. 1: *Unhinging Hinglish: The Languages and Politics of Fiction in English from the Indian Subcontinent.* MTP. [2001] pp. 152. pb. £14 ISBN 8 7728 9672 8, ISSN 0903 1723.

Hassumani, Sabrina. *Salman Rushdie: A Postmodern Reading of his Major Works.* FDUP. [2002] pp. 154. £28 ISBN 0 8386 3934 8.

Hewitt, Helen Verity. *Patrick White, Painter Manqué.* Miegunyah. [2002] pp. 200. $A49.95 ISBN 0 5228 5032 4.

Hill, Barry. *Broken Song: T.G.H. Strehlow and Aboriginal Possession.* RandomHAus. [2002] pp. xvii + 818. $A59.95 ISBN 1 7405 1065 8.

Holt, Elizabeth, and Elizabeth Perkins, eds. *The Poems of Charles Harpur: An Analytical Finding List.* ADFA. [2002] pp. 246. $A80 ISBN 0 7317 0371 5.

Innes, C.L. *A History of Black and Asian Writing in Britain, 1700–2000.* CUP. [2002] pp. xxii + 308. £45 ISBN 0 5216 4327 9.

Ivison, Douglas, ed. *Dictionary of Literary Biography,* vol. 251: *Canadian Fantasy and Science-Fiction Writers.* Gale. [2002] pp. 404. $175 ISBN 0 7876 4668 7.

Jain, Jasbir, and Avadesh Kumar Singh, eds. *Indian Feminisms.* CreativeB. [2001] pp. vii + 231. $25 ISBN 8 1863 1889 5.

Johnson-Woods, Toni. *Index to Serials in Australian Periodicals and Newspapers: Nineteenth Century.* Mulini. [2001] pp. 153. pb. $A25 ISBN 0 9499 1068 6.

Jordan, Robert. *The Convict Theatres of Early Australia, 1788–1840.* Currency. [2002] pp. xiii + 370 + illus. $A49.95 ISBN 0 9581 2130 3.

Joshi, Priya. *In Another Country: Colonialism, Culture and the English Novel in India.* ColUP. [2002] pp. xix + 363. hb. £ 41.50($62) ISBN 0 2311 2584 4, pb. £16 ($23.50) ISBN 0 2311 2585 2.

Kaul, R.K., and Jasbir Jain. *Attia Hosain: A Diptych Volume.* Rawat. [2002] pp. 239. Rs450 ISBN 8 1703 3685 6.

King, Michael. *An Inward Sun: The World of Janet Frame.* PenguinNZ. [2002] pp. 160. pb. $NZ34.95 ISBN 0 1430 1838 8.

Kumar, Amitava. *Bombay–London–New York.* Routledge. [2002] pp. 280. hb. $85 ISBN 0 4159 4210 1, pb. $19.95 ISBN 0 4159 4211 X.

Kuortti, Joel. *Indian Women's Writing in English: A Bibliography.* Rawat. [2002] pp. xvi + 383. Rs725 ISBN 8 1703 3727 5.

Laugesen, Amanda. *Convict Words: Language in Early Colonial Australia.* OUP. [2002] pp. xxiv + 208. pb. $A34.95 ISBN 0 1955 1655 9.

Liddelow, Eden. *After Electra: Rage, Grief and Hope in Twentieth-Century Fiction.* ASP. [2002] pp. 211. pb. $A49.95 ISBN 1 7409 7005 5.

Lokugé, Chandani, ed. *India Calling: The Memories of Cornelia Sorabji, India's First Woman Barrister.* OUPI. [2002] pp. xxxvi + 262. £22 ISBN 0 1956 4974 5.

Luyat, Anne, and Francine Tolron, eds. *Flight from Certainty: The Dilemma of Identity and Exile.* Rodopi. [2001] pp. 254. hb. $71 (€57) ISBN 9 0420 1595 0, pb. $29 (€23) 9 0420 1585 3.

Mittapalli, Rajeshwar, and Alessandro Monti, eds. *Commonwealth Fictions: Twenty-First Century Readings.* Atlantic. [2002] pp. vi + 280. Rs550 ISBN 8 1269 0176 4.

Modjeska, Drusilla. *Timepieces*. Macmillan. [2002] pp. 240. pb. $A22 ISBN 0 3303 6372 7.

Monti, Alessandro, and R.K. Dhawan, eds. *Discussing Indian Women Writers: Some Feminist Issues*. PrestigeB. [2002] pp. 294. $20 ISBN 8 1755 1128 1.

Mukherjee, Meenakshi. *The Twice-Born Fiction: Themes and Techniques of the Indian Novel in English* [1971]. PencraftI. [2001] pp. 215. Rs350 ISBN 8 1857 5346 6.

Mukherjee, Meenakshi, ed. *Early Novels in India*. SA. [2002] pp. xix + 278. Rs140 ISBN 8 1260 1342 7.

Muponde, Robert, and Mandi Taruvinga, eds. *Sign and Taboo: Perspectives on the Poetic Fiction of Yvonne Vera*. Weaver & Currey. [2002] pp. 236. $49.95 ISBN 1 7792 2004 9.

Naik, M. K., and Shyamala A. Narayan. *Indian English Literature, 1980–2000: A Critical Survey*. PencraftI. [2001] pp. 303. Rs495 ISBN 8 1857 5343 1.

Nair, Rama. *'Of Variegated Hues': The Poetry and Translations of A.K. Ramanujan*. PrestigeB. [2002] pp. 104. Rs300 ISBN 8 1755 1119 2.

Nair, Rukmini Bhaya. *Lying on the Postcolonial Couch: The Idea of Indifference*. UMinnP. [2002] pp. 320 hb. $68.95 ISBN 0 8166 3365 7, pb. $22.95 ISBN 0 8166 3366 5.

Nair, Rukmini Bhaya, ed. *Translation, Text and Theory: The Paradigm of India*. Sage. [2002] pp. 348. $62.95 ISBN 0 7619 9587 0.

Nasta, Susheila. *Home Truths: Fictions of the South Asian Diaspora in Britain*. Palgrave. [2002] pp. xii + 305. hb. £52.50 ISBN 0 3336 7005 1, pb. £17.50 ISBN 0 3336 7005 X.

Natarajan, Nalini. *Woman and Indian Modernity: Readings of Colonial and Postcolonial Novels*. UPSouth. [2002] pp. vi + 138. pb. $49.95 ISBN 1 8894 3182 6.

New, W.H., ed. *Encyclopedia of Literature in Canada*. UTorP. [2002] pp. 1347. £50 ($75) ISBN 0 8020 0761 9.

Niall, Brenda. *The Boyds: A Family Biography*. Miegunyah. [2002] pp. xxiv + 437. $A49.95 ISBN 0 5228 4871 0.

Nile, Richard. *The Making of the Australian Literary Imagination*. UQP. [2002] pp. 315. pb. $A28 ISBN 0 7022 3165 7.

O'Leary, Michael. *Alternative Small Press Publishing in New Zealand: An Introduction with Particular Reference to the Years, 1969–1999*. Monographs of Aotearoa Literature 56. OriginalNZ. [2002] pp. 61. pb. NZ$35 ISBN 1 8693 3547 3.

Oliver, W.H. *Looking for the* Phoenix*: A Memoir*. BWilliamsNZ. [2002] pp. 178. pb. $NZ39.95 ISBN 1 9772 4298 5.

Oni, Duro, and Sunday E. Ododo, eds. *Larger than his Frame: Critical Studies and Reflections on Olu Obafemi*. Kraft. [2001] pp. 350. pb. $17.25 ISBN 9 7803 9024 3.

Pender, Anne. *Christina Stead: Satirist*. CG. [2002] pp. 246. pb. $A23 ISBN 1 8633 5089 6.

Piper, Karen. *Cartographic Fictions: Maps, Race and Identity*. RutgersUP. [2002] pp. xiv + 220. hb. $60 ISBN 0 8135 3072 5, pb. $23 ISBN 0 8135 3073 3.

Pollak, Michael, and Margaret McNabb. *Days Never Done: The Life and Work of Hesba Fay Brinsmead*. UnityP. [2002] pp. 232. pb. $A27.95 ISBN 0 9589 7593 0.

Pollak, Michael, and Margaret McNabb, eds. *Gothic Matilda: The Amazing Visions of Australian Crime Fiction*. UnityP. [2002] pp. 224. pb. $A27.95 ISBN 0 9589 7594 9.

Pons, Xavier, ed. *Departures: How Australia Reinvents Itself*. MelbourneUP. [2002] pp. 336. pb. $A34.95 ISBN 0 5228 4995 4.

Reif-Hulser, Monika, ed. *Borderlands: Negotiating Boundaries in Post-Colonial Writing*. Rodopi. [2000] pp. 293. hb. €89 ($83) ISBN 9 0420 0468 1, pb. €28 ($26.50) ISBN 9 0420 0458 4.

Ricou, Laurie. *The Arbutus/Madrone Files: Reading the Pacific Northwest*. NeWest. [2002] pp. 240. $CAN34.95 ISBN 1 8963 0043 X.

Russell, Elizabeth, ed. *Caught Between Cultures: Women, Writing and Subjectivities*. Cross/Cultures 52. Rodopi. [2002] pp. xxi + 152. pb. $21 ISBN 9 0420 1368 0.

Sabin, Margery. *Dissenters and Mavericks: Writings about India in English, 1765–2000*. OUPAm. [2002] pp. viii + 239. $29.95 (£25) ISBN 0 1951 5017 1.

Samuels, Selina, ed. *Dictionary of Literary Biography: Australian Literature, 1788–1914*, vol. 230. Gale. [2001] pp. xx + 499. $A150 ISBN 0 7876 4647 4.

Samuels, Selina, ed. *Dictionary of Literary Biography: Australian Literature, 1915–1950*, vol. 260. Gale. [2002] pp. xxi + 510. $A150 ISBN 0 7876 6004 3.

Schaub, Danielle, and Christyl Verduyn, eds. *Identity, Community, Nation: Essays on Canadian Writing*. Magnes. [2002] pp. 218. $25 ISBN 9 6549 3151 6.

Settar, S., and Indira B. Gupta, eds. *Pangs of Partition*, vol. 2: *The Human Dimension*. Manohar. [2002] pp. 358. £35 (Rs700) ISBN 8 1730 4307 8.

Sheahan-Bright, Robyn, and Stuart Glover, eds. *Hot Iron Corrugated Sky: 100 Years of Queensland Writing*. UQP. [2002] pp. xxxi + 235. pb. $A22.95 ISBN 0 7022 3344 7.

Siegel, Kristi, ed. *Issues in Travel Writing: Empire, Spectacle and Displacement*. Lang. [2002] pp. 303. pb. £23 ISBN 0 8204 4580 0.

Smith, Angela, ed. *Les Murray and Australian Poetry*. Menzies. [2002] pp. 103. pb. £6 ISBN 0 7022 3165 7.

Sougou, Omar. *Writing Across Cultures: Gender Politics and Difference in the Fiction of Buchi Emecheta*. Rodopi. [2002] pp. 243. €28 ($26.50) ISBN 9 0420 1308 7.

Stead, C.K. *Kin of Place: Essays on 20 New Zealand Writers*. AucklandUP. [2002] pp. 386. pb. $39.95 ISBN 1 8694 0272 3.

Steenman-Marcuse, Conny, ed. *The Rhetoric of Canadian Writing*. Rodopi. [2002] pp. 304. $65 ISBN 9 0420 1290 0.

Stewart, Ken, and Shirley Walker, eds. *'Unemployed at Last!' Essays on Australian Literature to 2002 for Julian Croft*. CALLS. [2002] pp. vi + 218. pb. $A30 ISBN 1 8638 9813 1.

Stilz, Gerhard, ed. *Missions of Interdependence: A Literary Directory*. Cross/Cultures 58. Rodopi. [2002] pp. xvii + 424. pb. $51 ISBN 9 0420 1419 9.

Vanita, Ruth, ed. *Queering India: Same-Sex Love and Eroticism in Indian Culture and Society*. Routledge. [2002] pp. 252. hb. £60 ISBN 0 4159 2949 0, pb. £8.99 ISBN 0 4159 2950 4.

Walker, Brenda, ed. *The Writer's Reader: A Guide to Writing Fiction and Poetry*. HalsteadP. [2002] pp. 207. pb. $A32.95 ISBN 1 8756 8475 1.

Wertheim, Albert. *The Dramatic Art of Athol Fugard: From South Africa to the World*. IndUP. [2002] pp. 273. pb. $17.95 ISBN 0 2532 1504 8.

Wisker, Gina. *Margaret Atwood's 'Alias Grace': A Reader's Guide*. Continuum. [2002] pp. 103. £5 ($9.95) ISBN 0 8264 5706 1.

York, Lorraine. *Rethinking Women's Collaborative Writing: Power, Difference, Property*. UTorP. [2002] pp. 205. hb. £32 ($50) ISBN 0 8020 3623 6, pb. £15 ($24.95) ISBN 0 8020 8465 6.

XVIII

Bibliography and Textual Criticism

WILLIAM BAKER AND PAUL WEBB

This year's work in bibliography and textual criticism continues the pattern of previous years. Monographs on editorial theory continue to flourish in a healthy manner and work on the history of the book demonstrates that it has become a fashionable field of activity. The review encompasses materials of interests to students of various areas of librarianship, book collecting, and antiquarianism as well as English literature.

As in previous years, the variety and quality of journals and journal articles devoted to bibliography and textual criticism grows and flourishes. *The Papers of the Bibliographical Society of America* 96[2002] includes the following articles in addition to reviews. David R. Carlson, in his 'Printed Superior Figures in Nicholas Jenson's Lawbooks, 1478–80' (*PBSA* 96[2002] 4–22), explores the evidence relating to the typographical practices found in Nicholas Jenson's *Lawbooks*. Carlson's article is well served by some interesting accompanying illustrations. Marvin Spevack, in his 'What Price Shakespeare? James Orchard Halliwell-Phillips and the Shilling Shakespeares of the 1860s' (*PBSA* 96[2002] 23–47), pursues familiar terrain in his explorations of the activities of Halliwell-Phillips. Sandra M. Donaldson's 'Versions of a Text: "A Drama of Exile" as a Test Case for a New Edition of Elizabeth Browning's Collected Poems' (*PBSA* 96[2002] 49–58) reworks the complicated terrain of editing Elizabeth Barrett Browning. In a somewhat lengthy article replete with 151 footnotes, David Alan Richards, 'Kipling and the Pirates' (*PBSA* 96[2002] 59–109), trawls through the Kipling archives located in various places to examine the fascinating area of Kipling piracies. In a bibliographical note, 'The Early Editions and Reception of John Tutchin's *The Tribe of Levi* (1691)' (*PBSA* 96[2002] 111–21), the distinguished Dryden scholar Alan Roper illuminates John Tutchin's 1691 'imitation' (p. 111) of John Dryden's *Absalom and Achitophel*. Gary Taylor's lengthy 'Middleton and Rowley—and Heywood: *The Old Law* and New Attribution Technologies' (*PBSA* 96[2002] 165–217) examines the complex issue of authorial attribution in *The Old Law: Or a New Way to Please You* [1656], and whether or not Massinger had a hand in its composition. Taylor draws upon the 'enormous database provided by Chadwyck-Healey ... "Literature Online" (LION)' (p. 192). Taylor's conclusions concerning the collaborators involved in the play are somewhat difficult to follow. It is too early to say whether Brian Vickers will enter into the fray! The First Folio and the issue of 'the procedures of those responsible for the placement of the act divisions found in that volume' (p. 219) preoccupy James Hirsh in his 'Act Divisions in the Shakespeare First Folio' (*PBSA* 96[2002] 219–56). Massimiliano Demata draws upon the John Murray archives to illuminate 'the history of Murray's publishing venture[s] in contemporary drama' (p. 278) in 'Between the Stage and the Book: John Murray and the Publication of Drama, 1812–19' (*PBSA* 96[2002] 257–78). Claire Hoertz Badaracco's bibliographical note '*The Autobiography of an Ex-Coloured Man* by James Weldon Johnson: The 1927 Knopf Edition' (*PBSA* 96[2002] 279–87) interestingly draws upon the archives of James Weldon Johnson (1871–1938), 'a senior African-American statesman' (p. 279). William Spawn and Thomas E. Kinsella, 'The Description of Bookcloth: Making a Case for More Precision' (*PBSA* 96[2002] 341–9) raises the issue of 'descriptive terminology' regarding the terms 'design' and 'shade' (p. 341). There is an account of the 'Chronology of Pattern Books' in the William Tomlinson Bookcloth Collection now at the Mariam Coffin Canaday Library at Bryn Mawr College (pp. 346–9).

Keith Arbour's 'Papermaking in New England before 1675? A Document and a Challenge' (*PBSA* 96[2002] 351–79) is a clear exposition drawn from the papers of 'the English polymath Sir William Petty (1623–87)' (p. 351) of paper-making activities in the New World. Arthur Sherbo's 'From the Sale Catalogues of the Libraries of Dr. Richard Farmer, George Steevens, and Isaac Reed' (*PBSA* 96[2002] 381–403) selects items of interest from the sale catalogues of the libraries of 'Dr. Richard Farmer (1735–97), Master of Emmanuel College, Cambridge … George Stevens (1736–1800) … and Isaac Reed (1742–1807), bachelor-scholar, editorial factotum, diarist' (p. 381). In his 'Uncertain Proofs: Alexander Pope, Lewis Theobald, and Questions of Patronage' (*PBSA* 96[2002] 404–34) Michael F. Suarez, SJ, usefully illuminates the relationship between Pope and Theobald. Suarez draws upon the autographed manuscript of Pope's *Epistle to Arbuthnot* now at the Huntington Library (HM 6006). In a bibliographical note Karen Nipps, 'Addenda to McDonald et al., Miller, and NAIP: Two Previously Unlocated *Pennsylvania Gazette* Carrier's Addresses for 1761 and 1762' (*PBSA* 96[2002] 435–8), draws upon 'the Harvard University Library's run of Benjamin Franklin and David Hall's Philadelphia newspaper *The Pennsylvania Gazette* (Houghton shelf-mark E-136)' (p. 435). Michael Winship (*PBSA* 96[2002] 488–91) briefly but succinctly describes the decision of the 'Council of the Bibliographical Society of America … to elect William B. Todd to honorary membership in recognition of his ground-breaking and wide-ranging contributions to bibliography over five decades of sustained work' (p. 488). Hope Mayo's 'Newspapers and Bibliography: The Importance of Artifacts' (*PBSA* 96[2002] 493–6) serves as an introduction to 'Nicholson Baker's address to the annual meeting of The Bibliographical Society of America, 24th of January 2002' (p. 493). The text of Baker's address is illustrated with five elaborate and rather expensive colour illustrations from the *New York World* of 1911, 1912, and 1913, and the *Chicago Daily Tribune* from 1945. Baker, in his 'Reading the Paper: Newsprint and Modern Memory' (*PBSA* 96[2002] 497–508), considers the 'constant assertion of nowness [which] is precisely what is so appealing and instructive about old newspapers, yellowing and fragile though they may be' (p. 498). Peter Caster's '*Go Down, Moses* [*and Other Stories*]: Bibliography as a Novel Approach to a Question of Genre' (*PBSA* 96[2002] 509–19) examines 'the diverse documentary evidence of letters, revisions, issues, editions, and dust jacket marketing' (p. 519) in the evolution of Faulkner's work. Joseph Chaves, '"A most exquisite Mechanic": Labor and Leisure, Printing and Authorship in the Periodical Essays of Benjamin Franklin' (*PBSA* 96[2002] 521–30), 'addresses one aspect of the relation between Franklin's activities as a printer and as an author' (p. 521). Lara Moore describes her 'investigations into the development of 'the École des Chartes' (p. 540) in her 'Restoring Order: The École des Chartes and the Organization of Archives and Libraries in France, 1820–1870' (*PBSA* 96[2002] 531–41).

The latest volume of *Studies in Bibliography*, 53[2002] contains its usual diverse and fascinating assortment of articles dealing with manuscripts, textual criticism, and bibliographies, among other topics. Contributors and contents include the hitherto unpublished lectures delivered at Cambridge University by the great R.B. McKerrow (1872–1940), edited by Carlo M. Bajetta, 'The Relationship of English Printed Books to Authors' Manuscripts during the Sixteenth and Seventeenth Centuries (the 1928 Sandars Lectures)' (*SB* 53[2002] 1–65); G. Thomas Tanselle, in his erudite and detailed 'The Concept of Format' (*SB* 53[2002] 67–115), considers the history and usage of the bibliographical term 'format'. As is to be expected from Tanselle, his prose provides a fine example of the clarity of expression when dealing with complicated matters. Joseph A. Dane and Rosemary A. Roberts, in their 'The Calculus of Calculus: W.W. Greg and the Mathematics of *Everyman* Editions' (*SB* 53[2002] 117–28), examine assumptions underlying Greg's 1910 observations on the numbers of editions of *Everyman* which 'might have been produced in the early sixteenth century' (p. 117). Steven Escar Smith's 'The Eternal Verities Verified: Charlton Hinman and the Roots of Mechanical Collation' (*SB* 53[2002] 129–61) is replete with eight photographic illustrations of Hinman at work, and of collators. There is an appendix, listing, by American states and three other countries (Canada, the United Kingdom, and Germany), the current locations of surviving Hinman Collators (pp. 154–6). Somewhat surprisingly one isn't recorded in a London location! Ralph Hanna's 'The Application of Thought to Textual Criticism in all Modes—with Apologies to A.E. Housman' (*SB* 53[2002] 163–72) consists of reflections on his examination of Peter Robinson's edition of *The Wife of Bath's Prologue* in CD-ROM format published by Cambridge in 1996. Robert Adams's 'Evidence for the Stemma of the *Piers Plowman* B Manuscripts' (*SB* 53[2002] 173–94), contains an elaborate and rather esoteric appendix. John A. Dussinger's 'Samuel Richardson's "Elegant Disquisitions": Anonymous Writing in the *True Briton* and Other Journals' (*SB* 53[2002] 195–226) adds to Richardson's bibliography and prints five texts with editorial notes from the *True Briton*. Keith Maslen's 'Fielding, Richardson, and William Strahan: A Bibliographical Puzzle' (*SB* 53[2002] 227–40) considers variance in 'two 1755 editions of Henry Fielding's *Journal of a Voyage to Lisbon*' (p. 227) and ornaments. There are appendices on ornaments and 'Works Jointly Printed by Richardson and Strahan 1745–54' (pp. 237–40). James E. May's 'Interrelating the Cancellantia and Partial Gatherings in the First Edition of Edward Young's *The Centaur Not Fabulous*' (*SB* 53[2002] 241–63) is a thorough 'bibliographical and textual scrutiny' of Edward Young's 'prose satire and homily' published in 1755 (p. 241), based upon a rigorous examination of forty-two copies listed in two extensive appendices (pp. 259–63). However, as B.J. McMullin remarks in his review of this issue of *SB*, one wonders whether 'every detail of [Edward Young's] working notes needs to be published'. McMullin is correct in saying that May's argument 'could also have been shortened and simplified by the reproduction of three imposition diagrams' (*BSANZSB* 27:iii–iv[2003] 125: an issue to be reviewed in next year's edition of *YWES*). Andrew M. Stauffer, 'Byron, Medwin, and the False Fiend: Remembering "Remember Thee"' (*SB* 53[2002] 265–76), is an elucidation of *Thomas Medwin's Journal of the Conversation of Lord Byron noted during a residence with his Lordship at Pisa in the years 1821 and 1822* [1824].

The *Library: The Transactions of the Bibliographical Society*, 7th series (24[2002]) maintains its distinguished reputation. In addition to extensive reviews it includes Peter Hinds, 'Roger L'Estrange, the Rye House Plot, and the Regulation of Political Discourse in Late Seventeenth-Century London' (*Library* 24[2002] 3–31). Hinds's essay 'considers Roger L'Estrange's efforts to control the circulation of political propaganda in London after the discovery of the Rye House Plot in June 1683' (p. 3). Hinds draws upon contemporary documentation and especially 'L'Estrange's serial half-sheet the *Observator*' (p. 5) to show the way in which L'Estrange manipulated his public position 'to regulate the circulation of political discourse' (p. 31). This is an important contribution to the history of censorship. Peter Lindenbaum's 'Authors and Publishers in the Late Seventeenth Century, II: Brabazon Aylmer and the Mysteries of the Trade' (*Library* 24[2002] 32–57) enlarges our knowledge of 'a figure on the margins of John Milton's life' (p. 32). Lindenbaum's essay has variable appendices on Aylmer's imprints and illuminates the contract for John Locke's *Essay Concerning Human Understanding*. Oliver Everett's 'The Royal Library at Windsor Castle as Developed by Prince Albert and B.B. Woodward' (*Library* 24[2002] 58–88) analyses 'four reports on the Library and Print Room that were produced in [1860–1862] by the then Librarian, Bernard Bolingbroke Woodward (1816–1869)' (p. 58). Carole Rawcliffe's '"Written in the Book of Life": Building the Libraries of Medieval English Hospitals and Almshouses' (*Library* 24[2002] 127–62) contains an extensive appendix replete with details of 'English Medieval Hospitals Discussed in the Text' (pp. 155–62). Christopher Decker's 'The Poet as Reader: Thomas Gray's Borrowings from Cambridge College Libraries' (*Library* 24[2002] 163–93) contains a listing of manuscripts, fifty-two volumes probably borrowed by Thomas Gray and four conjectural titles borrowed from the Peterhouse Library. Gray's borrowings from the Pembroke College Library are also outlined in what is a most helpful bibliography which will prove most useful to students of Thomas Gray and the study of eighteenth-century Cambridge University Library usage. Oliver Pickering, in a bibliographical note, 'Henry Hall of Hereford and Henry Purcell: A Postscript' (*Library* 24[2002] 194–8), draws upon hitherto unexamined materials in the Brotherton Collection at Leeds University Library to throw fresh light on the output of the songwriter and poet Henry Hall (*c*.1656–1707). Not to be ignored is Ashley Chantler's witty poem entitled 'Editing: A Can of Worms' (*Library* 24[2002] 199–200), on modern post- 'Greg, Bowers, Tanselle, McKenzie, Zeller' and McGann and the 'can of worms' (pp. 199–200) involved in editing.

R.A. Beddard's 'The Official Inauguration of the Bodleian Library on November 1602' (*Library* 24[2002] 255–81) is an interesting account of the official 'reinstitution' (p. 255) of the Bodleian Library. James Kelley's valuable 'Defoe's Library' (*Library* 24[2002] 284–301) is a welcome addition to our knowledge. Tom Buchanan's 'Three Lives of *Homage to Catalonia*' (*Library* 24[2002] 302–14) illuminates one of George Orwell's neglected works. There are two Bibliographical

Notes: Peter Beal's 'Sir George Etherege's Library at Ratisbon' (*Library* 24[2002] 315–16) is an addition to his 1988 *Library* article on the same subject (*Library* 6:x[1988] 122–44), and Stephen Rawles, 'More Sextos: Two Editions of Zincgref's *Emblematum Ethico-Politicorum Centuria*' (*Library* 24[2002] 317–19), throws light upon an exceedingly obscure early seventeenth-century emblem book. K.E. Attar's 'More than a Mythologist: Jacob Bryant as Book Collector' (*Library* 24[2002] 351–66) is a valuable addition to our knowledge of the intellectual activities of 'the scholar, mythologist, and bibliophile Jacob Bryant (1715–1804)' (p. 351). David Allan's 'Provincial Readers and Book Culture in the Scottish Enlightenment: The Perth Library, 1784–*c*.1800' (*Library* 24[2002] 367–89) adds to our knowledge of cultural activities in late eighteenth-century Scotland. Tom Lockwood's 'Francis Godolphin Waldron and Ben Jonson's *The Sad Shepherd*' (*Library* 24[2002] 390–412) is a clearly written account of the published texts of 'Ben Jonson's incomplete, late pastoral drama, *The Sad Shepherd*' (p. 390). Hedwig Gwosdek, in a Bibliographical Note, adds to our knowledge of 'The Copies of Wolsey's *Methodus*, Colet's *Aeditio*, and Lily's *Rudimenta Grammatices* in Chichester Cathedral Library' (*Library* 24[2002] 413–16).

There is much of interest in *Text: An Interdisciplinary Annual of Textual Studies*, 14[2002]. Jerome McGann's 'The Gutenberg Variations' (*Txt* 14[2002] 1–13) is a reflection upon the changes witnessed by members of the Society for Textual Scholarship since its 1981 inception. Mathew G. Kirschenbaum's 'Editing the Interface: Textual Studies and First Generation Electronic Objects' (*Txt* 14[2002] 15–51) is a lengthy explanation of a highly complicated technological process. Geert Lernout's 'Genetic Criticism and Philology' (*Txt* 14[2002] 53–75) attempts to explain developments in French genetic criticism, which has been active since the late 1960s. Marita Mathijsen, 'The Concept of Authorisation' (*Txt* 14[2002] 77–90) attempts to explain this highly controversial concept and differences between Anglo-American and German perceptions of it. Nancy B. Black's 'An Analysis and Transcription of the Latin Glosses Accompanying Gautier de Coinci's Miracle of "The Empress of Rome"' (*Txt* 14[2002] 91–108) is a fairly straightforward account and description of ninety-eight transcriptions of glosses of *The Empress of Rome*. Robert Adams's 'The R/F MSS of *Piers Plowman* and the Pattern of Alpha/Beta Complementary Omissions: Implications for Critical Editing' (*Txt* 14[2002] 109–37) contains three extensive appendices dealing with a 'Summary of Causes for BETA Omissions of RF Readings' (pp. 123–35). Patrizia Botta's 'The Epigraphs in *La Celestina*: Titles, Sub-titles, Rubrics, Arguments' (*Txt* 14[2002] 139–68) deals with a subject of the 'titling and rubrication of early texts' (p. 139). Dayton Haskin's 'No Edition Is an Island: The Place of the Nineteenth-Century American Editions within the History of Editing Donne's Poems' (*Txt* 14[2002] 169–207) belongs to 'a reappraisal of what the eighteenth and nineteenth-century editions [of Donne] contributed to the editorial tradition' (p. 169). R.G. Siemens, 'Shakespearean Apparatus? Explicit Textual Structures and the Implicit Navigation of Accumulated Knowledge' (*Txt* 14[2002] 209–40), is primarily concerned with the technology surrounding textual editing with particular focus upon Shakespeare's sonnets. There is an extensive enumerative listing of works cited (pp. 235–40). Gabrielle Dean's extensive 'Emily Dickinson's "Poetry of the Portfolio"' (*Txt* 14[2002] 241–76) investigates the 'little hand-sewn, handwritten pamphlets of poems' (p. 241) found amongst Dickinson's papers after her death.

Volume 14 of *Text* continues the tradition of extensive review essays. Rodger L. Tarr's review of Thomas Tanselle's *Literature and Artifacts* (*Txt* 14[2002] 279–92) is an incisive analysis of Tanselle's achievement and of the present state of 'our fading high culture' (p. 292). Russel Greer considers word by Jack Stillinger in his 'The Architectonics of Multiplicity: A Bakhtinian Critique of Three Books by Jack Stillinger' (*Txt* 14[2002] 293–304). Recent editions of Sir Walter Scott are the subject of Kathryn Sutherland's *'Made in Scotland*: The Edinburgh Edition of the Waverley Novels' (*Txt* 14[2002] 305–23). The recent edition of F. Scott Fitzgerald's *Trimalchio* is the subject of Richard Bucci's 'Serving Fitzgerald's Intentions without a Copy-Text' (*Txt* 14[2002] 324–33). These review essays are followed by reviews by Peter Robinson, H.T.M. van Vliet, Adriaan van der Weel, Graham Barwell, Duncan Wu, David Gants, William Hogan, Richard Bucci, Geert Lernout, W. Speed Hill, Evelyn B. Tribble, and R.J. Schoeck. In short, something of interest for us all in this issue of *Text*.

A journal which still fortunately survives even in the electronic age is the *Bulletin of Bibliography*, 59[2002]. The issues under review are as usual eclectic and include Philip C. Kolin and Maureen Curley, 'A Classified Adrienne Kennedy Bibliography' (*BB* 59[2002] 41–58); John A. Edens, 'Taylor Caldwell: A Bibliography' (*BB* 59[2002] 59–67); Catherine Klein, 'T.H. White: A Selected Enumerative Bibliography Supplementing Gallix' (*BB* 59[2002] 69–72); Kathy Campbell, 'Josephine Baker: Selected Resources' (*BB* 59[2002] 73–5); Peter Dollard, 'A Guide to Core Critical Studies of Adah Isaacs Menken' (*BB* 59[2002] 77–83); Alan Boehm and Roy Ziegler, 'A Julian Wehr Miscellany: Unrecorded Animated Books, Foreign-Language Animated Books, and Other Works' (*BB* 59[2002] 87–92); John A. Drobnicki, 'Holocaust-Denial Literature: A Fifth Bibliography' (*BB* 59[2002] 93–110); Craig Gable, 'Shafts and Darts: An Annotated Bibliography of George S. Schuyler's Contributions to *The Messenger*, 1923–1928' (*BB* 59[2002] 111–19); Charmaine N. Ijeoma, 'The African American Short Story, 1820–1899: An Annotated Bibliography' (*BB* 59[2002] 121–6); Joseph A. LaRose, 'Terrence Malick: A Bio-Bibliography' (*BB* 59[2002] 137–42); and Stephen Field, 'Shakespeare's Influence on the Drama of John Ford: An Annotated Bibliography of Ford Criticism from 1990–2001' (*BB* 59[2002] 143–50).

The *Antiquarian Book Monthly Review* is becoming rather glossy. There are fewer articles of bibliographical interest, and these have been replaced by photographs and general book and saleroom 'chat'. Fortunately some traditional features of this monthly publication have been retained, including reviews of recent catalogues, the auction diary, and the listing of book fairs, and there is now a useful Web Directory, although the book reviews seem to be getting shorter. In spite of these caveats, the 2002 issues have much to interest *YWES* readers. C. Thompson's 'Plastic Surgery Back to the 16th Century' (*ABM* 29:i[2002] 8–19) is a brief account of Renaissance plastic surgery and the role Gaspare Tagliacozzi played in its development; Anthony Lane, 'The Reel Story from the Birth-Pangs of Cinema to the Present Day' (*ABM* 29:i[2002] 20–4), deals with the continuing turf battle between books and film; Carol Grossman, 'Two Gentleman from Los Angeles: Ward Ritchie and Lawrence Clark Powell Were Boyhood Friends who Changed the World of Books Forever' (*ABM* 29:i[2002] 26–8), discusses the role of two important contributors towards the development of librarianship and the book arts in twentieth-century America; Richard Lan, 'California Dreaming' (*ABM* 29:i[2002]

30–4) provides lively commentary on how fantasy shaped representations of the West Coast in seventeenth-century cartography; Sally Mann, in an article devoted to prints and photography, illuminates the persistence of memory and the evocative image of a vanquished past in her article about the American South entitled simply 'Motherland' (*ABM* 29:iii[2002] 6–7); Philippe Garner discusses photography and the provocative power of Sotheby's 'Jammes Collection' in 'Celebrating the Art of Photography' (*ABM* 29:iii[2002] 18–24); architectural and archaeological books focusing on travel are highlighted in Kerry Bristol's 'The Remains of the Day'(*ABM* 29:iii[2002] 30–3), an investigation of the work of Robert Wood, the eighteenth-century British author and politician.

Lavishly illustrated books on the history of the American West are the subject of Hugo Worthy's 'How the West Was Won' (*ABM* 29:iv[2002] 8–9); the literary history of baseball, encompassing F. Scott Fitzgerald, Bernard Malamud, and Philip Roth, amongst others, is the subject of Alex Gordon's 'A League of their Own' (*ABM* 29:iv[2002]: the survey highlights collectable items on baseball. Eric Chaim Kline's 'The Haggadah' (*ABM* 29:iv[2002] 26–9) is a rather superficial account of a very important and fascinating area of book and manuscript history transcending many cultures and national boundaries. Godfrey Barker speculates on 'How Will the Book Trade Survive the 21st Century?' (*ABM* 29:iv[2002] 30–7); 'The Readership of Rabelais' (*ABM* 29:v[2002] 8), and the search for lost copies of early editions of Rabelais, is the subject of a very short reflection by Christine Thomson; Tom Lamb, in 'The Secret History' (*ABM* 29:v[2002] 24–8), tells the story of Beriah Botfield (1807–63), a collector whose clandestine library is interesting for its preoccupation with literary and antiquity and medieval and early English texts. Kathryn Hughes, author of a fine biography of George Eliot, in 'Behind the Mask' (*ABM* 29:v[2002] 31–5) explains why 'George Eliot and the Brontë sisters ... were forced to erase their identities and publish under pseudonyms' (p. 31). Her article is rather nicely illustrated, especially with a full-colour illustration of François d'Albert's 1849 painting of Marian Evans (p. 30) and a well-reproduced detail of a page from the diaries of Charlotte and Emily Brontë (p. 33). In the rather brief 'Never Ending Story' (*ABM* 29:v[2002] 35), Pam Harrington attempts to explain 'Why *Wuthering Heights* will remain the Holy Grail for collectors of Women's Literature' (p. 35); R.A. Gilbert, in his 'For We Be Brethren of the Rose Crosse' (*ABM* 29:v[2002] 36–40), outlines some rather esoteric works contained in Rosicrucian myth materials; David Roberts, the great Victorian painter, is the subject of Hugh Worthy's 'A River Runs Through It' (*ABM* 29:vi[2002] 8–9), which focuses on pictorial representations in books of mid-nineteenth-century London—half of Worthy's article consists of a coloured illustration. Not without interest is Tony Laywood's account of the development of the literature of association football and Nick Varley's reflections on great soccer players and their biographies (*ABM* 29:vi[2002] 24–31). This is a sub-literature which, sadly, has been ignored.

An article of interest to students of eighteenth-century English literature through to the present is Lucinda Boyle's 'Location, Location, Location' (*ABM* 29:vi[2002] 32–7), an illustrated account of how London came to be constituted cartographically; Mathew Sweet, in his 'Sin Cities' (*ABM* 29:vi[2002] 38–42), surveys fictional London—a most interesting subject. Sweet clearly hasn't the room to discuss post-Second World War evocations of London by writers such as Harold Pinter, Bernard Kops, and Alexander Baron; his focus is clearly with the late

Victorians. A hidden London Library is explored in Pamela Willis's 'The Knights of St. John' (*ABM* 29:vi[2002] 44–6) ; the library in Clerkenwell even has 'wide-ranging and multi-lingual' (p. 46) collections. Carol Grossman's 'Easy Riders' (*ABM* 29:vi[2002] 48–54) examines selected fine presses based in San Francisco, giving special attention to the Grabhorn Press. Paul Minet, 'Collecting in the Royal Field', as its title suggests, focuses upon the collecting of materials relating to the British royal family (*ABM* 29:vi[2002] 56–8). In 'Through the Looking Glass' (*ABM* 29:vii[2002] 24–9) Chiara Nicolini attempts to explain why children's books hold such a fascination for book collectors. Selwyn Goodacre describes 'The Trials and Tribulations of Collecting Macmillan Editions of *Alice* [*Adventures in Wonderland*]' (*ABM* 29:vii[2002] 31). Justin Schiller, the distinguished collector of children's books, in 'Welcome to Oz' (*ABM* 29:vii[2002] 32–7), traces the personal history of his obsession. Maurice Sendak is the subject of Joyce Y. Hanrahan's 'Wild Thing'(*ABM* 29:vii[2002] 38–41). Brian Lake's 'A View from the Lake (*ABM* 29:viii–ix[2002] 14) provocatively examines the whole question of what constitutes a 'first' edition, especially in regard to Charles Dickens and, in this particular instance, *Great Expectations*. Madelyn Short's deliciously illustrated 'The Small Hours' (*ABM* 29:viii–ix[2002] 27–32) investigates the history of collection miniatures from the fifteenth century to the present. The fascination with Napoleon which is found in Sir Walter Scott and others is the subject of Mark Urban's 'Little Big Man' (*ABM* 29:viii–ix[2002] 36–7). Collecting and the formation of a collection are the subject of 'A Private Affair' in which the British actor Jeremy Beadle talks to James Morton (*ABM* 29:viii–ix[2002] 48–52). Julian Mackenzie's 'In the Land of the Pharaohs' (*ABM* 29:x[2002] 20–6) explores perceptions of Egypt reflected in large plate volumes published during the nineteenth century. The world of books focusing on big-game hunting and sport goes well beyond Ernest Hemingway's *Green Hills of Africa* or Victorian works by Richard Burton in Ellen Enzler Herring's 'The Big Game' (*ABM* 29:x[2002] 30–3). Hugo Worthy's 'The History Man' (*ABM* 29:x[2002] 37–40) is a nicely illustrated history of the publication of Frank Herrmann's autobiography *Low Profile*, which is discussed later on in the present section. The well-illustrated fore-edged paintings and bindings, including copies of Sterne's *A Sentimental Journey*, are the subject of Paul Quarries, 'Silk Cut: Lingerie or Literature?' (*ABM* 29:x[2002] 42–4).

The November 2002 *ABM* is an effectively illustrated issue entitled 'The Erotic Issue'. Amongst works explored in Alex Gordon's 'French Letters' (*ABM* 29:xi[2002] 20–6)—a somewhat gaudily illustrated piece—are D.H. Lawrence's *Lady Chatterley's Lover*, Philip Roth's *Portnoy's Complaint*, and works by Anaïs Nin. Shoes as a collecting subject preoccupy Christine Thomson in her 'Walk on the Wild Side' (*ABM* 29:xi[2002] 28–32). Illustrations in books of eighteenth-century and Regency pornography are the subject of Lucy Harris's 'Bottoms Up!' (*ABM* 29:xi[2002] 34–7). Alex Comfort writes about his own book *The Joy of Sex* and the problems of its illustrations in his 'Read My Lips' (*ABM* 29:xi[2002] 38–42). The final issue of 2002 and the first for 2003 includes Jeremy M. Norman's 'The Fabric of History' (*ABM* 29:xii[2002/3] 22–6), which describes the Plotnick collection of works on the history of the foundation of physics. Plotnick's library 'contains an amazing number of incredibly rare offprints' (pp. 24–6). Shona Marran's 'Behind the Scenes at the Museum' (*ABM* 29:xii[2002/3] 28–32) somewhat briefly describes some of the treasures to be found in the newly opened library of the old Ashmolean building in Oxford. The collecting of early books on automobilia may appear to have little of interest for *YWES*. However, as Hugo Worthy explains in 'Riding in Cars with Boy' (*ABM* 29:xii[2002/3] 34–9), his discussion with Keith Fletcher, a collector of such materials, this superficial perception would ignore, for instance, *Tristram Shandy*: 'Sterne's masterpiece briefly mentions Simon Stevin's extraordinary wind carriage' (p. 36). Books on ancient cosmography are the subject of Adair Butchins, 'Heavens Above' (*ABM* 29:xii[2002/3] 40–4).

Another important journal, which continues to impress with the diversity and quality of its contents and contains important obituaries, sometimes reprinted from newspaper sources such as *The Independent*, is *The Book Collector*. Volume 51[2002] includes Richard Garnett, 'Rupert Hart-Davis Limited: A Brief History: Part 3' (*BC* 51[2002] 35–47); James Armstrong, 'The Obelisk Press Imprint, 1931–1950' (*BC* 51[2002] 48–75); Paul Morgan, 'An Oxford Binding of 1488–9: English and Foreign Bookbindings 93' (*BC* 51[2002] 77–82); 'Obituaries: Edith Finer' (*BC* 51[2002] 120–1); 'Obituaries: Hugh Amory' (*BC* 51[2002] 121–2); 'Obituaries: Albinia De La Mare' (*BC* 51[2002] 122–5); 'Obituaries: O.F. Snelling' (*BC* 51[2002] 125–7); 'Obituaries: Geoffrey Bill' (*BC* 51[2002] 128–9); K.E. Attar, 'Jane Austin at King's College, Cambridge' (*BC* 51[2002] 197–221); Karen Hodder, 'Dispersing the Atmosphere of Antiquity and Attempting the Impossible' (*BC* 51[2002] 222–39); Edmund King, 'A Zaehnsdorf Exhibition Piece' (*BC* 51[2002] 240–2); 'Obituaries: Robin Waterfield' (*BC* 51[2002] 279–82); 'Obituaries: Wilfrid Hodgson' (*BC* 51[2002] 282–3); 'Obituaries: Herbert Spencer' (*BC* 51[2002] 283–5); John Bidwell, 'Designs by Mr. J. Baskerville for Six Poems by Mr. T. Gray' (*BC* 51[2002] 355–71); A.S.G. Edwards, 'John Davy Hayward (1905–1965): Scholar, Bibliophile and Man of Letters' (*BC* 51[2002] 372–88); James S. Dearden, 'Ruskin's Bindings' (*BC* 51[2002] 389–412); 'Obituaries: Max Israel' (*BC* 51[2002] 450–2); 'Obituaries: Decherd Henry Turner, Jr.' (*BC* 51[2002] 452–4); Paul Breman, 'The Changing View: Illustrations of Towns in Foresti's Chronicle, 1481–1553' (*BC* 51[2002] 498–507); A.R.A. Hobson, 'Modern First Editions in the Fifties' (*BC* 51[2002] 508–10); Mirjam M. Foot, 'Fifty Years On: Bookbinding History Then and Now' (*BC* 51[2002] 511–19); Edmund King, 'Book Cover Designs Made by Burn for Macmillan: The First Forty Years' (*BC* 51[2002] 520–30); Nicolas Barker, 'Brian Sawyer Cron: Portrait of a Bibliophile XXXVI' (*BC* 51[2002] 531–52); 'Obituaries: Charles Ede' (*BC* 51[2002] 583–5); 'Obituaries: Ian Mowat' (*BC* 51[2002] 585).

James E. May of Penn State DuBois edits *The East Central Intelligencer*, of which issue number 16:i[2002] includes Dick Frautschi, 'The MMF Bibliography of French Prose Fiction, 1700–1800: A Progress Report' (*ECIntell* 16:i[2002] 12–15); Alexandra Mason, 'Eighteenth-Century Holdings in the Kenneth Spencer Research Library at the University of Kansas' (*ECIntell* 16:i[2002] 15–24); Hermann J. Real, 'Another Epitaph on Dean Swift' (*ECIntell* 16:i[2002] 24–6); D. Timothy Erwin, 'Of Surveys, Excursions, and 1650–1850' (*ECIntell* 16:i[2002] 26–8); 'In Memory of Hugh Amory' (*ECIntell* 16:i[2002] 42–5); Andrea M. Bashore, 'Joseph Priestley and his American Home' (*ECIntell* 16:ii[2002] 1–6); Hermann J. Real, '"Wise enough to play the fool": Swift's Flappers' (*ECIntell* 16:ii[2002] 8–11); Donald D. Eddy, '"Additional Copies Found in Cornell University Libraries": An Unprinted Appendix to J.D. Fleeman's *Bibliography*' (*ECIntell* 16:ii[2002] 27–8); Donald D. Eddy, 'Additional Copies of Richard Hurd Found at the University of Virginia'

(*ECIntell* 16:ii[2002] 29); John E. Mustain, 'Eighteenth-Century Highlights of the Kline/Roethke Collection at Stanford University' (*ECIntell* 16:iii[2002] 2–8); James E. May, 'Union List of [Emily Lorraine] De Montluzin's *Gentleman's Magazine* Work Coming to the Web from UVA's Electronic Text Center' (*ECIntell* 16:iii[2002] 10–11); James E. May, '[Eighteenth-Century] MSS & Rare Books, Listed and Acquired, 1999–2001' (*ECIntell* 16:iii[2002] 30–53); James E. May, 'Supplement to "Bibliographical Tools": Printed Sources (Part 3)' (*ECIntell* 16:iii[2002] 53–64).

The contents of the *Journal of Scholarly Publishing* 33[2002] are self-explanatory. They include Allen H. Pasco, 'Basic Advice for Novice Authors' (*JScholP* 33[2002] 75–89); John M. Budd, 'Serials Prices and Subscriptions in the Social Sciences' (*JScholP* 33[2002] 90–101); Scot Danforth, 'Toward a Phenomenology of Running a Book Exhibit' (*JScholP* 33[2002] 102–10); Hazel Bell, 'Personalities in Publishing: Jane Dorner' (*JScholP* 33[2002] 111–16); Michael Cornett, Robert Spoo, and Harold Orlans, 'Current Copyright Law and Fair Use: The Council of Editors of Learned Journals, Keynote Address, MLA Convention 2000' (*JScholP* 33[2002] 125–47); Rimi Chatterjee, 'Translation' (*JScholP* 33[2002] 148–65); Lynette Felber, 'The Book Review: Scholarly and Editorial Responsibility' (*JScholP* 33[2002] 166–72); Hazel Bell, 'Personalities in Publishing: Gervase Muller' (*JScholP* 33[2002] 173–8); Brenna Mclaughlin, 'Books for Understanding: The History So Far of AAUP's On-line Public Information Resource' (*JScholP* 33[2002] 181–8); Robin Derricourt, 'Scholarly Book Publishing in Australia: The Impact of the Last Decade' (*JScholP* 33[2002] 189–201); Dana Courtney, 'The Cloth-Paper Conundrum: The Economics of Simultaneous Publication' (*JScholP* 33[2002] 202–29); David Henige, 'Indexing: A User's Perspective' (*JScholP* 33[2002] 230–47); Hazel Bell, 'Personalities in Publishing: Jeremy Wilson' (*JScholP* 33[2002] 248–55); Michael Cornett, Patrick Harrison, and Ian Lancashire, 'The Electronic Muse: The Council of Editors of Learned Journals Keynote Address, MLA Convention 2001' (*JScholP* 34[2002] 4–30); Richard J. Cox, 'Unfair Use: Advice to Unwitting Authors' (*JScholP* 34[2002] 31–42); John P.M. Court, 'Bibliographies and Notes as a Separate Online Publication: A Novel Trend in Scholarly Publishing' (*JScholP* 34[2002] 43–52); Bob Paul, 'A Scholarly Book Marketing Fantasy' (*JScholP* 34[2002] 53–8).

Book History 5[2002], edited by Ezra Greenspan and Jonathan Rose, continues to contain contributions noted for their variety and depth. Matt Cohen's 'Morton's Maypole and the Indians: Publishing in Early New England' (*BoH* 5[2002] 1–18), replete with forty-one footnotes, uses 'Thomas Morton's Maypole and his *New English Canaan* [1637] ... to sketch out a conflict over information cultures and social power in pre-1637 New England' (p. 2); M.O. Grenby's 'Adults Only? Children and Children's Books in British Circulating Libraries, 1748–1848' (*BoH* 5[2002] 19–38) comes to 'somewhat contradictory conclusions' (p. 38) concerning the issue of children's literature and circulating books in British circulating libraries over the course of a century; Jyrki Hakapää's fascinating, 'Internationalizing Book Distribution in the Early Nineteenth Century: The Origins of Finnish Bookstores' (*BoH* 5[2002] 39–66) is documented with 108 supporting footnotes. Hakapää's text usefully contains an English translation from the Finnish, with the footnotes giving the original Finnish (see, for instance, note 81). Marija Dalbello's 'Franz Josef's Time Machine: Images of Modernity in the Era of Mechanical Reproduction' (*BoH*

5[2002] 67–103) focuses on 'the formation of modernity as expressed in print and from the point of view of the Central European book trade'. The article examines 'a publishing house in an industrial region of the Hapsburg Empire at the end of the nineteenth century and the beginning of the twentieth' (p. 68), and is documented with seventeen black and white illustrations, mainly from the national and university library of Croatia. Ingrid Satelmajer's 'Dickinson as Child's Fare: The Author Served Up in *St. Nicholas*' (*BoH* 5[2002] 105–42) also contains illustrations to aid its consideration of the marketing of Emily Dickinson's poetry in late nineteenth-century American children's magazines.

Christine Pawley's 'Seeking "Significance": Actual Readers, Specific Reading Communities' (*BoH* 5[2002] 143–60) examines 'theoretical and methodological issues' by drawing upon 'examples from two research projects: a study of late nineteenth century readers in Osage', a small Iowa town, and 'the mid-twentieth-century patrons of the Door-Kewaunee Regional Library, in rural Wisconsin'. The issues Pawley is concerned with are those attempting 'to link ... apparently disparate elements—reader and text—but also to elaborate on who readers were, and thus to shed light on how these specific readers read' (p. 144). Pawley's article contains two tables on reader borrowings by month and date, and a subject-based table. In spite of her quasi-scientific efforts, no conclusion is reached and the article is rather opaque. One of the more interesting contributions in the view of the present reviewers is Alistair McCleery's 'The Return of the Publisher to Book History: The Case of Allen Lane' (*BoH* 5[2002] 161–85), which draws upon the Alan Lane archives at the University of Bristol Library to illuminate what is a fascinating episode in mid-twentieth-century British book and legal history, *Regina* v. *Penguin Books* [1960]. Modern book historiography is also the concern of Sarah Brouillette. In 'Corporate Publishing and Canonization: *Necromancer* and Science-Fiction Publishing in the 1970s and Early 1980s' (*BoH* 5[2002] 187–208), she examines William Gibson's science fiction neo-romancer [1984] in the light of science fiction publishing of the 1970s and early 1980s. Paul C. Gutjahr uses evidence found on Amazon.com to consider the concept of 'a sacred text' (p. 226) in his 'No Longer Left Behind: Amazon.com, Reader Response, and the Changing Fortunes of the Christian Novel in America' (*BoH* 5[2002] 209–36).

This issue of *BoH* concludes with four essays reflecting upon 'The Epistemology of Publishing Statistics'. The first, Robert Darnton's 'Book Production in British India, 1850–1900' (*BoH* 5[2002] 239–62), uses nineteenth-century book catalogues and 'statistics drawn from the papers of the Indian Civil Service' (p. 259). Priya Joshi, in her 'Quantitative Method, Literary History' (*BoH* 5[2002] 263–74), uses the same documents and statistics as Darnton, but gives different results on Indian print production during the 1850–1900 period. Wendy Griswold's 'Number Magic in Nigeria' (*BoH* 5[2002] 275–82) attempts a 'statistical analysis of Nigerian novels' (p. 276). Simon Eliot's 'Very Necessary But Not Quite Sufficient: A Personal View of Quantitative Analysis in Book History' (*BoH* 5[2002] 283–93) concludes cautiously. His is 'simply an attempt to identify a number of different types of data derived from different sources, which, interpreted cautiously and used intelligently, can illuminate and explain processes within book history that are simply not visible by any other means' (p. 293).

Of interest to students of bibliographical and textual criticism are the following items in *Textual Practice* 16[2002]: Hugh Haughton's provocatively entitled, 'The

Bright Garbage on the Incoming Wave: Rubbish in the Poetry of Derek Mahon'
(*TPr* 16[2002] 323–43); Marcus Waithe, 'News from Nowhere, Utopia and
Bakhtin's Idyllic Chronotype' (*TPr* 16[2002] 459–72); Douglas Kerr, 'Orwell's
BBC Broadcasts: Colonial Discourse and the Rhetoric of Propaganda' (*TPr*
16[2002] 473–90); Rachel Seiffert, 'Inarticulacy, Identity and Silence: Annie
Proulx's *The Shipping News*' (*TPr* 16[2002] 511–25); and Deirdre Sabina Knight,
'Capitalist and Enlightenment Values in 1990s Chinese Fiction: The Case of Yu
Hua's *Blood Seller*' (*TPr* 16[2002] 547–68).

Of abiding interest are the clearly titled articles in the *Bibliographical Society of
Australia and New Zealand Bulletin* 26[2002]. They include Margaret Rees Jones,
'From Candles to Gas: *The Poverty Bay Herald* and Newspaper Production in
Gisborne, 1874–1884' (*BSANZSB* 26[2002] 2–28); Tiffany Donnelly, '"Trumpery
Stuff": Gender Politics in Australian Publishing, 1858' (*BSANZSB* 26[2002] 29–42);
Harriet Edquist, 'The Private Library of Harold Desbrow-Annear, Architect'
(*BSANZSB* 26[2002] 43–56); Patrick Buckridge, '"How to Read Books": Reading-
Advice Books in Britain and America, 1870–1960' (*BSANZSB* 26[2002] 67–80); Ruth
Lightbourne, 'The General Assembly Library of New Zealand and the Book Trade'
(*BSANZSB* 26[2002] 81–104); Roger Osborne, 'The Typescript Versions of Conrad's
Under Western Eyes: Motivations, Intentions, and Editorial Possibilities' (*BSANZSB*
26[2002] 105–17); Joost Daalder, 'A History of Confusion: The Two Earliest English
Translations of Oscar Wilde's *Salomé*' (*BSANZSB* 26[2002] 131–72); Ronald L.
Ravneberg, 'The Hawkesworth Copy: An Investigation into the Printer's Copy Used
for the Preparation of the 1773 Second Edition of John Hawkesworth's Account of
Captain Cook's First Voyage' (*BSANZSB* 26[2002] 173–92); Paul Tankard, 'Vive les
Paratexts: A Review Essay' (*BSANZSB* 26[2002] 195–219); B.J. McMullin, 'Getting
Acquainted with EEBO' (*BSANZSB* 26[2002] 220–30). *Review* 24[2002] contains
Michael Groden, 'Sunny Arrangements of Small Conveniences: Works, Texts,
Authors, Publishers, Readers, Editions' (*Review* 24[2002] 39–48), a review of Peter L.
Shillingsburg's *Resisting Texts: Authority and Submission in Construction of
Meaning*. *Library History*, series 3[2002] contains Frank Gibbons, 'Oral History
Created an Urban Myth: The Origins of the Liverpool Library' (*LH* series 3[2002] 14–
16).

Moving from serials to monographic publications and essay collections, David
Daniell's erudite *The Bible in English* provides a fascinating history of the multiple
translations of the Bible into the English language. Nearly 900 pages in length, this
exhausting study will serve as *the* source to consult for those interested in the
multifaceted tale of the Bible's appearance in English and its ongoing evolution in
the hands of modern translators. The work contains black and white illustrations as
well as chapters dealing with popular perceptions of the Bible in literature, music,
and painting.

Additional publications that will spark interest for biblical scholars, as well as
informed lay readers, are two publications from Oak Knoll Press and the British
Library, Herbert and Tov, eds., *The Bible as Book: The Hebrew Bible and the
Judaean Desert Discoveries* and *The Book of Hebrew Script: History,
Palaeography, Script Styles, Calligraphy and Design*. In *The Bible as Book*, Edward
D. Herbert and Emmanuel Tov edit essays reflecting the course of developments in
biblical studies following the chance discovery of the Dead Sea Scrolls in 1947. The
collection of articles they have assembled represents the best and latest research

efforts of international scholars working with the Dead Sea Scrolls, and topics
addressed include rethinking the meaning and importance of Scripture in light of the
discovery of the Scrolls, what the discovery of the Scrolls means for canonical
development, and the ramifications of the Qumran discoveries as related to biblical
textual criticism. The volume is the fourth in the Bible as Book series, and represents
another valuable contribution to a healthy, vibrant, and often controversial field of
research. In *The Book of Hebrew Script*, Ada Yardeni makes an important
contribution to the field of palaeography. Containing over 480 illustrations,
Yardeni's work begins in the eighth century bc and goes through the Second Temple
era and the periods that follow. In addition to discussing Hebrew palaeography,
Yardeni also reviews methods for the analysis of letter-forms, Hebrew calligraphy,
and the typefaces, design, and inscriptions related to Hebrew letters. Both biblical
scholars and students will find this a most useful resource. English literary scholars
and editors, especially those working in the medieval period, can also learn much
from Nicholas de Lange's English translation of Colette Sirat's *Hebrew
Manuscripts of the Middle Ages*. In this thorough and well-researched study, Sirat
identifies the literary genres and historical eras to which various Hebrew
manuscripts belong; the result is a comprehensive overview of Hebraic manuscript
culture. Richly illustrated, Sirat's work brings together different disciplines;
especially noteworthy is the third part of the book, which deals with the history of
books and texts. Overall, Sirat's efforts result in an all-encompassing study worthy
of a wide readership.

Pinnock, ed., *The Orion Center Bibliography of the Dead Sea Scrolls (1995–
2000)*, is the fourth official Scrolls bibliography. Like its predecessors, this latest
compilation fills a valuable role in recording the vast amount of secondary literature
regarding Dead Sea Scroll scholarship. The work itself contains over 3,000 entries
and over 600 reviews, and these entries represent reviews, journal articles, and
electronic publications. Useful text and subject indexes are located at the end of the
work. Religious scholars and general readers interested in prayer books will find
much value in David N. Griffith's *The Bibliography of the Book of Common Prayer,
1549–1999*. Griffith's aim was to record in one source the many different editions of
the Book of Common Prayer from its original appearance in 1549 up to 1999. In this
endeavour he has largely succeeded, and each entry contains a full bibliographic
citation along with a brief narrative regarding its publication history. There are many
illustrations, some in colour, and numerous indexes related to languages, printers,
promoters, publishers, scripts, and translators. This very fine effort reflects and
represents almost forty years of effort and research.

Scholars whose research encompasses the history of publishing religious books
will find much that is useful in Cassidy and Wright, eds., *Studies in the Illustration
of the Psalter*. This volume features six papers presented at a conference on the
illumination of the medieval Psalter, held in St Andrews in May 1997. Contributors
and contents include a general introduction by Mary Muir Wright, 'Introduction to
the Psalter'; Bernard Meehan, 'The Book of Kells and the Corbie Psalter (with a
note on Harley 2788)'; Heather Pulliam, 'Eloquent Ornament: Exegesis and
Entanglement in the Corbie Psalter'; William Noel, 'Medieval Charades and the
Visual Syntax of the Utrecht Psalter'; Peter Kidd, 'A Re-examination of the Date of
an Eleventh-Century Psalter from Winchester (British Library, MS Arundel 60)';
Janet Backhouse, '"A Very Old Book": The Burdett Psalter-Hours, Made for a

Thirteenth-Century Hospitaller'; Lucy Freeman Sandler, 'The Images of Words in English Gothic Psalters (the Saunders Lecture 1997)'. The book includes numerous illustrations and sixty-four pages of photographic plates.

John Manning's learned *The Emblem* is a beautifully produced book, lavishly illustrated, charting the growth and development of the emblem from the sixteenth to the seventeenth centuries and onwards. Discussing how local and regional influences shaped the development of the emblem, Manning also engages the role the Jesuits played in using the emblem to convey moral themes in a witty and instructive manner. The work contains many scholarly references and an exhaustive index, and will prove to be the definitive work on the subject.

This year a collection of notable works and bibliographies includes a number devoted to well-known authors. In *Joseph Heller: A Descriptive Bibliography*, Matthew J. Bruccoli and Park Bucker have completed the first comprehensive bibliography of Heller's literary output. This is the first work to be co-published by the University of Pittsburgh Press and Oak Knoll Press, and as such extends the distinguished Pittsburgh series in bibliography. Readers will find descriptions of all the printings of all editions of Heller's work in the English language. Bruccoli and Bucker have also included Heller's contributions towards other books, work by Heller that has appeared in the periodical literature, and his published interviews. Replete with black and white illustrations, of wrappers, dust jackets, and title pages, Bruccoli and Bucker's descriptive bibliography is primarily based on the Heller collection at the Thomas Cooper Library at the University of South Carolina. This is an important bibliography and a recommended purchase for all reference collections that deal with modern American authors.

Other major descriptive bibliographies to be published in 2002 include Baker and Ross, *George Eliot: A Bibliographical History*, which has 146 illustrations of title pages, the front and back of wrappers, spines, corrected proofs, advertisements, letters, and other material evidence. The 'primary aim is to present as complete an account as possible of the earlier British and American editions of the literary works and other writing of George Eliot, from first publication up to the time of her death' (p. v). There are five sections. The first, 'Major Works', encompasses George Eliot's eight book-length works of fiction, *Impressions of Theophrastus Such* [1879], and her translations from Strauss and Feuerbach. The second, 'Minor Literary Works', examines her two other novellas, *The Lifted Veil* and *Brother Jacob*, as well as a significant number of her short poems primarily published in the periodical press. The third, 'Essays and Reviews', examines periodical publications. The fourth section, 'Miscellaneous', deals broadly with four types of publications, those dealing with unpublished and often fragmentary writings, compilations of extracts from Eliot's published works, items co-authored by Eliot, and unpublished autobiographical writings. The fifth section, 'Collections and Collected Works', includes material related to *The Legend of Jubal and Other Poems* [1874], and editions of collected novels and works. There are two appendices. The first focuses on 'Eliotiana', detailing sequels, settings for songs, and collections of illustrations. The second enumerates, with some descriptions, George Eliot's 'non-literary writings subsequently published'. There are two indexes to conclude this exceedingly detailed and thorough bibliographical history. Carol A. Martin concludes her review of this book (in *George Eliot—George Henry Lewes Studies* [September 2003]) with the observation that 'it is a stupendous achievement, the result of many years of research, and a lasting and invaluable contribution to George Eliot studies' (p. 126).

In *Philip Larkin: A Bibliography, 1933–1994*, the late Barry C. Bloomfield extends his earlier bibliography of Larkin first published in 1975, and in doing so describes all of Larkin's published work up to 1994, including selected letters and collected poems. Included in this new 'second revised and enlarged edition' is an ample amount of scholarly materials published after Larkin's death. Bloomfield's descriptive bibliography is divided into thirteen sections: 'Books and Pamphlets', 'Works Edited with Contributions', 'Contributions by Philip Larkin to Periodicals', 'Larkin at the University of Hull', 'Interviews', 'Recordings', 'Radio and Television Appearances', 'Odds and Ends', 'Manuscripts', 'Published Letters', 'Translations', 'Anthologies', and 'Memento Mori' (listing commemorative poems and selective obituaries on Larkin's death in 1985). An appendix attempts to list 'all substantive criticism of Larkin's work that appeared to the end of 1993' (p. 173). Bloomfield's work is the most authoritative bibliography on Larkin to date and should be considered a mandatory purchase for libraries and scholars.

In *Alasdair Gray: Critical Appreciations and a Bibliography*, editor Phil Moores has created more than just a thorough and exhaustive bibliography of the eminent Scottish writer Alasdair Gray's output; he has also brought together a series of essays that discuss the many and diverse features of Gray's work. Contributors and contents include Moores's preface, followed by an introduction by Will Self; Philip Hobsbaum, 'Arcadia and Apocalypse: The Garden of Eden and the Triumph of Death'; 'Alasdair Gray's Personal Curriculum Vitae'; 'Alasdair Gray Interviewed by Kathy Acker: 1986'; Jonathan Coe, '1994, Janine'; S.B. Kelly, 'An Equal Acceptance of Larks and Cancer': The Poetry and Poetics of Alasdair Gray'; Elspeth King, 'Art for the Early Days of a Better Nation'; Angus Calder, 'Politics, Scotland, and Prefaces: Alasdair Gray's Non-Fiction'; Stephen Bernstein, 'Doing As Things Do With You: Alasdair Gray's Minor Novels'; Kevin Williamson, 'Under the Influence'; Phil Moores, 'An Alasdair Gray Bibliography'; Joe Murray, 'A Short Tale of Woe!'.

In *Jane Austen: A Companion*, Josephine Ross provides a useful general guide to the work and world of Austen. Ross's book will appeal to all readers of Austen, and particularly readers new to her work and wanting an interesting and not too sophisticated introduction. The second volume to be published in *The Cambridge History of the Book in Britain* is volume 4: *1557–1695*, edited by John Barnard and the late D.F. McKenzie, with the assistance of Maureen Bell. As expected, this is a major work replete with over thirty full-page black and white glossy illustrations. Solidly bound with a clean typeface, good margins, notation at the foot of the page, and an extensive enumerative bibliography and index, this valuable volume includes many distinguished contributors. Divided into eight sections, the first covers 'Religion and Politics' and includes two extensive essays: Patrick Collinson, Arnold Hunt, and Alexandra Walsham, 'Religious Publishing in England, 1557–1640', and Ian Green and Kate Peters, 'Religious Publishing in England, 1640–1695'. The second section, 'Oral Traditions and Scribal Culture', includes Harold Love, 'Oral and Scribal Texts in Early Modern England'; Peter Beal, 'John Donne and the Circulation of Manuscripts'; and Mary Chan, 'Music Books'. The third section, 'Literature of the Learned', includes Julian Roberts, 'The Latin Trade'; Graham Parry, 'Patronage and the Printing of Learned Works for the Author'; David

McKitterick, 'University Printing at Oxford and Cambridge'; Nicolas Barker, 'Editing the Past: Classical and Historical Scholarship'; Laurence Worms, 'Maps and Atlases'; Michael G. Brennan, 'The Literature of Travel'; Adrian Johns, 'Science and the Book'; M. Greengrass, 'Samuel Hartlib and the Commonwealth of Learning'; Elisabeth Leedham-Green and David McKitterick, 'Ownership: Private and Public Libraries'; and James P. Carley, 'Monastic Collections and their Dispersal'. Section 4 focuses on 'Literary Canons' and includes John Pitcher, 'Literature, the Playhouse and the Public'; Joad Raymond, 'Milton'; Paul Hammond, 'The Restoration Poetic and Dramatic Canon'; Nigel Smith, 'Non-Conformist Voices and Books'; and Maureen Bell, 'Women Writing and Women Written'. Section 5, 'Vernacular Traditions', includes B.J. McMullin, 'The Bible Trade'; J.H. Baker, 'English Law Books and Legal Publishing'; R.C. Simmons, 'ABCs, Almanacs, Ballads, Chapbooks, Popular Piety and Textbooks'; Lynette Hunter, 'Books for Daily Life: Household, Husbandry, Behaviour'; and Carolyn Nelson and Mathew Seccombe, 'The Creation of the Periodical Press 1620–1695'. Section 6, 'The Business of Print and the Space of Reading', includes D.F. McKenzie, 'Printing and Publishing 1557–1700: Constraints on the London Book Trades'; James Raven, 'The Economic Context'; John Bidwell, 'French Paper in English Books'; Nicolas Barker, 'The Old English Letter Foundries'; Mirjam M. Foot, 'Bookbinding'; Maureen Bell's short *'Mise-en-page*, Illustration, Expressive Form Introduction' (incorrectly described in the volume's table of contents), Randall Anderson, 'The Rhetoric of Paratext in Early Printed Books'; Peter Campbell, 'The Typography of Hobbes's *Leviathan*'; Nicolas Barker, 'The Polyglot Bible'; Harold Love, 'The Look of News: Popish Plot Narratives 1678–1680' and T.A. Birrell, 'Sir Roger L'Estrange: The Journalism of Orality'. Section 7, 'Beyond London: Production, Distribution, Reception', includes John Barnard and Maureen Bell, 'The English Provinces'; Jonquil Bevan, 'Scotland'; Robert Welch, 'The Book in Ireland from the Tudor Re-conquest to the Battle of the Boyne'; Philip Henry Jones, 'Wales'; P.G. Hoftijzer, 'British Books Abroad: the Continent'; and Hugh Amory, 'British Books Abroad: The American Colonies'. The final section, 'Disruption and Restructuring: The Late Seventeenth-Century Book Trade', consists of one contribution, Michael Treadwell on 'The Stationers and the Printing Acts at the End of the Seventeenth Century'.

This phenomenal piece of scholarship has three appendices. These include John Barnard and Maureen Bell's 'Statistical Tables', a compilation of nine tables ranging from statistics on 'Annual Book Production (1475–1700)' to a listing of 'Freemen in the Provincial Book Trade (1476–1695)'. D.F. McKenzie's 'Survey of Printing Presses 1668' is a transcription of Public Record Office SP29/243. The third appendix is C.Y. Ferdinand's 'Apprentices Bound in the Stationer's Company and What Became of Them (1557–1700)'. The volume also includes a detailed list of abbreviations, and an extensive index.

The latest edition of *English Manuscript Studies, 1100–1700*, volume 10, edited by A.S.G. Edwards, continues the fine tradition of bringing the latest research regarding the study of medieval and Renaissance manuscripts to the scholarly community. Contributors and contents include Nigel Morgan, 'The Decorative Ornament of the Text and Page in Thirteenth-Century England: Initials, Border Extensions and Line Fillers'; Michelle Brown, 'Marvels of the West: Giraldus Cambrensis and the Role of the Author in the Development of Marginal

Illustration'; Alixe Bovey, 'A Pictorial Ex Libris in the Smithfield Decretals'; Jessica Brantley, 'Images of the Vernacular in the Taymouth Hours'; Lucy Freeman Sandler, 'Political Imagery in the Bohun Manuscripts'; William Marx, 'Iconography and Meaning in The Sherbrooke Missal'; Kathleen Scott, 'Four Early Fifteenth-Century English Manuscripts of the *Speculum humanae salvationis* and a Fourteenth-Century Exemplar'; Peter M. Jones, 'Staying with the Programme: Illustrated Manuscripts of John Arderne *c*.1380–*c*.1550'. In conclusion there is A.S.G. Edwards's most informative 'Manuscripts at Auction: January 2000–December 2000'.

Finkelstein and McCleery, eds., *The Book History Reader*, reprints a series of important essays dealing with aspects of book history. Their volume will serve as a valuable resource for those interested in the history of publishing and the book, library studies, and literary cultural studies. The volume contains a useful introduction by the editors and is divided into three sections. In part 1, 'What is Book History?', reprinted articles include Robert Darnton, 'What is the History of Books?'; D.F. McKenzie, 'The Book as an Expressive Form', Jerome McGann, 'The Socialization of Texts'; Roger Chartier, 'Labourers and Voyagers: From the Text to the Reader'; Adrian Johns, 'The Book of Nature and the Nature of the Book'; Pierre Bourdieu, 'The Field of Cultural Production'. The second part, 'From Orality to Literacy', includes Walter Ong, 'Orality and Literacy: Writing Restructures Consciousness'; Roger Chartier, 'The Practical Impact of Writing'; Jan-Dirk Müller, 'The Body of the Book: The Media Transition from Manuscript to Print'; Elisabeth Eisenstein, 'Defining the Initial Shift: Some Features of Print Culture'; C.A. Bayly, 'The Indian Ecumene: An Indigenous Public Sphere', and D.F. McKenzie, 'The Sociology of a Text: Orality, Literacy and Print in Early New Zealand'. The third part, 'Commodifying Print: Books and Authors', includes Roland Barthes, 'The Death of the Author'; Michel Foucault, 'What is an Author?'; Mark Rose, 'Literary Property Determined'; John Brewer, 'Authors, Publishers and the Making of Literary Culture'; Jane Tompkins, 'Masterpiece Theater: The Politics of Hawthorne's Literary Reputation'; John Sutherland, 'The Victorian Novelists: Who Were They?'; James L.W. West III, 'The Magazine Market'; N.N. Feltes, 'Anyone of Everybody: Net Books and *Howards End*'. Part 4, 'Books and Readers', includes Wolfgang Iser, 'Interaction Between Text and Reader'; E. Jennifer Monaghan, 'Literacy Instruction and Gender in Colonial New England'; Kate Flint, 'Reading Practices'; Jonathan Rose, 'Rereading the English Common Reader: A Preface to a History of Audiences'; Richard Altick, 'The English Common Reader: From Caxton to the Eighteenth Century'; Stanley Fish, 'Interpreting the Variorum', and Janice Radway, 'A Feeling for Books: The Book-of-the-Month Club, Literary Taste and Middle Class Desire'. The work also includes an alphabetically arranged bibliography to each section and an index.

In *Samuel Richardson of London, Printer: A Study of his Printing Based on Ornament Use and Business Accounts*, Keith Maslen offers a thorough accounting of Samuel Richardson's career in the print trade. Maslen's work is divided into four main sections: Richardson's career as a printer; his printing house at work; his customers and categories of work; and his methods of discovery. Additional supplementary material includes books and pamphlets printed by Richardson, a parliamentary list of private, local, and public bills printed by Richardson, a newspaper list, and ornament data, including reproductions of 526 ornaments. This is an important and highly recommended monograph. The fourteen essays in Taylor, ed., *Foreign-Language Printing in London, 1500–1900*, 'represent the first systematic attempt', as Clive Field indicates in his preface, 'to document and to analyse the tradition of foreign-language printing in London during the period 1500 to 1900' (p. v). Contributions include Graham Jefcoate's 'German Printing and Bookselling in Eighteenth-Century London: Evidence and Interpretation'; Susan Reed's 'Printers, Publishers and Proletarians: Some Aspects of German Book Trades in Nineteenth-Century London'; Anna E.C. Simoni's 'Dutch Printing in London. I.A Survey. II. The Strange Case of Double-Dutch Double Vision: Bilingual Pamphlets of 1615'; Peter Hogg's 'Scandinavian Printing in London in the Eighteenth Century and its Social Background'; David J. Shaw's 'French-Language Publishing in London to 1900'; Morna Daniels's 'A King's Last Days: True and False Memoirs of Louis XVI's Valet'; Stephen Parkin's 'Italian Printing in London 1553–1900'; Denis V. Reidy's 'Early Italian Printing in London'; Barry Taylor's 'UnSpanish Practices: Spanish and Portuguese Jews, Protestants and Liberals [spelt with a small 'l': is this a typo?], 1500–1900'; Chris Michaelides' 'Greek Printing in England, 1500–1900. I.A Survey. II. Stephanos Xenos, a Greek Publisher in Nineteenth-Century London'; Kate Sealey Rahman's 'Russian Revolutionaries in London, 1853–70: Alexander Herzen and the Free Russian Press'; Janet Zmroczek's 'Poetry and Polemics: The Polish Book Trade in London, 1836–67'; Bridget Guzner's 'The Beginnings of Hungarian Printing in London'; and David Shaw's 'Statistical Survey'. The work concludes with an 'Index of Printers, Publishers and Booksellers'. This is a valuable publication, which could have benefited from more consistent proof-reading.

A number of works that might be best described as general reference works make their appearance this year. In the second edition of Peter Richard Wilkinson's absorbing and informative *Thesaurus of Traditional English Metaphors*, first published in 1993, readers will find over 1,500 new entries as well as an index of themes and an index of keywords to assist in locating entries. A massive volume at 870 pages, it stands as a basic and mandatory reference work. Wilkinson writes in his introduction that 'the main purpose of this collection is to trace the origins of folk metaphors in English' (p. xvii). Divided into eleven main sections which are then subdivided, it is not difficult to use. The sections (labelled A to K) consist of 'Tinker', 'Tailor', 'Soldier', 'Sailor', 'Richman', 'Poorman', 'Beggarman', 'Thief', 'At Home', 'At School', and 'At Play'. Illustrative of the comprehensive nature of this *Thesaurus* are the 'At Home', and 'At Play' sections, which consist of ninety-one and eighty-one subsections respectively.

Representing the most comprehensive work of its kind to date, *A Dictionary of Linguistics and Phonetics*, compiled by David Crystal, includes more than 5,000 terms grouped into over 3,000 entries. This new edition, the fifth, captures the latest developments in linguistics, and presents this new material in straightforward language comprehensible to scholars and general readers alike. A list of abbreviations used throughout the text is located at the beginning of the book and a table of symbols is a new feature in this latest edition. A new eighth edition of Partridge's *A Dictionary of Slang*, edited by Paul Beale, makes its appearance for the first time in paperback, and remains an essential reference source for its subject matter. Often considered one of the most authoritative single-volume dictionaries available, the latest edition of *The Chambers Biographical Dictionary*, by Una

McGovern, contains hundreds of new entries and continues to excel in providing unrivalled coverage in the area of popular culture, including film, music, radio, sport, and television. British-orientated, Chambers remains a valuable resource for generalized reference collections seeking a concise but informative source.

In *The British Museum: A History*, David M. Wilson, a former director of the British Museum, has written a superb book on the best-known publicly funded museum in the world. Wilson's research and his prose capture the spirit of the institution he profiles, as he takes the reader from the British Museum's inception through its growth in terms of collection size and international prestige, all the while being careful to place his narrative within its intellectual, political, and social contexts. Thirty-two black and white plates are included in the volume. Detailed notes are found at the back of the text. There are three appendices: 'Selective Plans', 'Departmental Structures', and Marjorie Coghill's 'Curatorial Staff 1756–May 2002'. The volume concludes with a 'List of Sources' divided into manuscripts and alphabetically arranged printed sources. There is an extensive index to this well-designed volume (typeset in Quadraat, p. 4).

In *Science Fiction Before 1900: Imagination Discovers Technology*, Paul K. Alkon makes a valuable contribution to the field of genre studies, focusing on the development of early science fiction texts in Europe and the United States. Alkon's work is divided into four main chapters: an introductory chapter recounts the early themes of science fiction, and the succeeding chapters deal with the history of science fiction in England, France, and the United States. Alkon's work also includes an analysis of quintessential science fiction texts, including Bellamy's *Looking Backward*, Shelley's *Frankenstein*, Twain's *A Connecticut Yankee in King Arthur's Court*, Verne's *20,000 Leagues Under the Sea*, and Wells's *The Time Machine*. Akron's work represents a valuable contribution to the genre of early science fiction studies.

In his solid and well-researched *King's Inn and the Battle of the Books, 1972: Cultural Controversy at a Dublin Library*, Colum Kenny presents the story of how the Bar Council of the Honourable Society of King's Inns made the agonizing decision to sell rare and valuable books in their collection to raise funds for the education and training of barristers. Book lovers of all sorts will find Kenny's work compelling reading. The book also includes an extensive bibliography and index as well as numerous illustrations.

In *The Publishing Industry in Colonial Australia: A Name Index to John Alexander Ferguson's 'Bibliography of Australia, 1784–1900'*, Ian Morrison provides a unique perspective for scholars and lay readers alike regarding the history of the book trade in colonial Australia. His labour-intensive index provides data related to Australian booksellers, and printers and publishers mentioned in Ferguson's *Bibliography*, and in doing so it enhances the use of Ferguson's work while making a major contribution to Australian bibliographic studies. In *'The World's Best Books': Taste, Culture, and the Modern Library*, Jay Satterfield has written an impressive study of one of the seminal events in American publishing history: the conception, marketing, and implementation of the inexpensive series, the Modern Library of the World's Best Books. Satterfield's fluid prose convincingly argues that the Modern Library series was a pioneering publishing phenomenon, representing the mass production of culture that was widely accepted by American literary and cultural elites. Included are a useful selected bibliography and an index. Providing coverage of more than 450 short stories, the *Thematic Guide to Popular Short Stories*, edited by Patrick Smith, contains brief annotations that are ordered alphabetically by author, and also detailed plot summaries related to each short story entry. Two very useful bibliographies are located at the end of the book, one listing the anthologies which the short story entries are originally taken from, and the other listing anthologies that have practical classroom use related to instruction. There are, in addition, author and subject indexes.

James Raven's *London Booksellers and American Customers: Transatlantic Literary Community and the Charleston Library Society, 1748–1811* is a valuable contribution in the field of book history. It is based largely on his annotated edition of the 'Charles Town Library Society Letterbook, 1758–1811', which consists primarily of letters written to numerous London booksellers. Raven's work is also significant in that it ranks as an important contribution towards moving book history studies into broader historical contexts. His achievement here suggests that book history practitioners should be willing to draw more extensively on the intellectual, political, religious, and economic currents of the periods they research. Book history studies can then move from a narrow preoccupation with books and publishing towards becoming a field characterized by the examination of the multiple factors influencing the production of books. This is a highly recommended work and clearly worthy of emulation regarding its arguments for broadening the scope of book history studies.

Published on the occasion of the exhibition 'Voyages: A Smithsonian Libraries Exhibition' (16 May–4 August 2001), Thomas, ed., *An Odyssey in Print: Adventures in the Smithsonian Libraries*, with a foreword by Nancy E. Gwinn, is a richly illustrated work that guides the reader through the exhibition, highlighting the beautiful and rare pieces of the Smithsonian Collection. Interested readers may also view the exhibition online at <www.sil.si.edu/Exhibitions>. In *British Author House Museums and other Memorials: A Guide to Sites in England, Scotland and Wales*, Shirley H. Biggers has produced a guidebook chronicling over 300 sites devoted to over forty authors. A representative sample of authors covered includes Jane Austen, Agatha Christie, Sir Arthur Conan Doyle, Thomas Hardy, James Joyce, and D.H. Lawrence. These sites include historical homes, memorial statues, and literary museums. Readers will find detailed entries containing information related to how the sites relate to a specific author's career, as well as information related to admission prices, directions, telephone numbers, and hours of operation.

In *Out of the Flames: The Remarkable Story of a Fearless Scholar, a Fatal Heresy, and One of the Rarest Books in the World*, Lawrence and Nancy Goldstone present the story of Michael Servetus and the heretical work that cost him his life, the *Christianismi Restitutio*, written in 1553. In examining Servetus's life and the era in which he lived, the authors not only reveal the religious politics of the era, but also present a fascinating tale regarding the survival and transmission of a text that serves as a powerful reminder of the force of ideas in history and how ideas have been transmitted through the medium of the book. Also included are an epilogue, a useful selected bibliography, and an index.

In the *Thematic Guide to British Poetry*, Ruth F. Glancy brings together a valuable guide offering interpretations of over 415 poems spanning 110 poets representing the best of British poetry. The bulk of the work centres around narrative essays regarding twenty-nine alphabetically arranged themes that the author considers sufficiently recurrent in the development and evolution of British poetry. Examples of these themes include beauty, death, duty, immortality, love, marriage, nature and country life, patriotism, rebellion and conformity, religion, and war. Scholars of British poetry will find Glancy's work a useful additional resource, and general readers will find the book clearly organized and practical for general research. Additional suggested readings are supplied, as well as biographical sketches of the poets whose work is discussed, along with an index. Scholars of Scottish literature, as well as students and general readers, will find Gifford, Dunnigan, and Macgillivray, eds., *Scottish Literature*, a useful and informative general resource. Spanning Scottish literature from medieval to modern, the book is divided into six main sections: 'Medieval and Renaissance', 'Eighteenth-Century', 'The Age of Scott', 'Victorian and Edwardian', 'The Twentieth-Century Scottish Literary Renaissance', and 'Scottish Literature since 1945'. Each section begins with an essay introducing the reader to the main themes and personalities of the period, and each section concludes with suggested further readings. Additional sections include extensive reading lists for each period, as well as other non-print resources, and title and name indexes are also included.

In the *Encyclopedia of Canadian Literature,* W.H. New has compiled an impressive reference work devoted to the unique richness of Canadian literature. Over 300 contributors examine the varieties of Canadian literature, resulting in over 2,000 entries, each dealing with the historical and cultural events that influenced each author examined, and how this interplay formed the fabric of Canadian literature. The entries are arranged alphabetically, and include extensive cross-referencing, and recommendations for further reading. There are numerous appendices, including a cultural chronology, an index by contributor, and a supplementary index of names and concepts not covered by a separate entry. This work should be considered the definitive source regarding its subject matter.

In his highly engaging and thoroughly engrossing study, *Author Unknown: On the Trail of Anonymous*, Don Foster provides insight into the field of literary forensics. Foster's work relates his efforts regarding how anonymous authors often leave telling clues that point to their hidden identity. Foster's work will appeal to literary scholars and general readers alike as he narrates the application of his methods regarding topics as diverse as Shakespeare's sonnets, the unmasking of Joel Klein as the author of *Primary Colors*, and his work involving the Unabomber case and the question of who was the author of the Lewinsky–Tripp 'Talking Points'. In *'Counterfeiting' Shakespeare: Evidence, Authorship, and John Ford's Funerall Elegye*, Brian Vickers addresses the ongoing issue of what Shakespeare actually wrote by specifically taking issue with the attribution to him of the authorship of two poems, 'Shall I die?' and *A Funerall Elegye*. Vickers argues that each work incorporates commonplace expressions, and in the case of *A Funerall Elegye* he argues that authorship should be attributed to John Ford. The study is divided into two parts. The first is 'Donald Foster's "Shakespearean Construct"', in which Vickers takes issue with many of Foster's analyses, assumptions, and conclusions. The second part is devoted to 'John Ford's *A Funerall Elegye*'. There are three appendices: 'The Text of *A Funerall Elegye*'; 'Verbal Parallels between *A Funerall Elegye* and Ford's Poems'; and 'Establishing Ford's Canon'. There are extensive notes, an enumerative, chronologically arranged bibliography, and an extensive index. This 568-page monograph is amongst the most notable textual studies of the year and will generate much debate within Shakespearian studies. Vickers's awareness of the strengths and limitations of linguistics and statistical research methods is unrivalled.

In *Peter Short: An Elizabethan Printer*, Akihiro Yamada examines the books printed by Short's printing house, to gauge its level of productivity, and to situate Short in the history of book publishing and printing. The book is divided into the following chapters: 'A Brief Biography of Peter Short'; 'Books Printed by Peter Short'; 'The Annual Output of Peter Short's Printing House'; 'Peter Short's Shared Printing'; and 'Peter Short's Ornament Stock'. Yamada has also compiled an impressive number of examples of reproductions of Short's title-page borders, decorative initials, and woodcuts and ornamental blocks. Readers will appreciate the inclusion of an index and a useful bibliography for further reading. In *Shakespeare's Words: A Glossary and Language Companion*, compiled by David and Ben Crystal with a preface by Stanley Wells, readers will find a more general work designed for those who have an abiding interest in Shakespeare and in the English language. A special feature is the way in which each play is presented to the reader through the use of conventional plot summaries, but also through the use of author-constructed 'Shakespearian Circles': informative illustrations representing the interactions between characters in the plays profiled. This work is particularly useful as an introductory resource for students becoming acquainted with Shakespeare and his work.

A recent publication in the Cambridge Studies in Renaissance Literature and Culture series is *Ben Jonson and Possessive Authorship* by Joseph Loewenstein. Loewenstein examines the history of authorship and the changing definition of intellectual property by examining the work of Ben Jonson, and describes the early copyright practices of London's dramatic troupes and the Stationers' Company. His research is specifically focused on the works of Jonson; however, he also takes great care to situate his arguments and conclusion within the Renaissance cultural heritage. This is a challenging and thought-provoking book designed to critically engage scholars of Renaissance literature and culture. Lisa Hopkins's *Writing Renaissance Queens: Texts by and about Elizabeth I and Mary, Queen of Scots* has relevance to bibliographical and textual studies. Hopkins analyses writings both by and about her subjects, incorporating the large volume of work both figures produced during their respective lifetimes. The book is divided into four main sections. The first analyses images of queenship. Hopkins then moves on to examine the writing of her subjects, and contrasts their view of their role with that of mostly male commentators. The third section deals with the avoidance of serious discussion regarding the role of queenship in the leading plays and works of the period. The concluding section deals with how the role of the queen was imagined in works ranging from *Hamlet* to *Paradise Lost*. In *Women, Reading, and Piety in Late Medieval England*, Mary C. Erler presents an interesting work dealing with female book-ownership patterns, particularly regarding devotional books. She uses bibliographic methods to mine the social and intellectual history of the period she analyses, approximately 350–1550. Additional material beyond the text includes an appendix listing books not previously attributed to female ownership. Lambdin and Lambdin, eds., *A Companion to Old and Middle English Literature*, focuses on particular genres, including allegorical verse, balladry, beast fable, chronicle, debate poetry, epic and heroic, lyric, Middle English parody/burlesque, religious and allegorical verse, and romance. Chapters include reviews of scholarship and detailed biographies, and an extensive bibliography closes the book. Another work dealing with medieval studies is *Absent Narratives, Manuscript Textuality, and Literary Structure in Late Medieval England* by Elizabeth Scala. Scala's work deals with the theme of the difference between medieval and modern stories, giving particular attention to the medieval narrative use of absent narratives, or the process of alluding to stories that appear fragmented by the larger narrative but which still play a vital role in medieval storytelling. Writers discussed and profiled in the book include Chaucer, Gower, and Malory.

Works published by the distinguished Grolier Club in New York provide five quality entries in this compilation of significant and notable work in bibliography and textual studies. The first of these, *Books, Manuscripts and Works on Paper from the Collections of Grolier Club Members*, is compiled and introduced by T. Peter Kraus and Eric Holzenberg, and edited by Carol Z. Rothkopf, and is a catalogue of an exhibition held at the Grolier Club from 11 December 2002 to 1 February 2003. Subjects covered include classic bibliophily, Americana, history, travel, literature, association copies, fine printing, bindings, book illustration, photography, other works on paper, bibliography, music, science and medicine, and children's literature. This well-illustrated volume, set in Aldus and Michelangelo types designed by Martino Mardersteig, and designed by Jerry Kelly (p. 178), contains an index of lenders and index of entries. The second Grolier Club publication is Stephenson and Currie, eds., *Iter Veneticum*. Containing many illustrations, in mottled binding, and with a sumptuous gilt-lettered spine, the work is a visual treat and record of 'a Grolier Club trip to Venice' (p. 1) in October 1998. Contributors and contents relevant to bibliography and textual studies include G. Scott Clemons, 'Early Italian Typography and the Tipoteca Italiana Fondazione' and Eric Holzenberg, 'Libraries'. This isn't to say that there are not many other fascinating contributions of interest in this volume. The third Grolier Club item is *'To Set the Darkness Echoing': An Exhibition of Irish Literature, 1950–2000*, curated by Stephen Enniss, James O'Halloran, and Ronald Schuchard. This exhibition, to be seen as a sequel to the first exhibition on Irish literature, brings together a wide variety of remarkable Irish literature devoted to the second half of the twentieth century. The fourth item is Zachs, ed., *Mary Hyde Eccles: A Miscellany of her Essays and Addresses*. The volume, printed in Baskerville type in an edition of 500 copies, represents a successful attempt to introduce to the reading public some of the lesser-known writings by Mary Hyde Eccles, the noted collector, scholar, and bibliophile. Seventeen of her pieces are included, some published for the first time. Apart from the sheer enjoyment of reading these products of a remarkable scholar, readers will also get a glimpse of an era of book-collecting that serves as an inspiration to us all. Especially noteworthy are essays on 'The History of the Johnson Papers', 'Samuel Johnson's Library', and, amongst others, reminiscences of the bibliophiles John Hayward (1905–65), and John F. Fleming (1910–87). The fifth item published by the Grolier Club is Helfand, ed., *Quack, Quack, Quack: The Sellers of Nostrums in Prints, Posters, Ephemera and Books*. Published to accompany an exhibition at the Grolier Club from 18 September to 23 November 2002, Helfand's book is an amusing, entertaining, and very informative look at the history of quackery in general, and specifically as represented in art and literature. The book also includes a brief bibliography and a useful index.

In *Books in the Blood: Memoirs of a Fourth Generation Bookseller*, Anthony Rota presents a fascinating and informative memoir that relates his vast experience in the world of antiquarian books. Scholars, book collectors, and general readers alike will find much of value in these pages, including chapters on the archives of Lawrence Durrell, Hilaire Belloc, the Sitwells, John Gawsworth, John Rodker, and many others. In *Low Profile: A Life in the World of Books*, Frank Herrmann provides a frank and telling autobiography that gives readers a glimpse into the worlds of book-designing, auction houses, and art- and book-collecting. Included are many fine illustrations and rare photographs of significant personalities of the British, and especially London, auction world. This is a powerful and detailed account of the post-Second World War London book world through to the end of the century. There are chapters on Herrmann's apprenticeship at Faber & Faber, including his encounters with T.S. Eliot, his time at Methuen's, his analysis of 'the English' as 'Collectors', his days at Sotheby's, and amongst others, the creation of Bloomsbury Book Auctions. Some of its sales included materials by John Braine, H.A. Manhood, T.S. Eliot, Graham Greene, and D.H. Lawrence among others. In *Patience and Fortitude: A Roving Chronicle of Book People, Book Places, and Book Culture*, Nicholas A. Basbanes narrates the changing form of the book over time and those individuals whose passion for books and collecting them informs the very fabric of their lives. Written in a manner that combines scholarly precision with an upbeat and almost investigative journalistic style, Basbanes carries readers through the pages and is a delight to read. Myers, Harris, and Mandelbrote, eds., *Under the Hammer: Book Auctions Since the Seventeenth Century*, assembles a collection of essays from specialists regarding the topic of book auctions. Contributions range from a discussion of the organization and structure of early book sales, to identifying those social groups and elements which participated in auctions, to the form and structure of the principal auctioneers. Contributors and contents include Michael Harris, 'Newspaper Advertising for Book Auctions Before 1700'; Giles Mandelbrote, 'The Organization of Book Auctions in Late Seventeenth-Century London'; T.A. Birrell, 'Books and Buyers in Seventeenth-Century English Auction Sales'; Otto S. Lankhorst, 'Dutch Book Auctions in the Seventeenth and Eighteenth Centuries'; Nigel Ramsay, 'English Book Collectors and the Salerooms in the Eighteenth Century'; Marc Vaulbert de Chantilly, 'Property of a Distinguished Poisoner: Thomas Griffiths Wainewright and the Griffiths Family Library'; Arnold Hunt, 'The Sale of Richard Heber's Library'; Paul Needham, 'William Morris's "Ancient Books" at Sale'; and Arthur Freeman, 'The Jazz Age Library of Jerome Kern'. There is also an appendix, 'Book Auctions at Christie's and Sotheby's', containing an account of early auction catalogues displayed at the London conference on 25–6 November 2000 at which the papers published in the volume were given.

In the *Illustrated Editions of the Works of William Morris in English: A Descriptive Bibliography*, Robert L.M. Coupe has created a richly detailed bibliography chronicling the efforts of those artists and illustrators whose skill and eye for detail added so much value to the works of William Morris. Coupe includes biographical information related to each artist, and extensive critical commentary related to the style of the illustrations and their relationship to the work represented. Apart from the sheer physical beauty of many of the illustrations in the book, scholars studying the history and art of the book and the relationship between illustration and text will find much of value in these pages. In *Christina Rossetti and*

Illustration: A Publishing History, Lorraine Janzen Kooistra has provided a thorough resource that should be of interest to Rossetti scholars and to scholars of the Victorian publishing industry. Her book chronicles Rossetti's perception of the relationship between the verbal and the visual that is an integral part of her work. The book contains illustrations and a useful index and bibliography. Those interested in the preservation and repair of books will find a compact but valuable resource in *The Repair of Cloth Bindings: A Manual*, written by the noted English bookbinder Arthur W. Johnson. Of particular value are the more than eighty hand-drawn illustrations by Johnson which outline procedures he has developed and used during his long and distinguished career. Essentially this book is a valuable resource that will soon take its place as a classic regarding the repair of cloth bindings. Along similar lines, Margot Rosenberg and Ben Marcowitz provide repair, restoration, and preservation advice geared toward the amateur bibliophile in their *The Care and Feeding of Books Old and New: A Simple Repair Manual for Book Lovers*. Additional material includes a helpful glossary, suggested readings, a list of suppliers related to the care and maintenance of books, and a listing of internet sources related to conservation. In Holliday, ed., *Eric Gill in Ditchling: Four Essays*, readers get a glimpse of a remarkable individual best known for working as a sculptor, wood-engraver, and type designer; he designed eleven typefaces, Gill Sans being his most famous. Contributors and contents include Peter Holliday, 'Eric Gill's Photograph Album: "Rome 1906"'; Timothy J. McCann, 'Eric Gill's Inscriptional Work in Ditchling'; Jill Lingen-Watson, 'Finding Gill Sculptures'; and Peter Holliday, 'Eric Gill, Amy Sawyer, and the "Gladys Panel"'.

In *The Cambridge Introduction to Modern British Fiction, 1950–2000*, Dominic Head demonstrates how the novel reflects post-war British social and cultural history in the latter half of the twentieth century. Head's work is divided into seven chapters: 'The State and the Novel'; 'Class and Social Change'; 'Gender and Sexual Identity'; 'National Identity'; 'Multicultural Personae'; 'Country and Suburb'; and 'Beyond 2000'. Head includes more than a hundred novelists and approximately 200 fictional works, and his book will serve as a useful and valuable source for students and critics. The work also includes an extensive bibliography and listing of other works cited. Another useful source is *Bryson's Dictionary of Troublesome Words: A Writer's Guide to Getting it Right*, by Bill Bryson. A new and updated version of Bryson's previous edition with the same name, this valuably fills a niche, particular for those whose command of the quirks of the English language could use a little extra help. Included are a punctuation appendix, a glossary, and a bibliography for suggested further reading.

The topic of bibliographic studies related to magazines receives meritorious treatment in *Irish Literary Magazines: An Outline History and Descriptive Bibliography* by Tom Clyde. This work, published by the Irish Academic Press, consists of three main parts. The first is an outline of the history of Irish literary magazines by decade, ranging from pre-history up to 1985. The second part is a descriptive bibliography. The third part consists of several appendices, including an alphabetical index, distribution maps, and chronological charts. Clyde's is a fine work and highly recommended.

Buranen and Roy, eds., *Perspectives on Plagiarism and Intellectual Property in a Postmodern World*, provides a very timely, important, and relevant work. It is divided into two main sections, dealing with definitions and applications. Contents and contributors include Laurie Stearns, 'Copy Wrong: Plagiarism, Process, Property, and the Law'; C. Jan Swearingen, 'Originality, Authenticity, Imitation, and Plagiarism: Augustine's Chinese Cousins'; James Thomas Zebroski, 'Intellectual Property, Authority, and Social Formation: Sociohistorical Perspectives on the Author Function'; Sue Carter Simmons, 'Competing Notions of Authorship: A Historical Look at Students and Textbooks on Plagiarism and Cheating'; Alice M. Roy, 'Whose Words These Are I Think I Know: Plagiarism, the Postmodern, and Faculty Attitudes'; Lisa Buranen, 'But I Wasn't Cheating: Plagiarism and Cross-Cultural Mythology'; L.M. Dryden, 'A Distant Mirror or Through the Looking Glass? Plagiarism and Intellectual Property in Japanese Education'; Rebecca Moore Howard, 'The New Abolitionism Come to Plagiarism'; Kevin J.H. Dettmar, 'The Illusion of Modernist Allusion and the Politics of Postmodern Plagiarism'; Debora Halbert, 'Poaching and Plagiarizing: Property, Plagiarism, and Feminist Futures'; Gilbert Larochelle, 'From Kant to Foucault: What Remains of the Author in Postmodernism'; Marilyn Randall, 'Imperial Plagiarism'; Robert André LaFleur, 'Literary Borrowing and Historical Compilation in Medieval China'; Irene L. Clark, 'Writing Centers and Plagiarism'; Carol Peterson Haviland and Joan Mullin, 'Writing Centers and Intellectual Property: Are Faculty Members and Students Differently Entitled?'; Linda Shamoon and Deborah H. Burns, 'Plagiarism, Rhetorical Theory, and the Writing Center: New Approaches, New Locations'; Terri LeClercq, 'Confusion and Conflict about Plagiarism in Law Schools and Law Practice'; Edward M. White, 'Student Plagiarism as an Institutional and Social Issue'; Henry L. Wilson, 'When Collaboration Becomes Plagiarism: The Administrative Perspective'; David Leight, 'Plagiarism as Metaphor'; Candace Spigelman, 'The Ethics of Appropriation in Peer Writing Groups'; Shirley K. Rose, 'The Role of Scholarly Citations in Disciplinary Economics'; Shawn M. Clankie, 'Brand Name Use in Creative Writing: Genericide or Language Right?'; and Joan Livingston-Webber, 'GenX Occupies the Cultural Commons: Ethical Practices and Perceptions of Fair Use'. Also present in this valuable work is a works cited section and a detailed index.

Hainsworth and Robey, eds., *The Oxford Companion to Italian Literature*, attempts to cover Italian literature from the thirteenth century to the present. The work covers the major luminaries of Italian literature, but also seeks to incorporate lesser-known minor figures. Much of the work is contextual in nature, seeking to place the writers profiled and their works in historical context. There are over 2,400 alphabetically arranged entries, making this a broad and expansive work suitable for both the specialist and general reader. Entries vary in length and depth. Types of categories covered include literary genres and types; literary movements, themes, and issues; cultural contexts and institutions; language; social and political context; non-Italian writing and influences; other arts; and sources for further reference. The entries vary somewhat in quality, and each concludes with the critical reception of each author's work.

In *Flannery O'Connor: An Annotated Reference Guide to Criticism*, R. Neil Scott has compiled and annotated a source designed to capture critical assessments of O'Connor's work from 1975 to 2000, supplementing earlier critical reference guides dealing with O'Connor's work. Entries are arranged alphabetically by author and the abstracts written for the work are primarily descriptive and not evaluative. In *A Zora Neale Hurston Companion*, Robert W. Croft provides a thorough and easily accessible guide to the work of a significant twentieth-century African American author who draws upon African American folklore. Croft presents an outline of the major events of Hurston's life and likewise provides a concise but informative biography that evaluates and assesses her literary output in its social context. The hundreds of entries are arranged alphabetically and deal with topics related to Hurston's acquaintances, characters, family members, themes, and works. Most major topics contain suggestions for further reading and the book has helpful and thorough primary and secondary bibliographies.

In *A Reader's Guide to J.D. Salinger*, Eberhard Alsen provides a detailed and thoroughly researched account of one of the most reclusive writers of the twentieth century. Alsen's efforts highlight not only Salinger's *The Catcher in the Rye*, but also give attention to the full range of his writing, including the numerous shorter works he produced. An introductory essay discusses autobiographical elements of Salinger's work; additional topics covered are characterization and style, critical reception, the interpretation given to Salinger's work, its narrative structure, settings and symbols, and the underlying themes Salinger chose to convey. Each chapter contains suggestions for further reading, and the book concludes with several useful appendices and an extensive but unannotated bibliography of primary and secondary sources. In *A Langston Hughes Encyclopedia*, Hans Ostrom provides a welcome and thorough introduction to the life and work of perhaps the most well-known of the Harlem Renaissance poets. In terms of structure and layout, entries are arranged in alphabetical order and tend to be in paragraph format and contain information related to the original publication of the work. General readers will find the layout and structure of the book conducive to research, and scholars will welcome the appearance of this resource.

Guiyou Huang's *Asian American Poets: A Bio-Bibliographical Critical Sourcebook* will benefit both scholars and interested readers. Entries are arranged alphabetically and include works related to poetry, essays, short stories, and studies devoted to individual authors. Each entry concludes with the critical reception of each author's work. Contemporary and modern American female authors make significant and lasting contributions to the post-Second World War American literary and cultural scene. Laurie Chapman and Rhonda Austin describe many of these authors in *Contemporary American Women Fiction Writers: An A to Z Guide*, published by Greenwood Press. Chapman and Austin profile more than sixty American women writers representing diverse ethnic backgrounds whose primary body of literature was published after the end of the Second World War. Entries are alphabetically arranged and include brief biographies, discussions related to major themes and works, an overview of the author's critical reception, and a bibliography of primary and secondary sources for each of the authors included. This work is a convenient and useful resource, valuable for scholars and general readers alike, and recommended for reference collections.

In *The Crux: A Novel by Charlotte Perkins Gilman*, editor Jennifer S. Tuttle brings to the reading public a fresh edition of Gilman's novel, which depicts her reformist ideas related to gender roles and social organization. In her introduction Tuttle examines the cultural context of the book, and she provides explanatory notes throughout. Issues covered relate to ideologies and views of white middle-class womanhood, and views regarding, for instance, sexually transmitted diseases prevalent in the nineteenth century and American myths associated with the western frontier. Joseph Fichtelberg's *Critical Fictions: Sentiment and the American Market, 1780–1870* is a valuable addition to criticism of sentimental literature. Fichtelberg examines the changing depiction of women and traces this evolution to the vacillations of American economic life. Both popular and canonical writers are discussed, and the overall presentation is tightly argued. This serves as a potentially groundbreaking work in its field.

In *Forgotten Readers: Recovering the Lost History of African American Literary Societies*, Elizabeth McHenry has created a unique and compelling work dealing with a largely ignored topic of African American reading and literary societies in the nineteenth century. McHenry focuses heavily on the period between the height of the anti-slavery movement and the Harlem Renaissance, and, considering the paucity of sources available for her subject, she should be commended for her diligent research and well-executed presentation.

In the lavishly illustrated *An Elegant Hand: The Golden Age of American Penmanship and Calligraphy*, edited by Paul Melzer and written by William E. Henning, readers experience an amazingly detailed study of styles of penmanship and calligraphy. Many of the more than 400 illustrations are original specimens collected by the author's father, and a useful and functional glossary assists the reader. In a preface written by Ross Green, a scholarly perspective is provided that situates this book in the field of American calligraphy. A thoroughly entertaining, visually stunning, and highly original piece of work.

Casper, Chaison, and Groves, eds., *Perspectives on American Book History: Artifacts and Commentary*, contains an impressive array of essays dealing with the history of the book industry and trade in the United States. Contributors and contents include Robert A. Gross, 'Texts for the Times: An Introduction to Book History'; Jill LePore, 'Literacy and Reading in Puritan New England'; Patricia Crain, 'Print and Everyday Life in the Eighteenth Century'; Russell L. Martin, 'Publishing the American Revolution'; Jeffrey D. Groves, 'The Book Trade Transformed'; Scott E. Casper, 'Antebellum Reading Prescribed and Described'; Susan S. Williams, 'Publishing an Emergent "American" Literature'; Alice Fahs, 'Northern and Southern Worlds of Print'; Nancy Cook, 'Reshaping Publishing and Authorship in the Gilded Age'; Jen A. Huntley-Smith, 'Print Cultures in the American West'; Ann Fabian, 'Laboring Classes, New Readers, and Print Cultures'; Charles Johanningsmeier, 'The Industrialization and Nationalization of American Periodical Publishing'; Trysh Travis, 'Print and the Creation of Middlebrow Culture'; Ellen Gruber Garvey, 'Out of the Mainstream and into the Streets: Small Press Magazines, the Underground Press, Zines, and Artists' Books'; Glenn Wallach, 'Newspapers since 1945'; Scott E. Casper, Joanne D. Chaison, and Jeffrey D. Groves, 'The Once and Future Book'; and Joanne D. Chaison, 'Resources for Studying American Book History: A Selective, Annotated Bibliography'.

In *American Literature and the Culture of Reprinting, 1834–1853*, Meredith L. McGill combines historical research with textual analysis; the result is a challenging and new interpretation of American literary culture in the early nineteenth century. In her work, McGill demonstrates how the perceived rampant piracy of largely European literary works, principally English ones, helped to create and sustain a literary culture in the United States that was often more regional than national in nature. She argues that the centralization of American literary culture in the 1850s destroyed the regional character of American literary culture and deposited instead an identifiable national literary culture. A timely and interesting book considering the modern preoccupation with copyright issues and author rights in an electronic age.

Finally, of interest is the neglected bibliographical study of Freemasonry. Weisberger, McLeod, and Morris, eds., *Freemasonry on Both Sides of the Atlantic: Essays Concerning the Craft in the British Isles, Europe, the United States, and Mexico*, examines the practice and evolution of Freemasonry in almost forty essays by a wide range of international scholars. Examples of contributors and contents include Lisa Kahler, 'The Grand Lodge of Scotland and the Establishment of the Masonic Community'; Zsuzsa L. Nagy, 'Freemasonry in Hungary between the Eighteenth and Twentieth Centuries'; Lynn Dumenil, 'Religion and Freemasonry in Late 19th-Century America'; and Paul Rich and Carlos Cruz, 'Civil Society and Freemasonry: The Cardenista Rite and Mexico'. A unique compilation of essays that will serve specialists in freemasonry scholarship well, and which has considerable relevance to a largely ignored area of literary exploration.

Books Reviewed

Alkon, Paul K. *Science Fiction Before 1900: Imagination Discovers Technology*. Routledge. [2002] pp. 176. £12.99 ISBN 0 4159 3887 2.

Alsen, Eberhard. *A Reader's Guide to J.D. Salinger*. Greenwood. [2002] pp. x + 270. $64.95 ISBN 0 3133 1078 5.

Baker, William, and John C. Ross, *George Eliot: A Bibliographical History*. BL. [2002] pp. 675. ISBN 0 7123 4765 8.

Barnard, John, and D.F. McKenzie, eds. *The Cambridge History of the Book in Britain*, vol. 4. CUP. [2002] pp. 800. $140 ISBN 0 5216 6182 X.

Basbanes, Nicholas A. *Patience and Fortitude: A Roving Chronicle of Book People, Book Places, and Book Culture*. HarperCollins. [2002] pp. xviii + 636. $35. ISBN 0 0601 9695 5.

Biggers, Shirley. *British Author House Museums and Other Memorials: A Guide to Sites in England, Ireland, Scotland and Wales*. McFarland. [2002] pp. 386. £31.95 ISBN 0 7864 1268 2.

Bloomfield, B.C. *Philip Larkin: A Bibliography, 1933–1994*. OakK. [2002] pp. 226. $70 ISBN 1 5845 6062 2.

Bruccoli, Matthew J., and Park Bucker. *Joseph Heller: A Descriptive Bibliography*. OakK. [2002] pp. 246. $100 ISBN 1 5700 3355 2.

Bryson, Bill. *Bryson's Dictionary of Troublesome Words: A Writer's Guide to Getting it Right*. Broadway. [2002] pp. xiii + 241. $19.95 ISBN 0 7679 1042 7.

Buranen, Lise, and Alice M. Roy, eds. *Perspectives on Plagiarism and Intellectual Property in a Postmodern World*. State University of New York. [2002] pp. xxii + 302. £19.50 ISBN 0 7914 4080 X.

Cassidy, Brendan, and Rosemary Muir Wright, eds. *Studies in the Illustration of the Psalter*. Shaun Tyas. [2000] pp. x + 86 + 64 pp. plates. £19.95 ISBN 1 9002 8942 3.

Casper, Scott, Joanne D. Chaison, and Jeffrey D. Groves. *Perspectives on American Book History: Artifacts and Commentary*. UMassP. [2002] pp. ix + 461. £49.50 ISBN 1 5584 9136 6.

Champion, Laurie, and Rhonda Austin. *Contemporary American Women Fiction Writers: An A to Z Guide*. Greenwood. [2002] pp. xiii + 407. $94.95 ISBN 0 3133 1627 9.

Clyde, Tom. *Irish Literary Magazines: An Outline History and Descriptive Bibliography*. IAP. [2002] pp. 256. $49.50 ISBN 0 7165 2751 0.

Coupe, Robert L.M. *Illustrated Editions of the Works of William Morris in English: A Descriptive Bibliography*. OakK. [2002] pp. 240. $49.95 ISBN 1 5845 6079 7.

Croft, Robert W. *A Zora Neale Hurston Companion*. Greenwood. [2002] pp. xxix + 256. $74.95 ISBN 0 3133 0707 5.

Crystal, David. *A Dictionary of Linguistics and Phonetics*, 5th edn. Blackwell. [2002] pp. xxiv + 508. £16.35 ISBN 0 6312 2663 X.

Crystal, David and Ben Crystal (comp.). *Shakespeare's Words: A Glossary and Language Companion*, preface by Stanley Wells. Penguin. [2002] pp. 676. £9.83 ISBN 0 1402 9117 2.

Daniell, David. *The Bible in English*. YaleUP. [2002] pp. xx + 899. £29.95 ISBN 0 3000 9930 4.

Enniss, Stephen, James O'Halloran, and Ronald Schuchard. *'To Set the Darkness Echoing': An Exhibition of Irish Literature, 1950–2000*. GroC. [2002] pp. 59. $17.50 ISBN 0 9106 7243 1.

Edwards, A.S.G., ed. *Decoration and Illustration in Medieval English Manuscripts: English Manuscript Studies, 1100–1700*, vol. 10. BL [2002] pp. 272. £31.50 ISBN 0 7123 4732 1.

Erler, Mary C. *Women, Reading, and Piety in Late Medieval England*. CUP. [2002] pp. xii + 226. £35.48 ISBN 0 5218 1221 6.

Fichtelberg, Joseph. *Critical Fictions: Sentiment and the American Market, 1780–1870*. University of Georgia. [2002] pp. x + 280. £30.50 ISBN 0 8203 2434 5.

Finkelstein, David, and Alistair McCleery, eds. *The Book History Reader*. Routledge. [2002] pp. 368. £11.89 ISBN 0 4152 2658 9.

Foster, Don. *Author Unknown: On the Trail of Anonymous*. Henry Holt. [2002] pp. 318. $16.95 ISBN 0 8050 6357 9.

Gifford, Douglas, Sarah Dunnigan, and Alan Macgillivray. *Scottish Literature*. EdinUP. [2002] pp. ix + 1269. £24.99 ISBN 0 7486 0825 7.

Glancy, Ruth. *Thematic Guide to British Poetry*. Greenwood. [2002] pp. xii + 303. $64.95 ISBN 0 3133 1379 2.

Goldstone, Lawrence, and Nancy Goldstone. *Out of the Flames: The Remarkable Story of a Fearless Scholar, a Fatal Heresy, and One of the Rarest Books in the World*. Broadway [2002] pp. 353. $24.95 ISBN 0 7679 0836 8.

Griffiths, David N. *The Bibliography of the Book of Common Prayer, 1549–1999*. OakK and BL. [2002] pp. 624. $95 ISBN 1 5845 6081 9.

Hainsworth, Peter, and David Robey, eds. *The Oxford Companion to Italian Literature*. OUP. [2002] pp. xli + 644. $95 ISBN 0 1981 8332 1.

Head, Dominic. *The Cambridge Introduction to Modern British Fiction, 1950–2000*. CUP. [2002] pp. viii + 307. £15.99 ISBN 0 5216 6014 9.

Helfand, William H., ed. *Quack, Quack, Quack: The Sellers of Nostrums in Prints, Posters, Ephemera & Books*. GroC. [2002] pp. 252. ISBN 0 9106 7240 7.

Henning, William E. *An Elegant Hand: The Golden Age of American Penmanship and Calligraphy*, edited by Paul Melzer. OakK. [2002] pp. xi + 307. ISBN 1 5845 6067 3.

Herbert, Edward, and Emanuel Tov, eds. *The Bible as Book: The Hebrew Bible and the Judaean Desert Discoveries.* OakK. [2002] pp. 336. $60 ISBN 1 5845 6083 5.

Herrmann, Frank. *Low Profile: A Life in the World of Books.* OakK. [2002] pp. 408. $39.95 ISBN 1 5845 6065 7.

Holliday, Peter. *Eric Gill in Ditchling: Four Essays.* OakK. [2002] pp. vii + 82. £16 ISBN 1 5845 6075 4.

Hopkins, Lisa. *Writing Renaissance Queens: Texts by and about Elizabeth I and Mary, Queen of Scots.* UDelP [2002] pp. 209. £30.50 ISBN 0 8741 3786 1.

Huang, Guiyou. *Asian American Poets: A Bio-Bibliographical Critical Sourcebook.* Greenwood [2002] pp. viii + 376. £64.50 ISBN 0 3133 1809 3.

Johnson, Arthur. *The Repair of Cloth Bindings: A Manual.* OakK. [2002] pp. 140. $35 ISBN 1 5845 6078 9.

Kenny, Colum. *King's Inns and the Battle of the Books, 1972: Cultural Controversy at a Dublin Library.* FCP. [2002] pp. xvii + 192. £30 ISBN 1 8518 2686 6.

Kooistra, Lorraine Janzen. *Christina Rossetti and Illustration: A Publishing History.* OhioUP. [2002] pp. xvi + 332. £41.95($55) ISBN 0 8214 1454 2.

Kraus, T. Peter, and Eric Holzenberg. *The* Grolier Club *Collects: Books, Manuscripts and Works on Paper from the Collections of* Grolier Club *Members,* edited by Carol Rothkopf. GroC. [2002] pp. xx + 178. ISBN 0 9196 7244 X.

Lambdin, Laura Cooner, and Robert Thomas Lambdin. *A Companion to Old and Middle English Literature.* Greenwood. [2002] pp. xi + 433. £48.50 ISBN 0 3133 1054 8.

Loewenstein, Joseph. *Ben Jonson and Possessive Authorship.* CUP [2002] pp. x + 349. £40.94 ISBN 0 5218 1217 8.

Manning, John. *The Emblem.* Reaktion. [2002] pp. 392. $35 ISBN 1 8618 9110 5.

Maslen, Keith. *Samuel Richardson of London, Printer: A Study of his Printing Based on Ornament Use and Business Accounts.* UOtagoP. [2002] ISBN 0 4730 7760 4.

McGill, Meredith L. *American Literature and the Culture of Reprinting, 1834–1853.* UPennP. [2002] pp. viii + 364. $39.95 ISBN 0 8122 3698 X.

McGovern, Una. *Chambers Biographical Dictionary.* Chambers. [2002] pp. xi + 1,650. £24.50 ISBN 0 5501 0051 2.

McHenry, Elizabeth. *Forgotten Readers: Recovering the Lost History of African American Literary Societies.* DukeUP. [2002] pp. 440. $59.95 ISBN 0 8223 2980 8.

Moores, Phil, ed. *Alasdair Gray: Critical Appreciations and a Bibliography.* BL. [2002] pp. xii + 241. £20 ISBN 0 7123 1129 7.

Morrison, Ian. *The Publishing Industry in Colonial Australia: A Name Index to John Alexander Ferguson's 'Bibliography of Australia, 1784–1900'.* BSANZ. [2002] pp. 162. ISBN 0 9598 2716 1.

Myers, Robin, Michael Harris, and Giles Mandelbrote. *Under the Hammer: Book Auctions since the Seventeenth Century.* OakK. [2002] pp. 248 $39.95 ISBN 1 5845 6066 5.

New, W.H. *Encyclopedia of Literature in Canada.* UTorP. [2002] pp. 1347. $75 ISBN 0 8020 0761 9.

Ostrom, Hans. *A Langston Hughes Encyclopedia.* Greenwood. [2002] pp. 440. $99.95 ISBN 0 3133 0392 4.

Partridge, Eric. *A Dictionary of Slang and Unconventional English*, 8th edn., edited by Paul Beale. Routledge. [2002] pp. 1,400. pb $39.95 ISBN 0 4152 9189 5.

Pinnock, Avital. *The Orion Center Bibliography of Dead Sea Scrolls (1995–2000)*. BrillA. [2002] pp. 228. £? ISBN 9 0041 2366 0.

Raven, James. *London Booksellers and American Customers: Transatlantic Literary Community and the Charleston Library Society, 1748–1811*. USCP. [2002] pp. xxii + 522. £49.95 ISBN 1 5700 3406 0.

Rosenberg, Margot, and Bern Marcowitz. *The Care and Feeding of Books, Old and New: A Simple Repair Manual for Book Lovers*. St Martin's Press. [2002] pp. xv + 190. $21.95 ISBN 0 3123 0067 0.

Ross, Josephine. *Jane Austen: A Companion*. RutgersUP. [2002] pp xi + 259. £11.89 ISBN 0 8135 3299 X.

Rota, Anthony. *Books in the Blood: Memoirs of a Fourth Generation Bookseller*. OakK. [2002] pp. 313. $35 ISBN 1 5845 6076 2.

Satterfield, Jay. *'The World's Best Books': Taste, Culture, and the* Modern Library. UMassP. [2002] pp. ix + 240. £21.50 ISBN 1 5584 9353 0.

Scala, Elizabeth. *Absent Narratives, Manuscript Textuality, and Literary Structure in Late Medieval England*. Palgrave. [2002] pp. xix + 284. £31.50 ISBN 0 3122 4043 0.

Scott, R. Neil. *Flannery O'Connor: An Annotated Reference Guide to Criticism*. Timberlane. [2002] pp. xx + 1,061. ISBN 0 9715 6280 5.

Sirat, Colette. *Hebrew Manuscripts of the Middle Ages*, edited and translated by Nicholas de Lange. CUP. [2002] pp. xvi + 349. £51.85 ISBN 0 5217 7079 3.

Smith, Patrick A. *Thematic Guide to Popular Short Stories*. Greenwood. [2002] pp. 318. £29 ISBN 0 3133 1897 2.

Stephenson, Jean, and Kit Currie, eds. *Iter Veneticum*. GroC. [2002] pp. viii + 126. $75 ISBN 0 9106 7237 7.

Taylor, Barry, ed. *Foreign-Language Printing in London 1500–1900*. BL. [2002] pp. vii + 273. £30 ISBN 0 7123 1128 9.

Thomas, Mary Augusta. *An Odyssey in Print: Adventures in the Smithsonian Libraries*. Smithsonian Institution. [2002] pp. 179. £16.35 ISBN 1 5883 4036 8.

Tuttle, Jennifer S., ed. *The Crux* by Charlotte Perkins Gilman. UDelP. [2002] pp. 184. $42.50 ISBN 0 8741 3771 3.

Vickers, Brian. *'Counterfeiting' Shakespeare: Evidence, Authorship, and John Ford's Funerall Elegye*. CUP. [2002] pp. 568. $75 ISBN 0 5217 7243 5.

Weisberger, R. William, Wallace McLeod, and S. Brent Morris. *Freemasonry on Both Sides of the Atlantic: Essays Concerning the Craft in the British Isles, Europe, the United States, and Mexico*. East European Monographs. [2002] pp. xxviii + 942. £48 ISBN 0 8803 3992 6.

Wilkinson, P.R. *Thesaurus of Traditional English Metaphors*, 2nd edn. Routledge. [2002] pp. xxvi + 870. £94.50 ISBN 0 4152 7685 3.

Wilson, David M. *The British Museum: A History*. BMP. [2002] pp. 416. £35 ISBN 0 7141 2764 7.

Yamada, Akihiro. *Peter Short: An Elizabethan Printer*. MIE University Press. [2002] pp. 263. ISBN 4 9440 6860 3.

Yardeni, Ada. *The Book of Hebrew Script: History, Palaeography, Script Styles, Calligraphy and Design*. BL. [2002] pp. 368. £40 ISBN 0 7123 4793 3.

Zachs, William, ed. *A Miscellany of her Essays and Addresses* by Mary Hyde Eccles. GroC. [2002] pp. xx + 300. $55 ISBN 0 9106 7242 3.

Index I. Critics

Notes

(1) Material which has not been seen by contributors is not indexed.

(2) Authors such as J.R.R. Tolkien and Doris Lessing, who are both authors of criticism and subjects of discussion, are listed in whichever index is appropriate for each reference.

(3) Contributors to multi-authored works, all of whom may not be mentioned in the text, are listed with the name of the first author in brackets.

Cheng, Winnie 25–6
Cherewatuk, Karen 185
Chernaik, Warren 452
Cheshire, Jenny 61, 69
Cheshire, Paul 587
Chevrefils, Mary 989–90
Chew, Dolores 1004
Chico, Tita 522
Childers, Joseph W. 649
Childs, Peter 65
Chirico, Paul 557
Chism, Christine 154, 165
Chittleborough, Anne 943
Chiwengo, Nagwarsungu 899
Chiwome, Emmanuel 938
Chon, Sooyoung 1011
Chowdhury, Arvind 1010
Christ, Carol 670
Christian, Barbara 907
Christian, George Scott 663
Christian, Margaret 250
Christiansen, Peter 970
Christie, William 557
Christopher, R.A. 730
Chua, Derrick 993
Churchill, Laurie J. 416–17
Ciccone, Nancy 220
Ciociola, Gail 886
Clankie, Shawn M. 58–9, 1051
Clapp-Itnyre, Alisa 638–9
Clare, Janet 403
Clark, Irene L. 1051
Clark, J.C.D. 496
Clark, Jonathan 495–6
Clark, Robert 943
Clark, Roger 1006–7
Clark, Sandra 424
Clark, Victoria 35
Clarke, Deborah 898–9
Clarke, Elizabeth 424
Clarke, George Elliott 981, 982, 996
Clarke, Graham 821–2
Clarke, Patricia 942
Clarke, Sandra 70
Claughton, J.S. 80
Clayton, Jay 867
Clayton, Mary 49, 134
Clayworth, Anya 641, 669
Cleary, Joe 723, 724
Clegg, Cyndia Susan 403
Clemoes, Peter 110
Clemons, G. Scott 1048
Clery, E.J. 557

Clingham, Greg 472, 496, 497–8
Clinton, Andrew 665
Close, Cecily 953
Clubb, Louise George 328
Clucas, Stephen 428
Clum, John M. 880, 884
Clyde, Tom 1050
Coates, Donna 954
Coates, Irene 764–5
Coates, John 653, 738
Cobern, Kathleen 587
Cochran, Kate 569
Cody, Lisa Forman 416
Coe, Jonathan 1040
Coelsch-Foisner, Sabine 688
Coffey, John 455
Coffler, Gail 825
Coghill, Marjorie 1044
Cogswell, Thomas 404
Cohen, Ariel 45
Cohen, Derek 344
Cohen, Edward H. 633
Cohen, Margaret 510, 511
Cohen, Matt 1035
Cohen, Milton A. 733
Cohen, Samuel 871
Cohen, William A. 652
Colatrella, Carol 825
Colbert, Benjamin 557, 561
Colby, Robert A. 667
Colby, Vineta 729
Colclough, David 412
Coldiron, A.E.B. 248
Colella, Silvana 695
Coleman, Deirdre 613
Coleman, Julie 114
Coleman, Peter 969
Coleridge, Kathleen 703
Collellmir, Dolors 959
Collet, Barry 188
Collier, Gordon 951, 1004–5
Collier, Patrick 787
Colligan, Mimi 972
Collingwood-Whittock, Sheila 960
Collini, Stefan 641, 790
Collins, Chris 18
Collins, Jeffrey R. 485
Collins, Peter 16; (Peters) 23, 26, 27, 39
Collins, Philip 655
Collinson, Patrick 1040
Collis, Steven 842
Colón, Christine 618–19, 623
Comfort, Alex 1033

Index II. Authors and Subjects Treated

Notes
(1) Material which has not been seen by contributors is not indexed.
(2) Authors such as J.R.R Tolkien and Doris Lessing, who are both authors of criticism and subjects of discussion, are listed in whichever index is appropriate for each reference.
(3) Author entries have subdivisions listed in the following order:
   (a) author's relationship with other authors
   (b) author's relationship with other subjects
   (c) author's characteristics
   (d) author's works (listed alphabetically)
(4) A page reference in **bold** represents a main entry for that particular subject.